JMBuchanan
and
Gordon Tullock

Index of Economic Articles

IN JOURNALS AND COLLECTIVE VOLUMES

Volume XI · 1969

Prepared under the auspices of

THE JOURNAL OF ECONOMIC LITERATURE

of the

AMERICAN ECONOMIC ASSOCIATION

MARK PERLMAN, *Managing Editor*
NAOMI PERLMAN, *Associate Editor*
DRUCILLA EKWURZEL, *Assistant Editor*

Assisted by
ASATOSHI MAESHIRO, *classification consultant*
AND STUDENTS FROM THE DEPARTMENT OF ECONOMICS, UNIVERSITY OF PITTSBURGH

Distributed by
RICHARD D. IRWIN, INC.
1818 RIDGE ROAD
HOMEWOOD, ILLINOIS 60430
1976

Executive Office
1313 21st Avenue South, Nashville, Tennessee 37212

Library of Congress Catalog Card Number: 61–8020
International Standard Book Number: 0–917290–02–X
Printed in the United States of America

TABLE OF CONTENTS

INTRODUCTORY DISCUSSION

The *Index of Economic Articles* has been continued after a lapse of some years with Volumes XI–XV, 1969–72, which are all scheduled to appear in 1976. It is linked to the earlier volumes, I–X, in scope and content. The actual classification system, however, differs and is coordinated with the system developed by the American Economic Association Classification Committee in 1967 and used in the sections in the *Journal of Economic Literature* relating to articles and books and in the field of specialization classifications in the *American Economic Association Directory.*

Scope

This volume of the *Index* lists, both by subject category and by author, articles in major economic journals and in collective volumes published during the year 1969. It also includes articles or testimony from selected congressional committee hearings or prints published in 1969. The articles listed include all articles published in English or with English summaries in the journals and books listed below (p. xi).

Relationship to JEL

This *Index* is prepared largely as an adjunct to the bibliographic activities of the *Journal of Economic Literature (JEL).* Economies of joint production are pursued throughout the production process. Journals included are those indexed in the *JEL* quarterly; collective volumes are selected from the annotated 1969 books; the classification system is a more detailed version of the *JEL* system.

The joint production process involved computerization of the article citations, for use both in *JEL* and in the *Index.* The data-base article citations are then run through various programs. The resultant gains from a reduction in production costs involve some small losses in flexibility in arrangement and data inclusion as well as some relatively small losses with regard to proofreading and classification.

Articles without individual author(s) are omitted, except in the documents part. Relevant testimony or reports to congressional committees written by an organization are presented under that name.

Journals Included

The 182 journals listed are drawn from 220 journals representing, in general, those journals that we believe will be most helpful to research workers and teachers of economics. These journals are listed below on p. xi. The coverage is more extensive than previous volumes of the *Index of Economic Articles,* although some foreign journals included therein have been omitted.

Generally, articles, notes, communications, comments, replies, rejoinders, as well as papers and formal discussions in proceedings and review articles in the included journals have been indexed. There are some exceptions; only articles in English or with English summaries are included—this practice results in a slightly reduced coverage compared with the *JEL* quarterly. For example, articles in foreign languages are indexed in the quarterly from any journal where we regularly print English abstracts; also in some years, available foreign language skills permitted classification of such articles. Articles lacking author identification are omitted, as are articles without economic content. Identical articles appearing in two different journals in 1969 are listed from both sources.

The journal issues included are those for 1969, usually falling within a single volume. When a volume of a journal overlaps two calendar years, for example, Fall 1968 to Summer 1969, we include the issues from the two volumes relating to 1969 as best we can determine. As will be noted in the journal listings, there are a few instances where issues of journals are not included because they had not been received at the *JEL* office despite repeated requests.

Collective Volumes

The collective volumes consist of the following:

1. *Festschriften*
2. Conference publications with individual papers
3. Collected essays, original, by one or more authors
4. Collected essays, reprinted, by one or more authors
5. Proceedings volumes with individual papers not included among the journal listings
6. Books of readings

All original articles in English are indexed with the exception of unsigned articles or articles without economic content. Reprinted articles are included if they have not been indexed in the volumes of the *Index of Economic Journals* or the *Index of Economic Articles* covering the period from 1950 on, that is in Volumes IV to X.

The rule of thumb followed for the inclusion of excerpts from printed articles or books is that the excerpt should represent a substantial portion of the article or of a chapter of a book. The same article or excerpt appearing for the first time in different collective volumes in the same year is cited from both publications.

In the article citation, reference to the book in which the article appeared is by author or editor of the volume. If the same person or persons wrote or edited more than one book included in the 1969 *Index*, it is indicated by a I or II appearing immediately after the name in both the source given in the article citation and the bibliographic reference in the book listing. If the same person wrote one book and edited another in 1969, the inclusion of editor in the reference indicates which book is being cited.

The collective volumes are listed alphabetically by author or editor on pp. xvi with a full bibliographic reference. If there is more than one edition, the publisher cited is the one on the copy the *JEL* received, usually from the American publisher.

Government Documents

Selected documents (hearings and/or prints) from the following committees were examined:

House Committee on Agriculture
House Committee on Banking and Currency
House Committee on Education and Labor
House Committee on Foreign Affairs
House Committee on Government Operations
House Committee on Interstate and Foreign Commerce
House Committee on the Judiciary
House Committee on Public Works
House Committee on Science and Astronautics
House Committee on Ways and Means
House Select Committee on Government Research
House Select Committee on Small Business
Joint Economic Committee (U.S. Congress)
Senate Committee on Agriculture and Forestry
Senate Committee on Banking and Currency
Senate Committee on Commerce
Senate Committee on Finance
Senate Committee on Foreign Relations
Senate Committee on Government Operations
Senate Committee on the Judiciary

Senate Committee on Labor and Public Welfare
Senate Committee on Public Works
Senate Committee on Small Business
Senate Select Committee on Small Business
Senate Special Committee on Aging

Material with economic content, including studies, submissions, and testimony before congressional committees and committee prints, were indexed. In general these were statements and submissions by economists. In some cases, they represent statements by an organization or a government department or organization. In a departure from our procedure with articles in books and journals, these statements, even when lacking identification of individual author(s), are also included.

The following abbreviations were used in the indexed materials to indicate the document:

HCH House Committe Hearings
HCP House Committee Prints
SCH Senate Committee Hearing
SCP Senate Committee Prints
JECH Joint Economic Committee Hearing
JECP Joint Economic Committee Print

Government documents are listed on pp. xxiv. They are arranged by Committee, Hearings and Prints, and then alphabetically by title.

Arrangement

The Index consists of two parts:

1. A Subject Index in which the articles are arranged by subject according to the detailed classification system developed by the *JEL* staff from the American Economic Association Classification Committee systems.
2. An Author Index.

Subject Index

All articles are listed alphabetically under each 4-digit category. The entries are arranged alphabetically, first by author and then under particular authors by title. Since the sort is by computer and the number of programs was constrained by cost compared to frequency of usage, Part II of a two-part article may appear before Part I, or a reply to a comment before the article in question. If an article is written by more than one author, up to three authors are listed; beyond that, only the first author and the term, *et al.*

There is one exception to the alphabetical author arrangement. In the 0322 category, a subdivision of **History of Thought** entitled **Individuals,** the arrangement is first alphabetical by the individual discussed in the article and then alphabetically by the article's author.

Articles with empirical content or discussing a particular geographic area carry a geographic descriptor (see discussion below). Articles listed under subject category 1230, **Comparative Economics Studies . . .**, involve several countries. Since the number of geographic descriptors in the program is limited to five, the subject category often serves as a substitute for selecting individual countries, and these articles may carry no geographic descriptors. All articles under this category involve some empirical content.

Author Index

The Author Index is arranged alphabetically. Wherever possible the full first names and middle initial or middle name(s) are used. Wherever it could be definitely ascertained, articles by the same person were grouped together with only one listing of the name and/or initial. Authors' first names and intials are listed differently in various journals and books; for example, an individual may be identified as John L. Smith, J. L. Smith, or John Smith. Thus, despite our best efforts, we were left in doubt in several instances. Joint authors are listed up to three; beyond that, only the first author is listed, followed by *et al.* Articles by joint authors appear more than once, listed under the name of each of its authors, unless it is an *et al.* grouping. Under each author, articles are listed alphabetically. Prefix names are alphabetized according to the first *capitalized* letter. Thus, van Arkadie appears under A and D'Alabro under D.

Geographic Descriptors

Geographic descriptors appear in brackets at the end of any article entry where the article cites data from a particular country or area or refers to a specific geographic area. Research workers interested in these countries thus are made aware of the empirical content in the article. The descriptors used are countries or broader areas, such as southeast Asia (S.E. Asia); articles referring to cities or regions within a country are classified under the country. In general, the country name is written out in full with some adaptations and abbreviations, *e.g.,* U.S. is used for United States, U.K. for United Kingdom, and U.S.S.R. for Union of Soviet Socialist Republics. Abbreviations include: W. for West, E. for East, S. for South, N. for North. A shortened name such as W. Germany is used rather than the correct, but longer, Federal Republic of Germany. When broader regions are used as descriptors, the article may or may not refer to the full unit. For example, O.E.C.D. has been used at times when most, but not all, of the O.E.C.D. member countries are referred to. E.E.C. has been used at times to refer to the six and at times to the nine constituent countries.

The fact that an article carries a geographic descriptor does not necessarily preclude its being primarily theoretical in nature. Any theoretical article drawing on empirical data to demonstrate its findings will carry a geographic descriptor.

Classification System

The classification system is an expansion of the 3-digit classification system with approximately 100 subcategories used in the *Journal of Economic Literature* to a 4-digit system with approximately 300 subcategories. The classification system, itself, is shown on p. xxviii. In most cases the classification heading is self-explanatory; however, in some cases notes have been added to explain where related topics are classified. The basic approach in classification is from the point of view of the researcher rather than from the teacher. Course content does not necessarily coincide with subfields of our classification system. In all cases where there are two or more 4-digit classifications under a 3-digit category, there is a zero classification; in most instances this is labeled "General." The zero or general category has been used both as an inclusive and a residual category; thus, when the subject matter of an article covers all or most of the subcategories, that article appears in the zero or general category. For example, an article discussing *all* aspects of international trade theory appears in the general category. There are also some articles that do not fall in any of the individual subcategories, and these, too, are classified in the general or zero category.

The criterion used in the classifying process is whether a person interested in this topic would wish to have the article drawn to their attention. Slightly over half of the articles are classified in more than one subcategory.

Topical Guide to the Classification System

At the back of this book there is an alphabetical listing of standard economic terms and concepts. References are to the appropriate 4-digit classification numbers, not to page numbers.

LIST OF JOURNALS INDEXED 1969

Accounting Review, Vol. 44.

Acta Oeconomica, Vol. 6, Issue nos. 2–4.

Agricultural Economics Research, Vol. 21.

Agriculture Finance Review, Vol. 30.

American Economic Review, Vol. 59.
Includes American Economic Association **Papers and Proceedings** of the annual meeting in *59*(2).

American Economist, Vol. 13.

American Historical Review, Vol. 74.

American Journal of Agricultural Economics, Vol. 51.
Title changed from **Journal of Farm Economics** in 1968.

American Journal of Economics and Sociology, Vol. 28.

American Political Science Review, Vol. 63.

American Statistician, Vol. 23.

Annals of the American Academy of Political and Social Science, Issue nos. 382–86.

Antitrust Bulletin, Vol. 14.

Applied Economics, Vol. 1, Issue nos. 2–3.

Arquivo de Instituto Gulbenkian de Ciência, Vol. 4.

Arthaniti, Vol. 12.

Artha-Vikas, Vol. 5.

Asian Economic Review, Vol. 71, Issue nos. 2–4.

Aussenwirtschaft, Vol. 24.

Australian Economic History Review, Vol. 9.
Title changed from **Business Archives and History in 1967**; prior to 1962 entitled **Bulletin of the Business Archives Council of Australia.**

Australian Economic Papers, Vol. 8.

Australian Journal of Agricultural Economics, Vol. 13.

Banca Nazionale del Lavoro-Quarterly Review, Issue nos. 88–91.

Bancaria, Vol. 25.

Bulletin for International Fiscal Documentation, Vol. 23, Issue nos. 1–5, 7–9, 11, 12.

Bulletin of the Institute of Economics and Statistics, Vol. 31.

Business History Review, Vol. 43.
Title Changed from **Bulletin of the Business Historical Society** in 1954.

Canadian Journal of Agricultural Economics, Vol. 17.

Chinese Economic Studies, Vol. 2, Issue nos. 2–4; Vol. 5, Issue no. 1.

Czechoslovak Economic Papers, Issue no. 11.

Eastern Africa Economic Review, Vol. 1.

Eastern European Economics, Vol. 7, Issue nos. 1–4; Vol. 8, Issue no. 1.

Econometrica, Vol. 37.

Economia Internazionale, Vol. 22.

Economía Política, Vol. 6, Issue nos. 2–4.

Economic Affairs, Vol. 14, Issue no. 1–2.

Economic and Business Bulletin, Vol. 22, Issue no. 1.

Economic Development and Cultural Change, Vol. 17, Issue nos. 2–4; Vol. 18, Issue no. 1.

Journal of Economic Education, Vol. 1, Issue no. 1.

Journal of Economic History, Vol. 29.

Journal of Economic Issues, Vol. 3.

Journal of Economic Literature, Vol. 7.

Journal of Economic Theory, Vol. 1.

Journal of Finance, Vol. 24.

Journal of Financial and Quantitative Analysis, Vol. 4.

Journal of Human Resources, Vol. 4.

Journal of Industrial Economics, Vol. 17, Issue nos. 2–3; Vol. 18, Issue no. 1.

Journal of Law and Economics, Vol. 12.

Journal of Marketing Research, Vol. 6.

Journal of Money, Credit and Banking, Vol. 1.

Journal of Political Economy, Vol. 77.

Journal of Regional Science, Vol. 9.

Journal of Risk and Insurance, Vol. 36.

Journal of Royal Statistical Society, Series A, Vol. 132.

Journal of Transport Economics and Policy, Vol. 3.

Kansantaloudellinen Aikakauskirja, Vol. 65.

Kobe Economic and Business Review, Vol. 16.

Kyklos, Vol. 22.

Kyoto University Economic Review, Vol. 39.

Labor History, Vol. 10.

Land Economics, Vol. 45.

Law and Contemporary Problems, Vol. 34.

Liiketaloudellinen Aikakauskirja, Vol. 18.

Lloyds Bank Review, Issue nos. 91–94.

Malayan Economic Review, Vol. 14.

Management Accounting, Vol. 50, Issue nos. 7–12; Vol. 51, Issue nos. 1–6.

Manchester School of Economics and Social Studies, Vol. 37.
Title changed from **The Manchester School** in 1939; prior to 1932 entitled **The Manchester School of Economics, Commerce and Administration.**

Marquette Business Review, Vol. 13.

Matekon, Vol. 6, Issue no. 1.
Title changed from **Mathematical Studies in Economics and Statistics in the USSR and Eastern Europe** in 1969.

Michigan Academician, Vol. 1, Issue nos. 1–4; Vol. 2, Issue no. 1.

Michigan Law Review, Vol. 67, Issue nos. 3–8; Vol. 68, Issue nos. 1–2.

Middle East Journal, Vol. 23.

Mississippi Valley Journal of Business and Economics, Vol. 4, Issue no. 2; Vol. 5, Issue no. 1.

Mondo Aperto, Vol. 23.

Monthly Labor Review, Vol. 92.

National Institute Economic Review, Issue nos. 48–50.

National Tax Journal, Vol. 22.

National Westminster Bank Quarterly Review, February, May, August, November, 1969.

Nationaløkonomisk Tidsskrift, Vol. 107.

Nebraska Journal of Economics and Business, Vol. 8, Issue no. 1.

New England Economic Review, January–October, 1969.

New Mexico Business, Vol. 22.

New Trends in Czechoslovak Economics, Issue nos. 1–8, 1969.

Ohio State University Bulletin of Business Research, Vol. 44, Issue nos. 5–12.

Oregon Business Review, Vol. 28.

Osaka Economic Papers, Vol. 18.

Oxford Economic Papers, N. S., Vol. 21.

Pakistan Development Review, Vol. 9.

Peace Research Society International Papers, Vol. 11; Vol. 12.

Philippine Economic Journal, Vol. 8.

Political Science Quarterly, Vol. 84.

Problems of Economics, Vol. 11, Issue nos. 9–12; Vol. 12, Issue nos. 1–8.

Public Choice, Vol. 6; Vol. 7.

Public Finance, Vol. 24.

Public Policy, Vol. 18, Issue no. 1.

Quarterly Journal of Economics, Vol. 83.

Quarterly Review of Agricultural Economics, Vol. 22.

Quarterly Review of Economics and Business, Vol. 9.

Recherches Économiques de Louvain, Vol. 35.

Review of the Economic Conditions in Italy, Vol. 23, Issue nos. 1–2, 4–6.

Review of Economic Studies, Vol. 36.

Review of Economics and Statistics, Vol. 51.
Title changed from The Review of Economic Statistics in 1948.

Review of Income and Wealth, Vol. 15, Issue nos. 2–4.

Review of Marketing and Agricultural Economics, Vol. 37.

Review of Radical Political Economics, Vol. 1.

Review of Social Economy, Vol. 27.

Rivista Internazionale di Scienze Economiche e Commerciali, Vol. 16.

Revue Économique, Vol. 20.

Revue Roumaine des Sciences Sociales; Série Sciences Économiques, Vol. 13.

Schmollers Jahrbuch für Wirtschafts und Sozialwissenschaften, Vol. 89.

Schweizerische Zeitschrift für Volkswirtschaft und Statistik, Vol. 105.

Science and Society, Vol. 33.

Scottish Journal of Political Economy, Vol. 16.

Social and Economic Studies, Vol. 18.

Social Research, Vol. 36.

Social Science Quarterly, Vol. 49, Issue no. 4; Vol. 50, Issue nos. 1–3.

South African Journal of Economics, Vol. 37.

Southern Economic Journal, Vol. 35, Issue nos. 3–4; Vol. 36, Issue nos. 1–2.

Southern Quarterly, Vol. 7, Issue nos. 2–4; Vol. 8, Issue no. 1.

Soviet Studies, Vol. 20, Issue nos. 3–4; Vol. 21, Issue nos. 1–2.

Statistica, Vol. 29.

Statsøkonomisk Tidsskrift, Vol. 83.

Studii şi Cercetări Economicè, Issue nos. 1–4, 1969.

Survey of Current Business, Vol. 49.

Swedish Journal of Economics, Vol. 71.
Title changed from **Ekonomisk Tidskrift** in 1965.

Tahqiqāt eqtesādi (Quarterly Journal of Economic Research), Vol. 6.

Tijdschrfit Voor Economie, Vol. 14.

University of Missouri Business and Government Review, Vol. 10.

University of Washington Business Review, Vol. 28, Issue nos. 2–4; Vol. 29, Issue no. 1.

Water Resources Research, Vol. 5.

Weltwirtschaftliches Archiv, Vol. 103, Issue nos. 1–2; Vol. 104, Issue nos. 1–2.

Western Economic Journal, Vol. 7.

Yale Economic Essays, Vol. 9.

Yale Law Journal, Vol. 78, Issue nos. 3–8, Vol. 79, Issue nos. 1–2.

Yorkshire Bulletin of Economic and Social Research, Vol. 21.

Zeitschrift für die gesamte Staatswissenschaft, Vol. 125.

Zeitschrift für Nationalökonomie, Vol. 29.

LIST OF COLLECTIVE VOLUMES INDEXED 1969

ABSHIRE, DAVID M. AND SAMUELS, MICHAEL A., eds. *Portuguese Africa: A Handbook.* Handbooks to the Modern World. New York and London: Praeger in cooperation with the Center for Strategic and International Studies, Georgetown University, 1969.

ADELMAN, IRMA, ed. *Practical Approaches to Development Planning: Korea's Second Five-Year Plan.* Baltimore: Johns Hopkins Press, 1969.

ALEXIS, MARCUS; HOLLOWAY, ROBERT J. AND HANCOCK, ROBERT S., eds. *Empirical Foundations of Marketing: Research Findings in the Behavioral and Management Sciences.* Markham Series in Marketing. Chicago: Markham, 1969.

ALIBER, ROBERT Z., ed. *The International Market for Foreign Exchange.* Foreword by WALTER D. FACKLER. Praeger Special Studies in International Economics and Development. New York and London: Praeger in cooperation with the Graduate School of Business of the University of Chicago, 1969.

ALTING VON GEUSAU, FRANS A. M., ed. *Economic Relations after the Kennedy Round.* A publication of the John F. Kennedy Institute, Center for Atlantic Studies, Tilburg. Leyden, The Netherlands: A. W. Sijthoff, 1969.

ARNFIELD, R. V., ed. *Technological Forecasting.* Edinburgh: Edinburgh University Press; Chicago: Aldine, 1969.

ARNHOFF, FRANKLYN N.; RUBINSTEIN, ELI A. AND SPEISMAN, JOSEPH C., eds. *Manpower for Mental Health: A Constructive Survey of Mental Health Manpower in the Broader Context of Professional Force Dynamics in America Today.* Chicago: Aldine, 1969.

ARROW, KENNETH J. AND SCITOVSKY, TIBOR, eds. *Readings in Welfare Economics.* Republished Articles on Economics, Volume 12. Homewood, Ill.: Irwin; Nobleton, Ontario: Irwin-Dorsey; for the American Economic Association, 1969.

ASSOCIATION OF CANADIAN SCHOOLS OF BUSINESS. *Proceedings of the Thirteenth Annual Conference.* Toronto: York University, 1969.

BAIER, KURT AND RESCHER, NICHOLAS, eds. *Values and the Future: The Impact of Technological Change on American Values.* New York: Macmillan, Free Press; Toronto: Collier-Macmillan Canada, 1969.

BAKLANOFF, ERIC N., ed. *The Shaping of Modern Brazil.* Baton Rouge: Louisiana State University Press for the Latin American Studies Institute, 1969.

BALL, R. J. AND DOYLE, PETER, eds. *Inflation: Selected Readings.* Penguin Modern Economic Readings. Baltimore; Harmondsworth, England and Ringwood, Australia: Penguin, 1969.

BARAN, PAUL A. *The Longer View: Essays toward a Critique of Political Economy.* Edited and with an Introduction by JOHN O'NEILL. Preface by PAUL M. SWEEZY. London and New York: Monthly Review Press, 1969.

BEARD, THOMAS R., ed. *The Louisiana Economy.* Baton Rouge: Louisiana State University Press, 1969.

BECHHOFER, F., ed. *Population Growth and the Brain Drain.* Edinburgh: Edinburgh University Press; Chicago: Aldine, 1969.

BECKER, ARTHUR P., ed. *Land and Building Taxes: Their Effect on Economic Development.* Committee on Taxation, Resources and Economic Development series, No. 4. Madison and London: The University of Wisconsin Press, 1969.

BEEBY, C. E., ed. *Qualitative Aspects of Educational Planning.* Paris: UNESCO, International Institute for Educational Planning, 1969.

BEHRMAN, S. J.; CORSA, LESLIE, JR. AND FREEDMAN, RONALD, eds. *Fertility and Family Planning: A World View.* Ann Arbor: University of Michigan Press, 1969.

BELL, RODERICK; EDWARDS, DAVID V. AND WAGNER, R. HARRISON, eds. *Political Power: A Reader in Theory and Research.* New York: Macmillan, Free Press; London: Collier-Macmillan, 1969.

BEREDAY, GEORGE Z. F., ed. *Essays on World Education: The Crisis of Supply and Demand.* New York; London and Toronto: Oxford University Press, 1969.

BERND, JOSEPH L., ed. *Mathematical Applications in Political Science, IV.* Charlottesville: University Press of Virginia, 1969.

BERNSTEIN, BARTON J., ed. *Towards a New Past: Dissenting Essays in American History.* Paperback edition. New York: Vintage Books, [1967] 1969.

BHAGWATI, JAGDISH, ed. *International Trade: Selected Readings.* Penguin Modern Economics Readings. Baltimore; Harmondsworth, England and Ringwood, Australia: Penguin, 1969.

BHULESHKAR, ASHOK V., ed. *Indian Economic Thought and Development.* Jawaharlal Nehru Memorial Volume. Foreword by LORD MOUNTBATTEN. Bombay: Popular Prakashan, 1969.

BLAUG, M., ed. *Economics of Education 2: Selected Readings.* Baltimore; Harmondsworth, England and Ringwood, Australia: Penguin, 1969.

BLUMNER, SIDNEY M., ed. *Readings in Microeconomics.* Scranton, Pa.: International Textbook, 1969.

BOBROW, DAVIS B., ed. *Weapons System Decisions: Political and Psychological Perspectives on Continental Defense.* Praeger Special Studies in U.S. Economic and Social Development. New York and London: Praeger, 1969.

BORNSTEIN, MORRIS, ed. *Comparative Economic Systems: Models and Cases.* Irwin Series in Economics. Homewood, Ill.: Irwin; Nobleton, Ontario: Irwin-Dorsey, 1969.

BRAIBANTI, RALPH, ed. *Political and Administrative Development.* Duke University Commonwealth Studies Center series, No. 36. Durham, N.C.: Duke University Press, 1969.

BRONFENBRENNER, MARTIN, ed. *Is the Business Cycle Obsolete? Based on a Conference of the Social Science Research Council Committee on Economic Stability.* New York; London; Sydney and Toronto: Wiley-Interscience, 1969.

BRUNNER, KARL, ed. *Targets and Indicators of Monetary Policy.* San Francisco: Chandler, 1969.

BUCHLER, IRA R. AND NUTINI, HUGO G., eds. *Game Theory in the Behavioral Sciences.* Pittsburgh: University of Pittsburgh Press, 1969.

BURNS, ARTHUR F. *The Business Cycle in a Changing World: Essays Reprinted to Honor Dr. Burns for His 38 Years of Active Involvement in the Research and Administration of the National Bureau of Economic Research and on the Occasion of His Election as Honorary Chairman of the Bureau's Board of Directors.* Studies in business cycles, No. 18. New York and London: National Bureau of Economic Research; distributed by Columbia University Press, 1969.

BURT, ROGER, ed. *Cornish Mining: Essays on the Organisation of Cornish Mines and the Cornish Mining Economy.* New York: Kelley, 1969.

BURTON, JOHN C., ed. *Corporate Financial Reporting: Conflicts and Challenges. A Symposium.* New York: American Institute of Certified Public Accountants, 1969.

CALLOW, ALEXANDER B., JR., ed. *American Urban History: An Interpretive Reader with Commentaries.* New York; London and Toronto: Oxford University Press, 1969.

CARSBERG, B. V. AND EDEY, H. C., eds. *Modern Financial Management: Selected Readings.* Penguin Modern Management Readings. Baltimore; Harmondsworth, England and Ringwood, Australia: Penguin, 1969.

CHALMERS, ERIC B., ed. *Readings in the Euro-dollar.* London: W. P. Griffith & Sons, 1969.

CHAMBERLAIN, NEIL W., ed. *Contemporary Economic Issues.* Homewood, Ill.: Irwin; Georgetown, Ontario: Irwin-Dorsey, 1969.

CLOWER, R. W., ed. *Monetary Theory: Selected Readings.* Penguin Modern Economics Readings. Baltimore; Harmondsworth, England; and Ringwood, Australia: Penguin, 1969.

COLEMAN, D. C., ed. *Revisions in Mercantilism.* Debates in Economic History series. New York: Barnes & Noble; London: Methuen, 1969.

CONNERY, ROBERT H. AND CARALEY, DEMETRIOS, eds. *Governing the City: Challenges and Options for New York. Proceedings of the Academy of Political Science.* New York: Columbia University, 1969.

COOPER, R. N., ed. *International Finance: Selected Readings.* Baltimore, Harmondsworth, England and Ringwood, Australia: Penguin, 1969.

CRAWFORD, ELISABETH T. AND BIDERMAN, ALBERT D., eds. *Social Scientists and International Affairs: A Case for a Sociology of Social Science.* New York; London; Sydney and Toronto: Wiley, 1969.

CROUZET, F.; CHALONER, W. H. AND STERN, W. M., eds. *Essays in European Economic History, 1789–1914.* London: Edward Arnold; New York: St. Martin's Press, 1969.

DAGLI, VADILAL, ed. *The Public Sector in India: A Survey.* Commerce Economic Studies, Vol II. Bombay: Vora, 1969.

DAGLI, VADILAL, ed. *Two Decades of Indo–U.S. Relations.* Commerce Economic Studies, Vol. III. Bombay: Vora, 1969.

DESAI, V. R. MUTALIK AND GHONASGI, B. D. *Monetary Policy and Central Banking in India.* With contributions from P. R. BRAHMANANDA, ALAK GHOSH, KERSI D. DOODHA AND M. S. JOSHI. Bombay: Popular Prakashan, 1969.

DEWEY, ORVILLE. *Moral Views of Commerce, Society and Politics in Twelve Discourses.* Reprints of Economic Classics. New York: Kelley, [1838] 1969.

DOGAN, MATTEI AND ROKKAN, STEIN, eds. *Quantitative Ecological Analysis in the Social Sciences.* MIT Studies in Comparative Politics. Cambridge, Mass.: MIT Press, 1969.

DOUGAL, MERWIN D., ed. *Flood Plain Management: Iowa's Experience: Papers Presented at the Conference on Flood Plain Management, Sixth Water Resources Design Conference, Iowa State University.* Ames: Iowa State University Press, 1969.

DUESENBERRY, JAMES S.; FROMM, GARY; KLEIN, LAWRENCE R. AND KUH, EDWIN, eds. *The Brookings Model: Some Further Results.* Amsterdam and London: North Holland; Chicago: Rand McNally, 1969.

DUQUESNE, L., ET AL. *Ten Years of European Integration: Papers Presented at the Colloquy Organized by the C.E.D.E. in Montreal, March 14 and 15, 1968.* The Annals of the Centre d'Etudes et de Documentation Européennes. Papers prepared by MAURICE TORRELLI. Translated by CAMERON NISH. Montreal: Les Presses de l'École des Hautes Études Commerciales, 1969.

[EDDING, FRIEDRICH] *Economics of Education in Transition.* Edited by KLAUS HUFNER AND JENS NAUMANN. Stuttgart: Ernst Klett Verlag, 1969.

ELLIS, HOWARD S., ed. *The Economy of Brazil.* Foreword by LINCOLN GORDON. Berkeley: University of California Press, 1969.

FEDERAL RESERVE BANK OF BOSTON. *Controlling Monetary Aggregates: Proceedings of the Monetary Conference on Nantucket Island, June 8–10, 1969.* Boston: Public Information Center of Federal Reserve Bank of Boston, 1969.

FEDERAL RESERVE BANK OF CHICAGO. *Proceedings of a Conference on Bank Structure and Competition Held at the Federal Reserve Bank of Chicago, May 13–14, 1968.* Chicago: Author, 1968. (I)

FEDERAL RESERVE BANK OF CHICAGO. *Proceedings of a Conference on Bank Structure and Competition.* Chicago: Research Department, Federal Reserve Bank of Chicago, 1969. (II)

FINNEY, JOSEPH C., ed. *Cultural Change, Mental Health, and Poverty.* Lexington: University of Kentucky Press, 1969.

FLEAGLE, ROBERT G., ed. *Weather Modification: Science & Public Policy.* Public Policy Issues in Resource Management. Seattle and London: University of Washington Press, 1969.

FOX, KARL A. AND JOHNSON, D. GALE, eds. *Readings in the Economics of Agriculture.* Republished Articles on Economics series. Homewood, Ill.: Irwin; Georgetown, Ontario: Irwin-Dorsey, 1969.

FRANK, ANDRE GUNDER. *Latin America: Underdevelopment or Revolution; Essays on the Development of Underdevelopment and the Immediate Enemy.* New York and London: Monthly Review Press, 1969.

FRIEDMAN, MILTON. *The Optimum Quantity of Money and Other Essays.* Chicago: Aldine, 1969.

FRYKENBERG, ROBERT ERIC, ed. *Land Control and Social Structure in Indian History.* Madison; Milwaukee and London: University of Wisconsin Press, 1969.

FUCHS, VICTOR R., ed. *Production and Productivity in the Service Industries.* Studies in Income and Wealth, Vol. 34. New York: National Bureau of Economic Research; distributed by Columbia University Press, 1969.

GAA, CHARLES J. *Contemporary Thought on Federal Income Taxation.* Dickenson Series on Contemporary Thought in Accounting. Belmont, Calif.: Dickenson, 1969.

GALVIN, CHARLES O. AND BITTKER, BORIS I. *The Income Tax: How Progressive Should It Be?* Rational Debate Seminars, Third Series, No. 2. Washington, D.C.: American Enterprise Institute for Public Policy Research, 1969.

GAROIAN, LEON, ed. *Economics of Conglomerate Growth.* Corvallis, Ore.: Agricultural Research Foundation, Oregon State University, 1969.

[GHOSAL, U. N.] *Growth and Choice: Essays in Honour of U. N. Ghosal.* Edited by TAPAS MAJUMDAR. London: Oxford University Press, 1969.

GILROY, THOMAS P., ed. *Professional and Technical Personnel: Recruitment, Compensation, and Development.* Conference Series No. 13. Iowa City: The University of Iowa, Center for Labor and Management, 1969.

GRUB, PHILLIP D. AND HOLBIK, KAREL. *American-East European Trade: Controversy, Progress, Prospects.* Washington, D.C.: National Press, 1969.

GRUBER, WILLIAM H. AND MARQUIS, DONALD G., eds. *Factors in the Transfer of Technology.* Cambridge, Mass. and London: MIT Press, 1969.

GULICK, LUTHER AND URWICK, L., eds. *Papers on the Science of Administration.* Reprints of Economic Classics. New York: Kelley, [1937] 1969.

GUTTENTAG, JACK M. AND CAGAN, PHILIP, eds. *Essays on Interest Rates.* Vol. I. National Bureau of Economic Research, General Series, No. 88. New York and London: Columbia University Press for the N.B.E.R., 1969.

HARBERGER, ARNOLD C. AND BAILEY, MARTIN J., eds. *The Taxation of Income from Capital.* Studies of Government Finance series. Washington, D.C.: Brookings Institution, 1969.

HARDIN, CLIFFORD M., ed. *Overcoming World Hunger.* Englewood Cliffs, N.J.: Prentice-Hall, 1969.

HARRIS, J. R., ed. *Liverpool and Merseyside: Essays in the Economic and Social History of the Port and Its Hinterland.* New York: Kelley; London: Cass, 1969.

HARVEY, JOHN L. AND NEWGARDEN, ALBERT, eds. *Management Guides to Mergers and Acquisitions.* New York; London; Sydney and Toronto: Wiley-Interscience, 1969.

HAUSER, PHILIP M., ed. *The Population Dilemma.* Second edition. A publication of the American Assembly, Columbia University. Englewood Cliffs, N.J.; Sydney; Toronto and London: Prentice-Hall, [1963] 1969.

[VON HAYEK, FRIEDRICH A.] *Roads to Freedom: Essays in Honor of Friedrich A. von Hayek.* Edited by ERICH STREISSLER, GOTTFRIED HABERLER, FRIEDRICH A. LUTZ, AND FRITZ MACHLUP. New York: Kelley, 1969.

HEILBRONER, ROBERT L., ed. *Economic Means and Social Ends: Essays in Political Economics.* Englewood Cliffs, N.J.: Prentice-Hall, 1969.

HILTON, RONALD, ed. *The Movement toward Latin American Unity.* Praeger Special Studies in International Economics and Development. New York and London: Praeger in cooperation with The California Institute of International Studies, 1969.

HOROWITZ, DAVID, ed. *Corporations and the Cold War.* New York and London: Monthly Review Press, 1969.

HUGHES, HELEN AND SENG, YOU POH, eds. *Foreign Investment and Industrialisation in Singapore.* Canberra: Australian National University Press; Madison: University of Wisconsin Press, 1969.

HUGH-JONES, E. M., ed. *Economics and Technical Change: Papers Presented to Section F (Economics) and Jointly to Sections F and G (Engineering) at the 1968 Annual Meeting of the British Association for the Advancement of Science.* New York: Kelley, 1969.

HUNTER, ALEX, ed. *Monopoly and Competition: Selected Readings.* Baltimore; Harmondsworth, England and Ringwood, Australia: Penguin, 1969.

HUTCHINSON, [SIR] JOSEPH, ed. *Population and Food Supply: Essays on Human Needs and Agricultural Prospects.* London and New York: Cambridge University Press, 1969.

INDIAN SOCIETY OF AGRICULTURAL ECONOMICS. *Seminar on Foodgrains Buffer Stocks in India.* Seminar Series VIII. Bombay: Author, 1969.

JESSUP, PAUL F. *Innovations in Bank Management: Selected Readings.* New York: Holt, Rinehart and Winston, 1969.

JOHNSON, HARRY G., ed. *New Trade Strategy for the World Economy.* The Atlantic Trade Study Programme. Toronto and Buffalo: University of Toronto Press; London: George Allen and Unwin, 1969.

JOHNSON, NORMAN L. AND SMITH, HARRY, JR., eds. *New Developments in Survey Sampling: A*

Symposium of the Foundations of Survey Sampling Held at the University of North Carolina, Chapel Hill, North Carolina. New York; London; Sydney and Toronto: Wiley-Interscience, 1969.

JOHRI, C. K., ed. *Issues in Indian Labour Policy: Papers and Conclusions of the Fourth National Seminar on Industrial Relations in a Developing Economy, 1968.* New Delhi: Shri Ram Centre for Industrial Relations, 1969.

JONES, E. L. AND WOOLF, S. J., eds. *Agrarian Change and Economic Development: The Historical Problems.* London: Methuen; New York: Barnes & Noble, 1969.

KAIN, JOHN F., ed. *Race and Poverty: The Economics of Discrimination.* Modern Economic Issues. Englewood Cliffs, N.J.; London; Sydney; Toronto and Tokyo: Prentice-Hall, 1969.

KATZ, IRWIN AND GURIN, PATRICIA, eds. *Race and the Social Sciences.* London and New York: Basic Books, 1969.

KEMPNER, THOMAS, ed. *A Guide to the Study of Management.* Association of Teachers of Management Occasional Papers, No. 6. Oxford: Basil Blackwell, 1969.

KENNEDY, CHARLES J., ed. *Papers of the Sixteenth Business History Conference, February 21–22, 1969.* Lincoln: College of Business Administration, University of Nebraska for the Business History Conference, 1969.

KERR, CLARK. *Marshall, Marx and Modern Times: The Multi-dimensional Society.* The Marshall Lectures, 1967–68. New York and London: Cambridge University Press, 1969.

KHAN, AZIZUR RAHMAN, ed. *Studies on the Strategy and Technique of Development Planning.* Readings in Development Economics, No. 1. Karachi: Pakistan Institute of Development Economics, 1969.

KIKER, B. F. AND CARLSSON, ROBERT J., eds. *South Carolina Economists: Essays on the Evolution of Antebellum Economic Thought.* Essays in Economics, No. 20. Columbia: Bureau of Business and Economic Research, College of Business Administration, University of South Carolina, 1969.

KUHLMAN, JOHN M., ed. *Economic Problems and Policies.* Pacific Palisades, Calif.: Goodyear, 1969.

LANDSBERGER, HENRY A., ed. *Latin American Peasant Movements.* Ithaca, N.Y. and London: Cornell University Press, 1969.

LERNER, SHIRLEY W.; CABLE, JOHN R. AND GUPTA, S., eds. *Workshop Wage Determination.* The Commonwealth and International Library, Industrial Relations Division. Oxford; Toronto; Paris and New York: Pergamon Press, 1969.

LEYS, COLIN, ed. *Politics and Change in Developing Countries: Studies in the Theory and Practice of Development.* Institute of Development Studies at the University of Sussex. New York and London: Cambridge University Press, 1969.

LING, A. G., ET AL. *Private Capital for New Towns.* Occasional Paper No. 28. London: The Institute of Economic Affairs, 1969.

LIPSET, SEYMOUR MARTIN, ed. *Politics and the Social Sciences.* New York: Oxford University Press, 1969.

LYNN, ARTHUR D., JR., ed. *The Property Tax and Its Administration.* Madison and London: University of Wisconsin Press, 1969.

MANNE, HENRY G., ed. *Economic Policy and the Regulation of Corporate Securities: A Symposium Sponsored by The National Law Center, The George Washington University and American Enterprise Institute for Public Policy Research.* Washington, D.C.: A.E.I., 1969.

MARGOLIS, J. AND GUITTON, H., eds. *Public Economics: An Analysis of Public Production and Consumption and Their Relations to the Private Sectors: Proceedings of a Conference Held by the International Economic Association at Biarritz.* London; Melbourne and Toronto: Macmillan; New York: St. Martin's Press, 1969.

MCGRATH, MARY JEAN, ed. *Guidelines for Cooperatives in Developing Economies: A Book of Readings.* Madison: International Cooperative Training Center, University of Wisconsin, 1969.

VAN MEERHAEGHE, M. A. G., ed. *Economics: Britain and the E.E.C.* London: Longmans, 1969.

MINAR, DAVID W. AND GREER, SCOTT, eds. *The Concept of Community: Readings with Interpretations.* Chicago: Aldine, 1969.

MINCER, JACOB, ed. *Economic Forecasts and Expectations: Analyses of Forecasting Behavior and Performance.* National Bureau of Economic Research, Studies in Business Cycles, No. 19. New York and London: Columbia University Press, 1969.

MINCHINTON, W. E., ed. *Industrial South Wales, 1750–1914. Essays in Welsh Economic History.* London: Cass; New York: Kelley, 1969.

MISHAN, E. J. *Welfare Economics: Ten Introductory Essays.* Second edition. New York and Toronto: Random House [1964] 1969.

MORGAN, THEODORE AND SPOELSTRA, NYLE, eds. *Economic Interdependence in Southeast Asia.* Madison and London: University of Wisconsin Press for the Center for International Economics and Economic Development, 1969.

MORSE, CHANDLER, ET AL. *Modernization by Design: Social Change in the Twentieth Century.* Ithaca and London: Cornell University Press, 1969.

MUNDELL, ROBERT A. AND SWOBODA, ALEXANDER K., eds. *Monetary Problems of the International Economy.* Chicago: University of Chicago Press, 1969.

NADER, CLAIRE AND ZAHLAN, A. B., eds. *Science and Technology in Developing Countries: Proceedings of a Conference Held at the American University of Beirut, Lebanon.* Assisted by SORAYA ANTONIUS. New York and London: Cambridge University Press, 1969.

NATIONAL ACADEMY OF SCIENCES, NATIONAL RESEARCH COUNCIL, COMMITTEE ON RESOURCES AND MAN. *Resources and Man: A Study and Recommendations.* San Francisco: W. H. Freeman, 1969.

NAYLOR, THOMAS H., ed. *The Design of Computer Simulation Experiments.* Durham, N.C.: Duke University Press, 1969.

NISBET, CHARLES T., ed. *Latin America: Problems in Economic Development.* New York: Free Press; London: Collier-Macmillan, 1969.

NOAH, HAROLD J., ed. *The Economics of Education in the U.S.S.R.* Translated by the editor. Praeger Special Studies in International Economics and Development. New York and London: Praeger, 1969.

NONOMURA, KAZUO. *Essays on Soviet Economy.* Economic Research Series No. 10, The Institute of Economic Research, Hitotsubashi University. Tokyo: Kinokuniya Bookstore, 1969.

OFFICER, LAWRENCE H. AND WILLETT, THOMAS D., eds. *The International Monetary System: Problems and Proposals.* Modern Economics Issues. Englewood Cliffs, N.J.: Prentice-Hall, 1969.

OHKAWA, KAZUSHI; JOHNSTON, BRUCE F. AND KANEDA, HIROMITSU, eds. *Agriculture and Economic Growth: Japan's Experience.* Princeton, N.J.: Princeton University Press; Tokyo: University of Tokyo Press, 1969.

ORGANISATION FOR ECONOMIC CO-OPERATION AND DEVELOPMENT. *Low Income Groups and Methods of Dealing with Their Problems: Papers for a Trade Union Seminar.* International Seminars 1965, No. 3. Paris: O.E.C.D. Manpower and Social Affairs Directorate, Social Affairs Division, 1969.

OWEN, WYN F., ed. *American Agriculture: The Changing Structure.* Heath Studies in Economics series. Lexington, Mass.: Heath, 1969.

OZBEKHAN, HASAN AND TALBERT, GENE E., eds. *Business and Government Long Range Planning: Impacts, Problems, Opportunities: Proceedings of the Eleventh Annual Symposium on Planning.* Providence: The Institute of Management Sciences, 1969.

PANDIT, H. N., ed. *Measurement of Cost Productivity and Efficiency of Education.* India: National Council of Educational Research and Training, 1969.

PAPI, UGO AND NUNN, CHARLES, eds. *Economic Problems of Agriculture in Industrial Societies: Proceedings of a Conference Held by the International Economic Association.* New York: St. Martin's Press; London; Melbourne and Toronto: Macmillan, 1969.

PARKER, R. H. AND HARCOURT, G. C., eds. *Readings in the Concept and Measurement of Income.* London and New York: Cambridge University Press, 1969.

PEACOCK, ALAN T., ed. *Quantitative Analysis in Public Finance.* Assisted by DIETER BIEHL. Praeger Special Studies in International Economics and Development. New York and London: Praeger in cooperation with the Foundation: *Journal of Public Finance,* The Hague, 1969.

PERLOFF, HARVEY S., ed. *The Quality of the Urban Environment: Essays on "New Resources" in an Urban Age.* Washington, D.C.: Resources for the Future; distributed by Johns Hopkins Press, 1969.

PRESTON, RICHARD, ed. *Contemporary Australia: Studies in History, Politics, and Economics.*

Duke University Commonwealth-Studies Center series, Book No. 35. Durham: Duke University Press, 1969.

PROCHNOW, HERBERT V., ed. *The One-Bank Holding Company.* Chicago: Rand McNally, 1969.

PRYBYLA, JAN S., ed. *Comparative Economic Systems.* New York: Appleton-Century-Crofts, 1969.

PURSELL, CARROLL W., JR. *Readings in Technology and American Life.* New York: Oxford University Press, 1969.

ROBSON, P. AND LURY, D. A., eds. *The Economies of Africa.* Evanston, Ill.: Northwestern University Press, 1969.

ROSE, RICHARD, ed. *Policy-Making in Britain: A Reader in Government.* New York: Free Press, 1969.

RUTTAN, VERNON W.; WALDO, ARLEY D. AND HOUCK, JAMES P., eds. *Agricultural Policy in an Affluent Society.* Problems of the Modern Economy series. New York: Norton; Toronto: George J. McLeod, 1969.

SALIN, EDGAR; STOHLER, JACQUES AND PAWLOWSKY, PETER. *Notwendigkeit und Gefahr der wirtschaftlichen Konzentration in nationaler und internationaler Sicht.* Veröffentlichungen der List Gesellschaft, Vol. 62. Basel: Kyklos-Verlag; Tübingen: J. C. B. Mohr (Paul Siebeck), 1969.

SAMUELSON, PAUL A., ed. *International Economic Relations: Proceedings of the Third Congress of the International Economic Association.* London; Melbourne and Toronto: Macmillan; New York: St. Martin's Press, 1969.

SCHMANDT, HENRY J. AND BLOOMBERG, WARNER, JR., eds. *The Quality of Urban Life.* Urban Affairs Annual Reviews, Vol. 3. Beverly Hills, Calif.: Sage Publications, 1969.

SCOVILLE, WARREN C. AND LA FORCE, J. CLAYBURN, eds. *The Economic Development of Western Europe.* Volume I. *The Middle Ages and the Renaissance.* Volume II. *The Sixteenth and Seventeenth Centuries.* Volume III. *The Eighteenth and Early Nineteenth Centuries.* Volume IV. *The Late Nineteenth and Early Twentieth Centuries.* Lexington, Mass.: Heath, 1969.

SHADE, WILLIAM G. AND HERRENKOHL, ROY C., eds. *Seven on Black: Reflections on the Negro Experience in America.* Philadelphia: Lippincott, 1969.

SHERIF, MUZAFER AND SHERIF, CAROLYN W., eds. *Interdisciplinary Relationships in the Social Sciences.* Chicago: Aldine, 1969.

SIEGEL, ABRAHAM J., ed. *The Impact of Computers on Collective Bargaining.* Cambridge, Mass. and London: MIT Press, 1969.

SINICROPI, ANTHONY V. AND GILROY, THOMAS P., eds. *Collective Bargaining in the Iowa Public Sector.* Conference Series No. 14. Iowa City: The University of Iowa, Center for Labor and Management, 1969.

SMITH, ANTHONY D., ed. *Wage Policy Issues in Economic Development: Proceedings of a Symposium Held at Egelund, Denmark, by the International Institute for Labor Studies.* London; Bombay; Melbourne and Toronto: Macmillan; Dublin: Gill and Macmillan; New York: St. Martin's Press, 1969.

SOMERS, GERALD G. AND WOOD, W. D., eds. *Cost-Benefit Analysis of Manpower Policies: Proceedings of a North American Conference under the Auspices of the Center for Studies in Vocational and Technical Education, the University of Wisconsin, and the Industrial Relations Centre, Queens University; Sponsored by the Canadian Department of Manpower and Immigration and the United States Department of Labor.* Kingston, Ont.: Industrial Relations Centre, Queens University, 1969.

SOMERS, GERALD G., ed. *Essays in Industrial Relations Theory.* Ames: The Iowa State University Press, 1969. (I)

SOMERS, GERALD G., ed. *Proceedings of the Twenty-First Annual Winter Meeting, Industrial Relations Research Association.* Illinois: Author, 1969. (II)

STARLEAF, DENNIS R., ed. *Economics: Readings in Analysis and Policy.* Glenview, Ill.: Scott, Foresman, 1969.

STEWART, I. G., ed. *Economic Development and Structural Change.* Edinburgh: Edinburgh University Press; Chicago: Aldine, 1969.

STURDIVANT, FREDERICK D., ed. *The Ghetto Marketplace.* New York: Free Press, 1969.

STYKOLT, STEFAN. *Efficiency in the Open Economy: Collected Writings on Canadian Economic*

Problems and Policies. Edited with an Introduction by Anthony Scott and James D. Rae. Toronto: Oxford University Press, 1969.

Task Force on Economic Growth and Opportunity. *Rural Poverty and Regional Progress in an Urban Society.* Washington, D.C.: Chamber of Commerce of the United States, 1969.

Tax Institute of America. *Tax Impacts on Compensation: A Symposium.* Princeton: Author, 1969.

Thorbecke, Erik, ed. *The Role of Agriculture in Economic Development: A Conference of the Universities—National Bureau Committee for Economic Research.* New York and London: National Bureau of Economic Research; distributed by Columbia University Press, 1969.

[Tinbergen, Jan] *Towards Balanced International Growth: Essays Presented to J. Tinbergen.* Edited by H. C. Bos. New York: Wiley, 1969.

Trebing, Harry M. and Howard, R. Hayden, eds. *Rates of Return under Regulation: New Directions and Perspectives.* M.S.U. Public Utilities Studies. East Lansing: Institute of Public Utilities, Michigan State University, 1969.

Viser, Festus Justin, ed. *The U.S.S.R. in Today's World.* The M. L. Seidman Memorial Town Hall Lecture Series. Memphis: Memphis State University Press, 1969.

Walsh, Robert E., ed. *Sorry . . . No Government Today: Unions vs. City Hall: An Anthology.* Boston: Beacon Press, 1969.

Watson, Donald Stevenson, ed. *Price Theory in Action: A Book of Readings.* Second edition. Boston: Houghton Mifflin, [1965] 1969.

Weaver, Thomas and Magid, Alvin, eds. *Poverty: New Interdisciplinary Perspectives.* San Francisco: Chandler, 1969.

Weston, J. Fred and Peltzman, Sam, eds. *Public Policy towards Mergers.* Pacific Palisades, Calif.: Goodyear, 1969.

[White, Charles P.] *State and Local Tax Problems.* Edited by Harry L. Johnson. Knoxville: University of Tennessee Press, 1969.

Wicksell, Knut. *Selected Papers on Economic Theory.* Edited with and Introduction by Erik Lindahl. Reprints of Economic Classics. New York: Kelley, [1958] 1969.

Williams, Harold R. and Huffnagle, John D., eds. *Macroeconomic Theory: Selected Readings.* New York: Appleton-Century-Crofts, 1969.

Willis, Arthur B., ed. *Studies in Substantive Tax Reform.* Chicago: American Bar Foundation; Dallas: Southern Methodist University, 1969.

Wilson, Charles. *Economic History and the Historians: Collected Essays.* New York: Praeger, 1969.

Wolfe, J. N., ed. *Government and Nationalism in Scotland: An Enquiry by Members of the University of Edinburgh.* Edinburgh: Edinburgh University Press; Chicago: Aldine, 1969.

Wortman, Max S., Jr. *Critical Issues in Labor: Text and Readings.* New York: Macmillan; London: Collier-Macmillan, 1969.

Yanowitch, Murray, ed. *Contemporary Soviet Economics: A Collection of Readings from Soviet Sources.* Two volumes. White Plains, N.Y.: International Arts and Sciences Press, 1969.

Yesufu, T. M., ed. *Manpower Problems and Economic Development in Nigeria.* Ibadan, Nigeria; London and New York: Oxford University Press, 1969.

LIST OF GOVERNMENT DOCUMENTS INDEXED 1969

House Committee on Agriculture

Hearing

National Timber Supply Act of 1969. Subcommittee on Forests, 91st Congress, 1st session on H.R. 10325 and other bills; Serial I, May 21–23, 1969.

House Committee on Banking and Currency

Hearings

Bank Holding Company Act Amendments. 91st Congress, 1st session on H.R. 6788; pt. 1, April 15–25, 1969; pt. 2, April 29–May 6, 1969; and pt. 3, May 7–9, 1969.

Consumer Credit Regulations (Proposed Uniform Consumer Credit Code). Subcommittee on Consumer Affairs, 91st Congress, 1st session; pt. 1, Feb. 25 and 26, 1969.

Investigation of Increase in Prime Interest Rate. 91st Congress, 1st session, June 19–July 1, 1969.

National Housing Goals. Subcommittee on Housing, 91st Congress, 1st session, May 12–June 12, 1969, including model cities, May 12, 1969.

Population Trends. Ad Hoc Subcommittee on Urban Growth, 91st Congress, 1st session; pt. 1, June 3–July 31, 1969.

To Extend and Amend the Export Control Act of 1949. Subcommittee on International Trade, 91st Congress, 1st session, on H.R. 4293, May 22–July 24, 1969.

House Committee on Education and Labor

Hearings

Economic Opportunity Amendments of 1969. Ad Hoc Task Force on Poverty, 91st Congress, 1st session, on H.R. 513; pt. 2, Apr. 19–29, 1969.

Extension of Elementary and Secondary Education Programs. 91st Congress, 1st session, on H.R. 514; pt. 4, Mar. 5–10, 1969.

House Committee on Foreign Affairs

Hearings

Foreign Assistance Act of 1969. 91st Congress, 1st session, on H.R. 11792; pt. 5, July 14–18, 1969.

New Directions for the 1970's: Toward a Strategy of Inter-American Development. Subcommittee on Inter-American Affairs, 91st Congress, 1st session; pt. 1–4, Mar. 11–May 8, 1969; pt. 5, Aid Programs in Selected Latin American Countries, Feb. 25–May 1, 1969.

Overseas Private Investment Corporation: Title 2 of H.R. 11792. Subcommittee on Foreign Economic Policy, 91st Congress, 1st session, Aug. 5–Sept. 18, 1969.

House Committee on Government Operations

Hearing

Effects of Population Growth on Natural Resources and the Environment. Subcommittee on Government Operations, 91st Congress, 1st session, Sept. 15 and 16, 1969.

House Committee on Public Works

Hearing

Highway Legislation. Subcommittee on Roads, 91st Congress, 1st session, on H.R. 9446, H.R. 4808, H.R. 6785, and other related bills, May 13–June 5, 1969.

House Committee on Science and Astronautics

Hearing

Panel on Science and Technology, 10th Meeting: Science & Technology and the Cities, Proceedings. 91st Congress, 1st session, Feb. 4–6, 1969.

HOUSE COMMITTEE ON WAYS AND MEANS

Hearing

Unemployment Compensation. 91st Congress, 1st session, on H.R. 12625, Oct. 1–7, 1969.

JOINT ECONOMIC COMMITTEE

Hearings

The 1969 Economic Report of the President. 91st Congress, 1st session; pt. 2, Feb. 17–24, 1969; pt. 3, Feb. 25–Mar. 6, 1969; pt. 4, Invited Comments.

Guidelines for Estimating the Benefits of Public Expenditures. Subcommittee on Economy in Government, 91st Congress, 1st session, May 12 and 14, 1969.

Linking Reserve Creation and Development Assistance. 91st Congress, 1st session, May 28, 1969.

Public Facility Requirements over the Next Decade. Subcommittee on Economic Progress, 90th Congress, 2d session, Dec. 3 and 4, 1968.

A Review of Balance of Payments Policies. Subcommittee on International Exchange and Payments, 91st Congress, 1st session, Jan. 13–15, 1969.

Review of Federal Statistical Programs. Subcommittee on Economic Statistics, 91st Congress, 1st session, Apr. 30–May 15, 1969.

Prints

The Analysis and Evaluation of Public Expenditures: The PPB System: A Compendium of Papers Submitted to the Subcommittee on Economy in Government. 91st Congress, 1st session, 1969; v. 1, pt. 1, The Appropriate Functions of Government in an Enterprise System; pt. 2, Institutional Factors Affecting Efficient Public Expenditure Policy; and pt. 3, Some Problems of Analysis in Evaluating Public Expenditure Alternatives; v. 2, pt. 4, The Current Status of the Planning-Programming-Budgeting System; v. 3, pt. 5, The Performance of Program Budgeting and Analysis in the Federal Government; and pt. 6, Analysis and Evaluation in Major Policy Areas: Unresolved Issues and Next Steps.

The Economics and Financing of Higher Education in the United States: A Compendium of Papers. 91st Congress, 1st session, 1969.

Industrialized Housing. Subcommittee on Urban Affairs, 91st Congress, 1st session, Apr. 1969.

Innovations in Planning, Programing, and Budgeting in State and Local Governments: A Compendium of Papers Submitted to the Subcommittee on Economy in Government. 91st Congress, 1st session, 1969.

On Linking Reserve Creation and Development Assistance: A Staff Study. Subcommittee on International Exchange and Payments, 91st Congress, 1st session, Apr. 1969.

SENATE COMMITTEE ON BANKING AND CURRENCY

Hearings

Export Expansion and Regulation. Subcommittee on International Finance, 91st Congress, 1st session, on S. 813 and S. 1940, Apr. 23–May 28, 1969.

High Interest Rates. 91st Congress, 1st session, on impact of high interest rates on the economy, Mar. 25–Apr. 1, 1969.

Investment Company Amendments Act of 1969. 91st Congress, 1st session, on S. 34 and S. 296, Apr. 15–18, 1969.

SENATE COMMITTEE ON FINANCE

Hearings

Interest Equalization Tax Extension Act of 1969. 91st Congress, 1st session, on H.R. 12829, Sept. 3, 1969.

Proposed Extension of the Surcharge and Repeal of the Investment Tax Credit. 91st Congress, 1st session, on H.R. 12290, July 8–15, 1969.

Tax Credits to Stimulate Job Opportunities in Rural Areas. 91st Congress, 1st session, on S. 15, May 21 and 22, 1969.

Prints

Tax Reform Act of 1969, H.R. 13270. 91st Congress, 1st session; pt. A, Testimony To Be Received Friday, Sept. 26, 1969; pt. B, Additional Statements. (Topics: Real Estate, Depreciation Deductions and Recapture; Public Utilities Depreciation, Earnings and Profits, *etc.*)

Tax Reform Act of 1969, H.R. 13270. 91st Congress, 1st session; pt. A, Testimony To Be Received Wednesday, Oct. 1, 1969; pt. B, Additional Statements. (Topics: Natural Resources, Depletion Allowances, Exploration Expenses, Production Payments—Oil and Gas.)

Tax Reform Act of 1969, H.R. 13270. 91st Congress, 1st session; pt. A, Testimony To Be Received Thursday, Oct. 2, 1969; pt. B, Additional Statements. (Topics: General, Standard Deductions, Tax Treatment of Retired Persons, Single Persons.)

SENATE COMMITTEE ON FOREIGN RELATIONS

Hearing

Foreign Assistance Act, 1969. 91st Congress, 1st session, on S. 2347, July 14–Aug. 6, 1969.

SENATE COMMITTEE ON GOVERNMENT OPERATIONS

Hearings

To Establish a Department of Consumer Affairs. Subcommittee on Executive Reorganization, 91st Congress, 1st session, on S. 860 and S. 2045, Mar. 17–July 15, 1969.

To Establish a Select Senate Committee on Technology and the Human Environment. Subcommittee on Intergovernmental Relations, 91st Congress, 1st session, on S. Res. 78, Mar. 4–May 7, 1969.

Health Care in America. Subcommittee on Executive Reorganization, 90th Congress, 2d session; pt. 1, Apr. 22–25, 1968.

Utility Consumers' Counsel Act of 1969. Subcommittee on Intergovernmental Relations, 91st Congress, 1st session, on S. 607; pt. 6A, June 26–July 9, 1969.

Print

Planning-Programming-Budgeting: Rescuing Policy Analysis from PPBS, Subcommittee on National Security and International Operations, 91st Congress, 1st session, pursuant to S. Res. 24, 1969.

SENATE COMMITTEE ON THE JUDICIARY

Hearings

Automotive Repair Industry. Subcommittee on Antitrust and Monopoly, 90th Congress, 2d session, pursuant to S. Res. 233; pt. 1, Dec. 3–5, 1968.

Competition in Defense Procurement. Subcommittee on Antitrust and Monopoly, 90th Congress, 2d session, pursuant to S. Res. 233, June 17–21; Sept. 10, 1968.

Economic Concentration. Subcommittee on Antitrust and Monopoly, 90th Congress, 2d session, pursuant to S. Res. 233, 1968; pt. 7A, Appendix to pt. 7.

Governmental Intervention in the Market Mechanism. Subcommittee on Antitrust and Monopoly, 91st Congress, 1st session, on S. Res. 40; pt. 1, Economist's Views, Mar. 11–26, Apr. 1 and 2, 1969.

SENATE COMMITTEE ON LABOR AND PUBLIC WELFARE

Hearings

Coal Mine Health and Safety. Subcommittee on Labor, 91st Congress, 1st session, on S. 355, S. 467, S. 1094, S. 1178, S. 1300, and S. 1907; pt. 1, Feb. 27, Mar. 7–26, and May 2, 1969.

Economic Opportunity Amendments of 1969. Subcommittee on Employment, Manpower, and Poverty, 91st Congress, 1st session, on S. 1809, Apr. 23–June 6, 1969.

Indian Education. Special Subcommittee on Indian Education, 90th Congress, 1st and 2d sessions, on the study of the education of Indian children; pt. 2, Twin Oaks, Calif., Feb. 19, 1968.

Indian Education, 1969. Subcommittee on Indian Education, 91st Congress, 1st session, 1969, on policy, organization, administration, and new legislation concerning the American Indians; pt. 2, Appendix.

SENATE COMMITTEE ON PUBLIC WORKS

Hearing

Highway Beautification. Subcommittee on Roads, 91st Congress, 1st session, on S. 561 and S. 1442, June 17 and 18, 1969.

SENATE SELECT COMMITTEE ON SMALL BUSINESS

Hearings

Impact of Crime on Small Business—1969. 91st Congress, 1st session, on the impact of crime on small business; pt. 1, May 21–July 22, 1969.

Role of Giant Corporations. Subcommittee on Monopoly, 91st Congress, 1st session, on the role of giant corporations in the American and world economies; pt. 1, Automobile Industry—1969, July 9–11, 1969.

Timber Management Policies. Subcommittee on Retailing, Distribution, and Marketing Practices, 90th Congress, 2d session, on the subject: What are the wood needs of the future, and how will they be met? Nov. 26, 1968.

SENATE SPECIAL COMMITTEE ON AGING

Hearings

Costs and Delivery of Health Services to Older Americans. Subcommittee on Health of the Elderly, 90th Congress, 2d session; pt. 3—Los Angeles, Calif., Oct. 16, 1968.

Economics of Aging: Toward a Full Share in Abundance. 91st Congress, 1st session; pt. 1, Survey Hearing, Apr. 29–30, 1969; Subcommittee on Consumer Interests of the Elderly, 91st Congress, 1st session; pt. 2, Consumer Aspects, Ann Arbor, Mich., June 9, 1969.

Usefulness of the Model Cities Program to the Elderly. 90th Congress, 2d session; pt. 1, Washington, D.C., July 23, 1968.

Prints

Health Aspects of the Economics of Aging: A Working Paper in Conjunction with the Overall Study of "Economics of Aging: Toward a Full Share in Abundance." 91st Congress, 1st session, Revised, July 1969.

Social Security for the Aged: International Perspectives: A Working Paper Prepared for a Hearing on "International Perspectives on the Economics of Aging," August 25, 1969. 91st Congress, 1st session, Aug. 1969.

CLASSIFICATION SYSTEM

N.B. Editor's note. Reading this description seems to be unavoidable for anyone seeking to use this classification system.

Subject Index of Articles in Current Periodicals, Collective Volumes, and Government Documents

Abbreviated titles for journals are the same as those used in the *Journal of Economic Literature.* Full titles of Journals may be found on pages xi–xv.

Books have been identified by author or editor (noted *ed.*). In rare cases where two books by the same author appear, volumes are distinguished by I or II after the name. In some cases there appear two books by the same person, once as author, once as editor. These may be distinguished by *ed.* noted for the edited volume. Full titles and bibliographic references for books may be found on pages xvi–xxiii.

Government Documents are identified by a shortened document title, followed by an abbreviation of document type:

HCH	House Committee Hearing	*SCP*	Senate Committee Print
HCP	House Committee Print	*JECH*	Joint Economic Committee Hearing
SCH	Senate Committee Hearing	*JECP*	Joint Economic Committee Print

op. cit. is used when article and document titles are the same.

Full titles and bibliographic references for documents may be found on pages xiv–xxvii.

Geographic Descriptors when appropriate appear in brackets at the end of the article citation.

000 General Economics; Theory; History; Systems

010 General Economics

011 General Economics

0110 General

Almond, Gabriel A. Rake's or Pilgrim's Progress: From ESS to IESS. *Soc. Sci. Quart.,* September 1969, *50*(2), pp. 234–42.

Bennis, Warren G. Values and Organization in a University Social Research Group. **In** *Crawford, E. T. and Biderman, A. D., eds.,* 1969, pp. 92–99.

Boulding, Kenneth E. The Grants Economy. *Mich. Academician,* Winter 1969, *1*(1–2), pp. 3–11.

Crawford, Elisabeth T. The Informal Organization of Policy-Oriented Social Science. **In** *Crawford, E. T. and Biderman, A. D., eds.,* 1969, pp. 69–81.

De Forest, Paul. The Social Sciences in the Foreign Policy Subsystem of Congress. **In** *Crawford, E. T. and Biderman, A. D., eds.,* 1969, pp. 135–50.

Fores, M. J. No More General Theories? *Econ. J.,* March 1969, *79*(313), pp. 11–22.

Guither, Harold D. Institution Building: Training Gap in Economic and Agricultural Development. *Amer. J. Agr. Econ.,* December 1969, *51*(5), pp. 1574–77. **[G: U.S.]**

Gulick, Luther. Science, Values and Public Administration. **In** *Gulick, L. and Urwick, L., eds.,* 1969, pp. 189–95.

Hauser, Philip M. The International Encyclopedia: An Assessment of Its Goals and a Consideration of Alternatives. *Soc. Sci. Quart.,* September 1969, *50*(2), pp. 222–33.

Hermann, Donald H. J., III. From Economic Theory to Public Policy. *Univ. Wash. Bus. Rev.,* Spring 1969, *28*(3), pp. 59–64.

Marquardt, Wilhelm. German Economic Research in Africa. *Ger. Econ. Rev.,* 1969, *7*(1), pp. 71–76. **[G: W. Germany; Africa]**

Nikolitch, Radoje. I See It Differently. *Amer. J. Agr. Econ.,* December 1969, *51*(5), pp. 1629–32. **[G: U.S.]**

Opp, Karl-Dieter. Das Experiment in den Sozialwissenschafter: Einige Probleme und Vorschläge für seine effektivere Verwendung. (With English summary.) *Z. ges. Staatswiss.,* January 1969, *125* (1), pp. 106–22.

Polopolus, Leo. On Institutional Obsolescense and Innovation. *Amer. J. Agr. Econ.,* December 1969, *51*(5), pp. 1624–28. **[G: U.S.]**

Prichard, M. F. Lloyd. Economic History in New Zealand Universities. *Australian Econ. Hist. Rev.,* March 1969, *9*(1), pp. 3–8. **[G: New Zealand]**

Puu, Tönu. Causal Versus Teleological Explanation in Economics. *Swedish J. Econ.,* June 1969, *71*(2), pp. 111–26.

Robertson, H. M. The Wealth of Nations: How the National Income Is Produced, Divided Up and Spent. *S. Afr. J. Econ.,* June 1969, *37*(2), pp. 87–97.

Salant, Walter S. Writing and Reading in Economics. *J. Polit. Econ.,* Part I, July/August 1969, *77*(4), pp. 545–58.

Schmid, A. Allan. Natural Resources and Growth: Towards a Non-Marginal Political Economics. *Amer. J. Agr. Econ.,* December 1969, *51*(5), pp. 1304–13. **[G: U.S.]**

Spaeth, David H. Institutional Engineering—Venture into Applied Behavioral Science. *Amer. J. Agr. Econ.,* December 1969, *51*(5), pp. 1633–36.

Spengler, Joseph J. The Social Sciences and the New Encyclopedia: Trends and a Forecast. *Soc. Sci. Quart.,* September 1969, *50*(2), pp. 213–21.

Staats, Elmer B. Industry-Government Relationships. *Calif. Manage. Rev.,* Fall 1969, *12*(1), pp. 83–90. **[G: U.S.]**

0111 Teaching of Economics

Albakin, L. Student Responses to a Questionnaire. *Prob. Econ.,* December 1969, *12*(8), pp. 75–80. **[G: U.S.S.R.]**

Attiyeh, Richard E.; Bach, George L. and Lumsden, Keith G. The Efficiency of Programmed Learning in Teaching Economics: The Results of a Nationwide Experiment. *Amer. Econ. Rev.,* May 1969, *59*(2), pp. 217–23.

Bach, George L. The Effectiveness of Teaching Methods: A Further Note on Programmed Learning in Economics. *J. Econ. Educ.,* Fall 1969, *1*(1), pp. 56–59.

Barr, Wallace. A Basic Framework for Policy Education: Discussion. *Amer. J. Agr. Econ.,* December 1969, *51*(5), pp. 1365–67. **[G: U.S.]**

Boulding, Kenneth E. Economic Education: The Stepchild Too Is Father of the Man. *J. Econ. Educ.,* Fall 1969, *1*(1), pp. 7–11.

Bradford, Lawrence. Can Better Teaching Be Learned? *Amer. J. Agr. Econ.,* December 1969, *51*(5), pp. 1075–77. **[G: U.S.]**

Corneel, Frederic G. Tax Planning—Teaching and Practice. **In** *Gaa, C. J.,* 1969, pp. 191–204. **[G: U.S.]**

Coussy, Jean. Adjusting Economics Curricula to African Needs. *Int. Soc. Sci. J.,* 1969, *21*(3), pp. 393–405. **[G: Africa]**

Dowdy, G. T., Sr. Toward Better Undergraduate Teaching. *Amer. J. Agr. Econ.,* December 1969, *51*(5), pp. 1078–80. **[G: U.S.]**

Drake, P. J. Economics and Development. *Econ. Rec.,* September 1969, *45*(111), pp. 449–61.

Fels, Rendigs. Hard Research on a Soft Subject: Hypothesis-Testing in Economic Education. *Southern Econ. J.,* July 1969, *36*(1), pp. 1–9.

Forgács, T. Post-Graduate Training of Economists in Hungary. *Acta Oecon.,* 1969, *4*(2), pp. 205–08. **[G: Hungary]**

Frank, Andre Gunder. Economic Politics or Political Economy. **In** *Frank, A. G.,* 1969, pp. 108–21. **[G: Latin America]**

Gordon, Sanford D. The Effectiveness of Teaching Methods: Optimizing the Use of Televised Instruction. *J. Econ. Educ.,* Fall 1969, *1*(1), pp. 46–50.

Hawkins, Murray H. Involvement in Undergraduate Education. *Amer. J. Agr. Econ.,* December 1969, *51*(5), pp. 1577–82. **[G: U.S.]**

Hess, Carroll V. Social Science Needs in Agriculture and Natural Resources Curricula—The CEANAR Report. *Amer. J. Agr. Econ.,* December 1969, *51*(5), pp. 1613–17. **[G: U.S.]**

Ionescu, Constantin. Retrospectivă şi perspectivă în statistica românească în cel de-al XXV-lea an de la eliberarea patriei. (Retrospection and Prospects in Romanian Statistics in the XXVth Year Since the Eliberation of Romania. With English summary.) *Stud. Cercet. Econ.,* 1969, *3,* pp. 43–49. **[G: Romania]**

Kempner, Thomas. Economics for Business Studies. **In** *Kempner, T., ed.,* 1969, pp. 48–53.

Klos, Joseph J. and Trenton, R. W. The Effectiveness of Teaching Methods: One Semester or Two. *J. Econ. Educ.,* Fall 1969, *1*(1), pp. 51–55.

Kohlmeyer, J. B. A Basic Framework for Policy Education. *Amer. J. Agr. Econ.,* December 1969, *51*(5), pp. 1357–64. **[G: U.S.]**

Lard, Curtis F. and Martin, J. Rod. At a Crossroad: Graduate Teaching in Agricultural Economics. *Amer. J. Agr. Econ.,* December 1969, *51*(5), pp. 1569–73. **[G: U.S.]**

Lumsden, Keith G. The Effectiveness of Teaching Methods: Where We Now Stand. *J. Econ. Educ.,* Fall 1969, *1*(1), pp. 12–19.

Maher, John E. DEEP: Strengthening Economics in the Schools. *Amer. Econ. Rev.,* May 1969, *59*(2), pp. 230–38.

Manderscheid, Lester V. Better Teaching—Some Curricular Aspects. *Amer. J. Agr. Econ.,* December 1969, *51*(5), pp. 1081–84. **[G: U.S.]**

Mănescu, Manea. Present Problems of Economists' Training. *Revue Roumaine Sci. Soc. Serie Sci. Econ.,* 1969, *13*(1), pp. 3–8. **[G: Romania]**

McConnell, Campbell R. and Lamphear, Charles. The Effectiveness of Teaching Methods: Teaching Principles of Economics without Lectures. *J. Econ. Educ.,* Fall 1969, *1*(1), pp. 20–32.

Morris, O. Richard. A View from the Middle Ground. *Amer. J. Agr. Econ.,* December 1969, *51*(5), pp. 1565–68. **[G: U.S.]**

Morrison, Rodney J. Teaching Hour-Load Assignments in Economics Departments in Larger Institutions Revisited. *Amer. Econ. Rev.,* December 1969, *59*(5), pp. 960–62. **[G: U.S.]**

Paden, Donald W. and Moyer, M. Eugene. The Effectiveness of Teaching Methods: The Relative Effectiveness of Three Methods of Teaching Principles of Economics. *J. Econ. Educ.,* Fall 1969, *1*(1), pp. 33–45.

Porter, Richard L. Report on a Questionnaire Concerning the Present State of an Economics Encyclicals Course. *Rev. Soc. Econ.,* March 1969, *27*(1), pp. 41–44.

Ratchford, C. Brice. Mission of Higher Educational Institutions in Today's World. *Amer. J. Agr. Econ.,* December 1969, *51*(5), pp. 1603–12. **[G: U.S.]**

Reynolds, Lloyd G. The Efficiency of Education in Economics: Discussion. *Amer. Econ. Rev.,* May 1969, *59*(2), pp. 239–40.

Rhodes, V. James. Inter-University Collaboration in Undergraduate Teaching. *Amer. J. Agr. Econ.,* December 1969, *51*(5), pp. 1085–88. **[G: U.S.]**

Snyder, James C. Trials, Errors, and Successes in Agribusiness Education at Purdue. *Amer. J. Agr. Econ.,* December 1969, *51*(5), pp. 1218–21. **[G: U.S.]**

Steiner, Peter O. The Efficiency of Education in Economics: Discussion. *Amer. Econ. Rev.,* May 1969, *59*(2), pp. 240–42.

Thompson, Carey C. The Efficiency of Education in Economics: Discussion. *Amer. Econ. Rev.,* May 1969, *59*(2), pp. 242–43.

Tul'chinskii, L. I. Concerning Lecture Courses in the Economics of Education. **In** *Noah, H. J., ed.,* 1969, pp. 36–44. **[G: U.S.S.R.]**

Villard, Henry H. The Evaluation of Teaching Effectiveness: Where We Now Stand. *J. Econ. Educ.,* Fall 1969, *1*(1), pp. 60–66.

Welsh, Arthur L. and Fels, Rendigs. Performance on the New Test of Understanding in College Economics. *Amer. Econ. Rev.,* May 1969, *59*(2), pp. 224–29.

Woods, W. Fred. A Basic Framework for Policy Education: Discussion. *Amer. J. Agr. Econ.,* December 1969, *51*(5), pp. 1367–68. **[G: U.S.]**

0112 Role of Economics; Role of Economists

Blum, Reinhard. Die Wechselwirkungen zwischen Wirtschaftspolitik und Wirtschaftstheorie. (The Relations between Economic Policy and Economic Theory. With English summary.) *Schmollers Jahr.,* 1969, *89*(4), pp. 385–407. **[G: Germany]**

Bohnet, Michael. Wissenschaft und Entwicklungspolitik. (Science and Development. With English summary.) *Ifo-Studien,* 1969, *15*(1/2), pp. 57–92.

Buchanan, James M. A Future for "Agricultural Economics"? *Amer. J. Agr. Econ.,* December 1969, *51* (5), pp. 1027–36. **[G: U.S.]**

Buchanan, James M. Is Economics the Science of Choice? **In** *[von Hayek, Friedrich A.],* 1969, pp. 47–64.

di Fenizio, Ferdinando. Possibili valori e metodi d'indagine per "consulenti di direzione" di grandi gruppi industriali. (The Value Judgements and the Analytical Tools of a Management Consultant to a Large Industrial Company. With English summary.) *L'Industria,* April–June 1969, (2), pp. 147–58. **[G: Italy]**

Kaysen, Carl. Model Makers and Decision Makers: Economists and the Policy Process. **In** *Heilbroner, R. L., ed.,* 1969, pp. 137–53.

Parish, R. M. Some Thoughts on the Role of the Agricultural Economics Profession in Australia. *Australian J. Agr. Econ.,* June 1969, *13*(1), pp. 1–7. **[G: Australia]**

Rusanov, E. S. Methodology. **In** *Noah, H. J., ed.,* 1969, pp. 20–22. **[G: U.S.S.R.]**

Shils, Edward A. Social Science and Social Policy. **In** *Crawford, E. T. and Biderman, A. D., eds.,* 1969, pp. 35–49.

Simkin, C. G. F. Keynes's Grandchildren. *Australian Econ. Pap.,* December 1969, *8*(13), pp. 122–33.

Timm, Tyrus R. The Meaning to Research and Extension. *Amer. J. Agr. Econ.,* December 1969, *51* (5), pp. 1618–23. **[G: U.S.]**

Weeks, John. Political Economy and the Politics of Economists. *Rev. Radical Polit. Econ.,* May 1969, *1*(1), pp. 1–10.

0113 Relation of Economics to Other Disciplines

Baran, Paul A. Marxism and Psychoanalysis. **In** *Baran, P. A.,* 1969, pp. 92–111.

D'Ambrosio, Charles A. Asset Pricing, Time, and Causality—An Introspective View of Capital Theory. *Rev. Soc. Econ.,* March 1969, *27*(1), pp. 1–12.

Davis, Otto A. Notes on Strategy and Methodology for a Scientific Political Science. **In** *Bernd, J. L., ed.,* 1969, pp. 22–38.

Gurwitsch, Aron. Social Science and Natural Science: Methodological Reflections on Lowe's *On Economic Knowledge.* **In** *Heilbroner, R. L., ed.,* 1969, pp. 37–55.

Hargreaves, Herbert W. Social Scientists and Economists. **In** *Finney, J. C., ed.,* 1969, pp. 222–33.

Linstromberg, R. C. The Philosophy of Science and Alternative Approaches to Economic Thought. *J. Econ. Issues,* June 1969, *3*(2), pp. 176–91.

Lipset, Seymour Martin. Politics and the Social Sciences: Introduction. **In** *Lipset, S. M., ed.,* 1969, pp. vii–xxii.

Mitchell, William C. The Shape of Political Theory to Come: From Political Sociology to Political Economy. **In** *Lipset, S. M., ed.,* 1969, pp. 101–36.

Nagel, Ernest. Method in Social and Natural Science. **In** *Heilbroner, R. L., ed.,* 1969, pp. 57–66.

Olson, Mancur, Jr. The Relationship Between Economics and the Other Social Sciences: The Province of a "Social Report." **In** *Lipset, S. M., ed.,* 1969, pp. 137–62.

Popper, Karl R. A Pluralist Approach to the Philosophy of History. **In** *[von Hayek, Friedrich A.],* 1969, pp. 181–200.

Spengler, Joseph J. Is Social Science Ready? *Soc. Sci. Quart.,* December 1969, *50*(3), pp. 449–68.

0114 Relation of Economics to Social Values

Boulding, Kenneth E. Economics as a Moral Science. *Amer. Econ. Rev.,* March 1969, *59*(1), pp. 1–12.

Boulding, Kenneth E. The Emerging Superculture. **In** *Baier, K. and Rescher, N., eds.,* 1969, pp. 336–50.

Braybrooke, David. Private Production of Public Goods. **In** *Baier, K. and Rescher, N., eds.,* 1969, pp. 368–88.

Breton, Albert and Breton, Raymond. An Economic Theory of Social Movements. *Amer. Econ. Rev.,* May 1969, *59*(2), pp. 198–205.

Bronfenbrenner, Martin. Economic Consequences of Technological Change. **In** *Baier, K. and Rescher, N., eds.,* 1969, pp. 453–71.

Covi, Antonio M. Ideologia, utopia e sottosviluppo contro la società capitalistica. (Ideology, Utopia and Underdevelopment versus the Capitalistic Society. With English summary.) *Rivista Int. Sci. Econ. Com.,* January 1969, *16*(1), pp. 79–99.

Dewey, Orville. On the Moral Laws of Contracts. **In** *Dewey, O.,* 1969, pp. 9–47.

Dewey, Orville. On the Moral Laws of Trade. **In** *Dewey, O.,* 1969, pp. 48–73.

Dewey, Orville. On the Moral Limits of Accumulation. **In** *Dewey, O.,* 1969, pp. 99–116.

Dewey, Orville. On the Natural and Artificial Relations of Society. **In** *Dewey, O.,* 1969, pp. 117–44.

Dewey, Orville. On the Uses of Labor, and a Passion for a Fortune. **In** *Dewey, O.,* 1969, pp. 74–98.

Edel, Abraham. Ends, Commitments, and the Place of Ignorance. **In** *Heilbroner, R. L., ed.,* 1969, pp. 89–97.

Flammang, Robert A. Communications. *J. Econ. Issues,* June 1969, *3*(2), pp. 213–18.

Galbraith, John Kenneth. Technology, Planning and Organization. **In** *Baier, K. and Rescher, N., eds.,* 1969, pp. 353–67.

Gold, Bela. The Framework of Decision for Major Technological Innovation. **In** *Baier, K. and Rescher, N., eds.,* 1969, pp. 389–430.

Gold, Sonia S. The Professional Commitment of Educated Women. **In** *Baier, K. and Rescher, N., eds.,* 1969, pp. 266–93.

Gordon, Theodore J. The Feedback between Technology and Values. **In** *Baier, K. and Rescher, N., eds.,* 1969, pp. 148–92.

Grether, E. T. Business Responsibility Toward the Market. *Calif. Manage. Rev.,* Fall 1969, *12*(1), pp. 33–42.

Gruchy, Allan G. Neoinstitutionalism and the Economics of Dissent. *J. Econ. Issues,* March 1969, *3* (1), pp. 3–17.

Hazard, Leland. Challenges for Urban Policy. **In** *Baier, K. and Rescher, N., eds.,* 1969, pp. 320–35.

Helmer, Olaf. Simulating the Values of the Future. **In** *Baier, K. and Rescher, N., eds.,* 1969, pp. 193–214.

Jonas, Hans. Economic Knowledge and the Critique of Goals. **In** *Heilbroner, R. L., ed.,* 1969, pp. 67–87.

de Jouvenel, Bertrand. Technology as a Means. **In** *Baier, K. and Rescher, N., eds.,* 1969, pp. 217–32.

Lowe, Adolph. Economic Means and Social Ends: A Rejoinder. **In** *Heilbroner, R. L., ed.,* 1969, pp. 167–99.

Lowe, Adolph. Toward a Science of Political Economics. **In** *Heilbroner, R. L., ed.,* 1969, pp. 1–36.

Machlup, Fritz. Liberalism and the Choice of Freedoms. **In** *[von Hayek, Friedrich A.],* 1969, pp. 117–46.

Powelson, John P. Economic Attitudes in Latin America and the United States. **In** *Baier, K. and Rescher, N., eds.,* 1969, pp. 233–65. **[G: Latin America; U.S.]**

Price, Don K. The Structure of Policy. **In** *Crawford, E. T. and Biderman, A. D., eds.,* 1969, pp. 61–68.

Schneewind, J. B. Technology, Ways of Living, and Values in 19th Century England. **In** *Baier, K. and Rescher, N., eds.,* 1969, pp. 110–32. **[G: U.K.]**

Schweitzer, Arthur. Goals in Social Economics. *J. Econ. Issues,* June 1969, *3*(2), pp. 147–65.

Sethi, S. Prakash and Votaw, Dow. Do We Need a New Corporate Response to a Changing Social Environment? Part II. *Calif. Manage. Rev.,* Fall 1969, *12*(1), pp. 17–31.

Votaw, Dow and Sethi, S. Prakash. Do We Need a New Corporate Response to a Changing Social Environment? Part I. *Calif. Manage. Rev.,* Fall 1969, *12*(1), pp. 3–16.

Ward, Benjamin. Problems in the Theory of Public Choice: Discussion. *Amer. Econ. Rev.,* May 1969, *59*(2), pp. 214–16.

Wilson, James A. Motivation underlying the Brain Drain. **In** *Baier, K. and Rescher, N., eds.,* 1969, pp. 431–52. **[G: U.K.]**

Zweig, Michael. Political Economy and the "National Interest." *Rev. Radical Polit. Econ.,* May 1969, *1*(1), pp. 11–35. **[G: U.S.]**

0115 Methods Used by Economists

Herman, Barry. On Muddled Methods and Their Meaning. *Rev. Radical Polit. Econ.,* May 1969, *1* (1), pp. 75–84.

Lerner, Abba P. On Instrumental Analysis. **In** *Heilbroner, R. L., ed.,* 1969, pp. 131–36.

Nagel, Ernest. Method in Social and Natural Science. **In** *Heilbroner, R. L., ed.,* 1969, pp. 57–66.

Wallich, Henry C. Instrumental Analysis and the Decisional Process: A Critique. **In** *Heilbroner, R. L., ed.,* 1969, pp. 155–65.

020 General Economic Theory

021 General Equilibrium Theory

0210 General

Alchian, Armen A. Information Costs, Pricing, and Resource Unemployment. *Western Econ. J.,* June 1969, *7*(2), pp. 109–28.

Ayres, Robert U. and Kneese, Allen V. Production, Consumption, and Externalities. *Amer. Econ. Rev.,* June 1969, *59*(3), pp. 282–97.

Balassa, Bela. Centralization and Decentralization in Economic Systems: Discussion. *Amer. Econ. Rev.,* May 1969, *59*(2), pp. 533–37.

Cornwall, Richard R. The Use of Prices to Characterize the Core of an Economy. *J. Econ. Theory,* December 1969, *1*(4), pp. 353–73.

Fourgeaud, Claude. Contribution à l'Étude du Rôle des Administrations dans la Théorie Mathématique de l'Équilibre et de l'Optimum. (With English summary.) *Econometrica,* April 1969, *37* (2), pp. 307–23.

Ganguly, Subrata K. The Perfectly Competitive Production of Collective Goods: Comment. *Rev. Econ. Statist.,* November 1969, *51*(4), pp. 478–79.

Grossman, Herschel I. Theories of Markets without Recontracting. *J. Econ. Theory,* December 1969, *1*(4), pp. 476–79.

Hansen, Terje. A Note on the Limit of the Core of an Exchange Economy. *Int. Econ. Rev.,* October 1969, *10*(3), pp. 479–83.

Hurwicz, Leonid. On the Concept and Possibility of Informational Decentralization. *Amer. Econ. Rev.,* May 1969, *59*(2), pp. 513–24.

Isard, Walter. Toward a More Adequate General Regional Theory and Approach to Conflict Resolution. *Peace Res. Soc. Internat. Pap.,* 1969, *11,* pp. 1–21.

Kamien, Morton I. and Schwartz, Nancy L. Induced Factor Augmenting Technical Progress from a Microeconomic Viewpoint. *Econometrica,* October 1969, *37*(4), pp. 668–84.

Levin, A. The Market in the System of Socialist Reproduction. The Equilibrium Price Principle. *Prob. Econ.,* November 1969, *12*(7), pp. 30–48.

Lloyd, Peter J. Qualitative Calculus and Comparative Static Analysis. *Econ. Rec.,* September 1969, *45*(111), pp. 343–53.

McFadden, Daniel. A Simple Remark on the Second Best Pareto Optimality of Market Equilibria. *J. Econ. Theory,* June 1969, *1*(1), pp. 26–38.

Mirrlees, James A. The Dynamic Nonsubstitution Theorem. *Rev. Econ. Stud.,* January 1969, *36* (105), pp. 67–76.

Morrison, Clarence C. Marginal Cost Pricing and the Theory of Second Best. *Western Econ. J.,* June 1969, *7*(2), pp. 145–52.

Nicola, Pier Carlo. Equilibrio economico generale di tipo concorrenziale in condizioni dinamiche. (General Competitive Equilibrium under Dynamic Conditions—Part I. With English summary.) *L'Industria,* January–March 1969, (1), pp. 3–16.

Niehans, Jürg. The Neoclassical Dichotomy as a Controlled Experiment. *J. Polit. Econ.,* Part I, July/August 1969, *77*(4), pp. 504–11.

Owen, Bruce M. The Perfectly Competitive Production of Collective Goods: Comment. *Rev. Econ. Statist.,* November 1969, *51*(4), pp. 475–76.

Pelikán, Pavel. Language as a Limiting Factor for Centralization. *Amer. Econ. Rev.,* Part I, September 1969, *59*(4), pp. 625–31.

Rodgers, James D. The Perfectly Competitive Production of Collective Goods: Comment. *Rev. Econ. Statist.,* November 1969, *51*(4), pp. 476–78.

Scarf, Herbert. An Example of an Algorithm for Calculating General Equilibrium Prices. *Amer. Econ. Rev.*, Part I, September 1969, *59*(4), pp. 669–77.

Schmeidler, David. Competitive Equilibria in Markets with a Continuum of Traders and Incomplete Preferences. *Econometrica,* October 1969, *37*(4), pp. 578–85.

Shapley, Lloyd S. and Shubik, Martin. On the Core of an Economic System with Externalities. *Amer. Econ. Rev.*, Part I, September 1969, *59*(4), pp. 678–84.

Starr, Ross M. Quasi-Equilibria in Markets with Non-Convex Preferences. *Econometrica,* January 1969, *37*(1), pp. 25–38.

Stigum, Bernt P. Competitive Equilibria under Uncertainty. *Quart. J. Econ.*, November 1969, *83*(4), pp. 533–61.

Takayama, Akira. On a 'Concave' Contract Curve. *Australian Econ. Pap.*, December 1969, *8*(13), pp. 232–38.

Thompson, Earl A. The Perfectly Competitive Production of Collective Goods: Reply. *Rev. Econ. Statist.*, November 1969, *51*(4), pp. 479–82.

Veendorp, E. C. H. A Theorem on Non-tâtonnement Stability: A Comment. *Econometrica,* January 1969, *37*(1), pp. 142–43.

Wegge, Leon L. F. and Kemp, Murray C. Generalizations of the Stolper-Samuelson and Samuelson-Rybczynski Theorems in Terms of Conditional Input-Output Coefficients. *Int. Econ. Rev.*, October 1969, *10*(3), pp. 414–25.

022 Microeconomic Theory

0220 General

Alchian, Armen A. Information Costs, Pricing, and Resource Unemployment. *Western Econ. J.*, June 1969, *7*(2), pp. 109–28.

Bagiotti, Tullio. Parole e fatti sulla massimizzazione del profitto. (Words and Facts on Profit Maximization. With English summary.) *Rivista Int. Sci. Econ. Com.*, July 1969, *16*(7), pp. 637–51.

Barten, A. P.; Kloek, T. and Lempers, F. B. A Note on a Class of Utility and Production Functions Yielding Everywhere Differentiable Demand Functions. *Rev. Econ. Stud.*, January 1969, *36* (105), pp. 109–11.

Brechling, Frank. Wage-Price Dynamics, Inflation, and Unemployment: Discussion. *Amer. Econ. Rev.*, May 1969, *59*(2), pp. 161–62.

Byerlee, D. R. and Anderson, James R. Value of Predictors of Uncontrolled Factors in Response Functions. *Australian J. Agr. Econ.*, December 1969, *13*(2), pp. 118–27.

Caselli, Lorenzo. Dal profitto alla sopravvivenza: considerazioni in tema di finalità d'impresa. (From Profit to Survival—Remarks on Firm's Aims. With English summary.) *L'Impresa,* March/April 1969, *11*(2), pp. 126–32.

Dickson, Harald. Marginal Cost and Marginal Revenue in Elementary Treatment of the Problem of Profit Maximization. *Swedish J. Econ.*, June 1969, *71*(2), pp. 127–31.

Eckstein, Otto. Wage-Price Dynamics, Inflation, and Unemployment: Discussion. *Amer. Econ. Rev.*, May 1969, *59*(2), pp. 162–64.

Edwards, John B. and Orcutt, Guy H. Should Aggregation Prior to Estimation Be the Rule? *Rev. Econ. Statist.*, November 1969, *51*(4), pp. 409–20.

Hadar, Josef. Optimality of Imperfectly Competitive Resource Allocation. *Western Econ. J.*, March 1969, *7*(1), pp. 51–56.

Kemp, Murray C. and Wegge, Leon L. F. On the Relation between Commodity Prices and Factor Rewards. *Int. Econ. Rev.*, October 1969, *10*(3), pp. 407–13.

Lester, Richard A. Wage-Price Dynamics, Inflation, and Unemployment: Discussion. *Amer. Econ. Rev.*, May 1969, *59*(2), pp. 164–67.

Levhari, David and Srinivasan, T. N. Durability of Consumption Goods: Competition Versus Monopoly. *Amer. Econ. Rev.*, March 1969, *59*(1), pp. 102–07.

Machol, Robert E. and Lerner, Eugene M. Risk, Ruin and Investment Analysis. *J. Financial Quant. Anal.*, December 1969, *4*(4), pp. 473–92.

Magnani, Italo. Professor Scitovsky on Profit Maximization. *Rivista Int. Sci. Econ. Com.*, July 1969, *16* (7), pp. 652–63.

Mainander, Nils. Den samhällsekonomiska lönsamheten—praktiska kalkylmöjligheter. (Profitability to the Community—Its Calculability in Practice. With English summary.) *Econ. Samfundets Tidskr.*, 1969, *22*(2), pp. 81–94.

McKean, John R. A Note on Administered Prices with Fluctuating Demand. *J. Financial Quant. Anal.*, March 1969, *4*(1), pp. 15–23.

Meinander, Nils. Den Samhällsekonomiska lönsamheten—analys av begreppet. (An Analysis of the Concept "Profitability to the Society." With English summary.) *Econ. Samfundets Tidskr.*, 1969, *22*(1), pp. 3–19.

Misra, P. N. A Note on Linear Aggregation of Economic Relations. *Int. Econ. Rev.*, June 1969, *10*(2), pp. 247–49.

Phelps, Edmund S. The New Microeconomics in Inflation and Employment Theory. *Amer. Econ. Rev.*, May 1969, *59*(2), pp. 147–60.

Rasmussen, Arne. How Sensitive are the Optimal Points of Micro-economics? *Liiketaloudellinen Aikak.*, 1969, *18*(1), pp. 61–67.

Rasmussen, P. Nørregaard. How to Behave—as a Speculator. *Weltwirtsch. Arch.*, 1969, *103*(2), pp. 328–32.

Schmeidler, David. Competitive Equilibria in Markets with a Continuum of Traders and Incomplete Preferences. *Econometrica,* October 1969, *37*(4), pp. 578–85.

Shapley, Lloyd S. and Shubik, Martin. Pure Competition, Coalitional Power, and Fair Division. *Int. Econ. Rev.*, October 1969, *10*(3), pp. 337–62.

Stigum, Bernt P. Competitive Equilibria under Uncertainty. *Quart. J. Econ.*, November 1969, *83*(4), pp. 533–61.

Takayama, Akira. On a 'Concave' Contract Curve. *Australian Econ. Pap.*, December 1969, *8*(13), pp. 232–38.

Typolt, Jiří. Economic Policy and Prices. *New Trends Czech. Econ.*, July 1969, (4), pp. 89–102. **[G: Czechoslovakia]**

Videnov, Ivan. Theoretical Problems of Wholesale Prices. *Eastern Europ. Econ.,* Summer 1969, *7*(4), pp. 3–12.

Weinschenck, G.; Henrichsmeyer, W. and Aldinger, F. The Theory of Spatial Equilibrium and Optimal Location in Agriculture: A Survey. *Rev. Marketing Agr. Econ.,* March 1969, *37*(1), pp. 3–70.

0222 Theory of the Household (consumer demand)

Arditti, Fred D. A Utility Function Depending on the First Three Moments: Reply. *J. Finance,* September 1969, *24*(4), pp. 720.

Arrow, Kenneth J. and Kurz, Mordecai. Optimal Consumer Allocation over an Infinite Horizon. *J. Econ. Theory,* June 1969, *1*(1), pp. 68–91.

Borch, Karl. A Note on Uncertainty and Indifference Curves. *Rev. Econ. Stud.,* January 1969, *36*(105), pp. 1–4.

Bower, Richard S. and Wippern, Ronald F. Risk-Return Measurement in Portfolio Selection and Performance Appraisal Models: Progress Report. *J. Financial Quant. Anal.,* December 1969, *4*(4), pp. 417–47.

Cass, David. Resource Allocation with Probabilistic Individual Preferences: Discussion. *Amer. Econ. Rev.,* May 1969, *59*(2), pp. 562–63.

Claassen, Emil M. Stock-Flow Decisions and Full Equilibrium. *Kyklos,* 1969, *22*(3), pp. 493–505.

Deaglio, Mario. La scelta tra maggior reddito e maggior tempo libero. Un'analisi del comportamento del lavoratore. (The Choice between Greater Income and More Leisure: A Study in the Behaviour of the Worker. With English summary.) *L'Industria,* July–September 1969, (3), pp. 358–82.

Feldstein, Martin S. Mean-Variance Analysis in the Theory of Liquidity Preference and Portfolio Selection. *Rev. Econ. Stud.,* January 1969, *36*(105), pp. 5–12.

Fishburn, Peter C. A Study of Independence in Multivariate Utility Theory. *Econometrica,* January 1969, *37*(1), pp. 107–21.

Flemming, J. S. The Utility of Wealth and the Utility of Windfalls. *Rev. Econ. Stud.,* January 1969, *36* (105), pp. 55–66.

Glückaufová, Dagmar. O jedné axiomatice teorie užitku vedoucí k tzv. nepřímé užitkové funkci. (One Axiomatics of the Utility Theory Tending to so Called Indirect Utility Function. With English summary.) *Ekon.-Mat. Obzor,* 1969, *5*(4), pp. 423–41.

Goodfellow, Gordon P., Jr. and Sweeney, Vernon E. Vertically Parallel Indifference Curves with a Non-Constant Marginal Utility of Money. *Amer. Econ.,* Fall 1969, *13*(2), pp. 81–86.

Gottinger, Hans-Werner. Beiträge zur funktionalen Separabilität bei Nutzenfunktionen (Teil I). (With English summary.) *Z. ges. Staatswiss.,* July 1969, *125*(3), pp. 406–46.

Gottinger, Hans-Werner. Beiträge zur funktionalen Separabilität bei Nutzenfunktionen (Teil II). (With English summary.) *Z. ges. Staatswiss.,* October 1969, *125*(4), pp. 606–23.

Gottinger, Hans-Werner. Die Existenz einiger Klassen deterministischer Nutzenfunktionen. (Existence of Some Classes of Deterministic Utility Functions. With English summary.) *Jahr. Nationalökon. Statist.,* July 1969, *183*(2), pp. 97–124.

Gould, John P. The Expected Utility Hypothesis and the Selection of Optimal Deductibles for a Given Insurance Policy. *J. Bus.,* April 1969, *42*(2), pp. 143–51.

Gould, John P. and Segall, Joel. The Substitution Effects of Transportation Costs. *J. Polit. Econ.,* January/February 1969, *77*(1), pp. 130–37.

Hadar, Josef and Russell, William R. Rules for Ordering Uncertain Prospects. *Amer. Econ. Rev.,* March 1969, *59*(1), pp. 25–34.

Hagen, Ole. Separation of Cardinal Utility and Specific Utility of Risk in Theory of Choices under Uncertainty. *Statsokon. Tidsskr.,* October 1969, *83*(3), pp. 81–107.

Hakansson, Nils H. Optimal Investment and Consumption Strategies under Risk, an Uncertain Lifetime, and Insurance. *Int. Econ. Rev.,* October 1969, *10*(3), pp. 443–66.

Hanoch, G. and Levy, Haim. The Efficiency Analysis of Choices Involving Risk. *Rev. Econ. Stud.,* July 1969, *36*(107), pp. 335–46.

Hansen, Terje. A Note on the Limit of the Core of an Exchange Economy. *Int. Econ. Rev.,* October 1969, *10*(3), pp. 479–83.

Hicks, John R. Direct and Indirect Additivity. *Econometrica,* April 1969, *37*(2), pp. 353–54.

Hillinger, C. The Measurement of Utility. *Rev. Econ. Stud.,* January 1969, *36*(105), pp. 111–16.

Hoa, Tran Van. Consumer Demand and Welfare Indexes: A Comparative Study for the United Kingdom and Australia. *Economica, N.S.,* November 1969, *36*(144), pp. 409–25. **[G: U.K.; Australia]**

Ichiishi, T. Directly Additive Utility and Constant Marginal Budget Shares. *Rev. Econ. Stud.,* April 1969, *36*(106), pp. 251–56.

Ireland, Thomas R. The Calculus of Philanthropy. *Public Choice,* Fall 1969, *7,* pp. 23–31.

Johansen, Leif. On the Relationships between Some Systems of Demand Functions. *Liiketaloudellinen Aikak.,* 1969, *18*(1), pp. 30–41.

Jones-Lee, Michael. Valuation of Reduction in Probability of Death by Road Accident. *J. Transp. Econ. Policy,* January 1969, *3*(1), pp. 37–47.

Kalman, P. J. Classes of Utility Functions Admitting Tyrni's Homogeneous Saving Function. *Rev. Econ. Stud.,* January 1969, *36*(105), pp. 122–24.

Koch, James V. The Homogeneity Assumption and Financial Asset Demand Functions. *Quart. Rev. Econ. Bus.,* Winter 1969, *9*(4), pp. 57–65. **[G: U.S.]**

Lau, Lawrence J. Duality and the Structure of Utility Functions. *J. Econ. Theory,* December 1969, *1*(4), pp. 374–96.

Lee, Dwight R. Utility Analysis and Repetitive Gambling. *Amer. Econ.,* Fall 1969, *13*(2), pp. 87–91.

Levy, Haim. A Utility Function Depending on the First Three Moments: Comment. *J. Finance,* September 1969, *24*(4), pp. 715–19.

Liebhafsky, H. H. New Thoughts About Inferior Goods. *Amer. Econ. Rev.,* December 1969, *59*(5), pp. 931–34.

Lin, Chi-Yuan and Berger, Paul D. On the Selling Price and Buying Price of a Lottery. *Amer. Statist.,* December 1969, *23*(5), pp. 25–26.

Lindsay, Cotton M. Option Demand and Consumer's Surplus. *Quart. J. Econ.,* May 1969, *83*(2), pp. 344–46.

MacCrimmon, K. R. and Toda, M. The Experimental Determination of Indifference Curves. *Rev. Econ. Stud.,* October 1969, *36*(108), pp. 433–51.

Majumdar, Tapas. Revealed Preference and the Demand Theorem in a Not Necessarily Competitive Market. *Quart. J. Econ.,* February 1969, *83*(1), pp. 167–70.

Martelli, Antonio. Vecchie e nuove teorie sul consumatore. (Old and New Theories on the Consumer: Present Situation. With English summary.) *L'Impresa,* March/April 1969, *11*(2), pp. 133–37.

Massell, Benton F. Consistent Estimation of Expenditure Elasticities from Cross-Section Data on Households Producing Partly for Subsistence. *Rev. Econ. Statist.,* May 1969, *51*(2), pp. 136–42. **[G: Kenya]**

Michelson, Stephan. Rational Income Decisions of Negroes and Everybody Else. *Ind. Lab. Relat. Rev.,* October 1969, *23*(1), pp. 15–28.

Mossin, Jan. A Note on Uncertainty and Preferences in a Temporal Context. *Amer. Econ. Rev.,* March 1969, *59*(1), pp. 172–74.

Murphy, K. T. A Note on the Measurement of Price Elasticity of Demand. *Amer. J. Agr. Econ.,* August 1969, *51*(3), pp. 691–92.

Nicosia, Francesco M. Perceived Risk, Information Processing, and Consumer Behavior: A Review Article. *J. Bus.,* April 1969, *42*(2), pp. 162–66.

Parks, Richard W. Systems of Demand Equations: An Empirical Comparison of Alternative Functional Forms. *Econometrica,* October 1969, *37*(4), pp. 629–50.

Pollak, Robert A. Conditional Demand Functions and Consumption Theory. *Quart. J. Econ.,* February 1969, *83*(1), pp. 60–78.

Rahman, Anisur. Intertemporal Equity and Elasticity of Marginal Utility from Consumption. *Oxford Econ. Pap.,* March 1969, *21*(1), pp. 29–34.

Samuelson, Paul A. Corrected Formulation of Direct and Indirect Additivity. *Econometrica,* April 1969, *37*(2), pp. 355–59.

Sandmo, Agnar. Capital Risk, Consumption, and Portfolio Choice. *Econometrica,* October 1969, *37* (4), pp. 586–99.

Schmidt, Wilson. Charitable Exploitation. *Public Choice,* Spring 1969, *6,* pp. 103–04.

Sen, Amartya K. Quasi-Transitivity, Rational Choice and Collective Decisions. *Rev. Econ. Stud.,* July 1969, *36*(107), pp. 381–93.

Smith, Vernon L. Measuring Nonmonetary Utilities in Uncertain Choices: The Ellsberg Urn. *Quart. J. Econ.,* May 1969, *83*(2), pp. 324–29.

Stiglitz, Joseph E. Behavior Towards Risk with Many Commodities. *Econometrica,* October 1969, *37* (4), pp. 660–67.

Stiglitz, Joseph E. The Effects of Income, Wealth, and Capital Gains Taxation on Risk-Taking. *Quart. J. Econ.,* May 1969, *83*(2), pp. 263–83.

Tobin, James. Comment on Borch and Feldstein. *Rev. Econ. Stud.,* January 1969, *36*(105), pp. 13–14.

Tomasini, Luigi M. Funzioni di utilità, teoria del consumo e stima della domanda (II). (Utility Functions, Consumption Theories and Demand Estimation (II). With English summary.) *L'Industria,* October–December 1969, (4), pp. 444–74.

Tomasini, Luigi M. Funzioni di utilità, teorie del consumo e stima della domanda (I). (Utility Functions Consumption Theories and Demand Estimation (I). With English summary.) *L'Industria,* July–September 1969, (3), pp. 269–96.

Yaari, Menahem E. Some Remarks on Measures of Risk Aversion and on Their Uses. *J. Econ. Theory,* October 1969, *1*(3), pp. 315–29.

Zeckhauser, Richard J. Resource Allocation with Probabilistic Individual Preferences. *Amer. Econ. Rev.,* May 1969, *59*(2), pp. 546–52.

0223 Theory of Production

Agarwala, R. Price Policy in a Multi-Product Firm: A Case Study. *Appl. Econ.,* August 1969, *1*(3), pp. 161–66. **[G: U.K.]**

Altman, Stuart H. and Fisher, Anthony C. Marginal Product of Labor, Wages and Disequilibrium: Comment. *Rev. Econ. Statist.,* November 1969, *51*(4), pp. 485–86.

Arrow, Kenneth J. and Levhari, David. Uniqueness of the Internal Rate of Return with Variable Life of Investment. *Econ. J.,* September 1969, *79*(315), pp. 560–66.

Atlas, M. and Vinokur, R. The Economic Essence of Profit and Profitability under Socialism. *Prob. Econ.,* May 1969, *12*(1), pp. 3–32.

Bagchi, Amiya K. A Note on the Theory of Fixed Capital. **In** *[Ghosal, U. N.],* 1969, pp. 18–25.

Bagiotti, Tullio. Die Preistheorie im Prozess wachsender inländischer und internationaler Institutionalisierung. (Price Theory in the Process of Growing Domestic and International Institutionalism. With English summary.) *Weltwirtsch. Arch.,* 1969, *103*(2), pp. 229–48.

Bain, Joe S. Survival-Ability as a Test of Efficiency. *Amer. Econ. Rev.,* May 1969, *59*(2), pp. 99–104.

Bassett, Lowell R. and Borcherding, Thomas E. "Inferior Factors" and the Theories of Production and Input Demand: Comment. *Economica, N.S.,* August 1969, *36*(143), pp. 321–22.

Bassett, Lowell R. Returns to Scale and Cost Curves. *Southern Econ. J.,* October 1969, *36*(2), pp. 189–90.

Black, J. Two-Level Production Functions. *Economica, N.S.,* August 1969, *36*(143), pp. 310–13.

Black, Stephen. Profit Maximization: Economics' Zombie Concept. *S. Afr. J. Econ.,* September 1969, *37*(3), pp. 264–67.

Borch, Karl. Equilibrium, Optimum and Prejudices in Capital Markets. *J. Financial Quant. Anal.,* March 1969, *4*(1), pp. 1–14.

Borch, Karl. The Capital Structure of a Firm. *Swedish J. Econ.,* March 1969, *71*(1), pp. 1–13.

Britto, R. On Putty-Clay: A Comment. *Rev. Econ. Stud.,* July 1969, *36*(107), pp. 395–98.

Brusilovskaia, N., et al. Conditions for Applying a System of Accounting Prices in a Socialist Economy. *Prob. Econ.,* September 1969, *12*(5), pp. 71–81.

Bumas, Lester O. The Effects of an Advance in Technology on Employment in an Industry: A Theoretical Model. *Eng. Econ.*, July–August 1969, *14* (4), pp. 215–20.

Burkart, A. J. Some Managerial Influences on a Firm's Pricing Policy. *J. Ind. Econ.*, July 1969, *17* (3), pp. 180–87.

Carleton, Willard T. Linear Programming and Capital Budgeting Models: A New Interpretation. *J. Finance*, December 1969, *24*(5), pp. 825–33.

Carlson, John A. and O'Keefe, Terrence B. Buffer Stocks and Reaction Coefficients: An Experiment with Decision Making under Risk. *Rev. Econ. Stud.*, October 1969, *36*(108), pp. 467–84.

Chang, Chen Fu. The Firm's Long-run Average Cost Curve. *Quart. Rev. Econ. Bus.*, Winter 1969, *9*(4), pp. 80–84.

Chetty, V. Karuppan and Sankar, U. Bayesian Estimation of the CES Production Function. *Rev. Econ. Stud.*, July 1969, *36*(107), pp. 289–94. **[G: India]**

Cheung, Steven N. S. Transaction Costs, Risk Aversion, and the Choice of Contractual Arrangements. *J. Law Econ.*, April 1969, *12*(1), pp. 23–42.

Clague, Christopher K. Capital-Labor Substitution in Manufacturing in Undeveloped Countries. *Econometrica*, July 1969, *37*(3), pp. 528–37. **[G: Peru]**

Comanor, William S. and Wilson, Thomas A. Advertising and the Advantages of Size. *Amer. Econ. Rev.*, May 1969, *59*(2), pp. 87–98.

Courchene, Thomas J. An Analysis of the Price-Inventory Nexus with Empirical Application to the Canadian Manufacturing Sector. *Int. Econ. Rev.*, October 1969, *10*(3), pp. 315–36. **[G: Canada]**

Cummings, Ronald G. and Burt, Oscar R. The Economics of Production from Natural Resources: Note. *Amer. Econ. Rev.*, December 1969, *59*(5), pp. 985–90.

Day, Richard H. Exact Aggregation with Linear Programming Model—A Note on the Sufficient Conditions Proposed by R. H. Day: Reply. *Amer. J. Agr. Econ.*, August 1969, *51*(3), pp. 686–88.

Day, Richard H. More On the Aggregation Problem: Some Suggestions. *Amer. J. Agr. Econ.*, August 1969, *51*(3), pp. 673–75.

van De Panne, C. and Whinston, Andrew. The Symmetric Formulation of the Simplex Method for Quadratic Programming. *Econometrica*, July 1969, *37*(3), pp. 507–27.

De Salvia, Donald N. An Application of Peak-Load Pricing. *J. Bus.*, October 1969, *42*(4), pp. 458–76. **[G: U.S.]**

De Vecchi, Nicolò. Genesi e sviluppi della funzione della produzione CES. (The CES Production Function. With English summary.) *L'Industria*, January–March 1969, (1), pp. 58–77.

Dean, Joel. Pricing Pioneering Products. *J. Ind. Econ.*, July 1969, *17*(3), pp. 165–79.

Dorfman, Robert. An Economic Interpretation of Optimal Control Theory. *Amer. Econ. Rev.*, December 1969, *59*(5), pp. 817–31.

Eads, George; Nerlove, Marc and Raduchel, William. A Long-Run Cost Function for the Local Service Airline Industry: An Experiment in Non-Linear Estimation. *Rev. Econ. Statist.*, August 1969, *51* (3), pp. 258–70. **[G: U.S.]**

Eiteman, Wilford J. Factors Determining the Least Cost Point. **In** *Blumner, S. M., ed.*, 1969, pp. 88–96.

Ellis, Howard S. and Fellner, William. External Economies and Diseconomies. **In** *Blumner, S. M., ed.*, 1969, pp. 163–79.

Fellner, William. Specific Interpretations of Learning by Doing. *J. Econ. Theory*, August 1969, *1*(2), pp. 119–40.

Finkel, Sidney R. and Tarascio, Vincent J. A Theoretical Integration of Production and Wage Theory. *Western Econ. J.*, December 1969, *7*(4), pp. 371–78.

Ford, J. L. and Warford, J. J. Cost Functions for the Water Industry. *J. Ind. Econ.*, November 1969, *18* (1), pp. 53–63. **[G: U.K.]**

Geithman, David T. and Stinson, Byron S. A Note on Diminishing Returns and Linear Homogeneity. *Amer. Econ.*, Spring 1969, *13*(1), pp. 77–79.

Goller, Stanislav. Příspěvek k teorii tvorby účelových časových rozvrhů. (A Contribution to the Theory of the Formation of Purposeful Timetables. With English summary.) *Ekon.-Mat. Obzor*, 1969, *5*(1), pp. 60–71.

Gort, Michael. An Economic Disturbance Theory of Mergers. *Quart. J. Econ.*, November 1969, *83*(4), pp. 624–42. **[G: U.S.]**

Gould, John P. The Use of Endogenous Variables in Dynamic Models of Investment. *Quart. J. Econ.*, November 1969, *83*(4), pp. 580–99.

Hawkins, Clark A. Optimum Growth of the Regulated Firm. *Western Econ. J.*, June 1969, *7*(2), pp. 187–89.

Heflebower, Richard B. Theory of the Firm and of Market Structures: Discussion. *Amer. Econ. Rev.*, May 1969, *59*(2), pp. 119–21.

Herberg, Horst. On the Shape of the Transformation Curve in the Case of Homogenous Production Functions. *Z. ges. Staatswiss.*, April 1969, *125*(2), pp. 202–10.

Heubes, Jürgen. Time-Series CES-Production Functions for Primary Production and Manufacturing, Federal Republic of Germany 1950–1965. *Ger. Econ. Rev.*, 1969, *7*(4), pp. 346–60. **[G: W. Germany]**

Hirsch, Werner Z. Technological Progress and Microeconomic Theory. *Amer. Econ. Rev.*, May 1969, *59*(2), pp. 36–43.

Hodges, Dorothy J. A Note on Estimation of Cobb-Douglas and CES Production Function Models. *Econometrica*, October 1969, *37*(4), pp. 721–25.

Horowitz, Ira. The Price-Quoter under Risk. *Western Econ. J.*, June 1969, *7*(2), pp. 129–36.

Hsiao, Frank S. T. Some Notes on the Elasticity of Substitution. *Amer. Econ. Rev.*, June 1969, *59*(3), pp. 432–35.

Hutcheson, Thomas L. Factor Intensity and the CES Production Function. *Rev. Econ. Statist.*, November 1969, *51*(4), pp. 468–70.

Jones-Lee, Michael. Managerial Expectations and Investment Behaviour. *Yorkshire Bull. Econ. Soc. Res.*, November 1969, *21*(2), pp. 85–93.

Jorgenson, Dale W. and Stephenson, James A. Issues in the Development of the Neoclassical Theory of Investment Behavior. *Rev. Econ. Statist.*, August 1969, *51*(3), pp. 346–53.

Kalmbach, Peter and Kuhbier, Peter. Beiträge des technischen Fortschritts zum Produktivitätswachstum in Industriebereichen. (The Contribution of Technical Progress to Productivity Growth in Manufacturing Industries. With English summary.) *Ifo-Studien,* 1969, *15*(1/2), pp. 19–55.

Kamien, Morton I. and Schwartz, Nancy L. Induced Factor Augmenting Technical Progress from a Microeconomic Viewpoint. *Econometrica,* October 1969, *37*(4), pp. 668–84.

Kelly, Jerry Stewart. Lancaster vs. Samuelson on the Shape of the Neoclassical Transformation Surface. *J. Econ. Theory,* October 1969, *1*(3), pp. 347–51.

Kl'učárová, Mária. Jedna metóda riešenia výrobno-rozmiestňovacieho modelu. (A Method for Solving Integrated Production and Distribution Model. With English summary.) *Ekon.-Mat. Obzor,* 1969, *5*(1), pp. 30–44.

Koch, Helmut. The Law of Diminishing Marginal Capacity and Its Significance for the Theory of the Firm. *Ger. Econ. Rev.,* 1969, *7*(1), pp. 1–24.

Kolm, Serge-Christophe. Les politiques dynamiques optimales d'investissement. (With English summary.) *Revue Écon.,* September 1969, *20*(5), pp. 753–82.

Kottke, Marvin. The Supply Function in Agriculture Revisited: Discussion. *Amer. Econ. Rev.,* May 1969, *59*(2), pp. 184–85.

Kuligin, P. Improvement of Price Formation under the Economic Reform. *Prob. Econ.,* October 1969, *12*(6), pp. 27–41. **[G: U.S.S.R.]**

Kurz, Mordecai. Tightness and Substitution in the Theory of Capital. *J. Econ. Theory,* October 1969, *1*(3), pp. 244–72.

Ladd, George W. Utility Maximization Sufficient for Competitive Survival. *J. Polit. Econ.,* Part I, July/August 1969, *77*(4), pp. 478–83.

Leibenstein, Harvey. Organizational or Frictional Equilibria, X-Efficiency, and the Rate of Innovation. *Quart. J. Econ.,* November 1969, *83*(4), pp. 600–23.

Lianos, Theodore P. A Comment on a Traditional Behavior Model. *Amer. J. Agr. Econ.,* November 1969, *51*(4), pp. 937.

Lieberman, S. Has the Marginalist Anti-Marginalist Controversy Regarding the Theory of the Firm Been Settled? *Schweiz. Z. Volkswirtsch. Statist.,* December 1969, *105*(4), pp. 535–49.

Lipowski, Adam. Interdependence Between Goals and Incentives in an Experimental System of Management. *Eastern Europ. Econ.,* Fall 1969, *8* (1), pp. 20–71. **[G: Poland]**

Litzenberger, Robert H. and Jones, Charles P. Adjusting for Risk in the Capital Budget of a Growth Oriented Company: Comment. *J. Financial Quant. Anal.,* September 1969, *4*(3), pp. 301–04.

Lucas, Robert E., Jr. Labor-Capital Substitution in U.S. Manufacturing. **In** *Harberger, A. C. and Bailey, M. J., eds.,* 1969, pp. 223–74. **[G: U.S.]**

Marenco, G. Exact Aggregation with Linear Programming Models—A Note on the Sufficient Conditions Proposed by R. H. Day. *Amer. J. Agr. Econ.,* August 1969, *51*(3), pp. 684–86.

Maxwell, W. David. Production Theory and Cost Curves. *Appl. Econ.,* August 1969, *1*(3), pp. 211–24.

Mayor, Thomas H. Some Theoretical Difficulties in the Estimation of the Elasticity of Substitution from Cross-section Data. *Western Econ. J.,* June 1969, *7*(2), pp. 153–63.

McElroy, F. W. Returns to Scale, Euler's Theorem, and the Form of Production Functions. *Econometrica,* April 1969, *37*(2), pp. 275–79.

de Meester, J.-C. Fonctions de production et données technologiques. (Production Functions and Technological Data. With English summary.) *Rivista Int. Sci. Econ. Com.,* January 1969, *16*(1), pp. 31–45.

Melvin, James R. Intermediate Goods and Technological Change. *Economica, N.S.,* November 1969, *36*(144), pp. 400–408.

Melvin, James R. Intermediate Goods in Production Theory: The Differentiable Case. *Rev. Econ. Stud.,* January 1969, *36*(105), pp. 124–31.

Minasian, Jora R. Research and Development, Production Functions, and Rates of Return. *Amer. Econ. Rev.,* May 1969, *59*(2), pp. 80–85. **[G: U.S.]**

Moag, Joseph S. and Lerner, Eugene M. Capital Budgeting Decisions under Imperfect Market Conditions—A Systems Framework. *J. Finance,* September 1969, *24*(4), pp. 613–21.

Montesano, Aldo. Per una teoria generale empirica della produzione. (Towards an Empirical Theory of Production. With English summary.) *Rivista Int. Sci. Econ. Com.,* March 1969, *16*(3), pp. 228–58.

Moroney, John R. Economies of Scale in Manufacturing. **In** *Watson, D. S., ed.,* 1969, pp. 116–24. **[G: U.S.]**

Mueller, Dennis C. A Theory of Conglomerate Mergers. *Quart. J. Econ.,* November 1969, *83*(4), pp. 643–59.

Nadiri, M. Ishag and Rosen, Sherwin. Interrelated Factor Demand Functions. *Amer. Econ. Rev.,* Part I, September 1969, *59*(4), pp. 457–71. **[G: U.S.]**

Ng, Y.-K. A Note on Profit Maximization. *Australian Econ. Pap.,* June 1969, *8*(12), pp. 106–110.

Nove, Alec. Internal Economics. *Econ. J.,* December 1969, *79*(316), pp. 847–60.

Pratten, C. F. Economies of Scale. **In** *Hugh-Jones, E. M., ed.,* 1969, pp. 89–98.

Riistama, Veijo. Kustannusteoria kustannuslaskennan perustana. (Cost Theory as a Basis for Cost Accounting. With English summary.) *Liiketaloudellinen Aikak.,* 1969, *18*(3), pp. 550–75.

Sato, Kazuo. Micro and Macro Constant-Elasticity-of-Substitution Production Functions in a Multifirm Industry. *J. Econ. Theory,* December 1969, *1*(4), pp. 438–53.

Sau, Ranjit K. The Optimal Rate of Investment in a Firm. *J. Finance,* March 1969, *24*(1), pp. 1–12.

Schaller, W. Neill. The Supply Function in Agriculture Revisited: Discussion. *Amer. Econ. Rev.,* May 1969, *59*(2), pp. 185–87.

Schöndorff, R. Verkenningen langs het micro-groeipad: facetten van enkele moderne groeitheorieën van de onderneming. (Explorations along the Microgrowthpath. With English summary.) *De Economist*, November/December 1969, *117*(6), pp. 658–94.

Seagraves, James A. and Pasour, E. C., Jr. On Defining Uneconomic Regions of the Production Function. *Amer. J. Agr. Econ.*, February 1969, *51*(1), pp. 195–202.

Sen, Amitava and Sengupta, Jati K. Optimal Capacity Models under Periodic Demand: A Survey of Peak Load Pricing Theory and Appraisal. *Z. ges. Staatswiss.*, July 1969, *125*(3), pp. 371–95.

Sharples, Jerry A. The Representative Farm Approach to Estimation of Supply Response. *Amer. Econ. Rev.*, May 1969, *59*(2), pp. 168–74. [G: U.S.]

Sherman, Roger. Risk Attitude and Cost Variability in a Capacity Choice Experiment. *Rev. Econ. Stud.*, October 1969, *36*(108), pp. 453–66.

Siebert, Horst. Lern- und suchtheoretische Aspekte neuen technischen Wissens. (Learn Theoretical and Search Theoretical Aspects of New Technical Knowledge. With English summary.) *Schmollers Jahr.*, 1969, *89*(5), pp. 513–39.

Silver, Morris and Auster, Richard. Entrepreneurship, Profit, and Limits on Firm Size. *J. Bus.*, July 1969, *42*(3), pp. 277–81.

Smith, V. Kerry. The CES Production Function: A Derivation. *Amer. Econ.*, Spring 1969, *13*(1), pp. 72–76.

Smyth, David J. Sales Maximization and Managerial Effort: Note. *Amer. Econ. Rev.*, Part I, September 1969, *59*(4), pp. 633–34.

Sojit, Alberto A. Renta de la tierra y asignación de recursos. (Land Rent and Allocation of Resources. With English summary.) *Económica*, May–August 1969, *15*(2), pp. 211–22.

Starrett, David A. Switching and Reswitching in a General Production Model. *Quart. J. Econ.*, November 1969, *83*(4), pp. 673–87.

Stigum, Bernt P. Entrepreneurial Choice Over Time under Conditions of Uncertainty. *Int. Econ. Rev.*, October 1969, *10*(3), pp. 426–42.

Stober, William J. Cost Constraints and Factor Inferiority. *Western Econ. J.*, December 1969, *7*(4), pp. 379–84.

Szakolczai, György and Stahl, János. Increasing or Decreasing Returns to Scale in the Constant Elasticity of Substitution Production Function. *Rev. Econ. Statist.*, February 1969, *51*(1), pp. 84–90. [G: U.S.; Hungary]

Telser, Lester G. Theory of the Firm and of Market Structures: Discussion. *Amer. Econ. Rev.*, May 1969, *59*(2), pp. 121–23.

Treadway, Arthur B. On Rational Entrepreneurial Behaviour and the Demand for Investment. *Rev. Econ. Stud.*, April 1969, *36*(106), pp. 227–39.

Turnovsky, Stephen J. A Bayesian Approach to the Theory of Expectations. *J. Econ. Theory*, August 1969, *1*(2), pp. 220–27.

Turvey, R. Marginal Cost. *Econ. J.*, June 1969, *79* (314), pp. 282–99.

Van Rompuy, P. Flexibility, Adaptability and Demand for Labour. *Tijdschr. Econ.*, 1969, *14*(3), pp. 436–48.

Vincent, Andre L.-A. La productivité globale clé de l'étude de la répartition. (With English summary.) *Revue Écon.*, September 1969, *20*(5), pp. 783–829.

White, James H. The Supply Function in Agriculture Revisited: Discussion. *Amer. Econ. Rev.*, May 1969, *59*(2), pp. 187–88.

Whitin, T. M. Optimal Plant under Conditions of Risk. *J. Ind. Econ.*, April 1969, *17*(2), pp. 81–85.

Worcester, Dean A., Jr. Optimal Pricing Policy for Public Utilities as Optimal Taxation: Electric Power and Water. *Philippine Econ. J.*, Second Semester 1969, *8*(2), pp. 145–65. [G: Philippines]

Worcester, Dean A., Jr. Pecuniary and Technological Externality, Factor Rents, and Social Costs. *Amer. Econ. Rev.*, December 1969, *59*(5), pp. 873–85.

Wu, S. Y. A Multi-period Monopoly Model. *Tijdschr. Econ.*, 1969, *14*(4), pp. 497–518.

Wu, S. Y. A Nonlinear Programming Production Model. *Western Econ. J.*, December 1969, *7*(4), pp. 319–33.

Yeung, Patrick. Unifying Elements in the Theories of the Firm. *Quart. Rev. Econ. Bus.*, Winter 1969, *9*(4), pp. 21–28.

Yotopoulos, Pan A. and Wise, John. Epilegomena on Traditional Behavior Models. *Amer. J. Agr. Econ.*, November 1969, *51*(4), pp. 928–39.

Zabel, Edward. The Competitive Firm and Price Expectations. *Int. Econ. Rev.*, October 1969, *10*(3), pp. 467–78.

Zanetti, Giovanni and Filippi, Enrico. Il processo di sviluppo dell'impresa: Fattori endogeni ed esogeni esperienza italiana 1958–1963. (The Process of Firm Growth: Endogenous and Exogenous Factors in the Italian Experience 1958–1963. With English summary.) *L'Impresa*, January/February 1969, *11*(1), pp. 29–39. [G: Italy]

Zellner, A. and Revankar, N. S. Generalized Production Functions. *Rev. Econ. Stud.*, April 1969, *36* (106), pp. 241–50.

Ziemba, William T. A Myopic Capital Budgeting Model. *J. Financial Quant. Anal.*, September 1969, *4*(3), pp. 305–27.

Zima, Petr. Řešení jedné modifikace řezného problému. (A Solution of One Modification of the "Cutting Problem." With English summary.) *Ekon.-Mat. Obzor*, 1969, *5*(1), pp. 72–76.

Županov, Josip. The Producer and Risk. *Eastern Europ. Econ.*, Spring 1969, *7*(3), pp. 12–28. [G: Yugoslavia]

0224 Theory of Distribution (factor) and Distributive Shares

Behman, Sara. Wage Changes, Institutions, and Relative Factor Prices in Manufacturing. *Rev. Econ. Statist.*, August 1969, *51*(3), pp. 227–38. [G: U.S.]

Brahmananda, P. R. Towards a General Theory of the Pure Rate of Interest. *Indian Econ. J.*, July–September 1969, *17*(1), pp. 57–92.

Dudley, Dean. The Goodwill Account: The Accounting Recognition of the Concept of Economic Rent. *Marquette Bus. Rev.*, Summer 1969, *13*(2), pp. 89–92.

Gramm, Warren S. The Distribution of Industrial Production. *J. Econ. Issues*, December 1969, *3*(4), pp. 39–65.

Hoch, Irving. Anticipated Profit in Cobb-Douglas Models. *Econometrica,* October 1969, *37*(4), pp. 720.

Johnson, Harry G. Notes on the Geometry of Income Distribution in a Two-Factor, Two-Commodity Model. *Osaka Econ. Pap.,* March 1969, *17* (32), pp. 31–38.

Kaun, David E. A Comment on the Work-Leisure Myth. *Rev. Radical Polit. Econ.,* May 1969, *1*(1), pp. 85–88.

Lovell, C. A. Knox. Biased Technical Change and Factor Shares in United States Manufacturing. *Quart. Rev. Econ. Bus.,* Autumn 1969, *9*(3), pp. 17–33. **[G: U.S.]**

Mabry, Bevars D. Income-Leisure Analysis and the Salaried Professional. *Ind. Relat.,* February 1969, *8*(2), pp. 162–73.

Mishan, E. J. Rent and Producer's Surplus: Reply. *Amer. Econ. Rev.,* Part I, September 1969, *59*(4), pp. 635–37.

Moroney, John R. and Allen, Bruce T. Monopoly Power and the Relative Share of Labor. *Ind. Lab. Relat. Rev.,* January 1969, *22*(2), pp. 167–78. **[G: U.S.]**

Pavlov, P. and Tsaga, V. The Marginalist Treatment of the Law of Value under Socialism. *Prob. Econ.,* July 1969, *12*(3), pp. 3–22.

Schmitt-Rink, Gerhard. Funktionelle Verteilung, personelle Verteilung und Multiplikatoreffekt. Überlegungen zum Kaldor-Ansatz in der Verteilungstheorie. (With English summary.) *Jahr. Nationalökon. Statist.,* December 1969, *183*(5), pp. 361–771.

Wessel, Robert H. What Is Producer's Surplus?—Comment. *Amer. Econ. Rev.,* Part I, September 1969, *59*(4), pp. 634–35.

Wilczynski, Jozef. Towards Rationality in Land Economics under Central Planning. *Econ. J.,* September 1969, *79*(315), pp. 540–59.

0225 Price and Market Theory of Firm and Industry in Competition; Single Market Equilibrium

Beckmann, Martin J. and Wallace, James P. Continuous Lags and the Stability of Market Equilibrium. *Economica, N.S.,* February 1969, *36*(141), pp. 58–68.

Beckmann, Martin J. and Ryder, Harl E., Jr. Simultaneous Price and Quantity Adjustment in a Single Market. *Econometrica,* July 1969, *37*(3), pp. 470–84.

Day, Richard H. and Tinney, E. Herbert. Cycles, Phases and Growth in a Generalised Cobweb Theory. *Econ. J.,* March 1969, *79*(313), pp. 90–108.

De Salvia, Donald N. An Application of Peak-Load Pricing. *J. Bus.,* October 1969, *42*(4), pp. 458–76. **[G: U.S.]**

Ferguson, C. E. and Saving, Thomas R. Long-Run Scale Adjustments of a Perfectly Competitive Firm and Industry. *Amer. Econ. Rev.,* December 1969, *59*(5), pp. 774–83.

Ganguly, Subrata K. The Perfectly Competitive Production of Collective Goods: Comment. *Rev. Econ. Statist.,* November 1969, *51*(4), pp. 478–79.

Mickwitz, Gösta. Product Quality as a Means of Competition. *Liiketaloudellinen Aikak.,* 1969, *18*(1), pp. 51–60.

Mossin, Jan. Security Pricing and Investment Criteria in Competitive Markets. *Amer. Econ. Rev.,* December 1969, *59*(5), pp. 749–56.

Nicola, Pier Carlo. Equilibrio economico generale di tipo concorrenziale in condizioni dinamiche (II). (General Competitive Equilibrium under Dynamic Conditions—Part II. With English summary.) *L'Industria,* April–June 1969, (2), pp. 197–207.

Olsen, Edgar O. A Competitive Theory of the Housing Market. *Amer. Econ. Rev.,* Part I, September 1969, *59*(4), pp. 612–22.

Owen, Bruce M. The Perfectly Competitive Production of Collective Goods: Comment. *Rev. Econ. Statist.,* November 1969, *51*(4), pp. 475–76.

Rädel, F. E. Profit Maximisation—Can It Be Justified? *S. Afr. J. Econ.,* March 1969, *37*(1), pp. 32–41.

Rodgers, James D. The Perfectly Competitive Production of Collective Goods: Comment. *Rev. Econ. Statist.,* November 1969, *51*(4), pp. 476–78.

Spandau, Arnt. Some Comments on Professor Rädel's "Profit Maximization—Can It Be Justified?" *S. Afr. J. Econ.,* September 1969, *37*(3), pp. 268–72.

Swamy, M. R. Kumara. An Econometric Analysis of Cost Curves and Supply Curves under Modern Dynamic Competitive Conditions. *Rivista Int. Sci. Econ. Com.,* March 1969, *16*(3), pp. 280–93.

Thompson, Earl A. The Perfectly Competitive Production of Collective Goods: Reply. *Rev. Econ. Statist.,* November 1969, *51*(4), pp. 479–82.

Walter, Helmut. Bemerkungen zum gegenwärtigen Stand der Wettbewerbstheorie. (Remarks about the Present State of the Theory of Competition. With English summary.) *Schmollers Jahr.,* 1969, *89*(5), pp. 541–56.

Whan, R. B. and Richardson, R. A. A Simulated Study of an Auction Market. *Australian J. Agr. Econ.,* December 1969, *13*(2), pp. 91–100. **[G: Australia]**

0226 Price and Market Theory of Firm and Industry in Noncompetitive Relations

Baxter, W. T. and Oxenfeldt, A. R. Approaches to Pricing: Economist *Versus* Accountant. **In** *Carsberg, B. V. and Edey, H. C., eds.,* 1969, pp. 184–208.

Beckmann, Martin J. Market Shares and Distance. *Swedish J. Econ.,* June 1969, *71*(2), pp. 53–63.

Bennathan, E. and Walters, A. A. Revenue Pooling and Cartels. *Oxford Econ. Pap.,* July 1969, *21*(2), pp. 161–76.

Berry, R. Albert. A Note on Welfare Comparisons between Monopoly and Pure Competition. *Manchester Sch. Econ. Soc. Stud.,* March 1969, *37*(1), pp. 39–57.

Bilas, Richard A. Third Degree Price Discrimination and the Multiple Plant Monopolist: A Note on the Allocation of Output. *Southern Econ. J.,* July 1969, *36*(1), pp. 82–86.

Bilsen, Robert. Marktbenadering, marktstructuur en ondernemingsdimensie. (Market Approach, Market Structure and the Dimension of the Firm. With English summary.) *Econ. Soc. Tijdschr.*, December 1969, *23*(6), pp. 537–45.

Bork, Robert H. Vertical Integration and Competitive Processes. **In** *Weston, J. F. and Peltzman, S., eds.*, 1969, pp. 139–49. **[G: U.S.]**

Buchanan, James M. External Diseconomies, Corrective Taxes, and Market Structure. *Amer. Econ. Rev.*, March 1969, *59*(1), pp. 174–77.

Cebula, Richard J. A Look at Long-Run Equilibrium under Multiplant Monopoly. *Amer. Econ.*, Fall 1969, *13*(2), pp. 92–93.

Comanor, William S. and Leibenstein, Harvey. Allocative Efficiency, X-Efficiency and the Measurement of Welfare Losses. *Economica, N.S.*, August 1969, *36*(143), pp. 304–09.

Cummings, L. L. and Harnett, D. L. Bargaining Behaviour in a Symmetric Bargaining Triad: The Impact of Risk-Taking Propensity, Information, Communication and Terminal Bid. *Rev. Econ. Stud.*, October 1969, *36*(108), pp. 485–501.

Cyert, Richard M. and George, Kenneth D. Competition, Growth, and Efficiency. *Econ. J.*, March 1969, *79*(313), pp. 23–41.

Davenport, David S. Collusive Competition in Major League Baseball: Its Theory and Institutional Development. *Amer. Econ.*, Fall 1969, *13*(2), pp. 6–30. **[G: U.S.]**

DePrano, Michael E. and Nugent, Jeffrey B. Economies as an Antitrust Defense: Comment. *Amer. Econ. Rev.*, December 1969, *59*(5), pp. 947–53.

Doll, John P. Credit in the Production Organization of the Firm: Comment. *Amer. J. Agr. Econ.*, May 1969, *51*(2), pp. 474–76.

Douglas, A. J. and Goldman, Steven M. Monopolistic Behavior in a Market for Durable Goods. *J. Polit. Econ.*, January/February 1969, *77*(1), pp. 49–59.

Ferguson, C. E. A Look at Long-Run Equilibrium under Multiplant Monopoly: Comment. *Amer. Econ.*, Fall 1969, *13*(2), pp. 94–96.

Friedman, J. W. On Experimental Research in Oligopoly. *Rev. Econ. Stud.*, October 1969, *36* (108), pp. 399–415.

Furubotn, Eiřik G. Quality Control, Expected Utility, and Product Equilibrium. *Western Econ. J.*, March 1969, *7*(1), pp. 9–26.

Galbraith, John Kenneth. The Development of Monopoly Theory. **In** *Hunter, A., ed.*, 1969, pp. 19–23.

Gustafsson, Kaj. Markkinoiden segmentoinnista ja sen vertailua tuotedifferointiin markkinointistrategiana. (About Market Segmentation and Its Comparison to Product Differentiation as a Marketing Strategy. With English summary.) *Liiketaloudellinen Aikak.*, 1969, *18*(2), pp. 133–44.

Hadar, Josef and Hillinger, C. Imperfect Competition with Unknown Demand. *Rev. Econ. Stud.*, October 1969, *36*(108), pp. 519–25.

Hadar, Josef. On the Predictive Content of Models of Monopolistic Competition. *Southern Econ. J.*, July 1969, *36*(1), pp. 67–74.

Harrod, Roy F. [Sir]. Doctrines of Imperfect Competition. **In** *Blumner, S. M., ed.*, 1969, pp. 183–202.

Hoggatt, A. C. Response of Paid Student Subjects to Differential Behaviour of Robots in Bifurcated Duopoly Games. *Rev. Econ. Stud.*, October 1969, *36*(108), pp. 417–32.

Hosomatsu, Yasu. A Note on the Stability Conditions in Cournot's Dynamic Market Solution when neither the Actual Market Demand Function nor the Production Levels of Rivals Are Known. *Rev. Econ. Stud.*, January 1969, *36*(105), pp. 117–22.

Hunter, Alex. Welfare Analysis and Monopoly. **In** *Hunter, A., ed.*, 1969, pp. 30–39.

Jen, Frank C. and Southwick, Lawrence, Jr. Implications of Dynamic Monopoly Behavior. *Amer. Econ. Rev.*, March 1969, *59*(1), pp. 149–58.

Kafoglis, Milton Z. Output of the Restrained Firm. *Amer. Econ. Rev.*, Part I, September 1969, *59*(4), pp. 583–89.

Levin, A. The Market in the System of Socialist Reproduction. The Equilibrium Price Principle. *Prob. Econ.*, November 1969, *12*(7), pp. 30–48.

Logan, Samuel H. A Conceptual Framework for Analyzing Economies of Vertical Integration. *Amer. J. Agr. Econ.*, November 1969, *51*(4), pp. 834–48.

Melrose, Kendrick B. An Empirical Study on Optimizing Advertising Policy. *J. Bus.*, July 1969, *42* (3), pp. 282–92. **[G: U.S.]**

Okuguchi, Koji. On the Stability of Price Adjusting Oligopoly Equilibrium under Product Differentiation. *Southern Econ. J.*, January 1969, *35*(3), pp. 244–46.

Orr, Daniel. The "Taxicab Problem": A Proposed Solution. *J. Polit. Econ.*, January/February 1969, *77* (1), pp. 141–47.

Pritchard, Norris T. Toward a Concrete Concept of Effective Competition: Comment. *Amer. J. Agr. Econ.*, May 1969, *51*(2), pp. 476–78.

Raina, M. K. A Note on Differentiation in Railway Rates. *Indian Econ. J.*, July–September 1969, *17* (1), pp. 129–36. **[G: India]**

Rethwisch, Kurt. A Note on the Presumed Social Desirability of Internal Over External Growth. *Antitrust Bull.*, Winter 1969, *14*, pp. 855–64.

Rothschild, K. W. Price Theory and Oligopoly. **In** *Hunter, A., ed.*, 1969, pp. 24–29.

Sahota, G. S. Economic Problems in Separating the Determinants of Relative Prices. *Int. Econ. Rev.*, June 1969, *10*(2), pp. 183–206. **[G: U.S.]**

Schendel, Dan E. and Balestra, Pietro. Rational Behavior and Gasoline Price Wars. *Appl. Econ.*, May 1969, *1*(2), pp. 89–101.

Schumpeter, J. A. The Dynamics of Competition and Monopoly. **In** *Hunter, A., ed.*, 1969, pp. 40–67.

Schuster, Helmut. Further Remarks on the Theory of Product Differentiation. *J. Polit. Econ.*, September/October 1969, *77*(5), pp. 827–33.

Seidel, Marquis R. The Margins of Spatial Monopoly. *J. Reg. Sci.*, December 1969, *9*(3), pp. 353–68.

Shapley, Lloyd S. and Shubik, Martin. On Market Games. *J. Econ. Theory*, June 1969, *1*(1), pp. 9–25.

Shapley, Lloyd S. and Shubik, Martin. Price Strategy Oligopoly with Product Variation. *Kyklos*, 1969, *22*(1), pp. 30–44.

Simon, Julian L. A Further Test of the Kinky Oligopoly Demand Curve. *Amer. Econ. Rev.*, December 1969, *59*(5), pp. 971–75. **[G: U.S.]**

Smith, Kenneth R. The Effect of Uncertainty on Monopoly Price, Capital Stock and Utilization of

Capital. *J. Econ. Theory,* June 1969, *1*(1), pp. 48–59.

Smith, Vernon L. On Models of Commercial Fishing. *J. Polit. Econ.,* March/April 1969, *77*(2), pp. 181–98.

Sosnick, Stephen H. Toward a Concrete Concept of Effective Competition: Reply. *Amer. J. Agr. Econ.,* May 1969, *51*(2), pp. 478–81.

Spaetling, Dieter. Umsatzmaximierung und Werbung bei fixem Mindestgewinn: Eine graphische Analyse. (With English summary.) *Z. ges. Staatswiss.,* January 1969, *125*(1), pp. 89–105.

di Tella, Guido. The Behavior of the Firm with a Financial Restriction. *J. Ind. Econ.,* April 1969, *17* (2), pp. 119–32.

Telser, Lester G. On the Regulation of Industry: A Note. *J. Polit. Econ.,* November/December 1969, *77*(6), pp. 937–52.

Turnovec, František. Nutné a postačující podmínky pro rovnovážné body v konvexní nekooperativní hře. (Necessary and Sufficient Conditions for Equilibrium Points of Noncooperative Convex Games. With English summary.) *Ekon.-Mat. Obzor,* 1969, *5*(3), pp. 343–53.

Vickrey, William S. Decreasing Costs, Publicly Administered Prices, and Economic Efficiency. **In** *The Analysis and Evaluation of Public Expenditures: The PPB System, Vol. 1, JECP,* 1969, pp. 119–48.

Weston, J. Fred. Structure, Performance, and Behavior. **In** *Weston, J. F. and Peltzman, S., eds.,* 1969, pp. 67–78. **[G: U.S.]**

Williamson, Oliver E. Economies as an Antitrust Defense: Reply. *Amer. Econ. Rev.,* December 1969, *59*(5), pp. 954–59.

Wright, J. C. G. Monopolistic Competition Theory. *Econ. Rec.,* June 1969, *45*(110), pp. 276–87.

Wu, S. Y. A Multi-period Monopoly Model. *Tijdschr. Econ.,* 1969, *14*(4), pp. 497–518.

023 Macroeconomic Theory

0230 General

Andersen, Leonall C. and Jordan, Jerry L. Monetary and Fiscal Actions: A Test of Their Relative Importance in Economic Stabilization—Reply. *Fed. Res. Bank St. Louis Rev.,* April 1969, *51*(4), pp. 12–16. **[G: U.S.]**

Andersen, Leonall C. Monetary Velocity in Empirical Analysis: Discussion. **In** *Federal Reserve Bank of Boston,* 1969, pp. 52–55.

Anderson, Paul S. Monetary Velocity in Empirical Analysis. **In** *Federal Reserve Bank of Boston,* 1969, pp. 37–51.

Andreatta, Nino. Il disegno della politica della Banca centrale e l'uso di modelli econometrici di flussi monetari. (The Framing of Central Bank Policy and the Use of Econometric Models of Money Flows. With English summary.) *Bancaria,* January 1969, *25*(1), pp. 9–18.

Argy, Victor. The Impact of Monetary Policy on Expenditure, with Particular Reference to the United Kingdom. *Int. Monet. Fund Staff Pap.,* November 1969, *16*(3), pp. 436–88. **[G: U.K.]**

Artis, M. J. Two Aspects of the Monetary Debate. *Nat. Inst. Econ. Rev.,* August 1969, (49), pp. 33–51.

Banks, F. E. A Note on a "Keynesian" Model of Aggregate Demand. *J. Finance,* March 1969, *24* (1), pp. 101–03.

Bolza, Hans. Il concetto di rinnovamento come principio guida in economia. (The Concept of Renewal as Leading Idea for All Economic Events. With English summary.) *Rivista Int. Sci. Econ. Com.,* September 1969, *16*(9), pp. 920–29.

Boulding, Kenneth E. David Fand's "Keynesian Monetary Theories, Stabilization Policy, and the Recent Inflation": A Comment. *J. Money, Credit, Banking,* August 1969, *1*(3), pp. 588–89. **[G: U.S.]**

Bronfenbrenner, Martin. Eine makroökonomische Auffassung von Marx' "Kapital." (With English summary.) *Jahr. Nationalökon. Statist.,* March 1969, *182*(4–5), pp. 347–65.

Burmeister, Edwin and Sheshinski, Eytan. A Nonsubstitution Theorem in a Model with Fixed Capital. *Southern Econ. J.,* January 1969, *35*(3), pp. 273–76.

Cagan, Phillip. The Influence of Interest Rates on the Duration of Business Cycles. **In** *Guttentag, J. M. and Cagan, P., eds.,* 1969, pp. 3–28. **[G: U.S.]**

Cagan, Phillip and Gandolfi, Arthur. The Lag in Monetary Policy as Implied by the Time Pattern of Monetary Effects on Interest Rates. *Amer. Econ. Rev.,* May 1969, *59*(2), pp. 277–84. **[G: U.S.]**

Christ, Carl F. A Model of Monetary and Fiscal Policy Effects on the Money Stock, Price Level, and Real Output. *J. Money, Credit, Banking,* November 1969, *1*(4), pp. 683–705. **[G: U.S.]**

Colaco, Francis X. Harberger's Inflation Model: A Critique and Test Using Data for Brazil and India. *Indian Econ. J.,* April–June 1969, *16*(4–5), pp. 434–44. **[G: Brazil; India]**

Cooper, Richard N. Macroeconomic Policy Adjustment in Interdependent Economies. *Quart. J. Econ.,* February 1969, *83*(1), pp. 1–24.

Dasgupta, Samir. A Note on Keynes's Analysis of Demand. *Econ. Int.,* May 1969, *22*(2), pp. 252–59.

Davidson, Paul. A Keynesian View of the Relationship between Accumulation, Money and the Money Wage-Rate. *Econ. J.,* June 1969, *79*(314), pp. 300–323.

Davis, Richard G. Monetary Theory: Discussion. *Amer. Econ. Rev.,* May 1969, *59*(2), pp. 315–21. **[G: U.S.]**

Draper, J. E. and Hawkins, Clark A. On the Transactions Demand for Cash: Comment. *J. Finance,* December 1969, *24*(5), pp. 942–49.

Fand, David I. Keynesian Monetary Theories, Stabilization Policy, and the Recent Inflation. *J. Money, Credit, Banking,* August 1969, *1*(3), pp. 556–87. **[G: U.S.]**

Fazio, Antonio. Monetary Base and the Control of Credit in Italy. *Banca Naz. Lavoro Quart. Rev.,* June 1969, (89), pp. 146–69. **[G: Italy]**

Floyd, John E. Monetary and Fiscal Policy in a World of Capital Mobility. *Rev. Econ. Stud.,* October 1969, *36*(108), pp. 503–17.

Friedman, Milton. Post-War Trends in Monetary

Theory and Policy. In *Friedman, M.*, 1969, pp. 69–79. **[G: U.S.]**

Fuerst, E. The Comprehensive Macro-economic Model. *Rivista Int. Sci. Econ. Com.*, May 1969, *16* (5), pp. 429–45.

Gørtz, Erik. Interest Determination in a Simultaneous Money and Credit Market Model for Denmark 1950–66. *Swedish J. Econ.*, December 1969, *71*(4), pp. 263–74. **[G: Denmark]**

Gupta, Kanhaya L. Money Supply, Cyclical Fluctuations, and Income Determination. *Jahr. Nationalökon. Statist.*, May 1969, *182*(6), pp. 465–78. **[G: Canada]**

Gupta, Suraj B. The Invalidity of the Dichotomy in the Pure Inside-Money Model. *J. Polit. Econ.*, January/February 1969, *77*(1), pp. 118–21.

Hawkins, Clark A. and McClain, J. M. A Note on the Short-Run Demand for Money. *Miss. Val. J. Bus. Econ.*, Fall 1969, *5*(1), pp. 73–79. **[G: U.S.]**

Heitman, George and Robinson, Warren C. A Suggested Reformulation of the Basic Keynesian Model. *Quart. Rev. Econ. Bus.*, Autumn 1969, *9* (3), pp. 51–55.

Hicks, John R. Automatists, Hawtreyans, and Keynesians. *J. Money, Credit, Banking,* August 1969, *1*(3), pp. 307–17.

Iyengar, Sampath S. Multiplier Analysis for India. *Indian Econ. J.*, April–June 1969, *16*(4–5), pp. 478–87. **[G: India]**

Keran, Michael W. Monetary and Fiscal Influences on Economic Activity—The Historical Evidence. *Fed. Res. Bank St. Louis Rev.*, November 1969, *51* (11), pp. 5–24. **[G: U.S.]**

Killingsworth, Charles C. Full Employment and the New Economics. *Scot. J. Polit. Econ.*, February 1969, *16*(1), pp. 1–19.

Klein, Lawrence R. and Preston, R. S. Stochastic Nonlinear Models. *Econometrica,* January 1969, *37*(1), pp. 95–106.

Kolm, Serge-Christophe. L'encombrement pluridimensionnel. (With English summary.) *Revue Écon.*, November 1969, *20*(6), pp. 954–67.

Konstas, Panos and Khouja, Mohamad W. The Keynesian Demand-for-Money Function: Another Look and Some Additional Evidence. *J. Money, Credit, Banking,* November 1969, *1*(4), pp. 765–77.

Kurihara, Kenneth K. The Antinomic Impact of Automation on Employment and Growth. *Econ. Int.*, August 1969, *22*(3), pp. 423–33.

Laumas, Prem S. The Role of Savings Deposits as Money: A Comment. *J. Money, Credit, Banking,* November 1969, *1*(4), pp. 789–95. **[G: Canada]**

de Leeuw, Frank and Kalchbrenner, John. Monetary and Fiscal Actions: A Test of Their Relative Importance in Economic Stabilization—Comment. *Fed. Res. Bank St. Louis Rev.*, April 1969, *51*(4), pp. 6–11. **[G: U.S.]**

de Leeuw, Frank and Gramlich, Edward M. The Channels of Monetary Policy. *Fed. Res. Bull.*, June 1969, *55*(6), pp. 472–91. **[G: U.S.]**

McCallum, B. T. The Instability of Kaldorian Models. *Oxford Econ. Pap.*, March 1969, *21*(1), pp. 56–65.

Meiselman, David. The Role of Money in National Economic Policy. In *Federal Reserve Bank of Boston,* 1969, pp. 15–19.

Meltzer, Allan H. Money, Intermediation, and Growth. *J. Econ. Lit.*, March 1969, *7*(1), pp. 27–56.

Meltzer, Allan H. The Role of Money in National Economic Policy. In *Federal Reserve Bank of Boston,* 1969, pp. 25–29.

Naylor, John A. A Note on the 'Traditional Theory' of the Term Structure of Interest Rates and Rates on Three- and Six-Month Treasury Bills: Comment. *Int. Econ. Rev.*, October 1969, *10*(3), pp. 484–87. **[G: U.S.]**

Olivera, Julio H. G. La posición monetaria neta: Observaciones complementarias. (The Net Monetary Position: Some Additional Remarks. With English summary.) *Económica,* September–December 1969, *15*(3), pp. 313–15.

Patinkin, Don. Money and Wealth: A Review Article. *J. Econ. Lit.*, December 1969, *7*(4), pp. 1140–60.

Patinkin, Don. The Chicago Tradition, the Quantity Theory, and Friedman. *J. Money, Credit, Banking,* February 1969, *1*(1), pp. 46–70.

Peltzman, Sam. The Structure of the Money-Expenditures Relationship. *Amer. Econ. Rev.*, March 1969, *59*(1), pp. 129–37. **[G: U.S.]**

Phillips, Keith E. The Short-Run Stability of Velocity and the Autonomous Spending Multiplier, 1946–1962. *J. Polit. Econ.*, May/June 1969, *77*(3), pp. 418–29.

Pigou, A. C. The Classical Stationary State. In *Williams, H. R. and Huffnagle, J. D., eds.*, 1969, pp. 327–34.

Polakoff, Murray E. and Rangarajan, C. A Note on a "Keynesian" Model of Aggregate Demand: Reply. *J. Finance,* March 1969, *24*(1), pp. 104–05.

Robinson, T. Russell. The Foreign Trade Sector and Domestic Stability: The Canadian Case. *Yale Econ. Essays,* Spring 1969, *9*(1), pp. 47–87. **[G: Canada]**

Salama, Elías. Sobre la posición monetaria neta. (On the Net Monetary Position. With English summary.) *Económica,* September–December 1969, *15*(3), pp. 299–311.

Samuelson, Paul A. The Role of Money in National Economic Policy. In *Federal Reserve Bank of Boston,* 1969, pp. 7–13.

Sargent, Thomas J. Commodity Price Expectations and the Interest Rate. *Quart. J. Econ.*, February 1969, *83*(1), pp. 127–40. **[G: U.S.]**

Schwartz, Anna J. Why Money Matters. *Lloyds Bank Rev.*, October 1969, (94), pp. 1–16. **[G: U.S.; U.K.]**

Shimazu, Ryoji. A Reconsideration of the Quantity Theory of Money. *Kyoto Univ. Econ. Rev.*, April 1969, *39*(1), pp. 45–62.

Smith, Warren L. A Neo-Keynesian View of Monetary Policy. In *Federal Reserve Bank of Boston,* 1969, pp. 105–26.

Sprenkle, Case M. The Uselessness of Transactions Demand Models. *J. Finance,* December 1969, *24* (5), pp. 835–47.

Starleaf, Dennis R. and Stephenson, James A. A Suggested Solution to the Monetary-Policy Indicator Problem: The Monetary Full Employment Interest Rate. *J. Finance,* September 1969, *24*(4), pp. 623–41. [G: U.S.]

Stein, Herbert. Where Stands the New Fiscal Policy? *J. Money, Credit, Banking,* August 1969, *1*(3), pp. 463–73. [G: U.S.]

Sufrin, Sidney C. and Wagner, Abraham R. Interest Rate Manipulation, Employment and Output—A Disaggregated Suggestion. *Rivista Int. Sci. Econ. Com.,* April 1969, *16*(4), pp. 327–41. [G: U.S.]

Swamy, M. R. Kumara. The Paradox of Full Capacity *Vs.* Full Employment Growth. *Asian Econ. Rev.,* August 1969, *11*(4), pp. 446–51.

Tobin, James. A General Equilibrium Approach to Monetary Theory. *J. Money, Credit, Banking,* February 1969, *1*(1), pp. 15–29.

Tobin, James and Swan, Craig. Money and Permanent Income: Some Empirical Tests. *Amer. Econ. Rev.,* May 1969, *59*(2), pp. 285–95. [G: U.S.]

Tobin, James. The Role of Money in National Economic Policy. **In** *Federal Reserve Bank of Boston,* 1969, pp. 21–24.

Trezza, Bruno. Produttività marginale del capitale e tasso di interesse nel modello keynesiano. (The Marginal Productivity of Capital and the Rate of Interest in the Keynesian Model. With English summary.) *L'Industria,* January–March 1969, (1), pp. 35–57.

Tsiang, S. C. The Precautionary Demand for Money: An Inventory Theoretical Analysis. *J. Polit. Econ.,* January/February 1969, *77*(1), pp. 99–117.

Tucker, Donald P. Monetary Theory: Discussion. *Amer. Econ. Rev.,* May 1969, *59*(2), pp. 321–23. [G: U.S.]

Wallich, Henry C. A Neo-Keynesian View of Monetary Policy: Discussion. **In** *Federal Reserve Bank of Boston,* 1969, pp. 127–131.

Wallich, Henry C. Keynesian Monetary Theories, Stabilization Policy, and the Recent Inflation: A Comment. *J. Money, Credit, Banking,* August 1969, *1*(3), pp. 590–99. [G: U.S.]

Wallich, Henry C. The Role of Money in National Economic Policy. **In** *Federal Reserve Bank of Boston,* 1969, pp. 31–36.

Whalen, Edward L. On the Transactions Demand for Cash: Reply. *J. Finance,* December 1969, *24* (5), pp. 950–53.

Woll, Artur. Die Theorie der Geldnachfrage: Analytische Ansätze und statische Ergebnisse für die Bundesrepublik Deutschland. (With English summary.) *Z. ges. Staatswiss.,* January 1969, *125*(1), pp. 56–81. [G: W. Germany]

0231 Developments in General Macroeconomic Theory 1930-45

Borch, Karl. Another Note on Keynesian Mathematics. *Econ. J.,* March 1969, *79*(313), pp. 182–83.

Gossling, W. F. A Note on User Cost. *Manchester Sch. Econ. Soc. Stud.,* September 1969, *37*(3), pp. 259–61.

Harris, Seymour E. Introduction: Keynes' Attack on *Laissez Faire* and Classical Economics and Wage Theory. **In** *Williams, H. R. and Huffnagle, J. D., eds.,* 1969, pp. 7–20.

Naylor, Thomas H. A Third Note on Keynesian Mathematics. *Econ. J.,* March 1969, *79*(313), pp. 183–84.

Streeten, Paul. Keynes and the Classical Tradition. **In** *Williams, H. R. and Huffnagle, J. D., eds.,* 1969, pp. 21–37.

0232 Theory of Aggregate Demand: Consumption

Barnhill, J. Allison. The Application of Engel's Laws of Personal Consumption (1857) to the European Common Market (1957–61). **In** *Alexis, M.; Holloway, R. J. and Hancock, R. S., eds.,* 1969, pp. 95–104. [G: E.E.C.]

Blumenthal, Tuvia. A Note on the Life-Cycle Pattern of Saving in Japan. *Hitotsubashi J. Econ.,* February 1969, *9*(2), pp. 61–67. [G: Japan]

Branson, William H. and Klevorick, Alvin K. Money Illusion and the Aggregate Consumption Function. *Amer. Econ. Rev.,* December 1969, *59*(5), pp. 832–49. [G: U.S.]

Cass, David and Stiglitz, Joseph E. The Implications of Alternative Saving and Expectations Hypotheses for Choices of Technique and Patterns of Growth. *J. Polit. Econ.,* Part II, July/August 1969, *77*(4), pp. 586–627.

Evans, Michael K. and Kisselgoff, Avram. Demand for Consumer Installment Credit and Its Effects on Consumption. **In** *Duesenberry, J. S., et al.,* 1969, pp. 39–84. [G: U.S.]

Folsom, Roger Nils. Real and Money Consumption as Functions of Money Income. *Western Econ. J.,* March 1969, *7*(1), pp. 96–99.

Friedman, Milton. The Permanent Income Hypothesis. **In** *Williams, H. R. and Huffnagle, J. D., eds.,* 1969, pp. 141–58.

Goldman, Steven M. Consumption Behavior and Time Preference. *J. Econ. Theory,* June 1969, *1* (1), pp. 39–47.

Kalman, P. J. Classes of Utility Functions Admitting Tyrni's Homogeneous Saving Function. *Rev. Econ. Stud.,* January 1969, *36*(105), pp. 122–24.

Kumar, T. Krishna. The Existence of an Optimal Economic Policy. *Econometrica,* October 1969, *37*(4), pp. 600–610.

Laumas, Prem S. A Test of the Permanent Income Hypothesis. *J. Polit. Econ.,* September/October 1969, *77*(5), pp. 857–61. [G: Canada]

Leff, Nathaniel H. Dependency Rates and Savings Rates. *Amer. Econ. Rev.,* December 1969, *59*(5), pp. 886–96.

Mizoguchi, Toshiyuki. Time-Series Analysis of the Consumption Function in Japan by Occupational Group. *Hitotsubashi J. Econ.,* February 1969, *9* (2), pp. 13–34. [G: Japan]

Modigliani, Franco and Brumberg, Richard. Utility Analysis and the Consumption Function: An Interpretation of Cross-section Data. **In** *Williams, H. R. and Huffnagle, J. D., eds.,* 1969, pp. 99–140.

Motley, Brian. Consumer Investment, Expectations, and Transitory Income. *Western Econ. J.,* September 1969, *7*(3), pp. 223–29.

Motley, Brian. The Consumer's Demand for Money: A Neoclassical Approach. *J. Polit. Econ.,* September/October 1969, *77*(5), pp. 817–26.

Parks, Richard W. Systems of Demand Equations:

An Empirical Comparison of Alternative Functional Forms. *Econometrica,* October 1969, *37*(4), pp. 629–50.

Ramsey, Frank P. A Mathematical Theory of Saving. In *Arrow, K. J. and Scitovsky, T., eds.,* 1969, pp. 619–33.

Shell, Karl; Sidrauski, Miguel and Stiglitz, Joseph E. Capital Gains, Income, and Saving. *Rev. Econ. Stud.,* January 1969, *36*(105), pp. 15–26.

Williamson, Jeffrey G. Income Growth and Savings. *Philippine Econ. J.,* First Semester 1969, *8*(1), pp. 54–74. **[G: Asia]**

Wright, Colin. Estimating Permanent Income: A Note. *J. Polit. Econ.,* September/October 1969, *77*(5), pp. 845–50.

Wright, Colin. Saving and the Rate of Interest. In *Harberger, A. C. and Bailey, M. J., eds.,* 1969, pp. 275–300. **[G: U.S.]**

0233 Theory of Aggregate Demand: Investment

Agarwala, R.; Burns, T. and Duffy, M. Forecasting Gross Private Fixed Investment Using Intentions Survey Data. *Manchester Sch. Econ. Soc. Stud.,* December 1969, *37*(4), pp. 279–93. **[G: U.K.]**

Bischoff, Charles W. Hypothesis Testing and the Demand for Capital Goods. *Rev. Econ. Statist.,* August 1969, *51*(3), pp. 354–68.

Bredov, V. and Levin, A. Prediction of the Population's Demand. *Prob. Econ.,* January 1969, *11*(9), pp. 34–44. **[G: U.S.S.R.]**

Brown, H. P. The Present Theory of Investment Appraisal: A Critical Analysis. *Bull. Oxford Univ. Inst. Econ. Statist.,* May 1969, *31*(2), pp. 105–31.

Burmeister, Edwin and Dobell, A. Rodney. Disembodied Technological Change with Several Factors. *J. Econ. Theory,* June 1969, *1*(1), pp. 1–8.

Čobeljič, Nikola and Stojanovič, Radmila. The Theory of Investment Cycles in a Socialist Economy. *Eastern Europ. Econ.,* Fall 1968/Winter 1968–69, *7*(1–2), pp. 1–168. **[G: Europe]**

Fishelson, Gideon. The Future Income Hypothesis. *Southern Econ. J.,* January 1969, *35*(3), pp. 268–69.

Fisher, Franklin M. Approximate Aggregation and the Leontief Conditions. *Econometrica,* July 1969, *37*(3), pp. 457–69.

Fleck, Florian H. Die CES-Funktion als Produktionsund Verteilungsfunktion. Ein Vergleich mit der COBB-DOUGLAS-Funktion. (The CES-Function as a Production- and Distribution-Function. A Comparison with the Cobb-Douglas-Function. With English summary.) *Jahr. Nationalökon. Statist.,* July 1969, *183*(2), pp. 125–40.

Gollop, Frank. Structural Inflation. *Amer. Econ.,* Fall 1969, *13*(2), pp. 31–39. **[G: U.S.]**

Hayek, F. A. Three Elucidations of the Ricardo Effect. *J. Polit. Econ.,* March/April 1969, *77*(2), pp. 274–85.

Jorgenson, Dale W. and Stephenson, James A. Issues in the Development of the Neoclassical Theory of Investment Behavior. *Rev. Econ. Statist.,* August 1969, *51*(3), pp. 346–53.

Koizumi, Susumu. Technical Progress and Investment. *Int. Econ. Rev.,* February 1969, *10*(1), pp. 68–81.

Laing, N. F. Two Notes on Pasinetti's Theorem. *Econ. Rec.,* September 1969, *45*(111), pp. 373–85.

Macesich, George and Close, F. Alan. Monetary Velocity and Investment Multiplier Stability Relativity for Norway and Sweden. *Statsokon. Tidsskr.,* March 1969, *83*(1), pp. 10–22. **[G: Norway; Sweden]**

Minsky, Hyman P. Private Sector Asset Management and the Effectiveness of Monetary Policy: Theory and Practice. *J. Finance,* May 1969, *24*(2), pp. 223–38. **[G: U.S.]**

Schreiber, Wilfrid. Die determinierte Investition: Kritik am neoklassischen Wachstums-Konzept. (With English summary.) *Jahr. Nationalökon. Statist.,* May 1969, *182*(6), pp. 530–41.

Soldofsky, Robert M. Asset Management and Monetary Policy: Discussion. *J. Finance,* May 1969, *24*(2), pp. 245–47. **[G: U.S.]**

Stiglitz, Joseph E. Allocation of Heterogeneous Capital Goods in a Two-Sector Economy. *Int. Econ. Rev.,* October 1969, *10*(3), pp. 373–90.

Thurow, Lester C. A Disequilibrium Neoclassical Investment Function. *Rev. Econ. Statist.,* November 1969, *51*(4), pp. 431–35.

Wittmann, Walter. Die Staatsausgaben in der makroökonomischen Produktionsfunktion. (With English summary.) *Kyklos,* 1969, *22*(2), pp. 297–313.

0234 Theory of Aggregate Supply

Beckmann, Martin J. and Sato, Ryuzo. Aggregate Production Functions and Types of Technical Progress: A Statistical Analysis. *Amer. Econ. Rev.,* March 1969, *59*(1), pp. 88–101. **[G: U.S.; Japan; Germany]**

Davidson, Paul. A Keynesian View of Patinkin's Theory of Employment: A Rejoinder. *Econ. J.,* March 1969, *79*(313), pp. 181–82.

Dhrymes, Phoebus J. A Model of Short-run Labor Adjustment. In *Duesenberry, J. S., et al.,* 1969, pp. 110–49. **[G: U.S.]**

Fisher, Franklin M. The Existence of Aggregate Production Functions. *Econometrica,* October 1969, *37*(4), pp. 553–77.

Gramm, William P. A Keynesian View of Patinkin's Theory of Employment: Comment. *Econ. J.,* March 1969, *79*(313), pp. 179–81.

Hansen, Terje. An Aggregated Production Function. *Statsokon. Tidsskr.,* March 1969, *83*(1), pp. 1–9.

Lucas, Robert E., Jr. and Rapping, Leonard A. Real Wages, Employment, and Inflation. *J. Polit. Econ.,* September/October 1969, *77*(5), pp. 721–54. **[G: U.S.]**

Pasinetti, Luigi L. Switches of Technique and the "Rate of Return" in Capital Theory. *Econ. J.,* September 1969, *79*(315), pp. 508–31.

Phelps, Edmund S. A Note on Short-Run Employment and Real Wage Rate under Competitive Commodity Markets. *Int. Econ. Rev.,* June 1969, *10*(2), pp. 220–32.

Sato, Kazuo. Micro and Macro Constant-Elasticity-of-Substitution Production Functions in a Multifirm Industry. *J. Econ. Theory,* December 1969, *1*(4), pp. 438–53.

Schreiber, Wilfrid. On Two Topical Questions of Distribution Theory and Policy. *Ger. Econ. Rev.,* 1969, *7*(3), pp. 199–215. **[G: W. Germany]**

Szakolczai, György and Stahl, János. Increasing or Decreasing Returns to Scale in the Constant Elasticity of Substitution Production Function. *Rev. Econ. Statist.,* February 1969, *51*(1), pp. 84–90. **[G: U.S.; Hungary]**

0235 Theory of Aggregate Distribution

Anderson, Robert W. A Note on Tax Incidence in a Macroeconomic Distribution Model. *Rivista Int. Sci. Econ. Com.,* December 1969, *16*(12), pp. 1164–73.

Bhaduri, Amit. On the Significance of Recent Controversies on Capital Theory: A Marxian View. *Econ. J.,* September 1969, *79*(315), pp. 532–39.

Conlisk, John. An Approach to the Theory of Inequality in the Size Distribution of Income. *Western Econ. J.,* June 1969, *7*(2), pp. 180–86. **[G: U.S.]**

Harcourt, G. C. Some Cambridge Controversies in the Theory of Capital. *J. Econ. Lit.,* June 1969, *7* (2), pp. 369–405.

Heidensohn, K. Labour's Share in National Income—A Constant? *Manchester Sch. Econ. Soc. Stud.,* December 1969, *37*(4), pp. 295–321.

McCarthy, Michael D. An Analysis of Non-wage Income Components. **In** *Duesenberry, J. S., et al.,* 1969, pp. 151–86. **[G: U.S.]**

Mieszkowski, Peter. Tax Incidence Theory: The Effects of Taxes on the Distribution of Income. *J. Econ. Lit.,* December 1969, *7*(4), pp. 1103–24.

Riach, P. A. A Framework for Macro-Distribution Analysis. *Kyklos,* 1969, *22*(3), pp. 542–65.

Schmitt-Rink, Gerhard. Funktionelle Verteilung, personelle Verteilung und Multiplikatoreffekt. Überlegungen zum Kaldor-Ansatz in der Verteilungstheorie. (With English summary.) *Jahr. Nationalökon. Statist.,* December 1969, *183*(5), pp. 361–771.

Schreiber, Wilfrid. On Two Topical Questions of Distribution Theory and Policy. *Ger. Econ. Rev.,* 1969, *7*(3), pp. 199–215. **[G: W. Germany]**

Streissler, Erich. Long Term Structural Changes in the Distribution of Income. *Z. Nationalökon.,* May 1969, *29*(1–2), pp. 39–110.

Walter, Helmut. Über einige Zusammenhänge zwischen Einkommensverteilung und globaler Beschäftigtenstruktur. (With English summary.) *Z. ges. Staatswiss.,* April 1969, *125*(2), pp. 248–60. **[G: W. Germany]**

024 Welfare Theory

0240 General

Balassa, Bela. Centralization and Decentralization in Economic Systems: Discussion. *Amer. Econ. Rev.,* May 1969, *59*(2), pp. 533–37.

Baumol, William J. On the Discount Rate for Public Projects. **In** *The Analysis and Evaluation of Public Expenditures: The PPB System, Vol. 1, JECP,* 1969, pp. 489–503.

Chenery, Hollis B. The Interdependence of Investment Decisions. **In** *Arrow, K. J. and Scitovsky, T., eds.,* 1969, pp. 336–71.

Crew, Michael A. Coinsurance and the Welfare Economics of Medical Care. *Amer. Econ. Rev.,* December 1969, *59*(5), pp. 906–08.

Debreu, Gerard. Valuation Equilibrium and Pareto Optimum. **In** *Arrow, K. J. and Scitovsky, T., eds.,* 1969, pp. 39–45.

Dorfman, Robert. General Equilibrium with Public Goods. **In** *Margolis, J. and Guitton, H., eds.,* 1969, pp. 247–75.

Dupuit, Jules. On the Measurement of the Utility of Public Works. **In** *Arrow, K. J. and Scitovsky, T., eds.,* 1969, pp. 255–83.

Encarnación, José, Jr. On Independence Postulates Concerning Choice. *Int. Econ. Rev.,* June 1969, *10*(2), pp. 134–40.

Haveman, Robert H. The Opportunity Cost of Displaced Private Spending and the Social Discount Rate. *Water Resources Res.,* October 1969, *5*(5), pp. 947–57. **[G: U.S.]**

Head, John G. and Shoup, Carl S. Public Goods, Private Goods, and Ambiguous Goods. *Econ. J.,* September 1969, *79*(315), pp. 567–72.

Hicks, John R. The Rehabilitation of Consumers' Surplus. **In** *Arrow, K. J. and Scitovsky, T., eds.,* 1969, pp. 325–35.

Hinich, Melvin J. and Ordeshook, Peter C. Abstentions and Equilibrium in the Electoral Process. *Public Choice,* Fall 1969, *7,* pp. 81–106.

Hirshleifer, Jack and Shapiro, David L. The Treatment of Risk and Uncertainty. **In** *The Analysis and Evaluation of Public Expenditures: The PPB System, Vol. 1, JECP,* 1969, pp. 505–30.

Hurwicz, Leonid. On the Concept and Possibility of Informational Decentralization. *Amer. Econ. Rev.,* May 1969, *59*(2), pp. 513–24.

Hurwicz, Leonid. Optimality and Informational Efficiency in Resource Allocation Processes. **In** *Arrow, K. J. and Scitovsky, T., eds.,* 1969, pp. 61–80.

Jochimsen, R. Performance and Respective Spheres of Public and Private Enterprise. **In** *Margolis, J. and Guitton, H., eds.,* 1969, pp. 406–23.

Johansen, Leif. An Examination of the Relevance of Kenneth Arrow's General Possibility Theorem for Economic Planning. *Econ. Planning,* 1969, *9* (1–2), pp. 5–41.

de Jouvenel, Bertrand. Efficiency and Amenity. **In** *Arrow, K. J. and Scitovsky, T., eds.,* 1969, pp. 100–112.

Kaldor, Nicholas. Welfare Propositions of Economics and Interpersonal Comparisons of Utility. **In** *Arrow, K. J. and Scitovsky, T., eds.,* 1969, pp. 387–89.

Kirman, Alan P. and Tomasini, Luigi M. Teoria delle scelte sociali e relativi concetti. (Social Choice Theory and Related Concepts. With English summary.) *L'Industria,* April–June 1969, (2), pp. 176–96.

Kolm, Serge-Christophe. The Optimal Production of Social Justice. **In** *Margolis, J. and Guitton, H., eds.,* 1969, pp. 145–200.

Lange, Oskar. The Foundations of Welfare Economics. **In** *Arrow, K. J. and Scitovsky, T., eds.,* 1969, pp. 26–38.

Lieberman, Bernhardt. Combining Individual Preferences into a Social Choice. **In** *Buchler, I. R. and Nutini, H. G., eds.*, 1969, pp. 95–115.

Mainander, Nils. Den samhällsekonomiska lönsamheten—praktiska kalkylmöjligheter. (Profitability to the Community—Its Calculability in Practice. With English summary.) *Econ. Samfundets Tidskr.*, 1969, *22*(2), pp. 81–94.

Majumdar, Tapas. A Note on Arrow's Postulates for a Social Welfare Function—A Comment. *J. Polit. Econ.*, Part I, July/August 1969, *77*(4), pp. 528–31.

McGuire, Martin C. and Aaron, Henry J. Efficiency and Equity in the Optimal Supply of a Public Good. *Rev. Econ. Statist.*, February 1969, *51*(1), pp. 31–39.

Meinander, Nils. Den Samhällsekonomiska lönsamheten—analys av begreppet. (An Analysis of the Concept "Profitability to the Society." With English summary.) *Econ. Samfundets Tidskr.*, 1969, *22*(1), pp. 3–19.

Misra, P. N. A Welfare Criterion for the Determination of Agricultural Prices. *Indian Econ. J.*, October–December 1969, *17*(2), pp. 273–78.

Moore, Thomas Gale. An Economic Analysis of the Concept of Freedom. *J. Polit. Econ.*, Part I, July/August 1969, *77*(4), pp. 532–44.

Musgrave, Richard A. Provision for Social Goods. **In** *Margolis, J. and Guitton, H., eds.*, 1969, pp. 124–44.

Niemi, Richard G. Majority Decision-Making with Partial Unidimensionality. *Amer. Polit. Sci. Rev.*, June 1969, *63*(2), pp. 488–97.

Olson, Mancur, Jr. The Principle of "Fiscal Equivalence": The Division of Responsibilities among Different Levels of Government. *Amer. Econ. Rev.*, May 1969, *59*(2), pp. 479–87. **[G: U.S.]**

Radomysler, A. Welfare Economics and Economic Policy. **In** *Arrow, K. J. and Scitovsky, T., eds.*, 1969, pp. 81–94.

Ramsey, Frank P. A Mathematical Theory of Saving. **In** *Arrow, K. J. and Scitovsky, T., eds.*, 1969, pp. 619–33.

Samuelson, Paul A. Contrast between Welfare Conditions for Joint Supply and for Public Goods. *Rev. Econ. Statist.*, February 1969, *51*(1), pp. 26–30.

Samuelson, Paul A. Pure Theory of Public Expenditure and Taxation. **In** *Margolis, J. and Guitton, H., eds.*, 1969, pp. 98–123.

Sen, Amartya K. Planners' Preferences: Optimality, Distribution and Social Welfare. **In** *Margolis, J. and Guitton, H., eds.*, 1969, pp. 201–21.

Steiner, Peter O. The Public Sector and the Public Interest. **In** *The Analysis and Evaluation of Public Expenditures: The PPB System, Vol. 1, JECP*, 1969, pp. 13–45.

Tarascio, Vincent J. Paretian Welfare Theory: Some Neglected Aspects. *J. Polit. Econ.*, January/February 1969, *77*(1), pp. 1–20.

Thompson, Proctor. Government and the Market. **In** *Starleaf, D. R., ed.*, 1969, pp. 179–95.

Turvey, R. The Second-best Case for Marginal Cost Pricing. **In** *Margolis, J. and Guitton, H., eds.*, 1969, pp. 336–43.

Weiss, Roger W. Mishan on Progress: A Review Note. *J. Polit. Econ.*, January/February 1969, *77* (1), pp. 138–40.

Weisskopf, Walter A. Mishan on Progress: A Rejoinder. *J. Polit. Econ.*, November/December 1969, *77*(6), pp. 1036–39.

0242 Allocative Efficiency Including Theory of Cost/Benefit

Aaron, Henry J. Local Public Expenditures and the "Migration Effect." *Western Econ. J.*, December 1969, *7*(4), pp. 385–90.

Arrow, Kenneth J. and Kurz, Mordecai. Optimal Consumer Allocation over an Infinite Horizon. *J. Econ. Theory*, June 1969, *1*(1), pp. 68–91.

Arrow, Kenneth J. and Kurz, Mordecai. Optimal Public Investment Policy and Controllability with Fixed Private Savings Ratio. *J. Econ. Theory*, August 1969, *1*(2), pp. 141–77.

Arrow, Kenneth J. The Organization of Economic Activity: Issues Pertinent to the Choice of Market Versus Nonmarket Allocation. **In** *The Analysis and Evaluation of Public Expenditures: The PPB System, Vol. 1, JECP*, 1969, pp. 47–64.

Arrow, Kenneth J. The Social Discount Rate. **In** *Somers, G. G. and Wood, W. D., eds.*, 1969, pp. 56–75.

Asanuma, Banri. Shadow Prices for Public Investment Criteria. *Kyoto Univ. Econ. Rev.*, October 1969, *39*(2), pp. 62–80.

Atsumi, H. The Efficient Capital Programme for a Maintainable Utility Level. *Rev. Econ. Stud.*, July 1969, *36*(107), pp. 263–87.

Barzel, Yoram. Two Propositions on the Optimum Level of Producing Collective Goods. *Public Choice*, Spring 1969, *6*, pp. 31–37.

Baumol, William J. On the Social Rate of Discount: Comment on the Comments. *Amer. Econ. Rev.*, December 1969, *59*(5), pp. 930.

Berry, R. Albert. A Note on Welfare Comparisons between Monopoly and Pure Competition. *Manchester Sch. Econ. Soc. Stud.*, March 1969, *37*(1), pp. 39–57.

Brewer, Durward and Kuehn, John A. Conflicts within Recreation: A Rejoinder. *Land Econ.*, February 1969, *45*(1), pp. 131–33.

Brown, Gardner, Jr. and Johnson, M. Bruce. Public Utility Pricing and Output under Risk. *Amer. Econ. Rev.*, March 1969, *59*(1), pp. 119–28.

Buchanan, James M. and Flowers, Marilyn. An Analytical Setting for a "Taxpayers' Revolution." *Western Econ. J.*, December 1969, *7*(4), pp. 349–59. **[G: U.S.]**

Buchanan, James M. External Diseconomies, Corrective Taxes, and Market Structure. *Amer. Econ. Rev.*, March 1969, *59*(1), pp. 174–77.

Cass, David. Resource Allocation with Probabilistic Individual Preferences: Discussion. *Amer. Econ. Rev.*, May 1969, *59*(2), pp. 562–63.

Childs, Gerald L. Efficient Reallocation of Land in Urban Renewal. *Western Econ. J.*, September 1969, *7*(3), pp. 211–22.

Christ, Carl F. Resource Allocation in a Private-Property, Free-Contract Economy. **In** *Starleaf, D. R., ed.*, 1969, pp. 46–55.

Comanor, William S. and Leibenstein, Harvey. Allocative Efficiency, X-Efficiency and the Measurement of Welfare Losses. *Economica, N.S.*, August 1969, *36*(143), pp. 304–09.

Cornwall, Richard R. The Use of Prices to Characterize the Core of an Economy. *J. Econ. Theory,* December 1969, *1*(4), pp. 353–73.

Cotner, Melvin L. A Policy for Public Investments in Natural Resources. *Amer. J. Agr. Econ.,* February 1969, *51*(1), pp. 87–99.

Crew, Michael A. Mr. Tipping on Road Pricing. *Econ. J.,* December 1969, *79*(316), pp. 975–77.

Crew, Michael A. The Optimality of Pure Competition in the Capacity Problem: Further Comment. *Quart. J. Econ.,* May 1969, *83*(2), pp. 341–43.

De Alessi, Louis. Implications of Property Rights for Government Investment Choices. *Amer. Econ. Rev.,* March 1969, *59*(1), pp. 13–24.

Demsetz, Harold. Contracting Cost and Public Policy. **In** *The Analysis and Evaluation of Public Expenditures: The PPB System, Vol. 1, JECP,* 1969, pp. 167–74.

Demsetz, Harold. Information and Efficiency: Another Viewpoint. *J. Law Econ.,* April 1969, *12*(1), pp. 1–22.

Dorfman, Robert and Jacoby, Henry D. A Model of Public Decisions Illustrated by a Water Pollution Policy Problem. **In** *The Analysis and Evaluation of Public Expenditures: The PPB System, Vol. 1, JECP,* 1969, pp. 226–74.

Fedorenko, N. and Shatalin, S. The Problem of Optimal Planning of the Socialist Economy. *Prob. Econ.,* November 1969, *12*(7), pp. 3–29.

Fourgeaud, Claude. Contribution à l'Étude du Rôle des Administrations dans la Théorie Mathématique de l'Équilibre et de l'Optimum. (With English summary.) *Econometrica,* April 1969, *37* (2), pp. 307–23.

Ganguly, Subrata K. The Perfectly Competitive Production of Collective Goods: Comment. *Rev. Econ. Statist.,* November 1969, *51*(4), pp. 478–79.

Glejser, H. Een toepassing van de kosten-batenanalyse: het project "Zeestad." (Cost-Benefit Analysis of the Project "Zeestad." With English summary.) *Tijdschr. Econ.,* 1969, *14*(4), pp. 519–48. **[G: Belgium]**

Hadar, Josef. Optimality of Imperfectly Competitive Resource Allocation. *Western Econ. J.,* March 1969, *7*(1), pp. 51–56.

Harberger, Arnold C. Professor Arrow on the Social Discount Rate: Discussion. **In** *Somers, G. G. and Wood, W. D., eds.,* 1969, pp. 76–88.

Head, John G. and Shoup, C. S. Excess Burden: The Corner Case. *Amer. Econ. Rev.,* March 1969, *59* (1), pp. 181–83.

Henderson, Alexander M. The Pricing of Public Utility Undertakings. **In** *Arrow, K. J. and Scitovsky, T., eds.,* 1969, pp. 541–60.

Hildenbrand, Werner. Pareto Optimality for a Measure Space of Economic Agents. *Int. Econ. Rev.,* October 1969, *10*(3), pp. 363–72.

Hirsch, Werner Z. and Marcus, Morton J. Intercommunity Spillovers and the Provision of Public Education. *Kyklos,* 1969, *22*(4), pp. 641–60. **[G: U.S.]**

Hotelling, Harold. The General Welfare in Relation to Problems of Taxation and of Railway and Utility Rates. **In** *Arrow, K. J. and Scitovsky, T., eds.,* 1969, pp. 284–308.

Isard, Walter. Toward a More Adequate General Regional Theory and Approach to Conflict Resolution. *Peace Res. Soc. Internat. Pap.,* 1969, *11,* pp. 1–21.

James, Estelle. On the Social Rate of Discount: Comment. *Amer. Econ. Rev.,* December 1969, *59*(5), pp. 912–16.

Kapp, K. William. On the Nature and Significance of Social Costs. *Kyklos,* 1969, *22*(2), pp. 334–47.

Kolm, Serge-Christophe. La vérité des prix dans un monde imparfait. (With English summary.) *Revue Écon.,* July 1969, *20*(4), pp. 727–40.

Krutilla, John V. Efficiency Goals, Market Failure, and the Substitution of Public for Private Action. **In** *The Analysis and Evaluation of Public Expenditures: The PPB System, Vol. 1, JECP,* 1969, pp. 277–89. **[G: U.S.]**

Landauer, Carl. On the Social Rate of Discount: Comment. *Amer. Econ. Rev.,* December 1969, *59* (5), pp. 917–18.

Long, Burl F. and Barron, James C. Conflicts within Recreation: Comment. *Land Econ.,* February 1969, *45*(1), pp. 128–31.

Magnani, Italo. Effetti di benessere derivanti da variazioni del saggio d'interesse e imposizione degli incrementi patrimoniali. (Welfare Effects of Changes in the Interest Rate and Capital Gains Taxation. With English summary.) *Rivista Int. Sci. Econ. Com.,* December 1969, *16*(12), pp. 1145–63.

Malinvaud, E. Risk-taking and Resource Allocation. **In** *Margolis, J. and Guitton, H., eds.,* 1969, pp. 222–46.

Margolis, Julius. Shadow Prices for Incorrect or Nonexistent Market Values. **In** *The Analysis and Evaluation of Public Expenditures: The PPB System, Vol. 1, JECP,* 1969, pp. 533–46.

McFadden, Daniel. A Simple Remark on the Second Best Pareto Optimality of Market Equilibria. *J. Econ. Theory,* June 1969, *1*(1), pp. 26–38.

McGuire, Martin C. and Garn, Harvey A. The Integration of Equity and Efficiency Criteria in Public Project Selection. *Econ. J.,* December 1969, *79* (316), pp. 882–93.

Meade, James E. and Fleming, J. Marcus. Price and Output Policy of State Enterprise: A Symposium. **In** *Arrow, K. J. and Scitovsky, T., eds.,* 1969, pp. 309–24.

Mera, Koichi. Experimental Determination of Relative Marginal Utilities. *Quart. J. Econ.,* August 1969, *83*(3), pp. 464–77.

Merton, Robert C. A Golden Golden-Rule for Welfare-Maximization in an Economy with a Varying Population Growth Rate. *Western Econ. J.,* December 1969, *7*(4), pp. 307–18.

Milliman, Jerome W. Beneficiary Charges and Efficient Public Expenditure Decisions. **In** *The Analysis and Evaluation of Public Expenditures: The PPB System, Vol. 1, JECP,* 1969, pp. 291–318.

Mishan, E. J. Normalisation of Public Investment Criteria: Erratum. *Econ. J.,* December 1969, *79* (316), pp. 980.

Mishan, E. J. The Relationship between Joint Products, Collective Goods, and External Effects. *J. Polit. Econ.,* May/June 1969, *77*(3), pp. 329–48.

Mobasheri, Fereidoun. A Criterion for Appraisal of Economic Development Projects. *Eng. Econ.,* October–November 1969, *15*(1), pp. 9–27.

Morrison, Clarence C. Marginal Cost Pricing and the

Theory of Second Best. *Western Econ. J.,* June 1969, *7*(2), pp. 145–52.

Musgrave, Richard A. Cost-Benefit Analysis and the Theory of Public Finance. *J. Econ. Lit.,* September 1969, *7*(3), pp. 797–806.

Naor, P. The Regulation of Queue Size by Levying Tolls. *Econometrica,* January 1969, *37*(1), pp. 15–24.

Nichols, Alan. On the Social Rate of Discount: Comment. *Amer. Econ. Rev.,* December 1969, *59*(5), pp. 909–11.

Oakland, William H. Joint Goods. *Economica, N.S.,* August 1969, *36*(143), pp. 253–68.

Olson, Mancur, Jr. The Optimal Allocation of Jurisdictional Responsibility: The Principle of "Fiscal Equivalence." **In** *The Analysis and Evaluation of Public Expenditures: The PPB System, Vol. 1, JECP,* 1969, pp. 321–31.

Owen, Bruce M. The Perfectly Competitive Production of Collective Goods: Comment. *Rev. Econ. Statist.,* November 1969, *51*(4), pp. 475–76.

Ramsey, David D. On the Social Rate of Discount: Comment. *Amer. Econ. Rev.,* December 1969, *59*(5), pp. 919–24.

Renko, Kyösti. Second best-teoria. (The Theory of Second Best. With English summary.) *Kansant. Aikak.,* 1969, *65*(1), pp. 41–56.

Reuber, Grant L. Professor Arrow on the Social Discount Rate: Discussion. **In** *Somers, G. G. and Wood, W. D., eds.,* 1969, pp. 88–94.

Rodgers, James D. The Perfectly Competitive Production of Collective Goods: Comment. *Rev. Econ. Statist.,* November 1969, *51*(4), pp. 476–78.

Rothenberg, Jerome. Strategic Interaction and Resource Allocation in Metropolitan Intergovernmental Relations. *Amer. Econ. Rev.,* May 1969, *59*(2), pp. 494–503.

Ruff, Larry E. Research and Technological Progress in a Cournot Economy. *J. Econ. Theory,* December 1969, *1*(4), pp. 397–415.

Sen, Amitava and Sengupta, Jati K. Optimal Capacity Models under Periodic Demand: A Survey of Peak Load Pricing Theory and Appraisal. *Z. ges. Staatswiss.,* July 1969, *125*(3), pp. 371–95.

Sharp, C. H. Congestion and Welfare—A Reply. *Econ. J.,* June 1969, *79*(314), pp. 407–12.

Telser, Lester G. On the Regulation of Industry: A Note. *J. Polit. Econ.,* November/December 1969, *77*(6), pp. 937–52.

Thompson, Earl A. The Perfectly Competitive Production of Collective Goods: Reply. *Rev. Econ. Statist.,* November 1969, *51*(4), pp. 479–82.

Tipping, David G. Mr. Tipping on Road Pricing —Reply. *Econ. J.,* December 1969, *79*(316), pp. 977–78.

Usher, Dan. On the Social Rate of Discount: Comment. *Amer. Econ. Rev.,* December 1969, *59*(5), pp. 925–29.

West, E. G. Welfare Economics and Emigration Taxes. *Southern Econ. J.,* July 1969, *36*(1), pp. 52–59.

Whipple, William, Jr. Optimizing Investment in Flood Control and Floodplain Zoning. *Water Resources Res.,* August 1969, *5*(4), pp. 761–66.

Whipple, William, Jr. Utility as a Surrogate for Value in Water Resources Analysis. *Eng. Econ.,* April–May 1969, *14*(3), pp. 159–67.

Williamson, Oliver E. Allocative Efficiency and the Limits of Antitrust. *Amer. Econ. Rev.,* May 1969, *59*(2), pp. 105–18.

Winter, Sidney G., Jr. A Simple Remark on the Second Optimality Theorem of Welfare Economics. *J. Econ. Theory,* June 1969, *1*(1), pp. 99–103.

Wright, J. C. G. 'Products' and Welfare. *Australian Econ. Pap.,* December 1969, *8*(13), pp. 134–53.

Zeckhauser, Richard J. Resource Allocation with Probabilistic Individual Preferences. *Amer. Econ. Rev.,* May 1969, *59*(2), pp. 546–52.

Zeckhauser, Richard J. Uncertainty and the Need for Collective Action. **In** *The Analysis and Evaluation of Public Expenditures: The PPB System, Vol. 1, JECP,* 1969, pp. 149–66.

0243 Redistributive Aspects

Barbosa, A. S. Pinto. A Note on Intermediate Public Expenditures. *Arquivo Inst.,* 1969, *4*(1&2), pp. 21–26.

Hochman, Harold M. and Rodgers, James D. Pareto Optimal Redistribution. *Amer. Econ. Rev.,* Part I, September 1969, *59*(4), pp. 542–57.

Ireland, Thomas R. The Calculus of Philanthropy. *Public Choice,* Fall 1969, *7,* pp. 23–31.

Massell, Benton F. Price Stabilization and Welfare. *Quart. J. Econ.,* May 1969, *83*(2), pp. 284–98.

Mirrlees, James A. The Evaluation of National Income in an Imperfect Economy. *Pakistan Develop. Rev.,* Spring 1969, *9*(1), pp. 1–13.

Mishan, E. J. A Note on the Costs of Tariffs, Monopolies and Thefts. *Western Econ. J.,* September 1969, *7*(3), pp. 230–33.

Mishan, E. J. Rent and Producer's Surplus: Reply. *Amer. Econ. Rev.,* Part I, September 1969, *59*(4), pp. 635–37.

Olsen, Edgar O. A Normative Theory of Transfers. *Public Choice,* Spring 1969, *6,* pp. 39–58.

Peacock, Alan T. Welfare Economics and Public Subsidies to the Arts. *Manchester Sch. Econ. Soc. Stud.,* December 1969, *37*(4), pp. 323–35.

Schmidt, Wilson. Charitable Exploitation. *Public Choice,* Spring 1969, *6,* pp. 103–04.

Tullock, Gordon. Federalism: Problems of Scale. *Public Choice,* Spring 1969, *6,* pp. 19–29.

Weisbrod, Burton A. Collective Action and the Distribution of Income: A Conceptual Approach. **In** *The Analysis and Evaluation of Public Expenditures: The PPB System, Vol. 1, JECP,* 1969, pp. 177–97.

Wessel, Robert H. What Is Producer's Surplus?—Comment. *Amer. Econ. Rev.,* Part I, September 1969, *59*(4), pp. 634–35.

White, Lawrence J. Gains from Trade and Income Distribution: Some New Geometric Tools. *Rivista Int. Sci. Econ. Com.,* September 1969, *16*(9), pp. 837–58.

Worcester, Dean A., Jr. Innovations in the Calculation of Welfare Loss to Monopoly. *Western Econ. J.,* September 1969, *7*(3), pp. 234–43.

0244 Externalities

Ayres, Robert U. and Kneese, Allen V. Production, Consumption, and Externalities. *Amer. Econ. Rev.,* June 1969, *59*(3), pp. 282–97.

Baird, Charles W. On the Publicness of Health Care. *Rev. Soc. Econ.*, September 1969, *27*(2), pp. 109–20.

Davis, Otto A. and Kamien, Morton I. Externalities, Information and Alternative Collective Action. **In** *The Analysis and Evaluation of Public Expenditures: The PPB System, Vol. 1, JECP,* 1969, pp. 67–86.

Ellis, Howard S. and Fellner, William. External Economies and Diseconomies. **In** *Blumner, S. M., ed.*, 1969, pp. 163–79.

Gramm, William P. A Theoretical Note on the Capacity of the Market System to Abate Pollution. *Land Econ.*, August 1969, *45*(3), pp. 365–68.

Kneese, Allen V. and d' Arge, Ralph C. Pervasive External Costs and the Response of Society. **In** *The Analysis and Evaluation of Public Expenditures: The PPB System, Vol. 1, JECP,* 1969, pp. 87–115.

Knight, Frank H. Some Fallacies in the Interpretation of Social Cost. **In** *Arrow, K. J. and Scitovsky, T., eds.*, 1969, pp. 213–27.

Mishan, E. J. Interpretation of the Benefits of Private Transport. **In** *Mishan, E. J.*, 1969, pp. 275–83.

Mishan, E. J. The Relationship between Joint Products, Collective Goods, and External Effects. *J. Polit. Econ.*, May/June 1969, *77*(3), pp. 329–48.

Schmid, A. Allan. Problems in the Theory of Public Choice: Discussion. *Amer. Econ. Rev.*, May 1969, *59*(2), pp. 212–14.

Sherman, Roger and Willett, Thomas D. Regional Development, Externalities and Tax-Subsidy Combinations. *Nat. Tax J.*, June 1969, *22*(2), pp. 291–93.

Tullock, Gordon. Social Cost and Government Action. *Amer. Econ. Rev.*, May 1969, *59*(2), pp. 189–97.

Vincent, Phillip E. Reciprocal Externalities and Optimal Input and Output Levels. *Amer. Econ. Rev.*, December 1969, *59*(5), pp. 976–84.

Worcester, Dean A., Jr. Pecuniary and Technological Externality, Factor Rents, and Social Costs. *Amer. Econ. Rev.*, December 1969, *59*(5), pp. 873–85.

025 Social Choice

0250 Social Choice

Black, Duncan. Lewis Carroll and the Theory of Games. *Amer. Econ. Rev.*, May 1969, *59*(2), pp. 206–10.

Black, Duncan. On Arrow's Impossibility Theorem. *J. Law Econ.*, October 1969, *12*(2), pp. 227–48.

Borcherding, Thomas E. Problems in the Theory of Public Choice: Discussion. *Amer. Econ. Rev.*, May 1969, *59*(2), pp. 211–12.

Boulding, Kenneth E. "Public Choice and the Grants Economy: The Intersecting Set." *Public Choice*, Fall 1969, *7*, pp. 1–2.

Bowen, Howard R. The Interpretation of Voting in the Allocation of Economic Resources. **In** *Arrow, K. J. and Scitovsky, T., eds.*, 1969, pp. 115–32.

Brandt, Karl. Voting Problems in Group Decisions. *Ger. Econ. Rev.*, 1969, *7*(4), pp. 273–94.

Breton, Albert and Breton, Raymond. An Economic Theory of Social Movements. *Amer. Econ. Rev.*, May 1969, *59*(2), pp. 198–205.

Emshoff, James R. and Ackoff, Russell L. Prediction, Explanation, and Control of Conflict. *Peace Res. Soc. Internat. Pap.*, 1969, *12*, pp. 109–15.

FitzLyon, K. Plan and Prediction. *Soviet Stud.*, October 1969, *21*(2), pp. 164–92. **[G: U.S.S.R.]**

Freeman, A. Myrick, III. Income Redistribution and Social Choice: A Pragmatic Approach. *Public Choice*, Fall 1969, *7*, pp. 3–21.

Garvey, Gerald. The Political Economy of Patronal Groups. *Public Choice*, Fall 1969, *7*, pp. 33–45.

Gleser, Leon Jay. The Paradox of Voting: Some Probabilistic Results. *Public Choice*, Fall 1969, *7*, pp. 47–63.

Grofman, Bernard. Some Notes on Voting Schemes and the Will of the Majority. *Public Choice*, Fall 1969, *7*, pp. 65–80.

Hansson, Bengt. Group Preferences. *Econometrica*, January 1969, *37*(1), pp. 50–54.

Hinich, Melvin J. and Ordeshook, Peter C. Abstentions and Equilibrium in the Electoral Process. *Public Choice*, Fall 1969, *7*, pp. 81–106.

Inada, Ken-Ichi. The Simple Majority Decision Rule. *Econometrica*, July 1969, *37*(3), pp. 490–506.

Isard, Walter. Toward a More Adequate General Regional Theory and Approach to Conflict Resolution. *Peace Res. Soc. Internat. Pap.*, 1969, *11*, pp. 1–21.

Kirman, Alan P. and Tomasini, Luigi M. Teoria delle scelte sociali e relativi concetti. (Social Choice Theory and Related Concepts. With English summary.) *L'Industria*, April–June 1969, (2), pp. 176–96.

Klingaman, David. A Note on a Cyclical Majority Problem. *Public Choice*, Spring 1969, *6*, pp. 99–101.

Lady, George M. A Note on "Graph-Theoretical Approaches to the Theory of Social Choice." *Public Choice*, Spring 1969, *6*, pp. 93–98.

Lieberman, Bernhardt. Combining Individual Preferences into a Social Choice. **In** *Buchler, I. R. and Nutini, H. G., eds.*, 1969, pp. 95–115.

Majumdar, Tapas. Sen's General Theorem on Transitivity of Majority Decisions—An Alternative Approach. **In** *[Ghosal, U. N.]*, 1969, pp. 26–29.

Meister, Ronald W. Equal Representation and the Weighted Voting Alternative. *Yale Law J.*, December 1969, *79*(2), pp. 311–21.

Miller, James C., III. A Program for Direct and Proxy Voting in the Legislative Process. *Public Choice*, Fall 1969, *7*, pp. 107–13.

Niemi, Richard G. Majority Decision-Making with Partial Unidimensionality. *Amer. Polit. Sci. Rev.*, June 1969, *63*(2), pp. 488–97.

Nordin, J. A. The Normalized Vote Margins Method of Committee Voting. *Rivista Int. Sci. Econ. Com.*, June 1969, *16*(6), pp. 529–49.

Owen, John D. Education for Majority Voting? *Public Choice*, Spring 1969, *6*, pp. 59–70.

Rosenthal, Howard and Sen, Subrata. Candidate Selection and Voting Behavior in France. *Public Choice*, Spring 1969, *6*, pp. 71–92. **[G: France]**

Schmid, A. Allan. Problems in the Theory of Public Choice: Discussion. *Amer. Econ. Rev.*, May 1969, *59*(2), pp. 212–14.

Scott, Anthony. Investing and Protesting. *J. Polit.*

Econ., November/December 1969, *77*(6), pp. 916–20.

Sen, Amartya K. A Game-Theoretic Analysis of Theories of Collectivism in Allocation. **In** *[Ghosal, U. N.]*, 1969, pp. 1–17.

Sen, Amartya K. and Pattanaik, Prasanta K. Necessary and Sufficient Conditions for Rational Choice under Majority Decision. *J. Econ. Theory*, August 1969, *1*(2), pp. 178–202.

Sen, Amartya K. Quasi-Transitivity, Rational Choice and Collective Decisions. *Rev. Econ. Stud.*, July 1969, *36*(107), pp. 381–93.

Simpson, Paul B. On Defining Areas of Voter Choice: Professor Tullock on Stable Voting. *Quart. J. Econ.*, August 1969, *83*(3), pp. 478–90.

Theil, Henri. The Desired Political Entropy. *Amer. Polit. Sci. Rev.*, June 1969, *63*(2), pp. 521–25.

in't Veld, R. J. Stemmenhandel. (On Explicit Logrolling. With English summary.) *De Economist*, January/February 1969, *117*(1), pp. 24–72.

Ward, Benjamin. Problems in the Theory of Public Choice: Discussion. *Amer. Econ. Rev.*, May 1969, *59*(2), pp. 214–16.

Wilson, Robert. An Axiomatic Model of Logrolling. *Amer. Econ. Rev.*, June 1969, *59*(3), pp. 331–41.

Zeckhauser, Richard. Majority Rule with Lotteries on Alternatives. *Quart. J. Econ.*, November 1969, *83*(4), pp. 696–703.

030 History of Thought; Methodology

031 History of Economic Thought

0310 General

Coats, A. W. Is There a "Structure of Scientific Revolutions" in Economics? *Kyklos*, 1969, *22*(2), pp. 289–96.

Coats, A. W. Research Priorities in the History of Economics. *Hist. Polit. Econ.*, Spring 1969, *1*(1), pp. 9–18.

Engelhardt, Werner Wilhelm. Utopien als Problem der Sozial- und Wirtschaftswissenschaften. (With English summary.) *Z. ges. Staatswiss.*, October 1969, *125*(4), pp. 661–76.

Gerschenkron, Alexander. History of Economic Doctrines and Economic History. *Amer. Econ. Rev.*, May 1969, *59*(2), pp. 1–17.

Jamison, Harold B. On "Disguised Conservatism in Evolutionary Development Theory": Comment. *Sci. Soc.*, Summer-Fall 1969, *33*(3), pp. 348–53.

Letiche, John M. The History of Economic Thought in the *International Encyclopedia of the Social Sciences. J. Econ. Lit.*, June 1969, *7*(2), pp. 406–25.

Nicolae-Văleanu, Ivanciu. Istoria gîndirii economice Româneşti—probleme şi preocupări. (History of Romanian Economic Thought—Problems and Preoccupations. With English summary.) *Stud. Cercet. Econ.*, 1969, *3*, pp. 185–98. **[G: Romania]**

Pavlov, P. and Tsaga, V. The Marginalist Treatment of the Law of Value under Socialism. *Prob. Econ.*, July 1969, *12*(3), pp. 3–22.

Rhodes, Robert I. On "Disguised Conservatism in Evolutionary Development Theory": Reply. *Sci. Soc.*, Summer-Fall 1969, *33*(3), pp. 353–58.

Robinson, Joan. The Theory of Value Reconsidered. *Australian Econ. Pap.*, June 1969, *8*(12), pp. 13–19.

Seligman, Ben B. The Impact of Positivism on Economic Thought. *Hist. Polit. Econ.*, Fall 1969, *1*(2), pp. 256–78.

Shimazu, Ryoji. A Reconsideration of the Quantity Theory of Money. *Kyoto Univ. Econ. Rev.*, April 1969, *39*(1), pp. 45–62.

Stigler, George J. Does Economics Have a Useful Past? *Hist. Polit. Econ.*, Fall 1969, *1*(2), pp. 217–30.

Stjernschantz, Göran. Van man trodde och hur det gick: Något om idéer och debatt i Ekonomiska Samfundet i Finland 1944–69. (Ideas and Debates in the Economic Society of Finland, 1944–69. With English summary.) *Econ. Samfundets Tidskr.*, 1969, *22*(4), pp. 223–40. **[G: Finland]**

0311 Ancient, Medieval

Lowry, S. Todd. Aristotle's Mathematical Analysis of Exchange. *Hist. Polit. Econ.*, Spring 1969, *1*(1), pp. 44–66.

Spandau, Arnt. Some Comments on Professor Rädel's "Profit Maximization—Can It Be Justified?" *S. Afr. J. Econ.*, September 1969, *37*(3), pp. 268–72.

0312 Pre-Classical Except Mercantilist

Eagly, Robert V. A Physiocratic Model of Dynamic Equilibrium. *J. Polit. Econ.*, January/February 1969, *77*(1), pp. 66–84.

Jackson, Andrew. The Position of Condillac in the History of Economic Thought. *Indian Econ. J.*, January–March 1969, *16*(3), pp. 312–26.

Samuels, Warren J. The Tableau Economique as a Simple Leontief Model: A Precursor to Phillips. *Indian Econ. J.*, July–September 1969, *17*(1), pp. 112–17.

0313 Mercantilist

Bog, Ingomar. Mercantilism in Germany. **In** *Coleman, D. C., ed.*, 1969, pp. 162–89. **[G: Germany]**

Hamilton, Earl J. The Political Economy of France at the Time of John Law. *Hist. Polit. Econ.*, Spring 1969, *1*(1), pp. 123–49. **[G: France]**

Heckscher, Eli F. Mercantilism. **In** *Coleman, D. C., ed.*, 1969, pp. 19–34.

Judges, A. V. The Idea of a Mercantile State. **In** *Coleman, D. C., ed.*, 1969, pp. 35–60.

van Klaveren, Jacob. Fiscalism, Mercantilism and Corruption. **In** *Coleman, D. C., ed.*, 1969, pp. 140–61.

Muchmore, Lynn. Gerrard de Malnes and Mercantile Economics. *Hist. Polit. Econ.*, Fall 1969, *1*(2), pp. 336–58.

Parsons, J. E., Jr. Locke's Doctrine of Property. *Soc. Res.*, Autumn 1969, *36*(3), pp. 389–411.

Viner, Jacob. Power Versus Plenty as Objectives of Foreign Policy in the Seventeenth and Eighteenth Centuries. **In** *Coleman, D. C., ed.*, 1969, pp.

61–91. [G: W. Europe]

Wilson, Charles. The Other Face of Mercantilism. **In** *Coleman, D. C., ed.,* 1969, pp. 118–39.

0314 Classical

Barkai, Haim. A Formal Outline of a Smithian Growth Model. *Quart. J. Econ.,* August 1969, *83* (3), pp. 396–414.

Brahmananda, P. R. Towards a General Theory of the Pure Rate of Interest. *Indian Econ. J.,* July–September 1969, *17*(1), pp. 57–92.

Cochrane, James L. English Classical Economics. **In** *Kiker, B. F. and Carlsson, R. J., eds.,* 1969, pp. 1–9.

D'Ambrosio, Charles A. Asset Pricing, Time, and Causality—An Introspective View of Capital Theory. *Rev. Soc. Econ.,* March 1969, *27*(1), pp. 1–12.

Das, Amritananda. Malthus on the General Glut: A Reinterpretation. *Indian Econ. J.,* July–September 1969, *17*(1), pp. 118–28.

Dickinson, H. D. Von Thünen's Economics. *Econ. J.,* December 1969, *79*(316), pp. 894–902.

Eagly, Robert V. Monetary Policy and Politics in Mid-Eighteenth-Century Sweden. *J. Econ. Hist.,* December 1969, *29*(4), pp. 739–57. [G: Sweden]

Ekelund, Robert B., Jr. A Note on Jules Dupuit and Neo-classical Monopoly Theory. *Southern Econ. J.,* January 1969, *35*(3), pp. 257–62.

Fetter, Frank W. The Rise and Decline of Ricardian Economics. *Hist. Polit. Econ.,* Spring 1969, *1*(1), pp. 67–84.

Gordon, Barry J. Criticism of Ricardian Views on Value and Distribution in the British Periodicals, 1820–1850. *Hist. Polit. Econ.,* Fall 1969, *1*(2), pp. 370–87.

Groenewegen, P. D. Turgot and Adam Smith. *Scot. J. Polit. Econ.,* November 1969, *16*(3), pp. 271–87.

Hollander, S. Classical Economic Views of the Role of the State in Victorian Education: Comment. *Southern Econ. J.,* April 1969, *35*(4), pp. 378.

Hollander, S. Malthus and the Post-Napoleonic Depression. *Hist. Polit. Econ.,* Fall 1969, *1*(2), pp. 306–35.

Hume, L. J. Myrdal on Jeremy Bentham: Laissez-Faire and Harmony of Interests. *Economica, N.S.,* August 1969, *36*(143), pp. 295–303.

Hutchinson, T. W. Economists and Economic Policy in Britain after 1870. *Hist. Polit. Econ.,* Fall 1969, *1*(2), pp. 231–55. [G: U.K.]

Lindgren, J. Ralph. Adam Smith's Theory of Inquiry. *J. Polit. Econ.,* November/December 1969, *77*(6), pp. 897–915.

McKinley, Erskine. Trifling with a Serious Subject. *Rivista Int. Sci. Econ. Com.,* August 1969, *16*(8), pp. 816–23.

Papola, T. S. A 'Primitive' Equilibrium System: A Neglected Aspect of Smith's Economics. *Indian Econ. J.,* July–September 1969, *17*(1), pp. 93–100.

Pedone, Antonio. The Ricardian Tax Incidence Analysis in the Light of Optimum Growth Theory. *Econ. Int.,* February 1969, *22*(1), pp. 63–83.

Skinner, A. S. Of Malthus, Lauderdale and Say's Law. *Scot. J. Polit. Econ.,* June 1969, *16*(2), pp. 177–95.

Smith, Robert S. The Reception of Malthus' Essay on Population in Spain. *Rivista Int. Sci. Econ. Com.,* June 1969, *16*(6), pp. 550–65. [G: Spain]

Tu, Pierre N. V. The Classical Economists and Education. *Kyklos,* 1969, *22*(4), pp. 691–718.

West, E. G. The Political Economy of Alienation: Karl Marx and Adam Smith. *Oxford Econ. Pap.,* March 1969, *21*(1), pp. 1–23.

0315 Austrian, Marshallian, Neoclassical

Brahmananda, P. R. Towards a General Theory of the Pure Rate of Interest. *Indian Econ. J.,* July–September 1969, *17*(1), pp. 57–92.

Hicks, John R. Automatists, Hawtreyans, and Keynesians. *J. Money, Credit, Banking,* August 1969, *1*(3), pp. 307–17.

Lloyd, Peter J. Elementary Geometric/Arithmetic Series and Early Production Theory. *J. Polit. Econ.,* January/February 1969, *77*(1), pp. 21–34.

Marshall, Alfred. Three Lectures on Progress and Poverty. *J. Law Econ.,* April 1969, *12*(1), pp. 184–226.

Nash, Robert T. and Gramm, William P. A Neglected Early Statement of the Paradox of Thrift. *Hist. Polit. Econ.,* Fall 1969, *1*(2), pp. 395–400.

Schaller, François. Qu'est-ce que la productivité? (What Is Productivity? With English summary.) *Rivista Int. Sci. Econ. Com.,* May 1969, *16*(5), pp. 411–28.

Streissler, Erich. Structural Economic Thought: On the Significance of the Austrian School Today. *Z. Nationalökon.,* December 1969, *29*(3–4), pp. 237–66.

Tarascio, Vincent J. Paretian Welfare Theory: Some Neglected Aspects. *J. Polit. Econ.,* January/February 1969, *77*(1), pp. 1–20.

Wicksell, Knut. Böhm-Bawerk's Theory of Capital. **In** *Wicksell, K.,* 1969, pp. 176–85.

Wicksell, Knut. Carl Menger. **In** *Wicksell, K.,* 1969, pp. 186–92.

Wicksell, Knut. Marginal Productivity as the Basis of Distribution in Economics. **In** *Wicksell, K.,* 1969, pp. 93–120.

Wicksell, Knut. On the Problem of Distribution. **In** *Wicksell, K.,* 1969, pp. 121–30.

Wicksell, Knut. The 'Critical Point' in the Law of Decreasing Agricultural Productivity. **In** *Wicksell, K.,* 1969, pp. 131–37.

Wicksell, Knut. The New Edition of Menger's *Grundsätze.* **In** *Wicksell, K.,* 1969, pp. 193–203.

0316 General Equilibrium until 1945

Jaffé, William. A. N. Isnard, Progenitor of the Walrasian General Equilibrium Model. *Hist. Polit. Econ.,* Spring 1969, *1*(1), pp. 19–43.

Mishra, S. N. A Model of Gandhian Economy. *Indian Econ. J.,* July–September 1969, *17*(1), pp. 101–11. [G: India]

Samuels, Warren J. The Tableau Economique as a Simple Leontief Model: A Precursor to Phillips. *Indian Econ. J.,* July–September 1969, *17*(1), pp. 112–17.

0317 Socialist until 1945

Bălan, M. Gh. Concepția lui Nicolae Bălcescu cu privire la dezvoltarea forțelor de producție în Țările Române. (Nicolae Bălcescu's Outlook on the Development of Production Forces in the Romanian Principalities. With English summary.) *Stud. Cercet. Econ.*, 1969, *1-2*, pp. 229–35.

Baran, Paul A. On the Nature of Marxism. **In** *Baran, P. A.*, 1969, pp. 19–42.

Belianova, A. M. The Problem of the Rates of Economic Development in the U.S.S.R. as Treated in the Soviet Economic Literature of the 1920's. *Prob. Econ.*, April 1969, *11*(12), pp. 47–55. **[G: U.S.S.R.]**

Bhaduri, Amit. On the Significance of Recent Controversies on Capital Theory: A Marxian View. *Econ. J.*, September 1969, *79*(315), pp. 532–39.

Bronfenbrenner, Martin. Eine makroökonomische Auffassung von Marx' "Kapital." (With English summary.) *Jahr. Nationalökon. Statist.*, March 1969, *182*(4–5), pp. 347–65.

Bulborea, I. Nicolae Bălcescu în context european. (Nicolae Bălcescu in a European Context. With English summary.) *Stud. Cercet. Econ.*, 1969, *1-2*, pp. 245–51.

Gemorah, Solomon. Laurence Gronlund—Utopian or Reformer? *Sci. Soc.*, Fall-Winter 1969, *33*(4), pp. 446–58.

Goldmann, Josef. Karl Marx, the Soviet Economists of the Twenties and Contemporary 'Konjunkturforschung' in a Socialist Country. *Czech. Econ. Pap.*, 1969, (11), pp. 43–50.

Haşigan, D. Statistica în operele lui Nicolae Bălcescu. (Statistics in the Works of Nicolae Bălcescu. With English summary.) *Stud. Cercet. Econ.*, 1969, *1-2*, pp. 215–20.

Ivanciu-Văleanu, Nicolae. Democratismul revoluţionar în opera lui Nicolae Bălcescu. (Revolutionary Democratism in Nicolae Bălcescu's Work. With English summary.) *Stud. Cercet. Econ.*, 1969, *1-2*, pp. 183–93.

Johnson, Orace E. The "Last Hour" of Senior and Marx. *Hist. Polit. Econ.*, Fall 1969, *1*(2), pp. 359–69.

Needleman, Martin and Needleman, Carolyn. Marx and the Problem of Causation. *Sci. Soc.*, Summer-Fall 1969, *33*(3), pp. 322–39.

O'Neill, John. Introduction: Marxism and the Sociological Imagination. **In** *Baran, P. A.*, 1969, pp. xiii–xxviii.

Parpală, O. Programul agrar al lui Nicolae Bălcescu în revoluţia de la 1848. (Nicolae Bălcescu's Agrarian Program in the 1848 Revolution. With English summary.) *Stud. Cercet. Econ.*, 1969, *1-2*, pp. 205–13. **[G: Romania]**

Rozorea, M. and Mureşan, D. Probleme ale rentei funciare în opera lui Nicolae Bălcescu. (Problems of Ground Rent in Nicolae Bălcescu's Work. With English summary.) *Stud. Cercet. Econ.*, 1969, *1-2*, pp. 221–27.

Serban, Sielu. Unitatea naţional-politică în concepţia lui Nicolae Bălcescu. (National Unity in Nicolae Bălcescu's Conception. With English summary.) *Stud. Cercet. Econ.*, 1969, *1-2*, pp. 237–43.

Singer, Morris. Marxian Economics and Contemporary Growth Analysis. *J. Econ. Issues*, June 1969, *3*(2), pp. 192–205.

Sută-Selejan, Sultana. Nicolae Bălcescu şi curentele de gîndire economică din timpul său. (Nicolae Bălcescu and the Currents of Economic Thought of His Time. With English summary.) *Stud. Cercet. Econ.*, 1969, *1-2*, pp. 195–203.

Tanaka, Masaharu. The Narodniki and Marx on Russian Capitalism in the 1870's–1880's. *Kyoto Univ. Econ. Rev.*, October 1969, *39*(2), pp. 1–25.

Treml, Vladimir G. Interaction of Economic Thought and Economic Policy in the Soviet Union. *Hist. Polit. Econ.*, Spring 1969, *1*(1), pp. 187–216. **[G: U.S.S.R.]**

West, E. G. The Political Economy of Alienation: Karl Marx and Adam Smith. *Oxford Econ. Pap.*, March 1969, *21*(1), pp. 1–23.

Zauberman, Alfred. The Rapprochement between East and West in Mathematical-Economic Thought. *Manchester Sch. Econ. Soc. Stud.*, March 1969, *37*(1), pp. 1–21. **[G: U.S.S.R.]**

0318 Historical and Institutional

von Böventer, Edwin. Walter Christaller's Central Places and Peripheral Areas: The Central Place Theory in Retrospect. *J. Reg. Sci.*, April 1969, *9*(1), pp. 117–24.

Cornehls, James V. On the Use and Misuse of Veblen's 'Evolutionary Economics.' *Oxford Econ. Pap.*, November 1969, *21*(3), pp. 433–37.

Hershlag, Z. Y. Theory of Stages of Economic Growth in Historical Perspective. *Kyklos*, 1969, *22*(4), pp. 661–90.

Hirsch, Abraham. Bray Hammond on Wesley Mitchell and the North's Empty Purse. *J. Econ. Issues*, June 1969, *3*(2), pp. 206–12.

Nichols, Alan. On Savings and Neo-Institutionalism. *J. Econ. Issues*, September 1969, *3*(3), pp. 63–66.

Samuels, Warren J. On the Future of Institutional Economics. *J. Econ. Issues*, September 1969, *3*(3), pp. 67–72.

Sowell, Thomas. Veblen's *Higher Learning* after Fifty Years. *J. Econ. Issues*, December 1969, *3*(4), pp. 66–78.

Tilly, Richard. Soll *und* Haben: Recent German Economic History and the Problem of Economic Development. *J. Econ. Hist.*, June 1969, *29*(2), pp. 298–319. **[G: Germany]**

032 History of Economic Thought (continued)

0321 Other Schools Since 1800

Boserup, Mogens. A Note on the Prehistory of the Kahn Multiplier. *Econ. J.*, September 1969, *79* (315), pp. 667–69.

0322 Individuals

Aristotle

Lowry, S. Todd. Aristotle's Mathematical Analysis of Exchange. *Hist. Polit. Econ.*, Spring 1969, *1*(1), pp. 44–66.

Ashton, Thomas Southcliffe

Heaton, Herbert. Thomas Southcliffe Ashton 1889–1968: A Memoir. *J. Econ. Hist.*, June 1969, *29*(2), pp. 264–67.

Bălcescu, Nicolae

Bălan, M. Gh. Concepţia lui Nicolae Bălcescu cu

privire la dezvoltarea forțelor de producție în Țările Române. (Nicolae Bălcescu's Outlook on the Development of Production Forces in the Romanian Principalities. With English summary.) *Stud. Cercet. Econ.*, 1969, *1-2*, pp. 229–35.

Bulborea, I. Nicolae Bălcescu în context european. (Nicolae Bălcescu in a European Context. With English summary.) *Stud. Cercet. Econ.*, 1969, *1-2*, pp. 245–51.

Hașigan, D. Statistica în operele lui Nicolae Bălcescu. (Statistics in the Works of Nicolae Bălcescu. With English summary.) *Stud. Cercet. Econ.*, 1969, *1-2*, pp. 215–20.

Ivanciu-Văleanu, Nicolae. Democratismul revoluționar în opera lui Nicolae Bălcescu. (Revolutionary Democratism in Nicolae Bălcescu's Work. With English summary.) *Stud. Cercet. Econ.*, 1969, *1-2*, pp. 183–93.

Lupu, Marin A. Geneza și formarea proprietății feudale oglindite în opera lui Nicolae Bălcescu. (Genesis and Forming of Feudal Property as Mirrored in the Work of Nicolae Bălcescu. With English summary.) *Stud. Cercet. Econ.*, 1969, *1-2*, pp. 173–82.

Parpală, O. Programul agrar al lui Nicolae Bălcescu în revoluția de la 1848. (Nicolae Bălcescu's Agrarian Program in the 1848 Revolution. With English summary.) *Stud. Cercet. Econ.*, 1969, *1-2*, pp. 205–13. **[G: Romania]**

Rozorea, M. and Mureșan, D. Probleme ale rentei funciare în opera lui Nicolae Bălcescu. (Problems of Ground Rent in Nicolae Bălcescu's Work. With English summary.) *Stud. Cercet. Econ.*, 1969, *1-2*, pp. 221–27.

Serban, Sielu. Unitatea național-politică în concepția lui Nicolae Bălcescu. (National Unity in Nicolae Bălcescu's Conception. With English summary.) *Stud. Cercet. Econ.*, 1969, *1-2*, pp. 237–43.

Sută-Selejan, Sultana. Nicolae Bălcescu și curentele de gîndire economică din timpul său. (Nicolae Bălcescu and the Currents of Economic Thought of His Time. With English summary.) *Stud. Cercet. Econ.*, 1969, *1-2*, pp. 195–203.

Baruch, Bernard

Cuff, Robert D. Bernard Baruch: Symbol and Myth in Industrial Mobilization. *Bus. Hist. Rev.*, Summer 1969, *43*(2), pp. 115–33. **[G: U.S.]**

Bentham, Jeremy

Hume, L. J. Myrdal on Jeremy Bentham: Laissez-Faire and Harmony of Interests. *Economica, N.S.*, August 1969, *36*(143), pp. 295–303.

Böhm-Bawerk, Eugen

Wicksell, Knut. Böhm-Bawerk's Theory of Capital. **In** *Wicksell, K.*, 1969, pp. 176–85.

Bonnot, Étienne

Jackson, Andrew. The Position of Condillac in the History of Economic Thought. *Indian Econ. J.*, January–March 1969, *16*(3), pp. 312–26.

Cardozo, Jacob N.

Leiman, Melvin M. The Economic Ideas of Jacob N. Cardozo. **In** *Kiker, B. F. and Carlsson, R. J., eds.*, 1969, pp. 10–43. **[G: U.S.]**

Carroll, Lewis

Black, Duncan. Lewis Carroll and the Theory of Games. *Amer. Econ. Rev.*, May 1969, *59*(2), pp. 206–10.

Borcherding, Thomas E. Problems in the Theory of Public Choice: Discussion. *Amer. Econ. Rev.*, May 1969, *59*(2), pp. 211–12.

Cassel, Gustav

Spengler, Joseph J. Cassel on Population. *Hist. Polit. Econ.*, Spring 1969, *1*(1), pp. 150–72.

Clark, John Bates

Ghandour, M. M. J. B. Clark's Theory of Economic Growth: Comment. *Amer. Econ.*, Spring 1969, *13*(1), pp. 14–15.

Pisciotta, John. J. B. Clark's Theory of Economic Growth. *Amer. Econ.*, Spring 1969, *13*(1), pp. 4–13.

Cooper, Thomas

Whitten, William C., Jr. The Economic Ideas of Thomas Cooper. **In** *Kiker, B. F. and Carlsson, R. J., eds.*, 1969, pp. 44–82. **[G: U.S.]**

Dupuit, Jules

Ekelund, Robert B., Jr. A Note on Jules Dupuit and Neo-classical Monopoly Theory. *Southern Econ. J.*, January 1969, *35*(3), pp. 257–62.

Ely, Richard T.

Groves, Harold M. Richard T. Ely: An Appreciation. *Land Econ.*, February 1969, *45*(1), pp. 1–9.

Morehouse, Edward W. Richard T. Ely: A Supplement. *Land Econ.*, February 1969, *45*(1), pp. 10–18.

Fisher, Irving

Cheung, Steven N. S. Irving Fisher and the Red Guards. *J. Polit. Econ.*, May/June 1969, *77*(3), pp. 430–33.

Gall, Heinrich Ludwig Lambert

Zinn, Karl Georg. Staatstätigkeit und Multiplikator in den Schriften Ludwig Galls—Eine dogmengeschichtliche Ergänzung zur Beschäftigungstheorie. (With English summary.) *Kyklos*, 1969, *22*(4), pp. 719–36.

Galloway, Samuel

Carlsson, Robert J. The Economic Ideas of Samuel Galloway. **In** *Kiker, B. F. and Carlsson, R. J., eds.*, 1969, pp. 120–39. **[G: U.S.]**

Gandhi, Mahatma

Ray, Hemen. Changing Soviet Views on Mahatma Gandhi. *J. Asian Stud.*, November 1969, *29*(1), pp. 85–106. **[G: India]**

Gandhiji

Lakdawala, D. T. Gandhiji and Growth Economics. *Indian Econ. J.*, October–December 1969, *17*(2), pp. 266–72.

Gronlund, Laurence

Gemorah, Solomon. Laurence Gronlund—Utopian or Reformer? *Sci. Soc.*, Fall-Winter 1969, *33*(4), pp. 446–58.

Hawtrey, Ralph George

Hicks, John R. Automatists, Hawtreyans, and Keynesians. *J. Money, Credit, Banking*, August 1969, *1*(3), pp. 307–17.

Hughes, John Joseph

Gordon, Barry J. An American Contribution to the Theory of Social Economy: John Joseph

Hughes (1797–1864). *Rev. Soc. Econ.*, September 1969, *27*(2), pp. 233–41.

Innis, Harold Adams

Neill, Robin F. Harold Adams Innis: Canadian Economics. *J. Econ. Issues*, September 1969, *3*(3), pp. 3–15.

Isnard, Achylle-Nicolas

Jaffé, William. A. N. Isnard, Progenitor of the Walrasian General Equilibrium Model. *Hist. Polit. Econ.*, Spring 1969, *1*(1), pp. 19–43.

Keynes, John Maynard

Davidson, Paul. A Keynesian View of the Relationship between Accumulation, Money and the Money Wage-Rate. *Econ. J.*, June 1969, *79* (314), pp. 300–323.

Harris, Seymour E. Introduction: Keynes' Attack on *Laissez Faire* and Classical Economics and Wage Theory. **In** *Williams, H. R. and Huffnagle, J. D., eds.*, 1969, pp. 7–20.

Hicks, John R. Automatists, Hawtreyans, and Keynesians. *J. Money, Credit, Banking*, August 1969, *1*(3), pp. 307–17.

Hishiyama, Izumi. The Logic of Uncertainty According to J. M. Keynes. *Kyoto Univ. Econ. Rev.*, April 1969, *39*(1), pp. 22–44.

Streeten, Paul. Keynes and the Classical Tradition. **In** *Williams, H. R. and Huffnagle, J. D., eds.*, 1969, pp. 21–37.

Vaizey, John. Keynes. *Irish Banking Rev.*, June 1969, pp. 10–19.

Lenin, Vladimir Il'ich

Pshelyaskovskiy, V. I. Elements of the Theory of Growth in Lenin's Plan for the Electrification of Russia (On the 50th Anniversary of the GOELRO Plan). *Matekon*, Fall 1969, *6*(1), pp. 98–116. **[G: U.S.S.R.]**

Lieber, Francis

Flora, A. C., Jr. The Economic Ideas of Francis Lieber. **In** *Kiker, B. F. and Carlsson, R. J., eds.*, 1969, pp. 83–104. **[G: U.S.]**

Locke, John

Parsons, J. E., Jr. Locke's Doctrine of Property. *Soc. Res.*, Autumn 1969, *36*(3), pp. 389–411.

Maitland, John

Skinner, A. S. Of Malthus, Lauderdale and Say's Law. *Scot. J. Polit. Econ.*, June 1969, *16*(2), pp. 177–95.

Malthus, Thomas Robert

Das, Amritananda. Malthus on the General Glut: A Reinterpretation. *Indian Econ. J.*, July–September 1969, *17*(1), pp. 118–28.

Hollander, S. Malthus and the Post-Napoleonic Depression. *Hist. Polit. Econ.*, Fall 1969, *1*(2), pp. 306–35.

Skinner, A. S. Of Malthus, Lauderdale and Say's Law. *Scot. J. Polit. Econ.*, June 1969, *16*(2), pp. 177–95.

de Malynes, Gerrard

Muchmore, Lynn. Gerrard de Malnes and Mercantile Economics. *Hist. Polit. Econ.*, Fall 1969, *1*(2), pp. 336–58.

Marshall, Alfred

Kerr, Clark. Marshall and Marx. **In** *Kerr, C.*, 1969, pp. 62–73.

Kerr, Clark. The Classless Society and the Perfectibility of Man. **In** *Kerr, C.*, 1969, pp. 8–18.

Stigler, George J. Alfred Marshall's Lectures on Progress and Poverty. *J. Law Econ.*, April 1969, *12*(1), pp. 181–83.

Marx, Karl

Goldmann, Josef. Karl Marx, the Soviet Economists of the Twenties and Contemporary 'Konjunkturforschung' in a Socialist Country. *Czech. Econ. Pap.*, 1969, (11), pp. 43–50.

Howard, Dick. On Deforming Marx: The French Translation of *Grundrisse*. *Sci. Soc.*, Summer-Fall 1969, *33*(3), pp. 358–65.

Jamison, Harold B. On "Disguised Conservatism in Evolutionary Development Theory": Comment. *Sci. Soc.*, Summer-Fall 1969, *33*(3), pp. 348–53.

Johnson, Orace E. The "Last Hour" of Senior and Marx. *Hist. Polit. Econ.*, Fall 1969, *1*(2), pp. 359–69.

Kerr, Clark. Marshall and Marx. **In** *Kerr, C.*,1969, pp. 62–73.

Kerr, Clark. The Classless Society and the Perfectibility of Man. **In** *Kerr, C.*, 1969, pp. 8–18.

Needleman, Martin and Needleman, Carolyn. Marx and the Problem of Causation. *Sci. Soc.*, Summer-Fall 1969, *33*(3), pp. 322–39.

Rhodes, Robert I. On "Disguised Conservatism in Evolutionary Development Theory": Reply. *Sci. Soc.*, Summer-Fall 1969, *33*(3), pp. 353–58.

Stefanov, I. Marx's Theory of Expanded Reproduction and Problems of Economic Growth. *Matekon*, Fall 1969, *6*(1), pp. 3–18.

Tanaka, Masaharu. The Narodniki and Marx on Russian Capitalism in the 1870's–1880's. *Kyoto Univ. Econ. Rev.*, October 1969, *39*(2), pp. 1–25.

West, E. G. The Political Economy of Alienation: Karl Marx and Adam Smith. *Oxford Econ. Pap.*, March 1969, *21*(1), pp. 1–23.

Menger, Karl

Wicksell, Knut. Carl Menger. **In** *Wicksell, K.*, 1969, pp. 186–92.

Wicksell, Knut. The New Edition of Menger's *Grundsätze*. **In** *Wicksell, K.*, 1969, pp. 193–203.

Mill, James

Barber, William J. James Mill and the Theory of Economic Policy in India. *Hist. Polit. Econ.*, Spring 1969, *1*(1), pp. 85–100. **[G: India]**

Mitchell, Wesley Clair

Hirsch, Abraham. Bray Hammond on Wesley Mitchell and the North's Empty Purse. *J. Econ. Issues*, June 1969, *3*(2), pp. 206–12.

Montesquieu, Charles Louis

Devletoglou, Nicos E. The Economic Philosophy of Montesquieu. *Kyklos*, 1969, *22*(3), pp. 530–41.

Nehru, Jawaharlal

Dantwala, M. L. The Economic Ideology of Nehru. **In** *Bhuleshkar, A. V., ed.*, 1969, pp. 11–16. **[G: India]**

Dhavamony, S. J. The Ultimate Objectives of

Nehru's Socialism. **In** *Bhuleshkar, A. V., ed.,* 1969, pp. 17–30. **[G: India]**

Mehta, Asoka. Jawaharlal Nehru—Social Justice and National Development. **In** *Bhuleshkar, A. V., ed.,* 1969, pp. 3–10. **[G: India]**

Pareto, Vilfredo

Tarascio, Vincent J. The Monetary and Employment Theories of Vilfredo Pareto. *Hist. Polit. Econ.,* Spring 1969, *1*(1), pp. 101–22.

Wicksell, Knut. Vilfredo Pareto's *Cours d'économie politique.* **In** *Wicksell, K.,* 1969, pp. 141–58.

Wicksell, Knut. Vilfredo Pareto's *Manuel d'économie politique.* **In** *Wicksell, K.,* 1969, pp. 159–75.

Patten, Simon Nelson

Stephenson, Matthew A. A Note on Simon Patten's Contribution to the Concept of Consumer's Surplus. *J. Polit. Econ.,* March/April 1969, *77*(2), pp. 242–44.

Senior, Nassau

Johnson, Orace E. The "Last Hour" of Senior and Marx. *Hist. Polit. Econ.,* Fall 1969, *1*(2), pp. 359–69.

Simons, Henry

Davis, J. Ronnie. Henry Simons, the Radical: Some Documentary Evidence. *Hist. Polit. Econ.,* Fall 1969, *1*(2), pp. 388–94.

Smith, Adam

Freeman, R. D. Adam Smith, Education and Laissez-Faire. *Hist. Polit. Econ.,* Spring 1969, *1*(1), pp. 173–86.

Groenewegen, P. D. Turgot and Adam Smith. *Scot. J. Polit. Econ.,* November 1969, *16*(3), pp. 271–87.

Lindgren, J. Ralph. Adam Smith's Theory of Inquiry. *J. Polit. Econ.,* November/December 1969, *77*(6), pp. 897–915.

Papola, T. S. A 'Primitive' Equilibrium System: A Neglected Aspect of Smith's Economics. *Indian Econ. J.,* July–September 1969, *17*(1), pp. 93–100.

West, E. G. The Political Economy of Alienation: Karl Marx and Adam Smith. *Oxford Econ. Pap.,* March 1969, *21*(1), pp. 1–23.

Tallqvist, Josef Verner

Pipping, Hugo E. J. V. Tallqvist 1862–1960, en minnesteckning. (J. V. Tallqvist 1862–1960, in Memoriam. With English summary.) *Econ. Samfundets Tidskr.,* 1969, *22*(4), pp. 241–89.

von Thünen, Johann Heinrich

Kiker, B. F. Von Thünen on Human Capital. *Oxford Econ. Pap.,* November 1969, *21*(3), pp. 339–43.

Dickinson, H. D. Von Thünen's Economics. *Econ. J.,* December 1969, *79*(316), pp. 894–902.

Turgot, Anne Robert Jacques

Groenewegen, P. D. Turgot and Adam Smith. *Scot. J. Polit. Econ.,* November 1969, *16*(3), pp. 271–87.

Veblen, Thorstein

Cornehls, James V. On the Use and Misuse of Veblen's 'Evolutionary Economics.' *Oxford Econ. Pap.,* November 1969, *21*(3), pp. 433–37.

Mayberry, Thomas C. Thorstein Veblen on Human Nature. *Amer. J. Econ. Soc.,* July 1969, *28*(3), pp. 315–23.

Sowell, Thomas. Veblen's *Higher Learning* after Fifty Years. *J. Econ. Issues,* December 1969, *3*(4), pp. 66–78.

Ware, Nathaniel A.

Kiker, B. F. The Economic Ideas of Nathaniel A. Ware. **In** *Kiker, B. F. and Carlsson, R. J., eds.,* 1969, pp. 105–19. **[G: U.S.]**

Weber, Max

Jamison, Harold B. On "Disguised Conservatism in Evolutionary Development Theory": Comment. *Sci. Soc.,* Summer-Fall 1969, *33*(3), pp. 348–53.

Rhodes, Robert I. On "Disguised Conservatism in Evolutionary Development Theory": Reply. *Sci. Soc.,* Summer-Fall 1969, *33*(3), pp. 353–58.

Weippert, Georg

Egner, Erich. Weippert's Vorstoss auf eine Ontologie der Wirtschaft. (With English summary.) *Jahr. Nationalökon. Statist.,* December 1969, *183*(5), pp. 401–34.

0329 Other Special Topics

Coats, A. W. The American Economic Association's Publications: An Historical Perspective. *J. Econ. Lit.,* March 1969, *7*(1), pp. 57–68.

D'Ambrosio, Charles A. Asset Pricing, Time, and Causality—An Introspective View of Capital Theory. *Rev. Soc. Econ.,* March 1969, *27*(1), pp. 1–12.

Gibson, N. J. Foundations of Monetary Theory: A Review Article. *Manchester Sch. Econ. Soc. Stud.,* March 1969, *37*(1), pp. 59–75.

Gruchy, Allan G. Neoinstitutionalism and the Economics of Dissent. *J. Econ. Issues,* March 1969, *3*(1), pp. 3–17.

Lesser, Arthur, Jr. Engineering Economy in the United States in Retrospect—An Analysis. *Eng. Econ.,* January–February 1969, *14*(2), pp. 109–15. **[G: U.S.]**

Letiche, John M. The History of Economic Thought in the *International Encyclopedia of the Social Sciences. J. Econ. Lit.,* June 1969, *7*(2), pp. 406–25.

Liebhafsky, H. H. A Note on the Origin of Slutsky's "Well-Known" Formula of the Theory of Determinants. *Z. ges. Staatswiss.,* April 1969, *125*(2), pp. 243–47.

Sauvy, Alfred. La Pensée Économique en France sur l'idée d'abondance et de besoin. (With English summary.) *Hist. Polit. Econ.,* Fall 1969, *1*(2), pp. 279–305. **[G: France]**

Solterer, Josef. Liquidity Norms for Development. *Rev. Soc. Econ.,* March 1969, *27*(1), pp. 13–22.

Vining, Rutledge. On Two Foundation Concepts of the Theory of Political Economy. *J. Polit. Econ.,* March/April 1969, *77*(2), pp. 199–218.

Wicksell, Knut. Mathematical Economics. **In** *Wicksell, K.,* 1969, pp. 204–26.

Wold, Herman O. E. P. Mackeprangs fråga om val

av regression. Ett nyckelproblem i ekonometrins utveckling. (E. P. Mackeprang's Question about the Choice of Regression: A Key Problem in the Evolution of Econometrics. With English summary.) *Liiketaloudellinen Aikak.*, 1969, *18*(1), pp. 79–89.

036 Economic Methodology

0360 Economic Methodology

Boland, L. A. Economic Understanding and Understanding Economics. *S. Afr. J. Econ.*, June 1969, *37*(2), pp. 144–60.

Coats, A. W. Is There a "Structure of Scientific Revolutions" in Economics? *Kyklos*, 1969, *22*(2), pp. 289–96.

Coats, A. W. Research Priorities in the History of Economics. *Hist. Polit. Econ.*, Spring 1969, *1*(1), pp. 9–18.

Cochran, Thomas C. Economic History, Old and New. *Amer. Hist. Rev.*, June 1969, *74*(5), pp. 1561–72.

Davis, Otto A. Notes on Strategy and Methodology for a Scientific Political Science. **In** *Bernd, J. L., ed.*, 1969, pp. 22–38.

Gurwitsch, Aron. Social Science and Natural Science: Methodological Reflections on Lowe's *On Economic Knowledge*. **In** *Heilbroner, R. L., ed.*, 1969, pp. 37–55.

Habr, Jaroslav. Ekonomicko-matematické metody v retrospektivě. (Economico-Mathematical Methods in Retrospective. With English summary.) *Ekon.-Mat. Obzor*, 1969, *5*(2), pp. 163–71.

Hishiyama, Izumi. The Logic of Uncertainty According to J. M. Keynes. *Kyoto Univ. Econ. Rev.*, April 1969, *39*(1), pp. 22–44.

Linstromberg, R. C. The Philosophy of Science and Alternative Approaches to Economic Thought. *J. Econ. Issues*, June 1969, *3*(2), pp. 176–91.

Machlup, Fritz. Positive and Normative Economics: An Analysis of the Ideas. **In** *Heilbroner, R. L., ed.*, 1969, pp. 99–129.

Nagel, Ernest. Method in Social and Natural Science. **In** *Heilbroner, R. L., ed.*, 1969, pp. 57–66.

Nichols, Alan. On Savings and Neo-Institutionalism. *J. Econ. Issues*, September 1969, *3*(3), pp. 63–66.

Puu, Tönu. Causal Versus Teleological Explanation in Economics. *Swedish J. Econ.*, June 1969, *71*(2), pp. 111–26.

Samuels, Warren J. On the Future of Institutional Economics. *J. Econ. Issues*, September 1969, *3*(3), pp. 67–72.

Seligman, Ben B. The Impact of Positivism on Economic Thought. *Hist. Polit. Econ.*, Fall 1969, *1*(2), pp. 256–78.

Stigler, George J. Does Economics Have a Useful Past? *Hist. Polit. Econ.*, Fall 1969, *1*(2), pp. 217–30.

Streissler, Erich. Structural Economic Thought: On the Significance of the Austrian School Today. *Z. Nationalökon.*, December 1969, *29*(3–4), pp. 237–66.

Wicksell, Knut. Ends and Means in Economics. **In** *Wicksell, K.*, 1969, pp. 51–66.

040 Economic History

041 Economic History: General

0410 General

Baldwin, Robert E. Economic Development: Discussion. *Amer. Econ. Rev.*, May 1969, *59*(2), pp. 427–29.

Cameron, Rondo E. The International Encyclopedia of the Social Sciences. *J. Econ. Hist.*, September 1969, *29*(3), pp. 537–41.

Fei, John C. H. and Ranis, Gustav. Economic Development in Historical Perspective. *Amer. Econ. Rev.*, May 1969, *59*(2), pp. 286–400.

Gerschenkron, Alexander. History of Economic Doctrines and Economic History. *Amer. Econ. Rev.*, May 1969, *59*(2), pp. 1–17.

Jones, E. L. and Woolf, S. J. Introduction: The Historical Role of Agrarian Change in Economic Development. **In** *Jones, E. L. and Woolf, S. J., eds.*, 1969, pp. 1–21.

Lane, Frederic C. Meanings of Capitalism. *J. Econ. Hist.*, March 1969, *29*(1), pp. 5–12.

Marshall, Leon S. The English and American Industrial City of the Nineteenth Century. **In** *Callow, A. B., Jr., ed.*, 1969, pp. 148–55. **[G: U.S.; U.K.]**

Prichard, M. F. Lloyd. Economic History in New Zealand Universities. *Australian Econ. Hist. Rev.*, March 1969, *9*(1), pp. 3–8. **[G: New Zealand]**

Wilson, Charles. Canon Demant's Economic History. **In** *Wilson, C.*, 1969, pp. 128–39.

Wilson, Charles. The Other Face of Mercantilism. **In** *Wilson, C.*, 1969, pp. 73–93.

0411 Development of the Discipline

Coats, A. W. Research Priorities in the History of Economics. *Hist. Polit. Econ.*, Spring 1969, *1*(1), pp. 9–18.

Cochran, Thomas C. Economic History, Old and New. *Amer. Hist. Rev.*, June 1969, *74*(5), pp. 1561–72.

Gould, J. D. Hypothetical History. *Econ. Hist. Rev.*, August 1969, *22*(2), pp. 1954–207.

Wilson, Charles. History in Special and in General. **In** *Wilson, C.*, 1969, pp. 201–15.

Winters, Stanley B. Trends in Labor Historiography in Czechoslovakia. *Labor Hist.*, Fall 1969, *10*(4), pp. 602–29. **[G: Czechoslovakia]**

0412 Comparative Intercountry or Intertemporal Economic History

Bowden, Witt; Karpovich, Michael and Usher, Abbott Payson. Agrarian Reorganization and Reform in the Eighteenth Century. **In** *Scoville, W. C. and La Force, J. C., eds., Vol. III*, 1969, pp. 66–89.

Cialdea, Basilio. Alcune riflessioni sulle relazioni internazionali negli ultimi cento anni. (Some Reflections on the Last Century's International Relations. With English summary.) *Mondo Aperto*, April 1969, *23*(2), pp. 123–35.

Cullity, John P. The Growth of Educational Employment in Three Countries, 1895–1964. *J. Human Res.*, Winter 1969, *4*(1), pp. 84–92. **[G: U.S.; U.K.; Germany]**

Davies, Robert B. "Peacefully Working to Conquer the World": The Singer Manufacturing Company in Foreign Markets, 1854–1889. *Bus. Hist. Rev.*, Autumn 1969, *43*(3), pp. 299–325.

Enthoven, Adolf J. H. The Changing Role of Accountancy. *Finance Develop.*, June 1969, *6*(2), pp. 16–22.

Evans, Archibald A. Work and Leisure, 1919–1969. *Int. Lab. Rev.*, January 1969, *99*(1), pp. 35–59.

Franklin, N. N. Employment and Unemployment: Views and Policies, 1919–1969. *Int. Lab. Rev.*, March 1969, *99*(3), pp. 293–314.

Hayami, Yūjirō. Resource Endowments and Technological Change in Agriculture: U.S. and Japanese Experiences in International Perspective. *Amer. J. Agr. Econ.*, December 1969, *51*(5), pp. 1293–1303. **[G: U.S.; Japan]**

Hoffmann, Walther G. Der tertiäre Sektor im Wachstumsprozess. (The Service Sector in the Growth Process. With English summary.) *Jahr. Nationalökon. Statist.*, June 1969, *183*(1), pp. 1–29. **[G: W. Europe; Japan; U.S.; Australia]**

Kerr, Clark. Class Conflict and Class Collaboration. **In** *Kerr, C.*, 1969, pp. 33–43.

Kerr, Clark. New 'Inherent Contradictions.' **In** *Kerr, C.*, 1969, pp. 115–21.

Kerr, Clark. The Multi-dimensional Society. **In** *Kerr, C.*, 1969, pp. 82–114.

Lawyer, John E. The ILO at 50: How It Began and How It Functions. *Mon. Lab. Rev.*, May 1969, *92* (5), pp. 32–36.

Mathias, Peter. Who Unbound Prometheus? Science and Technical Change, 1600–1800. *Yorkshire Bull. Econ. Soc. Res.*, May 1969, *21*(1), pp. 3–16.

Mouly, Jean. Changing Concepts of Wage Policy. *Int. Lab. Rev.*, July 1969, *100*(1), pp. 1–22.

Orizet, Jean. The Co-operative Movement Since the First World War. *Int. Lab. Rev.*, July 1969, *100*(1), pp. 23–50.

Peet, J. Richard. The Spatial Expansion of Commercial Agriculture in the Nineteenth Century: A von Thünen Interpretation. *Econ. Geogr.*, October 1969, *45*(4), pp. 283–301.

Perrin, Guy. Reflections on Fifty Years of Social Security. *Int. Lab. Rev.*, March 1969, *99*(3), pp. 249–92.

Sandberg, Lars G. American Rings and English Mules: The Role of Economic Rationality. *Quart. J. Econ.*, February 1969, *83*(1), pp. 25–43. **[G: U.S.; U.K.]**

Trotter, G. J. Personal Income Tax. *S. Afr. J. Econ.*, December 1969, *37*(4), pp. 306–44.

Valticos, Nicolas. Fifty Years of Standard-Setting Activities by the International Labour Organisation. *Int. Lab. Rev.*, September 1969, *100*(3), pp. 201–37.

Wallin, Michel. Labour Administration: Origins and Development. *Int. Lab. Rev.*, July 1969, *100*(1), pp. 51–110.

Wilkins, Mira. An American Enterprise Abroad: American Radiator Company in Europe, 1895–1914. *Bus. Hist. Rev.*, Autumn 1969, *43*(3), pp. 326–46.

042 Economic History: North America (excluding Mexico)

0420 General

Chase, Samuel B., Jr. Household Demand for Savings Deposits, 1921–1965. *J. Finance*, September 1969, *24*(4), pp. 643–58. **[G: U.S.]**

Cuff, Robert D. Bernard Baruch: Symbol and Myth in Industrial Mobilization. *Bus. Hist. Rev.*, Summer 1969, *43*(2), pp. 115–33. **[G: U.S.]**

David, Paul A. Transport Innovation and Economic Growth: Professor Fogel on and off the Rails. *Econ. Hist. Rev.*, December 1969, *22*(3), pp. 506–25.

Eliot, Jared. Farming a New Land, 1747. **In** *Pursell, C. W., Jr.*, 1969, pp. 9–18. **[G: U.S.]**

Fogel, Robert W. and Engerman, Stanley L. A Model for the Explanation of Industrial Expansion during the Nineteenth Century: With an Application to the American Iron Industry. *J. Polit. Econ.*, May/June 1969, *77*(3), pp. 306–28. **[G: U.S.]**

Genovese, Eugene D. Marxian Interpretations of the Slave South. **In** *Bernstein, B. J., ed.*, 1969, pp. 90–125. **[G: U.S.]**

Goodrich, Carter. On Rereading Harry J. Carman's *Social and Economic History of the United States. J. Econ. Lit.*, June 1969, *7*(2), pp. 426–27. **[G: U.S.]**

Gramm, William P. and Timberlake, Richard H., Jr. The Stock of Money and Investment in the United States, 1897-1966. *Amer. Econ. Rev.*, December 1969, *59*(5), pp. 991–96. **[G: U.S.]**

Harlan, Louis R. Booker T. Washington and the National Negro Business League. **In** *Schmertz, E. J. and Sirefman, J. P., eds., Part II*, 1969, pp. 73–91. **[G: U.S.]**

Higgs, Robert. The Growth of Cities in a Midwestern Region, 1870–1900. *J. Reg. Sci.*, December 1969, *9*(3), pp. 369–75. **[G: U.S.]**

Holt, W. Stull. Some Consequences of the Urban Movement in American History. **In** *Callow, A. B., Jr., ed.*, 1969, pp. 41–52. **[G: U.S.]**

Johnson, Benjamin P. America at the Crystal Palace, 1851. **In** *Pursell, C. W., Jr.*, 1969, pp. 96–101. **[G: U.S.]**

Krooss, Herman E. Economic History: Discussion. *Amer. Econ. Rev.*, May 1969, *59*(2), pp. 384–85. **[G: U.S.; U.K.]**

Larson, Henrietta M. Contours of Change: Standard Oil Company (New Jersey), 1882–1950. **In** *Kennedy, C. J., ed.*, 1969, pp. 3–19. **[G: U.S.]**

McClelland, Peter D. The Cost to America of British Imperial Policy. *Amer. Econ. Rev.*, May 1969, *59* (2), pp. 370–81. **[G: U.S.; U.K.]**

McPherson, James M. The Civil War and Reconstruction: A Revolution of Racial Equality? **In** *Shade, W. G. and Herrenkohl, R. C., eds.*, 1969, pp. 49–72. **[G: U.S.]**

Neal, Larry. Investment Behavior by American Railroads: 1897–1914. *Rev. Econ. Statist.*, May 1969, *51*(2), pp. 126–35. **[G: U.S.]**

Reid, Samuel Richardson. Mergers and the Economist. *Antitrust Bull.*, Summer 1969, *14*, pp. 371–84. **[G: U.S.]**

Shepherd, James F. and Walton, Gary M. Estimate

of "Invisible" Earnings in the Balance of Payments of the British North American Colonies, 1768–1772. *J. Econ. Hist.*, June 1969, *29*(2), pp. 230–63.

Soltow, Lee C. Evidence on Income Inequality in the United States, 1866–1965. *J. Econ. Hist.*, June 1969, *29*(2), pp. 279–86. [G: U.S.]

Stevenson, David. Internal Improvements, 1838. **In** *Pursell, C. W., Jr.*, 1969, pp. 53–66. [G: U.S.]

Still, Bayrd. Problems of Mid-Nineteenth Century Urbanization in the Middle West. **In** *Callow, A. B., Jr., ed.*, 1969, pp. 112–25. [G: U.S.]

Thernstrom, Stephan. Urbanization, Migration, and Social Mobility in Late Nineteenth-Century America. **In** *Bernstein, B. J., ed.*, 1969, pp. 158–75. [G: U.S.]

Trethewey, Richard J. The Economic Burden of the Sugar Act. *Amer. Econ.*, Spring 1969, *13*(1), pp. 63–71. [G: U.K.]

Vatter, Harold G. An Estimate of Import Substitution for Manufactured Products in the U.S. Economy, 1859 and 1899. *Econ. Develop. Cult. Change*, Part I, October 1969, *18*(1), pp. 40–43. [G: U.S.]

Whitworth, Joseph and Wallis, George. Overview of American Manufactures, 1854. **In** *Pursell, C. W., Jr.*, 1969, pp. 49–52. [G: U.S.]

0421 History of Product Prices and Markets

Chandler, Alfred D., Jr. The Structure of American Industry in the Twentieth Century: A Historical Overview. *Bus. Hist. Rev.*, Autumn 1969, *43*(3), pp. 255–98. [G: U.S.]

Clark, John G. The Business Elite of New Orleans before 1815. **In** *Kennedy, C. J., ed.*, 1969, pp. 94–103. [G: U.S.]

Easterlin, Richard A. and Lebergott, Stanley. The Service Industries in the Nineteenth Century: Discussion. **In** *Fuchs, V. R., ed.*, 1969, pp. 352–68. [G: U.S.]

Eis, Carl. The 1919–1930 Merger Movement in American Industry. *J. Law Econ.*, October 1969, *12*(2), pp. 267–96. [G: U.S.]

Fabricant, Solomon and Firestone, O. J. The Service Industries in the Nineteenth Century: Comment. **In** *Fuchs, V. R., ed.*, 1969, pp. 368–72. [G: U.S.]

Gabel, Richard. The Early Competitive Era in Telephone Communication, 1893–1920. *Law Contemp. Probl.*, Spring 1969, *34*(2), pp. 340–59. [G: U.S.]

Gallman, Robert E. and Weiss, Thomas J. The Service Industries in the Nineteenth Century. **In** *Fuchs, V. R., ed.*, 1969, pp. 287–352. [G: U.S.]

Gallman, Robert E. and Weiss, Thomas J. The Service Industries in the Nineteenth Century: Reply. **In** *Fuchs, V. R., ed.*, 1969, pp. 372–81. [G: U.S.]

Klein, Donald J. History of the Odd-Lot Stock Trading Theory. *Marquette Bus. Rev.*, Fall 1969, *13*(3), pp. 99–116. [G: U.S.]

Klingaman, David. The Significance of Grain in the Development of the Tobacco Colonies. *J. Econ. Hist.*, June 1969, *29*(2), pp. 268–78. [G: U.S.]

Porter, Patrick G. Origins of the American Tobacco Company. *Bus. Hist. Rev.*, Spring 1969, *43*(1), pp. 59–76. [G: U.S.]

Poulson, Barry W. Estimates of the Value of Manufacturing Output in the Early Nineteenth Century. *J. Econ. Hist.*, September 1969, *29*(3), pp. 521–25. [G: U.S.]

Puth, Robert C. Supreme Life: The History of A Negro Life Insurance Company, 1919–1962. *Bus. Hist. Rev.*, Spring 1969, *43*(1), pp. 1–20. [G: U.S.]

Scheiber, Harry N. World War I as Entrepreneurial Opportunity: Willard Straight and the American International Corporation. *Polit. Sci. Quart.*, September 1969, *84*(3), pp. 486–511. [G: U.S.]

Tucker, David M. Black Pride and Negro Business in the 1920's: George Washington Lee of Memphis. *Bus. Hist. Rev.*, Winter 1969, *43*(4), pp. 435–51. [G: U.S.]

Zerbe, Richard. The American Sugar Refinery Company, 1887–1914: The Story of a Monopoly. *J. Law Econ.*, October 1969, *12*(2), pp. 339–75. [G: U.S.]

0422 History of Factor Prices and Markets

Allais, Maurice. Growth and Inflation. *J. Money, Credit, Banking*, August 1969, *1*(3), pp. 355–426. [G: U.K.]

Ashenfelter, Orley and Pencavel, John H. American Trade Union Growth: 1900–1960. *Quart. J. Econ.*, August 1969, *83*(3), pp. 434–48. [G: U.S.]

Bateman, Fred. Issues in the Measurement of Efficiency of American Dairy Farming, 1850–1910: A Reply. *J. Econ. Hist.*, September 1969, *29*(3), pp. 506–11. [G: U.S.]

Bateman, Fred. Labor Inputs and Productivity in American Dairy Agriculture, 1850–1910. *J. Econ. Hist.*, June 1969, *29*(2), pp. 206–29. [G: U.S.]

Brook, Michael. Annual Bibliography of Periodical Articles on American Labor History: 1968. *Labor Hist.*, Fall 1969, *10*(4), pp. 639–55. [G: U.S.]

Cargill, Thomas F. An Empirical Investigation of the Wage-Lag Hypothesis. *Amer. Econ. Rev.*, December 1969, *59*(5), pp. 806–16. [G: U.S.]

Crockett, Norman L. The Westward Movement and the Transit of American Machine Technology: The Case of Wool Manufacturing. **In** *Kennedy, C. J., ed.*, 1969, pp. 111–20. [G: U.S.]

Fromm, Gary. Growth and Inflation: A Comment. *J. Money, Credit, Banking*, August 1969, *1*(3), pp. 439–40. [G: U.K.]

Gross, James A. Historians and the Literature of the Negro Worker. *Labor Hist.*, Summer 1969, *10*(3), pp. 536–46. [G: U.S.]

Gunderson, Gerald. Issues in the Measurement of Efficiency of American Dairy Farming, 1850–1910: A Comment. *J. Econ. Hist.*, September 1969, *29*(3), pp. 501–505. [G: U.S.]

Gutman, Herbert G. Black Coal Miners and the Greenback-Labor Party in Redeemer, Alabama: 1878–1879: The Letters of Warren D. Kelley, Willis Johnson Thomas, "Dawson," and Others. *Labor Hist.*, Summer 1969, *10*(3), pp. 506–35. [G: U.S.]

Harvey, Katherine A. The Knights of Labor in the Maryland Coal Fields, 1878–1882. *Labor Hist.*, Fall 1969, *10*(4), pp. 555–83. [G: U.S.]

Heffron, Paul T. Manuscript Sources in the Library

of Congress for a Study of Labor History. *Labor Hist.*, Fall 1969, *10*(4), pp. 630–38. [G: U.S.]

Livesay, Harold C. and Porter, Patrick G. Vertical Integration in American Manufacturing, 1899–1948. *J. Econ. Hist.*, September 1969, *29*(3), pp. 494–500. [G: U.S.]

Merrett, A. J. and Sykes, A. Return on Equities and Fixed Interest Securities: 1919–66. **In** *Carsberg, B. V. and Edey, H. C., eds.*, 1969, pp. 113–26. [G: U.S.]

Olson, James S. Organized Black Leadership and Industrial Unionism: The Racial Response, 1936–1945. *Labor Hist.*, Summer 1969, *10*(3), pp. 475–86. [G: U.S.]

Page, Walter P. A Study of the Fixed-Coefficients Model of Production for Agriculture in a Selected Region of the Great Plains, 1899–1903: Some Tentative Results. *Miss. Val. J. Bus. Econ.*, Fall 1969, *5*(1), pp. 34–42. [G: U.S.]

Porter, Kenneth W. Negro Labor in the Western Cattle Industry, 1866–1900. *Labor Hist.*, Summer 1969, *10*(3), pp. 346–74. [G: U.S.]

Primack, Martin L. Farm Fencing in the Nineteenth Century. *J. Econ. Hist.*, June 1969, *29*(2), pp. 287–91. [G: U.S.]

Rogers, William Warren. Negro Knights of Labor in Arkansas: A Case Study of the "Miscellaneous" Strike. *Labor Hist.*, Summer 1969, *10*(3), pp. 498–505. [G: U.S.]

Scheiber, Jane Lang and Scheiber, Harry N. The Wilson Administration and the Wartime Mobilization of Black Americans, 1917–18. *Labor Hist.*, Summer 1969, *10*(3), pp. 433–58. [G: U.S.]

Tuttle, William M., Jr. Labor Conflict and Racial Violence: The Black Worker in Chicago, 1894–1919. *Labor Hist.*, Summer 1969, *10*(3), pp. 408–32. [G: U.S.]

Wagstaff, Thomas. Call Your Old Master—"Master": Southern Political Leaders and Negro Labor during Presidential Reconstruction. *Labor Hist.*, Summer 1969, *10*(3), pp. 323–45. [G: U.S.]

Wakstein, Allen M. The National Association of Manufacturers and Labor Relations in the 1920s. *Labor Hist.*, Spring 1969, *10*(2), pp. 163–76. [G: U.S.]

Walker, Joseph E. A Comparison of Negro and White Labor in a Charcoal Iron Community. *Labor Hist.*, Summer 1969, *10*(3), pp. 487–97. [G: U.S.]

Wolters, Raymond. Section 7a and the Black Worker. *Labor Hist.*, Summer 1969, *10*(3), pp. 459–74. [G: U.S.]

Worthman, Paul B. Black Workers and Labor Unions in Birmingham, Alabama, 1897–1904. *Labor Hist.*, Summer 1969, *10*(3), pp. 375–407. [G: U.S.]

0423 History of Public Economic Policy (all levels)

Asher, Robert. Business and Workers' Welfare in the Progressive Era: Workmen's Compensation Reform in Massachusetts, 1880–1911. *Bus. Hist. Rev.*, Winter 1969, *43*(4), pp. 452–75. [G: U.S.]

Awalt, Francis Gloyd. Recollections of the Banking Crisis in 1933. *Bus. Hist. Rev.*, Autumn 1969, *43*(3), pp. 347–71. [G: U.S.]

Carlisle, Rodney. William Randolph Hearst's Reaction to the American Newspaper Guild: A Challenge to New Deal Labor Legislation. *Labor Hist.*, Winter 1969, *10*(1), pp. 74–99. [G: U.S.]

Chambers, John W. The Big Switch: Justice Roberts and the Minimum-Wage Cases. *Labor Hist.*, Winter 1969, *10*(1), pp. 44–73. [G: U.S.]

Courchene, Thomas J. An Analysis of the Canadian Money Supply: 1925–1934. *J. Polit. Econ.*, May/June 1969, *77*(3), pp. 363–91. [G: Canada]

Dillard, Dudley. Fiscal Policy from Hoover to Heller—A Review Essay. *Mon. Lab. Rev.*, August 1969, *92*(8), pp. 10–14. [G: U.S.]

Duggar, Jan Warren and Rost, Ronald F. National Bank Note Redemption and Treasury Cash. *J. Econ. Hist.*, September 1969, *29*(3), pp. 512–20. [G: U.S.]

Eakins, David W. Business Planners and America's Postwar Expansion. **In** *Horowitz, D., ed.*, 1969, pp. 143–71. [G: U.S.]

Eisner, J. M. Politics, Legislation, and the ILGWU. *Amer. J. Econ. Soc.*, July 1969, *28*(3), pp. 301–14. [G: U.S.]

Erickson, Erling A. Money and Banking in a "Bankless" State: Iowa, 1846–1857. *Bus. Hist. Rev.*, Summer 1969, *43*(2), pp. 171–91. [G: U.S.]

Gardner, Lloyd C. The New Deal, New Frontiers, and the Cold War: A Re-examination of American Expansion, 1933–1945. **In** *Horowitz, D., ed.*, 1969, pp. 105–41. [G: U.S.]

Gutfeld, Arnon. The Murder of Frank Little: Radical Labor Agitation in Butte, Montana, 1917. *Labor Hist.*, Spring 1969, *10*(2), pp. 177–92. [G: U.S.]

Hancock, John L. Planning in the Changing American City, 1900–1940. **In** *Callow, A. B., Jr., ed.*, 1969, pp. 549–67. [G: U.S.]

Jones, Byrd L. A Plan for Planning in the New Deal. *Soc. Sci. Quart.*, December 1969, *50*(3), pp. 525–34. [G: U.S.]

Kimball, Warren F. "Beggar My Neighbor": America and the British Interim Financial Crisis, 1940–41. *J. Econ. Hist.*, December 1969, *29*(4), pp. 758–72. [G: U.S.; U.K.]

Masten, John T. The Structure of Commercial Banking in the United States. *Rivista Int. Sci. Econ. Com.*, July 1969, *16*(7), pp. 688–709. [G: U.S.]

McClelland, Peter D. New Perspectives on the Disposal of Western Lands in Nineteenth Century America. *Bus. Hist. Rev.*, Spring 1969, *43*(1), pp. 77–83. [G: U.S.]

McFarland, C. K. and Neal, Nevin E. The Nascence of Protectionism: American Tariff Policies, 1816–1824. *Land Econ.*, February 1969, *45*(1), pp. 22–30. [G: U.S.]

Mercer, Lloyd J. Land Grants to American Railroads: Social Cost or Social Benefit? *Bus. Hist. Rev.*, Summer 1969, *43*(2), pp. 134–51. [G: U.S.]

Minasian, Jora R. The Political Economy of Broadcasting in the 1920's. *J. Law Econ.*, October 1969, *12*(2), pp. 391–403. [G: U.S.]

Morgan, George T., Jr. No Compromise—No Recognition: John Henry Kirby, the Southern Lumber Operators' Association, and Unionism in the Piney Woods, 1906–1916. *Labor Hist.*, Spring 1969, *10*(2), pp. 193–204. [G: U.S.]

Redlich, Fritz. On the Origin of Created Deposits in the Commonwealth of Massachusetts. *Bus. Hist. Rev.*, Summer 1969, *43*(2), pp. 204–08. **[G: U.S.]**

Roucek, Joseph S. The Image of the Slav in U.S. History and in Immigration Policy. *Amer. J. Econ. Soc.*, January 1969, *28*(1), pp. 29–48. **[G: U.S.]**

Spengler, Joseph J. Evolution of Public-Utility Industry Regulation: Economists and Other Determinants. *S. Afr. J. Econ.*, March 1969, *37*(1), pp. 3–31. **[G: U.S.]**

Sylla, Richard. Federal Policy, Banking Market Structure, and Capital Mobilization in the United States, 1863–1913. *J. Econ. Hist.*, December 1969, *29*(4), pp. 657–86. **[G: U.S.]**

Trattner, Walter I. The First Federal Child Labor Law (1916). *Soc. Sci. Quart.*, December 1969, *50* (3), pp. 507–24. **[G: U.S.]**

Wellington, Donald. The Case of the Superfluous Railroads: A Look at Changing Transportation Patterns. *Econ. Bus. Bull.*, Fall 1969, *22*(1), pp. 33–38. **[G: U.S.]**

Wicker, Elmus R. The World War II Policy of Fixing a Pattern of Interest Rates. *J. Finance*, June 1969, *24*(3), pp. 447–58. **[G: U.S.]**

Williams, William Appleman. The Large Corporation and American Foreign Policy. **In** *Horowitz, D., ed.*, 1969, pp. 71–104. **[G: U.S.]**

043 Economic History: Ancient and Medieval (until 1453)

0430 General

Bridbury, A. R. The Dark Ages. *Econ. Hist. Rev.*, December 1969, *22*(3), pp. 526–37. **[G: W. Europe]**

Harvey, Barbara. The Leasing of the Abbot of Westminster's Demesnes in the Later Middle Ages. *Econ. Hist. Rev.*, April 1969, *22*(1), pp. 17–27. **[G: U.K.]**

Hatcher, John. A Diversified Economy: Later Medieval Cornwall. *Econ. Hist. Rev.*, August 1969, *22* (2), pp. 208–27. **[G: U.K.]**

Inalcik, Halil. Capital Formation in the Ottoman Empire. *J. Econ. Hist.*, March 1969, *29*(1), pp. 97–140. **[G: Ottoman Empire]**

Labib, Subhi Y. Capitalism in Medieval Islam. *J. Econ. Hist.*, March 1969, *29*(1), pp. 79–96. **[G: Islamic States]**

Pirenne, Henri. The Place of the Netherlands in the Economic History of Mediaeval Europe. **In** *Scoville, W. C. and La Force, J. C., eds., Vol. I*, 1969, pp. 19–40. **[G: Netherlands]**

Postan, Michael M. The Fifteenth Century. **In** *Scoville, W. C. and La Force, J. C., eds., Vol. I*, 1969, pp. 130–38. **[G: U.K.]**

Power, Eileen E. English Craft Guilds in the Middle Ages. **In** *Scoville, W. C. and La Force, J. C., eds., Vol. I*, 1969, pp. 76–80. **[G: U.K.]**

Saltmarsh, John. Plague and Economic Decline in England in the Latter Middle Ages. **In** *Scoville, W. C. and La Force, J. C., eds., Vol. I*, 1969, pp. 111–29. **[G: U.K.]**

Usher, Abbott Payson. The Origins of Banking: The Primitive Bank of Deposit, 1200–1600. **In** *Scoville, W. C. and La Force, J. C., eds., Vol. I*, 1969, pp. 81–110.

van der Wee, Herman. International Business Finance and Monetary Policy in Western Europe, 1384–1410. *Bus. Hist. Rev.*, Autumn 1969, *43*(3), pp. 372–80.

White, Lynn T., Jr. The Medieval Roots of Modern Technology and Science. **In** *Scoville, W. C. and La Force, J. C., eds., Vol. I*, 1969, pp. 60–75.

0431 History of Product Prices and Markets

Carus-Wilson, E. M. An Industrial Revolution of the Thirteenth Century. **In** *Scoville, W. C. and La Force, J. C., eds., Vol. I*, 1969, pp. 41–59. **[G: U.K.]**

Farmer, D. L. Some Livestock Price Movements in Thirteenth-Century England. *Econ. Hist. Rev.*, April 1969, *22*(1), pp. 1–16. **[G: U.K.]**

Freudenberger, Herman. Records of the Bohemian Iron Industry, 1694–1875: The Basis for a Comprehensive Study of Modern Factories. *Bus. Hist. Rev.*, Autumn 1969, *43*(3), pp. 381–84.

0432 History of Factor Prices and Markets

Jordan, Terry G. The Origin of Anglo-American Cattle Ranching in Texas: A Documentation of Diffusion from the Lower South. *Econ. Geogr.*, January 1969, *45*(1), pp. 63–87. **[G: U.S.]**

0433 History of Public Economic Policy (all levels)

Nakagawa, Manabu. Some Problems of Population Movements in China under the T'ang Dynasty (I). *Hitotsubashi J. Econ.*, February 1969, *9*(2), pp. 35–42. **[G: China]**

Prestwich, Michael. Edward I's Monetary Policies and Their Consequences. *Econ. Hist. Rev.*, December 1969, *22*(3), pp. 406–16. **[G: U.K.]**

044 Economic History: Europe

0440 General

Aldcroft, Derek H. Innovation on the Railways: The Lag in Diesel and Electric Traction. *J. Transp. Econ. Policy*, January 1969, *3*(1), pp. 96–107. **[G: U.K.]**

Ashton, Robert. The Aristocracy in Transition. *Econ. Hist. Rev.*, August 1969, *22*(2), pp. 308–22. **[G: U.K.]**

Ashton, T. S. The Industrial Revolution, 1760–1830. **In** *Scoville, W. C. and La Force, J. C., eds., Vol. III*, 1969, pp. 40–65. **[G: U.K.]**

Barbour, Violet. Dutch and English Merchant Shipping in the Seventeenth Century. **In** *Scoville, W. C. and La Force, J. C., eds., Vol. II*, 1969, pp. 108–37. **[G: Netherlands; U.K.]**

Barsby, Steven L. Economic Backwardness and the Characteristics of Development. *J. Econ. Hist.*, September 1969, *29*(3), pp. 449–72.

Beales, H. L. The "Great Depression" in Industry and Trade. **In** *Scoville, W. C. and La Force, J. C.,* *eds., Vol. IV,* 1969, pp. 97–107. **[G: U.K.]**

Beales, H. L. The Industrial Revolution. **In** *Scoville, W. C. and La Force, J. C., eds., Vol. III,* 1969, pp. 17–23.

Bowden, Witt; Karpovich, Michael and Usher, Abbott Payson. Agrarian Reorganization and Reform in the Eighteenth Century. **In** *Scoville, W. C. and La Force, J. C., eds., Vol. III,* 1969, pp. 66–89.

Brown, Richard H. The Achievement Norm and Economic Growth: The Case of Elizabethan England. *Rev. Soc. Econ.,* September 1969, *27*(2), pp. 181–201. **[G: U.K.]**

Brugmans, I. J. Economic Fluctuations in the Netherlands in the Nineteenth Century. **In** *Crouzet, F.; Chaloner, W. H. and Stern, W. M., eds.,* 1969, pp. 128–54. **[G: Netherlands]**

Brugmans, I. J. Nederlands overgang van onderontwikkeld gebied tot industrieland. (The Transition from Underdevelopment to Industrialization in the Netherlands. With English summary.) *De Economist,* January/February 1969, *117*(1), pp. 73–85. **[G: Netherlands]**

Cameron, Rondo E. Economic Growth and Stagnation in France, 1815–1914. **In** *Scoville, W. C. and La Force, J. C., eds., Vol. IV,* 1969, pp. 43–59. **[G: France]**

Carne, Joseph. Statistics of the Tin Mines of Cornwall, and of the Consumption of Tin in Great Britain. **In** *Burt, R., ed.,* 1969, pp. 83–93. **[G: U.K.]**

Clapham, John [Sir]. Communication and Commerce in Western Europe before the Railway Age. **In** *Scoville, W. C. and La Force, J. C., eds., Vol. IV,* 1969, pp. 148–55. **[G: W. Europe]**

Clapham, John [Sir]. The Making of the First Railway and Telegraph Network, 1830–69. **In** *Scoville, W. C. and La Force, J. C., eds., Vol. IV,* 1969, pp. 156–70.

Coale, Ansley J. The Decline of Fertility in Europe from the French Revolution to World War II. **In** *Behrman, S. J.; Corsa, L., Jr. and Freedman, R., eds.,* 1969, pp. 3–24. **[G: Europe]**

Conze, Werner. The Effects of Nineteenth-Century Liberal Agrarian Reforms on Social Structure in Central Europe. **In** *Crouzet, F.; Chaloner, W. H. and Stern, W. M., eds.,* 1969, pp. 53–81. **[G: Central Europe]**

Craig, R. S. and Floud, R. C. List of Publications on the Economic History of Great Britain and Ireland Published in 1967. *Econ. Hist. Rev.,* August 1969, *22*(2), pp. 322–41. **[G: U.K.; Ireland]**

Davies, P. N. The African Steam Ship Company. **In** *Harris, J. R., ed.,* 1969, pp. 212–38. **[G: U.K.]**

Dodd, A. H. The Character of Welsh Emigration to the United States to 1840. **In** *Minchinton, W. E., ed.,* 1969, pp. 19–36. **[G: U.K.]**

Dooley, Oscar S. Britain Revisited: A Fresh Appraisal of the Industrial Revolution. *Econ. Bus. Bull.,* Fall 1969, *22*(1), pp. 44–48. **[G: U.K.]**

Drake, M. Age at Marriage in the Pre-industrial West. **In** *Bechhofer, F., ed.,* 1969, pp. 196–208.

Earle, Peter. The Commercial Development of Ancona, 1479–1551. *Econ. Hist. Rev.,* April 1969, *22* (1), pp. 28–44. **[G: Italy]**

Edwards, J. K. Norwich Bills of Mortality—1707–1830. *Yorkshire Bull. Econ. Soc. Res.,* November 1969, *21*(2), pp. 94–113. **[G: U.K.]**

Engelmann, Hugo O. and Wanner, Richard A. Population Size and Industrial Technology. *Amer. J. Econ. Soc.,* July 1969, *28*(3), pp. 249–56. **[G: U.K.]**

Fairlie, Susan. The Corn Laws and British Wheat Production, 1829–76. *Econ. Hist. Rev.,* April 1969, *22*(1), pp. 88–116. **[G: U.K.]**

Fearon, Peter. The Formative Years of the British Aircraft Industry, 1913–1924. *Bus. Hist. Rev.,* Winter 1969, *43*(4), pp. 476–95.

Feldman, Gerald D. The Social and Economic Policies of German Big Business, 1918–1929. *Amer. Hist. Rev.,* October 1969, *75*(1), pp. 47–55. **[G: Germany]**

Ford, A. G. British Economic Fluctuations, 1870–1914. *Manchester Sch. Econ. Soc. Stud.,* June 1969, *37*(2), pp. 99–130. **[G: U.K.]**

Fussell, G. E. The Classical Tradition in West European Farming: The Sixteenth Century. *Econ. Hist. Rev.,* December 1969, *22*(3), pp. 538–51. **[G: W. Europe]**

Gadiel, D. L. and Falkus, M. E. A Comment on the 'Price Revolution.' *Australian Econ. Hist. Rev.,* March 1969, *9*(1), pp. 9–16.

Gerschenkron, Alexander. Notes on the Rate of Industrial Growth in Italy, 1881–1913. **In** *Scoville, W. C. and La Force, J. C., eds., Vol. IV,* 1969, pp. 60–74. **[G: Italy]**

Gili, Adolfo. Popolosità e dinamica demografica di lungo periodo nei comuni dell'Emilia e del Veneto: Parte I. (With English summary.) *Statistica,* October-December 1969, *29*(4), pp. 603–49. **[G: Italy]**

Gillet, Marcel. The Coal Age and the Rise of Coalfields in the North and the Pas-de-Calais. **In** *Crouzet, F.; Chaloner, W. H. and Stern, W. M., eds.,* 1969, pp. 179–202. **[G: France]**

Gould, J. D. The 'Price Revolution': Comments on a Comment. *Australian Econ. Hist. Rev.,* September 1969, *9*(2), pp. 179–81.

Habakkuk, H. J. Historical Demography: Comment. **In** *Bechhofer, F., ed.,* 1969, pp. 221–26.

Hamilton, Earl J. The Decline of Spain. **In** *Scoville, W. C. and La Force, J. C., eds., Vol. II,* 1969, pp. 150–62. **[G: Spain]**

Harder, K. Peter. Major Factors in Business Formation and Development: Germany in the Early Industrial Period. **In** *Kennedy, C. J., ed.,* 1969, pp. 72–81. **[G: Germany]**

Harris, J. R. Early Liverpool Canal Controversies. **In** *Harris, J. R., ed.,* 1969, pp. 78–97. **[G: U.K.]**

Hartwell, Richard M. Business Management in England during the Period of Early Industrialization: Inducements and Obstacles. **In** *Kennedy, C. J., ed.,* 1969, pp. 59–71. **[G: U.K.]**

Hartwell, Richard M. Economic Growth in England before the Industrial Revolution: Some Methodological Issues. *J. Econ. Hist.,* March 1969, *29*(1), pp. 13–31. **[G: U.K.]**

Hauser, Henri. The Characteristic Features of French Economic History from the Middle of the Sixteenth to the Middle of the Eighteenth Century. **In** *Scoville, W. C. and La Force, J. C., eds.,*

Vol. II, 1969, pp. 163–78. **[G: France]**

Hexter, J. H. Storm over the Gentry. **In** *Scoville, W. C. and La Force, J. C., eds., Vol. II,* 1969, pp. 65–95. **[G: U.K.]**

Hodges, T. Mansel. Early Banking in Cardiff. **In** *Minchinton, W. E., ed.,* 1969, pp. 163–72. **[G: U.K.]**

Hodges, T. Mansel. The History of the Newport and Caerleon Savings Bank 1839–88. **In** *Minchinton, W. E., ed.,* 1969, pp. 190–205. **[G: U.K.]**

Hodges, T. Mansel. The Peopling of the Hinterland and Port of Cardiff, 1801–1914. **In** *Minchinton, W. E., ed.,* 1969, pp. 3–18. **[G: U.K.]**

Hoffmann, Walther G. The Take-off in Germany. **In** *Scoville, W. C. and La Force, J. C., eds., Vol. IV,* 1969, pp. 75–96. **[G: Germany]**

Hughes, Jonathan R. T. Henry Mayhew's London. *J. Econ. Hist.,* September 1969, *29*(3), pp. 526–36. **[G: U.K.]**

Jones, E. J. 'Scotch Cattle' and Early Trade Unionism in Wales. **In** *Minchinton, W. E., ed.,* 1969, pp. 209–17. **[G: U.K.]**

Jörberg, Lennart. Structural Change and Economic Growth: Sweden in the Nineteenth Century. **In** *Crouzet, F.; Chaloner, W. H. and Stern, W. M., eds.,* 1969, pp. 259–80. **[G: Sweden]**

Kamen, Henry. Galley Service and Crime in Sixteenth-Century Spain. *Econ. Hist. Rev.,* August 1969, *22*(2), pp. 304–05. **[G: Spain]**

Kemp, Tom. Aspects of French Capitalism between the Wars. *Sci. Soc.,* Winter 1969, *33*(1), pp. 1–19. **[G: France]**

Labrousse, E. 1848–1830–1789: How Revolutions Are Born. **In** *Crouzet, F.; Chaloner, W. H. and Stern, W. M., eds.,* 1969, pp. 1–14. **[G: France]**

Landes, D. The Old Bank and the New: The Financial Revolution of the Nineteenth Century. **In** *Crouzet, F.; Chaloner, W. H. and Stern, W. M., eds.,* 1969, pp. 112–27. **[G: Europe]**

Lipson, E. The National Economy (1815–1914). **In** *Scoville, W. C. and La Force, J. C., eds., Vol. IV,* 1969, pp. 16–42. **[G: U.K.]**

Lipson, E. The Revolution in Transport. **In** *Scoville, W. C. and La Force, J. C., eds., Vol. IV,* 1969, pp. 137–47. **[G: U.K.]**

Litchfield, R. Burr. Demographic Characteristics of Florentine Patrician Families, Sixteenth to Nineteenth Centuries. *J. Econ. Hist.,* June 1969, *29*(2), pp. 191–205. **[G: Italy]**

Loschky, David J. and Krier, Donald F. Income and Family Size in Three Eighteenth-Century Lancashire Parishes: A Reconstitution Study. *J. Econ. Hist.,* September 1969, *29*(3), pp. 429–48. **[G: U.K.]**

Luzzatto, G. The Italian Economy in the First Decade after Unification. **In** *Crouzet, F.; Chaloner, W. H. and Stern, W. M., eds.,* 1969, pp. 203–25. **[G: Italy]**

Matassi, Luigi. The Italian Economy in the Late Eighteenth and Nineteenth Century. *Rev. Econ. Cond. Italy,* March 1969, *23*(2), pp. 116–33. **[G: Italy]**

Minchinton, W. E. Industrial South Wales, 1750–1914. **In** *Minchinton, W. E., ed.,* 1969, pp. ix–xxxi. **[G: U.K.]**

Minchinton, W. E. The Tinplate Maker and Technical Change. **In** *Minchinton, W. E., ed.,* 1969, pp. 107–20. **[G: U.K.]**

Morris, J. H. and Williams, L. J. The South Wales Sliding Scale. **In** *Minchinton, W. E., ed.,* 1969, pp. 218–31. **[G: U.K.]**

Namier, L. B. Anthony Bacon, M. P., an Eighteenth-century Merchant. **In** *Minchinton, W. E., ed.,* 1969, pp. 59–106. **[G: U.K.]**

Neal, F. Liverpool Shipping in the Early Nineteenth Century. **In** *Harris, J. R., ed.,* 1969, pp. 147–81. **[G: U.K.]**

Nef, John U. The Progress of Technology and the Growth of Large-Scale Industry in Great Britain, 1540–1640. **In** *Scoville, W. C. and La Force, J. C., eds., Vol. II,* 1969, pp. 43–64. **[G: U.K.]**

Nolte, Ernst. Big Business and German Politics: A Comment. *Amer. Hist. Rev.,* October 1969, *75*(1), pp. 71–78. **[G: Germany]**

Roberts, R. O. The Development and Decline of the Non-ferrous Metal Smelting Industries in South Wales. **In** *Minchinton, W. E., ed.,* 1969, pp. 121–60. **[G: U.K.]**

Rowe, D. J. The Chartist Convention and the Regions. *Econ. Hist. Rev.,* April 1969, *22*(1), pp. 58–74. **[G: U.K.]**

Sauvy, Alfred. La Pensée Économique en France sur l'idée d'abondance et de besoin. (With English summary.) *Hist. Polit. Econ.,* Fall 1969, *1*(2), pp. 279–305. **[G: France]**

Schiaffino, Andrea. Interrelazioni tra manifestazioni demografiche e manifestazioni economico-sociali in Emilia e Veneto nell'ultimo secolo. Relazione illustrativa dell'attività svolta dal gruppo di ricerca C.N.R. diretto dal prof. Paolo Fortunati. (With English summary.) *Statistica,* October-December 1969, *29*(4), pp. 563–602.

Schneewind, J. B. Technology, Ways of Living, and Values in 19th Century England. **In** *Baier, K. and Rescher, N., eds.,* 1969, pp. 110–32. **[G: U.K.]**

Sée, Henri. The Economic and Social Origins of the French Revolution. **In** *Scoville, W. C. and La Force, J. C., eds., Vol. III,* 1969, pp. 209–23. **[G: France]**

Sigsworth, Eric M. Some Problems in British Business History, 1870–1914. **In** *Kennedy, C. J., ed.,* 1969, pp. 21–37. **[G: U.K.]**

Slicher van Bath, B. H. Contrasting Demographic Development in Some Parts of the Netherlands during the Depression Period of the Seventeenth and Eighteenth Centuries. **In** *Bechhofer, F., ed.,* 1969, pp. 209–19. **[G: Netherlands]**

Strumilin, S. Industrial Crises in Russia 1847–67. **In** *Crouzet, F.; Chaloner, W. H. and Stern, W. M., eds.,* 1969, pp. 155–78. **[G: U.S.S.R.]**

Teichova, Alice. The Development of Business in the United States during the Period of Early Industrialization: Inducements and Obstacles. **In** *Kennedy, C. J., ed.,* 1969, pp. 82–92. **[G: U.S.]**

Thomas, Brinley. The Migration of Labour into the Glamorganshire Coalfield, 1861–1911. **In** *Minchinton, W. E., ed.,* 1969, pp. 37–56. **[G: U.K.]**

Thompson, F. M. L. Landownership and Economic Growth in England in the Eighteenth Century. **In** *Jones, E. L. and Woolf, S. J., eds.,* 1969, pp. 41–60. **[G: U.K.]**

Thompson, I. A. A. Galley Service and Crime in Sixteenth-Century Spain: Rejoinder. *Econ. Hist. Rev.*, August 1969, *22*(2), pp. 305–07. **[G: Spain]**

Tilly, Richard. Soll *und* Haben: Recent German Economic History and the Problem of Economic Development. *J. Econ. Hist.*, June 1969, *29*(2), pp. 298–319. **[G: Germany]**

Timmer, C. Peter. The Turnip, the New Husbandry, and the English Agricultural Revolution. *Quart. J. Econ.*, August 1969, *83*(3), pp. 375–95. **[G: U.K.]**

Tolley, B. H. The Liverpool Campaign against the Order in Council and the War of 1812. **In** *Harris, J. R., ed.*, 1969, pp. 98–146. **[G: U.K.]**

Trebilcock, Clive. "Spin-Off" in British Economic History: Armaments and Industry, 1760–1914. *Econ. Hist. Rev.*, December 1969, *22*(3), pp. 474–90. **[G: U.K.]**

Turner, Henry Ashby, Jr. Big Business and the Rise of Hitler. *Amer. Hist. Rev.*, October 1969, *75*(1), pp. 56–70. **[G: Germany]**

Usher, Abbott Payson. The Industrialization of Modern Britain. **In** *Scoville, W. C. and La Force, J. C., eds., Vol. III*, 1969, pp. 24–39. **[G: U.K.]**

Wilson, Charles. The Entrepreneur in the Industrial Revolution in Britain. **In** *Wilson, C.*, 1969, pp. 156–77. **[G: U.K.]**

Winters, Stanley B. Trends in Labor Historiography in Czechoslovakia. *Labor Hist.*, Fall 1969, *10*(4), pp. 602–29. **[G: Czechoslovakia]**

Yeager, Leland B. Fluctuating Exchange Rates in the Nineteenth Century: The Experiences of Austria and Russia. **In** *Mundell, R. A. and Swoboda, A. K., eds.*, 1969, pp. 61–89. **[G: Austria; U.S.S.R.]**

Zangheri, R. The Historical Relationship between Agricultural and Economic Development in Italy. **In** *Jones, E. L. and Woolf, S. J., eds.*, 1969, pp. 23–39. **[G: Italy]**

0441 History of Product Prices and Markets

Adelmann, Gerhard. Structural Change in the Rhenish Linen and Cotton Trades at the Outset of Industrialization. **In** *Crouzet, F.; Chaloner, W. H. and Stern, W. M., eds.*, 1969, pp. 82–97. **[G: Central Europe]**

Bailey, F. A. and Barker, T. C. The Seventeenth-century Origins of Watchmaking in South-west Lancashire. **In** *Harris, J. R., ed.*, 1969, pp. 1–15. **[G: U.K.]**

Barber, William J. James Mill and the Theory of Economic Policy in India. *Hist. Polit. Econ.*, Spring 1969, *1*(1), pp. 85–100. **[G: India]**

Blaich, Fritz. Der private Wohnungsbau in den deutschen Grossstädten während der Krisenjahre 1929–1933. (With English summary.) *Jahr. Nationalökon. Statist.*, December 1969, *183*(5), pp. 435–48. **[G: Germany]**

Burt, Roger. Lead Production in England and Wales, 1700–1770. *Econ. Hist. Rev.*, August 1969, *22*(2), pp. 249–68. **[G: U.K.]**

Coleman, D. C. An Innovation and Its Diffusion: The "New Draperies." *Econ. Hist. Rev.*, December 1969, *22*(3), pp. 417–29.

Dhondt, J. The Cotton Industry at Ghent during the French Régime. **In** *Crouzet, F.; Chaloner, W. H. and Stern, W. M., eds.*, 1969, pp. 15–52. **[G: Belgium]**

Ford, A. G. A Note on British Export Performance, 1899–1913. *Econ. Hist. Rev.*, April 1969, *22*(1), pp. 120–21. **[G: U.K.]**

Harrison, A. E. The Competitiveness of the British Cycle Industry, 1890–1914. *Econ. Hist. Rev.*, August 1969, *22*(2), pp. 287–303. **[G: U.K.]**

Maizels, Alfred. A Note on British Export Performance, 1899–1913: Rejoinder. *Econ. Hist. Rev.*, April 1969, *22*(1), pp. 122. **[G: U.K.]**

Maschke, Erich. Outline of the History of German Cartels from 1873 to 1914. **In** *Crouzet, F.; Chaloner, W. H. and Stern, W. M., eds.*, 1969, pp. 226–58. **[G: Germany]**

Matassi, Luigi. The Great Depression and the New Recovery of Italian Industry. *Rev. Econ. Cond. Italy*, July 1969, *23*(4), pp. 304–22. **[G: Italy]**

Niemi, Albert W. Some Aspects of the Relative Decline of the British Steel Industry, 1870–1913. *Amer. Econ.*, Fall 1969, *13*(2), pp. 40–49. **[G: U.K.]**

Posthumus, N. W. The Tulip Mania in Holland in the Years 1636 and 1637. **In** *Scoville, W. C. and La Force, J. C., eds., Vol. II*, 1969, pp. 138–49. **[G: Netherlands]**

Rees, Graham and Wiseman, Jack. London's Commodity Markets. *Lloyds Bank Rev.*, January 1969, (91), pp. 22–45. **[G: U.K.]**

Slaven, Anthony. A Glasgow Firm in the Indian Market: John Lean and Sons, Muslin Weavers. *Bus. Hist. Rev.*, Winter 1969, *43*(4), pp. 496–522. **[G: U.K.]**

Stephens, W. B. The Cloth Exports of the Provincial Ports, 1600–1640. *Econ. Hist. Rev.*, August 1969, *22*(2), pp. 228–48. **[G: U.K.]**

Williams, D. M. Liverpool Merchants and the Cotton Trade 1820–1850. **In** *Harris, J. R., ed.*, 1969, pp. 182–211. **[G: U.K.]**

0442 History of Factor Prices and Markets

Anderson, B. L. The Attorney and the Early Capital Market in Lancashire. **In** *Harris, J. R., ed.*, 1969, pp. 50–77. **[G: U.K.]**

Baines, D. E. and Bean, R. The General Strike on Merseyside. **In** *Harris, J. R., ed.*, 1969, pp. 239–75. **[G: U.K.]**

Collins, E. J. T. Harvest Technology and Labour Supply in Britain, 1790–1870. *Econ. Hist. Rev.*, December 1969, *22*(3), pp. 453–73. **[G: U.K.]**

Collins, E. J. T. Labour Supply and Demand in European Agriculture 1800–1880. **In** *Jones, E. L. and Woolf, S. J., eds.*, 1969, pp. 61–94. **[G: Europe]**

Duckham, Baron F. The Emergence of the Professional Manager in the Scottish Coal Industry, 1760–1815. *Bus. Hist. Rev.*, Spring 1969, *43*(1), pp. 21–38. **[G: U.K.]**

Fullerton, Kemper. Calvinism and Capitalism. **In** *Scoville, W. C. and La Force, J. C., eds., Vol. II*, 1969, pp. 15–42.

Hawke, G. R. and Reed, M. C. Railway Capital in the United Kingdom in the Nineteenth Century.

Econ. Hist. Rev., August 1969, *22*(2), pp. 269–86. [G: U.K.]

Hoffmann, Walther G. Die Entwicklung der Sparkassen im Rahmen des Wachatums der deutschen Wirtschaft (1850–1967). (With English summary.) *Z. ges. Staatswiss.*, October 1969, *125*(4), pp. 561–605. [G: Germany]

Hunt, E. H. Labour Productivity in English Agriculture, 1850–1914: Rejoinder. *Econ. Hist. Rev.*, April 1969, *22*(1), pp. 118–19. [G: U.K.]

Lemon, Charles [Sir]. The Statistics of the Copper Mines of Cornwall. **In** *Burt, R., ed.*, 1969, pp. 49–82. [G: U.K.]

Metcalf, David. Labour Productivity in English Agriculture, 1850–1914: A Theoretical Comment. *Econ. Hist. Rev.*, April 1969, *22*(1), pp. 117–18. [G: U.K.]

Price, Langford Lovell. *'West Barbary'; or Notes on the System of Work and Wages in Cornish Mines.* **In** *Burt, R., ed.*, 1969, pp. 111–206. [G: U.K.]

Rădulescu, G. Rata profitului în economia românească în anii 1927–1938. (The Rate of Profit in Romanian Economy between 1927–1938. With English summary.) *Stud. Cercet. Econ.*, 1969, *4*, pp. 23–58. [G: Romania]

Sanderson, Michael. The Universities and Industry in England 1919–1939. *Yorkshire Bull. Econ. Soc. Res.*, May 1969, *21*(1), pp. 39–65. [G: U.K.]

Sims, James. On the Economy of Mining in Cornwall. **In** *Burt, R., ed.*, 1969, pp. 95–107. [G: U.K.]

Taylor, John. On the Economy of the Mines of Cornwall and Devon. **In** *Burt, R., ed.*, 1969, pp. 15–29. [G: U.K.]

Taylor, John. On the Economy of Mining. **In** *Burt, R., ed.*, 1969, pp. 31–48. [G: U.K.]

0443 History of Public Economic Policy (all levels)

Ashworth, William. Economic Aspects of Late Victorian Naval Administration. *Econ. Hist. Rev.*, December 1969, *22*(3), pp. 491–505. [G: U.K.]

Blanchard, M. The Railway Policy of the Second Empire. **In** *Crouzet, F.; Chaloner, W. H. and Stern, W. M., eds.*, 1969, pp. 98–111. [G: France]

Callahan, William J. Don Juan de Goyeneche: Industrialist of Eighteenth-Century Spain. *Bus. Hist. Rev.*, Summer 1969, *43*(2), pp. 152–70. [G: Spain]

Cooney, E. W. Public Opinion and Government Policy in Nineteenth Century British Economic History: A Review and a Study of the Building Industry. *Yorkshire Bull. Econ. Soc. Res.*, November 1969, *21*(2), pp. 141–54. [G: U.K.]

Eagly, Robert V. Monetary Policy and Politics in Mid-Eighteenth-Century Sweden. *J. Econ. Hist.*, December 1969, *29*(4), pp. 739–57. [G: Sweden]

Gordon, Nancy M. Britain and the Zollverein Iron Duties, 1842–5. *Econ. Hist. Rev.*, April 1969, *22* (1), pp. 75–87. [G: U.K.; Germany]

Gourvish, T. R. The Bank of Scotland, 1830–45. *Scot. J. Polit. Econ.*, November 1969, *16*(3), pp. 288–305. [G: U.K.]

Hamilton, Earl J. The Political Economy of France at the Time of John Law. *Hist. Polit. Econ.*, Spring 1969, *1*(1), pp. 123–49. [G: France]

Hughes, Jonathan R. T. Economic History: Discussion. *Amer. Econ. Rev.*, May 1969, *59*(2), pp. 382–84. [G: U.S.]

Hutchinson, T. W. Economists and Economic Policy in Britain after 1870. *Hist. Polit. Econ.*, Fall 1969, *1*(2), pp. 231–55. [G: U.K.]

Huzel, James P. Malthus, the Poor Law, and Population in Early Nineteenth-Century England. *Econ. Hist. Rev.*, December 1969, *22*(3), pp. 430–52. [G: U.K.]

Kimball, Warren F. "Beggar My Neighbor": America and the British Interim Financial Crisis, 1940–41. *J. Econ. Hist.*, December 1969, *29*(4), pp. 758–72. [G: U.S.; U.K.]

Krooss, Herman E. Economic History: Discussion. *Amer. Econ. Rev.*, May 1969, *59*(2), pp. 384–85. [G: U.S.; U.K.]

La Force, J. Clayburn. The Supply of Muskets and Spain's War of Independence. *Bus. Hist. Rev.*, Winter 1969, *43*(4), pp. 523–44. [G: Spain]

McClelland, Peter D. The Cost to America of British Imperial Policy. *Amer. Econ. Rev.*, May 1969, *59* (2), pp. 370–81. [G: U.S.; U.K.]

Oxley, G. W. The Permanent Poor in South-west Lancashire under the Old Poor Law. **In** *Harris, J. R., ed.*, 1969, pp. 16–49. [G: U.K.]

Pares, Richard. The Economic Factors in the History of the Empire. **In** *Scoville, W. C. and La Force, J. C., eds., Vol. II*, 1969, pp. 96–107. [G: U.K.]

Parpală, O. Programul agrar al lui Nicolae Bălcescu în revoluția de la 1848. (Nicolae Bălcescu's Agrarian Program in the 1848 Revolution. With English summary.) *Stud. Cercet. Econ.*, 1969, *1-2*, pp. 205–13. [G: Romania]

Ponko, Vincent, Jr. The Colonial Office and British Business before World War I: A Case Study. *Bus. Hist. Rev.*, Spring 1969, *43*(1), pp. 39–58. [G: U.K.]

Ringrose, David R. The Government and the Carters in Spain, 1476–1700. *Econ. Hist. Rev.*, April 1969, *22*(1), pp. 45–57. [G: Spain]

Roussakis, Emmanuel N. The Common Market and the Zollverein: Experiences in Integration. *Rech. Écon. Louvain*, August 1969, *35*(3), pp. 201–08. [G: Germany]

Tautscher, Anton. Die Entwicklung der österreichischen Staatswirtschaft. (The Development of the Austrian State Economy. With English summary.) *Schmollers Jahr.*, 1969, *89*(3), pp. 267–311. [G: Austria]

Taylor, James Stephen. The Mythology of the Old Poor Law. *J. Econ. Hist.*, June 1969, *29*(2), pp. 292–97. [G: U.K.]

Treml, Vladimir G. Interaction of Economic Thought and Economic Policy in the Soviet Union. *Hist. Polit. Econ.*, Spring 1969, *1*(1), pp. 187–216. [G: U.S.S.R.]

Viner, Jacob. Power Versus Plenty as Objectives of Foreign Policy in the Seventeenth and Eighteenth Centuries. **In** *Coleman, D. C., ed.*, 1969, pp. 61–91. [G: W. Europe]

Wilson, Charles. Economics and Politics in the

Seventeenth Century. In *Wilson, C.,* 1969, pp. 1–21. **[G: U.K.]**

Wilson, Charles. Government Policy and Private Interest in Modern English History. In *Wilson, C.,* 1969, pp. 140–55. **[G: U.K.]**

Wilson, Charles. Taxation and the Decline of Empires, an Unfashionable Theme. In *Wilson, C.,* 1969, pp. 114–27.

045 Economic History: Asia

0450 General

Brand, S. S. The Interindustry Relationships of Agriculture and Economic Development in South Africa. *Finance Trade Rev.,* June 1969, *8*(3), pp. 171–86. **[G: S. Africa]**

Habib, Irfan. Potentialities of Capitalistic Development in the Economy of Mughal India. *J. Econ. Hist.,* March 1969, *29*(1), pp. 32–78. **[G: India]**

Hao, Yen-P'ing. Cheng Kuan-ying: The Comprador as Reformer. *J. Asian Stud.,* November 1969, *29* (1), pp. 15–22. **[G: China]**

Murphey, Rhoads. Traditionalism and Colonialism: Changing Urban Roles in Asia. *J. Asian Stud.,* November 1969, *29*(1), pp. 67–84. **[G: Asia]**

Neale, Walter C. Land Is to Rule. In *Frykenberg, R. E., ed.,* 1969, pp. 3–15. **[G: India]**

Park, Sung-Jo. Das Autoritätsverhalten als Leistungsprinzip in der Sozial-Wirtschaftsentwicklung: das Beispiel Japan (bis zur Meiji-Restauration). (Authoritarian Attitudes in Social and Economic Development: The Japanese Experience Until the Meiji Reform Period. With English summary.) *Schmollers Jahr.,* 1969, *89*(4), pp. 451–65. **[G: Japan]**

Ray, Hemen. Changing Soviet Views on Mahatma Gandhi. *J. Asian Stud.,* November 1969, *29*(1), pp. 85–106. **[G: India]**

Saini, Krishan G. The Growth of the Indian Economy: 1860–1960. *Rev. Income Wealth,* September 1969, *15*(3), pp. 247–63. **[G: India]**

Sinha, R. P. Unresolved Issues in Japan's Early Economic Development—A Correction. *Scot. J. Polit. Econ.,* November 1969, *16*(3), pp. 319. **[G: Japan]**

Sinha, R. P. Unresolved Issues in Japan's Early Economic Development. *Scot. J. Polit. Econ.,* June 1969, *16*(2), pp. 109–51. **[G: Japan]**

Spengler, Joseph J. India's Prospects According to Jean-Baptiste Say, 1824. *J. Asian Stud.,* May 1969, *28*(3), pp. 595–600. **[G: India]**

Takenaka, Yasukazu. Endogenous Formation and Development of Capitalism in Japan. *J. Econ. Hist.,* March 1969, *29*(1), pp. 141–62. **[G: Japan]**

0451 History of Product Prices and Markets

Bhatia, B. M. Terms of Trade and Economic Development: A Case Study of India—1861–1939. *Indian Econ. J.,* April-June 1969, *16*(4–5), pp. 414–33. **[G: India]**

Roychowdhury, K. C. The Indian Economy and the Drain Theory. *Indian Econ. J.,* January-March 1969, *16*(3), pp. 327–40. **[G: India]**

0452 History of Factor Prices and Markets

Odaka, Konosuke. Indices of the Excess Demand for Labor in Prewar Japan, 1929–39: A Preliminary Study. *Hitotsubashi J. Econ.,* June 1969, *10*(1), pp. 33–55.

Smith, Thomas C. Farm Family By-employments in Preindustrial Japan. *J. Econ. Hist.,* December 1969, *29*(4), pp. 687–715. **[G: Japan]**

Umemura, Mataji. Agriculture and Labor Supply in the Meiji Era. In *Ohkawa, K.; Johnston, B. F. and Kaneda, H., eds.,* 1969, pp. 175–97. **[G: Japan]**

0453 History of Public Economic Policy (all levels)

Katō, Yuzuru. Development of Long-Term Agricultural Credit. In *Ohkawa, K.; Johnston, B. F. and Kaneda, H., eds.,* 1969, pp. 324–51. **[G: Japan]**

Schrecker, John. The Reform Movement, Nationalism, and China's Foreign Policy. *J. Asian Stud.,* November 1969, *29*(1), pp. 43–53. **[G: China]**

046 Economic History: Africa

0460 General

Abshire, David M. Early History, European Discovery, and Colonization. In *Abshire, D. M. and Samuels, M. A., eds.,* 1969, pp. 29–59. **[G: Mozambique; Angola; Portuguese Guinea]**

van Dongen, Irene S. Physical, Human, and Economic Setting. In *Abshire, D. M. and Samuels, M. A., eds.,* 1969, pp. 1–28. **[G: Mozambique; Angola; Portuguese Guinea]**

Elliott, C. M. Agriculture and Economic Development in Africa: Theory and Experience 1880–1914. In *Jones, E. L. and Woolf, S. J., eds.,* 1969, pp. 123–50. **[G: Africa]**

Frederick, Kenneth D. The Role of Market Forces and Planning in Uganda's Economic Development, 1900–1938. *East Afr. Econ. Rev.,* June 1969, *1*(1), pp. 47–62. **[G: Uganda]**

Goody, Jack. Economy and Feudalism in Africa. *Econ. Hist. Rev.,* December 1969, *22*(3), pp. 393–405. **[G: Africa]**

0461 History of Product Prices and Markets

Brits, R. N. The Marketing of South African Maize. *S. Afr. J. Econ.,* September 1969, *37*(3), pp. 198–218. **[G: S. Africa]**

Coleman, F. L. Some Notes on the Native Development of Copper-Ore Deposits in Central Africa. *S. Afr. J. Econ.,* September 1969, *37*(3), pp. 260–63. **[G: Central Africa]**

0462 History of Factor Prices and Markets

Bailey, Norman A. Native and Labor Policy. In *Abshire, D. M. and Samuels, M. A., eds.,* 1969, pp. 165–77. **[G: Mozambique; Angola; Portuguese Guinea]**

0463 History of Public Economic Policy (all levels)

Botha, D. J. J. Local Taxation in South Africa. *S. Afr. J. Econ.*, December 1969, *37*(4), pp. 393–438. **[G: S. Africa]**

047 Economic History: Latin America and Caribbean

0470 General

Baklanoff, Eric N. External Factors in the Economic Development of Brazil's Heartland: The Center-South, 1850–1930. **In** *Baklanoff, E. N., ed.*, 1969, pp. 19–35. **[G: Brazil]**

Cardozo, Manoel. The Modernization of Brazil, 1500–1808: An Interpretive Essay. **In** *Baklanoff, E. N., ed.*, 1969, pp. 3–18. **[G: Brazil]**

Dulles, John W. F. The Contribution of Getúlio Vargas to the Modernization of Brazil. **In** *Baklanoff, E. N., ed.*, 1969, pp. 36–57. **[G: Brazil]**

Frank, Andre Gunder. Capitalist Latifundio Growth in Latin America. **In** *Frank, A. G.*, 1969, pp. 231–47. **[G: Latin America]**

Leff, Nathaniel H. Long-Term Brazilian Economic Development. *J. Econ. Hist.*, September 1969, *29*(3), pp. 473–93. **[G: Brazil]**

Mauro, Frédéric. Latin American History and Integration. **In** *Hilton, R., ed.*, 1969, pp. 49–58. **[G: Latin America]**

Solnick, Bruce B. A Historian's View of Central America: Economic Integration and Political Unity. **In** *Hilton, R., ed.*, 1969, pp. 500–507. **[G: Central America]**

Winsberg, Morton D. Jewish Agricultural Colonization in Entre Rios, Argentina, III: Economic Problems of Townsmen Resettled on the Land. *Amer. J. Econ. Soc.*, April 1969, *28*(2), pp. 179–91. **[G: Argentina]**

0472 History of Factor Prices and Markets

Elkins, W. F. Black Power in the British West Indies: The Trinidad Longshoremen's Strike of 1919. *Sci. Soc.*, Winter 1969, *33*(1), pp. 71–75. **[G: Trinidad]**

Keesing, Donald B. Structural Change Early in Development: Mexico's Changing Industrial and Occupational Structure from 1895 to 1950. *J. Econ. Hist.*, December 1969, *29*(4), pp. 716–38. **[G: Mexico]**

Waever, F. Stirton. The Dynamics of U.S. Investment in Latin America. *Sci. Soc.*, Winter 1969, *33*(1), pp. 20–24. **[G: U.S.; Latin America]**

0473 History of Public Economic Policy (all levels)

Berson, Theodore M. "Dependência do Imperialismo": Foreign Investment in Brazil, 1935. *Bus. Hist. Rev.*, Summer 1969, *43*(2), pp. 192–203. **[G: Brazil]**

Carr, Raymond. Mexican Agrarian Reform 1910–1960. **In** *Jones, E. L. and Woolf, S. J., eds.*, 1969, pp. 151–68. **[G: Mexico]**

Halperin, Ricardo A. Estimación de series bancarias y monetarias argentinas para el período 1926–1940. (Estimation of Argentina Banking and Monetary Series for the Period 1926–1940. With English summary.) *Económica*, January-April 1969, *15*(1), pp. 15–37. **[G: Argentina]**

048 Economic History: Oceania

0480 General

Bentick, B. L. Foreign Borrowing, Wealth, and Consumption: Victoria 1873–93. *Econ. Rec.*, September 1969, *45*(111), pp. 415–31. **[G: Australia]**

Mitchell, Phyllis. Australian Patriots: A Study of the New Guard. *Australian Econ. Hist. Rev.*, September 1969, *9*(2), pp. 156–78. **[G: Australia]**

0481 History of Product Prices and Markets

Fogarty, John P. New South Wales Wool Prices in the 1820s: A Note. *Australian Econ. Hist. Rev.*, March 1969, *9*(1), pp. 71–77. **[G: Australia]**

Little, Barbara. The Sealing and Whaling Industry in Australia before 1850. *Australian Econ. Hist. Rev.*, September 1969, *9*(2), pp. 109–27. **[G: Australia]**

0482 History of Factor Prices and Markets

Butlin, N. G. and Dowie, J. A. Estimates of Australian Work Force and Employment, 1861–1961. *Australian Econ. Hist. Rev.*, September 1969, *9*(2), pp. 138–55. **[G: Australia]**

0483 History of Public Economic Policy (all levels)

Bambrick, Susan. The 'C' Series: It's Sins of Commission and Omission. *Australian Econ. Hist. Rev.*, March 1969, *9*(1), pp. 53–63. **[G: Australia]**

Beever, E. A. A Reply to Mr. Fogarty's Note. *Australian Econ. Hist. Rev.*, March 1969, *9*(1), pp. 78–80. **[G: Australia]**

Bolton, G. C. Broken Reeds and Smoking Flax. *Australian Econ. Hist. Rev.*, March 1969, *9*(1), pp. 64–70. **[G: Australia]**

Buxton, G. L. Land Settlement in New South Wales: Some Research Problems. *Australian Econ. Hist. Rev.*, September 1969, *9*(2), pp. 128–37. **[G: Australia]**

Macarthy, P. G. Justice Higgins and the Harvester Judgement. *Australian Econ. Hist. Rev.*, March 1969, *9*(1), pp. 17–38. **[G: Australia]**

Spaull, A. D. The Rise of the Victorian Briquette Industry, 1895–1935. *Australian Econ. Hist. Rev.*, March 1969, *9*(1), pp. 39–52. **[G: Australia]**

050 ECONOMIC SYSTEMS

051 Capitalist Economic Systems

0510 Market Economies; Includes Cooperatives in Predominantly Market Economies

Baran, Paul A. An Alternative to Marxism. **In** *Baran, P. A.*, 1969, pp. 43–51.

Baran, Paul A. Better Smaller but Better. In *Baran, P. A.,* 1969, pp. 203–09.

Baran, Paul A. Reflections on Underconsumption. In *Baran, P. A.,* 1969, pp. 185–202.

Baran, Paul A. The Theory of the Leisure Class. In *Baran, P. A.,* 1969, pp. 210–22.

Barkin, Solomon. Trade Unions Face a New Western Capitalist Society. *J. Econ. Issues,* March 1969, *3* (1), pp. 49–65.

Braybrooke, David. Private Production of Public Goods. In *Baier, K. and Rescher, N., eds.,* 1969, pp. 368–88.

Chamberlain, Neil W. Public Planning in Market Systems. In *Prybyla, J. S., ed.,* 1969, pp. 49–55.

Domhoff, G. William. Who Made American Foreign Policy, 1945–1963? In *Horowitz, D., ed.,* 1969, pp. 25–69. **[G: U.S.]**

Donaldson, Peter. British Planning. In *Prybyla, J. S., ed.,* 1969, pp. 173–78. **[G: U.K.]**

Dowd, Douglas F. Statement. In *Role of Giant Corporations, Pt. 1, SCH,* 1969, pp. 521–29. **[G: U.S.]**

Ederer, Rupert J. Capitalism, Socialism, and the Social Market Economy. *Rev. Soc. Econ.,* March 1969, *27*(1), pp. 23–36.

Feulner, Edwin J., Jr. Capitalism, Socialism, and the Social Market Economy: Comment. *Rev. Soc. Econ.,* March 1969, *27*(1), pp. 37–40.

Galbraith, John Kenneth. Professor Gordon on "The Close of the Galbraithian System." *J. Polit. Econ.,* Part I, July/August 1969, *77*(4), pp. 494–503.

Galbraith, John Kenneth. Technology, Planning and Organization. In *Baier, K. and Rescher, N., eds.,* 1969, pp. 353–67.

Gordon, Scott. "The Galbraithian System"—Rejoinder. *J. Polit. Econ.,* November/December 1969, *77*(6), pp. 953–56.

Grether, E. T. Business Responsibility Toward the Market. *Calif. Manage. Rev.,* Fall 1969, *12*(1), pp. 33–42.

Guerrero, Jiménez Rodolfo. Oferta y demanda, relacion basica en el dessarrollo. (Supply and Demand: A Basic Relationship in Development. With English summary.) *Econ. Polít.,* Second Semester 1969, *6*(2), pp. 223–28.

Hindley, Brian. Capitalism and the Corporation. *Economica, N.S.,* November 1969, *36*(144), pp. 426–38.

Hinterhuber, Hans. Der Staat als Unternehmer. (The State as Entrepreneur. With English summary.) *Weltwirtsch. Arch.,* 1969, *103*(1), pp. 58–76.

Iyengar, S. Kesava. The Co-operative Caravan: A Casual Causerie. *Asian Econ. Rev.,* August 1969, *11*(4), pp. 363–404. **[G: India]**

Kemp, Tom. Aspects of French Capitalism between the Wars. *Sci. Soc.,* Winter 1969, *33*(1), pp. 1–19. **[G: France]**

Knutson, Ronald D. Nonproducer Cooperative Interests and the Antitrust Laws. *Amer. J. Agr. Econ.,* May 1969, *51*(2), pp. 335–41. **[G: U.S.]**

Lachmann, Ludwig M. Methodological Individualism and the Market Economy. In *[von Hayek, Friedrich A.],* 1969, pp. 89–103.

von Lanzenauer, Christoph Haehling. A Model for Determining Optimal Profit Sharing Plans. *J. Financial Quant. Anal.,* March 1969, *4*(1), pp. 53–63.

Lockley, Lawrence C. A Dome of Many Colored Glass. *Marquette Bus. Rev.,* Winter 1969, *13*(4), pp. 168–73.

Loyo, Gilberto. Las cooperativas en el desarrollo economico y social de los países en proceso de desarrollo. (The Role of Cooperatives in the Economic and Social Development. With English summary.) *Econ. Polít.,* Fourth Semester 1969, *6* (4), pp. 439–52.

Means, Gardiner C. The Problems and Prospects of Collective Capitalism. *J. Econ. Issues,* March 1969, *3*(1), pp. 18–31.

Mekhanik, G. Social Costs of the Scientific-Technical Revolution under Capitalism. *Prob. Econ.,* December 1969, *12*(8), pp. 3–22. **[G: U.S.]**

Miller, Arjay. A Proposal for a National Goals Institute. *J. Finance,* May 1969, *24*(2), pp. 173–79. **[G: U.S.]**

Nikolitch, Radoje. I See It Differently. *Amer. J. Agr. Econ.,* December 1969, *51*(5), pp. 1629–32. **[G: U.S.]**

O'Connor, James. Scientific and Ideological Elements in the Economic Theory of Government Policy. *Sci. Soc.,* Fall-Winter 1969, *33*(4), pp. 385–414.

Orizet, Jean. The Co-operative Movement Since the First World War. *Int. Lab. Rev.,* July 1969, *100*(1), pp. 23–50.

Papi, G. U. The Role of the State in Mixed Economies. In *Margolis, J. and Guitton, H., eds.,* 1969, pp. 1–21.

Polopolus, Leo. On Institutional Obsolescense and Innovation. *Amer. J. Agr. Econ.,* December 1969, *51*(5), pp. 1624–28. **[G: U.S.]**

della Porta, Glauco. Planning and Growth under a Mixed Economy: The Italian Experience. In *Prybyla, J. S., ed.,* 1969, pp. 179–92. **[G: Italy]**

Salgado Rabadán, Abel. La planeación económica en el sistema capitalista (Primera parte). (Economic Planning in the Capitalist System: First Part. With English summary.) *Econ. Polít.,* Third Semester 1969, *6*(3), pp. 361–66.

Schweitzer, Arthur. Goals in Social Economics. *J. Econ. Issues,* June 1969, *3*(2), pp. 147–65.

Spandau, Arnt. Rate of Return, Profit-Sharing, and the Distribution of Incomes. *S. Afr. J. Econ.,* June 1969, *37*(2), pp. 105–16.

Sweet, Morris L. Decision Making and French Planning. In *Prybyla, J. S., ed.,* 1969, pp. 200–211. **[G: France]**

Tautscher, Anton. Die Entwicklung der österreichischen Staatswirtschaft. (The Development of the Austrian State Economy. With English summary.) *Schmollers Jahr.,* 1969, *89*(3), pp. 267–311. **[G: Austria]**

Van Houtte, J. De socialisering van het recht. (The Socialisation of the Law. With English summary.) *Econ. Soc. Tijdschr.,* June 1969, *23*(3), pp. 257–71.

Vatter, Harold G. Capitalism without Accumulation. *J. Econ. Issues,* March 1969, *3*(1), pp. 110–25.

Ward, Benjamin. What is Distinctive about Contemporary Capitalism? *J. Econ. Issues,* March 1969, *3* (1), pp. 32–48.

Wunderlich, Gene. A Concept of Property. *Agr. Econ. Res.,* January 1969, *21*(1), pp. 1–6.

Zweig, Michael. Political Economy and the "National Interest." *Rev. Radical Polit. Econ.,* May 1969, *1*(1), pp. 11–35. [G: U.S.]

052 Socialist and Communist Economic Systems

0520 Socialist and Communist Economic Systems

Al'ter, L. and Pochkin, P. The First Soviet Model of Economic Growth. *Prob. Econ.,* January 1969, *11* (9), pp. 3–13. [G: U.S.S.R.]

Albu, Al. and Puiu, Al. Comerţul exterior şi creşterea economică. (Foreign Trade and Economic Growth. With English summary.) *Stud. Cercet. Econ.,* 1969, *3,* pp. 199–211. [G: Romania]

Apostol, Gh. Unitate şi diversitate în conceptul de economie socialistă. (Unity and Variety in the Conception of Socialist Economy. With English summary.) *Stud. Cercet. Econ.,* 1969, *3,* pp. 67–78. [G: Romania]

Ărvay, János. Development of the National Accounting System in Hungary. *Rev. Income Wealth,* June 1969, *15*(2), pp. 185–95. [G: Hungary]

Aslanyan, R. G. Action to Ensure That Soviet Citizens Enjoy Equal Rights and Opportunities. *Int. Lab. Rev.,* December 1969, *100*(6), pp. 551–82. [G: U.S.S.R.]

Atlas, M. and Vinokur, R. The Economic Essence of Profit and Profitability under Socialism. *Prob. Econ.,* May 1969, *12*(1), pp. 3–32.

Bachurin, A. The Economic Reform in Operation. *Prob. Econ.,* April 1969, *11*(12), pp. 11–25. [G: U.S.S.R.]

Basora, Adrian A. Cuba: Castroist Command. **In** *Prybyla, J. S., ed.,* 1969, pp. 428–41. [G: Cuba]

Belianova, A. M. The Problem of the Rates of Economic Development in the U.S.S.R. as Treated in the Soviet Economic Literature of the 1920's. *Prob. Econ.,* April 1969, *11*(12), pp. 47–55. [G: U.S.S.R.]

Bernášek, Miloslav. The Czechoslovak Economic Recession, 1962–65. *Soviet Stud.,* April 1969, *20* (4), pp. 444–61. [G: Czechoslovakia]

Bićanić, Rudolf. Economics of Socialism in a Developed Country. **In** *Bornstein, M., ed.,* 1969, pp. 222–35. [G: Yugoslavia]

Böhme, Hans. Dynamische Preisbildung in der sozialistischen Planwirtschaft der DDR. (Dynamic Price Formation in the Socialist Planned Economy of the G[erman] D[emocratic] R[epublic]. With English summary.) *Jahr. Nationalökon. Statist.,* August 1969, *183*(3–4), pp. 193–242. [G: E. Germany]

Bornstein, Morris. The Soviet Debate on Agricultural Price and Procurement Reforms. *Soviet Stud.,* July 1969, *21*(1), pp. 1–20. [G: U.S.S.R.]

Bradley, Michael E. Marxism and Soviet Agricultural Problems. **In** *Prybyla, J. S., ed.,* 1969, pp. 89–95. [G: U.S.S.R.]

Bredov, V. and Levin, A. Prediction of the Population's Demand. *Prob. Econ.,* January 1969, *11*(9), pp. 34–44. [G: U.S.S.R.]

Brody, Andrew. The Rate of Economic Growth in Hungary. **In** *Bronfenbrenner, M., ed.,* 1969, pp. 312–27. [G: Hungary]

Brus, W. A Few General Remarks on the Changes in the System of Planning and Management. **In** *Economic Concentration, Pt. 7A, SCH,* 1969, pp. 4459–65. [G: Poland]

Brusilovskaia, N., et al. Conditions for Applying a System of Accounting Prices in a Socialist Economy. *Prob. Econ.,* September 1969, *12*(5), pp. 71–81.

Buonomo, Maurizio. Moneta e credito nelle economie socialiste: vecchi e nuovi orientamenti. (Money and Credit in Socialist Economies: Old Trends and New. With English summary.) *Bancaria,* April 1969, *25*(4), pp. 449–59.

Černík, Oldřich. Develop Socialism to the Advantage of the Present and Future Generations. *New Trends Czech. Econ.,* February 1969, (1), pp. 3–33. [G: Czechoslovakia]

Černík, Oldřich. We Are Setting Out on the Road Towards Economic Consolidation. *New Trends Czech. Econ.,* December 1969, (8), pp. 3–44. [G: Czechoslovakia]

Červinka, Antonín. What Is the Matter in Dispute? *New Trends Czech. Econ.,* May 1969, (3), pp. 64–75. [G: Czechoslovakia]

Cheung, Steven N. S. Irving Fisher and the Red Guards. *J. Polit. Econ.,* May/June 1969, *77*(3), pp. 430–33.

Churánek, Miloš. Foreign Trade, the Reproduction Process and Personal Consumption. *New Trends Czech. Econ.,* December 1969, (8), pp. 71–88. [G: Czechoslovakia]

Čobeljić, Nikola and Stojanović, Radmila. The Theory of Investment Cycles in a Socialist Economy. *Eastern Europ. Econ.,* Fall 1968/Winter 1968–69, *7*(1–2), pp. 1–168. [G: Europe]

Conklin, D. W. Barriers to Technological Change in the U.S.S.R.: A Study of Chemical Fertilizers. *Soviet Stud.,* January 1969, *20*(3), pp. 353–65. [G: U.S.S.R.]

Constantinescu, N. N. Dezvoltarea sistemului ştiinţelor economice în socialism. (Development of the System of Economic Sciences in Socialism. With English summary.) *Stud. Cercet. Econ.,* 1969, *3,* pp. 173–84. [G: Romania]

Danciu, C. Dezvoltarea planificată armonioasă a economiei naţionale. (Planned and Balanced Development of National Economy. With English summary.) *Stud. Cercet. Econ.,* 1969, *3,* pp. 79–87. [G: Romania]

Daněček, Jiří. New Monetary Banking System in Czechoslovakia. *New Trends Czech. Econ.,* May 1969, (3), pp. 47–63. [G: Czechoslovakia]

De Felice, Frank. Productivity Changes in Soviet Distribution. *Econ. J.,* March 1969, *79*(313), pp. 185–87. [G: U.S.S.R.]

Ellman, Michael. The Consistency of Soviet Plans. *Scot. J. Polit. Econ.,* February 1969, *16*(1), pp. 50–74. [G: U.S.S.R.]

Ernst, Wolfgang. The Foreign Trade Policy of the Mao Tse-Tung Clique. *Chinese Econ. Stud.,* Fall 1969, *3*(1), pp. 33–47. [G: China]

Falkowski, Mieczysław. Socialist Economists and the Developing Countries. **In** *Prybyla, J. S., ed.,* 1969, pp. 511–22.

Fedorenko, N. Questions Pertaining to Optimization of the Growth and Location of Production. *Prob. Econ.,* January 1969, *11*(9), pp. 14–23. **[G: U.S.S.R.]**

Fedorenko, N. and Shatalin, S. The Problem of Optimal Planning of the Socialist Economy. *Prob. Econ.,* November 1969, *12*(7), pp. 3–29.

Feiwel, George R. Czechoslovakia's Economic Dilemma. *Indian Econ. J.,* July–September 1969, *17*(1), pp. 1–27. **[G: Czechoslovakia]**

Feiwel, George R. The Era of Economic Reforms of Socialist Planning. *Econ. Int.,* February 1969, *22* (1), pp. 87–115. **[G: U.S.S.R.; Czechoslovakia]**

Garetovskii, N. The Role of Profit and Profitability under the New System for Economic Stimulation of Production. *Prob. Econ.,* August 1969, *12*(4), pp. 3–30. **[G: U.S.S.R.]**

Ghrist, Bruce. Roadblocks to Reform of the Soviet Economy. *Amer. Econ.,* Fall 1969, *13*(2), pp. 50–56. **[G: U.S.S.R.]**

Goldmann, Josef. Fluctuation in the Growth Rate in a Socialist Economy and the Inventory Cycle. **In** *Bronfenbrenner, M., ed.,* 1969, pp. 332–49. **[G: Czechoslovakia]**

Goldmann, Josef. Karl Marx, the Soviet Economists of the Twenties and Contemporary 'Konjunkturforschung' in a Socialist Country. *Czech. Econ. Pap.,* 1969, (11), pp. 43–50.

Gomberg, Ia. Certain Questions in Wage Theory under Socialism. *Prob. Econ.,* July 1969, *12*(3), pp. 23–42.

Hemer, Jiří. About Foreign Trade Activities—Without Illusions. *New Trends Czech. Econ.,* November 1969, (7), pp. 65–79. **[G: Czechoslovakia]**

Hetényi, I. Economic Development and Long-Term Planning. *Acta Oecon.,* 1969, *4*(2), pp. 155–68. **[G: Hungary]**

Húla, Václav. This Is No Time for a Comfortable Plan. *New Trends Czech. Econ.,* December 1969, (8), pp. 45–60. **[G: Czechoslovakia]**

Hutchings, Raymond. Periodic Fluctuation in Soviet Industrial Growth Rates. *Soviet Stud.,* January 1969, *20*(3), pp. 331–52. **[G: U.S.S.R.]**

Iţicovici, I. Mecanismul pieţei şi sistemul indicatorilor de plan ai întreprinderilor industriale. (Mechanism of the Market and the System of Plan Indicators of Industrial Enterprises. With English summary.) *Stud. Cercet. Econ.,* 1969, *1-2,* pp. 37–44.

Janus, Arnošt and Krajčovič, Josef. The First State Budget of Slovakia, and Problems of Its Fulfillment. *New Trends Czech. Econ.,* November 1969, (7), pp. 80–94. **[G: Czechoslovakia]**

Karcz, Jerzy F. An Organizational Model of Command Farming. **In** *Bornstein, M., ed.,* 1969, pp. 278–99. **[G: E. Europe]**

Kaser, Michael. A Volume Index of Soviet Foreign Trade. *Soviet Stud.,* April 1969, *20*(4), pp. 523–26. **[G: U.S.S.R.]**

Kassirov, L. Methodological Questions Pertaining to Net Income and the Profitability of Agricultural Production. *Prob. Econ.,* May 1969, *12*(1), pp. 45–66. **[G: U.S.S.R.]**

Khachaturov, T. Questions Concerning the Theory of Socialist Reproduction. *Prob. Econ.,* September 1969, *12*(5), pp. 3–28.

Kohoutek, Miloslav. Economic Aspects of the Federalization of Czechoslovakia. *New Trends Czech. Econ.,* February 1969, (1), pp. 50–65. **[G: Czechoslovakia]**

Konovalova, N. and Petrosian, K. Problems of Intensifying the Stimulating Role of Payments for Funds. *Prob. Econ.,* June 1969, *12*(2), pp. 25–47. **[G: U.S.S.R.]**

Kormnov, Iu. Economic Stimulation of the Development of International Production Specialization. *Prob. Econ.,* January 1969, *11*(9), pp. 45–54. **[G: COMECON]**

Kozák, Josef and Šimůnek, Vladimír. Pokus o modelování sezónních výkyvů v bilanční rovnici důchodu. (An Attempt of Mathematical Formulation of Seasonal Variations of Inputs, Outputs and Prices in the Definitional Equation of Income. With English summary.) *Ekon.-Mat. Obzor,* 1969, *5*(2), pp. 209–23. **[G: Czechoslovakia]**

Kuboleca, S. Review of Movements in Yugoslav Economy towards Decentralization. **In** *Economic Concentration, Pt. 7A, SCH,* 1969, pp. 4495–4506. **[G: Yugoslavia]**

Kudrna, A. Differentiation in Earnings. *Eastern Europ. Econ.,* Summer 1969, *7*(4), pp. 25–37. **[G: Czechoslovakia]**

Kunel'skii, L. The Socioeconomic Significance of Raising the Minimum Wage. *Prob. Econ.,* July 1969, *12*(3), pp. 43–57. **[G: U.S.S.R.]**

Levin, A. The Market in the System of Socialist Reproduction. The Equilibrium Price Principle. *Prob. Econ.,* November 1969, *12*(7), pp. 30–48.

Levine, Herbert S. and Seton, Francis. Cyclical Fluctuations under Socialism: Comment. **In** *Bronfenbrenner, M., ed.,* 1969, pp. 303–11.

Li-tien, Feng and Chien, Wen. A Quantitative Analysis of the Relationship Between the Rate of Growth of Productivity and the Average Wage. *Chinese Econ. Stud.,* Fall 1969, *3*(1), pp. 70–91. **[G: China]**

Liberman, Y. The Soviet Economic Reform. **In** *Economic Concentration, Pt. 7A, SCH,* 1969, pp. 4366–71. **[G: U.S.S.R.]**

Lipowski, Adam. Interdependence Between Goals and Incentives in an Experimental System of Management. *Eastern Europ. Econ.,* Fall 1969, *8* (1), pp. 20–71. **[G: Poland]**

Machonin, Pavel. The Social Structure of Contemporary Czechoslovak Society. *Czech. Econ. Pap.,* 1969, (11), pp. 153–59. **[G: Czechoslovakia]**

Maehnel, Klaus. The Economic Policy of the Mao Tse-Tung Clique. *Chinese Econ. Stud.,* Fall 1969, *3*(1), pp. 48–69. **[G: China]**

Mănescu, Manea. Present Problems of Economists' Training. *Revue Roumaine Sci. Soc. Serie Sci. Econ.,* 1969, *13*(1), pp. 3–8. **[G: Romania]**

Mănescu, Manea. Romania's Economy on Her 25th Liberation Anniversary. *Revue Roumaine Sci. Soc. Serie Sci. Econ.,* 1969, *13*(2), pp. 105–12. **[G: Romania]**

Marcus, Mildred Rendl. Questions and Problems Concerning the Expansion of East European Trade with the West and the Financing Methodology. *Marquette Bus. Rev.,* Fall 1969, *13*(3), pp. 125–36. **[G: E. Europe]**

Matejko, Alexander. The International Scene: Current Trends in the Social Sciences: Some Sociological Problems of Socialist Factories. *Soc. Res.*, Autumn 1969, *36*(3), pp. 448–80. [G: E. Europe]

Mesa-Lago, Carmelo. Economic Significance of Unpaid Labor in Socialist Cuba. *Ind. Lab. Relat. Rev.*, April 1969, *22*(3), pp. 339–57. [G: Cuba]

Moldovan, Roman. Structural Changes in the National Economy and the Profile of the Economist. *Revue Roumaine Sci. Soc. Serie Sci. Econ.*, 1969, *13*(1), pp. 9–16. [G: Romania]

Montias, John Michael. East European Economic Reforms. **In** *Bornstein, M., ed.*, 1969, pp. 324–36. [G: E. Europe]

Mueller, C. E. Antitrust and Centralization: A Look at the 'Planned' Economy. **In** *Economic Concentration, Pt. 7A, SCH,* 1969, pp. 4371–86.

Murgescu, Costin. Romania and the Promotion of the Principles of International Economic Cooperation. *Revue Roumaine Sci. Soc. Serie Sci. Econ.*, 1969, *13*(2), pp. 133–55. [G: Romania]

Nonomura, Kazuo. On So-Called Profit Dispute. **In** *Nonomura, K.*, 1969, pp. 137–54. [G: U.S.S.R.]

Nonomura, Kazuo. Transition to the New Economic System in the Soviet Union. **In** *Nonomura, K.*, 1969, pp. 155–75. [G: U.S.S.R.]

Nove, Alec. Cyclical Fluctuations under Socialism. **In** *Bronfenbrenner, M., ed.*, 1969, pp. 287–302.

Nyers, R. Theoretical and Practical Problems of Socialist Economic Integration. (In Russian. With English summary.) *Acta Oecon.*, 1969, *4*(2), pp. 119–53.

Ozsvald, László. Incentives for Management Personnel in Hungarian Industry. *Int. Lab. Rev.*, September 1969, *100*(3), pp. 257–72. [G: Hungary]

Pajestka, J. Central Planning and the Market. **In** *Economic Concentration, Pt. 7A, SCH,* 1969, pp. 4465–72. [G: Poland]

Palubinskas, Feliksas. The Role of Marketing Research in the Soviet Economy. *Univ. Missouri Bus. Govt. Rev.*, September–October 1969, *10*(5), pp. 17–24. [G: U.S.S.R.]

Pavlov, P. and Tsaga, V. The Marginalist Treatment of the Law of Value under Socialism. *Prob. Econ.*, July 1969, *12*(3), pp. 3–22.

Pejovich, Svetozar. Liberman's Reforms and Property Rights in the Soviet Union. *J. Law Econ.*, April 1969, *12*(1), pp. 155–62. [G: U.S.S.R.]

Pejovich, Svetozar. The Firm, Monetary Policy and Property Rights in a Planned Economy. *Western Econ. J.*, September 1969, *7*(3), pp. 193–200.

Petrov, Tsvetan and Kalinov, Stefan. The Economic Mechanism of the New System in 1969 and 1970. *Eastern Europ. Econ.*, Fall 1969, *8*(1), pp. 72–89. [G: Bulgaria]

Piňdák, F. Czechoslovakia and COMECON. *De Economist,* September/October 1969, *117*(5), pp. 516–42. [G: Czechoslovakia; COMECON]

Portes, Richard D. The Enterprise under Central Planning. *Rev. Econ. Stud.*, April 1969, *36*(106), pp. 197–212.

Portes, Richard D. The Rate of Economic Growth in Hungary: Comment. **In** *Bronfenbrenner, M., ed.*, 1969, pp. 328–31. [G: Hungary]

Price, Ralph B. Ideology and Indian Planning. **In** *Prybyla, J. S., ed.*, 1969, pp. 96–111. [G: India]

Prybyla, Jan S. Communist China's Economic System, 1961-66. **In** *Prybyla, J. S., ed.*, 1969, pp. 368–83. [G: China]

Prybyla, Jan S. Soviet Command: From Libermanism to Liberalism? **In** *Prybyla, J. S., ed.*, 1969, pp. 273–83. [G: U.S.S.R.]

Pusić, Eugen. Area and Administration in Yugoslav Development. *Int. Soc. Sci. J.*, 1969, *21*(1), pp. 68–82. [G: Yugoslavia]

Racz, Barnabas A. Hungary's New Economic Mechanism. *Mich. Academician,* Winter 1969, *1*(1–2), pp. 175–81. [G: Hungary]

Rankoff, Iwan. Grundzüge des bulgarischen Finanzsystems. (Principles of the Bulgarian Financial System. With English summary.) *Schmollers Jahr.*, 1969, *89*(2), pp. 185–210. [G: Bulgaria]

Răvar, I. Probleme ale industrializării socialiste a României. (Problems of Romania's Socialist Industrialization. With English summary.) *Stud. Cercet. Econ.*, 1969, *3*, pp. 51–58. [G: Romania]

Roberts, Paul Craig. The Polycentric Soviet Economy. *J. Law Econ.*, April 1969, *12*(1), pp. 163–79.

Rohlíček, Rudolf. Intentions and Reality. *New Trends Czech. Econ.*, November 1969, (7), pp. 3–14. [G: Czechoslovakia]

Rohlíček, Rudolf. Principles of the Present Finance and Tax Policy. *New Trends Czech. Econ.*, December 1969, (8), pp. 61–70. [G: Czechoslovakia]

Roosevelt, Frank. Market Socialism: A Humane Economy? *J. Econ. Issues,* December 1969, *3*(4), pp. 3–20.

Schenk, Karl-Ernst. Die Konvertibilität der Ostblockwährungen als komplexes Entscheidungsproblem der Wirtschaftspolitik. (Convertibility of East Bloc Currencies as a Complex Decision Problem of Economic Policy. With English summary.) *Schmollers Jahr.*, 1969, *89*(6), pp. 675–89. [G: COMECON]

Seton, Francis. Fluctuation in the Growth Rate in a Socialist Economy and the Inventory Cycle: Comment. **In** *Bronfenbrenner, M., ed.*, 1969, pp. 350–55. [G: Czechoslovakia]

Shkatov, V. Prices on Natural Resources and the Problem of Improving Planned Price Formation. *Prob. Econ.*, June 1969, *12*(2), pp. 67–89.

Šíba, Vladimír. Economic Reform and Income Policy. *New Trends Czech. Econ.*, May 1969, (3), pp. 26–46. [G: Czechoslovakia]

Sik, Ota. On the Economic Problems in Czechoslovakia. **In** *Economic Concentration, Pt. 7A, SCH,* 1969, pp. 4509–30. [G: Czechoslovakia]

Simush, P. I. The Impact of the Scientific and Technological Revolution on the Socialist Village. *Int. Soc. Sci. J.*, 1969, *21*(2), pp. 256–64. [G: U.S.S.R.]

Smirnov, V. V. Theoretical Problems Pertaining to the Management of the Economy of Developing Countries. *Prob. Econ.*, July 1969, *12*(3), pp. 83–94.

Sobota, Václav. Federative Arrangement of External Economic Relations. *New Trends Czech. Econ.*, July 1969, (4), pp. 53–64. [G: Czechoslovakia]

Sokol, Jaroslav. The Economic Reform Viewed as a Problem. *Eastern Europ. Econ.*, Summer 1969, *7* (4), pp. 13–24. [G: Czechoslovakia]

Sokol, Miroslav. Observations on Economic Development. *Eastern Europ. Econ.*, Fall 1969, *8*(1), pp.

3–19. [G: Czechoslovakia]

Spornic, A. Consideraţii privind perfecţionarea relaţiilor de proprietate în etapa actuală. (Considerations Regarding the Improvement of Property Relations at the Present Stage. With English summary.) *Stud. Cercet. Econ.*, 1969, *1-2*, pp. 13–22.

Stýblo, Jan. The Socialist Entrepreneurship and the Investor's Risk. *New Trends Czech. Econ.*, July 1969, (4), pp. 65–88.

Sută, N. Comerţul exterior al României în anii construcţiei socialismului. (Foreign Trade of Romania in the Years of Socialist Construction. With English summary.) *Stud. Cercet. Econ.*, 1969, *3*, pp. 213–24. [G: Romania]

Swamy, Subramanian. Retail Price Index in the Peoples' Republic of China. *Rev. Econ. Statist.*, August 1969, *51*(3), pp. 309–19. [G: China]

T'ing-tung, Chang. A Preliminary Study of the Problems in Drafting and Auditing a Final Budget. *Chinese Econ. Stud.*, Winter 1968/69, *2*(2), pp. 28–49. [G: China]

Tabaček, Ján. Slovakia and the Development of Her Economy. *New Trends Czech. Econ.*, July 1969, (4), pp. 21–34. [G: Czechoslovakia]

Tabaček, Ján. Trade Relations Between Czechoslovakia and the Soviet Union. *New Trends Czech. Econ.*, November 1969, (7), pp. 37–64. [G: Czechoslovakia; U.S.S.R.]

Tarnovskii, O. Price Formation on the World Socialist Market. *Prob. Econ.*, October 1969, *12*(6), pp. 42–57.

Tesař, Jiří. The Development of the System of Economic Planning. *New Trends Czech. Econ.*, May 1969, (3), pp. 3–25. [G: Czechoslovakia]

Timár, J. The Level of Employment and Its Equilibrium in Socialism. *Acta Oecon.*, 1969, *4*(2), pp. 169–79.

Treml, Vladimir G. Interaction of Economic Thought and Economic Policy in the Soviet Union. *Hist. Polit. Econ.*, Spring 1969, *1*(1), pp. 187–216. [G: U.S.S.R.]

Typolt, Jiří. Economic Policy and Prices. *New Trends Czech. Econ.*, July 1969, (4), pp. 89–102. [G: Czechoslovakia]

Vasilev, Dimitur. The International Socialist Division of Labor and Its Role in the Increased Profitability of Bulgaria's Foreign Trade. *Eastern Europ. Econ.*, Fall 1969, *8*(1), pp. 90–99. [G: Bulgaria]

Videnov, Ivan. Theoretical Problems of Wholesale Prices. *Eastern Europ. Econ.*, Summer 1969, *7*(4), pp. 3–12.

Vladimirov, Iu. V. The Question of Soviet-Chinese Economic Relations in 1950–1966. *Chinese Econ. Stud.*, Fall 1969, *3*(1), pp. 3–32. [G: China; U.S.S.R.]

Vlasák, František. What Next in the Economic Policy? *New Trends Czech. Econ.*, September 1969, (5–6), pp. 3–89. [G: Czechoslovakia]

Wädekin, Karl-Eugen. Manpower in Soviet Agriculture—Some Post-Khrushchev Developments and Problems. *Soviet Stud.*, January 1969, *20*(3), pp. 281–305. [G: U.S.S.R.]

Wesolowski, Zdzislaw P. The Role of Marketing in a Soviet Type Economy. *Marquette Bus. Rev.*, Spring 1969, *13*(1), pp. 15–21.

Wilber, Charles K. The Role of Agriculture in Soviet Economic Development. *Land Econ.*, February 1969, *45*(1), pp. 87–96. [G: U.S.S.R.]

Wilczynski, Jozef. Towards Rationality in Land Economics under Central Planning. *Econ. J.*, September 1969, *79*(315), pp. 540–59.

Ya-nan, Wang. The Marxist Population Theory and China's Population Problem. *Chinese Econ. Stud.*, Spring-Summer 1969, *2*(3–4), pp. 3–91. [G: China]

Yung, Shen. The Substance, Characteristics, and System of Socialist Public Finance. *Chinese Econ. Stud.*, Winter 1968/69, *2*(2), pp. 3–27. [G: China]

Zieliński, Janusz G. Economics and Politics of Economic Reforms in Eastern Europe. *Econ. Planning*, 1969, *9*(3), pp. 279–95. [G: E. Europe]

Zieliński, Janusz G. The Mechanism for Management of Socialist Industry. **In** *Margolis, J. and Guitton, H., eds.*, 1969, pp. 78–97.

Zinam, Oleg. The Economics of Command Economies. **In** *Prybyla, J. S., ed.*, 1969, pp. 19–46.

Županov, Josip. The Producer and Risk. *Eastern Europ. Econ.*, Spring 1969, *7*(3), pp. 12–28. [G: Yugoslavia]

053 Comparative Economic Systems

0530 Comparative Economic Systems

Bagiotti, Tullio. Die Preistheorie im Prozess wachsender inländischer und internationaler Institutionalisierung. (Price Theory in the Process of Growing Domestic and International Institutionalism. With English summary.) *Weltwirtsch. Arch.*, 1969, *103*(2), pp. 229–48.

Balassa, Bela. Centralization and Decentralization in Economic Systems: Discussion. *Amer. Econ. Rev.*, May 1969, *59*(2), pp. 533–37.

Baran, Paul A. Comments on *The Political Economy of Growth.* **In** *Baran, P. A.*, 1969, pp. 316–60.

Baran, Paul A. and Sweezy, Paul M. Economics of Two Worlds. **In** *Baran, P. A.*, 1969, pp. 68–91.

Bergson, Abram. Centralization and Decentralization in Economic Systems: Discussion. *Amer. Econ. Rev.*, May 1969, *59*(2), pp. 537.

Brubaker, Earl R. Some Effects of Policy on Productivity in Soviet and American Crude Petroleum Extraction. *J. Ind. Econ.*, November 1969, *18*(1), pp. 33–52. [G: U.S.; U.S.S.R.]

Celen, R. De beoordeling van de resultaten in de E.E.G.-landen, Groot-Brittannië en de V.S., wordt geconditioneerd door afwi jkende nationale belastingstelsels. (Differences in the National Tax Systems Are the Causes that the Profits of the Firms in the Countries of the E.E.C., Great Britain and the U.S. Have to Be Compared Cautiously. With English summary.) *Econ. Soc. Tijdschr.*, April 1969, *23*(2), pp. 185–204.

Dalrymple, Dana G. The Organization of Agriculture: Discussion. *Amer. J. Agr. Econ.*, December 1969, *51*(5), pp. 1286–88.

Dovring, Folke. Variants and Invariants in Comparative Agricultural Systems. *Amer. J. Agr. Econ.*, December 1969, *51*(5), pp. 1263–73.

Grossack, Irvin. The Nation—Reflections upon the American Economy. *Indiana Bus. Rev.*, January–February 1969, *44*, pp. 13–16. [G: U.S.; India]

Halm, George N. Will Market Economies and

Planned Economies Converge? In *[von Hayek, Friedrich A.]*, 1969, pp. 75–88.

Holzman, Franklyn D. Import Bottlenecks and the Foreign Trade Multiplier. *Western Econ. J.*, June 1969, *7*(2), pp. 101–08.

Hsing, Su. The Two-Way Struggle Between Socialism and Capitalism in China's Rural Areas After the Land Reform [Part III]. *Chinese Econ. Stud.*, Winter 1968/69, *2*(2), pp. 50–80. **[G: China]**

Hurwicz, Leonid. On the Concept and Possibility of Informational Decentralization. *Amer. Econ. Rev.*, May 1969, *59*(2), pp. 513–24.

Kantzenbach, Erhard. Social Co-ordination of Individual Economic Activities—Thoughts on Basic Economic Policy Decisions. *Ger. Econ. Rev.*, 1969, *7*(3), pp. 185–98.

Kerr, Clark. The Future of Capitalism. In *Kerr, C.*, 1969, pp. 19–32.

Kerr, Clark. The Future of Pluralism. In *Kerr, C.*, 1969, pp. 122–30.

Kouba, Karel. The Plan and Market in a Socialist Economy. *Czech. Econ. Pap.*, 1969, (11), pp. 27–42. **[G: Czechoslovakia]**

Leontiev, L. Myth about the "Rapprochement" of the Two Systems. In *Prybyla, J. S., ed.*, 1969, pp. 477–84.

Licari, Joseph A. Economic Fluctuations: A Comparative Study. *Amer. Econ.*, Spring 1969, *13*(1), pp. 42–57.

Maevskii, I. Socioeconomic Questions Relating to Automation. *Prob. Econ.*, October 1969, *12*(6), pp. 3–26.

Marschak, Thomas. On the Comparison of Centralized and Decentralized Economies. *Amer. Econ. Rev.*, May 1969, *59*(2), pp. 525–32.

Munsinger, Gary M. and Curtis, Thomas D. A Comparison of the Regrouping Process in the United States and the Soviet Union. *Univ. Wash. Bus. Rev.*, Winter 1969, *28*(2), pp. 50–61. **[G: U.S.; U.S.S.R.]**

Nonomura, Kazuo. Competition of Economic Growth. In *Nonomura, K.*, 1969, pp. 3–91.

Nove, Alec. Internal Economics. *Econ. J.*, December 1969, *79*(316), pp. 847–60.

Nutler, G. Warren. Lecture Two: The Soviet Citizen: Today's Forgotten Man. In *Viser, F. J., ed.*, 1969, pp. 19–44. **[G: U.S.S.R.]**

Polanyi, Michael. The Determinants of Social Action. In *[von Hayek, Friedrich A.]*, 1969, pp. 165–79.

Powelson, John P. Economic Attitudes in Latin America and the United States. In *Baier, K. and Rescher, N., eds.*, 1969, pp. 233–65. **[G: Latin America; U.S.]**

Prybyla, Jan S. Meaning and Classification of Economic Systems: An Outline. In *Prybyla, J. S., ed.*, 1969, pp. 9–18.

Prybyla, Jan S. The Convergence of Market-Oriented and Command-Oriented Systems: A Critical Estimate. In *Prybyla, J. S., ed.*, 1969, pp. 467–76.

Prybyla, Jan S. The Convergence of Western and Communist Economic Systems: A Critical Estimate. In *Bornstein, M., ed.*, 1969, pp. 442–52.

Rimlinger, Gaston V. Social Security and Society: An East-West Comparison. *Soc. Sci. Quart.*, December 1969, *50*(3), pp. 494–506.

Seidl, Christian. On Measurement of Convergence of Economic Systems. *Z. Nationalökon.*, December 1969, *29*(3–4), pp. 427–32.

Shaffer, Harry G. Do the U.S. and Soviet Economies Show Signs of Convergence? In *Prybyla, J. S., ed.*, 1969, pp. 453–66.

Toussaint, W. D. The Organization of Agriculture: Discussion. *Amer. J. Agr. Econ.*, December 1969, *51*(5), pp. 1283–85.

Vanek, Jaroslav. Decentralization Under Worker's Management: A Theoretical Appraisal. *Amer. Econ. Rev.*, December 1969, *59*(5), pp. 1006–14.

Walker, Douglas O. Economic Fluctuations: A Comparative Study: Comment. *Amer. Econ.*, Spring 1969, *13*(1), pp. 58–62.

Wunderlich, Gene. The Organization of Agriculture: An Epilogue. *Amer. J. Agr. Econ.*, December 1969, *51*(5), pp. 1289–92.

Zauberman, Alfred. The Rapprochement between East and West in Mathematical-Economic Thought. *Manchester Sch. Econ. Soc. Stud.*, March 1969, *37*(1), pp. 1–21. **[G: U.S.S.R.]**

100 Economic Growth; Development; Planning; Fluctuations

110 Economic Growth; Development; and Planning Theory and Policy

111 Economic Growth Theory and Models

1110 Growth Theories

Allais, Maurice. Growth and Inflation. *J. Money, Credit, Banking*, August 1969, *1*(3), pp. 355–426. **[G: U.K.]**

Allais, Maurice. Growth and Inflation: A Reply to the Observations of the Discussants. *J. Money, Credit, Banking*, August 1969, *1*(3), pp. 441–62. **[G: U.K.]**

Arrow, Kenneth J. Classificatory Notes on the Production and Transmission of Technological Knowledge. *Amer. Econ. Rev.*, May 1969, *59*(2), pp. 29–35.

Atkinson, Anthony B. and Stiglitz, Joseph E. A New View of Technological Change. *Econ. J.*, September 1969, *79*(315), pp. 573–78.

Baldwin, Robert E. Economic Development: Discussion. *Amer. Econ. Rev.*, May 1969, *59*(2), pp. 427–29.

Barber, Clarence L. The Capital-Labor Ratio in Underdeveloped Areas. *Philippine Econ. J.*, First Semester 1969, *8*(1), pp. 85–89.

Bardhan, Pranab. Equilibrium Growth in a Model with Economic Obsolescence of Machines. *Quart. J. Econ.*, May 1969, *83*(2), pp. 312–23.

Bhagwati, Jagdish N. Optimal Policies and Immiserizing Growth. *Amer. Econ. Rev.*, December 1969, *59*(5), pp. 967–70.

Boserup, Mogens. Warning against Optimistic ICOR Statistics. *Kyklos*, 1969, *22*(4), pp. 774–76.

Bottomley, Anthony. Wage Rate Determination in Underpopulated, Underdeveloped Rural Areas. *Econ. Int.*, February 1969, *22*(1), pp. 51–62.

Burmeister, Edwin and Dobell, A. Rodney. Disembodied Technological Change with Several Factors. *J. Econ. Theory,* June 1969, *1*(1), pp. 1–8.

Cagan, Phillip. Allais' Monetary Theory: Interpretation and Comment. *J. Money, Credit, Banking,* August 1969, *1*(3), pp. 427–32. [G: U.K.]

Chakravarty, Sukhamoy. Some Aspects of Optimal Investment Policy in an Underdeveloped Economy. **In** *[Tinbergen, J.],* 1969, pp. 1–18.

Ciriacy-Wantrup, S. V. Natural Resources in Economic Growth: The Role of Institutions and Policies. *Amer. J. Agr. Econ.,* December 1969, *51*(5), pp. 1314–24. [G: India]

Day, Richard H. and Tinney, E. Herbert. Cycles, Phases and Growth in a Generalised Cobweb Theory. *Econ. J.,* March 1969, *79*(313), pp. 90–108.

Domar, Evsey D. Theory of Innovation: Discussion. *Amer. Econ. Rev.,* May 1969, *59*(2), pp. 44–46.

Dorfman, Robert. An Economic Interpretation of Optimal Control Theory. *Amer. Econ. Rev.,* December 1969, *59*(5), pp. 817–31.

Drake, P. J. Economics and Development. *Econ. Rec.,* September 1969, *45*(111), pp. 449–61.

Fei, John C. H. and Ranis, Gustav. Economic Development in Historical Perspective. *Amer. Econ. Rev.,* May 1969, *59*(2), pp. 286–400.

Frank, Charles R., Jr. Economic Development: Discussion. *Amer. Econ. Rev.,* May 1969, *59*(2), pp. 429–32.

Fromm, Gary. Growth and Inflation: A Comment. *J. Money, Credit, Banking,* August 1969, *1*(3), pp. 439–40. [G: U.K.]

George, P. V. Secular Price Behaviour in a Dual Market Economy. *Indian Econ. J.,* April–June 1969, *16*(4–5), pp. 532–43.

Heertje, A. Enkele opmerkingen over groeimodellen. (Some Remarks on Growth Models. With English summary.) *De Economist,* July/August 1969, *117*(4), pp. 361–80.

Hershlag, Z. Y. Theory of Stages of Economic Growth in Historical Perspective. *Kyklos,* 1969, *22*(4), pp. 661–90.

Hicks, John R. Value and Volume of Capital. *Indian Econ. J.,* October–December 1969, *17*(2), pp. 161–71.

Hunter, Guy. Istituzioni e sviluppo economico. (Economic Institutions and Development. With English summary.) *Mondo Aperto,* February 1969, *23* (1), pp. 1–9.

Hymer, Stephen and Resnick, S. Interactions between the Government and the Private Sector: An Analysis of Government Expenditure Policy and the Reflection Ratio. **In** *Stewart, I. G., ed.,* 1969, pp. 155–80.

Inagaki, M. Efficient, Inefficient, and Critical Growth. **In** *[Tinbergen, J.],* 1969, pp. 29–42.

Johnson, Harry G. Comparative Cost and Commercial Policy Theory in a Developing Economy. *Pakistan Develop. Rev.,* Spring Supplement 1969, *9*(1), pp. 1–33.

Keesing, Donald B. Small Population as a Political Handicap to National Development. *Polit. Sci. Quart.,* March 1969, *84*(1), pp. 50–60.

Kim, Young Chin. Sectoral Output-Capital Ratios and Levels of Economic Development: A Cross-Sectional Comparison of Manufacturing Industry. *Rev. Econ. Statist.,* November 1969, *51*(4), pp. 453–58.

Kouwenhoven, A. Enkele opmerkingen over het tijdaspect der economische verschijnselen. (Some Remarks on the Time-Aspect of Economic Phenomena. With English summary.) *De Economist,* March/April 1969, *117*(2), pp. 121–38.

Krishnaswamy, K. S. Some Thoughts on a Drama. *Finance Develop.,* March 1969, *6*(1), pp. 43–50.

Kurz, Mordecai. Tightness and Substitution in the Theory of Capital. *J. Econ. Theory,* October 1969, *1*(3), pp. 244–72.

Laing, N. F. Two Notes on Pasinetti's Theorem. *Econ. Rec.,* September 1969, *45*(111), pp. 373–85.

Levhari, David and Sheshinski, Eytan. A Theorem on Returns to Scale and Steady-State Growth. *J. Polit. Econ.,* January/February 1969, *77*(1), pp. 60–65.

Li-tien, Feng and Chien, Wen. A Quantitative Analysis of the Relationship Between the Rate of Growth of Productivity and the Average Wage. *Chinese Econ. Stud.,* Fall 1969, *3*(1), pp. 70–91. [G: China]

Marsden, Keith. Towards a Synthesis of Economic Growth and Social Justice. *Int. Lab. Rev.,* November 1969, *100*(5), pp. 389–418.

McCallum, B. T. The Instability of Kaldorian Models. *Oxford Econ. Pap.,* March 1969, *21*(1), pp. 56–65.

Merton, Robert C. A Golden Golden-Rule for Welfare-Maximization in an Economy with a Varying Population Growth Rate. *Western Econ. J.,* December 1969, *7*(4), pp. 307–18.

Morgan, Theodore. Investment *versus* Economic Growth. *Econ. Develop. Cult. Change,* April 1969, *17*(3), pp. 392–414.

Morrison, J. Roger. Strategia per lo sviluppo. (How Managers Make Growth. With English summary.) *Mondo Aperto,* April 1969, *23*(2), pp. 116–22.

Niehans, Jürg. Growth and Inflation: A Comment. *J. Money, Credit, Banking,* August 1969, *1*(3), pp. 433–38. [G: U.K.]

Nordhaus, William D. An Economic Theory of Technological Change. *Amer. Econ. Rev.,* May 1969, *59*(2), pp. 18–28. [G: U.S.]

Patel, Surendra J. Rejoinder to Boserup's 'Warning against Optimistic ICOR Statistics'. *Kyklos,* 1969, *22*(4), pp. 777–79.

Pedone, Antonio. The Ricardian Tax Incidence Analysis in the Light of Optimum Growth Theory. *Econ. Int.,* February 1969, *22*(1), pp. 63–83.

Poole, Kenyon E. Three Aspects of Stable Growth Policy. *Rivista Int. Sci. Econ. Com.,* December 1969, *16*(12), pp. 1174–96.

Preston, Esme. Growth and Investment in the Market Economies. *Econ. Rec.,* December 1969, *45* (112), pp. 544–62.

Pritchard, Norris T. A Framework for Analysis of Agricultural Marketing Systems in Developing Countries. *Agr. Econ. Res.,* July 1969, *21*(3), pp. 78–85.

Pshelyaskovskiy, V. I. Elements of the Theory of Growth in Lenin's Plan for the Electrification of Russia (On the 50th Anniversary of the GOELRO Plan). *Matekon,* Fall 1969, *6*(1), pp. 98–116. [G: U.S.S.R.]

Román, Zoltán. A Note on Measuring Structural Changes. *Rev. Income Wealth,* September 1969, *15*(3), pp. 265–68.

Saigal, J. C. Optimum Savings Programme: A Note. **In** *[Tinbergen, J.]*, 1969, pp. 19–27.

Samuelson, Paul A. Local Proof of the Turnpike Theorem. *Western Econ. J.*, March 1969, *7*(1), pp. 1–8.

Saxén, Tryggwe. Note on the Barfod Epsilon Process. *Liiketaloudellinen Aikak.*, 1969, *18*(1), pp. 74–78.

Schneider, Erich. Economic Growth and Economic Order. *Ger. Econ. Rev.*, 1969, *7*(2), pp. 101–07.

Selowsky, Marcelo. On the Measurement of Education's Contribution to Growth. *Quart. J. Econ.*, August 1969, *83*(3), pp. 449–63.

Sidrauski, Miguel. Rational Choice and Patterns of Growth. *J. Polit. Econ.*, Part II, July/August 1969, *77*(4), pp. 575–85.

Singer, Morris. Marxian Economics and Contemporary Growth Analysis. *J. Econ. Issues*, June 1969, *3*(2), pp. 192–205.

Smith, V. Kerry. The Maximization Policies of Less Developed Exporting Countries. *Quart. Rev. Econ. Bus.*, Winter 1969, *4*(9), pp. 84–86.

Solow, Robert M. Sources of Economic Growth. **In** *Starleaf, D. R., ed.*, 1969, pp. 484–92.

Starrett, David A. Switching and Reswitching in a General Production Model. *Quart. J. Econ.*, November 1969, *83*(4), pp. 673–87.

Stiglitz, Joseph E. Theory of Innovation: Discussion. *Amer. Econ. Rev.*, May 1969, *59*(2), pp. 46–49.

Streissler, Erich. Hayek on Growth: A Reconsideration of His Early Theoretical Work. **In** *[von Hayek, Friedrich A.]*, 1969, pp. 245–85.

Strydom, P. D. F. Why Growth Rates Differ (A Review Note). *S. Afr. J. Econ.*, March 1969, *37*(1), pp. 76–80.

Sydsæter, Knut. Note on a Difference Equation Occurring in Growth Theory. *J. Econ. Theory*, June 1969, *1*(1), pp. 104–06.

Tilly, Richard. Soll *und* Haben: Recent German Economic History and the Problem of Economic Development. *J. Econ. Hist.*, June 1969, *29*(2), pp. 298–319. **[G: Germany]**

Tu, Pierre N. V. Externalities and Balanced Growth. *Australian Econ. Pap.*, June 1969, *8*(12), pp. 59–74.

Wassom, John C. Inflation as a Tool for Promoting Growth. *Nebr. J. Econ. Bus.*, Winter 1968–69, *8* (1), pp. 34–43.

Weiss, Roger W. Mishan on Progress: A Review Note. *J. Polit. Econ.*, January/February 1969, *77* (1), pp. 138–40.

von Weizsäcker, Carl Christian. Forschungsinvestitionen und makroökonomische Modelle—Ein wirtschaftstheoretisches Dilemma? (With English summary.) *Kyklos*, 1969, *22*(3), pp. 454–66.

1112 One and Two Sector Growth Models and Related Topics

Akerlof, George A. and Stiglitz, Joseph E. Capital, Wages and Structural Unemployment. *Econ. J.*, June 1969, *79*(314), pp. 269–81.

Al'ter, L. and Pochkin, P. The First Soviet Model of Economic Growth. *Prob. Econ.*, January 1969, *11* (9), pp. 3–13. **[G: U.S.S.R.]**

Anand, Vinod and Srivastava, D. K. On the Stability Theorem in Uzawa's Two-Sector Growth Model. *Indian Econ. J.*, January–March 1969, *16*(3), pp. 362–70.

Asimakopulos, A. A Robinsonian Growth Model in One-Sector Notation. *Australian Econ. Pap.*, June 1969, *8*(12), pp. 41–58.

Atkinson, Anthony B. The Timescale of Economic Models: How Long Is the Long Run? *Rev. Econ. Stud.*, April 1969, *36*(106), pp. 137–52.

Atsumi, H. The Efficient Capital Programme for a Maintainable Utility Level. *Rev. Econ. Stud.*, July 1969, *36*(107), pp. 263–87.

Bardhan, P. K. Optimum Investment for an Open Economy. **In** *[Ghosal, U. N.]*, 1969, pp. 74–88.

Barkai, Haim. A Formal Outline of a Smithian Growth Model. *Quart. J. Econ.*, August 1969, *83* (3), pp. 396–414.

Baumol, William J. Macroeconomics of Unbalanced Growth: Comment on the Comment. *Amer. Econ. Rev.*, Part I, September 1969, *59*(4), pp. 632.

Bertrand, T. J. and Vanek, Jaroslav. Growth with Technological Change, Variable Returns to Scale, and a General Saving Function. *Rivista Int. Sci. Econ. Com.*, August 1969, *16*(8), pp. 741–55.

Bierwag, G. O.; Grove, M. A. and Khang, Chulsoon. National Debt in a Neoclassical Growth Model: Comment. *Amer. Econ. Rev.*, March 1969, *59*(1), pp. 205–10.

Birg, Herwig. Zu einer allgemeinen Theorie des technischen Fortschritts—Kritik der Definitionen von J. R. Hicks und R. F. Harrod. (With English summary.) *Jahr. Nationalökon. Statist.*, March 1969, *182*(4–5), pp. 327–46.

Böhm, Volker. Einige Bemerkungen über ein Zwei-Sektoren-Wachstumsmodell mit fixen Produktionskoeffizienten. (With English summary.) *Jahr. Nationalökon. Statist.*, May 1969, *182* (6), pp. 542–50.

Bradford, David F. Balance on Unbalanced Growth. *Z. Nationalökon.*, December 1969, *29*(3–4), pp. 291–304.

Brems, Hans. Convergence and Stability in the Neoclassical Growth Model. *Nationalokon. Tidsskr.*, 1969, *107*(5–6), pp. 226–35.

Britsch, Klaus; Reichardt, Helmut and Schips, Bernd. Sind die Lohnempfänger gut beraten, wenn sie sich einer Lohnquotensenkung widersetzen? (With English summary.) *Jahr. Nationalökon. Statist.*, August 1969, *183*(3–4), pp. 300–305.

Britto, R. On Putty-Clay: A Comment. *Rev. Econ. Stud.*, July 1969, *36*(107), pp. 395–98.

Brock, William A. and Gale, David. Optimal Growth under Factor Augmenting Progress. *J. Econ. Theory*, October 1969, *1*(3), pp. 229–43.

Brown, M. Substitution-Composition Effects, Capital Intensity Uniqueness and Growth. *Econ. J.*, June 1969, *79*(314), pp. 334–47.

Bruno, M. Fundamental Duality Relations in the Pure Theory of Capital Growth. *Rev. Econ. Stud.*, January 1969, *36*(105), pp. 39–53.

Burmeister, Edwin and Sheshinski, Eytan. A Nonsubstitution Theorem in a Model with Fixed Capital. *Southern Econ. J.*, January 1969, *35*(3), pp. 273–76.

Cass, David and Stiglitz, Joseph E. The Implications

of Alternative Saving and Expectations Hypotheses for Choices of Technique and Patterns of Growth. *J. Polit. Econ.*, Part II, July/August 1969, *77*(4), pp. 586–627.

Chakravarty, Sukhamoy. The Optimal Growth Path for Finite Planning Horizons. **In** *[Ghosal, U. N.]*, 1969, pp. 40–68.

Chang, Winston W. The Theory of Saving and the Stability of Growth Equilibrium. *Quart. J. Econ.*, August 1969, *83*(3), pp. 491–503.

Charles, K. J. Inflation and Economic Growth. *Econ. Aff.*, January-February 1969, *14*(1–2), pp. 26–32.

Cochrane, James L. The Evolution and Generalization of the Golden-Age Modification of the Ramsey Proposal. *Indian Econ. J.*, January–March 1969, *16*(3), pp. 341–55.

Conlisk, John. A Neoclassical Growth Model with Endogenously Positioned Technical Change Frontier. *Econ. J.*, June 1969, *79*(314), pp. 348–62.

Conlisk, John and Huddle, Donald. Allocating Foreign Aid: An Appraisal of a Self-Help Model. *J. Devel. Stud.*, July 1969, *5*(4), pp. 245–51.

Dasgupta, Partha S. On the Concept of Optimum Population. *Rev. Econ. Stud.*, July 1969, *36*(107), pp. 295–318.

Dasgupta, Partha S. On the Optimum Rate of Accumulation in a Labour-Surplus Economy. *Indian Econ. J.*, January–March 1969, *16*(3), pp. 277–311.

Dasgupta, Partha S. Optimum Growth when Capital Is Non-transferable. *Rev. Econ. Stud.*, January 1969, *36*(105), pp. 77–88.

Davis, Eric. A Modified Golden Rule: The Case with Endogenous Labor Supply. *Amer. Econ. Rev.*, March 1969, *59*(1), pp. 177–81.

Ezekiel, Hannan. A Wage Goods Approach to the Problem of Investment Allocation in a Developing Economy. *Kansant. Aikak.*, 1969, *65*(3), pp. 181–90.

Fisher, Franklin M.; Levhari, David and Sheshinski, Eytan. On the Sensitivity of the Level of Output to Savings: Embodiment and Disembodiment: A Clarificatory Note. *Quart. J. Econ.*, May 1969, *83* (2), pp. 347–48.

Foley, Duncan K.; Shell, Karl and Sidrauski, Miguel. Optimal Fiscal and Monetary Policy and Economic Growth. *J. Polit. Econ.*, Part II, July/August 1969, *77*(4), pp. 698–719.

Francis, A. A. A Model of National Economic Growth under Perfect Enclavism. *Soc. Econ. Stud.*, December 1969, *18*(4), pp. 365–73.

Frey, Bruno S. Eine einfache Einführung zu Pontryagins Maximum-Prinzip in Wirtschaftswachstum. (A Simple Introduction to Pontryagin's Maximum Principle in Economic Growth. With English summary.) *Weltwirtsch. Arch.*, 1969, *103* (2), pp. 213–28.

Frey, Bruno S. Product and Process Innovations in Economic Growth. *Z. Nationalökon.*, May 1969, *29*(1–2), pp. 29–38.

Goldman, Steven M. Consumption Behavior and Time Preference. *J. Econ. Theory*, June 1969, *1* (1), pp. 39–47.

Goldman, Steven M. Sequential Planning and Continual Planning Revision. *J. Polit. Econ.*, Part II, July/August 1969, *77*(4), pp. 653–64.

Guha, Ashok S. Accumulation, Innovation, and Growth under Conditions of Disguised Unemployment. *Oxford Econ. Pap.*, November 1969, *21*(3), pp. 360–72.

Guha, Ashok S. The Stability of Neo-classical Growth —A Unified View. **In** *[Ghosal, U. N.]*, 1969, pp. 30–39.

Hamada, Koichi. Optimal Capital Accumulation by an Economy Facing an International Capital Market. *J. Polit. Econ.*, Part II, July/August 1969, *77* (4), pp. 684–97.

Hamberg, D. Saving and Economic Growth. *Econ. Develop. Cult. Change*, July 1969, *17*(4), pp. 460–82.

Holländer, Heinz. Eine einfache Begründung zur langfristigen Harrod-Neutralität des technischen Fortschritts. (With English summary.) *Z. ges. Staatswiss.*, April 1969, *125*(2), pp. 236–42.

Inada, Ken-Ichi. Endogenous Technical Progress and Steady Growth. *Rev. Econ. Stud.*, January 1969, *36*(105), pp. 99–107.

Inada, Ken-Ichi. Fixed Factor Coefficients and Harrod-Neutral Technical Progress. *Rev. Econ. Stud.*, January 1969, *36*(105), pp. 89–97.

Katano, Hikoji. On Mr. Stoleru's Optimal Policy for Economic Growth. *Kobe Econ. Bus. Rev.*, 1969, *16*(1), pp. 31–38.

Khang, Chulsoon. A Neoclassical Growth Model of Vertically Related International Trade. *Osaka Econ. Pap.*, March 1969, *17*(32), pp. 21–29.

Kim, Kwan S. Capital Imports, External Debts, and Growth in the Mahalanobis Model. *Indian Econ. J.*, April–June 1969, *16*(4–5), pp. 488–91.

Levhari, David and Srinivasan, T. N. Optimal Savings under Uncertainty. *Rev. Econ. Stud.*, April 1969, *36*(106), pp. 153–63.

Levhari, David and Sheshinski, Eytan. The Relation between the Rate of Return and the Rate of Technical Progress. *Rev. Econ. Stud.*, July 1969, *36* (107), pp. 363–79.

Liviatan, Nissan and Samuelson, Paul A. Notes on Turnpikes: Stable and Unstable. *J. Econ. Theory*, December 1969, *1*(4), pp. 454–75.

Lorentzen, Ralph. On Efficient Consumption Paths in a Class of Simple Growth Models. *J. Econ. Theory*, June 1969, *1*(1), pp. 92–98.

Lovell, C. A. Knox. Biased Technical Change and Factor Shares in United States Manufacturing. *Quart. Rev. Econ. Bus.*, Autumn 1969, *9*(3), pp. 17–33. **[G: U.S.]**

Lunghini, Giorgio. Ottimo economico e ottimo matematico. (Economic Optimum versus Mathematical Optimum. With English summary.) *L'Industria*, April–June 1969, (2), pp. 159–75.

Mera, Koichi. A Generalized Aggregative Model for Optimal Growth with Some Empirical Tests. *Int. Econ. Rev.*, June 1969, *10*(2), pp. 149–62. **[G: U.S.; Japan]**

Mundlak, Yair. The Terms of Trade of Agriculture in Context of Economic Growth. **In** *Papi, U. and Nunn, C., eds.*, 1969, pp. 634–57.

Näslund, Bertil. On the Road to the Golden Age. *Z. Nationalökon.*, December 1969, *29*(3–4), pp. 305–12.

Nuti, Domenico Mario. The Degree of Monopoly in the Kaldor-Mirrlees Growth Model. *Rev. Econ. Stud.*, April 1969, *36*(106), pp. 257–60.

Park, Seong Yawng. Surplus Labor, Technical Progress, Growth, and Distribution. *Int. Econ. Rev.,* February 1969, *10*(1), pp. 22–35.

Phelps, Edmund S. and Shell, Karl. Public Debt, Taxation, and Capital Intensiveness. *J. Econ. Theory,* October 1969, *1*(3), pp. 330–46.

Qayum, A. Models of Balanced and Maximum Growth in Dualistic Economies. **In** *[Tinbergen, J.],* 1969, pp. 43–63.

Racoveanu, N., et al. Modele de creştere a economiei nationale. (Models of Growth of the National Economy. With English summary.) *Stud. Cercet. Econ.,* 1969, *3,* pp. 89–100. **[G: Romania]**

Ramaswami, V. K. On Two-Sector Neo-classical Growth. *Oxford Econ. Pap.,* July 1969, *21*(2), pp. 142–60.

Robinson, Joan. A Model for Accumulation Proposed by J. E. Stiglitz. *Econ. J.,* June 1969, *79*(314), pp. 412–13.

Robinson, Joan. Macroeconomics of Unbalanced Growth: A Belated Comment. *Amer. Econ. Rev.,* Part I, September 1969, *59*(4), pp. 632.

Robinson, Joan. The Degree of Monopoly in the Kaldor-Mirrlees Growth Model: A Further Note. *Rev. Econ. Stud.,* April 1969, *36*(106), pp. 260–62.

Ryder, Harl E., Jr. Optimal Accumulation in a Two-Sector Neoclassical Economy with Non-Shiftable Capital. *J. Polit. Econ.,* Part II, July/August 1969, *77*(4), pp. 665–83.

Sato, Ryuzo. Stability Conditions in Two-Sector Models of Economic Growth. *J. Econ. Theory,* June 1969, *1*(1), pp. 107–17.

Schreiber, Wilfrid. Beziehungen zwischen den Zuwachsraten des Sozialprodukts, der Faktoreinsätze und der Faktorpreise im vereinfachten Modell. Notizen zur Wachstrumstheorie. (Relations between the Growth Rates of the National Product, the Factor Inputs, and the Factor Prices in a Simplified Model. With English summary.) *Jahr. Nationalökon. Statist.,* August 1969, *183* (3–4), pp. 243–53.

Schumann, Jochen. Zur Theorie optimalen wirtschaftlichen Wachstums. (With English summary.) *Z. ges. Staatswiss.,* January 1969, *125*(1), pp. 1–16.

Sheshinski, Eytan. Stability of Growth Equilibrium in a Neoclassical Vintage Model. *Int. Econ. Rev.,* June 1969, *10*(2), pp. 141–48.

Stacey, R. D. Uniformity in Output Growth Patterns in the Manufacturing Sector. *S. Afr. J. Econ.,* March 1969, *37*(1), pp. 55–75.

Stefanov, I. Marx's Theory of Expanded Reproduction and Problems of Economic Growth. *Matekon,* Fall 1969, *6*(1), pp. 3–18.

Stein, Jerome L. A Minimal Role of Government in Achieving Optimal Growth. *Economica, N.S.,* May 1969, *36*(142), pp. 139–50.

Stephens, J. Kirker. The Simple Analytics of Neoclassical Growth Theory: A Comment. *Quart. Rev. Econ. Bus.,* Summer 1969, *9*(2), pp. 70–71.

Stiglitz, Joseph E. Allocation of Heterogeneous Capital Goods in a Two-Sector Economy. *Int. Econ. Rev.,* October 1969, *10*(3), pp. 373–90.

Stiglitz, Joseph E. Distribution of Income and Wealth among Individuals. *Econometrica,* July 1969, *37*(3), pp. 382–97.

Stiglitz, Joseph E. Rural-Urban Migration, Surplus Labour, and the Relationship between Urban and Rural Wages. *East Afr. Econ. Rev.,* December 1969, *1*(2), pp. 1–27.

Taubman, Paul and Wales, Terence J. Impact of Investment Subsidies in a Neoclassical Growth Model. *Rev. Econ. Statist.,* August 1969, *51*(3), pp. 287–97.

Thage, Bent. Equilibrium and Stability in Harrod's Model. *Swedish J. Econ.,* December 1969, *71*(4), pp. 284–99.

Thirlwall, A. P. Okun's Law and the Natural Rate of Growth. *Southern Econ. J.,* July 1969, *36*(1), pp. 87–89. **[G: U.S.; U.K.]**

Tolkemitt, Georg. Volkswirtschaften mit unbeschränkt zunehmendem Konsumvorsprung gegenüber Golden-Rule-Konsumpfaden. (With English summary.) *Jahr. Nationalökon. Statist.,* March 1969, *182*(4–5), pp. 289–326.

Uzawa, H. Time Preference and the Penrose Effect in a Two-Class Model of Economic Growth. *J. Polit. Econ.,* Part II, July/August 1969, *77*(4), pp. 628–52.

Votey, Harold L., Jr. The Optimum Population and Growth: A New Look. A Modification to Include a Preference for Children in the Welfare Function. *J. Econ. Theory,* October 1969, *1*(3), pp. 273–90.

1113 Multisector Growth Models and Related Topics

Atkinson, Anthony B. Import Strategy and Growth under Conditions of Stagnant Export Earnings. *Oxford Econ. Pap.,* November 1969, *21*(3), pp. 325–38. **[G: U.K.]**

Herman, B.; Mennes, L. B. M. and Waardenburg, J. G. Some Exercises with a Simple Model for World Development Planning. **In** *[Tinbergen, J.],* 1969, pp. 65–92.

Nicola, Pier Carlo. Equilibrio economico generale di tipo concorrenziale in condizioni dinamiche. (General Competitive Equilibrium under Dynamic Conditions—Part I. With English summary.) *L'Industria,* January–March 1969, (1), pp. 3–16.

Thoss, Rainer. Ein Vorschlag zur Koordinierung der Regionalpolitik in einer wachsenden Wirtschaft. (With English summary.) *Jahr. Nationalökon. Statist.,* May 1969, *182*(6), pp. 490–529. **[G: Germany]**

1114 Monetary Growth Models

de Haan, H. and Kuipers, S. K. Een onderzoek naar de invloed van monetaire factoren op het reële groeiproces in enkele traditionele theorieën van economische groei (II). (An Investigation into the Influence of Monetary Factors on the Real Process of Growth in Some Traditional Theories of Economic Growth (II). With English summary.) *De Economist,* July/August 1969, *117*(4), pp. 381–401.

de Haan, H. and Kuipers, S. K. Een onderzoek naar de invloed van monetaire factoren op het reële groeiproces in enkele traditionele theorieën van economische groei (III). (An Investigation into the Influence of Monetary Factors on the Real Process of Growth in Some Traditional Theories of Economic Growth (III). With English summary.) *De Economist,* September/October 1969, *117*(5), pp. 493–515.

de Haan, H. and Kuipers, S. K. Een onderzoek naar de invloed van monetaire factoren op het reële groeiproces in enkele traditionele theorieën van economische groei (I). (An Investigation into the Influence of Monetary Factors on the Real Process of Growth in Some Traditional Theories of Economic Growth (I). With English summary.) *De Economist,* March/April 1969, *117*(2), pp. 139–60.

Hahn, Frank. On Money and Growth. *J. Money, Credit, Banking,* May 1969, *1*(2), pp. 172–87.

Johnson, Harry G. Inside Money, Outside Money, Income, Wealth, and Welfare in Monetary Theory. *J. Money, Credit, Banking,* February 1969, *1* (1), pp. 30–45.

Komiya, Ryutaro. Economic Growth and the Balance of Payments: A Monetary Approach. *J. Polit. Econ.,* January/February 1969, *77*(1), pp. 35–48.

Marty, Alvin L. Notes on Money and Economic Growth. *J. Money, Credit, Banking,* May 1969, *1* (2), pp. 252–65.

Meltzer, Allan H. Money, Intermediation, and Growth. *J. Econ. Lit.,* March 1969, *7*(1), pp. 27–56.

Monti, Mario. Moneta, sviluppo economico e progresso tecnico. (Money, Economic Growth and Technical Progress. With English summary.) *L'Industria,* October–December 1969, (4), pp. 475–92.

Nagatani, Keizo. A Monetary Growth Model with Variable Employment. *J. Money, Credit, Banking,* May 1969, *1*(2), pp. 188–206.

Rousseas, S. W. Monetary Equilibrium, Economic Development and the Economics of Xenophon Zolotas. **In** *Economic Concentration, Pt. 7A, SCH,* 1969, pp. 4197–4206. **[G: Greece]**

Stein, Jerome L. "Neoclassical" and "Keynes-Wicksell" Monetary Growth Models. *J. Money, Credit, Banking,* May 1969, *1*(2), pp. 153–71.

Stein, Jerome L. and Nagatani, Keizo. Stabilization Policies in a Growing Economy. *Rev. Econ. Stud.,* April 1969, *36*(106), pp. 165–83.

Wallich, Henry C. Money and Growth: A Country Cross-Section Analysis. *J. Money, Credit, Banking,* May 1969, *1*(2), pp. 281–302.

112 Economic Development Models and Theories

1120 Economic Development Models and Theories

Adelman, Irma; Geier, Marsha and Morris, Cynthia Taft. Instruments and Goals in Economic Development. *Amer. Econ. Rev.,* May 1969, *59*(2), pp. 409–26.

Aleshina, I. Planning in the Developing Countries: The Problem of Selecting Goals (Toward a Critique of Bourgeois Methodology). *Prob. Econ.,* December 1969, *12*(8), pp. 46–67.

Alpander, Guvenc G. The Business Leaders of Selected Countries. *Univ. Missouri Bus. Govt. Rev.,* May–June 1969, *10*(3), pp. 13–19.

Baldwin, Robert E. Economic Development: Discussion. *Amer. Econ. Rev.,* May 1969, *59*(2), pp. 427–29.

Baletić, Zvonimir. Agricultural Development and a Stable Growth of Output. *Eastern Europ. Econ.,* Summer 1969, *7*(4), pp. 41–48. **[G: Yugoslavia]**

Bardhan, Kalpana. A Note on Price-Elasticity of Demand for Foodgrain in a Peasant Economy. *Oxford Econ. Pap.,* March 1969, *21*(1), pp. 104–08. **[G: India]**

Bauer, Peter T. Development Economics: The Spurious Consensus and Its Background. **In** *[von Hayek, Friedrich A.],* 1969, pp. 5–45.

Bauer, Peter T. Dissent on Development. *Scot. J. Polit. Econ.,* February 1969, *16*(1), pp. 75–94.

Beckford, George L. The Economics of Agricultural Resource Use and Development in Plantation Economies. *Soc. Econ. Stud.,* December 1969, *18* (4), pp. 321–47.

Bićanić, Rudolf. Turning Points in Economic Development and Agricultural Policy. **In** *Papi, U. and Nunn, C., eds.,* 1969, pp. 555–73.

Bottomley, Anthony and Nudds, Donald. A Widow's Cruse Theory of Credit Supply in Underdeveloped Rural Areas. *Manchester Sch. Econ. Soc. Stud.,* June 1969, *37*(2), pp. 131–40.

Brand, S. S. The Interindustry Relationships of Agriculture and Economic Development in South Africa. *Finance Trade Rev.,* June 1969, *8*(3), pp. 171–86. **[G: S. Africa]**

Brewster, Havelock and Thomas, Clive Y. Aspects of the Theory of Economic Integration. *J. Common Market Stud.,* December 1969, *8*(2), pp. 110–32.

Brown, J. A. C. A Regional Model of Agricultural Development. **In** *Thorbecke, E., ed.,* 1969, pp. 75–92.

Bruck, Nicholas K. Higher Education and Economic Development in Central America. *Rev. Soc. Econ.,* September 1969, *27*(2), pp. 160–80. **[G: Central America]**

Bruton, Henry J. The Two Gap Approach to Aid and Development: Comment. *Amer. Econ. Rev.,* June 1969, *59*(3), pp. 439–46.

Caiden, Gerald E. Development Administration and Administrative Reform. *Int. Soc. Sci. J.,* 1969, *21* (1), pp. 9–22.

Campolongo, Alberto. Note sul sottosviluppo. (Notes on Underdevelopment. With English summary.) *Rivista Int. Sci. Econ. Com.,* December 1969, *16* (12), pp. 1197–1204.

Chenery, Hollis B. and Westphal, Larry E. Economies of Scale and Investment over Time. **In** *Margolis, J. and Guitton, H., eds.,* 1969, pp. 359–87.

Chenery, Hollis B. The Two Gap Approach to Aid and Development: Reply to Bruton. *Amer. Econ. Rev.,* June 1969, *59*(3), pp. 446–49.

Coper, Rudolf. Economics and the Family. *Miss. Val. J. Bus. Econ.,* Spring 1969, *4*(2), pp. 57–64.

Curtin, T. R. C. The Economics of Population Growth and Control in Developing Countries. *Rev. Soc. Econ.,* September 1969, *27*(2), pp. 139–53.

Das Gupta, A. Uncertainty and Balanced Growth. **In** *[Ghosal, U. N.]*, 1969, pp. 89–104.

Díaz-Alejandro, Carlos F. Economic Development: Discussion. *Amer. Econ. Rev.*, May 1969, *59*(2), pp. 432–34.

Dixit, Avinash K. Marketable Surplus and Dual Development. *J. Econ. Theory*, August 1969, *1*(2), pp. 203–19.

Dovring, Folke. Commentary on Agrarian Revolution and Economic Progress: A Primer for Development (by Rainer Schickele). *Land Econ.*, February 1969, *45*(1), pp. 125–28.

Drake, P. J. Economics and Development. *Econ. Rec.*, September 1969, *45*(111), pp. 449–61.

Ekelund, Robert B., Jr. Tax Reform in Latin America: The E.C.L.A. Proposals—A Critical Evaluation. *Amer. J. Econ. Soc.*, January 1969, *28* (1), pp. 93–106.

Enache, C. and Mehedinţu, M. Creşterea rolului Partidului Comunist Român în conducerea economiei în etapa actuală. (Increased Importance of the Part Played by the Romanian Communist Party in the Management of Economy at the Present Stage. With English summary.) *Stud. Cercet. Econ.*, 1969, *3*, pp. 9–17. **[G: Romania]**

Enke, Stephen. Correcting Some Confusions. *Rev. Soc. Econ.*, September 1969, *27*(2), pp. 154–59.

Enke, Stephen. Economists and Development: Rediscovering Old Truths. *J. Econ. Lit.*, December 1969, *7*(4), pp. 1125–39.

Ezekiel, Hannan. A Wage Goods Approach to the Problem of Investment Allocation in a Developing Economy. *Kansant. Aikak.*, 1969, *65*(3), pp. 181–90.

Fedorenko, N. Questions Pertaining to Optimization of the Growth and Location of Production. *Prob. Econ.*, January 1969, *11*(9), pp. 14–23. **[G: U.S.S.R.]**

Fei, John C. H. and Ranis, Gustav. Agriculture in the Open Economy: Reply. **In** *Thorbecke, E., ed.*, 1969, pp. 163–64.

Fei, John C. H. and Ranis, Gustav. Agriculture in the Open Economy. **In** *Thorbecke, E., ed.*, 1969, pp. 129–59.

Fei, John C. H. and Ranis, Gustav. Economic Development in Historical Perspective. *Amer. Econ. Rev.*, May 1969, *59*(2), pp. 286–400.

Flanders, M. June. Agriculture versus Industry in Development Policy: The Planner's Dilemma Re-examined. *J. Devel. Stud.*, April 1969, *5*(3), pp. 171–89.

Fox, Karl A. A Regional Model of Agricultural Development: Comment. **In** *Thorbecke, E., ed.*, 1969, pp. 93–94.

Fox, Karl A. Toward a Policy Model of World Economic Development with Special Attention to the Agricultural Sector. **In** *Thorbecke, E., ed.*, 1969, pp. 95–126.

Frank, Andre Gunder. The Development of Underdevelopment. **In** *Frank, A. G.*, 1969, pp. 3–17.

Frank, Charles R., Jr. Economic Development: Discussion. *Amer. Econ. Rev.*, May 1969, *59*(2), pp. 429–32.

Franklin, N. N. Employment and Unemployment: Views and Policies, 1919–1969. *Int. Lab. Rev.*, March 1969, *99*(3), pp. 293–314.

Galnoor, Itzhak and Gross, Bertram M. The New Systems Budgeting and the Developing Nations. *Int. Soc. Sci. J.*, 1969, *21*(1), pp. 23–44.

Georgescu-Roegen, Nicholas. Process in Farming Versus Process in Manufacturing: A Problem of Balanced Development. **In** *Papi, U. and Nunn, C., eds.*, 1969, pp. 497–528.

Ginor, Fanny. The Impact of Capital Imports on the Structure of Developing Countries. *Kyklos*, 1969, *22*(1), pp. 104–23.

Guerrero, Jiménez Rodolfo. Oferta y demanda, relacion basica en el dessarrollo. (Supply and Demand: A Basic Relationship in Development. With English summary.) *Econ. Polít.*, Second Semester 1969, *6*(2), pp. 223–28.

Harbison, Frederick H. Education and Economic Development in Advanced Countries. **In** *[Edding, Friedrich]*, 1969, pp. 223–30.

Hargreaves, Herbert W. Social Scientists and Economists. **In** *Finney, J. C., ed.*, 1969, pp. 222–33.

Herrick, Bruce. Research Needs in Labor and Economic Development. *Ind. Relat.*, May 1969, *8*(3), pp. 214–23.

Hopkins, Terence K. Third World Modernization in Transnational Perspective. *Ann. Amer. Acad. Polit. Soc. Sci.*, November 1969, *386*, pp. 126–36.

Hymer, Stephen H. and Resnick, Stephen. A Model of an Agrarian Economy with Nonagricultural Activities. *Amer. Econ. Rev.*, Part I, September 1969, *59*(4), pp. 493–506.

Ireri, Dunstan. A Proposed Model to Analyze Economic Interdependence among the Member Countries of the East African Community. *East Afr. Econ. Rev.*, December 1969, *1*(2), pp. 75–85. **[G: E. African Community]**

Jorgenson, Dale W. A Programming Model for a Dual Economy: Comment. **In** *Thorbecke, E., ed.*, 1969, pp. 231–34.

Karkal, G. L. A Note on Basics. *Arthaniti*, January & July 1969, *12*(1&2), pp. 78–83. **[G: India; U.S.]**

Kelley, Allen C. Demand Patterns, Demographic Change and Economic Growth. *Quart. J. Econ.*, February 1969, *83*(1), pp. 110–26. **[G: Philippines]**

Khalid, Rasheed O. Fiscal Policy, Development Planning, and Annual Budgeting. *Int. Monet. Fund Staff Pap.*, March 1969, *16*(1), pp. 53–84.

Kolinski, Ralph. Customs Unions of Undeveloped Nations: The Case of Central America. *Econ. Int.*, February 1969, *22*(1), pp. 116–33. **[G: Central America]**

Lewis, W. Arthur. Agriculture in the Open Economy: Comment. **In** *Thorbecke, E., ed.*, 1969, pp. 159–63.

Maitra, Priyatosh. Models of Economic Development with Unlimited Supplies of Labour—Some Fundamental Limitations. *Arthaniti*, January & July 1969, *12*(1&2), pp. 41–56.

Marsden, Keith. Integrated Regional Development: A Quantitative Approach. *Int. Lab. Rev.*, June 1969, *99*(6), pp. 621–46.

Marsden, Keith. Towards a Synthesis of Economic Growth and Social Justice. *Int. Lab. Rev.*, November 1969, *100*(5), pp. 389–418.

McLoughlin, Peter F. M. "Subsistence Agriculture"

and Technological Change: Further Discussion of the Theoretical Problem. *Amer. J. Agr. Econ.*, November 1969, *51*(4), pp. 957–60.

Meier, Gerald M. Development Without Employment. *Banca Naz. Lavoro Quart. Rev.*, September 1969, (90), pp. 309–19.

Mobasheri, Fereidoun. A Criterion for Appraisal of Economic Development Projects. *Eng. Econ.*, October–November 1969, *15*(1), pp. 9–27.

Morse, Chandler. Becoming Versus Being Modern: An Essay on Institutional Change and Economic Development. **In** *Morse, C., et al.*, 1969, pp. 238–382.

Morss, Elliott R. Fiscal Policy, Savings, and Economic Growth in Developing Countries: An Empirical Study. *Finanzarchiv*, August 1969, *28*(3), pp. 460–66.

Mukerjee, Sudhir. The Role of Fiscal Policy in Economic Development. **In** *Bhuleshkar, A. V., ed.*, 1969, pp. 406–16. **[G: India]**

Naqvi, Syed Nawab Haider. Protection and Economic Development. *Kyklos*, 1969, *22*(1), pp. 124–54.

Nicolae-Văleanu, Ivanciu. Istoria gîndirii economice Româneşti—probleme şi preocupări. (History of Romanian Economic Thought—Problems and Preoccupations. With English summary.) *Stud. Cercet. Econ.*, 1969, *3*, pp. 185–98. **[G: Romania]**

Nove, Alec. Soviet Political Organization and Development. **In** *Leys, C., ed.*, 1969, pp. 65–84. **[G: U.S.S.R.]**

Oury, Bernard. Weather and Economic Development. *Finance Develop.*, June 1969, *6*(2), pp. 24–29.

Paakkanen, Jouko. Vaikutelmia kehitysmaiden tilanteesta ja kehitysavusta. (The Developing Countries and Development Aid. With English summary.) *Kansant. Aikak.*, 1969, *65*(1), pp. 27–36.

Pack, Howard and Todaro, Michael P. Technological Transfer, Labour Absorption, and Economic Development. *Oxford Econ. Pap.*, November 1969, *21*(3), pp. 395–403.

Parikh, G. O. Integration of Farm and Non-Farm Employment, Part II: Effective Cooperativisation in a Labour Surplus Economy. *Artha-Vikas*, January 1969, *5*(1), pp. 68–76. **[G: India]**

Parsons, Kenneth H. Poverty as an Issue in Development Policy: A Comparison of United States and Underdeveloped Countries. *Land Econ.*, February 1969, *45*(1), pp. 52–65.

Peaslee, Alexander L. Education's Role in Development. *Econ. Develop. Cult. Change*, April 1969, *17*(3), pp. 293–318.

Preston, Esme. Growth and Investment in the Market Economies. *Econ. Rec.*, December 1969, *45* (112), pp. 544–62.

Reichardt, Manfred. Finding Domestic Finance for Industrialization. *Finance Develop.*, June 1969, *6* (2), pp. 39–43.

Reynolds, Lloyd G. Economic Development with Surplus Labour: Some Complications. *Oxford Econ. Pap.*, March 1969, *21*(1), pp. 89–103.

Reynolds, Lloyd G. Relative Earnings and Manpower Allocation in Developing Economies. *Pakistan Develop. Rev.*, Spring 1969, *9*(1), pp. 14–34.

Reynolds, Lloyd G. The Content of Development Economics. *Amer. Econ. Rev.*, May 1969, *59*(2), pp. 401–08.

Rimmer, Douglas. The Abstraction from Politics: A Critique of Economic Theory and Design with Reference to West Africa. *J. Devel. Stud.*, April 1969, *5*(3), pp. 190–204. **[G: W. Africa]**

Robinson, Warren C. Population Control and Development Strategy. *J. Devel. Stud.*, January 1969, *5* (2), pp. 104–17.

Robinson, Warren C. Types of Disguised Rural Unemployment and Some Policy Implications. *Oxford Econ. Pap.*, November 1969, *21*(3), pp. 373–86.

Rozen, Marvin E. Some Observations on the Efficiency of Industrialization. *Pakistan Develop. Rev.*, Winter 1969, *9*(4), pp. 357–79.

Sachs, Ignacy. Employment and Economic Development in a Dual Economy. **In** *Yesufu, T. M., ed.*, 1969, pp. 227–36.

Sandee, Jan. A Programming Model for a Dual Economy. **In** *Thorbecke, E., ed.*, 1969, pp. 219–30.

Schloss, Henry H. Two Views on Myrdal (II). *Indian Econ. J.*, July–September 1969, *17*(1), pp. 158–60.

Schmitt, Hans O. Integration and Conflict in the World Economy. *J. Common Market Stud.*, September 1969, *8*(1), pp. 1–18.

Simeone, Franco. Integrazione economica e Paesi in via di sviluppo. (Economic Integration and Developing Countries. With English summary.) *Mondo Aperto*, December 1969, *23*(6), pp. 423–43.

Simmons, John L. Technology and Education for Economic Development. **In** *Nader, C. and Zahlan, A. B., eds.*, 1969, pp. 41–59.

Simon, Herbert A. Effects of Increased Productivity upon the Ratio of Urban to Rural Population. **In** *Fox, K. A. and Johnson, D. G., eds.*, 1969, pp. 309–20.

Smirnov, V. V. Theoretical Problems Pertaining to the Management of the Economy of Developing Countries. *Prob. Econ.*, July 1969, *12*(3), pp. 83–94.

Solo, Robert. Capital and Labor Intensive Technology in Developing Countries. *J. Econ. Issues*, December 1969, *3*(4), pp. 96–103.

Solterer, Josef. Liquidity Norms for Development. *Rev. Soc. Econ.*, March 1969, *27*(1), pp. 13–22.

Spengler, Joseph J. Allocation and Development, Economic and Political. **In** *Braibanti, R., ed.*, 1969, pp. 588–637.

Stepanov, Lev. "One Percent": The Problem of Economic Aid. *Ann. Amer. Acad. Polit. Soc. Sci.*, November 1969, *386*, pp. 41–53.

Streeten, Paul. Economic Development and Education. **In** *[Edding, Friedrich]*, 1969, pp. 183–98.

Taylor, Lance J. Development Patterns: A Simulation Study. *Quart. J. Econ.*, May 1969, *83*(2), pp. 220–41.

Tévoédjré, Albert. A Strategy for Social Progress in Africa and the I.L.O.'s Contribution. *Int. Lab. Rev.*, January 1969, *99*(1), pp. 61–84. **[G: Africa]**

Tolley, George S. Review Article: Mellor on Agricultural Development. *Econ. Develop. Cult. Change,* January 1969, *17*(2), pp. 254–61.

Törnqvist, Erik. Nordek-planen. (The Nordek Plan. With English summary.) *Econ. Samfundets Tidskr.,* 1969, *22*(2), pp. 95–104. **[G: Scandanavia; EFTA]**

Uppal, J. S. Work Habits and Disguised Unemployment in Underdeveloped Countries—A Theoretical Analysis. *Oxford Econ. Pap.,* November 1969, *21*(3), pp. 387–94.

Vyas, V. S. Integration of Farm and Non-Farm Employment, Part I: Farm and Non-Farm Employment in an Economically Backward Region. *Artha-Vikas,* January 1969, *5*(1), pp. 54–67. **[G: India]**

Waldo, Dwight. Reflections on Public Administration and National Development. *Int. Soc. Sci. J.,* 1969, *21*(2), pp. 294–309.

Ward, Richard J. Alternative Means to Control Population Growth. *Rev. Soc. Econ.,* September 1969, *27*(2), pp. 121–38.

Ward, Richard J. Two Views on Myrdal (I). *Indian Econ. J.,* July–September 1969, *17*(1), pp. 143–57.

Wilson, J. S. G. Building the Financial System of a Developing Country. *Lloyds Bank Rev.,* July 1969, (93), pp. 36–48.

Wu, Chi-Yuen. Public Administration for National Development: An Analysis of the United Nations Public Administration Programme in the Past Two Decades and the Major Problems in the 1970s. *Int. Soc. Sci. J.,* 1969, *21*(1), pp. 116–34.

Zaidan, George C. Population Growth and Economic Development. *Finance Develop.,* March 1969, *6*(1), pp. 2–8.

113 Economic Planning Theory and Policy

1130 Economic Planning Theory and Policy

Aglietta, Michel and Seibel, Claude. The National Accounting System and the Preparation of the Fifth French Plan. *Rev. Income Wealth,* June 1969, *15*(2), pp. 121–69. **[G: France]**

Arrow, Kenneth J. and Kurz, Mordecai. Optimal Public Investment Policy and Controllability with Fixed Private Savings Ratio. *J. Econ. Theory,* August 1969, *1*(2), pp. 141–77.

Aujac, Henri. Technical Progress and French National Planning. **In** *Arnfield, R. V., ed.,* 1969, pp. 12–25. **[G: France]**

Bachurin, A. The Economic Reform in Operation. *Prob. Econ.,* April 1969, *11*(12), pp. 11–25. **[G: U.S.S.R.]**

Baletic Zvonimir. Agricultural Development and a Stable Growth of Output. *Eastern Europ. Econ.,* Summer 1969, *7*(4), pp. 41–48. **[G: Yugoslavia]**

Baqai, Moin and Brecher, Irving. Foreign-Aid Requirements: A Critique of Aid Projections with Special Reference to Pakistan. *Pakistan Develop. Rev.,* Winter 1969, *9*(4), pp. 380–99. **[G: Pakistan]**

Baran, Paul A. National Economic Planning. **In** *Baran, P. A.,* 1969, pp. 115–81.

Barrère, A. Internal Consistency in the Public Economy: The Plan and the Market. **In** *Margolis, J. and Guitton, H., eds.,* 1969, pp. 22–53.

Basora, Adrian A. Cuba: Castroist Command. **In** *Prybyla, J. S., ed.,* 1969, pp. 428–41. **[G: Cuba]**

Bhagwati, Jagdish N. and Chakravarty, Sukhamoy. Contributions to Indian Economic Analysis: A Survey. *Amer. Econ. Rev.,* Part II, September 1969, *59*(4), pp. 2–73. **[G: India]**

Brusilovskaia, N., et al. Conditions for Applying a System of Accounting Prices in a Socialist Economy. *Prob. Econ.,* September 1969, *12*(5), pp. 71–81.

Carli, Guido. Celebration of the "World Thrift Day." *Rev. Econ. Cond. Italy,* January 1969, *23*(1), pp. 5–12. **[G: Italy]**

Černík, Oldřich. Develop Socialism to the Advantage of the Present and Future Generations. *New Trends Czech. Econ.,* February 1969, (1), pp. 3–33. **[G: Czechoslovakia]**

Černík, Oldřich. We Are Setting Out on the Road Towards Economic Consolidation. *New Trends Czech. Econ.,* December 1969, (8), pp. 3–44. **[G: Czechoslovakia]**

Červinka, Antonín. What Is the Matter in Dispute? *New Trends Czech. Econ.,* May 1969, (3), pp. 64–75. **[G: Czechoslovakia]**

Cole, David C. and Nam, Young Woo. The Pattern and Significance of Economic Planning in Korea. **In** *Adelman, I., ed.,* 1969, pp. 11–37. **[G: S. Korea]**

Cukor, Gy. Long-Term Planning and Technical Progress. *Acta Oecon.,* 1969, *4*(3), pp. 239–58. **[G: Hungary]**

De Wit, Y. B. Stages in Planning: The Indonesian Case. **In** *[Tinbergen, J.],* 1969, pp. 157–74. **[G: Indonesia]**

Dimitrijević, Dimitrije. The Use of Flow-of-Funds Accounts in Monetary Planning in Yugoslavia. *Rev. Income Wealth,* March 1969, *15*(1), pp. 101–15. **[G: Yugoslavia]**

Ellman, Michael. The Consistency of Soviet Plans. *Scot. J. Polit. Econ.,* February 1969, *16*(1), pp. 50–74. **[G: U.S.S.R.]**

Ennuste, Ü. Uncertainty, Information and Decomposition in the Planning of a Production System. *Econ. Planning,* 1969, *9*(3), pp. 258–66.

Falkowski, Mieczysław. Socialist Economists and the Developing Countries. **In** *Prybyla, J. S., ed.,* 1969, pp. 511–22.

Feiwel, George R. The Era of Economic Reforms of Socialist Planning. *Econ. Int.,* February 1969, *22* (1), pp. 87–115. **[G: U.S.S.R.; Czechoslovakia]**

FitzLyon, K. Plan and Prediction. *Soviet Stud.,* October 1969, *21*(2), pp. 164–92. **[G: U.S.S.R.]**

Garetovskii, N. The Role of Profit and Profitability under the New System for Economic Stimulation of Production. *Prob. Econ.,* August 1969, *12*(4), pp. 3–30. **[G: U.S.S.R.]**

Geary, Patrick. Economic Policy and Planning in Ireland: A Review Article. *Irish Banking Rev.,* June 1969, pp. 20–25. **[G: Ireland]**

Gerchuk, Ia. On the Question of Applying Economic-Mathematical Methods in Practice. *Prob. Econ.,* September 1969, *12*(5), pp. 52–70. **[G: U.S.S.R.]**

Gloushkov, V. P. New Methods of Economic Management in the U.S.S.R.: Some Features of the Recent Economic Reform. **In** *Margolis, J. and*

Guitton, H., eds., 1969, pp. 344–58. **[G: U.S.S.R.]**

Hansen, Niles M. French Indicative Planning and the *New Industrial State. J. Econ. Issues*, December 1969, *3*(4), pp. 79–95. **[G: France]**

Hejl, Luboš, et al. Macroeconomic Decision Model for the Medium-term Optimal Planning: A Progress Report. *Czech. Econ. Pap.*, 1969, (11), pp. 51–67. **[G: Czechoslovakia]**

Hetényi, I. Economic Development and Long-Term Planning. *Acta Oecon.*, 1969, *4*(2), pp. 155–68. **[G: Hungary]**

Húla, Václav. This Is No Time for a Comfortable Plan. *New Trends Czech. Econ.*, December 1969, (8), pp. 45–60. **[G: Czechoslovakia]**

Iţicovici, I. Mecanismul pieţei şi sistemul indicatorilor de plan ai întreprinderilor industriale. (Mechanism of the Market and the System of Plan Indicators of Industrial Enterprises. With English summary.) *Stud. Cercet. Econ.*, 1969, *1-2*, pp. 37–44.

Jungk, Robert. Technological Forecasting as a Tool of Social Strategy. **In** *Arnfield, R. V., ed.*, 1969, pp. 3–11.

Kádár, B. Economic Plans and Problems of Their Implementation in Developing Countries. *Acta Oecon.*, 1969, *4*(3), pp. 315–21. **[G: Africa]**

Kade, Gerhard; Hujer, Reinhard and Ipsen, Dirk. Kybernetik und Wirtschaftsplanung. (With English summary.) *Z. ges. Staatswiss.*, January 1969, *125*(1), pp. 17–55.

Kanesa-Thasan, S. Stabilizing an Economy: The Korean Experience. **In** *Adelman, I., ed.*, 1969, pp. 257–76. **[G: S. Korea]**

Kantzenbach, Erhard. Social Co-ordination of Individual Economic Activities—Thoughts on Basic Economic Policy Decisions. *Ger. Econ. Rev.*, 1969, *7*(3), pp. 185–98.

Khachaturov, T. Questions Concerning the Theory of Socialist Reproduction. *Prob. Econ.*, September 1969, *12*(5), pp. 3–28.

Khan, Azizur Rahman. The Possibilities of the East Pakistan Economy during the Fourth Five-Year Plan. *Pakistan Develop. Rev.*, Summer 1969, *9*(2), pp. 144–211. **[G: E. Pakistan]**

Khan, Azizur Rahman. The Possibilities of the East Pakistan Economy during the Fourth Five Year Plan. **In** *Khan, A. R., ed.*, 1969, pp. 169–238. **[G: Pakistan]**

Kim, Joungwon Alexander. The "Peak of Socialism" in North Korea: The Five and Seven Year Plans. **In** *Prybyla, J. S., ed.*, 1969, pp. 412–27. **[G: N. Korea]**

Koudelka, Miroslav. Program of Economic Balance. *New Trends Czech. Econ.*, July 1969, (4), pp. 3–20. **[G: Czechoslovakia]**

Kuznets, P. W. Korea's Five-Year Plans. **In** *Adelman, I., ed.*, 1969, pp. 39–73. **[G: S. Korea]**

Leys, Colin. The Analysis of Planning. **In** *Leys, C., ed.*, 1969, pp. 247–75.

Linnamo, Jussi. Den ekonomiska planeringen som medel för ekonomisk politik. (Economic Planning as a Means of Economic Policy. With English summary.) *Econ. Samfundets Tidskr.*, 1969, *22*(1), pp. 38–47. **[G: Finland]**

Loznevaia, M. Mathematical Methods in Planning Wages. *Prob. Econ.*, June 1969, *12*(2), pp. 48–66. **[G: U.S.S.R.]**

Lupu, Marin A. Problemele perfecţionării conducerii economice în România. (Problems Concerning the Improvement of Economic Management in Romania. With English summary.) *Stud. Cercet. Econ.*, 1969, *4*, pp. 5–21. **[G: Romania]**

Mănescu, Manea. Romania's Economy on Her 25th Liberation Anniversary. *Revue Roumaine Sci. Soc. Serie Sci. Econ.*, 1969, *13*(2), pp. 105–12. **[G: Romania]**

McHale, Thomas R. Policies for the Private Sector: Discussion. *Philippine Econ. J.*, First Semester 1969, *8*(1), pp. 31–32. **[G: Philippines]**

Mickwitz, Gösta. Ekonomisk planering, en kommentar. (Economic Planning: A Commentary on Mr. Linnamo's Article. With English summary.) *Econ. Samfundets Tidskr.*, 1969, *22*(1), pp. 48–51. **[G: Finland]**

Molina Enríquez, Alvaro. Las vias de la transformación social. (Economic and Social Aspects of Development. With English summary.) *Econ. Polít.*, Third Semester 1969, *6*(3), pp. 351–60.

Morton, George and Zauberman, Alfred. Von Neumann's Model and Soviet Long-Term (Perspective) Planning. *Kyklos*, 1969, *22*(1), pp. 45–61.

Nandwani, S. C. Use of Shadow Prices in Plan Methodology. *Indian Econ. J.*, July–September 1969, *17*(1), pp. 137–42.

Nassmàcher, Karl-Heinz. Probleme und Voraussetzungen einer rationalen Wirtschaftspolitik in Grossbritannien. (With English summary.) *Z. ges. Staatswiss.*, October 1969, *125*(4), pp. 637–60. **[G: U.K.]**

Nichita, Nicolae and Anghel, Eliza. Cu privire la corelaţia dintre cererea şi oferta de mărfuri în socialism. (The Correlation between Demand and Offer of Produce in Socialism. With English summary.) *Stud. Cercet. Econ.*, 1969, *1-2*, pp. 23–36.

Nuti, Domenico Mario. On Incomes Policy. *Sci. Soc.*, Fall-Winter 1969, *33*(4), pp. 415–25.

de Oliveira Campos, Roberto. A Retrospect Over Brazilian Development Plans. **In** *Ellis, H. S., ed.*, 1969, pp. 317–44. **[G: Brazil]**

Pejovich, Svetozar. Liberman's Reforms and Property Rights in the Soviet Union. *J. Law Econ.*, April 1969, *12*(1), pp. 155–62. **[G: U.S.S.R.]**

Perkins, Dwight H. Market Control and Command in Communist China: The Early Years. **In** *Prybyla, J. S., ed.*, 1969, pp. 359–67. **[G: China]**

Peterson, Wallace. Planning and the Market Economy. *J. Econ. Issues,* March 1969, *3*(1), pp. 126–43.

Pokrovski, A. Socialist Planning and Capitalist Programming: An Analytical Comparison of the Procedures. **In** *Margolis, J. and Guitton, H., eds.*, 1969, pp. 475–84.

della Porta, Glauco. Planning and Growth under a Mixed Economy: The Italian Experience. **In** *Prybyla, J. S., ed.*, 1969, pp. 179–92. **[G: Italy]**

Prybyla, Jan S. Communist China's Economic System, 1961-66. **In** *Prybyla, J. S., ed.*, 1969, pp. 368–83. **[G: China]**

Prybyla, Jan S. Soviet Command: From Libermanism to Liberalism? In *Prybyla, J. S., ed.*, 1969, pp. 273–83. **[G: U.S.S.R.]**

Prybyla, Jan S. The Development of Economic Thought and Policy in Communist China. In *Prybyla, J. S., ed.*, 1969, pp. 350–58. **[G: China]**

Prybyla, Jan S. The Economic Cost of the Cultural Revolution. In *Prybyla, J. S., ed.*, 1969, pp. 393–411. **[G: China]**

Ramaer, J. C. From Macro to Micro—and Back: Some Thoughts of a B.I.G. Man Who Went into Big Business. In *[Tinbergen, J.]*, 1969, pp. 309–26.

Redding, A. David. Policies for the Private Sector: Discussion. *Philippine Econ. J.*, First Semester 1969, *8*(1), pp. 33–36. **[G: Philippines]**

van Rijckeghem, Willy. An Intersectoral Consistency Model for Economic Planning in Brazil. In *Ellis, H. S., ed.*, 1969, pp. 376–401. **[G: Brazil]**

Roberts, Paul Craig. The Polycentric Soviet Economy. *J. Law Econ.*, April 1969, *12*(1), pp. 163–79.

Rohlíček, Rudolf. Intentions and Reality. *New Trends Czech. Econ.*, November 1969, (7), pp. 3–14. **[G: Czechoslovakia]**

Roxas, Sixto K. Policies for the Private Sector. *Philippine Econ. J.*, First Semester 1969, *8*(1), pp. 16–30. **[G: Philippines]**

Salgado Rabadán, Abel. La planeación económica en el sistema capitalista (Segunda y última parte). (The Economic Planning in a Capitalist System: Second and Last Part. With English summary.) *Econ. Polít.*, Fourth Semester 1969, *6*(4), pp. 461-72.

Salgado Rabadán, Abel. La planeación económica en el sistema capitalista (Primera parte). (Economic Planning in the Capitalist System: First Part. With English summary.) *Econ. Polít.*, Third Semester 1969, *6*(3), pp. 361–66.

de Schweinitz, Karl, Jr. Growth, Development, and Political Monuments. In *Sherif, M. and Sherif, C. W., eds.*, 1969, pp. 209–24.

Shaffer, Harry G. Problems and Prospects of Czechoslovakia's New Economic Model (Including an Interview with Professor Ota Sik). In *Prybyla, J. S., ed.*, 1969, pp. 323–39. **[G: Czechoslovakia]**

Shkatov, V. Prices on Natural Resources and the Problem of Improving Planned Price Formation. *Prob. Econ.*, June 1969, *12*(2), pp. 67–89.

Sokol, Miroslav. Observations on Economic Development. *Eastern Europ. Econ.*, Fall 1969, *8*(1), pp. 3–19. **[G: Czechoslovakia]**

Sovani, N. V. Policy and Plan Implementation. *Indian Econ. J.*, October–December 1969, *17*(2), pp. 250–65.

Spencer, Daniel L. and Woroniak, Alexander. Valuing Transfer of Military-Acquired Skills to Civilian Employment. *Kyklos*, 1969, *22*(3), pp. 467–92. **[G: Japan]**

Stýblo, Jan. The Socialist Entrepreneurship and the Investor's Risk. *New Trends Czech. Econ.*, July 1969, (4), pp. 65–88.

Sweet, Morris L. Decision Making and French Planning. In *Prybyla, J. S., ed.*, 1969, pp. 200–211. **[G: France]**

Tănase, Gh. Perfecţionarea metodologiei de fundamentare a amplasării obiectivelor industriale. (Improvement of the Methodology in Substantiating the Location of Industrial Objectives. With English summary.) *Stud. Cercet. Econ.*, 1969, *1-2*, pp. 45–64.

Tesař, Jiří. The Development of the System of Economic Planning. *New Trends Czech. Econ.*, May 1969, (3), pp. 3–25. **[G: Czechoslovakia]**

Vartiainen, Henri J. Kokonaistaloudellinen suunnittelu osallistumisen ja tavoitteiden ongelmana. (Economic Planning as a Problem of Participation and Aims. With English summary.) *Kansant. Aikak.*, 1969, *65*(2), pp. 95–101. **[G: Finland]**

Vasconcellos, A. S. The French Plans: Character, Targets, Achievements. *Indian Econ. J.*, October–December 1969, *17*(2), pp. 172–204. **[G: France]**

Vasilev, Dimitur. The International Socialist Division of Labor and Its Role in the Increased Profitability of Bulgaria's Foreign Trade. *Eastern Europ. Econ.*, Fall 1969, *8*(1), pp. 90–99. **[G: Bulgaria]**

Vernon, Raymond. Mexico: Public Planning and Private Initiative. In *Prybyla, J. S., ed.*, 1969, pp. 525–40. **[G: Mexico]**

von Wangenheim, Eberhard. Developing Countries and Monetary Reform. *Weltwirtsch. Arch.*, 1969, *103*(1), pp. 95–109.

Wilczynski, Jozef. Towards Rationality in Land Economics under Central Planning. *Econ. J.*, September 1969, *79*(315), pp. 540–59.

Zieliński, Janusz G. Economics and Politics of Economic Reforms in Eastern Europe. *Econ. Planning*, 1969, *9*(3), pp. 279–95. **[G: E. Europe]]**

1132 Economic Planning Theory

Aleshina, I. Planning in the Developing Countries: The Problem of Selecting Goals (Toward a Critique of Bourgeois Methodology). *Prob. Econ.*, December 1969, *12*(8), pp. 46–67.

Barthelemy, Serge. La Methode de Projection à Moyen Terme des Circuits Financiers Utilisée dans la Préparation du Ve Plan Français. (With English summary.) *Rev. Income Wealth*, March 1969, *15*(1), pp. 77–100. **[G: France]**

Baturin, F. and Shemetov, P. Activities of Siberian Economists. *Prob. Econ.*, November 1969, *12*(7), pp. 67–77. **[G: U.S.S.R.]**

Bhagwati, Jagdish N. and Srinivasan, T. N. Optimal Intervention to Acheive Non-Economic Objectives. *Rev. Econ. Stud.*, January 1969, *36*(105), pp. 27–38.

Biolley, T. and Paelinck, J. A Dynamic Model for the Belgian Economy: Simulation and Optimization. *Econ. Planning*, 1969, *9*(1–2), pp. 155–207. **[G: Belgium]**

Bod, P. On a Possible Mathematical Model of Long-Term (15–20 Year) National Economic Planning. *Acta Oecon.*, 1969, *4*(3), pp. 259–67. **[G: Hungary]**

Chandavarkar, Anand G. Indian Monetary Policy and Economic Development. In *Bhuleshkar, A. V., ed.*, 1969, pp. 305–17. **[G: India]**

Collcutt, R. H. Planning Economic Development. In *Arnfield, R. V., ed.*, 1969, pp. 97–111.

Das Gupta, A. K. A Framework of Planning for India. *Indian Econ. J.*, January–March 1969, *16* (3), pp. 265–76. **[G: India]**

Donaldson, Peter. British Planning. In *Prybyla, J. S.,* *ed.*, 1969, pp. 173–78. **[G: U.K.]**

Ellman, Michael. Aggregation as a Cause of Inconsistent Plans. *Economica, N.S.*, February 1969, *36* (141), pp. 69–74.

Fedorenko, N. and Shatalin, S. The Problem of Optimal Planning of the Socialist Economy. *Prob. Econ.*, November 1969, *12*(7), pp. 3–29.

Fericelli, Jean. Programmation dynamique et planification macro-économique. (With English summary.) *Revue Écon.*, March 1969, *20*(2), pp. 235–71.

Goldman, Steven M. Sequential Planning and Continual Planning Revision. *J. Polit. Econ.*, Part II, July/August 1969, *77*(4), pp. 653–64.

Heal, G. M. Planning without Prices. *Rev. Econ. Stud.*, July 1969, *36*(107), pp. 347–62.

Johansen, Leif. An Examination of the Relevance of Kenneth Arrow's General Possibility Theorem for Economic Planning. *Econ. Planning*, 1969, *9* (1–2), pp. 5–41.

Klotzvog, F. N.; Ageeva, V. A. and Buzunov, R. A. Input-Output and National Economic Planning. *Matekon*, Fall 1969, *6*(1), pp. 19–29.

Kouba, Karel. The Plan and Market in a Socialist Economy. *Czech. Econ. Pap.*, 1969, (11), pp. 27–42. **[G: Czechoslovakia]**

Kuligin, P. Improvement of Price Formation under the Economic Reform. *Prob. Econ.*, October 1969, *12*(6), pp. 27–41. **[G: U.S.S.R.]**

Kumar, T. Krishna. The Existence of an Optimal Economic Policy. *Econometrica*, October 1969, *37*(4), pp. 600–610.

Kurihara, Kenneth K. and Bhuleshkar, A. V. Democratic Welfare Statecraft in a Developing Economy with an Empirical Application. **In** *Bhuleshkar, A. V., ed.*, 1969, pp. 288–302. **[G: India]**

Kushwaha, D. S. The Role of Industrial Policy in Economic Development. **In** *Bhuleshkar, A. V., ed.*, 1969, pp. 214–27. **[G: India]**

Leroux, Roger and Raffoul, Faouzi. An Essay in Simulating Economic Policies for the French Economy. *Econ. Planning*, 1969, *9*(1–2), pp. 95–153. **[G: France]**

Little, I. M. D. Public Sector Project Selection in Relation to Indian Development. **In** *Bhuleshkar, A. V., ed.*, 1969, pp. 228–58. **[G: India]**

Marglin, S. A. Information in Price and Command Systems of Planning. **In** *Margolis, J. and Guitton, H., eds.*, 1969, pp. 54–77.

Mennes, L. B. M. Planning for Regions and Centres. *Econ. Planning*, 1969, *9*(1–2), pp. 43–70.

Nathan, Dev. Some Aspects of the Rate of Interest in Planning. *Indian Econ. J.*, April–June 1969, *16* (4–5), pp. 544–53.

Owen, Wyn F. Structural Planning in Densely Populated Countries: An Introduction with Applications to Indonesia. *Malayan Econ. Rev.*, April 1969, *14*(1), pp. 97–114. **[G: Indonesia]**

Pajestka, J. Central Planning and the Market. **In** *Economic Concentration, Pt. 7A, SCH*, 1969, pp. 4465–72. **[G: Poland]**

Papi, G. U. The Role of the State in Mixed Economies. **In** *Margolis, J. and Guitton, H., eds.*, 1969, pp. 1–21.

Pejovich, Svetozar. The Firm, Monetary Policy and Property Rights in a Planned Economy. *Western Econ. J.*, September 1969, *7*(3), pp. 193–200.

Poole, Kenyon E. Three Aspects of Stable Growth Policy. *Rivista Int. Sci. Econ. Com.*, December 1969, *16*(12), pp. 1174–96.

Portes, Richard D. The Enterprise under Central Planning. *Rev. Econ. Stud.*, April 1969, *36*(106), pp. 197–212.

Price, Ralph B. Ideology and Indian Planning. **In** *Prybyla, J. S., ed.*, 1969, pp. 96–111. **[G: India]**

Ryder, Harl E., Jr. Optimal Accumulation in a Two-Sector Neoclassical Economy with Non-Shiftable Capital. *J. Polit. Econ.*, Part II, July/August 1969, *77*(4), pp. 665–83.

Siebert, Horst. Goal Conflicts in Regional Growth Policy. *Z. Nationalökon.*, May 1969, *29*(1–2), pp. 19–28.

Sokol, Jaroslav. The Economic Reform Viewed as a Problem. *Eastern Europ. Econ.*, Summer 1969, *7* (4), pp. 13–24. **[G: Czechoslovakia]**

Tavis, Irene. Futurology and the Problem of Values. *Int. Soc. Sci. J.*, 1969, *21*(4), pp. 574–84.

Vanoli, Andre. Le Système Actuel de Comptabilité Nationale et la Planification. (With English summary.) *Rev. Income Wealth*, June 1969, *15*(2), pp. 171–84. **[G: France]**

Waterston, Albert. An Operational Approach to Development Planning. *Finance Develop.*, December 1969, *6*(4), pp. 38–42.

1136 Economic Planning Policy

Albach, Horst. New Trends in the Economic Policy of the Federal Republic of Germany. *Ger. Econ. Rev.*, 1969, *7*(2), pp. 108–28. **[G: W. Germany]**

Ali, Mansoor. Inflation and Economic Development. **In** *Bhuleshkar, A. V., ed.*, 1969, pp. 318–26. **[G: India]**

Ann, Lee Soo. Financial Planning of Investment in Malaysia. *Malayan Econ. Rev.*, April 1969, *14*(1), pp. 48–64. **[G: Malaysia]**

Baran, Paul A. A Few Thoughts on the Great Debate. **In** *Baran, P. A.*, 1969, pp. 374–87. **[G: U.S.S.R.]**

Baran, Paul A. Reflections on Planning of the Economic Development of India. **In** *Baran, P. A.*, 1969, pp. 308–15. **[G: India]**

Baran, Paul A. Social and Economic Planning. **In** *Baran, P. A.*, 1969, pp. 236–46.

Bernášek, Miloslav. The Czechoslovak Economic Recession, 1962–65. *Soviet Stud.*, April 1969, *20* (4), pp. 444–61. **[G: Czechoslovakia]**

Bhatt, S. J. An Approach to the Problem of Creation of Employment Opportunities in Nigeria. **In** *Yesufu, T. M., ed.*, 1969, pp. 261–68. **[G: Nigeria]**

Bieda, K. Economic Planning in Japan. *Econ. Rec.*, June 1969, *45*(110), pp. 181–205. **[G: Japan]**

Böhme, Hans. Dynamische Preisbildung in der sozialistischen Planwirtschaft der DDR. (Dynamic Price Formation in the Socialist Planned Economy of the G[erman] D[emocratic] R[epublic]. With English summary.) *Jahr. Nationalökon. Statist.*, August 1969, *183*(3–4), pp. 193–242. **[G: E. Germany]**

Borkar, V. V. Prohibition: An Economic Analysis. **In**

Bhuleshkar, A. V., ed., 1969, pp. 395–405. **[G: India]**

Brus, W. A Few General Remarks on the Changes in the System of Planning and Management. **In** *Economic Concentration, Pt. 7A, SCH,* 1969, pp. 4459–65. **[G: Poland]**

Buchanan, Ronald H. Toward Netherlands 2000: The Dutch National Plan. *Econ. Geogr.,* July 1969, *45*(3), pp. 258–74. **[G: Netherlands]**

Catherwood, H. F. R. The Planning Dialogue. *Nat. Westminster Bank Quart. Rev.,* May 1969, pp. 2–9. **[G: U.K.]**

Chowdhury, S. B. Lessons from France. **In** *Dagli, V., ed., Vol. II,* 1969, pp. 218–34. **[G: France]**

Daněček, Jiří. New Monetary Banking System in Czechoslovakia. *New Trends Czech. Econ.,* May 1969, (3), pp. 47–63. **[G: Czechoslovakia]**

Ebrahimzadeh, Cyrus. The Economics of Hydro-Electric Power in Iran. *Tahq. Eq.,* November 1969, *6*(15&16), pp. 54–79. **[G: Iran]**

Edgren, Gösta; Faxén, Karl-Olof and Odhner, Clas-Erik. Wages, Growth and the Distribution of Income. *Swedish J. Econ.,* September 1969, *71*(3), pp. 133–60. **[G: Sweden]**

Elliott, John. The Challenge of Development: Africa and Asia. **In** *Ozbekhan, H. and Talbert, G. E., eds.,* 1969, pp. 163–81. **[G: Africa; Asia]**

Falcon, Walter P. Agricultural Planning: The Peruvian Experience: Comment. **In** *Thorbecke, E., ed.,* 1969, pp. 446–50. **[G: Peru]**

Feiwel, George R. Czechoslovakia's Economic Dilemma. *Indian Econ. J.,* July–September 1969, *17*(1), pp. 1–27. **[G: Czechoslovakia]**

Feldman, David. The Economics of Ideology: Some Problems of Achieving Rural Socialism in Tanzania. **In** *Leys, C., ed.,* 1969, pp. 85–111. **[G: Tanzania]**

Fromm, Erich. The Outlook: Integrated Planning—Problems and Opportunities. **In** *Ozbekhan, H. and Talbert, G. E., eds.,* 1969, pp. 223–33. **[G: U.S.]**

Gerakis, Andreas S. Some Aspects of the U.A.R.'s First Five-Year Plan. *Finance Develop.,* March 1969, *6*(1), pp. 9–15. **[G: U.A.R.; Egypt]**

Ghosh, Alak. The Role of Agriculture in the Fourth Plan. **In** *Bhuleshkar, A. V., ed.,* 1969, pp. 60–68. **[G: India]**

Ghrist, Bruce. Roadblocks to Reform of the Soviet Economy. *Amer. Econ.,* Fall 1969, *13*(2), pp. 50–56. **[G: U.S.S.R.]**

Gross, Norman. Convergence and the Emerging Framework: Discussion. **In** *Ozbekhan, H. and Talbert, G. E., eds.,* 1969, pp. 234–40. **[G: U.S.]**

Halevi, Nadav. Economic Policy Discussion and Research in Israel. *Amer. Econ. Rev.,* Part II, September 1969, *59*(4), pp. 74–118. **[G: Israel]**

Herman, Leon M. The Cult of Bigness in Soviet Economic Planning. **In** *Economic Concentration, Pt. 7A, SCH,* 1969, pp. 4346–58. **[G: U.S.S.R.]**

Hilliard, John. Toward an Integrated Manpower Policy for Accelerated National Development. **In** *Yesufu, T. M., ed.,* 1969, pp. 27–36. **[G: Nigeria]**

Hurd, G. E. and Johnson, T. J. Sociology in the Third World Situation. *Int. Soc. Sci. J.,* 1969, *21*(3), pp. 421–27.

Il, Lee Hee. Project Selection and Evaluation: Formulation of an Investment Program. **In** *Adelman, I., ed.,* 1969, pp. 241–56. **[G: S. Korea]**

Ivan'kov, M. Wages of Collective Farm Managerial Personnel and Specialists and the Matter of Increasing the Effectiveness of Production. *Prob. Econ.,* July 1969, *12*(3), pp. 58–82. **[G: U.S.S.R.]**

Jones, Byrd L. A Plan for Planning in the New Deal. *Soc. Sci. Quart.,* December 1969, *50*(3), pp. 525–34. **[G: U.S.]**

Kulkarni, Vijay G. The Growth of Indian Industries (1951–1965). **In** *Bhuleshkar, A. V., ed.,* 1969, pp. 259–70. **[G: India]**

Lázár, G. Regional Pattern of the Hungarian Economy: Development of Some Topical Problems. *Acta Oecon.,* 1969, *4*(3), pp. 223–37. **[G: Hungary]**

Lipowski, Adam. Interdependence Between Goals and Incentives in an Experimental System of Management. *Eastern Europ. Econ.,* Fall 1969, *8* (1), pp. 20–71. **[G: Poland]**

Loomba, N. Paul. National Planning: Problems and Goals—Discussion. **In** *Ozbekhan, H. and Talbert, G. E., eds.,* 1969, pp. 78–96.

Lukinov, I. Prices and Planned Economic Regulation of Agricultural Production. *Prob. Econ.,* May 1969, *12*(1), pp. 67–90. **[G: U.S.S.R.]**

Lutoslanski, Z. The Role of R and D Units in Long-Range Planning of Technological Development in Poland. **In** *Arnfield, R. V., ed.,* 1969, pp. 112–28. **[G: Poland]**

Maehnel, Klaus. The Economic Policy of the Mao Tse-Tung Clique. *Chinese Econ. Stud.,* Fall 1969, *3*(1), pp. 48–69. **[G: China]**

Maikov, A. Questions Pertaining to the Redistribution of Labor Resources. *Prob. Econ.,* May 1969, *12*(1), pp. 33–44. **[G: U.S.S.R.]**

Mamalakis, Markos. An Analysis of the Financial and Investment Activities of the Chilean Development Corporation: 1939–1964. *J. Devel. Stud.,* January 1969, *5*(2), pp. 118–37. **[G: Chile]**

Morales, Cecilio. Latin America: The Developmental Challenge. **In** *Ozbekhan, H. and Talbert, G. E., eds.,* 1969, pp. 147–62. **[G: Latin America]**

Mouly, Jean. Changing Concepts of Wage Policy. *Int. Lab. Rev.,* July 1969, *100*(1), pp. 1–22.

Mulvey, Charles. A Critical Examination of Prices and Incomes Policy in the U.K. *Irish Banking Rev.,* September 1969, pp. 10–16. **[G: U.K.]**

Nanus, B. B. National Planning: Problems and Goals —Introduction and State-of-the-Art. **In** *Ozbekhan, H. and Talbert, G. E., eds.,* 1969, pp. 32–34.

Ogunsheye, Ayo. Manpower Problems in the Context of Economic Planning. **In** *Yesufu, T. M., ed.,* 1969, pp. 14–26. **[G: Nigeria]**

Okuboyejo, N. A. A. Economic and Development Planning in Nigeria 1945–1968. **In** *Yesufu, T. M., ed.,* 1969, pp. 3–13. **[G: Nigeria]**

Petrov, Tsvetan and Kalinov, Stefan. The Economic Mechanism of the New System in 1969 and 1970. *Eastern Europ. Econ.,* Fall 1969, *8*(1), pp. 72–89. **[G: Bulgaria]**

Power, John H. Industrialization in Pakistan: A Case of Frustrated Take-off? **In** *Khan, A. R., ed.,* 1969, pp. 3–21. **[G: Pakistan]**

Ramana, D. V. Deficit Financing and Import Substitution: India, 1951–65. **In** *Morgan, T. and Spoel-*

stra, N., eds., 1969, pp. 307–31. [G: India]

Rohlíček, Rudolf. Principles of the Present Finance and Tax Policy. *New Trends Czech. Econ.*, December 1969, (8), pp. 61–70. [G: Czechoslovakia]

Ryavec, Karl W. Soviet Industrial Managers, Their Superiors and the Economic Reform: A Study of an Attempt at Planned Behavioural Change. *Soviet Stud.*, October 1969, *21*(2), pp. 208–29. [G: U.S.S.R.]

Schairer, Robert A. Looking beyond the U.S. Experience: Discussion. In *Ozbekhan, H. and Talbert, G. E., eds.*, 1969, pp. 196–203.

Schollhammer, Hans. National Economic Planning and Business Decisions: The French Experience. In *Ozbekhan, H. and Talbert, G. E., eds.*, 1969, pp. 35–69. [G: France]

Schollhammer, Hans. National Economic Planning and Business Decision-Making: The French Experience. *Calif. Manage. Rev.*, Winter 1969, *12* (2), pp. 74–88. [G: France]

Schroeder, Gertrude E. The 1966–67 Soviet Industrial Price Reform: A Study in Complications. *Soviet Stud.*, April 1969, *20*(4), pp. 462–77. [G: U.S.S.R.]

Sharma, L. R. Need for a Growth-Oriented Industrial Policy. *Asian Econ. Rev.*, August 1969, *11*(4), pp. 333–48. [G: India]

Shubik, Martin. Planning: Perspectives and Prospects. In *Ozbekhan, H. and Talbert, G. E., eds.*, 1969, pp. 182–95.

Šíba, Vladimír. Economic Reform and Income Policy. *New Trends Czech. Econ.*, May 1969, (3), pp. 26–46. [G: Czechoslovakia]

Sitnin, V. Results of the Reform of Wholesale Prices and Tasks in the Further Improvement of Price Formation in the U.S.S.R. *Prob. Econ.*, April 1969, *11*(12), pp. 26–36. [G: U.S.S.R.]

Snyder, Wayne W. Turkish Economic Development: The First Five Year Plan, 1963–67. *J. Devel. Stud.*, October 1969, *6*(1), pp. 58–71. [G: Turkey]

Staats, Elmer B. Industry-Government Relationships: Issues Facing the New Administration. In *Ozbekhan, H. and Talbert, G. E., eds.*, 1969, pp. 205–22. [G: U.S.]

Tobias, George. New Markets for Manpower Planning. In *Yesufu, T. M., ed.*, 1969, pp. 37–51. [G: Nigeria]

Treml, Vladimir G. A Note on Soviet Input-Output Tables. *Soviet Stud.*, July 1969, *21*(1), pp. 21–34. [G: U.S.S.R.]

Typolt, Jiří. Economic Policy and Prices. *New Trends Czech. Econ.*, July 1969, (4), pp. 89–102. [G: Czechoslovakia]

Vepa, Ram K. Planning of Resources. In *Dagli, V., ed., Vol. II*, 1969, pp. 153–60. [G: India]

Vlasák, František. What Next in the Economic Policy? *New Trends Czech. Econ.*, September 1969, (5–6), pp. 3–89. [G: Czechoslovakia]

Volodarskii, L. and Eidel'man, M. Basic Results of Elaboration of the Interbranch Balance of Production and Distribution of Output throughout the National Economy of the U.S.S.R. for 1966. *Prob. Econ.*, September 1969, *12*(5), pp. 29–51. [G: U.S.S.R.]

van de Wetering, Hylke. Agricultural Planning: The Peruvian Experience. In *Thorbecke, E., ed.*, 1969, pp. 387–446. [G: Peru]

White, William H. The Usefulness of Econometric Models for Policymakers. *Finance Develop.*, September 1969, *6*(3), pp. 8–13.

114 Economics of War, Defense, and Disarmament

1140 Economics of War and Defense

Altman, Stuart H. Earnings, Unemployment, and the Supply of Enlisted Volunteers. *J. Human Res.*, Winter 1969, *4*(1), pp. 38–59. [G: U.S.]

Anderson, Richard M. Anguish in the Defense Industry. *Harvard Bus. Rev.*, November–December 1969, *47*(6), pp. 162–70, 176–80. [G: U.S.]

Anderson, Richard M. Handling Risk in Defense Contracting. *Harvard Bus. Rev.*, July–August 1969, *47*(4), pp. 90–98. [G: U.S.]

Bailey, Duncan M. and Cargill, Thomas F. The Military Draft and Future Income. *Western Econ. J.*, December 1969, *7*(4), pp. 365–70. [G: U.S.]

Berney, Robert E. The Incidence of the Draft—Is It Progressive? *Western Econ. J.*, September 1969, *7*(3), pp. 244–47. [G: U.S.]

Bingham, Jonathan B. Can Military Spending Be Controlled? *Foreign Aff.*, October 1969, *48*(1), pp. 51–66. [G: U.S.]

Bobrow, Davis B. Improving the Bases for Decision. In *Bobrow, D. B., ed.*, 1969, pp. 3–18. [G: U.S.]

Bohi, Douglas R. War in Vietnam and United States Balance of Payments. *Rev. Econ. Statist.*, November 1969, *51*(4), pp. 471–74. [G: U.S.]

Brennan, D. G. The Case for Missile Defense. *Foreign Aff.*, April 1969, *47*(3), pp. 433–48. [G: U.S.]

Burns, Arthur E. The Government Renegotiates Profits. In *Watson, D. S., ed.*, 1969, pp. 288–96. [G: U.S.]

Cambern, John R. and Newton, David A. Skill Transfers: Can Defense Workers Adapt to Civilian Occupations? *Mon. Lab. Rev.*, June 1969, *92*(6), pp. 21–25. [G: U.S.]

Cartter, Allan M. and Farrell, Robert L. Academic Labor Market Projections and the Draft. In *the Economics and Financing of Higher Education in the United States, JECP*, 1969, pp. 357–74. [G: U.S.]

Chatterji, Manas. A Model of Resolution of Conflict between India and Pakistan. *Peace Res. Soc. Internat. Pap.*, 1969, *12*, pp. 87–102. [G: India; Pakistan]

Cuff, Robert D. Bernard Baruch: Symbol and Myth in Industrial Mobilization. *Bus. Hist. Rev.*, Summer 1969, *43*(2), pp. 115–33. [G: U.S.]

Dewey, Orville. On War. In *Dewey, O.*, 1969, pp. 235–56.

Dudley, Leonard and Passell, Peter. War in Vietnam and United States Balance of Payments: Reply to Comment by Douglas Bohi. *Rev. Econ. Statist.*, November 1969, *51*(4), pp. 474–75.

Enthoven, Alain C. and Smith, K. Wayne. What Forces for NATO? And from Whom? *Foreign Aff.*, October 1969, *48*(1), pp. 80–96.

Erickson, John. Scotland's Defence Commitment:

Some Problems of Cost, Capability, and Effectiveness. In *Wolfe, J. N., ed.*, 1969, pp. 71–91. [G: U.K.]

Evans, Robert, Jr. The Military Draft as a Slave System: An Economic View. *Soc. Sci. Quart.*, December 1969, *50*(3), pp. 535–43. [G: U.S.]

Fisher, Anthony C. The Cost of the Draft and the Cost of Ending the Draft. *Amer. Econ. Rev.*, June 1969, *59*(3), pp. 239–54. [G: U.S.]

Flower, J. F. The Case of the Profitable Bloodhound. In *Carsberg, B. V. and Edey, H. C., eds.*, 1969, pp. 218–45.

Ford, William Freithaler and Tollison, Robert. Note on the Color of the Volunteer Army. *Soc. Sci. Quart.*, December 1969, *50*(3), pp. 544–47. [G: U.S.]

Frank, Andre Gunder. The Economics of Military Government. In *Frank, A. G.*, 1969, pp. 192–200. [G: Brazil]

Friedman, Milton. Why Not a Volunteer Army? In *Starleaf, D. R., ed.*, 1969, pp. 209–15. [G: U.S.]

Galper, Harvey. The Impacts of the Vietnam War on Defense Spending: A Simulation Approach. *J. Bus.*, October 1969, *42*(4), pp. 401–15. [G: U.S.]

Hartley, Eugene L. Prediction of U.S. Public Response to a Damage-Limiting Program. In *Bobrow, D. B., ed.*, 1969, pp. 263–82. [G: U.S.]

Hartley, Keith. Estimating Military Aircraft Production Outlays: The British Experience. *Econ. J.*, December 1969, *79*(316), pp. 861–81. [G: U.K.]

Hoffmann, Walther G. The Share of Defence Expenditure in Gross National Product (GNP)—An International and Diachronic Comparison. *Ger. Econ. Rev.*, 1969, *7*(4), pp. 295–307.

Johnson, Robert E. Statement. In *Competition in Defense Procurement, SCH*, 1969, pp. 32–81. [G: U.S.]

Johnson, Robert E. Technology Licensing in Defense Procurement: A Proposal. In *Competition in Defense Procurement, SCH*, 1969, pp. 339–44. [G: U.S.]

Jordan, Raymond B. Negotiating Overhead Expense with Confidence. *Manage. Account.*, December 1969, *51*(6), pp. 35–39.

Lieberman, A. E. Updating Impressions of the Military-Industry Complex. *Calif. Manage. Rev.*, Summer 1969, *11*(4), pp. 51–62. [G: U.S.]

Mäler, Karl-Göran. Optimal Pricing in Agricultural Emergency Policies. *Swedish J. Econ.*, December 1969, *71*(4), pp. 247–62.

McCall, John and Wallace, Neil. A Supply Function of First-Term Re-enlistees to the Air Force. *J. Human Res.*, Summer 1969, *4*(3), pp. 293–310. [G: U.S.]

McGarrah, Robert E. Let's Internationalize Defense Marketing. *Harvard Bus. Rev.*, May–June 1969, *47*(3), pp. 146–55.

Nash, Ralph C., Jr. Pricing Policies in Government Contracts. In *Competition in Defense Procurement, SCH*, 1969, pp. 237–56. [G: U.S.]

Nathanson, Charles E. The Militarization of the American Economy. In *Horowitz, D., ed.*, 1969, pp. 205–35. [G: U.S.]

Phillips, Joseph D. Economic Effects of the Cold War. In *Horowitz, D., ed.*, 1969, pp. 173–203.

Ratoosh, Philburn. Defense Decision-Making: Cost-Effectiveness Models and Rationality. In *Bobrow, D. B., ed.*, 1969, pp. 21–34.

Russett, Bruce M. Who Pays for Defense? *Amer. Polit. Sci. Rev.*, June 1969, *63*(2), pp. 412–26. [G: U.S.]

Sarin, H. C. Civil Production in Defense Undertakings. In *Dagli, V., ed., Vol. II*, 1969, pp. 195–200. [G: India]

Scherer, Frederic M. Statement. In *Competition in Defense Procurement, SCH*, 1969, pp. 119–31. [G: U.S.]

Shepler, Cora E. and Campbell, Leonard G. United States Defense Expenditures Abroad. *Surv. Curr. Bus.*, December 1969, *49*(12), pp. 40–47. [G: U.S.]

Weidenbaum, Murray L. Statement. In *Competition in Defense Procurement, SCH*, 1969, pp. 3–32. [G: U.S.]

Weidenbaum, Murray L. The Effects of Government Contracting on Private Enterprise. In *Competition in Defense Procurement, SCH*, 1969, pp. 257–63. [G: U.S.]

Weidenbaum, Murray L. The Military/Space Market: The Intersection of the Public and Private Sectors. In *Competition in Defense Procurement, SCH*, 1969, pp. 883–916. [G: U.S.]

120 Economic Development Studies

121 Economic Studies of Less Industrialized Countries

1210 General

Adams, Dale W. and Rask, Norman. Economics of Cost-Share Leases: A Reply. *Amer. J. Agr. Econ.*, August 1969, *51*(3), pp. 695–97.

Adelman, Irma; Geier, Marsha and Morris, Cynthia Taft. Instruments and Goals in Economic Development. *Amer. Econ. Rev.*, May 1969, *59*(2), pp. 409–26.

Aziz, U. A. Wage, Fiscal, Social Security Policies and Institutional Changes as a Means of Redistributing Income in Developing Countries. In *Smith, A. D., ed.*, 1969, pp. 235–55.

Baletić, Zvonimir. Agricultural Development and a Stable Growth of Output. *Eastern Europ. Econ.*, Summer 1969, *7*(4), pp. 41–48. [G: Yugoslavia]

Becker, Arthur P. Principles of Taxing Land and Buildings for Economic Development. In *Becker, A. P., ed.*, 1969, pp. 11–47.

Belsare, S. K. International Liquidity Problems and the Developing Countries. In *Bhuleshkar, A. V., ed.*, 1969, pp. 425–45.

Berg, Elliot J. Wage Structures in Less Developed Countries. In *Smith, A. D., ed.*, 1969, pp. 294–337.

Conlisk, John and Huddle, Donald. Allocating Foreign Aid: An Appraisal of a Self-Help Model. *J. Devel. Stud.*, July 1969, *5*(4), pp. 245–51.

Danciu, C. Dezvoltarea planificată armonioasă a economiei naționale. (Planned and Balanced Development of National Economy. With English summary.) *Stud. Cercet. Econ.*, 1969, *3*, pp. 79–87. [G: Romania]

Dandekar, V. M. Repercussions of Food Surpluses

in Industrialized Countries on Economic Growth in Developing Countries. In *Papi, U. and Nunn, C., eds.*, 1969, pp. 182–99.

Davies, Cyril H. The Bank Group Meeting. *Finance Develop.*, December 1969, *6*(4), pp. 4–9.

Delivanis, D. J. Problems Arising for the Agriculture of a Developing Country by Virtue of Its Association with the European Economic Community. In *Papi, U. and Nunn, C., eds.*, 1969, pp. 130–42. **[G: E.E.C.]**

Díaz-Alejandro, Carlos F. Economic Development: Discussion. *Amer. Econ. Rev.*, May 1969, *59*(2), pp. 432–34.

Dorrance, Graeme S. The Role of Central Banks in Less Developed Countries. *Finance Develop.*, December 1969, *6*(4), pp. 22–26.

Erb, Guy F. and Schiavo-Campo, Salvatore. Export Instability, Level of Development, and Economic Size of Less Developed Countries. *Bull. Oxford Univ. Inst. Econ. Statist.*, November 1969, *31*(4), pp. 263–83.

Falkowski, Mieczysław. Socialist Economists and the Developing Countries. In *Prybyla, J. S., ed.*, 1969, pp. 511–22.

Florescu, C. and Mircioiu, V. Dezvoltarea comerțului interior în anii construcției socialiste. (Development of Home Trade during the Years of Building up Socialism. With English summary.) *Stud. Cercet. Econ.*, 1969, *3*, pp. 151–59. **[G: Romania]**

Fölscher, G. C. K. Some Thoughts on Modernizing a Relatively Large Backward Region in an Otherwise Developed Economy. *Finance Trade Rev.*, June 1969, *8*(3), pp. 198–205.

Frank, Andre Gunder. Dialectic, Not Dual Society. In *Frank, A. G.*, 1969, pp. 221–30.

Frank, Andre Gunder. Mr. Heilbroner's Rhetoric and Reality. In *Frank, A. G.*, 1969, pp. 125–36.

Frank, Charles R., Jr. Economic Development: Discussion. *Amer. Econ. Rev.*, May 1969, *59*(2), pp. 429–32.

Franklin, N. N. Minimum Wage Fixing and Economic Development. In *Smith, A. D., ed.*, 1969, pp. 338–53.

Ginor, Fanny. The Impact of Capital Imports on the Structure of Developing Countries. *Kyklos*, 1969, *22*(1), pp. 104–23.

Gisser, Micha. Economics of Cost-Share Leases: Comment. *Amer. J. Agr. Econ.*, August 1969, *51* (3), pp. 692–95.

Goreux, Louis M. Prospects for Agricultural Trade of Less Developed Countries. In *Thorbecke, E., ed.*, 1969, pp. 15–73.

Holbik, Karel. Development Banks: A Catalyst for Economic Progress. *Rivista Int. Sci. Econ. Com.*, November 1969, *16*(11), pp. 1053–73.

Knudsen, John W. International Trade Policies—The Export Performance of Developing Countries. *Fed. Res. Bank Kansas City Rev.*, July–August 1969, pp. 10–18.

Kojima, Kiyoshi. Asian Developing Countries and PAFTA: Development, Aid and Trade Preferences. *Hitotsubashi J. Econ.*, June 1969, *10*(1), pp. 1–17. **[G: U.S.; Canada; Japan; Australia; New Zealand]**

Kojima, Kiyoshi. Trade Preferences for Developing Countries: A Japanese Assessment. *Hitotsubashi J. Econ.*, February 1969, *9*(2), pp. 1–12. **[G: Japan]**

Kuz'min, S. A. The Developing Countries: Employment and Capital Investment. *Prob. Econ.*, February/March 1969, *11*(10–11), pp. 1–108.

Lall, Sanjaya. A Note on Government Expenditures in Developing Countries. *Econ. J.*, June 1969, *79* (314), pp. 413–17.

Leff, Nathaniel H. The "Exportable Surplus" Approach to Foreign Trade in Underdeveloped Countries. *Econ. Develop. Cult. Change*, April 1969, *17*(3), pp. 346–55.

Lianos, Theodore P. Governmental Deficit Financing and Growth in Underdeveloped Countries: A Comment. *Miss. Val. J. Bus. Econ.*, Fall 1969, *5*(1), pp. 90–92.

Loyo, Gilberto. Las cooperativas en el desarrollo economico y social de los países en proceso de desarrollo. (The Role of Cooperatives in the Economic and Social Development. With English summary.) *Econ. Polít.*, Fourth Semester 1969, *6* (4), pp. 439–52.

Maitra, Priyatosh. Models of Economic Development with Unlimited Supplies of Labour—Some Fundamental Limitations. *Arthaniti*, January & July 1969, *12*(1&2), pp. 41–56.

van Meerhaeghe, M. A. G. Observations sur la signification des termes d'échange des pays sous-développés. (With English summary.) *Kyklos*, 1969, *22*(3), pp. 566–84.

Mellor, John W. Production Economics and the Modernization of Traditional Agricultures. *Australian J. Agr. Econ.*, June 1969, *13*(1), pp. 25–34.

Mitra, Ashok. Wage Policy in Developing Countries. In *Smith, A. D., ed.*, 1969, pp. 371–82.

Morss, Elliott R. Fiscal Policy, Savings, and Economic Growth in Developing Countries: An Empirical Study. *Finanzarchiv*, August 1969, *28*(3), pp. 460–66.

Narayanan, P. P. Trade Union Attitudes to Wage Policy in Developing Countries. In *Smith, A. D., ed.*, 1969, pp. 383–94.

Reynolds, Lloyd G. Objectives of Wage Policy in Developing Countries. In *Smith, A. D., ed.*, 1969, pp. 217–34.

Richmond, David. Employer Attitudes to Wage Policies in Developing Countries. In *Smith, A. D., ed.*, 1969, pp. 395–97.

Samli, A. Coskun. Governmental Deficit Financing and Growth in Underdeveloped Countries: Reply. *Miss. Val. J. Bus. Econ.*, Fall 1969, *5*(1), pp. 93–96.

Short, Brock K. Export Promotion in Underdeveloped Countries. *Amer. Econ.*, Fall 1969, *13* (2), pp. 70–79.

Simon, Julian L. and Gardner, David M. World Food Needs and "New Proteins." *Econ. Develop. Cult. Change*, July 1969, *17*(4), pp. 520–26.

Smith, Anthony D. A Conspectus of Wage Trends in Developing Countries. In *Smith, A. D., ed.*, 1969, pp. 3–52.

Smith, Anthony D. An Analysis of the Proceedings. In *Smith, A. D., ed.*, 1969, pp. 163–214.

Sukhatme, P. V. and Sukhatme, B. V. On Some

Methodological Aspects of Sample Surveys of Agriculture in Developing Countries. **In** *Johnson, N. L. and Smith, H., Jr., eds.*, 1969, pp. 528–61.

Turner, H. A. The Formulation of Wage Policy. **In** *Smith, A. D., ed.*, 1969, pp. 354–70.

de Vries, Barend A. High Cost of Industry in Developing Countries—Causes and Remedies. *Finance Develop.*, December 1969, *6*(4), pp. 43–47.

Ward, Richard J. Absorbing More Labor in LDC Agriculture. *Econ. Develop. Cult. Change*, January 1969, *17*(2), pp. 178–88.

Weiss, Steven J. Factors Affecting the Government Revenue Share in Less Developed Countries. *Soc. Econ. Stud.*, December 1969, *18*(4), pp. 348–64.

Woodley, W. John R. Some Institutional Aspects of Exchange Markets in the Less-Developed Countries. **In** *Aliber, R. Z., ed.*, 1969, pp. 177–93.

1211 Comparative Country Studies

Colaco, Francis X. Harberger's Inflation Model: A Critique and Test Using Data for Brazil and India. *Indian Econ. J.*, April–June 1969, *16*(4–5), pp. 434–44. **[G: Brazil; India]**

Cornehls, James V. and Van Roy, Edward. Economic Development in Mexico and Thailand: An Institutional Analysis (Part I). *J. Econ. Issues*, September 1969, *3*(3), pp. 16–32. **[G: Mexico; Thailand]**

Daniels, Mark R. Differences in Efficiency among Industries in Developing Countries. *Amer. Econ. Rev.*, March 1969, *59*(1), pp. 159–71.

Harris, Edward R., Jr. Funding Land Redistribution in Developing Countries: Maintaining Fiscal Solvency in the Face of Heavy Costs. *Amer. J. Econ. Soc.*, April 1969, *28*(2), pp. 193–204.

Kelley, Allen C. Demographic Cycles and Economic Growth: The Long Swing Reconsidered. *J. Econ. Hist.*, December 1969, *29*(4), pp. 633–56.

Sabolo, Yves. Sectoral Employment Growth: The Outlook for 1980. *Int. Lab. Rev.*, November 1969, *100*(5), pp. 445–74.

Schutjer, Wayne and Weigel, Dale. The Contribution of Foreign Assistance to Agricultural Development. *Amer. J. Agr. Econ.*, November 1969, *51*(4), pp. 788–97.

Strout, Alan M. Korea's Use of Foreign and Domestic Resources: A Cross-Country Comparison. **In** *Adelman, I., ed.*, 1969, pp. 277–92. **[G: S. Korea]**

Van Roy, Edward and Cornehls, James V. Economic Development in Mexico and Thailand: An Institutional Analysis (Part II). *J. Econ. Issues*, December 1969, *3*(4), pp. 21–38. **[G: Mexico; Thailand]**

1213 European Countries

Green, Andrew Wilson. Portugal and the African Territories: Economic Implications. **In** *Abshire, D. M. and Samuels, M. A., eds.*, 1969, pp. 345–63. **[G: Portugal]**

Mănescu, Manea. Romania's Economy on Her 25th Liberation Anniversary. *Revue Roumaine Sci. Soc. Serie Sci. Econ.*, 1969, *13*(2), pp. 105–12. **[G: Romania]**

Moldovan, Roman. Structural Changes in the National Economy and the Profile of the Economist. *Revue Roumaine Sci. Soc. Serie Sci. Econ.*, 1969, *13*(1), pp. 9–16. **[G: Romania]**

Prybyla, Jan S. Albania: Dependent Command. **In** *Prybyla, J. S., ed.*, 1969, pp. 284–92. **[G: Albania]**

Pusić, Eugen. Area and Administration in Yugoslav Development. *Int. Soc. Sci. J.*, 1969, *21*(1), pp. 68–82. **[G: Yugoslavia]**

Racz, Barnabas A. Hungary's New Economic Mechanism. *Mich. Academician*, Winter 1969, *1*(1–2), pp. 175–81. **[G: Hungary]**

Shaffer, Harry G. Problems and Prospects of Czechoslovakia's New Economic Model (Including an Interview with Professor Ota Sik). **In** *Prybyla, J. S., ed.*, 1969, pp. 323–39. **[G: Czechoslovakia]**

Wise, John and Yotopoulos, Pan A. The Empirical Content of Economic Rationality: A Test for a Less Developed Economy. *J. Polit. Econ.*, November/December 1969, *77*(6), pp. 976–1004. **[G: Greece]**

1214 Asian Countries

Abraham, W. I. and Gill, M. S. The Growth and Composition of Malaysia's Capital Stock. *Malayan Econ. Rev.*, October 1969, *14*(2), pp. 44–54. **[G: Malaysia]**

Ahmad, Zubeida M. and Sternberg, Marvin J. Agrarian Reform and Employment, with Special Reference to Asia. *Int. Lab. Rev.*, February 1969, *99*(2), pp. 159–83. **[G: Asia]**

Ali, Aamir. Fifty Years of the ILO and Asia. *Int. Lab. Rev.*, March 1969, *99*(3), pp. 347–61.

Ali, Mansoor. Inflation and Economic Development. **In** *Bhuleshkar, A. V., ed.*, 1969, pp. 318–26. **[G: India]**

Ann, Lee Soo. Financial Planning of Investment in Malaysia. *Malayan Econ. Rev.*, April 1969, *14*(1), pp. 48–64. **[G: Malaysia]**

Anstey, Vera. A Fresh Approach to Agricultural Reconstruction in Indian Development. **In** *Bhuleshkar, A. V., ed.*, 1969, pp. 47–59. **[G: India]**

Baali, Fuad. Agrarian Reform in Iraq: Some Socioeconomic Aspects. *Amer. J. Econ. Soc.*, January 1969, *28*(1), pp. 61–76. **[G: Iraq]**

Beyer, John C. Regional Inequalities and Economic Growth in Malaysia. *Yorkshire Bull. Econ. Soc. Res.*, May 1969, *21*(1), pp. 17–30. **[G: Malaysia]**

Bhagwati, Jagdish N. and Chakravarty, Sukhamoy. Contributions to Indian Economic Analysis: A Survey. *Amer. Econ. Rev.*, Part II, September 1969, *59*(4), pp. 2–73. **[G: India]**

Bhatt, V. V. On the Magnitude and Allocation of Federal Assistance to the States in India: Some Rational Criteria. *Public Finance*, 1969, *24*(4), pp. 563–76. **[G: India]**

Bose, Swadesh R. and Clark, Edwin H., II. Some Basic Considerations on Agricultural Mechanization in West Pakistan. *Pakistan Develop. Rev.*, Autumn 1969, *9*(3), pp. 273–308. **[G: W. Pakistan]**

Burki, Shahid Javed. West Pakistan's Rural Works Program: A Study in Political and Administrative Response. *Middle East J.*, Summer 1969, *23*(3), pp. 321–42. **[G: W. Pakistan]**

Castro, Amado A. The Philippines and the Industrial Nations. *Philippine Econ. J.*, First Semester 1969, *8*(1), pp. 1–12. **[G: Philippines]**

Chandavarkar, Anand G. Indian Monetary Policy and Economic Development. **In** *Bhuleshkar, A. V., ed.*, 1969, pp. 305–17. **[G: India]**

Chapin, Emerson. Success Story in South Korea. *Foreign Aff.*, April 1969, *47*(3), pp. 560–74. **[G: S. Korea]**

Chauduri, A. Oligopoly and Economic Growth in India. **In** *Economic Concentration, Pt. 7A, SCH*, 1969, pp. 4242–51. **[G: India]**

Choldin, Harvey M. The Development Project as Natural Experiment: The Comilla, Pakistan, Projects. *Econ. Develop. Cult. Change*, July 1969, *17* (4), pp. 483–500. **[G: E. Pakistan]**

Chowdhury, A. H. M. Nuruddin. Some Reflections on Income Redistributive Intermediation in Pakistan. *Pakistan Develop. Rev.*, Summer 1969, *9* (2), pp. 95–110. **[G: Pakistan]**

Currie, Lauchlin. Myrdal on South Asia. *J. Econ. Issues*, June 1969, *3*(2), pp. 166–76.

Davies, Gethyn. United Kingdom Investment. **In** *Hughes, H. and Seng, Y. P., eds.*, 1969, pp. 46–61. **[G: Singapore]**

Dernberger, Robert F. Review Article: Another Piece of the Jigsaw Puzzle Called Communist China. *Econ. Develop. Cult. Change*, January 1969, *17*(2), pp. 262–66. **[G: China]**

Desai, Padma. Growth and Structural Change in the Indian Manufacturing Sector: 1951–1963. *Indian Econ. J.*, October–December 1969, *17*(2), pp. 205–33. **[G: India]**

DeVoretz, Don. Alternative Planning Models for Philippine Educational Investment. *Philippine Econ. J.*, Second Semester 1969, *8*(2), pp. 99–116. **[G: Philippines]**

Divatia, V. V. and Bhatt, V. V. On Measuring the Pace of Development. *Banca Naz. Lavoro Quart. Rev.*, June 1969, (89), pp. 190–206. **[G: India]**

Eapen, A. T. A Critique of Indian Fiscal Federalism. *Public Finance*, 1969, *24*(4), pp. 537–62. **[G: India]**

Ernst, Wolfgang. The Foreign Trade Policy of the Mao Tse-Tung Clique. *Chinese Econ. Stud.*, Fall 1969, *3*(1), pp. 33–47. **[G: China]**

Eysenbach, M. L. A Note on Growth and Structural Change in Pakistan's Manufacturing Industry 1954–1964. *Pakistan Develop. Rev.*, Spring 1969, *9*(1), pp. 58–65. **[G: Pakistan]**

Fabella, A. V. Policies for Long-Term Growth in the Philippines: The Public Sector. *Philippine Econ. J.*, First Semester 1969, *8*(1), pp. 37–48. **[G: Philippines]**

Fernea, Robert A. Land Reform and Ecology in Post-revolutionary Iraq. *Econ. Develop. Cult. Change*, April 1969, *17*(3), pp. 356–81. **[G: Iraq]**

Gupta, T. R. An Application of Inter-Industry Analysis to Demand Structure of the Indian Economy. *Asian Econ. Rev.*, May 1969, *11*(3), pp. 260–72. **[G: India]**

Halevi, Nadav. Economic Policy Discussion and Research in Israel. *Amer. Econ. Rev.*, Part II, September 1969, *59*(4), pp. 74–118. **[G: Israel]**

Hazari, R. K. The Implications of the Managing Agency System in Indian Development. **In** *Bhuleshkar, A. V., ed.*, 1969, pp. 193–213. **[G: India]**

Hiniker, Paul J. and Farace, R. Vincent. Approaches to National Development in China: 1949–1958. *Econ. Develop. Cult. Change*, Part I, October 1969, *18*(1), pp. 51–72. **[G: China]**

Hirono, Ryokichi. Japanese Investment. **In** *Hughes, H. and Seng, Y. P., eds.*, 1969, pp. 86–111. **[G: Singapore]**

Horvath, Janos. A Note on Economic Trends in Indonesia. *Polit. Sci. Quart.*, December 1969, *84*(4), pp. 638–42. **[G: Indonesia]**

Hsueh, S. S. Local Government and National Development in South-East Asia. *Int. Soc. Sci. J.*, 1969, *21*(1), pp. 45–55. **[G: S. E. Asia]**

Hughes, Helen. Australian Investment. **In** *Hughes, H. and Seng, Y. P., eds.*, 1969, pp. 62–85. **[G: Singapore]**

Hughes, Helen. Foreign Investment and Industrialization in Singapore: Conclusions. **In** *Hughes, H. and Seng, Y. P., eds.*, 1969, pp. 177–219. **[G: Singapore]**

Hughes, Helen. From Entrepôt Trade to Manufacturing. **In** *Hughes, H. and Seng, Y. P., eds.*, 1969, pp. 1–45. **[G: Singapore]**

Iloniemi, Jaakko. Miksi kehitysmaat eivät kehity: kasvun teoria ja todellisuus: Reunamerkintöjä Pentti Pajusen mietteisiin Myrdalin "Aasian Draaman" johdosta. (With English summary.) *Kansant. Aikak.*, 1969, *65*(1), pp. 57–62.

Islam, Nurul. Tariff Protection, Comparative Costs, and Industrialization in Pakistan. **In** *Morgan, T. and Spoelstra, N., eds.*, 1969, pp. 65–95. **[G: Pakistan]**

Johnston, Bruce F. and Cownie, John. The Seed-Fertilizer Revolution and Labor Force Absorption. *Amer. Econ. Rev.*, Part I, September 1969, *59*(4), pp. 569–82. **[G: W. Pakistan]**

Kaneda, Hiromitsu. Economic Implications of the "Green Revolution" and the Strategy of Agricultural Development in West Pakistan. *Pakistan Develop. Rev.*, Summer 1969, *9*(2), pp. 111–43. **[G: W. Pakistan]**

Kanesa-Thasan, S. Stabilizing an Economy—A Study of the Republic of Korea. *Int. Monet. Fund Staff Pap.*, March 1969, *16*(1), pp. 1–26. **[G: S. Korea]**

Khan, Mahmood Hasan. Development Alternatives and Problems in Dual Economies. *Econ. Int.*, November 1969, *22*(4), pp. 636–61. **[G: India; Pakistan]**

Khan, Mohammad Irshad. Aggregative Analysis of Food Consumption in Pakistan. *Pakistan Develop. Rev.*, Winter 1969, *9*(4), pp. 426–41. **[G: Pakistan]**

Kim, Hyung K. The Role of Foreign Aid in Assisting the Stabilization of the Korean Economy. *Univ. Wash. Bus. Rev.*, Winter 1969, *28*(2), pp. 62–67. **[G: Korea]**

Kim, Joungwon Alexander. The "Peak of Socialism" in North Korea: The Five and Seven Year Plans. **In** *Prybyla, J. S., ed.*, 1969, pp. 412–27. **[G: N. Korea]**

Krishnaswamy, K. S. Some Thoughts on a Drama.

Finance Develop., March 1969, *6*(1), pp. 43–50.

Kumar, Pushpendra. Domestic Terms of Trade and Inter-Sectoral Income Flows in India: 1952–53 to 1966–67. *Asian Econ. Rev.*, August 1969, *11*(4), pp. 349–62. **[G: India]**

Kushwaha, D. S. The Role of Industrial Policy in Economic Development. **In** *Bhuleshkar, A. V., ed.*, 1969, pp. 214–27. **[G: India]**

Legarda, Benito J. The Philippines and the Industrial Nations: Discussion. *Philippine Econ. J.*, First Semester 1969, *8*(1), pp. 13–15. **[G: Philippines]**

Leonard, Patrick L. A Note on the Demand for Fertilizer in West Pakistan. *Pakistan Develop. Rev.*, Winter 1969, *9*(4), pp. 419–25. **[G: W. Pakistan]**

Lewis, Stephen R., Jr. A Note on the Consistency of Pakistan's Cotton-Cloth Statistics for Recent Years. *Pakistan Develop. Rev.*, Winter 1969, *9*(4), pp. 442–46. **[G: Pakistan]**

Lilienthal, David E. Postwar Development in Viet Nam. *Foreign Aff.*, January 1969, *47*(2), pp. 321–33. **[G: Viet Nam]**

Lindert, Peter H. United States Investment. **In** *Hughes, H. and Seng, Y. P., eds.*, 1969, pp. 154–76. **[G: Singapore]**

Little, I. M. D. Public Sector Project Selection in Relation to Indian Development. **In** *Bhuleshkar, A. V., ed.*, 1969, pp. 228–58. **[G: India]**

Luey, Paul. Hong Kong Investment. **In** *Hughes, H. and Seng, Y. P., eds.*, 1969, pp. 112–39. **[G: Singapore]**

Luey, Paul and Sei, Ung Gim. Taiwan Investment. **In** *Hughes, H. and Seng, Y. P., eds.*, 1969, pp. 140–53. **[G: Singapore]**

Maehnel, Klaus. The Economic Policy of the Mao Tse-Tung Clique. *Chinese Econ. Stud.*, Fall 1969, *3*(1), pp. 48–69. **[G: China]**

Malenbaum, Wilfred. Indian Economic Growth: Comparison with China (1965). **In** *Bhuleshkar, A. V., ed.*, 1969, pp. 271–87. **[G: India; China]**

Malenbaum, Wilfred. Two Decades of India's Growth: Whither Now? **In** *Dagli, V., ed., Vol. III*, 1969, pp. 41–46. **[G: India]**

McHale, Thomas R. Policies for the Private Sector: Discussion. *Philippine Econ. J.*, First Semester 1969, *8*(1), pp. 31–32. **[G: Philippines]**

Mehta, B. V. Size and Capital Intensity in Indian Industry. *Bull. Oxford Univ. Inst. Econ. Statist.*, August 1969, *31*(3), pp. 189–204. **[G: India]**

Miller, William Green. Political Organization in Iran: From Dowreh to Political Party. *Middle East J.*, Spring 1969, *23*(2), pp. 159–67. **[G: Iran]**

Minocha, A. C. Inter-Sectoral Financial Flows in Indian Economy—Some Implications for Policy. *Econ. Aff.*, January-February 1969, *14*(1–2), pp. 33–38, 103–04. **[G: India]**

Mishra, S. N. A Model of Gandhian Economy. *Indian Econ. J.*, July–September 1969, *17*(1), pp. 101–11. **[G: India]**

Mukherjee, Chittapriya. Some Problems of the Indian Agricultural Sector. *Land Econ.*, February 1969, *45*(1), pp. 74–86. **[G: India]**

Nair, K. R. Some Responses of Rice Farmers to the Package Program in Tanjore District, India: Comment. *Amer. J. Agr. Econ.*, August 1969, *51*(3), pp. 699–701. **[G: India]**

Nair, Kusum. Asian Drama—A Critique. *Econ. Develop. Cult. Change*, July 1969, *17*(4), pp. 449–59.

Newell, Richard S. Afghanistan: The Dangers of Cold War Generosity. *Middle East J.*, Spring 1969, *23*(2), pp. 168–76. **[G: Afghanistan]**

Nouri, Clement J. Iraq Revisited. *Marquette Bus. Rev.*, Spring 1969, *13*(1), pp. 22–33. **[G: Iraq]**

Perera, S. E. G. Some Labour Problems of the National Textile Corporation of Ceylon. *Int. Lab. Rev.*, February 1969, *99*(2), pp. 185–207. **[G: Ceylon]**

Pillai, P. Purushothaman. An Inter-District, Inter-Crop Comparison of Growth Rates in Agriculture in Kerala. *Asian Econ. Rev.*, May 1969, *11*(3), pp. 249–59. **[G: India]**

Pirnia, Hossein. Scientific Thought and National Independence. *Tahq. Eq.*, November 1969, *6* (15&16), pp. 3–20. **[G: Iran]**

Prakash, Prem. Relationship Between Size and Productivity in Selected Indian Industries. *Asian Econ. Rev.*, May 1969, *11*(3), pp. 237–48. **[G: India]**

Prybyla, Jan S. Communist China's Economic System, 1961-66. **In** *Prybyla, J. S., ed.*, 1969, pp. 368–83. **[G: China]**

Prybyla, Jan S. The Economic Cost of the Cultural Revolution. **In** *Prybyla, J. S., ed.*, 1969, pp. 393–411. **[G: China]**

Rabbani, A. K. M. Ghulam. A Proposal for Fiscal Incentives for the Raw-Jute Exports. *Pakistan Develop. Rev.*, Winter 1969, *9*(4), pp. 400–418. **[G: Pakistan]**

Redding, A. David. Policies for the Private Sector: Discussion. *Philippine Econ. J.*, First Semester 1969, *8*(1), pp. 33–36. **[G: Philippines]**

Redding, A. David. The Philippine Economy: A Newcomer's Perspective. *Philippine Econ. J.*, Second Semester 1969, *8*(2), pp. 130–44. **[G: Philippines]**

Robinson, Warren C. "Disguised" Unemployment Once Again: East Pakistan, 1951-1961. *Amer. J. Agr. Econ.*, August 1969, *51*(3), pp. 592–604. **[G: E. Pakistan]**

Roos, Leslie L., Jr. Development *versus* Distribution: An Attitudinal Study of Turkish Local Administration. *Econ. Develop. Cult. Change*, July 1969, *17*(4), pp. 552–66. **[G: Turkey]**

Roxas, Sixto K. Policies for the Private Sector. *Philippine Econ. J.*, First Semester 1969, *8*(1), pp. 16–30. **[G: Philippines]**

Saini, Krishan G. The Growth of the Indian Economy: 1860–1960. *Rev. Income Wealth*, September 1969, *15*(3), pp. 247–63. **[G: India]**

Sandesara, J. C. Size and Capital-Intensity in Indian Industry: Some Comments. *Bull. Oxford Univ. Inst. Econ. Statist.*, November 1969, *31*(4), pp. 331–34. **[G: India]**

Sansom, Robert L. The Motor Pump: A Case Study of Innovation and Development. *Oxford Econ. Pap.*, March 1969, *21*(1), pp. 109–21. **[G: S. Vietnam]**

Sarma, L. V. L. N. and Rao, R. S. Hanumanta. Estimates of the Cost of Capital to the Indian Engineering Industry, 1962–65. *Yorkshire Bull. Econ. Soc. Res.*, November 1969, *21*(2), pp. 132–40. **[G: India]**

Schiller, Otto. An Appraisal of Co-operative Farming

and Its Significance in Indian Development. In *Bhuleshkar, A. V., ed.*, 1969, pp. 40–46. **[G: India]**

Schloss, Henry H. Two Views on Myrdal (II). *Indian Econ. J.*, July–September 1969, *17*(1), pp. 158–60.

Sharma, L. R. Need for a Growth-Oriented Industrial Policy. *Asian Econ. Rev.*, August 1969, *11*(4), pp. 333–48. **[G: India]**

Sherk, Donald R. The New International Trade Models and Their Relevance for Developing Asia. *Malayan Econ. Rev.*, October 1969, *14*(2), pp. 1–17. **[G: Asia]**

Snyder, Wayne W. Turkish Economic Development: The First Five Year Plan, 1963–67. *J. Devel. Stud.*, October 1969, *6*(1), pp. 58–71. **[G: Turkey]**

Srivastava, U. K. P. L. 480 Counterpart Funds and Inflation: Myth and Realty. *Asian Econ. Rev.*, February 1969, *11*(2), pp. 145–59. **[G: India]**

Stern, Joseph J. A Note on the Structure of Pakistan's Foreign Trade. *Pakistan Develop. Rev.*, Summer 1969, *9*(2), pp. 212–23. **[G: Pakistan]**

Sun, I-Shuan. Trade Policies and Economic Development in Taiwan. In *Morgan, T. and Spoelstra, N., eds.*, 1969, pp. 99–123. **[G: Taiwan]**

Trescott, Paul B. The Growth of Inputs and Output in Thailand, 1946–65. *Philippine Econ. J.*, First Semester 1969, *8*(1), pp. 75–84. **[G: Thailand]**

Turner, Robert C. Macro Forecasting in the Philippines: An Experiment. *Philippine Econ. J.*, Second Semester 1969, *8*(2), pp. 185–201. **[G: Philippines]**

Usher, Dan. Income as a Measure of Productivity: A Reply. *Economica, N.S.*, August 1969, *36*(143), pp. 317–20. **[G: Thailand]**

Vasudevan, A. Deficit Financing and Economic Development. In *Bhuleshkar, A. V., ed.*, 1969, pp. 327–44. **[G: India]**

Vladimirov, Iu. V. The Question of Soviet-Chinese Economic Relations in 1950–1966. *Chinese Econ. Stud.*, Fall 1969, *3*(1), pp. 3–32. **[G: China; U.S.S.R.]**

Ward, Richard J. Two Views on Myrdal (I). *Indian Econ. J.*, July–September 1969, *17*(1), pp. 143–57.

Ya-nan, Wang. The Marxist Population Theory and China's Population Problem. *Chinese Econ. Stud.*, Spring-Summer 1969, *2*(3–4), pp. 3–91. **[G: China]**

Yossundara, Suparb and Huntrakoon, Yune. Some Salient Aspects of Thailand's Trade, 1955–64. In *Morgan, T. and Spoelstra, N., eds.*, 1969, pp. 127–50. **[G: Thailand]**

1215 African Countries

Aboyade, O. The Economy of Nigeria. In *Robson, P. and Lury, D. A., eds.*, 1969, pp. 127–93. **[G: Nigeria]**

Abshire, David M. Minerals, Manufacturing, Power and Communications. In *Abshire, D. M. and Samuels, M. A., eds.*, 1969, pp. 294–319. **[G: Mozambique; Angola; Portuguese Guinea]**

Amin, Samir. Levels of Remuneration, Factor Proportions and Income Differentials with Special Reference to Developing Countries. In *Smith, A. D., ed.*, 1969, pp. 269–93.

Bocock, Peter W. Impact of Development: Telecommunications in Ethiopia. *Finance Develop.*, December 1969, *6*(4), pp. 15–21. **[G: Ethiopia]**

Brandenburg, Frank. Development, Finance, and Trade. In *Abshire, D. M. and Samuels, M. A., eds.*, 1969, pp. 219–52. **[G: Mozambique; Angola; Portuguese Guinea]**

Brandenburg, Frank. Transport Systems and Their External Ramifications. In *Abshire, D. M. and Samuels, M. A., eds.*, 1969, pp. 320–44. **[G: Mozambique; Angola; Portuguese Guinea]**

Dalton, George and Walters, A. A. The Economy of Liberia. In *Robson, P. and Lury, D. A., eds.*, 1969, pp. 287–315. **[G: Liberia]**

van Dongen, Irene S. Agriculture and Other Primary Production. In *Abshire, D. M. and Samuels, M. A., eds.*, 1969, pp. 253–93. **[G: Mozambique; Angola; Portuguese Guinea]**

Due, Jean M. What Has Happened to the Ghanaian State Farms? *Ill. Agr. Econ.*, July 1969, *9*(2), pp. 25–35. **[G: Ghana]**

Due, John F. The Uganda Sales Tax on Importation and Manufacture. *East Afr. Econ. Rev.*, June 1969, *1*(1), pp. 1–16. **[G: Uganda]**

El-Agraa, Ali M. The Sudan and the Arab Customs Union: A Conflict. *East Afr. Econ. Rev.*, December 1969, *1*(2), pp. 39–51. **[G: Sudan; Arab Customs Union]**

Engberg, Holger L. and Hance, William A. Growth and Dispersion of Branch Banking in Tropical Africa, 1950–1964. *Econ. Geogr.*, July 1969, *45*(3), pp. 195–208. **[G: Africa]**

Foster, Phillips and Yost, Larry. A Simulation Study of Population, Education, and Income Growth in Uganda. *Amer. J. Agr. Econ.*, August 1969, *51*(3), pp. 576–91. **[G: Uganda]**

Gerakis, Andreas S. Some Aspects of the U.A.R.'s First Five-Year Plan. *Finance Develop.*, March 1969, *6*(1), pp. 9–15. **[G: U.A.R.; Egypt]**

Godfrey, E. M. Labor-Surplus Models and Labor-Deficit Economies: The West African Case. *Econ. Develop. Cult. Change*, April 1969, *17*(3), pp. 382–91. **[G: W. Africa]**

Green, R. H. The Economy of Cameroon Federal Republic. In *Robson, P. and Lury, D. A., eds.*, 1969, pp. 236–86. **[G: Cameroon]**

Hansen, Bent. Employment and Wages in Rural Egypt. *Amer. Econ. Rev.*, June 1969, *59*(3), pp. 298–313. **[G: Egypt]**

Harris, John R. and Todaro, Michael P. Wages, Industrial Employment and Labour Productivity: The Kenyan Experience. *East Afr. Econ. Rev.*, June 1969, *1*(1), pp. 29–46. **[G: Kenya]**

Hazlewood, Arthur. An Approach to the Analysis of the Spatial Distribution of the Market in East Africa. *Bull. Oxford Univ. Inst. Econ. Statist.*, November 1969, *31*(4), pp. 243–61. **[G: E. Africa]**

Hollister, Robinson G. Manpower Problems and Policies in Sub-Saharan Africa. *Int. Lab. Rev.*, May 1969, *99*(5), pp. 515–32. **[G: Africa]**

Killick, A. and Szerszewski, Robert. The Economy of Ghana. In *Robson, P. and Lury, D. A., eds.*, 1969, pp. 79–126. **[G: Ghana]**

Mallakh, Ragaei El. La programmazione in un'economia con eccesso di capitali: il caso della Libia. (Planning in the Capital Surplus Economy: The

Case of Libya. With English summary.) *Rivista Int. Sci. Econ. Com.*, February 1969, *16*(2), pp. 148–65. **[G: Libya]**

Mallakh, Ragaei El. The Economics of Rapid Growth: Libya. *Middle East J.*, Summer 1969, *23* (3), pp. 308–20. **[G: Libya]**

Massell, Benton F. and Parnes, Andrew. Estimation of Expenditure Elasticities from a Sample of Rural Households in Uganda. *Bull. Oxford Univ. Inst. Econ. Statist.*, November 1969, *31*(4), pp. 313–29. **[G: Uganda]**

Miracle, Michael. The Economy of the Ivory Coast. **In** *Robson, P. and Lury, D. A., eds.*, 1969, pp. 194–235. **[G: Ivory Coast]**

Mueller, P. and Zevering, K. H. Employment Promotion through Rural Development: A Pilot Project in Western Nigeria. *Int. Lab. Rev.*, August 1969, *100*(2), pp. 111–30. **[G: Nigeria]**

Norbye, O. The Economy of Algeria. **In** *Robson, P. and Lury, D. A., eds.*, 1969, pp. 471–521. **[G: Algeria]**

Osman, Omar and Suleiman, A. A. The Economy of Sudan. **In** *Robson, P. and Lury, D. A., eds.*, 1969, pp. 436–70. **[G: Sudan]**

Rimmer, Douglas. The Abstraction from Politics: A Critique of Economic Theory and Design with Reference to West Africa. *J. Devel. Stud.*, April 1969, *5*(3), pp. 190–204. **[G: W. Africa]**

Robson, P. and Lury, D. A. Introduction: The Economies of Africa. **In** *Robson, P. and Lury, D. A., eds.*, 1969, pp. 23–78. **[G: Africa]**

Roe, Alan R. Terms of Trade and Transfer Effects in the East African Common Market: An Empirical Study. *Bull. Oxford Univ. Inst. Econ. Statist.*, August 1969, *31*(3), pp. 153–67. **[G: E. Africa]**

Scheepers, C. F. The Effect of Import Substitution on the Volume and Structure of South Africa's Imports, 1926/27–1963/64. *Finance Trade Rev.*, December 1969, *8*(4), pp. 258–71. **[G: S. Africa]**

Singer, H. W. and Doss, A. C. Technical Assistance to Kenya: Some Thoughts on Flows and Programming. *East Afr. Econ. Rev.*, June 1969, *1*(1), pp. 17–27. **[G: Kenya]**

Szerszewski, Robert. Some Features of the Economic Development of Tropical Africa. *J. Devel. Stud.*, July 1969, *5*(4), pp. 239–44.

Taylor, W. L. The Economy of Central Africa: Rhodesia, Malawi and Zambia. **In** *Robson, P. and Lury, D. A., eds.*, 1969, pp. 384–435. **[G: Rhodesia; Malawi; Zambia]**

Van Arkadie, B. and Ghai, D. The East African Economies: Kenya, Uganda and Tanzania. **In** *Robson, P. and Lury, D. A., eds.*, 1969, pp. 316–83. **[G: Kenya; Uganda; Tanzania]**

Wedderspoon, William M. Simplifying Taxes in East Africa. *Finance Develop.*, March 1969, *6*(1), pp. 51–56.

Young, A. Patterns of Development in Zambian Manufacturing Industry since Independence. *East Afr. Econ. Rev.*, December 1969, *1*(2), pp. 29–38. **[G: Zambia]**

1216 Latin American and Caribbean Countries

Adams, Dale W. Rural Migration and Agricultural Development in Colombia. *Econ. Develop. Cult. Change*, July 1969, *17*(4), pp. 527–39. **[G: Colombia]**

Andic, Fuat M. The Development Impact of the EEC on the French and Dutch Caribbean. *J. Common Market Stud.*, September 1969, *8*(1), pp. 19–49. **[G: Dutch Caribbean; French Caribbean; E.E.C.]**

Baer, Werner. Steel and the Brazilian Economy. **In** *Ellis, H. S., ed.*, 1969, pp. 74–102. **[G: Brazil]**

Baldovinos de la Peña, Gabriel. La agricultura al final de la década. (The State of Agriculture at the End of the Present Decade. With English summary.) *Econ. Polít.*, Fourth Semester 1969, *6*(4), pp. 453–60. **[G: Mexico]**

Basora, Adrian A. Cuba: Castroist Command. **In** *Prybyla, J. S., ed.*, 1969, pp. 428–41. **[G: Cuba]**

Beker, Víctor Alberto. Elasticidades de oferta de la producción agropecuaria: trigo, maíz y carne vacuna. (Elasticities of Supply in Agricultural Production: Wheat, Maize and Beef. With English summary.) *Económica*, May–August 1969, *15*(2), pp. 145–81. **[G: Argentina]**

Bergsman, Joel and Morley, Samuel A. Import Constraints and Development: Causes of the Recent Decline of Brazilian Economic Growth: A Comment. *Rev. Econ. Statist.*, February 1969, *51*(1), pp. 101–02. **[G: Brazil]**

Bergsman, Joel and Candal, Arthur. Industrialization: Past Success and Future Problems. **In** *Ellis, H. S., ed.*, 1969, pp. 29–73. **[G: Brazil]**

Boon, Gerard K. Factor Intensities in Mexico with Special Reference to Manufacturing. **In** *[Tinbergen, J.]*, 1969, pp. 201–18. **[G: Mexico]**

Brannon, Russell H. Low Investment Levels in Uruguayan Agriculture: Some Tentative Explanations. *Land Econ.*, August 1969, *45*(3), pp. 304–12. **[G: Uruguay]**

Brewster, Havelock. The Pattern of Change in Wages, Prices and Productivity in British Guiana, 1948 to 1962. *Soc. Econ. Stud.*, June 1969, *18*(2), pp. 107–36. **[G: British Guiana]**

Bruck, Nicholas K. Higher Education and Economic Development in Central America. *Rev. Soc. Econ.*, September 1969, *27*(2), pp. 160–80. **[G: Central America]**

Bryce, Herrington J. Regional Labor Earnings Differentials in a Small Developing Country: The Republic of Panama. *J. Reg. Sci.*, December 1969, *9*(3), pp. 405–15. **[G: Panama]**

Caballero Tamayo, Xavier. The ILO and Development in the Americas. *Int. Lab. Rev.*, December 1969, *100*(6), pp. 505–50. **[G: Latin America]**

Chacel, Julian. The Principal Characteristics of the Agrarian Structure and Agricultural Production in Brazil. **In** *Ellis, H. S., ed.*, 1969, pp. 103–29. **[G: Brazil]**

Clague, Christopher K. Capital-Labor Substitution in Manufacturing in Undeveloped Countries. *Econometrica*, July 1969, *37*(3), pp. 528–37. **[G: Peru]**

Edel, Matthew D. The Colombian Community Action Program: Costs and Benefits. *Yale Econ. Essays*, Fall 1969, *9*(2), pp. 3–55. **[G: Colombia]**

Felix, David. Economic Development: Take-Offs into Unsustained Growth. *Soc. Res.*, Summer 1969, *36*(2), pp. 267–93. **[G: Latin America]**

Frank, Andre Gunder. Capitalist Underdevelopment or Socialist Revolution. **In** *Frank, A. G.,* 1969, pp. 371–409. **[G: Latin America]**

Frank, Andre Gunder. Destroy Capitalism, Not Feudalism. **In** *Frank, A. G.,* 1969, pp. 350–61. **[G: Latin America]**

Frank, Andre Gunder. Mexico: The Janus Faces of Twentieth-Century Bourgeois Revolution. **In** *Frank, A. G.,* 1969, pp. 298–317. **[G: Mexico]**

Frank, Andre Gunder. Rural Economic Structure and Peasant Political Power. **In** *Frank, A. G.,* 1969, pp. 248–68. **[G: Latin America]**

Freebairn, Donald K. The Dichotomy of Prosperity and Poverty in Mexican Agriculture. *Land Econ.,* February 1969, *45*(1), pp. 31–42. **[G: Mexico]**

Frisch, Uwe G. and Malagón, Oscar M. La concentracion territorial de la industria en Mexico. (Territorial Concentration of Industry in Mexico. With English summary.) *Econ. Polít.,* Second Semester 1969, *6*(2), pp. 195–208. **[G: Mexico]**

Fulton, David C. A Road to the West. *Finance Develop.,* September 1969, *6*(3), pp. 2–7. **[G: Honduras]**

Glade, William P. The Employment Question and Development Policies in Latin America. *J. Econ. Issues,* September 1969, *3*(3), pp. 43–62. **[G: Latin America]**

Gordon, Jerome B. Labor Mobility and Economic Growth: The Central American Experience—Costa Rica and El Salvador. *Econ. Develop. Cult. Change,* April 1969, *17*(3), pp. 319–37. **[G: Costa Rica; El Salvador]**

Gordon, Wendell. Capitalism and Technological Adaptation in Latin America. *J. Econ. Issues,* March 1969, *3*(1), pp. 66–86. **[G: Latin America]**

Grunwald, Joseph. Statement. **In** *New Directions for the 1970's: Toward a Strategy of Inter-American Development, Pts. 1–5, HCH,* 1969, pp. 294–97. **[G: Latin America]**

Gudin, Eugenio. The Chief Characteristics of the Postwar Economic Development of Brazil. **In** *Ellis, H. S., ed.,* 1969, pp. 3–25. **[G: Brazil]**

Hicks, W. Whitney. Primary Exports and Economic Development: An Application of the Staple Theory to Sonora, Mexico. *Can. J. Agr. Econ.,* July 1969, *17*(2), pp. 46–62. **[G: Mexico]**

Huddle, Donald. Postwar Brazilian Industrialization: Growth Patterns, Inflation, and Sources of Stagnation. **In** *Baklanoff, E. N., ed.,* 1969, pp. 86–108. **[G: Brazil]**

Humphrey, David B. Changes in Protection and Inflation in Argentina, 1953–1966. *Oxford Econ. Pap.,* July 1969, *21*(2), pp. 196–219. **[G: Argentina]**

Keesing, Donald B. Structural Change Early in Development: Mexico's Changing Industrial and Occupational Structure from 1895 to 1950. *J. Econ. Hist.,* December 1969, *29*(4), pp. 716–38. **[G: Mexico]**

Leff, Nathaniel H. Import Constraints and Development: A Reply. *Rev. Econ. Statist.,* February 1969, *51*(1), pp. 102–04. **[G: Brazil]**

Leff, Nathaniel H. Long-Term Brazilian Economic Development. *J. Econ. Hist.,* September 1969, *29* (3), pp. 473–93. **[G: Brazil]**

Llosas, Hernán P. La política de promoción industrial y de desarrollo regional en la Argentina, 1959–1966. (The Argentinian Government's Policy for the Promotion of Particular Industrial Sectors and for the Development of Some of the Country's Regions, 1959–1966. With English summary.) *Económica,* January–April 1969, *15*(1), pp. 39–91. **[G: Argentina]**

Lodge, George C. U.S. Aid to Latin America: Funding Radical Change. *Foreign Aff.,* July 1969, *47* (4), pp. 735–49. **[G: U.S.; Latin America]**

Mamalakis, Markos. An Analysis of the Financial and Investment Activities of the Chilean Development Corporation: 1939–1964. *J. Devel. Stud.,* January 1969, *5*(2), pp. 118–37. **[G: Chile]**

Marwah, Kanta. An Econometric Model of Colombia: A Prototype Devaluation View. *Econometrica,* April 1969, *37*(2), pp. 228–51. **[G: Colombia]**

Massell, Benton F. and Yotopoulos, Pan A. The Relationships between the Volume of Investment, Its Productivity and the Growth of the South American Countries. *Kyklos,* 1969, *22*(2), pp. 328–33. **[G: S. America]**

Michalopoulos, Constantine. Productivity Growth in Latin America: Comment. *Amer. Econ. Rev.,* June 1969, *59*(3), pp. 435–39. **[G: U.S.; Brazil; Chile; Colombia; Argentina]**

Montuschi, Luisa. Progreso technológico y rendimientos crecientes en el sector manufacturero argentino: La productividad de las inversiones en la década del 50. (Technical Progress and Increasing Returns in the Manfacturing Sector of Argentina. With English summary.) *Económica,* January–April 1969, *15*(1), pp. 93–110. **[G: Argentina]**

Munk, Bernard. The Welfare Costs of Content Protection: The Automotive Industry in Latin America. *J. Polit. Econ.,* January/February 1969, *77*(1), pp. 85–98. **[G: Latin America]**

Nicholls, William H. The Transformation of Agriculture in a Presently Semi-Industrialized Country: The Case of Brazil. **In** *Thorbecke, E., ed.,* 1969, pp. 311–78. **[G: Brazil]**

Pinto, Aníbal. Economic Structure, Productivity and Wages in Latin America. **In** *Smith, A. D., ed.,* 1969, pp. 256–68. **[G: Latin America]**

Restrepo Fernández, Iván and Sánchez Cortés, José. El arrendamiento de tierras ejidales: El caso de Apatzingán. (The Leasing of Common Lands: The Case of Apatzingán. With English summary.) *Econ. Polít.,* Third Semester 1969, *6*(3), pp. 331–46. **[G: Mexico]**

Reyes, Osorio Sergio. La pobreza rural. (Rural Poverty. With English summary.) *Econ. Polít.,* Second Semester 1969, *6*(2), pp. 209–14. **[G: Mexico]**

Reynolds, Clark W. Relationships between Agriculture, Nonagriculture, and Foreign Trade in the Development of Argentina and Peru: Comment. **In** *Thorbecke, E., ed.,* 1969, pp. 213–17. **[G: Argentina; Peru]**

Roldan, Alfredo. The Latin American Economic Integration: Its Benefits and Obstacles. *Nebr. J. Econ. Bus.,* Winter 1968–69, *8*(1), pp. 16–33. **[G: Latin America]**

Rostro Plasencia, Francisco. Perspectivas de continuidad del desarrollo economico de Mexico. (Prospects of Economic Development in Mexico. With English summary.) *Econ. Polít.*, Second Semester 1969, *6*(2), pp. 241–50. **[G: Mexico]**

Santomé Figueroa, César. La viabilidad economica del puerto de Topolobampo. (Economic Viability of the Topolobampo Port. With English summary.) *Econ. Polít.*, Fourth Semester 1969, *6*(4), pp. 485–94. **[G: Mexico]**

Schuh, G. Edward. The Transformation of Agriculture in a Presently Semi-Industrialized Country: The Case of Brazil: Comment. **In** *Thorbecke, E., ed.*, 1969, pp. 379–85. **[G: Brazil]**

Schultz, T. Paul. Demographic Conditions of Economic Development in Latin America. **In** *Nisbet, C. T., ed.*, 1969, pp. 41–72. **[G: Latin America]**

Seers, Dudley. A Step Towards a Political Economy of Development (Illustrated by the Case of Trinidad/Tobago). *Soc. Econ. Stud.*, September 1969, *18*(3), pp. 218–53. **[G: Trinidad/Tobago]**

Sethi, Narendra K. Land Reform in Economic Development—A Case Study from Latin America. *Asian Econ. Rev.*, February 1969, *11*(2), pp. 221–26.

Steiner, Henry Malcolm and Seminario, Adan. Economic Aspects of the Bolivar Highway in Peru. *Eng. Econ.*, January–February 1969, *14*(2), pp. 101–07. **[G: Peru]**

Sunkel, Osvaldo. National Development Policy and External Dependence in Latin America. *J. Devel. Stud.*, October 1969, *6*(1), pp. 23–48. **[G: Latin America]**

Tanzi, Vito. Tax Incentives and Economic Development: The Ecuadorian Experience. *Finanzarchiv*, March 1969, *28*(2), pp. 226–35. **[G: Ecuador]**

Thiesenhusen, William C. Population Growth and Agricultural Employment in Latin America, with Some U.S. Comparisons. *Amer. J. Agr. Econ.*, November 1969, *51*(4), pp. 735–52. **[G: Latin America; U.S.]**

Thorbecke, Erik and Field, Alfred J. Relationships between Agriculture, Nonagriculture, and Foreign Trade in the Development of Argentina and Peru: Reply. **In** *Thorbecke, E., ed.*, 1969, pp. 217–18. **[G: Argentina; Peru]**

Thorbecke, Erik and Field, Alfred J. Relationships between Agriculture, Nonagriculture, and Foreign Trade in the Development of Argentina and Peru. **In** *Thorbecke, E., ed.*, 1969, pp. 165–213. **[G: Argentina; Peru]**

Thorp, Rosemary. A Note on Food Supplies, the Distribution of Income and National Income Accounting in Peru. *Bull. Oxford Univ. Inst. Econ. Statist.*, November 1969, *31*(4), pp. 229–41. **[G: Peru]**

Tokman, Victor E. An Evaluation of Foreign Aid: The Chilean Case. *Bull. Oxford Univ. Inst. Econ. Statist.*, May 1969, *31*(2), pp. 89–103. **[G: Chile]**

Vernon, Raymond. Mexico: Public Planning and Private Initiative. **In** *Prybyla, J. S., ed.*, 1969, pp. 525–40. **[G: Mexico]**

Whitehead, Laurence. Basic Data in Poor Countries: The Bolivian Case. *Bull. Oxford Univ. Inst. Econ. Statist.*, August 1969, *31*(3), pp. 205–27. **[G: Bolivia]**

1217 Oceanic Countries

Blyth, C. A. Primitive South Pacific Economies: Their Consumption Pattern and Propensity to Save Out of Cash Income. *Econ. Rec.*, September 1969, *45*(111), pp. 354–72. **[G: Samoa; Papua]**

Kelley, Allen C. Demand Patterns, Demographic Change and Economic Growth. *Quart. J. Econ.*, February 1969, *83*(1), pp. 110–26. **[G: Philippines]**

Lorenzo, A. Employment Effects of Rural and Community Development in the Philippines. *Int. Lab. Rev.*, November 1969, *100*(5), pp. 419–44. **[G: Philippines]**

Ward, M. The Effects of the U.K. Devaluation of Sterling on the Fiji Economy. *Econ. Rec.*, March 1969, *45*(109), pp. 92–115. **[G: Fiji]**

Williamson, Jeffrey G. Dimensions of Postwar Philippine Economic Progress. *Quart. J. Econ.*, February 1969, *83*(1), pp. 93–109. **[G: Philippines]**

122 Economic Studies of More Industrialized Countries

1220 General

Hill, T. P. Too Much Consumption. *Nat. Westminster Bank Quart. Rev.*, February 1969, pp. 18–39.

Kerr, Clark. Industrialism and Pluralism. **In** *Kerr, C.*, 1969, pp. 74–81.

Kravis, Irving B. and Lipsey, Robert E. International Price Comparisons by Regression Methods. *Int. Econ. Rev.*, June 1969, *10*(2), pp. 233–46.

Macesich, George and Falero, Frank, Jr. Permanent Income Hypothesis, Interest Rates and the Demand for Money. *Weltwirtsch. Arch.*, 1969, *103* (1), pp. 129–52.

Matthews, R. C. O. Why Growth Rates Differ. *Econ. J.*, June 1969, *79*(314), pp. 261–68. **[G: U.S.; W. Europe]**

Vatter, Harold G. Capitalism without Accumulation. *J. Econ. Issues*, March 1969, *3*(1), pp. 110–25.

1221 Comparative Country Studies

Barger, Harold. Growth in Developed Nations. *Rev. Econ. Statist.*, May 1969, *51*(2), pp. 143–48.

Haenni, Paul M. Managers' gap mondiale: analisi spettrale. (The Management Gap in a World Context: A Spectral Analysis. With English summary.) *L'Impresa*, November/December 1969, *11*(6), pp. 444–53.

Heidensohn, K. Labour's Share in National Income—A Constant? *Manchester Sch. Econ. Soc. Stud.*, December 1969, *37*(4), pp. 295–321.

Lambert, Rapporto. Perché le imprese europee non guadagnano come le americane. (Why European Firms Do Not Earn as Much as the Americans. With English summary.) *L'Impresa*, January/February 1969, *11*(1), pp. 18–28.

Lomax, David F. and Reading, Brian. Too Little Saving. *Nat. Westminster Bank Quart. Rev.*, August 1969, pp. 23–42. **[G: U.K.]**

Lotz, Joergen R. Some Economic Effects of Increasing Public Expenditures: An Empirical Study of Selected Developed Countries. *Public Finance,* 1969, *24*(4), pp. 577–96.

Rhodes, John B. 'The American Challenge' Challenged. *Harvard Bus. Rev.,* September–October 1969, *47*(5), pp. 45–56. **[G: E.E.C.; U.S.]**

Tucci, Giuseppe. Accostamenti economici tra Giappone e Italia; prospettive dell'esportazione calzaturiera in Giappone. (Economic Approaches between Japan and Italy. With English summary.) *Mondo Aperto,* October 1969, *23*(5), pp. 321–29. **[G: Japan; Italy]**

Yamaoka, Ryoichi. The "Modernisation" of Agriculture at the Present Stage. *Kyoto Univ. Econ. Rev.,* April 1969, *39*(1), pp. 1–21. **[G: U.S.; W. Germany]**

1223 European Countries

Albach, Horst. New Trends in the Economic Policy of the Federal Republic of Germany. *Ger. Econ. Rev.,* 1969, *7*(2), pp. 108–28. **[G: W. Germany]**

Bachurin, A. The Economic Reform in Operation. *Prob. Econ.,* April 1969, *11*(12), pp. 11–25. **[G: U.S.S.R.]**

Balassa, Bela. Industrial Development in an Open Economy: The Case of Norway. *Oxford Econ. Pap.,* November 1969, *21*(3), pp. 344–59. **[G: Norway; E.F.T.A.]**

Barsby, Steven L. Economic Backwardness and the Characteristics of Development. *J. Econ. Hist.,* September 1969, *29*(3), pp. 449–72.

Beskid, Lidia. Real Wages in Poland During 1956–1967. *Eastern Europ. Econ.,* Spring 1969, *7*(3), pp. 29–47. **[G: Poland]**

Brigida, Franco. Industria alimentare e sviluppo industriale in italia. (Food Industry and Growth in Italy. With English summary.) *L'Impresa,* March/April 1969, *11*(2), pp. 163–66. **[G: Italy]**

Brown, E. H. Phelps. The Brookings Study of the Poor Performance of the British Economy. *Economica, N.S.,* August 1969, *36*(143), pp. 235–52. **[G: U.K.]**

Brubaker, Earl R. Development of Soviet Agriculture under a Vintage Model of Production. *Amer. J. Agr. Econ.,* November 1969, *51*(4), pp. 882–902. **[G: U.S.S.R.]**

Brubaker, Earl R. Growth in Soviet Transport and Communications: Note. *Amer. Econ. Rev.,* Part I, September 1969, *59*(4), pp. 622–24. **[G: U.S.S.R.]**

Brugmans, I. J. Nederlands overgang van onderontwikkeld gebied tot industrieland. (The Transition from Underdevelopment to Industrialization in the Netherlands. With English summary.) *De Economist,* January/February 1969, *117*(1), pp. 73–85. **[G: Netherlands]**

Buchanan, Ronald H. Toward Netherlands 2000: The Dutch National Plan. *Econ. Geogr.,* July 1969, *45*(3), pp. 258–74. **[G: Netherlands]**

Burrascano, Francesco. Origine ed evoluzione del dualismo economico italiano. (Origin and Evolution of Italian Economic Dualism. With English summary.) *Mondo Aperto,* April 1969, *23*(2), pp. 104–15.

Catherwood, H. F. R. The Planning Dialogue. *Nat. Westminster Bank Quart. Rev.,* May 1969, pp. 2–9. **[G: U.K.]**

Černík, Oldřich. We Are Setting Out on the Road Towards Economic Consolidation. *New Trends Czech. Econ.,* December 1969, (8), pp. 3–44. **[G: Czechoslovakia]**

Edgren, Gösta; Faxén, Karl-Olof and Odhner, Clas-Erik. Wages, Growth and the Distribution of Income. *Swedish J. Econ.,* September 1969, *71*(3), pp. 133–60. **[G: Sweden]**

Eltis, W. A. Is Stop-Go Inevitable? *Nat. Westminster Bank Quart. Rev.,* November 1969, pp. 2–12. **[G: U.K.]**

Engelmann, Hugo O. and Wanner, Richard A. Population Size and Industrial Technology. *Amer. J. Econ. Soc.,* July 1969, *28*(3), pp. 249–56. **[G: U.K.]**

Hansen, Niles M. French Indicative Planning and the *New Industrial State. J. Econ. Issues,* December 1969, *3*(4), pp. 79–95. **[G: France]**

Linnamo, Jussi. Vakauttamispolitiikasta tasapainoisen kasvun politiikkaan. (From Stabilization Policy to a Policy of Balanced Economic Growth. With English summary.) *Kansant. Aikak.,* 1969, *65*(3), pp. 171–80. **[G: Finland]**

Lundberg, Erik. Structural Change and Market Efficiency. *Acta Oecon.,* 1969, *4*(4), pp. 337–50. **[G: Sweden]**

Makkonen, Veikko T. Palvelusektorin työllisyyden kehityksestä Suomessa vuosina 1948–1964. (The Development of Employment in the Finnish Service Sector 1948–1964. With English summary.) *Kansant. Aikak.,* 1969, *65*(2), pp. 110–21. **[G: Finland]**

Marasco, Enrico. Interpretazione di un boom: l'Export 1968. (1968 Export: A Boom Interpretation. With English summary.) *Mondo Aperto,* April 1969, *23*(2), pp. 97–103. **[G: Italy]**

Matassi, Luigi. Reconstruction and Economic Growth in Italy Up to Date. *Rev. Econ. Cond. Italy,* November 1969, *23*(6), pp. 544–63. **[G: Italy]**

Matassi, Luigi. The Italian Economy after World War II. *Rev. Econ. Cond. Italy,* September 1969, *23*(5), pp. 428–42. **[G: Italy]**

Mulvey, Charles. A Critical Examination of Prices and Incomes Policy in the U.K. *Irish Banking Rev.,* September 1969, pp. 10–16. **[G: U.K.]**

Nassmacher, Karl-Heinz. Probleme und Voraussetzungen einer rationalen Wirtschaftspolitik in Grossbritannien. (With English summary.) *Z. ges. Staatswiss.,* October 1969, *125*(4), pp. 637–60. **[G: U.K.]**

Paelinck, J. H. P. Un modèle dynamique de simulation et de contrôle pour l'économie belge. (A Dynamic Simulation and Control Model for Belgian Economy. With English summary.) *Rivista Int. Sci. Econ. Com.,* March 1969, *16*(3), pp. 202–27. **[G: Belgium]**

Rohlíček, Rudolf. Intentions and Reality. *New Trends Czech. Econ.,* November 1969, (7), pp. 3–14. **[G: Czechoslovakia]**

Rychetnik, Ludek. The Growth of Inflationary Pressure: 1955–1966. *Eastern Europ. Econ.,* Spring 1969, *7*(3), pp. 3–11. **[G: Czechoslovakia]**

Schroeder, Gertrude E. The 1966–67 Soviet Industrial Price Reform: A Study in Complications. *Soviet Stud.*, April 1969, *20*(4), pp. 462–77. [G: U.S.S.R.]

Sitnin, V. Results of the Reform of Wholesale Prices and Tasks in the Further Improvement of Price Formation in the U.S.S.R. *Prob. Econ.*, April 1969, *11*(12), pp. 26–36. [G: U.S.S.R.]

Stykolt, Stefan. A Rude Awakening. In *Stykolt, S.*, 1969, pp. 123–25. [G: France]

Tabaček, Ján. Slovakia and the Development of Her Economy. *New Trends Czech. Econ.*, July 1969, (4), pp. 21–34. [G: Czechoslovakia]

Tautscher, Anton. Die Entwicklung der österreichischen Staatswirtschaft. (The Development of the Austrian State Economy. With English summary.) *Schmollers Jahr.*, 1969, *89*(3), pp. 267–311. [G: Austria]

Vachel, Jan. 50 Years of Czechoslovak Economic Development. *Czech. Econ. Pap.*, 1969, (11), pp. 141–51. [G: Czechoslovakia]

Ventriglia, Ferdinando. The Balance of Payments and Italian Economic Growth. *Rev. Econ. Cond. Italy*, September 1969, *23*(5), pp. 381–96. [G: Italy]

Vlasák, František. What Next in the Economic Policy? *New Trends Czech. Econ.*, September 1969, (5–6), pp. 3–89. [G: Czechoslovakia]

Wilber, Charles K. The Role of Agriculture in Soviet Economic Development. *Land Econ.*, February 1969, *45*(1), pp. 87–96. [G: U.S.S.R.]

Zanetti, Giovanni and Filippi, Enrico. Il processo di sviluppo dell'impresa: Fattori endogeni ed esogeni esperienza italiana 1958–1963. (The Process of Firm Growth: Endogenous and Exogenous Factors in the Italian Experience 1958–1963. With English summary.) *L'Impresa*, January/February 1969, *11*(1), pp. 29–39. [G: Italy]

Zlatin, V. and Rutgaizer, V. Comparison of the Levels of Economic Development of Union Republics and Large Regions. *Prob. Econ.*, June 1969, *12*(2), pp. 3–24. [G: U.S.S.R.]

1224 Asian Countries

Hayami, Yūjirō and Yamada, Saburō. Agricultural Productivity at the Beginning of Industrialization. In *Ohkawa, K.; Johnston, B. F. and Kaneda, H., eds.*, 1969, pp. 105–35. [G: Japan]

Hemmi, Kenzō. Primary Product Exports and Economic Development: The Case of Silk. In *Ohkawa, K.; Johnston, B. F. and Kaneda, H., eds.*, 1969, pp. 303–23. [G: Japan]

Hollerman, Leon. Recent Difficulties in Japan's Economic Development. *Banca Naz. Lavoro Quart. Rev.*, March 1969, (88), pp. 66–90. [G: Japan]

Ide, Yoshinori. Administrative Reform and Innovation: The Japanese Case. *Int. Soc. Sci. J.*, 1969, *21*(1), pp. 56–67. [G: Japan]

Ohkawa, Kazushi. Phases of Agricultural Development and Economic Growth. In *Ohkawa, K.; Johnston, B. F. and Kaneda, H., eds.*, 1969, pp. 3–36. [G: Japan]

1225 African Countries

Krogh, D. C. Taxation in a Developing Economy. *S. Afr. J. Econ.*, December 1969, *37*(4), pp. 285–305. [G: S. Africa]

1227 Oceanic Countries

Gruen, Fred H. The Economy. In *Preston, R., ed.*, 1969, pp. 35–70. [G: Australia]

Shaw, B. D. The New Zealand Economy, 1967–68. *Econ. Rec.*, March 1969, *45*(109), pp. 1–16. [G: New Zealand]

1228 North American Countries

Chase, Richard X. and Laber, Gene. Economic Growth as an Anti-poverty Tool: A Further Consideration of the Backwash Debate. *Soc. Sci. Quart.*, December 1969, *50*(3), pp. 604–08. [G: U.S.]

Conley, Ronald W. Roma Remarks on Methods of Measuring the Importance of Sources of Economic Growth. *Southern Econ. J.*, January 1969, *35*(3), pp. 224–30. [G: U.S.]

Green, Alan G. Regional Inequality, Structural Change, and Economic Growth in Canada —1890–1956. *Econ. Develop. Cult. Change*, July 1969, *17*(4), pp. 567–83. [G: Canada]

Paterson, Robert W. The 1970 U.S. Economy. *Univ. Missouri Bus. Govt. Rev.*, November–December 1969, *10*(6), pp. 13–23. [G: U.S.]

Weidenbaum, Murray L. Fiscal Policy and the National Economy. *Univ. Missouri Bus. Govt. Rev.*, November–December 1969, *10*(6), pp. 24–32. [G: U.S.]

123 Comparative Economic Studies Involving Both More and Less Industrialized Countries; International Statistical Comparisons

1230 Comparative Economic Studies Involving More and Less Industrialized Countries; International Statistical Comparisons

Balassa, Bela. Country Size and Trade Patterns: Comment. *Amer. Econ. Rev.*, March 1969, *59*(1), pp. 201–04.

Barth, Peter S. Social Security and Economic Development: A Quantitative Approach—Comment. *Ind. Lab. Relat. Rev.*, January 1969, *22*(2), pp. 257–59.

Chandler, John H. Perspectives on Poverty 5: An International Comparison. *Mon. Lab. Rev.*, February 1969, *92*(2), pp. 55–62.

Cohen, Benjamin I. Less Developed Countries and U.S. Domestic Problems: Comment. *Public Policy*, Fall 1969, *18*(1), pp. 55–60.

Davenport, Michael. The Allocation of Foreign Aid: A Cross Section Study. *Indian Econ. J.*, April–June 1969, *16*(4–5), pp. 458–77. [G: U.S.]

Duggar, Jan Warren. International Comparisons of Income Levels: An Additional Measure. *Econ. J.*, March 1969, *79*(313), pp. 109–16.

Erb, Guy F. and Schiavo-Campo, Salvatore. Export Instability, Level of Development, and Economic Size of Less Developed Countries. *Bull. Oxford Univ. Inst. Econ. Statist.*, November 1969, *31*(4), pp. 263–83.

Ezekiel, Hannan and Adekunle, Joseph O. The Secular Behavior of Income Velocity: An International Cross-Section Study. *Int. Monet. Fund Staff Pap.*, July 1969, *16*(2), pp. 224–39.

Forrest, Matthew D. and Yoshihara, Kunio. Japan's Dependence in Contrast with That of Six Other Nations. *Hitotsubashi J. Econ.*, June 1969, *10*(1), pp. 56–62. **[G: Japan]**

Galenson, Walter. Social Security and Economic Development: A Quantitative Approach—Reply. *Ind. Lab. Relat. Rev.*, January 1969, *22*(2), pp. 260–63.

Gupta, Shibshankar P. Public Expenditure and Economic Development—A Cross-Section Analysis. *Finanzarchiv*, October 1968, *28*(1), pp. 26–41.

Hagen, Everett and Hawrylyshyn, Oli. Analysis of World Income and Growth, 1955–1965. *Econ. Develop. Cult. Change*, Part II, October 1969, *18* (1), pp. 1–96.

Hayami, Yūjirō. Sources of Agricultural Productivity Gap among Selected Countries. *Amer. J. Agr. Econ.*, August 1969, *51*(3), pp. 564–75.

Herbst, František. The Housing Situation in the CSSR in Terms of International Comparison. *Eastern Europ. Econ.*, Summer 1969, *7*(4), pp. 38–40. **[G: Czechoslovakia]**

Hoffmann, Walther G. The Share of Defence Expenditure in Gross National Product (GNP)—An International and Diachronic Comparison. *Ger. Econ. Rev.*, 1969, *7*(4), pp. 295–307.

Jackman, Patrick C. Unit Labor Costs of Iron and Steel Industries in Five Countries. *Mon. Lab. Rev.*, August 1969, *92*(8), pp. 15–22. **[G: W. Germany; France; U.K.; U.S.; Japan]**

Kamerschen, David R. Further Analysis of Overurbanization. *Econ. Develop. Cult. Change*, January 1969, *17*(2), pp. 235–53.

Karcz, Jerzy F. Comparative Study of Transformation of Agriculture in Centrally Planned Economies: The Soviet Union, Eastern Europe and Mainland China. **In** *Thorbecke, E., ed.*, 1969, pp. 237–66. **[G: U.S.S.R.; E. Europe; China]**

Karcz, Jerzy F. Comparative Study of Transformation of Agriculture in Centrally Planned Economies: The Soviet Union, Eastern Europe and Mainland China: Reply. **In** *Thorbecke, E., ed.*, 1969, pp. 274–76. **[G: U.S.S.R.; E. Europe; China]**

Karkal, G. L. A Note on Basics. *Arthaniti*, January & July 1969, *12*(1&2), pp. 78–83. **[G: India; U.S.]**

Keesing, Donald B. Country Size and Trade Patterns: Reply. *Amer. Econ. Rev.*, March 1969, *59* (1), pp. 204.

Kirman, Alan P. and Tomasini, Luigi M. A New Look at International Income Inequalities. *Econ. Int.*, August 1969, *22*(3), pp. 437–61.

Kux, Jaroslav; Mairesse, Jacques and Drechsler, László. Labour Productivity Comparison between Czechoslovakia and France. *Rev. Income Wealth*, September 1969, *15*(3), pp. 219–28. **[G: Czechoslovakia; France]**

Lago, Armando M. The Hoffman Industrial Growth Development Path: An International Comparison. *Weltwirtsch. Arch.*, 1969, *103*(1), pp. 41–57.

Lee, T. H. The Transferability of the Japanese Pattern of Modernizing Traditional Agriculture: Comment. **In** *Thorbecke, E., ed.*, 1969, pp. 303–10.

Leff, Nathaniel H. Dependency Rates and Savings Rates. *Amer. Econ. Rev.*, December 1969, *59*(5), pp. 886–96.

Lotz, Joergen R. and Morss, Elliott R. "Tax Effort" in Developing Countries. *Finance Develop.*, September 1969, *6*(3), pp. 36–39.

Marsden, Keith. Towards a Synthesis of Economic Growth and Social Justice. *Int. Lab. Rev.*, November 1969, *100*(5), pp. 389–418.

Montias, John Michael. Comparative Study of Transformation of Agriculture in Centrally Planned Economies: The Soviet Union, Eastern Europe and Mainland China: Comment. **In** *Thorbecke, E., ed.*, 1969, pp. 266–74. **[G: U.S.S.R.; E. Europe; China]**

Nesterov, L. Current Position of National Wealth Estimation in the World. *Rev. Income Wealth*, September 1969, *15*(3), pp. 271–83.

Nie, Norman H.; Powell, G. Bingham, Jr. and Prewitt, Kenneth. Social Structure and Political Participation: Developmental Relationships, Part I. *Amer. Polit. Sci. Rev.*, June 1969, *63*(2), pp. 361–78.

Ohkawa, Kazushi and Johnston, Bruce F. The Transferability of the Japanese Pattern of Modernizing Traditional Agriculture. **In** *Thorbecke, E., ed.*, 1969, pp. 277–303.

Palomba, Neil A. Stability and Real Economic Growth: An International Comparison. *Kyklos*, 1969, *22*(3), pp. 589–92.

Peaslee, Alexander L. Education's Role in Development. *Econ. Develop. Cult. Change*, April 1969, *17*(3), pp. 293–318.

Preston, Esme. Growth and Investment in the Market Economies. *Econ. Rec.*, December 1969, *45* (112), pp. 544–62.

Ranis, Gustav. Economic Dualism—At Home and Abroad. *Public Policy*, Fall 1969, *18*(1), pp. 41–53.

Redding, A. David. The Philippine Economy: A Newcomer's Perspective. *Philippine Econ. J.*, Second Semester 1969, *8*(2), pp. 130–44. **[G: Philippines]**

Román, Zoltán. A Note on Measuring Structural Changes. *Rev. Income Wealth*, September 1969, *15*(3), pp. 265–68.

Selowsky, Marcelo. On the Measurement of Education's Contribution to Growth. *Quart. J. Econ.*, August 1969, *83*(3), pp. 449–63.

Shin, Kilman. International Difference in Tax Ratio. *Rev. Econ. Statist.*, May 1969, *51*(2), pp. 213–20.

Sicat, Gerardo P. Intercountry Trade: The Effects of Bilateralism, Development, and Regional Advantage. *Malayan Econ. Rev.*, October 1969, *14*(2), pp. 94–112.

Stacey, R. D. Uniformity in Output Growth Patterns

in the Manufacturing Sector. *S. Afr. J. Econ.*, March 1969, *37*(1), pp. 55–75.

Strydom, P. D. F. Why Growth Rates Differ (A Review Note). *S. Afr. J. Econ.*, March 1969, *37*(1), pp. 76–80.

Szakolczai, György and Stahl, János. Increasing or Decreasing Returns to Scale in the Constant Elasticity of Substitution Production Function. *Rev. Econ. Statist.*, February 1969, *51*(1), pp. 84–90. **[G: U.S.; Hungary]**

Taira, Koji. Consumer Preferences, Poverty Norms, and Extent of Poverty. *Quart. Rev. Econ. Bus.*, Summer 1969, *9*(2), pp. 31–44.

Trotter, G. J. Personal Income Tax. *S. Afr. J. Econ.*, December 1969, *37*(4), pp. 306–44.

Wallich, Henry C. Money and Growth: A Country Cross-Section Analysis. *J. Money, Credit, Banking*, May 1969, *1*(2), pp. 281–302.

Williamson, Jeffrey G. Income Growth and Savings. *Philippine Econ. J.*, First Semester 1969, *8*(1), pp. 54–74. **[G: Asia]**

Wilson, T.; Sinha, R. P. and Castree, J. R. The Income Terms of Trade of Developed and Developing Countries. *Econ. J.*, December 1969, *79*(316), pp. 813–32.

130 Economic Fluctuations; Forecasting; Stabilization; and Inflation

131 Economic Fluctuations

1310 General

Berry, R. Albert and Hymer, Stephen H. A Note on the Capacity to Transform and the Welfare Costs of Foreign Trade Fluctuations. *Econ. J.*, December 1969, *79*(316), pp. 833–46.

Burns, Arthur Frank. The Nature and Causes of Business Cycles. **In** *Burns, A. F.*, 1969, pp. 3–53.

Cagan, Phillip. The Influence of Interest Rates on the Duration of Business Cycles. **In** *Guttentag, J. M. and Cagan, P., eds.*, 1969, pp. 3–28. **[G: U.S.]**

Čobeljić, Nikola and Stojanović, Radmila. The Theory of Investment Cycles in a Socialist Economy. *Eastern Europ. Econ.*, Fall 1968/Winter 1968–69, *7*(1–2), pp. 1–168. **[G: Europe]**

Day, Richard H. and Tinney, E. Herbert. Cycles, Phases and Growth in a Generalised Cobweb Theory. *Econ. J.*, March 1969, *79*(313), pp. 90–108.

DeLorme, Charles D., Jr. and Selby, Edward B., Jr. The Cost of Stabilization: A Comment. *Amer. Econ.*, Fall 1969, *13*(2), pp. 97–99.

Jones, Robert J. The Cost of Stabilization: Reply. *Amer. Econ.*, Fall 1969, *13*(2), pp. 100–104.

Kelley, Allen C. Demographic Cycles and Economic Growth: The Long Swing Reconsidered. *J. Econ. Hist.*, December 1969, *29*(4), pp. 633–56.

Klein, Lawrence R. and Preston, R. S. Stochastic Nonlinear Models. *Econometrica*, January 1969, *37*(1), pp. 95–106.

Licari, Joseph A. Economic Fluctuations: A Comparative Study. *Amer. Econ.*, Spring 1969, *13*(1), pp. 42–57.

Rose, Hugh. Real and Monetary Factors in the Business Cycle. *J. Money, Credit, Banking*, May 1969, *1*(2), pp. 138–52.

Scott, Anthony. Investing and Protesting. *J. Polit. Econ.*, November/December 1969, *77*(6), pp. 916–20.

Walker, Douglas O. Economic Fluctuations: A Comparative Study: Comment. *Amer. Econ.*, Spring 1969, *13*(1), pp. 58–62.

1313 Fluctuation: Studies

Abramovitz, Moses. The Passing of the Kuznets Cycle: A Correction. *Economica, N.S.*, February 1969, *36*(141), pp. 81.

Auld, Douglas A. L. Fiscal Policy Performance in Canada 1957–1967. *Public Finance*, 1969, *24*(3), pp. 427–40. **[G: Canada]**

Auld, Douglas A. L. The Economic Impact of Built-In Changes in Budget Components. *Australian Econ. Pap.*, June 1969, *8*(12), pp. 75–98. **[G: Australia]**

Brody, Andrew. The Rate of Economic Growth in Hungary. **In** *Bronfenbrenner, M., ed.*, 1969, pp. 312–27. **[G: Hungary]**

Bronfenbrenner, Martin. Is the Business Cycle Obsolete?: Summary of the Discussion. **In** *Bronfenbrenner, M., ed.*, 1969, pp. 505–58.

Bronfenbrenner, Martin. Postwar Business Cycles in Japan: Comment. **In** *Bronfenbrenner, M., ed.*, 1969, pp. 96–98. **[G: Japan]**

Burley, S. P. A Spectral Analysis of the Australian Business Cycle. *Australian Econ. Pap.*, December 1969, *8*(13), pp. 193–218. **[G: Australia]**

Cassidy, Henry J. The Rate of Change in the Size Distribution of Wages as a Vector. *Rev. Income Wealth*, December 1969, *15*(4), pp. 349–68. **[G: U.S.]**

Chow, Gregory C. and Levitan, Richard E. Nature of Business Cycles Implicit in a Linear Economic Model. *Quart. J. Econ.*, August 1969, *83*(3), pp. 504–17. **[G: U.S.]**

Daly, D. J. Business Cycles in Canada: Their Postwar Persistence. **In** *Bronfenbrenner, M., ed.*, 1969, pp. 45–65. **[G: Canada]**

Dow, J. C. R. Cyclical Developments in France, Germany, and Italy Since the Early Fifties. **In** *Bronfenbrenner, M., ed.*, 1969, pp. 140–96. **[G: France; W. Germany; Italy]**

Ekelund, Robert B., Jr. and Gramm, William P. A Reconsideration of Advertising Expenditures, Aggregate Demand, and Economic Stabilization. *Quart. Rev. Econ. Bus.*, Summer 1969, *9*(2), pp. 71–77. **[G: U.S.]**

Eltis, W. A. Is Stop-Go Inevitable? *Nat. Westminster Bank Quart. Rev.*, November 1969, pp. 2–12. **[G: U.K.]**

Fox, Karl A. Comparison of the Prewar and Postwar Business Cycles in the Netherlands: An Experiment in Econometrics: Comment. **In** *Bronfenbrenner, M., ed.*, 1969, pp. 467–74. **[G: Netherlands]**

Friedman, Milton. The Monetary Studies of the National Bureau. In *Friedman, M.,* 1969, pp. 261–84. **[G: U.S.]**

Gelting, Jørgen H. Denmark, Norway and Sweden. In *Bronfenbrenner, M., ed.,* 1969, pp. 200–20. **[G: Denmark; Norway; Sweden]**

Goldmann, Josef. Fluctuation in the Growth Rate in a Socialist Economy and the Inventory Cycle. In *Bronfenbrenner, M., ed.,* 1969, pp. 332–49. **[G: Czechoslovakia]**

Gordon, R. A. The Stability of the U.S. Economy. In *Bronfenbrenner, M., ed.,* 1969, pp. 3–34. **[G: U.S.]**

Gujarati, Damodar. Cyclical Behavior of Help-Wanted Index and the Unemployment Rate. *Rev. Econ. Statist.,* November 1969, *51*(4), pp. 482–84. **[G: U.S.]**

Gupta, Kanhaya L. Money Supply, Cyclical Fluctuations, and Income Determination. *Jahr. Nationalökon. Statist.,* May 1969, *182*(6), pp. 465–78. **[G: Canada]**

Hamermesh, Daniel S. Spectral Analysis of the Relation between Gross Employment Changes and Output Changes, 1958–1966. *Rev. Econ. Statist.,* February 1969, *51*(1), pp. 62–69. **[G: U.S.]**

Harkness, Jon P. Long Swings. *Rev. Econ. Statist.,* February 1969, *51*(1), pp. 94–96. **[G: U.S.]**

Hatanaka, Michio and Howrey, E. Philip. Low Frequency Variation in Economic Time Series. *Kyklos,* 1969, *22*(4), pp. 752–66. **[G: U.S.]**

Hollerman, Leon. Recent Difficulties in Japan's Economic Development. *Banca Naz. Lavoro Quart. Rev.,* March 1969, (88), pp. 66–90. **[G: Japan]**

Howenstine, E. Jay. Rising Construction Costs and Anti-Inflation Policies: A Report on Western Europe. *Mon. Lab. Rev.,* June 1969, *92*(6), pp. 3–10. **[G: W. Europe]**

Hutchings, Raymond. Periodic Fluctuation in Soviet Industrial Growth Rates. *Soviet Stud.,* January 1969, *20*(3), pp. 331–52. **[G: U.S.S.R.]**

Krislov, Joseph and Christian, Virgil L., Jr. Union Organizing and the Business Cycle, 1949–1966. *Southern Econ. J.,* October 1969, *36*(2), pp. 185–88. **[G: U.S.]**

Levine, Herbert S. and Seton, Francis. Cyclical Fluctuations under Socialism: Comment. In *Bronfenbrenner, M., ed.,* 1969, pp. 303–11.

Lotz, Joergen R. Some Economic Effects of Increasing Public Expenditures: An Empirical Study of Selected Developed Countries. *Public Finance,* 1969, *24*(4), pp. 577–96.

Matthews, R. C. O. Postwar Business Cycles in the United Kingdom. In *Bronfenbrenner, M., ed.,* 1969, pp. 99–135. **[G: U.K.]**

McCracken, Paul W. The Game Plan for Economic Policy. *Amer. Statist.,* October 1969, *23*(4), pp. 7–10. **[G: U.S.]**

Melnik, Arie and Kraus, Alan. Short-Run Interest Rate Cycles in the U.S.: 1954–1967. *J. Financial Quant. Anal.,* September 1969, *4*(3), pp. 291–99. **[G: U.S.]**

Menshikov, Stanislav M. The Stability of the U.S. Economy: Comment. In *Bronfenbrenner, M., ed.,* 1969, pp. 35–39. **[G: U.S.]**

Metcalf, Charles E. The Size Distribution of Personal Income during the Business Cycle. *Amer. Econ. Rev.,* Part I, September 1969, *59*(4), pp. 657–68. **[G: U.S.]**

Meyer zu Schlochtern, F. J. M. Transmission of Business Fluctuations from Developed to Developing Countries: Comment. In *Bronfenbrenner, M., ed.,* 1969, pp. 279–83.

Moore, Geoffrey H. The Stability of the U.S. Economy: Comment. In *Bronfenbrenner, M., ed.,* 1969, pp. 40–44. **[G: U.S.]**

Niehans, Jürg. Austria and Switzerland: Comment. In *Bronfenbrenner, M., ed.,* 1969, pp. 247–50. **[G: Austria; Switzerland]**

Nove, Alec. Cyclical Fluctuations under Socialism. In *Bronfenbrenner, M., ed.,* 1969, pp. 287–302.

Palomba, Neil A. Stability and Real Economic Growth: An International Comparison. *Kyklos,* 1969, *22*(3), pp. 589–92.

Portes, Richard D. The Rate of Economic Growth in Hungary: Comment. In *Bronfenbrenner, M., ed.,* 1969, pp. 328–31. **[G: Hungary]**

Rasmussen, P. Nørregaard. Denmark, Norway and Sweden: Comment. In *Bronfenbrenner, M., ed.,* 1969, pp. 221–24. **[G: Denmark; Norway; Sweden]**

Rhomberg, Rudolf R. Transmission of Business Fluctuations from Developed to Developing Countries. In *Bronfenbrenner, M., ed.,* 1969, pp. 253–78.

Robinson, T. Russell. The Foreign Trade Sector and Domestic Stability: The Canadian Case. *Yale Econ. Essays,* Spring 1969, *9*(1), pp. 47–87. **[G: Canada]**

Rosenbluth, Gideon. Business Cycles in Canada: Their Postwar Persistence: Comment. In *Bronfenbrenner, M., ed.,* 1969, pp. 66–72. **[G: Canada]**

Rothschild, Kurt W. Austria and Switzerland. In *Bronfenbrenner, M., ed.,* 1969, pp. 225–46. **[G: Austria; Switzerland]**

Seton, Francis. Fluctuation in the Growth Rate in a Socialist Economy and the Inventory Cycle: Comment. In *Bronfenbrenner, M., ed.,* 1969, pp. 350–55. **[G: Czechoslovakia]**

Shinohara, Miyōhei. Postwar Business Cycles in Japan. In *Bronfenbrenner, M., ed.,* 1969, pp. 73–95. **[G: Japan]**

Spaventa, Luigi. Cyclical Developments in France, Germany, and Italy Since the Early Fifties: Comment. In *Bronfenbrenner, M., ed.,* 1969, pp. 197–99. **[G: France; W. Germany; Italy]**

Stekler, Lois E. Effect of U.S. Business Fluctuations on Imports of Primary Commodities. *Yale Econ. Essays,* Fall 1969, *9*(2), pp. 209–49. **[G: U.S.]**

Verdoorn, P. J. and Post, J. J. Comparison of the Prewar and Postwar Business Cycles in the Netherlands: An Experiment in Econometrics. In *Bronfenbrenner, M., ed.,* 1969, pp. 436–66. **[G: Netherlands]**

Vipond, M. J. Fluctuations in Private Housebuilding in Great Britain, 1950–1966. *Scot. J. Polit. Econ.,* June 1969, *16*(2), pp. 196–211. **[G: U.K.]**

Weiller, Jean. Anti-Cyclical Policies in Relation to Foreign Trade Patterns and Tariffs (An Historical Approach). *Econ. Int.,* May 1969, *22*(2), pp. 225–44. **[G: France]**

Worswick, G. D. N. Postwar Business Cycles in the United Kingdom: Comment. **In** *Bronfenbrenner, M., ed.,* 1969, pp. 136–39. **[G: U.K.]**

132 Economic Forecasting and Econometric Models

1320 General

Adelman, Irma and Je, Kim Mahn. An Econometric Model of the Korean Economy (1956–66). **In** *Adelman, I., ed.,* 1969, pp. 77–108. **[G: S. Korea]**

Adelman, Irma, et al. The Korean Sectoral Model. **In** *Adelman, I., ed.,* 1969, pp. 109–35. **[G: S. Korea]**

Anderson, Henry. Choosing the Base Period for Economic Forecasts. *Miss. Val. J. Bus. Econ.,* Spring 1969, *4*(2), pp. 33–42.

Bergström, Stig-Erik. Prognoser som underkag för beslutsfattandet inom företaget. (Forecasting as a Basis for Decision-Making within the Enterprise. With English summary.) *Econ. Samfundets Tidskr.,* 1969, *22*(2), pp. 105–25.

Bieda, K. Economic Planning in Japan. *Econ. Rec.,* June 1969, *45*(110), pp. 181–205. **[G: Japan]**

Brown, H. James. Shift and Share Projections of Regional Economic Growth: An Empirical Test. *J. Reg. Sci.,* April 1969, *9*(1), pp. 1–18.

Cairncross, Alec K. [Sir]. Economic Forecasting. *Econ. J.,* December 1969, *79*(316), pp. 797–812.

Cole, Rosanne. Data Errors and Forecasting Accuracy. **In** *Mincer, J., ed.,* 1969, pp. 47–82.

Diller, Stanley. Expectations in the Term Structure of Interest Rates. **In** *Mincer, J., ed.,* 1969, pp. 112–66.

Driehuis, W. Experiments in Explaining and Forecasting the Invisible Trade of the Netherlands. *Bull. Oxford Univ. Inst. Econ. Statist.,* November 1969, *31*(4), pp. 335–51. **[G: Netherlands]**

FitzLyon, K. Plan and Prediction. *Soviet Stud.,* October 1969, *21*(2), pp. 164–92. **[G: U.S.S.R.]**

Fromm, Gary. An Evaluation of Monetary Policy Instruments. **In** *Duesenberry, J. S., et al.,* 1969, pp. 473–511. **[G: U.S.]**

Hickman, Bert G. Dynamic Properties of Macroeconometric Models: An International Comparison. **In** *Bronfenbrenner, M., ed.,* 1969, pp. 393–435.

Holden, Kenneth. The Effect of Revisions to Data on Two Econometric Studies. *Manchester Sch. Econ. Soc. Stud.,* March 1969, *37*(1), pp. 23–37. **[G: U.K.]**

Juster, F. Thomas. Consumer Anticipations and Models of Durable Goods Demand. **In** *Mincer, J., ed.,* 1969, pp. 167–242.

Kaskimies, Mika. Product Life Pattern as a Means of Business Forecasting. *Liiketaloudellinen Aikak.,* 1969, *18*(3), pp. 433–41.

Kendrick, David A. and Taylor, Lance J. A Dynamic Nonlinear Planning Model for Korea. **In** *Adelman, I., ed.,* 1969, pp. 213–37. **[G: S. Korea]**

Klein, Lawrence R. Econometric Analysis of the Tax Cut of 1964. **In** *Duesenberry, J. S., et al.,* 1969, pp. 458–72. **[G: U.S.]**

Klein, Lawrence R. Statement. **In** *The 1969 Economic Report of the President, Pt. 2, JECH,* 1969, pp. 489–94. **[G: U.S.]**

L'Esperance, Wilford L. Econometric Model Building for State Economic Development. *Ohio State U. Bull. Bus. Res.,* December 1969, *44*(12), pp. 1–3, 7–8. **[G: U.S.]**

May, Francis B. The Voice of Apollo: Historical Trends in Business Forecasting. *Soc. Sci. Quart.,* June 1969, *50*(1), pp. 153–60.

Mincer, Jacob. Models of Adaptive Forecasting. **In** *Mincer, J., ed.,* 1969, pp. 83–111.

Mincer, Jacob and Zarnowitz, Victor. The Evaluation of Economic Forecasts. **In** *Mincer, J., ed.,* 1969, pp. 3–46.

Moore, Geoffrey H. Forecasting Short-Term Economic Change. *J. Amer. Statist. Assoc.,* March 1969, *64*(325), pp. 1–22.

Nagar, A. L. Stochastic Simulation of the Brookings Econometric Model. **In** *Duesenberry, J. S., et al.,* 1969, pp. 423–56. **[G: U.S.]**

Norton, Roger D. Formal Approaches to Regional Planning in Korea. **In** *Adelman, I., ed.,* 1969, pp. 185–212. **[G: S. Korea]**

Očenášek, Radomir. Diskuse o národohospodářských modelech. (Discussion about Macroeconomic Models. With English summary.) *Ekon.-Mat. Obzor,* 1969, *5*(4), pp. 522–24.

Paul, P.-E. Företagens Prognosbehov, en kommentar. (The Enterprise's Need of Forecasting. With English summary.) *Econ. Samfundets Tidskr.,* 1969, *22*(2), pp. 126–29.

Sabolo, Yves. Sectoral Employment Growth: The Outlook for 1980. *Int. Lab. Rev.,* November 1969, *100*(5), pp. 445–74.

Shapiro, A. Model-Building and Extrapolation. *Prob. Econ.,* August 1969, *12*(4), pp. 31–51.

Smyth, David J. and Briscoe, G. Investment Plans and Realizations in United Kingdom Manufacturing. *Economica, N.S.,* August 1969, *36*(143), pp. 277–94. **[G: U.K.]**

Westphal, Larry E. Multisectoral Project Analysis Employing Mixed Integer Programming. **In** *Adelman, I., ed.,* 1969, pp. 145–83. **[G: S. Korea]**

Wold, Herman O. Econometrics as Pioneering in Nonexperimental Model Building. *Econometrica,* July 1969, *37*(3), pp. 369–81.

Wood, Marshall and Labovitz, David E. The Korean Sectoral Model: Appendix. **In** *Adelman, I., ed.,* 1969, pp. 135–43. **[G: S. Korea]**

1322 General Forecasts for a Country

Aglietta, Michel and Seibel, Claude. The National Accounting System and the Preparation of the Fifth French Plan. *Rev. Income Wealth,* June 1969, *15*(2), pp. 121–69. **[G: France]**

Bailey, Duncan M. and Hogan, Timothy D. Future Growth Patterns in South Africa. *S. Afr. J. Econ.,* September 1969, *37*(3), pp. 237–51. **[G: S. Africa]**

Dutta, M. and Su, V. An Econometric Model of Puerto Rico. *Rev. Econ. Stud.,* July 1969, *36*(107), pp. 319–33. **[G: Puerto Rico]**

Evans, Michael K. and Klein, Lawrence R. Experience with Econometric Analysis of the U.S. "Konjunktur" Position. **In** *Bronfenbrenner, M., ed.,*

1969, pp. 359–88. [G: U.S.]

Evans, Michael K. Reconstruction and Estimation of the Balanced Budget Multiplier. *Rev. Econ. Statist.*, February 1969, *51*(1), pp. 14–25. [G: U.S.]

Fox, Karl A. Comparison of the Prewar and Postwar Business Cycles in the Netherlands: An Experiment in Econometrics: Comment. **In** *Bronfenbrenner, M., ed.*, 1969, pp. 467–74. [G: Netherlands]

Fromm, Gary and Klein, Lawrence R. Solutions of the Complete System. **In** *Duesenberry, J. S., et al.*, 1969, pp. 362–421. [G: U.S.]

Galper, Harvey. The Impacts of the Vietnam War on Defense Spending: A Simulation Approach. *J. Bus.*, October 1969, *42*(4), pp. 401–15. [G: U.S.]

Kennedy, M. C. How Well Does the National Institute Forecast? *Nat. Inst. Econ. Rev.*, November 1969, (50), pp. 40–52. [G: U.K.]

Khan, Azizur Rahman. The Possibilities of the East Pakistan Economy during the Fourth Five-Year Plan. *Pakistan Develop. Rev.*, Summer 1969, *9*(2), pp. 144–211. [G: E. Pakistan]

Lacina, Otakar. The Long-Term Forecast of the Czechoslovak Economy. *Czech. Econ. Pap.*, 1969, (11), pp. 7–26. [G: Czechoslovakia]

de Leeuw, Frank and Gramlich, Edward M. The Channels of Monetary Policy. *Fed. Res. Bull.*, June 1969, *55*(6), pp. 472–91. [G: U.S.]

Liu, Ta-Chung. A Monthly Recursive Econometric Model of United States: A Test of Feasibility. *Rev. Econ. Statist.*, February 1969, *51*(1), pp. 1–13. [G: U.S.]

Miller, Glenn H., Jr. The Business Outlook for 1969. *Fed. Res. Bank Kansas City Rev.*, January 1969, pp. 11–20. [G: U.S.]

Moore, Geoffrey H. Generating Leading Indicators from Lagging Indicators. *Western Econ. J.*, June 1969, *7*(2), pp. 137–44. [G: U.S.]

Paelinck, J. H. P. Un modèle dynamique de simulation et de contrôle pour l'économie belge. (A Dynamic Simulation and Control Model for Belgian Economy. With English summary.) *Rivista Int. Sci. Econ. Com.*, March 1969, *16*(3), pp. 202–27. [G: Belgium]

Perry, George L. Statement. **In** *The 1969 Economic Report of the President, Pt. 2, JECH,* 1969, pp. 495–97. [G: U.S.]

du Plessis, T. A. and Strydom, P. D. F. Future Growth Patterns in South Africa—A Comment. *S. Afr. J. Econ.*, September 1969, *37*(3), pp. 252–59. [G: S. Africa]

Schweiger, Irving. 1969 Forecast of Gross National Product, Consumer Spending, Saving, and Housing. *J. Bus.*, January 1969, *42*(1), pp. 7–11. [G: U.S.]

Sprinkel, Beryl W. The Business Outlook for 1969: Moving toward Economic Stability. *J. Bus.*, January 1969, *42*(1), pp. 1–6. [G: U.S.]

Suits, Daniel B. Statement. **In** *The 1969 Economic Report of the President, Pt. 2, JECH,* 1969, pp. 497–500. [G: U.S.]

Turner, Robert C. Macro Forecasting in the Philippines: An Experiment. *Philippine Econ. J.*, Second Semester 1969, *8*(2), pp. 185–201. [G: Philippines]

Verdoorn, P. J. and Post, J. J. Comparison of the Prewar and Postwar Business Cycles in the Netherlands: An Experiment in Econometrics. **In** *Bronfenbrenner, M., ed.*, 1969, pp. 436–66. [G: Netherlands]

Weidenbaum, Murray L. Fiscal Policy and the National Economy. *Univ. Missouri Bus. Govt. Rev.*, November–December 1969, *10*(6), pp. 24–32. [G: U.S.]

Williams, Robert M. Statement. **In** *The 1969 Economic Report of the President, Pt. 2, JECH,* 1969, pp. 500–504. [G: U.S.]

de Wolff, Pieter. Experience with Econometric Analysis of the U.S. "Konjunktur" Position: Comment. **In** *Bronfenbrenner, M., ed.*, 1969, pp. 389–92. [G: U.S.]

Zarnowitz, Victor. The New ASA-NBER Survey of Forecasts by Economic Statisticians. *Amer. Statist.*, February 1969, *23*(1), pp. 12–16. [G: U.S.]

1323 Specific Forecasts for a Sector

Aczel, J. A. The Usefulness of the CBI Industrial Trends Survey for Forecasting in the Chemical Industry. *Appl. Econ.*, August 1969, *1*(3), pp. 205–10. [G: U.K.]

Bolton, Roger E. Predictive Models for State and Local Government Purchases. **In** *Duesenberry, J. S., et al.*, 1969, pp. 221–67. [G: U.S.]

Duthu, Marie-Françoise. La prévision des structures d'emploi par la méthode des comparaisons internationales et intersectorielles. (With English summary.) *Revue Écon.*, July 1969, *20*(4), pp. 684–701.

Evans, Michael K. and Kisselgoff, Avram. Demand for Consumer Installment Credit and Its Effects on Consumption. **In** *Duesenberry, J. S., et al.*, 1969, pp. 39–84. [G: U.S.]

Glynn, D. R. The CBI Industrial Trends Survey. *Appl. Econ.*, August 1969, *1*(3), pp. 183–96. [G: U.K.]

Goldfeld, Stephen H. An Extension of the Monetary Sector. **In** *Duesenberry, J. S., et al.*, 1969, pp. 317–59. [G: U.S.]

Koumarová, Miluše and Vaner, Josef. Long-term Projection of the Sectoral Structure of the Czechoslovak National Economy on the Basis of an Input-Output Model. *Czech. Econ. Pap.*, 1969, (11), pp. 69–82. [G: Czechoslovakia]

de Leeuw, Frank. A Condensed Model of Financial Behavior. **In** *Duesenberry, J. S., et al.*, 1969, pp. 270–315. [G: U.S.]

Lovell, Michael C. Department Store Inventory, Sales, Order Relationships. **In** *Duesenberry, J. S., et al.*, 1969, pp. 18–38. [G: U.S.]

Reid, David J. The CBI Industrial Trends Survey—A Statistical Note. *Appl. Econ.*, August 1969, *1*(3), pp. 197–203. [G: U.K.]

Saarsalmi, Meeri. Kuluttajain ostoaikomukset ja ostotodennäköisyydet kysyntäennusteissa. (Consumer Buying Intentions and Purchase Probability in Forecasting Demand. With English summary.) *Liiketaloudellinen Aikak.*, 1969, *18* (3), pp. 576–84.

Stekler, H. O. Evaluation of Econometric Inventory Forecasts. *Rev. Econ. Statist.*, February 1969, *51* (1), pp. 77–83.

Taubman, Paul. Econometric Functions for Government Receipts. In *Duesenberry, J. S., et al.*, 1969, pp. 188–220. **[G: U.S.]**

Wimsatt, Genevieve B. 1969 Business Investment Programs and Sales—Strong Advances Expected. *Surv. Curr. Bus.*, March 1969, *49*(3), pp. 17–22. **[G: U.S.]**

1324 Forecasting Models; Theory and Methodology

Ando, Albert and Modigliani, Franco. Econometric Analysis of Stabilization Policies. *Amer. Econ. Rev.*, May 1969, *59*(2), pp. 296–314. **[G: U.S.]**

Barthelemy, Serge. La Methode de Projection à Moyen Terme des Circuits Financiers Utilisée dans la Préparation du Ve Plan Français. (With English summary.) *Rev. Income Wealth*, March 1969, *15*(1), pp. 77–100. **[G: France]**

Baturin, F. and Shemetov, P. Activities of Siberian Economists. *Prob. Econ.*, November 1969, *12*(7), pp. 67–77. **[G: U.S.S.R.]**

Bestuzhev-Lada, Igor. Forecasting—An Approach to the Problems of the Future. *Int. Soc. Sci. J.*, 1969, *21*(4), pp. 526–34. **[G: U.S.S.R.]**

Biolley, T. and Paelinck, J. A Dynamic Model for the Belgian Economy: Simulation and Optimization. *Econ. Planning*, 1969, *9*(1–2), pp. 155–207. **[G: Belgium]**

Bródy, A. Methods of Analysis and Forecasting Applied in Hungary. *Acta Oecon.*, 1969, *4*(3), pp. 299–314.

Burch, S. W. and Stekler, H. O. The Forecasting Accuracy of Consumer Attitude Data. *J. Amer. Statist. Assoc.*, December 1969, *64*(328), pp. 1225–33.

Coen, P. J.; Gomme, E. D. and Kendall, M. G. Lagged Relationships in Economic Forecasting. *J. Roy. Statist. Soc.*, Part 2, 1969, *132*, pp. 133–52.

Cohen, Malcolm S. Married Women in the Labor Force: An Analysis of Participation Rates. *Mon. Lab. Rev.*, October 1969, *92*(10), pp. 31–35. **[G: U.S.]**

Davis, Richard G. Monetary Theory: Discussion. *Amer. Econ. Rev.*, May 1969, *59*(2), pp. 315–21. **[G: U.S.]**

Gupta, Kanhaya L. Money Supply, Cyclical Fluctuations, and Income Determination. *Jahr. Nationalökon. Statist.*, May 1969, *182*(6), pp. 465–78. **[G: Canada]**

Helliwell, John F., et al. Econometric Analysis of Policy Choices for an Open Economy. *Rev. Econ. Statist.*, November 1969, *51*(4), pp. 383–98. **[G: Canada]**

Horowitz, Irving Louis. Engineering and Sociological Perspectives on Development: Interdisciplinary Constraints in Social Forecasting. *Int. Soc. Sci. J.*, 1969, *21*(4), pp. 545–56.

Jeffrey, D.; Casetti, E. and King, L. Economic Fluctuations in a Multiregional Setting: A Bi-factor Analytic Approach. *J. Reg. Sci.*, December 1969, *9*(3), pp. 397–404. **[G: U.S.]**

Klein, Lawrence R. Estimation on Interdependent Systems in Macroeconometrics. *Econometrica*, April 1969, *37*(2), pp. 171–92.

L'Esperance, Wilford L.; Nestel, G. and Fromm, D. Gross State Product and an Econometric Model of a State. *J. Amer. Statist. Assoc.*, September 1969, *64*(327), pp. 787–807. **[G: U.S.]**

de Leeuw, Frank and Gramlich, Edward M. The Channels of Monetary Policy: A Further Report on the Federal Reserve-M.I.T. Model. *J. Finance*, May 1969, *24*(2), pp. 265–90. **[G: U.S.]**

Leroux, Roger and Raffoul, Faouzi. An Essay in Simulating Economic Policies for the French Economy. *Econ. Planning*, 1969, *9*(1–2), pp. 95–153. **[G: France]**

Loznevaia, M. Mathematical Methods in Planning Wages. *Prob. Econ.*, June 1969, *12*(2), pp. 48–66. **[G: U.S.S.R.]**

Marwah, Kanta. An Econometric Model of Colombia: A Prototype Devaluation View. *Econometrica*, April 1969, *37*(2), pp. 228–51. **[G: Colombia]**

Minsky, Hyman P. Financial Model Building and Federal Reserve Policy: Discussion. *J. Finance*, May 1969, *24*(2), pp. 295–97. **[G: U.S.]**

Moody, Harold T. and Puffer, Frank W. A Gross Regional Product Approach to Regional Model-Building. *Western Econ. J.*, December 1969, *7*(4), pp. 391–402. **[G: U.S.]**

Richta, Radovan and Šulc, Ota. Forecasting and the Scientific and Technological Revolution. *Int. Soc. Sci. J.*, 1969, *21*(4), pp. 563–73.

Thurow, Lester C. A Fiscal Policy Model of the United States. *Surv. Curr. Bus.*, June 1969, *49*(6), pp. 45–64. **[G: U.S.]**

Turner, Robert C. Macro Forecasting in the Philippines: An Experiment. *Philippine Econ. J.*, Second Semester 1969, *8*(2), pp. 185–201. **[G: Philippines]**

White, William H. The Usefulness of Econometric Models for Policymakers. *Finance Develop.*, September 1969, *6*(3), pp. 8–13.

van Winkel, E. G. F. Extrapolationen einer Zeitreihe durch exponentiell abnehmende Gewichtung. (Extrapolation of Time Series by Exponential Smoothing. With English summary.) *Ifo-Studien*, 1969, *15*(1/2), pp. 1–18.

133 General Outlook and Stabilization Theories and Policies

1330 General Outlook

Calmus, Thomas W. Current Trends in the National Economy. *Oregon Bus. Rev.*, February 1969, *28*(2), pp. 1, 4–8. **[G: U.S.]**

Feiwel, George R. Czechoslovakia's Economic Dilemma. *Indian Econ. J.*, July–September 1969, *17*(1), pp. 1–27. **[G: Czechoslovakia]**

Lall, Sanjaya. Countering Inflation: The Role of Value Linking. *Finance Develop.*, June 1969, *6*(2), pp. 10–15.

Madden, Carl H. Statement. In *The 1969 Economic Report of the President, Pt. 3, JECH*, 1969, pp. 931–36. **[G: U.S.]**

Mayo, Robert P. Statement. In *The 1969 Economic Report of the President, Pt. 2, JECH*, 1969, pp. 337–42. **[G: U.S.]**

McCracken, Paul W. Statement. **In** *The 1969 Economic Report of the President, Pt. 2, JECH,* 1969, pp. 284–304. **[G: U.S.]**

Reuther, Walter P. Statement. **In** *The 1969 Economic Report of the President, Pt. 4, JECH,* 1969, pp. 1156–84. **[G: U.S.]**

Shultz, George P. Statement. **In** *The 1969 Economic Report of the President, Pt. 2, JECH,* 1969, pp. 426–45. **[G: U.S.]**

Stans, Maurice H. Statement. **In** *The 1969 Economic Report of the President, Pt. 3, JECH,* 1969, pp. 726–32. **[G: U.S.]**

Turner, Robert C. The Nation—Is Government Policy Curbing Consumer Spending? *Indiana Bus. Rev.,* March–April 1969, *44,* pp. 14–16. **[G: U.S.]**

Volcker, Paul A. Statement. **In** *The 1969 Economic Report of the President, Pt. 3, JECH,* 1969, pp. 732–37. **[G: U.S.]**

Wimsatt, Genevieve B. 1969 Business Investment Programs and Sales—Strong Advances Expected. *Surv. Curr. Bus.,* March 1969, *49*(3), pp. 17–22. **[G: U.S.]**

1331 Stabilization Theories and Policies

Allen, Clark Lee. Are National Full-Employment Policies Consistent with Freer Trade? *Nebr. J. Econ. Bus.,* Winter 1968–69, *8*(1), pp. 3–15.

Andersen, Leonall C. and Jordan, Jerry L. Monetary and Fiscal Actions: A Test of Their Relative Importance in Economic Stabilization—Reply. *Fed. Res. Bank St. Louis Rev.,* April 1969, *51*(4), pp. 12–16. **[G: U.S.]**

Bach, George L. Statement. **In** *The 1969 Economic Report of the President, Pt. 3, JECH,* 1969, pp. 537–42. **[G: U.S.]**

Bhatia, Rattan J.; Szapary, Gyorgy and Quinn, Brian. Stabilization Program in Sierra Leone. *Int. Monet. Fund Staff Pap.,* November 1969, *16*(3), pp. 504–28. **[G: Sierra Leone]**

Boulding, Kenneth E. David Fand's "Keynesian Monetary Theories, Stabilization Policy, and the Recent Inflation": A Comment. *J. Money, Credit, Banking,* August 1969, *1*(3), pp. 588–89. **[G: U.S.]**

Bowsher, Norman N. 1969—Battle Against Inflation. *Fed. Res. Bank St. Louis Rev.,* December 1969, *51*(12), pp. 2–12. **[G: U.S.]**

Bronfenbrenner, Martin. Statement. **In** *The 1969 Economic Report of the President, Pt. 3, JECH,* 1969, pp. 542–45. **[G: U.S.]**

Brunner, Karl. The Monetary Fiscal Dilemma. *Ohio State U. Bull. Bus. Res.,* June 1969, *44*(6), pp. 1–5, 8. **[G: U.S.]**

Brunner, Karl. The Policy Discussions by Stein and Worswick: A Comment. *J. Money, Credit, Banking,* August 1969, *1*(3), pp. 496–502. **[G: U.S.; U.K.]**

Buonomo, Maurizio. La stabilità economica interna, presupposto dell'equilibrio monetario internazionale. (Internal Economic Stability, the Prerequisite for International Monetary Equilibrium. With English summary.) *Bancaria,* June 1969, *25*(6), pp. 725–30.

Burns, Arthur Frank. Heller's "New Dimensions of Political Economy." **In** *Burns, A. F.,* 1969, pp. 303–12. **[G: U.S.]**

Burns, Arthur Frank. The Nature and Causes of Business Cycles. **In** *Burns, A. F.,* 1969, pp. 3–53.

Carli, Guido. Programmi e prospettive della politica monetaria internazionale. (International Monetary Policy of the Moment—Programs and Outlooks. With English summary.) *Bancaria,* December 1969, *25*(12), pp. 1459–63.

Carlson, Keith M. A Program of Budget Restraint. *Fed. Res. Bank St. Louis Rev.,* March 1969, *51*(3), pp. 10–14. **[G: U.S.]**

Coen, Robert M. Tax Policy and Investment Behavior: Comment. *Amer. Econ. Rev.,* June 1969, *59*(3), pp. 370–79. **[G: U.S.]**

Collado, Emilio G. Statement. **In** *The 1969 Economic Report of the President, Pt. 4, JECH,* 1969, pp. 983–92. **[G: U.S.]**

Colombo, Emilio. Equilibrio della bilancia dei pagamenti e utilizzo delle risorse senza inflazione. (Equilibrium of the Balance of Payments and Internal Use of Resources without Inflation. With English summary.) *Bancaria,* October 1969, *25*(10), pp. 1221–24. **[G: Italy]**

Culbertson, John M. Statement. **In** *The 1969 Economic Report of the President, Pt. 3, JECH,* 1969, pp. 545–47. **[G: U.S.]**

Douty, H. M. Some Aspects of British Wage Policy. *Southern Econ. J.,* July 1969, *36*(1), pp. 74–81. **[G: U.K.]**

Eisner, Robert. Tax Policy and Investment Behavior: Comment. *Amer. Econ. Rev.,* June 1969, *59*(3), pp. 379–88. **[G: U.S.]**

Ekelund, Robert B., Jr. and Gramm, William P. A Reconsideration of Advertising Expenditures, Aggregate Demand, and Economic Stabilization. *Quart. Rev. Econ. Bus.,* Summer 1969, *9*(2), pp. 71–77. **[G: U.S.]**

Ellis, Howard S. Corrective Inflation in Brazil, 1964–1966. **In** *Ellis, H. S., ed.,* 1969, pp. 177–212. **[G: Brazil]**

Fand, David I. Keynesian Monetary Theories, Stabilization Policy, and the Recent Inflation. *J. Money, Credit, Banking,* August 1969, *1*(3), pp. 556–87. **[G: U.S.]**

Francis, Darryl R. Controlling Inflation. *Fed. Res. Bank St. Louis Rev.,* September 1969, *51*(9), pp. 8–12.

Geyer, Herbert. Linear Tax Variations in the Stabilization Law. *Finanzarchiv,* October 1968, *28*(1), pp. 96–99. **[G: W. Germany]**

Hagedorn, George G. Statement. **In** *The 1969 Economic Report of the President, Pt. 3, JECH,* 1969, pp. 919–28. **[G: U.S.]**

Hall, Robert E. and Jorgenson, Dale W. Tax Policy and Investment Behavior: Reply and Further Results. *Amer. Econ. Rev.,* June 1969, *59*(3), pp. 388–401. **[G: U.S.]**

Harrod, Roy F. [Sir]. Problemi monetari d'oggi. (Survey of Monetary Problems. With English summary.) *Bancaria,* July 1969, *25*(7), pp. 819–28.

Helliwell, John F. Monetary and Fiscal Policies for an Open Economy. *Oxford Econ. Pap.,* March 1969, *21*(1), pp. 35–55.

de Jongh, T. W. Review of the Financial and Economic Situation in South Africa. *S. Afr. J. Econ.*, September 1969, *37*(3), pp. 187–97. **[G: S. Africa]**

Kanesa-Thasan, S. Stabilizing an Economy—A Study of the Republic of Korea. *Int. Monet. Fund Staff Pap.*, March 1969, *16*(1), pp. 1–26. **[G: S. Korea]**

Kenen, Peter B. The New Fiscal Policy: A Comment. *J. Money, Credit, Banking,* August 1969, *1*(3), pp. 503–05. **[G: U.S.; U.K.]**

Keran, Michael W. Monetary and Fiscal Influences on Economic Activity—The Historical Evidence. *Fed. Res. Bank St. Louis Rev.*, November 1969, *51* (11), pp. 5–24. **[G: U.S.]**

Keyserling, Leon H. Statement. **In** *The 1969 Economic Report of the President, Pt. 4, JECH,* 1969, pp. 999–1056. **[G: U.S.]**

Khalid, Rasheed O. Fiscal Policy, Development Planning, and Annual Budgeting. *Int. Monet. Fund Staff Pap.*, March 1969, *16*(1), pp. 53–84.

Killingsworth, Charles C. Full Employment and the New Economics. *Scot. J. Polit. Econ.*, February 1969, *16*(1), pp. 1–19.

de Leeuw, Frank and Kalchbrenner, John. Monetary and Fiscal Actions: A Test of Their Relative Importance in Economic Stabilization—Comment. *Fed. Res. Bank St. Louis Rev.*, April 1969, *51*(4), pp. 6–11. **[G: U.S.]**

Linnamo, Jussi. Vakauttamispolitiikasta tasapainoisen kasvun politiikkaan. (From Stabilization Policy to a Policy of Balanced Economic Growth. With English summary.) *Kansant. Aikak.*, 1969, *65*(3), pp. 171–80. **[G: Finland]**

Logue, Ruth. Imported Inflation and the International Adjustment Process. (Study summary.) *Fed. Res. Bull.*, December 1969, *55*(12), pp. 920. **[G: Europe]**

Lundberg, Erik. Postwar Stabilization Policies. **In** *Bronfenbrenner, M., ed.*, 1969, pp. 477–98.

Maddison, Angus. Postwar Stabilization Policies: Comment. **In** *Bronfenbrenner, M., ed.*, 1969, pp. 499–501.

Martin, William McChesney, Jr. Statement. **In** *The 1969 Economic Report of the President, Pt. 3, JECH,* 1969, pp. 647–52. **[G: U.S.]**

Massell, Benton F. Price Stabilization and Welfare. *Quart. J. Econ.*, May 1969, *83*(2), pp. 284–98.

McKinnon, Ronald I. Portfolio Balance and International Payments Adjustment. **In** *Mundell, R. A. and Swoboda, A. K., eds.*, 1969, pp. 199–234.

Mitchell, Joan. Why We Need a Prices Policy. *Lloyds Bank Rev.*, April 1969, (92), pp. 1–14. **[G: U.K.]**

Paish, Frank W. The Control of Demand. **In** *[von Hayek, Friedrich A.]*, 1969, pp. 147–64.

Raunio, Eino. Näkökohtia vuoden 1969 budjettiesityksestä. (Government Budget Proposal for 1969. With English summary.) *Kansant. Aikak.*, 1969, *65*(1), pp. 1–5. **[G: Finland]**

Ristimäki, Juhani. Valtion tuki ja tulopolitiikka. (Government Support and Incomes Policy. With English summary.) *Kansant. Aikak.*, 1969, *65*(1), pp. 6–20. **[G: Finland]**

Šíba, Vladimír. Economic Reform and Income Policy. *New Trends Czech. Econ.*, May 1969, (3), pp. 26–46. **[G: Czechoslovakia]**

Sinha, J. N. Framework of Incomes and Wage Policy in India. **In** *Johri, C. K., ed.*, 1969, pp. 235–53. **[G: India]**

Snyder, Wayne W. La mésure des effets des politiques budgétaires françaises de 1955 à 1965. (With English summary.) *Revue Écon.*, November 1969, *20*(6), pp. 929–53. **[G: France]**

Sohmen, Egon. The Assignment Problem. **In** *Mundell, R. A. and Swoboda, A. K., eds.*, 1969, pp. 183–97.

Sokol, Miroslav. Observations on Economic Development. *Eastern Europ. Econ.*, Fall 1969, *8*(1), pp. 3–19. **[G: Czechoslovakia]**

Stefani, Giorgio. Politica fiscale a politica monetaria per la stabilità negli Stati Uniti-I. (Fiscal Policy and Monetary Policy for the Stability of the United States-I. With English summary.) *Bancaria,* February 1969, *25*(2), pp. 147–69. **[G: U.S.]**

Stefani, Giorgio. Politica fiscale e politica monetaria per la stabilità negli Stati Uniti-II. (Fiscal Policy and Monetary Policy for the Stability of the United States-II. With English summary.) *Bancaria,* March 1969, *25*(3), pp. 303–20. **[G: U.S.]**

Stein, Jerome L. and Nagatani, Keizo. Stabilization Policies in a Growing Economy. *Rev. Econ. Stud.*, April 1969, *36*(106), pp. 165–83.

Tait, Alan A. Deflation and Incomes Policy: The British Budget 1968/69. *Finanzarchiv,* October 1968, *28*(1), pp. 110–25. **[G: U.K.]**

Terborgh, George. The Inflation Dilemma. **In** *The 1969 Economic Report of the President, Pt. 4, JECH,* 1969, pp. 1066–1109. **[G: U.S.]**

Thirlwall, A. P. Unemployment Compensation as an Automatic Stabilizer. *Bull. Oxford Univ. Inst. Econ. Statist.*, February 1969, *31*(1), pp. 23–37. **[G: U.K.]**

Tobin, James. On Improving the Economic Status of the Negro. **In** *Starleaf, D. R., ed.*, 1969, pp. 429–35. **[G: U.S.]**

Turner, Robert C. Statement. **In** *The 1969 Economic Report of the President, Pt. 3, JECH,* 1969, pp. 548–50. **[G: U.S.]**

Typolt, Jiří. Economic Policy and Prices. *New Trends Czech. Econ.*, July 1969, (4), pp. 89–102. **[G: Czechoslovakia]**

Ulman, Lloyd. Wage-Price Policies: Some Lessons from Abroad. *Ind. Relat.*, May 1969, *8*(3), pp. 195–213.

Wallich, Henry C. Keynesian Monetary Theories, Stabilization Policy, and the Recent Inflation: A Comment. *J. Money, Credit, Banking,* August 1969, *1*(3), pp. 590–99. **[G: U.S.]**

Weidenbaum, Murray L. Statement. **In** *Unemployment Compensation, HCH,* 1969, pp. 221–25. **[G: U.S.]**

Worswick, G. D. N. Fiscal Policy and Stabilization in Britain. *J. Money, Credit, Banking,* August 1969, *1*(3), pp. 474–95. **[G: U.K.]**

1332 Wage and Price Controls

Burns, Arthur F. The Case Against the Guideposts. **In** *Starleaf, D. R., ed.*, 1969, pp. 338–46. **[G: U.S.]**

Eckstein, Otto. Alternatives to Guideposts. **In** *Wortman, M. S., Jr.*, 1969, pp. 420–21. **[G: U.S.]**

134 Inflation and Deflation

1340 General

Baggott, Nancy and Flanders, M. June. Economic Policy in an Open Economy: A Reader's Guide. *Econ. Int.*, November 1969, *22*(4), pp. 593–605.

Buonomo, Maurizio. Moneta e credito nelle economie socialiste: vecchi e nuovi orientamenti. (Money and Credit in Socialist Economies: Old Trends and New. With English summary.) *Bancaria*, April 1969, *25*(4), pp. 449–59.

Burns, Arthur F. The Case Against the Guideposts. In *Starleaf, D. R., ed.*, 1969, pp. 338–46. **[G: U.S.]**

Burns, Arthur Frank. Dealing with Recession and Inflation. In *Burns, A. F.*, 1969, pp. 129–50.

Francis, Darryl R. Controlling Inflation. *Fed. Res. Bank St. Louis Rev.*, September 1969, *51*(9), pp. 8–12.

Francis, Darryl R. Monetary Policy and Inflation. *Fed. Res. Bank St. Louis Rev.*, June 1969, *51*(6), pp. 8–11. **[G: U.S.]**

Keynes, John Maynard. The Inflationary Gap. In *Ball, R. J. and Doyle, P., eds.*, 1969, pp. 21–27.

McCracken, Paul W. The Game Plan for Economic Policy. *Amer. Statist.*, October 1969, *23*(4), pp. 7–10. **[G: U.S.]**

Neumann, Seev. Anticipated and Unanticipated Inflation—Implications to Life Insurance. *J. Risk Ins.*, June 1969, *36*(2), pp. 315–19. **[G: U.S.]**

Shaw, B. D. The New Zealand Economy, 1967–68. *Econ. Rec.*, March 1969, *45*(109), pp. 1–16. **[G: New Zealand]**

Srivastava, U. K. P. L. 480 Counterpart Funds and Inflation: Myth and Realty. *Asian Econ. Rev.*, February 1969, *11*(2), pp. 145–59. **[G: India]**

Stahl, Sheldon W. A Look at Some Measures of Inflation. In *Starleaf, D. R., ed.*, 1969, pp. 302–08. **[G: U.S.]**

Turner, Robert C. The Nation—Is Government Policy Curbing Consumer Spending? *Indiana Bus. Rev.*, March-April 1969, *44*, pp. 14–16. **[G: U.S.]**

Wassom, John C. Inflation as a Tool for Promoting Growth. *Nebr. J. Econ. Bus.*, Winter 1968–69, *8* (1), pp. 34–43.

1342 Inflation Theories; Studies Illustrating Inflation Theories

Akerlof, George A. Relative Wages and the Rate of Inflation. *Quart. J. Econ.*, August 1969, *83*(3), pp. 353–74.

Allais, Maurice. Growth and Inflation. *J. Money, Credit, Banking*, August 1969, *1*(3), pp. 355–426. **[G: U.K.]**

Anderson, Paul S. Wages and the Guideposts: Comment. *Amer. Econ. Rev.*, June 1969, *59*(3), pp. 351–54. **[G: U.S.]**

Archibald, G. C. The Phillips Curve and the Distribution of Unemployment. *Amer. Econ. Rev.*, May 1969, *59*(2), pp. 124–34. **[G: U.S.; U.K.]**

Birch, John I. and Cramer, Curtis. A Secular Theory of Inflation. *J. Econ. Theory*, December 1969, *1* (4), pp. 480–86.

Bird, Monroe M. Statement. In *Proposed Extension of the Surcharge and Repeal of the Investment Tax Credit, SCH*, 1969, pp. 486–88. **[G: U.S.]**

Boulding, Kenneth E. David Fand's "Keynesian Monetary Theories, Stabilization Policy, and the Recent Inflation": A Comment. *J. Money, Credit, Banking*, August 1969, *1*(3), pp. 588–89. **[G: U.S.]**

Bowen, William G. The Dilemma Model Re-examined. In *Ball, R. J. and Doyle, P., eds.*, 1969, pp. 255–73.

Brechling, Frank. Wage-Price Dynamics, Inflation, and Unemployment: Discussion. *Amer. Econ. Rev.*, May 1969, *59*(2), pp. 161–62.

Brunner, Karl. The Monetary Fiscal Dilemma. *Ohio State U. Bull. Bus. Res.*, June 1969, *44*(6), pp. 1–5, 8. **[G: U.S.]**

Burger, Albert E. The Effects of Inflation (1960–68). *Fed. Res. Bank St. Louis Rev.*, November 1969, *51* (11), pp. 25–36. **[G: U.S.]**

Burns, Arthur Frank. The New Environment of Monetary Policy. In *Burns, A. F.*, 1969, pp. 151–74. **[G: U.S.]**

Burns, Arthur Frank. The Perils of Inflation. In *Burns, A. F.*, 1969, pp. 286–302. **[G: U.S.]**

Cagan, P. The Theory of Hyperinflation. In *Ball, R. J. and Doyle, P., eds.*, 1969, pp. 117–35.

Charles, K. J. Inflation and Economic Growth. *Econ. Aff.*, January-February 1969, *14*(1–2), pp. 26–32.

Ciocca, Pierluigi. L'ipotesi del "ritardo" dei salari rispetto ai prezzi in periodi di inflazione: alcune considerazioni generali-II. (The Hypothesis of the Lag of Wages behind Prices during Inflation: General Considerations-II. With English summary.) *Bancaria*, May 1969, *25*(5), pp. 572–83.

Ciocca, Pierluigi. L'ipotesi del "ritardo" dei salari rispetto ai prezzi in periodi di inflazione: alcune considerazioni generali-I. (The Hypothesis of the "Lag" of Wages behind Prices during Inflation: General Considerations-I. With English summary.) *Bancaria*, April 1969, *25*(4), pp. 423–37.

Colaco, Francis X. Harberger's Inflation Model: A Critique and Test Using Data for Brazil and India. *Indian Econ. J.*, April-June 1969, *16*(4–5), pp. 434–44. **[G: Brazil; India]**

Courchene, Thomas J. An Analysis of the Price-Inventory Nexus with Empirical Application to the Canadian Manufacturing Sector. *Int. Econ. Rev.*, October 1969, *10*(3), pp. 315–36. **[G: Canada]**

Eckstein, Otto. Wage-Price Dynamics, Inflation, and Unemployment: Discussion. *Amer. Econ. Rev.*, May 1969, *59*(2), pp. 162–64.

Eisner, Robert. Fiscal and Monetary Policy Reconsidered. *Amer. Econ. Rev.*, December 1969, *59*(5), pp. 897–905. **[G: U.S.]**

Fand, David I. A Monetary Interpretation of the Post-1965 Inflation in the United States. *Banca Naz. Lavoro Quart. Rev.*, June 1969, (89), pp. 99–127. **[G: U.S.]**

Fand, David I. Keynesian Monetary Theories, Stabilization Policy, and the Recent Inflation. *J. Money, Credit, Banking*, August 1969, *1*(3), pp. 556–87. **[G: U.S.]**

George, P. V. Secular Price Behaviour in a Dual

Market Economy. *Indian Econ. J.*, April–June 1969, *16*(4–5), pp. 532–43.

Gollop, Frank. Structural Inflation. *Amer. Econ.*, Fall 1969, *13*(2), pp. 31–39. [G: U.S.]

Haberler, Gottfried. Wage-Push Inflation Once More. In *[von Hayek, Friedrich A.]*, 1969, pp. 65–73.

Hazard, John L. Transportation and the Public Utilities: Discussion. *Amer. Econ. Rev.*, May 1969, *59* (2), pp. 271–74.

Hess, Alan C. A Quantity Theory Approach to the Current Inflation. *Univ. Wash. Bus. Rev.*, Summer 1969, *28*(4), pp. 12–17. [G: U.S.]

Hines, A. G. Wage Inflation in the United Kingdom 1948–62: A Disaggregated Study. *Econ. J.*, March 1969, *79*(313), pp. 66–89. [G: U.K.]

Hoffmann, Walther G. Die "Phillips-Kurve" in Deutschland. (With English summary.) *Kyklos*, 1969, *22*(2), pp. 219–31. [G: W. Germany]

Holt, Charles C. Improving the Labor Market Trade-Off between Inflation and Unemployment. *Amer. Econ. Rev.*, May 1969, *59*(2), pp. 135–46.

Howrey, E. Philip. Distributed Lags and Effectiveness of Monetary Policy: Note. *Amer. Econ. Rev.*, December 1969, *59*(5), pp. 997–1001.

Humphrey, David B. Changes in Protection and Inflation in Argentina, 1953–1966. *Oxford Econ. Pap.*, July 1969, *21*(2), pp. 196–219. [G: Argentina]

Jacobsson, Lars and Lindbeck, Assar. Labor Market Condition, Wages and Inflation—Swedish Experiences 1955–67. *Swedish J. Econ.*, June 1969, *71* (2), pp. 64–103. [G: Sweden]

Johnson, Glenn L. Professor Johnson's Hedges: A Reply. *Miss. Val. J. Bus. Econ.*, Fall 1969, *5*(1), pp. 85–89.

Koot, Ronald S. Wage Changes, Unemployment, and Inflation in Chile. *Ind. Lab. Relat. Rev.*, July 1969, *22*(4), pp. 568–75. [G: Chile]

Lester, Richard A. Wage-Price Dynamics, Inflation, and Unemployment: Discussion. *Amer. Econ. Rev.*, May 1969, *59*(2), pp. 164–67.

Liebling, H. I. and Cluff, A. T. U.S. Postwar Inflation and Phillips Curves. *Kyklos*, 1969, *22*(2), pp. 232–50. [G: U.S.]

Lucas, Robert E., Jr. and Rapping, Leonard A. Price Expectations and the Phillips Curve. *Amer. Econ. Rev.*, June 1969, *59*(3), pp. 342–50. [G: U.S.]

Lucas, Robert E., Jr. and Rapping, Leonard A. Real Wages, Employment, and Inflation. *J. Polit. Econ.*, September/October 1969, *77*(5), pp. 721–54. [G: U.S.]

Meidner, Rudolf. Active Manpower Policy and the Inflation Unemployment-Dilemma. *Swedish J. Econ.*, September 1969, *71*(3), pp. 161–83.

Mikesell, Raymond F. Inflation in Latin America. In *Nisbet, C. T., ed.*, 1969, pp. 143–89. [G: Latin America]

Mitchell, Daniel J. B. A Simplified Approach to Incomes Policy. *Ind. Lab. Relat. Rev.*, July 1969, *22* (4), pp. 512–27.

Molander, Ahti. Inflaatiotutkimuksen vaiheista ja ongelmista. (Phases and Problems of Inflation Research. With English summary.) *Kansant. Aikak.*, 1969, *65*(4), pp. 269–73.

Neumann, Seev. Inflation and Saving through Life Insurance. *J. Risk Ins.*, December 1969, *36*(5), pp. 567–82. [G: U.S.]

Paish, Frank W. Unemployment and Price Stability. In *Ball, R. J. and Doyle, P., eds.*, 1969, pp. 219–54.

Perry, George L. Wages and the Guideposts: Reply. *Amer. Econ. Rev.*, June 1969, *59*(3), pp. 365–70. [G: U.S.]

Phelps, Edmund S. The New Microeconomics in Inflation and Employment Theory. *Amer. Econ. Rev.*, May 1969, *59*(2), pp. 147–60.

Phlips, Louis. Business Pricing Policies and Inflation—Some Evidence from E.E.C. Countries. *J. Ind. Econ.*, November 1969, *18*(1), pp. 1–14. [G: Belgium; Netherlands; France]

Rychetnik, Ludek. The Growth of Inflationary Pressure: 1955–1966. *Eastern Europ. Econ.*, Spring 1969, *7*(3), pp. 3–11. [G: Czechoslovakia]

Schröder, Jürgen. Zur partialanalytischen Darstellung des direkten internationalen Preiszusammenhangs. Bemerkungen zu einem Aufsatz von O. Issing. (With English summary.) *Jahr. Nationalökon. Statist.*, August 1969, *183*(3–4), pp. 306–15.

Simone, Dante. Sobre teoría monetaria en alta inflación. (On Monetary Theory in High Inflation. With English summary.) *Económica*, May–August 1969, *15*(2), pp. 183–209.

Spencer, Roger W. The Relation between Prices and Employment: Two Views. *Fed. Res. Bank St. Louis Rev.*, March 1969, *51*(3), pp. 15–21.

Sufrin, Sidney C. and Wagner, Abraham R. Disaggregate Employment: The Search for Short Run Demand and Labor Market Stability. *Rivista Int. Sci. Econ. Com.*, October 1969, *16*(10), pp. 965–92. [G: U.S.]

Sufrin, Sidney C. and Wagner, Abraham R. Interest Rate Manipulation, Employment and Output—A Disaggregated Suggestion. *Rivista Int. Sci. Econ. Com.*, April 1969, *16*(4), pp. 327–41. [G: U.S.]

Thirlwall, A. P. Demand Disequilibrium in the Labour Market and Wage Rate Inflation in the United Kingdom (1) *Yorkshire Bull. Econ. Soc. Res.*, May 1969, *21*(1), pp. 66–76. [G: U.K.]

Throop, Adrian W. Wages and the Guideposts: Comment. *Amer. Econ. Rev.*, June 1969, *59*(3), pp. 358–65. [G: U.S.]

Wachter, Michael L. Wages and the Guideposts: Comment. *Amer. Econ. Rev.*, June 1969, *59*(3), pp. 354–58. [G: U.S.]

Wallich, Henry C. Keynesian Monetary Theories, Stabilization Policy, and the Recent Inflation: A Comment. *J. Money, Credit, Banking*, August 1969, *1*(3), pp. 590–99. [G: U.S.]

Walsh, Cornelius F. Professor Johnson's Hedges. *Miss. Val. J. Bus. Econ.*, Fall 1969, *5*(1), pp. 80–84.

Wilson, George W. Transportation and Price Stability. *Amer. Econ. Rev.*, May 1969, *59*(2), pp. 261–69.

Yohe, William P. and Karnosky, Denis S. Interest Rates and Price Level Changes, 1952–69. *Fed. Res. Bank St. Louis Rev.*, December 1969, *51*(12), pp. 18–38. [G: U.S.]

Zaidi, Mahmood A. The Determinants of Money Wage Rate Changes and Unemployment-Inflation "Trade-Offs" in Canada. *Int. Econ. Rev.*, June 1969, *10*(2), pp. 207–19. [G: Canada]

200 Quantitative Economic Methods and Data

210 Econometric, Statistical, and Mathematical Methods and Models

211 Econometric and Statistical Methods and Models

2110 General

Biji, Mircea; Ivănescu, I. and Biji, El. Preocupări actuale în statistica social-economică. (Present Preoccupations in Socio-Economical Statistics. With English summary.) *Stud. Cercet. Econ.*, 1969, *1-2*, pp. 121–28.

Blischke, W. R.; Truelove, A. J. and Mundle, P. B. On Non-Regular Estimation, I. Variance Bounds for Estimators of Location Parameters. *J. Amer. Statist. Assoc.*, September 1969, *64*(327), pp. 1056–72.

Bródy, A. Methods of Analysis and Forecasting Applied in Hungary. *Acta Oecon.*, 1969, *4*(3), pp. 299–314.

Broemeling, L. D. Confidence for Variance Ratios of Random Models. *J. Amer. Statist. Assoc.*, June 1969, *64*(326), pp. 660–64.

Cassidy, Henry J. Maximum Likelihood Estimation in an *n-th* Order Autoregressive Disturbance Model. *Southern Econ. J.*, January 1969, *35*(3), pp. 263–64.

Dagum, Camilo. Structural Permanence: Its Role in the Analysis of Structural Dualisms and Dependences and for Prediction and Decision Purposes. *Z. ges. Staatswiss.*, April 1969, *125*(2), pp. 211–35.

De Floriani, Walter. Stima non negativa della varianza nel campionamento a due stadi. (A Nonnegative Estimate of the Variance in the Two-Stage Sampling. With English summary.) *Rivista Int. Sci. Econ. Com.*, September 1969, *16* (9), pp. 889–97.

Dhrymes, Phoebus J. Alternative Asymptotic Tests of Significance and Related Aspects of 2SLS and 3SLS Estimated Parameters. *Rev. Econ. Stud.*, April 1969, *36*(106), pp. 213–26.

Duchan, Alan I. A Relationship between the F and t Statistics and the Simple Correlation Coefficients in Classical Least Squares Regression. *Amer. Statist.*, June 1969, *23*(3), pp. 27–28.

Easterling, Robert G. Discrimination Intervals for Percentiles in Regression. *J. Amer. Statist. Assoc.*, September 1969, *64*(327), pp. 1031–41.

Elston, R. C. An Analogue to Fieller's Theorem Using Scheffé's Solution to the Fisher-Behrens Problem. *Amer. Statist.*, February 1969, *23*(1), pp. 26–28.

Guenther, William C. Shortest Confidence Intervals. *Amer. Statist.*, February 1969, *23*(1), pp. 22–25.

Herzberg, Agnes M. and Cox, D. R. Recent Work on the Design of Experiments: A Bibliography and a Review. *J. Roy. Statist. Soc.*, Part 1, 1969, *132*, pp. 29–67.

Howe, W. G. Two-Sided Tolerance Limits for Normal Populations—Some Improvements. *J. Amer. Statist. Assoc.*, June 1969, *64*(326), pp. 610–20.

Hoyt, John P. Two Instructive Examples of Maximum Likelihood Estimates. *Amer. Statist.*, April 1969, *23*(2), pp. 14.

Koch, Gary G. A Useful Lemma for Proving the Equality of Two Matrices with Applications to Least Squares Type Quadratic Forms. *J. Amer. Statist. Assoc.*, September 1969, *64*(327), pp. 969–70.

Mandelbrot, Benoit. Long-Run Linearity, Locally Gaussian Process, H-Spectra and Infinite Variances. *Int. Econ. Rev.*, February 1969, *10*(1), pp. 82–111.

Mantel, Nathan. Functional Averages of a Variable. *Amer. Statist.*, February 1969, *23*(1), pp. 21–22.

McGilchrist, C. A. Discrete Distribution Estimators from the Recurrence Equation for Probabilities. *J. Amer. Statist. Assoc.*, June 1969, *64*(326), pp. 602–609.

Mehta, J. S. and Gurland, John. Combinations of Unbiased Estimators of the Mean Which Consider Inequality of Unknown Variances. *J. Amer. Statist. Assoc.*, September 1969, *64*(327), pp. 1042–55.

Mustafi, Chandan Kumar. A Recurrence Relation for Distribution Functions of Order Statistics from Bivariate Distributions. *J. Amer. Statist. Assoc.*, June 1969, *64*(326), pp. 600–601.

Muzio, Giovanni B. Su di un metodo di classificazione numerica nel caso di variabili unidimensionali. (With English summary.) *Statistica*, October-December 1969, *29*(4), pp. 699–725.

Neudecker, H. Some Theorems on Matrix Differentiation with Special Reference to Kronecker Matrix Products. *J. Amer. Statist. Assoc.*, September 1969, *64*(327), pp. 953–63.

Oi, Walter Y. On the Relationship among Different Members of the k-Class. *Int. Econ. Rev.*, February 1969, *10*(1), pp. 36–46.

Rao, J. N. K. and Bayless, D. L. An Empirical Study of the Stabilities of Estimators and Variance Estimators in Unequal Probability Sampling of Two Units per Stratum. *J. Amer. Statist. Assoc.*, June 1969, *64*(326), pp. 540–59.

Rao, Poduri S. R. S. Comparison of Four Ratio-Type Estimates under a Model. *J. Amer. Statist. Assoc.*, June 1969, *64*(326), pp. 574–80.

Rosekrans, Frank M. Statistical Significance and Reporting Test Results. *J. Marketing Res.*, November 1969, *6*(4), pp. 451–55.

Sastry, M. V. Rama. A Note on the Moments and Cumulants of a Weighted Mean. *Statistica*, January-March 1969, *29*(1), pp. 109–12.

Smith, V. Kerry. "The Identification Problem and the Validity of Economic Models": A Comment. *S. Afr. J. Econ.*, March 1969, *37*(1), pp. 81.

Stanley, Julian C. and Glass, Gene V. An Algebraic Proof That the Sum of the Squared Errors in Estimating Y from X Via b_1 and b_0 Is Minimal. *Amer. Statist.*, February 1969, *23*(1), pp. 25–26.

Steffens, F. E. Critical Values for Bivariate Student

t-Tests. *J. Amer. Statist. Assoc.*, June 1969, *64*(326), pp. 637–46.

Wallis, Kenneth F. Some Recent Developments in Applied Econometrics: Dynamic Models and Simultaneous Equation Systems. *J. Econ. Lit.*, September 1969, *7*(3), pp. 771–96.

Walls, Robert C. and Weeks, David L. A Note on the Variance of a Predicted Response in Regression. *Amer. Statist.*, June 1969, *23*(3), pp. 24–26.

Wold, Herman O. E. P. Mackeprangs fråga om val av regression. Ett nyckelproblem i ekonometrins utveckling. (E. P. Mackeprang's Question about the Choice of Regression: A Key Problem in the Evolution of Econometrics. With English summary.) *Liiketaloudellinen Aikak.*, 1969, *18*(1), pp. 79–89.

2112 Inferential Problems in Simultaneous Equation Systems

Chetty, V. Karuppan. Econometrics of Joint Production: A Comment. *Econometrica*, October 1969, *37*(4), pp. 731.

Conlisk, John. The Equilibrium Covariance Matrix of Dynamic Econometric Models. *J. Amer. Statist. Assoc.*, March 1969, *64*(325), pp. 277–79.

De Floriani, Walter. Stima lineare e corretta della media nel campionamento a grappoli e in quello a due stadi. (A Linear and Unbiased Estimate of the Mean in the Cluster Sampling and in the Two-Stage Sampling. With English summary.) *Rivista Int. Sci. Econ. Com.*, October 1969, *16*(10), pp. 1016–28.

Dhrymes, Phoebus J. and Mitchell, B. M. Estimation of Joint Production Functions. *Econometrica*, October 1969, *37*(4), pp. 732–36.

Draper, Norman R. and Lawrence, Willard E. Distributions of Blocks of Signs. **In** *Naylor, T. H., ed.*, 1969, pp. 347–51.

Fuller, Wayne A. Grafted Polynomials as Approximating Functions. *Australian J. Agr. Econ.*, June 1969, *13*(1), pp. 35–46.

Handscomb, D. C. Monte Carlo Techniques: Theoretical. **In** *Naylor, T. H., ed.*, 1969, pp. 252–62.

Hayes, Robert H. The Value of Sample Information. **In** *Naylor, T. H., ed.*, 1969, pp. 298–319.

Howard, Nigel. Least Squares Classification and Principal Component Analysis: A Comparison. **In** *Dogan, M. and Rokkan, S., eds.*, 1969, pp. 397–412.

Kleijnen, Jack P. Monte Carlo Techniques: A Comment. **In** *Naylor, T. H., ed.*, 1969, pp. 289–97.

Klein, Lawrence R. Estimation on Interdependent Systems in Macroeconometrics. *Econometrica*, April 1969, *37*(2), pp. 171–92.

Liu, Ta-Chung and Breen, William J. The Covariance Matrix of the Limited Information Estimator and the Identification Test. *Econometrica*, April 1969, *37*(2), pp. 222–27.

Moy, William A. Monte Carlo Techniques: Practical. **In** *Naylor, T. H., ed.*, 1969, pp. 263–88.

Narayanan, R. Computation of Zellner-Theil's Three Stage Least Squares Estimates. *Econometrica*, April 1969, *37*(2), pp. 298–306.

Pieraccini, Luciano. Su di una interpretazione alternativa del metodo dei minimi quadrati a due stadi. (With English summary.) *Statistica*, October-December 1969, *29*(4), pp. 786–802.

Rao, Potluri. A Note on Econometrics of Joint Production. *Econometrica*, October 1969, *37*(4), pp. 737–38.

Sawa, Takamitsu. The Exact Sampling Distribution of Ordinary Least Squares and Two-Stage Least Squares Estimators. *J. Amer. Statist. Assoc.*, September 1969, *64*(327), pp. 923–37.

Searle, S. R. Correlation Between Means of Parts and Wholes. *Amer. Statist.*, April 1969, *23*(2), pp. 23–24.

Sewell, Wade P. Least Squares, Conditional Predictions, and Estimator Properties. *Econometrica*, January 1969, *37*(1), pp. 39–43.

Smith, Harry. Regression Analysis and Analysis of Variance. **In** *Naylor, T. H., ed.*, 1969, pp. 123–31.

Vinod, Hrishikesh D. Econometrics of Joint Production—A Reply. *Econometrica*, October 1969, *37*(4), pp. 739–40.

Wegge, Leon L. F. A Family of Functional Iterations and the Solution of Maximum Likelihood Estimating Equations. *Econometrica*, January 1969, *37*(1), pp. 122–30.

Wickens, M. R. The Consistency and Efficiency of Generalized Least Squares in Simultaneous Equation Systems with Autocorrelated Errors. *Econometrica*, October 1969, *37*(4), pp. 651–59.

2113 Distributed Lags and Serially Correlated Disturbance Terms; Miscellaneous Single Equation Inferential Problems

Abrahamse, A. P. J. and Koerts, J. A Comparison between the Power of the Durbin-Watson Test and the Power of the BLUS Test. *J. Amer. Statist. Assoc.*, September 1969, *64*(327), pp. 938–48.

Atiquallah, M. On a Restricted Least Squares Estimator. *J. Amer. Statist. Assoc.*, September 1969, *64*(327), pp. 964–68.

Colantoni, Marcello. Nota sulla distribuzione di uno stimatore compionario dell'indice 'Alfa' di Pareto. (With English summary.) *Statistica*, October-December 1969, *29*(4), pp. 768–78.

Dagenais, Marcel G. A Threshold Regression Model. *Econometrica*, April 1969, *37*(2), pp. 193–203.

Dhrymes, Phoebus J. An Identity between Double *k*-Class and Two Stage Least Squares Estimators. *Int. Econ. Rev.*, February 1969, *10*(1), pp. 114–17.

Dhrymes, Phoebus J. Efficient Estimation of Distributed Lags with Autocorrelated Errors. *Int. Econ. Rev.*, February 1969, *10*(1), pp. 47–67.

Draper, Norman R. and Guttman, I. The Value of Prior Information. **In** *Johnson, N. L. and Smith, H., Jr., eds.*, 1969, pp. 305–25.

Gupta, Y. P. Least Squares Variant of the Dhrymes Two-Step Estimation Procedure of the Distributed Lag Model. *Int. Econ. Rev.*, February 1969, *10*(1), pp. 112–13.

Haitovsky, Yoel. Multicollinearity in Regression Analysis: Comment. *Rev. Econ. Statist.*, November 1969, *51*(4), pp. 486–89.

Hannan, E. J. A Note on an Exact Test for Trend and Serial Correlation. *Econometrica*, July 1969, *37*(3), pp. 485–89.

Heien, Dale M. Income and Price Lags in Consumer-demand Analysis. *J. Roy. Statist. Soc.*, Part 2, 1969, *132*, pp. 265–71. [G: U.S.]

Kaufman, Gordon M. Conditional Prediction and Unbiasedness in Structural Equations. *Econometrica,* January 1969, *37*(1), pp. 44–49.

Kelejian, H. H. Missing Observations in Multivariate Regression: Efficiency of a First Order Method. *J. Amer. Statist. Assoc.,* December 1969, *64*(328), pp. 1609–16.

Koivisto, Heikki. Viivästysjakautumien approksimointikeinoista. (On New Methods for Approximating Distributed Lags. With English summary.) *Kansant. Aikak.,* 1969, *65*(4), pp. 304–10. [G: Finland]

Kramer, Giselbert. Ein Autokorrelationstest der von Neumann-Klasse und seine Signifikanzpunkte. (With English summary.) *Z. ges. Staatswiss.,* October 1969, *125*(4), pp. 624–36.

Naus, J. I. The Distribution of the Logarithm of the Sum of Two Log-Normal Variates. *J. Amer. Statist. Assoc.,* June 1969, *64*(326), pp. 655–59.

Neudecker, H. A Note on BLUS Estimation. *J. Amer. Statist. Assoc.,* September 1969, *64*(327), pp. 949–52.

Oi, Walter Y. A Bracketing Rule for the Estimation of Simple Distributed Lag Models. *Rev. Econ. Statist.,* November 1969, *51*(4), pp. 445–52.

Oliver, F. R. Another Generalisation of the Logistic Growth Function. *Econometrica,* January 1969, *37*(1), pp. 144–47.

Orcutt, Guy H. and Winokur, Herbert S., Jr. First Order Autoregression: Inference, Estimation, and Prediction. *Econometrica,* January 1969, *37* (1), pp. 1–14.

Pike, Eugene W. A Note on "Learning Curves." *J. Amer. Statist. Assoc.,* December 1969, *64*(328), pp. 1276–77.

Powell, Alan. Aitken Estimators as a Tool in Allocating Predetermined Aggregates. *J. Amer. Statist. Assoc.,* September 1969, *64*(327), pp. 913–22.

Rayner, A. C. Effect of the Length of the Time Period on Serial Correlation. *Rev. Econ. Statist.,* February 1969, *51*(1), pp. 107–08.

Sastry, M. V. Rama. Multicollinearity and Consumer Demand Elasticities. *Can. J. Agr. Econ.,* February 1969, *17*(1), pp. 50–60. [G: U.S.]

Scott, John T., Jr. Factor Analysis Regression Revisited. *Econometrica,* October 1969, *37*(4), pp. 719.

Thöni, Hanspeter. A Table for Estimating the Mean of a Lognormal Distribution. *J. Amer. Statist. Assoc.,* June 1969, *64*(326), pp. 632–36.

Valentine, Thomas J. A Note on Multicollinearity. *Australian Econ. Pap.,* June 1969, *8*(12), pp. 99–105.

Wahba, Grace. Estimation of the Coefficients in a Multidimensional Distributed Lag Model. *Econometrica,* July 1969, *37*(3), pp. 398–407.

Walker, David A. A Two-Stage Decision Process to Estimate Functions with Collinear Independent Variables. *Jahr. Nationalökon. Statist.,* June 1969, *183*(1), pp. 48–60.

Wallace, T. D. and Hussain, Ashiq. The Use of Error Components Models in Combining Cross Section with Time Series Data. *Econometrica,* January 1969, *37*(1), pp. 55–72.

2114 Multivariate Analysis, Information Theory, and Other Special Inferential Problems; Queuing Theory; Markov Chains

Anderson, James R. and Dillon, John L. A Comparison of Response Surface and Factorial Designs in Agricultural Research: Comment. *Rev. Marketing Agr. Econ.,* June 1969, *37*(2), pp. 130–32.

Bohrnstedt, George W. and Goldberger, Arthur S. On the Exact Covariance of Products of Random Variables. *J. Amer. Statist. Assoc.,* December 1969, *64*(328), pp. 1439–42.

Chakrabarti, S. K. A Note on the Relation Between Binary and Multiple Choice Probabilities. *Econometrica,* October 1969, *37*(4), pp. 726–27.

Georgescu-Roegen, Nicholas. The Relation Between Binary and Multiple Choices: Some Comments and Further Results. *Econometrica,* October 1969, *37*(4), pp. 728–30.

Glahn, Harry R. Some Relationships Derived from Canonical Correlation Theory. *Econometrica,* April 1969, *37*(2), pp. 252–56.

Green, Paul E. and Rao, Vithala R. A Note on Proximity Measures and Cluster Analysis. *J. Marketing Res.,* August 1969, *6*(3), pp. 359–64.

Green, Paul E. and Carmone, Frank J. Multidimensional Scaling: An Introduction and Comparison of Nonmetric Unfolding Techniques. *J. Marketing Res.,* August 1969, *6*(3), pp. 330–41.

Horsnell, Gareth. A Theory of Consumer Behaviour Derived from Repeat Paired Preference Testing. *J. Roy. Statist. Soc.,* Part 2, 1969, *132*, pp. 164–84.

Howard, Nigel. Least Squares Classification and Principal Component Analysis: A Comparison. **In** *Dogan, M. and Rokkan, S., eds.,* 1969, pp. 397–412.

Janson, Carl-Gunnar. Some Problems of Ecological Factor Analysis. **In** *Dogan, M. and Rokkan, S., eds.,* 1969, pp. 301–41.

King, Benjamin. Comment on "Factor Analysis and Regression." *Econometrica,* July 1969, *37*(3), pp. 538–40.

Lev, Baruch. An Information Theory Analysis of Budget Variances. *Accounting Rev.,* October 1969, *44*(4), pp. 704–10.

Naor, P. The Regulation of Queue Size by Levying Tolls. *Econometrica,* January 1969, *37*(1), pp. 15–24.

Niedereichholz, Joachim. Grundzüge einer Systemanalyse ökonomischer Modelle mittels Flussgraphen. (With English summary.) *Jahr. Nationalökon. Statist.,* June 1969, *183*(1), pp. 30–47.

Popescu, S. Falcan. Folosirea analizei factoriale în cercetarea fenomenelor în profil teritorial. (Use of Factorial Analysis in the Investigation of Phenomena in a Territorial Profile. With English summary.) *Stud. Cercet. Econ.,* 1969, *4,* pp. 159–63.

Schleifer, Arthur, Jr. Two-Stage Normal Sampling in Two-Action Problems with Linear Economics. *J. Amer. Statist. Assoc.,* December 1969, *64*(328), pp. 1504–41.

Scott, John T., Jr. Factor Analysis Regression Revisited. *Econometrica,* October 1969, *37*(4), pp. 719.

Shah, S. M. On the Minimum Property of the First

Absolute Moment. *Amer. Statist.*, June 1969, *23*(3), pp. 27.

Sheth, Jagdish N. Using Factor Analysis to Estimate Parameters. *J. Amer. Statist. Assoc.*, September 1969, *64*(327), pp. 808–22.

Theil, Henri. A Multinomial Extension of the Linear Logit Model. *Int. Econ. Rev.*, October 1969, *10*(3), pp. 251–59.

Tracy, Derrick S. and Dwyer, Paul S. Multivariate Maxima and Minima with Matrix Derivatives. *J. Amer. Statist. Assoc.*, December 1969, *64*(328), pp. 1576–94.

Vosyka, Miroslav. Model vícefázové soustavy hromadné obsluhy s respektováním priority požadavků. (Model of a Multiple Parallel and Series Queueing System with Preemptive Priorities. With English summary.) *Ekon.-Mat. Obzor,* 1969, *5*(3), pp. 354–77.

Wallace, T. D. and Toro-Vizcarrondo, C. E. Tables for the Mean Square Error Test for Exact Linear Restrictions in Regression. *J. Amer. Statist. Assoc.*, December 1969, *64*(328), pp. 1649–63.

Walter, Jaromír. Modely obnovy. (Models of Renewal. With English summary.) *Ekon.-Mat. Obzor,* 1969, *5*(2), pp. 137–62.

Williams, R. J. and Baker, J. R. A Comparison of Response Surface and Factorial Designs in Agricultural Research: Reply. *Rev. Marketing Agr. Econ.*, June 1969, *37*(2), pp. 132–33.

2115 Bayesian Statistics and Statistical Decision Theory

Bullock, J. Bruce and Logan, Samuel H. A Model for Decision Making under Uncertainty. *Agr. Econ. Res.*, October 1969, *21*(4), pp. 109–115.

Chetty, V. Karuppan. On the Long-Run and Short-Run Demand for Money: Some Further Evidence. *J. Polit. Econ.*, November/December 1969, *77*(6), pp. 921–31. [G: U.S.]

Chow, Gregory C. Reply: A Note on the Estimation of Long-Run Relationships in Stock Adjustment Models. *J. Polit. Econ.*, November/December 1969, *77*(6), pp. 932–36. [G: U.S.]

de Cristofaro, Rodolfo. Impiego delle distribuzioni beta ed F per ricavare intervalli di stima di una percentuale nel campionamento bernoulliano. (With English summary.) *Statistica,* October-December 1969, *29*(4), pp. 779–85.

Draper, Norman R. and Guttman, I. The Value of Prior Information. In *Johnson, N. L. and Smith, H., Jr., eds.*, 1969, pp. 305–25.

Goldschmidt, Walter. Game Theory, Cultural Values, and the Brideprice in Africa. In *Buchler, I. R. and Nutini, H. G., eds.*, 1969, pp. 61–74. [G: Africa]

Kozelka, Robert. A Bayesian Approach to Jamaican Fishing. In *Buchler, I. R. and Nutini, H. G., eds.*, 1969, pp. 117–25. [G: Jamaica]

Lieberman, Bernhardt. Combining Individual Preferences into a Social Choice. In *Buchler, I. R. and Nutini, H. G., eds.*, 1969, pp. 95–115.

Press, S. James. The *t*-Ratio Distribution. *J. Amer. Statist. Assoc.*, March 1969, *64*(325), pp. 242–52.

Salisbury, Richard F. Formal Analysis in Anthropological Economics: The Rossel Island Case. In *Buchler, I. R. and Nutini, H. G., eds.*, 1969, pp. 75–93.

Shubik, Martin. The Uses of Game Theory in Management Science. In *Carsberg, B. V. and Edey, H. C., eds.*, 1969, pp. 376–95.

Skala, Heinz J. Bemerkungen zur Bayesschen Entscheidungstheorie. (With English summary.) *Jahr. Nationalökon. Statist.*, July 1969, *183*(2), pp. 141–49.

Sorensen, James E. Bayesian Analysis in Auditing. *Accounting Rev.*, July 1969, *44*(3), pp. 555–61.

Tracy, John A. Bayesian Statistical Methods in Auditing. *Accounting Rev.*, January 1969, *44*(1), pp. 90–98.

Varde, S. D. Life Testing and Reliability Estimation for the Two Parameter Exponential Distribution. *J. Amer. Statist. Assoc.*, June 1969, *64*(326), pp. 621–31.

2116 Time Series and Spectral Analysis

Brillinger, David R. and Hatanaka, Michio. An Harmonic Analysis of Nonstationary Multivariate Economic Processes. *Econometrica,* January 1969, *37*(1), pp. 131–41.

Burley, S. P. A Spectral Analysis of the Australian Business Cycle. *Australian Econ. Pap.*, December 1969, *8*(13), pp. 193–218. [G: Australia]

Chow, Gregory C. and Levitan, Richard E. Spectral Properties of Non-Stationary Systems of Linear Stochastic Difference Equations. *J. Amer. Statist. Assoc.*, June 1969, *64*(326), pp. 581–90.

Granger, C. W. J. Investigating Causal Relations by Econometric Models and Cross-Spectral Methods. *Econometrica,* July 1969, *37*(3), pp. 424–38.

Hannan, E. J. A Note on an Exact Test for Trend and Serial Correlation. *Econometrica,* July 1969, *37*(3), pp. 485–89.

Hatanaka, Michio and Howrey, E. Philip. Low Frequency Variation in Economic Time Series. *Kyklos,* 1969, *22*(4), pp. 752–66. [G: U.S.]

Naylor, Thomas H.; Wertz, Kenneth and Wonnacott, Thomas H. Spectral Analysis of Data Generated by Simulation Experiments with Econometric Models. *Econometrica,* April 1969, *37*(2), pp. 333–52.

Rangarajan, C. and Chatterjee, S. A Note on Comparison between Correlation Coefficients of Original and Transformed Variables. *Amer. Statist.*, October 1969, *23*(4), pp. 28–29.

Watts, Donald. Time Series Analysis. In *Naylor, T. H., ed.*, 1969, pp. 165–79.

van Winkel, E. G. F. Extrapolationen einer Zeitreihe durch exponentiell abnehmende Gewichtung. (Extrapolation of Time Series by Exponential Smoothing. With English summary.) *Ifo-Studien,* 1969, *15*(1/2), pp. 1–18.

2117 Survey Methods; Sampling Methods

Bershad, Max A. and Tepping, Benjamin J. The Development of Household Sample Surveys. *J. Amer. Statist. Assoc.*, December 1969, *64*(328), pp. 1134–40.

Booth, Gordon and Sedransk, J. Planning Some Two-Factor Comparative Surveys. *J. Amer. Statist. Assoc.*, June 1969, *64*(326), pp. 560–73.

Burt, Richard C. How the 1970 Census Will Be Taken. *Mon. Lab. Rev.*, December 1969, *92*(12), pp. 38–42. [G: U.S.]

Cox, D. R. Some Sampling Problems in Technology. **In** *Johnson, N. L. and Smith, H., Jr., eds.*, 1969, pp. 506–27.

Dalenius, T. Designing Descriptive Sample Surveys. **In** *Johnson, N. L. and Smith, H., Jr., eds.*, 1969, pp. 390–415.

Daly, Joseph F. Some Basic Principles of Statistical Surveys. *J. Amer. Statist. Assoc.*, December 1969, *64*(328), pp. 1129–33.

Deming, W. E. Boundaries of Statistical Inference. **In** *Johnson, N. L. and Smith, H., Jr., eds.*, 1969, pp. 652–70.

Durbin, J. Inferential Aspects of the Randomness of Sample Size in Survey Sampling. **In** *Johnson, N. L. and Smith, H., Jr., eds.*, 1969, pp. 629–51.

Ericson, W. A. Subjective Bayesian Models in Sampling Finite Populations: Stratification. **In** *Johnson, N. L. and Smith, H., Jr., eds.*, 1969, pp. 326–57.

Ferber, Robert, et al. Validation of a National Survey of Consumer Financial Characteristics: Savings Accounts. *Rev. Econ. Statist.*, November 1969, *51* (4), pp. 436–44. [G: U.S.]

Ferber, Robert, et al. Validation of Consumer Financial Characteristics: Common Stock. *J. Amer. Statist. Assoc.*, June 1969, *64*(326), pp. 415–32.

Frankel, L. R. The Role of Accuracy and Precision of Response in Sample Surveys. **In** *Johnson, N. L. and Smith, H., Jr., eds.*, 1969, pp. 439–56.

Gorinson, Morris. How the Census Data Will be Processed. *Mon. Lab. Rev.*, December 1969, *92*(12), pp. 42–45. [G: U.S.]

Green, Gloria P. Comparing Employment Estimates from Household and Payroll Surveys. *Mon. Lab. Rev.*, December 1969, *92*(12), pp. 9–20. [G: U.S.]

Gupta, S. S. and Panchapakesan, S. Selection and Ranking Procedures. **In** *Naylor, T. H., ed.*, 1969, pp. 132–60.

Hansen, M. H. and Tepping, B. J. Progress and Problems in Survey Methods and Theory Illustrated by the Work of the United States Bureau of the Census. **In** *Johnson, N. L. and Smith, H., Jr., eds.*, 1969, pp. 1–26.

Hartley, H. O. and Rao, J. N. K. A New Estimation Theory for Sample Surveys, II. **In** *Johnson, N. L. and Smith, H., Jr., eds.*, 1969, pp. 147–69.

Hayes, Robert H. The Value of Sample Information. **In** *Naylor, T. H., ed.*, 1969, pp. 298–319.

Horvitz, D. G. and Koch, Gary G. The Effect of Response Errors on Measures of Association. **In** *Johnson, N. L. and Smith, H., Jr., eds.*, 1969, pp. 247–81.

Jessen, R. J. Some "Master" Sampling Frames for Social and Statistical Surveys in California. **In** *Johnson, N. L. and Smith, H., Jr., eds.*, 1969, pp. 457–81.

Joshi, V. M. Admissibility of Estimates of the Mean of a Finite Population. **In** *Johnson, N. L. and Smith, H., Jr., eds.*, 1969, pp. 188–212.

Kalbfleisch, J. D. and Sprott, D. A. Applications of Likelihood and Fiducial Probability to Sampling Finite Populations. **In** *Johnson, N. L. and Smith, H., Jr., eds.*, 1969, pp. 358–89.

Kempthorne, O. Some Remarks on Statistical Inference in Finite Sampling. **In** *Johnson, N. L. and Smith, H., Jr., eds.*, 1969, pp. 671–95.

Keyfitz, Nathan. Sampling for Demographic Variables. **In** *Johnson, N. L. and Smith, H., Jr., eds.*, 1969, pp. 562–77.

Kirkbride, John W. Response Problems in Probability Sampling. *Amer. J. Agr. Econ.*, December 1969, *51*(5), pp. 1214–17.

Kish, L. Design and Estimation for Subclasses, Comparisons, and Analytical Statistics. **In** *Johnson, N. L. and Smith, H., Jr., eds.*, 1969, pp. 416–38.

Minton, George. Inspection and Correction Error in Data Processing. *J. Amer. Statist. Assoc.*, December 1969, *64*(328), pp. 1256–75.

Nathan, G. Tests of Independence in Contingency Tables from Stratified Samples. **In** *Johnson, N. L. and Smith, H., Jr., eds.*, 1969, pp. 578–600.

Neyman, J. Bias in Surveys Due to Nonresponse (Closing Address). **In** *Johnson, N. L. and Smith, H., Jr., eds.*, 1969, pp. 712–32.

O'Reagan, Robert T. Relative Costs of Computerized Error Inspection Plans. *J. Amer. Statist. Assoc.*, December 1969, *64*(328), pp. 1245–55.

Perkins, Walter M. How the Census Will Be Evaluated. *Mon. Lab. Rev.*, December 1969, *92*(12), pp. 55–60. [G: U.S.]

Phillips, M. J. A Survey of Sampling Procedures for Continuous Production. *J. Roy. Statist. Soc.*, Part 2, 1969, *132*, pp. 205–28.

Ramberg, John S. Selection and Ranking Procedures: A Comment. **In** *Naylor, T. H., ed.*, 1969, pp. 161–64.

Rao, J. N. K. Ratio and Regression Estimators. **In** *Johnson, N. L. and Smith, H., Jr., eds.*, 1969, pp. 213–34.

Sampford, M. R. A Comparison of Some Possible Methods of Sampling from Smallish Populations, with Units of Unequal Size. **In** *Johnson, N. L. and Smith, H., Jr., eds.*, 1969, pp. 170–87.

Simmons, W. R. and Bean, Judy Ann. Impact of Design and Estimation Components on Inference. **In** *Johnson, N. L. and Smith, H., Jr., eds.*, 1969, pp. 601–28.

Stambler, Howard V. Problems in Analyzing Urban Employment Survey Data. *Mon. Lab. Rev.*, November 1969, *92*(11), pp. 51–54. [G: U.S.]

Stephan, Frederick F. Three Extensions of Sample Survey Technique: Hybrid, Nexus, and Graduated Sampling. **In** *Johnson, N. L. and Smith, H., Jr., eds.*, 1969, pp. 81–104.

Sukhatme, P. V. and Sukhatme, B. V. On Some Methodological Aspects of Sample Surveys of Agriculture in Developing Countries. **In** *Johnson, N. L. and Smith, H., Jr., eds.*, 1969, pp. 528–61.

Thionet, P. Item Analysis and Reweighting. **In** *Johnson, N. L. and Smith, H., Jr., eds.*, 1969, pp. 282–304.

Waksberg, Joseph and Pritzker, Leon. Changes in Census Methods. *J. Amer. Statist. Assoc.*, December 1969, *64*(328), pp. 1141–49.

2118 Theory of Index Numbers and Aggregation

Edwards, John B. and Orcutt, Guy H. Should Aggregation Prior to Estimation Be the Rule? *Rev. Econ. Statist.*, November 1969, *51*(4), pp. 409–20.

Hoa, Tran Van. Additive Preferences and Cost of Living Indexes: An Empirical Study of the Australian Consumer's Welfare. *Econ. Rec.*, September 1969, *45*(111), pp. 432–40. **[G: Australia]**

Jonas, Paul and Sardy, Hyman. Production Index Bias as a Measure of Economic Development: A Comment. *Oxford Econ. Pap.*, November 1969, *21*(3), pp. 428–32. **[G: U.S.]**

Kresge, David T. Price and Output Conversion: A Modified Approach. **In** *Duesenberry, J. S., et al.*, 1969, pp. 85–108. **[G: U.S.]**

Kuchenbecker, Horst. Zur Darstellung von Veränderungen der Weltwarenpreise durch arithmetische und geometrische Indizes am Beispiel des Moody-Index und des Reuter-Index. (On the Representation of World Commodity Price Changes by Arithmetic and Geometric Index Numbers, Illustrated in Moodys Index of Staple Commodities and Reuters Commodity Index. With English summary.) *Jahr. Nationalökon. Statist.*, August 1969, *183*(3–4), pp. 254–70.

Lydall, Harold. On Measuring Technical Progress. *Australian Econ. Pap.*, June 1969, *8*(12), pp. 1–12. **[G: U.K.]**

Pyun, Chong Soo. Local Business Activity Index: Its Construction and Uses—Comment. *J. Reg. Sci.*, April 1969, *9*(1), pp. 163–66.

Sims, Christopher A. Theoretical Basis for a Double Deflated Index of Real Value Added. *Rev. Econ. Statist.*, November 1969, *51*(4), pp. 470–71.

Singh, Ajmer. Local Business Activity Index: Its Construction and Uses—Reply. *J. Reg. Sci.*, April 1969, *9*(1), pp. 167–69.

Tolley, George S.; Wang, Yi and Fletcher, R. G. Reexamination of the Time Series Evidence on Food Demand. *Econometrica*, October 1969, *37*(4), pp. 695–705.

Young, Allan H. and Harkins, Claudia. Alternative Measures of Price Change for GNP. *Surv. Curr. Bus.*, March 1969, *49*(3), pp. 47–52. **[G: U.S.]**

212 Construction, Analysis, and Use of Econometric Models

2120 Construction, Analysis, and Use of Econometric Models

Agarwala, R. Tests and Uses of Macro-Econometric Models: A Critical Survey. *Econ. Planning*, 1969, *9*(3), pp. 235–57.

Anderson, Henry. Choosing the Base Period for Economic Forecasts. *Miss. Val. J. Bus. Econ.*, Spring 1969, *4*(2), pp. 33–42.

Biolley, T. and Paelinck, J. A Dynamic Model for the Belgian Economy: Simulation and Optimization. *Econ. Planning*, 1969, *9*(1–2), pp. 155–207. **[G: Belgium]**

Bischoff, Charles W. Hypothesis Testing and the Demand for Capital Goods. *Rev. Econ. Statist.*, August 1969, *51*(3), pp. 354–68.

Black, Stanley W. and Russell, R. Robert. An Alternative Estimate of Potential GNP. *Rev. Econ. Statist.*, February 1969, *51*(1), pp. 70–76. **[G: U.S.]**

Boughton, James M., et al. A Policy Model of the United States Monetary Sector. *Southern Econ. J.*, April 1969, *35*(4), pp. 333–46. **[G: U.S.]**

Burgio, Giuseppe. Sulla misura dell'eterogeneità di un collettivo statistico. (With English summary.) *Statistica*, January-March 1969, *29*(1), pp. 5–25.

Candler, Wilfred and Cartwright, Wayne. Estimation of Performance Functions for Budgeting and Simulation Studies. *Amer. J. Agr. Econ.*, February 1969, *51*(1), pp. 159–69.

Cassidy, Henry J. Maximum Likelihood Estimation in an *n-th* Order Autoregressive Disturbance Model. *Southern Econ. J.*, January 1969, *35*(3), pp. 263–64.

Chernoff, Herman. Sequential Designs. **In** *Naylor, T. H., ed.*, 1969, pp. 99–120.

Chetty, V. Karuppan and Sankar, U. Bayesian Estimation of the CES Production Function. *Rev. Econ. Stud.*, July 1969, *36*(107), pp. 289–94. **[G: India]**

Conlisk, John. The Equilibrium Covariance Matrix of Dynamic Econometric Models. *J. Amer. Statist. Assoc.*, March 1969, *64*(325), pp. 277–79.

Di Marco, Luis Eugenio. Expectativas de precios. (Price Expectation. With English summary.) *Económica*, September–December 1969, *15*(3), pp. 275–82.

Elias, Víctor J. Cambios en la calidad de los bienes. Una forma de estimarlos. (Changes in the Quality of Goods—A Way of Estimation. With English summary.) *Económica*, September–December 1969, *15*(3), pp. 283–90.

Evans, Michael K. Non-Linear Econometric Models. **In** *Naylor, T. H., ed.*, 1969, pp. 369–92.

Fromm, Gary. The Evaluation of Economic Policies. **In** *Naylor, T. H., ed.*, 1969, pp. 355–68.

Grove, Ernest W. Econometricians and the Data Gap: Comment. *Amer. J. Agr. Econ.*, February 1969, *51*(1), pp. 184–88.

Haitovsky, Yoel. A Note on the Maximization of $\bar{R}^2$ *Amer. Statist.*, February 1969, *23*(1), pp. 20–21.

Hall, Harry H.; Heady, Earl O. and Plessner, Yakir. Quadratic Programming Solution of Competitive Equilibrium for U.S. Agriculture: Reply. *Amer. J. Agr. Econ.*, May 1969, *51*(2), pp. 483–84. **[G: U.S.]**

Hallberg, M. C. Projecting the Size Distribution of Agricultural Firms—An Application of a Markov Process with Non-Stationary Transition Probabilities. *Amer. J. Agr. Econ.*, May 1969, *51*(2), pp. 289–302. **[G: U.S.]**

Harkness, Jon P. Long Swings. *Rev. Econ. Statist.*, February 1969, *51*(1), pp. 94–96. **[G: U.S.]**

Hejl, Luboš, et al. Macroeconomic Decision Model for the Medium-term Optimal Planning: A Progress Report. *Czech. Econ. Pap.*, 1969, (11), pp. 51–67. **[G: Czechoslovakia]**

Helliwell, John F., et al. Econometric Analysis of Policy Choices for an Open Economy. *Rev. Econ. Statist.*, November 1969, *51*(4), pp. 383–98. **[G: Canada]**

Herman, Barry. On Muddled Methods and Their Meaning. *Rev. Radical Polit. Econ.*, May 1969, *1*(1), pp. 75–84.

Holden, Kenneth. The Effect of Revisions to Data on Two Econometric Studies. *Manchester Sch. Econ. Soc. Stud.*, March 1969, *37*(1), pp. 23–37. **[G: U.K.]**

Howrey, E. Philip and Kelejian, Harry H. Simulation Versus Analytical Solutions. **In** *Naylor, T. H., ed.*, 1969, pp. 207–31.

Hunter, J. S. and Naylor, Thomas H. Experimental Designs. **In** *Naylor, T. H., ed.*, 1969, pp. 39–58.

Klein, Lawrence R. and Preston, R. S. Stochastic Nonlinear Models. *Econometrica*, January 1969, *37*(1), pp. 95–106.

Krasnow, Howard S. Simulation Languages. **In** *Naylor, T. H., ed.*, 1969, pp. 320–46.

Leroux, Roger and Raffoul, Faouzi. An Essay in Simulating Economic Policies for the French Economy. *Econ. Planning*, 1969, *9*(1–2), pp. 95–153. **[G: France]**

Ling, Timothy Y. Statics and Dynamics of Simulation. **In** *Naylor, T. H., ed.*, 1969, pp. 180–203.

Liu, Ta-Chung. A Monthly Recursive Econometric Model of United States: A Test of Feasibility. *Rev. Econ. Statist.*, February 1969, *51*(1), pp. 1–13. **[G: U.S.]**

Manderscheid, Lester V. and Nelson, Glenn L. A Framework for Viewing Simulation. *Can. J. Agr. Econ.*, February 1969, *17*(1), pp. 33–41.

Menzel, Jindřich and Möller, Miroslav. Použití diskriminační analýzy v ekonomickém výzkumu. (Ivanovičova metoda.) (Application of Discriminatory Analysis in Economic Research. With English summary.) *Ekon.-Mat. Obzor*, 1969, *5*(2), pp. 199–208.

Michelini, Claudio. Stima bayesiana di una funzione di Engel. (With English summary.) *Statistica*, January-March 1969, *29*(1), pp. 27–48. **[G: Italy]**

Morris, John. Nonparametric Statistics on the Computer. *J. Marketing Res.*, February 1969, *6*(1), pp. 86–92.

Morrison, Donald G. On the Interpretation of Discriminant Analysis. *J. Marketing Res.*, May 1969, *6*(2), pp. 156–63.

Murphy, James L. An Appraisal of Repeated Predictive Tests on an Econometric Model. *Southern Econ. J.*, April 1969, *35*(4), pp. 293–307.

Nadiri, M. Ishag and Rosen, Sherwin. Interrelated Factor Demand Functions. *Amer. Econ. Rev.*, Part I, September 1969, *59*(4), pp. 457–71. **[G: U.S.]**

Naylor, Thomas H.; Burdick, Donald S. and Sasser, W. Earl, Jr. The Design of Computer Simulation Experiments. **In** *Naylor, T. H., ed.*, 1969, pp. 3–35.

Nelson, Boyd L. Econometrics and Applied Economic Analysis in Regulatory Decisions. *Law Contemp. Probl.*, Spring 1969, *34*(2), pp. 330–39.

O'Dell, Charles A. Econometricians and the Data Gap: Reply—Comment. *Amer. J. Agr. Econ.*, August 1969, *51*(3), pp. 679–80.

Oakland, William H. Budgetary Measures of Fiscal Performance. *Southern Econ. J.*, April 1969, *35*(4), pp. 347–58. **[G: U.S.]**

Scott, John T., Jr. and Heady, Earl O. Econometricians and the Data Gap: Reply. *Amer. J. Agr. Econ.*, February 1969, *51*(1), pp. 188.

Smith, Blair J. and Purcell, Joseph C. Quadratic Programming Solution of Competitive Equilibrium for U.S. Agriculture: Comment. *Amer. J. Agr. Econ.*, May 1969, *51*(2), pp. 481–82. **[G: U.S.]**

Swamy, M. R. Kumara. An Econometric Analysis of Cost Curves and Supply Curves under Modern Dynamic Competitive Conditions. *Rivista Int. Sci. Econ. Com.*, March 1969, *16*(3), pp. 280–93.

Van Horn, Richard. Validation. **In** *Naylor, T. H., ed.*, 1969, pp. 232–51.

Ward, Joe H., Jr. Synthesizing Regression Models —An Aid to Learning Effective Problem Analysis. *Amer. Statist.*, April 1969, *23*(2), pp. 14–20.

White, William H. How Useful Are Econometric Models? *Finance Develop.*, March 1969, *6*(1), pp. 23–29.

White, William H. The Usefulness of Econometric Models for Policymakers. *Finance Develop.*, September 1969, *6*(3), pp. 8–13.

Willis, J. F.; Minden, A. J. and Snyder, James C. Monte Carlo Simulation of Management Systems. *Can. J. Agr. Econ.*, February 1969, *17*(1), pp. 42–49.

Wold, Herman O. Econometrics as Pioneering in Nonexperimental Model Building. *Econometrica*, July 1969, *37*(3), pp. 369–81.

Zerby, J. A. An Econometric Model of Monetary Interaction in Australia. *Australian Econ. Pap.*, December 1969, *8*(13), pp. 154–77. **[G: Australia]**

213 Mathematical Methods and Models

2130 General

Adelman, M. A. Comment on the "H" Concentration Measure as a Numbers-Equivalent. *Rev. Econ. Statist.*, February 1969, *51*(1), pp. 99–101.

Bródy, A. Methods of Analysis and Forecasting Applied in Hungary. *Acta Oecon.*, 1969, *4*(3), pp. 299–314.

Burdick, Donald S. and Naylor, Thomas H. Response Surface Designs. **In** *Naylor, T. H., ed.*, 1969, pp. 80–98.

Desaeyere, W. Schatting van een array door middel van de marginale totalen. (Estimation of an Array by Means of the Marginal Totals. With English summary.) *Tijdschr. Econ.*, 1969, *14*(1), pp. 28–73.

Frank, Charles R., Jr. A Generalization of the Koopmans-Gale Theorem on Pricing and Efficiency. *Int. Econ. Rev.*, October 1969, *10*(3), pp. 488–91.

Gerchuk, Ia. On the Question of Applying Economic-Mathematical Methods in Practice. *Prob. Econ.*, September 1969, *12*(5), pp. 52–70. **[G: U.S.S.R.]**

Jackson. Equilibrium Results for Queueing Processes with Both Erlang Input and Service Time Distribution with More Than One Server. *Ekon.-Mat. Obzor*, 1969, *5*(2), pp. 172–85.

Kaška, Josef. Duality in Linear Fractional Programming. *Ekon.-Mat. Obzor*, 1969, *5*(4), pp. 442–53.

Kelly, Jerry Stewart. Lancaster vs. Samuelson on the Shape of the Neoclassical Transformation Surface. *J. Econ. Theory*, October 1969, *1*(3), pp. 347–51.

Newman, Peter. Some Properties of Concave Functions. *J. Econ. Theory*, October 1969, *1*(3), pp. 291–314.

Overholt, John L. Factor Selection. In *Naylor, T. H., ed.*, 1969, pp. 59–79.

Vlček, Jaroslav. Systémová analýza a systémový přístup: Srovnavácí studie s návrhem metody. (System Analysis and System Approach. With English summary.) *Ekon.-Mat. Obzor,* 1969, *5*(4), pp. 409–22.

2132 Optimization Techniques

Carleton, Willard T. Linear Programming and Capital Budgeting Models: A New Interpretation. *J. Finance,* December 1969, *24*(5), pp. 825–33.

Chakravarty, Sukhamoy. The Optimal Growth Path for Finite Planning Horizons. In *[Ghosal, U. N.]*, 1969, pp. 40–68.

Chuev, Iu. V. and Stekhova, G. P. The Generalized Equipment Replacement Problem. *Matekon,* Fall 1969, *6*(1), pp. 75–90.

Dethoor, Jean-Marc. Au-delà de la programmation dynamique. (With English summary.) *Revue Écon.,* May 1969, *20*(3), pp. 515–35.

Dorfman, Robert. An Economic Interpretation of Optimal Control Theory. *Amer. Econ. Rev.,* December 1969, *59*(5), pp. 817–31.

Duharcourt, Pierre. Introduction à la programmation dynamique. (With English summary.) *Revue Écon.,* March 1969, *20*(2), pp. 182–234.

Fericelli, Jean. Programmation dynamique et planification macro-économique. (With English summary.) *Revue Écon.,* March 1969, *20*(2), pp. 235–71.

Gottinger, Hans-Werner. Beiträge zur funktionalen Separabilität bei Nutzenfunktionen (Teil I). (With English summary.) *Z. ges. Staatswiss.,* July 1969, *125*(3), pp. 406–46.

Hamala, Milan. Geometrické programovanie. (Geometric Programming. With English summary.) *Ekon.-Mat. Obzor,* 1969, *5*(1), pp. 1–12.

Inosov, V. L. and Sviatskaia, N. V. Some Problems in Optimal Inventory Control. *Matekon,* Fall 1969, *6*(1), pp. 44–56.

Lunghini, Giorgio. Ottimo economico e ottimo matematico. (Economic Optimum versus Mathematical Optimum. With English summary.) *L'Industria,* April–June 1969, (2), pp. 159–75.

Lüttgen, Horst. Das Problem des optimalen Testaments. (With English summary.) *Z. ges. Staatswiss.,* January 1969, *125*(1), pp. 123–37.

Malinvaud, E. First Order Certainty Equivalence. *Econometrica,* October 1969, *37*(4), pp. 706–18.

Melrose, Kendrick B. An Empirical Study on Optimizing Advertising Policy. *J. Bus.,* July 1969, *42* (3), pp. 282–92. [G: U.S.]

Schneider, Georges. Le choix des investissements dans l'entreprise. (With English summary.) *Revue Écon.,* March 1969, *20*(2), pp. 272–301.

Vergé, Jean-Marie. Un modèle séquentiel de financement optimal à long terme dans l'entreprise. (With English summary.) *Revue Écon.,* March 1969, *20*(2), pp. 302–36.

Zima, Petr. Řešení jedné modifikace řezného problému. (A Solution of One Modification of the "Cutting Problem." With English summary.) *Ekon.-Mat. Obzor,* 1969, *5*(1), pp. 72–76.

2133 Existence and Stability Conditions of Equilibrium

Hadar, Josef. Dominant Diagonals—A Correction. *Econometrica,* July 1969, *37*(3), pp. 541–43.

Starr, Ross M. Quasi-Equilibria in Markets with Non-Convex Preferences. *Econometrica,* January 1969, *37*(1), pp. 25–38.

Turnovec, František. Nutné a postačující podmínky pro rovnovážné body v konvexní nekooperativní hře. (Necessary and Sufficient Conditions for Equilibrium Points of Noncooperative Convex Games. With English summary.) *Ekon.-Mat. Obzor,* 1969, *5*(3), pp. 343–53.

Veendorp, E. C. H. A Theorem on Non-tâtonnement Stability: A Comment. *Econometrica,* January 1969, *37*(1), pp. 142–43.

2134 Computational Techniques

Cornelisse, Peter A. and Versluis, Jan. The Semi-Input-Output Method under Upper Bounds. In *[Tinbergen, J.]*, 1969, pp. 175–99.

2135 Construction, Analysis, and Use of Mathematical Programming Models

Arbuzova, N. I. Stochastic Stability of a Quadratic Programming Problem with Random Free Constraints. *Matekon,* Fall 1969, *6*(1), pp. 91–97.

Bellman, Richard and Roth, Robert. Curve Fitting by Segmented Straight Lines. *J. Amer. Statist. Assoc.,* September 1969, *64*(327), pp. 1079–84.

Bernhard, Richard H. Mathematical Programming Models for Capital Budgeting—A Survey, Generalization, and Critique. *J. Financial Quant. Anal.,* June 1969, *4*(2), pp. 111–58.

Butcher, William S.; Haimes, Yacov Y. and Hall, Warren A. Dynamic Programming for the Optimal Sequencing of Water Supply Projects. *Water Resources Res.,* December 1969, *5*(6), pp. 1196–1204.

Colantoni, Claude S.; Manes, Rene P. and Whinston, Andrew. Programming, Profit Rates and Pricing Decisions. *Accounting Rev.,* July 1969, *44*(3), pp. 467–81.

van De Panne, C. and Whinston, Andrew. The Symmetric Formulation of the Simplex Method for Quadratic Programming. *Econometrica,* July 1969, *37*(3), pp. 507–27.

Fučík, Ivan and Gál, Tomáš. K otázce degenerace ve výchozím řešení simplexových úloh lineárního programování. (On the Question of Degeneration in the Original Solution of Simplex LP-Problems. With English summary.) *Ekon.-Mat. Obzor,* 1969, *5*(3), pp. 295–303.

Gottinger, Hans-Werner. Die Existenz einiger Klassen deterministischer Nutzenfunktionen. (Existence of Some Classes of Deterministic Utility Functions. With English summary.) *Jahr. Nationalökon. Statist.,* July 1969, *183*(2), pp. 97–124.

Hall, Warren A.; Tauxe, G. W. and Yeh, W. W.-G. An Alternate Procedure for the Optimization of Operations for Planning with Multiple River,

Multiple Purpose Systems. *Water Resources Res.*, December 1969, *5*(6), pp. 1367–72.

Hawgood, John. Social Benefit Analysis by Inverse Linear Programming. In *Arnfield, R. V., ed.*, 1969, pp. 187–96.

Hrouda, Jaroslav. Jeden popis Balasova aditivního algoritmu se zřetelem k programování. (A Description of Balas' Additive Algorithm with Respect to Programming. With English summary.) *Ekon.-Mat. Obzor,* 1969, *5*(1), pp. 45–59.

Jääskeläinen, Veikko. A Goal Programming Model of Aggregate Production Planning. *Swedish J. Econ.*, March 1969, *71*(1), pp. 14–29.

Kendrick, David A. and Taylor, Lance J. A Dynamic Nonlinear Planning Model for Korea. In *Adelman, I., ed.*, 1969, pp. 213–37. [G: S. Korea]

Kornai, J. Man-Machine Planning. *Econ. Planning,* 1969, *9*(3), pp. 209–34.

Kronsjö, Tom. Decomposition of a Large Nonlinear Convex Separable Economic System in the Dual Direction. *Econ. Planning,* 1969, *9*(1–2), pp. 71–94.

Kronsjö, Tom. Optimal Coordination of a Large Convex Economic System. (Decomposition of a Nonlinear Convex Separable Economic System in Primal and Dual Directions to Obtain a Common Subproblem.) *Jahr. Nationalökon. Statist.*, December 1969, *183*(5), pp. 378–400.

Major, David C. Benefit-Cost Ratios for Projects in Multiple Objective Investment Programs. *Water Resources Res.*, December 1969, *5*(6), pp. 1174–78. [G: U.S.]

Maňas, Miroslav. Metody pro nalezení všech krajních bodů konvexního polyedru. (Methods for Finding All Vertices of a Convex Polyhedron. With English summary.) *Ekon.-Mat. Obzor,* 1969, *5*(3), pp. 325–42.

Mensch, Gerhard. Approximate Solutions for Digraph Models with Complementary Variables by Separable Programming with Restricted Pivoting. *Z. ges. Staatswiss.*, July 1969, *125*(3), pp. 437–45.

Moeseke, Paul V. and Ghellinck, Guy. Decentralization in Separable Programming. *Econometrica,* January 1969, *37*(1), pp. 73–78.

Nedoma, Josef. Modifikovaný Gomoryho algoritmus pro smíšené boolovské lineární úlohy. (Modified Gomory's Algorithm for Mixed Boolean Linear Programming Problems. With English summary.) *Ekon.-Mat. Obzor,* 1969, *5*(2), pp. 186–98.

Norton, Roger D. Formal Approaches to Regional Planning in Korea. In *Adelman, I., ed.*, 1969, pp. 185–212. [G: S. Korea]

Nuthall, P. L. Estimation of Supply Functions by Linear Programming: A Note. *Rev. Marketing Agr. Econ.*, September 1969, *37*(3), pp. 172–77.

Sengupta, Jati K. and Gruver, Gene. A Linear Reliability Analysis in Programming with Chance Constraints. *Swedish J. Econ.*, December 1969, *71*(4), pp. 221–46.

Shapley, Lloyd S. and Shubik, Martin. On Market Games. *J. Econ. Theory,* June 1969, *1*(1), pp. 9–25.

Strnad, Vladimír. Structural Matrix Model of Energy Balance. *Czech. Econ. Pap.*, 1969, (11), pp. 113–26.

Vepřek, Jaromír. Lineární plánovací modely a podniková praxe. (Linear Planning Models in Business Practice. With English summary.) *Ekon.-Mat. Obzor,* 1969, *5*(3), pp. 273–94. [G: Czechoslovakia]

Vinod, Hrishikesh D. Integer Programming and the Theory of Grouping. *J. Amer. Statist. Assoc.,* June 1969, *64*(326), pp. 506–19.

Westphal, Larry E. Multisectoral Project Analysis Employing Mixed Integer Programming. In *Adelman, I., ed.*, 1969, pp. 145–83. [G: S. Korea]

Wu, S. Y. A Nonlinear Programming Production Model. *Western Econ. J.*, December 1969, *7*(4), pp. 319–33.

214 Computer Programs

2140 Computer Programs

Krasnow, Howard S. Simulation Languages. In *Naylor, T. H., ed.*, 1969, pp. 320–46.

Naylor, Thomas H.; Burdick, Donald S. and Sasser, W. Earl, Jr. The Design of Computer Simulation Experiments. In *Naylor, T. H., ed.*, 1969, pp. 3–35.

220 Economic and Social Statistics

2200 General

Eckler, A. Ross. Statisticians and Shoemakers: Applying Their Skills. *Mon. Lab. Rev.*, November 1969, *92*(11), pp. 43–47.

Kaysen, Carl, et al. Report of the Task Force on the Storage of and Access to Government Statistics. *Amer. Statist.*, June 1969, *23*(3), pp. 11–19. [G: U.S.]

Kinov, D. A Useful Initiative to Follow. *Eastern Europ. Econ.*, Spring 1969, *7*(3), pp. 48–54. [G: Bulgaria]

Meixner, L. Activity of the Economic Research Institute. *Acta Oecon.*, 1969, *4*(3), pp. 321–26. [G: Hungary]

Moore, Geoffrey H. Long-Range Program Objectives for BLS. *Mon. Lab. Rev.*, October 1969, *92*(10), pp. 3–6. [G: U.S.]

221 National Income Accounting

2210 National Income Accounting Theory and Procedures

Aaron, Henry J. What Is a Comprehensive Tax Base Anyway? *Nat. Tax J.*, December 1969, *22*(4), pp. 543–49.

Aglietta, Michel and Seibel, Claude. The National Accounting System and the Preparation of the Fifth French Plan. *Rev. Income Wealth,* June 1969, *15*(2), pp. 121–69. [G: France]

Árvay, János. Development of the National Accounting System in Hungary. *Rev. Income Wealth,* June 1969, *15*(2), pp. 185–95. [G: Hungary]

Barbosa, A. S. Pinto. A Note on Intermediate Public

Expenditures. *Arquivo Inst.*, 1969, *4*(1&2), pp. 21–26.

Barnard, Jerald R. A Social Accounting System for Regional Development Planning. *J. Reg. Sci.*, April 1969, *9*(1), pp. 109–15. **[G: U.S.]**

Black, Stanley W. and Russell, R. Robert. An Alternative Estimate of Potential GNP. *Rev. Econ. Statist.*, February 1969, *51*(1), pp. 70–76. **[G: U.S.]**

Courbis, R. Compatabilité Nationale à Prix Constants et à Productivité Constante. (With English summary.) *Rev. Income Wealth*, March 1969, *15*(1), pp. 33–76.

Delange, Georges. Les méchanismes financiers et la comptabilité nationale. (With English summary.) *Revue Écon.*, May 1969, *20*(3), pp. 401–54.

Enthoven, Adolf J. H. Accountancy for Economic Development. *Finance Develop.*, September 1969, *6*(3), pp. 24–29.

Garston, Gordon J. and Kendrick, John W. Measuring Real Output for Industries Providing Services: OBE Concepts and Methods: Discussion. **In** *Fuchs, V. R., ed.*, 1969, pp. 41–49. **[G: U.S.]**

Gossling, W. F. A Note on User Cost. *Manchester Sch. Econ. Soc. Stud.*, September 1969, *37*(3), pp. 259–61.

Guerrero, Jiménez Rodolfo. Oferta y demanda, relacion basica en el dessarrollo. (Supply and Demand: A Basic Relationship in Development. With English summary.) *Econ. Polít.*, Second Semester 1969, *6*(2), pp. 223–28.

Holden, Kenneth. An Examination of Revisions to Selected Components of National Income. *Bull. Oxford Univ. Inst. Econ. Statist.*, May 1969, *31*(2), pp. 133–38. **[G: U.K.]**

Ionescu, Constantin. Retrospectivă şi perspectivă în statistica românească în cel de-al XXV-lea an de la eliberarea patriei. (Retrospection and Prospects in Romanian Statistics in the XXVth Year Since the Eliberation of Romania. With English summary.) *Stud. Cercet. Econ.*, 1969, *3*, pp. 43–49. **[G: Romania]**

Jacobs, Philip. Mr. Sunga's Treatment: A Fly in the Ointment. *Rev. Income Wealth*, September 1969, *15*(3), pp. 285–87.

Kindleberger, Charles P. Measuring Equilibrium in the Balance of Payments. *J. Polit. Econ.*, November/December 1969, *77*(6), pp. 873–91. **[G: U.S.]**

Kurabayashi, Yoshimasa. The Structure of Income Redistribution within the Framework of an Extended System of National Accounts. *Hitotsubashi J. Econ.*, June 1969, *10*(1), pp. 18–32. **[G: Japan]**

Ma, Ronald. Current Developments in Accounting Theory: Problems of Income Measurement. *Malayan Econ. Rev.*, April 1969, *14*(1), pp. 1–14.

Marimont, Martin L. Measuring Real Output for Industries Providing Services: OBE Concepts and Methods: Reply. **In** *Fuchs, V. R., ed.*, 1969, pp. 50–52. **[G: U.S.]**

Marimont, Martin L. Measuring Real Output for Industries Providing Services: OBE Concepts and Methods. **In** *Fuchs, V. R., ed.*, 1969, pp. 15–40. **[G: U.S.]**

Maskin, Balwant Singh. Some Reflections on Systems of Social Accounts—A Review Article. *Asian Econ. Rev.*, May 1969, *11*(3), pp. 273–89. **[G: India]**

Meade, James E. and Stone, J. R. N. The Construction of Tables of National Income, Expenditure, Savings and Investment. **In** *Parker, R. H. and Harcourt, G. C., eds.*, 1969, pp. 329–46.

Mirrlees, James A. The Evaluation of National Income in an Imperfect Economy. *Pakistan Develop. Rev.*, Spring 1969, *9*(1), pp. 1–13.

Nosé, Nobuko. Functions of Screen Accounts. *Kobe Econ. Bus. Rev.*, 1969, *16*(1), pp. 19–30.

Pikkemaat, G. F. Over de grenzen van de beschrijvende statistiek. (On the Scope of Descriptive Statistics. With English summary.) *De Economist*, May/June 1969, *117*(3), pp. 258–75.

Pyun, Chong Soo. The Monetary Value of a Housewife: An Economic Analysis for Use in Litigation. *Amer. J. Econ. Soc.*, July 1969, *28*(3), pp. 271–84.

Rinne, Horst. On Revisions in National Accounts Estimates. *Rev. Income Wealth*, September 1969, *15*(3), pp. 229–45. **[G: W. Germany]**

Robertson, H. M. The Wealth of Nations: How the National Income Is Produced, Divided Up and Spent. *S. Afr. J. Econ.*, June 1969, *37*(2), pp. 87–97.

Rostro Plasencia, Francisco. Perspectivas de continuidad del desarrollo economico de Mexico. (Prospects of Economic Development in Mexico. With English summary.) *Econ. Polít.*, Second Semester 1969, *6*(2), pp. 241–50. **[G: Mexico]**

Stiglitz, Joseph E. Distribution of Income and Wealth among Individuals. *Econometrica*, July 1969, *37*(3), pp. 382–97.

Tait, Alan A. Sensible Accounts and Control of Government Revenue and Expenditure. *Irish Banking Rev.*, December 1969, pp. 9–16. **[G: Ireland]**

Terleckyj, Nestor E. Measuring Real Output for Industries Providing Services: OBE Concepts and Methods: Comment. **In** *Fuchs, V. R., ed.*, 1969, pp. 49–50. **[G: U.S.]**

Thorp, Rosemary. A Note on Food Supplies, the Distribution of Income and National Income Accounting in Peru. *Bull. Oxford Univ. Inst. Econ. Statist.*, November 1969, *31*(4), pp. 229–41. **[G: Peru]**

Ulizzi, Adalberto. Income, Saving and Structure of Wealth in Italian Households in 1967. *Rev. Econ. Cond. Italy*, July 1969, *23*(4), pp. 275–303. **[G: Italy]**

Vanoli, Andre. Le Système Actuel de Comptabilité Nationale et la Planification. (With English summary.) *Rev. Income Wealth*, June 1969, *15*(2), pp. 171–84. **[G: France]**

Weisskopf, Walter A. Mishan on Progress: A Rejoinder. *J. Polit. Econ.*, November/December 1969, *77*(6), pp. 1036–39.

Wells, J. M. and Bates, W. R. A Note on Some Implications of Family Partnership Formation for Farm Income Comparisons. *Quart. Rev. Agr. Econ.*, July 1969, *22*(3), pp. 140–46. **[G: Australia]**

Whitehead, Laurence. Basic Data in Poor Countries:

The Bolivian Case. *Bull. Oxford Univ. Inst. Econ. Statist.*, August 1969, *31*(3), pp. 205–27. [G: Bolivia]

2212 National Income Accounts

Abraham, W. I. and Gill, M. S. New Measures of Economic Growth and Structural Change of the Malaysian Economy in the Post-1960 Period. *Malayan Econ. Rev.*, April 1969, *14*(1), pp. 65–79. [G: Malaysia]

Calmus, Thomas W. Current Trends in the National Economy. *Oregon Bus. Rev.*, February 1969, *28* (2), pp. 1, 4–8. [G: U.S.]

Christensen, Laurits R. and Jorgenson, Dale W. The Measurement of U.S. Real Capital Input, 1929–1967. *Rev. Income Wealth*, December 1969, *15* (4), pp. 293–320. [G: U.S.]

Clague, Christopher K. Capital-Labor Substitution in Manufacturing in Undeveloped Countries. *Econometrica*, July 1969, *37*(3), pp. 528–37. [G: Peru]

Gordon, Robert J. $45 Billion of U.S. Private Investment Has Been Mislaid. *Amer. Econ. Rev.*, June 1969, *59*(3), pp. 221–38. [G: U.S.]

Hoffmann, Walther G. The Share of Defence Expenditure in Gross National Product (GNP)—An International and Diachronic Comparison. *Ger. Econ. Rev.*, 1969, *7*(4), pp. 295–307.

Jalas, Kari. Mitä kasvua ajetaan takaa? (What Kind of Growth Are We Pursuing? With English summary.) *Kansant. Aikak.*, 1969, *65*(3), pp. 224–25. [G: Finland]

Keating, M. Employment and the Growth of Australian Gross National Product. *Econ. Rec.*, March 1969, *45*(109), pp. 27–47. [G: Australia]

Kennedy, R. V. Quarterly Estimates of National Income and Expenditure: 1950–51 to 1957–58. *Econ. Rec.*, June 1969, *45*(110), pp. 218–42. [G: Australia]

Kim, Young Chin. Sectoral Output-Capital Ratios and Levels of Economic Development: A Cross-Sectional Comparison of Manufacturing Industry. *Rev. Econ. Statist.*, November 1969, *51*(4), pp. 453–58.

Kumar, Pushpendra. Domestic Terms of Trade and Inter-Sectoral Income Flows in India: 1952–53 to 1966–67. *Asian Econ. Rev.*, August 1969, *11*(4), pp. 349–62. [G: India]

Lewis, Robert E. Corporate Profits—The First National City Bank's Series on Leading Corporations. *Univ. Missouri Bus. Govt. Rev.*, March–April 1969, *10*(2), pp. 33–40. [G: U.S.]

Lund, Unto. Ovatko tehdasteollisuus-investointimme olleet kokonaistaloudellisesti mielekkäitä? (Have Investments into Finnish Manufacturing Industry Been Economically Sensible? With English summary.) *Kansant. Aikak.*, 1969, *65*(3), pp. 220–23. [G: Finland]

Mukherjee, M. Certain Thoughts on Capital-output and Capital-labour Ratios. *Econ. Aff.*, January-February 1969, *14*(1–2), pp. 15–25. [G: India]

Pekonen, Kari. Investoinnit—työttömyys—taloudellinen kasvu. (Investment—Unemployment—Economic Growth. With English summary.) *Kansant. Aikak.*, 1969, *65*(3), pp. 215–19. [G: Finland]

Rudra, Ashok. National Income Statistics of India. *Arthaniti*, January & July 1969, *12*(1&2), pp. 69–77. [G: India]

Trescott, Paul B. The Growth of Inputs and Output in Thailand, 1946–65. *Philippine Econ. J.*, First Semester 1969, *8*(1), pp. 75–84. [G: Thailand]

White, William H. Lags between Actual and Reported Fixed Investment. *Int. Monet. Fund Staff Pap.*, July 1969, *16*(2), pp. 240–66.

Young, Allan H. and Harkins, Claudia. Alternative Measures of Price Change for GNP. *Surv. Curr. Bus.*, March 1969, *49*(3), pp. 47–52. [G: U.S.]

2213 Income Distribution

Bretzfelder, Robert B. and Dallavalle, Q. Francis. Total and *Per Capita* Personal Income by Regions and States, 1968. *Surv. Curr. Bus.*, August 1969, *49*(8), pp. 13, 24. [G: U.S.]

Britsch, Klaus; Reichardt, Helmut and Schips, Bernd. Sind die Lohnempfänger gut beraten, wenn sie sich einer Lohnquotensenkung widersetzen? (With English summary.) *Jahr. Nationalökon. Statist.*, August 1969, *183*(3–4), pp. 300–305.

Budd, Edward C. and Radner, Daniel B. The OBE Size Distribution Series: Methods and Tentative Results for 1964. *Amer. Econ. Rev.*, May 1969, *59* (2), pp. 435–49. [G: U.S.]

Burger, Albert E. The Effects of Inflation (1960–68). *Fed. Res. Bank St. Louis Rev.*, November 1969, *51* (11), pp. 25–36. [G: U.S.]

Cassidy, Henry J. The Rate of Change in the Size Distribution of Wages as a Vector. *Rev. Income Wealth*, December 1969, *15*(4), pp. 349–68. [G: U.S.]

Chiswick, Barry R. Minimum Schooling Legislation and the Cross-Sectional Distribution of Income. *Econ. J.*, September 1969, *79*(315), pp. 495–507. [G: U.S.; Netherlands; U.K.]

Chowdhury, A. H. M. Nuruddin. Some Reflections on Income Redistributive Intermediation in Pakistan. *Pakistan Develop. Rev.*, Summer 1969, *9* (2), pp. 95–110. [G: Pakistan]

Conlisk, John. An Approach to the Theory of Inequality in the Size Distribution of Income. *Western Econ. J.*, June 1969, *7*(2), pp. 180–86. [G: U.S.]

Devine, P. J. Inter-Regional Variations in the Degree of Inequality of Income Distribution: The United Kingdom, 1949–65. *Manchester Sch. Econ. Soc. Stud.*, June 1969, *37*(2), pp. 141–59. [G: U.K.]

Duggar, Jan Warren. International Comparisons of Income Levels: An Additional Measure. *Econ. J.*, March 1969, *79*(313), pp. 109–16.

Edgren, Gösta; Faxén, Karl-Olof and Odhner, Clas-Erik. Wages, Growth and the Distribution of Income. *Swedish J. Econ.*, September 1969, *71*(3), pp. 133–60. [G: Sweden]

Ferguson, C. E. and Moroney, John R. The Sources of Change in Labor's Relative Share: A Neoclassical Analysis. *Southern Econ. J.*, April 1969, *35*(4), pp. 308–22. [G: U.S.]

Gardner, Bruce L. Determinants of Farm Family Income Inequality. *Amer. J. Agr. Econ.*, November 1969, *51*(4), pp. 753–69. **[G: U.S.]**

Green, Christopher. Problems in the Area of Poverty: Discussion. *Amer. Econ. Rev.*, May 1969, *59* (2), pp. 473–75. **[G: U.S.]**

Gujarati, Damodar. Labor's Share in Manufacturing Industries, 1949–64. *Ind. Lab. Relat. Rev.*, October 1969, *23*(1), pp. 65–77. **[G: U.S.]**

Guthrie, Harold W. Problems in the Area of Poverty: Discussion. *Amer. Econ. Rev.*, May 1969, *59*(2), pp. 475–76. **[G: U.S.]**

Heidensohn, K. Labour's Share in National Income—A Constant? *Manchester Sch. Econ. Soc. Stud.*, December 1969, *37*(4), pp. 295–321.

Kayler, J. Allan. Personal Income in Urban Indiana. *Indiana Bus. Rev.*, March–April 1969, *44*, pp. 7–11. **[G: U.S.]**

Kurabayashi, Yoshimasa. The Structure of Income Redistribution within the Framework of an Extended System of National Accounts. *Hitotsubashi J. Econ.*, June 1969, *10*(1), pp. 18–32. **[G: Japan]**

Liu, Ben-Chieh. Regional Income Inequality and Federal Government Expenditures, 1948–63. *Quart. Rev. Econ. Bus.*, Winter 1969, *9*(4), pp. 67–76. **[G: U.S.]**

Loftus, P. J. Labour's Share in Manufacturing. *Lloyds Bank Rev.*, April 1969, (92), pp. 15–25.

Metcalf, Charles E. The Size Distribution of Personal Income during the Business Cycle. *Amer. Econ. Rev.*, Part I, September 1969, *59*(4), pp. 657–68. **[G: U.S.]**

Michalopoulos, Constantine. Productivity Growth in Latin America: Comment. *Amer. Econ. Rev.*, June 1969, *59*(3), pp. 435–39. **[G: U.S.; Brazil; Chile; Colombia; Argentina]**

Murray, Barbara B. Metropolitan Interpersonal Income Inequality. *Land Econ.*, February 1969, *45* (1), pp. 121–25. **[G: U.S.]**

Rao, V. M. Two Decompositions of Concentration Ratio. *J. Roy. Statist. Soc.*, Part 3, 1969, *132*, pp. 418–25.

Roby, Pamela. Inequality: A Trend Analysis. *Ann. Amer. Acad. Polit. Soc. Sci.*, September 1969, *385*, pp. 110–17. **[G: U.S.]**

Shabman, Leonard A. and Kalter, Robert J. Effects of Public Programs for Outdoor Recreation and Personal Income Distribution. *Amer. J. Agr. Econ.*, December 1969, *51*(5), pp. 1516–19. **[G: U.S.]**

Spandau, Arnt. Rate of Return, Profit-Sharing, and the Distribution of Incomes. *S. Afr. J. Econ.*, June 1969, *37*(2), pp. 105–16.

Spitz, John V. A Note on Relative-Wage Trends in Nine Southern States: The Case of Production and Non-Production Labor in Manufacturing. *J. Reg. Sci.*, August 1969, *9*(2), pp. 319–23. **[G: U.S.]**

Streissler, Erich. Long Term Structural Changes in the Distribution of Income. *Z. Nationalökon.*, May 1969, *29*(1–2), pp. 39–110.

Taira, Koji. Consumer Preferences, Poverty Norms, and Extent of Poverty. *Quart. Rev. Econ. Bus.*, Summer 1969, *9*(2), pp. 31–44.

Thorp, Rosemary. A Note on Food Supplies, the Distribution of Income and National Income Accounting in Peru. *Bull. Oxford Univ. Inst. Econ. Statist.*, November 1969, *31*(4), pp. 229–41. **[G: Peru]**

Thurow, Lester C. Problems in the Area of Poverty: Discussion. *Amer. Econ. Rev.*, May 1969, *59*(2), pp. 476–78. **[G: U.S.]**

Ulizzi, Adalberto. Income, Saving and Structure of Wealth in Italian Households in 1967. *Rev. Econ. Cond. Italy*, July 1969, *23*(4), pp. 275–303. **[G: Italy]**

Walter, Helmut. Über einige Zusammenhänge zwischen Einkommensverteilung und globaler Beschäftigtenstruktur. (With English summary.) *Z. ges. Staatswiss.*, April 1969, *125*(2), pp. 248–60. **[G: W. Germany]**

Wicks, John H. and McDonald, Patrick G. Income Distribution of Death Bequest Recipients. *Nat. Tax J.*, September 1969, *22*(3), pp. 408–10. **[G: U.S.]**

222 Input-Output

2220 Input-Output (including regional)

Bahl, Roy W. and Shellhammer, Kenneth L. Evaluating the State Business Tax Structure: An Application of Input-Output Analysis. *Nat. Tax J.*, June 1969, *22*(2), pp. 203–16. **[G: U.S.]**

Benet, I. and Berend, I. Relative Capital Intensity of Food Production and Industry. *Acta Oecon.*, 1969, *4*(4), pp. 379–402. **[G: Hungary]**

Billings, R. Bruce. The Mathematical Identity of the Multipliers Derived from the Economic Base Model and the Input-Output Model. *J. Reg. Sci.*, December 1969, *9*(3), pp. 471–73.

Bradley, Iver E. and Gander, James P. Input-Output Multipliers: Some Theoretical Comments. *J. Reg. Sci.*, August 1969, *9*(2), pp. 309–17.

Brand, S. S. The Interindustry Relationships of Agriculture and Economic Development in South Africa. *Finance Trade Rev.*, June 1969, *8*(3), pp. 171–86. **[G: S. Africa]**

Davis, H. Craig. Interregional Production and Water Resource Dependencies among the Western States. *Western Econ. J.*, March 1969, *7*(1), pp. 27–40. **[G: U.S.]**

Davis, H. Craig. Variations in the California and Pacific Northwest Input-Output Formats. *Univ. Wash. Bus. Rev.*, Autumn 1969, *29*(1), pp. 48–56. **[G: U.S.]**

Ellman, Michael. The Consistency of Soviet Plans. *Scot. J. Polit. Econ.*, February 1969, *16*(1), pp. 50–74. **[G: U.S.S.R.]**

Garnick, Daniel H. Disaggregated Basic-Service Models and Regional Input-Output Models in Multiregional Projections. *J. Reg. Sci.*, April 1969, *9*(1), pp. 87–100. **[G: U.S.]**

Gossling, W. F. A Note on User Cost. *Manchester Sch. Econ. Soc. Stud.*, September 1969, *37*(3), pp. 259–61.

Gupta, T. R. An Application of Inter-Industry Analysis to Demand Structure of the Indian Economy. *Asian Econ. Rev.*, May 1969, *11*(3), pp. 260–72. **[G: India]**

Ireri, Dunstan. A Proposed Model to Analyze Economic Interdependence among the Member Countries of the East African Community. *East Afr. Econ. Rev.*, December 1969, *1*(2), pp. 75–85. [G: E. African Community]

de Jong, F. J. De economische betekenis van de Rijksuniversiteit te Groningen voor de provincie. (The Economic Significance of the University of Groningen for the Province. With English summary.) *De Economist*, May/June 1969, *117*(3), pp. 193–226. [G: Netherlands]

Khachaturov, T. Questions Concerning the Theory of Socialist Reproduction. *Prob. Econ.*, September 1969, *12*(5), pp. 3–28.

Klotzvog, F. N.; Ageeva, V. A. and Buzunov, R. A. Input-Output and National Economic Planning. *Matekon*, Fall 1969, *6*(1), pp. 19–29.

Korte, Bernhard and Oberhofer, Walter. Zur Triangulation von Input-Output-Matrizen. (With English summary.) *Jahr. Nationalökon. Statist.*, March 1969, *182*(4–5), pp. 398–433.

Koumarová, Miluše and Vaner, Josef. Long-term Projection of the Sectoral Structure of the Czechoslovak National Economy on the Basis of an Input-Output Model. *Czech. Econ. Pap.*, 1969, (11), pp. 69–82. [G: Czechoslovakia]

Križková, Mária. Integrovatel'né štruktúrne modely s priestorovým prvkom. (Structural Models with Integration Capabilities and Regional Elements. With English summary.) *Ekon.-Mat. Obzor*, 1969, *5*(4), pp. 509–17.

Lago, Armando M. The Hoffman Industrial Growth Development Path: An International Comparison. *Weltwirtsch. Arch.*, 1969, *103*(1), pp. 41–57.

Lecomber, Richard. RAS Projections When Two or More Complete Matrices Are Known. *Econ. Planning*, 1969, *9*(3), pp. 267–78.

Livingstone, John Leslie. Input-Output Analysis for Cost Accounting, Planning and Control. *Accounting Rev.*, January 1969, *44*(1), pp. 48–64.

Long, Wesley H. An Examination of Linear Homogeneity of Trade and Production Functions in County Leontief Matrices. *J. Reg. Sci.*, April 1969, *9*(1), pp. 47–67. [G: U.S.]

Lunghini, Giorgio. Costi di produzione, prezzo delle merci e quote dei fattori primari. Alcuni risultati di un'analisi intersettoriale. (Production Costs, Commodity Prices, and Factor Shares—An Intersectoral Analysis. With English summary.) *L'Industria*, July–September 1969, (3), pp. 297–315. [G: Italy]

McGilvray, James and Simpson, David. Some Tests of Stability in Interindustry Coefficients. *Econometrica*, April 1969, *37*(2), pp. 204–21. [G: Ireland]

Miller, Ronald E. Interregional Feedbacks in Input-Output Models: Some Experimental Results. *Western Econ. J.*, March 1969, *7*(1), pp. 41–50.

Nambiar, R. G. Input-Output Analysis: Nature and Significance. *Artha-Vikas*, January 1969, *5*(1), pp. 9–28.

Preston, Esme. Direct and Indirect Relations of Australian Industries with Final Demand Sectors. *Econ. Rec.*, March 1969, *45*(109), pp. 84–91. [G: Australia]

Preston, Esme. Some Structural Comparisons: Australia and Neighbour Economies. *Australian Econ. Pap.*, December 1969, *8*(13), pp. 219–31.

Roskamp, Karl W. Fiscal Policy Objectives and Government Purchases by Industries: Towards an Input-Output Decision Model. *Z. ges. Staatswiss.*, January 1969, *125*(1), pp. 82–88.

Slome, Benjamin. The Interregional Input-Output Model and Interregional Public Finance. *Public Finance*, 1969, *24*(4), pp. 618–23.

Stone, Richard. Foreign Trade and Full Employment: An Input-output Analysis. *L'Industria*, October–December 1969, (4), pp. 431–43.

Tiebout, Charles M. An Empirical Regional Input-Output Projection Model: The State of Washington 1980. *Rev. Econ. Statist.*, August 1969, *51*(3), pp. 334–40. [G: U.S.]

Treml, Vladimir G. A Note on Soviet Input-Output Tables. *Soviet Stud.*, July 1969, *21*(1), pp. 21–34. [G: U.S.S.R.]

Volodarskii, L. and Eidel'man, M. Basic Results of Elaboration of the Interbranch Balance of Production and Distribution of Output throughout the National Economy of the U.S.S.R. for 1966. *Prob. Econ.*, September 1969, *12*(5), pp. 29–51. [G: U.S.S.R.]

Yamada, Hiroyuki and Ihara, Takeo. An Interindustrial Analysis of the Transportation Sector. *Kyoto Univ. Econ. Rev.*, October 1969, *39*(2), pp. 26–61.

Yeh, M. H. and Lin, Leon. Technological Change in the Canadian Livestock Industry: An Input-Output Approach. *Can. J. Agr. Econ.*, July 1969, *17*(2), pp. 63–84. [G: Canada]

223 Financial Accounts

2230 Financial Accounts; Financial Statistics

Barthelemy, Serge. La Methode de Projection à Moyen Terme des Circuits Financiers Utilisée dans la Préparation du Ve Plan Français. (With English summary.) *Rev. Income Wealth*, March 1969, *15*(1), pp. 77–100. [G: France]

Breton, Albert. A Stable Velocity Function for Canada? A Further Note. *Economica, N.S.*, August 1969, *36*(143), pp. 316. [G: Canada]

Burger, Albert E. Revision of the Money Supply Series. *Fed. Res. Bank St. Louis Rev.*, October 1969, *51*(10), pp. 6–9. [G: U.S.]

Cacy, J. A. Credit Flows in the 1960's. *Fed. Res. Bank Kansas City Rev.*, June 1969, pp. 11–16. [G: U.S.]

Carli, Guido. Celebration of the "World Thrift Day." *Rev. Econ. Cond. Italy*, January 1969, *23*(1), pp. 5–12. [G: Italy]

Delange, Georges. Les méchanismes financiers et la comptabilité nationale. (With English summary.) *Revue Écon.*, May 1969, *20*(3), pp. 401–54.

Dimitrijević, Dimitrije. The Use of Flow-of-Funds Accounts in Monetary Planning in Yugoslavia. *Rev. Income Wealth*, March 1969, *15*(1), pp. 101–15. [G: Yugoslavia]

Dorrance, Graeme S. The Role of Financial Accounts. *Rev. Income Wealth*, June 1969, *15*(2), pp. 197–207.

Fry, Edward R.; Beck, Darwin L. and Weaver, Mary

F. Revision of Money Stock Series. *Fed. Res. Bull.*, October 1969, *55*(10), pp. 787–803. **[G: U.S.]**

Gaines, Tilford C. Some Inadequacies of Financial Data and Theories. *Nat. Westminster Bank Quart. Rev.*, November 1969, pp. 35–44. **[G: U.S.]**

Ghafur, Abdul. Financial-Asset Accumulation by the Noncorporate Private Sector in Pakistan 1959/60 to 1965/66. *Pakistan Develop. Rev.*, Spring 1969, *9*(1), pp. 66–86. **[G: Pakistan]**

Goodhart, C. A. E. A Stable Velocity Function for Canada? A Note. *Economica, N.S.*, August 1969, *36*(143), pp. 314–15. **[G: Canada]**

Gramm, William P. and Timberlake, Richard H., Jr. The Stock of Money and Investment in the United States, 1897-1966. *Amer. Econ. Rev.*, December 1969, *59*(5), pp. 991–96. **[G: U.S.]**

Kozák, Josef and Šimůnek, Vladimír. Pokus o modelování sezónních výkyvů v bilanční rovnici důchodu. (An Attempt of Mathematical Formulation of Seasonal Variations of Inputs, Outputs and Prices in the Definitional Equation of Income. With English summary.) *Ekon.-Mat. Obzor*, 1969, *5*(2), pp. 209–23. **[G: Czechoslovakia]**

Krásová, Ludmila and Šimůnek, Vladimír. Soustava finančních účtů ČSSR. (A System of Financial Accounts in Czechoslovakia. With English summary.) *Ekon.-Mat. Obzor*, 1969, *5*(4), pp. 486–508. **[G: Czechoslovakia]**

Lees, Francis A. Interregional Flows of Funds through State and Local Government Securities (1957–1962). *J. Reg. Sci.*, April 1969, *9*(1), pp. 79–86. **[G: U.S.]**

Minocha, A. C. Inter-Sectoral Financial Flows in Indian Economy—Some Implications for Policy. *Econ. Aff.*, January-February 1969, *14*(1–2), pp. 33–38, 103–04. **[G: India]**

Rosen, L. S. and DeCoster, Don T. "Funds" Statements: A Historical Perspective. *Accounting Rev.*, January 1969, *44*(1), pp. 124–36.

Salvemini, Maria Teresa. Idee per un bilancio previsionale di cassa. (Ideas for a Cash Budget. With English summary.) *Bancaria*, September 1969, *25* (9), pp. 1088–99.

Srinivasan, E. S. Analysis of the Trends in the Sources of Funds of the Non-Financial Companies in India during 1951–66. *Asian Econ. Rev.*, February 1969, *11*(2), pp. 131–44. **[G: India]**

Wallich, Henry C. Uses of Financial Accounts in Monetary Analysis. *Rev. Income Wealth*, December 1969, *15*(4), pp. 321–34.

224 National Wealth and Balance Sheets

2240 National Wealth and Balance Sheets

Abraham, W. I. and Gill, M. S. The Growth and Composition of Malaysia's Capital Stock. *Malayan Econ. Rev.*, October 1969, *14*(2), pp. 44–54. **[G: Malaysia]**

Nesterov, L. Current Position of National Wealth Estimation in the World. *Rev. Income Wealth*, September 1969, *15*(3), pp. 271–83.

Trescott, Paul B. The Growth of Inputs and Output in Thailand, 1946–65. *Philippine Econ. J.*, First Semester 1969, *8*(1), pp. 75–84. **[G: Thailand]**

225 Social Indicators and Social Accounts

2250 Social Indicators and Social Accounts

Brown, A. J. and Woodward, V. H. Regional Social Accounts for the United Kingdom. *Rev. Income Wealth*, December 1969, *15*(4), pp. 335–47. **[G: U.K.]**

Byrne, Joycelin. Population Growth in St. Vincent. *Soc. Econ. Stud.*, June 1969, *18*(2), pp. 152–88. **[G: St. Vincent]**

Flaim, Paul O. Persons Not in the Labor Force: Who They Are and Why They Don't Work. *Mon. Lab. Rev.*, July 1969, *92*(7), pp. 3–14. **[G: U.S.]**

Gainsbrugh, Martin R. Statement. In *Review of Federal Statistical Programs, JECH*, 1969, pp. 131–37. **[G: U.S.]**

Gordon, Jerome B. Socioeconomic Status: A Re-examination of Its Dimensions. *J. Human Res.*, Summer 1969, *4*(3), pp. 343–59. **[G: U.S.]**

Hawes, Mary H. Measuring Retired Couples' Living Costs in Urban Areas. *Mon. Lab. Rev.*, November 1969, *92*(11), pp. 3–16. **[G: U.S.]**

Herbst, František. The Housing Situation in the CSSR in Terms of International Comparison. *Eastern Europ. Econ.*, Summer 1969, *7*(4), pp. 38–40. **[G: Czechoslovakia]**

Khachaturov, T. Questions Concerning the Theory of Socialist Reproduction. *Prob. Econ.*, September 1969, *12*(5), pp. 3–28.

McCracken, Paul W. Statement. In *Review of Federal Statistical Programs, JECH*, 1969, pp. 115–18. **[G: U.S.]**

Orshansky, Mollie. Perspectives on Poverty 2: How Poverty Is Measured. *Mon. Lab. Rev.*, February 1969, *92*(2), pp. 37–41. **[G: U.S.]**

Sawhill, Isabel V. The Role of Social Indicators and Social Reporting in Public Expenditure Decisions. In *The Analysis and Evaluation of Public Expenditures: The PPB System, Vol. 1, JECP*, 1969, pp. 473–85. **[G: U.S.]**

Taeuber, Conrad. Planning a New Inventory of the U.S.—Who Will Use the 1970 Census? *Univ. Missouri Bus. Govt. Rev.*, March–April 1969, *10*(2), pp. 5–13. **[G: U.S.]**

Taeuber, Karl E. Negro Population and Housing: Demographic Aspects of a Social Accounting Scheme. In *Katz, I. and Gurin, P., eds.*, 1969, pp. 145–93. **[G: U.S.]**

Taira, Koji. Consumer Preferences, Poverty Norms, and Extent of Poverty. *Quart. Rev. Econ. Bus.*, Summer 1969, *9*(2), pp. 31–44.

Turner, Marshall L., Jr. How Changes in Household Composition Affect Family Income. *Mon. Lab. Rev.*, November 1969, *92*(11), pp. 59–61. **[G: U.S.]**

Watts, Harold W. Statement. In *Review of Federal Statistical Programs, JECH*, 1969, pp. 140–44. **[G: U.S.]**

226 Productivity and Growth Indicators

2260 Productivity and Growth Indicators

Barger, Harold. Growth in Developed Nations. *Rev. Econ. Statist.*, May 1969, *51*(2), pp. 143–48.

Belianova, A. M. The Problem of the Rates of Economic Development in the U.S.S.R. as Treated in the Soviet Economic Literature of the 1920's. *Prob. Econ.*, April 1969, *11*(12), pp. 47–55. **[G: U.S.S.R.]**

Boserup, Mogens. Warning against Optimistic ICOR Statistics. *Kyklos*, 1969, *22*(4), pp. 774–76.

Brown, E. H. Phelps. The Brookings Study of the Poor Performance of the British Economy. *Economica, N.S.*, August 1969, *36*(143), pp. 235–52. **[G: U.K.]**

Christensen, Laurits R. and Jorgenson, Dale W. The Measurement of U.S. Real Capital Input, 1929–1967. *Rev. Income Wealth*, December 1969, *15* (4), pp. 293–320. **[G: U.S.]**

Conley, Ronald W. Roma Remarks on Methods of Measuring the Importance of Sources of Economic Growth. *Southern Econ. J.*, January 1969, *35*(3), pp. 224–30. **[G: U.S.]**

Courbis, R. Compatabilité Nationale à Prix Constants et à Productivité Constante. (With English summary.) *Rev. Income Wealth*, March 1969, *15* (1), pp. 33–76.

De Felice, Frank. Productivity Changes in Soviet Distribution. *Econ. J.*, March 1969, *79*(313), pp. 185–87. **[G: U.S.S.R.]**

Divatia, V. V. and Bhatt, V. V. On Measuring the Pace of Development. *Banca Naz. Lavoro Quart. Rev.*, June 1969, (89), pp. 190–206. **[G: India]**

Eysenbach, M. L. A Note on Growth and Structural Change in Pakistan's Manufacturing Industry 1954–1964. *Pakistan Develop. Rev.*, Spring 1969, *9*(1), pp. 58–65. **[G: Pakistan]**

Felix, David. Economic Development: Take-Offs into Unsustained Growth. *Soc. Res.*, Summer 1969, *36*(2), pp. 267–93. **[G: Latin America]**

George, K. D. Productivity in the Distributive Trades. *Bull. Oxford Univ. Inst. Econ. Statist.*, May 1969, *31*(2), pp. 61–75. **[G: U.K.]**

Gordon, Robert J. $45 Billion of U.S. Private Investment Has Been Mislaid. *Amer. Econ. Rev.*, June 1969, *59*(3), pp. 221–38. **[G: U.S.]**

Harris, John R. and Todaro, Michael P. Wages, Industrial Employment and Labour Productivity: The Kenyan Experience. *East Afr. Econ. Rev.*, June 1969, *1*(1), pp. 29–46. **[G: Kenya]**

Hayami, Yūjirō. Sources of Agricultural Productivity Gap among Selected Countries. *Amer. J. Agr. Econ.*, August 1969, *51*(3), pp. 564–75.

Herman, Shelby W. and Fulco, Lawrence J. Productivity and Unit Labor Costs in 1968. *Mon. Lab. Rev.*, June 1969, *92*(6), pp. 11–15. **[G: U.S.]**

Hoffmann, Walther G. Der tertiäre Sektor im Wachstumsprozess. (The Service Sector in the Growth Process. With English summary.) *Jahr. Nationalökon. Statist.*, June 1969, *183*(1), pp. 1–29. **[G: W. Europe; Japan; U.S.; Australia]**

Houssiaux, J. R. Annexes I, II, III to Statement. **In** *Economic Concentration, Pt. 7A, SCH*, 1969, pp. 3957–96. **[G: E.E.C.]**

Humphrey, Kenneth R. Retail Trade in Indiana and Surrounding States. *Indiana Bus. Rev.*, November/December 1969, *44*, pp. 11–15. **[G: U.S.]**

Jackman, Patrick C. Unit Labor Costs of Iron and Steel Industries in Five Countries. *Mon. Lab. Rev.*, August 1969, *92*(8), pp. 15–22. **[G: W. Germany; France; U.K.; U.S.; Japan]**

Jalas, Kari. Mitä kasvua ajetaan takaa? (What Kind of Growth Are We Pursuing? With English summary.) *Kansant. Aikak.*, 1969, *65*(3), pp. 224–25. **[G: Finland]**

Jonas, Paul and Sardy, Hyman. Production Index Bias as a Measure of Economic Development: A Comment. *Oxford Econ. Pap.*, November 1969, *21*(3), pp. 428–32. **[G: U.S.]**

Keating, M. Employment and the Growth of Australian Gross National Product. *Econ. Rec.*, March 1969, *45*(109), pp. 27–47. **[G: Australia]**

Kendrick, John W. An Evaluation of Productivity Statistics. **In** *Somers, G. G., ed. (II)*, 1969, pp. 129–35. **[G: U.S.]**

Kravis, Irving B. and Liu, Ta-Chung. What Is Output? Problems of Concept and Measurement: Discussion. **In** *Fuchs, V. R., ed.*, 1969, pp. 84–94.

Kux, Jaroslav; Mairesse, Jacques and Drechsler, Lászó. Labour Productivity Comparison between Czechoslovakia and France. *Rev. Income Wealth*, September 1969, *15*(3), pp. 219–28. **[G: Czechoslovakia; France]**

Lago, Armando M. The Hoffman Industrial Growth Development Path: An International Comparison. *Weltwirtsch. Arch.*, 1969, *103*(1), pp. 41–57.

Lydall, Harold. On Measuring Technical Progress. *Australian Econ. Pap.*, June 1969, *8*(12), pp. 1–12. **[G: U.K.]**

Mallakh, Ragaei El. The Economics of Rapid Growth: Libya. *Middle East J.*, Summer 1969, *23* (3), pp. 308–20. **[G: Libya]**

Massell, Benton F. and Yotopoulos, Pan A. The Relationships between the Volume of Investment, Its Productivity and the Growth of the South American Countries. *Kyklos*, 1969, *22*(2), pp. 328–33. **[G: S. America]**

Matthews, R. C. O. Why Growth Rates Differ. *Econ. J.*, June 1969, *79*(314), pp. 261–68. **[G: U.S.; W. Europe]**

Mera, Koichi. A Generalized Aggregative Model for Optimal Growth with Some Empirical Tests. *Int. Econ. Rev.*, June 1969, *10*(2), pp. 149–62. **[G: U.S.; Japan]**

Michalopoulos, Constantine. Productivity Growth in Latin America: Comment. *Amer. Econ. Rev.*, June 1969, *59*(3), pp. 435–39. **[G: U.S.; Brazil; Chile; Colombia; Argentina]**

Mundlak, Yair and Razin, Assaf. Aggregation, Index Numbers and the Measurement of Technical Change. *Rev. Econ. Statist.*, May 1969, *51*(2), pp. 166–75.

Palomba, Neil A. Stability and Real Economic Growth: An International Comparison. *Kyklos*, 1969, *22*(3), pp. 589–92.

Patel, Surendra J. Rejoinder to Boserup's 'Warning against Optimistic ICOR Statistics.' *Kyklos*, 1969, *22*(4), pp. 777–79.

Powers, John Anthony. Branch Versus Unit Banking: Bank Output and Cost Economies. *Southern Econ. J.*, October 1969, *36*(2), pp. 153–64. **[G: U.S.]**

Prakash, Prem. Relationship Between Size and Productivity in Selected Indian Industries. *Asian Econ. Rev.*, May 1969, *11*(3), pp. 237–48. **[G: India]**

Román, Zoltán. A Note on Measuring Structural Changes. *Rev. Income Wealth*, September 1969, *15*(3), pp. 265–68.

Roussakis, Emmanuel N. La Comunità Economica Europea: Bilancio economico e politico. (The European Economic Community: An Economic and Political Balance Sheet. With English summary.) *Rivista Int. Sci. Econ. Com.*, October 1969, *16*(10), pp. 993–1006. **[G: E.E.C.]**

Saini, Krishan G. The Growth of the Indian Economy: 1860–1960. *Rev. Income Wealth*, September 1969, *15*(3), pp. 247–63. **[G: India]**

Schreiber, Wilfrid. Beziehungen zwischen den Zuwachsraten des Sozialprodukts, der Faktoreinsätze und der Faktorpreise im vereinfachten Modell. Notizen zur Wachstrumstheorie. (Relations between the Growth Rates of the National Product, the Factor Inputs, and the Factor Prices in a Simplified Model. With English summary.) *Jahr. Nationalökon. Statist.*, August 1969, *183* (3–4), pp. 243–53.

Shultz, George P. Labor Statistics for National Decision Making. *Amer. Statist.*, October 1969, *23*(4), pp. 11–14. **[G: U.S.]**

Stacey, R. D. Uniformity in Output Growth Patterns in the Manufacturing Sector. *S. Afr. J. Econ.*, March 1969, *37*(1), pp. 55–75.

Thirlwall, A. P. Okun's Law and the Natural Rate of Growth. *Southern Econ. J.*, July 1969, *36*(1), pp. 87–89. **[G: U.S.; U.K.]**

Treadway, Arthur B. What Is Output? Problems of Concept and Measurement. **In** *Fuchs, V. R., ed.*, 1969, pp. 53–84.

Trescott, Paul B. The Growth of Inputs and Output in Thailand, 1946–65. *Philippine Econ. J.*, First Semester 1969, *8*(1), pp. 75–84. **[G: Thailand]**

Vincent, Andre L.-A. La productivité globale clé de l'étude de la répartition. (With English summary.) *Revue Écon.*, September 1969, *20*(5), pp. 783–829.

227 Prices

2270 Prices

Aggrey-Mensah, W. and Tuckwell, N. E. A Study of Banana Supply and Price Patterns on the Sydney Wholesale Market: An Application of Spectral Analysis. *Australian J. Agr. Econ.*, December 1969, *13*(2), pp. 101–17. **[G: Australia]**

Bambrick, Susan. The Reserve Bank Index of Australian Import Prices. *Econ. Rec.*, September 1969, *45*(111), pp. 399–414. **[G: Australia]**

Barzel, Yoram. Productivity and the Price of Medical Services. *J. Polit. Econ.*, November/December 1969, *77*(6), pp. 1014–27. **[G: U.S.]**

Bickel, Blaine W. Farm Real Estate Prices 1950–67. *Fed. Res. Bank Kansas City Rev.*, April 1969, pp. 3–9. **[G: U.S.]**

Brackett, Jean C. New BLS Budgets Provide Yardsticks for Measuring Family Living Costs. *Mon. Lab. Rev.*, April 1969, *92*(4), pp. 3–16. **[G: U.S.]**

Brewster, Havelock. The Pattern of Change in Wages, Prices and Productivity in British Guiana, 1948 to 1962. *Soc. Econ. Stud.*, June 1969, *18*(2), pp. 107–36. **[G: British Guiana]**

Christensen, Laurits R. and Jorgenson, Dale W. The Measurement of U.S. Real Capital Input, 1929–1967. *Rev. Income Wealth*, December 1969, *15* (4), pp. 293–320. **[G: U.S.]**

Davidson, F. G. Pricing Behaviour: Another Plea for More Statistics. *Econ. Rec.*, December 1969, *45* (112), pp. 582–88. **[G: Australia]**

Dryden, Myles M. A Source of Bias in Filter Tests of Share Prices. *J. Bus.*, July 1969, *42*(3), pp. 321–25.

Duewer, Lawrence A. Effects of Specials on Composite Meat Prices. *Agr. Econ. Res.*, July 1969, *21* (3), pp. 70–77. **[G: U.S.]**

Emerson, Peter M. and Tomek, William G. Did Futures Trading Influence Potato Prices? *Amer. J. Agr. Econ.*, August 1969, *51*(3), pp. 666–72. **[G: U.S.]**

Emery, Betty J. and Garston, Gordon J. The Measurement of Constant Price Aggregates in Canada. *Rev. Income Wealth*, March 1969, *15*(1), pp. 1–32. **[G: Canada]**

Fredman, Albert J. and Wert, James E. Secondary Distributions of American Stock Exchange Securities. *Marquette Bus. Rev.*, Fall 1969, *13*(3), pp. 137–41. **[G: U.S.]**

Ganguly, Swapan and Venugopal, Bhaskar. International Crude Oil Prices after World War II. *Indian Econ. J.*, January–March 1969, *16*(3), pp. 382–87.

Heien, Dale M. Income and Price Lags in Consumer-demand Analysis. *J. Roy. Statist. Soc.*, Part 2, 1969, *132*, pp. 265–71. **[G: U.S.]**

Kaser, Michael. A Volume Index of Soviet Foreign Trade. *Soviet Stud.*, April 1969, *20*(4), pp. 523–26. **[G: U.S.S.R.]**

Kravis, Irving B. and Lipsey, Robert E. International Price Comparisons by Regression Methods. *Int. Econ. Rev.*, June 1969, *10*(2), pp. 233–46.

Kravis, Irving B. Statement. **In** *Review of Federal Statistical Programs, JECH*, 1969, pp. 203–06. **[G: U.S.]**

Kuchenbecker, Horst. Zur Darstellung von Veränderungen der Weltwarenpreise durch arithmetische und geometrische Indizes am Beispiel des Moody-Index und des Reuter-Index. (On the Representation of World Commodity Price Changes by Arithmetic and Geometric Index Numbers, Illustrated in Moodys Index of Staple Commodities and Reuters Commodity Index. With English summary.) *Jahr. Nationalökon. Statist.*, August 1969, *183*(3–4), pp. 254–70.

Ladd, George W. Federal Milk Marketing Order Provisions: Effects on Producer Prices and Intermarket Price Relationships. *Amer. J. Agr. Econ.*, August 1969, *51*(3), pp. 625–41. **[G: U.S.]**

Layng, W. John and Nakayama, Toshiko. An Analysis of Price Changes in Second Quarter of 1969. *Mon. Lab. Rev.*, October 1969, *92*(10), pp. 36–41. **[G: U.S.]**

Luttrell, Clifton B. Meat Prices. *Fed. Res. Bank St. Louis Rev.*, August 1969, *51*(8), pp. 24–28. **[G: U.S.]**

McKenzie, C. J.; Philpot, B. P. and Woods, M. J. Price Formation in the Raw Wool Market. *Econ. Rec.*, September 1969, *45*(111), pp. 386–98.

van Meerhaeghe, M. A. G. Observations sur la signification des termes d'échange des pays sous-développés. (With English summary.) *Kyklos*, 1969, *22*(3), pp. 566–84.

Moore, Geoffrey H. Statement. In *Review of Federal Statistical Programs, JECH,* 1969, pp. 173–98. [G: U.S.]

Musgrave, John C. The Measurement of Price Changes in Construction. *J. Amer. Statist. Assoc.,* September 1969, *64*(327), pp. 771–86. [G: U.S.]

Ng, S. H. The Terms of Trade in the Case of Entrepôt Trade. *Econ. Rec.,* June 1969, *45*(110), pp. 288–90.

Pikkemaat, G. F. Over de grenzen van de beschrijvende statistiek. (On the Scope of Descriptive Statistics. With English summary.) *De Economist,* May/June 1969, *117*(3), pp. 258–75.

Popkin, Joel. Price Changes in the First Quarter of 1969 in Perspective. *Mon. Lab. Rev.,* July 1969, *92*(7), pp. 26–30. [G: U.S.]

Sahota, G. S. Economic Problems in Separating the Determinants of Relative Prices. *Int. Econ. Rev.,* June 1969, *10*(2), pp. 183–206. [G: U.S.]

Samli, A. Coskun. Differential Price Structures for the Rich and the Poor. *Univ. Wash. Bus. Rev.,* Summer 1969, *28*(4), pp. 36–43. [G: U.S.]

Schroeder, Gertrude E. The 1966–67 Soviet Industrial Price Reform: A Study in Complications. *Soviet Stud.,* April 1969, *20*(4), pp. 462–77. [G: U.S.S.R.]

Smith, Keith V. Stock Price and Economic Indexes for Generating Efficient Portfolios. *J. Bus.,* July 1969, *42*(3), pp. 326–36.

Swamy, Subramanian. Retail Price Index in the Peoples' Republic of China. *Rev. Econ. Statist.,* August 1969, *51*(3), pp. 309–19. [G: China]

Triplett, Jack E. Automobiles and Hedonic Quality Measurement. *J. Polit. Econ.,* May/June 1969, *77*(3), pp. 408–17. [G: U.S.]

Tritschler, Charles A. Statistical Criteria for Asset Valuation by Specific Price Index. *Accounting Rev.,* January 1969, *44*(1), pp. 99–123.

Videnov, Ivan. Theoretical Problems of Wholesale Prices. *Eastern Europ. Econ.,* Summer 1969, *7*(4), pp. 3–12.

Vigand, V. C. Once More on the World Price of Oil: A Comment. *Acta Oecon.,* 1969, *4*(2), pp. 211–14.

Willett, Helen E. and Whan, R. B. Price Variation within Wool Auction Sales. *Quart. Rev. Agr. Econ.,* April 1969, *22*(2), pp. 66–81. [G: Australia]

Yohe, William P. and Karnosky, Denis S. Interest Rates and Price Level Changes, 1952–69. *Fed. Res. Bank St. Louis Rev.,* December 1969, *51*(12), pp. 18–38. [G: U.S.]

Young, Allan H. and Harkins, Claudia. Alternative Measures of Price Change for GNP. *Surv. Curr. Bus.,* March 1969, *49*(3), pp. 47–52. [G: U.S.]

228 Regional Statistics

2280 Regional Statistics

Bahl, Roy W. and Shellhammer, Kenneth L. Evaluating the State Business Tax Structure: An Application of Input-Output Analysis. *Nat. Tax J.,* June 1969, *22*(2), pp. 203–16. [G: U.S.]

Barnard, Jerald R. A Social Accounting System for Regional Development Planning. *J. Reg. Sci.,* April 1969, *9*(1), pp. 109–15. [G: U.S.]

Bourque, Philip J. Income Multipliers for the Washington Economy. *Univ. Wash. Bus. Rev.,* Winter 1969, *28*(2), pp. 5–15. [G: U.S.]

Bretzfelder, Robert B.; Dallavalle, Q. Francis and Hirschberg, David A. Personal Income, 1968, and Disposable Income, 1929–68, by States and Regions. *Surv. Curr. Bus.,* April 1969, *49*(4), pp. 16–21, 32. [G: U.S.]

Bretzfelder, Robert B. and Dallavalle, Q. Francis. Total and *Per Capita* Personal Income by Regions and States, 1968. *Surv. Curr. Bus.,* August 1969, *49*(8), pp. 13, 24. [G: U.S.]

Brown, A. J. and Woodward, V. H. Regional Social Accounts for the United Kingdom. *Rev. Income Wealth,* December 1969, *15*(4), pp. 335–47. [G: U.K.]

Brown, H. James. Shift and Share Projections of Regional Economic Growth: An Empirical Test. *J. Reg. Sci.,* April 1969, *9*(1), pp. 1–18.

Edwards, Clark. A Rural Economic Indicator System. *Amer. J. Agr. Econ.,* December 1969, *51*(5), pp. 1202–05. [G: U.S.]

Hirsch, Werner Z. Regional Information Design for Public Decisions. *Rev. Income Wealth,* December 1969, *15*(4), pp. 369–80.

Humphrey, Kenneth R. Retail Trade in Indiana and Surrounding States. *Indiana Bus. Rev.,* November/December 1969, *44,* pp. 11–15. [G: U.S.]

de Jong, F. J. De economische betekenis van de Rijksuniversiteit te Groningen voor de provincie. (The Economic Significance of the University of Groningen for the Province. With English summary.) *De Economist,* May/June 1969, *117*(3), pp. 193–226. [G: Netherlands]

Kayler, J. Allan. Personal Income in Urban Indiana. *Indiana Bus. Rev.,* March–April 1969, *44,* pp. 7–11. [G: U.S.]

L'Esperance, Wilford L.; Nestel, G. and Fromm, D. Gross State Product and an Econometric Model of a State. *J. Amer. Statist. Assoc.,* September 1969, *64*(327), pp. 787–807. [G: U.S.]

Long, Wesley H. An Examination of Linear Homogeneity of Trade and Production Functions in County Leontief Matrices. *J. Reg. Sci.,* April 1969, *9*(1), pp. 47–67. [G: U.S.]

Moody, Harold T. and Puffer, Frank W. A Gross Regional Product Approach to Regional Model-Building. *Western Econ. J.,* December 1969, *7*(4), pp. 391–402. [G: U.S.]

Muse, William V. Indicators of Economic Progress in the Ohio Valley: 1963–1967. *Ohio State U. Bull. Bus. Res.,* August 1969, *44*(8), pp. 1–3, 5. [G: U.S.]

Pyun, Chong Soo. Local Business Activity Index: Its Construction and Uses—Comment. *J. Reg. Sci.,* April 1969, *9*(1), pp. 163–66.

Singh, Ajmer. Local Business Activity Index: Its Construction and Uses—Reply. *J. Reg. Sci.,* April 1969, *9*(1), pp. 167–69.

Stambler, Howard V. Problems in Analyzing Urban Employment Survey Data. *Mon. Lab. Rev.,* November 1969, *92*(11), pp. 51–54. [G: U.S.]

Terry, Edwin F. Public Finance and Regional Accounts. *Rev. Income Wealth,* June 1969, *15*(2), pp. 207–13. [G: U.S.]

Thoss, Rainer. Ein Vorschlag zur Koordinierung der Regionalpolitik in einer wachsenden Wirtschaft. (With English summary.) *Jahr. Nationalökon. Statist.*, May 1969, *182*(6), pp. 490–529. **[G: Germany]**

300 Domestic Monetary and Fiscal Theory and Institutions

310 DOMESTIC MONETARY AND FINANCIAL THEORY AND INSTITUTIONS

311 Domestic Monetary and Financial Theory and Institutions

3110 Monetary Theory and Policy

Argy, Victor. Monetary Variables and the Balance of Payments. *Int. Monet. Fund Staff Pap.*, July 1969, *16*(2), pp. 267–88.

Artis, M. J. Two Aspects of the Monetary Debate. *Nat. Inst. Econ. Rev.*, August 1969, (49), pp. 33–51.

Beltrame, Carlo. Le merchant banks britanniche. (British Merchant Banks. With English summary.) *L'Impresa*, January/February 1969, *11*(1), pp. 68–71. **[G: U.K.]**

Bronfenbrenner, Martin. Monetary Rules: A New Look. **In** *The 1969 Economic Report of the President, Pt. 3, JECH*, 1969, pp. 583–615. **[G: U.S.]**

Bulhoes, Octávio de Gouveia. Financial Recuperation for Economic Expansion. **In** *Ellis, H. S., ed.*, 1969, pp. 162–76. **[G: Brazil]**

Buonomo, Maurizio. Moneta e credito nelle economie socialiste: vecchi e nuovi orientamenti. (Money and Credit in Socialist Economies: Old Trends and New. With English summary.) *Bancaria*, April 1969, *25*(4), pp. 449–59.

Cohen, Kalman J. and Reid, Samuel Richardson. Effects of Regulation, Branching, and Mergers on Banking Structure and Performance: Reply. *Southern Econ. J.*, October 1969, *36*(2), pp. 204–09. **[G: U.S.]**

Cooper, Richard N. Macroeconomic Policy Adjustment in Interdependent Economies. *Quart. J. Econ.*, February 1969, *83*(1), pp. 1–24.

Davis, Richard G. Monetary Theory: Discussion. *Amer. Econ. Rev.*, May 1969, *59*(2), pp. 315–21. **[G: U.S.]**

Duisenberg, W. F. Problematiek rond de Britse betalingsbalans. (British Balance of Payments Problems. With English summary.) *De Economist*, November/December 1969, *117*(6), pp. 615–57. **[G: U.K.]**

Eltis, W. A. Are Interest Rates too High? *Lloyds Bank Rev.*, July 1969, (93), pp. 27–35. **[G: U.K.]**

Fand, David I. A Monetary Interpretation of the Post-1965 Inflation in the United States. *Banca Naz. Lavoro Quart. Rev.*, June 1969, (89), pp. 99–127. **[G: U.S.]**

Fand, David I. Monetary Theory and the Post-1965 Inflation. *Mich. Academician*, Summer 1969, *2* (1), pp. 13–22. **[G: U.S.]**

Fand, David I. Some Issues in Monetary Economics. *Banca Naz. Lavoro Quart. Rev.*, September 1969, (90), pp. 215–47.

Francis, Darryl R. Monetary Policy and Inflation. *Fed. Res. Bank St. Louis Rev.*, June 1969, *51*(6), pp. 8–11. **[G: U.S.]**

Francis, Darryl R. Selective Credit—No Substitute for Monetary Restraint. *Fed. Res. Bank St. Louis Rev.*, December 1969, *51*(12), pp. 13–17. **[G: U.S.]**

Friedman, Milton. Post-War Trends in Monetary Theory and Policy. **In** *Friedman, M.*, 1969, pp. 69–79. **[G: U.S.]**

Friedman, Milton. The Optimum Quantity of Money. **In** *Friedman, M.*, 1969, pp. 1–50.

Graff, Jan de V. The National Debt. *S. Afr. J. Econ.*, September 1969, *37*(3), pp. 170–86. **[G: S. Africa]**

Holland, Thomas E. 'Operation Twist' and the Movement of Interest Rates and Related Economic Time Series. *Int. Econ. Rev.*, October 1969, *10*(3), pp. 260–65. **[G: U.S.]**

Jevons, W. S. Barter. **In** *Clower, R. W., ed.*, 1969, pp. 25–29.

Johnson, Harry G. Inside Money, Outside Money, Income, Wealth, and Welfare in Monetary Theory. *J. Money, Credit, Banking*, February 1969, *1* (1), pp. 30–45.

Jordan, Jerry L. Relations among Monetary Aggregates. *Fed. Res. Bank St. Louis Rev.*, March 1969, *51*(3), pp. 8–9. **[G: U.S.]**

Käräva, Simo. Luotonannon selektiivisyys ja pankit. (The Selective Lending Policy and the Banks. With English summary.) *Kansant. Aikak.*, 1969, *65*(3), pp. 226–32. **[G: Finland]**

Lutz, Friedrich A. On Neutral Money. **In** *[von Hayek, Friedrich A.]*, 1969, pp. 105–16.

Maddala, G. S. and Vogel, Robert C. Estimating Lagged Relationships in Corporate Demand for Liquid Assets. *Rev. Econ. Statist.*, February 1969, *51*(1), pp. 53–61. **[G: U.S.]**

Marty, Alvin L. Inside Money, Outside Money, and the Wealth Effect. *J. Money, Credit, Banking*, February 1969, *1*(1), pp. 101–11.

Newlyn, W. T. Monetary Analysis and Policy in Financially Dependent Economies. **In** *Stewart, I. G., ed.*, 1969, pp. 71–82.

Niehans, Jürg. Efficient Monetary and Fiscal Policies in Balanced Growth. *J. Money, Credit, Banking*, May 1969, *1*(2), pp. 228–51.

Pigou, A. C. Money, a Veil? **In** *Clower, R. W., ed.*, 1969, pp. 30–36.

Silber, William L. Portfolio Substitutability, Regulations, and Monetary Policy. *Quart. J. Econ.*, May 1969, *83*(2), pp. 197–219. **[G: U.S.]**

Simonsen, Mário Henrique. Inflation and the Money and Capital Markets of Brazil. **In** *Ellis, H. S., ed.*, 1969, pp. 133–61. **[G: Brazil]**

Smith, Warren L. A Neo-Keynesian View of Monetary Policy. **In** *Federal Reserve Bank of Boston*, 1969, pp. 105–26.

Sohmen, Egon and Schneeweiss, Hans. Fiscal and Monetary Policies under Alternative Exchange Rate Systems: A Correction. *Quart. J. Econ.*, May 1969, *83*(2), pp. 336–40.

Solterer, Josef. Liquidity Norms for Development. *Rev. Soc. Econ.*, March 1969, *27*(1), pp. 13–22.

Velk, Thomas J. Chicago Campfires. *Quart. Rev. Econ. Bus.*, Winter 1969, *9*(4), pp. 39–45.

Wallich, Henry C. A Neo-Keynesian View of Monetary Policy: Discussion. **In** *Federal Reserve Bank of Boston*, 1969, pp. 127-131.

Weiss, Steven J. Effects of Regulation, Branching, and Mergers on Banking Structure and Performance: Comment. *Southern Econ. J.*, October 1969, *36*(2), pp. 202–04. **[G: U.S.]**

Willett, Thomas D. and Forte, Francesco. Interest Rate Policy and External Balance. *Quart. J. Econ.*, May 1969, *83*(2), pp. 242–62. **[G: U.S.]**

Zerby, J. A. An Econometric Model of Monetary Interaction in Australia. *Australian Econ. Pap.*, December 1969, *8*(13), pp. 154–77. **[G: Australia]**

3112 Monetary Theory; Empirical Studies

Allais, Maurice. Growth and Inflation. *J. Money, Credit, Banking*, August 1969, *1*(3), pp. 355–426. **[G: U.K.]**

Allais, Maurice. Growth and Inflation: A Reply to the Observations of the Discussants. *J. Money, Credit, Banking*, August 1969, *1*(3), pp. 441–62. **[G: U.K.]**

Andersen, Leonall C. and Jordan, Jerry L. Monetary and Fiscal Actions: A Test of Their Relative Importance in Economic Stabilization—Reply. *Fed. Res. Bank St. Louis Rev.*, April 1969, *51*(4), pp. 12–16. **[G: U.S.]**

Andersen, Leonall C. Monetary Velocity in Empirical Analysis: Discussion. **In** *Federal Reserve Bank of Boston*, 1969, pp. 52–55.

Anderson, Leslie P. and Roscoe, David L. The Term Structure of Interest Rates—An Alternative Hypothesis. *Miss. Val. J. Bus. Econ.*, Spring 1969, *4* (2), pp. 1-9.

Anderson, Paul S. and Morris, Frank E. Defining the Money Supply: The Case of Government Deposits. *New Eng. Econ. Rev.*, March/April 1969, pp. 21–31. **[G: U.S.]**

Anderson, Paul S. Monetary Velocity in Empirical Analysis. **In** *Federal Reserve Bank of Boston*, 1969, pp. 37–51.

Andreatta, Nino. Il disegno della politica della Banca centrale e l'uso di modelli econometrici di flussi monetari. (The Framing of Central Bank Policy and the Use of Econometric Models of Money Flows. With English summary.) *Bancaria*, January 1969, *25*(1), pp. 9–18.

Argy, Victor. The Impact of Monetary Policy on Expenditure, with Particular Reference to the United Kingdom. *Int. Monet. Fund Staff Pap.*, November 1969, *16*(3), pp. 436–88. **[G: U.K.]**

Banks, F. E. A Note on Income, Capital Mobility, and the Theory of Economic Policy. *Kyklos*, 1969, *22*(4), pp. 767–73.

Bonello, Frank J. and Russell, William R. Multiple Year Forecast Errors and the Terms Structure of Interest Rates. *Indian Econ. J.*, April–June 1969, *16*(4–5), pp. 554–60.

Borch, Karl. A Note on Uncertainty and Indifference Curves. *Rev. Econ. Stud.*, January 1969, *36*(105), pp. 1–4.

Boulding, Kenneth E. David Fand's "Keynesian Monetary Theories, Stabilization Policy, and the Recent Inflation": A Comment. *J. Money, Credit, Banking*, August 1969, *1*(3), pp. 588–89. **[G: U.S.]**

Breen, William J. An Exploratory Econometric Model of Financial Markets. *J. Financial Quant. Anal.*, September 1969, *4*(3), pp. 233–69. **[G: U.S.]**

Breton, Albert. A Stable Velocity Function for Canada? A Further Note. *Economica, N.S.*, August 1969, *36*(143), pp. 316. **[G: Canada]**

Burger, Albert E. Revision of the Money Supply Series. *Fed. Res. Bank St. Louis Rev.*, October 1969, *51*(10), pp. 6–9. **[G: U.S.]**

Burstein, M. L. The Quantity Theory of Money: A Critique. **In** *Clower, R. W., ed.*, 1969, pp. 112–19.

Cagan, Phillip. Allais' Monetary Theory: Interpretation and Comment. *J. Money, Credit, Banking*, August 1969, *1*(3), pp. 427–32. **[G: U.K.]**

Cagan, Phillip. Interest Rates and Bank Reserves—A Reinterpretation of the Statistical Association. **In** *Guttentag, J. M. and Cagan, P., eds.*, 1969, pp. 223–71. **[G: U.S.]**

Cagan, Phillip. The Influence of Interest Rates on the Duration of Business Cycles. **In** *Guttentag, J. M. and Cagan, P., eds.*, 1969, pp. 3–28. **[G: U.S.]**

Cagan, Phillip and Gandolfi, Arthur. The Lag in Monetary Policy as Implied by the Time Pattern of Monetary Effects on Interest Rates. *Amer. Econ. Rev.*, May 1969, *59*(2), pp. 277–84. **[G: U.S.]**

Cagan, Phillip. The Non-Neutrality of Money in the Long Run: A Discussion of the Critical Assumptions and Some Evidence. *J. Money, Credit, Banking*, May 1969, *1*(2), pp. 207–27.

Chetty, V. Karuppan. On the Long-Run and Short-Run Demand for Money: Some Further Evidence. *J. Polit. Econ.*, November/December 1969, *77*(6), pp. 921–31. **[G: U.S.]**

Chetty, V. Karuppan. On Measuring the Nearness of the Near-Moneys. *Amer. Econ. Rev.*, June 1969, *59*(3), pp. 270–81. **[G: U.S.]**

Chow, Gregory C. Reply: A Note on the Estimation of Long-Run Relationships in Stock Adjustment Models. *J. Polit. Econ.*, November/December 1969, *77*(6), pp. 932–36. **[G: U.S.]**

Christ, Carl F. A Model of Monetary and Fiscal Policy Effects on the Money Stock, Price Level, and Real Output. *J. Money, Credit, Banking*, November 1969, *1*(4), pp. 683–705. **[G: U.S.]**

Claassen, Emil M. Stock-Flow Decisions and Full Equilibrium. *Kyklos*, 1969, *22*(3), pp. 493–505.

Colaco, Francis X. Harberger's Inflation Model: A Critique and Test Using Data for Brazil and India. *Indian Econ. J.*, April–June 1969, *16*(4–5), pp. 434–44. **[G: Brazil; India]**

Daloz, Jean-Pierre. La fonction de demande de monnaie en France de 1920 à 1968: Analyse théorique et économétrique sur les données françaises annueles de 1920 à 1966 prolongée pour 1967 et 1968. (With English summary.) *Revue Écon.*, May 1969, *20*(3), pp. 468–96. **[G: France]**

Davidson, Paul. A Keynesian View of the Relationship between Accumulation, Money and the

Money Wage-Rate. *Econ. J.,* June 1969, *79*(314), pp. 300–323.

Dewald, William G. Multiple Expansion of Bank Deposits under Australian Institutional Conditions: Comment. *Econ. Rec.,* June 1969, *45*(110), pp. 293–96. **[G: Australia]**

Diller, Stanley. Expectations in the Term Structure of Interest Rates. **In** *Mincer, J., ed.,* 1969, pp. 112–66.

Doodha, Kersi D. Liquidity Preference Theory for India. **In** *Desai, V. R. M. and Ghonasgi, B. D.,* 1969, pp. 49–69. **[G: India]**

Draper, J. E. and Hawkins, Clark A. On the Transactions Demand for Cash: Comment. *J. Finance,* December 1969, *24*(5), pp. 942–49.

Egle, Walter P. Reflections on the Money Illusion. *Weltwirtsch. Arch.,* 1969, *103*(1), pp. 153–59.

Eisner, Robert. Factors Affecting the Level of Interest Rates—Part II. **In** *High Interest Rates, SCH,* 1969, pp. 102–13. **[G: U.S.]**

Eisner, Robert. Fiscal and Monetary Policy Reconsidered. *Amer. Econ. Rev.,* December 1969, *59*(5), pp. 897–905. **[G: U.S.]**

Eppen, Gary D. and Fama, Eugene F. Cash Balance and Simple Dynamic Portfolio Problems with Proportional Costs. *Int. Econ. Rev.,* June 1969, *10* (2), pp. 119–33.

Ezekiel, Hannan and Adekunle, Joseph O. The Secular Behavior of Income Velocity: An International Cross-Section Study. *Int. Monet. Fund Staff Pap.,* July 1969, *16*(2), pp. 224–39.

Fand, David I. Keynesian Monetary Theories, Stabilization Policy, and the Recent Inflation. *J. Money, Credit, Banking,* August 1969, *1*(3), pp. 556–87. **[G: U.S.]**

Fazio, Antonio. Monetary Base and the Control of Credit in Italy. *Banca Naz. Lavoro Quart. Rev.,* June 1969, (89), pp. 146–69. **[G: Italy]**

Floyd, John E. Monetary and Fiscal Policy in a World of Capital Mobility. *Rev. Econ. Stud.,* October 1969, *36*(108), pp. 503–17.

Foley, Duncan K.; Shell, Karl and Sidrauski, Miguel. Optimal Fiscal and Monetary Policy and Economic Growth. *J. Polit. Econ.,* Part II, July/August 1969, *77*(4), pp. 698–719.

Friedman, Milton and Schwartz, Anna J. The Definition of Money: Net Wealth and Neutrality as Criteria. *J. Money, Credit, Banking,* February 1969, *1*(1), pp. 1–14. **[G: U.S.]**

Friedman, Milton. The Monetary Studies of the National Bureau. **In** *Friedman, M.,* 1969, pp. 261–84. **[G: U.S.]**

Fromm, Gary. Growth and Inflation: A Comment. *J. Money, Credit, Banking,* August 1969, *1*(3), pp. 439–40. **[G: U.K.]**

Fry, Edward R.; Beck, Darwin L. and Weaver, Mary F. Revision of Money Stock Series. *Fed. Res. Bull.,* October 1969, *55*(10), pp. 787–803. **[G: U.S.]**

Furness, Eric L. Income Flows and Financial Asset Holdings. *Oxford Econ. Pap.,* March 1969, *21*(1), pp. 70–88.

Gaines, Tilford C. Some Inadequacies of Financial Data and Theories. *Nat. Westminster Bank Quart. Rev.,* November 1969, pp. 35–44. **[G: U.S.]**

Galper, Harvey. Alternative Interest Rates and the Demand for Money: Comment. *Amer. Econ. Rev.,* June 1969, *59*(3), pp. 401–12. **[G: U.S.]**

Gibson, N. J. Foundations of Monetary Theory: A Review Article. *Manchester Sch. Econ. Soc. Stud.,* March 1969, *37*(1), pp. 59–75.

Goodfellow, Gordon P., Jr. and Sweeney, Vernon E. Vertically Parallel Indifference Curves with a Non-Constant Marginal Utility of Money. *Amer. Econ.,* Fall 1969, *13*(2), pp. 81–86.

Goodhart, C. A. E. A Stable Velocity Function for Canada? A Note. *Economica, N.S.,* August 1969, *36*(143), pp. 314–15. **[G: Canada]**

Gørtz, Erik. Interest Determination in a Simultaneous Money and Credit Market Model for Denmark 1950–66. *Swedish J. Econ.,* December 1969, *71*(4), pp. 263–74. **[G: Denmark]**

Gramm, William P. and Timberlake, Richard H., Jr. The Stock of Money and Investment in the United States, 1897-1966. *Amer. Econ. Rev.,* December 1969, *59*(5), pp. 991–96. **[G: U.S.]**

Gupta, Kanhaya L. Money Supply, Cyclical Fluctuations, and Income Determination. *Jahr. Nationalökon. Statist.,* May 1969, *182*(6), pp. 465–78. **[G: Canada]**

Gupta, Suraj B. The Invalidity of the Dichotomy in the Pure Inside-Money Model. *J. Polit. Econ.,* January/February 1969, *77*(1), pp. 118–21.

de Gyor, P. G. Gschwindt. The Money Supply Question. *Nat. Westminster Bank Quart. Rev.,* August 1969, pp. 61–68.

de Haan, H. and Kuipers, S. K. Een onderzoek naar de invloed van monetaire factoren op het reële groeiproces in enkele traditionele theorieën van economische groei (I). (An Investigation into the Influence of Monetary Factors on the Real Process of Growth in Some Traditional Theories of Economic Growth (I). With English summary.) *De Economist,* March/April 1969, *117*(2), pp. 139–60.

de Haan, H. and Kuipers, S. K. Een onderzoek naar de invloed van monetaire factoren op het reële groeiproces in enkele traditionele theorieën van economische groei (III). (An Investigation into the Influence of Monetary Factors on the Real Process of Growth in Some Traditional Theories of Economic Growth (III). With English summary.) *De Economist,* September/October 1969, *117*(5), pp. 493–515.

de Haan, H. and Kuipers, S. K. Een onderzoek naar de invloed van monetaire factoren op het reële groeiproces in enkele traditionele theorieën van economische groei (II). (An Investigation into the Influence of Monetary Factors on the Real Process of Growth in Some Traditional Theories of Economic Growth (II). With English summary.) *De Economist,* July/August 1969, *117*(4), pp. 381–401.

Hahn, Frank. On Money and Growth. *J. Money, Credit, Banking,* May 1969, *1*(2), pp. 172–87.

Hakansson, Nils H. On the Dividend Capitalization Model under Uncertainty. *J. Financial Quant. Anal.,* March 1969, *4*(1), pp. 65–87.

Hamburger, Michael J. and Silber, William L. An Empirical Study of Interest Rate Determination. *Rev. Econ. Statist.,* August 1969, *51*(3), pp. 369–73. **[G: U.S.]**

Hamburger, Michael J. and Latta, Cynthia M. The Term Structure of Interest Rates: Some Additional Evidence. *J. Money, Credit, Banking,* February 1969, *1*(1), pp. 71–83. **[G: U.S.]**

Harris, Laurence. Professor Hicks and the Foundations of Monetary Economics. *Economica, N.S.,* May 1969, *36*(142), pp. 196–208.

Hawkins, Clark A. and McClain, J. M. A Note on the Short-Run Demand for Money. *Miss. Val. J. Bus. Econ.,* Fall 1969, *5*(1), pp. 73–79. **[G: U.S.]**

Hayek, F. A. Three Elucidations of the Ricardo Effect. *J. Polit. Econ.,* March/April 1969, *77*(2), pp. 274–85.

Helmstädter, Ernst. Patinkin-Kontroverse-Beitrag Nr. X. (With English summary.) *Kyklos,* 1969, *22* (3), pp. 506–18.

Hess, Alan C. A Quantity Theory Approach to the Current Inflation. *Univ. Wash. Bus. Rev.,* Summer 1969, *28*(4), pp. 12–17. **[G: U.S.]**

Hester, Donald D. Financial Disintermediation and Policy. *J. Money, Credit, Banking,* August 1969, *1*(3), pp. 600–17. **[G: U.S.]**

Hicks, John R. Automatists, Hawtreyans, and Keynesians. *J. Money, Credit, Banking,* August 1969, *1*(3), pp. 307–17.

Horton, Joseph J., Jr. Is There a Money Supply Function? *Quart. Rev. Econ. Bus.,* Summer 1969, *9*(2), pp. 67–70.

Howrey, E. Philip. Distributed Lags and Effectiveness of Monetary Policy: Note. *Amer. Econ. Rev.,* December 1969, *59*(5), pp. 997–1001.

Hunter, J. S. H. The Roosa Doctrine and the Shiftability Thesis: Application to Debt Management in the United States. *Weltwirtsch. Arch.,* 1969, *103* (1), pp. 110–30. **[G: U.S.]**

Iyengar, Sampath S. Multiplier Analysis for India. *Indian Econ. J.,* April–June 1969, *16*(4–5), pp. 478–87. **[G: India]**

Johnson, Harry G. Pesek and Saving's Theory of Money and Wealth: A Comment. *J. Money, Credit, Banking,* August 1969, *1*(3), pp. 535–37.

Jordan, Jerry L. Elements of Money Stock Determination. *Fed. Res. Bank St. Louis Rev.,* October 1969, *51*(10), pp. 10–19. **[G: U.S.]**

Kaminow, Ira. The Household Demand for Money: An Empirical Study. *J. Finance,* September 1969, *24*(4), pp. 679–96. **[G: U.S.]**

Kaufman, George G. More on an Empirical Definition of Money. *Amer. Econ. Rev.,* March 1969, *59* (1), pp. 78–87. **[G: U.S.]**

Kelly, Alex K. Sources of Change in the Canadian Money Stock, 1955–65. *Banca Naz. Lavoro Quart. Rev.,* December 1969, (91), pp. 395–407. **[G: Canada]**

Keran, Michael W. Monetary and Fiscal Influences on Economic Activity—The Historical Evidence. *Fed. Res. Bank St. Louis Rev.,* November 1969, *51* (11), pp. 5–24. **[G: U.S.]**

Knight, Robert E. An Alternative Approach to Liquidity: Part I. *Fed. Res. Bank Kansas City Rev.,* December 1969, pp. 11–21. **[G: U.S.]**

Koch, James V. Homogeneity in Wealth: Demand Functions for Liquid Financial Assets. *Rivista Int. Sci. Econ. Com.,* October 1969, *16*(10), pp. 950–64.

Koch, James V. The Homogeneity Assumption and Financial Asset Demand Functions. *Quart. Rev. Econ. Bus.,* Winter 1969, *9*(4), pp. 57–65. **[G: U.S.]**

Komiya, Ryutaro. Economic Growth and the Balance of Payments: A Monetary Approach. *J. Polit. Econ.,* January/February 1969, *77*(1), pp. 35–48.

Konstas, Panos and Khouja, Mohamad W. The Keynesian Demand-for-Money Function: Another Look and Some Additional Evidence. *J. Money, Credit, Banking,* November 1969, *1*(4), pp. 765–77.

Krainer, Robert E. Liquidity Preference and Stock Market Speculation. *J. Financial Quant. Anal.,* March 1969, *4*(1), pp. 89–97. **[G: U.S.]**

Laidler, David. The Definition of Money: Theoretical and Empirical Problems. *J. Money, Credit, Banking,* August 1969, *1*(3), pp. 508–25. **[G: U.S.; U.K.]**

Laumas, Gurcharan S. Savings Deposits in the Definition of Money. *J. Polit. Econ.,* November/-December 1969, *77*(6), pp. 892–96.

Laumas, Prem S. and Laumas, Gurcharan S. Interest-Elasticity of Demand for Money. *Southern Econ. J.,* July 1969, *36*(1), pp. 90–93. **[G: Canada]**

Laumas, Prem S. The Role of Savings Deposits as Money: A Comment. *J. Money, Credit, Banking,* November 1969, *1*(4), pp. 789–95. **[G: Canada]**

Lee, Tong Hun. Alternative Interest Rates and the Demand for Money: Reply. *Amer. Econ. Rev.,* June 1969, *59*(3), pp. 412–18. **[G: U.S.]**

de Leeuw, Frank and Kalchbrenner, John. Monetary and Fiscal Actions: A Test of Their Relative Importance in Economic Stabilization—Comment. *Fed. Res. Bank St. Louis Rev.,* April 1969, *51*(4), pp. 6–11. **[G: U.S.]**

de Leeuw, Frank and Gramlich, Edward M. The Channels of Monetary Policy. *Fed. Res. Bull.,* June 1969, *55*(6), pp. 472–91. **[G: U.S.]**

Levhari, David and Srinivasan, T. N. Optimal Savings under Uncertainty. *Rev. Econ. Stud.,* April 1969, *36*(106), pp. 153–63.

Macesich, George and Close, F. Alan. Monetary Velocity and Investment Multiplier Stability Relativity for Norway and Sweden. *Statsokon. Tidsskr.,* March 1969, *83*(1), pp. 10–22. **[G: Norway; Sweden]**

Macesich, George and Falero, Frank, Jr. Permanent Income Hypothesis, Interest Rates and the Demand for Money. *Weltwirtsch. Arch.,* 1969, *103* (1), pp. 129–52.

Malkiel, Burton G. and Kane, Edward J. Expectations and Interest Rates: A Cross-sectional Test of the Error-learning Hypothesis. *J. Polit. Econ.,* Part I, July/August 1969, *77*(4), pp. 453–70. **[G: U.S.]**

Marshall, A. The Total Currency Needed by a Country. **In** *Clower, R. W., ed.,* 1969, pp. 80–93.

Marty, Alvin L. Notes on Money and Economic Growth. *J. Money, Credit, Banking,* May 1969, *1* (2), pp. 252–65.

Mauer, Laurence Jay. Commercial Bank Maturity Demand for United States Government Securities and the Determinants of the Term Structure of Interest Rates. *J. Financial Quant. Anal.,* March 1969, *4*(1), pp. 37–52. **[G: U.S.]**

McCracken, Paul W. Statement. **In** *High Interest Rates, SCH,* 1969, pp. 13–17. **[G: U.S.]**

Meiselman, David. The Role of Money in National Economic Policy. **In** *Federal Reserve Bank of Boston,* 1969, pp. 15–19.

Melitz, Jacques. Open Market Operations and the Classical "Real" Theory of the Interest Rate. *Z. Nationalökon.,* May 1969, *29*(1–2), pp. 111–20.

Melnik, Arie and Kraus, Alan. Short-Run Interest Rate Cycles in the U.S.: 1954–1967. *J. Financial Quant. Anal.,* September 1969, *4*(3), pp. 291–99. **[G: U.S.]**

Meltzer, Allan H. A Comment on Hester's Paper. *J. Money, Credit, Banking,* August 1969, *1*(3), pp. 618–23. **[G: U.S.]**

Meltzer, Allan H. Money, Intermediation, and Growth. *J. Econ. Lit.,* March 1969, *7*(1), pp. 27–56.

Meltzer, Allan H. The Role of Money in National Economic Policy. **In** *Federal Reserve Bank of Boston,* 1969, pp. 25–29.

Mittra, Sid. The Central Bank as a Utility Maximizer: A Theoretical Model. *Econ. Aff.,* January-February 1969, *14*(1–2), pp. 9–14.

Modigliani, Franco and Sutch, Richard. The Term Structure of Interest Rates: A Re-examination of the Evidence. *J. Money, Credit, Banking,* February 1969, *1*(1), pp. 112–20. **[G: U.S.]**

Monti, Mario. Dimensioni dell'economia e domanda di moneta: I. Alcuni modelli. (Economies of Scale and Demand for Money: I. Some Models. With English summary.) *Rivista Int. Sci. Econ. Com.,* August 1969, *16*(8), pp. 781–806.

Monti, Mario. Dimensioni dell'economia e domanda di moneta: II. Problemi metodologici. (Economies of Scale in the Demand for Money: II. Methodological Issues. With English summary.) *Rivista Int. Sci. Econ. Com.,* September 1969, *16*(9), pp. 859–71.

Monti, Mario. Moneta, sviluppo economico e progresso tecnico. (Money, Economic Growth and Technical Progress. With English summary.) *L'Industria,* October–December 1969, (4), pp. 475–92.

Morgan, E. V. The Essential Qualities of Money. *Manchester Sch. Econ. Soc. Stud.,* September 1969, *37*(3), pp. 237–48.

Motley, Brian. The Consumer's Demand for Money: A Neoclassical Approach. *J. Polit. Econ.,* September/October 1969, *77*(5), pp. 817–26.

Nadiri, M. Ishag. The Determinants of Real Cash Balances in the U.S. Total Manufacturing Sector. *Quart. J. Econ.,* May 1969, *83*(2), pp. 173–96. **[G: U.S.]**

Nagatani, Keizo. A Monetary Growth Model with Variable Employment. *J. Money, Credit, Banking,* May 1969, *1*(2), pp. 188–206.

Naylor, John A. A Note on the 'Traditional Theory' of the Term Structure of Interest Rates and Rates on Three- and Six-Month Treasury Bills: Comment. *Int. Econ. Rev.,* October 1969, *10*(3), pp. 484–87. **[G: U.S.]**

Naylor, John A. Expectations, Portfolio Preferences and the Term Structure of Interest Rates. *Ohio State U. Bull. Bus. Res.,* September 1969, *44*(9), pp. 4–7. **[G: U.S.]**

Niehans, Jürg. Growth and Inflation: A Comment. *J. Money, Credit, Banking,* August 1969, *1*(3), pp. 433–38. **[G: U.K.]**

Niehans, Jürg. Money in a Static Theory of Optimal Payment Arrangements. *J. Money, Credit, Banking,* November 1969, *1*(4), pp. 706–26.

Niehans, Jürg. The Neoclassical Dichotomy as a Controlled Experiment. *J. Polit. Econ.,* Part I, July/August 1969, *77*(4), pp. 504–11.

Olivera, Julio H. G. La posición monetaria neta: Observaciones complementarias. (The Net Monetary Position: Some Additional Remarks. With English summary.) *Económica,* September–December 1969, *15*(3), pp. 313–15.

Olivera, Julio H. G. On the Asymptotic Theory of the Demand for Money. *Oxford Econ. Pap.,* March 1969, *21*(1), pp. 24–28.

Patinkin, Don. Money and Prices. **In** *Clower, R. W., ed.,* 1969, pp. 123–48.

Patinkin, Don. Money and Wealth: A Review Article. *J. Econ. Lit.,* December 1969, *7*(4), pp. 1140–60.

Patinkin, Don. The Chicago Tradition, the Quantity Theory, and Friedman. *J. Money, Credit, Banking,* February 1969, *1*(1), pp. 46–70.

Peltzman, Sam. The Structure of the Money-Expenditures Relationship. *Amer. Econ. Rev.,* March 1969, *59*(1), pp. 129–37. **[G: U.S.]**

Pesek, B. P. and Saving, Thomas R. The Demand for Money: Some Post-Keynesian Confusions. **In** *Clower, R. W., ed.,* 1969, pp. 247–53.

Phillips, Keith E. The Short-Run Stability of Velocity and the Autonomous Spending Multiplier, 1946–1962. *J. Polit. Econ.,* May/June 1969, *77*(3), pp. 418–29.

Pierce, James L. Commercial Bank Liquidity. **In** *Jessup, P. F.,* 1969, pp. 16–27.

Pifer, Howard W. A Nonlinear, Maximum Likelihood Estimate of the Liquidity Trap. *Econometrica,* April 1969, *37*(2), pp. 324–32.

Prasad, K. A Note on the Transactions Demand for Cash. *Indian Econ. J.,* April–June 1969, *16*(4–5), pp. 561–66.

Rakshit, M. K. Inflation, the Choice of Assets, and the Liquidity Trap. **In** *[Ghosal, U. N.],* 1969, pp. 69–73.

Rose, Hugh. Real and Monetary Factors in the Business Cycle. *J. Money, Credit, Banking,* May 1969, *1*(2), pp. 138–52.

Ross, Myron H. and Zelder, Raymond E. The Discount Rate: A Phantom Policy Tool? *Western Econ. J.,* December 1969, *7*(4), pp. 341–48. **[G: U.S.]**

Russell, William R. An Investigation of Commercial Banks' Aggregate Portfolio Adjustments. *Int. Econ. Rev.,* October 1969, *10*(3), pp. 266–90. **[G: U.S.]**

Salama, Elías. Sobre la posición monetaria neta. (On the Net Monetary Position. With English summary.) *Económica,* September–December 1969, *15*(3), pp. 299–311.

Samuelson, Paul A. The Role of Money in National Economic Policy. **In** *Federal Reserve Bank of Boston,* 1969, pp. 7–13.

Sargent, Thomas J. Commodity Price Expectations and the Interest Rate. *Quart. J. Econ.,* February 1969, *83*(1), pp. 127–40. **[G: U.S.]**

Schmölders, Günter. A Behavioral Approach to Monetary Theory. **In** *[von Hayek, Friedrich A.]*, 1969, pp. 201–43.

Schreiber, Wilfrid. On Two Topical Questions of Distribution Theory and Policy. *Ger. Econ. Rev.*, 1969, *7*(3), pp. 199–215. **[G: W. Germany]**

Schwartz, Anna J. Why Money Matters. *Lloyds Bank Rev.*, October 1969, (94), pp. 1–16. **[G: U.S.; U.K.]**

Senior, N. W. The Value of Money. **In** *Clower, R. W., ed.*, 1969, pp. 67–79.

Shimazu, Ryoji. A Reconsideration of the Quantity Theory of Money. *Kyoto Univ. Econ. Rev.*, April 1969, *39*(1), pp. 45–62.

Silber, William L. Liquidity Premium Theory: Some Observations. *Kyklos*, 1969, *22*(1), pp. 155–58.

Silber, William L. Monetary Channels and the Relative Importance of Money Supply and Bank Portfolios. *J. Finance*, March 1969, *24*(1), pp. 81–87.

Silber, William L. Velocity and Bank Portfolio Composition. *Southern Econ. J.*, October 1969, *36*(2), pp. 147–52. **[G: U.S.]**

Simone, Dante. Sobre teoría monetaria en alta inflación. (On Monetary Theory in High Inflation. With English summary.) *Económica*, May–August 1969, *15*(2), pp. 183–209.

Sprenkle, Case M. Laidler's "The Definition of Money": A Comment. *J. Money, Credit, Banking*, August 1969, *1*(3), pp. 526–30. **[G: U.K.; U.S.]**

Sprenkle, Case M. The Uselessness of Transactions Demand Models. *J. Finance*, December 1969, *24* (5), pp. 835–47.

Stanford, J. D. Multiple Expansion of Bank Deposits under Australian Institutional Conditions: A Reply. *Econ. Rec.*, June 1969, *45*(110), pp. 297–98. **[G: Australia]**

Starleaf, Dennis R. and Stephenson, James A. A Suggested Solution to the Monetary-Policy Indicator Problem: The Monetary Full Employment Interest Rate. *J. Finance*, September 1969, *24*(4), pp. 623–41. **[G: U.S.]**

Stein, Jerome L. "Neoclassical" and "Keynes-Wicksell" Monetary Growth Models. *J. Money, Credit, Banking*, May 1969, *1*(2), pp. 153–71.

Stroup, Robert H. and Frazer, William J., Jr. The Demand for Money by Households in South Vietnam: The Evidence from Cross-Section Data. *J. Polit. Econ.*, Part I, July/August 1969, *77*(4), pp. 489–93. **[G: S. Vietnam]**

Sufrin, Sidney C. and Wagner, Abraham R. Interest Rate Manipulation, Employment and Output—A Disaggregated Suggestion. *Rivista Int. Sci. Econ. Com.*, April 1969, *16*(4), pp. 327–41. **[G: U.S.]**

Taylor, Lester D. and Newhouse, Joseph P. On the Long-Run and Short-Run Demand for Money: A Comment. *J. Polit. Econ.*, September/October 1969, *77*(5), pp. 851–56. **[G: U.S.]**

Teigen, Ronald L. Laidler's "Definition of Money": A Comment. *J. Money, Credit, Banking*, August 1969, *1*(3), pp. 531–34.

Thore, Sten. Credit Networks. *Economica, N.S.*, February 1969, *36*(141), pp. 42–57.

Tobin, James. A General Equilibrium Approach to Monetary Theory. *J. Money, Credit, Banking*, February 1969, *1*(1), pp. 15–29.

Tobin, James and Swan, Craig. Money and Permanent Income: Some Empirical Tests. *Amer. Econ. Rev.*, May 1969, *59*(2), pp. 285–95. **[G: U.S.]**

Tobin, James. The Role of Money in National Economic Policy. **In** *Federal Reserve Bank of Boston*, 1969, pp. 21–24.

Tsiang, S. C. A Critical Note on the Optimum Supply of Money. *J. Money, Credit, Banking*, May 1969, *1*(2), pp. 266–80.

Tsiang, S. C. The Precautionary Demand for Money: An Inventory Theoretical Analysis. *J. Polit. Econ.*, January/February 1969, *77*(1), pp. 99–117.

Tucker, Donald P. Monetary Theory: Discussion. *Amer. Econ. Rev.*, May 1969, *59*(2), pp. 321–23. **[G: U.S.]**

Vasudevan, A. The Portfolio Approach: Its Relevance to Under-Developed Economies. *Indian Econ. J.*, April–June 1969, *16*(4–5), pp. 520–31.

Wallace, Neil. Buse on Meiselman—A Comment. *J. Polit. Econ.*, Part I, July/August 1969, *77*(4), pp. 524–27.

Wallich, Henry C. Keynesian Monetary Theories, Stabilization Policy, and the Recent Inflation: A Comment. *J. Money, Credit, Banking*, August 1969, *1*(3), pp. 590–99. **[G: U.S.]**

Wallich, Henry C. Money and Growth: A Country Cross-Section Analysis. *J. Money, Credit, Banking*, May 1969, *1*(2), pp. 281–302.

Wallich, Henry C. The Role of Money in National Economic Policy. **In** *Federal Reserve Bank of Boston*, 1969, pp. 31–36.

Waters, Judith A. Money Supply and Credit—Theory and Practice. *Nat. Westminster Bank Quart. Rev.*, November 1969, pp. 19–34.

Whalen, Edward L. On the Transactions Demand for Cash: Reply. *J. Finance*, December 1969, *24* (5), pp. 950–53.

Woll, Artur. Die Theorie der Geldnachfrage: Analytische Ansätze und statische Ergebnisse für die Bundesrepublik Deutschland. (With English summary.) *Z. ges. Staatswiss.*, January 1969, *125*(1), pp. 56–81. **[G: W. Germany]**

Wood, John H. Expectations and the Demand for Bonds. *Amer. Econ. Rev.*, Part I, September 1969, *59*(4), pp. 522–30.

Yohe, William P. and Karnosky, Denis S. Interest Rates and Price Level Changes, 1952–69. *Fed. Res. Bank St. Louis Rev.*, December 1969, *51*(12), pp. 18–38. **[G: U.S.]**

3116 Monetary Policy (including all central banking topics)

Andersen, Leonall C. Additional Empirical Evidence on the Reverse-Causation Argument. *Fed. Res. Bank St. Louis Rev.*, August 1969, *51*(8), pp. 19–23. **[G: U.S.]**

Andersen, Leonall C. Money Market Conditions as a Guide for Monetary Management. **In** *Brunner, K., ed.*, 1969, pp. 66–83. **[G: U.S.]**

Atkinson, Thomas R. Comment on Maurice Mann's Views on Monetary Policy. *J. Money, Credit, Banking*, August 1969, *1*(3), pp. 553–55. **[G: U.K.]**

Atkinson, Thomas R. Tone and Feel of the Market as a Guide for Open Market Operations. **In** *Brunner, K., ed.*, 1969, pp. 84–97. **[G: U.S.]**

Basno, C. Aplicarea creditării diferențiate a întreprinderilor. (Application of Differentiated Crediting of Enterprises. With English summary.) *Stud. Cercet. Econ.*, 1969, *1-2*, pp. 93–105.

Baxter, Nevins D. Why Federal Funds? In *Jessup, P. F.*, 1969, pp. 50–60. **[G: U.S.]**

Beard, Thomas R. and Duggar, Jan Warren. Federal Reserve Proposals for Reform of the Discount Mechanism. *Southern Econ. J.*, October 1969, *36*(2), pp. 122–33. **[G: U.S.]**

Beard, Thomas R. and Duggar, Jan Warren. Member Bank Borrowing. *Quart. Rev. Econ. Bus.*, Autumn 1969, *9*(3), pp. 72–77. **[G: U.S.]**

Benston, George J. An Analysis and Evaluation of Alternative Reserve Requirement Plans. *J. Finance*, December 1969, *24*(5), pp. 849–70. **[G: U.S.]**

Bernholz, Peter. Einige Bemerkungen zur Devisenterminpolitik der Deutschen Bundesbank. (Forward Exchange Policies of the German Bundesbank: Some Critical Comments. With English summary.) *Jahr. Nationalökon. Statist.*, May 1969, *182*(6), pp. 479–89. **[G: Germany]**

Bonomo, Vittorio and Schotta, Charles. A Spectral Analysis of Post-Accord Federal Open Market Operations. *Amer. Econ. Rev.*, March 1969, *59*(1), pp. 50–61. **[G: U.S.]**

Boughton, James M., et al. A Policy Model of the United States Monetary Sector. *Southern Econ. J.*, April 1969, *35*(4), pp. 333–46. **[G: U.S.]**

Brahmananda, P. R. The Bank Rate in General Setting. **In** *Desai, V. R. M. and Ghonasgi, B. D.*, 1969, pp. 29–48. **[G: India]**

Brimmer, Andrew F. Euro-Dollar Flows and the Efficiency of U.S. Monetary Policy. **In** *High Interest Rates, SCH,* 1969, pp. 181–95. **[G: U.S.]**

Brovedani, Bruno. Italy's Financial Policies in the 'Sixties. *Banca Naz. Lavoro Quart. Rev.*, June 1969, (89), pp. 170–89. **[G: Italy]**

Brunner, Karl. Monetary Analysis and Federal Reserve Policy. **In** *Brunner, K., ed.*, 1969, pp. 250–82. **[G: U.S.]**

Brunner, Karl and Meltzer, Allan H. The Nature of Policy Problem. **In** *Brunner, K., ed.*, 1969, pp. 1–26.

Buehler, John E. and Fand, David I. The Federal Reserve and Monetary Policy. *Mich. Academician*, Spring 1969, *1*(3–4), pp. 21–35. **[G: U.S.]**

Burger, Albert E. A Historical Analysis of the Credit Crunch of 1966. *Fed. Res. Bank St. Louis Rev.*, September 1969, *51*(9), pp. 13–30. **[G: U.S.]**

Burns, Arthur Frank. The New Environment of Monetary Policy. **In** *Burns, A. F.*, 1969, pp. 151–74. **[G: U.S.]**

Cacy, J. A. Credit Flows in the 1960's. *Fed. Res. Bank Kansas City Rev.*, June 1969, pp. 11–16. **[G: U.S.]**

Cagle, Caroline H. Member Bank Income, 1968. *Fed. Res. Bull.*, May 1969, *55*(5), pp. 419–24. **[G: U.S.]**

Canterbery, E. Ray. Exchange Rates, Capital Flows and Monetary Policy. *Amer. Econ. Rev.*, June 1969, *59*(3), pp. 426–32. **[G: U.S.; U.K.; Canada]**

Carli, Guido. Celebration of the "World Thrift Day." *Rev. Econ. Cond. Italy*, January 1969, *23*(1), pp. 5–12. **[G: Italy]**

Carli, Guido. Programmi e prospettive della politica monetaria internazionale. (International Monetary Policy of the Moment—Programs and Outlooks. With English summary.) *Bancaria,* December 1969, *25*(12), pp. 1459–63.

Carli, Guido. Sistema monetario internazionale e mercato monetario interno. (International Monetary System and Italian Money Market. With English summary.) *Bancaria,* May 1969, *25*(5), pp. 555–71. **[G: Italy]**

Cawthorne, D. R. Reserve Adjustments of City Banks. **In** *Jessup, P. F.*, 1969, pp. 42–50. **[G: U.S.]**

Chalmers, Eric B. Monetary Policy Aspects of the Euro-dollar. **In** *Chalmers, E. B., ed.*, 1969, pp. 84–109.

Chandavarkar, Anand G. Indian Monetary Policy and Economic Development. **In** *Bhuleshkar, A. V., ed.*, 1969, pp. 305–17. **[G: India]**

Chandavarkar, Anand G. Margini non utilizzati di fidi bancari: loro implicazioni per l'analisi e la politica monetaria. (Unused Bank Overdraughts: Their Implications for Monetary Analysis and Policy. With English summary.) *Bancaria,* December 1969, *25*(12), pp. 1464–72.

Christian, James W. and Mazek, Warren F. Corporate Debt Structure and the Differential Effects of Monetary Policy. *Southern Econ. J.*, April 1969, *35*(4), pp. 359–68. **[G: U.S.]**

Colombo, Emilio. Equilibrio della bilancia dei pagamenti e utilizzo delle risorse senza inflazione. (Equilibrium of the Balance of Payments and Internal Use of Resources without Inflation. With English summary.) *Bancaria,* October 1969, *25*(10), pp. 1221–24. **[G: Italy]**

Coombs, Charles A. Treasury and Federal Reserve Foreign Exchange Operations. *Fed. Res. Bull.*, March 1969, *55*(3), pp. 210–27. **[G: U.S.]**

Coombs, H. C. Central Banking—A Look Back and Forward. *Econ. Rec.*, December 1969, *45*(112), pp. 485–95. **[G: Australia]**

Cooper, Jack L. Continuous Borrowing from the Federal Reserve System: Some Empirical Evidence. *J. Finance,* March 1969, *24*(1), pp. 33–48. **[G: U.S.]**

Daněček, Jiří. New Monetary Banking System in Czechoslovakia. *New Trends Czech. Econ.*, May 1969, (3), pp. 47–63. **[G: Czechoslovakia]**

Dewald, William G. A Review of the Conference on Targets and Indicators of Monetary Policy. **In** *Brunner, K., ed.*, 1969, pp. 313–30. **[G: U.S.]**

Dorrance, Graeme S. The Role of Central Banks in Less Developed Countries. *Finance Develop.*, December 1969, *6*(4), pp. 22–26.

Duesenberry, James S. Tactics and Targets of Monetary Policy. **In** *Federal Reserve Bank of Boston,* 1969, pp. 83–95. **[G: U.S.]**

Duggar, Jan Warren and Rost, Ronald F. National Bank Note Redemption and Treasury Cash. *J. Econ. Hist.*, September 1969, *29*(3), pp. 512–20. **[G: U.S.]**

Desai, V. R. Mutalik. The Structure of the Money Market in India. **In** *Desai, V. R. M. and Ghonasgi, B. D.*, 1969, pp. 1–28. **[G: India]**

Desai, V. R. Mutalik and Ghonasgi, B. D. Selective Credit Controls in India. **In** *Desai, V. R. M. and*

Ghonasgi, B. D., 1969, pp. 84–122. [G: India]

Eisner, Robert. Statement. **In** *High Interest Rates, SCH,* 1969, pp. 97–101. [G: U.S.]

Ercolani, Mario. Strumenti della politica monetaria in Italia e schemi di analisi finanziaria. (Monetary Policy Instruments in Italy and Financial Analysis Schemes. With English summary.) *Bancaria,* March 1969, *25*(3), pp. 291–302. [G: Italy]

Fisher, Robert Moore. Monetary Policy: Its Relation to Mortgage Lending and Land Economics. *Land Econ.*, November 1969, *45*(4), pp. 418–24.

Fishman, Leo. The White House and the Fed. **In** *Starleaf, D. R., ed.*, 1969, pp. 290–95. [G: U.S.]

Friend, Irwin. Statement. **In** *High Interest Rates, SCH,* 1969, pp. 114–19. [G: U.S.]

Ghonasgi, B. D. The Monetary Policy in a Developing Economy: An Assessment. **In** *Desai, V. R. M. and Ghonasgi, B. D.*, 1969, pp. 145–72. [G: India]

Ghosh, Alak. Open Market Operations of the Reserve Bank of India: Theory and Practice. **In** *Desai, V. R. M. and Ghonasgi, B. D.*, 1969, pp. 70–83. [G: India]

Gramley, Lyle E. and Chase, Samuel B., Jr. Time Deposits in Monetary Analysis. **In** *Brunner, K., ed.*, 1969, pp. 219–49. [G: U.S.]

Guttentag, Jack M. Defensive and Dynamic Open Market Operations, Discounting, and the Federal Reserve System's Crisis-Prevention Responsibilities. *J. Finance,* May 1969, *24*(2), pp. 249–63. [G: U.S.]

Hagemann, Helmut A. Reserve Policies of Central Banks and Their Implications for U.S. Balance of Payments Policy. *Amer. Econ. Rev.*, March 1969, *59*(1), pp. 62–77.

Hastings, Delbert G. and Robertson, Ross M. The Mysterious World of the Fed. **In** *Starleaf, D. R., ed.*, 1969, pp. 279–86. [G: U.S.]

Helliwell, John F. Monetary and Fiscal Policies for an Open Economy. *Oxford Econ. Pap.*, March 1969, *21*(1), pp. 35–55.

Helliwell, John F., et al. Econometric Analysis of Policy Choices for an Open Economy. *Rev. Econ. Statist.*, November 1969, *51*(4), pp. 383–98. [G: Canada]

Hendershott, Patric H. Open Market Operations, the Money Stock, and Various Policy Issues. **In** *Brunner, K., ed.*, 1969, pp. 283–99. [G: U.S.]

Holbik, Karel. United States Balance of Payments Deficit and Monetary Policy. *Weltwirtsch. Arch.*, 1969, *103*(1), pp. 160–80. [G: U.S.]

Holmes, Alan R. Operational Constraints on the Stabilization of Money Supply Growth. **In** *Federal Reserve Bank of Boston,* 1969, pp. 65–77. [G: U.S.]

Horwich, George. A Framework for Monetary Policy. **In** *Brunner, K., ed.*, 1969, pp. 124–64.

Jacobs, Donald. The Framework of Commercial Bank Regulation: An Appraisal. **In** *Jessup, P. F.*, 1969, pp. 402–21. [G: U.S.]

de Jongh, T. W. Review of the Financial and Economic Situation in South Africa. *S. Afr. J. Econ.*, September 1969, *37*(3), pp. 187–97. [G: S. Africa]

Jordan, Jerry L. and Ruebling, Charlotte E. Federal Open Market Committee Decisions in 1968—A Year of Watchful Waiting. *Fed. Res. Bank St. Louis Rev.*, May 1969, *51*(5), pp. 6–15. [G: U.S.]

Joshi, M. S. Monetary Policy and the Non-Bank Financial Intermediaries. **In** *Desai, V. R. M. and Ghonasgi, B. D.*, 1969, pp. 123–44. [G: India]

Kamien, Morton I. and Schwartz, Nancy L. A Naive View of the Indicator Problem. **In** *Brunner, K., ed.*, 1969, pp. 98–112.

Käräva, Simo. Takaukset pankkiluottojen vakuutena. (Guarantees as Security for Bank Credits. With English summary.) *Liiketaloudellinen Aikak.*, 1969, *18*(3), pp. 443–59. [G: Finland]

Kareken, John H. The Federal Reserve's *Modus Operandi.* **In** *Federal Reserve Bank of Boston,* 1969, pp. 57–63. [G: U.S.]

Kaufmann, Hugo M. A Debate over Germany's Revaluation 1961: A Chapter in Political Economy. *Weltwirtsch. Arch.*, 1969, *103*(2), pp. 181–212. [G: Germany]

Keran, Michael W. and Babb, Christopher T. An Explanation of Federal Reserve Actions (1933–68). *Fed. Res. Bank St. Louis Rev.*, July 1969, *51*(7), pp. 7–20. [G: U.S.]

Keran, Michael W. Comments on the "St. Louis Position"—Reply. *Fed. Res. Bank St. Louis Rev.*, August 1969, *51*(8), pp. 15–18. [G: U.S.]

King, Donald A. Monetary Restraint in 1969. *Surv. Curr. Bus.*, Part I, May 1969, *49*(5), pp. 13–18. [G: U.S.]

de Leeuw, Frank and Gramlich, Edward M. The Channels of Monetary Policy: A Further Report on the Federal Reserve-M.I.T. Model. *J. Finance,* May 1969, *24*(2), pp. 265–90. [G: U.S.]

Little, Jane Sneddon. The Euro-dollar Market: Its Nature and Impact. *New Eng. Econ. Rev.*, May/June 1969, pp. 2–31.

Logue, Ruth. Imported Inflation and the International Adjustment Process. (Study summary.) *Fed. Res. Bull.*, December 1969, *55*(12), pp. 920. [G: Europe]

Luttrell, Clifton B. Interest Rate Controls: Perspective, Purpose, and Problems. **In** *Kuhlman, J. M., ed.*, 1969, pp. 275–88. [G: U.S.]

Maisel, Sherman J. Controlling Monetary Aggregates. **In** *Federal Reserve Bank of Boston,* 1969, pp. 152–74. [G: U.S.]

Mann, Maurice. How Does Monetary Policy Affect the Economy? *J. Money, Credit, Banking,* August 1969, *1*(3), pp. 538–48. [G: U.S.]

Martin, William McChesney, Jr. Statement. **In** *High Interest Rates, SCH,* 1969, pp. 6–13. [G: U.S.]

Martin, William McChesney, Jr. Statement to Congress. *Fed. Res. Bull.*, September 1969, *55*(9), pp. 719–26. [G: U.S.]

Martin, William McChesney, Jr. Statement to Congress. *Fed. Res. Bull.*, July 1969, *55*(7), pp. 591–95. [G: U.S.]

Martin, William McChesney, Jr. Statement to Congress. *Fed. Res. Bull.*, October 1969, *55*(10), pp. 819–22. [G: U.S.]

Mayne, Lucille Stringer. Federal Reserve System Membership, Bank Liquidity, and Bank Profitability. *Southern Econ. J.*, October 1969, *36*(2), pp. 181–84. [G: U.S.]

McMahon, Christopher. Monetary Policies in the United States and the United Kingdom: A Comment. *J. Money, Credit, Banking,* August 1969, *1* (3), pp. 549–52. [G: U.S.; U.K.]

Meiselman, David. Some Rules for the Conduct of Monetary Policy: Discussion. **In** *Federal Reserve Bank of Boston,* 1969, pp. 147–51.

Melichar, Emanuel. Comments on the "St. Louis Position." *Fed. Res. Bank St. Louis Rev.,* August 1969, *51*(8), pp. 9–14. [G: U.S.]

Melitz, Jacques. Open Market Operations and the Classical "Real" Theory of the Interest Rate. *Z. Nationalökon.,* May 1969, *29*(1–2), pp. 111–20.

Meltzer, Allan H. Controlling Money. *Fed. Res. Bank St. Louis Rev.,* May 1969, *51*(5), pp. 16–24. [G: U.S.]

Meltzer, Allan H. Tactics and Targets of Monetary Policy: Discussion. **In** *Federal Reserve Bank of Boston,* 1969, pp. 96–103. [G: U.S.]

Mickwitz, Gösta. Uudet pankkilait ja pankkiemme kilpailutoiminta. (The New Bank Laws and the Competition among the Banks. With English summary.) *Liiketaloudellinen Aikak.,* 1969, *18* (3), pp. 507–19. [G: Finland]

Minsky, Hyman P. Financial Model Building and Federal Reserve Policy: Discussion. *J. Finance,* May 1969, *24*(2), pp. 295–97. [G: U.S.]

Minsky, Hyman P. Private Sector Asset Management and the Effectiveness of Monetary Policy: Theory and Practice. *J. Finance,* May 1969, *24*(2), pp. 223–38. [G: U.S.]

Nadler, Paul S. Financial Model Building and Federal Reserve Policy: Discussion. *J. Finance,* May 1969, *24*(2), pp. 291–94. [G: U.S.]

Naylor, John A. The Rationale and Significance of the Proposed Discount Mechanism. *Quart. Rev. Econ. Bus.,* Winter 1969, *9*(4), pp. 7–19. [G: U.S.]

Nichols, Dorothy M. Banks, too, Post Collateral. **In** *Jessup, P. F.,* 1969, pp. 73–79. [G: U.S.]

Norton, W. E. Debt Management and Monetary Policy in the United Kingdom. *Econ. J.,* September 1969, *79*(315), pp. 475–94. [G: U.K.]

Pejovich, Svetozar. The Firm, Monetary Policy and Property Rights in a Planned Economy. *Western Econ. J.,* September 1969, *7*(3), pp. 193–200.

Peltzman, Sam. The Banking Structure and the Transmission of Monetary Policy. *J. Finance,* June 1969, *24*(3), pp. 387–411. [G: U.S.]

Pierce, James L. Some Rules for the Conduct of Monetary Policy. **In** *Federal Reserve Bank of Boston,* 1969, pp. 133–44.

Pritchard, Leland J. The Economics of the Commercial Bank. Savings-Investment Process in the United States. *Rivista Int. Sci. Econ. Com.,* July 1969, *16*(7), pp. 664–87. [G: U.S.]

Reagan, Michael D. Mr. Martin's Sacred Cow. **In** *Starleaf, D. R., ed.,* 1969, pp. 286–89. [G: U.S.]

Ross, Myron H. and Zelder, Raymond E. The Discount Rate: A Phantom Policy Tool? *Western Econ. J.,* December 1969, *7*(4), pp. 341–48. [G: U.S.]

Schwartz, Anna J. Short Term Targets of Three Foreign Central Banks. **In** *Brunner, K., ed.,* 1969, pp. 27–65.

Smith, Warren L. Statement. **In** *High Interest Rates, SCH,* 1969, pp. 151–58. [G: U.S.]

Soldofsky, Robert M. Asset Management and Monetary Policy: Discussion. *J. Finance,* May 1969, *24* (2), pp. 245–47. [G: U.S.]

Stefani, Giorgio. Politica fiscale a politica monetaria per la stabilità negli Stati Uniti-I. (Fiscal Policy and Monetary Policy for the Stability of the United States-I. With English summary.) *Bancaria,* February 1969, *25*(2), pp. 147–69. [G: U.S.]

Stefani, Giorgio. Politica fiscale e politica monetaria per la stabilità negli Stati Uniti-II. (Fiscal Policy and Monetary Policy for the Stability of the United States-II. With English summary.) *Bancaria,* March 1969, *25*(3), pp. 303–20. [G: U.S.]

Stykolt, Stefan. A Positive Monetary Policy. **In** *Stykolt, S.,* 1969, pp. 149–53. [G: Canada]

Stykolt, Stefan and Eastman, Harry C. The Economic Consequences of Mr. Coyne. **In** *Stykolt, S.,* 1969, pp. 146–48. [G: Canada]

Tanner, J. Ernest. Lags in the Effects of Monetary Policy: A Statistical Investigation. *Amer. Econ. Rev.,* December 1969, *59*(5), pp. 794–805. [G: U.S.]

Teigen, Ronald L. An Aggregated Quarterly Model of the U.S. Monetary Sector, 1953–1964. **In** *Brunner, K., ed.,* 1969, pp. 175–218. [G: U.S.]

Tobin, James. Monetary Semantics. **In** *Brunner, K., ed.,* 1969, pp. 165–74.

Tobin, James. The Federal Reserve's *Modus Operandi*: Discussion. **In** *Federal Reserve Bank of Boston,* 1969, pp. 78–82. [G: U.S.]

Van de Ven, Petrus J. and Wolfson, Dirk J. Problems of Budget Analysis and Treasury Management in French-Speaking Africa. *Int. Monet. Fund Staff Pap.,* March 1969, *16*(1), pp. 140–58. [G: Africa]

Weintraub, Robert. The Time Deposit-Money Supply Controversy. **In** *Brunner, K., ed.,* 1969, pp. 300–312. [G: U.S.]

Wilson, J. S. G. Regulation and Control of the United Kingdom Banking and Financial Structure. *Banca Naz. Lavoro Quart. Rev.,* June 1969, (89), pp. 128–45. [G: U.K.]

Wilson, Ruth V. Public Treasurers' Money. **In** *Jessup, P. F.,* 1969, pp. 123–29. [G: U.S.]

312 Commercial Banking

3120 Commercial Banking

Adams, E. Sherman. Are Bank Dividend Policies too Conservative? **In** *Jessup, P. F.,* 1969, pp. 205–15. [G: U.S.]

Andersen, Leonall C. and Burger, Albert E. Asset Management and Commercial Bank Portfolio Behavior: Theory and Practice. *J. Finance,* May 1969, *24*(2), pp. 207–22. [G: U.S.]

Arlt, Carl T. Background and History. **In** *Prochnow, H. V., ed.,* 1969, pp. 12–29. [G: U.S.]

Baker, Donald I. An Antitrust Look at the One-Bank Holding Company Problem. **In** *Federal Reserve Bank of Chicago (II),* 1969, pp. 125–31. [G: U.S.]

Barilla', Umberto. Le holdings bancarie negli Stati Uniti. (Bank Holding Companies in the United States. With English summary.) *Bancaria,* August 1969, *25*(8), pp. 963–67. [G: U.S.]

Baxter, Nevins D. Why Federal Funds? **In** *Jessup, P.*

F., 1969, pp. 50–60. [G: U.S.]

Beard, Thomas R. and Duggar, Jan Warren. Federal Reserve Proposals for Reform of the Discount Mechanism. *Southern Econ. J.*, October 1969, *36* (2), pp. 122–33. [G: U.S.]

Beard, Thomas R. and Selby, Edward B., Jr. Growth, Structure, and Adequacy of Commercial Banking in Louisiana. **In** *Beard, T. R., ed.*, 1969, pp. 105–32. [G: U.S.]

Beard, Thomas R. and Duggar, Jan Warren. Member Bank Borrowing. *Quart. Rev. Econ. Bus.*, Autumn 1969, *9*(3), pp. 72–77. [G: U.S.]

Bell, Frederick W. and Murphy, Neil B. Economies of Scale in Commercial Banking (Parts I and III). **In** *Jessup, P. F.*, 1969, pp. 265–82. [G: U.S.]

Bell, Frederick W. and Murphy, Neil B. Impact of Market Structure on the Price of a Commercial Banking Service. *Rev. Econ. Statist.*, May 1969, *51* (2), pp. 210–13. [G: U.S.]

Bell, Frederick W. and Murphy, Neil B. The Impact of Regulation on Inter- and Intraregional Variation in Commercial Banking Costs. *J. Reg. Sci.*, August 1969, *9*(2), pp. 225–38. [G: U.S.]

Beltrame, Carlo. Le merchant banks britanniche. (British Merchant Banks. With English summary.) *L'Impresa*, January/February 1969, *11*(1), pp. 68–71. [G: U.K.]

Benston, George J. An Analysis and Evaluation of Alternative Reserve Requirement Plans. *J. Finance*, December 1969, *24*(5), pp. 849–70. [G: U.S.]

Bontoux, Charles. Considerazioni sul credito documentario trasferibile. (Considerations Regarding Transferable Documentary Credit. With English summary.) *Bancaria*, June 1969, *25*(6), pp. 700–10.

Brandt, Harry and Wyand, Robert R., II. A Shift in Banking Philosophy? An Examination of Bank Investment Practices. **In** *Jessup, P. F.*, 1969, pp. 60–72. [G: U.S.]

Bronfenbrenner, Martin. The Japanese Experience. **In** *Federal Reserve Bank of Chicago (II)*, 1969, pp. 95–98. [G: Japan]

Bunting, John R., Jr. One-Bank Holding Companies: A Banker's View. *Harvard Bus. Rev.*, May–June 1969, *47*(3), pp. 99–106. [G: U.S.]

Burger, Albert E. A Historical Analysis of the Credit Crunch of 1966. *Fed. Res. Bank St. Louis Rev.*, September 1969, *51*(9), pp. 13–30. [G: U.S.]

Burns, Joseph M. The Relative Decline of Commercial Banks: A Note. *J. Polit. Econ.*, January/February 1969, *77*(1), pp. 122–29. [G: U.S.]

Byerly, Richard A. The Use of Mathematical Models in the Analysis and Improvement of Bank Operations. **In** *Jessup, P. F.*, 1969, pp. 346–59.

Cacy, J. A. Credit Flows in the 1960's. *Fed. Res. Bank Kansas City Rev.*, June 1969, pp. 11–16. [G: U.S.]

Cacy, J. A. Tenth District Banks in the Federal Funds Market. *Fed. Res. Bank Kansas City Rev.*, November 1969, pp. 10–20. [G: U.S.]

Cagle, Caroline H. Changes in Time and Savings Deposits, January–April 1969. *Fed. Res. Bull.*, July 1969, *55*(7), pp. 581–90. [G: U.S.]

Cagle, Caroline H. Changes in Time and Savings Deposits, October 1968–January 1969. *Fed. Res. Bull.*, May 1969, *55*(5), pp. 409–18. [G: U.S.]

Cagle, Caroline H. Changes in Time and Savings Deposits, April-October 1968. *Fed. Res. Bull.*, March 1969, *55*(3), pp. 189–209. [G: U.S.]

Cagle, Caroline H. Changes in Time and Savings Deposits, April–July 1969. *Fed. Res. Bull.*, October 1969, *55*(10), pp. 804–14. [G: U.S.]

Cagle, Caroline H. Member Bank Income, 1968. *Fed. Res. Bull.*, May 1969, *55*(5), pp. 419–24. [G: U.S.]

Cameron, C. C. A Breakthrough in Banking. **In** *Prochnow, H. V., ed.*, 1969, pp. 56–65. [G: U.S.]

Camp, William B. Need to Encourage the Pioneering Spirit. **In** *Prochnow, H. V., ed.*, 1969, pp. 30–47. [G: U.S.]

Cawthorne, D. R. Reserve Adjustments of City Banks. **In** *Jessup, P. F.*, 1969, pp. 42–50. [G: U.S.]

Chandavarkar, Anand G. Margini non utilizzati di fidi bancari: loro implicazioni per l'analisi e la politica monetaria. (Unused Bank Overdraughts: Their Implications for Monetary Analysis and Policy. With English summary.) *Bancaria*, December 1969, *25*(12), pp. 1464–72.

Chase, Samuel B., Jr. Bank Reactions to Securities Losses. **In** *Jessup, P. F.*, 1969, pp. 79–89. [G: U.S.]

Chase, Samuel B., Jr. Household Demand for Savings Deposits, 1921–1965. *J. Finance*, September 1969, *24*(4), pp. 643–58. [G: U.S.]

Cohen, Kalman J. and Reid, Samuel Richardson. Effects of Regulation, Branching, and Mergers on Banking Structure and Performance: Reply. *Southern Econ. J.*, October 1969, *36*(2), pp. 204–09. [G: U.S.]

Cohen, Kalman J. Risk Analysis and Branch Bank Location Decisions. **In** *Jessup, P. F.*, 1969, pp. 330–40. [G: U.S.]

Coombs, H. C. Central Banking—A Look Back and Forward. *Econ. Rec.*, December 1969, *45*(112), pp. 485–95. [G: Australia]

Cooper, Jack L. Continuous Borrowing from the Federal Reserve System: Some Empirical Evidence. *J. Finance*, March 1969, *24*(1), pp. 33–48. [G: U.S.]

Daellenbach, Hans G. and Archer, Stephen H. The Optimal Bank Liquidity: A Multi-Period Stochastic Model. *J. Financial Quant. Anal.*, September 1969, *4*(3), pp. 329–43.

Davids, Lewis E. and West, David A. Limited Market for Bank Data Processing—For the Medical and Dental Professions. *Univ. Missouri Bus. Govt. Rev.*, September–October 1969, *10*(5), pp. 11–16. [G: U.S.]

De Mattia, Renato. La politica elettronica della Banca d'Italia. (The Bank of Italy's Electronic Policy. With English summary.) *Bancaria*, January 1969, *25*(1), pp. 19–24. [G: Italy]

De Mattia, Renato. 1969: esperienze e prospettive dell'elaborazione automatica dei dati nelle banche. (The Use of Electronic Data Processing in the Banking System: An Outlook. With English summary.) *L'Industria*, April–June 1969, (2), pp. 208–21.

Desai, V. R. Mutalik. The Structure of the Money Market in India. **In** *Desai, V. R. M. and Ghonasgi,*

B. D., 1969, pp. 1–28. [G: India]

Dewald, William G. Statement. **In** *Bank Holding Company Act Amendments, Pts. 1–3, HCH,* 1969, pp. 637–46. [G: U.S.]

Dirlam, Joel. Review of Recent Legislative and Judicial Trends Affecting Bank Structure. **In** *Federal Reserve Bank of Chicago (I),* 1969, pp. 2–19. [G: U.S.]

Eccles, George S. Registered Bank Holding Companies. **In** *Prochnow, H. V., ed.,* 1969, pp. 82–103. [G: U.S.]

Edwards, Franklin R. Tie-In Sales in Banking and One Bank Holding Companies. *Antitrust Bull.,* Fall 1969, *14,* pp. 587–605. [G: U.S.]

Engberg, Holger L. and Hance, William A. Growth and Dispersion of Branch Banking in Tropical Africa, 1950–1964. *Econ. Geogr.,* July 1969, *45*(3), pp. 195–208. [G: Africa]

Federici, Vincenzo. L'automazione del servizio pegno alla luce dell'esperienza di un'Azienda credito. (Automation of Pledge Service in the Light of a Bank's Experience. With English summary.) *Bancaria,* February 1969, *25*(2), pp. 203–05.

Fischer, Gerald. Market Extension by Bank Holding Companies: History, Economic Implications, and Current Issues. **In** *Federal Reserve Bank of Chicago (II),* 1969, pp. 43–72. [G: U.S.]

Fisher, Robert Moore. The Availibility of Mortgage Lending Commitments. (Study summary.) *Fed. Res. Bull.,* December 1969, *55*(12), pp. 919–20. [G: U.S.]

Gies, Thomas G. Topics in Bank Capital: Comment. **In** *Federal Reserve Bank of Chicago (I),* 1969, pp. 110–12. [G: U.S.]

Goldfeld, Stephen H. An Extension of the Monetary Sector. **In** *Duesenberry, J. S., et al.,* 1969, pp. 317–59. [G: U.S.]

Goldfinger, Nathaniel. Statement. **In** *Investigation of Increase in Prime Interest Rate, HCH,* 1969, pp. 221–27. [G: U.S.]

Golembe, Carter H. One-Bank Holding Companies. **In** *Prochnow, H. V., ed.,* 1969, pp. 66–81. [G: U.S.]

Goodman, Oscar. A Survey of Judicial and Regulatory Opinions Affecting Banking Competition under the Bank Merger Acts of 1960 and 1966. **In** *Federal Reserve Bank of Chicago (II),* 1969, pp. 1–16. [G: U.S.]

Goodman, Oscar. Topics on Bank Capital: Comment. **In** *Federal Reserve Bank of Chicago (I),* 1969, pp. 114–16. [G: U.S.]

Gorman, John A. Alternative Measures of the Real Output and Productivity of Commercial Banks. **In** *Fuchs, V. R., ed.,* 1969, pp. 155–89. [G: U.S.]

Green, Johs. Il finanziamento dell-espansione e della ristrutturazione economica. (Financing of Expansion and Structural Change. With English summary.) *Bancaria,* August 1969, *25*(8), pp. 947–53.

Greenbaum, Stuart I. Correspondent Banking. **In** *Jessup, P. F.,* 1969, pp. 135–46.

Guy, Edward G. The Applicability of the Federal Antitrust Laws to Bank Mergers. **In** *Jessup, P. F.,* 1969, pp. 444–51. [G: U.S.]

Hall, George R. Some Impacts of One-Bank Holding Companies. **In** *Federal Reserve Bank of Chicago (II),* 1969, pp. 73–94. [G: U.S.]

Hammond, Robert. The Justice Department Views Bank Mergers. **In** *Federal Reserve Bank of Chicago (I),* 1969, pp. 55–62. [G: U.S.]

Haslem, John A. A Statistical Estimation of Commercial Bank Profitability. *J. Bus.,* January 1969, *42*(1), pp. 22–35. [G: U.S.]

Hodgman, Donald R. Alternative Measures of the Real Output and Productivity of Commercial Banks: Discussion. **In** *Fuchs, V. R., ed.,* 1969, pp. 189–95. [G: U.S.]

Hodgman, Donald R. Bank Holding Companies: Discussion. **In** *Federal Reserve Bank of Chicago (II),* 1969, pp. 99–100. [G: U.S.]

Hooven, Eckart. La concorrenza fra aziende di credito per la raccolta dei depositi. (Competition for Deposits. With English summary.) *Bancaria,* August 1969, *25*(8), pp. 954–62. [G: W. Germany]

Horvitz, Paul M. and Shull, Bernard. Branch Banking, Independent Banks and Geographic Price Discrimination. *Antitrust Bull.,* Winter 1969, *14,* pp. 827–44. [G: U.S.]

Horvitz, Paul M. Topics in Bank Capital: Comment. **In** *Federal Reserve Bank of Chicago (I),* 1969, pp. 112–14. [G: U.S.]

Hunter, J. S. H. The Roosa Doctrine and the Shiftability Thesis: Application to Debt Management in the United States. *Weltwirtsch. Arch.,* 1969, *103* (1), pp. 110–30. [G: U.S.]

Jacobs, Donald. The Framework of Commercial Bank Regulation: An Appraisal. **In** *Jessup, P. F.,* 1969, pp. 402–21. [G: U.S.]

Jaffee, Dwight M. and Modigliani, Franco. A Theory and Test of Credit Rationing. *Amer. Econ. Rev.,* December 1969, *59*(5), pp. 850–72. [G: U.S.]

Jessup, Paul F. Bank Debt Capital: Urchin of Adversity to Child of Prosperity. **In** *Jessup, P. F.,* 1969, pp. 186–205. [G: U.S.]

Jessup, Paul F. Changes in Bank Ownership: The Impact on Operating Performance. (Study summary.) *Fed. Res. Bull.,* April 1969, *55*(4), pp. 309–10. [G: U.S.]

Johnson, Walter L. The Theory and Practice of Window Dressing by Commercial Banks. *Miss. Val. J. Bus. Econ.,* Spring 1969, *4*(2), pp. 43–49. [G: U.S.]

Johnston, Robert A. Credit—and Credit Cards. **In** *Jessup, P. F.,* 1969, pp. 101–09. [G: U.S.]

Käräva, Simo. Luotonannon selektiivisyys ja pankit. (The Selective Lending Policy and the Banks. With English summary.) *Kansant. Aikak.,* 1969, *65*(3), pp. 226–32. [G: Finland]

Käräva, Simo. Takaukset pankkiluottojen vakuutena. (Guarantees as Security for Bank Credits. With English summary.) *Liiketaloudellinen Aikak.,* 1969, *18*(3), pp. 443–59. [G: Finland]

Kaufman, George. Topics on Bank Capital: Comment. **In** *Federal Reserve Bank of Chicago (I),* 1969, pp. 116–18. [G: U.S.]

Kaufman, George G. Bank Holding Companies: Discussion. **In** *Federal Reserve Bank of Chicago (II),* 1969, pp. 100–102. [G: U.S.]

Keefe, Harry V., Jr. The One-Bank Holding Company—A Result, Not a Revolution. **In** *Prochnow, H. V., ed.,* 1969, pp. 116–41. [G: U.S.]

King, Donald A. Monetary Restraint in 1969. *Surv. Curr. Bus.*, Part I, May 1969, *49*(5), pp. 13–18. [G: U.S.]

Klaman, Saul B. Statement. **In** *Investigation of Increase in Prime Interest Rate, HCH,* 1969, pp. 239–43. [G: U.S.]

Klopstock, Fred H. Euro-dollars in the Liquidity and Reserve Management of United States Banks. **In** *Jessup, P. F.,* 1969, pp. 491–506.

Krohmer, F. R. Deposit Growth in the Tenth District—1949–68. *Fed. Res. Bank Kansas City Rev.*, May 1969, pp. 11-16. [G: U.S.]

Lanzillotti, R. F. and Saving, Thomas R. State Branching Restrictions and the Availability of Branching Services: A Comment. *J. Money, Credit, Banking,* November 1969, *1*(4), pp. 778–88. [G: U.S.]

Lapidus, Leonard. Bank Holding Companies: Discussion. **In** *Federal Reserve Bank of Chicago (II),* 1969, pp. 102–04. [G: U.S.]

de Leeuw, Frank. A Condensed Model of Financial Behavior. **In** *Duesenberry, J. S., et al.,* 1969, pp. 270–315. [G: U.S.]

Lipfert, Helmut. Il sistema creditizio tedesco verso nuovo vie. (The German Credit System Moving Towards New Developments. With English summary.) *Bancaria,* September 1969, *25*(9), pp. 1082–87. [G: W. Germany]

Luttrell, Clifton B. Interest Rate Controls: Perspective, Purpose, and Problems. **In** *Kuhlman, J. M., ed.,* 1969, pp. 275–88. [G: U.S.]

Main, Jeremy. The First Real International Bankers. **In** *Jessup, P. F.,* 1969, pp. 481–90.

Martin, William McChesney. Statement to Congress. *Fed. Res. Bull.,* October 1969, *55*(10), pp. 819–22. [G: U.S.]

Masten, John T. The Structure of Commercial Banking in the United States. *Rivista Int. Sci. Econ. Com.,* July 1969, *16*(7), pp. 688–709. [G: U.S.]

Mauer, Laurence Jay. Commercial Bank Maturity Demand for United States Government Securities and the Determinants of the Term Structure of Interest Rates. *J. Financial Quant. Anal.,* March 1969, *4*(1), pp. 37–52. [G: U.S.]

Mayne, Lucille Stringer. Federal Reserve System Membership, Bank Liquidity, and Bank Profitability. *Southern Econ. J.,* October 1969, *36*(2), pp. 181–84. [G: U.S.]

Meimberg, R. About the Theory and Practice of the Participation of Deposit Banks in the Financing of Capital Projects (with Reference to the Conditions in Germany, England and India). *Indian Econ. J.,* April-June 1969, *16*(4–5), pp. 496–506. [G: Germany; U.K.; India]

Melichar, Emanuel. Seasonal Discount Assistance to Rural Banks: Evaluation of a Federal Reserve Proposal. *Agr. Finance Rev.,* July 1969, *30,* pp. 44–57. [G: U.S.]

Melvin, Donald J. Conglomerate Acquisitions of Banks. **In** *Prochnow, H. V., ed.,* 1969, pp. 104–15. [G: U.S.]

Mickwitz, Gösta. Uudet pankkilait ja pankkiemme kilpailutoiminta. (The New Bank Laws and the Competition among the Banks. With English summary.) *Liiketaloudellinen Aikak.,* 1969, *18* (3), pp. 507–19. [G: Finland]

Mitchell, George. What Can We Do about Bank Structure? **In** *Federal Reserve Bank of Chicago (II),* 1969, pp. 109–19. [G: U.S.]

Moore, Basil J. Asset Management and Monetary Policy: Discussion. *J. Finance,* May 1969, *24*(2), pp. 242–44. [G: U.S.]

Mote, Larry R. A Conceptual Optimal Banking Structure for the United States. **In** *Federal Reserve Bank of Chicago (II),* 1969, pp. 17–34. [G: U.S.]

Mote, Larry R. Competition in Banking: The Issues. **In** *Jessup, P. F.,* 1969, pp. 421–31. [G: U.S.]

Mote, Larry R. Competition in Banking: The Evidence. **In** *Jessup, P. F.,* 1969, pp. 432–44. [G: U.S.]

Mote, Larry R. Review of Federal Reserve Board Split Merger and Holding Company Decisions. **In** *Federal Reserve Bank of Chicago (I),* 1969, pp. 37–54. [G: U.S.]

Murphy, Neil B. A Cross-Sectional Analysis of the Cost of Operations of Trust Departments. *J. Money, Credit, Banking,* February 1969, *1*(1), pp. 84–100. [G: U.S.]

Murphy, Neil B. and Anderson, Paul S. Running the Bank's Money Position: A Study of Demand Deposit Fluctuations. **In** *Jessup, P. F.,* 1969, pp. 117–23. [G: U.S.]

Nadler, Paul S. One-Bank Holding Companies: The Public Interest. *Harvard Bus. Rev.,* May–June 1969, *47*(3), pp. 107–13.

Nadler, Paul S. The Coming Change in Correspondent Relationships. **In** *Jessup, P. F.,* 1969, pp. 147–51. [G: U.S.]

Nadler, Paul S. The Outlook for the One-Bank Holding Company. **In** *Prochnow, H. V., ed.,* 1969, pp. 142–57. [G: U.S.]

Orgler, Yair E. Selection of Bank Loans for Evaluation: An Analytic Approach. *J. Finance,* March 1969, *24*(1), pp. 75–80. [G: U.S.]

Pearce, W. O. Functional Cost Analysis: A Tool of Bank Management. **In** *Jessup, P. F.,* 1969, pp. 219–23. [G: U.S.]

Peltzman, Sam. Capital Investment in Commercial Banking. **In** *Federal Reserve Bank of Chicago (I),* 1969, pp. 67–98. [G: U.S.]

Peltzman, Sam. The Banking Structure and the Transmission of Monetary Policy. *J. Finance,* June 1969, *24*(3), pp. 387–411. [G: U.S.]

Phillips, Almarin. A Conceptual Optimal Banking Structure for the United States: Discussion. **In** *Federal Reserve Bank of Chicago (II),* 1969, pp. 35–40. [G: U.S.]

Pierce, James L. Commercial Bank Liquidity. **In** *Jessup, P. F.,* 1969, pp. 16–27.

Powers, John Anthony. Branch Versus Unit Banking: Bank Output and Cost Economies. *Southern Econ. J.,* October 1969, *36*(2), pp. 153–64. [G: U.S.]

Pritchard, Leland J. The Economics of the Commercial Bank. Savings-Investment Process in the United States. *Rivista Int. Sci. Econ. Com.,* July 1969, *16*(7), pp. 664–87. [G: U.S.]

Randall, K. A. An Evolutionary Process in Banking. **In** *Prochnow, H. V., ed.,* 1969, pp. 48–55. [G: U.S.]

Robinson, Roland I. and Pettway, Richard H. Policies for Optimum Bank Capital: Summary. In *Jessup, P. F.*, 1969, pp. 183–86. [G: U.S.]

Russell, William R. An Investigation of Commercial Banks' Aggregate Portfolio Adjustments. *Int. Econ. Rev.*, October 1969, *10*(3), pp. 266–90. [G: U.S.]

Ruta, Guido. Profili comparativistici del sistema bancario italiano nell'ambito della Comunità Economica Europea. (Comparative Aspects of the Italian Banking System within the European Economic Community. With English summary.) *Bancaria*, July 1969, *25*(7), pp. 829–41. [G: Italy; E.E.C.]

Saunders, Robert J. On the Interpretation of Models Explaining Cross Sectional Differences among Commercial Banks. *J. Financial Quant. Anal.*, March 1969, *4*(1), pp. 25–35. [G: U.S.]

Shull, Bernard. Bank Holding Companies: Discussion. In *Federal Reserve Bank of Chicago (II)*, 1969, pp. 104–07. [G: U.S.]

Shull, Bernard. Problems in Economic Analysis of Bank Merger and Holding Company Cases. In *Federal Reserve Bank of Chicago (I)*, 1969, pp. 20–36. [G: U.S.]

Silber, William L. Velocity and Bank Portfolio Composition. *Southern Econ. J.*, October 1969, *36*(2), pp. 147–52. [G: U.S.]

Smith, David L. Characteristics of Merging Banks. (Study summary.) *Fed. Res. Bull.*, July 1969, *55*(7), pp. 579–80. [G: U.S.]

Taylor, Charles T. Meeting Seasonal Loan Demands. In *Jessup, P. F.*, 1969, pp. 89–100. [G: U.S.]

Terleckyj, Nestor E. and Fabricant, Solomon. Alternative Measures of the Real Output and Productivity of Commercial Banks: Comment. In *Fuchs, V. R., ed.*, 1969, pp. 195–99. [G: U.S.]

Tussing, A. Dale. Bank "Failure": A Meaningful Competitive Force? In *Federal Reserve Bank of Chicago (I)*, 1969, pp. 99–109. [G: U.S.]

Waterman, Robert H., Jr. and Gee, Robert E. A New Tool for Bank Management: A Mathematical Model in Banking. In *Jessup, P. F.*, 1969, pp. 293–300.

Weiss, Steven J. Bank Holding Companies and Public Policy. *New Eng. Econ. Rev.*, January/February 1969, pp. 3–29. [G: U.S.]

Weiss, Steven J. Commercial Bank Price Competition: The Case of "Free" Checking Accounts. *New Eng. Econ. Rev.*, September/October 1969, pp. 3–22. [G: U.S.]

Weiss, Steven J. Effects of Regulation, Branching, and Mergers on Banking Structure and Performance: Comment. *Southern Econ. J.*, October 1969, *36*(2), pp. 202–04. [G: U.S.]

Wilson, J. S. G. Building the Financial System of a Developing Country. *Lloyds Bank Rev.*, July 1969, (93), pp. 36–48.

Wilson, J. S. G. Regulation and Control of the United Kingdom Banking and Financial Structure. *Banca Naz. Lavoro Quart. Rev.*, June 1969, (89), pp. 128–45. [G: U.K.]

Wilson, Ruth V. Public Treasurers' Money. In *Jessup, P. F.*, 1969, pp. 123–29. [G: U.S.]

Wolf, Charles R. A Model for Selecting Commercial Bank Government Security Portfolios. *Rev. Econ. Statist.*, February 1969, *51*(1), pp. 40–52.

Wu, Hsiu-Kwang. Bank Examiner Criticisms, Bank Loan Defaults, and Bank Loan Quality. *J. Finance*, September 1969, *24*(4), pp. 697–705. [G: U.S.]

Zoellner, John F. Bank Holding Companies—Tenth District States. *Fed. Res. Bank Kansas City Rev.*, February 1969, pp. 10–16. [G: U.S.]

313 Financial Markets

3130 General

Bower, Richard S. and Bower, Dorothy H. Risk and the Valuation of Common Stock. *J. Polit. Econ.*, May/June 1969, *77*(3), pp. 349–62.

Brigham, Eugene F. and Pappas, James L. Rates of Return on Common Stock. *J. Bus.*, July 1969, *42*(3), pp. 302–16. [G: U.S.]

Cacy, J. A. Tenth District Banks in the Federal Funds Market. *Fed. Res. Bank Kansas City Rev.*, November 1969, pp. 10–20. [G: U.S.]

Demsetz, Harold. Perfect Competition, Regulation, and the Stock Market. In *Manne, H. G., ed.*, 1969, pp. 1–22. [G: U.S.]

Deweirdt, E. Le marché des euro-obligations. (About Euro-Bonds. With English summary.) *Rivista Int. Sci. Econ. Com.*, November 1969, *16*(11), pp. 1033–52. [G: Europe]

Drake, P. J. The New-Issue Boom in Malaya and Singapore, 1961–1964. *Econ. Develop. Cult. Change*, Part I, October 1969, *18*(1), pp. 73–91. [G: Malaya; Singapore]

Dryden, Myles M. A Source of Bias in Filter Tests of Share Prices. *J. Bus.*, July 1969, *42*(3), pp. 321–25.

Hausman, Warren H. A Note on "The Value Line Contest: A Test of the Predictability of Stock-Price Changes." *J. Bus.*, July 1969, *42*(3), pp. 317–20.

Johnson, Glenn L. Professor Johnson's Hedges: A Reply. *Miss. Val. J. Bus. Econ.*, Fall 1969, *5*(1), pp. 85–89.

Lees, Francis A. Interregional Flows of Funds through State and Local Government Securities (1957–1962). *J. Reg. Sci.*, April 1969, *9*(1), pp. 79–86. [G: U.S.]

Pogue, Thomas F. and Soldofsky, Robert M. What's in a Bond Rating? *J. Financial Quant. Anal.*, June 1969, *4*(2), pp. 201–28. [G: U.S.]

Richebächer, Kurt. Problemi e prospettive di integrazione dei mercati europei dei capitali. (Problems and Prospects of Integrating European Capital Markets. With English summary.) *Bancaria*, February 1969, *25*(2), pp. 170–77.

Silber, William L. Portfolio Substitutability, Regulations, and Monetary Policy. *Quart. J. Econ.*, May 1969, *83*(2), pp. 197–219. [G: U.S.]

Smith, Keith V. Stock Price and Economic Indexes for Generating Efficient Portfolios. *J. Bus.*, July 1969, *42*(3), pp. 326–36.

Wallich, Henry C. Uses of Financial Accounts in Monetary Analysis. *Rev. Income Wealth*, December 1969, *15*(4), pp. 321–34.

Walsh, Cornelius F. Professor Johnson's Hedges. *Miss. Val. J. Bus. Econ.*, Fall 1969, *5*(1), pp. 80–84.

Williamson, Oliver E. Corporate Control and the

Theory of the Firm. In *Manne, H. G., ed.*, 1969, pp. 281–336.

3132 Financial Markets Studies and Regulation

Alchian, Armen A. Corporate Management and Property Rights. In *Manne, H. G., ed.*, 1969, pp. 337–60.

Archibald, T. R. Stock Market Reaction to Different Accounting Practices. In *Association of Canadian Schools of Business*, 1969, pp. 171–95.

Backer, Morton. Comments on "The Value of the SEC's Accounting Disclosure Requirements." *Accounting Rev.*, July 1969, *44*(3), pp. 533–38. [G: U.S.]

Bacon, Peter W. and Winn, Edward L., Jr. The Impact of Forced Conversion on Stock Prices. *J. Finance*, December 1969, *24*(5), pp. 871–74. [G: U.S.]

Baumol, William J. Performance of the Firm and Performance of Its Stocks. In *Manne, H. G., ed.*, 1969, pp. 127–41.

Bennett, J. W.; Graham, K. R. and Hoa, Tran Van. The Determination of Yields on Corporate Shares: An Empirical Study. *Econ. Rec.*, December 1969, *45*(112), pp. 496–512. [G: Australia]

Benston, George J. The Effectiveness and Effects of the SEC's Accounting Disclosure Requirements. In *Manne, H. G., ed.*, 1969, pp. 23–79. [G: U.S.]

Benston, George J. The Value of the SEC's Accounting Disclosure Requirements. *Accounting Rev.*, July 1969, *44*(3), pp. 515–32. [G: U.S.]

Breen, William J. An Exploratory Econometric Model of Financial Markets. *J. Financial Quant. Anal.*, September 1969, *4*(3), pp. 233–69. [G: U.S.]

Cagan, Phillip. A Study of Liquidity Premiums on Federal and Municipal Government Securities. In *Guttentag, J. M. and Cagan, P., eds.*, 1969, pp. 107–42. [G: U.S.]

Carleton, Willard T. and Lerner, Eugene M. Statistical Credit Scoring of Municipal Bonds. *J. Money, Credit, Banking*, November 1969, *1*(4), pp. 750–64.

Coen, P. J.; Gomme, E. D. and Kendall, M. G. Lagged Relationships in Economic Forecasting. *J. Roy. Statist. Soc.*, Part 2, 1969, *132*, pp. 133–52.

Conard, Joseph W. and Frankena, Mark W. The Yield Spread Between New and Seasoned Corporate Bonds, 1952–63. In *Guttentag, J. M. and Cagan, P., eds.*, 1969, pp. 143–222. [G: U.S.]

Dryden, Myles M. Share Price Movements: A Markovian Approach. *J. Finance*, March 1969, *24*(1), pp. 49–60. [G: U.S.]

Drzycimski, Eugene F. The Stock Repurchase Decision. *Marquette Bus. Rev.*, Winter 1969, *13*(4), pp. 159–67.

Eiteman, David K. and Tom, Franklin. The New California Blue-Sky Law. *Calif. Manage. Rev.*, Winter 1969, *12*(2), pp. 5–12. [G: U.S.]

Elsaid, Hussein H. Non-convertible Preferred Stock as a Financing Instrument 1950–65: Comment. *J. Finance*, December 1969, *24*(5), pp. 939–41. [G: U.S.]

Fairbairn, I. J. and McShane, R. W. The Return on Equities and Fixed Interest Securities on the Australian Capital Market. *Econ. Rec.*, March 1969, *45*(109), pp. 116–23. [G: Australia]

Fama, Eugene F., et al. The Adjustment of Stock Prices to New Information. *Int. Econ. Rev.*, February 1969, *10*(1), pp. 1–21. [G: U.S.]

Fredman, Albert J. and Wert, James E. Secondary Distributions of American Stock Exchange Securities. *Marquette Bus. Rev.*, Fall 1969, *13*(3), pp. 137–41. [G: U.S.]

Fredman, Albert J. Stockholders' Returns: Dividends or Earnings? *Miss. Val. J. Bus. Econ.*, Fall 1969, *5*(1), pp. 23–33. [G: U.S.]

Friend, Irwin. The SEC and the Economic Performance of Securities Markets. In *Manne, H. G., ed.*, 1969, pp. 185–216. [G: U.S.]

Goldfeld, Stephen H. An Extension of the Monetary Sector. In *Duesenberry, J. S., et al.*, 1969, pp. 317–59. [G: U.S.]

Haugen, Robert A. and Heins, A. James. The Effects of the Personal Income Tax on the Stability of Equity Value. *Nat. Tax J.*, December 1969, *22*(4), pp. 466–71.

Holland, Thomas E. 'Operation Twist' and the Movement of Interest Rates and Related Economic Time Series. *Int. Econ. Rev.*, October 1969, *10*(3), pp. 260–65. [G: U.S.]

Howard, Robert E. Local, National Municipal Bond Markets Are Uncertain. *Indiana Bus. Rev.*, September/October 1969, *44*, pp. 13–14. [G: U.S.]

Kahn, Douglas A. Mandatory Buy-Out Agreements for Stock of Closely Held Corporations. *Mich. Law Rev.*, November 1969, *68*(1), pp. 1–64.

Kassouf, Sheen T. An Econometric Model for Option Price with Implications for Investors' Expectations and Audacity. *Econometrica*, October 1969, *37*(4), pp. 685–94.

Klein, Donald J. History of the Odd-Lot Stock Trading Theory. *Marquette Bus. Rev.*, Fall 1969, *13*(3), pp. 99–116. [G: U.S.]

Krainer, Robert E. Structural Estimates of Supply and Demand in the USA Short Term Bank Loan Market. *Bull. Oxford Univ. Inst. Econ. Statist.*, February 1969, *31*(1), pp. 39–46. [G: U.S.]

Kuehn, D. A. Stock Market Valuation and Acquisitions: An Empirical Test of One Component of Managerial Utility. *J. Ind. Econ.*, April 1969, *17*(2), pp. 132–44. [G: U.K.]

de Leeuw, Frank. A Condensed Model of Financial Behavior. In *Duesenberry, J. S., et al.*, 1969, pp. 270–315. [G: U.S.]

Little, Jane Sneddon. The Euro-dollar Market: Its Nature and Impact. *New Eng. Econ. Rev.*, May/June 1969, pp. 2–31.

Maccarone, Salvatore. Considerazioni sulla natura giuridica dei fondi comuni di investimento mobiliare-I. (Remarks on the Legal Nature of Unit Trust-I. With English summary.) *Bancaria*, November 1969, *25*(11), pp. 1350–60.

Maccarone, Salvatore. Considerazioni sulla natura giuridica dei fondi comuni di investimento mobiliare. (Remarks on the Legal Nature of Unit Trust. With English summary.) *Bancaria*, December 1969, *25*(12), pp. 1473–89.

Malkiel, Burton G. and Kane, Edward J. Expectations and Interest Rates: A Cross-sectional Test of the Error-learning Hypothesis. *J. Polit. Econ.*, Part I, July/August 1969, *77*(4), pp. 453–70. [G: U.S.]

Masera, R. S. Least Squares Construction of the Yield Curves for Italian Government Securities, 1957–1967, Part I: General Introduction to the Italian Bond Market and Main Results. *Banca Naz. Lavoro Quart. Rev.*, December 1969, (91), pp. 347–71. [G: Italy]

Meltzer, Allan H. On Efficiency and Regulation of the Securities Industry. **In** *Manne, H. G., ed.*, 1969, pp. 217–38. [G: U.S.]

Merrett, A. J. and Sykes, A. Return on Equities and Fixed Interest Securities: 1919–66. **In** *Carsberg, B. V. and Edey, H. C., eds.*, 1969, pp. 113–26. [G: U.S.]

Morton, Walter A. Risk and Return: Instability of Earnings as a Measure of Risk. *Land Econ.*, May 1969, *45*(2), pp. 229–61. [G: U.S.]

Naylor, John A. A Note on the 'Traditional Theory' of the Term Structure of Interest Rates and Rates on Three- and Six-Month Treasury Bills: Comment. *Int. Econ. Rev.*, October 1969, *10*(3), pp. 484–87. [G: U.S.]

Pelleri, Paolo. Le Borse estere nel 1968. (Foreign Stock Exchanges in 1968. With English summary.) *Bancaria*, February 1969, *25*(2), pp. 178–202.

Pelleri, Paolo. Le Borse italiane nel 1968. (The Italian Stock Exchanges in 1968. With English summary.) *Bancaria*, January 1969, *25*(1), pp. 25–64. [G: Italy]

Rayner, A. C. Premium Bonds—The Effect of the Price Structure. *Bull. Oxford Univ. Inst. Econ. Statist.*, November 1969, *31*(4), pp. 303–11. [G: U.K.]

Rees, Graham and Wiseman, Jack. London's Commodity Markets. *Lloyds Bank Rev.*, January 1969, (91), pp. 22–45. [G: U.K.]

Robichek, Alexander A. Risk and the Value of Securities. *J. Financial Quant. Anal.*, December 1969, *4*(4), pp. 513–38.

Roll, Richard. Bias in Fitting the Sharpe Model to Time Series Data. *J. Financial Quant. Anal.*, September 1969, *4*(3), pp. 271–89. [G: U.S.]

Samuelson, Paul A. Statement. **In** *Investment Company Amendments Act of 1969, SCH*, 1969, pp. 53–57. [G: U.S.]

Shapiro, A. A. Interindustry Differentials in the Demand for Money and Government Securities. *Southern Econ. J.*, October 1969, *36*(2), pp. 165–70. [G: U.S.]

Singhvi, Surendra S. Corporate Financial Disclosure in the United States. *Miss. Val. J. Bus. Econ.*, Fall 1969, *5*(1), pp. 43–50. [G: U.S.]

Soldofsky, Robert M. and Miller, Roger L. Risk Premium Curves for Different Classes of Long-Term Securities, 1950–1966. *J. Finance*, June 1969, *24*(3), pp. 429–45. [G: U.S.]

Stoll, Hans R. The Relationship between Put and Call Option Prices. *J. Finance*, December 1969, *24*(5), pp. 801–24.

Terna, Pietro. Ricerca di uniformità di borsa di breve periodo: primi risultati. (Short Term Behaviour of Share Prices. With English summary.) *L'Industria*, October–December 1969, (4), pp. 493–505. [G: Italy]

Wagner, Carroll L., Jr. Deputization under Section 16(b): The Implications of *Feder v. Martin Marietta Corporation*. *Yale Law J.*, June 1969, *78*(7), pp. 1151–73. [G: U.S.]

Walker, John E. The "Net Interest Cost" Method of Issuing Tax Exempt Bonds: Is It Rational?—A Comment. *Public Finance*, 1969, *24*(4), pp. 624–26.

Wallace, Neil. Buse on Meiselman—A Comment. *J. Polit. Econ.*, Part I, July/August 1969, *77*(4), pp. 524–27.

Wallich, Henry C. Statement. **In** *Investment Company Amendments Act of 1969, SCH*, 1969, pp. 143–47. [G: U.S.]

West, Richard R. The "Net Interest Cost" Method of Issuing Tax Exempt Bonds: Is It Rational?—A Reply to Professor Walker. *Public Finance*, 1969, *24*(4), pp. 627–30.

Young, Allan. Exchange Market Effects of Stock Repurchases through Tender Offers. *Miss. Val. J. Bus. Econ.*, Spring 1969, *4*(2), pp. 65–77.

3135 Portfolio Selection: Theories and Studies

Adler, F. Michael. On the Risk-Return Trade-Off in the Valuation of Assets. *J. Financial Quant. Anal.*, December 1969, *4*(4), pp. 493–512.

Bower, Richard S. and Wippern, Ronald F. Risk-Return Measurement in Portfolio Selection and Performance Appraisal Models: Progress Report. *J. Financial Quant. Anal.*, December 1969, *4*(4), pp. 417–47.

Brief, Richard P. and Owen, Joel. A Note on Earnings Risk and the Coefficient of Variation. *J. Finance*, December 1969, *24*(5), pp. 901–04.

Briscoe, G.; Samuels, J. M. and Smyth, David J. The Treatment of Risk in the Stock Market. *J. Finance*, September 1969, *24*(4), pp. 707–13. [G: U.K.]

Claassen, Emil M. Stock-Flow Decisions and Full Equilibrium. *Kyklos*, 1969, *22*(3), pp. 493–505.

Corluy, M. Waarom de verstandige beurbelegger altijd winst boekt. (Why the Intelligent Investor in the Stock Exchange Will Always Make Profits. With English summary.) *Econ. Soc. Tijdschr.*, August 1969, *23*(4), pp. 379–90.

Douglas, George W. Risk in the Equity Markets: An Empirical Appraisal of Market Efficiency. *Yale Econ. Essays*, Spring 1969, *9*(1), pp. 3–45.

Edey, H. C. Income and the Valuation of Stock-In-Trade. **In** *Parker, R. H. and Harcourt, G. C., eds.*, 1969, pp. 230–38. [G: U.K.]

Eppen, Gary D. and Fama, Eugene F. Cash Balance and Simple Dynamic Portfolio Problems with Proportional Costs. *Int. Econ. Rev.*, June 1969, *10*(2), pp. 119–33.

Feldstein, Martin S. Mean-Variance Analysis in the Theory of Liquidity Preference and Portfolio Selection. *Rev. Econ. Stud.*, January 1969, *36*(105), pp. 5–12.

Feldstein, Martin S. The Effects on Taxation on Risk Taking. *J. Polit. Econ.*, September/October 1969, *77*(5), pp. 755–64.

Gentry, James A. and Pike, John R. Rates of Return on Common Stock Portfolios of Life Insurance Companies. *J. Risk Ins.*, December 1969, *36*(5),

pp. 545–52. [G: U.S.]

Green, Paul E. and Maheshwari, Arun. Common Stock Perception and Preference: An Application of Multidimensional Scaling. *J. Bus.*, October 1969, *42*(4), pp. 439–57. [G: U.S.]

Grossman, Herschel I. Expectations, Transactions Costs, and Asset Demands. *J. Finance,* June 1969, *24*(3), pp. 491–506.

Hakansson, Nils H. Risk Disposition and the Separation Property in Portfolio Selection. *J. Financial Quant. Anal.*, December 1969, *4*(4), pp. 401–16.

Haley, Charles W. The Valuation of Risk Assets and the Selection of Risky Investments in Stock Portfolios and Capital Budgets: A Comment. *Rev. Econ. Statist.*, May 1969, *51*(2), pp. 220–21.

Hanoch, G. and Levy, Haim. The Efficiency Analysis of Choices Involving Risk. *Rev. Econ. Stud.*, July 1969, *36*(107), pp. 335–46.

Hofflander, A. E. and Drandell, Milton. A Linear Programming Model of Profitability, Capacity and Regulation in Insurance Management. *J. Risk Ins.*, March 1969, *36*(1), pp. 41–54.

Huntsman, Blaine. Asset Management and Monetary Policy: Discussion. *J. Finance,* May 1969, *24* (2), pp. 239–41. [G: U.S.]

Iyengar, Sampath S. Multiplier Analysis for India. *Indian Econ. J.*, April–June 1969, *16*(4–5), pp. 478–87. [G: India]

Jeffers, James R. and Kwon, Jene. A Portfolio Approach to Corporate Demands for Government Securities. *J. Finance,* December 1969, *24*(5), pp. 905–19.

Jensen, Michael C. Risk, The Pricing of Capital Assets, and the Evaluation of Investment Portfolios. *J. Bus.*, April 1969, *42*(2), pp. 167–247.

Krainer, Robert E. Liquidity Preference and Stock Market Speculation. *J. Financial Quant. Anal.*, March 1969, *4*(1), pp. 89–97. [G: U.S.]

Latané, Henry A. and Young, William E. Test of Portfolio Building Rules. *J. Finance,* September 1969, *24*(4), pp. 595–612.

Lee, C. H. A Stock-Adjustment Analysis of Capital Movements: The United States-Canadian Case. *J. Polit. Econ.*, Part I, July/August 1969, *77*(4), pp. 512–23. [G: U.S.; Canada]

Lintner, John. A Model of a Perfectly Functioning Securities Market. **In** *Manne, H. G., ed.*, 1969, pp. 143–66.

Lintner, John. The Aggregation of Investor's Diverse Judgments and Preferences in Purely Competitive Security Markets. *J. Financial Quant. Anal.*, December 1969, *4*(4), pp. 347–400.

Lintner, John. The Valuation of Risk Assets and the Selection of Risky Investments in Stock Portfolios and Capital Budgets: A Reply. *Rev. Econ. Statist.*, May 1969, *51*(2), pp. 222–24.

Litzenberger, Robert H. Equilibrium in the Equity Market under Uncertainty. *J. Finance,* September 1969, *24*(4), pp. 663–71.

Machol, Robert E. and Lerner, Eugene M. Risk, Ruin and Investment Analysis. *J. Financial Quant. Anal.*, December 1969, *4*(4), pp. 473–92.

Merton, Robert C. Lifetime Portfolio Selection under Uncertainty: The Continuous-Time Case. *Rev. Econ. Statist.*, August 1969, *51*(3), pp. 247–57.

Metzger, Bert L. Insurance Industry Begins to Court Profit Sharing Funds with Equity-Based Products. *J. Risk Ins.*, September 1969, *36*(4), pp. 437–45. [G: U.S.]

Minsky, Hyman P. Private Sector Asset Management and the Effectiveness of Monetary Policy: Theory and Practice. *J. Finance,* May 1969, *24*(2), pp. 223–38. [G: U.S.]

Mossin, Jan. Security Pricing and Investment Criteria in Competitive Markets. *Amer. Econ. Rev.*, December 1969, *59*(5), pp. 749–56.

Naylor, John A. Expectations, Portfolio Preferences and the Term Structure of Interest Rates. *Ohio State U. Bull. Bus. Res.*, September 1969, *44*(9), pp. 4–7. [G: U.S.]

Oakland, William H. Effects of Taxation on Risk-Taking: Discussion. *Amer. Econ. Rev.*, May 1969, *59*(2), pp. 563–65.

Panati, Giovanni. L'investiment trust e la "nuova scienza" degli investimenti mobiliari. (The Investment Trust and the "New Science" of Investing. With English summary.) *L'Impresa,* March/April 1969, *11*(2), pp. 152–55.

Peltzman, Sam. Capital Investment in Commercial Banking. **In** *Federal Reserve Bank of Chicago (I),* 1969, pp. 67–98. [G: U.S.]

Pye, Gordon. On the Tax Structure of Interest Rates. *Quart. J. Econ.*, November 1969, *83*(4), pp. 562–79.

Rakshit, M. K. Inflation, the Choice of Assets, and the Liquidity Trap. **In** *[Ghosal, U. N.],* 1969, pp. 69–73.

Rapp, Wilbur A. Treasury Common Stock Financing as an Investment Process. *Miss. Val. J. Bus. Econ.*, Fall 1969, *5*(1), pp. 1–10. [G: U.S.]

Renwick, Fred B. Asset Management and Investor Portfolio Behavior: Theory and Practice. *J. Finance,* May 1969, *24*(2), pp. 181–206. [G: U.S.]

Russell, William R. An Investigation of Commercial Banks' Aggregate Portfolio Adjustments. *Int. Econ. Rev.*, October 1969, *10*(3), pp. 266–90. [G: U.S.]

Samuelson, Paul A. Lifetime Portfolio Selection by Dynamic Stochastic Programming. *Rev. Econ. Statist.*, August 1969, *51*(3), pp. 239–46.

Sandmo, Agnar. Capital Risk, Consumption, and Portfolio Choice. *Econometrica,* October 1969, *37* (4), pp. 586–99.

Shibata, Aiko N. Effects of Taxation on Risk-Taking. *Amer. Econ. Rev.*, May 1969, *59*(2), pp. 553–61.

Smith, Keith V. and Tito, Dennis A. Risk-Return Measures of Ex Post Portfolio Performance. *J. Financial Quant. Anal.*, December 1969, *4*(4), pp. 449–71. [G: U.S.]

Soldofsky, Robert M. Asset Management and Monetary Policy: Discussion. *J. Finance,* May 1969, *24* (2), pp. 245–47. [G: U.S.]

Tambini, Luigi. Financial Policy and the Corporation Income Tax. **In** *Harberger, A. C. and Bailey, M. J., eds.*, 1969, pp. 185–222. [G: U.S.]

Taylor, Basil. Investment: Art, Science or What? *Lloyds Bank Rev.*, January 1969, (91), pp. 10–21.

Tobin, James. Comment on Borch and Feldstein. *Rev. Econ. Stud.*, January 1969, *36*(105), pp. 13–14.

Vasudevan, A. The Portfolio Approach: Its Relevance to Under-Developed Economies. *Indian Econ. J.*, April–June 1969, *16*(4–5), pp. 520–31.

Whitmore, G. A. The Mathematical Structure of Investor Preferences. **In** *Association of Canadian Schools of Business,* 1969, pp. 196–218.

Wolf, Charles R. A Model for Selecting Commercial Bank Government Security Portfolios. *Rev. Econ. Statist.,* February 1969, *51*(1), pp. 40–52.

Wood, John H. Expectations and the Demand for Bonds. *Amer. Econ. Rev.,* Part I, September 1969, *59*(4), pp. 522–30.

Yaari, Menahem E. Some Remarks on Measures of Risk Aversion and on Their Uses. *J. Econ. Theory,* October 1969, *1*(3), pp. 315–29.

Young, William E. and Trent, Robert H. Geometric Mean Approximations of Individual Security and Portfolio Performance. *J. Financial Quant. Anal.,* June 1969, *4*(2), pp. 179–99. **[G: U.S.]**

314 Financial Intermediaries

3140 Financial Intermediaries

Cannata, Giuseppe. Factoring: un nuovo ausilio per la gestione delle medie a piccole imprese-II. (Factoring: A New Facility for Medium and Small Companies-II. With English summary.) *Bancaria,* July 1969, *25*(7), pp. 842–50.

Cannata, Giuseppe. Factoring: un nuovo ausilio per la gestione delle medie e piccole imprese-I. (Factoring: A New Facility for Medium and Small Companies-I. With English summary.) *Bancaria,* June 1969, *25*(6), pp. 711–24.

Chase, Samuel B., Jr. Household Demand for Savings Deposits, 1921–1965. *J. Finance,* September 1969, *24*(4), pp. 643–58. **[G: U.S.]**

Coombs, H. C. Central Banking—A Look Back and Forward. *Econ. Rec.,* December 1969, *45*(112), pp. 485–95. **[G: Australia]**

Fisher, Robert Moore. The Availibility of Mortgage Lending Commitments. (Study summary.) *Fed. Res. Bull.,* December 1969, *55*(12), pp. 919–20. **[G: U.S.]**

Galper, Harvey. Alternative Interest Rates and the Demand for Money: Comment. *Amer. Econ. Rev.,* June 1969, *59*(3), pp. 401–12. **[G: U.S.]**

Gentry, James A. and Pike, John R. Rates of Return on Common Stock Portfolios of Life Insurance Companies. *J. Risk Ins.,* December 1969, *36*(5), pp. 545–52. **[G: U.S.]**

Hester, Donald D. Financial Disintermediation and Policy. *J. Money, Credit, Banking,* August 1969, *1*(3), pp. 600–17. **[G: U.S.]**

Hoffmann, Walther G. Die Entwicklung der Sparkassen im Rahmen des Wachatums der deutschen Wirtschaft (1850–1967). (With English summary.) *Z. ges. Staatswiss.,* October 1969, *125*(4), pp. 561–605. **[G: Germany]**

Hunter, J. S. H. The Roosa Doctrine and the Shiftability Thesis: Application to Debt Management in the United States. *Weltwirtsch. Arch.,* 1969, *103* (1), pp. 110–30. **[G: U.S.]**

Joshi, M. S. Monetary Policy and the Non-Bank Financial Intermediaries. **In** *Desai, V. R. M. and Ghonasgi, B. D.,* 1969, pp. 123–44. **[G: India]**

Kammerer, Peter. La politica dei premi al risparmio nell'esperienza tedesca. (Savings Bonus Policy in German Experience. With English summary.) *Bancaria,* October 1969, *25*(10), pp. 1225–38. **[G: Germany]**

Knight, Robert E. The Quality of Mortgage Credit: Part II. *Fed. Res. Bank Kansas City Rev.,* April 1969, pp. 10–18. **[G: U.S.]**

Knight, Robert E. The Quality of Mortgage Credit: Part I. *Fed. Res. Bank Kansas City Rev.,* March 1969, pp. 13–20. **[G: U.S.]**

Laidler, David. The Definition of Money: Theoretical and Empirical Problems. *J. Money, Credit, Banking,* August 1969, *1*(3), pp. 508–25. **[G: U.S.; U.K.]**

Lall, Sanjaya. Countering Inflation: The Role of Value Linking. *Finance Develop.,* June 1969, *6*(2), pp. 10–15.

Lee, Tong Hun. Alternative Interest Rates and the Demand for Money: Reply. *Amer. Econ. Rev.,* June 1969, *59*(3), pp. 412–18. **[G: U.S.]**

Lent, George E. Taxation of Financial Intermediaries. *Nat. Tax J.,* March 1969, *22*(1), pp. 139–53. **[G: U.S.; Canada]**

Lipfert, Helmut. Il sistema creditizio tedesco verso nuovo vie. (The German Credit System Moving Towards New Developments. With English summary.) *Bancaria,* September 1969, *25*(9), pp. 1082–87. **[G: W. Germany]**

Luttrell, Clifton B. Interest Rate Controls: Perspective, Purpose, and Problems. **In** *Kuhlman, J. M., ed.,* 1969, pp. 275–88. **[G: U.S.]**

Maccarone, Salvatore. Considerazioni sulla natura giuridica dei fondi comuni di investimento mobiliare-I. (Remarks on the Legal Nature of Unit Trust-I. With English summary.) *Bancaria,* November 1969, *25*(11), pp. 1350–60.

Maccarone, Salvatore. Considerazioni sulla natura giuridica dei fondi comuni di investimento mobiliare. (Remarks on the Legal Nature of Unit Trust. With English summary.) *Bancaria,* December 1969, *25*(12), pp. 1473–89.

Meltzer, Allan H. A Comment on Hester's Paper. *J. Money, Credit, Banking,* August 1969, *1*(3), pp. 618–23. **[G: U.S.]**

Murphy, Neil B. A Cross-Sectional Analysis of the Cost of Operations of Trust Departments. *J. Money, Credit, Banking,* February 1969, *1*(1), pp. 84–100. **[G: U.S.]**

Murray, Roger F. An Overview of the Life Insurance—Mutual Fund Combination. *J. Risk Ins.,* September 1969, *36*(4), pp. 419–24. **[G: U.S.]**

Saravane, Mohandas. Some Issues Relating to Deposit Mobilisation by Non-Banking Companies. *Indian Econ. J.,* April–June 1969, *16*(4–5), pp. 445–57. **[G: India]**

Smith, Keith V. and Tito, Dennis A. Risk-Return Measures of Ex Post Portfolio Performance. *J. Financial Quant. Anal.,* December 1969, *4*(4), pp. 449–71. **[G: U.S.]**

Wilson, J. S. G. Building the Financial System of a Developing Country. *Lloyds Bank Rev.,* July 1969, (93), pp. 36–48.

Wilson, J. S. G. Regulation and Control of the United Kingdom Banking and Financial Structure.

Banca Naz. Lavoro Quart. Rev., June 1969, (89), pp. 128–45. **[G: U.K.]**

315 Credit to Business, Consumer, etc. (including mortgages)

3150 General

Bhide, M. R. Investment Policy of the L. I. C. **In** *Dagli, V., ed., Vol. II,* 1969, pp. 87–101. **[G: India]**

Burger, Albert E. A Historical Analysis of the Credit Crunch of 1966. *Fed. Res. Bank St. Louis Rev.*, September 1969, *51*(9), pp. 13–30. **[G: U.S.]**

Cacy, J. A. Credit Flows in the 1960's. *Fed. Res. Bank Kansas City Rev.*, June 1969, pp. 11–16. **[G: U.S.]**

Dell'Amore, Giordano. Il contributo del risparmio familiare al riscatto del mezzogiorno. (Contribution Made by Household Savings to the Development of Southern Italy. With English summary.) *Bancaria,* October 1969, *25*(10), pp. 1206–15. **[G: Italy]**

Johnston, Robert A. Credit—and Credit Cards. **In** *Jessup, P. F.,* 1969, pp. 101–09. **[G: U.S.]**

Meigs, A. James. Capital Flows to Public Utilities and the Structure of the Money and Capital Markets. **In** *Trebing, H. M. and Howard, R. H., eds.*, 1969, pp. 33–56. **[G: U.S.]**

Robinson, Roland I. Capital Flows to Public Utilities and the Structure of the Money and Capital Markets: Comment. **In** *Trebing, H. M. and Howard, R. H., eds.*, 1969, pp. 57–61. **[G: U.S.]**

Struble, Frederick M. Bank Credit Cards and Check Credit Plans in the Nation and the District. *Fed. Res. Bank Kansas City Rev.*, July–August 1969, pp. 3–9. **[G: U.S.]**

Talwar, R. K. Public Sector Banking. **In** *Dagli, V., ed., Vol. II,* 1969, pp. 77–86. **[G: India]**

Thore, Sten. Credit Networks. *Economica, N.S.*, February 1969, *36*(141), pp. 42–57.

Wrightsman, Dwayne. Optimal Credit Terms for Accounts Receivable. *Quart. Rev. Econ. Bus.*, Summer 1969, *9*(2), pp. 59–66.

3151 Consumer Finance

Brimmer, Andrew F. Statement to Congress. *Fed. Res. Bull.*, December 1969, *55*(12), pp. 923–27. **[G: U.S.]**

Bryson, John E. and Dunham, Stephen S. A Case Study of the Impact of Consumer Legislation: The Elimination of Negotiability and the Cooling-Off Period. *Yale Law J.*, March 1969, *78*(4), pp. 618–61. **[G: U.S.]**

Evans, Michael K. and Kisselgoff, Avram. Demand for Consumer Installment Credit and Its Effects on Consumption. **In** *Duesenberry, J. S., et al.*, 1969, pp. 39–84. **[G: U.S.]**

Goudzwaard, Maurice B. Consumer Credit Charges and Credit Availability. *Southern Econ. J.*, January 1969, *35*(3), pp. 214–23. **[G: U.S.]**

Goudzwaard, Maurice B. The Economic Impact of Credit Insurance Charges. *J. Risk Ins.*, December 1969, *36*(5), pp. 515–23. **[G: U.S.]**

Il'in, V. and Koriagin, B. The Sale of Goods to the Public on Credit. *Prob. Econ.*, December 1969, *12* (8), pp. 68–74. **[G: U.S.S.R.]**

Johnson, Robert W. and Comiskey, Eugene E. Breakeven Analysis in Installment Lending. **In** *Jessup, P. F.,* 1969, pp. 229–37. **[G: U.S.]**

Johnson, Robert W. Statement. **In** *Consumer Credit Regulations, Pt. 1, HCH,* 1969, pp. 179–81. **[G: U.S.]**

Kawaja, Michael. The Economic Effects of Regulation: A Case Study of the Consumer Finance Industry. *Southern Econ. J.*, January 1969, *35*(3), pp. 231–38. **[G: U.S.]**

Ladd, John C. Consumers and Antitrust Treble Damages: Credit-Furniture Tie-Ins in the Low Income Market. *Yale Law J.*, December 1969, *79* (2), pp. 254–83. **[G: U.S.]**

Pais, A. Op de Pof. (On Tick. With English summary.) *De Economist,* January/February 1969, *117*(1), pp. 1–23. **[G: Netherlands]**

Samuelson, Paul A. Statement. **In** *Consumer Credit Regulations, Pt. 1, HCH,* 1969, pp. 163–66. **[G: U.S.]**

Stafford, Frank P. and Dunkelberg, William. The Cost of Financing Automobile Purchases. *Rev. Econ. Statist.*, November 1969, *51*(4), pp. 459–64. **[G: U.S.]**

3152 Mortgage Market

Fisher, Robert Moore. Monetary Policy: Its Relation to Mortgage Lending and Land Economics. *Land Econ.*, November 1969, *45*(4), pp. 418–24.

Fisher, Robert Moore. The Availibility of Mortgage Lending Commitments. (Study summary.) *Fed. Res. Bull.*, December 1969, *55*(12), pp. 919–20. **[G: U.S.]**

Friend, Irwin. Statement. **In** *High Interest Rates, SCH,* 1969, pp. 114–19. **[G: U.S.]**

von Furstenberg, George M. Default Risk on FHA-Insured Home Mortgages as a Function of the Terms of Financing: A Quantitative Analysis. *J. Finance,* June 1969, *24*(3), pp. 459–77. **[G: U.S.]**

Guttentag, Jack M. The Bahavior of Residential Mortgage Yields Since 1951. **In** *Guttentag, J. M. and Cagan, P., eds.*, 1969, pp. 29–76. **[G: U.S.]**

Heimann, John G. The Necessary Revolution in Housing Finance. **In** *National Housing Goals, HCH,* 1969, pp. 319–37. **[G: U.S.]**

Herr, William McD. The Role of FHA's Farm Operating and Ownership Loan Programs as Indicated by Borrower Characteristics. *Agr. Finance Rev.*, July 1969, *30,* pp. 1–10. **[G: U.S.]**

King, Donald A. Homebuilding Activity in 1969. *Surv. Curr. Bus.*, October 1969, *49*(10), pp. 16–22. **[G: U.S.]**

Knight, Robert E. The Quality of Mortgage Credit: Part II. *Fed. Res. Bank Kansas City Rev.*, April 1969, pp. 10–18. **[G: U.S.]**

Knight, Robert E. The Quality of Mortgage Credit: Part I. *Fed. Res. Bank Kansas City Rev.*, March 1969, pp. 13–20. **[G: U.S.]**

Lindholm, Richard W. Home Ownership and the Income Tax: A Proposed Change. *Oregon Bus. Rev.*, September 1969, *28*(9), pp. 1–3.

Martin, William McChesney. Statement to Congress. *Fed. Res. Bull.*, October 1969, *55*(10), pp. 815–19. **[G: U.S.]**

Ricks, R. Bruce. Imputed Equity Returns on Real Estate Financed with Life Insurance Company Loans. *J. Finance*, December 1969, *24*(5), pp. 921–37. **[G: U.S.]**

Schaaf, A. H. Mortgage Interest Rate Controls and the Veterans' Housing Market. *Miss. Val. J. Bus. Econ.*, Fall 1969, *5*(1), pp. 11–22. **[G: U.S.]**

Shipp, Royal. The Structure of the Mortgage Market for Income-Property Mortgage Loans. **In** *Guttentag, J. M. and Cagan, P., eds.*, 1969, pp. 77–106. **[G: U.S.]**

Smith, Lawrence B. A Model of the Canadian Housing and Mortgage Markets. *J. Polit. Econ.*, September/October 1969, *77*(5), pp. 795–816. **[G: Canada]**

Voorhis, Jerry. Statement. **In** *The 1969 Economic Report of the President, Pt. 4, JECH*, 1969, pp. 1189–97. **[G: U.S.]**

Winger, Alan R. Regional Growth Disparities and the Mortgage Market. *J. Finance*, September 1969, *24*(4), pp. 659–62. **[G: U.S.]**

3153 Business Credit

Basno, C. Aplicarea creditării diferențiate a întreprinderilor. (Application of Differentiated Crediting of Enterprises. With English summary.) *Stud. Cercet. Econ.*, 1969, *1-2*, pp. 93–105.

Benson, Richard A. Trade Credit in the Fertilizer Industry: Theory and Practice. *Agr. Finance Rev.*, July 1969, *30*, pp. 21–33. **[G: U.S.]**

Christian, James W. and Mazek, Warren F. Corporate Debt Structure and the Differential Effects of Monetary Policy. *Southern Econ. J.*, April 1969, *35*(4), pp. 359–68. **[G: U.S.]**

Ferrari, Alberto. Società internazionali problemi di finanziamento e mercato dei capitali. (International Companies: Capital Market and Financing Problems. With English summary.) *Bancaria*, June 1969, *25*(6), pp. 691–99.

Friend, Irwin. Statement. **In** *High Interest Rates, SCH*, 1969, pp. 114–19. **[G: U.S.]**

Haymes, Harmon H. Equipment Leasing. **In** *Jessup, P. F.*, 1969, pp. 109–13. **[G: U.S.]**

Jaffee, Dwight M. and Modigliani, Franco. A Theory and Test of Credit Rationing. *Amer. Econ. Rev.*, December 1969, *59*(5), pp. 850–72. **[G: U.S.]**

Krainer, Robert E. Structural Estimates of Supply and Demand in the USA Short Term Bank Loan Market. *Bull. Oxford Univ. Inst. Econ. Statist.*, February 1969, *31*(1), pp. 39–46. **[G: U.S.]**

Mills, Edwin S. The Small Business Capital Gap. *Rivista Int. Sci. Econ. Com.*, March 1969, *16*(3), pp. 259–79. **[G: U.S.]**

Nadiri, M. Ishag. The Determinants of Trade Credit in the U.S. Total Manufacturing Sector. *Econometrica*, July 1969, *37*(3), pp. 408–23.

Sarma, L. V. L. N. and Roa, K. S. Hanumanta. Leverage and the Value of the Firm. *J. Finance*, September 1969, *24*(4), pp. 673–77. **[G: India]**

Siglienti, Stefano. Sulle possibilità di formazione del risparmio e di investimento produttivo. (Savings and Productive Investments. With English summary.) *Bancaria*, October 1969, *25*(10), pp. 1195–99. **[G: Italy]**

320 Fiscal Theory and Policy; Public Finance

3200 General

Dehejia, V. T. Financing the Public Sector. **In** *Dagli, V., ed., Vol. II*, 1969, pp. 4–9. **[G: India]**

321 Fiscal Theory and Policy

3210 Fiscal Theory and Policy

Arrow, Kenneth J. and Kurz, Mordecai. Optimal Public Investment Policy and Controllability with Fixed Private Savings Ratio. *J. Econ. Theory*, August 1969, *1*(2), pp. 141–77.

Banks, F. E. A Note on Income, Capital Mobility, and the Theory of Economic Policy. *Kyklos*, 1969, *22*(4), pp. 767–73.

Barlow, Robin. A Comment on Alternative Federal Policies for Stimulating State and Local Expenditures. *Nat. Tax J.*, June 1969, *22*(2), pp. 282–85.

Desai, Morarji. Public Sector in a Mixed Economy. **In** *Dagli, V., ed., Vol. II*, 1969, pp. 1–3. **[G: India]**

Duisenberg, W. F. Problematiek rond de Britse betalingsbalans. (British Balance of Payments Problems. With English summary.) *De Economist*, November/December 1969, *117*(6), pp. 615–57. **[G: U.K.]**

Edey, H. C. Income and the Valuation of Stock-In-Trade. **In** *Parker, R. H. and Harcourt, G. C., eds.*, 1969, pp. 230–38. **[G: U.K.]**

Fisher, Irving. Income and Capital. **In** *Parker, R. H. and Harcourt, G. C., eds.*, 1969, pp. 33–53.

Foley, Duncan K.; Shell, Karl and Sidrauski, Miguel. Optimal Fiscal and Monetary Policy and Economic Growth. *J. Polit. Econ.*, Part II, July/August 1969, *77*(4), pp. 698–719.

Francis, Darryl R. Monetary Policy and Inflation. *Fed. Res. Bank St. Louis Rev.*, June 1969, *51*(6), pp. 8–11. **[G: U.S.]**

Galbraith, John Kenneth. How Keynes Came to America. **In** *Starleaf, D. R., ed.*, 1969, pp. 355–60. **[G: U.S.]**

Geyer, Herbert. Linear Tax Variations in the Stabilization Law. *Finanzarchiv*, October 1968, *28*(1), pp. 96–99. **[G: W. Germany]**

Gramlich, Edward M. A Clarification and a Correction. *Nat. Tax J.*, June 1969, *22*(2), pp. 286–90.

Gramlich, Edward M. State and Local Governments and Their Budget Constraint. *Int. Econ. Rev.*, June 1969, *10*(2), pp. 163–82. **[G: U.S.]**

Harberger, Arnold C. In Defense of Carter: A Personal Overview. *Nat. Tax J.*, March 1969, *22*(1), pp. 164–77.

Lent, George E. Taxation of Financial Intermediaries. *Nat. Tax J.*, March 1969, *22*(1), pp. 139–53. **[G: U.S.; Canada]**

Lianos, Theodore P. Governmental Deficit Financing and Growth in Underdeveloped Countries: A

Comment. *Miss. Val. J. Bus. Econ.*, Fall 1969, *5*(1), pp. 90–92.

Lindahl, Erik. The Concept of Income. **In** *Parker, R. H. and Harcourt, G. C., eds.*, 1969, pp. 54–62.

Mukerjee, Sudhir. The Role of Fiscal Policy in Economic Development. **In** *Bhuleshkar, A. V., ed.*, 1969, pp. 406–16. **[G: India]**

Nevin, Edward. The Burden of the Public Debt: A Survey. *Rivista Int. Sci. Econ. Com.*, November 1969, *16*(11), pp. 1074–91.

Niehans, Jürg. Efficient Monetary and Fiscal Policies in Balanced Growth. *J. Money, Credit, Banking*, May 1969, *1*(2), pp. 228–51.

Nuti, Domenico Mario. On Incomes Policy. *Sci. Soc.*, Fall-Winter 1969, *33*(4), pp. 415–25.

Rankoff, Iwan. Grundzüge des bulgarischen Finanzsystems. (Principles of the Bulgarian Financial System. With English summary.) *Schmollers Jahr.*, 1969, *89*(2), pp. 185–210. **[G: Bulgaria]**

Reagan, Michael D. Why Government Grows. **In** *Starleaf, D. R., ed.*, 1969, pp. 200–204. **[G: U.S.]**

Recktenwald, Horst Claus. Die Finanzwissenschaft in der Gegenwart. (With English summary.) *Kyklos*, 1969, *22*(1), pp. 1–29.

Samli, A. Coskun. Governmental Deficit Financing and Growth in Underdeveloped Countries: Reply. *Miss. Val. J. Bus. Econ.*, Fall 1969, *5*(1), pp. 93–96.

Shoup, Carl S. Comments on the Paper by Andre Laurent, "L'Harmonisation des regimes de securite sociale dans la communaute economique Europeenne." *Public Finance*, 1969, *24*(2), pp. 321–25.

Sohmen, Egon and Schneeweiss, Hans. Fiscal and Monetary Policies under Alternative Exchange Rate Systems: A Correction. *Quart. J. Econ.*, May 1969, *83*(2), pp. 336–40.

Solomons, D. Economic and Accounting Concepts of Income. **In** *Parker, R. H. and Harcourt, G. C., eds.*, 1969, pp. 106–19.

Thurow, Lester C. A Fiscal Policy Model of the United States. *Surv. Curr. Bus.*, June 1969, *49*(6), pp. 45–64. **[G: U.S.]**

Vecci, Giovanni. Il Planning-Programming-Budgeting-System—P.P.B.S. (The Planning-Programming-Budgeting-System—P.P.B.S. With English summary.) *L'Impresa*, November/December 1969, *11*(6), pp. 422–28. **[G: Italy]**

van Waasdijk, T. Some Thoughts on Indirect Tax Effects in South Africa. *S. Afr. J. Econ.*, December 1969, *37*(4), pp. 372–92. **[G: S. Africa]**

van Waasdijk, T. The Budget and Economic Policy. *S. Afr. J. Econ.*, June 1969, *37*(2), pp. 98–104. **[G: S. Africa]**

Walker, Jack L. The Diffusion of Innovations among the American States. *Amer. Polit. Sci. Rev.*, September 1969, *63*(3), pp. 880–99. **[G: U.S.]**

Wueller, P. H. Concepts of Taxable Income: The German Contribution. **In** *Parker, R. H. and Harcourt, G. C., eds.*, 1969, pp. 141–60. **[G: Germany]**

Yung, Shen. The Substance, Characteristics, and System of Socialist Public Finance. *Chinese Econ. Stud.*, Winter 1968/69, *2*(2), pp. 3–27. **[G: China]**

3212 Fiscal Theory; Empirical Studies Illustrating Fiscal Theory

Aaron, Henry J. What Is a Comprehensive Tax Base Anyway? *Nat. Tax J.*, December 1969, *22*(4), pp. 543–49.

Adams, Esmond and Fish, Mary. Comments on the Impact of Federal Tax-Sharing on Economic Stabilization. *Nebr. J. Econ. Bus.*, Winter 1968–69, *8*(1), pp. 53–60.

Agria, Susan R. Special Tax Treatment of Mineral Industries. **In** *Harberger, A. C. and Bailey, M. J., eds.*, 1969, pp. 77–122. **[G: U.S.]**

Andel, Norbert. Zur these von den unsozialen verteilungswirkungen öffentlicher schulden. (Notes on the Unsocial Distributive Effect of Public Debt. With English summary.) *Public Finance*, 1969, *24*(1), pp. 69–79.

Andersen, Leonall C. and Jordan, Jerry L. Monetary and Fiscal Actions: A Test of Their Relative Importance in Economic Stabilization—Reply. *Fed. Res. Bank St. Louis Rev.*, April 1969, *51*(4), pp. 12–16. **[G: U.S.]**

Anderson, Robert W. A Note on Tax Incidence in a Macroeconomic Distribution Model. *Rivista Int. Sci. Econ. Com.*, December 1969, *16*(12), pp. 1164–73.

Arrow, Kenneth J. The Organization of Economic Activity: Issues Pertinent to the Choice of Market Versus Nonmarket Allocation. **In** *The Analysis and Evaluation of Public Expenditures: The PPB System, Vol. 1, JECP*, 1969, pp. 47–64.

Asanuma, Banri. Shadow Prices for Public Investment Criteria. *Kyoto Univ. Econ. Rev.*, October 1969, *39*(2), pp. 62–80.

Auld, Douglas A. L. The Economic Impact of Built-In Changes in Budget Components. *Australian Econ. Pap.*, June 1969, *8*(12), pp. 75–98. **[G: Australia]**

Bailey, Martin J. Capital Gains and Income Taxation. **In** *Harberger, A. C. and Bailey, M. J., eds.*, 1969, pp. 11–49. **[G: U.S.]**

Barzel, Yoram. Two Propositions on the Optimum Level of Producing Collective Goods. *Public Choice*, Spring 1969, *6*, pp. 31–37.

Baumol, William J. On the Social Rate of Discount: Comment on the Comments. *Amer. Econ. Rev.*, December 1969, *59*(5), pp. 930.

Baxter, Nevins D.; Howrey, E. Philip and Penner, R. G. Unemployment and Cost-Benefit Analysis. *Public Finance*, 1969, *24*(1), pp. 80–88.

Botha, D. J. J. Local Taxation in South Africa. *S. Afr. J. Econ.*, December 1969, *37*(4), pp. 393–438. **[G: S. Africa]**

Boulding, Kenneth E. "Public Choice and the Grants Economy: The Intersecting Set." *Public Choice*, Fall 1969, *7*, pp. 1–2.

Break, George F. Integration of the Corporate and Personal Income Taxes. *Nat. Tax J.*, March 1969, *22*(1), pp. 39–56. **[G: U.S.]**

Brennan, Geoffrey. The Optimal Provision of Public Goods: A Comment. *J. Polit. Econ.*, March/April 1969, *77*(2), pp. 237–41.

Breton, Albert. Some Problems of Major Tax Reforms. *Nat. Tax J.*, March 1969, *22*(1), pp. 154–63.

Bruno, James Edward. Achieving Property Tax Relief with a Minimum Disruption of State Programs. *Nat. Tax J.*, September 1969, *22*(3), pp. 379–89. [G: U.S.]

Buchanan, James M. and Flowers, Marilyn. An Analytical Setting for a "Taxpayers' Revolution." *Western Econ. J.*, December 1969, *7*(4), pp. 349–59. [G: U.S.]

Butcher, William S.; Haimes, Yacov Y. and Hall, Warren A. Dynamic Programming for the Optimal Sequencing of Water Supply Projects. *Water Resources Res.*, December 1969, *5*(6), pp. 1196–1204.

Cassidy, Henry J. The Employer Payroll Tax and the Labor Mix. *Quart. Rev. Econ. Bus.*, Spring 1969, *9*(1), pp. 39–43.

Chiancone, Aldo. Ancora sulla trasferibilità fra diverse generazioni dell'onere del debito pubblico. (A Note on the Shifting of the Burden of the Public Debt between Different Generations. With English summary.) *Rivista Int. Sci. Econ. Com.*, December 1969, *16*(12), pp. 1223–26.

Daly, George G. The Burden of the Debt and Future Generations in Local Finance. *Southern Econ. J.*, July 1969, *36*(1), pp. 44–51.

Davis, J. Ronnie and Meyer, Charles W. Budget Size in Democracy. *Southern Econ. J.*, July 1969, *36*(1), pp. 10–17.

Davis, Otto A. and Kamien, Morton I. Externalities, Information and Alternative Collective Action. **In** *The Analysis and Evaluation of Public Expenditures: The PPB System, Vol. 1, JECP,* 1969, pp. 67–86.

Demsetz, Harold. Contracting Cost and Public Policy. **In** *The Analysis and Evaluation of Public Expenditures: The PPB System, Vol. 1, JECP,* 1969, pp. 167–74.

Dillard, Dudley. Fiscal Policy from Hoover to Heller—A Review Essay. *Mon. Lab. Rev.*, August 1969, *92*(8), pp. 10–14. [G: U.S.]

Dorfman, Robert. General Equilibrium with Public Goods. **In** *Margolis, J. and Guitton, H., eds.*, 1969, pp. 247–75.

Dosser, Douglas. Comment on "The Incidence of Social Security Taxes" by J. Weitenberg. *Public Finance,* 1969, *24*(2), pp. 209–14. [G: Netherlands]

Due, John F. The Somers Solution to the Use Tax: A Comment. *Nat. Tax J.*, June 1969, *22*(2), pp. 301.

Eisner, Robert. Fiscal and Monetary Policy Reconsidered. *Amer. Econ. Rev.*, December 1969, *59*(5), pp. 897–905. [G: U.S.]

Ekelund, Robert B., Jr. Tax Reform in Latin America: The E.C.L.A. Proposals—A Critical Evaluation. *Amer. J. Econ. Soc.*, January 1969, *28*(1), pp. 93–106.

Evans, Michael K. Reconstruction and Estimation of the Balanced Budget Multiplier. *Rev. Econ. Statist.*, February 1969, *51*(1), pp. 14–25. [G: U.S.]

Feldstein, Martin S. The Effects on Taxation on Risk Taking. *J. Polit. Econ.*, September/October 1969, *77*(5), pp. 755–64.

Floyd, John E. Monetary and Fiscal Policy in a World of Capital Mobility. *Rev. Econ. Stud.*, October 1969, *36*(108), pp. 503–17.

Fourgeaud, Claude. Contribution à l'Étude du Rôle des Administrations dans la Théorie Mathématique de l'Équilibre et de l'Optimum. (With English summary.) *Econometrica,* April 1969, *37*(2), pp. 307–23.

Freeman, A. Myrick, III. Income Redistribution and Social Choice: A Pragmatic Approach. *Public Choice,* Fall 1969, *7,* pp. 3–21.

Frostman, Lars. Optimal Financing and Tax Policy of the Corporation—A Review Article. *Swedish J. Econ.*, March 1969, *71*(1), pp. 30–41.

Garvey, Gerald. The Political Economy of Patronal Groups. *Public Choice,* Fall 1969, *7,* pp. 33–45.

Gulati, I. S. and Kothari, V. N. Land Tax as an Incentive for Better Land Utilization. *Artha-Vikas,* July 1969, *5*(2), pp. 108–16.

Gupta, Shibshankar P. Using Various Statistical Measures to Analyze the Size of the Public Sector: Comment. **In** *Peacock, A. T., ed.*, 1969, pp. 57–64.

Haugen, Robert A. and Heins, A. James. The Effects of the Personal Income Tax on the Stability of Equity Value. *Nat. Tax J.*, December 1969, *22*(4), pp. 466–71.

Haveman, Robert H. The Opportunity Cost of Displaced Private Spending and the Social Discount Rate. *Water Resources Res.*, October 1969, *5*(5), pp. 947–57. [G: U.S.]

Head, John G. and Shoup, C. S. Excess Burden: The Corner Case. *Amer. Econ. Rev.*, March 1969, *59*(1), pp. 181–83.

Head, John G. Merit Goods Revisited. *Finanzarchiv,* March 1969, *28*(2), pp. 214–25.

Head, John G. and Shoup, Carl S. Public Goods, Private Goods, and Ambiguous Goods. *Econ. J.*, September 1969, *79*(315), pp. 567–72.

Helliwell, John F. Monetary and Fiscal Policies for an Open Economy. *Oxford Econ. Pap.*, March 1969, *21*(1), pp. 35–55.

Hettenhouse, George W. and Lewellen, Wilbur G. The Taxation of Restricted Stock Compensation Plans. *Nat. Tax J.*, September 1969, *22*(3), pp. 368–78. [G: U.S.]

Iyengar, Sampath S. Multiplier Analysis for India. *Indian Econ. J.*, April–June 1969, *16*(4–5), pp. 478–87. [G: India]

James, Estelle. On the Social Rate of Discount: Comment. *Amer. Econ. Rev.*, December 1969, *59*(5), pp. 912–16.

Johansson, Sven-Erik. Income Taxes and Investment Decisions. *Swedish J. Econ.*, June 1969, *71*(2), pp. 104–10.

Johnson, David B. and Pauly, Mark V. Excess Burden and the Voluntary Theory of Public Finance. *Economica, N.S.*, August 1969, *36*(143), pp. 269–76.

Johnson, James A. The Distribution of the Burden of Sewer User Charges under Various Charge Formulas. *Nat. Tax J.*, December 1969, *22*(4), pp. 472–85.

Kapp, K. William. On the Nature and Significance of Social Costs. *Kyklos,* 1969, *22*(2), pp. 334–47.

Keran, Michael W. Monetary and Fiscal Influences on Economic Activity—The Historical Evidence.

Fed. Res. Bank St. Louis Rev., November 1969, *51* (11), pp. 5–24. [G: U.S.]

Kosters, Marvin. Effects of an Income Tax on Labor Supply. In *Harberger, A. C. and Bailey, M. J., eds.*, 1969, pp. 301–24. [G: U.S.]

Krogh, D. C. Taxation in a Developing Economy. *S. Afr. J. Econ.*, December 1969, *37*(4), pp. 285–305. [G: S. Africa]

Krupp, Hans-Juergen. Econometric Analysis of Tax Incidence. In *Peacock, A. T., ed.*, 1969, pp. 111–35.

Krutilla, John V. Efficiency Goals, Market Failure, and the Substitution of Public for Private Action. In *The Analysis and Evaluation of Public Expenditures: The PPB System, Vol. 1, JECP*, 1969, pp. 277–89. [G: U.S.]

Lady, George M. A Note on "Graph-Theoretical Approaches to the Theory of Social Choice." *Public Choice*, Spring 1969, *6*, pp. 93–98.

Laidler, David. Income Tax Incentives for Owner-Occupied Housing. In *Harberger, A. C. and Bailey, M. J., eds.*, 1969, pp. 50–76. [G: U.S.]

Landauer, Carl. On the Social Rate of Discount: Comment. *Amer. Econ. Rev.*, December 1969, *59* (5), pp. 917–18.

de Leeuw, Frank and Kalchbrenner, John. Monetary and Fiscal Actions: A Test of Their Relative Importance in Economic Stabilization—Comment. *Fed. Res. Bank St. Louis Rev.*, April 1969, *51*(4), pp. 6–11. [G: U.S.]

Lüttgen, Horst. Das Problem des optimalen Testaments. (With English summary.) *Z. ges. Staatswiss.*, January 1969, *125*(1), pp. 123–37.

Lynch, P. J. and Witherell, William H. The Carter Commission and the Saving Behavior of Canadian Corporations. *Nat. Tax J.*, March 1969, *22*(1), pp. 57–65. [G: Canada]

Mabro, Robert. Normalisation Procedure for Public Investment Criteria: A Comment. *Econ. J.*, September 1969, *79*(315), pp. 669–72.

Major, David C. Benefit-Cost Ratios for Projects in Multiple Objective Investment Programs. *Water Resources Res.*, December 1969, *5*(6), pp. 1174–78. [G: U.S.]

Malinvaud, E. Risk-taking and Resource Allocation. In *Margolis, J. and Guitton, H., eds.*, 1969, pp. 222–46.

McGuire, Martin C. and Aaron, Henry J. Efficiency and Equity in the Optimal Supply of a Public Good. *Rev. Econ. Statist.*, February 1969, *51*(1), pp. 31–39.

McGuire, Martin C. and Garn, Harvey A. Problems in the Cooperative Allocation of Public Expenditures. *Quart. J. Econ.*, February 1969, *83*(1), pp. 44–59.

McGuire, Martin C. and Garn, Harvey A. The Integration of Equity and Efficiency Criteria in Public Project Selection. *Econ. J.*, December 1969, *79* (316), pp. 882–93.

McLure, Charles E., Jr. The Inter-regional Incidence of General Regional Taxes. *Public Finance*, 1969, *24*(3), pp. 457–85.

Meek, Ronald L. A New Bulk Supply Tariff—Reply. *Econ. J.*, December 1969, *79*(316), pp. 974.

Mera, Koichi. Experimental Determination of Relative Marginal Utilities. *Quart. J. Econ.*, August 1969, *83*(3), pp. 464–77.

Mieszkowski, Peter. Tax Incidence Theory: The Effects of Taxes on the Distribution of Income. *J. Econ. Lit.*, December 1969, *7*(4), pp. 1103–24.

Miller, James C., III. A Program for Direct and Proxy Voting in the Legislative Process. *Public Choice*, Fall 1969, *7*, pp. 107–13.

Milliman, Jerome W. Beneficiary Charges and Efficient Public Expenditure Decisions. In *The Analysis and Evaluation of Public Expenditures: The PPB System, Vol. 1, JECP*, 1969, pp. 291–318.

Mishan, E. J. Normalisation of Public Investment Criteria: Erratum. *Econ. J.*, December 1969, *79* (316), pp. 980.

Mishan, E. J. Normalisation of Public Investment Criteria: An Amendment. *Econ. J.*, September 1969, *79*(315), pp. 672–74.

Morss, Elliott R. Fiscal Policy, Savings, and Economic Growth in Developing Countries: An Empirical Study. *Finanzarchiv*, August 1969, *28*(3), pp. 460–66.

Morss, Elliott R. Using Various Statistical Measures to Analyze the Size of the Public Sector. In *Peacock, A. T., ed.*, 1969, pp. 39–56.

Musgrave, Richard A. Cost-Benefit Analysis and the Theory of Public Finance. *J. Econ. Lit.*, September 1969, *7*(3), pp. 797–806.

Musgrave, Richard A. Provision for Social Goods. In *Margolis, J. and Guitton, H., eds.*, 1969, pp. 124–44.

Musgrave, Richard A. Theories of Fiscal Federalism. *Public Finance*, 1969, *24*(4), pp. 521–36.

Nathan, Dev. Some Aspects of the Rate of Interest in Planning. *Indian Econ. J.*, April–June 1969, *16* (4–5), pp. 544–53.

Nichols, Alan. On the Social Rate of Discount: Comment. *Amer. Econ. Rev.*, December 1969, *59*(5), pp. 909–11.

Niinimäki, Rauno. Kansallisen finanssi- ja sosiaalipolitiikan vaikutuksesta taloudelliseen integraatioon. (The Effect of National Fiscal and Social Policy on Economic Integration. With English summary.) *Kansant. Aikak.*, 1969, *65*(4), pp. 280–303.

O'Connor, James. Scientific and Ideological Elements in the Economic Theory of Government Policy. *Sci. Soc.*, Fall-Winter 1969, *33*(4), pp. 385–414.

Oakland, William H. Joint Goods. *Economica, N.S.*, August 1969, *36*(143), pp. 253–68.

Olsen, Edgar O. A Normative Theory of Transfers. *Public Choice*, Spring 1969, *6*, pp. 39–58.

Olson, Mancur, Jr. The Principle of "Fiscal Equivalence": The Division of Responsibilities among Different Levels of Government. *Amer. Econ. Rev.*, May 1969, *59*(2), pp. 479–87. [G: U.S.]

Owen, John D. Education for Majority Voting? *Public Choice*, Spring 1969, *6*, pp. 59–70.

Peacock, Alan T. Welfare Economics and Public Subsidies to the Arts. *Manchester Sch. Econ. Soc. Stud.*, December 1969, *37*(4), pp. 323–35.

Pedone, Antonio. The Ricardian Tax Incidence Analysis in the Light of Optimum Growth Theory. *Econ. Int.*, February 1969, *22*(1), pp. 63–83.

Phelps, Edmund S. and Shell, Karl. Public Debt, Taxation, and Capital Intensiveness. *J. Econ. Theory,* October 1969, *1*(3), pp. 330–46.

Prest, Alan R. The Finances of Small Countries. **In** *Stewart, I. G., ed.,* 1969, pp. 138–54.

Pye, Gordon. On the Tax Structure of Interest Rates. *Quart. J. Econ.,* November 1969, *83*(4), pp. 562–79.

Ramsey, David D. On the Social Rate of Discount: Comment. *Amer. Econ. Rev.,* December 1969, *59* (5), pp. 919–24.

Rees, R. A New Bulk Supply Tariff—Comment. *Econ. J.,* December 1969, *79*(316), pp. 973–74.

Rosenberg, Leonard Gerson. Taxation of Income from Capital, by Industry Group. **In** *Harberger, A. C. and Bailey, M. J., eds.,* 1969, pp. 123–84. **[G: U.S.]**

Rothenberg, Jerome. Strategic Interaction and Resource Allocation in Metropolitan Intergovernmental Relations. *Amer. Econ. Rev.,* May 1969, *59* (2), pp. 494–503.

Sadie, J. L. Company Taxation. *S. Afr. J. Econ.,* December 1969, *37*(4), pp. 345–71.

Samuelson, Paul A. Contrast between Welfare Conditions for Joint Supply and for Public Goods. *Rev. Econ. Statist.,* February 1969, *51*(1), pp. 26–30.

Samuelson, Paul A. Pure Theory of Public Expenditure and Taxation. **In** *Margolis, J. and Guitton, H., eds.,* 1969, pp. 98–123.

Sandee, Jan and van der Pas, J. H. The Effect of Fluctuations in Public Expenditure and Taxation on Economic Growth. **In** *Margolis, J. and Guitton, H., eds.,* 1969, pp. 388–405.

Schmid, A. Allan. Problems in the Theory of Public Choice: Discussion. *Amer. Econ. Rev.,* May 1969, *59*(2), pp. 212–14.

Schwartz, Eli and Aronson, J. Richard. The Preference for Accumulation vs. Spending: Gift and Estate Taxation, and the Timing of Wealth Transfers. *Nat. Tax J.,* September 1969, *22*(3), pp. 390–98. **[G: U.S.]**

Sharp, C. H. Congestion and Welfare—A Reply. *Econ. J.,* June 1969, *79*(314), pp. 407–12.

Sherman, Roger and Willett, Thomas D. Regional Development, Externalities and Tax-Subsidy Combinations. *Nat. Tax J.,* June 1969, *22*(2), pp. 291–93.

Slome, Benjamin. The Interregional Input-Output Model and Interregional Public Finance. *Public Finance,* 1969, *24*(4), pp. 618–23.

Smith, Vernon L. Taxes and Share Valuation in Competitive Markets. *Rev. Econ. Statist.,* February 1969, *51*(1), pp. 96–99.

Somers, Harold M. The Somers Solution to the Use Tax: Reply. *Nat. Tax J.,* June 1969, *22*(2), pp. 302.

Steiner, Peter O. The Public Sector and the Public Interest. **In** *The Analysis and Evaluation of Public Expenditures: The PPB System, Vol. 1, JECP,* 1969, pp. 13–45.

Stiglitz, Joseph E. The Effects of Income, Wealth, and Capital Gains Taxation on Risk-Taking. *Quart. J. Econ.,* May 1969, *83*(2), pp. 263–83.

Stone, Lawrence M. A Comprehensive Income Tax Base for the U.S.?: Implications of the Report of the Royal Commission on Taxation. *Nat. Tax J.,* March 1969, *22*(1), pp. 24–38. **[G: U.S.]**

Tambini, Luigi. Financial Policy and the Corporation Income Tax. **In** *Harberger, A. C. and Bailey, M. J., eds.,* 1969, pp. 185–222. **[G: U.S.]**

Tanzi, Vito. Measuring the Sensitivity of the Federal Income Tax from Cross-Section Data: A New Approach. *Rev. Econ. Statist.,* May 1969, *51*(2), pp. 206–09. **[G: U.S.]**

Taubman, Paul and Rasche, R. H. Economic and Tax Depreciation of Office Buildings. *Nat. Tax J.,* September 1969, *22*(3), pp. 334–46. **[G: U.S.]**

Teeples, Ronald K. A Model of a Matching Grant-in-Aid Program with External Tax Effects. *Nat. Tax J.,* December 1969, *22*(4), pp. 486–95.

Theiler, Donald F. Effects of Flood Protection on Land Use in the Coon Creek, Wisconsin, Watershed. *Water Resources Res.,* December 1969, *5*(6), pp. 1216–22. **[G: U.S.]**

Thys-Clement, F. Econometric Analysis of Tax Incidence: Comment. **In** *Peacock, A. T., ed.,* 1969, pp. 136–39.

Trestrail, Richard W. Forests and the Property Tax —Unsound Accepted Theory. *Nat. Tax J.,* September 1969, *22*(3), pp. 347–56.

Trotter, G. J. Personal Income Tax. *S. Afr. J. Econ.,* December 1969, *37*(4), pp. 306–44.

Tullock, Gordon. Federalism: Problems of Scale. *Public Choice,* Spring 1969, *6,* pp. 19–29.

Tullock, Gordon. Social Cost and Government Action. *Amer. Econ. Rev.,* May 1969, *59*(2), pp. 189–97.

Usher, Dan. On the Social Rate of Discount: Comment. *Amer. Econ. Rev.,* December 1969, *59*(5), pp. 925–29.

Walker, John E. The "Net Interest Cost" Method of Issuing Tax Exempt Bonds: Is It Rational?—A Comment. *Public Finance,* 1969, *24*(4), pp. 624–26.

Weisbrod, Burton A. Collective Action and the Distribution of Income: A Conceptual Approach. **In** *The Analysis and Evaluation of Public Expenditures: The PPB System, Vol. 1, JECP,* 1969, pp. 177–97.

Weitenberg, Johannes. The Incidence of Social Security Taxes. *Public Finance,* 1969, *24*(2), pp. 193–208. **[G: Netherlands]**

West, Richard R. The "Net Interest Cost" Method of Issuing Tax Exempt Bonds: Is It Rational?—A Reply to Professor Walker. *Public Finance,* 1969, *24*(4), pp. 627–30.

Wright, Colin. Saving and the Rate of Interest. **In** *Harberger, A. C. and Bailey, M. J., eds.,* 1969, pp. 275–300. **[G: U.S.]**

3216 Fiscal Policy; Studies

Anderson, Paul S. Wages and the Guideposts: Comment. *Amer. Econ. Rev.,* June 1969, *59*(3), pp. 351–54. **[G: U.S.]**

Auld, Douglas A. L. An Application of Econometrics to Evaluate Fiscal Tax Policy. *Econ. Rec.,* June 1969, *45*(110), pp. 147–57. **[G: Australia]**

Auld, Douglas A. L. Fiscal Policy Performance in Canada 1957-1967. *Public Finance,* 1969, *24*(3), pp. 427–40. **[G: Canada]**

Auld, Douglas A. L. The Measurement of Fiscal

Performance: A Reply. *Econ. Rec.*, June 1969, *45* (110), pp. 291–92.

Balopoulos, Elias T. Measuring the Effects of the Budget on Aggregate Demand and/or Balance of Payments. **In** *Peacock, A. T., ed.*, 1969, pp. 141–62.

Bhatia, Rattan J.; Szapary, Gyorgy and Quinn, Brian. Stabilization Program in Sierra Leone. *Int. Monet. Fund Staff Pap.*, November 1969, *16*(3), pp. 504–28. **[G: Sierra Leone]**

Biehl, Dieter. Measuring the Effects of the Budget on Aggregate Demand and/or Balance of Payments: Comment. **In** *Peacock, A. T., ed.*, 1969, pp. 163–69.

Bonnen, James T. The Absence of Knowledge of Distributional Impacts: An Obstacle to Effective Public Program Analysis and Decisions. **In** *The Analysis and Evaluation of Public Expenditures: The PPB System, Vol. 1, JECP,* 1969, pp. 419–49. **[G: U.S.]**

Brovedani, Bruno. Italy's Financial Policies in the 'Sixties. *Banca Naz. Lavoro Quart. Rev.*, June 1969, (89), pp. 170–89. **[G: Italy]**

Brunner, Karl. The Policy Discussions by Stein and Worswick: A Comment. *J. Money, Credit, Banking,* August 1969, *1*(3), pp. 496–502. **[G: U.S.; U.K.]**

Christ, Carl F. A Model of Monetary and Fiscal Policy Effects on the Money Stock, Price Level, and Real Output. *J. Money, Credit, Banking,* November 1969, *1*(4), pp. 683–705. **[G: U.S.]**

Coen, Robert M. Tax Policy and Investment Behavior: Comment. *Amer. Econ. Rev.*, June 1969, *59* (3), pp. 370–79. **[G: U.S.]**

Dorfman, Robert and Jacoby, Henry D. A Model of Public Decisions Illustrated by a Water Pollution Policy Problem. **In** *The Analysis and Evaluation of Public Expenditures: The PPB System, Vol. 1, JECP,* 1969, pp. 226–74.

Eisner, Robert. Tax Policy and Investment Behavior: Comment. *Amer. Econ. Rev.*, June 1969, *59*(3), pp. 379–88. **[G: U.S.]**

Enthoven, Adolf J. H. Accountancy for Economic Development. *Finance Develop.*, September 1969, *6*(3), pp. 24–29.

Fabella, A. V. Policies for Long-Term Growth in the Philippines: The Public Sector. *Philippine Econ. J.*, First Semester 1969, *8*(1), pp. 37–48. **[G: Philippines]**

Friedman, Milton. Worswick's Criticism of the Correlation Criterion: A Comment. *J. Money, Credit, Banking,* August 1969, *1*(3), pp. 506.

Goldstein, Henry N. Does It Necessarily Cost Anything to Be the "World Banker"? **In** *Officer, L. H. and Willett, T. D., eds.*, 1969, pp. 68–74. **[G: U.S.]**

Goodsell, Charles T. Trends in the Interrelationship of Polity and Economy in the United States. *Amer. J. Econ. Soc.*, January 1969, *28*(1), pp. 1–16. **[G: U.S.]**

Groves, Harold M. Taxing the Family Unit: The Carter Commission's Proposals and U.S. Practice. *Nat. Tax J.*, March 1969, *22*(1), pp. 109–20. **[G: U.S.; Canada]**

Grubel, Herbert G. The Benefits and Costs of Being the World Banker. **In** *Officer, L. H. and Willett, T. D., eds.*, 1969, pp. 59–67. **[G: U.S.]**

Hall, Robert E. and Jorgenson, Dale W. Tax Policy and Investment Behavior: Reply and Further Results. *Amer. Econ. Rev.*, June 1969, *59*(3), pp. 388–401. **[G: U.S.]**

Hamburger, Michael J. and Silber, William L. An Empirical Study of Interest Rate Determination. *Rev. Econ. Statist.*, August 1969, *51*(3), pp. 369–73. **[G: U.S.]**

Helliwell, John F., et al. Econometric Analysis of Policy Choices for an Open Economy. *Rev. Econ. Statist.*, November 1969, *51*(4), pp. 383–98. **[G: Canada]**

Jantscher, Gerald R. Death and Gift Taxation in the United States after the Report of the Royal Commission. *Nat. Tax J.*, March 1969, *22*(1), pp. 121–38. **[G: U.S.]**

Kenen, Peter B. The New Fiscal Policy: A Comment. *J. Money, Credit, Banking,* August 1969, *1*(3), pp. 503–05. **[G: U.S.; U.K.]**

Lomax, David F. and Reading, Brian. Too Little Saving. *Nat. Westminster Bank Quart. Rev.*, August 1969, pp. 23–42. **[G: U.K.]**

Maxwell, James A. Federal Grants in Canada and Australia. *Econ. Rec.*, September 1969, *45*(111), pp. 441–48. **[G: Canada; Australia]**

Mieszkowski, Peter. Carter on the Taxation of International Income Flows. *Nat. Tax J.*, March 1969, *22*(1), pp. 97–108. **[G: Canada]**

Morss, Elliott R. and Peacock, Alan T. The Measurement of Fiscal Performance in Developing Countries. **In** *Peacock, A. T., ed.*, 1969, pp. 171–97.

Oakland, William H. Budgetary Measures of Fiscal Performance. *Southern Econ. J.*, April 1969, *35* (4), pp. 347–58. **[G: U.S.]**

Ojha, P. D. and Lent, George E. Sales Taxes in Countries of the Far East. *Int. Monet. Fund Staff Pap.*, November 1969, *16*(3), pp. 529–81. **[G: Far East]**

Pechman, Joseph A. and Okner, Benjamin A. Simulation of the Carter Commission Tax Proposals for the United States. *Nat. Tax J.*, March 1969, *22*(1), pp. 2–23. **[G: U.S.]**

Pechman, Joseph A. Tax Policies for the 1970's. *Public Policy,* Fall 1969, *18*(1), pp. 75–93. **[G: U.S.]**

Perry, George L. Wages and the Guideposts: Reply. *Amer. Econ. Rev.*, June 1969, *59*(3), pp. 365–70. **[G: U.S.]**

Polsby, Nelson W. Policy Analysis and Congress. **In** *The Analysis and Evaluation of Public Expenditures: The PPB System, Vol. 3, JECP,* 1969, pp. 943–52. **[G: U.S.]**

Prest, A. R. Compulsory Lending Schemes. *Int. Monet. Fund Staff Pap.*, March 1969, *16*(1), pp. 27–52.

Ristimäki, Juhani. Valtion tuki ja tulopolitiikka. (Government Support and Incomes Policy. With English summary.) *Kansant. Aikak.*, 1969, *65*(1), pp. 6–20. **[G: Finland]**

Roskamp, Karl W. Fiscal Policy and Effects of Government Purchases: An Input-Output Analysis. *Public Finance,* 1969, *24*(1), pp. 33–47. **[G: W. Germany]**

Roskamp, Karl W. Fiscal Policy Objectives and Government Purchases by Industries: Towards an Input-Output Decision Model. *Z. ges. Staatswiss.*, January 1969, *125*(1), pp. 82–88.

Schultze, Charles L. The Role of Incentives, Penalties, and Rewards in Attaining Effective Policy. **In** *The Analysis and Evaluation of Public Expenditures: The PPB System, Vol. 1, JECP,* 1969, pp. 201–25.

Slitor, Richard E. The Carter Proposals on Capital Gains: Economic Effects and Policy Implications for the United States. *Nat. Tax J.,* March 1969, *22* (1), pp. 66–78. **[G: U.S.]**

Snyder, Wayne W. La mésure des effets des politiques budgétaires françaises de 1955 à 1965. (With English summary.) *Revue Écon.,* November 1969, *20*(6), pp. 929–53. **[G: France]**

Snyder, Wayne W. Una valutazione degli effetti delle politiche italiane di bilancio nel periodo 1955–65. (Measuring the Effects of Italian Budget Policies, 1955–65. With English summary.) *Econ. Int.,* November 1969, *22*(4), pp. 681–704. **[G: Italy]**

Stefani, Giorgio. Politica fiscale a politica monetaria per la stabilità negli Stati Uniti-I. (Fiscal Policy and Monetary Policy for the Stability of the United States-I. With English summary.) *Bancaria,* February 1969, *25*(2), pp. 147–69. **[G: U.S.]**

Stefani, Giorgio. Politica fiscale e politica monetaria per la stabilità negli Stati Uniti-II. (Fiscal Policy and Monetary Policy for the Stability of the United States-II. With English summary.) *Bancaria,* March 1969, *25*(3), pp. 303–20. **[G: U.S.]**

Stein, Herbert. Where Stands the New Fiscal Policy? *J. Money, Credit, Banking,* August 1969, *1*(3), pp. 463–73. **[G: U.S.]**

Steve, Sergio. Public Finance and Social Security. *Public Finance,* 1969, *24*(2), pp. 101–13.

Throop, Adrian W. Wages and the Guideposts: Comment. *Amer. Econ. Rev.,* June 1969, *59*(3), pp. 358–65. **[G: U.S.]**

Tillinghast, David R. The Carter Commission Report and International Investment Transactions; Integration and Ambiguous Intentions. *Nat. Tax J.,* March 1969, *22*(1), pp. 79–96. **[G: Canada]**

Van de Ven, Petrus J. and Wolfson, Dirk J. Problems of Budget Analysis and Treasury Management in French-Speaking Africa. *Int. Monet. Fund Staff Pap.,* March 1969, *16*(1), pp. 140–58. **[G: Africa]**

Wachter, Michael L. Wages and the Guideposts: Comment. *Amer. Econ. Rev.,* June 1969, *59*(3), pp. 354–58. **[G: U.S.]**

Weidenbaum, Murray L. Fiscal Policy and the National Economy. *Univ. Missouri Bus. Govt. Rev.,* November–December 1969, *10*(6), pp. 24–32. **[G: U.S.]**

Worswick, G. D. N. Fiscal Policy and Stabilization in Britain. *J. Money, Credit, Banking,* August 1969, *1*(3), pp. 474–95. **[G: U.K.]**

Wright, L. C. Some Fiscal Problems of Devolution in Scotland. **In** *Wolfe, J. N., ed.,* 1969, pp. 140–52. **[G: U.K.]**

322 National Government Expenditures and Budgeting

3220 General

Văcărel, Iulian. Finanțele—instrument activ în opera de edificare a socialismului în România. (Finance—An Active Instrument in the Work of Building up Socialism in Romania. With English summary.) *Stud. Cercet. Econ.,* 1969, *3,* pp. 131–41. **[G: Romania]**

3221 National Government Expenditures

Achinstein, Asher. Constraints on Policy Analysis and Policy Implementation in the Federal Agencies. **In** *The Analysis and Evaluation of Public Expenditures: The PPB System, Vol. 1, JECP,* 1969, pp. 369–80. **[G: U.S.]**

Bacchus, M. K. Patterns of Educational Expenditure in an Emergent Nation—A Study of Guyana 1945–65. *Soc. Econ. Stud.,* September 1969, *18* (3), pp. 282–301. **[G: Guyana]**

Barlow, Robin. A Comment on Alternative Federal Policies for Stimulating State and Local Expenditures. *Nat. Tax J.,* June 1969, *22*(2), pp. 282–85.

Baumol, William J. On the Social Rate of Discount: Comment on the Comments. *Amer. Econ. Rev.,* December 1969, *59*(5), pp. 930.

Bonin, Joseph M.; Finch, B. W. and Waters, Joseph B. Alternative Tests of the "Displacement Effect" Hypothesis. *Public Finance,* 1969, *24*(3), pp. 441–56. **[G: U.K.]**

Brunn, Stanley D. and Hoffman, Wayne L. The Geography of Federal Grants-in-Aid to States. *Econ. Geogr.,* July 1969, *45*(3), pp. 226–38. **[G: U.S.]**

Campbell, Colin D. Social Insurance in the United States: A Program in Search of an Explanation. *J. Law Econ.,* October 1969, *12*(2), pp. 249–65. **[G: U.S.]**

Carlson, Jack W. Statement. **In** *Guidelines for Estimating the Benefits of Public Expenditures, JECH,* 1969, pp. 23–30. **[G: U.S.]**

Cauley, Troy J. Public Expenditures in Our Federal System. *Rivista Int. Sci. Econ. Com.,* September 1969, *16*(9), pp. 898–919. **[G: U.S.]**

Chamberlain, Neil W. Government Investment: How Scientific Can It Be? **In** *Starleaf, D. R., ed.,* 1969, pp. 205–09. **[G: U.S.]**

Contini, Bruno. A Critical Survey of Use of Cost-Benefit Analysis in Public Finance. **In** *Peacock, A. T., ed.,* 1969, pp. 65–85.

Day, H. J., et al. Evaluation of Benefits of a Flood Warning System. *Water Resources Res.,* October 1969, *5*(5), pp. 937–46. **[G: U.S.]**

De Alessi, Louis. Implications of Property Rights for Government Investment Choices. *Amer. Econ. Rev.,* March 1969, *59*(1), pp. 13–24.

Dolman, Dirk. A Critical Survey of Use of Cost-Benefit Analysis in Public Finance: Comment. **In** *Peacock, A. T., ed.,* 1969, pp. 86–89.

Dorfman, Robert. Statement. **In** *Guidelines for Estimating the Benefits of Public Expenditures, JECH,* 1969, pp. 98–102. **[G: U.S.]**

Friedman, Milton. Why Not a Volunteer Army? **In** *Starleaf, D. R., ed.,* 1969, pp. 209–15. **[G: U.S.]**

Gramlich, Edward M. A Clarification and a Correction. *Nat. Tax J.,* June 1969, *22*(2), pp. 286–90.

Gupta, Shibshankar P. Public Expenditure and Economic Development—A Cross-Section Analysis. *Finanzarchiv,* October 1968, *28*(1), pp. 26–41.

Harmston, Floyd K. The Impact of Federal Expenditures on Missouri, Fiscal Year 1967. *Univ. Mis-*

souri Bus. Govt. Rev., November–December 1969, *10*(6), pp. 5–12. [G: U.S.]

Haveman, Robert H. Evaluating Public Expenditures under Conditions of Unemployment. *Mon. Lab. Rev.*, September 1969, *92*(9), pp. 30–33. [G: U.S.]

Haveman, Robert H. Evaluating Public Expenditures under Conditions of Unemployment. **In** *The Analysis and Evaluation of Public Expenditures: The PPB System, Vol. 1, JECP,* 1969, pp. 547–61. [G: U.S.]

Hicks, Ursula K. La finanza pubblica nel quadro della politica economica e sociale della Gran Bretagna. (The Finance of the British Government. With English summary.) *Bancaria,* September 1969, *25*(9), pp. 1067–81. [G: U.K.]

Howard, Dick. The Regional Development Commission—A Second Look at a New Concept. *Univ. Missouri Bus. Govt. Rev.,* July–August 1969, *10*(4), pp. 27–35. [G: U.S.]

Hufschmidt, Maynard M.; Krutilla, John V. and Margolis, Julius. Standards and Criteria for Formulating and Evaluating Federal Water Resources Development. **In** *Guidelines for Estimating the Benefits of Public Expenditures, JECH,* 1969, pp. 135–212. [G: U.S.]

James, Estelle. On the Social Rate of Discount: Comment. *Amer. Econ. Rev.,* December 1969, *59*(5), pp. 912–16.

Kaim-Caudle, P. R. Selectivity and the Social Services. *Lloyds Bank Rev.,* April 1969, (92), pp. 26–45. [G: U.K.]

Knetsch, Jack L., et al. Federal Natural Resources Development: Basic Issues in Benefit and Cost Measurement. **In** *Guidelines for Estimating the Benefits of Public Expenditures, JECH,* 1969, pp. 109–15. [G: U.S.]

Lall, Sanjaya. A Note on Government Expenditures in Developing Countries. *Econ. J.,* June 1969, *79* (314), pp. 413–17.

Landauer, Carl. On the Social Rate of Discount: Comment. *Amer. Econ. Rev.,* December 1969, *59* (5), pp. 917–18.

Landynski, Jacob W. Governmental Aid to Non-public Schools: The Constitutional Conflict Sharpens. *Soc. Res.,* Autumn 1969, *36*(3), pp. 333–56. [G: U.S.]

Levitan, Sar A. The Community Action Program: A Strategy to Fight Poverty. *Ann. Amer. Acad. Polit. Soc. Sci.,* September 1969, *385,* pp. 63–75. [G: U.S.]

Liu, Ben-Chieh. Regional Income Inequality and Federal Government Expenditures, 1948–63. *Quart. Rev. Econ. Bus.,* Winter 1969, *9*(4), pp. 67–76. [G: U.S.]

Lotz, Joergen R. Some Economic Effects of Increasing Public Expenditures: An Empirical Study of Selected Developed Countries. *Public Finance,* 1969, *24*(4), pp. 577–96.

McGuire, Martin C. and Garn, Harvey A. Problems in the Cooperative Allocation of Public Expenditures. *Quart. J. Econ.,* February 1969, *83*(1), pp. 44–59.

Nichols, Alan. On the Social Rate of Discount: Comment. *Amer. Econ. Rev.,* December 1969, *59*(5), pp. 909–11.

Patel, H. M. Why Public Sector Projects Are Not Profitable. **In** *Dagli, V., ed., Vol. II,* 1969, pp. 10–17. [G: India]

Raja, S. T. Project Planning and Execution. **In** *Dagli, V., ed., Vol. II,* 1969, pp. 140–45. [G: India]

Ramsey, David D. On the Social Rate of Discount: Comment. *Amer. Econ. Rev.,* December 1969, *59* (5), pp. 919–24.

Raunio, Eino. Näkökohtia vuoden 1969 budjettiesityksestä. (Government Budget Proposal for 1969. With English summary.) *Kansant. Aikak.,* 1969, *65*(1), pp. 1–5. [G: Finland]

Roskamp, Karl W. Fiscal Policy and Effects of Government Purchases: An Input-Output Analysis. *Public Finance,* 1969, *24*(1), pp. 33–47. [G: W. Germany]

Russett, Bruce M. Who Pays for Defense? *Amer. Polit. Sci. Rev.,* June 1969, *63*(2), pp. 412–26. [G: U.S.]

Schultze, Charles L. Using Incentives to Improve the Effectiveness of Government. *Mon. Lab. Rev.,* September 1969, *92*(9), pp. 34–38.

Silva, Donald H. State Technical Service—An Emerging Social System. *Amer. J. Econ. Soc.,* October 1969, *28*(4), pp. 399–403. [G: U.S.]

Staats, Elmer B. Statement. **In** *Guidelines for Estimating the Benefits of Public Expenditures, JECH,* 1969, pp. 3–15. [G: U.S.]

Terry, Edwin F. Public Finance and Regional Accounts. *Rev. Income Wealth,* June 1969, *15*(2), pp. 207–13. [G: U.S.]

Usher, Dan. On the Social Rate of Discount: Comment. *Amer. Econ. Rev.,* December 1969, *59*(5), pp. 925–29.

Weidenbaum, Murray L. Budget "Uncontrollability" as an Obstacle to Improving the Allocation of Government Resources. **In** *The Analysis and Evaluation of Public Expenditures: The PPB System, Vol. 1, JECP,* 1969, pp. 357–68. [G: U.S.]

Weidenbaum, Murray L. Federal Aid to the States: An Analytical Examination of the Alternatives. *Amer. J. Econ. Soc.,* October 1969, *28*(4), pp. 367–83. [G: U.S.]

Whipple, William, Jr. Optimizing Investment in Flood Control and Floodplain Zoning. *Water Resources Res.,* August 1969, *5*(4), pp. 761–66.

Wholey, Joseph S. The Absence of Program Evaluation as an Obstacle to Effective Public Expenditure Policy: A Case Study of Child Health Care Programs. **In** *The Analysis and Evaluation of Public Expenditures: The PPB System, Vol. 1, JECP,* 1969, pp. 451–71. [G: U.S.]

3226 National Government Budgeting

Augenstein, Bruno W. Policy Analysis in the National Space Program. **In** *The Analysis and Evaluation of Public Expenditures: The PPB System, Vol. 3, JECP,* 1969, pp. 1020–68. [G: U.S.]

Bhandari, M. C. Budgeting and Materials Management. **In** *Dagli, V., ed., Vol. II,* 1969, pp. 146–52. [G: India]

Bingham, Jonathan B. Can Military Spending Be Controlled? *Foreign Aff.,* October 1969, *48*(1), pp. 51–66. [G: U.S.]

Bittker, Boris I. Accounting for Federal "Tax Subsidies" in the National Budget. *Nat. Tax J.,* June

1969, *22*(2), pp. 244–61. [G: U.S.]

Bittker, Boris I. The Tax Expenditure Budget—A Reply to Professors Surrey and Hellmuth. *Nat. Tax J.,* December 1969, *22*(4), pp. 538–42. [G: U.S.]

Carlson, Jack W. The Status and Next Steps for Planning, Programing, and Budgeting. **In** *The Analysis and Evaluation of Public Expenditures: The PPB System, Vol. 2, JECP,* 1969, pp. 613–34. [G: U.S.]

Davis, J. Ronnie and Meyer, Charles W. Budget Size in Democracy. *Southern Econ. J.,* July 1969, *36*(1), pp. 10–17.

Enthoven, Adolf J. H. Accountancy for Economic Development. *Finance Develop.,* September 1969, *6*(3), pp. 24–29.

Enthoven, Alain C. The Planning, Programing, and Budgeting System in the Department of Defense: Some Lessons from Experience. **In** *The Analysis and Evaluation of Public Expenditures: The PPB System, Vol. 3, JECP,* 1969, pp. 901–08. [G: U.S.]

Enthoven, Alain C. and Smith, K. Wayne. The Planning, Programing, and Budgeting System in the Department of Defense: Current Status and Next Steps. **In** *The Analysis and Evaluation of Public Expenditures: The PPB System, Vol. 3, JECP,* 1969, pp. 955–69. [G: U.S.]

Evans, Michael K. Reconstruction and Estimation of the Balanced Budget Multiplier. *Rev. Econ. Statist.,* February 1969, *51*(1), pp. 14–25. [G: U.S.]

Feldman, Paul. Prescription for an Effective Government: Ethics, Economics, and PPBS. **In** *The Analysis and Evaluation of Public Expenditures: The PPB System, Vol. 3, JECP,* 1969, pp. 865–85. [G: U.S.]

di Fenizio, Ferdinando. Relazione al Ministro del Tesoro del Presidente del Gruppo residui nel bilancio dello Stato. (The Report of the President of the Commission on Residual Assets and Liabilities of the National Budget to the Minister of the Treasury. With English summary.) *L'Industria,* July–September 1969, (3), pp. 347–57. [G: Italy]

Freeman, A. Myrick, III. Project Design and Evaluation with Multiple Objectives. **In** *The Analysis and Evaluation of Public Expenditures: The PPB System, Vol. 1, JECP,* 1969, pp. 565–78.

Galnoor, Itzhak and Gross, Bertram M. The New Systems Budgeting and the Developing Nations. *Int. Soc. Sci. J.,* 1969, *21*(1), pp. 23–44.

Greenhouse, Samuel M. Today's PPBS: The Fatal Triumph of Financial Management over Economics. **In** *The Analysis and Evaluation of Public Expenditures: The PPB System, Vol. 3, JECP,* 1969, pp. 886–98. [G: U.S.]

Hauser, G. Measuring Efficiency in Government Services: Comment. **In** *Peacock, A. T., ed.,* 1969, pp. 104–09.

Haveman, Robert H. The Analysis and Evaluation of Public Expenditures: An Overview. **In** *The Analysis and Evaluation of Public Expenditures: The PPB System, Vol. 1, JECP,* 1969, pp. 1–10. [G: U.S.]

Henderson, P. D. Political and Budgetary Constraints: Some Characteristics and Implications. **In** *Margolis, J. and Guitton, H., eds.,* 1969, pp. 310–25.

Hoffman, Fred S. Public Expenditure Analysis and the Institutions of the Executive Branch. **In** *The Analysis and Evaluation of Public Expenditures: The PPB System, Vol. 3, JECP,* 1969, pp. 925–42. [G: U.S.]

Hutton J. P. Measuring Efficiency in Government Services. **In** *Peacock, A. T., ed.,* 1969, pp. 91–103.

Jones, Roger H. Program Budgeting: Fiscal Facts And Federal Fancy. *Quart. Rev. Econ. Bus.,* Summer 1969, *9*(2), pp. 45–57. [G: U.S.]

Khalid, Rasheed O. Fiscal Policy, Development Planning, and Annual Budgeting. *Int. Monet. Fund Staff Pap.,* March 1969, *16*(1), pp. 53–84.

Laris Casillas, Jorge. El proceso administrativo del presupuesto. (The Administrative Process of Drawing up a Budget. With English summary.) *Econ. Polít.,* Second Semester 1969, *6*(2), pp. 229–40.

Levine, Robert A. Policy Analysis and Economic Opportunity Programs. **In** *The Analysis and Evaluation of Public Expenditures: The PPB System, Vol. 3, JECP,* 1969, pp. 1181–96. [G: U.S.]

Lord, William B. and Smith, Stephen C. Tools of the Trade in Policy Decision—PPBS, A Case in Point. *Amer. J. Agr. Econ.,* December 1969, *51*(5), pp. 1427–33. [G: U.S.]

Marshall, Don C. Disclosure of Federal Tax Concessions—Billions in Implicit Subsidies. *Univ. Missouri Bus. Govt. Rev.,* January–February 1969, *10* (1), pp. 23–29. [G: U.S.]

Marvin, Keith E. and Rouse, Andrew M. The Status of PPB in Federal Agencies: A Comparative Perspective. **In** *The Analysis and Evaluation of Public Expenditures: The PPB System, Vol. 3, JECP,* 1969, pp. 801–14. [G: U.S.]

McGuire, Martin C. Program Analysis and Regional Economic Objectives. **In** *The Analysis and Evaluation of Public Expenditures: The PPB System, Vol. 1, JECP,* 1969, pp. 592–610. [G: U.S.]

Oakland, William H. Budgetary Measures of Fiscal Performance. *Southern Econ. J.,* April 1969, *35* (4), pp. 347–58. [G: U.S.]

Rivlin, Alice M. The Planning, Programing, and Budgeting System in the Department of Health, Education, and Welfare: Some Lessons from Experience. **In** *The Analysis and Evaluation of Public Expenditures: The PPB System, Vol. 3, JECP,* 1969, pp. 909–22. [G: U.S.]

Rowen, Henry S. and Williams, Albert P., Jr. Policy Analysis in International Affairs. **In** *The Analysis and Evaluation of Public Expenditures: The PPB System, Vol. 3, JECP,* 1969, pp. 970–1002. [G: U.S.]

Salvemini, Maria Teresa. Idee per un bilancio previsionale di cassa. (Ideas for a Cash Budget. With English summary.) *Bancaria,* September 1969, *25* (9), pp. 1088–99.

Sawhill, Isabel V. The Role of Social Indicators and Social Reporting in Public Expenditure Decisions. **In** *The Analysis and Evaluation of Public Expenditures: The PPB System, Vol. 1, JECP,* 1969, pp. 473–85. [G: U.S.]

Schick, Allen. Systems for Analysis: PPB and Its Alternatives. In *The Analysis and Evaluation of Public Expenditures: The PPB System, Vol. 3, JECP,* 1969, pp. 817–34. [G: U.S.]

Schmid, A. Allan. Effective Public Policy and the Government Budget: A Uniform Treatment of Public Expenditures and Public Rules. In *The Analysis and Evaluation of Public Expenditures: The PPB System, Vol. 1, JECP,* 1969, pp. 579–91. [G: U.S.]

Searl, Milton F. Prospects for PPB at AEC. In *The Analysis and Evaluation of Public Expenditures: The PPB System, Vol. 3, JECP,* 1969, pp. 1005–19. [G: U.S.]

Sewell, Wade P. Some Policy Issues in the Analysis of Research and Development Programs. In *The Analysis and Evaluation of Public Expenditures: The PPB System, Vol. 3, JECP,* 1969, pp. 1069–84. [G: U.S.]

Stammati, Gaetano. The Italian Budget. *Rev. Econ. Cond. Italy,* January 1969, *23*(1), pp. 13–27. [G: Italy]

Surrey, Stanley S. and Hellmuth, William F. The Tax Expenditure Budget—Response to Professor Bittker. *Nat. Tax J.,* December 1969, *22*(4), pp. 528–37. [G: U.S.]

T'ing-tung, Chang. A Preliminary Study of the Problems in Drafting and Auditing a Final Budget. *Chinese Econ. Stud.,* Winter 1968/69, *2*(2), pp. 28–49. [G: China]

Tait, Alan A. Deflation and Incomes Policy: The British Budget 1968/69. *Finanzarchiv,* October 1968, *28*(1), pp. 110–25. [G: U.K.]

Tait, Alan A. Sensible Accounts and Control of Government Revenue and Expenditure. *Irish Banking Rev.,* December 1969, pp. 9–16. [G: Ireland]

Van de Ven, Petrus J. and Wolfson, Dirk J. Problems of Budget Analysis and Treasury Management in French-Speaking Africa. *Int. Monet. Fund Staff Pap.,* March 1969, *16*(1), pp. 140–58. [G: Africa]

Vecci, Giovanni. Il Planning-Programming-Budgeting-System—P.P.B.S. (The Planning-Programming-Budgeting-System—P.P.B.S. With English summary.) *L'Impresa,* November/December 1969, *11*(6), pp. 422–28. [G: Italy]

van Waasdijk, T. The Budget and Economic Policy. *S. Afr. J. Econ.,* June 1969, *37*(2), pp. 98–104. [G: S. Africa]

Waite, Charles A. and Wakefield, Joseph C. Federal Programs for Fiscal 1970. *Surv. Curr. Bus.,* February 1969, *49*(2), pp. 13–20. [G: U.S.]

Wildavsky, Aaron. Planning-Programing-Budgeting: Rescuing Policy Analysis from PPBS. In *op. cit., SCP,* 1969, pp. 1–18.

Wildavsky, Aaron. Rescuing Policy Analysis from PPBS. In *The Analysis and Evaluation of Public Expenditures: The PPB System, Vol. 3, JECP,* 1969, pp. 835–64. [G: U.S.]

Yoingco, Angel Q. and Casem, Antonio O. Performance Budgeting in the Philippines. *Philippine Econ. J.,* Second Semester 1969, *8*(2), pp. 166–84. [G: Philippines]

Zverev, A. Role of the State Budget in the Distribution of the Social Product and National Income. In *Yanowitch, M., ed.,* 1969, pp. 189–96. [G: U.S.S.R.]

3228 National Government Debt Management

Chiancone, Aldo. Ancora sulla trasferibilità fra diverse generazioni dell'onere del debito pubblico. (A Note on the Shifting of the Burden of the Public Debt between Different Generations. With English summary.) *Rivista Int. Sci. Econ. Com.,* December 1969, *16*(12), pp. 1223–26.

Graaff, Jan de V. The National Debt. *S. Afr. J. Econ.,* September 1969, *37*(3), pp. 170–86. [G: S. Africa]

Hunter, J. S. H. The Roosa Doctrine and the Shiftability Thesis: Application to Debt Management in the United States. *Weltwirtsch. Arch.,* 1969, *103* (1), pp. 110–30. [G: U.S.]

McCalmont, David B. Why a Rising Federal Debt Is No Cause for Alarm. In *Starleaf, D. R., ed.,* 1969, pp. 247–54. [G: U.S.]

Nevin, Edward. The Burden of the Public Debt: A Survey. *Rivista Int. Sci. Econ. Com.,* November 1969, *16*(11), pp. 1074–91.

Norton, W. E. Debt Management and Monetary Policy in the United Kingdom. *Econ. J.,* September 1969, *79*(315), pp. 475–94. [G: U.K.]

Vasudevan, A. Deficit Financing and Economic Development. In *Bhuleshkar, A. V., ed.,* 1969, pp. 327–44. [G: India]

323 National Taxation and Subsidies

3230 National Taxation and Subsidies

Aaron, Henry J. Perspectives on Poverty 4: Income Transfer Programs. *Mon. Lab. Rev.,* February 1969, *92*(2), pp. 50–54. [G: U.S.]

Aaron, Henry J. What Is a Comprehensive Tax Base Anyway? *Nat. Tax J.,* December 1969, *22*(4), pp. 543–49.

Abeelen, Marc J. and Hammond, Robert C. The Fiscal Aspects of International Co-operation in Africa—The Experience of the UDEAC and the EAC. *Bull. Int. Fiscal Doc.,* March 1969, *23*(3), pp. 95–115. [G: Africa]

Agarwala, R. and Goodson, G. C. An Analysis of the Effects of Investment Incentives on Investment Behaviour in the British Economy. *Economica, N.S.,* November 1969, *36*(144), pp. 377–88. [G: U.K.]

Al-Nimry, Saad. Recent Developments in Taxation in the Hashemite Kingdom of Jordan. *Bull. Int. Fiscal Doc.,* January 1969, *23*(1), pp. 27–36. [G: Jordan]

Amin, R. B. Taxing Agricultural Incomes. *Artha-Vikas,* July 1969, *5*(2), pp. 106–07. [G: India]

Andersson, Edward. Skattepolitiken efter Företagsbeskattningsreformen. (Taxation Policy after the Reforms in Company Tax. With English summary.) *Econ. Samfundets Tidskr.,* 1969, *22* (1), pp. 52–61. [G: Finland]

Angrish, A. C. Rationalized Agricultural Tax Structures in India and Some Policy Implications. *Artha-Vikas,* July 1969, *5*(2), pp. 154–70. [G: India]

Arnett, Harold E. Taxable Income vs. Financial Income: How Much Uniformity Can We Stand? *Accounting Rev.,* July 1969, *44*(3), pp. 482–94.

Auld, Douglas A. L. An Application of Econometrics to Evaluate Fiscal Tax Policy. *Econ. Rec.,* June 1969, *45*(110), pp. 147–57. **[G: Australia]**

Auld, Douglas A. L. The Economic Impact of Built-In Changes in Budget Components. *Australian Econ. Pap.,* June 1969, *8*(12), pp. 75–98. **[G: Australia]**

Bailey, Duncan M. and Cargill, Thomas F. The Military Draft and Future Income. *Western Econ. J.,* December 1969, *7*(4), pp. 365–70. **[G: U.S.]**

Baumol, William J. On the Social Rate of Discount: Comment on the Comments. *Amer. Econ. Rev.,* December 1969, *59*(5), pp. 930.

Berney, Robert E. The Incidence of the Draft—Is It Progressive? *Western Econ. J.,* September 1969, *7*(3), pp. 244–47. **[G: U.S.]**

Bhatt, Mahesh. Some Implications of Agricultural Income Tax. *Artha-Vikas,* July 1969, *5*(2), pp. 138–45. **[G: India]**

Bichi, C. Repartitia rentei diferentiale. (Distribution of Differential Rent. With English summary.) *Stud. Cercet. Econ.,* 1969, *4,* pp. 59–70. **[G: Romania]**

Bierman, Harold, Jr. Accelerated Depreciation and Rate Regulation. *Accounting Rev.,* January 1969, *44*(1), pp. 65–78.

Bird, Monroe M. Statement. **In** *Proposed Extension of the Surcharge and Repeal of the Investment Tax Credit, SCH,* 1969, pp. 486–88. **[G: U.S.]**

Bittker, Boris I. Accounting for Federal "Tax Subsidies" in the National Budget. *Nat. Tax J.,* June 1969, *22*(2), pp. 244–61. **[G: U.S.]**

Bittker, Boris I. Churches, Taxes and the Constitution. *Yale Law J.,* July 1969, *78*(8), pp. 1285–1310. **[G: U.S.]**

Bittker, Boris I. The Income Tax: How Progressive Should It Be?: Rebuttal. **In** *Galvin, C. O. and Bittker, B. I.,* 1969, pp. 61–72. **[G: U.S.]**

Bittker, Boris I. The Income Tax: How Progressive Should It Be?: Second Lecture. **In** *Galvin, C. O. and Bittker, B. I.,* 1969, pp. 27–58. **[G: U.S.]**

Bittker, Boris I. The Tax Expenditure Budget—A Reply to Professors Surrey and Hellmuth. *Nat. Tax J.,* December 1969, *22*(4), pp. 538–42. **[G: U.S.]**

Blough, Roy. Basic Tax Issues. **In** *Gaa, C. J.,* 1969, pp. 26–39. **[G: U.S.]**

Boskin, Michael J. The Negative Income Tax and the Supply of Work Effort: Reply. *Nat. Tax J.,* September 1969, *22*(3), pp. 417.

Bouwsma, J. Unilateral Relief from Double Taxation in the Netherlands. *Bull. Int. Fiscal Doc.,* July, August, September 1969, *23*(7–8–9), pp. 407–37. **[G: Netherlands]**

Break, George F. Integrating Corporate and Personal Income Taxes: The Carter Commission Proposals. *Law Contemp. Probl.,* Autumn 1969, *34*(4), pp. 726–35. **[G: Canada]**

Break, George F. Integration of the Corporate and Personal Income Taxes. *Nat. Tax J.,* March 1969, *22*(1), pp. 39–56. **[G: U.S.]**

Breton, Albert. Some Problems of Major Tax Reforms. *Nat. Tax J.,* March 1969, *22*(1), pp. 154–63.

Brighton, Gerald D. Accrued Expense Tax Reform—Not Ready in 1954—Ready in 1969? *Accounting Rev.,* January 1969, *44*(1), pp. 137–44. **[G: U.S.]**

Bross, Steward R., Jr. The United States Borrower in the Eurobond Market—A Lawyer's Point of View. *Law Contemp. Probl.,* Winter 1969, *34*(1), pp. 172–202. **[G: U.S.]**

Buchanan, James M. and Flowers, Marilyn. An Analytical Setting for a "Taxpayers' Revolution." *Western Econ. J.,* December 1969, *7*(4), pp. 349–59. **[G: U.S.]**

Campbell, Colin D. Social Insurance in the United States: A Program in Search of an Explanation. *J. Law Econ.,* October 1969, *12*(2), pp. 249–65. **[G: U.S.]**

Carroll, Mitchell B. The U.N. Reenacts a Tax Drama. *Bull. Int. Fiscal Doc.,* April 1969, *23*(4), pp. 163–65.

Cassidy, Henry J. The Employer Payroll Tax and the Labor Mix. *Quart. Rev. Econ. Bus.,* Spring 1969, *9*(1), pp. 39–43.

Celen, R. De beoordeling van de resultaten in de E.E.G.-landen, Groot-Brittannië en de V.S., wordt geconditioneerd door afwi jkende nationale belastingstelsels. (Differences in the National Tax Systems Are the Causes that the Profits of the Firms in the Countries of the E.E.C., Great Britain and the U.S. Have to Be Compared Cautiously. With English summary.) *Econ. Soc. Tijdschr.,* April 1969, *23*(2), pp. 185–204.

Char, S. V. Agricultural Income Tax and the Indian Constitution. *Artha-Vikas,* July 1969, *5*(2), pp. 177–82. **[G: India]**

Cook, David E. Inter-Unit Pricing and Your New Pricing Expert: The IRS. *Manage. Account.,* August 1969, *51*(2), pp. 9–11. **[G: U.S.]**

Corneel, Frederic G. Tax Planning—Teaching and Practice. **In** *Gaa, C. J.,* 1969, pp. 191–204. **[G: U.S.]**

Corner, D. C. and Fletcher, C. H. Some Effects of Selective Employment Tax on the Construction and Service Industries. *Bull. Oxford Univ. Inst. Econ. Statist.,* February 1969, *31*(1), pp. 47–54. **[G: U.K.]**

Crumbley, D. Larry. How Long Will the Commissioner and the Courts Ignore Accounting Standards on the Accrual of Prepaid Income? *Nat. Tax J.,* December 1969, *22*(4), pp. 559–61. **[G: U.S.]**

Crystal, John. Canada Banker's 'Interest'. *Bull. Int. Fiscal Doc.,* March 1969, *23*(3), pp. 137–40. **[G: Canada]**

Crystal, John. The Curious Nature of "Know-How": Part II. *Bull. Int. Fiscal Doc.,* February 1969, *23* (2), pp. 73–75. **[G: Canada]**

Delano, Myles S. The Effects of Leverage and Corporate Taxes on the Shareholders of Regulated Utilities: Comment. **In** *Trebing, H. M. and Howard, R. H., eds.,* 1969, pp. 98–105. **[G: U.S.]**

Devers, M. De B.T.W.-aangifte en de factuur. (The Value Added Tax Declaration and the Invoice. With English summary.) *Econ. Soc. Tijdschr.,* June 1969, *23*(3), pp. 287–303. **[G: Belgium]**

Dosser, Douglas. Comment on "The Incidence of Social Security Taxes" by J. Weitenberg. *Public Finance,* 1969, *24*(2), pp. 209–14. **[G: Netherlands]**

Dosser, Douglas; Han, S. S. and Hitiris, Theodore. Trade Effects of Tax Harmonisation: Harmonisation of the Value-added Tax in E.E.C. *Manchester*

Sch. Econ. Soc. Stud., December 1969, *37*(4), pp. 337–46. **[G: E.E.C.]**

Due, John F. The Somers Solution to the Use Tax: A Comment. *Nat. Tax J.*, June 1969, *22*(2), pp. 301.

Due, John F. The Uganda Sales Tax on Importation and Manufacture. *East Afr. Econ. Rev.*, June 1969, *1*(1), pp. 1–16. **[G: Uganda]**

Durand, Patrick and Latscha, Jacques. The New Tax Treaty between the United Kingdom and France. *Bull. Int. Fiscal Doc.*, March 1969, *23*(3), pp. 131–36. **[G: U.K.; France]**

Ecker-Racz, L. L. Tax Simplification in this Federal System. *Law Contemp. Probl.*, Autumn 1969, *34* (4), pp. 769–81. **[G: U.S.]**

Eilbott, Peter. The Revenue Gain from Taxation of Decedents' Unrealized Capital Gains. *Nat. Tax J.*, December 1969, *22*(4), pp. 506–15. **[G: U.S.]**

Ekelund, Robert B., Jr. Tax Reform in Latin America: The E.C.L.A. Proposals—A Critical Evaluation. *Amer. J. Econ. Soc.*, January 1969, *28* (1), pp. 93–106.

Evans, Michael K. Reconstruction and Estimation of the Balanced Budget Multiplier. *Rev. Econ. Statist.*, February 1969, *51*(1), pp. 14–25. **[G: U.S.]**

Fabella, A. V. Policies for Long-Term Growth in the Philippines: The Public Sector. *Philippine Econ. J.*, First Semester 1969, *8*(1), pp. 37–48. **[G: Philippines]**

Feldstein, Martin S. The Effects on Taxation on Risk Taking. *J. Polit. Econ.*, September/October 1969, *77*(5), pp. 755–64.

Fernandes, L. Santos. Comments on Professor Reviglio's Paper on the "Finance of Social Security in Developing Countries." *Public Finance*, 1969, *24* (2), pp. 278–79.

Forte, Francesco. Summary of the Discussion on Policy Problems. *Public Finance*, 1969, *24*(2), pp. 405–13.

Freeman, Roger A. Federal Assistance to Higher Education through Income Tax Credits. **In** *the Economics and Financing of Higher Education in the United States, JECP*, 1969, pp. 665–83. **[G: U.S.]**

Frostman, Lars. Optimal Financing and Tax Policy of the Corporation—A Review Article. *Swedish J. Econ.*, March 1969, *71*(1), pp. 30–41.

Galvin, Charles O. The Income Tax: How Progressive Should It Be?: Rebuttal. **In** *Galvin, C. O. and Bittker, B. I.*, 1969, pp. 73–84. **[G: U.S.]**

Galvin, Charles O. The Income Tax: How Progressive Should It Be?: First Lecture. **In** *Galvin, C. O. and Bittker, B. I.*, 1969, pp. 1–23. **[G: U.S.]**

Gandhi, Ved P. Agricultural Taxation Policy: Search for a Direction. *Artha-Vikas*, July 1969, *5*(2), pp. 3–49. **[G: India]**

Giddy, R. V. An Outline of Taxes under the Hong Kong Inland Revenue Ordinance. *Bull. Int. Fiscal Doc.*, December 1969, *23*(12), pp. 574–83. **[G: Hong Kong]**

Goetz, Charles J. and Magnani, Italo. Automobile Taxation Based on Mechanical Characteristics: Evidence from the Italian Case. *Public Finance*, 1969, *24*(3), pp. 486–98. **[G: Italy]**

Goldin, Hyman H. Financing Public Broadcasting. *Law Contemp. Probl.*, Summer 1969, *34*(3), pp. 650–70. **[G: U.S.]**

Graaff, Jan de V. The National Debt. *S. Afr. J. Econ.*, September 1969, *37*(3), pp. 170–86. **[G: S. Africa]**

Green, Christopher and Tella, Alfred. Effect of Nonemployment Income and Wage Rates on the Work Incentives of the Poor. *Rev. Econ. Statist.*, November 1969, *51*(4), pp. 399–408. **[G: U.S.]**

Green, Christopher. Problems in the Area of Poverty: Discussion. *Amer. Econ. Rev.*, May 1969, *59* (2), pp. 473–75. **[G: U.S.]**

Groves, Harold M. Taxing the Family Unit: The Carter Commission's Proposals and U.S. Practice. *Nat. Tax J.*, March 1969, *22*(1), pp. 109–20. **[G: U.S.; Canada]**

Gulati, I. S. and Kothari, V. N. Land Tax as an Incentive for Better Land Utilization. *Artha-Vikas*, July 1969, *5*(2), pp. 108–16.

Guthrie, Harold W. Problems in the Area of Poverty: Discussion. *Amer. Econ. Rev.*, May 1969, *59*(2), pp. 475–76. **[G: U.S.]**

Hale, Carl W. The Optimality of Local Subsidies in Regional Development Programs. *Quart. Rev. Econ. Bus.*, Autumn 1969, *9*(3), pp. 35–50. **[G: U.S.]**

Hamada, Robert S. The Effects of Leverage and Corporate Taxes on the Shareholders of Regulated Utilities. **In** *Trebing, H. M. and Howard, R. H., eds.*, 1969, pp. 73–97. **[G: U.S.]**

Harberger, Arnold C. In Defense of Carter: A Personal Overview. *Nat. Tax J.*, March 1969, *22*(1), pp. 164–77.

Harriss, C. Lowell. Progression Reconsidered. **In** *Gaa, C. J.*, 1969, pp. 54–66. **[G: U.S.]**

Haugen, Robert A. and Heins, A. James. The Effects of the Personal Income Tax on the Stability of Equity Value. *Nat. Tax J.*, December 1969, *22*(4), pp. 466–71.

Hayes, William A. The Guaranteed Annual Income: An Appraisal. *Rev. Soc. Econ.*, March 1969, *27*(1), pp. 74–83. **[G: U.S.]**

Henderson, William L. and Ledebur, Larry C. Government Incentives and Black Economic Development. *Rev. Soc. Econ.*, September 1969, *27*(2), pp. 202–21. **[G: U.S.]**

Hettenhouse, George W. and Lewellen, Wilbur G. The Taxation of Restricted Stock Compensation Plans. *Nat. Tax J.*, September 1969, *22*(3), pp. 368–78. **[G: U.S.]**

af Heurlin, Lauri O. Vuokra-asunnon ja asunnonvuokran ongelma. (The Problem of Rented Accommodation and the Rent Level. With English summary.) *Kansant. Aikak.*, 1969, *65*(4), pp. 251–68. **[G: Finland]**

Hobbet, Richard D. Transitional Mechanisms to Facilitate Tax Reform. *Law Contemp. Probl.*, Autumn 1969, *34*(4), pp. 818–40. **[G: U.S.]**

Hochman, Harold M. and Rodgers, James D. Pareto Optimal Redistribution. *Amer. Econ. Rev.*, Part I, September 1969, *59*(4), pp. 542–57.

Hogan, William T. Statement. **In** *Proposed Extension of the Surcharge and Repeal of the Investment Tax Credit, SCH*, 1969, pp. 390–404. **[G: U.S.]**

Huefner, Ronald J. Taxation and the Disposition of

Depreciable Assets. *Eng. Econ.*, April–May 1969, *14*(3), pp. 141–50. **[G: U.S.]**

Huiskamp, J. C. L. Some General Principles of Dutch Tax Law. *Bull. Int. Fiscal Doc.*, July, August, September 1969, *23*(7–8–9), pp. 285–96. **[G: Netherlands]**

Husni, Muhd. The New System of Collecting Income Tax, Property Tax and Company Tax in Indonesia. *Bull. Int. Fiscal Doc.*, April 1969, *23*(4), pp. 151–59. **[G: Indonesia]**

James, Estelle. On the Social Rate of Discount: Comment. *Amer. Econ. Rev.*, December 1969, *59*(5), pp. 912–16.

Jantscher, Gerald R. Death and Gift Taxation in the United States after the Report of the Royal Commission. *Nat. Tax J.*, March 1969, *22*(1), pp. 121–38. **[G: U.S.]**

Jap, K. S. The Concept of Delivery of Goods by a Manufacturer under the Indonesian Sales Tax Act (1951–1968) *Bull. Int. Fiscal Doc.*, May 1969, *23* (5), pp. 223–28. **[G: Indonesia]**

Johansson, Sven-Erik. Income Taxes and Investment Decisions. *Swedish J. Econ.*, June 1969, *71*(2), pp. 104–10.

Johnson, James A. The Distribution of the Burden of Sewer User Charges under Various Charge Formulas. *Nat. Tax J.*, December 1969, *22*(4), pp. 472–85.

Kahlon, A. S. and Kahlon, S. S. Enhancement of Agricultural Taxation Will Not Sustain the Green Revolution in Agriculture. *Artha-Vikas,* July 1969, *5*(2), pp. 63–70. **[G: India]**

Kesselman, Jonathan. The Negative Income Tax and the Supply of Work Effort: Comment. *Nat. Tax J.*, September 1969, *22*(3), pp. 411–16.

Keyserling, Leon H. Statement. **In** *Tax Reform Act of 1969, Testimony, Sept. 26, SCP,* 1969, pp. 85–191. **[G: U.S.]**

Kosh, David A. The Effects of Leverage and Corporate Taxes on the Shareholders of Regulated Utilities: Comment. **In** *Trebing, H. M. and Howard, R. H., eds.*, 1969, pp. 106–10. **[G: U.S.]**

Krogh, D. C. Taxation in a Developing Economy. *S. Afr. J. Econ.*, December 1969, *37*(4), pp. 285–305. **[G: S. Africa]**

Landauer, Carl. On the Social Rate of Discount: Comment. *Amer. Econ. Rev.*, December 1969, *59* (5), pp. 917–18.

Laumas, Gurcharan S. The Shifting of the Corporation Income Tax in India. *Econ. Int.*, May 1969, *22*(2), pp. 283–91. **[G: India]**

Lees, Dennis. Controversy Surrounding Negative Income Taxation: Comment. *Public Finance,* 1969, *24*(2), pp. 362–66. **[G: U.K.]**

Leith, James Clark. The Customs Revenue Loss in a Southeast Asian Customs Union. *J. Devel. Stud.*, January 1969, *5*(2), pp. 142–46. **[G: Malaya]**

Lent, George E. Taxation of Financial Intermediaries. *Nat. Tax J.*, March 1969, *22*(1), pp. 139–53. **[G: U.S.; Canada]**

Lewellen, Wilbur G. Tax Minimization and Executive Compensation Plans. **In** *Tax Institute of America,* 1969, pp. 104–17. **[G: U.S.]**

Lindholm, Richard W. Home Ownership and the Income Tax: A Proposed Change. *Oregon Bus. Rev.*, September 1969, *28*(9), pp. 1–3.

Lomax, David F. and Reading, Brian. Too Little Saving. *Nat. Westminster Bank Quart. Rev.*, August 1969, pp. 23–42. **[G: U.K.]**

Lotz, Joergen R. and Morss, Elliott R. "Tax Effort" in Developing Countries. *Finance Develop.*, September 1969, *6*(3), pp. 36–39.

Lüttgen, Horst. Das Problem des optimalen Testaments. (With English summary.) *Z. ges. Staatswiss.*, January 1969, *125*(1), pp. 123–37.

Lynch, P. J. and Witherell, William H. The Carter Commission and the Saving Behavior of Canadian Corporations. *Nat. Tax J.*, March 1969, *22*(1), pp. 57–65. **[G: Canada]**

Magnani, Italo. Effetti di benessere derivanti da variazioni del saggio d'interesse e imposizione degli incrementi patrimoniali. (Welfare Effects of Changes in the Interest Rate and Capital Gains Taxation. With English summary.) *Rivista Int. Sci. Econ. Com.*, December 1969, *16*(12), pp. 1145–63.

Mahler, Walter, Jr. Elimination of the Sales Tax Burden on Exports. *Asian Econ. Rev.*, February 1969, *11*(2), pp. 227–32. **[G: India]**

Malluhi, Haytham. Tax System in Kuwait. *Bull. Int. Fiscal Doc.*, April 1969, *23*(4), pp. 160–62. **[G: Kuwait]**

Marshall, Don C. Disclosure of Federal Tax Concessions—Billions in Implicit Subsidies. *Univ. Missouri Bus. Govt. Rev.*, January–February 1969, *10* (1), pp. 23–29. **[G: U.S.]**

Mathai, M. K. Incentives for Investment in Malaysia. *Bull. Int. Fiscal Doc.*, November 1969, *23*(11), pp. 503–15. **[G: Malaysia]**

Mathew, E. T. Proposals for an Integrated System of Agricultural Taxation. *Artha-Vikas,* July 1969, *5*(2), pp. 146–53. **[G: India]**

Maxwell, James A. Federal Grant Elasticity and Distortion. *Nat. Tax J.*, December 1969, *22*(4), pp. 550–51. **[G: U.S.]**

Mayo, Robert P. Statement. **In** *Proposed Extension of the Surcharge and Repeal of the Investment Tax Credit, SCH,* 1969, pp. 71–75. **[G: U.S.]**

McArthur, A. T. G. Extra Tax Resulting from Income Variation with Particular Reference to New Zealand. *Australian J. Agr. Econ.*, June 1969, *13*(1), pp. 68–73. **[G: New Zealand]**

McLeod, Donald. The Personal Income Tax in Jamaica. *Soc. Econ. Stud.*, September 1969, *18*(3), pp. 254–62. **[G: Jamaica]**

Mendelson, Morris. Some Tax Considerations in American Eurobond Flotations. *Nat. Tax J.*, June 1969, *22*(2), pp. 303–10. **[G: U.S.]**

Mieszkowski, Peter. Carter on the Taxation of International Income Flows. *Nat. Tax J.*, March 1969, *22*(1), pp. 97–108. **[G: Canada]**

Mieszkowski, Peter. Tax Incidence Theory: The Effects of Taxes on the Distribution of Income. *J. Econ. Lit.*, December 1969, *7*(4), pp. 1103–24.

Mistry, Thakore. Land-Based vs. Income-Based Taxation in Indian Agriculture. *Artha-Vikas,* July 1969, *5*(2), pp. 117–29. **[G: India]**

de Moor, A. E. International Trade of Goods and Services with the TVA in Operation. *Bull. Int. Fiscal Doc.*, July, August, September 1969, *23*(7–8–9), pp. 297–334. **[G: Netherlands]**

Morris, Reginald Edward. Fiscal Controls of Land

Monopoly. *Amer. J. Econ. Soc.*, January 1969, *28*(1), pp. 77–92.

Nichols, Alan. On the Social Rate of Discount: Comment. *Amer. Econ. Rev.*, December 1969, *59*(5), pp. 909–11.

Nosé, Tetsuya. A Statistical Approach to Personal Taxation. *Oxford Econ. Pap.*, July 1969, *21*(2), pp. 177–95. **[G: U.K.]**

Oakland, William H. Effects of Taxation on Risk-Taking: Discussion. *Amer. Econ. Rev.*, May 1969, *59*(2), pp. 563–65.

Ojha, P. D. and Lent, George E. Sales Taxes in Countries of the Far East. *Int. Monet. Fund Staff Pap.*, November 1969, *16*(3), pp. 529–81. **[G: Far East]**

Ojha, P. D. Taxation of Agricultural Land and Income. *Artha-Vikas*, July 1969, *5*(2), pp. 50–62. **[G: India]**

Olsen, Edgar O. A Normative Theory of Transfers. *Public Choice*, Spring 1969, *6*, pp. 39–58.

Ott, Attiat F.; Ott, David J. and Turner, J. Scott. Burden Distribution of a Broad-Based Personal Income Tax System and Its Implications for Tax Reform Discussions. *Law Contemp. Probl.*, Autumn 1969, *34*(4), pp. 805–17. **[G: U.S.]**

Ott, Attiat F.; Ott, David J. and Turner, J. Scott. Simulation of Costs of a Negative Income Tax Plan and Its Implications for the Poor. **In** *Willis, A. B., ed.*, 1969, pp. 168–83. **[G: U.S.]**

Ott, Attiat F. and Ott, David J. Simulation of Revenue and Tax Structure: Implications of Broadening the Federal Income Tax Base. **In** *Willis, A. B., ed.*, 1969, pp. 27–106. **[G: U.S.]**

Patel, A. G. A Case for Income Tax on Agricultural Income. *Artha-Vikas*, July 1969, *5*(2), pp. 171–76. **[G: India]**

Patel, Shivabhai J. Taxation of Agricultural Land and Income. *Artha-Vikas*, July 1969, *5*(2), pp. 98–105. **[G: India]**

Pathak, Mahesh and Patel, Arun. Reform of Agricultural Taxation. *Artha-Vikas*, July 1969, *5*(2), pp. 71–78. **[G: India]**

Peacock, Alan T. Welfare Economics and Public Subsidies to the Arts. *Manchester Sch. Econ. Soc. Stud.*, December 1969, *37*(4), pp. 323–35.

Pechman, Joseph A. and Okner, Benjamin A. Simulation of the Carter Commission Tax Proposals for the United States. *Nat. Tax J.*, March 1969, *22*(1), pp. 2–23. **[G: U.S.]**

Pechman, Joseph A. Tax Policies for the 1970's. *Public Policy*, Fall 1969, *18*(1), pp. 75–93. **[G: U.S.]**

Pedone, Antonio. The Ricardian Tax Incidence Analysis in the Light of Optimum Growth Theory. *Econ. Int.*, February 1969, *22*(1), pp. 63–83.

Peeters, Frans. De B.T.W. in de onderneming. (The Value Added Tax and the Enterprise. With English summary.) *Econ. Soc. Tijdschr.*, August 1969, *23*(4), pp. 391–403. **[G: Belgium]**

Pennock, J. Roland. Agricultural Subsidies in Britain and America. **In** *Rose, R., ed.*, 1969, pp. 199–220. **[G: U.K.; U.S.]**

Pepper, H. W. T. and Huiskamp, J. C. L. Guilt and Innocence of Taxpayers—Including Some Small Notes on Tax Collection Practices in Certain Countries. *Bull. Int. Fiscal Doc.*, November 1969, *23*(11), pp. 516–20.

Pepper, H. W. T. Poll Taxes, Payroll Taxation, and Social Security (Part I). *Bull. Int. Fiscal Doc.*, January 1969, *23*(1), pp. 4–26.

Pepper, H. W. T. Poll Taxes, Payroll Taxation, and Social Security (Part II). *Bull. Int. Fiscal Doc.*, February 1969, *23*(2), pp. 55–65.

Phelps, Edmund S. and Shell, Karl. Public Debt, Taxation, and Capital Intensiveness. *J. Econ. Theory*, October 1969, *1*(3), pp. 330–46.

Philips, G. Edward. Income Concepts. **In** *Gaa, C. J.*, 1969, pp. 106–25.

Popkin, William D. Administration of a Negative Income Tax. *Yale Law J.*, January 1969, *78*(3), pp. 388–431. **[G: U.S.]**

Prest, A. R. Comments on "Social Insurance in a Growing Economy: A Proposal for Radical Reform." *Nat. Tax J.*, December 1969, *22*(4), pp. 554–56. **[G: U.S.]**

Projector, Dorothy S. Should the Payroll Tax Finance Higher Benefits under OASDI? A Review of the Issues. *J. Human Res.*, Winter 1969, *4*(1), pp. 60–75. **[G: U.S.]**

Pye, Gordon. On the Tax Structure of Interest Rates. *Quart. J. Econ.*, November 1969, *83*(4), pp. 562–79.

Quigley, Joseph M. The Effects of Leverage and Corporate Taxes on the Shareholders of Regulated Utilities: Comment. **In** *Trebing, H. M. and Howard, R. H., eds.*, 1969, pp. 111–16. **[G: U.S.]**

Ramsey, David D. On the Social Rate of Discount: Comment. *Amer. Econ. Rev.*, December 1969, *59*(5), pp. 919–24.

Reviglio, Franco. Finance of Social Security in Developing Countries. *Public Finance*, 1969, *24*(2), pp. 264–77.

Rice, Ralph S. Tax Reform and Tax Incentives. *Law Contemp. Probl.*, Autumn 1969, *34*(4), pp. 782–804.

Robbins, Gary A. Alternative Treatment of Corporate Income. **In** *Willis, A. B., ed.*, 1969, pp. 138–56. **[G: U.S.]**

Rohlíček, Rudolf. Principles of the Present Finance and Tax Policy. *New Trends Czech. Econ.*, December 1969, (8), pp. 61–70. **[G: Czechoslovakia]**

Rolph, Earl R. Controversy Surrounding Negative Income Taxation. *Public Finance*, 1969, *24*(2), pp. 352–61. **[G: U.S.]**

van Rooijen, M. J. The Substantial Holding Privilege in Netherlands Corporate Income Tax. *Bull. Int. Fiscal Doc.*, July, August, September 1969, *23*(7–8–9), pp. 337–405. **[G: Netherlands]**

Sadie, J. L. Company Taxation. *S. Afr. J. Econ.*, December 1969, *37*(4), pp. 345–71.

Schwab, Bernhard and Nicol, Robert E. G. From Double-Declining-Balance to Sum-of-the-Years'-Digits Depreciation: An Optimum Switching Rule. *Accounting Rev.*, April 1969, *44*(2), pp. 292–96. **[G: U.S.]**

Schwartz, Eli and Aronson, J. Richard. The Preference for Accumulation vs. Spending: Gift and Estate Taxation, and the Timing of Wealth Transfers. *Nat. Tax J.*, September 1969, *22*(3), pp. 390–98. **[G: U.S.]**

Seltzer, Lawrence H. Background of the Controversy. **In** *Gaa, C. J.*, 1969, pp. 126–45. **[G: U.S.]**

Seltzer, Lawrence H. Competing Proposals for the Tax Treatment of Gains and Losses. **In** *Gaa, C. J.*, 1969, pp. 146–53. **[G: U.S.]**

Sessa, Giuseppe. Il problema delle esenzioni nell' I.V.A. e gli scambi internazionali. (The Problem of the Exemptions in New Italian Taxation System. With English summary.) *Mondo Aperto,* February 1969, *23*(1), pp. 10–35. **[G: Italy]**

Shah, C. H. Agricultural Taxation: A Plea for Caution and a Proposal for a Positive Approach. *Artha-Vikas,* July 1969, *5*(2), pp. 79–97. **[G: India]**

Shibata, Aiko N. Effects of Taxation on Risk-Taking. *Amer. Econ. Rev.*, May 1969, *59*(2), pp. 553–61.

Shin, Kilman. International Difference in Tax Ratio. *Rev. Econ. Statist.*, May 1969, *51*(2), pp. 213–20.

Shoup, Carl S. Experience with the Value-Added Tax in Denmark, and Prospects in Sweden. *Finanzarchiv,* March 1969, *28*(2), pp. 236–52. **[G: Denmark; Sweden]**

Slitor, Richard E. The Carter Proposals on Capital Gains: Economic Effects and Policy Implications for the United States. *Nat. Tax J.*, March 1969, *22* (1), pp. 66–78. **[G: U.S.]**

Smith, Dan Throop. Federal Tax Reform—Conclusions. **In** *Gaa, C. J.*, 1969, pp. 85–90. **[G: U.S.]**

Smith, Dan Throop. Statement. **In** *Tax Reform Act of 1969, Testimony, Oct. 2, SCP,* 1969, pp. 9–22. **[G: U.S.]**

Smith, Dan Throop. Tax Alternatives for the Next Decade. **In** *Gaa, C. J.*, 1969, pp. 96–103. **[G: U.S.]**

Smith, Dan Throop. Tax Policy and Foreign Investment. *Law Contemp. Probl.*, Winter 1969, *34*(1), pp. 146–56. **[G: U.S.]**

Smith, Dan Throop. The Effects of Taxation of Executive Compensation on Economic Activity. **In** *Tax Institute of America,* 1969, pp. 34–43. **[G: U.S.]**

Smith, Dan Throop. The Nature of Taxation and the Objectives of Tax Policy. **In** *Gaa, C. J.*, 1969, pp. 6–12. **[G: U.S.]**

Smith, David L. Federal Grant Elasticity and Distortion: A Reply. *Nat. Tax J.*, December 1969, *22*(4), pp. 552–53. **[G: U.S.]**

Smith, Vernon L. Taxes and Share Valuation in Competitive Markets. *Rev. Econ. Statist.*, February 1969, *51*(1), pp. 96–99.

Snowbarger, Marvin and Shervais, Steve. A Study of Factors Influencing the Average Effective Tax Rate on Personal Income, 1954–1965. *Nat. Tax J.*, June 1969, *22*(2), pp. 217–31. **[G: U.S.]**

Snyder, Wayne W. La mésure des effets des politiques budgétaires françaises de 1955 à 1965. (With English summary.) *Revue Écon.*, November 1969, *20*(6), pp. 929–53. **[G: France]**

Somers, Harold M. The Somers Solution to the Use Tax: Reply. *Nat. Tax J.*, June 1969, *22*(2), pp. 302.

Steve, Sergio. Public Finance and Social Security. *Public Finance,* 1969, *24*(2), pp. 101–13.

Stiglitz, Joseph E. The Effects of Income, Wealth, and Capital Gains Taxation on Risk-Taking. *Quart. J. Econ.*, May 1969, *83*(2), pp. 263–83.

Stilz, Dieter. Die Auswirkungen der öffentlichen Hilfen für den Ruhrbergbau auf dessen Wettbewerbsbedingungen. (The Influence of Fiscal Support on the Conditions of Competition in the Ruhr Coal Mining Industry. With English summary.) *Schmollers Jahr.*, 1969, *89*(4), pp. 427–49. **[G: W. Germany]**

Stilz, Dieter. Die Begünstigung des Steinkohlenbergbaus des Ruhrgebiets durch die öffentliche Finanzwirtschaft. (Fiscal Support of the Ruhr Coal Mining Industry 1958–1967. With English summary.) *Schmollers Jahr.*, 1969, *89*(2), pp. 151–84. **[G: W. Germany]**

Stockfisch, J. A. The Influence of the Property Tax on Investment and Employment. **In** *Becker, A. P., ed.*, 1969, pp. 49–62. **[G: U.S.]**

Stolk, Leonard. Taxation of International Consolidations into a "European Corporation." *Bull. Int. Fiscal Doc.*, November 1969, *23*(11), pp. 521–44. **[G: E.E.C.]**

Stone, Lawrence M. A Comprehensive Income Tax Base for the U.S.?: Implications of the Report of the Royal Commission on Taxation. *Nat. Tax J.*, March 1969, *22*(1), pp. 24–38. **[G: U.S.]**

Strasma, John. Property Taxation in Chile. **In** *Becker, A. P., ed.*, 1969, pp. 187–200. **[G: Chile]**

Strümpel, Burkhard. The Contribution of Survey Research to Public Finance. **In** *Peacock, A. T., ed.*, 1969, pp. 13–32.

Sunley, Emil M., Jr. The Present Value of Depreciation Allowances. *Quart. Rev. Econ. Bus.*, Winter 1969, *9*(4), pp. 77–79.

Surrey, Stanley S. Complexity and the Internal Revenue Code: The Problem of the Management of Tax Detail. *Law Contemp. Probl.*, Autumn 1969, *34*(4), pp. 673–710. **[G: U.S.]**

Surrey, Stanley S. and Hellmuth, William F. The Tax Expenditure Budget—Response to Professor Bittker. *Nat. Tax J.*, December 1969, *22*(4), pp. 528–37. **[G: U.S.]**

Tabb, William K. Government Incentives to Private Industry to Locate in Urban Poverty Areas. *Land Econ.*, November 1969, *45*(4), pp. 392–99. **[G: U.S.]**

Tait, Alan A. Deflation and Incomes Policy: The British Budget 1968/69. *Finanzarchiv,* October 1968, *28*(1), pp. 110–25. **[G: U.K.]**

Tanzi, Vito. Measuring the Sensitivity of the Federal Income Tax from Cross-Section Data: A New Approach. *Rev. Econ. Statist.*, May 1969, *51*(2), pp. 206–09. **[G: U.S.]**

Tanzi, Vito. Tax Incentives and Economic Development: The Ecuadorian Experience. *Finanzarchiv,* March 1969, *28*(2), pp. 226–35. **[G: Ecuador]**

Taubman, Paul. Econometric Functions for Government Receipts. **In** *Duesenberry, J. S., et al.*, 1969, pp. 188–220. **[G: U.S.]**

Taubman, Paul and Wales, Terence J. Impact of Investment Subsidies in a Neoclassical Growth Model. *Rev. Econ. Statist.*, August 1969, *51*(3), pp. 287–97.

Tillinghast, David R. The Carter Commission Report and International Investment Transactions; Integration and Ambiguous Intentions. *Nat. Tax J.*, March 1969, *22*(1), pp. 79–96. **[G: Canada]**

Tinney, Robert W. Taxing Imputed Rental Income on Owner-Occupied Homes. **In** *Willis, A. B., ed.*,

1969, pp. 125–37. [G: U.S.]

Trotter, G. J. Personal Income Tax. *S. Afr. J. Econ.*, December 1969, *37*(4), pp. 306–44.

Uckmar, V. and Durand, Patrick. The Tax Treaty between Italy and France. *Bull. Int. Fiscal Doc.*, May 1969, *23*(5), pp. 191–203. [G: Italy; France]

Usher, Dan. On the Social Rate of Discount: Comment. *Amer. Econ. Rev.*, December 1969, *59*(5), pp. 925–29.

Van Houtte, J. B.T.W., een instrument van conjunctuur-politiek? (The Belgian V.A.T.-Bill and Economic Policy. With English summary.) *Econ. Soc. Tijdschr.*, February 1969, *23*(1), pp. 1–8. [G: E.E.C.]

Vandenhouten, F. De invoering van de B.T.W. in de ondernemingen. (The Value Added Tax in the Administration of the Firms. With English summary.) *Econ. Soc. Tijdschr.*, April 1969, *23*(2), pp. 159–71. [G: Belgium]

Vessillier, Elisabeth. L'instrument fiscal dans la politique française d'amenagement du territoire. (The Fiscal Instrument in the Regional Economic Policy of France. With English summary.) *Public Finance,* 1969, *24*(3), pp. 499–509. [G: France]

Vickrey, William S. Tax Simplification through Cumulative Averaging. *Law Contemp. Probl.*, Autumn 1969, *34*(4), pp. 736–50. [G: U.S.]

Vyas, V. S. and Pathak, Mahesh. A Case for Taxation of Agricultural Income. *Artha-Vikas,* July 1969, *5*(2), pp. 130–37. [G: India]

van Waasdijk, T. Some Thoughts on Indirect Tax Effects in South Africa. *S. Afr. J. Econ.*, December 1969, *37*(4), pp. 372–92. [G: S. Africa]

Walmsley, David J. The Less Developed Country Exclusion from Subpart F. *Nat. Tax J.*, September 1969, *22*(3), pp. 425–30. [G: U.S.]

Walters, A. A. The Cost of Using Roads. *Finance Develop.*, March 1969, *6*(1), pp. 16–22.

Watt, Melvin L. Tax Exemption for Organizations Investing in Black Businesses. *Yale Law J.*, June 1969, *78*(7), pp. 1212–27. [G: U.S.]

Watts, Harold W. Graduated Works Incentives: An Experiment in Negative Taxation. *Amer. Econ. Rev.*, May 1969, *59*(2), pp. 463–72. [G: U.S.]

Wedderspoon, William M. Simplifying Taxes in East Africa. *Finance Develop.*, March 1969, *6*(1), pp. 51–56.

Weinwurm, Ernest H. Discussion of Eugene L. Grant's "Tax Depreciation Restudied." *Eng. Econ.*, July–August 1969, *14*(4), pp. 237–38. [G: U.S.]

Weiss, Leonard W. Advertising, Profits, and Corporate Taxes. *Rev. Econ. Statist.*, November 1969, *51*(4), pp. 421–30. [G: U.S.]

Weiss, Steven J. Factors Affecting the Government Revenue Share in Less Developed Countries. *Soc. Econ. Stud.*, December 1969, *18*(4), pp. 348–64.

Weitenberg, Johannes. The Incidence of Social Security Taxes. *Public Finance,* 1969, *24*(2), pp. 193–208. [G: Netherlands]

Weston, J. Fred. The Effects of Leverage and Corporate Taxes on the Shareholders of Regulated Utilities: Comment. **In** *Trebing, H. M. and Howard, R. H., eds.*, 1969, pp. 117–25. [G: U.S.]

Wheatcroft, G. S. A. Inequity in Britain's Tax Structure. *Lloyds Bank Rev.*, July 1969, (93), pp. 11–26. [G: U.K.]

Wilson, A. G. and Wood, A. W. Regional Livestock Production and Feed Freight Assistance. *Can. J. Agr. Econ.*, February 1969, *17*(1), pp. 77–90. [G: Canada]

Woodworth, Laurence N. Tax Simplification and the Tax Reform Act of 1969. *Law Contemp. Probl.*, Autumn 1969, *34*(4), pp. 711–25. [G: U.S.]

Wright, Arthur W. Statement. **In** *Tax Reform Act of 1969, Testimony, Oct. 1, SCP,* 1969, pp. 347–68. [G: U.S.]

Zeitlin, Sherwin S. and Rosso, David J. United States Taxation of Foreign Enterprises—Structures for Doing Business in the United States and the Western Hemisphere. *Bull. Int. Fiscal Doc.*, December 1969, *23*(12), pp. 555–73. [G: U.S.]

324 State and Local Government Finance

3240 General

Adams, Esmond and Fish, Mary. Comments on the Impact of Federal Tax-Sharing on Economic Stabilization. *Nebr. J. Econ. Bus.*, Winter 1968–69, *8*(1), pp. 53–60.

Beard, Thomas R. Government Revenues and Expenditures in Louisiana. **In** *Beard, T. R., ed.*, 1969, pp. 173–230. [G: U.S.]

Botner, Stanley B. Municipal Budgeting: Problems and Developments. *Univ. Missouri Bus. Govt. Rev.*, March–April 1969, *10*(2), pp. 14–26. [G: U.S.]

Bowman, John H. City-Suburban Differentials in Local Government Fiscal Effort: A Comment. *Nat. Tax J.*, September 1969, *22*(3), pp. 418–21. [G: U.S.]

Braschler, Curtis and Klindt, Thomas. Theoretical and Empirical Problems in Local Government Consolidation. *Can. J. Agr. Econ.*, February 1969, *17*(1), pp. 141–50.

Childs, Gerald L. Efficient Reallocation of Land in Urban Renewal. *Western Econ. J.*, September 1969, *7*(3), pp. 211–22.

Cho, Yong Hyo. Fiscal Implications of Annexation: The Case of Metropolitan Central Cities in Texas. *Land Econ.*, August 1969, *45*(3), pp. 368–72. [G: U.S.]

Davies, David. City-Suburban Differentials in Local Government Fiscal Effort: A Comment. *Nat. Tax J.*, September 1969, *22*(3), pp. 422–23. [G: U.S.]

Gold, Ronald B. Fiscal Capacities and Welfare Expenditures of States. *Nat. Tax J.*, December 1969, *22*(4), pp. 496–505. [G: U.S.]

Gramlich, Edward M. State and Local Governments and Their Budget Constraint. *Int. Econ. Rev.*, June 1969, *10*(2), pp. 163–82. [G: U.S.]

Hady, Thomas F. Cost of Local Government Services. *Agr. Finance Rev.*, July 1969, *30,* pp. 11–20. [G: U.S.]

Haskell, Mark A. and Leshinski, Stephen. Fiscal Influences on Residential Choice: A Study of the New York Region. *Quart. Rev. Econ. Bus.*, Winter 1969, *9*(4), pp. 47–55. [G: U.S.]

Hicks, Ursula K. Economic and Financial Problems of Metropolitan Areas. *Z. Nationalökon.,* May 1969, *29*(1–2), pp. 1–18.

Hoffman, Ronald F. A Systematic Approach to a Practicable Plan for State Aid to Local Governments. *Public Finance,* 1969, *24*(1), pp. 1–32.

Hollenhorst, Jerry. Alternative Uses and Yields of Idle Public Funds: Comment. *Nat. Tax J.,* December 1969, *22*(4), pp. 557–58.

Holtmann, A. G. Correction to Migration to the Suburbs, Human Capital and City Income Tax Losses: A Case Study. *Nat. Tax J.,* September 1969, *22*(3), pp. 424. **[G: U.S.]**

Janus, Arnošt and Krajčovič, Josef. The First State Budget of Slovakia, and Problems of Its Fulfillment. *New Trends Czech. Econ.,* November 1969, (7), pp. 80–94. **[G: Czechoslovakia]**

Oates, Wallace E. The Effects of Property Taxes and Local Public Spending on Property Values: An Empirical Study of Tax Capitalization and the Tiebout Hypothesis. *J. Polit. Econ.,* November/December 1969, *77*(6), pp. 957–71. **[G: U.S.]**

Pechman, Joseph A. Tax Policies for the 1970's. *Public Policy,* Fall 1969, *18*(1), pp. 75–93. **[G: U.S.]**

Peck, John E. Financing State Expenditures in a Prospering Economy. *Indiana Bus. Rev.,* July/August 1969, *44,* pp. 7–15. **[G: U.S.]**

Phelps, Charlotte D. Real and Monetary Determinants of State and Local Highway Investment, 1951–66. *Amer. Econ. Rev.,* Part I, September 1969, *59*(4), pp. 507–21. **[G: U.S.]**

Pianese, Luigi. Local Finance. *Rev. Econ. Cond. Italy,* January 1969, *23*(1), pp. 28–50. **[G: Italy]**

Pidot, George B., Jr. A Principal Components Analysis of the Determinants of Local Government Fiscal Patterns. *Rev. Econ. Statist.,* May 1969, *51* (2), pp. 176–88. **[G: U.S.]**

Prakash, Ved. A Suggested Approach to Municipal Investment Planning. *Land Econ.,* August 1969, *45*(3), pp. 350–58.

Sharkansky, Ira and Hofferbert, Richard I. Dimensions of State Politics, Economics, and Public Policy. *Amer. Polit. Sci. Rev.,* September 1969, *63* (3), pp. 867–79. **[G: U.S.]**

Sims, Kent. Crisis in the State House. *Oregon Bus. Rev.,* December 1969, *28*(12), pp. 1–6. **[G: U.S.]**

Watters, Elsie M. Fiscal Outlook for State and Local Government. **In** *[White, Charles P.],* 1969, pp. 112–23. **[G: U.S.]**

3241 State and Local Government Expenditures and Budgeting

Aaron, Henry J. Local Public Expenditures and the "Migration Effect." *Western Econ. J.,* December 1969, *7*(4), pp. 385–90.

Barlow, Robin. A Comment on Alternative Federal Policies for Stimulating State and Local Expenditures. *Nat. Tax J.,* June 1969, *22*(2), pp. 282–85.

Basso, Louis G. PPBS in Wayne County, Michigan. **In** *Innovations in Planning, Programming, and Budgeting in State and Local Governments, JECP,* 1969, pp. 191–211. **[G: U.S.]**

Beach, Edwin W. California's Programing and Budgeting System. **In** *Innovations in Planning, Programming, and Budgeting in State and Local Governments, JECP,* 1969, pp. 27–35. **[G: U.S.]**

Bolton, Roger E. Predictive Models for State and Local Government Purchases. **In** *Duesenberry, J. S., et al.,* 1969, pp. 221–67. **[G: U.S.]**

Bradford, David F.; Malt, R. A. and Oates, Wallace E. The Rising Cost of Local Public Services: Some Evidence and Reflections. *Nat. Tax J.,* June 1969, *22*(2), pp. 185–202. **[G: U.S.]**

Brown, Paul L. An Evaluation of PPBS Developments in Wisconsin. **In** *Innovations in Planning, Programming, and Budgeting in State and Local Governments, JECP,* 1969, pp. 53–61. **[G: U.S.]**

Brunn, Stanley D. and Hoffman, Wayne L. The Geography of Federal Grants-in-Aid to States. *Econ. Geogr.,* July 1969, *45*(3), pp. 226–38. **[G: U.S.]**

Burns, Joseph M. and Chiswick, Barry R. An Economic Analysis of State Support for Higher Education. *Western Econ. J.,* March 1969, *7*(1), pp. 84–95.

Carlson, Jack W. Federal Support of State and Local Government Planning, Programing, and Budgeting. **In** *Innovations in Planning, Programming, and Budgeting in State and Local Governments, JECP,* 1969, pp. 15–26. **[G: U.S.]**

Cauley, Troy J. Public Expenditures in Our Federal System. *Rivista Int. Sci. Econ. Com.,* September 1969, *16*(9), pp. 898–919. **[G: U.S.]**

Crew, Robert E., Jr. Dimensions of Public Policy: A Factor Analysis of State Expenditures. *Soc. Sci. Quart.,* September 1969, *50*(2), pp. 381–88. **[G: U.S.]**

Gabler, L. R. Economies and Diseconomies of Scale in Urban Public Sectors. *Land Econ.,* November 1969, *45*(4), pp. 425–34. **[G: U.S.]**

Gramlich, Edward M. A Clarification and a Correction. *Nat. Tax J.,* June 1969, *22*(2), pp. 286–90.

Grizzle, Gloria. PPBS in Dade County: Status of Development and Implementation. **In** *Innovations in Planning, Programming, and Budgeting in State and Local Governments, JECP,* 1969, pp. 63–73. **[G: U.S.]**

Hauser, G. Measuring Efficiency in Government Services: Comment. **In** *Peacock, A. T., ed.,* 1969, pp. 104–09.

Hirsch, Werner Z. and Marcus, Morton J. Intercommunity Spillovers and the Provision of Public Education. *Kyklos,* 1969, *22*(4), pp. 641–60. **[G: U.S.]**

Hollinger, L. S. Changing Rules of the Budget Game: The Development of a Planning-Programing-Budgeting-System for Los Angeles County. **In** *Innovations in Planning, Programming, and Budgeting in State and Local Governments, JECP,* 1969, pp. 75–90. **[G: U.S.]**

Horton, Robert A. Planning, Programing, and Budgeting in Metropolitan Nashville-Davidson County, Tennessee. **In** *Innovations in Planning, Programming, and Budgeting in State and Local Governments, JECP,* 1969, pp. 91–103. **[G: U.S.]**

Hutton J. P. Measuring Efficiency in Government Services. **In** *Peacock, A. T., ed.,* 1969, pp. 91–103.

Jones, Roger H. Program Budgeting: Fiscal Facts And Federal Fancy. *Quart. Rev. Econ. Bus.,* Summer 1969, *9*(2), pp. 45–57. **[G: U.S.]**

Landynski, Jacob W. Governmental Aid to Non-public Schools: The Constitutional Conflict Sharpens. *Soc. Res.*, Autumn 1969, *36*(3), pp. 333–56. [G: U.S.]

Maxwell, James A. Federal Grant Elasticity and Distortion. *Nat. Tax J.*, December 1969, *22*(4), pp. 550–51. [G: U.S.]

Mc Intyre, M. Charles. Determinants of Expenditures for Public Higher Education. *Nat. Tax J.*, June 1969, *22*(2), pp. 262–72. [G: U.S.]

Meiszer, Nicholas M. Developing a Planning-Programing-Budgeting System in the City of Dayton, Ohio. **In** *Innovations in Planning, Programming, and Budgeting in State and Local Governments, JECP,* 1969, pp. 213–18. [G: U.S.]

Michas, Nicholas A. Variations in the Level of Provincial-Municipal Expenditures in Canada: An Econometric Analysis. *Public Finance,* 1969, *24* (4), pp. 597–617. [G: Canada]

Mushkin, Selma J. PPBS in City, State, and County: An Overview. **In** *Innovations in Planning, Programming, and Budgeting in State and Local Governments, JECP,* 1969, pp. 1–14. [G: U.S.]

Schultze, Charles L. Using Incentives to Improve the Effectiveness of Government. *Mon. Lab. Rev.*, September 1969, *92*(9), pp. 34–38.

Seyler, David A. The New York State Planning, Programing, and Budgeting System. **In** *Innovations in Planning, Programming, and Budgeting in State and Local Governments, JECP,* 1969, pp. 48–52. [G: U.S.]

Shoup, Donald C. Advance Land Acquisition by Local Governments: A Cost-Benefit Analysis. *Yale Econ. Essays,* Fall 1969, *9*(2), pp. 147–207. [G: U.S.]

Smith, David L. Federal Grant Elasticity and Distortion: A Reply. *Nat. Tax J.*, December 1969, *22*(4), pp. 552–53. [G: U.S.]

Sternberger, H.; Renz, J. and Fasolina, G. Planning-Programing-Budgeting System (PPBS) in Nassau County, N.Y. **In** *Innovations in Planning, Programming, and Budgeting in State and Local Governments, JECP,* 1969, pp. 105–89. [G: U.S.]

Stewart, I. G. Statistics on Expenditures in Scotland. **In** *Wolfe, J. N., ed.*, 1969, pp. 123–39. [G: U.K.]

Walker, Jack L. The Diffusion of Innovations among the American States. *Amer. Polit. Sci. Rev.*, September 1969, *63*(3), pp. 880–99. [G: U.S.]

Wileden, Paul H. Development of a PPB System in the State of Michigan. **In** *Innovations in Planning, Programming, and Budgeting in State and Local Governments, JECP,* 1969, pp. 36–47. [G: U.S.]

3242 State and Local Government Taxation, Subsidies, and Revenue

Aaron, Henry J. Some Observations on Property Tax Valuation and the Significance of Full Value Assessment. **In** *Lynn, A. D., Jr., ed.*, 1969, pp. 153–66. [G: U.S.]

Back, Kenneth C. Potential for Organizational Improvement of Property Tax Administration. **In** *Lynn, A. D., Jr., ed.*, 1969, pp. 31–43. [G: U.S.]

Bahl, Roy W. and Shellhammer, Kenneth L. Evaluating the State Business Tax Structure: An Application of Input-Output Analysis. *Nat. Tax J.*, June 1969, *22*(2), pp. 203–16. [G: U.S.]

Becker, Arthur P. Principles of Taxing Land and Buildings for Economic Development. **In** *Becker, A. P., ed.*, 1969, pp. 11–47.

Becker, Arthur P. Property Tax Problems Confronting State and Local Governments. **In** *[White, Charles P.]*, 1969, pp. 34–47. [G: U.S.]

Bittker, Boris I. Churches, Taxes and the Constitution. *Yale Law J.*, July 1969, *78*(8), pp. 1285–1310. [G: U.S.]

Botha, D. J. J. Local Taxation in South Africa. *S. Afr. J. Econ.*, December 1969, *37*(4), pp. 393–438. [G: S. Africa]

Brown, Elizabeth Read and Brown, Harry Gunnison. An Attack on Tax Reform in Hawaii. *Amer. J. Econ. Soc.*, January 1969, *28*(1), pp. 106–08. [G: U.S.]

Bruno, James Edward. Achieving Property Tax Relief with a Minimum Disruption of State Programs. *Nat. Tax J.*, September 1969, *22*(3), pp. 379–89. [G: U.S.]

Carleton, Willard T. and Lerner, Eugene M. Statistical Credit Scoring of Municipal Bonds. *J. Money, Credit, Banking,* November 1969, *1*(4), pp. 750–64.

Char, S. V. Agricultural Income Tax and the Indian Constitution. *Artha-Vikas,* July 1969, *5*(2), pp. 177–82. [G: India]

Chase, Richard X. State Sales Taxation as a Budget Balancing Device. *Amer. J. Econ. Soc.*, October 1969, *28*(4), pp. 405–07. [G: U.S.]

Davis, Otto A. and Wertz, Kenneth L. The Consistency of the Assessment of Property: Some Empirical Results and Managerial Suggestions. *Appl. Econ.*, May 1969, *1*(2), pp. 151–57. [G: U.S.]

Donovan, C. H. Recent Developments in Property Taxation in Florida: A Case Study. **In** *[White, Charles P.]*, 1969, pp. 48–59. [G: U.S.]

Due, John F. The Somers Solution to the Use Tax: A Comment. *Nat. Tax J.*, June 1969, *22*(2), pp. 301.

Eilers, Robert D. Minimum Premium Health Plans: Insured Non-Insurance. *J. Risk Ins.*, March 1969, *36*(1), pp. 63–84. [G: U.S.]

Engelbert, Ernest A. The Political Aspects of Real Estate Taxation in Relation to Metropolitan Growth and Planning. **In** *Becker, A. P., ed.*, 1969, pp. 97–114. [G: U.S.]

Ferraro, Anthony G. Valuation of Property Interests for *Ad Valorem* Taxation of Extractive Industry and Agricultural Realty: Problems and Solutions. **In** *Lynn, A. D., Jr., ed.*, 1969, pp. 119–39. [G: U.S.]

Fryman, Richard F. Sales Taxation of Producers' Goods in Illinois. *Nat. Tax J.*, June 1969, *22*(2), pp. 273–81. [G: U.S.]

Grey, Arthur L., Jr. Urban Renewal and Land Value Taxation. **In** *Becker, A. P., ed.*, 1969, pp. 81–96. [G: U.S.]

Groves, Harold M. Is the Property Tax Conceptually and Practically Administrable? **In** *Lynn, A. D., Jr., ed.*, 1969, pp. 15–28. [G: U.S.]

Hady, Thomas F. Tax Structure and Regional Economic Growth: A Comment. *J. Reg. Sci.*, August 1969, *9*(2), pp. 325–26. [G: U.S.]

Hale, Carl W. The Optimality of Local Subsidies in Regional Development Programs. *Quart. Rev. Econ. Bus.,* Autumn 1969, *9*(3), pp. 35–50. **[G: U.S.]**

Heilbrun, James. Reforming the Real Estate Tax to Encourage Housing Maintenance and Rehabilitation. **In** *Becker, A. P., ed.,* 1969, pp. 63–79. **[G: U.S.]**

Henley, Albert T. Land Value Taxation by California Irrigation Districts. **In** *Becker, A. P., ed.,* 1969, pp. 137–45. **[G: U.S.]**

Holland, Daniel M. A Study of Land Taxation in Jamaica. **In** *Becker, A. P., ed.,* 1969, pp. 239–86. **[G: Jamaica]**

Holland, Daniel M. and Vaughn, William M. An Evaluation of Self-Assessment under a Property Tax. **In** *Lynn, A. D., Jr., ed.,* 1969, pp. 79–118. **[G: U.S.]**

Huiskamp, J. C. L. Some General Principles of Dutch Tax Law. *Bull. Int. Fiscal Doc.,* July, August, September 1969, *23*(7–8–9), pp. 285–96. **[G: Netherlands]**

Johnson, James A. The Distribution of the Burden of Sewer User Charges under Various Charge Formulas. *Nat. Tax J.,* December 1969, *22*(4), pp. 472–85.

Kafoglis, Milton Z. Local Service Charges: Theory and Practice. **In** *[White, Charles P.],* 1969, pp. 164–86. **[G: U.S.]**

Kafoglis, Milton Z. and Keig, Norman G. New Policies of the Federal Power Commission. *Land Econ.,* November 1969, *45*(4), pp. 385–91. **[G: U.S.]**

Laird, William E. and Rinehart, James R. A Refinement of Local Industrial Subsidy Techniques: Reply. *Miss. Val. J. Bus. Econ.,* Spring 1969, *4*(2), pp. 82–88.

Legler, John B. and Shapiro, Perry. The Responsiveness of State Tax Revenue to Economic Growth: A Reply. *Nat. Tax J.,* June 1969, *22*(2), pp. 299–300.

Leong, Y. S. and Rhyne, Iola. Hawaii's Inversely Graduated Tax Credits. *Nat. Tax J.,* December 1969, *22*(4), pp. 446–65. **[G: U.S.]**

Lile, Stephen E. and Soule, Don M. Interstate Differences in Family Tax Burdens. *Nat. Tax J.,* December 1969, *22*(4), pp. 433–45. **[G: U.S.]**

Liu, Ben-Chieh. Comments on the Responsiveness of State Tax Revenue to Economic Growth. *Nat. Tax J.,* June 1969, *22*(2), pp. 294–98.

Low, Richard E. A Refinement of Local Industrial Subsidy Techniques: Comment. *Miss. Val. J. Bus. Econ.,* Spring 1969, *4*(2), pp. 78–81.

Lynn, Arthur D., Jr. Reform of Property Tax Systems: Substance or Semantics. **In** *[White, Charles P.],* 1969, pp. 23–33. **[G: U.S.]**

Lynn, Arthur D., Jr. The Institutional Context of Property Tax Administration. **In** *Lynn, A. D., Jr., ed.,* 1969, pp. 3–14. **[G: U.S.]**

Mark, Shelley M. Property Tax Administration and Hawaii's Land Use Law. **In** *Lynn, A. D., Jr., ed.,* 1969, pp. 187–202. **[G: U.S.]**

Martin, James W. New Dimensions of the Capitalization of Earnings in Appraising Public Utility Property. **In** *[White, Charles P.],* 1969, pp. 148–63. **[G: U.S.]**

McLure, Charles E., Jr. The Inter-regional Incidence of General Regional Taxes. *Public Finance,* 1969, *24*(3), pp. 457–85.

Mikesell, John. A Look at Local Sales Tax Costs. *Indiana Bus. Rev.,* March–April 1969, *44,* pp. 17–22. **[G: U.S.]**

Netzer, Dick. The Property Tax Case for Federal Tax Sharing. **In** *[White, Charles P.],* 1969, pp. 88–102. **[G: U.S.]**

Neutze, Max. Property Taxation and Multiple-Family Housing. **In** *Becker, A. P., ed.,* 1969, pp. 115–28.

Ojha, P. D. and Lent, George E. Sales Taxes in Countries of the Far East. *Int. Monet. Fund Staff Pap.,* November 1969, *16*(3), pp. 529–81. **[G: Far East]**

Prentice, P. I. The Case for Taxing Location Values: A Memorandum for a Metropolis Considering Property Tax Reform. *Amer. J. Econ. Soc.,* April 1969, *28*(2), pp. 145–58. **[G: U.S.]**

Prescott, James R. and Lewis, William C. State and Municipal Locational Incentives: A Discriminant Analysis. *Nat. Tax J.,* September 1969, *22*(3), pp. 399–407. **[G: U.S.]**

Quindry, Kenneth E. and Cook, Billy D. Humanization of the Property Tax for Low Income Households. *Nat. Tax J.,* September 1969, *22*(3), pp. 357–67. **[G: U.S.]**

Ray, Cadwell L. The Yield and Distribution of Potential Business Taxes: Texas as a Case Study. *Soc. Sci. Quart.,* March 1969, *49*(4), pp. 853–63. **[G: U.S.]**

Rhoads, William G. and Bird, Richard M. The Valorization Tax in Colombia: An Example for other Developing Countries? **In** *Becker, A. P., ed.,* 1969, pp. 201–37. **[G: Colombia]**

Schaaf, A. H. Effects of Property Taxation on Slums and Renewal: A Study of Land-Improvement Assessment Ratios. *Land Econ.,* February 1969, *45* (1), pp. 111–17. **[G: U.S.]**

Schaefer, Jeffrey M. Clothing Exemptions and Sales Tax Regressivity. *Amer. Econ. Rev.,* Part I, September 1969, *59*(4), pp. 596–99. **[G: U.S.]**

Schaefer, Jeffrey M. Sales Tax Regressivity under Alternative Tax Bases and Income Concepts. *Nat. Tax J.,* December 1969, *22*(4), pp. 516–27. **[G: U.S.]**

Schaefer, Jeffrey M. The Regressivity of State-Local Taxation: A Case Study of New Jersey. *Quart. Rev. Econ. Bus.,* Spring 1969, *9*(1), pp. 7–18. **[G: U.S.]**

Sehgal, R. K. Tax Efforts of States. *Asian Econ. Rev.,* August 1969, *11*(4), pp. 438–45. **[G: India]**

Shannon, John. Ways the Federal Government May Strengthen State and Local Financing. **In** *[White, Charles P.],* 1969, pp. 103–11. **[G: U.S.]**

Sherman, Roger and Willett, Thomas D. Regional Development, Externalities and Tax-Subsidy Combinations. *Nat. Tax J.,* June 1969, *22*(2), pp. 291–93.

Singhvi, Surendra S. and Slamka, John G. Industrial Revenue Bonds: A Source of Long-Term Financing. *Calif. Manage. Rev.,* Spring 1969, *11*(3), pp. 53–60. **[G: U.S.]**

Somers, Harold M. The Somers Solution to the Use Tax: Reply. *Nat. Tax J.,* June 1969, *22*(2), pp. 302.

Stephens, G. Ross. The Suburban Impact of Earnings Tax Policies. *Nat. Tax J.*, September 1969, *22*(3), pp. 313–33. **[G: U.S.]**

Stocker, Frederick D. Assessment of Land in Urban-Rural Fringe Areas. **In** *Lynn, A. D., Jr., ed.*, 1969, pp. 141–52. **[G: U.S.]**

Struyk, Raymond J. Tax Structure and Regional Economic Growth: A Reply. *J. Reg. Sci.*, August 1969, *9*(2), pp. 327–28. **[G: U.S.]**

Tarbet, Joseph R. Present and Proposed Direct Federal, State, and Local Taxes in Washington Compared with Idaho and Oregon. *Univ. Wash. Bus. Rev.*, Autumn 1969, *29*(1), pp. 5–17. **[G: U.S.]**

Tarbet, Joseph R. Washington's 1969 Income Tax Proposal and Its Effect on Individuals and Families. *Univ. Wash. Bus. Rev.*, Summer 1969, *28*(4), pp. 18–24. **[G: U.S.]**

Taubman, Paul. Econometric Functions for Government Receipts. **In** *Duesenberry, J. S., et al.*, 1969, pp. 188–220. **[G: U.S.]**

Trestrail, Richard W. Forests and the Property Tax —Unsound Accepted Theory. *Nat. Tax J.*, September 1969, *22*(3), pp. 347–56.

Weidenbaum, Murray L. Federal Aid to the States: An Analytical Examination of the Alternatives. *Amer. J. Econ. Soc.*, October 1969, *28*(4), pp. 367–83. **[G: U.S.]**

Welch, Ronald B. Property Taxation: Policy Potentials and Probabilities. **In** *Lynn, A. D., Jr., ed.*, 1969, pp. 203–14. **[G: U.S.]**

Wicks, John H. and McDonald, Patrick G. Income Distribution of Death Bequest Recipients. *Nat. Tax J.*, September 1969, *22*(3), pp. 408–10. **[G: U.S.]**

Wolff, Carole E. and Landis, Judson R. Dr. Irene Hickman and Tax Reform in Sacramento County, Calif. *Amer. J. Econ. Soc.*, October 1969, *28*(4), pp. 409–21. **[G: U.S.]**

Woodruff, A. M. Assessment Standards: Highest and Best Use as a Basis for Land Appraisal and Assessment. **In** *Lynn, A. D., Jr., ed.*, 1969, pp. 167–83. **[G: U.S.]**

Woodruff, A. M. and Ecker-Racz, L. L. Property Taxes and Land-Use Patterns in Australia and New Zealand. **In** *Becker, A. P., ed.*, 1969, pp. 147–86. **[G: Australia; New Zealand]**

3243 State and Local Government Borrowing

Daly, George G. The Burden of the Debt and Future Generations in Local Finance. *Southern Econ. J.*, July 1969, *36*(1), pp. 44–51.

Howard, Robert E. Local, National Municipal Bond Markets Are Uncertain. *Indiana Bus. Rev.*, September/October 1969, *44*, pp. 13–14. **[G: U.S.]**

Lees, Francis A. Interregional Flows of Funds through State and Local Government Securities (1957–1962). *J. Reg. Sci.*, April 1969, *9*(1), pp. 79–86. **[G: U.S.]**

Ross, William D. and Bonin, Joseph M. Economic Criteria for Sound State Debt Financing. **In** *[White, Charles P.]*, 1969, pp. 127–47. **[G: U.S.]**

Stober, William J. and Falk, Laurence H. Industrial Development Bonds as a Subsidy to Industry. *Nat. Tax J.*, June 1969, *22*(2), pp. 232–43. **[G: U.S.]**

Walker, John E. The "Net Interest Cost" Method of Issuing Tax Exempt Bonds: Is It Rational?—A Comment. *Public Finance*, 1969, *24*(4), pp. 624–26.

West, Richard R. The "Net Interest Cost" Method of Issuing Tax Exempt Bonds: Is It Rational?—A Reply to Professor Walker. *Public Finance*, 1969, *24*(4), pp. 627–30.

325 Intergovernmental Financial Relationships

3250 Intergovernmental Financial Relationships

Adams, Esmond and Fish, Mary. Comments on the Impact of Federal Tax-Sharing on Economic Stabilization. *Nebr. J. Econ. Bus.*, Winter 1968–69, *8*(1), pp. 53–60.

Barlow, Robin. A Comment on Alternative Federal Policies for Stimulating State and Local Expenditures. *Nat. Tax J.*, June 1969, *22*(2), pp. 282–85.

Bhatt, V. V. On the Magnitude and Allocation of Federal Assistance to the States in India: Some Rational Criteria. *Public Finance*, 1969, *24*(4), pp. 563–76. **[G: India]**

Brown, Sue Ellen and Lynn, Arthur D., Jr. Federal Revenue Sharing with the States: Implications for Effective Federalism. *Ohio State U. Bull. Bus. Res.*, November 1969, *44*(11), pp. 6–8. **[G: U.S.]**

Brunn, Stanley D. and Hoffman, Wayne L. The Geography of Federal Grants-in-Aid to States. *Econ. Geogr.*, July 1969, *45*(3), pp. 226–38. **[G: U.S.]**

Buchanan, James M. Financing a Viable Federalism. **In** *[White, Charles P.]*, 1969, pp. 3–19. **[G: U.S.]**

Campfield, W. L. Administration of Grants—Is the Federalist Partnership Synergistic or Symbiotic? *Univ. Missouri Bus. Govt. Rev.*, July–August 1969, *10*(4), pp. 7–12. **[G: U.S.]**

Eapen, A. T. A Critique of Indian Fiscal Federalism. *Public Finance*, 1969, *24*(4), pp. 537–62. **[G: India]**

Ecker-Racz, L. L. Tax Simplification in this Federal System. *Law Contemp. Probl.*, Autumn 1969, *34*(4), pp. 769–81. **[G: U.S.]**

Graaff, Jan de V. The National Debt. *S. Afr. J. Econ.*, September 1969, *37*(3), pp. 170–86. **[G: S. Africa]**

Gramlich, Edward M. A Clarification and a Correction. *Nat. Tax J.*, June 1969, *22*(2), pp. 286–90.

Harmston, Floyd K. The Impact of Federal Expenditures on Missouri, Fiscal Year 1967. *Univ. Missouri Bus. Govt. Rev.*, November–December 1969, *10*(6), pp. 5–12. **[G: U.S.]**

Hoffman, Ronald F. A Systematic Approach to a Practicable Plan for State Aid to Local Governments. *Public Finance*, 1969, *24*(1), pp. 1–32.

Kullmer, Lore. Problems of the Financial Reform in the Federal Republic of Germany. *Ger. Econ. Rev.*, 1969, *7*(1), pp. 63–71. **[G: W. Germany]**

Levitan, Sar A. The Community Action Program: A Strategy to Fight Poverty. *Ann. Amer. Acad. Po-*

lit. Soc. Sci., September 1969, *385*, pp. 63–75. [G: U.S.]

Maxwell, James A. Federal Grant Elasticity and Distortion. *Nat. Tax J.*, December 1969, *22*(4), pp. 550–51. [G: U.S.]

Maxwell, James A. Federal Grants in Canada and Australia. *Econ. Rec.*, September 1969, *45*(111), pp. 441–48. [G: Canada; Australia]

Musgrave, Richard A. Theories of Fiscal Federalism. *Public Finance*, 1969, *24*(4), pp. 521–36.

Mushkin, Selma J. and Cotton, John. Systematic Analysis and Grants-in-Aid in a Federal System. **In** *The Analysis and Evaluation of Public Expenditures: The PPB System, Vol. 1, JECP*, 1969, pp. 332–54. [G: U.S.]

Netzer, Dick. The Property Tax Case for Federal Tax Sharing. **In** *[White, Charles P.]*, 1969, pp. 88–102. [G: U.S.]

Pechman, Joseph A. Tax Policies for the 1970's. *Public Policy*, Fall 1969, *18*(1), pp. 75–93. [G: U.S.]

Rothenberg, Jerome. Strategic Interaction and Resource Allocation in Metropolitan Intergovernmental Relations. *Amer. Econ. Rev.*, May 1969, *59* (2), pp. 494–503.

Rubin, Lillian B. Maximum Feasible Participation: The Origins, Implications, and Present Status. *Ann. Amer. Acad. Polit. Soc. Sci.*, September 1969, *385*, pp. 14–29. [G: U.S.]

Shannon, John. Ways the Federal Government May Strengthen State and Local Financing. **In** *[White, Charles P.]*, 1969, pp. 103–11. [G: U.S.]

Shearer, John. Statement. **In** *Tax Credits to Stimulate Job Opportunities in Rural Areas, SCH*, 1969, pp. 157–62. [G: U.S.]

Smith, David L. Federal Grant Elasticity and Distortion: A Reply. *Nat. Tax J.*, December 1969, *22*(4), pp. 552–53. [G: U.S.]

Stone, Lawrence M. Tax Incentives as a Solution to Urban Problems. **In** *Tax Credits to Stimulate Job Opportunities in Rural Areas, SCH*, 1969, pp. 185–91. [G: U.S.]

Sundquist, James L. Co-ordinating the War on Poverty. *Ann. Amer. Acad. Polit. Soc. Sci.*, September 1969, *385*, pp. 41–49. [G: U.S.]

Teeples, Ronald K. A Model of a Matching Grant-in-Aid Program with External Tax Effects. *Nat. Tax J.*, December 1969, *22*(4), pp. 486–95.

Weidenbaum, Murray L. Federal Aid to the States: An Analytical Examination of the Alternatives. *Amer. J. Econ. Soc.*, October 1969, *28*(4), pp. 367–83. [G: U.S.]

Wolfe, J. N. Problems of Federal Financial Arrangements. **In** *Wolfe, J. N., ed.*, 1969, pp. 92–107. [G: U.K.]

Wright, Deil S. The Politics and Economics of Intergovernmental Fiscal Relations: Federal Grants, Tax Credits, and Revenue Sharing. **In** *[White, Charles P.]*, 1969, pp. 63–87. [G: U.S.]

400 International Economics

4000 General

Bloomfield, Arthur I. Recent Trends in International Economics. *Ann. Amer. Acad. Polit. Soc. Sci.*, November 1969, *386*, pp. 148–67.

410 International Trade Theory

411 International Trade Theory

4110 General

Armington, Paul S. The Geographic Pattern of Trade and the Effects of Price Changes. *Int. Monet. Fund Staff Pap.*, July 1969, *16*(2), pp. 179–201. [G: E.E.C.; U.K.; Canada; U.S.; Japan]

Inada, Ken-Ichi and Kemp, Murray C. International Capital Movements and the Theory of Tariffs and Trade: Comment. *Quart. J. Econ.*, August 1969, *83*(3), pp. 524–28.

Johnson, Harry G. Comparative Cost and Commercial Policy Theory in a Developing Economy. *Pakistan Develop. Rev.*, Spring Supplement 1969, *9* (1), pp. 1–33.

Leontief, W. W. The Use of Indifference Curves in the Analysis of Foreign Trade. **In** *Bhagwati, J., ed.*, 1969, pp. 21–29.

Melvin, James R. Demand Conditions and Immiserizing Growth. *Amer. Econ. Rev.*, Part I, September 1969, *59*(4), pp. 604–06.

Samuelson, Paul A. Presidential Address. **In** *Samuelson, P. A., ed.*, 1969, pp. 1–11.

Zandano, Gianni. The Heckscher-Ohlin Model and the Tariff Structures of the Industrial Countries. *Banca Naz. Lavoro Quart. Rev.*, March 1969, (88), pp. 46–65.

4112 Theory of International Trade: Prices, Comparative Advantage, etc.

Armington, Paul S. A Theory of Demand for Products Distinguished by Place of Production. *Int. Monet. Fund Staff Pap.*, March 1969, *16*(1), pp. 159–78.

Atkinson, Anthony B. Import Strategy and Growth under Conditions of Stagnant Export Earnings. *Oxford Econ. Pap.*, November 1969, *21*(3), pp. 325–38. [G: U.K.]

Batra, Raveendra N. Activity Analysis and the Pure Theory of International Trade. *Amer. Econ.*, Spring 1969, *13*(1), pp. 16–27.

Batra, Raveendra N. Changes in Factor-Endowment, the Terms of Trade, and Factor-Price Equalisation. *Amer. Econ.*, Fall 1969, *13*(2), pp. 57–69.

Berry, R. Albert and Hymer, Stephen H. A Note on the Capacity to Transform and the Welfare Costs of Foreign Trade Fluctuations. *Econ. J.*, December 1969, *79*(316), pp. 833–46.

Berry, R. Albert and Soligo, Ronald. Some Welfare Aspects of International Migration. *J. Polit. Econ.*, September/October 1969, *77*(5), pp. 778–94.

Black, J. Foreign Trade and Real Wages. *Econ. J.*, March 1969, *79*(313), pp. 184–85.

Boon, Gerard K. Factor Intensities in Mexico with Special Reference to Manufacturing. **In** *[Tinbergen, J.]*, 1969, pp. 201–18. [G: Mexico]

Borchert, Manfred. An Empirical Investigation of the Heckscher-Ohlin Theory: A Comment. *Economica, N.S.*, May 1969, *36*(142), pp. 193–95.

Caves, Richard E. The Theory of International Trade: Comment. **In** *Samuelson, P. A., ed.,* 1969, pp. 66–70.

Chipman, John S. Factor Price Equalization and the Stolper-Samuelson Theorem. *Int. Econ. Rev.,* October 1969, *10*(3), pp. 399–406.

Csáki, N. Competitive and Complementary International Division of Labour in the Agriculture of Socialist Countries. (In Russian. With English summary.) *Acta Oecon.,* 1969, *4*(3), pp. 283–97. **[G: E. Europe]**

de Dagum, Estela María Bee. An Econometric Model for the Foreign Trade Multiplier of Argentina. *Weltwirtsch. Arch.,* 1969, *103*(1), pp. 26–40. **[G: Argentina]**

Daniels, Mark R. Differences in Efficiency among Industries in Developing Countries. *Amer. Econ. Rev.,* March 1969, *59*(1), pp. 159–71.

Dasgupta, Manas. A Note on the Possibility of Creating Export Surplus in Manufactures from the Underdeveloped Countries. *Econ. Aff.,* January-February 1969, *14*(1–2), pp. 68–70.

Diamond, Peter. On the Economics of Tourism. *East Afr. Econ. Rev.,* December 1969, *1*(2), pp. 53–62.

Finger, J. M. Factor Intensity and "Leontief Type" Tests of the Factor Proportions Theory. *Econ. Int.,* August 1969, *22*(3), pp. 405–22.

Ford, J. L. Specific Factors of Production and the Ricardian and Ohlinian Doctrines. *Yorkshire Bull. Econ. Soc. Res.,* November 1969, *21*(2), pp. 119–31.

Ford, J. L. Variable Returns to Scale and the Factor-Price Equalisation Theorem. *Rivista Int. Sci. Econ. Com.,* August 1969, *16*(8), pp. 756–80.

Herberg, Horst. On the Shape of the Transformation Curve in the Case of Homogenous Production Functions. *Z. ges. Staatswiss.,* April 1969, *125*(2), pp. 202–10.

Holzman, Franklyn D. Import Bottlenecks and the Foreign Trade Multiplier. *Western Econ. J.,* June 1969, *7*(2), pp. 101–08.

Hong, Wontack. A Global Equilibrium Pattern of Specialization: A Model to Approximate Linder's World of Production and Trade. *Swedish J. Econ.,* December 1969, *71*(4), pp. 275–83.

Houthakker, Hendrik S. and Magee, Stephen P. Income and Price Elasticities in World Trade. *Rev. Econ. Statist.,* May 1969, *51*(2), pp. 111–25.

Hutcheson, Thomas L. Factor Intensity and the CES Production Function. *Rev. Econ. Statist.,* November 1969, *51*(4), pp. 468–70.

Johnson, Harry G. The Theory of International Trade. **In** *Samuelson, P. A., ed.,* 1969, pp. 55–66.

Johnson, Harry G. The Theory of International Trade: Reply. **In** *Samuelson, P. A., ed.,* 1969, pp. 78–80.

Katrak, Homi. An Empirical Test of Comparative Cost Theories: Japan, Peru, the United Kingdom and the United States. *Economica, N.S.,* November 1969, *36*(144), pp. 389–99. **[G: Japan; Peru; U.K.; U.S.]**

Kemp, Murray C. and Wegge, Leon L. F. On the Relation between Commodity Prices and Factor Rewards. *Int. Econ. Rev.,* October 1969, *10*(3), pp. 407–13.

Kemp, Murray C. The Theory of International Trade: Comment. **In** *Samuelson, P. A., ed.,* 1969, pp. 71–73.

Khang, Chulsoon. A Dynamic Model of Trade Between the Final and the Intermediate Products. *J. Econ. Theory,* December 1969, *1*(4), pp. 416–37.

Kreinin, Mordechai E. The Theory of Comparative Cost—Further Empirical Evidence. *Econ. Int.,* November 1969, *22*(4), pp. 662–74.

Mäler, Karl-Göran. Optimal Pricing in Agricultural Emergency Policies. *Swedish J. Econ.,* December 1969, *71*(4), pp. 247–62.

Melvin, James R. Intermediate Goods, the Production Possibility Curve, and Gains from Trade. *Quart. J. Econ.,* February 1969, *83*(1), pp. 141–51.

Melvin, James R. Mill's Law of International Value. *Southern Econ. J.,* October 1969, *36*(2), pp. 107–16.

Melvin, James R. On a Demand Assumption Made by Graham. *Southern Econ. J.,* July 1969, *36*(1), pp. 36–43.

Minabe, Nobuo. A Note on the Marshall Condition: Comment. *Southern Econ. J.,* October 1969, *36* (2), pp. 210–14.

Murray, Tracy W. Activity Analysis and the Pure Theory of International Trade: Comment. *Amer. Econ.,* Spring 1969, *13*(1), pp. 27–29.

Negishi, Takashi. Marshallian External Economies and Gains from Trade between Similar Countries. *Rev. Econ. Stud.,* January 1969, *36*(105), pp. 131–35.

Norton, W. E.; Jackson, G. H. and Sweeny, K. M. A Demand Equation for Imports. *Econ. Rec.,* December 1969, *45*(112), pp. 589–95. **[G: Australia]**

Officer, Lawrence H. A Comparison of the Effects of Monopoly and Competition in Commodity Markets upon the Foreign-Exchange Market. *Western Econ. J.,* December 1969, *7*(4), pp. 360–64.

Olivera, Julio H. G. Is Labour Mobility a Substitute for Trade?—A Reply. *Econ. J.,* March 1969, *79* (313), pp. 178–79.

Pitchford, J. D. A Note on International Trade and Factor Mobility. *Econ. Rec.,* December 1969, *45* (112), pp. 616–17.

Rakowski, James. Is Labour Mobility a Substitute for Trade? *Econ. J.,* March 1969, *79*(313), pp. 174–78.

Ranki, Risto. Kauppavirta-analyysi ja trendimatriisi. (Trend Matrix in Markov Analysis of Trade Flows. With English summary.) *Kansant. Aikak.,* 1969, *65*(2), pp. 122–32. **[G: Finland; E.F.T.A.; Japan; E.E.C.; N. America]**

Schlieper, Ulrich. Eine Verallgemeinerung des Optimalzolltheorems. (With English summary.) *Z. ges. Staatswiss.,* July 1969, *125*(3), pp. 296–405.

Schröder, Jürgen. Zur partialanalytischen Darstellung des direkten internationalen Preiszusammenhangs. Bemerkungen zu einem Aufsatz von O. Issing. (With English summary.) *Jahr. Nationalökon. Statist.,* August 1969, *183*(3–4), pp. 306–15.

Sherk, Donald R. The New International Trade Models and Their Relevance for Developing Asia. *Malayan Econ. Rev.,* October 1969, *14*(2), pp. 1–17. **[G: Asia]**

Sirotti, Vittorio. Sulla stabilita' dell'equilibrio nella teoria pura dello scambio internazionale-II. (On the Stability in the Pure Theory of International Trade-II. With English summary.) *Econ. Int.*, May 1969, *22*(2), pp. 203–24.

Tarnovskii, O. Price Formation on the World Socialist Market. *Prob. Econ.*, October 1969, *12*(6), pp. 42–57.

Tyler, William G. Export Promotion with Increasing Returns to Scale under Imperfect Domestic Market Conditions. *Soc. Econ. Stud.*, December 1969, *18*(4), pp. 402–07.

Vasilev, Dimitur. The International Socialist Division of Labor and Its Role in the Increased Profitability of Bulgaria's Foreign Trade. *Eastern Europ. Econ.*, Fall 1969, *8*(1), pp. 90–99. **[G: Bulgaria]**

Villanueva, Javier. Inversión privada extranjera, desarrollo industrial y comercio internacional. (Direct Foreign Investment in Industry. With English summary.) *Económica,* May–August 1969, *15*(2), pp. 223–42.

Wegge, Leon L. F. and Kemp, Murray C. Generalizations of the Stolper-Samuelson and Samuelson-Rybczynski Theorems in Terms of Conditional Input-Output Coefficients. *Int. Econ. Rev.*, October 1969, *10*(3), pp. 414–25.

Wells, Louis T., Jr. Test of a Product Cycle Model of International Trade: U.S. Exports of Consumer Durables. *Quart. J. Econ.*, February 1969, *83*(1), pp. 152–62. **[G: U.S.]**

Wemelsfelder, J. The Theory of International Trade: Comment. **In** *Samuelson, P. A., ed.*, 1969, pp. 73–78.

White, Lawrence J. Gains from Trade and Income Distribution: Some New Geometric Tools. *Rivista Int. Sci. Econ. Com.*, September 1969, *16*(9), pp. 837–58.

Yamazawa, Ippei. Factor-Proportions Theory Reconsidered. *Hitotsubashi J. Econ.*, February 1969, *9* (2), pp. 43–60.

Yeh, Yeong-Her. A Note on the Marshall Condition: Reply. *Southern Econ. J.*, October 1969, *36*(2), pp. 215–16.

4113 Theory of Protection

Allen, Clark Lee. Are National Full-Employment Policies Consistent with Freer Trade? *Nebr. J. Econ. Bus.*, Winter 1968–69, *8*(1), pp. 3–15.

Anderson, James and Naya, Seiji. Substitution and Two Concepts of Effective Rate of Protection. *Amer. Econ. Rev.*, Part I, September 1969, *59*(4), pp. 607–12.

Arndt, Sven W. Customs Union and the Theory of Tariffs. *Amer. Econ. Rev.*, March 1969, *59*(1), pp. 108–18.

Baldwin, Robert E. The Case against Infant-Industry Tariff Protection. *J. Polit. Econ.*, May/June 1969, *77*(3), pp. 295–305.

Bhagwati, Jagdish N.; Ramaswami, V. K. and Srinivasan, T. N. Domestic Distortions, Tariffs, and the Theory of Optimum Subsidy: Some Further Results. *J. Polit. Econ.*, November/December 1969, *77*(6), pp. 1005–10.

Bhagwati, Jagdish N. and Srinivasan, T. N. Optimal Intervention to Acheive Non-Economic Objectives. *Rev. Econ. Stud.*, January 1969, *36*(105), pp. 27–38.

Bhagwati, Jagdish N. Optimal Policies and Immiserizing Growth. *Amer. Econ. Rev.*, December 1969, *59*(5), pp. 967–70.

Bhagwati, Jagdish N. and Kemp, Murray C. Ranking of Tariffs under Monopoly Power in Trade. *Quart. J. Econ.*, May 1969, *83*(2), pp. 330–35.

Corden, W. M. Effective Protective Rates in the General Equilibrium Model: A Geometric Note. *Oxford Econ. Pap.*, July 1969, *21*(2), pp. 135–41.

Dosser, Douglas; Han, S. S. and Hitiris, Theodore. Trade Effects of Tax Harmonisation: Harmonisation of the Value-added Tax in E.E.C. *Manchester Sch. Econ. Soc. Stud.*, December 1969, *37*(4), pp. 337–46. **[G: E.E.C.]**

Dutta, Amita. Domestic Market Distortions and Customs Union: A Geometrical Analysis. *J. Devel. Stud.*, January 1969, *5*(2), pp. 87–103.

Eckstein, Peter. Uniform versus Differentiated Protective Tariffs. *J. Devel. Stud.*, July 1969, *5*(4), pp. 262–69.

Finger, J. M. Substitution and the Effective Rate of Protection. *J. Polit. Econ.*, November/December 1969, *77*(6), pp. 972–75.

Graaff, Jan de V. On Optimum Tariff Structures. **In** *Arrow, K. J. and Scitovsky, T., eds.*, 1969, pp. 523–40.

Grubel, Herbert G.; Johnson, Harry G. and Rapp, William V. Excise Taxes and Effective Protection: A Note. *Econ. J.*, September 1969, *79*(315), pp. 674–75.

Guisinger, Stephen E. Negative Value Added and the Theory of Effective Protection. *Quart. J. Econ.*, August 1969, *83*(3), pp. 415–33.

Hogan, W. P. Economic Effects of the Australian Protection System. *Econ. Rec.*, December 1969, *45*(112), pp. 513–25. **[G: Australia]**

Humphrey, David B. Measuring the Effective Rate of Protection: Direct and Indirect Effects. *J. Polit. Econ.*, September/October 1969, *77*(5), pp. 834–44. **[G: Argentina]**

Johnson, Harry G. The Theory of Effective Protection and Preferences. *Economica, N.S.*, May 1969, *36*(142), pp. 119–38.

Jones, Ronald W. Tariffs and Trade in General Equilibrium: Comment. *Amer. Econ. Rev.*, June 1969, *59*(3), pp. 418–24.

Kemp, Murray C. and Nagishi, Takashi. Domestic Distortions, Tariffs, and the Theory of Optimum Subsidy. *J. Polit. Econ.*, November/December 1969, *77*(6), pp. 1011–13.

Kreinin, Mordechai E. "Price" vs. "Tariff" Elasticities in International Trade: Reply. *Amer. Econ. Rev.*, March 1969, *59*(1), pp. 200.

Lacroix, Y. and Schouwenaars, W. Effectieve bescherming aan de grenzen van de E.E.G. en het Verenigd Koninkrijk, voor en na de Kennedy-ronde. (Effective Protection at the Borders of the E.E.C. and the United Kingdom before and after the Kennedy-Round. With English summary.) *Tijdschr. Econ.*, 1969, *14*(2), pp. 158–87. **[G: E.E.C.]**

Leith, James Clark and Reuber, Grant L. The Impact of the Industrial Countries' Tariff Structure on Their Imports of Manufactures from Less-

Developed Areas: A Comment. *Economica, N.S.*, February 1969, *36*(141), pp. 75–80.

Melvin, James R. Comments on the Theory of Customs Unions. *Manchester Sch. Econ. Soc. Stud.*, June 1969, *37*(2), pp. 161–68.

Mishan, E. J. A Note on the Costs of Tariffs, Monopolies and Thefts. *Western Econ. J.*, September 1969, *7*(3), pp. 230–33.

Naqvi, Syed Nawab Haider. Protection and Economic Development. *Kyklos*, 1969, *22*(1), pp. 124–54.

Negishi, Takashi. The Customs Union and the Theory of Second Best. *Int. Econ. Rev.*, October 1969, *10*(3), pp. 391–98.

Ophir, Tsvi. The Interaction of Tariffs and Quotas. *Amer. Econ. Rev.*, December 1969, *59*(5), pp. 1002–05.

Ruffin, Roy J. Tariffs, Intermediate Goods, and Domestic Protection. *Amer. Econ. Rev.*, June 1969, *59*(3), pp. 261–69.

Schlieper, Ulrich. Eine Verallgemeinerung des Optimalzolltheorems. (With English summary.) *Z. ges. Staatswiss.*, July 1969, *125*(3), pp. 296–405.

Södersten, Bo and Vind, Karl. Tariffs and Trade in General Equilibrium: Reply. *Amer. Econ. Rev.*, June 1969, *59*(3), pp. 424–26.

Stolper, W. F. and Samuelson, Paul A. Protection and Real Wages. **In** *Bereday, G. Z. F., ed.*, 1969, pp. 245–68.

Streeten, Paul. The Case for Export Subsidies. *J. Devel. Stud.*, July 1969, *5*(4), pp. 270–73.

Walker, Franklin V. The Restrictive Effect of the U.S. Tariff: Comment. *Amer. Econ. Rev.*, December 1969, *59*(5), pp. 963–66. **[G: U.S.]**

Wicksell, Knut. An Object-Lesson in the Tariff Question. **In** *Wicksell, K.*, 1969, pp. 267–87.

Wicksell, Knut. Protection and Free Trade. **In** *Wicksell, K.*, 1969, pp. 250–66.

Wood, G. Donald, Jr. "Price" vs. "Tariff" Elasticities in International Trade: Comment. *Amer. Econ. Rev.*, March 1969, *59*(1), pp. 198–200.

4114 Theory of International Trade and Economic Development

Balassa, Bela. Country Size and Trade Patterns: Comment. *Amer. Econ. Rev.*, March 1969, *59*(1), pp. 201–04.

Bardhan, P. K. Optimum Investment for an Open Economy. **In** *[Ghosal, U. N.]*, 1969, pp. 74–88.

Beckford, George L. The Economics of Agricultural Resource Use and Development in Plantation Economies. *Soc. Econ. Stud.*, December 1969, *18*(4), pp. 321–47.

Berry, R. Albert and Hymer, Stephen H. A Note on the Capacity to Transform and the Welfare Costs of Foreign Trade Fluctuations. *Econ. J.*, December 1969, *79*(316), pp. 833–46.

Bhagwati, Jagdish N. Optimal Policies and Immiserizing Growth. *Amer. Econ. Rev.*, December 1969, *59*(5), pp. 967–70.

Brewster, Havelock and Thomas, Clive Y. Aspects of the Theory of Economic Integration. *J. Common Market Stud.*, December 1969, *8*(2), pp. 110–32.

Bruton, Henry J. The Two Gap Approach to Aid and Development: Comment. *Amer. Econ. Rev.*, June 1969, *59*(3), pp. 439–46.

Chenery, Hollis B. The Two Gap Approach to Aid and Development: Reply to Bruton. *Amer. Econ. Rev.*, June 1969, *59*(3), pp. 446–49.

Dasgupta, Manas. A Note on the Possibility of Creating Export Surplus in Manufactures from the Underdeveloped Countries. *Econ. Aff.*, January-February 1969, *14*(1–2), pp. 68–70.

Desai, Padma. Alternative Measures of Import Substitution. *Oxford Econ. Pap.*, November 1969, *21*(3), pp. 312–24. **[G: India]**

Ezekiel, Hannan. A Wage Goods Approach to the Problem of Investment Allocation in a Developing Economy. *Kansant. Aikak.*, 1969, *65*(3), pp. 181–90.

Gulhati, Ravi. Debt-Servicing as an Aid to Promotion of Trade of Developing Countries: Comment. *Oxford Econ. Pap.*, November 1969, *21*(3), pp. 409–15.

Hemmi, Kenzō. Primary Product Exports and Economic Development: The Case of Silk. **In** *Ohkawa, K.; Johnston, B. F. and Kaneda, H., eds.*, 1969, pp. 303–23. **[G: Japan]**

Hicks, W. Whitney. Primary Exports and Economic Development: An Application of the Staple Theory to Sonora, Mexico. *Can. J. Agr. Econ.*, July 1969, *17*(2), pp. 46–62. **[G: Mexico]**

Honavar, R. M. Debt-Servicing as an Aid to Promotion of Trade of Developing Countries: Comment. *Oxford Econ. Pap.*, November 1969, *21*(3), pp. 416–19.

Hopkins, Terence K. Third World Modernization in Transnational Perspective. *Ann. Amer. Acad. Polit. Soc. Sci.*, November 1969, *386*, pp. 126–36.

Hufbauer, G. C.; Aziz, Nayyara and Ali, Asghar. Cotton Textile and Leather Exports: What Cost Foreign Exchange? *Pakistan Develop. Rev.*, Autumn 1969, *9*(3), pp. 330–42. **[G: Pakistan]**

Ikema, Makoto. The Effect of Economic Growth on the Demand for Imports: A Simple Diagram. *Oxford Econ. Pap.*, March 1969, *21*(1), pp. 66–69.

Keesing, Donald B. Country Size and Trade Patterns: Reply. *Amer. Econ. Rev.*, March 1969, *59*(1), pp. 204.

Khang, Chulsoon. A Neoclassical Growth Model of Vertically Related International Trade. *Osaka Econ. Pap.*, March 1969, *17*(32), pp. 21–29.

Khatkhate, Deena R. Debt-Servicing as an Aid to Promotion of Trade of Developing Countries: A Reply. *Oxford Econ. Pap.*, November 1969, *21*(3), pp. 424–27.

Kolm, Serge-Christophe. L'exploitation des nations par les nations. (With English summary.) *Revue Écon.*, September 1969, *20*(5), pp. 851–72.

Komiya, Ryutaro. Economic Growth and the Balance of Payments: A Monetary Approach. *J. Polit. Econ.*, January/February 1969, *77*(1), pp. 35–48.

Leff, Nathaniel H. The "Exportable Surplus" Approach to Foreign Trade in Underdeveloped Countries. *Econ. Develop. Cult. Change*, April 1969, *17*(3), pp. 346–55.

MacBean, A. I. Foreign Trade Aspects of Development Planning. **In** *Stewart, I. G., ed.*, 1969, pp. 13–25.

van Meerhaeghe, M. A. G. Observations sur la signification des termes d'échange des pays sous-développés. (With English summary.) *Kyklos,* 1969, *22*(3), pp. 566–84.

Myint, H. International Trade and the Developing Countries: Reply. **In** *Samuelson, P. A., ed.,* 1969, pp. 46.

Myint, H. International Trade and the Developing Countries. **In** *Samuelson, P. A., ed.,* 1969, pp. 15–35.

Myint, H. Trade, Education and Economic Development. **In** *Stewart, I. G., ed.,* 1969, pp. 1–12.

Narasimham, M. Debt-Servicing as an Aid to Promotion of Trade of Developing Countries: Comment. *Oxford Econ. Pap.,* November 1969, *21*(3), pp. 404–08.

Newlyn, W. T. Monetary Analysis and Policy in Financially Dependent Economies. **In** *Stewart, I. G., ed.,* 1969, pp. 71–82.

Onitiri, H. M. A. International Trade and the Developing Countries: Comment. **In** *Samuelson, P. A., ed.,* 1969, pp. 35–41.

Sakamoto, Jorge. Industrial Development and Integration of Underdeveloped Countries. *J. Common Market Stud.,* June 1969, *7*(4), pp. 283–304.

Scheepers, C. F. The Effect of Import Substitution on the Volume and Structure of South Africa's Imports, 1926/27–1963/64. *Finance Trade Rev.,* December 1969, *8*(4), pp. 258–71. **[G: S. Africa]**

Sherk, Donald R. The New International Trade Models and Their Relevance for Developing Asia. *Malayan Econ. Rev.,* October 1969, *14*(2), pp. 1–17. **[G: Asia]**

Short, Brock K. Export Promotion in Underdeveloped Countries. *Amer. Econ.,* Fall 1969, *13* (2), pp. 70–79.

Smith, V. Kerry. The Maximization Policies of Less Developed Exporting Countries. *Quart. Rev. Econ. Bus.,* Winter 1969, *4*(9), pp. 84–86.

Sunkel, Osvaldo. National Development Policy and External Dependence in Latin America. *J. Devel. Stud.,* October 1969, *6*(1), pp. 23–48. **[G: Latin America]**

Sutcliffe, R. B. Debt-Servicing as an Aid to Promotion of Trade of Developing Countries: A Further Comment. *Oxford Econ. Pap.,* November 1969, *21*(3), pp. 420–23.

Tyler, William G. Export Promotion with Increasing Returns to Scale under Imperfect Domestic Market Conditions. *Soc. Econ. Stud.,* December 1969, *18*(4), pp. 402–07.

Urquidi, Victor L. International Trade and the Developing Countries: Comment. **In** *Samuelson, P. A., ed.,* 1969, pp. 41–45.

420 Trade Relations; Commercial Policy; International Economic Integration

421 Trade Relations

4210 Trade Relations

Andic, Fuat M. The Development Impact of the EEC on the French and Dutch Caribbean. *J. Common Market Stud.,* September 1969, *8*(1), pp. 19–49. **[G: Dutch Caribbean; French Caribbean; E.E.C.]**

Armington, Paul S. The Geographic Pattern of Trade and the Effects of Price Changes. *Int. Monet. Fund Staff Pap.,* July 1969, *16*(2), pp. 179–201. **[G: E.E.C.; U.K.; Canada; U.S.; Japan]**

Balassa, Bela. Country Size and Trade Patterns: Comment. *Amer. Econ. Rev.,* March 1969, *59*(1), pp. 201–04.

Bambrick, Susan. The Reserve Bank Index of Australian Import Prices. *Econ. Rec.,* September 1969, *45*(111), pp. 399–414. **[G: Australia]**

Berry, R. Albert and Hymer, Stephen H. A Note on the Capacity to Transform and the Welfare Costs of Foreign Trade Fluctuations. *Econ. J.,* December 1969, *79*(316), pp. 833–46.

Bjarnason, Harold F.; McGarry, Michael J. and Schmitz, Andrew. Converting Price Series of Internationally Traded Commodities to a Common Currency Prior to Estimating National Supply and Demand Equations. *Amer. J. Agr. Econ.,* February 1969, *51*(1), pp. 189–92.

Bowman, Charles T. Report on Employment Related to Exports. *Mon. Lab. Rev.,* June 1969, *92* (6), pp. 16–20. **[G: U.S.]**

Bradshaw, Marie T. U.S. Exports to Foreign Affiliates of U.S. Firms. *Surv. Curr. Bus.,* Part I, May 1969, *49*(5), pp. 34–51. **[G: U.S.]**

Brandenburg, Frank. Development, Finance, and Trade. **In** *Abshire, D. M. and Samuels, M. A., eds.,* 1969, pp. 219–52. **[G: Mozambique; Angola; Portuguese Guinea]**

Brigida, Franco. Industria alimentare e sviluppo industriale in italia. (Food Industry and Growth in Italy. With English summary.) *L'Impresa,* March/April 1969, *11*(2), pp. 163–66. **[G: Italy]**

Castro, Amado A. The Philippines and the Industrial Nations. *Philippine Econ. J.,* First Semester 1969, *8*(1), pp. 1–12. **[G: Philippines]**

Chibrikov, G. Exporting Private Capital: Impact on the Exporting Country's Economy. *Prob. Econ.,* December 1969, *12*(8), pp. 23–45. **[G: U.S.]**

Chou, K. R. Hong Kong's Changing Pattern of Trade and Economic Interdependence in Southeast Asia. **In** *Morgan, T. and Spoelstra, N., eds.,* 1969, pp. 155–77. **[G: Hong Kong]**

Churánek, Miloš. Foreign Trade, the Reproduction Process and Personal Consumption. *New Trends Czech. Econ.,* December 1969, (8), pp. 71–88. **[G: Czechoslovakia]**

Clavaux, F. J. The Import Elasticity as a Yardstick for Measuring Trade Creation. *Econ. Int.,* November 1969, *22*(4), pp. 606–12.

Cordell, Arthur J. The Brazilian Soluble Coffee Problem: A Review. *Quart. Rev. Econ. Bus.,* Spring 1969, *9*(1), pp. 29–38. **[G: Brazil]**

Cristureanu, T. Mutații în structura comerțului exterior al României socialiste, expresie a realizărilor în 25 de ani de construire a socialismului. (Changes in the Structure of Romania's Foreign Trade, an Expression of the Achievements Made in 25 Years' Construction of Socialism. With English summary.) *Stud. Cercet. Econ.,* 1969, *3,* pp. 161–71. **[G: Romania]**

Curry, Robert L., Jr. Trade Restraints Injuring the

United States Government. *Quart. Rev. Econ. Bus.*, Autumn 1969, *9*(3), pp. 77–80. [G: U.S.]

de Dagum, Estela María Bee. An Econometric Model for the Foreign Trade Multiplier of Argentina. *Weltwirtsch. Arch.*, 1969, *103*(1), pp. 26–40. [G: Argentina]

Del Gaudio, Vincenzo. Problems and Prospects of Italian Tourism. *Rev. Econ. Cond. Italy*, November 1969, *23*(6), pp. 505–18. [G: Italy]

Driehuis, W. Experiments in Explaining and Forecasting the Invisible Trade of the Netherlands. *Bull. Oxford Univ. Inst. Econ. Statist.*, November 1969, *31*(4), pp. 335–51. [G: Netherlands]

Drysdale, Peter. Japan, Australia, New Zealand: The Prospect for Western Pacific Economic Integration. *Econ. Rec.*, September 1969, *45*(111), pp. 321–42. [G: Japan; Australia; New Zealand]

Dubois-Pelerin, P. E. Le Marché Commun et le commerce international des Six. (Common Market and Its International Trade. With English summary.) *Rivista Int. Sci. Econ. Com.*, June 1969, *16*(6), pp. 568–89.

El-Agraa, Ali M. The Sudan and the Arab Customs Union: A Conflict. *East Afr. Econ. Rev.*, December 1969, *1*(2), pp. 39–51. [G: Sudan; Arab Customs Union]

Erb, Guy F. and Schiavo-Campo, Salvatore. Export Instability, Level of Development, and Economic Size of Less Developed Countries. *Bull. Oxford Univ. Inst. Econ. Statist.*, November 1969, *31*(4), pp. 263–83.

Ernst, Wolfgang. The Foreign Trade Policy of the Mao Tse-Tung Clique. *Chinese Econ. Stud.*, Fall 1969, *3*(1), pp. 33–47. [G: China]

Fan, Liang-Shing. Note on Trade and Distribution of International Reserves. *Indian Econ. J.*, April–June 1969, *16*(4–5), pp. 492–95.

Finger, J. M. Factor Intensity and "Leontief Type" Tests of the Factor Proportions Theory. *Econ. Int.*, August 1969, *22*(3), pp. 405–22.

Flammang, Robert A. Louisiana and the World Economy. **In** *Beard, T. R., ed.*, 1969, pp. 133–47. [G: U.S.]

Forrest, Matthew D. and Yoshihara, Kunio. Japan's Dependence in Contrast with That of Six Other Nations. *Hitotsubashi J. Econ.*, June 1969, *10*(1), pp. 56–62. [G: Japan]

Francuz, Henryk. The International Bank for Economic Cooperation. *Int. Monet. Fund Staff Pap.*, November 1969, *16*(3), pp. 489–503.

Goldman, Marshall I. The East Reaches for Markets. *Foreign Aff.*, July 1969, *47*(4), pp. 721–34. [G: E. Europe]

Goodman, Seymour S. Turkey's Trade Prospects in the Common Market: An Exploratory Study. *J. Common Market Stud.*, June 1969, *7*(4), pp. 305–26. [G: Turkey]

Goreux, Louis M. Prospects for Agricultural Trade of Less Developed Countries. **In** *Thorbecke, E., ed.*, 1969, pp. 15–73.

Graham, Anila. The Export Growth of Agricultural Commodities in Indian International Trade. **In** *Bhuleshkar, A. V., ed.*, 1969, pp. 157–72. [G: India]

Greenwald, Joseph A. Statement. **In** *New Directions for the 1970's: Toward a Strategy of Inter-American Development, Pts. 1-5, HCH*, 1969, pp. 208–09. [G: Latin America]

Hays, S.; Hemming, M. F. W. and Ray, G. F. The Office Machinery Industry in the United Kingdom. *Nat. Inst. Econ. Rev.*, August 1969, (49), pp. 52–73. [G: U.K.]

Herman, Leon M. The Recent Course of East-West Trade. **In** *Grub, P. D. and Holbik, K.*, 1969, pp. 76–80.

Hicks, W. Whitney. Primary Exports and Economic Development: An Application of the Staple Theory to Sonora, Mexico. *Can. J. Agr. Econ.*, July 1969, *17*(2), pp. 46–62. [G: Mexico]

Horsefield, J. Keith. The Fund's Compensatory Financing. *Finance Develop.*, December 1969, *6*(4), pp. 34–37.

Houthakker, Hendrik S. and Magee, Stephen P. Income and Price Elasticities in World Trade. *Rev. Econ. Statist.*, May 1969, *51*(2), pp. 111–25.

Hufbauer, G. C.; Aziz, Nayyara and Ali, Asghar. Cotton Textile and Leather Exports: What Cost Foreign Exchange? *Pakistan Develop. Rev.*, Autumn 1969, *9*(3), pp. 330–42. [G: Pakistan]

Huff, H. Bruce. Canada's Future Role in the World Wheat Market. *Can. J. Agr. Econ.*, February 1969, *17*(1), pp. 1–14. [G: Canada]

Hughes, John J. U.S. Import Demand for Green Coffee by Variety: Comment. *Amer. J. Agr. Econ.*, November 1969, *51*(4), pp. 926–28. [G: U.S.]

Jansen, F. P. and Janssen, L. H. Imports from Developing Countries: A Comparison between EEC, EFTA and USA. **In** *[Tinbergen, J.]*, 1969, pp. 129–56. [G: E.E.C.; E.F.T.A.; U.S.]

Johnson, James F. The Influence of Cost Distance Factors on the Overseas Export of Corn from the United States Midwest. *Econ. Geogr.*, April 1969, *45*(2), pp. 170–79. [G: U.S.]

Kaser, Michael. A Volume Index of Soviet Foreign Trade. *Soviet Stud.*, April 1969, *20*(4), pp. 523–26. [G: U.S.S.R.]

Keesing, Donald B. Country Size and Trade Patterns: Reply. *Amer. Econ. Rev.*, March 1969, *59*(1), pp. 204.

Knudsen, John W. International Trade Policies—The Export Performance of Developing Countries. *Fed. Res. Bank Kansas City Rev.*, July–August 1969, pp. 10–18.

Kouwenhoven, A. De Noordse economische integratie. (Nordic Economic Integration. With English summary.) *De Economist*, September/October 1969, *117*(5), pp. 543–62. [G: Scandanavia]

Kravis, Irving B. and Lipsey, Robert E. International Price Comparisons by Regression Methods. *Int. Econ. Rev.*, June 1969, *10*(2), pp. 233–46.

Kreinin, Mordechai E. The Theory of Comparative Cost—Further Empirical Evidence. *Econ. Int.*, November 1969, *22*(4), pp. 662–74.

Lacroix, Y. and Schouwenaars, W. Effectieve bescherming aan de grenzen van de E.E.G. en het Verenigd Koninkrijk, voor en na de Kennedy-ronde. (Effective Protection at the Borders of the E.E.C. and the United Kingdom before and after the Kennedy-Round. With English summary.) *Tijdschr. Econ.*, 1969, *14*(2), pp. 158–87. [G: E.E.C.]

Legarda, Benito J. The Philippines and the Industrial Nations: Discussion. *Philippine Econ. J.*, First Semester 1969, *8*(1), pp. 13–15. **[G: Philippines]**

Linnemann, Hans. Trade Flows and Geographical Distance or the Importance of Being Neighbours. **In** *[Tinbergen, J.]*, 1969, pp. 111–28.

Major, R. L. The Competitiveness of British Exports since Devaluation. *Nat. Inst. Econ. Rev.*, May 1969, (48), pp. 31–39. **[G: U.K.]**

Manderscheid, Lester V. U.S. Import Demand for Green Coffee by Variety: Reply. *Amer. J. Agr. Econ.*, November 1969, *51*(4), pp. 929. **[G: U.S.]**

Marasco, Enrico. Interpretazione di un boom: l'Export 1968. (1968 Export: A Boom Interpretation. With English summary.) *Mondo Aperto*, April 1969, *23*(2), pp. 97–103. **[G: Italy]**

Marcus, Mildred Rendl. Questions and Problems Concerning the Expansion of East European Trade with the West and the Financing Methodology. *Marquette Bus. Rev.*, Fall 1969, *13*(3), pp. 125–36. **[G: E. Europe]**

Martinov, V. The Changing Character of International Trade and the Problems of Underdeveloped Regions. **In** *Papi, U. and Nunn, C., eds.*, 1969, pp. 163–74.

McQuade, Lawrence C. Statement. **In** *A Review of Balance of Payments Policies, JECH*, 1969, pp. 3–29. **[G: U.S.]**

van Meerhaeghe, M. A. G. Observations sur la signification des termes d'échange des pays sous-développés. (With English summary.) *Kyklos*, 1969, *22*(3), pp. 566–84.

Miller, Etienne H. Foreign Earnings from U.S. Travelers in 1968 Decline Slightly to $3.9 Billion. *Surv. Curr. Bus.*, June 1969, *49*(6), pp. 17–20.

Morgan, A. D. Re-Imports and Imports for Process and Repair. *Nat. Inst. Econ. Rev.*, November 1969, (50), pp. 53–56. **[G: U.K.]**

Mueller, Hans G. Recent Costs Trends in the Steel Industries of the United States, Japan and the European Community. *Econ. Int.*, August 1969, *22*(3), pp. 499–526. **[G: U.S.; Japan; E.E.C.]**

Naya, Seiji and Morgan, Theodore. The Accuracy of International Trade Data: The Case of Southeast Asian Countries. *J. Amer. Statist. Assoc.*, June 1969, *64*(326), pp. 452–67. **[G: S.E. Asia]**

Ng, S. H. The Terms of Trade in the Case of Entrepôt Trade. *Econ. Rec.*, June 1969, *45*(110), pp. 288–90.

Nicolae-Văleanu, Ivanciu. Istoria gîndirii economice Româneşti—probleme şi preocupări. (History of Romanian Economic Thought—Problems and Preoccupations. With English summary.) *Stud. Cercet. Econ.*, 1969, *3*, pp. 185–98. **[G: Romania]**

Norton, W. E.; Jackson, G. H. and Sweeny, K. M. A Demand Equation for Imports. *Econ. Rec.*, December 1969, *45*(112), pp. 589–95. **[G: Australia]**

Officer, Lawrence H. and Hurtubise, Jules R. Price Effects of the Kennedy Round on Canadian Trade. *Rev. Econ. Statist.*, August 1969, *51*(3), pp. 320–33. **[G: U.S.; Canada]**

Piňdák, F. Czechoslovakia and COMECON. *De Economist*, September/October 1969, *117*(5), pp. 516–42. **[G: Czechoslovakia; COMECON]**

Porter, R. C. Who Destabilizes Primary Product Prices? *Indian Econ. J.*, April–June 1969, *16*(4–5), pp. 389–418.

Ranki, Risto. Kauppavirta-analyysi ja trendimatriisi. (Trend Matrix in Markov Analysis of Trade Flows. With English summary.) *Kansant. Aikak.*, 1969, *65*(2), pp. 122–32. **[G: Finland; EFTA; Japan; E.E.C.; N. America]**

Rees, Richard D. U.S. Foreign Agricultural Trade in the 1970's: Growth or Contraction? *Fed. Res. Bank Kansas City Rev.*, September–October 1969, pp. 11–19. **[G: U.S.]**

Reynolds, Clark W. Relationships between Agriculture, Nonagriculture, and Foreign Trade in the Development of Argentina and Peru: Comment. **In** *Thorbecke, E., ed.*, 1969, pp. 213–17. **[G: Argentina; Peru]**

Rhodes, John B. 'The American Challenge' Challenged. *Harvard Bus. Rev.*, September–October 1969, *47*(5), pp. 45–56. **[G: E.E.C.; U.S.]**

Richter, J. H. The Changing Patterns of International Trade Problems of Under-developed Areas. **In** *Papi, U. and Nunn, C., eds.*, 1969, pp. 151–62.

Robinson, T. Russell. The Foreign Trade Sector and Domestic Stability: The Canadian Case. *Yale Econ. Essays*, Spring 1969, *9*(1), pp. 47–87. **[G: Canada]**

Roe, Alan R. Terms of Trade and Transfer Effects in the East African Common Market: An Empirical Study. *Bull. Oxford Univ. Inst. Econ. Statist.*, August 1969, *31*(3), pp. 153–67. **[G: E. Africa]**

Ruist, Erik. Den nordiska stålindustrin inför världsmarknaden. (The Scandanavian Steel Industry and the World Market. With English summary.) *Econ. Samfundets Tidskr.*, 1969, *22*(3), pp. 164–80. **[G: Scandanavia]**

Sault, J. L. and Hellier, W. L. The New International Sugar Agreement and the Australian Sugar Industry. *Quart. Rev. Agr. Econ.*, October 1969, *22* (4), pp. 210–29. **[G: Australia]**

Short, Brock K. Export Promotion in Underdeveloped Countries. *Amer. Econ.*, Fall 1969, *13* (2), pp. 70–79.

Sicat, Gerardo P. An Abstract of an Inventory of Philippine Exports, 1961–1967: Comment. *Philippine Econ. J.*, First Semester 1969, *8*(1), pp. 90–94. **[G: Philippines]**

Sicat, Gerardo P. Intercountry Trade: The Effects of Bilateralism, Development, and Regional Advantage. *Malayan Econ. Rev.*, October 1969, *14*(2), pp. 94–112.

Simpson, Robert E. Statement. **In** *New Directions for the 1970's: Toward a Strategy of Inter-American Development, Pts. 1–5, HCH*, 1969, pp. 211–12. **[G: U.S.]**

Smith, John S. World Summary of International Transactions, 1961–66. *Int. Monet. Fund Staff Pap.*, March 1969, *16*(1), pp. 85–102.

Snyder, Wayne W. Turkish Economic Development: The First Five Year Plan, 1963–67. *J. Devel. Stud.*, October 1969, *6*(1), pp. 58–71. **[G: Turkey]**

Stekler, Lois E. Effect of U.S. Business Fluctuations on Imports of Primary Commodities. *Yale Econ. Essays*, Fall 1969, *9*(2), pp. 209–49. **[G: U.S.]**

Stern, Joseph J. A Note on the Structure of Pakistan's Foreign Trade. *Pakistan Develop. Rev.*, Summer

1969, *9*(2), pp. 212–23. [G: Pakistan]

Stone, Richard. Foreign Trade and Full Employment: An Input-output Analysis. *L'Industria,* October–December 1969, (4), pp. 431–43.

Stonham, P. E. The Demand for Overseas Shipping in the Australian Export Trade. *J. Transp. Econ. Policy,* September 1969, *3*(3), pp. 333–49. [G: Australia]

Sturrock, F. G. A Policy for British Sugar Supplies. *Nat. Westminster Bank Quart. Rev.,* August 1969, pp. 54–60. [G: U.K.]

Sută, N. Comerțul exterior al României în anii construcției socialismului. (Foreign Trade of Romania in the Years of Socialist Construction. With English summary.) *Stud. Cercet. Econ.,* 1969, *3,* pp. 213–24. [G: Romania]

Tabaček, Ján. Trade Relations Between Czechoslovakia and the Soviet Union. *New Trends Czech. Econ.,* November 1969, (7), pp. 37–64. [G: Czechoslovakia; U.S.S.R.]

Tarnovskii, O. Price Formation on the World Socialist Market. *Prob. Econ.,* October 1969, *12*(6), pp. 42–57.

Tasker, Antony. British Sugar Supplies: An Alternative View. *Nat. Westminster Bank Quart. Rev.,* November 1969, pp. 45–51. [G: U.K.]

Thorbecke, Erik and Field, Alfred J. Relationships between Agriculture, Nonagriculture, and Foreign Trade in the Development of Argentina and Peru. **In** *Thorbecke, E., ed.,* 1969, pp. 165–213. [G: Argentina; Peru]

Thorbecke, Erik and Field, Alfred J. Relationships between Agriculture, Nonagriculture, and Foreign Trade in the Development of Argentina and Peru: Reply. **In** *Thorbecke, E., ed.,* 1969, pp. 217–18. [G: Argentina; Peru]

Tollet, C. G. Exportfrämjandets mål och medel—diskussion om ett modeords innehåll. (The Ends and Means of Export Drives—A Discussion of the Content of a Fashionable Phrase. With English summary.) *Econ. Samfundets Tidskr.,* 1969, *22* (1), pp. 20–37. [G: Finland]

Vasilev, Dimitur. The International Socialist Division of Labor and Its Role in the Increased Profitability of Bulgaria's Foreign Trade. *Eastern Europ. Econ.,* Fall 1969, *8*(1), pp. 90–99. [G: Bulgaria]

Verheirstraeten, A. Nominale tariefhoogte, effectieve bescherming en douane-opbrengsten met een toepassing op gegevens van het Beneluxdouanetarief. (Nominal Tarifflevel, Effective Protection and Customs Duties with an Application to data of the Benelux Customs Tariff. With English summary.) *Tijdschr. Econ.,* 1969, *14*(2), pp. 188–234. [G: E.E.C.]

Walgreen, John A. Liner Nationality and Steamship Conference Rate-Making. *J. Ind. Econ.,* July 1969, *17*(3), pp. 205–09.

Ward, M. The Effects of the U.K. Devaluation of Sterling on the Fiji Economy. *Econ. Rec.,* March 1969, *45*(109), pp. 92–115. [G: Fiji]

Wasowski, Stanislaw. The Fuel Situation in Eastern Europe. *Soviet Stud.,* July 1969, *21*(1), pp. 35–51. [G: E. Europe]

Weiller, Jean. Anti-Cyclical Policies in Relation to Foreign Trade Patterns and Tariffs (An Historical Approach). *Econ. Int.,* May 1969, *22*(2), pp. 225–44. [G: France]

Wells, Louis T., Jr. Test of a Product Cycle Model of International Trade: U.S. Exports of Consumer Durables. *Quart. J. Econ.,* February 1969, *83*(1), pp. 152–62. [G: U.S.]

Wells, Sidney. Paesi in sviluppo e commercio internazionale. (The Developing Countries, GATT and UNCTAD. With English summary.) *Mondo Aperto,* June–August 1969, *23*(3–4), pp. 189–204.

Whitman, Marina v. N. Economic Openness and International Financial Flows. *J. Money, Credit, Banking,* November 1969, *1*(4), pp. 727–49.

Wilson, T.; Sinha, R. P. and Castree, J. R. The Income Terms of Trade of Developed and Developing Countries. *Econ. J.,* December 1969, *79*(316), pp. 813–32.

Woolwine, Phil C. The South Pacific as a Source of Timber. *Oregon Bus. Rev.,* August 1969, *28*(8), pp. 1–5. [G: S. Pacific]

Yah, Lim Chong. West Malaysian External Trade, 1947–65. **In** *Morgan, T. and Spoelstra, N., eds.,* 1969, pp. 203–37. [G: Malaysia]

422 Commercial Policy

4220 Commercial Policy and Trade Regulations; Empirical Studies

Adelman, M. A. Statement. **In** *Governmental Intervention in the Market Mechanism, Pt. 1, SCH,* 1969, pp. 6–20.

Ady, Peter. International Commodity Agreements. **In** *Stewart, I. G., ed.,* 1969, pp. 26–46.

Albregts, A. H. M. and van de Gevel, A. J. W. Negotiating Techniques and Issues in the Kennedy Round. **In** *Alting von Geusau, F. A. M., ed.,* 1969, pp. 20–47. [G: E.E.C.; U.S.]

Allen, Robert Loring and Walter, Ingo. Statement. **In** *Export Expansion and Regulation, SCH,* 1969, pp. 427–28. [G: U.S.]

Atkinson, Anthony B. Import Strategy and Growth under Conditions of Stagnant Export Earnings. *Oxford Econ. Pap.,* November 1969, *21*(3), pp. 325–38. [G: U.K.]

Augenthaler, Zdenek. The Socialist Countries and GATT. **In** *Alting von Geusau, F. A. M., ed.,* 1969, pp. 75–82.

Baker, James C. and Verschuur, Jan B. The Versatile Combination Export Manager. *Marquette Bus. Rev.,* Winter 1969, *13*(4), pp. 143–50. [G: U.S.]

Balassa, Bela. Industrial Development in an Open Economy: The Case of Norway. *Oxford Econ. Pap.,* November 1969, *21*(3), pp. 344–59. [G: Norway; E.F.T.A.]

Behrman, Jack N. Statement. **In** *To Extend and Amend the Export Control Act of 1949, HCH,* 1969, pp. 14–16. [G: U.S.]

Bénard, J. Comments on the Papers on East-West Trade. **In** *Samuelson, P. A., ed.,* 1969, pp. 134–38.

Bergsman, Joel and Morley, Samuel A. Import Constraints and Development: Causes of the Recent Decline of Brazilian Economic Growth: A Comment. *Rev. Econ. Statist.,* February 1969, *51*(1), pp. 101–02. [G: Brazil]

Bhagwati, Jagdish N. and Chakravarty, Sukhamoy. Contributions to Indian Economic Analysis: A

Survey. *Amer. Econ. Rev.,* Part II, September 1969, *59*(4), pp. 2–73. [G: India]

Blainey, Geoffrey. Mining—And Undermining. *Econ. Rec.,* December 1969, *45*(112), pp. 607–15. [G: Australia]

Blough, Roy. The Adjustment Process and the International Role of the Dollar. *J. Finance,* May 1969, *24*(2), pp. 345–59. [G: U.S.]

Bontoux, Charles. Considerazioni sul credito documentario trasferibile. (Considerations Regarding Transferable Documentary Credit. With English summary.) *Bancaria,* June 1969, *25*(6), pp. 700–10.

Brash, Donald T. American Investment and Australian Sovereignty. **In** *Preston, R., ed.,* 1969, pp. 539–52. [G: Australia]

Cairncross, Alec K. [Sir]. Comments on the Papers by Goran Ohlin and André Marchal. **In** *Samuelson, P. A., ed.,* 1969, pp. 218–21.

Casadio, Gian Paolo. Ritorno al protezionismo? (Does the Protectionism Return? With English summary.) *Mondo Aperto,* December 1969, *23*(6), pp. 434–43.

Castrén, Kari. Kilpailun edistämisen nykyongelmia. (Some Contemporary Problems of Competition Policy. With English summary.) *Liiketaloudellinen Aikak.,* 1969, *18*(3), pp. 341–46.

Castro, Amado A. Philippine Export Development 1950–65. **In** *Morgan, T. and Spoelstra, N., eds.,* 1969, pp. 181–200. [G: Philippines]

Conan, A. R. Does Britain Pay Its Way? *Nat. Westminster Bank Quart. Rev.,* February 1969, pp. 2–17. [G: U.K.]

Cordell, Arthur J. The Brazilian Soluble Coffee Problem: A Review. *Quart. Rev. Econ. Bus.,* Spring 1969, *9*(1), pp. 29–38. [G: Brazil]

Dardis, Rachel and Dennisson, Janet. The Welfare Cost of Alternative Methods of Protecting Raw Wool in the United States. *Amer. J. Agr. Econ.,* May 1969, *51*(2), pp. 303–19. [G: U.S.]

Davis, Kenneth N. Statement. **In** *Export Expansion and Regulation, SCH,* 1969, pp. 62–65. [G: U.S.]

Davis, Kenneth N. Statement. **In** *Export Expansion and Regulation, SCH,* 1969, pp. 307–33. [G: U.S.]

Dellin, Lubomir. Statement. **In** *To Extend and Amend the Export Control Act of 1949, HCH,* 1969, pp. 343–48. [G: U.S.]

Diamond, Peter. On the Economics of Tourism. *East Afr. Econ. Rev.,* December 1969, *1*(2), pp. 53–62.

Diebold, William, Jr. Future Negotiating Issues and Policies in Foreign Trade. **In** *Alting von Geusau, F. A. M., ed.,* 1969, pp. 123–45.

Dixon, J. The Cost of Dumping Butter: A Comment. *J. Common Market Stud.,* March 1969, *7*(3), pp. 243–52. [G: France; U.K.]

Dolmans, D. Het aardgas zijn prijsvorming. (Natural Gas and Its Price Determination. With English summary.) *Tijdschr. Econ.,* 1969, *14*(1), pp. 3–27. [G: Netherlands]

Domar, Evsey D. Comments on the Papers on East-West Trade. **In** *Samuelson, P. A., ed.,* 1969, pp. 138–42.

Due, John F. The Uganda Sales Tax on Importation and Manufacture. *East Afr. Econ. Rev.,* June 1969, *1*(1), pp. 1–16. [G: Uganda]

Dymsza, William A. Statement. **In** *Export Expansion and Regulation, SCH,* 1969, pp. 412–20. [G: U.S.]

Eysenbach, M. L. A Note on Growth and Structural Change in Pakistan's Manufacturing Industry 1954–1964. *Pakistan Develop. Rev.,* Spring 1969, *9*(1), pp. 58–65. [G: Pakistan]

Fieleke, Norman S. The Buy-American Policy of the United States Government: Its Balance-of-Payments and Welfare Effects. *New Eng. Econ. Rev.,* July/August 1969, pp. 2–18. [G: U.S.]

Franks, Alison. Does Britain Pay Its Way?—A Rejoinder. *Nat. Westminster Bank Quart. Rev.,* May 1969, pp. 42–44. [G: U.K.]

Ghose, B. C. The Borooah Committee on Tea. *Econ. Aff.,* January-February 1969, *14*(1–2), pp. 71–73. [G: India]

Goodman, Richard J. Policy and Non-Policy in Foreign Trade: Discussion. *Amer. J. Agr. Econ.,* December 1969, *51*(5), pp. 1354–56. [G: U.S.; E.E.C.]

Greenwald, Joseph A. Statement. **In** *Export Expansion and Regulation, SCH,* 1969, pp. 269–72. [G: U.S.]

Greenwald, Joseph A. Statement. **In** *To Extend and Amend the Export Control Act of 1949, HCH,* 1969, pp. 114–17. [G: U.S.]

Grubel, Herbert G.; Johnson, Harry G. and Rapp, William V. Excise Taxes and Effective Protection: A Note. *Econ. J.,* September 1969, *79*(315), pp. 674–75.

Guisinger, Stephen E. Negative Value Added and the Theory of Effective Protection. *Quart. J. Econ.,* August 1969, *83*(3), pp. 415–33.

Gundelach, Finn. The Kennedy Round of Trade Negotiations: Results and Lessons. **In** *Alting von Geusau, F. A. M., ed.,* 1969, pp. 146–98.

Haberler, Gottfried. Institutional Arrangements: Appendix: Taxes on Imports and Subsidies on Exports as a Tool of Adjustment. **In** *Mundell, R. A. and Swoboda, A. K., eds.,* 1969, pp. 173–79.

Handke, Werner. Zielkonflikte in der Entwicklungshilfe zwischen Geber- und Nehmerländern. (With English summary.) *Z. ges. Staatswiss.,* April 1969, *125*(2), pp. 261–78.

Hemer, Jiří. About Foreign Trade Activities—Without Illusions. *New Trends Czech. Econ.,* November 1969, (7), pp. 65–79. [G: Czechoslovakia]

Hijzen, Th. C. Thoughts on Commercial Relations after the Kennedy Round. **In** *Alting von Geusau, F. A. M., ed.,* 1969, pp. 113–22.

Hinton, W. L. The Contribution of Horticulture. *Nat. Westminster Bank Quart. Rev.,* May 1969, pp. 33–41. [G: U.K.]

Hogan, W. P. Economic Effects of the Australian Protection System. *Econ. Rec.,* December 1969, *45*(112), pp. 513–25. [G: Australia]

Hollerman, Leon. Recent Difficulties in Japan's Economic Development. *Banca Naz. Lavoro Quart. Rev.,* March 1969, (88), pp. 66–90. [G: Japan]

Holzman, Franklyn D. Comparison of Different Forms of Trade Barriers. *Rev. Econ. Statist.,* May 1969, *51*(2), pp. 159–65.

Homan, Paul T. Statement. **In** *Governmental Intervention in the Market Mechanism, Pt. 1, SCH,* 1969, pp. 103–31. [G: U.S.]

Horn, Johan. Nationalism versus Internationalism in

Shipping. *J. Transp. Econ. Policy,* September 1969, *3*(3), pp. 245–50.

Humphrey, David B. Changes in Protection and Inflation in Argentina, 1953–1966. *Oxford Econ. Pap.,* July 1969, *21*(2), pp. 196–219. **[G: Argentina]**

Humphrey, David B. Measuring the Effective Rate of Protection: Direct and Indirect Effects. *J. Polit. Econ.,* September/October 1969, *77*(5), pp. 834–44. **[G: Argentina]**

Islam, Nurul. Export Incentive and Effective Subsidy in Pakistan: An Evaluation. *Bull. Oxford Univ. Inst. Econ. Statist.,* August 1969, *31*(3), pp. 169–88. **[G: Pakistan]**

Islam, Nurul. Export Policy in Pakistan. **In** *[Tinbergen, J.],* 1969, pp. 219–43. **[G: Pakistan]**

Islam, Nurul. Tariff Protection, Comparative Costs, and Industrialization in Pakistan. **In** *Morgan, T. and Spoelstra, N., eds.,* 1969, pp. 65–95. **[G: Pakistan]**

Jap, K. S. The Concept of Delivery of Goods by a Manufacturer under the Indonesian Sales Tax Act (1951–1968). *Bull. Int. Fiscal Doc.,* May 1969, *23* (5), pp. 223–28. **[G: Indonesia]**

Johnson, D. Gale. The New Agricultural Protectionism in the Industrial Countries. *Rivista Int. Sci. Econ. Com.,* January 1969, *16*(1), pp. 46–62.

Johnson, Harry G. Comparative Cost and Commercial Policy Theory in a Developing Economy. *Pakistan Develop. Rev.,* Spring Supplement 1969, *9* (1), pp. 1–33.

Johnson, Harry G. Current International Economic Policy Issues. *J. Bus.,* January 1969, *42*(1), pp. 12–21. **[G: U.S.]**

Johnson, Harry G. Some Aspects of the Multilateral Free Trade Association Proposal. *Manchester Sch. Econ. Soc. Stud.,* September 1969, *37*(3), pp. 189–212.

Johnson, Harry G. The Theory of Effective Protection and Preferences. *Economica, N.S.,* May 1969, *36*(142), pp. 119–38.

Kahn, Alfred E. Statement. **In** *Governmental Intervention in the Market Mechanism, Pt. 1, SCH,* 1969, pp. 132–54. **[G: U.S.]**

Karunatilake, H. N. S. The Impact of Import and Exchange Controls and Bilateral Trade Agreements on Trade and Production in Ceylon. **In** *Morgan, T. and Spoelstra, N., eds.,* 1969, pp. 285–303. **[G: Ceylon]**

Kaufmann, Hugo M. A Debate over Germany's Revaluation 1961: A Chapter in Political Economy. *Weltwirtsch. Arch.,* 1969, *103*(2), pp. 181–212. **[G: Germany]**

Kaufmann, Johan and Alting von Geusau, A. M. The Institutional Framework for International Trade Relations. **In** *Alting von Geusau, F. A. M., ed.,* 1969, pp. 94–112.

Kayoumy, Abdul Hay. Monopoly Pricing of Afghan Karakul in International Markets. *J. Polit. Econ.,* March/April 1969, *77*(2), pp. 219–36. **[G: Afghanistan]**

Kendrick, James G. Policy and Non-Policy in Foreign Trade: Discussion. *Amer. J. Agr. Econ.,* December 1969, *51*(5), pp. 1349–51. **[G: U.S.; E.E.C.]**

Khachaturov, T. S. The Development of the External Economic Relations of the Soviet Union. **In** *Samuelson, P. A., ed.,* 1969, pp. 89–99. **[G: U.S.S.R.]**

Khachaturov, T. S.; Nove, Alec and Vajda, Imre. Replies to Comments. **In** *Samuelson, P. A., ed.,* 1969, pp. 147–49.

Kojima, Kiyoshi. Trade Preferences for Developing Countries: A Japanese Assessment. *Hitotsubashi J. Econ.,* February 1969, *9*(2), pp. 1–12. **[G: Japan]**

Kronsten, Joseph A. East-West Trade: Myth and Matter. **In** *Grub, P. D. and Holbik, K.,* 1969, pp. 117–24.

Lacroix, Y. and Schouwenaars, W. Effectieve bescherming aan de grenzen van de E.E.G. en het Verenigd Koninkrijk, voor en na de Kennedyronde. (Effective Protection at the Borders of the E.E.C. and the United Kingdom before and after the Kennedy-Round. With English summary.) *Tijdschr. Econ.,* 1969, *14*(2), pp. 158–87. **[G: E.E.C.]**

Łączkowski, Bohdan. Poland's Participation in the Kennedy Round. **In** *Alting von Geusau, F. A. M., ed.,* 1969, pp. 83–93. **[G: Poland]**

Lakdawala, D. T. and Patil, R. H. Prospects of India's Trade with ECAFE Countries. **In** *Morgan, T. and Spoelstra, N., eds.,* 1969, pp. 241–73. **[G: India]**

Leff, Nathaniel H. Import Constraints and Development: A Reply. *Rev. Econ. Statist.,* February 1969, *51*(1), pp. 102–04. **[G: Brazil]**

Leff, Nathaniel H. The "Exportable Surplus" Approach to Foreign Trade in Underdeveloped Countries. *Econ. Develop. Cult. Change,* April 1969, *17*(3), pp. 346–55.

Leith, James Clark and Reuber, Grant L. The Impact of the Industrial Countries' Tariff Structure on Their Imports of Manufactures from Less-Developed Areas: A Comment. *Economica, N.S.,* February 1969, *36*(141), pp. 75–80.

Lichtblau, John H. Statement. **In** *Governmental Intervention in the Market Mechanism, Pt. 1, SCH,* 1969, pp. 317–27. **[G: U.S.]**

Llosas, Hernán P. La política de promoción industrial y de desarrollo regional en la Argentina, 1959–1966. (The Argentinian Government's Policy for the Promotion of Particular Industrial Sectors and for the Development of Some of the Country's Regions, 1959–1966. With English summary.) *Económica,* January–April 1969, *15*(1), pp. 39–91. **[G: Argentina]**

Lobato Løpez, Ernesto. Las normas de calidad y el desarrollo de la industria: Segunda parte y última. (Quality Standards and Industrial Development: Second and Last Part. With English summary.) *Econ. Polít.,* Third Semester 1969, *6*(3), pp. 317–30. **[G: Mexico]**

MacEachern, G. A. and Huff, H. Bruce. Policy and Non-Policy in Foreign Trade: Discussion. *Amer. J. Agr. Econ.,* December 1969, *51*(5), pp. 1352–54. **[G: U.S.; E.E.C.]**

Mahler, Walter, Jr. Elimination of the Sales Tax Burden on Exports. *Asian Econ. Rev.,* February 1969, *11*(2), pp. 227–32. **[G: India]**

Malluhi, Haytham. Tax System in Kuwait. *Bull. Int. Fiscal Doc.,* April 1969, *23*(4), pp. 160–62. **[G: Kuwait]**

Malmgren, H. B. and Schlechty, D. L. Technology

and Neo-Mercantilism in International Agricultural Trade. **In** *Interest Equalization Tax Extension Act of 1969, SCH,* 1969, pp. 35–42.

Marasco, Enrico. Politica degli scambi. (Foreign Trade Policy. With English summary.) *Mondo Aperto,* December 1969, *23*(6), pp. 417–22.

Markert, K. E. The Application of German Antitrust Law to International Restraints on Trade. **In** *Economic Concentration, Pt. 7A, SCH,* 1969, pp. 4091–4103. **[G: W. Germany]**

Mathai, M. K. Incentives for Investment in Malaysia. *Bull. Int. Fiscal Doc.,* November 1969, *23*(11), pp. 503–15. **[G: Malaysia]**

Matthews, Roy A. A New Atlantic Role for Canada. *Foreign Aff.,* January 1969, *47*(2), pp. 334–47. **[G: Canada]**

McColl, Gregory D. The Tariff: A Century of Debate. **In** *Preston, R., ed.,* 1969, pp. 71–90. **[G: Australia]**

McHale, Thomas R. Policies for the Private Sector: Discussion. *Philippine Econ. J.,* First Semester 1969, *8*(1), pp. 31–32. **[G: Philippines]**

Mestmäcker, E.-J. State Trading Monopolies in the European Economic Community. **In** *Economic Concentration, Pt. 7A, SCH,* 1969, pp. 3925–44. **[G: E.E.C.]**

Michael, Franz. Statement. **In** *To Extend and Amend the Export Control Act of 1949, HCH,* 1969, pp. 348–51. **[G: U.S.]**

Michl, H. E. Statement. **In** *To Extend and Amend the Export Control Act of 1949, HCH,* 1969, pp. 351–59. **[G: U.S.]**

Mieszkowski, Peter. Carter on the Taxation of International Income Flows. *Nat. Tax J.,* March 1969, *22*(1), pp. 97–108. **[G: Canada]**

Mikesell, Raymond F. Changing World Trade Patterns and America's Leadership Role. *Ann. Amer. Acad. Polit. Soc. Sci.,* July 1969, *384,* pp. 35–44. **[G: U.S.]**

Montias, John Michael. Comments on the Papers on East-West Trade. **In** *Samuelson, P. A., ed.,* 1969, pp. 142–47.

Morley, Samuel A. Import Demand and Import Substitution in Brazil. **In** *Ellis, H. S., ed.,* 1969, pp. 283–313. **[G: Brazil]**

Morrisse, Kathryn A. Automotive Trade between the United States and Canada. (Study summary.) *Fed. Res. Bull.,* November 1969, *55*(11), pp. 877–78. **[G: U.S.; Canada]**

Munk, Bernard. The Welfare Costs of Content Protection: The Automotive Industry in Latin America. *J. Polit. Econ.,* January/February 1969, *77*(1), pp. 85–98. **[G: Latin America]**

Murgescu, Costin. Romania and the Promotion of the Principles of International Economic Cooperation. *Revue Roumaine Sci. Soc. Serie Sci. Econ.,* 1969, *13*(2), pp. 133–55. **[G: Romania]**

Norwood, Bernard. The Kennedy Round: A Try at Linear Trade Negotiations. *J. Law Econ.,* October 1969, *12*(2), pp. 297–319. **[G: U.S.]**

Nove, Alec. East-West Trade. **In** *Samuelson, P. A., ed.,* 1969, pp. 100–120.

Nutter, G. Warren. Statement. **In** *To Extend and Amend the Export Control Act of 1949, HCH,* 1969, pp. 117–19. **[G: U.S.]**

Officer, Lawrence H. and Hurtubise, Jules R. Price Effects of the Kennedy Round on Canadian Trade. *Rev. Econ. Statist.,* August 1969, *51*(3), pp. 320–33. **[G: U.S.; Canada]**

Ohlin, Goran and Bienaymé, A. Replies to Comments. **In** *Samuelson, P. A., ed.,* 1969, pp. 230–31.

Ohlin, Goran. Trade in a Non-*Laissez-Faire* World. **In** *Samuelson, P. A., ed.,* 1969, pp. 157–75.

Oppenheimer, Peter M. Import Deposits. *Nat. Westminster Bank Quart. Rev.,* February 1969, pp. 69–72.

Panglaykim, J. and Thomas, Kenneth D. Indonesian Exports: Performance and Prospects. **In** *Morgan, T. and Spoelstra, N., eds.,* 1969, pp. 337–70. **[G: Indonesia]**

Patel, B. P. Twelve Years of the S. T. C. **In** *Dagli, V., ed., Vol. II,* 1969, pp. 102–10. **[G: India]**

Patil, S. M. Prospects for Machine Tool Exports. **In** *Dagli, V., ed., Vol. II,* 1969, pp. 180–89. **[G: India]**

Paunio, J. J. Comments on the Papers by Goran Ohlin and André Marchal. **In** *Samuelson, P. A., ed.,* 1969, pp. 221–26.

Pleva, Jan. Foreign Trade and the New System of Management. **In** *Grub, P. D. and Holbik, K.,* 1969, pp. 187–93. **[G: Yugoslavia]**

Rabbani, A. K. M. Ghulam. A Proposal for Fiscal Incentives for the Raw-Jute Exports. *Pakistan Develop. Rev.,* Winter 1969, *9*(4), pp. 400–418. **[G: Pakistan]**

Ramana, D. V. Deficit Financing and Import Substitution: India, 1951–65. **In** *Morgan, T. and Spoelstra, N., eds.,* 1969, pp. 307–31. **[G: India]**

Rattigan, G. A. The Tariff Board: Some Reflections. *Econ. Rec.,* March 1969, *45*(109), pp. 17–26. **[G: Australia]**

Redding, A. David. Policies for the Private Sector: Discussion. *Philippine Econ. J.,* First Semester 1969, *8*(1), pp. 33–36. **[G: Philippines]**

Rees, Richard D. U.S. Foreign Agricultural Trade in the 1970's: Growth or Contraction? *Fed. Res. Bank Kansas City Rev.,* September–October 1969, pp. 11–19. **[G: U.S.]**

Richebächer, Kurt. Problemi e prospettive di integrazione dei mercati europei dei capitali. (Problems and Prospects of Integrating European Capital Markets. With English summary.) *Bancaria,* February 1969, *25*(2), pp. 170–77.

Rieber, Michael. Statement. **In** *Governmental Intervention in the Market Mechanism, Pt. 1, SCH,* 1969, pp. 181–92. **[G: U.S.]**

Rogers, Christopher D. Consumer Participation in the International Tin Agreements. *Malayan Econ. Rev.,* October 1969, *14*(2), pp. 113–29.

van Rooijen, M. J. The Substantial Holding Privilege in Netherlands Corporate Income Tax. *Bull. Int. Fiscal Doc.,* July, August, September 1969, *23*(7–8–9), pp. 337–405. **[G: Netherlands]**

Roth, William M. Future U.S. Foreign Trade Policy: Report to the President. **In** *The 1969 Economic Report of the President, Pt. 3, JECH,* 1969, pp. 759–871. **[G: U.S.]**

Rowan, David C. Towards a Rational Exchange Policy: Some Reflections on the British Experience. *Fed. Res. Bank St. Louis Rev.,* April 1969, *51*(4), pp. 17–26. **[G: U.K.]**

Roxas, Sixto K. Policies for the Private Sector. *Phil-*

ippine Econ. J., First Semester 1969, *8*(1), pp. 16–30. **[G: Philippines]**

Ruffin, Roy J. Tariffs, Intermediate Goods, and Domestic Protection. *Amer. Econ. Rev.*, June 1969, *59*(3), pp. 261–69.

Schwenger, Robert B. New Concepts and Methods in Foreign Trade Negotiation. *Amer. J. Agr. Econ.*, December 1969, *51*(5), pp. 1338–48. **[G: U.S.]**

Snape, R. H. Sugar: Costs of Protection and Taxation. *Economica, N.S.*, February 1969, *36*(141), pp. 29–41.

Sobota, Václav. Federative Arrangement of External Economic Relations. *New Trends Czech. Econ.*, July 1969, (4), pp. 53–64. **[G: Czechoslovakia]**

Solomon, Robert. International Financial Problems and the Role of the Dollar: Discussion. *J. Finance*, May 1969, *24*(2), pp. 371–74. **[G: U.S.]**

Spulber, Nicolas. East-West Trade and the Paradoxes of the Strategic Embargo. **In** *To Extend and Amend the Export Control Act of 1949, HCH*, 1969, pp. 322–41.

Stermann, Walter. Austria as a Model for East-West Trade. **In** *Grub, P. D. and Holbik, K.*, 1969, pp. 132–34. **[G: Austria]**

Stonham, P. E. The Demand for Overseas Shipping in the Australian Export Trade. *J. Transp. Econ. Policy*, September 1969, *3*(3), pp. 333–49. **[G: Australia]**

Streeten, Paul. The Case for Export Subsidies. *J. Devel. Stud.*, July 1969, *5*(4), pp. 270–73.

Stykolt, Stefan and Eastman, Harry C. Disturbing Prospects. **In** *Stykolt, S.*, 1969, pp. 129–32. **[G: Canada]**

Stykolt, Stefan. Enquiry into What? **In** *Stykolt, S.*, 1969, pp. 126–28. **[G: Canada]**

Subocz, V. The Cargo Cult, or the 'Cinderella' Cult, in Mineral Policy? *Econ. Rec.*, December 1969, *45* (112), pp. 596–606. **[G: Australia]**

Sun, I-Shuan. Trade Policies and Economic Development in Taiwan. **In** *Morgan, T. and Spoelstra, N., eds.*, 1969, pp. 99–123. **[G: Taiwan]**

Sutton, Anthony C. Statement. **In** *Export Expansion and Regulation, SCH*, 1969, pp. 420–25. **[G: U.S.]**

Sutton, Anthony C. Technology, Trade and Peace with Communist Countries. **In** *To Extend and Amend the Export Control Act of 1949, HCH*, 1969, pp. 359–62. **[G: U.S.]**

Swidrowski, Jozef. Exchange Restrictions in 1969. *Finance Develop.*, December 1969, *6*(4), pp. 27–33.

Szabados, Joseph. Hungary's NEM: Reorganization or Basic Reform? **In** *Grub, P. D. and Holbik, K.*, 1969, pp. 194–98. **[G: Hungary]**

Tillinghast, David R. The Carter Commission Report and International Investment Transactions; Integration and Ambiguous Intentions. *Nat. Tax J.*, March 1969, *22*(1), pp. 79–96. **[G: Canada]**

Tollet, C. G. Exportfrämjandets mål och medel—diskussion om ett modeords innehåll. (The Ends and Means of Export Drives—A Discussion of the Content of a Fashionable Phrase. With English summary.) *Econ. Samfundets Tidskr.*, 1969, *22* (1), pp. 20–37. **[G: Finland]**

Törnqvist, Erik. Nordek-planen. (The Nordek Plan. With English summary.) *Econ. Samfundets Tidskr.*, 1969, *22*(2), pp. 95–104. **[G: Scandanavia; E.F.T.A.]**

Tucci, Giuseppe. Accostamenti economici tra Giappone e Italia; prospettive dell'esportazione calzaturiera in Giappone. (Economic Approaches between Japan and Italy. With English summary.) *Mondo Aperto*, October 1969, *23*(5), pp. 321–29. **[G: Japan; Italy]**

Tyler, William G. Export Promotion with Increasing Returns to Scale under Imperfect Domestic Market Conditions. *Soc. Econ. Stud.*, December 1969, *18*(4), pp. 402–07.

Uckmar, V. and Durand, Patrick. The Tax Treaty between Italy and France. *Bull. Int. Fiscal Doc.*, May 1969, *23*(5), pp. 191–203. **[G: Italy; France]**

Vaivo, Fedi. Ajatuksia Euroopan integraatiokehityksestä ja suomalaisten yritysten strategiasta. (Impressions on the Development of European Integration and the Strategy of Finnish Firms. With English summary.) *Kansant. Aikak.*, 1969, *65*(2), pp. 82–90. **[G: Finland; E.E.C.]**

Vajda, Imre. The Problems of East-West Trade. **In** *Samuelson, P. A., ed.*, 1969, pp. 121–33.

Verheirstraeten, A. Nominale tariefhoogte, effectieve bescherming en douane-opbrengsten met een toepassing op gegevens van het Beneluxdouanetarief. (Nominal Tarifflevel, Effective Protection and Customs Duties with an Application to data of the Benelux Customs Tariff. With English summary.) *Tijdschr. Econ.*, 1969, *14*(2), pp. 188–234. **[G: E.E.C.]**

Vingerhoets, J. The Kennedy Round and the Developing Countries. **In** *Alting von Geusau, F. A. M., ed.*, 1969, pp. 48–74.

Walker, Franklin V. The Restrictive Effect of the U.S. Tariff: Comment. *Amer. Econ. Rev.*, December 1969, *59*(5), pp. 963–66. **[G: U.S.]**

Wall, David. After UNCTAD II. **In** *Stewart, I. G., ed.*, 1969, pp. 181–84.

Walter, Ingo. Nontariff Barriers and the Free-Trade Area Option. *Banca Naz. Lavoro Quart. Rev.*, March 1969, (88), pp. 16–45.

Wells, Sidney. Paesi in sviluppo e commercio internazionale. (The Developing Countries, GATT and UNCTAD. With English summary.) *Mondo Aperto*, June–August 1969, *23*(3–4), pp. 189–204.

Wesolowski, Zdzislaw P. An Inquiry into the Administration and Utilization of the Webb-Pomerene Act. *Marquette Bus. Rev.*, Winter 1969, *13* (4), pp. 174–88. **[G: U.S.]**

Westerman, P. A. Changes in the World Wheat Situation and the 1967 International Grains Arrangement. *Quart. Rev. Agr. Econ.*, January 1969, *22*(1), pp. 20–34.

Wilczynski, Jozef. Does the Western Strategic Embargo Work? **In** *To Extend and Amend the Export Control Act of 1949, HCH*, 1969, pp. 303–14.

Yossundara, Suparb and Huntrakoon, Yune. Some Salient Aspects of Thailand's Trade, 1955–64. **In** *Morgan, T. and Spoelstra, N., eds.*, 1969, pp. 127–50. **[G: Thailand]**

Young, John H. Comments on the Papers by Goran Ohlin and André Marchal. **In** *Samuelson, P. A., ed.*, 1969, pp. 226–29.

Zandano, Gianni. The Heckscher-Ohlin Model and the Tariff Structures of the Industrial Countries. *Banca Naz. Lavoro Quart. Rev.,* March 1969, (88), pp. 46–65.

423 Economic Integration

4230 General

Albregts, A. H. M. and van de Gevel, A. J. W. Negotiating Techniques and Issues in the Kennedy Round. In *Alting von Geusau, F. A. M., ed.,* 1969, pp. 20–47. **[G: E.E.C.; U.S.]**

Carli, Guido. Problemi dell'adesione della Gran Bretagna al Mercato Comune relativamente alle questioni monetarie. (Monetary Aspects of British Entry into the Common Market. With English summary.) *Bancaria,* June 1969, *25*(6), pp. 768–72. **[G: U.K.; E.E.C.]**

Church, R. J. Harrision. Some Problems of Regional Economic Development in West Africa. *Econ. Geogr.,* January 1969, *45*(1), pp. 53–62. **[G: W. Africa]**

Cohen, Alvin. Monetarism vs. Structuralism: Conflict in U.S. Economic Aid to Latin America. In *Hilton, R., ed.,* 1969, pp. 173–84. **[G: Latin America]**

Curzon, Gerard and Curzon, Victoria. Options after the Kennedy Round. In *Johnson, H. G., ed.,* 1969, pp. 19–73.

Diebold, William, Jr. Future Negotiating Issues and Policies in Foreign Trade. In *Alting von Geusau, F. A. M., ed.,* 1969, pp. 123–45.

Edel, Matthew D. Regional Integration and Income Redistribution: Complements or Substitutes? In *Hilton, R., ed.,* 1969, pp. 185–202.

Fox, Hugh. Latin American Unity: A Socio-Economic Overview. In *Hilton, R., ed.,* 1969, pp. 454–59. **[G: Latin America]**

Frank, Andre Gunder. Latin American Economic Integration. In *Frank, A. G.,* 1969, pp. 175–80. **[G: Latin America]**

Goldstein, Henry N. Gresham's Law and the Demand for NRU's and SDR's. *Quart. J. Econ.,* February 1969, *83*(1), pp. 163–66.

Hansen, Roger D. Political Theory and Regional Integration: The First Ten Years. In *Hilton, R., ed.,* 1969, pp. 11–38.

Hijzen, Th. C. Thoughts on Commercial Relations after the Kennedy Round. In *Alting von Geusau, F. A. M., ed.,* 1969, pp. 113–22.

Huelin, David. Inflation as an Obstacle to Latin American Economic Integration. In *Hilton, R., ed.,* 1969, pp. 210–21. **[G: Latin America]**

Johnson, Harry G. Time for Change in Trade Strategy. In *Johnson, H. G., ed.,* 1969, pp. 1–18.

Kafka, Alexandre. Regional Monetary Integration of the Developing Countries. In *Mundell, R. A. and Swoboda, A. K., eds.,* 1969, pp. 135–43.

Kindleberger, Charles P. The Euro-Dollar and the Internationalization of United States Monetary Policy. *Banca Naz. Lavoro Quart. Rev.,* March 1969, (88), pp. 3–15.

Kormnov, Iu. Economic Stimulation of the Development of International Production Specialization. *Prob. Econ.,* January 1969, *11*(9), pp. 45–54. **[G: COMECON]**

Leith, James Clark. The Customs Revenue Loss in a Southeast Asian Customs Union. *J. Devel. Stud.,* January 1969, *5*(2), pp. 142–46. **[G: Malaya]**

Mauro, Frédéric. Latin American History and Integration. In *Hilton, R., ed.,* 1969, pp. 49–58. **[G: Latin America]**

Nowzad, Bahram. Economic Integration in Central and West Africa. *Int. Monet. Fund Staff Pap.,* March 1969, *16*(1), pp. 103–39. **[G: Central Africa; W. Africa]**

Nyers, R. Theoretical and Practical Problems of Socialist Economic Integration. (In Russian. With English summary.) *Acta Oecon.,* 1969, *4*(2), pp. 119–53.

Reynolds, S. E. Customs Union among Developing Countries. *Malayan Econ. Rev.,* April 1969, *14*(1), pp. 15–28.

Richebächer, Kurt. Problemi e prospettive di integrazione dei mercati europei dei capitali. (Problems and Prospects of Integrating European Capital Markets. With English summary.) *Bancaria,* February 1969, *25*(2), pp. 170–77.

Robertson, David. Scope for New Trade Strategy. In *Johnson, H. G., ed.,* 1969, pp. 255–344.

Roldan, Alfredo. Latin American Economic Integration: Its Benefits and Obstacles. In *Hilton, R., ed.,* 1969, pp. 80–96. **[G: Latin America]**

Roldan, Alfredo. The Latin American Economic Integration: Its Benefits and Obstacles. *Nebr. J. Econ. Bus.,* Winter 1968–69, *8*(1), pp. 16–33. **[G: Latin America]**

Roussakis, Emmanuel N. The Common Market and the Zollverein: Experiences in Integration. *Rech. Écon. Louvain,* August 1969, *35*(3), pp. 201–08. **[G: Germany]**

Ruist, Erik. Den nordiska stålindustrin inför världsmarknaden. (The Scandanavian Steel Industry and the World Market. With English summary.) *Econ. Samfundets Tidskr.,* 1969, *22*(3), pp. 164–80. **[G: Scandanavia]**

Stamp, Maxwell and Cowie, Harry. Britain and the Free Trade Area Option. In *Johnson, H. G., ed.,* 1969, pp. 165–253. **[G: U.K.]**

Stolk, Leonard. Taxation of International Consolidations into a "European Corporation." *Bull. Int. Fiscal Doc.,* November 1969, *23*(11), pp. 521–44. **[G: E.E.C.]**

Street, James H. Latin American Economic Integration: Some Historic Guideposts. In *Hilton, R., ed.,* 1969, pp. 39–48. **[G: Latin America]**

Tarnovskii, O. Price Formation on the World Socialist Market. *Prob. Econ.,* October 1969, *12*(6), pp. 42–57.

Törnqvist, Erik. Nordek-planen. (The Nordek Plan. With English summary.) *Econ. Samfundets Tidskr.,* 1969, *22*(2), pp. 95–104. **[G: Scandanavia; E.F.T.A.]**

Triffin, Robert. On the Creation of a European Reserve Fund. *Banca Naz. Lavoro Quart. Rev.,* December 1969, (91), pp. 327–46. **[G: E.E.C.]**

Truitt, George A. Participation as a Component of Integration: A Rationale for Regional Integration Centers. In *Hilton, R., ed.,* 1969, pp. 133–40.

Vaivo, Fedi. Ajatuksia Euroopan integraatiokehityksestä ja suomalaisten yritysten strategiasta. (Impressions on the Development of European

Integration and the Strategy of Finnish Firms. With English summary.) *Kansant. Aikak.*, 1969, *65*(2), pp. 82–90. [G: Finland; E.E.C.]

Van Houtte, J. B.T.W., een instrument van conjunctuur-politiek? (The Belgian V.A.T.-Bill and Economic Policy. With English summary.) *Econ. Soc. Tijdschr.*, February 1969, *23*(1), pp. 1–8. [G: E.E.C.]

Wood, Harold A. The Regional Implication of Economic Integration. **In** *Hilton, R., ed.*, 1969, pp. 141–48.

4232 Theory of Economic Integration

Arndt, Sven W. Customs Union and the Theory of Tariffs. *Amer. Econ. Rev.*, March 1969, *59*(1), pp. 108–18.

Bos, H. C. and Kuyvenhoven, A. Economic Integration and the Optimum International Distribution of Production. **In** *[Tinbergen, J.]*, 1969, pp. 93–110.

Brewster, Havelock and Thomas, Clive Y. Aspects of the Theory of Economic Integration. *J. Common Market Stud.*, December 1969, *8*(2), pp. 110–32.

Dutta, Amita. Domestic Market Distortions and Customs Union: A Geometrical Analysis. *J. Devel. Stud.*, January 1969, *5*(2), pp. 87–103.

Grewe, Klaus. Wirtschaftsunion bei flexiblen Wechselkursen. (Economic Union under a System of Flexible Exchange Rates. With English summary.) *Schmollers Jahr.*, 1969, *89*(1), pp. 1–32.

Ireri, Dunstan. A Proposed Model to Analyze Economic Interdependence among the Member Countries of the East African Community. *East Afr. Econ. Rev.*, December 1969, *1*(2), pp. 75–85. [G: E. African Community]

Melvin, James R. Comments on the Theory of Customs Unions. *Manchester Sch. Econ. Soc. Stud.*, June 1969, *37*(2), pp. 161–68.

Negishi, Takashi. The Customs Union and the Theory of Second Best. *Int. Econ. Rev.*, October 1969, *10*(3), pp. 391–98.

Sakamoto, Jorge. Industrial Development and Integration of Underdeveloped Countries. *J. Common Market Stud.*, June 1969, *7*(4), pp. 283–304.

Schmitt, Hans O. Integration and Conflict in the World Economy. *J. Common Market Stud.*, September 1969, *8*(1), pp. 1–18.

Simeone, Franco. Integrazione economica e Paesi in via di sviluppo. (Economic Integration and Developing Countries. With English summary.) *Mondo Aperto*, December 1969, *23*(6), pp. 423–43.

Slome, Benjamin. The Interregional Input-Output Model and Interregional Public Finance. *Public Finance*, 1969, *24*(4), pp. 618–23.

4233 Economic Integration: Policy and Empirical Studies

Abeelen, Marc J. and Hammond, Robert C. The Fiscal Aspects of International Co-operation in Africa—The Experience of the UDEAC and the EAC. *Bull. Int. Fiscal Doc.*, March 1969, *23*(3), pp. 95–115. [G: Africa]

Alexander, Willy. The Establishment of the Common Market and the Problem of Parallel Patents. *Antitrust Bull.*, Spring 1969, *14*, pp. 181–220. [G: E.E.C.]

Ameloot, W. De algemene evolutie van het baanvervoer. (The General Evolution of Road Transport. With English summary.) *Econ. Soc. Tijdschr.*, October 1969, *23*(5), pp. 441–54. [G: E.E.C.]

Andic, Fuat M. The Development Impact of the EEC on the French and Dutch Caribbean. *J. Common Market Stud.*, September 1969, *8*(1), pp. 19–49. [G: Dutch Caribbean; French Caribbean; E.E.C.]

d'Arge, Ralph C. Note on Customs Unions and Direct Foreign Investment. *Econ. J.*, June 1969, *79* (314), pp. 324–33. [G: E.E.C.; E.F.T.A.; U.S.]

Augenthaler, Zdenek. The Socialist Countries and GATT. **In** *Alting von Geusau, F. A. M., ed.*, 1969, pp. 75–82.

Bachmann, Hans. The Prospect of a European Monetary Union Restated. *Aussenwirtschaft*, March 1969, *24*(1), pp. 27–44. [G: E.E.C.]

Baerresen, Donald W. Brazil's Participation in LAFTA, 1962–1965. **In** *Ellis, H. S., ed.*, 1969, pp. 266–82. [G: Brazil]

Balassa, Bela. Industrial Development in an Open Economy: The Case of Norway. *Oxford Econ. Pap.*, November 1969, *21*(3), pp. 344–59. [G: Norway; E.F.T.A.]

Barall, Milton. Statement. **In** *New Directions for the 1970's: Toward a Strategy of Inter-American Development, Pts. 1–5, HCH*, 1969, pp. 227–29. [G: Latin America]

Baranson, Jack. Integration Prospects for the Automotive Industry under LAFTA. **In** *Hilton, R., ed.*, 1969, pp. 261–71. [G: LAFTA]

Barnes, William S. Legal Aspects of Economic Integration in Latin America. **In** *Hilton, R., ed.*, 1969, pp. 275–90. [G: Latin America]

Barre, Raymond. La Communità Europea e i problemi monetari internazionali. (The European Economic Community and International Monetary Problems. With English summary.) *Bancaria*, July 1969, *25*(7), pp. 897–901. [G: E.E.C.]

Bertrand, Raymond. Prospects for Integration of European Capital Markets: A Comment. *J. Money, Credit, Banking*, August 1969, *1*(3), pp. 347–49. [G: E.E.C.]

Bolin, William H. Commercial Banks and Latin American Integration. **In** *Hilton, R., ed.*, 1969, pp. 203–09. [G: Latin America]

Bradbury, Robert W. Socio-Economic Perspectives for a Latin American Common Market. **In** *Hilton, R., ed.*, 1969, pp. 72–79. [G: Latin America]

Buxbaum, Richard M. The Group Exemption and Exculsive Distributorships in the Common Market—Procedural Technicalities. *Antitrust Bull.*, Summer 1969, *14*, pp. 499–514. [G: E.E.C.]

Cairncross, Alec K. [Sir]. Comments on the Papers by Goran Ohlin and André Marchal. **In** *Samuelson, P. A., ed.*, 1969, pp. 218–21.

Carnoy, Martin. A Welfare Analysis of Latin American Economic Union: Six Industry Studies. **In** *Hilton, R., ed.*, 1969, pp. 237–60. [G: Latin America]

Cavin, James P. The International Encyclopedia of

the Social Sciences: A Review Article. *Amer. J. Agr. Econ.*, May 1969, *51*(2), pp. 268–78.

Chou, K. R. Hong Kong's Changing Pattern of Trade and Economic Interdependence in Southeast Asia. In *Morgan, T. and Spoelstra, N., eds.*, 1969, pp. 155–77. [G: Hong Kong]

Cleveland, Harold van B. The Common Market after De Gaulle. *Foreign Aff.*, July 1969, *47*(4), pp. 697–710. [G: E.E.C.]

Damm, Walter. The Obstacles to a Regional Integration of Capital Markets: A Comment. *J. Money, Credit, Banking*, August 1969, *1*(3), pp. 328–31.

Dell, Sidney. Obstacles to Latin American Integration. In *Hilton, R., ed.*, 1969, pp. 61–71. [G: Latin America]

Denham, Robert Edwin. The Role of the U.S. as an External Actor in the Integration of Latin America. *J. Common Market Stud.*, March 1969, *7*(3), pp. 199–216. [G: LAFTA]

Dosser, Douglas; Han, S. S. and Hitiris, Theodore. Trade Effects of Tax Harmonisation: Harmonisation of the Value-added Tax in E.E.C. *Manchester Sch. Econ. Soc. Stud.*, December 1969, *37*(4), pp. 337–46. [G: E.E.C.]

Drysdale, Peter. Japan, Australia, New Zealand: The Prospect for Western Pacific Economic Integration. *Econ. Rec.*, September 1969, *45*(111), pp. 321–42. [G: Japan; Australia; New Zealand]

Dubois-Pelerin, P. E. Le Marché Commun et le commerce international des Six. (Common Market and Its International Trade. With English summary.) *Rivista Int. Sci. Econ. Com.*, June 1969, *16*(6), pp. 568–89.

Dupuis, M. Great Britain and the Common Market. In *Duquesne, L., et al.*, 1969, pp. 105–15. [G: E.E.C.; U.K.]

Duquesne de la Vinelle, L. Common Monetary Policy. In *Duquesne, L., et al.*, 1969, pp. 83–91. [G: E.E.C.]

Duquesne de la Vinelle, L. Common Policy for Regional Development. In *Duquesne, L., et al.*, 1969, pp. 72–82. [G: E.E.C.]

Duquesne de la Vinelle, L. European Integration and Common Economic Policies. In *Duquesne, L., et al.*, 1969, pp. 54–61. [G: E.E.C.]

Duquesne de la Vinelle, L. The Common Market: An Evaluation of its First Ten Years. In *Duquesne, L., et al.*, 1969, pp. 15–29. [G: E.E.C.]

Eder, George Jackson. Economic Integration in Latin America: The Next Fifty Years. In *Hilton, R., ed.*, 1969, pp. 157–69. [G: Latin America]

El-Agraa, Ali M. The Sudan and the Arab Customs Union: A Conflict. *East Afr. Econ. Rev.*, December 1969, *1*(2), pp. 39–51. [G: Sudan; Arab Customs Union]

Erhard, Ludwig. Prospects for European Integration. *Lloyds Bank Rev.*, January 1969, (91), pp. 1–9. [G: E.E.C.]

Fazekas, B. and Öri, J. On the Formulation of a Common Agricultural Policy for CMEA Countries. (In Russian. With English summary.) *Acta Oecon.*, 1969, *4*(4), pp. 403–15. [G: CMEA]

Goodman, Richard J. Policy and Non-Policy in Foreign Trade: Discussion. *Amer. J. Agr. Econ.*, December 1969, *51*(5), pp. 1354–56. [G: U.S.; E.E.C.]

Goodman, Seymour S. Turkey's Trade Prospects in the Common Market: An Exploratory Study. *J. Common Market Stud.*, June 1969, *7*(4), pp. 305–26. [G: Turkey]

Goodman, Stephen H. E.E.C.: The Economics of Associate Membership. *J. Devel. Stud.*, January 1969, *5*(2), pp. 138–41. [G: E.E.C.]

Gundelach, Finn. The Kennedy Round of Trade Negotiations: Results and Lessons. In *Alting von Geusau, F. A. M., ed.*, 1969, pp. 146–98.

Hazlewood, Arthur. An Approach to the Analysis of the Spatial Distribution of the Market in East Africa. *Bull. Oxford Univ. Inst. Econ. Statist.*, November 1969, *31*(4), pp. 243–61. [G: E. Africa]

Heraud, Jorge and Pomalaza, José. An Educational Television and Communications System for Latin America. In *Hilton, R., ed.*, 1969, pp. 381–400. [G: Latin America]

Hildebrand, John R. LAFTA and Paraguay: Economic and Social Development. In *Hilton, R., ed.*, 1969, pp. 551–61. [G: LAFTA; Paraguay]

Hoan, Buu. Regionalism: Limitations and Possibilities. *Malayan Econ. Rev.*, October 1969, *14*(2), pp. 18–25. [G: Asia]

Holbik, Karel. An Economic Profile of Eastern Europe. In *Grub, P. D. and Holbik, K.*, 1969, pp. 140–47. [G: E. Europe]

Islam, Nurul. Comment on Part I: The Context of Economic Cooperation. In *Morgan, T. and Spoelstra, N., eds.*, 1969, pp. 59–61. [G: S. E. Asia]

Jansen, F. P. and Janssen, L. H. Imports from Developing Countries: A Comparison between EEC, EFTA and USA. In *[Tinbergen, J.]*, 1969, pp. 129–56. [G: E.E.C.; E.F.T.A.; U.S.]

Johnson, Harry G. Financial and Monetary Problems: Britain and the EEC. In *van Meerhaeghe, M. A. G., ed.*, 1969, pp. 21–32. [G: E.E.C.; U.K.]

Johnson, Harry G. Some Aspects of the Multilateral Free Trade Association Proposal. *Manchester Sch. Econ. Soc. Stud.*, September 1969, *37*(3), pp. 189–212.

de Jong, H. W. Concentration in the Common Market. In *Economic Concentration, Pt. 7A, SCH*, 1969, pp. 3907–15. [G: E.E.C.]

Kaufmann, Johan and Alting von Geusau, A. M. The Institutional Framework for International Trade Relations. In *Alting von Geusau, F. A. M., ed.*, 1969, pp. 94–112.

Kendrick, James G. Policy and Non-Policy in Foreign Trade: Discussion. *Amer. J. Agr. Econ.*, December 1969, *51*(5), pp. 1349–51. [G: U.S.; E.E.C.]

Kitamura, Hiroshi and Bhagat, A. N. Aspects of Regional Harmonization of National Development Plans. In *Morgan, T. and Spoelstra, N., eds.*, 1969, pp. 39–56. [G: S. E. Asia]

Kojima, Kiyoshi. Asian Developing Countries and PAFTA: Development, Aid and Trade Preferences. *Hitotsubashi J. Econ.*, June 1969, *10*(1), pp. 1–17. [G: U.S.; Canada; Japan; Australia; New Zealand]

Kolinski, Ralph. Customs Unions of Undeveloped Nations: The Case of Central America. *Econ. Int.*, February 1969, *22*(1), pp. 116–33. [G: Central America]

Kouwenhoven, A. De Noordse economische integratie. (Nordic Economic Integration. With English summary.) *De Economist,* September/October 1969, *117*(5), pp. 543–62. [G: Scandanavia]

Krause, Walter and Mathis, F. John. The Status of "Lesser Developed" Countries within a Latin American Common Market. **In** *Hilton, R., ed.,* 1969, pp. 471–84. [G: Latin America]

Kreinin, Mordechai E. Trade Creation and Diversion by the EEC and EFTA. *Econ. Int.,* May 1969, *22*(2), pp. 273–80. [G: E.E.C.; E.F.T.A.]

Łączkowski, Bohdan. Poland's Participation in the Kennedy Round. **In** *Alting von Geusau, F. A. M., ed.,* 1969, pp. 83–93. [G: Poland]

Larre, René. Facts of Life about the Integration of National Capital Markets. *J. Money, Credit, Banking,* August 1969, *1*(3), pp. 319–27.

Lipinski, Andrew J. Integration of Latin American Communications. **In** *Hilton, R., ed.,* 1969, pp. 343–54. [G: Latin America]

MacEachern, G. A. and Huff, H. Bruce. Policy and Non-Policy in Foreign Trade: Discussion. *Amer. J. Agr. Econ.,* December 1969, *51*(5), pp. 1352–54. [G: U.S.; E.E.C.]

Malmgren, H. B. and Schlechty, D. L. Technology and Neo-Mercantilism in International Agricultural Trade. *Amer. J. Agr. Econ.,* December 1969, *51*(5), pp. 1325–37. [G: E.E.C.]

Marchal, André. The Problems of the Common Market. **In** *Samuelson, P. A., ed.,* 1969, pp. 176–217. [G: E.E.C.]

Markert, Kurt E. The Dyestuff Case: A Contribution to the Relationship between the Antitrust Laws of the European Economic Community and Its Member States. *Antitrust Bull.,* Winter 1969, *14,* pp. 869–99. [G: E.E.C.]

Mathis, F. John. The Latin American Common Market: Problems and Progress. *Quart. Rev. Econ. Bus.,* Autumn 1969, *9*(3), pp. 5–16. [G: LAFTA]

McClelland, Donald H. The Common Market's Contribution to Central American Economic Growth: A First Approximation. **In** *Hilton, R., ed.,* 1969, pp. 508–36. [G: Central America]

van Meerhaeghe, M. A. G. Economics: Britain and the EEC—An Introduction. **In** *van Meerhaeghe, M. A. G., ed.,* 1969, pp. 1–20. [G: E.E.C.; U.K.]

Mikesell, Raymond F. Changing World Trade Patterns and America's Leadership Role. *Ann. Amer. Acad. Polit. Soc. Sci.,* July 1969, *384,* pp. 35–44. [G: U.S.]

Milano, Armando. The Autonomous State Tobacco Concern. *Rev. Econ. Cond. Italy,* September 1969, *23*(5), pp. 409–27. [G: Italy]

Mookerjee, Subimal; Chandavarkar, Anand G. and Cleary, D. J. Existing International Banking and Credit Facilities in the ECAFE Region. *Int. Monet. Fund Staff Pap.,* November 1969, *16*(3), pp. 391–435. [G: Far East]

de Moor, A. E. International Trade of Goods and Services with the TVA in Operation. *Bull. Int. Fiscal Doc.,* July, August, September 1969, *23*(7–8–9), pp. 297–334. [G: Netherlands]

Mouton, Claude. The European Common Market and the Move Towards Self-sufficiency in Food Production. **In** *Papi, U. and Nunn, C., eds.,* 1969, pp. 92–120. [G: E.E.C.]

Mueller, Hans G. The Policy of the European Coal and Steel Community Towards Mergers and Agreements by Steel Companies. *Antitrust Bull.,* Summer 1969, *14,* pp. 413–48. [G: E.E.C.]

Nasini, P. The Reconciliation of Fiscal Legislation. **In** *Duquesne, L., et al.,* 1969, pp. 44–53. [G: E.E.C.]

Niinimäki, Rauno. Kansallisen finanssi- ja sosiaalipolitiikan vaikutuksesta taloudelliseen integraatioon. (The Effect of National Fiscal and Social Policy on Economic Integration. With English summary.) *Kansant. Aikak.,* 1969, *65*(4), pp. 280–303.

Nonomura, Kazuo. Socialist International Division of Labor and Integration Project—A Brief Outline. **In** *Nonomura, K.,* 1969, pp. 95–116. [G: E. Europe; COMECON]

Nonomura, Kazuo. Trade Pricing within SEV Bloc. **In** *Nonomura, K.,* 1969, pp. 117–33. [G: E. Europe; COMECON]

O'Grada, Cormac. The Vocational Training Policy of the EEC and the Free Movement of Skilled Labour. *J. Common Market Stud.,* December 1969, *8*(2), pp. 79–109. [G: E.E.C.]

Ohlin, Goran and Bienaymé, A. Replies to Comments. **In** *Samuelson, P. A., ed.,* 1969, pp. 230–31.

Ohlin, Goran. Trade in a Non-*Laissez-Faire* World. **In** *Samuelson, P. A., ed.,* 1969, pp. 157–75.

Oliver, Covey T. Physical Integration and the Future of Latin America. *Soc. Res.,* Summer 1969, *36*(2), pp. 253–66. [G: Latin America]

Orrego Vicuña, Francisco. The Dynamics of the Subregional Agreements within the LAFTA Movement. **In** *Hilton, R., ed.,* 1969, pp. 485–99. [G: LAFTA]

Paunio, J. J. Comments on the Papers by Goran Ohlin and André Marchal. **In** *Samuelson, P. A., ed.,* 1969, pp. 221–26.

Piňdák, F. Czechoslovakia and COMECON. *De Economist,* September/October 1969, *117*(5), pp. 516–42. [G: Czechoslovakia; COMECON]

Pinder, J. Advanced Technology: Britain and the EEC. **In** *van Meerhaeghe, M. A. G., ed.,* 1969, pp. 58–76. [G: E.E.C.; U.K.]

Richebächer, Kurt. The Problems and Prospects of Integrating European Capital Markets. *J. Money, Credit, Banking,* August 1969, *1*(3), pp. 336–46. [G: E.E.C.]

Rizzoni, Eitel M. Development and Integration of Latin American Telecommunications. **In** *Hilton, R., ed.,* 1969, pp. 355–80. [G: Latin America]

Robinson, H. Leslie. Electric Power Integration in Latin America. **In** *Hilton, R., ed.,* 1969, pp. 335–42. [G: Latin America]

Roe, Alan R. Terms of Trade and Transfer Effects in the East African Common Market: An Empirical Study. *Bull. Oxford Univ. Inst. Econ. Statist.,* August 1969, *31*(3), pp. 153–67. [G: E. Africa]

Rolfe, Sidney E. The Capital Market Phenomena: A Comment. *J. Money, Credit, Banking,* August 1969, *1*(3), pp. 332–35.

van Rooijen, M. J. The Substantial Holding Privilege in Netherlands Corporate Income Tax. *Bull. Int. Fiscal Doc.,* July, August, September 1969, *23*(7–8–9), pp. 337–405. [G: Netherlands]

Roussakis, Emmanuel N. La Comunità Economica Europea: Bilancio economico e politico. (The European Economic Community: An Economic and Political Balance Sheet. With English summary.) *Rivista Int. Sci. Econ. Com.*, October 1969, *16*(10), pp. 993–1006. [G: E.E.C.]

Ruta, Guido. Profili comparativistici del sistema bancario italiano nell'ambito della Comunità Economica Europea. (Comparative Aspects of the Italian Banking System within the European Economic Community. With English summary.) *Bancaria*, July 1969, *25*(7), pp. 829–41. [G: Italy; E.E.C.]

Sarabia, Antonio R. A Comparison between European and Latin American Integration. In *Hilton, R., ed.*, 1969, pp. 97–109. [G: Europe; Latin America]

Scaperlanda, Anthony E. The Political Economy of Economic Integration. In *Hilton, R., ed.*, 1969, pp. 291–310. [G: Latin America]

Scott, Ira O., Jr. The Problems and Prospects of Integrating European Capital Markets: A Comment. *J. Money, Credit, Banking*, August 1969, *1* (3), pp. 350–53. [G: E.E.C.]

Sessa, Giuseppe. Il problema delle esenzioni nell' I.V.A. e gli scambi internazionali. (The Problem of the Exemptions in New Italian Taxation System. With English summary.) *Mondo Aperto*, February 1969, *23*(1), pp. 10–35. [G: Italy]

Snell, Hampton K. Transportation Integration: A Variety of Problems. In *Hilton, R., ed.*, 1969, pp. 321–34. [G: Latin America]

Solar, Donald. The Case against Latin American Integration: Economic and Political Factors. In *Hilton, R., ed.*, 1969, pp. 110–32. [G: Latin America]

Sunkel, Osvaldo. National Development Policy and External Dependence in Latin America. *J. Devel. Stud.*, October 1969, *6*(1), pp. 23–48. [G: Latin America]

Swann, D. Competition and Price Policies: Britain and the EEC. In *van Meerhaeghe, M. A. G., ed.*, 1969, pp. 33–57. [G: E.E.C.; U.K.]

Triffin, Robert. On the Creation of a European Reserve Fund. *Banca Naz. Lavoro Quart. Rev.*, December 1969, (91), pp. 327–46. [G: E.E.C.]

Truman, Edwin M. The European Economic Community: Trade Creation and Trade Diversion. *Yale Econ. Essays*, Spring 1969, *9*(1), pp. 201–57. [G: E.E.C.]

Vasilev, Dimitur. The International Socialist Division of Labor and Its Role in the Increased Profitability of Bulgaria's Foreign Trade. *Eastern Europ. Econ.*, Fall 1969, *8*(1), pp. 90–99. [G: Bulgaria]

Vingerhoets, J. The Kennedy Round and the Developing Countries. In *Alting von Geusau, F. A. M., ed.*, 1969, pp. 48–74.

de Vries, Barend A. High Cost of Industry in Developing Countries—Causes and Remedies. *Finance Develop.*, December 1969, *6*(4), pp. 43–47.

Wadhva, Charan D. Reserve Pooling in Asia and the Far East. *Pakistan Develop. Rev.*, Autumn 1969, *9*(3), pp. 309–29. [G: Asia; Far East]

Walter, Ingo. Nontariff Barriers and the Free-Trade Area Option. *Banca Naz. Lavoro Quart. Rev.*, March 1969, (88), pp. 16–45.

Woodruff, William and Woodruff, Helga. The Role of the United States in Latin American Economic Integration. In *Hilton, R., ed.*, 1969, pp. 149–56. [G: U.S.; Latin America]

Wu, Ta-Yeh. Problems and Prospects of Economic Cooperation in Southeast Asia. In *Morgan, T. and Spoelstra, N., eds.*, 1969, pp. 15–36. [G: S. E. Asia]

Young, John H. Comments on the Papers by Goran Ohlin and André Marchal. In *Samuelson, P. A., ed.*, 1969, pp. 226–29.

430 Balance of Payments; International Finance

431 Balance of Payments; Mechanisms of Adjustment; Exchange Rates

4310 General

Adler, F. Michael. The Framework for Investigating Direct Manufacturing Investment Overseas. *Law Contemp. Probl.*, Winter 1969, *34*(1), pp. 3–17. [G: U.S.]

Aliber, Robert Z. Exchange Risk, Yield Curves, and the Pattern of Capital Flows. *J. Finance*, May 1969, *24*(2), pp. 361–70. [G: U.S.]

Blough, Roy. The Adjustment Process and the International Role of the Dollar. *J. Finance*, May 1969, *24*(2), pp. 345–59. [G: U.S.]

Carli, Guido. Problemi dell'adesione della Gran Bretagna al Mercato Comune relativamente alle questioni monetarie. (Monetary Aspects of British Entry into the Common Market. With English summary.) *Bancaria*, June 1969, *25*(6), pp. 768–72. [G: U.K.; E.E.C.]

Conan, A. R. Does Britain Pay Its Way? *Nat. Westminster Bank Quart. Rev.*, February 1969, pp. 2–17. [G: U.K.]

Enthoven, Alain C. and Smith, K. Wayne. What Forces for NATO? And from Whom? *Foreign Aff.*, October 1969, *48*(1), pp. 80–96.

Franks, Alison. Does Britain Pay Its Way?—A Rejoinder. *Nat. Westminster Bank Quart. Rev.*, May 1969, pp. 42–44. [G: U.K.]

Gaud, William S. Statement. In *A Review of Balance of Payments Policies, JECH*, 1969, pp. 90–97. [G: U.S.]

Gulhati, Ravi. Debt-Servicing as an Aid to Promotion of Trade of Developing Countries: Comment. *Oxford Econ. Pap.*, November 1969, *21*(3), pp. 409–15.

Haberler, G. The Market for Foreign Exchange and the Stability of the Balance of Payments: A Theoretical Analysis. In *Cooper, R. N., ed.*, 1969, pp. 107–34.

Haberler, Gottfried. Institutional Arrangements: Appendix: Taxes on Imports and Subsidies on Exports as a Tool of Adjustment. In *Mundell, R. A. and Swoboda, A. K., eds.*, 1969, pp. 173–79.

Honavar, R. M. Debt-Servicing as an Aid to Promotion of Trade of Developing Countries: Comment. *Oxford Econ. Pap.*, November 1969, *21*(3), pp. 416–19.

Johnson, Harry G. Current International Economic Policy Issues. *J. Bus.*, January 1969, *42*(1), pp. 12–21. [G: U.S.]

Kaufmann, Hugo M. A Debate over Germany's Revaluation 1961: A Chapter in Political Economy. *Weltwirtsch. Arch.*, 1969, *103*(2), pp. 181–212. **[G: Germany]**

Kay, John A. and Hole, Peter C. The Fund Meeting. *Finance Develop.*, December 1969, *6*(4), pp. 10–14.

Khatkhate, Deena R. Debt-Servicing as an Aid to Promotion of Trade of Developing Countries: A Reply. *Oxford Econ. Pap.*, November 1969, *21*(3), pp. 424–27.

Kimball, Warren F. "Beggar My Neighbor": America and the British Interim Financial Crisis, 1940–41. *J. Econ. Hist.*, December 1969, *29*(4), pp. 758–72. **[G: U.S.; U.K.]**

Kindleberger, Charles P. Measuring Equilibrium in the Balance of Payments. *J. Polit. Econ.*, November/December 1969, *77*(6), pp. 873–91. **[G: U.S.]**

Kindleberger, Charles P. Princeton Essays in International Finance. *J. Econ. Lit.*, September 1969, *7*(3), pp. 807–10.

Laffer, Arthur B. The U.S. Balance of Payments—A Financial Center View. *Law Contemp. Probl.*, Winter 1969, *34*(1), pp. 33–46. **[G: U.S.]**

Manser, W. A. P. Professor Reddaway's Last Word? *Nat. Westminster Bank Quart. Rev.*, February 1969, pp. 40–52. **[G: U.K.]**

McQuade, Lawrence C. Statement. **In** *A Review of Balance of Payments Policies, JECH,* 1969, pp. 3–29. **[G: U.S.]**

Mikesell, Raymond F. Changing World Trade Patterns and America's Leadership Role. *Ann. Amer. Acad. Polit. Soc. Sci.*, July 1969, *384,* pp. 35–44. **[G: U.S.]**

Moot, Robert C. Statement. **In** *A Review of Balance of Payments Policies, JECH,* 1969, pp. 97–108. **[G: U.S.]**

Mundell, Robert A. Real Gold, Dollars, and Paper Gold. *Amer. Econ. Rev.*, May 1969, *59*(2), pp. 324–31.

Narasimham, M. Debt-Servicing as an Aid to Promotion of Trade of Developing Countries: Comment. *Oxford Econ. Pap.*, November 1969, *21*(3), pp. 404–08.

Nuti, Domenico Mario. On Incomes Policy. *Sci. Soc.*, Fall-Winter 1969, *33*(4), pp. 415–25.

Oppenheimer, Peter M. Import Deposits. *Nat. Westminster Bank Quart. Rev.*, February 1969, pp. 69–72.

Polasek, M. and Barattieri, V. U. S. Gold Policy and the Gold Exchange Standard. *Econ. Rec.*, March 1969, *45*(109), pp. 48–68. **[G: U.S.]**

Roosa, Robert V. The American Share in the Stream of International Payments. *Ann. Amer. Acad. Polit. Soc. Sci.*, July 1969, *384,* pp. 21–34. **[G: U.S.]**

Salant, Walter S. International Reserves and Payments Adjustment. *Banca Naz. Lavoro Quart. Rev.*, September 1969, (90), pp. 281–308.

Shapiro, Eli. International Financial Problems and the Role of the Dollar: Discussion. *J. Finance,* May 1969, *24*(2), pp. 375–78. **[G: U.S.]**

Shaw, B. D. The New Zealand Economy, 1967–68. *Econ. Rec.*, March 1969, *45*(109), pp. 1–16. **[G: New Zealand]**

Smith, John S. and Bouter, Arie C. The Treatment of Reserves and of Reserve Creation in the Balance of Payments Accounts. *Int. Monet. Fund Staff Pap.*, July 1969, *16*(2), pp. 202–23.

Solomon, Robert. International Financial Problems and the Role of the Dollar: Discussion. *J. Finance,* May 1969, *24*(2), pp. 371–74. **[G: U.S.]**

Spraos, John. Some Aspects of Sterling in the Decade 1957–66. **In** *Aliber, R. Z., ed.*, 1969, pp. 158–73.

Streissler, Erich. A Stochastic Model of International Reserve Requirements during Growth of World Trade. *Z. Nationalökon.*, December 1969, *29* (3–4), pp. 347–70.

Surrey, Stanley S. Statement. **In** *A Review of Balance of Payments Policies, JECH,* 1969, pp. 40–49. **[G: U.S.]**

Sutcliffe, R. B. Debt-Servicing as an Aid to Promotion of Trade of Developing Countries: A Further Comment. *Oxford Econ. Pap.*, November 1969, *21*(3), pp. 420–23.

Viita, Pentti. Investoinnit ja maksutase. (Investments and the Balance of Payments. With English summary.) *Kansant. Aikak.*, 1969, *65*(3), pp. 233. **[G: Finland]**

Ward, M. The Effects of the U.K. Devaluation of Sterling on the Fiji Economy. *Econ. Rec.*, March 1969, *45*(109), pp. 92–115. **[G: Fiji]**

Weiller, Jean. Anti-Cyclical Policies in Relation to Foreign Trade Patterns and Tariffs (An Historical Approach). *Econ. Int.*, May 1969, *22*(2), pp. 225–44. **[G: France]**

Wicksell, Knut. The Riddle of Foreign Exchanges. **In** *Wicksell, K.*, 1969, pp. 229–49.

4312 Balance of Payments and Adjustment Mechanisms: Theory

Argy, Victor. Monetary Variables and the Balance of Payments. *Int. Monet. Fund Staff Pap.*, July 1969, *16*(2), pp. 267–88.

Baffi, Paolo. International Liquidity and the Reform of the Adjustment Mechanism: Comment. **In** *Samuelson, P. A., ed.*, 1969, pp. 254–58.

Baggott, Nancy and Flanders, M. June. Economic Policy in an Open Economy: A Reader's Guide. *Econ. Int.*, November 1969, *22*(4), pp. 593–605.

Banks, F. E. A Note on Income, Capital Mobility, and the Theory of Economic Policy. *Kyklos,* 1969, *22*(4), pp. 767–73.

Belsare, S. K. International Liquidity Problems and the Developing Countries. **In** *Bhuleshkar, A. V., ed.*, 1969, pp. 425–45.

Branson, William H. The Minimum Covered Interest Differential Needed for International Arbitrage Activity. *J. Polit. Econ.*, November/December 1969, *77*(6), pp. 1028–35. **[G: U.S.; Canada; U.K.]**

Brown, E. H. Phelps. Balancing External Payments by Adjusting Domestic Income. *Australian Econ. Pap.*, December 1969, *8*(13), pp. 111–21.

Buonomo, Maurizio. La stabilità economica interna, presupposto dell'equilibrio monetario internazionale. (Internal Economic Stability, the Prerequisite for International Monetary Equilibrium. With English summary.) *Bancaria,* June 1969, *25*(6), pp. 725–30.

Cooper, Richard N. Macroeconomic Policy Adjustment in Interdependent Economies. *Quart. J. Econ.*, February 1969, *83*(1), pp. 1–24.

Fernandez Lopez, Manuel. Análisis gráfico de las devaluaciones cambiarias. (A Geometric Approach to Finite Devaluation. With English summary.) *Económica*, September–December 1969, *15*(3), pp. 291–98.

Flanders, M. June. International Liquidity Is Always Inadequate. *Kyklos*, 1969, *22*(3), pp. 519–29.

Furth, J. Herbert. Barriers to Investment Abroad as Tools of Payments Policy. *Law Contemp. Probl.*, Winter 1969, *34*(1), pp. 64–83. **[G: U.S.]**

Furth, J. Herbert. International Monetary Reform and the "Crawling Peg"—Comment. *Fed. Res. Bank St. Louis Rev.*, July 1969, *51*(7), pp. 21–25.

Grewe, Klaus. Wirtschaftsunion bei flexiblen Wechselkursen. (Economic Union under a System of Flexible Exchange Rates. With English summary.) *Schmollers Jahr.*, 1969, *89*(1), pp. 1–32.

Harrod, Roy F. [Sir]. Problemi monetari d'oggi. (Survey of Monetary Problems. With English summary.) *Bancaria*, July 1969, *25*(7), pp. 819–28.

Helliwell, John F. Monetary and Fiscal Policies for an Open Economy. *Oxford Econ. Pap.*, March 1969, *21*(1), pp. 35–55.

Hollerman, Leon. Recent Difficulties in Japan's Economic Development. *Banca Naz. Lavoro Quart. Rev.*, March 1969, (88), pp. 66–90. **[G: Japan]**

Hume, D. Of the Balance of Trade. **In** *Cooper, R. N., ed.*, 1969, pp. 25–37.

Ingram, J. C. Some Implications of Puerto Rican Experience. **In** *Cooper, R. N., ed.*, 1969, pp. 87–104. **[G: Puerto Rico]**

Johnson, Harry G. The Case for Flexible Exchange Rates, 1969. *Fed. Res. Bank St. Louis Rev.*, June 1969, *51*(6), pp. 12–24.

Klopstock, Fred H. Impact of Euro-Markets on the United States Balance of Payments. *Law Contemp. Probl.*, Winter 1969, *34*(1), pp. 157–71. **[G: U.S.]**

Krueger, Anne O. Balance-of-Payments Theory. *J. Econ. Lit.*, March 1969, *7*(1), pp. 1–26.

Letiche, John M. I pagamenti internazionali. (International Payments. With English summary.) *Rivista Int. Sci. Econ. Com.*, January 1969, *16*(1), pp. 1–30.

Levin, Jonathan. A Sectoral Approach to Balance of Payments Analysis. *Finance Develop.*, March 1969, *6*(1), pp. 57–61.

Lindbeck, Assar. International Liquidity and the Reform of the Adjustment Mechanism: Comment. **In** *Samuelson, P. A., ed.*, 1969, pp. 258–63.

Lorensen, Gunter. Untersuchungen zur Theorie des intervalutarischen Gleichgewichts. (On the Theory of Intermonetary Equilibrium. With English summary.) *Weltwirtsch. Arch.*, 1969, *103*(2), pp. 249–320.

McKenzie, George W. International Monetary Reform and the "Crawling Peg"—Reply. *Fed. Res. Bank St. Louis Rev.*, July 1969, *51*(7), pp. 26–31.

McKinnon, Ronald I. Portfolio Balance and International Payments Adjustment. **In** *Mundell, R. A. and Swoboda, A. K., eds.*, 1969, pp. 199–234.

Mundell, Robert A. The Problem of World Stability: Appendix: The Redundancy Problem and the World Price Level. **In** *Mundell, R. A. and Swoboda, A. K., eds.*, 1969, pp. 379–82.

Mundell, Robert A. Toward a Better International Monetary System. *J. Money, Credit, Banking*, August 1969, *1*(3), pp. 625–48.

Olivera, Julio H. G. A Note on the Optimal Rate of Growth of International Reserves. *J. Polit. Econ.*, March/April 1969, *77*(2), pp. 245–48.

Oppenheimer, Peter M. The Case for Raising the Price of Gold. *J. Money, Credit, Banking*, August 1969, *1*(3), pp. 649–65.

Pelleri, Paolo. Le Borse estere nel 1968. (Foreign Stock Exchanges in 1968. With English summary.) *Bancaria*, February 1969, *25*(2), pp. 178–202.

Rousseaux, R. La réévaluation larvée des monnaies des pays industrialisés par rapport à celles des pays en voie de développement. (The Disguised Revaluation of Money in the Industrialised Countries if Exchange Rates Are Compared with the Parities in the Underdeveloped Countries. With English summary.) *Econ. Soc. Tijdschr.*, June 1969, *23*(3), pp. 273–86.

Scitovsky, Tibor. International Liquidity and the Reform of the Adjustment Mechanism: Reply. **In** *Samuelson, P. A., ed.*, 1969, pp. 268–69.

Scitovsky, Tibor. International Liquidity and the Reform of the Adjustment Mechanism. **In** *Samuelson, P. A., ed.*, 1969, pp. 241–54.

Sohmen, Egon and Schneeweiss, Hans. Fiscal and Monetary Policies under Alternative Exchange Rate Systems: A Correction. *Quart. J. Econ.*, May 1969, *83*(2), pp. 336–40.

Sohmen, Egon. International Liquidity and the Reform of the Adjustment Mechanism: Comment. **In** *Samuelson, P. A., ed.*, 1969, pp. 263–68.

Sohmen, Egon. The Assignment Problem. **In** *Mundell, R. A. and Swoboda, A. K., eds.*, 1969, pp. 183–97.

Stone, Richard. Foreign Trade and Full Employment: An Input-output Analysis. *L'Industria*, October–December 1969, (4), pp. 431–43.

Ventriglia, Ferdinando. The Balance of Payments and Italian Economic Growth. *Rev. Econ. Cond. Italy*, September 1969, *23*(5), pp. 381–96. **[G: Italy]**

Willett, Thomas D. and Forte, Francesco. Interest Rate Policy and External Balance. *Quart. J. Econ.*, May 1969, *83*(2), pp. 242–62. **[G: U.S.]**

Willett, Thomas D. The Influence of the Trade Balance and Export Financing on International Short-Term Capital Movements: A Theoretical Analysis. *Kyklos*, 1969, *22*(2), pp. 314–27.

4313 Balance of Payments and Adjustment Mechanisms: Studies

Arey, Will. Statement. **In** *A Review of Balance of Payments Policies, JECH*, 1969, pp. 29–35. **[G: U.S.]**

Behrman, Jack N. Assessing the Foreign Investment Controls. *Law Contemp. Probl.*, Winter 1969, *34*(1), pp. 84–94. **[G: U.S.]**

Bhatia, Rattan J.; Szapary, Gyorgy and Quinn, Brian. Stabilization Program in Sierra Leone. *Int. Monet. Fund Staff Pap.*, November 1969, *16*(3), pp.

504–28. [G: Sierra Leone]

Bohi, Douglas R. War in Vietnam and United States Balance of Payments. *Rev. Econ. Statist.*, November 1969, *51*(4), pp. 471–74. [G: U.S.]

Botsas, Eleutherios N. A Note on Migration and the Balance of Payments. *Econ. Int.*, May 1969, *22*(2), pp. 247–51. [G: Greece]

Brimmer, Andrew F. Statement. In *A Review of Balance of Payments Policies, JECH,* 1969, pp. 155–68. [G: U.S.]

Canterbery, E. Ray. Exchange Rates, Capital Flows and Monetary Policy. *Amer. Econ. Rev.*, June 1969, *59*(3), pp. 426–32. [G: U.S.; U.K.; Canada]

Carli, Guido. Mobilità internazionale dei capitali e stabilità monetaria interna. (International Mobility of Capital and Internal Monetary Stability. With English summary.) *Bancaria,* October 1969, *25*(10), pp. 1216–20. [G: U.S.; Italy]

Carli, Guido. Programmi e prospettive della politica monetaria internazionale. (International Monetary Policy of the Moment—Programs and Outlooks. With English summary.) *Bancaria,* December 1969, *25*(12), pp. 1459–63.

de Carlo, G. R. Interest Sensitivity of Short-Term Capital Movements: Some Recent Statistical Studies. *Kyklos,* 1969, *22*(4), pp. 737–51. [G: U.S.]

de Cecco, Marcello. The Problem of World Stability: Appendix: The Italian Payments Crisis of 1963–64. In *Mundell, R. A. and Swoboda, A. K., eds.,* 1969, pp. 383–89. [G: Italy]

Chibrikov, G. Exporting Private Capital: Impact on the Exporting Country's Economy. *Prob. Econ.*, December 1969, *12*(8), pp. 23–45. [G: U.S.]

Christie, Herbert. Euro-dollars and the Balance of Payments. In *Chalmers, E. B., ed.,* 1969, pp. 57–71.

Clark, Peter B. The Effects of International Monetary Developments on Capital Movements. *Law Contemp. Probl.*, Winter 1969, *34*(1), pp. 18–32.

Colombo, Emilio. Equilibrio della bilancia dei pagamenti e utilizzo delle risorse senza inflazione. (Equilibrium of the Balance of Payments and Internal Use of Resources without Inflation. With English summary.) *Bancaria,* October 1969, *25* (10), pp. 1221–24. [G: Italy]

Constanzo, G. A. Statement. In *A Review of Balance of Payments Policies, JECH,* 1969, pp. 187–91. [G: U.S.]

Danielian, N. R. Statement. In *A Review of Balance of Payments Policies, JECH,* 1969, pp. 212–33. [G: U.S.]

Davenport, John. The Continuing Crisis of the Dollar. In *Starleaf, D. R., ed.,* 1969, pp. 379–86. [G: U.S.]

Deming, Frederick L. Statement. In *A Review of Balance of Payments Policies, JECH,* 1969, pp. 168–87. [G: U.S.]

Devlin, David T. The U.S. Balance of Payments: Third Quarter 1969. *Surv. Curr. Bus.*, December 1969, *49*(12), pp. 18–39. [G: U.S.]

Deweirdt, E. Le marché des euro-obligations. (About Euro-Bonds. With English summary.) *Rivista Int. Sci. Econ. Com.*, November 1969, *16* (11), pp. 1033–52. [G: Europe]

Dudley, Leonard and Passell, Peter. War in Vietnam and United States Balance of Payments: Reply to Comment by Douglas Bohi. *Rev. Econ. Statist.*, November 1969, *51*(4), pp. 474–75.

Duisenberg, W. F. Problematiek rond de Britse betalingsbalans. (British Balance of Payments Problems. With English summary.) *De Economist,* November/December 1969, *117*(6), pp. 615–57. [G: U.K.]

Ellicott, John. United States Controls on Foreign Direct Investment: The 1969 Program. *Law Contemp. Probl.*, Winter 1969, *34*(1), pp. 47–63. [G: U.S.]

Fieleke, Norman S. The Buy-American Policy of the United States Government: Its Balance-of-Payments and Welfare Effects. *New Eng. Econ. Rev.*, July/August 1969, pp. 2–18. [G: U.S.]

Fiero, Charles E. Statement. In *A Review of Balance of Payments Policies, JECH,* 1969, pp. 141–55. [G: U.S.]

Goldstein, Henry N. Does It Necessarily Cost Anything to Be the "World Banker"? In *Officer, L. H. and Willett, T. D., eds.,* 1969, pp. 68–74. [G: U.S.]

Gray, H. Peter. A Keynesian Framework for the International Accounts. *Weltwirtsch. Arch.*, 1969, *103*(1), pp. 1–25.

Grubel, Herbert G. The Benefits and Costs of Being the World Banker. In *Officer, L. H. and Willett, T. D., eds.,* 1969, pp. 59–67. [G: U.S.]

Hagemann, Helmut A. Reserve Policies of Central Banks and Their Implications for U.S. Balance of Payments Policy. *Amer. Econ. Rev.*, March 1969, *59*(1), pp. 62–77.

Helliwell, John F., et al. Econometric Analysis of Policy Choices for an Open Economy. *Rev. Econ. Statist.*, November 1969, *51*(4), pp. 383–98. [G: Canada]

Hodjera, Zoran. Basic Balances, Short-Term Capital Flow, and International Reserves of Industrial Countries. *Int. Monet. Fund Staff Pap.*, November 1969, *16*(3), pp. 582–612.

Holbik, Karel. United States Balance of Payments Deficit and Monetary Policy. *Weltwirtsch. Arch.*, 1969, *103*(1), pp. 160–80. [G: U.S.]

Holland, Thomas E. 'Operation Twist' and the Movement of Interest Rates and Related Economic Time Series. *Int. Econ. Rev.*, October 1969, *10*(3), pp. 260–65. [G: U.S.]

Islam, Nurul. Export Policy in Pakistan. In *[Tinbergen, J.],* 1969, pp. 219–43. [G: Pakistan]

Jalan, Bimal. Gains to Donor Countries from Tied Aid. *Finance Develop.*, September 1969, *6*(3), pp. 14–18.

Johnson, Harry G. Financial and Monetary Problems: Britain and the EEC. In *van Meerhaeghe, M. A. G., ed.,* 1969, pp. 21–32. [G: E.E.C.; U.K.]

Killick, Tony and During, R. W. A Structural Approach to the Balance of Payments of a Low-Income Country. *J. Devel. Stud.*, July 1969, *5*(4), pp. 274–98. [G: Sierra Leone]

Laber, Gene. International Travel in the Canadian Balance of Payments, 1949–1966. *Econ. Int.*, August 1969, *22*(3), pp. 487–98. [G: Canada]

Lederer, Walther and Parrish, Evelyn M. The U.S. Balance of Payments—Fourth Quarter and Year

1968. *Surv. Curr. Bus.*, March 1969, *49*(3), pp. 23–31, 45–46. [G: U.S.]

Lederer, Walther and Parrish, Evelyn M. The U.S. Balance of Payments: First Quarter, 1969. *Surv. Curr. Bus.*, June 1969, *49*(6), pp. 21–25, 37, 44. [G: U.S.]

Lederer, Walther and Parrish, Evelyn M. The U.S. Balance of Payments: Second Quarter 1969. *Surv. Curr. Bus.*, September 1969, *49*(9), pp. 27–35. [G: U.S.]

Logue, Ruth. Imported Inflation and the International Adjustment Process. (Study summary.) *Fed. Res. Bull.*, December 1969, *55*(12), pp. 920. [G: Europe]

Machlup, Fritz. The Adjustment Problem and the Balance of Payments Policy of the United States. **In** *Officer, L. H. and Willett, T. D., eds.*, 1969, pp. 92–106. [G: U.S.]

Marwah, Kanta. An Econometric Model of Colombia: A Prototype Devaluation View. *Econometrica*, April 1969, *37*(2), pp. 228–51. [G: Colombia]

McColl, Gregory D. The Balance-of-Payments Problems. **In** *Preston, R., ed.*, 1969, pp. 91–119. [G: Australia]

Miller, Etienne H. Foreign Earnings from U.S. Travelers in 1968 Decline Slightly to $3.9 Billion. *Surv. Curr. Bus.*, June 1969, *49*(6), pp. 17–20.

Morris, Frank E. Pax Americana and the U.S. Balance of Payments. *New Eng. Econ. Rev.*, January/February 1969, pp. 41–47. [G: U.S.]

Mossé, Robert. International Transactions of the United States (1946–1968) *Banca Naz. Lavoro Quart. Rev.*, September 1969, (90), pp. 248–80. [G: U.S.]

Reddaway, W. B. The Future of the Ghanian Economy. **In** *Stewart, I. G., ed.*, 1969, pp. 104–14. [G: Ghana]

Schelbert, Heidi. Einige Gedanken zum amerikanischen Zahlungsbilanzdefizit. (Some Reflections on the Deficit in the American Balance of Payments. With English summary.) *Schweiz. Z. Volkswirtsch. Statist.*, December 1969, *105*(4), pp. 497–514. [G: U.S.]

Shepler, Cora E. and Campbell, Leonard G. United States Defense Expenditures Abroad. *Surv. Curr. Bus.*, December 1969, *49*(12), pp. 40–47. [G: U.S.]

Smith, John S. World Summary of International Transactions, 1961–66. *Int. Monet. Fund Staff Pap.*, March 1969, *16*(1), pp. 85–102.

Solomon, Anthony M. Foreign Investment Controls: Policy and Response. *Law Contemp. Probl.*, Winter 1969, *34*(1), pp. 118–25. [G: U.S.]

Stans, Maurice H. Statement. **In** *The 1969 Economic Report of the President, Pt. 3, JECH*, 1969, pp. 726–32. [G: U.S.]

Swann, D. Competition and Price Policies: Britain and the EEC. **In** *van Meerhaeghe, M. A. G., ed.*, 1969, pp. 33–57. [G: E.E.C.; U.K.]

Tanzi, Vito. Tax Incentives and Economic Development: The Ecuadorian Experience. *Finanzarchiv*, March 1969, *28*(2), pp. 226–35. [G: Ecuador]

Volcker, Paul A. Statement. **In** *The 1969 Economic Report of the President, Pt. 3, JECH*, 1969, pp. 732–37. [G: U.S.]

Willett, Thomas D. Adequacy of International Means of Payments. *Rev. Econ. Statist.*, August 1969, *51*(3), pp. 373–74.

4314 Exchange Rates and Markets

Aliber, Robert Z. Central Bank Intervention in the Foreign Exchange Market. **In** *Aliber, R. Z., ed.*, 1969, pp. 222–35.

Altman, Oscar L. Eurodollar and Foreign Exchange Markets. **In** *Aliber, R. Z., ed.*, 1969, pp. 20–29.

Bernholz, Peter. Einige Bemerkungen zur Devisenterminpolitik der Deutschen Bundesbank. (Forward Exchange Policies of the German Bundesbank: Some Critical Comments. With English summary.) *Jahr. Nationalökon. Statist.*, May 1969, *182*(6), pp. 479–89. [G: Germany]

Bhuleshkar, A. V. Devaluation of the Indian Rupee: A Step in the Right Direction. **In** *Bhuleshkar, A. V., ed.*, 1969, pp. 345–50. [G: India]

Coombs, Charles A. Treasury and Federal Reserve Foreign Exchange Operations. *Fed. Res. Bull.*, March 1969, *55*(3), pp. 210–27. [G: U.S.]

Coombs, Charles A. Treasury and Federal Reserve Foreign Exchange Operations. *Fed. Res. Bull.*, September 1969, *55*(9), pp. 697–718.

Dansey, Cyril M. Non-Official Transactions in Gold—Their Effect upon Exchange Markets. **In** *Aliber, R. Z., ed.*, 1969, pp. 13–19.

Dasgupta, Manas. A Note on the Possibility of Creating Export Surplus in Manufactures from the Underdeveloped Countries. *Econ. Aff.*, January-February 1969, *14*(1–2), pp. 68–70.

Davis, Thomas E. Exchange Rate Adjustments Under the Par Value System 1946–68. *Fed. Res. Bank Kansas City Rev.*, September–October 1969, pp. 3–10.

Friedman, Milton. Round Table on Exchange Rate Policy. *Amer. Econ. Rev.*, May 1969, *59*(2), pp. 364–66.

Friedman, Milton. The Advantages of Flexible Exchange Rates. **In** *Starleaf, D. R., ed.*, 1969, pp. 387–92.

Haberler, Gottfried. Round Table on Exchange Rate Policy. *Amer. Econ. Rev.*, May 1969, *59*(2), pp. 357–60.

Johnson, Harry G. The Case for Flexible Exchange Rates, 1969. *Fed. Res. Bank St. Louis Rev.*, June 1969, *51*(6), pp. 12–24.

Kenen, Peter B. Round Table on Exchange Rate Policy. *Amer. Econ. Rev.*, May 1969, *59*(2), pp. 362–64.

Kenen, Peter B. The Theory of Optimum Currency Areas: An Eclectic View. **In** *Mundell, R. A. and Swoboda, A. K., eds.*, 1969, pp. 41–60.

Lipfert, Helmut. Measures to Improve the Depth, Breadth, and Resiliency of the Exchange Markets. **In** *Aliber, R. Z., ed.*, 1969, pp. 235–43.

Lipfert, Helmut. Psychology of the Exchange Market. **In** *Aliber, R. Z., ed.*, 1969, pp. 123–37.

Machlup, Fritz. Round Table on Exchange Rate Policy. *Amer. Econ. Rev.*, May 1969, *59*(2), pp. 366–69.

Marsh, Donald B. Canada's Experience with a Floating Exchange Rate: A Vindication of Free Markets in Exchange. **In** *Aliber, R. Z., ed.*, 1969, pp. 138–55. **[G: Canada]**

Mundell, Robert A. The Cost of Exchange Crises and the Problem of Sterling. **In** *Aliber, R. Z., ed.*, 1969, pp. 209–20.

Officer, Lawrence H. A Comparison of the Effects of Monopoly and Competition in Commodity Markets upon the Foreign-Exchange Market. *Western Econ. J.*, December 1969, *7*(4), pp. 360–64.

Rowan, David C. Towards a Rational Exchange Policy: Some Reflections on the British Experience. *Fed. Res. Bank St. Louis Rev.*, April 1969, *51*(4), pp. 17–26. **[G: U.K.]**

Schenk, Karl-Ernst. Die Konvertibilität der Ostblockwährungen als komplexes Entscheidungsproblem der Wirtschaftspolitik. (Convertibility of East Bloc Currencies as a Complex Decision Problem of Economic Policy. With English summary.) *Schmollers Jahr.*, 1969, *89*(6), pp. 675–89. **[G: COMECON]**

Schilling, Don. Forward Exchange and Currency Position. *J. Finance*, December 1969, *24*(5), pp. 875–85.

Swidrowski, Jozef. Exchange Restrictions in 1969. *Finance Develop.*, December 1969, *6*(4), pp. 27–33.

Swoboda, Alexander. Vehicle Currencies and the Foreign Exchange Market: The Case of the Dollar. **In** *Aliber, R. Z., ed.*, 1969, pp. 30–40.

Timberlake, Richard H., Jr. The Fixation with Fixed Exchange Rates. *Southern Econ. J.*, October 1969, *36*(2), pp. 134–46. **[G: U.S.]**

de Vries, Margaret G. Exchange Restrictions: Progress Toward Liberalization. *Finance Develop.*, September 1969, *6*(3), pp. 40–44.

de Vries, Margaret G. Fluctuating Exchange Rates: The Fund's Approach. *Finance Develop.*, June 1969, *6*(2), pp. 44–48.

Wallich, Henry C. In Defense of Fixed Exchange Rates. **In** *Starleaf, D. R., ed.*, 1969, pp. 392–95.

Wallich, Henry C. Round Table on Exchange Rate Policy. *Amer. Econ. Rev.*, May 1969, *59*(2), pp. 360–62.

Willeke, Franz-Ulrich. An Exchange-Rate Policy of Medium-Term Guaranteed Upward Parity Adjustment. *Ger. Econ. Rev.*, 1969, *7*(3), pp. 263–66. **[G: W. Germany]**

Woodley, W. John R. Some Institutional Aspects of Exchange Markets in the Less-Developed Countries. **In** *Aliber, R. Z., ed.*, 1969, pp. 177–93.

Yeager, Leland B. Fluctuating Exchange Rates in the Nineteenth Century: The Experiences of Austria and Russia. **In** *Mundell, R. A. and Swoboda, A. K., eds.*, 1969, pp. 61–89. **[G: Austria; U.S.S.R.]**

432 International Monetary Arrangements

4320 International Monetary Arrangements

Aliber, Robert Z. Exchange Risk, Yield Curves, and the Pattern of Capital Flows. *J. Finance*, May 1969, *24*(2), pp. 361–70. **[G: U.S.]**

Aliber, Robert Z. Gresham's Law and the Demand for NRU's and SDR's: A Reply. *Quart. J. Econ.*, November 1969, *83*(4), pp. 704–05.

Aliber, Robert Z. Improving the Bretton Woods System. **In** *Mundell, R. A. and Swoboda, A. K., eds.*, 1969, pp. 121–33.

Allais, Maurice. The Views of Mundell and Oppenheimer: A Comment. *J. Money, Credit, Banking*, August 1969, *1*(3), pp. 679–80.

Altman, Oscar L. Euro-dollars. **In** *Chalmers, E. B., ed.*, 1969, pp. 1–14.

Bachmann, Hans. The Prospect of a European Monetary Union Restated. *Aussenwirtschaft*, March 1969, *24*(1), pp. 27–44. **[G: E.E.C.]**

Barre, Raymond. La Communità Europea e i problemi monetari internazionali. (The European Economic Community and International Monetary Problems. With English summary.) *Bancaria*, July 1969, *25*(7), pp. 897–901. **[G: E.E.C.]**

Barrett, Martin and Greene, Margaret L. Special Drawing Rights: A Major Step in the Evolution of the World's Monetary System. **In** *Officer, L. H. and Willett, T. D., eds.*, 1969, pp. 143–50.

Baumgartner, Wilfrid. La funzione monetaria dell'oro nei prossimi dieci anni: Intervento. (The Role of Monetary Gold Over the Next Ten Years: Discussion. With English summary.) *Bancaria*, November 1969, *25*(11), pp. 1342–43.

Bell, Geoffrey L. Credit Creation through Euro-dollars? **In** *Chalmers, E. B., ed.*, 1969, pp. 38–50.

Bernstein, Edward M. The Future of Gold: Discussion. *Amer. Econ. Rev.*, May 1969, *59*(2), pp. 349–51.

Bertrand, Raymond. Prospects for Integration of European Capital Markets: A Comment. *J. Money, Credit, Banking*, August 1969, *1*(3), pp. 347–49. **[G: E.E.C.]**

Bhattacharya, D. Indicatori della scarsità di liquidità internazionale. (Indicators of International Liquidity Shortage. With English summary.) *Rivista Int. Sci. Econ. Com.*, October 1969, *16*(10), pp. 1007–15.

Brimmer, Andrew F. Euro-Dollar Flows and the Efficiency of U.S. Monetary Policy. **In** *High Interest Rates, SCH*, 1969, pp. 181–95. **[G: U.S.]**

Carli, Guido. La funzione monetaria dell'oro nei prossimi dieci anni: Intervento. (The Role of Monetary Gold Over the Next Ten Years: Discussion. With English summary.) *Bancaria*, November 1969, *25*(11), pp. 1344–47.

Carli, Guido. Sistema monetario internazionale e mercato monetario interno. (International Monetary System and Italian Money Market. With English summary.) *Bancaria*, May 1969, *25*(5), pp. 555–71. **[G: Italy]**

Chalmers, Eric B. Monetary Policy Aspects of the Euro-dollar. **In** *Chalmers, E. B., ed.*, 1969, pp. 84–109.

Christie, Herbert. Euro-dollars and the Balance of Payments. **In** *Chalmers, E. B., ed.*, 1969, pp. 57–71.

Clark, Peter B. The Effects of International Monetary Developments on Capital Movements. *Law Contemp. Probl.*, Winter 1969, *34*(1), pp. 18–32.

Clendenning, E. Wayne. Euro-dollars: The Problem of Control. In *Chalmers, E. B., ed.*, 1969, pp. 110–26.

Corden, W. M. International Monetary Reform and the Developing Countries: A Mainly Theoretical Paper. In *Mundell, R. A. and Swoboda, A. K., eds.*, 1969, pp. 283–304.

Damm, Walter. The Obstacles to a Regional Integration of Capital Markets: A Comment. *J. Money, Credit, Banking*, August 1969, *1*(3), pp. 328–31.

Davis, Thomas E. Exchange Rate Adjustments Under the Par Value System 1946–68. *Fed. Res. Bank Kansas City Rev.*, September–October 1969, pp. 3–10.

Day, A. C. L. Institutional Constraints and the International Monetary System. In *Mundell, R. A. and Swoboda, A. K., eds.*, 1969, pp. 333–42.

Dell, Sidney. Statement. In *Linking Reserve Creation and Development Assistance, JECH*, 1969, pp. 5–12. [G: U.S.]

Fan, Liang-Shing. Note on Trade and Distribution of International Reserves. *Indian Econ. J.*, April–June 1969, *16*(4–5), pp. 492–95.

Ferrari, Alberto. Società internazionali problemi di finanziamento e mercato dei capitali. (International Companies: Capital Market and Financing Problems. With English summary.) *Bancaria*, June 1969, *25*(6), pp. 691–99.

Flanders, M. June. International Liquidity Is Always Inadequate. *Kyklos*, 1969, *22*(3), pp. 519–29.

Francuz, Henryk. The International Bank for Economic Cooperation. *Int. Monet. Fund Staff Pap.*, November 1969, *16*(3), pp. 489–503.

Fried, Edward R. International Liquidity and Foreign Aid. *Foreign Aff.*, October 1969, *48*(1), pp. 139–49.

Furth, J. Herbert. International Monetary Reform and the "Crawling Peg"—Comment. *Fed. Res. Bank St. Louis Rev.*, July 1969, *51*(7), pp. 21–25.

Giscard d'Estaing, Valéry. The International Monetary Order. In *Mundell, R. A. and Swoboda, A. K., eds.*, 1969, pp. 7–19.

Grubel, Herbert G. The Distribution of Seigniorage from International Liquidity Creation. In *Mundell, R. A. and Swoboda, A. K., eds.*, 1969, pp. 269–82.

Harrod, Roy F. [Sir]. Problemi monetari d'oggi. (Survey of Monetary Problems. With English summary.) *Bancaria*, July 1969, *25*(7), pp. 819–28.

Hirsch, Fred. The Future of Gold: Discussion. *Amer. Econ. Rev.*, May 1969, *59*(2), pp. 351–53.

Horsefield, J. Keith. The Fund's Charges. *Finance Develop.*, September 1969, *6*(3), pp. 19–23.

Horsefield, J. Keith. The Fund's Compensatory Financing. *Finance Develop.*, December 1969, *6*(4), pp. 34–37.

Iyengar, S. Kesava. The International Financial Imbroglio: The Indian Quandry. *Asian Econ. Rev.*, February 1969, *11*(2), pp. 173–200. [G: India]

Jha, Shri L. K. La funzione monetaria dell'oro nei prossimi dieci anni: Intervento. (The Role of Monetary Gold Over the Next Ten Years: Discussion. With English summary.) *Bancaria*, November 1969, *25*(11), pp. 1348–49.

Johnson, Byron L. Statement. In *Linking Reserve Creation and Development Assistance, JECH*, 1969, pp. 94–102. [G: U.S.]

Johnson, Harry G. Current International Economic Policy Issues. *J. Bus.*, January 1969, *42*(1), pp. 12–21. [G: U.S.]

Johnson, Harry G. Statement. In *Linking Reserve Creation and Development Assistance, JECH*, 1969, pp. 19–21. [G: U.S.]

Johnson, Harry G. The "Problems" Approach to International Monetary Reform. In *Mundell, R. A. and Swoboda, A. K., eds.*, 1969, pp. 393–99.

Johnson, Harry G. The Gold Rush of 1968 in Retrospect and Prospect. *Amer. Econ. Rev.*, May 1969, *59*(2), pp. 344–48.

Johnson, Harry G. The International Monetary Problem: Gold, Dollars, Special Drawing Rights, Wider Bands and Crawling Pegs. In *Linking Reserve Creation and Development Assistance, JECH*, 1969, pp. 21–28. [G: U.S.]

Johnson, Harry G. The Seigniorage Problem and International Liquidity: Appendix: A Note on Seigniorage and the Social Saving from Substituting Credit for Commodity Money. In *Mundell, R. A. and Swoboda, A. K., eds.*, 1969, pp. 323–29.

de Jongh, T. W. Review of the Financial and Economic Situation in South Africa. *S. Afr. J. Econ.*, September 1969, *37*(3), pp. 187–97. [G: S. Africa]

Kafka, Alexandre. Regional Monetary Integration of the Developing Countries. In *Mundell, R. A. and Swoboda, A. K., eds.*, 1969, pp. 135–43.

Kay, John A. and Hole, Peter C. The Fund Meeting. *Finance Develop.*, December 1969, *6*(4), pp. 10–14.

Klopstock, Fred H. Euro-dollars in the Liquidity and Reserve Management of United States Banks. In *Jessup, P. F.*, 1969, pp. 491–506.

Krieger, Ronald A. Problems of Currency Unification in Latin America: Theory and Policy. In *Hilton, R., ed.*, 1969, pp. 222–33. [G: Latin America]

Kriz, Miroslav A. The Future of Gold: Discussion. *Amer. Econ. Rev.*, May 1969, *59*(2), pp. 353–56.

Laidler, David. The Case for Raising the Price of Gold: A Comment. *J. Money, Credit, Banking*, August 1969, *1*(3), pp. 675–78.

Lalwani, Gita. Battle for Franc—A New Crisis in the International Monetary System—I. *Econ. Aff.*, January-February 1969, *14*(1–2), pp. 49–56.

Lamfalussy, Alexandre. La funzione monetaria dell'oro nei prossimi dieci anni. (The Role of Monetary Gold Over the Next Ten Years. With English summary.) *Bancaria*, November 1969, *25*(11), pp. 1331–41.

Larre, René. Facts of Life about the Integration of National Capital Markets. *J. Money, Credit, Banking*, August 1969, *1*(3), pp. 319–27.

Lipfert, Helmut. Problems and Developments of the International Monetary System. *Rev. Econ. Cond. Italy*, November 1969, *23*(6), pp. 519–43.

Little, Jane Sneddon. The Euro-dollar Market: Its Nature and Impact. *New Eng. Econ. Rev.*, May/June 1969, pp. 2–31.

Machlup, Fritz. Speculations on Gold Speculation. *Amer. Econ. Rev.*, May 1969, *59*(2), pp. 332–43.

Madan, B. K. Echoes of Bretton Woods. *Finance Develop.*, June 1969, *6*(2), pp. 30–38.

Martin, William McChesney, Jr. The Price of Gold Is Not the Problem. In *Kuhlman, J. M., ed.*, 1969, pp. 326–33.

McKenzie, George W. International Monetary Reform and the "Crawling Peg"—Reply. *Fed. Res. Bank St. Louis Rev.*, July 1969, *51*(7), pp. 26–31.

McKenzie, George W. International Monetary Reform and the "Crawling Peg." *Fed. Res. Bank St. Louis Rev.*, February 1969, *51*(2), pp. 15–23.

Meigs, A. James. Managing the World's Money Supply: A Comment. *J. Money, Credit, Banking,* August 1969, *1*(3), pp. 668–74.

Montanaro, Silvano. I diritti speciali di prelievo e i problemi della cooperazione monetaria e finanziaria internazionale. (Special Drawing Rights and the Problem of International Monetary and Financial Cooperation. With English summary.) *Bancaria,* November 1969, *25*(11), pp. 1361–66.

Mookerjee, Subimal; Chandavarkar, Anand G. and Cleary, D. J. Existing International Banking and Credit Facilities in the ECAFE Region. *Int. Monet. Fund Staff Pap.*, November 1969, *16*(3), pp. 391–435. **[G: Far East]**

Mundell, Robert A. Problems of the International Monetary System. In *Mundell, R. A. and Swoboda, A. K., eds.*, 1969, pp. 21–38.

Mundell, Robert A. Real Gold, Dollars, and Paper Gold. *Amer. Econ. Rev.*, May 1969, *59*(2), pp. 324–31.

Mundell, Robert A. The Crisis Problem. In *Mundell, R. A. and Swoboda, A. K., eds.*, 1969, pp. 343–49.

Mundell, Robert A. Toward a Better International Monetary System. *J. Money, Credit, Banking,* August 1969, *1*(3), pp. 625–48.

Officer, Lawrence H. and Willett, Thomas D. Reserve-Asset Preferences and the Confidence Problem in the Crisis Zone. *Quart. J. Econ.*, November 1969, *83*(4), pp. 688–95.

Oppenheimer, Peter M. The Case for Raising the Price of Gold. *J. Money, Credit, Banking,* August 1969, *1*(3), pp. 649–65.

Polasek, M. and Barattieri, V. U. S. Gold Policy and the Gold Exchange Standard. *Econ. Rec.*, March 1969, *45*(109), pp. 48–68. **[G: U.S.]**

Prebisch, Raul. Statement. In *Linking Reserve Creation and Development Assistance, JECH,* 1969, pp. 30–31. **[G: U.S.]**

Reading, Brian. Euro-dollars—Tonic or Toxic? In *Chalmers, E. B., ed.*, 1969, pp. 72–83.

Reitsma, A. J. Internationale monetaire problemen. (International Monetary Problems. With English summary.) *De Economist,* November/December 1969, *117*(6), pp. 599–614.

Richebächer, Kurt. The Problems and Prospects of Integrating European Capital Markets. *J. Money, Credit, Banking,* August 1969, *1*(3), pp. 336–46. **[G: E.E.C.]**

Rolfe, Sidney E. The Capital Market Phenomena: A Comment. *J. Money, Credit, Banking,* August 1969, *1*(3), pp. 332–35.

Roosa, Robert V. The American Share in the Stream of International Payments. *Ann. Amer. Acad. Polit. Soc. Sci.*, July 1969, *384,* pp. 21–34. **[G: U.S.]**

Salant, Walter S. International Reserves and Payments Adjustment. *Banca Naz. Lavoro Quart. Rev.*, September 1969, (90), pp. 281–308.

Schenk, Karl-Ernst. Die Konvertibilität der Ostblockwährungen als komplexes Entscheidungsproblem der Wirtschaftspolitik. (Convertibility of East Bloc Currencies as a Complex Decision Problem of Economic Policy. With English summary.) *Schmollers Jahr.*, 1969, *89*(6), pp. 675–89. **[G: COMECON]**

Schmitt, Hans O. Integration and Conflict in the World Economy. *J. Common Market Stud.*, September 1969, *8*(1), pp. 1–18.

Scitovsky, Tibor. Statement. In *Linking Reserve Creation and Development Assistance, JECH,* 1969, pp. 32–34. **[G: U.S.]**

Scott, Ira O., Jr. That Controversial Euro-Dollar Market. *Nat. Westminster Bank Quart. Rev.*, August 1969, pp. 2–22.

Scott, Ira O., Jr. The Problems and Prospects of Integrating European Capital Markets: A Comment. *J. Money, Credit, Banking,* August 1969, *1* (3), pp. 350–53. **[G: E.E.C.]**

Shapiro, Eli. International Financial Problems and the Role of the Dollar: Discussion. *J. Finance,* May 1969, *24*(2), pp. 375–78. **[G: U.S.]**

Swidrowski, Jozef. Exchange Restrictions in 1969. *Finance Develop.*, December 1969, *6*(4), pp. 27–33.

Swoboda, Alexander. Vehicle Currencies and the Foreign Exchange Market: The Case of the Dollar. In *Aliber, R. Z., ed.*, 1969, pp. 30–40.

Tew, Brian. Comments on the Papers by Oppenheimer and Mundell. *J. Money, Credit, Banking,* August 1969, *1*(3), pp. 666–67.

Timberlake, Richard H., Jr. The Fixation with Fixed Exchange Rates. *Southern Econ. J.*, October 1969, *36*(2), pp. 134–46. **[G: U.S.]**

Triffin, Robert. Neither Gold Nor the Dollar. In *Officer, L. H. and Willett, T. D., eds.*, 1969, pp. 3–11.

Triffin, Robert. Statement. In *Linking Reserve Creation and Development Assistance, JECH,* 1969, pp. 37–42. **[G: U.S.]**

Triffin, Robert. The Thrust of History in International Monetary Reform. *Foreign Aff.*, April 1969, *47*(3), pp. 477–92.

U.S. Joint Economic Comm. On Linking Reserve Creation and Development Assistance: Staff Study. In *op. cit., JECP,* 1969, pp. 1–14.

de Vries, Margaret G. Exchange Restrictions: Progress Toward Liberalization. *Finance Develop.*, September 1969, *6*(3), pp. 40–44.

de Vries, Margaret G. Fluctuating Exchange Rates: The Fund's Approach. *Finance Develop.*, June 1969, *6*(2), pp. 44–48.

Wadhva, Charan D. Reserve Pooling in Asia and the Far East. *Pakistan Develop. Rev.*, Autumn 1969, *9*(3), pp. 309–29. **[G: Asia; Far East]**

von Wangenheim, Eberhard. Developing Countries and Monetary Reform. *Weltwirtsch. Arch.*, 1969, *103*(1), pp. 95–109.

Watanabe, Taro. The Economics of SDR's. *Osaka Econ. Pap.*, March 1969, *17*(32), pp. 1–20.

Young, Ralph A. Making Peace with Gold. In *Starleaf, D. R., ed.*, 1969, pp. 401–12.

Zaharescu, Barbu. On Some Theoretical Aspects of the Crisis of the World Monetary System. *Revue Roumaine Sci. Soc. Serie Sci. Econ.*, 1969, *13*(2), pp. 157–70.

440 International Investment and Foreign Aid

441 International Investment and Capital Markets

4410 Theory of International Investment and Capital Flows

Bardhan, P. K. Optimum Investment for an Open Economy. **In** *[Ghosal, U. N.]*, 1969, pp. 74–88.

Bauer, Peter T. Dissent on Development. *Scot. J. Polit. Econ.*, February 1969, *16*(1), pp. 75–94.

Floyd, John E. International Capital Movements and Monetary Equilibrium. *Amer. Econ. Rev.*, Part I, September 1969, *59*(4), pp. 472–92.

Floyd, John E. Monetary and Fiscal Policy in a World of Capital Mobility. *Rev. Econ. Stud.*, October 1969, *36*(108), pp. 503–17.

Hamada, Koichi. Optimal Capital Accumulation by an Economy Facing an International Capital Market. *J. Polit. Econ.*, Part II, July/August 1969, *77* (4), pp. 684–97.

Heckerman, Donald G. "Inefficient" European Capital Markets as an Explanation of International Capital Movements. *J. Money, Credit, Banking*, February 1969, *1*(1), pp. 121–23.

Inada, Ken-Ichi and Kemp, Murray C. International Capital Movements and the Theory of Tariffs and Trade: Comment. *Quart. J. Econ.*, August 1969, *83*(3), pp. 524–28.

Kim, Kwan S. Capital Imports, External Debts, and Growth in the Mahalanobis Model. *Indian Econ. J.*, April–June 1969, *16*(4–5), pp. 488–91.

MacDougall, G. A. D. The Benefits and Costs of Private Investment from Abroad: A Theoretical Approach. **In** *Bhagwati, J., ed.*, 1969, pp. 341–69.

Mendelson, Morris. Some Tax Considerations in American Eurobond Flotations. *Nat. Tax J.*, June 1969, *22*(2), pp. 303–10. [G: U.S.]

Schilling, Don. Forward Exchange and Currency Position. *J. Finance*, December 1969, *24*(5), pp. 875–85.

Whitman, Marina v. N. Economic Openness and International Financial Flows. *J. Money, Credit, Banking*, November 1969, *1*(4), pp. 727–49.

Willett, Thomas D. The Influence of the Trade Balance and Export Financing on International Short-Term Capital Movements: A Theoretical Analysis. *Kyklos*, 1969, *22*(2), pp. 314–27.

4412 International Investment and Capital Flows: Studies

Adler, F. Michael. The Framework for Investigating Direct Manufacturing Investment Overseas. *Law Contemp. Probl.*, Winter 1969, *34*(1), pp. 3–17. [G: U.S.]

d'Arge, Ralph C. Note on Customs Unions and Direct Foreign Investment. *Econ. J.*, June 1969, *79* (314), pp. 324–33. [G: E.E.C.; E.F.T.A.; U.S.]

Behrman, Jack N. Assessing the Foreign Investment Controls. *Law Contemp. Probl.*, Winter 1969, *34* (1), pp. 84–94. [G: U.S.]

Bouwsma, J. Unilateral Relief from Double Taxation in the Netherlands. *Bull. Int. Fiscal Doc.*, July, August, September 1969, *23*(7–8–9), pp. 407–37. [G: Netherlands]

Brimmer, Andrew F. Statement to Congress. *Fed. Res. Bull.*, January 1969, *55*(1), pp. 21–33. [G: U.S.]

Bross, Steward R., Jr. The United States Borrower in the Eurobond Market—A Lawyer's Point of View. *Law Contemp. Probl.*, Winter 1969, *34*(1), pp. 172–202. [G: U.S.]

Carli, Guido. Mobilità internazionale dei capitali e stabilità monetaria interna. (International Mobility of Capital and Internal Monetary Stability. With English summary.) *Bancaria*, October 1969, *25*(10), pp. 1216–20. [G: U.S.; Italy]

Chibrikov, G. Exporting Private Capital: Impact on the Exporting Country's Economy. *Prob. Econ.*, December 1969, *12*(8), pp. 23–45. [G: U.S.]

Clark, Peter B. The Effects of International Monetary Developments on Capital Movements. *Law Contemp. Probl.*, Winter 1969, *34*(1), pp. 18–32.

Deane, R. S. Import Licensing: A Stimulus to Foreign Investment. *Econ. Rec.*, December 1969, *45* (112), pp. 526–43. [G: New Zealand]

Devlin, David T. and Cutler, Frederick. The International Investment Position of the United States: Developments in 1968. *Surv. Curr. Bus.*, October 1969, *49*(10), pp. 23–36. [G: U.S.]

Deweirdt, E. Le marché des euro-obligations. (About Euro-Bonds. With English summary.) *Rivista Int. Sci. Econ. Com.*, November 1969, *16* (11), pp. 1033–52. [G: Europe]

Durand, Patrick and Latscha, Jacques. The New Tax Treaty between the United Kingdom and France. *Bull. Int. Fiscal Doc.*, March 1969, *23*(3), pp. 131–36. [G: U.K.; France]

Ellicott, John. United States Controls on Foreign Direct Investment: The 1969 Program. *Law Contemp. Probl.*, Winter 1969, *34*(1), pp. 47–63. [G: U.S.]

Frank, Andre Gunder. Aid or Exploitation? **In** *Frank, A. G.*, 1969, pp. 149–61. [G: Brazil]

Frank, Andre Gunder. Invisible Foreign Services or National Economic Development? **In** *Frank, A. G.*, 1969, pp. 181–91. [G: Latin America]

Frank, Andre Gunder. Mechanisms of Imperialism. **In** *Frank, A. G.*, 1969, pp. 162–74.

Froozan, Mansur. E.R.A.P.-Type Versus Fifty-Fifty Agreements. *Tahq. Eq.*, November 1969, *6* (15&16), pp. 21–53. [G: Iran]

Fugate, Wilbur L. Antitrust Aspects of Transatlantic Investment. *Law Contemp. Probl.*, Winter 1969, *34*(1), pp. 135–45. [G: U.S.]

Furth, J. Herbert. Barriers to Investment Abroad as Tools of Payments Policy. *Law Contemp. Probl.*, Winter 1969, *34*(1), pp. 64–83. [G: U.S.]

Ginor, Fanny. The Impact of Capital Imports on the Structure of Developing Countries. *Kyklos*, 1969, *22*(1), pp. 104–23.

Holbik, Karel. Development Banks: A Catalyst for Economic Progress. *Rivista Int. Sci. Econ. Com.*, November 1969, *16*(11), pp. 1053–73.

Hughes, Helen. Foreign Investment and Industrialization in Singapore: Conclusions. **In** *Hughes, H. and Seng, Y. P., eds.*, 1969, pp. 177–219. [G: Singapore]

Iyengar, S. Kesava. The International Financial Imbroglio: The Indian Quandry. *Asian Econ. Rev.*, February 1969, *11*(2), pp. 173–200. **[G: India]**

Kim, Hyung K. The Role of Foreign Aid in Assisting the Stabilization of the Korean Economy. *Univ. Wash. Bus. Rev.*, Winter 1969, *28*(2), pp. 62–67. **[G: Korea]**

Klopstock, Fred H. Impact of Euro-Markets on the United States Balance of Payments. *Law Contemp. Probl.*, Winter 1969, *34*(1), pp. 157–71. **[G: U.S.]**

Lee, C. H. A Stock-Adjustment Analysis of Capital Movements: The United States-Canadian Case. *J. Polit. Econ.*, Part I, July/August 1969, *77*(4), pp. 512–23. **[G: U.S.; Canada]**

Lorensen, Gunter. Untersuchungen zur Theorie des intervalutarischen Gleichgewichts. (On the Theory of Intermonetary Equilibrium. With English summary.) *Weltwirtsch. Arch.*, 1969, *103*(2), pp. 249–320.

Manser, W. A. P. Professor Reddaway's Last Word? *Nat. Westminster Bank Quart. Rev.*, February 1969, pp. 40–52. **[G: U.K.]**

Mathai, M. K. Incentives for Investment in Malaysia. *Bull. Int. Fiscal Doc.*, November 1969, *23*(11), pp. 503–15. **[G: Malaysia]**

Mieszkowski, Peter. Carter on the Taxation of International Income Flows. *Nat. Tax J.*, March 1969, *22*(1), pp. 97–108. **[G: Canada]**

Murthy, A. P. Srinivasa. India's External Public Debt Servicing Capacity. *Indian Econ. J.*, April–June 1969, *16*(4–5), pp. 507–19. **[G: India]**

Rahman, Anisur. Foreign Capital Requirements for Economic Development: The Year of Independence for the Case of Foreign Loans. *Oxford Econ. Pap.*, November 1969, *21*(3), pp. 438–41.

Rehbinder, Eckard. The Foreign Direct Investment Regulations: A European Legal Point of View. *Law Contemp. Probl.*, Winter 1969, *34*(1), pp. 95–117. **[G: Germany; France; U.S.]**

Richebächer, Kurt. Problemi e prospettive di integrazione dei mercati europei dei capitali. (Problems and Prospects of Integrating European Capital Markets. With English summary.) *Bancaria*, February 1969, *25*(2), pp. 170–77.

Scaperlanda, Anthony E. and Mauer, Laurence J. The Determinants of U.S. Direct Investment in the E.E.C. *Amer. Econ. Rev.*, Part I, September 1969, *59*(4), pp. 558–68. **[G: U.S.; E.E.C.]**

Shepler, Cora E. and Campbell, Leonard G. United States Defense Expenditures Abroad. *Surv. Curr. Bus.*, December 1969, *49*(12), pp. 40–47. **[G: U.S.]**

Smith, Dan Throop. Tax Policy and Foreign Investment. *Law Contemp. Probl.*, Winter 1969, *34*(1), pp. 146–56. **[G: U.S.]**

Solomon, Anthony M. Foreign Investment Controls: Policy and Response. *Law Contemp. Probl.*, Winter 1969, *34*(1), pp. 118–25. **[G: U.S.]**

Tillinghast, David R. The Carter Commission Report and International Investment Transactions; Integration and Ambiguous Intentions. *Nat. Tax J.*, March 1969, *22*(1), pp. 79–96. **[G: Canada]**

Villanueva, Javier. Inversión privada extranjera, desarrollo industrial y comercio internacional. (Direct Foreign Investment in Industry. With English summary.) *Económica*, May–August 1969, *15*(2), pp. 223–42.

Waever, F. Stirton. The Dynamics of U.S. Investment in Latin America. *Sci. Soc.*, Winter 1969, *33*(1), pp. 20–24. **[G: U.S.; Latin America]**

Walmsley, David J. The Less Developed Country Exclusion from Subpart F. *Nat. Tax J.*, September 1969, *22*(3), pp. 425–30. **[G: U.S.]**

Watkins, Melville H. The Canadian Experience with Foreign Direct Investment. *Law Contemp. Probl.*, Winter 1969, *34*(1), pp. 126–34. **[G: Canada]**

Zeitlin, Sherwin S. and Rosso, David J. United States Taxation of Foreign Enterprises—Structures for Doing Business in the United States and the Western Hemisphere. *Bull. Int. Fiscal Doc.*, December 1969, *23*(12), pp. 555–73. **[G: U.S.]**

442 International Business

4420 International Business; Management and Policies; Economic Imperialism and Host Country Policies

Arey, Will. Statement. **In** *A Review of Balance of Payments Policies, JECH*, 1969, pp. 29–35. **[G: U.S.]**

Ashley, George E. International Communications: What Shape to Come? *Law Contemp. Probl.*, Spring 1969, *34*(2), pp. 417–28.

Baker, James C. and Verschuur, Jan B. The Versatile Combination Export Manager. *Marquette Bus. Rev.*, Winter 1969, *13*(4), pp. 143–50. **[G: U.S.]**

Behrman, Jack N. Statement. **In** *Overseas Private Investment Corporation, HCH*, 1969, pp. 164–71. **[G: U.S.]**

Bozzola, G. B. Strutture organizzative e politiche commerciali su scala internazionale. (Organizational Structures and Commercial Policies at an International Level. With English summary.) *L'Impresa*, July/October 1969, *11*(4–5), pp. 311–19.

Bradshaw, Marie T. U.S. Exports to Foreign Affiliates of U.S. Firms. *Surv. Curr. Bus.*, Part I, May 1969, *49*(5), pp. 34–51. **[G: U.S.]**

Brief, Bernard. Per un marketing multinazionale. (For a Multinational Marketing. With English summary.) *Mondo Aperto*, October 1969, *23*(5), pp. 343–56.

Brimmer, Andrew F. Statement. **In** *A Review of Balance of Payments Policies, JECH*, 1969, pp. 155–68. **[G: U.S.]**

Carroll, Mitchell B. The U.N. Reenacts a Tax Drama. *Bull. Int. Fiscal Doc.*, April 1969, *23*(4), pp. 163–65.

Constanzo, G. A. Statement. **In** *A Review of Balance of Payments Policies, JECH*, 1969, pp. 187–91. **[G: U.S.]**

Corigliano, Giorgio. La funzione del "product manager" nella realtà industriale italiana. (The Product Manager's Function in the Italian Industrial Situation. With English summary.) *L'Impresa*, July/October 1969, *11*(4–5), pp. 343–46. **[G: Italy]**

Daidola, Giorgio. Formazione e trasferimento

quadri nelle imprese multinazionali. (Development and Transfer of Managers in Multinational Firms. With English summary.) *L'Impresa,* July/October 1969, *11*(4–5), pp. 373–75.

Davies, Gethyn. United Kingdom Investment. **In** *Hughes, H. and Seng, Y. P., eds.,* 1969, pp. 46–61. **[G: Singapore]**

Davis, Stanley M. U.S. versus Latin America: Business & Culture. *Harvard Bus. Rev.,* November–December 1969, *47*(6), pp. 88–98. **[G: U.S.; Latin America]**

De Cugis, Carlo. A Commentary on Jean-Jacques Servan-Schreiber's Book, *The American Challenge.* **In** *Kennedy, C. J., ed.,* 1969, pp. 123–45.

Deane, R. S. Import Licensing: A Stimulus to Foreign Investment. *Econ. Rec.,* December 1969, *45* (112), pp. 526–43. **[G: New Zealand]**

Díaz-Alejandro, Carlos. Statement. **In** *Overseas Private Investment Corporation, HCH,* 1969, pp. 115–16. **[G: U.S.]**

Donnelly, James H., Jr. and Ryans, John K., Jr. The Role of Culture in Organizing Overseas Operations: The Advertising Experience. *Univ. Wash. Bus. Rev.,* Autumn 1969, *29*(1), pp. 35–41.

Dunning, John H. The Study of International Direct Investment. *Rivista Int. Sci. Econ. Com.,* December 1969, *16*(12), pp. 1129–44.

Ebert, Robert R. Multinational Coordination of Labor Objectives in the Automobile Unions. *Ohio State U. Bull. Bus. Res.,* September 1969, *44*(9), pp. 1–3, 7–8.

Ellicott, John. United States Controls on Foreign Direct Investment: The 1969 Program. *Law Contemp. Probl.,* Winter 1969, *34*(1), pp. 47–63. **[G: U.S.]**

Ende, Asher H. International Telecommunications: Dynamics of Regulation of a Rapidly Expanding Service. *Law Contemp. Probl.,* Spring 1969, *34* (2), pp. 389–416. **[G: U.S.]**

Ferrari, Alberto. Società internazionali problemi di finanziamento e mercato dei capitali. (International Companies: Capital Market and Financing Problems. With English summary.) *Bancaria,* June 1969, *25*(6), pp. 691–99.

Ferrer-Pacces. L'internazionale dell imprese. (Multinational Firm. With English summary.) *L'Impresa,* March/April 1969, *11*(2), pp. 115–17.

Fiero, Charles E. Statement. **In** *A Review of Balance of Payments Policies, JECH,* 1969, pp. 141–55. **[G: U.S.]**

Francis, A. A. A Model of National Economic Growth under Perfect Enclavism. *Soc. Econ. Stud.,* December 1969, *18*(4), pp. 365–73.

Frank, Andre Gunder. Invisible Foreign Services or National Economic Development? **In** *Frank, A. G.,* 1969, pp. 181–91. **[G: Latin America]**

Frank, Andre Gunder. Mechanisms of Imperialism. **In** *Frank, A. G.,* 1969, pp. 162–74.

Froozan, Mansur. E.R.A.P.-Type Versus Fifty-Fifty Agreements. *Tahq. Eq.,* November 1969, *6* (15&16), pp. 21–53. **[G: Iran]**

Fugate, Wilbur L. Antitrust Aspects of Transatlantic Investment. *Law Contemp. Probl.,* Winter 1969, *34*(1), pp. 135–45. **[G: U.S.]**

Gamarnikow, Michael. Eastern Partners for Western Businessmen. **In** *Grub, P. D. and Holbik, K.,* 1969, pp. 148–53. **[G: E. Europe]**

Gekker, Paul. Financial Aspects of United States Trade with the Socialist World. **In** *Grub, P. D. and Holbik, K.,* 1969, pp. 180–86. **[G: U.S.S.R.]**

George, J. Mishell. Views East-West Trade Effect of Reforms, Controls. **In** *Grub, P. D. and Holbik, K.,* 1969, pp. 205–07. **[G: E. Europe]**

Gloor, Max. Il caso di un'impresa multinazionale: la Nestlè. (Nestlè's Multinational Mode. With English summary.) *Mondo Aperto,* June–August 1969, *23*(3–4), pp. 205–16.

Grub, Phillip D. Doing Business with and in East Europe: The Present and a Look toward the Future. **In** *Grub, P. D. and Holbik, K.,* 1969, pp. 208–13. **[G: E. Europe]**

Grunwald, Joseph. Statement. **In** *Overseas Private Investment Corporation, HCH,* 1969, pp. 104–07. **[G: U.S.]**

Hirono, Ryokichi. Japanese Investment. **In** *Hughes, H. and Seng, Y. P., eds.,* 1969, pp. 86–111. **[G: Singapore]**

Hughes, Helen. Australian Investment. **In** *Hughes, H. and Seng, Y. P., eds.,* 1969, pp. 62–85. **[G: Singapore]**

Ivancevich, John M. A Study of American Expatriate On-the-Job Performance Failures. *Univ. Wash. Bus. Rev.,* Winter 1969, *28*(2), pp. 42–49.

Kilcarr, Andrew J. United States v. Concentrated Phosphate Export Association: A Small Case in the Big Court. *Antitrust Bull.,* Spring 1969, *14,* pp. 37–61. **[G: U.S.]**

King, Alfred M. Budgeting Foreign Exchange Losses. *Manage. Account.,* October 1969, *51*(4), pp. 39–41, 46.

Lagioni, Iginio. Dal "commercio" internazionale alla "mercatistica" internazionale. (From "International Trade" to International "Marketing." With English summary.) *L'Impresa,* January/February 1969, *11*(1), pp. 61–67.

Liander, Bertil. Mercatistica internazionale analisi comparate. (Comparative Analysis for International Marketing. With English summary.) *L'Impresa,* July/October 1969, *11*(4–5), pp. 320–26.

Lindert, Peter H. United States Investment. **In** *Hughes, H. and Seng, Y. P., eds.,* 1969, pp. 154–76. **[G: Singapore]**

Luey, Paul. Hong Kong Investment. **In** *Hughes, H. and Seng, Y. P., eds.,* 1969, pp. 112–39. **[G: Singapore]**

Luey, Paul and Sei, Ung Gim. Taiwan Investment. **In** *Hughes, H. and Seng, Y. P., eds.,* 1969, pp. 140–53. **[G: Singapore]**

Main, Jeremy. The First Real International Bankers. **In** *Jessup, P. F.,* 1969, pp. 481–90.

Manser, W. A. P. Professor Reddaway's Last Word? *Nat. Westminster Bank Quart. Rev.,* February 1969, pp. 40–52. **[G: U.K.]**

Maule, C. J. Antitrust and the Takeover Activity of American Firms in Canada: A Rejoinder. *J. Law Econ.,* October 1969, *12*(2), pp. 419–24. **[G: U.S.; Canada]**

McNamara, Robert S. Esplosione demografica e sviluppo economico. (Demographic Increase and Economic Development. With English summary.) *Mondo Aperto,* October 1969, *23*(5), pp. 330–42.

Parks, F. Newton. Survival of the European Headquarters. *Harvard Bus. Rev.*, March–April 1969, *47*(2), pp. 79–84. [G: W. Europe]

Penrose, Edith T. OPEC and the Changing Structure of the International Petroleum Industry. **In** *Governmental Intervention in the Market Mechanism, Pt. 1, SCH,* 1969, pp. 429–47.

Petry, Horst. Technischer Fortschritt, Integration, internationale Wettbewerbsfähigkeit und Unternehmensgrösse. (With English summary.) *Jahr. Nationalökon. Statist.*, August 1969, *183*(3–4), pp. 271–99.

Pirnia, Hossein. Scientific Thought and National Independence. *Tahq. Eq.*, November 1969, *6* (15&16), pp. 3–20. [G: Iran]

Quinn, James Brian. Technology Transfer by Multinational Companies. *Harvard Bus. Rev.*, November–December 1969, *47*(6), pp. 147–61.

Rehbinder, Eckard. The Foreign Direct Investment Regulations: A European Legal Point of View. *Law Contemp. Probl.*, Winter 1969, *34*(1), pp. 95–117. [G: Germany; France; U.S.]

Reuber, Grant L. Antitrust and the Takeover Activity of American Firms in Canada: A Further Analysis. *J. Law Econ.*, October 1969, *12*(2), pp. 405–17. [G: U.S.; Canada]

Schooler, Robert D. and Sunoo, Don H. Consumer Preceptions of International Products: Regional vs. National Labeling. *Soc. Sci. Quart.*, March 1969, *49*(4), pp. 886–90.

Scott, John C. and Yablonski, Steven K. Transnational Mergers and Joint Ventures Affecting American Exports. *Antitrust Bull.*, Spring 1969, *14*, pp. 1–36. [G: U.S.]

Stevens, Guy V. G. Fixed Investment Expenditures of Foreign Manufacturing Affiliates of U.S. Firms: Theoretical Models and Empirical Evidence. *Yale Econ. Essays*, Spring 1969, *9*(1), pp. 137–98.

Stobaugh, Robert B., Jr. How to Analyze Foreign Investment Climates. *Harvard Bus. Rev.*, September–October 1969, *47*(5), pp. 100–108.

Stobaugh, Robert B., Jr. Where in the World Should We Put that Plant? *Harvard Bus. Rev.*, January–February 1969, *47*(1), pp. 129–36.

Stonehill, Arthur and Stitzel, Thomas. Financial Structure and Multinational Corporations. *Calif. Manage. Rev.*, Fall 1969, *12*(1), pp. 91–96.

Sturdivant, Frederick D. The Limits of Black Capitalism. *Harvard Bus. Rev.*, January–February 1969, *47*(1), pp. 122–28. [G: U.S.]

Stykolt, Stefan. Anti-U.S. Trends in Canadian Economic Policy. **In** *Stykolt, S.*, 1969, pp. 154–57. [G: Canada]

Surrey, Stanley S. Statement. **In** *A Review of Balance of Payments Policies, JECH,* 1969, pp. 40–49. [G: U.S.]

Vernon, Raymond. Multinational Enterprise and the Nation State: Project Report from the Harvard Business School. *J. Common Market Stud.*, December 1969, *8*(2), pp. 160–70.

Vigand, V. C. Once More on the World Price of Oil: A Comment. *Acta Oecon.*, 1969, *4*(2), pp. 211–14.

de Vries, Barend A. High Cost of Industry in Developing Countries—Causes and Remedies. *Finance Develop.*, December 1969, *6*(4), pp. 43–47.

Walker, Geoffrey de Q. The Australian Plaintiff and the Sherman Act. *Antitrust Bull.*, Winter 1969, *14*, pp. 901–32.

Walmsley, David J. The Less Developed Country Exclusion from Subpart F. *Nat. Tax J.*, September 1969, *22*(3), pp. 425–30. [G: U.S.]

Watkins, Melville H. The Canadian Experience with Foreign Direct Investment. *Law Contemp. Probl.*, Winter 1969, *34*(1), pp. 126–34. [G: Canada]

Wesolowski, Zdzislaw P. An Inquiry into the Administration and Utilization of the Webb-Pomerene Act. *Marquette Bus. Rev.*, Winter 1969, *13* (4), pp. 174–88. [G: U.S.]

Zeitlin, Sherwin S. and Rosso, David J. United States Taxation of Foreign Enterprises—Structures for Doing Business in the United States and the Western Hemisphere. *Bull. Int. Fiscal Doc.*, December 1969, *23*(12), pp. 555–73. [G: U.S.]

443 International Aid

4430 International Aid

Abdel-Rahman, I. H. The United Nations Organization for Industrial Development—Its Organization and Functions. *Kansant. Aikak.*, 1969, *65*(3), pp. 155–70.

Asher, Robert E. Foreign Aid: The Postwar Record and Targets for the 1970's. *Mon. Lab. Rev.*, November 1969, *92*(11), pp. 23–30. [G: U.S.]

Baqai, Moin and Brecher, Irving. Foreign-Aid Requirements: A Critique of Aid Projections with Special Reference to Pakistan. *Pakistan Develop. Rev.*, Winter 1969, *9*(4), pp. 380–99. [G: Pakistan]

Bauer, Peter T. Dissent on Development. *Scot. J. Polit. Econ.*, February 1969, *16*(1), pp. 75–94.

Behrman, Jack N. Statement. **In** *Overseas Private Investment Corporation, HCH,* 1969, pp. 164–71. [G: U.S.]

Bell, David E.; Hardin, Lowell S. and Hill, F. F. Hope for the Hungry: Fulfillment or Frustration? **In** *Hardin, C. M., ed.*, 1969, pp. 137–70. [G: U.S.]

Caballero Tamayo, Xavier. The ILO and Development in the Americas. *Int. Lab. Rev.*, December 1969, *100*(6), pp. 505–50. [G: Latin America]

Campolongo, Alberto. Note sul sottosviluppo. (Notes on Underdevelopment. With English summary.) *Rivista Int. Sci. Econ. Com.*, December 1969, *16* (12), pp. 1197–1204.

Chapin, Emerson. Success Story in South Korea. *Foreign Aff.*, April 1969, *47*(3), pp. 560–74. [G: S. Korea]

Cohen, Alvin. Monetarism vs. Structuralism: Conflict in U.S. Economic Aid to Latin America. **In** *Hilton, R., ed.*, 1969, pp. 173–84. [G: Latin America]

Conlisk, John and Huddle, Donald. Allocating Foreign Aid: An Appraisal of a Self-Help Model. *J. Devel. Stud.*, July 1969, *5*(4), pp. 245–51.

Danielian, N. R. Statement. **In** *Foreign Assistance Act, 1969, SCH,* 1969, pp. 237–48. [G: U.S.]

Danielian, N. R. Statement. **In** *Foreign Assistance Act of 1969, Pt. 5, HCH,* 1969, pp. 1104–20. [G: U.S.]

Davenport, Michael. The Allocation of Foreign Aid: A Cross Section Study. *Indian Econ. J.*, April–June 1969, *16*(4–5), pp. 458–77. **[G: U.S.]**

Davies, Cyril H. The Bank Group Meeting. *Finance Develop.*, December 1969, *6*(4), pp. 4–9.

Dell, Sidney. Statement. **In** *Linking Reserve Creation and Development Assistance, JECH,* 1969, pp. 5–12. **[G: U.S.]**

Denham, Robert Edwin. The Role of the U.S. as an External Actor in the Integration of Latin America. *J. Common Market Stud.*, March 1969, *7*(3), pp. 199–216. **[G: LAFTA]**

Díaz-Alejandro, Carlos. Statement. **In** *Overseas Private Investment Corporation, HCH,* 1969, pp. 115–16. **[G: U.S.]**

Evans, James Gilbert, Sr. Foreign Aid for Agricultural Development. *Amer. J. Agr. Econ.*, December 1969, *51*(5), pp. 1402–12.

Freeman, Orville L. Malthus, Marx, and the North American Breadbasket. **In** *Ruttan, V. W.; Waldo, A. D. and Houck, J. P., eds.*, 1969, pp. 282–98. **[G: U.S.]**

Fried, Edward R. International Liquidity and Foreign Aid. *Foreign Aff.*, October 1969, *48*(1), pp. 139–49.

Gaud, William S. Statement. **In** *A Review of Balance of Payments Policies, JECH,* 1969, pp. 90–97. **[G: U.S.]**

Gaud, William S. The Current Effect of the American Aid Program. *Ann. Amer. Acad. Polit. Soc. Sci.*, July 1969, *384,* pp. 73–84. **[G: U.S.]**

Gish, Oscar. A Note on Aid for Nursing Training in Britain. *J. Devel. Stud.*, April 1969, *5*(3), pp. 220–22. **[G: U.K.]**

Gowda, K. Venkatagiri. U.S. Aid: A Critical Evaluation. **In** *Dagli, V., ed., Vol. III,* 1969, pp. 31–40. **[G: India]**

Guither, Harold D. Institution Building: Training Gap in Economic and Agricultural Development. *Amer. J. Agr. Econ.*, December 1969, *51*(5), pp. 1574–77. **[G: U.S.]**

Gulhati, Ravi. Debt-Servicing as an Aid to Promotion of Trade of Developing Countries: Comment. *Oxford Econ. Pap.*, November 1969, *21*(3), pp. 409–15.

Handke, Werner. Zielkonflikte in der Entwicklungshilfe zwischen Geber- und Nehmerländern. (With English summary.) *Z. ges. Staatswiss.*, April 1969, *125*(2), pp. 261–78.

Holbik, Karel. Development Banks: A Catalyst for Economic Progress. *Rivista Int. Sci. Econ. Com.*, November 1969, *16*(11), pp. 1053–73.

Honavar, R. M. Debt-Servicing as an Aid to Promotion of Trade of Developing Countries: Comment. *Oxford Econ. Pap.*, November 1969, *21*(3), pp. 416–19.

Horsefield, J. Keith. The Fund's Compensatory Financing. *Finance Develop.*, December 1969, *6*(4), pp. 34–37.

Iyengar, S. Kesava. The International Financial Imbroglio: The Indian Quandry. *Asian Econ. Rev.*, February 1969, *11*(2), pp. 173–200. **[G: India]**

Jalan, Bimal. Gains to Donor Countries from Tied Aid. *Finance Develop.*, September 1969, *6*(3), pp. 14–18.

Johnson, Byron L. Statement. **In** *Linking Reserve Creation and Development Assistance, JECH,* 1969, pp. 94–102. **[G: U.S.]**

Johnson, Harry G. Current International Economic Policy Issues. *J. Bus.*, January 1969, *42*(1), pp. 12–21. **[G: U.S.]**

Johnson, Harry G. Statement. **In** *Linking Reserve Creation and Development Assistance, JECH,* 1969, pp. 19–21. **[G: U.S.]**

Khatkhate, Deena R. Debt-Servicing as an Aid to Promotion of Trade of Developing Countries: A Reply. *Oxford Econ. Pap.*, November 1969, *21*(3), pp. 424–27.

Kilcarr, Andrew J. United States v. Concentrated Phosphate Export Association: A Small Case in the Big Court. *Antitrust Bull.*, Spring 1969, *14,* pp. 37–61. **[G: U.S.]**

Kim, Hyung K. The Role of Foreign Aid in Assisting the Stabilization of the Korean Economy. *Univ. Wash. Bus. Rev.*, Winter 1969, *28*(2), pp. 62–67. **[G: Korea]**

Kojima, Kiyoshi. Asian Developing Countries and PAFTA: Development, Aid and Trade Preferences. *Hitotsubashi J. Econ.*, June 1969, *10*(1), pp. 1–17. **[G: U.S.; Canada; Japan; Australia; New Zealand]**

Lilienthal, David E. Postwar Development in Viet Nam. *Foreign Aff.*, January 1969, *47*(2), pp. 321–33. **[G: Viet Nam]**

Lodge, George C. U.S. Aid to Latin America: Funding Radical Change. *Foreign Aff.*, July 1969, *47*(4), pp. 735–49. **[G: U.S.; Latin America]**

Marquardt, Wilhelm. German Economic Research in Africa. *Ger. Econ. Rev.*, 1969, *7*(1), pp. 71–76. **[G: W. Germany; Africa]**

Marsden, Keith. Integrated Regional Development: A Quantitative Approach. *Int. Lab. Rev.*, June 1969, *99*(6), pp. 621–46.

Moot, Robert C. Statement. **In** *A Review of Balance of Payments Policies, JECH,* 1969, pp. 97–108. **[G: U.S.]**

Murthy, A. P. Srinivasa. India's External Public Debt Servicing Capacity. *Indian Econ. J.*, April–June 1969, *16*(4–5), pp. 507–19. **[G: India]**

Narasimham, M. Debt-Servicing as an Aid to Promotion of Trade of Developing Countries: Comment. *Oxford Econ. Pap.*, November 1969, *21*(3), pp. 404–08.

Newell, Richard S. Afghanistan: The Dangers of Cold War Generosity. *Middle East J.*, Spring 1969, *23*(2), pp. 168–76. **[G: Afghanistan]**

Paakkanen, Jouko. Vaikutelmia kehitysmaiden tilanteesta ja kehitysavusta. (The Developing Countries and Development Aid. With English summary.) *Kansant. Aikak.*, 1969, *65*(1), pp. 27–36.

Patel, H. M. Two Views on Foreign Aid. *Artha-Vikas,* January 1969, *5*(1), pp. 77–80.

Phillips, Richard. Inducing Economic Development in Less Developed Countries: Discussion. *Amer. J. Agr. Econ.*, December 1969, *51*(5), pp. 1424–26.

Prebisch, Raul. Statement. **In** *Linking Reserve Creation and Development Assistance, JECH,* 1969, pp. 30–31. **[G: U.S.]**

Pronk, J. P. and Schreuel, E. J. Some Reflections on the Effectiveness of Project Versus Plan Aid. **In** *[Tinbergen, J.],* 1969, pp. 283–307.

Rahman, Anisur. Foreign Capital Requirements for Economic Development: The Year of Independence for the Case of Foreign Loans. *Oxford Econ. Pap.*, November 1969, *21*(3), pp. 438–41.

Reddaway, W. B. The Importance of External Assistance and Self-help in Indian Development. **In** *Bhuleshkar, A. V., ed.*, 1969, pp. 353–67. **[G: India]**

Schutjer, Wayne and Weigel, Dale. The Contribution of Foreign Assistance to Agricultural Development. *Amer. J. Agr. Econ.*, November 1969, *51* (4), pp. 788–97.

Scitovsky, Tibor. Statement. **In** *Linking Reserve Creation and Development Assistance, JECH*, 1969, pp. 32–34. **[G: U.S.]**

Seevers, Gary L. The Cost of Food Aid to Recipient Countries. *Amer. J. Agr. Econ.*, December 1969, *51*(5), pp. 1588–92. **[G: U.S.]**

Shepler, Cora E. and Campbell, Leonard G. United States Defense Expenditures Abroad. *Surv. Curr. Bus.*, December 1969, *49*(12), pp. 40–47. **[G: U.S.]**

Singer, H. W. and Doss, A. C. Technical Assistance to Kenya: Some Thoughts on Flows and Programming. *East Afr. Econ. Rev.*, June 1969, *1*(1), pp. 17–27. **[G: Kenya]**

Smethurst, Richard G. Direct Commodity Aid: A Multilateral Experiment. *J. Devel. Stud.*, April 1969, *5*(3), pp. 205–19.

Soper, Tom. Western Attitudes to Aid. *Lloyds Bank Rev.*, October 1969, (94), pp. 17–33.

Srivastava, U. K. P. L. 480 Counterpart Funds and Inflation: Myth and Realty. *Asian Econ. Rev.*, February 1969, *11*(2), pp. 145–59. **[G: India]**

Stepanov, Lev. "One Percent": The Problem of Economic Aid. *Ann. Amer. Acad. Polit. Soc. Sci.*, November 1969, *386*, pp. 41–53.

Stern, Robert M. International Financial Issues in Foreign Economic Assistance to the Less Developed Countries. **In** *Stewart, I. G., ed.*, 1969, pp. 47–70.

Stolk, Leonard. Taxation of International Consolidations into a "European Corporation." *Bull. Int. Fiscal Doc.*, November 1969, *23*(11), pp. 521–44. **[G: E.E.C.]**

Sutcliffe, R. B. Debt-Servicing as an Aid to Promotion of Trade of Developing Countries: A Further Comment. *Oxford Econ. Pap.*, November 1969, *21*(3), pp. 420–23.

Thornton, Thomas Perry. A View from Washington. *Ann. Amer. Acad. Polit. Soc. Sci.*, November 1969, *386*, pp. 19–30. **[G: U.S.]**

Tokman, Victor E. An Evaluation of Foreign Aid: The Chilean Case. *Bull. Oxford Univ. Inst. Econ. Statist.*, May 1969, *31*(2), pp. 89–103. **[G: Chile]**

Triffin, Robert. Statement. **In** *Linking Reserve Creation and Development Assistance, JECH*, 1969, pp. 37–42. **[G: U.S.]**

U.S. Joint Economic Comm. On Linking Reserve Creation and Development Assistance: Staff Study. **In** *op. cit., JECP*, 1969, pp. 1–14.

Veldkamp, Gerald M. J. A New Dimension for International Co-operation in Social Security. *Int. Lab. Rev.*, August 1969, *100*(2), pp. 131–39.

Vladimirov, Iu. V. The Question of Soviet-Chinese Economic Relations in 1950–1966. *Chinese Econ. Stud.*, Fall 1969, *3*(1), pp. 3–32. **[G: China; U.S.S.R.]**

von Wangenheim, Eberhard. Developing Countries and Monetary Reform. *Weltwirtsch. Arch.*, 1969, *103*(1), pp. 95–109.

500 Administration; Business Finance; Marketing; Accounting

510 Administration

511 Organization and Decision Theory

5110 Organization and Decision Theory

Bliss, Charles A. Absolutism in the Realm of Uncertainty. *Calif. Manage. Rev.*, Spring 1969, *11*(3), pp. 35–42.

Bobrow, Davis B. Improving the Bases for Decision. **In** *Bobrow, D. B., ed.*, 1969, pp. 3–18. **[G: U.S.]**

Brandt, Louis K. Quantitative Tools for Financial Management. *Southern Quart.*, April 1969, *7*(3), pp. 261–81.

Brus, W. A Few General Remarks on the Changes in the System of Planning and Management. **In** *Economic Concentration, Pt. 7A, SCH*, 1969, pp. 4459–65. **[G: Poland]**

Burch, John G., Jr. Business Games and Simulation Techniques. *Manage. Account.*, December 1969, *51*(6), pp. 49–52.

Chester, T. E. Mergers and Opportunities for Managers. *Nat. Westminster Bank Quart. Rev.*, May 1969, pp. 10–21. **[G: U.K.]**

Cummings, L. L. and Harnett, D. L. Bargaining Behaviour in a Symmetric Bargaining Triad: The Impact of Risk-Taking Propensity, Information, Communication and Terminal Bid. *Rev. Econ. Stud.*, October 1969, *36*(108), pp. 485–501.

Cyert, Richard M. and George, Kenneth D. Competition, Growth, and Efficiency. *Econ. J.*, March 1969, *79*(313), pp. 23–41.

D'Iribarne, Alain. Les besoins d'emploi des entreprises. (With English summary.) *Revue Écon.*, July 1969, *20*(4), pp. 601–57.

Dadák, Zdeněk. Strojírenský výrobní proces a jeho operativní řízení jako kybernetický systém. (Production Process in Engineering and Operative Control of This Process as a Cybernetic System. With English summary.) *Ekon.-Mat. Obzor*, 1969, *5*(4), pp. 518–20.

Davis, J. Ronnie and Palomba, Neil A. The National Farmers Organization and the Prisoner's Dilemma: A Game Theory Prediction of Failure. *Soc. Sci. Quart.*, December 1969, *50*(3), pp. 742–48.

Demeyere, R. Doelmatig bedrijfsbeleid: een eis voor de toekomst. (Appropriate Management Is a Requirement for the Future. With English summary.) *Econ. Soc. Tijdschr.*, April 1969, *23*(2), pp. 143–58.

Demski, Joel S. Decision-Performance Control. *Accounting Rev.*, October 1969, *44*(4), pp. 669–79.

Dethoor, Jean-Marc. Au-delà de la programmation dynamique. (With English summary.) *Revue Écon.*, May 1969, *20*(3), pp. 515–35.

Evans, Campbell K. Model of Certain Relationships within the Structure of Insurance Agencies. *J. Risk Ins.,* December 1969, *36*(5), pp. 535–44.

Fayol, Henri. The Administrative Theory in the State. **In** *Gulick, L. and Urwick, L., eds.,* 1969, pp. 99–114.

Field, John E. Toward a Multi-Level, Multi-Goal Information System. *Accounting Rev.,* July 1969, *44*(3), pp. 593–99.

Filley, Alan C. New Directions in Organization Theory. **In** *Somers, G. G., ed. (I),* 1969, pp. 79–108.

Fleming, John E. A Decision Model of Control. *Miss. Val. J. Bus. Econ.,* Spring 1969, *4*(2), pp. 23–32.

Follett, Mary Parker. The Process of Control. **In** *Gulick, L. and Urwick, L., eds.,* 1969, pp. 159–69.

Fontela, E. Technological Forecasting and Corporate Strategy. **In** *Arnfield, R. V., ed.,* 1969, pp. 26–33.

French, Wendell. Organization Development Objectives, Assumptions and Strategies. *Calif. Manage. Rev.,* Winter 1969, *12*(2), pp. 23–34.

Gershefski, George W. Building a Corporate Financial Model. *Harvard Bus. Rev.,* July–August 1969, *47*(4), pp. 61–72. **[G: U.S.]**

Goetz, Billy E. Perplexing Problems in Decision Theory. *Eng. Econ.,* April–May 1969, *14*(3), pp. 129–40.

Goldschmidt, Y. and Smidt, S. Valuing the Firm's Durable Assets for Managerial Information. *Accounting Rev.,* April 1969, *44*(2), pp. 317–29.

Gross, Jack L. and McGinley, John J. Need for a Marketing Intelligence System . . . in Petroleum Marketing: Integration of Information Systems into the Decision-Making Process. *Econ. Bus. Bull.,* Fall 1969, *22*(1), pp. 25–32.

Guise, John W. B. and Ryland, G. J. Production Scheduling and Allocation: A Normative Decision Model for Sugar Milling. *Australian J. Agr. Econ.,* June 1969, *13*(1), pp. 8–24.

Gulick, Luther. Notes on the Theory of Organization. **In** *Gulick, L. and Urwick, L., eds.,* 1969, pp. 1–45.

Hadar, Josef and Hillinger, C. Imperfect Competition with Unknown Demand. *Rev. Econ. Stud.,* October 1969, *36*(108), pp. 519–25.

Hakansson, Nils H. An Induced Theory of Accounting under Risk. *Accounting Rev.,* July 1969, *44*(3), pp. 495–514.

Hanan, Mack. Corporate Growth through Internal Spin-outs. *Harvard Bus. Rev.,* November–December 1969, *47*(6), pp. 55–66.

Harsanyi, John C. Measurement of Social Power in *n*-Person Reciprocal Power Situations. **In** *Bell, R.; Edwards, D. V. and Wagner, R. H., eds.,* 1969, pp. 239–48.

Harsanyi, John C. Measurement of Social Power, Opportunity Costs, and the Theory of Two-Person Bargaining Games. **In** *Bell, R.; Edwards, D. V. and Wagner, R. H., eds.,* 1969, pp. 226–38.

Hoffman, L. Richard. Commitment and Conflict in Group Problem Solving. **In** *Association of Canadian Schools of Business,* 1969, pp. 5–21.

Honko, Jaakko. Some Basic Problems and Future Trends in Management. *Liiketaloudellinen Aikak.,* 1969, *18*(2), pp. 145–52.

Jääskeläinen, Veikko. Traditional and Ex Post Variance Analysis: A Reconciliation. *Liiketaloudellinen Aikak.,* 1969, *18*(2), pp. 153–70.

Johnsen, Erik. A Remark on Some Analytical Problems in a Normative Marketing Systems Model. *Liiketaloudellinen Aikak.,* 1969, *18*(1), pp. 42–50.

Kamerschen, David R. The Effect of Separation of Ownership and Control on the Performance of the Large Firm in the U.S. Economy. *Rivista Int. Sci. Econ. Com.,* May 1969, *16*(5), pp. 489–93.

Kedzie, Daniel P. Corporate Planning and the Holding Company. *J. Risk Ins.,* March 1969, *36*(1), pp. 85–91.

Kochen, Manfred and Deutsch, Karl W. Toward a Rational Theory of Decentralization: Some Implications of a Mathematical Approach. *Amer. Polit. Sci. Rev.,* September 1969, *63*(3), pp. 734–49.

Kolm, Serge-Christophe. Structuration informationnelle centralisée et hiérarchisée: Une contribution à la théorie des organisations. (With English summary.) *Revue Écon.,* May 1969, *20*(3), pp. 455–67.

Kronsjö, Tom. Decomposition of a Large Nonlinear Convex Separable Economic System in the Dual Direction. *Econ. Planning,* 1969, *9*(1–2), pp. 71–94.

Kuboleca, S. Review of Movements in Yugoslav Economy towards Decentralization. **In** *Economic Concentration, Pt. 7A, SCH,* 1969, pp. 4495–4506. **[G: Yugoslavia]**

Lee, John. The Pros and Cons of Functionalization. **In** *Gulick, L. and Urwick, L., eds.,* 1969, pp. 171–79.

Lee, Lucy C. and Bedford, Norton M. An Information Theory Analysis of the Accounting Process. *Accounting Rev.,* April 1969, *44*(2), pp. 256–75.

Lehtovuori, Jouko. Organisaatioteorian osa-alueista. (On Sub-Areas of Organization Theory. With English summary.) *Liiketaloudellinen Aikak.,* 1969, *18*(3), pp. 477–89.

Levy, Haim and Sarnat, Marshall. A Note on Indifference Curves and Uncertainty. *Swedish J. Econ.,* September 1969, *71*(3), pp. 206–08.

Lundstedt, Sven. Recognizing Organizational Diversity: A Problem of Fine Tuning. *Ohio State U. Bull. Bus. Res.,* November 1969, *44*(11), pp. 1–5.

Milligan, Bruce L. Contribution Margin in Decision Making. *Manage. Account.,* October 1969, *51*(4), pp. 33–38.

Monsen, R. J. Proprietà ed efficienza della grande impresa. (Ownership and Performance of the Large Firm. With English summary.) *Rivista Int. Sci. Econ. Com.,* May 1969, *16*(5), pp. 479–88.

Moore, David G. Toward More Comprehensive Human Relations in Industry. **In** *Somers, G. G., ed. (I),* 1969, pp. 137–46.

Naylor, R. D. Planning for the '70's. *Econ. Soc. Tijdschr.,* December 1969, *23*(6), pp. 567–85.

Paul, P.-E. Företagens Prognosbehov, en kommentar. (The Enterprise's Need of Forecasting. With English summary.) *Econ. Samfundets Tidskr.,* 1969, *22*(2), pp. 126–29.

Pfaff, Martin. Complex Organizational Processes. **In** *Naylor, T. H., ed.,* 1969, pp. 393–410.

Pintilie, Constanti and Vraca, Alexandru. Un concept nou: conducerea integrată a întreprinderilor. (A New Conception: Integrated Management of Enterprises. With English summary.) *Stud. Cercet. Econ.*, 1969, *1-2*, pp. 65–75.

Pugh, Derek. Organization Theory. **In** *Kempner, T., ed.*, 1969, pp. 98–103.

Pulkkinen, Kyösti. Asiakaspiirin vaikutus markkinointitoimen hajautukseen. (Effect of the Customers in the Decentralization of the Marketing Objective. With English summary.) *Liiketaloudellinen Aikak.*, 1969, *18*(2), pp. 192–205.

Rasmussen, Arne. How Sensitive are the Optimal Points of Micro-economics? *Liiketaloudellinen Aikak.*, 1969, *18*(1), pp. 61–67.

Ratoosh, Philburn. Defense Decision-Making: Cost-Effectiveness Models and Rationality. **In** *Bobrow, D. B., ed.*, 1969, pp. 21–34.

van Rest, E. D. Operational Research. **In** *Kempner, T., ed.*, 1969, pp. 71–74.

van Rest, E. D. Quantitative Foundations (Statistical Methods and Applicable Mathematics). **In** *Kempner, T., ed.*, 1969, pp. 33–42.

Robinson, David M. Some Comments on the Nature of the Scholarly Assumption as a Bias for Model Construction. *Liiketaloudellinen Aikak.*, 1969, *18*(1), pp. 68–73.

Sardi, Paolo. Interazione fra decisioni e sistema. (Inter-action between Decisions and Systems. With English summary.) *L'Impresa*, May/June 1969, *11* (3), pp. 231–36.

Särkisilta, Martti. Markkinointistrategian valinta suunnittelu- ja päätöksentekotapahtumana. (Choice of Marketing Strategy as a Planning and Decision-making Event. With English summary.) *Liiketaloudellinen Aikak.*, 1969, *18*(2), pp. 251–62.

Sayles, Leonard. Industrial Relations and Organization Behavior: Parent and Child? **In** *Somers, G. G., ed. (I)*, 1969, pp. 123–36.

Schleifer, Arthur, Jr. Two-Stage Normal Sampling in Two-Action Problems with Linear Economics. *J. Amer. Statist. Assoc.*, December 1969, *64*(328), pp. 1504–41.

Schneck, R. E., et al. A Strategic Contingencies' Model of Sub-unit Power. **In** *Association of Canadian Schools of Business*, 1969, pp. 66–79.

Schollhammer, Hans. National Economic Planning and Business Decision-Making: The French Experience. *Calif. Manage. Rev.*, Winter 1969, *12* (2), pp. 74–88. **[G: France]**

Schrier, Elliot. Production Planning in a Multiplant System. *Calif. Manage. Rev.*, Summer 1969, *11* (4), pp. 69–78.

Schwartzbaum, Allan M. Lateral Interaction and Effectiveness in Vertical Organizations. **In** *Somers, G. G., ed. (II)*, 1969, pp. 360–71.

Shapley, Lloyd S. and Shubik, Martin. A Method for Evaluating the Distribution of Power in a Committee System. **In** *Bell, R.; Edwards, D. V. and Wagner, R. H., eds.*, 1969, pp. 209–13.

Shubik, Martin. The Uses of Game Theory in Management Science. **In** *Carsberg, B. V. and Edey, H. C., eds.*, 1969, pp. 376–95.

Skala, Heinz J. Bemerkungen zur Bayesschen Entscheidungstheorie. (With English summary.) *Jahr. Nationalökon. Statist.*, July 1969, *183*(2), pp. 141–49.

Stigum, Bernt P. Entrepreneurial Choice Over Time under Conditions of Uncertainty. *Int. Econ. Rev.*, October 1969, *10*(3), pp. 426–42.

Stýblo, Jan. The Socialist Entrepreneurship and the Investor's Risk. *New Trends Czech. Econ.*, July 1969, (4), pp. 65–88.

Stykolt, Stefan. A Note on the Parametric Approach. **In** *Stykolt, S.*, 1969, pp. 196–98.

Swadener, Paul. The Loss Ratio Method of Rating and the Feedback Control Loop Concept. *J. Risk Ins.*, December 1969, *36*(5), pp. 615–27.

Theil, Henri. How to Worry About Increased Expenditures. *Accounting Rev.*, January 1969, *44*(1), pp. 27–37.

Tinsley, P. A. Optimal Factor Adjustment Paths: A Generalization of "Stock Adjustment" Decision Rules. (Study summary.) *Fed. Res. Bull.*, July 1969, *55*(7), pp. 580.

Tomasini, Luigi M. Il valore dell'informazione nella teoria dell'impresa. (The Value of Information in the Theory of the Firm. With English summary.) *L'Industria*, January–March 1969, (1), pp. 17–34.

Traimond, Pierre. La capacité excéndentaire stratégique dans l'entreprise. (With English summary.) *Revue Écon.*, September 1969, *20*(5), pp. 830–50.

Trapeznikov, V. For Flexible Economic Management of Enterprises. **In** *Economic Concentration, Pt. 7A, SCH*, 1969, pp. 4412–16. **[G: U.S.S.R.]**

Turnovsky, Stephen J. A Bayesian Approach to the Theory of Expectations. *J. Econ. Theory*, August 1969, *1*(2), pp. 220–27.

Urwick, Lyndall F. Organization as a Technical Problem. **In** *Gulick, L. and Urwick, L., eds.*, 1969, pp. 47–88.

Urwick, Lyndall F. The Function of Administration: With Special Reference to the Work of Henri Fayol. **In** *Gulick, L. and Urwick, L., eds.*, 1969, pp. 115–30.

Van Horne, James C. A Risk-Return Analysis of a Firm's Working-Capital Position. *Eng. Econ.*, January–February 1969, *14*(2), pp. 71–89.

Vepřek, Jaromír. Lineární plánovací modely a podniková praxe. (Linear Planning Models in Business Practice. With English summary.) *Ekon.-Mat. Obzor*, 1969, *5*(3), pp. 273–94. **[G: Czechoslovakia]**

Walker, James W. Forecasting Manpower Needs. *Harvard Bus. Rev.*, March–April 1969, *47*(2), pp. 152–64.

Whyte, William Foote. Building Better Organizational Models. **In** *Somers, G. G., ed. (I)*, 1969, pp. 109–21.

Will, Hartmut J. Management Information Systems: Educational Implications. **In** *Association of Canadian Schools of Business*, 1969, pp. 359–404.

Williams, Edward E. Selecting the Appropriate Form of Business Organization: A Decision Model. *Eng. Econ.*, July–August 1969, *14*(4), pp. 221–27.

Williamson, Oliver E. Corporate Control and the Theory of the Firm. **In** *Manne, H. G., ed.*, 1969, pp. 281–336.

Woodside, Arch G. Analysis of General System Theory. *Marquette Bus. Rev.,* Summer 1969, *13*(2), pp. 45–64.

Wright, A. and Dent, J. B. The Application of Simulation Techniques to the Study of Grazing Systems. *Australian J. Agr. Econ.,* December 1969, *13*(2), pp. 144–53.

Yoshihara, Hideki. A Note on the Behavioral Theory of Innovation. *Kobe Econ. Bus. Rev.,* 1969, *16*(1), pp. 55–61.

Zangwill, Willard I. Top Management and the Selection of Major Contractors at NASA. *Calif. Manage. Rev.,* Fall 1969, *12*(1), pp. 43–52. **[G: U.S.]**

512 Managerial Economics

5120 Managerial Economics

Acampora, Giovanni. Il "real time" per il servizio conti correnti di corrispondenza: una soluzione organizzativa che offre sicurezza opertiva. ("Real Time" for the Current Accounts Service: An Organizational Solution Affording Operational Reliability. With English summary.) *Bancaria,* April 1969, *25*(4), pp. 438–48.

Agarwala, R. Price Policy in a Multi-Product Firm: A Case Study. *Appl. Econ.,* August 1969, *1*(3), pp. 161–66. **[G: U.K.]**

Allen, Brandt. Time Sharing Takes Off. *Harvard Bus. Rev.,* March–April 1969, *47*(2), pp. 128–36. **[G: U.S.]**

Ammer, Dean S. Materials Management as a Profit Center. *Harvard Bus. Rev.,* January–February 1969, *47*(1), pp. 72–82.

Amstutz, Arnold E. Market-Oriented Management Systems: The Current Status. *J. Marketing Res.,* November 1969, *6*(4), pp. 481–96.

Barclay, William D. Factorial Design in a Pricing Experiment. *J. Marketing Res.,* November 1969, *6*(4), pp. 427–29.

Bierman, Harold, Jr. Accelerated Depreciation and Rate Regulation. *Accounting Rev.,* January 1969, *44*(1), pp. 65–78.

Bozzola, G. B. Strutture organizzative e politiche commerciali su scala internazionale. (Organizational Structures and Commercial Policies at an International Level. With English summary.) *L'Impresa,* July/October 1969, *11*(4–5), pp. 311–19.

Bradley, Hugh E. Setting and Controlling Budgets with Regression Analysis. *Manage. Account.,* November 1969, *51*(5), pp. 31–34.

Brighi, Massimo. Note sulla struttura dei sistemi. (Remarks on the Structures of Systems. With English summary.) *L'Impresa,* May/June 1969, *11*(3), pp. 258–60. **[G: Italy]**

Bunich, P. G.; Perlamutrov, V. L. and Sokolovskii, L. Kh. An Inventory Model in Physical and Monetary Terms. *Matekon,* Fall 1969, *6*(1), pp. 30–43. **[G: U.S.S.R.]**

Burkart, A. J. Some Managerial Influences on a Firm's Pricing Policy. *J. Ind. Econ.,* July 1969, *17*(3), pp. 180–87.

Bussetti, Giancarlo. Il ruolo della r.o. nell'economia del sistema. (The Role of Operation Research in the Economic Use of Systems. With English summary.) *L'Impresa,* May/June 1969, *11*(3), pp. 242–47.

Byerly, Richard A. The Use of Mathematical Models in the Analysis and Improvement of Bank Operations. **In** *Jessup, P. F.,* 1969, pp. 346–59.

Call, Dwight V. Some Salient Factors Often Overlooked in Stock Options. *Accounting Rev.,* October 1969, *44*(4), pp. 711–19. **[G: U.S.]**

Carlson, John A. and O'Keefe, Terrence B. Buffer Stocks and Reaction Coefficients: An Experiment with Decision Making under Risk. *Rev. Econ. Stud.,* October 1969, *36*(108), pp. 467–84.

Chuev, Iu. V. and Stekhova, G. P. The Generalized Equipment Replacement Problem. *Matekon,* Fall 1969, *6*(1), pp. 75–90.

Claycamp, Henry J. and Liddy, Lucien E. Prediction of New Product Performance: An Analytical Approach. *J. Marketing Res.,* November 1969, *6*(4), pp. 414–20. **[G: U.S.]**

Colantoni, Claude S.; Manes, Rene P. and Whinston, Andrew. Programming, Profit Rates and Pricing Decisions. *Accounting Rev.,* July 1969, *44*(3), pp. 467–81.

Cook, S. L. Scientific Approaches to Business Problems or the Advancement of Science in Management. **In** *Hugh-Jones, E. M., ed.,* 1969, pp. 62–88.

Cramer, Joe J., Jr. and Iwand, Thomas. Financial Reporting for Conglomerates: An Economic Analysis. *Calif. Manage. Rev.,* Spring 1969, *11*(3), pp. 25–34.

Crowther, John F. Peril-Point Acquisition Prices. *Harvard Bus. Rev.,* September–October 1969, *47*(5), pp. 58–62.

Dean, Joel. Pricing Pioneering Products. *J. Ind. Econ.,* July 1969, *17*(3), pp. 165–79.

Donaldson, Gordon. Strategy for Financial Emergencies. *Harvard Bus. Rev.,* November–December 1969, *47*(6), pp. 67–79.

Dudick, Thomas S. Use of Indicators in Planning for Profits. *Manage. Account.,* November 1969, *51*(5), pp. 16–18.

di Fenizio, Ferdinando. Possibili valori e metodi d'indagine per "consulenti di direzione" di grandi gruppi industriali. (The Value Judgements and the Analytical Tools of a Management Consultant to a Large Industrial Company. With English summary.) *L'Industria,* April–June 1969, (2), pp. 147–58. **[G: Italy]**

Flippo, Edwin B. La riscoperta del lavoro nella teoria del management. (The Rediscovery of Work in Management Theory. With English summary.) *Rivista Int. Sci. Econ. Com.,* May 1969, *16*(5), pp. 446–56.

Freed, Roy N. Get the Computer System You Want. *Harvard Bus. Rev.,* November–December 1969, *47*(6), pp. 99–108.

Glover, Fred. Management Decision and Integer Programming. *Accounting Rev.,* April 1969, *44*(2), pp. 300–303.

Gonedes, Nicholas J. A Test of the Equivalent-Risk Class Hypothesis. *J. Financial Quant. Anal.,* June 1969, *4*(2), pp. 159–77. **[G: U.S.]**

Haenni, Paul M. Managers' gap mondiale: analisi

spettrale. (The Management Gap in a World Context: A Spectral Analysis. With English summary.) *L'Impresa,* November/December 1969, *11*(6), pp. 444–53.

Hartley, Ronald V. Linear Programming: Some Implications for Management Accounting. *Manage. Account.,* November 1969, *51*(5), pp. 48–51.

Hayes, Robert H. Qualitative Insights from Quantitative Methods. *Harvard Bus. Rev.,* July–August 1969, *47*(4), pp. 108–17.

Hennessy, John H., Jr. AD HOC Research in Small Companies. *Manage. Account.,* July 1969, *51*(1), pp. 27–30.

Honko, Jaakko. Some Basic Problems and Future Trends in Management. *Liiketaloudellinen Aikak.,* 1969, *18*(2), pp. 145–52.

Horngren, Charles T. Capacity Utilization and the Efficiency Variance. *Accounting Rev.,* January 1969, *44*(1), pp. 86–89.

Houston, William S., Jr. A Model for Working Capital Management: Comment. *Miss. Val. J. Bus. Econ.,* Spring 1969, *4*(2), pp. 89–95.

Inosov, V. L. and Sviatskaia, N. V. Some Problems in Optimal Inventory Control. *Matekon,* Fall 1969, *6*(1), pp. 44–56.

Ivancevich, John M. A Study of American Expatriate On-the-Job Performance Failures. *Univ. Wash. Bus. Rev.,* Winter 1969, *28*(2), pp. 42–49.

Jääskeläinen, Veikko. Traditional and Ex Post Variance Analysis: A Reconciliation. *Liiketaloudellinen Aikak.,* 1969, *18*(2), pp. 153–70.

Jackson. Equilibrium Results for Queueing Processes with Both Erlang Input and Service Time Distribution with More Than One Server. *Ekon.-Mat. Obzor,* 1969, *5*(2), pp. 172–85.

Kellison, Stephen G. A Linear Programming Model of Profitability, Capacity and Regulation in Insurance Management: Comment. *J. Risk Ins.,* December 1969, *36*(5), pp. 637–39.

Koehler, Robert W. Statistical Variance Control: Through Performance Reports and On-the-Spot Observation. *Manage. Account.,* December 1969, *51*(6), pp. 42–46.

Kuehn, Alfred A. and Hamburger, Michael J. A Hueristic Program for Locating Warehouses. In *Alexis, M.; Holloway, R. J. and Hancock, R. S., eds.,* 1969, pp. 472–85.

Kuehn, D. A. Stock Market Valuation and Acquisitions: An Empirical Test of One Component of Managerial Utility. *J. Ind. Econ.,* April 1969, *17*(2), pp. 132–44. **[G: U.K.]**

Kuosa, Aarno. Suksessiivisten suoritevalintojen optimointi. (Optimization of Successive Choices of Products. With English summary.) *Liiketaloudellinen Aikak.,* 1969, *18*(4), pp. 716–27.

Lalonde, Bernard J.; Robeson, James F. and Grabner, John R., Jr. The Business Logistics Concept. *Ohio State U. Bull. Bus. Res.,* May 1969, *44*(5), pp. 1–3, 8.

Livingstone, John Leslie. Input-Output Analysis for Cost Accounting, Planning and Control. *Accounting Rev.,* January 1969, *44*(1), pp. 48–64.

Manole, M. Reţelele de transport în analiza utilizării timpului de muncă. (Transportation Networks as a Factor in the Analysis of the Utilization of Working Time. With English summary.) *Stud. Cercet. Econ.,* 1969, *4,* pp. 125–30.

Mărgulescu, D. and Işfănescu, A. Rentabilitatea ca indicator de sinteză economică. (Profitableness as an Indicator of Economic Synthesis. With English summary.) *Stud. Cercet. Econ.,* 1969, *4,* pp. 173–83.

Massy, William F. Forecasting the Demand for New Convenience Products. *J. Marketing Res.,* November 1969, *6*(4), pp. 405–12.

Mensch, Gerhard. Approximate Solutions for Digraph Models with Complementary Variables by Separable Programming with Restricted Pivoting. *Z. ges. Staatswiss.,* July 1969, *125*(3), pp. 437–45.

Mercer, A. Operational Marketing Research. *J. Ind. Econ.,* November 1969, *18*(1), pp. 15–32.

Miller, Irvin M. Computer Graphics for Decision Making. *Harvard Bus. Rev.,* November–December 1969, *47*(6), pp. 120–32.

Milligan, Bruce L. Contribution Margin in Decision Making. *Manage. Account.,* October 1969, *51*(4), pp. 33–38.

Morrison, Thomas A. and Kaczka, Eugene. A New Application of Calculus and Risk Analysis to Cost-Volume-Profit Changes. *Accounting Rev.,* April 1969, *44*(2), pp. 330–43.

Myers, James H. and Samli, A. Coskun. Management Control of Marketing Research. *J. Marketing Res.,* August 1969, *6*(3), pp. 267–77.

Nielsen, Oswald. The Role of Variance in Managerial Control. *Manage. Account.,* October 1969, *51*(4), pp. 26–28.

Oatman, Floyd W. How to Stimulate Innovation in Physical Distribution. *Oregon Bus. Rev.,* March 1969, *28*(3), pp. 1–4.

Panati, Giovanni. L'imprenditore del futuro: archetipi manageriali. (The Future Entrepreneur: Managerial Archetypes. With English summary.) *L'Impresa,* November/December 1969, *11*(6), pp. 454–60.

Petillon, Jack. Budgettering en direct costing. (Budgeting and Direct Costing. With English summary.) *Econ. Soc. Tijdschr.,* April 1969, *23*(2), pp. 129–42.

Pirasteh, Ross. Prevent Blunders in Supply and Distribution. *Harvard Bus. Rev.,* March–April 1969, *47*(2), pp. 113–27.

Rappaport, Alfred. Integer Programming and Managerial Analysis. *Accounting Rev.,* April 1969, *44*(2), pp. 297–99.

Ravazzi, Giancarlo. Una problematica nuova per la direzione commerciale la concezione mercatistica della direzione d'impresa. (New Problems for Commercial Management: The Marketing Conception of Firm Management. With English summary.) *L'Impresa,* July/October 1969, *11*(4–5), pp. 304–10. **[G: Italy]**

Reilly, Frank K. An Analysis and Reconciliation of Bond Refunding Decision Models. *Marquette Bus. Rev.,* Summer 1969, *13*(2), pp. 76–88.

Rowland, Kendrith M. and Sovereign, Michael G. Markov-Chain Analysis of Internal Manpower Supply. *Ind. Relat.,* October 1969, *9*(1), pp. 88–99.

Saitow, Arnold R. CSPC: Reporting Project Progress to the Top. *Harvard Bus. Rev.,* January–February 1969, *47*(1), pp. 88–97.

Sandbulte, Arend J. Sales and Revenue Forecasting. *Manage. Account.,* December 1969, *51*(6), pp. 17–23.

Searby, Frederick Wright. Control Postmerger Change. *Harvard Bus. Rev.,* September–October 1969, *47*(5), pp. 4–12, 154–55.

Sjöblom, Veikko. Havaintoja toimialarationalisoinnista useammalla alalla toimivassa yrityksessä. (Remarks on Rationalization in the Operational Field in a Firm Operating in Several Fields. With English summary.) *Liiketaloudellinen Aikak.,* 1969, *18*(2), pp. 243–50.

Stoicescu, V. and Bădin, V. O aplicaţie a lanţurilor Markov la controlul calităţii producţiei. (An Application of Markov Chains to the Control of Production Quality. With English summary.) *Stud. Cercet. Econ.,* 1969, *1-2,* pp. 159–72.

Stoichită, I. V. and Vasilescu, Floarea. Analiza critică a metodologiei statistice de caracterizare a vitezei de rotaţie a fondurilor circulante. (Critical Analysis of the Statistical Methodology Used in Characterizing the Turnover Rate of the Circulation Means. With English summary.) *Stud. Cercet. Econ.,* 1969, *4,* pp. 137–58.

Urrila, Matti. Kommunikaatiopanos markkinoinnissa. (Communication Effort in Marketing. With English summary.) *Liiketaloudellinen Aikak.,* 1969, *18*(2), pp. 263–67.

Vanni, Lido. La direzione del personale: un primo bilancio italiano. (Personnel Management: A Preliminary Italian Survey. With English summary.) *L'Impresa,* November/December 1969, *11*(6), pp. 461–68. **[G: Italy]**

Vosyka, Miroslav. Model vícefázové soustavy hromadné obsluhy s respektováním priority požadavků. (Model of a Multiple Parallel and Series Queueing System with Preemptive Priorities. With English summary.) *Ekon.-Mat. Obzor,* 1969, *5*(3), pp. 354–77.

Wasserman, Joseph J. Plugging the Leaks in Computer Security. *Harvard Bus. Rev.,* September–October 1969, *47*(5), pp. 119–29.

Wild, R. Production Management. **In** *Kempner, T., ed.,* 1969, pp. 104–11.

Willet, Ronald P. and Stephenson, P. Ronald. Determinants of Buyer Response to Physical Distribution Service. *J. Marketing Res.,* August 1969, *6*(3), pp. 279–83. **[G: U.S.]**

Willis, J. F.; Minden, A. J. and Snyder, James C. Monte Carlo Simulation of Management Systems. *Can. J. Agr. Econ.,* February 1969, *17*(1), pp. 42–49.

Wilson, Cyrus C. and Greenidge, Charles D. Classification Merchandising: An Overlooked Opportunity for Increasing Merchandising Profitability. *Calif. Manage. Rev.,* Fall 1969, *12*(1), pp. 53–61.

Windal, Floyd W. Dynamic Programming: An Introduction. *Manage. Account.,* July 1969, *51*(1), pp. 47–49.

Witte, Eberhard. Organization of Management Decision-Making Processes: A Research Report. *Ger. Econ. Rev.,* 1969, *7*(3), pp. 256–62.

513 Business and Public Administration

5130 Business and Public Administration

Allen, William M. The Requirement for Management Talent. *Univ. Wash. Bus. Rev.,* Spring 1969, *28*(3), pp. 21–25. **[G: U.S.]**

America, Richard F., Jr. 'What Do You People Want?' *Harvard Bus. Rev.,* March–April 1969, *47*(2), pp. 103–12. **[G: U.S.]**

Andrews, Kenneth R. Toward Professionalism in Business Management. *Harvard Bus. Rev.,* March–April 1969, *47*(2), pp. 49–60. **[G: U.S.]**

Anshen, Melvin. The Management of Ideas. *Harvard Bus. Rev.,* July–August 1969, *47*(4), pp. 99–107.

Ansoff, H. Igor and Brandenburg, R. G. The General Manager of the Future. *Calif. Manage. Rev.,* Spring 1969, *11*(3), pp. 61–72.

Artioli, Roberto. Linee per una ricerca documentaria. (Outlines for a Research-Work on Economic Information. With English summary.) *L'Impresa,* January/February 1969, *11*(1), pp. 56–58. **[G: Italy]**

Avots, Ivars. Why Does Project Management Fail? *Calif. Manage. Rev.,* Fall 1969, *12*(1), pp. 77–82.

Bansal, B. L. Financial Control: Checks and Balances. **In** *Dagli, V., ed., Vol. II,* 1969, pp. 65–76. **[G: India]**

Bassett, Glenn A. The Qualifications of a Manager. *Calif. Manage. Rev.,* Winter 1969, *12*(2), pp. 35–44.

Battistel, Ezio. Collocazione organizzativa della direzione commerciale. (The Status of Commercial Management within the Organization. With English summary.) *L'Impresa,* July/October 1969, *11*(4–5), pp. 336–39.

Belcher, D. W. The Changing Nature of Compensation Administration. *Calif. Manage. Rev.,* Summer 1969, *11*(4), pp. 89–94.

Belli, Claudio. Il dirigente potere centrale dell' impresa. (The Manager: Central Power in the Firm. With English summary.) *L'Impresa,* July/October 1969, *11*(4–5), pp. 365–72. **[G: Italy]**

Berg, Norman A. What's Different about Conglomerate Management? *Harvard Bus. Rev.,* November–December 1969, *47*(6), pp. 112–20. **[G: U.S.]**

Billia, Gianni. Inserimento dell'uomodirigente nel sistema. (How a Manager Becomes a Part of the System. With English summary.) *L'Impresa,* May/June 1969, *11*(3), pp. 237–41.

Block, Carl E. and Maddox, Robert C. The "Trickle Effect"—A New Management Tool. *Marquette Bus. Rev.,* Spring 1969, *13*(1), pp. 11–14.

Bonaparte, Tony H. The Influence of Culture on Business in a Pluralistic Society: A Study of Trinidad, West Indies. *Amer. J. Econ. Soc.,* July 1969, *28*(3), pp. 285–300. **[G: Trinidad]**

Brodrick, John. Management and Technology. **In** *Hugh-Jones, E. M., ed.,* 1969, pp. 48–61.

Brummet, R. Lee; Flamholtz, Eric G. and Pyle, William C. Human Resource Accounting: A Tool to Increase Managerial Effectiveness. *Manage. Account.,* August 1969, *51*(2), pp. 12–15.

Caiden, Gerald E. Development Administration and

Administrative Reform. *Int. Soc. Sci. J.*, 1969, *21* (1), pp. 9–22.

Carroll, Daniel T. What Future for the Conglomerate? *Harvard Bus. Rev.*, May–June 1969, *47*(3), pp. 4–12, 167–68.

Chevalier, Jean-Marie. The Problem of Control in Large American Corporations. *Antitrust Bull.*, Spring 1969, *14*, pp. 163–80.

Daidola, Giorgio. Formazione e trasferimento quadri nelle imprese multinazionali. (Development and Transfer of Managers in Multinational Firms. With English summary.) *L'Impresa*, July/October 1969, *11*(4–5), pp. 373–75.

Dearden, John. The Case Against ROI Control. *Harvard Bus. Rev.*, May–June 1969, *47*(3), pp. 124–35.

Diebold, John. Bad Decisions on Computer Use. *Harvard Bus. Rev.*, January–February 1969, *47* (1), pp. 14–28, 176.

Dooley, Peter C. The Interlocking Directorate. *Amer. Econ. Rev.*, June 1969, *59*(3), pp. 314–23. **[G: U.S.]**

Drucker, Peter F. Management's New Role. *Harvard Bus. Rev.*, November–December 1969, *47* (6), pp. 49–54.

Evans, John W. Evaluating Social Action Programs. *Soc. Sci. Quart.*, December 1969, *50*(3), pp. 568–81. **[G: U.S.]**

Fazal, Mohd. Management of Personnel. **In** *Dagli, V., ed., Vol. II*, 1969, pp. 161–65. **[G: India]**

Foster, Kenneth E. Accounting for Management Pay Differentials. *Ind. Relat.*, October 1969, *9*(1), pp. 80–87. **[G: U.S.]**

Fried, Louis. The Twilight of the Mechanical Technology. *Calif. Manage. Rev.*, Summer 1969, *11*(4), pp. 63–68.

Gellerman, Saul. Behavioral Strategies. *Calif. Manage. Rev.*, Winter 1969, *12*(2), pp. 45–51.

Goodman, Richard Alan. A Hidden Issue in Minority Employment. *Calif. Manage. Rev.*, Summer 1969, *11*(4), pp. 27–30.

Goolsby, John L. Integrated Accounting Systems: A Practical Approach. *Manage. Account.*, September 1969, *51*(3), pp. 11–13, 28.

Heinemann, Klaus. Stabilität und Wandel bürokratischer Organisationen. (Stability and Change in Bureaucratic Organizations. With English summary.) *Schmollers Jahr.*, 1969, *89*(3), pp. 313–31.

Helle, Tapani. Arvoanalyysistä ja sen käytöstä hallinnon rationalisoinnissa. (Value Analysis and Its Use in Rationalizing Administration. With English summary.) *Liiketaloudellinen Aikak.*, 1969, *18* (3), pp. 388–92.

Henderson, P. D. Political and Budgetary Constraints: Some Characteristics and Implications. **In** *Margolis, J. and Guitton, H., eds.*, 1969, pp. 310–25.

Hsueh, S. S. Local Government and National Development in South-East Asia. *Int. Soc. Sci. J.*, 1969, *21*(1), pp. 45–55. **[G: S. E. Asia]**

Ide, Yoshinori. Administrative Reform and Innovation: The Japanese Case. *Int. Soc. Sci. J.*, 1969, *21* (1), pp. 56–67. **[G: Japan]**

Khera, S. S. Efficiency in the Public Sector. **In** *Dagli, V., ed., Vol. II*, 1969, pp. 18–30. **[G: India]**

King, Alfred M. Budgeting Foreign Exchange Losses. *Manage. Account.*, October 1969, *51*(4), pp. 39–41, 46.

Kolbin, V. V. and Syroezhin, I. M. Computer Analysis of a Business Game. *Matekon*, Fall 1969, *6*(1), pp. 57–74.

Leighton, Charles M. and Tod, G. Robert. After the Acquisition: Continuing Challenge. *Harvard Bus. Rev.*, March–April 1969, *47*(2), pp. 90–102. **[G: U.S.]**

Levinson, Harry. On Being a Middle-Aged Manager. *Harvard Bus. Rev.*, July–August 1969, *47*(4), pp. 51–60.

Levitt, Theodore. The New Markets—Think before You Leap. *Harvard Bus. Rev.*, May–June 1969, *47* (3), pp. 53–67.

Levy, Sidney J. and Kotler, Philip. Beyond Marketing: The Furthering Concept. *Calif. Manage. Rev.*, Winter 1969, *12*(2), pp. 67–73.

Livingston, J. Sterling. Pygmalion in Management. *Harvard Bus. Rev.*, July–August 1969, *47*(4), pp. 81–89.

Mărgulescu, D. and Işfănescu, A. Rentabilitatea ca indicator de sinteză economică. (Profitableness as an Indicator of Economic Synthesis. With English summary.) *Stud. Cercet. Econ.*, 1969, *4*, pp. 173–83.

Marquis, Lloyd K. A Comprehensive Framework for Analyzing the Management of a Business Enterprise. **In** *Kennedy, C. J., ed.*, 1969, pp. 38–48.

May, Phillip T., Jr. System Control: Computers the Weak Link? *Accounting Rev.*, July 1969, *44*(3), pp. 583–92.

McDonald, Howard E. and Stromberger, T. L. Cost Control for the Professional Service Firm. *Harvard Bus. Rev.*, January–February 1969, *47*(1), pp. 109–21.

McGivering, Ian. Personnel Management. **In** *Kempner, T., ed.*, 1969, pp. 54–59.

Nally, Robert V. The Computer and Home Office Management Development in Life Insurance. *J. Risk Ins.*, September 1969, *36*(4), pp. 393–400.

Olson, Mancur, Jr. The Principle of "Fiscal Equivalence": The Division of Responsibilities among Different Levels of Government. *Amer. Econ. Rev.*, May 1969, *59*(2), pp. 479–87. **[G: U.S.]**

Ozsvald, László. Incentives for Management Personnel in Hungarian Industry. *Int. Lab. Rev.*, September 1969, *100*(3), pp. 257–72. **[G: Hungary]**

Paul, William J., Jr.; Robertson, Keith B. and Herzberg, Frederick. Job Enrichment Pays Off. *Harvard Bus. Rev.*, March–April 1969, *47*(2), pp. 61–78. **[G: U.K.]**

Phatak, Arvind. American Managers' Philosophies: Authoritarian or Permissive? *Univ. Wash. Bus. Rev.*, Winter 1969, *28*(2), pp. 33–39. **[G: U.S.]**

Pintilie, C. Folosirea metodelor moderne de conducere în întreprinderile industriale din România. (Use of Up-to-Date Methods in Industrial Enterprises of Romania. With English summary.) *Stud. Cercet. Econ.*, 1969, *3*, pp. 101–10. **[G: Romania]**

Porter, W. Thomas. Professional Education for Management. *Univ. Wash. Bus. Rev.*, Summer 1969, *28*(4), pp. 44–48.

Protopopescu, V. V. Organizarea şi raţionalizarea

muncii de administrație în intreprinderi și organizații economice. (Organizing and Rationalizing Administrative Work in Economic Organizations and Enterprises. With English summary.) *Stud. Cercet. Econ.*, 1969, *4*, pp. 71–83.

Pruden, Henry O. The Outside Salesman: Interorganizational Link. *Calif. Manage. Rev.*, Winter 1969, *12*(2), pp. 57–66.

Pulkkinen, Kyösti. Arkisto yrityksen tiedonvälityksessä. (Records Storage as a Part of the Communication of the Enterprise. With English summary.) *Liiketaloudellinen Aikak.*, 1969, *18*(3), pp. 541–49.

Pusić, Eugen. Area and Administration in Yugoslav Development. *Int. Soc. Sci. J.*, 1969, *21*(1), pp. 68–82. **[G: Yugoslavia]**

Rajesh. Efficient Management: A. R. C. Report. **In** *Dagli, V., ed., Vol. II*, 1969, pp. 41–49. **[G: India]**

Reavis, Marshall W. The Corporate Risk Manager's Contribution to Profit. *J. Risk Ins.*, September 1969, *36*(4), pp. 473–79.

Revelle, Charles; Joeres, Erhard and Kirby, William. The Linear Decision Rule in Reservoir Management and Design. 1. Development of the Stochastic Model. *Water Resources Res.*, August 1969, *5* (4), pp. 767–77.

Ryavec, Karl W. Soviet Industrial Managers, Their Superiors and the Economic Reform: A Study of an Attempt at Planned Behavioural Change. *Soviet Stud.*, October 1969, *21*(2), pp. 208–29. **[G: U.S.S.R.]**

Schnur, Roman. Area and Administration. *Int. Soc. Sci. J.*, 1969, *21*(1), pp. 83–99.

Schoen, Donald R. Managing Technological Innovation. *Harvard Bus. Rev.*, May–June 1969, *47*(3), pp. 156–67.

Schrier, Elliot. Production Planning in a Multiplant System. *Calif. Manage. Rev.*, Summer 1969, *11* (4), pp. 69–78.

Schultze, Charles L. Using Incentives to Improve the Effectiveness of Government. *Mon. Lab. Rev.*, September 1969, *92*(9), pp. 34–38.

Searby, Frederick Wright. Control Postmerger Change. *Harvard Bus. Rev.*, September–October 1969, *47*(5), pp. 4–12, 154–55.

Sherman, George. An Executive Looks at—The Corporate Will. *Calif. Manage. Rev.*, Spring 1969, *11* (3), pp. 3–6.

Skinner, Wickham. Manufacturing—Missing Link in Corporate Strategy. *Harvard Bus. Rev.*, May–June 1969, *47*(3), pp. 136–45.

Sokolik, Stanley L. Reorganize the Personnel Department? *Calif. Manage. Rev.*, Spring 1969, *11* (3), pp. 43–52.

Stoichită, I. V. and Vasilescu, Floarea. Analiza critică a metodologiei statistice de caracterizare a vitezei de rotație a fondurilor circulante. (Critical Analysis of the Statistical Methodology Used in Characterizing the Turnover Rate of the Circulation Means. With English summary.) *Stud. Cercet. Econ.*, 1969, *4*, pp. 137–58.

Tilli, Kalevi. Työntekijäin asenteisiin vaikuttavista tekijöistä. (Factors Influencing the Attitudes of Employees. With English summary.) *Liiketaloudellinen Aikak.*, 1969, *18*(3), pp. 616–23.

Tiwary, D. N. Control By Parliament. **In** *Dagli, V., ed., Vol. II*, 1969, pp. 60–64. **[G: India]**

Todd, Jerry D. The Risk Management Function in Municipal Government. *J. Risk Ins.*, June 1969, *36*(2), pp. 285–95. **[G: U.S.]**

Tripathi, B. N. Watchdog for Public Undertakings. **In** *Dagli, V., ed., Vol. II*, 1969, pp. 50–59. **[G: India]**

Tull, Donald S. The Man in the President's Chair: Oregon and Elsewhere. *Oregon Bus. Rev.*, May 1969, *28*(5), pp. 1–4. **[G: U.S.]**

Tullock, Gordon. Federalism: Problems of Scale. *Public Choice*, Spring 1969, *6*, pp. 19–29.

Urwick, Lyndall F. Integration and Integrity. *Calif. Manage. Rev.*, Winter 1969, *12*(2), pp. 53–56.

Vanni, Lido. La direzione del personale: un primo bilancio italiano. (Personnel Management: A Preliminary Italian Survey. With English summary.) *L'Impresa*, November/December 1969, *11*(6), pp. 461–68. **[G: Italy]**

Verhaegen, Jozef. Beleidsboekhouden. (Management Accounting. With English summary.) *Econ. Soc. Tijdschr.*, April 1969, *23*(2), pp. 113–28.

Waldo, Dwight. Reflections on Public Administration and National Development. *Int. Soc. Sci. J.*, 1969, *21*(2), pp. 294–309.

Walker, James W. Forecasting Manpower Needs. *Harvard Bus. Rev.*, March–April 1969, *47*(2), pp. 152–64.

Weller, Oren H. Touch-Tone Attendance and Labor Reporting. *Manage. Account.*, August 1969, *51* (2), pp. 27–28, 32.

Williams, Roger. Administrative Modernization in British Government. *Int. Soc. Sci. J.*, 1969, *21*(1), pp. 100–15. **[G: U.K.]**

Wright, Albert W. Maintaining Balance in Financial Position. *Manage. Account.*, September 1969, *51* (3), pp. 14–16, 28.

Wu, Chi-Yuen. Public Administration for National Development: An Analysis of the United Nations Public Administration Programme in the Past Two Decades and the Major Problems in the 1970s. *Int. Soc. Sci. J.*, 1969, *21*(1), pp. 116–34.

Zinkin, Maurice. A Child's Guide to Planning. *Appl. Econ.*, May 1969, *1*(2), pp. 81–88.

514 Goals and Objectives of Firms

5140 Goals and Objectives of Firms

Anshen, Melvin. The Management of Ideas. *Harvard Bus. Rev.*, July–August 1969, *47*(4), pp. 99–107.

Bagiotti, Tullio. Parole e fatti sulla massimizzazione del profitto. (Words and Facts on Profit Maximization. With English summary.) *Rivista Int. Sci. Econ. Com.*, July 1969, *16*(7), pp. 637–51.

Bowman, Dean A. How Corporations Plan: Introduction and State-of-the-Art. **In** *Ozbekhan, H. and Talbert, G. E., eds.*, 1969, pp. 97–101.

Case, Fred E. Business and the Urban Scene. *Calif. Manage. Rev.*, Summer 1969, *11*(4), pp. 3. **[G: U.S.]**

Caselli, Lorenzo. Dal profitto alla sopravvivenza: considerazioni in tema di finalità d'impresa. (From Profit to Survival—Remarks on Firm's

Aims. With English summary.) *L'Impresa*, March/April 1969, *11*(2), pp. 126–32.

Červinka, Antonín. What Is the Matter in Dispute? *New Trends Czech. Econ.,* May 1969, (3), pp. 64–75. **[G: Czechoslovakia]**

Drucker, Peter F. Management's New Role. *Harvard Bus. Rev.,* November–December 1969, *47* (6), pp. 49–54.

Dupuy, Yves. Les objectifs de la firme et l'analyse de l'effectif. (With English summary.) *Revue Écon.,* July 1969, *20*(4), pp. 658–83.

Fromm, Erich. The Outlook: Integrated Planning—Problems and Opportunities. **In** *Ozbekhan, H. and Talbert, G. E., eds.,* 1969, pp. 223–33. **[G: U.S.]**

Goeke, Joseph R. and Weymar, Caroline S. Barriers to Hiring the Blacks. *Harvard Bus. Rev.,* September–October 1969, *47*(5), pp. 144–52. **[G: U.S.]**

Goldston, Eli. BURP and Make Money. *Harvard Bus. Rev.,* September–October 1969, *47*(5), pp. 84–99. **[G: U.S.]**

Gross, Edwin J. An Industrial Approach to Consumerism: Ombudsmen. *Ohio State U. Bull. Bus. Res.,* October 1969, *44*(10), pp. 6–7. **[G: U.S.]**

Gross, Norman. Convergence and the Emerging Framework: Discussion. **In** *Ozbekhan, H. and Talbert, G. E., eds.,* 1969, pp. 234–40. **[G: U.S.]**

Hanan, Mack. Corporate Growth through Internal Spin-outs. *Harvard Bus. Rev.,* November–December 1969, *47*(6), pp. 55–66.

Jääskeläinen, Veikko. A Goal Programming Model of Aggregate Production Planning. *Swedish J. Econ.,* March 1969, *71*(1), pp. 14–29.

Lipowski, Adam. Interdependence Between Goals and Incentives in an Experimental System of Management. *Eastern Europ. Econ.,* Fall 1969, *8* (1), pp. 20–71. **[G: Poland]**

Lobato López, Ernesto. Las normas de calidad y el desarrollo de la industria (Primera parte). (Quality Standards and Industrial Development: First Part. With English summary.) *Econ. Polít.,* Second Semester 1969, *6*(2), pp. 183–94. **[G: Mexico]**

Long, Norton E. The Corporation, Its Satellites, and the Local Community. **In** *Minar, D. W. and Greer, S., eds.,* 1969, pp. 163–76. **[G: U.S.]**

Lord, A. Matthew. Government and Business Planning at the Crossroads: Discussion. **In** *Ozbekhan, H. and Talbert, G. E., eds.,* 1969, pp. 14–31. **[G: U.S.]**

Miller, Irwin. Business Has a War to Win. *Harvard Bus. Rev.,* March–April 1969, *47*(2), pp. 4–12, 164–68. **[G: U.S.]**

Miller, Richard A. Market Structure and Industrial Performance: Relation of Profit Rates to Concentration, Advertising Intensity, and Diversity. *J. Ind. Econ.,* April 1969, *17*(2), pp. 104–18. **[G: U.S.]**

Naylor, R. D. Planning for the '70's. *Econ. Soc. Tijdschr.,* December 1969, *23*(6), pp. 567–85.

Paul, William J., Jr.; Robertson, Keith B. and Herzberg, Frederick. Job Enrichment Pays Off. *Harvard Bus. Rev.,* March–April 1969, *47*(2), pp. 61–78. **[G: U.K.]**

Peterson, Russell K. The Role and Responsibility of Business in the Growth of American Society. **In** *Ozbekhan, H. and Talbert, G. E., eds.,* 1969, pp. 70–77. **[G: U.S.]**

Rozet, A. Bruce. The Complex World of the American Corporation: Priorities, Goals, and Strategies. **In** *Ozbekhan, H. and Talbert, G. E., eds.,* 1969, pp. 118–26. **[G: U.S.]**

Schaffir, Walter B. How Corporations Plan: Discussion. **In** *Ozbekhan, H. and Talbert, G. E., eds.,* 1969, pp. 127–44.

Schlusberg, Malcolm D. Corporate Legitimacy and Social Responsibility: The Role of Law. *Calif. Manage. Rev.,* Fall 1969, *12*(1), pp. 65–76.

Schriever, Bernard A. The Role and Responsibility of Business in the Growth of American Society. **In** *Ozbekhan, H. and Talbert, G. E., eds.,* 1969, pp. 5–13. **[G: U.S.]**

Sethi, S. Prakash and Votaw, Dow. Do We Need a New Corporate Response to a Changing Social Environment? Part II. *Calif. Manage. Rev.,* Fall 1969, *12*(1), pp. 17–31.

Smiddy, Harold F. Planning as a Fundamental Component of Management: Background and Perspective. **In** *Ozbekhan, H. and Talbert, G. E., eds.,* 1969, pp. 102–17.

Staats, Elmer B. Industry-Government Relationships: Issues Facing the New Administration. **In** *Ozbekhan, H. and Talbert, G. E., eds.,* 1969, pp. 205–22. **[G: U.S.]**

Staats, Elmer B. Industry-Government Relationships. *Calif. Manage. Rev.,* Fall 1969, *12*(1), pp. 83–90. **[G: U.S.]**

Teresi, Salvatore. The Formation of Marketing Men. *Econ. Soc. Tijdschr.,* December 1969, *23*(6), pp. 555–65.

Votaw, Dow and Sethi, S. Prakash. Do We Need a New Corporate Response to a Changing Social Environment? Part I. *Calif. Manage. Rev.,* Fall 1969, *12*(1), pp. 3–16.

Walton, Clarence C. The Role of Ethical Standards in Business. **In** *Burton, J. C., ed.,* 1969, pp. 59–69. **[G: U.S.]**

Yeung, Patrick. Unifying Elements in the Theories of the Firm. *Quart. Rev. Econ. Bus.,* Winter 1969, *9*(4), pp. 21–28.

520 Business Finance and Investment

5200 Business Finance and Investment

Altman, Edward I. Corporate Bankruptcy Potential, Stockholder Returns and Share Valuation. *J. Finance,* December 1969, *24*(5), pp. 887–900.

Bernhard, Richard H. Mathematical Programming Models for Capital Budgeting—A Survey, Generalization, and Critique. *J. Financial Quant. Anal.,* June 1969, *4*(2), pp. 111–58.

Celen, R. De beoordeling van de resultaten in de E.E.G.-landen, Groot-Brittannië en de V.S., wordt geconditioneerd door afwi jkende nationale belastingstelsels. (Differences in the National Tax Systems Are the Causes that the Profits of the Firms in the Countries of the E.E.C., Great Britain and the U.S. Have to Be Compared Cautiously. With English summary.) *Econ. Soc. Tijdschr.,* April 1969, *23*(2), pp. 185–204.

Christian, James W. and Mazek, Warren F. Corporate Debt Structure and the Differential Effects of Monetary Policy. *Southern Econ. J.*, April 1969, *35*(4), pp. 359–68. **[G: U.S.]**

Drzycimski, Eugene F. The Stock Repurchase Decision. *Marquette Bus. Rev.*, Winter 1969, *13*(4), pp. 159–67.

Furst, Richard W. and Markland, Robert E. Evaluating Merger-Acquisition Opportunities—A Risk Incorporation Model. *Univ. Missouri Bus. Govt. Rev.*, July–August 1969, *10*(4), pp. 21–26.

Green, Johs. Il finanziamento dell-espansione e della ristrutturazione economica. (Financing of Expansion and Structural Change. With English summary.) *Bancaria*, August 1969, *25*(8), pp. 947–53.

Hamada, Robert S. Portfolio Analysis, Market Equilibrium and Corporation Finance. *J. Finance*, March 1969, *24*(1), pp. 13–31.

Huefner, Ronald J. Taxation and the Disposition of Depreciable Assets. *Eng. Econ.*, April–May 1969, *14*(3), pp. 141–50. **[G: U.S.]**

Huntsman, Blaine. Asset Management and Monetary Policy: Discussion. *J. Finance*, May 1969, *24* (2), pp. 239–41. **[G: U.S.]**

Konovalova, N. and Petrosian, K. Problems of Intensifying the Stimulating Role of Payments for Funds. *Prob. Econ.*, June 1969, *12*(2), pp. 25–47. **[G: U.S.S.R.]**

Lambert, Rapporto. Perché le imprese europee non guadagnano come le americane. (Why European Firms Do Not Earn as Much as the Americans. With English summary.) *L'Impresa*, January/February 1969, *11*(1), pp. 18–28.

McConnell, Thomas P. Hidden Resources in the Dues Dollar. *Manage. Account.*, December 1969, *51*(6), pp. 24–26.

Mills, Edwin S. The Small Business Capital Gap. *Rivista Int. Sci. Econ. Com.*, March 1969, *16*(3), pp. 259–79. **[G: U.S.]**

Mossin, Jan. Security Pricing and Investment Criteria in Competitive Markets. *Amer. Econ. Rev.*, December 1969, *59*(5), pp. 749–56.

Plattner, Robert H. Fund Administration and Dividend Policy. *Quart. Rev. Econ. Bus.*, Summer 1969, *9*(2), pp. 21–29.

Rapp, Wilbur A. Treasury Common Stock Financing as an Investment Process. *Miss. Val. J. Bus. Econ.*, Fall 1969, *5*(1), pp. 1–10. **[G: U.S.]**

Renwick, Fred B. Asset Management and Investor Portfolio Behavior: Theory and Practice. *J. Finance*, May 1969, *24*(2), pp. 181–206. **[G: U.S.]**

Ricks, R. Bruce. Imputed Equity Returns on Real Estate Financed with Life Insurance Company Loans. *J. Finance*, December 1969, *24*(5), pp. 921–37. **[G: U.S.]**

Sarma, L. V. L. N. and Rao, R. S. Hanumanta. Estimates of the Cost of Capital to the Indian Engineering Industry, 1962–65. *Yorkshire Bull. Econ. Soc. Res.*, November 1969, *21*(2), pp. 132–40. **[G: India]**

Siglienti, Stefano. Sulle possibilità di formazione del risparmio e di investimento produttivo. (Savings and Productive Investments. With English summary.) *Bancaria*, October 1969, *25*(10), pp. 1195–99. **[G: Italy]**

Stober, William J. and Falk, Laurence H. The Effect of Financial Inducements on the Location of Firms. *Southern Econ. J.*, July 1969, *36*(1), pp. 25–35.

Zanetti, Giovanni and Filippi, Enrico. Il processo di sviluppo dell'impresa: Fattori endogeni ed esogeni esperienza italiana 1958–1963. (The Process of Firm Growth: Endogenous and Exogenous Factors in the Italian Experience 1958–1963. With English summary.) *L'Impresa*, January/February 1969, *11*(1), pp. 29–39. **[G: Italy]**

521 Business Finance

5210 Business Finance

Ansoff, H. I. A Quasi-analytic Method for Long-Range Planning. In *Carsberg, B. V. and Edey, H. C., eds.*, 1969, pp. 303–22.

Beechy, Thomas H. Quasi-Debt Analysis of Financial Leases. *Accounting Rev.*, April 1969, *44*(2), pp. 375–81.

Borch, Karl. The Capital Structure of a Firm. *Swedish J. Econ.*, March 1969, *71*(1), pp. 1–13.

Bower, Richard S. Problems and Progress in the Applications of Recent Developments in the Theory of Finance: Discussion. *J. Finance*, May 1969, *24*(2), pp. 339–41. **[G: U.S.]**

Brandt, Louis K. Quantitative Tools for Financial Management. *Southern Quart.*, April 1969, *7*(3), pp. 261–81.

Call, Dwight V. Some Salient Factors Often Overlooked in Stock Options. *Accounting Rev.*, October 1969, *44*(4), pp. 711–19. **[G: U.S.]**

Cannata, Giuseppe. Factoring: un nuovo ausilio per la gestione delle medie e piccole imprese-I. (Factoring: A New Facility for Medium and Small Companies-I. With English summary.) *Bancaria*, June 1969, *25*(6), pp. 711–24.

Cannata, Giuseppe. Factoring: un nuovo ausilio per la gestione delle medie a piccole imprese-II. (Factoring: A New Facility for Medium and Small Companies-II. With English summary.) *Bancaria*, July 1969, *25*(7), pp. 842–50.

Dodge, Robert H. How Leverage Affects the Cost of Capital to a Public Utility. *Manage. Account.*, August 1969, *51*(2), pp. 39–44.

Donaldson, Gordon. Strategy for Financial Emergencies. *Harvard Bus. Rev.*, November–December 1969, *47*(6), pp. 67–79.

Eiteman, David K. and Tom, Franklin. The New California Blue-Sky Law. *Calif. Manage. Rev.*, Winter 1969, *12*(2), pp. 5–12. **[G: U.S.]**

Elsaid, Hussein H. Non-convertible Preferred Stock as a Financing Instrument 1950–65: Comment. *J. Finance*, December 1969, *24*(5), pp. 939–41. **[G: U.S.]**

Frostman, Lars. Optimal Financing and Tax Policy of the Corporation—A Review Article. *Swedish J. Econ.*, March 1969, *71*(1), pp. 30–41.

Gershefski, George W. Building a Corporate Financial Model. *Harvard Bus. Rev.*, July–August 1969, *47*(4), pp. 61–72. **[G: U.S.]**

Ghafur, Abdul. Financial-Asset Accumulation by the

Noncorporate Private Sector in Pakistan 1959/60 to 1965/66. *Pakistan Develop. Rev.*, Spring 1969, *9*(1), pp. 66–86. [G: Pakistan]

Goudzwaard, Maurice B. Conglomerate Mergers, Convertibles, and Cash Dividends. *Quart. Rev. Econ. Bus.*, Spring 1969, *9*(1), pp. 53–62.

Gupta, Manak C. The Effect of Size, Growth, and Industry on the Financial Structure of Manufacturing Companies. *J. Finance*, June 1969, *24*(3), pp. 517–29. [G: U.S.]

Hakansson, Nils H. On the Dividend Capitalization Model under Uncertainty. *J. Financial Quant. Anal.*, March 1969, *4*(1), pp. 65–87.

Haves, Samuel L., III and Reiling, Henry B. Sophisticated Financing Tool: The Warrant. *Harvard Bus. Rev.*, January–February 1969, *47*(1), pp. 137–50.

Heamon, John W. Inventory and Financing Procedures for a Mortgage Banker. *Manage. Account.*, December 1969, *51*(6), pp. 32–34.

Heins, A. James and Sprenkle, Case M. A Comment on the Modigliani-Miller Cost of Capital Thesis. *Amer. Econ. Rev.*, Part I, September 1969, *59*(4), pp. 590–92.

Houston, William S., Jr. A Model for Working Capital Management: Comment. *Miss. Val. J. Bus. Econ.*, Spring 1969, *4*(2), pp. 89–95.

Jaffee, Dwight M. and Modigliani, Franco. A Theory and Test of Credit Rationing. *Amer. Econ. Rev.*, December 1969, *59*(5), pp. 850–72. [G: U.S.]

Jeffers, James R. and Kwon, Jene. A Portfolio Approach to Corporate Demands for Government Securities. *J. Finance*, December 1969, *24*(5), pp. 905–19.

Johnson, R. A.; Kast, F. E. and Rosenzweig, J. E. Systems Theory and Management. **In** *Carsberg, B. V. and Edey, H. C., eds.*, 1969, pp. 279–302.

Kahn, Douglas A. Mandatory Buy-Out Agreements for Stock of Closely Held Corporations. *Mich. Law Rev.*, November 1969, *68*(1), pp. 1–64.

Käräva, Simo. Luotonannon selektiivisyys ja pankit. (The Selective Lending Policy and the Banks. With English summary.) *Kansant. Aikak.*, 1969, *65*(3), pp. 226–32. [G: Finland]

Larson, Kermit D. and Gonedes, Nicholas J. Business Combinations: An Exchange Ratio Determination Model. *Accounting Rev.*, October 1969, *44*(4), pp. 720–28.

Lewellen, Wilbur G. Management and Ownership in the Large Firm. *J. Finance*, May 1969, *24*(2), pp. 299–322. [G: U.S.]

Lieberman, A. E. Updating Impressions of the Military-Industry Complex. *Calif. Manage. Rev.*, Summer 1969, *11*(4), pp. 51–62. [G: U.S.]

Maddala, G. S. and Vogel, Robert C. Estimating Lagged Relationships in Corporate Demand for Liquid Assets. *Rev. Econ. Statist.*, February 1969, *51*(1), pp. 53–61. [G: U.S.]

Meimberg, R. About the Theory and Practice of the Participation of Deposit Banks in the Financing of Capital Projects (with Reference to the Conditions in Germany, England and India). *Indian Econ. J.*, April–June 1969, *16*(4–5), pp. 496–506. [G: Germany; U.K.; India]

Modigliani, Franco and Miller, Merton H. A Comment on the Modigliani-Miller Cost of Capital Thesis: Reply. *Amer. Econ. Rev.*, Part I, September 1969, *59*(4), pp. 592–95.

Nadiri, M. Ishag. The Determinants of Trade Credit in the U.S. Total Manufacturing Sector. *Econometrica*, July 1969, *37*(3), pp. 408–23.

Paton, W. A. Postscript on "Treasury" Shares. *Accounting Rev.*, April 1969, *44*(2), pp. 276–83.

Perrin, J. R. Financial Management. **In** *Kempner, T., ed.*, 1969, pp. 75–83.

Reilly, Frank K. An Analysis and Reconciliation of Bond Refunding Decision Models. *Marquette Bus. Rev.*, Summer 1969, *13*(2), pp. 76–88.

Rickey, Kenneth R. Earnings per Share: Management and the Investor. *Manage. Account.*, December 1969, *51*(6), pp. 9–11.

Saravane, Mohandas. Some Issues Relating to Deposit Mobilisation by Non-Banking Companies. *Indian Econ. J.*, April–June 1969, *16*(4–5), pp. 445–57. [G: India]

Sarma, L. V. L. N. and Roa, K. S. Hanumanta. Leverage and the Value of the Firm. *J. Finance*, September 1969, *24*(4), pp. 673–77. [G: India]

Shad, John S. R. The Financial Realities of Mergers. *Harvard Bus. Rev.*, November–December 1969, *47*(6), pp. 132–46. [G: U.S.]

Simpson, Richard H. An Empirical Study of Possible Income Manipulation. *Accounting Rev.*, October 1969, *44*(4), pp. 806–17.

Singhvi, Surendra S. Corporate Financial Disclosure in the United States. *Miss. Val. J. Bus. Econ.*, Fall 1969, *5*(1), pp. 43–50. [G: U.S.]

Singhvi, Surendra S. and Slamka, John G. Industrial Revenue Bonds: A Source of Long-Term Financing. *Calif. Manage. Rev.*, Spring 1969, *11*(3), pp. 53–60. [G: U.S.]

Smith, Vernon L. Taxes and Share Valuation in Competitive Markets. *Rev. Econ. Statist.*, February 1969, *51*(1), pp. 96–99.

Sprenkle, Case M. The Uselessness of Transactions Demand Models. *J. Finance*, December 1969, *24*(5), pp. 835–47.

Srinivasan, E. S. Analysis of the Trends in the Sources of Funds of the Non-Financial Companies in India during 1951–66. *Asian Econ. Rev.*, February 1969, *11*(2), pp. 131–44. [G: India]

Stiglitz, Joseph E. A Re-Examination of the Modigliani-Miller Theorem. *Amer. Econ. Rev.*, December 1969, *59*(5), pp. 784–93.

Stonehill, Arthur and Stitzel, Thomas. Financial Structure and Multinational Corporations. *Calif. Manage. Rev.*, Fall 1969, *12*(1), pp. 91–96.

Tambini, Luigi. Financial Policy and the Corporation Income Tax. **In** *Harberger, A. C. and Bailey, M. J., eds.*, 1969, pp. 185–222. [G: U.S.]

di Tella, Guido. The Behavior of the Firm with a Financial Restriction. *J. Ind. Econ.*, April 1969, *17*(2), pp. 119–32.

Van Horne, James C. A Risk-Return Analysis of a Firm's Working-Capital Position. *Eng. Econ.*, January–February 1969, *14*(2), pp. 71–89.

Vance, Jack O. Is Your Company a Take-Over Target? *Harvard Bus. Rev.*, May–June 1969, *47*(3), pp. 93–98.

Wilhelm, Maurice F., Jr. Purchase or Lease: That Is

the Question. *Manage. Account.*, July 1969, *51*(1), pp. 43–46.

Wrightsman, Dwayne. Optimal Credit Terms for Accounts Receivable. *Quart. Rev. Econ. Bus.*, Summer 1969, *9*(2), pp. 59–66.

522 Business Investment

5220 Business Investment

Adler, F. Michael. On the Risk-Return Trade-Off in the Valuation of Assets. *J. Financial Quant. Anal.*, December 1969, *4*(4), pp. 493–512.

Agarwala, R. and Goodson, G. C. An Analysis of the Effects of Investment Incentives on Investment Behaviour in the British Economy. *Economica, N.S.*, November 1969, *36*(144), pp. 377–88. **[G: U.K.]**

Agarwala, R.; Burns, T. and Duffy, M. Forecasting Gross Private Fixed Investment Using Intentions Survey Data. *Manchester Sch. Econ. Soc. Stud.*, December 1969, *37*(4), pp. 279–93. **[G: U.K.]**

Ammer, Dean S. Materials Management as a Profit Center. *Harvard Bus. Rev.*, January–February 1969, *47*(1), pp. 72–82.

Andersson, Edward. Skattepolitiken efter Företagsbeskattningsreformen. (Taxation Policy after the Reforms in Company Tax. With English summary.) *Econ. Samfundets Tidskr.*, 1969, *22* (1), pp. 52–61. **[G: Finland]**

Arrow, Kenneth J. and Levhari, David. Uniqueness of the Internal Rate of Return with Variable Life of Investment. *Econ. J.*, September 1969, *79*(315), pp. 560–66.

Baldwin, George B. What Does It Really Mean? Discounted Cash Flow. *Finance Develop.*, September 1969, *6*(3), pp. 30–35.

Baumol, William J. Performance of the Firm and Performance of Its Stocks. **In** *Manne, H. G., ed.*, 1969, pp. 127–41.

Birkinsha, Jack E. Investment Income: The Legal Part. *J. Risk Ins.*, September 1969, *36*(4), pp. 463–64. **[G: U.S.]**

Borch, Karl. Equilibrium, Optimum and Prejudices in Capital Markets. *J. Financial Quant. Anal.*, March 1969, *4*(1), pp. 1–14.

Brennan, J. F. A Short Cut to Capital Budget Forecasting for Public Utilities. *Eng. Econ.*, April–May 1969, *14*(3), pp. 151–58.

Brief, Richard P. and Owen, Joel. A Note on Earnings Risk and the Coefficient of Variation. *J. Finance*, December 1969, *24*(5), pp. 901–04.

Brigham, Eugene F. and Pappas, James L. Rates of Return on Common Stock. *J. Bus.*, July 1969, *42* (3), pp. 302–16. **[G: U.S.]**

Brigham, Eugene F. and Pappas, James L. The Effect of Liberalized Depreciation on the Cost of Equity Capital. **In** *Trebing, H. M. and Howard, R. H., eds.*, 1969, pp. 129–58. **[G: U.S.]**

Brown, H. P. The Present Theory of Investment Appraisal: A Critical Analysis. *Bull. Oxford Univ. Inst. Econ. Statist.*, May 1969, *31*(2), pp. 105–31.

Carleton, Willard T. Linear Programming and Capital Budgeting Models: A New Interpretation. *J. Finance*, December 1969, *24*(5), pp. 825–33.

Chandra, Mahesh. Profitability and Investment Criteria. **In** *Dagli, V., ed., Vol. II*, 1969, pp. 31–40. **[G: India]**

Childress, Robert L. and Yost, Robert C. An Investigation of the Determinants of Investment Expenditures in Large, Multiproduct Corporations. *Western Econ. J.*, June 1969, *7*(2), pp. 173–79. **[G: U.S.]**

Curry, H. E. Investment Income in Fire and Casualty Rate Making. *J. Risk Ins.*, September 1969, *36*(4), pp. 447–53.

Delano, Myles S. The Effects of Leverage and Corporate Taxes on the Shareholders of Regulated Utilities: Comment. **In** *Trebing, H. M. and Howard, R. H., eds.*, 1969, pp. 98–105. **[G: U.S.]**

Diebold, John. Bad Decisions on Computer Use. *Harvard Bus. Rev.*, January–February 1969, *47* (1), pp. 14–28, 176.

Dyl, Edward A. and Long, Hugh W. Abandonment Value and Capital Budgeting: Comment. *J. Finance*, March 1969, *24*(1), pp. 88–95.

Edey, H. C. Income and the Valuation of Stock-In-Trade. **In** *Parker, R. H. and Harcourt, G. C., eds.*, 1969, pp. 230–38. **[G: U.K.]**

Eisner, Robert. Investment and the Frustrations of Econometricians. *Amer. Econ. Rev.*, May 1969, *59* (2), pp. 50–64. **[G: U.S.]**

Eltis, W. A. Are Interest Rates too High? *Lloyds Bank Rev.*, July 1969, (93), pp. 27–35. **[G: U.K.]**

Felt, Howard M. and Barsky, Donald T. Purchase vs. Lease: Computer Obsolescence. *Manage. Account.*, October 1969, *51*(4), pp. 29–32.

Fisher, I. N. and Hall, George R. Risk and Corporate Rates of Return. *Quart. J. Econ.*, February 1969, *83*(1), pp. 79–92.

Fredman, Albert J. Stockholders' Returns: Dividends or Earnings? *Miss. Val. J. Bus. Econ.*, Fall 1969, *5*(1), pp. 23–33. **[G: U.S.]**

Gordon, Myron J. Rate of Return on Equity Capital under Regulation. **In** *Trebing, H. M. and Howard, R. H., eds.*, 1969, pp. 65–72. **[G: U.S.]**

Gould, John P. The Use of Endogenous Variables in Dynamic Models of Investment. *Quart. J. Econ.*, November 1969, *83*(4), pp. 580–99.

Hamada, Robert S. The Effects of Leverage and Corporate Taxes on the Shareholders of Regulated Utilities. **In** *Trebing, H. M. and Howard, R. H., eds.*, 1969, pp. 73–97. **[G: U.S.]**

Hayek, Friedrich A. Maintaining Capital Intact: A Reply. **In** *Parker, R. H. and Harcourt, G. C., eds.*, 1969, pp. 127–31.

Hedges, Bob A. Insurance Rates and Investment Earnings Considered Together. *J. Risk Ins.*, September 1969, *36*(4), pp. 455–61.

Hicks, John R. Maintaining Capital Intact: A Further Suggestion. **In** *Parker, R. H. and Harcourt, G. C., eds.*, 1969, pp. 132–38.

Hirshleifer, Jack. On Multiple Rates of Return: Comment. *J. Finance*, March 1969, *24*(1), pp. 98.

Hotelling, Harold. A General Mathematical Theory of Depreciation. **In** *Parker, R. H. and Harcourt, G. C., eds.*, 1969, pp. 261–75.

Jean, William H. On Multiple Rates of Return: Reply. *J. Finance*, March 1969, *24*(1), pp. 99–100.

Jen, Frank C. Problems and Progress in the Applications of Recent Developments in the Theory of

Finance: Discussion. *J. Finance,* May 1969, *24*(2), pp. 342–44.

Johansson, Sven-Erik. Income Taxes and Investment Decisions. *Swedish J. Econ.,* June 1969, *71*(2), pp. 104–10.

Johnson, Glenn L. Professor Johnson's Hedges: A Reply. *Miss. Val. J. Bus. Econ.,* Fall 1969, *5*(1), pp. 85–89.

Jones-Lee, Michael. Managerial Expectations and Investment Behaviour. *Yorkshire Bull. Econ. Soc. Res.,* November 1969, *21*(2), pp. 85–93.

Jorgenson, Dale W. and Stephenson, James A. Anticipations and Investment Behavior in U.S. Manufacturing, 1947–1960. *J. Amer. Statist. Assoc.,* March 1969, *64*(325), pp. 67–89. **[G: U.S.]**

Klausner, Robert F. The Evaluation of Risk in Marine Capital Investments. *Eng. Econ.,* July–August 1969, *14*(4), pp. 183–214.

Kolm, Serge-Christophe. Les politiques dynamiques optimales d'investissement. (With English summary.) *Revue Écon.,* September 1969, *20*(5), pp. 753–82.

Kosh, David A. The Effects of Leverage and Corporate Taxes on the Shareholders of Regulated Utilities: Comment. **In** *Trebing, H. M. and Howard, R. H., eds.,* 1969, pp. 106–10. **[G: U.S.]**

Kostiainen, Seppo and Pekonen, Kari. Investointivaihtoehtojen optimaalinen valinta. (The Optimal Choice of Investment Projects. With English summary.) *Kansant. Aikak.,* 1969, *65*(3), pp. 191–205.

Lesso, William G. An Extension of the Net Present Value Concept to Intertemporal Investments. *Eng. Econ.,* October–November 1969, *15*(1), pp. 1–8.

Lewis, Robert E. Corporate Profits—The First National City Bank's Series on Leading Corporations. *Univ. Missouri Bus. Govt. Rev.,* March–April 1969, *10*(2), pp. 33–40. **[G: U.S.]**

Litzenberger, Robert H. and Jones, Charles P. Adjusting for Risk in the Capital Budget of a Growth Oriented Company: Comment. *J. Financial Quant. Anal.,* September 1969, *4*(3), pp. 301–04.

Long, John D. Comments on the Plotkin Paper. *J. Risk Ins.,* June 1969, *36*(2), pp. 201–16. **[G: U.S.]**

Loshing, Clement T. The Effect of Liberalized Depreciation on the Cost of Equity Capital: Comment. **In** *Trebing, H. M. and Howard, R. H., eds.,* 1969, pp. 159–63. **[G: U.S.]**

Lund, Unto. Ovatko tehdasteollisuus-investointimme olleet kokonaistaloudellisesti mielekkäitä? (Have Investments into Finnish Manufacturing Industry Been Economically Sensible? With English summary.) *Kansant. Aikak.,* 1969, *65*(3), pp. 220–23. **[G: Finland]**

Machol, Robert E. and Lerner, Eugene M. Risk, Ruin and Investment Analysis. *J. Financial Quant. Anal.,* December 1969, *4*(4), pp. 473–92.

Mansfield, Edwin. Industrial Research and Development: Characteristics, Costs, and Diffusion of Results. *Amer. Econ. Rev.,* May 1969, *59*(2), pp. 65–71. **[G: U.S.]**

Mao, James C. T. and Helliwell, John F. Investment Decisions under Uncertainty: Theory and Practice. *J. Finance,* May 1969, *24*(2), pp. 323–38.

Marcus, Matityahu. Profitability and Size of Firm: Some Further Evidence. *Rev. Econ. Statist.,* February 1969, *51*(1), pp. 104–07. **[G: U.S.]**

McCarthy, Michael D. An Analysis of Non-wage Income Components. **In** *Duesenberry, J. S., et al.,* 1969, pp. 151–86. **[G: U.S.]**

Mead, Walter J. Instantaneous Merger Profit as a Conglomerate Merger Motive. *Western Econ. J.,* December 1969, *7*(4), pp. 295–306. **[G: U.S.]**

Melody, William H. The Effect of Liberalized Depreciation on the Cost of Equity Capital: Comment. **In** *Trebing, H. M. and Howard, R. H., eds.,* 1969, pp. 164–75. **[G: U.S.]**

Minasian, Jora R. Research and Development and Other Determinants of Investment: Discussion. *Amer. Econ. Rev.,* May 1969, *59*(2), pp. 86.

Moag, Joseph S. and Lerner, Eugene M. Capital Budgeting Decisions under Imperfect Market Conditions—A Systems Framework. *J. Finance,* September 1969, *24*(4), pp. 613–21.

Morris, Peter F. Widget Pricing. *Manage. Account.,* December 1969, *51*(6), pp. 12–14.

Morton, Walter A. Risk and Return: Instability of Earnings as a Measure of Risk. *Land Econ.,* May 1969, *45*(2), pp. 229–61. **[G: U.S.]**

Motley, Brian. Inflation and Common Stock Values: Comment. *J. Finance,* June 1969, *24*(3), pp. 530–35.

Newnan, Donald G. Determining Rate of Return by Means of Payback Period and Useful Life. *Eng. Econ.,* October–November 1969, *15*(1), pp. 29–39.

Panati, Giovanni. L'investiment trust e la "nuova scienza" degli investimenti mobiliari. (The Investment Trust and the "New Science" of Investing. With English summary.) *L'Impresa,* March/April 1969, *11*(2), pp. 152–55.

Parker, R. H. Lower of Cost and Market in Britain and the United States: A Historical Survey. **In** *Parker, R. H. and Harcourt, G. C., eds.,* 1969, pp. 239–58. **[G: U.S.; U.K.]**

Pekonen, Kari. Investoinnit—työttömyys—taloudellinen kasvu. (Investment—Unemployment—Economic Growth. With English summary.) *Kansant. Aikak.,* 1969, *65*(3), pp. 215–19. **[G: Finland]**

Petri, Enrico. Use of Capitalized Cost in Repeated Replacement Problems. *Manage. Account.,* September 1969, *51*(3), pp. 49–53, 56.

Pigou, A. C. Maintaining Capital Intact. **In** *Parker, R. H. and Harcourt, G. C., eds.,* 1969, pp. 123–26.

Plotkin, Irving H. Rates of Return in the Property and Liability Insurance Industry: A Comparative Analysis. *J. Risk Ins.,* June 1969, *36*(2), pp. 173–200. **[G: U.S.]**

Prest, Alan R. Replacement Cost Depreciation. **In** *Parker, R. H. and Harcourt, G. C., eds.,* 1969, pp. 290–309.

Quigley, Joseph M. The Effects of Leverage and Corporate Taxes on the Shareholders of Regulated Utilities: Comment. **In** *Trebing, H. M. and Howard, R. H., eds.,* 1969, pp. 111–16. **[G: U.S.]**

Robichek, Alexander A. and Van Horne, James C. Abandonment Value and Capital Budgeting: Reply. *J. Finance,* March 1969, *24*(1), pp. 96–97.

Sampson, Anthony A. Measuring the Rate of Return

on Capital. *J. Finance,* March 1969, *24*(1), pp. 61–74. [G: U.K.]

Sarnat, Marshall and Levy, Haim. The Relationship of Rules of Thumb to the Internal Rate of Return: A Restatement and Generalization. *J. Finance,* June 1969, *24*(3), pp. 479–90.

Sau, Ranjit K. The Optimal Rate of Investment in a Firm. *J. Finance,* March 1969, *24*(1), pp. 1–12.

Scherer, Frederic M. Market Structure and the Stability of Investment. *Amer. Econ. Rev.,* May 1969, *59*(2), pp. 72–79. [G: U.S.]

Schneider, Georges. Le choix des investissements dans l'entreprise. (With English summary.) *Revue Écon.,* March 1969, *20*(2), pp. 272–301.

Schreiber, Wilfrid. Die determinierte Investition: Kritik am neoklassischen Wachstums-Konzept. (With English summary.) *Jahr. Nationalökon. Statist.,* May 1969, *182*(6), pp. 530–41.

Schwab, Bernhard and Lusztig, Peter. A Comparative Analysis of the Net Present Value and the Benefit-Cost Ratio as Measures of the Economic Desirability of Investment. *J. Finance,* June 1969, *24*(3), pp. 507–16.

Sharma, L. R. Need for a Growth-Oriented Industrial Policy. *Asian Econ. Rev.,* August 1969, *11*(4), pp. 333–48. [G: India]

Shaw, David C. The Cost of "Going Public" in Canada. **In** *Association of Canadian Schools of Business,* 1969, pp. 144–70. [G: Canada]

Smith, Keith V. and Schreiner, John C. A Portfolio Analysis of Conglomerate Diversification. *J. Finance,* June 1969, *24*(3), pp. 413–27. [G: U.S.]

Smyth, David J. and Briscoe, G. Investment Plans and Realizations in United Kingdom Manufacturing. *Economica, N.S.,* August 1969, *36*(143), pp. 277–94. [G: U.K.]

Smyth, David J.; Briscoe, G. and Samuels, J. M. The Variability of Industry Profit Rates. *Appl. Econ.,* May 1969, *1*(2), pp. 137–49. [G: U.K.]

Stevens, Guy V. G. Fixed Investment Expenditures of Foreign Manufacturing Affiliates of U.S. Firms: Theoretical Models and Empirical Evidence. *Yale Econ. Essays,* Spring 1969, *9*(1), pp. 137–98.

Stýblo, Jan. The Socialist Entrepreneurship and the Investor's Risk. *New Trends Czech. Econ.,* July 1969, (4), pp. 65–88.

Treadway, Arthur B. On Rational Entrepreneurial Behaviour and the Demand for Investment. *Rev. Econ. Stud.,* April 1969, *36*(106), pp. 227–39.

Tullock, Gordon. The New Theory of Corporations. **In** *[von Hayek, Friedrich A.],* 1969, pp. 287–307.

Vergé, Jean-Marie. Un modèle séquentiel de financement optimal à long terme dans l'entreprise. (With English summary.) *Revue Écon.,* March 1969, *20*(2), pp. 302–36.

Viita, Pentti. Investoinnit ja maksutase. (Investments and the Balance of Payments. With English summary.) *Kansant. Aikak.,* 1969, *65*(3), pp. 233. [G: Finland]

Walsh, Cornelius F. Professor Johnson's Hedges. *Miss. Val. J. Bus. Econ.,* Fall 1969, *5*(1), pp. 80–84.

Weiss, Leonard W. Advertising, Profits, and Corporate Taxes. *Rev. Econ. Statist.,* November 1969, *51*(4), pp. 421–30. [G: U.S.]

Weston, J. Fred. The Effects of Leverage and Corporate Taxes on the Shareholders of Regulated Utilities: Comment. **In** *Trebing, H. M. and Howard, R. H., eds.,* 1969, pp. 117–25. [G: U.S.]

White, William H. Lags between Actual and Reported Fixed Investment. *Int. Monet. Fund Staff Pap.,* July 1969, *16*(2), pp. 240–66.

Winfield, Richard A. The Rising Cost of Mergers. **In** *Harvey, J. L. and Newgarden, A., eds.,* 1969, pp. 133–45. [G: U.S.]

Wright, Frank K. Towards a General Theory of Depreciation. **In** *Parker, R. H. and Harcourt, G. C., eds.,* 1969, pp. 276–89.

Young, William E. and Trent, Robert H. Geometric Mean Approximations of Individual Security and Portfolio Performance. *J. Financial Quant. Anal.,* June 1969, *4*(2), pp. 179–99. [G: U.S.]

Ziemba, William T. A Myopic Capital Budgeting Model. *J. Financial Quant. Anal.,* September 1969, *4*(3), pp. 305–27.

530 MARKETING

531 Marketing and Advertising

5310 Marketing and Advertising

Aaltonen, Aimo O. Mainonnassa suoritetuista vertailuista silmällä pitäen vilpillisen kilpailun ehkäisemislakia. (Comparisons in Advertising with Reference to the Law for the Prevention of Unfair Competition. With English summary.) *Liiketaloudellinen Aikak.,* 1969, *18*(3), pp. 301–10.

Abrams, Jack. Reducing the Risk of New Product Marketing Strategies Testing. *J. Marketing Res.,* May 1969, *6*(2), pp. 216–20.

Alexis, Marcus; Simon, Leonard S. and Smith, Kenneth M. Some Determinants of Food Buying Behavior. **In** *Alexis, M.; Holloway, R. J. and Hancock, R. S., eds.,* 1969, pp. 20–32. [G: U.S.]

Alexis, Marcus. Some Differences in Household Consumption—Negroes and Whites. **In** *Alexis, M.; Holloway, R. J. and Hancock, R. S., eds.,* 1969, pp. 142–53. [G: U.S.]

Andrus, Roman R. Marketing Research in a Developing Nation—Taiwan: A Case Example. *Univ. Wash. Bus. Rev.,* Spring 1969, *28*(3), pp. 40–44. [G: Taiwan]

Andrus, Roman R. and Knutsen, John A. The Impact of Personal Information Sources on Retailer Success. *Oregon Bus. Rev.,* November 1969, *28*(11), pp. 1–3. [G: U.S.]

Barach, Jeffrey A. Advertising Effectiveness and Risk in the Consumer Decision Process. *J. Marketing Res.,* August 1969, *6*(3), pp. 314–20.

Barban, Arnold M. The Dilemma of "Integrated" Advertising. *J. Bus.,* October 1969, *42*(4), pp. 477–96. [G: U.S.]

Barclay, William D. Factorial Design in a Pricing Experiment. *J. Marketing Res.,* November 1969, *6*(4), pp. 427–29.

Barnett, Norman L. Beyond Market Segmentation. *Harvard Bus. Rev.,* January–February 1969, *47* (1), pp. 152–66.

Bass, Frank M. A Simultaneous Equation Regression Study of Advertising and Sale of Cigarettes. *J.*

Marketing Res., August 1969, *6*(3), pp. 291–300.

Bass, Frank M.; Pessemier, E. A. and Tigert, D. J. A Taxonomy of Magazine Readership Applied to Problems in Marketing Strategy and Media Selection. *J. Bus.*, July 1969, *42*(3), pp. 337–63.

Bass, Frank M. and Parsons, Leonard J. Simultaneous-Equation Regression Analysis of Sales and Advertising. *Appl. Econ.*, May 1969, *1*(2), pp. 103–24.

Battistel, Ezio. Collocazione organizzativa della direzione commerciale. (The Status of Commercial Management within the Organization. With English summary.) *L'Impresa*, July/October 1969, *11*(4–5), pp. 336–39.

Beernaert, Luc and Laevaert, Ludo. De Tienermarkt: Analyse van enkele karakteristieken. (The Teenager Market: An Analysis of Some Characteristics. With English summary.) *Econ. Soc. Tijdschr.*, December 1969, *23*(6), pp. 663–74.

Bennett, Peter D. and Mandell, Robert M. Prepurpose Information Seeking Behavior of New Car Purchasers—The Learning Hypothesis. *J. Marketing Res.*, November 1969, *6*(4), pp. 430–33. **[G: U.S.]**

Bilsen, Robert. Marktbenadering, marktstructuur en ondernemingsdimensie. (Market Approach, Market Structure and the Dimension of the Firm. With English summary.) *Econ. Soc. Tijdschr.*, December 1969, *23*(6), pp. 537–45.

Bither, Stewart W. Comments on Venkatesan and Haaland's Test of the Festinger-Maccoby Divided Attention Hypothesis. *J. Marketing Res.*, May 1969, *6*(2), pp. 237–38.

Blank, David M. Tonypandy once Again. *J. Bus.*, January 1969, *42*(1), pp. 104–12. **[G: U.S.]**

Bloede, Victor G. The Advertising Agency of the Future. *Econ. Soc. Tijdschr.*, December 1969, *23* (6), pp. 641–46.

Bozzola, G. B. Strutture organizzative e politiche commerciali su scala internazionale. (Organizational Structures and Commercial Policies at an International Level. With English summary.) *L'Impresa*, July/October 1969, *11*(4–5), pp. 311–19.

Brief, Bernard. Per un marketing multinazionale. (For a Multinational Marketing. With English summary.) *Mondo Aperto*, October 1969, *23*(5), pp. 343–56.

Brown, F. E. Price Image versus Price Reality. *J. Marketing Res.*, May 1969, *6*(2), pp. 185–91.

Bruce, Grady D. The Ecological Structure of Retail Institutions. *J. Marketing Res.*, February 1969, *6* (1), pp. 48–53. **[G: U.S.]**

Bucklin, Louis P. Consumer Search, Role Enactment, and Market Efficiency. *J. Bus.*, October 1969, *42*(4), pp. 416–38. **[G: U.S.]**

Cannata, Giuseppe. Factoring: un nuovo ausilio per la gestione delle medie a piccole imprese-II. (Factoring: A New Facility for Medium and Small Companies-II. With English summary.) *Bancaria*, July 1969, *25*(7), pp. 842–50.

Cannata, Giuseppe. Factoring: un nuovo ausilio per la gestione delle medie e piccole imprese-I. (Factoring: A New Facility for Medium and Small Companies-I. With English summary.) *Bancaria*, June 1969, *25*(6), pp. 711–24.

Caplovitz, David. The Merchant and the Low-Income Consumer. **In** *Sturdivant, F. D., ed.*, 1969, pp. 61–75. **[G: U.S.]**

Claycamp, Henry J. and Liddy, Lucien E. Prediction of New Product Performance: An Analytical Approach. *J. Marketing Res.*, November 1969, *6*(4), pp. 414–20. **[G: U.S.]**

Comanor, William S. and Wilson, Thomas A. Advertising and the Advantages of Size. *Amer. Econ. Rev.*, May 1969, *59*(2), pp. 87–98.

Corigliano, Giorgio. La funzione del "product manager" nella realtà industriale italiana. (The Product Manager's Function in the Italian Industrial Situation. With English summary.) *L'Impresa*, July/October 1969, *11*(4–5), pp. 343–46. **[G: Italy]**

Crosby, Richard W. Attitude Measurement in a Bilingual Culture. *J. Marketing Res.*, November 1969, *6*(4), pp. 421–26. **[G: Canada]**

Day, Ralph L. Position Bias in Paired Product Tests. *J. Marketing Res.*, February 1969, *6*(1), pp. 98–100.

De Baere, G. Marketing: Invloed op de verkooporganisatie en de verkooppraktijk. (The Influence of Marketing on Sales Organization and Sales Practice. With English summary.) *Econ. Soc. Tijdschr.*, December 1969, *23*(6), pp. 613–18.

De Vleeshouwer, Eduard. Aspecten van de distributie-ontwikkeling in België. (Aspects of the Development of Distribution in Belgium. With English summary.) *Econ. Soc. Tijdschr.*, December 1969, *23*(6), pp. 619–40. **[G: Belgium]**

Dean, Joel. Pricing Pioneering Products. *J. Ind. Econ.*, July 1969, *17*(3), pp. 165–79.

Dolan, Paul. Citizens Complaints in St. Louis—The Case for an Ombudsman? *Univ. Missouri Bus. Govt. Rev.*, September–October 1969, *10*(5), pp. 25–31. **[G: U.S.]**

Dolich, Ira J. Congruence Relationships between Self Images and Product Brands. *J. Marketing Res.*, February 1969, *6*(1), pp. 80–84.

Dommermuth, William P. and Bruce, Grady D. Dissonance and Satisfaction—Some Prepurchase Aspects. *Univ. Wash. Bus. Rev.*, Spring 1969, *28*(3), pp. 45–51.

Donnelly, James H., Jr. Cross-Cultural Communications Theory: Implications for International Advertising. *Univ. Wash. Bus. Rev.*, Spring 1969, *28* (3), pp. 52–58.

Donnelly, James H., Jr. and Ryans, John K., Jr. The Role of Culture in Organizing Overseas Operations: The Advertising Experience. *Univ. Wash. Bus. Rev.*, Autumn 1969, *29*(1), pp. 35–41.

Draper, Norman R.; Hunter, William G. and Tierney, David E. Analyzing Paired Comparison Tests. *J. Marketing Res.*, November 1969, *6*(4), pp. 477–80.

Ekelund, Robert B., Jr. and Gramm, William P. A Reconsideration of Advertising Expenditures, Aggregate Demand, and Economic Stabilization. *Quart. Rev. Econ. Bus.*, Summer 1969, *9*(2), pp. 71–77. **[G: U.S.]**

Ekelund, Robert B., Jr. and Maurice, Charles. An Empirical Investigation of Advertising and Concentration: Comment. *J. Ind. Econ.*, November 1969, *18*(1), pp. 76–80. **[G: U.S.]**

Fabricius, P. J. The Marketing Manager of Tomorrow. *Econ. Soc. Tijdschr.*, December 1969, *23*(6), pp. 547–54.

Feldstein, Martin S. Advertising, Research and Profits in the Drug Industry. *Southern Econ. J.*, January 1969, *35*(3), pp. 239–43. **[G: U.S.]**

Ferber, Robert. Contributions of Economics to the Study of Consumer Market Behavior. *Appl. Econ.*, May 1969, *1*(2), pp. 125–36.

Fitzhugh, H. Naylor. Ethnic Challenges to Marketing Management. *Univ. Wash. Bus. Rev.*, Spring 1969, *28*(3), pp. 26–32.

Fournis, Yves. Le implicazioni concrete del marketing sull'impresa. (Practical Implications of Marketing for the Firm. With English summary.) *L'Impresa,* July/October 1969, *11*(4–5), pp. 327–31.

French, Norman D. and Brooksher, William R. Marketing New Products—By Segmenting Product Lines. *Univ. Missouri Bus. Govt. Rev.*, September–October 1969, *10*(5), pp. 5–10.

Gensch, Dennis H. A Computer Simulation Model for Selecting Advertising Schedules. *J. Marketing Res.*, May 1969, *6*(2), pp. 203–14.

Gijs, Robert. Het onderzoek van de motivatie van de verbruiker in het raam van Marketing Informatie Systemen. (The Motivations Research of the Consumer in the Marketing Information Systems. With English summary.) *Econ. Soc. Tijdschr.*, December 1969, *23*(6), pp. 675–85.

Grabner, John R., Jr. Legal Limits of Competition. *Harvard Bus. Rev.*, November–December 1969, *47*(6), pp. 4–24, 182. **[G: U.S.]**

Grahn, Gary L. NBD Model of Repeat-Purchase Loyalty: An Empirical Investigation. *J. Marketing Res.*, February 1969, *6*(1), pp. 72–78.

Green, Paul E. and Carmone, Frank J. Multidimensional Scaling: An Introduction and Comparison of Nonmetric Unfolding Techniques. *J. Marketing Res.*, August 1969, *6*(3), pp. 330–41.

Greene, Mark R. How to Rationalize Your Marketing Risks. *Harvard Bus. Rev.*, May–June 1969, *47*(3), pp. 114–23.

Gross, Jack L. and McGinley, John J. Need for a Marketing Intelligence System . . . in Petroleum Marketing: Integration of Information Systems into the Decision-Making Process. *Econ. Bus. Bull.*, Fall 1969, *22*(1), pp. 25–32.

Gruber, Alin and Lindberg, Barbara. Sensitivity, Reliability, and Consumer Taste Testing: Reaffirmation and a Reply. *J. Marketing Res.*, February 1969, *6*(1), pp. 105–06.

Gruber, Alin. Top-of-Mind Awareness and Share of Families: An Observation. *J. Marketing Res.*, May 1969, *6*(2), pp. 227–31.

Guest, Lester. Brand Loyalty Revisited: A Twenty-Year Report. **In** *Alexis, M.; Holloway, R. J. and Hancock, R. S., eds.*, 1969, pp. 54–59. **[G: U.S.]**

Gupta, Shiv K. and Maier-Rothe, Christoph. A Note on the Partitioning of a Single Product Market into Territories of Outlets. *J. Marketing Res.*, May 1969, *6*(2), pp. 232–36.

Gustafsson, Kaj. Markkinoiden segmentoinnista ja sen vertailua tuotedifferointiin markkinointistrategiana. (About Market Segmentation and Its Comparison to Product Differentiation as a Marketing Strategy. With English summary.) *Liiketaloudellinen Aikak.*, 1969, *18*(2), pp. 133–44.

Hamm, B. Curtis and Cundiff, Edward W. Self-Actualization and Product Perception. *J. Marketing Res.*, November 1969, *6*(4), pp. 470–72.

Hanan, Mack. Corporate Growth through Venture Management. *Harvard Bus. Rev.*, January–February 1969, *47*(1), pp. 43–61.

Hansen, Flemming. Consumer Choice Behavior: An Experimental Approach. *J. Marketing Res.*, November 1969, *6*(4), pp. 436–43.

Hawkins, Murray H. Alternative Methods of Marketing Livestock. *Can. J. Agr. Econ.*, November 1969, *17*(3), pp. 104–110.

Hill, Conrad R. Another Look at Two Instant Coffee Studies. **In** *Alexis, M.; Holloway, R. J. and Hancock, R. S., eds.*, 1969, pp. 433–37.

Holmes, John H. A Note on the Product-Adoption Process. *Ohio State U. Bull. Bus. Res.*, July 1969, *44*(7), pp. 1–3, 5.

Jeanteur, Robert. La mercatistica nell'era dell'informatica. (Marketing in the Age of Information Theory. With English summary.) *L'Impresa,* July/October 1969, *11*(4–5), pp. 347–51.

Johnsen, Erik. A Remark on Some Analytical Problems in a Normative Marketing Systems Model. *Liiketaloudellinen Aikak.*, 1969, *18*(1), pp. 42–50.

Kaskimies, Mika. Product Life Pattern as a Means of Business Forecasting. *Liiketaloudellinen Aikak.*, 1969, *18*(3), pp. 433–41.

Kassarjian, Harold H. The Negro and American Advertising, 1946–1965. *J. Marketing Res.*, February 1969, *6*(1), pp. 29–39. **[G: U.S.]**

Kelly, Robert F. Predicting New Product Adoption Levels. **In** *Association of Canadian Schools of Business,* 1969, pp. 234–77.

Kerby, Joe Kent. Borrowing from the Behavioral Sciences. *J. Bus.*, April 1969, *42*(2), pp. 152–61.

Kotzan, Jeffrey A. and Evanson, Robert V. Responsiveness of Drug Store Sales to Shelf Space Allocations. *J. Marketing Res.*, November 1969, *6*(4), pp. 465–69. **[G: U.S.]**

Krum, James R. Perceptions and Evaluation of the Role of the Corporate Marketing Research Department. *J. Marketing Res.*, November 1969, *6* (4), pp. 459–64.

Lagioni, Iginio. Dal "commercio" internazionale alla "mercatistica" internazionale. (From "International Trade" to International "Marketing." With English summary.) *L'Impresa,* January/February 1969, *11*(1), pp. 61–67.

Lambin, Jean-Jacques. Measuring the Profitability of Advertising: An Empirical Study. *J. Ind. Econ.*, April 1969, *17*(2), pp. 86–103.

Lawrence, Raymond J. Patterns of Buyer Behavior: Time for a New Approach? *J. Marketing Res.*, May 1969, *6*(2), pp. 137–44.

Leonard, William N. Network Television Pricing: A Comment. *J. Bus.*, January 1969, *42*(1), pp. 93–103. **[G: U.S.]**

Levitt, Theodore. The New Markets—Think before You Leap. *Harvard Bus. Rev.*, May–June 1969, *47* (3), pp. 53–67.

Lewis, Edwin H. Sales Promotion Decisions. **In** *Alexis, M.; Holloway, R. J. and Hancock, R. S.,* *eds.*, 1969, pp. 315–23. [G: U.S.]

Liander, Bertil. Mercatistica internazionale analisi comparate. (Comparative Analysis for International Marketing. With English summary.) *L'Impresa,* July/October 1969, *11*(4–5), pp. 320–26.

Lippitt, Vernon G. Determinants of Consumer Demand for House Furnishings and Equipment. **In** *Alexis, M.; Holloway, R. J. and Hancock, R. S., eds.*, 1969, pp. 3–19. [G: U.S.]

Mann, H. Michael; Henning, John A. and Meehan, James W., Jr. Statistical Testing in Industrial Economics: A Reply on Measurement Error and Sampling Procedure. *J. Ind. Econ.*, November 1969, *18*(1), pp. 95–100.

Mann, H. Michael; Henning, John A. and Meehan, James W., Jr. Testing Hypothesis in Industrial Economics: A Reply. *J. Ind. Econ.*, November 1969, *18*(1), pp. 81–84. [G: U.S.]

Marcus, Matityahu. Advertising and Changes in Concentration. *Southern Econ. J.*, October 1969, *36*(2), pp. 117–21. [G: U.S.]

Massy, William F. Forecasting the Demand for New Convenience Products. *J. Marketing Res.*, November 1969, *6*(4), pp. 405–12.

Matsusaki, Hirofumi. The Potential of Comparative Marketing: A Methodological Review. **In** *Association of Canadian Schools of Business,* 1969, pp. 278–307.

May, Frederick E. Adaptive Behavior in Automobile Brand Choices. *J. Marketing Res.*, February 1969, *6*(1), pp. 62–65.

Mehr, Robert I. Channels of Distribution in Insurance. *J. Risk Ins.*, December 1969, *36*(5), pp. 583–95.

Melrose, Kendrick B. An Empirical Study on Optimizing Advertising Policy. *J. Bus.*, July 1969, *42*(3), pp. 282–92. [G: U.S.]

Mercer, A. Operational Marketing Research. *J. Ind. Econ.*, November 1969, *18*(1), pp. 15–32.

Mickwitz, Gösta. Product Quality as a Means of Competition. *Liiketaloudellinen Aikak.*, 1969, *18*(1), pp. 51–60.

Miller, Richard A. Market Structure and Industrial Performance: Relation of Profit Rates to Concentration, Advertising Intensity, and Diversity. *J. Ind. Econ.*, April 1969, *17*(2), pp. 104–18. [G: U.S.]

Mittelstaedt, Robert. A Dissonance Approach to Repeat Purchasing Behavior. *J. Marketing Res.*, November 1969, *6*(4), pp. 444–46.

Morrison, Donald G. Conditional Trend Analysis: A Model That Allows for Nonusers. *J. Marketing Res.*, August 1969, *6*(3), pp. 342–46.

Murray, J. Alex. Canadian Consumer Expectational Data: An Evaluation. *J. Marketing Res.*, February 1969, *6*(1), pp. 54–61. [G: Canada]

Myers, James H. and Samli, A. Coskun. Management Control of Marketing Research. *J. Marketing Res.*, August 1969, *6*(3), pp. 267–77.

Nel, P. A. The Standard Industrial Classification and Industrial Marketing. *Finance Trade Rev.*, December 1969, *8*(4), pp. 231–57.

Newton, Derek A. Get the Most Out of Your Sales Force. *Harvard Bus. Rev.*, September–October 1969, *47*(5), pp. 130–43.

Nicosia, Francesco M. Perceived Risk, Information Processing, and Consumer Behavior: A Review Article. *J. Bus.*, April 1969, *42*(2), pp. 162–66.

Nicosia, Francesco M. Ricerche sui consumatori: problemi e prospettive. (Consumer Research: Problems and Perspectives. With English summary.) *L'Impresa,* November/December 1969, *11*(6), pp. 429–35. [G: Italy]

Palubinskas, Feliksas. The Role of Marketing Research in the Soviet Economy. *Univ. Missouri Bus. Govt. Rev.*, September–October 1969, *10*(5), pp. 17–24. [G: U.S.S.R.]

Pennington, Allan L. and Peterson, Robert A. Interest Patterns and Product Preferences: An Exploratory Analysis. *J. Marketing Res.*, August 1969, *6*(3), pp. 284–90.

Perry, Michael and Hamm, B. Curtis. Canonical Analysis of Relations between Socioeconomic Risk and Personal Influence in Purchase Decisions. *J. Marketing Res.*, August 1969, *6*(3), pp. 351–54.

Peterson, R. D. and Leister, D. V. Market Structure-Conduct Relations: Some Evidence from Biomedical Electronic Firms. *Univ. Wash. Bus. Rev.*, Summer 1969, *28*(4), pp. 49–65. [G: U.S.]

Peterson, Robin T. Experimental Analysis of Theory of Promotion at Point of Consumption. *J. Marketing Res.*, August 1969, *6*(3), pp. 347–50.

Pollay, Richard W. and Swinth, Robert L. A Behavioral Simulation of the Agency-Client Relationship. *J. Marketing Res.*, May 1969, *6*(2), pp. 198–202.

Pollay, Richard W. and Churchill, Geoffrey. A Simple Method for Estimating Consumer Acceptance. *Miss. Val. J. Bus. Econ.*, Spring 1969, *4*(2), pp. 50–56.

Pollay, Richard W. Consumer Protection and Advertising. *Ohio State U. Bull. Bus. Res.*, July 1969, *44*(7), pp. 4–8.

Polli, Rolando and Cook, Victor. Validity of the Product Life Cycle. *J. Bus.*, October 1969, *42*(4), pp. 385–400. [G: U.S.]

Pulkkinen, Kyösti. Asiakaspiirin vaikutus markkinointitoimen hajautukseen. (Effect of the Customers in the Decentralization of the Marketing Objective. With English summary.) *Liiketaloudellinen Aikak.*, 1969, *18*(2), pp. 192–205.

Rao, Tanniru R. Are Some Consumers More Prone to Purchase Private Brands? *J. Marketing Res.*, November 1969, *6*(4), pp. 447–50. [G: U.S.]

Rao, Tanniru R. Consumer's Purchase Decision Process: Stochastic Models. *J. Marketing Res.*, August 1969, *6*(3), pp. 321–29.

Ravazzi, Giancarlo. Una problematica nuova per la direzione commerciale la concezione mercatistica della direzione d'impresa. (New Problems for Commercial Management: The Marketing Conception of Firm Management. With English summary.) *L'Impresa,* July/October 1969, *11*(4–5), pp. 304–10. [G: Italy]

Reitter, Robert N. Product Testing in Segmented Markets. *J. Marketing Res.*, May 1969, *6*(2), pp. 179–84.

Robarts, A. O. A Revised Look at Selected Determinants of Consumer Spatial Behavior. **In** *Association of Canadian Schools of Business,* 1969, pp. 219–33.

Robertson, Thomas S. and Myers, James H. Personality Correlates of Opinion Leadership and Innovative Buying Behavior. *J. Marketing Res.*, May 1969, *6*(2), pp. 164–68.

Robinson, David M. Some Comments on the Nature of the Scholarly Assumption as a Bias for Model Construction. *Liiketaloudellinen Aikak.*, 1969, *18*(1), pp. 68–73.

Roman, Hope S. Semantic Generalization in Formation of Consumer Attitudes. *J. Marketing Res.*, August 1969, *6*(3), pp. 369–73.

Roper, Burns W. Sensitivity, Reliability, and Consumer Taste Testing: Some "Rights" and "Wrongs." *J. Marketing Res.*, February 1969, *6*(1), pp. 102–05.

Ross, Ivan. Handling the Neutral Vote in Product Testing. *J. Marketing Res.*, May 1969, *6*(2), pp. 221–22.

Saarsalmi, Meeri. Kuluttajan käyttäytymisen tutkiminen markkinoinnin päätöksenteon kannalta tarkasteltuna. (The Study of Consumer Behavior from the Viewpoint of Decision-Making in Marketing. With English summary.) *Liiketaloudellinen Aikak.*, 1969, *18*(2), pp. 220–32.

Särkisilta, Martti. Markkinointistrategian valinta suunnittelu- ja päätöksentekotapahtumana. (Choice of Marketing Strategy as a Planning and Decision-making Event. With English summary.) *Liiketaloudellinen Aikak.*, 1969, *18*(2), pp. 251–62.

Shuchman, Abe and Perry, Michael. Self-Confidence and Persuasibility in Marketing: A Reappraisal. *J. Marketing Res.*, May 1969, *6*(2), pp. 146–54.

Siimestö, Orvo. Markovin ketjut ostosarjojen stokastisena mallina. (Markov Chains as a Stochastic Model of Buying Series. With English summary.) *Liiketaloudellinen Aikak.*, 1969, *18*(2), pp. 233–42.

Simon, Julian L. The Effect of Advertising on Liquor Brand Sales. *J. Marketing Res.*, August 1969, *6*(3), pp. 301–13.

Stafford, James E. and Enis, Ben M. The Price-Quality Relationship: An Extension. *J. Marketing Res.*, November 1969, *6*(4), pp. 456–58.

Stephenson, William. Evaluation of Public Relations Programs. *Rivista Int. Sci. Econ. Com.*, February 1969, *16*(2), pp. 166–84.

Swan, John E. Experimental Analysis of Predecision Information Seeking. *J. Marketing Res.*, May 1969, *6*(2), pp. 192–97.

Tartara, Giovanni. Programmazione e sviluppo del prodotto. (Product Planning and Development. With English summary.) *L'Impresa*, July/October 1969, *11*(4–5), pp. 340–42.

Telser, Lester G. Another Look at Advertising and Concentration. *J. Ind. Econ.*, November 1969, *18* (1), pp. 85–94. **[G: U.S.]**

Telser, Lester G. Theory of the Firm and of Market Structures: Discussion. *Amer. Econ. Rev.*, May 1969, *59*(2), pp. 121–23.

Teresi, Salvatore. The Formation of Marketing Men. *Econ. Soc. Tijdschr.*, December 1969, *23*(6), pp. 555–65.

Trabucchi, Romano and Santoro, Gaetano. Un'esperienza di addestramento mediante audiovisivi: il centro audiovisivi de la "rinascente-upim." (Training Experience through Audiovisual Methods. With English summary.) *L'Impresa*, November/December 1969, *11*(6), pp. 469–72.

Urban, Glen L. A Mathematical Modeling Approach to Product Line Decisions. *J. Marketing Res.*, February 1969, *6*(1), pp. 40–47.

Urrila, Matti. Kommunikaatiopanos markkinoinnissa. (Communication Effort in Marketing. With English summary.) *Liiketaloudellinen Aikak.*, 1969, *18*(2), pp. 263–67.

Valentini, Gilberto. Strategie di mercato. (Market Strategies. With English summary.) *L'Impresa*, July/October 1969, *11*(4–5), pp. 332–35.

Wall, Kelvin A. Marketing to Low-Income Neighborhoods: A Systems Approach. *Univ. Wash. Bus. Rev.*, Autumn 1969, *29*(1), pp. 18–26.

Walters, J. Hart. Pressures of Growth on the Polish Marketing System. **In** *Grub, P. D. and Holbik, K.*, 1969, pp. 164–70. **[G: Poland]**

Wasson, Chester R. Le previsioni sulla moda e sugli altri aspetti del ciclo di vita del prodotto. (How Predictable Are Fashion and Other Product Life Cycles. With English summary.) *Mondo Aperto*, October 1969, *23*(5), pp. 357–70.

Weale, W. Bruce. Creative Problem-Solving in Marketing. *Rivista Int. Sci. Econ. Com.*, January 1969, *16*(1), pp. 63–78.

Weiss, Leonard W. Advertising, Profits, and Corporate Taxes. *Rev. Econ. Statist.*, November 1969, *51*(4), pp. 421–30. **[G: U.S.]**

Wesolowski, Zdzislaw P. The Role of Marketing in a Soviet Type Economy. *Marquette Bus. Rev.*, Spring 1969, *13*(1), pp. 15–21.

Wills, Gordon. Marketing. **In** *Kempner, T., ed.*, 1969, pp. 65–70.

Wilson, Aubrey. Industrial Marketing Research in Britain. *J. Marketing Res.*, February 1969, *6*(1), pp. 15–27. **[G: U.K.]**

Wilson, Cyrus C. and Greenidge, Charles D. Classification Merchandising: An Overlooked Opportunity for Increasing Merchandising Profitability. *Calif. Manage. Rev.*, Fall 1969, *12*(1), pp. 53–61.

Wind, Yoram and Frank, Ronald E. Interproduct Household Loyalty to Brands. *J. Marketing Res.*, November 1969, *6*(4), pp. 434–35. **[G: U.S.]**

Winston, Clement. Trade and Services Outlays Related to Income. **In** *Alexis, M.; Holloway, R. J. and Hancock, R. S., eds.*, 1969, pp. 33–38. **[G: U.S.]**

Witt, Robert E. Informal Social Group Influence on Consumer Brand Choice. *J. Marketing Res.*, November 1969, *6*(4), pp. 473–76.

540 ACCOUNTING

541 Accounting

5410 Accounting

Acampora, Giovanni. Il "real time" per il servizio conti correnti di corrispondenza: una soluzione organizzativa che offre sicurezza opertiva. ("Real Time" for the Current Accounts Service: An

Organizational Solution Affording Operational Reliability. With English summary.) *Bancaria,* April 1969, *25*(4), pp. 438–48.

Archibald, T. R. Stock Market Reaction to Different Accounting Practices. **In** *Association of Canadian Schools of Business,* 1969, pp. 171–95.

Armstrong, Dale. The Flow of Funds Statement—An Effective Tool. *J. Risk Ins.,* March 1969, *36*(1), pp. 151–57.

Arnett, Harold E. Taxable Income vs. Financial Income: How Much Uniformity Can We Stand? *Accounting Rev.,* July 1969, *44*(3), pp. 482–94.

Backer, Morton. Comments on "The Value of the SEC's Accounting Disclosure Requirements." *Accounting Rev.,* July 1969, *44*(3), pp. 533–38. **[G: U.S.]**

Baker, Samuel H. Executive Incomes, Profits and Revenues: A Comment of Functional Specification. *Southern Econ. J.,* April 1969, *35*(4), pp. 379–83. **[G: U.S.]**

Baker, Samuel W. The Credibility Gap in Financial Communications. *Manage. Account.,* September 1969, *51*(3), pp. 58–59.

Baxter, W. T. Inflation and Accounts. **In** *Carsberg, B. V. and Edey, H. C., eds.,* 1969, pp. 50–72.

Bell, Philip W. Price Changes and Income Measurement. **In** *Parker, R. H. and Harcourt, G. C., eds.,* 1969, pp. 185–92.

Benston, George J. The Value of the SEC's Accounting Disclosure Requirements. *Accounting Rev.,* July 1969, *44*(3), pp. 515–32. **[G: U.S.]**

Bhandari, M. C. Budgeting and Materials Management. **In** *Dagli, V., ed., Vol. II,* 1969, pp. 146–52. **[G: India]**

Bierman, Harold, Jr. Accelerated Depreciation and Rate Regulation. *Accounting Rev.,* January 1969, *44*(1), pp. 65–78.

Bierman, Harold, Jr. and Davidson, Sidney. The Income Concept—Value Increment or Earnings Predictor. *Accounting Rev.,* April 1969, *44*(2), pp. 239–46.

Blakely, Edward J. and Thompson, Howard E. Technological Change and Its Effects on Dollar-Value LIFO. *Manage. Account.,* August 1969, *51*(2), pp. 33–38.

Brief, Richard P. An Econometric Analysis of Goodwill: Some Findings in a Search for Valuation Rules. *Accounting Rev.,* January 1969, *44*(1), pp. 20–26.

Brigham, Eugene F. and Pappas, James L. The Effect of Liberalized Depreciation on the Cost of Equity Capital. **In** *Trebing, H. M. and Howard, R. H., eds.,* 1969, pp. 129–58. **[G: U.S.]**

Brighton, Gerald D. Accrued Expense Tax Reform—Not Ready in 1954—Ready in 1969? *Accounting Rev.,* January 1969, *44*(1), pp. 137–44. **[G: U.S.]**

Brown, James J. Control in Multi-Division Operations. *Manage. Account.,* August 1969, *51*(2), pp. 18–20.

Brown, R. Gene. Ethical and Other Problems in Publishing Financial Forecasts. **In** *Burton, J. C., ed.,* 1969, pp. 225–38. **[G: U.S.]**

Brown, Robert O. Using Appraisal Information. *Manage. Account.,* October 1969, *51*(4), pp. 47–48.

Browne, Dudley E. Progress in Corporate Financial Reporting. *Manage. Account.,* July 1969, *51*(1), pp. 7–9, 14.

Brummet, R. Lee; Flamholtz, Eric G. and Pyle, William C. Human Resource Accounting: A Tool to Increase Managerial Effectiveness. *Manage. Account.,* August 1969, *51*(2), pp. 12–15.

Cannata, Giuseppe. Factoring: un nuovo ausilio per la gestione delle medie e piccole imprese-I. (Factoring: A New Facility for Medium and Small Companies-I. With English summary.) *Bancaria,* June 1969, *25*(6), pp. 711–24.

Cannata, Giuseppe. Factoring: un nuovo ausilio per la gestione delle medie a piccole imprese-II. (Factoring: A New Facility for Medium and Small Companies-II. With English summary.) *Bancaria,* July 1969, *25*(7), pp. 842–50.

Casal, José. Barter Accounting in the Puerto Rican Sugar Industry. *Manage. Account.,* August 1969, *51*(2), pp. 48–50, 53.

Cook, David E. Inter-Unit Pricing and Your New Pricing Expert: The IRS. *Manage. Account.,* August 1969, *51*(2), pp. 9–11. **[G: U.S.]**

Cramer, Joe J., Jr. and Iwand, Thomas. Financial Reporting for Conglomerates: An Economic Analysis. *Calif. Manage. Rev.,* Spring 1969, *11*(3), pp. 25–34.

Crandall, Robert H. Information Economics and Its Implications for the Further Development of Accounting Theory. *Accounting Rev.,* July 1969, *44* (3), pp. 457–66.

Crumbley, D. Larry. How Long Will the Commissioner and the Courts Ignore Accounting Standards on the Accrual of Prepaid Income? *Nat. Tax J.,* December 1969, *22*(4), pp. 559–61. **[G: U.S.]**

David, Herbert K. Control of In-Process Inventory. *Manage. Account.,* December 1969, *51*(6), pp. 27–31.

Devers, M. De B.T.W.-aangifte en de factuur. (The Value Added Tax Declaration and the Invoice. With English summary.) *Econ. Soc. Tijdschr.,* June 1969, *23*(3), pp. 287–303. **[G: Belgium]**

Dockweiler, Raymond C. The Practicability of Developing Multiple Financial Statements: A Case Study. *Accounting Rev.,* October 1969, *44*(4), pp. 729–42.

Dudley, Dean. The Goodwill Account: The Accounting Recognition of the Concept of Economic Rent. *Marquette Bus. Rev.,* Summer 1969, *13*(2), pp. 89–92.

Edey, H. C. Accounting Principles and Business Reality. **In** *Carsberg, B. V. and Edey, H. C., eds.,* 1969, pp. 21–49.

Enache, Gh., et al. Perfecţionarea contabilităţii în Republica Socialistă România. (Improvement of Accounting in the Socialist Republic of Romania. With English summary.) *Stud. Cercet. Econ.,* 1969, *3,* pp. 143–50. **[G: Romania]**

Enthoven, Adolf J. H. Accountancy for Economic Development. *Finance Develop.,* September 1969, *6*(3), pp. 24–29.

Enthoven, Adolf J. H. The Changing Role of Accountancy. *Finance Develop.,* June 1969, *6*(2), pp. 16–22.

Fagerberg, Dixon, Jr. Accounting for Vacation Expense. *Manage. Account.*, December 1969, *51*(6), pp. 47–48.

Federici, Vincenzo. L'automazione del servizio pegno alla luce dell'esperienza di un'Azienda credito. (Automation of Pledge Service in the Light of a Bank's Experience. With English summary.) *Bancaria*, February 1969, *25*(2), pp. 203–05.

Felt, Howard M. and Barsky, Donald T. Purchase vs. Lease: Computer Obsolescence. *Manage. Account.*, October 1969, *51*(4), pp. 29–32.

Fertakis, John P. On Communication, Understanding, and Relevance in Accounting Reporting. *Accounting Rev.*, October 1969, *44*(4), pp. 680–91.

Field, John E. Toward a Multi-Level, Multi-Goal Information System. *Accounting Rev.*, July 1969, *44*(3), pp. 593–99.

Flanders, David P. Mechanized Intercompany Transfer System. *Manage. Account.*, October 1969, *51*(4), pp. 49–52.

Ford, Allen. Should Cost Be Assigned to Conversion Value? *Accounting Rev.*, October 1969, *44*(4), pp. 818–22.

Frank, Werner. A Comparison and Evaluation of Three Interim Income Concepts. *Soc. Sci. Quart.*, March 1969, *49*(4), pp. 864–75.

Goldschmidt, Y. and Smidt, S. Valuing the Firm's Durable Assets for Managerial Information. *Accounting Rev.*, April 1969, *44*(2), pp. 317–29.

Goolsby, John L. Integrated Accounting Systems: A Practical Approach. *Manage. Account.*, September 1969, *51*(3), pp. 11–13, 28.

Hakansson, Nils H. An Induced Theory of Accounting under Risk. *Accounting Rev.*, July 1969, *44*(3), pp. 495–514.

Halliwell, Paul D. Basic Principles of Pension Funding and APB Opinion No. 8. *Manage. Account.*, July 1969, *51*(1), pp. 15–19, 23.

Hancke, P. De economische betekenis van het boekhouden. (The Economic Sense of Accounting. With English summary.) *Econ. Soc. Tijdschr.*, April 1969, *23*(2), pp. 97–112.

Hartley, Ronald V. Linear Programming: Some Implications for Management Accounting. *Manage. Account.*, November 1969, *51*(5), pp. 48–51.

Hawkins, David F. Behavioral Implications of Generally Accepted Accounting Principles. *Calif. Manage. Rev.*, Winter 1969, *12*(2), pp. 13–21.

Hayes, Douglas A. Ethical Standards in Financial Reporting: A Critical Review. **In** *Burton, J. C., ed.*, 1969, pp. 73–86. **[G: U.S.]**

Herring, Dora R. Statistical Estimations of Historical Distribution Cost. *Manage. Account.*, October 1969, *51*(4), pp. 42–46.

Heuser, Forrest L. The Question of Uniform Accounting Standards. *Manage. Account.*, July 1969, *51*(1), pp. 20–23.

Hotelling, Harold. A General Mathematical Theory of Depreciation. **In** *Parker, R. H. and Harcourt, G. C., eds.*, 1969, pp. 261–75.

Ijiri, Yuji and Kaplan, Robert S. Probabilistic Depreciation and Its Implications for Group Depreciation. *Accounting Rev.*, October 1969, *44*(4), pp. 743–56.

Imdieke, Leroy F. and Weygandt, Jerry J. Classification of Convertible Debt. *Accounting Rev.*, October 1969, *44*(4), pp. 798–805.

Jääskeläinen, Veikko. Traditional and Ex Post Variance Analysis: A Reconciliation. *Liiketaloudellinen Aikak.*, 1969, *18*(2), pp. 153–70.

Jägerhorn, Reginald. Perspektiv på högskoleutbildning av redovisare. (Perspective on College Training of Accounts. With English summary.) *Econ. Samfundets Tidskr.*, 1969, *22*(3), pp. 181–88.

Jordan, Raymond B. Negotiating Overhead Expense with Confidence. *Manage. Account.*, December 1969, *51*(6), pp. 35–39.

King, Alfred M. Budgeting Foreign Exchange Losses. *Manage. Account.*, October 1969, *51*(4), pp. 39–41, 46.

Korf, Jack H. Management Accounting Control by Remote Output. *Manage. Account.*, November 1969, *51*(5), pp. 44–47.

Kypris, Phidias C. Greece: The New Code on Financial Books and Documents—The Salient Points. *Bull. Int. Fiscal Doc.*, February 1969, *23*(2), pp. 66–72. **[G: Greece]**

Lee, Lucy C. and Bedford, Norton M. An Information Theory Analysis of the Accounting Process. *Accounting Rev.*, April 1969, *44*(2), pp. 256–75.

Lev, Baruch. An Information Theory Analysis of Budget Variances. *Accounting Rev.*, October 1969, *44*(4), pp. 704–10.

Livingstone, John Leslie. Input-Output Analysis for Cost Accounting, Planning and Control. *Accounting Rev.*, January 1969, *44*(1), pp. 48–64.

Loshing, Clement T. The Effect of Liberalized Depreciation on the Cost of Equity Capital: Comment. **In** *Trebing, H. M. and Howard, R. H., eds.*, 1969, pp. 159–63. **[G: U.S.]**

Ma, Ronald. Current Developments in Accounting Theory: Problems of Income Measurement. *Malayan Econ. Rev.*, April 1969, *14*(1), pp. 1–14.

Mallery, Gary. Statistical Sampling and Auditing. *Manage. Account.*, August 1969, *51*(2), pp. 51–53.

Mathews, R. and Grant, J. McB. Profit Measurement and Inflation. **In** *Parker, R. H. and Harcourt, G. C., eds.*, 1969, pp. 201–14.

Mauldon, R. G.; Schapper, H. P. and Treloar, D. W. G. Operational Accounting for Farm Management. *Australian J. Agr. Econ.*, June 1969, *13*(1), pp. 47–57.

Mautz, R. K. and Skousen, K. Fred. Some Problems in Empirical Research in Accounting. *Accounting Rev.*, July 1969, *44*(3), pp. 447–56.

McLaney, James P. Asset Forecasting: A Defense Industry Technique. *Manage. Account.*, September 1969, *51*(3), pp. 33–35.

Medford, William L. Key Item Reporting. *Manage. Account.*, August 1969, *51*(2), pp. 21–26.

Melody, William H. The Effect of Liberalized Depreciation on the Cost of Equity Capital: Comment. **In** *Trebing, H. M. and Howard, R. H., eds.*, 1969, pp. 164–75. **[G: U.S.]**

Morris, Peter F. Widget Pricing. *Manage. Account.*, December 1969, *51*(6), pp. 12–14.

Most, Kenneth S. Two Forms of Experimental Accounts. *Accounting Rev.*, January 1969, *44*(1), pp. 145–52.

Motley, Brian. Inflation and Common Stock Values:

Comment. *J. Finance,* June 1969, *24*(3), pp. 530–35.

Nakano, Isao. Objectivity Reexamined. *Kobe Econ. Bus. Rev.,* 1969, *16*(1), pp. 47–54.

Neumann, Frederick L. The Incidence and Nature of Consistency Exceptions. *Accounting Rev.,* July 1969, *44*(3), pp. 546–54.

Nichols, Donald R. PPBS: A Challenge to Non-Profit Accounting. *Manage. Account.,* November 1969, *51*(5), pp. 12–13.

Olson, Wallace E. Ethical Problems of the Auditor in Financial Reporting. **In** *Burton, J. C., ed.,* 1969, pp. 145–58. **[G: U.S.]**

Orton, Bryce B. and Bradish, Richard D. The Treatment and Disclosure of Research and Development Expenditures. *Manage. Account.,* July 1969, *51*(1), pp. 31–34.

Paish, Frank W. The Estimation of Business Profits in Periods of Changing Prices. **In** *Parker, R. H. and Harcourt, G. C., eds.,* 1969, pp. 193–200.

Parker, C. Reed. Ethical Issues for the Financial Analyst. **In** *Burton, J. C., ed.,* 1969, pp. 159–71. **[G: U.S.]**

Parker, R. H. Lower of Cost and Market in Britain and the United States: A Historical Survey. **In** *Parker, R. H. and Harcourt, G. C., eds.,* 1969, pp. 239–58. **[G: U.S.; U.K.]**

Peeters, Frans. De B.T.W. in de onderneming. (The Value Added Tax and the Enterprise. With English summary.) *Econ. Soc. Tijdschr.,* August 1969, *23*(4), pp. 391–403. **[G: Belgium]**

Perrin, J. R. Management Accounting. **In** *Kempner, T., ed.,* 1969, pp. 21–32.

Petillon, Jack. Budgettering en direct costing. (Budgeting and Direct Costing. With English summary.) *Econ. Soc. Tijdschr.,* April 1969, *23*(2), pp. 129–42.

Petri, Enrico. Use of Capitalized Cost in Repeated Replacement Problems. *Manage. Account.,* September 1969, *51*(3), pp. 49–53, 56.

Prest, Alan R. Replacement Cost Depreciation. **In** *Parker, R. H. and Harcourt, G. C., eds.,* 1969, pp. 290–309.

Raby, William L. Tax Allocation and Non-Historical Financial Statements. *Accounting Rev.,* January 1969, *44*(1), pp. 1–11.

Restall, Lawrence J. and Czajkowski, Peter. Computation of LIFO Index: A Statistical Sampling Approach. *Manage. Account.,* September 1969, *51* (3), pp. 43–48.

Revsine, Lawrence. Some Controversy Concerning "Controversial Accounting Changes" *Accounting Rev.,* April 1969, *44*(2), pp. 354–58.

Rickey, Kenneth R. Earnings per Share: Management and the Investor. *Manage. Account.,* December 1969, *51*(6), pp. 9–11.

Riistama, Veijo. Kustannusteoria kustannuslaskennan perustana. (Cost Theory as a Basis for Cost Accounting. With English summary.) *Liiketaloudellinen Aikak.,* 1969, *18*(3), pp. 550–75.

Rose, J., et al. Toward an Empirical Measure of Materiality. **In** *Association of Canadian Schools of Business,* 1969, pp. 22–46.

Rosen, L. S. and DeCoster, Don T. "Funds" Statements: A Historical Perspective. *Accounting Rev.,* January 1969, *44*(1), pp. 124–36.

Rosenfield, Paul. Reporting Subjective Gains and Losses. *Accounting Rev.,* October 1969, *44*(4), pp. 788–97.

Rossman, William H. Allocation of Equipment Cost in the Heavy Construction Industry. *Manage. Account.,* November 1969, *51*(5), pp. 14–15.

Schwab, Bernhard and Nicol, Robert E. G. From Double-Declining-Balance to Sum-of-the-Years'-Digits Depreciation: An Optimum Switching Rule. *Accounting Rev.,* April 1969, *44*(2), pp. 292–96. **[G: U.S.]**

Scott, Donald A. Enforcement of Ethical Standards in Corporate Financial Reporting. **In** *Burton, J. C., ed.,* 1969, pp. 107–32. **[G: U.S.]**

Shwayder, Keith. The Capital Maintenance Rule and the Net Asset Valuation Rule. *Accounting Rev.,* April 1969, *44*(2), pp. 304–16.

Simmons, John K. and Gray, Jack. An Investigation of the Effect of Differing Accounting Frameworks on the Prediction of Net Income. *Accounting Rev.,* October 1969, *44*(4), pp. 757–76.

Simpson, Richard H. An Empirical Study of Possible Income Manipulation. *Accounting Rev.,* October 1969, *44*(4), pp. 806–17.

Slutzker, David R. A Proposal to Computerize the Accounting System. *Manage. Account.,* September 1969, *51*(3), pp. 23–28.

Smith, Alan F. Purchased Goodwill Is an Investment: Treat It as Such. *Manage. Account.,* November 1969, *51*(5), pp. 19–22.

Snavely, Howard J. Current Cost for Long-Lived Assets: A Critical View. *Accounting Rev.,* April 1969, *44*(2), pp. 344–53.

Sommer, A. A., Jr. The Accountant's Changing Legal Environment. **In** *Burton, J. C., ed.,* 1969, pp. 87–106. **[G: U.S.]**

Sorensen, James E. Bayesian Analysis in Auditing. *Accounting Rev.,* July 1969, *44*(3), pp. 555–61.

Sorter, George H. An "Events" Approach to Basic Accounting Theory. *Accounting Rev.,* January 1969, *44*(1), pp. 12–19.

Sunley, Emil M., Jr. The Present Value of Depreciation Allowances. *Quart. Rev. Econ. Bus.,* Winter 1969, *9*(4), pp. 77–79.

Taubman, Paul and Rasche, R. H. Economic and Tax Depreciation of Office Buildings. *Nat. Tax J.,* September 1969, *22*(3), pp. 334–46. **[G: U.S.]**

Theil, Henri. How to Worry About Increased Expenditures. *Accounting Rev.,* January 1969, *44*(1), pp. 27–37.

Tracy, John A. Bayesian Statistical Methods in Auditing. *Accounting Rev.,* January 1969, *44*(1), pp. 90–98.

Tritschler, Charles A. Statistical Criteria for Asset Valuation by Specific Price Index. *Accounting Rev.,* January 1969, *44*(1), pp. 99–123.

Tyran, Michael R. Computerized Communication and Control of Backlog Commitments: The 'Lifeblood' of an Organization's Survival. *Manage. Account.,* November 1969, *51*(5), pp. 23–30.

Van Damme, G. De accountant in het Europa 1970. (The Accountant of the Seventies. With English summary.) *Econ. Soc. Tijdschr.,* April 1969, *23*(2), pp. 173–84.

Van Tatenhove, James M. Managing Indirect Costs

in the Aerospace Industry. *Manage. Account.*, September 1969, *51*(3), pp. 36–42, 48.

Vance, Lawrence L. The Road to Reform of Accounting Principles. *Accounting Rev.*, October 1969, *44*(4), pp. 692–703. [G: U.S.]

Vandenhouten, F. De invoering van de B.T.W. in de ondernemingen. (The Value Added Tax in the Administration of the Firms. With English summary.) *Econ. Soc. Tijdschr.*, April 1969, *23*(2), pp. 159–71. [G: Belgium]

Verhaegen, Jozef. Beleidsboekhouden. (Management Accounting. With English summary.) *Econ. Soc. Tijdschr.*, April 1969, *23*(2), pp. 113–28.

Weinwurm, Ernest H. Discussion of Eugene L. Grant's "Tax Depreciation Restudied." *Eng. Econ.*, July–August 1969, *14*(4), pp. 237–38. [G: U.S.]

Weiss, Leonard W. Advertising, Profits, and Corporate Taxes. *Rev. Econ. Statist.*, November 1969, *51*(4), pp. 421–30. [G: U.S.]

Weller, Oren H. Touch-Tone Attendance and Labor Reporting. *Manage. Account.*, August 1969, *51*(2), pp. 27–28, 32.

Wilhelm, Maurice F., Jr. Purchase or Lease: That Is the Question. *Manage. Account.*, July 1969, *51*(1), pp. 43–46.

Willard, Bruce K. Cost Distribution Using Infinitely Variable Averages. *Manage. Account.*, October 1969, *51*(4), pp. 12–15.

Windal, Floyd W. Dynamic Programming: An Introduction. *Manage. Account.*, July 1969, *51*(1), pp. 47–49.

Wojdak, Joseph F. A Theoretical Foundation for Leases and Other Executory Contracts. *Accounting Rev.*, July 1969, *44*(3), pp. 562–70.

Wright, Albert W. Maintaining Balance in Financial Position. *Manage. Account.*, September 1969, *51*(3), pp. 14–16, 28.

Wright, Frank K. Towards a General Theory of Depreciation. **In** *Parker, R. H. and Harcourt, G. C., eds.*, 1969, pp. 276–89.

Wuchina, Stephen W. Program Control Network: A Tool for Month End Closing. *Manage. Account.*, July 1969, *51*(1), pp. 38–42.

Yu, S. C. A Flow-of-Resources Statement for Business Enterprises. *Accounting Rev.*, July 1969, *44*(3), pp. 571–82.

600 Industrial Organization; Technological Change; Industry Studies

610 Industrial Organization and Public Policy

611 Industrial Organization and Market Structure

6110 Industrial Organization and Market Structure

Adams, Walter. Planning, Regulation, and Competition. **In** *Kuhlman, J. M., ed.*, 1969, pp. 233–38. [G: U.S.]

Adams, Walter. Statement. **In** *Governmental Intervention in the Market Mechanism, Pt. 1, SCH*, 1969, pp. 304–08. [G: U.S.]

Adams, Walter. The Case for Structural Tests. **In** *Weston, J. F. and Peltzman, S., eds.*, 1969, pp. 13–26. [G: U.S.]

Adelman, M. A. Comment on the "H" Concentration Measure as a Numbers-Equivalent. *Rev. Econ. Statist.*, February 1969, *51*(1), pp. 99–101.

Aines, Ronald. Rationale for Conglomerate Growth in the Farm Input Sector. **In** *Garoian, L., ed.*, 1969, pp. 63–68. [G: U.S.]

Airamo, Martti M. Toimialarationalisointi kartellin näkökulmasta tarkasteltuna. (Rationalization According to the Field of Operation Examined from the Point of View of the Cartel. With English summary.) *Liiketaloudellinen Aikak.*, 1969, *18*(3), pp. 316–23.

Alemson, M. A. Demand, Entry, and the Game of Conflict in Oligopoly over Time: Recent Australian Experience. *Oxford Econ. Pap.*, July 1969, *21*(2), pp. 220–47. [G: Australia]

Allen, Bruce T. Concentration and Economic Progress: Note. *Amer. Econ. Rev.*, Part I, September 1969, *59*(4), pp. 600–604. [G: U.S.]

Alzona, Gianluigi. Fusioni di macroimprese 1967: ricerche sullo sviluppo industriale. (Merger of Large Corporations, 1967. With English summary.) *L'Impresa*, May/June 1969, *11*(3), pp. 205–21. [G: Italy]

Ansoff, H. Igor. Issues in National Policy on Growth of Firms. **In** *Weston, J. F. and Peltzman, S., eds.*, 1969, pp. 197–207. [G: U.S.]

Arnould, Richard. Conglomerate Growth and Profitability. **In** *Garoian, L., ed.*, 1969, pp. 72–80. [G: U.S.]

Attiyeh, Robert S. The Bashful Conglomerates. *Univ. Wash. Bus. Rev.*, Summer 1969, *28*(4), pp. 5–11.

Bain, Joe S. Survival-Ability as a Test of Efficiency. *Amer. Econ. Rev.*, May 1969, *59*(2), pp. 99–104.

Baldwin, William L. and Childs, Gerald L. The Fast Second and Rivalry in Research and Development. *Southern Econ. J.*, July 1969, *36*(1), pp. 18–24.

Barilla', Umberto. Le holdings bancarie negli Stati Uniti. (Bank Holding Companies in the United States. With English summary.) *Bancaria*, August 1969, *25*(8), pp. 963–67. [G: U.S.]

Bennathan, E. and Walters, A. A. Revenue Pooling and Cartels. *Oxford Econ. Pap.*, July 1969, *21*(2), pp. 161–76.

Bilas, Richard A. Third Degree Price Discrimination and the Multiple Plant Monopolist: A Note on the Allocation of Output. *Southern Econ. J.*, July 1969, *36*(1), pp. 82–86.

Bilsen, Robert. Marktbenadering, marktstructuur en ondernemingsdimensie. (Market Approach, Market Structure and the Dimension of the Firm. With English summary.) *Econ. Soc. Tijdschr.*, December 1969, *23*(6), pp. 537–45.

Blair, John M. An Overall View of Conglomerate Concentration. **In** *Garoian, L., ed.*, 1969, pp. 1–20. [G: U.S.]

Blank, David M. Tonypandy once Again. *J. Bus.*, January 1969, *42*(1), pp. 104–12. [G: U.S.]

Bohnemann, Volker. Preismeldestellen und Wettbewerb. (Open Price Systems and Competition. With English summary.) *Schmollers Jahr.*, 1969, *89*(6), pp. 641–74.

Bork, Robert H. Vertical Integration and Competitive Processes. **In** *Weston, J. F. and Peltzman, S., eds.*, 1969, pp. 139–49. **[G: U.S.]**

Brandow, G. E. Market Power and Its Sources in the Food Industry. *Amer. J. Agr. Econ.*, February 1969, *51*(1), pp. 1–12.

Briloff, Abraham J. Financial Motives for Conglomerate Growth. **In** *Garoian, L., ed.*, 1969, pp. 81–87. **[G: U.S.]**

Brozen, Yale. Barriers Facilitate Entry. *Antitrust Bull.*, Winter 1969, *14*, pp. 851–54. **[G: U.S.]**

Brozen, Yale. Significance of Profit Data for Antitrust Policy. *Antitrust Bull.*, Spring 1969, *14*, pp. 119–39. **[G: U.S.]**

Buchanan, James M. External Diseconomies, Corrective Taxes, and Market Structure. *Amer. Econ. Rev.*, March 1969, *59*(1), pp. 174–77.

Bushch, Arnd. Vertical Restrictions in German Consumer Goods Industries. *Antitrust Bull.*, Summer 1969, *14*, pp. 473–97. **[G: Germany]**

Carroll, Daniel T. What Future for the Conglomerate? *Harvard Bus. Rev.*, May–June 1969, *47*(3), pp. 4–12, 167–68.

Chandler, Alfred D., Jr. The Structure of American Industry in the Twentieth Century: A Historical Overview. *Bus. Hist. Rev.*, Autumn 1969, *43*(3), pp. 255–98. **[G: U.S.]**

Chauduri, A. Oligopoly and Economic Growth in India. **In** *Economic Concentration, Pt. 7A, SCH*, 1969, pp. 4242–51. **[G: India]**

Chester, T. E. Mergers and Opportunities for Managers. *Nat. Westminster Bank Quart. Rev.*, May 1969, pp. 10–21. **[G: U.K.]**

Chevalier, Jean-Marie. The Problem of Control in Large American Corporations. *Antitrust Bull.*, Spring 1969, *14*, pp. 163–80.

Cobia, David W. and Farris, Paul L. Mergers and Diversified Growth of Large Grain Firms. *Amer. J. Agr. Econ.*, August 1969, *51*(3), pp. 619–24. **[G: U.S.]**

Collins, Norman R. and Preston, Lee E. Industry Structure and Price-Cost Margins. **In** *Weston, J. F. and Peltzman, S., eds.*, 1969, pp. 81–109. **[G: U.S.]**

Collins, Norman R. and Preston, Lee E. Price-Cost Margins and Industry Structure. *Rev. Econ. Statist.*, August 1969, *51*(3), pp. 271–86. **[G: U.S.]**

Comanor, William S. and Wilson, Thomas A. Advertising and the Advantages of Size. *Amer. Econ. Rev.*, May 1969, *59*(2), pp. 87–98.

Costello, P. M. Economics of the Ethical Drug Industry: A Reply to Whitney. *Antitrust Bull.*, Summer 1969, *14*, pp. 397–403. **[G: U.S.]**

Cyert, Richard M. and George, Kenneth D. Competition, Growth, and Efficiency. *Econ. J.*, March 1969, *79*(313), pp. 23–41.

Di Tella, Guido and Baccino, Osvaldo. Análisis teórico de los efectos de la intermediación comercial. El caso de la industria del automóvil en Argentina. (Theoretical Analysis of the Effects of Commercial Intermediation: The Case of Automobile Industry in Argentina. With English summary.) *Económica*, January–April 1969, *15*(1), pp. 1–14. **[G: Argentina]**

Dirlam, Joel. Problems of Market Power and Public Policy in Yugoslavia. **In** *Bornstein, M., ed.*, 1969, pp. 236–51. **[G: Yugoslavia]**

Dirlam, Joel. Statement. **In** *Governmental Intervention in the Market Mechanism, Pt. 1, SCH*, 1969, pp. 249–67. **[G: U.S.]**

Doll, John P. Credit in the Production Organization of the Firm: Comment. *Amer. J. Agr. Econ.*, May 1969, *51*(2), pp. 474–76.

Dooley, Peter C. The Interlocking Directorate. *Amer. Econ. Rev.*, June 1969, *59*(3), pp. 314–23. **[G: U.S.]**

Douglas, E. J. Apparent and Real Levels of Concentration in Australian Manufacturing Industry. *Econ. Rec.*, June 1969, *45*(110), pp. 251–57. **[G: Australia]**

Dowd, Douglas F. Statement. **In** *Role of Giant Corporations, Pt. 1, SCH*, 1969, pp. 521–29. **[G: U.S.]**

Dubois, Jean-Pierre. French Economic Interest Groups and the Rules of Competition. *Antitrust Bull.*, Fall 1969, *14*, pp. 667–703. **[G: France]**

Edwards, C. Concentration Data and Concentration Concepts in Japan. **In** *Economic Concentration, Pt. 7A, SCH*, 1969, pp. 4252–56. **[G: Japan]**

Ekelund, Robert B., Jr. and Maurice, Charles. An Empirical Investigation of Advertising and Concentration: Comment. *J. Ind. Econ.*, November 1969, *18*(1), pp. 76–80. **[G: U.S.]**

Farris, Paul L. Information Gaps and Research Problems. **In** *Garoian, L., ed.*, 1969, pp. 123–24.

Filippi, Enrico. Le duecento maggiori società industriali italiane. (The 200 Largest Italian Industrial Corporations. With English summary.) *L'Impresa*, January/February 1969, *11*(1), pp. 41–55. **[G: Italy]**

Galbraith, John Kenneth. Planning, Regulation, and Competition. **In** *Kuhlman, J. M., ed.*, 1969, pp. 227–33. **[G: U.S.]**

Galbraith, John Kenneth. Professor Gordon on "The Close of the Galbraithian System." *J. Polit. Econ.*, Part I, July/August 1969, *77*(4), pp. 494–503.

Ghosh, Arabinda and Sarkar, Anil Kumar. Size Structure of Indian Engineering Industries, 1948–61. *Indian Econ. J.*, January–March 1969, *16*(3), pp. 375–81. **[G: India]**

Gonzalez, Richard J. Interfuel Competition for Future Energy Markets. **In** *Governmental Intervention in the Market Mechanism, Pt. 1, SCH*, 1969, pp. 393–99. **[G: U.S.]**

Gordon, Scott. "The Galbraithian System"—Rejoinder. *J. Polit. Econ.*, November/December 1969, *77*(6), pp. 953–56.

Gort, Michael. An Economic Disturbance Theory of Mergers. *Quart. J. Econ.*, November 1969, *83*(4), pp. 624–42. **[G: U.S.]**

Goudzwaard, Maurice B. Conglomerate Mergers, Convertibles, and Cash Dividends. *Quart. Rev. Econ. Bus.*, Spring 1969, *9*(1), pp. 53–62.

Grether, E. T. Business Responsibility Toward the Market. *Calif. Manage. Rev.*, Fall 1969, *12*(1), pp. 33–42.

Gupta, Manak C. The Effect of Size, Growth, and Industry on the Financial Structure of Manufacturing Companies. *J. Finance*, June 1969, *24*(3),

pp. 517–29. [G: U.S.]

Hale, Rosemary D. Cookware and Vertical Integration: A Rejoinder. *J. Law Econ.*, October 1969, *12* (2), pp. 439–40. [G: U.S.]

Hammer, Marius. Binnenmärkte und Mafia in Sizilien. (Market Organization and Mafia in Sicily. With English summary.) *Jahr. Nationalökon. Statist.*, July 1969, *183*(2), pp. 150–58. [G: Italy]

Harwood, Kenneth. Broadcasting and the Theory of the Firm. *Law Contemp. Probl.*, Summer 1969, *34*(3), pp. 485–504.

Havrilesky, Thomas and Barth, Richard. Tests of Market Share Stability in the Cigarette Industry 1950–66. *J. Ind. Econ.*, April 1969, *17*(2), pp. 145–50.

Havrilesky, T. and Barth, Richard. Non-Price Competition in the Cigarette Industry. *Antitrust Bull.*, Fall 1969, *14*, pp. 607–28. [G: U.S.]

Hazari, R. K. The Implications of the Managing Agency System in Indian Development. **In** *Bhuleshkar, A. V., ed.*, 1969, pp. 193–213. [G: India]

Heflebower, Richard B. Theory of the Firm and of Market Structures: Discussion. *Amer. Econ. Rev.*, May 1969, *59*(2), pp. 119–21.

Henning, John A. Marginal Concentration Ratios: Some Statistical Implications—Comment. *Southern Econ. J.*, October 1969, *36*(2), pp. 196–98. [G: U.S.]

Hettena, Ran and Ruchlin, Hirsch S. The U.S. Tanker Industry: A Structural and Behavioral Analysis. *J. Ind. Econ.*, July 1969, *17*(3), pp. 188–204. [G: U.S.]

Hill, Lowell D. Information Gaps and Research Problems. **In** *Garoian, L., ed.*, 1969, pp. 125–27.

Hoa, Tran Van. Marketing Imperfections and Increasing Returns to Scale in Australian Manufacturing Industry. *Econ. Rec.*, June 1969, *45*(110), pp. 243–50. [G: Australia]

Hoffman, A. C. The Economic Rationale for Conglomerate Growth from a Management Perspective. **In** *Garoian, L., ed.*, 1969, pp. 57–62. [G: U.S.]

Hunter, Alex. Mergers and Industry Concentration in Britain. *Banca Naz. Lavoro Quart. Rev.*, December 1969, (91), pp. 372–94. [G: U.K.]

Hunter, Alex. The Measurement of Monopoly Power. **In** *Hunter, A., ed.*, 1969, pp. 92–121.

Hurnanen, R.; Devine, G. and Hawkins, Murray H. Industrial Organization and Policy Development in a Dynamic World. *Can. J. Agr. Econ.*, July 1969, *17*(2), pp. 106–17.

Institute of Econ., Acad. of Sci. Optimal Sizes for Enterprises. **In** *Economic Concentration, Pt. 7A, SCH*, 1969, pp. 4362–66. [G: U.S.S.R.]

Irwin, Manley R. The Computer Utility: Market Entry in Search of Public Policy. *J. Ind. Econ.*, July 1969, *17*(3), pp. 239–52. [G: U.S.]

Jacoby, Neil H. Statement. **In** *Role of Giant Corporations, Pt. 1, SCH*, 1969, pp. 502–13. [G: U.S.]

Johnson, Harold W. and Simon, Julian L. The Success of Mergers: The Case of Advertising Agencies. *Bull. Oxford Univ. Inst. Econ. Statist.*, May 1969, *31*(2), pp. 139–44.

de Jong, H. W. Concentration in the Common Market. **In** *Economic Concentration, Pt. 7A, SCH*, 1969, pp. 3907–15. [G: E.E.C.]

de Jong, H. W. The Direction, Relatedness, and Strategy of Mergers: Appendix. **In** *Economic Concentration, Pt. 7A, SCH*, 1969, pp. 3893–97. [G: E.E.C.]

de Jong, H. W. The European Brewing Industry: Appendix. **In** *Economic Concentration, Pt. 7A, SCH*, 1969, pp. 3897–3907. [G: E.E.C.]

Kafoglis, Milton Z. and Keig, Norman G. New Policies of the Federal Power Commission. *Land Econ.*, November 1969, *45*(4), pp. 385–91. [G: U.S.]

Kamerschen, David R. The Determination of Profit Rates in "Oligopolistic Industries." *J. Bus.*, July 1969, *42*(3), pp. 293–301. [G: U.S.]

Karssen, W. J. Concentration of the Automobile Industry of the E.E.C. **In** *Economic Concentration, Pt. 7A, SCH*, 1969, pp. 3915–25. [G: E.E.C.]

Kunnas, Heikki J. EFO-tutkimus. (EFO Survey. With English summary.) *Kansant. Aikak.*, 1969, *65*(3), pp. 206–13. [G: Sweden]

Kvasha, Ya. Concentration of Production and Small Scale Industry. **In** *Economic Concentration, Pt. 7A, SCH*, 1969, pp. 4358–62. [G: U.S.S.R.]

Laffer, Arthur B. Vertical Integration by Corporations, 1929–1965. *Rev. Econ. Statist.*, February 1969, *51*(1), pp. 91–93. [G: U.S.]

Leonard, William N. Network Television Pricing: A Comment. *J. Bus.*, January 1969, *42*(1), pp. 93–103. [G: U.S.]

Levin, Harvey J. Broadcast Structure, Technology, and the ABC-ITT Merger Decision. *Law Contemp. Probl.*, Summer 1969, *34*(3), pp. 452–84. [G: U.S.]

Lipfert, Helmut. Il sistema creditizio tedesco verso nuovo vie. (The German Credit System Moving Towards New Developments. With English summary.) *Bancaria*, September 1969, *25*(9), pp. 1082–87. [G: W. Germany]

Livesay, Harold C. and Porter, Patrick G. Vertical Integration in American Manufacturing, 1899–1948. *J. Econ. Hist.*, September 1969, *29*(3), pp. 494–500. [G: U.S.]

Logan, Samuel H. A Conceptual Framework for Analyzing Economies of Vertical Integration. *Amer. J. Agr. Econ.*, November 1969, *51*(4), pp. 834–48.

Madsen, Albert G. and Walsh, Richard G. Conglomerates: Economic Conduct and Performance. *Amer. J. Agr. Econ.*, December 1969, *51*(5), pp. 1495–1505. [G: U.S.]

Mann, H. Michael. A Note on Barriers to Entry and Long Run Profitability. *Antitrust Bull.*, Winter 1969, *14*, pp. 845–49. [G: U.S.]

Mann, H. Michael and Meehan, James W., Jr. Concentration and Profitability: An Examination of a Recent Study. *Antitrust Bull.*, Summer 1969, *14*, pp. 385–95. [G: U.S.]

Mann, H. Michael; Henning, John A. and Meehan, James W., Jr. Statistical Testing in Industrial Economics: A Reply on Measurement Error and Sampling Procedure. *J. Ind. Econ.*, November 1969, *18*(1), pp. 95–100.

Mann, H. Michael; Henning, John A. and Meehan, James W., Jr. Testing Hypothesis in Industrial Economics: A Reply. *J. Ind. Econ.*, November

1969, *18*(1), pp. 81–84. [G: U.S.]

Marcus, Matityahu. Advertising and Changes in Concentration. *Southern Econ. J.*, October 1969, *36*(2), pp. 117–21. [G: U.S.]

Marcus, Matityahu. Profitability and Size of Firm: Some Further Evidence. *Rev. Econ. Statist.*, February 1969, *51*(1), pp. 104–07. [G: U.S.]

Markert, Kurt E. The Dyestuff Case: A Contribution to the Relationship between the Antitrust Laws of the European Economic Community and Its Member States. *Antitrust Bull.*, Winter 1969, *14*, pp. 869–99. [G: E.E.C.]

Markham, Jesse W. Competition in the Nuclear Power Supply Industry—A Reply to Mr. Netschert. *Antitrust Bull.*, Fall 1969, *14*, pp. 657–63. [G: U.S.]

Masters, Stanley H. An Interindustry Analysis of Wages and Plant Size. *Rev. Econ. Statist.*, August 1969, *51*(3), pp. 341–45. [G: U.S.]

McKean, John R. A Note on Administered Prices with Fluctuating Demand. *J. Financial Quant. Anal.*, March 1969, *4*(1), pp. 15–23.

Mehta, B. V. Size and Capital Intensity in Indian Industry. *Bull. Oxford Univ. Inst. Econ. Statist.*, August 1969, *31*(3), pp. 189–204. [G: India]

Mermelstein, David. Large Industrial Corporations and Asset Shares. *Amer. Econ. Rev.*, Part I, September 1969, *59*(4), pp. 531–41. [G: U.S.]

Mestmäcker, E.-J. State Trading Monopolies in the European Economic Community. **In** *Economic Concentration, Pt. 7A, SCH*, 1969, pp. 3925–44. [G: E.E.C.]

Miller, Richard A. Marginal Concentration Ratios: Some Statistical Implications—Reply. *Southern Econ. J.*, October 1969, *36*(2), pp. 199–201. [G: U.S.]

Miller, Richard A. Market Structure and Industrial Performance: Relation of Profit Rates to Concentration, Advertising Intensity, and Diversity. *J. Ind. Econ.*, April 1969, *17*(2), pp. 104–18. [G: U.S.]

Minasian, Jora R. Research and Development and Other Determinants of Investment: Discussion. *Amer. Econ. Rev.*, May 1969, *59*(2), pp. 86.

Mohring, Herbert and Williamson, Harold F., Jr. Scale and "Industrial Reorganisation" Economies of Transport Improvements. *J. Transp. Econ. Policy*, September 1969, *3*(3), pp. 251–71. [G: U.S.]

Moroney, John R. and Allen, Bruce T. Monopoly Power and the Relative Share of Labor. *Ind. Lab. Relat. Rev.*, January 1969, *22*(2), pp. 167–78. [G: U.S.]

Mueller, Dennis C. A Theory of Conglomerate Mergers. *Quart. J. Econ.*, November 1969, *83*(4), pp. 643–59.

Mueller, Hans G. The Policy of the European Coal and Steel Community Towards Mergers and Agreements by Steel Companies. *Antitrust Bull.*, Summer 1969, *14*, pp. 413–48. [G: E.E.C.]

Mueller, Willard F. Firm Conglomeration as a Market Structure Variable. *Amer. J. Agr. Econ.*, December 1969, *51*(5), pp. 1488–94. [G: U.S.]

Narver, John. Conglomeration in the Food Industries. **In** *Garoian, L., ed.*, 1969, pp. 21–41. [G: U.S.]

Nel, P. A. The Standard Industrial Classification and Industrial Marketing. *Finance Trade Rev.*, December 1969, *8*(4), pp. 231–57.

Nelson, Paul E. Research Problems and Information Gaps Relating to Conglomerate Growth. **In** *Garoian, L., ed.*, 1969, pp. 128–30.

Netschert, Bruce C. Competition in the Nuclear Power Supply Industry—A Rejoinder to Professor Markham. *Antitrust Bull.*, Fall 1969, *14*, pp. 665–66. [G: U.S.]

Netschert, Bruce C. Competition in the Nuclear Power Supply Industry: A Review. *Antitrust Bull.*, Fall 1969, *14*, pp. 629–55. [G: U.S.]

Okuguchi, Koji. On the Stability of Price Adjusting Oligopoly Equilibrium under Product Differentiation. *Southern Econ. J.*, January 1969, *35*(3), pp. 244–46.

Pashigian, Peter. The Effect of Market Size on Concentration. *Int. Econ. Rev.*, October 1969, *10*(3), pp. 291–314. [G: U.S.]

Peltzman, Sam. Profit Data and Public Policy. **In** *Weston, J. F. and Peltzman, S., eds.*, 1969, pp. 128–36. [G: U.S.]

Peterson, R. D. and Leister, D. V. Market Structure-Conduct Relations: Some Evidence from Biomedical Electronic Firms. *Univ. Wash. Bus. Rev.*, Summer 1969, *28*(4), pp. 49–65. [G: U.S.]

Petry, Horst. Technischer Fortschritt, Integration, internationale Wettbewerbsfähigkeit und Unternehmensgrösse. (With English summary.) *Jahr. Nationalökon. Statist.*, August 1969, *183*(3–4), pp. 271–99.

Phlips, Louis. Business Pricing Policies and Inflation—Some Evidence from E.E.C. Countries. *J. Ind. Econ.*, November 1969, *18*(1), pp. 1–14. [G: Belgium; Netherlands; France]

Pogosov, I. Questions of the Economic Effectiveness in Concentrating Industrial Production. **In** *Economic Concentration, Pt. 7A, SCH*, 1969, pp. 4395–4404. [G: U.S.S.R.]

Prakash, Prem. Relationship Between Size and Productivity in Selected Indian Industries. *Asian Econ. Rev.*, May 1969, *11*(3), pp. 237–48. [G: India]

Probst, A. Optimal Dimensions of an Enterprise and Regional Factors. **In** *Economic Concentration, Pt. 7A, SCH*, 1969, pp. 4404–12. [G: U.S.S.R.]

Reid, Samuel Richardson. Conglomerate Growth: Consistency with Economic Theory of Growth. **In** *Garoian, L., ed.*, 1969, pp. 44–56.

Reid, Samuel Richardson. Mergers and the Economist. *Antitrust Bull.*, Summer 1969, *14*, pp. 371–84. [G: U.S.]

Rethwisch, Kurt. A Note on the Presumed Social Desirability of Internal Over External Growth. *Antitrust Bull.*, Winter 1969, *14*, pp. 855–64.

Rock, James M. Cookware and Vertical Integration: A Reply. *J. Law Econ.*, October 1969, *12*(2), pp. 441–43. [G: U.S.]

Rock, James M. Cookware: A Study in Vertical Integration—A Reexamination. *J. Law Econ.*, October 1969, *12*(2), pp. 425–38. [G: U.S.]

Rubel, John H. Systems Management and Industry Behavior. **In** *Weston, J. F. and Peltzman, S., eds.*, 1969, pp. 208–18. [G: U.S.]

Sahota, G. S. Economic Problems in Separating the

Determinants of Relative Prices. *Int. Econ. Rev.*, June 1969, *10*(2), pp. 183–206. [G: U.S.]

Sandesara, J. C. Size and Capital-Intensity in Indian Industry: Some Comments. *Bull. Oxford Univ. Inst. Econ. Statist.*, November 1969, *31*(4), pp. 331–34. [G: India]

Schendel, Dan E. and Balestra, Pietro. Rational Behavior and Gasoline Price Wars. *Appl. Econ.*, May 1969, *1*(2), pp. 89–101.

Scherer, Frederic M. Market Structure and the Stability of Investment. *Amer. Econ. Rev.*, May 1969, *59*(2), pp. 72–79. [G: U.S.]

Schlusberg, Malcolm D. Corporate Legitimacy and Social Responsibility: The Role of Law. *Calif. Manage. Rev.*, Fall 1969, *12*(1), pp. 65–76.

Schwartz, Hugh H. Concerning the Contention That Efficiency in the Allocation of Resources Really Doesn't Matter Very Much after All. *Econ. Develop. Cult. Change,* Part I, October 1969, *18* (1), pp. 44–50.

Shad, John S. R. The Financial Realities of Mergers. *Harvard Bus. Rev.*, November–December 1969, *47*(6), pp. 132–46. [G: U.S.]

Shaffer, James Duncan. Some Research Problems Concerning Conglomerate Firm Growth. **In** *Garoian, L., ed.*, 1969, pp. 131–32.

Shepherd, William G. Market Power and Racial Discrimination in White Collar Employment. *Antitrust Bull.*, Spring 1969, *14*, pp. 141–61. [G: U.S.]

Simon, Julian L. A Further Test of the Kinky Oligopoly Demand Curve. *Amer. Econ. Rev.*, December 1969, *59*(5), pp. 971–75. [G: U.S.]

Sjöblom, Veikko. Havaintoja toimialarationalisoinnista useammalla alalla toimivassa yrityksessä. (Remarks on Rationalization in the Operational Field in a Firm Operating in Several Fields. With English summary.) *Liiketaloudellinen Aikak.*, 1969, *18*(2), pp. 243–50.

Smith, David L. Characteristics of Merging Banks. (Study summary.) *Fed. Res. Bull.*, July 1969, *55*(7), pp. 579–80. [G: U.S.]

Smith, Keith V. and Schreiner, John C. A Portfolio Analysis of Conglomerate Diversification. *J. Finance,* June 1969, *24*(3), pp. 413–27. [G: U.S.]

Smyth, David J.; Briscoe, G. and Samuels, J. M. The Variability of Industry Profit Rates. *Appl. Econ.*, May 1969, *1*(2), pp. 137–49. [G: U.K.]

Spencer, Daniel L. Japan's Industrial Concentration and Technological Pattern in Secular Perspective. **In** *Salin, E.; Stohler, J. and Pawlowsky, P.*, 1969, pp. 242–64. [G: Japan]

Stern, Louis W. Mergers under Scrutiny. *Harvard Bus. Rev.*, July–August 1969, *47*(4), pp. 18–36, 160–63. [G: U.S.]

Telser, Lester G. Another Look at Advertising and Concentration. *J. Ind. Econ.*, November 1969, *18* (1), pp. 85–94. [G: U.S.]

Telser, Lester G. Theory of the Firm and of Market Structures: Discussion. *Amer. Econ. Rev.*, May 1969, *59*(2), pp. 121–23.

Tolksdorf, Michael. Hoppmanns neoklassische Wettbewerbstheorie als grundlage der Wettbewerbspolitik. (Hoppmann's Neoclassic Theory of Competition as a Basis for Competition Policy. With English summary.) *Jahr. Nationalökon. Statist.*, June 1969, *183*(1), pp. 61–72.

Trebing, Harry M. Government Regulation and Modern Capitalism. *J. Econ. Issues,* March 1969, *3*(1), pp. 87–109.

Van Cise, Jerrold G. A Franchise Contract. *Antitrust Bull.*, Summer 1969, *14*, pp. 325–46.

Venturini, V. G. Monopolies and Restrictive Trade Practices in Italy. **In** *Economic Concentration, Pt. 7A, SCH,* 1969, pp. 4207–34. [G: Italy]

Villanueva, Javier. Inversión privada extranjera, desarrollo industrial y comercio internacional. (Direct Foreign Investment in Industry. With English summary.) *Económica,* May–August 1969, *15*(2), pp. 223–42.

Walter, Helmut. Bemerkungen zum gegenwärtigen Stand der Wettbewerbstheorie. (Remarks about the Present State of the Theory of Competition. With English summary.) *Schmollers Jahr.*, 1969, *89*(5), pp. 541–56.

Weston, J. Fred. Summary of Discussions on Conglomerate Mergers. **In** *Weston, J. F. and Peltzman, S., eds.*, 1969, pp. 219–24. [G: U.S.]

Whitney, Simon N. Ethical Drugs: Comments on Professor Schifrin's Rejoinder and Professor Costello's Reply. *Antitrust Bull.*, Summer 1969, *14*, pp. 405–09. [G: U.S.]

Wilhelmy, Odin, Jr. Factors Underlying Business Interest in Conglomerate Mergers. *Amer. J. Agr. Econ.*, December 1969, *51*(5), pp. 1482–87. [G: U.S.]

Williamson, Oliver E. Allocative Efficiency and the Limits of Antitrust. *Amer. Econ. Rev.*, May 1969, *59*(2), pp. 105–18.

Worcester, Dean A., Jr. Innovations in the Calculation of Welfare Loss to Monopoly. *Western Econ. J.*, September 1969, *7*(3), pp. 234–43.

Woroniak, Alexander. Industrial Concentration in Eastern Europe: The Search for Optimum Size and Efficiency. **In** *Salin, E.; Stohler, J. and Pawlowsky, P.*, 1969, pp. 265–84. [G: E. Europe]

612 Public Policy Towards Monopoly and Competition

6120 Public Policy Towards Monopoly and Competition

Aaltonen, Aimo O. Mainonnassa suoritetuista vertailuista silmällä pitäen vilpillisen kilpailun ehkäisemislakia. (Comparisons in Advertising with Reference to the Law for the Prevention of Unfair Competition. With English summary.) *Liiketaloudellinen Aikak.*, 1969, *18*(3), pp. 301–10.

Adams, Walter. Planning, Regulation, and Competition. **In** *Kuhlman, J. M., ed.*, 1969, pp. 233–38. [G: U.S.]

Adams, Walter. Public Policy in a Free Enterprise Economy. **In** *Starleaf, D. R., ed.*, 1969, pp. 79–93. [G: U.S.]

Airamo, Martti M. Toimialarationalisointi kartellin näkökulmasta tarkasteltuna. (Rationalization According to the Field of Operation Examined from the Point of View of the Cartel. With English summary.) *Liiketaloudellinen Aikak.*, 1969, *18* (3), pp. 316–23.

Alexander, Willy. The Establishment of the Common Market and the Problem of Parallel Patents.

Antitrust Bull., Spring 1969, *14,* pp. 181–220. [G: E.E.C.]

Ansoff, H. Igor. Issues in National Policy on Growth of Firms. **In** *Weston, J. F. and Peltzman, S., eds.,* 1969, pp. 197–207. [G: U.S.]

Areeda, Phillip. Structure-Performance Assumptions in Recent Merger Cases. **In** *Weston, J. F. and Peltzman, S., eds.,* 1969, pp. 27–44. [G: U.S.]

Baker, Donald I. Another Look at Franchise Tie-Ins After Texaco and Fortner. *Antitrust Bull.,* Winter 1969, *14,* pp. 767–83. [G: U.S.]

Baker, James E. S. Combinations and Conspiracies —Is There a Difference? *Antitrust Bull.,* Spring 1969, *14,* pp. 71–90. [G: U.S.]

Baldwin, William L. The Feedback Effect of Business Conduct on Industry Structure. *J. Law Econ.,* April 1969, *12*(1), pp. 123–53. [G: U.S.]

Barnikel, Hans-Heinrich. Abuse of Power by Dominant Firms: Application of the German Law. *Antitrust Bull.,* Spring 1969, *14,* pp. 221–47. [G: W. Germany]

Bieberstein, J. The German Cartel Law and Its Administration: Role of the Federal Cartel Office in Regard to the E.E.C. Antitrust Provisions. **In** *Economic Concentration, Pt. 7A, SCH,* 1969, pp. 4038–58. [G: W. Germany]

Biedenkopt, K. H. Ordnungspolitische Probleme der Konzentration. (With English summary.) **In** *Economic Concentration, Pt. 7A, SCH,* 1969, pp. 4058–65. [G: W. Germany]

Blair, John M. Conglomerate Mergers—Theory and Congressional Intent. **In** *Weston, J. F. and Peltzman, S., eds.,* 1969, pp. 179–96. [G: U.S.]

Blake, Harland M. and Jones, William K. In Defense of Antitrust. **In** *Starleaf, D. R., ed.,* 1969, pp. 102–09. [G: U.S.]

Bork, Robert H. and Bowman, Ward S., Jr. The Crisis in Antitrust. **In** *Starleaf, D. R., ed.,* 1969, pp. 93–102. [G: U.S.]

Brozen, Yale. Barriers Facilitate Entry. *Antitrust Bull.,* Winter 1969, *14,* pp. 851–54. [G: U.S.]

Brozen, Yale. Significance of Profit Data for Antitrust Policy. *Antitrust Bull.,* Spring 1969, *14,* pp. 119–39. [G: U.S.]

Brozen, Yale. Significance of Profit Data for Antitrust Policy. **In** *Weston, J. F. and Peltzman, S., eds.,* 1969, pp. 110–27. [G: U.S.]

Brubaker, Earl R. Some Effects of Policy on Productivity in Soviet and American Crude Petroleum Extraction. *J. Ind. Econ.,* November 1969, *18*(1), pp. 33–52. [G: U.S.; U.S.S.R.]

Bushch, Arnd. Vertical Restrictions in German Consumer Goods Industries. *Antitrust Bull.,* Summer 1969, *14,* pp. 473–97. [G: Germany]

Buxbaum, Richard M. The Group Exemption and Exculsive Distributorships in the Common Market—Procedural Technicalities. *Antitrust Bull.,* Summer 1969, *14,* pp. 499–514. [G: E.E.C.]

Castrén, Kari. Kilpailun edistämisen nykyongelmia. (Some Contemporary Problems of Competition Policy. With English summary.) *Liiketaloudellinen Aikak.,* 1969, *18*(3), pp. 341–46.

Colwell, B. Joe. Antitrust and Efficiency: Product Extension Mergers. *Southern Econ. J.,* April 1969, *35*(4), pp. 369–75. [G: U.S.]

Curry, Robert L., Jr. The "Failing Company" Doctrine and Competition as an Antitrust Standard. *Oregon Bus. Rev.,* October 1969, *28*(10), pp. 1–5. [G: U.S.]

Curry, Robert L., Jr. Trade Restraints Injuring the United States Government. *Quart. Rev. Econ. Bus.,* Autumn 1969, *9*(3), pp. 77–80. [G: U.S.]

Dahl, Dale C. Conglomerate Growth: Policy Implications for Agriculture and Agribusiness. **In** *Garoian, L., ed.,* 1969, pp. 115–16. [G: U.S.]

DePrano, Michael E. and Nugent, Jeffrey B. Economies as an Antitrust Defense: Comment. *Amer. Econ. Rev.,* December 1969, *59*(5), pp. 947–53.

Dewey, Donald. The Shaky Case for Antitrust. **In** *Starleaf, D. R., ed.,* 1969, pp. 110–14. [G: U.S.]

Dirlam, Joel. Problems of Market Power and Public Policy in Yugoslavia. **In** *Bornstein, M., ed.,* 1969, pp. 236–51. [G: Yugoslavia]

Donnem, Roland W. The Antitrust Attack on Restrictive Patent License Provisions. *Antitrust Bull.,* Winter 1969, *14,* pp. 749–66. [G: U.S.]

Dubois, Jean-Pierre. French Economic Interest Groups and the Rules of Competition. *Antitrust Bull.,* Fall 1969, *14,* pp. 667–703. [G: France]

Elliott, Robert M. An SEC Primer. **In** *Harvey, J. L. and Newgarden, A., eds.,* 1969, pp. 62–78. [G: U.S.]

Elzinga, Kenneth G. The Antimerger Law: Pyrrhic Victories? *J. Law Econ.,* April 1969, *12*(1), pp. 43–78. [G: U.S.]

Erickson, W. Bruce. Costs and Conspiracy: The Uses of Cost Data in Private Antitrust Litigation. *Antitrust Bull.,* Summer 1969, *14,* pp. 347–70. [G: U.S.]

Fugate, Wilbur L. Antitrust Aspects of Transatlantic Investment. *Law Contemp. Probl.,* Winter 1969, *34*(1), pp. 135–45. [G: U.S.]

Galbraith, John Kenneth. Planning, Regulation, and Competition. **In** *Kuhlman, J. M., ed.,* 1969, pp. 227–33. [G: U.S.]

Grabner, John R., Jr. Legal Limits of Competition. *Harvard Bus. Rev.,* November–December 1969, *47*(6), pp. 4–24, 182. [G: U.S.]

Griesback, Bernard. The German Policy on Competition Within the Scope of General Economic Policy. *Antitrust Bull.,* Summer 1969, *14,* pp. 449–72. [G: Germany]

Hale, G. E. Communication Among Competitors. *Antitrust Bull.,* Spring 1969, *14,* pp. 63–70. [G: U.S.]

Handy, C. R. and Padberg, D. I. Conglomerate Growth: Policy Implications for Agriculture and Agribusiness. **In** *Garoian, L., ed.,* 1969, pp. 117–20. [G: U.S.]

Heflebower, Richard B. Theory of the Firm and of Market Structures: Discussion. *Amer. Econ. Rev.,* May 1969, *59*(2), pp. 119–21.

Helmberger, Peter. Who's Afraid of Conglomerate Firms? **In** *Garoian, L., ed.,* 1969, pp. 113–14. [G: U.S.]

Heyman, Thomas V. Patent Licensing and the Antitrust Laws—A Reappraisal at the Close of the Decade. *Antitrust Bull.,* Fall 1969, *14,* pp. 537–56. [G: U.S.]

Hoffman, Gerhard. The Austrian Cartel Law: Principles and Background. *Antitrust Bull.,* Spring 1969, *14,* pp. 249–78. [G: Austria]

Horowitz, Ann and Horowitz, Ira. Concentration, Competition, and Mergers in Brewing. **In** *Wes-*

ton, J. F. and Peltzman, S., eds., 1969, pp. 45–56. **[G: U.S.]**

Karber, James W. Competition and the Regulatory Process. *Quart. Rev. Econ. Bus.*, Autumn 1969, *9* (3), pp. 57–64. **[G: U.S.]**

Kilcarr, Andrew J. United States v. Concentrated Phosphate Export Association: A Small Case in the Big Court. *Antitrust Bull.*, Spring 1969, *14*, pp. 37–61. **[G: U.S.]**

Knutson, Ronald D. Nonproducer Cooperative Interests and the Antitrust Laws. *Amer. J. Agr. Econ.*, May 1969, *51*(2), pp. 335–41. **[G: U.S.]**

Knutson, Ronald D. The Economic Consequences of the Minnesota Dairy Industry Unfair Trade Practices Act. *J. Law Econ.*, October 1969, *12*(2), pp. 377–89. **[G: U.S.]**

Kornstein, Daniel J. Insurance Mergers and the Clayton Act. *Yale Law J.*, July 1969, *78*(8), pp. 1404–17. **[G: U.S.]**

Ladd, John C. Consumers and Antitrust Treble Damages: Credit-Furniture Tie-Ins in the Low Income Market. *Yale Law J.*, December 1969, *79* (2), pp. 254–83. **[G: U.S.]**

Ladd, John C. The Logic of Foreclosure: Tie-In Doctrine after *Fortner v. U. S. Steel. Yale Law J.*, November 1969, *79*(1), pp. 86–101. **[G: U.S.]**

Lobato López, Ernesto. Las normas de calidad y el desarrollo de la industria (Primera parte). (Quality Standards and Industrial Development: First Part. With English summary.) *Econ. Polít.*, Second Semester 1969, *6*(2), pp. 183–94. **[G: Mexico]**

Loevinger, Lee. Lexonomic Analysis and Antitrust. *Antitrust Bull.*, Summer 1969, *14*, pp. 313–24.

Lundberg, Erik. Structural Change and Market Efficiency. *Acta Oecon.*, 1969, *4*(4), pp. 337–50. **[G: Sweden]**

MacIntyre, A. Everette. The Public Policy of the Robinson-Patman Act and the Commission's New Guides for Advertising Allowances and Other Merchandising Payments and Services. *Antitrust Bull.*, Winter 1969, *14*, pp. 789–802. **[G: U.S.]**

Mann, H. Michael. A Note on Barriers to Entry and Long Run Profitability. *Antitrust Bull.*, Winter 1969, *14*, pp. 845–49. **[G: U.S.]**

Markert, K. E. International Cartels and Legal Order. **In** *Economic Concentration, Pt. 7A, SCH*, 1969, pp. 4103–20. **[G: W. Germany]**

Markert, K. E. The Application of German Antitrust Law to International Restraints on Trade. **In** *Economic Concentration, Pt. 7A, SCH*, 1969, pp. 4091–4103. **[G: W. Germany]**

Markert, Kurt E. The Dyestuff Case: A Contribution to the Relationship between the Antitrust Laws of the European Economic Community and Its Member States. *Antitrust Bull.*, Winter 1969, *14*, pp. 869–99. **[G: E.E.C.]**

Maule, C. J. Antitrust and the Takeover Activity of American Firms in Canada: A Rejoinder. *J. Law Econ.*, October 1969, *12*(2), pp. 419–24. **[G: U.S.; Canada]**

Mead, Walter J. Instantaneous Merger Profit as a Conglomerate Merger Motive. *Western Econ. J.*, December 1969, *7*(4), pp. 295–306. **[G: U.S.]**

Mezines, Basil J. The Robinson-Patman Act: Current Developments. *Antitrust Bull.*, Winter 1969, *14*, pp. 803–12. **[G: U.S.]**

Mickwitz, Gösta. Uudet pankkilait ja pankkiemme kilpailutoiminta. (The New Bank Laws and the Competition among the Banks. With English summary.) *Liiketaloudellinen Aikak.*, 1969, *18* (3), pp. 507–19. **[G: Finland]**

Mouton, D. J. Resale Price Maintenance in the Republic of South Africa. *Antitrust Bull.*, Winter 1969, *14*, pp. 981–1017. **[G: S. Africa]**

Mueller, C. E. Antitrust and Centralization: A Look at the 'Planned' Economy. **In** *Economic Concentration, Pt. 7A, SCH*, 1969, pp. 4371–86.

Mueller, Willard F. Public Policy Toward Mergers in Food Retailing. **In** *Ruttan, V. W.; Waldo, A. D. and Houck, J. P., eds.*, 1969, pp. 186–91. **[G: U.S.]**

Mueller, Willard F. Public Policy Toward Vertical Mergers. **In** *Weston, J. F. and Peltzman, S., eds.*, 1969, pp. 150–66. **[G: U.S.]**

Neale, A. D. The Policy Content of Anti-trust. **In** *Hunter, A., ed.*, 1969, pp. 202–29. **[G: U.S.]**

Nelson, Saul. Antitrust and Economic Efficiency. **In** *Weston, J. F. and Peltzman, S., eds.*, 1969, pp. 57–66. **[G: U.S.]**

Nourse, Edwin G. Government Discipline of Private Economic Power. **In** *Kuhlman, J. M., ed.*, 1969, pp. 240–56. **[G: U.S.]**

O'Brien, Francis A. The Federal Trade Commission's Pre-Merger Notification Requirements. *Antitrust Bull.*, Fall 1969, *14*, pp. 557–85. **[G: U.S.]**

Peltzman, Sam. Issues in Vertical Integration Policy. **In** *Weston, J. F. and Peltzman, S., eds.*, 1969, pp. 167–76. **[G: U.S.]**

Peltzman, Sam. Profit Data and Public Policy. **In** *Weston, J. F. and Peltzman, S., eds.*, 1969, pp. 128–36. **[G: U.S.]**

Pickering, J. F. Would Prices Rise without R.P.M.? *Oxford Econ. Pap.*, July 1969, *21*(2), pp. 248–67. **[G: U.K.]**

Reboul, John W. Horizontal Restraints under the French Antitrust Laws: Competition and Economic Progress. **In** *Economic Concentration, Pt. 7A, SCH*, 1969, pp. 3997–4037. **[G: France]**

Rethwisch, Kurt. A Note on the Presumed Social Desirability of Internal Over External Growth. *Antitrust Bull.*, Winter 1969, *14*, pp. 855–64.

Reuber, Grant L. Antitrust and the Takeover Activity of American Firms in Canada: A Further Analysis. *J. Law Econ.*, October 1969, *12*(2), pp. 405–17. **[G: U.S.; Canada]**

Richardson, J. E. Australian Antitrust and the Decline of American Influence: The Trade Practices Act. **In** *Preston, R., ed.*, 1969, pp. 458–97. **[G: Australia]**

Rill, James F. Robinson-Patman Developments: The Approach of Business Counsel. *Antitrust Bull.*, Winter 1969, *14*, pp. 813–26. **[G: U.S.]**

Robson, Edwin A. Multi-District Litigation: §1407 in Operation. *Antitrust Bull.*, Spring 1969, *14*, pp. 109–18. **[G: U.S.]**

Rostow, E. V. The Development of Law on Monopoly and Competition. **In** *Hunter, A., ed.*, 1969, pp. 161–82.

Rowley, C. K. The Monopolies Commission and Rate of Return on Capital. *Econ. J.*, March 1969,

79(313), pp. 42–65. [G: U.K.]

Schneidau, R. E. and Knutson, Ronald D. Price Discrimination in the Food Industry: A Competitive Stimulant or Tranquilizer? *Amer. J. Agr. Econ.*, December 1969, *51*(5), pp. 1143–48. [G: U.S.]

Schupack, Mark B. Statement. **In** *Role of Giant Corporations, Pt. 1, SCH,* 1969, pp. 492–501. [G: U.S.]

Scott, John C. and Yablonski, Steven K. Transnational Mergers and Joint Ventures Affecting American Exports. *Antitrust Bull.*, Spring 1969, *14*, pp. 1–36. [G: U.S.]

Spector, N. J. Use of FTC's Investigative Function in Antitrust. *Univ. Missouri Bus. Govt. Rev.*, July–August 1969, *10*(4), pp. 13–20. [G: U.S.]

Stern, Louis W. Mergers under Scrutiny. *Harvard Bus. Rev.*, July–August 1969, *47*(4), pp. 18–36, 160–63. [G: U.S.]

Stevens, R. B. and Yamey, B. S. The Justiciability of Restrictive Practices. **In** *Hunter, A., ed.*, 1969, pp. 183–201. [G: U.K.]

Stout, Thomas T. Economics of Conglomerate Growth: Policy Implications for Agriculture. **In** *Garoian, L., ed.*, 1969, pp. 121–22. [G: U.S.]

Stykolt, Stefan. A Note on Economic Activity in the Administrative State. **In** *Stykolt, S.*, 1969, pp. 193–95.

Stykolt, Stefan and Eastman, Harry C. An Evaluation of Trading Stamp Schemes. **In** *Stykolt, S.*, 1969, pp. 141–43. [G: Canada]

Stykolt, Stefan and Bladen, V. W. Combines Policy and the Public Interest: An Economist's Evaluation. **In** *Stykolt, S.*, 1969, pp. 19–54. [G: Canada]

Stykolt, Stefan. Economic Policy and Effective Competition in the Canadian Economy. **In** *Stykolt, S.*, 1969, pp. 3–8. [G: Canada]

Stykolt, Stefan. Federal Government Policy Concerning Market Organization and Regulation. **In** *Stykolt, S.*, 1969, pp. 103–19. [G: Canada]

Stykolt, Stefan. In Defence of the Canadian Consumer. **In** *Stykolt, S.*, 1969, pp. 133–40. [G: Canada]

Stykolt, Stefan. Resale Price Maintenance and the New 'Escape Clause'. **In** *Stykolt, S.*, 1969, pp. 144–45. [G: Canada]

Swann, D. Competition and Price Policies: Britain and the EEC. **In** *van Meerhaeghe, M. A. G., ed.*, 1969, pp. 33–57. [G: E.E.C.; U.K.]

Telser, Lester G. On the Regulation of Industry: A Note. *J. Polit. Econ.*, November/December 1969, *77*(6), pp. 937–52.

Trebing, Harry M. Government Regulation and Modern Capitalism. *J. Econ. Issues*, March 1969, *3*(1), pp. 87–109.

Turner, Donald F. Agricultural Cooperatives and the Antitrust Laws. **In** *Ruttan, V. W.; Waldo, A. D. and Houck, J. P., eds.*, 1969, pp. 192–200. [G: U.S.]

Vacha, S. Against Monopoly Administratively or by Economic Means? **In** *Economic Concentration, Pt. 7A, SCH,* 1969, pp. 4430–33. [G: Czechoslovakia]

Venturini, V. G. Monopolies and Restrictive Trade Practices in Italy. **In** *Economic Concentration, Pt. 7A, SCH,* 1969, pp. 4207–34. [G: Italy]

Vickrey, William S. Decreasing Costs, Publicly Administered Prices, and Economic Efficiency. **In** *The Analysis and Evaluation of Public Expenditures: The PPB System, Vol. 1, JECP,* 1969, pp. 119–48.

Walker, Geoffrey de Q. The Australian Plaintiff and the Sherman Act. *Antitrust Bull.*, Winter 1969, *14*, pp. 901–32.

Weiss, Leonard W. Conglomerate Mergers and Public Policy. **In** *Garoian, L., ed.*, 1969, pp. 88–95. [G: U.S.]

Werner, Robert L. and Hill, John D. Corporate Expansion and the Law. **In** *Harvey, J. L. and Newgarden, A., eds.*, 1969, pp. 49–61. [G: U.S.]

Wesolowski, Zdzislaw P. An Inquiry into the Administration and Utilization of the Webb-Pomerene Act. *Marquette Bus. Rev.*, Winter 1969, *13* (4), pp. 174–88. [G: U.S.]

Weston, J. Fred and Peltzman, Sam. Issues in Public Policy Toward Mergers. **In** *Weston, J. F. and Peltzman, S., eds.*, 1969, pp. 3–9. [G: U.S.]

Weston, J. Fred. Structure, Performance, and Behavior. **In** *Weston, J. F. and Peltzman, S., eds.*, 1969, pp. 67–78. [G: U.S.]

Weston, J. Fred and Peltzman, Sam. Unresolved Issues and an Agenda for Future Research. **In** *Weston, J. F. and Peltzman, S., eds.*, 1969, pp. 227–31. [G: U.S.]

Williamson, Oliver E. Allocative Efficiency and the Limits of Antitrust. *Amer. Econ. Rev.*, May 1969, *59*(2), pp. 105–18.

Williamson, Oliver E. Economies as an Antitrust Defense: Reply. *Amer. Econ. Rev.*, December 1969, *59*(5), pp. 954–59.

Wolf, E. Cartel and Monopoly Legislation: Its Application in the European Economic Community. **In** *Economic Concentration, Pt. 7A, SCH,* 1969, pp. 3944–56. [G: E.E.C.]

Yamamura, K. The Development of Anti-monopoly Policy in Japan: The Erosion of Japanese Antimonopoly Policy, 1947–1967. **In** *Economic Concentration, Pt. 7A, SCH,* 1969, pp. 4273–87. [G: Japan]

613 Public Utilities and Government Regulation of Other Industries in the Private Sector

6130 Public Utilities and Government Regulation of Other Industries in the Private Sector

Aymond, A. H. Reassessment of Economic Standards for the Rate of Return under Regulation: Comment. **In** *Trebing, H. M. and Howard, R. H., eds.*, 1969, pp. 21–25. [G: U.S.]

Barnett, Harold J. and Greenberg, Edward. Regulating CATV Systems: An Analysis of FCC Policy and an Alternative. *Law Contemp. Probl.*, Summer 1969, *34*(3), pp. 562–85. [G: U.S.]

Barrow, Roscoe L. and Manelli, Daniel J. Communications Technology—A Forecast of Change (Part II). *Law Contemp. Probl.*, Summer 1969, *34*(3), pp. 431–51. [G: U.S.]

Barrow, Roscoe L. and Manelli, Daniel J. Communications Technology—A Forecast of Change (Part

I). *Law Contemp. Probl.*, Spring 1969, *34*(2), pp. 205–43.

Berle, A. A. Statement. **In** *Bank Holding Company Act Amendments, Pts. 1–3, HCH,* 1969, pp. 15–20. **[G: U.S.]**

Bertrand, Robert J. Comments on the Williams Paper. *J. Risk Ins.*, June 1969, *36*(2), pp. 237–38. **[G: U.S.]**

Brennan, J. F. A Short Cut to Capital Budget Forecasting for Public Utilities. *Eng. Econ.*, April–May 1969, *14*(3), pp. 151–58.

Brigham, Eugene F. and Pappas, James L. The Effect of Liberalized Depreciation on the Cost of Equity Capital. **In** *Trebing, H. M. and Howard, R. H., eds.*, 1969, pp. 129–58. **[G: U.S.]**

Brown, Gardner, Jr. and Johnson, M. Bruce. Public Utility Pricing and Output under Risk. *Amer. Econ. Rev.*, March 1969, *59*(1), pp. 119–28.

Bryant, Ashbrook P. Historical and Social Aspects of Concentration of Program Control in Television. *Law Contemp. Probl.*, Summer 1969, *34*(3), pp. 610–35. **[G: U.S.]**

Bushnell, Curtis M. Development of Separations Principles in the Telephone Industry (Review Article). *Land Econ.*, August 1969, *45*(3), pp. 381–83. **[G: U.S.]**

Clark, John J. Flags of Convenience and U.S. Maritime Policy. *Rivista Int. Sci. Econ. Com.*, April 1969, *16*(4), pp. 306–26. **[G: U.S.]**

De Salvia, Donald N. An Application of Peak-Load Pricing. *J. Bus.*, October 1969, *42*(4), pp. 458–76. **[G: U.S.]**

Delano, Myles S. The Effects of Leverage and Corporate Taxes on the Shareholders of Regulated Utilities: Comment. **In** *Trebing, H. M. and Howard, R. H., eds.*, 1969, pp. 98–105. **[G: U.S.]**

Dewald, William G. Statement. **In** *Bank Holding Company Act Amendments, Pts. 1–3, HCH,* 1969, pp. 637–46. **[G: U.S.]**

Dodge, Robert H. How Leverage Affects the Cost of Capital to a Public Utility. *Manage. Account.*, August 1969, *51*(2), pp. 39–44.

Dolmans, D. Het aardgas zijn prijsvorming. (Natural Gas and Its Price Determination. With English summary.) *Tijdschr. Econ.*, 1969, *14*(1), pp. 3–27. **[G: Netherlands]**

Dunn, Donald A. Policy Issues Presented by the Interdependence of Computer and Communications Services. *Law Contemp. Probl.*, Spring 1969, *34*(2), pp. 369–88.

Ende, Asher H. International Telecommunications: Dynamics of Regulation of a Rapidly Expanding Service. *Law Contemp. Probl.*, Spring 1969, *34* (2), pp. 389–416. **[G: U.S.]**

Farris, Martin T. Transportation Regulation and Economic Efficiency. *Amer. Econ. Rev.*, May 1969, *59*(2), pp. 244–50.

Fienga, Ruben. Situation and Prospects of the Italian State Railways. *Rev. Econ. Cond. Italy*, September 1969, *23*(5), pp. 397–408. **[G: Italy]**

Fine, Phil David. Statement. **In** *Bank Holding Company Act Amendments, Pts. 1–3, HCH,* 1969, pp. 924–29. **[G: U.S.]**

Ford, J. L. and Warford, J. J. Cost Functions for the Water Industry. *J. Ind. Econ.*, November 1969, *18* (1), pp. 53–63. **[G: U.K.]**

Gaffney, Mason. Economic Aspects of Water Resource Policy. *Amer. J. Econ. Soc.*, April 1969, *28* (2), pp. 131–44. **[G: U.S.]**

Gies, Thomas G. Inflation and the Rate of Return: Comment. **In** *Trebing, H. M. and Howard, R. H., eds.*, 1969, pp. 187–91. **[G: U.S.]**

Goldin, Hyman H. Financing Public Broadcasting. *Law Contemp. Probl.*, Summer 1969, *34*(3), pp. 650–70. **[G: U.S.]**

Gonzalez, Richard J. Federal Policies Dominating U.S. Energy Supplies. **In** *Governmental Intervention in the Market Mechanism, Pt. 1, SCH,* 1969, pp. 385–90. **[G: U.S.]**

Gordon, Myron J. Rate of Return on Equity Capital under Regulation. **In** *Trebing, H. M. and Howard, R. H., eds.*, 1969, pp. 65–72. **[G: U.S.]**

Gray, J. L. Economics of Scale—Generation of Electrical Power. **In** *Hugh-Jones, E. M., ed.*, 1969, pp. 99–112.

Greenberg, Edward. Television Station Profitability and FCC Regulatory Policy. *J. Ind. Econ.*, July 1969, *17*(3), pp. 210–38. **[G: U.S.]**

Gutmann, Peter M. Statement. **In** *Bank Holding Company Act Amendments, Pts. 1–3, HCH,* 1969, pp. 360–64. **[G: U.S.]**

Hamada, Robert S. The Effects of Leverage and Corporate Taxes on the Shareholders of Regulated Utilities. **In** *Trebing, H. M. and Howard, R. H., eds.*, 1969, pp. 73–97. **[G: U.S.]**

Harper, Donald V. Transportation and the Public Utilities: Discussion. *Amer. Econ. Rev.*, May 1969, *59*(2), pp. 270–71.

Harwood, Kenneth. Broadcasting and the Theory of the Firm. *Law Contemp. Probl.*, Summer 1969, *34*(3), pp. 485–504.

Hawkins, Clark A. Optimum Growth of the Regulated Firm. *Western Econ. J.*, June 1969, *7*(2), pp. 187–89.

Henderson, Alexander M. The Pricing of Public Utility Undertakings. **In** *Arrow, K. J. and Scitovsky, T., eds.*, 1969, pp. 541–60.

Hotelling, Harold. The General Welfare in Relation to Problems of Taxation and of Railway and Utility Rates. **In** *Arrow, K. J. and Scitovsky, T., eds.*, 1969, pp. 284–308.

Houghton, Harrison F. Statement. **In** *Bank Holding Company Act Amendments, Pts. 1–3, HCH,* 1969, pp. 350–53. **[G: U.S.]**

Irwin, Manley R. Computers and Communications: The Economics of Interdependence. *Law Contemp. Probl.*, Spring 1969, *34*(2), pp. 360–68.

Irwin, Manley R. The Computer Utility: Market Entry in Search of Public Policy. *J. Ind. Econ.*, July 1969, *17*(3), pp. 239–52. **[G: U.S.]**

Jackson, Raymond. Regulation and Electric Utility Rate Levels. *Land Econ.*, August 1969, *45*(3), pp. 372–76. **[G: U.S.]**

Johnson, Nicholas. Statement. **In** *Bank Holding Company Act Amendments, Pts. 1–3, HCH,* 1969, pp. 240–49. **[G: U.S.]**

Johnson, Nicholas. Towers of Babel: The Chaos in Radio Spectrum Utilization and Allocation. *Law Contemp. Probl.*, Summer 1969, *34*(3), pp. 505–34. **[G: U.S.]**

Kafoglis, Milton Z. and Keig, Norman G. New Policies of the Federal Power Commission. *Land*

Econ., November 1969, *45*(4), pp. 385–91. [G: U.S.]

Karber, James W. Competition and the Regulatory Process. *Quart. Rev. Econ. Bus.*, Autumn 1969, *9* (3), pp. 57–64. [G: U.S.]

Klebaner, Benjamin J. Statement. **In** *Bank Holding Company Act Amendments, Pts. 1–3, HCH,* 1969, pp. 651–54. [G: U.S.]

Kosh, David A. The Effects of Leverage and Corporate Taxes on the Shareholders of Regulated Utilities: Comment. **In** *Trebing, H. M. and Howard, R. H., eds.,* 1969, pp. 106–10. [G: U.S.]

Lerner, Eugene M. and Moag, Joseph S. Information Requirements for Regulatory Decisions. **In** *Trebing, H. M. and Howard, R. H., eds.,* 1969, pp. 195–204. [G: U.S.]

Levin, Harvey J. Broadcast Structure, Technology, and the ABC-ITT Merger Decision. *Law Contemp. Probl.,* Summer 1969, *34*(3), pp. 452–84. [G: U.S.]

Lewis, Ben W. *Performance under Regulation* (Review Article). *Land Econ.,* November 1969, *45*(4), pp. 477. [G: U.S.]

Loescher, Samuel M. Statement. **In** *Bank Holding Company Act Amendments, Pts. 1–3, HCH,* 1969, pp. 370–77. [G: U.S.]

Loevinger, Lee. Lexonomic Analysis and Antitrust. *Antitrust Bull.,* Summer 1969, *14,* pp. 313–24.

Loshing, Clement T. The Effect of Liberalized Depreciation on the Cost of Equity Capital: Comment. **In** *Trebing, H. M. and Howard, R. H., eds.,* 1969, pp. 159–63. [G: U.S.]

Macy, John W., Jr. Public Broadcasting: A Medium in Search of Solutions. *Law Contemp. Probl.,* Summer 1969, *34*(3), pp. 636–49. [G: U.S.]

Markham, Jesse W. Competition in the Nuclear Power Supply Industry—A Reply to Mr. Netschert. *Antitrust Bull.,* Fall 1969, *14,* pp. 657–63. [G: U.S.]

Martin, James W. New Dimensions of the Capitalization of Earnings in Appraising Public Utility Property. **In** *[White, Charles P.],* 1969, pp. 148–63. [G: U.S.]

Martin, William McChesney, Jr. Statement. **In** *Bank Holding Company Act Amendments, Pts. 1–3, HCH,* 1969, pp. 196–202. [G: U.S.]

Meek, Ronald L. A New Bulk Supply Tariff—Reply. *Econ. J.,* December 1969, *79*(316), pp. 974.

Meigs, A. James. Capital Flows to Public Utilities and the Structure of the Money and Capital Markets. **In** *Trebing, H. M. and Howard, R. H., eds.,* 1969, pp. 33–56. [G: U.S.]

Melody, William H. The Effect of Liberalized Depreciation on the Cost of Equity Capital: Comment. **In** *Trebing, H. M. and Howard, R. H., eds.,* 1969, pp. 164–75. [G: U.S.]

Mendelson, Morris. Regulation and Utility Financing. *Land Econ.,* May 1969, *45*(2), pp. 288–92. [G: U.S.]

Minasian, Jora R. The Political Economy of Broadcasting in the 1920's. *J. Law Econ.,* October 1969, *12*(2), pp. 391–403. [G: U.S.]

Morton, Walter A. Risk and Return: Instability of Earnings as a Measure of Risk. *Land Econ.,* May 1969, *45*(2), pp. 229–61. [G: U.S.]

Mueller, Willard F. Statement. **In** *Bank Holding Company Act Amendments, Pts. 1–3, HCH,* 1969, pp. 338–45. [G: U.S.]

Nader, Ralph. Statement. **In** *Bank Holding Company Act Amendments, Pts. 1–3, HCH,* 1969, pp. 262–70. [G: U.S.]

Nelson, Boyd L. Econometrics and Applied Economic Analysis in Regulatory Decisions. *Law Contemp. Probl.,* Spring 1969, *34*(2), pp. 330–39.

Nelson, James R. Reassessment of Economic Standards for the Rate of Return under Regulation. **In** *Trebing, H. M. and Howard, R. H., eds.,* 1969, pp. 3–20. [G: U.S.]

Netschert, Bruce C. Competition in the Nuclear Power Supply Industry—A Rejoinder to Professor Markham. *Antitrust Bull.,* Fall 1969, *14,* pp. 665–66. [G: U.S.]

Netschert, Bruce C. Competition in the Nuclear Power Supply Industry: A Review. *Antitrust Bull.,* Fall 1969, *14,* pp. 629–55. [G: U.S.]

Parsons, Donald H. Statement. **In** *Bank Holding Company Act Amendments, Pts. 1–3, HCH,* 1969, pp. 758–66. [G: U.S.]

Payne, James P., Jr. Regulation of Public Utilities in Louisiana. **In** *Beard, T. R., ed.,* 1969, pp. 148–69. [G: U.S.]

Quigley, Joseph M. The Effects of Leverage and Corporate Taxes on the Shareholders of Regulated Utilities: Comment. **In** *Trebing, H. M. and Howard, R. H., eds.,* 1969, pp. 111–16. [G: U.S.]

Rees, R. A New Bulk Supply Tariff—Comment. *Econ. J.,* December 1969, *79*(316), pp. 973–74.

Robertson, J. L. Statement. **In** *Bank Holding Company Act Amendments, Pts. 1–3, HCH,* 1969, pp. 204–10. [G: U.S.]

Robinson, Roland I. Capital Flows to Public Utilities and the Structure of the Money and Capital Markets: Comment. **In** *Trebing, H. M. and Howard, R. H., eds.,* 1969, pp. 57–61. [G: U.S.]

Scanlon, John J. Inflation and the Rate of Return. **In** *Trebing, H. M. and Howard, R. H., eds.,* 1969, pp. 176–86. [G: U.S.]

Scarato, Russell F. Time-Capacity Expansion of Urban Water Systems. *Water Resources Res.,* October 1969, *5*(5), pp. 929–36.

Schupack, Mark B. Statement. **In** *Bank Holding Company Act Amendments, Pts. 1–3, HCH,* 1969, pp. 1381–87. [G: U.S.]

Spengler, Joseph J. Evolution of Public-Utility Industry Regulation: Economists and Other Determinants. *S. Afr. J. Econ.,* March 1969, *37*(1), pp. 3–31. [G: U.S.]

Spivak, Peter B. Reassessment of Economic Standards for the Rate of Return under Regulation: Comment. **In** *Trebing, H. M. and Howard, R. H., eds.,* 1969, pp. 26–29. [G: U.S.]

Stewart, Richard E. The End of Isolationism in Insurance Regulation. *J. Risk Ins.,* September 1969, *36* (4), pp. 489–92. [G: U.S.]

Stewart, Samuel B. Statement. **In** *Bank Holding Company Act Amendments, Pts. 1–3, HCH,* 1969, pp. 881–99. [G: U.S.]

Takayama, Akira. Behavior of the Firm under Regulatory Constraint. *Amer. Econ. Rev.,* June 1969, *59*(3), pp. 255–60.

Trebing, Harry M. Common Carrier Regulation—The Silent Crisis. *Law Contemp. Probl.,* Spring

1969, *34*(2), pp. 299–329. [G: U.S.]

Verrill, Charles O., Jr. CATV's Emerging Role: Cablecaster or Common Carrier? *Law Contemp. Probl.*, Summer 1969, *34*(3), pp. 586–609. [G: U.S.]

Wald, Haskell P. Information Requirements for Regulatory Decisions: Comment. **In** *Trebing, H. M. and Howard, R. H., eds.*, 1969, pp. 205–11. [G: U.S.]

Webbink, Douglas W. The Impact of UHF Promotion: The All-Channel Television Receiver Law. *Law Contemp. Probl.*, Summer 1969, *34*(3), pp. 535–61. [G: U.S.]

Weston, J. Fred. The Effects of Leverage and Corporate Taxes on the Shareholders of Regulated Utilities: Comment. **In** *Trebing, H. M. and Howard, R. H., eds.*, 1969, pp. 117–25. [G: U.S.]

Williams, C. Arthur, Jr. Insurer Views on Property and Liability Insurance Rate Regulation. *J. Risk Ins.*, June 1969, *36*(2), pp. 217–36. [G: U.S.]

Worcester, Dean A., Jr. Optimal Pricing Policy for Public Utilities as Optimal Taxation: Electric Power and Water. *Philippine Econ. J.*, Second Semester 1969, *8*(2), pp. 145–65. [G: Philippines]

614 Public Enterprises

6140 Public Enterprises

Bailey, Richard. Investment Requirements in Energy. *Nat. Westminster Bank Quart. Rev.*, August 1969, pp. 43–53. [G: U.K.]

Banerji, A. N. Problems of Public Sector Steel Plants. **In** *Dagli, V., ed., Vol. II*, 1969, pp. 126–29. [G: India]

Bauchet, P. The Coherence of Public Enterprises: Planning v. Market Forces. **In** *Margolis, J. and Guitton, H., eds.*, 1969, pp. 462–74.

Edey, H. C. Equity Capital and the Public Corporation. **In** *Carsberg, B. V. and Edey, H. C., eds.*, 1969, pp. 325–33.

Haldi, John. Policy Analysis in the Post Office. **In** *The Analysis and Evaluation of Public Expenditures: The PPB System, Vol. 3, JECP*, 1969, pp. 1151–67. [G: U.S.]

Hinterhuber, Hans. Der Staat als Unternehmer. (The State as Entrepreneur. With English summary.) *Weltwirtsch. Arch.*, 1969, *103*(1), pp. 58–76.

Houssiaux, J. R. Consistency of Action: The Compatibility of Decision-taking by Private and Public Enterprises. **In** *Margolis, J. and Guitton, H., eds.*, 1969, pp. 424–61.

Jochimsen, R. Performance and Respective Spheres of Public and Private Enterprise. **In** *Margolis, J. and Guitton, H., eds.*, 1969, pp. 406–23.

Lal, H. Reflections on Steel Pricing. **In** *Dagli, V., ed., Vol. II*, 1969, pp. 130–39. [G: India]

Mahanti, P. C. Steel: A Balance Sheet. **In** *Dagli, V., ed., Vol. II*, 1969, pp. 171–79. [G: India]

Meade, James E. and Fleming, J. Marcus. Price and Output Policy of State Enterprise: A Symposium. **In** *Arrow, K. J. and Scitovsky, T., eds.*, 1969, pp. 309–24.

Milano, Armando. The Autonomous State Tobacco Concern. *Rev. Econ. Cond. Italy*, September 1969, *23*(5), pp. 409–27. [G: Italy]

Nigam, Raj K. State Government Undertakings. **In** *Dagli, V., ed., Vol. II*, 1969, pp. 207–17. [G: India]

Pellegrini, Giorgio. Toll Motorways. *Rev. Econ. Cond. Italy*, March 1969, *23*(2), pp. 95–105. [G: Italy]

Peston, M. H. Aspects of the Pricing Policy of the Nationalised Industries. **In** *Margolis, J. and Guitton, H., eds.*, 1969, pp. 298–309. [G: U.K.]

Ramanadham, V. V. Softening of Monopoly Power. **In** *Dagli, V., ed., Vol. II*, 1969, pp. 166–70. [G: India]

Stoleru, L. Investment Behaviour Rules and Practices of Public Enterprises. **In** *Margolis, J. and Guitton, H., eds.*, 1969, pp. 276–97. [G: France]

Wickham, S. P. Management and Financial Constraints in Public Enterprise. **In** *Margolis, J. and Guitton, H., eds.*, 1969, pp. 326–35. [G: France]

Zangwill, Willard I. Top Management and the Selection of Major Contractors at NASA. *Calif. Manage. Rev.*, Fall 1969, *12*(1), pp. 43–52. [G: U.S.]

615 Economics of Transportation

6150 Economics of Transportation

Abouchar, Alan. Inflation and Transportation Policy in Brazil. *Econ. Develop. Cult. Change*, Part I, October 1969, *18*(1), pp. 92–109. [G: Brazil]

Abouchar, Alan. Public Investment Allocation and Pricing Policy for Transportation. **In** *Ellis, H. S., ed.*, 1969, pp. 345–75. [G: Brazil]

Abrahamsson, B. J. Recent Developments in International Shipping with Reference to Singapore. *Malayan Econ. Rev.*, October 1969, *14*(2), pp. 26–39. [G: Singapore]

Adler, Hans A. Notes on Feasibility Studies: III. Some Thoughts on Feasibility Studies. *J. Transp. Econ. Policy*, May 1969, *3*(2), pp. 231–36. [G: Thailand]

Aldcroft, Derek H. Innovation on the Railways: The Lag in Diesel and Electric Traction. *J. Transp. Econ. Policy*, January 1969, *3*(1), pp. 96–107. [G: U.K.]

Ameloot, W. De algemene evolutie van het baanvervoer. (The General Evolution of Road Transport. With English summary.) *Econ. Soc. Tijdschr.*, October 1969, *23*(5), pp. 441–54. [G: E.E.C.]

Barsness, Richard W. Policy Challenges and Objectives of the Department of Transportation. *Quart. Rev. Econ. Bus.*, Spring 1969, *9*(1), pp. 63–76. [G: U.S.]

Beesley, M. E. and Politi, Janet. A Study of the Profits of Bus Companies, 1960–1966. *Economica, N.S.*, May 1969, *36*(142), pp. 151–71. [G: U.K.]

Blauwens, G. Haveninvesteringen en kostenbatenanalyse: met een toepassing op Antwerpen L.O. (Port Investments and the Costs Benefit Analysis with Special Reference to the Extension of the Port of Antwerp. With English summary.) *Econ. Soc. Tijdschr.*, October 1969, *23*(5), pp. 495–525.

Boyce, Byrl N. Excess Acquisition Revisited: Control of Land Use at the Interstate Interchange. *Land Econ.*, August 1969, *45*(3), pp. 293–303. [G: U.S.]

Brewer, Stanley H. The Pacific Northwest Battles for

Air Routes. *Univ. Wash. Bus. Rev.*, Spring 1969, *28*(3), pp. 5–20. [G: U.S.]

Brubaker, Earl R. Growth in Soviet Transport and Communications: Note. *Amer. Econ. Rev.*, Part I, September 1969, *59*(4), pp. 622–24. [G: U.S.S.R.]

Burns, Robert E. Transport Planning: Selection of Analytical Techniques. *J. Transp. Econ. Policy*, September 1969, *3*(3), pp. 306–21. [G: W. Pakistan]

Clark, John J. Flags of Convenience and U.S. Maritime Policy. *Rivista Int. Sci. Econ. Com.*, April 1969, *16*(4), pp. 306–26. [G: U.S.]

Córdova, Efrén. Collective Labour Relations in Latin American Ports. *Int. Lab. Rev.*, October 1969, *100*(4), pp. 315–39. [G: Latin America]

Crew, Michael A. Mr. Tipping on Road Pricing. *Econ. J.*, December 1969, *79*(316), pp. 975–77.

David, Paul A. Transport Innovation and Economic Growth: Professor Fogel on and off the Rails. *Econ. Hist. Rev.*, December 1969, *22*(3), pp. 506–25.

Del Viscovo, Mario. Land Transport in 1968. *Rev. Econ. Cond. Italy*, March 1969, *23*(2), pp. 106–15. [G: Italy]

DeSalvo, Joseph S. A Process Function for Rail Linehaul Operations. *J. Transp. Econ. Policy*, January 1969, *3*(1), pp. 3–27.

Eads, George; Nerlove, Marc and Raduchel, William. A Long-Run Cost Function for the Local Service Airline Industry: An Experiment in Non-Linear Estimation. *Rev. Econ. Statist.*, August 1969, *51* (3), pp. 258–70. [G: U.S.]

Edwards, S. L. Transport Costs in the Wholesale Trades. *J. Transp. Econ. Policy*, September 1969, *3*(3), pp. 272–78. [G: U.K.]

Else, P. K. and Howe, M. Cost-Benefit Analysis and the Withdrawal of Railway Services. *J. Transp. Econ. Policy*, May 1969, *3*(2), pp. 178–94. [G: U.K.]

Evans, Andrew W. Intercity Travel and the London Midland Electrification. *J. Transp. Econ. Policy*, January 1969, *3*(1), pp. 69–95. [G: U.K.]

Falkson, Louis Michael. Airline Overbooking: Some Comments. *J. Transp. Econ. Policy*, September 1969, *3*(3), pp. 352–54.

Farris, Martin T. Transportation Regulation and Economic Efficiency. *Amer. Econ. Rev.*, May 1969, *59*(2), pp. 244–50.

Fieleke, Norman S. Toward a More Efficient Railroad System. *New Eng. Econ. Rev.*, March/April 1969, pp. 2–20. [G: U.S.]

Fienga, Ruben. Situation and Prospects of the Italian State Railways. *Rev. Econ. Cond. Italy*, September 1969, *23*(5), pp. 397–408. [G: Italy]

Foss, B. A Cost Model for Coastal Shipping: A Norwegian Example. *J. Transp. Econ. Policy*, May 1969, *3*(2), pp. 195–221. [G: Norway]

Fulton, David C. A Road to the West. *Finance Develop.*, September 1969, *6*(3), pp. 2–7. [G: Honduras]

Gerald, John O. Role of Transportation in Agricultural Marketing and Development: Discussion. *Amer. J. Agr. Econ.*, December 1969, *51*(5), pp. 1478–81. [G: U.S.]

Gifford, J. Morris. Some Considerations Involved in Port Planning Policy. *Econ. Soc. Tijdschr.*, February 1969, *23*(1), pp. 23–32. [G: U.K.]

Gleditsch, Nils Petter. The International Airline Network: A Test of the Zipf and Stouffer Hypotheses. *Peace Res. Soc. Internat. Pap.*, 1969, *11*, pp. 123–53.

Glejser, H. Een toepassing van de kosten–batenanalyse: het project "Zeestad". (Cost-Benefit Analysis of the Project "Zeestad." With English summary.) *Tijdschr. Econ.*, 1969, *14*(4), pp. 519–48. [G: Belgium]

Granfelt, Jarmo. Näkökohtia liikenteen koordinointiongelmasta. (Aspects of the Traffic Coordination Problem. With English summary.) *Liiketaloudellinen Aikak.*, 1969, *18*(2), pp. 121–32.

Gronau, Reuben and Alcaly, Roger E. The Demand for Abstract Transport Modes: Some Misgivings. *J. Reg. Sci.*, April 1969, *9*(1), pp. 153–57.

Hammarskjöld, Knut. The Air Transport Industry—Some Economic Aspects. *Nationalokon. Tidsskr.*, 1969, *107*(1–2), pp. 20–32.

Harbeson, Robert W. Toward Better Resource Allocation in Transport. *J. Law Econ.*, October 1969, *12*(2), pp. 321–38. [G: U.S.]

Harper, Donald V. Transportation and the Public Utilities: Discussion. *Amer. Econ. Rev.*, May 1969, *59*(2), pp. 270–71.

Hazard, John L. Transportation and the Public Utilities: Discussion. *Amer. Econ. Rev.*, May 1969, *59* (2), pp. 271–74.

Hazlewood, Arthur. An Approach to the Analysis of the Spatial Distribution of the Market in East Africa. *Bull. Oxford Univ. Inst. Econ. Statist.*, November 1969, *31*(4), pp. 243–61. [G: E. Africa]

Heggie, Ian G. Notes on Feasibility Studies: I. Road Investment Criteria. *J. Transp. Econ. Policy*, May 1969, *3*(2), pp. 222–24. [G: U.K.]

Hettena, Ran and Ruchlin, Hirsch S. The U.S. Tanker Industry: A Structural and Behavioral Analysis. *J. Ind. Econ.*, July 1969, *17*(3), pp. 188–204. [G: U.S.]

Horn, Johan. Nationalism versus Internationalism in Shipping. *J. Transp. Econ. Policy*, September 1969, *3*(3), pp. 245–50.

Howrey, E. Philip. On the Choice of Forecasting Models for Air Travel. *J. Reg. Sci.*, August 1969, *9*(2), pp. 215–24. [G: U.S.]

Jansson, Jan Owen. Optimal Congestion Tolls for Car Commuters: A Note on Current Theory. *J. Transp. Econ. Policy*, September 1969, *3*(3), pp. 300–305.

Johnson, James F. The Influence of Cost Distance Factors on the Overseas Export of Corn from the United States Midwest. *Econ. Geogr.*, April 1969, *45*(2), pp. 170–79. [G: U.S.]

Jones-Lee, Michael. Valuation of Reduction in Probability of Death by Road Accident. *J. Transp. Econ. Policy*, January 1969, *3*(1), pp. 37–47.

Keith-Lucas, D. The Prospects of 1,000-Passenger Aircraft. In *Hugh-Jones, E. M., ed.*, 1969, pp. 120–34.

Kl'učárová, Mária. Jedna metóda riešenia výrobnorozmiestňovacieho modelu. (A Method for Solving Integrated Production and Distribution Model. With English summary.) *Ekon.-Mat. Obzor*, 1969, *5*(1), pp. 30–44.

Klausner, Robert F. The Evaluation of Risk in Marine Capital Investments. *Eng. Econ.*, July–August 1969, *14*(4), pp. 183–214.

Knowles, J. W. A Process Function for Rail Linehaul Operations: A Note. *J. Transp. Econ. Policy,* September 1969, *3*(3), pp. 350–51.

Knowles, J. W. The Economics of Branch Line Railway Operation in Queensland. *Econ. Rec.*, December 1969, *45*(112), pp. 563–77. **[G: Australia]**

Lauth, James H. Economic Considerations in Rate Making and Rate Structures for Farm Products. *Amer. J. Agr. Econ.*, December 1969, *51*(5), pp. 1464–70. **[G: U.S.]**

Lee, N. and Dalvi, M. Q. Variations in the Value of Travel Time. *Manchester Sch. Econ. Soc. Stud.*, September 1969, *37*(3), pp. 213–36.

Levine, Michael E. Landing Fees and the Airport Congestion Problem. *J. Law Econ.*, April 1969, *12* (1), pp. 79–108. **[G: U.S.]**

Levine, Morton. Adjusting to Technology on the Railroads. *Mon. Lab. Rev.*, November 1969, *92* (11), pp. 36–42. **[G: U.S.]**

Little, Wallace I. An Appraisal of Transportation Regulation in the United States. *Rivista Int. Sci. Econ. Com.*, September 1969, *16*(9), pp. 872–88. **[G: U.S.]**

Lock, Eric Khoo Cheng. Recent Developments in International Shipping with Reference to Singapore: Comment. *Malayan Econ. Rev.*, October 1969, *14*(2), pp. 40–43. **[G: Singapore]**

Long, Wesley H. Airline Service and the Demand for Intercity Air Travel. *J. Transp. Econ. Policy,* September 1969, *3*(3), pp. 287–99. **[G: U.S.]**

Mansfield, N. W. Recreational Trip Generation: A Cross Section Analysis of Weekend Pleasure Trips to the Lake District National Park. *J. Transp. Econ. Policy,* May 1969, *3*(2), pp. 152–64. **[G: U.K.]**

Mercer, Lloyd J. Land Grants to American Railroads: Social Cost or Social Benefit? *Bus. Hist. Rev.*, Summer 1969, *43*(2), pp. 134–51. **[G: U.S.]**

Miklius, Walter. Estimating Freight Traffic of Competing Transportation Modes: An Application of the Linear Discriminant Function. *Land Econ.*, May 1969, *45*(2), pp. 267–73.

Minasian, Jora R. and Eckert, Ross D. The Economics of Airport Use, Congestion, and Safety. *Calif. Manage. Rev.*, Spring 1969, *11*(3), pp. 11–24. **[G: U.S.]**

Mohring, Herbert and Williamson, Harold F., Jr. Scale and "Industrial Reorganisation" Economies of Transport Improvements. *J. Transp. Econ. Policy,* September 1969, *3*(3), pp. 251–71. **[G: U.S.]**

Munro, John M. Planning the Appalachian Development Highway System: Some Critical Questions. *Land Econ.*, May 1969, *45*(2), pp. 149–61. **[G: U.S.]**

Nelson, James R. Policy Analysis in Transportation Programs. **In** *The Analysis and Evaluation of Public Expenditures: The PPB System, Vol. 3, JECP,* 1969, pp. 1102–27. **[G: U.S.]**

Nichols, T. E., Jr. Transportation and Regional Development in Agriculture. *Amer. J. Agr. Econ.*, December 1969, *51*(5), pp. 1455–63.

Ody, J. G. Application of Cost-Benefit Analysis to Airports: The Case of Nicosia, Cyprus. *J. Transp. Econ. Policy,* September 1969, *3*(3), pp. 322–32. **[G: Cyprus]**

Oort, C. J. The Evaluation of Travelling Time. *J. Transp. Econ. Policy,* September 1969, *3*(3), pp. 279–86.

Owen, John D. The Value of Commuter Speed. *Western Econ. J.*, June 1969, *7*(2), pp. 164–72.

Pellegrini, Giorgio. Toll Motorways. *Rev. Econ. Cond. Italy,* March 1969, *23*(2), pp. 95–105. **[G: Italy]**

Perlberg, Arye and Shaal, Gil. An Interdisciplinary Approach to Manpower Planning and Development. *Int. Lab. Rev.*, April 1969, *99*(4), pp. 363–80. **[G: Israel]**

Quandt, Richard E. and Young, Kan Hua. Cross-sectional Travel Demand Models: Estimates and Tests. *J. Reg. Sci.*, August 1969, *9*(2), pp. 201–14. **[G: U.S.]**

Quandt, Richard E. and Baumol, William J. The Demand for Abstract Transport Modes: Some Hopes. *J. Reg. Sci.*, April 1969, *9*(1), pp. 159–62.

Raina, M. K. A Note on Differentiation in Railway Rates. *Indian Econ. J.*, July–September 1969, *17* (1), pp. 129–36. **[G: India]**

Richardson, J. E. American Influence on the Air Transport Industry. **In** *Preston, R., ed.*, 1969, pp. 521–38. **[G: Australia]**

Roberts, Merrill J. Transport Coordination and Distribution Efficiency: Pricing Norms and Profit Potential. *J. Transp. Econ. Policy,* May 1969, *3*(2), pp. 165–77.

Roosens, Paul. De lichte luchtvaart. (The Light Aviation. With English summary.) *Econ. Soc. Tijdschr.*, October 1969, *23*(5), pp. 481–87.

Rust, Charles H. and St. George, George. Transportation Pricing as a Factor in Commodity Marketing: Montana Wheat, A Case Study. *Amer. J. Agr. Econ.*, December 1969, *51*(5), pp. 1471–77. **[G: U.S.]**

Santomé Figueroa, César. La viabilidad economica del puerto de Topolobampo. (Economic Viability of the Topolobampo Port. With English summary.) *Econ. Polít.*, Fourth Semester 1969, *6*(4), pp. 485–94. **[G: Mexico]**

Schneider, Lewis M. The Fallacy of Free Transportation. *Harvard Bus. Rev.*, January–February 1969, *47*(1), pp. 83–87.

Sharp, C. H. Congestion and Welfare—A Reply. *Econ. J.*, June 1969, *79*(314), pp. 407–12.

Sivula, Tarmo. Huolitsijan oikeudellisesta ja taloudellisesta asemasta. (Forwarding Agent's Legal and Economic Position. With English summary.) *Liiketaloudellinen Aikak.*, 1969, *18*(3), pp. 598–607. **[G: Finland]**

Snell, Hampton K. Transportation Integration: A Variety of Problems. **In** *Hilton, R., ed.*, 1969, pp. 321–34. **[G: Latin America]**

Spottiswoode, R. A. Note on Feasibility Studies: II. The Western Nigeria Road Development Survey. *J. Transp. Econ. Policy,* May 1969, *3*(2), pp. 225–30. **[G: Nigeria]**

Srivastava, C. P. Public Sector in Shipping Industry. **In** *Dagli, V., ed., Vol. II,* 1969, pp. 111–16. **[G: India]**

Steiner, Henry Malcolm and Seminario, Adan. Economic Aspects of the Bolivar Highway in Peru. *Eng. Econ.*, January–February 1969, *14*(2), pp. 101–07. **[G: Peru]**

Stonham, P. E. The Demand for Overseas Shipping in the Australian Export Trade. *J. Transp. Econ. Policy,* September 1969, *3*(3), pp. 333–49. **[G: Australia]**

Stonham, P. E. User Costs in Port: An Australian Study. *Australian Econ. Pap.*, December 1969, *8* (13), pp. 178–92. **[G: Australia]**

Suykens, F. Containerization, the Unit Load, the Combination Ship. *Econ. Soc. Tijdschr.*, October 1969, *23*(5), pp. 455–70.

Tipping, David G. Mr. Tipping on Road Pricing—Reply. *Econ. J.*, December 1969, *79*(316), pp. 977–78.

Troy, Patrick and Neutze, Max. Urban Road Planning in Theory and Practice. *J. Transp. Econ. Policy,* May 1969, *3*(2), pp. 139–51. **[G: U.K.]**

Vickrey, William S. Congestion Theory and Transport Investment. *Amer. Econ. Rev.*, May 1969, *59* (2), pp. 251–60.

Vickrey, William S. Current Issues in Transportation. **In** *Chamberlain, N. W., ed.*, 1969, pp. 185–240. **[G: U.S.]**

Wabe, J. S. Commuter Travel into Central London. *J. Transp. Econ. Policy,* January 1969, *3*(1), pp. 48–68. **[G: U.K.]**

Walgreen, John A. Liner Nationality and Steamship Conference Rate-Making. *J. Ind. Econ.*, July 1969, *17*(3), pp. 205–09.

Walters, A. A. The Cost of Using Roads. *Finance Develop.*, March 1969, *6*(1), pp. 16–22.

Wellington, Donald. The Case of the Superfluous Railroads: A Look at Changing Transportation Patterns. *Econ. Bus. Bull.*, Fall 1969, *22*(1), pp. 33–38. **[G: U.S.]**

Wilson, A. G. The Use of Entropy Maximising Models: In the Theory of Trip Distribution, Mode Split and Route Split. *J. Transp. Econ. Policy,* January 1969, *3*(1), pp. 108–26.

Wilson, George W. Transportation and Price Stability. *Amer. Econ. Rev.*, May 1969, *59*(2), pp. 261–69.

Yamada, Hiroyuki and Ihara, Takeo. An Interindustrial Analysis of the Transportation Sector. *Kyoto Univ. Econ. Rev.*, October 1969, *39*(2), pp. 26–61.

Yance, Joseph V. Movement Time as a Cost in Airport Operations. *J. Transp. Econ. Policy,* January 1969, *3*(1), pp. 28–36.

Yance, Joseph V. Transportation and the Public Utilities: Discussion. *Amer. Econ. Rev.*, May 1969, *59*(2), pp. 274–76.

620 Economics of Technological Change

621 Technological Change; Innovation; Research and Development

6210 General

Aldcroft, Derek H. Innovation on the Railways: The Lag in Diesel and Electric Traction. *J. Transp. Econ. Policy,* January 1969, *3*(1), pp. 96–107. **[G: U.K.]**

Arrow, Kenneth J. Classificatory Notes on the Production and Transmission of Technological Knowledge. *Amer. Econ. Rev.*, May 1969, *59*(2), pp. 29–35.

Barrow, Roscoe L. and Manelli, Daniel J. Communications Technology—A Forecast of Change (Part I). *Law Contemp. Probl.*, Spring 1969, *34*(2), pp. 205–43.

Barrow, Roscoe L. and Manelli, Daniel J. Communications Technology—A Forecast of Change (Part II). *Law Contemp. Probl.*, Summer 1969, *34*(3), pp. 431–51. **[G: U.S.]**

Batra, Raveendra N. Activity Analysis and the Pure Theory of International Trade. *Amer. Econ.*, Spring 1969, *13*(1), pp. 16–27.

Biji, Mircea. Dezvoltarea științei în R. S. România. (Development of Science on the Socialist Republic of Romania. With English summary.) *Stud. Cercet. Econ.*, 1969, *3*, pp. 19–28. **[G: Romania]**

Brighi, Massimo. Note sulla struttura dei sistemi. (Remarks on the Structures of Systems. With English summary.) *L'Impresa,* May/June 1969, *11*(3), pp. 258–60. **[G: Italy]**

Brodrick, John. Management and Technology. **In** *Hugh-Jones, E. M., ed.*, 1969, pp. 48–61.

Bronfenbrenner, Martin. Economic Consequences of Technological Change. **In** *Baier, K. and Rescher, N., eds.*, 1969, pp. 453–71.

Brooks, Harvey. Statement. **In** *To Establish a Select Senate Committee on Technology and the Human Environment, SCH,* 1969, pp. 189–95. **[G: U.S.]**

Burns, Tom. Models, Images, and Myths. **In** *Gruber, W. H. and Marquis, D. G., eds.*, 1969, pp. 11–23.

Carli, Guido. La scuola di automazione per dirigenti bancari. (School of Automation for Bank Executives. With English summary.) *Bancaria,* January 1969, *25*(1), pp. 7–8. **[G: Italy]**

Comanor, William S. and Scherer, Frederic M. Patent Statistics as a Measure of Technical Change. *J. Polit. Econ.*, May/June 1969, *77*(3), pp. 392–98. **[G: U.S.]**

Curnow, R. The Innovation Cycle in the Manufacture and Application of Computer Systems. **In** *Arnfield, R. V., ed.*, 1969, pp. 314–20.

David, Lily Mary. Recent Collective Bargaining and Technological Change. **In** *Wortman, M. S., Jr.*, 1969, pp. 194–205. **[G: U.S.]**

De Mattia, Renato. La politica elettronica della Banca d'Italia. (The Bank of Italy's Electronic Policy. With English summary.) *Bancaria,* January 1969, *25*(1), pp. 19–24. **[G: Italy]**

Demsetz, Harold. Information and Efficiency: Another Viewpoint. *J. Law Econ.*, April 1969, *12*(1), pp. 1–22.

Donnem, Roland W. The Antitrust Attack on Restrictive Patent License Provisions. *Antitrust Bull.*, Winter 1969, *14,* pp. 749–66. **[G: U.S.]**

Fried, Louis. The Twilight of the Mechanical Technology. *Calif. Manage. Rev.*, Summer 1969, *11*(4), pp. 63–68.

Gold, Bela. The Framework of Decision for Major Technological Innovation. **In** *Baier, K. and Rescher, N., eds.*, 1969, pp. 389–430.

Gordon, Wendell. Capitalism and Technological

Adaptation in Latin America. *J. Econ. Issues,* March 1969, *3*(1), pp. 66–86. [G: Latin America]

Gruber, William H. The Development and Utilization of Technology in Industry. **In** *Gruber, W. H. and Marquis, D. G., eds.,* 1969, pp. 39–60.

Herman, Leon M. The Cult of Bigness in Soviet Economic Planning. **In** *Economic Concentration, Pt. 7A, SCH,* 1969, pp. 4346–58. [G: U.S.S.R.]

Heyman, Thomas V. Patent Licensing and the Antitrust Laws—A Reappraisal at the Close of the Decade. *Antitrust Bull.,* Fall 1969, *14,* pp. 537–56. [G: U.S.]

Hill, Roger B. The Improvement of Returns from Research and Development Investment. **In** *Hugh-Jones, E. M., ed.,* 1969, pp. 29–47.

Horowitz, Irving Louis. Engineering and Sociological Perspectives on Development: Interdisciplinary Constraints in Social Forecasting. *Int. Soc. Sci. J.,* 1969, *21*(4), pp. 545–56.

Hunter, Maxwell W., II. Are Technological Upheavals Inevitable? *Harvard Bus. Rev.,* September–October 1969, *47*(5), pp. 73–83.

Isenson, Raymond S. Project Hindsight: An Empirical Study of the Sources of Ideas Utilized in Operational Weapon Systems. **In** *Gruber, W. H. and Marquis, D. G., eds.,* 1969, pp. 155–76. [G: U.S.]

Kurihara, Kenneth K. The Antinomic Impact of Automation on Employment and Growth. *Econ. Int.,* August 1969, *22*(3), pp. 423–33.

Le Bihan, Joseph. Vertical Integration and Development of Farms: The Perfecting and Diffusion of Innovations in Integrated Systems. **In** *Papi, U. and Nunn, C., eds.,* 1969, pp. 325–43.

Levin, Harvey J. Broadcast Structure, Technology, and the ABC-ITT Merger Decision. *Law Contemp. Probl.,* Summer 1969, *34*(3), pp. 452–84. [G: U.S.]

Lobato Løpez, Ernesto. Las normas de calidad y el desarrollo de la industria: Segunda parte y última. (Quality Standards and Industrial Development: Second and Last Part. With English summary.) *Econ. Polít.,* Third Semester 1969, *6*(3), pp. 317–30. [G: Mexico]

Marzi, Giorgio. Attualita' dell'ufficio studi. (The Studies Department in the Modern Firm. With English summary.) *L'Impresa,* March/April 1969, *11*(2), pp. 149–51.

Mayo, Louis H. Statement. **In** *To Establish a Select Senate Committee on Technology and the Human Environment, SCH,* 1969, pp. 96–121. [G: U.S.]

Mesthene, Emanuel G. Statement. **In** *To Establish a Select Senate Committee on Technology and the Human Environment, SCH,* 1969, pp. 74–94.

Minasian, Jora R. Research and Development and Other Determinants of Investment: Discussion. *Amer. Econ. Rev.,* May 1969, *59*(2), pp. 86.

Monti, Mario. Moneta, sviluppo economico e progresso tecnico. (Money, Economic Growth and Technical Progress. With English summary.) *L'Industria,* October–December 1969, (4), pp. 475–92.

Mundlak, Yair and Razin, Assaf. Aggregation, Index Numbers and the Measurement of Technical Change. *Rev. Econ. Statist.,* May 1969, *51*(2), pp. 166–75.

Murray, Tracy W. Activity Analysis and the Pure Theory of International Trade: Comment. *Amer. Econ.,* Spring 1969, *13*(1), pp. 27–29.

North, Harper Q. and Pyke, Donald L. 'Probes' of the Technological Future. *Harvard Bus. Rev.,* May–June 1969, *47*(3), pp. 68–82.

Olken, Hyman. Technological Growth and the Evolution of New Industries: The Implications for an Industrial Society. *Econ. Bus. Bull.,* Fall 1969, *22*(1), pp. 15–24.

Petry, Horst. Technischer Fortschritt, Integration, internationale Wettbewerbsfähigkeit und Unternehmensgrösse. (With English summary.) *Jahr. Nationalökon. Statist.,* August 1969, *183*(3–4), pp. 271–99.

Pinder, J. Advanced Technology: Britain and the EEC. **In** *van Meerhaeghe, M. A. G., ed.,* 1969, pp. 58–76. [G: E.E.C.; U.K.]

de Price, Derek J. S. The Structures of Publication in Science and Technology. **In** *Gruber, W. H. and Marquis, D. G., eds.,* 1969, pp. 91–104.

Ray, G. F. The Diffusion of New Technology: A Study of Ten Processes in Nine Industries. *Nat. Inst. Econ. Rev.,* May 1969, (48), pp. 40–83.

Rosenberg, Nathan. The Direction of Technological Change: Inducement Mechanisms and Focusing Devices. *Econ. Develop. Cult. Change,* Part I, October 1969, *18*(1), pp. 1–24.

Schoen, Donald R. Managing Technological Innovation. *Harvard Bus. Rev.,* May–June 1969, *47*(3), pp. 156–67.

Sharma, Baldev R. Technology and Socio-Economic Change. **In** *Johri, C. K., ed.,* 1969, pp. 123–41.

Siebert, Horst. Lern- und suchtheoretische Aspekte neuen technischen Wissens. (Learn Theoretical and Search Theoretical Aspects of New Technical Knowledge. With English summary.) *Schmollers Jahr.,* 1969, *89*(5), pp. 513–39.

Simmons, John L. Technology and Education for Economic Development. **In** *Nader, C. and Zahlan, A. B., eds.,* 1969, pp. 41–59.

Simon, Herbert A. Statement. **In** *To Establish a Select Senate Committee on Technology and the Human Environment, SCH,* 1969, pp. 201–06.

Swackhamer, Gene L. Synthetics and Substitutes: Challenge to Agriculture. *Fed. Res. Bank Kansas City Rev.,* March 1969, pp. 3–12. [G: U.S.]

Tavis, Irene. Futurology and the Problem of Values. *Int. Soc. Sci. J.,* 1969, *21*(4), pp. 574–84.

Wharton, Clifton R., Jr. The Green Revolution: Cornucopia or Pandora's Box? *Foreign Aff.,* April 1969, *47*(3), pp. 464–76.

Wiener, Anthony J. Statement. **In** *To Establish a Select Senate Committee on Technology and the Human Environment, SCH,* 1969, pp. 34–68. [G: U.S.]

6211 Technological Change and Innovation

Acampora, Giovanni. Il "real time" per il servizio conti correnti di corrispondenza: una soluzione organizzativa che offre sicurezza opertiva. ("Real Time" for the Current Accounts Service: An

Organizational Solution Affording Operational Reliability. With English summary.) *Bancaria,* April 1969, *25*(4), pp. 438–48.

Atkinson, Anthony B. and Stiglitz, Joseph E. A New View of Technological Change. *Econ. J.,* September 1969, *79*(315), pp. 573–78.

Baldwin, Robert E. The Case against Infant-Industry Tariff Protection. *J. Polit. Econ.,* May/June 1969, *77*(3), pp. 295–305.

Bardhan, Pranab. Equilibrium Growth in a Model with Economic Obsolescence of Machines. *Quart. J. Econ.,* May 1969, *83*(2), pp. 312–23.

Barger, Harold. Growth in Developed Nations. *Rev. Econ. Statist.,* May 1969, *51*(2), pp. 143–48.

Beckmann, Martin J. and Sato, Ryuzo. Aggregate Production Functions and Types of Technical Progress: A Statistical Analysis. *Amer. Econ. Rev.,* March 1969, *59*(1), pp. 88–101. **[G: U.S.; Japan; Germany]**

Bertrand, T. J. and Vanek, Jaroslav. Growth with Technological Change, Variable Returns to Scale, and a General Saving Function. *Rivista Int. Sci. Econ. Com.,* August 1969, *16*(8), pp. 741–55.

Birg, Herwig. Zu einer allgemeinen Theorie des technischen Fortschritts—Kritik der Definitionen von J. R. Hicks und R. F. Harrod. (With English summary.) *Jahr. Nationalökon. Statist.,* March 1969, *182*(4–5), pp. 327–46.

Britto, R. On Putty-Clay: A Comment. *Rev. Econ. Stud.,* July 1969, *36*(107), pp. 395–98.

Brock, William A. and Gale, David. Optimal Growth under Factor Augmenting Progress. *J. Econ. Theory,* October 1969, *1*(3), pp. 229–43.

Bumas, Lester O. The Effects of an Advance in Technology on Employment in an Industry: A Theoretical Model. *Eng. Econ.,* July–August 1969, *14* (4), pp. 215–20.

Burmeister, Edwin and Dobell, A. Rodney. Disembodied Technological Change with Several Factors. *J. Econ. Theory,* June 1969, *1*(1), pp. 1–8.

Coleman, James; Katz, Elihu and Menzel, Herbert. The Diffusion of an Innovation among Physicians. **In** *Alexis, M.; Holloway, R. J. and Hancock, R. S., eds.,* 1969, pp. 154–67. **[G: U.S.]**

Conklin, D. W. Barriers to Technological Change in the U.S.S.R.: A Study of Chemical Fertilizers. *Soviet Stud.,* January 1969, *20*(3), pp. 353–65. **[G: U.S.S.R.]**

Cukor, Gy. Long-Term Planning and Technical Progress. *Acta Oecon.,* 1969, *4*(3), pp. 239–58. **[G: Hungary]**

Daddario, Emilio Q. Predicting Effects, 1967. **In** *Pursell, C. W., Jr.,* 1969, pp. 447–55. **[G: U.S.]**

Domar, Evsey D. Theory of Innovation: Discussion. *Amer. Econ. Rev.,* May 1969, *59*(2), pp. 44–46.

Fellner, William. Specific Interpretations of Learning by Doing. *J. Econ. Theory,* August 1969, *1*(2), pp. 119–40.

Ferguson, C. E. and Moroney, John R. The Sources of Change in Labor's Relative Share: A Neoclassical Analysis. *Southern Econ. J.,* April 1969, *35*(4), pp. 308–22. **[G: U.S.]**

Fisher, Franklin M.; Levhari, David and Sheshinski, Eytan. On the Sensitivity of the Level of Output to Savings: Embodiment and Disembodiment: A Clarificatory Note. *Quart. J. Econ.,* May 1969, *83* (2), pp. 347–48.

Fleck, Florian H. Wechselwirkungen zwischen dem technischen Fortschritt und den Skalenerträgen—noch einmal unter Berücksichtigung der VES-Produktionsfunktion. (Relationship between Technical Progress and Marginal Returns to Scale. With English summary.) *Schweiz. Z. Volkswirtsch. Statist.,* December 1969, *105*(4), pp. 551–56.

Fransman, Martin J. Technological Change in South African Manufacturing Industry, 1955–1964: A Comment. *S. Afr. J. Econ.,* June 1969, *37*(2), pp. 161–63. **[G: S. Africa]**

Frey, Bruno S. Product and Process Innovations in Economic Growth. *Z. Nationalökon.,* May 1969, *29*(1–2), pp. 29–38.

Grant-Suttie, R. I. Copper Substitution. *Finance Develop.,* June 1969, *6*(2), pp. 49–55.

Greenwald, William. The Multiple Role of Technology in Advanced Industrial Economies. *Rivista Int. Sci. Econ. Com.,* June 1969, *16*(6), pp. 590–97.

Grossfield, Karl. National Interest Aspects of Innovation. **In** *Hugh-Jones, E. M., ed.,* 1969, pp. 14–28. **[G: U.K.]**

Gruber, William H. and Marquis, Donald G. Research on the Human Factor in the Transfer of Technology. **In** *Gruber, W. H. and Marquis, D. G., eds.,* 1969, pp. 255–82.

Guise, John W. B. Factors Associated with Variation in the Aggregate Average Yield of New Zealand Wheat (1918–1967) *Amer. J. Agr. Econ.,* November 1969, *51*(4), pp. 866–81. **[G: New Zealand]**

Hawthorne, E. P. and Willis, R. J. Forecasting the Market for Certain Machine Tools, 1974–1999. **In** *Arnfield, R. V., ed.,* 1969, pp. 241–52.

Hayami, Yūjirō. Resource Endowments and Technological Change in Agriculture: U.S. and Japanese Experiences in International Perspective. *Amer. J. Agr. Econ.,* December 1969, *51*(5), pp. 1293–1303. **[G: U.S.; Japan]**

Heubes, Jürgen. Time-Series CES-Production Functions for Primary Production and Manufacturing, Federal Republic of Germany 1950–1965. *Ger. Econ. Rev.,* 1969, *7*(4), pp. 346–60. **[G: W. Germany]**

Hirsch, Werner Z. Technological Progress and Microeconomic Theory. *Amer. Econ. Rev.,* May 1969, *59*(2), pp. 36–43.

Hoa, Tran Van. Marketing Imperfections and Increasing Returns to Scale in Australian Manufacturing Industry. *Econ. Rec.,* June 1969, *45*(110), pp. 243–50. **[G: Australia]**

Hobbs, J. A. Trend Projection. **In** *Arnfield, R. V., ed.,* 1969, pp. 231–40.

Holländer, Heinz. Eine einfache Begründung zur langfristigen Harrod-Neutralität des technischen Fortschritts. (With English summary.) *Z. ges. Staatswiss.,* April 1969, *125*(2), pp. 236–42.

Hugh-Jones, E. M. The Impact of Technical Change. **In** *Hugh-Jones, E. M., ed.,* 1969, pp. 1–13.

Inada, Ken-Ichi. Endogenous Technical Progress and Steady Growth. *Rev. Econ. Stud.,* January 1969, *36*(105), pp. 99–107.

Inada, Ken-Ichi. Fixed Factor Coefficients and Harrod-Neutral Technical Progress. *Rev. Econ. Stud.*, January 1969, *36*(105), pp. 89–97.

Johnson, Robert E. Technology Licensing in Defense Procurement: A Proposal. **In** *Competition in Defense Procurement, SCH,* 1969, pp. 339–44. **[G: U.S.]**

Kaldor, Nicholas. The Choice of Technology in Less Developed Countries. *Mon. Lab. Rev.*, August 1969, *92*(8), pp. 50–53.

Kalmbach, Peter and Kuhbier, Peter. Beiträge des technischen Fortschritts zum Produktivitätswachstum in Industriebereichen. (The Contribution of Technical Progress to Productivity Growth in Manufacturing Industries. With English summary.) *Ifo-Studien*, 1969, *15*(1/2), pp. 19–55.

Koizumi, Susumu. Technical Progress and Investment. *Int. Econ. Rev.*, February 1969, *10*(1), pp. 68–81.

Leibenstein, Harvey. Organizational or Frictional Equilibria, X-Efficiency, and the Rate of Innovation. *Quart. J. Econ.*, November 1969, *83*(4), pp. 600–23.

Levhari, David and Sheshinski, Eytan. The Relation between the Rate of Return and the Rate of Technical Progress. *Rev. Econ. Stud.*, July 1969, *36* (107), pp. 363–79.

Levine, Morton. Adjusting to Technology on the Railroads. *Mon. Lab. Rev.*, November 1969, *92* (11), pp. 36–42. **[G: U.S.]**

Li-tien, Feng and Chien, Wen. A Quantitative Analysis of the Relationship Between the Rate of Growth of Productivity and the Average Wage. *Chinese Econ. Stud.*, Fall 1969, *3*(1), pp. 70–91. **[G: China]**

Lovell, C. A. Knox. Biased Technical Change and Factor Shares in United States Manufacturing. *Quart. Rev. Econ. Bus.*, Autumn 1969, *9*(3), pp. 17–33. **[G: U.S.]**

Lydall, Harold. On Measuring Technical Progress. *Australian Econ. Pap.*, June 1969, *8*(12), pp. 1–12. **[G: U.K.]**

Maevskii, I. Socioeconomic Questions Relating to Automation. *Prob. Econ.*, October 1969, *12*(6), pp. 3–26.

de Meester, J.-C. Fonctions de production et données technologiques. (Production Functions and Technological Data. With English summary.) *Rivista Int. Sci. Econ. Com.*, January 1969, *16*(1), pp. 31–45.

Mekhanik, G. Social Costs of the Scientific-Technical Revolution under Capitalism. *Prob. Econ.*, December 1969, *12*(8), pp. 3–22. **[G: U.S.]**

Melvin, James R. Intermediate Goods and Technological Change. *Economica, N.S.*, November 1969, *36*(144), pp. 400–408.

Montuschi, Luisa. Progreso technológico y rendimientos crecientes en el sector manufacturero argentino: La productividad de las inversiones en la década del 50. (Technical Progress and Increasing Returns in the Manfacturing Sector of Argentina. With English summary.) *Económica*, January–April 1969, *15*(1), pp. 93–110. **[G: Argentina]**

Murray, Lionel. Trade Unions and Technical Change. **In** *Hugh-Jones, E. M., ed.*, 1969, pp. 135–50. **[G: U.K.]**

Nevel, Robert O. Technological Change in Agriculture. *Agr. Econ. Res.*, January 1969, *21*(1), pp. 13–18. **[G: U.S.]**

Nikolitch, Radoje. Family-Operated Farms: Their Compatibility with Technological Advance. *Amer. J. Agr. Econ.*, August 1969, *51*(3), pp. 530–45. **[G: U.S.]**

Nordhaus, William D. An Economic Theory of Technological Change. *Amer. Econ. Rev.*, May 1969, *59*(2), pp. 18–28. **[G: U.S.]**

Pack, Howard and Todaro, Michael P. Technological Transfer, Labour Absorption, and Economic Development. *Oxford Econ. Pap.*, November 1969, *21*(3), pp. 395–403.

Palmerio, Giovanni. Economie di scala e progresso tecnico incorporato nel settore industriale in Italia nel periodo 1951–1965. (Economies of Scale and Embodied Technical Progress in the Italian Industry—1951–1965. With English summary.) *L'Industria*, July–September 1969, (3), pp. 316–46. **[G: Italy]**

Piganiol, Pierre. Introduction: Futurology and Prospective Study. *Int. Soc. Sci. J.*, 1969, *21*(4), pp. 515–25.

Price, William J.; Ashley, William G. and Martino, Joseph P. Science-Technology Coupling: Experience of the Air Force Office of Scientific Research. **In** *Gruber, W. H. and Marquis, D. G., eds.*, 1969, pp. 117–36. **[G: U.S.]**

Quinn, James Brian. Technology Transfer by Multinational Companies. *Harvard Bus. Rev.*, November–December 1969, *47*(6), pp. 147–61.

Reiss, Howard. Human Factors at the Science-Technology Interface. **In** *Gruber, W. H. and Marquis, D. G., eds.*, 1969, pp. 105–16.

Richta, Radovan and Šulc, Ota. Forecasting and the Scientific and Technological Revolution. *Int. Soc. Sci. J.*, 1969, *21*(4), pp. 563–73.

Roberts, Edward B. Entrepreneurship and Technology. **In** *Gruber, W. H. and Marquis, D. G., eds.*, 1969, pp. 219–37. **[G: U.S.]**

Rothberg, Herman J. A Study of the Impact of Office Automation in the IRS. *Mon. Lab. Rev.*, October 1969, *92*(10), pp. 26–30. **[G: U.S.]**

Sansom, Robert L. The Motor Pump: A Case Study of Innovation and Development. *Oxford Econ. Pap.*, March 1969, *21*(1), pp. 109–21. **[G: S. Vietnam]**

Scott, John T., Jr. and Reiss, Franklin J. Changing Technology and Lease Adjustment: Theory and Practice. *Land Econ.*, November 1969, *45*(4), pp. 400–405.

Simush, P. I. The Impact of the Scientific and Technological Revolution on the Socialist Village. *Int. Soc. Sci. J.*, 1969, *21*(2), pp. 256–64. **[G: U.S.S.R.]**

Singh, Tarlok. On Planning Technological Change in Indian Agriculture. *Int. Soc. Sci. J.*, 1969, *21*(2), pp. 265–71. **[G: India]**

Slen, S. B. and Cameron, M. A. Prospects and Potentials in Canadian Beef Production. *Can. J. Agr. Econ.*, November 1969, *17*(3), pp. 80–89. **[G: Canada]**

Stiglitz, Joseph E. Theory of Innovation: Discussion.

Amer. Econ. Rev., May 1969, *59*(2), pp. 46–49.

Streissler, Erich. Long Term Structural Changes in the Distribution of Income. *Z. Nationalökon.,* May 1969, *29*(1–2), pp. 39–110.

Verma, Pramod. Patents in British Industry: A Note. *Yorkshire Bull. Econ. Soc. Res.,* November 1969, *21*(2), pp. 114–18. [G: U.K.]

von Weizsäcker, Carl Christian. Forschungsinvestitionen und makroökonomische Modelle—Ein wirtschaftstheoretisches Dilemma? (With English summary.) *Kyklos,* 1969, *22*(3), pp. 454–66.

Wright, Philip. Government Efforts to Facilitate Technical Transfer: The NASA Experience. **In** *Gruber, W. H. and Marquis, D. G., eds.,* 1969, pp. 238–51. [G: U.S.]

Yeh, M. H. and Lin, Leon. Technological Change in the Canadian Livestock Industry: An Input-Output Approach. *Can. J. Agr. Econ.,* July 1969, *17*(2), pp. 63–84. [G: Canada]

Yoshihara, Hideki. A Note on the Behavioral Theory of Innovation. *Kobe Econ. Bus. Rev.,* 1969, *16*(1), pp. 55–61.

6212 Research and Development

Andarawewa, A. B. Evaluation of Public Research Programs in Agriculture. *Can. J. Agr. Econ.,* November 1969, *17*(3), pp. 157–69. [G: Canada]

Baldwin, William L. and Childs, Gerald L. The Fast Second and Rivalry in Research and Development. *Southern Econ. J.,* July 1969, *36*(1), pp. 18–24.

Bauer, Larry L. The Effect of Technology on the Farm Labor Market. *Amer. J. Agr. Econ.,* August 1969, *51*(3), pp. 605–18. [G: U.S.]

Black, Guy. The Effect of Government Funding on Commercial R and D. **In** *Gruber, W. H. and Marquis, D. G., eds.,* 1969, pp. 202–18. [G: U.S.]

Brown, A. W. The Economic Benefits to Australia from Atomic Absorption Spectroscopy. *Econ. Rec.,* June 1969, *45*(110), pp. 158–80. [G: Australia]

Burley, S. Peter and Morgenstern, Oskar. Insiders and Outsiders in Industrial Research. *Z. ges. Staatswiss.,* April 1969, *125*(2), pp. 193–201.

Coates, David R. Technological Forecasting and the Planning of R and D. **In** *Arnfield, R. V., ed.,* 1969, pp. 83–96.

Davies, R. W. Science and the Soviet Economy. **In** *Economic Concentration, Pt. 7A, SCH,* 1969, pp. 4332–45. [G: U.S.S.R.]

Feldstein, Martin S. Advertising, Research and Profits in the Drug Industry. *Southern Econ. J.,* January 1969, *35*(3), pp. 239–43. [G: U.S.]

Golosovskii, S. Determination of the Economic Effect of Scientific Research and New Technology. *Prob. Econ.,* January 1969, *11*(9), pp. 24–33. [G: U.S.S.R.]

Hollomon, J. Herbert. Keeping the Economy Strong, 1963. **In** *Pursell, C. W., Jr.,* 1969, pp. 424–30. [G: U.S.]

Johnson, P. S. Research in Britain Today. *Lloyds Bank Rev.,* October 1969, (94), pp. 34–49. [G: U.K.]

Lutoslanski, Z. The Role of R and D Units in Long-Range Planning of Technological Development in Poland. **In** *Arnfield, R. V., ed.,* 1969, pp. 112–28. [G: Poland]

Mansfield, Edwin. Industrial Research and Development: Characteristics, Costs, and Diffusion of Results. *Amer. Econ. Rev.,* May 1969, *59*(2), pp. 65–71. [G: U.S.]

Minasian, Jora R. Research and Development, Production Functions, and Rates of Return. *Amer. Econ. Rev.,* May 1969, *59*(2), pp. 80–85. [G: U.S.]

Orton, Bryce B. and Bradish, Richard D. The Treatment and Disclosure of Research and Development Expenditures. *Manage. Account.,* July 1969, *51*(1), pp. 31–34.

Shapero, Albert. Effects of Government R and D Contracting on Mobility and Regional Resources. **In** *Gruber, W. H. and Marquis, D. G., eds.,* 1969, pp. 179–201. [G: U.S.]

Silva, Donald H. State Technical Service—An Emerging Social System. *Amer. J. Econ. Soc.,* October 1969, *28*(4), pp. 399–403. [G: U.S.]

630 INDUSTRY STUDIES

6300 General

Beika, Minoru. The Change in Regional Characteristics of Industries in Japan. *Kobe Econ. Bus. Rev.,* 1969, *16*(1), pp. 1–18. [G: Japan]

Chandler, Alfred D., Jr. The Structure of American Industry in the Twentieth Century: A Historical Overview. *Bus. Hist. Rev.,* Autumn 1969, *43*(3), pp. 255–98. [G: U.S.]

Filippi, Enrico. Le duecento maggiori società industriali italiane. (The 200 Largest Italian Industrial Corporations. With English summary.) *L'Impresa,* January/February 1969, *11*(1), pp. 41–55. [G: Italy]

Fredman, Albert J. Stockholders' Returns: Dividends or Earnings? *Miss. Val. J. Bus. Econ.,* Fall 1969, *5*(1), pp. 23–33. [G: U.S.]

Frisch, Uwe G. and Malagón, Oscar M. La concentracion territorial de la industria en Mexico. (Territorial Concentration of Industry in Mexico. With English summary.) *Econ. Polít.,* Second Semester 1969, *6*(2), pp. 195–208. [G: Mexico]

Gibbins, Ronald W. American Influence on Commercial Practice. **In** *Preston, R., ed.,* 1969, pp. 498–520. [G: Australia]

Heubes, Jürgen. Time-Series CES-Production Functions for Primary Production and Manufacturing, Federal Republic of Germany 1950–1965. *Ger. Econ. Rev.,* 1969, *7*(4), pp. 346–60. [G: W. Germany]

Kulkarni, Vijay G. The Growth of Indian Industries (1951–1965). **In** *Bhuleshkar, A. V., ed.,* 1969, pp. 259–70. [G: India]

Ray, G. F. The Diffusion of New Technology: A Study of Ten Processes in Nine Industries. *Nat. Inst. Econ. Rev.,* May 1969, (48), pp. 40–83.

Rosenberg, Leonard Gerson. Taxation of Income from Capital, by Industry Group. **In** *Harberger, A. C. and Bailey, M. J., eds.,* 1969, pp. 123–84. [G: U.S.]

de Vries, Barend A. High Cost of Industry in Developing Countries—Causes and Remedies. *Finance Develop.*, December 1969, *6*(4), pp. 43–47.

631 Industry Studies: Manufacturing

6310 General

Benet, I. and Berend, I. Relative Capital Intensity of Food Production and Industry. *Acta Oecon.*, 1969, *4*(4), pp. 379–402. **[G: Hungary]**

Brozen, Yale. Barriers Facilitate Entry. *Antitrust Bull.*, Winter 1969, *14*, pp. 851–54. **[G: U.S.]**

Childress, Robert L. and Yost, Robert C. An Investigation of the Determinants of Investment Expenditures in Large, Multiproduct Corporations. *Western Econ. J.*, June 1969, *7*(2), pp. 173–79. **[G: U.S.]**

Clague, Christopher K. Capital-Labor Substitution in Manufacturing in Undeveloped Countries. *Econometrica*, July 1969, *37*(3), pp. 528–37. **[G: Peru]**

Courchene, Thomas J. An Analysis of the Price-Inventory Nexus with Empirical Application to the Canadian Manufacturing Sector. *Int. Econ. Rev.*, October 1969, *10*(3), pp. 315–36. **[G: Canada]**

Desai, Padma. Growth and Structural Change in the Indian Manufacturing Sector: 1951–1963. *Indian Econ. J.*, October–December 1969, *17*(2), pp. 205–33. **[G: India]**

Eisner, Robert. Investment and the Frustrations of Econometricians. *Amer. Econ. Rev.*, May 1969, *59*(2), pp. 50–64. **[G: U.S.]**

Eysenbach, M. L. A Note on Growth and Structural Change in Pakistan's Manufacturing Industry 1954–1964. *Pakistan Develop. Rev.*, Spring 1969, *9*(1), pp. 58–65. **[G: Pakistan]**

Ferguson, C. E. and Moroney, John R. The Sources of Change in Labor's Relative Share: A Neoclassical Analysis. *Southern Econ. J.*, April 1969, *35*(4), pp. 308–22. **[G: U.S.]**

Fransman, Martin J. Technological Change in South African Manufacturing Industry, 1955–1964: A Comment. *S. Afr. J. Econ.*, June 1969, *37*(2), pp. 161–63. **[G: S. Africa]**

Glynn, D. R. The CBI Industrial Trends Survey. *Appl. Econ.*, August 1969, *1*(3), pp. 183–96. **[G: U.K.]**

Gujarati, Damodar. Labor's Share in Manufacturing Industries, 1949–64. *Ind. Lab. Relat. Rev.*, October 1969, *23*(1), pp. 65–77. **[G: U.S.]**

Gupta, Manak C. The Effect of Size, Growth, and Industry on the Financial Structure of Manufacturing Companies. *J. Finance*, June 1969, *24*(3), pp. 517–29. **[G: U.S.]**

Hoa, Tran Van. Marketing Imperfections and Increasing Returns to Scale in Australian Manufacturing Industry. *Econ. Rec.*, June 1969, *45*(110), pp. 243–50. **[G: Australia]**

Kinyon, John. A Report on Wage Developments in Manufacturing, 1968. *Mon. Lab. Rev.*, August 1969, *92*(8), pp. 33–39. **[G: U.S.]**

Lieberman, A. E. Updating Impressions of the Military-Industry Complex. *Calif. Manage. Rev.*, Summer 1969, *11*(4), pp. 51–62. **[G: U.S.]**

Llosas, Hernán P. La política de promoción industrial y de desarrollo regional en la Argentina, 1959–1966. (The Argentinian Government's Policy for the Promotion of Particular Industrial Sectors and for the Development of Some of the Country's Regions, 1959–1966. With English summary.) *Económica*, January–April 1969, *15*(1), pp. 39–91. **[G: Argentina]**

Lovell, C. A. Knox. Biased Technical Change and Factor Shares in United States Manufacturing. *Quart. Rev. Econ. Bus.*, Autumn 1969, *9*(3), pp. 17–33. **[G: U.S.]**

Lucas, Robert E., Jr. Labor-Capital Substitution in U.S. Manufacturing. **In** *Harberger, A. C. and Bailey, M. J., eds.*, 1969, pp. 223–74. **[G: U.S.]**

Mann, H. Michael. A Note on Barriers to Entry and Long Run Profitability. *Antitrust Bull.*, Winter 1969, *14*, pp. 845–49. **[G: U.S.]**

Masters, Stanley H. An Interindustry Analysis of Wages and Plant Size. *Rev. Econ. Statist.*, August 1969, *51*(3), pp. 341–45. **[G: U.S.]**

Matassi, Luigi. The Italian Economy after World War II. *Rev. Econ. Cond. Italy*, September 1969, *23*(5), pp. 428–42. **[G: Italy]**

Mehta, B. V. Size and Capital Intensity in Indian Industry. *Bull. Oxford Univ. Inst. Econ. Statist.*, August 1969, *31*(3), pp. 189–204. **[G: India]**

Moroney, John R. Economies of Scale in Manufacturing. **In** *Watson, D. S., ed.*, 1969, pp. 116–24. **[G: U.S.]**

Moroney, John R. and Allen, Bruce T. Monopoly Power and the Relative Share of Labor. *Ind. Lab. Relat. Rev.*, January 1969, *22*(2), pp. 167–78. **[G: U.S.]**

Nadiri, M. Ishag and Rosen, Sherwin. Interrelated Factor Demand Functions. *Amer. Econ. Rev.*, Part I, September 1969, *59*(4), pp. 457–71. **[G: U.S.]**

Nadiri, M. Ishag. The Determinants of Real Cash Balances in the U.S. Total Manufacturing Sector. *Quart. J. Econ.*, May 1969, *83*(2), pp. 173–96. **[G: U.S.]**

Nadiri, M. Ishag. The Determinants of Trade Credit in the U.S. Total Manufacturing Sector. *Econometrica*, July 1969, *37*(3), pp. 408–23.

Palmerio, Giovanni. Economie di scala e progresso tecnico incorporato nel settore industriale in Italia nel periodo 1951–1965. (Economies of Scale and Embodied Technical Progress in the Italian Industry—1951–1965. With English summary.) *L'Industria*, July–September 1969, (3), pp. 316–46. **[G: Italy]**

Phipps, Anthony J. The Roles of Labour Productivity and Demand in the Pricing Process: An Inter-Industry Study Using Time-Series Data. *Bull. Oxford Univ. Inst. Econ. Statist.*, November 1969, *31*(4), pp. 285–301. **[G: U.K.]**

Pratten, C. F. Economies of Scale. **In** *Hugh-Jones, E. M., ed.*, 1969, pp. 89–98.

Reid, David J. The CBI Industrial Trends Survey—A Statistical Note. *Appl. Econ.*, August 1969, *1*(3), pp. 197–203. **[G: U.K.]**

Román, Zoltán. Pattern of the Hungarian Industry. *Acta Oecon.*, 1969, *4*(2), pp. 181–95. **[G: Hungary]**

Sandesara, J. C. Size and Capital-Intensity in Indian

Industry: Some Comments. *Bull. Oxford Univ. Inst. Econ. Statist.*, November 1969, *31*(4), pp. 331–34. [G: India]

Scully, Gerald W. Human Capital and Productivity in U.S. Manufacturing. *Western Econ. J.*, December 1969, *7*(4), pp. 334–40. [G: U.S.]

Smyth, David J. and Briscoe, G. Investment Plans and Realizations in United Kingdom Manufacturing. *Economica, N.S.*, August 1969, *36*(143), pp. 277–94. [G: U.K.]

Stelluto, George L. Report on Incentive Pay in Manufacturing Industries. *Mon. Lab. Rev.*, July 1969, *92*(7), pp. 49–53. [G: U.S.]

Verma, Pramod. Patents in British Industry: A Note. *Yorkshire Bull. Econ. Soc. Res.*, November 1969, *21*(2), pp. 114–18. [G: U.K.]

Viita, Pentti. Investoinnit ja maksutase. (Investments and the Balance of Payments. With English summary.) *Kansant. Aikak.*, 1969, *65*(3), pp. 233. [G: Finland]

Weiss, Leonard W. Advertising, Profits, and Corporate Taxes. *Rev. Econ. Statist.*, November 1969, *51*(4), pp. 421–30. [G: U.S.]

Young, A. Patterns of Development in Zambian Manufacturing Industry since Independence. *East Afr. Econ. Rev.*, December 1969, *1*(2), pp. 29–38. [G: Zambia]

Zaidi, Mahmood A. The Determinants of Money Wage Rate Changes and Unemployment-Inflation "Trade-Offs" in Canada. *Int. Econ. Rev.*, June 1969, *10*(2), pp. 207–19. [G: Canada]

6312 Metals (iron, steel, and other)

Baer, Werner. Steel and the Brazilian Economy. **In** *Ellis, H. S., ed.*, 1969, pp. 74–102. [G: Brazil]

Banerji, A. N. Problems of Public Sector Steel Plants. **In** *Dagli, V., ed., Vol. II*, 1969, pp. 126–29. [G: India]

Blomqvist, Ingvar. Strukturproblem inom metallindustrin. (Structural Problems in the Metal Industry. With English summary.) *Econ. Samfundets Tidskr.*, 1969, *22*(3), pp. 151–63. [G: Finland]

Grant-Suttie, R. I. Copper Substitution. *Finance Develop.*, June 1969, *6*(2), pp. 49–55.

Gray, Irwin. Employment Effect of a New Industry in a Rural Area. *Mon. Lab. Rev.*, June 1969, *92*(6), pp. 26–30. [G: U.S.]

Heineke, J. M. Demand for Refined Lead. *Rev. Econ. Statist.*, August 1969, *51*(3), pp. 374–78. [G: U.S.]

Jackman, Patrick C. Unit Labor Costs of Iron and Steel Industries in Five Countries. *Mon. Lab. Rev.*, August 1969, *92*(8), pp. 15–22. [G: W. Germany; France; U.K.; U.S.; Japan]

Lomax, Alfred L. Big Steel Mill Comes to Portland. *Oregon Bus. Rev.*, April 1969, *28*(4), pp. 1, 3. [G: U.S.]

Mahanti, P. C. Steel: A Balance Sheet. **In** *Dagli, V., ed., Vol. II*, 1969, pp. 171–79. [G: India]

Mueller, Hans G. Recent Costs Trends in the Steel Industries of the United States, Japan and the European Community. *Econ. Int.*, August 1969, *22*(3), pp. 499–526. [G: U.S.; Japan; E.E.C.]

Mueller, Hans G. The Policy of the European Coal and Steel Community Towards Mergers and Agreements by Steel Companies. *Antitrust Bull.*, Summer 1969, *14*, pp. 413–48. [G: E.E.C.]

Rowan, Richard L. Negro Employment in the Basic Steel Industry. *Ind. Lab. Relat. Rev.*, October 1969, *23*(1), pp. 29–39. [G: U.S.]

Ruist, Erik. Den nordiska stålindustrin inför världsmarknaden. (The Scandanavian Steel Industry and the World Market. With English summary.) *Econ. Samfundets Tidskr.*, 1969, *22*(3), pp. 164–80. [G: Scandanavia]

Smith, C. Selby. Benefits to British Employers from Post-secondary Education. *J. Roy. Statist. Soc.*, Part 3, 1969, *132*, pp. 408–17. [G: U.K.]

6313 Machinery (tools, electrical equipment, and appliances)

Ghosh, Arabinda and Sarkar, Anil Kumar. Size Structure of Indian Engineering Industries, 1948–61. *Indian Econ. J.*, January–March 1969, *16*(3), pp. 375–81. [G: India]

Hays, S.; Hemming, M. F. W. and Ray, G. F. The Office Machinery Industry in the United Kingdom. *Nat. Inst. Econ. Rev.*, August 1969, (49), pp. 52–73. [G: U.K.]

Patil, S. M. Prospects for Machine Tool Exports. **In** *Dagli, V., ed., Vol. II*, 1969, pp. 180–89. [G: India]

Peterson, R. D. and Leister, D. V. Market Structure-Conduct Relations: Some Evidence from Biomedical Electronic Firms. *Univ. Wash. Bus. Rev.*, Summer 1969, *28*(4), pp. 49–65. [G: U.S.]

Sampson, Anthony A. Measuring the Rate of Return on Capital. *J. Finance*, March 1969, *24*(1), pp. 61–74. [G: U.K.]

Sarma, L. V. L. N. and Rao, R. S. Hanumanta. Estimates of the Cost of Capital to the Indian Engineering Industry, 1962–65. *Yorkshire Bull. Econ. Soc. Res.*, November 1969, *21*(2), pp. 132–40. [G: India]

Swayambu, S. Role of H. E. L. in Power Development. **In** *Dagli, V., ed., Vol. II*, 1969, pp. 190–94. [G: India]

Walter, Emil J. Statistische Erhebungen über die Verbreitung von elektronischen Datenverarbeitungsanlagen (EDV) in der Schweiz. (Statistical Enquiries in Regard to the Diffusion in Switzerland of Electronic Installations for the Analysis of Information (IED). With English summary.) *Schweiz. Z. Volkswirtsch. Statist.*, December 1969, *105*(4), pp. 515–33. [G: Switzerland]

6314 Transportation and Communication Equipment

Adams, Walter. Planning, Regulation, and Competition. **In** *Kuhlman, J. M., ed.*, 1969, pp. 233–38. [G: U.S.]

Cordtz, Dan. How Auto Firms Figure Their Cost to Reckon the Price Dealers Pay. **In** *Alexis, M.; Holloway, R. J. and Hancock, R. S., eds.*, 1969, pp. 335–42. [G: U.S.]

Dempsey, Richard E. and Schmude, Douglas F. How Consumer Spending for Automobiles Creates Jobs. *Mon. Lab. Rev.*, March 1969, *92*(3), pp.

33–36. [G: U.S.]

Galbraith, John Kenneth. Planning, Regulation, and Competition. In *Kuhlman, J. M., ed.,* 1969, pp. 227–33. [G: U.S.]

Henneberger, John E. Productivity Rises as Radio-TV Output Triples in 8 Years. *Mon. Lab. Rev.,* March 1969, *92*(3), pp. 40–42. [G: U.S.]

Karssen, W. J. Concentration of the Automobile Industry of the E.E.C. In *Economic Concentration, Pt. 7A, SCH,* 1969, pp. 3915–25. [G: E.E.C.]

Kravis, Irving B. and Lipsey, Robert E. International Price Comparisons by Regression Methods. *Int. Econ. Rev.,* June 1969, *10*(2), pp. 233–46.

Leonard, William N. Statement. In *Automotive Repair Industry, Pt. 1, SCH,* 1969, pp. 4–50. [G: U.S.]

Morrisse, Kathryn A. Automotive Trade between the United States and Canada. (Study summary.) *Fed. Res. Bull.,* November 1969, *55*(11), pp. 877–78. [G: U.S.; Canada]

Munk, Bernard. The Welfare Costs of Content Protection: The Automotive Industry in Latin America. *J. Polit. Econ.,* January/February 1969, *77*(1), pp. 85–98. [G: Latin America]

Myslicki, Chester. Report on Productivity Increases in the Auto Industry. *Mon. Lab. Rev.,* March 1969, *92*(3), pp. 37–39. [G: U.S.]

Northrup, Herbert R. The Negro in Aerospace Work. *Calif. Manage. Rev.,* Summer 1969, *11*(4), pp. 11–26. [G: U.S.]

Pike, Eugene W. A Note on "Learning Curves." *J. Amer. Statist. Assoc.,* December 1969, *64*(328), pp. 1276–77.

Quintero Briseño, Jesús. La integración de la industria automovilística en Mexico. (Integration of the Automotive Industry in Mexico. With English summary.) *Econ. Polít.,* Fourth Semester 1969, *6*(4), pp. 473–84. [G: Mexico]

Van Tatenhove, James M. Managing Indirect Costs in the Aerospace Industry. *Manage. Account.,* September 1969, *51*(3), pp. 36–42, 48.

6315 Chemicals, Drugs, Plastics, Ceramics, Glass, and Rubber

Aczel, J. A. The Usefulness of the CBI Industrial Trends Survey for Forecasting in the Chemical Industry. *Appl. Econ.,* August 1969, *1*(3), pp. 205–10. [G: U.K.]

Bain, Trevor. Flat Glass: "Industrial Peace" Revisited. *Ind. Relat.,* May 1969, *8*(3), pp. 259–68. [G: U.S.]

Benson, Richard A. Trade Credit in the Fertilizer Industry: Theory and Practice. *Agr. Finance Rev.,* July 1969, *30,* pp. 21–33. [G: U.S.]

Chatterji, M. Chemical Fertilisers: Rapid Growth. In *Dagli, V., ed., Vol. II,* 1969, pp. 201–03. [G: India]

Comanor, William S. and Scherer, Frederic M. Patent Statistics as a Measure of Technical Change. *J. Polit. Econ.,* May/June 1969, *77*(3), pp. 392–98. [G: U.S.]

Conklin, D. W. Barriers to Technological Change in the U.S.S.R.: A Study of Chemical Fertilizers. *Soviet Stud.,* January 1969, *20*(3), pp. 353–65. [G: U.S.S.R.]

Costello, P. M. Economics of the Ethical Drug Industry: A Reply to Whitney. *Antitrust Bull.,* Summer 1969, *14,* pp. 397–403. [G: U.S.]

Feldstein, Martin S. Advertising, Research and Profits in the Drug Industry. *Southern Econ. J.,* January 1969, *35*(3), pp. 239–43. [G: U.S.]

Mansfield, Edwin. Industrial Research and Development: Characteristics, Costs, and Diffusion of Results. *Amer. Econ. Rev.,* May 1969, *59*(2), pp. 65–71. [G: U.S.]

Minasian, Jora R. Research and Development, Production Functions, and Rates of Return. *Amer. Econ. Rev.,* May 1969, *59*(2), pp. 80–85. [G: U.S.]

Nakamura, Tsutomu. The Organization of the Ceramic Industry around the Nagoya Area of Japan. *J. Ind. Econ.,* April 1969, *17*(2), pp. 151–62. [G: Japan]

Whitney, Simon N. Ethical Drugs: Comments on Professor Schifrin's Rejoinder and Professor Costello's Reply. *Antitrust Bull.,* Summer 1969, *14,* pp. 405–09. [G: U.S.]

6316 Textiles, Leather, and Clothing

Bray, Jennifer M. The Economics of Traditional Cloth Production in Iseyin, Nigeria. *Econ. Develop. Cult. Change,* July 1969, *17*(4), pp. 540–51. [G: Nigeria]

Bryan, Robert G. Wages in the Shirt and Nightwear Manufacturing Industry. *Mon. Lab. Rev.,* November 1969, *92*(11), pp. 66–67. [G: U.S.]

Chetty, V. Karuppan and Sankar, U. Bayesian Estimation of the CES Production Function. *Rev. Econ. Stud.,* July 1969, *36*(107), pp. 289–94. [G: India]

Leponiemi, Arvi. Vaatetusteollisuuden tuotanto- ja kustannusfunktioista. (On the Production and Cost Functions of the Clothing Industry. With English summary.) *Liiketaloudellinen Aikak.,* 1969, *18*(2), pp. 183–91. [G: Finland]

Lewis, Stephen R., Jr. A Note on the Consistency of Pakistan's Cotton-Cloth Statistics for Recent Years. *Pakistan Develop. Rev.,* Winter 1969, *9*(4), pp. 442–46. [G: Pakistan]

McGilvray, James and Simpson, David. Some Tests of Stability in Interindustry Coefficients. *Econometrica,* April 1969, *37*(2), pp. 204–21. [G: Ireland]

Perera, S. E. G. Some Labour Problems of the National Textile Corporation of Ceylon. *Int. Lab. Rev.,* February 1969, *99*(2), pp. 185–207. [G: Ceylon]

Rayner, A. C. The Wool Price and the Production of Synthetics. *Yorkshire Bull. Econ. Soc. Res.,* May 1969, *21*(1), pp. 31–38.

6317 Forest Products, Building Materials, and Paper

Cliff, Edward P. Statement. In *Timber Management Policies, SCH,* 1969, pp. 234–70. [G: U.S.]

Douglas, E. J. Apparent and Real Levels of Concentration in Australian Manufacturing Industry. *Econ. Rec.,* June 1969, *45*(110), pp. 251–57. [G: Australia]

Shaffer, Leslie L. D. The Myrtlewood Industry of Oregon. *Oregon Bus. Rev.*, April 1969, *28*(4), pp. 1–3. **[G: U.S.]**

Woolwine, Phil C. The South Pacific as a Source of Timber. *Oregon Bus. Rev.*, August 1969, *28*(8), pp. 1–5. **[G: S. Pacific]**

Young, Charles E. Statement. **In** *Timber Management Policies, SCH,* 1969, pp. 71–110. **[G: U.S.]**

6318 Food Processing (excluding agribusiness), Tobacco, and Beverages

Babb, E. M.; Belden, S. A. and Saathoff, C. R. An Analysis of Cooperative Bargaining in the Processing Tomato Industry. *Amer. J. Agr. Econ.*, February 1969, *51*(1), pp. 13–25. **[G: U.S.]**

Brigida, Franco. Industria alimentare e sviluppo industriale in italia. (Food Industry and Growth in Italy. With English summary.) *L'Impresa,* March/April 1969, *11*(2), pp. 163–66. **[G: Italy]**

Cloutier, Raymond. Structural Relationships in Industrial Milk Production in Ontario. *Can. J. Agr. Econ.*, February 1969, *17*(1), pp. 157–58. **[G: Canada]**

Guise, John W. B. and Ryland, G. J. Production Scheduling and Allocation: A Normative Decision Model for Sugar Milling. *Australian J. Agr. Econ.*, June 1969, *13*(1), pp. 8–24.

Hallberg, M. C. Projecting the Size Distribution of Agricultural Firms—An Application of a Markov Process with Non-Stationary Transition Probabilities. *Amer. J. Agr. Econ.*, May 1969, *51*(2), pp. 289–302. **[G: U.S.]**

Havrilesky, Thomas and Barth, Richard. Tests of Market Share Stability in the Cigarette Industry 1950–66. *J. Ind. Econ.*, April 1969, *17*(2), pp. 145–50.

Havrilesky, Thomas and Barth, Richard. Non-Price Competition in the Cigarette Industry. *Antitrust Bull.*, Fall 1969, *14*, pp. 607–28. **[G: U.S.]**

Horowitz, Ann and Horowitz, Ira. Concentration, Competition, and Mergers in Brewing. **In** *Weston, J. F. and Peltzman, S., eds.*, 1969, pp. 45–56. **[G: U.S.]**

de Jong, H. W. The European Brewing Industry: Appendix. **In** *Economic Concentration, Pt. 7A, SCH,* 1969, pp. 3897–3907. **[G: E.E.C.]**

Juris, Hervey A. Union Crisis Wage Decisions. *Ind. Relat.*, May 1969, *8*(3), pp. 247–58. **[G: U.S.]**

Madsen, Albert G. and Walsh, Richard G. Conglomerates: Economic Conduct and Performance. *Amer. J. Agr. Econ.*, December 1969, *51*(5), pp. 1495–1505. **[G: U.S.]**

Manhertz, Huntley G. Statistical Evaluation of Regional Differences in the Market for Processed Food Commodities. *Rev. Econ. Statist.*, May 1969, *51*(2), pp. 195–201. **[G: U.S.]**

Milano, Armando. The Autonomous State Tobacco Concern. *Rev. Econ. Cond. Italy,* September 1969, *23*(5), pp. 409–27. **[G: Italy]**

Murphy, K. T. A Note on the Measurement of Price Elasticity of Demand. *Amer. J. Agr. Econ.*, August 1969, *51*(3), pp. 691–92.

Narver, John. Conglomeration in the Food Industries. **In** *Garoian, L., ed.*, 1969, pp. 21–41. **[G: U.S.]**

Parsons, S. A. The Capacity and Utilisation of Cattle and Sheep Slaughtering Establishments in Australia. *Quart. Rev. Agr. Econ.*, January 1969, *22*(1), pp. 34–46. **[G: Australia]**

Rotaru, V. Determinarea mărimii optime a întreprinderii în industria alimentară. (Determining the Optimum Size of an Enterprise in the Food Industry. With English summary.) *Stud. Cercet. Econ.*, 1969, *4*, pp. 85–101.

Schneidau, R. E. and Knutson, Ronald D. Price Discrimination in the Food Industry: A Competitive Stimulant or Tranquilizer? *Amer. J. Agr. Econ.*, December 1969, *51*(5), pp. 1143–48. **[G: U.S.]**

Simon, Julian L. and Gardner, David M. World Food Needs and "New Proteins." *Econ. Develop. Cult. Change,* July 1969, *17*(4), pp. 520–26.

Vernon, John M.; Rives, Norfleet W., Jr. and Naylor, Thomas H. An Econometric Model of the Tobacco Industry. *Rev. Econ. Statist.*, May 1969, *51*(2), pp. 149–58. **[G: U.S.]**

Welden, William C. Milk Production and Utilization in the East. *Amer. J. Agr. Econ.*, November 1969, *51*(4), pp. 964–66. **[G: U.S.]**

6319 Other Industries

Hale, Rosemary D. Cookware and Vertical Integration: A Rejoinder. *J. Law Econ.*, October 1969, *12*(2), pp. 439–40. **[G: U.S.]**

Rock, James M. Cookware and Vertical Integration: A Reply. *J. Law Econ.*, October 1969, *12*(2), pp. 441–43. **[G: U.S.]**

Rock, James M. Cookware: A Study in Vertical Integration—A Reexamination. *J. Law Econ.*, October 1969, *12*(2), pp. 425–38. **[G: U.S.]**

632 Industry Studies: Extractive Industries

6320 General

Agria, Susan R. Special Tax Treatment of Mineral Industries. **In** *Harberger, A. C. and Bailey, M. J., eds.*, 1969, pp. 77–122. **[G: U.S.]**

Stykolt, Stefan and Eastman, Harry C. The Performance of Two Protected Oligopolies in Canada. **In** *Stykolt, S.*, 1969, pp. 83–102. **[G: Canada]**

6322 Mining (metal, coal, and other nonmetallic minerals)

Blainey, Geoffrey. Mining—And Undermining. *Econ. Rec.*, December 1969, *45*(112), pp. 607–15. **[G: Australia]**

Hakala, Donald R. The Iron Ore Industry: A Study of Shifts in Ownership and Control. *Quart. Rev. Econ. Bus.*, Spring 1969, *9*(1), pp. 45–51. **[G: U.S.; Canada]**

Sahota, G. S. Economic Problems in Separating the Determinants of Relative Prices. *Int. Econ. Rev.*, June 1969, *10*(2), pp. 183–206. **[G: U.S.]**

Shaffer, Leslie L. D. and Hashimoto, Steve T. The Semi-Precious Gem Industry of Oregon. *Oregon Bus. Rev.*, July 1969, *28*(7), pp. 1–4. **[G: U.S.]**

Stilz, Dieter. Die Auswirkungen der öffentlichen Hilfen für den Ruhrbergbau auf dessen Wettbewerbsbedingungen. (The Influence of Fiscal

Support on the Conditions of Competition in the Ruhr Coal Mining Industry. With English summary.) *Schmollers Jahr.*, 1969, *89*(4), pp. 427–49. [G: W. Germany]

Stilz, Dieter. Die Begünstigung des Steinkohlenbergbaus des Ruhrgebiets durch die öffentliche Finanzwirtschaft. (Fiscal Support of the Ruhr Coal Mining Industry 1958–1967. With English summary.) *Schmollers Jahr.*, 1969, *89*(2), pp. 151–84. [G: W. Germany]

Subocz, V. The Cargo Cult, or the 'Cinderella' Cult, in Mineral Policy? *Econ. Rec.*, December 1969, *45* (112), pp. 596–606. [G: Australia]

Thompson, B. C. Recent Trends in the Coal Mining Industry. In *Coal Mine Health and Safety, Pt. 1, SCH,* 1969, pp. 510–14. [G: U.S.]

6323 Oil, Gas, and Other Fuels

Adams, Walter. Statement. In *Governmental Intervention in the Market Mechanism, Pt. 1, SCH,* 1969, pp. 304–08. [G: U.S.]

Adelman, M. A. Statement. In *Governmental Intervention in the Market Mechanism, Pt. 1, SCH,* 1969, pp. 6–20.

Bailey, Richard. Investment Requirements in Energy. *Nat. Westminster Bank Quart. Rev.*, August 1969, pp. 43–53. [G: U.K.]

Bradley, Paul G. Statement. In *Governmental Intervention in the Market Mechanism, Pt. 1, SCH,* 1969, pp. 284–301.

Brubaker, Earl R. Some Effects of Policy on Productivity in Soviet and American Crude Petroleum Extraction. *J. Ind. Econ.*, November 1969, *18*(1), pp. 33–52. [G: U.S.; U.S.S.R.]

Dirlam, Joel. Statement. In *Governmental Intervention in the Market Mechanism, Pt. 1, SCH,* 1969, pp. 249–67. [G: U.S.]

Dolmans, D. Het aardgas zijn prijsvorming. (Natural Gas and Its Price Determination. With English summary.) *Tijdschr. Econ.*, 1969, *14*(1), pp. 3–27. [G: Netherlands]

Frank, Helmut J. Statement. In *Governmental Intervention in the Market Mechanism, Pt. 1, SCH,* 1969, pp. 339–51.

Froozan, Mansur. E.R.A.P.-Type Versus Fifty-Fifty Agreements. *Tahq. Eq.*, November 1969, *6* (15&16), pp. 21–53. [G: Iran]

Ganguly, Swapan and Venugopal, Bhaskar. International Crude Oil Prices after World War II. *Indian Econ. J.*, January–March 1969, *16*(3), pp. 382–87.

Gonzalez, Richard J. Federal Policies Dominating U.S. Energy Supplies. In *Governmental Intervention in the Market Mechanism, Pt. 1, SCH,* 1969, pp. 385–90. [G: U.S.]

Gonzalez, Richard J. Interfuel Competition for Future Energy Markets. In *Governmental Intervention in the Market Mechanism, Pt. 1, SCH,* 1969, pp. 393–99. [G: U.S.]

Homan, Paul T. Statement. In *Governmental Intervention in the Market Mechanism, Pt. 1, SCH,* 1969, pp. 103–31. [G: U.S.]

Kahn, Alfred E. Statement. In *Governmental Intervention in the Market Mechanism, Pt. 1, SCH,* 1969, pp. 132–54. [G: U.S.]

Kashyap, N. N. Oil: Its Strategic Role in a Growth-Oriented Economy. In *Dagli, V., ed., Vol. II,* 1969, pp. 117–25. [G: India]

Leeman, Wayne A. Statement. In *Governmental Intervention in the Market Mechanism, Pt. 1, SCH,* 1969, pp. 268–84.

Lichtblau, John H. Statement. In *Governmental Intervention in the Market Mechanism, Pt. 1, SCH,* 1969, pp. 317–27. [G: U.S.]

Mansfield, Edwin. Industrial Research and Development: Characteristics, Costs, and Diffusion of Results. *Amer. Econ. Rev.*, May 1969, *59*(2), pp. 65–71. [G: U.S.]

Mead, Walter J. Statement. In *Governmental Intervention in the Market Mechanism, Pt. 1, SCH,* 1969, pp. 77–102. [G: U.S.]

Odell, Peter R. Natural Gas in Western Europe: A Case Study in the Economic Geography of Energy Resources. *De Economist,* May/June 1969, *117*(3), pp. 227–57. [G: W. Europe]

Penrose, Edith T. OPEC and the Changing Structure of the International Petroleum Industry. In *Governmental Intervention in the Market Mechanism, Pt. 1, SCH,* 1969, pp. 429–47.

Penrose, Edith T. Statement. In *Governmental Intervention in the Market Mechanism, Pt. 1, SCH,* 1969, pp. 156–66.

Rieber, Michael. Statement. In *Governmental Intervention in the Market Mechanism, Pt. 1, SCH,* 1969, pp. 181–92. [G: U.S.]

Steele, Henry. Statement. In *Governmental Intervention in the Market Mechanism, Pt. 1, SCH,* 1969, pp. 208–22. [G: U.S.]

Vigand, V. C. Once More on the World Price of Oil: A Comment. *Acta Oecon.*, 1969, *4*(2), pp. 211–14.

Wasowski, Stanislaw. The Fuel Situation in Eastern Europe. *Soviet Stud.*, July 1969, *21*(1), pp. 35–51. [G: E. Europe]

633 Industry Studies: Distributive Trades

6330 General

Baker, Donald I. Another Look at Franchise Tie-Ins After Texaco and Fortner. *Antitrust Bull.*, Winter 1969, *14*, pp. 767–83. [G: U.S.]

Bushch, Arnd. Vertical Restrictions in German Consumer Goods Industries. *Antitrust Bull.*, Summer 1969, *14*, pp. 473–97. [G: Germany]

Buxbaum, Richard M. The Group Exemption and Exculsive Distributorships in the Common Market—Procedural Technicalities. *Antitrust Bull.*, Summer 1969, *14*, pp. 499–514. [G: E.E.C.]

Cobia, David W. and Farris, Paul L. Mergers and Diversified Growth of Large Grain Firms. *Amer. J. Agr. Econ.*, August 1969, *51*(3), pp. 619–24. [G: U.S.]

David, Michel. La distribuzione alimentare in Francia: oggli e domani. (Food Distribution in France: To-day and Tomorrow. With English summary.) *L'Impresa,* March/April 1969, *11*(2), pp. 156–62. [G: France]

David, Michel. Nuovi tipi di punti di vendita per la periferia dell citta'. (New Types of Suburban Selling Points. With English summary.) *L'Impresa,* November/December 1969, *11*(6), pp. 436–43.

De Vleeshouwer, Eduard. Aspecten van de distributie-ontwikkeling in België. (Aspects of the Development of Distribution in Belgium. With English summary.) *Econ. Soc. Tijdschr.*, December 1969, *23*(6), pp. 619–40. **[G: Belgium]**

George, K. D. Productivity in the Distributive Trades. *Bull. Oxford Univ. Inst. Econ. Statist.*, May 1969, *31*(2), pp. 61–75. **[G: U.K.]**

Gross, Jack L. and McGinley, John J. Need for a Marketing Intelligence System . . . in Petroleum Marketing: Integration of Information Systems into the Decision-Making Process. *Econ. Bus. Bull.*, Fall 1969, *22*(1), pp. 25–32.

Knutson, Ronald D. The Economic Consequences of the Minnesota Dairy Industry Unfair Trade Practices Act. *J. Law Econ.*, October 1969, *12*(2), pp. 377–89. **[G: U.S.]**

Simon, Julian L. The Effect of Advertising on Liquor Brand Sales. *J. Marketing Res.*, August 1969, *6*(3), pp. 301–13.

Williams, T. David. Commodity Distribution in Malawi: A Case Study. **In** *Stewart, I. G., ed.*, 1969, pp. 83–103. **[G: Malawi]**

6332 Wholesale Trade

Edwards, S. L. Transport Costs in the Wholesale Trades. *J. Transp. Econ. Policy*, September 1969, *3*(3), pp. 272–78. **[G: U.K.]**

Lopata, Richard S. Faster Pace in Wholesaling. *Harvard Bus. Rev.*, July–August 1969, *47*(4), pp. 130–43. **[G: U.S.]**

6333 Retail Trade

Andrus, Roman R. and Knutsen, John A. The Impact of Personal Information Sources on Retailer Success. *Oregon Bus. Rev.*, November 1969, *28*(11), pp. 1–3. **[G: U.S.]**

Barzel, Yoram. The Growth of Sales *Per* Man-Hour in Retail Trade, 1929–1963: Discussion. **In** *Fuchs, V. R., ed.*, 1969, pp. 230–33. **[G: U.S.]**

Bruce, Grady D. The Ecological Structure of Retail Institutions. *J. Marketing Res.*, February 1969, *6* (1), pp. 48–53. **[G: U.S.]**

Corner, D. C. Recent Trends in Retail Distribution. *Nat. Westminster Bank Quart. Rev.*, May 1969, pp. 22–32. **[G: U.K.]**

Di Tella, Guido and Baccino, Osvaldo. Análisis teórico de los efectos de la intermediación comercial. El caso de la industria del automóvil en Argentina. (Theoretical Analysis of the Effects of Commercial Intermediation: The Case of Automobile Industry in Argentina. With English summary.) *Económica*, January–April 1969, *15*(1), pp. 1–14. **[G: Argentina]**

Gray, Roger W. and Anderson, Roice. Advertised Specials and Local Competition among Supermarkets. **In** *Alexis, M.; Holloway, R. J. and Hancock, R. S., eds.*, 1969, pp. 343–57. **[G: U.S.]**

Humphrey, Kenneth R. Retail Trade in Indiana and Surrounding States. *Indiana Bus. Rev.*, November/December 1969, *44*, pp. 11–15. **[G: U.S.]**

Il'in, V. and Koriagin, B. The Sale of Goods to the Public on Credit. *Prob. Econ.*, December 1969, *12* (8), pp. 68–74. **[G: U.S.S.R.]**

Kotzan, Jeffrey A. and Evanson, Robert V. Responsiveness of Drug Store Sales to Shelf Space Allocations. *J. Marketing Res.*, November 1969, *6*(4), pp. 465–69. **[G: U.S.]**

Lavidge, Robert J. The Ghetto Challenge to Marketing People. *Ohio State U. Bull. Bus. Res.*, August 1969, *44*(8), pp. 4, 6–7. **[G: U.S.]**

Markin, Rom J. The Supermarket—A Study of Size, Profits, and Concentration. **In** *Alexis, M.; Holloway, R. J. and Hancock, R. S., eds.*, 1969, pp. 201–13. **[G: U.S.]**

Mason, Joseph Barry and Moore, Charles Thomas. A Note on the Reliability of Census Data in Trading Area Analysis. *Miss. Val. J. Bus. Econ.*, Fall 1969, *5*(1), pp. 68–72. **[G: U.S.]**

Mueller, Willard F. Public Policy Toward Mergers in Food Retailing. **In** *Ruttan, V. W.; Waldo, A. D. and Houck, J. P., eds.*, 1969, pp. 186–91. **[G: U.S.]**

Perkins, Frederick A. Showing a Retailer that Meat Sanitation Pays—An Economic Approach. *Amer. J. Agr. Econ.*, December 1969, *51*(5), pp. 1259–62. **[G: U.S.]**

Rao, Tanniru R. Are Some Consumers More Prone to Purchase Private Brands? *J. Marketing Res.*, November 1969, *6*(4), pp. 447–50. **[G: U.S.]**

Rao, Tanniru R. Consumer's Purchase Decision Process: Stochastic Models. *J. Marketing Res.*, August 1969, *6*(3), pp. 321–29.

Ryans, John K., Jr. and Hise, Richard T. Retailing's Unfortunate Image: Problems of Attracting College Graduates. *Econ. Bus. Bull.*, Fall 1969, *22*(1), pp. 39–43. **[G: U.S.]**

Schendel, Dan E. and Balestra, Pietro. Rational Behavior and Gasoline Price Wars. *Appl. Econ.*, May 1969, *1*(2), pp. 89–101.

Schwartzman, David. The Growth of Sales *Per* Man-Hour in Retail Trade, 1929–1963: Reply. **In** *Fuchs, V. R., ed.*, 1969, pp. 233–35. **[G: U.S.]**

Schwartzman, David. The Growth of Sales *Per* Man-Hour in Retail Trade, 1929–1963. **In** *Fuchs, V. R., ed.*, 1969, pp. 201–29. **[G: U.S.]**

Sherman, Roger. A Note on Trading Stamp Strategy. *Appl. Econ.*, August 1969, *1*(3), pp. 225–28.

Skinner, R. W. Hidden Consumer Motives in Supermarket Selection. *Amer. J. Agr. Econ.*, December 1969, *51*(5), pp. 1154–58. **[G: U.S.]**

Willet, Ronald P. and Stephenson, P. Ronald. Determinants of Buyer Response to Physical Distribution Service. *J. Marketing Res.*, August 1969, *6*(3), pp. 279–83. **[G: U.S.]**

Wilson, Cyrus C. and Greenidge, Charles D. Classification Merchandising: An Overlooked Opportunity for Increasing Merchandising Profitability. *Calif. Manage. Rev.*, Fall 1969, *12*(1), pp. 53–61.

Zusman, Pinhas. Welfare Implication and Evaluation of Buyers' Travel Inputs and Nonprice Offer Variations in Networks of Retail Food Stores. *Econometrica*, July 1969, *37*(3), pp. 439–56. **[G: Israel]**

634 Industry Studies: Construction

6340 Construction

Howenstine, E. Jay. Rising Construction Costs and Anti-Inflation Policies: A Report on Western Europe. *Mon. Lab. Rev.*, June 1969, *92*(6), pp. 3–10. **[G: W. Europe]**

King, Donald A. Homebuilding Activity in 1969. *Surv. Curr. Bus.*, October 1969, *49*(10), pp. 16–22. **[G: U.S.]**

Miller, Glenn H., Jr. Housing in the 60's: A Survey of Some Nonfinancial Factors. *Fed. Res. Bank Kansas City Rev.*, May 1969, pp. 3–10. **[G: U.S.]**

Musgrave, John C. The Measurement of Price Changes in Construction. *J. Amer. Statist. Assoc.*, September 1969, *64*(327), pp. 771–86. **[G: U.S.]**

Roberts, Higdon C. A Private Approach to Public Problems: Unions and Contractors Create Job Training Program. *Indiana Bus. Rev.*, July/August 1969, *44*, pp. 16–20. **[G: U.S.]**

Rossman, William H. Allocation of Equipment Cost in the Heavy Construction Industry. *Manage. Account.*, November 1969, *51*(5), pp. 14–15.

Russell, Joe L. and Pilot, Michael J. Seasonality in Construction: A Continuing Problem. *Mon. Lab. Rev.*, December 1969, *92*(12), pp. 3–8. **[G: U.S.]**

Smith, C. Selby. Benefits to British Employers from Post-secondary Education. *J. Roy. Statist. Soc.*, Part 3, 1969, *132*, pp. 408–17. **[G: U.K.]**

Vipond, M. J. Fluctuations in Private Housebuilding in Great Britain, 1950–1966. *Scot. J. Polit. Econ.*, June 1969, *16*(2), pp. 196–211. **[G: U.K.]**

Weinberg, Edgar. Reducing Skill Shortages in Construction. *Mon. Lab. Rev.*, February 1969, *92*(2), pp. 3–9. **[G: U.S.]**

635 Industry Studies: Services and Related Industries

6350 General

Driehuis, W. Experiments in Explaining and Forecasting the Invisible Trade of the Netherlands. *Bull. Oxford Univ. Inst. Econ. Statist.*, November 1969, *31*(4), pp. 335–51. **[G: Netherlands]**

Garston, Gordon J. and Kendrick, John W. Measuring Real Output for Industries Providing Services: OBE Concepts and Methods: Discussion. **In** *Fuchs, V. R., ed.*, 1969, pp. 41–49. **[G: U.S.]**

Hoffmann, Walther G. Der tertiäre Sektor im Wachstumsprozess. (The Service Sector in the Growth Process. With English summary.) *Jahr. Nationalökon. Statist.*, June 1969, *183*(1), pp. 1–29. **[G: W. Europe; Japan; U.S.; Australia]**

Marimont, Martin L. Measuring Real Output for Industries Providing Services: OBE Concepts and Methods. **In** *Fuchs, V. R., ed.*, 1969, pp. 15–40. **[G: U.S.]**

Marimont, Martin L. Measuring Real Output for Industries Providing Services: OBE Concepts and Methods: Reply. **In** *Fuchs, V. R., ed.*, 1969, pp. 50–52. **[G: U.S.]**

Terleckyj, Nestor E. Measuring Real Output for Industries Providing Services: OBE Concepts and Methods: Comment. **In** *Fuchs, V. R., ed.*, 1969, pp. 49–50. **[G: U.S.]**

Terleckyj, Nestor E. The Service Industries in Canada, 1946–66: Discussion. **In** *Fuchs, V. R., ed.*, 1969, pp. 282–86. **[G: Canada]**

Worton, David A. The Service Industries in Canada, 1946–66. **In** *Fuchs, V. R., ed.*, 1969, pp. 237–82. **[G: Canada]**

6352 Electrical, Communication, and Information Services

Ashley, George E. International Communications: What Shape to Come? *Law Contemp. Probl.*, Spring 1969, *34*(2), pp. 417–28.

Bailey, Richard. Investment Requirements in Energy. *Nat. Westminster Bank Quart. Rev.*, August 1969, pp. 43–53. **[G: U.K.]**

Barnett, Harold J. and Greenberg, Edward. Regulating CATV Systems: An Analysis of FCC Policy and an Alternative. *Law Contemp. Probl.*, Summer 1969, *34*(3), pp. 562–85. **[G: U.S.]**

Barr, Brenton M. and Bater, James H. The Electricity Industry of Central Siberia. *Econ. Geogr.*, October 1969, *45*(4), pp. 349–69. **[G: U.S.S.R.]**

Barrow, Roscoe L. and Manelli, Daniel J. Communications Technology—A Forecast of Change (Part II). *Law Contemp. Probl.*, Summer 1969, *34*(3), pp. 431–51. **[G: U.S.]**

Bateman, Merrill J. Statement. **In** *Highway Legislation, HCH*, 1969, pp. 169–73. **[G: U.S.]**

Blank, David M. Tonypandy once Again. *J. Bus.*, January 1969, *42*(1), pp. 104–12. **[G: U.S.]**

Bocock, Peter W. Impact of Development: Telecommunications in Ethiopia. *Finance Develop.*, December 1969, *6*(4), pp. 15–21. **[G: Ethiopia]**

Bryant, Ashbrook P. Historical and Social Aspects of Concentration of Program Control in Television. *Law Contemp. Probl.*, Summer 1969, *34*(3), pp. 610–35. **[G: U.S.]**

Dunn, Donald A. Policy Issues Presented by the Interdependence of Computer and Communications Services. *Law Contemp. Probl.*, Spring 1969, *34*(2), pp. 369–88.

Ebrahimzadeh, Cyrus. The Economics of Hydro-Electric Power in Iran. *Tahq. Eq.*, November 1969, *6*(15&16), pp. 54–79. **[G: Iran]**

Goldin, Hyman H. Financing Public Broadcasting. *Law Contemp. Probl.*, Summer 1969, *34*(3), pp. 650–70. **[G: U.S.]**

Goodhardt, G. J. and Ehrenberg, A. S. C. Duplication of Television Viewing between and within Channels. *J. Marketing Res.*, May 1969, *6*(2), pp. 169–78.

Gray, J. L. Economics of Scale—Generation of Electrical Power. **In** *Hugh-Jones, E. M., ed.*, 1969, pp. 99–112.

Greenberg, Edward. Television Station Profitability and FCC Regulatory Policy. *J. Ind. Econ.*, July 1969, *17*(3), pp. 210–38. **[G: U.S.]**

Harwood, Kenneth. Broadcasting and the Theory of the Firm. *Law Contemp. Probl.*, Summer 1969, *34*(3), pp. 485–504.

Heraud, Jorge and Pomalaza, José. An Educational Television and Communications System for Latin America. **In** *Hilton, R., ed.*, 1969, pp. 381–400. **[G: Latin America]**

Irwin, Manley R. Computers and Communications: The Economics of Interdependence. *Law Contemp. Probl.*, Spring 1969, *34*(2), pp. 360–68.

Irwin, Manley R. The Computer Utility: Market Entry in Search of Public Policy. *J. Ind. Econ.*, July 1969, *17*(3), pp. 239–52. **[G: U.S.]**

Johnson, Harold W. and Simon, Julian L. The Success of Mergers: The Case of Advertising Agencies. *Bull. Oxford Univ. Inst. Econ. Statist.*, May 1969, *31*(2), pp. 139–44.

Johnson, Nicholas. Towers of Babel: The Chaos in Radio Spectrum Utilization and Allocation. *Law Contemp. Probl.*, Summer 1969, *34*(3), pp. 505–34. [G: U.S.]

Kaimann, Richard A. Milwaukee Electronic Data Processing User Profile. *Marquette Bus. Rev.*, Fall 1969, *13*(3), pp. 117–24. [G: U.S.]

Leonard, William N. Network Television Pricing: A Comment. *J. Bus.*, January 1969, *42*(1), pp. 93–103. [G: U.S.]

Levin, Harvey J. Broadcast Structure, Technology, and the ABC-ITT Merger Decision. *Law Contemp. Probl.*, Summer 1969, *34*(3), pp. 452–84. [G: U.S.]

Lipinski, Andrew J. Integration of Latin American Communications. **In** *Hilton, R., ed.*, 1969, pp. 343–54. [G: Latin America]

Macy, John W., Jr. Public Broadcasting: A Medium in Search of Solutions. *Law Contemp. Probl.*, Summer 1969, *34*(3), pp. 636–49. [G: U.S.]

Markham, Jesse W. Competition in the Nuclear Power Supply Industry—A Reply to Mr. Netschert. *Antitrust Bull.*, Fall 1969, *14*, pp. 657–63. [G: U.S.]

Minasian, Jora R. The Political Economy of Broadcasting in the 1920's. *J. Law Econ.*, October 1969, *12*(2), pp. 391–403. [G: U.S.]

Netschert, Bruce C. Competition in the Nuclear Power Supply Industry—A Rejoinder to Professor Markham. *Antitrust Bull.*, Fall 1969, *14*, pp. 665–66. [G: U.S.]

Netschert, Bruce C. Competition in the Nuclear Power Supply Industry: A Review. *Antitrust Bull.*, Fall 1969, *14*, pp. 629–55. [G: U.S.]

Rizzoni, Eitel M. Development and Integration of Latin American Telecommunications. **In** *Hilton, R., ed.*, 1969, pp. 355–80. [G: Latin America]

Robinson, H. Leslie. Electric Power Integration in Latin America. **In** *Hilton, R., ed.*, 1969, pp. 335–42. [G: Latin America]

Sandbulte, Arend J. Sales and Revenue Forecasting. *Manage. Account.*, December 1969, *51*(6), pp. 17–23.

Sarnoff, Thomas W. Television—Focus on the Future. *Calif. Manage. Rev.*, Fall 1969, *12*(1), pp. 62–64.

Seneca, Joseph J. and Cicchetti, Charles J. A Gravity Model Analysis of the Demand for Public Communication. *J. Reg. Sci.*, December 1969, *9*(3), pp. 459–70. [G: U.S.]

Simpson, E. S. Electricity Production in Nigeria. *Econ. Geogr.*, July 1969, *45*(3), pp. 239–57. [G: Nigeria]

Thomas, G. R. The Economics of Scale of Computing Systems. **In** *Hugh-Jones, E. M., ed.*, 1969, pp. 113–19. [G: U.K.]

Trebing, Harry M. Common Carrier Regulation—The Silent Crisis. *Law Contemp. Probl.*, Spring 1969, *34*(2), pp. 299–329. [G: U.S.]

Verrill, Charles O., Jr. CATV's Emerging Role: Cablecaster or Common Carrier? *Law Contemp. Probl.*, Summer 1969, *34*(3), pp. 586–609. [G: U.S.]

Webbink, Douglas W. The Impact of UHF Promotion: The All-Channel Television Receiver Law. *Law Contemp. Probl.*, Summer 1969, *34*(3), pp. 535–61. [G: U.S.]

Wimmer, Larry. Statement. **In** *Highway Beautification, SCH*, 1969, pp. 23–27. [G: U.S.]

6353 Personal Services

Welch, John M. Education for Institutional Food Service—On Wheels. *Amer. J. Agr. Econ.*, December 1969, *51*(5), pp. 1229–32. [G: U.S.]

6354 Business and Legal Services

Skeels, Jack W. Perspectives on Private Employment Agencies. *Ind. Relat.*, February 1969, *8*(2), pp. 151–61. [G: U.S.]

6355 Repair Services

Leonard, William N. Statement. **In** *Automotive Repair Industry, Pt. 1, SCH*, 1969, pp. 4–50. [G: U.S.]

6356 Insurance

Belth, Joseph M. The Relationship between Benefits and Premiums in Life Insurance. *J. Risk Ins.*, March 1969, *36*(1), pp. 19–39.

Belth, Joseph M. The Retail Price Structure in American Life Insurance: Reply. *J. Risk Ins.*, September 1969, *36*(4), pp. 495–96. [G: U.S.]

Bertrand, Robert J. Comments on the Williams Paper. *J. Risk Ins.*, June 1969, *36*(2), pp. 237–38. [G: U.S.]

Birkinsha, Jack E. Investment Income: The Legal Part. *J. Risk Ins.*, September 1969, *36*(4), pp. 463–64. [G: U.S.]

Curry, H. E. Investment Income in Fire and Casualty Rate Making. *J. Risk Ins.*, September 1969, *36*(4), pp. 447–53.

Denenberg, Herbert S. Insurance Regulation: The Search for Countervailing Power and Consumer Protection. **In** *Impact of Crime on Small Business—1969, Pt. 1, SCH*, 1969, pp. 57–63. [G: U.S.]

Denenberg, Herbert S. Statement. **In** *Impact of Crime on Small Business—1969, Pt. 1, SCH*, 1969, pp. 47–55. [G: U.S.]

Duker, Jacob M. Expenditures for Life Insurance among Working-Wife Families. *J. Risk Ins.*, December 1969, *36*(5), pp. 525–33. [G: U.S.]

Eilers, Robert D. Minimum Premium Health Plans: Insured Non-Insurance. *J. Risk Ins.*, March 1969, *36*(1), pp. 63–84. [G: U.S.]

Evans, Campbell K. Model of Certain Relationships within the Structure of Insurance Agencies. *J. Risk Ins.*, December 1969, *36*(5), pp. 535–44.

Ferrari, J. Robert. Implications of Viewing Interest Foregone as an Opportunity Cost of Life Insurance. *J. Risk Ins.*, June 1969, *36*(2), pp. 253–65.

Forbes, Stephen W. Automobile Bodily Injury Liability Loss Reserving Techniques and Simulation. *J. Risk Ins.*, December 1969, *36*(5), pp. 597–614. [G: U.S.]

Gentry, James A. and Pike, John R. Rates of Return on Common Stock Portfolios of Life Insurance Companies. *J. Risk Ins.,* December 1969, *36*(5), pp. 545–52. [G: U.S.]

Goudzwaard, Maurice B. The Economic Impact of Credit Insurance Charges. *J. Risk Ins.,* December 1969, *36*(5), pp. 515–23. [G: U.S.]

Greene, Mark R. Doctoral Education for Risk and Insurance in Leading U.S. Universities. *J. Risk Ins.,* December 1969, *36*(5), pp. 505–13. [G: U.S.]

Hammond, J. D. and Shilling, N. A Review Article: The Little Report on Prices and Profits in the Property and Liability Insurance Industry. *J. Risk Ins.,* March 1969, *36*(1), pp. 129–45. [G: U.S.]

Harwayne, Frank. Personal Premium Saving under Basic Protection. *J. Risk Ins.,* June 1969, *36*(2), pp. 239–51. [G: U.S.]

Hedges, Bob A. Insurance Rates and Investment Earnings Considered Together. *J. Risk Ins.,* September 1969, *36*(4), pp. 455–61.

Hedges, Bob A. Substandard Automobile Insurers: Comment. *J. Risk Ins.,* December 1969, *36*(5), pp. 640–42. [G: U.S.]

Hofflander, A. E. and Drandell, Milton. A Linear Programming Model of Profitability, Capacity and Regulation in Insurance Management. *J. Risk Ins.,* March 1969, *36*(1), pp. 41–54.

Hold, William T. A Review Article on Basic Protection for the Traffic Victim: Comment. *J. Risk Ins.,* June 1969, *36*(2), pp. 310–13. [G: U.S.]

Kamerschen, David R. and Pascucci, John J. The Retail Price Structure in American Life Insurance: Comment. *J. Risk Ins.,* September 1969, *36* (4), pp. 493–95. [G: U.S.]

Kedzie, Daniel P. Corporate Planning and the Holding Company. *J. Risk Ins.,* March 1969, *36*(1), pp. 85–91.

Kellison, Stephen G. A Linear Programming Model of Profitability, Capacity and Regulation in Insurance Management: Comment. *J. Risk Ins.,* December 1969, *36*(5), pp. 637–39.

Klarman, Herbert E. Reimbursing the Hospital—The Differences the Third Party Makes. *J. Risk Ins.,* December 1969, *36*(5), pp. 553–66. [G: U.S.]

Kornstein, Daniel J. Insurance Mergers and the Clayton Act. *Yale Law J.,* July 1969, *78*(8), pp. 1404–17. [G: U.S.]

Lange, Jeffrey T. Application of a Mathematical Concept of Risk to Property-Liability Insurance Ratemaking. *J. Risk Ins.,* September 1969, *36*(4), pp. 383–91.

Launie, J. J. The Supply Function of Urban Property Insurance. *J. Risk Ins.,* June 1969, *36*(2), pp. 269–83. [G: U.S.]

Lee, J. Finley. The Competitive Role of the Associated Factory Mutuals. *J. Risk Ins.,* September 1969, *36*(4), pp. 401–18. [G: U.S.]

Long, John D. Comments on the Plotkin Paper. *J. Risk Ins.,* June 1969, *36*(2), pp. 201–16. [G: U.S.]

Mehr, Robert I. Channels of Distribution in Insurance. *J. Risk Ins.,* December 1969, *36*(5), pp. 583–95.

Metzger, Bert L. Insurance Industry Begins to Court Profit Sharing Funds with Equity-Based Products. *J. Risk Ins.,* September 1969, *36*(4), pp. 437–45. [G: U.S.]

Moeller, Charles, Jr. Economic Implications of the Life Insurance Industry's Investment Program in the Central Cities. *J. Risk Ins.,* March 1969, *36*(1), pp. 93–101. [G: U.S.]

Moorhead, E. J. The Impact of Lapse Rates on Life Insurance Prices: Comment. *J. Risk Ins.,* March 1969, *36*(1), pp. 163–64.

Murray, Roger F. An Overview of the Life Insurance—Mutual Fund Combination. *J. Risk Ins.,* September 1969, *36*(4), pp. 419–24. [G: U.S.]

Nally, Robert V. The Computer and Home Office Management Development in Life Insurance. *J. Risk Ins.,* September 1969, *36*(4), pp. 393–400.

Neumann, Seev. Anticipated and Unanticipated Inflation—Implications to Life Insurance. *J. Risk Ins.,* June 1969, *36*(2), pp. 315–19. [G: U.S.]

Neumann, Seev. Inflation and Saving through Life Insurance. *J. Risk Ins.,* December 1969, *36*(5), pp. 567–82. [G: U.S.]

Plotkin, Irving H. Rates of Return in the Property and Liability Insurance Industry: A Comparative Analysis. *J. Risk Ins.,* June 1969, *36*(2), pp. 173–200. [G: U.S.]

Reavis, Marshall W. The Corporate Risk Manager's Contribution to Profit. *J. Risk Ins.,* September 1969, *36*(4), pp. 473–79.

Ricks, R. Bruce. Imputed Equity Returns on Real Estate Financed with Life Insurance Company Loans. *J. Finance,* December 1969, *24*(5), pp. 921–37. [G: U.S.]

Ross, H. Laurence. A Review Article on Basic Protection for the Traffic Victim: Reply. *J. Risk Ins.,* June 1969, *36*(2), pp. 313–14. [G: U.S.]

Rottman, Dick L. Analysis of Perpetual Insurance. *J. Risk Ins.,* September 1969, *36*(4), pp. 365–82. [G: U.S.]

Scotton, R. B. and Deeble, J. S. The Nimmo Report. *Econ. Rec.,* June 1969, *45*(110), pp. 258–75. [G: Australia]

Stewart, Richard E. The End of Isolationism in Insurance Regulation. *J. Risk Ins.,* September 1969, *36* (4), pp. 489–92. [G: U.S.]

Swadener, Paul. The Loss Ratio Method of Rating and the Feedback Control Loop Concept. *J. Risk Ins.,* December 1969, *36*(5), pp. 615–27.

Todd, Jerry D. The Risk Management Function in Municipal Government. *J. Risk Ins.,* June 1969, *36*(2), pp. 285–95. [G: U.S.]

Vanderbeek, Robert E. Auto Insurance as a Fringe Benefit. *J. Risk Ins.,* September 1969, *36*(4), pp. 481–85.

Webb, Bernard L. Collective Merchandising of Automobile Insurance. *J. Risk Ins.,* September 1969, *36*(4), pp. 465–71. [G: U.S.]

Williams, C. Arthur, Jr. Insurer Views on Property and Liability Insurance Rate Regulation. *J. Risk Ins.,* June 1969, *36*(2), pp. 217–36. [G: U.S.]

6357 Real Estate

Conger, John Stoy. Conglomerate Land Acquisition: Reasons and Use. In *Garoian, L., ed.,* 1969, pp. 98–105. [G: U.S.]

6358 Entertainment, Recreation, Tourism

Davenport, David S. Collusive Competition in Major League Baseball: Its Theory and Institutional Development. *Amer. Econ.*, Fall 1969, *13*(2), pp. 6–30. **[G: U.S.]**

Del Gaudio, Vincenzo. Problems and Prospects of Italian Tourism. *Rev. Econ. Cond. Italy*, November 1969, *23*(6), pp. 505–18. **[G: Italy]**

Scaglia, Giovanni Battista. Features of a Tourist Development Policy in Italy. *Rev. Econ. Cond. Italy*, November 1969, *23*(6), pp. 501–04. **[G: Italy]**

640 Economic Capacity

641 Economic Capacity

6410 Economic Capacity

Hogan, W. P. Some New Results in the Measurement of Capacity Utilization. *Amer. Econ. Rev.*, March 1969, *59*(1), pp. 183–84.

Horngren, Charles T. Capacity Utilization and the Efficiency Variance. *Accounting Rev.*, January 1969, *44*(1), pp. 86–89.

700 Agriculture; Natural Resources

710 Agriculture

7100 Agriculture

Adams, Dale W. Rural Migration and Agricultural Development in Colombia. *Econ. Develop. Cult. Change*, July 1969, *17*(4), pp. 527–39. **[G: Colombia]**

Ahmad, Zubeida M. and Sternberg, Marvin J. Agrarian Reform and Employment, with Special Reference to Asia. *Int. Lab. Rev.*, February 1969, *99*(2), pp. 159–83. **[G: Asia]**

Andarawewa, A. B. Evaluation of Public Research Programs in Agriculture. *Can. J. Agr. Econ.*, November 1969, *17*(3), pp. 157–69. **[G: Canada]**

Baletić, Zvonimir. Agricultural Development and a Stable Growth of Output. *Eastern Europ. Econ.*, Summer 1969, *7*(4), pp. 41–48. **[G: Yugoslavia]**

Bhagwati, Jagdish N. and Chakravarty, Sukhamoy. Contributions to Indian Economic Analysis: A Survey. *Amer. Econ. Rev.*, Part II, September 1969, *59*(4), pp. 2–73. **[G: India]**

Bhuleshkar, A. V. The Ideas and Goals of Co-operation in Indian Agricultural Development. **In** *Bhuleshkar, A. V., ed.*, 1969, pp. 33–39. **[G: India]**

Bićanić, Rudolf. Turning Points in Economic Development and Agricultural Policy. **In** *Papi, U. and Nunn, C., eds.*, 1969, pp. 555–73.

Blase, Melvin G. The World Food-Population Problem: 1969. *Univ. Missouri Bus. Govt. Rev.*, May–June 1969, *10*(3), pp. 20–27.

Brand, S. S. The Interindustry Relationships of Agriculture and Economic Development in South Africa. *Finance Trade Rev.*, June 1969, *8*(3), pp. 171–86. **[G: S. Africa]**

Brubaker, Earl R. Development of Soviet Agriculture under a Vintage Model of Production. *Amer. J. Agr. Econ.*, November 1969, *51*(4), pp. 882–902. **[G: U.S.S.R.]**

Carr, Raymond. Mexican Agrarian Reform 1910–1960. **In** *Jones, E. L. and Woolf, S. J., eds.*, 1969, pp. 151–68. **[G: Mexico]**

Chacel, Julian. The Principal Characteristics of the Agrarian Structure and Agricultural Production in Brazil. **In** *Ellis, H. S., ed.*, 1969, pp. 103–29. **[G: Brazil]**

Cumming, J. N. The Sheep Industry in Tasmania. *Quart. Rev. Agr. Econ.*, July 1969, *22*(3), pp. 165–78. **[G: Australia]**

Dalrymple, Dana G. The Organization of Agriculture: Discussion. *Amer. J. Agr. Econ.*, December 1969, *51*(5), pp. 1286–88.

van Dongen, Irene S. Agriculture and Other Primary Production. **In** *Abshire, D. M. and Samuels, M. A., eds.*, 1969, pp. 253–93. **[G: Mozambique; Angola; Portuguese Guinea]**

Dovring, Folke. Commentary on Agrarian Revolution and Economic Progress: A Primer for Development (by Rainer Schickele). *Land Econ.*, February 1969, *45*(1), pp. 125–28.

Dovring, Folke. Underemployment in Agriculture: A Rejoinder. *Econ. Develop. Cult. Change*, January 1969, *17*(2), pp. 273–76. **[G: Greece]**

Dovring, Folke. Variants and Invariants in Comparative Agricultural Systems. *Amer. J. Agr. Econ.*, December 1969, *51*(5), pp. 1263–73.

Elliott, C. M. Agriculture and Economic Development in Africa: Theory and Experience 1880–1914. **In** *Jones, E. L. and Woolf, S. J., eds.*, 1969, pp. 123–50. **[G: Africa]**

Evans, James Gilbert, Sr. Foreign Aid for Agricultural Development. *Amer. J. Agr. Econ.*, December 1969, *51*(5), pp. 1402–12.

Fei, John C. H. and Ranis, Gustav. Agriculture in the Open Economy. **In** *Thorbecke, E., ed.*, 1969, pp. 129–59.

Fei, John C. H. and Ranis, Gustav. Agriculture in the Open Economy: Reply. **In** *Thorbecke, E., ed.*, 1969, pp. 163–64.

Fox, Karl A. Toward a Policy Model of World Economic Development with Special Attention to the Agricultural Sector. **In** *Thorbecke, E., ed.*, 1969, pp. 95–126.

Georgescu-Roegen, Nicholas. Process in Farming Versus Process in Manufacturing: A Problem of Balanced Development. **In** *Papi, U. and Nunn, C., eds.*, 1969, pp. 497–528.

Gerald, John O. Role of Transportation in Agricultural Marketing and Development: Discussion. *Amer. J. Agr. Econ.*, December 1969, *51*(5), pp. 1478–81. **[G: U.S.]**

Ghosh, Alak. The Role of Agriculture in the Fourth Plan. **In** *Bhuleshkar, A. V., ed.*, 1969, pp. 60–68. **[G: India]**

Gilson, J. C. The Demand for Agricultural Economists by Canadian Universities and Governments. *Can. J. Agr. Econ.*, November 1969, *17*(3), pp. 124–32. **[G: Canada]**

Graham, Anila. The Export Growth of Agricultural Commodities in Indian International Trade.

In *Bhuleshkar, A. V., ed.,* 1969, pp. 157–72. [G: India]

Grigg, David. The Agricultural Regions of the World: Review and Reflections. *Econ. Geogr.,* April 1969, *45*(2), pp. 95–132.

Hardin, Charles M. The Bureau of Agricultural Economics under Fire: A Study in Valuation Conflicts. In *Fox, K. A. and Johnson, D. G., eds.,* 1969, pp. 423–52. [G: U.S.]

Hathaway, Dale E. The Economics of Agricultural Economics. *Amer. J. Agr. Econ.,* December 1969, *51*(5), pp. 1011–26. [G: U.S.]

Hemmi, Kenzō. Primary Product Exports and Economic Development: The Case of Silk. In *Ohkawa, K.; Johnston, B. F. and Kaneda, H., eds.,* 1969, pp. 303–23. [G: Japan]

Hsing, Su. The Two-Way Struggle Between Socialism and Capitalism in China's Rural Areas After the Land Reform [Part III]. *Chinese Econ. Stud.,* Winter 1968/69, *2*(2), pp. 50–80. [G: China]

Hymer, Stephen H. and Resnick, Stephen. A Model of an Agrarian Economy with Nonagricultural Activities. *Amer. Econ. Rev.,* Part I, September 1969, *59*(4), pp. 493–506.

Jones, E. L. and Woolf, S. J. Introduction: The Historical Role of Agrarian Change in Economic Development. In *Jones, E. L. and Woolf, S. J., eds.,* 1969, pp. 1–21.

Jorgenson, Dale W. A Programming Model for a Dual Economy: Comment. In *Thorbecke, E., ed.,* 1969, pp. 231–34.

Karcz, Jerzy F. Comparative Study of Transformation of Agriculture in Centrally Planned Economies: The Soviet Union, Eastern Europe and Mainland China: Reply. In *Thorbecke, E., ed.,* 1969, pp. 274–76. [G: U.S.S.R.; E. Europe; China]

Karcz, Jerzy F. Comparative Study of Transformation of Agriculture in Centrally Planned Economies: The Soviet Union, Eastern Europe and Mainland China. In *Thorbecke, E., ed.,* 1969, pp. 237–66. [G: U.S.S.R.; E. Europe; China]

Kassirov, L. Methodological Questions Pertaining to Net Income and the Profitability of Agricultural Production. *Prob. Econ.,* May 1969, *12*(1), pp. 45–66. [G: U.S.S.R.]

Khan, Mahmood Hasan. Development Alternatives and Problems in Dual Economies. *Econ. Int.,* November 1969, *22*(4), pp. 636–61. [G: India; Pakistan]

Lee, T. H. The Transferability of the Japanese Pattern of Modernizing Traditional Agriculture: Comment. In *Thorbecke, E., ed.,* 1969, pp. 303–10.

Lewis, W. Arthur. Agriculture in the Open Economy: Comment. In *Thorbecke, E., ed.,* 1969, pp. 159–63.

Manderscheid, Lester V. and Nelson, Glenn L. A Framework for Viewing Simulation. *Can. J. Agr. Econ.,* February 1969, *17*(1), pp. 33–41.

McLoughlin, Peter F. M. "Subsistence Agriculture" and Technological Change: Further Discussion of the Theoretical Problem. *Amer. J. Agr. Econ.,* November 1969, *51*(4), pp. 957–60.

McRorie, H. D. The Demand for Agricultural Economists by Agri-Business to 1980. *Can. J. Agr. Econ.,* November 1969, *17*(3), pp. 114–23. [G: Canada]

Mellor, John W. Agricultural Price Policy in the Context of Economic Development. *Amer. J. Agr. Econ.,* December 1969, *51*(5), pp. 1413–19.

Mellor, John W. Production Economics and the Modernization of Traditional Agricultures. *Australian J. Agr. Econ.,* June 1969, *13*(1), pp. 25–34.

Montias, John Michael. Comparative Study of Transformation of Agriculture in Centrally Planned Economies: The Soviet Union, Eastern Europe and Mainland China: Comment. In *Thorbecke, E., ed.,* 1969, pp. 266–74. [G: U.S.S.R.; E. Europe; China]

Mueller, P. and Zevering, K. H. Employment Promotion through Rural Development: A Pilot Project in Western Nigeria. *Int. Lab. Rev.,* August 1969, *100*(2), pp. 111–30. [G: Nigeria]

Nicholls, William H. The Transformation of Agriculture in a Presently Semi-Industrialized Country: The Case of Brazil. In *Thorbecke, E., ed.,* 1969, pp. 311–78. [G: Brazil]

Nichols, T. E., Jr. Transportation and Regional Development in Agriculture. *Amer. J. Agr. Econ.,* December 1969, *51*(5), pp. 1455–63.

Ohkawa, Kazushi. Phases of Agricultural Development and Economic Growth. In *Ohkawa, K.; Johnston, B. F. and Kaneda, H., eds.,* 1969, pp. 3–36. [G: Japan]

Ohkawa, Kazushi and Johnston, Bruce F. The Transferability of the Japanese Pattern of Modernizing Traditional Agriculture. In *Thorbecke, E., ed.,* 1969, pp. 277–303.

Parish, R. M. Some Thoughts on the Role of the Agricultural Economics Profession in Australia. *Australian J. Agr. Econ.,* June 1969, *13*(1), pp. 1–7. [G: Australia]

Pepelasis, A. Underemployment in Agriculture: A Comment. *Econ. Develop. Cult. Change,* January 1969, *17*(2), pp. 267–72. [G: Greece]

Peterson, Willis L. The Allocation of Research, Teaching, and Extension Personnel in U.S. Colleges of Agriculture. *Amer. J. Agr. Econ.,* February 1969, *51*(1), pp. 41–56. [G: U.S.]

Phillips, Richard. Inducing Economic Development in Less Developed Countries: Discussion. *Amer. J. Agr. Econ.,* December 1969, *51*(5), pp. 1424–26.

Puri, I. C. and Srinivasan, R. Agency for Operation of Buffer Stocks. In *Indian Society of Agricultural Economics,* 1969, pp. 118–27. [G: India]

Reynolds, Clark W. Relationships between Agriculture, Nonagriculture, and Foreign Trade in the Development of Argentina and Peru: Comment. In *Thorbecke, E., ed.,* 1969, pp. 213–17. [G: Argentina; Peru]

Sandee, Jan. A Programming Model for a Dual Economy. In *Thorbecke, E., ed.,* 1969, pp. 219–30.

Schuh, G. Edward. The Transformation of Agriculture in a Presently Semi-Industrialized Country: The Case of Brazil: Comment. In *Thorbecke, E., ed.,* 1969, pp. 379–85. [G: Brazil]

Schutjer, Wayne and Weigel, Dale. The Contribution of Foreign Assistance to Agricultural Development. *Amer. J. Agr. Econ.,* November 1969, *51* (4), pp. 788–97.

Shaffer, James Duncan. On Institutional Obsolescence and Innovation—Background for Professional Dialogue on Public Policy. *Amer. J. Agr. Econ.*, May 1969, *51*(2), pp. 245–67. [G: U.S.]

Simon, Julian L. and Gardner, David M. World Food Needs and "New Proteins." *Econ. Develop. Cult. Change*, July 1969, *17*(4), pp. 520–26.

Smith, T. Lynn. Some Major Current Rural Social Trends in the United States of America. *Int. Soc. Sci. J.*, 1969, *21*(2), pp. 272–85. [G: U.S.]

Steeper, N. J. Some Results of an Economic Survey of the Dried Vine Fruit Industry, 1965–66 to 1967–68. *Quart. Rev. Agr. Econ.*, April 1969, *22* (2), pp. 82–102. [G: Australia]

Sukhatme, P. V. The Dimensions of India's Food Problem in Economic Development. **In** *Bhuleshkar, A. V., ed.*, 1969, pp. 69–87. [G: India]

Thorbecke, Erik and Field, Alfred J. Relationships between Agriculture, Nonagriculture, and Foreign Trade in the Development of Argentina and Peru. **In** *Thorbecke, E., ed.*, 1969, pp. 165–213. [G: Argentina; Peru]

Thorbecke, Erik and Field, Alfred J. Relationships between Agriculture, Nonagriculture, and Foreign Trade in the Development of Argentina and Peru: Reply. **In** *Thorbecke, E., ed.*, 1969, pp. 217–18. [G: Argentina; Peru]

Tolley, George S. Review Article: Mellor on Agricultural Development. *Econ. Develop. Cult. Change*, January 1969, *17*(2), pp. 254–61.

Toussaint, W. D. The Organization of Agriculture: Discussion. *Amer. J. Agr. Econ.*, December 1969, *51*(5), pp. 1283–85.

Ward, Richard J. Absorbing More Labor in LDC Agriculture. *Econ. Develop. Cult. Change*, January 1969, *17*(2), pp. 178–88.

Wells, Oris V. Some Problems of Agricultural Development. *Amer. J. Agr. Econ.*, December 1969, *51* (5), pp. 1037–45.

Wiegmann, Fred H. Agriculture in the Louisiana Economy. **In** *Beard, T. R., ed.*, 1969, pp. 55–81. [G: U.S.]

Wilber, Charles K. The Role of Agriculture in Soviet Economic Development. *Land Econ.*, February 1969, *45*(1), pp. 87–96. [G: U.S.S.R.]

Williams, F. A. Agricultural Price Policy in the Context of Economic Development: Discussion. *Amer. J. Agr. Econ.*, December 1969, *51*(5), pp. 1420–23.

Wunderlich, Gene. The Organization of Agriculture: An Epilogue. *Amer. J. Agr. Econ.*, December 1969, *51*(5), pp. 1289–92.

Zangheri, R. The Historical Relationship between Agricultural and Economic Development in Italy. **In** *Jones, E. L. and Woolf, S. J., eds.*, 1969, pp. 23–39. [G: Italy]

711 Agricultural Supply and Demand Analysis

7110 Agricultural Supply and Demand Analysis

Adhvaryu, J. H. and Patel, A. S. Determinants and Development Implications of Foodgrain Prices in India: Comment. *Amer. J. Agr. Econ.*, November 1969, *51*(4), pp. 939–40. [G: India]

Agarwala, R. Price Policy in a Multi-Product Firm: A Case Study. *Appl. Econ.*, August 1969, *1*(3), pp. 161–66. [G: U.K.]

Aggrey-Mensah, W. and Tuckwell, N. E. A Study of Banana Supply and Price Patterns on the Sydney Wholesale Market: An Application of Spectral Analysis. *Australian J. Agr. Econ.*, December 1969, *13*(2), pp. 101–17. [G: Australia]

Allan, William. Land Tenure and Productivity. **In** *Hutchinson, J. [Sir], ed.*, 1969, pp. 96–114.

Arak, Marcelle. Estimation of Assymetric Longrun Supply Functions: The Case of Coffee. *Can. J. Agr. Econ.*, February 1969, *17*(1), pp. 15–22. [G: Brazil]

Arromdee, Virach. Can West Malaysia Become Self-Sufficient in Rice by 1975? *Malayan Econ. Rev.*, October 1969, *14*(2), pp. 79–93. [G: Malaysia]

Babb, E. M.; Belden, S. A. and Saathoff, C. R. An Analysis of Cooperative Bargaining in the Processing Tomato Industry. *Amer. J. Agr. Econ.*, February 1969, *51*(1), pp. 13–25. [G: U.S.]

Baldovinos de la Peña, Gabriel. El sector ejidal y el plan agricola nacional. (The Ejidal Sector and the National Agricultural Plan. With English summary.) *Econ. Polít.*, Second Semester 1969, *6*(2), pp. 215–22. [G: Mexico]

Bardhan, Kalpana. A Note on Price-Elasticity of Demand for Foodgrain in a Peasant Economy. *Oxford Econ. Pap.*, March 1969, *21*(1), pp. 104–08. [G: India]

Beighley, H. Prescott and Mak, James. The Effect of a Marketing Order on Winter Carrot Prices: Comment. *Amer. J. Agr. Econ.*, November 1969, *51*(4), pp. 929–33. [G: U.S.]

Beker, Víctor Alberto. Elasticidades de oferta de la producción agropecuaria: trigo, maíz y carne vacuna. (Elasticities of Supply in Agricultural Production: Wheat, Maize and Beef. With English summary.) *Económica*, May–August 1969, *15*(2), pp. 145–81. [G: Argentina]

Bell, Peter F. and Tai, Janet. Markets, Middlemen and Technology: Agricultural Supply Response in the Dualistic Economies of Southeast Asia. *Malayan Econ. Rev.*, April 1969, *14*(1), pp. 29–47. [G: S.E. Asia]

Benet, I. and Berend, I. Relative Capital Intensity of Food Production and Industry. *Acta Oecon.*, 1969, *4*(4), pp. 379–402. [G: Hungary]

Bhuleshkar, A. V. An Analysis of the Price Movements of Certain Agricultural Commodities Since 1939: Food for Peace and Its Effects of Economic Development. **In** *Bhuleshkar, A. V., ed.*, 1969, pp. 117–36. [G: India]

Bhuleshkar, A. V. The Problem of Productivity and Technical Change in Indian Agriculture: A Theoretical Analysis. **In** *Bhuleshkar, A. V., ed.*, 1969, pp. 103–16. [G: India]

Bose, Swadesh R. and Clark, Edwin H., II. Some Basic Considerations on Agricultural Mechanization in West Pakistan. *Pakistan Develop. Rev.*, Autumn 1969, *9*(3), pp. 273–308. [G: W. Pakistan]

Brandow, G. E. Market Power and Its Sources in the Food Industry. *Amer. J. Agr. Econ.*, February 1969, *51*(1), pp. 1–12.

Brown, Joseph D. Effect of a Health Hazard "Scare" on Consumer Demand. *Amer. J. Agr. Econ.*, August 1969, *51*(3), pp. 676–79. [G: U.S.]

Buller, Orlan and Lin, Wuu-Long. Measuring the Effect of Weather on Crop Production. *Can. J. Agr. Econ.*, February 1969, *17*(1), pp. 91–98. **[G: U.S.]**

Chatterji, M. Chemical Fertilisers: Rapid Growth. **In** *Dagli, V., ed., Vol. II*, 1969, pp. 201–03. **[G: India]**

Chaudhri, D. P. Education of Farmers and Productivity. **In** *Pandit, H. N., ed.*, 1969, pp. 337–48. **[G: India]**

Cliff, Edward P. Statement. **In** *Timber Management Policies, SCH*, 1969, pp. 234–70. **[G: U.S.]**

Cloutier, Raymond. Structural Relationships in Industrial Milk Production in Ontario. *Can. J. Agr. Econ.*, February 1969, *17*(1), pp. 157–58. **[G: Canada]**

Conneman, George J. and Harrington, D. H. Implications of Exit and Entry of Farm Firms in Agricultural Supply Analysis. *Agr. Econ. Res.*, April 1969, *21*(2), pp. 40–44. **[G: U.S.]**

Coondoo, Dipankor. The Effect of Relative Prices on Engel Elasticity of Cereals in India. *Arthaniti*, January & July 1969, *12*(1&2), pp. 57–68. **[G: India]**

Day, Richard H. Recursive Programming and Supply Prediction. **In** *Fox, K. A. and Johnson, D. G., eds.*, 1969, pp. 107–22.

Desai, M. D. Experience of Hybrid Bajra Farming in the Kaira District. *Artha-Vikas*, January 1969, *5*(1), pp. 95–103. **[G: India]**

Dixit, Avinash K. Marketable Surplus and Dual Development. *J. Econ. Theory*, August 1969, *1*(2), pp. 203–19.

Egbert, Alvin C. An Aggregate Model of Agriculture—Empirical Estimates and Some Policy Implications. *Amer. J. Agr. Econ.*, February 1969, *51* (1), pp. 71–86. **[G: U.S.]**

Ehrich, R. L. Cash-Futures Price Relationships for Live Beef Cattle. *Amer. J. Agr. Econ.*, February 1969, *51*(1), pp. 26–40. **[G: U.S.]**

Engel, N. Eugene and Johnson, Stanley R. Spatial Price Equilibrium and Price Variability: An Application to the Fall Potato Industry. *Can. J. Agr. Econ.*, February 1969, *17*(1), pp. 23–32. **[G: U.S.]**

Folwell, Raymond J. A New Look at Demand Analysis for Beef: Comment. *Amer. J. Agr. Econ.*, November 1969, *51*(4), pp. 947–49. **[G: U.S.]**

Fox, Karl A. Factors Affecting Farm Income, Farm Prices, and Food Consumption. **In** *Fox, K. A. and Johnson, D. G., eds.*, 1969, pp. 37–63. **[G: U.S.]**

Guise, John W. B. Factors Associated with Variation in the Aggregate Average Yield of New Zealand Wheat (1918–1967) *Amer. J. Agr. Econ.*, November 1969, *51*(4), pp. 866–81. **[G: New Zealand]**

Hall, Harry H.; Heady, Earl O. and Plessner, Yakir. Quadratic Programming Solution of Competitive Equilibrium for U.S. Agriculture: Reply. *Amer. J. Agr. Econ.*, May 1969, *51*(2), pp. 483–84. **[G: U.S.]**

Hartman, L. M.; Holland, David and Giddings, Marvin. Effects of Hurricane Storms on Agriculture. *Water Resources Res.*, June 1969, *5*(3), pp. 555–62. **[G: U.S.]**

Hayami, Yūjirō. Resource Endowments and Technological Change in Agriculture: U.S. and Japanese Experiences in International Perspective. *Amer. J. Agr. Econ.*, December 1969, *51*(5), pp. 1293–1303. **[G: U.S.; Japan]**

Hayami, Yūjirō. Sources of Agricultural Productivity Gap among Selected Countries. *Amer. J. Agr. Econ.*, August 1969, *51*(3), pp. 564–75.

Hayami, Yūjirō and Yamada, Saburō. Agricultural Productivity at the Beginning of Industrialization. **In** *Ohkawa, K.; Johnston, B. F. and Kaneda, H., eds.*, 1969, pp. 105–35. **[G: Japan]**

Hirvonen, Martti J. Balanced Dairy Production—Interregional Linear Programming Approach. *Kansant. Aikak.*, 1969, *65*(4), pp. 274–79.

Houck, James P. and Subotnik, Abraham. The U.S. Supply of Soybeans: Regional Acreage Functions. *Agr. Econ. Res.*, October 1969, *21*(4), pp. 99–108. **[G: U.S.]**

Hughes, John J. Note on the U.S. Demand for Coffee. *Amer. J. Agr. Econ.*, November 1969, *51*(4), pp. 912–14. **[G: U.S.]**

Hussain, Sayed Mushtaq. The Effect of the Growing Constraint of Subsistence Farming on Farmer Response to Price: A Case Study of Jute in Pakistan. *Pakistan Develop. Rev.*, Autumn 1969, *9*(3), pp. 235–72. **[G: Pakistan]**

Johnson, Paul R. On Testing Competing Hypotheses: Economic Rationality versus Traditional Behavior: Reply. *Amer. J. Agr. Econ.*, February 1969, *51*(1), pp. 208–09.

Johnston, Bruce F. and Cownie, John. The Seed-Fertilizer Revolution and Labor Force Absorption. *Amer. Econ. Rev.*, Part I, September 1969, *59*(4), pp. 569–82. **[G: W. Pakistan]**

Kahlon, A. S. and Kahlon, S. S. Enhancement of Agricultural Taxation Will Not Sustain the Green Revolution in Agriculture. *Artha-Vikas*, July 1969, *5*(2), pp. 63–70. **[G: India]**

Kaneda, Hiromitsu. Economic Implications of the "Green Revolution" and the Strategy of Agricultural Development in West Pakistan. *Pakistan Develop. Rev.*, Summer 1969, *9*(2), pp. 111–43. **[G: W. Pakistan]**

Knutson, Ronald D. The Economic Consequences of the Minnesota Dairy Industry Unfair Trade Practices Act. *J. Law Econ.*, October 1969, *12*(2), pp. 377–89. **[G: U.S.]**

Kottke, Marvin. The Supply Function in Agriculture Revisited: Discussion. *Amer. Econ. Rev.*, May 1969, *59*(2), pp. 184–85.

Kuchenbecker, Horst. Zur Darstellung von Veränderungen der Weltwarenpreise durch arithmetische und geometrische Indizes am Beispiel des Moody-Index und des Reuter-Index. (On the Representation of World Commodity Price Changes by Arithmetic and Geometric Index Numbers, Illustrated in Moodys Index of Staple Commodities and Reuters Commodity Index. With English summary.) *Jahr. Nationalökon. Statist.*, August 1969, *183*(3–4), pp. 254–70.

Leonard, Patrick L. A Note on the Demand for Fertilizer in West Pakistan. *Pakistan Develop. Rev.*, Winter 1969, *9*(4), pp. 419–25. **[G: W. Pakistan]**

Leuthold, Raymond M. An Analysis of Daily Fluctuations in the Hog Economy. *Amer. J. Agr. Econ.*, November 1969, *51*(4), pp. 849–65. **[G: U.S.]**

Lindner, R. K. The Economics of Increased Beef

Production on Dairy Farms in Western Australia. *Quart. Rev. Agr. Econ.*, July 1969, *22*(3), pp. 147–64. **[G: Australia]**

Loyns, R. M. A. Are Beef Prices Too High? *Can. J. Agr. Econ.*, July 1969, *17*(2), pp. 124–31. **[G: Canada]**

Lukinov, I. Prices and Planned Economic Regulation of Agricultural Production. *Prob. Econ.*, May 1969, *12*(1), pp. 67–90. **[G: U.S.S.R.]**

Maitha, J. K. A Supply Function for Kenyan Coffee. *East Afr. Econ. Rev.*, June 1969, *1*(1), pp. 63–72. **[G: Kenya]**

Marshall, R. G. The Size and Structure of the Livestock Industry in Canada, 1980. *Can. J. Agr. Econ.*, November 1969, *17*(3), pp. 90–103. **[G: Canada]**

McKenzie, C. J.; Philpot, B. P. and Woods, M. J. Price Formation in the Raw Wool Market. *Econ. Rec.*, September 1969, *45*(111), pp. 386–98.

Mehta, Parkash. Different Inputs as Related to Apple Output in Kulu District. *Asian Econ. Rev.*, May 1969, *11*(3), pp. 325–28. **[G: India]**

Mellor, John W. Determinants and Development Implications of Foodgrain Prices in India: Reply. *Amer. J. Agr. Econ.*, November 1969, *51*(4), pp. 941–42. **[G: India]**

Misawa, Takeo. An Analysis of Part-time Farming in the Postwar Period. **In** *Ohkawa, K.; Johnston, B. F. and Kaneda, H., eds.*, 1969, pp. 250–69. **[G: Japan]**

Mukerji, V. and Mukerji, K. Substitution between Superior and Inferior Foodgrains in India between 1900–1958. **In** *Bhuleshkar, A. V., ed.*, 1969, pp. 137–56. **[G: India]**

Nayar, M. K. K. Fertilisers and Farm Revolution. **In** *Dagli, V., ed., Vol. II*, 1969, pp. 204–06. **[G: India]**

Nevel, Robert O. Technological Change in Agriculture. *Agr. Econ. Res.*, January 1969, *21*(1), pp. 13–18. **[G: U.S.]**

Nuthall, P. L. Estimation of Supply Functions by Linear Programming: A Note. *Rev. Marketing Agr. Econ.*, September 1969, *37*(3), pp. 172–77.

Patel, G. A. and Shah, R. L. Cultivation of Hybrid Bajri in Gujarat State. *Artha-Vikas*, January 1969, *5*(1), pp. 81–94. **[G: India]**

Pillai, P. Purushothaman. An Inter-District, Inter-Crop Comparison of Growth Rates in Agriculture in Kerala. *Asian Econ. Rev.*, May 1969, *11*(3), pp. 249–59. **[G: India]**

Pincock, M. Glade. Assessing Impacts of Declining Water Quality on Gross Value Output of Agriculture, A Case Study. *Water Resources Res.*, February 1969, *5*(1), pp. 1–12. **[G: U.S.]**

Porter, R. C. Who Destabilizes Primary Product Prices? *Indian Econ. J.*, April–June 1969, *16*(4–5), pp. 389–418.

Rabbani, A. K. M. Ghulam. A Proposal for Fiscal Incentives for the Raw-Jute Exports. *Pakistan Develop. Rev.*, Winter 1969, *9*(4), pp. 400–418. **[G: Pakistan]**

Rayner, A. C. The Wool Price and the Production of Synthetics. *Yorkshire Bull. Econ. Soc. Res.*, May 1969, *21*(1), pp. 31–38.

Riahi, Ebrahim. Factors Causing Declines in the Sugar Content of Beets in Iran. *Tahq. Eq.*, November 1969, *6*(15&16), pp. 80–97. **[G: Iran]**

Ruttan, Vernon W. Agricultural Product and Factor Markets in Southeast Asia. *Econ. Develop. Cult. Change*, July 1969, *17*(4), pp. 501–19. **[G: Asia]**

Sault, J. L. Recent Developments Affecting the Market Outlook for Australian Raw Cotton. *Quart. Rev. Agr. Econ.*, July 1969, *22*(3), pp. 123–39. **[G: Australia]**

Sawada, Shūjirō. Technological Change in Japanese Agriculture: A Long-Term Analysis. **In** *Ohkawa, K.; Johnston, B. F. and Kaneda, H., eds.*, 1969, pp. 136–54. **[G: Japan]**

Schaller, W. Neill. The Supply Function in Agriculture Revisited: Discussion. *Amer. Econ. Rev.*, May 1969, *59*(2), pp. 185–87.

Scobie, G. M. Trends in Production from Sheep Properties: A Brief Review and Medium Term Projection of Sheep Numbers. *Quart. Rev. Agr. Econ.*, October 1969, *22*(4), pp. 185–98. **[G: Australia]**

Seagraves, James A. Capitalized Values of Tobacco Allotments and the Rate of Return to Allotment Owners. *Amer. J. Agr. Econ.*, May 1969, *51*(2), pp. 320–34. **[G: U.S.]**

Sengupta, Jati K. and Sen, Amitava. Econometric Supply Functions for Rice and Jute. *Arthaniti*, January & July 1969, *12*(1&2), pp. 1–40. **[G: India]**

Shafer, Carl E. The Effect of a Marketing Order on Winter Carrot Prices: Reply. *Amer. J. Agr. Econ.*, November 1969, *51*(4), pp. 933–34. **[G: U.S.]**

Sharples, Jerry A. The Representative Farm Approach to Estimation of Supply Response. *Amer. Econ. Rev.*, May 1969, *59*(2), pp. 168–74. **[G: U.S.]**

Simush, P. I. The Impact of the Scientific and Technological Revolution on the Socialist Village. *Int. Soc. Sci. J.*, 1969, *21*(2), pp. 256–64. **[G: U.S.S.R.]**

Sinha, Randhir and Singh, D. K. A Study of Potato Price Behaviour in Selected Markets of Bihar. *Econ. Aff.*, January-February 1969, *14*(1–2), pp. 93–102. **[G: India]**

Slaughter, Rudie W., Jr. Payment Limitation: Effect on Supply Adjustment and Income Distribution. *Amer. J. Agr. Econ.*, December 1969, *51*(5), pp. 1233–36. **[G: U.S.]**

Smith, Blair J. and Purcell, Joseph C. Quadratic Programming Solution of Competitive Equilibrium for U.S. Agriculture: Comment. *Amer. J. Agr. Econ.*, May 1969, *51*(2), pp. 481–82. **[G: U.S.]**

Solverson, Lyle. Consumer Knowledge for Sovereignty: Apples. *Amer. J. Agr. Econ.*, December 1969, *51*(5), pp. 1247–50. **[G: U.S.]**

Swackhamer, Gene L. Synthetics and Substitutes: Challenge to Agriculture. *Fed. Res. Bank Kansas City Rev.*, March 1969, pp. 3–12. **[G: U.S.]**

Swanson, Earl R. and Dunlap, R. D. Influence of Prices on Production Potential for Beef and Hogs on Farms with Fixed Acreages. *Ill. Agr. Econ.*, January 1969, *9*(1), pp. 10–17. **[G: U.S.]**

Taplin, J. and Ryan, W. The Prospects for Wine in Australia. *Quart. Rev. Agr. Econ.*, October 1969, *22*(4), pp. 198–209. **[G: Australia]**

Thorp, Rosemary. A Note on Food Supplies, the Distribution of Income and National Income Accounting in Peru. *Bull. Oxford Univ. Inst. Econ. Statist.*, November 1969, *31*(4), pp. 229–41. [G: Peru]

Tintner, Gerhard and Patel, Malvika. A Lognormal Diffusion Process Applied to the Growth of Yields of Some Agricultural Crops in India. *J. Devel. Stud.*, October 1969, *6*(1), pp. 49–57. [G: India]

Tsuchiya, Keizō. Economics of Mechanization in Small-scale Agriculture. In *Ohkawa, K.; Johnston, B. F. and Kaneda, H., eds.*, 1969, pp. 155–72. [G: Japan]

Tweeten, Luther G. and Quance, C. Leroy. Positivistic Measures of Aggregate Supply Elasticities: Some New Approaches. *Amer. Econ. Rev.*, May 1969, *59*(2), pp. 175–83. [G: U.S.]

Tyrchniewicz, Edward W. and Schuh, G. Edward. Econometric Analysis of the Agricultural Labor Market. *Amer. J. Agr. Econ.*, November 1969, *51* (4), pp. 770–87. [G: U.S.]

Uvacek, Edward, Jr. A New Look at Demand Analysis for Beef: Reply. *Amer. J. Agr. Econ.*, November 1969, *51*(4), pp. 949–52. [G: U.S.]

Vosloo, J. J. and Groenewald, J. A. An Analysis of the Demand for Apples in the Republic of South Africa. *Finance Trade Rev.*, June 1969, *8*(3), pp. 187–97. [G: S. Africa]

Weisenborn, David E. Allocation of Florida Orange Production among Alternative Product Forms and Market Sectors. *Amer. J. Agr. Econ.*, December 1969, *51*(5), pp. 1134–37. [G: U.S.]

Whan, R. B. and Richardson, R. A. A Simulated Study of an Auction Market. *Australian J. Agr. Econ.*, December 1969, *13*(2), pp. 91–100. [G: Australia]

White, James H. The Supply Function in Agriculture Revisited: Discussion. *Amer. Econ. Rev.*, May 1969, *59*(2), pp. 187–88.

Willett, Helen E. and Whan, R. B. Price Variation within Wool Auction Sales. *Quart. Rev. Agr. Econ.*, April 1969, *22*(2), pp. 66–81. [G: Australia]

Williams, G. D. V. Weather and Prairie Wheat Production. *Can. J. Agr. Econ.*, February 1969, *17*(1), pp. 99–109. [G: Canada]

Wilson, A. G. and Wood, A. W. Regional Livestock Production and Feed Freight Assistance. *Can. J. Agr. Econ.*, February 1969, *17*(1), pp. 77–90. [G: Canada]

Wipf, Larry J. and Bawden, D. Lee. Reliability of Supply Equations Derived from Production Functions. *Amer. J. Agr. Econ.*, February 1969, *51* (1), pp. 170–78. [G: U.S.]

Witherell, William H. A Comparison of the Determinants of Wool Production in the Six Leading Producing Countries: 1949–1965. *Amer. J. Agr. Econ.*, February 1969, *51*(1), pp. 138–58.

Woolwine, Phil C. The South Pacific as a Source of Timber. *Oregon Bus. Rev.*, August 1969, *28*(8), pp. 1–5. [G: S. Pacific]

Yeh, M. H. and Lin, Leon. Technological Change in the Canadian Livestock Industry: An Input-Output Approach. *Can. J. Agr. Econ.*, July 1969, *17*(2), pp. 63–84. [G: Canada]

Yotopoulos, Pan A. and Wise, John. On Testing Competing Hypotheses: Economic Rationality versus Traditional Behavior—A Further Development. *Amer. J. Agr. Econ.*, February 1969, *51*(1), pp. 203–08.

Yotopoulos, Pan A. and Wise, John. On Testing Competing Hypotheses: Economic Rationality versus Traditional Behavior: Rejoinder. *Amer. J. Agr. Econ.*, February 1969, *51*(1), pp. 209–10.

Young, Charles E. Statement. In *Timber Management Policies, SCH*, 1969, pp. 71–110. [G: U.S.]

712 Agricultural Situation and Outlook

7120 Agricultural Situation and Outlook

Anstey, Vera. A Fresh Approach to Agricultural Reconstruction in Indian Development. **In** *Bhuleshkar, A. V., ed.*, 1969, pp. 47–59. [G: India]

Baldovinos de la Peña, Gabriel. La agricultura al final de la década. (The State of Agriculture at the End of the Present Decade. With English summary.) *Econ. Polít.*, Fourth Semester 1969, *6*(4), pp. 453–60. [G: Mexico]

Bell, Peter F. and Tai, Janet. Markets, Middlemen and Technology: Agricultural Supply Response in the Dualistic Economies of Southeast Asia. *Malayan Econ. Rev.*, April 1969, *14*(1), pp. 29–47. [G: S.E. Asia]

Bishop, C. E. The Mobility of Rural Manpower. **In** *Papi, U. and Nunn, C., eds.*, 1969, pp. 283–92.

Blase, Melvin G. The World Food-Population Problem: 1969. *Univ. Missouri Bus. Govt. Rev.*, May–June 1969, *10*(3), pp. 20–27.

Boden, E. A. The Canadian Livestock Industry: Comment. *Can. J. Agr. Econ.*, November 1969, *17* (3), pp. 111–13. [G: Canada]

Boulding, Kenneth E. The Old Agricultural Lag. **In** *Ruttan, V. W.; Waldo, A. D. and Houck, J. P., eds.*, 1969, pp. 317–18.

Breimyer, Harold F. Future Organization and Control of U.S. Agricultural Production and Marketing. **In** *Owen, W. F., ed.*, 1969, pp. 14–25. [G: U.S.]

Brown, J. A. C. A Regional Model of Agricultural Development. **In** *Thorbecke, E., ed.*, 1969, pp. 75–92.

Campbell, D. R. and MacGregor, M. A. Guidelines for Agricultural Policy Over the Next Decade. *Can. J. Agr. Econ.*, November 1969, *17*(3), pp. 57–64. [G: Canada]

Engel, N. Eugene and Johnson, Stanley R. Spatial Price Equilibrium and Price Variability: An Application to the Fall Potato Industry. *Can. J. Agr. Econ.*, February 1969, *17*(1), pp. 23–32. [G: U.S.]

Fox, Karl A. A Regional Model of Agricultural Development: Comment. **In** *Thorbecke, E., ed.*, 1969, pp. 93–94.

Freebairn, Donald K. The Dichotomy of Prosperity and Poverty in Mexican Agriculture. *Land Econ.*, February 1969, *45*(1), pp. 31–42. [G: Mexico]

Harrar, J. George and Wortman, Sterling. Expanding Food Production in Hungry Nations: The Promise, the Problems. **In** *Hardin, C. M., ed.*, 1969, pp. 89–135.

Havlíček, Jaromír and Jeníček, Vladimír. Estimates

of Long-term Development of Agriculture by Means of the Global Factorial Model: Reply. *Czech. Econ. Pap.*, 1969, (11), pp. 109–111. **[G: Czechoslovakia]**

Havlíček, Jaromír and Jeníček, Vladimír. Model of the Long-term Development of Czechoslovak Agriculture. *Czech. Econ. Pap.*, 1969, (11), pp. 83–102. **[G: Czechoslovakia]**

Heady, Earl O. The Future Structure of U.S. Agriculture. **In** *Owen, W. F., ed.*, 1969, pp. 113–28. **[G: U.S.]**

Hieronymus, T. A. Soybeans: End of an Era? *Ill. Agr. Econ.*, July 1969, *9*(2), pp. 1–18. **[G: U.S.]**

Hinton, W. L. The Contribution of Horticulture. *Nat. Westminster Bank Quart. Rev.*, May 1969, pp. 33–41. **[G: U.K.]**

Huff, H. Bruce. Canada's Future Role in the World Wheat Market. *Can. J. Agr. Econ.*, February 1969, *17*(1), pp. 1–14. **[G: Canada]**

Johnson, Glenn L. The Modern Family Farm and Its Problems: With Particular Reference to the United States of America. **In** *Papi, U. and Nunn, C., eds.*, 1969, pp. 234–50. **[G: U.S.]**

Le Bihan, Joseph. Vertical Integration and Development of Farms: The Perfecting and Diffusion of Innovations in Integrated Systems. **In** *Papi, U. and Nunn, C., eds.*, 1969, pp. 325–43.

Lindsey, Quentin W. The Problem of Periodic Reorganization in American Agriculture. **In** *Owen, W. F., ed.*, 1969, pp. 1–14. **[G: U.S.]**

MacEachern, G. A. Guidelines for Agricultural Policy Over the Next Decade: Discussion. *Can. J. Agr. Econ.*, November 1969, *17*(3), pp. 64–69. **[G: Canada]**

Manning, Travis W. Economic Guidelines for Land and Water Resource Use in Agriculture. *Can. J. Agr. Econ.*, November 1969, *17*(3), pp. 1–8. **[G: Canada]**

Marshall, R. G. The Size and Structure of the Livestock Industry in Canada, 1980. *Can. J. Agr. Econ.*, November 1969, *17*(3), pp. 90–103. **[G: Canada]**

Mazumder, Debkumar Dutta. Estimates of Increase in Demand for Specific Items of Milk and Milk Products during Fourth and Fifth Five Year Plans. *Econ. Aff.*, January-February 1969, *14* (1–2), pp. 81–87. **[G: India]**

McCalla, Alex F. Whither Goest U.S. Agricultural Policy: An Exercise in Naive Prophesy. *Can. J. Agr. Econ.*, July 1969, *17*(2), pp. 1–16. **[G: U.S.]**

Melichar, Emanuel. Farm Capital and Credit Projections to 1980. *Amer. J. Agr. Econ.*, December 1969, *51*(5), pp. 1172–77. **[G: U.S.]**

Mujumdar, N. A. Agricultural Growth in India: Performance and Prospects. **In** *Bhuleshkar, A. V., ed.*, 1969, pp. 173–89. **[G: India]**

Nikl, Josef. Estimates of Long-term Development of Agriculture by Means of the Global Factorial Model. *Czech. Econ. Pap.*, 1969, (11), pp. 103–07. **[G: Czechoslovakia]**

Nikolitch, Radoje. The Adequate Family Farm—Mainstay of the Farm Economy. **In** *Owen, W. F., ed.*, 1969, pp. 26–37. **[G: U.S.]**

Ojala, E. M. Agriculture in the World of 1975: General Picture of Trends. **In** *Papi, U. and Nunn, C., eds.*, 1969, pp. 3–20.

Oury, Bernard. Weather and Economic Development. *Finance Develop.*, June 1969, *6*(2), pp. 24–29.

Paarlberg, Don. Food for More People and Better Nutrition. **In** *Hardin, C. M., ed.*, 1969, pp. 41–87.

Parpală, O. Experienţa României în făurirea unei agriculturi moderne. (The Experience of Romania in Creating a Modern Agriculture. With English summary.) *Stud. Cercet. Econ.*, 1969, *3*, pp. 121–29. **[G: Romania]**

Priebe, H. The Modern Family Farm and Its Problems: With Particular Reference to the Federal German Republic. **In** *Papi, U. and Nunn, C., eds.*, 1969, pp. 251–64. **[G: W. Germany]**

Rees, Richard D. U.S. Foreign Agricultural Trade in the 1970's: Growth or Contraction? *Fed. Res. Bank Kansas City Rev.*, September–October 1969, pp. 11–19. **[G: U.S.]**

Sault, J. L. Recent Developments Affecting the Market Outlook for Australian Raw Cotton. *Quart. Rev. Agr. Econ.*, July 1969, *22*(3), pp. 123–39. **[G: Australia]**

Sault, J. L. and Hellier, W. L. The New International Sugar Agreement and the Australian Sugar Industry. *Quart. Rev. Agr. Econ.*, October 1969, *22* (4), pp. 210–29. **[G: Australia]**

Simon, Herbert A. Effects of Increased Productivity upon the Ratio of Urban to Rural Population. **In** *Fox, K. A. and Johnson, D. G., eds.*, 1969, pp. 309–20.

Slen, S. B. and Cameron, M. A. Prospects and Potentials in Canadian Beef Production. *Can. J. Agr. Econ.*, November 1969, *17*(3), pp. 80–89. **[G: Canada]**

Sullivan, Gene D. Some Thoughts on Bargaining. *Amer. J. Agr. Econ.*, November 1969, *51*(4), pp. 960–61.

Swackhamer, Gene L. Agricultural Outlook: Approach of the 1970's. *Fed. Res. Bank Kansas City Rev.*, January 1969, pp. 3–11. **[G: U.S.]**

Taplin, J. and Ryan, W. The Prospects for Wine in Australia. *Quart. Rev. Agr. Econ.*, October 1969, *22*(4), pp. 198–209. **[G: Australia]**

Wädekin, Karl-Eugen. Manpower in Soviet Agriculture—Some Post-Khrushchev Developments and Problems. *Soviet Stud.*, January 1969, *20*(3), pp. 281–305. **[G: U.S.S.R.]**

Welden, William C. Milk Production and Utilization in the East. *Amer. J. Agr. Econ.*, November 1969, *51*(4), pp. 964–66. **[G: U.S.]**

Westerman, P. A. Changes in the World Wheat Situation and the 1967 International Grains Arrangement. *Quart. Rev. Agr. Econ.*, January 1969, *22*(1), pp. 20–34.

Wharton, Clifton R., Jr. The Green Revolution: Cornucopia or Pandora's Box? *Foreign Aff.*, April 1969, *47*(3), pp. 464–76.

Yamaoka, Ryoichi. The "Modernisation" of Agriculture at the Present Stage. *Kyoto Univ. Econ. Rev.*, April 1969, *39*(1), pp. 1–21. **[G: U.S.; W. Germany]**

Yeh, M. H. and Lin, Leon. Technological Change in the Canadian Livestock Industry: An Input-Output Approach. *Can. J. Agr. Econ.*, July 1969, *17*(2), pp. 63–84. **[G: Canada]**

Zepp, Glenn A. and McAlexander, Robert H. Predicting Aggregate Milk Production: An Empirical Study. *Amer. J. Agr. Econ.*, August 1969, *51*(3), pp. 642–49. [G: U.S.]

713 Agricultural Policy, Domestic and International

7130 Agricultural Policy, Domestic and International

Amin, R. B. Taxing Agricultural Incomes. *Artha-Vikas,* July 1969, *5*(2), pp. 106–07. [G: India]

Andal, Melvin E. Economic Guidelines for Present and Future Capital Use in Canadian Agriculture. *Can. J. Agr. Econ.*, November 1969, *17*(3), pp. 9–19. [G: Canada]

Angrish, A. C. Rationalized Agricultural Tax Structures in India and Some Policy Implications. *Artha-Vikas,* July 1969, *5*(2), pp. 154–70. [G: India]

Astrand, H. The Income Objective in Agricultural Policies. **In** *Papi, U. and Nunn, C., eds.*, 1969, pp. 397–408. [G: Sweden]

Baldovinos de la Peña, Gabriel. El sector ejidal y el plan agricola nacional. (The Ejidal Sector and the National Agricultural Plan. With English summary.) *Econ. Polít.*, Second Semester 1969, *6*(2), pp. 215–22. [G: Mexico]

Bandini, Mario. Free Trade and Planning in the Common Agricultural Policy. **In** *Papi, U. and Nunn, C., eds.*, 1969, pp. 77–84.

Bell, David E.; Hardin, Lowell S. and Hill, F. F. Hope for the Hungry: Fulfillment or Frustration? **In** *Hardin, C. M., ed.*, 1969, pp. 137–70. [G: U.S.]

Bhatt, Mahesh. Some Implications of Agricultural Income Tax. *Artha-Vikas,* July 1969, *5*(2), pp. 138–45. [G: India]

Bhuleshkar, A. V. An Analysis of the Price Movements of Certain Agricultural Commodities Since 1939: Food for Peace and Its Effects of Economic Development. **In** *Bhuleshkar, A. V., ed.*, 1969, pp. 117–36. [G: India]

Bichi, C. Reparţitia rentei diferenţiale. (Distribution of Differential Rent. With English summary.) *Stud. Cercet. Econ.*, 1969, *4*, pp. 59–70. [G: Romania]

Bonnen, James T. The Crises in the Traditional Roles of Agricultural Institutions. **In** *Ruttan, V. W.; Waldo, A. D. and Houck, J. P., eds.*, 1969, pp. 48–62. [G: U.S.]

Bornstein, Morris. The Soviet Debate on Agricultural Price and Procurement Reforms. *Soviet Stud.*, July 1969, *21*(1), pp. 1–20. [G: U.S.S.R.]

Bradley, Michael E. Marxism and Soviet Agricultural Problems. **In** *Prybyla, J. S., ed.*, 1969, pp. 89–95. [G: U.S.S.R.]

Brown, Harrison. Population, Food and the Energy Transition. **In** *Behrman, S. J.; Corsa, L., Jr. and Freedman, R., eds.*, 1969, pp. 180–88.

Burki, Shahid Javed. West Pakistan's Rural Works Program: A Study in Political and Administrative Response. *Middle East J.*, Summer 1969, *23*(3), pp. 321–42. [G: W. Pakistan]

Campbell, D. R. and MacGregor, M. A. Guidelines for Agricultural Policy Over the Next Decade. *Can. J. Agr. Econ.*, November 1969, *17*(3), pp. 57–64. [G: Canada]

Carr, A. Barry. Long-Term Versus Short-Term Land Retirement. *Amer. J. Agr. Econ.*, December 1969, *51*(5), pp. 1524–27. [G: U.S.]

Crutchfield, James A. Economic Evaluation of Weather Modification. **In** *Fleagle, R. G., ed.*, 1969, pp. 105–17. [G: U.S.]

Cummings, Ralph W., Jr. Buffer Stocks. **In** *Indian Society of Agricultural Economics,* 1969, pp. 49–84. [G: India]

Dandekar, V. M. Repercussions of Food Surpluses in Industrialized Countries on Economic Growth in Developing Countries. **In** *Papi, U. and Nunn, C., eds.*, 1969, pp. 182–99.

Dardis, Rachel and Dennisson, Janet. The Welfare Cost of Alternative Methods of Protecting Raw Wool in the United States. *Amer. J. Agr. Econ.*, May 1969, *51*(2), pp. 303–19. [G: U.S.]

Davidson, Malcolm. Directions for Ontario Agriculture. *Can. J. Agr. Econ.*, November 1969, *17*(3), pp. 170–74. [G: Canada]

Dawson, John A. Obstacles Expected and Steps Required in Implementation of a Sound Policy for Canadian Agriculture. *Can. J. Agr. Econ.*, November 1969, *17*(3), pp. 70–76. [G: Canada]

Delivanis, D. J. Problems Arising for the Agriculture of a Developing Country by Virtue of Its Association with the European Economic Community. **In** *Papi, U. and Nunn, C., eds.*, 1969, pp. 130–42. [G: E.E.C.]

Due, Jean M. What Has Happened to the Ghanaian State Farms? *Ill. Agr. Econ.*, July 1969, *9*(2), pp. 25–35. [G: Ghana]

Easter, K. William. Changing the ACP Investment. *Land Econ.*, May 1969, *45*(2), pp. 218–28. [G: U.S.]

Egbert, Alvin C. and Hiemstra, Stephen J. Shifting Direct Government Payments from Agriculture to Poor People: Impacts on Food Consumption and Farm Income. *Agr. Econ. Res.*, July 1969, *21*(3), pp. 61–69. [G: U.S.]

Epp, Donald J. Some Implications of the EEC's Agricultural Price Policy. *Amer. J. Agr. Econ.*, May 1969, *51*(2), pp. 279–88. [G: E.E.C.]

Falcon, Walter P. Agricultural Planning: The Peruvian Experience: Comment. **In** *Thorbecke, E., ed.*, 1969, pp. 446–50. [G: Peru]

Fazekas, B. and Ôri, J. On the Formulation of a Common Agricultural Policy for CMEA Countries. (In Russian. With English summary.) *Acta Oecon.*, 1969, *4*(4), pp. 403–15. [G: CMEA]

Flanders, M. June. Agriculture versus Industry in Development Policy: The Planner's Dilemma Reexamined. *J. Devel. Stud.*, April 1969, *5*(3), pp. 171–89.

Fleagle, Robert G. Background and Present Status of Weather Modification. **In** *Fleagle, R. G., ed.*, 1969, pp. 3–17. [G: 7310]

Fleagle, Robert G. Implications for Public Policy. **In** *Fleagle, R. G., ed.*, 1969, pp. 138–42.

Freebairn, Donald K. The Dichotomy of Prosperity and Poverty in Mexican Agriculture. *Land Econ.*, February 1969, *45*(1), pp. 31–42. [G: Mexico]

Freeman, Orville L. Malthus, Marx, and the North American Breadbasket. **In** *Ruttan, V. W.; Waldo,*

A. D. and Houck, J. P., eds., 1969, pp. 282–98. [G: U.S.]

Fuller, Varden. Political Pressures and Income Distribution in Agriculture. **In** *Ruttan, V. W.; Waldo, A. D. and Houck, J. P., eds.*, 1969, pp. 255–63. [G: U.S.]

Gaarder, Raymond O. The Unseen—and Unfeeling —Hand. *Amer. J. Agr. Econ.*, November 1969, *51* (4), pp. 952–53. [G: U.S.]

Gandhi, Ved P. Agricultural Taxation Policy: Search for a Direction. *Artha-Vikas*, July 1969, *5*(2), pp. 3–49. [G: India]

Ghose, B. C. The Borooah Committee on Tea. *Econ. Aff.*, January-February 1969, *14*(1–2), pp. 71–73. [G: India]

Gisser, Micha. The Pure Theory of Government Aid to Agriculture. *Amer. J. Agr. Econ.*, December 1969, *51*(5), pp. 1511–15.

Goodman, Richard J. Policy and Non-Policy in Foreign Trade: Discussion. *Amer. J. Agr. Econ.*, December 1969, *51*(5), pp. 1354–56. [G: U.S.; E.E.C.]

Gordon, Kermit. How Much Should Government Do? **In** *Ruttan, V. W.; Waldo, A. D. and Houck, J. P., eds.*, 1969, pp. 129–36. [G: U.S.]

Grant, Walter V. Economic Guidelines for Resource Use: Discussion. *Can. J. Agr. Econ.*, November 1969, *17*(3), pp. 38–40. [G: Canada]

Gronsdahl, John. Agricultural Policy in a Dynamic Economy: Symposium. *Can. J. Agr. Econ.*, November 1969, *17*(3), pp. 50–52. [G: Canada]

Guither, Harold D. Direct Payments: An Increasing Proportion of Farm Income and a Changing Geographic Distribution. *Amer. J. Agr. Econ.*, November 1969, *51*(4), pp. 915–20. [G: U.S.]

Gulati, I. S. and Kothari, V. N. Land Tax as an Incentive for Better Land Utilization. *Artha-Vikas*, July 1969, *5*(2), pp. 108–16.

Gulbrandsen, Odd. Swedish Experience in Agricultural Policy. **In** *Papi, U. and Nunn, C., eds.*, 1969, pp. 409–19. [G: Sweden]

Hamilton, W. E. Payment Limitation: Pros and Cons as Seen by Farm Organizations. *Amer. J. Agr. Econ.*, December 1969, *51*(5), pp. 1243–46. [G: U.S.]

Hammond, Jerome W. and Graf, Truman F. Pricing Milk in Federal Order Markets. *Amer. J. Agr. Econ.*, December 1969, *51*(5), pp. 1506–10. [G: U.S.]

Hardin, Clifford M. For Humanity, New Hope: Introduction. **In** *Hardin, C. M., ed.*, 1969, pp. 1–7.

Hathaway, Dale E. The Implications of Changing Political Power on Agriculture. **In** *Ruttan, V. W.; Waldo, A. D. and Houck, J. P., eds.*, 1969, pp. 63–68. [G: U.S.]

Hathaway, Dale E. The Search for New International Arrangements to Deal with the Agricultural Problems of Industrialized Countries. **In** *Papi, U. and Nunn, C., eds.*, 1969, pp. 51–69.

Haviland, William E., et al. Agricultural Policy in a Dynamic Economy: Symposium. *Can. J. Agr. Econ.*, November 1969, *17*(3), pp. 41. [G: Canada]

Hendricks, Sterling B. Food from the Land. **In** *National Academy of Sciences*, 1969, pp. 65–85.

Hiscocks, Geoffrey. Agricultural Policy in a Dynamic Economy: Symposium. *Can. J. Agr. Econ.*, November 1969, *17*(3), pp. 47–50. [G: Canada]

Hoos, Sidney. Joint Decision-making Processes in Present-Day Agriculture. **In** *Papi, U. and Nunn, C., eds.*, 1969, pp. 379–89.

Houthakker, Hendrik S. The Causes of the Farm Problem. **In** *Starleaf, D. R., ed.*, 1969, pp. 164–68. [G: U.S.]

Hurd, Lorne. Agricultural Policy in a Dynamic Economy: Symposium. *Can. J. Agr. Econ.*, November 1969, *17*(3), pp. 42–46. [G: Canada]

Jacobson, Robert E. Criteria for Defining Federal Milk Order Market Areas. *Amer. J. Agr. Econ.*, December 1969, *51*(5), pp. 1138–42. [G: U.S.]

Kaneda, Hiromitsu. Economic Implications of the "Green Revolution" and the Strategy of Agricultural Development in West Pakistan. *Pakistan Develop. Rev.*, Summer 1969, *9*(2), pp. 111–43. [G: W. Pakistan]

Karcz, Jerzy F. An Organizational Model of Command Farming. **In** *Bornstein, M., ed.*, 1969, pp. 278–99. [G: E. Europe]

Kayoumy, Abdul Hay. Monopoly Pricing of Afghan Karakul in International Markets. *J. Polit. Econ.*, March/April 1969, *77*(2), pp. 219–36. [G: Afghanistan]

Kendrick, James G. Policy and Non-Policy in Foreign Trade: Discussion. *Amer. J. Agr. Econ.*, December 1969, *51*(5), pp. 1349–51. [G: U.S.; E.E.C.]

Krishna, Jai and Jha, S. C. Buffer Stock—Concepts and Objectives. **In** *Indian Society of Agricultural Economics*, 1969, pp. 35–48. [G: India]

Kulshreshtha, S. N. Age and Efficiency in Public Agricultural Policy: The Case of Ontario. *Can. J. Agr. Econ.*, July 1969, *17*(2), pp. 85–91. [G: Canada]

Ladd, George W. Federal Milk Marketing Order Provisions: Effects on Producer Prices and Intermarket Price Relationships. *Amer. J. Agr. Econ.*, August 1969, *51*(3), pp. 625–41. [G: U.S.]

Lee, Alvin T. M. Regional Research—Further Analysis and Reflections. *Amer. J. Agr. Econ.*, November 1969, *51*(4), pp. 953–57. [G: U.S.]

Leonard, Patrick L. A Note on the Demand for Fertilizer in West Pakistan. *Pakistan Develop. Rev.*, Winter 1969, *9*(4), pp. 419–25. [G: W. Pakistan]

Lerohl, M. L. Obstacles Expected and Steps Required in Implementation of a Sound Policy for Canadian Agriculture: Discussion. *Can. J. Agr. Econ.*, November 1969, *17*(3), pp. 76–79. [G: Canada]

Leuthold, Raymond M. Government Payments and the Distribution of Income in Agriculture. *Amer. J. Agr. Econ.*, December 1969, *51*(5), pp. 1520–23. [G: U.S.]

Lukinov, I. Prices and Planned Economic Regulation of Agricultural Production. *Prob. Econ.*, May 1969, *12*(1), pp. 67–90. [G: U.S.S.R.]

Macdonald, Gordon J. F. Federal Government Programs in Weather Modification. **In** *Fleagle, R. G., ed.*, 1969, pp. 69–86. [G: U.S.]

MacEachern, G. A. Guidelines for Agricultural Policy Over the Next Decade: Discussion. *Can. J. Agr. Econ.*, November 1969, *17*(3), pp. 64–69. [G: Canada]

MacEachern, G. A. and Huff, H. Bruce. Policy and Non-Policy in Foreign Trade: Discussion. *Amer. J. Agr. Econ.*, December 1969, *51*(5), pp. 1352–54. **[G: U.S.; E.E.C.]**

Malassis, Louis. Education and Agricultural Development. *Int. Soc. Sci. J.*, 1969, *21*(2), pp. 244–55.

Mäler, Karl-Göran. Optimal Pricing in Agricultural Emergency Policies. *Swedish J. Econ.*, December 1969, *71*(4), pp. 247–62.

Malmgren, H. B. and Schlechty, D. L. Technology and Neo-Mercantilism in International Agricultural Trade. *Amer. J. Agr. Econ.*, December 1969, *51*(5), pp. 1325–37. **[G: E.E.C.]**

Malmgren, H. B. and Schlechty, D. L. Technology and Neo-Mercantilism in International Agricultural Trade. **In** *Interest Equalization Tax Extension Act of 1969, SCH,* 1969, pp. 35–42.

Mathew, E. T. Proposals for an Integrated System of Agricultural Taxation. *Artha-Vikas,* July 1969, *5*(2), pp. 146–53. **[G: India]**

McCalla, Alex F. Whither Goest U.S. Agricultural Policy: An Exercise in Naive Prophesy. *Can. J. Agr. Econ.*, July 1969, *17*(2), pp. 1–16. **[G: U.S.]**

Mellor, John W. Agricultural Price Policy in the Context of Economic Development. *Amer. J. Agr. Econ.*, December 1969, *51*(5), pp. 1413–19.

Misra, P. N. A Welfare Criterion for the Determination of Agricultural Prices. *Indian Econ. J.*, October–December 1969, *17*(2), pp. 273–78.

Montigaud, J. C. Les Plans Conjoints au Québec. (Marketing Boards in Quebec. With English summary.) *Can. J. Agr. Econ.*, July 1969, *17*(2), pp. 17–35. **[G: Canada]**

Moszer, Max. An Analysis of the 1964 Wheat Option. *Amer. J. Agr. Econ.*, February 1969, *51*(1), pp. 100–118. **[G: U.S.]**

Mouton, Claude. The European Common Market and the Move Towards Self-sufficiency in Food Production. **In** *Papi, U. and Nunn, C., eds.*, 1969, pp. 92–120. **[G: E.E.C.]**

Mukherjee, Chittapriya. Some Problems of the Indian Agricultural Sector. *Land Econ.*, February 1969, *45*(1), pp. 74–86. **[G: India]**

Nicholls, William H. The U.S. South as an Underdeveloped Region. **In** *Papi, U. and Nunn, C., eds.*, 1969, pp. 469–88. **[G: U.S.]**

Obolenski, K. P. Agricultural Planning in U.S.S.R. **In** *Papi, U. and Nunn, C., eds.*, 1969, pp. 449–63. **[G: U.S.S.R.]**

Ojha, P. D. Taxation of Agricultural Land and Income. *Artha-Vikas,* July 1969, *5*(2), pp. 50–62. **[G: India]**

Owen, Wyn F. Structural Planning in Densely Populated Countries: An Introduction with Applications to Indonesia. *Malayan Econ. Rev.*, April 1969, *14*(1), pp. 97–114. **[G: Indonesia]**

Parikh, G. O. Integration of Farm and Non-Farm Employment, Part II: Effective Cooperativisation in a Labour Surplus Economy. *Artha-Vikas,* January 1969, *5*(1), pp. 68–76. **[G: India]**

Patel, A. G. A Case for Income Tax on Agricultural Income. *Artha-Vikas,* July 1969, *5*(2), pp. 171–76. **[G: India]**

Patel, Shivabhai J. Taxation of Agricultural Land and Income. *Artha-Vikas,* July 1969, *5*(2), pp. 98–105. **[G: India]**

Pathak, Mahesh and Patel, Arun. Reform of Agricultural Taxation. *Artha-Vikas,* July 1969, *5*(2), pp. 71–78. **[G: India]**

Paulsen, Arnold. Payment Limitations: The Economic and Political Feasibility. *Amer. J. Agr. Econ.*, December 1969, *51*(5), pp. 1237–42. **[G: U.S.]**

Pennock, J. Roland. Agricultural Subsidies in Britain and America. **In** *Rose, R., ed.*, 1969, pp. 199–220. **[G: U.K.; U.S.]**

Phillips, Richard. Inducing Economic Development in Less Developed Countries: Discussion. *Amer. J. Agr. Econ.*, December 1969, *51*(5), pp. 1424–26.

Plaunt, Darrel. Economic Guidelines for Mobilizing Labour and Management in Canadian Agriculture. *Can. J. Agr. Econ.*, November 1969, *17*(3), pp. 20–33. **[G: Canada]**

Pohorille, M. Purchasing Contracts and Price Policy as Means of Planning Agricultural Production. **In** *Papi, U. and Nunn, C., eds.*, 1969, pp. 430–41.

Rabbani, A. K. M. Ghulam. A Proposal for Fiscal Incentives for the Raw-Jute Exports. *Pakistan Develop. Rev.*, Winter 1969, *9*(4), pp. 400–418. **[G: Pakistan]**

Ramachandran, C. V. Cost of Buffer Stock Operations: Desirability or Otherwise of Subsidising Cost. **In** *Indian Society of Agricultural Economics,* 1969, pp. 100–117. **[G: India]**

Rasmussen, Wayne D. and Baker, Gladys L. Programs for Agriculture, 1933–1965. **In** *Ruttan, V. W.; Waldo, A. D. and Houck, J. P., eds.*, 1969, pp. 69–88. **[G: U.S.]**

Richter, J. H. The Changing Patterns of International Trade Problems of Under-developed Areas. **In** *Papi, U. and Nunn, C., eds.*, 1969, pp. 151–62.

Robinson, E. A. G. The Desirable Level of Agriculture in the Advanced Industrial Economies. **In** *Papi, U. and Nunn, C., eds.*, 1969, pp. 26–44.

Rogers, S. J. Political Algebra and U.K. Agricultural Policy. *Nat. Westminster Bank Quart. Rev.*, February 1969, pp. 53–68. **[G: U.K.]**

Runciman, A. M. Agricultural Policy in a Dynamic Economy: Symposium. *Can. J. Agr. Econ.*, November 1969, *17*(3), pp. 52–56. **[G: Canada]**

Ruttan, Vernon W. Program Analysis and Agricultural Policy. **In** *The Analysis and Evaluation of Public Expenditures: The PPB System, Vol. 3, JECP,* 1969, pp. 1128–50. **[G: U.S.]**

Saran, Ram. Buffer Stock in Foodgrains. **In** *Indian Society of Agricultural Economics,* 1969, pp. 85–99. **[G: India]**

Sault, J. L. Recent Developments Affecting the Market Outlook for Australian Raw Cotton. *Quart. Rev. Agr. Econ.*, July 1969, *22*(3), pp. 123–39. **[G: Australia]**

Schultz, Theodore W. What Ails World Agriculture? **In** *Ruttan, V. W.; Waldo, A. D. and Houck, J. P., eds.*, 1969, pp. 299–316.

Schwenger, Robert B. New Concepts and Methods in Foreign Trade Negotiation. *Amer. J. Agr. Econ.*, December 1969, *51*(5), pp. 1338–48. **[G: U.S.]**

Seagraves, James A. Capitalized Values of Tobacco Allotments and the Rate of Return to Allotment Owners. *Amer. J. Agr. Econ.*, May 1969, *51*(2), pp.

320–34. [G: U.S.]

Seevers, Gary L. The Cost of Food Aid to Recipient Countries. *Amer. J. Agr. Econ.,* December 1969, *51*(5), pp. 1588–92. [G: U.S.]

Sewell, W. R. Derrick. Weather Modification: When Should We Do It and How Far Should We Go? **In** *Fleagle, R. G., ed.,* 1969, pp. 94–104. [G: U.S.]

Shah, C. H. Agricultural Taxation: A Plea for Caution and a Proposal for a Positive Approach. *Artha-Vikas,* July 1969, *5*(2), pp. 79–97. [G: India]

Shah, C. H. Problems of Buffer Stock—A Theoretical Framework. **In** *Indian Society of Agricultural Economics,* 1969, pp. 15–34. [G: India]

Shuffett, Milton and Hoskins, Josiah. Capitalization of Burley Tobacco Allotment Rights into Farmland Values. *Amer. J. Agr. Econ.,* May 1969, *51*(2), pp. 471–74. [G: U.S.]

Sinclair, Sol. Economic Guidelines for Resource Use: Discussion. *Can. J. Agr. Econ.,* November 1969, *17*(3), pp. 34–38. [G: Canada]

Singh, Tarlok. On Planning Technological Change in Indian Agriculture. *Int. Soc. Sci. J.,* 1969, *21*(2), pp. 265–71. [G: India]

Slaughter, Rudie W., Jr. Payment Limitation: Effect on Supply Adjustment and Income Distribution. *Amer. J. Agr. Econ.,* December 1969, *51*(5), pp. 1233–36. [G: U.S.]

Smethurst, Richard G. Direct Commodity Aid: A Multilateral Experiment. *J. Devel. Stud.,* April 1969, *5*(3), pp. 205–19.

Smirnov, V. V. Movement and Utilization of Rural Labor Resources (in the Non-black Soil Zone of the RSFSR). *Prob. Econ.,* October 1969, *12*(6), pp. 68–81. [G: U.S.S.R.]

Smith, George W. Brazilian Agricultural Policy, 1950–1967. **In** *Ellis, H. S., ed.,* 1969, pp. 213–65. [G: Brazil]

Sobering, Fred; Quance, C. Leroy and Tweeten, Luther G. An Economic Model for Determining Cotton Allotments and Prices to Maximize Net Farm Income. *Amer. J. Agr. Econ.,* December 1969, *51*(5), pp. 1124–28. [G: U.S.]

Stover, Stephen L. The Government as Farmer in New Zealand. *Econ. Geogr.,* October 1969, *45*(4), pp. 324–38. [G: New Zealand]

Sturrock, F. G. A Policy for British Sugar Supplies. *Nat. Westminster Bank Quart. Rev.,* August 1969, pp. 54–60. [G: U.K.]

Tasker, Antony. British Sugar Supplies: An Alternative View. *Nat. Westminster Bank Quart. Rev.,* November 1969, pp. 45–51. [G: U.K.]

Tepicht, J. Problems of the Re-structuring of Agriculture in the Light of the Polish Experience. **In** *Papi, U. and Nunn, C., eds.,* 1969, pp. 534–47. [G: Poland]

Thomsen, F. L. and Foote, R. J. Parity Price. **In** *Ruttan, V. W.; Waldo, A. D. and Houck, J. P., eds.,* 1969, pp. 90–95. [G: U.S.]

Traylor, Harold D. and Gandy, Dewell R. Caloric Cost of Rice and Wheat Programs. *Amer. J. Agr. Econ.,* November 1969, *51*(4), pp. 962–63. [G: U.S.]

Tweeten, Luther G. Commodity Programs for Agriculture. **In** *Ruttan, V. W.; Waldo, A. D. and Houck, J. P., eds.,* 1969, pp. 99–115. [G: U.S.]

Tweeten, Luther G. Theories Explaining the Persistence of Low Resource Returns in a Growing Farm Economy. *Amer. J. Agr. Econ.,* November 1969, *51*(4), pp. 798–817. [G: U.S.]

Vasil'ev, N. The Distribution of Agricultural Enterprises and Increased Specialization of Agriculture. *Prob. Econ.,* April 1969, *11*(12), pp. 37–46. [G: U.S.S.R.]

Vyas, V. S. Integration of Farm and Non-Farm Employment, Part I: Farm and Non-Farm Employment in an Economically Backward Region. *Artha-Vikas,* January 1969, *5*(1), pp. 54–67. [G: India]

Vyas, V. S. and Pathak, Mahesh. A Case for Taxation of Agricultural Income. *Artha-Vikas,* July 1969, *5*(2), pp. 130–37. [G: India]

Warrack, Allan A. The Challenge of Abundance: Comment. *Can. J. Agr. Econ.,* July 1969, *17*(2), pp. 118–23. [G: Canada]

van Wetering, Hylke. Agricultural Planning: The Peruvian Experience. **In** *Thorbecke, E., ed.,* 1969, pp. 387–446. [G: Peru]

White, W. James. Conventional Wisdom and Agricultural Policy. *Can. J. Agr. Econ.,* November 1969, *17*(3), pp. 175–80. [G: Canada]

White, W. James. Farm Income Policy in Ontario: Review and Analysis. *Can. J. Agr. Econ.,* February 1969, *17*(1), pp. 132–40. [G: Canada]

Williams, F. A. Agricultural Price Policy in the Context of Economic Development: Discussion. *Amer. J. Agr. Econ.,* December 1969, *51*(5), pp. 1420–23.

Wilson, A. G. and Wood, A. W. Regional Livestock Production and Feed Freight Assistance. *Can. J. Agr. Econ.,* February 1969, *17*(1), pp. 77–90. [G: Canada]

Yamaoka, Ryoichi. The "Modernisation" of Agriculture at the Present Stage. *Kyoto Univ. Econ. Rev.,* April 1969, *39*(1), pp. 1–21. [G: U.S.; W. Germany]

714 Agricultural Finance

7140 Agricultural Finance

Andal, Melvin E. Economic Guidelines for Present and Future Capital Use in Canadian Agriculture. *Can. J. Agr. Econ.,* November 1969, *17*(3), pp. 9–19. [G: Canada]

Baker, C. B. and Hopkin, John A. Concepts of Finance Capital for a Capital-Using Agriculture. *Amer. J. Agr. Econ.,* December 1969, *51*(5), pp. 1055–64. [G: U.S.]

Benson, Richard A. Trade Credit in the Fertilizer Industry: Theory and Practice. *Agr. Finance Rev.,* July 1969, *30,* pp. 21–33. [G: U.S.]

Bottomley, Anthony and Nudds, Donald. A Widow's Cruse Theory of Credit Supply in Underdeveloped Rural Areas. *Manchester Sch. Econ. Soc. Stud.,* June 1969, *37*(2), pp. 131–40.

Diesslin, Harold C. Evaluation of the Credit Market and Credit Institutions. **In** *Owen, W. F., ed.,* 1969, pp. 95–112. [G: U.S.]

Doll, John P. Credit in the Production Organization of the Firm: Comment. *Amer. J. Agr. Econ.,* May 1969, *51*(2), pp. 474–76.

Ehrich, R. L. Cash-Futures Price Relationships for

Live Beef Cattle. *Amer. J. Agr. Econ.*, February 1969, *51*(1), pp. 26–40. [G: U.S.]

Gandhi, Ved P. Agricultural Taxation Policy: Search for a Direction. *Artha-Vikas*, July 1969, *5*(2), pp. 3–49. [G: India]

Herbst, J. H. Net Worth Projections for a Period of Farm Business Expansion. *Ill. Agr. Econ.*, July 1969, *9*(2), pp. 36–47.

Herr, William McD. The Role of FHA's Farm Operating and Ownership Loan Programs as Indicated by Borrower Characteristics. *Agr. Finance Rev.*, July 1969, *30*, pp. 1–10. [G: U.S.]

Iyengar, S. Kesava. The Co-operative Caravan: A Casual Causerie. *Asian Econ. Rev.*, August 1969, *11*(4), pp. 363–404. [G: India]

Katō, Yuzuru. Development of Long-Term Agricultural Credit. **In** *Ohkawa, K.; Johnston, B. F. and Kaneda, H., eds.*, 1969, pp. 324–51. [G: Japan]

McArthur, D. A. Educational Efforts in Farm Credit Management. *Can. J. Agr. Econ.*, November 1969, *17*(3), pp. 181–85. [G: Canada]

Melichar, Emanuel. Farm Capital and Credit Projections to 1980. *Amer. J. Agr. Econ.*, December 1969, *51*(5), pp. 1172–77. [G: U.S.]

Melichar, Emanuel. Seasonal Discount Assistance to Rural Banks: Evaluation of a Federal Reserve Proposal. *Agr. Finance Rev.*, July 1969, *30*, pp. 44–57. [G: U.S.]

Nisbet, Charles T. The Relationship between Institutional and Informal Credit Markets in Rural Chile. *Land Econ.*, May 1969, *45*(2), pp. 162–73. [G: Chile]

Rodewald, Gordon E., Jr. A Method for Analyzing the Effect of Taxes and Financing on Investment Decisions. *Amer. J. Agr. Econ.*, December 1969, *51*(5), pp. 1178–81.

Sarkar, K. K. Development of Indian Agriculture: Role of Institutional Credit Agencies. *Econ. Aff.*, January-February 1969, *14*(1–2), pp. 57–67. [G: India]

Smith, Allen G. Corporate and Noncorporate Farm Borrowers—Some Financial Aspects. *Agr. Finance Rev.*, July 1969, *30*, pp. 70–75. [G: U.S.]

Smith, Allen G. and Baker, C. B. The Effect of Real Estate Debt Commitments on Nonreal Estate Credit and Liquidity of the Farm. *Ill. Agr. Econ.*, January 1969, *9*(1), pp. 1–6.

Varshneya, J. S. Financing of Buffer Stock Operations: Role of Commercial Banks with Special Reference to the State Bank of India. **In** *Indian Society of Agricultural Economics*, 1969, pp. 128–33. [G: India]

715 Agricultural Marketing and Agribusiness

7150 Agricultural Marketing; Cooperatives

Aggrey-Mensah, W. and Tuckwell, N. E. A Study of Banana Supply and Price Patterns on the Sydney Wholesale Market: An Application of Spectral Analysis. *Australian J. Agr. Econ.*, December 1969, *13*(2), pp. 101–17. [G: Australia]

Araji, Ahmed A. and Walsh, Richard G. Effect of Assembly Costs on Optimum Grain Elevator Size and Location. *Can. J. Agr. Econ.*, July 1969, *17*(2), pp. 36–45. [G: U.S.]

Boden, E. A. The Canadian Livestock Industry: Comment. *Can. J. Agr. Econ.*, November 1969, *17* (3), pp. 111–13. [G: Canada]

Bornstein, Morris. The Soviet Debate on Agricultural Price and Procurement Reforms. *Soviet Stud.*, July 1969, *21*(1), pp. 1–20. [G: U.S.S.R.]

Breimyer, Harold F. Future Organization and Control of U.S. Agricultural Production and Marketing. **In** *Owen, W. F., ed.*, 1969, pp. 14–25. [G: U.S.]

Brits, R. N. The Marketing of South African Maize. *S. Afr. J. Econ.*, September 1969, *37*(3), pp. 198–218. [G: S. Africa]

Cole, David L. Effect of Merchandising Methods on Prices Paid at Cooperative Feeder Cattle Sales. *Amer. J. Agr. Econ.*, December 1969, *51*(5), pp. 1129–33. [G: U.S.]

Costache, Sandu. Valorificarea producției cooperativelor agricole. (Turning to Account Agricultural Cooperative Farm Production. With English summary.) *Stud. Cercet. Econ.*, 1969, *1-2*, pp. 107–19.

Dahl, Dale C. Structure of Input Supplying Industries and Techniques of Analysis. *Amer. J. Agr. Econ.*, December 1969, *51*(5), pp. 1046–53. [G: U.S.]

Davis, J. Ronnie and Palomba, Neil A. The National Farmers Organization and the Prisoner's Dilemma: A Game Theory Prediction of Failure. *Soc. Sci. Quart.*, December 1969, *50*(3), pp. 742–48.

Emerson, Peter M. and Tomek, William G. Did Futures Trading Influence Potato Prices? *Amer. J. Agr. Econ.*, August 1969, *51*(3), pp. 666–72. [G: U.S.]

Flek, Josef. Life and Income of Czechoslovak Cooperatives. **In** *Papi, U. and Nunn, C., eds.*, 1969, pp. 304–15. [G: Czechoslovakia]

Gerald, John O. Role of Transportation in Agricultural Marketing and Development: Discussion. *Amer. J. Agr. Econ.*, December 1969, *51*(5), pp. 1478–81. [G: U.S.]

Hammer, Marius. Binnenmärkte und Mafia in Sizilien. (Market Organization and Mafia in Sicily. With English summary.) *Jahr. Nationalökon. Statist.*, July 1969, *183*(2), pp. 150–58. [G: Italy]

Hammond, Jerome W. and Graf, Truman F. Pricing Milk in Federal Order Markets. *Amer. J. Agr. Econ.*, December 1969, *51*(5), pp. 1506–10. [G: U.S.]

Hammond, Jerome W.; Anthony, Willis E. and Christiansen, Martin K. Why the Growing Farm-Retail Price Spread? **In** *Ruttan, V. W.; Waldo, A. D. and Houck, J. P., eds.*, 1969, pp. 165–85. [G: U.S.]

Hardie, Ian W. Shadow Prices as Member Returns for a Marketing Cooperative. *Amer. J. Agr. Econ.*, November 1969, *51*(4), pp. 818–33.

Hawkins, Murray H. Alternative Methods of Marketing Livestock. *Can. J. Agr. Econ.*, November 1969, *17*(3), pp. 104–110.

Heady, Earl O. The Future Structure of U.S. Agriculture. **In** *Owen, W. F., ed.*, 1969, pp. 113–28. [G: U.S.]

Hoos, Sidney. Joint Decision-making Processes in

Present-Day Agriculture. In *Papi, U. and Nunn, C., eds.*, 1969, pp. 379–89.

Ikerd, John E. and Schupp, Alvin R. A Decision Model for Continuous Sequence Production Processes of Variable Length: An Application to Hog Marketing. *Amer. J. Agr. Econ.*, December 1969, *51*(5), pp. 1159–63.

Iyengar, S. Kesava. The Co-operative Caravan: A Casual Causerie. *Asian Econ. Rev.*, August 1969, *11*(4), pp. 363–404. **[G: India]**

Jacobson, Robert E. Criteria for Defining Federal Milk Order Market Areas. *Amer. J. Agr. Econ.*, December 1969, *51*(5), pp. 1138–42. **[G: U.S.]**

Johnson, James F. The Influence of Cost Distance Factors on the Overseas Export of Corn from the United States Midwest. *Econ. Geogr.*, April 1969, *45*(2), pp. 170–79. **[G: U.S.]**

Kahlon, A. S. Cost of Storage and Replacement of Buffer Stock in Foodgrains. In *Indian Society of Agricultural Economics*, 1969, pp. 148–58. **[G: India]**

Khusro, A. M. Stocks and Storage of Major Foodgrains. In *Indian Society of Agricultural Economics*, 1969, pp. 134–47. **[G: India]**

Knutson, Ronald D. Nonproducer Cooperative Interests and the Antitrust Laws. *Amer. J. Agr. Econ.*, May 1969, *51*(2), pp. 335–41. **[G: U.S.]**

Komló, László. The Problems of Vertical Integration in Agriculture: The Hungarian Case. In *Papi, U. and Nunn, C., eds.*, 1969, pp. 365–76. **[G: Hungary]**

Kriebel, Wesley R. Extension Transportation Programs to Improve Marketing Efficiency. *Amer. J. Agr. Econ.*, December 1969, *51*(5), pp. 1226–28. **[G: U.S.]**

Lauth, James H. Economic Considerations in Rate Making and Rate Structures for Farm Products. *Amer. J. Agr. Econ.*, December 1969, *51*(5), pp. 1464–70. **[G: U.S.]**

Lindsey, Quentin W. The Problem of Periodic Reorganization in American Agriculture. In *Owen, W. F., ed.*, 1969, pp. 1–14. **[G: U.S.]**

Loyo, Gilberto. Las cooperativas en el desarrollo economico y social de los países en proceso de desarrollo. (The Role of Cooperatives in the Economic and Social Development. With English summary.) *Econ. Polít.*, Fourth Semester 1969, *6*(4), pp. 439–52.

Maddock, Wallace J. Financing Cooperatives in Developing Countries. In *McGrath, M. J., ed.*, 1969, pp. 47–91.

Manchester, Alden C. Some Thoughts on Agricultural Marketing Research. *Agr. Econ. Res.*, April 1969, *21*(2), pp. 29–34. **[G: U.S.]**

Murri, D. G. and Hawkins, Murray H. Organizational Structure and Collective Bargaining. *Can. J. Agr. Econ.*, November 1969, *17*(3), pp. 150–56.

Paarlberg, Don. Proposed and Existing Organizational Efforts for Farmers. In *Ruttan, V. W.; Waldo, A. D. and Houck, J. P., eds.*, 1969, pp. 201–05. **[G: U.S.]**

Perkins, Frederick A. Showing a Retailer that Meat Sanitation Pays—An Economic Approach. *Amer. J. Agr. Econ.*, December 1969, *51*(5), pp. 1259–62. **[G: U.S.]**

Pritchard, Norris T. A Framework for Analysis of Agricultural Marketing Systems in Developing Countries. *Agr. Econ. Res.*, July 1969, *21*(3), pp. 78–85.

Purcell, Wayne D. Marketing, Price, and the Theory of Communication. *Amer. J. Agr. Econ.*, December 1969, *51*(5), pp. 1110–13. **[G: U.S.]**

Rayner, A. C. The Wool Price and the Production of Synthetics. *Yorkshire Bull. Econ. Soc. Res.*, May 1969, *21*(1), pp. 31–38.

Robertson, B. Russell and Love, Harold G. Louisville Produce Terminal: Its Changing Trends and Potentials, 1966–1975. *Amer. J. Agr. Econ.*, December 1969, *51*(5), pp. 1251–54. **[G: U.S.]**

Rust, Charles H. and St. George, George. Transportation Pricing as a Factor in Commodity Marketing: Montana Wheat, A Case Study. *Amer. J. Agr. Econ.*, December 1969, *51*(5), pp. 1471–77. **[G: U.S.]**

Sault, J. L. and Hellier, W. L. The New International Sugar Agreement and the Australian Sugar Industry. *Quart. Rev. Agr. Econ.*, October 1969, *22*(4), pp. 210–29. **[G: Australia]**

Turner, Donald F. Agricultural Cooperatives and the Antitrust Laws. In *Ruttan, V. W.; Waldo, A. D. and Houck, J. P., eds.*, 1969, pp. 192–200. **[G: U.S.]**

Valarché, Jean. Innovations in Stock Farming: Information Flow from the Agricultural and Animal Food Industries. In *Papi, U. and Nunn, C., eds.*, 1969, pp. 344–56. **[G: Switzerland]**

Ward, Gordon H. The Structure and Organization of Cooperatives in Developing Nations. In *McGrath, M. J., ed.*, 1969, pp. 5–41.

Weinschenck, G.; Henrichsmeyer, W. and Aldinger, F. The Theory of Spatial Equilibrium and Optimal Location in Agriculture: A Survey. *Rev. Marketing Agr. Econ.*, March 1969, *37*(1), pp. 3–70.

Weisenborn, David E. Allocation of Florida Orange Production among Alternative Product Forms and Market Sectors. *Amer. J. Agr. Econ.*, December 1969, *51*(5), pp. 1134–37. **[G: U.S.]**

Welch, John M. Education for Institutional Food Service—On Wheels. *Amer. J. Agr. Econ.*, December 1969, *51*(5), pp. 1229–32. **[G: U.S.]**

7151 Agribusiness

Boulding, Kenneth E. Does Absence of Monopoly Power in Agriculture Influence the Stability and Level of Farm Income? In *Owen, W. F., ed.*, 1969, pp. 85–94. **[G: U.S.]**

Dahl, Dale C. Conglomerate Growth: Policy Implications for Agriculture and Agribusiness. In *Garoian, L., ed.*, 1969, pp. 115–16. **[G: U.S.]**

Hady, Thomas F. Agriculture and the Law: Discussion. *Amer. J. Agr. Econ.*, December 1969, *51*(5), pp. 1399–1401. **[G: U.S.]**

Halcrow, Harold G. The Illinois Agricultural Industries Forum. *Amer. J. Agr. Econ.*, December 1969, *51*(5), pp. 1222–25. **[G: U.S.]**

Handy, C. R. and Padberg, D. I. Conglomerate Growth: Policy Implications for Agriculture and Agribusiness. In *Garoian, L., ed.*, 1969, pp. 117–20. **[G: U.S.]**

Harl, Neil E. Do Legal and Tax Rules Favor Large-Scale Agricultural Firms? *Amer. J. Agr. Econ.*, December 1969, *51*(5), pp. 1381–92. **[G: U.S.]**

Luttrell, Clifton B. Agribusiness—A Growth Analysis. *Univ. Missouri Bus. Govt. Rev.*, November–December 1969, *10*(6), pp. 33–42. **[G: U.S.]**

Maharja, Madhukar. Economics of Ghee Manufacture: A Study at Micro Level—A Reply. *Artha-Vikas*, January 1969, *5*(1), pp. 109–10.

Mighell, Ronald L. Concentration in Farming and Transition Bias. *Amer. J. Agr. Econ.*, December 1969, *51*(5), pp. 1114–18. **[G: U.S.]**

Murty, A. G. K. and Patel, D. A. Economics of Ghee Manufacture: A Study at Micro Level—A Comment. *Artha-Vikas*, January 1969, *5*(1), pp. 104–08.

Raup, Philip M. Economies and Diseconomies of Large-Scale Agriculture. *Amer. J. Agr. Econ.*, December 1969, *51*(5), pp. 1274–82.

Schermerhorn, Richard W. The Economic Feasibility of an Integrated Broiler Operation. *Amer. J. Agr. Econ.*, December 1969, *51*(5), pp. 1255–58.

Schiller, Otto. An Appraisal of Co-operative Farming and Its Significance in Indian Development. **In** *Bhuleshkar, A. V., ed.*, 1969, pp. 40–46. **[G: India]**

Schiopu, Bucur. Elemente agro-industriale în agricultura Republicii Socialiste România. (Agro-Industrial Elements in the Agriculture of the Socialist Republic of Romania. With English summary.) *Stud. Cercet. Econ.*, 1969, *3*, pp. 59–66. **[G: Romania]**

Scofield, William. Corporate Farm Ownership and Operation. **In** *Garoian, L., ed.*, 1969, pp. 106–10. **[G: U.S.]**

Snyder, James C. Trials, Errors, and Successes in Agribusiness Education at Purdue. *Amer. J. Agr. Econ.*, December 1969, *51*(5), pp. 1218–21. **[G: U.S.]**

Stout, Thomas T. Economics of Conglomerate Growth: Policy Implications for Agriculture. **In** *Garoian, L., ed.*, 1969, pp. 121–22. **[G: U.S.]**

716 Farm Management

7160 Farm Management; Allocative Efficiency

Andal, Melvin E. Economic Guidelines for Present and Future Capital Use in Canadian Agriculture. *Can. J. Agr. Econ.*, November 1969, *17*(3), pp. 9–19. **[G: Canada]**

Andarawewa, A. B. Tenure Patterns and the Commercialization of Canadian Agriculture. *Can. J. Agr. Econ.*, February 1969, *17*(1), pp. 110–20. **[G: Canada]**

Anderson, James R. and Dillon, John L. A Comparison of Response Surface and Factorial Designs in Agricultural Research: Comment. *Rev. Marketing Agr. Econ.*, June 1969, *37*(2), pp. 130–32.

Asopa, V. N. and Swanson, Earl R. Profitability of Supplemental Irrigation of Corn. *Ill. Agr. Econ.*, January 1969, *9*(1), pp. 7–9.

Baldovinos de la Peña, Gabriel. El sector ejidal y el plan agricola nacional. (The Ejidal Sector and the National Agricultural Plan. With English summary.) *Econ. Polít.*, Second Semester 1969, *6*(2), pp. 215–22. **[G: Mexico]**

Boehlje, Michael D. and White, T. Kelley. A Production-Investment Decision Model of Farm Firm Growth. *Amer. J. Agr. Econ.*, August 1969, *51*(3), pp. 546–63.

Bostwick, Don. Effects of Machinery Control Strategies on Income. *Agr. Finance Rev.*, July 1969, *30*, pp. 34–43.

Bostwick, Don. Financial Returns in Agriculture. *Amer. J. Agr. Econ.*, August 1969, *51*(3), pp. 662–65.

Bostwick, Don. Returns to Farm Resources. *Amer. J. Agr. Econ.*, December 1969, *51*(5), pp. 1528–35. **[G: U.S.]**

Brannon, Russell H. Low Investment Levels in Uruguayan Agriculture: Some Tentative Explanations. *Land Econ.*, August 1969, *45*(3), pp. 304–12. **[G: Uruguay]**

Breimyer, Harold F. Future Organization and Control of U.S. Agricultural Production and Marketing. **In** *Owen, W. F., ed.*, 1969, pp. 14–25. **[G: U.S.]**

Bretthauer, G. L. and Swanson, Earl R. Supplemental Irrigation of Corn: A Break-Even Analysis. *Ill. Agr. Econ.*, July 1969, *9*(2), pp. 19–24.

Brooks, Scott E. and Constable, G. A. Minimum Resource Requirements for Specified Resource Returns on Ontario Farms. *Can. J. Agr. Econ.*, November 1969, *17*(3), pp. 133–43. **[G: Canada]**

Bullock, J. Bruce and Logan, Samuel H. A Model for Decision Making under Uncertainty. *Agr. Econ. Res.*, October 1969, *21*(4), pp. 109–115.

Byerlee, D. R. and Anderson, James R. Value of Predictors of Uncontrolled Factors in Response Functions. *Australian J. Agr. Econ.*, December 1969, *13*(2), pp. 118–27.

Byrne, P. F. and Healy, A. T. A. A Note on Livestock Breeding Policies in Stable and Development Situations. *Australian J. Agr. Econ.*, December 1969, *13*(2), pp. 154–61.

Carlsson, Mårten; Hovmark, Bertil and Lindgren, Ingvar. Recent Developments in Farm Planning: 1: A Monte Carlo Method for the Study of Farm Planning Problems. *Rev. Marketing Agr. Econ.*, June 1969, *37*(2), pp. 80–103.

Carman, Hoy F. Income Tax Planning for Farmers. *Amer. J. Agr. Econ.*, December 1969, *51*(5), pp. 1543–47. **[G: U.S.]**

Casler, George L. Development of a Two-Stage Equipment-Enterprise Selection Method. *Can. J. Agr. Econ.*, February 1969, *17*(1), pp. 61–76.

Colyer, D. Fertilization Strategy Under Uncertainty. *Can. J. Agr. Econ.*, November 1969, *17*(3), pp. 144–49.

Conneman, George J. Farm Panels as a Source of Farm Management Data: The Cornell Producer Panel. *Amer. J. Agr. Econ.*, December 1969, *51* (5), pp. 1206–10. **[G: U.S.]**

Constandse, A. K. The Social Impact of Farm Mechanization: Some Findings of Cross-National Research. *Int. Soc. Sci. J.*, 1969, *21*(2), pp. 235–43.

Day, Richard H. Exact Aggregation with Linear Programming Model—A Note on the Sufficient Conditions Proposed by R. H. Day: Reply. *Amer. J. Agr. Econ.*, August 1969, *51*(3), pp. 686–88.

Day, Richard H. More On the Aggregation Problem: Some Suggestions. *Amer. J. Agr. Econ.*, August 1969, *51*(3), pp. 673–75.

Dent, J. B. and Byrne, P. F. Recent Developments in Farm Planning: 2: Investment Planning by Monte Carlo Simulation. *Rev. Marketing Agr. Econ.*, June 1969, *37*(2), pp. 104–20.

Duvick, Richard D. and Uhl, Joseph N. Large Farms and Above Parity Returns: Inseparable or Just Good Friends? *Amer. J. Agr. Econ.*, February 1969, *51*(1), pp. 179–82. **[G: U.S.]**

Flinn, J. C. The Demand for Irrigation Water in an Intensive Irrigation Area. *Australian J. Agr. Econ.*, December 1969, *13*(2), pp. 128–43.

Gregor, Howard F. Farm Structure in Regional Comparison: California and New Jersey Vegetable Farms. *Econ. Geogr.*, July 1969, *45*(3), pp. 209–25. **[G: U.S.]**

Guise, John W. B. and Ryland, G. J. Production Scheduling and Allocation: A Normative Decision Model for Sugar Milling. *Australian J. Agr. Econ.*, June 1969, *13*(1), pp. 8–24.

Hady, Thomas F. Agriculture and the Law: Discussion. *Amer. J. Agr. Econ.*, December 1969, *51*(5), pp. 1399–1401. **[G: U.S.]**

Hallberg, M. C. Projecting the Size Distribution of Agricultural Firms—An Application of a Markov Process with Non-Stationary Transition Probabilities. *Amer. J. Agr. Econ.*, May 1969, *51*(2), pp. 289–302. **[G: U.S.]**

Harris, Marshall. Shifts in Entrepreneurial Functions in Agriculture. *Amer. J. Agr. Econ.*, August 1969, *51*(3), pp. 517–29. **[G: U.S.]**

Heady, Earl O. Elementary Models in Farm Production Economics Research. **In** *Fox, K. A. and Johnson, D. G., eds.*, 1969, pp. 181–202.

Heady, Earl O. The Future Structure of U.S. Agriculture. **In** *Owen, W. F., ed.*, 1969, pp. 113–28. **[G: U.S.]**

Herbst, J. H. Net Worth Projections for a Period of Farm Business Expansion. *Ill. Agr. Econ.*, July 1969, *9*(2), pp. 36–47.

Huffman, Donald C. and Stanton, Lynn A. Application of Linear Programming to Individual Farm Planning. *Amer. J. Agr. Econ.*, December 1969, *51*(5), pp. 1168–71.

Ikerd, John E. and Schupp, Alvin R. A Decision Model for Continuous Sequence Production Processes of Variable Length: An Application to Hog Marketing. *Amer. J. Agr. Econ.*, December 1969, *51*(5), pp. 1159–63.

Ismail, A. Halim. Some Considerations Regarding the Optimum Ages for Replanting Rubber Trees on Smallholdings in Malaya. *Malayan Econ. Rev.*, October 1969, *14*(2), pp. 55–78. **[G: Malaysia]**

Ivan'kov, M. Wages of Collective Farm Managerial Personnel and Specialists and the Matter of Increasing the Effectiveness of Production. *Prob. Econ.*, July 1969, *12*(3), pp. 58–82. **[G: U.S.S.R.]**

Johnson, Glenn L. Stress on Production Economics. **In** *Fox, K. A. and Johnson, D. G., eds.*, 1969, pp. 203–20.

Johnson, Glenn L. The Modern Family Farm and Its Problems: With Particular Reference to the United States of America. **In** *Papi, U. and Nunn, C., eds.*, 1969, pp. 234–50. **[G: U.S.]**

Kahlon, A. S. and Sharma, A. C. Role of Farm and Family Size in Determining Cropping Patterns in the Punjab. *Asian Econ. Rev.*, February 1969, *11*(2), pp. 117–30. **[G: India]**

Krause, Kenneth R. Application of the Financial Management Function in the Family Size Farm Firm. *Amer. J. Agr. Econ.*, December 1969, *51*(5), pp. 1536–42. **[G: U.S.]**

Krausz, N. G. P. and Reiss, Franklin J. Institutions and Instruments—Management Alternatives. *Amer. J. Agr. Econ.*, December 1969, *51*(5), pp. 1369–80. **[G: U.S.]**

Kulshreshtha, S. N. Age and Efficiency in Public Agricultural Policy: The Case of Ontario. *Can. J. Agr. Econ.*, July 1969, *17*(2), pp. 85–91. **[G: Canada]**

Kulshreshtha, S. N. Part-Time Farming in Ontario Agriculture. *Can. J. Agr. Econ.*, February 1969, *17*(1), pp. 151–56. **[G: Canada]**

Langham, Max R. and Edwards, W. F. Externalities in Pesticide Use. *Amer. J. Agr. Econ.*, December 1969, *51*(5), pp. 1195–1201.

Levi, Donald R. and Allwood, James K. Legal-Economic Models as a Tool for Optimizing Intergeneration Property Transfers. *Amer. J. Agr. Econ.*, December 1969, *51*(5), pp. 1393–98. **[G: U.S.]**

Lindner, R. K. The Economics of Increased Beef Production on Dairy Farms in Western Australia. *Quart. Rev. Agr. Econ.*, July 1969, *22*(3), pp. 147–64. **[G: Australia]**

Lindsey, Quentin W. The Problem of Periodic Reorganization in American Agriculture. **In** *Owen, W. F., ed.*, 1969, pp. 1–14. **[G: U.S.]**

Lins, David A. An Empirical Comparison of Simulation and Recursive Linear Programming Firm Growth Models. *Agr. Econ. Res.*, January 1969, *21*(1), pp. 7–12.

Longworth, John W. Management Games and the Teaching of Farm Management. *Australian J. Agr. Econ.*, June 1969, *13*(1), pp. 58–67.

Marenco, G. Exact Aggregation with Linear Programming Models—A Note on the Sufficient Conditions Proposed by R. H. Day. *Amer. J. Agr. Econ.*, August 1969, *51*(3), pp. 684–86.

Mauldon, R. G.; Schapper, H. P. and Treloar, D. W. G. Operational Accounting for Farm Management. *Australian J. Agr. Econ.*, June 1969, *13*(1), pp. 47–57.

McArthur, D. A. Educational Efforts in Farm Credit Management. *Can. J. Agr. Econ.*, November 1969, *17*(3), pp. 181–85. **[G: Canada]**

Michalson, E. L. Impact of Weather and Technology on Net Return Estimates. *Agr. Econ. Res.*, January 1969, *21*(1), pp. 19–22. **[G: U.S.]**

Moore, C. V. and Snyder, J. H. Crop Selection in High-Risk Agriculture. *Agr. Econ. Res.*, October 1969, *21*(4), pp. 89–98. **[G: U.S.]**

Moszer, Max. An Analysis of the 1964 Wheat Option. *Amer. J. Agr. Econ.*, February 1969, *51*(1), pp. 100–118. **[G: U.S.]**

Nair, K. R. Some Responses of Rice Farmers to the Package Program in Tanjore District, India: Comment. *Amer. J. Agr. Econ.*, August 1969, *51*(3), pp. 699–701. **[G: India]**

Nikolitch, Radoje. The Adequate Family Farm—Mainstay of the Farm Economy. **In** *Owen, W.*

F., ed., 1969, pp. 26–37. [G: U.S.]

Plaunt, Darrel. Economic Guidelines for Mobilizing Labour and Management in Canadian Agriculture. *Can. J. Agr. Econ.*, November 1969, *17*(3), pp. 20–33. [G: Canada]

Powell, R. A. and Hardaker, J. B. Recent Developments in Farm Planning: 3: Sub-optimal Programming Methods for Practical Farm Planning. *Rev. Marketing Agr. Econ.*, June 1969, *37*(2), pp. 121–29.

Priebe, H. The Modern Family Farm and Its Problems: With Particular Reference to the Federal German Republic. **In** *Papi, U. and Nunn, C., eds.*, 1969, pp. 251–64. [G: W. Germany]

Randall, Alan J. Integration of Irrigated and Dry Land Agriculture—Profitability and Product Mix. *Rev. Marketing Agr. Econ.*, September 1969, *37* (3), pp. 141–52. [G: Australia]

Rodewald, Gorden E., Jr. and Baker, C. B. Interim Period Asset Valuation: A Method for Making Investment Decisions. *Agr. Econ. Res.*, April 1969, *21*(2), pp. 35–39. [G: U.S.]

Rodewald, Gordon E., Jr. and Baker, C. B. Economics of Investment in Cattle Feeding. *Ill. Agr. Econ.*, January 1969, *9*(1), pp. 18–25.

Ryan, J. G. Optimum Programmes for Irrigation Farms. *Rev. Marketing Agr. Econ.*, September 1969, *37*(3), pp. 153–71. [G: Australia]

Scott, John T., Jr. and Reiss, Franklin J. Changing Technology and Lease Adjustment: Theory and Practice. *Land Econ.*, November 1969, *45*(4), pp. 400–405.

Shaudys, E. T. Farm Panels as a Source of Farm Management Data: The Ohio Plan. *Amer. J. Agr. Econ.*, December 1969, *51*(5), pp. 1211–13. [G: U.S.]

Smith, Allen G. and Baker, C. B. The Effect of Real Estate Debt Commitments on Nonreal Estate Credit and Liquidity of the Farm. *Ill. Agr. Econ.*, January 1969, *9*(1), pp. 1–6.

Sobering, Fred; Quance, C. Leroy and Tweeten, Luther G. An Economic Model for Determining Cotton Allotments and Prices to Maximize Net Farm Income. *Amer. J. Agr. Econ.*, December 1969, *51*(5), pp. 1124–28. [G: U.S.]

Sojit, Alberto A. Renta de la tierra y asignación de recursos. (Land Rent and Allocation of Resources. With English summary.) *Económica*, May–August 1969, *15*(2), pp. 211–22.

Swanson, Earl R. and Dunlap, R. D. Influence of Prices on Production Potential for Beef and Hogs on Farms with Fixed Acreages. *Ill. Agr. Econ.*, January 1969, *9*(1), pp. 10–17. [G: U.S.]

Tadros, Mahfouz E. and Casler, George L. A Game Theoretic Model for Farm Planning under Uncertainty. *Amer. J. Agr. Econ.*, December 1969, *51*(5), pp. 1164–67.

Topor, V. V. and Şotan, S. Determinarea influenţei nivelului de organizare şi conducere asupra rezultatelor economice ale I.A.S. (Determining the Influence of the Level of Organization and Management on the Economic Results of State Agricultural Enterprises. With English summary.) *Stud. Cercet. Econ.*, 1969, *1-2*, pp. 77–91. [G: Romania]

Tsuchiya, Keizō. Economics of Mechanization in Small-scale Agriculture. **In** *Ohkawa, K.; Johnston, B. F. and Kaneda, H., eds.*, 1969, pp. 155–72. [G: Japan]

Tweeten, Luther G. Theories Explaining the Persistence of Low Resource Returns in a Growing Farm Economy. *Amer. J. Agr. Econ.*, November 1969, *51*(4), pp. 798–817. [G: U.S.]

Venugopalacharyulu, N. Allocation Efficiency in Agriculture in Madras State. *Asian Econ. Rev.*, February 1969, *11*(2), pp. 216–20. [G: India]

Weinschenck, G.; Henrichsmeyer, W. and Aldinger, F. The Theory of Spatial Equilibrium and Optimal Location in Agriculture: A Survey. *Rev. Marketing Agr. Econ.*, March 1969, *37*(1), pp. 3–70.

Wells, J. M. and Bates, W. R. A Note on Some Implications of Family Partnership Formation for Farm Income Comparisons. *Quart. Rev. Agr. Econ.*, July 1969, *22*(3), pp. 140–46. [G: Australia]

Wells, J. M. and Bates, W. R. Changes in Farm Business Organisation in Australia. *Quart. Rev. Agr. Econ.*, April 1969, *22*(2), pp. 53–65. [G: Australia]

Williams, Donald B. Production Economics, Farm Management, and Extension. *Amer. J. Agr. Econ.*, February 1969, *51*(1), pp. 57–70.

Williams, R. J. and Baker, J. R. A Comparison of Response Surface and Factorial Designs in Agricultural Research: Reply. *Rev. Marketing Agr. Econ.*, June 1969, *37*(2), pp. 132–33.

Wise, John and Yotopoulos, Pan A. The Empirical Content of Economic Rationality: A Test for a Less Developed Economy. *J. Polit. Econ.*, November/December 1969, *77*(6), pp. 976–1004. [G: Greece]

Wright, A. and Dent, J. B. The Application of Simulation Techniques to the Study of Grazing Systems. *Australian J. Agr. Econ.*, December 1969, *13*(2), pp. 144–53.

717 Land Reform and Land Use

7170 General

Beckford, George L. The Economics of Agricultural Resource Use and Development in Plantation Economies. *Soc. Econ. Stud.*, December 1969, *18* (4), pp. 321–47.

Burki, Shahid Javed. West Pakistan's Rural Works Program: A Study in Political and Administrative Response. *Middle East J.*, Summer 1969, *23*(3), pp. 321–42. [G: W. Pakistan]

Flores, Edmundo. Latin American Land Reform: Meaning and Experience. **In** *Nisbet, C. T., ed.*, 1969, pp. 132–40. [G: Latin America]

Gregor, Howard F. Farm Structure in Regional Comparison: California and New Jersey Vegetable Farms. *Econ. Geogr.*, July 1969, *45*(3), pp. 209–25. [G: U.S.]

Gulati, I. S. and Kothari, V. N. Land Tax as an Incentive for Better Land Utilization. *Artha-Vikas*, July 1969, *5*(2), pp. 108–16.

Harris, Edward R., Jr. The Process of Land Reform in Developing Countries: The Background and Basic Legal Strategy. *Amer. J. Econ. Soc.*, January 1969, *28*(1), pp. 49–58.

Harris, Marshall. Shifts in Entrepreneurial Functions in Agriculture. *Amer. J. Agr. Econ.*, August 1969, *51*(3), pp. 517–29. **[G: U.S.]**

Kahlon, A. S. and Sharma, A. C. Role of Farm and Family Size in Determining Cropping Patterns in the Punjab. *Asian Econ. Rev.*, February 1969, *11* (2), pp. 117–30. **[G: India]**

Mistry, Thakore. Land-Based vs. Income-Based Taxation in Indian Agriculture. *Artha-Vikas*, July 1969, *5*(2), pp. 117–29. **[G: India]**

Mitchell, Edward J. Some Econometrics of the Huk Rebellion. *Amer. Polit. Sci. Rev.*, December 1969, *63*(4), pp. 1159–71. **[G: Philippines]**

Pearse, P. H. Principles of Allocating Wildland Among Alternative Uses. *Can. J. Agr. Econ.*, February 1969, *17*(1), pp. 121–31.

Restrepo Fernández, Iván and Sánchez Cortés, José. El arrendamiento de tierras ejidales: El caso de Apatzingán. (The Leasing of Common Lands: The Case of Apatzingán. With English summary.) *Econ. Polít.*, Third Semester 1969, *6*(3), pp. 331–46. **[G: Mexico]**

Ruttan, Vernon W. Equity and Productivity Issues in Modern Agrarian Reform Legislation. **In** *Papi, U. and Nunn, C., eds.*, 1969, pp. 581–600.

Sethi, Narendra K. Land Reform in Economic Development—A Case Study from Latin America. *Asian Econ. Rev.*, February 1969, *11*(2), pp. 221–26.

Sojit, Alberto A. Renta de la tierra y asignación de recursos. (Land Rent and Allocation of Resources. With English summary.) *Económica*, May–August 1969, *15*(2), pp. 211–22.

Wilczynski, Jozef. Towards Rationality in Land Economics under Central Planning. *Econ. J.*, September 1969, *79*(315), pp. 540–59.

7171 Land Ownership and Tenure; Land Reform

Adams, Dale W. and Rask, Norman. Economics of Cost-Share Leases: A Reply. *Amer. J. Agr. Econ.*, August 1969, *51*(3), pp. 695–97.

Ahmad, Zubeida M. and Sternberg, Marvin J. Agrarian Reform and Employment, with Special Reference to Asia. *Int. Lab. Rev.*, February 1969, *99*(2), pp. 159–83. **[G: Asia]**

Allan, William. Land Tenure and Productivity. **In** *Hutchinson, J. [Sir], ed.*, 1969, pp. 96–114.

Andarawewa, A. B. Tenure Patterns and the Commercialization of Canadian Agriculture. *Can. J. Agr. Econ.*, February 1969, *17*(1), pp. 110–20. **[G: Canada]**

Baali, Fuad. Agrarian Reform in Iraq: Some Socioeconomic Aspects. *Amer. J. Econ. Soc.*, January 1969, *28*(1), pp. 61–76. **[G: Iraq]**

Cheung, Steven N. S. Transaction Costs, Risk Aversion, and the Choice of Contractual Arrangements. *J. Law Econ.*, April 1969, *12*(1), pp. 23–42.

Due, Jean M. What Has Happened to the Ghanaian State Farms? *Ill. Agr. Econ.*, July 1969, *9*(2), pp. 25–35. **[G: Ghana]**

Feder, Ernest. Societal Opposition to Peasant Movements and Its Effects on Farm People in Latin America. **In** *Landsberger, H. A., ed.*, 1969, pp. 399–450. **[G: Latin America]**

Fernea, Robert A. Land Reform and Ecology in Postrevolutionary Iraq. *Econ. Develop. Cult. Change*, April 1969, *17*(3), pp. 356–81. **[G: Iraq]**

Foland, Frances M. Agrarian Reform in Latin America. *Foreign Aff.*, October 1969, *48*(1), pp. 97–112. **[G: Latin America]**

Frank, Andre Gunder. Varieties of Land Reform. **In** *Frank, A. G.*, 1969, pp. 269–75. **[G: Latin America]**

Frisch, Uwe G. and Malagón, Oscar M. La concentracion territorial de la industria en Mexico. (Territorial Concentration of Industry in Mexico. With English summary.) *Econ. Polít.*, Second Semester 1969, *6*(2), pp. 195–208. **[G: Mexico]**

George, P. T. Land Tenures in India—Results of 1961 Census. *Asian Econ. Rev.*, May 1969, *11*(3), pp. 317–24. **[G: India]**

Gisser, Micha. Economics of Cost-Share Leases: Comment. *Amer. J. Agr. Econ.*, August 1969, *51* (3), pp. 692–95.

Harris, Edward R., Jr. Funding Land Redistribution in Developing Countries: Maintaining Fiscal Solvency in the Face of Heavy Costs. *Amer. J. Econ. Soc.*, April 1969, *28*(2), pp. 193–204.

Harris, Edward R., Jr. The Role of Bonds as Compensation in Modern Land Reform Programs: Characteristics of Landowner Payments Converting Landlords into Producers. *Amer. J. Econ. Soc.*, July 1969, *28*(3), pp. 325–32.

Huizer, Gerrit. Community Development, Land Reform, and Political Participation: Preliminary Observations on Some Cases in Latin America. *Amer. J. Econ. Soc.*, April 1969, *28*(2), pp. 159–78. **[G: Latin America]**

Kawano, Shigeto. Effects of the Land Reform on Consumption and Investment of Farmers. **In** *Ohkawa, K.; Johnston, B. F. and Kaneda, H., eds.*, 1969, pp. 374–97. **[G: Japan]**

Mehta, Parkash. Different Inputs as Related to Apple Output in Kulu District. *Asian Econ. Rev.*, May 1969, *11*(3), pp. 325–28. **[G: India]**

Morris, Reginald Edward. Fiscal Controls of Land Monopoly. *Amer. J. Econ. Soc.*, January 1969, *28* (1), pp. 77–92.

Morris, Reginald Edward. Problems in the Reform of Land Tenure. *Amer. J. Econ. Soc.*, April 1969, *28*(2), pp. 205–09.

Nikolitch, Radoje. Family-Operated Farms: Their Compatibility with Technological Advance. *Amer. J. Agr. Econ.*, August 1969, *51*(3), pp. 530–45. **[G: U.S.]**

Parthasarthy, G. Tenancy Legislation in Labour Surplus Economies and Economic Analysis—A Note. *Indian Econ. J.*, January–March 1969, *16*(3), pp. 371–74.

Renborg, Ulf. Tendencies Towards Concentration and Specialization in Agriculture. **In** *Papi, U. and Nunn, C., eds.*, 1969, pp. 209–33.

Reyes, Osorio Sergio. La pobreza rural. (Rural Poverty. With English summary.) *Econ. Polít.*, Second Semester 1969, *6*(2), pp. 209–14. **[G: Mexico]**

Rutman, Gilbert L. Innovation in the Land Tenure System of the Transkei, South Africa. *Land Econ.*, November 1969, *45*(4), pp. 467–71. **[G: S. Africa]**

Scott, John T., Jr. and Reiss, Franklin J. Changing

Technology and Lease Adjustment: Theory and Practice. *Land Econ.*, November 1969, *45*(4), pp. 400–405.

Winsberg, Morton D. Jewish Agricultural Colonization in Entre Rios, Argentina, III: Economic Problems of Townsmen Resettled on the Land. *Amer. J. Econ. Soc.*, April 1969, *28*(2), pp. 179–91. **[G: Argentina]**

7172 Land Development; Land Use; Irrigation Policy

Baldovinos de la Peña, Gabriel. El sector ejidal y el plan agricola nacional. (The Ejidal Sector and the National Agricultural Plan. With English summary.) *Econ. Polít.*, Second Semester 1969, *6*(2), pp. 215–22. **[G: Mexico]**

Bickel, Blaine W. Farm Real Estate Prices 1950–67. *Fed. Res. Bank Kansas City Rev.*, April 1969, pp. 3–9. **[G: U.S.]**

Bretthauer, G. L. and Swanson, Earl R. Supplemental Irrigation of Corn: A Break-Even Analysis. *Ill. Agr. Econ.*, July 1969, *9*(2), pp. 19–24.

Conger, John Stoy. Conglomerate Land Acquisition: Reasons and Use. **In** *Garoian, L., ed.*, 1969, pp. 98–105. **[G: U.S.]**

Csáki, N. Competitive and Complementary International Division of Labour in the Agriculture of Socialist Countries. (In Russian. With English summary.) *Acta Oecon.*, 1969, *4*(3), pp. 283–97. **[G: E. Europe]**

David, E. J. L. The Exploding Demand for Recreational Property. *Land Econ.*, May 1969, *45*(2), pp. 206–17. **[G: U.S.]**

Deaconu, V. and Parpală, E. Eficienţa economică a culturilor de proumb la I.A.S. Fundeni şi Mihăileşti. (Economic Efficiency of the Culture of Maize for Grain at the Fundeni and Mihăileşti I.A.S. (State Farms). With English summary.) *Stud. Cercet. Econ.*, 1969, *4*, pp. 103–13. **[G: Romania]**

Delphendahl, J. Environmental Effects of Rural Land Use. *Amer. J. Agr. Econ.*, December 1969, *51*(5), pp. 1189–94. **[G: U.S.]**

Dincu, I. and Sandu, Gh. Implicaţiile economice ale unor măsuri de valorificare a solurilor slab productive. (Economic Implications of Some Measures Taken in View of Turning to Account Weakly Productive Soils. With English summary.) *Stud. Cercet. Econ.*, 1969, *4*, pp. 115–23. **[G: Romania]**

Dougal, Merwin D. Techniques for Developing a Comprehensive Program for Flood Plain Management. **In** *Dougal, M. D., ed.*, 1969, pp. 53–75.

Easter, K. William. Changing the ACP Investment. *Land Econ.*, May 1969, *45*(2), pp. 218–28. **[G: U.S.]**

Flinn, J. C. The Demand for Irrigation Water in an Intensive Irrigation Area. *Australian J. Agr. Econ.*, December 1969, *13*(2), pp. 128–43.

Gardner, Donald K. The Role of Open Spaces in Flood Plain Management. **In** *Dougal, M. D., ed.*, 1969, pp. 137–46. **[G: U.S.]**

Hammill, Anne E. Variables Related to Farm Real Estate Values in Minnesota Counties. *Agr. Econ. Res.*, April 1969, *21*(2), pp. 45–50. **[G: U.S.]**

Henley, Albert T. Land Value Taxation by California Irrigation Districts. **In** *Becker, A. P., ed.*, 1969, pp. 137–45. **[G: U.S.]**

Higbee, Edward. Other Traditions: The Advance of the Hacienda. **In** *Owen, W. F., ed.*, 1969, pp. 43–51. **[G: U.S.]**

Holland, Daniel M. A Study of Land Taxation in Jamaica. **In** *Becker, A. P., ed.*, 1969, pp. 239–86. **[G: Jamaica]**

Leonard, Patrick L. Farm Planning and Land Development Schemes. *Malayan Econ. Rev.*, April 1969, *14*(1), pp. 80–96. **[G: Indonesia]**

Manning, Travis W. Economic Guidelines for Land and Water Resource Use in Agriculture. *Can. J. Agr. Econ.*, November 1969, *17*(3), pp. 1–8. **[G: Canada]**

Mark, Shelley M. Property Tax Administration and Hawaii's Land Use Law. **In** *Lynn, A. D., Jr., ed.*, 1969, pp. 187–202. **[G: U.S.]**

Martin, William E.; Burdak, Thomas G. and Young, Robert A. Projecting Hydrologic and Economic Interrelationships in Groundwater Basin Management. *Amer. J. Agr. Econ.*, December 1969, *51*(5), pp. 1593–97. **[G: U.S.]**

Parks, Burl A. A Brief Background of the Planning Process. **In** *Dougal, M. D., ed.*, 1969, pp. 79–83.

Pine, Wilfred H. and Sirohi, Amar S. Irrigation with Restraints on Land and Water Resources. *Land Econ.*, May 1969, *45*(2), pp. 285–87.

Randall, Alan J. Integration of Irrigated and Dry Land Agriculture—Profitability and Product Mix. *Rev. Marketing Agr. Econ.*, September 1969, *37*(3), pp. 141–52. **[G: Australia]**

Rhoads, William G. and Bird, Richard M. The Valorization Tax in Colombia: An Example for other Developing Countries? **In** *Becker, A. P., ed.*, 1969, pp. 201–37. **[G: Colombia]**

Ryan, J. G. Optimum Programmes for Irrigation Farms. *Rev. Marketing Agr. Econ.*, September 1969, *37*(3), pp. 153–71. **[G: Australia]**

Sansom, Robert L. The Motor Pump: A Case Study of Innovation and Development. *Oxford Econ. Pap.*, March 1969, *21*(1), pp. 109–21. **[G: S. Vietnam]**

Sheaffer, John R. The Interaction of Urban Redevelopment and Flood Plain Management in Waterloo, Iowa. **In** *Dougal, M. D., ed.*, 1969, pp. 123–35. **[G: U.S.]**

Shuffett, Milton and Hoskins, Josiah. Capitalization of Burley Tobacco Allotment Rights into Farmland Values. *Amer. J. Agr. Econ.*, May 1969, *51*(2), pp. 471–74. **[G: U.S.]**

Snyder, Robert W. Using Local Comprehensive Planning to Control Lakewater Pollution in Seasonal Home Communities. *Amer. J. Agr. Econ.*, December 1969, *51*(5), pp. 1583–87. **[G: U.S.]**

Strasma, John. Property Taxation in Chile. **In** *Becker, A. P., ed.*, 1969, pp. 187–200. **[G: Chile]**

Theiler, Donald F. Effects of Flood Protection on Land Use in the Coon Creek, Wisconsin, Watershed. *Water Resources Res.*, December 1969, *5*(6), pp. 1216–22. **[G: U.S.]**

Tintner, Gerhard and Patel, Malvika. A Lognormal Diffusion Process Applied to the Growth of Yields of Some Agricultural Crops in India. *J. Devel.*

Stud., October 1969, *6*(1), pp. 49–57. [G: India]

Trock, Warren L. Institutional Factors Affecting Land and Water Development, Lower Rio Grande Valley, Texas. *Water Resources Res.*, December 1969, *5*(6), pp. 1364–66. [G: U.S.]

Woodruff, A. M. Assessment Standards: Highest and Best Use as a Basis for Land Appraisal and Assessment. In *Lynn, A. D., Jr., ed.*, 1969, pp. 167–83. [G: U.S.]

Woodruff, A. M. and Ecker-Racz, L. L. Property Taxes and Land-Use Patterns in Australia and New Zealand. In *Becker, A. P., ed.*, 1969, pp. 147–86. [G: Australia; New Zealand]

718 Rural Economics

7180 Rural Economics

Buchanan, James M. A Future for "Agricultural Economics"? *Amer. J. Agr. Econ.*, December 1969, *51* (5), pp. 1027–36. [G: U.S.]

Edwards, Clark. A Rural Economic Indicator System. *Amer. J. Agr. Econ.*, December 1969, *51*(5), pp. 1202–05. [G: U.S.]

Folse, C. I. and Riffe, W. W. Changing Patterns of Business Services and Population in Illinois Rural Villages. *Ill. Agr. Econ.*, January 1969, *9*(1), pp. 26–32. [G: U.S.]

Gardner, Bruce L. Determinants of Farm Family Income Inequality. *Amer. J. Agr. Econ.*, November 1969, *51*(4), pp. 753–69. [G: U.S.]

Hansen, Bent. Employment and Wages in Rural Egypt. *Amer. Econ. Rev.*, June 1969, *59*(3), pp. 298–313. [G: Egypt]

Holmes, O. Wendell. The Farm Poor: Counted, Miscounted, or Discounted? *Amer. J. Agr. Econ.*, December 1969, *51*(5), pp. 1557–60.

Jesness, O. B. Poverty among American Farmers. In *Task Force on Economic Growth and Opportunity*, 1969, pp. 229–43. [G: U.S.]

Kahlon, A. S. and Sharma, A. C. Role of Farm and Family Size in Determining Cropping Patterns in the Punjab. *Asian Econ. Rev.*, February 1969, *11* (2), pp. 117–30. [G: India]

Leuthold, Raymond M. Government Payments and the Distribution of Income in Agriculture. *Amer. J. Agr. Econ.*, December 1969, *51*(5), pp. 1520–23. [G: U.S.]

Lorenzo, A. Employment Effects of Rural and Community Development in the Philippines. *Int. Lab. Rev.*, November 1969, *100*(5), pp. 419–44. [G: Philippines]

Muehlbeier, John. Problems That Persist in the Great Plains. *Amer. J. Agr. Econ.*, December 1969, *51*(5), pp. 1089–96. [G: U.S.]

Newman, Monroe and March, Eli P. Rural Areas in the Urban Economy. *Amer. J. Agr. Econ.*, December 1969, *51*(5), pp. 1097–1109. [G: U.S.]

Stevenson, Russell. The United States Graduate Training of Asian Rural Social Scientists. *Land Econ.*, August 1969, *45*(3), pp. 334–43.

Tendulkar, Suresh D. Econometric Study of Monthly Consumption Expenditures in Rural Uttar Pradesh. *Amer. J. Agr. Econ.*, February 1969, *51*(1), pp. 119–37. [G: India]

720 Natural Resources

721 Natural Resources

7210 General (for agricultural irrigation aspects see 7172)

Back, W. B. Estimating Contributions of Natural Resource Investments to Objectives in Regional Economic Development. *Amer. J. Agr. Econ.*, December 1969, *51*(5), pp. 1442–48. [G: U.S.]

Barr, Brenton M. and Bater, James H. The Electricity Industry of Central Siberia. *Econ. Geogr.*, October 1969, *45*(4), pp. 349–69. [G: U.S.S.R.]

Baumann, Duane D. Perception and Public Policy in the Recreational Use of Domestic Water Supply Reservoirs. *Water Resources Res.*, June 1969, *5*(3), pp. 543–54. [G: U.S.]

Blainey, Geoffrey. Mining—And Undermining. *Econ. Rec.*, December 1969, *45*(112), pp. 607–15. [G: Australia]

Brown, Richard E. and Weber, Glen D. Tributary Area Development: TVA's Approach to Sub-Regional Development. *Land Econ.*, February 1969, *45*(1), pp. 141–46. [G: U.S.]

Buller, Orlan and Lin, Wuu-Long. Measuring the Effect of Weather on Crop Production. *Can. J. Agr. Econ.*, February 1969, *17*(1), pp. 91–98. [G: U.S.]

Butcher, William S.; Haimes, Yacov Y. and Hall, Warren A. Dynamic Programming for the Optimal Sequencing of Water Supply Projects. *Water Resources Res.*, December 1969, *5*(6), pp. 1196–1204.

Ciriacy-Wantrup, S. V. Natural Resources in Economic Growth: The Role of Institutions and Policies. *Amer. J. Agr. Econ.*, December 1969, *51*(5), pp. 1314–24. [G: India]

Cloud, Preston E., Jr. Mineral Resources from the Sea. In *National Academy of Sciences*, 1969, pp. 135–55.

Cloud, Preston E., Jr. Realities in Mineral Distribution. In *Effects of Population Growth on Natural Resources and the Environment, HCH*, 1969, pp. 219–42.

Comm. on Resources and Man, Nat'l. Acad. of Sci. Introduction and Recommendations from *Resources and Man.* In *Effects of Population Growth on Natural Resources and the Environment, HCH*, 1969, pp. 120–30.

Cotner, Melvin L. A Policy for Public Investments in Natural Resources. *Amer. J. Agr. Econ.*, February 1969, *51*(1), pp. 87–99.

Crutchfield, James A. Economic Evaluation of Weather Modification. In *Fleagle, R. G., ed.*, 1969, pp. 105–17. [G: U.S.]

Cummings, Ronald G. Some Extensions of the Economic Theory of Exhaustible Resources. *Western Econ. J.*, September 1969, *7*(3), pp. 201–10.

Cummings, Ronald G. and Burt, Oscar R. The Economics of Production from Natural Resources: Note. *Amer. Econ. Rev.*, December 1969, *59*(5), pp. 985–90.

Davis, H. Craig. Interregional Production and Water

Resource Dependencies among the Western States. *Western Econ. J.*, March 1969, *7*(1), pp. 27–40. [G: U.S.]

Day, H. J., et al. Evaluation of Benefits of a Flood Warning System. *Water Resources Res.*, October 1969, *5*(5), pp. 937–46. [G: U.S.]

Ebrahimzadeh, Cyrus. The Economics of Hydro-Electric Power in Iran. *Tahq. Eq.*, November 1969, *6*(15&16), pp. 54–79. [G: Iran]

Eddleman, B. R. Estimating the Effects of Resource Development Programs on Regional Employment. *Amer. J. Agr. Econ.*, December 1969, *51*(5), pp. 1434–41. [G: U.S.]

Fleagle, Robert G. Implications for Public Policy. **In** *Fleagle, R. G., ed.*, 1969, pp. 138–42.

Ford, J. L. and Warford, J. J. Cost Functions for the Water Industry. *J. Ind. Econ.*, November 1969, *18* (1), pp. 53–63. [G: U.K.]

Fox, Irving K. *The Nation's Water Resources* (Review Article). *Land Econ.*, November 1969, *45*(4), pp. 474–76. [G: U.S.]

Gaffney, Mason. Economic Aspects of Water Resource Policy. *Amer. J. Econ. Soc.*, April 1969, *28* (2), pp. 131–44. [G: U.S.]

Giurovich, Gualtiero. L'impresa di acquedotto: una condizione di minimo costo fra la condotta addut-trice e il serbatoio. (With English summary.) *Statistica*, July-September 1969, *29*(3), pp. 385–421.

Grant, Walter V. Economic Guidelines for Resource Use: Discussion. *Can. J. Agr. Econ.*, November 1969, *17*(3), pp. 38–40. [G: Canada]

Grant-Suttie, R. I. Copper Substitution. *Finance Develop.*, June 1969, *6*(2), pp. 49–55.

Hall, Warren A.; Tauxe, G. W. and Yeh, W. W.-G. An Alternate Procedure for the Optimization of Operations for Planning with Multiple River, Multiple Purpose Systems. *Water Resources Res.*, December 1969, *5*(6), pp. 1367–72.

Hartman, L. M.; Holland, David and Giddings, Marvin. Effects of Hurricane Storms on Agriculture. *Water Resources Res.*, June 1969, *5*(3), pp. 555–62. [G: U.S.]

Hines, Lawrence G. The Long-Run Cost Function of Water Production for Selected Wisconsin Communities. *Land Econ.*, February 1969, *45*(1), pp. 133–40. [G: U.S.]

Hubbert, M. King. Energy Resources. **In** *National Academy of Sciences*, 1969, pp. 157–242.

James, I. C., II; Bower, B. T. and Matalas, N. C. Relative Importance of Variables in Water Resources Planning. *Water Resources Res.*, December 1969, *5*(6), pp. 1165–73.

Khachaturov, T. On the Economic Evaluation of Natural Resources. *Prob. Econ.*, August 1969, *12* (4), pp. 52–67. [G: U.S.S.R.]

Knetsch, Jack L. Economic Analysis in Natural Resource Programs. **In** *The Analysis and Evaluation of Public Expenditures: The PPB System, Vol. 3, JECP*, 1969, pp. 1087–1101. [G: U.S.]

Kozelka, Robert. A Bayesian Approach to Jamaican Fishing. **In** *Buchler, I. R. and Nutini, H. G., eds.*, 1969, pp. 117–25. [G: Jamaica]

Levi, Donald R. A Lawyer Looks at Water Resource Economists. *Amer. J. Agr. Econ.*, February 1969, *51*(1), pp. 182–83.

Lord, William B. and Smith, Stephen C. Tools of the Trade in Policy Decision—PPBS, A Case in Point. *Amer. J. Agr. Econ.*, December 1969, *51*(5), pp. 1427–33. [G: U.S.]

Lovering, Thomas S. Mineral Resources from the Land. **In** *National Academy of Sciences*, 1969, pp. 109–34.

Major, David C. Benefit-Cost Ratios for Projects in Multiple Objective Investment Programs. *Water Resources Res.*, December 1969, *5*(6), pp. 1174–78. [G: U.S.]

Manning, Travis W. Economic Guidelines for Land and Water Resource Use in Agriculture. *Can. J. Agr. Econ.*, November 1969, *17*(3), pp. 1–8. [G: Canada]

McGee, Dean A. Treasures of Energy: Natural Resources of the Ninth and Tenth Federal Reserve Districts. *Fed. Res. Bank Kansas City Rev.*, February 1969, pp. 3–9. [G: U.S.]

Miller, S. F. and Halter, A. N. Computer Simulation of the Substitution between Project Size and Management. *Amer. J. Agr. Econ.*, December 1969, *51*(5), pp. 1119–23. [G: U.S.]

Pearse, P. H. Principles of Allocating Wildland Among Alternative Uses. *Can. J. Agr. Econ.*, February 1969, *17*(1), pp. 121–31.

Pine, Wilfred H. and Sirohi, Amar S. Irrigation with Restraints on Land and Water Resources. *Land Econ.*, May 1969, *45*(2), pp. 285–87.

Revelle, Charles; Joeres, Erhard and Kirby, William. The Linear Decision Rule in Reservoir Management and Design. 1. Development of the Stochastic Model. *Water Resources Res.*, August 1969, *5* (4), pp. 767–77.

Ricker, William E. Food from the Sea. **In** *National Academy of Sciences*, 1969, pp. 87–108.

Robinson, Warren C. A Critical Note on the New Conservationism. *Land Econ.*, November 1969, *45*(4), pp. 453–56.

Rogers, Peter. A Game Theory Approach to the Problems of International River Basins. *Water Resources Res.*, August 1969, *5*(4), pp. 749–60. [G: India; Pakistan]

Saunders, Robert J. Urban Area Water Consumption: Analysis and Projections. *Quart. Rev. Econ. Bus.*, Summer 1969, *9*(2), pp. 5–20. [G: U.S.]

Schmid, A. Allan. Natural Resources and Growth: Towards a Non-Marginal Political Economics. *Amer. J. Agr. Econ.*, December 1969, *51*(5), pp. 1304–13. [G: U.S.]

Sewell, W. R. Derrick. Weather Modification: When Should We Do It and How Far Should We Go? **In** *Fleagle, R. G., ed.*, 1969, pp. 94–104. [G: U.S.]

Shkatov, V. Prices on Natural Resources and the Problem of Improving Planned Price Formation. *Prob. Econ.*, June 1969, *12*(2), pp. 67–89.

Simpson, E. S. Electricity Production in Nigeria. *Econ. Geogr.*, July 1969, *45*(3), pp. 239–57. [G: Nigeria]

Sinclair, Sol. Economic Guidelines for Resource Use: Discussion. *Can. J. Agr. Econ.*, November 1969, *17*(3), pp. 34–38. [G: Canada]

Smith, Vernon L. On Models of Commercial Fishing. *J. Polit. Econ.*, March/April 1969, *77*(2), pp. 181–98.

Sokoloski, Adam A. A Water Resource Economist

Looks Back at a Lawyer. *Amer. J. Agr. Econ.,* August 1969, *51*(3), pp. 680–84.

Stoevener, Herbert H. Estimating the Effects of Water Policies in the West. *Amer. J. Agr. Econ.,* December 1969, *51*(5), pp. 1449–54. [G: U.S.]

Subocz, V. The Cargo Cult, or the 'Cinderella' Cult, in Mineral Policy? *Econ. Rec.,* December 1969, *45* (112), pp. 596–606. [G: Australia]

Theiler, Donald F. Effects of Flood Protection on Land Use in the Coon Creek, Wisconsin, Watershed. *Water Resources Res.,* December 1969, *5*(6), pp. 1216–22. [G: U.S.]

Trestrail, Richard W. Forests and the Property Tax —Unsound Accepted Theory. *Nat. Tax J.,* September 1969, *22*(3), pp. 347–56.

Trock, Warren L. Institutional Factors Affecting Land and Water Development, Lower Rio Grande Valley, Texas. *Water Resources Res.,* December 1969, *5*(6), pp. 1364–66. [G: U.S.]

Turnovsky, Stephen J. The Demand for Water: Some Empirical Evidence on Consumers' Response to a Commodity Uncertain in Supply. *Water Resources Res.,* April 1969, *5*(2), pp. 350–61. [G: U.S.]

Wasowski, Stanislaw. The Fuel Situation in Eastern Europe. *Soviet Stud.,* July 1969, *21*(1), pp. 35–51. [G: E. Europe]

Whipple, William, Jr. Optimizing Investment in Flood Control and Floodplain Zoning. *Water Resources Res.,* August 1969, *5*(4), pp. 761–66.

Whipple, William, Jr. Utility as a Surrogate for Value in Water Resources Analysis. *Eng. Econ.,* April–May 1969, *14*(3), pp. 159–67.

Wood, Douglas. The Water Supply System up to A.D. 2001. *J. Ind. Econ.,* November 1969, *18*(1), pp. 64–75. [G: U.K.]

Woolwine, Phil C. The South Pacific as a Source of Timber. *Oregon Bus. Rev.,* August 1969, *28*(8), pp. 1–5. [G: S. Pacific]

Wright, Arthur W. Statement. **In** *Tax Reform Act of 1969, Testimony, Oct. 1, SCP,* 1969, pp. 347–68. [G: U.S.]

7211 Recreational Aspects of Natural Resources

Bateman, Merrill J. Statement. **In** *Highway Legislation, HCH,* 1969, pp. 169–73. [G: U.S.]

Baumann, Duane D. Perception and Public Policy in the Recreational Use of Domestic Water Supply Reservoirs. *Water Resources Res.,* June 1969, *5*(3), pp. 543–54. [G: U.S.]

Brewer, Durward and Kuehn, John A. Conflicts within Recreation: A Rejoinder. *Land Econ.,* February 1969, *45*(1), pp. 131–33.

Brewer, Durward and Gillespie, Glenn A. Effects of Nonprice Variables upon Participation in Water-Oriented Outdoor Recreation: Reply. *Amer. J. Agr. Econ.,* February 1969, *51*(1), pp. 194–95.

Burt, Oscar R. Comments on 'Recreation Benefits from Water Pollution Control' by Joe B. Stevens. *Water Resources Res.,* August 1969, *5*(4), pp. 905–07.

Clawson, Marion. Open (Uncovered) Space as a New Urban Resource. **In** *Perloff, H. S., ed.,* 1969, pp. 139–75.

David, E. J. L. Effects of Nonprice Variables upon Participation in Water-Oriented Outdoor Recreation: Comment. *Amer. J. Agr. Econ.,* November 1969, *51*(4), pp. 942–45.

David, E. J. L. The Exploding Demand for Recreational Property. *Land Econ.,* May 1969, *45*(2), pp. 206–17. [G: U.S.]

Gardner, Donald K. The Role of Open Spaces in Flood Plain Management. **In** *Dougal, M. D., ed.,* 1969, pp. 137–46. [G: U.S.]

Long, Burl F. and Barron, James C. Conflicts within Recreation: Comment. *Land Econ.,* February 1969, *45*(1), pp. 128–31.

McClellan, Keith and Medrich, Elliot A. Outdoor Recreation: Economic Consideration for Optimal Site Selection and Development. *Land Econ.,* May 1969, *45*(2), pp. 174–82.

Seneca, Joseph J. Water Recreation, Demand, and Supply. *Water Resources Res.,* December 1969, *5* (6), pp. 1179–85. [G: U.S.]

Shabman, Leonard A. and Kalter, Robert J. Effects of Public Programs for Outdoor Recreation and Personal Income Distribution. *Amer. J. Agr. Econ.,* December 1969, *51*(5), pp. 1516–19. [G: U.S.]

Stevens, Joe B. Effects of Nonprice Variables upon Participation in Water-Oriented Outdoor Recreation: Comment. *Amer. J. Agr. Econ.,* February 1969, *51*(1), pp. 192–93.

Stevens, Joe B. Recreation Benefits from Water Pollution Control: Reply. *Water Resources Res.,* August 1969, *5*(4), pp. 908–09.

722 Conservation and Pollution

7220 Conservation and Pollution

Anderson, Dewey. Statement. **In** *National Timber Supply Act of 1969, HCH,* 1969, pp. 182–96. [G: U.S.]

Ayres, Robert U. and Kneese, Allen V. Pollution and Environmental Quality. **In** *Perloff, H. S., ed.,* 1969, pp. 35–71. [G: U.S.]

Boyle, W. A. Statement. **In** *The 1969 Economic Report of the President, Pt. 4, JECH,* 1969, pp. 1185–88. [G: U.S.]

Chapman, John D. Interactions between Man and His Resources. **In** *National Academy of Sciences,* 1969, pp. 31–42.

Cook, Jack L. Conservation by Bulldozer. *Mich. Academician,* Spring 1969, *1*(3–4), pp. 179–91.

Delphendahl, J. Environmental Effects of Rural Land Use. *Amer. J. Agr. Econ.,* December 1969, *51*(5), pp. 1189–94. [G: U.S.]

Dorfman, Robert and Jacoby, Henry D. A Model of Public Decisions Illustrated by a Water Pollution Policy Problem. **In** *The Analysis and Evaluation of Public Expenditures: The PPB System, Vol. 1, JECP,* 1969, pp. 226–74.

Edmondson, W. T. Ecology and Weather Modification. **In** *Fleagle, R. G., ed.,* 1969, pp. 87–93. [G: U.S.]

Fisher, Joseph L. and Potter, Neal. Natural Resource Adequacy for the United States and the World. **In** *Hauser, P. M., ed.,* 1969, pp. 106–38. [G: U.S.]

Gramm, William P. A Theoretical Note on the Capacity of the Market System to Abate Pollution. *Land Econ.*, August 1969, *45*(3), pp. 365–68.

Graves, G. W.; Hatfield, G. B. and Whinston, Andrew. Water Pollution Control Using By-Pass Piping. *Water Resources Res.*, February 1969, *5* (1), pp. 13–47.

Havlicek, Joseph, Jr.; Tolley, George S. and Wang, Yi. "Solid Wastes"—A Resource? *Amer. J. Agr. Econ.*, December 1969, *51*(5), pp. 1598–1602. **[G: U.S.]**

Hufschmidt, Maynard M.; Krutilla, John V. and Margolis, Julius. Standards and Criteria for Formulating and Evaluating Federal Water Resources Development. **In** *Guidelines for Estimating the Benefits of Public Expenditures, JECH,* 1969, pp. 135–212. **[G: U.S.]**

Kelly, William C., Jr. Water Quality Standards in Private Nuisance Actions. *Yale Law J.*, November 1969, *79*(1), pp. 102–10. **[G: U.S.]**

Kneese, Allen V. and d' Arge, Ralph C. Pervasive External Costs and the Response of Society. **In** *The Analysis and Evaluation of Public Expenditures: The PPB System, Vol. 1, JECP,* 1969, pp. 87–115.

Knetsch, Jack L. Economic Analysis in Natural Resource Programs. **In** *The Analysis and Evaluation of Public Expenditures: The PPB System, Vol. 3, JECP,* 1969, pp. 1087–1101. **[G: U.S.]**

Knetsch, Jack L., et al. Federal Natural Resources Development: Basic Issues in Benefit and Cost Measurement. **In** *Guidelines for Estimating the Benefits of Public Expenditures, JECH,* 1969, pp. 109–15. **[G: U.S.]**

Langham, Max R. and Edwards, W. F. Externalities in Pesticide Use. *Amer. J. Agr. Econ.*, December 1969, *51*(5), pp. 1195–1201.

Merritt, Lavere B. and Mar, Brian W. Marginal Values of Dilution Waters. *Water Resources Res.*, December 1969, *5*(6), pp. 1186–95. **[G: U.S.]**

Pincock, M. Glade. Assessing Impacts of Declining Water Quality on Gross Value Output of Agriculture, A Case Study. *Water Resources Res.*, February 1969, *5*(1), pp. 1–12. **[G: U.S.]**

Robinson, Warren C. A Critical Note on the New Conservationism. *Land Econ.*, November 1969, *45*(4), pp. 453–56.

Shaffer, Leslie L. D. The Myrtlewood Industry of Oregon. *Oregon Bus. Rev.*, April 1969, *28*(4), pp. 1–3. **[G: U.S.]**

Snyder, Robert W. Using Local Comprehensive Planning to Control Lakewater Pollution in Seasonal Home Communities. *Amer. J. Agr. Econ.*, December 1969, *51*(5), pp. 1583–87. **[G: U.S.]**

Taylor, Gary C. Economic Issues in Controlling Agricultural Pollution. *Amer. J. Agr. Econ.*, December 1969, *51*(5), pp. 1182–88. **[G: U.S.]**

730 ECONOMIC GEOGRAPHY

731 Economic Geography

7310 Economic Geography

Barr, Brenton M. and Bater, James H. The Electricity Industry of Central Siberia. *Econ. Geogr.*, October 1969, *45*(4), pp. 349–69. **[G: U.S.S.R.]**

von Böventer, Edwin. Walter Christaller's Central Places and Peripheral Areas: The Central Place Theory in Retrospect. *J. Reg. Sci.*, April 1969, *9*(1), pp. 117–24.

Brunn, Stanley D. and Hoffman, Wayne L. The Geography of Federal Grants-in-Aid to States. *Econ. Geogr.*, July 1969, *45*(3), pp. 226–38. **[G: U.S.]**

Buchanan, Ronald H. Toward Netherlands 2000: The Dutch National Plan. *Econ. Geogr.*, July 1969, *45*(3), pp. 258–74. **[G: Netherlands]**

Crutchfield, James A. Economic Evaluation of Weather Modification. **In** *Fleagle, R. G., ed.,* 1969, pp. 105–17. **[G: U.S.]**

Edmondson, W. T. Ecology and Weather Modification. **In** *Fleagle, R. G., ed.,* 1969, pp. 87–93. **[G: U.S.]**

Eriksson, Gösta A. Models in Human Geography. *Liiketaloudellinen Aikak.*, 1969, *18*(1), pp. 13–23.

Fleagle, Robert G. Background and Present Status of Weather Modification. **In** *Fleagle, R. G., ed.,* 1969, pp. 3–17.

Fleagle, Robert G. Implications for Public Policy. **In** *Fleagle, R. G., ed.,* 1969, pp. 138–42.

Forward, C. N. A Comparison of Waterfront Land Use in Four Canadian Ports: St. John's, St. John, Halifax, and Victoria. *Econ. Geogr.*, April 1969, *45* (2), pp. 155–69. **[G: Canada]**

Fox, Karl A. The New Synthesis of Rural and Urban Society in the United States. **In** *Papi, U. and Nunn, C., eds.,* 1969, pp. 606–28. **[G: U.S.]**

Glassner, Martin I. Feeding a Desert City: Antofagasta, Chile. *Econ. Geogr.*, October 1969, *45* (4), pp. 339–48. **[G: Chile]**

Gregor, Howard F. Farm Structure in Regional Comparison: California and New Jersey Vegetable Farms. *Econ. Geogr.*, July 1969, *45*(3), pp. 209–25. **[G: U.S.]**

Grigg, David. The Agricultural Regions of the World: Review and Reflections. *Econ. Geogr.*, April 1969, *45*(2), pp. 95–132.

Hazlewood, Arthur. An Approach to the Analysis of the Spatial Distribution of the Market in East Africa. *Bull. Oxford Univ. Inst. Econ. Statist.*, November 1969, *31*(4), pp. 243–61. **[G: E. Africa]**

Hudson, John C. Pattern Recognition in Empirical Map Analysis. *J. Reg. Sci.*, August 1969, *9*(2), pp. 189–99. **[G: U.S.]**

Jensen, Robert G. and Karaska, Gerald J. The Mathematical Thrust in Soviet Economic Geography—Its Nature and Significance. *J. Reg. Sci.*, April 1969, *9*(1), pp. 141–52. **[G: U.S.S.R.]**

Krumme, Günter. Toward a Geography of Enterprise. *Econ. Geogr.*, January 1969, *45*(1), pp. 30–40.

Macdonald, Gordon J. F. Federal Government Programs in Weather Modification. **In** *Fleagle, R. G., ed.,* 1969, pp. 69–86. **[G: U.S.]**

Mathieson, R. S. The Soviet Contribution to Regional Science: A Review Article. *J. Reg. Sci.*, April 1969, *9*(1), pp. 125–40. **[G: U.S.S.R.]**

Niedercorn, J. H. and Bechdolt, B. V., Jr. An Economic Derivation of the "Gravity Law" of Spatial

Interaction. *J. Reg. Sci.,* August 1969, *9*(2), pp. 273–82.

Odell, Peter R. Natural Gas in Western Europe: A Case Study in the Economic Geography of Energy Resources. *De Economist,* May/June 1969, *117*(3), pp. 227–57. **[G: W. Europe]**

Parr, John B. City Hierarchies and the Distribution of City Size: A Reconsideration of Beckmann's Contribution. *J. Reg. Sci.,* August 1969, *9*(2), pp. 239–53.

Sewell, W. R. Derrick. Weather Modification: When Should We Do It and How Far Should We Go? **In** *Fleagle, R. G., ed.,* 1969, pp. 94–104. **[G: U.S.]**

Simpson, E. S. Electricity Production in Nigeria. *Econ. Geogr.,* July 1969, *45*(3), pp. 239–57. **[G: Nigeria]**

Solomon, R. J. Property Values as a Structural Element of Urban Evolution. *Econ. Geogr.,* January 1969, *45*(1), pp. 1–29. **[G: Australia]**

Van Cleef, Eugene. "Things Are Not Always What They Seem" for the Economic Geographer. *Econ. Geogr.,* January 1969, *45*(1), pp. 41–44.

Webb, Kempton E. The Geography of Brazil's Modernization and Implications for the Years 1980 and 2000 A.D. **In** *Baklanoff, E. N., ed.,* 1969, pp. 142–56. **[G: Brazil]**

Wilkins, C. A. and Shaw, J. A. An Example to Illustrate the "Average" Nature of Clark's Law of Urban Populations. *J. Reg. Sci.,* August 1969, *9*(2), pp. 255–59.

Wolf, Laurence G. The Metropolitan Tidal Wave in Ohio, 1900–2000. *Econ. Geogr.,* April 1969, *45*(2), pp. 133–54. **[G: U.S.]**

800 Manpower; Labor; Population

8000 General

Herrick, Bruce. Research Needs in Labor and Economic Development. *Ind. Relat.,* May 1969, *8*(3), pp. 214–23.

810 Manpower Training and Allocation; Labor Force and Supply

811 Manpower Training and Development

8110 Manpower Training and Development

Awokoya, Stephen O. The Structure and Development of Nigerian Education. **In** *Yesufu, T. M., ed.,* 1969, pp. 157–82. **[G: Nigeria]**

Battistel, Ezio. I quadri direttivi nella "media" azienda industriale italiana. (Middle Management in the Italian "Medium-Sized" Industrial Firm. With English summary.) *L'Impresa,* March/April 1969, *11*(2), pp. 143–46. **[G: Italy]**

Blackburn, John O. An Optimal Unemployment Rate: Comment. *Quart. J. Econ.,* August 1969, *83*(3), pp. 518–20.

Boyd, Thomas. Planning the Recruitment of Professional Personnel. **In** *Gilroy, T. P., ed.,* 1969, pp. 18–23.

Brummet, R. Lee; Flamholtz, Eric G. and Pyle, William C. Human Resource Accounting: A Tool to Increase Managerial Effectiveness. *Manage. Account.,* August 1969, *51*(2), pp. 12–15.

Brummet, R. Lee; Flamholtz, Eric G. and Pyle, William C. Human Resource Myopia. *Mon. Lab. Rev.,* January 1969, *92*(1), pp. 29–30.

Bumas, Lester O. and Stein, Bruno. The Economic Rationale of Occupational Choice: Comment. *Ind. Lab. Relat. Rev.,* April 1969, *22*(3), pp. 422–28.

Cain, Glen G. and Hollister, Robinson G. Evaluating Manpower Programs for the Disadvantaged. **In** *Somers, G. G. and Wood, W. D., eds.,* 1969, pp. 119–51. **[G: U.S.]**

Carli, Guido. La scuola di automazione per dirigenti bancari. (School of Automation for Bank Executives. With English summary.) *Bancaria,* January 1969, *25*(1), pp. 7–8. **[G: Italy]**

Carol, Arthur and Parry, Samuel. The Economic Rationale of Occupational Choice: Reply. *Ind. Lab. Relat. Rev.,* April 1969, *22*(3), pp. 428–30.

Carr, Julian L., Jr. and Estafen, Bernard D. M.B.A. Salary Expectations: Fact or Fantasy? *Indiana Bus. Rev.,* September/October 1969, *44,* pp. 9–12.

Chung, Kae H. Toward a General Theory of Motivation and Performance. *Calif. Manage. Rev.,* Spring 1969, *11*(3), pp. 81–88.

Clark, Kenneth B. Efficiency as a Prod to Social Action. *Mon. Lab. Rev.,* August 1969, *92*(8), pp. 54–56.

Cohen, Malcolm S. The Direct Effects of Federal Manpower Programs in Reducing Unemployment. *J. Human Res.,* Fall 1969, *4*(4), pp. 491–507. **[G: U.S.]**

Conley, Ronald W. A Benefit-Cost Analysis of the Vocational Rehabilitation Program. *J. Human Res.,* Spring 1969, *4*(2), pp. 226–52. **[G: U.S.]**

Daidola, Giorgio. Formazione e trasferimento quadri nelle imprese multinazionali. (Development and Transfer of Managers in Multinational Firms. With English summary.) *L'Impresa,* July/October 1969, *11*(4–5), pp. 373–75.

Dayal, Ishwar. Role Analysis Technique in Job Descriptions. *Calif. Manage. Rev.,* Summer 1969, *11*(4), pp. 47–50.

Diatchenko, V. P. The Financial Problems of Professional Retraining of Personnel in the U.S.S.R. *Public Finance,* 1969, *24*(2), pp. 391–404. **[G: U.S.S.R.]**

Dobell, A. Rodney. An Optimal Unemployment Rate: Reply. *Quart. J. Econ.,* August 1969, *83*(3), pp. 521–23.

Doeringer, Peter B. Manpower Programs for Ghetto Labor Markets. **In** *Somers, G. G., ed. (II),* 1969, pp. 257–67. **[G: U.S.]**

Dunnette, Marvin D. and Campbell, John R. Laboratory Training: Reply. *Ind. Relat.,* May 1969, *8*(3), pp. 289–90.

Dupuy, Yves and Loustau, M. Etude des carrières des ingénieurs E.N.S.T.C. (With English summary.) *Revue Écon.,* July 1969, *20*(4), pp. 702–26.

Dupuy, Yves. Les objectifs de la firme et l'analyse de l'effectif. (With English summary.) *Revue Écon.,* July 1969, *20*(4), pp. 658–83.

Dymond, William R. The Role of Benefit/Cost Analysis in Formulating Manpower Policy. **In** *Somers, G. G. and Wood, W. D., eds.,* 1969, pp. 42–55.

Erickson, Edsel L., et al. Differences between Economically Disadvantaged Students Who Volunteer and Do Not Volunteer for Economic Opportunity Programs. *J. Human Res.,* Winter 1969, *4*(1), pp. 76–83. **[G: U.S.]**

Fafunwa, A. Babs. Educational Philosophy and Structure for Economic Development. **In** *Yesufu, T. M., ed.,* 1969, pp. 137–56. **[G: Nigeria]**

Fougstedt, Gunnar. Ekonomien tuleva kysyntä ja tarjonta vuoteen 1985. (The Demand for and the Supply of People with B.Sc. (Econ.) Degree in Finland up to 1985. With English summary.) *Liiketaloudellinen Aikak.,* 1969, *18*(4), pp. 692–715. **[G: Finland]**

Freedman, Marcia. Youth Employment Programmes in the United States. *Int. Lab. Rev.,* May 1969, *99* (5), pp. 493–513. **[G: U.S.]**

George, Roy E. Immobility of Redundant Labour. **In** *Association of Canadian Schools of Business,* 1969, pp. 126–43.

Gish, Oscar. A Note on Aid for Nursing Training in Britain. *J. Devel. Stud.,* April 1969, *5*(3), pp. 220–22. **[G: U.K.]**

Goldfarb, Robert S. The Evaluation of Government Programs: The Case of New Haven's Manpower Training Activities. *Yale Econ. Essays,* Fall 1969, *9*(2), pp. 59–104. **[G: U.S.]**

Goodman, Paul S. Hiring, Training, and Retaining the Hard-Core. *Ind. Relat.,* October 1969, *9*(1), pp. 54–66. **[G: U.S.]**

Hansen, Niles M. Improving Economic Opportunity for the Mexican Americans: A Critical Evaluation of Public Policy, with Assessment of the Problem in South Texas. *Econ. Bus. Bull.,* Fall 1969, *22*(1), pp. 1–14. **[G: U.S.]**

Harbison, Frederick H. The Objectives, Machinery and Methodology of Manpower Planning. **In** *Yesufu, T. M., ed.,* 1969, pp. 63–89.

Hardin, Einar. Benefit/Cost Analyses of Occupational Training Programs: A Comparison of Recent Studies. **In** *Somers, G. G. and Wood, W. D., eds.,* 1969, pp. 97–118. **[G: U.S.]**

Hilliard, John. Toward an Integrated Manpower Policy for Accelerated National Development. **In** *Yesufu, T. M., ed.,* 1969, pp. 27–36. **[G: Nigeria]**

Hollister, Robinson G. Manpower Problems and Policies in Sub-Saharan Africa. *Int. Lab. Rev.,* May 1969, *99*(5), pp. 515–32. **[G: Africa]**

Judy, Richard W. Costs: Theoretical and Methodological Issues. **In** *Somers, G. G. and Wood, W. D., eds.,* 1969, pp. 16–29.

Kaplan, I. I. The Influence of Education on Labor Output. **In** *Noah, H. J., ed.,* 1969, pp. 101–13. **[G: U.S.S.R.]**

Keig, Norman G. The Occupational Aspirations and Labor Force Experience of Negro Youth: A Case Study. *Amer. J. Econ. Soc.,* April 1969, *28*(2), pp. 113–30. **[G: U.S.]**

Khaikin, N. M. Technical-Economic Indexes of the Labor of Workers with Different Vocational Preparation. **In** *Noah, H. J., ed.,* 1969, pp. 141–49. **[G: U.S.S.R.]**

Kleingartner, Archie. The Characteristics and Work Adjustment of Engineering Technicians. *Calif. Manage. Rev.,* Spring 1969, *11*(3), pp. 89–96.

Kozlova, D. I. The Influence of Education on the Labor of Textile Workers. **In** *Noah, H. J., ed.,* 1969, pp. 114–18. **[G: U.S.S.R.]**

Lester, Richard A. Some Investment-Like Aspects of Employment and Pay. *Mon. Lab. Rev.,* November 1969, *92*(11), pp. 62–65.

Levine, Robert A. Manpower Programs in the War on Poverty. **In** *Somers, G. G. and Wood, W. D., eds.,* 1969, pp. 170–83. **[G: U.S.]**

Levitan, Sar A. and Mangum, Garth L. A Functional Manpower Policy. **In** *Wortman, M. S., Jr.,* 1969, pp. 125–32. **[G: U.S.]**

Levitan, Sar A. and Mangum, Garth L. The Changing Goals of Federal Manpower Policy. **In** *Wortman, M. S., Jr.,* 1969, pp. 122–24. **[G: U.S.]**

Lisitsyn, V. and Popov, G. On Administrative Cadres. *Prob. Econ.,* April 1969, *11*(12), pp. 3–10. **[G: U.S.S.R.]**

Loyo, Gilberto. Las cooperativas en el desarrollo economico y social de los países en proceso de desarrollo. (The Role of Cooperatives in the Economic and Social Development. With English summary.) *Econ. Polít.,* Fourth Semester 1969, *6* (4), pp. 439–52.

MacDonald, John S. Benefits and Costs: Theoretical and Methodological Issues: Discussion. **In** *Somers, G. G. and Wood, W. D., eds.,* 1969, pp. 30–36.

Maikov, A. Questions Pertaining to the Redistribution of Labor Resources. *Prob. Econ.,* May 1969, *12*(1), pp. 33–44. **[G: U.S.S.R.]**

Mănescu, Manea. Present Problems of Economists' Training. *Revue Roumaine Sci. Soc. Serie Sci. Econ.,* 1969, *13*(1), pp. 3–8. **[G: Romania]**

Mangum, Garth L. Determining the Results of Manpower and Antipoverty Programs. **In** *The Analysis and Evaluation of Public Expenditures: The PPB System, Vol. 3, JECP,* 1969, pp. 1171–80. **[G: U.S.]**

Mangum, Garth L. The Why, How, and Whence of Manpower Programs. *Ann. Amer. Acad. Polit. Soc. Sci.,* September 1969, *385,* pp. 50–62. **[G: U.S.]**

Marks, Samuel B. Employer Techniques for Upgrading Low-Skill Workers. **In** *Somers, G. G., ed. (II),* 1969, pp. 217–27. **[G: U.S.]**

Maton, J. Experience on the Job and Formal Training as Alternative Means of Skill Acquisition: An Empirical Study. *Int. Lab. Rev.,* September 1969, *100*(3), pp. 239–55. **[G: Belgium; Argentina]**

McLennan, Kenneth. Education and Training for Managerial Jobs. *Amer. J. Econ. Soc.,* October 1969, *28*(4), pp. 423–36. **[G: U.S.]**

Melnik, Arie R. Hedging in the Labor Market. *Southern Econ. J.,* January 1969, *35*(3), pp. 270–72.

Moldovan, Roman. Structural Changes in the National Economy and the Profile of the Economist. *Revue Roumaine Sci. Soc. Serie Sci. Econ.,* 1969, *13*(1), pp. 9–16. **[G: Romania]**

Moore, Geoffrey H. Long-Range Program Objectives for BLS. *Mon. Lab. Rev.,* October 1969, *92* (10), pp. 3–6. **[G: U.S.]**

Nafziger, E. Wayne. The Effect of the Nigerian Extended Family on Entrepreneurial Activity.

Econ. Develop. Cult. Change, Part I, October 1969, *18*(1), pp. 25–33. [G: Nigeria]

Niklasson, Harald. Problems of Method in Cost-Benefit Analyses of Retraining. *Swedish J. Econ.,* September 1969, *71*(3), pp. 184–97.

O'Grada, Cormac. The Vocational Training Policy of the EEC and the Free Movement of Skilled Labour. *J. Common Market Stud.,* December 1969, *8*(2), pp. 79–109. [G: E.E.C.]

Ogunsheye, Ayo. Manpower Problems in the Context of Economic Planning. **In** *Yesufu, T. M., ed.,* 1969, pp. 14–26. [G: Nigeria]

Onwuka Dike, K. Manpower Training for Economic Development: Professional and Managerial Staff. **In** *Yesufu, T. M., ed.,* 1969, pp. 200–216. [G: Nigeria]

Parkinson, C. Northcote. Our Overheads Are Overhigh. *Manage. Account.,* November 1969, *51*(5), pp. 9–11.

Patten, Thomas H., Jr. Laboratory Training: Comment. *Ind. Relat.,* May 1969, *8*(3), pp. 286–89.

Perera, S. E. G. Some Labour Problems of the National Textile Corporation of Ceylon. *Int. Lab. Rev.,* February 1969, *99*(2), pp. 185–207. [G: Ceylon]

Perlberg, Arye and Shaal, Gil. An Interdisciplinary Approach to Manpower Planning and Development. *Int. Lab. Rev.,* April 1969, *99*(4), pp. 363–80. [G: Israel]

Porter, W. Thomas. Professional Education for Management. *Univ. Wash. Bus. Rev.,* Summer 1969, *28*(4), pp. 44–48.

Powell, Walter H. Employing Negroes in Urban Labor Markets. **In** *Kain, J. F., ed.,* 1969, pp. 74–77. [G: U.S.]

Raynauld, André. Benefits and Costs: Theoretical and Methodological Issues: Discussion. **In** *Somers, G. G. and Wood, W. D., eds.,* 1969, pp. 37–41.

Roberts, Higdon C. A Private Approach to Public Problems: Unions and Contractors Create Job Training Program. *Indiana Bus. Rev.,* July/August 1969, *44,* pp. 16–20. [G: U.S.]

Rowland, Kendrith M. and Sovereign, Michael G. Markov-Chain Analysis of Internal Manpower Supply. *Ind. Relat.,* October 1969, *9*(1), pp. 88–99.

Samoilova, I. D. The Returns from Various Types of Specialist Training. **In** *Noah, H. J., ed.,* 1969, pp. 159–66. [G: U.S.S.R.]

Schmidt, Fred H. A Repair Shop for Unemployables. *Ind. Relat.,* May 1969, *8*(3), pp. 280–85. [G: U.S.]

Scoville, James G. A Theory of Jobs and Training. *Ind. Relat.,* October 1969, *9*(1), pp. 36–53.

Sewell, David O. Occupational Training Programs and Manpower Programs for the Disadvantaged: Discussion. **In** *Somers, G. G. and Wood, W. D., eds.,* 1969, pp. 160–69. [G: U.S.]

Shaffer, Charles L. Educational Problems in Economic Development. **In** *Yesufu, T. M., ed.,* 1969, pp. 183–99. [G: Nigeria]

Shrimali, P. D. Pattern of Employment and Earnings Among University Graduates in Lucknow, India. *Ind. Lab. Relat. Rev.,* January 1969, *22*(2), pp. 249–56. [G: India]

Shultz, George P. Statement. **In** *Economic Opportunity Amendments of 1969, Pt. 2, HCH,* 1969, pp. 935–45. [G: U.S.]

Smith, C. Selby. Benefits to British Employers from Post-secondary Education. *J. Roy. Statist. Soc.,* Part 3, 1969, *132,* pp. 408–17. [G: U.K.]

Somers, Gerald G. Data Needs for Monitoring and Evaluating Manpower Programs. **In** *Somers, G. G., ed. (II),* 1969, pp. 97–104.

Sonin, M. Ia. Training Personnel and Labor Turnover. **In** *Noah, H. J., ed.,* 1969, pp. 32–35. [G: U.S.S.R.]

Sorkin, Alan L. Education and Manpower Programs for Indian Americans. **In** *Indian Education 1969, Pt. 2, Appendix, SCH,* 1969, pp. 1559–98. [G: U.S.]

Spasibenko, S. G. Labor Productivity and Worker Qualifications. **In** *Noah, H. J., ed.,* 1969, pp. 119–31. [G: U.S.S.R.]

Spencer, Daniel L. and Woroniak, Alexander. Valuing Transfer of Military-Acquired Skills to Civilian Employment. *Kyklos,* 1969, *22*(3), pp. 467–92. [G: Japan]

Stern, James L. Evolution of Private Manpower Planning in Armour's Plant Closings. *Mon. Lab. Rev.,* December 1969, *92*(12), pp. 21–28. [G: U.S.]

Stevenson, Russell. The United States Graduate Training of Asian Rural Social Scientists. *Land Econ.,* August 1969, *45*(3), pp. 334–43.

Striver, Herbert E. Toward a Fundamental Program for the Training, Employment, and Economic Equality of the American Indian. **In** *Indian Education, Pt. 2, SCH,* 1969, pp. 608–32. [G: U.S.]

Stromsdorfer, Ernst W. Occupational Training Programs and Manpower Programs for the Disadvantaged: Discussion. **In** *Somers, G. G. and Wood, W. D., eds.,* 1969, pp. 152–59. [G: U.S.]

Tan, Edita Abella. Implications of Private Demand for Education on Manpower Planning. *Philippine Econ. J.,* Second Semester 1969, *8*(2), pp. 117–29.

Tévoédjré, Albert. A Strategy for Social Progress in Africa and the I.L.O.'s Contribution. *Int. Lab. Rev.,* January 1969, *99*(1), pp. 61–84. [G: Africa]

Tobias, George. New Markets for Manpower Planning. **In** *Yesufu, T. M., ed.,* 1969, pp. 37–51. [G: Nigeria]

Ullman, Joseph C. Helping Workers Locate Jobs Following a Plant Shutdown. *Mon. Lab. Rev.,* April 1969, *92*(4), pp. 35–40. [G: U.S.]

Van Rompuy, P. Note on the Optimum Period of Employment. *Tijdschr. Econ.,* 1969, *14*(4), pp. 584–86.

Walker, James W. Forecasting Manpower Needs. *Harvard Bus. Rev.,* March–April 1969, *47*(2), pp. 152–64.

Weinberg, Edgar. Reducing Skill Shortages in Construction. *Mon. Lab. Rev.,* February 1969, *92*(2), pp. 3–9. [G: U.S.]

Weisbrod, Burton A. Benefits of Manpower Programs: Theoretical and Methodological Issues. **In** *Somers, G. G. and Wood, W. D., eds.,* 1969, pp. 3–15.

Wortman, Max S., Jr. National Policies and Programs for Human Resources Management. *Ohio State U. Bull. Bus. Res.,* December 1969, *44*(12), pp. 4–6. [G: U.S.]

Yesufu, T. M. Organization for Manpower Planning in Nigeria. **In** *Yesufu, T. M., ed.,* 1969, pp. 90–103. **[G: Nigeria]**

Ziderman, Adrian. Costs and Benefits of Adult Retraining in the United Kingdom. *Economica, N.S.,* November 1969, *36*(144), pp. 363–76. **[G: U.K.]**

812 Occupation

8120 Occupation

Allen, William M. The Requirement for Management Talent. *Univ. Wash. Bus. Rev.,* Spring 1969, *28*(3), pp. 21–25. **[G: U.S.]**

Ambannavar, Jaipal P. Upward Occupational Mobility Through Education and Age. *Asian Econ. Rev.,* May 1969, *11*(3), pp. 290–99. **[G: India]**

Andrews, Edith Wall and Moylan, Maurice. Scientific and Professional Employment by State Governments. *Mon. Lab. Rev.,* August 1969, *92*(8), pp. 40–45. **[G: U.S.]**

Broom, Leonard and Maynard, Betty J. Prestige and Socioeconomic Ranking of Occupations. *Soc. Sci. Quart.,* September 1969, *50*(2), pp. 369–73. **[G: U.S.]**

Buckley, John E. Intraoccupational Wage Dispersion in Metropolitan Areas, 1967–68. *Mon. Lab. Rev.,* September 1969, *92*(9), pp. 24–29. **[G: U.S.]**

Bumas, Lester O. and Stein, Bruno. The Economic Rationale of Occupational Choice: Comment. *Ind. Lab. Relat. Rev.,* April 1969, *22*(3), pp. 422–28.

Cambern, John R. and Newton, David A. Skill Transfers: Can Defense Workers Adapt to Civilian Occupations? *Mon. Lab. Rev.,* June 1969, *92*(6), pp. 21–25. **[G: U.S.]**

Carol, Arthur and Parry, Samuel. The Economic Rationale of Occupational Choice: Reply. *Ind. Lab. Relat. Rev.,* April 1969, *22*(3), pp. 428–30.

Carol, Arthur and Parry, Samuel. The Economic Rationale of Occupational Choice: Reply. *Ind. Lab. Relat. Rev.,* July 1969, *22*(4), pp. 587–88. **[G: U.S.]**

Carr, Julian L., Jr. and Estafen, Bernard D. M.B.A. Salary Expectations: Fact or Fantasy? *Indiana Bus. Rev.,* September/October 1969, *44,* pp. 9–12.

D'Iribarne, Alain. Les besoins d'emploi des entreprises. (With English summary.) *Revue Écon.,* July 1969, *20*(4), pp. 601–57.

Desaeyere, W. Het inkomen van de economisten, analyse van de U.N.A. enquête. (The Income of the Economists, Analysis of the U.N.A. Questionnaire Study. With English summary.) *Tijdschr. Econ.,* 1969, *14*(3), pp. 375–435. **[G: Belgium]**

Diatchenko, V. P. The Financial Problems of Professional Retraining of Personnel in the U.S.S.R. *Public Finance,* 1969, *24*(2), pp. 391–404. **[G: U.S.S.R.]**

Dufty, Norman F. A Model of Choice in an Australian Labor Market. *J. Human Res.,* Summer 1969, *4*(3), pp. 328–42. **[G: Australia]**

Duthu, Marie-Françoise. La prévision des structures d'emploi par la méthode des comparaisons internationales et intersectorielles. (With English summary.) *Revue Écon.,* July 1969, *20*(4), pp. 684–701.

Fenlon, John. Patterns in Overtime Hours and Premium Pay. *Mon. Lab. Rev.,* October 1969, *92* (10), pp. 42–46. **[G: U.S.]**

Fougstedt, Gunnar. Ekonomien tuleva kysyntä ja tarjonta vuoteen 1985. (The Demand for and the Supply of People with B.Sc. (Econ.) Degree in Finland up to 1985. With English summary.) *Liiketaloudellinen Aikak.,* 1969, *18*(4), pp. 692–715. **[G: Finland]**

Gilson, J. C. The Demand for Agricultural Economists by Canadian Universities and Governments. *Can. J. Agr. Econ.,* November 1969, *17*(3), pp. 124–32. **[G: Canada]**

Glasgow, John M. The Economic Rationale of Occupational Choice: Comment. *Ind. Lab. Relat. Rev.,* July 1969, *22*(4), pp. 584–87. **[G: U.S.]**

Glueck, William F. Executive Mobility in Missouri. *Univ. Missouri Bus. Govt. Rev.,* March–April 1969, *10*(2), pp. 27–32. **[G: U.S.]**

Goldsmith, Harold F. and Stockwell, Edward G. Interrelationship of Occupational Selectivity Patterns among City, Suburban and Fringe Areas of Major Metropolitan Centers. *Land Econ.,* May 1969, *45*(2), pp. 194–205. **[G: U.S.]**

Gross, Andrew C. Patterns and Determinants of Income of Canadian Engineering Graduates. *Ind. Lab. Relat. Rev.,* October 1969, *23*(1), pp. 52–64. **[G: Canada]**

Hilaski, Harvey J. and Willacy, Hazel M. Employment Patterns and Place of Residence. *Mon. Lab. Rev.,* October 1969, *92*(10), pp. 18–25. **[G: U.S.]**

Hodge, Claire C. The Negro Job Situation: Has It Improved? *Mon. Lab. Rev.,* January 1969, *92*(1), pp. 20–28. **[G: U.S.]**

Johnson, David B. and Stern, James L. Why and How Workers Shift from Blue-Collar to White-Collar Jobs. *Mon. Lab. Rev.,* October 1969, *92* (10), pp. 7–13. **[G: U.S.]**

Katzman, Martin T. Opportunity, Subculture and the Economic Performance of Urban Ethnic Groups. *Amer. J. Econ. Soc.,* October 1969, *28*(4), pp. 351–66. **[G: U.S.]**

Keig, Norman G. The Occupational Aspirations and Labor Force Experience of Negro Youth: A Case Study. *Amer. J. Econ. Soc.,* April 1969, *28*(2), pp. 113–30. **[G: U.S.]**

Kleingartner, Archie. Professionalism and Engineering Unionism. *Ind. Relat.,* May 1969, *8*(3), pp. 224–35.

Kleingartner, Archie. The Characteristics and Work Adjustment of Engineering Technicians. *Calif. Manage. Rev.,* Spring 1969, *11*(3), pp. 89–96.

Kordaszewski, Jan. A Polish Contribution to Job Evaluation for Non-Manual Workers. *Int. Lab. Rev.,* August 1969, *100*(2), pp. 141–58.

McRorie, H. D. The Demand for Agricultural Economists by Agri-Business to 1980. *Can. J. Agr. Econ.,* November 1969, *17*(3), pp. 114–23. **[G: Canada]**

Melichar, Emanuel. Characteristics and Salaries of Agricultural Economists. *Amer. J. Agr. Econ.,* November 1969, *51*(4), pp. 903–11. **[G: U.S.]**

Newsom, Robert T. Metropolitan and Nonmetropolitan Employment Changes: The Case of Texas. *Soc. Sci. Quart.,* September 1969, *50*(2),

pp. 354–68. [G: U.S.]

Parish, R. M. Some Thoughts on the Role of the Agricultural Economics Profession in Australia. *Australian J. Agr. Econ.*, June 1969, *13*(1), pp. 1–7. [G: Australia]

Peitchinis, S. G. Occupational Wage Differentials in Canada 1939–1965. *Australian Econ. Pap.*, June 1969, *8*(12), pp. 20–40. [G: Canada]

Rowan, Richard L. Negro Employment in the Basic Steel Industry. *Ind. Lab. Relat. Rev.*, October 1969, *23*(1), pp. 29–39. [G: U.S.]

Ryans, John K., Jr. and Hise, Richard T. Retailing's Unfortunate Image: Problems of Attracting College Graduates. *Econ. Bus. Bull.*, Fall 1969, *22*(1), pp. 39–43. [G: U.S.]

Schmidt, Fred H. Job Caste in the Southwest. *Ind. Relat.*, October 1969, *9*(1), pp. 100–110. [G: U.S.]

Scoville, James G. A Theory of Jobs and Training. *Ind. Relat.*, October 1969, *9*(1), pp. 36–53.

Smirnov, V. V. Movement and Utilization of Rural Labor Resources (in the Non-black Soil Zone of the RSFSR). *Prob. Econ.*, October 1969, *12*(6), pp. 68–81. [G: U.S.S.R.]

Sorkin, Alan L. Some Factors Associated with Earnings and Unemployment Differences between Occupations. *Nebr. J. Econ. Bus.*, Winter 1968–69, *8*(1), pp. 44–52. [G: U.S.]

Swerdloff, Sol. How Good Were Manpower Projections for the 1960's. *Mon. Lab. Rev.*, November 1969, *92*(11), pp. 17–22. [G: U.S.]

Troy, Leo. Trade Union Growth in a Changing Economy. *Mon. Lab. Rev.*, September 1969, *92*(9), pp. 3–7. [G: U.S.]

Vincens, Jean. Les prévisions par professions. (With English summary.) *Revue Écon.*, July 1969, *20*(4), pp. 561–600.

Waldman, Elizabeth. Educational Attainment of Workers. *Mon. Lab. Rev.*, February 1969, *92*(2), pp. 14–22. [G: U.S.]

Watanabe, S. The Brain Drain from Developing to Developed Countries. *Int. Lab. Rev.*, April 1969, *99*(4), pp. 401–33.

Wheeler, James O. Some Effects of Occupational Status on Work Trips. *J. Reg. Sci.*, April 1969, *9*(1), pp. 69–77. [G: U.S.]

813 Labor Force

8130 General

Alpander, Guvenc G. The Business Leaders of Selected Countries. *Univ. Missouri Bus. Govt. Rev.*, May–June 1969, *10*(3), pp. 13–19.

Biggeri, Luigi. Su un metodo di previsione della popolazione attiva a livello regionale. (With English summary.) *Statistica*, July-September 1969, *29*(3), pp. 343–76. [G: Italy]

Bogan, Forrest A. Work Experience of the Population: Spotlight on Women and Youths. *Mon. Lab. Rev.*, June 1969, *92*(6), pp. 44–50. [G: U.S.]

Cohen, Malcolm S. The Micro Approach to Manpower Research. In *Somers, G. G., ed. (II)*, 1969, pp. 120–28.

Flaim, Paul O. Persons Not in the Labor Force: Who They Are and Why They Don't Work. *Mon. Lab. Rev.*, July 1969, *92*(7), pp. 3–14. [G: U.S.]

Fougstedt, Gunnar. Ekonomien tuleva kysyntä ja tarjonta vuoteen 1985. (The Demand for and the Supply of People with B.Sc. (Econ.) Degree in Finland up to 1985. With English summary.) *Liiketaloudellinen Aikak.*, 1969, *18*(4), pp. 692–715. [G: Finland]

Gray, Irwin. Employment Effect of a New Industry in a Rural Area. *Mon. Lab. Rev.*, June 1969, *92*(6), pp. 26–30. [G: U.S.]

Hoyle, Kathryn D. Job Losers, Leavers, and Entrants—A Report on the Unemployed. *Mon. Lab. Rev.*, April 1969, *92*(4), pp. 24–29. [G: U.S.]

Johnston, Denis F. and Wetzel, James R. Effect of the Census Undercount on Labor Force Estimates. *Mon. Lab. Rev.*, March 1969, *92*(3), pp. 3–13. [G: U.S.]

Kosters, Marvin. Effects of an Income Tax on Labor Supply. In *Harberger, A. C. and Bailey, M. J., eds.*, 1969, pp. 301–24. [G: U.S.]

Maikov, A. Questions Pertaining to the Redistribution of Labor Resources. *Prob. Econ.*, May 1969, *12*(1), pp. 33–44. [G: U.S.S.R.]

Maitra, Priyatosh. Models of Economic Development with Unlimited Supplies of Labour—Some Fundamental Limitations. *Arthaniti*, January & July 1969, *12*(1&2), pp. 41–56.

Marion, Gérald. Fonction d'emploi, taux de participation de la main-d'oeuvre et demande excédentaire de travil. (With English summary.) *Revue Écon.*, November 1969, *20*(6), pp. 968–1005. [G: Canada]

Mazek, Warren F. Unemployment and the Efficacy of Migration: The Case of Laborers. *J. Reg. Sci.*, April 1969, *9*(1), pp. 101–07. [G: U.S.]

Nag, A. Estimation and Projection of the Working Force in Greater Bombay. *Asian Econ. Rev.*, February 1969, *11*(2), pp. 160–72. [G: India]

O'Boyle, Edward J. Job Tenure: How It Relates to Race and Age. *Mon. Lab. Rev.*, September 1969, *92*(9), pp. 16–23. [G: U.S.]

Parikh, G. O. Integration of Farm and Non-Farm Employment, Part II: Effective Cooperativisation in a Labour Surplus Economy. *Artha-Vikas*, January 1969, *5*(1), pp. 68–76. [G: India]

Perrella, Vera C. Employment of High School Graduates and Dropouts. *Mon. Lab. Rev.*, June 1969, *92*(6), pp. 36–43. [G: U.S.]

Reynolds, Lloyd G. Relative Earnings and Manpower Allocation in Developing Economies. *Pakistan Develop. Rev.*, Spring 1969, *9*(1), pp. 14–34.

Ryscavage, Paul M. Employment Developments in Urban Poverty Neighborhoods. *Mon. Lab. Rev.*, June 1969, *92*(6), pp. 51–56. [G: U.S.]

Sabolo, Yves. Sectoral Employment Growth: The Outlook for 1980. *Int. Lab. Rev.*, November 1969, *100*(5), pp. 445–74.

Stambler, Howard V. New Directions in Area Labor Force Statistics. *Mon. Lab. Rev.*, August 1969, *92*(8), pp. 3–9. [G: U.S.]

Swerdloff, Sol. How Good Were Manpower Projections for the 1960's. *Mon. Lab. Rev.*, November 1969, *92*(11), pp. 17–22. [G: U.S.]

Timár, J. The Level of Employment and Its Equilibrium in Socialism. *Acta Oecon.*, 1969, *4*(2), pp. 169–79.

Valentei, D. Current Population Problems in the U.S.S.R. *Prob. Econ.*, November 1969, *12*(7), pp. 49–60. **[G: U.S.S.R.]**

Vyas, V. S. Integration of Farm and Non-Farm Employment, Part I: Farm and Non-Farm Employment in an Economically Backward Region. *Artha-Vikas*, January 1969, *5*(1), pp. 54–67. **[G: India]**

Waldman, Elizabeth. Employment Status of School Age Youth. *Mon. Lab. Rev.*, August 1969, *92*(8), pp. 23–32. **[G: U.S.]**

Weller, Robert H. Role Conflict and Fertility. *Soc. Econ. Stud.*, September 1969, *18*(3), pp. 263–72.

Willacy, Hazel M. Men in Poverty Neighborhoods: A Status Report. *Mon. Lab. Rev.*, February 1969, *92*(2), pp. 23–27. **[G: U.S.]**

Yamamoto, Hiromasa. A Note on Shorter Working Hours for Seamen. *Kobe Econ. Bus. Rev.*, 1969, *16* (1), pp. 39–45.

Yesufu, T. M. Forecasting Nigeria's Manpower Needs 1963–68: A Note on Methodology. **In** *Yesufu, T. M., ed.*, 1969, pp. 104–29. **[G: Nigeria]**

8131 Agriculture

Adams, Dale W. Rural Migration and Agricultural Development in Colombia. *Econ. Develop. Cult. Change*, July 1969, *17*(4), pp. 527–39. **[G: Colombia]**

Coffey, Joseph D. National Labor Relations Legislation: Possible Impact on American Agriculture. *Amer. J. Agr. Econ.*, December 1969, *51*(5), pp. 1065–74. **[G: U.S.]**

Dasgupta, Partha S. On the Optimum Rate of Accumulation in a Labour-Surplus Economy. *Indian Econ. J.*, January–March 1969, *16*(3), pp. 277–311.

Dovring, Folke. Underemployment in Agriculture: A Rejoinder. *Econ. Develop. Cult. Change*, January 1969, *17*(2), pp. 273–76. **[G: Greece]**

Godfrey, E. M. Labor-Surplus Models and Labor-Deficit Economies: The West African Case. *Econ. Develop. Cult. Change*, April 1969, *17*(3), pp. 382–91. **[G: W. Africa]**

Gordon, Jerome B. Labor Mobility and Economic Growth: The Central American Experience—Costa Rica and El Salvador. *Econ. Develop. Cult. Change*, April 1969, *17*(3), pp. 319–37. **[G: Costa Rica; El Salvador]**

Guha, Ashok S. Accumulation, Innovation, and Growth under Conditions of Disguised Unemployment. *Oxford Econ. Pap.*, November 1969, *21*(3), pp. 360–72.

Hansen, Bent. Employment and Wages in Rural Egypt. *Amer. Econ. Rev.*, June 1969, *59*(3), pp. 298–313. **[G: Egypt]**

Henry, G. C. Farm Labor. **In** *Task Force on Economic Growth and Opportunity*, 1969, pp. 217–27. **[G: U.S.]**

Meier, Gerald M. Development Without Employment. *Banca Naz. Lavoro Quart. Rev.*, September 1969, (90), pp. 309–19.

Misawa, Takeo. An Analysis of Part-time Farming in the Postwar Period. **In** *Ohkawa, K.; Johnston, B. F. and Kaneda, H., eds.*, 1969, pp. 250–69. **[G: Japan]**

Pepelasis, A. Underemployment in Agriculture: A Comment. *Econ. Develop. Cult. Change*, January 1969, *17*(2), pp. 267–72. **[G: Greece]**

Reynolds, Lloyd G. Economic Development with Surplus Labour: Some Complications. *Oxford Econ. Pap.*, March 1969, *21*(1), pp. 89–103.

Robinson, Warren C. "Disguised" Unemployment Once Again: East Pakistan, 1951–1961. *Amer. J. Agr. Econ.*, August 1969, *51*(3), pp. 592–604. **[G: E. Pakistan]**

Robinson, Warren C. Types of Disguised Rural Unemployment and Some Policy Implications. *Oxford Econ. Pap.*, November 1969, *21*(3), pp. 373–86.

Stiglitz, Joseph E. Rural-Urban Migration, Surplus Labour, and the Relationship between Urban and Rural Wages. *East Afr. Econ. Rev.*, December 1969, *1*(2), pp. 1–27.

Thiesenhusen, William C. Population Growth and Agricultural Employment in Latin America, with Some U.S. Comparisons. *Amer. J. Agr. Econ.*, November 1969, *51*(4), pp. 735–52. **[G: Latin America; U.S.]**

Tyrchniewicz, Edward W. and Schuh, G. Edward. Econometric Analysis of the Agricultural Labor Market. *Amer. J. Agr. Econ.*, November 1969, *51* (4), pp. 770–87. **[G: U.S.]**

Uppal, J. S. Measurement of Disguised Unemployment in an Underdeveloped Economy—An Economic Approach. *Asian Econ. Rev.*, August 1969, *11*(4), pp. 405–11. **[G: India]**

Uppal, J. S. Work Habits and Disguised Unemployment in Underdeveloped Countries—A Theoretical Analysis. *Oxford Econ. Pap.*, November 1969, *21*(3), pp. 387–94.

Wädekin, Karl-Eugen. Manpower in Soviet Agriculture—Some Post-Khrushchev Developments and Problems. *Soviet Stud.*, January 1969, *20*(3), pp. 281–305. **[G: U.S.S.R.]**

8132 Manufacturing

de Menil, George. Nonlinearity in a Wage Equation for United States Manufacturing. *Rev. Econ. Statist.*, May 1969, *51*(2), pp. 202–06. **[G: U.S.]**

8134 Professional

Andrews, Edith Wall and Moylan, Maurice. Scientific and Professional Employment by State Governments. *Mon. Lab. Rev.*, August 1969, *92*(8), pp. 40–45. **[G: U.S.]**

Chew, David C. E. Wastage Patterns in the Nursing Profession in Singapore: A Study of Manpower Utilisation. *Int. Lab. Rev.*, December 1969, *100* (6), pp. 583–94. **[G: Singapore]**

Daly, D. J. The Changing Environment for Management in Canada. **In** *Association of Canadian Schools of Business*, 1969, pp. 308–22. **[G: Canada]**

Dupuy, Yves and Loustau, M. Etude des carrières des ingénieurs E.N.S.T.C. (With English summary.) *Revue Écon.*, July 1969, *20*(4), pp. 702–26.

Grubel, Herbert G. The M.B.A. Education Myth. *J. Bus.*, January 1969, *42*(1), pp. 42–49.

Klarman, Herbert E. Economic Aspects of Projecting Requirements for Health Manpower. *J. Human Res.*, Summer 1969, *4*(3), pp. 360–76. [G: U.S.]

Lurie, Melvin. Aspetti economici dell'abilitazione alla professione medica negli Stati Uniti. (Physician Licensing in the United States and the Supply of Physician Service by Graduates of Foreign Medical Schools. With English summary.) *Rivista Int. Sci. Econ. Com.*, April 1969, *16*(4), pp. 371–89. [G: U.S.]

8135 Government Employees

Andrews, Edith Wall and Moylan, Maurice. Scientific and Professional Employment by State Governments. *Mon. Lab. Rev.*, August 1969, *92*(8), pp. 40–45. [G: U.S.]

Devine, Eugene J. Manpower Shortages in Local Government Employment. *Amer. Econ. Rev.*, May 1969, *59*(2), pp. 538–45. [G: U.S.]

Pauly, Mark V. Manpower Shortages in Local Government Employment: Discussion. *Amer. Econ. Rev.*, May 1969, *59*(2), pp. 565–67.

820 Labor Markets; Public Policy

821 Theory of Labor Markets and Leisure

8210 Theory of Labor Markets and Leisure: Empirical Studies Illustrating Theories

Adams, Dale W. Rural Migration and Agricultural Development in Colombia. *Econ. Develop. Cult. Change*, July 1969, *17*(4), pp. 527–39. [G: Colombia]

Akerlof, George A. and Stiglitz, Joseph E. Capital, Wages and Structural Unemployment. *Econ. J.*, June 1969, *79*(314), pp. 269–81.

Akerlof, George A. Relative Wages and the Rate of Inflation. *Quart. J. Econ.*, August 1969, *83*(3), pp. 353–74.

Akerlof, George A. Structural Unemployment in a Neoclassical Framework. *J. Polit. Econ.*, May/June 1969, *77*(3), pp. 399–407.

Alchian, Armen A. Information Costs, Pricing, and Resource Unemployment. *Western Econ. J.*, June 1969, *7*(2), pp. 109–28.

Ambannavar, Jaipal P. Upward Occupational Mobility Through Education and Age. *Asian Econ. Rev.*, May 1969, *11*(3), pp. 290–99. [G: India]

Archibald, G. C. The Phillips Curve and the Distribution of Unemployment. *Amer. Econ. Rev.*, May 1969, *59*(2), pp. 124–34. [G: U.S.; U.K.]

Ashenfelter, Orley and Johnson, George E. Bargaining Theory, Trade Unions, and Industrial Strike Activity. *Amer. Econ. Rev.*, March 1969, *59*(1), pp. 35–49. [G: U.S.]

Behman, Sara. Wage Changes, Institutions, and Relative Factor Prices in Manufacturing. *Rev. Econ. Statist.*, August 1969, *51*(3), pp. 227–38. [G: U.S.]

Berg, Elliot J. Wage Structures in Less Developed Countries. In *Smith, A. D., ed.*, 1969, pp. 294–337.

Bienefeld, M. A. The Normal Week under Collective Bargaining. *Economica, N.S.*, May 1969, *36* (142), pp. 172–92.

Boskin, Michael J. The Negative Income Tax and the Supply of Work Effort: Reply. *Nat. Tax J.*, September 1969, *22*(3), pp. 417.

Bottomley, Anthony. Wage Rate Determination in Underpopulated, Underdeveloped Rural Areas. *Econ. Int.*, February 1969, *22*(1), pp. 51–62.

Brechling, Frank. Wage-Price Dynamics, Inflation, and Unemployment: Discussion. *Amer. Econ. Rev.*, May 1969, *59*(2), pp. 161–62.

Carlsson, Robert J. and Robinson, James W. Toward a Public Employment Wage Theory. *Ind. Lab. Relat. Rev.*, January 1969, *22*(2), pp. 243–48.

Carlsson, Robert J. and Robinson, James W. Toward a Public Employment Wage Theory: Reply. *Ind. Lab. Relat. Rev.*, October 1969, *23*(1), pp. 95–100. [G: U.S.]

Cassidy, Henry J. The Employer Payroll Tax and the Labor Mix. *Quart. Rev. Econ. Bus.*, Spring 1969, *9*(1), pp. 39–43.

Craft, James A. Toward a Public Employment Wage Theory: Comment. *Ind. Lab. Relat. Rev.*, October 1969, *23*(1), pp. 89–95. [G: U.S.]

Davidson, Paul. A Keynesian View of Patinkin's Theory of Employment: A Rejoinder. *Econ. J.*, March 1969, *79*(313), pp. 181–82.

Deaglio, Mario. La scelta tra maggior reddito e maggior tempo libero. Un'analisi del comportamento del lavoratore. (The Choice between Greater Income and More Leisure: A Study in the Behaviour of the Worker. With English summary.) *L'Industria*, July–September 1969, (3), pp. 358–82.

Dhrymes, Phoebus J. A Model of Short-run Labor Adjustment. In *Duesenberry, J. S., et al.*, 1969, pp. 110–49. [G: U.S.]

Dovring, Folke. Underemployment in Agriculture: A Rejoinder. *Econ. Develop. Cult. Change*, January 1969, *17*(2), pp. 273–76. [G: Greece]

Eckstein, Otto. Wage-Price Dynamics, Inflation, and Unemployment: Discussion. *Amer. Econ. Rev.*, May 1969, *59*(2), pp. 162–64.

Egle, Walter P. Recessional Unemployment and Leisure. *Rivista Int. Sci. Econ. Com.*, April 1969, *16* (4), pp. 363–70.

Finkel, Sidney R. and Tarascio, Vincent J. A Theoretical Integration of Production and Wage Theory. *Western Econ. J.*, December 1969, *7*(4), pp. 371–78.

Gallaway, Lowell E. One Last Word. *Southern Econ. J.*, January 1969, *35*(3), pp. 267.

Godfrey, E. M. Labor-Surplus Models and Labor-Deficit Economies: The West African Case. *Econ. Develop. Cult. Change*, April 1969, *17*(3), pp. 382–91. [G: W. Africa]

Gold, Sonia S. The Professional Commitment of Educated Women. In *Baier, K. and Rescher, N., eds.*, 1969, pp. 266–93.

Gomberg, Ia. Certain Questions in Wage Theory under Socialism. *Prob. Econ.*, July 1969, *12*(3), pp. 23–42.

Goodwin, Leonard. Work Orientations of the Underemployed Poor: Report on a Pilot Study. *J.*

Human Res., Fall 1969, *4*(4), pp. 508–19. [G: U.S.]

Gramm, William P. A Keynesian View of Patinkin's Theory of Employment: Comment. *Econ. J.*, March 1969, *79*(313), pp. 179–81.

Guha, Ashok S. Accumulation, Innovation, and Growth under Conditions of Disguised Unemployment. *Oxford Econ. Pap.*, November 1969, *21*(3), pp. 360–72.

Harris, John R. and Todaro, Michael P. Wages, Industrial Employment and Labour Productivity: The Kenyan Experience. *East Afr. Econ. Rev.*, June 1969, *1*(1), pp. 29–46. [G: Kenya]

Hoffmann, Walther G. Die "Phillips-Kurve" in Deutschland. (With English summary.) *Kyklos*, 1969, *22*(2), pp. 219–31. [G: W. Germany]

Holt, Charles C. Improving the Labor Market Trade-Off between Inflation and Unemployment. *Amer. Econ. Rev.*, May 1969, *59*(2), pp. 135–46.

Jacobsson, Lars and Lindbeck, Assar. Labor Market Condition, Wages and Inflation—Swedish Experiences 1955–67. *Swedish J. Econ.*, June 1969, *71*(2), pp. 64–103. [G: Sweden]

Kaun, David E. A Comment on the Work-Leisure Myth. *Rev. Radical Polit. Econ.*, May 1969, *1*(1), pp. 85–88.

Kesselman, Jonathan. Labor-Supply Effects of Income, Income-Work, and Wage Subsidies. *J. Human Res.*, Summer 1969, *4*(3), pp. 275–92.

Kesselman, Jonathan. The Negative Income Tax and the Supply of Work Effort: Comment. *Nat. Tax J.*, September 1969, *22*(3), pp. 411–16.

Koot, Ronald S. Wage Changes, Unemployment, and Inflation in Chile. *Ind. Lab. Relat. Rev.*, July 1969, *22*(4), pp. 568–75. [G: Chile]

Kreps, Juanita M. Lifetime Tradeoffs between Work and Play. **In** *Somers, G. G., ed. (II)*, 1969, pp. 307–16.

Lester, Richard A. Wage-Price Dynamics, Inflation, and Unemployment: Discussion. *Amer. Econ. Rev.*, May 1969, *59*(2), pp. 164–67.

Liebling, H. I. and Cluff, A. T. U.S. Postwar Inflation and Phillips Curves. *Kyklos*, 1969, *22*(2), pp. 232–50. [G: U.S.]

Lorenzo, A. Employment Effects of Rural and Community Development in the Philippines. *Int. Lab. Rev.*, November 1969, *100*(5), pp. 419–44. [G: Philippines]

Lucas, Robert E., Jr. and Rapping, Leonard A. Price Expectations and the Phillips Curve. *Amer. Econ. Rev.*, June 1969, *59*(3), pp. 342–50. [G: U.S.]

Lucas, Robert E., Jr. and Rapping, Leonard A. Real Wages, Employment, and Inflation. *J. Polit. Econ.*, September/October 1969, *77*(5), pp. 721–54. [G: U.S.]

Mabry, Bevars D. Income-Leisure Analysis and the Salaried Professional. *Ind. Relat.*, February 1969, *8*(2), pp. 162–73.

Meidner, Rudolf. Active Manpower Policy and the Inflation Unemployment-Dilemma. *Swedish J. Econ.*, September 1969, *71*(3), pp. 161–83.

Melnik, Arie R. Hedging in the Labor Market. *Southern Econ. J.*, January 1969, *35*(3), pp. 270–72.

de Menil, George. Nonlinearity in a Wage Equation for United States Manufacturing. *Rev. Econ. Statist.*, May 1969, *51*(2), pp. 202–06. [G: U.S.]

van der Merwe, P. J. The Economic Influence of the Bantu Labour Bureau System on the Bantu Labour Market. *S. Afr. J. Econ.*, March 1969, *37*(1), pp. 42–54. [G: S. Africa]

Molander, Ahti. Inflaatiotutkimuksen vaiheista ja ongelmista. (Phases and Problems of Inflation Research. With English summary.) *Kansant. Aikak.*, 1969, *65*(4), pp. 269–73.

Nagatani, Keizo. A Monetary Growth Model with Variable Employment. *J. Money, Credit, Banking*, May 1969, *1*(2), pp. 188–206.

Paish, Frank W. Unemployment and Price Stability. **In** *Ball, R. J. and Doyle, P., eds.*, 1969, pp. 219–54.

Pepelasis, A. Underemployment in Agriculture: A Comment. *Econ. Develop. Cult. Change*, January 1969, *17*(2), pp. 267–72. [G: Greece]

Phelps, Edmund S. A Note on Short-Run Employment and Real Wage Rate under Competitive Commodity Markets. *Int. Econ. Rev.*, June 1969, *10*(2), pp. 220–32.

Phelps, Edmund S. The New Microeconomics in Inflation and Employment Theory. *Amer. Econ. Rev.*, May 1969, *59*(2), pp. 147–60.

Rayner, A. C. On the Identification of the Supply Curve of Working Hours. *Oxford Econ. Pap.*, July 1969, *21*(2), pp. 293–98.

Reder, M. W. The Theory of Frictional Unemployment. *Economica, N.S.*, February 1969, *36*(141), pp. 1–28.

Reynolds, Lloyd G. Economic Development with Surplus Labour: Some Complications. *Oxford Econ. Pap.*, March 1969, *21*(1), pp. 89–103.

Roberts, Paul Craig and Brown, Norman L. The Economics of the Right to Work Controversy: Revisited. *Southern Econ. J.*, January 1969, *35*(3), pp. 265–66.

Robinson, Warren C. Types of Disguised Rural Unemployment and Some Policy Implications. *Oxford Econ. Pap.*, November 1969, *21*(3), pp. 373–86.

Rosen, Sherwin. On the Interindustry Wage and Hours Structure. *J. Polit. Econ.*, March/April 1969, *77*(2), pp. 249–73. [G: U.S.]

Rosen, Sherwin. Trade Union Power, Threat Effects and the Extent of Organization. *Rev. Econ. Stud.*, April 1969, *36*(106), pp. 185–96. [G: U.S.]

Sachs, Ignacy. Employment and Economic Development in a Dual Economy. **In** *Yesufu, T. M., ed.*, 1969, pp. 227–36.

Spencer, Roger W. The Relation between Prices and Employment: Two Views. *Fed. Res. Bank St. Louis Rev.*, March 1969, *51*(3), pp. 15–21.

Stiglitz, Joseph E. Rural-Urban Migration, Surplus Labour, and the Relationship between Urban and Rural Wages. *East Afr. Econ. Rev.*, December 1969, *1*(2), pp. 1–27.

Stoikov, Vladimir. The Allocation of the Cost of Displaced Labor and Severance Pay. *J. Human Res.*, Spring 1969, *4*(2), pp. 192–204.

Sufrin, Sidney C. and Wagner, Abraham R. Disaggregate Employment: The Search for Short Run Demand and Labor Market Stability. *Rivista Int. Sci. Econ. Com.*, October 1969, *16*(10), pp. 965–92. [G: U.S.]

Tauchman, Josef and Novozámský, Jiří. The Nature

of the International Division of Labour under Socialism. *Czech. Econ. Pap.*, 1969, (11), pp. 127–39. **[G: Czechoslovakia]**

Thirlwall, A. P. Demand Disequilibrium in the Labour Market and Wage Rate Inflation in the United Kingdom (1) *Yorkshire Bull. Econ. Soc. Res.*, May 1969, *21*(1), pp. 66–76. **[G: U.K.]**

Thirlwall, A. P. Types of Unemployment: With Special Reference to 'Non Demand-Deficient' Unemployment in Great Britain. *Scot. J. Polit. Econ.*, February 1969, *16*(1), pp. 20–49. **[G: U.K.]**

Timár, J. The Level of Employment and Its Equilibrium in Socialism. *Acta Oecon.*, 1969, *4*(2), pp. 169–79.

Todaro, Michael P. A Theoretical Note on Labour as an 'Inferior' Factor in Less Developed Economies. *J. Devel. Stud.*, July 1969, *5*(4), pp. 252–61.

Uppal, J. S. Measurement of Disguised Unemployment in an Underdeveloped Economy—An Economic Approach. *Asian Econ. Rev.*, August 1969, *11*(4), pp. 405–11. **[G: India]**

Uppal, J. S. Work Habits and Disguised Unemployment in Underdeveloped Countries—A Theoretical Analysis. *Oxford Econ. Pap.*, November 1969, *21*(3), pp. 387–94.

Van Rompuy, P. Flexibility, Adaptability and Demand for Labour. *Tijdschr. Econ.*, 1969, *14*(3), pp. 436–48.

Watts, Harold W. Graduated Works Incentives: An Experiment in Negative Taxation. *Amer. Econ. Rev.*, May 1969, *59*(2), pp. 463–72. **[G: U.S.]**

Zaidi, Mahmood A. The Determinants of Money Wage Rate Changes and Unemployment-Inflation "Trade-Offs" in Canada. *Int. Econ. Rev.*, June 1969, *10*(2), pp. 207–19. **[G: Canada]**

822 Public Policy; Role of Government

8220 General

Aaron, Benjamin. Individual Employee Rights and Union Democracy. **In** *Somers, G. G., ed. (II)*, 1969, pp. 275–82. **[G: U.S.]**

Agarwal, D. K. The Purpose and Future Direction of Legislation on Standing Orders. **In** *Johri, C. K., ed.*, 1969, pp. 189–200. **[G: India]**

Aziz, U. A. Wage, Fiscal, Social Security Policies and Institutional Changes as a Means of Redistributing Income in Developing Countries. **In** *Smith, A. D., ed.*, 1969, pp. 235–55.

Barbash, Jack. Federal Regulation and the Unions: Discussion. **In** *Somers, G. G., ed. (II)*, 1969, pp. 303–05. **[G: U.S.]**

Baxter, Nevins D.; Howrey, E. Philip and Penner, R. G. Unemployment and Cost-Benefit Analysis. *Public Finance*, 1969, *24*(1), pp. 80–88.

Bhatt, S. J. An Approach to the Problem of Creation of Employment Opportunities in Nigeria. **In** *Yesufu, T. M., ed.*, 1969, pp. 261–68. **[G: Nigeria]**

Bhatty, I. Z. Conflict and Reconciliation between the Economic, Social, and Industrial Relations Policies. **In** *Johri, C. K., ed.*, 1969, pp. 105–22. **[G: India]**

Blumrosen, Alfred W. A Survey of Remedies for Discrimination in the Union and on the Job. **In** *Somers, G. G., ed. (II)*, 1969, pp. 283–91. **[G: U.S.]**

Callaway, Archibald. Creating Employment for Africa's Youth. **In** *Yesufu, T. M., ed.*, 1969, pp. 237–60. **[G: Africa]**

Dhyani, S. N. Anatomy of Trade Union Law and Purpose and Future Direction of Trade Union Legislation in India. **In** *Johri, C. K., ed.*, 1969, pp. 201–20. **[G: India]**

Drotning, John E. and Lipsky, David B. The Effectiveness of Reinstatement as a Public Policy Remedy: The Kohler Case. *Ind. Lab. Relat. Rev.*, January 1969, *22*(2), pp. 179–98. **[G: U.S.]**

Goldfarb, Robert S. The Evaluation of Government Programs: The Case of New Haven's Manpower Training Activities. *Yale Econ. Essays*, Fall 1969, *9*(2), pp. 59–104. **[G: U.S.]**

Hilgert, Raymond L. and Young, Jerry D. Right-to-Work Legislation—Examination of Related Issues and Effects. **In** *Wortman, M. S., Jr.*, 1969, pp. 377–87. **[G: U.S.]**

Hodgson, James D. Federal Regulation of Unions—Impact on Management. **In** *Somers, G. G., ed. (II)*, 1969, pp. 292–302. **[G: U.S.]**

Hubbard, Russell H. The Role of Government Regulation. **In** *Tax Institute of America*, 1969, pp. 180–85. **[G: U.S.]**

Johri, C. K. Labour Policy in Perspective. **In** *Johri, C. K., ed.*, 1969, pp. 1–22. **[G: India]**

Kruger, Daniel H. Statement. **In** *Unemployment Compensation, HCH*, 1969, pp. 319–26. **[G: U.S.]**

Laird, William E. Statement. **In** *Tax Credits to Stimulate Job Opportunities in Rural Areas, SCH*, 1969, pp. 191–95. **[G: U.S.]**

Liggett, Malcolm H. The Efficacy of State Fair Employment Practices Commissions. *Ind. Lab. Relat. Rev.*, July 1969, *22*(4), pp. 559–67. **[G: U.S.]**

Moore, Mack A. Much Ado about 14b. **In** *Starleaf, D. R., ed.*, 1969, pp. 134–37. **[G: U.S.]**

Perrin, Guy. Reflections on Fifty Years of Social Security. *Int. Lab. Rev.*, March 1969, *99*(3), pp. 249–92.

Plata-Castilla, Alfonso. International Labour Standards and Colombian Legislation. *Int. Lab. Rev.*, February 1969, *99*(2), pp. 137–58. **[G: Colombia]**

Prakash, Anand. The Purpose and Future Direction of Industrial Disputes Legislation in India. **In** *Johri, C. K., ed.*, 1969, pp. 172–88. **[G: India]**

Pylee, M. V. Is Further Centralization of Labour Policy Desirable? **In** *Johri, C. K., ed.*, 1969, pp. 221–34. **[G: India]**

Shaw, Lee. Public Policy and the Strategy and Tactics of Collective Bargaining: Discussion. **In** *Somers, G. G., ed. (II)*, 1969, pp. 201–05. **[G: U.S.]**

Sheth, N. R. The Tripartite System: Past, Present, and Future. **In** *Johri, C. K., ed.*, 1969, pp. 142–59. **[G: India]**

Shultz, George P. Priorities in Policy and Research for Industrial Relations. **In** *Somers, G. G., ed. (II)*, 1969, pp. 1–13. **[G: U.S.]**

Sinha, G. P. and Sinha, P. R. N. Working of the Central Wage Boards. **In** *Johri, C. K., ed.*, 1969, pp. 270–86. **[G: India]**

Sorenson, Clara T. Review of State Labor Laws Enacted in 1968. *Mon. Lab. Rev.*, January 1969, *92*(1), pp. 41–46. [G: U.S.]
Thomson, Andrew W. J. The Next Step in Industrial Relations. *Scot. J. Polit. Econ.*, June 1969, *16*(2), pp. 212–24. [G: U.K.]
Thurow, Lester C. and Rappaport, Carl. Law Enforcement and Cost-Benefit Analysis. *Public Finance*, 1969, *24*(1), pp. 48–68. [G: U.S.]
Turner, H. A. The Donovan Report. *Econ. J.*, March 1969, *79*(313), pp. 1–10. [G: U.K.]
Valticos, Nicolas. Fifty Years of Standard-Setting Activities by the International Labour Organisation. *Int. Lab. Rev.*, September 1969, *100*(3), pp. 201–37.
Wallin, Michel. Labour Administration: Origins and Development. *Int. Lab. Rev.*, July 1969, *100*(1), pp. 51–110.
Wellington, Harry H. and Winter, Ralph K., Jr. The Limits of Collective Bargaining in Public Employment. *Yale Law J.*, June 1969, *78*(7), pp. 1107–27.
Ziderman, Adrian. Costs and Benefits of Adult Retraining in the United Kingdom. *Economica, N.S.*, November 1969, *36*(144), pp. 363–76. [G: U.K.]

8221 Wages and Hours

Brozen, Yale. The Effect of Statutory Minimum Wage Increases on Teen-Age Employment. *J. Law Econ.*, April 1969, *12*(1), pp. 109–22. [G: U.S.]
Campbell, Colin D. and Campbell, Rosemary G. State Minimum Wage Laws as a Cause of Unemployment. *Southern Econ. J.*, April 1969, *35*(4), pp. 323–32. [G: U.S.]
Carlsson, Robert J. and Robinson, James W. Toward a Public Employment Wage Theory: Reply. *Ind. Lab. Relat. Rev.*, October 1969, *23*(1), pp. 95–100. [G: U.S.]
Clague, Ewan. Statement on Hours of Work. **In** *Wortman, M. S., Jr.*, 1969, pp. 238–39. [G: U.S.]
Craft, James A. Toward a Public Employment Wage Theory: Comment. *Ind. Lab. Relat. Rev.*, October 1969, *23*(1), pp. 89–95. [G: U.S.]
Douty, H. M. Some Aspects of British Wage Policy. *Southern Econ. J.*, July 1969, *36*(1), pp. 74–81. [G: U.K.]
Foenander, Orwell de R. Australian Wage Fixation and a Change in Its Method. *Ind. Lab. Relat. Rev.*, January 1969, *22*(2), pp. 226–42. [G: Australia]
Franklin, N. N. Minimum Wage Fixing and Economic Development. **In** *Smith, A. D., ed.*, 1969, pp. 338–53.
Goldberg, Stephen B. Current Decisions of the NLRB and of the Courts. **In** *Somers, G. G., ed. (II)*, 1969, pp. 195–200. [G: U.S.]
Gomberg, Ia. Certain Questions in Wage Theory under Socialism. *Prob. Econ.*, July 1969, *12*(3), pp. 23–42.
Henle, Peter. Leisure and the Long Workweek. **In** *Wortman, M. S., Jr.*, 1969, pp. 247–57. [G: U.S.]
Johri, C. K. Some Aspects of Wage Policy in India. **In** *Johri, C. K., ed.*, 1969, pp. 254–69. [G: India]
Kunel'skii, L. The Socioeconomic Significance of Raising the Minimum Wage. *Prob. Econ.*, July 1969, *12*(3), pp. 43–57. [G: U.S.S.R.]
Mitchell, Daniel J. B. A Simplified Approach to Incomes Policy. *Ind. Lab. Relat. Rev.*, July 1969, *22*(4), pp. 512–27.
Mitra, Ashok. Wage Policy in Developing Countries. **In** *Smith, A. D., ed.*, 1969, pp. 371–82.
Mouly, Jean. Changing Concepts of Wage Policy. *Int. Lab. Rev.*, July 1969, *100*(1), pp. 1–22.
Pinto, Aníbal. Economic Structure, Productivity and Wages in Latin America. **In** *Smith, A. D., ed.*, 1969, pp. 256–68. [G: Latin America]
Pursell, Donald E. The Impact of the South African Wage Board on Skilled/Unskilled Wage Differentials. *East Afr. Econ. Rev.*, June 1969, *1*(1), pp. 73–81. [G: S. Africa]
Reynolds, Lloyd G. Objectives of Wage Policy in Developing Countries. **In** *Smith, A. D., ed.*, 1969, pp. 217–34.
Smith, Anthony D. An Analysis of the Proceedings. **In** *Smith, A. D., ed.*, 1969, pp. 163–214.
Trattner, Walter I. The First Federal Child Labor Law (1916). *Soc. Sci. Quart.*, December 1969, *50*(3), pp. 507–24. [G: U.S.]
Turner, H. A. The Formulation of Wage Policy. **In** *Smith, A. D., ed.*, 1969, pp. 354–70.

8223 Factory Act and Safety Legislation

Robert, Marcel and Parmeggiani, Luigi. Fifty Years of International Collaboration in Occupational Safety and Health. *Int. Lab. Rev.*, January 1969, *99*(1), pp. 85–136.

8224 Unemployment Insurance

Hickey, Joseph A. Status Report on Unemployment Insurance Laws. *Mon. Lab. Rev.*, January 1969, *92*(1), pp. 47–51. [G: U.S.]
van der Merwe, P. J. The Economic Influence of the Bantu Labour Bureau System on the Bantu Labour Market. *S. Afr. J. Econ.*, March 1969, *37*(1), pp. 42–54. [G: S. Africa]
Thirlwall, A. P. Unemployment Compensation as an Automatic Stabilizer. *Bull. Oxford Univ. Inst. Econ. Statist.*, February 1969, *31*(1), pp. 23–37. [G: U.K.]
Weidenbaum, Murray L. Statement. **In** *Unemployment Compensation, HCH*, 1969, pp. 221–25. [G: U.S.]

8225 Employment Services

Davies, Gordon K. Needed: A National Job-Matching Network. *Harvard Bus. Rev.*, September–October 1969, *47*(5), pp. 63–72. [G: U.S.]
Ullman, Joseph C. Helping Workers Locate Jobs Following a Plant Shutdown. *Mon. Lab. Rev.*, April 1969, *92*(4), pp. 35–40. [G: U.S.]

8226 Employment in Public Sector

Abner, Willoughby. The FMCS and Dispute Mediation in the Federal Government. *Mon. Lab. Rev.*, May 1969, *92*(5), pp. 27–29. [G: U.S.]
Anderson, Arvid. Strikes and Impasse Resolution in

Public Employment. *Mich. Law Rev.*, March 1969, *67*(5), pp. 943–70. [G: U.S.]

Arthurs, H. W. Collective Bargaining in the Public Service of Canada: Bold Experiment or Act of Folly? *Mich. Law Rev.*, March 1969, *67*(5), pp. 971–1000. [G: Canada]

Craft, James A. Public Employee Negotiations Legislation: The Paradox of Labor Divided. *Quart. Rev. Econ. Bus.*, Winter 1969, *9*(4), pp. 29–37. [G: U.S.]

Donoian, Harry A. A New Approach to Setting the Pay of Federal Blue-collar Workers. *Mon. Lab. Rev.*, April 1969, *92*(4), pp. 30–34. [G: U.S.]

Kheel, Theodore W. Strikes and Public Employment. *Mich. Law Rev.*, March 1969, *67*(5), pp. 931–42. [G: U.S.]

Lewis, L. Earl. Federal Pay Comparability Procedures. *Mon. Lab. Rev.*, February 1969, *92*(2), pp. 10–13. [G: U.S.]

Lutz, Carl F. Quantitative Job Evaluation in Local Government in the United States. *Int. Lab. Rev.*, June 1969, *99*(6), pp. 607–19. [G: U.S.]

Mesa-Lago, Carmelo. Economic Significance of Unpaid Labor in Socialist Cuba. *Ind. Lab. Relat. Rev.*, April 1969, *22*(3), pp. 339–57. [G: Cuba]

Rehmus, Charles M. Constraints on Local Governments in Public Employee Bargaining. *Mich. Law Rev.*, March 1969, *67*(5), pp. 919–30. [G: U.S.]

Rock, Eli. The Appropriate Unit Question in the Public Service: The Problem of Proliferation. *Mich. Law Rev.*, March 1969, *67*(5), pp. 1001–16. [G: U.S.]

Ross, Anne M. Public Employee Unions and the Right to Strike. *Mon. Lab. Rev.*, March 1969, *92*(3), pp. 14–18. [G: U.S.]

Seidman, Joel. Collective Bargaining in the Postal Service. *Ind. Relat.*, October 1969, *9*(1), pp. 11–26. [G: U.S.]

Smith, Russell A. State and Local Advisory Reports on Public Employment Labor Legislation: A Comparative Analysis. *Mich. Law Rev.*, March 1969, *67*(5), pp. 891–918. [G: U.S.]

White, Sheila C. Work Stoppages of Government Employees. *Mon. Lab. Rev.*, December 1969, *92*(12), pp. 29–34. [G: U.S.]

Woolf, Donald A. Labor Problems in the Post Office. *Ind. Relat.*, October 1969, *9*(1), pp. 27–35. [G: U.S.]

823 Labor Mobility; National and International Migration

8230 Labor Mobility; National and International Migration

Adams, Dale W. Rural Migration and Agricultural Development in Colombia. *Econ. Develop. Cult. Change*, July 1969, *17*(4), pp. 527–39. [G: Colombia]

Adams, Nassau A. Internal Migration in Jamaica: An Economic Analysis. *Soc. Econ. Stud.*, June 1969, *18*(2), pp. 137–51. [G: Jamaica]

Adebahr, Hubertus. Binnenwanderung und Lohnhöhe. Eine Analyse der Binnenwanderungen in der Bundesrepublik in den Jahren 1957–1967 im Hinblick auf die Frage ob Wanderungen "lohngerichtet" sind. (Internal Migration and Regional Wage Levels. An Analysis of Internal Migrations in the Federal Republic of Germany 1957–1967. With English summary.) *Schmollers Jahr.*, 1969, *89*(5), pp. 557–78. [G: W. Germany]

Bachmura, Frank T. Latin American Brain Drainage. In *Hilton, R., ed.*, 1969, pp. 426–44. [G: Latin America]

Beijer, G. Brain Drain as a Burden, a Stimulus and a Challenge to European Integration. In *Bechhofer, F., ed.*, 1969, pp. 3–30. [G: Europe]

Berry, R. Albert and Soligo, Ronald. Some Welfare Aspects of International Migration. *J. Polit. Econ.*, September/October 1969, *77*(5), pp. 778–94.

Bishop, C. E. The Mobility of Rural Manpower. In *Papi, U. and Nunn, C., eds.*, 1969, pp. 283–92.

Bishop, C. E. The Need for Improved Mobility Policy. In *Ruttan, V. W.; Waldo, A. D. and Houck, J. P., eds.*, 1969, pp. 242–54. [G: U.S.]

Blevins, Audie L., Jr. Migration Rates in Twelve Southern Metropolitan Areas: A "Push-Pull" Analysis. *Soc. Sci. Quart.*, September 1969, *50*(2), pp. 337–53. [G: U.S.]

Botsas, Eleutherios N. A Note on Migration and the Balance of Payments. *Econ. Int.*, May 1969, *22*(2), pp. 247–51. [G: Greece]

Bramhall, David F. and Bryce, Herrington J. Interstate Migration of Labor-Force Age Population. *Ind. Lab. Relat. Rev.*, July 1969, *22*(4), pp. 576–83. [G: U.S.]

Burton, John F., Jr. Interindustry Variations in Voluntary Labor Mobility: Reply. *Ind. Lab. Relat. Rev.*, October 1969, *23*(1), pp. 84–88. [G: U.S.]

Burton, John F., Jr. and Parker, John E. Interindustry Variations in Voluntary Labor Mobility. *Ind. Lab. Relat. Rev.*, January 1969, *22*(2), pp. 199–216. [G: U.S.]

Chesler, Herbert A. Labor Utilization and Earnings in the Johnstown Labor Market. *Land Econ.*, May 1969, *45*(2), pp. 273–77. [G: U.S.]

Corner, D. C. and Fletcher, C. H. Some Effects of Selective Employment Tax on the Construction and Service Industries. *Bull. Oxford Univ. Inst. Econ. Statist.*, February 1969, *31*(1), pp. 47–54. [G: U.K.]

Fillerup, O. W. Migratory Labor in California Agriculture. In *Task Force on Economic Growth and Opportunity*, 1969, pp. 145–52. [G: U.S.]

Flek, Josef. Life and Income of Czechoslovak Cooperatives. In *Papi, U. and Nunn, C., eds.*, 1969, pp. 304–15. [G: Czechoslovakia]

Gallaway, Lowell E. Age and Labor Mobility Patterns. *Southern Econ. J.*, October 1969, *36*(2), pp. 171–80. [G: U.S.]

Gallaway, Lowell E. The Effect of Geographic Labor Mobility on Income: A Brief Comment. *J. Human Res.*, Winter 1969, *4*(1), pp. 103–09. [G: U.S.]

George, Roy E. Immobility of Redundant Labour. In *Association of Canadian Schools of Business*, 1969, pp. 126–43.

Gish, Oscar. A Note on Aid for Nursing Training in Britain. *J. Devel. Stud.*, April 1969, *5*(3), pp. 220–22. [G: U.K.]

Glueck, William F. Executive Mobility in Missouri. *Univ. Missouri Bus. Govt. Rev.*, March–April

1969, *10*(2), pp. 27–32. [G: U.S.]

Gordon, Jerome B. Labor Mobility and Economic Growth: The Central American Experience—Costa Rica and El Salvador. *Econ. Develop. Cult. Change,* April 1969, *17*(3), pp. 319–37. [G: Costa Rica; El Salvador]

Greenwood, Michael J. An Analysis of the Determinants of Geographic Labor Mobility in the United States. *Rev. Econ. Statist.,* May 1969, *51*(2), pp. 189–94. [G: U.S.]

Greenwood, Michael J. The Determinants of Labor Migration in Egypt. *J. Reg. Sci.,* August 1969, *9*(2), pp. 283–90. [G: Egypt]

Hansen, Niles M. Improving Economic Opportunity for the Mexican Americans: A Critical Evaluation of Public Policy, with Assessment of the Problem in South Texas. *Econ. Bus. Bull.,* Fall 1969, *22*(1), pp. 1–14. [G: U.S.]

Jenness, Robert A. Manpower Mobility Programs. **In** *Somers, G. G. and Wood, W. D., eds.,* 1969, pp. 184–220. [G: U.S.; Canada]

Johnson, David B. and Stern, James L. Why and How Workers Shift from Blue-Collar to White-Collar Jobs. *Mon. Lab. Rev.,* October 1969, *92* (10), pp. 7–13. [G: U.S.]

Johnson, Harry G.; Scott, A. D. and Thomas, Brinley. Criticisms of Thomas's Analysis of Brain Drain. **In** *Blaug, M., ed.,* 1969, pp. 281–301.

Jones, R. M. A Case Study in Labour Mobility. *Manchester Sch. Econ. Soc. Stud.,* June 1969, *37*(2), pp. 169–74. [G: U.K.]

Kelley, Allen C. and Weiss, Leonard W. Markov Processes and Economic Analysis: The Case of Migration. *Econometrica,* April 1969, *37*(2), pp. 280–97.

Last, J. M. International Mobility in the Medical Profession. **In** *Bechhofer, F., ed.,* 1969, pp. 31–42. [G: U.K.]

Lavagne, Pierre. Conséquences de la liberté de mouvement du facteur travail en économie internationale. (With English summary.) *Revue Écon.,* September 1969, *20*(5), pp. 873–87.

Lianos, Theodore P. South-Nonsouth Migration, 1955–1960. *Miss. Val. J. Bus. Econ.,* Spring 1969, *4*(2), pp. 10–22. [G: U.S.]

Maikov, A. Questions Pertaining to the Redistribution of Labor Resources. *Prob. Econ.,* May 1969, *12*(1), pp. 33–44. [G: U.S.S.R.]

Mazek, Warren F. Unemployment and the Efficacy of Migration: The Case of Laborers. *J. Reg. Sci.,* April 1969, *9*(1), pp. 101–07. [G: U.S.]

McDonald, James R. Contemporary Patterns of Internal Migration in France. *Mich. Academician,* Spring 1969, *1*(3–4), pp. 101–11. [G: France]

McKechnie, Graeme H. Manpower Mobility Programs: Discussion. **In** *Somers, G. G. and Wood, W. D., eds.,* 1969, pp. 224–29. [G: U.S.; Canada]

Murphy, George and Fannin, Paul I. The Migratory Farm Labor Problem in the United States. **In** *Kuhlman, J. M., ed.,* 1969, pp. 151–73. [G: U.S.]

Murray, Barbara B. Central City Expenditures and Out-Migration to the Fringe. *Land Econ.,* November 1969, *45*(4), pp. 471–74.

Newsom, Robert T. Metropolitan and Nonmetropolitan Employment Changes: The Case of Texas. *Soc. Sci. Quart.,* September 1969, *50*(2), pp. 354–68. [G: U.S.]

O'Grada, Cormac. The Vocational Training Policy of the EEC and the Free Movement of Skilled Labour. *J. Common Market Stud.,* December 1969, *8*(2), pp. 79–109. [G: E.E.C.]

Parnes, Herbert S. and Spitz, Ruth S. A Conceptual Framework for Studying Labor Mobility. *Mon. Lab. Rev.,* November 1969, *92*(11), pp. 55–58.

Parnes, Herbert S. Manpower Mobility Programs: Discussion. **In** *Somers, G. G. and Wood, W. D., eds.,* 1969, pp. 221–24. [G: U.S.; Canada]

Pencavel, John H. Interindustry Variations in Voluntary Labor Mobility: Comment. *Ind. Lab. Relat. Rev.,* October 1969, *23*(1), pp. 78–83. [G: U.S.]

Raymond, Richard. Mobility and Economic Progress of Negro Americans during the 1940's. *Amer. J. Econ. Soc.,* October 1969, *28*(4), pp. 337–50. [G: U.S.]

Rogers, Tommy W. Migration Attractiveness of Southern Metropolitan Areas. *Soc. Sci. Quart.,* September 1969, *50*(2), pp. 325–36. [G: U.S.]

Sanders, John. The Depressed Area and Labor Mobility: The Eastern Kentucky Case. *J. Human Res.,* Fall 1969, *4*(4), pp. 437–50. [G: U.S.]

Shapero, Albert. Effects of Government R and D Contracting on Mobility and Regional Resources. **In** *Gruber, W. H. and Marquis, D. G., eds.,* 1969, pp. 179–201. [G: U.S.]

Smirnov, V. V. Movement and Utilization of Rural Labor Resources (in the Non-black Soil Zone of the RSFSR). *Prob. Econ.,* October 1969, *12*(6), pp. 68–81. [G: U.S.S.R.]

Stiglitz, Joseph E. Rural-Urban Migration, Surplus Labour, and the Relationship between Urban and Rural Wages. *East Afr. Econ. Rev.,* December 1969, *1*(2), pp. 1–27.

Tarver, James D. Migration Differentials in Southern Cities and Suburbs. *Soc. Sci. Quart.,* September 1969, *50*(2), pp. 298–324. [G: U.S.]

Thomas, Brinley. Brain Drain Again. **In** *Blaug, M., ed.,* 1969, pp. 250–80.

Todaro, Michael P. A Model for Labor Migration and Urban Unemployment in Less Developed Countries. *Amer. Econ. Rev.,* March 1969, *59*(1), pp. 138–48.

Vechkanov, G. Raising the Effectiveness of the Territorial Redistribution of Labor Resources. *Prob. Econ.,* October 1969, *12*(6), pp. 58–67. [G: U.S.S.R.]

Watanabe, S. The Brain Drain from Developing to Developed Countries. *Int. Lab. Rev.,* April 1969, *99*(4), pp. 401–33.

West, E. G. Regional Planning: Fact and Fallacy. **In** *Task Force on Economic Growth and Opportunity,* 1969, pp. 249–68.

Wilson, James A. Motivation underlying the Brain Drain. **In** *Baier, K. and Rescher, N., eds.,* 1969, pp. 431–52. [G: U.K.]

Wolf, Laurence G. The Metropolitan Tidal Wave in Ohio, 1900–2000. *Econ. Geogr.,* April 1969, *45*(2), pp. 133–54. [G: U.S.]

Yocum, James C. Recent Changes in Interstate and Interregional Population Flows. *Ohio State U. Bull. Bus. Res.,* May 1969, *44*(5), pp. 4–7. [G: U.S.]

824 Labor Market Studies, Wages, Employment

8240 General

Altman, Stuart H. Earnings, Unemployment, and the Supply of Enlisted Volunteers. *J. Human Res.*, Winter 1969, *4*(1), pp. 38–59. [G: U.S.]

Amin, Samir. Levels of Remuneration, Factor Proportions and Income Differentials with Special Reference to Developing Countries. In *Smith, A. D., ed.*, 1969, pp. 269–93.

Anderson, Paul S. Wages and the Guideposts: Comment. *Amer. Econ. Rev.*, June 1969, *59*(3), pp. 351–54. [G: U.S.]

Aslanyan, R. G. Action to Ensure That Soviet Citizens Enjoy Equal Rights and Opportunities. *Int. Lab. Rev.*, December 1969, *100*(6), pp. 551–82. [G: U.S.S.R.]

Belcher, D. W. The Changing Nature of Compensation Administration. *Calif. Manage. Rev.*, Summer 1969, *11*(4), pp. 89–94.

Bienefeld, M. A. The Normal Week under Collective Bargaining. *Economica, N.S.*, May 1969, *36* (142), pp. 172–92.

Bogan, Forrest A. Work Experience of the Population: Spotlight on Women and Youths. *Mon. Lab. Rev.*, June 1969, *92*(6), pp. 44–50. [G: U.S.]

Bose, Swadesh R. and Clark, Edwin H., II. Some Basic Considerations on Agricultural Mechanization in West Pakistan. *Pakistan Develop. Rev.*, Autumn 1969, *9*(3), pp. 273–308. [G: W. Pakistan]

Carlsson, Robert J. and Robinson, James W. Compensation Decisions in Public Organizations: Comment. *Ind. Relat.*, October 1969, *9*(1), pp. 111–13. [G: U.S.]

Ciocca, Pierluigi. L'ipotesi del "ritardo" dei salari rispetto ai prezzi in periodi di inflazione: alcune considerazioni generali-II. (The Hypothesis of the Lag of Wages behind Prices during Inflation: General Considerations-II. With English summary.) *Bancaria*, May 1969, *25*(5), pp. 572–83.

Ciocca, Pierluigi. L'ipotesi del "ritardo" dei salari rispetto ai prezzi in periodi di inflazione: alcune considerazioni generali-I. (The Hypothesis of the "Lag" of Wages behind Prices during Inflation: General Considerations-I. With English summary.) *Bancaria*, April 1969, *25*(4), pp. 423–37.

Egle, Walter P. Recessional Unemployment and Leisure. *Rivista Int. Sci. Econ. Com.*, April 1969, *16* (4), pp. 363–70.

Evans, Archibald A. Work and Leisure, 1919–1969. *Int. Lab. Rev.*, January 1969, *99*(1), pp. 35–59.

Ferguson, C. E. and Moroney, John R. The Sources of Change in Labor's Relative Share: A Neoclassical Analysis. *Southern Econ. J.*, April 1969, *35*(4), pp. 308–22. [G: U.S.]

Foenander, Orwell de R. Australian Wage Fixation and a Change in Its Method. *Ind. Lab. Relat. Rev.*, January 1969, *22*(2), pp. 226–42. [G: Australia]

Franklin, N. N. Employment and Unemployment: Views and Policies, 1919–1969. *Int. Lab. Rev.*, March 1969, *99*(3), pp. 293–314.

Gallaway, Lowell E. The Effect of Geographic Labor Mobility on Income: A Brief Comment. *J. Human Res.*, Winter 1969, *4*(1), pp. 103–09. [G: U.S.]

Gerwin, Donald. Compensation Decisions in Public Organizations: Reply. *Ind. Relat.*, October 1969, *9*(1), pp. 114–16. [G: U.S.]

Goodman, Richard Alan. A Hidden Issue in Minority Employment. *Calif. Manage. Rev.*, Summer 1969, *11*(4), pp. 27–30.

Goodwin, Leonard. Work Orientations of the Underemployed Poor: Report on a Pilot Study. *J. Human Res.*, Fall 1969, *4*(4), pp. 508–19. [G: U.S.]

Hathaway, Dale E. Poverty in the Hired Farm Work Force. In *Task Force on Economic Growth and Opportunity*, 1969, pp. 177–98. [G: U.S.]

Heidensohn, K. Labour's Share in National Income—A Constant? *Manchester Sch. Econ. Soc. Stud.*, December 1969, *37*(4), pp. 295–321.

Hellriegel, Don and French, Wendell. A Critique of Jaques' Equitable Payment System. *Ind. Relat.*, May 1969, *8*(3), pp. 269–79.

Henry, G. C. Farm Labor. In *Task Force on Economic Growth and Opportunity*, 1969, pp. 217–27. [G: U.S.]

Herman, Shelby W. and Fulco, Lawrence J. Productivity and Unit Labor Costs in 1968. *Mon. Lab. Rev.*, June 1969, *92*(6), pp. 11–15. [G: U.S.]

Hines, A. G. Wage Inflation in the United Kingdom 1948–62: A Disaggregated Study. *Econ. J.*, March 1969, *79*(313), pp. 66–89. [G: U.K.]

Jacobsson, Lars and Lindbeck, Assar. Labor Market Condition, Wages and Inflation—Swedish Experiences 1955–67. *Swedish J. Econ.*, June 1969, *71* (2), pp. 64–103. [G: Sweden]

Jesness, O. B. Poverty among American Farmers. In *Task Force on Economic Growth and Opportunity*, 1969, pp. 229–43. [G: U.S.]

Joseph, Myron L. State of the Art in Labor Statistics. In *Somers, G. G., ed. (II)*, 1969, pp. 105–19. [G: U.S.]

Kalachek, Edward. Determinants of Teenage Employment. *J. Human Res.*, Winter 1969, *4*(1), pp. 3–21. [G: U.S.]

Keshava, G. P. Incentives for Industrial Labour: A Survey. *Artha-Vikas*, January 1969, *5*(1), pp. 29–53.

Killingsworth, Charles C. Full Employment and the New Economics. *Scot. J. Polit. Econ.*, February 1969, *16*(1), pp. 1–19.

Kunnas, Heikki J. EFO-tutkimus. (EFO Survey. With English summary.) *Kansant. Aikak.*, 1969, *65*(3), pp. 206–13. [G: Sweden]

Liebling, H. I. and Cluff, A. T. U.S. Postwar Inflation and Phillips Curves. *Kyklos*, 1969, *22*(2), pp. 232–50. [G: U.S.]

Loftus, P. J. Labour's Share in Manufacturing. *Lloyds Bank Rev.*, April 1969, (92), pp. 15–25.

Lucas, Robert E., Jr. and Rapping, Leonard A. Real Wages, Employment, and Inflation. *J. Polit. Econ.*, September/October 1969, *77*(5), pp. 721–54. [G: U.S.]

Makkonen, Veikko T. Palvelusektorin työllisyyden kehityksestä Suomessa vuosina 1948–1964. (The Development of Employment in the Finnish Service Sector 1948–1964. With English summary.) *Kansant. Aikak.*, 1969, *65*(2), pp. 110–21. **[G: Finland]**

Marion, Gérald. Fonction d'emploi, taux de participation de la main-d'oeuvre et demande excédentaire de travil. (With English summary.) *Revue Écon.*, November 1969, *20*(6), pp. 968–1005. **[G: Canada]**

Mesa-Lago, Carmelo. Economic Significance of Unpaid Labor in Socialist Cuba. *Ind. Lab. Relat. Rev.*, April 1969, *22*(3), pp. 339–57. **[G: Cuba]**

Moore, Geoffrey H. Long-Range Program Objectives for BLS. *Mon. Lab. Rev.*, October 1969, *92*(10), pp. 3–6. **[G: U.S.]**

Moore, L. W. Urban Unrest—Whose Problem Is It? *Calif. Manage. Rev.*, Summer 1969, *11*(4), pp. 7–10.

Moroney, John R. and Allen, Bruce T. Monopoly Power and the Relative Share of Labor. *Ind. Lab. Relat. Rev.*, January 1969, *22*(2), pp. 167–78. **[G: U.S.]**

Mueller, P. and Zevering, K. H. Employment Promotion through Rural Development: A Pilot Project in Western Nigeria. *Int. Lab. Rev.*, August 1969, *100*(2), pp. 111–30. **[G: Nigeria]**

Murray, Lionel. Trade Unions and Technical Change. **In** *Hugh-Jones, E. M., ed.*, 1969, pp. 135–50. **[G: U.K.]**

Perry, George L. Wages and the Guideposts: Reply. *Amer. Econ. Rev.*, June 1969, *59*(3), pp. 365–70. **[G: U.S.]**

Reynolds, Lloyd G. Relative Earnings and Manpower Allocation in Developing Economies. *Pakistan Develop. Rev.*, Spring 1969, *9*(1), pp. 14–34.

Rosen, Sherwin. On the Interindustry Wage and Hours Structure. *J. Polit. Econ.*, March/April 1969, *77*(2), pp. 249–73. **[G: U.S.]**

Schreiber, Wilfrid. On Two Topical Questions of Distribution Theory and Policy. *Ger. Econ. Rev.*, 1969, *7*(3), pp. 199–215. **[G: W. Germany]**

Shultz, George P. Labor Statistics for National Decision Making. *Amer. Statist.*, October 1969, *23*(4), pp. 11–14. **[G: U.S.]**

Shultz, George P. The Use of Labor Statistics in National Decisionmaking. *Mon. Lab. Rev.*, November 1969, *92*(11), pp. 48–50. **[G: U.S.]**

Smith, Anthony D. A Conspectus of Wage Trends in Developing Countries. **In** *Smith, A. D., ed.*, 1969, pp. 3–52.

Sorkin, Alan L. Some Factors Associated with Earnings and Unemployment Differences between Occupations. *Nebr. J. Econ. Bus.*, Winter 1968–69, *8*(1), pp. 44–52. **[G: U.S.]**

Thirlwall, A. P. Demand Disequilibrium in the Labour Market and Wage Rate Inflation in the United Kingdom (1) *Yorkshire Bull. Econ. Soc. Res.*, May 1969, *21*(1), pp. 66–76. **[G: U.K.]**

Thormann, Peter H. Employment and Earnings in Portugal, 1953–1967. *Int. Lab. Rev.*, June 1969, *99*(6), pp. 589–606. **[G: Portugal]**

Throop, Adrian W. Wages and the Guideposts: Comment. *Amer. Econ. Rev.*, June 1969, *59*(3), pp. 358–65. **[G: U.S.]**

Ulman, Lloyd. Wage-Price Policies: Some Lessons from Abroad. *Ind. Relat.*, May 1969, *8*(3), pp. 195–213.

Wachter, Michael L. Wages and the Guideposts: Comment. *Amer. Econ. Rev.*, June 1969, *59*(3), pp. 354–58. **[G: U.S.]**

Walter, Helmut. Über einige Zusammenhänge zwischen Einkommensverteilung und globaler Beschäftigtenstruktur. (With English summary.) *Z. ges. Staatswiss.*, April 1969, *125*(2), pp. 248–60. **[G: W. Germany]**

Ward, Cordelia T. and Davis, William M. Negotiations and Wage Calendar for 1969. *Mon. Lab. Rev.*, January 1969, *92*(1), pp. 52–64.

Welch, Finis. Linear Synthesis of Skill Distribution. *J. Human Res.*, Summer 1969, *4*(3), pp. 311–27. **[G: U.S.]**

Zaidi, Mahmood A. The Determinants of Money Wage Rate Changes and Unemployment-Inflation "Trade-Offs" in Canada. *Int. Econ. Rev.*, June 1969, *10*(2), pp. 207–19. **[G: Canada]**

8241 Specific Labor Market Studies

Bauer, Larry L. The Effect of Technology on the Farm Labor Market. *Amer. J. Agr. Econ.*, August 1969, *51*(3), pp. 605–18. **[G: U.S.]**

Bryce, Herrington J. Regional Labor Earnings Differentials in a Small Developing Country: The Republic of Panama. *J. Reg. Sci.*, December 1969, *9*(3), pp. 405–15. **[G: Panama]**

Chesler, Herbert A. Labor Utilization and Earnings in the Johnstown Labor Market. *Land Econ.*, May 1969, *45*(2), pp. 273–77. **[G: U.S.]**

Dasso, Jerome J. Economic Outlook for Oregon in 1969. *Oregon Bus. Rev.*, February 1969, *28*(2), pp. 1–4. **[G: U.S.]**

Franke, Walter H. Research on Big City Labor Markets: Discussion. **In** *Somers, G. G., ed. (II)*, 1969, pp. 272–74. **[G: U.S.]**

Guthrie, Harold W. Teachers in the Moonlight. *Mon. Lab. Rev.*, February 1969, *92*(2), pp. 28–31. **[G: U.S.]**

Hildebrand, George H. Research on Big City Labor Markets: Discussion. **In** *Somers, G. G., ed. (II)*, 1969, pp. 268–71. **[G: U.S.]**

Hunter, J. B. K. The Development of the Labour Market in Kenya. **In** *Stewart, I. G., ed.*, 1969, pp. 115–37. **[G: Kenya]**

Johnson, David B. and Stern, James L. Why and How Workers Shift from Blue-Collar to White-Collar Jobs. *Mon. Lab. Rev.*, October 1969, *92*(10), pp. 7–13. **[G: U.S.]**

Katzman, Martin T. Opportunity, Subculture and the Economic Performance of Urban Ethnic Groups. *Amer. J. Econ. Soc.*, October 1969, *28*(4), pp. 351–66. **[G: U.S.]**

Kpedekpo, G. M. K. On Working Life Tables in Ghana with Particular Reference to the Female Working Population. *J. Roy. Statist. Soc.*, Part 3, 1969, *132*, pp. 431–41. **[G: Ghana]**

Lurie, Melvin and Rayack, Elton. Employment Opportunities for Negro Families in "Satellite" Cities. *Southern Econ. J.*, October 1969, *36*(2), pp. 191–95. **[G: U.S.]**

McCall, John and Wallace, Neil. A Supply Function of First-Term Re-enlistees to the Air Force. *J. Human Res.*, Summer 1969, *4*(3), pp. 293–310. **[G: U.S.]**

Nag, A. Estimation and Projection of the Working Force in Greater Bombay. *Asian Econ. Rev.*, February 1969, *11*(2), pp. 160–72. **[G: India]**

Ryscavage, Paul M. Employment Developments in Urban Poverty Neighborhoods. *Mon. Lab. Rev.*, June 1969, *92*(6), pp. 51–56. **[G: U.S.]**

Thal-Larsen, Margaret. Changing Employer Policies in a Large Urban Labor Market. **In** *Somers, G. G., ed. (II)*, 1969, pp. 248–56. **[G: U.S.]**

Wabe, J. S. Labour Force Participation Rates in the London Metropolitan Region. *J. Roy. Statist. Soc.*, Part 2, 1969, *132*, pp. 245–64. **[G: U.K.]**

Yamamoto, Hiromasa. A Note on Shorter Working Hours for Seamen. *Kobe Econ. Bus. Rev.*, 1969, *16* (1), pp. 39–45.

8242 Wage and Fringe Benefit Studies

Albert, Linzy D. and Kellow, James H. Decision-Makers' Reactions to Plant Location Factors: An Appraisal. *Land Econ.*, August 1969, *45*(3), pp. 376–81.

Behman, Sara. Wage Changes, Institutions, and Relative Factor Prices in Manufacturing. *Rev. Econ. Statist.*, August 1969, *51*(3), pp. 227–38. **[G: U.S.]**

Berg, Elliot J. Urban Real Wages and the Nigerian Trade Union Movement, 1939–60: A Comment. *Econ. Develop. Cult. Change*, July 1969, *17*(4), pp. 604–17. **[G: Nigeria]**

Beskid, Lidia. Real Wages in Poland During 1956–1967. *Eastern Europ. Econ.*, Spring 1969, *7*(3), pp. 29–47. **[G: Poland]**

Bower, Richard S. Problems and Progress in the Applications of Recent Developments in the Theory of Finance: Discussion. *J. Finance*, May 1969, *24*(2), pp. 339–41. **[G: U.S.]**

Britsch, Klaus; Reichardt, Helmut and Schips, Bernd. Sind die Lohnempfänger gut beraten, wenn sie sich einer Lohnquotensenkung widersetzen? (With English summary.) *Jahr. Nationalökon. Statist.*, August 1969, *183*(3–4), pp. 300–305.

Brown, E. H. Phelps. Balancing External Payments by Adjusting Domestic Income. *Australian Econ. Pap.*, December 1969, *8*(13), pp. 111–21.

Brozen, Yale. The Effect of Statutory Minimum Wage Increases on Teen-Age Employment. *J. Law Econ.*, April 1969, *12*(1), pp. 109–22. **[G: U.S.]**

Bryan, Robert G. Wages in the Shirt and Nightwear Manufacturing Industry. *Mon. Lab. Rev.*, November 1969, *92*(11), pp. 66–67. **[G: U.S.]**

Buchenroth, Kenneth J. Motivation: Financial and Nonfinancial. *Manage. Account.*, December 1969, *51*(6), pp. 15–16, 48. **[G: U.S.]**

Buckley, John E. Intraoccupational Wage Dispersion in Metropolitan Areas, 1967–68. *Mon. Lab. Rev.*, September 1969, *92*(9), pp. 24–29. **[G: U.S.]**

Call, Dwight V. Some Salient Factors Often Overlooked in Stock Options. *Accounting Rev.*, October 1969, *44*(4), pp. 711–19. **[G: U.S.]**

Caramela, Edward J. Salary Levels Continue Sharp Rise in White-collar Occupations. *Mon. Lab. Rev.*, April 1969, *92*(4), pp. 46–48.

Cargill, Thomas F. An Empirical Investigation of the Wage-Lag Hypothesis. *Amer. Econ. Rev.*, December 1969, *59*(5), pp. 806–16. **[G: U.S.]**

Cassidy, Henry J. The Rate of Change in the Size Distribution of Wages as a Vector. *Rev. Income Wealth*, December 1969, *15*(4), pp. 349–68. **[G: U.S.]**

Childs, A. R. A Compensation Program for Managers of Professional, Technical and Non-Technical Personnel. **In** *Gilroy, T. P., ed.*, 1969, pp. 24–32.

Czarnecki, Edgar R. Profit Sharing and Union Organizing. *Mon. Lab. Rev.*, December 1969, *92* (12), pp. 61–62. **[G: U.S.]**

Daniels, Wilbur. Uses of the Computer in Contract Enforcement: The ILGWU Experience. **In** *Siegel, A. J., ed.*, 1969, pp. 189–202. **[G: U.S.]**

Daubigney, Jean-Pierre. Actualité du système "Parodi" dans les comportements salariaux des entreprises. (With English summary.) *Revue Écon.*, May 1969, *20*(3), pp. 497–514. **[G: France]**

David, Lily Mary and Sheifer, Victor J. Estimating the Cost of Collective Bargaining Settlements. *Mon. Lab. Rev.*, May 1969, *92*(5), pp. 16–26. **[G: U.S.]**

Desaeyere, W. Het inkomen van de economisten, analyse van de U.N.A. enquête. (The Income of the Economists, Analysis of the U.N.A. Questionnaire Study. With English summary.) *Tijdschr. Econ.*, 1969, *14*(3), pp. 375–435. **[G: Belgium]**

Fefferman, Arthur S. Private Pension Plans: A 1968 Prospectus. *J. Risk Ins.*, September 1969, *36*(4), pp. 433–36. **[G: U.S.]**

Fenlon, John. Patterns in Overtime Hours and Premium Pay. *Mon. Lab. Rev.*, October 1969, *92* (10), pp. 42–46. **[G: U.S.]**

Foster, Kenneth E. Accounting for Management Pay Differentials. *Ind. Relat.*, October 1969, *9*(1), pp. 80–87. **[G: U.S.]**

Gerwin, Donald. Compensation Decisions in Public Organizations. *Ind. Relat.*, February 1969, *8*(2), pp. 174–84. **[G: U.S.]**

Green, Christopher and Tella, Alfred. Effect of Nonemployment Income and Wage Rates on the Work Incentives of the Poor. *Rev. Econ. Statist.*, November 1969, *51*(4), pp. 399–408. **[G: U.S.]**

Gross, Andrew C. Patterns and Determinants of Income of Canadian Engineering Graduates. *Ind. Lab. Relat. Rev.*, October 1969, *23*(1), pp. 52–64. **[G: Canada]**

Hamermesh, Daniel S. A Disaggregative Econometric Model of Gross Changes in Employment. *Yale Econ. Essays*, Fall 1969, *9*(2), pp. 107–45. **[G: U.S.]**

Hendon, William S. Faculty Compensation and the Cost of Living. *Soc. Sci. Quart.*, September 1969, *50*(2), pp. 396–400. **[G: U.S.]**

Hettenhouse, George W. and Lewellen, Wilbur G. The Taxation of Restricted Stock Compensation Plans. *Nat. Tax J.*, September 1969, *22*(3), pp. 368–78. **[G: U.S.]**

Holland, Daniel M. Pension Fund Growth and Its Economic Implications. **In** *Tax Institute of America*, 1969, pp. 3–33. **[G: U.S.]**

Holtmann, A. G. Teacher Salaries and the Economic Benefits of Search. *J. Human Res.*, Winter 1969, *4*(1), pp. 99–103.

Houff, James N. Area Wages and Living Costs. *Mon. Lab. Rev.,* March 1969, *92*(3), pp. 43–46. **[G: U.S.]**

Hubbard, Russell H. The Role of Government Regulation. **In** *Tax Institute of America,* 1969, pp. 180–85. **[G: U.S.]**

Ivan'kov, M. Wages of Collective Farm Managerial Personnel and Specialists and the Matter of Increasing the Effectiveness of Production. *Prob. Econ.,* July 1969, *12*(3), pp. 58–82. **[G: U.S.S.R.]**

Kaufman, G. M. and Penchansky, R. Simulation of Union Health and Welfare Funds. **In** *Siegel, A. J., ed.,* 1969, pp. 121–75. **[G: U.S.]**

Kinyon, John. A Report on Wage Developments in Manufacturing, 1968. *Mon. Lab. Rev.,* August 1969, *92*(8), pp. 33–39. **[G: U.S.]**

Knight, K. G. The Baking Industry. **In** *Lerner, S. W.; Cable, J. R. and Gupta, S., eds.,* 1969, pp. 199–243. **[G: U.K.]**

Knowles, K. G. J. C. and Robinson, D. Wage Movements in Coventry. *Bull. Oxford Univ. Inst. Econ. Statist.,* February 1969, *31*(1), pp. 1–21. **[G: U.K.]**

Knowles, K. G. J. C. and Robinson, D. Wage Movements in Coventry—Appendix II. *Bull. Oxford Univ. Inst. Econ. Statist.,* May 1969, *31*(2), pp. 145–52. **[G: U.K.]**

Kudrna, A. Differentiation in Earnings. *Eastern Europ. Econ.,* Summer 1969, *7*(4), pp. 25–37. **[G: Czechoslovakia]**

Kunel'skii, L. The Socioeconomic Significance of Raising the Minimum Wage. *Prob. Econ.,* July 1969, *12*(3), pp. 43–57. **[G: U.S.S.R.]**

Lewellen, Wilbur G. Management and Ownership in the Large Firm. *J. Finance,* May 1969, *24*(2), pp. 299–322. **[G: U.S.]**

Lewellen, Wilbur G. Tax Minimization and Executive Compensation Plans. **In** *Tax Institute of America,* 1969, pp. 104–17. **[G: U.S.]**

Lewis, L. Earl. Federal Pay Comparability Procedures. *Mon. Lab. Rev.,* February 1969, *92*(2), pp. 10–13. **[G: U.S.]**

Li-tien, Feng and Chien, Wen. A Quantitative Analysis of the Relationship Between the Rate of Growth of Productivity and the Average Wage. *Chinese Econ. Stud.,* Fall 1969, *3*(1), pp. 70–91. **[G: China]**

Loznevaia, M. Mathematical Methods in Planning Wages. *Prob. Econ.,* June 1969, *12*(2), pp. 48–66. **[G: U.S.S.R.]**

Lukaczer, Moses. The Farm Wage Worker in the Social Security Program: An Introduction to His Earnings Profile. *J. Risk Ins.,* March 1969, *36*(1), pp. 103–15. **[G: U.S.]**

Lunden, Leon E. Bargaining in Major Symphony Orchestras. *Mon. Lab. Rev.,* July 1969, *92*(7), pp. 15–19. **[G: U.S.]**

Lundgren, Earl F. and Myers, Doyle F. A Survey of Foremen Incentive Systems in Wisconsin. *Marquette Bus. Rev.,* Spring 1969, *13*(1), pp. 1–10.

Masters, Stanley H. An Interindustry Analysis of Wages and Plant Size. *Rev. Econ. Statist.,* August 1969, *51*(3), pp. 341–45. **[G: U.S.]**

Masui, Yukio. The Supply Price of Labor: Farm Family Workers. **In** *Ohkawa, K.; Johnston, B. F. and Kaneda, H., eds.,* 1969, pp. 222–49. **[G: Japan]**

McClung, Nelson. The Economics of Pension Finance. *J. Risk Ins.,* September 1969, *36*(4), pp. 425–32.

McGill, Dan M. Critical Issues in Pension Planning. **In** *Tax Institute of America,* 1969, pp. 167–71. **[G: U.S.]**

Metzger, Bert L. Insurance Industry Begins to Court Profit Sharing Funds with Equity-Based Products. *J. Risk Ins.,* September 1969, *36*(4), pp. 437–45. **[G: U.S.]**

Mouly, Jean. Changing Concepts of Wage Policy. *Int. Lab. Rev.,* July 1969, *100*(1), pp. 1–22.

Muthuchidambaram, S. P. Factors Determining Earnings of Selected Blue Collar Workers in India and Japan. **In** *Somers, G. G., ed. (II),* 1969, pp. 337–47. **[G: India; Japan]**

Ozsvald, László. Incentives for Management Personnel in Hungarian Industry. *Int. Lab. Rev.,* September 1969, *100*(3), pp. 257–72. **[G: Hungary]**

Peitchinis, S. G. Occupational Wage Differentials in Canada 1939–1965. *Australian Econ. Pap.,* June 1969, *8*(12), pp. 20–40. **[G: Canada]**

Pursell, Donald E. The Impact of the South African Wage Board on Skilled/Unskilled Wage Differentials. *East Afr. Econ. Rev.,* June 1969, *1*(1), pp. 73–81. **[G: S. Africa]**

Raimon, Robert L. and Stoikov, Vladimir. The Effect of Blue-Collar Unionism on White-Collar Earnings. *Ind. Lab. Relat. Rev.,* April 1969, *22*(3), pp. 358–74. **[G: U.S.]**

Ramachandran, V. A. Fringe Benefit and Its Role in Productivity. **In** *Johri, C. K., ed.,* 1969, pp. 302–20. **[G: India]**

Rees, Albert. Spatial Wage Differentials in a Large City Labor Market. **In** *Somers, G. G., ed. (II),* 1969, pp. 237–47. **[G: U.S.]**

Rose, Arthur. Wage Differentials in the Building Trades. *Mon. Lab. Rev.,* October 1969, *92*(10), pp. 14–17. **[G: U.S.]**

Sawhney, P. K. Inter-Industry Wage Differentials in India. *Indian Econ. J.,* July–September 1969, *17*(1), pp. 28–56. **[G: India]**

Schweitzer, Stuart O. Factors Determining the Interindustry Structure of Wages. *Ind. Lab. Relat. Rev.,* January 1969, *22*(2), pp. 217–25. **[G: U.S.]**

Scoville, James G. Remuneration in Afghan Industry. *Int. Lab. Rev.,* April 1969, *99*(4), pp. 381–400. **[G: Afghanistan]**

Scully, Gerald W. Interstate Wage Differentials: A Cross Section Analysis. *Amer. Econ. Rev.,* December 1969, *59*(5), pp. 757–73. **[G: U.S.]**

Smith, Dan Throop. The Effects of Taxation of Executive Compensation on Economic Activity. **In** *Tax Institute of America,* 1969, pp. 34–43. **[G: U.S.]**

Sproull, Mary. A Report on Salary Changes for Teachers in Urban Areas. *Mon. Lab. Rev.,* April 1969, *92*(4), pp. 49–52.

Stelluto, George L. Report on Incentive Pay in Manufacturing Industries. *Mon. Lab. Rev.,* July 1969, *92*(7), pp. 49–53. **[G: U.S.]**

Umezawa, Tadashi and Honjo, Masahiko. Company Housing in Japan. *Int. Lab. Rev.,* June 1969, *99*(6), pp. 579–87. **[G: Japan]**

Usher, Dan. Income as a Measure of Productivity: A Reply. *Economica, N.S.,* August 1969, *36*(143), pp. 317–20. **[G: Thailand]**

Vanderbeek, Robert E. Auto Insurance as a Fringe Benefit. *J. Risk Ins.*, September 1969, *36*(4), pp. 481–85.

Verma, Pramod. The Chemical Industry. **In** *Lerner, S. W.; Cable, J. R. and Gupta, S., eds.*, 1969, pp. 95–157. **[G: U.K.]**

Waldman, Elizabeth. Employment Status of School Age Youth. *Mon. Lab. Rev.*, August 1969, *92*(8), pp. 23–32. **[G: U.S.]**

Warren, W. M. Urban Real Wages and the Nigerian Trade Union Movement, 1939–60: Rejoinder. *Econ. Develop. Cult. Change*, July 1969, *17*(4), pp. 618–33. **[G: Nigeria]**

Willacy, Hazel M. Men in Poverty Neighborhoods: A Status Report. *Mon. Lab. Rev.*, February 1969, *92*(2), pp. 23–27. **[G: U.S.]**

Willis, E. S. and Kaimer, Fred R. Employee Benefit Options. **In** *Somers, G. G., ed. (II)*, 1969, pp. 317–25. **[G: U.S.]**

8243 Employment Studies; Unemployment and Vacancies

Andrews, Edith Wall and Moylan, Maurice. Scientific and Professional Employment by State Governments. *Mon. Lab. Rev.*, August 1969, *92*(8), pp. 40–45. **[G: U.S.]**

Aventur, Jacques. Origine et nature du chômage dans l'économie française. (Origin and Nature of Unemployment in the French Economy. With English summary.) *Rivista Int. Sci. Econ. Com.*, April 1969, *16*(4), pp. 342–62. **[G: France]**

Beier, Emerson H. Financing Supplemental Unemployment Benefit Plans. *Mon. Lab. Rev.*, November 1969, *92*(11), pp. 31–35. **[G: U.S.]**

Blackburn, John O. An Optimal Unemployment Rate: Comment. *Quart. J. Econ.*, August 1969, *83*(3), pp. 518–20.

Bowman, Charles T. Report on Employment Related to Exports. *Mon. Lab. Rev.*, June 1969, *92*(6), pp. 16–20. **[G: U.S.]**

Cambern, John R. and Newton, David A. Skill Transfers: Can Defense Workers Adapt to Civilian Occupations? *Mon. Lab. Rev.*, June 1969, *92*(6), pp. 21–25. **[G: U.S.]**

Campbell, Colin D. and Campbell, Rosemary G. State Minimum Wage Laws as a Cause of Unemployment. *Southern Econ. J.*, April 1969, *35*(4), pp. 323–32. **[G: U.S.]**

Corner, D. C. and Fletcher, C. H. Some Effects of Selective Employment Tax on the Construction and Service Industries. *Bull. Oxford Univ. Inst. Econ. Statist.*, February 1969, *31*(1), pp. 47–54. **[G: U.K.]**

Dasgupta, Partha S. On the Optimum Rate of Accumulation in a Labour-Surplus Economy. *Indian Econ. J.*, January–March 1969, *16*(3), pp. 277–311.

Dempsey, Richard E. and Schmude, Douglas F. How Consumer Spending for Automobiles Creates Jobs. *Mon. Lab. Rev.*, March 1969, *92*(3), pp. 33–36. **[G: U.S.]**

Dobell, A. Rodney. An Optimal Unemployment Rate: Reply. *Quart. J. Econ.*, August 1969, *83*(3), pp. 521–23.

Dovring, Folke. Underemployment in Agriculture: A Rejoinder. *Econ. Develop. Cult. Change*, January 1969, *17*(2), pp. 273–76. **[G: Greece]**

Eddleman, B. R. Estimating the Effects of Resource Development Programs on Regional Employment. *Amer. J. Agr. Econ.*, December 1969, *51*(5), pp. 1434–41. **[G: U.S.]**

Flaim, Paul O. Persons Not in the Labor Force: Who They Are and Why They Don't Work. *Mon. Lab. Rev.*, July 1969, *92*(7), pp. 3–14. **[G: U.S.]**

Fulco, Lawrence J. How Mechanization of Harvesting Is Affecting Jobs. *Mon. Lab. Rev.*, March 1969, *92*(3), pp. 26–32. **[G: U.S.]**

Gallaway, Lowell E. A Note on the Incidence of Hidden Unemployment in the United States. *Western Econ. J.*, March 1969, *7*(1), pp. 71–83. **[G: U.S.]**

Gallaway, Lowell E. Unemployment Levels among Nonwhite Teen-agers. *J. Bus.*, July 1969, *42*(3), pp. 265–76. **[G: U.S.]**

Glade, William P. The Employment Question and Development Policies in Latin America. *J. Econ. Issues*, September 1969, *3*(3), pp. 43–62. **[G: Latin America]**

Gray, Irwin. Employment Effect of a New Industry in a Rural Area. *Mon. Lab. Rev.*, June 1969, *92*(6), pp. 26–30. **[G: U.S.]**

Green, Gloria P. Comparing Employment Estimates from Household and Payroll Surveys. *Mon. Lab. Rev.*, December 1969, *92*(12), pp. 9–20. **[G: U.S.]**

Gujarati, Damodar. Cyclical Behavior of Help-Wanted Index and the Unemployment Rate. *Rev. Econ. Statist.*, November 1969, *51*(4), pp. 482–84. **[G: U.S.]**

Hamermesh, Daniel S. Spectral Analysis of the Relation between Gross Employment Changes and Output Changes, 1958–1966. *Rev. Econ. Statist.*, February 1969, *51*(1), pp. 62–69. **[G: U.S.]**

Hansen, Bent. Employment and Wages in Rural Egypt. *Amer. Econ. Rev.*, June 1969, *59*(3), pp. 298–313. **[G: Egypt]**

Harris, John R. and Todaro, Michael P. Wages, Industrial Employment and Labour Productivity: The Kenyan Experience. *East Afr. Econ. Rev.*, June 1969, *1*(1), pp. 29–46. **[G: Kenya]**

Hilaski, Harvey J. and Willacy, Hazel M. Employment Patterns and Place of Residence. *Mon. Lab. Rev.*, October 1969, *92*(10), pp. 18–25. **[G: U.S.]**

Hodge, Claire C. The Negro Job Situation: Has It Improved? *Mon. Lab. Rev.*, January 1969, *92*(1), pp. 20–28. **[G: U.S.]**

Hoyle, Kathryn D. Job Losers, Leavers, and Entrants—A Report on the Unemployed. *Mon. Lab. Rev.*, April 1969, *92*(4), pp. 24–29. **[G: U.S.]**

Hoyt, Homer. Importance of Manufacturing in Basic Employment. *Land Econ.*, August 1969, *45*(3), pp. 344–49. **[G: U.S.]**

Jeffrey, D.; Casetti, E. and King, L. Economic Fluctuations in a Multiregional Setting: A Bi-factor Analytic Approach. *J. Reg. Sci.*, December 1969, *9*(3), pp. 397–404. **[G: U.S.]**

Jensen, Vernon H. Decasualizing a Labor Market: The Longshore Experience. **In** *Siegel, A. J., ed.*, 1969, pp. 226–59. **[G: U.S.]**

Kelley, Allen C. and Weiss, Leonard W. Markov Processes and Economic Analysis: The Case of Migration. *Econometrica*, April 1969, *37*(2), pp. 280–97.

Koot, Ronald S. Wage Changes, Unemployment,

and Inflation in Chile. *Ind. Lab. Relat. Rev.*, July 1969, *22*(4), pp. 568–75. **[G: Chile]**

Kulshreshtha, S. N. Part-Time Farming in Ontario Agriculture. *Can. J. Agr. Econ.*, February 1969, *17* (1), pp. 151–56. **[G: Canada]**

Lurie, Melvin and Rayack, Elton. Employment Opportunities for Negro Families in "Satellite" Cities. *Southern Econ. J.*, October 1969, *36*(2), pp. 191–95. **[G: U.S.]**

Maevskii, I. Socioeconomic Questions Relating to Automation. *Prob. Econ.*, October 1969, *12*(6), pp. 3–26.

Mazek, Warren F. Unemployment and the Efficacy of Migration: The Case of Laborers. *J. Reg. Sci.*, April 1969, *9*(1), pp. 101–07. **[G: U.S.]**

Molander, Ahti. Inflaatiotutkimuksen vaiheista ja ongelmista. (Phases and Problems of Inflation Research. With English summary.) *Kansant. Aikak.*, 1969, *65*(4), pp. 269–73.

Mooney, Joseph D. Housing Segregation, Negro Employment and Metropolitan Decentralization: An Alternative Perspective. *Quart. J. Econ.*, May 1969, *83*(2), pp. 299–311. **[G: U.S.]**

Newsom, Robert T. Metropolitan and Nonmetropolitan Employment Changes: The Case of Texas. *Soc. Sci. Quart.*, September 1969, *50*(2), pp. 354–68. **[G: U.S.]**

Northrup, Herbert R. The Negro in Aerospace Work. *Calif. Manage. Rev.*, Summer 1969, *11*(4), pp. 11–26. **[G: U.S.]**

O'Boyle, Edward J. Job Tenure: How It Relates to Race and Age. *Mon. Lab. Rev.*, September 1969, *92*(9), pp. 16–23. **[G: U.S.]**

Pack, Howard and Todaro, Michael P. Technological Transfer, Labour Absorption, and Economic Development. *Oxford Econ. Pap.*, November 1969, *21*(3), pp. 395–403.

Pepelasis, A. Underemployment in Agriculture: A Comment. *Econ. Develop. Cult. Change*, January 1969, *17*(2), pp. 267–72. **[G: Greece]**

Perrella, Vera C. Employment of High School Graduates and Dropouts. *Mon. Lab. Rev.*, June 1969, *92*(6), pp. 36–43. **[G: U.S.]**

Robinson, Warren C. "Disguised" Unemployment Once Again: East Pakistan, 1951–1961. *Amer. J. Agr. Econ.*, August 1969, *51*(3), pp. 592–604. **[G: E. Pakistan]**

Robinson, Warren C. Types of Disguised Rural Unemployment and Some Policy Implications. *Oxford Econ. Pap.*, November 1969, *21*(3), pp. 373–86.

Rothberg, Herman J. A Study of the Impact of Office Automation in the IRS. *Mon. Lab. Rev.*, October 1969, *92*(10), pp. 26–30. **[G: U.S.]**

Rowan, Richard L. Negro Employment in the Basic Steel Industry. *Ind. Lab. Relat. Rev.*, October 1969, *23*(1), pp. 29–39. **[G: U.S.]**

Russell, Joe L. and Pilot, Michael J. Seasonality in Construction: A Continuing Problem. *Mon. Lab. Rev.*, December 1969, *92*(12), pp. 3–8. **[G: U.S.]**

Sawers, Larry. Unemployment and the Structure of Labor Demand. *Rev. Radical Polit. Econ.*, May 1969, *1*(1), pp. 56–74. **[G: U.S.]**

Schmidt, Fred H. Job Caste in the Southwest. *Ind. Relat.*, October 1969, *9*(1), pp. 100–110. **[G: U.S.]**

Shrimali, P. D. Pattern of Employment and Earnings Among University Graduates in Lucknow, India. *Ind. Lab. Relat. Rev.*, January 1969, *22*(2), pp. 249–56. **[G: India]**

Stern, James L. Evolution of Private Manpower Planning in Armour's Plant Closings. *Mon. Lab. Rev.*, December 1969, *92*(12), pp. 21–28. **[G: U.S.]**

Sufrin, Sidney C. and Wagner, Abraham R. Disaggregate Employment: The Search for Short Run Demand and Labor Market Stability. *Rivista Int. Sci. Econ. Com.*, October 1969, *16*(10), pp. 965–92. **[G: U.S.]**

Talbot, Joseph E., Jr. An Analysis of 1968 Changes in Wages and Benefits. *Mon. Lab. Rev.*, July 1969, *92*(7), pp. 43–48. **[G: U.S.]**

Thirlwall, A. P. Okun's Law and the Natural Rate of Growth. *Southern Econ. J.*, July 1969, *36*(1), pp. 87–89. **[G: U.S.; U.K.]**

Thirlwall, A. P. Types of Unemployment: With Special Reference to 'Non Demand-Deficient' Unemployment in Great Britain. *Scot. J. Polit. Econ.*, February 1969, *16*(1), pp. 20–49. **[G: U.K.]**

Uppal, J. S. Measurement of Disguised Unemployment in an Underdeveloped Economy—An Economic Approach. *Asian Econ. Rev.*, August 1969, *11*(4), pp. 405–11. **[G: India]**

Wabe, J. S. Labour Force Participation Rates in the London Metropolitan Region. *J. Roy. Statist. Soc.*, Part 2, 1969, *132*, pp. 245–64. **[G: U.K.]**

White, Rudolph A. Measuring Unemployment and Subemployment in the Mississippi Delta. *Mon. Lab. Rev.*, April 1969, *92*(4), pp. 17–23. **[G: U.S.]**

Zaidi, Mahmood A. Structural Unemployment, Labor Market Efficiency and the Intrafactor Allocation Mechanism in the United States and Canada. *Southern Econ. J.*, January 1969, *35*(3), pp. 205–13. **[G: U.S.; Canada]**

Zeisel, Rose N. The Workweek for Production Workers in the Private Economy. *Surv. Curr. Bus.*, September 1969, *49*(9), pp. 21–26. **[G: U.S.]**

825 Labor Productivity

8250 Labor Productivity

Barzel, Yoram. The Growth of Sales *Per* Man-Hour in Retail Trade, 1929–1963: Discussion. **In** *Fuchs, V. R., ed.*, 1969, pp. 230–33. **[G: U.S.]**

Behrend, Hilde; Knowles, Ann and Davies, Jean. 'Have You Heard the Phrase "Productivity Agreements"?' Findings from Two National Sample Surveys. *Scot. J. Polit. Econ.*, November 1969, *16*(3), pp. 256–70. **[G: U.K.]**

Brewster, Havelock. The Pattern of Change in Wages, Prices and Productivity in British Guiana, 1948 to 1962. *Soc. Econ. Stud.*, June 1969, *18*(2), pp. 107–36. **[G: British Guiana]**

Chukwumah, P. A. L. Developments in the Search for Higher Productivity. **In** *Yesufu, T. M., ed.*, 1969, pp. 300–312. **[G: Africa]**

D'Iribarne, Alain. Les besoins d'emploi des entreprises. (With English summary.) *Revue Écon.*, July 1969, *20*(4), pp. 601–57.

Denison, Edward F. The Contribution of Education

to the Quality of Labor: Comment. *Amer. Econ. Rev.*, December 1969, *59*(5), pp. 935–43. [G: U.S.]

Fabricant, Solomon and Hirsch, Werner Z. Some Problems in the Measurement of Productivity in the Medical Care Industry: Comment. **In** *Fuchs, V. R., ed.*, 1969, pp. 146–47. [G: U.S.]

George, K. D. Productivity in the Distributive Trades. *Bull. Oxford Univ. Inst. Econ. Statist.*, May 1969, *31*(2), pp. 61–75. [G: U.K.]

Gorman, John A. Alternative Measures of the Real Output and Productivity of Commercial Banks. **In** *Fuchs, V. R., ed.*, 1969, pp. 155–89. [G: U.S.]

Gujarati, Damodar. Labor's Share in Manufacturing Industries, 1949–64. *Ind. Lab. Relat. Rev.*, October 1969, *23*(1), pp. 65–77. [G: U.S.]

Hamermesh, Daniel S. A Disaggregative Econometric Model of Gross Changes in Employment. *Yale Econ. Essays*, Fall 1969, *9*(2), pp. 107–45. [G: U.S.]

Harris, John R. and Todaro, Michael P. Wages, Industrial Employment and Labour Productivity: The Kenyan Experience. *East Afr. Econ. Rev.*, June 1969, *1*(1), pp. 29–46. [G: Kenya]

Henneberger, John E. Productivity Rises as Radio-TV Output Triples in 8 Years. *Mon. Lab. Rev.*, March 1969, *92*(3), pp. 40–42. [G: U.S.]

Herman, Shelby W. and Fulco, Lawrence J. Productivity and Unit Labor Costs in 1968. *Mon. Lab. Rev.*, June 1969, *92*(6), pp. 11–15. [G: U.S.]

Hodgman, Donald R. Alternative Measures of the Real Output and Productivity of Commercial Banks: Discussion. **In** *Fuchs, V. R., ed.*, 1969, pp. 189–95. [G: U.S.]

Ivan'kov, M. Wages of Collective Farm Managerial Personnel and Specialists and the Matter of Increasing the Effectiveness of Production. *Prob. Econ.*, July 1969, *12*(3), pp. 58–82. [G: U.S.S.R.]

Jackman, Patrick C. Unit Labor Costs of Iron and Steel Industries in Five Countries. *Mon. Lab. Rev.*, August 1969, *92*(8), pp. 15–22. [G: W. Germany; France; U.K.; U.S.; Japan]

Kaplan, I. I. The Influence of Education on Labor Output. **In** *Noah, H. J., ed.*, 1969, pp. 101–13. [G: U.S.S.R.]

Kapustin, E. I. Training Personnel and Comparing Types of Labor. **In** *Noah, H. J., ed.*, 1969, pp. 63–74. [G: U.S.S.R.]

Keating, M. Employment and the Growth of Australian Gross National Product. *Econ. Rec.*, March 1969, *45*(109), pp. 27–47. [G: Australia]

Kendrick, John W. An Evaluation of Productivity Statistics. **In** *Somers, G. G., ed. (II)*, 1969, pp. 129–35. [G: U.S.]

Klarman, Herbert E. and Feldstein, Martin S. Some Problems in the Measurement of Productivity in the Medical Care Industry: Discussion. **In** *Fuchs, V. R., ed.*, 1969, pp. 132–46. [G: U.S.]

Kravis, Irving B. and Liu, Ta-Chung. What Is Output? Problems of Concept and Measurement: Discussion. **In** *Fuchs, V. R., ed.*, 1969, pp. 84–94.

Kunnas, Heikki J. EFO-tutkimus. (EFO Survey. With English summary.) *Kansant. Aikak.*, 1969, *65*(3), pp. 206–13. [G: Sweden]

Kux, Jaroslav; Mairesse, Jacques and Drechsler, László. Labour Productivity Comparison between Czechoslovakia and France. *Rev. Income Wealth*, September 1969, *15*(3), pp. 219–28. [G: Czechoslovakia; France]

Li-tien, Feng and Chien, Wen. A Quantitative Analysis of the Relationship Between the Rate of Growth of Productivity and the Average Wage. *Chinese Econ. Stud.*, Fall 1969, *3*(1), pp. 70–91. [G: China]

Loftus, P. J. Labour's Share in Manufacturing. *Lloyds Bank Rev.*, April 1969, (92), pp. 15–25.

Mikulich, A. P. The Influence of Different Levels of Education on Labor Productivity: A Calculation. **In** *Noah, H. J., ed.*, 1969, pp. 132–40. [G: U.S.S.R.]

Myslicki, Chester. Report on Productivity Increases in the Auto Industry. *Mon. Lab. Rev.*, March 1969, *92*(3), pp. 37–39. [G: U.S.]

Palmerio, Giovanni. Economie di scala e progresso tecnico incorporato nel settore industriale in Italia nel periodo 1951–1965. (Economies of Scale and Embodied Technical Progress in the Italian Industry—1951–1965. With English summary.) *L'Industria*, July–September 1969, (3), pp. 316–46. [G: Italy]

Phipps, Anthony J. The Roles of Labour Productivity and Demand in the Pricing Process: An Inter-Industry Study Using Time-Series Data. *Bull. Oxford Univ. Inst. Econ. Statist.*, November 1969, *31*(4), pp. 285–301. [G: U.K.]

Ramachandran, V. A. Fringe Benefit and Its Role in Productivity. **In** *Johri, C. K., ed.*, 1969, pp. 302–20. [G: India]

Reder, M. W. Some Problems in the Measurement of Productivity in the Medical Care Industry: Reply. **In** *Fuchs, V. R., ed.*, 1969, pp. 148–53. [G: U.S.]

Reder, M. W. Some Problems in the Measurement of Productivity in the Medical Care Industry. **In** *Fuchs, V. R., ed.*, 1969, pp. 95–131. [G: U.S.]

Schwartzman, David. The Contribution of Education to the Quality of Labor: Reply. *Amer. Econ. Rev.*, December 1969, *59*(5), pp. 944–46. [G: U.S.]

Schwartzman, David. The Growth of Sales *Per* Man-Hour in Retail Trade, 1929–1963. **In** *Fuchs, V. R., ed.*, 1969, pp. 201–29. [G: U.S.]

Schwartzman, David. The Growth of Sales *Per* Man-Hour in Retail Trade, 1929–1963: Reply. **In** *Fuchs, V. R., ed.*, 1969, pp. 233–35. [G: U.S.]

Scully, Gerald W. Human Capital and Productivity in U.S. Manufacturing. *Western Econ. J.*, December 1969, *7*(4), pp. 334–40. [G: U.S.]

Sheriff, Don R. and West, Jude P. The Changing Motivational Patterns of Professional Personnel. **In** *Gilroy, T. P., ed.*, 1969, pp. 9–17.

Spasibenko, S. G. Labor Productivity and Worker Qualifications. **In** *Noah, H. J., ed.*, 1969, pp. 119–31. [G: U.S.S.R.]

Terleckyj, Nestor E. and Fabricant, Solomon. Alternative Measures of the Real Output and Productivity of Commercial Banks: Comment. **In** *Fuchs, V. R., ed.*, 1969, pp. 195–99. [G: U.S.]

Terleckyj, Nestor E. The Service Industries in Canada, 1946–66: Discussion. **In** *Fuchs, V. R., ed.*, 1969, pp. 282–86. [G: Canada]

Thakur, C. P. Obstacles to Productivity. **In** *Johri, C. K., ed.*, 1969, pp. 287–301. [G: India]

Treadway, Arthur B. What Is Output? Problems of Concept and Measurement. In *Fuchs, V. R., ed.*, 1969, pp. 53–84.

Usher, Dan. Income as a Measure of Productivity: A Reply. *Economica, N.S.*, August 1969, *36*(143), pp. 317–20. **[G: Thailand]**

Vasilev, Dimitur. The International Socialist Division of Labor and Its Role in the Increased Profitability of Bulgaria's Foreign Trade. *Eastern Europ. Econ.*, Fall 1969, *8*(1), pp. 90–99. **[G: Bulgaria]**

Weinberg, Edgar. Reducing Skill Shortages in Construction. *Mon. Lab. Rev.*, February 1969, *92*(2), pp. 3–9. **[G: U.S.]**

Wolf, S. K. Concepts and Measurement of Productivity in Developing Economies. In *Yesufu, T. M., ed.*, 1969, pp. 279–99. **[G: Nigeria]**

Worton, David A. The Service Industries in Canada, 1946–66. In *Fuchs, V. R., ed.*, 1969, pp. 237–82. **[G: Canada]**

Zhil'tsov, E. N. Statistical Methods of Evaluating the Complexity of Labor. In *Noah, H. J., ed.*, 1969, pp. 75–86. **[G: U.S.S.R.]**

826 Labor Markets: Demographic Characteristics

8260 Labor Markets: Demographic Characteristics

Ahearn, Frederick L., Jr. Correlates of Job Status Among Indigenous Nonprofessionals in Community Action Programs. *Soc. Sci. Quart.*, December 1969, *50*(3), pp. 668–75. **[G: U.S.]**

Ambannavar, Jaipal P. Upward Occupational Mobility Through Education and Age. *Asian Econ. Rev.*, May 1969, *11*(3), pp. 290–99. **[G: India]**

Blevins, Audie L., Jr. Migration Rates in Twelve Southern Metropolitan Areas: A "Push-Pull" Analysis. *Soc. Sci. Quart.*, September 1969, *50*(2), pp. 337–53. **[G: U.S.]**

Bogan, Forrest A. Work Experience of the Population: Spotlight on Women and Youths. *Mon. Lab. Rev.*, June 1969, *92*(6), pp. 44–50. **[G: U.S.]**

Brozen, Yale. The Effect of Statutory Minimum Wage Increases on Teen-Age Employment. *J. Law Econ.*, April 1969, *12*(1), pp. 109–22. **[G: U.S.]**

Cain, Glen G. and Mincer, Jacob. Urban Poverty and Labor Force Participation: Comment. *Amer. Econ. Rev.*, March 1969, *59*(1), pp. 185–94. **[G: U.S.]**

Cohen, Malcolm S. Married Women in the Labor Force: An Analysis of Participation Rates. *Mon. Lab. Rev.*, October 1969, *92*(10), pp. 31–35. **[G: U.S.]**

Ford, William Freithaler and Tollison, Robert. Note on the Color of the Volunteer Army. *Soc. Sci. Quart.*, December 1969, *50*(3), pp. 544–47. **[G: U.S.]**

Hilaski, Harvey J. and Willacy, Hazel M. Employment Patterns and Place of Residence. *Mon. Lab. Rev.*, October 1969, *92*(10), pp. 18–25. **[G: U.S.]**

Katzman, Martin T. Opportunity, Subculture and the Economic Performance of Urban Ethnic Groups. *Amer. J. Econ. Soc.*, October 1969, *28*(4), pp. 351–66. **[G: U.S.]**

Kpedekpo, G. M. K. On Working Life Tables in Ghana with Particular Reference to the Female Working Population. *J. Roy. Statist. Soc.*, Part 3, 1969, *132*, pp. 431–41. **[G: Ghana]**

Kpedekpo, G. M. K. Working Life Tables for Males in Ghana 1960. *J. Amer. Statist. Assoc.*, March 1969, *64*(325), pp. 102–10. **[G: Ghana]**

Maton, J. Experience on the Job and Formal Training as Alternative Means of Skill Acquisition: An Empirical Study. *Int. Lab. Rev.*, September 1969, *100*(3), pp. 239–55. **[G: Belgium; Argentina]**

Montanari, Antonio. A propositio di sociologia e storia del lavoro femminile. (With English summary.) *Statistica*, October-December 1969, *29*(4), pp. 803–21. **[G: Italy]**

Mooney, Joseph D. Urban Poverty and Labor Force Participation: Reply. *Amer. Econ. Rev.*, March 1969, *59*(1), pp. 194–98. **[G: U.S.]**

Schmidt, Fred H. Job Caste in the Southwest. *Ind. Relat.*, October 1969, *9*(1), pp. 100–110. **[G: U.S.]**

Scully, Gerald W. Human Capital and Productivity in U.S. Manufacturing. *Western Econ. J.*, December 1969, *7*(4), pp. 334–40. **[G: U.S.]**

Shepherd, William G. Market Power and Racial Discrimination in White Collar Employment. *Antitrust Bull.*, Spring 1969, *14*, pp. 141–61. **[G: U.S.]**

Sufrin, Sidney C. and Wagner, Abraham R. Disaggregate Employment: The Search for Short Run Demand and Labor Market Stability. *Rivista Int. Sci. Econ. Com.*, October 1969, *16*(10), pp. 965–92. **[G: U.S.]**

Tarver, James D. Migration Differentials in Southern Cities and Suburbs. *Soc. Sci. Quart.*, September 1969, *50*(2), pp. 298–324. **[G: U.S.]**

Thiesenhusen, William C. Population Growth and Agricultural Employment in Latin America, with Some U.S. Comparisons. *Amer. J. Agr. Econ.*, November 1969, *51*(4), pp. 735–52. **[G: Latin America; U.S.]**

Thormann, Peter H. Employment and Earnings in Portugal, 1953–1967. *Int. Lab. Rev.*, June 1969, *99*(6), pp. 589–606. **[G: Portugal]**

Tyrchniewicz, Edward W. and Schuh, G. Edward. Econometric Analysis of the Agricultural Labor Market. *Amer. J. Agr. Econ.*, November 1969, *51* (4), pp. 770–87. **[G: U.S.]**

Wabe, J. S. Labour Force Participation Rates in the London Metropolitan Region. *J. Roy. Statist. Soc.*, Part 2, 1969, *132*, pp. 245–64. **[G: U.K.]**

Weller, Robert H. Role Conflict and Fertility. *Soc. Econ. Stud.*, September 1969, *18*(3), pp. 263–72.

Yancey, William L. Intervention as a Strategy of Social Inquiry: An Exploratory Study with Unemployed Negro Men. *Soc. Sci. Quart.*, December 1969, *50*(3), pp. 582–88. **[G: U.S.]**

830 Trade Unions; Collective Bargaining; Labor Management Relations

831 Trade Unions

8310 Trade Unions

Aaron, Benjamin. Individual Employee Rights and Union Democracy. In *Somers, G. G., ed. (II),*

1969, pp. 275–82. [G: U.S.]

Ali, Aamir. Fifty Years of the ILO and Asia. *Int. Lab. Rev.,* March 1969, *99*(3), pp. 347–61.

Ashenfelter, Orley and Pencavel, John H. American Trade Union Growth: 1900–1960. *Quart. J. Econ.,* August 1969, *83*(3), pp. 434–48. [G: U.S.]

Ashenfelter, Orley and Johnson, George E. Bargaining Theory, Trade Unions, and Industrial Strike Activity. *Amer. Econ. Rev.,* March 1969, *59*(1), pp. 35–49. [G: U.S.]

Baer, Walter E. Arbitrating the Discharge and Discipline of Union Officials. *Mon. Lab. Rev.,* September 1969, *92*(9), pp. 39–45.

Bakke, E. Wight. Union Leadership and the Public Interest. **In** *Somers, G. G., ed. (II),* 1969, pp. 173–82. [G: U.S.]

Barbash, Jack. Federal Regulation and the Unions: Discussion. **In** *Somers, G. G., ed. (II),* 1969, pp. 303–05. [G: U.S.]

Barbash, Jack. Rationalization in the American Union. **In** *Somers, G. G., ed. (I),* 1969, pp. 147–62. [G: U.S.]

Barkin, Solomon. Trade Unions Face a New Western Capitalist Society. *J. Econ. Issues,* March 1969, *3* (1), pp. 49–65.

Barkin, Solomon and Blum, Albert A. What's to Be Done for Labor? The Trade Unionists' Answer. **In** *Wortman, M. S., Jr.,* 1969, pp. 73–81. [G: U.S.]

Berg, Elliot J. Urban Real Wages and the Nigerian Trade Union Movement, 1939–60: A Comment. *Econ. Develop. Cult. Change,* July 1969, *17*(4), pp. 604–17. [G: Nigeria]

Bienefeld, M. A. The Normal Week under Collective Bargaining. *Economica, N.S.,* May 1969, *36* (142), pp. 172–92.

Blumrosen, Alfred W. A Survey of Remedies for Discrimination in the Union and on the Job. **In** *Somers, G. G., ed. (II),* 1969, pp. 283–91. [G: U.S.]

Caballero Tamayo, Xavier. The ILO and Development in the Americas. *Int. Lab. Rev.,* December 1969, *100*(6), pp. 505–50. [G: Latin America]

Coffey, Joseph D. National Labor Relations Legislation: Possible Impact on American Agriculture. *Amer. J. Agr. Econ.,* December 1969, *51*(5), pp. 1065–74. [G: U.S.]

Cole, David L. The AFL-CIO's Internal Disputes Plan. *Mon. Lab. Rev.,* September 1969, *92*(9), pp. 12–15.

Cook, Alice H. The ILO and Japanese Politics, II: Gain or Loss for Labor? *Ind. Lab. Relat. Rev.,* April 1969, *22*(3), pp. 375–98. [G: Japan]

Córdova, Efrén. The Check-Off System: A Comparative Study. *Int. Lab. Rev.,* May 1969, *99*(5), pp. 463–91.

Craypo, Charles. The National Union Convention as an Internal Appeal Tribunal. *Ind. Lab. Relat. Rev.,* July 1969, *22*(4), pp. 487–511. [G: U.S.]

Czarnecki, Edgar R. Profit Sharing and Union Organizing. *Mon. Lab. Rev.,* December 1969, *92* (12), pp. 61–62. [G: U.S.]

Dhyani, S. N. Anatomy of Trade Union Law and Purpose and Future Direction of Trade Union Legislation in India. **In** *Johri, C. K., ed.,* 1969, pp. 201–20. [G: India]

Douty, H. M. Prospects for White-collar Unionism. *Mon. Lab. Rev.,* January 1969, *92*(1), pp. 31–34.

Ebert, Robert R. Multinational Coordination of Labor Objectives in the Automobile Unions. *Ohio State U. Bull. Bus. Res.,* September 1969, *44*(9), pp. 1–3, 7–8.

Eisner, J. M. Politics, Legislation, and the ILGWU. *Amer. J. Econ. Soc.,* July 1969, *28*(3), pp. 301–14. [G: U.S.]

Evans, Archibald A. Work and Leisure, 1919–1969. *Int. Lab. Rev.,* January 1969, *99*(1), pp. 35–59.

Faupl, Rudolph. The ILO at 50: A Trade Union Perspective. *Mon. Lab. Rev.,* May 1969, *92*(5), pp. 44–46.

Finkel, Sidney R. and Tarascio, Vincent J. A Theoretical Integration of Production and Wage Theory. *Western Econ. J.,* December 1969, *7*(4), pp. 371–78.

Gilroy, Thomas P. Recent Developments in the Unionization of Professional/Technical Personnel. **In** *Gilroy, T. P., ed.,* 1969, pp. 33–37.

Givry, Jean. Developments in Labour-Management Relations in the Undertaking. *Int. Lab. Rev.,* January 1969, *99*(1), pp. 1–33.

Goldfinger, Nathaniel. The Growth of the AFL-CIO. **In** *Walsh, R. E., ed.,* 1969, pp. 12–20. [G: U.S.]

Goodman, Stephen H. Trade Unions and Political Parties: The Case of East Africa. *Econ. Develop. Cult. Change,* April 1969, *17*(3), pp. 338–45. [G: E. Africa]

Gould, William B. Black Power in the Unions: The Impact upon Collective Bargaining Relationships. *Yale Law J.,* November 1969, *79*(1), pp. 46–84. [G: U.S.]

Gould, William B. Racial Equality in Jobs and Unions, Collective Bargaining, and the Burger Court. *Mich. Law Rev.,* December 1969, *68*(2), pp. 237–58. [G: U.S.]

Graham, Harry. Asset Forfeiture Clauses: Should They Be Enforced? *Univ. Wash. Bus. Rev.,* Autumn 1969, *29*(1), pp. 42–47.

Gross, James A. Historians and the Literature of the Negro Worker. *Labor Hist.,* Summer 1969, *10*(3), pp. 536–46. [G: U.S.]

Hardbeck, George W. Unionism again at a Crossroads. **In** *Wortman, M. S., Jr.,* 1969, pp. 65–72. [G: U.S.]

Helfgott, Roy B. The Computer and Prospects for Office Unionism. *Quart. Rev. Econ. Bus.,* Spring 1969, *9*(1), pp. 19–28. [G: U.S.]

Henle, Peter. Some Reflections on Organized Labor and the New Militants. *Mon. Lab. Rev.,* July 1969, *92*(7), pp. 20–25. [G: U.S.]

Hines, A. G. Wage Inflation in the United Kingdom 1948–62: A Disaggregated Study. *Econ. J.,* March 1969, *79*(313), pp. 66–89. [G: U.K.]

Hutchinson, John. Hoffa. *Calif. Manage. Rev.,* Summer 1969, *11*(4), pp. 79–88.

Hutchinson, John. The Anatomy of Corruption in Trade Unions. *Ind. Relat.,* February 1969, *8*(2), pp. 135–50. [G: U.S.]

Kassalow, Everett M. Professional Unionism in Sweden. *Ind. Relat.,* February 1969, *8*(2), pp. 119–34. [G: Sweden]

Kerr, Clark. Trade Unions and Group Interests. **In** *Kerr, C.,* 1969, pp. 44–61.

Kilroy-Silk, Robert. The Royal Commission on Trade Unions and Employers' Associations. *Ind. Lab.*

Relat. Rev., July 1969, *22*(4), pp. 544–58. **[G: U.K.]**

Kleingartner, Archie. Professionalism and Engineering Unionism. *Ind. Relat.,* May 1969, *8*(3), pp. 224–35.

Krislov, Joseph and Christian, Virgil L., Jr. Union Organizing and the Business Cycle, 1949–1966. *Southern Econ. J.,* October 1969, *36*(2), pp. 185–88. **[G: U.S.]**

Lacroix, Henri. The ILO at 50: Its Role in Improving Labor Statistics. *Mon. Lab. Rev.,* May 1969, *92*(5), pp. 47–50.

Lahne, Herbert J. Coalition Bargaining and the Future of Union Structure. **In** *Wortman, M. S., Jr.,* 1969, pp. 46–52. **[G: U.S.]**

Lawyer, John E. The ILO at 50: How It Began and How It Functions. *Mon. Lab. Rev.,* May 1969, *92* (5), pp. 32–36.

Masters, Stanley H. An Interindustry Analysis of Wages and Plant Size. *Rev. Econ. Statist.,* August 1969, *51*(3), pp. 341–45. **[G: U.S.]**

Millen, Bruce H. Factions of the Turkish Labor Movement Differ over Political Role. *Mon. Lab. Rev.,* June 1969, *92*(6), pp. 31–35. **[G: Turkey]**

Morse, David A. The ILO at 50: Its Hopes for Social Progress. *Mon. Lab. Rev.,* May 1969, *92*(5), pp. 51–53.

Muir, J. Douglas. Canada's Experience with the Right of Public Employees to Strike. *Mon. Lab. Rev.,* July 1969, *92*(7), pp. 54–59. **[G: Canada]**

Murray, Lionel. Trade Unions and Technical Change. **In** *Hugh-Jones, E. M., ed.,* 1969, pp. 135–50. **[G: U.K.]**

Neilan, Edwin P. The ILO at 50: A Management Assessment. *Mon. Lab. Rev.,* May 1969, *92*(5), pp. 41–43.

Öhman, Berndt. A Note on the "Solidarity Wage Policy" of the Swedish Labor Movement. *Swedish J. Econ.,* September 1969, *71*(3), pp. 198–205. **[G: Sweden]**

Ozsvald, László. Incentives for Management Personnel in Hungarian Industry. *Int. Lab. Rev.,* September 1969, *100*(3), pp. 257–72. **[G: Hungary]**

Palomba, Neil A. Strike Activity and Union Membership: An Empirical Approach. *Univ. Wash. Bus. Rev.,* Winter 1969, *28*(2), pp. 16–22.

Perlman, David L. Public Employees: An Emerging Force. **In** *Walsh, R. E., ed.,* 1969, pp. 20–27. **[G: U.S.]**

Prickett, James R. Some Aspects of the Communist Controversy in the CIO. *Sci. Soc.,* Summer-Fall 1969, *33*(3), pp. 299–321. **[G: U.S.]**

Raimon, Robert L. and Stoikov, Vladimir. The Effect of Blue-Collar Unionism on White-Collar Earnings. *Ind. Lab. Relat. Rev.,* April 1969, *22*(3), pp. 358–74. **[G: U.S.]**

Robert, Marcel and Parmeggiani, Luigi. Fifty Years of International Collaboration in Occupational Safety and Health. *Int. Lab. Rev.,* January 1969, *99*(1), pp. 85–136.

Rose, Arthur. Wage Differentials in the Building Trades. *Mon. Lab. Rev.,* October 1969, *92*(10), pp. 14–17. **[G: U.S.]**

Rosen, Sherwin. Trade Union Power, Threat Effects and the Extent of Organization. *Rev. Econ. Stud.,* April 1969, *36*(106), pp. 185–96. **[G: U.S.]**

Snyder, Carl Dean. White Collars and the U.A.W. *Mich. Academician,* Winter 1969, *1*(1–2), pp. 43–54.

Strauss, George. Union Bargaining Strength: Goliath or Paper Tiger. **In** *Wortman, M. S., Jr.,* 1969, pp. 315–22. **[G: U.S.]**

Sulg, Madis. Individual Rights under Collective Agreements. *Mon. Lab. Rev.,* July 1969, *92*(7), pp. 40–42. **[G: U.S.]**

Taft, Philip. A Labor Historian Views Changes in the Trade Union Movement. *Mon. Lab. Rev.,* September 1969, *92*(9), pp. 8–11. **[G: U.S.]**

Thomson, Andrew W. J. The Next Step in Industrial Relations. *Scot. J. Polit. Econ.,* June 1969, *16*(2), pp. 212–24. **[G: U.K.]**

Tillery, Winston L. Local and Single-Employer Unions. *Mon. Lab. Rev.,* September 1969, *92*(9), pp. 46–47. **[G: U.S.]**

Toth, Barbara V. Labor in a Year of Expansion. *Mon. Lab. Rev.,* January 1969, *92*(1), pp. 11–19. **[G: U.S.]**

Troy, Leo. Trade Union Growth in a Changing Economy. *Mon. Lab. Rev.,* September 1969, *92*(9), pp. 3–7. **[G: U.S.]**

Truman, Thomas C. Political Ideology, Belief Systems, and Parties: The Australian Labor Party. **In** *Preston, R., ed.,* 1969, pp. 255–91. **[G: Australia]**

Turner, H. A. The Donovan Report. *Econ. J.,* March 1969, *79*(313), pp. 1–10. **[G: U.K.]**

Walsh, Robert E. Labor in Private Industry. **In** *Walsh, R. E., ed.,* 1969, pp. 5–12. **[G: U.S.]**

Ward, Cordelia T. and Davis, William M. Negotiations and Wage Calendar for 1969. *Mon. Lab. Rev.,* January 1969, *92*(1), pp. 52–64.

Warren, W. M. Urban Real Wages and the Nigerian Trade Union Movement, 1939–60: Rejoinder. *Econ. Develop. Cult. Change,* July 1969, *17*(4), pp. 618–33. **[G: Nigeria]**

Ways, Max. Labor Unions Are Worth the Price. **In** *Starleaf, D. R., ed.,* 1969, pp. 153–63. **[G: U.S.]**

Weaver, George L.-P. The ILO at 50: A Government Delegate's View. *Mon. Lab. Rev.,* May 1969, *92* (5), pp. 37–40.

Whitty, M. D. Kohler on Strike. *Marquette Bus. Rev.,* Summer 1969, *13*(2), pp. 65–75. **[G: U.S.]**

Wolfe, Arthur C. Trends in Labor Union Voting Behavior, 1948–1968. *Ind. Relat.,* October 1969, *9*(1), pp. 1–10. **[G: U.S.]**

Woolf, Donald A. Labor Problems in the Post Office. *Ind. Relat.,* October 1969, *9*(1), pp. 27–35. **[G: U.S.]**

832 Collective Bargaining

8320 General

Baitsell, John M.; Sprague, Christopher R. and Taylor, David P. A Computer-Based Negotiation: Uses and Limitations as a Training Device. **In** *Siegel, A. J., ed.,* 1969, pp. 260–85.

Belli, Claudio. Direzione del personale: un'ipotesi sociologica. (A Sociological Hypothesis on the Function of Personnel Management in the Firm. With English summary.) *L'Impresa,* March/April 1969, *11*(2), pp. 138–42. **[G: Italy]**

Bienefeld, M. A. The Normal Week under Collective Bargaining. *Economica, N.S.,* May 1969, *36* (142), pp. 172–92.

Caples, William G. The Computer's Uses and Potential in Bargaining: A Management View. **In** *Siegel, A. J., ed.,* 1969, pp. 69–120.

Conway, Jack T. and Ginsburg, Woodrow L. The Extension of Collective Bargaining to New Fields. **In** *Wortman, M. S., Jr.,* 1969, pp. 148–50. **[G: U.S.]**

Córdova, Efrén. Collective Labour Relations in Latin American Ports. *Int. Lab. Rev.,* October 1969, *100*(4), pp. 315–39. **[G: Latin America]**

David, Lily Mary and Sheifer, Victor J. Estimating the Cost of Collective Bargaining Settlements. *Mon. Lab. Rev.,* May 1969, *92*(5), pp. 16–26. **[G: U.S.]**

Davis, Harry E. Negotiated Retirement Plans—A Decade of Benefit Improvements. *Mon. Lab. Rev.,* May 1969, *92*(5), pp. 11–15.

Davison, J. P. The Ultimate State in Disputes: St. James' Square or Downing Street? **In** *Hugh-Jones, E. M., ed.,* 1969, pp. 169–76. **[G: U.K.]**

Fraser, Douglas A. A Union View of Government Intervention in Bargaining. **In** *Wortman, M. S., Jr.,* 1969, pp. 423–28. **[G: U.S.]**

Gallaway, Lowell E. One Last Word. *Southern Econ. J.,* January 1969, *35*(3), pp. 267.

Ginsburg, Woodrow L. The Computer's Uses and Potential in Bargaining: A Trade Union View. **In** *Siegel, A. J., ed.,* 1969, pp. 26–68.

Goldberg, Stephen B. Current Decisions of the NLRB and of the Courts. **In** *Somers, G. G., ed. (II),* 1969, pp. 195–200. **[G: U.S.]**

Gomberg, William. Collective Bargaining and the New Industrial Engineering. **In** *Somers, G. G., ed. (I),* 1969, pp. 69–78.

Howard, William A. Wage Adjustment and Profit Rates: An Error-Learning Approach to Collective Bargaining. *Ind. Lab. Relat. Rev.,* April 1969, *22* (3), pp. 416–21.

Isaac, J. E. Compulsory Arbitration: National Wage Policy. **In** *Preston, R., ed.,* 1969, pp. 173–95. **[G: Australia]**

Jackson, Samuel C. A New Center for Dispute Settlement. *Mon. Lab. Rev.,* January 1969, *92*(1), pp. 10.

Jacobs, Paul. Old before Its Time: Collective Bargaining at 28. **In** *Wortman, M. S., Jr.,* 1969, pp. 60–65. **[G: U.S.]**

Joseph, Myron L. Approaches to Collective Bargaining in Industrial Relations Theory. **In** *Somers, G. G., ed. (I),* 1969, pp. 55–67.

Kilroy-Silk, Robert. The Royal Commission on Trade Unions and Employers' Associations. *Ind. Lab. Relat. Rev.,* July 1969, *22*(4), pp. 544–58. **[G: U.K.]**

Kleingartner, Archie. Nurses, Collective Bargaining, and Labor Legislation. **In** *Wortman, M. S., Jr.,* 1969, pp. 94–102. **[G: U.S.]**

Laffer, Kingsley. Compulsory Arbitration: A New Province for Law and Order. **In** *Preston, R., ed.,* 1969, pp. 153–72. **[G: Australia]**

Landay, Donald M. Trends in Negotiated Health Plans; Broader Coverage, Higher Quality Care. *Mon. Lab. Rev.,* May 1969, *92*(5), pp. 3–10.

Lerner, Shirley W. The Report of the Royal Commission on Trade Unions and Employers' Associations, 1965–68. **In** *Hugh-Jones, E. M., ed.,* 1969, pp. 151–68. **[G: U.K.]**

Mead, John F. and Krislov, Joseph. Drawing Jurisdictional Lines in Mediation. *Mon. Lab. Rev.,* April 1969, *92*(4), pp. 41–45. **[G: U.S.]**

Narayanan, P. P. Trade Union Attitudes to Wage Policy in Developing Countries. **In** *Smith, A. D., ed.,* 1969, pp. 383–94.

O'Connell, Francis A., Jr. A Management View of Government Intervention in Bargaining. **In** *Wortman, M. S., Jr.,* 1969, pp. 429–35. **[G: U.S.]**

Richmond, David. Employer Attitudes to Wage Policies in Developing Countries. **In** *Smith, A. D., ed.,* 1969, pp. 395–97.

Roberts, Harold S. Compulsory Arbitration. **In** *Wortman, M. S., Jr.,* 1969, pp. 403–08. **[G: U.S.]**

Roberts, Paul Craig and Brown, Norman L. The Economics of the Right to Work Controversy: Revisited. *Southern Econ. J.,* January 1969, *35*(3), pp. 265–66.

Sadler, Marion. Who Speaks for the People in Collective Bargaining? **In** *Starleaf, D. R., ed.,* 1969, pp. 148–52. **[G: U.S.]**

Summers, Clyde W. Collective Agreements and the Law of Contracts. *Yale Law J.,* March 1969, *78*(4), pp. 525–75.

Wellington, Harry H. and Winter, Ralph K., Jr. The Limits of Collective Bargaining in Public Employment. *Yale Law J.,* June 1969, *78*(7), pp. 1107–27.

8321 Collective Bargaining in the Private Sector

Babb, E. M.; Belden, S. A. and Saathoff, C. R. An Analysis of Cooperative Bargaining in the Processing Tomato Industry. *Amer. J. Agr. Econ.,* February 1969, *51*(1), pp. 13–25. **[G: U.S.]**

Bowen, Charles L. Preventive Mediation. **In** *Somers, G. G., ed. (II),* 1969, pp. 160–64. **[G: U.S.]**

Conant, Eaton H. Report and Appraisal: The Armour Fund's Sioux City Project. **In** *Wortman, M. S., Jr.,* 1969, pp. 205–11. **[G: U.S.]**

David, Lily Mary. Recent Collective Bargaining and Technological Change. **In** *Wortman, M. S., Jr.,* 1969, pp. 194–205. **[G: U.S.]**

Drotning, John E. and Lipsky, David B. The Effectiveness of Reinstatement as a Public Policy Remedy: The Kohler Case. *Ind. Lab. Relat. Rev.,* January 1969, *22*(2), pp. 179–98. **[G: U.S.]**

Feller, David E. The Steel Experience: Myth and Reality. **In** *Somers, G. G., ed. (II),* 1969, pp. 152–59. **[G: U.S.]**

Gomberg, William. Featherbedding: An Assertion of Property Rights. **In** *Wortman, M. S., Jr.,* 1969, pp. 225–34. **[G: U.S.]**

Gould, William B. Black Power in the Unions: The Impact upon Collective Bargaining Relationships. *Yale Law J.,* November 1969, *79*(1), pp. 46–84. **[G: U.S.]**

Gould, William B. Racial Equality in Jobs and Unions, Collective Bargaining, and the Burger Court. *Mich. Law Rev.,* December 1969, *68*(2), pp. 237–58. **[G: U.S.]**

Hirsch, John S., Jr. Strike Insurance and Collective Bargaining. *Ind. Lab. Relat. Rev.,* April 1969, *22*

(3), pp. 399–415. [G: U.S.]

Juris, Hervey A. Union Crisis Wage Decisions. *Ind. Relat.,* May 1969, *8*(3), pp. 247–58. [G: U.S.]

Kossoris, Max D. 1966 West Coast Longshore Negotiations. **In** *Wortman, M. S., Jr.,* 1969, pp. 175–86. [G: U.S.]

Lunden, Leon E. Bargaining in Major Symphony Orchestras. *Mon. Lab. Rev.,* July 1969, *92*(7), pp. 15–19. [G: U.S.]

Mason, Charles. Scheduling and Seniority: The United Airlines Experience. **In** *Siegel, A. J., ed.,* 1969, pp. 203–25.

Murri, D. G. and Hawkins, Murray H. Organizational Structure and Collective Bargaining. *Can. J. Agr. Econ.,* November 1969, *17*(3), pp. 150–56.

Rose, Arthur. Wage Differentials in the Building Trades. *Mon. Lab. Rev.,* October 1969, *92*(10), pp. 14–17. [G: U.S.]

Shaw, Lee. Public Policy and the Strategy and Tactics of Collective Bargaining: Discussion. **In** *Somers, G. G., ed. (II),* 1969, pp. 201–05. [G: U.S.]

Stieglitz, Harold. The Kaiser-Steel Union Sharing Plan. **In** *Wortman, M. S., Jr.,* 1969, pp. 186–94. [G: U.S.]

8322 Collective Bargaining in the Public Sector

Abner, Willoughby. The FMCS and Dispute Mediation in the Federal Government. *Mon. Lab. Rev.,* May 1969, *92*(5), pp. 27–29. [G: U.S.]

Anderson, Arvid. Strikes and Impasse Resolution in Public Employment. *Mich. Law Rev.,* March 1969, *67*(5), pp. 943–70. [G: U.S.]

Arthurs, H. W. Collective Bargaining in the Public Service of Canada: Bold Experiment or Act of Folly? *Mich. Law Rev.,* March 1969, *67*(5), pp. 971–1000. [G: Canada]

Bain, Trevor. Flat Glass: "Industrial Peace" Revisited. *Ind. Relat.,* May 1969, *8*(3), pp. 259–68. [G: U.S.]

Belasco, James A. and Alutto, Joseph A. Organizational Impacts of Teacher Negotiations. *Ind. Relat.,* October 1969, *9*(1), pp. 67–79. [G: U.S.]

Bloedorn, John. The Strike in the Public Sector. **In** *Walsh, R. E., ed.,* 1969, pp. 250–65. [G: U.S.]

Brown, Ralph S., Jr. Collective Bargaining in Higher Education. *Mich. Law Rev.,* March 1969, *67*(5), pp. 1067–82. [G: U.S.]

Capozzola, John M. Citizens' Concern with Municipal Collective Bargaining. **In** *Walsh, R. E., ed.,* 1969, pp. 301–10. [G: U.S.]

Craft, James A. Proportional Representation for Teacher Negotiations. *Ind. Relat.,* May 1969, *8*(3), pp. 236–46. [G: U.S.]

Craft, James A. Public Employee Negotiations Legislation: The Paradox of Labor Divided. *Quart. Rev. Econ. Bus.,* Winter 1969, *9*(4), pp. 29–37. [G: U.S.]

Dole, Richard F., Jr. The Role of Public Officials and Administrators: Remarks. **In** *Sinicropi, A. V. and Gilroy, T. P., eds.,* 1969, pp. 47–51.

Donoian, Harry A. A New Approach to Setting the Pay of Federal Blue-collar Workers. *Mon. Lab. Rev.,* April 1969, *92*(4), pp. 30–34. [G: U.S.]

Friedman, Harvey L. The Role of the AFL-CIO in the Growth of the Public Sector Collective Bargaining. **In** *Walsh, R. E., ed.,* 1969, pp. 27–33. [G: U.S.]

Gilroy, Thomas P. Public Sector Negotiations in Iowa. **In** *Sinicropi, A. V. and Gilroy, T. P., eds.,* 1969, pp. 17–26. [G: U.S.]

Gold, Samuel M. Strikes by Public Workers. **In** *Walsh, R. E., ed.,* 1969, pp. 225–32. [G: U.S.]

Graham, Harry. Public Employees and Collective Negotiations: Remarks. **In** *Sinicropi, A. V. and Gilroy, T. P., eds.,* 1969, pp. 41–44.

Helsby, Robert D. Disputes in the Public Sector—New York's Experience. **In** *Sinicropi, A. V. and Gilroy, T. P., eds.,* 1969, pp. 9–16. [G: U.S.]

Kassalow, Everett M. Public Employee Bargaining in Europe: What Lessons for the United States? **In** *Somers, G. G., ed. (II),* 1969, pp. 48–58. [G: U.S.; Europe]

Kheel, Theodore W. Strikes and Public Employment. *Mich. Law Rev.,* March 1969, *67*(5), pp. 931–42. [G: U.S.]

Klaus, Ida. The Evolution of a Collective Bargaining Relationship in Public Education: New York City's Changing Seven-Year History. *Mich. Law Rev.,* March 1969, *67*(5), pp. 1033–66. [G: U.S.]

Lane, Willard R. School Administration and Negotiations: Remarks. **In** *Sinicropi, A. V. and Gilroy, T. P., eds.,* 1969, pp. 34–40.

McKelvey, Jean T. Fact Finding in Public Employment Disputes: Promise or Illusion? *Ind. Lab. Relat. Rev.,* July 1969, *22*(4), pp. 528–43. [G: U.S.]

McKelvey, Jean T. Fact Finding in Public Employment Disputes: Promise or Illusion? **In** *Somers, G. G., ed. (II),* 1969, pp. 41–47. [G: U.S.]

McLaughlin, Richard P. Public Employee Collective Bargaining. **In** *Walsh, R. E., ed.,* 1969, pp. 290–301. [G: U.S.]

McLennan, Kenneth and Moskow, Michael H. Multilateral Bargaining in the Public Sector. **In** *Somers, G. G., ed. (II),* 1969, pp. 31–40. [G: U.S.]

Moskow, Michael H. Collective Bargaining for Public School Teachers. **In** *Wortman, M. S., Jr.,* 1969, pp. 87–94. [G: U.S.]

Muir, J. Douglas. Canada's Experience with the Right of Public Employees to Strike. *Mon. Lab. Rev.,* July 1969, *92*(7), pp. 54–59. [G: Canada]

Rehmus, Charles M. Impasse Resolution: The Community and Bargaining in the Public Sector: Discussion. **In** *Somers, G. G., ed. (II),* 1969, pp. 59–63.

Rock, Eli. The Appropriate Unit Question in the Public Service: The Problem of Proliferation. *Mich. Law Rev.,* March 1969, *67*(5), pp. 1001–16. [G: U.S.]

Ross, Anne M. Public Employee Unions and the Right to Strike. *Mon. Lab. Rev.,* March 1969, *92*(3), pp. 14–18. [G: U.S.]

Ross, David B. The Arbitration of Public Employee Wage Disputes. *Ind. Lab. Relat. Rev.,* October 1969, *23*(1), pp. 3–14.

Seidman, Joel. Collective Bargaining in the Postal Service. *Ind. Relat.,* October 1969, *9*(1), pp. 11–26. [G: U.S.]

Sinicropi, Anthony V. Collective Negotiations and

Teachers: Remarks. **In** *Sinicropi, A. V. and Gilroy, T. P., eds.*, 1969, pp. 29–31.

Slavney, Morris. Experiences with Current Substantive Practices in Administering. **In** *Sinicropi, A. V. and Gilroy, T. P., eds.*, 1969, pp. 52–59. **[G: U.S.]**

Stieber, Jack. A New Approach to Strikes in Public Employment. **In** *Walsh, R. E., ed.*, 1969, pp. 242–50. **[G: U.S.]**

Thompson, Duane E. School Administration and Negotiations: Introduction. **In** *Sinicropi, A. V. and Gilroy, T. P., eds.*, 1969, pp. 32–33.

Warner, Kenneth O. Cities at the Bargaining Table. **In** *Walsh, R. E., ed.*, 1969, pp. 34–41. **[G: U.S.]**

Weber, Arnold R. Paradise Lost; or Whatever Happened to the Chicago Social Workers? *Ind. Lab. Relat. Rev.*, April 1969, *22*(3), pp. 323–38. **[G: U.S.]**

West, Jude P. The Role of Public Officials and Administrators: Introduction. **In** *Sinicropi, A. V. and Gilroy, T. P., eds.*, 1969, pp. 45–46.

White, Sheila C. Work Stoppages of Government Employees. *Mon. Lab. Rev.*, December 1969, *92* (12), pp. 29–34. **[G: U.S.]**

Wildman, Wesley. Impasse Resolution: The Community and Bargaining in the Public Sector: Discussion. **In** *Somers, G. G., ed. (II)*, 1969, pp. 64–69.

Wollett, Donald H. The Coming Revolution in Public School Management. *Mich. Law Rev.*, March 1969, *67*(5), pp. 1017–32.

Woolf, Donald A. Labor Problems in the Post Office. *Ind. Relat.*, October 1969, *9*(1), pp. 27–35. **[G: U.S.]**

Wortman, Max S., Jr. Collective Bargaining Strategies and Tactics in the Federal Civil Service. **In** *Wortman, M. S., Jr.*, 1969, pp. 102–12. **[G: U.S.]**

Wurf, Jerry. The Use of Factfinding in Dispute Settlement. **In** *Walsh, R. E., ed.*, 1969, pp. 80–92. **[G: U.S.]**

833 Labor Management Relations

8330 General

Barbash, Jack. Rationalization in the American Union. **In** *Somers, G. G., ed. (I)*, 1969, pp. 147–62. **[G: U.S.]**

Behrend, Hilde; Knowles, Ann and Davies, Jean. 'Have You Heard the Phrase "Productivity Agreements"?' Findings from Two National Sample Surveys. *Scot. J. Polit. Econ.*, November 1969, *16*(3), pp. 256–70. **[G: U.K.]**

Belli, Claudio. Il dirigente potere centrale dell' impresa. (The Manager: Central Power in the Firm. With English summary.) *L'Impresa*, July/October 1969, *11*(4–5), pp. 365–72. **[G: Italy]**

Bhatty, I. Z. Conflict and Reconciliation between the Economic, Social, and Industrial Relations Policies. **In** *Johri, C. K., ed.*, 1969, pp. 105–22. **[G: India]**

Blake, Robert R. and Mouton, Jane S. Union-Management Relations: From Conflict to Collaboration. **In** *Wortman, M. S., Jr.*, 1969, pp. 300–309.

De, Nitish R. An Approach to the Problem of Industrial Relations: The Indian Case. **In** *Johri, C. K., ed.*, 1969, pp. 64–104. **[G: India]**

Derber, Milton. "Industrial Democracy" as an Organizing Concept for a Theory of Industrial Relations. **In** *Somers, G. G., ed. (I)*, 1969, pp. 177–90.

Dunlop, John T. Industrial Relations Systems at Work. **In** *Somers, G. G., ed. (I)*, 1969, pp. 25–37.

Dunlop, John T. Industrial Relations Systems. **In** *Wortman, M. S., Jr.*, 1969, pp. 23–30.

Edelman, Murray. The Conservative Political Consequences of Labor Conflict. **In** *Somers, G. G., ed. (I)*, 1969, pp. 163–76.

Filley, Alan C. New Directions in Organization Theory. **In** *Somers, G. G., ed. (I)*, 1969, pp. 79–108.

Givry, Jean. Developments in Labour-Management Relations in the Undertaking. *Int. Lab. Rev.*, January 1969, *99*(1), pp. 1–33.

Heneman, Herbert G., Jr. Toward a General Conceptual System of Industrial Relations: How Do We Get There? **In** *Somers, G. G., ed. (I)*, 1969, pp. 3–24.

Hodgson, James D. Federal Regulation of Unions—Impact on Management. **In** *Somers, G. G., ed. (II)*, 1969, pp. 292–302. **[G: U.S.]**

Kerr, Clark. Industrial Relations and University Relations. **In** *Somers, G. G., ed. (II)*, 1969, pp. 15–25. **[G: U.S.]**

Kheel, Theodore W. Collective Bargaining and Community Disputes. *Mon. Lab. Rev.*, January 1969, *92*(1), pp. 3–8.

Kilroy-Silk, Robert. The Problem of Industrial Relations. *Manchester Sch. Econ. Soc. Stud.*, September 1969, *37*(3), pp. 249–58. **[G: U.K.]**

Kress, A. L. Job Evaluation for White-Collar Workers in Private Sector Employment in the United States. *Int. Lab. Rev.*, October 1969, *100*(4), pp. 341–57. **[G: U.S.]**

Lawrence, Paul R. How to Deal with Resistance to Change. *Harvard Bus. Rev.*, January–February 1969, *47*(1), pp. 4–12, 166–76.

Lesieur, Frederick G. and Puckett, Elbridge S. The Scanlon Plan: Past, Present and Future. **In** *Somers, G. G., ed. (II)*, 1969, pp. 71–80.

Lester, Richard A. Labor Policy in a Changing World. **In** *Wortman, M. S., Jr.*, 1969, pp. 449–59.

Livingston, Frederick R. Union-Management Cooperation Revisited: Discussion. **In** *Somers, G. G., ed. (II)*, 1969, pp. 90–92.

McConnell, John W. Industrial Relations and University Relations: Discussion. **In** *Somers, G. G., ed. (II)*, 1969, pp. 26–28. **[G: U.S.]**

Moore, David G. Toward More Comprehensive Human Relations in Industry. **In** *Somers, G. G., ed. (I)*, 1969, pp. 137–46.

Pylee, M. V. Is Further Centralization of Labour Policy Desirable? **In** *Johri, C. K., ed.*, 1969, pp. 221–34. **[G: India]**

Robertson, N. and Sams, K. I. Industrial Relations Reform in Great Britain. *Mon. Lab. Rev.*, January 1969, *92*(1), pp. 35–40. **[G: U.K.]**

Rosen, Sumner M. Union-Management Cooperation: Is There an Agenda for Tomorrow? **In** *Somers, G. G., ed. (II)*, 1969, pp. 81–89. **[G: U.S.]**

Sadler, Marion. Who Speaks for the People in Collective Bargaining? **In** *Starleaf, D. R., ed.*, 1969, pp. 148–52. **[G: U.S.]**

Sayles, Leonard. Industrial Relations and Organization Behavior: Parent and Child? **In** *Somers, G. G., ed. (I),* 1969, pp. 123–36.

Somers, Gerald G. Bargaining Power and Industrial Relations Theory. **In** *Somers, G. G., ed. (I),* 1969, pp. 39–53.

Spaniol, Roland D. Computers and Electronic Data Processing in Industrial Relations. *Ohio State U. Bull. Bus. Res.,* June 1969, *44*(6), pp. 6–7.

Spyropoulos, Georges. An Outline of Developments and Trends in Labour Relations. *Int. Lab. Rev.,* March 1969, *99*(3), pp. 315–46.

Sturmthal, Adolf. Union-Management Cooperation Revisited: Discussion. **In** *Somers, G. G., ed. (II),* 1969, pp. 93–95.

Thomason, George F. Industrial Relations. **In** *Kempner, T., ed.,* 1969, pp. 60–64.

Vanek, Jaroslav. Decentralization Under Worker's Management: A Theoretical Appraisal. *Amer. Econ. Rev.,* December 1969, *59*(5), pp. 1006–14.

Ways, Max. Labor Unions Are Worth the Price. **In** *Starleaf, D. R., ed.,* 1969, pp. 153–63. **[G: U.S.]**

Whyte, William Foote. Building Better Organizational Models. **In** *Somers, G. G., ed. (I),* 1969, pp. 109–21.

Witney, Fred. The Era of Sophisticated Labor Relations. **In** *Starleaf, D. R., ed.,* 1969, pp. 128–34. **[G: U.S.]**

Witney, Fred. The Era of Sophisticated Labor Relations. **In** *Wortman, M. S., Jr.,* 1969, pp. 442–48. **[G: U.S.]**

Young, Edwin. Industrial Relations and University Relations: Discussion. **In** *Somers, G. G., ed. (II),* 1969, pp. 29–30. **[G: U.S.]**

Zand, Dale E. and Steckman, William E. Resolving Industrial Conflict—An Experimental Study of the Effects of Attitudes and Precedent. **In** *Somers, G. G., ed. (II),* 1969, pp. 348–59.

8331 Labor Management Relations in Private Sector

Baer, Walter E. Arbitrating the Discharge and Discipline of Union Officials. *Mon. Lab. Rev.,* September 1969, *92*(9), pp. 39–45.

Brooks, Harold E. The Armour Automation Committee Experience. **In** *Somers, G. G., ed. (II),* 1969, pp. 137–43. **[G: U.S.]**

Horvitz, Wayne L. The ILWU-PMA Mechanization and Modernization Agreement. **In** *Somers, G. G., ed. (II),* 1969, pp. 144–51. **[G: U.S.]**

Joshi, N. K. Normative Aspects of Industrial Relations. **In** *Johri, C. K., ed.,* 1969, pp. 160–71. **[G: India]**

Sheth, N. R. The Tripartite System: Past, Present, and Future. **In** *Johri, C. K., ed.,* 1969, pp. 142–59. **[G: India]**

Sinha, G. P. and Sinha, P. R. N. Working of the Central Wage Boards. **In** *Johri, C. K., ed.,* 1969, pp. 270–86. **[G: India]**

Stern, James L. Evolution of Private Manpower Planning in Armour's Plant Closings. *Mon. Lab. Rev.,* December 1969, *92*(12), pp. 21–28. **[G: U.S.]**

Stone, Morris. Why Arbitrators Reinstate Discharged Employees. *Mon. Lab. Rev.,* October 1969, *92* (10), pp. 47–50.

8332 Labor Management Relations in Public Sector

Cogen, Charles. Collective Negotiations in Public Education. **In** *Walsh, R. E., ed.,* 1969, pp. 141–53. **[G: U.S.]**

Doherty, Robert E. and Oberer, Walter E. The Public School Teacher as Organization Man. **In** *Walsh, R. E., ed.,* 1969, pp. 115–40. **[G: U.S.]**

Matejko, Alexander. The International Scene: Current Trends in the Social Sciences: Some Sociological Problems of Socialist Factories. *Soc. Res.,* Autumn 1969, *36*(3), pp. 448–80. **[G: E. Europe]**

Perera, S. E. G. Some Labour Problems of the National Textile Corporation of Ceylon. *Int. Lab. Rev.,* February 1969, *99*(2), pp. 185–207. **[G: Ceylon]**

Rehmus, Charles M. Constraints on Local Governments in Public Employee Bargaining. *Mich. Law Rev.,* March 1969, *67*(5), pp. 919–30. **[G: U.S.]**

Smith, Russell A. State and Local Advisory Reports on Public Employment Labor Legislation: A Comparative Analysis. *Mich. Law Rev.,* March 1969, *67*(5), pp. 891–918. **[G: U.S.]**

Warner, Kenneth O. Financial Implications of Employee Bargaining in the Public Service. **In** *Walsh, R. E., ed.,* 1969, pp. 189–97.

Zeidler, Frank P. Rethinking the Philosophy of Employee Relations in the Public Service. **In** *Walsh, R. E., ed.,* 1969, pp. 198–213.

840 Demographic Economics

841 Demographic Economics

8410 Demographic Economics

Aaron, Henry J. Local Public Expenditures and the "Migration Effect." *Western Econ. J.,* December 1969, *7*(4), pp. 385–90.

Adams, Nassau A. Internal Migration in Jamaica: An Economic Analysis. *Soc. Econ. Stud.,* June 1969, *18*(2), pp. 137–51. **[G: Jamaica]**

Alpander, Guvenc G. The Business Leaders of Selected Countries. *Univ. Missouri Bus. Govt. Rev.,* May–June 1969, *10*(3), pp. 13–19.

Amato, Peter W. Population Densities, Land Values, and Socioeconomic Class in Bogotá, Colombia. *Land Econ.,* February 1969, *45*(1), pp. 66–73. **[G: Colombia]**

Auster, Richard; Leveson, Irving and Sarachek, Deborah. The Production of Health, an Exploratory Study. *J. Human Res.,* Fall 1969, *4*(4), pp. 411–36. **[G: U.S.]**

Bachmura, Frank T. Latin American Brain Drainage. **In** *Hilton, R., ed.,* 1969, pp. 426–44. **[G: Latin America]**

Bates, Marston. The Human Ecosystem. **In** *National Academy of Sciences,* 1969, pp. 21–30.

Baumgartner, Leona. Governmental Responsibility for Family Planning in the United States. **In** *Behrman, S. J.; Corsa, L., Jr. and Freedman, R., eds.,* 1969, pp. 435–48. **[G: U.S.]**

Beale, Calvin L. Statement. **In** *Population Trends,*

Pt. 1, HCH, 1969, pp. 473–97. **[G: U.S.]**

Bean, Lee L. and Bhatti, A. D. Three Years on Pakistan's New National Family-Planning Programme. *Pakistan Develop. Rev.,* Spring 1969, *9*(1), pp. 35–57. **[G: Pakistan]**

Beijer, G. Brain Drain as a Burden, a Stimulus and a Challenge to European Integration. **In** *Bechhofer, F., ed.,* 1969, pp. 3–30. **[G: Europe]**

Bell, David E.; Hardin, Lowell S. and Hill, F. F. Hope for the Hungry: Fulfillment or Frustration? **In** *Hardin, C. M., ed.,* 1969, pp. 137–70. **[G: U.S.]**

Bellettini, Athos. L'analisi della struttura e della dinamica della popolazione urbana attraverso la gestione automatizzata dell'anagrafe comunale. (With English summary.) *Statistica,* October-December 1969, *29*(4), pp. 535–62. **[G: Italy]**

Berelson, Bernard. National Family Planning Programs: Where We Stand. **In** *Behrman, S. J.; Corsa, L., Jr. and Freedman, R., eds.,* 1969, pp. 341–87.

Bernardo, Robert M. Why It Is Cheap, Not Dear, to Marry a Ph.D. *J. Polit. Econ.,* September/October 1969, *77*(5), pp. 862.

Blake, Judith. Population Policy for Americans: Is the Government Being Misled? **In** *Effects of Population Growth on Natural Resources and the Environment, HCH,* 1969, pp. 189–201. **[G: U.S.]**

Bonaguidi, Alberto. L'aumento del coniugio e la sua influenza sul rialzo della fecondità in Italia. (With English summary.) *Statistica,* October-December 1969, *29*(4), pp. 754–67.

Brand, W. Population Growth and Economic Development. **In** *Bechhofer, F., ed.,* 1969, pp. 145–54.

Braschler, Curtis and Klindt, Thomas. Theoretical and Empirical Problems in Local Government Consolidation. *Can. J. Agr. Econ.,* February 1969, *17*(1), pp. 141–50.

Brass, W. A Generation Method for Projecting Death Rates. **In** *Bechhofer, F., ed.,* 1969, pp. 75–91.

Brown, Harrison. Population, Food and the Energy Transition. **In** *Behrman, S. J.; Corsa, L., Jr. and Freedman, R., eds.,* 1969, pp. 180–88.

Burford, Roger L. Louisiana's Population: Its Growth and Distribution. **In** *Beard, T. R., ed.,* 1969, pp. 41–54. **[G: U.S.]**

Burt, Richard C. How the 1970 Census Will Be Taken. *Mon. Lab. Rev.,* December 1969, *92*(12), pp. 38–42. **[G: U.S.]**

Byrne, Joycelin. Population Growth in St. Vincent. *Soc. Econ. Stud.,* June 1969, *18*(2), pp. 152–88. **[G: St. Vincent]**

Carrier, N. Calculation of Family Structure as a Demographic Example of the Organizational Power of Matrix Notation in Mass Arithmetical Operations. **In** *Bechhofer, F., ed.,* 1969, pp. 92–105.

Carstairs, G. M. Population Growth and Economic Development: Comment. **In** *Bechhofer, F., ed.,* 1969, pp. 155–64.

Chiassino, Giuseppe. Vita probabile e vita media. (With English summary.) *Statistica,* April-June 1969, *29*(2), pp. 149–83. **[G: Italy]**

Chow, L. P. and Hsu, S. C. A Chinese View of Family Planning in the Developing World. **In** *Behrman, S. J.; Corsa, L., Jr. and Freedman, R., eds.,* 1969, pp. 451–66.

Coale, Ansley J. The Decline of Fertility in Europe from the French Revolution to World War II. **In** *Behrman, S. J.; Corsa, L., Jr. and Freedman, R., eds.,* 1969, pp. 3–24. **[G: Europe]**

Coale, Ansley J. Population and Economic Development. **In** *Hauser, P. M., ed.,* 1969, pp. 59–84.

Cole, H. J. D. The Contribution of Demography to Physical and Spatial Planning: Comment. **In** *Bechhofer, F., ed.,* 1969, pp. 131–33.

Comm. on Resources and Man, Nat'l. Acad. of Sci. Introduction and Recommendations from *Resources and Man.* **In** *Effects of Population Growth on Natural Resources and the Environment, HCH,* 1969, pp. 120–30.

Conlisk, John. Determinants of School Enrollment and School Performance. *J. Human Res.,* Spring 1969, *4*(2), pp. 140–57. **[G: U.S.]**

Cox, P. Calculation of Family Structure as a Demographic Example of the Organizational Power of Matrix Notation in Mass Arithmetical Operations: Comment. **In** *Bechhofer, F., ed.,* 1969, pp. 107–11.

Curtin, T. R. C. The Economics of Population Growth and Control in Developing Countries. *Rev. Soc. Econ.,* September 1969, *27*(2), pp. 139–53.

Dasgupta, Partha S. On the Concept of Optimum Population. *Rev. Econ. Stud.,* July 1969, *36*(107), pp. 295–318.

Day, Lincoln H. and Day, Alice Taylor. *Too many Americans*: Excerpts. **In** *Effects of Population Growth on Natural Resources and the Environment, HCH,* 1969, pp. 160–88. **[G: U.S.]**

Day, Lincoln H. The Population Problem in the United States. **In** *Effects of Population Growth on Natural Resources and the Environment, HCH,* 1969, pp. 152–59. **[G: U.S.]**

Di Comite, Luigi. Ipotesi di Gompertz e di Makeham e popolazione stabile. (With English summary.) *Statistica,* July-September 1969, *29*(3), pp. 483–87.

Di Comite, Luigi. Sulla rappresentazione analitica delle curve integrali di fecondità. (With English summary.) *Statistica,* January-March 1969, *29*(1), pp. 113–18.

Drakatos, Constantine G. The Determinants of Birth Rate in Developing Countries: An Econometric Study of Greece. *Econ. Develop. Cult. Change,* July 1969, *17*(4), pp. 596–603. **[G: Greece]**

Easterlin, Richard A. Population. **In** *Chamberlain, N. W., ed.,* 1969, pp. 241–72.

Easterlin, Richard A. Towards a Socioeconomic Theory of Fertility: Survey of Recent Research on Economic Factors in American Fertility. **In** *Behrman, S. J.; Corsa, L., Jr. and Freedman, R., eds.,* 1969, pp. 127–56. **[G: U.S.]**

Ebanks, G. Edward. Social and Demographic Characteristics of Family Planning Clients in Barbados. *Soc. Econ. Stud.,* December 1969, *18*(4), pp. 391–401. **[G: Barbados]**

El-Badry, M. A. Higher Female than Male Mortality in Some Countries of South Asia: A Digest. *J. Amer. Statist. Assoc.,* December 1969, *64*(328), pp. 1234–44. **[G: S. Asia]**

Engelmann, Hugo O. and Wanner, Richard A. Population Size and Industrial Technology. *Amer. J. Econ. Soc.*, July 1969, *28*(3), pp. 249–56. **[G: U.K.]**

Enke, Stephen. Correcting Some Confusions. *Rev. Soc. Econ.*, September 1969, *27*(2), pp. 154–59.

Evans, Francis C. Space Relations in Ecology: An Overview. *Mich. Academician*, Summer 1969, *2* (1), pp. 69–76.

Eversley, D. E. C. The Validity of Family and Group Statistics as Indicators of Secular Population Trends. **In** *Bechhofer, F., ed.*, 1969, pp. 179–95.

Farmer, B. H. Available Food Supplies. **In** *Hutchinson, J. [Sir], ed.*, 1969, pp. 75–95.

Fisek, Nusret H. Prospects for Fertility Planning in Turkey. **In** *Behrman, S. J.; Corsa, L., Jr. and Freedman, R., eds.*, 1969, pp. 467–77. **[G: Turkey]**

Fisher, Joseph L. and Potter, Neal. Natural Resource Adequacy for the United States and the World. **In** *Hauser, P. M., ed.*, 1969, pp. 106–38. **[G: U.S.]**

Folse, C. I. and Riffe, W. W. Changing Patterns of Business Services and Population in Illinois Rural Villages. *Ill. Agr. Econ.*, January 1969, *9*(1), pp. 26–32. **[G: U.S.]**

Forstall, Richard L. Economic Classification of Places over 10,000, 1960–1963. **In** *Population Trends, Pt. 1, HCH*, 1969, pp. 452–70. **[G: U.S.]**

Forstall, Richard L. Population Change in American Cities, 1960–1965. **In** *Population Trends, Pt. 1, HCH*, 1969, pp. 433–51. **[G: U.S.]**

Forstall, Richard L. Statement. **In** *Population Trends, Pt. 1, HCH*, 1969, pp. 411–22. **[G: U.S.]**

Foster, Phillips and Yost, Larry. A Simulation Study of Population, Education, and Income Growth in Uganda. *Amer. J. Agr. Econ.*, August 1969, *51*(3), pp. 576–91. **[G: Uganda]**

Gabler, L. R. Economies and Diseconomies of Scale in Urban Public Sectors. *Land Econ.*, November 1969, *45*(4), pp. 425–34. **[G: U.S.]**

Gili, Adolfo. Popolosità e dinamica demografica di lungo periodo nei comuni dell'Emilia e del Veneto: Parte I. (With English summary.) *Statistica*, October-December 1969, *29*(4), pp. 603–49. **[G: Italy]**

Glass, D. V. Fertility Trends in Europe Since the Second World War. **In** *Behrman, S. J.; Corsa, L., Jr. and Freedman, R., eds.*, 1969, pp. 25–74. **[G: Europe]**

Goldstone, Stephen E. Family Planning, Population Policies, and Mental Health. **In** *Effects of Population Growth on Natural Resources and the Environment, HCH*, 1969, pp. 140–51.

Gordon, Jerome B. Labor Mobility and Economic Growth: The Central American Experience—Costa Rica and El Salvador. *Econ. Develop. Cult. Change*, April 1969, *17*(3), pp. 319–37. **[G: Costa Rica; El Salvador]**

Gorinson, Morris. How the Census Data Will be Processed. *Mon. Lab. Rev.*, December 1969, *92*(12), pp. 42–45. **[G: U.S.]**

Greenwood, Michael J. An Analysis of the Determinants of Geographic Labor Mobility in the United States. *Rev. Econ. Statist.*, May 1969, *51*(2), pp. 189–94. **[G: U.S.]**

Greenwood, Michael J. The Determinants of Labor Migration in Egypt. *J. Reg. Sci.*, August 1969, *9*(2), pp. 283–90. **[G: Egypt]**

Habakkuk, H. J. Historical Demography: Comment. **In** *Bechhofer, F., ed.*, 1969, pp. 221–26.

Hardin, Clifford M. For Humanity, New Hope: Introduction. **In** *Hardin, C. M., ed.*, 1969, pp. 1–7.

Hauser, Philip M. Statement. **In** *Population Trends, Pt. 1, HCH*, 1969, pp. 509–22. **[G: U.S.]**

Hauser, Philip M. The Population of the United States, Retrospect and Prospect. **In** *Hauser, P. M., ed.*, 1969, pp. 85–105. **[G: U.S.]**

Hauser, Philip M. World Population Growth. **In** *Hauser, P. M., ed.*, 1969, pp. 12–33.

Hawley, Amos H. Population and Society: An Essay on Growth. **In** *Behrman, S. J.; Corsa, L., Jr. and Freedman, R., eds.*, 1969, pp. 189–209.

Husain, I. Z. Unemployment Implications of Population Growth in India. **In** *Bhuleshkar, A. V., ed.*, 1969, pp. 88–102. **[G: India]**

Illsley, R. The Economic and Political Consequences of Selective Migrations from One Country to Another: Comment. **In** *Bechhofer, F., ed.*, 1969, pp. 57–62.

Jaffe, A. J. Statement. **In** *Economics of Aging: Toward a Full Share in Abundance, Pt. 2, SCH*, 1969, pp. 388–409. **[G: U.S.]**

Johnson-Marshall, P. The Contribution of Demography to Physical and Spatial Planning: Comment. **In** *Bechhofer, F., ed.*, 1969, pp. 134–36.

Johnson, Harry G.; Scott, A. D. and Thomas, Brinley. Criticisms of Thomas's Analysis of Brain Drain. **In** *Blaug, M., ed.*, 1969, pp. 281–301.

Johnston, Denis F. and Wetzel, James R. Effect of the Census Undercount on Labor Force Estimates. *Mon. Lab. Rev.*, March 1969, *92*(3), pp. 3–13. **[G: U.S.]**

Johnston, R. J. Zonal and Sectoral Patterns in Melbourne's Residential Structure: 1961. *Land Econ.*, November 1969, *45*(4), pp. 463–67. **[G: Australia]**

Jones, L. W. Rapid Population Growth in Baghdad and Amman. *Middle East J.*, Spring 1969, *23*(2), pp. 209–15. **[G: Iraq; Jordan]**

Josowitz, Aaron. Housing Statistics: Published and Unpublished. *Mon. Lab. Rev.*, December 1969, *92*(12), pp. 50–55. **[G: U.S.]**

Katz, Michael. Legal Dimensions of Population Policy. *Soc. Sci. Quart.*, December 1969, *50*(3), pp. 731–41. **[G: U.S.]**

Katzman, Martin T. Ethnic Geography and Regional Economies, 1880–1960. *Econ. Geogr.*, January 1969, *45*(1), pp. 45–52. **[G: U.S.]**

Keele, David L. Economic Growth Outside Metropolitan Areas: The Tenth District Experience. *Fed. Res. Bank Kansas City Rev.*, June 1969, pp. 3–10. **[G: U.S.]**

Keesing, Donald B. Small Population as a Political Handicap to National Development. *Polit. Sci. Quart.*, March 1969, *84*(1), pp. 50–60.

Kelley, Allen C. Demand Patterns, Demographic Change and Economic Growth. *Quart. J. Econ.*, February 1969, *83*(1), pp. 110–26. **[G: Philippines]**

Kelley, Allen C. Demographic Cycles and Economic Growth: The Long Swing Reconsidered. *J. Econ. Hist.*, December 1969, *29*(4), pp. 633–56.

Keyfitz, Nathan. Sampling for Demographic Variables. **In** *Johnson, N. L. and Smith, H., Jr., eds.,* 1969, pp. 562–77.

Keyfitz, Nathan. United States and World Populations. **In** *National Academy of Sciences,* 1969, pp. 43–64.

Khan, Mahmood Hasan. Development Alternatives and Problems in Dual Economies. *Econ. Int.,* November 1969, *22*(4), pp. 636–61. **[G: India; Pakistan]**

King, R. F. T. Population, Food Supplies and Economic Growth. **In** *Hutchinson, J. [Sir], ed.,* 1969, pp. 28–46.

Kirk, Dudley. Natality in the Developing Countries: Recent Trends and Prospects. **In** *Behrman, S. J.; Corsa, L., Jr. and Freedman, R., eds.,* 1969, pp. 75–98.

Kpedekpo, G. M. K. On Working Life Tables in Ghana with Particular Reference to the Female Working Population. *J. Roy. Statist. Soc.,* Part 3, 1969, *132,* pp. 431–41. **[G: Ghana]**

Kpedekpo, G. M. K. Working Life Tables for Males in Ghana 1960. *J. Amer. Statist. Assoc.,* March 1969, *64*(325), pp. 102–10. **[G: Ghana]**

Kuznets, Simon. Economic Aspects of Fertility Trends in the Less Developed Countries. **In** *Behrman, S. J.; Corsa, L., Jr. and Freedman, R., eds.,* 1969, pp. 157–79.

Lavagne, Pierre. Conséquences de la liberté de mouvement du facteur travail en économie internationale. (With English summary.) *Revue Écon.,* September 1969, *20*(5), pp. 873–87.

Lee, Everett. Education and Migration in the United States. **In** *[Edding, Friedrich],* 1969, pp. 231–37. **[G: U.S.]**

Leff, Nathaniel H. Dependency Rates and Savings Rates. *Amer. Econ. Rev.,* December 1969, *59*(5), pp. 886–96.

Leyhausen, Paul. Human Nature and Modern Society. *Soc. Res.,* Winter 1969, *36*(4), pp. 510–29.

Lianos, Theodore P. South-Nonsouth Migration, 1955–1960. *Miss. Val. J. Bus. Econ.,* Spring 1969, *4*(2), pp. 10–22. **[G: U.S.]**

Lindberg, Carolyn G. A Note on Population Estimates and Their Meaning. *N. Mex. Bus.,* November–December 1969, *22*(11&12), pp. 6–10. **[G: U.S.]**

Lorimer, Frank. Issues of Population Policy. **In** *Hauser, P. M., ed.,* 1969, pp. 168–206.

Mayer, Jean. Toward a Non-Malthusian Population Policy. **In** *Effects of Population Growth on Natural Resources and the Environment, HCH,* 1969, pp. 111–19.

McDonald, James R. Contemporary Patterns of Internal Migration in France. *Mich. Academician,* Spring 1969, *1*(3–4), pp. 101–11. **[G: France]**

McNamara, Robert S. Esplosione demografica e sviluppo economico. (Demographic Increase and Economic Development. With English summary.) *Mondo Aperto,* October 1969, *23*(5), pp. 330–42.

Merton, Robert C. A Golden Golden-Rule for Welfare-Maximization in an Economy with a Varying Population Growth Rate. *Western Econ. J.,* December 1969, *7*(4), pp. 307–18.

Miller, Glenn H., Jr. Some Demographic Influences on the Future Market for Housing. *Fed. Res. Bank Kansas City Rev.,* November 1969, pp. 3–9. **[G: U.S.]**

Montanari, Antonio. Considerazioni in margine ad una indagine motivazionale sul controllo delle nascite. (With English summary.) *Statistica,* July-September 1969, *29*(3), pp. 488–505. **[G: Italy]**

Moran, William E., Jr. Statement. **In** *Population Trends, Pt. 1, HCH,* 1969, pp. 67–71. **[G: U.S.]**

Murray, Barbara B. Central City Expenditures and Out-Migration to the Fringe. *Land Econ.,* November 1969, *45*(4), pp. 471–74.

Nafziger, E. Wayne. The Effect of the Nigerian Extended Family on Entrepreneurial Activity. *Econ. Develop. Cult. Change,* Part I, October 1969, *18*(1), pp. 25–33. **[G: Nigeria]**

Nakagawa, Manabu. Some Problems of Population Movements in China under the T'ang Dynasty (I). *Hitotsubashi J. Econ.,* February 1969, *9*(2), pp. 35–42. **[G: China]**

Newman, Monroe and March, Eli P. Rural Areas in the Urban Economy. *Amer. J. Agr. Econ.,* December 1969, *51*(5), pp. 1097–1109. **[G: U.S.]**

Northam, Ray M. Population Size, Relative Location, and Declining Urban Centers: Conterminous United States, 1940–1960. *Land Econ.,* August 1969, *45*(3), pp. 313–22. **[G: U.S.]**

Notestein, Frank W. Population Growth and Its Control. **In** *Hardin, C. M., ed.,* 1969, pp. 9–39.

Notestein, Frank W.; Kirk, Dudley and Segal, Sheldon. The Problem of Population Control. **In** *Hauser, P. M., ed.,* 1969, pp. 139–67.

Paarlberg, Don. Food for More People and Better Nutrition. **In** *Hardin, C. M., ed.,* 1969, pp. 41–87.

Parmeggiani, Antonio. Evoluzione del peso alla nascita in una popolazione isolana durante un intervallo venticinquennale. (With English summary.) *Statistica,* April-June 1969, *29*(2), pp. 241–73. **[G: Italy]**

Parmeggiani, Antonio. Evoluzione della mortalità perinatale in una compagine demografica isolana. (With English summary.) *Statistica,* April-June 1969, *29*(2), pp. 185–239. **[G: Italy]**

Perkins, Walter M. How the Census Will Be Evaluated. *Mon. Lab. Rev.,* December 1969, *92*(12), pp. 55–60. **[G: U.S.]**

Phillips, Llad; Votey, Harold L., Jr. and Maxwell, Darold E. A Synthesis of the Economic and Demographic Models of Fertility: An Econometric Test. *Rev. Econ. Statist.,* August 1969, *51*(3), pp. 298–308.

Pickard, Jerome P. Statement. **In** *Population Trends, Pt. 1, HCH,* 1969, pp. 656–68. **[G: U.S.]**

Pidot, George B., Jr. A Principal Components Analysis of the Determinants of Local Government Fiscal Patterns. *Rev. Econ. Statist.,* May 1969, *51* (2), pp. 176–88. **[G: U.S.]**

Pollard, J. H. Continuous-time and Discrete-time Models of Population Growth. *J. Roy. Statist. Soc.,* Part 1, 1969, *132,* pp. 80–88.

Potter, Robert G., Jr. Estimating Births Averted in a Family Planning Program. **In** *Behrman, S. J.; Corsa, L., Jr. and Freedman, R., eds.,* 1969, pp. 413–34.

Potts, Georgena R. The Decennial Census: Its Purpose and Its Uses. *Mon. Lab. Rev.,* December

1969, *92*(12), pp. 35–38. [G: U.S.]

Requena B., Mariano. Chilean Program of Abortion Control and Fertility Planning: Present Situation and Forecast for the Next Decade. **In** *Behrman, S. J.; Corsa, L., Jr. and Freedman, R., eds.,* 1969, pp. 478–89. [G: Chile]

Robinson, Warren C. Population Control and Development Strategy. *J. Devel. Stud.,* January 1969, *5* (2), pp. 104–17.

Rockefeller, John D., III. The Citizen's View of Public Programs for Family Limitation. **In** *Behrman, S. J.; Corsa, L., Jr. and Freedman, R., eds.,* 1969, pp. 493–98.

Rogers, Andrei. On Perfect Aggregation in the Matrix Cohort-Survival Model of Interregional Population Growth. *J. Reg. Sci.,* December 1969, *9*(3), pp. 417–24.

Rogers, Tommy W. Factors in the Net Migration Rates of Southern SMSA's: A Comparison of the Subregional Influence of Selected Variables. *Miss. Val. J. Bus. Econ.,* Fall 1969, *5*(1), pp. 51–67. [G: U.S.]

Rogers, Tommy W. Migration Attractiveness of Southern Metropolitan Areas. *Soc. Sci. Quart.,* September 1969, *50*(2), pp. 325–36. [G: U.S.]

Ruzavina, E. Economic Aspects in the Urbanization Process. *Prob. Econ.,* August 1969, *12*(4), pp. 68–79. [G: U.S.S.R.]

Ryder, Norman B. The Emergence of a Modern Fertility Pattern: United States 1917–66. **In** *Behrman, S. J.; Corsa, L., Jr. and Freedman, R., eds.,* 1969, pp. 99–123. [G: U.S.]

Sabolo, Yves. Sectoral Employment Growth: The Outlook for 1980. *Int. Lab. Rev.,* November 1969, *100*(5), pp. 445–74.

Santoro, Vincenzo. Considerazioni sul movimento demografico in Campania, per gruppi di comuni. (With English summary.) *Statistica,* January-March 1969, *29*(1), pp. 73–105. [G: Italy]

Schiaffino, Andrea. Interrelazioni tra manifestazioni demografiche e manifestazioni economico-sociali in Emilia e Veneto nell'ultimo secolo. Relazione illustrativa dell'attività svolta dal gruppo di ricerca C.N.R. diretto dal prof. Paolo Fortunati. (With English summary.) *Statistica,* October-December 1969, *29*(4), pp. 563–602.

Schultz, T. Paul. An Economic Model of Family Planning and Fertility. *J. Polit. Econ.,* March/April 1969, *77*(2), pp. 153–80. [G: Puerto Rico]

Schultz, T. Paul. Demographic Conditions of Economic Development in Latin America. **In** *Nisbet, C. T., ed.,* 1969, pp. 41–72. [G: Latin America]

Sheldon, Henry D. Population Statistics: Published and Unpublished. *Mon. Lab. Rev.,* December 1969, *92*(12), pp. 45–49. [G: U.S.]

Simon, Herbert A. Effects of Increased Productivity upon the Ratio of Urban to Rural Population. **In** *Fox, K. A. and Johnson, D. G., eds.,* 1969, pp. 309–20.

Sivamurthy, M. Errors in the Estimation of Net Migration Rate in the Studies of Internal Migration. *J. Amer. Statist. Assoc.,* December 1969, *64*(328), pp. 1434–38.

Spencer, Geraldine. Recent Trends in Marriages in Australia. *Econ. Rec.,* June 1969, *45*(110), pp. 206–17. [G: Australia]

Stafford, Frank P. Student Family Size in Relation to Current and Expected Income. *J. Polit. Econ.,* Part I, July/August 1969, *77*(4), pp. 471–77. [G: U.S.]

Steigenga, W. The Contribution of Demography to Physical and Spatial Planning. **In** *Bechhofer, F., ed.,* 1969, pp. 117–26.

Stigler, George J. Opportunity Cost of Marriage: Comment. *J. Polit. Econ.,* September/October 1969, *77*(5), pp. 863.

Suavy, A. The Economic and Political Consequences of Selective Migrations from One Country to Another. **In** *Bechhofer, F., ed.,* 1969, pp. 43–56.

Sukhatme, P. V. The Dimensions of India's Food Problem in Economic Development. **In** *Bhuleshkar, A. V., ed.,* 1969, pp. 69–87. [G: India]

Sutter, Jean. The Effect of Birth Limitation on Genetic Composition of Populations. **In** *Behrman, S. J.; Corsa, L., Jr. and Freedman, R., eds.,* 1969, pp. 213–51.

Swerdloff, Sol. How Good Were Manpower Projections for the 1960's. *Mon. Lab. Rev.,* November 1969, *92*(11), pp. 17–22. [G: U.S.]

Sykes, Z. M. Some Stochastic Versions of the Matrix Model for Population Dynamics. *J. Amer. Statist. Assoc.,* March 1969, *64*(325), pp. 111–30.

Taagepera, Rein. National Differences within Soviet Demographic Trends. *Soviet Stud.,* April 1969, *20* (4), pp. 478–89. [G: U.S.S.R.]

Tabah, L. Population Growth and Economic Development: Comment. **In** *Bechhofer, F., ed.,* 1969, pp. 165–69.

Taeuber, Conrad. Planning a New Inventory of the U.S.—Who Will Use the 1970 Census? *Univ. Missouri Bus. Govt. Rev.,* March–April 1969, *10*(2), pp. 5–13. [G: U.S.]

Taeuber, Irene B. Population Growth in Less-Developed Countries. **In** *Hauser, P. M., ed.,* 1969, pp. 34–58.

Taeuber, Karl E. Negro Population and Housing: Demographic Aspects of a Social Accounting Scheme. **In** *Katz, I. and Gurin, P., eds.,* 1969, pp. 145–93. [G: U.S.]

Tarver, James D. Migration Differentials in Southern Cities and Suburbs. *Soc. Sci. Quart.,* September 1969, *50*(2), pp. 298–324. [G: U.S.]

Thomas, Brinley. Brain Drain Again. **In** *Blaug, M., ed.,* 1969, pp. 250–80.

Thomas, V. J. A Stochastic Population Model Related to Human Populations. *J. Roy. Statist. Soc.,* Part 1, 1969, *132,* pp. 89–104.

Tietze, Christopher. Induced Abortion as a Method of Fertility Control. **In** *Behrman, S. J.; Corsa, L., Jr. and Freedman, R., eds.,* 1969, pp. 311–37.

Tobier, Emanuel. People and Jobs. **In** *Connery, R. H. and Caraley, D., eds.,* 1969, pp. 7–19. [G: U.S.]

Trebici, Vladimir. Metode moderne de analiză demografică. (Modern Methods of Demographic Analysis. With English summary.) *Stud. Cercet. Econ.,* 1969, *4,* pp. 165–71. [G: Romania]

Turner, Marshall L., Jr. How Changes in Household Composition Affect Family Income. *Mon. Lab. Rev.,* November 1969, *92*(11), pp. 59–61. [G: U.S.]

Valentei, D. Current Population Problems in the U.S.S.R. *Prob. Econ.,* November 1969, *12*(7), pp.

49–60. [G: U.S.S.R.]

Vechkanov, G. Raising the Effectiveness of the Territorial Redistribution of Labor Resources. *Prob. Econ.*, October 1969, *12*(6), pp. 58–67. [G: U.S.S.R.]

Votey, Harold L., Jr. The Optimum Population and Growth: A New Look. A Modification to Include a Preference for Children in the Welfare Function. *J. Econ. Theory*, October 1969, *1*(3), pp. 273–90.

Ward, Richard J. Alternative Means to Control Population Growth. *Rev. Soc. Econ.*, September 1969, *27*(2), pp. 121–38.

Watanabe, S. The Brain Drain from Developing to Developed Countries. *Int. Lab. Rev.*, April 1969, *99*(4), pp. 401–33.

Weller, Robert H. Role Conflict and Fertility. *Soc. Econ. Stud.*, September 1969, *18*(3), pp. 263–72.

West, E. G. Welfare Economics and Emigration Taxes. *Southern Econ. J.*, July 1969, *36*(1), pp. 52–59.

Westoff, Charles F. and Ryder, Norman B. Recent Trends in Attitudes Toward Fertility Control and in the Practice of Contraception in the United States. **In** *Behrman, S. J.; Corsa, L., Jr. and Freedman, R., eds.*, 1969, pp. 388–412. [G: U.S.]

Wilkins, C. A. and Shaw, J. A. An Example to Illustrate the "Average" Nature of Clark's Law of Urban Populations. *J. Reg. Sci.*, August 1969, *9*(2), pp. 255–59.

Wolf, Laurence G. The Metropolitan Tidal Wave in Ohio, 1900–2000. *Econ. Geogr.*, April 1969, *45*(2), pp. 133–54. [G: U.S.]

Wolfe, J. N. The Contribution of Demography to Physical and Spatial Planning: Comment. **In** *Bechhofer, F., ed.*, 1969, pp. 127–30.

Ya-nan, Wang. The Marxist Population Theory and China's Population Problem. *Chinese Econ. Stud.*, Spring-Summer 1969, *2*(3–4), pp. 3–91. [G: China]

Yocum, James C. Recent Changes in Interstate and Interregional Population Flows. *Ohio State U. Bull. Bus. Res.*, May 1969, *44*(5), pp. 4–7. [G: U.S.]

Zaidan, George C. Population Growth and Economic Development. *Finance Develop.*, March 1969, *6*(1), pp. 2–8.

Zelnik, Marvin. Age Patterns of Mortality of American Negroes: 1900–02 to 1959–61. *J. Amer. Statist. Assoc.*, June 1969, *64*(326), pp. 433–51. [G: U.S.]

850 Human Capital

851 Human Capital

8510 Human Capital

Adhvaryu, J. H. The Theory of Investment in Human Capital. **In** *Pandit, H. N., ed.*, 1969, pp. 136–45. [G: India]

Altman, Stuart H. and Fisher, Anthony C. Marginal Product of Labor, Wages and Disequilibrium: Comment. *Rev. Econ. Statist.*, November 1969, *51*(4), pp. 485–86.

Ambannavar, Jaipal P. Upward Occupational Mobility Through Education and Age. *Asian Econ. Rev.*, May 1969, *11*(3), pp. 290–99. [G: India]

Ashenfelter, Orley and Mooney, Joseph D. Some Evidence on the Private Returns to Graduate Education. *Southern Econ. J.*, January 1969, *35*(3), pp. 247–56.

Baird, Leonard L. and Holland, John L. The Flow of High School Students to Schools, Colleges, and Jobs: A Re-examination of Some Old Questions by the Use of Multiple Indices of Talent. *J. Human Res.*, Winter 1969, *4*(1), pp. 22–37. [G: U.S.]

Balogh, Thomas. Education and Agrarian Progress in Developing Countries. **In** *[Edding, Friedrich]*, 1969, pp. 259–68.

Berls, Robert H. An Exploration of the Determinants of Effectiveness in Higher Education. **In** *the Economics and Financing of Higher Education in the United States, JECP*, 1969, pp. 207–60. [G: U.S.]

Bishop, C. E. The Need for Improved Mobility Policy. **In** *Ruttan, V. W.; Waldo, A. D. and Houck, J. P., eds.*, 1969, pp. 242–54. [G: U.S.]

Bolton, Roger E. The Economics and Public Financing of Higher Education: An Overview. **In** *the Economics and Financing of Higher Education in the United States, JECP*, 1969, pp. 11–104. [G: U.S.]

Bowman, Mary Jean and Anderson, C. Arnold. Relationship among Schooling, "Ability," and Income in Industrialized Societies. **In** *[Edding, Friedrich]*, 1969, pp. 97–119.

Buniaev, M. F. The Role of Education in the Training of Qualified Personnel for Agriculture. **In** *Noah, H. J., ed.*, 1969, pp. 23–26. [G: U.S.S.R.]

Cartter, Allan M. The Economics of Higher Education. **In** *Chamberlain, N. W., ed.*, 1969, pp. 145–84. [G: U.S.]

Chamberlain, Neil W. Some Further Thoughts on the Concept of Human Capital. **In** *Somers, G. G. and Wood, W. D., eds.*, 1969, pp. 230–48.

Chaudhri, D. P. Education of Farmers and Productivity. **In** *Pandit, H. N., ed.*, 1969, pp. 337–48. [G: India]

Chiswick, Barry R. Minimum Schooling Legislation and the Cross-Sectional Distribution of Income. *Econ. J.*, September 1969, *79*(315), pp. 495–507. [G: U.S.; Netherlands; U.K.]

Chomchai, Prachoom. Implantation and Acclimatization of the Social Sciences in Thailand. *Int. Soc. Sci. J.*, 1969, *21*(3), pp. 383–92. [G: Thailand]

Daniere, Andre. The Benefits and Costs of Alternative Federal Programs of Financial Aid to College Students. **In** *the Economics and Financing of Higher Education in the United States, JECP*, 1969, pp. 556–98. [G: U.S.]

Denison, Edward F. The Contribution of Education to the Quality of Labor: Comment. *Amer. Econ. Rev.*, December 1969, *59*(5), pp. 935–43. [G: U.S.]

DeVoretz, Don. Alternative Planning Models for Philippine Educational Investment. *Philippine Econ. J.*, Second Semester 1969, *8*(2), pp. 99–116. [G: Philippines]

Dorai, G. C. A Cost-Benefit Analysis of the International Flow of Students. *Indian Econ. J.*,

October–December 1969, *17*(2), pp. 234–49. **[G: India]**

Dyar, Robert and Gaffey, William R. Current Challenges to Health Statisticians. *Amer. Statist.*, December 1969, *23*(5), pp. 19–22. **[G: U.S.]**

Elvin, H. L. The Idea of Quality in Education and the Difficulty of Costing It. **In** *Beeby, C. E., ed.*, 1969, pp. 89–102.

Feldman, Paul and Hoenack, Stephen A. Private Demand for Higher Education in the United States. **In** *the Economics and Financing of Higher Education in the United States, JECP*, 1969, pp. 375–95. **[G: U.S.]**

Foster, Phillips and Yost, Larry. A Simulation Study of Population, Education, and Income Growth in Uganda. *Amer. J. Agr. Econ.*, August 1969, *51*(3), pp. 576–91. **[G: Uganda]**

Galper, Harvey and Dunn, Robert M., Jr. A Short-Run Demand Function for Higher Education in the United States. *J. Polit. Econ.*, September/October 1969, *77*(5), pp. 765–77. **[G: U.S.]**

Griliches, Zvi. Capital-Skill Complementarity. *Rev. Econ. Statist.*, November 1969, *51*(4), pp. 465–68. **[G: U.S.]**

Grossack, Irvin. The Nation—Economic Benefits of Higher Education Distribution. *Indiana Bus. Rev.*, September/October 1969, *44*, pp. 14–16. **[G: U.S.]**

Hajela, P. D. Investment in Education—A Point of View. **In** *Pandit, H. N., ed.*, 1969, pp. 387–91. **[G: India]**

Hansen, Niles M. Improving Economic Opportunity for the Mexican Americans: A Critical Evaluation of Public Policy, with Assessment of the Problem in South Texas. *Econ. Bus. Bull.*, Fall 1969, *22*(1), pp. 1–14. **[G: U.S.]**

Harbison, Frederick H. Education and Economic Development in Advanced Countries. **In** *[Edding, Friedrich]*, 1969, pp. 223–30.

Harbison, Frederick H. and Myers, C. A. Strategies of Human Resource Development. **In** *Blaug, M., ed.*, 1969, pp. 13–60.

Hines, Fred K. Propensities to Invest in Schooling in the South and Non-South. *Amer. J. Agr. Econ.*, December 1969, *51*(5), pp. 1561–64. **[G: U.S.]**

Holtmann, A. G. Correction to Migration to the Suburbs, Human Capital and City Income Tax Losses: A Case Study. *Nat. Tax J.*, September 1969, *22*(3), pp. 424. **[G: U.S.]**

Hussain, I. Z. Returns Approach to Educational Planning. **In** *Pandit, H. N., ed.*, 1969, pp. 280–93. **[G: India]**

Kamat, A. R. Efficiency of Education. **In** *Pandit, H. N., ed.*, 1969, pp. 123–30. **[G: India]**

Kaplan, I. I. The Influence of Education on Labor Output. **In** *Noah, H. J., ed.*, 1969, pp. 101–13. **[G: U.S.S.R.]**

Kaser, Michael. Some Macroeconomics of Education. **In** *[Edding, Friedrich]*, 1969, pp. 139–53.

Khaikin, N. M. Technical-Economic Indexes of the Labor of Workers with Different Vocational Preparation. **In** *Noah, H. J., ed.*, 1969, pp. 141–49. **[G: U.S.S.R.]**

Kozlova, D. I. The Influence of Education on the Labor of Textile Workers. **In** *Noah, H. J., ed.*, 1969, pp. 114–18. **[G: U.S.S.R.]**

Kudrna, A. Differentiation in Earnings. *Eastern Europ. Econ.*, Summer 1969, *7*(4), pp. 25–37. **[G: Czechoslovakia]**

Lee, Everett. Education and Migration in the United States. **In** *[Edding, Friedrich]*, 1969, pp. 231–37. **[G: U.S.]**

Lester, Richard A. Some Investment-Like Aspects of Employment and Pay. *Mon. Lab. Rev.*, November 1969, *92*(11), pp. 62–65.

Lewis, A. B. Training Foreign Graduate Students in Agricultural Economics: Further Comment. *Amer. J. Agr. Econ.*, August 1969, *51*(3), pp. 697–99.

Lewis, W. Arthur. Economic Aspects of Quality in Education. **In** *Beeby, C. E., ed.*, 1969, pp. 71–88.

Meyer, A. J. The Harvard Tunisia Project: An Experiment in Field Research. **In** *Nader, C. and Zahlan, A. B., eds.*, 1969, pp. 31–39. **[G: Tunisia]**

Mikulich, A. P. The Influence of Different Levels of Education on Labor Productivity: A Calculation. **In** *Noah, H. J., ed.*, 1969, pp. 132–40. **[G: U.S.S.R.]**

Myint, H. Trade, Education and Economic Development. **In** *Stewart, I. G., ed.*, 1969, pp. 1–12.

Padmanabhan, C. B. Problems Involved in Measuring Cost, Efficiency and Productivity of the Indian Educational System. **In** *Pandit, H. N., ed.*, 1969, pp. 416–24. **[G: India]**

Panchamukhi, V. R. and Panchamukhi, P. R. Socio-Economic Variables and Urban Incomes. **In** *Pandit, H. N., ed.*, 1969, pp. 306–36. **[G: India]**

Parish, R. M. Some Thoughts on the Role of the Agricultural Economics Profession in Australia. *Australian J. Agr. Econ.*, June 1969, *13*(1), pp. 1–7. **[G: Australia]**

Patel, M. L. Rationale of Human Capital and Its Productivity Analysis. **In** *Pandit, H. N., ed.*, 1969, pp. 349–55. **[G: India]**

Roy, M. Sinha. Productivity of Education with Special Reference to Under-developed Countries. **In** *Pandit, H. N., ed.*, 1969, pp. 294–303. **[G: India]**

Samoilova, I. D. The Returns from Various Types of Specialist Training. **In** *Noah, H. J., ed.*, 1969, pp. 159–66. **[G: U.S.S.R.]**

Saunders, John V. D. Education and Modernization in Brazil. **In** *Baklanoff, E. N., ed.*, 1969, pp. 109–41. **[G: Brazil]**

Schwartzman, David. The Contribution of Education to the Quality of Labor: Reply. *Amer. Econ. Rev.*, December 1969, *59*(5), pp. 944–46. **[G: U.S.]**

Scully, Gerald W. Human Capital and Productivity in U.S. Manufacturing. *Western Econ. J.*, December 1969, *7*(4), pp. 334–40. **[G: U.S.]**

Segal, David. "Equity" Versus "Efficiency" in Higher Education. **In** *The Economics and Financing of Higher Education in the United States, JECP*, 1969, pp. 135–44. **[G: U.S.]**

Sharma, R. C. Benefit-Cost Analysis of Educational Projects: A Review of Researches. **In** *Pandit, H. N., ed.*, 1969, pp. 393–415. **[G: India]**

Simmons, John L. Technology and Education for Economic Development. **In** *Nader, C. and Zahlan, A. B., eds.*, 1969, pp. 41–59.

Singer, Neil and Feldman, Paul. Criteria for Public

Investment in Higher Education. **In** *The Economics and Financing of Higher Education in the United States, JECP,* 1969, pp. 124–34. **[G: U.S.]**

Sinha, Laksminarayan. Cost and Efficiency of Education. **In** *Pandit, H. N., ed.,* 1969, pp. 131–35. **[G: India]**

Smith, C. Selby. Benefits to British Employers from Post-secondary Education. *J. Roy. Statist. Soc.,* Part 3, 1969, *132,* pp. 408–17. **[G: U.K.]**

Stevenson, Russell. The United States Graduate Training of Asian Rural Social Scientists. *Land Econ.,* August 1969, *45*(3), pp. 334–43.

Streeten, Paul. Economic Development and Education. **In** *[Edding, Friedrich],* 1969, pp. 183–98.

Tan, Edita Abella. Implications of Private Demand for Education on Manpower Planning. *Philippine Econ. J.,* Second Semester 1969, *8*(2), pp. 117–29.

Van Rompuy, P. Note on the Optimum Period of Employment. *Tijdschr. Econ.,* 1969, *14*(4), pp. 584–86.

Venkateshwar Rao, H. Educational Costs: Concepts and Issues. **In** *Pandit, H. N., ed.,* 1969, pp. 46–56. **[G: India]**

Waldman, Elizabeth. Educational Attainment of Workers. *Mon. Lab. Rev.,* February 1969, *92*(2), pp. 14–22. **[G: U.S.]**

Welch, Finis. Linear Synthesis of Skill Distribution. *J. Human Res.,* Summer 1969, *4*(3), pp. 311–27. **[G: U.S.]**

Wortman, Max S., Jr. National Policies and Programs for Human Resources Management. *Ohio State U. Bull. Bus. Res.,* December 1969, *44*(12), pp. 4–6. **[G: U.S.]**

Zhamin, V. A. Contemporary Problems of the Economics of Education. **In** *Noah, H. J., ed.,* 1969, pp. 3–19. **[G: U.S.S.R.]**

Ziderman, Adrian. Costs and Benefits of Adult Retraining in the United Kingdom. *Economica, N.S.,* November 1969, *36*(144), pp. 363–76. **[G: U.K.]**

900 Welfare Programs; Consumer Economics; Urban and Regional Economics

910 Welfare, Health, and Education

911 General Welfare Programs

9110 General Welfare Programs

Aaron, Henry J. Perspectives on Poverty 4: Income Transfer Programs. *Mon. Lab. Rev.,* February 1969, *92*(2), pp. 50–54. **[G: U.S.]**

Barth, Peter S. An Economist Looks at Welfare Programs. *Ohio State U. Bull. Bus. Res.,* October 1969, *44*(10), pp. 1–5. **[G: U.S.]**

Brockelbank, W. J. The Family Desertion Problems across State Lines. *Ann. Amer. Acad. Polit. Soc. Sci.,* May 1969, *383,* pp. 23–33. **[G: U.S.]**

Caballero Tamayo, Xavier. The ILO and Development in the Americas. *Int. Lab. Rev.,* December 1969, *100*(6), pp. 505–50. **[G: Latin America]**

Cnudde, Charles F. and McCrone, Donald J. Party Competition and Welfare Policies in the American States. *Amer. Polit. Sci. Rev.,* September 1969, *63*(3), pp. 858–66. **[G: U.S.]**

Cox, Eli P. Guaranteed Annual Income and Consumer Demand. **In** *Extension of Elementary and Secondary Education Programs, Pt. 4, HCH,* 1969, pp. 2848–74. **[G: U.S.]**

Egbert, Alvin C. and Hiemstra, Stephen J. Shifting Direct Government Payments from Agriculture to Poor People: Impacts on Food Consumption and Farm Income. *Agr. Econ. Res.,* July 1969, *21* (3), pp. 61–69. **[G: U.S.]**

Faltermayer, Edmund K. A Way Out of the Welfare Mess. **In** *Starleaf, D. R., ed.,* 1969, pp. 439–48. **[G: U.S.]**

Gold, Ronald B. Fiscal Capacities and Welfare Expenditures of States. *Nat. Tax J.,* December 1969, *22*(4), pp. 496–505. **[G: U.S.]**

Hausman, Leonard J. Potential for Financial Self-Support among AFDC and AFDC-UP Recipients. *Southern Econ. J.,* July 1969, *36*(1), pp. 60–66. **[G: U.S.]**

Hayes, William A. The Guaranteed Annual Income: An Appraisal. *Rev. Soc. Econ.,* March 1969, *27*(1), pp. 74–83. **[G: U.S.]**

Hicks, Ursula K. La finanza pubblica nel quadro della politica economica e sociale della Gran Bretagna. (The Finance of the British Government. With English summary.) *Bancaria,* September 1969, *25*(9), pp. 1067–81. **[G: U.K.]**

Johnson, Orace E. Beyond the Illfare State. *Univ. Missouri Bus. Govt. Rev.,* May–June 1969, *10*(3), pp. 28–36. **[G: U.S.]**

Kaim-Caudle, P. R. Selectivity and the Social Services. *Lloyds Bank Rev.,* April 1969, (92), pp. 26–45. **[G: U.K.]**

Kunel'skii, L. The Socioeconomic Significance of Raising the Minimum Wage. *Prob. Econ.,* July 1969, *12*(3), pp. 43–57. **[G: U.S.S.R.]**

Loyd, Harold J. and Breimyer, Harold F. Food Donation Programs. *Amer. J. Agr. Econ.,* November 1969, *51*(4), pp. 934–36. **[G: U.S.]**

Oeter, Ferdinand. Familienlastenausgleich und Angleichung der sozialen Startbedingungen: Analysen und Vorschläge. (Equilization of Family Burdens and Social Starting Conditions: Analysis and Proposals. With English summary.) *Schmollers Jahr.,* 1969, *89*(1), pp. 33–59. **[G: W. Germany]**

Ott, Attiat F.; Ott, David J. and Turner, J. Scott. Simulation of Costs of a Negative Income Tax Plan and Its Implications for the Poor. **In** *Willis, A. B., ed.,* 1969, pp. 168–83. **[G: U.S.]**

Paulson, Wayne; Butler, Edgar W. and Pope, Hallowell. Community Power and Public Welfare. *Amer. J. Econ. Soc.,* January 1969, *28*(1), pp. 17–28. **[G: U.S.]**

Popkin, William D. Administration of a Negative Income Tax. *Yale Law J.,* January 1969, *78*(3), pp. 388–431. **[G: U.S.]**

Rein, Martin. Choice and Change in the American Welfare System. *Ann. Amer. Acad. Polit. Soc. Sci.,* September 1969, *385,* pp. 89–109. **[G: U.S.]**

Rohrlich, George F. The Place of Social Insurance

in the Pursuit of the General Welfare. *J. Risk Ins.*, September 1969, *36*(4), pp. 333–53.

Tévoédjré, Albert. A Strategy for Social Progress in Africa and the I.L.O.'s Contribution. *Int. Lab. Rev.*, January 1969, *99*(1), pp. 61–84. **[G: Africa]**

Tobin, James. The Negative Income Tax. **In** *Starleaf, D. R., ed.*, 1969, pp. 435–38. **[G: U.S.]**

912 Economics of Education

9120 Economics of Education

Aaron, Henry J. Local Public Expenditures and the "Migration Effect." *Western Econ. J.*, December 1969, *7*(4), pp. 385–90.

Amin, R. B. University and Industry. *Artha-Vikas,* January 1969, *5*(1), pp. 1–8.

Armitage, P. and Smith, C. Selby. Computable Models of the British Educational System. **In** *Blaug, M., ed.*, 1969, pp. 202–37. **[G: U.K.]**

Awokoya, Stephen O. The Structure and Development of Nigerian Education. **In** *Yesufu, T. M., ed.*, 1969, pp. 157–82. **[G: Nigeria]**

Bacchus, M. K. Patterns of Educational Expenditure in an Emergent Nation—A Study of Guyana 1945–65. *Soc. Econ. Stud.*, September 1969, *18* (3), pp. 282–301. **[G: Guyana]**

Baird, Leonard L. and Holland, John L. The Flow of High School Students to Schools, Colleges, and Jobs: A Re-examination of Some Old Questions by the Use of Multiple Indices of Talent. *J. Human Res.*, Winter 1969, *4*(1), pp. 22–37. **[G: U.S.]**

Bauman, W. Scott. The School Calendar Dilemma—A Solution for the Approaching Crisis. *Oregon Bus. Rev.*, June 1969, *28*(6), pp. 1–5. **[G: U.S.]**

Becker, Hellmut. Friedrich Edding's Contribution to the Economics of Education and to Educational Research. **In** *[Edding, Friedrich]*, 1969, pp. 17–23.

Belasco, James A. and Alutto, Joseph A. Organizational Impacts of Teacher Negotiations. *Ind. Relat.*, October 1969, *9*(1), pp. 67–79. **[G: U.S.]**

Berezniak, E. S. Structuring the Network of Schools in the Ukrainian S.S.R. **In** *Noah, H. J., ed.*, 1969, pp. 196–204. **[G: U.S.S.R.]**

Berls, Robert H. Higher Education Opportunity and Achievement in the United States. **In** *the Economics and Financing of Higher Education in the United States, JECP,* 1969, pp. 145–204. **[G: U.S.]**

Betancur-Mejia, Gabriel. Latin America. **In** *Bereday, G. Z. F., ed.*, 1969, pp. 264–76. **[G: Latin America]**

Blaug, Mark. The Productivity of Universities. **In** *Blaug, M., ed.*, 1969, pp. 313–25.

Bowen, Howard R. Tuitions and Student Loans in the Finance of Higher Education. **In** *the Economics and Financing of Higher Education in the United States, JECP,* 1969, pp. 618–31. **[G: U.S.]**

Bowen, William G. Economic Pressures on the Major Private Universities. **In** *the Economics and Financing of Higher Education in the United States, JECP,* 1969, pp. 399–439. **[G: U.S.]**

Brandl, John E. Education Program Analysis at HEW. **In** *The Analysis and Evaluation of Public Expenditures: The PPB System, Vol. 3, JECP,* 1969, pp. 1224–32. **[G: U.S.]**

Braun, Hubert; Hammer, Gerald and Schmid, Karl. Ein Verfahren zur Ermittlung der Ausbildungskapazität wissenschaftlicher Hochschulen. (With English summary.) *Jahr. Nationalökon. Statist.*, March 1969, *182*(4–5), pp. 381–97.

Brown, Ralph S., Jr. Collective Bargaining in Higher Education. *Mich. Law Rev.*, March 1969, *67*(5), pp. 1067–82. **[G: U.S.]**

Bruck, Nicholas K. Higher Education and Economic Development in Central America. *Rev. Soc. Econ.*, September 1969, *27*(2), pp. 160–80. **[G: Central America]**

Bruno, James Edward. Achieving Property Tax Relief with a Minimum Disruption of State Programs. *Nat. Tax J.*, September 1969, *22*(3), pp. 379–89. **[G: U.S.]**

Burns, Joseph M. and Chiswick, Barry R. An Economic Analysis of State Support for Higher Education. *Western Econ. J.*, March 1969, *7*(1), pp. 84–95.

Butenko, A. M. The Economics of Education: Some Observations. **In** *Noah, H. J., ed.*, 1969, pp. 27–31. **[G: U.S.S.R.]**

Carter, Charles F. Can We Get British Higher Education Cheaper? **In** *Blaug, M., ed.*, 1969, pp. 326–39. **[G: U.K.]**

Cartter, Allan M. and Farrell, Robert L. Academic Labor Market Projections and the Draft. **In** *the Economics and Financing of Higher Education in the United States, JECP,* 1969, pp. 357–74. **[G: U.S.]**

Cerych, Ladislav. Accelerating the Innovation Process in Education. **In** *Bereday, G. Z. F., ed.*, 1969, pp. 34–50.

Chiswick, Barry R. Minimum Schooling Legislation and the Cross-Sectional Distribution of Income. *Econ. J.*, September 1969, *79*(315), pp. 495–507. **[G: U.S.; Netherlands; U.K.]**

Chomchai, Prachoom. Implantation and Acclimatization of the Social Sciences in Thailand. *Int. Soc. Sci. J.*, 1969, *21*(3), pp. 383–92. **[G: Thailand]**

Clurman, Michael. Does Higher Education Need More Money? **In** *the Economics and Financing of Higher Education in the United States, JECP,* 1969, pp. 632–64. **[G: U.S.]**

Cnudde, Charles F. and McCrone, Donald J. Party Competition and Welfare Policies in the American States. *Amer. Polit. Sci. Rev.*, September 1969, *63*(3), pp. 858–66. **[G: U.S.]**

Conlisk, John. Determinants of School Enrollment and School Performance. *J. Human Res.*, Spring 1969, *4*(2), pp. 140–57. **[G: U.S.]**

Coussy, Jean. Adjusting Economics Curricula to African Needs. *Int. Soc. Sci. J.*, 1969, *21*(3), pp. 393–405. **[G: Africa]**

Cross, Malcolm and Schwartzbaum, Allan M. Social Mobility and Secondary School Selection in Trinidad and Tobago. *Soc. Econ. Stud.*, June 1969, *18*(2), pp. 189–207. **[G: Trinidad; Tobago]**

Cullity, John P. The Growth of Educational Employment in Three Countries, 1895–1964. *J. Human Res.*, Winter 1969, *4*(1), pp. 84–92. **[G: U.S.; U.K.; Germany]**

Datt, Ruddar. Unit Costs of Education—A Case

Study of Haryana Colleges. **In** *Pandit, H. N., ed.*, 1969, pp. 92–113. **[G: India]**

Dey, B. On Costing of Education. **In** *Pandit, H. N., ed.*, 1969, pp. 14–26. **[G: India]**

Edding, Friedrich. Educational Resources and Productivity. **In** *Bereday, G. Z. F., ed.*, 1969, pp. 19–33.

Feitel'man, N. G. The Tasks of Planning Education. **In** *Noah, H. J., ed.*, 1969, pp. 169–76. **[G: U.S.S.R.]**

de Franz, Marie-Anne. Implanting the Social Sciences—A Review of UNESCO's Endeavours. *Int. Soc. Sci. J.*, 1969, *21*(3), pp. 406–20.

Freeman, Roger A. Federal Assistance to Higher Education through Income Tax Credits. **In** *the Economics and Financing of Higher Education in the United States, JECP*, 1969, pp. 665–83. **[G: U.S.]**

Galper, Harvey and Dunn, Robert M., Jr. A Short-Run Demand Function for Higher Education in the United States. *J. Polit. Econ.*, September/October 1969, *77*(5), pp. 765–77. **[G: U.S.]**

Gass, James Ronald. Reflections on Equality, Quantity and Quality in Education. **In** *[Edding, Friedrich]*, 1969, pp. 215–22.

Gilson, J. C. The Demand for Agricultural Economists by Canadian Universities and Governments. *Can. J. Agr. Econ.*, November 1969, *17*(3), pp. 124–32. **[G: Canada]**

Greene, Mark R. Doctoral Education for Risk and Insurance in Leading U.S. Universities. *J. Risk Ins.*, December 1969, *36*(5), pp. 505–13. **[G: U.S.]**

Grossack, Irvin. The Nation—Economic Benefits of Higher Education Distribution. *Indiana Bus. Rev.*, September/October 1969, *44*, pp. 14–16. **[G: U.S.]**

Hajela, D. and Tikkiwal, B. D. Wastage in Education and Measures to Prevent It. **In** *Pandit, H. N., ed.*, 1969, pp. 146–63. **[G: India]**

Hansen, W. Lee and Weisbrod, Burton A. The Distribution of Costs and Direct Benefits of Public Higher Education: The Case of California. *J. Human Res.*, Spring 1969, *4*(2), pp. 176–91. **[G: U.S.]**

Hansen, W. Lee and Weisbrod, Burton A. The Search for Equity in the Provision and Finance of Higher Education. **In** *the Economics and Financing of Higher Education in the United States, JECP*, 1969, pp. 107–23. **[G: U.S.]**

Harris, Seymour E. Financing Higher Education: An Overview. **In** *the Economics and Financing of Higher Education in the United States, JECP*, 1969, pp. 467–506. **[G: U.S.]**

Hendon, William S. Faculty Compensation and the Cost of Living. *Soc. Sci. Quart.*, September 1969, *50*(2), pp. 396–400. **[G: U.S.]**

Hettich, Walter. Mixed Public and Private Financing of Education: Comment. *Amer. Econ. Rev.*, March 1969, *59*(1), pp. 210–12.

Hicks, Ursula K. Educational Expansion in Low Income Countries with Special Reference to India. **In** *Bhuleshkar, A. V., ed.*, 1969, pp. 368–94. **[G: India]**

Hirsch, Werner Z. and Marcus, Morton J. Intercommunity Spillovers and the Provision of Public Education. *Kyklos*, 1969, *22*(4), pp. 641–60. **[G: U.S.]**

Holtmann, A. G. Teacher Salaries and the Economic Benefits of Search. *J. Human Res.*, Winter 1969, *4*(1), pp. 99–103.

Hüfner, Klaus and Naumann, Jens. Economics of Education in Transition: Summary of the Contribution. **In** *[Edding, Friedrich]*, 1969, pp. 39–50.

Hurd, G. E. and Johnson, T. J. Sociology in the Third World Situation. *Int. Soc. Sci. J.*, 1969, *21*(3), pp. 421–27.

Husén, Torsten. Some Views of Cross-National Assessment of the "Quality of Education." **In** *[Edding, Friedrich]*, 1969, pp. 87–95.

Idenburg, Philip J. Europe—In Search of New Forms of Education. **In** *Bereday, G. Z. F., ed.*, 1969, pp. 277–96. **[G: Europe]**

Jenny, Hans H. and Wynn, G. Richard. Expenditure Expectations for Private Colleges. **In** *The Economics and Financing of Higher Education in the United States, JECP*, 1969, pp. 440–64. **[G: U.S.]**

Jenny, Hans H. and Wynn, G. Richard. Short-Run Cost Variations in Institutions of Higher Learning. **In** *The Economics and Financing of Higher Education in the United States, JECP*, 1969, pp. 261–94. **[G: U.S.]**

de Jong, F. J. De economische betekenis van de Rijksuniversiteit te Groningen voor de provincie. (The Economic Significance of the University of Groningen for the Province. With English summary.) *De Economist*, May/June 1969, *117*(3), pp. 193–226. **[G: Netherlands]**

Kaverau, T. A. Consolidating Small Schools—An Essential Task. **In** *Noah, H. J., ed.*, 1969, pp. 192–95. **[G: U.S.S.R.]**

Kerr, Clark. Education in the United States: Past Accomplishments and Present Problems. **In** *Bereday, G. Z. F., ed.*, 1969, pp. 297–311. **[G: U.S.]**

Kerr, Clark. Federal Aid to Higher Education through 1976. **In** *the Economics and Financing of Higher Education in the United States, JECP*, 1969, pp. 599–617. **[G: U.S.]**

Khan, Q. U. Efficiency Coefficients for School Stage Education. **In** *Pandit, H. N., ed.*, 1969, pp. 164–72. **[G: India]**

Klaus, Ida. The Evolution of a Collective Bargaining Relationship in Public Education: New York City's Changing Seven-Year History. *Mich. Law Rev.*, March 1969, *67*(5), pp. 1033–66. **[G: U.S.]**

Komarov, V. E. The Efficiency of Day, Correspondence, and Evening Education. **In** *Noah, H. J., ed.*, 1969, pp. 153–58. **[G: U.S.S.R.]**

Kulkarni, G. B. Unit Costs of Education in Commerce Colleges of Bombay: 1962–63 to 1966–67. **In** *Pandit, H. N., ed.*, 1969, pp. 114–20. **[G: India]**

Landynski, Jacob W. Governmental Aid to Non-public Schools: The Constitutional Conflict Sharpens. *Soc. Res.*, Autumn 1969, *36*(3), pp. 333–56. **[G: U.S.]**

Leont'ev, E. A. Expenditures in the Tatar Autonomous Republic for Vocational Training in Secondary Schools and Directly in Enterprises: A Comparison. **In** *Noah, H. J., ed.*, 1969, pp. 187–91. **[G: U.S.S.R.]**

Lerman, L. M. Education and the Development of Production in the Uzbek S. S. R. **In** *Noah, H. J., ed.,* 1969, pp. 45–62. **[G: U.S.S.R.]**

Levy, Ferdinand K. Sources of Economies of Scale in Universities. **In** *the Economics and Financing of Higher Education in the United States, JECP,* 1969, pp. 295–302. **[G: U.S.]**

Malassis, Louis. Education and Agricultural Development. *Int. Soc. Sci. J.,* 1969, *21*(2), pp. 244–55.

Malhotra, P. C. The Economics of Correspondence Course for Higher Education. **In** *Pandit, H. N., ed.,* 1969, pp. 379–86. **[G: India]**

Masters, Stanley H. The Effect of Family Income on Children's Education: Some Findings on Inequality of Opportunity. *J. Human Res.,* Spring 1969, *4*(2), pp. 158–75. **[G: U.S.]**

Mc Intyre, M. Charles. Determinants of Expenditures for Public Higher Education. *Nat. Tax J.,* June 1969, *22*(2), pp. 262–72. **[G: U.S.]**

Mushkin, Selma J. A Note on State and Local Financing of Higher Education. **In** *the Economics and Financing of Higher Education in the United States, JECP,* 1969, pp. 518–40. **[G: U.S.]**

Oates, Wallace E. The Effects of Property Taxes and Local Public Spending on Property Values: An Empirical Study of Tax Capitalization and the Tiebout Hypothesis. *J. Polit. Econ.,* November/December 1969, *77*(6), pp. 957–71. **[G: U.S.]**

Onwuka Dike, K. Manpower Training for Economic Development: Professional and Managerial Staff. **In** *Yesufu, T. M., ed.,* 1969, pp. 200–216. **[G: Nigeria]**

Owen, John D. Education for Majority Voting? *Public Choice,* Spring 1969, *6,* pp. 59–70.

Panchamukhi, P. R. Economic Analysis and Planning of Education Industry. **In** *Pandit, H. N., ed.,* 1969, pp. 215–43. **[G: India]**

Pandit, H. N. A Study in Unit Cost at the School Stage in India: A Design of the Research Project. **In** *Pandit, H. N., ed.,* 1969, pp. 3–13. **[G: India]**

Panschar, William. Businessmen, Educators, Move to Enlist Black Grads. *Indiana Bus. Rev.,* May/June 1969, *44,* pp. 12–16. **[G: U.S.]**

Pauly, Mark V. Mixed Public and Private Financing of Education: Reply. *Amer. Econ. Rev.,* March 1969, *59*(1), pp. 212–13.

Peacock, Alan T. and Wiseman, Jack. Principles of Educational Finance in Developed Countries. **In** *Blaug, M., ed.,* 1969, pp. 343–59.

Peaslee, Alexander L. Education's Role in Development. *Econ. Develop. Cult. Change,* April 1969, *17*(3), pp. 293–318.

Porter, Arthur T. Africa. **In** *Bereday, G. Z. F., ed.,* 1969, pp. 225–43. **[G: Africa]**

Prest, Wilfred. Federalism and Education. **In** *Preston, R., ed.,* 1969, pp. 292–315. **[G: Australia]**

Queener, R. S. The Use of Economic Criteria for Educational Decision Making. **In** *Pandit, H. N., ed.,* 1969, pp. 205–14. **[G: India]**

Ramamoorthy, B. and Prakasa Rao, M. S. Terminalization Approach to Pre-University Education. **In** *Pandit, H. N., ed.,* 1969, pp. 356–74. **[G: India]**

Ramamoorthy, B. The Economics of Education. *Econ. Aff.,* January-February 1969, *14*(1–2), pp. 74–80.

Ramanujam, M. S. Planning Models for Optimum Allocation of Resources in Education. **In** *Pandit, H. N., ed.,* 1969, pp. 244–59. **[G: India]**

Rivlin, Alice M. and Weiss, Jeffrey H. Social Goals and Federal Support of Higher Education—The Implications of Various Strategies. **In** *The Economics and Financing of Higher Education in the United States, JECP,* 1969, pp. 543–55. **[G: U.S.]**

Rogers, Daniel C. Private Rates of Return to Education in the United States: A Case Study. *Yale Econ. Essays,* Spring 1969, *9*(1), pp. 89–134. **[G: U.S.]**

Romulo, Carlos P. Symposium on Asian Education. **In** *Bereday, G. Z. F., ed.,* 1969, pp. 244–63. **[G: Asia]**

Rowley, C. K. The Political Economy of British Education. *Scot. J. Polit. Econ.,* June 1969, *16*(2), pp. 152–76. **[G: U.K.]**

Saenko, Iu. I. The Allocation of Capital Investment for School Construction. **In** *Noah, H. J., ed.,* 1969, pp. 87–98. **[G: U.S.S.R.]**

Samoilova, I. D. The Returns from Various Types of Specialist Training. **In** *Noah, H. J., ed.,* 1969, pp. 159–66. **[G: U.S.S.R.]**

Sau, R. K. Some Notes on Resource Allocation in Education. **In** *Pandit, H. N., ed.,* 1969, pp. 260–73. **[G: India]**

Segal, David. "Equity" Versus "Efficiency" in Higher Education. **In** *The Economics and Financing of Higher Education in the United States, JECP,* 1969, pp. 135–44. **[G: U.S.]**

Shah, K. R. Expenditure on Professional School Education in India, 1950–51 to 1960–61. **In** *Pandit, H. N., ed.,* 1969, pp. 75–91. **[G: India]**

Shah, K. R. Private Costs of Elementary Education. **In** *Pandit, H. N., ed.,* 1969, pp. 57–74. **[G: India]**

Sharma, D. L. Unit Costs of Educations, Our Knowledge, Gaps and Our Need. **In** *Pandit, H. N., ed.,* 1969, pp. 27–41. **[G: India]**

Simon, Kenneth A. The Planning of U.S. Higher Education: Projections of Enrollment, Degrees, Staff, and Expenditures to 1977–78. **In** *The Economics and Financing of Higher Education in the United States, JECP,* 1969, pp. 321–56. **[G: U.S.]**

Singh, V. B. and Papola, T. S. Investment Effectiveness and Educational Planning in India. **In** *Pandit, H. N., ed.,* 1969, pp. 274–79. **[G: India]**

Solomon, Gregory L. Public School Systems in Indiana and Its Bordering States. *Indiana Bus. Rev.,* January–February 1969, *44,* pp. 17–24. **[G: U.S.]**

Sonin, M. Ia. Training Personnel and Labor Turnover. **In** *Noah, H. J., ed.,* 1969, pp. 32–35. **[G: U.S.S.R.]**

Sorkin, Alan L. Education and Manpower Programs for Indian Americans. **In** *Indian Education 1969, Pt. 2, Appendix, SCH,* 1969, pp. 1559–98. **[G: U.S.]**

Southwick, Lawrence, Jr. Cost Trends in Land Grant Colleges and Universities. *Appl. Econ.,* August 1969, *1*(3), pp. 167–82. **[G: U.S.]**

Stauss, James H. Endowment as a Source of Increased Revenue. **In** *the Economics and Financing of Higher Education in the United States, JECP,* 1969, pp. 507–17. **[G: U.S.]**

Stepaniuk, V. I. The Use of Classroom Space in Urban Schools: The Case of the Ukraine. **In** *Noah, H. J., ed.,* 1969, pp. 205–15. **[G: U.S.S.R.]**

Stepanov, B. V. Determining Future Requirements for Labor in the Planning Period. **In** *Noah, H. J., ed.,* 1969, pp. 177–86. **[G: U.S.S.R.]**

Stinson, Thomas F. and Krahmer, Edward F. Local School Expenditures and Educational Quality: A Correlation Analysis. *Amer. J. Agr. Econ.,* December 1969, *51*(5), pp. 1553–56. **[G: U.S.]**

Streeten, Paul. Economic Development and Education. **In** *[Edding, Friedrich],* 1969, pp. 183–98.

Stroup, Robert H. and Hargrove, Michael B. Earnings and Education in Rural South Vietnam. *J. Human Res.,* Spring 1969, *4*(2), pp. 215–25. **[G: S. Vietnam]**

Tan, Edita Abella. Implications of Private Demand for Education on Manpower Planning. *Philippine Econ. J.,* Second Semester 1969, *8*(2), pp. 117–29.

Tauchar, William F. Cross Elasticities of Collegiate Demand. *Rev. Soc. Econ.,* September 1969, *27*(2), pp. 222–32. **[G: U.S.]**

Tyler, Ralph W. The Changing Structure of American Institutions of Higher Education. **In** *the Economics and Financing of Higher Education in the United States, JECP,* 1969, pp. 305–20. **[G: U.S.]**

Venkateshwar Rao, H. Educational Costs: Concepts and Issues. **In** *Pandit, H. N., ed.,* 1969, pp. 46–56. **[G: India]**

Waldman, Elizabeth. Educational Attainment of Workers. *Mon. Lab. Rev.,* February 1969, *92*(2), pp. 14–22. **[G: U.S.]**

Wolf, Eleanor P. Community Control of Schools as an Ideology and Social Mechanism. *Soc. Sci. Quart.,* December 1969, *50*(3), pp. 713–22. **[G: U.S.]**

Wollett, Donald H. The Coming Revolution in Public School Management. *Mich. Law Rev.,* March 1969, *67*(5), pp. 1017–32.

Woodhall, Maureen and Blaug, Mark. Variations in Costs and Productivity of British Primary and Secondary Education. **In** *[Edding, Friedrich],* 1969, pp. 69–85. **[G: U.K.]**

Zacharias, Jerrold R. Educational Opportunity through Student Loans: An Approach to Higher Education Financing. **In** *the Economics and Financing of Higher Education in the United States, JECP,* 1969, pp. 652–64. **[G: U.S.]**

Zhamin, V. A. Contemporary Problems of the Economics of Education. **In** *Noah, H. J., ed.,* 1969, pp. 3–19. **[G: U.S.S.R.]**

913 Economics of Health

9130 Economics of Health

Auster, Richard; Leveson, Irving and Sarachek, Deborah. The Production of Health, an Exploratory Study. *J. Human Res.,* Fall 1969, *4*(4), pp. 411–36. **[G: U.S.]**

Baird, Charles W. On the Publicness of Health Care. *Rev. Soc. Econ.,* September 1969, *27*(2), pp. 109–20.

Barzel, Yoram. Productivity and the Price of Medical Services. *J. Polit. Econ.,* November/December 1969, *77*(6), pp. 1014–27. **[G: U.S.]**

Battistella, Roger and Southby, Richard McK. Crisis in American Medicine. **In** *Health Care in America, Pt. 1, SCH,* 1969, pp. 139–47. **[G: U.S.]**

Baumann, Duane D. Perception and Public Policy in the Recreational Use of Domestic Water Supply Reservoirs. *Water Resources Res.,* June 1969, *5*(3), pp. 543–54. **[G: U.S.]**

Breslow, Lester. Statement. **In** *Costs and Delivery of Health Services to Older Americans, Pt. 3, SCH,* 1969, pp. 638–45. **[G: U.S.]**

Brewster, Agnes W. Statement. **In** *Economics of Aging: Toward a Full Share in Abundance, Pt. 1, SCH,* 1969, pp. 9–11. **[G: U.S.]**

Brewster, Agnes W., et al. Health Aspects of the Economics of Aging: A Working Paper. **In** *op. cit., SCP,* 1969, pp. 1–41. **[G: U.S.]**

Brown, Joseph D. Effect of a Health Hazard "Scare" on Consumer Demand. *Amer. J. Agr. Econ.,* August 1969, *51*(3), pp. 676–79. **[G: U.S.]**

Bryant, John H. The Gap between Biomedical Technology and Health Needs in Developing Countries. **In** *Nader, C. and Zahlan, A. B., eds.,* 1969, pp. 1–26.

Cherkasky, Martin. Statement. **In** *Health Care in America, Pt. 1, SCH,* 1969, pp. 4–23. **[G: U.S.]**

Chew, David C. E. Wastage Patterns in the Nursing Profession in Singapore: A Study of Manpower Utilisation. *Int. Lab. Rev.,* December 1969, *100*(6), pp. 583–94. **[G: Singapore]**

Conforti, Joseph M. Attitudes Toward Health and Health Care Facilities Among Low Income Youth. *Soc. Sci. Quart.,* December 1969, *50*(3), pp. 687–94. **[G: U.S.]**

Crew, Michael A. Coinsurance and the Welfare Economics of Medical Care. *Amer. Econ. Rev.,* December 1969, *59*(5), pp. 906–08.

Dyar, Robert and Gaffey, William R. Current Challenges to Health Statisticians. *Amer. Statist.,* December 1969, *23*(5), pp. 19–22. **[G: U.S.]**

Eckstein, Harry. Planning: The National Health Service. **In** *Rose, R., ed.,* 1969, pp. 221–37. **[G: U.K.]**

Ehreneich, Joseph W. Creating Competition in the Health-Care Industry: Some Reflections on Possible Impacts of Major Group Purchasers on Costs and Quality of Health Care. **In** *Costs and Delivery of Health Services to Older Americans, Pt. 3, SCH,* 1969, pp. 746–56. **[G: U.S.]**

Fabricant, Solomon and Hirsch, Werner Z. Some Problems in the Measurement of Productivity in the Medical Care Industry: Comment. **In** *Fuchs, V. R., ed.,* 1969, pp. 146–47. **[G: U.S.]**

Fuchs, Victor. Statement. **In** *Health Care in America, Pt. 1, SCH,* 1969, pp. 275–90. **[G: U.S.]**

Fuchs, Victor. The Basic Forces Influencing Costs of Medical Care. **In** *Health Care in America, Pt. 1, SCH,* 1969, pp. 291–306. **[G: U.S.]**

Fuchs, Victor. The Contribution of Health Services to the American Economy. **In** *Health Care in America, Pt. 1, SCH,* 1969, pp. 313–51. **[G: U.S.]**

Fuchs, Victor. The Growing Demand for Medical Care. **In** *Health Care in America, Pt. 1, SCH,* 1969, pp. 307–12. **[G: U.S.]**

Fullerton, William D. The Problem of Rising Hospital Costs. **In** *Health Care in America, Pt. 1, SCH,* 1969, pp. 165–79. **[G: U.S.]**

Grosse, Robert N. Problems of Resource Allocation in Health. **In** *The Analysis and Evaluation of Public Expenditures: The PPB System, Vol. 3, JECP,* 1969, pp. 1197–1223. **[G: U.S.]**

Harris, Seymour E. Statement. **In** *Costs and Delivery of Health Services to Older Americans, Pt. 3, SCH,* 1969, pp. 766–70. **[G: U.S.]**

Klarman, Herbert E. Economic Aspects of Mental Health Manpower. **In** *Arnhoff, F. N.; Rubinstein, E. A. and Speisman, J. C., eds.,* 1969, pp. 67–92.

Klarman, Herbert E. Economic Aspects of Projecting Requirements for Health Manpower. *J. Human Res.,* Summer 1969, *4*(3), pp. 360–76. **[G: U.S.]**

Klarman, Herbert E. Reimbursing the Hospital—The Differences the Third Party Makes. *J. Risk Ins.,* December 1969, *36*(5), pp. 553–66. **[G: U.S.]**

Klarman, Herbert E. and Feldstein, Martin S. Some Problems in the Measurement of Productivity in the Medical Care Industry: Discussion. **In** *Fuchs, V. R., ed.,* 1969, pp. 132–46. **[G: U.S.]**

Kramer, Morton. Statistics of Mental Disorders in the United States: Current Status, Some Urgent Needs and Suggested Solutions. *J. Roy. Statist. Soc.,* Part 3, 1969, *132,* pp. 353–97. **[G: U.S.]**

Landay, Donald M. Trends in Negotiated Health Plans; Broader Coverage, Higher Quality Care. *Mon. Lab. Rev.,* May 1969, *92*(5), pp. 3–10.

Last, J. M. International Mobility in the Medical Profession. **In** *Bechhofer, F., ed.,* 1969, pp. 31–42. **[G: U.K.]**

Lindner, Forrest. The Health of the American People. **In** *Health Care in America, Pt. 1, SCH,* 1969, pp. 360–65. **[G: U.S.]**

Lindsay, Cotton M. Medical Care and the Economics of Sharing. *Economica, N.S.,* November 1969, *36*(144), pp. 351–62. **[G: U.K.]**

Lurie, Melvin. Aspetti economici dell'abilitazione alla professione medica negli Stati Uniti. (Physician Licensing in the United States and the Supply of Physician Service by Graduates of Foreign Medical Schools. With English summary.) *Rivista Int. Sci. Econ. Com.,* April 1969, *16*(4), pp. 371–89. **[G: U.S.]**

Meyer, A. J. The Harvard Tunisia Project: An Experiment in Field Research. **In** *Nader, C. and Zahlan, A. B., eds.,* 1969, pp. 31–39. **[G: Tunisia]**

Perkinson, Leon B. General Hospital Facilities in Michigan, 1965. *Amer. J. Agr. Econ.,* December 1969, *51*(5), pp. 1548–52. **[G: U.S.]**

Reder, M. W. Some Problems in the Measurement of Productivity in the Medical Care Industry: Reply. **In** *Fuchs, V. R., ed.,* 1969, pp. 148–53. **[G: U.S.]**

Reder, M. W. Some Problems in the Measurement of Productivity in the Medical Care Industry. **In** *Fuchs, V. R., ed.,* 1969, pp. 95–131. **[G: U.S.]**

Rees, M. S. The Inflation of National Health Service Registers of Patients and Its Effect on the Remuneration of General Practitioners. *J. Roy. Statist. Soc.,* Part 4, 1969, *132,* pp. 526–42. **[G: U.K.]**

Scotton, R. B. Membership of Voluntary Health Insurance. *Econ. Rec.,* March 1969, *45*(109), pp. 69–83. **[G: Australia]**

Scotton, R. B. and Deeble, J. S. The Nimmo Report. *Econ. Rec.,* June 1969, *45*(110), pp. 258–75. **[G: Australia]**

Simon, Julian L. and Gardner, David M. World Food Needs and "New Proteins." *Econ. Develop. Cult. Change,* July 1969, *17*(4), pp. 520–26.

Somers, Herman M. Economic Issues in Health Services. **In** *Chamberlain, N. W., ed.,* 1969, pp. 109–44. **[G: U.S.]**

Thomas, William C., Jr. Keeping the City Healthy. **In** *Connery, R. H. and Caraley, D., eds.,* 1969, pp. 121–32. **[G: U.S.]**

White, Kerr. Improved Medical Care Statistics and the Health Service System. **In** *Health Care in America, Pt. 1, SCH,* 1969, pp. 352–59. **[G: U.S.]**

White, Kerr. Organization and Delivery of Personal Health Services. **In** *Health Care in America, Pt. 1, SCH,* 1969, pp. 203–36. **[G: U.S.]**

White, Kerr. Statement. **In** *Health Care in America, Pt. 1, SCH,* 1969, pp. 181–202. **[G: U.S.]**

Wholey, Joseph S. The Absence of Program Evaluation as an Obstacle to Effective Public Expenditure Policy: A Case Study of Child Health Care Programs. **In** *The Analysis and Evaluation of Public Expenditures: The PPB System, Vol. 1, JECP,* 1969, pp. 451–71. **[G: U.S.]**

914 Economics of Poverty

9140 Economics of Poverty

Aaron, Henry J. Perspectives on Poverty 4: Income Transfer Programs. *Mon. Lab. Rev.,* February 1969, *92*(2), pp. 50–54. **[G: U.S.]**

Ahearn, Frederick L., Jr. Correlates of Job Status Among Indigenous Nonprofessionals in Community Action Programs. *Soc. Sci. Quart.,* December 1969, *50*(3), pp. 668–75. **[G: U.S.]**

Allen, Louis L. Making Capitalism Work in the Ghettos. *Harvard Bus. Rev.,* May–June 1969, *47* (3), pp. 83–92. **[G: U.S.]**

Barkin, Solomon. The American Debate on the Poor. **In** *O.E.C.D.,* 1969, pp. 121–28. **[G: U.S.]**

Barth, Peter S. An Economist Looks at Welfare Programs. *Ohio State U. Bull. Bus. Res.,* October 1969, *44*(10), pp. 1–5. **[G: U.S.]**

Bee, Robert L. Tribal Leadership in the War on Poverty: A Case Study. *Soc. Sci. Quart.,* December 1969, *50*(3), pp. 676–86. **[G: U.S.]**

Bishop, C. E. Rural Poverty in the Southeast. **In** *Task Force on Economic Growth and Opportunity,* 1969, pp. 75–92. **[G: U.S.]**

Boskin, Michael J. The Negative Income Tax and the Supply of Work Effort: Reply. *Nat. Tax J.,* September 1969, *22*(3), pp. 417.

Boulanger, Raymond P. Public Utilities and the Poor: The Requirement of Cash Deposits from Domestic Consumers. *Yale Law J.,* January 1969, *78*(3), pp. 448–63.

Bowman, Mary Jean. Poverty in an Affluent Society. **In** *Chamberlain, N. W., ed.,* 1969, pp. 49–107. **[G: U.S.]**

Bressler, Barry. Relative Poverty, Absolute Poverty, and Policy Implications. *Quart. Rev. Econ. Bus.*, Autumn 1969, *9*(3), pp. 65–71. **[G: U.S.]**

Bronfenbrenner, Martin. A Working Library on Riots and Hunger. *J. Human Res.*, Summer 1969, *4*(3), pp. 377–90. **[G: U.S.]**

Bryant, W. Keith. Rural Poverty. **In** *Ruttan, V. W.; Waldo, A. D. and Houck, J. P., eds.*, 1969, pp. 226–34. **[G: U.S.]**

Budd, Edward C. and Radner, Daniel B. The OBE Size Distribution Series: Methods and Tentative Results for 1964. *Amer. Econ. Rev.*, May 1969, *59*(2), pp. 435–49. **[G: U.S.]**

Cain, Glen G. and Mincer, Jacob. Urban Poverty and Labor Force Participation: Comment. *Amer. Econ. Rev.*, March 1969, *59*(1), pp. 185–94. **[G: U.S.]**

Caplovitz, David. The Merchant and the Low-Income Consumer. **In** *Sturdivant, F. D., ed.*, 1969, pp. 61–75. **[G: U.S.]**

Chandler, John H. Perspectives on Poverty 5: An International Comparison. *Mon. Lab. Rev.*, February 1969, *92*(2), pp. 55–62.

Chase, Richard X. and Laber, Gene. Economic Growth as an Anti-poverty Tool: A Further Consideration of the Backwash Debate. *Soc. Sci. Quart.*, December 1969, *50*(3), pp. 604–08. **[G: U.S.]**

Chinitz, Benjamin. The Regional Aspects of Poverty. **In** *Task Force on Economic Growth and Opportunity*, 1969, pp. 93–104. **[G: U.S.]**

Cohen, Benjamin I. Less Developed Countries and U.S. Domestic Problems: Comment. *Public Policy*, Fall 1969, *18*(1), pp. 55–60.

Conway, Jack T. and Ginsburg, Woodrow L. The Extension of Collective Bargaining to New Fields. **In** *Wortman, M. S., Jr.*, 1969, pp. 148–50. **[G: U.S.]**

Dahl, Dale C. The Upper Midwest Region. **In** *Task Force on Economic Growth and Opportunity*, 1969, pp. 105–23. **[G: U.S.]**

Doeringer, Peter B. Manpower Programs for Ghetto Labor Markets. **In** *Somers, G. G., ed. (II)*, 1969, pp. 257–67. **[G: U.S.]**

Eisenmenger, Robert W. The Regional Poor. **In** *Task Force on Economic Growth and Opportunity*, 1969, pp. 125–43. **[G: U.S.]**

Erickson, Edsel L., et al. Differences between Economically Disadvantaged Students Who Volunteer and Do Not Volunteer for Economic Opportunity Programs. *J. Human Res.*, Winter 1969, *4*(1), pp. 76–83. **[G: U.S.]**

Fillerup, O. W. Migratory Labor in California Agriculture. **In** *Task Force on Economic Growth and Opportunity*, 1969, pp. 145–52. **[G: U.S.]**

Ford, Thomas R. Rural Poverty in the United States. **In** *Task Force on Economic Growth and Opportunity*, 1969, pp. 153–76. **[G: U.S.]**

Ford, Thomas R. The Psychiatric Perspective on Poverty: Comment. **In** *Weaver, T. and Magid, A., eds.*, 1969, pp. 129–32. **[G: U.S.]**

Forte, Francesco. Summary of the Discussion on Policy Problems. *Public Finance*, 1969, *24*(2), pp. 405–13.

Fuchs, Estelle. Education and the Culture of Poverty. **In** *Weaver, T. and Magid, A., eds.*, 1969, pp. 162–76. **[G: U.S.]**

Fuller, Varden. Political Pressures and Income Distribution in Agriculture. **In** *Ruttan, V. W.; Waldo, A. D. and Houck, J. P., eds.*, 1969, pp. 255–63. **[G: U.S.]**

Gardner, John W. Statement. **In** *Economic Opportunity Amendments of 1969, SCH*, 1969, pp. 21–28. **[G: U.S.]**

Gove, Walter and Costner, Herbert. Organizing the Poor: An Evaluation of a Strategy. *Soc. Sci. Quart.*, December 1969, *50*(3), pp. 643–56. **[G: U.S.]**

Green, Christopher and Tella, Alfred. Effect of Nonemployment Income and Wage Rates on the Work Incentives of the Poor. *Rev. Econ. Statist.*, November 1969, *51*(4), pp. 399–408. **[G: U.S.]**

Green, Christopher. Problems in the Area of Poverty: Discussion. *Amer. Econ. Rev.*, May 1969, *59*(2), pp. 473–75. **[G: U.S.]**

Greene, John W., Jr. Fighting Poverty with Family Planning: Comment. **In** *Weaver, T. and Magid, A., eds.*, 1969, pp. 54–56. **[G: U.S.]**

Groom, Phyllis. Prices in Poor Neighborhoods. **In** *Sturdivant, F. D., ed.*, 1969, pp. 118–28. **[G: U.S.]**

Guthrie, Harold W. Problems in the Area of Poverty: Discussion. *Amer. Econ. Rev.*, May 1969, *59*(2), pp. 475–76. **[G: U.S.]**

Hall, Mildred and Williams, Bill. The Retailers, the Ghetto, and the Government. **In** *Sturdivant, F. D., ed.*, 1969, pp. 210–20. **[G: U.S.]**

Hansen, Niles M. Urban Alternatives for Eliminating Poverty. *Mon. Lab. Rev.*, August 1969, *92*(8), pp. 46–47.

Hathaway, Dale E. Poverty in the Hired Farm Work Force. **In** *Task Force on Economic Growth and Opportunity*, 1969, pp. 177–98. **[G: U.S.]**

Hencke, Paul. Is War on Poverty Becoming War on Business? **In** *Sturdivant, F. D., ed.*, 1969, pp. 162–70. **[G: U.S.]**

Holmes, O. Wendell. The Farm Poor: Counted, Miscounted, or Discounted? *Amer. J. Agr. Econ.*, December 1969, *51*(5), pp. 1557–60.

Irelan, Lola M. and Besner, Arthur. Low-Income Life Styles. **In** *Sturdivant, F. D., ed.*, 1969, pp. 17–26.

Jesness, O. B. Poverty among American Farmers. **In** *Task Force on Economic Growth and Opportunity*, 1969, pp. 229–43. **[G: U.S.]**

Johnson, Orace E. Beyond the Illfare State. *Univ. Missouri Bus. Govt. Rev.*, May-June 1969, *10*(3), pp. 28–36. **[G: U.S.]**

Jones, Mary Gardiner. Deception in the Marketplace of the Poor: The Role of the Federal Trade Commission. **In** *Sturdivant, F. D., ed.*, 1969, pp. 244–56. **[G: U.S.]**

Kain, John F. Race and Poverty: The Economics of Discrimination. **In** *Kain, J. F., ed.*, 1969, pp. 1–32. **[G: U.S.]**

Kaun, David E. A Comment on the Work-Leisure Myth. *Rev. Radical Polit. Econ.*, May 1969, *1*(1), pp. 85–88.

Kee, Woo Sik. The Causes of Urban Poverty. *J. Human Res.*, Winter 1969, *4*(1), pp. 93–99. **[G: U.S.]**

Kennedy, Robert F. A Business Development Program for Our Poverty Areas. **In** *Sturdivant, F. D.,* *ed.*, 1969, pp. 193–209. [G: U.S.]

Kesselman, Jonathan. The Negative Income Tax and the Supply of Work Effort: Comment. *Nat. Tax J.*, September 1969, *22*(3), pp. 411–16.

Kohl, Schuyler G. Fighting Poverty with Family Planning. **In** *Weaver, T. and Magid, A., eds.*, 1969, pp. 48–54. [G: U.S.]

Kravitz, Sanford and Kolodner, Ferne K. Community Action: Where Has It Been? Where Will It Go? *Ann. Amer. Acad. Polit. Soc. Sci.*, September 1969, *385*, pp. 30–40. [G: U.S.]

Krislov, Joseph. The Economics of Poverty: Comment. **In** *Weaver, T. and Magid, A., eds.*, 1969, pp. 39–43. [G: U.S.]

Lamale, Helen H. Poverty: The Word and the Reality. **In** *Wortman, M. S., Jr.*, 1969, pp. 133–40. [G: U.S.]

Lees, Dennis. Controversy Surrounding Negative Income Taxation: Comment. *Public Finance*, 1969, *24*(2), pp. 362–66. [G: U.K.]

Levine, Robert A. Manpower Programs in the War on Poverty. **In** *Somers, G. G. and Wood, W. D., eds.*, 1969, pp. 170–83. [G: U.S.]

Levine, Robert A. Policy Analysis and Economic Opportunity Programs. **In** *The Analysis and Evaluation of Public Expenditures: The PPB System, Vol. 3, JECP*, 1969, pp. 1181–96. [G: U.S.]

Levitan, Sar A. The Community Action Program: A Strategy to Fight Poverty. *Ann. Amer. Acad. Polit. Soc. Sci.*, September 1969, *385*, pp. 63–75. [G: U.S.]

Little, Alan. Low Wage Earners. **In** *O.E.C.D.*, 1969, pp. 250–72. [G: U.K.]

Looff, David H. The Psychiatric Perspective on Poverty. **In** *Weaver, T. and Magid, A., eds.*, 1969, pp. 110–29. [G: U.S.]

Lowe, Jeanne. The End of the Line: Race and Poverty in Cities. **In** *Callow, A. B., Jr., ed.*, 1969, pp. 519–40. [G: U.S.]

Lyden, Fremont James and Thomas, Jerry V. Citizen Participation in Policy-Making: A Study of a Community Action Program. *Soc. Sci. Quart.*, December 1969, *50*(3), pp. 631–42. [G: U.S.]

Marshall, Alfred. Three Lectures on Progress and Poverty. *J. Law Econ.*, April 1969, *12*(1), pp. 184–226.

McCamman, Dorothy, et al. Facts and Findings. **In** *Economics of Aging: Toward a Full Share in Abundance, Pt. 1, SCH*, 1969, pp. 149–228. [G: U.S.]

Mooney, Joseph D. Urban Poverty and Labor Force Participation: Reply. *Amer. Econ. Rev.*, March 1969, *59*(1), pp. 194–98. [G: U.S.]

Morgan, James N. and Smith, James D. Measures of Economic Well-Offness and Their Correlates. *Amer. Econ. Rev.*, May 1969, *59*(2), pp. 450–62. [G: U.S.]

Murray, Barbara B. An Economic Profile of a Potential Ghetto. *Marquette Bus. Rev.*, Summer 1969, *13*(2), pp. 93–97. [G: U.S.]

Paillat, Paul. Old People. **In** *O.E.C.D.*, 1969, pp. 179–90.

Parsons, Kenneth H. Poverty as an Issue in Development Policy: A Comparison of United States and Underdeveloped Countries. *Land Econ.*, February 1969, *45*(1), pp. 52–65.

Popkin, William D. Administration of a Negative Income Tax. *Yale Law J.*, January 1969, *78*(3), pp. 388–431. [G: U.S.]

Powell, Walter H. Employing Negroes in Urban Labor Markets. **In** *Kain, J. F., ed.*, 1969, pp. 74–77. [G: U.S.]

Ranis, Gustav. Economic Dualism—At Home and Abroad. *Public Policy*, Fall 1969, *18*(1), pp. 41–53.

Reyes, Osorio Sergio. La pobreza rural. (Rural Poverty. With English summary.) *Econ. Polít.*, Second Semester 1969, *6*(2), pp. 209–14. [G: Mexico]

Richards, Louise G. Consumer Practices of the Poor. **In** *Sturdivant, F. D., ed.*, 1969, pp. 42–60. [G: U.S.]

Roby, Pamela. Inequality: A Trend Analysis. *Ann. Amer. Acad. Polit. Soc. Sci.*, September 1969, *385*, pp. 110–17. [G: U.S.]

Rolph, Earl R. Controversy Surrounding Negative Income Taxation. *Public Finance*, 1969, *24*(2), pp. 352–61. [G: U.S.]

Rossi, Peter H. No Good Idea Goes Unpunished: Moynihan's Misunderstandings and the Proper Role of Social Science in Policy Making. *Soc. Sci. Quart.*, December 1969, *50*(3), pp. 469–79. [G: U.S.]

Rubin, Lillian B. Maximum Feasible Participation: The Origins, Implications, and Present Status. *Ann. Amer. Acad. Polit. Soc. Sci.*, September 1969, *385*, pp. 14–29. [G: U.S.]

Ryscavage, Paul M. Employment Developments in Urban Poverty Neighborhoods. *Mon. Lab. Rev.*, June 1969, *92*(6), pp. 51–56. [G: U.S.]

Samli, A. Coskun. Differential Price Structures for the Rich and the Poor. *Univ. Wash. Bus. Rev.*, Summer 1969, *28*(4), pp. 36–43. [G: U.S.]

Schneider, Lewis M. The Fallacy of Free Transportation. *Harvard Bus. Rev.*, January–February 1969, *47*(1), pp. 83–87.

Schwarzweller, Harry K. The Problem of Conceptualizing Poverty: Comment. **In** *Weaver, T. and Magid, A., eds.*, 1969, pp. 18–21.

de Schweinitz, Karl, Jr. The Economics of Poverty. **In** *Weaver, T. and Magid, A., eds.*, 1969, pp. 24–39. [G: U.S.]

Sheppard, Harold L. Some Broader Reality Frameworks for Anti-poverty Intervention. *Soc. Sci. Quart.*, December 1969, *50*(3), pp. 487–93. [G: U.S.]

Shultz, George P. Statement. **In** *Economic Opportunity Amendments of 1969, Pt. 2, HCH*, 1969, pp. 935–45. [G: U.S.]

Sorkin, Alan L. American Indians Industrialize to Combat Poverty. *Mon. Lab. Rev.*, March 1969, *92*(3), pp. 19–25. [G: U.S.]

Straus, Robert. The Problem of Conceptualizing Poverty. **In** *Weaver, T. and Magid, A., eds.*, 1969, pp. 7–18.

Sturdivant, Frederick D. Business and the Mexican-American Community. *Calif. Manage. Rev.*, Spring 1969, *11*(3), pp. 73–80. [G: U.S.]

Sturdivant, Frederick D. and Wilhelm, Walter T. Poverty, Minorities, and Consumer Exploitation. **In** *Sturdivant, F. D., ed.*, 1969, pp. 108–17. [G: U.S.]

Sturdivant, Frederick D. The Limits of Black Capitalism. *Harvard Bus. Rev.*, January–February

1969, *47*(1), pp. 122–28. [G: U.S.]

Sundquist, James L. Co-ordinating the War on Poverty. *Ann. Amer. Acad. Polit. Soc. Sci.*, September 1969, *385*, pp. 41–49. [G: U.S.]

Sutton, Willis A., Jr. Differential Perceptions of Impact of a Rural Anti-poverty Campaign. *Soc. Sci. Quart.*, December 1969, *50*(3), pp. 657–67. [G: U.S.]

Tabb, William K. Government Incentives to Private Industry to Locate in Urban Poverty Areas. *Land Econ.*, November 1969, *45*(4), pp. 392–99. [G: U.S.]

Taira, Koji. Consumer Preferences, Poverty Norms, and Extent of Poverty. *Quart. Rev. Econ. Bus.*, Summer 1969, *9*(2), pp. 31–44.

Thurow, Lester C. Problems in the Area of Poverty: Discussion. *Amer. Econ. Rev.*, May 1969, *59*(2), pp. 476–78. [G: U.S.]

Vanecko, James J. Community Mobilization and Institutional Change: The Influence of the Community Action Program in Large Cities. *Soc. Sci. Quart.*, December 1969, *50*(3), pp. 609–30. [G: U.S.]

Watt, Melvin L. Tax Exemption for Organizations Investing in Black Businesses. *Yale Law J.*, June 1969, *78*(7), pp. 1212–27. [G: U.S.]

Watts, Harold W. Graduated Works Incentives: An Experiment in Negative Taxation. *Amer. Econ. Rev.*, May 1969, *59*(2), pp. 463–72. [G: U.S.]

Willacy, Hazel M. Men in Poverty Neighborhoods: A Status Report. *Mon. Lab. Rev.*, February 1969, *92*(2), pp. 23–27. [G: U.S.]

Yancey, William L. Intervention as a Strategy of Social Inquiry: An Exploratory Study with Unemployed Negro Men. *Soc. Sci. Quart.*, December 1969, *50*(3), pp. 582–88. [G: U.S.]

915 Social Security

9150 Social Security (public superannuation and survivors benefits)

Ball, Robert M. Statement. **In** *Economics of Aging: Toward a Full Share in Abundance, Pt. 1, SCH,* 1969, pp. 12–25. [G: U.S.]

Barth, Peter S. Social Security and Economic Development: A Quantitative Approach—Comment. *Ind. Lab. Relat. Rev.*, January 1969, *22*(2), pp. 257–59.

Burns, Eveline M. Social Security in Evolution: Towards What? **In** *O.E.C.D.*, 1969, pp. 110–20. [G: U.S.]

Campbell, Colin D. Social Insurance in the United States: A Program in Search of an Explanation. *J. Law Econ.*, October 1969, *12*(2), pp. 249–65. [G: U.S.]

David, Martin. Comment on "Social Insurance and Economic Incentives" by M. Kucharski and Z. Pirozynski. *Public Finance,* 1969, *24*(2), pp. 256–63. [G: Poland]

Davis, Harry E. Negotiated Retirement Plans—A Decade of Benefit Improvements. *Mon. Lab. Rev.*, May 1969, *92*(5), pp. 11–15.

Fefferman, Arthur S. Private Pension Plans: A 1968 Prospectus. *J. Risk Ins.*, September 1969, *36*(4), pp. 433–36. [G: U.S.]

Fernandes, L. Santos. Comments on Professor Reviglio's Paper on the "Finance of Social Security in Developing Countries." *Public Finance,* 1969, *24* (2), pp. 278–79.

Forte, Francesco. Summary of the Discussion on Policy Problems. *Public Finance,* 1969, *24*(2), pp. 405–13.

Galenson, Walter. Social Security and Economic Development: A Quantitative Approach—Reply. *Ind. Lab. Relat. Rev.*, January 1969, *22*(2), pp. 260–63.

Jaffe, A. J. Statement. **In** *Economics of Aging: Toward a Full Share in Abundance, Pt. 2, SCH,* 1969, pp. 388–409. [G: U.S.]

Klarman, Herbert E. Reimbursing the Hospital—The Differences the Third Party Makes. *J. Risk Ins.*, December 1969, *36*(5), pp. 553–66. [G: U.S.]

Kreps, Juanita M. Statement. **In** *Economics of Aging: Toward a Full Share in Abundance, Pt. 1, SCH,* 1969, pp. 4–5. [G: U.S.]

Kucharski, Mieczyslaw and Pirozynski, Zbigniew. Social Insurance and Economic Incentives. *Public Finance,* 1969, *24*(2), pp. 238–55. [G: Poland]

Lukaczer, Moses. The Farm Wage Worker in the Social Security Program: An Introduction to His Earnings Profile. *J. Risk Ins.*, March 1969, *36*(1), pp. 103–15. [G: U.S.]

McCamman, Dorothy, et al. Facts and Findings. **In** *Economics of Aging: Toward a Full Share in Abundance, Pt. 1, SCH,* 1969, pp. 149–228. [G: U.S.]

McClung, Nelson. The Economics of Pension Finance. *J. Risk Ins.*, September 1969, *36*(4), pp. 425–32.

Myers, Robert J. Various Proposals to Change the Financing of Social Security. *J. Risk Ins.*, September 1969, *36*(4), pp. 355–63. [G: U.S.]

Pechman, Joseph A.; Aaron, Henry J. and Taussig, Michael K. Improving Social Security Benefits and Financing: Brookings Research Report 94. **In** *Economics of Aging: Toward a Full Share in Abundance, Pt. 1, SCH,* 1969, pp. 253–63. [G: U.S.]

Pechman, Joseph A. Statement. **In** *Economics of Aging: Toward a Full Share in Abundance, Pt. 1, SCH,* 1969, pp. 112–17. [G: U.S.]

Pepper, H. W. T. Poll Taxes, Payroll Taxation, and Social Security (Part II). *Bull. Int. Fiscal Doc.*, February 1969, *23*(2), pp. 55–65.

Pepper, H. W. T. Poll Taxes, Payroll Taxation, and Social Security (Part I). *Bull. Int. Fiscal Doc.*, January 1969, *23*(1), pp. 4–26.

Perrin, Guy. Reflections on Fifty Years of Social Security. *Int. Lab. Rev.*, March 1969, *99*(3), pp. 249–92.

Prest, A. R. Comments on "Social Insurance in a Growing Economy: A Proposal for Radical Reform." *Nat. Tax J.*, December 1969, *22*(4), pp. 554–56. [G: U.S.]

Projector, Dorothy S. Should the Payroll Tax Finance Higher Benefits under OASDI? A Review of the Issues. *J. Human Res.*, Winter 1969, *4*(1), pp. 60–75. [G: U.S.]

Reviglio, Franco. Finance of Social Security in Developing Countries. *Public Finance,* 1969, *24*(2), pp. 264–77.

Rimlinger, Gaston V. Social Security and Society: An East-West Comparison. *Soc. Sci. Quart.,* December 1969, *50*(3), pp. 494–506.

Rohrlich, George F. The Place of Social Insurance in the Pursuit of the General Welfare. *J. Risk Ins.,* September 1969, *36*(4), pp. 333–53.

Rohrlich, George F. Social Security for the Aged: International Perspectives—A Working Paper. **In** *op. cit., SCP,* 1969, pp. 1–14.

Schottland, Charles I. Statement. **In** *Economics of Aging: Toward a Full Share in Abundance, Pt. 1, SCH,* 1969, pp. 97–107. **[G: U.S.]**

Schulz, James H. Statement. **In** *Economics of Aging: Toward a Full Share in Abundance, Pt. 1, SCH,* 1969, pp. 7–9. **[G: U.S.]**

Sheppard, Harold L. Statement. **In** *Economics of Aging: Toward a Full Share in Abundance, Pt. 1, SCH,* 1969, pp. 5–7. **[G: U.S.]**

Shoup, Carl S. Comments on the Paper by Andre Laurent, "L'Harmonisation des regimes de securite sociale dans la communaute economique Europeenne." *Public Finance,* 1969, *24*(2), pp. 321–25.

Steve, Sergio. Public Finance and Social Security. *Public Finance,* 1969, *24*(2), pp. 101–13.

Thirlwall, A. P. Unemployment Compensation as an Automatic Stabilizer. *Bull. Oxford Univ. Inst. Econ. Statist.,* February 1969, *31*(1), pp. 23–37. **[G: U.K.]**

Turner, J. Scott. Profile of Nonfilers. **In** *Willis, A. B., ed.,* 1969, pp. 157–67. **[G: U.S.]**

Veldkamp, Gerald M. J. A New Dimension for International Co-operation in Social Security. *Int. Lab. Rev.,* August 1969, *100*(2), pp. 131–39.

916 Economics of Crime

9160 Economics of Crime

Caplan, Nathan S. and Paige, Jeffrey M. A Study of Ghetto Rioters. **In** *Callow, A. B., Jr., ed.,* 1969, pp. 541–48. **[G: U.S.]**

Crowther, Carol. Crimes, Penalties, and Legislatures. *Ann. Amer. Acad. Polit. Soc. Sci.,* January 1969, *381,* pp. 147–58.

Denenberg, Herbert S. Law and Order—A Modest Program for Immediate Action: Some Comments on the SBA's Report on the Impact of Crime on Small Business. **In** *Impact of Crime on Small Business—1969, Pt. 1, SCH,* 1969, pp. 55–57. **[G: U.S.]**

Denenberg, Herbert S. Statement. **In** *Impact of Crime on Small Business—1969, Pt. 1, SCH,* 1969, pp. 47–55. **[G: U.S.]**

Downs, Anthony. Round Table on Allocation of Resources in Law Enforcement. *Amer. Econ. Rev.,* May 1969, *59*(2), pp. 504–05.

Erickson, Edward. The Social Costs of the Discovery and Suppression of the Clandestine Distribution of Heroin. *J. Polit. Econ.,* Part I, July/August 1969, *77*(4), pp. 484–86.

Fernandez, Raul A. The Clandestine Distribution of Heroin, Its Discovery and Suppression: A Comment. *J. Polit. Econ.,* Part I, July/August 1969, *77* (4), pp. 487–88.

Firey, Walter. Limits to Economy in Crime and Punishment. *Soc. Sci. Quart.,* June 1969, *50*(1), pp. 72–77.

Hoffman, Richard B. Round Table on Allocation of Resources in Law Enforcement. *Amer. Econ. Rev.,* May 1969, *59*(2), pp. 510–12.

Landes, William M. Round Table on Allocation of Resources in Law Enforcement. *Amer. Econ. Rev.,* May 1969, *59*(2), pp. 505–08.

Mishan, E. J. A Note on the Costs of Tariffs, Monopolies and Thefts. *Western Econ. J.,* September 1969, *7*(3), pp. 230–33.

Reiss, Albert J., Jr. Statement. **In** *Impact of Crime on Small Business—1969, Pt. 1, SCH,* 1969, pp. 29–44. **[G: U.S.]**

Rottenberg, Simon. Round Table on Allocation of Resources in Law Enforcement. *Amer. Econ. Rev.,* May 1969, *59*(2), pp. 508–10.

Schmidt, Kurt. Zur Ökonomik der Korruption. (On the Economics of Corruption. With English summary.) *Schmollers Jahr.,* 1969, *89*(2), pp. 129–49.

Thurow, Lester C. and Rappaport, Carl. Law Enforcement and Cost-Benefit Analysis. *Public Finance,* 1969, *24*(1), pp. 48–68. **[G: U.S.]**

Tullock, Gordon. An Economic Approach to Crime. *Soc. Sci. Quart.,* June 1969, *50*(1), pp. 59–71.

917 Economics of Discrimination

9170 Economics of Discrimination

Allen, Louis L. Making Capitalism Work in the Ghettos. *Harvard Bus. Rev.,* May–June 1969, *47* (3), pp. 83–92. **[G: U.S.]**

America, Richard F., Jr. 'What Do You People Want?' *Harvard Bus. Rev.,* March–April 1969, *47* (2), pp. 103–12. **[G: U.S.]**

Aslanyan, R. G. Action to Ensure That Soviet Citizens Enjoy Equal Rights and Opportunities. *Int. Lab. Rev.,* December 1969, *100*(6), pp. 551–82. **[G: U.S.S.R.]**

Birren, James E. The Aged in Cities. **In** *Usefulness of the Model Cities Program to the Elderly, Pt. 1, SCH,* 1969, pp. 138–45. **[G: U.S.]**

Bluestone, Barry. Black Capitalism: The Path to Black Liberation? *Rev. Radical Polit. Econ.,* May 1969, *1*(1), pp. 36–55. **[G: U.S.]**

Blumrosen, Alfred W. A Survey of Remedies for Discrimination in the Union and on the Job. **In** *Somers, G. G., ed. (II),* 1969, pp. 283–91. **[G: U.S.]**

Brimmer, Andrew F. The Negro in the National Economy. **In** *Kain, J. F., ed.,* 1969, pp. 89–99. **[G: U.S.]**

Case, Fred E. Business and the Urban Scene. *Calif. Manage. Rev.,* Summer 1969, *11*(4), pp. 3. **[G: U.S.]**

Clark, Kenneth B. Efficiency as a Prod to Social Action. *Mon. Lab. Rev.,* August 1969, *92*(8), pp. 54–56.

Farmer, Richard N. The Dilemma of the Black Businessman: Clarification of the Current Situation. *Indiana Bus. Rev.,* March–April 1969, *44,* pp. 13,

27–28. [G: U.S.]

Gallaway, Lowell E. Unemployment Levels among Nonwhite Teen-agers. *J. Bus.*, July 1969, *42*(3), pp. 265–76. [G: U.S.]

Goeke, Joseph R. and Weymar, Caroline S. Barriers to Hiring the Blacks. *Harvard Bus. Rev.*, September–October 1969, *47*(5), pp. 144–52. [G: U.S.]

Goodman, Richard Alan. A Hidden Issue in Minority Employment. *Calif. Manage. Rev.*, Summer 1969, *11*(4), pp. 27–30.

Gould, William B. Black Power in the Unions: The Impact upon Collective Bargaining Relationships. *Yale Law J.*, November 1969, *79*(1), pp. 46–84. [G: U.S.]

Gould, William B. Racial Equality in Jobs and Unions, Collective Bargaining, and the Burger Court. *Mich. Law Rev.*, December 1969, *68*(2), pp. 237–58. [G: U.S.]

Groom, Phyllis. Prices in Poor Neighborhoods. **In** *Sturdivant, F. D., ed.*, 1969, pp. 118–28. [G: U.S.]

Gross, James A. Historians and the Literature of the Negro Worker. *Labor Hist.*, Summer 1969, *10*(3), pp. 536–46. [G: U.S.]

Hamilton, Charles V. Black Power: An Alternative. **In** *Shade, W. G. and Herrenkohl, R. C., eds.*, 1969, pp. 134–48. [G: U.S.]

Hansen, Niles M. Improving Economic Opportunity for the Mexican Americans: A Critical Evaluation of Public Policy, with Assessment of the Problem in South Texas. *Econ. Bus. Bull.*, Fall 1969, *22*(1), pp. 1–14. [G: U.S.]

Haugen, Robert A. and Heins, A. James. A Market Separation Theory of Rent Differentials in Metropolitan Areas. *Quart. J. Econ.*, November 1969, *83*(4), pp. 660–72. [G: U.S.]

Henderson, William L. and Ledebur, Larry C. Government Incentives and Black Economic Development. *Rev. Soc. Econ.*, September 1969, *27*(2), pp. 202–21. [G: U.S.]

Hiestand, Dale L. The Changing Position of Negro Workers. **In** *Kain, J. F., ed.*, 1969, pp. 68–73. [G: U.S.]

Hill, Herbert. Racial Inequality in Employment: The Patterns of Discrimination. **In** *Kain, J. F., ed.*, 1969, pp. 78–88. [G: U.S.]

Kain, John F. and Persky, Joseph J. Alternatives to the Gilded Ghetto. **In** *Kain, J. F., ed.*, 1969, pp. 167–74. [G: U.S.]

Kain, John F. Race and Poverty: The Economics of Discrimination. **In** *Kain, J. F., ed.*, 1969, pp. 1–32. [G: U.S.]

Kennedy, Robert F. Industrial Investment in Urban Poverty Areas. **In** *Kain, J. F., ed.*, 1969, pp. 153–63. [G: U.S.]

Killingsworth, Charles C. Jobs and Income for Negroes. **In** *Katz, I. and Gurin, P., eds.*, 1969, pp. 194–273. [G: U.S.]

Kramer, Daniel C. White Versus Colored in Britain: An Explosive Confrontation? *Soc. Res.*, Winter 1969, *36*(4), pp. 585–605. [G: U.K.]

Lavidge, Robert J. The Ghetto Challenge to Marketing People. *Ohio State U. Bull. Bus. Res.*, August 1969, *44*(8), pp. 4, 6–7. [G: U.S.]

Levine, Charles H. The Dilemma of the Black Businessman: A New Approach? *Indiana Bus. Rev.*, March–April 1969, *44*, pp. 12, 22–26. [G: U.S.]

Liggett, Malcolm H. The Efficacy of State Fair Employment Practices Commissions. *Ind. Lab. Relat. Rev.*, July 1969, *22*(4), pp. 559–67. [G: U.S.]

Lowe, Jeanne. The End of the Line: Race and Poverty in Cities. **In** *Callow, A. B., Jr., ed.*, 1969, pp. 519–40. [G: U.S.]

Lurie, Melvin and Rayack, Elton. Employment Opportunities for Negro Families in "Satellite" Cities. *Southern Econ. J.*, October 1969, *36*(2), pp. 191–95. [G: U.S.]

Marcus, Burton H. Similarity of Ghetto and Nonghetto Food Costs. *J. Marketing Res.*, August 1969, *6*(3), pp. 365–68. [G: U.S.]

Marshall, Ray. Equal Employment Opportunities: Problems and Prospects. **In** *Wortman, M. S., Jr.*, 1969, pp. 364–71. [G: U.S.]

Michelson, Stephan. Rational Income Decisions of Negroes and Everybody Else. *Ind. Lab. Relat. Rev.*, October 1969, *23*(1), pp. 15–28.

Moore, L. W. Urban Unrest—Whose Problem Is It? *Calif. Manage. Rev.*, Summer 1969, *11*(4), pp. 7–10.

Northrup, Herbert R. The Negro in Aerospace Work. *Calif. Manage. Rev.*, Summer 1969, *11*(4), pp. 11–26. [G: U.S.]

O'Boyle, Edward J. Job Tenure: How It Relates to Race and Age. *Mon. Lab. Rev.*, September 1969, *92*(9), pp. 16–23. [G: U.S.]

Petrof, John V. Negro Entrepreneurship: Myth or Reality? *Marquette Bus. Rev.*, Spring 1969, *13*(1), pp. 34–37.

Piven, Frances Fox and Cloward, Richard A. Desegregated Housing: Who Pays for the Reformers' Ideal? **In** *Kain, J. F., ed.*, 1969, pp. 175–83. [G: U.S.]

Raymond, Richard. Changes in the Relative Economic Status of Nonwhites: 1950–1960. *Western Econ. J.*, March 1969, *7*(1), pp. 57–70. [G: U.S.]

Raymond, Richard. Mobility and Economic Progress of Negro Americans during the 1940's. *Amer. J. Econ. Soc.*, October 1969, *28*(4), pp. 337–50. [G: U.S.]

Ritter, Lawrence S. A Capital Market Plan for the Urban Areas. *Calif. Manage. Rev.*, Summer 1969, *11*(4), pp. 37–46.

Rothman, Jack. The Ghetto Makers. **In** *Kain, J. F., ed.*, 1969, pp. 122–27. [G: U.S.]

Schelling, Thomas C. Models of Segregation. *Amer. Econ. Rev.*, May 1969, *59*(2), pp. 488–93.

Sheatsley, Paul B. White Attitudes Toward the Negro. **In** *Kain, J. F., ed.*, 1969, pp. 128–38. [G: U.S.]

Shepherd, William G. Market Power and Racial Discrimination in White Collar Employment. *Antitrust Bull.*, Spring 1969, *14*, pp. 141–61. [G: U.S.]

Siegel, Paul M. On the Cost of Being a Negro. **In** *Kain, J. F., ed.*, 1969, pp. 60–67. [G: U.S.]

Sorkin, Alan L. Education and Manpower Programs for Indian Americans. **In** *Indian Education 1969, Pt. 2, Appendix, SCH*, 1969, pp. 1559–98. [G: U.S.]

Striver, Herbert E. Toward a Fundamental Program for the Training, Employment, and Economic Equality of the American Indian. **In** *Indian Education, Pt. 2, SCH,* 1969, pp. 608–32. **[G: U.S.]**

Sturdivant, Frederick D. Business and the Mexican-American Community. *Calif. Manage. Rev.,* Spring 1969, *11*(3), pp. 73–80. **[G: U.S.]**

Sturdivant, Frederick D. and Wilhelm, Walter T. Poverty, Minorities, and Consumer Exploitation. **In** *Sturdivant, F. D., ed.,* 1969, pp. 108–17. **[G: U.S.]**

Sturdivant, Frederick D. The Limits of Black Capitalism. **In** *Sturdivant, F. D., ed.,* 1969, pp. 257–68. **[G: U.S.]**

Sturdivant, Frederick D. The Limits of Black Capitalism. *Harvard Bus. Rev.,* January–February 1969, *47*(1), pp. 122–28. **[G: U.S.]**

Taeuber, Karl E. and Taeuber, Alma F. The Negro as an Immigrant Group: Recent Trends in Racial and Ethnic Segregation in Chicago. **In** *Kain, J. F., ed.,* 1969, pp. 100–111. **[G: U.S.]**

Tobin, James. On Improving the Economic Status of the Negro. **In** *Starleaf, D. R., ed.,* 1969, pp. 429–35. **[G: U.S.]**

Watt, Melvin L. Tax Exemption for Organizations Investing in Black Businesses. *Yale Law J.,* June 1969, *78*(7), pp. 1212–27. **[G: U.S.]**

Williams, J. Allen, Jr. The Effects of Urban Renewal upon a Black Community: Evaluation and Recommendations. *Soc. Sci. Quart.,* December 1969, *50*(3), pp. 703–12. **[G: U.S.]**

Yancey, William L. Intervention as a Strategy of Social Inquiry: An Exploratory Study with Unemployed Negro Men. *Soc. Sci. Quart.,* December 1969, *50*(3), pp. 582–88. **[G: U.S.]**

Yessian, Mark R. Statement. **In** *Usefulness of the Model Cities Program to the Elderly, Pt. 1, SCH,* 1969, pp. 78–82. **[G: U.S.]**

920 Consumer Economics

921 Consumer Economics; Levels and Standards of Living

9210 General

Branson, William H. and Klevorick, Alvin K. Money Illusion and the Aggregate Consumption Function. *Amer. Econ. Rev.,* December 1969, *59*(5), pp. 832–49. **[G: U.S.]**

Dagenais, Marcel G. A Threshold Regression Model. *Econometrica,* April 1969, *37*(2), pp. 193–203.

Gorkin, Stefan. Shearson, Hammill & Co. and the Ghetto. *Univ. Wash. Bus. Rev.,* Autumn 1969, *29* (1), pp. 27–34. **[G: U.S.]**

Jaffe, A. J. Statement. **In** *Economics of Aging: Toward a Full Share in Abundance, Pt. 2, SCH,* 1969, pp. 388–409. **[G: U.S.]**

Mansfield, N. W. Recreational Trip Generation: A Cross Section Analysis of Weekend Pleasure Trips to the Lake District National Park. *J. Transp. Econ. Policy,* May 1969, *3*(2), pp. 152–64. **[G: U.K.]**

Martelli, Antonio. Vecchie e nuove teorie sul consumatore. (Old and New Theories on the Consumer: Present Situation. With English summary.) *L'Impresa,* March/April 1969, *11*(2), pp. 133–37.

McClellan, Keith and Medrich, Elliot A. Outdoor Recreation: Economic Consideration for Optimal Site Selection and Development. *Land Econ.,* May 1969, *45*(2), pp. 174–82.

Murray, J. Alex. Canadian Consumer Expectational Data: An Evaluation. *J. Marketing Res.,* February 1969, *6*(1), pp. 54–61. **[G: Canada]**

Saarsalmi, Meeri. Kuluttajan käyttäytymisen tutkiminen markkinoinnin päätöksenteon kannalta tarkasteltuna. (The Study of Consumer Behavior from the Viewpoint of Decision-Making in Marketing. With English summary.) *Liiketaloudellinen Aikak.,* 1969, *18*(2), pp. 220–32.

Seneca, Joseph J. Water Recreation, Demand, and Supply. *Water Resources Res.,* December 1969, *5* (6), pp. 1179–85. **[G: U.S.]**

Skinner, R. W. Hidden Consumer Motives in Supermarket Selection. *Amer. J. Agr. Econ.,* December 1969, *51*(5), pp. 1154–58. **[G: U.S.]**

Triplett, Jack E. Automobiles and Hedonic Quality Measurement. *J. Polit. Econ.,* May/June 1969, *77* (3), pp. 408–17. **[G: U.S.]**

9211 Living Standards Studies and Composition of Over-all Expenditures

Alexis, Marcus. Some Differences in Household Consumption—Negroes and Whites. **In** *Alexis, M.; Holloway, R. J. and Hancock, R. S., eds.,* 1969, pp. 142–53. **[G: U.S.]**

Auld, Douglas A. L. An Application of Econometrics to Evaluate Fiscal Tax Policy. *Econ. Rec.,* June 1969, *45*(110), pp. 147–57. **[G: Australia]**

Barach, Jeffrey A. Advertising Effectiveness and Risk in the Consumer Decision Process. *J. Marketing Res.,* August 1969, *6*(3), pp. 314–20.

Blumenthal, Tuvia. A Note on the Life-Cycle Pattern of Saving in Japan. *Hitotsubashi J. Econ.,* February 1969, *9*(2), pp. 61–67. **[G: Japan]**

Blyth, C. A. Primitive South Pacific Economies: Their Consumption Pattern and Propensity to Save Out of Cash Income. *Econ. Rec.,* September 1969, *45*(111), pp. 354–72. **[G: Samoa; Papua]**

Brackett, Jean C. New BLS Budgets Provide Yardsticks for Measuring Family Living Costs. *Mon. Lab. Rev.,* April 1969, *92*(4), pp. 3–16. **[G: U.S.]**

Burger, Albert E. The Effects of Inflation (1960–68). *Fed. Res. Bank St. Louis Rev.,* November 1969, *51* (11), pp. 25–36. **[G: U.S.]**

Chase, Samuel B., Jr. Household Demand for Savings Deposits, 1921–1965. *J. Finance,* September 1969, *24*(4), pp. 643–58. **[G: U.S.]**

Chowdhury, A. H. M. Nuruddin. Some Reflections on Income Redistributive Intermediation in Pakistan. *Pakistan Develop. Rev.,* Summer 1969, *9* (2), pp. 95–110. **[G: Pakistan]**

Churánek, Miloš. Foreign Trade, the Reproduction Process and Personal Consumption. *New Trends Czech. Econ.,* December 1969, (8), pp. 71–88. **[G: Czechoslovakia]**

Conlisk, John. An Approach to the Theory of Inequality in the Size Distribution of Income. *Western Econ. J.*, June 1969, *7*(2), pp. 180–86. **[G: U.S.]**

Ferber, Robert. Contributions of Economics to the Study of Consumer Market Behavior. *Appl. Econ.*, May 1969, *1*(2), pp. 125–36.

Flek, Josef. Life and Income of Czechoslovak Cooperatives. **In** *Papi, U. and Nunn, C., eds.*, 1969, pp. 304–15. **[G: Czechoslovakia]**

Green, Christopher. Problems in the Area of Poverty: Discussion. *Amer. Econ. Rev.*, May 1969, *59* (2), pp. 473–75. **[G: U.S.]**

Guthrie, Harold W. Problems in the Area of Poverty: Discussion. *Amer. Econ. Rev.*, May 1969, *59*(2), pp. 475–76. **[G: U.S.]**

Hawes, Mary H. Measuring Retired Couples' Living Costs in Urban Areas. *Mon. Lab. Rev.*, November 1969, *92*(11), pp. 3–16. **[G: U.S.]**

Hewett, Edward A. A Note on Soviet Standards. *Bull. Oxford Univ. Inst. Econ. Statist.*, February 1969, *31*(1), pp. 55–60. **[G: U.S.S.R.]**

Hill, T. P. Too Much Consumption. *Nat. Westminster Bank Quart. Rev.*, February 1969, pp. 18–39.

Hoa, Tran Van. Additive Preferences and Cost of Living Indexes: An Empirical Study of the Australian Consumer's Welfare. *Econ. Rec.*, September 1969, *45*(111), pp. 432–40. **[G: Australia]**

Hoa, Tran Van. Consumer Demand and Welfare Indexes: A Comparative Study for the United Kingdom and Australia. *Economica, N.S.*, November 1969, *36*(144), pp. 409–25. **[G: U.K.; Australia]**

Horsnell, Gareth. A Theory of Consumer Behaviour Derived from Repeat Paired Preference Testing. *J. Roy. Statist. Soc.*, Part 2, 1969, *132*, pp. 164–84.

Houff, James N. Area Wages and Living Costs. *Mon. Lab. Rev.*, March 1969, *92*(3), pp. 43–46. **[G: U.S.]**

Iyengar, Sampath S. Multiplier Analysis for India. *Indian Econ. J.*, April–June 1969, *16*(4–5), pp. 478–87. **[G: India]**

Juster, F. Thomas. Consumer Anticipations and Models of Durable Goods Demand. **In** *Mincer, J., ed.*, 1969, pp. 167–242.

Kammerer, Peter. La politica dei premi al risparmio nell'esperienza tedesca. (Savings Bonus Policy in German Experience. With English summary.) *Bancaria*, October 1969, *25*(10), pp. 1225–38. **[G: Germany]**

Kawano, Shigeto. Effects of the Land Reform on Consumption and Investment of Farmers. **In** *Ohkawa, K.; Johnston, B. F. and Kaneda, H., eds.*, 1969, pp. 374–97. **[G: Japan]**

Kelley, Allen C. Demand Patterns, Demographic Change and Economic Growth. *Quart. J. Econ.*, February 1969, *83*(1), pp. 110–26. **[G: Philippines]**

Laumas, Prem S. A Test of the Permanent Income Hypothesis. *J. Polit. Econ.*, September/October 1969, *77*(5), pp. 857–61. **[G: Canada]**

Lee, Feng-Yao. An Analysis of Farm Household Expenditures on Basic Living Materials in Japan. *Amer. J. Agr. Econ.*, August 1969, *51*(3), pp. 650–61. **[G: Japan]**

Leff, Nathaniel H. Dependency Rates and Savings Rates. *Amer. Econ. Rev.*, December 1969, *59*(5), pp. 886–96.

Lockley, Lawrence C. A Dome of Many Colored Glass. *Marquette Bus. Rev.*, Winter 1969, *13*(4), pp. 168–73.

Lomax, David F. and Reading, Brian. Too Little Saving. *Nat. Westminster Bank Quart. Rev.*, August 1969, pp. 23–42. **[G: U.K.]**

MacMillan, James A. and Loyns, R. M. A. A Cross-Section Analysis of Farm Household Expenditures. *Can. J. Agr. Econ.*, July 1969, *17*(2), pp. 92–105. **[G: Canada]**

Massell, Benton F. and Parnes, Andrew. Estimation of Expenditure Elasticities from a Sample of Rural Households in Uganda. *Bull. Oxford Univ. Inst. Econ. Statist.*, November 1969, *31*(4), pp. 313–29. **[G: Uganda]**

Mieszkowski, Peter. Tax Incidence Theory: The Effects of Taxes on the Distribution of Income. *J. Econ. Lit.*, December 1969, *7*(4), pp. 1103–24.

Mizoguchi, Toshiyuki. Time-Series Analysis of the Consumption Function in Japan by Occupational Group. *Hitotsubashi J. Econ.*, February 1969, *9* (2), pp. 13–34. **[G: Japan]**

Morgan, James N. and Smith, James D. Measures of Economic Well-Offness and Their Correlates. *Amer. Econ. Rev.*, May 1969, *59*(2), pp. 450–62. **[G: U.S.]**

Nichita, Nicolae and Anghel, Eliza. Cu privire la corelația dintre cererea și oferta de mărfuri în socialism. (The Correlation between Demand and Offer of Produce in Socialism. With English summary.) *Stud. Cercet. Econ.*, 1969, *1-2*, pp. 23–36.

Noda, Tsutomu. Savings of Farm Households. **In** *Ohkawa, K.; Johnston, B. F. and Kaneda, H., eds.*, 1969, pp. 352–73. **[G: Japan]**

Ostby, Ivar and Gulilat, Taye. A Statistical Study of Household Expenditure in Addis Ababa. *East Afr. Econ. Rev.*, December 1969, *1*(2), pp. 63–74. **[G: Ethiopia]**

Ramanathan, R. An Econometric Exploration of Indian Saving Behavior. *J. Amer. Statist. Assoc.*, March 1969, *64*(325), pp. 90–101. **[G: India]**

Richards, Louise G. Consumer Practices of the Poor. **In** *Sturdivant, F. D., ed.*, 1969, pp. 42–60. **[G: U.S.]**

Rostro Plasencia, Francisco. Perspectivas de continuidad del desarrollo economico de Mexico. (Prospects of Economic Development in Mexico. With English summary.) *Econ. Polit.*, Second Semester 1969, *6*(2), pp. 241–50. **[G: Mexico]**

Sastry, M. V. Rama. Multicollinearity and Consumer Demand Elasticities. *Can. J. Agr. Econ.*, February 1969, *17*(1), pp. 50–60. **[G: U.S.]**

Schaefer, Jeffrey M. Clothing Exemptions and Sales Tax Regressivity. *Amer. Econ. Rev.*, Part I, September 1969, *59*(4), pp. 596–99. **[G: U.S.]**

Schaefer, Jeffrey M. Sales Tax Regressivity under Alternative Tax Bases and Income Concepts. *Nat. Tax J.*, December 1969, *22*(4), pp. 516–27. **[G: U.S.]**

Stafford, Frank P. Student Family Size in Relation to Current and Expected Income. *J. Polit. Econ.*,

Part I, July/August 1969, *77*(4), pp. 471–77. [G: U.S.]

Stafford, James E. and Enis, Ben M. The Price-Quality Relationship: An Extension. *J. Marketing Res.,* November 1969, *6*(4), pp. 456–58.

Taylor, Lester D. and Newhouse, Joseph P. On the Long-Run and Short-Run Demand for Money: A Comment. *J. Polit. Econ.,* September/October 1969, *77*(5), pp. 851–56. [G: U.S.]

Thurow, Lester C. Problems in the Area of Poverty: Discussion. *Amer. Econ. Rev.,* May 1969, *59*(2), pp. 476–78. [G: U.S.]

Thurow, Lester C. The Optimum Lifetime Distribution of Consumption Expenditures. *Amer. Econ. Rev.,* June 1969, *59*(3), pp. 324–30. [G: U.S.]

Turner, Marshall L., Jr. How Changes in Household Composition Affect Family Income. *Mon. Lab. Rev.,* November 1969, *92*(11), pp. 59–61. [G: U.S.]

Ulizzi, Adalberto. Income, Saving and Structure of Wealth in Italian Households in 1967. *Rev. Econ. Cond. Italy,* July 1969, *23*(4), pp. 275–303. [G: Italy]

Williamson, Jeffrey G. Income Growth and Savings. *Philippine Econ. J.,* First Semester 1969, *8*(1), pp. 54–74. [G: Asia]

Wright, Colin. Estimating Permanent Income: A Note. *J. Polit. Econ.,* September/October 1969, *77*(5), pp. 845–50.

Yoshihara, Kunio. Demand Functions: An Application to the Japanese Expenditure Pattern. *Econometrica,* April 1969, *37*(2), pp. 257–74. [G: Japan]

Zusman, Pinhas. Welfare Implication and Evaluation of Buyers' Travel Inputs and Nonprice Offer Variations in Networks of Retail Food Stores. *Econometrica,* July 1969, *37*(3), pp. 439–56. [G: Israel]

9212 Expenditure Patterns and Consumption of Expenditure on Specific Items

Alexis, Marcus; Simon, Leonard S. and Smith, Kenneth M. Some Determinants of Food Buying Behavior. **In** *Alexis, M.; Holloway, R. J. and Hancock, R. S., eds.,* 1969, pp. 20–32. [G: U.S.]

Angus, Robert C. and Stull, J. Warren. Consumer Attitudes toward Milk Substitutes. *Amer. J. Agr. Econ.,* December 1969, *51*(5), pp. 1149–53. [G: U.S.]

Ayanian, Robert. A Comparison of Barten's Estimated Demand Elasticities with Those Obtained Using Frisch's Method. *Econometrica,* January 1969, *37*(1), pp. 79–94. [G: Netherlands; U.K.]

Barban, Arnold M. The Dilemma of "Integrated" Advertising. *J. Bus.,* October 1969, *42*(4), pp. 477–96. [G: U.S.]

Barnhill, J. Allison. An Empirical Analysis of the "Culturation Impact" on Patterns of Food Consumption. *Univ. Wash. Bus. Rev.,* Spring 1969, *28* (3), pp. 33–39. [G: U.S.]

Beernaert, Luc and Laevaert, Ludo. De Tienermarkt: Analyse van enkele karakteristieken. (The Teenager Market: An Analysis of Some Characteristics. With English summary.) *Econ. Soc. Tijdschr.,* December 1969, *23*(6), pp. 663–74.

Bennett, Peter D. and Mandell, Robert M. Prepurpose Information Seeking Behavior of New Car Purchasers—The Learning Hypothesis. *J. Marketing Res.,* November 1969, *6*(4), pp. 430–33. [G: U.S.]

Blyth, C. A. Primitive South Pacific Economies: Their Consumption Pattern and Propensity to Save Out of Cash Income. *Econ. Rec.,* September 1969, *45*(111), pp. 354–72. [G: Samoa; Papua]

Borkar, V. V. Prohibition: An Economic Analysis. **In** *Bhuleshkar, A. V., ed.,* 1969, pp. 395–405. [G: India]

Bredov, V. and Levin, A. Prediction of the Population's Demand. *Prob. Econ.,* January 1969, *11*(9), pp. 34–44. [G: U.S.S.R.]

Brown, Joseph D. Effect of a Health Hazard "Scare" on Consumer Demand. *Amer. J. Agr. Econ.,* August 1969, *51*(3), pp. 676–79. [G: U.S.]

Bucklin, Louis P. Consumer Search, Role Enactment, and Market Efficiency. *J. Bus.,* October 1969, *42*(4), pp. 416–38. [G: U.S.]

Burch, S. W. and Stekler, H. O. The Forecasting Accuracy of Consumer Attitude Data. *J. Amer. Statist. Assoc.,* December 1969, *64*(328), pp. 1225–33.

Claycamp, Henry J. and Liddy, Lucien E. Prediction of New Product Performance: An Analytical Approach. *J. Marketing Res.,* November 1969, *6*(4), pp. 414–20. [G: U.S.]

Coondoo, Dipankor. The Effect of Relative Prices on Engel Elasticity of Cereals in India. *Arthaniti,* January & July 1969, *12*(1&2), pp. 57–68. [G: India]

David, Michel. La distribuzione alimentare in Francia: oggli e domani. (Food Distribution in France: To-day and Tomorrow. With English summary.) *L'Impresa,* March/April 1969, *11*(2), pp. 156–62. [G: France]

Dempsey, Richard E. and Schmude, Douglas F. How Consumer Spending for Automobiles Creates Jobs. *Mon. Lab. Rev.,* March 1969, *92*(3), pp. 33–36. [G: U.S.]

Dowd, Douglas F. Statement. **In** *Role of Giant Corporations, Pt. 1, SCH,* 1969, pp. 521–29. [G: U.S.]

Duewer, Lawrence A. Effects of Specials on Composite Meat Prices. *Agr. Econ. Res.,* July 1969, *21* (3), pp. 70–77. [G: U.S.]

Duker, Jacob M. Expenditures for Life Insurance among Working-Wife Families. *J. Risk Ins.,* December 1969, *36*(5), pp. 525–33. [G: U.S.]

Fabricius, P. J. The Marketing Manager of Tomorrow. *Econ. Soc. Tijdschr.,* December 1969, *23*(6), pp. 547–54.

Ferber, Robert, et al. Validation of a National Survey of Consumer Financial Characteristics: Savings Accounts. *Rev. Econ. Statist.,* November 1969, *51* (4), pp. 436–44. [G: U.S.]

Ferber, Robert, et al. Validation of Consumer Financial Characteristics: Common Stock. *J. Amer. Statist. Assoc.,* June 1969, *64*(326), pp. 415–32.

Folwell, Raymond J. A New Look at Demand Analysis for Beef: Comment. *Amer. J. Agr. Econ.,* November 1969, *51*(4), pp. 947–49. [G: U.S.]

Fox, Karl A. Factors Affecting Farm Income, Farm

Prices, and Food Consumption. In *Fox, K. A. and Johnson, D. G., eds.*, 1969, pp. 37–63. **[G: U.S.]**

Galper, Harvey and Dunn, Robert M., Jr. A Short-Run Demand Function for Higher Education in the United States. *J. Polit. Econ.*, September/October 1969, *77*(5), pp. 765–77. **[G: U.S.]**

Gustafson, Albert W. Consumer Preference for "Imitation" Milk Beverages. *Amer. J. Agr. Econ.*, December 1969, *51*(5), pp. 1637–44. **[G: U.S.]**

Hansen, Flemming. Consumer Choice Behavior: An Experimental Approach. *J. Marketing Res.*, November 1969, *6*(4), pp. 436–43.

Harmston, Floyd K. The Importance of 1967 Tourism to Missouri. *Univ. Missouri Bus. Govt. Rev.*, May–June 1969, *10*(3), pp. 6–12. **[G: U.S.]**

Hawes, Mary H. Measuring Retired Couples' Living Costs in Urban Areas. *Mon. Lab. Rev.*, November 1969, *92*(11), pp. 3–16. **[G: U.S.]**

Heien, Dale M. Income and Price Lags in Consumer-demand Analysis. *J. Roy. Statist. Soc.*, Part 2, 1969, *132*, pp. 265–71. **[G: U.S.]**

Hughes, John J. Note on the U.S. Demand for Coffee. *Amer. J. Agr. Econ.*, November 1969, *51*(4), pp. 912–14. **[G: U.S.]**

Khan, Mohammad Irshad. Aggregative Analysis of Food Consumption in Pakistan. *Pakistan Develop. Rev.*, Winter 1969, *9*(4), pp. 426–41. **[G: Pakistan]**

Koch, James V. The Homogeneity Assumption and Financial Asset Demand Functions. *Quart. Rev. Econ. Bus.*, Winter 1969, *9*(4), pp. 57–65. **[G: U.S.]**

Leoni, Renato. A proposito dell'impiego del modello di Theil-Barten nell'analisi della domanda di beni di consumo in Italia. (With English summary.) *Statistica*, April-June 1969, *29*(2), pp. 277–86. **[G: Italy]**

Lewis, Stephen R., Jr. A Note on the Consistency of Pakistan's Cotton-Cloth Statistics for Recent Years. *Pakistan Develop. Rev.*, Winter 1969, *9*(4), pp. 442–46. **[G: Pakistan]**

Lippitt, Vernon G. Determinants of Consumer Demand for House Furnishings and Equipment. In *Alexis, M.; Holloway, R. J. and Hancock, R. S., eds.*, 1969, pp. 3–19. **[G: U.S.]**

Luttrell, Clifton B. Meat Prices. *Fed. Res. Bank St. Louis Rev.*, August 1969, *51*(8), pp. 24–28. **[G: U.S.]**

Manhertz, Huntley G. Statistical Evaluation of Regional Differences in the Market for Processed Food Commodities. *Rev. Econ. Statist.*, May 1969, *51*(2), pp. 195–201. **[G: U.S.]**

Marcus, Burton H. Similarity of Ghetto and Nonghetto Food Costs. *J. Marketing Res.*, August 1969, *6*(3), pp. 365–68. **[G: U.S.]**

Martelli, Antonio. Gli errori nelle previsioni dei consumi. (Mistakes in Consumer Forecasting. With English summary.) *L'Impresa*, July/October 1969, *11*(4–5), pp. 357–64.

Massell, Benton F. Consistent Estimation of Expenditure Elasticities from Cross-Section Data on Households Producing Partly for Subsistence. *Rev. Econ. Statist.*, May 1969, *51*(2), pp. 136–42. **[G: Kenya]**

Massell, Benton F. and Heyer, Judith. Household Expenditure in Nairobi: A Statistical Analysis in Consumer Behavior. *Econ. Develop. Cult. Change*, January 1969, *17*(2), pp. 212–34. **[G: Nairobi]**

Massy, William F. Forecasting the Demand for New Convenience Products. *J. Marketing Res.*, November 1969, *6*(4), pp. 405–12.

Mazumder, Debkumar Dutta. Estimates of Increase in Demand for Specific Items of Milk and Milk Products during Fourth and Fifth Five Year Plans. *Econ. Aff.*, January-February 1969, *14* (1–2), pp. 81–87. **[G: India]**

Michelini, Claudio. Stima bayesiana di una funzione di Engel. (With English summary.) *Statistica*, January-March 1969, *29*(1), pp. 27–48. **[G: Italy]**

Mittelstaedt, Robert. A Dissonance Approach to Repeat Purchasing Behavior. *J. Marketing Res.*, November 1969, *6*(4), pp. 444–46.

Mizoguchi, Toshiyuki. A Comparison of Levels of Consumption of Urban Households in Japan and in Mainland China—A Summary. *Rev. Income Wealth*, June 1969, *15*(2), pp. 215–17. **[G: Japan; China]**

Murphy, K. T. A Note on the Measurement of Price Elasticity of Demand. *Amer. J. Agr. Econ.*, August 1969, *51*(3), pp. 691–92.

Neter, J. Measurement Errors in Anticipated Consumer Expenditures. In *Johnson, N. L. and Smith, H., Jr., eds.*, 1969, pp. 482–505.

Neumann, Seev. Inflation and Saving through Life Insurance. *J. Risk Ins.*, December 1969, *36*(5), pp. 567–82. **[G: U.S.]**

Nicosia, Francesco M. Ricerche sui consumatori: problemi e prospettive. (Consumer Research: Problems and Perspectives. With English summary.) *L'Impresa*, November/December 1969, *11*(6), pp. 429–35. **[G: Italy]**

Parks, Richard W. Systems of Demand Equations: An Empirical Comparison of Alternative Functional Forms. *Econometrica*, October 1969, *37*(4), pp. 629–50.

Perry, Michael and Hamm, B. Curtis. Canonical Analysis of Relations between Socioeconomic Risk and Personal Influence in Purchase Decisions. *J. Marketing Res.*, August 1969, *6*(3), pp. 351–54.

Pollak, Robert A. and Wales, Terrence J. Estimation of the Linear Expenditure System. *Econometrica*, October 1969, *37*(4), pp. 611–28.

Rao, Tanniru R. Are Some Consumers More Prone to Purchase Private Brands? *J. Marketing Res.*, November 1969, *6*(4), pp. 447–50. **[G: U.S.]**

Rao, Tanniru R. Consumer's Purchase Decision Process: Stochastic Models. *J. Marketing Res.*, August 1969, *6*(3), pp. 321–29.

Saarsalmi, Meeri. Kuluttajain ostoaikomukset ja ostotodennäköisyydet kysyntäennusteissa. (Consumer Buying Intentions and Purchase Probability in Forecasting Demand. With English summary.) *Liiketaloudellinen Aikak.*, 1969, *18* (3), pp. 576–84.

Samli, A. Coskun. Differential Price Structures for the Rich and the Poor. *Univ. Wash. Bus. Rev.*, Summer 1969, *28*(4), pp. 36–43. **[G: U.S.]**

Siimestö, Orvo. Markovin ketjut ostosarjojen stokastisena mallina. (Markov Chains as a Stochastic

Model of Buying Series. With English summary.) *Liiketaloudellinen Aikak.*, 1969, *18*(2), pp. 233–42.

Sleeman, John F. A New Look at the Distribution of Private Cars in Britain. *Scot. J. Polit. Econ.*, November 1969, *16*(3), pp. 306–18. **[G: U.K.]**

Solverson, Lyle. Consumer Knowledge for Sovereignty: Apples. *Amer. J. Agr. Econ.*, December 1969, *51*(5), pp. 1247–50. **[G: U.S.]**

Stafford, Frank P. and Dunkelberg, William. The Cost of Financing Automobile Purchases. *Rev. Econ. Statist.*, November 1969, *51*(4), pp. 459–64. **[G: U.S.]**

Swackhamer, Gene L. Synthetics and Substitutes: Challenge to Agriculture. *Fed. Res. Bank Kansas City Rev.*, March 1969, pp. 3–12. **[G: U.S.]**

Taplin, J. and Ryan, W. The Prospects for Wine in Australia. *Quart. Rev. Agr. Econ.*, October 1969, *22*(4), pp. 198–209. **[G: Australia]**

Tendulkar, Suresh D. Econometric Study of Monthly Consumption Expenditures in Rural Uttar Pradesh. *Amer. J. Agr. Econ.*, February 1969, *51*(1), pp. 119–37. **[G: India]**

Tolley, George S.; Wang, Yi and Fletcher, R. G. Reexamination of the Time Series Evidence on Food Demand. *Econometrica*, October 1969, *37* (4), pp. 695–705.

Turnovsky, Stephen J. The Demand for Water: Some Empirical Evidence on Consumers' Response to a Commodity Uncertain in Supply. *Water Resources Res.*, April 1969, *5*(2), pp. 350–61. **[G: U.S.]**

Uvacek, Edward, Jr. A New Look at Demand Analysis for Beef: Reply. *Amer. J. Agr. Econ.*, November 1969, *51*(4), pp. 949–52. **[G: U.S.]**

Wasson, Chester R. Le previsioni sulla moda e sugli altri aspetti del ciclo di vita del prodotto. (How Predictable Are Fashion and Other Product Life Cycles. With English summary.) *Mondo Aperto*, October 1969, *23*(5), pp. 357–70.

Wind, Yoram and Frank, Ronald E. Interproduct Household Loyalty to Brands. *J. Marketing Res.*, November 1969, *6*(4), pp. 434–35. **[G: U.S.]**

Winston, Clement. Trade and Services Outlays Related to Income. **In** *Alexis, M.; Holloway, R. J. and Hancock, R. S., eds.*, 1969, pp. 33–38. **[G: U.S.]**

Witt, Robert E. Informal Social Group Influence on Consumer Brand Choice. *J. Marketing Res.*, November 1969, *6*(4), pp. 473–76.

9213 Consumer Protection

Angevine, Erma. Statement. **In** *Utility Consumers' Counsel Act of 1969, Pt. 6A, SCH*, 1969, pp. 1462–66. **[G: U.S.]**

Brimmer, Andrew F. Statement to Congress. *Fed. Res. Bull.*, December 1969, *55*(12), pp. 923–27. **[G: U.S.]**

Bryson, John E. and Dunham, Stephen S. A Case Study of the Impact of Consumer Legislation: The Elimination of Negotiability and the Cooling-Off Period. *Yale Law J.*, March 1969, *78*(4), pp. 618–61. **[G: U.S.]**

Cox, Edward; Fellmeth, Robert and Schulz, John. The Consumer and the Federal Trade Commission, a Critique of the Consumer Protection Record of the FTC. **In** *To Establish a Department of Consumer Affairs, SCH*, 1969, pp. 123–312. **[G: U.S.]**

Denenberg, Herbert S. Insurance Regulation: The Search for Countervailing Power and Consumer Protection. **In** *Impact of Crime on Small Business—1969, Pt. 1, SCH*, 1969, pp. 57–63. **[G: U.S.]**

Furness, Betty. Statement. **In** *To Establish a Department of Consumer Affairs, SCH*, 1969, pp. 343–61. **[G: U.S.]**

Goudzwaard, Maurice B. Consumer Credit Charges and Credit Availability. *Southern Econ. J.*, January 1969, *35*(3), pp. 214–23. **[G: U.S.]**

Grabner, John R., Jr. Legal Limits of Competition. *Harvard Bus. Rev.*, November–December 1969, *47*(6), pp. 4–24, 182. **[G: U.S.]**

Gross, Edwin J. An Industrial Approach to Consumerism: Ombudsmen. *Ohio State U. Bull. Bus. Res.*, October 1969, *44*(10), pp. 6–7. **[G: U.S.]**

Kawaja, Michael. The Economic Effects of Regulation: A Case Study of the Consumer Finance Industry. *Southern Econ. J.*, January 1969, *35*(3), pp. 231–38. **[G: U.S.]**

Ladd, John C. The Logic of Foreclosure: Tie-In Doctrine after *Fortner v. U. S. Steel. Yale Law J.*, November 1969, *79*(1), pp. 86–101. **[G: U.S.]**

Lobato López, Ernesto. Las normas de calidad y el desarrollo de la industria (Primera parte). (Quality Standards and Industrial Development: First Part. With English summary.) *Econ. Polít.*, Second Semester 1969, *6*(2), pp. 183–94. **[G: Mexico]**

Nader, Ralph. Statement. **In** *To Establish a Department of Consumer Affairs, SCH*, 1969, pp. 365–97. **[G: U.S.]**

Nader, Ralph. The Great American Gyp and Taming the Corporate Tiger. **In** *To Establish a Department of Consumer Affairs, SCH*, 1969, pp. 473–81. **[G: U.S.]**

Pollay, Richard W. Consumer Protection and Advertising. *Ohio State U. Bull. Bus. Res.*, July 1969, *44*(7), pp. 4–8.

Rados, David L. Product Liability: Tougher Ground Rules. *Harvard Bus. Rev.*, July–August 1969, *47* (4), pp. 144–52. **[G: U.S.]**

Raymond, Robert S. Consumer Protection in Great Britain and in the United States. *Marquette Bus. Rev.*, Winter 1969, *13*(4), pp. 151–58. **[G: U.K.; U.S.]**

930 URBAN ECONOMICS

931 Urban Economics and Public Policy

9310 Urban Economics and Public Policy

Aaron, Henry J. Local Public Expenditures and the "Migration Effect." *Western Econ. J.*, December 1969, *7*(4), pp. 385–90.

Allen, Louis L. Making Capitalism Work in the Ghettos. *Harvard Bus. Rev.*, May–June 1969, *47* (3), pp. 83–92. **[G: U.S.]**

Andrews, Richard B. Economia del suolo urbano:

sommario della disciplina e delle sue tendenze. (Urban Land Economics: A Summary View. With English summary.) *Rivista Int. Sci. Econ. Com.*, August 1969, *16*(8), pp. 807–15.

Archer, R. W. From New Towns to Metrotowns and Regional Cities. *Amer. J. Econ. Soc.*, July 1969, *28* (3), pp. 257–70. **[G: Australia; U.K.; U.S.]**

Archer, R. W. From New Towns to Metrotowns and Regional Cities, II. *Amer. J. Econ. Soc.*, October 1969, *28*(4), pp. 385–98. **[G: Sweden]**

Atkisson, Arthur A. and Robinson, Ira M. Amenity Resources for Urban Living. **In** *Perloff, H. S., ed.*, 1969, pp. 179–201.

Bell, Frederick W. and Murphy, Neil B. The Impact of Regulation on Inter- and Intraregional Variation in Commercial Banking Costs. *J. Reg. Sci.*, August 1969, *9*(2), pp. 225–38. **[G: U.S.]**

Benjamin, B. Statistics in Town Planning. *J. Roy. Statist. Soc.*, Part 1, 1969, *132*, pp. 1–15.

Bergmann, Barbara R. The Urban Economy and the "Urban Crisis." *Amer. Econ. Rev.*, Part I, September 1969, *59*(4), pp. 639–45.

Birren, James E. The Aged in Cities. **In** *Usefulness of the Model Cities Program to the Elderly, Pt. 1, SCH*, 1969, pp. 138–45. **[G: U.S.]**

Bish, Robert L. Public Housing: The Magnitude and Distribution of Direct Benefits and Effects on Housing Consumption. *J. Reg. Sci.*, December 1969, *9*(3), pp. 425–38. **[G: U.S.]**

Blevins, Audie L., Jr. Migration Rates in Twelve Southern Metropolitan Areas: A "Push-Pull" Analysis. *Soc. Sci. Quart.*, September 1969, *50*(2), pp. 337–53. **[G: U.S.]**

Blumenfeld, Hans. Criteria for Judging the Quality of the Urban Environment. **In** *Schmandt, H. J. and Bloomberg, W., Jr., eds.*, 1969, pp. 137–64.

Blumenfeld, Hans. The Modern Metropolis. **In** *Callow, A. B., Jr., ed.*, 1969, pp. 166–77.

Bourne, L. S. A Spatial Allocation-Land Use Conversion Model of Urban Growth. *J. Reg. Sci.*, August 1969, *9*(2), pp. 261–72.

Bourne, L. S. Location Factors in the Redevelopment Process: A Model of Residential Change. *Land Econ.*, May 1969, *45*(2), pp. 183–93. **[G: Canada]**

Bowley, Marian. Constraints on the Freedom of the Profit Motive. **In** *Ling, A. G., et al.*, 1969, pp. 43–46. **[G: U.K.]**

Bowman, John H. City-Suburban Differentials in Local Government Fiscal Effort: A Comment. *Nat. Tax J.*, September 1969, *22*(3), pp. 418–21. **[G: U.S.]**

Bronfenbrenner, Martin. A Working Library on Riots and Hunger. *J. Human Res.*, Summer 1969, *4*(3), pp. 377–90. **[G: U.S.]**

Brown, Robert Kevin. City Cybernetics. *Land Econ.*, November 1969, *45*(4), pp. 406–12.

Caplan, Nathan S. and Paige, Jeffrey M. A Study of Ghetto Rioters. **In** *Callow, A. B., Jr., ed.*, 1969, pp. 541–48. **[G: U.S.]**

Chapin, F. Stuart, Jr. and Logan, Thomas H. Patterns of Time and Space Use. **In** *Perloff, H. S., ed.*, 1969, pp. 305–32.

Childs, Gerald L. Efficient Reallocation of Land in Urban Renewal. *Western Econ. J.*, September 1969, *7*(3), pp. 211–22.

Cho, Yong Hyo. Fiscal Implications of Annexation: The Case of Metropolitan Central Cities in Texas. *Land Econ.*, August 1969, *45*(3), pp. 368–72. **[G: U.S.]**

Clarke, James W. Environment, Process and Policy: A Reconsideration. *Amer. Polit. Sci. Rev.*, December 1969, *63*(4), pp. 1172–82. **[G: U.S.]**

Clawson, Marion. Open (Uncovered) Space as a New Urban Resource. **In** *Perloff, H. S., ed.*, 1969, pp. 139–75.

Cohen, Henry. Planning Rationally for the City. **In** *Connery, R. H. and Caraley, D., eds.*, 1969, pp. 179–92. **[G: U.S.]**

Connery, Robert H. Governing the City. **In** *Connery, R. H. and Caraley, D., eds.*, 1969, pp. 1–6.

Davies, David. City-Suburban Differentials in Local Government Fiscal Effort: A Comment. *Nat. Tax J.*, September 1969, *22*(3), pp. 422–23. **[G: U.S.]**

Davis, Otto A. and Wertz, Kenneth L. The Consistency of the Assessment of Property: Some Empirical Results and Managerial Suggestions. *Appl. Econ.*, May 1969, *1*(2), pp. 151–57. **[G: U.S.]**

Devine, Eugene J. Manpower Shortages in Local Government Employment. *Amer. Econ. Rev.*, May 1969, *59*(2), pp. 538–45. **[G: U.S.]**

Dolan, Paul. Citizens Complaints in St. Louis—The Case for an Ombudsman? *Univ. Missouri Bus. Govt. Rev.*, September–October 1969, *10*(5), pp. 25–31. **[G: U.S.]**

Downing, Paul B. Extension of Sewer Service at the Urban-Rural Fringe. *Land Econ.*, February 1969, *45*(1), pp. 103–11.

Doxiadis, Constantinos. A City for Human Development. **In** *Population Trends, Pt. 1, HCH*, 1969, pp. 374–94.

Doxiadis, Constantinos. Man's Movement and His City. **In** *Population Trends, Pt. 1, HCH*, 1969, pp. 398–406.

Doxiadis, Constantinos. Statement. **In** *Population Trends, Pt. 1, HCH*, 1969, pp. 341–69. **[G: U.S.]**

Doxiadis, Constantinos. Statement. **In** *Panel on Science and Technology: Science and Technology and the Cities, HCH*, 1969, pp. 19–35. **[G: U.S.]**

Dyos, H. J. Some Historical Reflections on the Quality of Urban Life. **In** *Schmandt, H. J. and Bloomberg, W., Jr., eds.*, 1969, pp. 31–60.

Engelbert, Ernest A. The Political Aspects of Real Estate Taxation in Relation to Metropolitan Growth and Planning. **In** *Becker, A. P., ed.*, 1969, pp. 97–114. **[G: U.S.]**

Farmer, Richard N. The Dilemma of the Black Businessman: Clarification of the Current Situation. *Indiana Bus. Rev.*, March–April 1969, *44*, pp. 13, 27–28. **[G: U.S.]**

Forward, C. N. A Comparison of Waterfront Land Use in Four Canadian Ports: St. John's, St. John, Halifax, and Victoria. *Econ. Geogr.*, April 1969, *45* (2), pp. 155–69. **[G: Canada]**

Frank, Andre Gunder. Instability and Integration in Urban Latin America. **In** *Frank, A. G.*, 1969, pp. 276–97. **[G: Latin America]**

Frankel, Richard J. and Frankel, Beverly F. A Framework for Dealing with the Urban Environment: Appendix: Microenvironmental Responses to Changes in the Urban Environment. **In** *Perloff, H. S., ed.*, 1969, pp. 26–31.

Gabler, L. R. Economies and Diseconomies of Scale in Urban Public Sectors. *Land Econ.,* November 1969, *45*(4), pp. 425–34. **[G: U.S.]**

Gans, Herbert J. The Failure of Urban Renewal. **In** *Callow, A. B., Jr., ed.,* 1969, pp. 567–81. **[G: U.S.]**

Gardner, John W. Statement. **In** *Panel on Science and Technology: Science and Technology and the Cities, HCH,* 1969, pp. 3–11. **[G: U.S.]**

Goldston, Eli. BURP and Make Money. *Harvard Bus. Rev.,* September–October 1969, *47*(5), pp. 84–99. **[G: U.S.]**

Greenwald, Carol S. and Syron, Richard. Increasing Job Opportunities in Boston's Urban Core. *New Eng. Econ. Rev.,* January/February 1969, pp. 30–40.

Greer, Scott. The City in Crisis. **In** *Callow, A. B., Jr., ed.,* 1969, pp. 401–15.

Greer, Scott. Waiting for Reality: Birth of the Megalopolis. **In** *Callow, A. B., Jr., ed.,* 1969, pp. 597–604. **[G: U.S.]**

Grey, Arthur L., Jr. Urban Renewal and Land Value Taxation. **In** *Becker, A. P., ed.,* 1969, pp. 81–96. **[G: U.S.]**

Hady, Thomas F. Tax Structure and Regional Economic Growth: A Comment. *J. Reg. Sci.,* August 1969, *9*(2), pp. 325–26. **[G: U.S.]**

Hansen, Niles M. Urban Alternatives for Eliminating Poverty. *Mon. Lab. Rev.,* August 1969, *92*(8), pp. 46–47.

Harris, Walter D. Urban Quality in the Context of the Developing Society. **In** *Schmandt, H. J. and Bloomberg, W., Jr., eds.,* 1969, pp. 187–210. **[G: Latin America]**

Hazard, Leland. Challenges for Urban Policy. **In** *Baier, K. and Rescher, N., eds.,* 1969, pp. 320–35.

Heideman, M. Lawrence, Jr. Public Implementation and Incentive Devices for Innovation and Experiment in Planned Urban Development. *Land Econ.,* May 1969, *45*(2), pp. 262–67.

Hicks, Ursula K. Economic and Financial Problems of Metropolitan Areas. *Z. Nationalökon.,* May 1969, *29*(1–2), pp. 1–18.

Hirsch, Werner Z. and Marcus, Morton J. Intercommunity Spillovers and the Provision of Public Education. *Kyklos,* 1969, *22*(4), pp. 641–60. **[G: U.S.]**

Hoch, Irving. The Three-dimensional City: Contained Urban Space. **In** *Perloff, H. S., ed.,* 1969, pp. 75–135.

Holt, W. Stull. Some Consequences of the Urban Movement in American History. **In** *Callow, A. B., Jr., ed.,* 1969, pp. 41–52. **[G: U.S.]**

Holtmann, A. G. Correction to Migration to the Suburbs, Human Capital and City Income Tax Losses: A Case Study. *Nat. Tax J.,* September 1969, *22*(3), pp. 424. **[G: U.S.]**

Hoyt, Homer. Importance of Manufacturing in Basic Employment. *Land Econ.,* August 1969, *45*(3), pp. 344–49. **[G: U.S.]**

Isomura, Eiichi. The Urban Crisis in Japan. **In** *Panel on Science and Technology: Science and Technology and the Cities, HCH,* 1969, pp. 157–62. **[G: Japan]**

Jacobs, Jane. Strategies for Helping Cities. *Amer. Econ. Rev.,* Part I, September 1969, *59*(4), pp. 652–56.

Jeffrey, D.; Casetti, E. and King, L. Economic Fluctuations in a Multiregional Setting: A Bi-factor Analytic Approach. *J. Reg. Sci.,* December 1969, *9*(3), pp. 397–404. **[G: U.S.]**

Johnston, R. J. Zonal and Sectoral Patterns in Melbourne's Residential Structure: 1961. *Land Econ.,* November 1969, *45*(4), pp. 463–67. **[G: Australia]**

Kamerschen, David R. Further Analysis of Overurbanization. *Econ. Develop. Cult. Change,* January 1969, *17*(2), pp. 235–53.

Katzman, Martin T. Opportunity, Subculture and the Economic Performance of Urban Ethnic Groups. *Amer. J. Econ. Soc.,* October 1969, *28*(4), pp. 351–66. **[G: U.S.]**

Kee, Woo Sik. The Causes of Urban Poverty. *J. Human Res.,* Winter 1969, *4*(1), pp. 93–99. **[G: U.S.]**

Kelliher, Walter J. Statement. **In** *Population Trends, Pt. 1, HCH,* 1969, pp. 681–86. **[G: U.S.]**

Kravitz, Sanford and Kolodner, Ferne K. Community Action: Where Has It Been? Where Will It Go? *Ann. Amer. Acad. Polit. Soc. Sci.,* September 1969, *385,* pp. 30–40. **[G: U.S.]**

Launie, J. J. The Supply Function of Urban Property Insurance. *J. Risk Ins.,* June 1969, *36*(2), pp. 269–83. **[G: U.S.]**

Lavidge, Robert J. The Ghetto Challenge to Marketing People. *Ohio State U. Bull. Bus. Res.,* August 1969, *44*(8), pp. 4, 6–7. **[G: U.S.]**

Levine, Charles H. The Dilemma of the Black Businessman: A New Approach? *Indiana Bus. Rev.,* March–April 1969, *44,* pp. 12, 22–26. **[G: U.S.]**

Lewis, David. New Urban Structures. **In** *Baier, K. and Rescher, N., eds.,* 1969, pp. 294–319.

Lichfield, Nathaniel. Problems of Obtaining Private Capital for New Towns. **In** *Ling, A. G., et al.,* 1969, pp. 47–51. **[G: U.K.]**

Lineberry, Robert L. Community Structure and Planning Commitment: A Note on the Correlates of Agency Expenditures. *Soc. Sci. Quart.,* December 1969, *50*(3), pp. 723–30. **[G: U.S.]**

Llewelyn-Davies, Richard. New Cities—A British Example: Milton Keynes. **In** *Panel on Science and Technology: Science and Technology and the Cities, HCH,* 1969, pp. 56–67. **[G: U.K.]**

Lomax, Alfred L. Big Steel Mill Comes to Portland. *Oregon Bus. Rev.,* April 1969, *28*(4), pp. 1, 3. **[G: U.S.]**

Lowe, Jeanne. The End of the Line: Race and Poverty in Cities. **In** *Callow, A. B., Jr., ed.,* 1969, pp. 519–40. **[G: U.S.]**

Lurie, Melvin and Rayack, Elton. Employment Opportunities for Negro Families in "Satellite" Cities. *Southern Econ. J.,* October 1969, *36*(2), pp. 191–95. **[G: U.S.]**

Mason, Joseph Barry and Moore, Charles Thomas. A Note on the Reliability of Census Data in Trading Area Analysis. *Miss. Val. J. Bus. Econ.,* Fall 1969, *5*(1), pp. 68–72. **[G: U.S.]**

Meyerson, Martin. Statement. **In** *Panel on Science and Technology: Science and Technology and the Cities, HCH,* 1969, pp. 17–19. **[G: U.S.]**

Mills, Edwin S. The Value of Urban Land. **In** *Perloff, H. S., ed.,* 1969, pp. 231–53.

Moeller, Charles, Jr. Economic Implications of the Life Insurance Industry's Investment Program in the Central Cities. *J. Risk Ins.*, March 1969, *36*(1), pp. 93–101. [G: U.S.]

Murphy, Thomas P. and Eurman, Stuart. Intergovernmental Cooperation in the Kansas City Region. *Univ. Missouri Bus. Govt. Rev.*, January–February 1969, *10*(1), pp. 5–13. [G: U.S.]

Murray, Barbara B. An Economic Profile of a Potential Ghetto. *Marquette Bus. Rev.*, Summer 1969, *13*(2), pp. 93–97. [G: U.S.]

Murray, Barbara B. Central City Expenditures and Out-Migration to the Fringe. *Land Econ.*, November 1969, *45*(4), pp. 471–74.

Murray, Barbara B. Metropolitan Interpersonal Income Inequality. *Land Econ.*, February 1969, *45* (1), pp. 121–25. [G: U.S.]

Nag, A. Estimation and Projection of the Working Force in Greater Bombay. *Asian Econ. Rev.*, February 1969, *11*(2), pp. 160–72. [G: India]

Neutze, Max. Property Taxation and Multiple-Family Housing. **In** *Becker, A. P., ed.*, 1969, pp. 115–28.

Nieburg, H. L. The Tech-Fix and the City. **In** *Schmandt, H. J. and Bloomberg, W., Jr., eds.*, 1969, pp. 211–43.

Northam, Ray M. Population Size, Relative Location, and Declining Urban Centers: Conterminous United States, 1940–1960. *Land Econ.*, August 1969, *45*(3), pp. 313–22. [G: U.S.]

Paterson, Robert W. Metropolitan Fragments v. Urban Order. *Univ. Missouri Bus. Govt. Rev.*, January–February 1969, *10*(1), pp. 14–22. [G: U.S.]

Pauly, Mark V. Manpower Shortages in Local Government Employment: Discussion. *Amer. Econ. Rev.*, May 1969, *59*(2), pp. 565–67.

Perloff, Harvey S. A Framework for Dealing with the Urban Environment: Introductory Statement. **In** *Perloff, H. S., ed.*, 1969, pp. 3–25.

Perloff, Harvey S. Statement. **In** *Panel on Science and Technology: Science and Technology and the Cities, HCH,* 1969, pp. 149–55. [G: U.S.]

Pidot, George B., Jr. A Principal Components Analysis of the Determinants of Local Government Fiscal Patterns. *Rev. Econ. Statist.*, May 1969, *51* (2), pp. 176–88. [G: U.S.]

Prakash, Ved. A Suggested Approach to Municipal Investment Planning. *Land Econ.*, August 1969, *45*(3), pp. 350–58.

Prentice, P. I. The Case for Taxing Location Values: A Memorandum for a Metropolis Considering Property Tax Reform. *Amer. J. Econ. Soc.*, April 1969, *28*(2), pp. 145–58. [G: U.S.]

Raymond, George M.; Rivkin, Malcolm D. and Gans, Herbert J. Urban Renewal: A Controversy. **In** *Callow, A. B., Jr., ed.*, 1969, pp. 582–96. [G: U.S.]

Ritter, Lawrence S. A Capital Market Plan for the Urban Areas. *Calif. Manage. Rev.*, Summer 1969, *11*(4), pp. 37–46.

Rothenberg, Jerome. Strategic Interaction and Resource Allocation in Metropolitan Intergovernmental Relations. *Amer. Econ. Rev.*, May 1969, *59* (2), pp. 494–503.

Rouse, James W. Columbia: A New Town Built with Private Capital. **In** *Ling, A. G., et al.*, 1969, pp. 13–29. [G: U.S.]

Ruzavina, E. Economic Aspects in the Urbanization Process. *Prob. Econ.*, August 1969, *12*(4), pp. 68–79. [G: U.S.S.R.]

Scarato, Russell F. Time-Capacity Expansion of Urban Water Systems. *Water Resources Res.*, October 1969, *5*(5), pp. 929–36.

Schlesinger, Arthur M. The City in American Civilization. **In** *Callow, A. B., Jr., ed.*, 1969, pp. 25–41. [G: U.S.]

Schlesinger, Arthur M. The Urban World. **In** *Callow, A. B., Jr., ed.*, 1969, pp. 186–209.

Schmandt, Henry J. and Goldbach, John C. The Urban Paradox. **In** *Schmandt, H. J. and Bloomberg, W., Jr., eds.*, 1969, pp. 473–98.

Schmid, A. Allan. Natural Resources and Growth: Towards a Non-Marginal Political Economics. *Amer. J. Agr. Econ.*, December 1969, *51*(5), pp. 1304–13. [G: U.S.]

Schnore, Leo F. City-Suburban Income Differentials in Metropolitan Areas. **In** *Population Trends, Pt. 1, HCH,* 1969, pp. 242–45. [G: U.S.]

Schnore, Leo F. Metropolitan Development in the United Kingdom. **In** *Population Trends, Pt. 1, HCH,* 1969, pp. 245–64. [G: U.K.]

Schnore, Leo F. Municipal Annexations and the Growth of Metropolitan Suburbs, 1950–1960. **In** *Population Trends, Pt. 1, HCH,* 1969, pp. 264–76. [G: U.S.]

Schnore, Leo F. Some Correlates of Urban Size: A Replication. **In** *Population Trends, Pt. 1, HCH,* 1969, pp. 292–300. [G: U.S.]

Schnore, Leo F. The City as a Social Organism. **In** *Callow, A. B., Jr., ed.*, 1969, pp. 53–60.

Schnore, Leo F. The Rural-Urban Variable: An Urbanite's Perspective. **In** *Population Trends, Pt. 1, HCH,* 1969, pp. 301–25. [G: U.S.]

Schnore, Leo F. Urban Structure and Suburban Selectivity. **In** *Population Trends, Pt. 1, HCH,* 1969, pp. 326–38. [G: U.S.]

Schoenbrod, David. Large Lot Zoning. *Yale Law J.*, July 1969, *78*(8), pp. 1418–41.

Schultz, George P. Facility Planning for a Public Service System: Domestic Solid Waste Collection. *J. Reg. Sci.*, August 1969, *9*(2), pp. 291–307.

Scott, Allen J. Spatial Equilibrium of the Central City. *J. Reg. Sci.*, April 1969, *9*(1), pp. 29–45. [G: U.K.]

Self, Peter J. O. Urban Systems and the Quality of Life. **In** *Schmandt, H. J. and Bloomberg, W., Jr., eds.*, 1969, pp. 165–86.

Seneca, Joseph J. and Cicchetti, Charles J. A Gravity Model Analysis of the Demand for Public Communication. *J. Reg. Sci.*, December 1969, *9*(3), pp. 459–70. [G: U.S.]

Sheaffer, John R. The Interaction of Urban Redevelopment and Flood Plain Management in Waterloo, Iowa. **In** *Dougal, M. D., ed.*, 1969, pp. 123–35. [G: U.S.]

Shoup, Donald C. Advance Land Acquisition by Local Governments: A Cost-Benefit Analysis. *Yale Econ. Essays*, Fall 1969, *9*(2), pp. 147–207. [G: U.S.]

Solzman, David M. The Value of Inland Waterfront Industrial Sites. *Land Econ.*, November 1969, *45* (4), pp. 456–62. [G: U.S.]

Spiegel, Hans B. C. and Alicea, Victor G. The Trade-Off Strategy in Community Research. *Soc. Sci. Quart.*, December 1969, *50*(3), pp. 598–603.

Spilhaus, Athelstan. Technology, Living Cities, and Human Environment. In *Panel on Science and Technology: Science and Technology and the Cities, HCH,* 1969, pp. 47–54. [G: U.S.]

Stambler, Howard V. New Directions in Area Labor Force Statistics. *Mon. Lab. Rev.,* August 1969, *92* (8), pp. 3–9. [G: U.S.]

Stambler, Howard V. Problems in Analyzing Urban Employment Survey Data. *Mon. Lab. Rev.,* November 1969, *92*(11), pp. 51–54. [G: U.S.]

Stephens, G. Ross. The Suburban Impact of Earnings Tax Policies. *Nat. Tax J.,* September 1969, *22*(3), pp. 313–33. [G: U.S.]

Stone, Lawrence M. Tax Incentives as a Solution to Urban Problems. In *Tax Credits to Stimulate Job Opportunities in Rural Areas, SCH,* 1969, pp. 185–91. [G: U.S.]

Struyk, Raymond J. Tax Structure and Regional Economic Growth: A Reply. *J. Reg. Sci.,* August 1969, *9*(2), pp. 327–28. [G: U.S.]

Sundquist, James L. Co-ordinating the War on Poverty. *Ann. Amer. Acad. Polit. Soc. Sci.,* September 1969, *385,* pp. 41–49. [G: U.S.]

Tabb, William K. Government Incentives to Private Industry to Locate in Urban Poverty Areas. *Land Econ.,* November 1969, *45*(4), pp. 392–99. [G: U.S.]

Tarver, James D. Migration Differentials in Southern Cities and Suburbs. *Soc. Sci. Quart.,* September 1969, *50*(2), pp. 298–324. [G: U.S.]

Taubman, Paul and Rasche, R. H. Economic and Tax Depreciation of Office Buildings. *Nat. Tax J.,* September 1969, *22*(3), pp. 334–46. [G: U.S.]

Thiesenhusen, William C. Population Growth and Agricultural Employment in Latin America, with Some U.S. Comparisons. *Amer. J. Agr. Econ.,* November 1969, *51*(4), pp. 735–52. [G: Latin America; U.S.]

Thomas, William C., Jr. Keeping the City Healthy. In *Connery, R. H. and Caraley, D., eds.,* 1969, pp. 121–32. [G: U.S.]

Thompson, Wilbur R. Statement. In *Population Trends, Pt. 1, HCH,* 1969, pp. 565–96. [G: U.S.]

Thompson, Wilbur R. The Economic Base of Urban Problems. In *Chamberlain, N. W., ed.,* 1969, pp. 1–47.

Tobier, Emanuel. People and Jobs. In *Connery, R. H. and Caraley, D., eds.,* 1969, pp. 7–19. [G: U.S.]

Todd, Jerry D. The Risk Management Function in Municipal Government. *J. Risk Ins.,* June 1969, *36*(2), pp. 285–95. [G: U.S.]

Turnovsky, Stephen J. The Demand for Water: Some Empirical Evidence on Consumers' Response to a Commodity Uncertain in Supply. *Water Resources Res.,* April 1969, *5*(2), pp. 350–61. [G: U.S.]

Vanecko, James J. Community Mobilization and Institutional Change: The Influence of the Community Action Program in Large Cities. *Soc. Sci. Quart.,* December 1969, *50*(3), pp. 609–30. [G: U.S.]

Walter, Ingo and Kramer, John E. Political Autonomy and Economic Dependence in an All-Negro Municipality. *Amer. J. Econ. Soc.,* July 1969, *28*(3), pp. 225–48. [G: U.S.]

West, W. A. Planning. In *Ling, A. G., et al.,* 1969, pp. 38–42. [G: U.K.]

Widner, Ralph B. Statement. In *Population Trends, Pt. 1, HCH,* 1969, pp. 598–605. [G: U.S.]

Williams, J. Allen, Jr. The Effects of Urban Renewal upon a Black Community: Evaluation and Recommendations. *Soc. Sci. Quart.,* December 1969, *50*(3), pp. 703–12. [G: U.S.]

Wood, Robert C. Statement. In *Public Facility Requirements over the Next Decade, JECH,* 1969, pp. 27–35. [G: U.S.]

932 Housing Economics

9320 Housing Economics (including nonurban housing)

Àdams, John S. Directional Bias in Intra-Urban Migration. *Econ. Geogr.,* October 1969, *45*(4), pp. 302–23.

Amato, Peter W. Population Densities, Land Values, and Socioeconomic Class in Bogotá, Colombia. *Land Econ.,* February 1969, *45*(1), pp. 66–73. [G: Colombia]

Bates, A. Allen. Low Cost Housing in the Soviet Union. In *Industrialized Housing, JECP,* 1969, pp. 1–21. [G: U.S.S.R.]

Beckmann, Martin J. On the Distribution of Urban Rent and Residential Density. *J. Econ. Theory,* June 1969, *1*(1), pp. 60–67.

Bish, Robert L. Public Housing: The Magnitude and Distribution of Direct Benefits and Effects on Housing Consumption. *J. Reg. Sci.,* December 1969, *9*(3), pp. 425–38. [G: U.S.]

Bishop, D. The Economics of Industrialized Building. In *Industrialized Housing, JECP,* 1969, pp. 201–19. [G: U.S.]

Bourne, L. S. Location Factors in the Redevelopment Process: A Model of Residential Change. *Land Econ.,* May 1969, *45*(2), pp. 183–93. [G: Canada]

Downs, Anthony. Housing the Urban Poor: The Economics of Various Strategies. *Amer. Econ. Rev.,* Part I, September 1969, *59*(4), pp. 646–51.

Drennan, Matthew P. Household Location Decisions and Local Public Benefits and Costs. *Amer. Econ.,* Spring 1969, *13*(1), pp. 30–39. [G: U.S.]

Fisher, Robert Moore. Monetary Policy: Its Relation to Mortgage Lending and Land Economics. *Land Econ.,* November 1969, *45*(4), pp. 418–24.

Fisher, Robert Moore. The Availibility of Mortgage Lending Commitments. (Study summary.) *Fed. Res. Bull.,* December 1969, *55*(12), pp. 919–20. [G: U.S.]

Gardner, John W. Statement. In *Panel on Science and Technology: Science and Technology and the Cities, HCH,* 1969, pp. 3–11. [G: U.S.]

Goldsmith, Harold F. and Stockwell, Edward G. Interrelationship of Occupational Selectivity Patterns among City, Suburban and Fringe Areas of Major Metropolitån Centers. *Land Econ.,* May 1969, *45*(2), pp. 194–205. [G: U.S.]

Greenbie, Barrie Barstow. New House or New Neighborhood? A Survey of Priorities among Home Owners in Madison, Wisconsin. *Land Econ.,* August 1969, *45*(3), pp. 359–65. [G: U.S.]

Greenfield, R. J. and Lewis, J. F. An Alternative to

a Density Function Definition of Overcrowding. *Land Econ.*, May 1969, *45*(2), pp. 282–85.

Guy, R. B., et al. The State of the Art of Prefabrication in the Construction Industry to the Building and Construction Trades Department: Final Report. **In** *Industrialized Housing, JECP,* 1969, pp. 190–200. **[G: U.S.]**

Haugen, Robert A. and Heins, A. James. A Market Separation Theory of Rent Differentials in Metropolitan Areas. *Quart. J. Econ.*, November 1969, *83*(4), pp. 660–72. **[G: U.S.]**

Heilbrun, James. Reforming the Real Estate Tax to Encourage Housing Maintenance and Rehabilitation. **In** *Becker, A. P., ed.*, 1969, pp. 63–79. **[G: U.S.]**

Heimann, John G. The Necessary Revolution in Housing Finance. **In** *National Housing Goals, HCH,* 1969, pp. 319–37. **[G: U.S.]**

Herbst, František. The Housing Situation in the CSSR in Terms of International Comparison. *Eastern Europ. Econ.*, Summer 1969, *7*(4), pp. 38–40. **[G: Czechoslovakia]**

Herman, Leon M. Urbanization and New Housing Construction in the U.S.S.R. **In** *Industrialized Housing, JECP,* 1969, pp. 22–40. **[G: U.S.S.R.]**

Hesburgh, Theodore M. Statement. **In** *National Housing Goals, HCH,* 1969, pp. 404–12. **[G: U.S.]**

af Heurlin, Lauri O. Vuokra-asunnon ja asunnonvuokran ongelma. (The Problem of Rented Accommodation and the Rent Level. With English summary.) *Kansant. Aikak.*, 1969, *65*(4), pp. 251–68. **[G: Finland]**

Hills, Stuart L. The Planned Suburban Community. *Land Econ.*, May 1969, *45*(2), pp. 277–82. **[G: U.S.]**

Johnston, R. J. Zonal and Sectoral Patterns in Melbourne's Residential Structure: 1961. *Land Econ.*, November 1969, *45*(4), pp. 463–67. **[G: Australia]**

Josowitz, Aaron. Housing Statistics: Published and Unpublished. *Mon. Lab. Rev.*, December 1969, *92*(12), pp. 50–55. **[G: U.S.]**

Keenan, Joseph D. Housing and Community Development Policy Paper. **In** *National Housing Goals, HCH,* 1969, pp. 519–25. **[G: U.S.]**

Keyserling, Leon H. Statement. **In** *Tax Reform Act of 1969, Testimony, Sept. 26, SCP,* 1969, pp. 85–191. **[G: U.S.]**

King, Donald A. Homebuilding Activity in 1969. *Surv. Curr. Bus.*, October 1969, *49*(10), pp. 16–22. **[G: U.S.]**

Knight, Robert E. The Quality of Mortgage Credit: Part II. *Fed. Res. Bank Kansas City Rev.*, April 1969, pp. 10–18. **[G: U.S.]**

Knight, Robert E. The Quality of Mortgage Credit: Part I. *Fed. Res. Bank Kansas City Rev.*, March 1969, pp. 13–20. **[G: U.S.]**

Lindholm, Richard W. Home Ownership and the Income Tax: A Proposed Change. *Oregon Bus. Rev.*, September 1969, *28*(9), pp. 1–3.

Mandelker, Daniel R. Housing Codes, Building Demolition, and Just Compensation: A Rationale for the Exercise of Public Powers over Slum Housing. *Mich. Law Rev.*, February 1969, *67*(4), pp. 635–78. **[G: U.S.]**

Meadows, Richard. Household Location Decisions and Local Public Benefits and Costs: Comment. *Amer. Econ.*, Spring 1969, *13*(1), pp. 40–41. **[G: U.S.]**

Miller, Glenn H., Jr. Housing in the 60's: A Survey of Some Nonfinancial Factors. *Fed. Res. Bank Kansas City Rev.*, May 1969, pp. 3–10. **[G: U.S.]**

Miller, Glenn H., Jr. Some Demographic Influences on the Future Market for Housing. *Fed. Res. Bank Kansas City Rev.*, November 1969, pp. 3–9. **[G: U.S.]**

Mizoguchi, Toshiyuki. A Comparison of Levels of Consumption of Urban Households in Japan and in Mainland China—A Summary. *Rev. Income Wealth,* June 1969, *15*(2), pp. 215–17. **[G: Japan; China]**

Mooney, Joseph D. Housing Segregation, Negro Employment and Metropolitan Decentralization: An Alternative Perspective. *Quart. J. Econ.*, May 1969, *83*(2), pp. 299–311. **[G: U.S.]**

Neutze, Max. Property Taxation and Multiple-Family Housing. **In** *Becker, A. P., ed.*, 1969, pp. 115–28.

Oates, Wallace E. The Effects of Property Taxes and Local Public Spending on Property Values: An Empirical Study of Tax Capitalization and the Tiebout Hypothesis. *J. Polit. Econ.*, November/December 1969, *77*(6), pp. 957–71. **[G: U.S.]**

Olsen, Edgar O. A Competitive Theory of the Housing Market. *Amer. Econ. Rev.*, Part I, September 1969, *59*(4), pp. 612–22.

Patman, Philip F., et al. Industrialized Building—A Comparative Analysis of European Experience. **In** *Industrialized Housing, JECP,* 1969, pp. 80–145. **[G: Europe]**

Piven, Frances Fox and Cloward, Richard A. Desegregated Housing: Who Pays for the Reformers' Ideal? **In** *Kain, J. F., ed.*, 1969, pp. 175–83. **[G: U.S.]**

Quindry, Kenneth E. and Cook, Billy D. Humanization of the Property Tax for Low Income Households. *Nat. Tax J.*, September 1969, *22*(3), pp. 357–67. **[G: U.S.]**

Ross, William B. Policy Analysis and Housing and Urban Development Programs. **In** *The Analysis and Evaluation of Public Expenditures: The PPB System, Vol. 3, JECP,* 1969, pp. 1233–41. **[G: U.S.]**

Rothman, Jack. The Ghetto Makers. **In** *Kain, J. F., ed.*, 1969, pp. 122–27. **[G: U.S.]**

Schaaf, A. H. Effects of Property Taxation on Slums and Renewal: A Study of Land-Improvement Assessment Ratios. *Land Econ.*, February 1969, *45* (1), pp. 111–17. **[G: U.S.]**

Schaaf, A. H. Mortgage Interest Rate Controls and the Veterans' Housing Market. *Miss. Val. J. Bus. Econ.*, Fall 1969, *5*(1), pp. 11–22. **[G: U.S.]**

Schlefer, Marion. Industrialization in Housing: Today's Potential. **In** *Industrialized Housing, JECP,* 1969, pp. 145–63. **[G: U.S.]**

Schoenbrod, David. Large Lot Zoning. *Yale Law J.*, July 1969, *78*(8), pp. 1418–41.

Smith, Lawrence B. A Model of the Canadian Housing and Mortgage Markets. *J. Polit. Econ.*, September/October 1969, *77*(5), pp. 795–816. **[G: Canada]**

Sternlieb, George and Indik, Bernard. Housing Vacancy Analysis. *Land Econ.,* February 1969, *45* (1), pp. 117–21. **[G: U.S.]**

Sudman, Seymour; Bradburn, Norman M. and Gockel, Galen. The Extent and Characteristics of Racially Integrated Housing in the United States. *J. Bus.,* January 1969, *42*(1), pp. 50–92. **[G: U.S.]**

Taeuber, Karl E. Negro Population and Housing: Demographic Aspects of a Social Accounting Scheme. **In** *Katz, I. and Gurin, P., eds.,* 1969, pp. 145–93. **[G: U.S.]**

Umezawa, Tadashi and Honjo, Masahiko. Company Housing in Japan. *Int. Lab. Rev.,* June 1969, *99*(6), pp. 579–87. **[G: Japan]**

Wendt, Paul F. The Determination of National Housing Policies. *Land Econ.,* August 1969, *45*(3), pp. 323–32. **[G: Chile]**

Wilkins, C. A. and Shaw, J. A. An Example to Illustrate the "Average" Nature of Clark's Law of Urban Populations. *J. Reg. Sci.,* August 1969, *9*(2), pp. 255–59.

Wilson, A. G. Developments of Some Elementary Residential Location Models. *J. Reg. Sci.,* December 1969, *9*(3), pp. 377–85.

Winger, Alan R. Regional Growth Disparities and the Mortgage Market. *J. Finance,* September 1969, *24*(4), pp. 659–62. **[G: U.S.]**

Winger, Alan R. Trade-Offs in Housing. *Land Econ.,* November 1969, *45*(4), pp. 413–17. **[G: U.S.]**

Wood, Robert C. Statement. **In** *Public Facility Requirements over the Next Decade, JECH,* 1969, pp. 27–35. **[G: U.S.]**

Yessian, Mark R. Statement. **In** *Usefulness of the Model Cities Program to the Elderly, Pt. 1, SCH,* 1969, pp. 78–82. **[G: U.S.]**

933 Urban Transportation Economics

9330 Urban Transportation Economics

Àdams, John S. Directional Bias in Intra-Urban Migration. *Econ. Geogr.,* October 1969, *45*(4), pp. 302–23.

Adler, Hans A. Notes on Feasibility Studies: III. Some Thoughts on Feasibility Studies. *J. Transp. Econ. Policy,* May 1969, *3*(2), pp. 231–36. **[G: Thailand]**

Else, P. K. and Howe, M. Cost-Benefit Analysis and the Withdrawal of Railway Services. *J. Transp. Econ. Policy,* May 1969, *3*(2), pp. 178–94. **[G: U.K.]**

Evans, Andrew W. Intercity Travel and the London Midland Electrification. *J. Transp. Econ. Policy,* January 1969, *3*(1), pp. 69–95. **[G: U.K.]**

Glejser, H. Een toepassing van de kosten–baten-analyse: het project "Zeestad". (Cost-Benefit Analysis of the Project "Zeestad." With English summary.) *Tijdschr. Econ.,* 1969, *14*(4), pp. 519–48. **[G: Belgium]**

Goel, H. C. Econometric Models for Traffic Projections. *Econ. Aff.,* January-February 1969, *14*(1–2), pp. 88–92.

Greenwald, Carol S. and Syron, Richard. Increasing Job Opportunities in Boston's Urban Core. *New Eng. Econ. Rev.,* January/February 1969, pp. 30–40.

Gronau, Reuben and Alcaly, Roger E. The Demand for Abstract Transport Modes: Some Misgivings. *J. Reg. Sci.,* April 1969, *9*(1), pp. 153–57.

Heggie, Ian G. Notes on Feasibility Studies: I. Road Investment Criteria. *J. Transp. Econ. Policy,* May 1969, *3*(2), pp. 222–24. **[G: U.K.]**

Howrey, E. Philip. On the Choice of Forecasting Models for Air Travel. *J. Reg. Sci.,* August 1969, *9*(2), pp. 215–24. **[G: U.S.]**

Jansson, Jan Owen. Optimal Congestion Tolls for Car Commuters: A Note on Current Theory. *J. Transp. Econ. Policy,* September 1969, *3*(3), pp. 300–305.

Lee, N. and Dalvi, M. Q. Variations in the Value of Travel Time. *Manchester Sch. Econ. Soc. Stud.,* September 1969, *37*(3), pp. 213–36.

Long, Wesley H. Airline Service and the Demand for Intercity Air Travel. *J. Transp. Econ. Policy,* September 1969, *3*(3), pp. 287–99. **[G: U.S.]**

Mishan, E. J. Interpretation of the Benefits of Private Transport. **In** *Mishan, E. J.,* 1969, pp. 275–83.

Ochs, Jack. An Application of Linear Programming to Urban Spatial Organization. *J. Reg. Sci.,* December 1969, *9*(3), pp. 451–57.

Owen, John D. The Value of Commuter Speed. *Western Econ. J.,* June 1969, *7*(2), pp. 164–72.

Owen, Wilfred. Transport: Key to the Future of Cities. **In** *Perloff, H. S., ed.,* 1969, pp. 205–27.

Quandt, Richard E. and Young, Kan Hua. Cross-sectional Travel Demand Models: Estimates and Tests. *J. Reg. Sci.,* August 1969, *9*(2), pp. 201–14. **[G: U.S.]**

Quandt, Richard E. and Baumol, William J. The Demand for Abstract Transport Modes: Some Hopes. *J. Reg. Sci.,* April 1969, *9*(1), pp. 159–62.

Schneider, Lewis M. The Fallacy of Free Transportation. *Harvard Bus. Rev.,* January–February 1969, *47*(1), pp. 83–87.

Seifert, William W. Transportation Development—A National Challenge. **In** *Panel on Science and Technology: Science and Technology and the Cities, HCH,* 1969, pp. 119–30. **[G: U.S.]**

Solzman, David M. The Value of Inland Waterfront Industrial Sites. *Land Econ.,* November 1969, *45* (4), pp. 456–62. **[G: U.S.]**

Spottiswoode, R. A. Note on Feasibility Studies: II. The Western Nigeria Road Development Survey. *J. Transp. Econ. Policy,* May 1969, *3*(2), pp. 225–30. **[G: Nigeria]**

Troy, Patrick and Neutze, Max. Urban Road Planning in Theory and Practice. *J. Transp. Econ. Policy,* May 1969, *3*(2), pp. 139–51. **[G: U.K.]**

Vickrey, William S. Current Issues in Transportation. **In** *Chamberlain, N. W., ed.,* 1969, pp. 185–240. **[G: U.S.]**

Wabe, J. S. Commuter Travel into Central London. *J. Transp. Econ. Policy,* January 1969, *3*(1), pp. 48–68. **[G: U.K.]**

Webber, Melvin M. Statement. **In** *Panel on Science and Technology: Science and Technology and the Cities, HCH,* 1969, pp. 97–114. **[G: U.S.]**

Wheeler, James O. Some Effects of Occupational Status on Work Trips. *J. Reg. Sci.,* April 1969, *9*(1), pp. 69–77. **[G: U.S.]**

940 Regional Economics

941 Regional Economics

9410 General

Archer, R. W. From New Towns to Metrotowns and Regional Cities, II. *Amer. J. Econ. Soc.*, October 1969, *28*(4), pp. 385–98. **[G: Sweden]**

Back, W. B. Estimating Contributions of Natural Resource Investments to Objectives in Regional Economic Development. *Amer. J. Agr. Econ.*, December 1969, *51*(5), pp. 1442–48. **[G: U.S.]**

Braschler, Curtis and Klindt, Thomas. Theoretical and Empirical Problems in Local Government Consolidation. *Can. J. Agr. Econ.*, February 1969, *17*(1), pp. 141–50.

Breton, Albert. The Political Economy of Regional Balance. *Rech. Écon. Louvain*, August 1969, *35* (3), pp. 175–99.

Brown, A. J. Surveys of Applied Economics: Regional Economics, with Special Reference to the United Kingdom. *Econ. J.*, December 1969, *79* (316), pp. 759–96. **[G: U.K.]**

Burrascano, Francesco. Origine ed evoluzione del dualismo economico italiano. (Origin and Evolution of Italian Economic Dualism. With English summary.) *Mondo Aperto*, April 1969, *23*(2), pp. 104–15.

Cole, H. J. D. The Contribution of Demography to Physical and Spatial Planning: Comment. **In** *Bechhofer, F., ed.*, 1969, pp. 131–33.

Cunningham, N. J. A Note on the 'Proper Distribution of Industry.' *Oxford Econ. Pap.*, March 1969, *21*(1), pp. 122–27. **[G: U.K.]**

Doxiadis, Constantinos. Statement. **In** *Panel on Science and Technology: Science and Technology and the Cities, HCH*, 1969, pp. 19–35. **[G: U.S.]**

Eriksson, Gösta A. Models in Human Geography. *Liiketaloudellinen Aikak.*, 1969, *18*(1), pp. 13–23.

Fedorenko, N. Questions Pertaining to Optimization of the Growth and Location of Production. *Prob. Econ.*, January 1969, *11*(9), pp. 14–23. **[G: U.S.S.R.]**

Fölscher, G. C. K. Some Thoughts on Modernizing a Relatively Large Backward Region in an Otherwise Developed Economy. *Finance Trade Rev.*, June 1969, *8*(3), pp. 198–205.

Fox, Karl A. The New Synthesis of Rural and Urban Society in the United States. **In** *Papi, U. and Nunn, C., eds.*, 1969, pp. 606–28. **[G: U.S.]**

Gifford, J. Morris. Some Considerations Involved in Port Planning Policy. *Econ. Soc. Tijdschr.*, February 1969, *23*(1), pp. 23–32. **[G: U.K.]**

Gili, Adolfo. Popolosità e dinamica demografica di lungo periodo nei comuni dell'Emilia e del Veneto: Parte I. (With English summary.) *Statistica*, October-December 1969, *29*(4), pp. 603–49. **[G: Italy]**

Herzog, Elizabeth. Perspectives on Poverty 3: Facts and Fictions about the Poor. *Mon. Lab. Rev.*, February 1969, *92*(2), pp. 42–49.

Jensen, Robert G. and Karaska, Gerald J. The Mathematical Thrust in Soviet Economic Geography—Its Nature and Significance. *J. Reg. Sci.*, April 1969, *9*(1), pp. 141–52. **[G: U.S.S.R.]**

Johnson-Marshall, P. The Contribution of Demography to Physical and Spatial Planning: Comment. **In** *Bechhofer, F., ed.*, 1969, pp. 134–36.

Katzman, Martin T. Ethnic Geography and Regional Economies, 1880–1960. *Econ. Geogr.*, January 1969, *45*(1), pp. 45–52. **[G: U.S.]**

Kohoutek, Miloslav. Economic Aspects of the Federalization of Czechoslovakia. *New Trends Czech. Econ.*, February 1969, (1), pp. 50–65. **[G: Czechoslovakia]**

Križková, Mária. Integrovatel'né štruktúrne modely s priestorovým prvkom. (Structural Models with Integration Capabilities and Regional Elements. With English summary.) *Ekon.-Mat. Obzor*, 1969, *5*(4), pp. 509–17.

Krumme, Günter. Toward a Geography of Enterprise. *Econ. Geogr.*, January 1969, *45*(1), pp. 30–40.

Mason, Joseph Barry and Moore, Charles Thomas. A Note on the Reliability of Census Data in Trading Area Analysis. *Miss. Val. J. Bus. Econ.*, Fall 1969, *5*(1), pp. 68–72. **[G: U.S.]**

Mathieson, R. S. The Soviet Contribution to Regional Science: A Review Article. *J. Reg. Sci.*, April 1969, *9*(1), pp. 125–40. **[G: U.S.S.R.]**

McGuire, Martin C. and Garn, Harvey A. The Integration of Equity and Efficiency Criteria in Public Project Selection. *Econ. J.*, December 1969, *79* (316), pp. 882–93.

Mennes, L. B. M. Planning for Regions and Centres. *Econ. Planning*, 1969, *9*(1–2), pp. 43–70.

Newman, Dorothy K. Perspectives on Poverty 1: Changing Attitudes about the Poor. *Mon. Lab. Rev.*, February 1969, *92*(2), pp. 32–36.

Nichols, T. E., Jr. Transportation and Regional Development in Agriculture. *Amer. J. Agr. Econ.*, December 1969, *51*(5), pp. 1455–63.

Orshansky, Mollie. Perspectives on Poverty 2: How Poverty Is Measured. *Mon. Lab. Rev.*, February 1969, *92*(2), pp. 37–41. **[G: U.S.]**

Parker, Alfred L. Economic Growth for New Mexico. *N. Mex. Bus.*, October 1969, *22*(10), pp. 1–7. **[G: U.S.]**

Popescu, S. Falcan. Folosirea analizei factoriale în cercetarea fenomenelor în profil teritorial. (Use of Factorial Analysis in the Investigation of Phenomena in a Territorial Profile. With English summary.) *Stud. Cercet. Econ.*, 1969, *4*, pp. 159–63.

Ryan, Bruce. Metropolitan Growth. **In** *Preston, R., ed.*, 1969, pp. 196–225. **[G: Australia]**

Schiaffino, Andrea. Interrelazioni tra manifestazioni demografiche e manifestazioni economico-sociali in Emilia e Veneto nell'ultimo secolo. Relazione illustrativa dell'attività svolta dal gruppo di ricerca C.N.R. diretto dal prof. Paolo Fortunati. (With English summary.) *Statistica*, October-December 1969, *29*(4), pp. 563–602.

Steigenga, W. The Contribution of Demography to Physical and Spatial Planning. **In** *Bechhofer, F., ed.*, 1969, pp. 117–26.

Stobaugh, Robert B., Jr. Where in the World Should We Put that Plant? *Harvard Bus. Rev.*, January–February 1969, *47*(1), pp. 129–36.

Swackhamer, Gene L. Concepts of Rural Economic

Development. *Fed. Res. Bank Kansas City Rev.*, December 1969, pp. 3–10. [G: U.S.]

Thirlwall, A. P. Weighting Systems and Regional Analysis: A Reply to Mr. Cunningham. *Oxford Econ. Pap.*, March 1969, *21*(1), pp. 128–33.

Thomas, Morgan D. Regional Economic Growth: Some Conceptual Aspects. *Land Econ.*, February 1969, *45*(1), pp. 43–51.

Van Cleef, Eugene. "Things Are Not Always What They Seem" for the Economic Geographer. *Econ. Geogr.*, January 1969, *45*(1), pp. 41–44.

Veblen, Thorstein. The Case of America: The Country Town. **In** *Minar, D. W. and Greer, S., eds.*, 1969, pp. 91–106. [G: U.S.]

West, E. G. Regional Planning: Fact and Fallacy. **In** *Task Force on Economic Growth and Opportunity*, 1969, pp. 249–68.

Wilson, A. G. and Wood, A. W. Regional Livestock Production and Feed Freight Assistance. *Can. J. Agr. Econ.*, February 1969, *17*(1), pp. 77–90. [G: Canada]

Wolfe, J. N. The Contribution of Demography to Physical and Spatial Planning: Comment. **In** *Bechhofer, F., ed.*, 1969, pp. 127–30.

9411 Theory of Regional Economics

Archibald, G. C. The Phillips Curve and the Distribution of Unemployment. *Amer. Econ. Rev.*, May 1969, *59*(2), pp. 124–34. [G: U.S.; U.K.]

Barnard, Jerald R. A Social Accounting System for Regional Development Planning. *J. Reg. Sci.*, April 1969, *9*(1), pp. 109–15. [G: U.S.]

Baxter, Nevins D.; Howrey, E. Philip and Penner, R. G. Unemployment and Cost-Benefit Analysis. *Public Finance*, 1969, *24*(1), pp. 80–88.

Beckmann, Martin J. Market Shares and Distance. *Swedish J. Econ.*, June 1969, *71*(2), pp. 53–63.

Berry, Brian J. L. and Neils, Elaine. Location, Size, and Shape of Cities as Influenced by Environmental Factors: The Urban Environment Writ Large. **In** *Perloff, H. S., ed.*, 1969, pp. 257–302.

von Böventer, Edwin. Walter Christaller's Central Places and Peripheral Areas: The Central Place Theory in Retrospect. *J. Reg. Sci.*, April 1969, *9*(1), pp. 117–24.

Brown, A. J. and Woodward, V. H. Regional Social Accounts for the United Kingdom. *Rev. Income Wealth*, December 1969, *15*(4), pp. 335–47. [G: U.K.]

David, Michel. Nuovi tipi di punti di vendita per la periferia dell citta'. (New Types of Suburban Selling Points. With English summary.) *L'Impresa*, November/December 1969, *11*(6), pp. 436–43.

Hirsch, Werner Z. Regional Information Design for Public Decisions. *Rev. Income Wealth*, December 1969, *15*(4), pp. 369–80.

Isard, Walter. Toward a More Adequate General Regional Theory and Approach to Conflict Resolution. *Peace Res. Soc. Internat. Pap.*, 1969, *11*, pp. 1–21.

Kelley, Allen C. and Weiss, Leonard W. Markov Processes and Economic Analysis: The Case of Migration. *Econometrica*, April 1969, *37*(2), pp. 280–97.

Laird, William E. and Rinehart, James R. A Refinement of Local Industrial Subsidy Techniques: Reply. *Miss. Val. J. Bus. Econ.*, Spring 1969, *4*(2), pp. 82–88.

Legler, John B. and Shapiro, Perry. The Responsiveness of State Tax Revenue to Economic Growth: A Reply. *Nat. Tax J.*, June 1969, *22*(2), pp. 299–300.

Little, Wallace I. Location Selection through Integrated Systems Management. *Land Econ.*, February 1969, *45*(1), pp. 97–103.

Liu, Ben-Chieh. Comments on the Responsiveness of State Tax Revenue to Economic Growth. *Nat. Tax J.*, June 1969, *22*(2), pp. 294–98.

Low, Richard E. A Refinement of Local Industrial Subsidy Techniques: Comment. *Miss. Val. J. Bus. Econ.*, Spring 1969, *4*(2), pp. 78–81.

Marsden, Keith. Integrated Regional Development: A Quantitative Approach. *Int. Lab. Rev.*, June 1969, *99*(6), pp. 621–46.

McLure, Charles E., Jr. The Inter-regional Incidence of General Regional Taxes. *Public Finance*, 1969, *24*(3), pp. 457–85.

Niedercorn, J. H. and Bechdolt, B. V., Jr. An Economic Derivation of the "Gravity Law" of Spatial Interaction. *J. Reg. Sci.*, August 1969, *9*(2), pp. 273–82.

Parr, John B. City Hierarchies and the Distribution of City Size: A Reconsideration of Beckmann's Contribution. *J. Reg. Sci.*, August 1969, *9*(2), pp. 239–53.

Pyun, Chong Soo. Local Business Activity Index: Its Construction and Uses—Comment. *J. Reg. Sci.*, April 1969, *9*(1), pp. 163–66.

Seidel, Marquis R. The Margins of Spatial Monopoly. *J. Reg. Sci.*, December 1969, *9*(3), pp. 353–68.

Serck-Hanssen, Jan. The Optimal Number of Factories in a Spatial Market. **In** *[Tinbergen, J.]*, 1969, pp. 269–81.

Sherman, Roger and Willett, Thomas D. Regional Development, Externalities and Tax-Subsidy Combinations. *Nat. Tax J.*, June 1969, *22*(2), pp. 291–93.

Siebert, Horst. Goal Conflicts in Regional Growth Policy. *Z. Nationalökon.*, May 1969, *29*(1–2), pp. 19–28.

Singh, Ajmer. Local Business Activity Index: Its Construction and Uses—Reply. *J. Reg. Sci.*, April 1969, *9*(1), pp. 167–69.

Stober, William J. and Falk, Laurence H. The Effect of Financial Inducements on the Location of Firms. *Southern Econ. J.*, July 1969, *36*(1), pp. 25–35.

Tănase, Gh. Perfecţionarea metodologiei de fundamentare a amplasării obiectivelor industriale. (Improvement of the Methodology in Substantiating the Location of Industrial Objectives. With English summary.) *Stud. Cercet. Econ.*, 1969, *1-2*, pp. 45–64.

Terry, Edwin F. Public Finance and Regional Accounts. *Rev. Income Wealth*, June 1969, *15*(2), pp. 207–13. [G: U.S.]

Weinschenck, G.; Henrichsmeyer, W. and Aldinger, F. The Theory of Spatial Equilibrium and Optimal Location in Agriculture: A Survey. *Rev. Marketing Agr. Econ.*, March 1969, *37*(1), pp. 3–70.

Wolf, Laurence G. The Metropolitan Tidal Wave in

Ohio, 1900–2000. *Econ. Geogr.*, April 1969, *45*(2), pp. 133–54. [G: U.S.]

9412 Regional Economic Studies

Adams, Nassau A. Internal Migration in Jamaica: An Economic Analysis. *Soc. Econ. Stud.*, June 1969, *18*(2), pp. 137–51. [G: Jamaica]

Albert, Linzy D. and Kellow, James H. Decision-Makers' Reactions to Plant Location Factors: An Appraisal. *Land Econ.*, August 1969, *45*(3), pp. 376–81.

Bahl, Roy W. and Shellhammer, Kenneth L. Evaluating the State Business Tax Structure: An Application of Input-Output Analysis. *Nat. Tax J.*, June 1969, *22*(2), pp. 203–16. [G: U.S.]

Barr, Brenton M. and Bater, James H. The Electricity Industry of Central Siberia. *Econ. Geogr.*, October 1969, *45*(4), pp. 349–69. [G: U.S.S.R.]

Beika, Minoru. The Change in Regional Characteristics of Industries in Japan. *Kobe Econ. Bus. Rev.*, 1969, *16*(1), pp. 1–18. [G: Japan]

Bell, Frederick W. and Murphy, Neil B. The Impact of Regulation on Inter- and Intraregional Variation in Commercial Banking Costs. *J. Reg. Sci.*, August 1969, *9*(2), pp. 225–38. [G: U.S.]

Beyer, John C. Regional Inequalities and Economic Growth in Malaysia. *Yorkshire Bull. Econ. Soc. Res.*, May 1969, *21*(1), pp. 17–30. [G: Malaysia]

Bishop, C. E. Rural Poverty in the Southeast. **In** *Task Force on Economic Growth and Opportunity*, 1969, pp. 75–92. [G: U.S.]

Blevins, Audie L., Jr. Migration Rates in Twelve Southern Metropolitan Areas: A "Push-Pull" Analysis. *Soc. Sci. Quart.*, September 1969, *50*(2), pp. 337–53. [G: U.S.]

Bourque, Philip J. Income Multipliers for the Washington Economy. *Univ. Wash. Bus. Rev.*, Winter 1969, *28*(2), pp. 5–15. [G: U.S.]

Boyce, Byrl N. Excess Acquisition Revisited: Control of Land Use at the Interstate Interchange. *Land Econ.*, August 1969, *45*(3), pp. 293–303. [G: U.S.]

Boyle, Gerald J. The Economic Progress of New Mexico Since 1948. *N. Mex. Bus.*, September 1969, *22*(9), pp. 3–10. [G: U.S.]

Brackett, Jean C. New BLS Budgets Provide Yardsticks for Measuring Family Living Costs. *Mon. Lab. Rev.*, April 1969, *92*(4), pp. 3–16. [G: U.S.]

Bretzfelder, Robert B.; Dallavalle, Q. Francis and Hirschberg, David A. Personal Income, 1968, and Disposable Income, 1929–68, by States and Regions. *Surv. Curr. Bus.*, April 1969, *49*(4), pp. 16–21, 32. [G: U.S.]

Bretzfelder, Robert B. and Dallavalle, Q. Francis. Total and *Per Capita* Personal Income by Regions and States, 1968. *Surv. Curr. Bus.*, August 1969, *49*(8), pp. 13, 24. [G: U.S.]

Brown, A. J. Some English Thoughts on the Scottish Economy. *Scot. J. Polit. Econ.*, November 1969, *16*(3), pp. 233–47. [G: U.K.]

Brown, Richard E. and Weber, Glen D. Tributary Area Development: TVA's Approach to Sub-Regional Development. *Land Econ.*, February 1969, *45*(1), pp. 141–46. [G: U.S.]

Bruce, Grady D. The Ecological Structure of Retail Institutions. *J. Marketing Res.*, February 1969, *6* (1), pp. 48–53. [G: U.S.]

Brunn, Stanley D. and Hoffman, Wayne L. The Geography of Federal Grants-in-Aid to States. *Econ. Geogr.*, July 1969, *45*(3), pp. 226–38. [G: U.S.]

Bryce, Herrington J. Regional Labor Earnings Differentials in a Small Developing Country: The Republic of Panama. *J. Reg. Sci.*, December 1969, *9*(3), pp. 405–15. [G: Panama]

Carter, Charles F. The Hunt Report. *Scot. J. Polit. Econ.*, November 1969, *16*(3), pp. 248–55. [G: U.K.]

Chinitz, Benjamin. The Regional Aspects of Poverty. **In** *Task Force on Economic Growth and Opportunity*, 1969, pp. 93–104. [G: U.S.]

Church, R. J. Harrision. Some Problems of Regional Economic Development in West Africa. *Econ. Geogr.*, January 1969, *45*(1), pp. 53–62. [G: W. Africa]

Cohen, Kalman J. Risk Analysis and Branch Bank Location Decisions. **In** *Jessup, P. F.*, 1969, pp. 330–40. [G: U.S.]

Costello, Edward T. The Terms of Trade of the Southeast (1947–1958). *Southern Econ. J.*, April 1969, *35*(4), pp. 376–77. [G: U.S.]

Covell, James. Some Economic Needs and Programs in New Mexico. *N. Mex. Bus.*, November–December 1969, *22*(11&12), pp. 1–5. [G: U.S.]

Dahl, Dale C. The Upper Midwest Region. **In** *Task Force on Economic Growth and Opportunity*, 1969, pp. 105–23. [G: U.S.]

Dasso, Jerome J. Economic Outlook for Oregon in 1969. *Oregon Bus. Rev.*, February 1969, *28*(2), pp. 1–4. [G: U.S.]

Davis, H. Craig. Interregional Production and Water Resource Dependencies among the Western States. *Western Econ. J.*, March 1969, *7*(1), pp. 27–40. [G: U.S.]

Davis, Howard W. A Case Study in Industrial Location. *Land Econ.*, November 1969, *45*(4), pp. 444–52. [G: U.S.]

Dell'Amore, Giordano. Il contributo del risparmio familiare al riscatto del mezzogiorno. (Contribution Made by Household Savings to the Development of Southern Italy. With English summary.) *Bancaria*, October 1969, *25*(10), pp. 1206–15. [G: Italy]

Devine, P. J. Inter-Regional Variations in the Degree of Inequality of Income Distribution: The United Kingdom, 1949–65. *Manchester Sch. Econ. Soc. Stud.*, June 1969, *37*(2), pp. 141–59. [G: U.K.]

Duquesne de la Vinelle, L. Common Policy for Regional Development. **In** *Duquesne, L., et al.*, 1969, pp. 72–82. [G: E.E.C.]

Eisenmenger, Robert W. The Regional Poor. **In** *Task Force on Economic Growth and Opportunity*, 1969, pp. 125–43. [G: U.S.]

Folse, C. I. and Riffe, W. W. Changing Patterns of Business Services and Population in Illinois Rural Villages. *Ill. Agr. Econ.*, January 1969, *9*(1), pp. 26–32. [G: U.S.]

Ford, Thomas R. Rural Poverty in the United States. **In** *Task Force on Economic Growth and Oppor-*

tunity, 1969, pp. 153–76. [G: U.S.]

Frisch, Uwe G. and Malagón, Oscar M. La concentracion territorial de la industria en Mexico. (Territorial Concentration of Industry in Mexico. With English summary.) *Econ. Polít.,* Second Semester 1969, *6*(2), pp. 195–208. [G: Mexico]

Gallaway, Lowell E. A Note on the Incidence of Hidden Unemployment in the United States. *Western Econ. J.,* March 1969, *7*(1), pp. 71–83. [G: U.S.]

Glassner, Martin I. Feeding a Desert City: Antofagasta, Chile. *Econ. Geogr.,* October 1969, *45* (4), pp. 339–48. [G: Chile]

Gleditsch, Nils Petter. The International Airline Network: A Test of the Zipf and Stouffer Hypotheses. *Peace Res. Soc. Internat. Pap.,* 1969, *11,* pp. 123–53.

Gray, Irwin. Employment Effect of a New Industry in a Rural Area. *Mon. Lab. Rev.,* June 1969, *92*(6), pp. 26–30. [G: U.S.]

Greenwood, Michael J. The Determinants of Labor Migration in Egypt. *J. Reg. Sci.,* August 1969, *9*(2), pp. 283–90. [G: Egypt]

Gregor, Howard F. Farm Structure in Regional Comparison: California and New Jersey Vegetable Farms. *Econ. Geogr.,* July 1969, *45*(3), pp. 209–25. [G: U.S.]

Hady, Thomas F. Tax Structure and Regional Economic Growth: A Comment. *J. Reg. Sci.,* August 1969, *9*(2), pp. 325–26. [G: U.S.]

Hale, Carl W. The Optimality of Local Subsidies in Regional Development Programs. *Quart. Rev. Econ. Bus.,* Autumn 1969, *9*(3), pp. 35–50. [G: U.S.]

Hammill, Anne E. Variables Related to Farm Real Estate Values in Minnesota Counties. *Agr. Econ. Res.,* April 1969, *21*(2), pp. 45–50. [G: U.S.]

Hampton, P. Empirical Evidence on the Determinants of Interregional Trade Flows. *Econ. Develop. Cult. Change,* Part I, October 1969, *18*(1), pp. 34–39. [G: New Zealand]

Hampton, P. Regional Import Functions in New Zealand. *J. Common Market Stud.,* June 1969, *7* (4), pp. 327–35. [G: New Zealand]

Hansen, Niles M. Regional Development and the Rural Poor. *J. Human Res.,* Spring 1969, *4*(2), pp. 205–14.

Harmston, Floyd K. Post-War Trends in the Missouri Economy. *Univ. Missouri Bus. Govt. Rev.,* January–February 1969, *10*(1), pp. 30–36.

Harmston, Floyd K. The Impact of Federal Expenditures on Missouri, Fiscal Year 1967. *Univ. Missouri Bus. Govt. Rev.,* November–December 1969, *10*(6), pp. 5–12. [G: U.S.]

Harmston, Floyd K. The Importance of 1967 Tourism to Missouri. *Univ. Missouri Bus. Govt. Rev.,* May–June 1969, *10*(3), pp. 6–12. [G: U.S.]

Harris, Curtis C., Jr. and McGuire, Martin C. Planning Techniques for Regional Development Policy. *J. Human Res.,* Fall 1969, *4*(4), pp. 466–90. [G: U.S.]

Haskell, Mark A. and Leshinski, Stephen. Fiscal Influences on Residential Choice: A Study of the New York Region. *Quart. Rev. Econ. Bus.,* Winter 1969, *9*(4), pp. 47–55. [G: U.S.]

Hellickson, George C. A Regional Self-Help Program. In *Task Force on Economic Growth and Opportunity,* 1969, pp. 199–216. [G: U.S.]

Houff, James N. Area Wages and Living Costs. *Mon. Lab. Rev.,* March 1969, *92*(3), pp. 43–46. [G: U.S.]

Howard, Dick. The Regional Development Commission—A Second Look at a New Concept. *Univ. Missouri Bus. Govt. Rev.,* July–August 1969, *10*(4), pp. 27–35. [G: U.S.]

Humphrey, Kenneth R. Retail Trade in Indiana and Surrounding States. *Indiana Bus. Rev.,* November/December 1969, *44,* pp. 11–15. [G: U.S.]

Jackson, Samuel C. Statement. In *Tax Credits to Stimulate Job Opportunities in Rural Areas, SCH,* 1969, pp. 177–82. [G: U.S.]

Jeffrey, D.; Casetti, E. and King, L. Economic Fluctuations in a Multiregional Setting: A Bi-factor Analytic Approach. *J. Reg. Sci.,* December 1969, *9*(3), pp. 397–404. [G: U.S.]

Johnson, James F. The Influence of Cost Distance Factors on the Overseas Export of Corn from the United States Midwest. *Econ. Geogr.,* April 1969, *45*(2), pp. 170–79. [G: U.S.]

de Jong, F. J. De economische betekenis van de Rijksuniversiteit te Groningen voor de provincie. (The Economic Significance of the University of Groningen for the Province. With English summary.) *De Economist,* May/June 1969, *117*(3), pp. 193–226. [G: Netherlands]

Kayler, J. Allan. Personal Income in Urban Indiana. *Indiana Bus. Rev.,* March–April 1969, *44,* pp. 7–11. [G: U.S.]

Keele, David L. Economic Growth Outside Metropolitan Areas: The Tenth District Experience. *Fed. Res. Bank Kansas City Rev.,* June 1969, pp. 3–10. [G: U.S.]

Krohmer, F. R. Deposit Growth in the Tenth District—1949–68. *Fed. Res. Bank Kansas City Rev.,* May 1969, pp. 11–16. [G: U.S.]

Kuehn, John A. and Bender, Lloyd D. An Empirical Identification of Growth Centers. *Land Econ.,* November 1969, *45*(4), pp. 435–43. [G: U.S.]

L'Esperance, Wilford L.; Nestel, G. and Fromm, D. Gross State Product and an Econometric Model of a State. *J. Amer. Statist. Assoc.,* September 1969, *64*(327), pp. 787–807. [G: U.S.]

Laird, William E. Statement. In *Tax Credits to Stimulate Job Opportunities in Rural Areas, SCH,* 1969, pp. 191–95. [G: U.S.]

Lázár, G. Regional Pattern of the Hungarian Economy: Development of SomeTopical Problems. *Acta Oecon.,* 1969, *4*(3), pp. 223–37. [G: Hungary]

Lees, Francis A. Interregional Flows of Funds through State and Local Government Securities (1957–1962). *J. Reg. Sci.,* April 1969, *9*(1), pp. 79–86. [G: U.S.]

Lile, Stephen E. and Soule, Don M. Interstate Differences in Family Tax Burdens. *Nat. Tax J.,* December 1969, *22*(4), pp. 433–45. [G: U.S.]

Lindberg, Carolyn G. A Note on Population Estimates and Their Meaning. *N. Mex. Bus.,* November–December 1969, *22*(11&12), pp. 6–10. [G: U.S.]

Liu, Ben-Chieh. Regional Income Inequality and Federal Government Expenditures, 1948–63.

Quart. Rev. Econ. Bus., Winter 1969, *9*(4), pp. 67–76. [G: U.S.]

Llosas, Hernán P. La política de promoción industrial y de desarrollo regional en la Argentina, 1959–1966. (The Argentinian Government's Policy for the Promotion of Particular Industrial Sectors and for the Development of Some of the Country's Regions, 1959–1966. With English summary.) *Económica,* January–April 1969, *15*(1), pp. 39–91. [G: Argentina]

Luttrell, Clifton B. and Armentrout, Claire. Growth—Metropolitan vs. Nonmetropolitan Areas in the Central Mississippi Valley. *Fed. Res. Bank St. Louis Rev.*, January 1969, *51*(1), pp. 8–15. [G: U.S.]

Macgregor, D. R. On the Importance of the Regions to Scotland. **In** *Wolfe, J. N., ed.*, 1969, pp. 153–66. [G: U.K.]

Manhertz, Huntley G. Statistical Evaluation of Regional Differences in the Market for Processed Food Commodities. *Rev. Econ. Statist.*, May 1969, *51*(2), pp. 195–201. [G: U.S.]

McDonald, Stephen L. Postwar Economic Growth and Fluctuations in Louisiana. **In** *Beard, T. R., ed.*, 1969, pp. 82–102. [G: U.S.]

McGee, Dean A. Treasures of Energy: Natural Resources of the Ninth and Tenth Federal Reserve Districts. *Fed. Res. Bank Kansas City Rev.*, February 1969, pp. 3–9. [G: U.S.]

McGuire, Martin C. Program Analysis and Regional Economic Objectives. **In** *The Analysis and Evaluation of Public Expenditures: The PPB System, Vol. 1, JECP,* 1969, pp. 592–610. [G: U.S.]

Melton, Lee J., Jr. Some Factors Affecting the Economic Development of Louisiana. **In** *Beard, T. R., ed.*, 1969, pp. 21–40. [G: U.S.]

Miernyk, William H. British Regional Development Policy. *J. Econ. Issues,* September 1969, *3*(3), pp. 33–42. [G: U.K.]

Moutsanides, Demetrius T. Idaho Economic Activity in 1968 and Prospects for 1969. *Univ. Wash. Bus. Rev.*, Winter 1969, *28*(2), pp. 23–32. [G: U.S.]

Muehlbeier, John. Problems That Persist in the Great Plains. *Amer. J. Agr. Econ.*, December 1969, *51*(5), pp. 1089–96. [G: U.S.]

Mueller, P. and Zevering, K. H. Employment Promotion through Rural Development: A Pilot Project in Western Nigeria. *Int. Lab. Rev.*, August 1969, *100*(2), pp. 111–30. [G: Nigeria]

Munro, John M. Planning the Appalachian Development Highway System: Some Critical Questions. *Land Econ.*, May 1969, *45*(2), pp. 149–61. [G: U.S.]

Muse, William V. Indicators of Economic Progress in the Ohio Valley: 1963–1967. *Ohio State U. Bull. Bus. Res.*, August 1969, *44*(8), pp. 1–3, 5. [G: U.S.]

Newman, Monroe and March, Eli P. Rural Areas in the Urban Economy. *Amer. J. Agr. Econ.*, December 1969, *51*(5), pp. 1097–1109. [G: U.S.]

Newsom, Robert T. Metropolitan and Nonmetropolitan Employment Changes: The Case of Texas. *Soc. Sci. Quart.*, September 1969, *50*(2), pp. 354–68. [G: U.S.]

Ody, J. G. Application of Cost-Benefit Analysis to Airports: The Case of Nicosia, Cyprus. *J. Transp. Econ. Policy,* September 1969, *3*(3), pp. 322–32. [G: Cyprus]

Parikh, G. O. Integration of Farm and Non-Farm Employment, Part II: Effective Cooperativisation in a Labour Surplus Economy. *Artha-Vikas,* January 1969, *5*(1), pp. 68–76. [G: India]

Pillai, P. Purushothaman. An Inter-District, Inter-Crop Comparison of Growth Rates in Agriculture in Kerala. *Asian Econ. Rev.*, May 1969, *11*(3), pp. 249–59. [G: India]

Prescott, James R. and Lewis, William C. State and Municipal Locational Incentives: A Discriminant Analysis. *Nat. Tax J.*, September 1969, *22*(3), pp. 399–407. [G: U.S.]

Pusić, Eugen. Area and Administration in Yugoslav Development. *Int. Soc. Sci. J.*, 1969, *21*(1), pp. 68–82. [G: Yugoslavia]

Quindry, Kenneth E. and Cook, Billy D. Humanization of the Property Tax for Low Income Households. *Nat. Tax J.*, September 1969, *22*(3), pp. 357–67. [G: U.S.]

Quinn, Gerard. The Buchanan Report. *Irish Banking Rev.*, September 1969, pp. 3–9. [G: Ireland]

Raymond, Richard. Changes in the Relative Economic Status of Nonwhites: 1950–1960. *Western Econ. J.*, March 1969, *7*(1), pp. 57–70. [G: U.S.]

Richter, Charles E. The Impact of Industrial Linkages on Geographic Association. *J. Reg. Sci.*, April 1969, *9*(1), pp. 19–28. [G: U.S.]

Robarts, A. O. A Revised Look at Selected Determinants of Consumer Spatial Behavior. **In** *Association of Canadian Schools of Business,* 1969, pp. 219–33.

Rogers, Tommy W. Migration Attractiveness of Southern Metropolitan Areas. *Soc. Sci. Quart.*, September 1969, *50*(2), pp. 325–36. [G: U.S.]

Sanders, John. The Depressed Area and Labor Mobility: The Eastern Kentucky Case. *J. Human Res.*, Fall 1969, *4*(4), pp. 437–50. [G: U.S.]

Schnur, Roman. Area and Administration. *Int. Soc. Sci. J.*, 1969, *21*(1), pp. 83–99.

Scoville, James G. Remuneration in Afghan Industry. *Int. Lab. Rev.*, April 1969, *99*(4), pp. 381–400. [G: Afghanistan]

Scully, Gerald W. Interstate Wage Differentials: A Cross Section Analysis. *Amer. Econ. Rev.*, December 1969, *59*(5), pp. 757–73. [G: U.S.]

Shearer, John. Statement. **In** *Tax Credits to Stimulate Job Opportunities in Rural Areas, SCH,* 1969, pp. 157–62. [G: U.S.]

Shelton, David H. The Pace of Income Equalization in a Market Economy: Some Evidence from Experience in the United States. *Rivista Int. Sci. Econ. Com.*, February 1969, *16*(2), pp. 131–47. [G: U.S.]

Simpson, E. S. Electricity Production in Nigeria. *Econ. Geogr.*, July 1969, *45*(3), pp. 239–57. [G: Nigeria]

Sleeman, John F. A New Look at the Distribution of Private Cars in Britain. *Scot. J. Polit. Econ.*, November 1969, *16*(3), pp. 306–18. [G: U.K.]

Solomon, R. J. Property Values as a Structural Element of Urban Evolution. *Econ. Geogr.*, January 1969, *45*(1), pp. 1–29. [G: Australia]

Sorkin, Alan L. American Indians Industrialize to

Combat Poverty. *Mon. Lab. Rev.*, March 1969, *92*(3), pp. 19–25. [G: U.S.]

Spitz, John V. A Note on Relative-Wage Trends in Nine Southern States: The Case of Production and Non-Production Labor in Manufacturing. *J. Reg. Sci.*, August 1969, *9*(2), pp. 319–23. [G: U.S.]

Steele, D. B. Regional Multipliers in Great Britain. *Oxford Econ. Pap.*, July 1969, *21*(2), pp. 268–92. [G: U.K.]

Stober, William J. and Falk, Laurence H. Industrial Development Bonds as a Subsidy to Industry. *Nat. Tax J.*, June 1969, *22*(2), pp. 232–43. [G: U.S.]

Stoevener, Herbert H. Estimating the Effects of Water Policies in the West. *Amer. J. Agr. Econ.*, December 1969, *51*(5), pp. 1449–54. [G: U.S.]

Streit, M. E. Spatial Associations and Economic Linkages between Industries. *J. Reg. Sci.*, August 1969, *9*(2), pp. 177–88. [G: W. Germany; France]

Struyk, Raymond J. Tax Structure and Regional Economic Growth: A Reply. *J. Reg. Sci.*, August 1969, *9*(2), pp. 327–28. [G: U.S.]

Sutton, Willis A., Jr. Differential Perceptions of Impact of a Rural Anti-poverty Campaign. *Soc. Sci. Quart.*, December 1969, *50*(3), pp. 657–67. [G: U.S.]

Tatai, Z. Tools of Regional Development under the New System of Economic Control and Management. *Acta Oecon.*, 1969, *4*(4), pp. 417–22. [G: Hungary]

Thomas, Roy. The Financial Benefits of Expanding in the Development Areas. *Bull. Oxford Univ. Inst. Econ. Statist.*, May 1969, *31*(2), pp. 77–87. [G: U.K.]

Trock, Warren L. Institutional Factors Affecting Land and Water Development, Lower Rio Grande Valley, Texas. *Water Resources Res.*, December 1969, *5*(6), pp. 1364–66. [G: U.S.]

Vapnarsky, Cesar A. On Rank-Size Distributions of Cities: An Ecological Approach. *Econ. Develop. Cult. Change*, July 1969, *17*(4), pp. 584–95.

Vasil'ev, N. The Distribution of Agricultural Enterprises and Increased Specialization of Agriculture. *Prob. Econ.*, April 1969, *11*(12), pp. 37–46. [G: U.S.S.R.]

Vechkanov, G. Raising the Effectiveness of the Territorial Redistribution of Labor Resources. *Prob. Econ.*, October 1969, *12*(6), pp. 58–67. [G: U.S.S.R.]

Vessillier, Elisabeth. L'instrument fiscal dans la politique française d'amenagement du territoire. (The Fiscal Instrument in the Regional Economic Policy of France. With English summary.) *Public Finance*, 1969, *24*(3), pp. 499–509. [G: France]

Vyas, V. S. Integration of Farm and Non-Farm Employment, Part I: Farm and Non-Farm Employment in an Economically Backward Region. *Artha-Vikas*, January 1969, *5*(1), pp. 54–67. [G: India]

Wheatley, John J. and Randall, Gary B. Industrial Specialization in Washington. *Univ. Wash. Bus. Rev.*, Summer 1969, *28*(4), pp. 25–35. [G: U.S.]

White, Rudolph A. Measuring Unemployment and Subemployment in the Mississippi Delta. *Mon. Lab. Rev.*, April 1969, *92*(4), pp. 17–23. [G: U.S.]

Winger, Alan R. Regional Growth Disparities and the Mortgage Market. *J. Finance*, September 1969, *24*(4), pp. 659–62. [G: U.S.]

Yocum, James C. Recent Changes in Interstate and Interregional Population Flows. *Ohio State U. Bull. Bus. Res.*, May 1969, *44*(5), pp. 4–7. [G: U.S.]

Zaidi, Mahmood A. Structural Unemployment, Labor Market Efficiency and the Intrafactor Allocation Mechanism in the United States and Canada. *Southern Econ. J.*, January 1969, *35*(3), pp. 205–13. [G: U.S.; Canada]

Zlatin, V. and Rutgaizer, V. Comparison of the Levels of Economic Development of Union Republics and Large Regions. *Prob. Econ.*, June 1969, *12*(2), pp. 3–24. [G: U.S.S.R.]

9413 Regional Economic Models and Forecasts

Billings, R. Bruce. The Mathematical Identity of the Multipliers Derived from the Economic Base Model and the Input-Output Model. *J. Reg. Sci.*, December 1969, *9*(3), pp. 471–73.

Bourne, L. S. A Spatial Allocation-Land Use Conversion Model of Urban Growth. *J. Reg. Sci.*, August 1969, *9*(2), pp. 261–72.

Bradley, Iver E. and Gander, James P. Input-Output Multipliers: Some Theoretical Comments. *J. Reg. Sci.*, August 1969, *9*(2), pp. 309–17.

Brown, H. James. Shift and Share Projections of Regional Economic Growth: An Empirical Test. *J. Reg. Sci.*, April 1969, *9*(1), pp. 1–18.

Davis, H. Craig. Variations in the California and Pacific Northwest Input-Output Formats. *Univ. Wash. Bus. Rev.*, Autumn 1969, *29*(1), pp. 48–56. [G: U.S.]

Eddleman, B. R. Estimating the Effects of Resource Development Programs on Regional Employment. *Amer. J. Agr. Econ.*, December 1969, *51*(5), pp. 1434–41. [G: U.S.]

Farrish, Raymond O. P. and Hardie, Ian W. Mysterious Multipliers: Comment. *Amer. J. Agr. Econ.*, August 1969, *51*(3), pp. 689. [G: U.S.]

Garnick, Daniel H. Disaggregated Basic-Service Models and Regional Input-Output Models in Multiregional Projections. *J. Reg. Sci.*, April 1969, *9*(1), pp. 87–100. [G: U.S.]

Glejser, H. and Dramais, A. A Gravity Model of Interdependent Equations to Estimate Flow Creation and Diversion. *J. Reg. Sci.*, December 1969, *9*(3), pp. 439–49.

Greytak, David. A Statistical Analysis of Regional Export Estimating Techniques. *J. Reg. Sci.*, December 1969, *9*(3), pp. 387–95. [G: U.S.]

Hirvonen, Martti J. Balanced Dairy Production—Interregional Linear Programming Approach. *Kansant. Aikak.*, 1969, *65*(4), pp. 274–79.

Holzheu, Franz. Regionales Wachstum und interregionale Kapitalbewegungen. (With English summary.) *Kyklos*, 1969, *22*(3), pp. 417–53.

Howrey, E. Philip. On the Choice of Forecasting Models for Air Travel. *J. Reg. Sci.*, August 1969, *9*(2), pp. 215–24. [G: U.S.]

Hudson, John C. Pattern Recognition in Empirical Map Analysis. *J. Reg. Sci.*, August 1969, *9*(2), pp. 189–99. [G: U.S.]

Klaassen, L. H. and Van Wickeren, A. C. Interindustry Relations: An Attraction Model: A Progress Report. **In** *[Tinbergen, J.]*, 1969, pp. 245–68.

L'Esperance, Wilford L. Econometric Model Building for State Economic Development. *Ohio State U. Bull. Bus. Res.*, December 1969, *44*(12), pp. 1–3, 7–8. **[G: U.S.]**

Long, Wesley H. An Examination of Linear Homogeneity of Trade and Production Functions in County Leontief Matrices. *J. Reg. Sci.*, April 1969, *9*(1), pp. 47–67. **[G: U.S.]**

MacKay, D. I. Industrial Structure and Regional Economic Growth—A Further Comment. *Scot. J. Polit. Econ.*, February 1969, *16*(1), pp. 99. **[G: U.K.]**

Miller, Ronald E. Interregional Feedbacks in Input-Output Models: Some Experimental Results. *Western Econ. J.*, March 1969, *7*(1), pp. 41–50.

Mirakhor, Abbas and Orazem, Frank. Mysterious Multipliers: Reply. *Amer. J. Agr. Econ.*, August 1969, *51*(3), pp. 689–90. **[G: U.S.]**

Moody, Harold T. and Puffer, Frank W. A Gross Regional Product Approach to Regional Model-Building. *Western Econ. J.*, December 1969, *7*(4), pp. 391–402. **[G: U.S.]**

Ochs, Jack. An Application of Linear Programming to Urban Spatial Organization. *J. Reg. Sci.*, December 1969, *9*(3), pp. 451–57.

Quandt, Richard E. and Young, Kan Hua. Cross-sectional Travel Demand Models: Estimates and Tests. *J. Reg. Sci.*, August 1969, *9*(2), pp. 201–14. **[G: U.S.]**

Rogers, Andrei. On Perfect Aggregation in the Matrix Cohort-Survival Model of Interregional Population Growth. *J. Reg. Sci.*, December 1969, *9*(3), pp. 417–24.

Rogers, Tommy W. Factors in the Net Migration Rates of Southern SMSA's: A Comparison of the Subregional Influence of Selected Variables. *Miss. Val. J. Bus. Econ.*, Fall 1969, *5*(1), pp. 51–67. **[G: U.S.]**

Saunders, Robert J. Urban Area Water Consumption: Analysis and Projections. *Quart. Rev. Econ. Bus.*, Summer 1969, *9*(2), pp. 5–20. **[G: U.S.]**

Scott, Allen J. Spatial Equilibrium of the Central City. *J. Reg. Sci.*, April 1969, *9*(1), pp. 29–45. **[G: U.K.]**

Tabaček, Ján. Slovakia and the Development of Her Economy. *New Trends Czech. Econ.*, July 1969, (4), pp. 21–34. **[G: Czechoslovakia]**

Thoss, Rainer. Ein Vorschlag zur Koordinierung der Regionalpolitik in einer wachsenden Wirtschaft. (With English summary.) *Jahr. Nationalökon. Statist.*, May 1969, *182*(6), pp. 490–529. **[G: Germany]**

Tiebout, Charles M. An Empirical Regional Input-Output Projection Model: The State of Washington 1980. *Rev. Econ. Statist.*, August 1969, *51*(3), pp. 334–40. **[G: U.S.]**

Townroe, P. M. Industrial Structure and Regional Economic Growth—A Comment. *Scot. J. Polit. Econ.*, February 1969, *16*(1), pp. 95–98. **[G: U.K.]**

Author Index of Articles in Current Periodicals, Collective Volumes, and Government Documents

Abbreviated titles for journals are the same as those used in the *Journal of Economic Literature*. Full titles of Journals may be found on pages xi–xv.

Books have been identified by author or editor (noted *ed.*). In rare cases where two books by the same author appear, volumes are distinguished by I or II after the name. In some cases there appear two books by the same person, once as author, once as editor. These may be distinguished by *ed.* noted for the edited volume. Full titles and bibliographic references for books may be found on pages xvi–xxiii.

Government Documents are identified by a shortened document title, followed by an abbreviation of document type:

HCH	House Committee Hearing	*SCP*	Senate Committee Print
HCP	House Committee Print	*JECH*	Joint Economic Committee Hearing
SCH	Senate Committee Hearing	*JECP*	Joint Economic Committee Print

op. cit. is used when article and document titles are the same.

Full titles and bibliographic references for documents may be found on pages xiv–xxvii.

Aaltonen, Aimo O. Mainonnassa suoritetuista vertailuista silmällä pitäen vilpillisen kilpailun ehkäisemislakia. (Comparisons in Advertising with Reference to the Law for the Prevention of Unfair Competition. With English summary.) *Liiketaloudellinen Aikak.*, 1969, *18*(3), pp. 301–10.

Aaron, Benjamin. Individual Employee Rights and Union Democracy. **In** *Somers, G. G., ed. (II)*, 1969, pp. 275–82.

Aaron, Henry J. Local Public Expenditures and the "Migration Effect." *Western Econ. J.*, December 1969, *7*(4), pp. 385–90.

______ Perspectives on Poverty 4: Income Transfer Programs. *Mon. Lab. Rev.*, February 1969, *92*(2), pp. 50–54.

______ Some Observations on Property Tax Valuation and the Significance of Full Value Assessment. **In** *Lynn, A. D., Jr., ed.*, 1969, pp. 153–66.

______ What Is a Comprehensive Tax Base Anyway? *Nat. Tax J.*, December 1969, *22*(4), pp. 543–49.

______ **and McGuire, Martin C.** Efficiency and Equity in the Optimal Supply of a Public Good. *Rev. Econ. Statist.*, February 1969, *51*(1), pp. 31–39.

______**; Taussig, Michael K. and Pechman, Joseph A.** Improving Social Security Benefits and Financing: Brookings Research Report 94. **In** *Economics of Aging: Toward a Full Share in Abundance, Pt. 1, SCH*, 1969, pp. 253–63.

Abdel-Rahman, I. H. The United Nations Organization for Industrial Development—Its Organization and Functions. *Kansant. Aikak.*, 1969, *65*(3), pp. 155–70.

Abeelen, Marc J. and Hammond, Robert C. The Fiscal Aspects of International Co-operation in Africa—The Experience of the UDEAC and the EAC. *Bull. Int. Fiscal Doc.*, March 1969, *23*(3), pp. 95–115.

Abner, Willoughby. The FMCS and Dispute Mediation in the Federal Government. *Mon. Lab. Rev.*, May 1969, *92*(5), pp. 27–29.

Abouchar, Alan. Inflation and Transportation Policy in Brazil. *Econ. Develop. Cult. Change*, Part I, October 1969, *18*(1), pp. 92–109.

______ Public Investment Allocation and Pricing Policy for Transportation. **In** *Ellis, H. S., ed.*, 1969, pp. 345–75.

Aboyade, O. The Economy of Nigeria. **In** *Robson, P. and Lury, D. A., eds.*, 1969, pp. 127–93.

Abraham, W. I. and Gill, M. S. The Growth and Composition of Malaysia's Capital Stock. *Malayan Econ. Rev.*, October 1969, *14*(2), pp. 44–54.

______ New Measures of Economic Growth and Structural Change of the Malaysian Economy in the Post-1960 Period. *Malayan Econ. Rev.*, April 1969, *14*(1), pp. 65–79.

Abrahamse, A. P. J. and Koerts, J. A Comparison between the Power of the Durbin-Watson Test and the Power of the BLUS Test. *J. Amer. Statist. Assoc.*, September 1969, *64*(327), pp. 938–48.

Abrahamsson, B. J. Recent Developments in International Shipping with Reference to Singapore. *Malayan Econ. Rev.*, October 1969, *14*(2), pp. 26–39.

Abramovitz, Moses. The Passing of the Kuznets Cycle: A Correction. *Economica, N.S.*, February 1969, *36*(141), pp. 81.

Abrams, Jack. Reducing the Risk of New Product Marketing Strategies Testing. *J. Marketing Res.*, May 1969, *6*(2), pp. 216–20.

Abshire, David M. Early History, European Discovery, and Colonization. **In** *Abshire, D. M. and Samuels, M. A., eds.*, 1969, pp. 29–59.

______ Minerals, Manufacturing, Power and Communications. **In** *Abshire, D. M. and Samuels, M. A., eds.*, 1969, pp. 294–319.

Acampora, Giovanni. Il "real time" per il servizio conti correnti di corrispondenza: una soluzione organizzativa che offre sicurezza opertiva. ("Real Time" for the Current Accounts Service: An Organizational Solution Affording Operational Reliability. With English summary.) *Bancaria*, April 1969, *25*(4), pp. 438–48.

Achinstein, Asher. Constraints on Policy Analysis and Policy Implementation in the Federal Agencies. **In** *The Analysis and Evaluation of Public Expenditures: The PPB System, Vol. 1, JECP*, 1969, pp. 369–80.

Ackoff, Russell L. and Emshoff, James R. Prediction,

Explanation, and Control of Conflict. *Peace Res. Soc. Internat. Pap.*, 1969, *12*, pp. 109–15.

Aczel, J. A. The Usefulness of the CBI Industrial Trends Survey for Forecasting in the Chemical Industry. *Appl. Econ.*, August 1969, *1*(3), pp. 205–10.

Adams, Dale W. Rural Migration and Agricultural Development in Colombia. *Econ. Develop. Cult. Change*, July 1969, *17*(4), pp. 527–39.

Adams, Dale W. and Rask, Norman. Economics of Cost-Share Leases: A Reply. *Amer. J. Agr. Econ.*, August 1969, *51*(3), pp. 695–97.

Adams, E. Sherman. Are Bank Dividend Policies too Conservative? **In** *Jessup, P. F.*, 1969, pp. 205–15.

Adams, Esmond and Fish, Mary. Comments on the Impact of Federal Tax-Sharing on Economic Stabilization. *Nebr. J. Econ. Bus.*, Winter 1968–69, *8*(1), pp. 53–60.

Adams, John S. Directional Bias in Intra-Urban Migration. *Econ. Geogr.*, October 1969, *45*(4), pp. 302–23.

Adams, Nassau A. Internal Migration in Jamaica: An Economic Analysis. *Soc. Econ. Stud.*, June 1969, *18*(2), pp. 137–51.

Adams, Walter. The Case for Structural Tests. **In** *Weston, J. F. and Peltzman, S., eds.*, 1969, pp. 13–26.

______ Planning, Regulation, and Competition. **In** *Kuhlman, J. M., ed.*, 1969, pp. 233–38.

______ Public Policy in a Free Enterprise Economy. **In** *Starleaf, D. R., ed.*, 1969, pp. 79–93.

______ Statement. **In** *Governmental Intervention in the Market Mechanism, Pt. 1, SCH*, 1969, pp. 304–08.

Adebahr, Hubertus. Binnenwanderung und Lohnhöhe. Eine Analyse der Binnenwanderungen in der Bundesrepublik in den Jahren 1957–1967 im Hinblick auf die Frage ob Wanderungen "lohngerichtet" sind. (Internal Migration and Regional Wage Levels. An Analysis of Internal Migrations in the Federal Republic of Germany 1957–1967. With English summary.) *Schmollers Jahr.*, 1969, *89*(5), pp. 557–78.

Adekunle, Joseph O. and Ezekiel, Hannan. The Secular Behavior of Income Velocity: An International Cross-Section Study. *Int. Monet. Fund Staff Pap.*, July 1969, *16*(2), pp. 224–39.

Adelman, Irma; Geier, Marsha and Morris, Cynthia Taft. Instruments and Goals in Economic Development. *Amer. Econ. Rev.*, May 1969, *59*(2), pp. 409–26.

______ **and Je, Kim Mahn.** An Econometric Model of the Korean Economy (1956–66). **In** *Adelman, I., ed.*, 1969, pp. 77–108.

Adelman, Irma, et al. The Korean Sectoral Model. **In** *Adelman, I., ed.*, 1969, pp. 109–35.

Adelman, M. A. Comment on the "H" Concentration Measure as a Numbers-Equivalent. *Rev. Econ. Statist.*, February 1969, *51*(1), pp. 99–101.

______ Statement. **In** *Governmental Intervention in the Market Mechanism, Pt. 1, SCH*, 1969, pp. 6–20.

Adelmann, Gerhard. Structural Change in the Rhenish Linen and Cotton Trades at the Outset of Industrialization. **In** *Crouzet, F.; Chaloner, W. H. and Stern, W. M., eds.*, 1969, pp. 82–97.

Adhvaryu, J. H. The Theory of Investment in Human Capital. **In** *Pandit, H. N., ed.*, 1969, pp. 136–45.

______ **and Patel, A. S.** Determinants and Development Implications of Foodgrain Prices in India: Comment. *Amer. J. Agr. Econ.*, November 1969, *51*(4), pp. 939–40.

Adler, F. Michael. The Framework for Investigating Direct Manufacturing Investment Overseas. *Law Contemp. Probl.*, Winter 1969, *34*(1), pp. 3–17.

______ On the Risk-Return Trade-Off in the Valuation of Assets. *J. Financial Quant. Anal.*, December 1969, *4*(4), pp. 493–512.

Adler, Hans A. Notes on Feasibility Studies: III. Some Thoughts on Feasibility Studies. *J. Transp. Econ. Policy*, May 1969, *3*(2), pp. 231–36.

Ady, Peter. International Commodity Agreements. **In** *Stewart, I. G., ed.*, 1969, pp. 26–46.

Agarwal, D. K. The Purpose and Future Direction of Legislation on Standing Orders. **In** *Johri, C. K., ed.*, 1969, pp. 189–200.

Agarwala, R. Price Policy in a Multi-Product Firm: A Case Study. *Appl. Econ.*, August 1969, *1*(3), pp. 161–66.

______ Tests and Uses of Macro-Econometric Models: A Critical Survey. *Econ. Planning*, 1969, *9*(3), pp. 235–57.

______**; Burns, T. and Duffy, M.** Forecasting Gross Private Fixed Investment Using Intentions Survey Data. *Manchester Sch. Econ. Soc. Stud.*, December 1969, *37*(4), pp. 279–93.

______ **and Goodson, G. C.** An Analysis of the Effects of Investment Incentives on Investment Behaviour in the British Economy. *Economica, N.S.*, November 1969, *36*(144), pp. 377–88.

Ageeva, V. A.; Buzunov, R. A. and Klotzvog, F. N. Input-Output and National Economic Planning. *Matekon*, Fall 1969, *6*(1), pp. 19–29.

Aggrey-Mensah, W. and Tuckwell, N. E. A Study of Banana Supply and Price Patterns on the Sydney Wholesale Market: An Application of Spectral Analysis. *Australian J. Agr. Econ.*, December 1969, *13*(2), pp. 101–17.

Aglietta, Michel and Seibel, Claude. The National Accounting System and the Preparation of the Fifth French Plan. *Rev. Income Wealth*, June 1969, *15*(2), pp. 121–69.

Agria, Susan R. Special Tax Treatment of Mineral Industries. **In** *Harberger, A. C. and Bailey, M. J., eds.*, 1969, pp. 77–122.

Ahearn, Frederick L., Jr. Correlates of Job Status Among Indigenous Nonprofessionals in Community Action Programs. *Soc. Sci. Quart.*, December 1969, *50*(3), pp. 668–75.

Ahmad, Zubeida M. and Sternberg, Marvin J. Agrarian Reform and Employment, with Special Reference to Asia. *Int. Lab. Rev.*, February 1969, *99*(2), pp. 159–83.

Aines, Ronald. Rationale for Conglomerate Growth in the Farm Input Sector. **In** *Garoian, L., ed.*, 1969, pp. 63–68.

Airamo, Martti M. Toimialarationalisointi kartellin näkökulmasta tarkasteltuna. (Rationalization According to the Field of Operation Examined from the Point of View of the Cartel. With English summary.) *Liiketaloudellinen Aikak.*, 1969, *18* (3), pp. 316–23.

Altman, Edward I. Corporate Bankruptcy Potential, Stockholder Returns and Share Valuation. *J. Finance,* December 1969, *24*(5), pp. 887–900.

Altman, Oscar L. Euro-dollars. **In** *Chalmers, E. B., ed.,* 1969, pp. 1-14.

——— Eurodollar and Foreign Exchange Markets. **In** *Aliber, R. Z., ed.,* 1969, pp. 20–29.

Altman, Stuart H. Earnings, Unemployment, and the Supply of Enlisted Volunteers. *J. Human Res.,* Winter 1969, *4*(1), pp. 38–59.

——— **and Fisher, Anthony C.** Marginal Product of Labor, Wages and Disequilibrium: Comment. *Rev. Econ. Statist.,* November 1969, *51*(4), pp. 485–86.

Alutto, Joseph A. and Belasco, James A. Organizational Impacts of Teacher Negotiations. *Ind. Relat.,* October 1969, *9*(1), pp. 67–79.

Alzona, Gianluigi. Fusioni di macroimprese 1967: ricerche sullo sviluppo industriale. (Merger of Large Corporations, 1967. With English summary.) *L'Impresa,* May/June 1969, *11*(3), pp. 205–21.

Amato, Peter W. Population Densities, Land Values, and Socioeconomic Class in Bogotá, Colombia. *Land Econ.,* February 1969, *45*(1), pp. 66–73.

Ambannavar, Jaipal P. Upward Occupational Mobility Through Education and Age. *Asian Econ. Rev.,* May 1969, *11*(3), pp. 290–99.

Ameloot, W. De algemene evolutie van het baanvervoer. (The General Evolution of Road Transport. With English summary.) *Econ. Soc. Tijdschr.,* October 1969, *23*(5), pp. 441–54.

America, Richard F., Jr. 'What Do You People Want?' *Harvard Bus. Rev.,* March–April 1969, *47* (2), pp. 103–12.

Amin, R. B. Taxing Agricultural Incomes. *Artha-Vikas,* July 1969, *5*(2), pp. 106–07.

——— University and Industry. *Artha-Vikas,* January 1969, *5*(1), pp. 1–8.

Amin, Samir. Levels of Remuneration, Factor Proportions and Income Differentials with Special Reference to Developing Countries. **In** *Smith, A. D., ed.,* 1969, pp. 269–93.

Ammer, Dean S. Materials Management as a Profit Center. *Harvard Bus. Rev.,* January–February 1969, *47*(1), pp. 72–82.

Amstutz, Arnold E. Market-Oriented Management Systems: The Current Status. *J. Marketing Res.,* November 1969, *6*(4), pp. 481–96.

Anand, Vinod and Srivastava, D. K. On the Stability Theorem in Uzawa's Two-Sector Growth Model. *Indian Econ. J.,* January–March 1969, *16*(3), pp. 362–70.

Andal, Melvin E. Economic Guidelines for Present and Future Capital Use in Canadian Agriculture. *Can. J. Agr. Econ.,* November 1969, *17*(3), pp. 9–19.

Andarawewa, A. B. Evaluation of Public Research Programs in Agriculture. *Can. J. Agr. Econ.,* November 1969, *17*(3), pp. 157–69.

——— Tenure Patterns and the Commercialization of Canadian Agriculture. *Can. J. Agr. Econ.,* February 1969, *17*(1), pp. 110–20.

Andel, Norbert. Zur these von den unsozialen verteilungswirkungen öffentlicher schulden. (Notes on the Unsocial Distributive Effect of Public Debt. With English summary.) *Public Finance,* 1969, *24*(1), pp. 69–79.

Andersen, Leonall C. Additional Empirical Evidence on the Reverse-Causation Argument. *Fed. Res. Bank St. Louis Rev.,* August 1969, *51*(8), pp. 19–23.

——— Monetary Velocity in Empirical Analysis: Discussion. **In** *Federal Reserve Bank of Boston,* 1969, pp. 52–55.

——— Money Market Conditions as a Guide for Monetary Management. **In** *Brunner, K., ed.,* 1969, pp. 66–83.

——— **and Burger, Albert E.** Asset Management and Commercial Bank Portfolio Behavior: Theory and Practice. *J. Finance,* May 1969, *24*(2), pp. 207–22.

——— **and Jordan, Jerry L.** Monetary and Fiscal Actions: A Test of Their Relative Importance in Economic Stabilization—Reply. *Fed. Res. Bank St. Louis Rev.,* April 1969, *51*(4), pp. 12–16.

Anderson, Arvid. Strikes and Impasse Resolution in Public Employment. *Mich. Law Rev.,* March 1969, *67*(5), pp. 943–70.

Anderson, B. L. The Attorney and the Early Capital Market in Lancashire. **In** *Harris, J. R., ed.,* 1969, pp. 50–77.

Anderson, C. Arnold and Bowman, Mary Jean. Relationship among Schooling, "Ability," and Income in Industrialized Societies. **In** *[Edding, Friedrich],* 1969, pp. 97–119.

Anderson, Dewey. Statement. **In** *National Timber Supply Act of 1969, HCH,* 1969, pp. 182–96.

Anderson, Henry. Choosing the Base Period for Economic Forecasts. *Miss. Val. J. Bus. Econ.,* Spring 1969, *4*(2), pp. 33–42.

Anderson, James and Naya, Seiji. Substitution and Two Concepts of Effective Rate of Protection. *Amer. Econ. Rev.,* Part I, September 1969, *59*(4), pp. 607–12.

Anderson, James R. and Byerlee, D. R. Value of Predictors of Uncontrolled Factors in Response Functions. *Australian J. Agr. Econ.,* December 1969, *13*(2), pp. 118–27.

——— **and Dillon, John L.** A Comparison of Response Surface and Factorial Designs in Agricultural Research: Comment. *Rev. Marketing Agr. Econ.,* June 1969, *37*(2), pp. 130–32.

Anderson, Leslie P. and Roscoe, David L. The Term Structure of Interest Rates—An Alternative Hypothesis. *Miss. Val. J. Bus. Econ.,* Spring 1969, *4* (2), pp. 1–9.

Anderson, Paul S. Monetary Velocity in Empirical Analysis. **In** *Federal Reserve Bank of Boston,* 1969, pp. 37–51.

——— Wages and the Guideposts: Comment. *Amer. Econ. Rev.,* June 1969, *59*(3), pp. 351–54.

——— **and Morris, Frank E.** Defining the Money Supply: The Case of Government Deposits. *New Eng. Econ. Rev.,* March/April 1969, pp. 21–31.

——— **and Murphy, Neil B.** Running the Bank's Money Position: A Study of Demand Deposit Fluctuations. **In** *Jessup, P. F.,* 1969, pp. 117–23.

Anderson, Richard M. Anguish in the Defense Industry. *Harvard Bus. Rev.,* November–December 1969, *47*(6), pp. 162–70, 176–80.

——— Handling Risk in Defense Contracting. *Har-*

vard Bus. Rev., July–August 1969, *47*(4), pp. 90–98.

Anderson, Robert W. A Note on Tax Incidence in a Macroeconomic Distribution Model. *Rivista Int. Sci. Econ. Com.*, December 1969, *16*(12), pp. 1164–73.

Anderson, Roice and Gray, Roger W. Advertised Specials and Local Competition among Supermarkets. **In** *Alexis, M.; Holloway, R. J. and Hancock, R. S., eds.*, 1969, pp. 343–57.

Andersson, Edward. Skattepolitiken efter Företagsbeskattningsreformen. (Taxation Policy after the Reforms in Company Tax. With English summary.) *Econ. Samfundets Tidskr.*, 1969, *22* (1), pp. 52–61.

Andic, Fuat M. The Development Impact of the EEC on the French and Dutch Caribbean. *J. Common Market Stud.*, September 1969, *8*(1), pp. 19–49.

Ando, Albert and Modigliani, Franco. Econometric Analysis of Stabilization Policies. *Amer. Econ. Rev.*, May 1969, *59*(2), pp. 296–314.

Andreatta, Nino. Il disegno della politica della Banca centrale e l'uso di modelli econometrici di flussi monetari. (The Framing of Central Bank Policy and the Use of Econometric Models of Money Flows. With English summary.) *Bancaria*, January 1969, *25*(1), pp. 9–18.

Andrews, Edith Wall and Moylan, Maurice. Scientific and Professional Employment by State Governments. *Mon. Lab. Rev.*, August 1969, *92*(8), pp. 40–45.

Andrews, Kenneth R. Toward Professionalism in Business Management. *Harvard Bus. Rev.*, March–April 1969, *47*(2), pp. 49–60.

Andrews, Richard B. Economia del suolo urbano: sommario della disciplina e delle sue tendenze. (Urban Land Economics: A Summary View. With English summary.) *Rivista Int. Sci. Econ. Com.*, August 1969, *16*(8), pp. 807–15.

Andrus, Roman R. Marketing Research in a Developing Nation—Taiwan: A Case Example. *Univ. Wash. Bus. Rev.*, Spring 1969, *28*(3), pp. 40–44.

______ **and Knutsen, John A.** The Impact of Personal Information Sources on Retailer Success. *Oregon Bus. Rev.*, November 1969, *28*(11), pp. 1–3.

Angevine, Erma. Statement. **In** *Utility Consumers' Counsel Act of 1969, Pt. 6A, SCH*, 1969, pp. 1462–66.

Anghel, Eliza and Nichita, Nicolae. Cu privire la corelaţia dintre cererea şi oferta de mărfuri în socialism. (The Correlation between Demand and Offer of Produce in Socialism. With English summary.) *Stud. Cercet. Econ.*, 1969, *1-2*, pp. 23–36.

Angrish, A. C. Rationalized Agricultural Tax Structures in India and Some Policy Implications. *Artha-Vikas*, July 1969, *5*(2), pp. 154–70.

Angus, Robert C. and Stull, J. Warren. Consumer Attitudes toward Milk Substitutes. *Amer. J. Agr. Econ.*, December 1969, *51*(5), pp. 1149–53.

Ann, Lee Soo. Financial Planning of Investment in Malaysia. *Malayan Econ. Rev.*, April 1969, *14*(1), pp. 48–64.

Anshen, Melvin. The Management of Ideas. *Harvard Bus. Rev.*, July–August 1969, *47*(4), pp. 99–107.

Ansoff, H. I. A Quasi-analytic Method for Long-Range Planning. **In** *Carsberg, B. V. and Edey, H. C., eds.*, 1969, pp. 303–22.

Ansoff, H. Igor. Issues in National Policy on Growth of Firms. **In** *Weston, J. F. and Peltzman, S., eds.*, 1969, pp. 197–207.

______ **and Brandenburg, R. G.** The General Manager of the Future. *Calif. Manage. Rev.*, Spring 1969, *11*(3), pp. 61–72.

Anstey, Vera. A Fresh Approach to Agricultural Reconstruction in Indian Development. **In** *Bhuleshkar, A. V., ed.*, 1969, pp. 47–59.

Anthony, Willis E.; Christiansen, Martin K. and Hammond, Jerome W. Why the Growing Farm-Retail Price Spread? **In** *Ruttan, V. W.; Waldo, A. D. and Houck, J. P., eds.*, 1969, pp. 165–85.

Apostol, Gh. Unitate şi diversitate în conceptul de economie socialistă. (Unity and Variety in the Conception of Socialist Economy. With English summary.) *Stud. Cercet. Econ.*, 1969, *3*, pp. 67–78.

Araji, Ahmed A. and Walsh, Richard G. Effect of Assembly Costs on Optimum Grain Elevator Size and Location. *Can. J. Agr. Econ.*, July 1969, *17*(2), pp. 36–45.

Arak, Marcelle. Estimation of Assymetric Longrun Supply Functions: The Case of Coffee. *Can. J. Agr. Econ.*, February 1969, *17*(1), pp. 15–22.

Arbuzova, N. I. Stochastic Stability of a Quadratic Programming Problem with Random Free Constraints. *Matekon*, Fall 1969, *6*(1), pp. 91–97.

Archer, R. W. From New Towns to Metrotowns and Regional Cities. *Amer. J. Econ. Soc.*, July 1969, *28* (3), pp. 257–70.

______ From New Towns to Metrotowns and Regional Cities, II. *Amer. J. Econ. Soc.*, October 1969, *28*(4), pp. 385–98.

Archer, Stephen H. and Daellenbach, Hans G. The Optimal Bank Liquidity: A Multi-Period Stochastic Model. *J. Financial Quant. Anal.*, September 1969, *4*(3), pp. 329–43.

Archibald, G. C. The Phillips Curve and the Distribution of Unemployment. *Amer. Econ. Rev.*, May 1969, *59*(2), pp. 124–34.

Archibald, T. R. Stock Market Reaction to Different Accounting Practices. **In** *Association of Canadian Schools of Business*, 1969, pp. 171–95.

Arditti, Fred D. A Utility Function Depending on the First Three Moments: Reply. *J. Finance*, September 1969, *24*(4), pp. 720.

Areeda, Phillip. Structure-Performance Assumptions in Recent Merger Cases. **In** *Weston, J. F. and Peltzman, S., eds.*, 1969, pp. 27–44.

Arey, Will. Statement. **In** *A Review of Balance of Payments Policies, JECH*, 1969, pp. 29–35.

d'Arge, Ralph C. Note on Customs Unions and Direct Foreign Investment. *Econ. J.*, June 1969, *79* (314), pp. 324–33.

______ **and Kneese, Allen V.** Pervasive External Costs and the Response of Society. **In** *The Analysis and Evaluation of Public Expenditures: The PPB System, Vol. 1, JECP*, 1969, pp. 87–115.

Argy, Victor. The Impact of Monetary Policy on Expenditure, with Particular Reference to the United Kingdom. *Int. Monet. Fund Staff Pap.*, November 1969, *16*(3), pp. 436–88.

______ Monetary Variables and the Balance of Pay-

ments. *Int. Monet. Fund Staff Pap.,* July 1969, *16* (2), pp. 267–88.
Arlt, Carl T. Background and History. **In** *Prochnow, H. V., ed.,* 1969, pp. 12–29.
Armentrout, Claire and Luttrell, Clifton B. Growth —Metropolitan vs. Nonmetropolitan Areas in the Central Mississippi Valley. *Fed. Res. Bank St. Louis Rev.,* January 1969, *51*(1), pp. 8–15.
Armington, Paul S. The Geographic Pattern of Trade and the Effects of Price Changes. *Int. Monet. Fund Staff Pap.,* July 1969, *16*(2), pp. 179–201.
______ A Theory of Demand for Products Distinguished by Place of Production. *Int. Monet. Fund Staff Pap.,* March 1969, *16*(1), pp. 159–78.
Armitage, P. and Smith, C. Selby. Computable Models of the British Educational System. **In** *Blaug, M., ed.,* 1969, pp. 202–37.
Armstrong, Dale. The Flow of Funds Statement —An Effective Tool. *J. Risk Ins.,* March 1969, *36* (1), pp. 151–57.
Arndt, Sven W. Customs Union and the Theory of Tariffs. *Amer. Econ. Rev.,* March 1969, *59*(1), pp. 108–18.
Arnett, Harold E. Taxable Income vs. Financial Income: How Much Uniformity Can We Stand? *Accounting Rev.,* July 1969, *44*(3), pp. 482–94.
Arnould, Richard. Conglomerate Growth and Profitability. **In** *Garoian, L., ed.,* 1969, pp. 72–80.
Aronson, J. Richard and Schwartz, Eli. The Preference for Accumulation vs. Spending: Gift and Estate Taxation, and the Timing of Wealth Transfers. *Nat. Tax J.,* September 1969, *22*(3), pp. 390–98.
Arromdee, Virach. Can West Malaysia Become Self-Sufficient in Rice by 1975? *Malayan Econ. Rev.,* October 1969, *14*(2), pp. 79–93.
Arrow, Kenneth J. Classificatory Notes on the Production and Transmission of Technological Knowledge. *Amer. Econ. Rev.,* May 1969, *59*(2), pp. 29–35.
______ The Organization of Economic Activity: Issues Pertinent to the Choice of Market Versus Nonmarket Allocation. **In** *The Analysis and Evaluation of Public Expenditures: The PPB System, Vol. 1, JECP,* 1969, pp. 47–64.
______ The Social Discount Rate. **In** *Somers, G. G. and Wood, W. D., eds.,* 1969, pp. 56–75.
______ **and Kurz, Mordecai.** Optimal Consumer Allocation over an Infinite Horizon. *J. Econ. Theory,* June 1969, *1*(1), pp. 68–91.
______ **and Kurz, Mordecai.** Optimal Public Investment Policy and Controllability with Fixed Private Savings Ratio. *J. Econ. Theory,* August 1969, *1*(2), pp. 141–77.
______ **and Levhari, David.** Uniqueness of the Internal Rate of Return with Variable Life of Investment. *Econ. J.,* September 1969, *79*(315), pp. 560–66.
Arthurs, H. W. Collective Bargaining in the Public Service of Canada: Bold Experiment or Act of Folly? *Mich. Law Rev.,* March 1969, *67*(5), pp. 971–1000.
Artioli, Roberto. Linee per una ricerca documentaria. (Outlines for a Research-Work on Economic Information. With English summary.) *L'Impresa,* January/February 1969, *11*(1), pp. 56–58.
Artis, M. J. Two Aspects of the Monetary Debate. *Nat. Inst. Econ. Rev.,* August 1969, (49), pp. 33–51.
Ărvay, János. Development of the National Accounting System in Hungary. *Rev. Income Wealth,* June 1969, *15*(2), pp. 185–95.
Asanuma, Banri. Shadow Prices for Public Investment Criteria. *Kyoto Univ. Econ. Rev.,* October 1969, *39*(2), pp. 62–80.
Ashenfelter, Orley and Johnson, George E. Bargaining Theory, Trade Unions, and Industrial Strike Activity. *Amer. Econ. Rev.,* March 1969, *59*(1), pp. 35–49.
______ **and Mooney, Joseph D.** Some Evidence on the Private Returns to Graduate Education. *Southern Econ. J.,* January 1969, *35*(3), pp. 247–56.
______ **and Pencavel, John H.** American Trade Union Growth: 1900–1960. *Quart. J. Econ.,* August 1969, *83*(3), pp. 434–48.
Asher, Robert. Business and Workers' Welfare in the Progressive Era: Workmen's Compensation Reform in Massachusetts, 1880–1911. *Bus. Hist. Rev.,* Winter 1969, *43*(4), pp. 452–75.
Asher, Robert E. Foreign Aid: The Postwar Record and Targets for the 1970's. *Mon. Lab. Rev.,* November 1969, *92*(11), pp. 23–30.
Ashley, George E. International Communications: What Shape to Come? *Law Contemp. Probl.,* Spring 1969, *34*(2), pp. 417–28.
Ashley, William G.; Martino, Joseph P. and Price, William J. Science-Technology Coupling: Experience of the Air Force Office of Scientific Research. **In** *Gruber, W. H. and Marquis, D. G., eds.,* 1969, pp. 117–36.
Ashton, Robert. The Aristocracy in Transition. *Econ. Hist. Rev.,* August 1969, *22*(2), pp. 308–22.
Ashton, T. S. The Industrial Revolution, 1760–1830. **In** *Scoville, W. C. and La Force, J. C., eds., Vol. III,* 1969, pp. 40–65.
Ashworth, William. Economic Aspects of Late Victorian Naval Administration. *Econ. Hist. Rev.,* December 1969, *22*(3), pp. 491–505.
Asimakopulos, A. A Robinsonian Growth Model in One-Sector Notation. *Australian Econ. Pap.,* June 1969, *8*(12), pp. 41–58.
Aslanyan, R. G. Action to Ensure That Soviet Citizens Enjoy Equal Rights and Opportunities. *Int. Lab. Rev.,* December 1969, *100*(6), pp. 551–82.
Asopa, V. N. and Swanson, Earl R. Profitability of Supplemental Irrigation of Corn. *Ill. Agr. Econ.,* January 1969, *9*(1), pp. 7–9.
Astrand, H. The Income Objective in Agricultural Policies. **In** *Papi, U. and Nunn, C., eds.,* 1969, pp. 397–408.
Atiquallah, M. On a Restricted Least Squares Estimator. *J. Amer. Statist. Assoc.,* September 1969, *64*(327), pp. 964–68.
Atkinson, Anthony B. Import Strategy and Growth under Conditions of Stagnant Export Earnings. *Oxford Econ. Pap.,* November 1969, *21*(3), pp. 325–38.
______ The Timescale of Economic Models: How

Long Is the Long Run? *Rev. Econ. Stud.,* April 1969, *36*(106), pp. 137–52.

______ **and Stiglitz, Joseph E.** A New View of Technological Change. *Econ. J.,* September 1969, *79* (315), pp. 573–78.

Atkinson, Thomas R. Comment on Maurice Mann's Views on Monetary Policy. *J. Money, Credit, Banking,* August 1969, *1*(3), pp. 553–55.

______ Tone and Feel of the Market as a Guide for Open Market Operations. **In** *Brunner, K., ed.,* 1969, pp. 84–97.

Atkisson, Arthur A. and Robinson, Ira M. Amenity Resources for Urban Living. **In** *Perloff, H. S., ed.,* 1969, pp. 179–201.

Atlas, M. and Vinokur, R. The Economic Essence of Profit and Profitability under Socialism. *Prob. Econ.,* May 1969, *12*(1), pp. 3–32.

Atsumi, H. The Efficient Capital Programme for a Maintainable Utility Level. *Rev. Econ. Stud.,* July 1969, *36*(107), pp. 263–87.

Attiyeh, Richard E.; Bach, George L. and Lumsden, Keith G. The Efficiency of Programmed Learning in Teaching Economics: The Results of a Nationwide Experiment. *Amer. Econ. Rev.,* May 1969, *59*(2), pp. 217–23.

Attiyeh, Robert S. The Bashful Conglomerates. *Univ. Wash. Bus. Rev.,* Summer 1969, *28*(4), pp. 5–11.

Augenstein, Bruno W. Policy Analysis in the National Space Program. **In** *The Analysis and Evaluation of Public Expenditures: The PPB System, Vol. 3, JECP,* 1969, pp. 1020–68.

Augenthaler, Zdenek. The Socialist Countries and GATT. **In** *Alting von Geusau, F. A. M., ed.,* 1969, pp. 75–82.

Aujac, Henri. Technical Progress and French National Planning. **In** *Arnfield, R. V., ed.,* 1969, pp. 12–25.

Auld, Douglas A. L. An Application of Econometrics to Evaluate Fiscal Tax Policy. *Econ. Rec.,* June 1969, *45*(110), pp. 147–57.

______ The Economic Impact of Built-In Changes in Budget Components. *Australian Econ. Pap.,* June 1969, *8*(12), pp. 75–98.

______ Fiscal Policy Performance in Canada 1957–1967. *Public Finance,* 1969, *24*(3), pp. 427–40.

______ The Measurement of Fiscal Performance: A Reply. *Econ. Rec.,* June 1969, *45*(110), pp. 291–92.

Auster, Richard; Leveson, Irving and Sarachek, Deborah. The Production of Health, an Exploratory Study. *J. Human Res.,* Fall 1969, *4*(4), pp. 411–36.

______ **and Silver, Morris.** Entrepreneurship, Profit, and Limits on Firm Size. *J. Bus.,* July 1969, *42*(3), pp. 277–81.

Aventur, Jacques. Origine et nature du chômage dans l'économie française. (Origin and Nature of Unemployment in the French Economy. With English summary.) *Rivista Int. Sci. Econ. Com.,* April 1969, *16*(4), pp. 342–62.

Avots, Ivars. Why Does Project Management Fail? *Calif. Manage. Rev.,* Fall 1969, *12*(1), pp. 77–82.

Awalt, Francis Gloyd. Recollections of the Banking Crisis in 1933. *Bus. Hist. Rev.,* Autumn 1969, *43* (3), pp. 347–71.

Awokoya, Stephen O. The Structure and Development of Nigerian Education. **In** *Yesufu, T. M., ed.,* 1969, pp. 157–82.

Ayanian, Robert. A Comparison of Barten's Estimated Demand Elasticities with Those Obtained Using Frisch's Method. *Econometrica,* January 1969, *37*(1), pp. 79–94.

Aymond, A. H. Reassessment of Economic Standards for the Rate of Return under Regulation: Comment. **In** *Trebing, H. M. and Howard, R. H., eds.,* 1969, pp. 21–25.

Ayres, Robert U. and Kneese, Allen V. Pollution and Environmental Quality. **In** *Perloff, H. S., ed.,* 1969, pp. 35–71.

______ Production, Consumption, and Externalities. *Amer. Econ. Rev.,* June 1969, *59*(3), pp. 282–97.

Aziz, Nayyara; Ali, Asghar and Hufbauer, G. C. Cotton Textile and Leather Exports: What Cost Foreign Exchange? *Pakistan Develop. Rev.,* Autumn 1969, *9*(3), pp. 330–42.

Aziz, U. A. Wage, Fiscal, Social Security Policies and Institutional Changes as a Means of Redistributing Income in Developing Countries. **In** *Smith, A. D., ed.,* 1969, pp. 235–55.

Baali, Fuad. Agrarian Reform in Iraq: Some Socioeconomic Aspects. *Amer. J. Econ. Soc.,* January 1969, *28*(1), pp. 61–76.

Babb, Christopher T. and Keran, Michael W. An Explanation of Federal Reserve Actions (1933–68). *Fed. Res. Bank St. Louis Rev.,* July 1969, *51*(7), pp. 7–20.

Babb, E. M.; Belden, S. A. and Saathoff, C. R. An Analysis of Cooperative Bargaining in the Processing Tomato Industry. *Amer. J. Agr. Econ.,* February 1969, *51*(1), pp. 13–25.

Bacchus, M. K. Patterns of Educational Expenditure in an Emergent Nation—A Study of Guyana 1945–65. *Soc. Econ. Stud.,* September 1969, *18* (3), pp. 282–301.

Baccino, Osvaldo and Di Tella, Guido. Análisis teórico de los efectos de la intermediación comercial. El caso de la industria del automóvil en Argentina. (Theoretical Analysis of the Effects of Commercial Intermediation: The Case of Automobile Industry in Argentina. With English summary.) *Económica,* January–April 1969, *15*(1), pp. 1–14.

Bach, George L. The Effectiveness of Teaching Methods: A Further Note on Programmed Learning in Economics. *J. Econ. Educ.,* Fall 1969, *1*(1), pp. 56–59.

______ Statement. **In** *The 1969 Economic Report of the President, Pt. 3, JECH,* 1969, pp. 537–42.

______**; Lumsden, Keith G. and Attiyeh, Richard E.** The Efficiency of Programmed Learning in Teaching Economics: The Results of a Nationwide Experiment. *Amer. Econ. Rev.,* May 1969, *59*(2), pp. 217–23.

Bachmann, Hans. The Prospect of a European Monetary Union Restated. *Aussenwirtschaft,* March 1969, *24*(1), pp. 27–44.

Bachmura, Frank T. Latin American Brain Drainage. **In** *Hilton, R., ed.,* 1969, pp. 426–44.

Bachurin, A. The Economic Reform in Operation. *Prob. Econ.,* April 1969, *11*(12), pp. 11–25.

Back, Kenneth C. Potential for Organizational Improvement of Property Tax Administration. **In** *Lynn, A. D., Jr., ed.,* 1969, pp. 31–43.

Back, W. B. Estimating Contributions of Natural Resource Investments to Objectives in Regional Economic Development. *Amer. J. Agr. Econ.,* December 1969, *51*(5), pp. 1442–48.

Backer, Morton. Comments on "The Value of the SEC's Accounting Disclosure Requirements." *Accounting Rev.,* July 1969, *44*(3), pp. 533–38.

Bacon, Peter W. and Winn, Edward L., Jr. The Impact of Forced Conversion on Stock Prices. *J. Finance,* December 1969, *24*(5), pp. 871–74.

Bădin, V. and Stoicescu, V. O aplicaţie a lanţurilor Markov la controlul calităţii producţiei. (An Application of Markov Chains to the Control of Production Quality. With English summary.) *Stud. Cercet. Econ.,* 1969, *1-2,* pp. 159–72.

Baer, Walter E. Arbitrating the Discharge and Discipline of Union Officials. *Mon. Lab. Rev.,* September 1969, *92*(9), pp. 39–45.

Baer, Werner. Steel and the Brazilian Economy. **In** *Ellis, H. S., ed.,* 1969, pp. 74–102.

Baerresen, Donald W. Brazil's Participation in LAFTA, 1962–1965. **In** *Ellis, H. S., ed.,* 1969, pp. 266–82.

Baffi, Paolo. International Liquidity and the Reform of the Adjustment Mechanism: Comment. **In** *Samuelson, P. A., ed.,* 1969, pp. 254–58.

Bagchi, Amiya K. A Note on the Theory of Fixed Capital. **In** *[Ghosal, U. N.],* 1969, pp. 18–25.

Baggott, Nancy and Flanders, M. June. Economic Policy in an Open Economy: A Reader's Guide. *Econ. Int.,* November 1969, *22*(4), pp. 593–605.

Bagiotti, Tullio. Die Preistheorie im Prozess wachsender inländischer und internationaler Institutionalisierung. (Price Theory in the Process of Growing Domestic and International Institutionalism. With English summary.) *Weltwirtsch. Arch.,* 1969, *103*(2), pp. 229–48.

______ Parole e fatti sulla massimizzazione del profitto. (Words and Facts on Profit Maximization. With English summary.) *Rivista Int. Sci. Econ. Com.,* July 1969, *16*(7), pp. 637–51.

Bahl, Roy W. and Shellhammer, Kenneth L. Evaluating the State Business Tax Structure: An Application of Input-Output Analysis. *Nat. Tax J.,* June 1969, *22*(2), pp. 203–16.

Bailey, Duncan M. and Cargill, Thomas F. The Military Draft and Future Income. *Western Econ. J.,* December 1969, *7*(4), pp. 365–70.

______ **and Hogan, Timothy D.** Future Growth Patterns in South Africa. *S. Afr. J. Econ.,* September 1969, *37*(3), pp. 237–51.

Bailey, F. A. and Barker, T. C. The Seventeenth-century Origins of Watchmaking in South-west Lancashire. **In** *Harris, J. R., ed.,* 1969, pp. 1–15.

Bailey, Martin J. Capital Gains and Income Taxation. **In** *Harberger, A. C. and Bailey, M. J., eds.,* 1969, pp. 11–49.

Bailey, Norman A. Native and Labor Policy. **In** *Abshire, D. M. and Samuels, M. A., eds.,* 1969, pp. 165–77.

Bailey, Richard. Investment Requirements in Energy. *Nat. Westminster Bank Quart. Rev.,* August 1969, pp. 43–53.

Bain, Joe S. Survival-Ability as a Test of Efficiency. *Amer. Econ. Rev.,* May 1969, *59*(2), pp. 99–104.

Bain, Trevor. Flat Glass: "Industrial Peace" Revisited. *Ind. Relat.,* May 1969, *8*(3), pp. 259–68.

Baines, D. E. and Bean, R. The General Strike on Merseyside. **In** *Harris, J. R., ed.,* 1969, pp. 239–75.

Baird, Charles W. On the Publicness of Health Care. *Rev. Soc. Econ.,* September 1969, *27*(2), pp. 109–20.

Baird, Leonard L. and Holland, John L. The Flow of High School Students to Schools, Colleges, and Jobs: A Re-examination of Some Old Questions by the Use of Multiple Indices of Talent. *J. Human Res.,* Winter 1969, *4*(1), pp. 22–37.

Baitsell, John M.; Sprague, Christopher R. and Taylor, David P. A Computer-Based Negotiation: Uses and Limitations as a Training Device. **In** *Siegel, A. J., ed.,* 1969, pp. 260–85.

Baker, C. B. and Hopkin, John A. Concepts of Finance Capital for a Capital-Using Agriculture. *Amer. J. Agr. Econ.,* December 1969, *51*(5), pp. 1055–64.

______ **and Rodewald, Gordon E., Jr.** Interim Period Asset Valuation: A Method for Making Investment Decisions. *Agr. Econ. Res.,* April 1969, *21*(2), pp. 35–39.

______ **and Rodewald, Gordon E., Jr.** Economics of Investment in Cattle Feeding. *Ill. Agr. Econ.,* January 1969, *9*(1), pp. 18–25.

______ **and Smith, Allen G.** The Effect of Real Estate Debt Commitments on Nonreal Estate Credit and Liquidity of the Farm. *Ill. Agr. Econ.,* January 1969, *9*(1), pp. 1–6.

Baker, Donald I. An Antitrust Look at the One-Bank Holding Company Problem. **In** *Federal Reserve Bank of Chicago (II),* 1969, pp. 125–31.

______ Another Look at Franchise Tie-Ins After Texaco and Fortner. *Antitrust Bull.,* Winter 1969, *14,* pp. 767–83.

Baker, Gladys L. and Rasmussen, Wayne D. Programs for Agriculture, 1933–1965. **In** *Ruttan, V. W.; Waldo, A. D. and Houck, J. P., eds.,* 1969, pp. 69–88.

Baker, J. R. and Williams, R. J. A Comparison of Response Surface and Factorial Designs in Agricultural Research: Reply. *Rev. Marketing Agr. Econ.,* June 1969, *37*(2), pp. 132–33.

Baker, James C. and Verschuur, Jan B. The Versatile Combination Export Manager. *Marquette Bus. Rev.,* Winter 1969, *13*(4), pp. 143–50.

Baker, James E. S. Combinations and Conspiracies —Is There a Difference? *Antitrust Bull.,* Spring 1969, *14,* pp. 71–90.

Baker, Samuel H. Executive Incomes, Profits and Revenues: A Comment of Functional Specification. *Southern Econ. J.,* April 1969, *35*(4), pp. 379–83.

Baker, Samuel W. The Credibility Gap in Financial Communications. *Manage. Account.,* September 1969, *51*(3), pp. 58–59.

Bakke, E. Wight. Union Leadership and the Public Interest. **In** *Somers, G. G., ed. (II),* 1969, pp. 173–82.

Baklanoff, Eric N. External Factors in the Economic Development of Brazil's Heartland: The Center-

South, 1850–1930. In *Baklanoff, E. N., ed.,* 1969, pp. 19–35.

Bălan, M. Gh. Concepţia lui Nicolae Bălcescu cu privire la dezvoltarea forţelor de producţie în Tările Române. (Nicolae Bălcescu's Outlook on the Development of Production Forces in the Romanian Principalities. With English summary.) *Stud. Cercet. Econ.,* 1969, *1-2,* pp. 229–35.

Balassa, Bela. Centralization and Decentralization in Economic Systems: Discussion. *Amer. Econ. Rev.,* May 1969, *59*(2), pp. 533–37.

______ Country Size and Trade Patterns: Comment. *Amer. Econ. Rev.,* March 1969, *59*(1), pp. 201–04.

______ Industrial Development in an Open Economy: The Case of Norway. *Oxford Econ. Pap.,* November 1969, *21*(3), pp. 344–59.

Baldovinos de la Peña, Gabriel. El sector ejidal y el plan agricola nacional. (The Ejidal Sector and the National Agricultural Plan. With English summary.) *Econ. Polít.,* Second Semester 1969, *6*(2), pp. 215–22.

______ La agricultura al final de la década. (The State of Agriculture at the End of the Present Decade. With English summary.) *Econ. Polít.,* Fourth Semester 1969, *6*(4), pp. 453–60.

Baldwin, George B. What Does It Really Mean? Discounted Cash Flow. *Finance Develop.,* September 1969, *6*(3), pp. 30–35.

Baldwin, Robert E. The Case against Infant-Industry Tariff Protection. *J. Polit. Econ.,* May/June 1969, *77*(3), pp. 295–305.

______ Economic Development: Discussion. *Amer. Econ. Rev.,* May 1969, *59*(2), pp. 427–29.

Baldwin, William L. The Feedback Effect of Business Conduct on Industry Structure. *J. Law Econ.,* April 1969, *12*(1), pp. 123–53.

______ **and Childs, Gerald L.** The Fast Second and Rivalry in Research and Development. *Southern Econ. J.,* July 1969, *36*(1), pp. 18–24.

Balestra, Pietro and Schendel, Dan E. Rational Behavior and Gasoline Price Wars. *Appl. Econ.,* May 1969, *1*(2), pp. 89–101.

Baletić, Zvonimir. Agricultural Development and a Stable Growth of Output. *Eastern Europ. Econ.,* Summer 1969, *7*(4), pp. 41–48.

Ball, Robert M. Statement. In *Economics of Aging: Toward a Full Share in Abundance, Pt. 1, SCH,* 1969, pp. 12–25.

Balogh, Thomas. Education and Agrarian Progress in Developing Countries. In *[Edding, Friedrich],* 1969, pp. 259–68.

Balopoulos, Elias T. Measuring the Effects of the Budget on Aggregate Demand and/or Balance of Payments. In *Peacock, A. T., ed.,* 1969, pp. 141–62.

Bambrick, Susan. The 'C' Series: It's Sins of Commission and Omission. *Australian Econ. Hist. Rev.,* March 1969, *9*(1), pp. 53–63.

______ The Reserve Bank Index of Australian Import Prices. *Econ. Rec.,* September 1969, *45*(111), pp. 399–414.

Bandini, Mario. Free Trade and Planning in the Common Agricultural Policy. In *Papi, U. and Nunn, C., eds.,* 1969, pp. 77–84.

Banerji, A. N. Problems of Public Sector Steel Plants. In *Dagli, V., ed., Vol. II,* 1969, pp. 126–29.

Banks, F. E. A Note on a "Keynesian" Model of Aggregate Demand. *J. Finance,* March 1969, *24* (1), pp. 101–03.

______ A Note on Income, Capital Mobility, and the Theory of Economic Policy. *Kyklos,* 1969, *22*(4), pp. 767–73.

Bansal, B. L. Financial Control: Checks and Balances. In *Dagli, V., ed., Vol. II,* 1969, pp. 65–76.

Baqai, Moin and Brecher, Irving. Foreign-Aid Requirements: A Critique of Aid Projections with Special Reference to Pakistan. *Pakistan Develop. Rev.,* Winter 1969, *9*(4), pp. 380–99.

Barach, Jeffrey A. Advertising Effectiveness and Risk in the Consumer Decision Process. *J. Marketing Res.,* August 1969, *6*(3), pp. 314–20.

Barall, Milton. Statement. In *New Directions for the 1970's: Toward a Strategy of Inter-American Development, Pts. 1–5, HCH,* 1969, pp. 227–29.

Baran, Paul A. An Alternative to Marxism. In *Baran, P. A.,* 1969, pp. 43–51.

______ Better Smaller but Better. In *Baran, P. A.,* 1969, pp. 203–09.

______ Comments on *The Political Economy of Growth.* In *Baran, P. A.,* 1969, pp. 316–60.

______ A Few Thoughts on the Great Debate. In *Baran, P. A.,* 1969, pp. 374–87.

______ Marxism and Psychoanalysis. In *Baran, P. A.,* 1969, pp. 92–111.

______ National Economic Planning. In *Baran, P. A.,* 1969, pp. 115–81.

______ On the Nature of Marxism. In *Baran, P. A.,* 1969, pp. 19–42.

______ Reflections on Planning of the Economic Development of India. In *Baran, P. A.,* 1969, pp. 308–15.

______ Reflections on Underconsumption. In *Baran, P. A.,* 1969, pp. 185–202.

______ Social and Economic Planning. In *Baran, P. A.,* 1969, pp. 236–46.

______ The Theory of the Leisure Class. In *Baran, P. A.,* 1969, pp. 210–22.

______ **and Sweezy, Paul M.** Economics of Two Worlds. In *Baran, P. A.,* 1969, pp. 68–91.

Baranson, Jack. Integration Prospects for the Automotive Industry under LAFTA. In *Hilton, R., ed.,* 1969, pp. 261–71.

Barattieri, V. and Polasek, M. U. S. Gold Policy and the Gold Exchange Standard. *Econ. Rec.,* March 1969, *45*(109), pp. 48–68.

Barban, Arnold M. The Dilemma of "Integrated" Advertising. *J. Bus.,* October 1969, *42*(4), pp. 477–96.

Barbash, Jack. Federal Regulation and the Unions: Discussion. In *Somers, G. G., ed. (II),* 1969, pp. 303–05.

______ Rationalization in the American Union. In *Somers, G. G., ed. (I),* 1969, pp. 147–62.

Barber, Clarence L. The Capital-Labor Ratio in Underdeveloped Areas. *Philippine Econ. J.,* First Semester 1969, *8*(1), pp. 85–89.

Barber, William J. James Mill and the Theory of Economic Policy in India. *Hist. Polit. Econ.,* Spring 1969, *1*(1), pp. 85–100.

Barbosa, A. S. Pinto. A Note on Intermediate Public Expenditures. *Arquivo Inst.,* 1969, *4*(1&2), pp. 21–26.

Barbour, Violet. Dutch and English Merchant Shipping in the Seventeenth Century. **In** *Scoville, W. C. and La Force, J. C., eds., Vol. II,* 1969, pp. 108–37.

Barclay, William D. Factorial Design in a Pricing Experiment. *J. Marketing Res.,* November 1969, *6*(4), pp. 427–29.

Bardhan, Kalpana. A Note on Price-Elasticity of Demand for Foodgrain in a Peasant Economy. *Oxford Econ. Pap.,* March 1969, *21*(1), pp. 104–08.

Bardhan, P. K. Optimum Investment for an Open Economy. **In** *[Ghosal, U. N.],* 1969, pp. 74–88.

Bardhan, Pranab. Equilibrium Growth in a Model with Economic Obsolescence of Machines. *Quart. J. Econ.,* May 1969, *83*(2), pp. 312–23.

Barger, Harold. Growth in Developed Nations. *Rev. Econ. Statist.,* May 1969, *51*(2), pp. 143–48.

Barilla', Umberto. Le holdings bancarie negli Stati Uniti. (Bank Holding Companies in the United States. With English summary.) *Bancaria,* August 1969, *25*(8), pp. 963–67.

Barkai, Haim. A Formal Outline of a Smithian Growth Model. *Quart. J. Econ.,* August 1969, *83* (3), pp. 396–414.

Barker, T. C. and Bailey, F. A. The Seventeenth-century Origins of Watchmaking in South-west Lancashire. **In** *Harris, J. R., ed.,* 1969, pp. 1–15.

Barkin, Solomon. The American Debate on the Poor. **In** *O.E.C.D.,* 1969, pp. 121–28.

______ Trade Unions Face a New Western Capitalist Society. *J. Econ. Issues,* March 1969, *3*(1), pp. 49–65.

______ **and Blum, Albert A.** What's to Be Done for Labor? The Trade Unionists' Answer. **In** *Wortman, M. S., Jr.,* 1969, pp. 73–81.

Barlow, Robin. A Comment on Alternative Federal Policies for Stimulating State and Local Expenditures. *Nat. Tax J.,* June 1969, *22*(2), pp. 282–85.

Barnard, Jerald R. A Social Accounting System for Regional Development Planning. *J. Reg. Sci.,* April 1969, *9*(1), pp. 109–15.

Barnes, William S. Legal Aspects of Economic Integration in Latin America. **In** *Hilton, R., ed.,* 1969, pp. 275–90.

Barnett, Harold J. and Greenberg, Edward. Regulating CATV Systems: An Analysis of FCC Policy and an Alternative. *Law Contemp. Probl.,* Summer 1969, *34*(3), pp. 562–85.

Barnett, Norman L. Beyond Market Segmentation. *Harvard Bus. Rev.,* January–February 1969, *47* (1), pp. 152–66.

Barnhill, J. Allison. An Empirical Analysis of the "Culturation Impact" on Patterns of Food Consumption. *Univ. Wash. Bus. Rev.,* Spring 1969, *28* (3), pp. 33–39.

______ The Application of Engel's Laws of Personal Consumption (1857) to the European Common Market (1957–61). **In** *Alexis, M.; Holloway, R. J. and Hancock, R. S., eds.,* 1969, pp. 95–104.

Barnikel, Hans-Heinrich. Abuse of Power by Dominant Firms: Application of the German Law. *Antitrust Bull.,* Spring 1969, *14,* pp. 221–47.

Barr, Brenton M. and Bater, James H. The Electricity Industry of Central Siberia. *Econ. Geogr.,* October 1969, *45*(4), pp. 349–69.

Barr, Wallace. A Basic Framework for Policy Education: Discussion. *Amer. J. Agr. Econ.,* December 1969, *51*(5), pp. 1365–67.

Barre, Raymond. La Communità Europea e i problemi monetari internazionali. (The European Economic Community and International Monetary Problems. With English summary.) *Bancaria,* July 1969, *25*(7), pp. 897–901.

Barrère, A. Internal Consistency in the Public Economy: The Plan and the Market. **In** *Margolis, J. and Guitton, H., eds.,* 1969, pp. 22–53.

Barrett, Martin and Greene, Margaret L. Special Drawing Rights: A Major Step in the Evolution of the World's Monetary System. **In** *Officer, L. H. and Willett, T. D., eds.,* 1969, pp. 143–50.

Barron, James C. and Long, Burl F. Conflicts within Recreation: Comment. *Land Econ.,* February 1969, *45*(1), pp. 128–31.

Barrow, Roscoe L. and Manelli, Daniel J. Communications Technology—A Forecast of Change (Part II). *Law Contemp. Probl.,* Summer 1969, *34*(3), pp. 431–51.

______ Communications Technology—A Forecast of Change (Part I). *Law Contemp. Probl.,* Spring 1969, *34*(2), pp. 205–43.

Barsby, Steven L. Economic Backwardness and the Characteristics of Development. *J. Econ. Hist.,* September 1969, *29*(3), pp. 449–72.

Barsky, Donald T. and Felt, Howard M. Purchase vs. Lease: Computer Obsolescence. *Manage. Account.,* October 1969, *51*(4), pp. 29–32.

Barsness, Richard W. Policy Challenges and Objectives of the Department of Transportation. *Quart. Rev. Econ. Bus.,* Spring 1969, *9*(1), pp. 63–76.

Barten, A. P.; Kloek, T. and Lempers, F. B. A Note on a Class of Utility and Production Functions Yielding Everywhere Differentiable Demand Functions. *Rev. Econ. Stud.,* January 1969, *36* (105), pp. 109–11.

Barth, Peter S. An Economist Looks at Welfare Programs. *Ohio State U. Bull. Bus. Res.,* October 1969, *44*(10), pp. 1–5.

______ Social Security and Economic Development: A Quantitative Approach—Comment. *Ind. Lab. Relat. Rev.,* January 1969, *22*(2), pp. 257–59.

Barth, Richard and Havrilesky, Thomas. Tests of Market Share Stability in the Cigarette Industry 1950–66. *J. Ind. Econ.,* April 1969, *17*(2), pp. 145–50.

______ **and Havrilesky, Thomas.** Non-Price Competition in the Cigarette Industry. *Antitrust Bull.,* Fall 1969, *14,* pp. 607–28.

Barthelemy, Serge. La Methode de Projection à Moyen Terme des Circuits Financiers Utilisée dans la Préparation du Ve Plan Français. (With English summary.) *Rev. Income Wealth,* March 1969, *15*(1), pp. 77–100.

Barzel, Yoram. The Growth of Sales *Per* Man-Hour in Retail Trade, 1929–1963: Discussion. **In** *Fuchs, V. R., ed.,* 1969, pp. 230–33.

______ Productivity and the Price of Medical Services. *J. Polit. Econ.,* November/December 1969, *77*(6), pp. 1014–27.

______ Two Propositions on the Optimum Level of

Producing Collective Goods. *Public Choice,* Spring 1969, *6,* pp. 31–37.

Basno, C. Aplicarea creditării diferențiate a întreprinderilor. (Application of Differentiated Crediting of Enterprises. With English summary.) *Stud. Cercet. Econ.,* 1969, *1-2,* pp. 93–105.

Basora, Adrian A. Cuba: Castroist Command. **In** *Prybyla, J. S., ed.,* 1969, pp. 428–41.

Bass, Frank M. A Simultaneous Equation Regression Study of Advertising and Sale of Cigarettes. *J. Marketing Res.,* August 1969, *6*(3), pp. 291–300.

______ **and Parsons, Leonard J.** Simultaneous-Equation Regression Analysis of Sales and Advertising. *Appl. Econ.,* May 1969, *1*(2), pp. 103–24.

______**; Pessemier, E. A. and Tigert, D. J.** A Taxonomy of Magazine Readership Applied to Problems in Marketing Strategy and Media Selection. *J. Bus.,* July 1969, *42*(3), pp. 337–63.

Bassett, Glenn A. The Qualifications of a Manager. *Calif. Manage. Rev.,* Winter 1969, *12*(2), pp. 35–44.

Bassett, Lowell R. Returns to Scale and Cost Curves. *Southern Econ. J.,* October 1969, *36*(2), pp. 189–90.

______ **and Borcherding, Thomas E.** "Inferior Factors" and the Theories of Production and Input Demand: Comment. *Economica, N.S.,* August 1969, *36*(143), pp. 321–22.

Basso, Louis G. PPBS in Wayne County, Michigan. **In** *Innovations in Planning, Programming, and Budgeting in State and Local Governments, JECP,* 1969, pp. 191–211.

Bateman, Fred. Issues in the Measurement of Efficiency of American Dairy Farming, 1850–1910: A Reply. *J. Econ. Hist.,* September 1969, *29*(3), pp. 506–11.

______ Labor Inputs and Productivity in American Dairy Agriculture, 1850–1910. *J. Econ. Hist.,* June 1969, *29*(2), pp. 206–29.

Bateman, Merrill J. Statement. **In** *Highway Legislation, HCH,* 1969, pp. 169–73.

Bater, James H. and Barr, Brenton M. The Electricity Industry of Central Siberia. *Econ. Geogr.,* October 1969, *45*(4), pp. 349–69.

Bates, A. Allen. Low Cost Housing in the Soviet Union. **In** *Industrialized Housing, JECP,* 1969, pp. 1–21.

Bates, Marston. The Human Ecosystem. **In** *National Academy of Sciences,* 1969, pp. 21–30.

Bates, W. R. and Wells, J. M. Changes in Farm Business Organisation in Australia. *Quart. Rev. Agr. Econ.,* April 1969, *22*(2), pp. 53–65.

______ A Note on Some Implications of Family Partnership Formation for Farm Income Comparisons. *Quart. Rev. Agr. Econ.,* July 1969, *22*(3), pp. 140–46.

Batra, Raveendra N. Activity Analysis and the Pure Theory of International Trade. *Amer. Econ.,* Spring 1969, *13*(1), pp. 16–27.

______ Changes in Factor-Endowment, the Terms of Trade, and Factor-Price Equalisation. *Amer. Econ.,* Fall 1969, *13*(2), pp. 57–69.

Battistel, Ezio. Collocazione organizzativa della direzione commerciale. (The Status of Commercial Management within the Organization. With English summary.) *L'Impresa,* July/October 1969, *11*(4–5), pp. 336–39.

______ I quadri direttivi nella "media" azienda industriale italiana. (Middle Management in the Italian "Medium-Sized" Industrial Firm. With English summary.) *L'Impresa,* March/April 1969, *11*(2), pp. 143–46.

Battistella, Roger and Southby, Richard McK. Crisis in American Medicine. **In** *Health Care in America, Pt. 1, SCH,* 1969, pp. 139–47.

Baturin, F. and Shemetov, P. Activities of Siberian Economists. *Prob. Econ.,* November 1969, *12*(7), pp. 67–77.

Bauchet, P. The Coherence of Public Enterprises: Planning v. Market Forces. **In** *Margolis, J. and Guitton, H., eds.,* 1969, pp. 462–74.

Bauer, Larry L. The Effect of Technology on the Farm Labor Market. *Amer. J. Agr. Econ.,* August 1969, *51*(3), pp. 605–18.

Bauer, Peter T. Development Economics: The Spurious Consensus and Its Background. **In** *[von Hayek, Friedrich A.],* 1969, pp. 5–45.

______ Dissent on Development. *Scot. J. Polit. Econ.,* February 1969, *16*(1), pp. 75–94.

Bauman, W. Scott. The School Calendar Dilemma—A Solution for the Approaching Crisis. *Oregon Bus. Rev.,* June 1969, *28*(6), pp. 1–5.

Baumann, Duane D. Perception and Public Policy in the Recreational Use of Domestic Water Supply Reservoirs. *Water Resources Res.,* June 1969, *5*(3), pp. 543–54.

Baumgartner, Leona. Governmental Responsibility for Family Planning in the United States. **In** *Behrman, S. J.; Corsa, L., Jr. and Freedman, R., eds.,* 1969, pp. 435–48.

Baumgartner, Wilfrid. La funzione monetaria dell'oro nei prossimi dieci anni: Intervento. (The Role of Monetary Gold Over the Next Ten Years: Discussion. With English summary.) *Bancaria,* November 1969, *25*(11), pp. 1342–43.

Baumol, William J. Macroeconomics of Unbalanced Growth: Comment on the Comment. *Amer. Econ. Rev.,* Part I, September 1969, *59*(4), pp. 632.

______ On the Discount Rate for Public Projects. **In** *The Analysis and Evaluation of Public Expenditures: The PPB System, Vol. 1, JECP,* 1969, pp. 489–503.

______ On the Social Rate of Discount: Comment on the Comments. *Amer. Econ. Rev.,* December 1969, *59*(5), pp. 930.

______ Performance of the Firm and Performance of Its Stocks. **In** *Manne, H. G., ed.,* 1969, pp. 127–41.

______ **and Quandt, Richard E.** The Demand for Abstract Transport Modes: Some Hopes. *J. Reg. Sci.,* April 1969, *9*(1), pp. 159–62.

Bawden, D. Lee and Wipf, Larry J. Reliability of Supply Equations Derived from Production Functions. *Amer. J. Agr. Econ.,* February 1969, *51* (1), pp. 170–78.

Baxter, Nevins D. Why Federal Funds? **In** *Jessup, P. F.,* 1969, pp. 50–60.

______**; Howrey, E. Philip and Penner, R. G.** Unemployment and Cost-Benefit Analysis. *Public Finance,* 1969, *24*(1), pp. 80–88.

Baxter, W. T. Inflation and Accounts. **In** *Carsberg, B. V. and Edey, H. C., eds.,* 1969, pp. 50–72.

______ **and Oxenfeldt, A. R.** Approaches to Pricing: Economist *Versus* Accountant. **In** *Carsberg, B. V. and Edey, H. C., eds.,* 1969, pp. 184–208.

Bayless, D. L. and Rao, J. N. K. An Empirical Study of the Stabilities of Estimators and Variance Estimators in Unequal Probability Sampling of Two Units per Stratum. *J. Amer. Statist. Assoc.,* June 1969, *64*(326), pp. 540–59.

Beach, Edwin W. California's Programing and Budgeting System. **In** *Innovations in Planning, Programming, and Budgeting in State and Local Governments, JECP,* 1969, pp. 27–35.

Beale, Calvin L. Statement. **In** *Population Trends, Pt. 1, HCH,* 1969, pp. 473–97.

Beales, H. L. The Industrial Revolution. **In** *Scoville, W. C. and La Force, J. C., eds., Vol. III,* 1969, pp. 17–23.

______ The "Great Depression" in Industry and Trade. **In** *Scoville, W. C. and La Force, J. C., eds., Vol. IV,* 1969, pp. 97–107.

Bean, Judy Ann and Simmons, W. R. Impact of Design and Estimation Components on Inference. **In** *Johnson, N. L. and Smith, H., Jr., eds.,* 1969, pp. 601–28.

Bean, Lee L. and Bhatti, A. D. Three Years on Pakistan's New National Family-Planning Programme. *Pakistan Develop. Rev.,* Spring 1969, *9*(1), pp. 35–57.

Bean, R. and Baines, D. E. The General Strike on Merseyside. **In** *Harris, J. R., ed.,* 1969, pp. 239–75.

Beard, Thomas R. Government Revenues and Expenditures in Louisiana. **In** *Beard, T. R., ed.,* 1969, pp. 173–230.

______ **and Duggar, Jan Warren.** Federal Reserve Proposals for Reform of the Discount Mechanism. *Southern Econ. J.,* October 1969, *36*(2), pp. 122–33.

______ **and Duggar, Jan Warren.** Member Bank Borrowing. *Quart. Rev. Econ. Bus.,* Autumn 1969, *9* (3), pp. 72–77.

______ **and Selby, Edward B., Jr.** Growth, Structure, and Adequacy of Commercial Banking in Louisiana. **In** *Beard, T. R., ed.,* 1969, pp. 105–32.

Bechdolt, B. V., Jr. and Niedercorn, J. H. An Economic Derivation of the "Gravity Law" of Spatial Interaction. *J. Reg. Sci.,* August 1969, *9*(2), pp. 273–82.

Beck, Darwin L.; Weaver, Mary F. and Fry, Edward R. Revision of Money Stock Series. *Fed. Res. Bull.,* October 1969, *55*(10), pp. 787–803.

Becker, Arthur P. Principles of Taxing Land and Buildings for Economic Development. **In** *Becker, A. P., ed.,* 1969, pp. 11–47.

______ Property Tax Problems Confronting State and Local Governments. **In** *[White, Charles P.],* 1969, pp. 34–47.

Becker, Hellmut. Friedrich Edding's Contribution to the Economics of Education and to Educational Research. **In** *[Edding, Friedrich],* 1969, pp. 17–23.

Beckford, George L. The Economics of Agricultural Resource Use and Development in Plantation Economies. *Soc. Econ. Stud.,* December 1969, *18* (4), pp. 321–47.

Beckmann, Martin J. Market Shares and Distance. *Swedish J. Econ.,* June 1969, *71*(2), pp. 53–63.

______ On the Distribution of Urban Rent and Residential Density. *J. Econ. Theory,* June 1969, *1*(1), pp. 60–67.

______ **and Ryder, Harl E., Jr.** Simultaneous Price and Quantity Adjustment in a Single Market. *Econometrica,* July 1969, *37*(3), pp. 470–84.

______ **and Sato, Ryuzo.** Aggregate Production Functions and Types of Technical Progress: A Statistical Analysis. *Amer. Econ. Rev.,* March 1969, *59*(1), pp. 88–101.

______ **and Wallace, James P.** Continuous Lags and the Stability of Market Equilibrium. *Economica, N.S.,* February 1969, *36*(141), pp. 58–68.

Bedford, Norton M. and Lee, Lucy C. An Information Theory Analysis of the Accounting Process. *Accounting Rev.,* April 1969, *44*(2), pp. 256–75.

Bee, Robert L. Tribal Leadership in the War on Poverty: A Case Study. *Soc. Sci. Quart.,* December 1969, *50*(3), pp. 676–86.

Beechy, Thomas H. Quasi-Debt Analysis of Financial Leases. *Accounting Rev.,* April 1969, *44*(2), pp. 375–81.

Beernaert, Luc and Laevaert, Ludo. De Tienermarkt: Analyse van enkele karakteristieken. (The Teenager Market: An Analysis of Some Characteristics. With English summary.) *Econ. Soc. Tijdschr.,* December 1969, *23*(6), pp. 663–74.

Beesley, M. E. and Politi, Janet. A Study of the Profits of Bus Companies, 1960–1966. *Economica, N.S.,* May 1969, *36*(142), pp. 151–71.

Beever, E. A. A Reply to Mr. Fogarty's Note. *Australian Econ. Hist. Rev.,* March 1969, *9*(1), pp. 78–80.

Behman, Sara. Wage Changes, Institutions, and Relative Factor Prices in Manufacturing. *Rev. Econ. Statist.,* August 1969, *51*(3), pp. 227–38.

Behrend, Hilde; Knowles, Ann and Davies, Jean. 'Have You Heard the Phrase "Productivity Agreements"?' Findings from Two National Sample Surveys. *Scot. J. Polit. Econ.,* November 1969, *16*(3), pp. 256–70.

Behrman, Jack N. Assessing the Foreign Investment Controls. *Law Contemp. Probl.,* Winter 1969, *34* (1), pp. 84–94.

______ Statement. **In** *To Extend and Amend the Export Control Act of 1949, HCH,* 1969, pp. 14–16.

______ Statement. **In** *Overseas Private Investment Corporation, HCH,* 1969, pp. 164–71.

Beier, Emerson H. Financing Supplemental Unemployment Benefit Plans. *Mon. Lab. Rev.,* November 1969, *92*(11), pp. 31–35.

Beighley, H. Prescott and Mak, James. The Effect of a Marketing Order on Winter Carrot Prices: Comment. *Amer. J. Agr. Econ.,* November 1969, *51*(4), pp. 929–33.

Beijer, G. Brain Drain as a Burden, a Stimulus and a Challenge to European Integration. **In** *Bechhofer, F., ed.,* 1969, pp. 3–30.

Beika, Minoru. The Change in Regional Characteristics of Industries in Japan. *Kobe Econ. Bus. Rev.,* 1969, *16*(1), pp. 1–18.

Beker, Víctor Alberto. Elasticidades de oferta de la producción agropecuaria: trigo, maíz y carne vacuna. (Elasticities of Supply in Agricultural Production: Wheat, Maize and Beef. With English summary.) *Económica,* May–August 1969, *15*(2), pp. 145–81.

Belasco, James A. and Alutto, Joseph A. Organizational Impacts of Teacher Negotiations. *Ind. Relat.,* October 1969, *9*(1), pp. 67–79.

Belcher, D. W. The Changing Nature of Compensation Administration. *Calif. Manage. Rev.,* Summer 1969, *11*(4), pp. 89–94.

Belden, S. A.; Saathoff, C. R. and Babb, E. M. An Analysis of Cooperative Bargaining in the Processing Tomato Industry. *Amer. J. Agr. Econ.,* February 1969, *51*(1), pp. 13–25.

Belianova, A. M. The Problem of the Rates of Economic Development in the U.S.S.R. as Treated in the Soviet Economic Literature of the 1920's. *Prob. Econ.,* April 1969, *11*(12), pp. 47–55.

Bell, David E.; Hardin, Lowell S. and Hill, F. F. Hope for the Hungry: Fulfillment or Frustration? **In** *Hardin, C. M., ed.,* 1969, pp. 137–70.

Bell, Frederick W. and Murphy, Neil B. Economies of Scale in Commercial Banking (Parts I and III). **In** *Jessup, P. F.,* 1969, pp. 265–82.

_____ Impact of Market Structure on the Price of a Commercial Banking Service. *Rev. Econ. Statist.,* May 1969, *51*(2), pp. 210–13.

_____ The Impact of Regulation on Inter- and Intraregional Variation in Commercial Banking Costs. *J. Reg. Sci.,* August 1969, *9*(2), pp. 225–38.

Bell, Geoffrey L. Credit Creation through Euro-dollars? **In** *Chalmers, E. B., ed.,* 1969, pp. 38–50.

Bell, Peter F. and Tai, Janet. Markets, Middlemen and Technology: Agricultural Supply Response in the Dualistic Economies of Southeast Asia. *Malayan Econ. Rev.,* April 1969, *14*(1), pp. 29–47.

Bell, Philip W. Price Changes and Income Measurement. **In** *Parker, R. H. and Harcourt, G. C., eds.,* 1969, pp. 185–92.

Bellettini, Athos. L'analisi della struttura e della dinamica della popolazione urbana attraverso la gestione automatizzata dell'anagrafe comunale. (With English summary.) *Statistica,* October-December 1969, *29*(4), pp. 535–62.

Belli, Claudio. Direzione del personale: un'ipotesi sociologica. (A Sociological Hypothesis on the Function of Personnel Management in the Firm. With English summary.) *L'Impresa,* March/April 1969, *11*(2), pp. 138–42.

_____ Il dirigente potere centrale dell' impresa. (The Manager: Central Power in the Firm. With English summary.) *L'Impresa,* July/October 1969, *11*(4–5), pp. 365–72.

Bellman, Richard and Roth, Robert. Curve Fitting by Segmented Straight Lines. *J. Amer. Statist. Assoc.,* September 1969, *64*(327), pp. 1079–84.

Belsare, S. K. International Liquidity Problems and the Developing Countries. **In** *Bhuleshkar, A. V., ed.,* 1969, pp. 425–45.

Belth, Joseph M. The Relationship between Benefits and Premiums in Life Insurance. *J. Risk Ins.,* March 1969, *36*(1), pp. 19–39.

_____ The Retail Price Structure in American Life Insurance: Reply. *J. Risk Ins.,* September 1969, *36* (4), pp. 495–96.

Beltrame, Carlo. Le merchant banks britanniche. (British Merchant Banks. With English summary.) *L'Impresa,* January/February 1969, *11*(1), pp. 68–71.

Bénard, J. Comments on the Papers on East-West Trade. **In** *Samuelson, P. A., ed.,* 1969, pp. 134–38.

Bender, Lloyd D. and Kuehn, John A. An Empirical Identification of Growth Centers. *Land Econ.,* November 1969, *45*(4), pp. 435–43.

Benet, I. and Berend, I. Relative Capital Intensity of Food Production and Industry. *Acta Oecon.,* 1969, *4*(4), pp. 379–402.

Benjamin, B. Statistics in Town Planning. *J. Roy. Statist. Soc.,* Part 1, 1969, *132,* pp. 1–15.

Bennathan, E. and Walters, A. A. Revenue Pooling and Cartels. *Oxford Econ. Pap.,* July 1969, *21*(2), pp. 161–76.

Bennett, J. W.; Graham, K. R. and Hoa, Tran Van. The Determination of Yields on Corporate Shares: An Empirical Study. *Econ. Rec.,* December 1969, *45*(112), pp. 496–512.

Bennett, Peter D. and Mandell, Robert M. Prepurpose Information Seeking Behavior of New Car Purchasers—The Learning Hypothesis. *J. Marketing Res.,* November 1969, *6*(4), pp. 430–33.

Bennis, Warren G. Values and Organization in a University Social Research Group. **In** *Crawford, E. T. and Biderman, A. D., eds.,* 1969, pp. 92–99.

Benson, Richard A. Trade Credit in the Fertilizer Industry: Theory and Practice. *Agr. Finance Rev.,* July 1969, *30,* pp. 21–33.

Benston, George J. An Analysis and Evaluation of Alternative Reserve Requirement Plans. *J. Finance,* December 1969, *24*(5), pp. 849–70.

_____ The Effectiveness and Effects of the SEC's Accounting Disclosure Requirements. **In** *Manne, H. G., ed.,* 1969, pp. 23–79.

_____ The Value of the SEC's Accounting Disclosure Requirements. *Accounting Rev.,* July 1969, *44*(3), pp. 515–32.

Bentick, B. L. Foreign Borrowing, Wealth, and Consumption: Victoria 1873–93. *Econ. Rec.,* September 1969, *45*(111), pp. 415–31.

Berelson, Bernard. National Family Planning Programs: Where We Stand. **In** *Behrman, S. J.; Corsa, L., Jr. and Freedman, R., eds.,* 1969, pp. 341–87.

Berend, I. and Benet, I. Relative Capital Intensity of Food Production and Industry. *Acta Oecon.,* 1969, *4*(4), pp. 379–402.

Berezniak, E. S. Structuring the Network of Schools in the Ukrainian S.S.R. **In** *Noah, H. J., ed.,* 1969, pp. 196–204.

Berg, Elliot J. Urban Real Wages and the Nigerian Trade Union Movement, 1939–60: A Comment. *Econ. Develop. Cult. Change,* July 1969, *17*(4), pp. 604–17.

_____ Wage Structures in Less Developed Countries. **In** *Smith, A. D., ed.,* 1969, pp. 294–337.

Berg, Norman A. What's Different about Conglomerate Management? *Harvard Bus. Rev.,* November–December 1969, *47*(6), pp. 112–20.

Berger, Paul D. and Lin, Chi-Yuan. On the Selling Price and Buying Price of a Lottery. *Amer. Statist.,* December 1969, *23*(5), pp. 25–26.

Bergmann, Barbara R. The Urban Economy and the "Urban Crisis." *Amer. Econ. Rev.,* Part I, September 1969, *59*(4), pp. 639–45.

Bergsman, Joel and Candal, Arthur. Industrialization: Past Success and Future Problems. **In** *Ellis, H. S., ed.,* 1969, pp. 29–73.

——— **and Morley, Samuel A.** Import Constraints and Development: Causes of the Recent Decline of Brazilian Economic Growth: A Comment. *Rev. Econ. Statist.,* February 1969, *51*(1), pp. 101–02.

Bergson, Abram. Centralization and Decentralization in Economic Systems: Discussion. *Amer. Econ. Rev.,* May 1969, *59*(2), pp. 537.

Bergström, Stig-Erik. Prognoser som underkag för beslutsfattandet inom företaget. (Forecasting as a Basis for Decision-Making within the Enterprise. With English summary.) *Econ. Samfundets Tidskr.,* 1969, *22*(2), pp. 105–25.

Berle, A. A. Statement. **In** *Bank Holding Company Act Amendments, Pts. 1–3, HCH,* 1969, pp. 15–20.

Berls, Robert H. An Exploration of the Determinants of Effectiveness in Higher Education. **In** *the Economics and Financing of Higher Education in the United States, JECP,* 1969, pp. 207–60.

——— Higher Education Opportunity and Achievement in the United States. **In** *the Economics and Financing of Higher Education in the United States, JECP,* 1969, pp. 145–204.

Bernardo, Robert M. Why It Is Cheap, Not Dear, to Marry a Ph.D. *J. Polit. Econ.,* September/October 1969, *77*(5), pp. 862.

Bernášek, Miloslav. The Czechoslovak Economic Recession, 1962–65. *Soviet Stud.,* April 1969, *20*(4), pp. 444–61.

Berney, Robert E. The Incidence of the Draft—Is It Progressive? *Western Econ. J.,* September 1969, *7*(3), pp. 244–47.

Bernhard, Richard H. Mathematical Programming Models for Capital Budgeting—A Survey, Generalization, and Critique. *J. Financial Quant. Anal.,* June 1969, *4*(2), pp. 111–58.

Bernholz, Peter. Einige Bemerkungen zur Devisenterminpolitik der Deutschen Bundesbank. (Forward Exchange Policies of the German Bundesbank: Some Critical Comments. With English summary.) *Jahr. Nationalökon. Statist.,* May 1969, *182*(6), pp. 479–89.

Bernstein, Edward M. The Future of Gold: Discussion. *Amer. Econ. Rev.,* May 1969, *59*(2), pp. 349–51.

Berry, Brian J. L. and Neils, Elaine. Location, Size, and Shape of Cities as Influenced by Environmental Factors: The Urban Environment Writ Large. **In** *Perloff, H. S., ed.,* 1969, pp. 257–302.

Berry, R. Albert. A Note on Welfare Comparisons between Monopoly and Pure Competition. *Manchester Sch. Econ. Soc. Stud.,* March 1969, *37*(1), pp. 39–57.

——— **and Hymer, Stephen H.** A Note on the Capacity to Transform and the Welfare Costs of Foreign Trade Fluctuations. *Econ. J.,* December 1969, *79*(316), pp. 833–46.

——— **and Soligo, Ronald.** Some Welfare Aspects of International Migration. *J. Polit. Econ.,* September/October 1969, *77*(5), pp. 778–94.

Bershad, Max A. and Tepping, Benjamin J. The Development of Household Sample Surveys. *J. Amer. Statist. Assoc.,* December 1969, *64*(328), pp. 1134–40.

Berson, Theodore M. "Dependência do Imperialismo": Foreign Investment in Brazil, 1935. *Bus. Hist. Rev.,* Summer 1969, *43*(2), pp. 192–203.

Bertrand, Raymond. Prospects for Integration of European Capital Markets: A Comment. *J. Money, Credit, Banking,* August 1969, *1*(3), pp. 347–49.

Bertrand, Robert J. Comments on the Williams Paper. *J. Risk Ins.,* June 1969, *36*(2), pp. 237–38.

Bertrand, T. J. and Vanek, Jaroslav. Growth with Technological Change, Variable Returns to Scale, and a General Saving Function. *Rivista Int. Sci. Econ. Com.,* August 1969, *16*(8), pp. 741–55.

Beskid, Lidia. Real Wages in Poland During 1956–1967. *Eastern Europ. Econ.,* Spring 1969, *7*(3), pp. 29–47.

Besner, Arthur and Irelan, Lola M. Low-Income Life Styles. **In** *Sturdivant, F. D., ed.,* 1969, pp. 17–26.

Bestuzhev-Lada, Igor. Forecasting—An Approach to the Problems of the Future. *Int. Soc. Sci. J.,* 1969, *21*(4), pp. 526–34.

Betancur-Mejia, Gabriel. Latin America. **In** *Bereday, G. Z. F., ed.,* 1969, pp. 264–76.

Beyer, John C. Regional Inequalities and Economic Growth in Malaysia. *Yorkshire Bull. Econ. Soc. Res.,* May 1969, *21*(1), pp. 17–30.

Bhaduri, Amit. On the Significance of Recent Controversies on Capital Theory: A Marxian View. *Econ. J.,* September 1969, *79*(315), pp. 532–39.

Bhagat, A. N. and Kitamura, Hiroshi. Aspects of Regional Harmonization of National Development Plans. **In** *Morgan, T. and Spoelstra, N., eds.,* 1969, pp. 39–56.

Bhagwati, Jagdish N. Optimal Policies and Immiserizing Growth. *Amer. Econ. Rev.,* December 1969, *59*(5), pp. 967–70.

——— **and Chakravarty, Sukhamoy.** Contributions to Indian Economic Analysis: A Survey. *Amer. Econ. Rev.,* Part II, September 1969, *59*(4), pp. 2–73.

——— **and Kemp, Murray C.** Ranking of Tariffs under Monopoly Power in Trade. *Quart. J. Econ.,* May 1969, *83*(2), pp. 330–35.

———**; Ramaswami, V. K. and Srinivasan, T. N.** Domestic Distortions, Tariffs, and the Theory of Optimum Subsidy: Some Further Results. *J. Polit. Econ.,* November/December 1969, *77*(6), pp. 1005–10.

——— **and Srinivasan, T. N.** Optimal Intervention to Acheive Non-Economic Objectives. *Rev. Econ. Stud.,* January 1969, *36*(105), pp. 27–38.

Bhandari, M. C. Budgeting and Materials Management. **In** *Dagli, V., ed., Vol. II,* 1969, pp. 146–52.

Bhatia, B. M. Terms of Trade and Economic Development: A Case Study of India—1861–1939. *Indian Econ. J.,* April–June 1969, *16*(4–5), pp. 414–33.

Bhatia, Rattan J.; Szapary, Gyorgy and Quinn, Brian. Stabilization Program in Sierra Leone. *Int. Monet. Fund Staff Pap.,* November 1969, *16*(3), pp. 504–28.

Bhatt, Mahesh. Some Implications of Agricultural Income Tax. *Artha-Vikas,* July 1969, *5*(2), pp. 138–45.

Bhatt, S. J. An Approach to the Problem of Creation of Employment Opportunities in Nigeria. **In** *Yesufu, T. M., ed.,* 1969, pp. 261–68.

Bhatt, V. V. On the Magnitude and Allocation of Federal Assistance to the States in India: Some

Rational Criteria. *Public Finance,* 1969, *24*(4), pp. 563–76.

______ **and Divatia, V. V.** On Measuring the Pace of Development. *Banca Naz. Lavoro Quart. Rev.,* June 1969, (89), pp. 190–206.

Bhattacharya, D. Indicatori della scarsità di liquidità internazionale. (Indicators of International Liquidity Shortage. With English summary.) *Rivista Int. Sci. Econ. Com.,* October 1969, *16*(10), pp. 1007–15.

Bhatti, A. D. and Bean, Lee L. Three Years on Pakistan's New National Family-Planning Programme. *Pakistan Develop. Rev.,* Spring 1969, *9*(1), pp. 35–57.

Bhatty, I. Z. Conflict and Reconciliation between the Economic, Social, and Industrial Relations Policies. **In** *Johri, C. K., ed.,* 1969, pp. 105–22.

Bhide, M. R. Investment Policy of the L. I. C. **In** *Dagli, V., ed., Vol. II,* 1969, pp. 87–101.

Bhuleshkar, A. V. An Analysis of the Price Movements of Certain Agricultural Commodities Since 1939: Food for Peace and Its Effects of Economic Development. **In** *Bhuleshkar, A. V., ed.,* 1969, pp. 117–36.

______ Devaluation of the Indian Rupee: A Step in the Right Direction. **In** *Bhuleshkar, A. V., ed.,* 1969, pp. 345–50.

______ The Ideas and Goals of Co-operation in Indian Agricultural Development. **In** *Bhuleshkar, A. V., ed.,* 1969, pp. 33–39.

______ The Problem of Productivity and Technical Change in Indian Agriculture: A Theoretical Analysis. **In** *Bhuleshkar, A. V., ed.,* 1969, pp. 103–16.

______ **and Kurihara, Kenneth K.** Democratic Welfare Statecraft in a Developing Economy with an Empirical Application. **In** *Bhuleshkar, A. V., ed.,* 1969, pp. 288–302.

Bićanić, Rudolf. Economics of Socialism in a Developed Country. **In** *Bornstein, M., ed.,* 1969, pp. 222–35.

______ Turning Points in Economic Development and Agricultural Policy. **In** *Papi, U. and Nunn, C., eds.,* 1969, pp. 555–73.

Bichi, C. Repartitia rentei diferențiale. (Distribution of Differential Rent. With English summary.) *Stud. Cercet. Econ.,* 1969, *4,* pp. 59–70.

Bickel, Blaine W. Farm Real Estate Prices 1950–67. *Fed. Res. Bank Kansas City Rev.,* April 1969, pp. 3–9.

Bieberstein, J. The German Cartel Law and Its Administration: Role of the Federal Cartel Office in Regard to the E.E.C. Antitrust Provisions. **In** *Economic Concentration, Pt. 7A, SCH,* 1969, pp. 4038–58.

Bieda, K. Economic Planning in Japan. *Econ. Rec.,* June 1969, *45*(110), pp. 181–205.

Biedenkopt, K. H. Ordnungspolitische Probleme der Konzentration. (With English summary.) **In** *Economic Concentration, Pt. 7A, SCH,* 1969, pp. 4058–65.

Biehl, Dieter. Measuring the Effects of the Budget on Aggregate Demand and/or Balance of Payments: Comment. **In** *Peacock, A. T., ed.,* 1969, pp. 163–69.

Bienaymé, A. and Ohlin, Goran. Replies to Comments. **In** *Samuelson, P. A., ed.,* 1969, pp. 230–31.

Bienefeld, M. A. The Normal Week under Collective Bargaining. *Economica, N.S.,* May 1969, *36* (142), pp. 172–92.

Bierman, Harold, Jr. Accelerated Depreciation and Rate Regulation. *Accounting Rev.,* January 1969, *44*(1), pp. 65–78.

______ **and Davidson, Sidney.** The Income Concept—Value Increment or Earnings Predictor. *Accounting Rev.,* April 1969, *44*(2), pp. 239–46.

Bierwag, G. O.; Grove, M. A. and Khang, Chulsoon. National Debt in a Neoclassical Growth Model: Comment. *Amer. Econ. Rev.,* March 1969, *59*(1), pp. 205–10.

Biggeri, Luigi. Su un metodo di previsione della popolazione attiva a livello regionale. (With English summary.) *Statistica,* July-September 1969, *29*(3), pp. 343–76.

Biji, El.; Biji, Mircea and Ivănescu, I. Preocupări actuale în statistica social-economică. (Present Preoccupations in Socio-Economical Statistics. With English summary.) *Stud. Cercet. Econ.,* 1969, *1-2,* pp. 121–28.

Biji, Mircea. Dezvoltarea științei în R. S. România. (Development of Science on the Socialist Republic of Romania. With English summary.) *Stud. Cercet. Econ.,* 1969, *3,* pp. 19–28.

______**; Ivănescu, I. and Biji, El.** Preocupări actuale în statistica social-economică. (Present Preoccupations in Socio-Economical Statistics. With English summary.) *Stud. Cercet. Econ.,* 1969, *1-2,* pp. 121–28.

Bilas, Richard A. Third Degree Price Discrimination and the Multiple Plant Monopolist: A Note on the Allocation of Output. *Southern Econ. J.,* July 1969, *36*(1), pp. 82–86.

Billia, Gianni. Inserimento dell'uomodirigente nel sistema. (How a Manager Becomes a Part of the System. With English summary.) *L'Impresa,* May/June 1969, *11*(3), pp. 237–41.

Billings, R. Bruce. The Mathematical Identity of the Multipliers Derived from the Economic Base Model and the Input-Output Model. *J. Reg. Sci.,* December 1969, *9*(3), pp. 471–73.

Bilsen, Robert. Marktbenadering, marktstructuur en ondernemingsdimensie. (Market Approach, Market Structure and the Dimension of the Firm. With English summary.) *Econ. Soc. Tijdschr.,* December 1969, *23*(6), pp. 537–45.

Bingham, Jonathan B. Can Military Spending Be Controlled? *Foreign Aff.,* October 1969, *48*(1), pp. 51–66.

Biolley, T. and Paelinck, J. A Dynamic Model for the Belgian Economy: Simulation and Optimization. *Econ. Planning,* 1969, *9*(1–2), pp. 155–207.

Birch, John I. and Cramer, Curtis. A Secular Theory of Inflation. *J. Econ. Theory,* December 1969, *1* (4), pp. 480–86.

Bird, Monroe M. Statement. **In** *Proposed Extension of the Surcharge and Repeal of the Investment Tax Credit, SCH,* 1969, pp. 486–88.

Bird, Richard M. and Rhoads, William G. The Valorization Tax in Colombia: An Example for other Developing Countries? **In** *Becker, A. P., ed.,* 1969, pp. 201–37.

Birg, Herwig. Zu einer allgemeinen Theorie des technischen Fortschritts—Kritik der Definitionen von J. R. Hicks und R. F. Harrod. (With

English summary.) *Jahr. Nationalökon. Statist.*, March 1969, *182*(4–5), pp. 327–46.

Birkinsha, Jack E. Investment Income: The Legal Part. *J. Risk Ins.*, September 1969, *36*(4), pp. 463–64.

Birren, James E. The Aged in Cities. **In** *Usefulness of the Model Cities Program to the Elderly, Pt. 1, SCH*, 1969, pp. 138–45.

Bischoff, Charles W. Hypothesis Testing and the Demand for Capital Goods. *Rev. Econ. Statist.*, August 1969, *51*(3), pp. 354–68.

Bish, Robert L. Public Housing: The Magnitude and Distribution of Direct Benefits and Effects on Housing Consumption. *J. Reg. Sci.*, December 1969, *9*(3), pp. 425–38.

Bishop, C. E. The Mobility of Rural Manpower. **In** *Papi, U. and Nunn, C., eds.*, 1969, pp. 283–92.

______ The Need for Improved Mobility Policy. **In** *Ruttan, V. W.; Waldo, A. D. and Houck, J. P., eds.*, 1969, pp. 242–54.

______ Rural Poverty in the Southeast. **In** *Task Force on Economic Growth and Opportunity*, 1969, pp. 75–92.

Bishop, D. The Economics of Industrialized Building. **In** *Industrialized Housing, JECP*, 1969, pp. 201–19.

Bither, Stewart W. Comments on Venkatesan and Haaland's Test of the Festinger-Maccoby Divided Attention Hypothesis. *J. Marketing Res.*, May 1969, *6*(2), pp. 237–38.

Bittker, Boris I. Accounting for Federal "Tax Subsidies" in the National Budget. *Nat. Tax J.*, June 1969, *22*(2), pp. 244–61.

______ Churches, Taxes and the Constitution. *Yale Law J.*, July 1969, *78*(8), pp. 1285–1310.

______ The Income Tax: How Progressive Should It Be?: Rebuttal. **In** *Galvin, C. O. and Bittker, B. I.*, 1969, pp. 61–72.

______ The Income Tax: How Progressive Should It Be?: Second Lecture. **In** *Galvin, C. O. and Bittker, B. I.*, 1969, pp. 27–58.

______ The Tax Expenditure Budget—A Reply to Professors Surrey and Hellmuth. *Nat. Tax J.*, December 1969, *22*(4), pp. 538–42.

Bjarnason, Harold F.; McGarry, Michael J. and Schmitz, Andrew. Converting Price Series of Internationally Traded Commodities to a Common Currency Prior to Estimating National Supply and Demand Equations. *Amer. J. Agr. Econ.*, February 1969, *51*(1), pp. 189–92.

Black, Duncan. Lewis Carroll and the Theory of Games. *Amer. Econ. Rev.*, May 1969, *59*(2), pp. 206–10.

______ On Arrow's Impossibility Theorem. *J. Law Econ.*, October 1969, *12*(2), pp. 227–48.

Black, Guy. The Effect of Government Funding on Commercial R and D. **In** *Gruber, W. H. and Marquis, D. G., eds.*, 1969, pp. 202–18.

Black, J. Foreign Trade and Real Wages. *Econ. J.*, March 1969, *79*(313), pp. 184–85.

______ Two-Level Production Functions. *Economica, N.S.*, August 1969, *36*(143), pp. 310–13.

Black, Stanley W. and Russell, R. Robert. An Alternative Estimate of Potential GNP. *Rev. Econ. Statist.*, February 1969, *51*(1), pp. 70–76.

Black, Stephen. Profit Maximization: Economics' Zombie Concept. *S. Afr. J. Econ.*, September 1969, *37*(3), pp. 264–67.

Blackburn, John O. An Optimal Unemployment Rate: Comment. *Quart. J. Econ.*, August 1969, *83*(3), pp. 518–20.

Bladen, V. W. and Stykolt, Stefan. Combines Policy and the Public Interest: An Economist's Evaluation. **In** *Stykolt, S.*, 1969, pp. 19–54.

Blaich, Fritz. Der private Wohnungsbau in den deutschen Grossstädten während der Krisenjahre 1929–1933. (With English summary.) *Jahr. Nationalökon. Statist.*, December 1969, *183*(5), pp. 435–48.

Blainey, Geoffrey. Mining—And Undermining. *Econ. Rec.*, December 1969, *45*(112), pp. 607–15.

Blair, John M. An Overall View of Conglomerate Concentration. **In** *Garoian, L., ed.*, 1969, pp. 1–20.

______ Conglomerate Mergers—Theory and Congressional Intent. **In** *Weston, J. F. and Peltzman, S., eds.*, 1969, pp. 179–96.

Blake, Harland M. and Jones, William K. In Defense of Antitrust. **In** *Starleaf, D. R., ed.*, 1969, pp. 102–09.

Blake, Judith. Population Policy for Americans: Is the Government Being Misled? **In** *Effects of Population Growth on Natural Resources and the Environment, HCH*, 1969, pp. 189–201.

Blake, Robert R. and Mouton, Jane S. Union-Management Relations: From Conflict to Collaboration. **In** *Wortman, M. S., Jr.*, 1969, pp. 300–309.

Blakely, Edward J. and Thompson, Howard E. Technological Change and Its Effects on Dollar-Value LIFO. *Manage. Account.*, August 1969, *51*(2), pp. 33–38.

Blanchard, M. The Railway Policy of the Second Empire. **In** *Crouzet, F.; Chaloner, W. H. and Stern, W. M., eds.*, 1969, pp. 98–111.

Blank, David M. Tonypandy once Again. *J. Bus.*, January 1969, *42*(1), pp. 104–12.

Blase, Melvin G. The World Food-Population Problem: 1969. *Univ. Missouri Bus. Govt. Rev.*, May–June 1969, *10*(3), pp. 20–27.

Blaug, Mark. The Productivity of Universities. **In** *Blaug, M., ed.*, 1969, pp. 313–25.

______ **and Woodhall, Maureen.** Variations in Costs and Productivity of British Primary and Secondary Education. **In** *[Edding, Friedrich]*, 1969, pp. 69–85.

Blauwens, G. Haveninvesteringen en kostenbatenanalyse: met een toepassing op Antwerpen L.O. (Port Investments and the Costs Benefit Analysis with Special Reference to the Extension of the Port of Antwerp. With English summary.) *Econ. Soc. Tijdschr.*, October 1969, *23*(5), pp. 495–525.

Blevins, Audie L., Jr. Migration Rates in Twelve Southern Metropolitan Areas: A "Push-Pull" Analysis. *Soc. Sci. Quart.*, September 1969, *50*(2), pp. 337–53.

Blischke, W. R.; Truelove, A. J. and Mundle, P. B. On Non-Regular Estimation, I. Variance Bounds for Estimators of Location Parameters. *J. Amer. Statist. Assoc.*, September 1969, *64*(327), pp. 1056–72.

Bliss, Charles A. Absolutism in the Realm of Uncertainty. *Calif. Manage. Rev.*, Spring 1969, *11*(3), pp. 35–42.

Block, Carl E. and Maddox, Robert C. The "Trickle Effect"—A New Management Tool. *Marquette Bus. Rev.*, Spring 1969, *13*(1), pp. 11–14.

Bloede, Victor G. The Advertising Agency of the Future. *Econ. Soc. Tijdschr.*, December 1969, *23* (6), pp. 641–46.

Bloedorn, John. The Strike in the Public Sector. **In** *Walsh, R. E., ed.*, 1969, pp. 250–65.

Blomqvist, Ingvar. Strukturproblem inom metallindustrin. (Structural Problems in the Metal Industry. With English summary.) *Econ. Samfundets Tidskr.*, 1969, *22*(3), pp. 151–63.

Bloomfield, Arthur I. Recent Trends in International Economics. *Ann. Amer. Acad. Polit. Soc. Sci.*, November 1969, *386*, pp. 148–67.

Blough, Roy. The Adjustment Process and the International Role of the Dollar. *J. Finance*, May 1969, *24*(2), pp. 345–59.

______ Basic Tax Issues. **In** *Gaa, C. J.*, 1969, pp. 26–39.

Bluestone, Barry. Black Capitalism: The Path to Black Liberation? *Rev. Radical Polit. Econ.*, May 1969, *1*(1), pp. 36–55.

Blum, Albert A. and Barkin, Solomon. What's to Be Done for Labor? The Trade Unionists' Answer. **In** *Wortman, M. S., Jr.*, 1969, pp. 73–81.

Blum, Reinhard. Die Wechselwirkungen zwischen Wirtschaftspolitik und Wirtschaftstheorie. (The Relations between Economic Policy and Economic Theory. With English summary.) *Schmollers Jahr.*, 1969, *89*(4), pp. 385–407.

Blumenfeld, Hans. Criteria for Judging the Quality of the Urban Environment. **In** *Schmandt, H. J. and Bloomberg, W., Jr., eds.*, 1969, pp. 137–64.

______ The Modern Metropolis. **In** *Callow, A. B., Jr., ed.*, 1969, pp. 166–77.

Blumenthal, Tuvia. A Note on the Life-Cycle Pattern of Saving in Japan. *Hitotsubashi J. Econ.*, February 1969, *9*(2), pp. 61–67.

Blumrosen, Alfred W. A Survey of Remedies for Discrimination in the Union and on the Job. **In** *Somers, G. G., ed. (II)*, 1969, pp. 283–91.

Blyth, C. A. Primitive South Pacific Economies: Their Consumption Pattern and Propensity to Save Out of Cash Income. *Econ. Rec.*, September 1969, *45*(111), pp. 354–72.

Bobrow, Davis B. Improving the Bases for Decision. **In** *Bobrow, D. B., ed.*, 1969, pp. 3–18.

Bocock, Peter W. Impact of Development: Telecommunications in Ethiopia. *Finance Develop.*, December 1969, *6*(4), pp. 15–21.

Bod, P. On a Possible Mathematical Model of Long-Term (15–20 Year) National Economic Planning. *Acta Oecon.*, 1969, *4*(3), pp. 259–67.

Boden, E. A. The Canadian Livestock Industry: Comment. *Can. J. Agr. Econ.*, November 1969, *17* (3), pp. 111–13.

Boehlje, Michael D. and White, T. Kelley. A Production-Investment Decision Model of Farm Firm Growth. *Amer. J. Agr. Econ.*, August 1969, *51*(3), pp. 546–63.

Bog, Ingomar. Mercantilism in Germany. **In** *Coleman, D. C., ed.*, 1969, pp. 162–89.

Bogan, Forrest A. Work Experience of the Population: Spotlight on Women and Youths. *Mon. Lab. Rev.*, June 1969, *92*(6), pp. 44–50.

Bohi, Douglas R. War in Vietnam and United States Balance of Payments. *Rev. Econ. Statist.*, November 1969, *51*(4), pp. 471–74.

Böhm, Volker. Einige Bemerkungen über ein Zwei-Sektoren-Wachstumsmodell mit fixen Produktionskoeffizienten. (With English summary.) *Jahr. Nationalökon. Statist.*, May 1969, *182* (6), pp. 542–50.

Böhme, Hans. Dynamische Preisbildung in der sozialistischen Planwirtschaft der DDR. (Dynamic Price Formation in the Socialist Planned Economy of the G[erman] D[emocratic] R[epublic]. With English summary.) *Jahr. Nationalökon. Statist.*, August 1969, *183*(3–4), pp. 193–242.

Bohnemann, Volker. Preismeldestellen und Wettbewerb. (Open Price Systems and Competition. With English summary.) *Schmollers Jahr.*, 1969, *89*(6), pp. 641–74.

Bohnet, Michael. Wissenschaft und Entwicklungspolitik. (Science and Development. With English summary.) *Ifo-Studien*, 1969, *15*(1/2), pp. 57–92.

Bohrnstedt, George W. and Goldberger, Arthur S. On the Exact Covariance of Products of Random Variables. *J. Amer. Statist. Assoc.*, December 1969, *64*(328), pp. 1439–42.

Boland, L. A. Economic Understanding and Understanding Economics. *S. Afr. J. Econ.*, June 1969, *37*(2), pp. 144–60.

Bolin, William H. Commercial Banks and Latin American Integration. **In** *Hilton, R., ed.*, 1969, pp. 203–09.

Bolton, G. C. Broken Reeds and Smoking Flax. *Australian Econ. Hist. Rev.*, March 1969, *9*(1), pp. 64–70.

Bolton, Roger E. The Economics and Public Financing of Higher Education: An Overview. **In** *the Economics and Financing of Higher Education in the United States, JECP*, 1969, pp. 11–104.

______ Predictive Models for State and Local Government Purchases. **In** *Duesenberry, J. S., et al.*, 1969, pp. 221–67.

Bolza, Hans. Il concetto di rinnovamento come principio guida in economia. (The Concept of Renewal as Leading Idea for All Economic Events. With English summary.) *Rivista Int. Sci. Econ. Com.*, September 1969, *16*(9), pp. 920–29.

Bonaguidi, Alberto. L'aumento del coniugio e la sua influenza sul rialzo della fecondità in Italia. (With English summary.) *Statistica*, October-December 1969, *29*(4), pp. 754–67.

Bonaparte, Tony H. The Influence of Culture on Business in a Pluralistic Society: A Study of Trinidad, West Indies. *Amer. J. Econ. Soc.*, July 1969, *28*(3), pp. 285–300.

Bonello, Frank J. and Russell, William R. Multiple Year Forecast Errors and the Terms Structure of Interest Rates. *Indian Econ. J.*, April–June 1969, *16*(4–5), pp. 554–60.

Bonin, Joseph M.; Finch, B. W. and Waters, Joseph B. Alternative Tests of the "Displacement Effect" Hypothesis. *Public Finance*, 1969, *24*(3), pp. 441–56.

______ **and Ross, William D.** Economic Criteria for

Sound State Debt Financing. **In** *[White, Charles P.],* 1969, pp. 127–47.

Bonnen, James T. The Absence of Knowledge of Distributional Impacts: An Obstacle to Effective Public Program Analysis and Decisions. **In** *The Analysis and Evaluation of Public Expenditures: The PPB System, Vol. 1, JECP,* 1969, pp. 419–49.

——— The Crises in the Traditional Roles of Agricultural Institutions. **In** *Ruttan, V. W.; Waldo, A. D. and Houck, J. P., eds.,* 1969, pp. 48–62.

Bonomo, Vittorio and Schotta, Charles. A Spectral Analysis of Post-Accord Federal Open Market Operations. *Amer. Econ. Rev.,* March 1969, *59*(1), pp. 50–61.

Bontoux, Charles. Considerazioni sul credito documentario trasferibile. (Considerations Regarding Transferable Documentary Credit. With English summary.) *Bancaria,* June 1969, *25*(6), pp. 700–10.

Boon, Gerard K. Factor Intensities in Mexico with Special Reference to Manufacturing. **In** *[Tinbergen, J.],* 1969, pp. 201–18.

Booth, Gordon and Sedransk, J. Planning Some Two-Factor Comparative Surveys. *J. Amer. Statist. Assoc.,* June 1969, *64*(326), pp. 560–73.

Borch, Karl. Another Note on Keynesian Mathematics. *Econ. J.,* March 1969, *79*(313), pp. 182–83.

——— The Capital Structure of a Firm. *Swedish J. Econ.,* March 1969, *71*(1), pp. 1–13.

——— Equilibrium, Optimum and Prejudices in Capital Markets. *J. Financial Quant. Anal.,* March 1969, *4*(1), pp. 1–14.

——— A Note on Uncertainty and Indifference Curves. *Rev. Econ. Stud.,* January 1969, *36*(105), pp. 1–4.

Borcherding, Thomas E. Problems in the Theory of Public Choice: Discussion. *Amer. Econ. Rev.,* May 1969, *59*(2), pp. 211–12.

——— **and Bassett, Lowell R.** "Inferior Factors" and the Theories of Production and Input Demand: Comment. *Economica, N.S.,* August 1969, *36* (143), pp. 321–22.

Borchert, Manfred. An Empirical Investigation of the Heckscher-Ohlin Theory: A Comment. *Economica, N.S.,* May 1969, *36*(142), pp. 193–95.

Bork, Robert H. Vertical Integration and Competitive Processes. **In** *Weston, J. F. and Peltzman, S., eds.,* 1969, pp. 139–49.

——— **and Bowman, Ward S., Jr.** The Crisis in Antitrust. **In** *Starleaf, D. R., ed.,* 1969, pp. 93–102.

Borkar, V. V. Prohibition: An Economic Analysis. **In** *Bhuleshkar, A. V., ed.,* 1969, pp. 395–405.

Bornstein, Morris. The Soviet Debate on Agricultural Price and Procurement Reforms. *Soviet Stud.,* July 1969, *21*(1), pp. 1–20.

Bos, H. C. and Kuyvenhoven, A. Economic Integration and the Optimum International Distribution of Production. **In** *[Tinbergen, J.],* 1969, pp. 93–110.

Bose, Swadesh R. and Clark, Edwin H., II. Some Basic Considerations on Agricultural Mechanization in West Pakistan. *Pakistan Develop. Rev.,* Autumn 1969, *9*(3), pp. 273–308.

Boserup, Mogens. A Note on the Prehistory of the Kahn Multiplier. *Econ. J.,* September 1969, *79* (315), pp. 667–69.

——— Warning against Optimistic ICOR Statistics. *Kyklos,* 1969, *22*(4), pp. 774–76.

Boskin, Michael J. The Negative Income Tax and the Supply of Work Effort: Reply. *Nat. Tax J.,* September 1969, *22*(3), pp. 417.

Bostwick, Don. Effects of Machinery Control Strategies on Income. *Agr. Finance Rev.,* July 1969, *30,* pp. 34–43.

——— Financial Returns in Agriculture. *Amer. J. Agr. Econ.,* August 1969, *51*(3), pp. 662–65.

——— Returns to Farm Resources. *Amer. J. Agr. Econ.,* December 1969, *51*(5), pp. 1528–35.

Botha, D. J. J. Local Taxation in South Africa. *S. Afr. J. Econ.,* December 1969, *37*(4), pp. 393–438.

Botner, Stanley B. Municipal Budgeting: Problems and Developments. *Univ. Missouri Bus. Govt. Rev.,* March–April 1969, *10*(2), pp. 14–26.

Botsas, Eleutherios N. A Note on Migration and the Balance of Payments. *Econ. Int.,* May 1969, *22*(2), pp. 247–51.

Bottomley, Anthony. Wage Rate Determination in Underpopulated, Underdeveloped Rural Areas. *Econ. Int.,* February 1969, *22*(1), pp. 51–62.

——— **and Nudds, Donald.** A Widow's Cruse Theory of Credit Supply in Underdeveloped Rural Areas. *Manchester Sch. Econ. Soc. Stud.,* June 1969, *37*(2), pp. 131–40.

Boughton, James M., et al. A Policy Model of the United States Monetary Sector. *Southern Econ. J.,* April 1969, *35*(4), pp. 333–46.

Boulanger, Raymond P. Public Utilities and the Poor: The Requirement of Cash Deposits from Domestic Consumers. *Yale Law J.,* January 1969, *78*(3), pp. 448–63.

Boulding, Kenneth E. David Fand's "Keynesian Monetary Theories, Stabilization Policy, and the Recent Inflation": A Comment. *J. Money, Credit, Banking,* August 1969, *1*(3), pp. 588–89.

——— Does Absence of Monopoly Power in Agriculture Influence the Stability and Level of Farm Income? **In** *Owen, W. F., ed.,* 1969, pp. 85–94.

——— Economic Education: The Stepchild Too Is Father of the Man. *J. Econ. Educ.,* Fall 1969, *1*(1), pp. 7–11.

——— Economics as a Moral Science. *Amer. Econ. Rev.,* March 1969, *59*(1), pp. 1–12.

——— The Emerging Superculture. **In** *Baier, K. and Rescher, N., eds.,* 1969, pp. 336–50.

——— The Grants Economy. *Mich. Academician,* Winter 1969, *1*(1–2), pp. 3–11.

——— The Old Agricultural Lag. **In** *Ruttan, V. W.; Waldo, A. D. and Houck, J. P., eds.,* 1969, pp. 317–18.

——— "Public Choice and the Grants Economy: The Intersecting Set." *Public Choice,* Fall 1969, *7,* pp. 1–2.

Bourne, L. S. Location Factors in the Redevelopment Process: A Model of Residential Change. *Land Econ.,* May 1969, *45*(2), pp. 183–93.

——— A Spatial Allocation-Land Use Conversion Model of Urban Growth. *J. Reg. Sci.,* August 1969, *9*(2), pp. 261–72.

Bourque, Philip J. Income Multipliers for the Washington Economy. *Univ. Wash. Bus. Rev.,* Winter 1969, *28*(2), pp. 5–15.

Bouter, Arie C. and Smith, John S. The Treatment

of Reserves and of Reserve Creation in the Balance of Payments Accounts. *Int. Monet. Fund Staff Pap.*, July 1969, *16*(2), pp. 202–23.

Bouwsma, J. Unilateral Relief from Double Taxation in the Netherlands. *Bull. Int. Fiscal Doc.*, July, August, September 1969, *23*(7–8–9), pp. 407–37.

von Böventer, Edwin. Walter Christaller's Central Places and Peripheral Areas: The Central Place Theory in Retrospect. *J. Reg. Sci.*, April 1969, *9*(1), pp. 117–24.

Bowden, Witt; Karpovich, Michael and Usher, Abbott Payson. Agrarian Reorganization and Reform in the Eighteenth Century. **In** *Scoville, W. C. and La Force, J. C., eds., Vol. III*, 1969, pp. 66–89.

Bowen, Charles L. Preventive Mediation. **In** *Somers, G. G., ed. (II)*, 1969, pp. 160–64.

Bowen, Howard R. The Interpretation of Voting in the Allocation of Economic Resources. **In** *Arrow, K. J. and Scitovsky, T., eds.*, 1969, pp. 115–32.

_____ Tuitions and Student Loans in the Finance of Higher Education. **In** *the Economics and Financing of Higher Education in the United States, JECP*, 1969, pp. 618–31.

Bowen, William G. The Dilemma Model Re-examined. **In** *Ball, R. J. and Doyle, P., eds.*, 1969, pp. 255–73.

_____ Economic Pressures on the Major Private Universities. **In** *the Economics and Financing of Higher Education in the United States, JECP*, 1969, pp. 399–439.

Bower, B. T.; Matalas, N. C. and James, I. C., II. Relative Importance of Variables in Water Resources Planning. *Water Resources Res.*, December 1969, *5*(6), pp. 1165–73.

Bower, Dorothy H. and Bower, Richard S. Risk and the Valuation of Common Stock. *J. Polit. Econ.*, May/June 1969, *77*(3), pp. 349–62.

Bower, Richard S. Problems and Progress in the Applications of Recent Developments in the Theory of Finance: Discussion. *J. Finance*, May 1969, *24*(2), pp. 339–41.

_____ **and Bower, Dorothy H.** Risk and the Valuation of Common Stock. *J. Polit. Econ.*, May/June 1969, *77*(3), pp. 349–62.

_____ **and Wippern, Ronald F.** Risk-Return Measurement in Portfolio Selection and Performance Appraisal Models: Progress Report. *J. Financial Quant. Anal.*, December 1969, *4*(4), pp. 417–47.

Bowley, Marian. Constraints on the Freedom of the Profit Motive. **In** *Ling, A. G., et al.*, 1969, pp. 43–46.

Bowman, Charles T. Report on Employment Related to Exports. *Mon. Lab. Rev.*, June 1969, *92* (6), pp. 16–20.

Bowman, Dean A. How Corporations Plan: Introduction and State-of-the-Art. **In** *Ozbekhan, H. and Talbert, G. E., eds.*, 1969, pp. 97–101.

Bowman, John H. City-Suburban Differentials in Local Government Fiscal Effort: A Comment. *Nat. Tax J.*, September 1969, *22*(3), pp. 418–21.

Bowman, Mary Jean. Poverty in an Affluent Society. **In** *Chamberlain, N. W., ed.*, 1969, pp. 49–107.

_____ **and Anderson, C. Arnold.** Relationship among Schooling, "Ability," and Income in Industrialized Societies. **In** *[Edding, Friedrich]*, 1969, pp. 97–119.

Bowman, Ward S., Jr. and Bork, Robert H. The Crisis in Antitrust. **In** *Starleaf, D. R., ed.*, 1969, pp. 93–102.

Bowsher, Norman N. 1969—Battle Against Inflation. *Fed. Res. Bank St. Louis Rev.*, December 1969, *51* (12), pp. 2–12.

Boyce, Byrl N. Excess Acquisition Revisited: Control of Land Use at the Interstate Interchange. *Land Econ.*, August 1969, *45*(3), pp. 293–303.

Boyd, Thomas. Planning the Recruitment of Professional Personnel. **In** *Gilroy, T. P., ed.*, 1969, pp. 18–23.

Boyle, Gerald J. The Economic Progress of New Mexico Since 1948. *N. Mex. Bus.*, September 1969, *22*(9), pp. 3–10.

Boyle, W. A. Statement. **In** *The 1969 Economic Report of the President, Pt. 4, JECH*, 1969, pp. 1185–88.

Bozzola, G. B. Strutture organizzative e politiche commerciali su scala internazionale. (Organizational Structures and Commercial Policies at an International Level. With English summary.) *L'Impresa*, July/October 1969, *11*(4–5), pp. 311–19.

Brackett, Jean C. New BLS Budgets Provide Yardsticks for Measuring Family Living Costs. *Mon. Lab. Rev.*, April 1969, *92*(4), pp. 3–16.

Bradburn, Norman M.; Gockel, Galen and Sudman, Seymour. The Extent and Characteristics of Racially Integrated Housing in the United States. *J. Bus.*, January 1969, *42*(1), pp. 50–92.

Bradbury, Robert W. Socio-Economic Perspectives for a Latin American Common Market. **In** *Hilton, R., ed.*, 1969, pp. 72–79.

Bradford, David F. Balance on Unbalanced Growth. *Z. Nationalökon.*, December 1969, *29*(3–4), pp. 291–304.

_____**; Malt, R. A. and Oates, Wallace E.** The Rising Cost of Local Public Services: Some Evidence and Reflections. *Nat. Tax J.*, June 1969, *22*(2), pp. 185–202.

Bradford, Lawrence. Can Better Teaching Be Learned? *Amer. J. Agr. Econ.*, December 1969, *51*(5), pp. 1075–77.

Bradish, Richard D. and Orton, Bryce B. The Treatment and Disclosure of Research and Development Expenditures. *Manage. Account.*, July 1969, *51*(1), pp. 31–34.

Bradley, Hugh E. Setting and Controlling Budgets with Regression Analysis. *Manage. Account.*, November 1969, *51*(5), pp. 31–34.

Bradley, Iver E. and Gander, James P. Input-Output Multipliers: Some Theoretical Comments. *J. Reg. Sci.*, August 1969, *9*(2), pp. 309–17.

Bradley, Michael E. Marxism and Soviet Agricultural Problems. **In** *Prybyla, J. S., ed.*, 1969, pp. 89–95.

Bradley, Paul G. Statement. **In** *Governmental Intervention in the Market Mechanism, Pt. 1, SCH*, 1969, pp. 284–301.

Bradshaw, Marie T. U.S. Exports to Foreign Affiliates of U.S. Firms. *Surv. Curr. Bus.*, Part I, May 1969, *49*(5), pp. 34–51.

Brahmananda, P. R. The Bank Rate in General Setting. In *Desai, V. R. M. and Ghonasgi, B. D.*, 1969, pp. 29–48.

——— Towards a General Theory of the Pure Rate of Interest. *Indian Econ. J.*, July–September 1969, *17*(1), pp. 57–92.

Bramhall, David F. and Bryce, Herrington J. Interstate Migration of Labor-Force Age Population. *Ind. Lab. Relat. Rev.*, July 1969, *22*(4), pp. 576–83.

Brand, S. S. The Interindustry Relationships of Agriculture and Economic Development in South Africa. *Finance Trade Rev.*, June 1969, *8*(3), pp. 171–86.

Brand, W. Population Growth and Economic Development. In *Bechhofer, F., ed.*, 1969, pp. 145–54.

Brandenburg, Frank. Development, Finance, and Trade. In *Abshire, D. M. and Samuels, M. A., eds.*, 1969, pp. 219–52.

——— Transport Systems and Their External Ramifications. In *Abshire, D. M. and Samuels, M. A., eds.*, 1969, pp. 320–44.

Brandenburg, R. G. and Ansoff, H. Igor. The General Manager of the Future. *Calif. Manage. Rev.*, Spring 1969, *11*(3), pp. 61–72.

Brandl, John E. Education Program Analysis at HEW. In *The Analysis and Evaluation of Public Expenditures: The PPB System, Vol. 3, JECP*, 1969, pp. 1224–32.

Brandow, G. E. Market Power and Its Sources in the Food Industry. *Amer. J. Agr. Econ.*, February 1969, *51*(1), pp. 1–12.

Brandt, Harry and Wyand, Robert R., II. A Shift in Banking Philosophy? An Examination of Bank Investment Practices. In *Jessup, P. F.*, 1969, pp. 60–72.

Brandt, Karl. Voting Problems in Group Decisions. *Ger. Econ. Rev.*, 1969, *7*(4), pp. 273–94.

Brandt, Louis K. Quantitative Tools for Financial Management. *Southern Quart.*, April 1969, *7*(3), pp. 261–81.

Brannon, Russell H. Low Investment Levels in Uruguayan Agriculture: Some Tentative Explanations. *Land Econ.*, August 1969, *45*(3), pp. 304–12.

Branson, William H. The Minimum Covered Interest Differential Needed for International Arbitrage Activity. *J. Polit. Econ.*, November/December 1969, *77*(6), pp. 1028–35.

——— **and Klevorick, Alvin K.** Money Illusion and the Aggregate Consumption Function. *Amer. Econ. Rev.*, December 1969, *59*(5), pp. 832–49.

Braschler, Curtis and Klindt, Thomas. Theoretical and Empirical Problems in Local Government Consolidation. *Can. J. Agr. Econ.*, February 1969, *17*(1), pp. 141–50.

Brash, Donald T. American Investment and Australian Sovereignty. In *Preston, R., ed.*, 1969, pp. 539–52.

Brass, W. A Generation Method for Projecting Death Rates. In *Bechhofer, F., ed.*, 1969, pp. 75–91.

Braun, Hubert; Hammer, Gerald and Schmid, Karl. Ein Verfahren zur Ermittlung der Ausbildungskapazität wissenschaftlicher Hochschulen. (With English summary.) *Jahr. Nationalökon. Statist.*, March 1969, *182*(4–5), pp. 381–97.

Bray, Jennifer M. The Economics of Traditional Cloth Production in Iseyin, Nigeria. *Econ. Develop. Cult. Change*, July 1969, *17*(4), pp. 540–51.

Braybrooke, David. Private Production of Public Goods. In *Baier, K. and Rescher, N., eds.*, 1969, pp. 368–88.

Break, George F. Integrating Corporate and Personal Income Taxes: The Carter Commission Proposals. *Law Contemp. Probl.*, Autumn 1969, *34*(4), pp. 726–35.

——— Integration of the Corporate and Personal Income Taxes. *Nat. Tax J.*, March 1969, *22*(1), pp. 39–56.

Brecher, Irving and Baqai, Moin. Foreign-Aid Requirements: A Critique of Aid Projections with Special Reference to Pakistan. *Pakistan Develop. Rev.*, Winter 1969, *9*(4), pp. 380–99.

Brechling, Frank. Wage-Price Dynamics, Inflation, and Unemployment: Discussion. *Amer. Econ. Rev.*, May 1969, *59*(2), pp. 161–62.

Bredov, V. and Levin, A. Prediction of the Population's Demand. *Prob. Econ.*, January 1969, *11*(9), pp. 34–44.

Breen, William J. An Exploratory Econometric Model of Financial Markets. *J. Financial Quant. Anal.*, September 1969, *4*(3), pp. 233–69.

——— **and Liu, Ta-Chung.** The Covariance Matrix of the Limited Information Estimator and the Identification Test. *Econometrica*, April 1969, *37*(2), pp. 222–27.

Breimyer, Harold F. Future Organization and Control of U.S. Agricultural Production and Marketing. In *Owen, W. F., ed.*, 1969, pp. 14–25.

——— **and Loyd, Harold J.** Food Donation Programs. *Amer. J. Agr. Econ.*, November 1969, *51*(4), pp. 934–36.

Brems, Hans. Convergence and Stability in the Neoclassical Growth Model. *Nationalokon. Tidsskr.*, 1969, *107*(5–6), pp. 226–35.

Brennan, D. G. The Case for Missile Defense. *Foreign Aff.*, April 1969, *47*(3), pp. 433–48.

Brennan, Geoffrey. The Optimal Provision of Public Goods: A Comment. *J. Polit. Econ.*, March/April 1969, *77*(2), pp. 237–41.

Brennan, J. F. A Short Cut to Capital Budget Forecasting for Public Utilities. *Eng. Econ.*, April–May 1969, *14*(3), pp. 151–58.

Breslow, Lester. Statement. In *Costs and Delivery of Health Services to Older Americans, Pt. 3, SCH*, 1969, pp. 638–45.

Bressler, Barry. Relative Poverty, Absolute Poverty, and Policy Implications. *Quart. Rev. Econ. Bus.*, Autumn 1969, *9*(3), pp. 65–71.

Breton, Albert. The Political Economy of Regional Balance. *Rech. Écon. Louvain*, August 1969, *35*(3), pp. 175–99.

——— Some Problems of Major Tax Reforms. *Nat. Tax J.*, March 1969, *22*(1), pp. 154–63.

——— A Stable Velocity Function for Canada? A Further Note. *Economica, N.S.*, August 1969, *36*(143), pp. 316.

——— **and Breton, Raymond.** An Economic Theory of Social Movements. *Amer. Econ. Rev.*, May 1969, *59*(2), pp. 198–205.

Breton, Raymond and Breton, Albert. An Economic Theory of Social Movements. *Amer. Econ. Rev.*, May 1969, *59*(2), pp. 198–205.

Bretthauer, G. L. and Swanson, Earl R. Supplemental Irrigation of Corn: A Break-Even Analysis. *Ill. Agr. Econ.,* July 1969, *9*(2), pp. 19–24.

Bretzfelder, Robert B. and Dallavalle, Q. Francis. Total and *Per Capita* Personal Income by Regions and States, 1968. *Surv. Curr. Bus.,* August 1969, *49*(8), pp. 13, 24.

______**; Dallavalle, Q. Francis and Hirschberg, David A.** Personal Income, 1968, and Disposable Income, 1929–68, by States and Regions. *Surv. Curr. Bus.,* April 1969, *49*(4), pp. 16–21, 32.

Brewer, Durward and Gillespie, Glenn A. Effects of Nonprice Variables upon Participation in Water-Oriented Outdoor Recreation: Reply. *Amer. J. Agr. Econ.,* February 1969, *51*(1), pp. 194–95.

______ **and Kuehn, John A.** Conflicts within Recreation: A Rejoinder. *Land Econ.,* February 1969, *45*(1), pp. 131–33.

Brewer, Stanley H. The Pacific Northwest Battles for Air Routes. *Univ. Wash. Bus. Rev.,* Spring 1969, *28*(3), pp. 5–20.

Brewster, Agnes W. Statement. **In** *Economics of Aging: Toward a Full Share in Abundance, Pt. 1, SCH,* 1969, pp. 9–11.

Brewster, Agnes W., et al. Health Aspects of the Economics of Aging: A Working Paper. **In** *op. cit., SCP,* 1969, pp. 1–41.

Brewster, Havelock. The Pattern of Change in Wages, Prices and Productivity in British Guiana, 1948 to 1962. *Soc. Econ. Stud.,* June 1969, *18*(2), pp. 107–36.

______ **and Thomas, Clive Y.** Aspects of the Theory of Economic Integration. *J. Common Market Stud.,* December 1969, *8*(2), pp. 110–32.

Bridbury, A. R. The Dark Ages. *Econ. Hist. Rev.,* December 1969, *22*(3), pp. 526–37.

Brief, Bernard. Per un marketing multinazionale. (For a Multinational Marketing. With English summary.) *Mondo Aperto,* October 1969, *23*(5), pp. 343–56.

Brief, Richard P. An Econometric Analysis of Goodwill: Some Findings in a Search for Valuation Rules. *Accounting Rev.,* January 1969, *44*(1), pp. 20–26.

______ **and Owen, Joel.** A Note on Earnings Risk and the Coefficient of Variation. *J. Finance,* December 1969, *24*(5), pp. 901–04.

Brigham, Eugene F. and Pappas, James L. The Effect of Liberalized Depreciation on the Cost of Equity Capital. **In** *Trebing, H. M. and Howard, R. H., eds.,* 1969, pp. 129–58.

______ Rates of Return on Common Stock. *J. Bus.,* July 1969, *42*(3), pp. 302–16.

Brighi, Massimo. Note sulla struttura dei sistemi. (Remarks on the Structures of Systems. With English summary.) *L'Impresa,* May/June 1969, *11*(3), pp. 258–60.

Brighton, Gerald D. Accrued Expense Tax Reform—Not Ready in 1954—Ready in 1969? *Accounting Rev.,* January 1969, *44*(1), pp. 137–44.

Brigida, Franco. Industria alimentare e sviluppo industriale in italia. (Food Industry and Growth in Italy. With English summary.) *L'Impresa,* March/April 1969, *11*(2), pp. 163–66.

Brillinger, David R. and Hatanaka, Michio. An Harmonic Analysis of Nonstationary Multivariate Economic Processes. *Econometrica,* January 1969, *37*(1), pp. 131–41.

Briloff, Abraham J. Financial Motives for Conglomerate Growth. **In** *Garoian, L., ed.,* 1969, pp. 81–87.

Brimmer, Andrew F. Euro-Dollar Flows and the Efficiency of U.S. Monetary Policy. **In** *High Interest Rates, SCH,* 1969, pp. 181–95.

______ The Negro in the National Economy. **In** *Kain, J. F., ed.,* 1969, pp. 89–99.

______ Statement. **In** *A Review of Balance of Payments Policies, JECH,* 1969, pp. 155–68.

______ Statement to Congress. *Fed. Res. Bull.,* January 1969, *55*(1), pp. 21–33.

______ Statement to Congress. *Fed. Res. Bull.,* December 1969, *55*(12), pp. 923–27.

Briscoe, G.; Samuels, J. M. and Smyth, David J. The Treatment of Risk in the Stock Market. *J. Finance,* September 1969, *24*(4), pp. 707–13.

______ The Variability of Industry Profit Rates. *Appl. Econ.,* May 1969, *1*(2), pp. 137–49.

______ **and Smyth, David J.** Investment Plans and Realizations in United Kingdom Manufacturing. *Economica, N.S.,* August 1969, *36*(143), pp. 277–94.

Brits, R. N. The Marketing of South African Maize. *S. Afr. J. Econ.,* September 1969, *37*(3), pp. 198–218.

Britsch, Klaus; Reichardt, Helmut and Schips, Bernd. Sind die Lohnempfänger gut beraten, wenn sie sich einer Lohnquotensenkung widersetzen? (With English summary.) *Jahr. Nationalökon. Statist.,* August 1969, *183*(3–4), pp. 300–305.

Britto, R. On Putty-Clay: A Comment. *Rev. Econ. Stud.,* July 1969, *36*(107), pp. 395–98.

Brock, William A. and Gale, David. Optimal Growth under Factor Augmenting Progress. *J. Econ. Theory,* October 1969, *1*(3), pp. 229–43.

Brockelbank, W. J. The Family Desertion Problems across State Lines. *Ann. Amer. Acad. Polit. Soc. Sci.,* May 1969, *383,* pp. 23–33.

Brodrick, John. Management and Technology. **In** *Hugh-Jones, E. M., ed.,* 1969, pp. 48–61.

Bródy, A. Methods of Analysis and Forecasting Applied in Hungary. *Acta Oecon.,* 1969, *4*(3), pp. 299–314.

Brody, Andrew. The Rate of Economic Growth in Hungary. **In** *Bronfenbrenner, M., ed.,* 1969, pp. 312–27.

Broemeling, L. D. Confidence for Variance Ratios of Random Models. *J. Amer. Statist. Assoc.,* June 1969, *64*(326), pp. 660–64.

Bronfenbrenner, Martin. Economic Consequences of Technological Change. **In** *Baier, K. and Rescher, N., eds.,* 1969, pp. 453–71.

______ Eine makroökonomische Auffassung von Marx' "Kapital." (With English summary.) *Jahr. Nationalökon. Statist.,* March 1969, *182*(4–5), pp. 347–65.

______ Is the Business Cycle Obsolete?: Summary of the Discussion. **In** *Bronfenbrenner, M., ed.,* 1969, pp. 505–58.

______ The Japanese Experience. **In** *Federal Reserve Bank of Chicago (II),* 1969, pp. 95–98.

______ Monetary Rules: A New Look. **In** *The 1969 Economic Report of the President, Pt. 3, JECH,* 1969, pp. 583–615.

______ Postwar Business Cycles in Japan: Comment. **In** *Bronfenbrenner, M., ed.,* 1969, pp. 96–98.

——— Statement. In *The 1969 Economic Report of the President, Pt. 3, JECH,* 1969, pp. 542–45.

——— A Working Library on Riots and Hunger. *J. Human Res.,* Summer 1969, *4*(3), pp. 377–90.

Brook, Michael. Annual Bibliography of Periodical Articles on American Labor History: 1968. *Labor Hist.,* Fall 1969, *10*(4), pp. 639–55.

Brooks, Harold E. The Armour Automation Committee Experience. In *Somers, G. G., ed. (II),* 1969, pp. 137–43.

Brooks, Harvey. Statement. In *To Establish a Select Senate Committee on Technology and the Human Environment, SCH,* 1969, pp. 189–95.

Brooks, Scott E. and Constable, G. A. Minimum Resource Requirements for Specified Resource Returns on Ontario Farms. *Can. J. Agr. Econ.,* November 1969, *17*(3), pp. 133–43.

Brooksher, William R. and French, Norman D. Marketing New Products—By Segmenting Product Lines. *Univ. Missouri Bus. Govt. Rev.,* September–October 1969, *10*(5), pp. 5–10.

Broom, Leonard and Maynard, Betty J. Prestige and Socioeconomic Ranking of Occupations. *Soc. Sci. Quart.,* September 1969, *50*(2), pp. 369–73.

Bross, Steward R., Jr. The United States Borrower in the Eurobond Market—A Lawyer's Point of View. *Law Contemp. Probl.,* Winter 1969, *34*(1), pp. 172–202.

Brovedani, Bruno. Italy's Financial Policies in the 'Sixties. *Banca Naz. Lavoro Quart. Rev.,* June 1969, (89), pp. 170–89.

Brown, Elizabeth Read and Brown, Harry Gunnison. An Attack on Tax Reform in Hawaii. *Amer. J. Econ. Soc.,* January 1969, *28*(1), pp. 106–08.

Brown, A. J. Some English Thoughts on the Scottish Economy. *Scot. J. Polit. Econ.,* November 1969, *16*(3), pp. 233–47.

——— Surveys of Applied Economics: Regional Economics, with Special Reference to the United Kingdom. *Econ. J.,* December 1969, *79*(316), pp. 759–96.

——— **and Woodward, V. H.** Regional Social Accounts for the United Kingdom. *Rev. Income Wealth,* December 1969, *15*(4), pp. 335–47.

Brown, A. W. The Economic Benefits to Australia from Atomic Absorption Spectroscopy. *Econ. Rec.,* June 1969, *45*(110), pp. 158–80.

Brown, E. H. Phelps. Balancing External Payments by Adjusting Domestic Income. *Australian Econ. Pap.,* December 1969, *8*(13), pp. 111–21.

——— The Brookings Study of the Poor Performance of the British Economy. *Economica, N.S.,* August 1969, *36*(143), pp. 235–52.

Brown, F. E. Price Image versus Price Reality. *J. Marketing Res.,* May 1969, *6*(2), pp. 185–91.

Brown, Gardner, Jr. and Johnson, M. Bruce. Public Utility Pricing and Output under Risk. *Amer. Econ. Rev.,* March 1969, *59*(1), pp. 119–28.

Brown, H. James. Shift and Share Projections of Regional Economic Growth: An Empirical Test. *J. Reg. Sci.,* April 1969, *9*(1), pp. 1–18.

Brown, H. P. The Present Theory of Investment Appraisal: A Critical Analysis. *Bull. Oxford Univ. Inst. Econ. Statist.,* May 1969, *31*(2), pp. 105–31.

Brown, Harrison. Population, Food and the Energy Transition. In *Behrman, S. J.; Corsa, L., Jr. and Freedman, R., eds.,* 1969, pp. 180–88.

Brown, Harry Gunnison and Brown, Elizabeth Read. An Attack on Tax Reform in Hawaii. *Amer. J. Econ. Soc.,* January 1969, *28*(1), pp. 106–08.

Brown, J. A. C. A Regional Model of Agricultural Development. In *Thorbecke, E., ed.,* 1969, pp. 75–92.

Brown, James J. Control in Multi-Division Operations. *Manage. Account.,* August 1969, *51*(2), pp. 18–20.

Brown, Joseph D. Effect of a Health Hazard "Scare" on Consumer Demand. *Amer. J. Agr. Econ.,* August 1969, *51*(3), pp. 676–79.

Brown, M. Substitution-Composition Effects, Capital Intensity Uniqueness and Growth. *Econ. J.,* June 1969, *79*(314), pp. 334–47.

Brown, Norman L. and Roberts, Paul Craig. The Economics of the Right to Work Controversy: Revisited. *Southern Econ. J.,* January 1969, *35*(3), pp. 265–66.

Brown, Paul L. An Evaluation of PPBS Developments in Wisconsin. In *Innovations in Planning, Programming, and Budgeting in State and Local Governments, JECP,* 1969, pp. 53–61.

Brown, R. Gene. Ethical and Other Problems in Publishing Financial Forecasts. In *Burton, J. C., ed.,* 1969, pp. 225–38.

Brown, Ralph S., Jr. Collective Bargaining in Higher Education. *Mich. Law Rev.,* March 1969, *67*(5), pp. 1067–82.

Brown, Richard E. and Weber, Glen D. Tributary Area Development: TVA's Approach to Sub-Regional Development. *Land Econ.,* February 1969, *45*(1), pp. 141–46.

Brown, Richard H. The Achievement Norm and Economic Growth: The Case of Elizabethan England. *Rev. Soc. Econ.,* September 1969, *27*(2), pp. 181–201.

Brown, Robert Kevin. City Cybernetics. *Land Econ.,* November 1969, *45*(4), pp. 406–12.

Brown, Robert O. Using Appraisal Information. *Manage. Account.,* October 1969, *51*(4), pp. 47–48.

Brown, Sue Ellen and Lynn, Arthur D., Jr. Federal Revenue Sharing with the States: Implications for Effective Federalism. *Ohio State U. Bull. Bus. Res.,* November 1969, *44*(11), pp. 6–8.

Browne, Dudley E. Progress in Corporate Financial Reporting. *Manage. Account.,* July 1969, *51*(1), pp. 7–9, 14.

Brozen, Yale. Barriers Facilitate Entry. *Antitrust Bull.,* Winter 1969, *14,* pp. 851–54.

——— The Effect of Statutory Minimum Wage Increases on Teen-Age Employment. *J. Law Econ.,* April 1969, *12*(1), pp. 109–22.

——— Significance of Profit Data for Antitrust Policy. *Antitrust Bull.,* Spring 1969, *14,* pp. 119–39.

——— Significance of Profit Data for Antitrust Policy. In *Weston, J. F. and Peltzman, S., eds.,* 1969, pp. 110–27.

Brubaker, Earl R. Development of Soviet Agriculture under a Vintage Model of Production. *Amer. J. Agr. Econ.,* November 1969, *51*(4), pp. 882–902.

——— Growth in Soviet Transport and Communications: Note. *Amer. Econ. Rev.,* Part I, September 1969, *59*(4), pp. 622–24.

——— Some Effects of Policy on Productivity in

Soviet and American Crude Petroleum Extraction. *J. Ind. Econ.*, November 1969, *18*(1), pp. 33–52.

Bruce, Grady D. The Ecological Structure of Retail Institutions. *J. Marketing Res.*, February 1969, *6* (1), pp. 48–53.

______ **and Dommermuth, William P.** Dissonance and Satisfaction—Some Prepurchase Aspects. *Univ. Wash. Bus. Rev.*, Spring 1969, *28*(3), pp. 45–51.

Bruck, Nicholas K. Higher Education and Economic Development in Central America. *Rev. Soc. Econ.*, September 1969, *27*(2), pp. 160–80.

Brugmans, I. J. Economic Fluctuations in the Netherlands in the Nineteenth Century. **In** *Crouzet, F.; Chaloner, W. H. and Stern, W. M., eds.*, 1969, pp. 128–54.

______ Nederlands overgang van onderontwikkeld gebied tot industrieland. (The Transition from Underdevelopment to Industrialization in the Netherlands. With English summary.) *De Economist*, January/February 1969, *117*(1), pp. 73–85.

Brumberg, Richard and Modigliani, Franco. Utility Analysis and the Consumption Function: An Interpretation of Cross-section Data. **In** *Williams, H. R. and Huffnagle, J. D., eds.*, 1969, pp. 99–140.

Brummet, R. Lee; Flamholtz, Eric G. and Pyle, William C. Human Resource Accounting: A Tool to Increase Managerial Effectiveness. *Manage. Account.*, August 1969, *51*(2), pp. 12–15.

______ Human Resource Myopia. *Mon. Lab. Rev.*, January 1969, *92*(1), pp. 29–30.

Brunn, Stanley D. and Hoffman, Wayne L. The Geography of Federal Grants-in-Aid to States. *Econ. Geogr.*, July 1969, *45*(3), pp. 226–38.

Brunner, Karl. Monetary Analysis and Federal Reserve Policy. **In** *Brunner, K., ed.*, 1969, pp. 250–82.

______ The Monetary Fiscal Dilemma. *Ohio State U. Bull. Bus. Res.*, June 1969, *44*(6), pp. 1–5, 8.

______ The Policy Discussions by Stein and Worswick: A Comment. *J. Money, Credit, Banking*, August 1969, *1*(3), pp. 496–502.

______ **and Meltzer, Allan H.** The Nature of Policy Problem. **In** *Brunner, K., ed.*, 1969, pp. 1–26.

Bruno, James Edward. Achieving Property Tax Relief with a Minimum Disruption of State Programs. *Nat. Tax J.*, September 1969, *22*(3), pp. 379–89.

Bruno, M. Fundamental Duality Relations in the Pure Theory of Capital Growth. *Rev. Econ. Stud.*, January 1969, *36*(105), pp. 39–53.

Brus, W. A Few General Remarks on the Changes in the System of Planning and Management. **In** *Economic Concentration, Pt. 7A, SCH*, 1969, pp. 4459–65.

Brusilovskaia, N., et al. Conditions for Applying a System of Accounting Prices in a Socialist Economy. *Prob. Econ.*, September 1969, *12*(5), pp. 71–81.

Bruton, Henry J. The Two Gap Approach to Aid and Development: Comment. *Amer. Econ. Rev.*, June 1969, *59*(3), pp. 439–46.

Bryan, Robert G. Wages in the Shirt and Nightwear Manufacturing Industry. *Mon. Lab. Rev.*, November 1969, *92*(11), pp. 66–67.

Bryant, Ashbrook P. Historical and Social Aspects of Concentration of Program Control in Television. *Law Contemp. Probl.*, Summer 1969, *34*(3), pp. 610–35.

Bryant, John H. The Gap between Biomedical Technology and Health Needs in Developing Countries. **In** *Nader, C. and Zahlan, A. B., eds.*, 1969, pp. 1–26.

Bryant, W. Keith. Rural Poverty. **In** *Ruttan, V. W.; Waldo, A. D. and Houck, J. P., eds.*, 1969, pp. 226–34.

Bryce, Herrington J. Regional Labor Earnings Differentials in a Small Developing Country: The Republic of Panama. *J. Reg. Sci.*, December 1969, *9*(3), pp. 405–15.

______ **and Bramhall, David F.** Interstate Migration of Labor-Force Age Population. *Ind. Lab. Relat. Rev.*, July 1969, *22*(4), pp. 576–83.

Bryson, John E. and Dunham, Stephen S. A Case Study of the Impact of Consumer Legislation: The Elimination of Negotiability and the Cooling-Off Period. *Yale Law J.*, March 1969, *78*(4), pp. 618–61.

Buchanan, James M. External Diseconomies, Corrective Taxes, and Market Structure. *Amer. Econ. Rev.*, March 1969, *59*(1), pp. 174–77.

______ Financing a Viable Federalism. **In** *[White, Charles P.]*, 1969, pp. 3–19.

______ A Future for "Agricultural Economics"? *Amer. J. Agr. Econ.*, December 1969, *51*(5), pp. 1027–36.

______ Is Economics the Science of Choice? **In** *[von Hayek, Friedrich A.]*, 1969, pp. 47–64.

______ **and Flowers, Marilyn.** An Analytical Setting for a "Taxpayers' Revolution." *Western Econ. J.*, December 1969, *7*(4), pp. 349–59.

Buchanan, Ronald H. Toward Netherlands 2000: The Dutch National Plan. *Econ. Geogr.*, July 1969, *45*(3), pp. 258–74.

Buchenroth, Kenneth J. Motivation: Financial and Nonfinancial. *Manage. Account.*, December 1969, *51*(6), pp. 15–16, 48.

Buckley, John E. Intraoccupational Wage Dispersion in Metropolitan Areas, 1967–68. *Mon. Lab. Rev.*, September 1969, *92*(9), pp. 24–29.

Bucklin, Louis P. Consumer Search, Role Enactment, and Market Efficiency. *J. Bus.*, October 1969, *42*(4), pp. 416–38.

Budd, Edward C. and Radner, Daniel B. The OBE Size Distribution Series: Methods and Tentative Results for 1964. *Amer. Econ. Rev.*, May 1969, *59* (2), pp. 435–49.

Buehler, John E. and Fand, David I. The Federal Reserve and Monetary Policy. *Mich. Academician*, Spring 1969, *1*(3–4), pp. 21–35.

Bulborea, I. Nicolae Bălcescu în context european. (Nicolae Bălcescu in a European Context. With English summary.) *Stud. Cercet. Econ.*, 1969, *1-2*, pp. 245–51.

Bulhoes, Octávio de Gouveia. Financial Recuperation for Economic Expansion. **In** *Ellis, H. S., ed.*, 1969, pp. 162–76.

Buller, Orlan and Lin, Wuu-Long. Measuring the Effect of Weather on Crop Production. *Can. J. Agr. Econ.*, February 1969, *17*(1), pp. 91–98.

Bullock, J. Bruce and Logan, Samuel H. A Model for Decision Making under Uncertainty. *Agr. Econ. Res.*, October 1969, *21*(4), pp. 109–115.

Bumas, Lester O. The Effects of an Advance in Technology on Employment in an Industry: A Theoretical Model. *Eng. Econ.,* July–August 1969, *14* (4), pp. 215–20.

——— **and Stein, Bruno.** The Economic Rationale of Occupational Choice: Comment. *Ind. Lab. Relat. Rev.,* April 1969, *22*(3), pp. 422–28.

Buniaev, M. F. The Role of Education in the Training of Qualified Personnel for Agriculture. **In** *Noah, H. J., ed.,* 1969, pp. 23–26.

Bunich, P. G.; Perlamutrov, V. L. and Sokolovskii, L. Kh. An Inventory Model in Physical and Monetary Terms. *Matekon,* Fall 1969, *6*(1), pp. 30–43.

Bunting, John R., Jr. One-Bank Holding Companies: A Banker's View. *Harvard Bus. Rev.,* May–June 1969, *47*(3), pp. 99–106.

Buonomo, Maurizio. La stabilità economica interna, presupposto dell'equilibrio monetario internazionale. (Internal Economic Stability, the Prerequisite for International Monetary Equilibrium. With English summary.) *Bancaria,* June 1969, *25*(6), pp. 725–30.

——— Moneta e credito nelle economie socialiste: vecchi e nuovi orientamenti. (Money and Credit in Socialist Economies: Old Trends and New. With English summary.) *Bancaria,* April 1969, *25* (4), pp. 449–59.

Burch, John G., Jr. Business Games and Simulation Techniques. *Manage. Account.,* December 1969, *51*(6), pp. 49–52.

Burch, S. W. and Stekler, H. O. The Forecasting Accuracy of Consumer Attitude Data. *J. Amer. Statist. Assoc.,* December 1969, *64*(328), pp. 1225–33.

Burdak, Thomas G.; Young, Robert A. and Martin, William E. Projecting Hydrologic and Economic Interrelationships in Groundwater Basin Management. *Amer. J. Agr. Econ.,* December 1969, *51* (5), pp. 1593–97.

Burdick, Donald S. and Naylor, Thomas H. Response Surface Designs. **In** *Naylor, T. H., ed.,* 1969, pp. 80–98.

———**; Sasser, W. Earl, Jr. and Naylor, Thomas H.** The Design of Computer Simulation Experiments. **In** *Naylor, T. H., ed.,* 1969, pp. 3–35.

Burford, Roger L. Louisiana's Population: Its Growth and Distribution. **In** *Beard, T. R., ed.,* 1969, pp. 41–54.

Burger, Albert E. The Effects of Inflation (1960–68). *Fed. Res. Bank St. Louis Rev.,* November 1969, *51* (11), pp. 25–36.

——— A Historical Analysis of the Credit Crunch of 1966. *Fed. Res. Bank St. Louis Rev.,* September 1969, *51*(9), pp. 13–30.

——— Revision of the Money Supply Series. *Fed. Res. Bank St. Louis Rev.,* October 1969, *51*(10), pp. 6–9.

——— **and Andersen, Leonall C.** Asset Management and Commercial Bank Portfolio Behavior: Theory and Practice. *J. Finance,* May 1969, *24*(2), pp. 207–22.

Burgio, Giuseppe. Sulla misura dell'eterogeneità di un collettivo statistico. (With English summary.) *Statistica,* January-March 1969, *29*(1), pp. 5–25.

Burkart, A. J. Some Managerial Influences on a Firm's Pricing Policy. *J. Ind. Econ.,* July 1969, *17* (3), pp. 180–87.

Burki, Shahid Javed. West Pakistan's Rural Works Program: A Study in Political and Administrative Response. *Middle East J.,* Summer 1969, *23*(3), pp. 321–42.

Burley, S. P. A Spectral Analysis of the Australian Business Cycle. *Australian Econ. Pap.,* December 1969, *8*(13), pp. 193–218.

Burley, S. Peter and Morgenstern, Oskar. Insiders and Outsiders in Industrial Research. *Z. ges. Staatswiss.,* April 1969, *125*(2), pp. 193–201.

Burmeister, Edwin and Dobell, A. Rodney. Disembodied Technological Change with Several Factors. *J. Econ. Theory,* June 1969, *1*(1), pp. 1–8.

——— **and Sheshinski, Eytan.** A Nonsubstitution Theorem in a Model with Fixed Capital. *Southern Econ. J.,* January 1969, *35*(3), pp. 273–76.

Burns, Arthur E. The Government Renegotiates Profits. **In** *Watson, D. S., ed.,* 1969, pp. 288–96.

Burns, Arthur F. The Case Against the Guideposts. **In** *Starleaf, D. R., ed.,* 1969, pp. 338–46.

Burns, Arthur Frank. Dealing with Recession and Inflation. **In** *Burns, A. F.,* 1969, pp. 129–50.

——— Heller's "New Dimensions of Political Economy." **In** *Burns, A. F.,* 1969, pp. 303–12.

——— The Nature and Causes of Business Cycles. **In** *Burns, A. F.,* 1969, pp. 3–53.

——— The New Environment of Monetary Policy. **In** *Burns, A. F.,* 1969, pp. 151–74.

——— The Perils of Inflation. **In** *Burns, A. F.,* 1969, pp. 286–302.

Burns, Eveline M. Social Security in Evolution: Towards What? **In** *O.E.C.D.,* 1969, pp. 110–20.

Burns, Joseph M. The Relative Decline of Commercial Banks: A Note. *J. Polit. Econ.,* January/February 1969, *77*(1), pp. 122–29.

——— **and Chiswick, Barry R.** An Economic Analysis of State Support for Higher Education. *Western Econ. J.,* March 1969, *7*(1), pp. 84–95.

Burns, Robert E. Transport Planning: Selection of Analytical Techniques. *J. Transp. Econ. Policy,* September 1969, *3*(3), pp. 306–21.

Burns, T.; Duffy, M. and Agarwala, R. Forecasting Gross Private Fixed Investment Using Intentions Survey Data. *Manchester Sch. Econ. Soc. Stud.,* December 1969, *37*(4), pp. 279–93.

Burns, Tom. Models, Images, and Myths. **In** *Gruber, W. H. and Marquis, D. G., eds.,* 1969, pp. 11–23.

Burrascano, Francesco. Origine ed evoluzione del dualismo economico italiano. (Origin and Evolution of Italian Economic Dualism. With English summary.) *Mondo Aperto,* April 1969, *23*(2), pp. 104–15.

Burstein, M. L. The Quantity Theory of Money: A Critique. **In** *Clower, R. W., ed.,* 1969, pp. 112–19.

Burt, Oscar R. Comments on 'Recreation Benefits from Water Pollution Control' by Joe B. Stevens. *Water Resources Res.,* August 1969, *5*(4), pp. 905–07.

——— **and Cummings, Ronald G.** The Economics of Production from Natural Resources: Note. *Amer. Econ. Rev.,* December 1969, *59*(5), pp. 985–90.

Burt, Richard C. How the 1970 Census Will Be

Taken. *Mon. Lab. Rev.*, December 1969, *92*(12), pp. 38–42.

Burt, Roger. Lead Production in England and Wales, 1700–1770. *Econ. Hist. Rev.*, August 1969, *22*(2), pp. 249–68.

Burton, John F., Jr. Interindustry Variations in Voluntary Labor Mobility: Reply. *Ind. Lab. Relat. Rev.*, October 1969, *23*(1), pp. 84–88.

______ **and Parker, John E.** Interindustry Variations in Voluntary Labor Mobility. *Ind. Lab. Relat. Rev.*, January 1969, *22*(2), pp. 199–216.

Bushch, Arnd. Vertical Restrictions in German Consumer Goods Industries. *Antitrust Bull.*, Summer 1969, *14*, pp. 473–97.

Bushnell, Curtis M. Development of Separations Principles in the Telephone Industry (Review Article). *Land Econ.*, August 1969, *45*(3), pp. 381–83.

Bussetti, Giancarlo. Il ruolo della r.o. nell'economia del sistema. (The Role of Operation Research in the Economic Use of Systems. With English summary.) *L'Impresa*, May/June 1969, *11*(3), pp. 242–47.

Butcher, William S.; Haimes, Yacov Y. and Hall, Warren A. Dynamic Programming for the Optimal Sequencing of Water Supply Projects. *Water Resources Res.*, December 1969, *5*(6), pp. 1196–1204.

Butenko, A. M. The Economics of Education: Some Observations. **In** *Noah, H. J., ed.*, 1969, pp. 27–31.

Butler, Edgar W.; Pope, Hallowell and Paulson, Wayne. Community Power and Public Welfare. *Amer. J. Econ. Soc.*, January 1969, *28*(1), pp. 17–28.

Butlin, N. G. and Dowie, J. A. Estimates of Australian Work Force and Employment, 1861–1961. *Australian Econ. Hist. Rev.*, September 1969, *9*(2), pp. 138–55.

Buxbaum, Richard M. The Group Exemption and Exculsive Distributorships in the Common Market—Procedural Technicalities. *Antitrust Bull.*, Summer 1969, *14*, pp. 499–514.

Buxton, G. L. Land Settlement in New South Wales: Some Research Problems. *Australian Econ. Hist. Rev.*, September 1969, *9*(2), pp. 128–37.

Buzunov, R. A.; Klotzvog, F. N. and Ageeva, V. A. Input-Output and National Economic Planning. *Matekon*, Fall 1969, *6*(1), pp. 19–29.

Byerlee, D. R. and Anderson, James R. Value of Predictors of Uncontrolled Factors in Response Functions. *Australian J. Agr. Econ.*, December 1969, *13*(2), pp. 118–27.

Byerly, Richard A. The Use of Mathematical Models in the Analysis and Improvement of Bank Operations. **In** *Jessup, P. F.*, 1969, pp. 346–59.

Byrne, Joycelin. Population Growth in St. Vincent. *Soc. Econ. Stud.*, June 1969, *18*(2), pp. 152–88.

Byrne, P. F. and Dent, J. B. Recent Developments in Farm Planning: 2: Investment Planning by Monte Carlo Simulation. *Rev. Marketing Agr. Econ.*, June 1969, *37*(2), pp. 104–20.

______ **and Healy, A. T. A.** A Note on Livestock Breeding Policies in Stable and Development Situations. *Australian J. Agr. Econ.*, December 1969, *13*(2), pp. 154–61.

Caballero Tamayo, Xavier. The ILO and Development in the Americas. *Int. Lab. Rev.*, December 1969, *100*(6), pp. 505–50.

Cacy, J. A. Credit Flows in the 1960's. *Fed. Res. Bank Kansas City Rev.*, June 1969, pp. 11–16.

______ Tenth District Banks in the Federal Funds Market. *Fed. Res. Bank Kansas City Rev.*, November 1969, pp. 10–20.

Cagan, Phillip. Allais' Monetary Theory: Interpretation and Comment. *J. Money, Credit, Banking*, August 1969, *1*(3), pp. 427–32.

______ The Influence of Interest Rates on the Duration of Business Cycles. **In** *Guttentag, J. M. and Cagan, P., eds.*, 1969, pp. 3–28.

______ Interest Rates and Bank Reserves—A Reinterpretation of the Statistical Association. **In** *Guttentag, J. M. and Cagan, P., eds.*, 1969, pp. 223–71.

______ The Non-Neutrality of Money in the Long Run: A Discussion of the Critical Assumptions and Some Evidence. *J. Money, Credit, Banking*, May 1969, *1*(2), pp. 207–27.

______ A Study of Liquidity Premiums on Federal and Municipal Government Securities. **In** *Guttentag, J. M. and Cagan, P., eds.*, 1969, pp. 107–42.

______ The Theory of Hyperinflation. **In** *Ball, R. J. and Doyle, P., eds.*, 1969, pp. 117–35.

______ **and Gandolfi, Arthur.** The Lag in Monetary Policy as Implied by the Time Pattern of Monetary Effects on Interest Rates. *Amer. Econ. Rev.*, May 1969, *59*(2), pp. 277–84.

Cagle, Caroline H. Changes in Time and Savings Deposits, April–July 1969. *Fed. Res. Bull.*, October 1969, *55*(10), pp. 804–14.

______ Changes in Time and Savings Deposits, April-October 1968. *Fed. Res. Bull.*, March 1969, *55*(3), pp. 189–209.

______ Changes in Time and Savings Deposits, January–April 1969. *Fed. Res. Bull.*, July 1969, *55* (7), pp. 581–90.

______ Changes in Time and Savings Deposits, October 1968–January 1969. *Fed. Res. Bull.*, May 1969, *55*(5), pp. 409–18.

______ Member Bank Income, 1968. *Fed. Res. Bull.*, May 1969, *55*(5), pp. 419–24.

Caiden, Gerald E. Development Administration and Administrative Reform. *Int. Soc. Sci. J.*, 1969, *21* (1), pp. 9–22.

Cain, Glen G. and Hollister, Robinson G. Evaluating Manpower Programs for the Disadvantaged. **In** *Somers, G. G. and Wood, W. D., eds.*, 1969, pp. 119–51.

______ **and Mincer, Jacob.** Urban Poverty and Labor Force Participation: Comment. *Amer. Econ. Rev.*, March 1969, *59*(1), pp. 185–94.

Cairncross, Alec K. [Sir]. Comments on the Papers by Goran Ohlin and André Marchal. **In** *Samuelson, P. A., ed.*, 1969, pp. 218–21.

______ Economic Forecasting. *Econ. J.*, December 1969, *79*(316), pp. 797–812.

Call, Dwight V. Some Salient Factors Often Overlooked in Stock Options. *Accounting Rev.*, October 1969, *44*(4), pp. 711–19.

Callahan, William J. Don Juan de Goyeneche: Industrialist of Eighteenth-Century Spain. *Bus. Hist. Rev.*, Summer 1969, *43*(2), pp. 152–70.

Callaway, Archibald. Creating Employment for

Africa's Youth. In *Yesufu, T. M., ed.,* 1969, pp. 237–60.

Calmus, Thomas W. Current Trends in the National Economy. *Oregon Bus. Rev.,* February 1969, *28* (2), pp. 1, 4–8.

Cambern, John R. and Newton, David A. Skill Transfers: Can Defense Workers Adapt to Civilian Occupations? *Mon. Lab. Rev.,* June 1969, *92*(6), pp. 21–25.

Cameron, C. C. A Breakthrough in Banking. **In** *Prochnow, H. V., ed.,* 1969, pp. 56–65.

Cameron, M. A. and Slen, S. B. Prospects and Potentials in Canadian Beef Production. *Can. J. Agr. Econ.,* November 1969, *17*(3), pp. 80–89.

Cameron, Rondo E. Economic Growth and Stagnation in France, 1815–1914. **In** *Scoville, W. C. and La Force, J. C., eds., Vol. IV,* 1969, pp. 43–59.

——— The International Encyclopedia of the Social Sciences. *J. Econ. Hist.,* September 1969, *29*(3), pp. 537–41.

Camp, William B. Need to Encourage the Pioneering Spirit. **In** *Prochnow, H. V., ed.,* 1969, pp. 30–47.

Campbell, Colin D. Social Insurance in the United States: A Program in Search of an Explanation. *J. Law Econ.,* October 1969, *12*(2), pp. 249–65.

——— **and Campbell, Rosemary G.** State Minimum Wage Laws as a Cause of Unemployment. *Southern Econ. J.,* April 1969, *35*(4), pp. 323–32.

Campbell, D. R. and MacGregor, M. A. Guidelines for Agricultural Policy Over the Next Decade. *Can. J. Agr. Econ.,* November 1969, *17*(3), pp. 57–64.

Campbell, John R. and Dunnette, Marvin D. Laboratory Training: Reply. *Ind. Relat.,* May 1969, *8*(3), pp. 289–90.

Campbell, Leonard G. and Shepler, Cora E. United States Defense Expenditures Abroad. *Surv. Curr. Bus.,* December 1969, *49*(12), pp. 40–47.

Campbell, Rosemary G. and Campbell, Colin D. State Minimum Wage Laws as a Cause of Unemployment. *Southern Econ. J.,* April 1969, *35*(4), pp. 323–32.

Campfield, W. L. Administration of Grants—Is the Federalist Partnership Synergistic or Symbiotic? *Univ. Missouri Bus. Govt. Rev.,* July–August 1969, *10*(4), pp. 7–12.

Campolongo, Alberto. Note sul sottosviluppo. (Notes on Underdevelopment. With English summary.) *Rivista Int. Sci. Econ. Com.,* December 1969, *16* (12), pp. 1197–1204.

Candal, Arthur and Bergsman, Joel. Industrialization: Past Success and Future Problems. **In** *Ellis, H. S., ed.,* 1969, pp. 29–73.

Candler, Wilfred and Cartwright, Wayne. Estimation of Performance Functions for Budgeting and Simulation Studies. *Amer. J. Agr. Econ.,* February 1969, *51*(1), pp. 159–69.

Cannata, Giuseppe. Factoring: un nuovo ausilio per la gestione delle medie a piccole imprese-II. (Factoring: A New Facility for Medium and Small Companies-II. With English summary.) *Bancaria,* July 1969, *25*(7), pp. 842–50.

——— Factoring: un nuovo ausilio per la gestione delle medie e piccole imprese-I. (Factoring: A New Facility for Medium and Small Companies-I. With English summary.) *Bancaria,* June 1969, *25* (6), pp. 711–24.

Canterbery, E. Ray. Exchange Rates, Capital Flows and Monetary Policy. *Amer. Econ. Rev.,* June 1969, *59*(3), pp. 426–32.

Caplan, Nathan S. and Paige, Jeffrey M. A Study of Ghetto Rioters. **In** *Callow, A. B., Jr., ed.,* 1969, pp. 541–48.

Caples, William G. The Computer's Uses and Potential in Bargaining: A Management View. **In** *Siegel, A. J., ed.,* 1969, pp. 69–120.

Caplovitz, David. The Merchant and the Low-Income Consumer. **In** *Sturdivant, F. D., ed.,* 1969, pp. 61–75.

Capozzola, John M. Citizens' Concern with Municipal Collective Bargaining. **In** *Walsh, R. E., ed.,* 1969, pp. 301–10.

Caramela, Edward J. Salary Levels Continue Sharp Rise in White-collar Occupations. *Mon. Lab. Rev.,* April 1969, *92*(4), pp. 46–48.

Cardozo, Manoel. The Modernization of Brazil, 1500–1808: An Interpretive Essay. **In** *Baklanoff, E. N., ed.,* 1969, pp. 3–18.

Cargill, Thomas F. An Empirical Investigation of the Wage-Lag Hypothesis. *Amer. Econ. Rev.,* December 1969, *59*(5), pp. 806–16.

——— **and Bailey, Duncan M.** The Military Draft and Future Income. *Western Econ. J.,* December 1969, *7*(4), pp. 365–70.

Carleton, Willard T. Linear Programming and Capital Budgeting Models: A New Interpretation. *J. Finance,* December 1969, *24*(5), pp. 825–33.

——— **and Lerner, Eugene M.** Statistical Credit Scoring of Municipal Bonds. *J. Money, Credit, Banking,* November 1969, *1*(4), pp. 750–64.

Carli, Guido. Celebration of the "World Thrift Day." *Rev. Econ. Cond. Italy,* January 1969, *23*(1), pp. 5–12.

——— La funzione monetaria dell'oro nei prossimi dieci anni: Intervento. (The Role of Monetary Gold Over the Next Ten Years: Discussion. With English summary.) *Bancaria,* November 1969, *25* (11), pp. 1344–47.

——— La scuola di automazione per dirigenti bancari. (School of Automation for Bank Executives. With English summary.) *Bancaria,* January 1969, *25*(1), pp. 7–8.

——— Mobilità internazionale dei capitali e stabilità monetaria interna. (International Mobility of Capital and Internal Monetary Stability. With English summary.) *Bancaria,* October 1969, *25* (10), pp. 1216–20.

——— Problemi dell'adesione della Gran Bretagna al Mercato Comune relativamente alle questioni monetarie. (Monetary Aspects of British Entry into the Common Market. With English summary.) *Bancaria,* June 1969, *25*(6), pp. 768–72.

——— Programmi e prospettive della politica monetaria internazionale. (International Monetary Policy of the Moment—Programs and Outlooks. With English summary.) *Bancaria,* December 1969, *25*(12), pp. 1459–63.

——— Sistema monetario internazionale e mercato monetario interno. (International Monetary System and Italian Money Market. With English summary.) *Bancaria,* May 1969, *25*(5), pp. 555–71.

Carlisle, Rodney. William Randolph Hearst's Reaction to the American Newspaper Guild: A Challenge to New Deal Labor Legislation. *Labor Hist.,* Winter 1969, *10*(1), pp. 74–99.

de Carlo, G. R. Interest Sensitivity of Short-Term Capital Movements: Some Recent Statistical Studies. *Kyklos,* 1969, *22*(4), pp. 737–51.

Carlson, Jack W. Federal Support of State and Local Government Planning, Programming, and Budgeting. **In** *Innovations in Planning, Programming, and Budgeting in State and Local Governments, JECP,* 1969, pp. 15–26.

______ Statement. **In** *Guidelines for Estimating the Benefits of Public Expenditures, JECH,* 1969, pp. 23–30.

______ The Status and Next Steps for Planning, Programing, and Budgeting. **In** *The Analysis and Evaluation of Public Expenditures: The PPB System, Vol. 2, JECP,* 1969, pp. 613–34.

Carlson, John A. and O'Keefe, Terrence B. Buffer Stocks and Reaction Coefficients: An Experiment with Decision Making under Risk. *Rev. Econ. Stud.,* October 1969, *36*(108), pp. 467–84.

Carlson, Keith M. A Program of Budget Restraint. *Fed. Res. Bank St. Louis Rev.,* March 1969, *51*(3), pp. 10–14.

Carlsson, Mårten; Hovmark, Bertil and Lindgren, Ingvar. Recent Developments in Farm Planning: 1: A Monte Carlo Method for the Study of Farm Planning Problems. *Rev. Marketing Agr. Econ.,* June 1969, *37*(2), pp. 80–103.

Carlsson, Robert J. The Economic Ideas of Samuel Galloway. **In** *Kiker, B. F. and Carlsson, R. J., eds.,* 1969, pp. 120–39.

______ **and Robinson, James W.** Compensation Decisions in Public Organizations: Comment. *Ind. Relat.,* October 1969, *9*(1), pp. 111–13.

______ **and Robinson, James W.** Toward a Public Employment Wage Theory. *Ind. Lab. Relat. Rev.,* January 1969, *22*(2), pp. 243–48.

______ **and Robinson, James W.** Toward a Public Employment Wage Theory: Reply. *Ind. Lab. Relat. Rev.,* October 1969, *23*(1), pp. 95–100.

Carman, Hoy F. Income Tax Planning for Farmers. *Amer. J. Agr. Econ.,* December 1969, *51*(5), pp. 1543–47.

Carmone, Frank J. and Green, Paul E. Multidimensional Scaling: An Introduction and Comparison of Nonmetric Unfolding Techniques. *J. Marketing Res.,* August 1969, *6*(3), pp. 330–41.

Carne, Joseph. Statistics of the Tin Mines of Cornwall, and of the Consumption of Tin in Great Britain. **In** *Burt, R., ed.,* 1969, pp. 83–93.

Carnoy, Martin. A Welfare Analysis of Latin American Economic Union: Six Industry Studies. **In** *Hilton, R., ed.,* 1969, pp. 237–60.

Carol, Arthur and Parry, Samuel. The Economic Rationale of Occupational Choice: Reply. *Ind. Lab. Relat. Rev.,* April 1969, *22*(3), pp. 428–30.

______ The Economic Rationale of Occupational Choice: Reply. *Ind. Lab. Relat. Rev.,* July 1969, *22*(4), pp. 587–88.

Carr, A. Barry. Long-Term Versus Short-Term Land Retirement. *Amer. J. Agr. Econ.,* December 1969, *51*(5), pp. 1524–27.

Carr, Julian L., Jr. and Estafen, Bernard D. M.B.A. Salary Expectations: Fact or Fantasy? *Indiana Bus. Rev.,* September/October 1969, *44,* pp. 9–12.

Carr, Raymond. Mexican Agrarian Reform 1910–1960. **In** *Jones, E. L. and Woolf, S. J., eds.,* 1969, pp. 151–68.

Carrier, N. Calculation of Family Structure as a Demographic Example of the Organizational Power of Matrix Notation in Mass Arithmetical Operations. **In** *Bechhofer, F., ed.,* 1969, pp. 92–105.

Carroll, Daniel T. What Future for the Conglomerate? *Harvard Bus. Rev.,* May-June 1969, *47*(3), pp. 4–12, 167–68.

Carroll, Mitchell B. The U.N. Reenacts a Tax Drama. *Bull. Int. Fiscal Doc.,* April 1969, *23*(4), pp. 163–65.

Carstairs, G. M. Population Growth and Economic Development: Comment. **In** *Bechhofer, F., ed.,* 1969, pp. 155–64.

Carter, Charles F. Can We Get British Higher Education Cheaper? **In** *Blaug, M., ed.,* 1969, pp. 326–39.

______ The Hunt Report. *Scot. J. Polit. Econ.,* November 1969, *16*(3), pp. 248–55.

Cartter, Allan M. The Economics of Higher Education. **In** *Chamberlain, N. W., ed.,* 1969, pp. 145–84.

______ **and Farrell, Robert L.** Academic Labor Market Projections and the Draft. **In** *the Economics and Financing of Higher Education in the United States, JECP,* 1969, pp. 357–74.

Cartwright, Wayne and Candler, Wilfred. Estimation of Performance Functions for Budgeting and Simulation Studies. *Amer. J. Agr. Econ.,* February 1969, *51*(1), pp. 159–69.

Carus-Wilson, E. M. An Industrial Revolution of the Thirteenth Century. **In** *Scoville, W. C. and La Force, J. C., eds., Vol. I,* 1969, pp. 41–59.

Casadio, Gian Paolo. Ritorno al protezionismo? (Does the Protectionism Return? With English summary.) *Mondo Aperto,* December 1969, *23*(6), pp. 434–43.

Casal, José. Barter Accounting in the Puerto Rican Sugar Industry. *Manage. Account.,* August 1969, *51*(2), pp. 48–50, 53.

Case, Fred E. Business and the Urban Scene. *Calif. Manage. Rev.,* Summer 1969, *11*(4), pp. 3.

Caselli, Lorenzo. Dal profitto alla sopravvivenza: considerazioni in tema di finalità d'impresa. (From Profit to Survival—Remarks on Firm's Aims. With English summary.) *L'Impresa,* March/April 1969, *11*(2), pp. 126–32.

Casem, Antonio O. and Yoingco, Angel Q. Performance Budgeting in the Philippines. *Philippine Econ. J.,* Second Semester 1969, *8*(2), pp. 166–84.

Casetti, E.; King, L. and Jeffrey, D. Economic Fluctuations in a Multiregional Setting: A Bi-factor Analytic Approach. *J. Reg. Sci.,* December 1969, *9*(3), pp. 397–404.

Casler, George L. Development of a Two-Stage

Equipment-Enterprise Selection Method. *Can. J. Agr. Econ.*, February 1969, *17*(1), pp. 61–76.

——— **and Tadros, Mahfouz E.** A Game Theoretic Model for Farm Planning under Uncertainty. *Amer. J. Agr. Econ.*, December 1969, *51*(5), pp. 1164–67.

Cass, David. Resource Allocation with Probabilistic Individual Preferences: Discussion. *Amer. Econ. Rev.*, May 1969, *59*(2), pp. 562–63.

——— **and Stiglitz, Joseph E.** The Implications of Alternative Saving and Expectations Hypotheses for Choices of Technique and Patterns of Growth. *J. Polit. Econ.*, Part II, July/August 1969, *77*(4), pp. 586–627.

Cassidy, Henry J. The Employer Payroll Tax and the Labor Mix. *Quart. Rev. Econ. Bus.*, Spring 1969, *9*(1), pp. 39–43.

——— Maximum Likelihood Estimation in an *n-th* Order Autoregressive Disturbance Model. *Southern Econ. J.*, January 1969, *35*(3), pp. 263–64.

——— The Rate of Change in the Size Distribution of Wages as a Vector. *Rev. Income Wealth*, December 1969, *15*(4), pp. 349–68.

Castree, J. R.; Wilson, T. and Sinha, R. P. The Income Terms of Trade of Developed and Developing Countries. *Econ. J.*, December 1969, *79*(316), pp. 813–32.

Castrén, Kari. Kilpailun edistämisen nykyongelmia. (Some Contemporary Problems of Competition Policy. With English summary.) *Liiketaloudellinen Aikak.*, 1969, *18*(3), pp. 341–46.

Castro, Amado A. Philippine Export Development 1950–65. **In** *Morgan, T. and Spoelstra, N., eds.*, 1969, pp. 181–200.

——— The Philippines and the Industrial Nations. *Philippine Econ. J.*, First Semester 1969, *8*(1), pp. 1–12.

Catherwood, H. F. R. The Planning Dialogue. *Nat. Westminster Bank Quart. Rev.*, May 1969, pp. 2–9.

Cauley, Troy J. Public Expenditures in Our Federal System. *Rivista Int. Sci. Econ. Com.*, September 1969, *16*(9), pp. 898–919.

Caves, Richard E. The Theory of International Trade: Comment. **In** *Samuelson, P. A., ed.*, 1969, pp. 66–70.

Cavin, James P. The International Encyclopedia of the Social Sciences: A Review Article. *Amer. J. Agr. Econ.*, May 1969, *51*(2), pp. 268–78.

Cawthorne, D. R. Reserve Adjustments of City Banks. **In** *Jessup, P. F.*, 1969, pp. 42–50.

Cebula, Richard J. A Look at Long-Run Equilibrium under Multiplant Monopoly. *Amer. Econ.*, Fall 1969, *13*(2), pp. 92–93.

de Cecco, Marcello. The Problem of World Stability: Appendix: The Italian Payments Crisis of 1963–64. **In** *Mundell, R. A. and Swoboda, A. K., eds.*, 1969, pp. 383–89.

Celen, R. De beoordeling van de resultaten in de E.E.G.-landen, Groot-Brittannië en de V.S., wordt geconditioneerd door afwi jkende nationale belastingstelsels. (Differences in the National Tax Systems Are the Causes that the Profits of the Firms in the Countries of the E.E.C., Great Britain and the U.S. Have to Be Compared Cautiously. With English summary.) *Econ. Soc. Tijdschr.*, April 1969, *23*(2), pp. 185–204.

Černík, Oldřich. Develop Socialism to the Advantage of the Present and Future Generations. *New Trends Czech. Econ.*, February 1969, (1), pp. 3–33.

——— We Are Setting Out on the Road Towards Economic Consolidation. *New Trends Czech. Econ.*, December 1969, (8), pp. 3–44.

Červinka, Antonín. What Is the Matter in Dispute? *New Trends Czech. Econ.*, May 1969, (3), pp. 64–75.

Cerych, Ladislav. Accelerating the Innovation Process in Education. **In** *Bereday, G. Z. F., ed.*, 1969, pp. 34–50.

Chacel, Julian. The Principal Characteristics of the Agrarian Structure and Agricultural Production in Brazil. **In** *Ellis, H. S., ed.*, 1969, pp. 103–29.

Chakrabarti, S. K. A Note on the Relation Between Binary and Multiple Choice Probabilities. *Econometrica*, October 1969, *37*(4), pp. 726–27.

Chakravarty, Sukhamoy. The Optimal Growth Path for Finite Planning Horizons. **In** *[Ghosal, U. N.]*, 1969, pp. 40–68.

——— Some Aspects of Optimal Investment Policy in an Underdeveloped Economy. **In** *[Tinbergen, J.]*, 1969, pp. 1–18.

——— **and Bhagwati, Jagdish N.** Contributions to Indian Economic Analysis: A Survey. *Amer. Econ. Rev.*, Part II, September 1969, *59*(4), pp. 2–73.

Chalmers, Eric B. Monetary Policy Aspects of the Euro-dollar. **In** *Chalmers, E. B., ed.*, 1969, pp. 84–109.

Chamberlain, Neil W. Government Investment: How Scientific Can It Be? **In** *Starleaf, D. R., ed.*, 1969, pp. 205–09.

——— Public Planning in Market Systems. **In** *Prybyla, J. S., ed.*, 1969, pp. 49–55.

——— Some Further Thoughts on the Concept of Human Capital. **In** *Somers, G. G. and Wood, W. D., eds.*, 1969, pp. 230–48.

Chambers, John W. The Big Switch: Justice Roberts and the Minimum-Wage Cases. *Labor Hist.*, Winter 1969, *10*(1), pp. 44–73.

Chandavarkar, Anand G. Indian Monetary Policy and Economic Development. **In** *Bhuleshkar, A. V., ed.*, 1969, pp. 305–17.

——— Margini non utilizzati di fidi bancari: loro implicazioni per l'analisi e la politica monetaria. (Unused Bank Overdraughts: Their Implications for Monetary Analysis and Policy. With English summary.) *Bancaria*, December 1969, *25*(12), pp. 1464–72.

———**; Cleary, D. J. and Mookerjee, Subimal.** Existing International Banking and Credit Facilities in the ECAFE Region. *Int. Monet. Fund Staff Pap.*, November 1969, *16*(3), pp. 391–435.

Chandler, Alfred D., Jr. The Structure of American Industry in the Twentieth Century: A Historical Overview. *Bus. Hist. Rev.*, Autumn 1969, *43*(3), pp. 255–98.

Chandler, John H. Perspectives on Poverty 5: An International Comparison. *Mon. Lab. Rev.*, February 1969, *92*(2), pp. 55–62.

Chandra, Mahesh. Profitability and Investment Criteria. **In** *Dagli, V., ed., Vol. II,* 1969, pp. 31–40.

Chang, Chen Fu. The Firm's Long-run Average Cost Curve. *Quart. Rev. Econ. Bus.,* Winter 1969, *9*(4), pp. 80–84.

Chang, Winston W. The Theory of Saving and the Stability of Growth Equilibrium. *Quart. J. Econ.,* August 1969, *83*(3), pp. 491–503.

Chapin, Emerson. Success Story in South Korea. *Foreign Aff.,* April 1969, *47*(3), pp. 560–74.

Chapin, F. Stuart, Jr. and Logan, Thomas H. Patterns of Time and Space Use. **In** *Perloff, H. S., ed.,* 1969, pp. 305–32.

Chapman, John D. Interactions between Man and His Resources. **In** *National Academy of Sciences,* 1969, pp. 31–42.

Char, S. V. Agricultural Income Tax and the Indian Constitution. *Artha-Vikas,* July 1969, *5*(2), pp. 177–82.

Charles, K. J. Inflation and Economic Growth. *Econ. Aff.,* January-February 1969, *14*(1–2), pp. 26–32.

Chase, Richard X. State Sales Taxation as a Budget Balancing Device. *Amer. J. Econ. Soc.,* October 1969, *28*(4), pp. 405–07.

______ **and Laber, Gene.** Economic Growth as an Anti-poverty Tool: A Further Consideration of the Backwash Debate. *Soc. Sci. Quart.,* December 1969, *50*(3), pp. 604–08.

Chase, Samuel B., Jr. Bank Reactions to Securities Losses. **In** *Jessup, P. F.,* 1969, pp. 79–89.

______ Household Demand for Savings Deposits, 1921–1965. *J. Finance,* September 1969, *24*(4), pp. 643–58.

______ **and Gramley, Lyle E.** Time Deposits in Monetary Analysis. **In** *Brunner, K., ed.,* 1969, pp. 219–49.

Chatterjee, S. and Rangarajan, C. A Note on Comparison between Correlation Coefficients of Original and Transformed Variables. *Amer. Statist.,* October 1969, *23*(4), pp. 28–29.

Chatterji, M. Chemical Fertilisers: Rapid Growth. **In** *Dagli, V., ed., Vol. II,* 1969, pp. 201–03.

Chatterji, Manas. A Model of Resolution of Conflict between India and Pakistan. *Peace Res. Soc. Internat. Pap.,* 1969, *12,* pp. 87–102.

Chaudhri, D. P. Education of Farmers and Productivity. **In** *Pandit, H. N., ed.,* 1969, pp. 337–48.

Chauduri, A. Oligopoly and Economic Growth in India. **In** *Economic Concentration, Pt. 7A, SCH,* 1969, pp. 4242–51.

Chenery, Hollis B. The Interdependence of Investment Decisions. **In** *Arrow, K. J. and Scitovsky, T., eds.,* 1969, pp. 336–71.

______ The Two Gap Approach to Aid and Development: Reply to Bruton. *Amer. Econ. Rev.,* June 1969, *59*(3), pp. 446–49.

______ **and Westphal, Larry E.** Economies of Scale and Investment over Time. **In** *Margolis, J. and Guitton, H., eds.,* 1969, pp. 359–87.

Cherkasky, Martin. Statement. **In** *Health Care in America, Pt. 1, SCH,* 1969, pp. 4–23.

Chernoff, Herman. Sequential Designs. **In** *Naylor, T. H., ed.,* 1969, pp. 99–120.

Chesler, Herbert A. Labor Utilization and Earnings in the Johnstown Labor Market. *Land Econ.,* May 1969, *45*(2), pp. 273–77.

Chester, T. E. Mergers and Opportunities for Managers. *Nat. Westminster Bank Quart. Rev.,* May 1969, pp. 10–21.

Chetty, V. Karuppan. Econometrics of Joint Production: A Comment. *Econometrica,* October 1969, *37*(4), pp. 731.

______ On Measuring the Nearness of the Near-Moneys. *Amer. Econ. Rev.,* June 1969, *59*(3), pp. 270–81.

______ On the Long-Run and Short-Run Demand for Money: Some Further Evidence. *J. Polit. Econ.,* November/December 1969, *77*(6), pp. 921–31.

______ **and Sankar, U.** Bayesian Estimation of the CES Production Function. *Rev. Econ. Stud.,* July 1969, *36*(107), pp. 289–94.

Cheung, Steven N. S. Irving Fisher and the Red Guards. *J. Polit. Econ.,* May/June 1969, *77*(3), pp. 430–33.

______ Transaction Costs, Risk Aversion, and the Choice of Contractual Arrangements. *J. Law Econ.,* April 1969, *12*(1), pp. 23–42.

Chevalier, Jean-Marie. The Problem of Control in Large American Corporations. *Antitrust Bull.,* Spring 1969, *14,* pp. 163–80.

Chew, David C. E. Wastage Patterns in the Nursing Profession in Singapore: A Study of Manpower Utilisation. *Int. Lab. Rev.,* December 1969, *100* (6), pp. 583–94.

Chiancone, Aldo. Ancora sulla trasferibilità fra diverse generazioni dell'onere del debito pubblico. (A Note on the Shifting of the Burden of the Public Debt between Different Generations. With English summary.) *Rivista Int. Sci. Econ. Com.,* December 1969, *16*(12), pp. 1223–26.

Chiassino, Giuseppe. Vita probabile e vita media. (With English summary.) *Statistica,* April-June 1969, *29*(2), pp. 149–83.

Chibrikov, G. Exporting Private Capital: Impact on the Exporting Country's Economy. *Prob. Econ.,* December 1969, *12*(8), pp. 23–45.

Chien, Wen and Li-tien, Feng. A Quantitative Analysis of the Relationship Between the Rate of Growth of Productivity and the Average Wage. *Chinese Econ. Stud.,* Fall 1969, *3*(1), pp. 70–91.

Childress, Robert L. and Yost, Robert C. An Investigation of the Determinants of Investment Expenditures in Large, Multiproduct Corporations. *Western Econ. J.,* June 1969, *7*(2), pp. 173–79.

Childs, A. R. A Compensation Program for Managers of Professional, Technical and Non-Technical Personnel. **In** *Gilroy, T. P., ed.,* 1969, pp. 24–32.

Childs, Gerald L. Efficient Reallocation of Land in Urban Renewal. *Western Econ. J.,* September 1969, *7*(3), pp. 211–22.

______ **and Baldwin, William L.** The Fast Second and Rivalry in Research and Development. *Southern Econ. J.,* July 1969, *36*(1), pp. 18–24.

Chinitz, Benjamin. The Regional Aspects of Poverty. **In** *Task Force on Economic Growth and Opportunity,* 1969, pp. 93–104.

Chipman, John S. Factor Price Equalization and the Stolper-Samuelson Theorem. *Int. Econ. Rev.,* October 1969, *10*(3), pp. 399–406.

Chiswick, Barry R. Minimum Schooling Legislation and the Cross-Sectional Distribution of Income.

Econ. J., September 1969, *79*(315), pp. 495–507.

——— **and Burns, Joseph M.** An Economic Analysis of State Support for Higher Education. *Western Econ. J.*, March 1969, *7*(1), pp. 84–95.

Cho, Yong Hyo. Fiscal Implications of Annexation: The Case of Metropolitan Central Cities in Texas. *Land Econ.*, August 1969, *45*(3), pp. 368–72.

Choldin, Harvey M. The Development Project as Natural Experiment: The Comilla, Pakistan, Projects. *Econ. Develop. Cult. Change*, July 1969, *17* (4), pp. 483–500.

Chomchai, Prachoom. Implantation and Acclimatization of the Social Sciences in Thailand. *Int. Soc. Sci. J.*, 1969, *21*(3), pp. 383–92.

Chou, K. R. Hong Kong's Changing Pattern of Trade and Economic Interdependence in Southeast Asia. **In** *Morgan, T. and Spoelstra, N., eds.*, 1969, pp. 155–77.

Chow, Gregory C. Reply: A Note on the Estimation of Long-Run Relationships in Stock Adjustment Models. *J. Polit. Econ.*, November/December 1969, *77*(6), pp. 932–36.

——— **and Levitan, Richard E.** Nature of Business Cycles Implicit in a Linear Economic Model. *Quart. J. Econ.*, August 1969, *83*(3), pp. 504–17.

——— **and Levitan, Richard E.** Spectral Properties of Non-Stationary Systems of Linear Stochastic Difference Equations. *J. Amer. Statist. Assoc.*, June 1969, *64*(326), pp. 581–90.

Chow, L. P. and Hsu, S. C. A Chinese View of Family Planning in the Developing World. **In** *Behrman, S. J.; Corsa, L., Jr. and Freedman, R., eds.*, 1969, pp. 451–66.

Chowdhury, A. H. M. Nuruddin. Some Reflections on Income Redistributive Intermediation in Pakistan. *Pakistan Develop. Rev.*, Summer 1969, *9* (2), pp. 95–110.

Chowdhury, S. B. Lessons from France. **In** *Dagli, V., ed., Vol. II*, 1969, pp. 218–34.

Christ, Carl F. A Model of Monetary and Fiscal Policy Effects on the Money Stock, Price Level, and Real Output. *J. Money, Credit, Banking*, November 1969, *1*(4), pp. 683–705.

——— Resource Allocation in a Private-Property, Free-Contract Economy. **In** *Starleaf, D. R., ed.*, 1969, pp. 46–55.

Christensen, Laurits R. and Jorgenson, Dale W. The Measurement of U.S. Real Capital Input, 1929–1967. *Rev. Income Wealth*, December 1969, *15* (4), pp. 293–320.

Christian, James W. and Mazek, Warren F. Corporate Debt Structure and the Differential Effects of Monetary Policy. *Southern Econ. J.*, April 1969, *35*(4), pp. 359–68.

Christian, Virgil L., Jr. and Krislov, Joseph. Union Organizing and the Business Cycle, 1949–1966. *Southern Econ. J.*, October 1969, *36*(2), pp. 185–88.

Christiansen, Martin K.; Hammond, Jerome W. and Anthony, Willis E. Why the Growing Farm-Retail Price Spread? **In** *Ruttan, V. W.; Waldo, A. D. and Houck, J. P., eds.*, 1969, pp. 165–85.

Christie, Herbert. Euro-dollars and the Balance of Payments. **In** *Chalmers, E. B., ed.*, 1969, pp. 57–71.

Chuev, Iu. V. and Stekhova, G. P. The Generalized Equipment Replacement Problem. *Matekon*, Fall 1969, *6*(1), pp. 75–90.

Chukwumah, P. A. L. Developments in the Search for Higher Productivity. **In** *Yesufu, T. M., ed.*, 1969, pp. 300–312.

Chung, Kae H. Toward a General Theory of Motivation and Performance. *Calif. Manage. Rev.*, Spring 1969, *11*(3), pp. 81–88.

Churánek, Miloš. Foreign Trade, the Reproduction Process and Personal Consumption. *New Trends Czech. Econ.*, December 1969, (8), pp. 71–88.

Church, R. J. Harrision. Some Problems of Regional Economic Development in West Africa. *Econ. Geogr.*, January 1969, *45*(1), pp. 53–62.

Churchill, Geoffrey and Pollay, Richard W. A Simple Method for Estimating Consumer Acceptance. *Miss. Val. J. Bus. Econ.*, Spring 1969, *4*(2), pp. 50–56.

Cialdea, Basilio. Alcune riflessioni sulle relazioni internazionali negli ultimi cento anni. (Some Reflections on the Last Century's International Relations. With English summary.) *Mondo Aperto*, April 1969, *23*(2), pp. 123–35.

Cicchetti, Charles J. and Seneca, Joseph J. A Gravity Model Analysis of the Demand for Public Communication. *J. Reg. Sci.*, December 1969, *9*(3), pp. 459–70.

Ciocca, Pierluigi. L'ipotesi del "ritardo" dei salari rispetto ai prezzi in periodi di inflazione: alcune considerazioni generali-II. (The Hypothesis of the Lag of Wages behind Prices during Inflation: General Considerations-II. With English summary.) *Bancaria*, May 1969, *25*(5), pp. 572–83.

——— L'ipotesi del "ritardo" dei salari rispetto ai prezzi in periodi di inflazione: alcune considerazioni generali-I. (The Hypothesis of the "Lag" of Wages behind Prices during Inflation: General Considerations-I. With English summary.) *Bancaria*, April 1969, *25*(4), pp. 423–37.

Ciriacy-Wantrup, S. V. Natural Resources in Economic Growth: The Role of Institutions and Policies. *Amer. J. Agr. Econ.*, December 1969, *51*(5), pp. 1314–24.

Claassen, Emil M. Stock-Flow Decisions and Full Equilibrium. *Kyklos*, 1969, *22*(3), pp. 493–505.

Clague, Christopher K. Capital-Labor Substitution in Manufacturing in Undeveloped Countries. *Econometrica*, July 1969, *37*(3), pp. 528–37.

Clague, Ewan. Statement on Hours of Work. **In** *Wortman, M. S., Jr.*, 1969, pp. 238–39.

Clapham, John [Sir]. Communication and Commerce in Western Europe before the Railway Age. **In** *Scoville, W. C. and La Force, J. C., eds., Vol. IV*, 1969, pp. 148–55.

——— The Making of the First Railway and Telegraph Network, 1830–69. **In** *Scoville, W. C. and La Force, J. C., eds., Vol. IV*, 1969, pp. 156–70.

Clark, Edwin H., II and Bose, Swadesh R. Some Basic Considerations on Agricultural Mechanization in West Pakistan. *Pakistan Develop. Rev.*, Autumn 1969, *9*(3), pp. 273–308.

Clark, John G. The Business Elite of New Orleans before 1815. **In** *Kennedy, C. J., ed.*, 1969, pp. 94–103.

Clark, John J. Flags of Convenience and U.S. Maritime Policy. *Rivista Int. Sci. Econ. Com.*, April 1969, *16*(4), pp. 306–26.

Clark, Kenneth B. Efficiency as a Prod to Social Action. *Mon. Lab. Rev.*, August 1969, *92*(8), pp. 54–56.

Clark, Peter B. The Effects of International Monetary Developments on Capital Movements. *Law Contemp. Probl.*, Winter 1969, *34*(1), pp. 18–32.

Clarke, James W. Environment, Process and Policy: A Reconsideration. *Amer. Polit. Sci. Rev.*, December 1969, *63*(4), pp. 1172–82.

Clavaux, F. J. The Import Elasticity as a Yardstick for Measuring Trade Creation. *Econ. Int.*, November 1969, *22*(4), pp. 606–12.

Clawson, Marion. Open (Uncovered) Space as a New Urban Resource. **In** *Perloff, H. S., ed.*, 1969, pp. 139–75.

Claycamp, Henry J. and Liddy, Lucien E. Prediction of New Product Performance: An Analytical Approach. *J. Marketing Res.*, November 1969, *6*(4), pp. 414–20.

Cleary, D. J.; Mookerjee, Subimal and Chandavarkar, Anand G. Existing International Banking and Credit Facilities in the ECAFE Region. *Int. Monet. Fund Staff Pap.*, November 1969, *16*(3), pp. 391–435.

Clendenning, E. Wayne. Euro-dollars: The Problem of Control. **In** *Chalmers, E. B., ed.*, 1969, pp. 110–26.

Cleveland, Harold van B. The Common Market after De Gaulle. *Foreign Aff.*, July 1969, *47*(4), pp. 697–710.

Cliff, Edward P. Statement. **In** *Timber Management Policies, SCH,* 1969, pp. 234–70.

Close, F. Alan and Macesich, George. Monetary Velocity and Investment Multiplier Stability Relativity for Norway and Sweden. *Statsokon. Tidsskr.*, March 1969, *83*(1), pp. 10–22.

Cloud, Preston E., Jr. Mineral Resources from the Sea. **In** *National Academy of Sciences,* 1969, pp. 135–55.

______ Realities in Mineral Distribution. **In** *Effects of Population Growth on Natural Resources and the Environment, HCH,* 1969, pp. 219–42.

Cloutier, Raymond. Structural Relationships in Industrial Milk Production in Ontario. *Can. J. Agr. Econ.*, February 1969, *17*(1), pp. 157–58.

Cloward, Richard A. and Piven, Frances Fox. Desegregated Housing: Who Pays for the Reformers' Ideal? **In** *Kain, J. F., ed.*, 1969, pp. 175–83.

Cluff, A. T. and Liebling, H. I. U.S. Postwar Inflation and Phillips Curves. *Kyklos,* 1969, *22*(2), pp. 232–50.

Clurman, Michael. Does Higher Education Need More Money? **In** *the Economics and Financing of Higher Education in the United States, JECP,* 1969, pp. 632–64.

Cnudde, Charles F. and McCrone, Donald J. Party Competition and Welfare Policies in the American States. *Amer. Polit. Sci. Rev.*, September 1969, *63*(3), pp. 858–66.

Coale, Ansley J. The Decline of Fertility in Europe from the French Revolution to World War II. **In** *Behrman, S. J.; Corsa, L., Jr. and Freedman, R., eds.*, 1969, pp. 3–24.

______ Population and Economic Development. **In** *Hauser, P. M., ed.*, 1969, pp. 59–84.

Coates, David R. Technological Forecasting and the Planning of R and D. **In** *Arnfield, R. V., ed.*, 1969, pp. 83–96.

Coats, A. W. The American Economic Association's Publications: An Historical Perspective. *J. Econ. Lit.*, March 1969, *7*(1), pp. 57–68.

______ Is There a "Structure of Scientific Revolutions" in Economics? *Kyklos,* 1969, *22*(2), pp. 289–96.

______ Research Priorities in the History of Economics. *Hist. Polit. Econ.*, Spring 1969, *1*(1), pp. 9–18.

Čobeljić, Nikola and Stojanović, Radmila. The Theory of Investment Cycles in a Socialist Economy. *Eastern Europ. Econ.*, Fall 1968/Winter 1968–69, *7*(1–2), pp. 1–168.

Cobia, David W. and Farris, Paul L. Mergers and Diversified Growth of Large Grain Firms. *Amer. J. Agr. Econ.*, August 1969, *51*(3), pp. 619–24.

Cochran, Thomas C. Economic History, Old and New. *Amer. Hist. Rev.*, June 1969, *74*(5), pp. 1561–72.

Cochrane, James L. English Classical Economics. **In** *Kiker, B. F. and Carlsson, R. J., eds.*, 1969, pp. 1–9.

______ The Evolution and Generalization of the Golden-Age Modification of the Ramsey Proposal. *Indian Econ. J.*, January–March 1969, *16*(3), pp. 341–55.

Coen, P. J.; Gomme, E. D. and Kendall, M. G. Lagged Relationships in Economic Forecasting. *J. Roy. Statist. Soc.*, Part 2, 1969, *132,* pp. 133–52.

Coen, Robert M. Tax Policy and Investment Behavior: Comment. *Amer. Econ. Rev.*, June 1969, *59* (3), pp. 370–79.

Coffey, Joseph D. National Labor Relations Legislation: Possible Impact on American Agriculture. *Amer. J. Agr. Econ.*, December 1969, *51*(5), pp. 1065–74.

Cogen, Charles. Collective Negotiations in Public Education. **In** *Walsh, R. E., ed.*, 1969, pp. 141–53.

Cohen, Alvin. Monetarism vs. Structuralism: Conflict in U.S. Economic Aid to Latin America. **In** *Hilton, R., ed.*, 1969, pp. 173–84.

Cohen, Benjamin I. Less Developed Countries and U.S. Domestic Problems: Comment. *Public Policy,* Fall 1969, *18*(1), pp. 55–60.

Cohen, Henry. Planning Rationally for the City. **In** *Connery, R. H. and Caraley, D., eds.*, 1969, pp. 179–92.

Cohen, Kalman J. Risk Analysis and Branch Bank Location Decisions. **In** *Jessup, P. F.,* 1969, pp. 330–40.

______ **and Reid, Samuel Richardson.** Effects of Regulation, Branching, and Mergers on Banking Structure and Performance: Reply. *Southern Econ. J.*, October 1969, *36*(2), pp. 204–09.

Cohen, Malcolm S. The Direct Effects of Federal Manpower Programs in Reducing Unemployment. *J. Human Res.*, Fall 1969, *4*(4), pp. 491–507.

______ Married Women in the Labor Force: An Analysis of Participation Rates. *Mon. Lab. Rev.*, October 1969, *92*(10), pp. 31–35.

______ The Micro Approach to Manpower Research. **In** *Somers, G. G., ed. (II),* 1969, pp. 120–28.

Colaco, Francis X. Harberger's Inflation Model: A

Critique and Test Using Data for Brazil and India. *Indian Econ. J.*, April–June 1969, *16*(4–5), pp. 434–44.

Colantoni, Claude S.; Manes, Rene P. and Whinston, Andrew. Programming, Profit Rates and Pricing Decisions. *Accounting Rev.*, July 1969, *44*(3), pp. 467–81.

Colantoni, Marcello. Nota sulla distribuzione di uno stimatore compionario dell'indice 'Alfa' di Pareto. (With English summary.) *Statistica*, October-December 1969, *29*(4), pp. 768–78.

Cole, David C. and Nam, Young Woo. The Pattern and Significance of Economic Planning in Korea. **In** *Adelman, I., ed.*, 1969, pp. 11–37.

Cole, David L. The AFL-CIO's Internal Disputes Plan. *Mon. Lab. Rev.*, September 1969, *92*(9), pp. 12–15.

______ Effect of Merchandising Methods on Prices Paid at Cooperative Feeder Cattle Sales. *Amer. J. Agr. Econ.*, December 1969, *51*(5), pp. 1129–33.

Cole, H. J. D. The Contribution of Demography to Physical and Spatial Planning: Comment. **In** *Bechhofer, F., ed.*, 1969, pp. 131–33.

Cole, Rosanne. Data Errors and Forecasting Accuracy. **In** *Mincer, J., ed.*, 1969, pp. 47–82.

Coleman, D. C. An Innovation and Its Diffusion: The "New Draperies." *Econ. Hist. Rev.*, December 1969, *22*(3), pp. 417–29.

Coleman, F. L. Some Notes on the Native Development of Copper-Ore Deposits in Central Africa. *S. Afr. J. Econ.*, September 1969, *37*(3), pp. 260–63.

Coleman, James; Katz, Elihu and Menzel, Herbert. The Diffusion of an Innovation among Physicians. **In** *Alexis, M.; Holloway, R. J. and Hancock, R. S., eds.*, 1969, pp. 154–67.

Collado, Emilio G. Statement. **In** *The 1969 Economic Report of the President, Pt. 4, JECH*, 1969, pp. 983–92.

Collcutt, R. H. Planning Economic Development. **In** *Arnfield, R. V., ed.*, 1969, pp. 97–111.

Collins, E. J. T. Harvest Technology and Labour Supply in Britain, 1790–1870. *Econ. Hist. Rev.*, December 1969, *22*(3), pp. 453–73.

______ Labour Supply and Demand in European Agriculture 1800–1880. **In** *Jones, E. L. and Woolf, S. J., eds.*, 1969, pp. 61–94.

Collins, Norman R. and Preston, Lee E. Industry Structure and Price-Cost Margins. **In** *Weston, J. F. and Peltzman, S., eds.*, 1969, pp. 81–109.

______ Price-Cost Margins and Industry Structure. *Rev. Econ. Statist.*, August 1969, *51*(3), pp. 271–86.

Colombo, Emilio. Equilibrio della bilancia dei pagamenti e utilizzo delle risorse senza inflazione. (Equilibrium of the Balance of Payments and Internal Use of Resources without Inflation. With English summary.) *Bancaria*, October 1969, *25* (10), pp. 1221–24.

Colwell, B. Joe. Antitrust and Efficiency: Product Extension Mergers. *Southern Econ. J.*, April 1969, *35*(4), pp. 369–75.

Colyer, D. Fertilization Strategy Under Uncertainty. *Can. J. Agr. Econ.*, November 1969, *17*(3), pp. 144–49.

Comanor, William S. and Leibenstein, Harvey. Allocative Efficiency, X-Efficiency and the Measurement of Welfare Losses. *Economica, N.S.*, August 1969, *36*(143), pp. 304–09.

______ **and Scherer, Frederic M.** Patent Statistics as a Measure of Technical Change. *J. Polit. Econ.*, May/June 1969, *77*(3), pp. 392–98.

______ **and Wilson, Thomas A.** Advertising and the Advantages of Size. *Amer. Econ. Rev.*, May 1969, *59*(2), pp. 87–98.

Comiskey, Eugene E. and Johnson, Robert W. Breakeven Analysis in Installment Lending. **In** *Jessup, P. F.*, 1969, pp. 229–37.

Comm. on Resources and Man, Nat'l. Acad. of Sci. Introduction and Recommendations from *Resources and Man.* **In** *Effects of Population Growth on Natural Resources and the Environment, HCH*, 1969, pp. 120–30.

Conan, A. R. Does Britain Pay Its Way? *Nat. Westminster Bank Quart. Rev.*, February 1969, pp. 2–17.

Conant, Eaton H. Report and Appraisal: The Armour Fund's Sioux City Project. **In** *Wortman, M. S., Jr.*, 1969, pp. 205–11.

Conard, Joseph W. and Frankena, Mark W. The Yield Spread Between New and Seasoned Corporate Bonds, 1952–63. **In** *Guttentag, J. M. and Cagan, P., eds.*, 1969, pp. 143–222.

Conforti, Joseph M. Attitudes Toward Health and Health Care Facilities Among Low Income Youth. *Soc. Sci. Quart.*, December 1969, *50*(3), pp. 687–94.

Conger, John Stoy. Conglomerate Land Acquisition: Reasons and Use. **In** *Garoian, L., ed.*, 1969, pp. 98–105.

Conklin, D. W. Barriers to Technological Change in the U.S.S.R.: A Study of Chemical Fertilizers. *Soviet Stud.*, January 1969, *20*(3), pp. 353–65.

Conley, Ronald W. A Benefit-Cost Analysis of the Vocational Rehabilitation Program. *J. Human Res.*, Spring 1969, *4*(2), pp. 226–52.

______ Roma Remarks on Methods of Measuring the Importance of Sources of Economic Growth. *Southern Econ. J.*, January 1969, *35*(3), pp. 224–30.

Conlisk, John. An Approach to the Theory of Inequality in the Size Distribution of Income. *Western Econ. J.*, June 1969, *7*(2), pp. 180–86.

______ Determinants of School Enrollment and School Performance. *J. Human Res.*, Spring 1969, *4*(2), pp. 140–57.

______ The Equilibrium Covariance Matrix of Dynamic Econometric Models. *J. Amer. Statist. Assoc.*, March 1969, *64*(325), pp. 277–79.

______ A Neoclassical Growth Model with Endogenously Positioned Technical Change Frontier. *Econ. J.*, June 1969, *79*(314), pp. 348–62.

______ **and Huddle, Donald.** Allocating Foreign Aid: An Appraisal of a Self-Help Model. *J. Devel. Stud.*, July 1969, *5*(4), pp. 245–51.

Conneman, George J. Farm Panels as a Source of Farm Management Data: The Cornell Producer Panel. *Amer. J. Agr. Econ.*, December 1969, *51* (5), pp. 1206–10.

______ **and Harrington, D. H.** Implications of Exit

and Entry of Farm Firms in Agricultural Supply Analysis. *Agr. Econ. Res.*, April 1969, *21*(2), pp. 40–44.

Connery, Robert H. Governing the City. **In** *Connery, R. H. and Caraley, D., eds.*, 1969, pp. 1–6.

Constable, G. A. and Brooks, Scott E. Minimum Resource Requirements for Specified Resource Returns on Ontario Farms. *Can. J. Agr. Econ.*, November 1969, *17*(3), pp. 133–43.

Constandse, A. K. The Social Impact of Farm Mechanization: Some Findings of Cross-National Research. *Int. Soc. Sci. J.*, 1969, *21*(2), pp. 235–43.

Constantinescu, N. N. Dezvoltarea sistemului științelor economice în socialism. (Development of the System of Economic Sciences in Socialism. With English summary.) *Stud. Cercet. Econ.*, 1969, *3*, pp. 173–84.

Constanzo, G. A. Statement. **In** *A Review of Balance of Payments Policies, JECH*, 1969, pp. 187–91.

Contini, Bruno. A Critical Survey of Use of Cost-Benefit Analysis in Public Finance. **In** *Peacock, A. T., ed.*, 1969, pp. 65–85.

Conway, Jack T. and Ginsburg, Woodrow L. The Extension of Collective Bargaining to New Fields. **In** *Wortman, M. S., Jr.*, 1969, pp. 148–50.

Conze, Werner. The Effects of Nineteenth-Century Liberal Agrarian Reforms on Social Structure in Central Europe. **In** *Crouzet, F.; Chaloner, W. H. and Stern, W. M., eds.*, 1969, pp. 53–81.

Cook, Alice H. The ILO and Japanese Politics, II: Gain or Loss for Labor? *Ind. Lab. Relat. Rev.*, April 1969, *22*(3), pp. 375–98.

Cook, Billy D. and Quindry, Kenneth E. Humanization of the Property Tax for Low Income Households. *Nat. Tax J.*, September 1969, *22*(3), pp. 357–67.

Cook, David E. Inter-Unit Pricing and Your New Pricing Expert: The IRS. *Manage. Account.*, August 1969, *51*(2), pp. 9–11.

Cook, Jack L. Conservation by Bulldozer. *Mich. Academician*, Spring 1969, *1*(3–4), pp. 179–91.

Cook, S. L. Scientific Approaches to Business Problems or the Advancement of Science in Management. **In** *Hugh-Jones, E. M., ed.*, 1969, pp. 62–88.

Cook, Victor and Polli, Rolando. Validity of the Product Life Cycle. *J. Bus.*, October 1969, *42*(4), pp. 385–400.

Coombs, Charles A. Treasury and Federal Reserve Foreign Exchange Operations. *Fed. Res. Bull.*, September 1969, *55*(9), pp. 697–718.

______ Treasury and Federal Reserve Foreign Exchange Operations. *Fed. Res. Bull.*, March 1969, *55*(3), pp. 210–27.

Coombs, H. C. Central Banking—A Look Back and Forward. *Econ. Rec.*, December 1969, *45*(112), pp. 485–95.

Coondoo, Dipankor. The Effect of Relative Prices on Engel Elasticity of Cereals in India. *Arthaniti*, January & July 1969, *12*(1&2), pp. 57–68.

Cooney, E. W. Public Opinion and Government Policy in Nineteenth Century British Economic History: A Review and a Study of the Building Industry. *Yorkshire Bull. Econ. Soc. Res.*, November 1969, *21*(2), pp. 141–54.

Cooper, Jack L. Continuous Borrowing from the Federal Reserve System: Some Empirical Evidence. *J. Finance*, March 1969, *24*(1), pp. 33–48.

Cooper, Richard N. Macroeconomic Policy Adjustment in Interdependent Economies. *Quart. J. Econ.*, February 1969, *83*(1), pp. 1–24.

Coper, Rudolf. Economics and the Family. *Miss. Val. J. Bus. Econ.*, Spring 1969, *4*(2), pp. 57–64.

Cordell, Arthur J. The Brazilian Soluble Coffee Problem: A Review. *Quart. Rev. Econ. Bus.*, Spring 1969, *9*(1), pp. 29–38.

Corden, W. M. Effective Protective Rates in the General Equilibrium Model: A Geometric Note. *Oxford Econ. Pap.*, July 1969, *21*(2), pp. 135–41.

______ International Monetary Reform and the Developing Countries: A Mainly Theoretical Paper. **In** *Mundell, R. A. and Swoboda, A. K., eds.*, 1969, pp. 283–304.

Córdova, Efrén. The Check-Off System: A Comparative Study. *Int. Lab. Rev.*, May 1969, *99*(5), pp. 463–91.

______ Collective Labour Relations in Latin American Ports. *Int. Lab. Rev.*, October 1969, *100*(4), pp. 315–39.

Cordtz, Dan. How Auto Firms Figure Their Cost to Reckon the Price Dealers Pay. **In** *Alexis, M.; Holloway, R. J. and Hancock, R. S., eds.*, 1969, pp. 335–42.

Corigliano, Giorgio. La funzione del "product manager" nella realtà industriale italiana. (The Product Manager's Function in the Italian Industrial Situation. With English summary.) *L'Impresa*, July/October 1969, *11*(4–5), pp. 343–46.

Corluy, M. Waarom de verstandige beurbelegger altijd winst boekt. (Why the Intelligent Investor in the Stock Exchange Will Always Make Profits. With English summary.) *Econ. Soc. Tijdschr.*, August 1969, *23*(4), pp. 379–90.

Corneel, Frederic G. Tax Planning—Teaching and Practice. **In** *Gaa, C. J.*, 1969, pp. 191–204.

Cornehls, James V. On the Use and Misuse of Veblen's 'Evolutionary Economics'. *Oxford Econ. Pap.*, November 1969, *21*(3), pp. 433–37.

______ **and Van Roy, Edward.** Economic Development in Mexico and Thailand: An Institutional Analysis (Part I). *J. Econ. Issues*, September 1969, *3*(3), pp. 16–32.

______ **and Van Roy, Edward.** Economic Development in Mexico and Thailand: An Institutional Analysis (Part II). *J. Econ. Issues*, December 1969, *3*(4), pp. 21–38.

Cornelisse, Peter A. and Versluis, Jan. The Semi-Input-Output Method under Upper Bounds. **In** *[Tinbergen, J.]*, 1969, pp. 175–99.

Corner, D. C. Recent Trends in Retail Distribution. *Nat. Westminster Bank Quart. Rev.*, May 1969, pp. 22–32.

______ **and Fletcher, C. H.** Some Effects of Selective Employment Tax on the Construction and Service Industries. *Bull. Oxford Univ. Inst. Econ. Statist.*, February 1969, *31*(1), pp. 47–54.

Cornwall, Richard R. The Use of Prices to Characterize the Core of an Economy. *J. Econ. Theory*, December 1969, *1*(4), pp. 353–73.

Costache, Sandu. Valorificarea producției cooperativelor agricole. (Turning to Account Agricultural

Cooperative Farm Production. With English summary.) *Stud. Cercet. Econ.*, 1969, *1-2*, pp. 107–19.

Costello, Edward T. The Terms of Trade of the Southeast (1947–1958). *Southern Econ. J.*, April 1969, *35*(4), pp. 376–77.

Costello, P. M. Economics of the Ethical Drug Industry: A Reply to Whitney. *Antitrust Bull.*, Summer 1969, *14*, pp. 397–403.

Costner, Herbert and Gove, Walter. Organizing the Poor: An Evaluation of a Strategy. *Soc. Sci. Quart.*, December 1969, *50*(3), pp. 643–56.

Cotner, Melvin L. A Policy for Public Investments in Natural Resources. *Amer. J. Agr. Econ.*, February 1969, *51*(1), pp. 87–99.

Cotton, John and Mushkin, Selma J. Systematic Analysis and Grants-in-Aid in a Federal System. **In** *The Analysis and Evaluation of Public Expenditures: The PPB System, Vol. 1, JECP*, 1969, pp. 332–54.

Courbis, R. Compatabilité Nationale à Prix Constants et à Productivité Constante. (With English summary.) *Rev. Income Wealth*, March 1969, *15* (1), pp. 33–76.

Courchene, Thomas J. An Analysis of the Canadian Money Supply: 1925–1934. *J. Polit. Econ.*, May/June 1969, *77*(3), pp. 363–91.

______ An Analysis of the Price-Inventory Nexus with Empirical Application to the Canadian Manufacturing Sector. *Int. Econ. Rev.*, October 1969, *10*(3), pp. 315–36.

Coussy, Jean. Adjusting Economics Curricula to African Needs. *Int. Soc. Sci. J.*, 1969, *21*(3), pp. 393–405.

Covell, James. Some Economic Needs and Programs in New Mexico. *N. Mex. Bus.*, November–December 1969, *22*(11&12), pp. 1–5.

Covi, Antonio M. Ideologia, utopia e sottosviluppo contro la società capitalistica. (Ideology, Utopia and Underdevelopment versus the Capitalistic Society. With English summary.) *Rivista Int. Sci. Econ. Com.*, January 1969, *16*(1), pp. 79–99.

Cowie, Harry and Stamp, Maxwell. Britain and the Free Trade Area Option. **In** *Johnson, H. G., ed.*, 1969, pp. 165–253.

Cownie, John and Johnston, Bruce F. The Seed-Fertilizer Revolution and Labor Force Absorption. *Amer. Econ. Rev.*, Part I, September 1969, *59*(4), pp. 569–82.

Cox, D. R. Some Sampling Problems in Technology. **In** *Johnson, N. L. and Smith, H., Jr., eds.*, 1969, pp. 506–27.

______ **and Herzberg, Agnes M.** Recent Work on the Design of Experiments: A Bibliography and a Review. *J. Roy. Statist. Soc.*, Part 1, 1969, *132*, pp. 29–67.

Cox, Edward; Fellmeth, Robert and Schulz, John. The Consumer and the Federal Trade Commission, a Critique of the Consumer Protection Record of the FTC. **In** *To Establish a Department of Consumer Affairs, SCH*, 1969, pp. 123–312.

Cox, Eli P. Guaranteed Annual Income and Consumer Demand. **In** *Extension of Elementary and Secondary Education Programs, Pt. 4, HCH*, 1969, pp. 2848–74.

Cox, P. Calculation of Family Structure as a Demographic Example of the Organizational Power of Matrix Notation in Mass Arithmetical Operations: Comment. **In** *Bechhofer, F., ed.*, 1969, pp. 107–11.

Craft, James A. Proportional Representation for Teacher Negotiations. *Ind. Relat.*, May 1969, *8*(3), pp. 236–46.

______ Public Employee Negotiations Legislation: The Paradox of Labor Divided. *Quart. Rev. Econ. Bus.*, Winter 1969, *9*(4), pp. 29–37.

______ Toward a Public Employment Wage Theory: Comment. *Ind. Lab. Relat. Rev.*, October 1969, *23*(1), pp. 89–95.

Craig, R. S. and Floud, R. C. List of Publications on the Economic History of Great Britain and Ireland Published in 1967. *Econ. Hist. Rev.*, August 1969, *22*(2), pp. 322–41.

Cramer, Curtis and Birch, John I. A Secular Theory of Inflation. *J. Econ. Theory*, December 1969, *1* (4), pp. 480–86.

Cramer, Joe J., Jr. and Iwand, Thomas. Financial Reporting for Conglomerates: An Economic Analysis. *Calif. Manage. Rev.*, Spring 1969, *11*(3), pp. 25–34.

Crandall, Robert H. Information Economics and Its Implications for the Further Development of Accounting Theory. *Accounting Rev.*, July 1969, *44* (3), pp. 457–66.

Crawford, Elisabeth T. The Informal Organization of Policy-Oriented Social Science. **In** *Crawford, E. T. and Biderman, A. D., eds.*, 1969, pp. 69–81.

Craypo, Charles. The National Union Convention as an Internal Appeal Tribunal. *Ind. Lab. Relat. Rev.*, July 1969, *22*(4), pp. 487–511.

Crew, Michael A. Coinsurance and the Welfare Economics of Medical Care. *Amer. Econ. Rev.*, December 1969, *59*(5), pp. 906–08.

______ Mr. Tipping on Road Pricing. *Econ. J.*, December 1969, *79*(316), pp. 975–77.

______ The Optimality of Pure Competition in the Capacity Problem: Further Comment. *Quart. J. Econ.*, May 1969, *83*(2), pp. 341–43.

Crew, Robert E., Jr. Dimensions of Public Policy: A Factor Analysis of State Expenditures. *Soc. Sci. Quart.*, September 1969, *50*(2), pp. 381–88.

de Cristofaro, Rodolfo. Impiego delle distribuzioni beta ed F per ricavare intervalli di stima di una percentuale nel campionamento bernoulliano. (With English summary.) *Statistica*, October-December 1969, *29*(4), pp. 779–85.

Cristureanu, T. Mutații în structura comerțului exterior al României socialiste, expresie a realizărilor în 25 de ani de construire a socialismului. (Changes in the Structure of Romania's Foreign Trade, an Expression of the Achievements Made in 25 Years' Construction of Socialism. With English summary.) *Stud. Cercet. Econ.*, 1969, *3*, pp. 161–71.

Crockett, Norman L. The Westward Movement and the Transit of American Machine Technology: The Case of Wool Manufacturing. **In** *Kennedy, C. J., ed.*, 1969, pp. 111–20.

Crosby, Richard W. Attitude Measurement in a Bilingual Culture. *J. Marketing Res.*, November 1969, *6*(4), pp. 421–26.

Cross, Malcolm and Schwartzbaum, Allan M. Social

Mobility and Secondary School Selection in Trinidad and Tobago. *Soc. Econ. Stud.*, June 1969, *18* (2), pp. 189–207.

Crowther, Carol. Crimes, Penalties, and Legislatures. *Ann. Amer. Acad. Polit. Soc. Sci.*, January 1969, *381*, pp. 147–58.

Crowther, John F. Peril-Point Acquisition Prices. *Harvard Bus. Rev.*, September–October 1969, *47* (5), pp. 58–62.

Crumbley, D. Larry. How Long Will the Commissioner and the Courts Ignore Accounting Standards on the Accrual of Prepaid Income? *Nat. Tax J.*, December 1969, *22*(4), pp. 559–61.

Crutchfield, James A. Economic Evaluation of Weather Modification. **In** *Fleagle, R. G., ed.*, 1969, pp. 105–17.

Crystal, John. Canada Banker's 'Interest'. *Bull. Int. Fiscal Doc.*, March 1969, *23*(3), pp. 137–40.

______ The Curious Nature of "Know-How": Part II. *Bull. Int. Fiscal Doc.*, February 1969, *23*(2), pp. 73–75.

Csáki, N. Competitive and Complementary International Division of Labour in the Agriculture of Socialist Countries. (In Russian. With English summary.) *Acta Oecon.*, 1969, *4*(3), pp. 283–97.

Cuff, Robert D. Bernard Baruch: Symbol and Myth in Industrial Mobilization. *Bus. Hist. Rev.*, Summer 1969, *43*(2), pp. 115–33.

Cukor, Gy. Long-Term Planning and Technical Progress. *Acta Oecon.*, 1969, *4*(3), pp. 239–58.

Culbertson, John M. Statement. **In** *The 1969 Economic Report of the President, Pt. 3, JECH*, 1969, pp. 545–47.

Cullity, John P. The Growth of Educational Employment in Three Countries, 1895–1964. *J. Human Res.*, Winter 1969, *4*(1), pp. 84–92.

Cumming, J. N. The Sheep Industry in Tasmania. *Quart. Rev. Agr. Econ.*, July 1969, *22*(3), pp. 165–78.

Cummings, L. L. and Harnett, D. L. Bargaining Behaviour in a Symmetric Bargaining Triad: The Impact of Risk-Taking Propensity, Information, Communication and Terminal Bid. *Rev. Econ. Stud.*, October 1969, *36*(108), pp. 485–501.

Cummings, Ralph W., Jr. Buffer Stocks. **In** *Indian Society of Agricultural Economics*, 1969, pp. 49–84.

Cummings, Ronald G. Some Extensions of the Economic Theory of Exhaustible Resources. *Western Econ. J.*, September 1969, *7*(3), pp. 201–10.

______ **and Burt, Oscar R.** The Economics of Production from Natural Resources: Note. *Amer. Econ. Rev.*, December 1969, *59*(5), pp. 985–90.

Cundiff, Edward W. and Hamm, B. Curtis. Self-Actualization and Product Perception. *J. Marketing Res.*, November 1969, *6*(4), pp. 470–72.

Cunningham, N. J. A Note on the 'Proper Distribution of Industry.' *Oxford Econ. Pap.*, March 1969, *21*(1), pp. 122–27.

Curnow, R. The Innovation Cycle in the Manufacture and Application of Computer Systems. **In** *Arnfield, R. V., ed.*, 1969, pp. 314–20.

Currie, Lauchlin. Myrdal on South Asia. *J. Econ. Issues*, June 1969, *3*(2), pp. 166–76.

Curry, H. E. Investment Income in Fire and Casualty Rate Making. *J. Risk Ins.*, September 1969, *36*(4), pp. 447–53.

Curry, Robert L., Jr. The "Failing Company" Doctrine and Competition as an Antitrust Standard. *Oregon Bus. Rev.*, October 1969, *28*(10), pp. 1–5.

______ Trade Restraints Injuring the United States Government. *Quart. Rev. Econ. Bus.*, Autumn 1969, *9*(3), pp. 77–80.

Curtin, T. R. C. The Economics of Population Growth and Control in Developing Countries. *Rev. Soc. Econ.*, September 1969, *27*(2), pp. 139–53.

Curtis, Thomas D. and Munsinger, Gary M. A Comparison of the Regrouping Process in the United States and the Soviet Union. *Univ. Wash. Bus. Rev.*, Winter 1969, *28*(2), pp. 50–61.

Curzon, Gerard and Curzon, Victoria. Options after the Kennedy Round. **In** *Johnson, H. G., ed.*, 1969, pp. 19–73.

Curzon, Victoria and Curzon, Gerard. Options after the Kennedy Round. **In** *Johnson, H. G., ed.*, 1969, pp. 19–73.

Cutler, Frederick and Devlin, David T. The International Investment Position of the United States: Developments in 1968. *Surv. Curr. Bus.*, October 1969, *49*(10), pp. 23–36.

Cyert, Richard M. and George, Kenneth D. Competition, Growth, and Efficiency. *Econ. J.*, March 1969, *79*(313), pp. 23–41.

Czajkowski, Peter and Restall, Lawrence J. Computation of LIFO Index: A Statistical Sampling Approach. *Manage. Account.*, September 1969, *51* (3), pp. 43–48.

Czarnecki, Edgar R. Profit Sharing and Union Organizing. *Mon. Lab. Rev.*, December 1969, *92* (12), pp. 61–62.

D'Ambrosio, Charles A. Asset Pricing, Time, and Causality—An Introspective View of Capital Theory. *Rev. Soc. Econ.*, March 1969, *27*(1), pp. 1–12.

D'Iribarne, Alain. Les besoins d'emploi des entreprises. (With English summary.) *Revue Écon.*, July 1969, *20*(4), pp. 601–57.

Dadák, Zdeněk. Strojírenský výrobní proces a jeho operativní řízení jako kybernetický systém. (Production Process in Engineering and Operative Control of This Process as a Cybernetic System. With English summary.) *Ekon.-Mat. Obzor*, 1969, *5*(4), pp. 518–20.

Daddario, Emilio Q. Predicting Effects, 1967. **In** *Pursell, C. W., Jr.*, 1969, pp. 447–55.

Daellenbach, Hans G. and Archer, Stephen H. The Optimal Bank Liquidity: A Multi-Period Stochastic Model. *J. Financial Quant. Anal.*, September 1969, *4*(3), pp. 329–43.

Dagenais, Marcel G. A Threshold Regression Model. *Econometrica*, April 1969, *37*(2), pp. 193–203.

Dagum, Camilo. Structural Permanence: Its Role in the Analysis of Structural Dualisms and Dependences and for Prediction and Decision Purposes. *Z. ges. Staatswiss.*, April 1969, *125*(2), pp. 211–35.

de Dagum, Estela María Bee. An Econometric Model for the Foreign Trade Multiplier of Argentina. *Weltwirtsch. Arch.*, 1969, *103*(1), pp. 26–40.

Dahl, Dale C. Conglomerate Growth: Policy Implications for Agriculture and Agribusiness. **In** *Garoian, L., ed.*, 1969, pp. 115–16.

______ Structure of Input Supplying Industries and Techniques of Analysis. *Amer. J. Agr. Econ.*, December 1969, *51*(5), pp. 1046–53.

______ The Upper Midwest Region. In *Task Force on Economic Growth and Opportunity*, 1969, pp. 105–23.

Daidola, Giorgio. Formazione e trasferimento quadri nelle imprese multinazionali. (Development and Transfer of Managers in Multinational Firms. With English summary.) *L'Impresa*, July/October 1969, *11*(4–5), pp. 373–75.

Dalenius, T. Designing Descriptive Sample Surveys. In *Johnson, N. L. and Smith, H., Jr., eds.*, 1969, pp. 390–415.

Dallavalle, Q. Francis and Bretzfelder, Robert B. Total and *Per Capita* Personal Income by Regions and States, 1968. *Surv. Curr. Bus.*, August 1969, *49*(8), pp. 13, 24.

______**; Hirschberg, David A. and Bretzfelder, Robert B.** Personal Income, 1968, and Disposable Income, 1929–68, by States and Regions. *Surv. Curr. Bus.*, April 1969, *49*(4), pp. 16–21, 32.

Daloz, Jean-Pierre. La fonction de demande de monnaie en France de 1920 à 1968: Analyse théorique et économétrique sur les données françaises annueles de 1920 à 1966 prolongée pour 1967 et 1968. (With English summary.) *Revue Écon.*, May 1969, *20*(3), pp. 468–96.

Dalrymple, Dana G. The Organization of Agriculture: Discussion. *Amer. J. Agr. Econ.*, December 1969, *51*(5), pp. 1286–88.

Dalton, George and Walters, A. A. The Economy of Liberia. In *Robson, P. and Lury, D. A., eds.*, 1969, pp. 287–315.

Dalvi, M. Q. and Lee, N. Variations in the Value of Travel Time. *Manchester Sch. Econ. Soc. Stud.*, September 1969, *37*(3), pp. 213–36.

Daly, D. J. Business Cycles in Canada: Their Postwar Persistence. In *Bronfenbrenner, M., ed.*, 1969, pp. 45–65.

______ The Changing Environment for Management in Canada. In *Association of Canadian Schools of Business*, 1969, pp. 308–22.

Daly, George G. The Burden of the Debt and Future Generations in Local Finance. *Southern Econ. J.*, July 1969, *36*(1), pp. 44–51.

Daly, Joseph F. Some Basic Principles of Statistical Surveys. *J. Amer. Statist. Assoc.*, December 1969, *64*(328), pp. 1129–33.

Damm, Walter. The Obstacles to a Regional Integration of Capital Markets: A Comment. *J. Money, Credit, Banking*, August 1969, *1*(3), pp. 328–31.

Danciu, C. Dezvoltarea planificată armonioasă a economiei naționale. (Planned and Balanced Development of National Economy. With English summary.) *Stud. Cercet. Econ.*, 1969, *3*, pp. 79–87.

Dandekar, V. M. Repercussions of Food Surpluses in Industrialized Countries on Economic Growth in Developing Countries. In *Papi, U. and Nunn, C., eds.*, 1969, pp. 182–99.

Daněček, Jiří. New Monetary Banking System in Czechoslovakia. *New Trends Czech. Econ.*, May 1969, (3), pp. 47–63.

Danielian, N. R. Statement. In *Foreign Assistance Act, 1969, SCH*, 1969, pp. 237–48.

______ Statement. In *A Review of Balance of Payments Policies, JECH*, 1969, pp. 212–33.

______ Statement. In *Foreign Assistance Act of 1969, Pt. 5, HCH*, 1969, pp. 1104–20.

Daniels, Mark R. Differences in Efficiency among Industries in Developing Countries. *Amer. Econ. Rev.*, March 1969, *59*(1), pp. 159–71.

Daniels, Wilbur. Uses of the Computer in Contract Enforcement: The ILGWU Experience. In *Siegel, A. J., ed.*, 1969, pp. 189–202.

Daniere, Andre. The Benefits and Costs of Alternative Federal Programs of Financial Aid to College Students. In *the Economics and Financing of Higher Education in the United States, JECP*, 1969, pp. 556–98.

Dansey, Cyril M. Non-Official Transactions in Gold—Their Effect upon Exchange Markets. In *Aliber, R. Z., ed.*, 1969, pp. 13–19.

Dantwala, M. L. The Economic Ideology of Nehru. In *Bhuleshkar, A. V., ed.*, 1969, pp. 11–16.

Dardis, Rachel and Dennisson, Janet. The Welfare Cost of Alternative Methods of Protecting Raw Wool in the United States. *Amer. J. Agr. Econ.*, May 1969, *51*(2), pp. 303–19.

Das Gupta, A. Uncertainty and Balanced Growth. In *[Ghosal, U. N.]*, 1969, pp. 89–104.

Das Gupta, A. K. A Framework of Planning for India. *Indian Econ. J.*, January–March 1969, *16*(3), pp. 265–76.

Das, Amritananda. Malthus on the General Glut: A Reinterpretation. *Indian Econ. J.*, July–September 1969, *17*(1), pp. 118–28.

Dasgupta, Manas. A Note on the Possibility of Creating Export Surplus in Manufactures from the Underdeveloped Countries. *Econ. Aff.*, January–February 1969, *14*(1–2), pp. 68–70.

Dasgupta, Partha S. On the Concept of Optimum Population. *Rev. Econ. Stud.*, July 1969, *36*(107), pp. 295–318.

______ On the Optimum Rate of Accumulation in a Labour-Surplus Economy. *Indian Econ. J.*, January–March 1969, *16*(3), pp. 277–311.

______ Optimum Growth when Capital Is Non-transferable. *Rev. Econ. Stud.*, January 1969, *36*(105), pp. 77–88.

Dasgupta, Samir. A Note on Keynes's Analysis of Demand. *Econ. Int.*, May 1969, *22*(2), pp. 252–59.

Dasso, Jerome J. Economic Outlook for Oregon in 1969. *Oregon Bus. Rev.*, February 1969, *28*(2), pp. 1–4.

Datt, Ruddar. Unit Costs of Education—A Case Study of Haryana Colleges. In *Pandit, H. N., ed.*, 1969, pp. 92–113.

Daubigney, Jean-Pierre. Actualité du système "Parodi" dans les comportements salariaux des entreprises. (With English summary.) *Revue Écon.*, May 1969, *20*(3), pp. 497–514.

Davenport, David S. Collusive Competition in Major League Baseball: Its Theory and Institutional Development. *Amer. Econ.*, Fall 1969, *13*(2), pp. 6–30.

Davenport, John. The Continuing Crisis of the Dollar. In *Starleaf, D. R., ed.*, 1969, pp. 379–86.

Davenport, Michael. The Allocation of Foreign Aid: A Cross Section Study. *Indian Econ. J.*, April–June 1969, *16*(4–5), pp. 458–77.

David, E. J. L. Effects of Nonprice Variables upon Participation in Water-Oriented Outdoor Recreation: Comment. *Amer. J. Agr. Econ.*, November 1969, *51*(4), pp. 942–45.

______ The Exploding Demand for Recreational Property. *Land Econ.*, May 1969, *45*(2), pp. 206–17.

David, Herbert K. Control of In-Process Inventory. *Manage. Account.*, December 1969, *51*(6), pp. 27–31.

David, Lily Mary. Recent Collective Bargaining and Technological Change. **In** *Wortman, M. S., Jr.*, 1969, pp. 194–205.

______ **and Sheifer, Victor J.** Estimating the Cost of Collective Bargaining Settlements. *Mon. Lab. Rev.*, May 1969, *92*(5), pp. 16–26.

David, Martin. Comment on "Social Insurance and Economic Incentives" by M. Kucharski and Z. Pirozynski. *Public Finance*, 1969, *24*(2), pp. 256–63.

David, Michel. La distribuzione alimentare in Francia: oggli e domani. (Food Distribution in France: To-day and Tomorrow. With English summary.) *L'Impresa*, March/April 1969, *11*(2), pp. 156–62.

______ Nuovi tipi di punti di vendita per la periferia dell citta'. (New Types of Suburban Selling Points. With English summary.) *L'Impresa*, November/December 1969, *11*(6), pp. 436–43.

David, Paul A. Transport Innovation and Economic Growth: Professor Fogel on and off the Rails. *Econ. Hist. Rev.*, December 1969, *22*(3), pp. 506–25.

Davids, Lewis E. and West, David A. Limited Market for Bank Data Processing—For the Medical and Dental Professions. *Univ. Missouri Bus. Govt. Rev.*, September–October 1969, *10*(5), pp. 11–16.

Davidson, F. G. Pricing Behaviour: Another Plea for More Statistics. *Econ. Rec.*, December 1969, *45* (112), pp. 582–88.

Davidson, Malcolm. Directions for Ontario Agriculture. *Can. J. Agr. Econ.*, November 1969, *17*(3), pp. 170–74.

Davidson, Paul. A Keynesian View of Patinkin's Theory of Employment: A Rejoinder. *Econ. J.*, March 1969, *79*(313), pp. 181–82.

______ A Keynesian View of the Relationship between Accumulation, Money and the Money Wage-Rate. *Econ. J.*, June 1969, *79*(314), pp. 300–323.

Davidson, Sidney and Bierman, Harold, Jr. The Income Concept—Value Increment or Earnings Predictor. *Accounting Rev.*, April 1969, *44*(2), pp. 239–46.

Davies, Cyril H. The Bank Group Meeting. *Finance Develop.*, December 1969, *6*(4), pp. 4–9.

Davies, David. City-Suburban Differentials in Local Government Fiscal Effort: A Comment. *Nat. Tax J.*, September 1969, *22*(3), pp. 422–23.

Davies, Gethyn. United Kingdom Investment. **In** *Hughes, H. and Seng, Y. P., eds.*, 1969, pp. 46–61.

Davies, Gordon K. Needed: A National Job-Matching Network. *Harvard Bus. Rev.*, September–October 1969, *47*(5), pp. 63–72.

Davies, Jean; Behrend, Hilde and Knowles, Ann. 'Have You Heard the Phrase "Productivity Agreements"?' Findings from Two National Sample Surveys. *Scot. J. Polit. Econ.*, November 1969, *16*(3), pp. 256–70.

Davies, P. N. The African Steam Ship Company. **In** *Harris, J. R., ed.*, 1969, pp. 212–38.

Davies, R. W. Science and the Soviet Economy. **In** *Economic Concentration, Pt. 7A, SCH*, 1969, pp. 4332–45.

Davies, Robert B. "Peacefully Working to Conquer the World": The Singer Manufacturing Company in Foreign Markets, 1854–1889. *Bus. Hist. Rev.*, Autumn 1969, *43*(3), pp. 299–325.

Davis, Eric. A Modified Golden Rule: The Case with Endogenous Labor Supply. *Amer. Econ. Rev.*, March 1969, *59*(1), pp. 177–81.

Davis, H. Craig. Interregional Production and Water Resource Dependencies among the Western States. *Western Econ. J.*, March 1969, *7*(1), pp. 27–40.

______ Variations in the California and Pacific Northwest Input-Output Formats. *Univ. Wash. Bus. Rev.*, Autumn 1969, *29*(1), pp. 48–56.

Davis, Harry E. Negotiated Retirement Plans—A Decade of Benefit Improvements. *Mon. Lab. Rev.*, May 1969, *92*(5), pp. 11–15.

Davis, Howard W. A Case Study in Industrial Location. *Land Econ.*, November 1969, *45*(4), pp. 444–52.

Davis, J. Ronnie. Henry Simons, the Radical: Some Documentary Evidence. *Hist. Polit. Econ.*, Fall 1969, *1*(2), pp. 388–94.

______ **and Meyer, Charles W.** Budget Size in Democracy. *Southern Econ. J.*, July 1969, *36*(1), pp. 10–17.

______ **and Palomba, Neil A.** The National Farmers Organization and the Prisoner's Dilemma: A Game Theory Prediction of Failure. *Soc. Sci. Quart.*, December 1969, *50*(3), pp. 742–48.

Davis, Kenneth N. Statement. **In** *Export Expansion and Regulation, SCH*, 1969, pp. 307–33.

______ Statement. **In** *Export Expansion and Regulation, SCH*, 1969, pp. 62–65.

Davis, Otto A. Notes on Strategy and Methodology for a Scientific Political Science. **In** *Bernd, J. L., ed.*, 1969, pp. 22–38.

______ **and Kamien, Morton I.** Externalities, Information and Alternative Collective Action. **In** *The Analysis and Evaluation of Public Expenditures: The PPB System, Vol. 1, JECP*, 1969, pp. 67–86.

______ **and Wertz, Kenneth L.** The Consistency of the Assessment of Property: Some Empirical Results and Managerial Suggestions. *Appl. Econ.*, May 1969, *1*(2), pp. 151–57.

Davis, Richard G. Monetary Theory: Discussion. *Amer. Econ. Rev.*, May 1969, *59*(2), pp. 315–21.

Davis, Stanley M. U.S. versus Latin America: Business & Culture. *Harvard Bus. Rev.*, November–December 1969, *47*(6), pp. 88–98.

Davis, Thomas E. Exchange Rate Adjustments Under the Par Value System 1946–68. *Fed. Res. Bank Kansas City Rev.*, September–October 1969, pp. 3–10.

Davis, William M. and Ward, Cordelia T. Negotiations and Wage Calendar for 1969. *Mon. Lab. Rev.*, January 1969, *92*(1), pp. 52–64.

Davison, J. P. The Ultimate State in Disputes: St.

James' Square or Downing Street? In *Hugh-Jones, E. M., ed.,* 1969, pp. 169–76.

Dawson, John A. Obstacles Expected and Steps Required in Implementation of a Sound Policy for Canadian Agriculture. *Can. J. Agr. Econ.,* November 1969, *17*(3), pp. 70–76.

Day, A. C. L. Institutional Constraints and the International Monetary System. In *Mundell, R. A. and Swoboda, A. K., eds.,* 1969, pp. 333–42.

Day, Alice Taylor and Day, Lincoln H. *Too many Americans*: Excerpts. In *Effects of Population Growth on Natural Resources and the Environment, HCH,* 1969, pp. 160–88.

Day, H. J., et al. Evaluation of Benefits of a Flood Warning System. *Water Resources Res.,* October 1969, *5*(5), pp. 937–46.

Day, Lincoln H. The Population Problem in the United States. In *Effects of Population Growth on Natural Resources and the Environment, HCH,* 1969, pp. 152–59.

______ **and Day, Alice Taylor.** *Too many Americans:* Excerpts. In *Effects of Population Growth on Natural Resources and the Environment, HCH,* 1969, pp. 160–88.

Day, Ralph L. Position Bias in Paired Product Tests. *J. Marketing Res.,* February 1969, *6*(1), pp. 98–100.

Day, Richard H. Exact Aggregation with Linear Programming Model—A Note on the Sufficient Conditions Proposed by R. H. Day: Reply. *Amer. J. Agr. Econ.,* August 1969, *51*(3), pp. 686–88.

______ Flexible Utility and Myopic Expectations in Economic Growth. *Oxford Econ. Pap.,* November 1969, *21*(3), pp. 299–311.

______ More On the Aggregation Problem: Some Suggestions. *Amer. J. Agr. Econ.,* August 1969, *51* (3), pp. 673–75.

______ Recursive Programming and Supply Prediction. In *Fox, K. A. and Johnson, D. G., eds.,* 1969, pp. 107–22.

______ **and Tinney, E. Herbert.** Cycles, Phases and Growth in a Generalised Cobweb Theory. *Econ. J.,* March 1969, *79*(313), pp. 90–108.

Dayal, Ishwar. Role Analysis Technique in Job Descriptions. *Calif. Manage. Rev.,* Summer 1969, *11* (4), pp. 47–50.

De Alessi, Louis. Implications of Property Rights for Government Investment Choices. *Amer. Econ. Rev.,* March 1969, *59*(1), pp. 13–24.

De Baere, G. Marketing: Invloed op de verkooporganisatie en de verkooppraktijk. (The Influence of Marketing on Sales Organization and Sales Practice. With English summary.) *Econ. Soc. Tijdschr.,* December 1969, *23*(6), pp. 613–18.

De Cugis, Carlo. A Commentary on Jean-Jacques Servan-Schreiber's Book, *The American Challenge.* In *Kennedy, C. J., ed.,* 1969, pp. 123–45.

De Felice, Frank. Productivity Changes in Soviet Distribution. *Econ. J.,* March 1969, *79*(313), pp. 185–87.

De Floriani, Walter. Stima lineare e corretta della media nel campionamento a grappoli e in quello a due stadi. (A Linear and Unbiased Estimate of the Mean in the Cluster Sampling and in the Two-Stage Sampling. With English summary.) *Rivista Int. Sci. Econ. Com.,* October 1969, *16*(10), pp. 1016–28.

______ Stima non negativa della varianza nel campionamento a due stadi. (A Non-negative Estimate of the Variance in the Two-Stage Sampling. With English summary.) *Rivista Int. Sci. Econ. Com.,* September 1969, *16*(9), pp. 889–97.

De Forest, Paul. The Social Sciences in the Foreign Policy Subsystem of Congress. In *Crawford, E. T. and Biderman, A. D., eds.,* 1969, pp. 135–50.

De Mattia, Renato. La politica elettronica della Banca d'Italia. (The Bank of Italy's Electronic Policy. With English summary.) *Bancaria,* January 1969, *25*(1), pp. 19–24.

______ 1969: esperienze e prospettive dell'elaborazione automatica dei dati nelle banche. (The Use of Electronic Data Processing in the Banking System: An Outlook. With English summary.) *L'Industria,* April–June 1969, (2), pp. 208–21.

van De Panne, C. and Whinston, Andrew. The Symmetric Formulation of the Simplex Method for Quadratic Programming. *Econometrica,* July 1969, *37*(3), pp. 507–27.

De Salvia, Donald N. An Application of Peak-Load Pricing. *J. Bus.,* October 1969, *42*(4), pp. 458–76.

De Vecchi, Nicolò. Genesi e sviluppi della funzione della produzione CES. (The CES Production Function. With English summary.) *L'Industria,* January–March 1969, (1), pp. 58–77.

De Vleeshouwer, Eduard. Aspecten van de distributie-ontwikkeling in België. (Aspects of the Development of Distribution in Belgium. With English summary.) *Econ. Soc. Tijdschr.,* December 1969, *23*(6), pp. 619–40.

De Wit, Y. B. Stages in Planning: The Indonesian Case. In *[Tinbergen, J.],* 1969, pp. 157–74.

De, Nitish R. An Approach to the Problem of Industrial Relations: The Indian Case. In *Johri, C. K., ed.,* 1969, pp. 64–104.

Deaconu, V. and Parpală, E. Eficienţa economică a culturilor de proumb la I.A.S. Fundeni şi Mihăileşti. (Economic Efficiency of the Culture of Maize for Grain at the Fundeni and Mihăileşti I.A.S. (State Farms). With English summary.) *Stud. Cercet. Econ.,* 1969, *4,* pp. 103–13.

Deaglio, Mario. La scelta tra maggior reddito e maggior tempo libero. Un'analisi del comportamento del lavoratore. (The Choice between Greater Income and More Leisure: A Study in the Behaviour of the Worker. With English summary.) *L'Industria,* July–September 1969, (3), pp. 358–82.

Dean, Joel. Pricing Pioneering Products. *J. Ind. Econ.,* July 1969, *17*(3), pp. 165–79.

Deane, R. S. Import Licensing: A Stimulus to Foreign Investment. *Econ. Rec.,* December 1969, *45* (112), pp. 526–43.

Dearden, John. The Case Against ROI Control. *Harvard Bus. Rev.,* May–June 1969, *47*(3), pp. 124–35.

Debreu, Gerard. Valuation Equilibrium and Pareto Optimum. In *Arrow, K. J. and Scitovsky, T., eds.,* 1969, pp. 39–45.

DeCoster, Don T. and Rosen, L. S. "Funds" Statements: A Historical Perspective. *Accounting Rev.,* January 1969, *44*(1), pp. 124–36.

Deeble, J. S. and Scotton, R. B. The Nimmo Report. *Econ. Rec.,* June 1969, *45*(110), pp. 258–75.
Dehejia, V. T. Financing the Public Sector. **In** *Dagli, V., ed., Vol. II,* 1969, pp. 4–9.
Del Gaudio, Vincenzo. Problems and Prospects of Italian Tourism. *Rev. Econ. Cond. Italy,* November 1969, *23*(6), pp. 505–18.
Del Viscovo, Mario. Land Transport in 1968. *Rev. Econ. Cond. Italy,* March 1969, *23*(2), pp. 106–15.
Delange, Georges. Les méchanismes financiers et la comptabilité nationale. (With English summary.) *Revue Écon.,* May 1969, *20*(3), pp. 401–54.
Delano, Myles S. The Effects of Leverage and Corporate Taxes on the Shareholders of Regulated Utilities: Comment. **In** *Trebing, H. M. and Howard, R. H., eds.,* 1969, pp. 98–105.
Delivanis, D. J. Problems Arising for the Agriculture of a Developing Country by Virtue of Its Association with the European Economic Community. **In** *Papi, U. and Nunn, C., eds.,* 1969, pp. 130–42.
Dell, Sidney. Obstacles to Latin American Integration. **In** *Hilton, R., ed.,* 1969, pp. 61–71.
______ Statement. **In** *Linking Reserve Creation and Development Assistance, JECH,* 1969, pp. 5–12.
Dell'Amore, Giordano. Il contributo del risparmio familiare al riscatto del mezzogiorno. (Contribution Made by Household Savings to the Development of Southern Italy. With English summary.) *Bancaria,* October 1969, *25*(10), pp. 1206–15.
Dellin, Lubomir. Statement. **In** *To Extend and Amend the Export Control Act of 1949, HCH,* 1969, pp. 343–48.
DeLorme, Charles D., Jr. and Selby, Edward B., Jr. The Cost of Stabilization: A Comment. *Amer. Econ.,* Fall 1969, *13*(2), pp. 97–99.
Delphendahl, J. Environmental Effects of Rural Land Use. *Amer. J. Agr. Econ.,* December 1969, *51*(5), pp. 1189–94.
Demeyere, R. Doelmatig bedrijfsbeleid: een eis voor de toekomst. (Appropriate Management Is a Requirement for the Future. With English summary.) *Econ. Soc. Tijdschr.,* April 1969, *23*(2), pp. 143–58.
Deming, Frederick L. Statement. **In** *A Review of Balance of Payments Policies, JECH,* 1969, pp. 168–87.
Deming, W. E. Boundaries of Statistical Inference. **In** *Johnson, N. L. and Smith, H., Jr., eds.,* 1969, pp. 652–70.
Dempsey, Richard E. and Schmude, Douglas F. How Consumer Spending for Automobiles Creates Jobs. *Mon. Lab. Rev.,* March 1969, *92*(3), pp. 33–36.
Demsetz, Harold. Contracting Cost and Public Policy. **In** *The Analysis and Evaluation of Public Expenditures: The PPB System, Vol. 1, JECP,* 1969, pp. 167–74.
______ Information and Efficiency: Another Viewpoint. *J. Law Econ.,* April 1969, *12*(1), pp. 1–22.
______ Perfect Competition, Regulation, and the Stock Market. **In** *Manne, H. G., ed.,* 1969, pp. 1–22.
Demski, Joel S. Decision-Performance Control. *Accounting Rev.,* October 1969, *44*(4), pp. 669–79.
Denenberg, Herbert S. Insurance Regulation: The Search for Countervailing Power and Consumer Protection. **In** *Impact of Crime on Small Business—1969, Pt. 1, SCH,* 1969, pp. 57–63.
______ Law and Order—A Modest Program for Immediate Action: Some Comments on the SBA's Report on the Impact of Crime on Small Business. **In** *Impact of Crime on Small Business—1969, Pt. 1, SCH,* 1969, pp. 55–57.
______ Statement. **In** *Impact of Crime on Small Business—1969, Pt. 1, SCH,* 1969, pp. 47–55.
Denham, Robert Edwin. The Role of the U.S. as an External Actor in the Integration of Latin America. *J. Common Market Stud.,* March 1969, *7*(3), pp. 199–216.
Denison, Edward F. The Contribution of Education to the Quality of Labor: Comment. *Amer. Econ. Rev.,* December 1969, *59*(5), pp. 935–43.
Dennisson, Janet and Dardis, Rachel. The Welfare Cost of Alternative Methods of Protecting Raw Wool in the United States. *Amer. J. Agr. Econ.,* May 1969, *51*(2), pp. 303–19.
Dent, J. B. and Byrne, P. F. Recent Developments in Farm Planning: 2: Investment Planning by Monte Carlo Simulation. *Rev. Marketing Agr. Econ.,* June 1969, *37*(2), pp. 104–20.
______ **and Wright, A.** The Application of Simulation Techniques to the Study of Grazing Systems. *Australian J. Agr. Econ.,* December 1969, *13*(2), pp. 144–53.
DePrano, Michael E. and Nugent, Jeffrey B. Economies as an Antitrust Defense: Comment. *Amer. Econ. Rev.,* December 1969, *59*(5), pp. 947–53.
Derber, Milton. "Industrial Democracy" as an Organizing Concept for a Theory of Industrial Relations. **In** *Somers, G. G., ed. (I),* 1969, pp. 177–90.
Dernberger, Robert F. Review Article: Another Piece of the Jigsaw Puzzle Called Communist China. *Econ. Develop. Cult. Change,* January 1969, *17*(2), pp. 262–66.
Desaeyere, W. Het inkomen van de economisten, analyse van de U.N.A. enquête. (The Income of the Economists, Analysis of the U.N.A. Questionnaire Study. With English summary.) *Tijdschr. Econ.,* 1969, *14*(3), pp. 375–435.
______ Schatting van een array door middel van de marginale totalen. (Estimation of an Array by Means of the Marginal Totals. With English summary.) *Tijdschr. Econ.,* 1969, *14*(1), pp. 28–73.
Desai, M. D. Experience of Hybrid Bajra Farming in the Kaira District. *Artha-Vikas,* January 1969, *5*(1), pp. 95–103.
Desai, Morarji. Public Sector in a Mixed Economy. **In** *Dagli, V., ed., Vol. II,* 1969, pp. 1–3.
Desai, Padma. Alternative Measures of Import Substitution. *Oxford Econ. Pap.,* November 1969, *21* (3), pp. 312–24.
______ Growth and Structural Change in the Indian Manufacturing Sector: 1951–1963. *Indian Econ. J.,* October–December 1969, *17*(2), pp. 205–33.
Desai, V. R. Mutalik. The Structure of the Money Market in India. **In** *Desai, V. R. M. and Ghonasgi, B. D.,* 1969, pp. 1–28.
______ **and Ghonasgi, B. D.** Selective Credit Controls in India. **In** *Desai, V. R. M. and Ghonasgi, B. D.,* 1969, pp. 84–122.

DeSalvo, Joseph S. A Process Function for Rail Linehaul Operations. *J. Transp. Econ. Policy,* January 1969, *3*(1), pp. 3–27.

Dethoor, Jean-Marc. Au-delà de la programmation dynamique. (With English summary.) *Revue Écon.,* May 1969, *20*(3), pp. 515–35.

Deutsch, Karl W. and Kochen, Manfred. Toward a Rational Theory of Decentralization: Some Implications of a Mathematical Approach. *Amer. Polit. Sci. Rev.,* September 1969, *63*(3), pp. 734–49.

Devers, M. De B.T.W.-aangifte en de factuur. (The Value Added Tax Declaration and the Invoice. With English summary.) *Econ. Soc. Tijdschr.,* June 1969, *23*(3), pp. 287–303.

Devine, Eugene J. Manpower Shortages in Local Government Employment. *Amer. Econ. Rev.,* May 1969, *59*(2), pp. 538–45.

Devine, G.; Hawkins, Murray H. and Hurnanen, R. Industrial Organization and Policy Development in a Dynamic World. *Can. J. Agr. Econ.,* July 1969, *17*(2), pp. 106–17.

Devine, P. J. Inter-Regional Variations in the Degree of Inequality of Income Distribution: The United Kingdom, 1949–65. *Manchester Sch. Econ. Soc. Stud.,* June 1969, *37*(2), pp. 141–59.

Devletoglou, Nicos E. The Economic Philosophy of Montesquieu. *Kyklos,* 1969, *22*(3), pp. 530–41.

Devlin, David T. The U.S. Balance of Payments: Third Quarter 1969. *Surv. Curr. Bus.,* December 1969, *49*(12), pp. 18–39.

——— **and Cutler, Frederick.** The International Investment Position of the United States: Developments in 1968. *Surv. Curr. Bus.,* October 1969, *49* (10), pp. 23–36.

DeVoretz, Don. Alternative Planning Models for Philippine Educational Investment. *Philippine Econ. J.,* Second Semester 1969, *8*(2), pp. 99–116.

Dewald, William G. Multiple Expansion of Bank Deposits under Australian Institutional Conditions: Comment. *Econ. Rec.,* June 1969, *45*(110), pp. 293–96.

——— A Review of the Conference on Targets and Indicators of Monetary Policy. **In** *Brunner, K., ed.,* 1969, pp. 313–30.

——— Statement. **In** *Bank Holding Company Act Amendments, Pts. 1–3, HCH,* 1969, pp. 637–46.

Deweirdt, E. Le marché des euro-obligations. (About Euro-Bonds. With English summary.) *Rivista Int. Sci. Econ. Com.,* November 1969, *16* (11), pp. 1033–52.

Dewey, Donald. The Shaky Case for Antitrust. **In** *Starleaf, D. R., ed.,* 1969, pp. 110–14.

Dewey, Orville. On the Moral Laws of Contracts. **In** *Dewey, O.,* 1969, pp. 9–47.

——— On the Moral Laws of Trade. **In** *Dewey, O.,* 1969, pp. 48–73.

——— On the Moral Limits of Accumulation. **In** *Dewey, O.,* 1969, pp. 99–116.

——— On the Natural and Artificial Relations of Society. **In** *Dewey, O.,* 1969, pp. 117–44.

——— On the Uses of Labor, and a Passion for a Fortune. **In** *Dewey, O.,* 1969, pp. 74–98.

——— On War. **In** *Dewey, O.,* 1969, pp. 235–56.

Dey, B. On Costing of Education. **In** *Pandit, H. N., ed.,* 1969, pp. 14–26.

Dhavamony, S. J. The Ultimate Objectives of Nehru's Socialism. **In** *Bhuleshkar, A. V., ed.,* 1969, pp. 17–30.

Dhondt, J. The Cotton Industry at Ghent during the French Régime. **In** *Crouzet, F.; Chaloner, W. H. and Stern, W. M., eds.,* 1969, pp. 15–52.

Dhrymes, Phoebus J. Alternative Asymptotic Tests of Significance and Related Aspects of 2SLS and 3SLS Estimated Parameters. *Rev. Econ. Stud.,* April 1969, *36*(106), pp. 213–26.

——— An Identity between Double *k*-Class and Two Stage Least Squares Estimators. *Int. Econ. Rev.,* February 1969, *10*(1), pp. 114–17.

——— Efficient Estimation of Distributed Lags with Autocorrelated Errors. *Int. Econ. Rev.,* February 1969, *10*(1), pp. 47–67.

——— A Model of Short-run Labor Adjustment. **In** *Duesenberry, J. S., et al.,* 1969, pp. 110–49.

——— **and Mitchell, B. M.** Estimation of Joint Production Functions. *Econometrica,* October 1969, *37*(4), pp. 732–36.

Dhyani, S. N. Anatomy of Trade Union Law and Purpose and Future Direction of Trade Union Legislation in India. **In** *Johri, C. K., ed.,* 1969, pp. 201–20.

Di Comite, Luigi. Ipotesi di Gompertz e di Makeham e popolazione stabile. (With English summary.) *Statistica,* July-September 1969, *29*(3), pp. 483–87.

——— Sulla rappresentazione analitica delle curve integrali di fecondità. (With English summary.) *Statistica,* January-March 1969, *29*(1), pp. 113–18.

Di Marco, Luis Eugenio. Expectativas de precios. (Price Expectation. With English summary.) *Económica,* September–December 1969, *15*(3), pp. 275–82.

Di Tella, Guido and Baccino, Osvaldo. Análisis teórico de los efectos de la intermediación comercial. El caso de la industria del automóvil en Argentina. (Theoretical Analysis of the Effects of Commercial Intermediation: The Case of Automobile Industry in Argentina. With English summary.) *Económica,* January–April 1969, *15*(1), pp. 1–14.

Diamond, Peter. On the Economics of Tourism. *East Afr. Econ. Rev.,* December 1969, *1*(2), pp. 53–62.

Diatchenko, V. P. The Financial Problems of Professional Retraining of Personnel in the U.S.S.R. *Public Finance,* 1969, *24*(2), pp. 391–404.

Díaz-Alejandro, Carlos F. Economic Development: Discussion. *Amer. Econ. Rev.,* May 1969, *59*(2), pp. 432–34.

——— Statement. **In** *Overseas Private Investment Corporation, HCH,* 1969, pp. 115–16.

Dickinson, H. D. Von Thünen's Economics. *Econ. J.,* December 1969, *79*(316), pp. 894–902.

Dickson, Harald. Marginal Cost and Marginal Revenue in Elementary Treatment of the Problem of Profit Maximization. *Swedish J. Econ.,* June 1969, *71*(2), pp. 127–31.

Diebold, John. Bad Decisions on Computer Use. *Harvard Bus. Rev.,* January–February 1969, *47* (1), pp. 14–28, 176.

Diebold, William, Jr. Future Negotiating Issues and Policies in Foreign Trade. **In** *Alting von Geusau, F. A. M., ed.,* 1969, pp. 123–45.

Diesslin, Harold C. Evaluation of the Credit Market

and Credit Institutions. **In** *Owen, W. F., ed.,* 1969, pp. 95–112.

Dillard, Dudley. Fiscal Policy from Hoover to Heller—A Review Essay. *Mon. Lab. Rev.,* August 1969, *92*(8), pp. 10–14.

Diller, Stanley. Expectations in the Term Structure of Interest Rates. **In** *Mincer, J., ed.,* 1969, pp. 112–66.

Dillon, John L. and Anderson, James R. A Comparison of Response Surface and Factorial Designs in Agricultural Research: Comment. *Rev. Marketing Agr. Econ.,* June 1969, *37*(2), pp. 130–32.

Dimitrijević, Dimitrije. The Use of Flow-of-Funds Accounts in Monetary Planning in Yugoslavia. *Rev. Income Wealth,* March 1969, *15*(1), pp. 101–15.

Dincu, I. and Sandu, Gh. Implicațiile economice ale unor măsuri de valorificare a solurilor slab productive. (Economic Implications of Some Measures Taken in View of Turning to Account Weakly Productive Soils. With English summary.) *Stud. Cercet. Econ.,* 1969, *4,* pp. 115–23.

Dirlam, Joel. Problems of Market Power and Public Policy in Yugoslavia. **In** *Bornstein, M., ed.,* 1969, pp. 236–51.

______ Review of Recent Legislative and Judicial Trends Affecting Bank Structure. **In** *Federal Reserve Bank of Chicago (I),* 1969, pp. 2–19.

______ Statement. **In** *Governmental Intervention in the Market Mechanism, Pt. 1, SCH,* 1969, pp. 249–67.

Divatia, V. V. and Bhatt, V. V. On Measuring the Pace of Development. *Banca Naz. Lavoro Quart. Rev.,* June 1969, (89), pp. 190–206.

Dixit, Avinash K. Marketable Surplus and Dual Development. *J. Econ. Theory,* August 1969, *1*(2), pp. 203–19.

Dixon, J. The Cost of Dumping Butter: A Comment. *J. Common Market Stud.,* March 1969, *7*(3), pp. 243–52.

Dobell, A. Rodney. An Optimal Unemployment Rate: Reply. *Quart. J. Econ.,* August 1969, *83*(3), pp. 521–23.

______ **and Burmeister, Edwin.** Disembodied Technological Change with Several Factors. *J. Econ. Theory,* June 1969, *1*(1), pp. 1–8.

Dockweiler, Raymond C. The Practicability of Developing Multiple Financial Statements: A Case Study. *Accounting Rev.,* October 1969, *44*(4), pp. 729–42.

Dodd, A. H. The Character of Welsh Emigration to the United States to 1840. **In** *Minchinton, W. E., ed.,* 1969, pp. 19–36.

Dodge, Robert H. How Leverage Affects the Cost of Capital to a Public Utility. *Manage. Account.,* August 1969, *51*(2), pp. 39–44.

Doeringer, Peter B. Manpower Programs for Ghetto Labor Markets. **In** *Somers, G. G., ed. (II),* 1969, pp. 257–67.

Doherty, Robert E. and Oberer, Walter E. The Public School Teacher as Organization Man. **In** *Walsh, R. E., ed.,* 1969, pp. 115–40.

Dolan, Paul. Citizens Complaints in St. Louis—The Case for an Ombudsman? *Univ. Missouri Bus. Govt. Rev.,* September–October 1969, *10*(5), pp. 25–31.

Dole, Richard F., Jr. The Role of Public Officials and Administrators: Remarks. **In** *Sinicropi, A. V. and Gilroy, T. P., eds.,* 1969, pp. 47–51.

Dolich, Ira J. Congruence Relationships between Self Images and Product Brands. *J. Marketing Res.,* February 1969, *6*(1), pp. 80–84.

Doll, John P. Credit in the Production Organization of the Firm: Comment. *Amer. J. Agr. Econ.,* May 1969, *51*(2), pp. 474–76.

Dolman, Dirk. A Critical Survey of Use of Cost-Benefit Analysis in Public Finance: Comment. **In** *Peacock, A. T., ed.,* 1969, pp. 86–89.

Dolmans, D. Het aardgas zijn prijsvorming. (Natural Gas and Its Price Determination. With English summary.) *Tijdschr. Econ.,* 1969, *14*(1), pp. 3–27.

Domar, Evsey D. Comments on the Papers on East-West Trade. **In** *Samuelson, P. A., ed.,* 1969, pp. 138–42.

______ Theory of Innovation: Discussion. *Amer. Econ. Rev.,* May 1969, *59*(2), pp. 44–46.

Domhoff, G. William. Who Made American Foreign Policy, 1945–1963? **In** *Horowitz, D., ed.,* 1969, pp. 25–69.

Dommermuth, William P. and Bruce, Grady D. Dissonance and Satisfaction—Some Prepurchase Aspects. *Univ. Wash. Bus. Rev.,* Spring 1969, *28*(3), pp. 45–51.

Donaldson, Gordon. Strategy for Financial Emergencies. *Harvard Bus. Rev.,* November–December 1969, *47*(6), pp. 67–79.

Donaldson, Peter. British Planning. **In** *Prybyla, J. S., ed.,* 1969, pp. 173–78.

van Dongen, Irene S. Agriculture and Other Primary Production. **In** *Abshire, D. M. and Samuels, M. A., eds.,* 1969, pp. 253–93.

______ Physical, Human, and Economic Setting. **In** *Abshire, D. M. and Samuels, M. A., eds.,* 1969, pp. 1–28.

Donnelly, James H., Jr. Cross-Cultural Communications Theory: Implications for International Advertising. *Univ. Wash. Bus. Rev.,* Spring 1969, *28* (3), pp. 52–58.

______ **and Ryans, John K., Jr.** The Role of Culture in Organizing Overseas Operations: The Advertising Experience. *Univ. Wash. Bus. Rev.,* Autumn 1969, *29*(1), pp. 35–41.

Donnem, Roland W. The Antitrust Attack on Restrictive Patent License Provisions. *Antitrust Bull.,* Winter 1969, *14,* pp. 749–66.

Donoian, Harry A. A New Approach to Setting the Pay of Federal Blue-collar Workers. *Mon. Lab. Rev.,* April 1969, *92*(4), pp. 30–34.

Donovan, C. H. Recent Developments in Property Taxation in Florida: A Case Study. **In** *[White, Charles P.],* 1969, pp. 48–59.

Doodha, Kersi D. Liquidity Preference Theory for India. **In** *Desai, V. R. M. and Ghonasgi, B. D.,* 1969, pp. 49–69.

Dooley, Oscar S. Britain Revisited: A Fresh Appraisal of the Industrial Revolution. *Econ. Bus. Bull.,* Fall 1969, *22*(1), pp. 44–48.

Dooley, Peter C. The Interlocking Directorate. *Amer. Econ. Rev.,* June 1969, *59*(3), pp. 314–23.

Dorai, G. C. A Cost-Benefit Analysis of the International Flow of Students. *Indian Econ. J.,* October–December 1969, *17*(2), pp. 234–49.

Dorfman, Robert. An Economic Interpretation of Optimal Control Theory. *Amer. Econ. Rev.,* December 1969, *59*(5), pp. 817–31.

______ General Equilibrium with Public Goods. **In** *Margolis, J. and Guitton, H., eds.,* 1969, pp. 247–75.

______ Statement. **In** *Guidelines for Estimating the Benefits of Public Expenditures, JECH,* 1969, pp. 98–102.

______ **and Jacoby, Henry D.** A Model of Public Decisions Illustrated by a Water Pollution Policy Problem. **In** *The Analysis and Evaluation of Public Expenditures: The PPB System, Vol. 1, JECP,* 1969, pp. 226–74.

Dorrance, Graeme S. The Role of Central Banks in Less Developed Countries. *Finance Develop.,* December 1969, *6*(4), pp. 22–26.

______ The Role of Financial Accounts. *Rev. Income Wealth,* June 1969, *15*(2), pp. 197–207.

Doss, A. C. and Singer, H. W. Technical Assistance to Kenya: Some Thoughts on Flows and Programming. *East Afr. Econ. Rev.,* June 1969, *1*(1), pp. 17–27.

Dosser, Douglas. Comment on "The Incidence of Social Security Taxes" by J. Weitenberg. *Public Finance,* 1969, *24*(2), pp. 209–14.

______**; Han, S. S. and Hitiris, Theodore.** Trade Effects of Tax Harmonisation: Harmonisation of the Value-added Tax in E.E.C. *Manchester Sch. Econ. Soc. Stud.,* December 1969, *37*(4), pp. 337–46.

Dougal, Merwin D. Techniques for Developing a Comprehensive Program for Flood Plain Management. **In** *Dougal, M. D., ed.,* 1969, pp. 53–75.

Douglas, A. J. and Goldman, Steven M. Monopolistic Behavior in a Market for Durable Goods. *J. Polit. Econ.,* January/February 1969, *77*(1), pp. 49–59.

Douglas, E. J. Apparent and Real Levels of Concentration in Australian Manufacturing Industry. *Econ. Rec.,* June 1969, *45*(110), pp. 251–57.

Douglas, George W. Risk in the Equity Markets: An Empirical Appraisal of Market Efficiency. *Yale Econ. Essays,* Spring 1969, *9*(1), pp. 3–45.

Douty, H. M. Prospects for White-collar Unionism. *Mon. Lab. Rev.,* January 1969, *92*(1), pp. 31–34.

______ Some Aspects of British Wage Policy. *Southern Econ. J.,* July 1969, *36*(1), pp. 74–81.

Dovring, Folke. Commentary on Agrarian Revolution and Economic Progress: A Primer for Development (by Rainer Schickele). *Land Econ.,* February 1969, *45*(1), pp. 125–28.

______ Underemployment in Agriculture: A Rejoinder. *Econ. Develop. Cult. Change,* January 1969, *17*(2), pp. 273–76.

______ Variants and Invariants in Comparative Agricultural Systems. *Amer. J. Agr. Econ.,* December 1969, *51*(5), pp. 1263–73.

Dow, J. C. R. Cyclical Developments in France, Germany, and Italy Since the Early Fifties. **In** *Bronfenbrenner, M., ed.,* 1969, pp. 140–96.

Dowd, Douglas F. Statement. **In** *Role of Giant Corporations, Pt. 1, SCH,* 1969, pp. 521–29.

Dowdy, G. T., Sr. Toward Better Undergraduate Teaching. *Amer. J. Agr. Econ.,* December 1969, *51*(5), pp. 1078–80.

Dowie, J. A. and Butlin, N. G. Estimates of Australian Work Force and Employment, 1861–1961. *Australian Econ. Hist. Rev.,* September 1969, *9*(2), pp. 138–55.

Downing, Paul B. Extension of Sewer Service at the Urban-Rural Fringe. *Land Econ.,* February 1969, *45*(1), pp. 103–11.

Downs, Anthony. Housing the Urban Poor: The Economics of Various Strategies. *Amer. Econ. Rev.,* Part I, September 1969, *59*(4), pp. 646–51.

______ Round Table on Allocation of Resources in Law Enforcement. *Amer. Econ. Rev.,* May 1969, *59*(2), pp. 504–05.

Doxiadis, Constantinos. A City for Human Development. **In** *Population Trends, Pt. 1, HCH,* 1969, pp. 374–94.

______ Man's Movement and His City. **In** *Population Trends, Pt. 1, HCH,* 1969, pp. 398–406.

______ Statement. **In** *Population Trends, Pt. 1, HCH,* 1969, pp. 341–69.

______ Statement. **In** *Panel on Science and Technology: Science and Technology and the Cities, HCH,* 1969, pp. 19–35.

Drakatos, Constantine G. The Determinants of Birth Rate in Developing Countries: An Econometric Study of Greece. *Econ. Develop. Cult. Change,* July 1969, *17*(4), pp. 596–603.

Drake, M. Age at Marriage in the Pre-industrial West. **In** *Bechhofer, F., ed.,* 1969, pp. 196–208.

Drake, P. J. Economics and Development. *Econ. Rec.,* September 1969, *45*(111), pp. 449–61.

______ The New-Issue Boom in Malaya and Singapore, 1961–1964. *Econ. Develop. Cult. Change,* Part I, October 1969, *18*(1), pp. 73–91.

Dramais, A. and Glejser, H. A Gravity Model of Interdependent Equations to Estimate Flow Creation and Diversion. *J. Reg. Sci.,* December 1969, *9*(3), pp. 439–49.

Drandell, Milton and Hofflander, A. E. A Linear Programming Model of Profitability, Capacity and Regulation in Insurance Management. *J. Risk Ins.,* March 1969, *36*(1), pp. 41–54.

Draper, J. E. and Hawkins, Clark A. On the Transactions Demand for Cash: Comment. *J. Finance,* December 1969, *24*(5), pp. 942–49.

Draper, Norman R. and Guttman, I. The Value of Prior Information. **In** *Johnson, N. L. and Smith, H., Jr., eds.,* 1969, pp. 305–25.

______**; Hunter, William G. and Tierney, David E.** Analyzing Paired Comparison Tests. *J. Marketing Res.,* November 1969, *6*(4), pp. 477–80.

______ **and Lawrence, Willard E.** Distributions of Blocks of Signs. **In** *Naylor, T. H., ed.,* 1969, pp. 347–51.

Drechsler, László; Kux, Jaroslav and Mairesse, Jacques. Labour Productivity Comparison between Czechoslovakia and France. *Rev. Income Wealth,* September 1969, *15*(3), pp. 219–28.

Drennan, Matthew P. Household Location Decisions and Local Public Benefits and Costs. *Amer. Econ.,* Spring 1969, *13*(1), pp. 30–39.

Driehuis, W. Experiments in Explaining and Forecasting the Invisible Trade of the Netherlands. *Bull. Oxford Univ. Inst. Econ. Statist.,* November 1969, *31*(4), pp. 335–51.

Drotning, John E. and Lipsky, David B. The Effectiveness of Reinstatement as a Public Policy

Remedy: The Kohler Case. *Ind. Lab. Relat. Rev.*, January 1969, *22*(2), pp. 179–98.

Drucker, Peter F. Management's New Role. *Harvard Bus. Rev.*, November–December 1969, *47* (6), pp. 49–54.

Dryden, Myles M. Share Price Movements: A Markovian Approach. *J. Finance*, March 1969, *24*(1), pp. 49–60.

______ A Source of Bias in Filter Tests of Share Prices. *J. Bus.*, July 1969, *42*(3), pp. 321–25.

Drysdale, Peter. Japan, Australia, New Zealand: The Prospect for Western Pacific Economic Integration. *Econ. Rec.*, September 1969, *45*(111), pp. 321–42.

Drzycimski, Eugene F. The Stock Repurchase Decision. *Marquette Bus. Rev.*, Winter 1969, *13*(4), pp. 159–67.

Dubois-Pelerin, P. E. Le Marché Commun et le commerce international des Six. (Common Market and Its International Trade. With English summary.) *Rivista Int. Sci. Econ. Com.*, June 1969, *16*(6), pp. 568–89.

Dubois, Jean-Pierre. French Economic Interest Groups and the Rules of Competition. *Antitrust Bull.*, Fall 1969, *14*, pp. 667–703.

Duchan, Alan I. A Relationship between the *F* and *t* Statistics and the Simple Correlation Coefficients in Classical Least Squares Regression. *Amer. Statist.*, June 1969, *23*(3), pp. 27–28.

Duckham, Baron F. The Emergence of the Professional Manager in the Scottish Coal Industry, 1760–1815. *Bus. Hist. Rev.*, Spring 1969, *43*(1), pp. 21–38.

Dudick, Thomas S. Use of Indicators in Planning for Profits. *Manage. Account.*, November 1969, *51* (5), pp. 16–18.

Dudley, Dean. The Goodwill Account: The Accounting Recognition of the Concept of Economic Rent. *Marquette Bus. Rev.*, Summer 1969, *13*(2), pp. 89–92.

Dudley, Leonard and Passell, Peter. War in Vietnam and United States Balance of Payments: Reply to Comment by Douglas Bohi. *Rev. Econ. Statist.*, November 1969, *51*(4), pp. 474–75.

Due, Jean M. What Has Happened to the Ghanaian State Farms? *Ill. Agr. Econ.*, July 1969, *9*(2), pp. 25–35.

Due, John F. The Somers Solution to the Use Tax: A Comment. *Nat. Tax J.*, June 1969, *22*(2), pp. 301.

______ The Uganda Sales Tax on Importation and Manufacture. *East Afr. Econ. Rev.*, June 1969, *1* (1), pp. 1–16.

Duesenberry, James S. Tactics and Targets of Monetary Policy. **In** *Federal Reserve Bank of Boston*, 1969, pp. 83–95.

Duewer, Lawrence A. Effects of Specials on Composite Meat Prices. *Agr. Econ. Res.*, July 1969, *21* (3), pp. 70–77.

Duffy, M.; Agarwala, R. and Burns, T. Forecasting Gross Private Fixed Investment Using Intentions Survey Data. *Manchester Sch. Econ. Soc. Stud.*, December 1969, *37*(4), pp. 279–93.

Dufty, Norman F. A Model of Choice in an Australian Labor Market. *J. Human Res.*, Summer 1969, *4*(3), pp. 328–42.

Duggar, Jan Warren. International Comparisons of Income Levels: An Additional Measure. *Econ. J.*, March 1969, *79*(313), pp. 109–16.

______ **and Beard, Thomas R.** Federal Reserve Proposals for Reform of the Discount Mechanism. *Southern Econ. J.*, October 1969, *36*(2), pp. 122–33.

______ **and Beard, Thomas R.** Member Bank Borrowing. *Quart. Rev. Econ. Bus.*, Autumn 1969, *9* (3), pp. 72–77.

______ **and Rost, Ronald F.** National Bank Note Redemption and Treasury Cash. *J. Econ. Hist.*, September 1969, *29*(3), pp. 512–20.

Duharcourt, Pierre. Introduction à la programmation dynamique. (With English summary.) *Revue Écon.*, March 1969, *20*(2), pp. 182–234.

Duisenberg, W. F. Problematiek rond de Britse betalingsbalans. (British Balance of Payments Problems. With English summary.) *De Economist*, November/December 1969, *117*(6), pp. 615–57.

Duker, Jacob M. Expenditures for Life Insurance among Working-Wife Families. *J. Risk Ins.*, December 1969, *36*(5), pp. 525–33.

Dulles, John W. F. The Contribution of Getúlio Vargas to the Modernization of Brazil. **In** *Baklanoff, E. N., ed.*, 1969, pp. 36–57.

Dunham, Stephen S. and Bryson, John E. A Case Study of the Impact of Consumer Legislation: The Elimination of Negotiability and the Cooling-Off Period. *Yale Law J.*, March 1969, *78*(4), pp. 618–61.

Dunkelberg, William and Stafford, Frank P. The Cost of Financing Automobile Purchases. *Rev. Econ. Statist.*, November 1969, *51*(4), pp. 459–64.

Dunlap, R. D. and Swanson, Earl R. Influence of Prices on Production Potential for Beef and Hogs on Farms with Fixed Acreages. *Ill. Agr. Econ.*, January 1969, *9*(1), pp. 10–17.

Dunlop, John T. Industrial Relations Systems. **In** *Wortman, M. S., Jr.*, 1969, pp. 23–30.

______ Industrial Relations Systems at Work. **In** *Somers, G. G., ed. (I)*, 1969, pp. 25–37.

Dunn, Donald A. Policy Issues Presented by the Interdependence of Computer and Communications Services. *Law Contemp. Probl.*, Spring 1969, *34*(2), pp. 369–88.

Dunn, Robert M., Jr. and Galper, Harvey. A Short-Run Demand Function for Higher Education in the United States. *J. Polit. Econ.*, September/October 1969, *77*(5), pp. 765–77.

Dunnette, Marvin D. and Campbell, John R. Laboratory Training: Reply. *Ind. Relat.*, May 1969, *8*(3), pp. 289–90.

Dunning, John H. The Study of International Direct Investment. *Rivista Int. Sci. Econ. Com.*, December 1969, *16*(12), pp. 1129–44.

Dupuis, M. Great Britain and the Common Market. **In** *Duquesne, L., et al.*, 1969, pp. 105–15.

Dupuit, Jules. On the Measurement of the Utility of Public Works. **In** *Arrow, K. J. and Scitovsky, T., eds.*, 1969, pp. 255–83.

Dupuy, Yves. Les objectifs de la firme et l'analyse de l'effectif. (With English summary.) *Revue Écon.*, July 1969, *20*(4), pp. 658–83.

______ **and Loustau, M.** Etude des carrières des ingénieurs E.N.S.T.C. (With English summary.) *Revue Écon.*, July 1969, *20*(4), pp. 702–26.

Duquesne de la Vinelle, L. The Common Market: An Evaluation of its First Ten Years. **In** *Duquesne, L., et al.*, 1969, pp. 15–29.

——— Common Monetary Policy. **In** *Duquesne, L., et al.*, 1969, pp. 83–91.

——— Common Policy for Regional Development. **In** *Duquesne, L., et al.*, 1969, pp. 72–82.

——— European Integration and Common Economic Policies. **In** *Duquesne, L., et al.*, 1969, pp. 54–61.

Durand, Patrick and Latscha, Jacques. The New Tax Treaty between the United Kingdom and France. *Bull. Int. Fiscal Doc.*, March 1969, *23*(3), pp. 131–36.

——— **and Uckmar, V.** The Tax Treaty between Italy and France. *Bull. Int. Fiscal Doc.*, May 1969, *23*(5), pp. 191–203.

Durbin, J. Inferential Aspects of the Randomness of Sample Size in Survey Sampling. **In** *Johnson, N. L. and Smith, H., Jr., eds.*, 1969, pp. 629–51.

During, R. W. and Killick, Tony. A Structural Approach to the Balance of Payments of a Low-Income Country. *J. Devel. Stud.*, July 1969, *5*(4), pp. 274–98.

Duthu, Marie-Françoise. La prévision des structures d'emploi par la méthode des comparaisons internationales et intersectorielles. (With English summary.) *Revue Écon.*, July 1969, *20*(4), pp. 684–701.

Dutta, Amita. Domestic Market Distortions and Customs Union: A Geometrical Analysis. *J. Devel. Stud.*, January 1969, *5*(2), pp. 87–103.

Dutta, M. and Su, V. An Econometric Model of Puerto Rico. *Rev. Econ. Stud.*, July 1969, *36*(107), pp. 319–33.

Duvick, Richard D. and Uhl, Joseph N. Large Farms and Above Parity Returns: Inseparable or Just Good Friends? *Amer. J. Agr. Econ.*, February 1969, *51*(1), pp. 179–82.

Dwyer, Paul S. and Tracy, Derrick S. Multivariate Maxima and Minima with Matrix Derivatives. *J. Amer. Statist. Assoc.*, December 1969, *64*(328), pp. 1576–94.

Dyar, Robert and Gaffey, William R. Current Challenges to Health Statisticians. *Amer. Statist.*, December 1969, *23*(5), pp. 19–22.

Dyl, Edward A. and Long, Hugh W. Abandonment Value and Capital Budgeting: Comment. *J. Finance*, March 1969, *24*(1), pp. 88–95.

Dymond, William R. The Role of Benefit/Cost Analysis in Formulating Manpower Policy. **In** *Somers, G. G. and Wood, W. D., eds.*, 1969, pp. 42–55.

Dymsza, William A. Statement. **In** *Export Expansion and Regulation, SCH*, 1969, pp. 412–20.

Dyos, H. J. Some Historical Reflections on the Quality of Urban Life. **In** *Schmandt, H. J. and Bloomberg, W., Jr., eds.*, 1969, pp. 31–60.

Eads, George; Nerlove, Marc and Raduchel, William. A Long-Run Cost Function for the Local Service Airline Industry: An Experiment in Non-Linear Estimation. *Rev. Econ. Statist.*, August 1969, *51*(3), pp. 258–70.

Eagly, Robert V. Monetary Policy and Politics in Mid-Eighteenth-Century Sweden. *J. Econ. Hist.*, December 1969, *29*(4), pp. 739–57.

——— A Physiocratic Model of Dynamic Equilibrium. *J. Polit. Econ.*, January/February 1969, *77*(1), pp. 66–84.

Eakins, David W. Business Planners and America's Postwar Expansion. **In** *Horowitz, D., ed.*, 1969, pp. 143–71.

Eapen, A. T. A Critique of Indian Fiscal Federalism. *Public Finance*, 1969, *24*(4), pp. 537–62.

Earle, Peter. The Commercial Development of Ancona, 1479–1551. *Econ. Hist. Rev.*, April 1969, *22*(1), pp. 28–44.

Easter, K. William. Changing the ACP Investment. *Land Econ.*, May 1969, *45*(2), pp. 218–28.

Easterlin, Richard A. Population. **In** *Chamberlain, N. W., ed.*, 1969, pp. 241–72.

——— Towards a Socioeconomic Theory of Fertility: Survey of Recent Research on Economic Factors in American Fertility. **In** *Behrman, S. J.; Corsa, L., Jr. and Freedman, R., eds.*, 1969, pp. 127–56.

——— **and Lebergott, Stanley.** The Service Industries in the Nineteenth Century: Discussion. **In** *Fuchs, V. R., ed.*, 1969, pp. 352–68.

Easterling, Robert G. Discrimination Intervals for Percentiles in Regression. *J. Amer. Statist. Assoc.*, September 1969, *64*(327), pp. 1031–41.

Eastman, Harry C. and Stykolt, Stefan. An Evaluation of Trading Stamp Schemes. **In** *Stykolt, S.*, 1969, pp. 141–43.

——— Disturbing Prospects. **In** *Stykolt, S.*, 1969, pp. 129–32.

——— The Economic Consequences of Mr. Coyne. **In** *Stykolt, S.*, 1969, pp. 146–48.

——— The Performance of Two Protected Oligopolies in Canada. **In** *Stykolt, S.*, 1969, pp. 83–102.

Ebanks, G. Edward. Social and Demographic Characteristics of Family Planning Clients in Barbados. *Soc. Econ. Stud.*, December 1969, *18*(4), pp. 391–401.

Ebert, Robert R. Multinational Coordination of Labor Objectives in the Automobile Unions. *Ohio State U. Bull. Bus. Res.*, September 1969, *44*(9), pp. 1–3, 7–8.

Ebrahimzadeh, Cyrus. The Economics of Hydro-Electric Power in Iran. *Tahq. Eq.*, November 1969, *6*(15&16), pp. 54–79.

Eccles, George S. Registered Bank Holding Companies. **In** *Prochnow, H. V., ed.*, 1969, pp. 82–103.

Ecker-Racz, L. L. Tax Simplification in this Federal System. *Law Contemp. Probl.*, Autumn 1969, *34*(4), pp. 769–81.

——— **and Woodruff, A. M.** Property Taxes and Land-Use Patterns in Australia and New Zealand. **In** *Becker, A. P., ed.*, 1969, pp. 147–86.

Eckert, Ross D. and Minasian, Jora R. The Economics of Airport Use, Congestion, and Safety. *Calif. Manage. Rev.*, Spring 1969, *11*(3), pp. 11–24.

Eckler, A. Ross. Statisticians and Shoemakers: Applying Their Skills. *Mon. Lab. Rev.*, November 1969, *92*(11), pp. 43–47.

Eckstein, Harry. Planning: The National Health Service. **In** *Rose, R., ed.*, 1969, pp. 221–37.

Eckstein, Otto. Alternatives to Guideposts. **In** *Wortman, M. S., Jr.*, 1969, pp. 420–21.

——— Wage-Price Dynamics, Inflation, and Unemployment: Discussion. *Amer. Econ. Rev.*, May 1969, *59*(2), pp. 162–64.

Eiteman, Wilford J. Factors Determining the Least Cost Point. **In** *Blumner, S. M., ed.*, 1969, pp. 88–96.

Ekelund, Robert B., Jr. A Note on Jules Dupuit and Neo-classical Monopoly Theory. *Southern Econ. J.*, January 1969, *35*(3), pp. 257–62.

______ Tax Reform in Latin America: The E.C.L.A. Proposals—A Critical Evaluation. *Amer. J. Econ. Soc.*, January 1969, *28*(1), pp. 93–106.

______ **and Gramm, William P.** A Reconsideration of Advertising Expenditures, Aggregate Demand, and Economic Stabilization. *Quart. Rev. Econ. Bus.*, Summer 1969, *9*(2), pp. 71–77.

______ **and Maurice, Charles.** An Empirical Investigation of Advertising and Concentration: Comment. *J. Ind. Econ.*, November 1969, *18*(1), pp. 76–80.

El-Agraa, Ali M. The Sudan and the Arab Customs Union: A Conflict. *East Afr. Econ. Rev.*, December 1969, *1*(2), pp. 39–51.

El-Badry, M. A. Higher Female than Male Mortality in Some Countries of South Asia: A Digest. *J. Amer. Statist. Assoc.*, December 1969, *64*(328), pp. 1234–44.

Elias, Víctor J. Cambios en la calidad de los bienes. Una forma de estimarlos. (Changes in the Quality of Goods—A Way of Estimation. With English summary.) *Económica*, September–December 1969, *15*(3), pp. 283–90.

Eliot, Jared. Farming a New Land, 1747. **In** *Pursell, C. W., Jr.*, 1969, pp. 9–18.

Elkins, W. F. Black Power in the British West Indies: The Trinidad Longshoremen's Strike of 1919. *Sci. Soc.*, Winter 1969, *33*(1), pp. 71–75.

Ellicott, John. United States Controls on Foreign Direct Investment: The 1969 Program. *Law Contemp. Probl.*, Winter 1969, *34*(1), pp. 47–63.

Elliott, C. M. Agriculture and Economic Development in Africa: Theory and Experience 1880–1914. **In** *Jones, E. L. and Woolf, S. J., eds.*, 1969, pp. 123–50.

Elliott, John. The Challenge of Development: Africa and Asia. **In** *Ozbekhan, H. and Talbert, G. E., eds.*, 1969, pp. 163–81.

Elliott, Robert M. An SEC Primer. **In** *Harvey, J. L. and Newgarden, A., eds.*, 1969, pp. 62–78.

Ellis, Howard S. Corrective Inflation in Brazil, 1964–1966. **In** *Ellis, H. S., ed.*, 1969, pp. 177–212.

______ **and Fellner, William.** External Economies and Diseconomies. **In** *Blumner, S. M., ed.*, 1969, pp. 163–79.

Ellman, Michael. Aggregation as a Cause of Inconsistent Plans. *Economica, N.S.*, February 1969, *36* (141), pp. 69–74.

______ The Consistency of Soviet Plans. *Scot. J. Polit. Econ.*, February 1969, *16*(1), pp. 50–74.

Elsaid, Hussein H. Non-convertible Preferred Stock as a Financing Instrument 1950–65: Comment. *J. Finance*, December 1969, *24*(5), pp. 939–41.

Else, P. K. and Howe, M. Cost-Benefit Analysis and the Withdrawal of Railway Services. *J. Transp. Econ. Policy*, May 1969, *3*(2), pp. 178–94.

Elston, R. C. An Analogue to Fieller's Theorem Using Scheffé's Solution to the Fisher-Behrens Problem. *Amer. Statist.*, February 1969, *23*(1), pp. 26–28.

Eltis, W. A. Are Interest Rates too High? *Lloyds Bank Rev.*, July 1969, (93), pp. 27–35.

______ Is Stop-Go Inevitable? *Nat. Westminster Bank Quart. Rev.*, November 1969, pp. 2–12.

Elvin, H. L. The Idea of Quality in Education and the Difficulty of Costing It. **In** *Beeby, C. E., ed.*, 1969, pp. 89–102.

Elzinga, Kenneth G. The Antimerger Law: Pyrrhic Victories? *J. Law Econ.*, April 1969, *12*(1), pp. 43–78.

Emerson, Peter M. and Tomek, William G. Did Futures Trading Influence Potato Prices? *Amer. J. Agr. Econ.*, August 1969, *51*(3), pp. 666–72.

Emery, Betty J. and Garston, Gordon J. The Measurement of Constant Price Aggregates in Canada. *Rev. Income Wealth*, March 1969, *15*(1), pp. 1–32.

Emshoff, James R. and Ackoff, Russell L. Prediction, Explanation, and Control of Conflict. *Peace Res. Soc. Internat. Pap.*, 1969, *12*, pp. 109–15.

Enache, C. and Mehedinţu, M. Creşterea rolului Partidului Comunist Român în conducerea economiei în etapa actuală. (Increased Importance of the Part Played by the Romanian Communist Party in the Management of Economy at the Present Stage. With English summary.) *Stud. Cercet. Econ.*, 1969, *3*, pp. 9–17.

Enache, Gh., et al. Perfecţionarea contabilităţii în Republica Socialistă România. (Improvement of Accounting in the Socialist Republic of Romania. With English summary.) *Stud. Cercet. Econ.*, 1969, *3*, pp. 143–50.

Encarnación, José, Jr. On Independence Postulates Concerning Choice. *Int. Econ. Rev.*, June 1969, *10*(2), pp. 134–40.

Ende, Asher H. International Telecommunications: Dynamics of Regulation of a Rapidly Expanding Service. *Law Contemp. Probl.*, Spring 1969, *34* (2), pp. 389–416.

Engberg, Holger L. and Hance, William A. Growth and Dispersion of Branch Banking in Tropical Africa, 1950–1964. *Econ. Geogr.*, July 1969, *45*(3), pp. 195–208.

Engel, N. Eugene and Johnson, Stanley R. Spatial Price Equilibrium and Price Variability: An Application to the Fall Potato Industry. *Can. J. Agr. Econ.*, February 1969, *17*(1), pp. 23–32.

Engelbert, Ernest A. The Political Aspects of Real Estate Taxation in Relation to Metropolitan Growth and Planning. **In** *Becker, A. P., ed.*, 1969, pp. 97–114.

Engelhardt, Werner Wilhelm. Utopien als Problem der Sozial- und Wirtschaftswissenschaften. (With English summary.) *Z. ges. Staatswiss.*, October 1969, *125*(4), pp. 661–76.

Engelmann, Hugo O. and Wanner, Richard A. Population Size and Industrial Technology. *Amer. J. Econ. Soc.*, July 1969, *28*(3), pp. 249–56.

Engerman, Stanley L. and Fogel, Robert W. A Model for the Explanation of Industrial Expansion during the Nineteenth Century: With an Application to the American Iron Industry. *J. Polit. Econ.*, May/June 1969, *77*(3), pp. 306–28.

Enis, Ben M. and Stafford, James E. The Price-Quality Relationship: An Extension. *J. Marketing Res.*, November 1969, *6*(4), pp. 456–58.

Enke, Stephen. Correcting Some Confusions. *Rev.*

Soc. Econ., September 1969, 27(2), pp. 154–59.
______ Economists and Development: Rediscovering Old Truths. *J. Econ. Lit.*, December 1969, 7(4), pp. 1125–39.
Ennuste, Ü. Uncertainty, Information and Decomposition in the Planning of a Production System. *Econ. Planning,* 1969, 9(3), pp. 258–66.
Enthoven, Adolf J. H. Accountancy for Economic Development. *Finance Develop.,* September 1969, 6(3), pp. 24–29.
______ The Changing Role of Accountancy. *Finance Develop.,* June 1969, 6(2), pp. 16–22.
Enthoven, Alain C. The Planning, Programing, and Budgeting System in the Department of Defense: Some Lessons from Experience. **In** *The Analysis and Evaluation of Public Expenditures: The PPB System, Vol. 3, JECP,* 1969, pp. 901–08.
______ **and Smith, K. Wayne.** The Planning, Programing, and Budgeting System in the Department of Defense: Current Status and Next Steps. **In** *The Analysis and Evaluation of Public Expenditures: The PPB System, Vol. 3, JECP,* 1969, pp. 955–69.
______ **and Smith, K. Wayne.** What Forces for NATO? And from Whom? *Foreign Aff.,* October 1969, 48(1), pp. 80–96.
Epp, Donald J. Some Implications of the EEC's Agricultural Price Policy. *Amer. J. Agr. Econ.,* May 1969, 51(2), pp. 279–88.
Eppen, Gary D. and Fama, Eugene F. Cash Balance and Simple Dynamic Portfolio Problems with Proportional Costs. *Int. Econ. Rev.,* June 1969, 10 (2), pp. 119–33.
Erb, Guy F. and Schiavo-Campo, Salvatore. Export Instability, Level of Development, and Economic Size of Less Developed Countries. *Bull. Oxford Univ. Inst. Econ. Statist.,* November 1969, 31(4), pp. 263–83.
Ercolani, Mario. Strumenti della politica monetaria in Italia e schemi di analisi finanziaria. (Monetary Policy Instruments in Italy and Financial Analysis Schemes. With English summary.) *Bancaria,* March 1969, 25(3), pp. 291–302.
Erhard, Ludwig. Prospects for European Integration. *Lloyds Bank Rev.,* January 1969, (91), pp. 1–9.
Erickson, Edsel L., et al. Differences between Economically Disadvantaged Students Who Volunteer and Do Not Volunteer for Economic Opportunity Programs. *J. Human Res.,* Winter 1969, 4(1), pp. 76–83.
Erickson, Edward. The Social Costs of the Discovery and Suppression of the Clandestine Distribution of Heroin. *J. Polit. Econ.,* Part I, July/August 1969, 77(4), pp. 484–86.
Erickson, Erling A. Money and Banking in a "Bankless" State: Iowa, 1846–1857. *Bus. Hist. Rev.,* Summer 1969, 43(2), pp. 171–91.
Erickson, John. Scotland's Defence Commitment: Some Problems of Cost, Capability, and Effectiveness. **In** *Wolfe, J. N., ed.,* 1969, pp. 71–91.
Erickson, W. Bruce. Costs and Conspiracy: The Uses of Cost Data in Private Antitrust Litigation. *Antitrust Bull.,* Summer 1969, 14, pp. 347–70.
Ericson, W. A. Subjective Bayesian Models in Sampling Finite Populations: Stratification. **In** *Johnson, N. L. and Smith, H., Jr., eds.,* 1969, pp. 326–57.
Eriksson, Gösta A. Models in Human Geography. *Liiketaloudellinen Aikak.,* 1969, 18(1), pp. 13–23.
Ernst, Wolfgang. The Foreign Trade Policy of the Mao Tse-Tung Clique. *Chinese Econ. Stud.,* Fall 1969, 3(1), pp. 33–47.
Estafen, Bernard D. and Carr, Julian L., Jr. M.B.A. Salary Expectations: Fact or Fantasy? *Indiana Bus. Rev.,* September/October 1969, 44, pp. 9–12.
Eurman, Stuart and Murphy, Thomas P. Intergovernmental Cooperation in the Kansas City Region. *Univ. Missouri Bus. Govt. Rev.,* January–February 1969, 10(1), pp. 5–13.
Evans, Andrew W. Intercity Travel and the London Midland Electrification. *J. Transp. Econ. Policy,* January 1969, 3(1), pp. 69–95.
Evans, Archibald A. Work and Leisure, 1919–1969. *Int. Lab. Rev.,* January 1969, 99(1), pp. 35–59.
Evans, Campbell K. Model of Certain Relationships within the Structure of Insurance Agencies. *J. Risk Ins.,* December 1969, 36(5), pp. 535–44.
Evans, Francis C. Space Relations in Ecology: An Overview. *Mich. Academician,* Summer 1969, 2 (1), pp. 69–76.
Evans, James Gilbert, Sr. Foreign Aid for Agricultural Development. *Amer. J. Agr. Econ.,* December 1969, 51(5), pp. 1402–12.
Evans, John W. Evaluating Social Action Programs. *Soc. Sci. Quart.,* December 1969, 50(3), pp. 568–81.
Evans, Michael K. Non-Linear Econometric Models. **In** *Naylor, T. H., ed.,* 1969, pp. 369–92.
______ Reconstruction and Estimation of the Balanced Budget Multiplier. *Rev. Econ. Statist.,* February 1969, 51(1), pp. 14–25.
______ **and Kisselgoff, Avram.** Demand for Consumer Installment Credit and Its Effects on Consumption. **In** *Duesenberry, J. S., et al.,* 1969, pp. 39–84.
______ **and Klein, Lawrence R.** Experience with Econometric Analysis of the U.S. "Konjunktur" Position. **In** *Bronfenbrenner, M., ed.,* 1969, pp. 359–88.
Evans, Robert, Jr. The Military Draft as a Slave System: An Economic View. *Soc. Sci. Quart.,* December 1969, 50(3), pp. 535–43.
Evanson, Robert V. and Kotzan, Jeffrey A. Responsiveness of Drug Store Sales to Shelf Space Allocations. *J. Marketing Res.,* November 1969, 6(4), pp. 465–69.
Eversley, D. E. C. The Validity of Family and Group Statistics as Indicators of Secular Population Trends. **In** *Bechhofer, F., ed.,* 1969, pp. 179–95.
Eysenbach, M. L. A Note on Growth and Structural Change in Pakistan's Manufacturing Industry 1954–1964. *Pakistan Develop. Rev.,* Spring 1969, 9(1), pp. 58–65.
Ezekiel, Hannan. A Wage Goods Approach to the Problem of Investment Allocation in a Developing Economy. *Kansant. Aikak.,* 1969, 65(3), pp. 181–90.
______ **and Adekunle, Joseph O.** The Secular Behavior of Income Velocity: An International Cross-

Section Study. *Int. Monet. Fund Staff Pap.*, July 1969, *16*(2), pp. 224–39.

Fabella, A. V. Policies for Long-Term Growth in the Philippines: The Public Sector. *Philippine Econ. J.*, First Semester 1969, *8*(1), pp. 37–48.

Fabricant, Solomon and Firestone, O. J. The Service Industries in the Nineteenth Century: Comment. **In** *Fuchs, V. R., ed.*, 1969, pp. 368–72.

——— **and Hirsch, Werner Z.** Some Problems in the Measurement of Productivity in the Medical Care Industry: Comment. **In** *Fuchs, V. R., ed.*, 1969, pp. 146–47.

——— **and Terleckyj, Nestor E.** Alternative Measures of the Real Output and Productivity of Commercial Banks: Comment. **In** *Fuchs, V. R., ed.*, 1969, pp. 195–99.

Fabricius, P. J. The Marketing Manager of Tomorrow. *Econ. Soc. Tijdschr.*, December 1969, *23*(6), pp. 547–54.

Fafunwa, A. Babs. Educational Philosophy and Structure for Economic Development. **In** *Yesufu, T. M., ed.*, 1969, pp. 137–56.

Fagerberg, Dixon, Jr. Accounting for Vacation Expense. *Manage. Account.*, December 1969, *51*(6), pp. 47–48.

Fairbairn, I. J. and McShane, R. W. The Return on Equities and Fixed Interest Securities on the Australian Capital Market. *Econ. Rec.*, March 1969, *45*(109), pp. 116–23.

Fairlie, Susan. The Corn Laws and British Wheat Production, 1829–76. *Econ. Hist. Rev.*, April 1969, *22*(1), pp. 88–116.

Falcon, Walter P. Agricultural Planning: The Peruvian Experience: Comment. **In** *Thorbecke, E., ed.*, 1969, pp. 446–50.

Falero, Frank, Jr. and Macesich, George. Permanent Income Hypothesis, Interest Rates and the Demand for Money. *Weltwirtsch. Arch.*, 1969, *103* (1), pp. 129–52.

Falk, Laurence H. and Stober, William J. The Effect of Financial Inducements on the Location of Firms. *Southern Econ. J.*, July 1969, *36*(1), pp. 25–35.

——— Industrial Development Bonds as a Subsidy to Industry. *Nat. Tax J.*, June 1969, *22*(2), pp. 232–43.

Falkowski, Mieczysław. Socialist Economists and the Developing Countries. **In** *Prybyla, J. S., ed.*, 1969, pp. 511–22.

Falkson, Louis Michael. Airline Overbooking: Some Comments. *J. Transp. Econ. Policy*, September 1969, *3*(3), pp. 352–54.

Falkus, M. E. and Gadiel, D. L. A Comment on the 'Price Revolution.' *Australian Econ. Hist. Rev.*, March 1969, *9*(1), pp. 9–16.

Faltermayer, Edmund K. A Way Out of the Welfare Mess. **In** *Starleaf, D. R., ed.*, 1969, pp. 439–48.

Fama, Eugene F. and Eppen, Gary D. Cash Balance and Simple Dynamic Portfolio Problems with Proportional Costs. *Int. Econ. Rev.*, June 1969, *10* (2), pp. 119–33.

Fama, Eugene F., et al. The Adjustment of Stock Prices to New Information. *Int. Econ. Rev.*, February 1969, *10*(1), pp. 1–21.

Fan, Liang-Shing. Note on Trade and Distribution of International Reserves. *Indian Econ. J.*, April–June 1969, *16*(4–5), pp. 492–95.

Fand, David I. Keynesian Monetary Theories, Stabilization Policy, and the Recent Inflation. *J. Money, Credit, Banking*, August 1969, *1*(3), pp. 556–87.

——— A Monetary Interpretation of the Post-1965 Inflation in the United States. *Banca Naz. Lavoro Quart. Rev.*, June 1969, (89), pp. 99–127.

——— Monetary Theory and the Post-1965 Inflation. *Mich. Academician*, Summer 1969, *2*(1), pp. 13–22.

——— Some Issues in Monetary Economics. *Banca Naz. Lavoro Quart. Rev.*, September 1969, (90), pp. 215–47.

——— **and Buehler, John E.** The Federal Reserve and Monetary Policy. *Mich. Academician*, Spring 1969, *1*(3–4), pp. 21–35.

Fannin, Paul I. and Murphy, George. The Migratory Farm Labor Problem in the United States. **In** *Kuhlman, J. M., ed.*, 1969, pp. 151–73.

Farace, R. Vincent and Hiniker, Paul J. Approaches to National Development in China: 1949–1958. *Econ. Develop. Cult. Change*, Part I, October 1969, *18*(1), pp. 51–72.

Farmer, B. H. Available Food Supplies. **In** *Hutchinson, J. [Sir], ed.*, 1969, pp. 75–95.

Farmer, D. L. Some Livestock Price Movements in Thirteenth-Century England. *Econ. Hist. Rev.*, April 1969, *22*(1), pp. 1–16.

Farmer, Richard N. The Dilemma of the Black Businessman: Clarification of the Current Situation. *Indiana Bus. Rev.*, March–April 1969, *44*, pp. 13, 27–28.

Farrell, Robert L. and Cartter, Allan M. Academic Labor Market Projections and the Draft. **In** *the Economics and Financing of Higher Education in the United States, JECP*, 1969, pp. 357–74.

Farris, Martin T. Transportation Regulation and Economic Efficiency. *Amer. Econ. Rev.*, May 1969, *59*(2), pp. 244–50.

Farris, Paul L. Information Gaps and Research Problems. **In** *Garoian, L., ed.*, 1969, pp. 123–24.

——— **and Cobia, David W.** Mergers and Diversified Growth of Large Grain Firms. *Amer. J. Agr. Econ.*, August 1969, *51*(3), pp. 619–24.

Farrish, Raymond O. P. and Hardie, Ian W. Mysterious Multipliers: Comment. *Amer. J. Agr. Econ.*, August 1969, *51*(3), pp. 689.

Fasolina, G.; Sternberger, H. and Renz, J. Planning-Programing-Budgeting System (PPBS) in Nassau County, N.Y. **In** *Innovations in Planning, Programming, and Budgeting in State and Local Governments, JECP*, 1969, pp. 105–89.

Faupl, Rudolph. The ILO at 50: A Trade Union Perspective. *Mon. Lab. Rev.*, May 1969, *92*(5), pp. 44–46.

Faxén, Karl-Olof; Odhner, Clas-Erik and Edgren, Gösta. Wages, Growth and the Distribution of Income. *Swedish J. Econ.*, September 1969, *71*(3), pp. 133–60.

Fayol, Henri. The Administrative Theory in the State. **In** *Gulick, L. and Urwick, L., eds.*, 1969, pp. 99–114.

Fazal, Mohd. Management of Personnel. **In** *Dagli, V., ed., Vol. II*, 1969, pp. 161–65.

Fazekas, B. and Öri, J. On the Formulation of a Common Agricultural Policy for CMEA Countries. (In Russian. With English summary.) *Acta Oecon.*, 1969, *4*(4), pp. 403–15.

Fazio, Antonio. Monetary Base and the Control of Credit in Italy. *Banca Naz. Lavoro Quart. Rev.,* June 1969, (89), pp. 146–69.

Fearon, Peter. The Formative Years of the British Aircraft Industry, 1913–1924. *Bus. Hist. Rev.,* Winter 1969, *43*(4), pp. 476–95.

Feder, Ernest. Societal Opposition to Peasant Movements and Its Effects on Farm People in Latin America. **In** *Landsberger, H. A., ed.,* 1969, pp. 399–450.

Federici, Vincenzo. L'automazione del servizio pegno alla luce dell'esperienza di un'Azienda credito. (Automation of Pledge Service in the Light of a Bank's Experience. With English summary.) *Bancaria,* February 1969, *25*(2), pp. 203–05.

Fedorenko, N. Questions Pertaining to Optimization of the Growth and Location of Production. *Prob. Econ.,* January 1969, *11*(9), pp. 14–23.

______ **and Shatalin, S.** The Problem of Optimal Planning of the Socialist Economy. *Prob. Econ.,* November 1969, *12*(7), pp. 3–29.

Fefferman, Arthur S. Private Pension Plans: A 1968 Prospectus. *J. Risk Ins.,* September 1969, *36*(4), pp. 433–36.

Fei, John C. H. and Ranis, Gustav. Agriculture in the Open Economy. **In** *Thorbecke, E., ed.,* 1969, pp. 129–59.

______ Agriculture in the Open Economy: Reply. **In** *Thorbecke, E., ed.,* 1969, pp. 163–64.

______ Economic Development in Historical Perspective. *Amer. Econ. Rev.,* May 1969, *59*(2), pp. 286–400.

Feitel'man, N. G. The Tasks of Planning Education. **In** *Noah, H. J., ed.,* 1969, pp. 169–76.

Feiwel, George R. Czechoslovakia's Economic Dilemma. *Indian Econ. J.,* July–September 1969, *17*(1), pp. 1–27.

______ The Era of Economic Reforms of Socialist Planning. *Econ. Int.,* February 1969, *22*(1), pp. 87–115.

Feldman, David. The Economics of Ideology: Some Problems of Achieving Rural Socialism in Tanzania. **In** *Leys, C., ed.,* 1969, pp. 85–111.

Feldman, Gerald D. The Social and Economic Policies of German Big Business, 1918–1929. *Amer. Hist. Rev.,* October 1969, *75*(1), pp. 47–55.

Feldman, Paul. Prescription for an Effective Government: Ethics, Economics, and PPBS. **In** *The Analysis and Evaluation of Public Expenditures: The PPB System, Vol. 3, JECP,* 1969, pp. 865–85.

______ **and Hoenack, Stephen A.** Private Demand for Higher Education in the United States. **In** *the Economics and Financing of Higher Education in the United States, JECP,* 1969, pp. 375–95.

______ **and Singer, Neil.** Criteria for Public Investment in Higher Education. **In** *the Economics and Financing of Higher Education in the United States, JECP,* 1969, pp. 124–34.

Feldstein, Martin S. Advertising, Research and Profits in the Drug Industry. *Southern Econ. J.,* January 1969, *35*(3), pp. 239–43.

______ The Effects on Taxation on Risk Taking. *J. Polit. Econ.,* September/October 1969, *77*(5), pp. 755–64.

______ Mean-Variance Analysis in the Theory of Liquidity Preference and Portfolio Selection. *Rev. Econ. Stud.,* January 1969, *36*(105), pp. 5–12.

______ **and Klarman, Herbert E.** Some Problems in the Measurement of Productivity in the Medical Care Industry: Discussion. **In** *Fuchs, V. R., ed.,* 1969, pp. 132–46.

Felix, David. Economic Development: Take-Offs into Unsustained Growth. *Soc. Res.,* Summer 1969, *36*(2), pp. 267–93.

Feller, David E. The Steel Experience: Myth and Reality. **In** *Somers, G. G., ed. (II),* 1969, pp. 152–59.

Fellmeth, Robert; Schulz, John and Cox, Edward. The Consumer and the Federal Trade Commission, a Critique of the Consumer Protection Record of the FTC. **In** *To Establish a Department of Consumer Affairs, SCH,* 1969, pp. 123–312.

Fellner, William. Specific Interpretations of Learning by Doing. *J. Econ. Theory,* August 1969, *1*(2), pp. 119–40.

______ **and Ellis, Howard S.** External Economies and Diseconomies. **In** *Blumner, S. M., ed.,* 1969, pp. 163–79.

Fels, Rendigs. Hard Research on a Soft Subject: Hypothesis-Testing in Economic Education. *Southern Econ. J.,* July 1969, *36*(1), pp. 1–9.

______ **and Welsh, Arthur L.** Performance on the New Test of Understanding in College Economics. *Amer. Econ. Rev.,* May 1969, *59*(2), pp. 224–29.

Felt, Howard M. and Barsky, Donald T. Purchase vs. Lease: Computer Obsolescence. *Manage. Account.,* October 1969, *51*(4), pp. 29–32.

di Fenizio, Ferdinando. Possibili valori e metodi d'indagine per "consulenti di direzione" di grandi gruppi industriali. (The Value Judgements and the Analytical Tools of a Management Consultant to a Large Industrial Company. With English summary.) *L'Industria,* April–June 1969, (2), pp. 147–58.

______ Relazione al Ministro del Tesoro del Presidente del Gruppo residui nel bilancio dello Stato. (The Report of the President of the Commission on Residual Assets and Liabilities of the National Budget to the Minister of the Treasury. With English summary.) *L'Industria,* July–September 1969, (3), pp. 347–57.

Fenlon, John. Patterns in Overtime Hours and Premium Pay. *Mon. Lab. Rev.,* October 1969, *92*(10), pp. 42–46.

Ferber, Robert. Contributions of Economics to the Study of Consumer Market Behavior. *Appl. Econ.,* May 1969, *1*(2), pp. 125–36.

Ferber, Robert, et al. Validation of a National Survey of Consumer Financial Characteristics: Savings Accounts. *Rev. Econ. Statist.,* November 1969, *51*(4), pp. 436–44.

______ Validation of Consumer Financial Characteristics: Common Stock. *J. Amer. Statist. Assoc.,* June 1969, *64*(326), pp. 415–32.

Ferguson, C. E. A Look at Long-Run Equilibrium under Multiplant Monopoly: Comment. *Amer. Econ.,* Fall 1969, *13*(2), pp. 94–96.

______ **and Moroney, John R.** The Sources of Change in Labor's Relative Share: A Neoclassical Analysis. *Southern Econ. J.,* April 1969, *35*(4), pp. 308–22.

______ **and Saving, Thomas R.** Long-Run Scale Adjustments of a Perfectly Competitive Firm and

Industry. *Amer. Econ. Rev.*, December 1969, *59* (5), pp. 774–83.

Fericelli, Jean. Programmation dynamique et planification macro-économique. (With English summary.) *Revue Écon.*, March 1969, *20*(2), pp. 235–71.

Fernandes, L. Santos. Comments on Professor Reviglio's Paper on the "Finance of Social Security in Developing Countries." *Public Finance*, 1969, *24* (2), pp. 278–79.

Fernandez Lopez, Manuel. Análisis gráfico de las devaluaciones cambiarias. (A Geometric Approach to Finite Devaluation. With English summary.) *Económica*, September–December 1969, *15*(3), pp. 291–98.

Fernandez, Raul A. The Clandestine Distribution of Heroin, Its Discovery and Suppression: A Comment. *J. Polit. Econ.*, Part I, July/August 1969, *77* (4), pp. 487–88.

Fernea, Robert A. Land Reform and Ecology in Postrevolutionary Iraq. *Econ. Develop. Cult. Change*, April 1969, *17*(3), pp. 356–81.

Ferrari, Alberto. Società internazionali problemi di finanziamento e mercato dei capitali. (International Companies: Capital Market and Financing Problems. With English summary.) *Bancaria*, June 1969, *25*(6), pp. 691–99.

Ferrari, J. Robert. Implications of Viewing Interest Foregone as an Opportunity Cost of Life Insurance. *J. Risk Ins.*, June 1969, *36*(2), pp. 253–65.

Ferraro, Anthony G. Valuation of Property Interests for *Ad Valorem* Taxation of Extractive Industry and Agricultural Realty: Problems and Solutions. **In** *Lynn, A. D., Jr., ed.*, 1969, pp. 119–39.

Ferrer-Pacces. L'internazionale dell imprese. (Multinational Firm. With English summary.) *L'Impresa*, March/April 1969, *11*(2), pp. 115–17.

Fertakis, John P. On Communication, Understanding, and Relevance in Accounting Reporting. *Accounting Rev.*, October 1969, *44*(4), pp. 680–91.

Fetter, Frank W. The Rise and Decline of Ricardian Economics. *Hist. Polit. Econ.*, Spring 1969, *1*(1), pp. 67–84.

Feulner, Edwin J., Jr. Capitalism, Socialism, and the Social Market Economy: Comment. *Rev. Soc. Econ.*, March 1969, *27*(1), pp. 37–40.

Field, Alfred J. and Thorbecke, Erik. Relationships between Agriculture, Nonagriculture, and Foreign Trade in the Development of Argentina and Peru: Reply. **In** *Thorbecke, E., ed.*, 1969, pp. 217–18.

______ Relationships between Agriculture, Nonagriculture, and Foreign Trade in the Development of Argentina and Peru. **In** *Thorbecke, E., ed.*, 1969, pp. 165–213.

Field, John E. Toward a Multi-Level, Multi-Goal Information System. *Accounting Rev.*, July 1969, *44*(3), pp. 593–99.

Fieleke, Norman S. The Buy-American Policy of the United States Government: Its Balance-of-Payments and Welfare Effects. *New Eng. Econ. Rev.*, July/August 1969, pp. 2–18.

______ Toward a More Efficient Railroad System. *New Eng. Econ. Rev.*, March/April 1969, pp. 2–20.

Fienga, Ruben. Situation and Prospects of the Italian State Railways. *Rev. Econ. Cond. Italy*, September 1969, *23*(5), pp. 397–408.

Fiero, Charles E. Statement. **In** *A Review of Balance of Payments Policies, JECH*, 1969, pp. 141–55.

Filippi, Enrico. Le duecento maggiori società industriali italiane. (The 200 Largest Italian Industrial Corporations. With English summary.) *L'Impresa*, January/February 1969, *11*(1), pp. 41–55.

______ **and Zanetti, Giovanni.** Il processo di sviluppo dell'impresa: Fattori endogeni ed esogeni esperienza italiana 1958–1963. (The Process of Firm Growth: Endogenous and Exogenous Factors in the Italian Experience 1958–1963. With English summary.) *L'Impresa*, January/February 1969, *11*(1), pp. 29–39.

Fillerup, O. W. Migratory Labor in California Agriculture. **In** *Task Force on Economic Growth and Opportunity*, 1969, pp. 145–52.

Filley, Alan C. New Directions in Organization Theory. **In** *Somers, G. G., ed. (I)*, 1969, pp. 79–108.

Finch, B. W.; Waters, Joseph B. and Bonin, Joseph M. Alternative Tests of the "Displacement Effect" Hypothesis. *Public Finance*, 1969, *24*(3), pp. 441–56.

Fine, Phil David. Statement. **In** *Bank Holding Company Act Amendments, Pts. 1–3, HCH*, 1969, pp. 924–29.

Finger, J. M. Factor Intensity and "Leontief Type" Tests of the Factor Proportions Theory. *Econ. Int.*, August 1969, *22*(3), pp. 405–22.

______ Substitution and the Effective Rate of Protection. *J. Polit. Econ.*, November/December 1969, *77*(6), pp. 972–75.

Finkel, Sidney R. and Tarascio, Vincent J. A Theoretical Integration of Production and Wage Theory. *Western Econ. J.*, December 1969, *7*(4), pp. 371–78.

Firestone, O. J. and Fabricant, Solomon. The Service Industries in the Nineteenth Century: Comment. **In** *Fuchs, V. R., ed.*, 1969, pp. 368–72.

Firey, Walter. Limits to Economy in Crime and Punishment. *Soc. Sci. Quart.*, June 1969, *50*(1), pp. 72–77.

Fischer, Gerald. Market Extension by Bank Holding Companies: History, Economic Implications, and Current Issues. **In** *Federal Reserve Bank of Chicago (II)*, 1969, pp. 43–72.

Fisek, Nusret H. Prospects for Fertility Planning in Turkey. **In** *Behrman, S. J.; Corsa, L., Jr. and Freedman, R., eds.*, 1969, pp. 467–77.

Fish, Mary and Adams, Esmond. Comments on the Impact of Federal Tax-Sharing on Economic Stabilization. *Nebr. J. Econ. Bus.*, Winter 1968–69, *8*(1), pp. 53–60.

Fishburn, Peter C. A Study of Independence in Multivariate Utility Theory. *Econometrica*, January 1969, *37*(1), pp. 107–21.

Fishelson, Gideon. The Future Income Hypothesis. *Southern Econ. J.*, January 1969, *35*(3), pp. 268–69.

Fisher, Anthony C. The Cost of the Draft and the Cost of Ending the Draft. *Amer. Econ. Rev.*, June 1969, *59*(3), pp. 239–54.

______ **and Altman, Stuart H.** Marginal Product of Labor, Wages and Disequilibrium: Comment.

Rev. Econ. Statist., November 1969, *51*(4), pp. 485–86.

Fisher, Franklin M. Approximate Aggregation and the Leontief Conditions. *Econometrica,* July 1969, *37*(3), pp. 457–69.

______ The Existence of Aggregate Production Functions. *Econometrica,* October 1969, *37*(4), pp. 553–77.

______; **Levhari, David and Sheshinski, Eytan.** On the Sensitivity of the Level of Output to Savings: Embodiment and Disembodiment: A Clarificatory Note. *Quart. J. Econ.,* May 1969, *83*(2), pp. 347–48.

Fisher, I. N. and Hall, George R. Risk and Corporate Rates of Return. *Quart. J. Econ.,* February 1969, *83*(1), pp. 79–92.

Fisher, Irving. Income and Capital. **In** *Parker, R. H. and Harcourt, G. C., eds.,* 1969, pp. 33–53.

Fisher, Joseph L. and Potter, Neal. Natural Resource Adequacy for the United States and the World. **In** *Hauser, P. M., ed.,* 1969, pp. 106–38.

Fisher, Robert Moore. The Availibility of Mortgage Lending Commitments. (Study summary.) *Fed. Res. Bull.,* December 1969, *55*(12), pp. 919–20.

______ Monetary Policy: Its Relation to Mortgage Lending and Land Economics. *Land Econ.,* November 1969, *45*(4), pp. 418–24.

Fishman, Leo. The White House and the Fed. **In** *Starleaf, D. R., ed.,* 1969, pp. 290–95.

Fitzhugh, H. Naylor. Ethnic Challenges to Marketing Management. *Univ. Wash. Bus. Rev.,* Spring 1969, *28*(3), pp. 26–32.

FitzLyon, K. Plan and Prediction. *Soviet Stud.,* October 1969, *21*(2), pp. 164–92.

Flaim, Paul O. Persons Not in the Labor Force: Who They Are and Why They Don't Work. *Mon. Lab. Rev.,* July 1969, *92*(7), pp. 3–14.

Flamholtz, Eric G.; Pyle, William C. and Brummet, R. Lee. Human Resource Accounting: A Tool to Increase Managerial Effectiveness. *Manage. Account.,* August 1969, *51*(2), pp. 12–15.

______ Human Resource Myopia. *Mon. Lab. Rev.,* January 1969, *92*(1), pp. 29–30.

Flammang, Robert A. Communications. *J. Econ. Issues,* June 1969, *3*(2), pp. 213–18.

______ Louisiana and the World Economy. **In** *Beard, T. R., ed.,* 1969, pp. 133–47.

Flanders, David P. Mechanized Intercompany Transfer System. *Manage. Account.,* October 1969, *51*(4), pp. 49–52.

Flanders, M. June. Agriculture versus Industry in Development Policy: The Planner's Dilemma Reexamined. *J. Devel. Stud.,* April 1969, *5*(3), pp. 171–89.

______ International Liquidity Is Always Inadequate. *Kyklos,* 1969, *22*(3), pp. 519–29.

______ **and Baggott, Nancy.** Economic Policy in an Open Economy: A Reader's Guide. *Econ. Int.,* November 1969, *22*(4), pp. 593–605.

Fleagle, Robert G. Background and Present Status of Weather Modification. **In** *Fleagle, R. G., ed.,* 1969, pp. 3–17.

______ Implications for Public Policy. **In** *Fleagle, R. G., ed.,* 1969, pp. 138–42.

Fleck, Florian H. Die CES-Funktion als Produktionsund Verteilungsfunktion. Ein Vergleich mit der COBB-DOUGLAS-Funktion. (The CES-Function as a Production- and Distribution-Function. A Comparison with the Cobb-Douglas-Function. With English summary.) *Jahr. Nationalökon. Statist.,* July 1969, *183*(2), pp. 125–40.

______ Wechselwirkungen zwischen dem technischen Fortschritt und den Skalenerträgen—noch einmal unter Berücksichtigung der VES-Produktionsfunktion. (Relationship between Technical Progress and Marginal Returns to Scale. With English summary.) *Schweiz. Z. Volkswirtsch. Statist.,* December 1969, *105*(4), pp. 551–56.

Flek, Josef. Life and Income of Czechoslovak Cooperatives. **In** *Papi, U. and Nunn, C., eds.,* 1969, pp. 304–15.

Fleming, J. Marcus and Meade, James E. Price and Output Policy of State Enterprise: A Symposium. **In** *Arrow, K. J. and Scitovsky, T., eds.,* 1969, pp. 309–24.

Fleming, John E. A Decision Model of Control. *Miss. Val. J. Bus. Econ.,* Spring 1969, *4*(2), pp. 23–32.

Flemming, J. S. The Utility of Wealth and the Utility of Windfalls. *Rev. Econ. Stud.,* January 1969, *36* (105), pp. 55–66.

Fletcher, C. H. and Corner, D. C. Some Effects of Selective Employment Tax on the Construction and Service Industries. *Bull. Oxford Univ. Inst. Econ. Statist.,* February 1969, *31*(1), pp. 47–54.

Fletcher, R. G.; Tolley, George S. and Wang, Yi. Reexamination of the Time Series Evidence on Food Demand. *Econometrica,* October 1969, *37* (4), pp. 695–705.

Flinn, J. C. The Demand for Irrigation Water in an Intensive Irrigation Area. *Australian J. Agr. Econ.,* December 1969, *13*(2), pp. 128–43.

Flippo, Edwin B. La riscoperta del lavoro nella teoria del management. (The Rediscovery of Work in Management Theory. With English summary.) *Rivista Int. Sci. Econ. Com.,* May 1969, *16*(5), pp. 446–56.

Flora, A. C., Jr. The Economic Ideas of Francis Lieber. **In** *Kiker, B. F. and Carlsson, R. J., eds.,* 1969, pp. 83–104.

Flores, Edmundo. Latin American Land Reform: Meaning and Experience. **In** *Nisbet, C. T., ed.,* 1969, pp. 132–40.

Florescu, C. and Mircioiu, V. Dezvoltarea comerțului interior în anii construcției socialiste. (Development of Home Trade during the Years of Building up Socialism. With English summary.) *Stud. Cercet. Econ.,* 1969, *3,* pp. 151–59.

Floud, R. C. and Craig, R. S. List of Publications on the Economic History of Great Britain and Ireland Published in 1967. *Econ. Hist. Rev.,* August 1969, *22*(2), pp. 322–41.

Flower, J. F. The Case of the Profitable Bloodhound. **In** *Carsberg, B. V. and Edey, H. C., eds.,* 1969, pp. 218–45.

Flowers, Marilyn and Buchanan, James M. An Analytical Setting for a "Taxpayers' Revolution." *Western Econ. J.,* December 1969, *7*(4), pp. 349–59.

Floyd, John E. International Capital Movements and Monetary Equilibrium. *Amer. Econ. Rev.,* Part I, September 1969, *59*(4), pp. 472–92.

______ Monetary and Fiscal Policy in a World of

Capital Mobility. *Rev. Econ. Stud.*, October 1969, *36*(108), pp. 503–17.

Foenander, Orwell de R. Australian Wage Fixation and a Change in Its Method. *Ind. Lab. Relat. Rev.*, January 1969, *22*(2), pp. 226–42.

Fogarty, John P. New South Wales Wool Prices in the 1820s: A Note. *Australian Econ. Hist. Rev.*, March 1969, *9*(1), pp. 71–77.

Fogel, Robert W. and Engerman, Stanley L. A Model for the Explanation of Industrial Expansion during the Nineteenth Century: With an Application to the American Iron Industry. *J. Polit. Econ.*, May/June 1969, *77*(3), pp. 306–28.

Foland, Frances M. Agrarian Reform in Latin America. *Foreign Aff.*, October 1969, *48*(1), pp. 97–112.

Foley, Duncan K.; Shell, Karl and Sidrauski, Miguel. Optimal Fiscal and Monetary Policy and Economic Growth. *J. Polit. Econ.*, Part II, July/August 1969, *77*(4), pp. 698–719.

Follett, Mary Parker. The Process of Control. **In** *Gulick, L. and Urwick, L., eds.*, 1969, pp. 159–69.

Fölscher, G. C. K. Some Thoughts on Modernizing a Relatively Large Backward Region in an Otherwise Developed Economy. *Finance Trade Rev.*, June 1969, *8*(3), pp. 198–205.

Folse, C. I. and Riffe, W. W. Changing Patterns of Business Services and Population in Illinois Rural Villages. *Ill. Agr. Econ.*, January 1969, *9*(1), pp. 26–32.

Folsom, Roger Nils. Real and Money Consumption as Functions of Money Income. *Western Econ. J.*, March 1969, *7*(1), pp. 96–99.

Folwell, Raymond J. A New Look at Demand Analysis for Beef: Comment. *Amer. J. Agr. Econ.*, November 1969, *51*(4), pp. 947–49.

Fontela, E. Technological Forecasting and Corporate Strategy. **In** *Arnfield, R. V., ed.*, 1969, pp. 26–33.

Foote, R. J. and Thomsen, F. L. Parity Price. **In** *Ruttan, V. W.; Waldo, A. D. and Houck, J. P., eds.*, 1969, pp. 90–95.

Forbes, Stephen W. Automobile Bodily Injury Liability Loss Reserving Techniques and Simulation. *J. Risk Ins.*, December 1969, *36*(5), pp. 597–614.

Ford, A. G. British Economic Fluctuations, 1870–1914. *Manchester Sch. Econ. Soc. Stud.*, June 1969, *37*(2), pp. 99–130.

——— A Note on British Export Performance, 1899–1913. *Econ. Hist. Rev.*, April 1969, *22*(1), pp. 120–21.

Ford, Allen. Should Cost Be Assigned to Conversion Value? *Accounting Rev.*, October 1969, *44*(4), pp. 818–22.

Ford, J. L. Specific Factors of Production and the Ricardian and Ohlinian Doctrines. *Yorkshire Bull. Econ. Soc. Res.*, November 1969, *21*(2), pp. 119–31.

——— Variable Returns to Scale and the Factor-Price Equalisation Theorem. *Rivista Int. Sci. Econ. Com.*, August 1969, *16*(8), pp. 756–80.

——— **and Warford, J. J.** Cost Functions for the Water Industry. *J. Ind. Econ.*, November 1969, *18*(1), pp. 53–63.

Ford, Thomas R. The Psychiatric Perspective on Poverty: Comment. **In** *Weaver, T. and Magid, A., eds.*, 1969, pp. 129–32.

——— Rural Poverty in the United States. **In** *Task Force on Economic Growth and Opportunity*, 1969, pp. 153–76.

Ford, William Freithaler and Tollison, Robert. Note on the Color of the Volunteer Army. *Soc. Sci. Quart.*, December 1969, *50*(3), pp. 544–47.

Fores, M. J. No More General Theories? *Econ. J.*, March 1969, *79*(313), pp. 11–22.

Forgács, T. Post-Graduate Training of Economists in Hungary. *Acta Oecon.*, 1969, *4*(2), pp. 205–08.

Forrest, Matthew D. and Yoshihara, Kunio. Japan's Dependence in Contrast with That of Six Other Nations. *Hitotsubashi J. Econ.*, June 1969, *10*(1), pp. 56–62.

Forstall, Richard L. Economic Classification of Places over 10,000, 1960–1963. **In** *Population Trends, Pt. 1, HCH*, 1969, pp. 452–70.

——— Population Change in American Cities, 1960–1965. **In** *Population Trends, Pt. 1, HCH*, 1969, pp. 433–51.

——— Statement. **In** *Population Trends, Pt. 1, HCH*, 1969, pp. 411–22.

Forte, Francesco. Summary of the Discussion on Policy Problems. *Public Finance*, 1969, *24*(2), pp. 405–13.

——— **and Willet, Thomas D.** Interest Rate Policy and External Balance. *Quart. J. Econ.*, May 1969, *83*(2), pp. 242–62.

Forward, C. N. A Comparison of Waterfront Land Use in Four Canadian Ports: St. John's, St. John, Halifax, and Victoria. *Econ. Geogr.*, April 1969, *45*(2), pp. 155–69.

Foss, B. A Cost Model for Coastal Shipping: A Norwegian Example. *J. Transp. Econ. Policy*, May 1969, *3*(2), pp. 195–221.

Foster, Kenneth E. Accounting for Management Pay Differentials. *Ind. Relat.*, October 1969, *9*(1), pp. 80–87.

Foster, Phillips and Yost, Larry. A Simulation Study of Population, Education, and Income Growth in Uganda. *Amer. J. Agr. Econ.*, August 1969, *51*(3), pp. 576–91.

Fougstedt, Gunnar. Ekonomien tuleva kysyntä ja tarjonta vuoteen 1985. (The Demand for and the Supply of People with B.Sc. (Econ.) Degree in Finland up to 1985. With English summary.) *Liiketaloudellinen Aikak.*, 1969, *18*(4), pp. 692–715.

Fourgeaud, Claude. Contribution à l'Étude du Rôle des Administrations dans la Théorie Mathématique de l'Équilibre et de l'Optimum. (With English summary.) *Econometrica*, April 1969, *37*(2), pp. 307–23.

Fournis, Yves. Le implicazioni concrete del marketing sull'impresa. (Practical Implications of Marketing for the Firm. With English summary.) *L'Impresa*, July/October 1969, *11*(4–5), pp. 327–31.

Fox, Hugh. Latin American Unity: A Socio-Economic Overview. **In** *Hilton, R., ed.*, 1969, pp. 454–59.

Fox, Irving K. *The Nation's Water Resources* (Review Article). *Land Econ.*, November 1969, *45*(4), pp. 474–76.

Fox, Karl A. Comparison of the Prewar and Postwar Business Cycles in the Netherlands: An Experiment in Econometrics: Comment. **In** *Bronfenbrenner, M., ed.,* 1969, pp. 467–74.

______ Factors Affecting Farm Income, Farm Prices, and Food Consumption. **In** *Fox, K. A. and Johnson, D. G., eds.,* 1969, pp. 37–63.

______ The New Synthesis of Rural and Urban Society in the United States. **In** *Papi, U. and Nunn, C., eds.,* 1969, pp. 606–28.

______ A Regional Model of Agricultural Development: Comment. **In** *Thorbecke, E., ed.,* 1969, pp. 93–94.

______ Toward a Policy Model of World Economic Development with Special Attention to the Agricultural Sector. **In** *Thorbecke, E., ed.,* 1969, pp. 95–126.

Francis, A. A. A Model of National Economic Growth under Perfect Enclavism. *Soc. Econ. Stud.,* December 1969, *18*(4), pp. 365–73.

Francis, Darryl R. Controlling Inflation. *Fed. Res. Bank St. Louis Rev.,* September 1969, *51*(9), pp. 8–12.

______ Monetary Policy and Inflation. *Fed. Res. Bank St. Louis Rev.,* June 1969, *51*(6), pp. 8–11.

______ Selective Credit—No Substitute for Monetary Restraint. *Fed. Res. Bank St. Louis Rev.,* December 1969, *51*(12), pp. 13–17.

Francuz, Henryk. The International Bank for Economic Cooperation. *Int. Monet. Fund Staff Pap.,* November 1969, *16*(3), pp. 489–503.

Frank, Andre Gunder. Aid or Exploitation? **In** *Frank, A. G.,* 1969, pp. 149–61.

______ Capitalist Latifundio Growth in Latin America. **In** *Frank, A. G.,* 1969, pp. 231–47.

______ Capitalist Underdevelopment or Socialist Revolution. **In** *Frank, A. G.,* 1969, pp. 371–409.

______ Destroy Capitalism, Not Feudalism. **In** *Frank, A. G.,* 1969, pp. 350–61.

______ The Development of Underdevelopment. **In** *Frank, A. G.,* 1969, pp. 3–17.

______ Dialectic, Not Dual Society. **In** *Frank, A. G.,* 1969, pp. 221–30.

______ Economic Politics or Political Economy. **In** *Frank, A. G.,* 1969, pp. 108–21.

______ The Economics of Military Government. **In** *Frank, A. G.,* 1969, pp. 192–200.

______ Instability and Integration in Urban Latin America. **In** *Frank, A. G.,* 1969, pp. 276–97.

______ Invisible Foreign Services or National Economic Development? **In** *Frank, A. G.,* 1969, pp. 181–91.

______ Latin American Economic Integration. **In** *Frank, A. G.,* 1969, pp. 175–80.

______ Mechanisms of Imperialism. **In** *Frank, A. G.,* 1969, pp. 162–74.

______ Mexico: The Janus Faces of Twentieth-Century Bourgeois Revolution. **In** *Frank, A. G.,* 1969, pp. 298–317.

______ Mr. Heilbroner's Rhetoric and Reality. **In** *Frank, A. G.,* 1969, pp. 125–36.

______ Rural Economic Structure and Peasant Political Power. **In** *Frank, A. G.,* 1969, pp. 248–68.

______ Varieties of Land Reform. **In** *Frank, A. G.,* 1969, pp. 269–75.

Frank, Charles R., Jr. Economic Development: Discussion. *Amer. Econ. Rev.,* May 1969, *59*(2), pp. 429–32.

______ A Generalization of the Koopmans-Gale Theorem on Pricing and Efficiency. *Int. Econ. Rev.,* October 1969, *10*(3), pp. 488–91.

Frank, Helmut J. Statement. **In** *Governmental Intervention in the Market Mechanism, Pt. 1, SCH,* 1969, pp. 339–51.

Frank, Ronald E. and Wind, Yoram. Interproduct Household Loyalty to Brands. *J. Marketing Res.,* November 1969, *6*(4), pp. 434–35.

Frank, Werner. A Comparison and Evaluation of Three Interim Income Concepts. *Soc. Sci. Quart.,* March 1969, *49*(4), pp. 864–75.

Franke, Walter H. Research on Big City Labor Markets: Discussion. **In** *Somers, G. G., ed. (II),* 1969, pp. 272–74.

Frankel, Beverly F. and Frankel, Richard J. A Framework for Dealing with the Urban Environment: Appendix: Microenvironmental Responses to Changes in the Urban Environment. **In** *Perloff, H. S., ed.,* 1969, pp. 26–31.

Frankel, L. R. The Role of Accuracy and Precision of Response in Sample Surveys. **In** *Johnson, N. L. and Smith, H., Jr., eds.,* 1969, pp. 439–56.

Frankel, Richard J. and Frankel, Beverly F. A Framework for Dealing with the Urban Environment: Appendix: Microenvironmental Responses to Changes in the Urban Environment. **In** *Perloff, H. S., ed.,* 1969, pp. 26–31.

Frankena, Mark W. and Conard, Joseph W. The Yield Spread Between New and Seasoned Corporate Bonds, 1952–63. **In** *Guttentag, J. M. and Cagan, P., eds.,* 1969, pp. 143–222.

Franklin, N. N. Employment and Unemployment: Views and Policies, 1919–1969. *Int. Lab. Rev.,* March 1969, *99*(3), pp. 293–314.

______ Minimum Wage Fixing and Economic Development. **In** *Smith, A. D., ed.,* 1969, pp. 338–53.

Franks, Alison. Does Britain Pay Its Way?—A Rejoinder. *Nat. Westminster Bank Quart. Rev.,* May 1969, pp. 42–44.

Fransman, Martin J. Technological Change in South African Manufacturing Industry, 1955–1964: A Comment. *S. Afr. J. Econ.,* June 1969, *37*(2), pp. 161–63.

de Franz, Marie-Anne. Implanting the Social Sciences—A Review of UNESCO's Endeavours. *Int. Soc. Sci. J.,* 1969, *21*(3), pp. 406–20.

Fraser, Douglas A. A Union View of Government Intervention in Bargaining. **In** *Wortman, M. S., Jr.,* 1969, pp. 423–28.

Frazer, William J., Jr. and Stroup, Robert H. The Demand for Money by Households in South Vietnam: The Evidence from Cross-Section Data. *J. Polit. Econ.,* Part I, July/August 1969, *77*(4), pp. 489–93.

Frederick, Kenneth D. The Role of Market Forces and Planning in Uganda's Economic Development, 1900–1938. *East Afr. Econ. Rev.,* June 1969, *1*(1), pp. 47–62.

Fredman, Albert J. Stockholders' Returns: Dividends or Earnings? *Miss. Val. J. Bus. Econ.,* Fall 1969, *5*(1), pp. 23–33.

______ **and Wert, James E.** Secondary Distributions of American Stock Exchange Securities. *Mar-*

quette Bus. Rev., Fall 1969, *13*(3), pp. 137–41.

Freebairn, Donald K. The Dichotomy of Prosperity and Poverty in Mexican Agriculture. *Land Econ.*, February 1969, *45*(1), pp. 31–42.

Freed, Roy N. Get the Computer System You Want. *Harvard Bus. Rev.*, November–December 1969, *47*(6), pp. 99–108.

Freedman, Marcia. Youth Employment Programmes in the United States. *Int. Lab. Rev.*, May 1969, *99*(5), pp. 493–513.

Freeman, A. Myrick, III. Income Redistribution and Social Choice: A Pragmatic Approach. *Public Choice*, Fall 1969, *7*, pp. 3–21.

______ Project Design and Evaluation with Multiple Objectives. In *The Analysis and Evaluation of Public Expenditures: The PPB System, Vol. 1, JECP*, 1969, pp. 565–78.

Freeman, Orville L. Malthus, Marx, and the North American Breadbasket. In *Ruttan, V. W.; Waldo, A. D. and Houck, J. P., eds.*, 1969, pp. 282–98.

Freeman, R. D. Adam Smith, Education and Laissez-Faire. *Hist. Polit. Econ.*, Spring 1969, *1*(1), pp. 173–86.

Freeman, Roger A. Federal Assistance to Higher Education through Income Tax Credits. In *the Economics and Financing of Higher Education in the United States, JECP*, 1969, pp. 665–83.

French, Norman D. and Brooksher, William R. Marketing New Products—By Segmenting Product Lines. *Univ. Missouri Bus. Govt. Rev.*, September -October 1969, *10*(5), pp. 5–10.

French, Wendell. Organization Development Objectives, Assumptions and Strategies. *Calif. Manage. Rev.*, Winter 1969, *12*(2), pp. 23–34.

______ **and Hellriegel, Don.** A Critique of Jaques' Equitable Payment System. *Ind. Relat.*, May 1969, *8*(3), pp. 269–79.

Freudenberger, Herman. Records of the Bohemian Iron Industry, 1694–1875: The Basis for a Comprehensive Study of Modern Factories. *Bus. Hist. Rev.*, Autumn 1969, *43*(3), pp. 381–84.

Frey, Bruno S. Eine einfache Einführung zu Pontryagins Maximum-Prinzip in Wirtschaftswachstum. (A Simple Introduction to Pontryagin's Maximum Principle in Economic Growth. With English summary.) *Weltwirtsch. Arch.*, 1969, *103* (2), pp. 213–28.

______ Product and Process Innovations in Economic Growth. *Z. Nationalökon.*, May 1969, *29*(1–2), pp. 29–38.

Fried, Edward R. International Liquidity and Foreign Aid. *Foreign Aff.*, October 1969, *48*(1), pp. 139–49.

Fried, Louis. The Twilight of the Mechanical Technology. *Calif. Manage. Rev.*, Summer 1969, *11*(4), pp. 63–68.

Friedman, Harvey L. The Role of the AFL-CIO in the Growth of the Public Sector Collective Bargaining. In *Walsh, R. E., ed.*, 1969, pp. 27–33.

Friedman, J. W. On Experimental Research in Oligopoly. *Rev. Econ. Stud.*, October 1969, *36* (108), pp. 399–415.

Friedman, Milton. The Advantages of Flexible Exchange Rates. In *Starleaf, D. R., ed.*, 1969, pp. 387–92.

______ The Monetary Studies of the National Bureau. In *Friedman, M.*, 1969, pp. 261–84.

______ The Optimum Quantity of Money. In *Friedman, M.*, 1969, pp. 1–50.

______ The Permanent Income Hypothesis. In *Williams, H. R. and Huffnagle, J. D., eds.*, 1969, pp. 141–58.

______ Post-War Trends in Monetary Theory and Policy. In *Friedman, M.*, 1969, pp. 69–79.

______ Round Table on Exchange Rate Policy. *Amer. Econ. Rev.*, May 1969, *59*(2), pp. 364–66.

______ Why Not a Volunteer Army? In *Starleaf, D. R., ed.*, 1969, pp. 209–15.

______ Worswick's Criticism of the Correlation Criterion: A Comment. *J. Money, Credit, Banking*, August 1969, *1*(3), pp. 506.

______ **and Schwartz, Anna J.** The Definition of Money: Net Wealth and Neutrality as Criteria. *J. Money, Credit, Banking*, February 1969, *1*(1), pp. 1–14.

Friend, Irwin. The SEC and the Economic Performance of Securities Markets. In *Manne, H. G., ed.*, 1969, pp. 185–216.

______ Statement. In *High Interest Rates, SCH*, 1969, pp. 114–19.

Frisch, Uwe G. and Malagón, Oscar M. La concentracion territorial de la industria en Mexico. (Territorial Concentration of Industry in Mexico. With English summary.) *Econ. Polít.*, Second Semester 1969, *6*(2), pp. 195–208.

Fromm, D.; L'Esperance, Wilford L. and Nestel, G. Gross State Product and an Econometric Model of a State. *J. Amer. Statist. Assoc.*, September 1969, *64*(327), pp. 787–807.

Fromm, Erich. The Outlook: Integrated Planning—Problems and Opportunities. In *Ozbekhan, H. and Talbert, G. E., eds.*, 1969, pp. 223–33.

Fromm, Gary. An Evaluation of Monetary Policy Instruments. In *Duesenberry, J. S., et al.*, 1969, pp. 473–511.

______ The Evaluation of Economic Policies. In *Naylor, T. H., ed.*, 1969, pp. 355–68.

______ Growth and Inflation: A Comment. *J. Money, Credit, Banking*, August 1969, *1*(3), pp. 439–40.

______ **and Klein, Lawrence R.** Solutions of the Complete System. In *Duesenberry, J. S., et al.*, 1969, pp. 362–421.

Froozan, Mansur. E.R.A.P.-Type Versus Fifty-Fifty Agreements. *Tahq. Eq.*, November 1969, *6* (15&16), pp. 21–53.

Frostman, Lars. Optimal Financing and Tax Policy of the Corporation—A Review Article. *Swedish J. Econ.*, March 1969, *71*(1), pp. 30–41.

Fry, Edward R.; Beck, Darwin L. and Weaver, Mary F. Revision of Money Stock Series. *Fed. Res. Bull.*, October 1969, *55*(10), pp. 787–803.

Fryman, Richard F. Sales Taxation of Producers' Goods in Illinois. *Nat. Tax J.*, June 1969, *22*(2), pp. 273–81.

Fuchs, Estelle. Education and the Culture of Poverty. In *Weaver, T. and Magid, A., eds.*, 1969, pp. 162–76.

Fuchs, Victor. The Basic Forces Influencing Costs of Medical Care. In *Health Care in America, Pt. 1, SCH*, 1969, pp. 291–306.

______ The Contribution of Health Services to the American Economy. In *Health Care in America, Pt. 1, SCH*, 1969, pp. 313–51.

______ The Growing Demand for Medical Care. In

Health Care in America, Pt. 1, SCH, 1969, pp. 307–12.

——— Statement. In *Health Care in America, Pt. 1, SCH,* 1969, pp. 275–90.

Fučík, Ivan and Gál, Tomáš. K otázce degenerace ve výchozím řešení simplexových úloh lineárního programování. (On the Question of Degeneration in the Original Solution of Simplex LP-Problems. With English summary.) *Ekon.-Mat. Obzor,* 1969, *5*(3), pp. 295–303.

Fuerst, E. The Comprehensive Macro-economic Model. *Rivista Int. Sci. Econ. Com.,* May 1969, *16* (5), pp. 429–45.

Fugate, Wilbur L. Antitrust Aspects of Transatlantic Investment. *Law Contemp. Probl.,* Winter 1969, *34*(1), pp. 135–45.

Fulco, Lawrence J. How Mechanization of Harvesting Is Affecting Jobs. *Mon. Lab. Rev.,* March 1969, *92*(3), pp. 26–32.

——— **and Herman, Shelby W.** Productivity and Unit Labor Costs in 1968. *Mon. Lab. Rev.,* June 1969, *92*(6), pp. 11–15.

Fuller, Varden. Political Pressures and Income Distribution in Agriculture. In *Ruttan, V. W.; Waldo, A. D. and Houck, J. P., eds.,* 1969, pp. 255–63.

Fuller, Wayne A. Grafted Polynomials as Approximating Functions. *Australian J. Agr. Econ.,* June 1969, *13*(1), pp. 35–46.

Fullerton, Kemper. Calvinism and Capitalism. In *Scoville, W. C. and La Force, J. C., eds., Vol. II,* 1969, pp. 15–42.

Fullerton, William D. The Problem of Rising Hospital Costs. In *Health Care in America, Pt. 1, SCH,* 1969, pp. 165–79.

Fulton, David C. A Road to the West. *Finance Develop.,* September 1969, *6*(3), pp. 2–7.

Furness, Betty. Statement. In *To Establish a Department of Consumer Affairs, SCH,* 1969, pp. 343–61.

Furness, Eric L. Income Flows and Financial Asset Holdings. *Oxford Econ. Pap.,* March 1969, *21*(1), pp. 70–88.

Furst, Richard W. and Markland, Robert E. Evaluating Merger-Acquisition Opportunities—A Risk Incorporation Model. *Univ. Missouri Bus. Govt. Rev.,* July–August 1969, *10*(4), pp. 21–26.

von Furstenberg, George M. Default Risk on FHA-Insured Home Mortgages as a Function of the Terms of Financing: A Quantitative Analysis. *J. Finance,* June 1969, *24*(3), pp. 459–77.

Furth, J. Herbert. Barriers to Investment Abroad as Tools of Payments Policy. *Law Contemp. Probl.,* Winter 1969, *34*(1), pp. 64–83.

——— International Monetary Reform and the "Crawling Peg"—Comment. *Fed. Res. Bank St. Louis Rev.,* July 1969, *51*(7), pp. 21–25.

Furubotn, Eirik G. Quality Control, Expected Utility, and Product Equilibrium. *Western Econ. J.,* March 1969, *7*(1), pp. 9–26.

Fussell, G. E. The Classical Tradition in West European Farming: The Sixteenth Century. *Econ. Hist. Rev.,* December 1969, *22*(3), pp. 538–51.

Gaarder, Raymond O. The Unseen—and Unfeeling—Hand. *Amer. J. Agr. Econ.,* November 1969, *51*(4), pp. 952–53.

Gabel, Richard. The Early Competitive Era in Telephone Communication, 1893–1920. *Law Contemp. Probl.,* Spring 1969, *34*(2), pp. 340–59.

Gabler, L. R. Economies and Diseconomies of Scale in Urban Public Sectors. *Land Econ.,* November 1969, *45*(4), pp. 425–34.

Gadiel, D. L. and Falkus, M. E. A Comment on the 'Price Revolution.' *Australian Econ. Hist. Rev.,* March 1969, *9*(1), pp. 9–16.

Gaffey, William R. and Dyar, Robert. Current Challenges to Health Statisticians. *Amer. Statist.,* December 1969, *23*(5), pp. 19–22.

Gaffney, Mason. Economic Aspects of Water Resource Policy. *Amer. J. Econ. Soc.,* April 1969, *28* (2), pp. 131–44.

Gaines, Tilford C. Some Inadequacies of Financial Data and Theories. *Nat. Westminster Bank Quart. Rev.,* November 1969, pp. 35–44.

Gainsbrugh, Martin R. Statement. In *Review of Federal Statistical Programs, JECH,* 1969, pp. 131–37.

Gál, Tomáš and Fučík, Ivan. K otázce degenerace ve výchozím řešení simplexových úloh lineárního programování. (On the Question of Degeneration in the Original Solution of Simplex LP-Problems. With English summary.) *Ekon.-Mat. Obzor,* 1969, *5*(3), pp. 295–303.

Galbraith, John Kenneth. The Development of Monopoly Theory. In *Hunter, A., ed.,* 1969, pp. 19–23.

——— How Keynes Came to America. In *Starleaf, D. R., ed.,* 1969, pp. 355–60.

——— Planning, Regulation, and Competition. In *Kuhlman, J. M., ed.,* 1969, pp. 227–33.

——— Professor Gordon on "The Close of the Galbraithian System." *J. Polit. Econ.,* Part I, July/August 1969, *77*(4), pp. 494–503.

——— Technology, Planning and Organization. In *Baier, K. and Rescher, N., eds.,* 1969, pp. 353–67.

Gale, David and Brock, William A. Optimal Growth under Factor Augmenting Progress. *J. Econ. Theory,* October 1969, *1*(3), pp. 229–43.

Galenson, Walter. Social Security and Economic Development: A Quantitative Approach—Reply. *Ind. Lab. Relat. Rev.,* January 1969, *22*(2), pp. 260–63.

Gallaway, Lowell E. Age and Labor Mobility Patterns. *Southern Econ. J.,* October 1969, *36*(2), pp. 171–80.

——— The Effect of Geographic Labor Mobility on Income: A Brief Comment. *J. Human Res.,* Winter 1969, *4*(1), pp. 103–09.

——— A Note on the Incidence of Hidden Unemployment in the United States. *Western Econ. J.,* March 1969, *7*(1), pp. 71–83.

——— One Last Word. *Southern Econ. J.,* January 1969, *35*(3), pp. 267.

——— Unemployment Levels among Nonwhite Teen-agers. *J. Bus.,* July 1969, *42*(3), pp. 265–76.

Gallman, Robert E. and Weiss, Thomas J. The Service Industries in the Nineteenth Century. In *Fuchs, V. R., ed.,* 1969, pp. 287–352.

——— The Service Industries in the Nineteenth Century: Reply. In *Fuchs, V. R., ed.,* 1969, pp. 372–81.

Galnoor, Itzhak and Gross, Bertram M. The New Systems Budgeting and the Developing Nations. *Int. Soc. Sci. J.,* 1969, *21*(1), pp. 23–44.

Galper, Harvey. Alternative Interest Rates and the

Demand for Money: Comment. *Amer. Econ. Rev.*, June 1969, *59*(3), pp. 401–12.

——— The Impacts of the Vietnam War on Defense Spending: A Simulation Approach. *J. Bus.*, October 1969, *42*(4), pp. 401–15.

——— **and Dunn, Robert M., Jr.** A Short-Run Demand Function for Higher Education in the United States. *J. Polit. Econ.*, September/October 1969, *77*(5), pp. 765–77.

Galvin, Charles O. The Income Tax: How Progressive Should It Be?: First Lecture. **In** *Galvin, C. O. and Bittker, B. I.*, 1969, pp. 1–23.

——— The Income Tax: How Progressive Should It Be?: Rebuttal. **In** *Galvin, C. O. and Bittker, B. I.*, 1969, pp. 73–84.

Gamarnikow, Michael. Eastern Partners for Western Businessmen. **In** *Grub, P. D. and Holbik, K.*, 1969, pp. 148–53.

Gander, James P. and Bradley, Iver E. Input-Output Multipliers: Some Theoretical Comments. *J. Reg. Sci.*, August 1969, *9*(2), pp. 309–17.

Gandhi, Ved P. Agricultural Taxation Policy: Search for a Direction. *Artha-Vikas*, July 1969, *5*(2), pp. 3–49.

Gandolfi, Arthur and Cagan, Phillip. The Lag in Monetary Policy as Implied by the Time Pattern of Monetary Effects on Interest Rates. *Amer. Econ. Rev.*, May 1969, *59*(2), pp. 277–84.

Gandy, Dewell R. and Traylor, Harold D. Caloric Cost of Rice and Wheat Programs. *Amer. J. Agr. Econ.*, November 1969, *51*(4), pp. 962–63.

Ganguly, Subrata K. The Perfectly Competitive Production of Collective Goods: Comment. *Rev. Econ. Statist.*, November 1969, *51*(4), pp. 478–79.

Ganguly, Swapan and Venugopal, Bhaskar. International Crude Oil Prices after World War II. *Indian Econ. J.*, January–March 1969, *16*(3), pp. 382–87.

Gans, Herbert J. The Failure of Urban Renewal. **In** *Callow, A. B., Jr., ed.*, 1969, pp. 567–81.

———**; Raymond, George M. and Rivkin, Malcolm D.** Urban Renewal: A Controversy. **In** *Callow, A. B., Jr., ed.*, 1969, pp. 582–96.

Gardner, Bruce L. Determinants of Farm Family Income Inequality. *Amer. J. Agr. Econ.*, November 1969, *51*(4), pp. 753–69.

Gardner, David M. and Simon, Julian L. World Food Needs and "New Proteins." *Econ. Develop. Cult. Change*, July 1969, *17*(4), pp. 520–26.

Gardner, Donald K. The Role of Open Spaces in Flood Plain Management. **In** *Dougal, M. D., ed.*, 1969, pp. 137–46.

Gardner, John W. Statement. **In** *Panel on Science and Technology: Science and Technology and the Cities, HCH*, 1969, pp. 3–11.

——— Statement. **In** *Economic Opportunity Amendments of 1969, SCH*, 1969, pp. 21–28.

Gardner, Lloyd C. The New Deal, New Frontiers, and the Cold War: A Re-examination of American Expansion, 1933–1945. **In** *Horowitz, D., ed.*, 1969, pp. 105–41.

Garetovskii, N. The Role of Profit and Profitability under the New System for Economic Stimulation of Production. *Prob. Econ.*, August 1969, *12*(4), pp. 3–30.

Garn, Harvey A. and McGuire, Martin C. The Integration of Equity and Efficiency Criteria in Public Project Selection. *Econ. J.*, December 1969, *79* (316), pp. 882–93.

——— Problems in the Cooperative Allocation of Public Expenditures. *Quart. J. Econ.*, February 1969, *83*(1), pp. 44–59.

Garnick, Daniel H. Disaggregated Basic-Service Models and Regional Input-Output Models in Multiregional Projections. *J. Reg. Sci.*, April 1969, *9*(1), pp. 87–100.

Garston, Gordon J. and Emery, Betty J. The Measurement of Constant Price Aggregates in Canada. *Rev. Income Wealth*, March 1969, *15*(1), pp. 1–32.

——— **and Kendrick, John W.** Measuring Real Output for Industries Providing Services: OBE Concepts and Methods: Discussion. **In** *Fuchs, V. R., ed.*, 1969, pp. 41–49.

Garvey, Gerald. The Political Economy of Patronal Groups. *Public Choice*, Fall 1969, *7*, pp. 33–45.

Gass, James Ronald. Reflections on Equality, Quantity and Quality in Education. **In** *[Edding, Friedrich]*, 1969, pp. 215–22.

Gaud, William S. The Current Effect of the American Aid Program. *Ann. Amer. Acad. Polit. Soc. Sci.*, July 1969, *384*, pp. 73–84.

——— Statement. **In** *A Review of Balance of Payments Policies, JECH*, 1969, pp. 90–97.

Geary, Patrick. Economic Policy and Planning in Ireland: A Review Article. *Irish Banking Rev.*, June 1969, pp. 20–25.

Gee, Robert E. and Waterman, Robert H., Jr. A New Tool for Bank Management: A Mathematical Model in Banking. **In** *Jessup, P. F.*, 1969, pp. 293–300.

Geier, Marsha; Morris, Cynthia Taft and Adelman, Irma. Instruments and Goals in Economic Development. *Amer. Econ. Rev.*, May 1969, *59*(2), pp. 409–26.

Geithman, David T. and Stinson, Byron S. A Note on Diminishing Returns and Linear Homogeneity. *Amer. Econ.*, Spring 1969, *13*(1), pp. 77–79.

Gekker, Paul. Financial Aspects of United States Trade with the Socialist World. **In** *Grub, P. D. and Holbik, K.*, 1969, pp. 180–86.

Gellerman, Saul. Behavioral Strategies. *Calif. Manage. Rev.*, Winter 1969, *12*(2), pp. 45–51.

Gelting, Jørgen H. Denmark, Norway and Sweden. **In** *Bronfenbrenner, M., ed.*, 1969, pp. 200–20.

Gemorah, Solomon. Laurence Gronlund—Utopian or Reformer? *Sci. Soc.*, Fall-Winter 1969, *33*(4), pp. 446–58.

Genovese, Eugene D. Marxian Interpretations of the Slave South. **In** *Bernstein, B. J., ed.*, 1969, pp. 90–125.

Gensch, Dennis H. A Computer Simulation Model for Selecting Advertising Schedules. *J. Marketing Res.*, May 1969, *6*(2), pp. 203–14.

Gentry, James A. and Pike, John R. Rates of Return on Common Stock Portfolios of Life Insurance Companies. *J. Risk Ins.*, December 1969, *36*(5), pp. 545–52.

George, J. Mishell. Views East-West Trade Effect of Reforms, Controls. **In** *Grub, P. D. and Holbik, K.*, 1969, pp. 205–07.

George, Kenneth D. Productivity in the Distributive Trades. *Bull. Oxford Univ. Inst. Econ. Statist.*, May 1969, *31*(2), pp. 61–75.

——— **and Cyert, Richard M.** Competition, Growth,

and Efficiency. *Econ. J.*, March 1969, *79*(313), pp. 23–41.

George, P. T. Land Tenures in India—Results of 1961 Census. *Asian Econ. Rev.*, May 1969, *11*(3), pp. 317–24.

George, P. V. Secular Price Behaviour in a Dual Market Economy. *Indian Econ. J.*, April–June 1969, *16*(4–5), pp. 532–43.

George, Roy E. Immobility of Redundant Labour. **In** *Association of Canadian Schools of Business*, 1969, pp. 126–43.

Georgescu-Roegen, Nicholas. Process in Farming Versus Process in Manufacturing: A Problem of Balanced Development. **In** *Papi, U. and Nunn, C., eds.*, 1969, pp. 497–528.

______ The Relation Between Binary and Multiple Choices: Some Comments and Further Results. *Econometrica*, October 1969, *37*(4), pp. 728–30.

Gerakis, Andreas S. Some Aspects of the U.A.R.'s First Five-Year Plan. *Finance Develop.*, March 1969, *6*(1), pp. 9–15.

Gerald, John O. Role of Transportation in Agricultural Marketing and Development: Discussion. *Amer. J. Agr. Econ.*, December 1969, *51*(5), pp. 1478–81.

Gerchuk, Ia. On the Question of Applying Economic-Mathematical Methods in Practice. *Prob. Econ.*, September 1969, *12*(5), pp. 52–70.

Gerschenkron, Alexander. History of Economic Doctrines and Economic History. *Amer. Econ. Rev.*, May 1969, *59*(2), pp. 1–17.

______ Notes on the Rate of Industrial Growth in Italy, 1881–1913. **In** *Scoville, W. C. and La Force, J. C., eds., Vol. IV*, 1969, pp. 60–74.

Gershefski, George W. Building a Corporate Financial Model. *Harvard Bus. Rev.*, July–August 1969, *47*(4), pp. 61–72.

Gerwin, Donald. Compensation Decisions in Public Organizations. *Ind. Relat.*, February 1969, *8*(2), pp. 174–84.

______ Compensation Decisions in Public Organizations: Reply. *Ind. Relat.*, October 1969, *9*(1), pp. 114–16.

van de Gevel, A. J. W. and Albregts, A. H. M. Negotiating Techniques and Issues in the Kennedy Round. **In** *Alting von Geusau, F. A. M., ed.*, 1969, pp. 20–47.

Geyer, Herbert. Linear Tax Variations in the Stabilization Law. *Finanzarchiv*, October 1968, *28*(1), pp. 96–99.

Ghafur, Abdul. Financial-Asset Accumulation by the Noncorporate Private Sector in Pakistan 1959/60 to 1965/66. *Pakistan Develop. Rev.*, Spring 1969, *9*(1), pp. 66–86.

Ghai, D. and Van Arkadie, B. The East African Economies: Kenya, Uganda and Tanzania. **In** *Robson, P. and Lury, D. A., eds.*, 1969, pp. 316–83.

Ghandour, M. M. J. B. Clark's Theory of Economic Growth: Comment. *Amer. Econ.*, Spring 1969, *13* (1), pp. 14–15.

Ghellinck, Guy and Moeseke, Paul V. Decentralization in Separable Programming. *Econometrica*, January 1969, *37*(1), pp. 73–78.

Ghonasgi, B. D. The Monetary Policy in a Developing Economy: An Assessment. **In** *Desai, V. R. M. and Ghonasgi, B. D.*, 1969, pp. 145–72.

______ **and Mutalik Desai, V. R.** Selective Credit Controls in India. **In** *Desai, V. R. M. and Ghonasgi, B. D.*, 1969, pp. 84–122.

Ghose, B. C. The Borooah Committee on Tea. *Econ. Aff.*, January–February 1969, *14*(1–2), pp. 71–73.

Ghosh, Alak. Open Market Operations of the Reserve Bank of India: Theory and Practice. **In** *Desai, V. R. M. and Ghonasgi, B. D.*, 1969, pp. 70–83.

______ The Role of Agriculture in the Fourth Plan. **In** *Bhuleshkar, A. V., ed.*, 1969, pp. 60–68.

Ghosh, Arabinda and Sarkar, Anil Kumar. Size Structure of Indian Engineering Industries, 1948–61. *Indian Econ. J.*, January–March 1969, *16*(3), pp. 375–81.

Ghrist, Bruce. Roadblocks to Reform of the Soviet Economy. *Amer. Econ.*, Fall 1969, *13*(2), pp. 50–56.

Gibbins, Ronald W. American Influence on Commercial Practice. **In** *Preston, R., ed.*, 1969, pp. 498–520.

Gibson, N. J. Foundations of Monetary Theory: A Review Article. *Manchester Sch. Econ. Soc. Stud.*, March 1969, *37*(1), pp. 59–75.

Giddings, Marvin; Hartman, L. M. and Holland, David. Effects of Hurricane Storms on Agriculture. *Water Resources Res.*, June 1969, *5*(3), pp. 555–62.

Giddy, R. V. An Outline of Taxes under the Hong Kong Inland Revenue Ordinance. *Bull. Int. Fiscal Doc.*, December 1969, *23*(12), pp. 574–83.

Gies, Thomas G. Inflation and the Rate of Return: Comment. **In** *Trebing, H. M. and Howard, R. H., eds.*, 1969, pp. 187–91.

______ Topics in Bank Capital: Comment. **In** *Federal Reserve Bank of Chicago (I)*, 1969, pp. 110–12.

Gifford, J. Morris. Some Considerations Involved in Port Planning Policy. *Econ. Soc. Tijdschr.*, February 1969, *23*(1), pp. 23–32.

Gijs, Robert. Het onderzoek van de motivatie van de verbruiker in het raam van Marketing Informatie Systemen. (The Motivations Research of the Consumer in the Marketing Information Systems. With English summary.) *Econ. Soc. Tijdschr.*, December 1969, *23*(6), pp. 675–85.

Gili, Adolfo. Popolosità e dinamica demografica di lungo periodo nei comuni dell'Emilia e del Veneto: Parte I. (With English summary.) *Statistica*, October-December 1969, *29*(4), pp. 603–49.

Gill, M. S. and Abraham, W. I. The Growth and Composition of Malaysia's Capital Stock. *Malayan Econ. Rev.*, October 1969, *14*(2), pp. 44–54.

______ New Measures of Economic Growth and Structural Change of the Malaysian Economy in the Post-1960 Period. *Malayan Econ. Rev.*, April 1969, *14*(1), pp. 65–79.

Gillespie, Glenn A. and Brewer, Durward. Effects of Nonprice Variables upon Participation in Water-Oriented Outdoor Recreation: Reply. *Amer. J. Agr. Econ.*, February 1969, *51*(1), pp. 194–95.

Gillet, Marcel. The Coal Age and the Rise of Coalfields in the North and the Pas-de-Calais. **In** *Crouzet, F.; Chaloner, W. H. and Stern, W. M., eds.*, 1969, pp. 179–202.

Gilroy, Thomas P. Public Sector Negotiations in Iowa. **In** *Sinicropi, A. V. and Gilroy, T. P., eds.*, 1969, pp. 17–26.

______ Recent Developments in the Unionization of

Professional/Technical Personnel. In *Gilroy, T. P., ed.*, 1969, pp. 33–37.

Gilson, J. C. The Demand for Agricultural Economists by Canadian Universities and Governments. *Can. J. Agr. Econ.*, November 1969, *17*(3), pp. 124–32.

Ginor, Fanny. The Impact of Capital Imports on the Structure of Developing Countries. *Kyklos*, 1969, *22*(1), pp. 104–23.

Ginsburg, Woodrow L. The Computer's Uses and Potential in Bargaining: A Trade Union View. In *Siegel, A. J., ed.*, 1969, pp. 26–68.

——— **and Conway, Jack T.** The Extension of Collective Bargaining to New Fields. In *Wortman, M. S., Jr.*, 1969, pp. 148–50.

Giscard d'Estaing, Valéry. The International Monetary Order. In *Mundell, R. A. and Swoboda, A. K., eds.*, 1969, pp. 7–19.

Gish, Oscar. A Note on Aid for Nursing Training in Britain. *J. Devel. Stud.*, April 1969, *5*(3), pp. 220–22.

Gisser, Micha. Economics of Cost-Share Leases: Comment. *Amer. J. Agr. Econ.*, August 1969, *51* (3), pp. 692–95.

——— The Pure Theory of Government Aid to Agriculture. *Amer. J. Agr. Econ.*, December 1969, *51*(5), pp. 1511–15.

Giurovich, Gualtiero. L'impresa di acquedotto: una condizione di minimo costo fra la condotta adduttrice e il serbatoio. (With English summary.) *Statistica*, July-September 1969, *29*(3), pp. 385–421.

Givry, Jean. Developments in Labour-Management Relations in the Undertaking. *Int. Lab. Rev.*, January 1969, *99*(1), pp. 1–33.

Glade, William P. The Employment Question and Development Policies in Latin America. *J. Econ. Issues*, September 1969, *3*(3), pp. 43–62.

Glahn, Harry R. Some Relationships Derived from Canonical Correlation Theory. *Econometrica*, April 1969, *37*(2), pp. 252–56.

Glasgow, John M. The Economic Rationale of Occupational Choice: Comment. *Ind. Lab. Relat. Rev.*, July 1969, *22*(4), pp. 584–87.

Glass, D. V. Fertility Trends in Europe Since the Second World War. In *Behrman, S. J.; Corsa, L., Jr. and Freedman, R., eds.*, 1969, pp. 25–74.

Glass, Gene V. and Stanley, Julian C. An Algebraic Proof That the Sum of the Squared Errors in Estimating Y from X Via b_1 and b_0 Is Minimal. *Amer. Statist.*, February 1969, *23*(1), pp. 25–26.

Glassner, Martin I. Feeding a Desert City: Antofagasta, Chile. *Econ. Geogr.*, October 1969, *45* (4), pp. 339–48.

Gleditsch, Nils Petter. The International Airline Network: A Test of the Zipf and Stouffer Hypotheses. *Peace Res. Soc. Internat. Pap.*, 1969, *11*, pp. 123–53.

Glejser, H. Een toepassing van de kosten-batenanalyse: het project "Zeestad". (Cost-Benefit Analysis of the Project "Zeestad." With English summary.) *Tijdschr. Econ.*, 1969, *14*(4), pp. 519–48.

——— **and Dramais, A.** A Gravity Model of Interdependent Equations to Estimate Flow Creation and Diversion. *J. Reg. Sci.*, December 1969, *9*(3), pp. 439–49.

Gleser, Leon Jay. The Paradox of Voting: Some Probabilistic Results. *Public Choice*, Fall 1969, *7*, pp. 47–63.

Gloor, Max. Il caso di un'impresa multinazionale: la Nestlè. (Nestlè's Multinational Mode. With English summary.) *Mondo Aperto*, June–August 1969, *23*(3–4), pp. 205–16.

Gloushkov, V. P. New Methods of Economic Management in the U.S.S.R.: Some Features of the Recent Economic Reform. In *Margolis, J. and Guitton, H., eds.*, 1969, pp. 344–58.

Glover, Fred. Management Decision and Integer Programming. *Accounting Rev.*, April 1969, *44* (2), pp. 300–303.

Glückaufová, Dagmar. O jedné axiomatice teorie užitku vedoucí k tzv. nepřímé užitkové funkci. (One Axiomatics of the Utility Theory Tending to so Called Indirect Utility Function. With English summary.) *Ekon.-Mat. Obzor*, 1969, *5*(4), pp. 423–41.

Glueck, William F. Executive Mobility in Missouri. *Univ. Missouri Bus. Govt. Rev.*, March–April 1969, *10*(2), pp. 27–32.

Glynn, D. R. The CBI Industrial Trends Survey. *Appl. Econ.*, August 1969, *1*(3), pp. 183–96.

Gockel, Galen; Sudman, Seymour and Bradburn, Norman M. The Extent and Characteristics of Racially Integrated Housing in the United States. *J. Bus.*, January 1969, *42*(1), pp. 50–92.

Godfrey, E. M. Labor-Surplus Models and Labor-Deficit Economies: The West African Case. *Econ. Develop. Cult. Change*, April 1969, *17*(3), pp. 382–91.

Goeke, Joseph R. and Weymar, Caroline S. Barriers to Hiring the Blacks. *Harvard Bus. Rev.*, September–October 1969, *47*(5), pp. 144–52.

Goel, H. C. Econometric Models for Traffic Projections. *Econ. Aff.*, January-February 1969, *14*(1–2), pp. 88–92.

Goetz, Billy E. Perplexing Problems in Decision Theory. *Eng. Econ.*, April–May 1969, *14*(3), pp. 129–40.

Goetz, Charles J. and Magnani, Italo. Automobile Taxation Based on Mechanical Characteristics: Evidence from the Italian Case. *Public Finance*, 1969, *24*(3), pp. 486–98.

Gold, Bela. The Framework of Decision for Major Technological Innovation. In *Baier, K. and Rescher, N., eds.*, 1969, pp. 389–430.

Gold, Ronald B. Fiscal Capacities and Welfare Expenditures of States. *Nat. Tax J.*, December 1969, *22*(4), pp. 496–505.

Gold, Samuel M. Strikes by Public Workers. In *Walsh, R. E., ed.*, 1969, pp. 225–32.

Gold, Sonia S. The Professional Commitment of Educated Women. In *Baier, K. and Rescher, N., eds.*, 1969, pp. 266–93.

Goldbach, John C. and Schmandt, Henry J. The Urban Paradox. In *Schmandt, H. J. and Bloomberg, W., Jr., eds.*, 1969, pp. 473–98.

Goldberg, Stephen B. Current Decisions of the NLRB and of the Courts. In *Somers, G. G., ed. (II)*, 1969, pp. 195–200.

Goldberger, Arthur S. and Bohrnstedt, George W. On the Exact Covariance of Products of Random Variables. *J. Amer. Statist. Assoc.*, December 1969, *64*(328), pp. 1439–42.

Goldfarb, Robert S. The Evaluation of Government

Programs: The Case of New Haven's Manpower Training Activities. *Yale Econ. Essays,* Fall 1969, *9*(2), pp. 59–104.

Goldfeld, Stephen H. An Extension of the Monetary Sector. **In** *Duesenberry, J. S., et al.,* 1969, pp. 317–59.

Goldfinger, Nathaniel. The Growth of the AFL-CIO. **In** *Walsh, R. E., ed.,* 1969, pp. 12–20.

______ Statement. **In** *Investigation of Increase in Prime Interest Rate, HCH,* 1969, pp. 221–27.

Goldin, Hyman H. Financing Public Broadcasting. *Law Contemp. Probl.,* Summer 1969, *34*(3), pp. 650–70.

Goldman, Marshall I. The East Reaches for Markets. *Foreign Aff.,* July 1969, *47*(4), pp. 721–34.

Goldman, Steven M. Consumption Behavior and Time Preference. *J. Econ. Theory,* June 1969, *1* (1), pp. 39–47.

______ Sequential Planning and Continual Planning Revision. *J. Polit. Econ.,* Part II, July/August 1969, *77*(4), pp. 653–64.

______ **and Douglas, A. J.** Monopolistic Behavior in a Market for Durable Goods. *J. Polit. Econ.,* January/February 1969, *77*(1), pp. 49–59.

Goldmann, Josef. Fluctuation in the Growth Rate in a Socialist Economy and the Inventory Cycle. **In** *Bronfenbrenner, M., ed.,* 1969, pp. 332–49.

______ Karl Marx, the Soviet Economists of the Twenties and Contemporary 'Konjunkturforschung' in a Socialist Country. *Czech. Econ. Pap.,* 1969, (11), pp. 43–50.

Goldschmidt, Walter. Game Theory, Cultural Values, and the Brideprice in Africa. **In** *Buchler, I. R. and Nutini, H. G., eds.,* 1969, pp. 61–74.

Goldschmidt, Y. and Smidt, S. Valuing the Firm's Durable Assets for Managerial Information. *Accounting Rev.,* April 1969, *44*(2), pp. 317–29.

Goldsmith, Harold F. and Stockwell, Edward G. Interrelationship of Occupational Selectivity Patterns among City, Suburban and Fringe Areas of Major Metropolitan Centers. *Land Econ.,* May 1969, *45*(2), pp. 194–205.

Goldstein, Henry N. Does It Necessarily Cost Anything to Be the "World Banker"? **In** *Officer, L. H. and Willett, T. D., eds.,* 1969, pp. 68–74.

______ Gresham's Law and the Demand for NRU's and SDR's. *Quart. J. Econ.,* February 1969, *83*(1), pp. 163–66.

Goldston, Eli. BURP and Make Money. *Harvard Bus. Rev.,* September–October 1969, *47*(5), pp. 84–99.

Goldstone, Stephen E. Family Planning, Population Policies, and Mental Health. **In** *Effects of Population Growth on Natural Resources and the Environment, HCH,* 1969, pp. 140–51.

Golembe, Carter H. One-Bank Holding Companies. **In** *Prochnow, H. V., ed.,* 1969, pp. 66–81.

Goller, Stanislav. Příspěvek k teorii tvorby účelových časových rozvrhů. (A Contribution to the Theory of the Formation of Purposeful Timetables. With English summary.) *Ekon.-Mat. Obzor,* 1969, *5*(1), pp. 60–71.

Gollop, Frank. Structural Inflation. *Amer. Econ.,* Fall 1969, *13*(2), pp. 31–39.

Golosovskii, S. Determination of the Economic Effect of Scientific Research and New Technology. *Prob. Econ.,* January 1969, *11*(9), pp. 24–33.

Gomberg, Ia. Certain Questions in Wage Theory under Socialism. *Prob. Econ.,* July 1969, *12*(3), pp. 23–42.

Gomberg, William. Collective Bargaining and the New Industrial Engineering. **In** *Somers, G. G., ed. (I),* 1969, pp. 69–78.

______ Featherbedding: An Assertion of Property Rights. **In** *Wortman, M. S., Jr.,* 1969, pp. 225–34.

Gomme, E. D.; Kendall, M. G. and Coen, P. J. Lagged Relationships in Economic Forecasting. *J. Roy. Statist. Soc.,* Part 2, 1969, *132,* pp. 133–52.

Gonedes, Nicholas J. A Test of the Equivalent-Risk Class Hypothesis. *J. Financial Quant. Anal.,* June 1969, *4*(2), pp. 159–77.

______ **and Larson, Kermit D.** Business Combinations: An Exchange Ratio Determination Model. *Accounting Rev.,* October 1969, *44*(4), pp. 720–28.

Gonzalez, Richard J. Federal Policies Dominating U.S. Energy Supplies. **In** *Governmental Intervention in the Market Mechanism, Pt. 1, SCH,* 1969, pp. 385–90.

______ Interfuel Competition for Future Energy Markets. **In** *Governmental Intervention in the Market Mechanism, Pt. 1, SCH,* 1969, pp. 393–99.

Goodfellow, Gordon P., Jr. and Sweeney, Vernon E. Vertically Parallel Indifference Curves with a Non-Constant Marginal Utility of Money. *Amer. Econ.,* Fall 1969, *13*(2), pp. 81–86.

Goodhardt, G. J. and Ehrenberg, A. S. C. Duplication of Television Viewing between and within Channels. *J. Marketing Res.,* May 1969, *6*(2), pp. 169–78.

Goodhart, C. A. E. A Stable Velocity Function for Canada? A Note. *Economica, N.S.,* August 1969, *36*(143), pp. 314–15.

Goodman, Oscar. A Survey of Judicial and Regulatory Opinions Affecting Banking Competition under the Bank Merger Acts of 1960 and 1966. **In** *Federal Reserve Bank of Chicago (II),* 1969, pp. 1–16.

______ Topics on Bank Capital: Comment. **In** *Federal Reserve Bank of Chicago (I),* 1969, pp. 114–16.

Goodman, Paul S. Hiring, Training, and Retaining the Hard-Core. *Ind. Relat.,* October 1969, *9*(1), pp. 54–66.

Goodman, Richard Alan. A Hidden Issue in Minority Employment. *Calif. Manage. Rev.,* Summer 1969, *11*(4), pp. 27–30.

Goodman, Richard J. Policy and Non-Policy in Foreign Trade: Discussion. *Amer. J. Agr. Econ.,* December 1969, *51*(5), pp. 1354–56.

Goodman, Seymour S. Turkey's Trade Prospects in the Common Market: An Exploratory Study. *J. Common Market Stud.,* June 1969, *7*(4), pp. 305–26.

Goodman, Stephen H. E.E.C.: The Economics of Associate Membership. *J. Devel. Stud.,* January 1969, *5*(2), pp. 138–41.

______ Trade Unions and Political Parties: The Case of East Africa. *Econ. Develop. Cult. Change,* April 1969, *17*(3), pp. 338–45.

Goodrich, Carter. On Rereading Harry J. Carman's *Social and Economic History of the United States. J. Econ. Lit.,* June 1969, *7*(2), pp. 426–27.

Goodsell, Charles T. Trends in the Interrelationship of Polity and Economy in the United States.

Amer. J. Econ. Soc., January 1969, *28*(1), pp. 1–16.

Goodson, G. C. and Agarwala, R. An Analysis of the Effects of Investment Incentives on Investment Behaviour in the British Economy. *Economica, N.S.,* November 1969, *36*(144), pp. 377–88.

Goodwin, Leonard. Work Orientations of the Underemployed Poor: Report on a Pilot Study. *J. Human Res.,* Fall 1969, *4*(4), pp. 508–19.

Goody, Jack. Economy and Feudalism in Africa. *Econ. Hist. Rev.,* December 1969, *22*(3), pp. 393–405.

Goolsby, John L. Integrated Accounting Systems: A Practical Approach. *Manage. Account.,* September 1969, *51*(3), pp. 11–13, 28.

Gordon, Barry J. An American Contribution to the Theory of Social Economy: John Joseph Hughes (1797–1864). *Rev. Soc. Econ.,* September 1969, *27*(2), pp. 233–41.

——— Criticism of Ricardian Views on Value and Distribution in the British Periodicals, 1820–1850. *Hist. Polit. Econ.,* Fall 1969, *1*(2), pp. 370–87.

Gordon, Jerome B. Labor Mobility and Economic Growth: The Central American Experience—Costa Rica and El Salvador. *Econ. Develop. Cult. Change,* April 1969, *17*(3), pp. 319–37.

——— Socioeconomic Status: A Re-examination of Its Dimensions. *J. Human Res.,* Summer 1969, *4*(3), pp. 343–59.

Gordon, Kermit. How Much Should Government Do? **In** *Ruttan, V. W.; Waldo, A. D. and Houck, J. P., eds.,* 1969, pp. 129–36.

Gordon, Myron J. Rate of Return on Equity Capital under Regulation. **In** *Trebing, H. M. and Howard, R. H., eds.,* 1969, pp. 65–72.

Gordon, Nancy M. Britain and the Zollverein Iron Duties, 1842–5. *Econ. Hist. Rev.,* April 1969, *22*(1), pp. 75–87.

Gordon, R. A. The Stability of the U.S. Economy. **In** *Bronfenbrenner, M., ed.,* 1969, pp. 3–34.

Gordon, Robert J. $45 Billion of U.S. Private Investment Has Been Mislaid. *Amer. Econ. Rev.,* June 1969, *59*(3), pp. 221–38.

Gordon, Sanford D. The Effectiveness of Teaching Methods: Optimizing the Use of Televised Instruction. *J. Econ. Educ.,* Fall 1969, *1*(1), pp. 46–50.

Gordon, Scott. "The Galbraithian System"—Rejoinder. *J. Polit. Econ.,* November/December 1969, *77*(6), pp. 953–56.

Gordon, Theodore J. The Feedback between Technology and Values. **In** *Baier, K. and Rescher, N., eds.,* 1969, pp. 148–92.

Gordon, Wendell. Capitalism and Technological Adaptation in Latin America. *J. Econ. Issues,* March 1969, *3*(1), pp. 66–86.

Goreux, Louis M. Prospects for Agricultural Trade of Less Developed Countries. **In** *Thorbecke, E., ed.,* 1969, pp. 15–73.

Gorinson, Morris. How the Census Data Will be Processed. *Mon. Lab. Rev.,* December 1969, *92*(12), pp. 42–45.

Gorkin, Stefan. Shearson, Hammill & Co. and the Ghetto. *Univ. Wash. Bus. Rev.,* Autumn 1969, *29*(1), pp. 27–34.

Gorman, John A. Alternative Measures of the Real Output and Productivity of Commercial Banks. **In** *Fuchs, V. R., ed.,* 1969, pp. 155–89.

Gort, Michael. An Economic Disturbance Theory of Mergers. *Quart. J. Econ.,* November 1969, *83*(4), pp. 624–42.

Gørtz, Erik. Interest Determination in a Simultaneous Money and Credit Market Model for Denmark 1950–66. *Swedish J. Econ.,* December 1969, *71*(4), pp. 263–74.

Gossling, W. F. A Note on User Cost. *Manchester Sch. Econ. Soc. Stud.,* September 1969, *37*(3), pp. 259–61.

Gottinger, Hans-Werner. Beiträge zur funktionalen Separabilität bei Nutzenfunktionen (Teil I). (With English summary.) *Z. ges. Staatswiss.,* July 1969, *125*(3), pp. 406–46.

——— Beiträge zur funktionalen Separabilität bei Nutzenfunktionen (Teil II). (With English summary.) *Z. ges. Staatswiss.,* October 1969, *125*(4), pp. 606–23.

——— Die Existenz einiger Klassen deterministischer Nutzenfunktionen. (Existence of Some Classes of Deterministic Utility Functions. With English summary.) *Jahr. Nationalökon. Statist.,* July 1969, *183*(2), pp. 97–124.

Goudzwaard, Maurice B. Conglomerate Mergers, Convertibles, and Cash Dividends. *Quart. Rev. Econ. Bus.,* Spring 1969, *9*(1), pp. 53–62.

——— Consumer Credit Charges and Credit Availability. *Southern Econ. J.,* January 1969, *35*(3), pp. 214–23.

——— The Economic Impact of Credit Insurance Charges. *J. Risk Ins.,* December 1969, *36*(5), pp. 515–23.

Gould, J. D. Hypothetical History. *Econ. Hist. Rev.,* August 1969, *22*(2), pp. 1954–207.

——— The 'Price Revolution': Comments on a Comment. *Australian Econ. Hist. Rev.,* September 1969, *9*(2), pp. 179–81.

Gould, John P. The Expected Utility Hypothesis and the Selection of Optimal Deductibles for a Given Insurance Policy. *J. Bus.,* April 1969, *42*(2), pp. 143–51.

——— The Use of Endogenous Variables in Dynamic Models of Investment. *Quart. J. Econ.,* November 1969, *83*(4), pp. 580–99.

——— **and Segall, Joel.** The Substitution Effects of Transportation Costs. *J. Polit. Econ.,* January/February 1969, *77*(1), pp. 130–37.

Gould, William B. Black Power in the Unions: The Impact upon Collective Bargaining Relationships. *Yale Law J.,* November 1969, *79*(1), pp. 46–84.

——— Racial Equality in Jobs and Unions, Collective Bargaining, and the Burger Court. *Mich. Law Rev.,* December 1969, *68*(2), pp. 237–58.

Gourvish, T. R. The Bank of Scotland, 1830–45. *Scot. J. Polit. Econ.,* November 1969, *16*(3), pp. 288–305.

Gove, Walter and Costner, Herbert. Organizing the Poor: An Evaluation of a Strategy. *Soc. Sci. Quart.,* December 1969, *50*(3), pp. 643–56.

Gowda, K. Venkatagiri. U.S. Aid: A Critical Evaluation. **In** *Dagli, V., ed., Vol. III,* 1969, pp. 31–40.

Graaff, Jan de V. The National Debt. *S. Afr. J. Econ.,* September 1969, *37*(3), pp. 170–86.

______ On Optimum Tariff Structures. **In** *Arrow, K. J. and Scitovsky, T., eds.,* 1969, pp. 523–40.

Grabner, John R., Jr. Legal Limits of Competition. *Harvard Bus. Rev.,* November–December 1969, *47*(6), pp. 4–24, 182.

______**; Lalonde, Bernard J. and Robeson, James F.** The Business Logistics Concept. *Ohio State U. Bull. Bus. Res.,* May 1969, *44*(5), pp. 1–3, 8.

Graf, Truman F. and Hammond, Jerome W. Pricing Milk in Federal Order Markets. *Amer. J. Agr. Econ.,* December 1969, *51*(5), pp. 1506–10.

Graham, Anila. The Export Growth of Agricultural Commodities in Indian International Trade. **In** *Bhuleshkar, A. V., ed.,* 1969, pp. 157–72.

Graham, Harry. Asset Forfeiture Clauses: Should They Be Enforced? *Univ. Wash. Bus. Rev.,* Autumn 1969, *29*(1), pp. 42–47.

______ Public Employees and Collective Negotiations: Remarks. **In** *Sinicropi, A. V. and Gilroy, T. P., eds.,* 1969, pp. 41–44.

Graham, K. R.; Hoa, Tran Van and Bennett, J. W. The Determination of Yields on Corporate Shares: An Empirical Study. *Econ. Rec.,* December 1969, *45*(112), pp. 496–512.

Grahn, Gary L. NBD Model of Repeat-Purchase Loyalty: An Empirical Investigation. *J. Marketing Res.,* February 1969, *6*(1), pp. 72–78.

Gramley, Lyle E. and Chase, Samuel B., Jr. Time Deposits in Monetary Analysis. **In** *Brunner, K., ed.,* 1969, pp. 219–49.

Gramlich, Edward M. A Clarification and a Correction. *Nat. Tax J.,* June 1969, *22*(2), pp. 286–90.

______ State and Local Governments and Their Budget Constraint. *Int. Econ. Rev.,* June 1969, *10* (2), pp. 163–82.

______ **and de Leeuw, Frank.** The Channels of Monetary Policy. *Fed. Res. Bull.,* June 1969, *55*(6), pp. 472–91.

______ **and de Leeuw, Frank.** The Channels of Monetary Policy: A Further Report on the Federal Reserve-M.I.T. Model. *J. Finance,* May 1969, *24*(2), pp. 265–90.

Gramm, Warren S. The Distribution of Industrial Production. *J. Econ. Issues,* December 1969, *3*(4), pp. 39–65.

Gramm, William P. A Keynesian View of Patinkin's Theory of Employment: Comment. *Econ. J.,* March 1969, *79*(313), pp. 179–81.

______ A Theoretical Note on the Capacity of the Market System to Abate Pollution. *Land Econ.,* August 1969, *45*(3), pp. 365–68.

______ **and Ekelund, Robert B., Jr.** A Reconsideration of Advertising Expenditures, Aggregate Demand, and Economic Stabilization. *Quart. Rev. Econ. Bus.,* Summer 1969, *9*(2), pp. 71–77.

______ **and Nash, Robert T.** A Neglected Early Statement of the Paradox of Thrift. *Hist. Polit. Econ.,* Fall 1969, *1*(2), pp. 395–400.

______ **and Timberlake, Richard H., Jr.** The Stock of Money and Investment in the United States, 1897-1966. *Amer. Econ. Rev.,* December 1969, *59* (5), pp. 991–96.

Granfelt, Jarmo. Näkökohtia liikenteen koordinointiongelmasta. (Aspects of the Traffic Coordination Problem. With English summary.) *Liiketaloudellinen Aikak.,* 1969, *18*(2), pp. 121–32.

Granger, C. W. J. Investigating Causal Relations by Econometric Models and Cross-Spectral Methods. *Econometrica,* July 1969, *37*(3), pp. 424–38.

Grant, J. McB. and Mathews, R. Profit Measurement and Inflation. **In** *Parker, R. H. and Harcourt, G. C., eds.,* 1969, pp. 201–14.

Grant, Walter V. Economic Guidelines for Resource Use: Discussion. *Can. J. Agr. Econ.,* November 1969, *17*(3), pp. 38–40.

Grant-Suttie, R. I. Copper Substitution. *Finance Develop.,* June 1969, *6*(2), pp. 49–55.

Graves, G. W.; Hatfield, G. B. and Whinston, Andrew. Water Pollution Control Using By-Pass Piping. *Water Resources Res.,* February 1969, *5* (1), pp. 13–47.

Gray, H. Peter. A Keynesian Framework for the International Accounts. *Weltwirtsch. Arch.,* 1969, *103*(1), pp. 1–25.

Gray, Irwin. Employment Effect of a New Industry in a Rural Area. *Mon. Lab. Rev.,* June 1969, *92*(6), pp. 26–30.

Gray, J. L. Economics of Scale—Generation of Electrical Power. **In** *Hugh-Jones, E. M., ed.,* 1969, pp. 99–112.

Gray, Jack and Simmons, John K. An Investigation of the Effect of Differing Accounting Frameworks on the Prediction of Net Income. *Accounting Rev.,* October 1969, *44*(4), pp. 757–76.

Gray, Roger W. and Anderson, Roice. Advertised Specials and Local Competition among Supermarkets. **In** *Alexis, M.; Holloway, R. J. and Hancock, R. S., eds.,* 1969, pp. 343–57.

Green, Alan G. Regional Inequality, Structural Change, and Economic Growth in Canada —1890–1956. *Econ. Develop. Cult. Change,* July 1969, *17*(4), pp. 567–83.

Green, Andrew Wilson. Portugal and the African Territories: Economic Implications. **In** *Abshire, D. M. and Samuels, M. A., eds.,* 1969, pp. 345–63.

Green, Christopher. Problems in the Area of Poverty: Discussion. *Amer. Econ. Rev.,* May 1969, *59* (2), pp. 473–75.

______ **and Tella, Alfred.** Effect of Nonemployment Income and Wage Rates on the Work Incentives of the Poor. *Rev. Econ. Statist.,* November 1969, *51*(4), pp. 399–408.

Green, Gloria P. Comparing Employment Estimates from Household and Payroll Surveys. *Mon. Lab. Rev.,* December 1969, *92*(12), pp. 9–20.

Green, Johs. Il finanziamento dell-espansione e della ristrutturazione economica. (Financing of Expansion and Structural Change. With English summary.) *Bancaria,* August 1969, *25*(8), pp. 947–53.

Green, Paul E. and Carmone, Frank J. Multidimensional Scaling: An Introduction and Comparison of Nonmetric Unfolding Techniques. *J. Marketing Res.,* August 1969, *6*(3), pp. 330–41.

______ **and Maheshwari, Arun.** Common Stock Perception and Preference: An Application of Multidimensional Scaling. *J. Bus.,* October 1969, *42* (4), pp. 439–57.

______ **and Rao, Vithala R.** A Note on Proximity Measures and Cluster Analysis. *J. Marketing Res.,* August 1969, *6*(3), pp. 359–64.

Green, R. H. The Economy of Cameroon Federal

Republic. **In** *Robson, P. and Lury, D. A., eds.,* 1969, pp. 236–86.

Greenbaum, Stuart I. Correspondent Banking. **In** *Jessup, P. F.,* 1969, pp. 135–46.

Greenberg, Edward. Television Station Profitability and FCC Regulatory Policy. *J. Ind. Econ.,* July 1969, *17*(3), pp. 210–38.

______ **and Barnett, Harold J.** Regulating CATV Systems: An Analysis of FCC Policy and an Alternative. *Law Contemp. Probl.,* Summer 1969, *34*(3), pp. 562–85.

Greenbie, Barrie Barstow. New House or New Neighborhood? A Survey of Priorities among Home Owners in Madison, Wisconsin. *Land Econ.,* August 1969, *45*(3), pp. 359–65.

Greene, John W., Jr. Fighting Poverty with Family Planning: Comment. **In** *Weaver, T. and Magid, A., eds.,* 1969, pp. 54–56.

Greene, Margaret L. and Barrett, Martin. Special Drawing Rights: A Major Step in the Evolution of the World's Monetary System. **In** *Officer, L. H. and Willett, T. D., eds.,* 1969, pp. 143–50.

Greene, Mark R. Doctoral Education for Risk and Insurance in Leading U.S. Universities. *J. Risk Ins.,* December 1969, *36*(5), pp. 505–13.

______ How to Rationalize Your Marketing Risks. *Harvard Bus. Rev.,* May–June 1969, *47*(3), pp. 114–23.

Greenfield, R. J. and Lewis, J. F. An Alternative to a Density Function Definition of Overcrowding. *Land Econ.,* May 1969, *45*(2), pp. 282–85.

Greenhouse, Samuel M. Today's PPBS: The Fatal Triumph of Financial Management over Economics. **In** *The Analysis and Evaluation of Public Expenditures: The PPB System, Vol. 3, JECP,* 1969, pp. 886–98.

Greenidge, Charles D. and Wilson, Cyrus C. Classification Merchandising: An Overlooked Opportunity for Increasing Merchandising Profitability. *Calif. Manage. Rev.,* Fall 1969, *12*(1), pp. 53–61.

Greenwald, Carol S. and Syron, Richard. Increasing Job Opportunities in Boston's Urban Core. *New Eng. Econ. Rev.,* January/February 1969, pp. 30–40.

Greenwald, Joseph A. Statement. **In** *Export Expansion and Regulation, SCH,* 1969, pp. 269–72.

______ Statement. **In** *New Directions for the 1970's: Toward a Strategy of Inter-American Development, Pts. 1–5, HCH,* 1969, pp. 208–09.

______ Statement. **In** *To Extend and Amend the Export Control Act of 1949, HCH,* 1969, pp. 114–17.

Greenwald, William. The Multiple Role of Technology in Advanced Industrial Economies. *Rivista Int. Sci. Econ. Com.,* June 1969, *16*(6), pp. 590–97.

Greenwood, Michael J. An Analysis of the Determinants of Geographic Labor Mobility in the United States. *Rev. Econ. Statist.,* May 1969, *51*(2), pp. 189–94.

______ The Determinants of Labor Migration in Egypt. *J. Reg. Sci.,* August 1969, *9*(2), pp. 283–90.

Greer, Scott. The City in Crisis. **In** *Callow, A. B., Jr., ed.,* 1969, pp. 401–15.

______ Waiting for Reality: Birth of the Megalopolis. **In** *Callow, A. B., Jr., ed.,* 1969, pp. 597–604.

Gregor, Howard F. Farm Structure in Regional Comparison: California and New Jersey Vegetable Farms. *Econ. Geogr.,* July 1969, *45*(3), pp. 209–25.

Grether, E. T. Business Responsibility Toward the Market. *Calif. Manage. Rev.,* Fall 1969, *12*(1), pp. 33–42.

Grewe, Klaus. Wirtschaftsunion bei flexiblen Wechselkursen. (Economic Union under a System of Flexible Exchange Rates. With English summary.) *Schmollers Jahr.,* 1969, *89*(1), pp. 1–32.

Grey, Arthur L., Jr. Urban Renewal and Land Value Taxation. **In** *Becker, A. P., ed.,* 1969, pp. 81–96.

Greytak, David. A Statistical Analysis of Regional Export Estimating Techniques. *J. Reg. Sci.,* December 1969, *9*(3), pp. 387–95.

Griesback, Bernard. The German Policy on Competition Within the Scope of General Economic Policy. *Antitrust Bull.,* Summer 1969, *14,* pp. 449–72.

Grigg, David. The Agricultural Regions of the World: Review and Reflections. *Econ. Geogr.,* April 1969, *45*(2), pp. 95–132.

Griliches, Zvi. Capital-Skill Complementarity. *Rev. Econ. Statist.,* November 1969, *51*(4), pp. 465–68.

Grizzle, Gloria. PPBS in Dade County: Status of Development and Implementation. **In** *Innovations in Planning, Programming, and Budgeting in State and Local Governments, JECP,* 1969, pp. 63–73.

Groenewald, J. A. and Vosloo, J. J. An Analysis of the Demand for Apples in the Republic of South Africa. *Finance Trade Rev.,* June 1969, *8*(3), pp. 187–97.

Groenewegen, P. D. Turgot and Adam Smith. *Scot. J. Polit. Econ.,* November 1969, *16*(3), pp. 271–87.

Grofman, Bernard. Some Notes on Voting Schemes and the Will of the Majority. *Public Choice,* Fall 1969, *7,* pp. 65–80.

Gronau, Reuben and Alcaly, Roger E. The Demand for Abstract Transport Modes: Some Misgivings. *J. Reg. Sci.,* April 1969, *9*(1), pp. 153–57.

Gronsdahl, John. Agricultural Policy in a Dynamic Economy: Symposium. *Can. J. Agr. Econ.,* November 1969, *17*(3), pp. 50–52.

Groom, Phyllis. Prices in Poor Neighborhoods. **In** *Sturdivant, F. D., ed.,* 1969, pp. 118–28.

Gross, Andrew C. Patterns and Determinants of Income of Canadian Engineering Graduates. *Ind. Lab. Relat. Rev.,* October 1969, *23*(1), pp. 52–64.

Gross, Bertram M. and Galnoor, Itzhak. The New Systems Budgeting and the Developing Nations. *Int. Soc. Sci. J.,* 1969, *21*(1), pp. 23–44.

Gross, Edwin J. An Industrial Approach to Consumerism: Ombudsmen. *Ohio State U. Bull. Bus. Res.,* October 1969, *44*(10), pp. 6–7.

Gross, Jack L. and McGinley, John J. Need for a Marketing Intelligence System . . . in Petroleum Marketing: Integration of Information Systems into the Decision-Making Process. *Econ. Bus. Bull.,* Fall 1969, *22*(1), pp. 25–32.

Gross, James A. Historians and the Literature of the Negro Worker. *Labor Hist.,* Summer 1969, *10*(3), pp. 536–46.

Gross, Norman. Convergence and the Emerging Framework: Discussion. **In** *Ozbekhan, H. and Talbert, G. E., eds.,* 1969, pp. 234–40.

Grossack, Irvin. The Nation—Economic Benefits of Higher Education Distribution. *Indiana Bus.*

Rev., September/October 1969, *44*, pp. 14–16.

_____ The Nation—Reflections upon the American Economy. *Indiana Bus. Rev.*, January–February 1969, *44*, pp. 13–16.

Grosse, Robert N. Problems of Resource Allocation in Health. **In** *The Analysis and Evaluation of Public Expenditures: The PPB System, Vol. 3, JECP,* 1969, pp. 1197–1223.

Grossfield, Karl. National Interest Aspects of Innovation. **In** *Hugh-Jones, E. M., ed.*, 1969, pp. 14–28.

Grossman, Herschel I. Expectations, Transactions Costs, and Asset Demands. *J. Finance,* June 1969, *24*(3), pp. 491–506.

_____ Theories of Markets without Recontracting. *J. Econ. Theory,* December 1969, *1*(4), pp. 476–79.

Grove, Ernest W. Econometricians and the Data Gap: Comment. *Amer. J. Agr. Econ.*, February 1969, *51*(1), pp. 184–88.

Grove, M. A.; Khang, Chulsoon and Bierwag, G. O. National Debt in a Neoclassical Growth Model: Comment. *Amer. Econ. Rev.*, March 1969, *59*(1), pp. 205–10.

Groves, Harold M. Is the Property Tax Conceptually and Practically Administrable? **In** *Lynn, A. D., Jr., ed.*, 1969, pp. 15–28.

_____ Richard T. Ely: An Appreciation. *Land Econ.*, February 1969, *45*(1), pp. 1–9.

_____ Taxing the Family Unit: The Carter Commission's Proposals and U.S. Practice. *Nat. Tax J.*, March 1969, *22*(1), pp. 109–20.

Grub, Phillip D. Doing Business with and in East Europe: The Present and a Look toward the Future. **In** *Grub, P. D. and Holbik, K.*, 1969, pp. 208–13.

Grubel, Herbert G. The Benefits and Costs of Being the World Banker. **In** *Officer, L. H. and Willett, T. D., eds.*, 1969, pp. 59–67.

_____ The Distribution of Seigniorage from International Liquidity Creation. **In** *Mundell, R. A. and Swoboda, A. K., eds.*, 1969, pp. 269–82.

_____ The M.B.A. Education Myth. *J. Bus.*, January 1969, *42*(1), pp. 42–49.

_____**; Johnson, Harry G. and Rapp, William V.** Excise Taxes and Effective Protection: A Note. *Econ. J.*, September 1969, *79*(315), pp. 674–75.

Gruber, Alin. Top-of-Mind Awareness and Share of Families: An Observation. *J. Marketing Res.*, May 1969, *6*(2), pp. 227–31.

_____ **and Lindberg, Barbara.** Sensitivity, Reliability, and Consumer Taste Testing: Reaffirmation and a Reply. *J. Marketing Res.*, February 1969, *6* (1), pp. 105–06.

Gruber, William H. The Development and Utilization of Technology in Industry. **In** *Gruber, W. H. and Marquis, D. G., eds.*, 1969, pp. 39–60.

_____ **and Marquis, Donald G.** Research on the Human Factor in the Transfer of Technology. **In** *Gruber, W. H. and Marquis, D. G., eds.*, 1969, pp. 255–82.

Gruchy, Allan G. Neoinstitutionalism and the Economics of Dissent. *J. Econ. Issues,* March 1969, *3* (1), pp. 3–17.

Gruen, Fred H. The Economy. **In** *Preston, R., ed.*, 1969, pp. 35–70.

Grunwald, Joseph. Statement. **In** *New Directions for the 1970's: Toward a Strategy of Inter-American Development, Pts. 1–5, HCH,* 1969, pp. 294–97.

_____ Statement. **In** *Overseas Private Investment Corporation, HCH,* 1969, pp. 104–07.

Gruver, Gene and Sengupta, Jati K. A Linear Reliability Analysis in Programming with Chance Constraints. *Swedish J. Econ.*, December 1969, *71*(4), pp. 221–46.

Gudin, Eugenio. The Chief Characteristics of the Postwar Economic Development of Brazil. **In** *Ellis, H. S., ed.*, 1969, pp. 3–25.

Guenther, William C. Shortest Confidence Intervals. *Amer. Statist.*, February 1969, *23*(1), pp. 22–25.

Guerrero, Jiménez Rodolfo. Oferta y demanda, relacion basica en el dessarrollo. (Supply and Demand: A Basic Relationship in Development. With English summary.) *Econ. Polít.*, Second Semester 1969, *6*(2), pp. 223–28.

Guest, Lester. Brand Loyalty Revisited: A Twenty-Year Report. **In** *Alexis, M.; Holloway, R. J. and Hancock, R. S., eds.*, 1969, pp. 54–59.

Guha, Ashok S. Accumulation, Innovation, and Growth under Conditions of Disguised Unemployment. *Oxford Econ. Pap.*, November 1969, *21*(3), pp. 360–72.

_____ The Stability of Neo-classical Growth—A Unified View. **In** *[Ghosal, U. N.]*, 1969, pp. 30–39.

Guise, John W. B. Factors Associated with Variation in the Aggregate Average Yield of New Zealand Wheat (1918–1967) *Amer. J. Agr. Econ.*, November 1969, *51*(4), pp. 866–81.

_____ **and Ryland, G. J.** Production Scheduling and Allocation: A Normative Decision Model for Sugar Milling. *Australian J. Agr. Econ.*, June 1969, *13*(1), pp. 8–24.

Guisinger, Stephen E. Negative Value Added and the Theory of Effective Protection. *Quart. J. Econ.*, August 1969, *83*(3), pp. 415–33.

Guither, Harold D. Direct Payments: An Increasing Proportion of Farm Income and a Changing Geographic Distribution. *Amer. J. Agr. Econ.*, November 1969, *51*(4), pp. 915–20.

_____ Institution Building: Training Gap in Economic and Agricultural Development. *Amer. J. Agr. Econ.*, December 1969, *51*(5), pp. 1574–77.

Gujarati, Damodar. Cyclical Behavior of Help-Wanted Index and the Unemployment Rate. *Rev. Econ. Statist.*, November 1969, *51*(4), pp. 482–84.

_____ Labor's Share in Manufacturing Industries, 1949–64. *Ind. Lab. Relat. Rev.*, October 1969, *23* (1), pp. 65–77.

Gulati, I. S. and Kothari, V. N. Land Tax as an Incentive for Better Land Utilization. *Artha-Vikas,* July 1969, *5*(2), pp. 108–16.

Gulbrandsen, Odd. Swedish Experience in Agricultural Policy. **In** *Papi, U. and Nunn, C., eds.*, 1969, pp. 409–19.

Gulhati, Ravi. Debt-Servicing as an Aid to Promotion of Trade of Developing Countries: Comment. *Oxford Econ. Pap.*, November 1969, *21*(3), pp. 409–15.

Gulick, Luther. Notes on the Theory of Organization. **In** *Gulick, L. and Urwick, L., eds.*, 1969, pp. 1–45.

_____ Science, Values and Public Administration. **In** *Gulick, L. and Urwick, L., eds.*, 1969, pp. 189–95.

Gulilat, Taye and Ostby, Ivar. A Statistical Study of Household Expenditure in Addis Ababa. *East Afr.*

Econ. Rev., December 1969, *1*(2), pp. 63–74.

Gundelach, Finn. The Kennedy Round of Trade Negotiations: Results and Lessons. **In** *Alting von Geusau, F. A. M., ed.*, 1969, pp. 146–98.

Gunderson, Gerald. Issues in the Measurement of Efficiency of American Dairy Farming, 1850–1910: A Comment. *J. Econ. Hist.*, September 1969, *29*(3), pp. 501-505.

Gupta, Kanhaya L. Money Supply, Cyclical Fluctuations, and Income Determination. *Jahr. Nationalökon. Statist.*, May 1969, *182*(6), pp. 465–78.

Gupta, Manak C. The Effect of Size, Growth, and Industry on the Financial Structure of Manufacturing Companies. *J. Finance*, June 1969, *24*(3), pp. 517–29.

Gupta, S. S. and Panchapakesan, S. Selection and Ranking Procedures. **In** *Naylor, T. H., ed.*, 1969, pp. 132–60.

Gupta, Shibshankar P. Public Expenditure and Economic Development—A Cross-Section Analysis. *Finanzarchiv*, October 1968, *28*(1), pp. 26–41.

——— Using Various Statistical Measures to Analyze the Size of the Public Sector: Comment. **In** *Peacock, A. T., ed.*, 1969, pp. 57–64.

Gupta, Shiv K. and Maier-Rothe, Christoph. A Note on the Partitioning of a Single Product Market into Territories of Outlets. *J. Marketing Res.*, May 1969, *6*(2), pp. 232–36.

Gupta, Suraj B. The Invalidity of the Dichotomy in the Pure Inside-Money Model. *J. Polit. Econ.*, January/February 1969, *77*(1), pp. 118–21.

Gupta, T. R. An Application of Inter-Industry Analysis to Demand Structure of the Indian Economy. *Asian Econ. Rev.*, May 1969, *11*(3), pp. 260–72.

Gupta, Y. P. Least Squares Variant of the Dhrymes Two-Step Estimation Procedure of the Distributed Lag Model. *Int. Econ. Rev.*, February 1969, *10*(1), pp. 112–13.

Gurland, John and Mehta, J. S. Combinations of Unbiased Estimators of the Mean Which Consider Inequality of Unknown Variances. *J. Amer. Statist. Assoc.*, September 1969, *64*(327), pp. 1042–55.

Gurwitsch, Aron. Social Science and Natural Science: Methodological Reflections on Lowe's *On Economic Knowledge*. **In** *Heilbroner, R. L., ed.*, 1969, pp. 37–55.

Gustafson, Albert W. Consumer Preference for "Imitation" Milk Beverages. *Amer. J. Agr. Econ.*, December 1969, *51*(5), pp. 1637–44.

Gustafsson, Kaj. Markkinoiden segmentoinnista ja sen vertailua tuotedifferointiin markkinointistrategiana. (About Market Segmentation and Its Comparison to Product Differentiation as a Marketing Strategy. With English summary.) *Liiketaloudellinen Aikak.*, 1969, *18*(2), pp. 133–44.

Gutfeld, Arnon. The Murder of Frank Little: Radical Labor Agitation in Butte, Montana, 1917. *Labor Hist.*, Spring 1969, *10*(2), pp. 177–92.

Guthrie, Harold W. Problems in the Area of Poverty: Discussion. *Amer. Econ. Rev.*, May 1969, *59*(2), pp. 475–76.

——— Teachers in the Moonlight. *Mon. Lab. Rev.*, February 1969, *92*(2), pp. 28–31.

Gutman, Herbert G. Black Coal Miners and the Greenback-Labor Party in Redeemer, Alabama: 1878–1879: The Letters of Warren D. Kelley, Willis Johnson Thomas, "Dawson," and Others. *Labor Hist.*, Summer 1969, *10*(3), pp. 506–35.

Gutmann, Peter M. Statement. **In** *Bank Holding Company Act Amendments, Pts. 1–3, HCH*, 1969, pp. 360–64.

Guttentag, Jack M. The Bahavior of Residential Mortgage Yields Since 1951. **In** *Guttentag, J. M. and Cagan, P., eds.*, 1969, pp. 29–76.

——— Defensive and Dynamic Open Market Operations, Discounting, and the Federal Reserve System's Crisis-Prevention Responsibilities. *J. Finance*, May 1969, *24*(2), pp. 249–63.

Guttman, I. and Draper, Norman R. The Value of Prior Information. **In** *Johnson, N. L. and Smith, H., Jr., eds.*, 1969, pp. 305–25.

Guy, Edward G. The Applicability of the Federal Antitrust Laws to Bank Mergers. **In** *Jessup, P. F.*, 1969, pp. 444–51.

Guy, R. B., et al. The State of the Art of Prefabrication in the Construction Industry to the Building and Construction Trades Department: Final Report. **In** *Industrialized Housing, JECP*, 1969, pp. 190–200.

de Gyor, P. G. Gschwindt. The Money Supply Question. *Nat. Westminster Bank Quart. Rev.*, August 1969, pp. 61–68.

de Haan, H. and Kuipers, S. K. Een onderzoek naar de invloed van monetaire factoren op het reële groeiproces in enkele traditionele theorieën van economische groei (II). (An Investigation into the Influence of Monetary Factors on the Real Process of Growth in Some Traditional Theories of Economic Growth (II). With English summary.) *De Economist*, July/August 1969, *117*(4), pp. 381–401.

——— Een onderzoek naar de invloed van monetaire factoren op het reële groeiproces in enkele traditionele theorieën van economische groei (III). (An Investigation into the Influence of Monetary Factors on the Real Process of Growth in Some Traditional Theories of Economic Growth (III). With English summary.) *De Economist*, September/October 1969, *117*(5), pp. 493–515.

——— Een onderzoek naar de invloed van monetaire factoren op het reële groeiproces in enkele traditionele theorieën van economische groei (I). (An Investigation into the Influence of Monetary Factors on the Real Process of Growth in Some Traditional Theories of Economic Growth (I). With English summary.) *De Economist*, March/April 1969, *117*(2), pp. 139–60.

Habakkuk, H. J. Historical Demography: Comment. **In** *Bechhofer, F., ed.*, 1969, pp. 221–26.

Haberler, Gottfried. Institutional Arrangements: Appendix: Taxes on Imports and Subsidies on Exports as a Tool of Adjustment. **In** *Mundell, R. A. and Swoboda, A. K., eds.*, 1969, pp. 173–79.

——— The Market for Foreign Exchange and the Stability of the Balance of Payments: A Theoretical Analysis. **In** *Cooper, R. N., ed.*, 1969, pp. 107–34.

______ Round Table on Exchange Rate Policy. *Amer. Econ. Rev.*, May 1969, *59*(2), pp. 357–60.

______ Wage-Push Inflation Once More. **In** *[von Hayek, Friedrich A.]*, 1969, pp. 65–73.

Habib, Irfan. Potentialities of Capitalistic Development in the Economy of Mughal India. *J. Econ. Hist.*, March 1969, *29*(1), pp. 32–78.

Habr, Jaroslav. Ekonomicko-matematické metody v retrospektivě. (Economico-Mathematical Methods in Retrospective. With English summary.) *Ekon.-Mat. Obzor,* 1969, *5*(2), pp. 163–71.

Hadar, Josef. Dominant Diagonals—A Correction. *Econometrica,* July 1969, *37*(3), pp. 541–43.

______ On the Predictive Content of Models of Monopolistic Competition. *Southern Econ. J.,* July 1969, *36*(1), pp. 67–74.

______ Optimality of Imperfectly Competitive Resource Allocation. *Western Econ. J.*, March 1969, *7*(1), pp. 51–56.

______ **and Hillinger, C.** Imperfect Competition with Unknown Demand. *Rev. Econ. Stud.*, October 1969, *36*(108), pp. 519–25.

______ **and Russell, William R.** Rules for Ordering Uncertain Prospects. *Amer. Econ. Rev.*, March 1969, *59*(1), pp. 25–34.

Hady, Thomas F. Agriculture and the Law: Discussion. *Amer. J. Agr. Econ.*, December 1969, *51*(5), pp. 1399–1401.

______ Cost of Local Government Services. *Agr. Finance Rev.*, July 1969, *30,* pp. 11–20.

______ Tax Structure and Regional Economic Growth: A Comment. *J. Reg. Sci.*, August 1969, *9*(2), pp. 325–26.

Haenni, Paul M. Managers' gap mondiale: analisi spettrale. (The Management Gap in a World Context: A Spectral Analysis. With English summary.) *L'Impresa,* November/December 1969, *11*(6), pp. 444–53.

Hagedorn, George G. Statement. **In** *The 1969 Economic Report of the President, Pt. 3, JECH,* 1969, pp. 919–28.

Hagemann, Helmut A. Reserve Policies of Central Banks and Their Implications for U.S. Balance of Payments Policy. *Amer. Econ. Rev.*, March 1969, *59*(1), pp. 62–77.

Hagen, Everett and Hawrylyshyn, Oli. Analysis of World Income and Growth, 1955–1965. *Econ. Develop. Cult. Change,* Part II, October 1969, *18* (1), pp. 1–96.

Hagen, Ole. Separation of Cardinal Utility and Specific Utility of Risk in Theory of Choices under Uncertainty. *Statsokon. Tidsskr.*, October 1969, *83*(3), pp. 81–107.

Hahn, Frank. On Money and Growth. *J. Money, Credit, Banking,* May 1969, *1*(2), pp. 172–87.

Haimes, Yacov Y.; Hall, Warren A. and Butcher, William S. Dynamic Programming for the Optimal Sequencing of Water Supply Projects. *Water Resources Res.*, December 1969, *5*(6), pp. 1196–1204.

Haitovsky, Yoel. Multicollinearity in Regression Analysis: Comment. *Rev. Econ. Statist.*, November 1969, *51*(4), pp. 486–89.

______ A Note on the Maximization of $\bar{R}^2$. *Amer. Statist.*, February 1969, *23*(1), pp. 20–21.

Hajela, D. and Tikkiwal, B. D. Wastage in Education and Measures to Prevent It. **In** *Pandit, H. N., ed.*, 1969, pp. 146–63.

Hajela, P. D. Investment in Education—A Point of View. **In** *Pandit, H. N., ed.*, 1969, pp. 387–91.

Hakala, Donald R. The Iron Ore Industry: A Study of Shifts in Ownership and Control. *Quart. Rev. Econ. Bus.*, Spring 1969, *9*(1), pp. 45–51.

Hakansson, Nils H. An Induced Theory of Accounting under Risk. *Accounting Rev.,* July 1969, *44*(3), pp. 495–514.

______ On the Dividend Capitalization Model under Uncertainty. *J. Financial Quant. Anal.*, March 1969, *4*(1), pp. 65–87.

______ Optimal Investment and Consumption Strategies under Risk, an Uncertain Lifetime, and Insurance. *Int. Econ. Rev.*, October 1969, *10*(3), pp. 443–66.

______ Risk Disposition and the Separation Property in Portfolio Selection. *J. Financial Quant. Anal.*, December 1969, *4*(4), pp. 401–16.

Halcrow, Harold G. The Illinois Agricultural Industries Forum. *Amer. J. Agr. Econ.*, December 1969, *51*(5), pp. 1222–25.

Haldi, John. Policy Analysis in the Post Office. **In** *The Analysis and Evaluation of Public Expenditures: The PPB System, Vol. 3, JECP,* 1969, pp. 1151–67.

Hale, Carl W. The Optimality of Local Subsidies in Regional Development Programs. *Quart. Rev. Econ. Bus.*, Autumn 1969, *9*(3), pp. 35–50.

Hale, G. E. Communication Among Competitors. *Antitrust Bull.*, Spring 1969, *14,* pp. 63–70.

Hale, Rosemary D. Cookware and Vertical Integration: A Rejoinder. *J. Law Econ.*, October 1969, *12* (2), pp. 439–40.

Halevi, Nadav. Economic Policy Discussion and Research in Israel. *Amer. Econ. Rev.*, Part II, September 1969, *59*(4), pp. 74–118.

Haley, Charles W. The Valuation of Risk Assets and the Selection of Risky Investments in Stock Portfolios and Capital Budgets: A Comment. *Rev. Econ. Statist.*, May 1969, *51*(2), pp. 220–21.

Hall, George R. Some Impacts of One-Bank Holding Companies. **In** *Federal Reserve Bank of Chicago (II),* 1969, pp. 73–94.

______ **and Fisher, I. N.** Risk and Corporate Rates of Return. *Quart. J. Econ.*, February 1969, *83*(1), pp. 79–92.

Hall, Harry H.; Heady, Earl O. and Plessner, Yakir. Quadratic Programming Solution of Competitive Equilibrium for U.S. Agriculture: Reply. *Amer. J. Agr. Econ.*, May 1969, *51*(2), pp. 483–84.

Hall, Mildred and Williams, Bill. The Retailers, the Ghetto, and the Government. **In** *Sturdivant, F. D., ed.*, 1969, pp. 210–20.

Hall, Robert E. and Jorgenson, Dale W. Tax Policy and Investment Behavior: Reply and Further Results. *Amer. Econ. Rev.,* June 1969, *59*(3), pp. 388–401.

Hall, Warren A.; Butcher, William S. and Haimes, Yacov Y. Dynamic Programming for the Optimal Sequencing of Water Supply Projects. *Water Resources Res.*, December 1969, *5*(6), pp. 1196–1204.

______**; Tauxe, G. W. and Yeh, W. W.-G.** An Alternate Procedure for the Optimization of Operations for Planning with Multiple River, Multiple

Purpose Systems. *Water Resources Res.*, December 1969, *5*(6), pp. 1367–72.

Hallberg, M. C. Projecting the Size Distribution of Agricultural Firms—An Application of a Markov Process with Non-Stationary Transition Probabilities. *Amer. J. Agr. Econ.*, May 1969, *51*(2), pp. 289–302.

Halliwell, Paul D. Basic Principles of Pension Funding and APB Opinion No. 8. *Manage. Account.*, July 1969, *51*(1), pp. 15–19, 23.

Halm, George N. Will Market Economies and Planned Economies Converge? **In** *[von Hayek, Friedrich A.]*, 1969, pp. 75–88.

Halperin, Ricardo A. Estimación de series bancarias y monetarias argentinas para el período 1926–1940. (Estimation of Argentina Banking and Monetary Series for the Period 1926–1940. With English summary.) *Económica*, January–April 1969, *15*(1), pp. 15–37.

Halter, A. N. and Miller, S. F. Computer Simulation of the Substitution between Project Size and Management. *Amer. J. Agr. Econ.*, December 1969, *51*(5), pp. 1119–23.

Hamada, Koichi. Optimal Capital Accumulation by an Economy Facing an International Capital Market. *J. Polit. Econ.*, Part II, July/August 1969, *77* (4), pp. 684–97.

Hamada, Robert S. The Effects of Leverage and Corporate Taxes on the Shareholders of Regulated Utilities. **In** *Trebing, H. M. and Howard, R. H., eds.*, 1969, pp. 73–97.

______ Portfolio Analysis, Market Equilibrium and Corporation Finance. *J. Finance*, March 1969, *24* (1), pp. 13–31.

Hamala, Milan. Geometrické programovanie. (Geometric Programming. With English summary.) *Ekon.-Mat. Obzor*, 1969, *5*(1), pp. 1–12.

Hamberg, D. Saving and Economic Growth. *Econ. Develop. Cult. Change*, July 1969, *17*(4), pp. 460–82.

Hamburger, Michael J. and Kuehn, Alfred A. A Heuristic Program for Locating Warehouses. **In** *Alexis, M.; Holloway, R. J. and Hancock, R. S., eds.*, 1969, pp. 472–85.

______ **and Latta, Cynthia M.** The Term Structure of Interest Rates: Some Additional Evidence. *J. Money, Credit, Banking*, February 1969, *1*(1), pp. 71–83.

______ **and Silber, William L.** An Empirical Study of Interest Rate Determination. *Rev. Econ. Statist.*, August 1969, *51*(3), pp. 369–73.

Hamermesh, Daniel S. A Disaggregative Econometric Model of Gross Changes in Employment. *Yale Econ. Essays*, Fall 1969, *9*(2), pp. 107–45.

______ Spectral Analysis of the Relation between Gross Employment Changes and Output Changes, 1958–1966. *Rev. Econ. Statist.*, February 1969, *51*(1), pp. 62–69.

Hamilton, Charles V. Black Power: An Alternative. **In** *Shade, W. G. and Herrenkohl, R. C., eds.*, 1969, pp. 134–48.

Hamilton, Earl J. The Decline of Spain. **In** *Scoville, W. C. and La Force, J. C., eds., Vol. II*, 1969, pp. 150–62.

______ The Political Economy of France at the Time of John Law. *Hist. Polit. Econ.*, Spring 1969, *1*(1), pp. 123–49.

Hamilton, W. E. Payment Limitation: Pros and Cons as Seen by Farm Organizations. *Amer. J. Agr. Econ.*, December 1969, *51*(5), pp. 1243–46.

Hamm, B. Curtis and Cundiff, Edward W. Self-Actualization and Product Perception. *J. Marketing Res.*, November 1969, *6*(4), pp. 470–72.

______ **and Perry, Michael.** Canonical Analysis of Relations between Socioeconomic Risk and Personal Influence in Purchase Decisions. *J. Marketing Res.*, August 1969, *6*(3), pp. 351–54.

Hammarskjöld, Knut. The Air Transport Industry—Some Economic Aspects. *Nationalokon. Tidsskr.*, 1969, *107*(1–2), pp. 20–32.

Hammer, Gerald; Schmid, Karl and Braun, Hubert. Ein Verfahren zur Ermittlung der Ausbildungskapazität wissenschaftlicher Hochschulen. (With English summary.) *Jahr. Nationalökon. Statist.*, March 1969, *182*(4–5), pp. 381–97.

Hammer, Marius. Binnenmärkte und Mafia in Sizilien. (Market Organization and Mafia in Sicily. With English summary.) *Jahr. Nationalökon. Statist.*, July 1969, *183*(2), pp. 150–58.

Hammill, Anne E. Variables Related to Farm Real Estate Values in Minnesota Counties. *Agr. Econ. Res.*, April 1969, *21*(2), pp. 45–50.

Hammond, J. D. and Shilling, N. A Review Article: The Little Report on Prices and Profits in the Property and Liability Insurance Industry. *J. Risk Ins.*, March 1969, *36*(1), pp. 129–45.

Hammond, Jerome W.; Anthony, Willis E. and Christiansen, Martin K. Why the Growing Farm-Retail Price Spread? **In** *Ruttan, V. W.; Waldo, A. D. and Houck, J. P., eds.*, 1969, pp. 165–85.

______ **and Graf, Truman F.** Pricing Milk in Federal Order Markets. *Amer. J. Agr. Econ.*, December 1969, *51*(5), pp. 1506–10.

Hammond, Robert. The Justice Department Views Bank Mergers. **In** *Federal Reserve Bank of Chicago (I)*, 1969, pp. 55–62.

Hammond, Robert C. and Abeelen, Marc J. The Fiscal Aspects of International Co-operation in Africa—The Experience of the UDEAC and the EAC. *Bull. Int. Fiscal Doc.*, March 1969, *23*(3), pp. 95–115.

Hampton, P. Empirical Evidence on the Determinants of Interregional Trade Flows. *Econ. Develop. Cult. Change*, Part I, October 1969, *18*(1), pp. 34–39.

______ Regional Import Functions in New Zealand. *J. Common Market Stud.*, June 1969, *7*(4), pp. 327–35.

Han, S. S.; Hitiris, Theodore and Dosser, Douglas. Trade Effects of Tax Harmonisation: Harmonisation of the Value-added Tax in E.E.C. *Manchester Sch. Econ. Soc. Stud.*, December 1969, *37*(4), pp. 337–46.

Hanan, Mack. Corporate Growth through Internal Spin-outs. *Harvard Bus. Rev.*, November–December 1969, *47*(6), pp. 55–66.

______ Corporate Growth through Venture Management. *Harvard Bus. Rev.*, January–February 1969, *47*(1), pp. 43–61.

Hance, William A. and Engberg, Holger L. Growth and Dispersion of Branch Banking in Tropical Africa, 1950–1964. *Econ. Geogr.*, July 1969, *45*(3), pp. 195–208.

Hancke, P. De economische betekenis van het boekhouden. (The Economic Sense of Accounting. With English summary.) *Econ. Soc. Tijdschr.*, April 1969, *23*(2), pp. 97–112.

Hancock, John L. Planning in the Changing American City, 1900–1940. **In** *Callow, A. B., Jr., ed.*, 1969, pp. 549–67.

Handke, Werner. Zielkonflikte in der Entwicklungshilfe zwischen Geber- und Nehmerländern. (With English summary.) *Z. ges. Staatswiss.*, April 1969, *125*(2), pp. 261–78.

Handscomb, D. C. Monte Carlo Techniques: Theoretical. **In** *Naylor, T. H., ed.*, 1969, pp. 252–62.

Handy, C. R. and Padberg, D. I. Conglomerate Growth: Policy Implications for Agriculture and Agribusiness. **In** *Garoian, L., ed.*, 1969, pp. 117–20.

Hannan, E. J. A Note on an Exact Test for Trend and Serial Correlation. *Econometrica*, July 1969, *37*(3), pp. 485–89.

Hanoch, G. and Levy, Haim. The Efficiency Analysis of Choices Involving Risk. *Rev. Econ. Stud.*, July 1969, *36*(107), pp. 335–46.

Hansen, Bent. Employment and Wages in Rural Egypt. *Amer. Econ. Rev.*, June 1969, *59*(3), pp. 298–313.

Hansen, Flemming. Consumer Choice Behavior: An Experimental Approach. *J. Marketing Res.*, November 1969, *6*(4), pp. 436–43.

Hansen, M. H. and Tepping, B. J. Progress and Problems in Survey Methods and Theory Illustrated by the Work of the United States Bureau of the Census. **In** *Johnson, N. L. and Smith, H., Jr., eds.*, 1969, pp. 1–26.

Hansen, Niles M. French Indicative Planning and the *New Industrial State. J. Econ. Issues*, December 1969, *3*(4), pp. 79–95.

______ Improving Economic Opportunity for the Mexican Americans: A Critical Evaluation of Public Policy, with Assessment of the Problem in South Texas. *Econ. Bus. Bull.*, Fall 1969, *22*(1), pp. 1–14.

______ Regional Development and the Rural Poor. *J. Human Res.*, Spring 1969, *4*(2), pp. 205–14.

______ Urban Alternatives for Eliminating Poverty. *Mon. Lab. Rev.*, August 1969, *92*(8), pp. 46–47.

Hansen, Roger D. Political Theory and Regional Integration: The First Ten Years. **In** *Hilton, R., ed.*, 1969, pp. 11–38.

Hansen, Terje. An Aggregated Production Function. *Statsokon. Tidsskr.*, March 1969, *83*(1), pp. 1–9.

______ A Note on the Limit of the Core of an Exchange Economy. *Int. Econ. Rev.*, October 1969, *10*(3), pp. 479–83.

Hansen, W. Lee and Weisbrod, Burton A. The Distribution of Costs and Direct Benefits of Public Higher Education: The Case of California. *J. Human Res.*, Spring 1969, *4*(2), pp. 176–91.

______ The Search for Equity in the Provision and Finance of Higher Education. **In** *the Economics and Financing of Higher Education in the United States, JECP*, 1969, pp. 107–23.

Hansson, Bengt. Group Preferences. *Econometrica*, January 1969, *37*(1), pp. 50–54.

Hao, Yen-P'ing. Cheng Kuan-ying: The Comprador as Reformer. *J. Asian Stud.*, November 1969, *29*(1), pp. 15–22.

Harberger, Arnold C. In Defense of Carter: A Personal Overview. *Nat. Tax J.*, March 1969, *22*(1), pp. 164–77.

______ Professor Arrow on the Social Discount Rate: Discussion. **In** *Somers, G. G. and Wood, W. D., eds.*, 1969, pp. 76–88.

Harbeson, Robert W. Toward Better Resource Allocation in Transport. *J. Law Econ.*, October 1969, *12*(2), pp. 321–38.

Harbison, Frederick H. Education and Economic Development in Advanced Countries. **In** *[Edding, Friedrich]*, 1969, pp. 223–30.

______ The Objectives, Machinery and Methodology of Manpower Planning. **In** *Yesufu, T. M., ed.*, 1969, pp. 63–89.

______ **and Myers, C. A.** Strategies of Human Resource Development. **In** *Blaug, M., ed.*, 1969, pp. 13–60.

Harcourt, G. C. Some Cambridge Controversies in the Theory of Capital. *J. Econ. Lit.*, June 1969, *7*(2), pp. 369–405.

Hardaker, J. B. and Powell, R. A. Recent Developments in Farm Planning: 3: Sub-optimal Programming Methods for Practical Farm Planning. *Rev. Marketing Agr. Econ.*, June 1969, *37*(2), pp. 121–29.

Hardbeck, George W. Unionism again at a Crossroads. **In** *Wortman, M. S., Jr.*, 1969, pp. 65–72.

Harder, K. Peter. Major Factors in Business Formation and Development: Germany in the Early Industrial Period. **In** *Kennedy, C. J., ed.*, 1969, pp. 72–81.

Hardie, Ian W. Shadow Prices as Member Returns for a Marketing Cooperative. *Amer. J. Agr. Econ.*, November 1969, *51*(4), pp. 818–33.

______ **and Farrish, Raymond O. P.** Mysterious Multipliers: Comment. *Amer. J. Agr. Econ.*, August 1969, *51*(3), pp. 689.

Hardin, Charles M. The Bureau of Agricultural Economics under Fire: A Study in Valuation Conflicts. **In** *Fox, K. A. and Johnson, D. G., eds.*, 1969, pp. 423–52.

Hardin, Clifford M. For Humanity, New Hope: Introduction. **In** *Hardin, C. M., ed.*, 1969, pp. 1–7.

Hardin, Einar. Benefit/Cost Analyses of Occupational Training Programs: A Comparison of Recent Studies. **In** *Somers, G. G. and Wood, W. D., eds.*, 1969, pp. 97–118.

Hardin, Lowell S.; Hill, F. F. and Bell, David E. Hope for the Hungry: Fulfillment or Frustration? **In** *Hardin, C. M., ed.*, 1969, pp. 137–70.

Hargreaves, Herbert W. Social Scientists and Economists. **In** *Finney, J. C., ed.*, 1969, pp. 222–33.

Hargrove, Michael B. and Stroup, Robert H. Earnings and Education in Rural South Vietnam. *J. Human Res.*, Spring 1969, *4*(2), pp. 215–25.

Harkins, Claudia and Young, Allan H. Alternative Measures of Price Change for GNP. *Surv. Curr. Bus.*, March 1969, *49*(3), pp. 47–52.

Harkness, Jon P. Long Swings. *Rev. Econ. Statist.*, February 1969, *51*(1), pp. 94–96.

Harl, Neil E. Do Legal and Tax Rules Favor Large-Scale Agricultural Firms? *Amer. J. Agr. Econ.*, December 1969, *51*(5), pp. 1381–92.

Harlan, Louis R. Booker T. Washington and the National Negro Business League. **In** *Schmertz, E.*

J. and Sirefman, J. P., eds., Part II, 1969, pp. 73–91.

Harmston, Floyd K. The Impact of Federal Expenditures on Missouri, Fiscal Year 1967. *Univ. Missouri Bus. Govt. Rev.,* November–December 1969, *10*(6), pp. 5–12.

——— The Importance of 1967 Tourism to Missouri. *Univ. Missouri Bus. Govt. Rev.,* May–June 1969, *10*(3), pp. 6–12.

——— Post-War Trends in the Missouri Economy. *Univ. Missouri Bus. Govt. Rev.,* January–February 1969, *10*(1), pp. 30–36.

Harnett, D. L. and Cummings, L. L. Bargaining Behaviour in a Symmetric Bargaining Triad: The Impact of Risk-Taking Propensity, Information, Communication and Terminal Bid. *Rev. Econ. Stud.,* October 1969, *36*(108), pp. 485–501.

Harper, Donald V. Transportation and the Public Utilities: Discussion. *Amer. Econ. Rev.,* May 1969, *59*(2), pp. 270–71.

Harrar, J. George and Wortman, Sterling. Expanding Food Production in Hungry Nations: The Promise, the Problems. **In** *Hardin, C. M., ed.,* 1969, pp. 89–135.

Harrington, D. H. and Conneman, George J. Implications of Exit and Entry of Farm Firms in Agricultural Supply Analysis. *Agr. Econ. Res.,* April 1969, *21*(2), pp. 40–44.

Harris, Curtis C., Jr. and McGuire, Martin C. Planning Techniques for Regional Development Policy. *J. Human Res.,* Fall 1969, *4*(4), pp. 466–90.

Harris, Edward R., Jr. Funding Land Redistribution in Developing Countries: Maintaining Fiscal Solvency in the Face of Heavy Costs. *Amer. J. Econ. Soc.,* April 1969, *28*(2), pp. 193–204.

——— The Process of Land Reform in Developing Countries: The Background and Basic Legal Strategy. *Amer. J. Econ. Soc.,* January 1969, *28*(1), pp. 49–58.

——— The Role of Bonds as Compensation in Modern Land Reform Programs: Characteristics of Landowner Payments Converting Landlords into Producers. *Amer. J. Econ. Soc.,* July 1969, *28*(3), pp. 325–32.

Harris, J. R. Early Liverpool Canal Controversies. **In** *Harris, J. R., ed.,* 1969, pp. 78–97.

Harris, John R. and Todaro, Michael P. Wages, Industrial Employment and Labour Productivity: The Kenyan Experience. *East Afr. Econ. Rev.,* June 1969, *1*(1), pp. 29–46.

Harris, Laurence. Professor Hicks and the Foundations of Monetary Economics. *Economica, N.S.,* May 1969, *36*(142), pp. 196–208.

Harris, Marshall. Shifts in Entrepreneurial Functions in Agriculture. *Amer. J. Agr. Econ.,* August 1969, *51*(3), pp. 517–29.

Harris, Seymour E. Financing Higher Education: An Overview. **In** *the Economics and Financing of Higher Education in the United States, JECP,* 1969, pp. 467–506.

——— Introduction: Keynes' Attack on *Laissez Faire* and Classical Economics and Wage Theory. **In** *Williams, H. R. and Huffnagle, J. D., eds.,* 1969, pp. 7–20.

——— Statement. **In** *Costs and Delivery of Health Services to Older Americans, Pt. 3, SCH,* 1969, pp. 766–70.

Harris, Walter D. Urban Quality in the Context of the Developing Society. **In** *Schmandt, H. J. and Bloomberg, W., Jr., eds.,* 1969, pp. 187–210.

Harrison, A. E. The Competitiveness of the British Cycle Industry, 1890–1914. *Econ. Hist. Rev.,* August 1969, *22*(2), pp. 287–303.

Harriss, C. Lowell. Progression Reconsidered. **In** *Gaa, C. J.,* 1969, pp. 54–66.

Harrod, Roy F. [Sir]. Doctrines of Imperfect Competition. **In** *Blumner, S. M., ed.,* 1969, pp. 183–202.

——— Problemi monetari d'oggi. (Survey of Monetary Problems. With English summary.) *Bancaria,* July 1969, *25*(7), pp. 819–28.

Harsanyi, John C. Measurement of Social Power in *n*-Person Reciprocal Power Situations. **In** *Bell, R.; Edwards, D. V. and Wagner, R. H., eds.,* 1969, pp. 239–48.

——— Measurement of Social Power, Opportunity Costs, and the Theory of Two-Person Bargaining Games. **In** *Bell, R.; Edwards, D. V. and Wagner, R. H., eds.,* 1969, pp. 226–38.

Hartley, Eugene L. Prediction of U.S. Public Response to a Damage-Limiting Program. **In** *Bobrow, D. B., ed.,* 1969, pp. 263–82.

Hartley, H. O. and Rao, J. N. K. A New Estimation Theory for Sample Surveys, II. **In** *Johnson, N. L. and Smith, H., Jr., eds.,* 1969, pp. 147–69.

Hartley, Keith. Estimating Military Aircraft Production Outlays: The British Experience. *Econ. J.,* December 1969, *79*(316), pp. 861–81.

Hartley, Ronald V. Linear Programming: Some Implications for Management Accounting. *Manage. Account.,* November 1969, *51*(5), pp. 48–51.

Hartman, L. M.; Holland, David and Giddings, Marvin. Effects of Hurricane Storms on Agriculture. *Water Resources Res.,* June 1969, *5*(3), pp. 555–62.

Hartwell, Richard M. Business Management in England during the Period of Early Industrialization: Inducements and Obstacles. **In** *Kennedy, C. J., ed.,* 1969, pp. 59–71.

——— Economic Growth in England before the Industrial Revolution: Some Methodological Issues. *J. Econ. Hist.,* March 1969, *29*(1), pp. 13–31.

Harvey, Barbara. The Leasing of the Abbot of Westminster's Demesnes in the Later Middle Ages. *Econ. Hist. Rev.,* April 1969, *22*(1), pp. 17–27.

Harvey, Katherine A. The Knights of Labor in the Maryland Coal Fields, 1878–1882. *Labor Hist.,* Fall 1969, *10*(4), pp. 555–83.

Harwayne, Frank. Personal Premium Saving under Basic Protection. *J. Risk Ins.,* June 1969, *36*(2), pp. 239–51.

Harwood, Kenneth. Broadcasting and the Theory of the Firm. *Law Contemp. Probl.,* Summer 1969, *34*(3), pp. 485–504.

Hashimoto, Steve T. and Shaffer, Leslie L. D. The Semi-Precious Gem Industry of Oregon. *Oregon Bus. Rev.,* July 1969, *28*(7), pp. 1–4.

Haşigan, D. Statistica în operele lui Nicolae Bălcescu. (Statistics in the Works of Nicolae Bălcescu. With English summary.) *Stud. Cercet. Econ.,* 1969, *1-2,* pp. 215–20.

Haskell, Mark A. and Leshinski, Stephen. Fiscal Influences on Residential Choice: A Study of the New York Region. *Quart. Rev. Econ. Bus.,* Winter 1969, *9*(4), pp. 47–55.

Haslem, John A. A Statistical Estimation of Commercial Bank Profitability. *J. Bus.*, January 1969, *42*(1), pp. 22–35.

Hastings, Delbert G. and Robertson, Ross M. The Mysterious World of the Fed. **In** *Starleaf, D. R., ed.*, 1969, pp. 279–86.

Hatanaka, Michio and Brillinger, David R. An Harmonic Analysis of Nonstationary Multivariate Economic Processes. *Econometrica,* January 1969, *37*(1), pp. 131–41.

______ **and Howrey, E. Philip.** Low Frequency Variation in Economic Time Series. *Kyklos,* 1969, *22*(4), pp. 752–66.

Hatcher, John. A Diversified Economy: Later Medieval Cornwall. *Econ. Hist. Rev.*, August 1969, *22* (2), pp. 208–27.

Hatfield, G. B.; Whinston, Andrew and Graves, G. W. Water Pollution Control Using By-Pass Piping. *Water Resources Res.*, February 1969, *5*(1), pp. 13–47.

Hathaway, Dale E. The Economics of Agricultural Economics. *Amer. J. Agr. Econ.*, December 1969, *51*(5), pp. 1011–26.

______ The Implications of Changing Political Power on Agriculture. **In** *Ruttan, V. W.; Waldo, A. D. and Houck, J. P., eds.*, 1969, pp. 63–68.

______ Poverty in the Hired Farm Work Force. **In** *Task Force on Economic Growth and Opportunity,* 1969, pp. 177–98.

______ The Search for New International Arrangements to Deal with the Agricultural Problems of Industrialized Countries. **In** *Papi, U. and Nunn, C., eds.*, 1969, pp. 51–69.

Haugen, Robert A. and Heins, A. James. The Effects of the Personal Income Tax on the Stability of Equity Value. *Nat. Tax J.*, December 1969, *22*(4), pp. 466–71.

______ A Market Separation Theory of Rent Differentials in Metropolitan Areas. *Quart. J. Econ.*, November 1969, *83*(4), pp. 660–72.

Hauser, G. Measuring Efficiency in Government Services: Comment. **In** *Peacock, A. T., ed.*, 1969, pp. 104–09.

Hauser, Henri. The Characteristic Features of French Economic History from the Middle of the Sixteenth to the Middle of the Eighteenth Century. **In** *Scoville, W. C. and La Force, J. C., eds., Vol. II,* 1969, pp. 163–78.

Hauser, Philip M. The International Encyclopedia: An Assessment of Its Goals and a Consideration of Alternatives. *Soc. Sci. Quart.*, September 1969, *50*(2), pp. 222–33.

______ The Population of the United States, Retrospect and Prospect. **In** *Hauser, P. M., ed.*, 1969, pp. 85–105.

______ Statement. **In** *Population Trends, Pt. 1, HCH,* 1969, pp. 509–22.

______ World Population Growth. **In** *Hauser, P. M., ed.*, 1969, pp. 12–33.

Hausman, Leonard J. Potential for Financial Self-Support among AFDC and AFDC-UP Recipients. *Southern Econ. J.*, July 1969, *36*(1), pp. 60–66.

Hausman, Warren H. A Note on "The Value Line Contest: A Test of the Predictability of Stock-Price Changes." *J. Bus.*, July 1969, *42*(3), pp. 317–20.

Haveman, Robert H. The Analysis and Evaluation of Public Expenditures: An Overview. **In** *The Analysis and Evaluation of Public Expenditures: The PPB System, Vol. 1, JECP,* 1969, pp. 1–10.

______ Evaluating Public Expenditures under Conditions of Unemployment. **In** *The Analysis and Evaluation of Public Expenditures: The PPB System, Vol. 1, JECP,* 1969, pp. 547–61.

______ Evaluating Public Expenditures under Conditions of Unemployment. *Mon. Lab. Rev.*, September 1969, *92*(9), pp. 30–33.

______ The Opportunity Cost of Displaced Private Spending and the Social Discount Rate. *Water Resources Res.*, October 1969, *5*(5), pp. 947–57.

Haves, Samuel L., III and Reiling, Henry B. Sophisticated Financing Tool: The Warrant. *Harvard Bus. Rev.*, January–February 1969, *47*(1), pp. 137–50.

Haviland, William E., et al. Agricultural Policy in a Dynamic Economy: Symposium. *Can. J. Agr. Econ.*, November 1969, *17*(3), pp. 41.

Havlíček, Jaromír and Jeníček, Vladimír. Estimates of Long-term Development of Agriculture by Means of the Global Factorial Model: Reply. *Czech. Econ. Pap.*, 1969, (11), pp. 109–111.

______ Model of the Long-term Development of Czechoslovak Agriculture. *Czech. Econ. Pap.*, 1969, (11), pp. 83–102.

Havlicek, Joseph, Jr.; Tolley, George S. and Wang, Yi. "Solid Wastes"—A Resource? *Amer. J. Agr. Econ.*, December 1969, *51*(5), pp. 1598–1602.

Havrilesky, Thomas and Barth, Richard. Tests of Market Share Stability in the Cigarette Industry 1950–66. *J. Ind. Econ.*, April 1969, *17*(2), pp. 145–50.

______ Non-Price Competition in the Cigarette Industry. *Antitrust Bull.*, Fall 1969, *14,* pp. 607–28.

Hawes, Mary H. Measuring Retired Couples' Living Costs in Urban Areas. *Mon. Lab. Rev.*, November 1969, *92*(11), pp. 3–16.

Hawgood, John. Social Benefit Analysis by Inverse Linear Programming. **In** *Arnfield, R. V., ed.*, 1969, pp. 187–96.

Hawke, G. R. and Reed, M. C. Railway Capital in the United Kingdom in the Nineteenth Century. *Econ. Hist. Rev.*, August 1969, *22*(2), pp. 269–86.

Hawkins, Clark A. Optimum Growth of the Regulated Firm. *Western Econ. J.*, June 1969, *7*(2), pp. 187–89.

______ **and Draper, J. E.** On the Transactions Demand for Cash: Comment. *J. Finance,* December 1969, *24*(5), pp. 942–49.

______ **and McClain, J. M.** A Note on the Short-Run Demand for Money. *Miss. Val. J. Bus. Econ.*, Fall 1969, *5*(1), pp. 73–79.

Hawkins, David F. Behavioral Implications of Generally Accepted Accounting Principles. *Calif. Manage. Rev.*, Winter 1969, *12*(2), pp. 13–21.

Hawkins, Murray H. Alternative Methods of Marketing Livestock. *Can. J. Agr. Econ.*, November 1969, *17*(3), pp. 104–110.

______ Involvement in Undergraduate Education. *Amer. J. Agr. Econ.*, December 1969, *51*(5), pp. 1577–82.

______**; Hurnanen, R. and Devine, G.** Industrial Organization and Policy Development in a Dynamic World. *Can. J. Agr. Econ.*, July 1969, *17*(2), pp. 106–17.

______ **and Murri, D. G.** Organizational Structure

and Collective Bargaining. *Can. J. Agr. Econ.*, November 1969, *17*(3), pp. 150–56.

Hawley, Amos H. Population and Society: An Essay on Growth. **In** *Behrman, S. J.; Corsa, L., Jr. and Freedman, R., eds.*, 1969, pp. 189–209.

Hawrylyshyn, Oli and Hagen, Everett. Analysis of World Income and Growth, 1955–1965. *Econ. Develop. Cult. Change*, Part II, October 1969, *18* (1), pp. 1–96.

Hawthorne, E. P. and Willis, R. J. Forecasting the Market for Certain Machine Tools, 1974–1999. **In** *Arnfield, R. V., ed.*, 1969, pp. 241–52.

Hayami, Yūjirō. Resource Endowments and Technological Change in Agriculture: U.S. and Japanese Experiences in International Perspective. *Amer. J. Agr. Econ.*, December 1969, *51*(5), pp. 1293–1303.

______ Sources of Agricultural Productivity Gap among Selected Countries. *Amer. J. Agr. Econ.*, August 1969, *51*(3), pp. 564–75.

______ **and Yamada, Saburō.** Agricultural Productivity at the Beginning of Industrialization. **In** *Ohkawa, K.; Johnston, B. F. and Kaneda, H., eds.*, 1969, pp. 105–35.

Hayek, Friedrich A. Maintaining Capital Intact: A Reply. **In** *Parker, R. H. and Harcourt, G. C., eds.*, 1969, pp. 127–31.

______ Three Elucidations of the Ricardo Effect. *J. Polit. Econ.*, March/April 1969, *77*(2), pp. 274–85.

Hayes, Douglas A. Ethical Standards in Financial Reporting: A Critical Review. **In** *Burton, J. C., ed.*, 1969, pp. 73–86.

Hayes, Robert H. Qualitative Insights from Quantitative Methods. *Harvard Bus. Rev.*, July–August 1969, *47*(4), pp. 108–17.

______ The Value of Sample Information. **In** *Naylor, T. H., ed.*, 1969, pp. 298–319.

Hayes, William A. The Guaranteed Annual Income: An Appraisal. *Rev. Soc. Econ.*, March 1969, *27*(1), pp. 74–83.

Haymes, Harmon H. Equipment Leasing. **In** *Jessup, P. F.*, 1969, pp. 109–13.

Hays, S.; Hemming, M. F. W. and Ray, G. F. The Office Machinery Industry in the United Kingdom. *Nat. Inst. Econ. Rev.*, August 1969, (49), pp. 52–73.

Hazard, John L. Transportation and the Public Utilities: Discussion. *Amer. Econ. Rev.*, May 1969, *59* (2), pp. 271–74.

Hazard, Leland. Challenges for Urban Policy. **In** *Baier, K. and Rescher, N., eds.*, 1969, pp. 320–35.

Hazari, R. K. The Implications of the Managing Agency System in Indian Development. **In** *Bhuleshkar, A. V., ed.*, 1969, pp. 193–213.

Hazlewood, Arthur. An Approach to the Analysis of the Spatial Distribution of the Market in East Africa. *Bull. Oxford Univ. Inst. Econ. Statist.*, November 1969, *31*(4), pp. 243–61.

Head, John G. Merit Goods Revisited. *Finanzarchiv*, March 1969, *28*(2), pp. 214–25.

______ **and Shoup, Carl S.** Excess Burden: The Corner Case. *Amer. Econ. Rev.*, March 1969, *59*(1), pp. 181–83.

______ **and Shoup, Carl S.** Public Goods, Private Goods, and Ambiguous Goods. *Econ. J.*, September 1969, *79*(315), pp. 567–72.

Heady, Earl O. Elementary Models in Farm Production Economics Research. **In** *Fox, K. A. and Johnson, D. G., eds.*, 1969, pp. 181–202.

______ The Future Structure of U.S. Agriculture. **In** *Owen, W. F., ed.*, 1969, pp. 113–28.

______**; Plessner, Yakir and Hall, Harry H.** Quadratic Programming Solution of Competitive Equilibrium for U.S. Agriculture: Reply. *Amer. J. Agr. Econ.*, May 1969, *51*(2), pp. 483–84.

______ **and Scott, John T., Jr.** Econometricians and the Data Gap: Reply. *Amer. J. Agr. Econ.*, February 1969, *51*(1), pp. 188.

Heal, G. M. Planning without Prices. *Rev. Econ. Stud.*, July 1969, *36*(107), pp. 347–62.

Healy, A. T. A. and Byrne, P. F. A Note on Livestock Breeding Policies in Stable and Development Situations. *Australian J. Agr. Econ.*, December 1969, *13*(2), pp. 154–61.

Heamon, John W. Inventory and Financing Procedures for a Mortgage Banker. *Manage. Account.*, December 1969, *51*(6), pp. 32–34.

Heaton, Herbert. Thomas Southcliffe Ashton 1889–1968: A Memoir. *J. Econ. Hist.*, June 1969, *29*(2), pp. 264–67.

Heckerman, Donald G. "Inefficient" European Capital Markets as an Explanation of International Capital Movements. *J. Money, Credit, Banking*, February 1969, *1*(1), pp. 121–23.

Heckscher, Eli F. Mercantilism. **In** *Coleman, D. C., ed.*, 1969, pp. 19–34.

Hedges, Bob A. Insurance Rates and Investment Earnings Considered Together. *J. Risk Ins.*, September 1969, *36*(4), pp. 455–61.

______ Substandard Automobile Insurers: Comment. *J. Risk Ins.*, December 1969, *36*(5), pp. 640–42.

Heertje, A. Enkele opmerkingen over groeimodellen. (Some Remarks on Growth Models. With English summary.) *De Economist*, July/August 1969, *117*(4), pp. 361–80.

Heffron, Paul T. Manuscript Sources in the Library of Congress for a Study of Labor History. *Labor Hist.*, Fall 1969, *10*(4), pp. 630–38.

Heflebower, Richard B. Theory of the Firm and of Market Structures: Discussion. *Amer. Econ. Rev.*, May 1969, *59*(2), pp. 119–21.

Heggie, Ian G. Notes on Feasibility Studies: I. Road Investment Criteria. *J. Transp. Econ. Policy*, May 1969, *3*(2), pp. 222–24.

Heideman, M. Lawrence, Jr. Public Implementation and Incentive Devices for Innovation and Experiment in Planned Urban Development. *Land Econ.*, May 1969, *45*(2), pp. 262–67.

Heidensohn, K. Labour's Share in National Income—A Constant? *Manchester Sch. Econ. Soc. Stud.*, December 1969, *37*(4), pp. 295–321.

Heien, Dale M. Income and Price Lags in Consumer-demand Analysis. *J. Roy. Statist. Soc.*, Part 2, 1969, *132*, pp. 265–71.

Heilbrun, James. Reforming the Real Estate Tax to Encourage Housing Maintenance and Rehabilitation. **In** *Becker, A. P., ed.*, 1969, pp. 63–79.

Heimann, John G. The Necessary Revolution in Housing Finance. **In** *National Housing Goals, HCH*, 1969, pp. 319–37.

Heineke, J. M. Demand for Refined Lead. *Rev. Econ. Statist.*, August 1969, *51*(3), pp. 374–78.

Heinemann, Klaus. Stabilität und Wandel bürokratischer Organisationen. (Stability and Change in Bureaucratic Organizations. With English summary.) *Schmollers Jahr.*, 1969, *89*(3), pp. 313–31.

Heins, A. James and Haugen, Robert A. The Effects of the Personal Income Tax on the Stability of Equity Value. *Nat. Tax J.*, December 1969, *22*(4), pp. 466–71.

______ A Market Separation Theory of Rent Differentials in Metropolitan Areas. *Quart. J. Econ.*, November 1969, *83*(4), pp. 660–72.

______ **and Sprenkle, Case M.** A Comment on the Modigliani-Miller Cost of Capital Thesis. *Amer. Econ. Rev.*, Part I, September 1969, *59*(4), pp. 590–92.

Heitman, George and Robinson, Warren C. A Suggested Reformulation of the Basic Keynesian Model. *Quart. Rev. Econ. Bus.*, Autumn 1969, *9*(3), pp. 51–55.

Hejl, Luboš, et al. Macroeconomic Decision Model for the Medium-term Optimal Planning: A Progress Report. *Czech. Econ. Pap.*, 1969, (11), pp. 51–67.

Helfgott, Roy B. The Computer and Prospects for Office Unionism. *Quart. Rev. Econ. Bus.*, Spring 1969, *9*(1), pp. 19–28.

Helle, Tapani. Arvoanalyysistä ja sen käytöstä hallinnon rationalisoinnissa. (Value Analysis and Its Use in Rationalizing Administration. With English summary.) *Liiketaloudellinen Aikak.*, 1969, *18*(3), pp. 388–92.

Hellickson, George C. A Regional Self-Help Program. **In** *Task Force on Economic Growth and Opportunity,* 1969, pp. 199–216.

Hellier, W. L. and Sault, J. L. The New International Sugar Agreement and the Australian Sugar Industry. *Quart. Rev. Agr. Econ.*, October 1969, *22*(4), pp. 210–29.

Helliwell, John F. Monetary and Fiscal Policies for an Open Economy. *Oxford Econ. Pap.*, March 1969, *21*(1), pp. 35–55.

______ **and Mao, James C. T.** Investment Decisions under Uncertainty: Theory and Practice. *J. Finance,* May 1969, *24*(2), pp. 323–38.

Helliwell, John F., et al. Econometric Analysis of Policy Choices for an Open Economy. *Rev. Econ. Statist.*, November 1969, *51*(4), pp. 383–98.

Hellmuth, William F. and Surrey, Stanley S. The Tax Expenditure Budget—Response to Professor Bittker. *Nat. Tax J.*, December 1969, *22*(4), pp. 528–37.

Hellriegel, Don and French, Wendell. A Critique of Jaques' Equitable Payment System. *Ind. Relat.*, May 1969, *8*(3), pp. 269–79.

Helmberger, Peter. Who's Afraid of Conglomerate Firms? **In** *Garoian, L., ed.*, 1969, pp. 113–14.

Helmer, Olaf. Simulating the Values of the Future. **In** *Baier, K. and Rescher, N., eds.*, 1969, pp. 193–214.

Helmstädter, Ernst. Patinkin-Kontroverse-Beitrag Nr. X. (With English summary.) *Kyklos,* 1969, *22*(3), pp. 506–18.

Helsby, Robert D. Disputes in the Public Sector—New York's Experience. **In** *Sinicropi, A. V. and Gilroy, T. P., eds.*, 1969, pp. 9–16.

Hemer, Jiří. About Foreign Trade Activities—Without Illusions. *New Trends Czech. Econ.*, November 1969, (7), pp. 65–79.

Hemmi, Kenzō. Primary Product Exports and Economic Development: The Case of Silk. **In** *Ohkawa, K.; Johnston, B. F. and Kaneda, H., eds.*, 1969, pp. 303–23.

Hemming, M. F. W.; Ray, G. F. and Hays, S. The Office Machinery Industry in the United Kingdom. *Nat. Inst. Econ. Rev.*, August 1969, (49), pp. 52–73.

Hencke, Paul. Is War on Poverty Becoming War on Business? **In** *Sturdivant, F. D., ed.*, 1969, pp. 162–70.

Hendershott, Patric H. Open Market Operations, the Money Stock, and Various Policy Issues. **In** *Brunner, K., ed.*, 1969, pp. 283–99.

Henderson, Alexander M. The Pricing of Public Utility Undertakings. **In** *Arrow, K. J. and Scitovsky, T., eds.*, 1969, pp. 541–60.

Henderson, P. D. Political and Budgetary Constraints: Some Characteristics and Implications. **In** *Margolis, J. and Guitton, H., eds.*, 1969, pp. 310–25.

Henderson, William L. and Ledebur, Larry C. Government Incentives and Black Economic Development. *Rev. Soc. Econ.*, September 1969, *27*(2), pp. 202–21.

Hendon, William S. Faculty Compensation and the Cost of Living. *Soc. Sci. Quart.*, September 1969, *50*(2), pp. 396–400.

Hendricks, Sterling B. Food from the Land. **In** *National Academy of Sciences,* 1969, pp. 65–85.

Heneman, Herbert G., Jr. Toward a General Conceptual System of Industrial Relations: How Do We Get There? **In** *Somers, G. G., ed. (I),* 1969, pp. 3–24.

Henle, Peter. Leisure and the Long Workweek. **In** *Wortman, M. S., Jr.*, 1969, pp. 247–57.

______ Some Reflections on Organized Labor and the New Militants. *Mon. Lab. Rev.*, July 1969, *92*(7), pp. 20–25.

Henley, Albert T. Land Value Taxation by California Irrigation Districts. **In** *Becker, A. P., ed.*, 1969, pp. 137–45.

Henneberger, John E. Productivity Rises as Radio-TV Output Triples in 8 Years. *Mon. Lab. Rev.*, March 1969, *92*(3), pp. 40–42.

Hennessy, John H., Jr. AD HOC Research in Small Companies. *Manage. Account.*, July 1969, *51*(1), pp. 27–30.

Henning, John A. Marginal Concentration Ratios: Some Statistical Implications—Comment. *Southern Econ. J.*, October 1969, *36*(2), pp. 196–98.

______**; Meehan, James W., Jr. and Mann, H. Michael.** Statistical Testing in Industrial Economics: A Reply on Measurement Error and Sampling Procedure. *J. Ind. Econ.*, November 1969, *18*(1), pp. 95–100.

______**; Meehan, James W., Jr. and Mann, H. Michael.** Testing Hypothesis in Industrial Economics: A Reply. *J. Ind. Econ.*, November 1969, *18*(1), pp. 81–84.

Henrichsmeyer, W.; Aldinger, F. and Weinschenck, G. The Theory of Spatial Equilibrium and Optimal Location in Agriculture: A Survey. *Rev. Marketing Agr. Econ.*, March 1969, *37*(1), pp. 3–70.

Henry, G. C. Farm Labor. **In** *Task Force on Economic Growth and Opportunity,* 1969, pp. 217–27.

Heraud, Jorge and Pomalaza, José. An Educational Television and Communications System for Latin America. **In** *Hilton, R., ed.,* 1969, pp. 381–400.

Herberg, Horst. On the Shape of the Transformation Curve in the Case of Homogenous Production Functions. *Z. ges. Staatswiss.,* April 1969, *125*(2), pp. 202–10.

Herbst, František. The Housing Situation in the CSSR in Terms of International Comparison. *Eastern Europ. Econ.,* Summer 1969, *7*(4), pp. 38–40.

Herbst, J. H. Net Worth Projections for a Period of Farm Business Expansion. *Ill. Agr. Econ.,* July 1969, *9*(2), pp. 36–47.

Herman, B.; Mennes, L. B. M. and Waardenburg, J. G. Some Exercises with a Simple Model for World Development Planning. **In** *[Tinbergen, J.],* 1969, pp. 65–92.

Herman, Barry. On Muddled Methods and Their Meaning. *Rev. Radical Polit. Econ.,* May 1969, *1* (1), pp. 75–84.

Herman, Leon M. The Cult of Bigness in Soviet Economic Planning. **In** *Economic Concentration, Pt. 7A, SCH,* 1969, pp. 4346–58.

——— The Recent Course of East-West Trade. **In** *Grub, P. D. and Holbik, K.,* 1969, pp. 76–80.

——— Urbanization and New Housing Construction in the U.S.S.R. **In** *Industrialized Housing, JECP,* 1969, pp. 22–40.

Herman, Shelby W. and Fulco, Lawrence J. Productivity and Unit Labor Costs in 1968. *Mon. Lab. Rev.,* June 1969, *92*(6), pp. 11–15.

Hermann, Donald H. J., III. From Economic Theory to Public Policy. *Univ. Wash. Bus. Rev.,* Spring 1969, *28*(3), pp. 59–64.

Herr, William McD. The Role of FHA's Farm Operating and Ownership Loan Programs as Indicated by Borrower Characteristics. *Agr. Finance Rev.,* July 1969, *30,* pp. 1–10.

Herrick, Bruce. Research Needs in Labor and Economic Development. *Ind. Relat.,* May 1969, *8*(3), pp. 214–23.

Herring, Dora R. Statistical Estimations of Historical Distribution Cost. *Manage. Account.,* October 1969, *51*(4), pp. 42–46.

Hershlag, Z. Y. Theory of Stages of Economic Growth in Historical Perspective. *Kyklos,* 1969, *22*(4), pp. 661–90.

Herzberg, Agnes M. and Cox, D. R. Recent Work on the Design of Experiments: A Bibliography and a Review. *J. Roy. Statist. Soc.,* Part 1, 1969, *132,* pp. 29–67.

Herzberg, Frederick; Paul, William J., Jr. and Robertson, Keith B. Job Enrichment Pays Off. *Harvard Bus. Rev.,* March–April 1969, *47*(2), pp. 61–78.

Herzog, Elizabeth. Perspectives on Poverty 3: Facts and Fictions about the Poor. *Mon. Lab. Rev.,* February 1969, *92*(2), pp. 42–49.

Hesburgh, Theodore M. Statement. **In** *National Housing Goals, HCH,* 1969, pp. 404–12.

Hess, Alan C. A Quantity Theory Approach to the Current Inflation. *Univ. Wash. Bus. Rev.,* Summer 1969, *28*(4), pp. 12–17.

Hess, Carroll V. Social Science Needs in Agriculture and Natural Resources Curricula—The CEANAR Report. *Amer. J. Agr. Econ.,* December 1969, *51* (5), pp. 1613–17.

Hester, Donald D. Financial Disintermediation and Policy. *J. Money, Credit, Banking,* August 1969, *1*(3), pp. 600–17.

Hetényi, I. Economic Development and Long-Term Planning. *Acta Oecon.,* 1969, *4*(2), pp. 155–68.

Hettena, Ran and Ruchlin, Hirsch S. The U.S. Tanker Industry: A Structural and Behavioral Analysis. *J. Ind. Econ.,* July 1969, *17*(3), pp. 188–204.

Hettenhouse, George W. and Lewellen, Wilbur G. The Taxation of Restricted Stock Compensation Plans. *Nat. Tax J.,* September 1969, *22*(3), pp. 368–78.

Hettich, Walter. Mixed Public and Private Financing of Education: Comment. *Amer. Econ. Rev.,* March 1969, *59*(1), pp. 210–12.

Heubes, Jürgen. Time-Series CES-Production Functions for Primary Production and Manufacturing, Federal Republic of Germany 1950–1965. *Ger. Econ. Rev.,* 1969, *7*(4), pp. 346–60.

af Heurlin, Lauri O. Vuokra-asunnon ja asunnonvuokran ongelma. (The Problem of Rented Accommodation and the Rent Level. With English summary.) *Kansant. Aikak.,* 1969, *65*(4), pp. 251–68.

Heuser, Forrest L. The Question of Uniform Accounting Standards. *Manage. Account.,* July 1969, *51*(1), pp. 20–23.

Hewett, Edward A. A Note on Soviet Standards. *Bull. Oxford Univ. Inst. Econ. Statist.,* February 1969, *31*(1), pp. 55–60.

Hexter, J. H. Storm over the Gentry. **In** *Scoville, W. C. and La Force, J. C., eds., Vol. II,* 1969, pp. 65–95.

Heyer, Judith and Massell, Benton F. Household Expenditure in Nairobi: A Statistical Analysis in Consumer Behavior. *Econ. Develop. Cult. Change,* January 1969, *17*(2), pp. 212–34.

Heyman, Thomas V. Patent Licensing and the Antitrust Laws—A Reappraisal at the Close of the Decade. *Antitrust Bull.,* Fall 1969, *14,* pp. 537–56.

Hickey, Joseph A. Status Report on Unemployment Insurance Laws. *Mon. Lab. Rev.,* January 1969, *92* (1), pp. 47–51.

Hickman, Bert G. Dynamic Properties of Macroeconometric Models: An International Comparison. **In** *Bronfenbrenner, M., ed.,* 1969, pp. 393–435.

Hicks, John R. [Sir] Automatists, Hawtreyans, and Keynesians. *J. Money, Credit, Banking,* August 1969, *1*(3), pp. 307–17.

——— Direct and Indirect Additivity. *Econometrica,* April 1969, *37*(2), pp. 353–54.

——— Maintaining Capital Intact: A Further Suggestion. **In** *Parker, R. H. and Harcourt, G. C., eds.,* 1969, pp. 132–38.

——— The Rehabilitation of Consumers' Surplus. **In** *Arrow, K. J. and Scitovsky, T., eds.,* 1969, pp. 325–35.

______ Value and Volume of Capital. *Indian Econ. J.*, October–December 1969, *17*(2), pp. 161–71.

Hicks, Ursula K. Economic and Financial Problems of Metropolitan Areas. *Z. Nationalökon.*, May 1969, *29*(1–2), pp. 1–18.

______ Educational Expansion in Low Income Countries with Special Reference to India. **In** *Bhuleshkar, A. V., ed.*, 1969, pp. 368–94.

______ La finanza pubblica nel quadro della politica economica e sociale della Gran Bretagna. (The Finance of the British Government. With English summary.) *Bancaria*, September 1969, *25*(9), pp. 1067–81.

Hicks, W. Whitney. Primary Exports and Economic Development: An Application of the Staple Theory to Sonora, Mexico. *Can. J. Agr. Econ.*, July 1969, *17*(2), pp. 46–62.

Hiemstra, Stephen J. and Egbert, Alvin C. Shifting Direct Government Payments from Agriculture to Poor People: Impacts on Food Consumption and Farm Income. *Agr. Econ. Res.*, July 1969, *21*(3), pp. 61–69.

Hieronymus, T. A. Soybeans: End of an Era? *Ill. Agr. Econ.*, July 1969, *9*(2), pp. 1–18.

Hiestand, Dale L. The Changing Position of Negro Workers. **In** *Kain, J. F., ed.*, 1969, pp. 68–73.

Higbee, Edward. Other Traditions: The Advance of the Hacienda. **In** *Owen, W. F., ed.*, 1969, pp. 43–51.

Higgs, Robert. The Growth of Cities in a Midwestern Region, 1870–1900. *J. Reg. Sci.*, December 1969, *9*(3), pp. 369–75.

Hijzen, Th. C. Thoughts on Commercial Relations after the Kennedy Round. **In** *Alting von Geusau, F. A. M., ed.*, 1969, pp. 113–22.

Hilaski, Harvey J. and Willacy, Hazel M. Employment Patterns and Place of Residence. *Mon. Lab. Rev.*, October 1969, *92*(10), pp. 18–25.

Hildebrand, George H. Research on Big City Labor Markets: Discussion. **In** *Somers, G. G., ed. (II)*, 1969, pp. 268–71.

Hildebrand, John R. LAFTA and Paraguay: Economic and Social Development. **In** *Hilton, R., ed.*, 1969, pp. 551–61.

Hildenbrand, Werner. Pareto Optimality for a Measure Space of Economic Agents. *Int. Econ. Rev.*, October 1969, *10*(3), pp. 363–72.

Hilgert, Raymond L. and Young, Jerry D. Right-to-Work Legislation—Examination of Related Issues and Effects. **In** *Wortman, M. S., Jr.*, 1969, pp. 377–87.

Hill, Conrad R. Another Look at Two Instant Coffee Studies. **In** *Alexis, M.; Holloway, R. J. and Hancock, R. S., eds.*, 1969, pp. 433–37.

Hill, F. F.; Bell, David E. and Hardin, Lowell S. Hope for the Hungry: Fulfillment or Frustration? **In** *Hardin, C. M., ed.*, 1969, pp. 137–70.

Hill, Herbert. Racial Inequality in Employment: The Patterns of Discrimination. **In** *Kain, J. F., ed.*, 1969, pp. 78–88.

Hill, John D. and Werner, Robert L. Corporate Expansion and the Law. **In** *Harvey, J. L. and Newgarden, A., eds.*, 1969, pp. 49–61.

Hill, Lowell D. Information Gaps and Research Problems. **In** *Garoian, L., ed.*, 1969, pp. 125–27.

Hill, Roger B. The Improvement of Returns from Research and Development Investment. **In** *Hugh-Jones, E. M., ed.*, 1969, pp. 29–47.

Hill, T. P. Too Much Consumption. *Nat. Westminster Bank Quart. Rev.*, February 1969, pp. 18–39.

Hilliard, John. Toward an Integrated Manpower Policy for Accelerated National Development. **In** *Yesufu, T. M., ed.*, 1969, pp. 27–36.

Hillinger, C. The Measurement of Utility. *Rev. Econ. Stud.*, January 1969, *36*(105), pp. 111–16.

______ **and Hadar, Josef.** Imperfect Competition with Unknown Demand. *Rev. Econ. Stud.*, October 1969, *36*(108), pp. 519–25.

Hills, Stuart L. The Planned Suburban Community. *Land Econ.*, May 1969, *45*(2), pp. 277–82.

Hindley, Brian. Capitalism and the Corporation. *Economica, N.S.*, November 1969, *36*(144), pp. 426–38.

Hines, A. G. Wage Inflation in the United Kingdom 1948–62: A Disaggregated Study. *Econ. J.*, March 1969, *79*(313), pp. 66–89.

Hines, Fred K. Propensities to Invest in Schooling in the South and Non-South. *Amer. J. Agr. Econ.*, December 1969, *51*(5), pp. 1561–64.

Hines, Lawrence G. The Long-Run Cost Function of Water Production for Selected Wisconsin Communities. *Land Econ.*, February 1969, *45*(1), pp. 133–40.

Hinich, Melvin J. and Ordeshook, Peter C. Abstentions and Equilibrium in the Electoral Process. *Public Choice*, Fall 1969, *7*, pp. 81–106.

Hiniker, Paul J. and Farace, R. Vincent. Approaches to National Development in China: 1949–1958. *Econ. Develop. Cult. Change*, Part I, October 1969, *18*(1), pp. 51–72.

Hinterhuber, Hans. Der Staat als Unternehmer. (The State as Entrepreneur. With English summary.) *Weltwirtsch. Arch.*, 1969, *103*(1), pp. 58–76.

Hinton, W. L. The Contribution of Horticulture. *Nat. Westminster Bank Quart. Rev.*, May 1969, pp. 33–41.

Hirono, Ryokichi. Japanese Investment. **In** *Hughes, H. and Seng, Y. P., eds.*, 1969, pp. 86–111.

Hirsch, Abraham. Bray Hammond on Wesley Mitchell and the North's Empty Purse. *J. Econ. Issues*, June 1969, *3*(2), pp. 206–12.

Hirsch, Fred. The Future of Gold: Discussion. *Amer. Econ. Rev.*, May 1969, *59*(2), pp. 351–53.

Hirsch, John S., Jr. Strike Insurance and Collective Bargaining. *Ind. Lab. Relat. Rev.*, April 1969, *22*(3), pp. 399–415.

Hirsch, Werner Z. Regional Information Design for Public Decisions. *Rev. Income Wealth*, December 1969, *15*(4), pp. 369–80.

______ Technological Progress and Microeconomic Theory. *Amer. Econ. Rev.*, May 1969, *59*(2), pp. 36–43.

______ **and Fabricant, Solomon.** Some Problems in the Measurement of Productivity in the Medical Care Industry: Comment. **In** *Fuchs, V. R., ed.*, 1969, pp. 146–47.

______ **and Marcus, Morton J.** Intercommunity Spillovers and the Provision of Public Education. *Kyklos*, 1969, *22*(4), pp. 641–60.

Hirschberg, David A.; Bretzfelder, Robert B. and Dallavalle, Q. Francis. Personal Income, 1968, and Disposable Income, 1929–68, by States and Regions. *Surv. Curr. Bus.*, April 1969, *49*(4), pp. 16–21, 32.

Hirshleifer, Jack. On Multiple Rates of Return: Comment. *J. Finance,* March 1969, *24*(1), pp. 98.

_____ **and Shapiro, David L.** The Treatment of Risk and Uncertainty. **In** *The Analysis and Evaluation of Public Expenditures: The PPB System, Vol. 1, JECP,* 1969, pp. 505–30.

Hirvonen, Martti J. Balanced Dairy Production—Interregional Linear Programming Approach. *Kansant. Aikak.*, 1969, *65*(4), pp. 274–79.

Hiscocks, Geoffrey. Agricultural Policy in a Dynamic Economy: Symposium. *Can. J. Agr. Econ.*, November 1969, *17*(3), pp. 47–50.

Hise, Richard T. and Ryans, John K., Jr. Retailing's Unfortunate Image: Problems of Attracting College Graduates. *Econ. Bus. Bull.*, Fall 1969, *22*(1), pp. 39–43.

Hishiyama, Izumi. The Logic of Uncertainty According to J. M. Keynes. *Kyoto Univ. Econ. Rev.*, April 1969, *39*(1), pp. 22–44.

Hitiris, Theodore; Dosser, Douglas and Han, S. S. Trade Effects of Tax Harmonisation: Harmonisation of the Value-added Tax in E.E.C. *Manchester Sch. Econ. Soc. Stud.*, December 1969, *37*(4), pp. 337–46.

Hoa, Tran Van. Additive Preferences and Cost of Living Indexes: An Empirical Study of the Australian Consumer's Welfare. *Econ. Rec.*, September 1969, *45*(111), pp. 432–40.

_____ Consumer Demand and Welfare Indexes: A Comparative Study for the United Kingdom and Australia. *Economica, N.S.*, November 1969, *36* (144), pp. 409–25.

_____ Marketing Imperfections and Increasing Returns to Scale in Australian Manufacturing Industry. *Econ. Rec.*, June 1969, *45*(110), pp. 243–50.

_____**; Bennett, J. W. and Graham, K. R.** The Determination of Yields on Corporate Shares: An Empirical Study. *Econ. Rec.*, December 1969, *45* (112), pp. 496–512.

Hoan, Buu. Regionalism: Limitations and Possibilities. *Malayan Econ. Rev.*, October 1969, *14*(2), pp. 18–25.

Hobbet, Richard D. Transitional Mechanisms to Facilitate Tax Reform. *Law Contemp. Probl.*, Autumn 1969, *34*(4), pp. 818–40.

Hobbs, J. A. Trend Projection. **In** *Arnfield, R. V., ed.*, 1969, pp. 231–40.

Hoch, Irving. Anticipated Profit in Cobb-Douglas Models. *Econometrica*, October 1969, *37*(4), pp. 720.

_____ The Three-dimensional City: Contained Urban Space. **In** *Perloff, H. S., ed.*, 1969, pp. 75–135.

Hochman, Harold M. and Rodgers, James D. Pareto Optimal Redistribution. *Amer. Econ. Rev.*, Part I, September 1969, *59*(4), pp. 542–57.

Hodge, Claire C. The Negro Job Situation: Has It Improved? *Mon. Lab. Rev.*, January 1969, *92*(1), pp. 20–28.

Hodges, Dorothy J. A Note on Estimation of Cobb-Douglas and CES Production Function Models. *Econometrica*, October 1969, *37*(4), pp. 721–25.

Hodges, T. Mansel. Early Banking in Cardiff. **In** *Minchinton, W. E., ed.*, 1969, pp. 163–72.

_____ The History of the Newport and Caerleon Savings Bank 1839–88. **In** *Minchinton, W. E., ed.*, 1969, pp. 190–205.

_____ The Peopling of the Hinterland and Port of Cardiff, 1801–1914. **In** *Minchinton, W. E., ed.*, 1969, pp. 3–18.

Hodgman, Donald R. Alternative Measures of the Real Output and Productivity of Commercial Banks: Discussion. **In** *Fuchs, V. R., ed.*, 1969, pp. 189–95.

_____ Bank Holding Companies: Discussion. **In** *Federal Reserve Bank of Chicago (II),* 1969, pp. 99–100.

Hodgson, James D. Federal Regulation of Unions —Impact on Management. **In** *Somers, G. G., ed. (II),* 1969, pp. 292–302.

Hodjera, Zoran. Basic Balances, Short-Term Capital Flow, and International Reserves of Industrial Countries. *Int. Monet. Fund Staff Pap.*, November 1969, *16*(3), pp. 582–612.

Hoenack, Stephen A. and Feldman, Paul. Private Demand for Higher Education in the United States. **In** *the Economics and Financing of Higher Education in the United States, JECP,* 1969, pp. 375–95.

Hofferbert, Richard I. and Sharkansky, Ira. Dimensions of State Politics, Economics, and Public Policy. *Amer. Polit. Sci. Rev.*, September 1969, *63* (3), pp. 867–79.

Hofflander, A. E. and Drandell, Milton. A Linear Programming Model of Profitability, Capacity and Regulation in Insurance Management. *J. Risk Ins.*, March 1969, *36*(1), pp. 41–54.

Hoffman, A. C. The Economic Rationale for Conglomerate Growth from a Management Perspective. **In** *Garoian, L., ed.*, 1969, pp. 57–62.

Hoffman, Fred S. Public Expenditure Analysis and the Institutions of the Executive Branch. **In** *The Analysis and Evaluation of Public Expenditures: The PPB System, Vol. 3, JECP,* 1969, pp. 925–42.

Hoffman, Gerhard. The Austrian Cartel Law: Principles and Background. *Antitrust Bull.*, Spring 1969, *14,* pp. 249–78.

Hoffman, L. Richard. Commitment and Conflict in Group Problem Solving. **In** *Association of Canadian Schools of Business,* 1969, pp. 5–21.

Hoffman, Richard B. Round Table on Allocation of Resources in Law Enforcement. *Amer. Econ. Rev.*, May 1969, *59*(2), pp. 510–12.

Hoffman, Ronald F. A Systematic Approach to a Practicable Plan for State Aid to Local Governments. *Public Finance,* 1969, *24*(1), pp. 1–32.

Hoffman, Wayne L. and Brunn, Stanley D. The Geography of Federal Grants-in-Aid to States. *Econ. Geogr.*, July 1969, *45*(3), pp. 226–38.

Hoffmann, Walther G. Der tertiäre Sektor im Wachstumsprozess. (The Service Sector in the Growth Process. With English summary.) *Jahr. Nationalökon. Statist.*, June 1969, *183*(1), pp. 1–29.

_____ Die Entwicklung der Sparkassen im Rahmen des Wachatums der deutschen Wirtschaft (1850–1967). (With English summary.) *Z. ges. Staatswiss.*, October 1969, *125*(4), pp. 561–605.

——— Die "Phillips-Kurve" in Deutschland. (With English summary.) *Kyklos,* 1969, *22*(2), pp. 219–31.

——— The Share of Defence Expenditure in Gross National Product (GNP)—An International and Diachronic Comparison. *Ger. Econ. Rev.,* 1969, *7* (4), pp. 295–307.

——— The Take-off in Germany. **In** *Scoville, W. C. and La Force, J. C., eds., Vol. IV,* 1969, pp. 75–96.

Hogan, Timothy D. and Bailey, Duncan M. Future Growth Patterns in South Africa. *S. Afr. J. Econ.,* September 1969, *37*(3), pp. 237–51.

Hogan, W. P. Economic Effects of the Australian Protection System. *Econ. Rec.,* December 1969, *45*(112), pp. 513–25.

——— Some New Results in the Measurement of Capacity Utilization. *Amer. Econ. Rev.,* March 1969, *59*(1), pp. 183–84.

Hogan, William T. Statement. **In** *Proposed Extension of the Surcharge and Repeal of the Investment Tax Credit, SCH,* 1969, pp. 390–404.

Hoggatt, A. C. Response of Paid Student Subjects to Differential Behaviour of Robots in Bifurcated Duopoly Games. *Rev. Econ. Stud.,* October 1969, *36*(108), pp. 417–32.

Holbik, Karel. An Economic Profile of Eastern Europe. **In** *Grub, P. D. and Holbik, K.,* 1969, pp. 140–47.

——— Development Banks: A Catalyst for Economic Progress. *Rivista Int. Sci. Econ. Com.,* November 1969, *16*(11), pp. 1053–73.

——— United States Balance of Payments Deficit and Monetary Policy. *Weltwirtsch. Arch.,* 1969, *103*(1), pp. 160–80.

Hold, William T. A Review Article on Basic Protection for the Traffic Victim: Comment. *J. Risk Ins.,* June 1969, *36*(2), pp. 310–13.

Holden, Kenneth. An Examination of Revisions to Selected Components of National Income. *Bull. Oxford Univ. Inst. Econ. Statist.,* May 1969, *31*(2), pp. 133–38.

——— The Effect of Revisions to Data on Two Econometric Studies. *Manchester Sch. Econ. Soc. Stud.,* March 1969, *37*(1), pp. 23–37.

Hole, Peter C. and Kay, John A. The Fund Meeting. *Finance Develop.,* December 1969, *6*(4), pp. 10–14.

Holland, Daniel M. Pension Fund Growth and Its Economic Implications. **In** *Tax Institute of America,* 1969, pp. 3–33.

——— A Study of Land Taxation in Jamaica. **In** *Becker, A. P., ed.,* 1969, pp. 239–86.

——— **and Vaughn, William M.** An Evaluation of Self-Assessment under a Property Tax. **In** *Lynn, A. D., Jr., ed.,* 1969, pp. 79–118.

Holland, David; Giddings, Marvin and Hartman, L. M. Effects of Hurricane Storms on Agriculture. *Water Resources Res.,* June 1969, *5*(3), pp. 555–62.

Holland, John L. and Baird, Leonard L. The Flow of High School Students to Schools, Colleges, and Jobs: A Re-examination of Some Old Questions by the Use of Multiple Indices of Talent. *J. Human Res.,* Winter 1969, *4*(1), pp. 22–37.

Holland, Thomas E. 'Operation Twist' and the Movement of Interest Rates and Related Economic Time Series. *Int. Econ. Rev.,* October 1969, *10*(3), pp. 260–65.

Holländer, Heinz. Eine einfache Begründung zur langfristigen Harrod-Neutralität des technischen Fortschritts. (With English summary.) *Z. ges. Staatswiss.,* April 1969, *125*(2), pp. 236–42.

Hollander, S. Classical Economic Views of the Role of the State in Victorian Education: Comment. *Southern Econ. J.,* April 1969, *35*(4), pp. 378.

——— Malthus and the Post-Napoleonic Depression. *Hist. Polit. Econ.,* Fall 1969, *1*(2), pp. 306–35.

Hollenhorst, Jerry. Alternative Uses and Yields of Idle Public Funds: Comment. *Nat. Tax J.,* December 1969, *22*(4), pp. 557–58.

Hollerman, Leon. Recent Difficulties in Japan's Economic Development. *Banca Naz. Lavoro Quart. Rev.,* March 1969, (88), pp. 66–90.

Hollinger, L. S. Changing Rules of the Budget Game: The Development of a Planning-Programing-Budgeting-System for Los Angeles County. **In** *Innovations in Planning, Programming, and Budgeting in State and Local Governments, JECP,* 1969, pp. 75–90.

Hollister, Robinson G. Manpower Problems and Policies in Sub-Saharan Africa. *Int. Lab. Rev.,* May 1969, *99*(5), pp. 515–32.

——— **and Cain, Glen G.** Evaluating Manpower Programs for the Disadvantaged. **In** *Somers, G. G. and Wood, W. D., eds.,* 1969, pp. 119–51.

Hollomon, J. Herbert. Keeping the Economy Strong, 1963. **In** *Pursell, C. W., Jr.,* 1969, pp. 424–30.

Holmes, Alan R. Operational Constraints on the Stabilization of Money Supply Growth. **In** *Federal Reserve Bank of Boston,* 1969, pp. 65–77.

Holmes, John H. A Note on the Product-Adoption Process. *Ohio State U. Bull. Bus. Res.,* July 1969, *44*(7), pp. 1–3, 5.

Holmes, O. Wendell. The Farm Poor: Counted, Miscounted, or Discounted? *Amer. J. Agr. Econ.,* December 1969, *51*(5), pp. 1557–60.

Holt, Charles C. Improving the Labor Market Trade-Off between Inflation and Unemployment. *Amer. Econ. Rev.,* May 1969, *59*(2), pp. 135–46.

Holt, W. Stull. Some Consequences of the Urban Movement in American History. **In** *Callow, A. B., Jr., ed.,* 1969, pp. 41–52.

Holtmann, A. G. Correction to Migration to the Suburbs, Human Capital and City Income Tax Losses: A Case Study. *Nat. Tax J.,* September 1969, *22*(3), pp. 424.

——— Teacher Salaries and the Economic Benefits of Search. *J. Human Res.,* Winter 1969, *4*(1), pp. 99–103.

Holzheu, Franz. Regionales Wachstum und interregionale Kapitalbewegungen. (With English summary.) *Kyklos,* 1969, *22*(3), pp. 417–53.

Holzman, Franklyn D. Comparison of Different Forms of Trade Barriers. *Rev. Econ. Statist.,* May 1969, *51*(2), pp. 159–65.

——— Import Bottlenecks and the Foreign Trade Multiplier. *Western Econ. J.,* June 1969, *7*(2), pp. 101–08.

Homan, Paul T. Statement. **In** *Governmental Intervention in the Market Mechanism, Pt. 1, SCH,* 1969, pp. 103–31.

Honavar, R. M. Debt-Servicing as an Aid to Promotion of Trade of Developing Countries: Comment. *Oxford Econ. Pap.*, November 1969, *21*(3), pp. 416–19.

Hong, Wontack. A Global Equilibrium Pattern of Specialization: A Model to Approximate Linder's World of Production and Trade. *Swedish J. Econ.*, December 1969, *71*(4), pp. 275–83.

Honjo, Masahiko and Umezawa, Tadashi. Company Housing in Japan. *Int. Lab. Rev.*, June 1969, *99*(6), pp. 579–87.

Honko, Jaakko. Some Basic Problems and Future Trends in Management. *Liiketaloudellinen Aikak.*, 1969, *18*(2), pp. 145–52.

Hoos, Sidney. Joint Decision-making Processes in Present-Day Agriculture. **In** *Papi, U. and Nunn, C., eds.*, 1969, pp. 379–89.

Hooven, Eckart. La concorrenza fra aziende di credito per la raccolta dei depositi. (Competition for Deposits. With English summary.) *Bancaria*, August 1969, *25*(8), pp. 954–62.

Hopkin, John A. and Baker, C. B. Concepts of Finance Capital for a Capital-Using Agriculture. *Amer. J. Agr. Econ.*, December 1969, *51*(5), pp. 1055–64.

Hopkins, Terence K. Third World Modernization in Transnational Perspective. *Ann. Amer. Acad. Polit. Soc. Sci.*, November 1969, *386*, pp. 126–36.

Horn, Johan. Nationalism versus Internationalism in Shipping. *J. Transp. Econ. Policy*, September 1969, *3*(3), pp. 245–50.

Horngren, Charles T. Capacity Utilization and the Efficiency Variance. *Accounting Rev.*, January 1969, *44*(1), pp. 86–89.

Horowitz, Ann and Horowitz, Ira. Concentration, Competition, and Mergers in Brewing. **In** *Weston, J. F. and Peltzman, S., eds.*, 1969, pp. 45–56.

Horowitz, Ira. The Price-Quoter under Risk. *Western Econ. J.*, June 1969, *7*(2), pp. 129–36.

______ **and Horowitz, Ann.** Concentration, Competition, and Mergers in Brewing. **In** *Weston, J. F. and Peltzman, S., eds.*, 1969, pp. 45–56.

Horowitz, Irving Louis. Engineering and Sociological Perspectives on Development: Interdisciplinary Constraints in Social Forecasting. *Int. Soc. Sci. J.*, 1969, *21*(4), pp. 545–56.

Horsefield, J. Keith. The Fund's Charges. *Finance Develop.*, September 1969, *6*(3), pp. 19–23.

______ The Fund's Compensatory Financing. *Finance Develop.*, December 1969, *6*(4), pp. 34–37.

Horsnell, Gareth. A Theory of Consumer Behaviour Derived from Repeat Paired Preference Testing. *J. Roy. Statist. Soc.*, Part 2, 1969, *132*, pp. 164–84.

Horton, Joseph J., Jr. Is There a Money Supply Function? *Quart. Rev. Econ. Bus.*, Summer 1969, *9*(2), pp. 67–70.

Horton, Robert A. Planning, Programing, and Budgeting in Metropolitan Nashville-Davidson County, Tennessee. **In** *Innovations in Planning, Programming, and Budgeting in State and Local Governments, JECP*, 1969, pp. 91–103.

Horvath, Janos. A Note on Economic Trends in Indonesia. *Polit. Sci. Quart.*, December 1969, *84*(4), pp. 638–42.

Horvitz, D. G. and Koch, Gary G. The Effect of Response Errors on Measures of Association. **In** *Johnson, N. L. and Smith, H., Jr., eds.*, 1969, pp. 247–81.

Horvitz, Paul M. Topics in Bank Capital: Comment. **In** *Federal Reserve Bank of Chicago (I)*, 1969, pp. 112–14.

______ **and Shull, Bernard.** Branch Banking, Independent Banks and Geographic Price Discrimination. *Antitrust Bull.*, Winter 1969, *14*, pp. 827–44.

Horvitz, Wayne L. The ILWU-PMA Mechanization and Modernization Agreement. **In** *Somers, G. G., ed. (II)*, 1969, pp. 144–51.

Horwich, George. A Framework for Monetary Policy. **In** *Brunner, K., ed.*, 1969, pp. 124–64.

Hoskins, Josiah and Shuffett, Milton. Capitalization of Burley Tobacco Allotment Rights into Farmland Values. *Amer. J. Agr. Econ.*, May 1969, *51*(2), pp. 471–74.

Hosomatsu, Yasu. A Note on the Stability Conditions in Cournot's Dynamic Market Solution when neither the Actual Market Demand Function nor the Production Levels of Rivals Are Known. *Rev. Econ. Stud.*, January 1969, *36*(105), pp. 117–22.

Hotelling, Harold. A General Mathematical Theory of Depreciation. **In** *Parker, R. H. and Harcourt, G. C., eds.*, 1969, pp. 261–75.

______ The General Welfare in Relation to Problems of Taxation and of Railway and Utility Rates. **In** *Arrow, K. J. and Scitovsky, T., eds.*, 1969, pp. 284–308.

Houck, James P. and Subotnik, Abraham. The U.S. Supply of Soybeans: Regional Acreage Functions. *Agr. Econ. Res.*, October 1969, *21*(4), pp. 99–108.

Houff, James N. Area Wages and Living Costs. *Mon. Lab. Rev.*, March 1969, *92*(3), pp. 43–46.

Houghton, Harrison F. Statement. **In** *Bank Holding Company Act Amendments, Pts. 1–3, HCH*, 1969, pp. 350–53.

Houssiaux, J. R. Annexes I, II, III to Statement. **In** *Economic Concentration, Pt. 7A, SCH*, 1969, pp. 3957–96.

______ Consistency of Action: The Compatibility of Decision-taking by Private and Public Enterprises. **In** *Margolis, J. and Guitton, H., eds.*, 1969, pp. 424–61.

Houston, William S., Jr. A Model for Working Capital Management: Comment. *Miss. Val. J. Bus. Econ.*, Spring 1969, *4*(2), pp. 89–95.

Houthakker, Hendrik S. The Causes of the Farm Problem. **In** *Starleaf, D. R., ed.*, 1969, pp. 164–68.

______ **and Magee, Stephen P.** Income and Price Elasticities in World Trade. *Rev. Econ. Statist.*, May 1969, *51*(2), pp. 111–25.

Hovmark, Bertil; Lindgren, Ingvar and Carlsson, Mårten. Recent Developments in Farm Planning: 1: A Monte Carlo Method for the Study of Farm Planning Problems. *Rev. Marketing Agr. Econ.*, June 1969, *37*(2), pp. 80–103.

Howard, Dick. On Deforming Marx: The French Translation of *Grundrisse. Sci. Soc.*, Summer-Fall 1969, *33*(3), pp. 358–65.

______ The Regional Development Commission—A Second Look at a New Concept. *Univ. Missouri Bus. Govt. Rev.*, July–August 1969, *10*(4), pp. 27–35.

Howard, Nigel. Least Squares Classification and

Tax Collection Practices in Certain Countries. *Bull. Int. Fiscal Doc.*, November 1969, *23*(11), pp. 516–20.

Huizer, Gerrit. Community Development, Land Reform, and Political Participation: Preliminary Observations on Some Cases in Latin America. *Amer. J. Econ. Soc.*, April 1969, *28*(2), pp. 159–78.

Hujer, Reinhard; Ipsen, Dirk and Kade, Gerhard. Kybernetik und Wirtschaftsplanung. (With English summary.) *Z. ges. Staatswiss.*, January 1969, *125*(1), pp. 17–55.

Hůla, Václav. This Is No Time for a Comfortable Plan. *New Trends Czech. Econ.*, December 1969, (8), pp. 45–60.

Hume, D. Of the Balance of Trade. **In** *Cooper, R. N., ed.*, 1969, pp. 25–37.

Hume, L. J. Myrdal on Jeremy Bentham: Laissez-Faire and Harmony of Interests. *Economica, N.S.*, August 1969, *36*(143), pp. 295–303.

Humphrey, David B. Changes in Protection and Inflation in Argentina, 1953–1966. *Oxford Econ. Pap.*, July 1969, *21*(2), pp. 196–219.

——— Measuring the Effective Rate of Protection: Direct and Indirect Effects. *J. Polit. Econ.*, September/October 1969, *77*(5), pp. 834–44.

Humphrey, Kenneth R. Retail Trade in Indiana and Surrounding States. *Indiana Bus. Rev.*, November/December 1969, *44*, pp. 11–15.

Hunt, E. H. Labour Productivity in English Agriculture, 1850–1914: Rejoinder. *Econ. Hist. Rev.*, April 1969, *22*(1), pp. 118–19.

Hunter, Alex. The Measurement of Monopoly Power. **In** *Hunter, A., ed.*, 1969, pp. 92–121.

——— Mergers and Industry Concentration in Britain. *Banca Naz. Lavoro Quart. Rev.*, December 1969, (91), pp. 372–94.

——— Welfare Analysis and Monopoly. **In** *Hunter, A., ed.*, 1969, pp. 30–39.

Hunter, Guy. Istituzioni e sviluppo economico. (Economic Institutions and Development. With English summary.) *Mondo Aperto*, February 1969, *23* (1), pp. 1–9.

Hunter, J. B. K. The Development of the Labour Market in Kenya. **In** *Stewart, I. G., ed.*, 1969, pp. 115–37.

Hunter, J. S. and Naylor, Thomas H. Experimental Designs. **In** *Naylor, T. H., ed.*, 1969, pp. 39–58.

Hunter, J. S. H. The Roosa Doctrine and the Shiftability Thesis: Application to Debt Management in the United States. *Weltwirtsch. Arch.*, 1969, *103* (1), pp. 110–30.

Hunter, Maxwell W., II. Are Technological Upheavals Inevitable? *Harvard Bus. Rev.*, September–October 1969, *47*(5), pp. 73–83.

Hunter, William G.; Tierney, David E. and Draper, Norman R. Analyzing Paired Comparison Tests. *J. Marketing Res.*, November 1969, *6*(4), pp. 477–80.

Huntrakoon, Yune and Yossundara, Suparb. Some Salient Aspects of Thailand's Trade, 1955–64. **In** *Morgan, T. and Spoelstra, N., eds.*, 1969, pp. 127–50.

Huntsman, Blaine. Asset Management and Monetary Policy: Discussion. *J. Finance*, May 1969, *24* (2), pp. 239–41.

Hurd, G. E. and Johnson, T. J. Sociology in the Third World Situation. *Int. Soc. Sci. J.*, 1969, *21*(3), pp. 421–27.

Hurd, Lorne. Agricultural Policy in a Dynamic Economy: Symposium. *Can. J. Agr. Econ.*, November 1969, *17*(3), pp. 42–46.

Hurnanen, R.; Devine, G. and Hawkins, Murray H. Industrial Organization and Policy Development in a Dynamic World. *Can. J. Agr. Econ.*, July 1969, *17*(2), pp. 106–17.

Hurtubise, Jules R. and Officer, Lawrence H. Price Effects of the Kennedy Round on Canadian Trade. *Rev. Econ. Statist.*, August 1969, *51*(3), pp. 320–33.

Hurwicz, Leonid. On the Concept and Possibility of Informational Decentralization. *Amer. Econ. Rev.*, May 1969, *59*(2), pp. 513–24.

——— Optimality and Informational Efficiency in Resource Allocation Processes. **In** *Arrow, K. J. and Scitovsky, T., eds.*, 1969, pp. 61–80.

Husain, I. Z. Unemployment Implications of Population Growth in India. **In** *Bhuleshkar, A. V., ed.*, 1969, pp. 88–102.

Husén, Torsten. Some Views of Cross-National Assessment of the "Quality of Education." **In** *[Edding, Friedrich]*, 1969, pp. 87–95.

Husni, Muhd. The New System of Collecting Income Tax, Property Tax and Company Tax in Indonesia. *Bull. Int. Fiscal Doc.*, April 1969, *23* (4), pp. 151–59.

Hussain, Ashiq and Wallace, T. D. The Use of Error Components Models in Combining Cross Section with Time Series Data. *Econometrica*, January 1969, *37*(1), pp. 55–72.

Hussain, I. Z. Returns Approach to Educational Planning. **In** *Pandit, H. N., ed.*, 1969, pp. 280–93.

Hussain, Sayed Mushtaq. The Effect of the Growing Constraint of Subsistence Farming on Farmer Response to Price: A Case Study of Jute in Pakistan. *Pakistan Develop. Rev.*, Autumn 1969, *9*(3), pp. 235–72.

Hutcheson, Thomas L. Factor Intensity and the CES Production Function. *Rev. Econ. Statist.*, November 1969, *51*(4), pp. 468–70.

Hutchings, Raymond. Periodic Fluctuation in Soviet Industrial Growth Rates. *Soviet Stud.*, January 1969, *20*(3), pp. 331–52.

Hutchinson, John. The Anatomy of Corruption in Trade Unions. *Ind. Relat.*, February 1969, *8*(2), pp. 135–50.

——— Hoffa. *Calif. Manage. Rev.*, Summer 1969, *11* (4), pp. 79–88.

Hutchinson, T. W. Economists and Economic Policy in Britain after 1870. *Hist. Polit. Econ.*, Fall 1969, *1*(2), pp. 231–55.

Hutton J. P. Measuring Efficiency in Government Services. **In** *Peacock, A. T., ed.*, 1969, pp. 91–103.

Huzel, James P. Malthus, the Poor Law, and Population in Early Nineteenth-Century England. *Econ. Hist. Rev.*, December 1969, *22*(3), pp. 430–52.

Hymer, Stephen H. and Berry, R. Albert. A Note on the Capacity to Transform and the Welfare Costs of Foreign Trade Fluctuations. *Econ. J.*, December 1969, *79*(316), pp. 833–46.

——— **and Resnick, S.** Interactions between the Government and the Private Sector: An Analysis of Government Expenditure Policy and the Reflection Ratio. In *Stewart, I. G., ed.,* 1969, pp. 155–80.

_____ and **Resnick, Stephen.** A Model of an Agrarian Economy with Nonagricultural Activities. *Amer. Econ. Rev.,* Part I, September 1969, *59* (4), pp. 493–506.

Ichiishi, T. Directly Additive Utility and Constant Marginal Budget Shares. *Rev. Econ. Stud.,* April 1969, *36*(106), pp. 251–56.

Ide, Yoshinori. Administrative Reform and Innovation: The Japanese Case. *Int. Soc. Sci. J.,* 1969, *21* (1), pp. 56–67.

Idenburg, Philip J. Europe—In Search of New Forms of Education. In *Bereday, G. Z. F., ed.,* 1969, pp. 277–96.

Ihara, Takeo and Yamada, Hiroyuki. An Interindustrial Analysis of the Transportation Sector. *Kyoto Univ. Econ. Rev.,* October 1969, *39*(2), pp. 26–61.

Ijiri, Yuji and Kaplan, Robert S. Probabilistic Depreciation and Its Implications for Group Depreciation. *Accounting Rev.,* October 1969, *44*(4), pp. 743–56.

Ikema, Makoto. The Effect of Economic Growth on the Demand for Imports: A Simple Diagram. *Oxford Econ. Pap.,* March 1969, *21*(1), pp. 66–69.

Ikerd, John E. and Schupp, Alvin R. A Decision Model for Continuous Sequence Production Processes of Variable Length: An Application to Hog Marketing. *Amer. J. Agr. Econ.,* December 1969, *51*(5), pp. 1159–63.

Il, Lee Hee. Project Selection and Evaluation: Formulation of an Investment Program. In *Adelman, I., ed.,* 1969, pp. 241–56.

Il'in, V. and Koriagin, B. The Sale of Goods to the Public on Credit. *Prob. Econ.,* December 1969, *12* (8), pp. 68–74.

Illsley, R. The Economic and Political Consequences of Selective Migrations from One Country to Another: Comment. In *Bechhofer, F., ed.,* 1969, pp. 57–62.

Iloniemi, Jaakko. Miksi kehitysmaat eivät kehity: kasvun teoria ja todellisuus: Reunamerkintöjä Pentti Pajusen mietteisiin Myrdalin "Aasian Draaman" johdosta. (With English summary.) *Kansant. Aikak.,* 1969, *65*(1), pp. 57–62.

Imdieke, Leroy F. and Weygandt, Jerry J. Classification of Convertible Debt. *Accounting Rev.,* October 1969, *44*(4), pp. 798–805.

Inada, Ken-Ichi. Endogenous Technical Progress and Steady Growth. *Rev. Econ. Stud.,* January 1969, *36*(105), pp. 99–107.

_____ Fixed Factor Coefficients and Harrod-Neutral Technical Progress. *Rev. Econ. Stud.,* January 1969, *36*(105), pp. 89–97.

_____ The Simple Majority Decision Rule. *Econometrica,* July 1969, *37*(3), pp. 490–506.

_____ and **Kemp, Murray C.** International Capital Movements and the Theory of Tariffs and Trade: Comment. *Quart. J. Econ.,* August 1969, *83*(3), pp. 524–28.

Inagaki, M. Efficient, Inefficient, and Critical Growth. In *[Tinbergen, J.],* 1969, pp. 29–42.

Inalcik, Halil. Capital Formation in the Ottoman Empire. *J. Econ. Hist.,* March 1969, *29*(1), pp. 97–140.

Indik, Bernard and Sternlieb, George. Housing Vacancy Analysis. *Land Econ.,* February 1969, *45* (1), pp. 117–21.

Ingram, J. C. Some Implications of Puerto Rican Experience. In *Cooper, R. N., ed.,* 1969, pp. 87–104.

Inosov, V. L. and Sviatskaia, N. V. Some Problems in Optimal Inventory Control. *Matekon,* Fall 1969, *6*(1), pp. 44–56.

Institute of Econ., Acad. of Sci. Optimal Sizes for Enterprises. In *Economic Concentration, Pt. 7A, SCH,* 1969, pp. 4362–66.

Ionescu, Constantin. Retrospectivă şi perspectivă în statistica românească în cel de-al XXV-lea an de la eliberarea patriei. (Retrospection and Prospects in Romanian Statistics in the XXVth Year Since the Eliberation of Romania. With English summary.) *Stud. Cercet. Econ.,* 1969, *3,* pp. 43–49.

Ipsen, Dirk; Kade, Gerhard and Hujer, Reinhard. Kybernetik und Wirtschaftsplanung. (With English summary.) *Z. ges. Staatswiss.,* January 1969, *125*(1), pp. 17–55.

Irelan, Lola M. and Besner, Arthur. Low-Income Life Styles. In *Sturdivant, F. D., ed.,* 1969, pp. 17–26.

Ireland, Thomas R. The Calculus of Philanthropy. *Public Choice,* Fall 1969, *7,* pp. 23–31.

Ireri, Dunstan. A Proposed Model to Analyze Economic Interdependence among the Member Countries of the East African Community. *East Afr. Econ. Rev.,* December 1969, *1*(2), pp. 75–85.

Irwin, Manley R. The Computer Utility: Market Entry in Search of Public Policy. *J. Ind. Econ.,* July 1969, *17*(3), pp. 239–52.

_____ Computers and Communications: The Economics of Interdependence. *Law Contemp. Probl.,* Spring 1969, *34*(2), pp. 360–68.

Isaac, J. E. Compulsory Arbitration: National Wage Policy. In *Preston, R., ed.,* 1969, pp. 173–95.

Isard, Walter. Toward a More Adequate General Regional Theory and Approach to Conflict Resolution. *Peace Res. Soc. Internat. Pap.,* 1969, *11,* pp. 1–21.

Isenson, Raymond S. Project Hindsight: An Empirical Study of the Sources of Ideas Utilized in Operational Weapon Systems. In *Gruber, W. H. and Marquis, D. G., eds.,* 1969, pp. 155–76.

Işfănescu, A. and Mărgulescu, D. Rentabilitatea ca indicator de sinteză economică. (Profitableness as an Indicator of Economic Synthesis. With English summary.) *Stud. Cercet. Econ.,* 1969, *4,* pp. 173–83.

Islam, Nurul. Comment on Part I: The Context of Economic Cooperation. In *Morgan, T. and Spoelstra, N., eds.,* 1969, pp. 59–61.

_____ Export Incentive and Effective Subsidy in Pakistan: An Evaluation. *Bull. Oxford Univ. Inst. Econ. Statist.,* August 1969, *31*(3), pp. 169–88.

_____ Export Policy in Pakistan. In *[Tinbergen, J.],* 1969, pp. 219–43.

_____ Tariff Protection, Comparative Costs, and Industrialization in Pakistan. In *Morgan, T. and Spoelstra, N., eds.,* 1969, pp. 65–95.

Ismail, A. Halim. Some Considerations Regarding the Optimum Ages for Replanting Rubber Trees on Smallholdings in Malaya. *Malayan Econ. Rev.,* October 1969, *14*(2), pp. 55–78.

Isomura, Eiichi. The Urban Crisis in Japan. In *Panel on Science and Technology: Science and Technology and the Cities, HCH,* 1969, pp. 157–62.

Ițicovici, I. Mecanismul pieței și sistemul indicatorilor de plan ai întreprinderilor industriale. (Mechanism of the Market and the System of Plan Indicators of Industrial Enterprises. With English summary.) *Stud. Cercet. Econ.,* 1969, *1-2,* pp. 37–44.

Ivancevich, John M. A Study of American Expatriate On-the-Job Performance Failures. *Univ. Wash. Bus. Rev.,* Winter 1969, *28*(2), pp. 42–49.

Ivanciu-Văleanu, Nicolae. Democratismul revoluționar în opera lui Nicolae Bălcescu. (Revolutionary Democratism in Nicolae Bălcescu's Work. With English summary.) *Stud. Cercet. Econ.,* 1969, *1-2,* pp. 183–93.

Ivănescu, I.; Biji, El. and Biji, Mircea. Preocupări actuale în statistica social-economică. (Present Preoccupations in Socio-Economical Statistics. With English summary.) *Stud. Cercet. Econ.,* 1969, *1-2,* pp. 121–28.

Ivan'kov, M. Wages of Collective Farm Managerial Personnel and Specialists and the Matter of Increasing the Effectiveness of Production. *Prob. Econ.,* July 1969, *12*(3), pp. 58–82.

Iwand, Thomas and Cramer, Joe J., Jr. Financial Reporting for Conglomerates: An Economic Analysis. *Calif. Manage. Rev.,* Spring 1969, *11*(3), pp. 25–34.

Iyengar, S. Kesava. The Co-operative Caravan: A Casual Causerie. *Asian Econ. Rev.,* August 1969, *11*(4), pp. 363–404.

——— The International Financial Imbroglio: The Indian Quandry. *Asian Econ. Rev.,* February 1969, *11*(2), pp. 173–200.

Iyengar, Sampath S. Multiplier Analysis for India. *Indian Econ. J.,* April–June 1969, *16*(4–5), pp. 478–87.

Jääskeläinen, Veikko. A Goal Programming Model of Aggregate Production Planning. *Swedish J. Econ.,* March 1969, *71*(1), pp. 14–29.

——— Traditional and Ex Post Variance Analysis: A Reconciliation. *Liiketaloudellinen Aikak.,* 1969, *18*(2), pp. 153–70.

Jackman, Patrick C. Unit Labor Costs of Iron and Steel Industries in Five Countries. *Mon. Lab. Rev.,* August 1969, *92*(8), pp. 15–22.

Jackson. Equilibrium Results for Queueing Processes with Both Erlang Input and Service Time Distribution with More Than One Server. *Ekon.-Mat. Obzor,* 1969, *5*(2), pp. 172–85.

Jackson, Andrew. The Position of Condillac in the History of Economic Thought. *Indian Econ. J.,* January–March 1969, *16*(3), pp. 312–26.

Jackson, G. H.; Sweeny, K. M. and Norton, W. E. A Demand Equation for Imports. *Econ. Rec.,* December 1969, *45*(112), pp. 589–95.

Jackson, Raymond. Regulation and Electric Utility Rate Levels. *Land Econ.,* August 1969, *45*(3), pp. 372–76.

Jackson, Samuel C. A New Center for Dispute Settlement. *Mon. Lab. Rev.,* January 1969, *92*(1), pp. 10.

——— Statement. In *Tax Credits to Stimulate Job Opportunities in Rural Areas, SCH,* 1969, pp. 177–82.

Jacobs, Donald. The Framework of Commercial Bank Regulation: An Appraisal. In *Jessup, P. F.,* 1969, pp. 402–21.

Jacobs, Jane. Strategies for Helping Cities. *Amer. Econ. Rev.,* Part I, September 1969, *59*(4), pp. 652–56.

Jacobs, Paul. Old before Its Time: Collective Bargaining at 28. In *Wortman, M. S., Jr.,* 1969, pp. 60–65.

Jacobs, Philip. Mr. Sunga's Treatment: A Fly in the Ointment. *Rev. Income Wealth,* September 1969, *15*(3), pp. 285–87.

Jacobson, Robert E. Criteria for Defining Federal Milk Order Market Areas. *Amer. J. Agr. Econ.,* December 1969, *51*(5), pp. 1138–42.

Jacobsson, Lars and Lindbeck, Assar. Labor Market Condition, Wages and Inflation—Swedish Experiences 1955–67. *Swedish J. Econ.,* June 1969, *71* (2), pp. 64–103.

Jacoby, Henry D. and Dorfman, Robert. A Model of Public Decisions Illustrated by a Water Pollution Policy Problem. In *The Analysis and Evaluation of Public Expenditures: The PPB System, Vol. 1, JECP,* 1969, pp. 226–74.

Jacoby, Neil H. Statement. In *Role of Giant Corporations, Pt. 1, SCH,* 1969, pp. 502–13.

Jaffe, A. J. Statement. In *Economics of Aging: Toward a Full Share in Abundance, Pt. 2, SCH,* 1969, pp. 388–409.

Jaffé, William. A. N. Isnard, Progenitor of the Walrasian General Equilibrium Model. *Hist. Polit. Econ.,* Spring 1969, *1*(1), pp. 19–43.

Jaffee, Dwight M. and Modigliani, Franco. A Theory and Test of Credit Rationing. *Amer. Econ. Rev.,* December 1969, *59*(5), pp. 850–72.

Jägerhorn, Reginald. Perspektiv på högskoleutbildning av redovisare. (Perspective on College Training of Accounts. With English summary.) *Econ. Samfundets Tidskr.,* 1969, *22*(3), pp. 181–88.

Jalan, Bimal. Gains to Donor Countries from Tied Aid. *Finance Develop.,* September 1969, *6*(3), pp. 14–18.

Jalas, Kari. Mitä kasvua ajetaan takaa? (What Kind of Growth Are We Pursuing? With English summary.) *Kansant. Aikak.,* 1969, *65*(3), pp. 224–25.

James, Estelle. On the Social Rate of Discount: Comment. *Amer. Econ. Rev.,* December 1969, *59*(5), pp. 912–16.

James, I. C., II; Bower, B. T. and Matalas, N. C. Relative Importance of Variables in Water Resources Planning. *Water Resources Res.,* December 1969, *5*(6), pp. 1165–73.

Jamison, Harold B. On "Disguised Conservatism in Evolutionary Development Theory": Comment. *Sci. Soc.,* Summer-Fall 1969, *33*(3), pp. 348–53.

Jansen, F. P. and Janssen, L. H. Imports from Developing Countries: A Comparison between EEC, EFTA and USA. In *[Tinbergen, J.],* 1969, pp. 129–56.

Janson, Carl-Gunnar. Some Problems of Ecological Factor Analysis. In *Dogan, M. and Rokkan, S., eds.,* 1969, pp. 301–41.

Janssen, L. H. and Jansen, F. P. Imports from Developing Countries: A Comparison between EEC, EFTA and USA. In *[Tinbergen, J.]*, 1969, pp. 129–56.

Jansson, Jan Owen. Optimal Congestion Tolls for Car Commuters: A Note on Current Theory. *J. Transp. Econ. Policy*, September 1969, *3*(3), pp. 300–305.

Jantscher, Gerald R. Death and Gift Taxation in the United States after the Report of the Royal Commission. *Nat. Tax J.*, March 1969, *22*(1), pp. 121–38.

Janus, Arnošt and Krajčovič, Josef. The First State Budget of Slovakia, and Problems of Its Fulfillment. *New Trends Czech. Econ.*, November 1969, (7), pp. 80–94.

Jap, K. S. The Concept of Delivery of Goods by a Manufacturer under the Indonesian Sales Tax Act (1951–1968). *Bull. Int. Fiscal Doc.*, May 1969, *23* (5), pp. 223–28.

Je, Kim Mahn and Adelman, Irma. An Econometric Model of the Korean Economy (1956–66). **In** *Adelman, I., ed.*, 1969, pp. 77–108.

Jean, William H. On Multiple Rates of Return: Reply. *J. Finance*, March 1969, *24*(1), pp. 99–100.

Jeanteur, Robert. La mercatistica nell'era dell'informatica. (Marketing in the Age of Information Theory. With English summary.) *L'Impresa*, July-/October 1969, *11*(4–5), pp. 347–51.

Jeffers, James R. and Kwon, Jene. A Portfolio Approach to Corporate Demands for Government Securities. *J. Finance*, December 1969, *24*(5), pp. 905–19.

Jeffrey, D.; Casetti, E. and King, L. Economic Fluctuations in a Multiregional Setting: A Bi-factor Analytic Approach. *J. Reg. Sci.*, December 1969, *9*(3), pp. 397–404.

Jen, Frank C. Problems and Progress in the Applications of Recent Developments in the Theory of Finance: Discussion. *J. Finance*, May 1969, *24*(2), pp. 342–44.

______ **and Southwick, Lawrence, Jr.** Implications of Dynamic Monopoly Behavior. *Amer. Econ. Rev.*, March 1969, *59*(1), pp. 149–58.

Jeníček, Vladimír and Havlíček, Jaromír. Estimates of Long-term Development of Agriculture by Means of the Global Factorial Model: Reply. *Czech. Econ. Pap.*, 1969, (11), pp. 109–111.

______ **and Havlíček, Jaromír.** Model of the Long-term Development of Czechoslovak Agriculture. *Czech. Econ. Pap.*, 1969, (11), pp. 83–102.

Jenness, Robert A. Manpower Mobility Programs. **In** *Somers, G. G. and Wood, W. D., eds.*, 1969, pp. 184–220.

Jenny, Hans H. and Wynn, G. Richard. Expenditure Expectations for Private Colleges. **In** *the Economics and Financing of Higher Education in the United States, JECP*, 1969, pp. 440–64.

______ Short-Run Cost Variations in Institutions of Higher Learning. **In** *the Economics and Financing of Higher Education in the United States, JECP*, 1969, pp. 261–94.

Jensen, Michael C. Risk, The Pricing of Capital Assets, and the Evaluation of Investment Portfolios. *J. Bus.*, April 1969, *42*(2), pp. 167–247.

Jensen, Robert G. and Karaska, Gerald J. The Mathematical Thrust in Soviet Economic Geography—Its Nature and Significance. *J. Reg. Sci.*, April 1969, *9*(1), pp. 141–52.

Jensen, Vernon H. Decasualizing a Labor Market: The Longshore Experience. **In** *Siegel, A. J., ed.*, 1969, pp. 226–59.

Jesness, O. B. Poverty among American Farmers. **In** *Task Force on Economic Growth and Opportunity*, 1969, pp. 229–43.

Jessen, R. J. Some "Master" Sampling Frames for Social and Statistical Surveys in California. **In** *Johnson, N. L. and Smith, H., Jr., eds.*, 1969, pp. 457–81.

Jessup, Paul F. Bank Debt Capital: Urchin of Adversity to Child of Prosperity. **In** *Jessup, P. F.*, 1969, pp. 186–205.

______ Changes in Bank Ownership: The Impact on Operating Performance. (Study summary.) *Fed. Res. Bull.*, April 1969, *55*(4), pp. 309–10.

Jevons, W. S. Barter. **In** *Clower, R. W., ed.*, 1969, pp. 25–29.

Jha, S. C. and Krishna, Jai. Buffer Stock—Concepts and Objectives. **In** *Indian Society of Agricultural Economics*, 1969, pp. 35–48.

Jha, Shri L. K. La funzione monetaria dell'oro nei prossimi dieci anni: Intervento. (The Role of Monetary Gold Over the Next Ten Years: Discussion. With English summary.) *Bancaria*, November 1969, *25*(11), pp. 1348–49.

Jochimsen, R. Performance and Respective Spheres of Public and Private Enterprise. **In** *Margolis, J. and Guitton, H., eds.*, 1969, pp. 406–23.

Joeres, Erhard; Kirby, William and Revelle, Charles. The Linear Decision Rule in Reservoir Management and Design. 1. Development of the Stochastic Model. *Water Resources Res.*, August 1969, *5* (4), pp. 767–77.

Johansen, Leif. An Examination of the Relevance of Kenneth Arrow's General Possibility Theorem for Economic Planning. *Econ. Planning*, 1969, *9* (1–2), pp. 5–41.

______ On the Relationships between Some Systems of Demand Functions. *Liiketaloudellinen Aikak.*, 1969, *18*(1), pp. 30–41.

Johansson, Sven-Erik. Income Taxes and Investment Decisions. *Swedish J. Econ.*, June 1969, *71*(2), pp. 104–10.

Johnsen, Erik. A Remark on Some Analytical Problems in a Normative Marketing Systems Model. *Liiketaloudellinen Aikak.*, 1969, *18*(1), pp. 42–50.

Johnson, Benjamin P. America at the Crystal Palace, 1851. **In** *Pursell, C. W., Jr.*, 1969, pp. 96–101.

Johnson, Byron L. Statement. **In** *Linking Reserve Creation and Development Assistance, JECH*, 1969, pp. 94–102.

Johnson, D. Gale. The New Agricultural Protectionism in the Industrial Countries. *Rivista Int. Sci. Econ. Com.*, January 1969, *16*(1), pp. 46–62.

Johnson, David B. and Pauly, Mark V. Excess Burden and the Voluntary Theory of Public Finance. *Economica, N.S.*, August 1969, *36*(143), pp. 269–76.

______ **and Stern, James L.** Why and How Workers

Shift from Blue-Collar to White-Collar Jobs. *Mon. Lab. Rev.*, October 1969, *92*(10), pp. 7–13.
Johnson, George E. and Ashenfelter, Orley. Bargaining Theory, Trade Unions, and Industrial Strike Activity. *Amer. Econ. Rev.*, March 1969, *59*(1), pp. 35–49.
Johnson, Glenn L. The Modern Family Farm and Its Problems: With Particular Reference to the United States of America. **In** *Papi, U. and Nunn, C., eds.*, 1969, pp. 234–50.
______ Professor Johnson's Hedges: A Reply. *Miss. Val. J. Bus. Econ.*, Fall 1969, *5*(1), pp. 85–89.
______ Stress on Production Economics. **In** *Fox, K. A. and Johnson, D. G., eds.*, 1969, pp. 203–20.
Johnson, Harold W. and Simon, Julian L. The Success of Mergers: The Case of Advertising Agencies. *Bull. Oxford Univ. Inst. Econ. Statist.*, May 1969, *31*(2), pp. 139–44.
Johnson, Harry G. The Case for Flexible Exchange Rates, 1969. *Fed. Res. Bank St. Louis Rev.*, June 1969, *51*(6), pp. 12–24.
______ Comparative Cost and Commercial Policy Theory in a Developing Economy. *Pakistan Develop. Rev.*, Spring Supplement 1969, *9*(1), pp. 1–33.
______ Current International Economic Policy Issues. *J. Bus.*, January 1969, *42*(1), pp. 12–21.
______ Financial and Monetary Problems: Britain and the EEC. **In** *van Meerhaeghe, M. A. G., ed.*, 1969, pp. 21–32.
______ The Gold Rush of 1968 in Retrospect and Prospect. *Amer. Econ. Rev.*, May 1969, *59*(2), pp. 344–48.
______ Inside Money, Outside Money, Income, Wealth, and Welfare in Monetary Theory. *J. Money, Credit, Banking,* February 1969, *1*(1), pp. 30–45.
______ The International Monetary Problem: Gold, Dollars, Special Drawing Rights, Wider Bands and Crawling Pegs. **In** *Linking Reserve Creation and Development Assistance, JECH,* 1969, pp. 21–28.
______ Notes on the Geometry of Income Distribution in a Two-Factor, Two-Commodity Model. *Osaka Econ. Pap.*, March 1969, *17*(32), pp. 31–38.
______ The "Problems" Approach to International Monetary Reform. **In** *Mundell, R. A. and Swoboda, A. K., eds.*, 1969, pp. 393–99.
______ Pesek and Saving's Theory of Money and Wealth: A Comment. *J. Money, Credit, Banking,* August 1969, *1*(3), pp. 535–37.
______ The Seigniorage Problem and International Liquidity: Appendix: A Note on Seigniorage and the Social Saving from Substituting Credit for Commodity Money. **In** *Mundell, R. A. and Swoboda, A. K., eds.*, 1969, pp. 323–29.
______ Some Aspects of the Multilateral Free Trade Association Proposal. *Manchester Sch. Econ. Soc. Stud.*, September 1969, *37*(3), pp. 189–212.
______ Statement. **In** *Linking Reserve Creation and Development Assistance, JECH,* 1969, pp. 19–21.
______ The Theory of Effective Protection and Preferences. *Economica, N.S.*, May 1969, *36*(142), pp. 119–38.
______ The Theory of International Trade. **In** *Samuelson, P. A., ed.*, 1969, pp. 55–66.
______ The Theory of International Trade: Reply. **In** *Samuelson, P. A., ed.*, 1969, pp. 78–80.
______ Time for Change in Trade Strategy. **In** *Johnson, H. G., ed.*, 1969, pp. 1–18.
______**; Rapp, William V. and Grubel, Herbert G.** Excise Taxes and Effective Protection: A Note. *Econ. J.*, September 1969, *79*(315), pp. 674–75.
______**; Scott, A. D. and Thomas, Brinley.** Criticisms of Thomas's Analysis of Brain Drain. **In** *Blaug, M., ed.*, 1969, pp. 281–301.
Johnson, James A. The Distribution of the Burden of Sewer User Charges under Various Charge Formulas. *Nat. Tax J.*, December 1969, *22*(4), pp. 472–85.
Johnson, James F. The Influence of Cost Distance Factors on the Overseas Export of Corn from the United States Midwest. *Econ. Geogr.*, April 1969, *45*(2), pp. 170–79.
Johnson, M. Bruce and Brown, Gardner, Jr. Public Utility Pricing and Output under Risk. *Amer. Econ. Rev.*, March 1969, *59*(1), pp. 119–28.
Johnson, Nicholas. Statement. **In** *Bank Holding Company Act Amendments, Pts. 1–3, HCH,* 1969, pp. 240–49.
______ Towers of Babel: The Chaos in Radio Spectrum Utilization and Allocation. *Law Contemp. Probl.*, Summer 1969, *34*(3), pp. 505–34.
Johnson, Orace E. Beyond the Illfare State. *Univ. Missouri Bus. Govt. Rev.*, May–June 1969, *10*(3), pp. 28–36.
______ The "Last Hour" of Senior and Marx. *Hist. Polit. Econ.*, Fall 1969, *1*(2), pp. 359–69.
Johnson, P. S. Research in Britain Today. *Lloyds Bank Rev.*, October 1969, (94), pp. 34–49.
Johnson, Paul R. On Testing Competing Hypotheses: Economic Rationality versus Traditional Behavior: Reply. *Amer. J. Agr. Econ.*, February 1969, *51*(1), pp. 208–09.
Johnson, R. A.; Kast, F. E. and Rosenzweig, J. E. Systems Theory and Management. **In** *Carsberg, B. V. and Edey, H. C., eds.*, 1969, pp. 279–302.
Johnson, Robert E. Statement. **In** *Competition in Defense Procurement, SCH,* 1969, pp. 32–81.
______ Technology Licensing in Defense Procurement: A Proposal. **In** *Competition in Defense Procurement, SCH,* 1969, pp. 339–44.
Johnson, Robert W. Statement. **In** *Consumer Credit Regulations, Pt. 1, HCH,* 1969, pp. 179–81.
______ **and Comiskey, Eugene E.** Breakeven Analysis in Installment Lending. **In** *Jessup, P. F.*, 1969, pp. 229–37.
Johnson, Stanley R. and Engel, N. Eugene. Spatial Price Equilibrium and Price Variability: An Application to the Fall Potato Industry. *Can. J. Agr. Econ.*, February 1969, *17*(1), pp. 23–32.
Johnson, T. J. and Hurd, G. E. Sociology in the Third World Situation. *Int. Soc. Sci. J.*, 1969, *21*(3), pp. 421–27.
Johnson, Walter L. The Theory and Practice of Window Dressing by Commercial Banks. *Miss. Val. J. Bus. Econ.*, Spring 1969, *4*(2), pp. 43–49.
Johnson-Marshall, P. The Contribution of Demography to Physical and Spatial Planning: Comment. **In** *Bechhofer, F., ed.*, 1969, pp. 134–36.
Johnston, Bruce F. and Cownie, John. The Seed-Fertilizer Revolution and Labor Force Absorp-

tion. *Amer. Econ. Rev.*, Part I, September 1969, *59*(4), pp. 569–82.

______ **and Ohkawa, Kazushi.** The Transferability of the Japanese Pattern of Modernizing Traditional Agriculture. **In** *Thorbecke, E., ed.*, 1969, pp. 277–303.

Johnston, Denis F. and Wetzel, James R. Effect of the Census Undercount on Labor Force Estimates. *Mon. Lab. Rev.*, March 1969, *92*(3), pp. 3–13.

Johnston, R. J. Zonal and Sectoral Patterns in Melbourne's Residential Structure: 1961. *Land Econ.*, November 1969, *45*(4), pp. 463–67.

Johnston, Robert A. Credit—and Credit Cards. **In** *Jessup, P. F.*, 1969, pp. 101–09.

Johri, C. K. Labour Policy in Perspective. **In** *Johri, C. K., ed.*, 1969, pp. 1–22.

______ Some Aspects of Wage Policy in India. **In** *Johri, C. K., ed.*, 1969, pp. 254–69.

Jonas, Hans. Economic Knowledge and the Critique of Goals. **In** *Heilbroner, R. L., ed.*, 1969, pp. 67–87.

Jonas, Paul and Sardy, Hyman. Production Index Bias as a Measure of Economic Development: A Comment. *Oxford Econ. Pap.*, November 1969, *21*(3), pp. 428–32.

Jones, Byrd L. A Plan for Planning in the New Deal. *Soc. Sci. Quart.*, December 1969, *50*(3), pp. 525–34.

Jones, Charles P. and Litzenberger, Robert H. Adjusting for Risk in the Capital Budget of a Growth Oriented Company: Comment. *J. Financial Quant. Anal.*, September 1969, *4*(3), pp. 301–04.

Jones, E. J. 'Scotch Cattle' and Early Trade Unionism in Wales. **In** *Minchinton, W. E., ed.*, 1969, pp. 209–17.

Jones, E. L. and Woolf, S. J. Introduction: The Historical Role of Agrarian Change in Economic Development. **In** *Jones, E. L. and Woolf, S. J., eds.*, 1969, pp. 1–21.

Jones, L. W. Rapid Population Growth in Baghdad and Amman. *Middle East J.*, Spring 1969, *23*(2), pp. 209–15.

Jones, Mary Gardiner. Deception in the Marketplace of the Poor: The Role of the Federal Trade Commission. **In** *Sturdivant, F. D., ed.*, 1969, pp. 244–56.

Jones, R. M. A Case Study in Labour Mobility. *Manchester Sch. Econ. Soc. Stud.*, June 1969, *37*(2), pp. 169–74.

Jones, Robert J. The Cost of Stabilization: Reply. *Amer. Econ.*, Fall 1969, *13*(2), pp. 100–104.

Jones, Roger H. Program Budgeting: Fiscal Facts And Federal Fancy. *Quart. Rev. Econ. Bus.*, Summer 1969, *9*(2), pp. 45–57.

Jones, Ronald W. Tariffs and Trade in General Equilibrium: Comment. *Amer. Econ. Rev.*, June 1969, *59*(3), pp. 418–24.

Jones, William K. and Blake, Harland M. In Defense of Antitrust. **In** *Starleaf, D. R., ed.*, 1969, pp. 102–09.

Jones-Lee, Michael. Managerial Expectations and Investment Behaviour. *Yorkshire Bull. Econ. Soc. Res.*, November 1969, *21*(2), pp. 85–93.

______ Valuation of Reduction in Probability of Death by Road Accident. *J. Transp. Econ. Policy*, January 1969, *3*(1), pp. 37–47.

de Jong, F. J. De economische betekenis van de Rijksuniversiteit te Groningen voor de provincie. (The Economic Significance of the University of Groningen for the Province. With English summary.) *De Economist*, May/June 1969, *117*(3), pp. 193–226.

de Jong, H. W. Concentration in the Common Market. **In** *Economic Concentration, Pt. 7A, SCH*, 1969, pp. 3907–15.

______ The Direction, Relatedness, and Strategy of Mergers: Appendix. **In** *Economic Concentration, Pt. 7A, SCH*, 1969, pp. 3893–97.

______ The European Brewing Industry: Appendix. **In** *Economic Concentration, Pt. 7A, SCH*, 1969, pp. 3897–3907.

de Jongh, T. W. Review of the Financial and Economic Situation in South Africa. *S. Afr. J. Econ.*, September 1969, *37*(3), pp. 187–97.

Jörberg, Lennart. Structural Change and Economic Growth: Sweden in the Nineteenth Century. **In** *Crouzet, F.; Chaloner, W. H. and Stern, W. M., eds.*, 1969, pp. 259–80.

Jordan, Jerry L. Elements of Money Stock Determination. *Fed. Res. Bank St. Louis Rev.*, October 1969, *51*(10), pp. 10–19.

______ Relations among Monetary Aggregates. *Fed. Res. Bank St. Louis Rev.*, March 1969, *51*(3), pp. 8–9.

______ **and Andersen, Leonall C.** Monetary and Fiscal Actions: A Test of Their Relative Importance in Economic Stabilization—Reply. *Fed. Res. Bank St. Louis Rev.*, April 1969, *51*(4), pp. 12–16.

______ **and Ruebling, Charlotte E.** Federal Open Market Committee Decisions in 1968—A Year of Watchful Waiting. *Fed. Res. Bank St. Louis Rev.*, May 1969, *51*(5), pp. 6–15.

Jordan, Raymond B. Negotiating Overhead Expense with Confidence. *Manage. Account.*, December 1969, *51*(6), pp. 35–39.

Jordan, Terry G. The Origin of Anglo-American Cattle Ranching in Texas: A Documentation of Diffusion from the Lower South. *Econ. Geogr.*, January 1969, *45*(1), pp. 63–87.

Jorgenson, Dale W. A Programming Model for a Dual Economy: Comment. **In** *Thorbecke, E., ed.*, 1969, pp. 231–34.

______ **and Christensen, Laurits R.** The Measurement of U.S. Real Capital Input, 1929–1967. *Rev. Income Wealth*, December 1969, *15*(4), pp. 293–320.

______ **and Hall, Robert E.** Tax Policy and Investment Behavior: Reply and Further Results. *Amer. Econ. Rev.*, June 1969, *59*(3), pp. 388–401.

______ **and Stephenson, James A.** Anticipations and Investment Behavior in U.S. Manufacturing, 1947–1960. *J. Amer. Statist. Assoc.*, March 1969, *64*(325), pp. 67–89.

______ **and Stephenson, James A.** Issues in the Development of the Neoclassical Theory of Investment Behavior. *Rev. Econ. Statist.*, August 1969, *51*(3), pp. 346–53.

Joseph, Myron L. Approaches to Collective Bargaining in Industrial Relations Theory. **In** *Somers, G. G., ed. (I)*, 1969, pp. 55–67.

Control on the Performance of the Large Firm in the U.S. Economy. *Rivista Int. Sci. Econ. Com.*, May 1969, *16*(5), pp. 489–93.

_____ Further Analysis of Overurbanization. *Econ. Develop. Cult. Change*, January 1969, *17*(2), pp. 235–53.

_____ **and Pascucci, John J.** The Retail Price Structure in American Life Insurance: Comment. *J. Risk Ins.*, September 1969, *36*(4), pp. 493–95.

Kamien, Morton I. and Davis, Otto A. Externalities, Information and Alternative Collective Action. **In** *The Analysis and Evaluation of Public Expenditures: The PPB System, Vol. 1, JECP*, 1969, pp. 67–86.

_____ **and Schwartz, Nancy L.** Induced Factor Augmenting Technical Progress from a Microeconomic Viewpoint. *Econometrica*, October 1969, *37*(4), pp. 668–84.

_____ **and Schwartz, Nancy L.** A Naive View of the Indicator Problem. **In** *Brunner, K., ed.*, 1969, pp. 98–112.

Kaminow, Ira. The Household Demand for Money: An Empirical Study. *J. Finance*, September 1969, *24*(4), pp. 679–96.

Kammerer, Peter. La politica dei premi al risparmio nell'esperienza tedesca. (Savings Bonus Policy in German Experience. With English summary.) *Bancaria*, October 1969, *25*(10), pp. 1225–38.

Kane, Edward J. and Malkiel, Burton G. Expectations and Interest Rates: A Cross-sectional Test of the Error-learning Hypothesis. *J. Polit. Econ.*, Part I, July/August 1969, *77*(4), pp. 453–70.

Kaneda, Hiromitsu. Economic Implications of the "Green Revolution" and the Strategy of Agricultural Development in West Pakistan. *Pakistan Develop. Rev.*, Summer 1969, *9*(2), pp. 111–43.

Kanesa-Thasan, S. Stabilizing an Economy—A Study of the Republic of Korea. *Int. Monet. Fund Staff Pap.*, March 1969, *16*(1), pp. 1–26.

_____ Stabilizing an Economy: The Korean Experience. **In** *Adelman, I., ed.*, 1969, pp. 257–76.

Kantzenbach, Erhard. Social Co-ordination of Individual Economic Activities—Thoughts on Basic Economic Policy Decisions. *Ger. Econ. Rev.*, 1969, *7*(3), pp. 185–98.

Kaplan, I. I. The Influence of Education on Labor Output. **In** *Noah, H. J., ed.*, 1969, pp. 101–13.

Kaplan, Robert S. and Ijiri, Yuji. Probabilistic Depreciation and Its Implications for Group Depreciation. *Accounting Rev.*, October 1969, *44*(4), pp. 743–56.

Kapp, K. William. On the Nature and Significance of Social Costs. *Kyklos*, 1969, *22*(2), pp. 334–47.

Kapustin, E. I. Training Personnel and Comparing Types of Labor. **In** *Noah, H. J., ed.*, 1969, pp. 63–74.

Karaska, Gerald J. and Jensen, Robert G. The Mathematical Thrust in Soviet Economic Geography—Its Nature and Significance. *J. Reg. Sci.*, April 1969, *9*(1), pp. 141–52.

Kärävä, Simo. Luotonannon selektiivisyys ja pankit. (The Selective Lending Policy and the Banks. With English summary.) *Kansant. Aikak.*, 1969, *65*(3), pp. 226–32.

_____ Takaukset pankkiluottojen vakuutena. (Guarantees as Security for Bank Credits. With English summary.) *Liiketaloudellinen Aikak.*, 1969, *18*(3), pp. 443–59.

Karber, James W. Competition and the Regulatory Process. *Quart. Rev. Econ. Bus.*, Autumn 1969, *9*(3), pp. 57–64.

Karcz, Jerzy F. An Organizational Model of Command Farming. **In** *Bornstein, M., ed.*, 1969, pp. 278–99.

_____ Comparative Study of Transformation of Agriculture in Centrally Planned Economies: The Soviet Union, Eastern Europe and Mainland China: Reply. **In** *Thorbecke, E., ed.*, 1969, pp. 274–76.

_____ Comparative Study of Transformation of Agriculture in Centrally Planned Economies: The Soviet Union, Eastern Europe and Mainland China. **In** *Thorbecke, E., ed.*, 1969, pp. 237–66.

Kareken, John H. The Federal Reserve's *Modus Operandi.* **In** *Federal Reserve Bank of Boston*, 1969, pp. 57–63.

Karkal, G. L. A Note on Basics. *Arthaniti*, January & July 1969, *12*(1&2), pp. 78–83.

Karnosky, Denis S. and Yohe, William P. Interest Rates and Price Level Changes, 1952–69. *Fed. Res. Bank St. Louis Rev.*, December 1969, *51*(12), pp. 18–38.

Karpovich, Michael; Usher, Abbott Payson and Bowden, Witt. Agrarian Reorganization and Reform in the Eighteenth Century. **In** *Scoville, W. C. and La Force, J. C., eds., Vol. III*, 1969, pp. 66–89.

Karssen, W. J. Concentration of the Automobile Industry of the E.E.C. **In** *Economic Concentration, Pt. 7A, SCH*, 1969, pp. 3915–25.

Karunatilake, H. N. S. The Impact of Import and Exchange Controls and Bilateral Trade Agreements on Trade and Production in Ceylon. **In** *Morgan, T. and Spoelstra, N., eds.*, 1969, pp. 285–303.

Kaser, Michael. Some Macroeconomics of Education. **In** *[Edding, Friedrich]*, 1969, pp. 139–53.

_____ A Volume Index of Soviet Foreign Trade. *Soviet Stud.*, April 1969, *20*(4), pp. 523–26.

Kashyap, N. N. Oil: Its Strategic Role in a Growth-Oriented Economy. **In** *Dagli, V., ed., Vol. II*, 1969, pp. 117–25.

Kaška, Josef. Duality in Linear Fractional Programming. *Ekon.-Mat. Obzor*, 1969, *5*(4), pp. 442–53.

Kaskimies, Mika. Product Life Pattern as a Means of Business Forecasting. *Liiketaloudellinen Aikak.*, 1969, *18*(3), pp. 433–41.

Kassalow, Everett M. Professional Unionism in Sweden. *Ind. Relat.*, February 1969, *8*(2), pp. 119–34.

_____ Public Employee Bargaining in Europe: What Lessons for the United States? **In** *Somers, G. G., ed. (II)*, 1969, pp. 48–58.

Kassarjian, Harold H. The Negro and American Advertising, 1946–1965. *J. Marketing Res.*, February 1969, *6*(1), pp. 29–39.

Kassirov, L. Methodological Questions Pertaining to Net Income and the Profitability of Agricultural Production. *Prob. Econ.*, May 1969, *12*(1), pp. 45–66.

Kassouf, Sheen T. An Econometric Model for Option Price with Implications for Investors' Expectations and Audacity. *Econometrica,* October 1969, *37*(4), pp. 685–94.

Kast, F. E.; Rosenzweig, J. E. and Johnson, R. A. Systems Theory and Management. **In** *Carsberg, B. V. and Edey, H. C., eds.,* 1969, pp. 279–302.

Katano, Hikoji. On Mr. Stoleru's Optimal Policy for Economic Growth. *Kobe Econ. Bus. Rev.,* 1969, *16*(1), pp. 31–38.

Katō, Yuzuru. Development of Long-Term Agricultural Credit. **In** *Ohkawa, K.; Johnston, B. F. and Kaneda, H., eds.,* 1969, pp. 324–51.

Katrak, Homi. An Empirical Test of Comparative Cost Theories: Japan, Peru, the United Kingdom and the United States. *Economica, N.S.,* November 1969, *36*(144), pp. 389–99.

Katz, Elihu; Menzel, Herbert and Coleman, James. The Diffusion of an Innovation among Physicians. **In** *Alexis, M.; Holloway, R. J. and Hancock, R. S., eds.,* 1969, pp. 154–67.

Katz, Michael. Legal Dimensions of Population Policy. *Soc. Sci. Quart.,* December 1969, *50*(3), pp. 731–41.

Katzman, Martin T. Ethnic Geography and Regional Economies, 1880–1960. *Econ. Geogr.,* January 1969, *45*(1), pp. 45–52.

______ Opportunity, Subculture and the Economic Performance of Urban Ethnic Groups. *Amer. J. Econ. Soc.,* October 1969, *28*(4), pp. 351–66.

Kaufman, G. M. and Penchansky, R. Simulation of Union Health and Welfare Funds. **In** *Siegel, A. J., ed.,* 1969, pp. 121–75.

Kaufman, George G. Bank Holding Companies: Discussion. **In** *Federal Reserve Bank of Chicago (II),* 1969, pp. 100–102.

______ More on an Empirical Definition of Money. *Amer. Econ. Rev.,* March 1969, *59*(1), pp. 78–87.

______ Topics on Bank Capital: Comment. **In** *Federal Reserve Bank of Chicago (I),* 1969, pp. 116–18.

Kaufman, Gordon M. Conditional Prediction and Unbiasedness in Structural Equations. *Econometrica,* January 1969, *37*(1), pp. 44–49.

Kaufmann, Hugo M. A Debate over Germany's Revaluation 1961: A Chapter in Political Economy. *Weltwirtsch. Arch.,* 1969, *103*(2), pp. 181–212.

Kaufmann, Johan and Alting von Geusau, A. M. The Institutional Framework for International Trade Relations. **In** *Alting von Geusau, F. A. M., ed.,* 1969, pp. 94–112.

Kaun, David E. A Comment on the Work-Leisure Myth. *Rev. Radical Polit. Econ.,* May 1969, *1*(1), pp. 85–88.

Kaverau, T. A. Consolidating Small Schools—An Essential Task. **In** *Noah, H. J., ed.,* 1969, pp. 192–95.

Kawaja, Michael. The Economic Effects of Regulation: A Case Study of the Consumer Finance Industry. *Southern Econ. J.,* January 1969, *35*(3), pp. 231–38.

Kawano, Shigeto. Effects of the Land Reform on Consumption and Investment of Farmers. **In** *Ohkawa, K.; Johnston, B. F. and Kaneda, H., eds.,* 1969, pp. 374–97.

Kay, John A. and Hole, Peter C. The Fund Meeting. *Finance Develop.,* December 1969, *6*(4), pp. 10–14.

Kayler, J. Allan. Personal Income in Urban Indiana. *Indiana Bus. Rev.,* March–April 1969, *44,* pp. 7–11.

Kayoumy, Abdul Hay. Monopoly Pricing of Afghan Karakul in International Markets. *J. Polit. Econ.,* March/April 1969, *77*(2), pp. 219–36.

Kaysen, Carl. Model Makers and Decision Makers: Economists and the Policy Process. **In** *Heilbroner, R. L., ed.,* 1969, pp. 137–53.

Kaysen, Carl, et al. Report of the Task Force on the Storage of and Access to Government Statistics. *Amer. Statist.,* June 1969, *23*(3), pp. 11–19.

Keating, M. Employment and the Growth of Australian Gross National Product. *Econ. Rec.,* March 1969, *45*(109), pp. 27–47.

Kedzie, Daniel P. Corporate Planning and the Holding Company. *J. Risk Ins.,* March 1969, *36*(1), pp. 85–91.

Kee, Woo Sik. The Causes of Urban Poverty. *J. Human Res.,* Winter 1969, *4*(1), pp. 93–99.

Keefe, Harry V., Jr. The One-Bank Holding Company—A Result, Not a Revolution. **In** *Prochnow, H. V., ed.,* 1969, pp. 116–41.

Keele, David L. Economic Growth Outside Metropolitan Areas: The Tenth District Experience. *Fed. Res. Bank Kansas City Rev.,* June 1969, pp. 3–10.

Keenan, Joseph D. Housing and Community Development Policy Paper. **In** *National Housing Goals, HCH,* 1969, pp. 519–25.

Keesing, Donald B. Country Size and Trade Patterns: Reply. *Amer. Econ. Rev.,* March 1969, *59* (1), pp. 204.

______ Small Population as a Political Handicap to National Development. *Polit. Sci. Quart.,* March 1969, *84*(1), pp. 50–60.

______ Structural Change Early in Development: Mexico's Changing Industrial and Occupational Structure from 1895 to 1950. *J. Econ. Hist.,* December 1969, *29*(4), pp. 716–38.

Keig, Norman G. The Occupational Aspirations and Labor Force Experience of Negro Youth: A Case Study. *Amer. J. Econ. Soc.,* April 1969, *28*(2), pp. 113–30.

______ **and Kafoglis, Milton Z.** New Policies of the Federal Power Commission. *Land Econ.,* November 1969, *45*(4), pp. 385–91.

Keith-Lucas, D. The Prospects of 1,000-Passenger Aircraft. **In** *Hugh-Jones, E. M., ed.,* 1969, pp. 120–34.

Kelejian, H. H. Missing Observations in Multivariate Regression: Efficiency of a First Order Method. *J. Amer. Statist. Assoc.,* December 1969, *64*(328), pp. 1609–16.

Kelejian, Harry H. and Howrey, E. Philip. Simulation Versus Analytical Solutions. **In** *Naylor, T. H., ed.,* 1969, pp. 207–31.

Kelley, Allen C. Demand Patterns, Demographic Change and Economic Growth. *Quart. J. Econ.,* February 1969, *83*(1), pp. 110–26.

______ Demographic Cycles and Economic Growth: The Long Swing Reconsidered. *J. Econ. Hist.,* December 1969, *29*(4), pp. 633–56.

______ **and Weiss, Leonard W.** Markov Processes and Economic Analysis: The Case of Migration.

Econometrica, April 1969, *37*(2), pp. 280–97.

Kelliher, Walter J. Statement. **In** *Population Trends, Pt. 1, HCH,* 1969, pp. 681–86.

Kellison, Stephen G. A Linear Programming Model of Profitability, Capacity and Regulation in Insurance Management: Comment. *J. Risk Ins.,* December 1969, *36*(5), pp. 637–39.

Kellow, James H. and Albert, Linzy D. Decision-Makers' Reactions to Plant Location Factors: An Appraisal. *Land Econ.,* August 1969, *45*(3), pp. 376–81.

Kelly, Alex K. Sources of Change in the Canadian Money Stock, 1955–65. *Banca Naz. Lavoro Quart. Rev.,* December 1969, (91), pp. 395–407.

Kelly, Jerry Stewart. Lancaster vs. Samuelson on the Shape of the Neoclassical Transformation Surface. *J. Econ. Theory,* October 1969, *1*(3), pp. 347–51.

Kelly, Robert F. Predicting New Product Adoption Levels. **In** *Association of Canadian Schools of Business,* 1969, pp. 234–77.

Kelly, William C., Jr. Water Quality Standards in Private Nuisance Actions. *Yale Law J.,* November 1969, *79*(1), pp. 102–10.

Kemp, Murray C. The Theory of International Trade: Comment. **In** *Samuelson, P. A., ed.,* 1969, pp. 71–73.

_____ **and Bhagwati, Jagdish N.** Ranking of Tariffs under Monopoly Power in Trade. *Quart. J. Econ.,* May 1969, *83*(2), pp. 330–35.

_____ **and Inada, Ken-Ichi.** International Capital Movements and the Theory of Tariffs and Trade: Comment. *Quart. J. Econ.,* August 1969, *83*(3), pp. 524–28.

_____ **and Nagishi, Takashi.** Domestic Distortions, Tariffs, and the Theory of Optimum Subsidy. *J. Polit. Econ.,* November/December 1969, *77*(6), pp. 1011–13.

_____ **and Wegge, Leon L. F.** Generalizations of the Stolper-Samuelson and Samuelson-Rybczynski Theorems in Terms of Conditional Input-Output Coefficients. *Int. Econ. Rev.,* October 1969, *10*(3), pp. 414–25.

_____ **and Wegge, Leon L. F.** On the Relation between Commodity Prices and Factor Rewards. *Int. Econ. Rev.,* October 1969, *10*(3), pp. 407–13.

Kemp, Tom. Aspects of French Capitalism between the Wars. *Sci. Soc.,* Winter 1969, *33*(1), pp. 1–19.

Kempner, Thomas. Economics for Business Studies. **In** *Kempner, T., ed.,* 1969, pp. 48–53.

Kempthorne, O. Some Remarks on Statistical Inference in Finite Sampling. **In** *Johnson, N. L. and Smith, H., Jr., eds.,* 1969, pp. 671–95.

Kendall, M. G.; Coen, P. J. and Gomme, E. D. Lagged Relationships in Economic Forecasting. *J. Roy. Statist. Soc.,* Part 2, 1969, *132,* pp. 133–52.

Kendrick, David A. and Taylor, Lance J. A Dynamic Nonlinear Planning Model for Korea. **In** *Adelman, I., ed.,* 1969, pp. 213–37.

Kendrick, James G. Policy and Non-Policy in Foreign Trade: Discussion. *Amer. J. Agr. Econ.,* December 1969, *51*(5), pp. 1349–51.

Kendrick, John W. An Evaluation of Productivity Statistics. **In** *Somers, G. G., ed. (II),* 1969, pp. 129–35.

_____ **and Garston, Gordon J.** Measuring Real Output for Industries Providing Services: OBE Concepts and Methods: Discussion. **In** *Fuchs, V. R., ed.,* 1969, pp. 41–49.

Kenen, Peter B. The New Fiscal Policy: A Comment. *J. Money, Credit, Banking,* August 1969, *1*(3), pp. 503–05.

_____ Round Table on Exchange Rate Policy. *Amer. Econ. Rev.,* May 1969, *59*(2), pp. 362–64.

_____ The Theory of Optimum Currency Areas: An Eclectic View. **In** *Mundell, R. A. and Swoboda, A. K., eds.,* 1969, pp. 41–60.

Kennedy, M. C. How Well Does the National Institute Forecast? *Nat. Inst. Econ. Rev.,* November 1969, (50), pp. 40–52.

Kennedy, R. V. Quarterly Estimates of National Income and Expenditure: 1950–51 to 1957–58. *Econ. Rec.,* June 1969, *45*(110), pp. 218–42.

Kennedy, Robert F. A Business Development Program for Our Poverty Areas. **In** *Sturdivant, F. D., ed.,* 1969, pp. 193–209.

_____ Industrial Investment in Urban Poverty Areas. **In** *Kain, J. F., ed.,* 1969, pp. 153–63.

Keran, Michael W. Comments on the "St. Louis Position"—Reply. *Fed. Res. Bank St. Louis Rev.,* August 1969, *51*(8), pp. 15–18.

_____ Monetary and Fiscal Influences on Economic Activity—The Historical Evidence. *Fed. Res. Bank St. Louis Rev.,* November 1969, *51*(11), pp. 5–24.

_____ **and Babb, Christopher T.** An Explanation of Federal Reserve Actions (1933–68). *Fed. Res. Bank St. Louis Rev.,* July 1969, *51*(7), pp. 7–20.

Kerby, Joe Kent. Borrowing from the Behavioral Sciences. *J. Bus.,* April 1969, *42*(2), pp. 152–61.

Kerr, Clark. Class Conflict and Class Collaboration. **In** *Kerr, C.,* 1969, pp. 33–43.

_____ The Classless Society and the Perfectibility of Man. **In** *Kerr, C.,* 1969, pp. 8–18.

_____ Education in the United States: Past Accomplishments and Present Problems. **In** *Bereday, G. Z. F., ed.,* 1969, pp. 297–311.

_____ Federal Aid to Higher Education through 1976. **In** *the Economics and Financing of Higher Education in the United States, JECP,* 1969, pp. 599–617.

_____ The Future of Capitalism. **In** *Kerr, C.,* 1969, pp. 19–32.

_____ The Future of Pluralism. **In** *Kerr, C.,* 1969, pp. 122–30.

_____ Industrial Relations and University Relations. **In** *Somers, G. G., ed. (II),* 1969, pp. 15–25.

_____ Industrialism and Pluralism. **In** *Kerr, C.,* 1969, pp. 74–81.

_____ Marshall and Marx. **In** *Kerr, C.,* 1969, pp. 62–73.

_____ The Multi-dimensional Society. **In** *Kerr, C.,* 1969, pp. 82–114.

_____ New 'Inherent Contradictions.' **In** *Kerr, C.,* 1969, pp. 115–21.

_____ Trade Unions and Group Interests. **In** *Kerr, C.,* 1969, pp. 44–61.

Keshava, G. P. Incentives for Industrial Labour: A Survey. *Artha-Vikas,* January 1969, *5*(1), pp. 29–53.

Kesselman, Jonathan. Labor-Supply Effects of Income, Income-Work, and Wage Subsidies. *J. Human Res.*, Summer 1969, *4*(3), pp. 275–92.

——— The Negative Income Tax and the Supply of Work Effort: Comment. *Nat. Tax J.*, September 1969, *22*(3), pp. 411–16.

Keyfitz, Nathan. Sampling for Demographic Variables. **In** *Johnson, N. L. and Smith, H., Jr., eds.*, 1969, pp. 562–77.

——— United States and World Populations. **In** *National Academy of Sciences*, 1969, pp. 43–64.

Keynes, John Maynard. The Inflationary Gap. **In** *Ball, R. J. and Doyle, P., eds.*, 1969, pp. 21–27.

Keyserling, Leon H. Statement. **In** *The 1969 Economic Report of the President, Pt. 4, JECH*, 1969, pp. 999–1056.

——— Statement. **In** *Tax Reform Act of 1969, Testimony, Sept. 26, SCP*, 1969, pp. 85–191.

Khachaturov, T. On the Economic Evaluation of Natural Resources. *Prob. Econ.*, August 1969, *12* (4), pp. 52–67.

——— Questions Concerning the Theory of Socialist Reproduction. *Prob. Econ.*, September 1969, *12* (5), pp. 3–28.

Khachaturov, T. S. The Development of the External Economic Relations of the Soviet Union. **In** *Samuelson, P. A., ed.*, 1969, pp. 89–99.

———**; Nove, Alec and Vajda, Imre.** Replies to Comments. **In** *Samuelson, P. A., ed.*, 1969, pp. 147–49.

Khaikin, N. M. Technical-Economic Indexes of the Labor of Workers with Different Vocational Preparation. **In** *Noah, H. J., ed.*, 1969, pp. 141–49.

Khalid, Rasheed O. Fiscal Policy, Development Planning, and Annual Budgeting. *Int. Monet. Fund Staff Pap.*, March 1969, *16*(1), pp. 53–84.

Khan, Azizur Rahman. The Possibilities of the East Pakistan Economy during the Fourth Five-Year Plan. *Pakistan Develop. Rev.*, Summer 1969, *9*(2), pp. 144–211.

——— The Possibilities of the East Pakistan Economy during the Fourth Five Year Plan. **In** *Khan, A. R., ed.*, 1969, pp. 169–238.

Khan, Mahmood Hasan. Development Alternatives and Problems in Dual Economies. *Econ. Int.*, November 1969, *22*(4), pp. 636–61.

Khan, Mohammad Irshad. Aggregative Analysis of Food Consumption in Pakistan. *Pakistan Develop. Rev.*, Winter 1969, *9*(4), pp. 426–41.

Khan, Q. U. Efficiency Coefficients for School Stage Education. **In** *Pandit, H. N., ed.*, 1969, pp. 164–72.

Khang, Chulsoon. A Dynamic Model of Trade Between the Final and the Intermediate Products. *J. Econ. Theory*, December 1969, *1*(4), pp. 416–37.

——— A Neoclassical Growth Model of Vertically Related International Trade. *Osaka Econ. Pap.*, March 1969, *17*(32), pp. 21–29.

———**; Bierwag, G. O. and Grove, M. A.** National Debt in a Neoclassical Growth Model: Comment. *Amer. Econ. Rev.*, March 1969, *59*(1), pp. 205–10.

Khatkhate, Deena R. Debt-Servicing as an Aid to Promotion of Trade of Developing Countries: A Reply. *Oxford Econ. Pap.*, November 1969, *21*(3), pp. 424–27.

Kheel, Theodore W. Collective Bargaining and Community Disputes. *Mon. Lab. Rev.*, January 1969, *92*(1), pp. 3–8.

——— Strikes and Public Employment. *Mich. Law Rev.*, March 1969, *67*(5), pp. 931–42.

Khera, S. S. Efficiency in the Public Sector. **In** *Dagli, V., ed., Vol. II*, 1969, pp. 18–30.

Khouja, Mohamad W. and Konstas, Panos. The Keynesian Demand-for-Money Function: Another Look and Some Additional Evidence. *J. Money, Credit, Banking*, November 1969, *1*(4), pp. 765–77.

Khusro, A. M. Stocks and Storage of Major Foodgrains. **In** *Indian Society of Agricultural Economics*, 1969, pp. 134–47.

Kiker, B. F. The Economic Ideas of Nathaniel A. Ware. **In** *Kiker, B. F. and Carlsson, R. J., eds.*, 1969, pp. 105–19.

——— Von Thünen on Human Capital. *Oxford Econ. Pap.*, November 1969, *21*(3), pp. 339–43.

Kilcarr, Andrew J. United States v. Concentrated Phosphate Export Association: A Small Case in the Big Court. *Antitrust Bull.*, Spring 1969, *14*, pp. 37–61.

Killick, A. and Szerszewski, Robert. The Economy of Ghana. **In** *Robson, P. and Lury, D. A., eds.*, 1969, pp. 79–126.

Killick, Tony and During, R. W. A Structural Approach to the Balance of Payments of a Low-Income Country. *J. Devel. Stud.*, July 1969, *5*(4), pp. 274–98.

Killingsworth, Charles C. Full Employment and the New Economics. *Scot. J. Polit. Econ.*, February 1969, *16*(1), pp. 1–19.

——— Jobs and Income for Negroes. **In** *Katz, I. and Gurin, P., eds.*, 1969, pp. 194–273.

Kilroy-Silk, Robert. The Problem of Industrial Relations. *Manchester Sch. Econ. Soc. Stud.*, September 1969, *37*(3), pp. 249–58.

——— The Royal Commission on Trade Unions and Employers' Associations. *Ind. Lab. Relat. Rev.*, July 1969, *22*(4), pp. 544–58.

Kim, Hyung K. The Role of Foreign Aid in Assisting the Stabilization of the Korean Economy. *Univ. Wash. Bus. Rev.*, Winter 1969, *28*(2), pp. 62–67.

Kim, Joungwon Alexander. The "Peak of Socialism" in North Korea: The Five and Seven Year Plans. **In** *Prybyla, J. S., ed.*, 1969, pp. 412–27.

Kim, Kwan S. Capital Imports, External Debts, and Growth in the Mahalanobis Model. *Indian Econ. J.*, April–June 1969, *16*(4–5), pp. 488–91.

Kim, Young Chin. Sectoral Output-Capital Ratios and Levels of Economic Development: A Cross-Sectional Comparison of Manufacturing Industry. *Rev. Econ. Statist.*, November 1969, *51*(4), pp. 453–58.

Kimball, Warren F. "Beggar My Neighbor": America and the British Interim Financial Crisis, 1940–41. *J. Econ. Hist.*, December 1969, *29*(4), pp. 758–72.

Kindleberger, Charles P. The Euro-Dollar and the Internationalization of United States Monetary

Policy. *Banca Naz. Lavoro Quart. Rev.*, March 1969, (88), pp. 3–15.

_____ Measuring Equilibrium in the Balance of Payments. *J. Polit. Econ.*, November/December 1969, *77*(6), pp. 873–91.

_____ Princeton Essays in International Finance. *J. Econ. Lit.*, September 1969, *7*(3), pp. 807–10.

King, Alfred M. Budgeting Foreign Exchange Losses. *Manage. Account.*, October 1969, *51*(4), pp. 39–41, 46.

King, Benjamin. Comment on "Factor Analysis and Regression." *Econometrica*, July 1969, *37*(3), pp. 538–40.

King, Donald A. Homebuilding Activity in 1969. *Surv. Curr. Bus.*, October 1969, *49*(10), pp. 16–22.

_____ Monetary Restraint in 1969. *Surv. Curr. Bus.*, Part I, May 1969, *49*(5), pp. 13–18.

King, L.; Jeffrey, D. and Casetti, E. Economic Fluctuations in a Multiregional Setting: A Bi-factor Analytic Approach. *J. Reg. Sci.*, December 1969, *9*(3), pp. 397–404.

King, R. F. T. Population, Food Supplies and Economic Growth. **In** *Hutchinson, J. [Sir], ed.*, 1969, pp. 28–46.

Kinov, D. A Useful Initiative to Follow. *Eastern Europ. Econ.*, Spring 1969, *7*(3), pp. 48–54.

Kinyon, John. A Report on Wage Developments in Manufacturing, 1968. *Mon. Lab. Rev.*, August 1969, *92*(8), pp. 33–39.

Kirby, William; Revelle, Charles and Joeres, Erhard. The Linear Decision Rule in Reservoir Management and Design. 1. Development of the Stochastic Model. *Water Resources Res.*, August 1969, *5* (4), pp. 767–77.

Kirk, Dudley. Natality in the Developing Countries: Recent Trends and Prospects. **In** *Behrman, S. J.; Corsa, L., Jr. and Freedman, R., eds.*, 1969, pp. 75–98.

_____**; Segal, Sheldon and Notestein, Frank W.** The Problem of Population Control. **In** *Hauser, P. M., ed.*, 1969, pp. 139–67.

Kirkbride, John W. Response Problems in Probability Sampling. *Amer. J. Agr. Econ.*, December 1969, *51*(5), pp. 1214–17.

Kirman, Alan P. and Tomasini, Luigi M. A New Look at International Income Inequalities. *Econ. Int.*, August 1969, *22*(3), pp. 437–61.

_____ Teoria delle scelte sociali e relativi concetti. (Social Choice Theory and Related Concepts. With English summary.) *L'Industria*, April–June 1969, (2), pp. 176–96.

Kish, L. Design and Estimation for Subclasses, Comparisons, and Analytical Statistics. **In** *Johnson, N. L. and Smith, H., Jr., eds.*, 1969, pp. 416–38.

Kisselgoff, Avram and Evans, Michael K. Demand for Consumer Installment Credit and Its Effects on Consumption. **In** *Duesenberry, J. S., et al.*, 1969, pp. 39–84.

Kitamura, Hiroshi and Bhagat, A. N. Aspects of Regional Harmonization of National Development Plans. **In** *Morgan, T. and Spoelstra, N., eds.*, 1969, pp. 39–56.

Klaassen, L. H. and Van Wickeren, A. C. Interindustry Relations: An Attraction Model: A Progress Report. **In** *[Tinbergen, J.]*, 1969, pp. 245–68.

Klaman, Saul B. Statement. **In** *Investigation of Increase in Prime Interest Rate, HCH*, 1969, pp. 239–43.

Klarman, Herbert E. Economic Aspects of Mental Health Manpower. **In** *Arnhoff, F. N.; Rubinstein, E. A. and Speisman, J. C., eds.*, 1969, pp. 67–92.

_____ Economic Aspects of Projecting Requirements for Health Manpower. *J. Human Res.*, Summer 1969, *4*(3), pp. 360–76.

_____ Reimbursing the Hospital—The Differences the Third Party Makes. *J. Risk Ins.*, December 1969, *36*(5), pp. 553–66.

_____ **and Feldstein, Martin S.** Some Problems in the Measurement of Productivity in the Medical Care Industry: Discussion. **In** *Fuchs, V. R., ed.*, 1969, pp. 132–46.

Klaus, Ida. The Evolution of a Collective Bargaining Relationship in Public Education: New York City's Changing Seven-Year History. *Mich. Law Rev.*, March 1969, *67*(5), pp. 1033–66.

Klausner, Robert F. The Evaluation of Risk in Marine Capital Investments. *Eng. Econ.*, July–August 1969, *14*(4), pp. 183–214.

van Klaveren, Jacob. Fiscalism, Mercantilism and Corruption. **In** *Coleman, D. C., ed.*, 1969, pp. 140–61.

Klebaner, Benjamin J. Statement. **In** *Bank Holding Company Act Amendments, Pts. 1–3, HCH*, 1969, pp. 651–54.

Kleijnen, Jack P. Monte Carlo Techniques: A Comment. **In** *Naylor, T. H., ed.*, 1969, pp. 289–97.

Klein, Donald J. History of the Odd-Lot Stock Trading Theory. *Marquette Bus. Rev.*, Fall 1969, *13*(3), pp. 99–116.

Klein, Lawrence R. Econometric Analysis of the Tax Cut of 1964. **In** *Duesenberry, J. S., et al.*, 1969, pp. 458–72.

_____ Estimation on Interdependent Systems in Macroeconometrics. *Econometrica*, April 1969, *37*(2), pp. 171–92.

_____ Statement. **In** *The 1969 Economic Report of the President, Pt. 2, JECH*, 1969, pp. 489–94.

_____ **and Evans, Michael K.** Experience with Econometric Analysis of the U.S. "Konjunktur" Position. **In** *Bronfenbrenner, M., ed.*, 1969, pp. 359–88.

_____ **and Fromm, Gary.** Solutions of the Complete System. **In** *Duesenberry, J. S., et al.*, 1969, pp. 362–421.

_____ **and Preston, R. S.** Stochastic Nonlinear Models. *Econometrica*, January 1969, *37*(1), pp. 95–106.

Kleingartner, Archie. The Characteristics and Work Adjustment of Engineering Technicians. *Calif. Manage. Rev.*, Spring 1969, *11*(3), pp. 89–96.

_____ Nurses, Collective Bargaining, and Labor Legislation. **In** *Wortman, M. S., Jr.*, 1969, pp. 94–102.

_____ Professionalism and Engineering Unionism. *Ind. Relat.*, May 1969, *8*(3), pp. 224–35.

Klevorick, Alvin K. and Branson, William H. Money Illusion and the Aggregate Consumption Function. *Amer. Econ. Rev.*, December 1969, *59*(5), pp. 832–49.

Klindt, Thomas and Braschler, Curtis. Theoretical

and Empirical Problems in Local Government Consolidation. *Can. J. Agr. Econ.*, February 1969, *17*(1), pp. 141–50.

Klingaman, David. A Note on a Cyclical Majority Problem. *Public Choice*, Spring 1969, *6*, pp. 99–101.

——— The Significance of Grain in the Development of the Tobacco Colonies. *J. Econ. Hist.*, June 1969, *29*(2), pp. 268–78.

Kloek, T.; Lempers, F. B. and Barten, A. P. A Note on a Class of Utility and Production Functions Yielding Everywhere Differentiable Demand Functions. *Rev. Econ. Stud.*, January 1969, *36* (105), pp. 109–11.

Klopstock, Fred H. Euro-dollars in the Liquidity and Reserve Management of United States Banks. **In** *Jessup, P. F.*, 1969, pp. 491–506.

——— Impact of Euro-Markets on the United States Balance of Payments. *Law Contemp. Probl.*, Winter 1969, *34*(1), pp. 157–71.

Klos, Joseph J. and Trenton, R. W. The Effectiveness of Teaching Methods: One Semester or Two. *J. Econ. Educ.*, Fall 1969, *1*(1), pp. 51–55.

Klotzvog, F. N.; Ageeva, V. A. and Buzunov, R. A. Input-Output and National Economic Planning. *Matekon*, Fall 1969, *6*(1), pp. 19–29.

Kl'učárová, Mária. Jedna metóda riešenia výrobnorozmiestňovacieho modelu. (A Method for Solving Integrated Production and Distribution Model. With English summary.) *Ekon.-Mat. Obzor*, 1969, *5*(1), pp. 30–44.

Kneese, Allen V. and d' Arge, Ralph C. Pervasive External Costs and the Response of Society. **In** *The Analysis and Evaluation of Public Expenditures: The PPB System, Vol. 1, JECP*, 1969, pp. 87–115.

——— **and Ayres, Robert U.** Pollution and Environmental Quality. **In** *Perloff, H. S., ed.*, 1969, pp. 35–71.

——— **and Ayres, Robert U.** Production, Consumption, and Externalities. *Amer. Econ. Rev.*, June 1969, *59*(3), pp. 282–97.

Knetsch, Jack L. Economic Analysis in Natural Resource Programs. **In** *The Analysis and Evaluation of Public Expenditures: The PPB System, Vol. 3, JECP*, 1969, pp. 1087–1101.

Knetsch, Jack L., et al. Federal Natural Resources Development: Basic Issues in Benefit and Cost Measurement. **In** *Guidelines for Estimating the Benefits of Public Expenditures, JECH*, 1969, pp. 109–15.

Knight, Frank H. Some Fallacies in the Interpretation of Social Cost. **In** *Arrow, K. J. and Scitovsky, T., eds.*, 1969, pp. 213–27.

Knight, K. G. The Baking Industry. **In** *Lerner, S. W.; Cable, J. R. and Gupta, S., eds.*, 1969, pp. 199–243.

Knight, Robert E. An Alternative Approach to Liquidity: Part I. *Fed. Res. Bank Kansas City Rev.*, December 1969, pp. 11–21.

——— The Quality of Mortgage Credit: Part I. *Fed. Res. Bank Kansas City Rev.*, March 1969, pp. 13–20.

——— The Quality of Mortgage Credit: Part II. *Fed. Res. Bank Kansas City Rev.*, April 1969, pp. 10–18.

Knowles, Ann; Davies, Jean and Behrend, Hilde. 'Have You Heard the Phrase "Productivity Agreements"?' Findings from Two National Sample Surveys. *Scot. J. Polit. Econ.*, November 1969, *16*(3), pp. 256–70.

Knowles, J. W. The Economics of Branch Line Railway Operation in Queensland. *Econ. Rec.*, December 1969, *45*(112), pp. 563–77.

——— A Process Function for Rail Linehaul Operations: A Note. *J. Transp. Econ. Policy*, September 1969, *3*(3), pp. 350–51.

Knowles, K. G. J. C. and Robinson, D. Wage Movements in Coventry. *Bull. Oxford Univ. Inst. Econ. Statist.*, February 1969, *31*(1), pp. 1–21.

——— Wage Movements in Coventry—Appendix II. *Bull. Oxford Univ. Inst. Econ. Statist.*, May 1969, *31*(2), pp. 145–52.

Knudsen, John W. International Trade Policies—The Export Performance of Developing Countries. *Fed. Res. Bank Kansas City Rev.*, July-August 1969, pp. 10–18.

Knutsen, John A. and Andrus, Roman R. The Impact of Personal Information Sources on Retailer Success. *Oregon Bus. Rev.*, November 1969, *28*(11), pp. 1–3.

Knutson, Ronald D. The Economic Consequences of the Minnesota Dairy Industry Unfair Trade Practices Act. *J. Law Econ.*, October 1969, *12*(2), pp. 377–89.

——— Nonproducer Cooperative Interests and the Antitrust Laws. *Amer. J. Agr. Econ.*, May 1969, *51* (2), pp. 335–41.

——— **and Schneidau, R. E.** Price Discrimination in the Food Industry: A Competitive Stimulant or Tranquilizer? *Amer. J. Agr. Econ.*, December 1969, *51*(5), pp. 1143–48.

Koch, Gary G. A Useful Lemma for Proving the Equality of Two Matrices with Applications to Least Squares Type Quadratic Forms. *J. Amer. Statist. Assoc.*, September 1969, *64*(327), pp. 969–70.

——— **and Horvitz, D. G.** The Effect of Response Errors on Measures of Association. **In** *Johnson, N. L. and Smith, H., Jr., eds.*, 1969, pp. 247–81.

Koch, Helmut. The Law of Diminishing Marginal Capacity and Its Significance for the Theory of the Firm. *Ger. Econ. Rev.*, 1969, *7*(1), pp. 1–24.

Koch, James V. The Homogeneity Assumption and Financial Asset Demand Functions. *Quart. Rev. Econ. Bus.*, Winter 1969, *9*(4), pp. 57–65.

——— Homogeneity in Wealth: Demand Functions for Liquid Financial Assets. *Rivista Int. Sci. Econ. Com.*, October 1969, *16*(10), pp. 950–64.

Kochen, Manfred and Deutsch, Karl W. Toward a Rational Theory of Decentralization: Some Implications of a Mathematical Approach. *Amer. Polit. Sci. Rev.*, September 1969, *63*(3), pp. 734–49.

Koehler, Robert W. Statistical Variance Control: Through Performance Reports and On-the-Spot Observation. *Manage. Account.*, December 1969, *51*(6), pp. 42–46.

Koerts, J. and Abrahamse, A. P. J. A Comparison between the Power of the Durbin-Watson Test and the Power of the BLUS Test. *J. Amer. Statist. Assoc.*, September 1969, *64*(327), pp. 938–48.

Kohl, Schuyler G. Fighting Poverty with Family Planning. In *Weaver, T. and Magid, A., eds.*, 1969, pp. 48–54.

Kohlmeyer, J. B. A Basic Framework for Policy Education. *Amer. J. Agr. Econ.*, December 1969, *51* (5), pp. 1357–64.

Kohoutek, Miloslav. Economic Aspects of the Federalization of Czechoslovakia. *New Trends Czech. Econ.*, February 1969, (1), pp. 50–65.

Koivisto, Heikki. Viivästysjakautumien approksimointikeinoista. (On New Methods for Approximating Distributed Lags. With English summary.) *Kansant. Aikak.*, 1969, *65*(4), pp. 304–10.

Koizumi, Susumu. Technical Progress and Investment. *Int. Econ. Rev.*, February 1969, *10*(1), pp. 68–81.

Kojima, Kiyoshi. Asian Developing Countries and PAFTA: Development, Aid and Trade Preferences. *Hitotsubashi J. Econ.*, June 1969, *10*(1), pp. 1–17.

______ Trade Preferences for Developing Countries: A Japanese Assessment. *Hitotsubashi J. Econ.*, February 1969, *9*(2), pp. 1–12.

Kolbin, V. V. and Syroezhin, I. M. Computer Analysis of a Business Game. *Matekon*, Fall 1969, *6*(1), pp. 57–74.

Kolinski, Ralph. Customs Unions of Undeveloped Nations: The Case of Central America. *Econ. Int.*, February 1969, *22*(1), pp. 116–33.

Kolm, Serge-Christophe. L'encombrement pluridimensionnel. (With English summary.) *Revue Écon.*, November 1969, *20*(6), pp. 954–67.

______ L'exploitation des nations par les nations. (With English summary.) *Revue Écon.*, September 1969, *20*(5), pp. 851–72.

______ La vérité des prix dans un monde imparfait. (With English summary.) *Revue Écon.*, July 1969, *20*(4), pp. 727–40.

______ Les politiques dynamiques optimales d'investissement. (With English summary.) *Revue Écon.*, September 1969, *20*(5), pp. 753–82.

______ The Optimal Production of Social Justice. In *Margolis, J. and Guitton, H., eds.*, 1969, pp. 145–200.

______ Structuration informationnelle centralisée et hiérarchisée: Une contribution à la théorie des organisations. (With English summary.) *Revue Écon.*, May 1969, *20*(3), pp. 455–67.

Kolodner, Ferne K. and Kravitz, Sanford. Community Action: Where Has It Been? Where Will It Go? *Ann. Amer. Acad. Polit. Soc. Sci.*, September 1969, *385*, pp. 30–40.

Komarov, V. E. The Efficiency of Day, Correspondence, and Evening Education. In *Noah, H. J., ed.*, 1969, pp. 153–58.

Komiya, Ryutaro. Economic Growth and the Balance of Payments: A Monetary Approach. *J. Polit. Econ.*, January/February 1969, *77*(1), pp. 35–48.

Komló, László. The Problems of Vertical Integration in Agriculture: The Hungarian Case. In *Papi, U. and Nunn, C., eds.*, 1969, pp. 365–76.

Konovalova, N. and Petrosian, K. Problems of Intensifying the Stimulating Role of Payments for Funds. *Prob. Econ.*, June 1969, *12*(2), pp. 25–47.

Konstas, Panos and Khouja, Mohamad W. The Keynesian Demand-for-Money Function: Another Look and Some Additional Evidence. *J. Money, Credit, Banking*, November 1969, *1*(4), pp. 765–77.

Koot, Ronald S. Wage Changes, Unemployment, and Inflation in Chile. *Ind. Lab. Relat. Rev.*, July 1969, *22*(4), pp. 568–75.

Kordaszewski, Jan. A Polish Contribution to Job Evaluation for Non-Manual Workers. *Int. Lab. Rev.*, August 1969, *100*(2), pp. 141–58.

Korf, Jack H. Management Accounting Control by Remote Output. *Manage. Account.*, November 1969, *51*(5), pp. 44–47.

Koriagin, B. and Il'in, V. The Sale of Goods to the Public on Credit. *Prob. Econ.*, December 1969, *12* (8), pp. 68–74.

Kormnov, Iu. Economic Stimulation of the Development of International Production Specialization. *Prob. Econ.*, January 1969, *11*(9), pp. 45–54.

Kornai, J. Man-Machine Planning. *Econ. Planning*, 1969, *9*(3), pp. 209–34.

Kornstein, Daniel J. Insurance Mergers and the Clayton Act. *Yale Law J.*, July 1969, *78*(8), pp. 1404–17.

Korte, Bernhard and Oberhofer, Walter. Zur Triangulation von Input-Output-Matrizen. (With English summary.) *Jahr. Nationalökon. Statist.*, March 1969, *182*(4–5), pp. 398–433.

Kosh, David A. The Effects of Leverage and Corporate Taxes on the Shareholders of Regulated Utilities: Comment. In *Trebing, H. M. and Howard, R. H., eds.*, 1969, pp. 106–10.

Kossoris, Max D. 1966 West Coast Longshore Negotiations. In *Wortman, M. S., Jr.*, 1969, pp. 175–86.

Kosters, Marvin. Effects of an Income Tax on Labor Supply. In *Harberger, A. C. and Bailey, M. J., eds.*, 1969, pp. 301–24.

Kostiainen, Seppo and Pekonen, Kari. Investointivaihtoehtojen optimaalinen valinta. (The Optimal Choice of Investment Projects. With English summary.) *Kansant. Aikak.*, 1969, *65*(3), pp. 191–205.

Kothari, V. N. and Gulati, I. S. Land Tax as an Incentive for Better Land Utilization. *Artha-Vikas*, July 1969, *5*(2), pp. 108–16.

Kotler, Philip and Levy, Sidney J. Beyond Marketing: The Furthering Concept. *Calif. Manage. Rev.*, Winter 1969, *12*(2), pp. 67–73.

Kottke, Marvin. The Supply Function in Agriculture Revisited: Discussion. *Amer. Econ. Rev.*, May 1969, *59*(2), pp. 184–85.

Kotzan, Jeffrey A. and Evanson, Robert V. Responsiveness of Drug Store Sales to Shelf Space Allocations. *J. Marketing Res.*, November 1969, *6*(4), pp. 465–69.

Kouba, Karel. The Plan and Market in a Socialist Economy. *Czech. Econ. Pap.*, 1969, (11), pp. 27–42.

Koudelka, Miroslav. Program of Economic Balance. *New Trends Czech. Econ.*, July 1969, (4), pp. 3–20.

Koumarová, Miluše and Vaner, Josef. Long-term Projection of the Sectoral Structure of the Czechoslovak National Economy on the Basis of an Input-Output Model. *Czech. Econ. Pap.*, 1969, (11), pp. 69–82.

Kouwenhoven, A. De Noordse economische integratie. (Nordic Economic Integration. With English summary.) *De Economist*, September/October 1969, *117*(5), pp. 543–62.

——— Enkele opmerkingen over het tijdaspect der economische verschijnselen. (Some Remarks on the Time-Aspect of Economic Phenomena. With English summary.) *De Economist*, March/April 1969, *117*(2), pp. 121–38.

Kozák, Josef and Šimůnek, Vladimír. Pokus o modelování sezónních výkyvů v bilanční rovnici důchodu. (An Attempt of Mathematical Formulation of Seasonal Variations of Inputs, Outputs and Prices in the Definitional Equation of Income. With English summary.) *Ekon.-Mat. Obzor*, 1969, *5*(2), pp. 209–23.

Kozelka, Robert. A Bayesian Approach to Jamaican Fishing. **In** *Buchler, I. R. and Nutini, H. G., eds.*, 1969, pp. 117–25.

Kozlova, D. I. The Influence of Education on the Labor of Textile Workers. **In** *Noah, H. J., ed.*, 1969, pp. 114–18.

Kpedekpo, G. M. K. On Working Life Tables in Ghana with Particular Reference to the Female Working Population. *J. Roy. Statist. Soc.*, Part 3, 1969, *132*, pp. 431–41.

——— Working Life Tables for Males in Ghana 1960. *J. Amer. Statist. Assoc.*, March 1969, *64*(325), pp. 102–10.

Krahmer, Edward F. and Stinson, Thomas F. Local School Expenditures and Educational Quality: A Correlation Analysis. *Amer. J. Agr. Econ.*, December 1969, *51*(5), pp. 1553–56.

Krainer, Robert E. Liquidity Preference and Stock Market Speculation. *J. Financial Quant. Anal.*, March 1969, *4*(1), pp. 89–97.

——— Structural Estimates of Supply and Demand in the USA Short Term Bank Loan Market. *Bull. Oxford Univ. Inst. Econ. Statist.*, February 1969, *31*(1), pp. 39–46.

Krajčovič, Josef and Janus, Arnošt. The First State Budget of Slovakia, and Problems of Its Fulfillment. *New Trends Czech. Econ.*, November 1969, (7), pp. 80–94.

Kramer, Daniel C. White Versus Colored in Britain: An Explosive Confrontation? *Soc. Res.*, Winter 1969, *36*(4), pp. 585–605.

Kramer, Giselbert. Ein Autokorrelationstest der von Neumann-Klasse und seine Signifikanzpunkte. (With English summary.) *Z. ges. Staatswiss.*, October 1969, *125*(4), pp. 624–36.

Kramer, John E. and Walter, Ingo. Political Autonomy and Economic Dependence in an All-Negro Municipality. *Amer. J. Econ. Soc.*, July 1969, *28*(3), pp. 225–48.

Kramer, Morton. Statistics of Mental Disorders in the United States: Current Status, Some Urgent Needs and Suggested Solutions. *J. Roy. Statist. Soc.*, Part 3, 1969, *132*, pp. 353–97.

Krasnow, Howard S. Simulation Languages. **In** *Naylor, T. H., ed.*, 1969, pp. 320–46.

Krásová, Ludmila and Šimůnek, Vladimír. Soustava finančních účtů ČSSR. (A System of Financial Accounts in Czechoslovakia. With English summary.) *Ekon.-Mat. Obzor*, 1969, *5*(4), pp. 486–508.

Kraus, Alan and Melnik, Arie. Short-Run Interest Rate Cycles in the U.S.: 1954–1967. *J. Financial Quant. Anal.*, September 1969, *4*(3), pp. 291–99.

Krause, Kenneth R. Application of the Financial Management Function in the Family Size Farm Firm. *Amer. J. Agr. Econ.*, December 1969, *51*(5), pp. 1536–42.

Krause, Walter and Mathis, F. John. The Status of "Lesser Developed" Countries within a Latin American Common Market. **In** *Hilton, R., ed.*, 1969, pp. 471–84.

Krausz, N. G. P. and Reiss, Franklin J. Institutions and Instruments—Management Alternatives. *Amer. J. Agr. Econ.*, December 1969, *51*(5), pp. 1369–80.

Kravis, Irving B. Statement. **In** *Review of Federal Statistical Programs, JECH*, 1969, pp. 203–06.

——— **and Lipsey, Robert E.** International Price Comparisons by Regression Methods. *Int. Econ. Rev.*, June 1969, *10*(2), pp. 233–46.

——— **and Liu, Ta-Chung.** What Is Output? Problems of Concept and Measurement: Discussion. **In** *Fuchs, V. R., ed.*, 1969, pp. 84–94.

Kravitz, Sanford and Kolodner, Ferne K. Community Action: Where Has It Been? Where Will It Go? *Ann. Amer. Acad. Polit. Soc. Sci.*, September 1969, *385*, pp. 30–40.

Kreinin, Mordechai E. "Price" vs. "Tariff" Elasticities in International Trade: Reply. *Amer. Econ. Rev.*, March 1969, *59*(1), pp. 200.

——— The Theory of Comparative Cost—Further Empirical Evidence. *Econ. Int.*, November 1969, *22*(4), pp. 662–74.

——— Trade Creation and Diversion by the EEC and EFTA. *Econ. Int.*, May 1969, *22*(2), pp. 273–80.

Kreps, Juanita M. Lifetime Tradeoffs between Work and Play. **In** *Somers, G. G., ed. (II)*, 1969, pp. 307–16.

——— Statement. **In** *Economics of Aging: Toward a Full Share in Abundance, Pt. 1, SCH*, 1969, pp. 4–5.

Kresge, David T. Price and Output Conversion: A Modified Approach. **In** *Duesenberry, J. S., et al.*, 1969, pp. 85–108.

Kress, A. L. Job Evaluation for White-Collar Workers in Private Sector Employment in the United States. *Int. Lab. Rev.*, October 1969, *100*(4), pp. 341–57.

Kriebel, Wesley R. Extension Transportation Programs to Improve Marketing Efficiency. *Amer. J. Agr. Econ.*, December 1969, *51*(5), pp. 1226–28.

Krieger, Ronald A. Problems of Currency Unification in Latin America: Theory and Policy. **In** *Hilton, R., ed.*, 1969, pp. 222–33.

Krier, Donald F. and Loschky, David J. Income and Family Size in Three Eighteenth-Century Lancashire Parishes: A Reconstitution Study. *J. Econ. Hist.*, September 1969, *29*(3), pp. 429–48.

Krishna, Jai and Jha, S. C. Buffer Stock—Concepts and Objectives. **In** *Indian Society of Agricultural Economics*, 1969, pp. 35–48.

Krishnaswamy, K. S. Some Thoughts on a Drama. *Finance Develop.*, March 1969, *6*(1), pp. 43–50.

Krislov, Joseph. The Economics of Poverty: Comment. **In** *Weaver, T. and Magid, A., eds.,* 1969, pp. 39–43.

______ **and Christian, Virgil L., Jr.** Union Organizing and the Business Cycle, 1949–1966. *Southern Econ. J.,* October 1969, *36*(2), pp. 185–88.

______ **and Mead, John F.** Drawing Jurisdictional Lines in Mediation. *Mon. Lab. Rev.,* April 1969, *92*(4), pp. 41–45.

Kriz, Miroslav A. The Future of Gold: Discussion. *Amer. Econ. Rev.,* May 1969, *59*(2), pp. 353–56.

Križková, Mária. Integrovatel'né štruktúrne modely s priestorovým prvkom. (Structural Models with Integration Capabilities and Regional Elements. With English summary.) *Ekon.-Mat. Obzor,* 1969, *5*(4), pp. 509–17.

Krogh, D. C. Taxation in a Developing Economy. *S. Afr. J. Econ.,* December 1969, *37*(4), pp. 285–305.

Krohmer, F. R. Deposit Growth in the Tenth District—1949–68. *Fed. Res. Bank Kansas City Rev.,* May 1969, pp. 11–16.

Kronsjö, Tom. Decomposition of a Large Nonlinear Convex Separable Economic System in the Dual Direction. *Econ. Planning,* 1969, *9*(1–2), pp. 71–94.

______ Optimal Coordination of a Large Convex Economic System. (Decomposition of a Nonlinear Convex Separable Economic System in Primal and Dual Directions to Obtain a Common Subproblem.) *Jahr. Nationalökon. Statist.,* December 1969, *183*(5), pp. 378–400.

Kronsten, Joseph A. East-West Trade: Myth and Matter. **In** *Grub, P. D. and Holbik, K.,* 1969, pp. 117–24.

Krooss, Herman E. Economic History: Discussion. *Amer. Econ. Rev.,* May 1969, *59*(2), pp. 384–85.

Krueger, Anne O. Balance-of-Payments Theory. *J. Econ. Lit.,* March 1969, *7*(1), pp. 1–26.

Kruger, Daniel H. Statement. **In** *Unemployment Compensation, HCH,* 1969, pp. 319–26.

Krum, James R. Perceptions and Evaluation of the Role of the Corporate Marketing Research Department. *J. Marketing Res.,* November 1969, *6* (4), pp. 459–64.

Krumme, Günter. Toward a Geography of Enterprise. *Econ. Geogr.,* January 1969, *45*(1), pp. 30–40.

Krupp, Hans-Juergen. Econometric Analysis of Tax Incidence. **In** *Peacock, A. T., ed.,* 1969, pp. 111–35.

Krutilla, John V. Efficiency Goals, Market Failure, and the Substitution of Public for Private Action. **In** *The Analysis and Evaluation of Public Expenditures: The PPB System, Vol. 1, JECP,* 1969, pp. 277–89.

______; **Margolis, Julius and Hufschmidt, Maynard M.** Standards and Criteria for Formulating and Evaluating Federal Water Resources Development. **In** *Guidelines for Estimating the Benefits of Public Expenditures, JECH,* 1969, pp. 135–212.

Kuboleca, S. Review of Movements in Yugoslav Economy towards Decentralization. **In** *Economic Concentration, Pt. 7A, SCH,* 1969, pp. 4495–4506.

Kucharski, Mieczyslaw and Pirozynski, Zbigniew. Social Insurance and Economic Incentives. *Public Finance,* 1969, *24*(2), pp. 238–55.

Kuchenbecker, Horst. Zur Darstellung von Veränderungen der Weltwarenpreise durch arithmetische und geometrische Indizes am Beispiel des Moody-Index und des Reuter-Index. (On the Representation of World Commodity Price Changes by Arithmetic and Geometric Index Numbers, Illustrated in Moodys Index of Staple Commodities and Reuters Commodity Index. With English summary.) *Jahr. Nationalökon. Statist.,* August 1969, *183*(3–4), pp. 254–70.

Kudrna, A. Differentiation in Earnings. *Eastern Europ. Econ.,* Summer 1969, *7*(4), pp. 25–37.

Kuehn, Alfred A. and Hamburger, Michael J. A Hueristic Program for Locating Warehouses. **In** *Alexis, M.; Holloway, R. J. and Hancock, R. S., eds.,* 1969, pp. 472–85.

Kuehn, D. A. Stock Market Valuation and Acquisitions: An Empirical Test of One Component of Managerial Utility. *J. Ind. Econ.,* April 1969, *17* (2), pp. 132–44.

Kuehn, John A. and Bender, Lloyd D. An Empirical Identification of Growth Centers. *Land Econ.,* November 1969, *45*(4), pp. 435–43.

______ **and Brewer, Durward.** Conflicts within Recreation: A Rejoinder. *Land Econ.,* February 1969, *45*(1), pp. 131–33.

Kuhbier, Peter and Kalmbach, Peter. Beiträge des technischen Fortschritts zum Produktivitätswachstum in Industriebereichen. (The Contribution of Technical Progress to Productivity Growth in Manufacturing Industries. With English summary.) *Ifo-Studien,* 1969, *15*(1/2), pp. 19–55.

Kuipers, S. K. and de Haan, H. Een onderzoek naar de invloed van monetaire factoren op het reële groeiproces in enkele traditionele theorieën van economische groei (II). (An Investigation into the Influence of Monetary Factors on the Real Process of Growth in Some Traditional Theories of Economic Growth (II). With English summary.) *De Economist,* July/August 1969, *117*(4), pp. 381–401.

______ Een onderzoek naar de invloed van monetaire factoren op het reële groeiproces in enkele traditionele theorieën van economische groei (III). (An Investigation into the Influence of Monetary Factors on the Real Process of Growth in Some Traditional Theories of Economic Growth (III). With English summary.) *De Economist,* September/October 1969, *117*(5), pp. 493–515.

______ Een onderzoek naar de invloed van monetaire factoren op het reële groeiproces in enkele traditionele theorieën van economische groei (I). (An Investigation into the Influence of Monetary Factors on the Real Process of Growth in Some Traditional Theories of Economic Growth (I). With English summary.) *De Economist,* March/April 1969, *117*(2), pp. 139–60.

Kuligin, P. Improvement of Price Formation under the Economic Reform. *Prob. Econ.,* October 1969, *12*(6), pp. 27–41.

Kulkarni, G. B. Unit Costs of Education in Commerce Colleges of Bombay: 1962–63 to 1966–67. **In** *Pandit, H. N., ed.,* 1969, pp. 114–20.

Kulkarni, Vijay G. The Growth of Indian Industries

(1951–1965). **In** *Bhuleshkar, A. V., ed.,* 1969, pp. 259–70.

Kullmer, Lore. Problems of the Financial Reform in the Federal Republic of Germany. *Ger. Econ. Rev.,* 1969, *7*(1), pp. 63–71.

Kulshreshtha, S. N. Age and Efficiency in Public Agricultural Policy: The Case of Ontario. *Can. J. Agr. Econ.,* July 1969, *17*(2), pp. 85–91.

——— Part-Time Farming in Ontario Agriculture. *Can. J. Agr. Econ.,* February 1969, *17*(1), pp. 151–56.

Kumar, Pushpendra. Domestic Terms of Trade and Inter-Sectoral Income Flows in India: 1952–53 to 1966–67. *Asian Econ. Rev.,* August 1969, *11*(4), pp. 349–62.

Kumar, T. Krishna. The Existence of an Optimal Economic Policy. *Econometrica,* October 1969, *37*(4), pp. 600–610.

Kunel'skii, L. The Socioeconomic Significance of Raising the Minimum Wage. *Prob. Econ.,* July 1969, *12*(3), pp. 43–57.

Kunnas, Heikki J. EFO-tutkimus. (EFO Survey. With English summary.) *Kansant. Aikak.,* 1969, *65*(3), pp. 206–13.

Kuosa, Aarno. Suksessiivisten suoritevalintojen optimointi. (Optimization of Successive Choices of Products. With English summary.) *Liiketaloudellinen Aikak.,* 1969, *18*(4), pp. 716–27.

Kurabayashi, Yoshimasa. The Structure of Income Redistribution within the Framework of an Extended System of National Accounts. *Hitotsubashi J. Econ.,* June 1969, *10*(1), pp. 18–32.

Kurihara, Kenneth K. The Antinomic Impact of Automation on Employment and Growth. *Econ. Int.,* August 1969, *22*(3), pp. 423–33.

——— **and Bhuleshkar, A. V.** Democratic Welfare Statecraft in a Developing Economy with an Empirical Application. **In** *Bhuleshkar, A. V., ed.,* 1969, pp. 288–302.

Kurz, Mordecai. Tightness and Substitution in the Theory of Capital. *J. Econ. Theory,* October 1969, *1*(3), pp. 244–72.

——— **and Arrow, Kenneth J.** Optimal Consumer Allocation over an Infinite Horizon. *J. Econ. Theory,* June 1969, *1*(1), pp. 68–91.

——— **and Arrow, Kenneth J.** Optimal Public Investment Policy and Controllability with Fixed Private Savings Ratio. *J. Econ. Theory,* August 1969, *1*(2), pp. 141–77.

Kushwaha, D. S. The Role of Industrial Policy in Economic Development. **In** *Bhuleshkar, A. V., ed.,* 1969, pp. 214–27.

Kux, Jaroslav; Mairesse, Jacques and Drechsler, László. Labour Productivity Comparison between Czechoslovakia and France. *Rev. Income Wealth,* September 1969, *15*(3), pp. 219–28.

Kuyvenhoven, A. and Bos, H. C. Economic Integration and the Optimum International Distribution of Production. **In** *[Tinbergen, J.],* 1969, pp. 93–110.

Kuz'min, S. A. The Developing Countries: Employment and Capital Investment. *Prob. Econ.,* February/March 1969, *11*(10–11), pp. 1–108.

Kuznets, P. W. Korea's Five-Year Plans. **In** *Adelman, I., ed.,* 1969, pp. 39–73.

Kuznets, Simon. Economic Aspects of Fertility Trends in the Less Developed Countries. **In** *Behrman, S. J.; Corsa, L., Jr. and Freedman, R., eds.,* 1969, pp. 157–79.

Kvasha, Ya. Concentration of Production and Small Scale Industry. **In** *Economic Concentration, Pt. 7A, SCH,* 1969, pp. 4358–62.

Kwon, Jene and Jeffers, James R. A Portfolio Approach to Corporate Demands for Government Securities. *J. Finance,* December 1969, *24*(5), pp. 905–19.

Kypris, Phidias C. Greece: The New Code on Financial Books and Documents—The Salient Points. *Bull. Int. Fiscal Doc.,* February 1969, *23*(2), pp. 66–72.

L'Esperance, Wilford L. Econometric Model Building for State Economic Development. *Ohio State U. Bull. Bus. Res.,* December 1969, *44*(12), pp. 1–3, 7–8.

———**; Nestel, G. and Fromm, D.** Gross State Product and an Econometric Model of a State. *J. Amer. Statist. Assoc.,* September 1969, *64*(327), pp. 787–807.

La Force, J. Clayburn. The Supply of Muskets and Spain's War of Independence. *Bus. Hist. Rev.,* Winter 1969, *43*(4), pp. 523–44.

Laber, Gene. International Travel in the Canadian Balance of Payments, 1949–1966. *Econ. Int.,* August 1969, *22*(3), pp. 487–98.

——— **and Chase, Richard X.** Economic Growth as an Anti-poverty Tool: A Further Consideration of the Backwash Debate. *Soc. Sci. Quart.,* December 1969, *50*(3), pp. 604–08.

Labib, Subhi Y. Capitalism in Medieval Islam. *J. Econ. Hist.,* March 1969, *29*(1), pp. 79–96.

Labovitz, David E. and Wood, Marshall. The Korean Sectoral Model: Appendix. **In** *Adelman, I., ed.,* 1969, pp. 135–43.

Labrousse, E. 1848–1830–1789: How Revolutions Are Born. **In** *Crouzet, F.; Chaloner, W. H. and Stern, W. M., eds.,* 1969, pp. 1–14.

Lachmann, Ludwig M. Methodological Individualism and the Market Economy. **In** *[von Hayek, Friedrich A.],* 1969, pp. 89–103.

Lacina, Otakar. The Long-Term Forecast of the Czechoslovak Economy. *Czech. Econ. Pap.,* 1969, (11), pp. 7–26.

Lacroix, Henri. The ILO at 50: Its Role in Improving Labor Statistics. *Mon. Lab. Rev.,* May 1969, *92*(5), pp. 47–50.

Lacroix, Y. and Schouwenaars, W. Effectieve bescherming aan de grenzen van de E.E.G. en het Verenigd Koninkrijk, voor en na de Kennedy-ronde. (Effective Protection at the Borders of the E.E.C. and the United Kingdom before and after the Kennedy-Round. With English summary.) *Tijdschr. Econ.,* 1969, *14*(2), pp. 158–87.

Łączkowski, Bohdan. Poland's Participation in the Kennedy Round. **In** *Alting von Geusau, F. A. M., ed.,* 1969, pp. 83–93.

Ladd, George W. Federal Milk Marketing Order Provisions: Effects on Producer Prices and Intermarket Price Relationships. *Amer. J. Agr. Econ.,* August 1969, *51*(3), pp. 625–41.

——— Utility Maximization Sufficient for Competitive Survival. *J. Polit. Econ.,* Part I, July/August 1969, *77*(4), pp. 478–83.

Ladd, John C. Consumers and Antitrust Treble Damages: Credit-Furniture Tie-Ins in the Low Income Market. *Yale Law J.,* December 1969, *79* (2), pp. 254–83.

______ The Logic of Foreclosure: Tie-In Doctrine after *Fortner v. U. S. Steel. Yale Law J.,* November 1969, *79*(1), pp. 86–101.

Lady, George M. A Note on "Graph-Theoretical Approaches to the Theory of Social Choice." *Public Choice,* Spring 1969, *6,* pp. 93–98.

Laevaert, Ludo and Beernaert, Luc. De Tienermarkt: Analyse van enkele karakteristieken. (The Teenager Market: An Analysis of Some Characteristics. With English summary.) *Econ. Soc. Tijdschr.,* December 1969, *23*(6), pp. 663–74.

Laffer, Arthur B. The U.S. Balance of Payments—A Financial Center View. *Law Contemp. Probl.,* Winter 1969, *34*(1), pp. 33–46.

______ Vertical Integration by Corporations, 1929–1965. *Rev. Econ. Statist.,* February 1969, *51*(1), pp. 91–93.

Laffer, Kingsley. Compulsory Arbitration: A New Province for Law and Order. **In** *Preston, R., ed.,* 1969, pp. 153–72.

Lagioni, Iginio. Dal "commercio" internazionale alla "mercatistica" internazionale. (From "International Trade" to International "Marketing." With English summary.) *L'Impresa,* January/February 1969, *11*(1), pp. 61–67.

Lago, Armando M. The Hoffman Industrial Growth Development Path: An International Comparison. *Weltwirtsch. Arch.,* 1969, *103*(1), pp. 41–57.

Lahne, Herbert J. Coalition Bargaining and the Future of Union Structure. **In** *Wortman, M. S., Jr.,* 1969, pp. 46–52.

Laidler, David. The Case for Raising the Price of Gold: A Comment. *J. Money, Credit, Banking,* August 1969, *1*(3), pp. 675–78.

______ The Definition of Money: Theoretical and Empirical Problems. *J. Money, Credit, Banking,* August 1969, *1*(3), pp. 508–25.

______ Income Tax Incentives for Owner-Occupied Housing. **In** *Harberger, A. C. and Bailey, M. J., eds.,* 1969, pp. 50–76.

Laing, N. F. Two Notes on Pasinetti's Theorem. *Econ. Rec.,* September 1969, *45*(111), pp. 373–85.

Laird, William E. Statement. **In** *Tax Credits to Stimulate Job Opportunities in Rural Areas, SCH,* 1969, pp. 191–95.

______ **and Rinehart, James R.** A Refinement of Local Industrial Subsidy Techniques: Reply. *Miss. Val. J. Bus. Econ.,* Spring 1969, *4*(2), pp. 82–88.

Lakdawala, D. T. Gandhiji and Growth Economics. *Indian Econ. J.,* October–December 1969, *17*(2), pp. 266–72.

______ **and Patil, R. H.** Prospects of India's Trade with ECAFE Countries. **In** *Morgan, T. and Spoelstra, N., eds.,* 1969, pp. 241–73.

Lal, H. Reflections on Steel Pricing. **In** *Dagli, V., ed., Vol. II,* 1969, pp. 130–39.

Lall, Sanjaya. Countering Inflation: The Role of Value Linking. *Finance Develop.,* June 1969, *6*(2), pp. 10–15.

______ A Note on Government Expenditures in Developing Countries. *Econ. J.,* June 1969, *79*(314), pp. 413–17.

Lalonde, Bernard J.; Robeson, James F. and Grabner, John R., Jr. The Business Logistics Concept. *Ohio State U. Bull. Bus. Res.,* May 1969, *44*(5), pp. 1–3, 8.

Lalwani, Gita. Battle for Franc—A New Crisis in the International Monetary System—I. *Econ. Aff.,* January-February 1969, *14*(1–2), pp. 49–56.

Lamale, Helen H. Poverty: The Word and the Reality. **In** *Wortman, M. S., Jr.,* 1969, pp. 133–40.

Lambert, Rapporto. Perché le imprese europee non guadagnano come le americane. (Why European Firms Do Not Earn as Much as the Americans. With English summary.) *L'Impresa,* January/February 1969, *11*(1), pp. 18–28.

Lambin, Jean-Jacques. Measuring the Profitability of Advertising: An Empirical Study. *J. Ind. Econ.,* April 1969, *17*(2), pp. 86–103.

Lamfalussy, Alexandre. La funzione monetaria dell'oro nei prossimi dieci anni. (The Role of Monetary Gold Over the Next Ten Years. With English summary.) *Bancaria,* November 1969, *25*(11), pp. 1331–41.

Lamphear, Charles and McConnell, Campbell R. The Effectiveness of Teaching Methods: Teaching Principles of Economics without Lectures. *J. Econ. Educ.,* Fall 1969, *1*(1), pp. 20–32.

Landauer, Carl. On the Social Rate of Discount: Comment. *Amer. Econ. Rev.,* December 1969, *59* (5), pp. 917–18.

Landay, Donald M. Trends in Negotiated Health Plans; Broader Coverage, Higher Quality Care. *Mon. Lab. Rev.,* May 1969, *92*(5), pp. 3–10.

Landes, D. The Old Bank and the New: The Financial Revolution of the Nineteenth Century. **In** *Crouzet, F.; Chaloner, W. H. and Stern, W. M., eds.,* 1969, pp. 112–27.

Landes, William M. Round Table on Allocation of Resources in Law Enforcement. *Amer. Econ. Rev.,* May 1969, *59*(2), pp. 505–08.

Landis, Judson R. and Wolff, Carole E. Dr. Irene Hickman and Tax Reform in Sacramento County, Calif. *Amer. J. Econ. Soc.,* October 1969, *28*(4), pp. 409–21.

Landynski, Jacob W. Governmental Aid to Non-public Schools: The Constitutional Conflict Sharpens. *Soc. Res.,* Autumn 1969, *36*(3), pp. 333–56.

Lane, Frederic C. Meanings of Capitalism. *J. Econ. Hist.,* March 1969, *29*(1), pp. 5–12.

Lane, Willard R. School Administration and Negotiations: Remarks. **In** *Sinicropi, A. V. and Gilroy, T. P., eds.,* 1969, pp. 34–40.

Lange, Jeffrey T. Application of a Mathematical Concept of Risk to Property-Liability Insurance Ratemaking. *J. Risk Ins.,* September 1969, *36*(4), pp. 383–91.

Lange, Oskar. The Foundations of Welfare Economics. **In** *Arrow, K. J. and Scitovsky, T., eds.,* 1969, pp. 26–38.

Langham, Max R. and Edwards, W. F. Externalities in Pesticide Use. *Amer. J. Agr. Econ.,* December 1969, *51*(5), pp. 1195–1201.

von Lanzenauer, Christoph Haehling. A Model for Determining Optimal Profit Sharing Plans. *J. Financial Quant. Anal.,* March 1969, *4*(1), pp. 53–63.

Lanzillotti, R. F. and Saving, Thomas R. State

Branching Restrictions and the Availability of Branching Services: A Comment. *J. Money, Credit, Banking,* November 1969, *1*(4), pp. 778–88.

Lapidus, Leonard. Bank Holding Companies: Discussion. **In** *Federal Reserve Bank of Chicago (II),* 1969, pp. 102–04.

Lard, Curtis F. and Martin, J. Rod. At a Crossroad: Graduate Teaching in Agricultural Economics. *Amer. J. Agr. Econ.,* December 1969, *51*(5), pp. 1569–73.

Laris Casillas, Jorge. El proceso administrativo del presupuesto. (The Administrative Process of Drawing up a Budget. With English summary.) *Econ. Polít.,* Second Semester 1969, *6*(2), pp. 229–40.

Larre, René. Facts of Life about the Integration of National Capital Markets. *J. Money, Credit, Banking,* August 1969, *1*(3), pp. 319–27.

Larson, Henrietta M. Contours of Change: Standard Oil Company (New Jersey), 1882–1950. **In** *Kennedy, C. J., ed.,* 1969, pp. 3–19.

Larson, Kermit D. and Gonedes, Nicholas J. Business Combinations: An Exchange Ratio Determination Model. *Accounting Rev.,* October 1969, *44* (4), pp. 720–28.

Last, J. M. International Mobility in the Medical Profession. **In** *Bechhofer, F., ed.,* 1969, pp. 31–42.

Latané, Henry A. and Young, William E. Test of Portfolio Building Rules. *J. Finance,* September 1969, *24*(4), pp. 595–612.

Latscha, Jacques and Durand, Patrick. The New Tax Treaty between the United Kingdom and France. *Bull. Int. Fiscal Doc.,* March 1969, *23*(3), pp. 131–36.

Latta, Cynthia M. and Hamburger, Michael J. The Term Structure of Interest Rates: Some Additional Evidence. *J. Money, Credit, Banking,* February 1969, *1*(1), pp. 71–83.

Lau, Lawrence J. Duality and the Structure of Utility Functions. *J. Econ. Theory,* December 1969, *1*(4), pp. 374–96.

Laumas, Gurcharan S. Savings Deposits in the Definition of Money. *J. Polit. Econ.,* November/December 1969, *77*(6), pp. 892–96.

______ The Shifting of the Corporation Income Tax in India. *Econ. Int.,* May 1969, *22*(2), pp. 283–91.

______ **and Laumas, Prem S.** Interest-Elasticity of Demand for Money. *Southern Econ. J.,* July 1969, *36*(1), pp. 90–93.

Laumas, Prem S. The Role of Savings Deposits as Money: A Comment. *J. Money, Credit, Banking,* November 1969, *1*(4), pp. 789–95.

______ A Test of the Permanent Income Hypothesis. *J. Polit. Econ.,* September/October 1969, *77*(5), pp. 857–61.

______ **and Laumas, Gurcharan S.** Interest-Elasticity of Demand for Money. *Southern Econ. J.,* July 1969, *36*(1), pp. 90–93.

Launie, J. J. The Supply Function of Urban Property Insurance. *J. Risk Ins.,* June 1969, *36*(2), pp. 269–83.

Lauth, James H. Economic Considerations in Rate Making and Rate Structures for Farm Products. *Amer. J. Agr. Econ.,* December 1969, *51*(5), pp. 1464–70.

Lavagne, Pierre. Conséquences de la liberté de mouvement du facteur travail en économie internationale. (With English summary.) *Revue Écon.,* September 1969, *20*(5), pp. 873–87.

Lavidge, Robert J. The Ghetto Challenge to Marketing People. *Ohio State U. Bull. Bus. Res.,* August 1969, *44*(8), pp. 4, 6–7.

Lawrence, Paul R. How to Deal with Resistance to Change. *Harvard Bus. Rev.,* January–February 1969, *47*(1), pp. 4–12, 166–76.

Lawrence, Raymond J. Patterns of Buyer Behavior: Time for a New Approach? *J. Marketing Res.,* May 1969, *6*(2), pp. 137–44.

Lawrence, Willard E. and Draper, Norman R. Distributions of Blocks of Signs. **In** *Naylor, T. H., ed.,* 1969, pp. 347–51.

Lawyer, John E. The ILO at 50: How It Began and How It Functions. *Mon. Lab. Rev.,* May 1969, *92* (5), pp. 32–36.

Layng, W. John and Nakayama, Toshiko. An Analysis of Price Changes in Second Quarter of 1969. *Mon. Lab. Rev.,* October 1969, *92*(10), pp. 36–41.

Lázár, G. Regional Pattern of the Hungarian Economy: Development of SomeTopical Problems. *Acta Oecon.,* 1969, *4*(3), pp. 223–37.

Le Bihan, Joseph. Vertical Integration and Development of Farms: The Perfecting and Diffusion of Innovations in Integrated Systems. **In** *Papi, U. and Nunn, C., eds.,* 1969, pp. 325–43.

Lebergott, Stanley and Easterlin, Richard A. The Service Industries in the Nineteenth Century: Discussion. **In** *Fuchs, V. R., ed.,* 1969, pp. 352–68.

Lecomber, Richard. RAS Projections When Two or More Complete Matrices Are Known. *Econ. Planning,* 1969, *9*(3), pp. 267–78.

Ledebur, Larry C. and Henderson, William L. Government Incentives and Black Economic Development. *Rev. Soc. Econ.,* September 1969, *27*(2), pp. 202–21.

Lederer, Walther and Parrish, Evelyn M. The U.S. Balance of Payments—Fourth Quarter and Year 1968. *Surv. Curr. Bus.,* March 1969, *49*(3), pp. 23–31, 45–46.

______ The U.S. Balance of Payments: First Quarter, 1969. *Surv. Curr. Bus.,* June 1969, *49*(6), pp. 21–25, 37, 44.

______ The U.S. Balance of Payments: Second Quarter 1969. *Surv. Curr. Bus.,* September 1969, *49*(9), pp. 27–35.

Lee, Alvin T. M. Regional Research—Further Analysis and Reflections. *Amer. J. Agr. Econ.,* November 1969, *51*(4), pp. 953–57.

Lee, C. H. A Stock-Adjustment Analysis of Capital Movements: The United States-Canadian Case. *J. Polit. Econ.,* Part I, July/August 1969, *77*(4), pp. 512–23.

Lee, Dwight R. Utility Analysis and Repetitive Gambling. *Amer. Econ.,* Fall 1969, *13*(2), pp. 87–91.

Lee, Everett. Education and Migration in the United States. **In** *[Edding, Friedrich],* 1969, pp. 231–37.

Lee, Feng-Yao. An Analysis of Farm Household Expenditures on Basic Living Materials in Japan. *Amer. J. Agr. Econ.,* August 1969, *51*(3), pp. 650–61.

Lee, J. Finley. The Competitive Role of the Associated Factory Mutuals. *J. Risk Ins.*, September 1969, *36*(4), pp. 401–18.

Lee, John. The Pros and Cons of Functionalization. **In** *Gulick, L. and Urwick, L., eds.*, 1969, pp. 171–79.

Lee, Lucy C. and Bedford, Norton M. An Information Theory Analysis of the Accounting Process. *Accounting Rev.*, April 1969, *44*(2), pp. 256–75.

Lee, N. and Dalvi, M. Q. Variations in the Value of Travel Time. *Manchester Sch. Econ. Soc. Stud.*, September 1969, *37*(3), pp. 213–36.

Lee, T. H. The Transferability of the Japanese Pattern of Modernizing Traditional Agriculture: Comment. **In** *Thorbecke, E., ed.*, 1969, pp. 303–10.

Lee, Tong Hun. Alternative Interest Rates and the Demand for Money: Reply. *Amer. Econ. Rev.*, June 1969, *59*(3), pp. 412–18.

Leeman, Wayne A. Statement. **In** *Governmental Intervention in the Market Mechanism, Pt. 1, SCH*, 1969, pp. 268–84.

Lees, Dennis. Controversy Surrounding Negative Income Taxation: Comment. *Public Finance*, 1969, *24*(2), pp. 362–66.

Lees, Francis A. Interregional Flows of Funds through State and Local Government Securities (1957–1962). *J. Reg. Sci.*, April 1969, *9*(1), pp. 79–86.

de Leeuw, Frank. A Condensed Model of Financial Behavior. **In** *Duesenberry, J. S., et al.*, 1969, pp. 270–315.

______ **and Gramlich, Edward M.** The Channels of Monetary Policy. *Fed. Res. Bull.*, June 1969, *55*(6), pp. 472–91.

______ **and Gramlich, Edward M.** The Channels of Monetary Policy: A Further Report on the Federal Reserve-M.I.T. Model. *J. Finance*, May 1969, *24*(2), pp. 265–90.

______ **and Kalchbrenner, John.** Monetary and Fiscal Actions: A Test of Their Relative Importance in Economic Stabilization—Comment. *Fed. Res. Bank St. Louis Rev.*, April 1969, *51*(4), pp. 6–11.

Leff, Nathaniel H. Dependency Rates and Savings Rates. *Amer. Econ. Rev.*, December 1969, *59*(5), pp. 886–96.

______ Import Constraints and Development: A Reply. *Rev. Econ. Statist.*, February 1969, *51*(1), pp. 102–04.

______ Long-Term Brazilian Economic Development. *J. Econ. Hist.*, September 1969, *29*(3), pp. 473–93.

______ The "Exportable Surplus" Approach to Foreign Trade in Underdeveloped Countries. *Econ. Develop. Cult. Change*, April 1969, *17*(3), pp. 346–55.

Legarda, Benito J. The Philippines and the Industrial Nations: Discussion. *Philippine Econ. J.*, First Semester 1969, *8*(1), pp. 13–15.

Legler, John B. and Shapiro, Perry. The Responsiveness of State Tax Revenue to Economic Growth: A Reply. *Nat. Tax J.*, June 1969, *22*(2), pp. 299–300.

Lehtovuori, Jouko. Organisaatioteorian osa-alueista. (On Sub-Areas of Organization Theory. With English summary.) *Liiketaloudellinen Aikak.*, 1969, *18*(3), pp. 477–89.

Leibenstein, Harvey. Organizational or Frictional Equilibria, X-Efficiency, and the Rate of Innovation. *Quart. J. Econ.*, November 1969, *83*(4), pp. 600–23.

______ **and Comanor, William S.** Allocative Efficiency, X-Efficiency and the Measurement of Welfare Losses. *Economica, N.S.*, August 1969, *36* (143), pp. 304–09.

Leighton, Charles M. and Tod, G. Robert. After the Acquisition: Continuing Challenge. *Harvard Bus. Rev.*, March–April 1969, *47*(2), pp. 90–102.

Leiman, Melvin M. The Economic Ideas of Jacob N. Cardozo. **In** *Kiker, B. F. and Carlsson, R. J., eds.*, 1969, pp. 10–43.

Leister, D. V. and Peterson, R. D. Market Structure-Conduct Relations: Some Evidence from Biomedical Electronic Firms. *Univ. Wash. Bus. Rev.*, Summer 1969, *28*(4), pp. 49–65.

Leith, James Clark. The Customs Revenue Loss in a Southeast Asian Customs Union. *J. Devel. Stud.*, January 1969, *5*(2), pp. 142–46.

______ **and Reuber, Grant L.** The Impact of the Industrial Countries' Tariff Structure on Their Imports of Manufactures from Less-Developed Areas: A Comment. *Economica, N.S.*, February 1969, *36*(141), pp. 75–80.

Lemon, Charles [Sir]. The Statistics of the Copper Mines of Cornwall. **In** *Burt, R., ed.*, 1969, pp. 49–82.

Lempers, F. B.; Barten, A. P. and Kloek, T. A Note on a Class of Utility and Production Functions Yielding Everywhere Differentiable Demand Functions. *Rev. Econ. Stud.*, January 1969, *36* (105), pp. 109–11.

Lent, George E. Taxation of Financial Intermediaries. *Nat. Tax J.*, March 1969, *22*(1), pp. 139–53.

______ **and Ojha, P. D.** Sales Taxes in Countries of the Far East. *Int. Monet. Fund Staff Pap.*, November 1969, *16*(3), pp. 529–81.

Leonard, Patrick L. Farm Planning and Land Development Schemes. *Malayan Econ. Rev.*, April 1969, *14*(1), pp. 80–96.

______ A Note on the Demand for Fertilizer in West Pakistan. *Pakistan Develop. Rev.*, Winter 1969, *9* (4), pp. 419–25.

Leonard, William N. Network Television Pricing: A Comment. *J. Bus.*, January 1969, *42*(1), pp. 93–103.

______ Statement. **In** *Automotive Repair Industry, Pt. 1, SCH*, 1969, pp. 4–50.

Leong, Y. S. and Rhyne, Iola. Hawaii's Inversely Graduated Tax Credits. *Nat. Tax J.*, December 1969, *22*(4), pp. 446–65.

Leoni, Renato. A proposito dell'impiego del modello di Theil-Barten nell'analisi della domanda di beni di consumo in Italia. (With English summary.) *Statistica*, April-June 1969, *29*(2), pp. 277–86.

Leont'ev, E. A. Expenditures in the Tatar Autonomous Republic for Vocational Training in Secondary Schools and Directly in Enterprises: A Comparison. **In** *Noah, H. J., ed.*, 1969, pp. 187–91.

Leontief, W. W. The Use of Indifference Curves in the Analysis of Foreign Trade. **In** *Bhagwati, J., ed.*, 1969, pp. 21–29.

Leontiev, L. Myth about the "Rapprochement" of

the Two Systems. In *Prybyla, J. S., ed.*, 1969, pp. 477–84.

Leponiemi, Arvi. Vaatetusteollisuuden tuotanto- ja kustannusfunktioista. (On the Production and Cost Functions of the Clothing Industry. With English summary.) *Liiketaloudellinen Aikak.*, 1969, *18*(2), pp. 183–91.

Lerman, L. M. Education and the Development of Production in the Uzbek S. S. R. In *Noah, H. J., ed.*, 1969, pp. 45–62.

Lerner, Abba P. On Instrumental Analysis. In *Heilbroner, R. L., ed.*, 1969, pp. 131–36.

Lerner, Eugene M. and Carleton, Willard T. Statistical Credit Scoring of Municipal Bonds. *J. Money, Credit, Banking*, November 1969, *1*(4), pp. 750–64.

______ **and Machol, Robert E.** Risk, Ruin and Investment Analysis. *J. Financial Quant. Anal.*, December 1969, *4*(4), pp. 473–92.

______ **and Moag, Joseph S.** Capital Budgeting Decisions under Imperfect Market Conditions—A Systems Framework. *J. Finance*, September 1969, *24* (4), pp. 613–21.

______ **and Moag, Joseph S.** Information Requirements for Regulatory Decisions. In *Trebing, H. M. and Howard, R. H., eds.*, 1969, pp. 195–204.

Lerner, Shirley W. The Report of the Royal Commission on Trade Unions and Employers' Associations, 1965–68. In *Hugh-Jones, E. M., ed.*, 1969, pp. 151–68.

Lerohl, M. L. Obstacles Expected and Steps Required in Implementation of a Sound Policy for Canadian Agriculture: Discussion. *Can. J. Agr. Econ.*, November 1969, *17*(3), pp. 76–79.

Leroux, Roger and Raffoul, Faouzi. An Essay in Simulating Economic Policies for the French Economy. *Econ. Planning*, 1969, *9*(1–2), pp. 95–153.

Leshinski, Stephen and Haskell, Mark A. Fiscal Influences on Residential Choice: A Study of the New York Region. *Quart. Rev. Econ. Bus.*, Winter 1969, *9*(4), pp. 47–55.

Lesieur, Frederick G. and Puckett, Elbridge S. The Scanlon Plan: Past, Present and Future. In *Somers, G. G., ed. (II)*, 1969, pp. 71–80.

Lesser, Arthur, Jr. Engineering Economy in the United States in Retrospect—An Analysis. *Eng. Econ.*, January–February 1969, *14*(2), pp. 109–15.

Lesso, William G. An Extension of the Net Present Value Concept to Intertemporal Investments. *Eng. Econ.*, October–November 1969, *15*(1), pp. 1–8.

Lester, Richard A. Labor Policy in a Changing World. In *Wortman, M. S., Jr.*, 1969, pp. 449–59.

______ Some Investment-Like Aspects of Employment and Pay. *Mon. Lab. Rev.*, November 1969, *92*(11), pp. 62–65.

______ Wage-Price Dynamics, Inflation, and Unemployment: Discussion. *Amer. Econ. Rev.*, May 1969, *59*(2), pp. 164–67.

Letiche, John M. The History of Economic Thought in the *International Encyclopedia of the Social Sciences*. *J. Econ. Lit.*, June 1969, *7*(2), pp. 406–25.

______ I pagamenti internazionali. (International Payments. With English summary.) *Rivista Int. Sci. Econ. Com.*, January 1969, *16*(1), pp. 1–30.

Leuthold, Raymond M. An Analysis of Daily Fluctuations in the Hog Economy. *Amer. J. Agr. Econ.*, November 1969, *51*(4), pp. 849–65.

______ Government Payments and the Distribution of Income in Agriculture. *Amer. J. Agr. Econ.*, December 1969, *51*(5), pp. 1520–23.

Lev, Baruch. An Information Theory Analysis of Budget Variances. *Accounting Rev.*, October 1969, *44*(4), pp. 704–10.

Leveson, Irving; Sarachek, Deborah and Auster, Richard. The Production of Health, an Exploratory Study. *J. Human Res.*, Fall 1969, *4*(4), pp. 411–36.

Levhari, David and Arrow, Kenneth J. Uniqueness of the Internal Rate of Return with Variable Life of Investment. *Econ. J.*, September 1969, *79*(315), pp. 560–66.

______ **and Sheshinski, Eytan.** The Relation between the Rate of Return and the Rate of Technical Progress. *Rev. Econ. Stud.*, July 1969, *36*(107), pp. 363–79.

______ **and Sheshinski, Eytan.** A Theorem on Returns to Scale and Steady-State Growth. *J. Polit. Econ.*, January/February 1969, *77*(1), pp. 60–65.

______**; Sheshinski, Eytan and Fisher, Franklin M.** On the Sensitivity of the Level of Output to Savings: Embodiment and Disembodiment: A Clarificatory Note. *Quart. J. Econ.*, May 1969, *83* (2), pp. 347–48.

______ **and Srinivasan, T. N.** Durability of Consumption Goods: Competition Versus Monopoly. *Amer. Econ. Rev.*, March 1969, *59*(1), pp. 102–07.

______ **and Srinivasan, T. N.** Optimal Savings under Uncertainty. *Rev. Econ. Stud.*, April 1969, *36* (106), pp. 153–63.

Levi, Donald R. A Lawyer Looks at Water Resource Economists. *Amer. J. Agr. Econ.*, February 1969, *51*(1), pp. 182–83.

______ **and Allwood, James K.** Legal-Economic Models as a Tool for Optimizing Intergeneration Property Transfers. *Amer. J. Agr. Econ.*, December 1969, *51*(5), pp. 1393–98.

Levin, A. The Market in the System of Socialist Reproduction. The Equilibrium Price Principle. *Prob. Econ.*, November 1969, *12*(7), pp. 30–48.

______ **and Bredov, V.** Prediction of the Population's Demand. *Prob. Econ.*, January 1969, *11*(9), pp. 34–44.

Levin, Harvey J. Broadcast Structure, Technology, and the ABC-ITT Merger Decision. *Law Contemp. Probl.*, Summer 1969, *34*(3), pp. 452–84.

Levin, Jonathan. A Sectoral Approach to Balance of Payments Analysis. *Finance Develop.*, March 1969, *6*(1), pp. 57–61.

Levine, Charles H. The Dilemma of the Black Businessman: A New Approach? *Indiana Bus. Rev.*, March–April 1969, *44*, pp. 12, 22–26.

Levine, Herbert S. and Seton, Francis. Cyclical Fluctuations under Socialism: Comment. In *Bronfenbrenner, M., ed.*, 1969, pp. 303–11.

Levine, Michael E. Landing Fees and the Airport Congestion Problem. *J. Law Econ.*, April 1969, *12* (1), pp. 79–108.

Levine, Morton. Adjusting to Technology on the

Railroads. *Mon. Lab. Rev.*, November 1969, *92* (11), pp. 36–42.

Levine, Robert A. Manpower Programs in the War on Poverty. **In** *Somers, G. G. and Wood, W. D., eds.*, 1969, pp. 170–83.

______ Policy Analysis and Economic Opportunity Programs. **In** *The Analysis and Evaluation of Public Expenditures: The PPB System, Vol. 3, JECP*, 1969, pp. 1181–96.

Levinson, Harry. On Being a Middle-Aged Manager. *Harvard Bus. Rev.*, July–August 1969, *47*(4), pp. 51–60.

Levitan, Richard E. and Chow, Gregory C. Nature of Business Cycles Implicit in a Linear Economic Model. *Quart. J. Econ.*, August 1969, *83*(3), pp. 504–17.

______ Spectral Properties of Non-Stationary Systems of Linear Stochastic Difference Equations. *J. Amer. Statist. Assoc.*, June 1969, *64*(326), pp. 581–90.

Levitan, Sar A. The Community Action Program: A Strategy to Fight Poverty. *Ann. Amer. Acad. Polit. Soc. Sci.*, September 1969, *385*, pp. 63–75.

______ **and Mangum, Garth L.** The Changing Goals of Federal Manpower Policy. **In** *Wortman, M. S., Jr.*, 1969, pp. 122–24.

______ **and Mangum, Garth L.** A Functional Manpower Policy. **In** *Wortman, M. S., Jr.*, 1969, pp. 125–32.

Levitt, Theodore. The New Markets—Think before You Leap. *Harvard Bus. Rev.*, May–June 1969, *47* (3), pp. 53–67.

Levy, Ferdinand K. Sources of Economies of Scale in Universities. **In** *the Economics and Financing of Higher Education in the United States, JECP*, 1969, pp. 295–302.

Levy, Haim. A Utility Function Depending on the First Three Moments: Comment. *J. Finance*, September 1969, *24*(4), pp. 715–19.

______ **and Hanoch, G.** The Efficiency Analysis of Choices Involving Risk. *Rev. Econ. Stud.*, July 1969, *36*(107), pp. 335–46.

______ **and Sarnat, Marshall.** A Note on Indifference Curves and Uncertainty. *Swedish J. Econ.*, September 1969, *71*(3), pp. 206–08.

______ **and Sarnat, Marshall.** The Relationship of Rules of Thumb to the Internal Rate of Return: A Restatement and Generalization. *J. Finance*, June 1969, *24*(3), pp. 479–90.

Levy, Sidney J. and Kotler, Philip. Beyond Marketing: The Furthering Concept. *Calif. Manage. Rev.*, Winter 1969, *12*(2), pp. 67–73.

Lewellen, Wilbur G. Management and Ownership in the Large Firm. *J. Finance*, May 1969, *24*(2), pp. 299–322.

______ Tax Minimization and Executive Compensation Plans. **In** *Tax Institute of America*, 1969, pp. 104–17.

______ **and Hettenhouse, George W.** The Taxation of Restricted Stock Compensation Plans. *Nat. Tax J.*, September 1969, *22*(3), pp. 368–78.

Lewis, A. B. Training Foreign Graduate Students in Agricultural Economics: Further Comment. *Amer. J. Agr. Econ.*, August 1969, *51*(3), pp. 697–99.

Lewis, Ben W. *Performance under Regulation* (Review Article). *Land Econ.*, November 1969, *45*(4), pp. 477.

Lewis, David. New Urban Structures. **In** *Baier, K. and Rescher, N., eds.*, 1969, pp. 294–319.

Lewis, Edwin H. Sales Promotion Decisions. **In** *Alexis, M.; Holloway, R. J. and Hancock, R. S., eds.*, 1969, pp. 315–23.

Lewis, J. F. and Greenfield, R. J. An Alternative to a Density Function Definition of Overcrowding. *Land Econ.*, May 1969, *45*(2), pp. 282–85.

Lewis, L. Earl. Federal Pay Comparability Procedures. *Mon. Lab. Rev.*, February 1969, *92*(2), pp. 10–13.

Lewis, Robert E. Corporate Profits—The First National City Bank's Series on Leading Corporations. *Univ. Missouri Bus. Govt. Rev.*, March–April 1969, *10*(2), pp. 33–40.

Lewis, Stephen R., Jr. A Note on the Consistency of Pakistan's Cotton-Cloth Statistics for Recent Years. *Pakistan Develop. Rev.*, Winter 1969, *9*(4), pp. 442–46.

Lewis, W. Arthur. Agriculture in the Open Economy: Comment. **In** *Thorbecke, E., ed.*, 1969, pp. 159–63.

______ Economic Aspects of Quality in Education. **In** *Beeby, C. E., ed.*, 1969, pp. 71–88.

Lewis, William C. and Prescott, James R. State and Municipal Locational Incentives: A Discriminant Analysis. *Nat. Tax J.*, September 1969, *22*(3), pp. 399–407.

Leyhausen, Paul. Human Nature and Modern Society. *Soc. Res.*, Winter 1969, *36*(4), pp. 510–29.

Leys, Colin. The Analysis of Planning. **In** *Leys, C., ed.*, 1969, pp. 247–75.

Li-tien, Feng and Chien, Wen. A Quantitative Analysis of the Relationship Between the Rate of Growth of Productivity and the Average Wage. *Chinese Econ. Stud.*, Fall 1969, *3*(1), pp. 70–91.

Liander, Bertil. Mercatistica internazionale analisi comparate. (Comparative Analysis for International Marketing. With English summary.) *L'Impresa*, July/October 1969, *11*(4–5), pp. 320–26.

Lianos, Theodore P. A Comment on a Traditional Behavior Model. *Amer. J. Agr. Econ.*, November 1969, *51*(4), pp. 937.

______ Governmental Deficit Financing and Growth in Underdeveloped Countries: A Comment. *Miss. Val. J. Bus. Econ.*, Fall 1969, *5*(1), pp. 90–92.

______ South-Nonsouth Migration, 1955–1960. *Miss. Val. J. Bus. Econ.*, Spring 1969, *4*(2), pp. 10–22.

Liberman, Y. The Soviet Economic Reform. **In** *Economic Concentration, Pt. 7A, SCH*, 1969, pp. 4366–71.

Licari, Joseph A. Economic Fluctuations: A Comparative Study. *Amer. Econ.*, Spring 1969, *13*(1), pp. 42–57.

Lichfield, Nathaniel. Problems of Obtaining Private Capital for New Towns. **In** *Ling, A. G., et al.*, 1969, pp. 47–51.

Lichtblau, John H. Statement. **In** *Governmental Intervention in the Market Mechanism, Pt. 1, SCH*, 1969, pp. 317–27.

Liddy, Lucien E. and Claycamp, Henry J. Prediction of New Product Performance: An Analytical Approach. *J. Marketing Res.*, November 1969, *6*(4), pp. 414–20.

Lieberman, A. E. Updating Impressions of the Military-Industry Complex. *Calif. Manage. Rev.*, Summer 1969, *11*(4), pp. 51–62.

Lieberman, Bernhardt. Combining Individual Preferences into a Social Choice. In *Buchler, I. R. and Nutini, H. G., eds.*, 1969, pp. 95–115.

Lieberman, S. Has the Marginalist Anti-Marginalist Controversy Regarding the Theory of the Firm Been Settled? *Schweiz. Z. Volkswirtsch. Statist.*, December 1969, *105*(4), pp. 535–49.

Liebhafsky, H. H. New Thoughts About Inferior Goods. *Amer. Econ. Rev.*, December 1969, *59*(5), pp. 931–34.

——— A Note on the Origin of Slutsky's "Well-Known" Formula of the Theory of Determinants. *Z. ges. Staatswiss.*, April 1969, *125*(2), pp. 243–47.

Liebling, H. I. and Cluff, A. T. U.S. Postwar Inflation and Phillips Curves. *Kyklos*, 1969, *22*(2), pp. 232–50.

Liggett, Malcolm H. The Efficacy of State Fair Employment Practices Commissions. *Ind. Lab. Relat. Rev.*, July 1969, *22*(4), pp. 559–67.

Lile, Stephen E. and Soule, Don M. Interstate Differences in Family Tax Burdens. *Nat. Tax J.*, December 1969, *22*(4), pp. 433–45.

Lilienthal, David E. Postwar Development in Viet Nam. *Foreign Aff.*, January 1969, *47*(2), pp. 321–33.

Lin, Chi-Yuan and Berger, Paul D. On the Selling Price and Buying Price of a Lottery. *Amer. Statist.*, December 1969, *23*(5), pp. 25–26.

Lin, Leon and Yeh, M. H. Technological Change in the Canadian Livestock Industry: An Input-Output Approach. *Can. J. Agr. Econ.*, July 1969, *17*(2), pp. 63–84.

Lin, Wuu-Long and Buller, Orlan. Measuring the Effect of Weather on Crop Production. *Can. J. Agr. Econ.*, February 1969, *17*(1), pp. 91–98.

Lindahl, Erik. The Concept of Income. In *Parker, R. H. and Harcourt, G. C., eds.*, 1969, pp. 54–62.

Lindbeck, Assar. International Liquidity and the Reform of the Adjustment Mechanism: Comment. In *Samuelson, P. A., ed.*, 1969, pp. 258–63.

——— **and Jacobsson, Lars.** Labor Market Condition, Wages and Inflation—Swedish Experiences 1955–67. *Swedish J. Econ.*, June 1969, *71*(2), pp. 64–103.

Lindberg, Barbara and Gruber, Alin. Sensitivity, Reliability, and Consumer Taste Testing: Reaffirmation and a Reply. *J. Marketing Res.*, February 1969, *6*(1), pp. 105–06.

Lindberg, Carolyn G. A Note on Population Estimates and Their Meaning. *N. Mex. Bus.*, November–December 1969, *22*(11&12), pp. 6–10.

Lindert, Peter H. United States Investment. In *Hughes, H. and Seng, Y. P., eds.*, 1969, pp. 154–76.

Lindgren, Ingvar; Carlsson, Mårten and Hovmark, Bertil. Recent Developments in Farm Planning: 1: A Monte Carlo Method for the Study of Farm Planning Problems. *Rev. Marketing Agr. Econ.*, June 1969, *37*(2), pp. 80–103.

Lindgren, J. Ralph. Adam Smith's Theory of Inquiry. *J. Polit. Econ.*, November/December 1969, *77*(6), pp. 897–915.

Lindholm, Richard W. Home Ownership and the Income Tax: A Proposed Change. *Oregon Bus. Rev.*, September 1969, *28*(9), pp. 1–3.

Lindner, Forrest. The Health of the American People. In *Health Care in America, Pt. 1, SCH*, 1969, pp. 360–65.

Lindner, R. K. The Economics of Increased Beef Production on Dairy Farms in Western Australia. *Quart. Rev. Agr. Econ.*, July 1969, *22*(3), pp. 147–64.

Lindsay, Cotton M. Medical Care and the Economics of Sharing. *Economica, N.S.*, November 1969, *36*(144), pp. 351–62.

——— Option Demand and Consumer's Surplus. *Quart. J. Econ.*, May 1969, *83*(2), pp. 344–46.

Lindsey, Quentin W. The Problem of Periodic Reorganization in American Agriculture. In *Owen, W. F., ed.*, 1969, pp. 1–14.

Lineberry, Robert L. Community Structure and Planning Commitment: A Note on the Correlates of Agency Expenditures. *Soc. Sci. Quart.*, December 1969, *50*(3), pp. 723–30.

Ling, Timothy Y. Statics and Dynamics of Simulation. In *Naylor, T. H., ed.*, 1969, pp. 180–203.

Linnamo, Jussi. Den ekonomiska planeringen som medel för ekonomisk politik. (Economic Planning as a Means of Economic Policy. With English summary.) *Econ. Samfundets Tidskr.*, 1969, *22*(1), pp. 38–47.

——— Vakauttamispolitiikasta tasapainoisen kasvun politiikkaan. (From Stabilization Policy to a Policy of Balanced Economic Growth. With English summary.) *Kansant. Aikak.*, 1969, *65*(3), pp. 171–80.

Linnemann, Hans. Trade Flows and Geographical Distance or the Importance of Being Neighbours. In *[Tinbergen, J.]*, 1969, pp. 111–28.

Lins, David A. An Empirical Comparison of Simulation and Recursive Linear Programming Firm Growth Models. *Agr. Econ. Res.*, January 1969, *21*(1), pp. 7–12.

Linstromberg, R. C. The Philosophy of Science and Alternative Approaches to Economic Thought. *J. Econ. Issues*, June 1969, *3*(2), pp. 176–91.

Lintner, John. The Aggregation of Investor's Diverse Judgments and Preferences in Purely Competitive Security Markets. *J. Financial Quant. Anal.*, December 1969, *4*(4), pp. 347–400.

——— A Model of a Perfectly Functioning Securities Market. In *Manne, H. G., ed.*, 1969, pp. 143–66.

——— The Valuation of Risk Assets and the Selection of Risky Investments in Stock Portfolios and Capital Budgets: A Reply. *Rev. Econ. Statist.*, May 1969, *51*(2), pp. 222–24.

Lipfert, Helmut. Il sistema creditizio tedesco verso nuovo vie. (The German Credit System Moving Towards New Developments. With English summary.) *Bancaria*, September 1969, *25*(9), pp. 1082–87.

——— Measures to Improve the Depth, Breadth, and Resiliency of the Exchange Markets. In *Aliber, R. Z., ed.*, 1969, pp. 235–43.

——— Problems and Developments of the International Monetary System. *Rev. Econ. Cond. Italy*, November 1969, *23*(6), pp. 519–43.

——— Psychology of the Exchange Market. **In** *Aliber, R. Z., ed.,* 1969, pp. 123–37.

Lipinski, Andrew J. Integration of Latin American Communications. **In** *Hilton, R., ed.,* 1969, pp. 343–54.

Lipowski, Adam. Interdependence Between Goals and Incentives in an Experimental System of Management. *Eastern Europ. Econ.,* Fall 1969, *8* (1), pp. 20–71.

Lippitt, Vernon G. Determinants of Consumer Demand for House Furnishings and Equipment. **In** *Alexis, M.; Holloway, R. J. and Hancock, R. S., eds.,* 1969, pp. 3–19.

Lipset, Seymour Martin. Politics and the Social Sciences: Introduction. **In** *Lipset, S. M., ed.,* 1969, pp. vii–xxii.

Lipsey, Robert E. and Kravis, Irving B. International Price Comparisons by Regression Methods. *Int. Econ. Rev.,* June 1969, *10*(2), pp. 233–46.

Lipsky, David B. and Drotning, John E. The Effectiveness of Reinstatement as a Public Policy Remedy: The Kohler Case. *Ind. Lab. Relat. Rev.,* January 1969, *22*(2), pp. 179–98.

Lipson, E. The National Economy (1815–1914). **In** *Scoville, W. C. and La Force, J. C., eds., Vol. IV,* 1969, pp. 16–42.

——— The Revolution in Transport. **In** *Scoville, W. C. and La Force, J. C., eds., Vol. IV,* 1969, pp. 137–47.

Lisitsyn, V. and Popov, G. On Administrative Cadres. *Prob. Econ.,* April 1969, *11*(12), pp. 3–10.

Litchfield, R. Burr. Demographic Characteristics of Florentine Patrician Families, Sixteenth to Nineteenth Centuries. *J. Econ. Hist.,* June 1969, *29*(2), pp. 191–205.

Little, Alan. Low Wage Earners. **In** *O.E.C.D.,* 1969, pp. 250–72.

Little, Barbara. The Sealing and Whaling Industry in Australia before 1850. *Australian Econ. Hist. Rev.,* September 1969, *9*(2), pp. 109–27.

Little, I. M. D. Public Sector Project Selection in Relation to Indian Development. **In** *Bhuleshkar, A. V., ed.,* 1969, pp. 228–58.

Little, Jane Sneddon. The Euro-dollar Market: Its Nature and Impact. *New Eng. Econ. Rev.,* May/June 1969, pp. 2–31.

Little, Wallace I. An Appraisal of Transportation Regulation in the United States. *Rivista Int. Sci. Econ. Com.,* September 1969, *16*(9), pp. 872–88.

——— Location Selection through Integrated Systems Management. *Land Econ.,* February 1969, *45*(1), pp. 97–103.

Litzenberger, Robert H. Equilibrium in the Equity Market under Uncertainty. *J. Finance,* September 1969, *24*(4), pp. 663–71.

——— **and Jones, Charles P.** Adjusting for Risk in the Capital Budget of a Growth Oriented Company: Comment. *J. Financial Quant. Anal.,* September 1969, *4*(3), pp. 301–04.

Liu, Ben-Chieh. Comments on the Responsiveness of State Tax Revenue to Economic Growth. *Nat. Tax J.,* June 1969, *22*(2), pp. 294–98.

——— Regional Income Inequality and Federal Government Expenditures, 1948–63. *Quart. Rev. Econ. Bus.,* Winter 1969, *9*(4), pp. 67–76.

Liu, Ta-Chung. A Monthly Recursive Econometric Model of United States: A Test of Feasibility. *Rev. Econ. Statist.,* February 1969, *51*(1), pp. 1–13.

——— **and Breen, William J.** The Covariance Matrix of the Limited Information Estimator and the Identification Test. *Econometrica,* April 1969, *37* (2), pp. 222–27.

——— **and Kravis, Irving B.** What Is Output? Problems of Concept and Measurement: Discussion. **In** *Fuchs, V. R., ed.,* 1969, pp. 84–94.

Livesay, Harold C. and Porter, Patrick G. Vertical Integration in American Manufacturing, 1899–1948. *J. Econ. Hist.,* September 1969, *29*(3), pp. 494–500.

Liviatan, Nissan and Samuelson, Paul A. Notes on Turnpikes: Stable and Unstable. *J. Econ. Theory,* December 1969, *1*(4), pp. 454–75.

Livingston, Frederick R. Union-Management Cooperation Revisited: Discussion. **In** *Somers, G. G., ed. (II),* 1969, pp. 90–92.

Livingston, J. Sterling. Pygmalion in Management. *Harvard Bus. Rev.,* July–August 1969, *47*(4), pp. 81–89.

Livingstone, John Leslie. Input-Output Analysis for Cost Accounting, Planning and Control. *Accounting Rev.,* January 1969, *44*(1), pp. 48–64.

Llewelyn-Davies, Richard. New Cities—A British Example: Milton Keynes. **In** *Panel on Science and Technology: Science and Technology and the Cities, HCH,* 1969, pp. 56–67.

Llosas, Hernán P. La política de promoción industrial y de desarrollo regional en la Argentina, 1959–1966. (The Argentinian Government's Policy for the Promotion of Particular Industrial Sectors and for the Development of Some of the Country's Regions, 1959–1966. With English summary.) *Económica,* January–April 1969, *15*(1), pp. 39–91.

Lloyd, Peter J. Elementary Geometric/Arithmetic Series and Early Production Theory. *J. Polit. Econ.,* January/February 1969, *77*(1), pp. 21–34.

——— Qualitative Calculus and Comparative Static Analysis. *Econ. Rec.,* September 1969, *45*(111), pp. 343–53.

Lobato Lopez, Ernesto. Las normas de calidad y el desarrollo de la industria: Segunda parte y última. (Quality Standards and Industrial Development: Second and Last Part. With English summary.) *Econ. Polít.,* Third Semester 1969, *6*(3), pp. 317–30.

——— Las normas de calidad y el desarrollo de la industria (Primera parte). (Quality Standards and Industrial Development: First Part. With English summary.) *Econ. Polít.,* Second Semester 1969, *6* (2), pp. 183–94.

Lock, Eric Khoo Cheng. Recent Developments in International Shipping with Reference to Singapore: Comment. *Malayan Econ. Rev.,* October 1969, *14*(2), pp. 40–43.

Lockley, Lawrence C. A Dome of Many Colored Glass. *Marquette Bus. Rev.,* Winter 1969, *13*(4), pp. 168–73.

Lodge, George C. U.S. Aid to Latin America: Funding Radical Change. *Foreign Aff.,* July 1969, *47* (4), pp. 735–49.

Loescher, Samuel M. Statement. **In** *Bank Holding*

Company Act Amendments, Pts. 1–3, HCH, 1969, pp. 370–77.

Loevinger, Lee. Lexonomic Analysis and Antitrust. *Antitrust Bull.,* Summer 1969, *14,* pp. 313–24.

Loftus, P. J. Labour's Share in Manufacturing. *Lloyds Bank Rev.,* April 1969, (92), pp. 15–25.

Logan, Samuel H. A Conceptual Framework for Analyzing Economies of Vertical Integration. *Amer. J. Agr. Econ.,* November 1969, *51*(4), pp. 834–48.

——— **and Bullock, J. Bruce.** A Model for Decision Making under Uncertainty. *Agr. Econ. Res.,* October 1969, *21*(4), pp. 109–115.

Logan, Thomas H. and Chapin, F. Stuart, Jr. Patterns of Time and Space Use. **In** *Perloff, H. S., ed.,* 1969, pp. 305–32.

Logue, Ruth. Imported Inflation and the International Adjustment Process. (Study summary.) *Fed. Res. Bull.,* December 1969, *55*(12), pp. 920.

Lomax, Alfred L. Big Steel Mill Comes to Portland. *Oregon Bus. Rev.,* April 1969, *28*(4), pp. 1, 3.

Lomax, David F. and Reading, Brian. Too Little Saving. *Nat. Westminster Bank Quart. Rev.,* August 1969, pp. 23–42.

Long, Burl F. and Barron, James C. Conflicts within Recreation: Comment. *Land Econ.,* February 1969, *45*(1), pp. 128–31.

Long, Hugh W. and Dyl, Edward A. Abandonment Value and Capital Budgeting: Comment. *J. Finance,* March 1969, *24*(1), pp. 88–95.

Long, John D. Comments on the Plotkin Paper. *J. Risk Ins.,* June 1969, *36*(2), pp. 201–16.

Long, Norton E. The Corporation, Its Satellites, and the Local Community. **In** *Minar, D. W. and Greer, S., eds.,* 1969, pp. 163–76.

Long, Wesley H. Airline Service and the Demand for Intercity Air Travel. *J. Transp. Econ. Policy,* September 1969, *3*(3), pp. 287–99.

——— An Examination of Linear Homogeneity of Trade and Production Functions in County Leontief Matrices. *J. Reg. Sci.,* April 1969, *9*(1), pp. 47–67.

Longworth, John W. Management Games and the Teaching of Farm Management. *Australian J. Agr. Econ.,* June 1969, *13*(1), pp. 58–67.

Looff, David H. The Psychiatric Perspective on Poverty. **In** *Weaver, T. and Magid, A., eds.,* 1969, pp. 110–29.

Loomba, N. Paul. National Planning: Problems and Goals—Discussion. **In** *Ozbekhan, H. and Talbert, G. E., eds.,* 1969, pp. 78–96.

Lopata, Richard S. Faster Pace in Wholesaling. *Harvard Bus. Rev.,* July–August 1969, *47*(4), pp. 130–43.

Lord, A. Matthew. Government and Business Planning at the Crossroads: Discussion. **In** *Ozbekhan, H. and Talbert, G. E., eds.,* 1969, pp. 14–31.

Lord, William B. and Smith, Stephen C. Tools of the Trade in Policy Decision—PPBS, A Case in Point. *Amer. J. Agr. Econ.,* December 1969, *51*(5), pp. 1427–33.

Lorensen, Gunter. Untersuchungen zur Theorie des intervalutarischen Gleichgewichts. (On the Theory of Intermonetary Equilibrium. With English summary.) *Weltwirtsch. Arch.,* 1969, *103*(2), pp. 249–320.

Lorentzen, Ralph. On Efficient Consumption Paths in a Class of Simple Growth Models. *J. Econ. Theory,* June 1969, *1*(1), pp. 92–98.

Lorenzo, A. Employment Effects of Rural and Community Development in the Philippines. *Int. Lab. Rev.,* November 1969, *100*(5), pp. 419–44.

Lorimer, Frank. Issues of Population Policy. **In** *Hauser, P. M., ed.,* 1969, pp. 168–206.

Loschky, David J. and Krier, Donald F. Income and Family Size in Three Eighteenth-Century Lancashire Parishes: A Reconstitution Study. *J. Econ. Hist.,* September 1969, *29*(3), pp. 429–48.

Loshing, Clement T. The Effect of Liberalized Depreciation on the Cost of Equity Capital: Comment. **In** *Trebing, H. M. and Howard, R. H., eds.,* 1969, pp. 159–63.

Lotz, Joergen R. Some Economic Effects of Increasing Public Expenditures: An Empirical Study of Selected Developed Countries. *Public Finance,* 1969, *24*(4), pp. 577–96.

——— **and Morss, Elliott R.** "Tax Effort" in Developing Countries. *Finance Develop.,* September 1969, *6*(3), pp. 36–39.

Loustau, M. and Dupuy, Yves. Etude des carrières des ingénieurs E.N.S.T.C. (With English summary.) *Revue Écon.,* July 1969, *20*(4), pp. 702–26.

Love, Harold G. and Robertson, B. Russell. Louisville Produce Terminal: Its Changing Trends and Potentials, 1966–1975. *Amer. J. Agr. Econ.,* December 1969, *51*(5), pp. 1251–54.

Lovell, C. A. Knox. Biased Technical Change and Factor Shares in United States Manufacturing. *Quart. Rev. Econ. Bus.,* Autumn 1969, *9*(3), pp. 17–33.

Lovell, Michael C. Department Store Inventory, Sales, Order Relationships. **In** *Duesenberry, J. S., et al.,* 1969, pp. 18–38.

Lovering, Thomas S. Mineral Resources from the Land. **In** *National Academy of Sciences,* 1969, pp. 109–34.

Low, Richard E. A Refinement of Local Industrial Subsidy Techniques: Comment. *Miss. Val. J. Bus. Econ.,* Spring 1969, *4*(2), pp. 78–81.

Lowe, Adolph. Economic Means and Social Ends: A Rejoinder. **In** *Heilbroner, R. L., ed.,* 1969, pp. 167–99.

——— Toward a Science of Political Economics. **In** *Heilbroner, R. L., ed.,* 1969, pp. 1–36.

Lowe, Jeanne. The End of the Line: Race and Poverty in Cities. **In** *Callow, A. B., Jr., ed.,* 1969, pp. 519–40.

Lowry, S. Todd. Aristotle's Mathematical Analysis of Exchange. *Hist. Polit. Econ.,* Spring 1969, *1*(1), pp. 44–66.

Loyd, Harold J. and Breimyer, Harold F. Food Donation Programs. *Amer. J. Agr. Econ.,* November 1969, *51*(4), pp. 934–36.

Loyns, R. M. A. Are Beef Prices Too High? *Can. J. Agr. Econ.,* July 1969, *17*(2), pp. 124–31.

——— **and MacMillan, James A.** A Cross-Section Analysis of Farm Household Expenditures. *Can. J. Agr. Econ.,* July 1969, *17*(2), pp. 92–105.

Loyo, Gilberto. Las cooperativas en el desarrollo economico y social de los países en proceso de desarrollo. (The Role of Cooperatives in the Economic and Social Development. With English summary.) *Econ. Polít.,* Fourth Semester 1969, *6* (4), pp. 439–52.

Loznevaia, M. Mathematical Methods in Planning Wages. *Prob. Econ.,* June 1969, *12*(2), pp. 48–66.

Lucas, Robert E., Jr. Labor-Capital Substitution in U.S. Manufacturing. **In** *Harberger, A. C. and Bailey, M. J., eds.,* 1969, pp. 223–74.

______ **and Rapping, Leonard A.** Price Expectations and the Phillips Curve. *Amer. Econ. Rev.,* June 1969, *59*(3), pp. 342–50.

______ **and Rapping, Leonard A.** Real Wages, Employment, and Inflation. *J. Polit. Econ.,* September/October 1969, *77*(5), pp. 721–54.

Luey, Paul. Hong Kong Investment. **In** *Hughes, H. and Seng, Y. P., eds.,* 1969, pp. 112–39.

______ **and Sei, Ung Gim.** Taiwan Investment. **In** *Hughes, H. and Seng, Y. P., eds.,* 1969, pp. 140–53.

Lukaczer, Moses. The Farm Wage Worker in the Social Security Program: An Introduction to His Earnings Profile. *J. Risk Ins.,* March 1969, *36*(1), pp. 103–15.

Lukinov, I. Prices and Planned Economic Regulation of Agricultural Production. *Prob. Econ.,* May 1969, *12*(1), pp. 67–90.

Lumsden, Keith G. The Effectiveness of Teaching Methods: Where We Now Stand. *J. Econ. Educ.,* Fall 1969, *1*(1), pp. 12–19.

______**; Attiyeh, Richard E. and Bach, George L.** The Efficiency of Programmed Learning in Teaching Economics: The Results of a Nationwide Experiment. *Amer. Econ. Rev.,* May 1969, *59*(2), pp. 217–23.

Lund, Unto. Ovatko tehdasteollisuus-investointimme olleet kokonaistaloudellisesti mielekkäitä? (Have Investments into Finnish Manufacturing Industry Been Economically Sensible? With English summary.) *Kansant. Aikak.,* 1969, *65*(3), pp. 220–23.

Lundberg, Erik. Postwar Stabilization Policies. **In** *Bronfenbrenner, M., ed.,* 1969, pp. 477–98.

______ Structural Change and Market Efficiency. *Acta Oecon.,* 1969, *4*(4), pp. 337–50.

Lunden, Leon E. Bargaining in Major Symphony Orchestras. *Mon. Lab. Rev.,* July 1969, *92*(7), pp. 15–19.

Lundgren, Earl F. and Myers, Doyle F. A Survey of Foremen Incentive Systems in Wisconsin. *Marquette Bus. Rev.,* Spring 1969, *13*(1), pp. 1–10.

Lundstedt, Sven. Recognizing Organizational Diversity: A Problem of Fine Tuning. *Ohio State U. Bull. Bus. Res.,* November 1969, *44*(11), pp. 1–5.

Lunghini, Giorgio. Costi di produzione, prezzo delle merci e quote dei fattori primari. Alcuni risultati di un'analisi intersettoriale. (Production Costs, Commodity Prices, and Factor Shares—An Intersectoral Analysis. With English summary.) *L'Industria,* July–September 1969, (3), pp. 297–315.

______ Ottimo economico e ottimo matematico. (Economic Optimum versus Mathematical Optimum. With English summary.) *L'Industria,* April–June 1969, (2), pp. 159–75.

Lupu, Marin A. Geneza şi formarea proprietăţii feudale oglindite în opera lui Nicolae Bălcescu. (Genesis and Forming of Feudal Property as Mirrored in the Work of Nicolae Bălcescu. With English summary.) *Stud. Cercet. Econ.,* 1969, *1-2,* pp. 173–82.

______ Problemele perfecţionării conducerii economice în România. (Problems Concerning the Improvement of Economic Management in Romania. With English summary.) *Stud. Cercet. Econ.,* 1969, *4,* pp. 5–21.

Lurie, Melvin. Aspetti economici dell'abilitazione alla professione medica negli Stati Uniti. (Physician Licensing in the United States and the Supply of Physician Service by Graduates of Foreign Medical Schools. With English summary.) *Rivista Int. Sci. Econ. Com.,* April 1969, *16*(4), pp. 371–89.

______ **and Rayack, Elton.** Employment Opportunities for Negro Families in "Satellite" Cities. *Southern Econ. J.,* October 1969, *36*(2), pp. 191–95.

Lury, D. A. and Robson, P. Introduction: The Economies of Africa. **In** *Robson, P. and Lury, D. A., eds.,* 1969, pp. 23–78.

Lusztig, Peter and Schwab, Bernhard. A Comparative Analysis of the Net Present Value and the Benefit-Cost Ratio as Measures of the Economic Desirability of Investment. *J. Finance,* June 1969, *24*(3), pp. 507–16.

Lutoslanski, Z. The Role of R and D Units in Long-Range Planning of Technological Development in Poland. **In** *Arnfield, R. V., ed.,* 1969, pp. 112–28.

Lüttgen, Horst. Das Problem des optimalen Testaments. (With English summary.) *Z. ges. Staatswiss.,* January 1969, *125*(1), pp. 123–37.

Luttrell, Clifton B. Agribusiness—A Growth Analysis. *Univ. Missouri Bus. Govt. Rev.,* November–December 1969, *10*(6), pp. 33–42.

______ Interest Rate Controls: Perspective, Purpose, and Problems. **In** *Kuhlman, J. M., ed.,* 1969, pp. 275–88.

______ Meat Prices. *Fed. Res. Bank St. Louis Rev.,* August 1969, *51*(8), pp. 24–28.

______ **and Armentrout, Claire.** Growth—Metropolitan vs. Nonmetropolitan Areas in the Central Mississippi Valley. *Fed. Res. Bank St. Louis Rev.,* January 1969, *51*(1), pp. 8–15.

Lutz, Carl F. Quantitative Job Evaluation in Local Government in the United States. *Int. Lab. Rev.,* June 1969, *99*(6), pp. 607–19.

Lutz, Friedrich A. On Neutral Money. **In** *[von Hayek, Friedrich A.],* 1969, pp. 105–16.

Luzzatto, G. The Italian Economy in the First Decade after Unification. **In** *Crouzet, F.; Chaloner, W. H. and Stern, W. M., eds.,* 1969, pp. 203–25.

Lydall, Harold. On Measuring Technical Progress. *Australian Econ. Pap.,* June 1969, *8*(12), pp. 1–12.

Lyden, Fremont James and Thomas, Jerry V. Citizen Participation in Policy-Making: A Study of a Community Action Program. *Soc. Sci. Quart.,* December 1969, *50*(3), pp. 631–42.

Lynch, P. J. and Witherell, William H. The Carter Commission and the Saving Behavior of Canadian Corporations. *Nat. Tax J.,* March 1969, *22*(1), pp. 57–65.

Lynn, Arthur D., Jr. The Institutional Context of Property Tax Administration. **In** *Lynn, A. D., Jr., ed.,* 1969, pp. 3–14.

______ Reform of Property Tax Systems: Substance or Semantics. **In** *[White, Charles P.],* 1969, pp. 23–33.

——— and **Brown, Sue Ellen.** Federal Revenue Sharing with the States: Implications for Effective Federalism. *Ohio State U. Bull. Bus. Res.*, November 1969, *44*(11), pp. 6–8.

Ma, Ronald. Current Developments in Accounting Theory: Problems of Income Measurement. *Malayan Econ. Rev.*, April 1969, *14*(1), pp. 1–14.

Mabro, Robert. Normalisation Procedure for Public Investment Criteria: A Comment. *Econ. J.*, September 1969, *79*(315), pp. 669–72.

Mabry, Bevars D. Income-Leisure Analysis and the Salaried Professional. *Ind. Relat.*, February 1969, *8*(2), pp. 162–73.

Macarthy, P. G. Justice Higgins and the Harvester Judgement. *Australian Econ. Hist. Rev.*, March 1969, *9*(1), pp. 17–38.

MacBean, A. I. Foreign Trade Aspects of Development Planning. **In** *Stewart, I. G., ed.*, 1969, pp. 13–25.

Maccarone, Salvatore. Considerazioni sulla natura giuridica dei fondi comuni di investimento mobiliare-I. (Remarks on the Legal Nature of Unit Trust-I. With English summary.) *Bancaria*, November 1969, *25*(11), pp. 1350–60.

——— Considerazioni sulla natura giuridica dei fondi comuni di investimento mobiliare. (Remarks on the Legal Nature of Unit Trust. With English summary.) *Bancaria*, December 1969, *25*(12), pp. 1473–89.

MacCrimmon, K. R. and Toda, M. The Experimental Determination of Indifference Curves. *Rev. Econ. Stud.*, October 1969, *36*(108), pp. 433–51.

Macdonald, Gordon J. F. Federal Government Programs in Weather Modification. **In** *Fleagle, R. G., ed.*, 1969, pp. 69–86.

MacDonald, John S. Benefits and Costs: Theoretical and Methodological Issues: Discussion. **In** *Somers, G. G. and Wood, W. D., eds.*, 1969, pp. 30–36.

MacDougall, G. A. D. The Benefits and Costs of Private Investment from Abroad: A Theoretical Approach. **In** *Bhagwati, J., ed.*, 1969, pp. 341–69.

MacEachern, G. A. Guidelines for Agricultural Policy Over the Next Decade: Discussion. *Can. J. Agr. Econ.*, November 1969, *17*(3), pp. 64–69.

——— and **Huff, H. Bruce.** Policy and Non-Policy in Foreign Trade: Discussion. *Amer. J. Agr. Econ.*, December 1969, *51*(5), pp. 1352–54.

Macesich, George and Close, F. Alan. Monetary Velocity and Investment Multiplier Stability Relativity for Norway and Sweden. *Statsokon. Tidsskr.*, March 1969, *83*(1), pp. 10–22.

——— and **Falero, Frank, Jr.** Permanent Income Hypothesis, Interest Rates and the Demand for Money. *Weltwirtsch. Arch.*, 1969, *103*(1), pp. 129–52.

Macgregor, D. R. On the Importance of the Regions to Scotland. **In** *Wolfe, J. N., ed.*, 1969, pp. 153–66.

MacGregor, M. A. and Campbell, D. R. Guidelines for Agricultural Policy Over the Next Decade. *Can. J. Agr. Econ.*, November 1969, *17*(3), pp. 57–64.

Machlup, Fritz. The Adjustment Problem and the Balance of Payments Policy of the United States. **In** *Officer, L. H. and Willett, T. D., eds.*, 1969, pp. 92–106.

——— Liberalism and the Choice of Freedoms. **In** *[von Hayek, Friedrich A.]*, 1969, pp. 117–46.

——— Positive and Normative Economics: An Analysis of the Ideas. **In** *Heilbroner, R. L., ed.*, 1969, pp. 99–129.

——— Round Table on Exchange Rate Policy. *Amer. Econ. Rev.*, May 1969, *59*(2), pp. 366–69.

——— Speculations on Gold Speculation. *Amer. Econ. Rev.*, May 1969, *59*(2), pp. 332–43.

Machol, Robert E. and Lerner, Eugene M. Risk, Ruin and Investment Analysis. *J. Financial Quant. Anal.*, December 1969, *4*(4), pp. 473–92.

Machonin, Pavel. The Social Structure of Contemporary Czechoslovak Society. *Czech. Econ. Pap.*, 1969, (11), pp. 153–59.

MacIntyre, A. Everette. The Public Policy of the Robinson-Patman Act and the Commission's New Guides for Advertising Allowances and Other Merchandising Payments and Services. *Antitrust Bull.*, Winter 1969, *14*, pp. 789–802.

MacKay, D. I. Industrial Structure and Regional Economic Growth—A Further Comment. *Scot. J. Polit. Econ.*, February 1969, *16*(1), pp. 99.

MacMillan, James A. and Loyns, R. M. A. A Cross-Section Analysis of Farm Household Expenditures. *Can. J. Agr. Econ.*, July 1969, *17*(2), pp. 92–105.

Macy, John W., Jr. Public Broadcasting: A Medium in Search of Solutions. *Law Contemp. Probl.*, Summer 1969, *34*(3), pp. 636–49.

Madan, B. K. Echoes of Bretton Woods. *Finance Develop.*, June 1969, *6*(2), pp. 30–38.

Maddala, G. S. and Vogel, Robert C. Estimating Lagged Relationships in Corporate Demand for Liquid Assets. *Rev. Econ. Statist.*, February 1969, *51*(1), pp. 53–61.

Madden, Carl H. Statement. **In** *The 1969 Economic Report of the President, Pt. 3, JECH*, 1969, pp. 931–36.

Maddison, Angus. Postwar Stabilization Policies: Comment. **In** *Bronfenbrenner, M., ed.*, 1969, pp. 499–501.

Maddock, Wallace J. Financing Cooperatives in Developing Countries. **In** *McGrath, M. J., ed.*, 1969, pp. 47–91.

Maddox, Robert C. and Block, Carl E. The "Trickle Effect"—A New Management Tool. *Marquette Bus. Rev.*, Spring 1969, *13*(1), pp. 11–14.

Madsen, Albert G. and Walsh, Richard G. Conglomerates: Economic Conduct and Performance. *Amer. J. Agr. Econ.*, December 1969, *51*(5), pp. 1495–1505.

Maehnel, Klaus. The Economic Policy of the Mao Tse-Tung Clique. *Chinese Econ. Stud.*, Fall 1969, *3*(1), pp. 48–69.

Maevskii, I. Socioeconomic Questions Relating to Automation. *Prob. Econ.*, October 1969, *12*(6), pp. 3–26.

Magee, Stephen P. and Houthakker, Hendrik S. Income and Price Elasticities in World Trade. *Rev. Econ. Statist.*, May 1969, *51*(2), pp. 111–25.

Magnani, Italo. Effetti di benessere derivanti da variazioni del saggio d'interesse e imposizione degli incrementi patrimoniali. (Welfare Effects of Changes in the Interest Rate and Capital Gains Taxation. With English summary.) *Rivista Int. Sci. Econ. Com.*, December 1969, *16*(12), pp. 1145–63.

——— Professor Scitovsky on Profit Maximization.

Rivista Int. Sci. Econ. Com., July 1969, *16*(7), pp. 652–63.

_____ **and Goetz, Charles J.** Automobile Taxation Based on Mechanical Characteristics: Evidence from the Italian Case. *Public Finance*, 1969, *24* (3), pp. 486–98.

Mahanti, P. C. Steel: A Balance Sheet. **In** *Dagli, V., ed., Vol. II*, 1969, pp. 171–79.

Maharja, Madhukar. Economics of Ghee Manufacture: A Study at Micro Level—A Reply. *Artha-Vikas*, January 1969, *5*(1), pp. 109–10.

Maher, John E. DEEP: Strengthening Economics in the Schools. *Amer. Econ. Rev.*, May 1969, *59*(2), pp. 230–38.

Maheshwari, Arun and Green, Paul E. Common Stock Perception and Preference: An Application of Multidimensional Scaling. *J. Bus.*, October 1969, *42*(4), pp. 439–57.

Mahler, Walter, Jr. Elimination of the Sales Tax Burden on Exports. *Asian Econ. Rev.*, February 1969, *11*(2), pp. 227–32.

Maier-Rothe, Christoph and Gupta, Shiv K. A Note on the Partitioning of a Single Product Market into Territories of Outlets. *J. Marketing Res.*, May 1969, *6*(2), pp. 232–36.

Maikov, A. Questions Pertaining to the Redistribution of Labor Resources. *Prob. Econ.*, May 1969, *12*(1), pp. 33–44.

Main, Jeremy. The First Real International Bankers. **In** *Jessup, P. F.*, 1969, pp. 481–90.

Mainander, Nils. Den samhällsekonomiska lönsamheten—praktiska kalkylmöjligheter. (Profitability to the Community—Its Calculability in Practice. With English summary.) *Econ. Samfundets Tidskr.*, 1969, *22*(2), pp. 81–94.

Mairesse, Jacques; Drechsler, László and Kux, Jaroslav. Labour Productivity Comparison between Czechoslovakia and France. *Rev. Income Wealth*, September 1969, *15*(3), pp. 219–28.

Maisel, Sherman J. Controlling Monetary Aggregates. **In** *Federal Reserve Bank of Boston*, 1969, pp. 152–74.

Maitha, J. K. A Supply Function for Kenyan Coffee. *East Afr. Econ. Rev.*, June 1969, *1*(1), pp. 63–72.

Maitra, Priyatosh. Models of Economic Development with Unlimited Supplies of Labour—Some Fundamental Limitations. *Arthaniti*, January & July 1969, *12*(1&2), pp. 41–56.

Maizels, Alfred. A Note on British Export Performance, 1899–1913: Rejoinder. *Econ. Hist. Rev.*, April 1969, *22*(1), pp. 122.

Major, David C. Benefit-Cost Ratios for Projects in Multiple Objective Investment Programs. *Water Resources Res.*, December 1969, *5*(6), pp. 1174–78.

Major, R. L. The Competitiveness of British Exports since Devaluation. *Nat. Inst. Econ. Rev.*, May 1969, (48), pp. 31–39.

Majumdar, Tapas. A Note on Arrow's Postulates for a Social Welfare Function—A Comment. *J. Polit. Econ.*, Part I, July/August 1969, *77*(4), pp. 528–31.

_____ Revealed Preference and the Demand Theorem in a Not Necessarily Competitive Market. *Quart. J. Econ.*, February 1969, *83*(1), pp. 167–70.

_____ Sen's General Theorem on Transitivity of Majority Decisions—An Alternative Approach. **In** *[Ghosal, U. N.]*, 1969, pp. 26–29.

Mak, James and Beighley, H. Prescott. The Effect of a Marketing Order on Winter Carrot Prices: Comment. *Amer. J. Agr. Econ.*, November 1969, *51*(4), pp. 929–33.

Makkonen, Veikko T. Palvelusektorin työllisyyden kehityksestä Suomessa vuosina 1948–1964. (The Development of Employment in the Finnish Service Sector 1948–1964. With English summary.) *Kansant. Aikak.*, 1969, *65*(2), pp. 110–21.

Malagón, Oscar M. and Frisch, Uwe G. La concentracion territorial de la industria en Mexico. (Territorial Concentration of Industry in Mexico. With English summary.) *Econ. Polít.*, Second Semester 1969, *6*(2), pp. 195–208.

Malassis, Louis. Education and Agricultural Development. *Int. Soc. Sci. J.*, 1969, *21*(2), pp. 244–55.

Malenbaum, Wilfred. Indian Economic Growth: Comparison with China (1965). **In** *Bhuleshkar, A. V., ed.*, 1969, pp. 271–87.

_____ Two Decades of India's Growth: Whither Now? **In** *Dagli, V., ed., Vol. III*, 1969, pp. 41–46.

Mäler, Karl-Göran. Optimal Pricing in Agricultural Emergency Policies. *Swedish J. Econ.*, December 1969, *71*(4), pp. 247–62.

Malhotra, P. C. The Economics of Correspondence Course for Higher Education. **In** *Pandit, H. N., ed.*, 1969, pp. 379–86.

Malinvaud, E. First Order Certainty Equivalence. *Econometrica*, October 1969, *37*(4), pp. 706–18.

_____ Risk-taking and Resource Allocation. **In** *Margolis, J. and Guitton, H., eds.*, 1969, pp. 222–46.

Malkiel, Burton G. and Kane, Edward J. Expectations and Interest Rates: A Cross-sectional Test of the Error-learning Hypothesis. *J. Polit. Econ.*, Part I, July/August 1969, *77*(4), pp. 453–70.

Mallakh, Ragaei El. The Economics of Rapid Growth: Libya. *Middle East J.*, Summer 1969, *23* (3), pp. 308–20.

_____ La programmazione in un'economia con eccesso di capitali: il caso della Libia. (Planning in the Capital Surplus Economy: The Case of Libya. With English summary.) *Rivista Int. Sci. Econ. Com.*, February 1969, *16*(2), pp. 148–65.

Mallery, Gary. Statistical Sampling and Auditing. *Manage. Account.*, August 1969, *51*(2), pp. 51–53.

Malluhi, Haytham. Tax System in Kuwait. *Bull. Int. Fiscal Doc.*, April 1969, *23*(4), pp. 160–62.

Malmgren, H. B. and Schlechty, D. L. Technology and Neo-Mercantilism in International Agricultural Trade. *Amer. J. Agr. Econ.*, December 1969, *51*(5), pp. 1325–37.

_____ Technology and Neo-Mercantilism in International Agricultural Trade. **In** *Interest Equalization Tax Extension Act of 1969, SCH*, 1969, pp. 35–42.

Malt, R. A.; Oates, Wallace E. and Bradford, David F. The Rising Cost of Local Public Services: Some Evidence and Reflections. *Nat. Tax J.*, June 1969, *22*(2), pp. 185–202.

Mamalakis, Markos. An Analysis of the Financial and Investment Activities of the Chilean Development Corporation: 1939–1964. *J. Devel. Stud.*, January 1969, *5*(2), pp. 118–37.

Mañas, Miroslav. Metody pro nalezení všech krajních bodů konvexního polyedru. (Methods for

Finding All Vertices of a Convex Polyhedron. With English summary.) *Ekon.-Mat. Obzor,* 1969, *5*(3), pp. 325–42.

Manchester, Alden C. Some Thoughts on Agricultural Marketing Research. *Agr. Econ. Res.,* April 1969, *21*(2), pp. 29–34.

Mandelbrot, Benoit. Long-Run Linearity, Locally Gaussian Process, H-Spectra and Infinite Variances. *Int. Econ. Rev.,* February 1969, *10*(1), pp. 82–111.

Mandelker, Daniel R. Housing Codes, Building Demolition, and Just Compensation: A Rationale for the Exercise of Public Powers over Slum Housing. *Mich. Law Rev.,* February 1969, *67*(4), pp. 635–78.

Mandell, Robert M. and Bennett, Peter D. Prepurpose Information Seeking Behavior of New Car Purchasers—The Learning Hypothesis. *J. Marketing Res.,* November 1969, *6*(4), pp. 430–33.

Manderscheid, Lester V. Better Teaching—Some Curricular Aspects. *Amer. J. Agr. Econ.,* December 1969, *51*(5), pp. 1081–84.

______ U.S. Import Demand for Green Coffee by Variety: Reply. *Amer. J. Agr. Econ.,* November 1969, *51*(4), pp. 929.

______ **and Nelson, Glenn L.** A Framework for Viewing Simulation. *Can. J. Agr. Econ.,* February 1969, *17*(1), pp. 33–41.

Manelli, Daniel J. and Barrow, Roscoe L. Communications Technology—A Forecast of Change (Part II). *Law Contemp. Probl.,* Summer 1969, *34*(3), pp. 431–51.

______ Communications Technology—A Forecast of Change (Part I). *Law Contemp. Probl.,* Spring 1969, *34*(2), pp. 205–43.

Manes, Rene P.; Whinston, Andrew and Colantoni, Claude S. Programming, Profit Rates and Pricing Decisions. *Accounting Rev.,* July 1969, *44*(3), pp. 467–81.

Mănescu, Manea. Present Problems of Economists' Training. *Revue Roumaine Sci. Soc. Serie Sci. Econ.,* 1969, *13*(1), pp. 3–8.

______ Romania's Economy on Her 25th Liberation Anniversary. *Revue Roumaine Sci. Soc. Serie Sci. Econ.,* 1969, *13*(2), pp. 105–12.

Mangum, Garth L. Determining the Results of Manpower and Antipoverty Programs. **In** *The Analysis and Evaluation of Public Expenditures: The PPB System, Vol. 3, JECP,* 1969, pp. 1171–80.

______ The Why, How, and Whence of Manpower Programs. *Ann. Amer. Acad. Polit. Soc. Sci.,* September 1969, *385,* pp. 50–62.

______ **and Levitan, Sar A.** The Changing Goals of Federal Manpower Policy. **In** *Wortman, M. S., Jr.,* 1969, pp. 122–24.

______ **and Levitan, Sar A.** A Functional Manpower Policy. **In** *Wortman, M. S., Jr.,* 1969, pp. 125–32.

Manhertz, Huntley G. Statistical Evaluation of Regional Differences in the Market for Processed Food Commodities. *Rev. Econ. Statist.,* May 1969, *51*(2), pp. 195–201.

Mann, H. Michael. A Note on Barriers to Entry and Long Run Profitability. *Antitrust Bull.,* Winter 1969, *14,* pp. 845–49.

______**; Henning, John A. and Meehan, James W., Jr.** Statistical Testing in Industrial Economics: A Reply on Measurement Error and Sampling Procedure. *J. Ind. Econ.,* November 1969, *18*(1), pp. 95–100.

______**; Henning, John A. and Meehan, James W., Jr.** Testing Hypothesis in Industrial Economics: A Reply. *J. Ind. Econ.,* November 1969, *18*(1), pp. 81–84.

______ **and Meehan, James W., Jr.** Concentration and Profitability: An Examination of a Recent Study. *Antitrust Bull.,* Summer 1969, *14,* pp. 385–95.

Mann, Maurice. How Does Monetary Policy Affect the Economy? *J. Money, Credit, Banking,* August 1969, *1*(3), pp. 538–48.

Manning, Travis W. Economic Guidelines for Land and Water Resource Use in Agriculture. *Can. J. Agr. Econ.,* November 1969, *17*(3), pp. 1–8.

Manole, M. Rețelele de transport în analiza utilizării timpului de muncă. (Transportation Networks as a Factor in the Analysis of the Utilization of Working Time. With English summary.) *Stud. Cercet. Econ.,* 1969, *4,* pp. 125–30.

Manser, W. A. P. Professor Reddaway's Last Word? *Nat. Westminster Bank Quart. Rev.,* February 1969, pp. 40–52.

Mansfield, Edwin. Industrial Research and Development: Characteristics, Costs, and Diffusion of Results. *Amer. Econ. Rev.,* May 1969, *59*(2), pp. 65–71.

Mansfield, N. W. Recreational Trip Generation: A Cross Section Analysis of Weekend Pleasure Trips to the Lake District National Park. *J. Transp. Econ. Policy,* May 1969, *3*(2), pp. 152–64.

Mantel, Nathan. Functional Averages of a Variable. *Amer. Statist.,* February 1969, *23*(1), pp. 21–22.

Mao, James C. T. and Helliwell, John F. Investment Decisions under Uncertainty: Theory and Practice. *J. Finance,* May 1969, *24*(2), pp. 323–38.

Mar, Brian W. and Merritt, Lavere B. Marginal Values of Dilution Waters. *Water Resources Res.,* December 1969, *5*(6), pp. 1186–95.

Marasco, Enrico. Interpretazione di un boom: l'Export 1968. (1968 Export: A Boom Interpretation. With English summary.) *Mondo Aperto,* April 1969, *23*(2), pp. 97–103.

______ Politica degli scambi. (Foreign Trade Policy. With English summary.) *Mondo Aperto,* December 1969, *23*(6), pp. 417–22.

March, Eli P. and Newman, Monroe. Rural Areas in the Urban Economy. *Amer. J. Agr. Econ.,* December 1969, *51*(5), pp. 1097–1109.

Marchal, André. The Problems of the Common Market. **In** *Samuelson, P. A., ed.,* 1969, pp. 176–217.

Marcus, Burton H. Similarity of Ghetto and Nonghetto Food Costs. *J. Marketing Res.,* August 1969, *6*(3), pp. 365–68.

Marcus, Matityahu. Advertising and Changes in Concentration. *Southern Econ. J.,* October 1969, *36*(2), pp. 117–21.

______ Profitability and Size of Firm: Some Further Evidence. *Rev. Econ. Statist.,* February 1969, *51* (1), pp. 104–07.

Marcus, Mildred Rendl. Questions and Problems Concerning the Expansion of East European Trade with the West and the Financing Methodology. *Marquette Bus. Rev.,* Fall 1969, *13*(3), pp. 125–36.

Marcus, Morton J. and Hirsch, Werner Z. Intercommunity Spillovers and the Provision of Public Education. *Kyklos,* 1969, *22*(4), pp. 641–60.

Marenco, G. Exact Aggregation with Linear Programming Models—A Note on the Sufficient Conditions Proposed by R. H. Day. *Amer. J. Agr. Econ.,* August 1969, *51*(3), pp. 684–86.

Marglin, S. A. Information in Price and Command Systems of Planning. **In** *Margolis, J. and Guitton, H., eds.,* 1969, pp. 54–77.

Margolis, Julius. Shadow Prices for Incorrect or Nonexistent Market Values. **In** *The Analysis and Evaluation of Public Expenditures: The PPB System, Vol. 1, JECP,* 1969, pp. 533–46.

______; **Hufschmidt, Maynard M. and Krutilla, John V.** Standards and Criteria for Formulating and Evaluating Federal Water Resources Development. **In** *Guidelines for Estimating the Benefits of Public Expenditures, JECH,* 1969, pp. 135–212.

Mărgulescu, D. and Ișfănescu, A. Rentabilitatea ca indicator de sinteză economică. (Profitableness as an Indicator of Economic Synthesis. With English summary.) *Stud. Cercet. Econ.,* 1969, *4,* pp. 173–83.

Marimont, Martin L. Measuring Real Output for Industries Providing Services: OBE Concepts and Methods: Reply. **In** *Fuchs, V. R., ed.,* 1969, pp. 50–52.

______ Measuring Real Output for Industries Providing Services: OBE Concepts and Methods. **In** *Fuchs, V. R., ed.,* 1969, pp. 15–40.

Marion, Gérald. Fonction d'emploi, taux de participation de la main-d'oeuvre et demande excédentaire de travil. (With English summary.) *Revue Écon.,* November 1969, *20*(6), pp. 968–1005.

Mark, Shelley M. Property Tax Administration and Hawaii's Land Use Law. **In** *Lynn, A. D., Jr., ed.,* 1969, pp. 187–202.

Markert, Kurt E. The Application of German Antitrust Law to International Restraints on Trade. **In** *Economic Concentration, Pt. 7A, SCH,* 1969, pp. 4091–4103.

______ International Cartels and Legal Order. **In** *Economic Concentration, Pt. 7A, SCH,* 1969, pp. 4103–20.

______ The Dyestuff Case: A Contribution to the Relationship between the Antitrust Laws of the European Economic Community and Its Member States. *Antitrust Bull.,* Winter 1969, *14,* pp. 869–99.

Markham, Jesse W. Competition in the Nuclear Power Supply Industry—A Reply to Mr. Netschert. *Antitrust Bull.,* Fall 1969, *14,* pp. 657–63.

Markin, Rom J. The Supermarket—A Study of Size, Profits, and Concentration. **In** *Alexis, M.; Holloway, R. J. and Hancock, R. S., eds.,* 1969, pp. 201–13.

Markland, Robert E. and Furst, Richard W. Evaluating Merger-Acquisition Opportunities—A Risk Incorporation Model. *Univ. Missouri Bus. Govt. Rev.,* July–August 1969, *10*(4), pp. 21–26.

Marks, Samuel B. Employer Techniques for Upgrading Low-Skill Workers. **In** *Somers, G. G., ed. (II),* 1969, pp. 217–27.

Marquardt, Wilhelm. German Economic Research in Africa. *Ger. Econ. Rev.,* 1969, *7*(1), pp. 71–76.

Marquis, Donald G. and Gruber, William H. Research on the Human Factor in the Transfer of Technology. **In** *Gruber, W. H. and Marquis, D. G., eds.,* 1969, pp. 255–82.

Marquis, Lloyd K. A Comprehensive Framework for Analyzing the Management of a Business Enterprise. **In** *Kennedy, C. J., ed.,* 1969, pp. 38–48.

Marschak, Thomas. On the Comparison of Centralized and Decentralized Economies. *Amer. Econ. Rev.,* May 1969, *59*(2), pp. 525–32.

Marsden, Keith. Integrated Regional Development: A Quantitative Approach. *Int. Lab. Rev.,* June 1969, *99*(6), pp. 621–46.

______ Towards a Synthesis of Economic Growth and Social Justice. *Int. Lab. Rev.,* November 1969, *100* (5), pp. 389–418.

Marsh, Donald B. Canada's Experience with a Floating Exchange Rate: A Vindication of Free Markets in Exchange. **In** *Aliber, R. Z., ed.,* 1969, pp. 138–55.

Marshall, A. The Total Currency Needed by a Country. **In** *Clower, R. W., ed.,* 1969, pp. 80–93.

Marshall, Alfred. Three Lectures on Progress and Poverty. *J. Law Econ.,* April 1969, *12*(1), pp. 184–226.

Marshall, Don C. Disclosure of Federal Tax Concessions—Billions in Implicit Subsidies. *Univ. Missouri Bus. Govt. Rev.,* January–February 1969, *10* (1), pp. 23–29.

Marshall, Leon S. The English and American Industrial City of the Nineteenth Century. **In** *Callow, A. B., Jr., ed.,* 1969, pp. 148–55.

Marshall, R. G. The Size and Structure of the Livestock Industry in Canada, 1980. *Can. J. Agr. Econ.,* November 1969, *17*(3), pp. 90–103.

Marshall, Ray. Equal Employment Opportunities: Problems and Prospects. **In** *Wortman, M. S., Jr.,* 1969, pp. 364–71.

Martelli, Antonio. Gli errori nelle previsioni dei consumi. (Mistakes in Consumer Forecasting. With English summary.) *L'Impresa,* July/October 1969, *11*(4–5), pp. 357–64.

______ Vecchie e nuove teorie sul consumatore. (Old and New Theories on the Consumer: Present Situation. With English summary.) *L'Impresa,* March/April 1969, *11*(2), pp. 133–37.

Martin, J. Rod and Lard, Curtis F. At a Crossroad: Graduate Teaching in Agricultural Economics. *Amer. J. Agr. Econ.,* December 1969, *51*(5), pp. 1569–73.

Martin, James W. New Dimensions of the Capitalization of Earnings in Appraising Public Utility Property. **In** *[White, Charles P.],* 1969, pp. 148–63.

Martin, William E.; Burdak, Thomas G. and Young, Robert A. Projecting Hydrologic and Economic Interrelationships in Groundwater Basin Management. *Amer. J. Agr. Econ.,* December 1969, *51* (5), pp. 1593–97.

Martin, William McChesney, Jr. Statement to Congress. *Fed. Res. Bull.,* October 1969, *55*(10), pp. 815–19.

______ Statement to Congress. *Fed. Res. Bull.,* October 1969, *55*(10), pp. 819–22.

______ The Price of Gold Is Not the Problem. **In** *Kuhlman, J. M., ed.,* 1969, pp. 326–33.

______ Statement. **In** *High Interest Rates, SCH,* 1969, pp. 6–13.

______ Statement. **In** *Bank Holding Company Act Amendments, Pts. 1–3, HCH,* 1969, pp. 196–202.

——— Statement. In *The 1969 Economic Report of the President, Pt. 3, JECH,* 1969, pp. 647–52.

——— Statement to Congress. *Fed. Res. Bull.,* July 1969, *55*(7), pp. 591–95.

——— Statement to Congress. *Fed. Res. Bull.,* September 1969, *55*(9), pp. 719–26.

Martino, Joseph P.; Price, William J. and Ashley, William G. Science-Technology Coupling: Experience of the Air Force Office of Scientific Research. In *Gruber, W. H. and Marquis, D. G., eds.,* 1969, pp. 117–36.

Martinov, V. The Changing Character of International Trade and the Problems of Underdeveloped Regions. In *Papi, U. and Nunn, C., eds.,* 1969, pp. 163–74.

Marty, Alvin L. Inside Money, Outside Money, and the Wealth Effect. *J. Money, Credit, Banking,* February 1969, *1*(1), pp. 101–11.

——— Notes on Money and Economic Growth. *J. Money, Credit, Banking,* May 1969, *1*(2), pp. 252–65.

Marvin, Keith E. and Rouse, Andrew M. The Status of PPB in Federal Agencies: A Comparative Perspective. In *The Analysis and Evaluation of Public Expenditures: The PPB System, Vol. 3, JECP,* 1969, pp. 801–14.

Marwah, Kanta. An Econometric Model of Colombia: A Prototype Devaluation View. *Econometrica,* April 1969, *37*(2), pp. 228–51.

Marzi, Giorgio. Attualita' dell'ufficio studi. (The Studies Department in the Modern Firm. With English summary.) *L'Impresa,* March/April 1969, *11*(2), pp. 149–51.

Maschke, Erich. Outline of the History of German Cartels from 1873 to 1914. In *Crouzet, F.; Chaloner, W. H. and Stern, W. M., eds.,* 1969, pp. 226–58.

Masera, R. S. Least Squares Construction of the Yield Curves for Italian Government Securities, 1957–1967, Part I: General Introduction to the Italian Bond Market and Main Results. *Banca Naz. Lavoro Quart. Rev.,* December 1969, (91), pp. 347–71.

Maskin, Balwant Singh. Some Reflections on Systems of Social Accounts—A Review Article. *Asian Econ. Rev.,* May 1969, *11*(3), pp. 273–89.

Mason, Charles. Scheduling and Seniority: The United Airlines Experience. In *Siegel, A. J., ed.,* 1969, pp. 203–25.

Mason, Joseph Barry and Moore, Charles Thomas. A Note on the Reliability of Census Data in Trading Area Analysis. *Miss. Val. J. Bus. Econ.,* Fall 1969, *5*(1), pp. 68–72.

Massell, Benton F. Consistent Estimation of Expenditure Elasticities from Cross-Section Data on Households Producing Partly for Subsistence. *Rev. Econ. Statist.,* May 1969, *51*(2), pp. 136–42.

——— Price Stabilization and Welfare. *Quart. J. Econ.,* May 1969, *83*(2), pp. 284–98.

——— **and Heyer, Judith.** Household Expenditure in Nairobi: A Statistical Analysis in Consumer Behavior. *Econ. Develop. Cult. Change,* January 1969, *17*(2), pp. 212–34.

——— **and Parnes, Andrew.** Estimation of Expenditure Elasticities from a Sample of Rural Households in Uganda. *Bull. Oxford Univ. Inst. Econ. Statist.,* November 1969, *31*(4), pp. 313–29.

——— **and Yotopoulos, Pan A.** The Relationships between the Volume of Investment, Its Productivity and the Growth of the South American Countries. *Kyklos,* 1969, *22*(2), pp. 328–33.

Massy, William F. Forecasting the Demand for New Convenience Products. *J. Marketing Res.,* November 1969, *6*(4), pp. 405–12.

Masten, John T. The Structure of Commercial Banking in the United States. *Rivista Int. Sci. Econ. Com.,* July 1969, *16*(7), pp. 688–709.

Masters, Stanley H. An Interindustry Analysis of Wages and Plant Size. *Rev. Econ. Statist.,* August 1969, *51*(3), pp. 341–45.

——— The Effect of Family Income on Children's Education: Some Findings on Inequality of Opportunity. *J. Human Res.,* Spring 1969, *4*(2), pp. 158–75.

Masui, Yukio. The Supply Price of Labor: Farm Family Workers. In *Ohkawa, K.; Johnston, B. F. and Kaneda, H., eds.,* 1969, pp. 222–49.

Matalas, N. C.; James, I. C., II and Bower, B. T. Relative Importance of Variables in Water Resources Planning. *Water Resources Res.,* December 1969, *5*(6), pp. 1165–73.

Matassi, Luigi. The Great Depression and the New Recovery of Italian Industry. *Rev. Econ. Cond. Italy,* July 1969, *23*(4), pp. 304–22.

——— The Italian Economy after World War II. *Rev. Econ. Cond. Italy,* September 1969, *23*(5), pp. 428–42.

——— The Italian Economy in the Late Eighteenth and Nineteenth Century. *Rev. Econ. Cond. Italy,* March 1969, *23*(2), pp. 116–33.

——— Reconstruction and Economic Growth in Italy Up to Date. *Rev. Econ. Cond. Italy,* November 1969, *23*(6), pp. 544–63.

Matejko, Alexander. The International Scene: Current Trends in the Social Sciences: Some Sociological Problems of Socialist Factories. *Soc. Res.,* Autumn 1969, *36*(3), pp. 448–80.

Mathai, M. K. Incentives for Investment in Malaysia. *Bull. Int. Fiscal Doc.,* November 1969, *23*(11), pp. 503–15.

Mathew, E. T. Proposals for an Integrated System of Agricultural Taxation. *Artha-Vikas,* July 1969, *5*(2), pp. 146–53.

Mathews, R. and Grant, J. McB. Profit Measurement and Inflation. In *Parker, R. H. and Harcourt, G. C., eds.,* 1969, pp. 201–14.

Mathias, Peter. Who Unbound Prometheus? Science and Technical Change, 1600–1800. *Yorkshire Bull. Econ. Soc. Res.,* May 1969, *21*(1), pp. 3–16.

Mathieson, R. S. The Soviet Contribution to Regional Science: A Review Article. *J. Reg. Sci.,* April 1969, *9*(1), pp. 125–40.

Mathis, F. John. The Latin American Common Market: Problems and Progress. *Quart. Rev. Econ. Bus.,* Autumn 1969, *9*(3), pp. 5–16.

——— **and Krause, Walter.** The Status of "Lesser Developed" Countries within a Latin American Common Market. In *Hilton, R., ed.,* 1969, pp. 471–84.

Maton, J. Experience on the Job and Formal Training as Alternative Means of Skill Acquisition: An

Empirical Study. *Int. Lab. Rev.*, September 1969, *100*(3), pp. 239–55.

Matsusaki, Hirofumi. The Potential of Comparative Marketing: A Methodological Review. **In** *Association of Canadian Schools of Business,* 1969, pp. 278–307.

Matthews, R. C. O. Postwar Business Cycles in the United Kingdom. **In** *Bronfenbrenner, M., ed.,* 1969, pp. 99–135.

_____ Why Growth Rates Differ. *Econ. J.,* June 1969, *79*(314), pp. 261–68.

Matthews, Roy A. A New Atlantic Role for Canada. *Foreign Aff.,* January 1969, *47*(2), pp. 334–47.

Mauer, Laurence J. and Scaperlanda, Anthony E. The Determinants of U.S. Direct Investment in the E.E.C. *Amer. Econ. Rev.,* Part I, September 1969, *59*(4), pp. 558–68.

Mauer, Laurence Jay. Commercial Bank Maturity Demand for United States Government Securities and the Determinants of the Term Structure of Interest Rates. *J. Financial Quant. Anal.,* March 1969, *4*(1), pp. 37–52.

Mauldon, R. G.; Schapper, H. P. and Treloar, D. W. G. Operational Accounting for Farm Management. *Australian J. Agr. Econ.,* June 1969, *13*(1), pp. 47–57.

Maule, C. J. Antitrust and the Takeover Activity of American Firms in Canada: A Rejoinder. *J. Law Econ.,* October 1969, *12*(2), pp. 419–24.

Maurice, Charles and Ekelund, Robert B., Jr. An Empirical Investigation of Advertising and Concentration: Comment. *J. Ind. Econ.,* November 1969, *18*(1), pp. 76–80.

Mauro, Frédéric. Latin American History and Integration. **In** *Hilton, R., ed.,* 1969, pp. 49–58.

Mautz, R. K. and Skousen, K. Fred. Some Problems in Empirical Research in Accounting. *Accounting Rev.,* July 1969, *44*(3), pp. 447–56.

Maxwell, Darold E.; Phillips, Llad and Votey, Harold L., Jr. A Synthesis of the Economic and Demographic Models of Fertility: An Econometric Test. *Rev. Econ. Statist.,* August 1969, *51*(3), pp. 298–308.

Maxwell, James A. Federal Grant Elasticity and Distortion. *Nat. Tax J.,* December 1969, *22*(4), pp. 550–51.

_____ Federal Grants in Canada and Australia. *Econ. Rec.,* September 1969, *45*(111), pp. 441–48.

Maxwell, W. David. Production Theory and Cost Curves. *Appl. Econ.,* August 1969, *1*(3), pp. 211–24.

May, Francis B. The Voice of Apollo: Historical Trends in Business Forecasting. *Soc. Sci. Quart.,* June 1969, *50*(1), pp. 153–60.

May, Frederick E. Adaptive Behavior in Automobile Brand Choices. *J. Marketing Res.,* February 1969, *6*(1), pp. 62–65.

May, Phillip T., Jr. System Control: Computers the Weak Link? *Accounting Rev.,* July 1969, *44*(3), pp. 583–92.

Mayberry, Thomas C. Thorstein Veblen on Human Nature. *Amer. J. Econ. Soc.,* July 1969, *28*(3), pp. 315–23.

Mayer, Jean. Toward a Non-Malthusian Population Policy. **In** *Effects of Population Growth on Natural Resources and the Environment, HCH,* 1969, pp. 111–19.

Maynard, Betty J. and Broom, Leonard. Prestige and Socioeconomic Ranking of Occupations. *Soc. Sci. Quart.,* September 1969, *50*(2), pp. 369–73.

Mayne, Lucille Stringer. Federal Reserve System Membership, Bank Liquidity, and Bank Profitability. *Southern Econ. J.,* October 1969, *36*(2), pp. 181–84.

Mayo, Louis H. Statement. **In** *To Establish a Select Senate Committee on Technology and the Human Environment, SCH,* 1969, pp. 96–121.

Mayo, Robert P. Statement. **In** *Proposed Extension of the Surcharge and Repeal of the Investment Tax Credit, SCH,* 1969, pp. 71–75.

_____ Statement. **In** *The 1969 Economic Report of the President, Pt. 2, JECH,* 1969, pp. 337–42.

Mayor, Thomas H. Some Theoretical Difficulties in the Estimation of the Elasticity of Substitution from Cross-section Data. *Western Econ. J.,* June 1969, *7*(2), pp. 153–63.

Mazek, Warren F. Unemployment and the Efficacy of Migration: The Case of Laborers. *J. Reg. Sci.,* April 1969, *9*(1), pp. 101–07.

_____ **and Christian, James W.** Corporate Debt Structure and the Differential Effects of Monetary Policy. *Southern Econ. J.,* April 1969, *35*(4), pp. 359–68.

Mazumder, Debkumar Dutta. Estimates of Increase in Demand for Specific Items of Milk and Milk Products during Fourth and Fifth Five Year Plans. *Econ. Aff.,* January-February 1969, *14* (1–2), pp. 81–87.

McAlexander, Robert H. and Zepp, Glenn A. Predicting Aggregate Milk Production: An Empirical Study. *Amer. J. Agr. Econ.,* August 1969, *51*(3), pp. 642–49.

McArthur, A. T. G. Extra Tax Resulting from Income Variation with Particular Reference to New Zealand. *Australian J. Agr. Econ.,* June 1969, *13*(1), pp. 68–73.

McArthur, D. A. Educational Efforts in Farm Credit Management. *Can. J. Agr. Econ.,* November 1969, *17*(3), pp. 181–85.

McCall, John and Wallace, Neil. A Supply Function of First-Term Re-enlistees to the Air Force. *J. Human Res.,* Summer 1969, *4*(3), pp. 293–310.

McCalla, Alex F. Whither Goest U.S. Agricultural Policy: An Exercise in Naive Prophesy. *Can. J. Agr. Econ.,* July 1969, *17*(2), pp. 1–16.

McCallum, B. T. The Instability of Kaldorian Models. *Oxford Econ. Pap.,* March 1969, *21*(1), pp. 56–65.

McCalmont, David B. Why a Rising Federal Debt Is No Cause for Alarm. **In** *Starleaf, D. R., ed.,* 1969, pp. 247–54.

McCamman, Dorothy, et al. Facts and Findings. **In** *Economics of Aging: Toward a Full Share in Abundance, Pt. 1, SCH,* 1969, pp. 149–228.

McCarthy, Michael D. An Analysis of Non-wage Income Components. **In** *Duesenberry, J. S., et al.,* 1969, pp. 151–86.

McClain, J. M. and Hawkins, Clark A. A Note on the Short-Run Demand for Money. *Miss. Val. J. Bus. Econ.,* Fall 1969, *5*(1), pp. 73–79.

McClellan, Keith and Medrich, Elliot A. Outdoor

Recreation: Economic Consideration for Optimal Site Selection and Development. *Land Econ.,* May 1969, *45*(2), pp. 174–82.

McClelland, Donald H. The Common Market's Contribution to Central American Economic Growth: A First Approximation. **In** *Hilton, R., ed.,* 1969, pp. 508–36.

McClelland, Peter D. The Cost to America of British Imperial Policy. *Amer. Econ. Rev.,* May 1969, *59* (2), pp. 370–81.

——— New Perspectives on the Disposal of Western Lands in Nineteenth Century America. *Bus. Hist. Rev.,* Spring 1969, *43*(1), pp. 77–83.

McClung, Nelson. The Economics of Pension Finance. *J. Risk Ins.,* September 1969, *36*(4), pp. 425–32.

McColl, Gregory D. The Balance-of-Payments Problems. **In** *Preston, R., ed.,* 1969, pp. 91–119.

——— The Tariff: A Century of Debate. **In** *Preston, R., ed.,* 1969, pp. 71–90.

McConnell, Campbell R. and Lamphear, Charles. The Effectiveness of Teaching Methods: Teaching Principles of Economics without Lectures. *J. Econ. Educ.,* Fall 1969, *1*(1), pp. 20–32.

McConnell, John W. Industrial Relations and University Relations: Discussion. **In** *Somers, G. G., ed. (II),* 1969, pp. 26–28.

McConnell, Thomas P. Hidden Resources in the Dues Dollar. *Manage. Account.,* December 1969, *51*(6), pp. 24–26.

McCracken, Paul W. The Game Plan for Economic Policy. *Amer. Statist.,* October 1969, *23*(4), pp. 7–10.

——— Statement. **In** *The 1969 Economic Report of the President, Pt. 2, JECH,* 1969, pp. 284–304.

——— Statement. **In** *Review of Federal Statistical Programs, JECH,* 1969, pp. 115–18.

——— Statement. **In** *High Interest Rates, SCH,* 1969, pp. 13–17.

McCrone, Donald J. and Cnudde, Charles F. Party Competition and Welfare Policies in the American States. *Amer. Polit. Sci. Rev.,* September 1969, *63*(3), pp. 858–66.

McDonald, Howard E. and Stromberger, T. L. Cost Control for the Professional Service Firm. *Harvard Bus. Rev.,* January–February 1969, *47*(1), pp. 109–21.

McDonald, James R. Contemporary Patterns of Internal Migration in France. *Mich. Academician,* Spring 1969, *1*(3–4), pp. 101–11.

McDonald, Patrick G. and Wicks, John H. Income Distribution of Death Bequest Recipients. *Nat. Tax J.,* September 1969, *22*(3), pp. 408–10.

McDonald, Stephen L. Postwar Economic Growth and Fluctuations in Louisiana. **In** *Beard, T. R., ed.,* 1969, pp. 82–102.

McElroy, F. W. Returns to Scale, Euler's Theorem, and the Form of Production Functions. *Econometrica,* April 1969, *37*(2), pp. 275–79.

McFadden, Daniel. A Simple Remark on the Second Best Pareto Optimality of Market Equilibria. *J. Econ. Theory,* June 1969, *1*(1), pp. 26–38.

McFarland, C. K. and Neal, Nevin E. The Nascence of Protectionism: American Tariff Policies, 1816–1824. *Land Econ.,* February 1969, *45*(1), pp. 22–30.

McGarrah, Robert E. Let's Internationalize Defense Marketing. *Harvard Bus. Rev.,* May–June 1969, *47*(3), pp. 146–55.

McGarry, Michael J.; Schmitz, Andrew and Bjarnason, Harold F. Converting Price Series of Internationally Traded Commodities to a Common Currency Prior to Estimating National Supply and Demand Equations. *Amer. J. Agr. Econ.,* February 1969, *51*(1), pp. 189–92.

McGee, Dean A. Treasures of Energy: Natural Resources of the Ninth and Tenth Federal Reserve Districts. *Fed. Res. Bank Kansas City Rev.,* February 1969, pp. 3–9.

McGilchrist, C. A. Discrete Distribution Estimators from the Recurrence Equation for Probabilities. *J. Amer. Statist. Assoc.,* June 1969, *64*(326), pp. 602–609.

McGill, Dan M. Critical Issues in Pension Planning. **In** *Tax Institute of America,* 1969, pp. 167–71.

McGilvray, James and Simpson, David. Some Tests of Stability in Interindustry Coefficients. *Econometrica,* April 1969, *37*(2), pp. 204–21.

McGinley, John J. and Gross, Jack L. Need for a Marketing Intelligence System . . . in Petroleum Marketing: Integration of Information Systems into the Decision-Making Process. *Econ. Bus. Bull.,* Fall 1969, *22*(1), pp. 25–32.

McGivering, Ian. Personnel Management. **In** *Kempner, T., ed.,* 1969, pp. 54–59.

McGuire, Martin C. Program Analysis and Regional Economic Objectives. **In** *The Analysis and Evaluation of Public Expenditures: The PPB System, Vol. 1, JECP,* 1969, pp. 592–610.

——— **and Aaron, Henry J.** Efficiency and Equity in the Optimal Supply of a Public Good. *Rev. Econ. Statist.,* February 1969, *51*(1), pp. 31–39.

——— **and Garn, Harvey A.** The Integration of Equity and Efficiency Criteria in Public Project Selection. *Econ. J.,* December 1969, *79*(316), pp. 882–93.

——— **and Garn, Harvey A.** Problems in the Cooperative Allocation of Public Expenditures. *Quart. J. Econ.,* February 1969, *83*(1), pp. 44–59.

——— **and Harris, Curtis C., Jr.** Planning Techniques for Regional Development Policy. *J. Human Res.,* Fall 1969, *4*(4), pp. 466–90.

McHale, Thomas R. Policies for the Private Sector: Discussion. *Philippine Econ. J.,* First Semester 1969, *8*(1), pp. 31–32.

McIntyre, M. Charles. Determinants of Expenditures for Public Higher Education. *Nat. Tax J.,* June 1969, *22*(2), pp. 262–72.

McKean, John R. A Note on Administered Prices with Fluctuating Demand. *J. Financial Quant. Anal.,* March 1969, *4*(1), pp. 15–23.

McKechnie, Graeme H. Manpower Mobility Programs: Discussion. **In** *Somers, G. G. and Wood, W. D., eds.,* 1969, pp. 224–29.

McKelvey, Jean T. Fact Finding in Public Employment Disputes: Promise or Illusion? **In** *Somers, G. G., ed. (II),* 1969, pp. 41–47.

——— Fact Finding in Public Employment Disputes: Promise or Illusion? *Ind. Lab. Relat. Rev.,* July 1969, *22*(4), pp. 528–43.

McKenzie, C. J.; Philpot, B. P. and Woods, M. J. Price Formation in the Raw Wool Market. *Econ. Rec.*, September 1969, *45*(111), pp. 386–98.

McKenzie, George W. International Monetary Reform and the "Crawling Peg"—Reply. *Fed. Res. Bank St. Louis Rev.*, July 1969, *51*(7), pp. 26–31.

______ International Monetary Reform and the "Crawling Peg." *Fed. Res. Bank St. Louis Rev.*, February 1969, *51*(2), pp. 15–23.

McKinley, Erskine. Trifling with a Serious Subject. *Rivista Int. Sci. Econ. Com.*, August 1969, *16*(8), pp. 816–23.

McKinnon, Ronald I. Portfolio Balance and International Payments Adjustment. **In** *Mundell, R. A. and Swoboda, A. K., eds.*, 1969, pp. 199–234.

McLaney, James P. Asset Forecasting: A Defense Industry Technique. *Manage. Account.*, September 1969, *51*(3), pp. 33–35.

McLaughlin, Richard P. Public Employee Collective Bargaining. **In** *Walsh, R. E., ed.*, 1969, pp. 290–301.

McLennan, Kenneth. Education and Training for Managerial Jobs. *Amer. J. Econ. Soc.*, October 1969, *28*(4), pp. 423–36.

______ **and Moskow, Michael H.** Multilateral Bargaining in the Public Sector. **In** *Somers, G. G., ed. (II)*, 1969, pp. 31–40.

McLeod, Donald. The Personal Income Tax in Jamaica. *Soc. Econ. Stud.*, September 1969, *18*(3), pp. 254–62.

McLoughlin, Peter F. M. "Subsistence Agriculture" and Technological Change: Further Discussion of the Theoretical Problem. *Amer. J. Agr. Econ.*, November 1969, *51*(4), pp. 957–60.

McLure, Charles E., Jr. The Inter-regional Incidence of General Regional Taxes. *Public Finance*, 1969, *24*(3), pp. 457–85.

McMahon, Christopher. Monetary Policies in the United States and the United Kingdom: A Comment. *J. Money, Credit, Banking*, August 1969, *1* (3), pp. 549–52.

McNamara, Robert S. Esplosione demografica e sviluppo economico. (Demographic Increase and Economic Development. With English summary.) *Mondo Aperto*, October 1969, *23*(5), pp. 330–42.

McPherson, James M. The Civil War and Reconstruction: A Revolution of Racial Equality? **In** *Shade, W. G. and Herrenkohl, R. C., eds.*, 1969, pp. 49–72.

McQuade, Lawrence C. Statement. **In** *A Review of Balance of Payments Policies, JECH*, 1969, pp. 3–29.

McRorie, H. D. The Demand for Agricultural Economists by Agri-Business to 1980. *Can. J. Agr. Econ.*, November 1969, *17*(3), pp. 114–23.

McShane, R. W. and Fairbairn, I. J. The Return on Equities and Fixed Interest Securities on the Australian Capital Market. *Econ. Rec.*, March 1969, *45*(109), pp. 116–23.

Mead, John F. and Krislov, Joseph. Drawing Jurisdictional Lines in Mediation. *Mon. Lab. Rev.*, April 1969, *92*(4), pp. 41–45.

Mead, Walter J. Instantaneous Merger Profit as a Conglomerate Merger Motive. *Western Econ. J.*, December 1969, *7*(4), pp. 295–306.

______ Statement. **In** *Governmental Intervention in the Market Mechanism, Pt. 1, SCH*, 1969, pp. 77–102.

Meade, James E. and Fleming, J. Marcus. Price and Output Policy of State Enterprise: A Symposium. **In** *Arrow, K. J. and Scitovsky, T., eds.*, 1969, pp. 309–24.

______ **and Stone, J. R. N.** The Construction of Tables of National Income, Expenditure, Savings and Investment. **In** *Parker, R. H. and Harcourt, G. C., eds.*, 1969, pp. 329–46.

Meadows, Richard. Household Location Decisions and Local Public Benefits and Costs: Comment. *Amer. Econ.*, Spring 1969, *13*(1), pp. 40–41.

Means, Gardiner C. The Problems and Prospects of Collective Capitalism. *J. Econ. Issues*, March 1969, *3*(1), pp. 18–31.

Medford, William L. Key Item Reporting. *Manage. Account.*, August 1969, *51*(2), pp. 21–26.

Medrich, Elliot A. and McClellan, Keith. Outdoor Recreation: Economic Consideration for Optimal Site Selection and Development. *Land Econ.*, May 1969, *45*(2), pp. 174–82.

Meehan, James W., Jr. and Mann, H. Michael. Concentration and Profitability: An Examination of a Recent Study. *Antitrust Bull.*, Summer 1969, *14*, pp. 385–95.

______**; Mann, H. Michael and Henning, John A.** Statistical Testing in Industrial Economics: A Reply on Measurement Error and Sampling Procedure. *J. Ind. Econ.*, November 1969, *18*(1), pp. 95–100.

______**; Mann, H. Michael and Henning, John A.** Testing Hypothesis in Industrial Economics: A Reply. *J. Ind. Econ.*, November 1969, *18*(1), pp. 81–84.

Meek, Ronald L. A New Bulk Supply Tariff—Reply. *Econ. J.*, December 1969, *79*(316), pp. 974.

van Meerhaeghe, M. A. G. Economics: Britain and the EEC—An Introduction. **In** *van Meerhaeghe, M. A. G., ed.*, 1969, pp. 1–20.

______ Observations sur la signification des termes d'échange des pays sous-développés. (With English summary.) *Kyklos*, 1969, *22*(3), pp. 566–84.

de Meester, J.-C. Fonctions de production et données technologiques. (Production Functions and Technological Data. With English summary.) *Rivista Int. Sci. Econ. Com.*, January 1969, *16*(1), pp. 31–45.

Mehedinţu, M. and Enache, C. Creşterea rolului Partidului Comunist Român în conducerea economiei în etapa actuală. (Increased Importance of the Part Played by the Romanian Communist Party in the Management of Economy at the Present Stage. With English summary.) *Stud. Cercet. Econ.*, 1969, *3*, pp. 9–17.

Mehr, Robert I. Channels of Distribution in Insurance. *J. Risk Ins.*, December 1969, *36*(5), pp. 583–95.

Mehta, Asoka. Jawaharlal Nehru—Social Justice and National Development. **In** *Bhuleshkar, A. V., ed.*, 1969, pp. 3–10.

Mehta, B. V. Size and Capital Intensity in Indian

Industry. *Bull. Oxford Univ. Inst. Econ. Statist.*, August 1969, *31*(3), pp. 189–204.

Mehta, J. S. and Gurland, John. Combinations of Unbiased Estimators of the Mean Which Consider Inequality of Unknown Variances. *J. Amer. Statist. Assoc.*, September 1969, *64*(327), pp. 1042–55.

Mehta, Parkash. Different Inputs as Related to Apple Output in Kulu District. *Asian Econ. Rev.*, May 1969, *11*(3), pp. 325–28.

Meidner, Rudolf. Active Manpower Policy and the Inflation Unemployment-Dilemma. *Swedish J. Econ.*, September 1969, *71*(3), pp. 161–83.

Meier, Gerald M. Development Without Employment. *Banca Naz. Lavoro Quart. Rev.*, September 1969, (90), pp. 309–19.

Meigs, A. James. Capital Flows to Public Utilities and the Structure of the Money and Capital Markets. **In** *Trebing, H. M. and Howard, R. H., eds.*, 1969, pp. 33–56.

——— Managing the World's Money Supply: A Comment. *J. Money, Credit, Banking,* August 1969, *1* (3), pp. 668–74.

Meimberg, R. About the Theory and Practice of the Participation of Deposit Banks in the Financing of Capital Projects (with Reference to the Conditions in Germany, England and India). *Indian Econ. J.*, April–June 1969, *16*(4–5), pp. 496–506.

Meinander, Nils. Den Samhällsekonomiska lönsamheten—analys av begreppet. (An Analysis of the Concept "Profitability to the Society." With English summary.) *Econ. Samfundets Tidskr.*, 1969, *22*(1), pp. 3–19.

Meiselman, David. The Role of Money in National Economic Policy. **In** *Federal Reserve Bank of Boston,* 1969, pp. 15–19.

——— Some Rules for the Conduct of Monetary Policy: Discussion. **In** *Federal Reserve Bank of Boston,* 1969, pp. 147–51.

Meister, Ronald W. Equal Representation and the Weighted Voting Alternative. *Yale Law J.*, December 1969, *79*(2), pp. 311–21.

Meiszer, Nicholas M. Developing a Planning-Programing-Budgeting System in the City of Dayton, Ohio. **In** *Innovations in Planning, Programming, and Budgeting in State and Local Governments, JECP,* 1969, pp. 213–18.

Meixner, L. Activity of the Economic Research Institute. *Acta Oecon.*, 1969, *4*(3), pp. 321–26.

Mekhanik, G. Social Costs of the Scientific-Technical Revolution under Capitalism. *Prob. Econ.*, December 1969, *12*(8), pp. 3–22.

Melichar, Emanuel. Characteristics and Salaries of Agricultural Economists. *Amer. J. Agr. Econ.*, November 1969, *51*(4), pp. 903–11.

——— Comments on the "St. Louis Position." *Fed. Res. Bank St. Louis Rev.*, August 1969, *51*(8), pp. 9–14.

——— Farm Capital and Credit Projections to 1980. *Amer. J. Agr. Econ.*, December 1969, *51*(5), pp. 1172–77.

——— Seasonal Discount Assistance to Rural Banks: Evaluation of a Federal Reserve Proposal. *Agr. Finance Rev.*, July 1969, *30*, pp. 44–57.

Melitz, Jacques. Open Market Operations and the Classical "Real" Theory of the Interest Rate. *Z. Nationalökon.*, May 1969, *29*(1–2), pp. 111–20.

Mellor, John W. Agricultural Price Policy in the Context of Economic Development. *Amer. J. Agr. Econ.*, December 1969, *51*(5), pp. 1413–19.

——— Determinants and Development Implications of Foodgrain Prices in India: Reply. *Amer. J. Agr. Econ.*, November 1969, *51*(4), pp. 941–42.

——— Production Economics and the Modernization of Traditional Agricultures. *Australian J. Agr. Econ.*, June 1969, *13*(1), pp. 25–34.

Melnik, Arie R. Hedging in the Labor Market. *Southern Econ. J.*, January 1969, *35*(3), pp. 270–72.

——— **and Kraus, Alan.** Short-Run Interest Rate Cycles in the U.S.: 1954–1967. *J. Financial Quant. Anal.*, September 1969, *4*(3), pp. 291–99.

Melody, William H. The Effect of Liberalized Depreciation on the Cost of Equity Capital: Comment. **In** *Trebing, H. M. and Howard, R. H., eds.*, 1969, pp. 164–75.

Melrose, Kendrick B. An Empirical Study on Optimizing Advertising Policy. *J. Bus.*, July 1969, *42* (3), pp. 282–92.

Melton, Lee J., Jr. Some Factors Affecting the Economic Development of Louisiana. **In** *Beard, T. R., ed.*, 1969, pp. 21–40.

Meltzer, Allan H. A Comment on Hester's Paper. *J. Money, Credit, Banking,* August 1969, *1*(3), pp. 618–23.

——— Controlling Money. *Fed. Res. Bank St. Louis Rev.*, May 1969, *51*(5), pp. 16–24.

——— Money, Intermediation, and Growth. *J. Econ. Lit.*, March 1969, *7*(1), pp. 27–56.

——— On Efficiency and Regulation of the Securities Industry. **In** *Manne, H. G., ed.*, 1969, pp. 217–38.

——— The Role of Money in National Economic Policy. **In** *Federal Reserve Bank of Boston,* 1969, pp. 25–29.

——— Tactics and Targets of Monetary Policy: Discussion. **In** *Federal Reserve Bank of Boston,* 1969, pp. 96–103.

——— **and Brunner, Karl.** The Nature of Policy Problem. **In** *Brunner, K., ed.*, 1969, pp. 1–26.

Melvin, Donald J. Conglomerate Acquisitions of Banks. **In** *Prochnow, H. V., ed.*, 1969, pp. 104–15.

Melvin, James R. Comments on the Theory of Customs Unions. *Manchester Sch. Econ. Soc. Stud.*, June 1969, *37*(2), pp. 161–68.

——— Demand Conditions and Immiserizing Growth. *Amer. Econ. Rev.*, Part I, September 1969, *59*(4), pp. 604–06.

——— Intermediate Goods and Technological Change. *Economica, N.S.*, November 1969, *36* (144), pp. 400–408.

——— Intermediate Goods in Production Theory: The Differentiable Case. *Rev. Econ. Stud.*, January 1969, *36*(105), pp. 124–31.

——— Intermediate Goods, the Production Possibility Curve, and Gains from Trade. *Quart. J. Econ.*, February 1969, *83*(1), pp. 141–51.

——— Mill's Law of International Value. *Southern Econ. J.*, October 1969, *36*(2), pp. 107–16.

——— On a Demand Assumption Made by Graham. *Southern Econ. J.*, July 1969, *36*(1), pp. 36–43.

Mendelson, Morris. Regulation and Utility Financing. *Land Econ.*, May 1969, *45*(2), pp. 288–92.

_____ Some Tax Considerations in American Eurobond Flotations. *Nat. Tax J.*, June 1969, *22*(2), pp. 303–10.

de Menil, George. Nonlinearity in a Wage Equation for United States Manufacturing. *Rev. Econ. Statist.*, May 1969, *51*(2), pp. 202–06.

Mennes, L. B. M. Planning for Regions and Centres. *Econ. Planning*, 1969, *9*(1–2), pp. 43–70.

_____; **Waardenburg, J. G. and Herman, B.** Some Exercises with a Simple Model for World Development Planning. **In** *[Tinbergen, J.]*, 1969, pp. 65–92.

Mensch, Gerhard. Approximate Solutions for Digraph Models with Complementary Variables by Separable Programming with Restricted Pivoting. *Z. ges. Staatswiss.*, July 1969, *125*(3), pp. 437–45.

Menshikov, Stanislav M. The Stability of the U.S. Economy: Comment. **In** *Bronfenbrenner, M., ed.*, 1969, pp. 35–39.

Menzel, Herbert; Coleman, James and Katz, Elihu. The Diffusion of an Innovation among Physicians. **In** *Alexis, M.; Holloway, R. J. and Hancock, R. S., eds.*, 1969, pp. 154–67.

Menzel, Jindřich and Möller, Miroslav. Použití diskriminační analýzy v ekonomickém výzkumu. (Ivanovičova metoda.) (Application of Discriminatory Analysis in Economic Research. With English summary.) *Ekon.-Mat. Obzor*, 1969, *5*(2), pp. 199–208.

Mera, Koichi. Experimental Determination of Relative Marginal Utilities. *Quart. J. Econ.*, August 1969, *83*(3), pp. 464–77.

_____ A Generalized Aggregative Model for Optimal Growth with Some Empirical Tests. *Int. Econ. Rev.*, June 1969, *10*(2), pp. 149–62.

Mercer, A. Operational Marketing Research. *J. Ind. Econ.*, November 1969, *18*(1), pp. 15–32.

Mercer, Lloyd J. Land Grants to American Railroads: Social Cost or Social Benefit? *Bus. Hist. Rev.*, Summer 1969, *43*(2), pp. 134–51.

Mermelstein, David. Large Industrial Corporations and Asset Shares. *Amer. Econ. Rev.*, Part I, September 1969, *59*(4), pp. 531–41.

Merrett, A. J. and Sykes, A. Return on Equities and Fixed Interest Securities: 1919–66. **In** *Carsberg, B. V. and Edey, H. C., eds.*, 1969, pp. 113–26.

Merritt, Lavere B. and Mar, Brian W. Marginal Values of Dilution Waters. *Water Resources Res.*, December 1969, *5*(6), pp. 1186–95.

Merton, Robert C. A Golden Golden-Rule for Welfare-Maximization in an Economy with a Varying Population Growth Rate. *Western Econ. J.*, December 1969, *7*(4), pp. 307–18.

_____ Lifetime Portfolio Selection under Uncertainty: The Continuous-Time Case. *Rev. Econ. Statist.*, August 1969, *51*(3), pp. 247–57.

van der Merwe, P. J. The Economic Influence of the Bantu Labour Bureau System on the Bantu Labour Market. *S. Afr. J. Econ.*, March 1969, *37*(1), pp. 42–54.

Mesa-Lago, Carmelo. Economic Significance of Unpaid Labor in Socialist Cuba. *Ind. Lab. Relat. Rev.*, April 1969, *22*(3), pp. 339–57.

Mesthene, Emanuel G. Statement. **In** *To Establish a Select Senate Committee on Technology and the Human Environment, SCH*, 1969, pp. 74–94.

Mestmäcker, E.-J. State Trading Monopolies in the European Economic Community. **In** *Economic Concentration, Pt. 7A, SCH*, 1969, pp. 3925–44.

Metcalf, Charles E. The Size Distribution of Personal Income during the Business Cycle. *Amer. Econ. Rev.*, Part I, September 1969, *59*(4), pp. 657–68.

Metcalf, David. Labour Productivity in English Agriculture, 1850–1914: A Theoretical Comment. *Econ. Hist. Rev.*, April 1969, *22*(1), pp. 117–18.

Metzger, Bert L. Insurance Industry Begins to Court Profit Sharing Funds with Equity-Based Products. *J. Risk Ins.*, September 1969, *36*(4), pp. 437–45.

Meyer zu Schlochtern, F. J. M. Transmission of Business Fluctuations from Developed to Developing Countries: Comment. **In** *Bronfenbrenner, M., ed.*, 1969, pp. 279–83.

Meyer, A. J. The Harvard Tunisia Project: An Experiment in Field Research. **In** *Nader, C. and Zahlan, A. B., eds.*, 1969, pp. 31–39.

Meyer, Charles W. and Davis, J. Ronnie. Budget Size in Democracy. *Southern Econ. J.*, July 1969, *36*(1), pp. 10–17.

Meyerson, Martin. Statement. **In** *Panel on Science and Technology: Science and Technology and the Cities, HCH*, 1969, pp. 17–19.

Mezines, Basil J. The Robinson-Patman Act: Current Developments. *Antitrust Bull.*, Winter 1969, *14*, pp. 803–12.

Michael, Franz. Statement. **In** *To Extend and Amend the Export Control Act of 1949, HCH*, 1969, pp. 348–51.

Michalopoulos, Constantine. Productivity Growth in Latin America: Comment. *Amer. Econ. Rev.*, June 1969, *59*(3), pp. 435–39.

Michalson, E. L. Impact of Weather and Technology on Net Return Estimates. *Agr. Econ. Res.*, January 1969, *21*(1), pp. 19–22.

Michas, Nicholas A. Variations in the Level of Provincial-Municipal Expenditures in Canada: An Econometric Analysis. *Public Finance*, 1969, *24* (4), pp. 597–617.

Michelini, Claudio. Stima bayesiana di una funzione di Engel. (With English summary.) *Statistica*, January-March 1969, *29*(1), pp. 27–48.

Michelson, Stephan. Rational Income Decisions of Negroes and Everybody Else. *Ind. Lab. Relat. Rev.*, October 1969, *23*(1), pp. 15–28.

Michl, H. E. Statement. **In** *To Extend and Amend the Export Control Act of 1949, HCH*, 1969, pp. 351–59.

Mickwitz, Gösta. Ekonomisk planering, en kommentar. (Economic Planning: A Commentary on Mr. Linnamo's Article. With English summary.) *Econ. Samfundets Tidskr.*, 1969, *22*(1), pp. 48–51.

_____ Product Quality as a Means of Competition. *Liiketaloudellinen Aikak.*, 1969, *18*(1), pp. 51–60.

_____ Uudet pankkilait ja pankkiemme kilpailutoiminta. (The New Bank Laws and the Competition among the Banks. With English summary.) *Liiketaloudellinen Aikak.*, 1969, *18* (3), pp. 507–19.

Miernyk, William H. British Regional Development

Policy. *J. Econ. Issues,* September 1969, *3*(3), pp. 33–42.

Mieszkowski, Peter. Carter on the Taxation of International Income Flows. *Nat. Tax J.,* March 1969, *22*(1), pp. 97–108.

——— Tax Incidence Theory: The Effects of Taxes on the Distribution of Income. *J. Econ. Lit.,* December 1969, *7*(4), pp. 1103–24.

Mighell, Ronald L. Concentration in Farming and Transition Bias. *Amer. J. Agr. Econ.,* December 1969, *51*(5), pp. 1114–18.

Mikesell, John. A Look at Local Sales Tax Costs. *Indiana Bus. Rev.,* March–April 1969, *44,* pp. 17–22.

Mikesell, Raymond F. Changing World Trade Patterns and America's Leadership Role. *Ann. Amer. Acad. Polit. Soc. Sci.,* July 1969, *384,* pp. 35–44.

——— Inflation in Latin America. **In** *Nisbet, C. T., ed.,* 1969, pp. 143–89.

Miklius, Walter. Estimating Freight Traffic of Competing Transportation Modes: An Application of the Linear Discriminant Function. *Land Econ.,* May 1969, *45*(2), pp. 267–73.

Mikulich, A. P. The Influence of Different Levels of Education on Labor Productivity: A Calculation. **In** *Noah, H. J., ed.,* 1969, pp. 132–40.

Milano, Armando. The Autonomous State Tobacco Concern. *Rev. Econ. Cond. Italy,* September 1969, *23*(5), pp. 409–27.

Millen, Bruce H. Factions of the Turkish Labor Movement Differ over Political Role. *Mon. Lab. Rev.,* June 1969, *92*(6), pp. 31–35.

Miller, Arjay. A Proposal for a National Goals Institute. *J. Finance,* May 1969, *24*(2), pp. 173–79.

Miller, Etienne H. Foreign Earnings from U.S. Travelers in 1968 Decline Slightly to $3.9 Billion. *Surv. Curr. Bus.,* June 1969, *49*(6), pp. 17–20.

Miller, Glenn H., Jr. The Business Outlook for 1969. *Fed. Res. Bank Kansas City Rev.,* January 1969, pp. 11–20.

——— Housing in the 60's: A Survey of Some Nonfinancial Factors. *Fed. Res. Bank Kansas City Rev.,* May 1969, pp. 3–10.

——— Some Demographic Influences on the Future Market for Housing. *Fed. Res. Bank Kansas City Rev.,* November 1969, pp. 3–9.

Miller, Irvin M. Computer Graphics for Decision Making. *Harvard Bus. Rev.,* November–December 1969, *47*(6), pp. 120–32.

Miller, Irwin. Business Has a War to Win. *Harvard Bus. Rev.,* March–April 1969, *47*(2), pp. 4–12, 164–68.

Miller, James C., III. A Program for Direct and Proxy Voting in the Legislative Process. *Public Choice,* Fall 1969, *7,* pp. 107–13.

Miller, Merton H. and Modigliani, Franco. A Comment on the Modigliani-Miller Cost of Capital Thesis: Reply. *Amer. Econ. Rev.,* Part I, September 1969, *59*(4), pp. 592–95.

Miller, Richard A. Marginal Concentration Ratios: Some Statistical Implications—Reply. *Southern Econ. J.,* October 1969, *36*(2), pp. 199–201.

——— Market Structure and Industrial Performance: Relation of Profit Rates to Concentration, Advertising Intensity, and Diversity. *J. Ind. Econ.,* April 1969, *17*(2), pp. 104–18.

Miller, Roger L. and Soldofsky, Robert M. Risk Premium Curves for Different Classes of Long-Term Securities, 1950–1966. *J. Finance,* June 1969, *24*(3), pp. 429–45.

Miller, Ronald E. Interregional Feedbacks in Input-Output Models: Some Experimental Results. *Western Econ. J.,* March 1969, *7*(1), pp. 41–50.

Miller, S. F. and Halter, A. N. Computer Simulation of the Substitution between Project Size and Management. *Amer. J. Agr. Econ.,* December 1969, *51*(5), pp. 1119–23.

Miller, William Green. Political Organization in Iran: From Dowreh to Political Party. *Middle East J.,* Spring 1969, *23*(2), pp. 159–67.

Milligan, Bruce L. Contribution Margin in Decision Making. *Manage. Account.,* October 1969, *51*(4), pp. 33–38.

Milliman, Jerome W. Beneficiary Charges and Efficient Public Expenditure Decisions. **In** *The Analysis and Evaluation of Public Expenditures: The PPB System, Vol. 1, JECP,* 1969, pp. 291–318.

Mills, Edwin S. The Small Business Capital Gap. *Rivista Int. Sci. Econ. Com.,* March 1969, *16*(3), pp. 259–79.

——— The Value of Urban Land. **In** *Perloff, H. S., ed.,* 1969, pp. 231–53.

Minabe, Nobuo. A Note on the Marshall Condition: Comment. *Southern Econ. J.,* October 1969, *36* (2), pp. 210–14.

Minasian, Jora R. The Political Economy of Broadcasting in the 1920's. *J. Law Econ.,* October 1969, *12*(2), pp. 391–403.

——— Research and Development and Other Determinants of Investment: Discussion. *Amer. Econ. Rev.,* May 1969, *59*(2), pp. 86.

——— Research and Development, Production Functions, and Rates of Return. *Amer. Econ. Rev.,* May 1969, *59*(2), pp. 80–85.

——— **and Eckert, Ross D.** The Economics of Airport Use, Congestion, and Safety. *Calif. Manage. Rev.,* Spring 1969, *11*(3), pp. 11–24.

Mincer, Jacob. Models of Adaptive Forecasting. **In** *Mincer, J., ed.,* 1969, pp. 83–111.

——— **and Cain, Glen G.** Urban Poverty and Labor Force Participation: Comment. *Amer. Econ. Rev.,* March 1969, *59*(1), pp. 185–94.

——— **and Zarnowitz, Victor.** The Evaluation of Economic Forecasts. **In** *Mincer, J., ed.,* 1969, pp. 3–46.

Minchinton, W. E. Industrial South Wales, 1750–1914. **In** *Minchinton, W. E., ed.,* 1969, pp. ix–xxxi.

——— The Tinplate Maker and Technical Change. **In** *Minchinton, W. E., ed.,* 1969, pp. 107–20.

Minden, A. J.; Snyder, James C. and Willis, J. F. Monte Carlo Simulation of Management Systems. *Can. J. Agr. Econ.,* February 1969, *17*(1), pp. 42–49.

Minocha, A. C. Inter-Sectoral Financial Flows in Indian Economy—Some Implications for Policy. *Econ. Aff.,* January-February 1969, *14*(1–2), pp. 33–38, 103–04.

Minsky, Hyman P. Financial Model Building and Federal Reserve Policy: Discussion. *J. Finance,* May 1969, *24*(2), pp. 295–97.

——— Private Sector Asset Management and the Effectiveness of Monetary Policy: Theory and Practice. *J. Finance,* May 1969, *24*(2), pp. 223–38.

Minton, George. Inspection and Correction Error in Data Processing. *J. Amer. Statist. Assoc.,* December 1969, *64*(328), pp. 1256–75.

Miracle, Michael. The Economy of the Ivory Coast. **In** *Robson, P. and Lury, D. A., eds.,* 1969, pp. 194–235.

Mirakhor, Abbas and Orazem, Frank. Mysterious Multipliers: Reply. *Amer. J. Agr. Econ.,* August 1969, *51*(3), pp. 689–90.

Mircioiu, V. and Florescu, C. Dezvoltarea comerţului interior în anii construcţiei socialiste. (Development of Home Trade during the Years of Building up Socialism. With English summary.) *Stud. Cercet. Econ.,* 1969, *3,* pp. 151–59.

Mirrlees, James A. The Dynamic Nonsubstitution Theorem. *Rev. Econ. Stud.,* January 1969, *36* (105), pp. 67–76.

______ The Evaluation of National Income in an Imperfect Economy. *Pakistan Develop. Rev.,* Spring 1969, *9*(1), pp. 1–13.

Misawa, Takeo. An Analysis of Part-time Farming in the Postwar Period. **In** *Ohkawa, K.; Johnston, B. F. and Kaneda, H., eds.,* 1969, pp. 250–69.

Mishan, E. J. Interpretation of the Benefits of Private Transport. **In** *Mishan, E. J.,* 1969, pp. 275–83.

______ Normalisation of Public Investment Criteria: An Amendment. *Econ. J.,* September 1969, *79* (315), pp. 672–74.

______ Normalisation of Public Investment Criteria: Erratum. *Econ. J.,* December 1969, *79*(316), pp. 980.

______ A Note on the Costs of Tariffs, Monopolies and Thefts. *Western Econ. J.,* September 1969, *7*(3), pp. 230–33.

______ The Relationship between Joint Products, Collective Goods, and External Effects. *J. Polit. Econ.,* May/June 1969, *77*(3), pp. 329–48.

______ Rent and Producer's Surplus: Reply. *Amer. Econ. Rev.,* Part I, September 1969, *59*(4), pp. 635–37.

Mishra, S. N. A Model of Gandhian Economy. *Indian Econ. J.,* July–September 1969, *17*(1), pp. 101–11.

Misra, P. N. A Note on Linear Aggregation of Economic Relations. *Int. Econ. Rev.,* June 1969, *10*(2), pp. 247–49.

______ A Welfare Criterion for the Determination of Agricultural Prices. *Indian Econ. J.,* October–December 1969, *17*(2), pp. 273–78.

Mistry, Thakore. Land-Based vs. Income-Based Taxation in Indian Agriculture. *Artha-Vikas,* July 1969, *5*(2), pp. 117–29.

Mitchell, B. M. and Dhrymes, Phoebus J. Estimation of Joint Production Functions. *Econometrica,* October 1969, *37*(4), pp. 732–36.

Mitchell, Daniel J. B. A Simplified Approach to Incomes Policy. *Ind. Lab. Relat. Rev.,* July 1969, *22* (4), pp. 512–27.

Mitchell, Edward J. Some Econometrics of the Huk Rebellion. *Amer. Polit. Sci. Rev.,* December 1969, *63*(4), pp. 1159–71.

Mitchell, George. What Can We Do about Bank Structure? **In** *Federal Reserve Bank of Chicago (II),* 1969, pp. 109–19.

Mitchell, Joan. Why We Need a Prices Policy. *Lloyds Bank Rev.,* April 1969, (92), pp. 1–14.

Mitchell, Phyllis. Australian Patriots: A Study of the New Guard. *Australian Econ. Hist. Rev.,* September 1969, *9*(2), pp. 156–78.

Mitchell, William C. The Shape of Political Theory to Come: From Political Sociology to Political Economy. **In** *Lipset, S. M., ed.,* 1969, pp. 101–36.

Mitra, Ashok. Wage Policy in Developing Countries. **In** *Smith, A. D., ed.,* 1969, pp. 371–82.

Mittelstaedt, Robert. A Dissonance Approach to Repeat Purchasing Behavior. *J. Marketing Res.,* November 1969, *6*(4), pp. 444–46.

Mittra, Sid. The Central Bank as a Utility Maximizer: A Theoretical Model. *Econ. Aff.,* January-February 1969, *14*(1–2), pp. 9–14.

Mizoguchi, Toshiyuki. A Comparison of Levels of Consumption of Urban Households in Japan and in Mainland China—A Summary. *Rev. Income Wealth,* June 1969, *15*(2), pp. 215–17.

______ Time-Series Analysis of the Consumption Function in Japan by Occupational Group. *Hitotsubashi J. Econ.,* February 1969, *9*(2), pp. 13–34.

Moag, Joseph S. and Lerner, Eugene M. Capital Budgeting Decisions under Imperfect Market Conditions—A Systems Framework. *J. Finance,* September 1969, *24*(4), pp. 613–21.

______ Information Requirements for Regulatory Decisions. **In** *Trebing, H. M. and Howard, R. H., eds.,* 1969, pp. 195–204.

Mobasheri, Fereidoun. A Criterion for Appraisal of Economic Development Projects. *Eng. Econ.,* October–November 1969, *15*(1), pp. 9–27.

Modigliani, Franco and Ando, Albert. Econometric Analysis of Stabilization Policies. *Amer. Econ. Rev.,* May 1969, *59*(2), pp. 296–314.

______ **and Brumberg, Richard.** Utility Analysis and the Consumption Function: An Interpretation of Cross-section Data. **In** *Williams, H. R. and Huffnagle, J. D., eds.,* 1969, pp. 99–140.

______ **and Jaffee, Dwight M.** A Theory and Test of Credit Rationing. *Amer. Econ. Rev.,* December 1969, *59*(5), pp. 850–72.

______ **and Miller, Merton H.** A Comment on the Modigliani-Miller Cost of Capital Thesis: Reply. *Amer. Econ. Rev.,* Part I, September 1969, *59*(4), pp. 592–95.

______ **and Sutch, Richard.** The Term Structure of Interest Rates: A Re-examination of the Evidence. *J. Money, Credit, Banking,* February 1969, *1*(1), pp. 112–20.

Moeller, Charles, Jr. Economic Implications of the Life Insurance Industry's Investment Program in the Central Cities. *J. Risk Ins.,* March 1969, *36*(1), pp. 93–101.

Moeseke, Paul V. and Ghellinck, Guy. Decentralization in Separable Programming. *Econometrica,* January 1969, *37*(1), pp. 73–78.

Mohring, Herbert and Williamson, Harold F., Jr. Scale and "Industrial Reorganisation" Economies of Transport Improvements. *J. Transp. Econ. Policy,* September 1969, *3*(3), pp. 251–71.

Molander, Ahti. Inflaatiotutkimuksen vaiheista ja ongelmista. (Phases and Problems of Inflation Research. With English summary.) *Kansant. Aikak.,* 1969, *65*(4), pp. 269–73.

Moldovan, Roman. Structural Changes in the National Economy and the Profile of the Economist.

Revue Roumaine Sci. Soc. Serie Sci. Econ., 1969, *13*(1), pp. 9–16.

Molina Enríquez, Alvaro. Las vias de la transformación social. (Economic and Social Aspects of Development. With English summary.) *Econ. Polít.*, Third Semester 1969, *6*(3), pp. 351–60.

Möller, Miroslav and Menzel, Jindřich. Použití diskriminační analýzy v ekonomickém výzkumu. (Ivanovičova metoda.) (Application of Discriminatory Analysis in Economic Research. With English summary.) *Ekon.-Mat. Obzor*, 1969, *5*(2), pp. 199–208.

Monsen, R. J. Proprietà ed efficienza della grande impresa. (Ownership and Performance of the Large Firm. With English summary.) *Rivista Int. Sci. Econ. Com.*, May 1969, *16*(5), pp. 479–88.

Montanari, Antonio. Considerazioni in margine ad una indagine motivazionale sul controllo delle nascite. (With English summary.) *Statistica*, July-September 1969, *29*(3), pp. 488–505.

——— A propositio di sociologia e storia del lavoro femminile. (With English summary.) *Statistica*, October-December 1969, *29*(4), pp. 803–21.

Montanaro, Silvano. I diritti speciali di prelievo e i problemi della cooperazione monetaria e finanziaria internazionale. (Special Drawing Rights and the Problem of International Monetary and Financial Cooperation. With English summary.) *Bancaria*, November 1969, *25*(11), pp. 1361–66.

Montesano, Aldo. Per una teoria generale empirica della produzione. (Towards an Empirical Theory of Production. With English summary.) *Rivista Int. Sci. Econ. Com.*, March 1969, *16*(3), pp. 228–58.

Monti, Mario. Dimensioni dell'economia e domanda di moneta: I. Alcuni modelli. (Economies of Scale and Demand for Money: I. Some Models. With English summary.) *Rivista Int. Sci. Econ. Com.*, August 1969, *16*(8), pp. 781–806.

——— Dimensioni dell'economia e domanda di moneta: II. Problemi metodologici. (Economies of Scale in the Demand for Money: II. Methodological Issues. With English summary.) *Rivista Int. Sci. Econ. Com.*, September 1969, *16*(9), pp. 859–71.

——— Moneta, sviluppo economico e progresso tecnico. (Money, Economic Growth and Technical Progress. With English summary.) *L'Industria*, October–December 1969, (4), pp. 475–92.

Montias, John Michael. Comments on the Papers on East-West Trade. **In** *Samuelson, P. A., ed.*, 1969, pp. 142–47.

——— Comparative Study of Transformation of Agriculture in Centrally Planned Economies: The Soviet Union, Eastern Europe and Mainland China: Comment. **In** *Thorbecke, E., ed.*, 1969, pp. 266–74.

——— East European Economic Reforms. **In** *Bornstein, M., ed.*, 1969, pp. 324–36.

Montigaud, J. C. Les Plans Conjoints au Québec. (Marketing Boards in Quebec. With English summary.) *Can. J. Agr. Econ.*, July 1969, *17*(2), pp. 17–35.

Montuschi, Luisa. Progreso technológico y rendimientos crecientes en el sector manufacturero argentino: La productividad de las inversiones en la década del 50. (Technical Progress and Increasing Returns in the Manfacturing Sector of Argentina. With English summary.) *Económica*, January-April 1969, *15*(1), pp. 93–110.

Moody, Harold T. and Puffer, Frank W. A Gross Regional Product Approach to Regional Model-Building. *Western Econ. J.*, December 1969, *7*(4), pp. 391–402.

Mookerjee, Subimal; Chandavarkar, Anand G. and Cleary, D. J. Existing International Banking and Credit Facilities in the ECAFE Region. *Int. Monet. Fund Staff Pap.*, November 1969, *16*(3), pp. 391–435.

Mooney, Joseph D. Housing Segregation, Negro Employment and Metropolitan Decentralization: An Alternative Perspective. *Quart. J. Econ.*, May 1969, *83*(2), pp. 299–311.

——— Urban Poverty and Labor Force Participation: Reply. *Amer. Econ. Rev.*, March 1969, *59*(1), pp. 194–98.

——— **and Ashenfelter, Orley.** Some Evidence on the Private Returns to Graduate Education. *Southern Econ. J.*, January 1969, *35*(3), pp. 247–56.

de Moor, A. E. International Trade of Goods and Services with the TVA in Operation. *Bull. Int. Fiscal Doc.*, July, August, September 1969, *23*(7–8–9), pp. 297–334.

Moore, Basil J. Asset Management and Monetary Policy: Discussion. *J. Finance*, May 1969, *24*(2), pp. 242–44.

Moore, C. V. and Snyder, J. H. Crop Selection in High-Risk Agriculture. *Agr. Econ. Res.*, October 1969, *21*(4), pp. 89–98.

Moore, Charles Thomas and Mason, Joseph Barry. A Note on the Reliability of Census Data in Trading Area Analysis. *Miss. Val. J. Bus. Econ.*, Fall 1969, *5*(1), pp. 68–72.

Moore, David G. Toward More Comprehensive Human Relations in Industry. **In** *Somers, G. G., ed. (I)*, 1969, pp. 137–46.

Moore, Geoffrey H. Forecasting Short-Term Economic Change. *J. Amer. Statist. Assoc.*, March 1969, *64*(325), pp. 1–22.

——— Generating Leading Indicators from Lagging Indicators. *Western Econ. J.*, June 1969, *7*(2), pp. 137–44.

——— Long-Range Program Objectives for BLS. *Mon. Lab. Rev.*, October 1969, *92*(10), pp. 3–6.

——— The Stability of the U.S. Economy: Comment. **In** *Bronfenbrenner, M., ed.*, 1969, pp. 40–44.

——— Statement. **In** *Review of Federal Statistical Programs, JECH*, 1969, pp. 173–98.

Moore, L. W. Urban Unrest—Whose Problem Is It? *Calif. Manage. Rev.*, Summer 1969, *11*(4), pp. 7–10.

Moore, Mack A. Much Ado about 14b. **In** *Starleaf, D. R., ed.*, 1969, pp. 134–37.

Moore, Thomas Gale. An Economic Analysis of the Concept of Freedom. *J. Polit. Econ.*, Part I, July/August 1969, *77*(4), pp. 532–44.

Moorhead, E. J. The Impact of Lapse Rates on Life Insurance Prices: Comment. *J. Risk Ins.*, March 1969, *36*(1), pp. 163–64.

Moot, Robert C. Statement. **In** *A Review of Balance of Payments Policies, JECH*, 1969, pp. 97–108.

Morales, Cecilio. Latin America: The Developmental Challenge. **In** *Ozbekhan, H. and Talbert, G. E., eds.,* 1969, pp. 147–62.

Moran, William E., Jr. Statement. **In** *Population Trends, Pt. 1, HCH,* 1969, pp. 67–71.

Morehouse, Edward W. Richard T. Ely: A Supplement. *Land Econ.,* February 1969, *45*(1), pp. 10–18.

Morgan, A. D. Re-Imports and Imports for Process and Repair. *Nat. Inst. Econ. Rev.,* November 1969, (50), pp. 53–56.

Morgan, E. V. The Essential Qualities of Money. *Manchester Sch. Econ. Soc. Stud.,* September 1969, *37*(3), pp. 237–48.

Morgan, George T., Jr. No Compromise—No Recognition: John Henry Kirby, the Southern Lumber Operators' Association, and Unionism in the Piney Woods, 1906–1916. *Labor Hist.,* Spring 1969, *10*(2), pp. 193–204.

Morgan, James N. and Smith, James D. Measures of Economic Well-Offness and Their Correlates. *Amer. Econ. Rev.,* May 1969, *59*(2), pp. 450–62.

Morgan, Theodore. Investment *versus* Economic Growth. *Econ. Develop. Cult. Change,* April 1969, *17*(3), pp. 392–414.

______ **and Naya, Seiji.** The Accuracy of International Trade Data: The Case of Southeast Asian Countries. *J. Amer. Statist. Assoc.,* June 1969, *64* (326), pp. 452–67.

Morgenstern, Oskar and Burley, S. Peter. Insiders and Outsiders in Industrial Research. *Z. ges. Staatswiss.,* April 1969, *125*(2), pp. 193–201.

Morley, Samuel A. Import Demand and Import Substitution in Brazil. **In** *Ellis, H. S., ed.,* 1969, pp. 283–313.

______ **and Bergsman, Joel.** Import Constraints and Development: Causes of the Recent Decline of Brazilian Economic Growth: A Comment. *Rev. Econ. Statist.,* February 1969, *51*(1), pp. 101–02.

Moroney, John R. Economies of Scale in Manufacturing. **In** *Watson, D. S., ed.,* 1969, pp. 116–24.

______ **and Allen, Bruce T.** Monopoly Power and the Relative Share of Labor. *Ind. Lab. Relat. Rev.,* January 1969, *22*(2), pp. 167–78.

______ **and Ferguson, C. E.** The Sources of Change in Labor's Relative Share: A Neoclassical Analysis. *Southern Econ. J.,* April 1969, *35*(4), pp. 308–22.

Morris, Cynthia Taft; Adelman, Irma and Geier, Marsha. Instruments and Goals in Economic Development. *Amer. Econ. Rev.,* May 1969, *59*(2), pp. 409–26.

Morris, Frank E. Pax Americana and the U.S. Balance of Payments. *New Eng. Econ. Rev.,* January/February 1969, pp. 41–47.

______ **and Anderson, Paul S.** Defining the Money Supply: The Case of Government Deposits. *New Eng. Econ. Rev.,* March/April 1969, pp. 21–31.

Morris, J. H. and Williams, L. J. The South Wales Sliding Scale. **In** *Minchinton, W. E., ed.,* 1969, pp. 218–31.

Morris, John. Nonparametric Statistics on the Computer. *J. Marketing Res.,* February 1969, *6*(1), pp. 86–92.

Morris, O. Richard. A View from the Middle Ground. *Amer. J. Agr. Econ.,* December 1969, *51* (5), pp. 1565–68.

Morris, Peter F. Widget Pricing. *Manage. Account.,* December 1969, *51*(6), pp. 12–14.

Morris, Reginald Edward. Fiscal Controls of Land Monopoly. *Amer. J. Econ. Soc.,* January 1969, *28* (1), pp. 77–92.

______ Problems in the Reform of Land Tenure. *Amer. J. Econ. Soc.,* April 1969, *28*(2), pp. 205–09.

Morrison, Clarence C. Marginal Cost Pricing and the Theory of Second Best. *Western Econ. J.,* June 1969, *7*(2), pp. 145–52.

Morrison, Donald G. Conditional Trend Analysis: A Model That Allows for Nonusers. *J. Marketing Res.,* August 1969, *6*(3), pp. 342–46.

______ On the Interpretation of Discriminant Analysis. *J. Marketing Res.,* May 1969, *6*(2), pp. 156–63.

Morrison, J. Roger. Strategia per lo sviluppo. (How Managers Make Growth. With English summary.) *Mondo Aperto,* April 1969, *23*(2), pp. 116–22.

Morrison, Rodney J. Teaching Hour-Load Assignments in Economics Departments in Larger Institutions Revisited. *Amer. Econ. Rev.,* December 1969, *59*(5), pp. 960–62.

Morrison, Thomas A. and Kaczka, Eugene. A New Application of Calculus and Risk Analysis to Cost-Volume-Profit Changes. *Accounting Rev.,* April 1969, *44*(2), pp. 330–43.

Morrisse, Kathryn A. Automotive Trade between the United States and Canada. (Study summary.) *Fed. Res. Bull.,* November 1969, *55*(11), pp. 877–78.

Morse, Chandler. Becoming Versus Being Modern: An Essay on Institutional Change and Economic Development. **In** *Morse, C., et al.,* 1969, pp. 238–382.

Morse, David A. The ILO at 50: Its Hopes for Social Progress. *Mon. Lab. Rev.,* May 1969, *92*(5), pp. 51–53.

Morss, Elliott R. Fiscal Policy, Savings, and Economic Growth in Developing Countries: An Empirical Study. *Finanzarchiv,* August 1969, *28*(3), pp. 460–66.

______ Using Various Statistical Measures to Analyze the Size of the Public Sector. **In** *Peacock, A. T., ed.,* 1969, pp. 39–56.

______ **and Lotz, Joergen R.** "Tax Effort" in Developing Countries. *Finance Develop.,* September 1969, *6*(3), pp. 36–39.

______ **and Peacock, Alan T.** The Measurement of Fiscal Performance in Developing Countries. **In** *Peacock, A. T., ed.,* 1969, pp. 171–97.

Morton, George and Zauberman, Alfred. Von Neumann's Model and Soviet Long-Term (Perspective) Planning. *Kyklos,* 1969, *22*(1), pp. 45–61.

Morton, Walter A. Risk and Return: Instability of Earnings as a Measure of Risk. *Land Econ.,* May 1969, *45*(2), pp. 229–61.

Moskow, Michael H. Collective Bargaining for Public School Teachers. **In** *Wortman, M. S., Jr.,* 1969, pp. 87–94.

______ **and McLennan, Kenneth.** Multilateral Bargaining in the Public Sector. **In** *Somers, G. G., ed. (II),* 1969, pp. 31–40.

Mossé, Robert. International Transactions of the United States (1946–1968) *Banca Naz. Lavoro Quart. Rev.,* September 1969, (90), pp. 248–80.

Mossin, Jan. A Note on Uncertainty and Preferences in a Temporal Context. *Amer. Econ. Rev.*, March 1969, *59*(1), pp. 172–74.

______ Security Pricing and Investment Criteria in Competitive Markets. *Amer. Econ. Rev.*, December 1969, *59*(5), pp. 749–56.

Most, Kenneth S. Two Forms of Experimental Accounts. *Accounting Rev.*, January 1969, *44*(1), pp. 145–52.

Moszer, Max. An Analysis of the 1964 Wheat Option. *Amer. J. Agr. Econ.*, February 1969, *51*(1), pp. 100–118.

Mote, Larry R. Competition in Banking: The Evidence. **In** *Jessup, P. F.*, 1969, pp. 432–44.

______ Competition in Banking: The Issues. **In** *Jessup, P. F.*, 1969, pp. 421–31.

______ A Conceptual Optimal Banking Structure for the United States. **In** *Federal Reserve Bank of Chicago (II)*, 1969, pp. 17–34.

______ Review of Federal Reserve Board Split Merger and Holding Company Decisions. **In** *Federal Reserve Bank of Chicago (I)*, 1969, pp. 37–54.

Motley, Brian. Consumer Investment, Expectations, and Transitory Income. *Western Econ. J.*, September 1969, *7*(3), pp. 223–29.

______ The Consumer's Demand for Money: A Neoclassical Approach. *J. Polit. Econ.*, September/October 1969, *77*(5), pp. 817–26.

______ Inflation and Common Stock Values: Comment. *J. Finance*, June 1969, *24*(3), pp. 530–35.

Mouly, Jean. Changing Concepts of Wage Policy. *Int. Lab. Rev.*, July 1969, *100*(1), pp. 1–22.

Mouton, Claude. The European Common Market and the Move Towards Self-sufficiency in Food Production. **In** *Papi, U. and Nunn, C., eds.*, 1969, pp. 92–120.

Mouton, D. J. Resale Price Maintenance in the Republic of South Africa. *Antitrust Bull.*, Winter 1969, *14*, pp. 981–1017.

Mouton, Jane S. and Blake, Robert R. Union-Management Relations: From Conflict to Collaboration. **In** *Wortman, M. S., Jr.*, 1969, pp. 300–309.

Moutsanides, Demetrius T. Idaho Economic Activity in 1968 and Prospects for 1969. *Univ. Wash. Bus. Rev.*, Winter 1969, *28*(2), pp. 23–32.

Moy, William A. Monte Carlo Techniques: Practical. **In** *Naylor, T. H., ed.*, 1969, pp. 263–88.

Moyer, M. Eugene and Paden, Donald W. The Effectiveness of Teaching Methods: The Relative Effectiveness of Three Methods of Teaching Principles of Economics. *J. Econ. Educ.*, Fall 1969, *1* (1), pp. 33–45.

Moylan, Maurice and Andrews, Edith Wall. Scientific and Professional Employment by State Governments. *Mon. Lab. Rev.*, August 1969, *92*(8), pp. 40–45.

Muchmore, Lynn. Gerrard de Malnes and Mercantile Economics. *Hist. Polit. Econ.*, Fall 1969, *1*(2), pp. 336–58.

Muehlbeier, John. Problems That Persist in the Great Plains. *Amer. J. Agr. Econ.*, December 1969, *51*(5), pp. 1089–96.

Mueller, C. E. Antitrust and Centralization: A Look at the 'Planned' Economy. **In** *Economic Concentration, Pt. 7A, SCH*, 1969, pp. 4371–86.

Mueller, Dennis C. A Theory of Conglomerate Mergers. *Quart. J. Econ.*, November 1969, *83*(4), pp. 643–59.

Mueller, Hans G. The Policy of the European Coal and Steel Community Towards Mergers and Agreements by Steel Companies. *Antitrust Bull.*, Summer 1969, *14*, pp. 413–48.

______ Recent Costs Trends in the Steel Industries of the United States, Japan and the European Community. *Econ. Int.*, August 1969, *22*(3), pp. 499–526.

Mueller, P. and Zevering, K. H. Employment Promotion through Rural Development: A Pilot Project in Western Nigeria. *Int. Lab. Rev.*, August 1969, *100*(2), pp. 111–30.

Mueller, Willard F. Firm Conglomeration as a Market Structure Variable. *Amer. J. Agr. Econ.*, December 1969, *51*(5), pp. 1488–94.

______ Public Policy Toward Mergers in Food Retailing. **In** *Ruttan, V. W.; Waldo, A. D. and Houck, J. P., eds.*, 1969, pp. 186–91.

______ Public Policy Toward Vertical Mergers. **In** *Weston, J. F. and Peltzman, S., eds.*, 1969, pp. 150–66.

______ Statement. **In** *Bank Holding Company Act Amendments, Pts. 1–3, HCH*, 1969, pp. 338–45.

Muir, J. Douglas. Canada's Experience with the Right of Public Employees to Strike. *Mon. Lab. Rev.*, July 1969, *92*(7), pp. 54–59.

Mujumdar, N. A. Agricultural Growth in India: Performance and Prospects. **In** *Bhuleshkar, A. V., ed.*, 1969, pp. 173–89.

Mukerjee, Sudhir. The Role of Fiscal Policy in Economic Development. **In** *Bhuleshkar, A. V., ed.*, 1969, pp. 406–16.

Mukerji, K. and Mukerji, V. Substitution between Superior and Inferior Foodgrains in India between 1900–1958. **In** *Bhuleshkar, A. V., ed.*, 1969, pp. 137–56.

Mukerji, V. and Mukerji, K. Substitution between Superior and Inferior Foodgrains in India between 1900–1958. **In** *Bhuleshkar, A. V., ed.*, 1969, pp. 137–56.

Mukherjee, Chittapriya. Some Problems of the Indian Agricultural Sector. *Land Econ.*, February 1969, *45*(1), pp. 74–86.

Mukherjee, M. Certain Thoughts on Capital-output and Capital-labour Ratios. *Econ. Aff.*, January–February 1969, *14*(1–2), pp. 15–25.

Mulvey, Charles. A Critical Examination of Prices and Incomes Policy in the U.K. *Irish Banking Rev.*, September 1969, pp. 10–16.

Mundell, Robert A. The Cost of Exchange Crises and the Problem of Sterling. **In** *Aliber, R. Z., ed.*, 1969, pp. 209–20.

______ The Crisis Problem. **In** *Mundell, R. A. and Swoboda, A. K., eds.*, 1969, pp. 343–49.

______ The Problem of World Stability: Appendix: The Redundancy Problem and the World Price Level. **In** *Mundell, R. A. and Swoboda, A. K., eds.*, 1969, pp. 379–82.

______ Problems of the International Monetary System. **In** *Mundell, R. A. and Swoboda, A. K., eds.*, 1969, pp. 21–38.

______ Real Gold, Dollars, and Paper Gold. *Amer. Econ. Rev.*, May 1969, *59*(2), pp. 324–31.

______ Toward a Better International Monetary Sys-

Muzio, Giovanni B. Su di un metodo di classificazione numerica nel caso di variabili unidimensionali. (With English summary.) *Statistica,* October-December 1969, *29*(4), pp. 699–725.

Myers, C. A. and Harbison, Frederick H. Strategies of Human Resource Development. **In** *Blaug, M., ed.,* 1969, pp. 13–60.

Myers, Doyle F. and Lundgren, Earl F. A Survey of Foremen Incentive Systems in Wisconsin. *Marquette Bus. Rev.,* Spring 1969, *13*(1), pp. 1–10.

Myers, James H. and Robertson, Thomas S. Personality Correlates of Opinion Leadership and Innovative Buying Behavior. *J. Marketing Res.,* May 1969, *6*(2), pp. 164–68.

______ **and Samli, A. Coskun.** Management Control of Marketing Research. *J. Marketing Res.,* August 1969, *6*(3), pp. 267–77.

Myers, Robert J. Various Proposals to Change the Financing of Social Security. *J. Risk Ins.,* September 1969, *36*(4), pp. 355–63.

Myint, H. International Trade and the Developing Countries. **In** *Samuelson, P. A., ed.,* 1969, pp. 15–35.

______ International Trade and the Developing Countries: Reply. **In** *Samuelson, P. A., ed.,* 1969, pp. 46.

______ Trade, Education and Economic Development. **In** *Stewart, I. G., ed.,* 1969, pp. 1–12.

Myslicki, Chester. Report on Productivity Increases in the Auto Industry. *Mon. Lab. Rev.,* March 1969, *92*(3), pp. 37–39.

Nader, Ralph. The Great American Gyp and Taming the Corporate Tiger. **In** *To Establish a Department of Consumer Affairs, SCH,* 1969, pp. 473–81.

______ Statement. **In** *To Establish a Department of Consumer Affairs, SCH,* 1969, pp. 365–97.

______ Statement. **In** *Bank Holding Company Act Amendments, Pts. 1–3, HCH,* 1969, pp. 262–70.

Nadiri, M. Ishag. The Determinants of Real Cash Balances in the U.S. Total Manufacturing Sector. *Quart. J. Econ.,* May 1969, *83*(2), pp. 173–96.

______ The Determinants of Trade Credit in the U.S. Total Manufacturing Sector. *Econometrica,* July 1969, *37*(3), pp. 408–23.

______ **and Rosen, Sherwin.** Interrelated Factor Demand Functions. *Amer. Econ. Rev.,* Part I, September 1969, *59*(4), pp. 457–71.

Nadler, Paul S. The Coming Change in Correspondent Relationships. **In** *Jessup, P. F.,* 1969, pp. 147–51.

______ Financial Model Building and Federal Reserve Policy: Discussion. *J. Finance,* May 1969, *24* (2), pp. 291–94.

______ One-Bank Holding Companies: The Public Interest. *Harvard Bus. Rev.,* May–June 1969, *47* (3), pp. 107–13.

______ The Outlook for the One-Bank Holding Company. **In** *Prochnow, H. V., ed.,* 1969, pp. 142–57.

Nafziger, E. Wayne. The Effect of the Nigerian Extended Family on Entrepreneurial Activity. *Econ. Develop. Cult. Change,* Part I, October 1969, *18*(1), pp. 25–33.

Nag, A. Estimation and Projection of the Working Force in Greater Bombay. *Asian Econ. Rev.,* February 1969, *11*(2), pp. 160–72.

Nagar, A. L. Stochastic Simulation of the Brookings Econometric Model. **In** *Duesenberry, J. S., et al.,* 1969, pp. 423–56.

Nagatani, Keizo. A Monetary Growth Model with Variable Employment. *J. Money, Credit, Banking,* May 1969, *1*(2), pp. 188–206.

______ **and Stein, Jerome L.** Stabilization Policies in a Growing Economy. *Rev. Econ. Stud.,* April 1969, *36*(106), pp. 165–83.

Nagel, Ernest. Method in Social and Natural Science. **In** *Heilbroner, R. L., ed.,* 1969, pp. 57–66.

Nagishi, Takashi and Kemp, Murray C. Domestic Distortions, Tariffs, and the Theory of Optimum Subsidy. *J. Polit. Econ.,* November/December 1969, *77*(6), pp. 1011–13.

Nair, K. R. Some Responses of Rice Farmers to the Package Program in Tanjore District, India: Comment. *Amer. J. Agr. Econ.,* August 1969, *51*(3), pp. 699–701.

Nair, Kusum. Asian Drama—A Critique. *Econ. Develop. Cult. Change,* July 1969, *17*(4), pp. 449–59.

Nakagawa, Manabu. Some Problems of Population Movements in China under the T'ang Dynasty (I). *Hitotsubashi J. Econ.,* February 1969, *9*(2), pp. 35–42.

Nakamura, Tsutomu. The Organization of the Ceramic Industry around the Nagoya Area of Japan. *J. Ind. Econ.,* April 1969, *17*(2), pp. 151–62.

Nakano, Isao. Objectivity Reexamined. *Kobe Econ. Bus. Rev.,* 1969, *16*(1), pp. 47–54.

Nakayama, Toshiko and Layng, W. John. An Analysis of Price Changes in Second Quarter of 1969. *Mon. Lab. Rev.,* October 1969, *92*(10), pp. 36–41.

Nally, Robert V. The Computer and Home Office Management Development in Life Insurance. *J. Risk Ins.,* September 1969, *36*(4), pp. 393–400.

Nam, Young Woo and Cole, David C. The Pattern and Significance of Economic Planning in Korea. **In** *Adelman, I., ed.,* 1969, pp. 11–37.

Nambiar, R. G. Input-Output Analysis: Nature and Significance. *Artha-Vikas,* January 1969, *5*(1), pp. 9–28.

Namier, L. B. Anthony Bacon, M. P., an Eighteenth-century Merchant. **In** *Minchinton, W. E., ed.,* 1969, pp. 59–106.

Nandwani, S. C. Use of Shadow Prices in Plan Methodology. *Indian Econ. J.,* July–September 1969, *17*(1), pp. 137–42.

Nanus, B. B. National Planning: Problems and Goals —Introduction and State-of-the-Art. **In** *Ozbekhan, H. and Talbert, G. E., eds.,* 1969, pp. 32–34.

Naor, P. The Regulation of Queue Size by Levying Tolls. *Econometrica,* January 1969, *37*(1), pp. 15–24.

Naqvi, Syed Nawab Haider. Protection and Economic Development. *Kyklos,* 1969, *22*(1), pp. 124–54.

Narasimham, M. Debt-Servicing as an Aid to Promotion of Trade of Developing Countries: Comment. *Oxford Econ. Pap.,* November 1969, *21*(3), pp. 404–08.

Narayanan, P. P. Trade Union Attitudes to Wage Policy in Developing Countries. **In** *Smith, A. D., ed.,* 1969, pp. 383–94.

Narayanan, R. Computation of Zellner-Theil's Three Stage Least Squares Estimates. *Econometrica,* April 1969, *37*(2), pp. 298–306.

Narver, John. Conglomeration in the Food Industries. **In** *Garoian, L., ed.,* 1969, pp. 21–41.

Nash, Ralph C., Jr. Pricing Policies in Government Contracts. **In** *Competition in Defense Procurement, SCH,* 1969, pp. 237–56.

Nash, Robert T. and Gramm, William P. A Neglected Early Statement of the Paradox of Thrift. *Hist. Polit. Econ.,* Fall 1969, *1*(2), pp. 395–400.

Nasini, P. The Reconciliation of Fiscal Legislation. **In** *Duquesne, L., et al.,* 1969, pp. 44–53.

Näslund, Bertil. On the Road to the Golden Age *Z. Nationalökon.,* December 1969, *29*(3–4), pp. 305–12.

Nassmacher, Karl-Heinz. Probleme und Voraussetzungen einer rationalen Wirtschaftspolitik in Grossbritannien. (With English summary.) *Z. ges. Staatswiss.,* October 1969, *125*(4), pp. 637–60.

Nathan, Dev. Some Aspects of the Rate of Interest in Planning. *Indian Econ. J.,* April–June 1969, *16* (4–5), pp. 544–53.

Nathan, G. Tests of Independence in Contingency Tables from Stratified Samples. **In** *Johnson, N. L. and Smith, H., Jr., eds.,* 1969, pp. 578–600.

Nathanson, Charles E. The Militarization of the American Economy. **In** *Horowitz, D., ed.,* 1969, pp. 205–35.

Naumann, Jens and Hüfner, Klaus. Economics of Education in Transition: Summary of the Contribution. **In** *[Edding, Friedrich],* 1969, pp. 39–50.

Naus, J. I. The Distribution of the Logarithm of the Sum of Two Log-Normal Variates. *J. Amer. Statist. Assoc.,* June 1969, *64*(326), pp. 655–59.

Naya, Seiji and Anderson, James. Substitution and Two Concepts of Effective Rate of Protection. *Amer. Econ. Rev.,* Part I, September 1969, *59*(4), pp. 607–12.

______ **and Morgan, Theodore.** The Accuracy of International Trade Data: The Case of Southeast Asian Countries. *J. Amer. Statist. Assoc.,* June 1969, *64*(326), pp. 452–67.

Nayar, M. K. K. Fertilisers and Farm Revolution. **In** *Dagli, V., ed., Vol. II,* 1969, pp. 204–06.

Naylor, John A. Expectations, Portfolio Preferences and the Term Structure of Interest Rates. *Ohio State U. Bull. Bus. Res.,* September 1969, *44*(9), pp. 4–7.

______ A Note on the 'Traditional Theory' of the Term Structure of Interest Rates and Rates on Three- and Six-Month Treasury Bills: Comment. *Int. Econ. Rev.,* October 1969, *10*(3), pp. 484–87.

______ The Rationale and Significance of the Proposed Discount Mechanism. *Quart. Rev. Econ. Bus.,* Winter 1969, *9*(4), pp. 7–19.

Naylor, R. D. Planning for the '70's. *Econ. Soc. Tijdschr.,* December 1969, *23*(6), pp. 567–85.

Naylor, Thomas H. A Third Note on Keynesian Mathematics. *Econ. J.,* March 1969, *79*(313), pp. 183–84.

______ **and Burdick, Donald S.** Response Surface Designs. **In** *Naylor, T. H., ed.,* 1969, pp. 80–98.

______; **Burdick, Donald S. and Sasser, W. Earl, Jr.** The Design of Computer Simulation Experiments. **In** *Naylor, T. H., ed.,* 1969, pp. 3–35.

______ **and Hunter, J. S.** Experimental Designs. **In** *Naylor, T. H., ed.,* 1969, pp. 39–58.

______; **Vernon, John M. and Rives, Norfleet W., Jr.** An Econometric Model of the Tobacco Industry. *Rev. Econ. Statist.,* May 1969, *51*(2), pp. 149–58.

______; **Wertz, Kenneth and Wonnacott, Thomas H.** Spectral Analysis of Data Generated by Simulation Experiments with Econometric Models. *Econometrica,* April 1969, *37*(2), pp. 333–52.

Neal, F. Liverpool Shipping in the Early Nineteenth Century. **In** *Harris, J. R., ed.,* 1969, pp. 147–81.

Neal, Larry. Investment Behavior by American Railroads: 1897–1914. *Rev. Econ. Statist.,* May 1969, *51*(2), pp. 126–35.

Neal, Nevin E. and McFarland, C. K. The Nascence of Protectionism: American Tariff Policies, 1816–1824. *Land Econ.,* February 1969, *45*(1), pp. 22–30.

Neale, A. D. The Policy Content of Anti-trust. **In** *Hunter, A., ed.,* 1969, pp. 202–29.

Neale, Walter C. Land Is to Rule. **In** *Frykenberg, R. E., ed.,* 1969, pp. 3–15.

Nedoma, Josef. Modifikovaný Gomoryho algoritmus pro smíšené boolovské lineární úlohy. (Modified Gomory's Algorithm for Mixed Boolean Linear Programming Problems. With English summary.) *Ekon.-Mat. Obzor,* 1969, *5*(2), pp. 186–98.

Needleman, Carolyn and Needleman, Martin. Marx and the Problem of Causation. *Sci. Soc.,* Summer-Fall 1969, *33*(3), pp. 322–39.

Needleman, Martin and Needleman, Carolyn. Marx and the Problem of Causation. *Sci. Soc.,* Summer-Fall 1969, *33*(3), pp. 322–39.

Nef, John U. The Progress of Technology and the Growth of Large-Scale Industry in Great Britain, 1540–1640. **In** *Scoville, W. C. and La Force, J. C., eds., Vol. II,* 1969, pp. 43–64.

Negishi, Takashi. The Customs Union and the Theory of Second Best. *Int. Econ. Rev.,* October 1969, *10*(3), pp. 391–98.

______ Marshallian External Economies and Gains from Trade between Similar Countries. *Rev. Econ. Stud.,* January 1969, *36*(105), pp. 131–35.

Neilan, Edwin P. The ILO at 50: A Management Assessment. *Mon. Lab. Rev.,* May 1969, *92*(5), pp. 41–43.

Neill, Robin F. Harold Adams Innis: Canadian Economics. *J. Econ. Issues,* September 1969, *3*(3), pp. 3–15.

Neils, Elaine and Berry, Brian J. L. Location, Size, and Shape of Cities as Influenced by Environmental Factors: The Urban Environment Writ Large. **In** *Perloff, H. S., ed.,* 1969, pp. 257–302.

Nel, P. A. The Standard Industrial Classification and Industrial Marketing. *Finance Trade Rev.,* December 1969, *8*(4), pp. 231–57.

Nelson, Boyd L. Econometrics and Applied Economic Analysis in Regulatory Decisions. *Law Contemp. Probl.,* Spring 1969, *34*(2), pp. 330–39.

Nelson, Glenn L. and Manderscheid, Lester V. A Framework for Viewing Simulation. *Can. J. Agr. Econ.,* February 1969, *17*(1), pp. 33–41.

Nelson, James R. Policy Analysis in Transportation Programs. **In** *The Analysis and Evaluation of Public Expenditures: The PPB System, Vol. 3, JECP,* 1969, pp. 1102–27.

______ Reassessment of Economic Standards for the Rate of Return under Regulation. **In** *Trebing, H. M. and Howard, R. H., eds.,* 1969, pp. 3–20.

Nelson, Paul E. Research Problems and Information

Gaps Relating to Conglomerate Growth. **In** *Garoian, L., ed.*, 1969, pp. 128–30.

Nelson, Saul. Antitrust and Economic Efficiency. **In** *Weston, J. F. and Peltzman, S., eds.*, 1969, pp. 57–66.

Nerlove, Marc; Raduchel, William and Eads, George. A Long-Run Cost Function for the Local Service Airline Industry: An Experiment in Non-Linear Estimation. *Rev. Econ. Statist.*, August 1969, *51* (3), pp. 258–70.

Nestel, G.; Fromm, D. and L'Esperance, Wilford L. Gross State Product and an Econometric Model of a State. *J. Amer. Statist. Assoc.*, September 1969, *64*(327), pp. 787–807.

Nesterov, L. Current Position of National Wealth Estimation in the World. *Rev. Income Wealth*, September 1969, *15*(3), pp. 271–83.

Neter, J. Measurement Errors in Anticipated Consumer Expenditures. **In** *Johnson, N. L. and Smith, H., Jr., eds.*, 1969, pp. 482–505.

Netschert, Bruce C. Competition in the Nuclear Power Supply Industry—A Rejoinder to Professor Markham. *Antitrust Bull.*, Fall 1969, *14*, pp. 665–66.

——— Competition in the Nuclear Power Supply Industry: A Review. *Antitrust Bull.*, Fall 1969, *14*, pp. 629–55.

Netzer, Dick. The Property Tax Case for Federal Tax Sharing. **In** *[White, Charles P.]*, 1969, pp. 88–102.

Neudecker, H. A Note on BLUS Estimation. *J. Amer. Statist. Assoc.*, September 1969, *64*(327), pp. 949–52.

——— Some Theorems on Matrix Differentiation with Special Reference to Kronecker Matrix Products. *J. Amer. Statist. Assoc.*, September 1969, *64*(327), pp. 953–63.

Neumann, Frederick L. The Incidence and Nature of Consistency Exceptions. *Accounting Rev.*, July 1969, *44*(3), pp. 546–54.

Neumann, Seev. Anticipated and Unanticipated Inflation—Implications to Life Insurance. *J. Risk Ins.*, June 1969, *36*(2), pp. 315–19.

——— Inflation and Saving through Life Insurance. *J. Risk Ins.*, December 1969, *36*(5), pp. 567–82.

Neutze, Max. Property Taxation and Multiple-Family Housing. **In** *Becker, A. P., ed.*, 1969, pp. 115–28.

——— **and Troy, Patrick.** Urban Road Planning in Theory and Practice. *J. Transp. Econ. Policy*, May 1969, *3*(2), pp. 139–51.

Nevel, Robert O. Technological Change in Agriculture. *Agr. Econ. Res.*, January 1969, *21*(1), pp. 13–18.

Nevin, Edward. The Burden of the Public Debt: A Survey. *Rivista Int. Sci. Econ. Com.*, November 1969, *16*(11), pp. 1074–91.

Newell, Richard S. Afghanistan: The Dangers of Cold War Generosity. *Middle East J.*, Spring 1969, *23*(2), pp. 168–76.

Newhouse, Joseph P. and Taylor, Lester D. On the Long-Run and Short-Run Demand for Money: A Comment. *J. Polit. Econ.*, September/October 1969, *77*(5), pp. 851–56.

Newlyn, W. T. Monetary Analysis and Policy in Financially Dependent Economies. **In** *Stewart, I. G., ed.*, 1969, pp. 71–82.

Newman, Dorothy K. Perspectives on Poverty 1: Changing Attitudes about the Poor. *Mon. Lab. Rev.*, February 1969, *92*(2), pp. 32–36.

Newman, Monroe and March, Eli P. Rural Areas in the Urban Economy. *Amer. J. Agr. Econ.*, December 1969, *51*(5), pp. 1097–1109.

Newman, Peter. Some Properties of Concave Functions. *J. Econ. Theory*, October 1969, *1*(3), pp. 291–314.

Newnan, Donald G. Determining Rate of Return by Means of Payback Period and Useful Life. *Eng. Econ.*, October–November 1969, *15*(1), pp. 29–39.

Newsom, Robert T. Metropolitan and Nonmetropolitan Employment Changes: The Case of Texas. *Soc. Sci. Quart.*, September 1969, *50*(2), pp. 354–68.

Newton, David A. and Cambern, John R. Skill Transfers: Can Defense Workers Adapt to Civilian Occupations? *Mon. Lab. Rev.*, June 1969, *92*(6), pp. 21–25.

Newton, Derek A. Get the Most Out of Your Sales Force. *Harvard Bus. Rev.*, September–October 1969, *47*(5), pp. 130–43.

Neyman, J. Bias in Surveys Due to Nonresponse (Closing Address). **In** *Johnson, N. L. and Smith, H., Jr., eds.*, 1969, pp. 712–32.

Ng, S. H. The Terms of Trade in the Case of Entrepôt Trade. *Econ. Rec.*, June 1969, *45*(110), pp. 288–90.

Ng, Y.-K. A Note on Profit Maximization. *Australian Econ. Pap.*, June 1969, *8*(12), pp. 106–110.

Nichita, Nicolae and Anghel, Eliza. Cu privire la corelația dintre cererea și oferta de mărfuri în socialism. (The Correlation between Demand and Offer of Produce in Socialism. With English summary.) *Stud. Cercet. Econ.*, 1969, *1-2*, pp. 23–36.

Nicholls, William H. The Transformation of Agriculture in a Presently Semi-Industrialized Country: The Case of Brazil. **In** *Thorbecke, E., ed.*, 1969, pp. 311–78.

——— The U.S. South as an Under-developed Region. **In** *Papi, U. and Nunn, C., eds.*, 1969, pp. 469–88.

Nichols, Alan. On Savings and Neo-Institutionalism. *J. Econ. Issues*, September 1969, *3*(3), pp. 63–66.

——— On the Social Rate of Discount: Comment. *Amer. Econ. Rev.*, December 1969, *59*(5), pp. 909–11.

Nichols, Donald R. PPBS: A Challenge to Non-Profit Accounting. *Manage. Account.*, November 1969, *51*(5), pp. 12–13.

Nichols, Dorothy M. Banks, too, Post Collateral. **In** *Jessup, P. F.*, 1969, pp. 73–79.

Nichols, T. E., Jr. Transportation and Regional Development in Agriculture. *Amer. J. Agr. Econ.*, December 1969, *51*(5), pp. 1455–63.

Nicol, Robert E. G. and Schwab, Bernhard. From Double-Declining-Balance to Sum-of-the-Years'-Digits Depreciation: An Optimum Switching Rule. *Accounting Rev.*, April 1969, *44*(2), pp. 292–96.

Nicola, Pier Carlo. Equilibrio economico generale di tipo concorrenziale in condizioni dinamiche. (General Competitive Equilibrium under Dynamic Conditions—Part I. With English summary.) *L'Industria,* January–March 1969, (1), pp. 3–16.

______ Equilibrio economico generale di tipo concorrenziale in condizioni dinamiche (II). (General Competitive Equilibrium under Dynamic Conditions—Part II. With English summary.) *L'Industria,* April–June 1969, (2), pp. 197–207.

Nicolae-Văleanu, Ivanciu. Istoria gîndirii economice Româneşti—probleme şi preocupări. (History of Romanian Economic Thought—Problems and Preoccupations. With English summary.) *Stud. Cercet. Econ.,* 1969, *3,* pp. 185–98.

Nicosia, Francesco M. Perceived Risk, Information Processing, and Consumer Behavior: A Review Article. *J. Bus.,* April 1969, *42*(2), pp. 162–66.

______ Ricerche sui consumatori: problemi e prospettive. (Consumer Research: Problems and Perspectives. With English summary.) *L'Impresa,* November/December 1969, *11*(6), pp. 429–35.

Nie, Norman H.; Powell, G. Bingham, Jr. and Prewitt, Kenneth. Social Structure and Political Participation: Developmental Relationships, Part I. *Amer. Polit. Sci. Rev.,* June 1969, *63*(2), pp. 361–78.

Nieburg, H. L. The Tech-Fix and the City. **In** *Schmandt, H. J. and Bloomberg, W., Jr., eds.,* 1969, pp. 211–43.

Niedercorn, J. H. and Bechdolt, B. V., Jr. An Economic Derivation of the "Gravity Law" of Spatial Interaction. *J. Reg. Sci.,* August 1969, *9*(2), pp. 273–82.

Niedereichholz, Joachim. Grundzüge einer Systemanalyse ökonomischer Modelle mittels Flussgraphen. (With English summary.) *Jahr. Nationalökon. Statist.,* June 1969, *183*(1), pp. 30–47.

Niehans, Jürg. Austria and Switzerland: Comment. **In** *Bronfenbrenner, M., ed.,* 1969, pp. 247–50.

______ Efficient Monetary and Fiscal Policies in Balanced Growth. *J. Money, Credit, Banking,* May 1969, *1*(2), pp. 228–51.

______ Growth and Inflation: A Comment. *J. Money, Credit, Banking,* August 1969, *1*(3), pp. 433–38.

______ Money in a Static Theory of Optimal Payment Arrangements. *J. Money, Credit, Banking,* November 1969, *1*(4), pp. 706–26.

______ The Neoclassical Dichotomy as a Controlled Experiment. *J. Polit. Econ.,* Part I, July/August 1969, *77*(4), pp. 504–11.

Nielsen, Oswald. The Role of Variance in Managerial Control. *Manage. Account.,* October 1969, *51*(4), pp. 26–28.

Niemi, Albert W. Some Aspects of the Relative Decline of the British Steel Industry, 1870–1913. *Amer. Econ.,* Fall 1969, *13*(2), pp. 40–49.

Niemi, Richard G. Majority Decision-Making with Partial Unidimensionality. *Amer. Polit. Sci. Rev.,* June 1969, *63*(2), pp. 488–97.

Nigam, Raj K. State Government Undertakings. **In** *Dagli, V., ed., Vol. II,* 1969, pp. 207–17.

Niinimäki, Rauno. Kansallisen finanssi- ja sosiaalipolitiikan vaikutuksesta taloudelliseen integraatioon. (The Effect of National Fiscal and Social Policy on Economic Integration. With English summary.) *Kansant. Aikak.,* 1969, *65*(4), pp. 280–303.

Nikl, Josef. Estimates of Long-term Development of Agriculture by Means of the Global Factorial Model. *Czech. Econ. Pap.,* 1969, (11), pp. 103–07.

Niklasson, Harald. Problems of Method in Cost-Benefit Analyses of Retraining. *Swedish J. Econ.,* September 1969, *71*(3), pp. 184–97.

Nikolitch, Radoje. The Adequate Family Farm—Mainstay of the Farm Economy. **In** *Owen, W. F., ed.,* 1969, pp. 26–37.

______ Family-Operated Farms: Their Compatibility with Technological Advance. *Amer. J. Agr. Econ.,* August 1969, *51*(3), pp. 530–45.

______ I See It Differently. *Amer. J. Agr. Econ.,* December 1969, *51*(5), pp. 1629–32.

Nisbet, Charles T. The Relationship between Institutional and Informal Credit Markets in Rural Chile. *Land Econ.,* May 1969, *45*(2), pp. 162–73.

Noda, Tsutomu. Savings of Farm Households. **In** *Ohkawa, K.; Johnston, B. F. and Kaneda, H., eds.,* 1969, pp. 352–73.

Nolte, Ernst. Big Business and German Politics: A Comment. *Amer. Hist. Rev.,* October 1969, *75*(1), pp. 71–78.

Nonomura, Kazuo. Competition of Economic Growth. **In** *Nonomura, K.,* 1969, pp. 3–91.

______ On So-Called Profit Dispute. **In** *Nonomura, K.,* 1969, pp. 137–54.

______ Socialist International Division of Labor and Integration Project—A Brief Outline. **In** *Nonomura, K.,* 1969, pp. 95–116.

______ Trade Pricing within SEV Bloc. **In** *Nonomura, K.,* 1969, pp. 117–33.

______ Transition to the New Economic System in the Soviet Union. **In** *Nonomura, K.,* 1969, pp. 155–75.

Norbye, O. The Economy of Algeria. **In** *Robson, P. and Lury, D. A., eds.,* 1969, pp. 471–521.

Nordhaus, William D. An Economic Theory of Technological Change. *Amer. Econ. Rev.,* May 1969, *59*(2), pp. 18–28.

Nordin, J. A. The Normalized Vote Margins Method of Committee Voting. *Rivista Int. Sci. Econ. Com.,* June 1969, *16*(6), pp. 529–49.

North, Harper Q. and Pyke, Donald L. 'Probes' of the Technological Future. *Harvard Bus. Rev.,* May–June 1969, *47*(3), pp. 68–82.

Northam, Ray M. Population Size, Relative Location, and Declining Urban Centers: Conterminous United States, 1940–1960. *Land Econ.,* August 1969, *45*(3), pp. 313–22.

Northrup, Herbert R. The Negro in Aerospace Work. *Calif. Manage. Rev.,* Summer 1969, *11*(4), pp. 11–26.

Norton, Roger D. Formal Approaches to Regional Planning in Korea. **In** *Adelman, I., ed.,* 1969, pp. 185–212.

Norton, W. E. Debt Management and Monetary Policy in the United Kingdom. *Econ. J.,* September 1969, *79*(315), pp. 475–94.

______**; Jackson, G. H. and Sweeny, K. M.** A Demand Equation for Imports. *Econ. Rec.,* December 1969, *45*(112), pp. 589–95.

Norwood, Bernard. The Kennedy Round: A Try at Linear Trade Negotiations. *J. Law Econ.,* October 1969, *12*(2), pp. 297–319.

Nosé, Nobuko. Functions of Screen Accounts. *Kobe Econ. Bus. Rev.,* 1969, *16*(1), pp. 19–30.

Nosé, Tetsuya. A Statistical Approach to Personal

Taxation. *Oxford Econ. Pap.,* July 1969, *21*(2), pp. 177–95.

Notestein, Frank W. Population Growth and Its Control. **In** *Hardin, C. M., ed.,* 1969, pp. 9–39.

———; Kirk, Dudley and Segal, Sheldon. The Problem of Population Control. **In** *Hauser, P. M., ed.,* 1969, pp. 139–67.

Nouri, Clement J. Iraq Revisited. *Marquette Bus. Rev.,* Spring 1969, *13*(1), pp. 22–33.

Nourse, Edwin G. Government Discipline of Private Economic Power. **In** *Kuhlman, J. M., ed.,* 1969, pp. 240–56.

Nove, Alec. Cyclical Fluctuations under Socialism. **In** *Bronfenbrenner, M., ed.,* 1969, pp. 287–302.

——— East-West Trade. **In** *Samuelson, P. A., ed.,* 1969, pp. 100–120.

——— Internal Economics. *Econ. J.,* December 1969, *79*(316), pp. 847–60.

——— Soviet Political Organization and Development. **In** *Leys, C., ed.,* 1969, pp. 65–84.

———; Vajda, Imre and Khachaturov, T. S. Replies to Comments. **In** *Samuelson, P. A., ed.,* 1969, pp. 147–49.

Novozámský, Jiří and Tauchman, Josef. The Nature of the International Division of Labour under Socialism. *Czech. Econ. Pap.,* 1969, (11), pp. 127–39.

Nowzad, Bahram. Economic Integration in Central and West Africa. *Int. Monet. Fund Staff Pap.,* March 1969, *16*(1), pp. 103–39.

Nudds, Donald and Bottomley, Anthony. A Widow's Cruse Theory of Credit Supply in Underdeveloped Rural Areas. *Manchester Sch. Econ. Soc. Stud.,* June 1969, *37*(2), pp. 131–40.

Nugent, Jeffrey B. and DePrano, Michael E. Economies as an Antitrust Defense: Comment. *Amer. Econ. Rev.,* December 1969, *59*(5), pp. 947–53.

Nuthall, P. L. Estimation of Supply Functions by Linear Programming: A Note. *Rev. Marketing Agr. Econ.,* September 1969, *37*(3), pp. 172–77.

Nuti, Domenico Mario. The Degree of Monopoly in the Kaldor-Mirrlees Growth Model. *Rev. Econ. Stud.,* April 1969, *36*(106), pp. 257–60.

——— On Incomes Policy. *Sci. Soc.,* Fall-Winter 1969, *33*(4), pp. 415–25.

Nutler, G. Warren. Lecture Two: The Soviet Citizen: Today's Forgotten Man. **In** *Viser, F. J., ed.,* 1969, pp. 19–44.

Nutter, G. Warren. Statement. **In** *To Extend and Amend the Export Control Act of 1949, HCH,* 1969, pp. 117–19.

Nyers, R. Theoretical and Practical Problems of Socialist Economic Integration. (In Russian. With English summary.) *Acta Oecon.,* 1969, *4*(2), pp. 119–53.

O'Boyle, Edward J. Job Tenure: How It Relates to Race and Age. *Mon. Lab. Rev.,* September 1969, *92*(9), pp. 16–23.

O'Brien, Francis A. The Federal Trade Commission's Pre-Merger Notification Requirements. *Antitrust Bull.,* Fall 1969, *14,* pp. 557–85.

O'Connell, Francis A., Jr. A Management View of Government Intervention in Bargaining. **In** *Wortman, M. S., Jr.,* 1969, pp. 429–35.

O'Connor, James. Scientific and Ideological Elements in the Economic Theory of Government Policy. *Sci. Soc.,* Fall-Winter 1969, *33*(4), pp. 385–414.

O'Dell, Charles A. Econometricians and the Data Gap: Reply—Comment. *Amer. J. Agr. Econ.,* August 1969, *51*(3), pp. 679–80.

O'Grada, Cormac. The Vocational Training Policy of the EEC and the Free Movement of Skilled Labour. *J. Common Market Stud.,* December 1969, *8*(2), pp. 79–109.

O'Keefe, Terrence B. and Carlson, John A. Buffer Stocks and Reaction Coefficients: An Experiment with Decision Making under Risk. *Rev. Econ. Stud.,* October 1969, *36*(108), pp. 467–84.

O'Neill, John. Introduction: Marxism and the Sociological Imagination. **In** *Baran, P. A.,* 1969, pp. xiii–xxviii.

O'Reagan, Robert T. Relative Costs of Computerized Error Inspection Plans. *J. Amer. Statist. Assoc.,* December 1969, *64*(328), pp. 1245–55.

Oakland, William H. Budgetary Measures of Fiscal Performance. *Southern Econ. J.,* April 1969, *35* (4), pp. 347–58.

——— Effects of Taxation on Risk-Taking: Discussion. *Amer. Econ. Rev.,* May 1969, *59*(2), pp. 563–65.

——— Joint Goods. *Economica, N.S.,* August 1969, *36* (143), pp. 253–68.

Oates, Wallace E. The Effects of Property Taxes and Local Public Spending on Property Values: An Empirical Study of Tax Capitalization and the Tiebout Hypothesis. *J. Polit. Econ.,* November/December 1969, *77*(6), pp. 957–71.

———; Bradford, David F. and Malt, R. A. The Rising Cost of Local Public Services: Some Evidence and Reflections. *Nat. Tax J.,* June 1969, *22*(2), pp. 185–202.

Oatman, Floyd W. How to Stimulate Innovation in Physical Distribution. *Oregon Bus. Rev.,* March 1969, *28*(3), pp. 1–4.

Oberer, Walter E. and Doherty, Robert E. The Public School Teacher as Organization Man. **In** *Walsh, R. E., ed.,* 1969, pp. 115–40.

Oberhofer, Walter and Korte, Bernhard. Zur Triangulation von Input-Output-Matrizen. (With English summary.) *Jahr. Nationalökon. Statist.,* March 1969, *182*(4–5), pp. 398–433.

Obolenski, K. P. Agricultural Planning in U.S.S.R. **In** *Papi, U. and Nunn, C., eds.,* 1969, pp. 449–63.

Očenášek, Radomir. Diskuse o národohospodářských modelech. (Discussion about Macroeconomic Models. With English summary.) *Ekon.-Mat. Obzor,* 1969, *5*(4), pp. 522–24.

Ochs, Jack. An Application of Linear Programming to Urban Spatial Organization. *J. Reg. Sci.,* December 1969, *9*(3), pp. 451–57.

Odaka, Konosuke. Indices of the Excess Demand for Labor in Prewar Japan, 1929–39: A Preliminary Study. *Hitotsubashi J. Econ.,* June 1969, *10*(1), pp. 33–55.

Odell, Peter R. Natural Gas in Western Europe: A Case Study in the Economic Geography of Energy Resources. *De Economist,* May/June 1969, *117*(3), pp. 227–57.

Odhner, Clas-Erik; Edgren, Gösta and Faxén, Karl-Olof. Wages, Growth and the Distribution of Income. *Swedish J. Econ.*, September 1969, *71*(3), pp. 133–60.

Ody, J. G. Application of Cost-Benefit Analysis to Airports: The Case of Nicosia, Cyprus. *J. Transp. Econ. Policy*, September 1969, *3*(3), pp. 322–32.

Oeter, Ferdinand. Familienlastenausgleich und Angleichung der sozialen Startbedingungen: Analysen und Vorschläge. (Equilization of Family Burdens and Social Starting Conditions: Analysis and Proposals. With English summary.) *Schmollers Jahr.*, 1969, *89*(1), pp. 33–59.

Officer, Lawrence H. A Comparison of the Effects of Monopoly and Competition in Commodity Markets upon the Foreign-Exchange Market. *Western Econ. J.*, December 1969, *7*(4), pp. 360–64.

______ **and Hurtubise, Jules R.** Price Effects of the Kennedy Round on Canadian Trade. *Rev. Econ. Statist.*, August 1969, *51*(3), pp. 320–33.

______ **and Willett, Thomas D.** Reserve-Asset Preferences and the Confidence Problem in the Crisis Zone. *Quart. J. Econ.*, November 1969, *83*(4), pp. 688–95.

Ogunsheye, Ayo. Manpower Problems in the Context of Economic Planning. **In** *Yesufu, T. M., ed.*, 1969, pp. 14–26.

Ohkawa, Kazushi. Phases of Agricultural Development and Economic Growth. **In** *Ohkawa, K.; Johnston, B. F. and Kaneda, H., eds.*, 1969, pp. 3–36.

______ **and Johnston, Bruce F.** The Transferability of the Japanese Pattern of Modernizing Traditional Agriculture. **In** *Thorbecke, E., ed.*, 1969, pp. 277–303.

Ohlin, Goran. Trade in a Non-*Laissez-Faire* World. **In** *Samuelson, P. A., ed.*, 1969, pp. 157–75.

______ **and Bienaymé, A.** Replies to Comments. **In** *Samuelson, P. A., ed.*, 1969, pp. 230–31.

Öhman, Berndt. A Note on the "Solidarity Wage Policy" of the Swedish Labor Movement. *Swedish J. Econ.*, September 1969, *71*(3), pp. 198–205.

Oi, Walter Y. A Bracketing Rule for the Estimation of Simple Distributed Lag Models. *Rev. Econ. Statist.*, November 1969, *51*(4), pp. 445–52.

______ On the Relationship among Different Members of the *k*-Class. *Int. Econ. Rev.*, February 1969, *10*(1), pp. 36–46.

Ojala, E. M. Agriculture in the World of 1975: General Picture of Trends. **In** *Papi, U. and Nunn, C., eds.*, 1969, pp. 3–20.

Ojha, P. D. Taxation of Agricultural Land and Income. *Artha-Vikas*, July 1969, *5*(2), pp. 50–62.

______ **and Lent, George E.** Sales Taxes in Countries of the Far East. *Int. Monet. Fund Staff Pap.*, November 1969, *16*(3), pp. 529–81.

Okner, Benjamin A. and Pechman, Joseph A. Simulation of the Carter Commission Tax Proposals for the United States. *Nat. Tax J.*, March 1969, *22*(1), pp. 2–23.

Okuboyejo, N. A. A. Economic and Development Planning in Nigeria 1945–1968. **In** *Yesufu, T. M., ed.*, 1969, pp. 3–13.

Okuguchi, Koji. On the Stability of Price Adjusting Oligopoly Equilibrium under Product Differentiation. *Southern Econ. J.*, January 1969, *35*(3), pp. 244–46.

de Oliveira Campos, Roberto. A Retrospect Over Brazilian Development Plans. **In** *Ellis, H. S., ed.*, 1969, pp. 317–44.

Oliver, Covey T. Physical Integration and the Future of Latin America. *Soc. Res.*, Summer 1969, *36*(2), pp. 253–66.

Oliver, F. R. Another Generalisation of the Logistic Growth Function. *Econometrica*, January 1969, *37*(1), pp. 144–47.

Olivera, Julio H. G. Is Labour Mobility a Substitute for Trade?—A Reply. *Econ. J.*, March 1969, *79* (313), pp. 178–79.

______ La posición monetaria neta: Observaciones complementarias. (The Net Monetary Position: Some Additional Remarks. With English summary.) *Económica*, September–December 1969, *15*(3), pp. 313–15.

______ A Note on the Optimal Rate of Growth of International Reserves. *J. Polit. Econ.*, March/April 1969, *77*(2), pp. 245–48.

______ On the Asymptotic Theory of the Demand for Money. *Oxford Econ. Pap.*, March 1969, *21*(1), pp. 24–28.

Olken, Hyman. Technological Growth and the Evolution of New Industries: The Implications for an Industrial Society. *Econ. Bus. Bull.*, Fall 1969, *22* (1), pp. 15–24.

Olsen, Edgar O. A Competitive Theory of the Housing Market. *Amer. Econ. Rev.*, Part I, September 1969, *59*(4), pp. 612–22.

______ A Normative Theory of Transfers. *Public Choice*, Spring 1969, *6*, pp. 39–58.

Olson, James S. Organized Black Leadership and Industrial Unionism: The Racial Response, 1936–1945. *Labor Hist.*, Summer 1969, *10*(3), pp. 475–86.

Olson, Mancur, Jr. The Optimal Allocation of Jurisdictional Responsibility: The Principle of "Fiscal Equivalence." **In** *The Analysis and Evaluation of Public Expenditures: The PPB System, Vol. 1, JECP*, 1969, pp. 321–31.

______ The Principle of "Fiscal Equivalence": The Division of Responsibilities among Different Levels of Government. *Amer. Econ. Rev.*, May 1969, *59*(2), pp. 479–87.

______ The Relationship Between Economics and the Other Social Sciences: The Province of a "Social Report." **In** *Lipset, S. M., ed.*, 1969, pp. 137–62.

Olson, Wallace E. Ethical Problems of the Auditor in Financial Reporting. **In** *Burton, J. C., ed.*, 1969, pp. 145–58.

Onitiri, H. M. A. International Trade and the Developing Countries: Comment. **In** *Samuelson, P. A., ed.*, 1969, pp. 35–41.

Onwuka Dike, K. Manpower Training for Economic Development: Professional and Managerial Staff. **In** *Yesufu, T. M., ed.*, 1969, pp. 200–216.

Oort, C. J. The Evaluation of Travelling Time. *J. Transp. Econ. Policy*, September 1969, *3*(3), pp. 279–86.

Ophir, Tsvi. The Interaction of Tariffs and Quotas. *Amer. Econ. Rev.*, December 1969, *59*(5), pp. 1002–05.

Opp, Karl-Dieter. Das Experiment in den Sozialwissenschafter: Einige Probleme und Vorschläge für seine effektivere Verwendung. (With English summary.) *Z. ges. Staatswiss.*, January 1969, *125* (1), pp. 106–22.

Oppenheimer, Peter M. The Case for Raising the Price of Gold. *J. Money, Credit, Banking*, August 1969, *1*(3), pp. 649–65.

——— Import Deposits. *Nat. Westminster Bank Quart. Rev.*, February 1969, pp. 69–72.

Orazem, Frank and Mirakhor, Abbas. Mysterious Multipliers: Reply. *Amer. J. Agr. Econ.*, August 1969, *51*(3), pp. 689–90.

Orcutt, Guy H. and Edwards, John B. Should Aggregation Prior to Estimation Be the Rule? *Rev. Econ. Statist.*, November 1969, *51*(4), pp. 409–20.

——— **and Winokur, Herbert S., Jr.** First Order Autoregression: Inference, Estimation, and Prediction. *Econometrica*, January 1969, *37*(1), pp. 1–14.

Ordeshook, Peter C. and Hinich, Melvin J. Abstentions and Equilibrium in the Electoral Process. *Public Choice*, Fall 1969, *7*, pp. 81–106.

Orgler, Yair E. Selection of Bank Loans for Evaluation: An Analytic Approach. *J. Finance*, March 1969, *24*(1), pp. 75–80.

Öri, J. and Fazekas, B. On the Formulation of a Common Agricultural Policy for CMEA Countries. (In Russian. With English summary.) *Acta Oecon.*, 1969, *4*(4), pp. 403–15.

Orizet, Jean. The Co-operative Movement Since the First World War. *Int. Lab. Rev.*, July 1969, *100*(1), pp. 23–50.

Orr, Daniel. The "Taxicab Problem": A Proposed Solution. *J. Polit. Econ.*, January/February 1969, *77*(1), pp. 141–47.

Orrego Vicuña, Francisco. The Dynamics of the Subregional Agreements within the LAFTA Movement. **In** *Hilton, R., ed.*, 1969, pp. 485–99.

Orshansky, Mollie. Perspectives on Poverty 2: How Poverty Is Measured. *Mon. Lab. Rev.*, February 1969, *92*(2), pp. 37–41.

Orton, Bryce B. and Bradish, Richard D. The Treatment and Disclosure of Research and Development Expenditures. *Manage. Account.*, July 1969, *51*(1), pp. 31–34.

Osman, Omar and Suleiman, A. A. The Economy of Sudan. **In** *Robson, P. and Lury, D. A., eds.*, 1969, pp. 436–70.

Ostby, Ivar and Gulilat, Taye. A Statistical Study of Household Expenditure in Addis Ababa. *East Afr. Econ. Rev.*, December 1969, *1*(2), pp. 63–74.

Ott, Attiat F. and Ott, David J. Simulation of Revenue and Tax Structure: Implications of Broadening the Federal Income Tax Base. **In** *Willis, A. B., ed.*, 1969, pp. 27–106.

———**; Ott, David J. and Turner, J. Scott.** Burden Distribution of a Broad-Based Personal Income Tax System and Its Implications for Tax Reform Discussions. *Law Contemp. Probl.*, Autumn 1969, *34*(4), pp. 805–17.

———**; Ott, David J. and Turner, J. Scott.** Simulation of Costs of a Negative Income Tax Plan and Its Implications for the Poor. **In** *Willis, A. B., ed.*, 1969, pp. 168–83.

Ott, David J. and Ott, Attiat F. Simulation of Revenue and Tax Structure: Implications of Broadening the Federal Income Tax Base. **In** *Willis, A. B., ed.*, 1969, pp. 27–106.

———**; Turner, J. Scott and Ott, Attiat F.** Burden Distribution of a Broad-Based Personal Income Tax System and Its Implications for Tax Reform Discussions. *Law Contemp. Probl.*, Autumn 1969, *34*(4), pp. 805–17.

———**; Turner, J. Scott and Ott, Attiat F.** Simulation of Costs of a Negative Income Tax Plan and Its Implications for the Poor. **In** *Willis, A. B., ed.*, 1969, pp. 168–83.

Oury, Bernard. Weather and Economic Development. *Finance Develop.*, June 1969, *6*(2), pp. 24–29.

Overholt, John L. Factor Selection. **In** *Naylor, T. H., ed.*, 1969, pp. 59–79.

Owen, Bruce M. The Perfectly Competitive Production of Collective Goods: Comment. *Rev. Econ. Statist.*, November 1969, *51*(4), pp. 475–76.

Owen, Joel and Brief, Richard P. A Note on Earnings Risk and the Coefficient of Variation. *J. Finance*, December 1969, *24*(5), pp. 901–04.

Owen, John D. Education for Majority Voting? *Public Choice*, Spring 1969, *6*, pp. 59–70.

——— The Value of Commuter Speed. *Western Econ. J.*, June 1969, *7*(2), pp. 164–72.

Owen, Wilfred. Transport: Key to the Future of Cities. **In** *Perloff, H. S., ed.*, 1969, pp. 205–27.

Owen, Wyn F. Structural Planning in Densely Populated Countries: An Introduction with Applications to Indonesia. *Malayan Econ. Rev.*, April 1969, *14*(1), pp. 97–114.

Oxenfeldt, A. R. and Baxter, W. T. Approaches to Pricing: Economist *Versus* Accountant. **In** *Carsberg, B. V. and Edey, H. C., eds.*, 1969, pp. 184–208.

Oxley, G. W. The Permanent Poor in South-west Lancashire under the Old Poor Law. **In** *Harris, J. R., ed.*, 1969, pp. 16–49.

Ozsvald, László. Incentives for Management Personnel in Hungarian Industry. *Int. Lab. Rev.*, September 1969, *100*(3), pp. 257–72.

Paakkanen, Jouko. Vaikutelmia kehitysmaiden tilanteesta ja kehitysavusta. (The Developing Countries and Development Aid. With English summary.) *Kansant. Aikak.*, 1969, *65*(1), pp. 27–36.

Paarlberg, Don. Food for More People and Better Nutrition. **In** *Hardin, C. M., ed.*, 1969, pp. 41–87.

——— Proposed and Existing Organizational Efforts for Farmers. **In** *Ruttan, V. W.; Waldo, A. D. and Houck, J. P., eds.*, 1969, pp. 201–05.

Pack, Howard and Todaro, Michael P. Technological Transfer, Labour Absorption, and Economic Development. *Oxford Econ. Pap.*, November 1969, *21*(3), pp. 395–403.

Padberg, D. I. and Handy, C. R. Conglomerate Growth: Policy Implications for Agriculture and Agribusiness. **In** *Garoian, L., ed.*, 1969, pp. 117–20.

Paden, Donald W. and Moyer, M. Eugene. The Effectiveness of Teaching Methods: The Relative Effectiveness of Three Methods of Teaching Principles of Economics. *J. Econ. Educ.*, Fall 1969, *1* (1), pp. 33–45.

Padmanabhan, C. B. Problems Involved in Measuring Cost, Efficiency and Productivity of the Indian Educational System. **In** *Pandit, H. N., ed.*, 1969, pp. 416–24.

Paelinck, J. and Biolley, T. A Dynamic Model for the

Belgian Economy: Simulation and Optimization. *Econ. Planning,* 1969, *9*(1–2), pp. 155–207.

Paelinck, J. H. P. Un modèle dynamique de simulation et de contrôle pour l'économie belge. (A Dynamic Simulation and Control Model for Belgian Economy. With English summary.) *Rivista Int. Sci. Econ. Com.,* March 1969, *16*(3), pp. 202–27.

Page, Walter P. A Study of the Fixed-Coefficients Model of Production for Agriculture in a Selected Region of the Great Plains, 1899–1903: Some Tentative Results. *Miss. Val. J. Bus. Econ.,* Fall 1969, *5*(1), pp. 34–42.

Paige, Jeffrey M. and Caplan, Nathan S. A Study of Ghetto Rioters. **In** *Callow, A. B., Jr., ed.,* 1969, pp. 541–48.

Paillat, Paul. Old People. **In** *O.E.C.D.,* 1969, pp. 179–90.

Pais, A. Op de Pof. (On Tick. With English summary.) *De Economist,* January/February 1969, *117*(1), pp. 1–23.

Paish, Frank W. The Control of Demand. **In** *[von Hayek, Friedrich A.],* 1969, pp. 147–64.

______ The Estimation of Business Profits in Periods of Changing Prices. **In** *Parker, R. H. and Harcourt, G. C., eds.,* 1969, pp. 193–200.

______ Unemployment and Price Stability. **In** *Ball, R. J. and Doyle, P., eds.,* 1969, pp. 219–54.

Pajestka, J. Central Planning and the Market. **In** *Economic Concentration, Pt. 7A, SCH,* 1969, pp. 4465–72.

Palmerio, Giovanni. Economie di scala e progresso tecnico incorporato nel settore industriale in Italia nel periodo 1951–1965. (Economies of Scale and Embodied Technical Progress in the Italian Industry—1951–1965. With English summary.) *L'Industria,* July–September 1969, (3), pp. 316–46.

Palomba, Neil A. Stability and Real Economic Growth: An International Comparison. *Kyklos,* 1969, *22*(3), pp. 589–92.

______ Strike Activity and Union Membership: An Empirical Approach. *Univ. Wash. Bus. Rev.,* Winter 1969, *28*(2), pp. 16–22.

______ **and Davis, J. Ronnie.** The National Farmers Organization and the Prisoner's Dilemma: A Game Theory Prediction of Failure. *Soc. Sci. Quart.,* December 1969, *50*(3), pp. 742–48.

Palubinskas, Feliksas. The Role of Marketing Research in the Soviet Economy. *Univ. Missouri Bus. Govt. Rev.,* September–October 1969, *10*(5), pp. 17–24.

Panati, Giovanni. L'imprenditore del futuro: archetipi manageriali. (The Future Entrepreneur: Managerial Archetypes. With English summary.) *L'Impresa,* November/December 1969, *11*(6), pp. 454–60.

______ L'investiment trust e la "nuova scienza" degli investimenti mobiliari. (The Investment Trust and the "New Science" of Investing. With English summary.) *L'Impresa,* March/April 1969, *11* (2), pp. 152–55.

Panchamukhi, P. R. Economic Analysis and Planning of Education Industry. **In** *Pandit, H. N., ed.,* 1969, pp. 215–43.

______ **and Panchamukhi, V. R.** Socio-Economic Variables and Urban Incomes. **In** *Pandit, H. N., ed.,* 1969, pp. 306–36.

Panchamukhi, V. R. and Panchamukhi, P. R. Socio-Economic Variables and Urban Incomes. **In** *Pandit, H. N., ed.,* 1969, pp. 306–36.

Panchapakesan, S. and Gupta, S. S. Selection and Ranking Procedures. **In** *Naylor, T. H., ed.,* 1969, pp. 132–60.

Pandit, H. N. A Study in Unit Cost at the School Stage in India: A Design of the Research Project. **In** *Pandit, H. N., ed.,* 1969, pp. 3–13.

Panglaykim, J. and Thomas, Kenneth D. Indonesian Exports: Performance and Prospects. **In** *Morgan, T. and Spoelstra, N., eds.,* 1969, pp. 337–70.

Panschar, William. Businessmen, Educators, Move to Enlist Black Grads. *Indiana Bus. Rev.,* May/June 1969, *44,* pp. 12–16.

Papi, G. U. The Role of the State in Mixed Economies. **In** *Margolis, J. and Guitton, H., eds.,* 1969, pp. 1–21.

Papola, T. S. A 'Primitive' Equilibrium System: A Neglected Aspect of Smith's Economics. *Indian Econ. J.,* July–September 1969, *17*(1), pp. 93–100.

______ **and Singh, V. B.** Investment Effectiveness and Educational Planning in India. **In** *Pandit, H. N., ed.,* 1969, pp. 274–79.

Pappas, James L. and Brigham, Eugene F. The Effect of Liberalized Depreciation on the Cost of Equity Capital. **In** *Trebing, H. M. and Howard, R. H., eds.,* 1969, pp. 129–58.

______ Rates of Return on Common Stock. *J. Bus.,* July 1969, *42*(3), pp. 302–16.

Pares, Richard. The Economic Factors in the History of the Empire. **In** *Scoville, W. C. and La Force, J. C., eds., Vol. II,* 1969, pp. 96–107.

Parikh, G. O. Integration of Farm and Non-Farm Employment, Part II: Effective Cooperativisation in a Labour Surplus Economy. *Artha-Vikas,* January 1969, *5*(1), pp. 68–76.

Parish, R. M. Some Thoughts on the Role of the Agricultural Economics Profession in Australia. *Australian J. Agr. Econ.,* June 1969, *13*(1), pp. 1–7.

Park, Seong Yawng. Surplus Labor, Technical Progress, Growth, and Distribution. *Int. Econ. Rev.,* February 1969, *10*(1), pp. 22–35.

Park, Sung-Jo. Das Autoritätsverhalten als Leistungsprinzip in der Sozial-Wirtschaftsentwicklung: das Beispiel Japan (bis zur Meiji-Restauration). (Authoritarian Attitudes in Social and Economic Development: The Japanese Experience Until the Meiji Reform Period. With English summary.) *Schmollers Jahr.,* 1969, *89*(4), pp. 451–65.

Parker, Alfred L. Economic Growth for New Mexico. *N. Mex. Bus.,* October 1969, *22*(10), pp. 1–7.

Parker, C. Reed. Ethical Issues for the Financial Analyst. **In** *Burton, J. C., ed.,* 1969, pp. 159–71.

Parker, John E. and Burton, John F., Jr. Interindustry Variations in Voluntary Labor Mobility. *Ind. Lab. Relat. Rev.,* January 1969, *22*(2), pp. 199–216.

Parker, R. H. Lower of Cost and Market in Britain and the United States: A Historical Survey. **In** *Parker, R. H. and Harcourt, G. C., eds.,* 1969, pp. 239–58.

Parkinson, C. Northcote. Our Overheads Are Overhigh. *Manage. Account.,* November 1969, *51*(5), pp. 9–11.

Parks, Burl A. A Brief Background of the Planning

Process. In *Dougal, M. D., ed.,* 1969, pp. 79–83.

Parks, F. Newton. Survival of the European Headquarters. *Harvard Bus. Rev.,* March–April 1969, *47*(2), pp. 79–84.

Parks, Richard W. Systems of Demand Equations: An Empirical Comparison of Alternative Functional Forms. *Econometrica,* October 1969, *37*(4), pp. 629–50.

Parmeggiani, Antonio. Evoluzione del peso alla nascita in una popolazione isolana durante un intervallo venticinquennale. (With English summary.) *Statistica,* April-June 1969, *29*(2), pp. 241–73.

——— Evoluzione della mortalità perinatale in una compagine demografica isolana. (With English summary.) *Statistica,* April-June 1969, *29*(2), pp. 185–239.

Parmeggiani, Luigi and Robert, Marcel. Fifty Years of International Collaboration in Occupational Safety and Health. *Int. Lab. Rev.,* January 1969, *99*(1), pp. 85–136.

Parnes, Andrew and Massell, Benton F. Estimation of Expenditure Elasticities from a Sample of Rural Households in Uganda. *Bull. Oxford Univ. Inst. Econ. Statist.,* November 1969, *31*(4), pp. 313–29.

Parnes, Herbert S. Manpower Mobility Programs: Discussion. In *Somers, G. G. and Wood, W. D., eds.,* 1969, pp. 221–24.

——— **and Spitz, Ruth S.** A Conceptual Framework for Studying Labor Mobility. *Mon. Lab. Rev.,* November 1969, *92*(11), pp. 55–58.

Parpală, E. and Deaconu, V. Eficienţa economică a culturilor de proumb la I.A.S. Fundeni şi Mihăileşti. (Economic Efficiency of the Culture of Maize for Grain at the Fundeni and Mihăileşti I.A.S. (State Farms). With English summary.) *Stud. Cercet. Econ.,* 1969, *4,* pp. 103–13.

Parpală, O. Experienţa României în făurirea unei agriculturi moderne. (The Experience of Romania in Creating a Modern Agriculture. With English summary.) *Stud. Cercet. Econ.,* 1969, *3,* pp. 121–29.

——— Programul agrar al lui Nicolae Bălcescu în revoluţia de la 1848. (Nicolae Bălcescu's Agrarian Program in the 1848 Revolution. With English summary.) *Stud. Cercet. Econ.,* 1969, *1-2,* pp. 205–13.

Parr, John B. City Hierarchies and the Distribution of City Size: A Reconsideration of Beckmann's Contribution. *J. Reg. Sci.,* August 1969, *9*(2), pp. 239–53.

Parrish, Evelyn M. and Lederer, Walther. The U.S. Balance of Payments—Fourth Quarter and Year 1968. *Surv. Curr. Bus.,* March 1969, *49*(3), pp. 23–31, 45–46.

——— The U.S. Balance of Payments: First Quarter, 1969. *Surv. Curr. Bus.,* June 1969, *49*(6), pp. 21–25, 37, 44.

——— The U.S. Balance of Payments: Second Quarter 1969. *Surv. Curr. Bus.,* September 1969, *49*(9), pp. 27–35.

Parry, Samuel and Carol, Arthur. The Economic Rationale of Occupational Choice: Reply. *Ind. Lab. Relat. Rev.,* April 1969, *22*(3), pp. 428–30.

——— The Economic Rationale of Occupational Choice: Reply. *Ind. Lab. Relat. Rev.,* July 1969, *22*(4), pp. 587–88.

Parsons, Donald H. Statement. In *Bank Holding Company Act Amendments, Pts. 1–3, HCH,* 1969, pp. 758–66.

Parsons, J. E., Jr. Locke's Doctrine of Property. *Soc. Res.,* Autumn 1969, *36*(3), pp. 389–411.

Parsons, Kenneth H. Poverty as an Issue in Development Policy: A Comparison of United States and Underdeveloped Countries. *Land Econ.,* February 1969, *45*(1), pp. 52–65.

Parsons, Leonard J. and Bass, Frank M. Simultaneous-Equation Regression Analysis of Sales and Advertising. *Appl. Econ.,* May 1969, *1*(2), pp. 103–24.

Parsons, S. A. The Capacity and Utilisation of Cattle and Sheep Slaughtering Establishments in Australia. *Quart. Rev. Agr. Econ.,* January 1969, *22* (1), pp. 34–46.

Parthasarthy, G. Tenancy Legislation in Labour Surplus Economies and Economic Analysis—A Note. *Indian Econ. J.,* January–March 1969, *16*(3), pp. 371–74.

van de Pas, J. H. and Sandee, Jan. The Effect of Fluctuations in Public Expenditure and Taxation on Economic Growth. In *Margolis, J. and Guitton, H., eds.,* 1969, pp. 388–405.

Pascucci, John J. and Kamerschen, David R. The Retail Price Structure in American Life Insurance: Comment. *J. Risk Ins.,* September 1969, *36* (4), pp. 493–95.

Pashigian, Peter. The Effect of Market Size on Concentration. *Int. Econ. Rev.,* October 1969, *10*(3), pp. 291–314.

Pasinetti, Luigi L. Switches of Technique and the "Rate of Return" in Capital Theory. *Econ. J.,* September 1969, *79*(315), pp. 508–31.

Pasour, E. C., Jr. and Seagraves, James A. On Defining Uneconomic Regions of the Production Function. *Amer. J. Agr. Econ.,* February 1969, *51*(1), pp. 195–202.

Passell, Peter and Dudley, Leonard. War in Vietnam and United States Balance of Payments: Reply to Comment by Douglas Bohi. *Rev. Econ. Statist.,* November 1969, *51*(4), pp. 474–75.

Patel, A. G. A Case for Income Tax on Agricultural Income. *Artha-Vikas,* July 1969, *5*(2), pp. 171–76.

Patel, A. S. and Adhvaryu, J. H. Determinants and Development Implications of Foodgrain Prices in India: Comment. *Amer. J. Agr. Econ.,* November 1969, *51*(4), pp. 939–40.

Patel, Arun and Pathak, Mahesh. Reform of Agricultural Taxation. *Artha-Vikas,* July 1969, *5*(2), pp. 71–78.

Patel, B. P. Twelve Years of the S. T. C. In *Dagli, V., ed., Vol. II,* 1969, pp. 102–10.

Patel, D. A. and Murty, A. G. K. Economics of Ghee Manufacture: A Study at Micro Level—A Comment. *Artha-Vikas,* January 1969, *5*(1), pp. 104–08.

Patel, G. A. and Shah, R. L. Cultivation of Hybrid Bajri in Gujarat State. *Artha-Vikas,* January 1969, *5*(1), pp. 81–94.

Patel, H. M. Two Views on Foreign Aid. *Artha-Vikas,* January 1969, *5*(1), pp. 77–80.

——— Why Public Sector Projects Are Not Profitable. **In** *Dagli, V., ed., Vol. II,* 1969, pp. 10–17.

Patel, M. L. Rationale of Human Capital and Its Productivity Analysis. **In** *Pandit, H. N., ed.,* 1969, pp. 349–55.

Patel, Malvika and Tintner, Gerhard. A Lognormal Diffusion Process Applied to the Growth of Yields of Some Agricultural Crops in India. *J. Devel. Stud.,* October 1969, *6*(1), pp. 49–57.

Patel, Shivabhai J. Taxation of Agricultural Land and Income. *Artha-Vikas,* July 1969, *5*(2), pp. 98–105.

Patel, Surendra J. Rejoinder to Boserup's 'Warning against Optimistic ICOR Statistics.' *Kyklos,* 1969, *22*(4), pp. 777–79.

Paterson, Robert W. Metropolitan Fragments v. Urban Order. *Univ. Missouri Bus. Govt. Rev.,* January–February 1969, *10*(1), pp. 14–22.

______ The 1970 U.S. Economy. *Univ. Missouri Bus. Govt. Rev.,* November–December 1969, *10*(6), pp. 13–23.

Pathak, Mahesh and Patel, Arun. Reform of Agricultural Taxation. *Artha-Vikas,* July 1969, *5*(2), pp. 71–78.

______ **and Vyas, V. S.** A Case for Taxation of Agricultural Income. *Artha-Vikas,* July 1969, *5*(2), pp. 130–37.

Patil, R. H. and Lakdawala, D. T. Prospects of India's Trade with ECAFE Countries. **In** *Morgan, T. and Spoelstra, N., eds.,* 1969, pp. 241–73.

Patil, S. M. Prospects for Machine Tool Exports. **In** *Dagli, V., ed., Vol. II,* 1969, pp. 180–89.

Patinkin, Don. The Chicago Tradition, the Quantity Theory, and Friedman. *J. Money, Credit, Banking,* February 1969, *1*(1), pp. 46–70.

______ Money and Prices. **In** *Clower, R. W., ed.,* 1969, pp. 123–48.

______ Money and Wealth: A Review Article. *J. Econ. Lit.,* December 1969, *7*(4), pp. 1140–60.

Patman, Philip F., et al. Industrialized Building—A Comparative Analysis of European Experience. **In** *Industrialized Housing, JECP,* 1969, pp. 80–145.

Paton, W. A. Postscript on "Treasury" Shares. *Accounting Rev.,* April 1969, *44*(2), pp. 276–83.

Pattanaik, Prasanta K. and Sen, Amartya K. Necessary and Sufficient Conditions for Rational Choice under Majority Decision. *J. Econ. Theory,* August 1969, *1*(2), pp. 178–202.

Patten, Thomas H., Jr. Laboratory Training: Comment. *Ind. Relat.,* May 1969, *8*(3), pp. 286–89.

Paul, P.-E. Företagens Prognosbehov, en kommentar. (The Enterprise's Need of Forecasting. With English summary.) *Econ. Samfundets Tidskr.,* 1969, *22*(2), pp. 126–29.

Paul, William J., Jr.; Robertson, Keith B. and Herzberg, Frederick. Job Enrichment Pays Off. *Harvard Bus. Rev.,* March–April 1969, *47*(2), pp. 61–78.

Paulsen, Arnold. Payment Limitations: The Economic and Political Feasibility. *Amer. J. Agr. Econ.,* December 1969, *51*(5), pp. 1237–42.

Paulson, Wayne; Butler, Edgar W. and Pope, Hallowell. Community Power and Public Welfare. *Amer. J. Econ. Soc.,* January 1969, *28*(1), pp. 17–28.

Pauly, Mark V. Manpower Shortages in Local Government Employment: Discussion. *Amer. Econ. Rev.,* May 1969, *59*(2), pp. 565–67.

______ Mixed Public and Private Financing of Education: Reply. *Amer. Econ. Rev.,* March 1969, *59*(1), pp. 212–13.

______ **and Johnson, David B.** Excess Burden and the Voluntary Theory of Public Finance. *Economica, N.S.,* August 1969, *36*(143), pp. 269–76.

Paunio, J. J. Comments on the Papers by Goran Ohlin and André Marchal. **In** *Samuelson, P. A., ed.,* 1969, pp. 221–26.

Pavlov, P. and Tsaga, V. The Marginalist Treatment of the Law of Value under Socialism. *Prob. Econ.,* July 1969, *12*(3), pp. 3–22.

Payne, James P., Jr. Regulation of Public Utilities in Louisiana. **In** *Beard, T. R., ed.,* 1969, pp. 148–69.

Peacock, Alan T. Welfare Economics and Public Subsidies to the Arts. *Manchester Sch. Econ. Soc. Stud.,* December 1969, *37*(4), pp. 323–35.

______ **and Morss, Elliott R.** The Measurement of Fiscal Performance in Developing Countries. **In** *Peacock, A. T., ed.,* 1969, pp. 171–97.

______ **and Wiseman, Jack.** Principles of Educational Finance in Developed Countries. **In** *Blaug, M., ed.,* 1969, pp. 343–59.

Pearce, W. O. Functional Cost Analysis: A Tool of Bank Management. **In** *Jessup, P. F.,* 1969, pp. 219–23.

Pearse, P. H. Principles of Allocating Wildland Among Alternative Uses. *Can. J. Agr. Econ.,* February 1969, *17*(1), pp. 121–31.

Peaslee, Alexander L. Education's Role in Development. *Econ. Develop. Cult. Change,* April 1969, *17*(3), pp. 293–318.

Pechman, Joseph A. Statement. **In** *Economics of Aging: Toward a Full Share in Abundance, Pt. 1, SCH,* 1969, pp. 112–17.

______ Tax Policies for the 1970's. *Public Policy,* Fall 1969, *18*(1), pp. 75–93.

______**; Aaron, Henry J. and Taussig, Michael K.** Improving Social Security Benefits and Financing: Brookings Research Report 94. **In** *Economics of Aging: Toward a Full Share in Abundance, Pt. 1, SCH,* 1969, pp. 253–63.

______ **and Okner, Benjamin A.** Simulation of the Carter Commission Tax Proposals for the United States. *Nat. Tax J.,* March 1969, *22*(1), pp. 2–23.

Peck, John E. Financing State Expenditures in a Prospering Economy. *Indiana Bus. Rev.,* July/August 1969, *44,* pp. 7–15.

Pedone, Antonio. The Ricardian Tax Incidence Analysis in the Light of Optimum Growth Theory. *Econ. Int.,* February 1969, *22*(1), pp. 63–83.

Peet, J. Richard. The Spatial Expansion of Commercial Agriculture in the Nineteenth Century: A von Thünen Interpretation. *Econ. Geogr.,* October 1969, *45*(4), pp. 283–301.

Peeters, Frans. De B.T.W. in de onderneming. (The Value Added Tax and the Enterprise. With English summary.) *Econ. Soc. Tijdschr.,* August 1969, *23*(4), pp. 391–403.

Peitchinis, S. G. Occupational Wage Differentials in Canada 1939–1965. *Australian Econ. Pap.,* June 1969, *8*(12), pp. 20–40.

Pejovich, Svetozar. The Firm, Monetary Policy and

Property Rights in a Planned Economy. *Western Econ. J.*, September 1969, *7*(3), pp. 193–200.

——— Liberman's Reforms and Property Rights in the Soviet Union. *J. Law Econ.*, April 1969, *12*(1), pp. 155–62.

Pekonen, Kari. Investoinnit—työttömyys—taloudellinen kasvu. (Investment—Unemployment—Economic Growth. With English summary.) *Kansant. Aikak.*, 1969, *65*(3), pp. 215–19.

——— **and Kostiainen, Seppo.** Investointivaihtoehtojen optimaalinen valinta. (The Optimal Choice of Investment Projects. With English summary.) *Kansant. Aikak.*, 1969, *65*(3), pp. 191–205.

Pelikán, Pavel. Language as a Limiting Factor for Centralization. *Amer. Econ. Rev.*, Part I, September 1969, *59*(4), pp. 625–31.

Pellegrini, Giorgio. Toll Motorways. *Rev. Econ. Cond. Italy*, March 1969, *23*(2), pp. 95–105.

Pelleri, Paolo. Le Borse estere nel 1968. (Foreign Stock Exchanges in 1968. With English summary.) *Bancaria*, February 1969, *25*(2), pp. 178–202.

——— Le Borse italiane nel 1968. (The Italian Stock Exchanges in 1968. With English summary.) *Bancaria*, January 1969, *25*(1), pp. 25–64.

Peltzman, Sam. The Banking Structure and the Transmission of Monetary Policy. *J. Finance*, June 1969, *24*(3), pp. 387–411.

——— Capital Investment in Commercial Banking. **In** *Federal Reserve Bank of Chicago (I)*, 1969, pp. 67–98.

——— Issues in Vertical Integration Policy. **In** *Weston, J. F. and Peltzman, S., eds.*, 1969, pp. 167–76.

——— Profit Data and Public Policy. **In** *Weston, J. F. and Peltzman, S., eds.*, 1969, pp. 128–36.

——— The Structure of the Money-Expenditures Relationship. *Amer. Econ. Rev.*, March 1969, *59*(1), pp. 129–37.

——— **and Weston, J. Fred.** Issues in Public Policy Toward Mergers. **In** *Weston, J. F. and Peltzman, S., eds.*, 1969, pp. 3–9.

——— **and Weston, J. Fred.** Unresolved Issues and an Agenda for Future Research. **In** *Weston, J. F. and Peltzman, S., eds.*, 1969, pp. 227–31.

Pencavel, John H. Interindustry Variations in Voluntary Labor Mobility: Comment. *Ind. Lab. Relat. Rev.*, October 1969, *23*(1), pp. 78–83.

——— **and Ashenfelter, Orley.** American Trade Union Growth: 1900–1960. *Quart. J. Econ.*, August 1969, *83*(3), pp. 434–48.

Penchansky, R. and Kaufman, G. M. Simulation of Union Health and Welfare Funds. **In** *Siegel, A. J., ed.*, 1969, pp. 121–75.

Penner, R. G.; Baxter, Nevins D. and Howrey, E. Philip. Unemployment and Cost-Benefit Analysis. *Public Finance*, 1969, *24*(1), pp. 80–88.

Pennington, Allan L. and Peterson, Robert A. Interest Patterns and Product Preferences: An Exploratory Analysis. *J. Marketing Res.*, August 1969, *6*(3), pp. 284–90.

Pennock, J. Roland. Agricultural Subsidies in Britain and America. **In** *Rose, R., ed.*, 1969, pp. 199–220.

Penrose, Edith T. OPEC and the Changing Structure of the International Petroleum Industry. **In** *Governmental Intervention in the Market Mechanism, Pt. 1, SCH*, 1969, pp. 429–47.

——— Statement. **In** *Governmental Intervention in the Market Mechanism, Pt. 1, SCH*, 1969, pp. 156–66.

Pepelasis, A. Underemployment in Agriculture: A Comment. *Econ. Develop. Cult. Change*, January 1969, *17*(2), pp. 267–72.

Pepper, H. W. T. Poll Taxes, Payroll Taxation, and Social Security (Part I). *Bull. Int. Fiscal Doc.*, January 1969, *23*(1), pp. 4–26.

——— Poll Taxes, Payroll Taxation, and Social Security (Part II). *Bull. Int. Fiscal Doc.*, February 1969, *23*(2), pp. 55–65.

——— **and Huiskamp, J. C. L.** Guilt and Innocence of Taxpayers—Including Some Small Notes on Tax Collection Practices in Certain Countries. *Bull. Int. Fiscal Doc.*, November 1969, *23*(11), pp. 516–20.

Perera, S. E. G. Some Labour Problems of the National Textile Corporation of Ceylon. *Int. Lab. Rev.*, February 1969, *99*(2), pp. 185–207.

Perkins, Dwight H. Market Control and Command in Communist China: The Early Years. **In** *Prybyla, J. S., ed.*, 1969, pp. 359–67.

Perkins, Frederick A. Showing a Retailer that Meat Sanitation Pays—An Economic Approach. *Amer. J. Agr. Econ.*, December 1969, *51*(5), pp. 1259–62.

Perkins, Walter M. How the Census Will Be Evaluated. *Mon. Lab. Rev.*, December 1969, *92*(12), pp. 55–60.

Perkinson, Leon B. General Hospital Facilities in Michigan, 1965. *Amer. J. Agr. Econ.*, December 1969, *51*(5), pp. 1548–52.

Perlamutrov, V. L.; Sokolovskii, L. Kh. and Bunich, P. G. An Inventory Model in Physical and Monetary Terms. *Matekon*, Fall 1969, *6*(1), pp. 30–43.

Perlberg, Arye and Shaal, Gil. An Interdisciplinary Approach to Manpower Planning and Development. *Int. Lab. Rev.*, April 1969, *99*(4), pp. 363–80.

Perlman, David L. Public Employees: An Emerging Force. **In** *Walsh, R. E., ed.*, 1969, pp. 20–27.

Perloff, Harvey S. A Framework for Dealing with the Urban Environment: Introductory Statement. **In** *Perloff, H. S., ed.*, 1969, pp. 3–25.

——— Statement. **In** *Panel on Science and Technology: Science and Technology and the Cities, HCH*, 1969, pp. 149–55.

Perrella, Vera C. Employment of High School Graduates and Dropouts. *Mon. Lab. Rev.*, June 1969, *92*(6), pp. 36–43.

Perrin, Guy. Reflections on Fifty Years of Social Security. *Int. Lab. Rev.*, March 1969, *99*(3), pp. 249–92.

Perrin, J. R. Financial Management. **In** *Kempner, T., ed.*, 1969, pp. 75–83.

——— Management Accounting. **In** *Kempner, T., ed.*, 1969, pp. 21–32.

Perry, George L. Statement. **In** *The 1969 Economic Report of the President, Pt. 2, JECH*, 1969, pp. 495–97.

——— Wages and the Guideposts: Reply. *Amer. Econ. Rev.*, June 1969, *59*(3), pp. 365–70.

Perry, Michael and Hamm, B. Curtis. Canonical Analysis of Relations between Socioeconomic Risk and Personal Influence in Purchase Decisions. *J. Marketing Res.*, August 1969, *6*(3), pp. 351–54.

——— **and Shuchman, Abe.** Self-Confidence and

Persuasibility in Marketing: A Reappraisal. *J. Marketing Res.,* May 1969, *6*(2), pp. 146–54.

Persky, Joseph J. and Kain, John F. Alternatives to the Gilded Ghetto. **In** *Kain, J. F., ed.,* 1969, pp. 167–74.

Pesek, B. P. and Saving, Thomas R. The Demand for Money: Some Post-Keynesian Confusions. **In** *Clower, R. W., ed.,* 1969, pp. 247–53.

Pessemier, E. A.; Tigert, D. J. and Bass, Frank M. A Taxonomy of Magazine Readership Applied to Problems in Marketing Strategy and Media Selection. *J. Bus.,* July 1969, *42*(3), pp. 337–63.

Peston, M. H. Aspects of the Pricing Policy of the Nationalised Industries. **In** *Margolis, J. and Guitton, H., eds.,* 1969, pp. 298–309.

Peterson, R. D. and Leister, D. V. Market Structure-Conduct Relations: Some Evidence from Biomedical Electronic Firms. *Univ. Wash. Bus. Rev.,* Summer 1969, *28*(4), pp. 49–65.

Peterson, Robert A. and Pennington, Allan L. Interest Patterns and Product Preferences: An Exploratory Analysis. *J. Marketing Res.,* August 1969, *6*(3), pp. 284–90.

Peterson, Robin T. Experimental Analysis of Theory of Promotion at Point of Consumption. *J. Marketing Res.,* August 1969, *6*(3), pp. 347–50.

Peterson, Russell K. The Role and Responsibility of Business in the Growth of American Society. **In** *Ozbekhan, H. and Talbert, G. E., eds.,* 1969, pp. 70–77.

Peterson, Wallace. Planning and the Market Economy. *J. Econ. Issues,* March 1969, *3*(1), pp. 126–43.

Peterson, Willis L. The Allocation of Research, Teaching, and Extension Personnel in U.S. Colleges of Agriculture. *Amer. J. Agr. Econ.,* February 1969, *51*(1), pp. 41–56.

Petillon, Jack. Budgettering en direct costing. (Budgeting and Direct Costing. With English summary.) *Econ. Soc. Tijdschr.,* April 1969, *23*(2), pp. 129–42.

Petri, Enrico. Use of Capitalized Cost in Repeated Replacement Problems. *Manage. Account.,* September 1969, *51*(3), pp. 49–53, 56.

Petrof, John V. Negro Entrepreneurship: Myth or Reality? *Marquette Bus. Rev.,* Spring 1969, *13*(1), pp. 34–37.

Petrosian, K. and Konovalova, N. Problems of Intensifying the Stimulating Role of Payments for Funds. *Prob. Econ.,* June 1969, *12*(2), pp. 25–47.

Petrov, Tsvetan and Kalinov, Stefan. The Economic Mechanism of the New System in 1969 and 1970. *Eastern Europ. Econ.,* Fall 1969, *8*(1), pp. 72–89.

Petry, Horst. Technischer Fortschritt, Integration, internationale Wettbewerbsfähigkeit und Unternehmensgrösse. (With English summary.) *Jahr. Nationalökon. Statist.,* August 1969, *183*(3–4), pp. 271–99.

Pettway, Richard H. and Robinson, Roland I. Policies for Optimum Bank Capital: Summary. **In** *Jessup, P. F.,* 1969, pp. 183–86.

Pfaff, Martin. Complex Organizational Processes. **In** *Naylor, T. H., ed.,* 1969, pp. 393–410.

Phatak, Arvind. American Managers' Philosophies: Authoritarian or Permissive? *Univ. Wash. Bus. Rev.,* Winter 1969, *28*(2), pp. 33–39.

Phelps, Charlotte D. Real and Monetary Determinants of State and Local Highway Investment, 1951–66. *Amer. Econ. Rev.,* Part I, September 1969, *59*(4), pp. 507–21.

Phelps, Edmund S. The New Microeconomics in Inflation and Employment Theory. *Amer. Econ. Rev.,* May 1969, *59*(2), pp. 147–60.

_____ A Note on Short-Run Employment and Real Wage Rate under Competitive Commodity Markets. *Int. Econ. Rev.,* June 1969, *10*(2), pp. 220–32.

_____ **and Shell, Karl.** Public Debt, Taxation, and Capital Intensiveness. *J. Econ. Theory,* October 1969, *1*(3), pp. 330–46.

Philips, G. Edward. Income Concepts. **In** *Gaa, C. J.,* 1969, pp. 106–25.

Phillips, Almarin. A Conceptual Optimal Banking Structure for the United States: Discussion. **In** *Federal Reserve Bank of Chicago (II),* 1969, pp. 35–40.

Phillips, Joseph D. Economic Effects of the Cold War. **In** *Horowitz, D., ed.,* 1969, pp. 173–203.

Phillips, Keith E. The Short-Run Stability of Velocity and the Autonomous Spending Multiplier, 1946–1962. *J. Polit. Econ.,* May/June 1969, *77*(3), pp. 418–29.

Phillips, Llad; Votey, Harold L., Jr. and Maxwell, Darold E. A Synthesis of the Economic and Demographic Models of Fertility: An Econometric Test. *Rev. Econ. Statist.,* August 1969, *51*(3), pp. 298–308.

Phillips, M. J. A Survey of Sampling Procedures for Continuous Production. *J. Roy. Statist. Soc.,* Part 2, 1969, *132,* pp. 205–28.

Phillips, Richard. Inducing Economic Development in Less Developed Countries: Discussion. *Amer. J. Agr. Econ.,* December 1969, *51*(5), pp. 1424–26.

Philpot, B. P.; Woods, M. J. and McKenzie, C. J. Price Formation in the Raw Wool Market. *Econ. Rec.,* September 1969, *45*(111), pp. 386–98.

Phipps, Anthony J. The Roles of Labour Productivity and Demand in the Pricing Process: An Inter-Industry Study Using Time-Series Data. *Bull. Oxford Univ. Inst. Econ. Statist.,* November 1969, *31*(4), pp. 285–301.

Phlips, Louis. Business Pricing Policies and Inflation—Some Evidence from E.E.C. Countries. *J. Ind. Econ.,* November 1969, *18*(1), pp. 1–14.

Pianese, Luigi. Local Finance. *Rev. Econ. Cond. Italy,* January 1969, *23*(1), pp. 28–50.

Pickard, Jerome P. Statement. **In** *Population Trends, Pt. 1, HCH,* 1969, pp. 656–68.

Pickering, J. F. Would Prices Rise without R.P.M.? *Oxford Econ. Pap.,* July 1969, *21*(2), pp. 248–67.

Pidot, George B., Jr. A Principal Components Analysis of the Determinants of Local Government Fiscal Patterns. *Rev. Econ. Statist.,* May 1969, *51* (2), pp. 176–88.

Pieraccini, Luciano. Su di una interpretazione alternativa del metodo dei minimi quadrati a due stadi. (With English summary.) *Statistica,* October-December 1969, *29*(4), pp. 786–802.

Pierce, James L. Commercial Bank Liquidity. **In** *Jessup, P. F.,* 1969, pp. 16–27.

_____ Some Rules for the Conduct of Monetary Policy. **In** *Federal Reserve Bank of Boston,* 1969, pp. 133–44.

Pifer, Howard W. A Nonlinear, Maximum Likelihood Estimate of the Liquidity Trap. *Econometrica,* April 1969, *37*(2), pp. 324–32.

Piganiol, Pierre. Introduction: Futurology and Prospective Study. *Int. Soc. Sci. J.,* 1969, *21*(4), pp. 515–25.

Pigou, A. C. The Classical Stationary State. **In** *Williams, H. R. and Huffnagle, J. D., eds.,* 1969, pp. 327–34.

——— Maintaining Capital Intact. **In** *Parker, R. H. and Harcourt, G. C., eds.,* 1969, pp. 123–26.

——— Money, a Veil? **In** *Clower, R. W., ed.,* 1969, pp. 30–36.

Pike, Eugene W. A Note on "Learning Curves." *J. Amer. Statist. Assoc.,* December 1969, *64*(328), pp. 1276–77.

Pike, John R. and Gentry, James A. Rates of Return on Common Stock Portfolios of Life Insurance Companies. *J. Risk Ins.,* December 1969, *36*(5), pp. 545–52.

Pikkemaat, G. F. Over de grenzen van de beschrijvende statistiek. (On the Scope of Descriptive Statistics. With English summary.) *De Economist,* May/June 1969, *117*(3), pp. 258–75.

Pillai, P. Purushothaman. An Inter-District, Inter-Crop Comparison of Growth Rates in Agriculture in Kerala. *Asian Econ. Rev.,* May 1969, *11*(3), pp. 249–59.

Pilot, Michael J. and Russell, Joe L. Seasonality in Construction: A Continuing Problem. *Mon. Lab. Rev.,* December 1969, *92*(12), pp. 3–8.

Pincock, M. Glade. Assessing Impacts of Declining Water Quality on Gross Value Output of Agriculture, A Case Study. *Water Resources Res.,* February 1969, *5*(1), pp. 1–12.

Piňdák, F. Czechoslovakia and COMECON. *De Economist,* September/October 1969, *117*(5), pp. 516–42.

Pinder, J. Advanced Technology: Britain and the EEC. **In** *van Meerhaeghe, M. A. G., ed.,* 1969, pp. 58–76.

Pine, Wilfred H. and Sirohi, Amar S. Irrigation with Restraints on Land and Water Resources. *Land Econ.,* May 1969, *45*(2), pp. 285–87.

Pintilie, Constanti. Folosirea metodelor moderne de conducere în întreprinderile industriale din România. (Use of Up-to-Date Methods in Industrial Enterprises of Romania. With English summary.) *Stud. Cercet. Econ.,* 1969, *3,* pp. 101–10.

——— **and Vraca, Alexandru.** Un concept nou: conducerea întegrată a întreprinderilor. (A New Conception: Integrated Management of Enterprises. With English summary.) *Stud. Cercet. Econ.,* 1969, *1-2,* pp. 65–75.

Pinto, Aníbal. Economic Structure, Productivity and Wages in Latin America. **In** *Smith, A. D., ed.,* 1969, pp. 256–68.

Pipping, Hugo E. J. V. Tallqvist 1862–1960, en minnesteckning. (J. V. Tallqvist 1862–1960, in Memoriam. With English summary.) *Econ. Samfundets Tidskr.,* 1969, *22*(4), pp. 241–89.

Pirasteh, Ross. Prevent Blunders in Supply and Distribution. *Harvard Bus. Rev.,* March–April 1969, *47*(2), pp. 113–27.

Pirenne, Henri. The Place of the Netherlands in the Economic History of Mediaeval Europe. **In** *Scoville, W. C. and La Force, J. C., eds., Vol. I,* 1969, pp. 19–40.

Pirnia, Hossein. Scientific Thought and National Independence. *Tahq. Eq.,* November 1969, *6* (15&16), pp. 3–20.

Pirozynski, Zbigniew and Kucharski, Mieczyslaw. Social Insurance and Economic Incentives. *Public Finance,* 1969, *24*(2), pp. 238–55.

Pisciotta, John. J. B. Clark's Theory of Economic Growth. *Amer. Econ.,* Spring 1969, *13*(1), pp. 4–13.

Pitchford, J. D. A Note on International Trade and Factor Mobility. *Econ. Rec.,* December 1969, *45* (112), pp. 616–17.

Piven, Frances Fox and Cloward, Richard A. Desegregated Housing: Who Pays for the Reformers' Ideal? **In** *Kain, J. F., ed.,* 1969, pp. 175–83.

Plata-Castilla, Alfonso. International Labour Standards and Colombian Legislation. *Int. Lab. Rev.,* February 1969, *99*(2), pp. 137–58.

Plattner, Robert H. Fund Administration and Dividend Policy. *Quart. Rev. Econ. Bus.,* Summer 1969, *9*(2), pp. 21–29.

Plaunt, Darrel. Economic Guidelines for Mobilizing Labour and Management in Canadian Agriculture. *Can. J. Agr. Econ.,* November 1969, *17*(3), pp. 20–33.

du Plessis, T. A. and Strydom, P. D. F. Future Growth Patterns in South Africa—A Comment. *S. Afr. J. Econ.,* September 1969, *37*(3), pp. 252–59.

Plessner, Yakir; Hall, Harry H. and Heady, Earl O. Quadratic Programming Solution of Competitive Equilibrium for U.S. Agriculture: Reply. *Amer. J. Agr. Econ.,* May 1969, *51*(2), pp. 483–84.

Pleva, Jan. Foreign Trade and the New System of Management. **In** *Grub, P. D. and Holbik, K.,* 1969, pp. 187–93.

Plotkin, Irving H. Rates of Return in the Property and Liability Insurance Industry: A Comparative Analysis. *J. Risk Ins.,* June 1969, *36*(2), pp. 173–200.

Pochkin, P. and Al'ter, L. The First Soviet Model of Economic Growth. *Prob. Econ.,* January 1969, *11* (9), pp. 3–13.

Pogosov, I. Questions of the Economic Effectiveness in Concentrating Industrial Production. **In** *Economic Concentration, Pt. 7A, SCH,* 1969, pp. 4395–4404.

Pogue, Thomas F. and Soldofsky, Robert M. What's in a Bond Rating? *J. Financial Quant. Anal.,* June 1969, *4*(2), pp. 201–28.

Pohorille, M. Purchasing Contracts and Price Policy as Means of Planning Agricultural Production. **In** *Papi, U. and Nunn, C., eds.,* 1969, pp. 430–41.

Pokrovski, A. Socialist Planning and Capitalist Programming: An Analytical Comparison of the Procedures. **In** *Margolis, J. and Guitton, H., eds.,* 1969, pp. 475–84.

Polakoff, Murray E. and Rangarajan, C. A Note on a "Keynesian" Model of Aggregate Demand: Reply. *J. Finance,* March 1969, *24*(1), pp. 104–05.

Polanyi, Michael. The Determinants of Social Action. **In** *[von Hayek, Friedrich A.],* 1969, pp. 165–79.

Polasek, M. and Barattieri, V. U. S. Gold Policy and the Gold Exchange Standard. *Econ. Rec.,* March 1969, *45*(109), pp. 48–68.

Politi, Janet and Beesley, M. E. A Study of the Profits of Bus Companies, 1960–1966. *Economica, N.S.,* May 1969, *36*(142), pp. 151–71.

Pollak, Robert A. Conditional Demand Functions and Consumption Theory. *Quart. J. Econ.,* February 1969, *83*(1), pp. 60–78.

______ **and Wales, Terrence J.** Estimation of the Linear Expenditure System. *Econometrica,* October 1969, *37*(4), pp. 611–28.

Pollard, J. H. Continuous-time and Discrete-time Models of Population Growth. *J. Roy. Statist. Soc.,* Part 1, 1969, *132,* pp. 80–88.

Pollay, Richard W. Consumer Protection and Advertising. *Ohio State U. Bull. Bus. Res.,* July 1969, *44*(7), pp. 4–8.

______ **and Churchill, Geoffrey.** A Simple Method for Estimating Consumer Acceptance. *Miss. Val. J. Bus. Econ.,* Spring 1969, *4*(2), pp. 50–56.

______ **and Swinth, Robert L.** A Behavioral Simulation of the Agency-Client Relationship. *J. Marketing Res.,* May 1969, *6*(2), pp. 198–202.

Polli, Rolando and Cook, Victor. Validity of the Product Life Cycle. *J. Bus.,* October 1969, *42*(4), pp. 385–400.

Polopolus, Leo. On Institutional Obsolescense and Innovation. *Amer. J. Agr. Econ.,* December 1969, *51*(5), pp. 1624–28.

Polsby, Nelson W. Policy Analysis and Congress. **In** *The Analysis and Evaluation of Public Expenditures: The PPB System, Vol. 3, JECP,* 1969, pp. 943–52.

Pomalaza, José and Heraud, Jorge. An Educational Television and Communications System for Latin America. **In** *Hilton, R., ed.,* 1969, pp. 381–400.

Ponko, Vincent, Jr. The Colonial Office and British Business before World War I: A Case Study. *Bus. Hist. Rev.,* Spring 1969, *43*(1), pp. 39–58.

Poole, Kenyon E. Three Aspects of Stable Growth Policy. *Rivista Int. Sci. Econ. Com.,* December 1969, *16*(12), pp. 1174–96.

Pope, Hallowell; Paulson, Wayne and Butler, Edgar W. Community Power and Public Welfare. *Amer. J. Econ. Soc.,* January 1969, *28*(1), pp. 17–28.

Popescu, S. Falcan. Folosirea analizei factoriale în cercetarea fenomenelor în profil teritorial. (Use of Factorial Analysis in the Investigation of Phenomena in a Territorial Profile. With English summary.) *Stud. Cercet. Econ.,* 1969, *4,* pp. 159–63.

Popkin, Joel. Price Changes in the First Quarter of 1969 in Perspective. *Mon. Lab. Rev.,* July 1969, *92*(7), pp. 26–30.

Popkin, William D. Administration of a Negative Income Tax. *Yale Law J.,* January 1969, *78*(3), pp. 388–431.

Popov, G. and Lisitsyn, V. On Administrative Cadres. *Prob. Econ.,* April 1969, *11*(12), pp. 3–10.

Popper, Karl R. A Pluralist Approach to the Philosophy of History. **In** *[von Hayek, Friedrich A.],* 1969, pp. 181–200.

della Porta, Glauco. Planning and Growth under a Mixed Economy: The Italian Experience. **In** *Prybyla, J. S., ed.,* 1969, pp. 179–92.

Porter, Arthur T. Africa. **In** *Bereday, G. Z. F., ed.,* 1969, pp. 225–43.

Porter, Kenneth W. Negro Labor in the Western Cattle Industry, 1866–1900. *Labor Hist.,* Summer 1969, *10*(3), pp. 346–74.

Porter, Patrick G. Origins of the American Tobacco Company. *Bus. Hist. Rev.,* Spring 1969, *43*(1), pp. 59–76.

______ **and Livesay, Harold C.** Vertical Integration in American Manufacturing, 1899–1948. *J. Econ. Hist.,* September 1969, *29*(3), pp. 494–500.

Porter, R. C. Who Destabilizes Primary Product Prices? *Indian Econ. J.,* April–June 1969, *16*(4–5), pp. 389–418.

Porter, Richard L. Report on a Questionnaire Concerning the Present State of an Economics Encyclicals Course. *Rev. Soc. Econ.,* March 1969, *27*(1), pp. 41–44.

Porter, W. Thomas. Professional Education for Management. *Univ. Wash. Bus. Rev.,* Summer 1969, *28*(4), pp. 44–48.

Portes, Richard D. The Enterprise under Central Planning. *Rev. Econ. Stud.,* April 1969, *36*(106), pp. 197–212.

______ The Rate of Economic Growth in Hungary: Comment. **In** *Bronfenbrenner, M., ed.,* 1969, pp. 328–31.

Post, J. J. and Verdoorn, P. J. Comparison of the Prewar and Postwar Business Cycles in the Netherlands: An Experiment in Econometrics. **In** *Bronfenbrenner, M., ed.,* 1969, pp. 436–66.

Postan, Michael M. The Fifteenth Century. **In** *Scoville, W. C. and La Force, J. C., eds., Vol. I,* 1969, pp. 130–38.

Posthumus, N. W. The Tulip Mania in Holland in the Years 1636 and 1637. **In** *Scoville, W. C. and La Force, J. C., eds., Vol. II,* 1969, pp. 138–49.

Potter, Neal and Fisher, Joseph L. Natural Resource Adequacy for the United States and the World. **In** *Hauser, P. M., ed.,* 1969, pp. 106–38.

Potter, Robert G., Jr. Estimating Births Averted in a Family Planning Program. **In** *Behrman, S. J.; Corsa, L., Jr. and Freedman, R., eds.,* 1969, pp. 413–34.

Potts, Georgena R. The Decennial Census: Its Purpose and Its Uses. *Mon. Lab. Rev.,* December 1969, *92*(12), pp. 35–38.

Poulson, Barry W. Estimates of the Value of Manufacturing Output in the Early Nineteenth Century. *J. Econ. Hist.,* September 1969, *29*(3), pp. 521–25.

Powell, Alan. Aitken Estimators as a Tool in Allocating Predetermined Aggregates. *J. Amer. Statist. Assoc.,* September 1969, *64*(327), pp. 913–22.

Powell, G. Bingham, Jr.; Prewitt, Kenneth and Nie, Norman H. Social Structure and Political Participation: Developmental Relationships, Part I. *Amer. Polit. Sci. Rev.,* June 1969, *63*(2), pp. 361–78.

Powell, R. A. and Hardaker, J. B. Recent Developments in Farm Planning: 3: Sub-optimal Programming Methods for Practical Farm Planning. *Rev. Marketing Agr. Econ.,* June 1969, *37*(2), pp. 121–29.

Powell, Walter H. Employing Negroes in Urban Labor Markets. **In** *Kain, J. F., ed.,* 1969, pp. 74–77.

Powelson, John P. Economic Attitudes in Latin America and the United States. **In** *Baier, K. and Rescher, N., eds.,* 1969, pp. 233–65.

Power, Eileen E. English Craft Guilds in the Middle

Ages. In *Scoville, W. C. and La Force, J. C., eds., Vol. I,* 1969, pp. 76–80.

Power, John H. Industrialization in Pakistan: A Case of Frustrated Take-off? In *Khan, A. R., ed.,* 1969, pp. 3–21.

Powers, John Anthony. Branch Versus Unit Banking: Bank Output and Cost Economies. *Southern Econ. J.,* October 1969, *36*(2), pp. 153–64.

Prakasa Rao, M. S. and Ramamoorthy, B. Terminalization Approach to Pre-University Education. In *Pandit, H. N., ed.,* 1969, pp. 356–74.

Prakash, Anand. The Purpose and Future Direction of Industrial Disputes Legislation in India. In *Johri, C. K., ed.,* 1969, pp. 172–88.

Prakash, Prem. Relationship Between Size and Productivity in Selected Indian Industries. *Asian Econ. Rev.,* May 1969, *11*(3), pp. 237–48.

Prakash, Ved. A Suggested Approach to Municipal Investment Planning. *Land Econ.,* August 1969, *45*(3), pp. 350–58.

Prasad, K. A Note on the Transactions Demand for Cash. *Indian Econ. J.,* April–June 1969, *16*(4–5), pp. 561–66.

Pratten, C. F. Economies of Scale. In *Hugh-Jones, E. M., ed.,* 1969, pp. 89–98.

Prebisch, Raul. Statement. In *Linking Reserve Creation and Development Assistance, JECH,* 1969, pp. 30–31.

Prentice, P. I. The Case for Taxing Location Values: A Memorandum for a Metropolis Considering Property Tax Reform. *Amer. J. Econ. Soc.,* April 1969, *28*(2), pp. 145–58.

Prescott, James R. and Lewis, William C. State and Municipal Locational Incentives: A Discriminant Analysis. *Nat. Tax J.,* September 1969, *22*(3), pp. 399–407.

Press, S. James. The *t*-Ratio Distribution. *J. Amer. Statist. Assoc.,* March 1969, *64*(325), pp. 242–52.

Prest, Alan R. Comments on "Social Insurance in a Growing Economy: A Proposal for Radical Reform." *Nat. Tax J.,* December 1969, *22*(4), pp. 554–56.

——— Compulsory Lending Schemes. *Int. Monet. Fund Staff Pap.,* March 1969, *16*(1), pp. 27–52.

——— The Finances of Small Countries. In *Stewart, I. G., ed.,* 1969, pp. 138–54.

——— Replacement Cost Depreciation. In *Parker, R. H. and Harcourt, G. C., eds.,* 1969, pp. 290–309.

Prest, Wilfred. Federalism and Education. In *Preston, R., ed.,* 1969, pp. 292–315.

Preston, Esme. Direct and Indirect Relations of Australian Industries with Final Demand Sectors. *Econ. Rec.,* March 1969, *45*(109), pp. 84–91.

——— Growth and Investment in the Market Economies. *Econ. Rec.,* December 1969, *45*(112), pp. 544–62.

——— Some Structural Comparisons: Australia and Neighbour Economies. *Australian Econ. Pap.,* December 1969, *8*(13), pp. 219–31.

Preston, Lee E. and Collins, Norman R. Industry Structure and Price-Cost Margins. In *Weston, J. F. and Peltzman, S., eds.,* 1969, pp. 81–109.

——— Price-Cost Margins and Industry Structure. *Rev. Econ. Statist.,* August 1969, *51*(3), pp. 271–86.

Preston, R. S. and Klein, Lawrence R. Stochastic Nonlinear Models. *Econometrica,* January 1969, *37*(1), pp. 95–106.

Prestwich, Michael. Edward I's Monetary Policies and Their Consequences. *Econ. Hist. Rev.,* December 1969, *22*(3), pp. 406–16.

Prewitt, Kenneth; Nie, Norman H. and Powell, G. Bingham, Jr. Social Structure and Political Participation: Developmental Relationships, Part I. *Amer. Polit. Sci. Rev.,* June 1969, *63*(2), pp. 361–78.

Price, Derek J. de The Structures of Publication in Science and Technology. In *Gruber, W. H. and Marquis, D. G., eds.,* 1969, pp. 91–104.

Price, Don K. The Structure of Policy. In *Crawford, E. T. and Biderman, A. D., eds.,* 1969, pp. 61–68.

Price, Langford Lovell. *'West Barbary'; or Notes on the System of Work and Wages in Cornish Mines.* In *Burt, R., ed.,* 1969, pp. 111–206.

Price, Ralph B. Ideology and Indian Planning. In *Prybyla, J. S., ed.,* 1969, pp. 96–111.

Price, William J.; Ashley, William G. and Martino, Joseph P. Science-Technology Coupling: Experience of the Air Force Office of Scientific Research. In *Gruber, W. H. and Marquis, D. G., eds.,* 1969, pp. 117–36.

Prichard, M. F. Lloyd. Economic History in New Zealand Universities. *Australian Econ. Hist. Rev.,* March 1969, *9*(1), pp. 3–8.

Prickett, James R. Some Aspects of the Communist Controversy in the CIO. *Sci. Soc.,* Summer-Fall 1969, *33*(3), pp. 299–321.

Priebe, H. The Modern Family Farm and Its Problems: With Particular Reference to the Federal German Republic. In *Papi, U. and Nunn, C., eds.,* 1969, pp. 251–64.

Primack, Martin L. Farm Fencing in the Nineteenth Century. *J. Econ. Hist.,* June 1969, *29*(2), pp. 287–91.

Pritchard, Leland J. The Economics of the Commercial Bank. Savings-Investment Process in the United States. *Rivista Int. Sci. Econ. Com.,* July 1969, *16*(7), pp. 664–87.

Pritchard, Norris T. A Framework for Analysis of Agricultural Marketing Systems in Developing Countries. *Agr. Econ. Res.,* July 1969, *21*(3), pp. 78–85.

——— Toward a Concrete Concept of Effective Competition: Comment. *Amer. J. Agr. Econ.,* May 1969, *51*(2), pp. 476–78.

Pritzker, Leon and Waksberg, Joseph. Changes in Census Methods. *J. Amer. Statist. Assoc.,* December 1969, *64*(328), pp. 1141–49.

Probst, A. Optimal Dimensions of an Enterprise and Regional Factors. In *Economic Concentration, Pt. 7A, SCH,* 1969, pp. 4404–12.

Projector, Dorothy S. Should the Payroll Tax Finance Higher Benefits under OASDI? A Review of the Issues. *J. Human Res.,* Winter 1969, *4*(1), pp. 60–75.

Pronk, J. P. and Schreuel, E. J. Some Reflections on the Effectiveness of Project Versus Plan Aid. In *[Tinbergen, J.],* 1969, pp. 283–307.

Protopopescu, V. V. Organizarea şi raţionalizarea muncii de administraţie în intreprinderi şi organizaţii economice. (Organizing and Rationalizing Administrative Work in Economic

Organizations and Enterprises. With English summary.) *Stud. Cercet. Econ.*, 1969, *4*, pp. 71–83.

Pruden, Henry O. The Outside Salesman: Interorganizational Link. *Calif. Manage. Rev.*, Winter 1969, *12*(2), pp. 57–66.

Prybyla, Jan S. Albania: Dependent Command. **In** *Prybyla, J. S., ed.*, 1969, pp. 284–92.

______ Communist China's Economic System, 1961-66. **In** *Prybyla, J. S., ed.*, 1969, pp. 368–83.

______ The Convergence of Market-Oriented and Command-Oriented Systems: A Critical Estimate. **In** *Prybyla, J. S., ed.*, 1969, pp. 467–76.

______ The Convergence of Western and Communist Economic Systems: A Critical Estimate. **In** *Bornstein, M., ed.*, 1969, pp. 442–52.

______ The Development of Economic Thought and Policy in Communist China. **In** *Prybyla, J. S., ed.*, 1969, pp. 350–58.

______ The Economic Cost of the Cultural Revolution. **In** *Prybyla, J. S., ed.*, 1969, pp. 393–411.

______ Meaning and Classification of Economic Systems: An Outline. **In** *Prybyla, J. S., ed.*, 1969, pp. 9–18.

______ Soviet Command: From Libermanism to Liberalism? **In** *Prybyla, J. S., ed.*, 1969, pp. 273–83.

Pshelyaskovskiy, V. I. Elements of the Theory of Growth in Lenin's Plan for the Electrification of Russia (On the 50th Anniversary of the GOELRO Plan). *Matekon*, Fall 1969, *6*(1), pp. 98–116.

Puckett, Elbridge S. and Lesieur, Frederick G. The Scanlon Plan: Past, Present and Future. **In** *Somers, G. G., ed. (II)*, 1969, pp. 71–80.

Puffer, Frank W. and Moody, Harold T. A Gross Regional Product Approach to Regional Model-Building. *Western Econ. J.*, December 1969, *7*(4), pp. 391–402.

Pugh, Derek. Organization Theory. **In** *Kempner, T., ed.*, 1969, pp. 98–103.

Puiu, Al. and Albu, Al. Comerţul exterior şi creşterea economică. (Foreign Trade and Economic Growth. With English summary.) *Stud. Cercet. Econ.*, 1969, *3*, pp. 199–211.

Pulkkinen, Kyösti. Arkisto yrityksen tiedonvälityksessä. (Records Storage as a Part of the Communication of the Enterprise. With English summary.) *Liiketaloudellinen Aikak.*, 1969, *18*(3), pp. 541–49.

______ Asiakaspiirin vaikutus markkinointitoimen hajautukseen. (Effect of the Customers in the Decentralization of the Marketing Objective. With English summary.) *Liiketaloudellinen Aikak.*, 1969, *18*(2), pp. 192–205.

Purcell, Joseph C. and Smith, Blair J. Quadratic Programming Solution of Competitive Equilibrium for U.S. Agriculture: Comment. *Amer. J. Agr. Econ.*, May 1969, *51*(2), pp. 481–82.

Purcell, Wayne D. Marketing, Price, and the Theory of Communication. *Amer. J. Agr. Econ.*, December 1969, *51*(5), pp. 1110–13.

Puri, I. C. and Srinivasan, R. Agency for Operation of Buffer Stocks. **In** *Indian Society of Agricultural Economics*, 1969, pp. 118–27.

Pursell, Donald E. The Impact of the South African Wage Board on Skilled/Unskilled Wage Differentials. *East Afr. Econ. Rev.*, June 1969, *1*(1), pp. 73–81.

Pusić, Eugen. Area and Administration in Yugoslav Development. *Int. Soc. Sci. J.*, 1969, *21*(1), pp. 68–82.

Puth, Robert C. Supreme Life: The History of A Negro Life Insurance Company, 1919–1962. *Bus. Hist. Rev.*, Spring 1969, *43*(1), pp. 1–20.

Puu, Tönu. Causal Versus Teleological Explanation in Economics. *Swedish J. Econ.*, June 1969, *71*(2), pp. 111–26.

Pye, Gordon. On the Tax Structure of Interest Rates. *Quart. J. Econ.*, November 1969, *83*(4), pp. 562–79.

Pyke, Donald L. and North, Harper Q. 'Probes' of the Technological Future. *Harvard Bus. Rev.*, May–June 1969, *47*(3), pp. 68–82.

Pyle, William C.; Brummet, R. Lee and Flamholtz, Eric G. Human Resource Accounting: A Tool to Increase Managerial Effectiveness. *Manage. Account.*, August 1969, *51*(2), pp. 12–15.

______ Human Resource Myopia. *Mon. Lab. Rev.*, January 1969, *92*(1), pp. 29–30.

Pylee, M. V. Is Further Centralization of Labour Policy Desirable? **In** *Johri, C. K., ed.*, 1969, pp. 221–34.

Pyun, Chong Soo. Local Business Activity Index: Its Construction and Uses—Comment. *J. Reg. Sci.*, April 1969, *9*(1), pp. 163–66.

______ The Monetary Value of a Housewife: An Economic Analysis for Use in Litigation. *Amer. J. Econ. Soc.*, July 1969, *28*(3), pp. 271–84.

Qayum, A. Models of Balanced and Maximum Growth in Dualistic Economies. **In** *[Tinbergen, J.]*, 1969, pp. 43–63.

Quance, C. Leroy and Tweeten, Luther G. Positivistic Measures of Aggregate Supply Elasticities: Some New Approaches. *Amer. Econ. Rev.*, May 1969, *59*(2), pp. 175–83.

______**; Tweeten, Luther G. and Sobering, Fred.** An Economic Model for Determining Cotton Allotments and Prices to Maximize Net Farm Income. *Amer. J. Agr. Econ.*, December 1969, *51*(5), pp. 1124–28.

Quandt, Richard E. and Baumol, William J. The Demand for Abstract Transport Modes: Some Hopes. *J. Reg. Sci.*, April 1969, *9*(1), pp. 159–62.

______ **and Young, Kan Hua.** Cross-sectional Travel Demand Models: Estimates and Tests. *J. Reg. Sci.*, August 1969, *9*(2), pp. 201–14.

Queener, R. S. The Use of Economic Criteria for Educational Decision Making. **In** *Pandit, H. N., ed.*, 1969, pp. 205–14.

Quigley, Joseph M. The Effects of Leverage and Corporate Taxes on the Shareholders of Regulated Utilities: Comment. **In** *Trebing, H. M. and Howard, R. H., eds.*, 1969, pp. 111–16.

Quindry, Kenneth E. and Cook, Billy D. Humanization of the Property Tax for Low Income Households. *Nat. Tax J.*, September 1969, *22*(3), pp. 357–67.

Quinn, Brian; Bhatia, Rattan J. and Szapary, Gyorgy. Stabilization Program in Sierra Leone. *Int. Monet. Fund Staff Pap.*, November 1969, *16*(3), pp. 504–28.

Quinn, Gerard. The Buchanan Report. *Irish Banking Rev.*, September 1969, pp. 3–9.

Quinn, James Brian. Technology Transfer by Multinational Companies. *Harvard Bus. Rev.,* November–December 1969, *47*(6), pp. 147–61.

Quintero Briseño, Jesús. La integración de la industria automovilística en Mexico. (Integration of the Automotive Industry in Mexico. With English summary.) *Econ. Polít.,* Fourth Semester 1969, *6* (4), pp. 473–84.

Rabbani, A. K. M. Ghulam. A Proposal for Fiscal Incentives for the Raw-Jute Exports. *Pakistan Develop. Rev.,* Winter 1969, *9*(4), pp. 400–418.

Raby, William L. Tax Allocation and Non-Historical Financial Statements. *Accounting Rev.,* January 1969, *44*(1), pp. 1–11.

Racoveanu, N., et al. Modele de creştere a economiei nationale. (Models of Growth of the National Economy. With English summary.) *Stud. Cercet. Econ.,* 1969, *3,* pp. 89–100.

Racz, Barnabas A. Hungary's New Economic Mechanism. *Mich. Academician,* Winter 1969, *1*(1–2), pp. 175–81.

Rädel, F. E. Profit Maximisation—Can It Be Justified? *S. Afr. J. Econ.,* March 1969, *37*(1), pp. 32–41.

Radner, Daniel B. and Budd, Edward C. The OBE Size Distribution Series: Methods and Tentative Results for 1964. *Amer. Econ. Rev.,* May 1969, *59* (2), pp. 435–49.

Radomysler, A. Welfare Economics and Economic Policy. **In** *Arrow, K. J. and Scitovsky, T., eds.,* 1969, pp. 81–94.

Rados, David L. Product Liability: Tougher Ground Rules. *Harvard Bus. Rev.,* July–August 1969, *47* (4), pp. 144–52.

Raduchel, William; Eads, George and Nerlove, Marc. A Long-Run Cost Function for the Local Service Airline Industry: An Experiment in Non-Linear Estimation. *Rev. Econ. Statist.,* August 1969, *51* (3), pp. 258–70.

Rădulescu, G. Rata profitului în economia românească în anii 1927–1938. (The Rate of Profit in Romanian Economy between 1927–1938. With English summary.) *Stud. Cercet. Econ.,* 1969, *4,* pp. 23–58.

Raffoul, Faouzi and Leroux, Roger. An Essay in Simulating Economic Policies for the French Economy. *Econ. Planning,* 1969, *9*(1–2), pp. 95–153.

Rahman, Anisur. Foreign Capital Requirements for Economic Development: The Year of Independence for the Case of Foreign Loans. *Oxford Econ. Pap.,* November 1969, *21*(3), pp. 438–41.

——— Intertemporal Equity and Elasticity of Marginal Utility from Consumption. *Oxford Econ. Pap.,* March 1969, *21*(1), pp. 29–34.

Raimon, Robert L. and Stoikov, Vladimir. The Effect of Blue-Collar Unionism on White-Collar Earnings. *Ind. Lab. Relat. Rev.,* April 1969, *22*(3), pp. 358–74.

Raina, M. K. A Note on Differentiation in Railway Rates. *Indian Econ. J.,* July–September 1969, *17* (1), pp. 129–36.

Raja, S. T. Project Planning and Execution. **In** *Dagli, V., ed., Vol. II,* 1969, pp. 140–45.

Rajesh. Efficient Management: A. R. C. Report. **In** *Dagli, V., ed., Vol. II,* 1969, pp. 41–49.

Rakowski, James. Is Labour Mobility a Substitute for Trade? *Econ. J.,* March 1969, *79*(313), pp. 174–78.

Rakshit, M. K. Inflation, the Choice of Assets, and the Liquidity Trap. **In** *[Ghosal, U. N.],* 1969, pp. 69–73.

Ramachandran, C. V. Cost of Buffer Stock Operations: Desirability or Otherwise of Subsidising Cost. **In** *Indian Society of Agricultural Economics,* 1969, pp. 100–117.

Ramachandran, V. A. Fringe Benefit and Its Role in Productivity. **In** *Johri, C. K., ed.,* 1969, pp. 302–20.

Ramaer, J. C. From Macro to Micro—and Back: Some Thoughts of a B.I.G. Man Who Went into Big Business. **In** *[Tinbergen, J.],* 1969, pp. 309–26.

Ramamoorthy, B. The Economics of Education. *Econ. Aff.,* January-February 1969, *14*(1–2), pp. 74–80.

——— **and Prakasa Rao, M. S.** Terminalization Approach to Pre-University Education. **In** *Pandit, H. N., ed.,* 1969, pp. 356–74.

Ramana, D. V. Deficit Financing and Import Substitution: India, 1951–65. **In** *Morgan, T. and Spoelstra, N., eds.,* 1969, pp. 307–31.

Ramanadham, V. V. Softening of Monopoly Power. **In** *Dagli, V., ed., Vol. II,* 1969, pp. 166–70.

Ramanathan, R. An Econometric Exploration of Indian Saving Behavior. *J. Amer. Statist. Assoc.,* March 1969, *64*(325), pp. 90–101.

Ramanujam, M. S. Planning Models for Optimum Allocation of Resources in Education. **In** *Pandit, H. N., ed.,* 1969, pp. 244–59.

Ramaswami, V. K. On Two-Sector Neo-classical Growth. *Oxford Econ. Pap.,* July 1969, *21*(2), pp. 142–60.

———**; Srinivasan, T. N. and Bhagwati, Jagdish N.** Domestic Distortions, Tariffs, and the Theory of Optimum Subsidy: Some Further Results. *J. Polit. Econ.,* November/December 1969, *77*(6), pp. 1005–10.

Ramberg, John S. Selection and Ranking Procedures: A Comment. **In** *Naylor, T. H., ed.,* 1969, pp. 161–64.

Ramsey, David D. On the Social Rate of Discount: Comment. *Amer. Econ. Rev.,* December 1969, *59* (5), pp. 919–24.

Ramsey, Frank P. A Mathematical Theory of Saving. **In** *Arrow, K. J. and Scitovsky, T., eds.,* 1969, pp. 619–33.

Randall, Alan J. Integration of Irrigated and Dry Land Agriculture—Profitability and Product Mix. *Rev. Marketing Agr. Econ.,* September 1969, *37* (3), pp. 141–52.

Randall, Gary B. and Wheatley, John J. Industrial Specialization in Washington. *Univ. Wash. Bus. Rev.,* Summer 1969, *28*(4), pp. 25–35.

Randall, K. A. An Evolutionary Process in Banking. **In** *Prochnow, H. V., ed.,* 1969, pp. 48–55.

Rangarajan, C. and Chatterjee, S. A Note on Comparison between Correlation Coefficients of Original and Transformed Variables. *Amer. Statist.,* October 1969, *23*(4), pp. 28–29.

——— **and Polakoff, Murray E.** A Note on a "Keynesian" Model of Aggregate Demand: Reply. *J. Finance,* March 1969, *24*(1), pp. 104–05.

Ranis, Gustav. Economic Dualism—At Home and Abroad. *Public Policy,* Fall 1969, *18*(1), pp. 41–53.

______ and **Fei, John C. H.** Agriculture in the Open Economy. **In** *Thorbecke, E., ed.,* 1969, pp. 129–59.

______ and **Fei, John C. H.** Agriculture in the Open Economy: Reply. **In** *Thorbecke, E., ed.,* 1969, pp. 163–64.

______ and **Fei, John C. H.** Economic Development in Historical Perspective. *Amer. Econ. Rev.,* May 1969, *59*(2), pp. 286–400.

Ranki, Risto. Kauppavirta-analyysi ja trendimatriisi. (Trend Matrix in Markov Analysis of Trade Flows. With English summary.) *Kansant. Aikak.,* 1969, *65*(2), pp. 122–32.

Rankoff, Iwan. Grundzüge des bulgarischen Finanzsystems. (Principles of the Bulgarian Financial System. With English summary.) *Schmollers Jahr.,* 1969, *89*(2), pp. 185–210.

Rao, J. N. K. Ratio and Regression Estimators. **In** *Johnson, N. L. and Smith, H., Jr., eds.,* 1969, pp. 213–34.

______ and **Bayless, D. L.** An Empirical Study of the Stabilities of Estimators and Variance Estimators in Unequal Probability Sampling of Two Units per Stratum. *J. Amer. Statist. Assoc.,* June 1969, *64*(326), pp. 540–59.

______ and **Hartley, H. O.** A New Estimation Theory for Sample Surveys, II. **In** *Johnson, N. L. and Smith, H., Jr., eds.,* 1969, pp. 147–69.

Rao, Poduri S. R. S. Comparison of Four Ratio-Type Estimates under a Model. *J. Amer. Statist. Assoc.,* June 1969, *64*(326), pp. 574–80.

Rao, Potluri. A Note on Econometrics of Joint Production. *Econometrica,* October 1969, *37*(4), pp. 737–38.

Rao, R. S. Hanumanta and Sarma, L. V. L. N. Estimates of the Cost of Capital to the Indian Engineering Industry, 1962–65. *Yorkshire Bull. Econ. Soc. Res.,* November 1969, *21*(2), pp. 132–40.

Rao, Tanniru R. Are Some Consumers More Prone to Purchase Private Brands? *J. Marketing Res.,* November 1969, *6*(4), pp. 447–50.

______ Consumer's Purchase Decision Process: Stochastic Models. *J. Marketing Res.,* August 1969, *6* (3), pp. 321–29.

Rao, V. M. Two Decompositions of Concentration Ratio. *J. Roy. Statist. Soc.,* Part 3, 1969, *132,* pp. 418–25.

Rao, Vithala R. and Green, Paul E. A Note on Proximity Measures and Cluster Analysis. *J. Marketing Res.,* August 1969, *6*(3), pp. 359–64.

Rapp, Wilbur A. Treasury Common Stock Financing as an Investment Process. *Miss. Val. J. Bus. Econ.,* Fall 1969, *5*(1), pp. 1–10.

Rapp, William V.; Grubel, Herbert G. and Johnson, Harry G. Excise Taxes and Effective Protection: A Note. *Econ. J.,* September 1969, *79*(315), pp. 674–75.

Rappaport, Alfred. Integer Programming and Managerial Analysis. *Accounting Rev.,* April 1969, *44*(2), pp. 297–99.

Rappaport, Carl and Thurow, Lester C. Law Enforcement and Cost-Benefit Analysis. *Public Finance,* 1969, *24*(1), pp. 48–68.

Rapping, Leonard A. and Lucas, Robert E., Jr. Price Expectations and the Phillips Curve. *Amer. Econ. Rev.,* June 1969, *59*(3), pp. 342–50.

______ Real Wages, Employment, and Inflation. *J. Polit. Econ.,* September/October 1969, *77*(5), pp. 721–54.

Rasche, R. H. and Taubman, Paul. Economic and Tax Depreciation of Office Buildings. *Nat. Tax J.,* September 1969, *22*(3), pp. 334–46.

Rask, Norman and Adams, Dale W. Economics of Cost-Share Leases: A Reply. *Amer. J. Agr. Econ.,* August 1969, *51*(3), pp. 695–97.

Rasmussen, Arne. How Sensitive are the Optimal Points of Micro-economics? *Liiketaloudellinen Aikak.,* 1969, *18*(1), pp. 61–67.

Rasmussen, P. Nørregaard. Denmark, Norway and Sweden: Comment. **In** *Bronfenbrenner, M., ed.,* 1969, pp. 221–24.

______ How to Behave—as a Speculator. *Weltwirtsch. Arch.,* 1969, *103*(2), pp. 328–32.

Rasmussen, Wayne D. and Baker, Gladys L. Programs for Agriculture, 1933–1965. **In** *Ruttan, V. W.; Waldo, A. D. and Houck, J. P., eds.,* 1969, pp. 69–88.

Ratchford, C. Brice. Mission of Higher Educational Institutions in Today's World. *Amer. J. Agr. Econ.,* December 1969, *51*(5), pp. 1603–12.

Ratoosh, Philburn. Defense Decision-Making: Cost-Effectiveness Models and Rationality. **In** *Bobrow, D. B., ed.,* 1969, pp. 21–34.

Rattigan, G. A. The Tariff Board: Some Reflections. *Econ. Rec.,* March 1969, *45*(109), pp. 17–26.

Raunio, Eino. Näkökohtia vuoden 1969 budjettiesityksestä. (Government Budget Proposal for 1969. With English summary.) *Kansant. Aikak.,* 1969, *65*(1), pp. 1–5.

Raup, Philip M. Economies and Diseconomies of Large-Scale Agriculture. *Amer. J. Agr. Econ.,* December 1969, *51*(5), pp. 1274–82.

Răvar, I. Probleme ale industrializării socialiste a României. (Problems of Romania's Socialist Industrialization. With English summary.) *Stud. Cercet. Econ.,* 1969, *3,* pp. 51–58.

Ravazzi, Giancarlo. Una problematica nuova per la direzione commerciale la concezione mercatistica della direzione d'impresa. (New Problems for Commercial Management: The Marketing Conception of Firm Management. With English summary.) *L'Impresa,* July/October 1969, *11*(4–5), pp. 304–10.

Ray, Cadwell L. The Yield and Distribution of Potential Business Taxes: Texas as a Case Study. *Soc. Sci. Quart.,* March 1969, *49*(4), pp. 853–63.

Ray, G. F. The Diffusion of New Technology: A Study of Ten Processes in Nine Industries. *Nat. Inst. Econ. Rev.,* May 1969, (48), pp. 40–83.

______; **Hays, S. and Hemming, M. F. W.** The Office Machinery Industry in the United Kingdom. *Nat. Inst. Econ. Rev.,* August 1969, (49), pp. 52–73.

Ray, Hemen. Changing Soviet Views on Mahatma Gandhi. *J. Asian Stud.,* November 1969, *29*(1), pp. 85–106.

Rayack, Elton and Lurie, Melvin. Employment Opportunities for Negro Families in "Satellite" Cities. *Southern Econ. J.,* October 1969, *36*(2), pp. 191–95.

Raymond, George M.; Rivkin, Malcolm D. and Gans, Herbert J. Urban Renewal: A Controversy. **In** *Callow, A. B., Jr., ed.,* 1969, pp. 582–96.

Raymond, Richard. Changes in the Relative Economic Status of Nonwhites: 1950–1960. *Western Econ. J.*, March 1969, *7*(1), pp. 57–70.

——— Mobility and Economic Progress of Negro Americans during the 1940's. *Amer. J. Econ. Soc.*, October 1969, *28*(4), pp. 337–50.

Raymond, Robert S. Consumer Protection in Great Britain and in the United States. *Marquette Bus. Rev.*, Winter 1969, *13*(4), pp. 151–58.

Raynauld, André. Benefits and Costs: Theoretical and Methodological Issues: Discussion. **In** *Somers, G. G. and Wood, W. D., eds.*, 1969, pp. 37–41.

Rayner, A. C. Effect of the Length of the Time Period on Serial Correlation. *Rev. Econ. Statist.*, February 1969, *51*(1), pp. 107–08.

——— On the Identification of the Supply Curve of Working Hours. *Oxford Econ. Pap.*, July 1969, *21* (2), pp. 293–98.

——— Premium Bonds—The Effect of the Price Structure. *Bull. Oxford Univ. Inst. Econ. Statist.*, November 1969, *31*(4), pp. 303–11.

——— The Wool Price and the Production of Synthetics. *Yorkshire Bull. Econ. Soc. Res.*, May 1969, *21*(1), pp. 31–38.

Razin, Assaf and Mundlak, Yair. Aggregation, Index Numbers and the Measurement of Technical Change. *Rev. Econ. Statist.*, May 1969, *51*(2), pp. 166–75.

Reading, Brian. Euro-dollars—Tonic or Toxic? **In** *Chalmers, E. B., ed.*, 1969, pp. 72–83.

——— **and Lomax, David F.** Too Little Saving. *Nat. Westminster Bank Quart. Rev.*, August 1969, pp. 23–42.

Reagan, Michael D. Mr. Martin's Sacred Cow. **In** *Starleaf, D. R., ed.*, 1969, pp. 286–89.

——— Why Government Grows. **In** *Starleaf, D. R., ed.*, 1969, pp. 200–204.

Reavis, Marshall W. The Corporate Risk Manager's Contribution to Profit. *J. Risk Ins.*, September 1969, *36*(4), pp. 473–79.

Reboul, John W. Horizontal Restraints under the French Antitrust Laws: Competition and Economic Progress. **In** *Economic Concentration, Pt. 7A, SCH,* 1969, pp. 3997–4037.

Recktenwald, Horst Claus. Die Finanzwissenschaft in der Gegenwart. (With English summary.) *Kyklos,* 1969, *22*(1), pp. 1–29.

Reddaway, W. B. The Future of the Ghanian Economy. **In** *Stewart, I. G., ed.*, 1969, pp. 104–14.

——— The Importance of External Assistance and Self-help in Indian Development. **In** *Bhuleshkar, A. V., ed.*, 1969, pp. 353–67.

Redding, A. David. The Philippine Economy: A Newcomer's Perspective. *Philippine Econ. J.*, Second Semester 1969, *8*(2), pp. 130–44.

——— Policies for the Private Sector: Discussion. *Philippine Econ. J.*, First Semester 1969, *8*(1), pp. 33–36.

Reder, M. W. Some Problems in the Measurement of Productivity in the Medical Care Industry. **In** *Fuchs, V. R., ed.*, 1969, pp. 95–131.

——— Some Problems in the Measurement of Productivity in the Medical Care Industry: Reply. **In** *Fuchs, V. R., ed.*, 1969, pp. 148–53.

——— The Theory of Frictional Unemployment. *Economica, N.S.*, February 1969, *36*(141), pp. 1–28.

Redlich, Fritz. On the Origin of Created Deposits in the Commonwealth of Massachusetts. *Bus. Hist. Rev.*, Summer 1969, *43*(2), pp. 204–08.

Reed, M. C. and Hawke, G. R. Railway Capital in the United Kingdom in the Nineteenth Century. *Econ. Hist. Rev.*, August 1969, *22*(2), pp. 269–86.

Rees, Albert. Spatial Wage Differentials in a Large City Labor Market. **In** *Somers, G. G., ed. (II),* 1969, pp. 237–47.

Rees, Graham and Wiseman, Jack. London's Commodity Markets. *Lloyds Bank Rev.*, January 1969, (91), pp. 22–45.

Rees, M. S. The Inflation of National Health Service Registers of Patients and Its Effect on the Remuneration of General Practitioners. *J. Roy. Statist. Soc.*, Part 4, 1969, *132*, pp. 526–42.

Rees, R. A New Bulk Supply Tariff—Comment. *Econ. J.*, December 1969, *79*(316), pp. 973–74.

Rees, Richard D. U.S. Foreign Agricultural Trade in the 1970's: Growth or Contraction? *Fed. Res. Bank Kansas City Rev.*, September–October 1969, pp. 11–19.

Rehbinder, Eckard. The Foreign Direct Investment Regulations: A European Legal Point of View. *Law Contemp. Probl.*, Winter 1969, *34*(1), pp. 95–117.

Rehmus, Charles M. Constraints on Local Governments in Public Employee Bargaining. *Mich. Law Rev.*, March 1969, *67*(5), pp. 919–30.

——— Impasse Resolution: The Community and Bargaining in the Public Sector: Discussion. **In** *Somers, G. G., ed. (II),* 1969, pp. 59–63.

Reichardt, Helmut; Schips, Bernd and Britsch, Klaus. Sind die Lohnempfänger gut beraten, wenn sie sich einer Lohnquotensenkung widersetzen? (With English summary.) *Jahr. Nationalökon. Statist.*, August 1969, *183*(3–4), pp. 300–305.

Reichardt, Manfred. Finding Domestic Finance for Industrialization. *Finance Develop.*, June 1969, *6* (2), pp. 39–43.

Reid, David J. The CBI Industrial Trends Survey—A Statistical Note. *Appl. Econ.*, August 1969, *1*(3), pp. 197–203.

Reid, Samuel Richardson. Conglomerate Growth: Consistency with Economic Theory of Growth. **In** *Garoian, L., ed.*, 1969, pp. 44–56.

——— Mergers and the Economist. *Antitrust Bull.*, Summer 1969, *14*, pp. 371–84.

——— **and Cohen, Kalman J.** Effects of Regulation, Branching, and Mergers on Banking Structure and Performance: Reply. *Southern Econ. J.*, October 1969, *36*(2), pp. 204–09.

Reiling, Henry B. and Haves, Samuel L., III. Sophisticated Financing Tool: The Warrant. *Harvard Bus. Rev.*, January–February 1969, *47*(1), pp. 137–50.

Reilly, Frank K. An Analysis and Reconciliation of Bond Refunding Decision Models. *Marquette Bus. Rev.*, Summer 1969, *13*(2), pp. 76–88.

Rein, Martin. Choice and Change in the American Welfare System. *Ann. Amer. Acad. Polit. Soc. Sci.*, September 1969, *385*, pp. 89–109.

Reiss, Albert J., Jr. Statement. **In** *Impact of Crime* *on Small Business—1969, Pt. 1, SCH,* 1969, pp. 29–44.

Reiss, Franklin J. and Krausz, N. G. P. Institutions and Instruments—Management Alternatives. *Amer. J. Agr. Econ.,* December 1969, *51*(5), pp. 1369–80.

______ **and Scott, John T., Jr.** Changing Technology and Lease Adjustment: Theory and Practice. *Land Econ.,* November 1969, *45*(4), pp. 400–405.

Reiss, Howard. Human Factors at the Science-Technology Interface. **In** *Gruber, W. H. and Marquis, D. G., eds.,* 1969, pp. 105–16.

Reitsma, A. J. Internationale monetaire problemen. (International Monetary Problems. With English summary.) *De Economist,* November/December 1969, *117*(6), pp. 599–614.

Reitter, Robert N. Product Testing in Segmented Markets. *J. Marketing Res.,* May 1969, *6*(2), pp. 179–84.

Renborg, Ulf. Tendencies Towards Concentration and Specialization in Agriculture. **In** *Papi, U. and Nunn, C., eds.,* 1969, pp. 209–33.

Renko, Kyösti. Second best-teoria. (The Theory of Second Best. With English summary.) *Kansant. Aikak.,* 1969, *65*(1), pp. 41–56.

Renwick, Fred B. Asset Management and Investor Portfolio Behavior: Theory and Practice. *J. Finance,* May 1969, *24*(2), pp. 181–206.

Renz, J.; Fasolina, G. and Sternberger, H. Planning-Programing-Budgeting System (PPBS) in Nassau County, N.Y. **In** *Innovations in Planning, Programming, and Budgeting in State and Local Governments, JECP,* 1969, pp. 105–89.

Requena B., Mariano. Chilean Program of Abortion Control and Fertility Planning: Present Situation and Forecast for the Next Decade. **In** *Behrman, S. J.; Corsa, L., Jr. and Freedman, R., eds.,* 1969, pp. 478–89.

Resnick, Stephen H. and Hymer, Stephen. Interactions between the Government and the Private Sector: An Analysis of Government Expenditure Policy and the Reflection Ratio. **In** *Stewart, I. G., ed.,* 1969, pp. 155–80.

______ **and Hymer, Stephen H.** A Model of an Agrarian Economy with Nonagricultural Activities. *Amer. Econ. Rev.,* Part I, September 1969, *59* (4), pp. 493–506.

van Rest, E. D. Operational Research. **In** *Kempner, T., ed.,* 1969, pp. 71–74.

______ Quantitative Foundations (Statistical Methods and Applicable Mathematics). **In** *Kempner, T., ed.,* 1969, pp. 33–42.

Restall, Lawrence J. and Czajkowski, Peter. Computation of LIFO Index: A Statistical Sampling Approach. *Manage. Account.,* September 1969, *51* (3), pp. 43–48.

Restrepo Fernández, Iván and Sánchez Cortés, José. El arrendamiento de tierras ejidales: El caso de Apatzingán. (The Leasing of Common Lands: The Case of Apatzingán. With English summary.) *Econ. Polít.,* Third Semester 1969, *6*(3), pp. 331–46.

Rethwisch, Kurt. A Note on the Presumed Social Desirability of Internal Over External Growth. *Antitrust Bull.,* Winter 1969, *14,* pp. 855–64.

Reuber, Grant L. Antitrust and the Takeover Activity of American Firms in Canada: A Further Analysis. *J. Law Econ.,* October 1969, *12*(2), pp. 405–17.

______ Professor Arrow on the Social Discount Rate: Discussion. **In** *Somers, G. G. and Wood, W. D., eds.,* 1969, pp. 88–94.

______ **and Leith, James Clark.** The Impact of the Industrial Countries' Tariff Structure on Their Imports of Manufactures from Less-Developed Areas: A Comment. *Economica, N.S.,* February 1969, *36*(141), pp. 75–80.

Reuther, Walter P. Statement. **In** *The 1969 Economic Report of the President, Pt. 4, JECH,* 1969, pp. 1156–84.

Revankar, N. S. and Zellner, A. Generalized Production Functions. *Rev. Econ. Stud.,* April 1969, *36* (106), pp. 241–50.

Revelle, Charles; Joeres, Erhard and Kirby, William. The Linear Decision Rule in Reservoir Management and Design. 1. Development of the Stochastic Model. *Water Resources Res.,* August 1969, *5* (4), pp. 767–77.

Reviglio, Franco. Finance of Social Security in Developing Countries. *Public Finance,* 1969, *24*(2), pp. 264–77.

Revsine, Lawrence. Some Controversy Concerning "Controversial Accounting Changes" *Accounting Rev.,* April 1969, *44*(2), pp. 354–58.

Reyes, Osorio Sergio. La pobreza rural. (Rural Poverty. With English summary.) *Econ. Polít.,* Second Semester 1969, *6*(2), pp. 209–14.

Reynolds, Clark W. Relationships between Agriculture, Nonagriculture, and Foreign Trade in the Development of Argentina and Peru: Comment. **In** *Thorbecke, E., ed.,* 1969, pp. 213–17.

Reynolds, Lloyd G. The Content of Development Economics. *Amer. Econ. Rev.,* May 1969, *59*(2), pp. 401–08.

______ Economic Development with Surplus Labour: Some Complications. *Oxford Econ. Pap.,* March 1969, *21*(1), pp. 89–103.

______ The Efficiency of Education in Economics: Discussion. *Amer. Econ. Rev.,* May 1969, *59*(2), pp. 239–40.

______ Objectives of Wage Policy in Developing Countries. **In** *Smith, A. D., ed.,* 1969, pp. 217–34.

______ Relative Earnings and Manpower Allocation in Developing Economies. *Pakistan Develop. Rev.,* Spring 1969, *9*(1), pp. 14–34.

Reynolds, S. E. Customs Union among Developing Countries. *Malayan Econ. Rev.,* April 1969, *14*(1), pp. 15–28.

Rhoads, William G. and Bird, Richard M. The Valorization Tax in Colombia: An Example for other Developing Countries? **In** *Becker, A. P., ed.,* 1969, pp. 201–37.

Rhodes, John B. 'The American Challenge' Challenged. *Harvard Bus. Rev.,* September–October 1969, *47*(5), pp. 45–56.

Rhodes, Robert I. On "Disguised Conservatism in Evolutionary Development Theory": Reply. *Sci. Soc.,* Summer-Fall 1969, *33*(3), pp. 353–58.

Rhodes, V. James. Inter-University Collaboration in

Undergraduate Teaching. *Amer. J. Agr. Econ.*, December 1969, *51*(5), pp. 1085–88.

Rhomberg, Rudolf R. Transmission of Business Fluctuations from Developed to Developing Countries. **In** *Bronfenbrenner, M., ed.*, 1969, pp. 253–78.

Rhyne, Iola and Leong, Y. S. Hawaii's Inversely Graduated Tax Credits. *Nat. Tax J.*, December 1969, *22*(4), pp. 446–65.

Riach, P. A. A Framework for Macro-Distribution Analysis. *Kyklos*, 1969, *22*(3), pp. 542–65.

Riahi, Ebrahim. Factors Causing Declines in the Sugar Content of Beets in Iran. *Tahq. Eq.*, November 1969, *6*(15&16), pp. 80–97.

Rice, Ralph S. Tax Reform and Tax Incentives. *Law Contemp. Probl.*, Autumn 1969, *34*(4), pp. 782–804.

Richards, Louise G. Consumer Practices of the Poor. **In** *Sturdivant, F. D., ed.*, 1969, pp. 42–60.

Richardson, J. E. American Influence on the Air Transport Industry. **In** *Preston, R., ed.*, 1969, pp. 521–38.

——— Australian Antitrust and the Decline of American Influence: The Trade Practices Act. **In** *Preston, R., ed.*, 1969, pp. 458–97.

Richardson, R. A. and Whan, R. B. A Simulated Study of an Auction Market. *Australian J. Agr. Econ.*, December 1969, *13*(2), pp. 91–100.

Richebächer, Kurt. Problemi e prospettive di integrazione dei mercati europei dei capitali. (Problems and Prospects of Integrating European Capital Markets. With English summary.) *Bancaria*, February 1969, *25*(2), pp. 170–77.

——— The Problems and Prospects of Integrating European Capital Markets. *J. Money, Credit, Banking*, August 1969, *1*(3), pp. 336–46.

Richmond, David. Employer Attitudes to Wage Policies in Developing Countries. **In** *Smith, A. D., ed.*, 1969, pp. 395–97.

Richta, Radovan and Šulc, Ota. Forecasting and the Scientific and Technological Revolution. *Int. Soc. Sci. J.*, 1969, *21*(4), pp. 563–73.

Richter, Charles E. The Impact of Industrial Linkages on Geographic Association. *J. Reg. Sci.*, April 1969, *9*(1), pp. 19–28.

Richter, J. H. The Changing Patterns of International Trade Problems of Under-developed Areas. **In** *Papi, U. and Nunn, C., eds.*, 1969, pp. 151–62.

Ricker, William E. Food from the Sea. **In** *National Academy of Sciences*, 1969, pp. 87–108.

Rickey, Kenneth R. Earnings per Share: Management and the Investor. *Manage. Account.*, December 1969, *51*(6), pp. 9–11.

Ricks, R. Bruce. Imputed Equity Returns on Real Estate Financed with Life Insurance Company Loans. *J. Finance*, December 1969, *24*(5), pp. 921–37.

Rieber, Michael. Statement. **In** *Governmental Intervention in the Market Mechanism, Pt. 1, SCH*, 1969, pp. 181–92.

Riffe, W. W. and Folse, C. I. Changing Patterns of Business Services and Population in Illinois Rural Villages. *Ill. Agr. Econ.*, January 1969, *9*(1), pp. 26–32.

Riistama, Veijo. Kustannusteoria kustannuslaskennan perustana. (Cost Theory as a Basis for Cost Accounting. With English summary.) *Liiketaloudellinen Aikak.*, 1969, *18*(3), pp. 550–75.

van Rijckeghem, Willy. An Intersectoral Consistency Model for Economic Planning in Brazil. **In** *Ellis, H. S., ed.*, 1969, pp. 376–401.

Rill, James F. Robinson-Patman Developments: The Approach of Business Counsel. *Antitrust Bull.*, Winter 1969, *14*, pp. 813–26.

Rimlinger, Gaston V. Social Security and Society: An East-West Comparison. *Soc. Sci. Quart.*, December 1969, *50*(3), pp. 494–506.

Rimmer, Douglas. The Abstraction from Politics: A Critique of Economic Theory and Design with Reference to West Africa. *J. Devel. Stud.*, April 1969, *5*(3), pp. 190–204.

Rinehart, James R. and Laird, William E. A Refinement of Local Industrial Subsidy Techniques: Reply. *Miss. Val. J. Bus. Econ.*, Spring 1969, *4*(2), pp. 82–88.

Ringrose, David R. The Government and the Carters in Spain, 1476–1700. *Econ. Hist. Rev.*, April 1969, *22*(1), pp. 45–57.

Rinne, Horst. On Revisions in National Accounts Estimates. *Rev. Income Wealth*, September 1969, *15*(3), pp. 229–45.

Ristimäki, Juhani. Valtion tuki ja tulopolitiikka. (Government Support and Incomes Policy. With English summary.) *Kansant. Aikak.*, 1969, *65*(1), pp. 6–20.

Ritter, Lawrence S. A Capital Market Plan for the Urban Areas. *Calif. Manage. Rev.*, Summer 1969, *11*(4), pp. 37–46.

Rives, Norfleet W., Jr.; Naylor, Thomas H. and Vernon, John M. An Econometric Model of the Tobacco Industry. *Rev. Econ. Statist.*, May 1969, *51*(2), pp. 149–58.

Rivkin, Malcolm D.; Gans, Herbert J. and Raymond, George M. Urban Renewal: A Controversy. **In** *Callow, A. B., Jr., ed.*, 1969, pp. 582–96.

Rivlin, Alice M. The Planning, Programing, and Budgeting System in the Department of Health, Education, and Welfare: Some Lessons from Experience. **In** *The Analysis and Evaluation of Public Expenditures: The PPB System, Vol. 3, JECP*, 1969, pp. 909–22.

——— **and Weiss, Jeffrey H.** Social Goals and Federal Support of Higher Education—The Implications of Various Strategies. **In** *the Economics and Financing of Higher Education in the United States, JECP*, 1969, pp. 543–55.

Rizzoni, Eitel M. Development and Integration of Latin American Telecommunications. **In** *Hilton, R., ed.*, 1969, pp. 355–80.

Roa, K. S. Hanumanta and Sarma, L. V. L. N. Leverage and the Value of the Firm. *J. Finance*, September 1969, *24*(4), pp. 673–77.

Robarts, A. O. A Revised Look at Selected Determinants of Consumer Spatial Behavior. **In** *Association of Canadian Schools of Business*, 1969, pp. 219–33.

Robbins, Gary A. Alternative Treatment of Corporate Income. **In** *Willis, A. B., ed.*, 1969, pp. 138–56.

Robert, Marcel and Parmeggiani, Luigi. Fifty Years of International Collaboration in Occupational Safety and Health. *Int. Lab. Rev.,* January 1969, *99*(1), pp. 85–136.

Roberts, Edward B. Entrepreneurship and Technology. **In** *Gruber, W. H. and Marquis, D. G., eds.,* 1969, pp. 219–37.

Roberts, Harold S. Compulsory Arbitration. **In** *Wortman, M. S., Jr.,* 1969, pp. 403–08.

Roberts, Higdon C. A Private Approach to Public Problems: Unions and Contractors Create Job Training Program. *Indiana Bus. Rev.,* July/August 1969, *44,* pp. 16–20.

Roberts, Merrill J. Transport Coordination and Distribution Efficiency: Pricing Norms and Profit Potential. *J. Transp. Econ. Policy,* May 1969, *3*(2), pp. 165–77.

Roberts, Paul Craig. The Polycentric Soviet Economy. *J. Law Econ.,* April 1969, *12*(1), pp. 163–79.

______ **and Brown, Norman L.** The Economics of the Right to Work Controversy: Revisited. *Southern Econ. J.,* January 1969, *35*(3), pp. 265–66.

Roberts, R. O. The Development and Decline of the Non-ferrous Metal Smelting Industries in South Wales. **In** *Minchinton, W. E., ed.,* 1969, pp. 121–60.

Robertson, B. Russell and Love, Harold G. Louisville Produce Terminal: Its Changing Trends and Potentials, 1966–1975. *Amer. J. Agr. Econ.,* December 1969, *51*(5), pp. 1251–54.

Robertson, David. Scope for New Trade Strategy. **In** *Johnson, H. G., ed.,* 1969, pp. 255–344.

Robertson, H. M. The Wealth of Nations: How the National Income Is Produced, Divided Up and Spent. *S. Afr. J. Econ.,* June 1969, *37*(2), pp. 87–97.

Robertson, J. L. Statement. **In** *Bank Holding Company Act Amendments, Pts. 1–3, HCH,* 1969, pp. 204–10.

Robertson, Keith B.; Herzberg, Frederick and Paul, William J., Jr. Job Enrichment Pays Off. *Harvard Bus. Rev.,* March–April 1969, *47*(2), pp. 61–78.

Robertson, N. and Sams, K. I. Industrial Relations Reform in Great Britain. *Mon. Lab. Rev.,* January 1969, *92*(1), pp. 35–40.

Robertson, Ross M. and Hastings, Delbert G. The Mysterious World of the Fed. **In** *Starleaf, D. R., ed.,* 1969, pp. 279–86.

Robertson, Thomas S. and Myers, James H. Personality Correlates of Opinion Leadership and Innovative Buying Behavior. *J. Marketing Res.,* May 1969, *6*(2), pp. 164–68.

Robeson, James F.; Grabner, John R., Jr. and Lalonde, Bernard J. The Business Logistics Concept. *Ohio State U. Bull. Bus. Res.,* May 1969, *44* (5), pp. 1–3, 8.

Robichek, Alexander A. Risk and the Value of Securities. *J. Financial Quant. Anal.,* December 1969, *4*(4), pp. 513–38.

______ **and Van Horne, James C.** Abandonment Value and Capital Budgeting: Reply. *J. Finance,* March 1969, *24*(1), pp. 96–97.

Robinson, D. and Knowles, K. G. J. C. Wage Movements in Coventry. *Bull. Oxford Univ. Inst. Econ. Statist.,* February 1969, *31*(1), pp. 1–21.

______ Wage Movements in Coventry—Appendix II. *Bull. Oxford Univ. Inst. Econ. Statist.,* May 1969, *31*(2), pp. 145–52.

Robinson, David M. Some Comments on the Nature of the Scholarly Assumption as a Bias for Model Construction. *Liiketaloudellinen Aikak.,* 1969, *18*(1), pp. 68–73.

Robinson, E. A. G. The Desirable Level of Agriculture in the Advanced Industrial Economies. **In** *Papi, U. and Nunn, C., eds.,* 1969, pp. 26–44.

Robinson, H. Leslie. Electric Power Integration in Latin America. **In** *Hilton, R., ed.,* 1969, pp. 335–42.

Robinson, Ira M. and Atkisson, Arthur A. Amenity Resources for Urban Living. **In** *Perloff, H. S., ed.,* 1969, pp. 179–201.

Robinson, James W. and Carlsson, Robert J. Compensation Decisions in Public Organizations: Comment. *Ind. Relat.,* October 1969, *9*(1), pp. 111–13.

______ Toward a Public Employment Wage Theory. *Ind. Lab. Relat. Rev.,* January 1969, *22*(2), pp. 243–48.

______ Toward a Public Employment Wage Theory: Reply. *Ind. Lab. Relat. Rev.,* October 1969, *23*(1), pp. 95–100.

Robinson, Joan. The Degree of Monopoly in the Kaldor-Mirrlees Growth Model: A Further Note. *Rev. Econ. Stud.,* April 1969, *36*(106), pp. 260–62.

______ Macroeconomics of Unbalanced Growth: A Belated Comment. *Amer. Econ. Rev.,* Part I, September 1969, *59*(4), pp. 632.

______ A Model for Accumulation Proposed by J. E. Stiglitz. *Econ. J.,* June 1969, *79*(314), pp. 412–13.

______ The Theory of Value Reconsidered. *Australian Econ. Pap.,* June 1969, *8*(12), pp. 13–19.

Robinson, Roland I. Capital Flows to Public Utilities and the Structure of the Money and Capital Markets: Comment. **In** *Trebing, H. M. and Howard, R. H., eds.,* 1969, pp. 57–61.

______ **and Pettway, Richard H.** Policies for Optimum Bank Capital: Summary. **In** *Jessup, P. F.,* 1969, pp. 183–86.

Robinson, T. Russell. The Foreign Trade Sector and Domestic Stability: The Canadian Case. *Yale Econ. Essays,* Spring 1969, *9*(1), pp. 47–87.

Robinson, Warren C. A Critical Note on the New Conservationism. *Land Econ.,* November 1969, *45*(4), pp. 453–56.

______ "Disguised" Unemployment Once Again: East Pakistan, 1951–1961. *Amer. J. Agr. Econ.,* August 1969, *51*(3), pp. 592–604.

______ Population Control and Development Strategy. *J. Devel. Stud.,* January 1969, *5*(2), pp. 104–17.

______ Types of Disguised Rural Unemployment and Some Policy Implications. *Oxford Econ. Pap.,* November 1969, *21*(3), pp. 373–86.

______ **and Heitman, George.** A Suggested Reformulation of the Basic Keynesian Model. *Quart. Rev. Econ. Bus.,* Autumn 1969, *9*(3), pp. 51–55.

Robson, Edwin A. Multi-District Litigation: §1407 in Operation. *Antitrust Bull.,* Spring 1969, *14,* pp. 109–18.

Robson, P. and Lury, D. A. Introduction: The Economies of Africa. In *Robson, P. and Lury, D. A., eds.*, 1969, pp. 23–78.

Roby, Pamela. Inequality: A Trend Analysis. *Ann. Amer. Acad. Polit. Soc. Sci.*, September 1969, *385*, pp. 110–17.

Rock, Eli. The Appropriate Unit Question in the Public Service: The Problem of Proliferation. *Mich. Law Rev.*, March 1969, *67*(5), pp. 1001–16.

Rock, James M. Cookware and Vertical Integration: A Reply. *J. Law Econ.*, October 1969, *12*(2), pp. 441–43.

______ Cookware: A Study in Vertical Integration—A Reexamination. *J. Law Econ.*, October 1969, *12*(2), pp. 425–38.

Rockefeller, John D., III. The Citizen's View of Public Programs for Family Limitation. In *Behrman, S. J.; Corsa, L., Jr. and Freedman, R., eds.*, 1969, pp. 493–98.

Rodewald, Gordon E., Jr. A Method for Analyzing the Effect of Taxes and Financing on Investment Decisions. *Amer. J. Agr. Econ.*, December 1969, *51*(5), pp. 1178–81.

______ **and Baker, C. B.** Economics of Investment in Cattle Feeding. *Ill. Agr. Econ.*, January 1969, *9*(1), pp. 18–25.

______ **and Baker, C. B.** Interim Period Asset Valuation: A Method for Making Investment Decisions. *Agr. Econ. Res.*, April 1969, *21*(2), pp. 35–39.

Rodgers, James D. The Perfectly Competitive Production of Collective Goods: Comment. *Rev. Econ. Statist.*, November 1969, *51*(4), pp. 476–78.

______ **and Hochman, Harold M.** Pareto Optimal Redistribution. *Amer. Econ. Rev.*, Part I, September 1969, *59*(4), pp. 542–57.

Roe, Alan R. Terms of Trade and Transfer Effects in the East African Common Market: An Empirical Study. *Bull. Oxford Univ. Inst. Econ. Statist.*, August 1969, *31*(3), pp. 153–67.

Rogers, Andrei. On Perfect Aggregation in the Matrix Cohort-Survival Model of Interregional Population Growth. *J. Reg. Sci.*, December 1969, *9*(3), pp. 417–24.

Rogers, Christopher D. Consumer Participation in the International Tin Agreements. *Malayan Econ. Rev.*, October 1969, *14*(2), pp. 113–29.

Rogers, Daniel C. Private Rates of Return to Education in the United States: A Case Study. *Yale Econ. Essays*, Spring 1969, *9*(1), pp. 89–134.

Rogers, Peter. A Game Theory Approach to the Problems of International River Basins. *Water Resources Res.*, August 1969, *5*(4), pp. 749–60.

Rogers, S. J. Political Algebra and U.K. Agricultural Policy. *Nat. Westminster Bank Quart. Rev.*, February 1969, pp. 53–68.

Rogers, Tommy W. Factors in the Net Migration Rates of Southern SMSA's: A Comparison of the Subregional Influence of Selected Variables. *Miss. Val. J. Bus. Econ.*, Fall 1969, *5*(1), pp. 51–67.

______ Migration Attractiveness of Southern Metropolitan Areas. *Soc. Sci. Quart.*, September 1969, *50*(2), pp. 325–36.

Rogers, William Warren. Negro Knights of Labor in Arkansas: A Case Study of the "Miscellaneous" Strike. *Labor Hist.*, Summer 1969, *10*(3), pp. 498–505.

Rohlíček, Rudolf. Intentions and Reality. *New Trends Czech. Econ.*, November 1969, (7), pp. 3–14.

______ Principles of the Present Finance and Tax Policy. *New Trends Czech. Econ.*, December 1969, (8), pp. 61–70.

Rohrlich, George F. The Place of Social Insurance in the Pursuit of the General Welfare. *J. Risk Ins.*, September 1969, *36*(4), pp. 333–53.

______ Social Security for the Aged: International Perspectives—A Working Paper. In *op. cit., SCP*, 1969, pp. 1–14.

Roldan, Alfredo. Latin American Economic Integration: Its Benefits and Obstacles. In *Hilton, R., ed.*, 1969, pp. 80–96.

______ The Latin American Economic Integration: Its Benefits and Obstacles. *Nebr. J. Econ. Bus.*, Winter 1968–69, *8*(1), pp. 16–33.

Rolfe, Sidney E. The Capital Market Phenomena: A Comment. *J. Money, Credit, Banking*, August 1969, *1*(3), pp. 332–35.

Roll, Richard. Bias in Fitting the Sharpe Model to Time Series Data. *J. Financial Quant. Anal.*, September 1969, *4*(3), pp. 271–89.

Rolph, Earl R. Controversy Surrounding Negative Income Taxation. *Public Finance*, 1969, *24*(2), pp. 352–61.

Roman, Hope S. Semantic Generalization in Formation of Consumer Attitudes. *J. Marketing Res.*, August 1969, *6*(3), pp. 369–73.

Román, Zoltán. A Note on Measuring Structural Changes. *Rev. Income Wealth*, September 1969, *15*(3), pp. 265–68.

______ Pattern of the Hungarian Industry. *Acta Oecon.*, 1969, *4*(2), pp. 181–95.

Romulo, Carlos P. Symposium on Asian Education. In *Bereday, G. Z. F., ed.*, 1969, pp. 244–63.

van Rooijen, M. J. The Substantial Holding Privilege in Netherlands Corporate Income Tax. *Bull. Int. Fiscal Doc.*, July, August, September 1969, *23*(7–8–9), pp. 337–405.

Roos, Leslie L., Jr. Development *versus* Distribution: An Attitudinal Study of Turkish Local Administration. *Econ. Develop. Cult. Change*, July 1969, *17*(4), pp. 552–66.

Roosa, Robert V. The American Share in the Stream of International Payments. *Ann. Amer. Acad. Polit. Soc. Sci.*, July 1969, *384*, pp. 21–34.

Roosens, Paul. De lichte luchtvaart. (The Light Aviation. With English summary.) *Econ. Soc. Tijdschr.*, October 1969, *23*(5), pp. 481–87.

Roosevelt, Frank. Market Socialism: A Humane Economy? *J. Econ. Issues*, December 1969, *3*(4), pp. 3–20.

Roper, Burns W. Sensitivity, Reliability, and Consumer Taste Testing: Some "Rights" and "Wrongs." *J. Marketing Res.*, February 1969, *6*(1), pp. 102–05.

Roscoe, David L. and Anderson, Leslie P. The Term Structure of Interest Rates—An Alternative Hypothesis. *Miss. Val. J. Bus. Econ.*, Spring 1969, *4*(2), pp. 1–9.

Rose, Arthur. Wage Differentials in the Building Trades. *Mon. Lab. Rev.*, October 1969, *92*(10), pp. 14–17.

Rose, Hugh. Real and Monetary Factors in the Business Cycle. *J. Money, Credit, Banking,* May 1969, *1*(2), pp. 138–52.

Rose, J., et al. Toward an Empirical Measure of Materiality. **In** *Association of Canadian Schools of Business,* 1969, pp. 22–46.

Rosekrans, Frank M. Statistical Significance and Reporting Test Results. *J. Marketing Res.,* November 1969, *6*(4), pp. 451–55.

Rosen, L. S. and DeCoster, Don T. "Funds" Statements: A Historical Perspective. *Accounting Rev.,* January 1969, *44*(1), pp. 124–36.

Rosen, Sherwin. On the Interindustry Wage and Hours Structure. *J. Polit. Econ.,* March/April 1969, *77*(2), pp. 249–73.

______ Trade Union Power, Threat Effects and the Extent of Organization. *Rev. Econ. Stud.,* April 1969, *36*(106), pp. 185–96.

______ **and Nadiri, M. Ishag.** Interrelated Factor Demand Functions. *Amer. Econ. Rev.,* Part I, September 1969, *59*(4), pp. 457–71.

Rosen, Sumner M. Union-Management Cooperation: Is There an Agenda for Tomorrow? **In** *Somers, G. G., ed. (II),* 1969, pp. 81–89.

Rosenberg, Leonard Gerson. Taxation of Income from Capital, by Industry Group. **In** *Harberger, A. C. and Bailey, M. J., eds.,* 1969, pp. 123–84.

Rosenberg, Nathan. The Direction of Technological Change: Inducement Mechanisms and Focusing Devices. *Econ. Develop. Cult. Change,* Part I, October 1969, *18*(1), pp. 1–24.

Rosenbluth, Gideon. Business Cycles in Canada: Their Postwar Persistence: Comment. **In** *Bronfenbrenner, M., ed.,* 1969, pp. 66–72.

Rosenfield, Paul. Reporting Subjective Gains and Losses. *Accounting Rev.,* October 1969, *44*(4), pp. 788–97.

Rosenthal, Howard and Sen, Subrata. Candidate Selection and Voting Behavior in France. *Public Choice,* Spring 1969, *6,* pp. 71–92.

Rosenzweig, J. E.; Johnson, R. A. and Kast, F. E. Systems Theory and Management. **In** *Carsberg, B. V. and Edey, H. C., eds.,* 1969, pp. 279–302.

Roskamp, Karl W. Fiscal Policy and Effects of Government Purchases: An Input-Output Analysis. *Public Finance,* 1969, *24*(1), pp. 33–47.

______ Fiscal Policy Objectives and Government Purchases by Industries: Towards an Input-Output Decision Model. *Z. ges. Staatswiss.,* January 1969, *125*(1), pp. 82–88.

Ross, Anne M. Public Employee Unions and the Right to Strike. *Mon. Lab. Rev.,* March 1969, *92*(3), pp. 14–18.

Ross, David B. The Arbitration of Public Employee Wage Disputes. *Ind. Lab. Relat. Rev.,* October 1969, *23*(1), pp. 3–14.

Ross, H. Laurence. A Review Article on Basic Protection for the Traffic Victim: Reply. *J. Risk Ins.,* June 1969, *36*(2), pp. 313–14.

Ross, Ivan. Handling the Neutral Vote in Product Testing. *J. Marketing Res.,* May 1969, *6*(2), pp. 221–22.

Ross, Myron H. and Zelder, Raymond E. The Discount Rate: A Phantom Policy Tool? *Western Econ. J.,* December 1969, *7*(4), pp. 341–48.

Ross, William B. Policy Analysis and Housing and Urban Development Programs. **In** *The Analysis and Evaluation of Public Expenditures: The PPB System, Vol. 3, JECP,* 1969, pp. 1233–41.

Ross, William D. and Bonin, Joseph M. Economic Criteria for Sound State Debt Financing. **In** *[White, Charles P.],* 1969, pp. 127–47.

Rossi, Peter H. No Good Idea Goes Unpunished: Moynihan's Misunderstandings and the Proper Role of Social Science in Policy Making. *Soc. Sci. Quart.,* December 1969, *50*(3), pp. 469–79.

Rossman, William H. Allocation of Equipment Cost in the Heavy Construction Industry. *Manage. Account.,* November 1969, *51*(5), pp. 14–15.

Rosso, David J. and Zeitlin, Sherwin S. United States Taxation of Foreign Enterprises—Structures for Doing Business in the United States and the Western Hemisphere. *Bull. Int. Fiscal Doc.,* December 1969, *23*(12), pp. 555–73.

Rost, Ronald F. and Duggar, Jan Warren. National Bank Note Redemption and Treasury Cash. *J. Econ. Hist.,* September 1969, *29*(3), pp. 512–20.

Rostow, E. V. The Development of Law on Monopoly and Competition. **In** *Hunter, A., ed.,* 1969, pp. 161–82.

Rostro Plasencia, Francisco. Perspectivas de continuidad del desarrollo economico de Mexico. (Prospects of Economic Development in Mexico. With English summary.) *Econ. Polít.,* Second Semester 1969, *6*(2), pp. 241–50.

Rotaru, V. Determinarea mărimii optime a întreprinderii în industria alimentară. (Determining the Optimum Size of an Enterprise in the Food Industry. With English summary.) *Stud. Cercet. Econ.,* 1969, *4,* pp. 85–101.

Roth, Robert and Bellman, Richard. Curve Fitting by Segmented Straight Lines. *J. Amer. Statist. Assoc.,* September 1969, *64*(327), pp. 1079–84.

Roth, William M. Future U.S. Foreign Trade Policy: Report to the President. **In** *The 1969 Economic Report of the President, Pt. 3, JECH,* 1969, pp. 759–871.

Rothberg, Herman J. A Study of the Impact of Office Automation in the IRS. *Mon. Lab. Rev.,* October 1969, *92*(10), pp. 26–30.

Rothenberg, Jerome. Strategic Interaction and Resource Allocation in Metropolitan Intergovernmental Relations. *Amer. Econ. Rev.,* May 1969, *59*(2), pp. 494–503.

Rothman, Jack. The Ghetto Makers. **In** *Kain, J. F., ed.,* 1969, pp. 122–27.

Rothschild, K. W. Price Theory and Oligopoly. **In** *Hunter, A., ed.,* 1969, pp. 24–29.

Rothschild, Kurt W. Austria and Switzerland. **In** *Bronfenbrenner, M., ed.,* 1969, pp. 225–46.

Rottenberg, Simon. Round Table on Allocation of Resources in Law Enforcement. *Amer. Econ. Rev.,* May 1969, *59*(2), pp. 508–10.

Rottman, Dick L. Analysis of Perpetual Insurance. *J. Risk Ins.,* September 1969, *36*(4), pp. 365–82.

Roucek, Joseph S. The Image of the Slav in U.S. History and in Immigration Policy. *Amer. J. Econ. Soc.,* January 1969, *28*(1), pp. 29–48.

Rouse, Andrew M. and Marvin, Keith E. The Status of PPB in Federal Agencies: A Comparative Perspective. **In** *The Analysis and Evaluation of Public Expenditures: The PPB System, Vol. 3, JECP,* 1969, pp. 801–14.

Rouse, James W. Columbia: A New Town Built with Private Capital. **In** *Ling, A. G., et al.,* 1969, pp. 13–29.

Roussakis, Emmanuel N. The Common Market and the Zollverein: Experiences in Integration. *Rech. Écon. Louvain,* August 1969, *35*(3), pp. 201–08.

——— La Comunità Economica Europea: Bilancio economico e politico. (The European Economic Community: An Economic and Political Balance Sheet. With English summary.) *Rivista Int. Sci. Econ. Com.,* October 1969, *16*(10), pp. 993–1006.

Rousseas, S. W. Monetary Equilibrium, Economic Development and the Economics of Xenophon Zolotas. **In** *Economic Concentration, Pt. 7A, SCH,* 1969, pp. 4197–4206.

Rousseaux, R. La réévaluation larvée des monnaies des pays industrialisés par rapport à celles des pays en voie de développement. (The Disguised Revaluation of Money in the Industrialised Countries if Exchange Rates Are Compared with the Parities in the Underdeveloped Countries. With English summary.) *Econ. Soc. Tijdschr.,* June 1969, *23*(3), pp. 273–86.

Rowan, David C. Towards a Rational Exchange Policy: Some Reflections on the British Experience. *Fed. Res. Bank St. Louis Rev.,* April 1969, *51*(4), pp. 17–26.

Rowan, Richard L. Negro Employment in the Basic Steel Industry. *Ind. Lab. Relat. Rev.,* October 1969, *23*(1), pp. 29–39.

Rowe, D. J. The Chartist Convention and the Regions. *Econ. Hist. Rev.,* April 1969, *22*(1), pp. 58–74.

Rowen, Henry S. and Williams, Albert P., Jr. Policy Analysis in International Affairs. **In** *The Analysis and Evaluation of Public Expenditures: The PPB System, Vol. 3, JECP,* 1969, pp. 970–1002.

Rowland, Kendrith M. and Sovereign, Michael G. Markov-Chain Analysis of Internal Manpower Supply. *Ind. Relat.,* October 1969, *9*(1), pp. 88–99.

Rowley, C. K. The Monopolies Commission and Rate of Return on Capital. *Econ. J.,* March 1969, *79*(313), pp. 42–65.

——— The Political Economy of British Education. *Scot. J. Polit. Econ.,* June 1969, *16*(2), pp. 152–76.

Roxas, Sixto K. Policies for the Private Sector. *Philippine Econ. J.,* First Semester 1969, *8*(1), pp. 16–30.

Roy, M. Sinha. Productivity of Education with Special Reference to Under-developed Countries. **In** *Pandit, H. N., ed.,* 1969, pp. 294–303.

Roychowdhury, K. C. The Indian Economy and the Drain Theory. *Indian Econ. J.,* January–March 1969, *16*(3), pp. 327–40.

Rozen, Marvin E. Some Observations on the Efficiency of Industrialization. *Pakistan Develop. Rev.,* Winter 1969, *9*(4), pp. 357–79.

Rozet, A. Bruce. The Complex World of the American Corporation: Priorities, Goals, and Strategies. **In** *Ozbekhan, H. and Talbert, G. E., eds.,* 1969, pp. 118–26.

Rozorea, M. and Mureşan, D. Probleme ale rentei funciare în opera lui Nicolae Bălcescu. (Problems of Ground Rent in Nicolae Bălcescu's Work. With English summary.) *Stud. Cercet. Econ.,* 1969, *1-2,* pp. 221–27.

Rubel, John H. Systems Management and Industry Behavior. **In** *Weston, J. F. and Peltzman, S., eds.,* 1969, pp. 208–18.

Rubin, Lillian B. Maximum Feasible Participation: The Origins, Implications, and Present Status. *Ann. Amer. Acad. Polit. Soc. Sci.,* September 1969, *385,* pp. 14–29.

Ruchlin, Hirsch S. and Hettena, Ran. The U.S. Tanker Industry: A Structural and Behavioral Analysis. *J. Ind. Econ.,* July 1969, *17*(3), pp. 188–204.

Rudra, Ashok. National Income Statistics of India. *Arthaniti,* January & July 1969, *12*(1&2), pp. 69–77.

Ruebling, Charlotte E. and Jordan, Jerry L. Federal Open Market Committee Decisions in 1968—A Year of Watchful Waiting. *Fed. Res. Bank St. Louis Rev.,* May 1969, *51*(5), pp. 6–15.

Ruff, Larry E. Research and Technological Progress in a Cournot Economy. *J. Econ. Theory,* December 1969, *1*(4), pp. 397–415.

Ruffin, Roy J. Tariffs, Intermediate Goods, and Domestic Protection. *Amer. Econ. Rev.,* June 1969, *59*(3), pp. 261–69.

Ruist, Erik. Den nordiska stålindustrin inför världsmarknaden. (The Scandanavian Steel Industry and the World Market. With English summary.) *Econ. Samfundets Tidskr.,* 1969, *22*(3), pp. 164–80.

Runciman, A. M. Agricultural Policy in a Dynamic Economy: Symposium. *Can. J. Agr. Econ.,* November 1969, *17*(3), pp. 52–56.

Rusanov, E. S. Methodology. **In** *Noah, H. J., ed.,* 1969, pp. 20–22.

Russell, Joe L. and Pilot, Michael J. Seasonality in Construction: A Continuing Problem. *Mon. Lab. Rev.,* December 1969, *92*(12), pp. 3–8.

Russell, R. Robert and Black, Stanley W. An Alternative Estimate of Potential GNP. *Rev. Econ. Statist.,* February 1969, *51*(1), pp. 70–76.

Russell, William R. An Investigation of Commercial Banks' Aggregate Portfolio Adjustments. *Int. Econ. Rev.,* October 1969, *10*(3), pp. 266–90.

——— **and Bonello, Frank J.** Multiple Year Forecast Errors and the Terms Structure of Interest Rates. *Indian Econ. J.,* April–June 1969, *16*(4–5), pp. 554–60.

——— **and Hadar, Josef.** Rules for Ordering Uncertain Prospects. *Amer. Econ. Rev.,* March 1969, *59* (1), pp. 25–34.

Russett, Bruce M. Who Pays for Defense? *Amer. Polit. Sci. Rev.,* June 1969, *63*(2), pp. 412–26.

Rust, Charles H. and St. George, George. Transportation Pricing as a Factor in Commodity Marketing: Montana Wheat, A Case Study. *Amer. J. Agr. Econ.,* December 1969, *51*(5), pp. 1471–77.

Ruta, Guido. Profili comparativistici del sistema bancario italiano nell'ambito della Comunità Economica Europea. (Comparative Aspects of the Italian Banking System within the European Economic Community. With English summary.) *Bancaria,* July 1969, *25*(7), pp. 829–41.

Rutgaizer, V. and Zlatin, V. Comparison of the Levels of Economic Development of Union Republics and Large Regions. *Prob. Econ.*, June 1969, *12*(2), pp. 3–24.

Rutman, Gilbert L. Innovation in the Land Tenure System of the Transkei, South Africa. *Land Econ.*, November 1969, *45*(4), pp. 467–71.

Ruttan, Vernon W. Agricultural Product and Factor Markets in Southeast Asia. *Econ. Develop. Cult. Change*, July 1969, *17*(4), pp. 501–19.

_____ Equity and Productivity Issues in Modern Agrarian Reform Legislation. **In** *Papi, U. and Nunn, C., eds.*, 1969, pp. 581–600.

_____ Program Analysis and Agricultural Policy. **In** *The Analysis and Evaluation of Public Expenditures: The PPB System, Vol. 3, JECP*, 1969, pp. 1128–50.

Ruzavina, E. Economic Aspects in the Urbanization Process. *Prob. Econ.*, August 1969, *12*(4), pp. 68–79.

Ryan, Bruce. Metropolitan Growth. **In** *Preston, R., ed.*, 1969, pp. 196–225.

Ryan, J. G. Optimum Programmes for Irrigation Farms. *Rev. Marketing Agr. Econ.*, September 1969, *37*(3), pp. 153–71.

Ryan, W. and Taplin, J. The Prospects for Wine in Australia. *Quart. Rev. Agr. Econ.*, October 1969, *22*(4), pp. 198–209.

Ryans, John K., Jr. and Donnelly, James H., Jr. The Role of Culture in Organizing Overseas Operations: The Advertising Experience. *Univ. Wash. Bus. Rev.*, Autumn 1969, *29*(1), pp. 35–41.

_____ **and Hise, Richard T.** Retailing's Unfortunate Image: Problems of Attracting College Graduates. *Econ. Bus. Bull.*, Fall 1969, *22*(1), pp. 39–43.

Ryavec, Karl W. Soviet Industrial Managers, Their Superiors and the Economic Reform: A Study of an Attempt at Planned Behavioural Change. *Soviet Stud.*, October 1969, *21*(2), pp. 208–29.

Rychetnik, Ludek. The Growth of Inflationary Pressure: 1955–1966. *Eastern Europ. Econ.*, Spring 1969, *7*(3), pp. 3–11.

Ryder, Harl E., Jr. Optimal Accumulation in a Two-Sector Neoclassical Economy with Non-Shiftable Capital. *J. Polit. Econ.*, Part II, July/August 1969, *77*(4), pp. 665–83.

_____ **and Beckmann, Martin J.** Simultaneous Price and Quantity Adjustment in a Single Market. *Econometrica*, July 1969, *37*(3), pp. 470–84.

Ryder, Norman B. The Emergence of a Modern Fertility Pattern: United States 1917–66. **In** *Behrman, S. J.; Corsa, L., Jr. and Freedman, R., eds.*, 1969, pp. 99–123.

_____ **and Westoff, Charles F.** Recent Trends in Attitudes Toward Fertility Control and in the Practice of Contraception in the United States. **In** *Behrman, S. J.; Corsa, L., Jr. and Freedman, R., eds.*, 1969, pp. 388–412.

Ryland, G. J. and Guise, John W. B. Production Scheduling and Allocation: A Normative Decision Model for Sugar Milling. *Australian J. Agr. Econ.*, June 1969, *13*(1), pp. 8–24.

Ryscavage, Paul M. Employment Developments in Urban Poverty Neighborhoods. *Mon. Lab. Rev.*, June 1969, *92*(6), pp. 51–56.

Saarsalmi, Meeri. Kuluttajain ostoaikomukset ja ostotodennäköisyydet kysyntäennusteissa. (Consumer Buying Intentions and Purchase Probability in Forecasting Demand. With English summary.) *Liiketaloudellinen Aikak.*, 1969, *18* (3), pp. 576–84.

_____ Kuluttajan käyttäytymisen tutkiminen markkinoinnin päätöksenteon kannalta tarkasteltuna. (The Study of Consumer Behavior from the Viewpoint of Decision-Making in Marketing. With English summary.) *Liiketaloudellinen Aikak.*, 1969, *18*(2), pp. 220–32.

Saathoff, C. R.; Babb, E. M. and Belden, S. A. An Analysis of Cooperative Bargaining in the Processing Tomato Industry. *Amer. J. Agr. Econ.*, February 1969, *51*(1), pp. 13–25.

Sabolo, Yves. Sectoral Employment Growth: The Outlook for 1980. *Int. Lab. Rev.*, November 1969, *100*(5), pp. 445–74.

Sachs, Ignacy. Employment and Economic Development in a Dual Economy. **In** *Yesufu, T. M., ed.*, 1969, pp. 227–36.

Sadie, J. L. Company Taxation. *S. Afr. J. Econ.*, December 1969, *37*(4), pp. 345–71.

Sadler, Marion. Who Speaks for the People in Collective Bargaining? **In** *Starleaf, D. R., ed.*, 1969, pp. 148–52.

Saenko, Iu. I. The Allocation of Capital Investment for School Construction. **In** *Noah, H. J., ed.*, 1969, pp. 87–98.

Sahota, G. S. Economic Problems in Separating the Determinants of Relative Prices. *Int. Econ. Rev.*, June 1969, *10*(2), pp. 183–206.

Saigal, J. C. Optimum Savings Programme: A Note. **In** *[Tinbergen, J.]*, 1969, pp. 19–27.

Saini, Krishan G. The Growth of the Indian Economy: 1860–1960. *Rev. Income Wealth*, September 1969, *15*(3), pp. 247–63.

Saitow, Arnold R. CSPC: Reporting Project Progress to the Top. *Harvard Bus. Rev.*, January–February 1969, *47*(1), pp. 88–97.

Sakamoto, Jorge. Industrial Development and Integration of Underdeveloped Countries. *J. Common Market Stud.*, June 1969, *7*(4), pp. 283–304.

Salama, Elías. Sobre la posición monetaria neta. (On the Net Monetary Position. With English summary.) *Económica*, September–December 1969, *15*(3), pp. 299–311.

Salant, Walter S. International Reserves and Payments Adjustment. *Banca Naz. Lavoro Quart. Rev.*, September 1969, (90), pp. 281–308.

_____ Writing and Reading in Economics. *J. Polit. Econ.*, Part I, July/August 1969, *77*(4), pp. 545–58.

Salgado Rabadán, Abel. La planeación económica en el sistema capitalista (Segunda y última parte). (The Economic Planning in a Capitalist System: Second and Last Part. With English summary.) *Econ. Polít.*, Fourth Semester 1969, *6*(4), pp. 461–72.

_____ La planeación económica en el sistema capitalista (Primera parte). (Economic Planning in the Capitalist System: First Part. With English summary.) *Econ. Polít.*, Third Semester 1969, *6* (3), pp. 361–66.

Salisbury, Richard F. Formal Analysis in Anthropological Economics: The Rossel Island Case. **In**

Buchler, I. R. and Nutini, H. G., eds., 1969, pp. 75–93.

Saltmarsh, John. Plague and Economic Decline in England in the Latter Middle Ages. **In** *Scoville, W. C. and La Force, J. C., eds., Vol. I*, 1969, pp. 111–29.

Salvemini, Maria Teresa. Idee per un bilancio previsionale di cassa. (Ideas for a Cash Budget. With English summary.) *Bancaria*, September 1969, *25* (9), pp. 1088–99.

Samli, A. Coskun. Differential Price Structures for the Rich and the Poor. *Univ. Wash. Bus. Rev.*, Summer 1969, *28*(4), pp. 36–43.

——— Governmental Deficit Financing and Growth in Underdeveloped Countries: Reply. *Miss. Val. J. Bus. Econ.*, Fall 1969, *5*(1), pp. 93–96.

——— **and Myers, James H.** Management Control of Marketing Research. *J. Marketing Res.*, August 1969, *6*(3), pp. 267–77.

Samoilova, I. D. The Returns from Various Types of Specialist Training. **In** *Noah, H. J., ed.*, 1969, pp. 159–66.

Sampford, M. R. A Comparison of Some Possible Methods of Sampling from Smallish Populations, with Units of Unequal Size. **In** *Johnson, N. L. and Smith, H., Jr., eds.*, 1969, pp. 170–87.

Sampson, Anthony A. Measuring the Rate of Return on Capital. *J. Finance*, March 1969, *24*(1), pp. 61–74.

Sams, K. I. and Robertson, N. Industrial Relations Reform in Great Britain. *Mon. Lab. Rev.*, January 1969, *92*(1), pp. 35–40.

Samuels, J. M.; Smyth, David J. and Briscoe, G. The Treatment of Risk in the Stock Market. *J. Finance*, September 1969, *24*(4), pp. 707–13.

——— The Variability of Industry Profit Rates. *Appl. Econ.*, May 1969, *1*(2), pp. 137–49.

Samuels, Warren J. On the Future of Institutional Economics. *J. Econ. Issues*, September 1969, *3*(3), pp. 67–72.

——— The Tableau Economique as a Simple Leontief Model: A Precursor to Phillips. *Indian Econ. J.*, July–September 1969, *17*(1), pp. 112–17.

Samuelson, Paul A. Contrast between Welfare Conditions for Joint Supply and for Public Goods. *Rev. Econ. Statist.*, February 1969, *51*(1), pp. 26–30.

——— Corrected Formulation of Direct and Indirect Additivity. *Econometrica*, April 1969, *37*(2), pp. 355–59.

——— Lifetime Portfolio Selection by Dynamic Stochastic Programming. *Rev. Econ. Statist.*, August 1969, *51*(3), pp. 239–46.

——— Local Proof of the Turnpike Theorem. *Western Econ. J.*, March 1969, *7*(1), pp. 1–8.

——— Presidential Address. **In** *Samuelson, P. A., ed.*, 1969, pp. 1–11.

——— Pure Theory of Public Expenditure and Taxation. **In** *Margolis, J. and Guitton, H., eds.*, 1969, pp. 98–123.

——— The Role of Money in National Economic Policy. **In** *Federal Reserve Bank of Boston*, 1969, pp. 7–13.

——— Statement. **In** *Consumer Credit Regulations, Pt. 1, HCH*, 1969, pp. 163–66.

——— Statement. **In** *Investment Company Amendments Act of 1969, SCH*, 1969, pp. 53–57.

——— **and Liviatan, Nissan.** Notes on Turnpikes: Stable and Unstable. *J. Econ. Theory*, December 1969, *1*(4), pp. 454–75.

——— **and Stolper, W. F.** Protection and Real Wages. **In** *Bereday, G. Z. F., ed.*, 1969, pp. 245–68.

Sánchez Cortés, José and Restrepo Fernández, Iván. El arrendamiento de tierras ejidales: El caso de Apatzingán. (The Leasing of Common Lands: The Case of Apatzingán. With English summary.) *Econ. Polít.*, Third Semester 1969, *6*(3), pp. 331–46.

Sandberg, Lars G. American Rings and English Mules: The Role of Economic Rationality. *Quart. J. Econ.*, February 1969, *83*(1), pp. 25–43.

Sandbulte, Arend J. Sales and Revenue Forecasting. *Manage. Account.*, December 1969, *51*(6), pp. 17–23.

Sandee, Jan. A Programming Model for a Dual Economy. **In** *Thorbecke, E., ed.*, 1969, pp. 219–30.

——— **and van de Pas, J. H.** The Effect of Fluctuations in Public Expenditure and Taxation on Economic Growth. **In** *Margolis, J. and Guitton, H., eds.*, 1969, pp. 388–405.

Sanders, John. The Depressed Area and Labor Mobility: The Eastern Kentucky Case. *J. Human Res.*, Fall 1969, *4*(4), pp. 437–50.

Sanderson, Michael. The Universities and Industry in England 1919–1939. *Yorkshire Bull. Econ. Soc. Res.*, May 1969, *21*(1), pp. 39–65.

Sandesara, J. C. Size and Capital-Intensity in Indian Industry: Some Comments. *Bull. Oxford Univ. Inst. Econ. Statist.*, November 1969, *31*(4), pp. 331–34.

Sandmo, Agnar. Capital Risk, Consumption, and Portfolio Choice. *Econometrica*, October 1969, *37* (4), pp. 586–99.

Sandu, Gh. and Dincu, I. Implicațiile economice ale unor măsuri de valorificare a solurilor slab productive. (Economic Implications of Some Measures Taken in View of Turning to Account Weakly Productive Soils. With English summary.) *Stud. Cercet. Econ.*, 1969, *4*, pp. 115–23.

Sankar, U. and Chetty, V. Karuppan. Bayesian Estimation of the CES Production Function. *Rev. Econ. Stud.*, July 1969, *36*(107), pp. 289–94.

Sansom, Robert L. The Motor Pump: A Case Study of Innovation and Development. *Oxford Econ. Pap.*, March 1969, *21*(1), pp. 109–21.

Santomé Figueroa, César. La viabilidad economica del puerto de Topolobampo. (Economic Viability of the Topolobampo Port. With English summary.) *Econ. Polít.*, Fourth Semester 1969, *6*(4), pp. 485–94.

Santoro, Gaetano and Trabucchi, Romano. Un'esperienza di addestramento mediante audiovisivi: il centro audiovisivi de la "rinascente-upim." (Training Experience through Audiovisual Methods. With English summary.) *L'Impresa*, November/December 1969, *11*(6), pp. 469–72.

Santoro, Vincenzo. Considerazioni sul movimento demografico in Campania, per gruppi di comuni. (With English summary.) *Statistica*, January–March 1969, *29*(1), pp. 73–105.

Sarabia, Antonio R. A Comparison between European and Latin American Integration. **In** *Hilton, R., ed.*, 1969, pp. 97–109.

Sarachek, Deborah; Auster, Richard and Leveson, Irving. The Production of Health, an Exploratory Study. *J. Human Res.*, Fall 1969, *4*(4), pp. 411–36.

Saran, Ram. Buffer Stock in Foodgrains. **In** *Indian Society of Agricultural Economics,* 1969, pp. 85–99.

Saravane, Mohandas. Some Issues Relating to Deposit Mobilisation by Non-Banking Companies. *Indian Econ. J.*, April–June 1969, *16*(4–5), pp. 445–57.

Sardi, Paolo. Interazione fra decisioni e sistema. (Inter-action between Decisions and Systems. With English summary.) *L'Impresa,* May/June 1969, *11* (3), pp. 231–36.

Sardy, Hyman and Jonas, Paul. Production Index Bias as a Measure of Economic Development: A Comment. *Oxford Econ. Pap.*, November 1969, *21*(3), pp. 428–32.

Sargent, Thomas J. Commodity Price Expectations and the Interest Rate. *Quart. J. Econ.*, February 1969, *83*(1), pp. 127–40.

Sarin, H. C. Civil Production in Defense Undertakings. **In** *Dagli, V., ed., Vol. II,* 1969, pp. 195–200.

Sarkar, Anil Kumar and Ghosh, Arabinda. Size Structure of Indian Engineering Industries, 1948–61. *Indian Econ. J.*, January–March 1969, *16*(3), pp. 375–81.

Sarkar, K. K. Development of Indian Agriculture: Role of Institutional Credit Agencies. *Econ. Aff.*, January-February 1969, *14*(1–2), pp. 57–67.

Särkisilta, Martti. Markkinointistrategian valinta suunnittelu- ja päätöksentekotapahtumana. (Choice of Marketing Strategy as a Planning and Decision-making Event. With English summary.) *Liiketaloudellinen Aikak.*, 1969, *18*(2), pp. 251–62.

Sarma, L. V. L. N. and Rao, R. S. Hanumanta. Estimates of the Cost of Capital to the Indian Engineering Industry, 1962–65. *Yorkshire Bull. Econ. Soc. Res.*, November 1969, *21*(2), pp. 132–40.

______ **and Roa, K. S. Hanumanta.** Leverage and the Value of the Firm. *J. Finance,* September 1969, *24*(4), pp. 673–77.

Sarnat, Marshall and Levy, Haim. A Note on Indifference Curves and Uncertainty. *Swedish J. Econ.*, September 1969, *71*(3), pp. 206–08.

______ The Relationship of Rules of Thumb to the Internal Rate of Return: A Restatement and Generalization. *J. Finance,* June 1969, *24*(3), pp. 479–90.

Sarnoff, Thomas W. Television—Focus on the Future. *Calif. Manage. Rev.*, Fall 1969, *12*(1), pp. 62–64.

Sasser, W. Earl, Jr.; Naylor, Thomas H. and Burdick, Donald S. The Design of Computer Simulation Experiments. **In** *Naylor, T. H., ed.*, 1969, pp. 3–35.

Sastry, M. V. Rama. Multicollinearity and Consumer Demand Elasticities. *Can. J. Agr. Econ.*, February 1969, *17*(1), pp. 50–60.

______ A Note on the Moments and Cumulants of a Weighted Mean. *Statistica,* January–March 1969, *29*(1), pp. 109–12.

Sato, Kazuo. Micro and Macro Constant-Elasticity-of-Substitution Production Functions in a Multifirm Industry. *J. Econ. Theory,* December 1969, *1*(4), pp. 438–53.

Sato, Ryuzo. Stability Conditions in Two-Sector Models of Economic Growth. *J. Econ. Theory,* June 1969, *1*(1), pp. 107–17.

______ **and Beckmann, Martin J.** Aggregate Production Functions and Types of Technical Progress: A Statistical Analysis. *Amer. Econ. Rev.*, March 1969, *59*(1), pp. 88–101.

Sau, R. K. Some Notes on Resource Allocation in Education. **In** *Pandit, H. N., ed.*, 1969, pp. 260–73.

Sau, Ranjit K. The Optimal Rate of Investment in a Firm. *J. Finance,* March 1969, *24*(1), pp. 1–12.

Sault, J. L. Recent Developments Affecting the Market Outlook for Australian Raw Cotton. *Quart. Rev. Agr. Econ.*, July 1969, *22*(3), pp. 123–39.

______ **and Hellier, W. L.** The New International Sugar Agreement and the Australian Sugar Industry. *Quart. Rev. Agr. Econ.*, October 1969, *22* (4), pp. 210–29.

Saunders, John V. D. Education and Modernization in Brazil. **In** *Baklanoff, E. N., ed.*, 1969, pp. 109–41.

Saunders, Robert J. On the Interpretation of Models Explaining Cross Sectional Differences among Commercial Banks. *J. Financial Quant. Anal.*, March 1969, *4*(1), pp. 25–35.

______ Urban Area Water Consumption: Analysis and Projections. *Quart. Rev. Econ. Bus.*, Summer 1969, *9*(2), pp. 5–20.

Sauvy, Alfred. La Pensée Économique en France sur l'idée d'abondance et de besoin. (With English summary.) *Hist. Polit. Econ.*, Fall 1969, *1*(2), pp. 279–305.

Saving, Thomas R. and Ferguson, C. E. Long-Run Scale Adjustments of a Perfectly Competitive Firm and Industry. *Amer. Econ. Rev.*, December 1969, *59*(5), pp. 774–83.

______ **and Lanzillotti, R. F.** State Branching Restrictions and the Availability of Branching Services: A Comment. *J. Money, Credit, Banking,* November 1969, *1*(4), pp. 778–88.

______ **and Pesek, B. P.** The Demand for Money: Some Post-Keynesian Confusions. **In** *Clower, R. W., ed.*, 1969, pp. 247–53.

Sawa, Takamitsu. The Exact Sampling Distribution of Ordinary Least Squares and Two-Stage Least Squares Estimators. *J. Amer. Statist. Assoc.*, September 1969, *64*(327), pp. 923–37.

Sawada, Shūjirō. Technological Change in Japanese Agriculture: A Long-Term Analysis. **In** *Ohkawa, K.; Johnston, B. F. and Kaneda, H., eds.*, 1969, pp. 136–54.

Sawers, Larry. Unemployment and the Structure of Labor Demand. *Rev. Radical Polit. Econ.*, May 1969, *1*(1), pp. 56–74.

Sawhill, Isabel V. The Role of Social Indicators and Social Reporting in Public Expenditure Decisions. **In** *The Analysis and Evaluation of Public Expenditures: The PPB System, Vol. 1, JECP,* 1969, pp. 473–85.

Sawhney, P. K. Inter-Industry Wage Differentials in India. *Indian Econ. J.*, July–September 1969, *17* (1), pp. 28–56.

Saxén, Tryggwe. Note on the Barfod Epsilon Process. *Liiketaloudellinen Aikak.*, 1969, *18*(1), pp. 74–78.

Sayles, Leonard. Industrial Relations and Organization Behavior: Parent and Child? In *Somers, G. G., ed. (I),* 1969, pp. 123–36.

Scaglia, Giovanni Battista. Features of a Tourist Development Policy in Italy. *Rev. Econ. Cond. Italy,* November 1969, *23*(6), pp. 501–04.

Scanlon, John J. Inflation and the Rate of Return. In *Trebing, H. M. and Howard, R. H., eds.,* 1969, pp. 176–86.

Scaperlanda, Anthony E. The Political Economy of Economic Integration. In *Hilton, R., ed.,* 1969, pp. 291–310.

——— **and Mauer, Laurence J.** The Determinants of U.S. Direct Investment in the E.E.C. *Amer. Econ. Rev.,* Part I, September 1969, *59*(4), pp. 558–68.

Scarato, Russell F. Time-Capacity Expansion of Urban Water Systems. *Water Resources Res.,* October 1969, *5*(5), pp. 929–36.

Scarf, Herbert. An Example of an Algorithm for Calculating General Equilibrium Prices. *Amer. Econ. Rev.,* Part I, September 1969, *59*(4), pp. 669–77.

Schaaf, A. H. Effects of Property Taxation on Slums and Renewal: A Study of Land-Improvement Assessment Ratios. *Land Econ.,* February 1969, *45* (1), pp. 111–17.

——— Mortgage Interest Rate Controls and the Veterans' Housing Market. *Miss. Val. J. Bus. Econ.,* Fall 1969, *5*(1), pp. 11–22.

Schaefer, Jeffrey M. Clothing Exemptions and Sales Tax Regressivity. *Amer. Econ. Rev.,* Part I, September 1969, *59*(4), pp. 596–99.

——— The Regressivity of State-Local Taxation: A Case Study of New Jersey. *Quart. Rev. Econ. Bus.,* Spring 1969, *9*(1), pp. 7–18.

——— Sales Tax Regressivity under Alternative Tax Bases and Income Concepts. *Nat. Tax J.,* December 1969, *22*(4), pp. 516–27.

Schaffir, Walter B. How Corporations Plan: Discussion. In *Ozbekhan, H. and Talbert, G. E., eds.,* 1969, pp. 127–44.

Schairer, Robert A. Looking beyond the U.S. Experience: Discussion. In *Ozbekhan, H. and Talbert, G. E., eds.,* 1969, pp. 196–203.

Schaller, François. Qu'est-ce que la productivité? (What Is Productivity? With English summary.) *Rivista Int. Sci. Econ. Com.,* May 1969, *16*(5), pp. 411–28.

Schaller, W. Neill. The Supply Function in Agriculture Revisited: Discussion. *Amer. Econ. Rev.,* May 1969, *59*(2), pp. 185–87.

Schapper, H. P.; Treloar, D. W. G. and Mauldon, R. G. Operational Accounting for Farm Management. *Australian J. Agr. Econ.,* June 1969, *13*(1), pp. 47–57.

Scheepers, C. F. The Effect of Import Substitution on the Volume and Structure of South Africa's Imports, 1926/27–1963/64. *Finance Trade Rev.,* December 1969, *8*(4), pp. 258–71.

Scheiber, Harry N. World War I as Entrepreneurial Opportunity: Willard Straight and the American International Corporation. *Polit. Sci. Quart.,* September 1969, *84*(3), pp. 486–511.

——— **and Scheiber, Jane Lang.** The Wilson Administration and the Wartime Mobilization of Black Americans, 1917–18. *Labor Hist.,* Summer 1969, *10*(3), pp. 433–58.

Scheiber, Jane Lang and Scheiber, Harry N. The Wilson Administration and the Wartime Mobilization of Black Americans, 1917–18. *Labor Hist.,* Summer 1969, *10*(3), pp. 433–58.

Schelbert, Heidi. Einige Gedanken zum amerikanischen Zahlungsbilanzdefizit. (Some Reflections on the Deficit in the American Balance of Payments. With English summary.) *Schweiz. Z. Volkswirtsch. Statist.,* December 1969, *105*(4), pp. 497–514.

Schelling, Thomas C. Models of Segregation. *Amer. Econ. Rev.,* May 1969, *59*(2), pp. 488–93.

Schendel, Dan E. and Balestra, Pietro. Rational Behavior and Gasoline Price Wars. *Appl. Econ.,* May 1969, *1*(2), pp. 89–101.

Schenk, Karl-Ernst. Die Konvertibilität der Ostblockwährungen als komplexes Entscheidungsproblem der Wirtschaftspolitik. (Convertibility of East Bloc Currencies as a Complex Decision Problem of Economic Policy. With English summary.) *Schmollers Jahr.,* 1969, *89*(6), pp. 675–89.

Scherer, Frederic M. Market Structure and the Stability of Investment. *Amer. Econ. Rev.,* May 1969, *59*(2), pp. 72–79.

——— Statement. In *Competition in Defense Procurement, SCH,* 1969, pp. 119–31.

——— **and Comanor, William S.** Patent Statistics as a Measure of Technical Change. *J. Polit. Econ.,* May/June 1969, *77*(3), pp. 392–98.

Schermerhorn, Richard W. The Economic Feasibility of an Integrated Broiler Operation. *Amer. J. Agr. Econ.,* December 1969, *51*(5), pp. 1255–58.

Schiaffino, Andrea. Interrelazioni tra manifestazioni demografiche e manifestazioni economico-sociali in Emilia e Veneto nell'ultimo secolo. Relazione illustrativa dell'attività svolta dal gruppo di ricerca C.N.R. diretto dal prof. Paolo Fortunati. (With English summary.) *Statistica,* October-December 1969, *29*(4), pp. 563–602.

Schiavo-Campo, Salvatore and Erb, Guy F. Export Instability, Level of Development, and Economic Size of Less Developed Countries. *Bull. Oxford Univ. Inst. Econ. Statist.,* November 1969, *31*(4), pp. 263–83.

Schick, Allen. Systems for Analysis: PPB and Its Alternatives. In *The Analysis and Evaluation of Public Expenditures: The PPB System, Vol. 3, JECP,* 1969, pp. 817–34.

Schiller, Otto. An Appraisal of Co-operative Farming and Its Significance in Indian Development. In *Bhuleshkar, A. V., ed.,* 1969, pp. 40–46.

Schilling, Don. Forward Exchange and Currency Position. *J. Finance,* December 1969, *24*(5), pp. 875–85.

Schiopu, Bucur. Elemente agro-industriale în agricultura Republicii Socialiste România. (Agro-Industrial Elements in the Agriculture of the Socialist Republic of Romania. With English summary.) *Stud. Cercet. Econ.,* 1969, *3,* pp. 59–66.

Schips, Bernd; Britsch, Klaus and Reichardt, Helmut. Sind die Lohnempfänger gut beraten, wenn sie sich einer Lohnquotensenkung widersetzen? (With English summary.) *Jahr. Nationalökon. Statist.,* August 1969, *183*(3–4), pp. 300–305.

Schlechty, D. L. and Malmgren, H. B. Technology and Neo-Mercantilism in International Agricultural Trade. *Amer. J. Agr. Econ.*, December 1969, *51*(5), pp. 1325–37.

_____ Technology and Neo-Mercantilism in International Agricultural Trade. In *Interest Equalization Tax Extension Act of 1969, SCH,* 1969, pp. 35–42.

Schlefer, Marion. Industrialization in Housing: Today's Potential. In *Industrialized Housing, JECP,* 1969, pp. 145–63.

Schleifer, Arthur, Jr. Two-Stage Normal Sampling in Two-Action Problems with Linear Economics. *J. Amer. Statist. Assoc.*, December 1969, *64*(328), pp. 1504–41.

Schlesinger, Arthur M. The City in American Civilization. In *Callow, A. B., Jr., ed.*, 1969, pp. 25–41.

_____ The Urban World. In *Callow, A. B., Jr., ed.*, 1969, pp. 186–209.

Schlieper, Ulrich. Eine Verallgemeinerung des Optimalzolltheorems. (With English summary.) *Z. ges. Staatswiss.*, July 1969, *125*(3), pp. 296–405.

Schloss, Henry H. Two Views on Myrdal (II). *Indian Econ. J.*, July–September 1969, *17*(1), pp. 158–60.

Schlusberg, Malcolm D. Corporate Legitimacy and Social Responsibility: The Role of Law. *Calif. Manage. Rev.*, Fall 1969, *12*(1), pp. 65–76.

Schmandt, Henry J. and Goldbach, John C. The Urban Paradox. In *Schmandt, H. J. and Bloomberg, W., Jr., eds.*, 1969, pp. 473–98.

Schmeidler, David. Competitive Equilibria in Markets with a Continuum of Traders and Incomplete Preferences. *Econometrica,* October 1969, *37*(4), pp. 578–85.

Schmid, A. Allan. Effective Public Policy and the Government Budget: A Uniform Treatment of Public Expenditures and Public Rules. In *The Analysis and Evaluation of Public Expenditures: The PPB System, Vol. 1, JECP,* 1969, pp. 579–91.

_____ Natural Resources and Growth: Towards a Non-Marginal Political Economics. *Amer. J. Agr. Econ.*, December 1969, *51*(5), pp. 1304–13.

_____ Problems in the Theory of Public Choice: Discussion. *Amer. Econ. Rev.*, May 1969, *59*(2), pp. 212–14.

Schmid, Karl; Braun, Hubert and Hammer, Gerald. Ein Verfahren zur Ermittlung der Ausbildungskapazität wissenschaftlicher Hochschulen. (With English summary.) *Jahr. Nationalökon. Statist.*, March 1969, *182*(4–5), pp. 381–97.

Schmidt, Fred H. Job Caste in the Southwest. *Ind. Relat.*, October 1969, *9*(1), pp. 100–110.

_____ A Repair Shop for Unemployables. *Ind. Relat.*, May 1969, *8*(3), pp. 280–85.

Schmidt, Kurt. Zur Ökonomik der Korruption. (On the Economics of Corruption. With English summary.) *Schmollers Jahr.*, 1969, *89*(2), pp. 129–49.

Schmidt, Wilson. Charitable Exploitation. *Public Choice,* Spring 1969, *6,* pp. 103–04.

Schmitt, Hans O. Integration and Conflict in the World Economy. *J. Common Market Stud.*, September 1969, *8*(1), pp. 1–18.

Schmitt-Rink, Gerhard. Funktionelle Verteilung, personelle Verteilung und Multiplikatoreffekt. Überlegungen zum Kaldor-Ansatz in der Verteilungstheorie. (With English summary.) *Jahr. Nationalökon. Statist.*, December 1969, *183*(5), pp. 361–771.

Schmitz, Andrew; Bjarnason, Harold F. and McGarry, Michael J. Converting Price Series of Internationally Traded Commodities to a Common Currency Prior to Estimating National Supply and Demand Equations. *Amer. J. Agr. Econ.*, February 1969, *51*(1), pp. 189–92.

Schmölders, Günter. A Behavioral Approach to Monetary Theory. In *[von Hayek, Friedrich A.],* 1969, pp. 201–43.

Schmude, Douglas F. and Dempsey, Richard E. How Consumer Spending for Automobiles Creates Jobs. *Mon. Lab. Rev.*, March 1969, *92*(3), pp. 33–36.

Schneck, R. E., et al. A Strategic Contingencies' Model of Sub-unit Power. In *Association of Canadian Schools of Business,* 1969, pp. 66–79.

Schneeweiss, Hans and Sohmen, Egon. Fiscal and Monetary Policies under Alternative Exchange Rate Systems: A Correction. *Quart. J. Econ.*, May 1969, *83*(2), pp. 336–40.

Schneewind, J. B. Technology, Ways of Living, and Values in 19th Century England. In *Baier, K. and Rescher, N., eds.*, 1969, pp. 110–32.

Schneidau, R. E. and Knutson, Ronald D. Price Discrimination in the Food Industry: A Competitive Stimulant or Tranquilizer? *Amer. J. Agr. Econ.*, December 1969, *51*(5), pp. 1143–48.

Schneider, Erich. Economic Growth and Economic Order. *Ger. Econ. Rev.*, 1969, *7*(2), pp. 101–07.

Schneider, Georges. Le choix des investissements dans l'entreprise. (With English summary.) *Revue Écon.*, March 1969, *20*(2), pp. 272–301.

Schneider, Lewis M. The Fallacy of Free Transportation. *Harvard Bus. Rev.*, January–February 1969, *47*(1), pp. 83–87.

Schnore, Leo F. The City as a Social Organism. In *Callow, A. B., Jr., ed.*, 1969, pp. 53–60.

_____ City-Suburban Income Differentials in Metropolitan Areas. In *Population Trends, Pt. 1, HCH,* 1969, pp. 242–45.

_____ Metropolitan Development in the United Kingdom. In *Population Trends, Pt. 1, HCH,* 1969, pp. 245–64.

_____ Municipal Annexations and the Growth of Metropolitan Suburbs, 1950–1960. In *Population Trends, Pt. 1, HCH,* 1969, pp. 264–76.

_____ The Rural-Urban Variable: An Urbanite's Perspective. In *Population Trends, Pt. 1, HCH,* 1969, pp. 301–25.

_____ Some Correlates of Urban Size: A Replication. In *Population Trends, Pt. 1, HCH,* 1969, pp. 292–300.

_____ Urban Structure and Suburban Selectivity. In *Population Trends, Pt. 1, HCH,* 1969, pp. 326–38.

Schnur, Roman. Area and Administration. *Int. Soc. Sci. J.*, 1969, *21*(1), pp. 83–99.

Schoen, Donald R. Managing Technological Innovation. *Harvard Bus. Rev.*, May–June 1969, *47*(3), pp. 156–67.

Schoenbrod, David. Large Lot Zoning. *Yale Law J.*, July 1969, *78*(8), pp. 1418–41.

Schollhammer, Hans. National Economic Planning and Business Decision-Making: The French Experience. *Calif. Manage. Rev.*, Winter 1969, *12* (2), pp. 74–88.

_____ National Economic Planning and Business

Decisions: The French Experience. **In** *Ozbekhan, H. and Talbert, G. E., eds.,* 1969, pp. 35–69.

Schöndorff, R. Verkenningen langs het micro-groeipad: facetten van enkele moderne groeitheorieën van de onderneming. (Explorations along the Microgrowthpath. With English summary.) *De Economist,* November/December 1969, *117*(6), pp. 658–94.

Schooler, Robert D. and Sunoo, Don H. Consumer Preceptions of International Products: Regional vs. National Labeling. *Soc. Sci. Quart.,* March 1969, *49*(4), pp. 886–90.

Schotta, Charles and Bonomo, Vittorio. A Spectral Analysis of Post-Accord Federal Open Market Operations. *Amer. Econ. Rev.,* March 1969, *59*(1), pp. 50–61.

Schottland, Charles I. Statement. **In** *Economics of Aging: Toward a Full Share in Abundance, Pt. 1, SCH,* 1969, pp. 97–107.

Schouwenaars, W. and Lacroix, Y. Effectieve bescherming aan de grenzen van de E.E.G. en het Verenigd Koninkrijk, voor en na de Kennedyronde. (Effective Protection at the Borders of the E.E.C. and the United Kingdom before and after the Kennedy-Round. With English summary.) *Tijdschr. Econ.,* 1969, *14*(2), pp. 158–87.

Schrecker, John. The Reform Movement, Nationalism, and China's Foreign Policy. *J. Asian Stud.,* November 1969, *29*(1), pp. 43–53.

Schreiber, Wilfrid. Beziehungen zwischen den Zuwachsraten des Sozialprodukts, der Faktoreinsätze und der Faktorpreise im vereinfachten Modell. Notizen zur Wachstrumstheorie. (Relations between the Growth Rates of the National Product, the Factor Inputs, and the Factor Prices in a Simplified Model. With English summary.) *Jahr. Nationalökon. Statist.,* August 1969, *183* (3–4), pp. 243–53.

——— Die determinierte Investition: Kritik am neoklassischen Wachstums-Konzept. (With English summary.) *Jahr. Nationalökon. Statist.,* May 1969, *182*(6), pp. 530–41.

——— On Two Topical Questions of Distribution Theory and Policy. *Ger. Econ. Rev.,* 1969, *7*(3), pp. 199–215.

Schreiner, John C. and Smith, Keith V. A Portfolio Analysis of Conglomerate Diversification. *J. Finance,* June 1969, *24*(3), pp. 413–27.

Schreuel, E. J. and Pronk, J. P. Some Reflections on the Effectiveness of Project Versus Plan Aid. **In** *[Tinbergen, J.],* 1969, pp. 283–307.

Schrier, Elliot. Production Planning in a Multiplant System. *Calif. Manage. Rev.,* Summer 1969, *11* (4), pp. 69–78.

Schriever, Bernard A. The Role and Responsibility of Business in the Growth of American Society. **In** *Ozbekhan, H. and Talbert, G. E., eds.,* 1969, pp. 5–13.

Schröder, Jürgen. Zur partialanalytischen Darstellung des direkten internationalen Preiszusammenhangs. Bemerkungen zu einem Aufsatz von O. Issing. (With English summary.) *Jahr. Nationalökon. Statist.,* August 1969, *183*(3–4), pp. 306–15.

Schroeder, Gertrude E. The 1966–67 Soviet Industrial Price Reform: A Study in Complications. *Soviet Stud.,* April 1969, *20*(4), pp. 462–77.

Schuh, G. Edward. The Transformation of Agriculture in a Presently Semi-Industrialized Country: The Case of Brazil: Comment. **In** *Thorbecke, E., ed.,* 1969, pp. 379–85.

——— **and Tyrchniewicz, Edward W.** Econometric Analysis of the Agricultural Labor Market. *Amer. J. Agr. Econ.,* November 1969, *51*(4), pp. 770–87.

Schultz, George P. Facility Planning for a Public Service System: Domestic Solid Waste Collection. *J. Reg. Sci.,* August 1969, *9*(2), pp. 291–307.

Schultz, T. Paul. An Economic Model of Family Planning and Fertility. *J. Polit. Econ.,* March/April 1969, *77*(2), pp. 153–80.

——— Demographic Conditions of Economic Development in Latin America. **In** *Nisbet, C. T., ed.,* 1969, pp. 41–72.

Schultz, Theodore W. What Ails World Agriculture? **In** *Ruttan, V. W.; Waldo, A. D. and Houck, J. P., eds.,* 1969, pp. 299–316.

Schultze, Charles L. The Role of Incentives, Penalties, and Rewards in Attaining Effective Policy. **In** *The Analysis and Evaluation of Public Expenditures: The PPB System, Vol. 1, JECP,* 1969, pp. 201–25.

——— Using Incentives to Improve the Effectiveness of Government. *Mon. Lab. Rev.,* September 1969, *92*(9), pp. 34–38.

Schulz, James H. Statement. **In** *Economics of Aging: Toward a Full Share in Abundance, Pt. 1, SCH,* 1969, pp. 7–9.

Schulz, John; Cox, Edward and Fellmeth, Robert. The Consumer and the Federal Trade Commission, a Critique of the Consumer Protection Record of the FTC. **In** *To Establish a Department of Consumer Affairs, SCH,* 1969, pp. 123–312.

Schumann, Jochen. Zur Theorie optimalen wirtschaftlichen Wachstums. (With English summary.) *Z. ges. Staatswiss.,* January 1969, *125*(1), pp. 1–16.

Schumpeter, J. A. The Dynamics of Competition and Monopoly. **In** *Hunter, A., ed.,* 1969, pp. 40–67.

Schupack, Mark B. Statement. **In** *Bank Holding Company Act Amendments, Pts. 1–3, HCH,* 1969, pp. 1381–87.

——— Statement. **In** *Role of Giant Corporations, Pt. 1, SCH,* 1969, pp. 492–501.

Schupp, Alvin R. and Ikerd, John E. A Decision Model for Continuous Sequence Production Processes of Variable Length: An Application to Hog Marketing. *Amer. J. Agr. Econ.,* December 1969, *51*(5), pp. 1159–63.

Schuster, Helmut. Further Remarks on the Theory of Product Differentiation. *J. Polit. Econ.,* September/October 1969, *77*(5), pp. 827–33.

Schutjer, Wayne and Weigel, Dale. The Contribution of Foreign Assistance to Agricultural Development. *Amer. J. Agr. Econ.,* November 1969, *51* (4), pp. 788–97.

Schwab, Bernhard and Lusztig, Peter. A Comparative Analysis of the Net Present Value and the Benefit-Cost Ratio as Measures of the Economic Desirability of Investment. *J. Finance,* June 1969, *24*(3), pp. 507–16.

——— **and Nicol, Robert E. G.** From Double-Declining-Balance to Sum-of-the-Years'-Digits Depreciation: An Optimum Switching Rule. *Accounting Rev.,* April 1969, *44*(2), pp. 292–96.

Schwartz, Anna J. Short Term Targets of Three Foreign Central Banks. **In** *Brunner, K., ed.,* 1969, pp. 27–65.

_____ Why Money Matters. *Lloyds Bank Rev.,* October 1969, (94), pp. 1–16.

_____ **and Friedman, Milton.** The Definition of Money: Net Wealth and Neutrality as Criteria. *J. Money, Credit, Banking,* February 1969, *1*(1), pp. 1–14.

Schwartz, Eli and Aronson, J. Richard. The Preference for Accumulation vs. Spending: Gift and Estate Taxation, and the Timing of Wealth Transfers. *Nat. Tax J.,* September 1969, *22*(3), pp. 390–98.

Schwartz, Hugh H. Concerning the Contention That Efficiency in the Allocation of Resources Really Doesn't Matter Very Much after All. *Econ. Develop. Cult. Change,* Part I, October 1969, *18* (1), pp. 44–50.

Schwartz, Nancy L. and Kamien, Morton I. Induced Factor Augmenting Technical Progress from a Microeconomic Viewpoint. *Econometrica,* October 1969, *37*(4), pp. 668–84.

_____ A Naive View of the Indicator Problem. **In** *Brunner, K., ed.,* 1969, pp. 98–112.

Schwartzbaum, Allan M. Lateral Interaction and Effectiveness in Vertical Organizations. **In** *Somers, G. G., ed. (II),* 1969, pp. 360–71.

_____ **and Cross, Malcolm.** Social Mobility and Secondary School Selection in Trinidad and Tobago. *Soc. Econ. Stud.,* June 1969, *18*(2), pp. 189–207.

Schwartzman, David. The Contribution of Education to the Quality of Labor: Reply. *Amer. Econ. Rev.,* December 1969, *59*(5), pp. 944–46.

_____ The Growth of Sales *Per* Man-Hour in Retail Trade, 1929–1963. **In** *Fuchs, V. R., ed.,* 1969, pp. 201–29.

_____ The Growth of Sales *Per* Man-Hour in Retail Trade, 1929–1963: Reply. **In** *Fuchs, V. R., ed.,* 1969, pp. 233–35.

Schwarzweller, Harry K. The Problem of Conceptualizing Poverty: Comment. **In** *Weaver, T. and Magid, A., eds.,* 1969, pp. 18–21.

Schweiger, Irving. 1969 Forecast of Gross National Product, Consumer Spending, Saving, and Housing. *J. Bus.,* January 1969, *42*(1), pp. 7–11.

de Schweinitz, Karl, Jr. The Economics of Poverty. **In** *Weaver, T. and Magid, A., eds.,* 1969, pp. 24–39.

_____ Growth, Development, and Political Monuments. **In** *Sherif, M. and Sherif, C. W., eds.,* 1969, pp. 209–24.

Schweitzer, Arthur. Goals in Social Economics. *J. Econ. Issues,* June 1969, *3*(2), pp. 147–65.

Schweitzer, Stuart O. Factors Determining the Interindustry Structure of Wages. *Ind. Lab. Relat. Rev.,* January 1969, *22*(2), pp. 217–25.

Schwenger, Robert B. New Concepts and Methods in Foreign Trade Negotiation. *Amer. J. Agr. Econ.,* December 1969, *51*(5), pp. 1338–48.

Scitovsky, Tibor. International Liquidity and the Reform of the Adjustment Mechanism. **In** *Samuelson, P. A., ed.,* 1969, pp. 241–54.

_____ International Liquidity and the Reform of the Adjustment Mechanism: Reply. **In** *Samuelson, P. A., ed.,* 1969, pp. 268–69.

_____ Statement. **In** *Linking Reserve Creation and Development Assistance, JECH,* 1969, pp. 32–34.

Scobie, G. M. Trends in Production from Sheep Properties: A Brief Review and Medium Term Projection of Sheep Numbers. *Quart. Rev. Agr. Econ.,* October 1969, *22*(4), pp. 185–98.

Scofield, William. Corporate Farm Ownership and Operation. **In** *Garoian, L., ed.,* 1969, pp. 106–10.

Scott, A. D.; Thomas, Brinley and Johnson, Harry G. Criticisms of Thomas's Analysis of Brain Drain. **In** *Blaug, M., ed.,* 1969, pp. 281–301.

Scott, Allen J. Spatial Equilibrium of the Central City. *J. Reg. Sci.,* April 1969, *9*(1), pp. 29–45.

Scott, Anthony. Investing and Protesting. *J. Polit. Econ.,* November/December 1969, *77*(6), pp. 916–20.

Scott, Donald A. Enforcement of Ethical Standards in Corporate Financial Reporting. **In** *Burton, J. C., ed.,* 1969, pp. 107–32.

Scott, Ira O., Jr. The Problems and Prospects of Integrating European Capital Markets: A Comment. *J. Money, Credit, Banking,* August 1969, *1* (3), pp. 350–53.

_____ That Controversial Euro-Dollar Market. *Nat. Westminster Bank Quart. Rev.,* August 1969, pp. 2–22.

Scott, John C. and Yablonski, Steven K. Transnational Mergers and Joint Ventures Affecting American Exports. *Antitrust Bull.,* Spring 1969, *14,* pp. 1–36.

Scott, John T., Jr. Factor Analysis Regression Revisited. *Econometrica,* October 1969, *37*(4), pp. 719.

_____ **and Heady, Earl O.** Econometricians and the Data Gap: Reply. *Amer. J. Agr. Econ.,* February 1969, *51*(1), pp. 188.

_____ **and Reiss, Franklin J.** Changing Technology and Lease Adjustment: Theory and Practice. *Land Econ.,* November 1969, *45*(4), pp. 400–405.

Scotton, R. B. Membership of Voluntary Health Insurance. *Econ. Rec.,* March 1969, *45*(109), pp. 69–83.

_____ **and Deeble, J. S.** The Nimmo Report. *Econ. Rec.,* June 1969, *45*(110), pp. 258–75.

Scoville, James G. Remuneration in Afghan Industry. *Int. Lab. Rev.,* April 1969, *99*(4), pp. 381–400.

_____ A Theory of Jobs and Training. *Ind. Relat.,* October 1969, *9*(1), pp. 36–53.

Scully, Gerald W. Human Capital and Productivity in U.S. Manufacturing. *Western Econ. J.,* December 1969, *7*(4), pp. 334–40.

_____ Interstate Wage Differentials: A Cross Section Analysis. *Amer. Econ. Rev.,* December 1969, *59* (5), pp. 757–73.

Seagraves, James A. Capitalized Values of Tobacco Allotments and the Rate of Return to Allotment Owners. *Amer. J. Agr. Econ.,* May 1969, *51*(2), pp. 320–34.

_____ **and Pasour, E. C., Jr.** On Defining Uneconomic Regions of the Production Function. *Amer. J. Agr. Econ.,* February 1969, *51*(1), pp. 195–202.

Searby, Frederick Wright. Control Postmerger Change. *Harvard Bus. Rev.,* September–October 1969, *47*(5), pp. 4–12, 154–55.

Searl, Milton F. Prospects for PPB at AEC. **In** *The Analysis and Evaluation of Public Expenditures: The PPB System, Vol. 3, JECP,* 1969, pp. 1005–19.

Searle, S. R. Correlation Between Means of Parts and Wholes. *Amer. Statist.*, April 1969, *23*(2), pp. 23–24.

Sedransk, J. and Booth, Gordon. Planning Some Two-Factor Comparative Surveys. *J. Amer. Statist. Assoc.*, June 1969, *64*(326), pp. 560–73.

Sée, Henri. The Economic and Social Origins of the French Revolution. **In** *Scoville, W. C. and La Force, J. C., eds., Vol. III,* 1969, pp. 209–23.

Seers, Dudley. A Step Towards a Political Economy of Development (Illustrated by the Case of Trinidad/Tobago). *Soc. Econ. Stud.*, September 1969, *18*(3), pp. 218–53.

Seevers, Gary L. The Cost of Food Aid to Recipient Countries. *Amer. J. Agr. Econ.*, December 1969, *51*(5), pp. 1588–92.

Segal, David. "Equity" Versus "Efficiency" in Higher Education. **In** *the Economics and Financing of Higher Education in the United States, JECP,* 1969, pp. 135–44.

Segal, Sheldon; Notestein, Frank W. and Kirk, Dudley. The Problem of Population Control. **In** *Hauser, P. M., ed.*, 1969, pp. 139–67.

Segall, Joel and Gould, John P. The Substitution Effects of Transportation Costs. *J. Polit. Econ.*, January/February 1969, *77*(1), pp. 130–37.

Sehgal, R. K. Tax Efforts of States. *Asian Econ. Rev.*, August 1969, *11*(4), pp. 438–45.

Sei, Ung Gim and Luey, Paul. Taiwan Investment. **In** *Hughes, H. and Seng, Y. P., eds.*, 1969, pp. 140–53.

Seibel, Claude and Aglietta, Michel. The National Accounting System and the Preparation of the Fifth French Plan. *Rev. Income Wealth,* June 1969, *15*(2), pp. 121–69.

Seidel, Marquis R. The Margins of Spatial Monopoly. *J. Reg. Sci.*, December 1969, *9*(3), pp. 353–68.

Seidl, Christian. On Measurement of Convergence of Economic Systems. *Z. Nationalökon.*, December 1969, *29*(3–4), pp. 427–32.

Seidman, Joel. Collective Bargaining in the Postal Service. *Ind. Relat.*, October 1969, *9*(1), pp. 11–26.

Seifert, William W. Transportation Development—A National Challenge. **In** *Panel on Science and Technology: Science and Technology and the Cities, HCH,* 1969, pp. 119–30.

Selby, Edward B., Jr. and Beard, Thomas R. Growth, Structure, and Adequacy of Commercial Banking in Louisiana. **In** *Beard, T. R., ed.*, 1969, pp. 105–32.

——— **and DeLorme, Charles D., Jr.** The Cost of Stabilization: A Comment. *Amer. Econ.*, Fall 1969, *13*(2), pp. 97–99.

Self, Peter J. O. Urban Systems and the Quality of Life. **In** *Schmandt, H. J. and Bloomberg, W., Jr., eds.*, 1969, pp. 165–86.

Seligman, Ben B. The Impact of Positivism on Economic Thought. *Hist. Polit. Econ.*, Fall 1969, *1*(2), pp. 256–78.

Selowsky, Marcelo. On the Measurement of Education's Contribution to Growth. *Quart. J. Econ.*, August 1969, *83*(3), pp. 449–63.

Seltzer, Lawrence H. Background of the Controversy. **In** *Gaa, C. J.*, 1969, pp. 126–45.

——— Competing Proposals for the Tax Treatment of Gains and Losses. **In** *Gaa, C. J.*, 1969, pp. 146–53.

Seminario, Adan and Steiner, Henry Malcolm. Economic Aspects of the Bolivar Highway in Peru. *Eng. Econ.*, January–February 1969, *14*(2), pp. 101–07.

Sen, Amartya K. A Game-Theoretic Analysis of Theories of Collectivism in Allocation. **In** *[Ghosal, U. N.]*, 1969, pp. 1–17.

——— Planners' Preferences: Optimality, Distribution and Social Welfare. **In** *Margolis, J. and Guitton, H., eds.*, 1969, pp. 201–21.

——— Quasi-Transitivity, Rational Choice and Collective Decisions. *Rev. Econ. Stud.*, July 1969, *36* (107), pp. 381–93.

——— **and Pattanaik, Prasanta K.** Necessary and Sufficient Conditions for Rational Choice under Majority Decision. *J. Econ. Theory,* August 1969, *1*(2), pp. 178–202.

Sen, Amitava and Sengupta, Jati K. Econometric Supply Functions for Rice and Jute. *Arthaniti,* January & July 1969, *12*(1&2), pp. 1–40.

——— Optimal Capacity Models under Periodic Demand: A Survey of Peak Load Pricing Theory and Appraisal. *Z. ges. Staatswiss.*, July 1969, *125*(3), pp. 371–95.

Sen, Subrata and Rosenthal, Howard. Candidate Selection and Voting Behavior in France. *Public Choice,* Spring 1969, *6,* pp. 71–92.

Seneca, Joseph J. Water Recreation, Demand, and Supply. *Water Resources Res.*, December 1969, *5* (6), pp. 1179–85.

——— **and Cicchetti, Charles J.** A Gravity Model Analysis of the Demand for Public Communication. *J. Reg. Sci.*, December 1969, *9*(3), pp. 459–70.

Sengupta, Jati K. and Gruver, Gene. A Linear Reliability Analysis in Programming with Chance Constraints. *Swedish J. Econ.*, December 1969, *71*(4), pp. 221–46.

——— **and Sen, Amitava.** Econometric Supply Functions for Rice and Jute. *Arthaniti,* January & July 1969, *12*(1&2), pp. 1–40.

——— **and Sen, Amitava.** Optimal Capacity Models under Periodic Demand: A Survey of Peak Load Pricing Theory and Appraisal. *Z. ges. Staatswiss.*, July 1969, *125*(3), pp. 371–95.

Senior, N. W. The Value of Money. **In** *Clower, R. W., ed.*, 1969, pp. 67–79.

Serban, Sielu. Unitatea național-politică în concepția lui Nicolae Bălcescu. (National Unity in Nicolae Bălcescu's Conception. With English summary.) *Stud. Cercet. Econ.*, 1969, *1-2,* pp. 237–43.

Serck-Hanssen, Jan. The Optimal Number of Factories in a Spatial Market. **In** *[Tinbergen, J.]*, 1969, pp. 269–81.

Sessa, Giuseppe. II problema delle esenzioni nell' I.V.A. e gli scambi internazionali. (The Problem of the Exemptions in New Italian Taxation System. With English summary.) *Mondo Aperto,* February 1969, *23*(1), pp. 10–35.

Sethi, Narendra K. Land Reform in Economic Development—A Case Study from Latin America. *Asian Econ. Rev.*, February 1969, *11*(2), pp. 221–26.

Sethi, S. Prakash and Votaw, Dow. Do We Need a

New Corporate Response to a Changing Social Environment? Part II. *Calif. Manage. Rev.*, Fall 1969, *12*(1), pp. 17–31.

______ Do We Need a New Corporate Response to a Changing Social Environment? Part I. *Calif. Manage. Rev.*, Fall 1969, *12*(1), pp. 3–16.

Seton, Francis. Fluctuation in the Growth Rate in a Socialist Economy and the Inventory Cycle: Comment. **In** *Bronfenbrenner, M., ed.*, 1969, pp. 350–55.

______ **and Levine, Herbert S.** Cyclical Fluctuations under Socialism: Comment. **In** *Bronfenbrenner, M., ed.*, 1969, pp. 303–11.

Sewell, David O. Occupational Training Programs and Manpower Programs for the Disadvantaged: Discussion. **In** *Somers, G. G. and Wood, W. D., eds.*, 1969, pp. 160–69.

Sewell, W. R. Derrick. Weather Modification: When Should We Do It and How Far Should We Go? **In** *Fleagle, R. G., ed.*, 1969, pp. 94–104.

Sewell, Wade P. Least Squares, Conditional Predictions, and Estimator Properties. *Econometrica*, January 1969, *37*(1), pp. 39–43.

______ Some Policy Issues in the Analysis of Research and Development Programs. **In** *The Analysis and Evaluation of Public Expenditures: The PPB System, Vol. 3, JECP*, 1969, pp. 1069–84.

Seyler, David A. The New York State Planning, Programing, and Budgeting System. **In** *Innovations in Planning, Programming, and Budgeting in State and Local Governments, JECP*, 1969, pp. 48–52.

Shaal, Gil and Perlberg, Arye. An Interdisciplinary Approach to Manpower Planning and Development. *Int. Lab. Rev.*, April 1969, *99*(4), pp. 363–80.

Shabman, Leonard A. and Kalter, Robert J. Effects of Public Programs for Outdoor Recreation and Personal Income Distribution. *Amer. J. Agr. Econ.*, December 1969, *51*(5), pp. 1516–19.

Shad, John S. R. The Financial Realities of Mergers. *Harvard Bus. Rev.*, November–December 1969, *47*(6), pp. 132–46.

Shafer, Carl E. The Effect of a Marketing Order on Winter Carrot Prices: Reply. *Amer. J. Agr. Econ.*, November 1969, *51*(4), pp. 933–34.

Shaffer, Charles L. Educational Problems in Economic Development. **In** *Yesufu, T. M., ed.*, 1969, pp. 183–99.

Shaffer, Harry G. Do the U.S. and Soviet Economies Show Signs of Convergence? **In** *Prybyla, J. S., ed.*, 1969, pp. 453–66.

______ Problems and Prospects of Czechoslovakia's New Economic Model (Including an Interview with Professor Ota Sik). **In** *Prybyla, J. S., ed.*, 1969, pp. 323–39.

Shaffer, James Duncan. On Institutional Obsolescence and Innovation—Background for Professional Dialogue on Public Policy. *Amer. J. Agr. Econ.*, May 1969, *51*(2), pp. 245–67.

______ Some Research Problems Concerning Conglomerate Firm Growth. **In** *Garoian, L., ed.*, 1969, pp. 131–32.

Shaffer, Leslie L. D. The Myrtlewood Industry of Oregon. *Oregon Bus. Rev.*, April 1969, *28*(4), pp. 1–3.

______ **and Hashimoto, Steve T.** The Semi-Precious Gem Industry of Oregon. *Oregon Bus. Rev.*, July 1969, *28*(7), pp. 1–4.

Shah, C. H. Agricultural Taxation: A Plea for Caution and a Proposal for a Positive Approach. *Artha-Vikas*, July 1969, *5*(2), pp. 79–97.

______ Problems of Buffer Stock—A Theoretical Framework. **In** *Indian Society of Agricultural Economics*, 1969, pp. 15–34.

Shah, K. R. Expenditure on Professional School Education in India, 1950–51 to 1960–61. **In** *Pandit, H. N., ed.*, 1969, pp. 75–91.

______ Private Costs of Elementary Education. **In** *Pandit, H. N., ed.*, 1969, pp. 57–74.

Shah, R. L. and Patel, G. A. Cultivation of Hybrid Bajri in Gujarat State. *Artha-Vikas*, January 1969, *5*(1), pp. 81–94.

Shah, S. M. On the Minimum Property of the First Absolute Moment. *Amer. Statist.*, June 1969, *23* (3), pp. 27.

Shannon, John. Ways the Federal Government May Strengthen State and Local Financing. **In** *[White, Charles P.]*, 1969, pp. 103–11.

Shapero, Albert. Effects of Government R and D Contracting on Mobility and Regional Resources. **In** *Gruber, W. H. and Marquis, D. G., eds.*, 1969, pp. 179–201.

Shapiro, A. Model-Building and Extrapolation. *Prob. Econ.*, August 1969, *12*(4), pp. 31–51.

Shapiro, A. A. Interindustry Differentials in the Demand for Money and Government Securities. *Southern Econ. J.*, October 1969, *36*(2), pp. 165–70.

Shapiro, David L. and Hirshleifer, Jack. The Treatment of Risk and Uncertainty. **In** *The Analysis and Evaluation of Public Expenditures: The PPB System, Vol. 1, JECP*, 1969, pp. 505–30.

Shapiro, Eli. International Financial Problems and the Role of the Dollar: Discussion. *J. Finance*, May 1969, *24*(2), pp. 375–78.

Shapiro, Perry and Legler, John B. The Responsiveness of State Tax Revenue to Economic Growth: A Reply. *Nat. Tax J.*, June 1969, *22*(2), pp. 299–300.

Shapley, Lloyd S. and Shubik, Martin. A Method for Evaluating the Distribution of Power in a Committee System. **In** *Bell, R.; Edwards, D. V. and Wagner, R. H., eds.*, 1969, pp. 209–13.

______ On Market Games. *J. Econ. Theory*, June 1969, *1*(1), pp. 9–25.

______ On the Core of an Economic System with Externalities. *Amer. Econ. Rev.*, Part I, September 1969, *59*(4), pp. 678–84.

______ Price Strategy Oligopoly with Product Variation. *Kyklos*, 1969, *22*(1), pp. 30–44.

______ Pure Competition, Coalitional Power, and Fair Division. *Int. Econ. Rev.*, October 1969, *10* (3), pp. 337–62.

Sharkansky, Ira and Hofferbert, Richard I. Dimensions of State Politics, Economics, and Public Policy. *Amer. Polit. Sci. Rev.*, September 1969, *63* (3), pp. 867–79.

Sharma, A. C. and Kahlon, A. S. Role of Farm and Family Size in Determining Cropping Patterns in the Punjab. *Asian Econ. Rev.*, February 1969, *11* (2), pp. 117–30.

Sharma, Baldev R. Technology and Socio-Economic Change. **In** *Johri, C. K., ed.,* 1969, pp. 123–41.

Sharma, D. L. Unit Costs of Educations, Our Knowledge, Gaps and Our Need. **In** *Pandit, H. N., ed.,* 1969, pp. 27–41.

Sharma, L. R. Need for a Growth-Oriented Industrial Policy. *Asian Econ. Rev.,* August 1969, *11*(4), pp. 333–48.

Sharma, R. C. Benefit-Cost Analysis of Educational Projects: A Review of Researches. **In** *Pandit, H. N., ed.,* 1969, pp. 393–415.

Sharp, C. H. Congestion and Welfare—A Reply. *Econ. J.,* June 1969, *79*(314), pp. 407–12.

Sharples, Jerry A. The Representative Farm Approach to Estimation of Supply Response. *Amer. Econ. Rev.,* May 1969, *59*(2), pp. 168–74.

Shatalin, S. and Fedorenko, N. The Problem of Optimal Planning of the Socialist Economy. *Prob. Econ.,* November 1969, *12*(7), pp. 3–29.

Shaudys, E. T. Farm Panels as a Source of Farm Management Data: The Ohio Plan. *Amer. J. Agr. Econ.,* December 1969, *51*(5), pp. 1211–13.

Shaw, B. D. The New Zealand Economy, 1967–68. *Econ. Rec.,* March 1969, *45*(109), pp. 1–16.

Shaw, David C. The Cost of "Going Public" in Canada. **In** *Association of Canadian Schools of Business,* 1969, pp. 144–70.

Shaw, J. A. and Wilkins, C. A. An Example to Illustrate the "Average" Nature of Clark's Law of Urban Populations. *J. Reg. Sci.,* August 1969, *9*(2), pp. 255–59.

Shaw, Lee. Public Policy and the Strategy and Tactics of Collective Bargaining: Discussion. **In** *Somers, G. G., ed. (II),* 1969, pp. 201–05.

Sheaffer, John R. The Interaction of Urban Redevelopment and Flood Plain Management in Waterloo, Iowa. **In** *Dougal, M. D., ed.,* 1969, pp. 123–35.

Shearer, John. Statement. **In** *Tax Credits to Stimulate Job Opportunities in Rural Areas, SCH,* 1969, pp. 157–62.

Sheatsley, Paul B. White Attitudes Toward the Negro. **In** *Kain, J. F., ed.,* 1969, pp. 128–38.

Sheifer, Victor J. and David, Lily Mary. Estimating the Cost of Collective Bargaining Settlements. *Mon. Lab. Rev.,* May 1969, *92*(5), pp. 16–26.

Sheldon, Henry D. Population Statistics: Published and Unpublished. *Mon. Lab. Rev.,* December 1969, *92*(12), pp. 45–49.

Shell, Karl and Phelps, Edmund S. Public Debt, Taxation, and Capital Intensiveness. *J. Econ. Theory,* October 1969, *1*(3), pp. 330–46.

______; Sidrauski, Miguel and Foley, Duncan K. Optimal Fiscal and Monetary Policy and Economic Growth. *J. Polit. Econ.,* Part II, July/August 1969, *77*(4), pp. 698–719.

______; Sidrauski, Miguel and Stiglitz, Joseph E. Capital Gains, Income, and Saving. *Rev. Econ. Stud.,* January 1969, *36*(105), pp. 15–26.

Shellhammer, Kenneth L. and Bahl, Roy W. Evaluating the State Business Tax Structure: An Application of Input-Output Analysis. *Nat. Tax J.,* June 1969, *22*(2), pp. 203–16.

Shelton, David H. The Pace of Income Equalization in a Market Economy: Some Evidence from Experience in the United States. *Rivista Int. Sci. Econ. Com.,* February 1969, *16*(2), pp. 131–47.

Shemetov, P. and Baturin, F. Activities of Siberian Economists. *Prob. Econ.,* November 1969, *12*(7), pp. 67–77.

Shepherd, James F. and Walton, Gary M. Estimate of "Invisible" Earnings in the Balance of Payments of the British North American Colonies, 1768–1772. *J. Econ. Hist.,* June 1969, *29*(2), pp. 230–63.

Shepherd, William G. Market Power and Racial Discrimination in White Collar Employment. *Antitrust Bull.,* Spring 1969, *14,* pp. 141–61.

Shepler, Cora E. and Campbell, Leonard G. United States Defense Expenditures Abroad. *Surv. Curr. Bus.,* December 1969, *49*(12), pp. 40–47.

Sheppard, Harold L. Some Broader Reality Frameworks for Anti-poverty Intervention. *Soc. Sci. Quart.,* December 1969, *50*(3), pp. 487–93.

______ Statement. **In** *Economics of Aging: Toward a Full Share in Abundance, Pt. 1, SCH,* 1969, pp. 5–7.

Sheriff, Don R. and West, Jude P. The Changing Motivational Patterns of Professional Personnel. **In** *Gilroy, T. P., ed.,* 1969, pp. 9–17.

Sherk, Donald R. The New International Trade Models and Their Relevance for Developing Asia. *Malayan Econ. Rev.,* October 1969, *14*(2), pp. 1–17.

Sherman, George. An Executive Looks at—The Corporate Will. *Calif. Manage. Rev.,* Spring 1969, *11* (3), pp. 3–6.

Sherman, Roger. A Note on Trading Stamp Strategy. *Appl. Econ.,* August 1969, *1*(3), pp. 225–28.

______ Risk Attitude and Cost Variability in a Capacity Choice Experiment. *Rev. Econ. Stud.,* October 1969, *36*(108), pp. 453–66.

______ and Willett, Thomas D. Regional Development, Externalities and Tax-Subsidy Combinations. *Nat. Tax J.,* June 1969, *22*(2), pp. 291–93.

Shervais, Steve and Snowbarger, Marvin. A Study of Factors Influencing the Average Effective Tax Rate on Personal Income, 1954–1965. *Nat. Tax J.,* June 1969, *22*(2), pp. 217–31.

Sheshinski, Eytan. Stability of Growth Equilibrium in a Neoclassical Vintage Model. *Int. Econ. Rev.,* June 1969, *10*(2), pp. 141–48.

______ and Burmeister, Edwin. A Nonsubstitution Theorem in a Model with Fixed Capital. *Southern Econ. J.,* January 1969, *35*(3), pp. 273–76.

______; Fisher, Franklin M. and Levhari, David. On the Sensitivity of the Level of Output to Savings: Embodiment and Disembodiment: A Clarificatory Note. *Quart. J. Econ.,* May 1969, *83*(2), pp. 347–48.

______ and Levhari, David. The Relation between the Rate of Return and the Rate of Technical Progress. *Rev. Econ. Stud.,* July 1969, *36*(107), pp. 363–79.

______ and Levhari, David. A Theorem on Returns to Scale and Steady-State Growth. *J. Polit. Econ.,* January/February 1969, *77*(1), pp. 60–65.

Sheth, Jagdish N. Using Factor Analysis to Estimate Parameters. *J. Amer. Statist. Assoc.,* September 1969, *64*(327), pp. 808–22.

Sheth, N. R. The Tripartite System: Past, Present, and Future. **In** *Johri, C. K., ed.,* 1969, pp. 142–59.

Shibata, Aiko N. Effects of Taxation on Risk-Taking.

Amer. Econ. Rev., May 1969, *59*(2), pp. 553–61.

Shilling, N. and Hammond, J. D. A Review Article: The Little Report on Prices and Profits in the Property and Liability Insurance Industry. *J. Risk Ins.*, March 1969, *36*(1), pp. 129–45.

Shils, Edward A. Social Science and Social Policy. **In** *Crawford, E. T. and Biderman, A. D., eds.*, 1969, pp. 35–49.

Shimazu, Ryoji. A Reconsideration of the Quantity Theory of Money. *Kyoto Univ. Econ. Rev.*, April 1969, *39*(1), pp. 45–62.

Shin, Kilman. International Difference in Tax Ratio. *Rev. Econ. Statist.*, May 1969, *51*(2), pp. 213–20.

Shinohara, Miyōhei. Postwar Business Cycles in Japan. **In** *Bronfenbrenner, M., ed.*, 1969, pp. 73–95.

Shipp, Royal. The Structure of the Mortgage Market for Income-Property Mortgage Loans. **In** *Guttentag, J. M. and Cagan, P., eds.*, 1969, pp. 77–106.

Shkatov, V. Prices on Natural Resources and the Problem of Improving Planned Price Formation. *Prob. Econ.*, June 1969, *12*(2), pp. 67–89.

Short, Brock K. Export Promotion in Underdeveloped Countries. *Amer. Econ.*, Fall 1969, *13* (2), pp. 70–79.

Shoup, Carl S. Comments on the Paper by Andre Laurent, "L'Harmonisation des regimes de securite sociale dans la communaute economique Europeenne." *Public Finance*, 1969, *24*(2), pp. 321–25.

______ Experience with the Value-Added Tax in Denmark, and Prospects in Sweden. *Finanzarchiv*, March 1969, *28*(2), pp. 236–52.

______ **and Head, John G.** Excess Burden: The Corner Case. *Amer. Econ. Rev.*, March 1969, *59*(1), pp. 181–83.

______ **and Head, John G.** Public Goods, Private Goods, and Ambiguous Goods. *Econ. J.*, September 1969, *79*(315), pp. 567–72.

Shoup, Donald C. Advance Land Acquisition by Local Governments: A Cost-Benefit Analysis. *Yale Econ. Essays*, Fall 1969, *9*(2), pp. 147–207.

Shrimali, P. D. Pattern of Employment and Earnings Among University Graduates in Lucknow, India. *Ind. Lab. Relat. Rev.*, January 1969, *22*(2), pp. 249–56.

Shubik, Martin. Planning: Perspectives and Prospects. **In** *Ozbekhan, H. and Talbert, G. E., eds.*, 1969, pp. 182–95.

______ The Uses of Game Theory in Management Science. **In** *Carsberg, B. V. and Edey, H. C., eds.*, 1969, pp. 376–95.

______ **and Shapley, Lloyd S.** A Method for Evaluating the Distribution of Power in a Committee System. **In** *Bell, R.; Edwards, D. V. and Wagner, R. H., eds.*, 1969, pp. 209–13.

______ **and Shapley, Lloyd S.** On Market Games. *J. Econ. Theory*, June 1969, *1*(1), pp. 9–25.

______ **and Shapley, Lloyd S.** On the Core of an Economic System with Externalities. *Amer. Econ. Rev.*, Part I, September 1969, *59*(4), pp. 678–84.

______ **and Shapley, Lloyd S.** Price Strategy Oligopoly with Product Variation. *Kyklos*, 1969, *22*(1), pp. 30–44.

______ **and Shapley, Lloyd S.** Pure Competition, Coalitional Power, and Fair Division. *Int. Econ. Rev.*, October 1969, *10*(3), pp. 337–62.

Shuchman, Abe and Perry, Michael. Self-Confidence and Persuasibility in Marketing: A Reappraisal. *J. Marketing Res.*, May 1969, *6*(2), pp. 146–54.

Shuffett, Milton and Hoskins, Josiah. Capitalization of Burley Tobacco Allotment Rights into Farmland Values. *Amer. J. Agr. Econ.*, May 1969, *51*(2), pp. 471–74.

Shull, Bernard. Bank Holding Companies: Discussion. **In** *Federal Reserve Bank of Chicago (II)*, 1969, pp. 104–07.

______ Problems in Economic Analysis of Bank Merger and Holding Company Cases. **In** *Federal Reserve Bank of Chicago (I)*, 1969, pp. 20–36.

______ **and Horvitz, Paul M.** Branch Banking, Independent Banks and Geographic Price Discrimination. *Antitrust Bull.*, Winter 1969, *14*, pp. 827–44.

Shultz, George P. Labor Statistics for National Decision Making. *Amer. Statist.*, October 1969, *23*(4), pp. 11–14.

______ Priorities in Policy and Research for Industrial Relations. **In** *Somers, G. G., ed. (II)*, 1969, pp. 1–13.

______ Statement. **In** *The 1969 Economic Report of the President, Pt. 2, JECH*, 1969, pp. 426–45.

______ Statement. **In** *Economic Opportunity Amendments of 1969, Pt. 2, HCH*, 1969, pp. 935–45.

______ The Use of Labor Statistics in National Decisionmaking. *Mon. Lab. Rev.*, November 1969, *92* (11), pp. 48–50.

Shwayder, Keith. The Capital Maintenance Rule and the Net Asset Valuation Rule. *Accounting Rev.*, April 1969, *44*(2), pp. 304–16.

Šíba, Vladimír. Economic Reform and Income Policy. *New Trends Czech. Econ.*, May 1969, (3), pp. 26–46.

Sicat, Gerardo P. An Abstract of an Inventory of Philippine Exports, 1961–1967: Comment. *Philippine Econ. J.*, First Semester 1969, *8*(1), pp. 90–94.

______ Intercountry Trade: The Effects of Bilateralism, Development, and Regional Advantage. *Malayan Econ. Rev.*, October 1969, *14*(2), pp. 94–112.

Sidrauski, Miguel. Rational Choice and Patterns of Growth. *J. Polit. Econ.*, Part II, July/August 1969, *77*(4), pp. 575–85.

______**; Foley, Duncan K. and Shell, Karl.** Optimal Fiscal and Monetary Policy and Economic Growth. *J. Polit. Econ.*, Part II, July/August 1969, *77*(4), pp. 698–719.

______**; Stiglitz, Joseph E. and Shell, Karl.** Capital Gains, Income, and Saving. *Rev. Econ. Stud.*, January 1969, *36*(105), pp. 15–26.

Siebert, Horst. Goal Conflicts in Regional Growth Policy. *Z. Nationalökon.*, May 1969, *29*(1–2), pp. 19–28.

______ Lern- und suchtheoretische Aspekte neuen technischen Wissens. (Learn Theoretical and Search Theoretical Aspects of New Technical Knowledge. With English summary.) *Schmollers Jahr.*, 1969, *89*(5), pp. 513–39.

Siegel, Paul M. On the Cost of Being a Negro. **In** *Kain, J. F., ed.*, 1969, pp. 60–67.

Siglienti, Stefano. Sulle possibilità di formazione del

risparmio e di investimento produttivo. (Savings and Productive Investments. With English summary.) *Bancaria,* October 1969, *25*(10), pp. 1195–99.

Sigsworth, Eric M. Some Problems in British Business History, 1870–1914. **In** *Kennedy, C. J., ed.,* 1969, pp. 21–37.

Siimestö, Orvo. Markovin ketjut ostosarjojen stokastisena mallina. (Markov Chains as a Stochastic Model of Buying Series. With English summary.) *Liiketaloudellinen Aikak.,* 1969, *18*(2), pp. 233–42.

Sik, Ota. On the Economic Problems in Czechoslovakia. **In** *Economic Concentration, Pt. 7A, SCH,* 1969, pp. 4509–30.

Silber, William L. Liquidity Premium Theory: Some Observations. *Kyklos,* 1969, *22*(1), pp. 155–58.

——— Monetary Channels and the Relative Importance of Money Supply and Bank Portfolios. *J. Finance,* March 1969, *24*(1), pp. 81–87.

——— Portfolio Substitutability, Regulations, and Monetary Policy. *Quart. J. Econ.,* May 1969, *83* (2), pp. 197–219.

——— Velocity and Bank Portfolio Composition. *Southern Econ. J.,* October 1969, *36*(2), pp. 147–52.

——— **and Hamburger, Michael J.** An Empirical Study of Interest Rate Determination. *Rev. Econ. Statist.,* August 1969, *51*(3), pp. 369–73.

Silva, Donald H. State Technical Service—An Emerging Social System. *Amer. J. Econ. Soc.,* October 1969, *28*(4), pp. 399–403.

Silver, Morris and Auster, Richard. Entrepreneurship, Profit, and Limits on Firm Size. *J. Bus.,* July 1969, *42*(3), pp. 277–81.

Simeone, Franco. Integrazione economica e Paesi in via di sviluppo. (Economic Integration and Developing Countries. With English summary.) *Mondo Aperto,* December 1969, *23*(6), pp. 423–43.

Simkin, C. G. F. Keynes's Grandchildren. *Australian Econ. Pap.,* December 1969, *8*(13), pp. 122–33.

Simmons, John K. and Gray, Jack. An Investigation of the Effect of Differing Accounting Frameworks on the Prediction of Net Income. *Accounting Rev.,* October 1969, *44*(4), pp. 757–76.

Simmons, John L. Technology and Education for Economic Development. **In** *Nader, C. and Zahlan, A. B., eds.,* 1969, pp. 41–59.

Simmons, W. R. and Bean, Judy Ann. Impact of Design and Estimation Components on Inference. **In** *Johnson, N. L. and Smith, H., Jr., eds.,* 1969, pp. 601–28.

Simon, Herbert A. Effects of Increased Productivity upon the Ratio of Urban to Rural Population. **In** *Fox, K. A. and Johnson, D. G., eds.,* 1969, pp. 309–20.

——— Statement. **In** *To Establish a Select Senate Committee on Technology and the Human Environment, SCH,* 1969, pp. 201–06.

Simon, Julian L. The Effect of Advertising on Liquor Brand Sales. *J. Marketing Res.,* August 1969, *6*(3), pp. 301–13.

——— A Further Test of the Kinky Oligopoly Demand Curve. *Amer. Econ. Rev.,* December 1969, *59*(5), pp. 971–75.

——— **and Gardner, David M.** World Food Needs and "New Proteins." *Econ. Develop. Cult. Change,* July 1969, *17*(4), pp. 520–26.

——— **and Johnson, Harold W.** The Success of Mergers: The Case of Advertising Agencies. *Bull. Oxford Univ. Inst. Econ. Statist.,* May 1969, *31*(2), pp. 139–44.

Simon, Kenneth A. The Planning of U.S. Higher Education: Projections of Enrollment, Degrees, Staff, and Expenditures to 1977–78. **In** *the Economics and Financing of Higher Education in the United States, JECP,* 1969, pp. 321–56.

Simon, Leonard S.; Smith, Kenneth M. and Alexis, Marcus. Some Determinants of Food Buying Behavior. **In** *Alexis, M.; Holloway, R. J. and Hancock, R. S., eds.,* 1969, pp. 20–32.

Simone, Dante. Sobre teoría monetaria en alta inflación. (On Monetary Theory in High Inflation. With English summary.) *Económica,* May–August 1969, *15*(2), pp. 183–209.

Simonsen, Mário Henrique. Inflation and the Money and Capital Markets of Brazil. **In** *Ellis, H. S., ed.,* 1969, pp. 133–61.

Simpson, David and McGilvray, James. Some Tests of Stability in Interindustry Coefficients. *Econometrica,* April 1969, *37*(2), pp. 204–21.

Simpson, E. S. Electricity Production in Nigeria. *Econ. Geogr.,* July 1969, *45*(3), pp. 239–57.

Simpson, Paul B. On Defining Areas of Voter Choice: Professor Tullock on Stable Voting. *Quart. J. Econ.,* August 1969, *83*(3), pp. 478–90.

Simpson, Richard H. An Empirical Study of Possible Income Manipulation. *Accounting Rev.,* October 1969, *44*(4), pp. 806–17.

Simpson, Robert E. Statement. **In** *New Directions for the 1970's: Toward a Strategy of Inter-American Development, Pts. 1–5, HCH,* 1969, pp. 211–12.

Sims, Christopher A. Theoretical Basis for a Double Deflated Index of Real Value Added. *Rev. Econ. Statist.,* November 1969, *51*(4), pp. 470–71.

Sims, James. On the Economy of Mining in Cornwall. **In** *Burt, R., ed.,* 1969, pp. 95–107.

Sims, Kent. Crisis in the State House. *Oregon Bus. Rev.,* December 1969, *28*(12), pp. 1–6.

Šimůnek, Vladimír and Kozák, Josef. Pokus o modelování sezónních výkyvů v bilanční rovnici důchodu. (An Attempt of Mathematical Formulation of Seasonal Variations of Inputs, Outputs and Prices in the Definitional Equation of Income. With English summary.) *Ekon.-Mat. Obzor,* 1969, *5*(2), pp. 209–23.

——— **and Krásová, Ludmila.** Soustava finančních účtů ČSSR. (A System of Financial Accounts in Czechoslovakia. With English summary.) *Ekon.-Mat. Obzor,* 1969, *5*(4), pp. 486–508.

Simush, P. I. The Impact of the Scientific and Technological Revolution on the Socialist Village. *Int. Soc. Sci. J.,* 1969, *21*(2), pp. 256–64.

Sinclair, Sol. Economic Guidelines for Resource Use: Discussion. *Can. J. Agr. Econ.,* November 1969, *17*(3), pp. 34–38.

Singer, H. W. and Doss, A. C. Technical Assistance to Kenya: Some Thoughts on Flows and Programming. *East Afr. Econ. Rev.,* June 1969, *1*(1), pp. 17–27.

Singer, Morris. Marxian Economics and Contemporary Growth Analysis. *J. Econ. Issues,* June 1969, *3*(2), pp. 192–205.

Singer, Neil and Feldman, Paul. Criteria for Public Investment in Higher Education. In *the Economics and Financing of Higher Education in the United States, JECP,* 1969, pp. 124–34.

Singh, Ajmer. Local Business Activity Index: Its Construction and Uses—Reply. *J. Reg. Sci.,* April 1969, *9*(1), pp. 167–69.

Singh, D. K. and Sinha, Randhir. A Study of Potato Price Behaviour in Selected Markets of Bihar. *Econ. Aff.,* January-February 1969, *14*(1–2), pp. 93–102.

Singh, Tarlok. On Planning Technological Change in Indian Agriculture. *Int. Soc. Sci. J.,* 1969, *21*(2), pp. 265–71.

Singh, V. B. and Papola, T. S. Investment Effectiveness and Educational Planning in India. In *Pandit, H. N., ed.,* 1969, pp. 274–79.

Singhvi, Surendra S. Corporate Financial Disclosure in the United States. *Miss. Val. J. Bus. Econ.,* Fall 1969, *5*(1), pp. 43–50.

______ **and Slamka, John G.** Industrial Revenue Bonds: A Source of Long-Term Financing. *Calif. Manage. Rev.,* Spring 1969, *11*(3), pp. 53–60.

Sinha, G. P. and Sinha, P. R. N. Working of the Central Wage Boards. In *Johri, C. K., ed.,* 1969, pp. 270–86.

Sinha, J. N. Framework of Incomes and Wage Policy in India. In *Johri, C. K., ed.,* 1969, pp. 235–53.

Sinha, Laksminarayan. Cost and Efficiency of Education. In *Pandit, H. N., ed.,* 1969, pp. 131–35.

Sinha, P. R. N. and Sinha, G. P. Working of the Central Wage Boards. In *Johri, C. K., ed.,* 1969, pp. 270–86.

Sinha, R. P. Unresolved Issues in Japan's Early Economic Development. *Scot. J. Polit. Econ.,* June 1969, *16*(2), pp. 109–51.

______ Unresolved Issues in Japan's Early Economic Development—A Correction. *Scot. J. Polit. Econ.,* November 1969, *16*(3), pp. 319.

______**; Castree, J. R. and Wilson, T.** The Income Terms of Trade of Developed and Developing Countries. *Econ. J.,* December 1969, *79*(316), pp. 813–32.

Sinha, Randhir and Singh, D. K. A Study of Potato Price Behaviour in Selected Markets of Bihar. *Econ. Aff.,* January-February 1969, *14*(1–2), pp. 93–102.

Sinicropi, Anthony V. Collective Negotiations and Teachers: Remarks. In *Sinicropi, A. V. and Gilroy, T. P., eds.,* 1969, pp. 29–31.

Sirohi, Amar S. and Pine, Wilfred H. Irrigation with Restraints on Land and Water Resources. *Land Econ.,* May 1969, *45*(2), pp. 285–87.

Sirotti, Vittorio. Sulla stabilita' dell'equilibrio nella teoria pura dello scambio internazionale-II. (On the Stability in the Pure Theory of International Trade-II. With English summary.) *Econ. Int.,* May 1969, *22*(2), pp. 203–24.

Sitnin, V. Results of the Reform of Wholesale Prices and Tasks in the Further Improvement of Price Formation in the U.S.S.R. *Prob. Econ.,* April 1969, *11*(12), pp. 26–36.

Sivamurthy, M. Errors in the Estimation of Net Migration Rate in the Studies of Internal Migration. *J. Amer. Statist. Assoc.,* December 1969, *64*(328), pp. 1434–38.

Sivula, Tarmo. Huolitsijan oikeudellisesta ja taloudellisesta asemasta. (Forwarding Agent's Legal and Economic Position. With English summary.) *Liiketaloudellinen Aikak.,* 1969, *18*(3), pp. 598–607.

Sjöblom, Veikko. Havaintoja toimialarationalisoinnista useammalla alalla toimivassa yrityksessä. (Remarks on Rationalization in the Operational Field in a Firm Operating in Several Fields. With English summary.) *Liiketaloudellinen Aikak.,* 1969, *18*(2), pp. 243–50.

Skala, Heinz J. Bemerkungen zur Bayesschen Entscheidungstheorie. (With English summary.) *Jahr. Nationalökon. Statist.,* July 1969, *183*(2), pp. 141–49.

Skeels, Jack W. Perspectives on Private Employment Agencies. *Ind. Relat.,* February 1969, *8*(2), pp. 151–61.

Skinner, A. S. Of Malthus, Lauderdale and Say's Law. *Scot. J. Polit. Econ.,* June 1969, *16*(2), pp. 177–95.

Skinner, R. W. Hidden Consumer Motives in Supermarket Selection. *Amer. J. Agr. Econ.,* December 1969, *51*(5), pp. 1154–58.

Skinner, Wickham. Manufacturing—Missing Link in Corporate Strategy. *Harvard Bus. Rev.,* May–June 1969, *47*(3), pp. 136–45.

Skousen, K. Fred and Mautz, R. K. Some Problems in Empirical Research in Accounting. *Accounting Rev.,* July 1969, *44*(3), pp. 447–56.

Slamka, John G. and Singhvi, Surendra S. Industrial Revenue Bonds: A Source of Long-Term Financing. *Calif. Manage. Rev.,* Spring 1969, *11*(3), pp. 53–60.

Slaughter, Rudie W., Jr. Payment Limitation: Effect on Supply Adjustment and Income Distribution. *Amer. J. Agr. Econ.,* December 1969, *51*(5), pp. 1233–36.

Slaven, Anthony. A Glasgow Firm in the Indian Market: John Lean and Sons, Muslin Weavers. *Bus. Hist. Rev.,* Winter 1969, *43*(4), pp. 496–522.

Slavney, Morris. Experiences with Current Substantive Practices in Administering. In *Sinicropi, A. V. and Gilroy, T. P., eds.,* 1969, pp. 52–59.

Sleeman, John F. A New Look at the Distribution of Private Cars in Britain. *Scot. J. Polit. Econ.,* November 1969, *16*(3), pp. 306–18.

Slen, S. B. and Cameron, M. A. Prospects and Potentials in Canadian Beef Production. *Can. J. Agr. Econ.,* November 1969, *17*(3), pp. 80–89.

Slicher van Bath, B. H. Contrasting Demographic Development in Some Parts of the Netherlands during the Depression Period of the Seventeenth and Eighteenth Centuries. In *Bechhofer, F., ed.,* 1969, pp. 209–19.

Slitor, Richard E. The Carter Proposals on Capital Gains: Economic Effects and Policy Implications for the United States. *Nat. Tax J.,* March 1969, *22* (1), pp. 66–78.

Slome, Benjamin. The Interregional Input-Output Model and Interregional Public Finance. *Public Finance,* 1969, *24*(4), pp. 618–23.

Slutzker, David R. A Proposal to Computerize the

Accounting System. *Manage. Account.*, September 1969, *51*(3), pp. 23–28.

Smethurst, Richard G. Direct Commodity Aid: A Multilateral Experiment. *J. Devel. Stud.*, April 1969, *5*(3), pp. 205–19.

Smiddy, Harold F. Planning as a Fundamental Component of Management: Background and Perspective. **In** *Ozbekhan, H. and Talbert, G. E., eds.*, 1969, pp. 102–17.

Smidt, S. and Goldschmidt, Y. Valuing the Firm's Durable Assets for Managerial Information. *Accounting Rev.*, April 1969, *44*(2), pp. 317–29.

Smirnov, V. V. Movement and Utilization of Rural Labor Resources (in the Non-black Soil Zone of the RSFSR). *Prob. Econ.*, October 1969, *12*(6), pp. 68–81.

______ Theoretical Problems Pertaining to the Management of the Economy of Developing Countries. *Prob. Econ.*, July 1969, *12*(3), pp. 83–94.

Smith, Alan F. Purchased Goodwill Is an Investment: Treat It as Such. *Manage. Account.*, November 1969, *51*(5), pp. 19–22.

Smith, Allen G. Corporate and Noncorporate Farm Borrowers—Some Financial Aspects. *Agr. Finance Rev.*, July 1969, *30*, pp. 70–75.

______ **and Baker, C. B.** The Effect of Real Estate Debt Commitments on Nonreal Estate Credit and Liquidity of the Farm. *Ill. Agr. Econ.*, January 1969, *9*(1), pp. 1–6.

Smith, Anthony D. An Analysis of the Proceedings. **In** *Smith, A. D., ed.*, 1969, pp. 163–214.

______ A Conspectus of Wage Trends in Developing Countries. **In** *Smith, A. D., ed.*, 1969, pp. 3–52.

Smith, Blair J. and Purcell, Joseph C. Quadratic Programming Solution of Competitive Equilibrium for U.S. Agriculture: Comment. *Amer. J. Agr. Econ.*, May 1969, *51*(2), pp. 481–82.

Smith, C. Selby. Benefits to British Employers from Post-secondary Education. *J. Roy. Statist. Soc.*, Part 3, 1969, *132*, pp. 408–17.

______ **and Armitage, P.** Computable Models of the British Educational System. **In** *Blaug, M., ed.*, 1969, pp. 202–37.

Smith, Dan Throop. The Effects of Taxation of Executive Compensation on Economic Activity. **In** *Tax Institute of America*, 1969, pp. 34–43.

______ Federal Tax Reform—Conclusions. **In** *Gaa, C. J.*, 1969, pp. 85–90.

______ The Nature of Taxation and the Objectives of Tax Policy. **In** *Gaa, C. J.*, 1969, pp. 6–12.

______ Statement. **In** *Tax Reform Act of 1969, Testimony, Oct. 2, SCP*, 1969, pp. 9–22.

______ Tax Alternatives for the Next Decade. **In** *Gaa, C. J.*, 1969, pp. 96–103.

______ Tax Policy and Foreign Investment. *Law Contemp. Probl.*, Winter 1969, *34*(1), pp. 146–56.

Smith, David L. Characteristics of Merging Banks. (Study summary.) *Fed. Res. Bull.*, July 1969, *55*(7), pp. 579–80.

______ Federal Grant Elasticity and Distortion: A Reply. *Nat. Tax J.*, December 1969, *22*(4), pp. 552–53.

Smith, George W. Brazilian Agricultural Policy, 1950–1967. **In** *Ellis, H. S., ed.*, 1969, pp. 213–65.

Smith, Harry. Regression Analysis and Analysis of Variance. **In** *Naylor, T. H., ed.*, 1969, pp. 123–31.

Smith, James D. and Morgan, James N. Measures of Economic Well-Offness and Their Correlates. *Amer. Econ. Rev.*, May 1969, *59*(2), pp. 450–62.

Smith, John S. World Summary of International Transactions, 1961–66. *Int. Monet. Fund Staff Pap.*, March 1969, *16*(1), pp. 85–102.

______ **and Bouter, Arie C.** The Treatment of Reserves and of Reserve Creation in the Balance of Payments Accounts. *Int. Monet. Fund Staff Pap.*, July 1969, *16*(2), pp. 202–23.

Smith, K. Wayne and Enthoven, Alain C. The Planning, Programing, and Budgeting System in the Department of Defense: Current Status and Next Steps. **In** *The Analysis and Evaluation of Public Expenditures: The PPB System, Vol. 3, JECP*, 1969, pp. 955–69.

______ What Forces for NATO? And from Whom? *Foreign Aff.*, October 1969, *48*(1), pp. 80–96.

Smith, Keith V. Stock Price and Economic Indexes for Generating Efficient Portfolios. *J. Bus.*, July 1969, *42*(3), pp. 326–36.

______ **and Schreiner, John C.** A Portfolio Analysis of Conglomerate Diversification. *J. Finance*, June 1969, *24*(3), pp. 413–27.

______ **and Tito, Dennis A.** Risk-Return Measures of Ex Post Portfolio Performance. *J. Financial Quant. Anal.*, December 1969, *4*(4), pp. 449–71.

Smith, Kenneth M.; Alexis, Marcus and Simon, Leonard S. Some Determinants of Food Buying Behavior. **In** *Alexis, M.; Holloway, R. J. and Hancock, R. S., eds.*, 1969, pp. 20–32.

Smith, Kenneth R. The Effect of Uncertainty on Monopoly Price, Capital Stock and Utilization of Capital. *J. Econ. Theory*, June 1969, *1*(1), pp. 48–59.

Smith, Lawrence B. A Model of the Canadian Housing and Mortgage Markets. *J. Polit. Econ.*, September/October 1969, *77*(5), pp. 795–816.

Smith, Robert S. The Reception of Malthus' Essay on Population in Spain. *Rivista Int. Sci. Econ. Com.*, June 1969, *16*(6), pp. 550–65.

Smith, Russell A. State and Local Advisory Reports on Public Employment Labor Legislation: A Comparative Analysis. *Mich. Law Rev.*, March 1969, *67*(5), pp. 891–918.

Smith, Stephen C. and Lord, William B. Tools of the Trade in Policy Decision—PPBS, A Case in Point. *Amer. J. Agr. Econ.*, December 1969, *51*(5), pp. 1427–33.

Smith, T. Lynn. Some Major Current Rural Social Trends in the United States of America. *Int. Soc. Sci. J.*, 1969, *21*(2), pp. 272–85.

Smith, Thomas C. Farm Family By-employments in Preindustrial Japan. *J. Econ. Hist.*, December 1969, *29*(4), pp. 687–715.

Smith, V. Kerry. The CES Production Function: A Derivation. *Amer. Econ.*, Spring 1969, *13*(1), pp. 72–76.

______ The Maximization Policies of Less Developed Exporting Countries. *Quart. Rev. Econ. Bus.*, Winter 1969, *4*(9), pp. 84–86.

______ "The Identification Problem and the Validity of Economic Models": A Comment. *S. Afr. J. Econ.*, March 1969, *37*(1), pp. 81.

Smith, Vernon L. Measuring Nonmonetary Utilities in Uncertain Choices: The Ellsberg Urn. *Quart. J. Econ.*, May 1969, *83*(2), pp. 324–29.

______ On Models of Commercial Fishing. *J. Polit. Econ.*, March/April 1969, *77*(2), pp. 181–98.

______ Taxes and Share Valuation in Competitive Markets. *Rev. Econ. Statist.*, February 1969, *51* (1), pp. 96–99.

Smith, Warren L. A Neo-Keynesian View of Monetary Policy. **In** *Federal Reserve Bank of Boston,* 1969, pp. 105–26.

______ Statement. **In** *High Interest Rates, SCH,* 1969, pp. 151–58.

Smyth, David J. Sales Maximization and Managerial Effort: Note. *Amer. Econ. Rev.*, Part I, September 1969, *59*(4), pp. 633–34.

______ **and Briscoe, G.** Investment Plans and Realizations in United Kingdom Manufacturing. *Economica, N.S.*, August 1969, *36*(143), pp. 277–94.

______**; Briscoe, G. and Samuels, J. M.** The Treatment of Risk in the Stock Market. *J. Finance*, September 1969, *24*(4), pp. 707–13.

______**; Briscoe, G. and Samuels, J. M.** The Variability of Industry Profit Rates. *Appl. Econ.*, May 1969, *1*(2), pp. 137–49.

Snape, R. H. Sugar: Costs of Protection and Taxation. *Economica, N.S.*, February 1969, *36*(141), pp. 29–41.

Snavely, Howard J. Current Cost for Long-Lived Assets: A Critical View. *Accounting Rev.*, April 1969, *44*(2), pp. 344–53.

Snell, Hampton K. Transportation Integration: A Variety of Problems. **In** *Hilton, R., ed.*, 1969, pp. 321–34.

Snowbarger, Marvin and Shervais, Steve. A Study of Factors Influencing the Average Effective Tax Rate on Personal Income, 1954–1965. *Nat. Tax J.*, June 1969, *22*(2), pp. 217–31.

Snyder, Carl Dean. White Collars and the U.A.W. *Mich. Academician,* Winter 1969, *1*(1–2), pp. 43–54.

Snyder, J. H. and Moore, C. V. Crop Selection in High-Risk Agriculture. *Agr. Econ. Res.*, October 1969, *21*(4), pp. 89–98.

Snyder, James C. Trials, Errors, and Successes in Agribusiness Education at Purdue. *Amer. J. Agr. Econ.*, December 1969, *51*(5), pp. 1218–21.

______**; Willis, J. F. and Minden, A. J.** Monte Carlo Simulation of Management Systems. *Can. J. Agr. Econ.*, February 1969, *17*(1), pp. 42–49.

Snyder, Robert W. Using Local Comprehensive Planning to Control Lakewater Pollution in Seasonal Home Communities. *Amer. J. Agr. Econ.*, December 1969, *51*(5), pp. 1583–87.

Snyder, Wayne W. La mésure des effets des politiques budgétaires françaises de 1955 à 1965. (With English summary.) *Revue Écon.*, November 1969, *20*(6), pp. 929–53.

______ Turkish Economic Development: The First Five Year Plan, 1963–67. *J. Devel. Stud.*, October 1969, *6*(1), pp. 58–71.

______ Una valutazione degli effetti delle politiche italiane di bilancio nel periodo 1955–65. (Measuring the Effects of Italian Budget Policies, 1955–65. With English summary.) *Econ. Int.*, November 1969, *22*(4), pp. 681–704.

Sobering, Fred; Quance, C. Leroy and Tweeten, Luther G. An Economic Model for Determining Cotton Allotments and Prices to Maximize Net Farm Income. *Amer. J. Agr. Econ.*, December 1969, *51*(5), pp. 1124–28.

Sobota, Václav. Federative Arrangement of External Economic Relations. *New Trends Czech. Econ.*, July 1969, (4), pp. 53–64.

Södersten, Bo and Vind, Karl. Tariffs and Trade in General Equilibrium: Reply. *Amer. Econ. Rev.*, June 1969, *59*(3), pp. 424–26.

Sohmen, Egon. The Assignment Problem. **In** *Mundell, R. A. and Swoboda, A. K., eds.*, 1969, pp. 183–97.

______ International Liquidity and the Reform of the Adjustment Mechanism: Comment. **In** *Samuelson, P. A., ed.*, 1969, pp. 263–68.

______ **and Schneeweiss, Hans.** Fiscal and Monetary Policies under Alternative Exchange Rate Systems: A Correction. *Quart. J. Econ.*, May 1969, *83* (2), pp. 336–40.

Sojit, Alberto A. Renta de la tierra y asignación de recursos. (Land Rent and Allocation of Resources. With English summary.) *Económica*, May–August 1969, *15*(2), pp. 211–22.

Sokol, Jaroslav. The Economic Reform Viewed as a Problem. *Eastern Europ. Econ.*, Summer 1969, *7* (4), pp. 13–24.

Sokol, Miroslav. Observations on Economic Development. *Eastern Europ. Econ.*, Fall 1969, *8*(1), pp. 3–19.

Sokolik, Stanley L. Reorganize the Personnel Department? *Calif. Manage. Rev.*, Spring 1969, *11* (3), pp. 43–52.

Sokoloski, Adam A. A Water Resource Economist Looks Back at a Lawyer. *Amer. J. Agr. Econ.*, August 1969, *51*(3), pp. 680–84.

Sokolovskii, L. Kh.; Bunich, P. G. and Perlamutrov, V. L. An Inventory Model in Physical and Monetary Terms. *Matekon*, Fall 1969, *6*(1), pp. 30–43.

Solar, Donald. The Case against Latin American Integration: Economic and Political Factors. **In** *Hilton, R., ed.*, 1969, pp. 110–32.

Soldofsky, Robert M. Asset Management and Monetary Policy: Discussion. *J. Finance*, May 1969, *24* (2), pp. 245–47.

______ **and Miller, Roger L.** Risk Premium Curves for Different Classes of Long-Term Securities, 1950–1966. *J. Finance,* June 1969, *24*(3), pp. 429–45.

______ **and Pogue, Thomas F.** What's in a Bond Rating? *J. Financial Quant. Anal.*, June 1969, *4*(2), pp. 201–28.

Soligo, Ronald and Berry, R. Albert. Some Welfare Aspects of International Migration. *J. Polit. Econ.*, September/October 1969, *77*(5), pp. 778–94.

Solnick, Bruce B. A Historian's View of Central America: Economic Integration and Political Unity. **In** *Hilton, R., ed.*, 1969, pp. 500–507.

Solo, Robert. Capital and Labor Intensive Technology in Developing Countries. *J. Econ. Issues,* December 1969, *3*(4), pp. 96–103.

Solomon, Anthony M. Foreign Investment Controls:

Policy and Response. *Law Contemp. Probl.*, Winter 1969, *34*(1), pp. 118–25.

Solomon, Gregory L. Public School Systems in Indiana and Its Bordering States. *Indiana Bus. Rev.*, January–February 1969, *44*, pp. 17–24.

Solomon, R. J. Property Values as a Structural Element of Urban Evolution. *Econ. Geogr.*, January 1969, *45*(1), pp. 1–29.

Solomon, Robert. International Financial Problems and the Role of the Dollar: Discussion. *J. Finance*, May 1969, *24*(2), pp. 371–74.

Solomons, D. Economic and Accounting Concepts of Income. **In** *Parker, R. H. and Harcourt, G. C., eds.*, 1969, pp. 106–19.

Solow, Robert M. Sources of Economic Growth. **In** *Starleaf, D. R., ed.*, 1969, pp. 484–92.

Solterer, Josef. Liquidity Norms for Development. *Rev. Soc. Econ.*, March 1969, *27*(1), pp. 13–22.

Soltow, Lee C. Evidence on Income Inequality in the United States, 1866–1965. *J. Econ. Hist.*, June 1969, *29*(2), pp. 279–86.

Solverson, Lyle. Consumer Knowledge for Sovereignty: Apples. *Amer. J. Agr. Econ.*, December 1969, *51*(5), pp. 1247–50.

Solzman, David M. The Value of Inland Waterfront Industrial Sites. *Land Econ.*, November 1969, *45* (4), pp. 456–62.

Somers, Gerald G. Bargaining Power and Industrial Relations Theory. **In** *Somers, G. G., ed. (I)*, 1969, pp. 39–53.

——— Data Needs for Monitoring and Evaluating Manpower Programs. **In** *Somers, G. G., ed. (II)*, 1969, pp. 97–104.

Somers, Harold M. The Somers Solution to the Use Tax: Reply. *Nat. Tax J.*, June 1969, *22*(2), pp. 302.

Somers, Herman M. Economic Issues in Health Services. **In** *Chamberlain, N. W., ed.*, 1969, pp. 109–44.

Sommer, A. A., Jr. The Accountant's Changing Legal Environment. **In** *Burton, J. C., ed.*, 1969, pp. 87–106.

Sonin, M. Ia. Training Personnel and Labor Turnover. **In** *Noah, H. J., ed.*, 1969, pp. 32–35.

Soper, Tom. Western Attitudes to Aid. *Lloyds Bank Rev.*, October 1969, (94), pp. 17–33.

Sorensen, James E. Bayesian Analysis in Auditing. *Accounting Rev.*, July 1969, *44*(3), pp. 555–61.

Sorenson, Clara T. Review of State Labor Laws Enacted in 1968. *Mon. Lab. Rev.*, January 1969, *92*(1), pp. 41–46.

Sorkin, Alan L. American Indians Industrialize to Combat Poverty. *Mon. Lab. Rev.*, March 1969, *92* (3), pp. 19–25.

——— Education and Manpower Programs for Indian Americans. **In** *Indian Education 1969, Pt. 2, Appendix, SCH*, 1969, pp. 1559–98.

——— Some Factors Associated with Earnings and Unemployment Differences between Occupations. *Nebr. J. Econ. Bus.*, Winter 1968–69, *8*(1), pp. 44–52.

Sorter, George H. An "Events" Approach to Basic Accounting Theory. *Accounting Rev.*, January 1969, *44*(1), pp. 12–19.

Sosnick, Stephen H. Toward a Concrete Concept of Effective Competition: Reply. *Amer. J. Agr. Econ.*, May 1969, *51*(2), pp. 478–81.

Șotan, S. and Topor, V. V. Determinarea influenței nivelului de organizare și conducere asupra rezultatelor economice ale I.A.S. (Determining the Influence of the Level of Organization and Management on the Economic Results of State Agricultural Enterprises. With English summary.) *Stud. Cercet. Econ.*, 1969, *1-2*, pp. 77–91.

Soule, Don M. and Lile, Stephen E. Interstate Differences in Family Tax Burdens. *Nat. Tax J.*, December 1969, *22*(4), pp. 433–45.

Southby, Richard McK. and Battistella, Roger. Crisis in American Medicine. **In** *Health Care in America, Pt. 1, SCH*, 1969, pp. 139–47.

Southwick, Lawrence, Jr. Cost Trends in Land Grant Colleges and Universities. *Appl. Econ.*, August 1969, *1*(3), pp. 167–82.

——— **and Jen, Frank C.** Implications of Dynamic Monopoly Behavior. *Amer. Econ. Rev.*, March 1969, *59*(1), pp. 149–58.

Sovani, N. V. Policy and Plan Implementation. *Indian Econ. J.*, October–December 1969, *17*(2), pp. 250–65.

Sovereign, Michael G. and Rowland, Kendrith M. Markov-Chain Analysis of Internal Manpower Supply. *Ind. Relat.*, October 1969, *9*(1), pp. 88–99.

Sowell, Thomas. Veblen's *Higher Learning* after Fifty Years. *J. Econ. Issues*, December 1969, *3*(4), pp. 66–78.

Spaeth, David H. Institutional Engineering—Venture into Applied Behavioral Science. *Amer. J. Agr. Econ.*, December 1969, *51*(5), pp. 1633–36.

Spaetling, Dieter. Umsatzmaximierung und Werbung bei fixem Mindestgewinn: Eine graphische Analyse. (With English summary.) *Z. ges. Staatswiss.*, January 1969, *125*(1), pp. 89–105.

Spandau, Arnt. Rate of Return, Profit-Sharing, and the Distribution of Incomes. *S. Afr. J. Econ.*, June 1969, *37*(2), pp. 105–16.

——— Some Comments on Professor Rädel's "Profit Maximization—Can It Be Justified?" *S. Afr. J. Econ.*, September 1969, *37*(3), pp. 268–72.

Spaniol, Roland D. Computers and Electronic Data Processing in Industrial Relations. *Ohio State U. Bull. Bus. Res.*, June 1969, *44*(6), pp. 6–7.

Spasibenko, S. G. Labor Productivity and Worker Qualifications. **In** *Noah, H. J., ed.*, 1969, pp. 119–31.

Spaull, A. D. The Rise of the Victorian Briquette Industry, 1895–1935. *Australian Econ. Hist. Rev.*, March 1969, *9*(1), pp. 39–52.

Spaventa, Luigi. Cyclical Developments in France, Germany, and Italy Since the Early Fifties: Comment. **In** *Bronfenbrenner, M., ed.*, 1969, pp. 197–99.

Spector, N. J. Use of FTC's Investigative Function in Antitrust. *Univ. Missouri Bus. Govt. Rev.*, July–August 1969, *10*(4), pp. 13–20.

Spencer, Daniel L. Japan's Industrial Concentration and Technological Pattern in Secular Perspective. **In** *Salin, E.; Stohler, J. and Pawlowsky, P.*, 1969, pp. 242–64.

——— **and Woroniak, Alexander.** Valuing Transfer of Military-Acquired Skills to Civilian Employment. *Kyklos*, 1969, *22*(3), pp. 467–92.

Spencer, Geraldine. Recent Trends in Marriages in

Australia. *Econ. Rec.*, June 1969, *45*(110), pp. 206–17.

Spencer, Roger W. The Relation between Prices and Employment: Two Views. *Fed. Res. Bank St. Louis Rev.*, March 1969, *51*(3), pp. 15–21.

Spengler, Joseph J. Allocation and Development, Economic and Political. **In** *Braibanti, R., ed.*, 1969, pp. 588–637.

______ Cassel on Population. *Hist. Polit. Econ.*, Spring 1969, *1*(1), pp. 150–72.

______ Evolution of Public-Utility Industry Regulation: Economists and Other Determinants. *S. Afr. J. Econ.*, March 1969, *37*(1), pp. 3–31.

______ India's Prospects According to Jean-Baptiste Say, 1824. *J. Asian Stud.*, May 1969, *28*(3), pp. 595–600.

______ Is Social Science Ready? *Soc. Sci. Quart.*, December 1969, *50*(3), pp. 449–68.

______ The Social Sciences and the New Encyclopedia: Trends and a Forecast. *Soc. Sci. Quart.*, September 1969, *50*(2), pp. 213–21.

Spiegel, Hans B. C. and Alicea, Victor G. The Trade-Off Strategy in Community Research. *Soc. Sci. Quart.*, December 1969, *50*(3), pp. 598–603.

Spilhaus, Athelstan. Technology, Living Cities, and Human Environment. **In** *Panel on Science and Technology: Science and Technology and the Cities, HCH*, 1969, pp. 47–54.

Spitz, John V. A Note on Relative-Wage Trends in Nine Southern States: The Case of Production and Non-Production Labor in Manufacturing. *J. Reg. Sci.*, August 1969, *9*(2), pp. 319–23.

Spitz, Ruth S. and Parnes, Herbert S. A Conceptual Framework for Studying Labor Mobility. *Mon. Lab. Rev.*, November 1969, *92*(11), pp. 55–58.

Spivak, Peter B. Reassessment of Economic Standards for the Rate of Return under Regulation: Comment. **In** *Trebing, H. M. and Howard, R. H., eds.*, 1969, pp. 26–29.

Spornic, A. Considerații privind perfecționarea relațiilor de proprietate în etapa actuală. (Considerations Regarding the Improvement of Property Relations at the Present Stage. With English summary.) *Stud. Cercet. Econ.*, 1969, *1-2*, pp. 13–22.

Spottiswoode, R. A. Note on Feasibility Studies: II. The Western Nigeria Road Development Survey. *J. Transp. Econ. Policy*, May 1969, *3*(2), pp. 225–30.

Sprague, Christopher R.; Taylor, David P. and Baitsell, John M. A Computer-Based Negotiation: Uses and Limitations as a Training Device. **In** *Siegel, A. J., ed.*, 1969, pp. 260–85.

Spraos, John. Some Aspects of Sterling in the Decade 1957–66. **In** *Aliber, R. Z., ed.*, 1969, pp. 158–73.

Sprenkle, Case M. Laidler's "The Definition of Money": A Comment. *J. Money, Credit, Banking*, August 1969, *1*(3), pp. 526–30.

______ The Uselessness of Transactions Demand Models. *J. Finance*, December 1969, *24*(5), pp. 835–47.

______ **and Heins, A. James.** A Comment on the Modigliani-Miller Cost of Capital Thesis. *Amer. Econ. Rev.*, Part I, September 1969, *59*(4), pp. 590–92.

Sprinkel, Beryl W. The Business Outlook for 1969: Moving toward Economic Stability. *J. Bus.*, January 1969, *42*(1), pp. 1–6.

Sprott, D. A. and Kalbfleisch, J. D. Applications of Likelihood and Fiducial Probability to Sampling Finite Populations. **In** *Johnson, N. L. and Smith, H., Jr., eds.*, 1969, pp. 358–89.

Sproull, Mary. A Report on Salary Changes for Teachers in Urban Areas. *Mon. Lab. Rev.*, April 1969, *92*(4), pp. 49–52.

Spulber, Nicolas. East-West Trade and the Paradoxes of the Strategic Embargo. **In** *To Extend and Amend the Export Control Act of 1949, HCH*, 1969, pp. 322–41.

Spyropoulos, Georges. An Outline of Developments and Trends in Labour Relations. *Int. Lab. Rev.*, March 1969, *99*(3), pp. 315–46.

Srinivasan, E. S. Analysis of the Trends in the Sources of Funds of the Non-Financial Companies in India during 1951–66. *Asian Econ. Rev.*, February 1969, *11*(2), pp. 131–44.

Srinivasan, R. and Puri, I. C. Agency for Operation of Buffer Stocks. **In** *Indian Society of Agricultural Economics*, 1969, pp. 118–27.

Srinivasan, T. N. and Bhagwati, Jagdish N. Optimal Intervention to Acheive Non-Economic Objectives. *Rev. Econ. Stud.*, January 1969, *36*(105), pp. 27–38.

______**; Bhagwati, Jagdish N. and Ramaswami, V. K.** Domestic Distortions, Tariffs, and the Theory of Optimum Subsidy: Some Further Results. *J. Polit. Econ.*, November/December 1969, *77*(6), pp. 1005–10.

______ **and Levhari, David.** Durability of Consumption Goods: Competition Versus Monopoly. *Amer. Econ. Rev.*, March 1969, *59*(1), pp. 102–07.

______ **and Levhari, David.** Optimal Savings under Uncertainty. *Rev. Econ. Stud.*, April 1969, *36* (106), pp. 153–63.

Srivastava, C. P. Public Sector in Shipping Industry. **In** *Dagli, V., ed., Vol. II*, 1969, pp. 111–16.

Srivastava, D. K. and Anand, Vinod. On the Stability Theorem in Uzawa's Two-Sector Growth Model. *Indian Econ. J.*, January–March 1969, *16*(3), pp. 362–70.

Srivastava, U. K. P. L. 480 Counterpart Funds and Inflation: Myth and Realty. *Asian Econ. Rev.*, February 1969, *11*(2), pp. 145–59.

St. George, George and Rust, Charles H. Transportation Pricing as a Factor in Commodity Marketing: Montana Wheat, A Case Study. *Amer. J. Agr. Econ.*, December 1969, *51*(5), pp. 1471–77.

Staats, Elmer B. Industry-Government Relationships. *Calif. Manage. Rev.*, Fall 1969, *12*(1), pp. 83–90.

______ Industry-Government Relationships: Issues Facing the New Administration. **In** *Ozbekhan, H. and Talbert, G. E., eds.*, 1969, pp. 205–22.

______ Statement. **In** *Guidelines for Estimating the Benefits of Public Expenditures, JECH*, 1969, pp. 3–15.

Stacey, R. D. Uniformity in Output Growth Patterns in the Manufacturing Sector. *S. Afr. J. Econ.*, March 1969, *37*(1), pp. 55–75.

Stafford, Frank P. Student Family Size in Relation to Current and Expected Income. *J. Polit. Econ.*, Part I, July/August 1969, *77*(4), pp. 471–77.

——— and Dunkelberg, William. The Cost of Financing Automobile Purchases. *Rev. Econ. Statist.*, November 1969, *51*(4), pp. 459–64.

Stafford, James E. and Enis, Ben M. The Price-Quality Relationship: An Extension. *J. Marketing Res.*, November 1969, *6*(4), pp. 456–58.

Stahl, János and Szakolczai, György. Increasing or Decreasing Returns to Scale in the Constant Elasticity of Substitution Production Function. *Rev. Econ. Statist.*, February 1969, *51*(1), pp. 84–90.

Stahl, Sheldon W. A Look at Some Measures of Inflation. **In** *Starleaf, D. R., ed.*, 1969, pp. 302–08.

Stambler, Howard V. New Directions in Area Labor Force Statistics. *Mon. Lab. Rev.*, August 1969, *92* (8), pp. 3–9.

——— Problems in Analyzing Urban Employment Survey Data. *Mon. Lab. Rev.*, November 1969, *92* (11), pp. 51–54.

Stammati, Gaetano. The Italian Budget. *Rev. Econ. Cond. Italy*, January 1969, *23*(1), pp. 13–27.

Stamp, Maxwell and Cowie, Harry. Britain and the Free Trade Area Option. **In** *Johnson, H. G., ed.*, 1969, pp. 165–253.

Stanford, J. D. Multiple Expansion of Bank Deposits under Australian Institutional Conditions: A Reply. *Econ. Rec.*, June 1969, *45*(110), pp. 297–98.

Stanley, Julian C. and Glass, Gene V. An Algebraic Proof That the Sum of the Squared Errors in Estimating Y from X Via b_1 and b_0 Is Minimal. *Amer. Statist.*, February 1969, *23*(1), pp. 25–26.

Stans, Maurice H. Statement. **In** *The 1969 Economic Report of the President, Pt. 3, JECH*, 1969, pp. 726–32.

Stanton, Lynn A. and Huffman, Donald C. Application of Linear Programming to Individual Farm Planning. *Amer. J. Agr. Econ.*, December 1969, *51*(5), pp. 1168–71.

Starleaf, Dennis R. and Stephenson, James A. A Suggested Solution to the Monetary-Policy Indicator Problem: The Monetary Full Employment Interest Rate. *J. Finance*, September 1969, *24*(4), pp. 623–41.

Starr, Ross M. Quasi-Equilibria in Markets with Non-Convex Preferences. *Econometrica*, January 1969, *37*(1), pp. 25–38.

Starrett, David A. Switching and Reswitching in a General Production Model. *Quart. J. Econ.*, November 1969, *83*(4), pp. 673–87.

Stauss, James H. Endowment as a Source of Increased Revenue. **In** *the Economics and Financing of Higher Education in the United States, JECP*, 1969, pp. 507–17.

Steckman, William E. and Zand, Dale E. Resolving Industrial Conflict—An Experimental Study of the Effects of Attitudes and Precedent. **In** *Somers, G. G., ed. (II)*, 1969, pp. 348–59.

Steele, D. B. Regional Multipliers in Great Britain. *Oxford Econ. Pap.*, July 1969, *21*(2), pp. 268–92.

Steele, Henry. Statement. **In** *Governmental Intervention in the Market Mechanism, Pt. 1, SCH*, 1969, pp. 208–22.

Steeper, N. J. Some Results of an Economic Survey of the Dried Vine Fruit Industry, 1965–66 to 1967–68. *Quart. Rev. Agr. Econ.*, April 1969, *22* (2), pp. 82–102.

Stefani, Giorgio. Politica fiscale a politica monetaria per la stabilità negli Stati Uniti-I. (Fiscal Policy and Monetary Policy for the Stability of the United States-I. With English summary.) *Bancaria*, February 1969, *25*(2), pp. 147–69.

——— Politica fiscale e politica monetaria per la stabilità negli Stati Uniti-II. (Fiscal Policy and Monetary Policy for the Stability of the United States-II. With English summary.) *Bancaria*, March 1969, *25*(3), pp. 303–20.

Stefanov, I. Marx's Theory of Expanded Reproduction and Problems of Economic Growth. *Matekon*, Fall 1969, *6*(1), pp. 3–18.

Steffens, F. E. Critical Values for Bivariate Student *t*-Tests. *J. Amer. Statist. Assoc.*, June 1969, *64* (326), pp. 637–46.

Steigenga, W. The Contribution of Demography to Physical and Spatial Planning. **In** *Bechhofer, F., ed.*, 1969, pp. 117–26.

Stein, Bruno and Bumas, Lester O. The Economic Rationale of Occupational Choice: Comment. *Ind. Lab. Relat. Rev.*, April 1969, *22*(3), pp. 422–28.

Stein, Herbert. Where Stands the New Fiscal Policy? *J. Money, Credit, Banking*, August 1969, *1*(3), pp. 463–73.

Stein, Jerome L. A Minimal Role of Government in Achieving Optimal Growth. *Economica, N.S.*, May 1969, *36*(142), pp. 139–50.

——— "Neoclassical" and "Keynes-Wicksell" Monetary Growth Models. *J. Money, Credit, Banking*, May 1969, *1*(2), pp. 153–71.

——— and Nagatani, Keizo. Stabilization Policies in a Growing Economy. *Rev. Econ. Stud.*, April 1969, *36*(106), pp. 165–83.

Steiner, Henry Malcolm and Seminario, Adan. Economic Aspects of the Bolivar Highway in Peru. *Eng. Econ.*, January–February 1969, *14*(2), pp. 101–07.

Steiner, Peter O. The Efficiency of Education in Economics: Discussion. *Amer. Econ. Rev.*, May 1969, *59*(2), pp. 240–42.

——— The Public Sector and the Public Interest. **In** *The Analysis and Evaluation of Public Expenditures: The PPB System, Vol. 1, JECP*, 1969, pp. 13–45.

Stekhova, G. P. and Chuev, Iu. V. The Generalized Equipment Replacement Problem. *Matekon*, Fall 1969, *6*(1), pp. 75–90.

Stekler, H. O. Evaluation of Econometric Inventory Forecasts. *Rev. Econ. Statist.*, February 1969, *51* (1), pp. 77–83.

——— and Burch, S. W. The Forecasting Accuracy of Consumer Attitude Data. *J. Amer. Statist. Assoc.*, December 1969, *64*(328), pp. 1225–33.

Stekler, Lois E. Effect of U.S. Business Fluctuations on Imports of Primary Commodities. *Yale Econ. Essays*, Fall 1969, *9*(2), pp. 209–49.

Stelluto, George L. Report on Incentive Pay in Manufacturing Industries. *Mon. Lab. Rev.*, July 1969, *92*(7), pp. 49–53.

Stepaniuk, V. I. The Use of Classroom Space in Urban Schools: The Case of the Ukraine. **In** *Noah, H. J., ed.*, 1969, pp. 205–15.

Stepanov, B. V. Determining Future Requirements for Labor in the Planning Period. **In** *Noah, H. J., ed.*, 1969, pp. 177–86.

Stepanov, Lev. "One Percent": The Problem of Economic Aid. *Ann. Amer. Acad. Polit. Soc. Sci.*, November 1969, *386*, pp. 41–53.

Stephan, Frederick F. Three Extensions of Sample Survey Technique: Hybrid, Nexus, and Graduated Sampling. **In** *Johnson, N. L. and Smith, H., Jr., eds.*, 1969, pp. 81–104.

Stephens, G. Ross. The Suburban Impact of Earnings Tax Policies. *Nat. Tax J.*, September 1969, *22*(3), pp. 313–33.

Stephens, J. Kirker. The Simple Analytics of Neoclassical Growth Theory: A Comment. *Quart. Rev. Econ. Bus.*, Summer 1969, *9*(2), pp. 70–71.

Stephens, W. B. The Cloth Exports of the Provincial Ports, 1600–1640. *Econ. Hist. Rev.*, August 1969, *22*(2), pp. 228–48.

Stephenson, James A. and Jorgenson, Dale W. Anticipations and Investment Behavior in U.S. Manufacturing, 1947–1960. *J. Amer. Statist. Assoc.*, March 1969, *64*(325), pp. 67–89.

______ Issues in the Development of the Neoclassical Theory of Investment Behavior. *Rev. Econ. Statist.*, August 1969, *51*(3), pp. 346–53.

______ **and Starleaf, Dennis R.** A Suggested Solution to the Monetary-Policy Indicator Problem: The Monetary Full Employment Interest Rate. *J. Finance*, September 1969, *24*(4), pp. 623–41.

Stephenson, Matthew A. A Note on Simon Patten's Contribution to the Concept of Consumer's Surplus. *J. Polit. Econ.*, March/April 1969, *77*(2), pp. 242–44.

Stephenson, P. Ronald and Willet, Ronald P. Determinants of Buyer Response to Physical Distribution Service. *J. Marketing Res.*, August 1969, *6*(3), pp. 279–83.

Stephenson, William. Evaluation of Public Relations Programs. *Rivista Int. Sci. Econ. Com.*, February 1969, *16*(2), pp. 166–84.

Stermann, Walter. Austria as a Model for East-West Trade. **In** *Grub, P. D. and Holbik, K.*, 1969, pp. 132–34.

Stern, James L. Evolution of Private Manpower Planning in Armour's Plant Closings. *Mon. Lab. Rev.*, December 1969, *92*(12), pp. 21–28.

______ **and Johnson, David B.** Why and How Workers Shift from Blue-Collar to White-Collar Jobs. *Mon. Lab. Rev.*, October 1969, *92*(10), pp. 7–13.

Stern, Joseph J. A Note on the Structure of Pakistan's Foreign Trade. *Pakistan Develop. Rev.*, Summer 1969, *9*(2), pp. 212–23.

Stern, Louis W. Mergers under Scrutiny. *Harvard Bus. Rev.*, July–August 1969, *47*(4), pp. 18–36, 160–63.

Stern, Robert M. International Financial Issues in Foreign Economic Assistance to the Less Developed Countries. **In** *Stewart, I. G., ed.*, 1969, pp. 47–70.

Sternberg, Marvin J. and Ahmad, Zubeida M. Agrarian Reform and Employment, with Special Reference to Asia. *Int. Lab. Rev.*, February 1969, *99*(2), pp. 159–83.

Sternberger, H.; Renz, J. and Fasolina, G. Planning-Programing-Budgeting System (PPBS) in Nassau County, N.Y. **In** *Innovations in Planning, Programming, and Budgeting in State and Local Governments, JECP*, 1969, pp. 105–89.

Sternlieb, George and Indik, Bernard. Housing Vacancy Analysis. *Land Econ.*, February 1969, *45*(1), pp. 117–21.

Steve, Sergio. Public Finance and Social Security. *Public Finance*, 1969, *24*(2), pp. 101–13.

Stevens, Guy V. G. Fixed Investment Expenditures of Foreign Manufacturing Affiliates of U.S. Firms: Theoretical Models and Empirical Evidence. *Yale Econ. Essays*, Spring 1969, *9*(1), pp. 137–98.

Stevens, Joe B. Effects of Nonprice Variables upon Participation in Water-Oriented Outdoor Recreation: Comment. *Amer. J. Agr. Econ.*, February 1969, *51*(1), pp. 192–93.

______ Recreation Benefits from Water Pollution Control: Reply. *Water Resources Res.*, August 1969, *5*(4), pp. 908–09.

Stevens, R. B. and Yamey, B. S. The Justiciability of Restrictive Practices. **In** *Hunter, A., ed.*, 1969, pp. 183–201.

Stevenson, David. Internal Improvements, 1838. **In** *Pursell, C. W., Jr.*, 1969, pp. 53–66.

Stevenson, Russell. The United States Graduate Training of Asian Rural Social Scientists. *Land Econ.*, August 1969, *45*(3), pp. 334–43.

Stewart, I. G. Statistics on Expenditures in Scotland. **In** *Wolfe, J. N., ed.*, 1969, pp. 123–39.

Stewart, Richard E. The End of Isolationism in Insurance Regulation. *J. Risk Ins.*, September 1969, *36*(4), pp. 489–92.

Stewart, Samuel B. Statement. **In** *Bank Holding Company Act Amendments, Pts. 1–3, HCH*, 1969, pp. 881–99.

Stieber, Jack. A New Approach to Strikes in Public Employment. **In** *Walsh, R. E., ed.*, 1969, pp. 242–50.

Stieglitz, Harold. The Kaiser-Steel Union Sharing Plan. **In** *Wortman, M. S., Jr.*, 1969, pp. 186–94.

Stigler, George J. Alfred Marshall's Lectures on Progress and Poverty. *J. Law Econ.*, April 1969, *12*(1), pp. 181–83.

______ Does Economics Have a Useful Past? *Hist. Polit. Econ.*, Fall 1969, *1*(2), pp. 217–30.

______ Opportunity Cost of Marriage: Comment. *J. Polit. Econ.*, September/October 1969, *77*(5), pp. 863.

Stiglitz, Joseph E. Allocation of Heterogeneous Capital Goods in a Two-Sector Economy. *Int. Econ. Rev.*, October 1969, *10*(3), pp. 373–90.

______ Behavior Towards Risk with Many Commodities. *Econometrica*, October 1969, *37*(4), pp. 660–67.

______ Distribution of Income and Wealth among Individuals. *Econometrica*, July 1969, *37*(3), pp. 382–97.

______ The Effects of Income, Wealth, and Capital Gains Taxation on Risk-Taking. *Quart. J. Econ.*, May 1969, *83*(2), pp. 263–83.

______ A Re-Examination of the Modigliani-Miller Theorem. *Amer. Econ. Rev.*, December 1969, *59*(5), pp. 784–93.

______ Rural-Urban Migration, Surplus Labour, and the Relationship between Urban and Rural Wages. *East Afr. Econ. Rev.*, December 1969, *1*(2), pp. 1–27.

______ Theory of Innovation: Discussion. *Amer. Econ. Rev.*, May 1969, *59*(2), pp. 46–49.

——— and Akerlof, George A. Capital, Wages and Structural Unemployment. *Econ. J.*, June 1969, *79* (314), pp. 269–81.

——— and Atkinson, Anthony B. A New View of Technological Change. *Econ. J.*, September 1969, *79*(315), pp. 573–78.

——— and Cass, David. The Implications of Alternative Saving and Expectations Hypotheses for Choices of Technique and Patterns of Growth. *J. Polit. Econ.*, Part II, July/August 1969, *77*(4), pp. 586–627.

———; Shell, Karl and Sidrauski, Miguel. Capital Gains, Income, and Saving. *Rev. Econ. Stud.*, January 1969, *36*(105), pp. 15–26.

Stigum, Bernt P. Competitive Equilibria under Uncertainty. *Quart. J. Econ.*, November 1969, *83*(4), pp. 533–61.

——— Entrepreneurial Choice Over Time under Conditions of Uncertainty. *Int. Econ. Rev.*, October 1969, *10*(3), pp. 426–42.

Still, Bayrd. Problems of Mid-Nineteenth Century Urbanization in the Middle West. In *Callow, A. B., Jr., ed.*, 1969, pp. 112–25.

Stilz, Dieter. Die Auswirkungen der öffentlichen Hilfen für den Ruhrbergbau auf dessen Wettbewerbsbedingungen. (The Influence of Fiscal Support on the Conditions of Competition in the Ruhr Coal Mining Industry. With English summary.) *Schmollers Jahr.*, 1969, *89*(4), pp. 427–49.

——— Die Begünstigung des Steinkohlenbergbaus des Ruhrgebiets durch die öffentliche Finanzwirtschaft. (Fiscal Support of the Ruhr Coal Mining Industry 1958–1967. With English summary.) *Schmollers Jahr.*, 1969, *89*(2), pp. 151–84.

Stinson, Byron S. and Geithman, David T. A Note on Diminishing Returns and Linear Homogeneity. *Amer. Econ.*, Spring 1969, *13*(1), pp. 77–79.

Stinson, Thomas F. and Krahmer, Edward F. Local School Expenditures and Educational Quality: A Correlation Analysis. *Amer. J. Agr. Econ.*, December 1969, *51*(5), pp. 1553–56.

Stitzel, Thomas and Stonehill, Arthur. Financial Structure and Multinational Corporations. *Calif. Manage. Rev.*, Fall 1969, *12*(1), pp. 91–96.

Stjernschantz, Göran. Van man trodde och hur det gick: Något om idéer och debatt i Ekonomiska Samfundet i Finland 1944–69. (Ideas and Debates in the Economic Society of Finland, 1944–69. With English summary.) *Econ. Samfundets Tidskr.*, 1969, *22*(4), pp. 223–40.

Stobaugh, Robert B., Jr. How to Analyze Foreign Investment Climates. *Harvard Bus. Rev.*, September–October 1969, *47*(5), pp. 100–108.

——— Where in the World Should We Put that Plant? *Harvard Bus. Rev.*, January–February 1969, *47*(1), pp. 129–36.

Stober, William J. Cost Constraints and Factor Inferiority. *Western Econ. J.*, December 1969, *7*(4), pp. 379–84.

——— and Falk, Laurence H. The Effect of Financial Inducements on the Location of Firms. *Southern Econ. J.*, July 1969, *36*(1), pp. 25–35.

——— and Falk, Laurence H. Industrial Development Bonds as a Subsidy to Industry. *Nat. Tax J.*, June 1969, *22*(2), pp. 232–43.

Stocker, Frederick D. Assessment of Land in Urban-Rural Fringe Areas. In *Lynn, A. D., Jr., ed.*, 1969, pp. 141–52.

Stockfisch, J. A. The Influence of the Property Tax on Investment and Employment. In *Becker, A. P., ed.*, 1969, pp. 49–62.

Stockwell, Edward G. and Goldsmith, Harold F. Interrelationship of Occupational Selectivity Patterns among City, Suburban and Fringe Areas of Major Metropolitan Centers. *Land Econ.*, May 1969, *45*(2), pp. 194–205.

Stoevener, Herbert H. Estimating the Effects of Water Policies in the West. *Amer. J. Agr. Econ.*, December 1969, *51*(5), pp. 1449–54.

Stoicescu, V. and Bădin, V. O aplicaţie a lanţurilor Markov la controlul calităţii producţiei. (An Application of Markov Chains to the Control of Production Quality. With English summary.) *Stud. Cercet. Econ.*, 1969, *1-2*, pp. 159–72.

Stoichită, I. V. and Vasilescu, Floarea. Analiza critică a metodologiei statistice de caracterizare a vitezei de rotaţie a fondurilor circulante. (Critical Analysis of the Statistical Methodology Used in Characterizing the Turnover Rate of the Circulation Means. With English summary.) *Stud. Cercet. Econ.*, 1969, *4*, pp. 137–58.

Stoikov, Vladimir. The Allocation of the Cost of Displaced Labor and Severance Pay. *J. Human Res.*, Spring 1969, *4*(2), pp. 192–204.

——— and Raimon, Robert L. The Effect of Blue-Collar Unionism on White-Collar Earnings. *Ind. Lab. Relat. Rev.*, April 1969, *22*(3), pp. 358–74.

Stojanović, Radmila and Čobeljić, Nikola. The Theory of Investment Cycles in a Socialist Economy. *Eastern Europ. Econ.*, Fall 1968/Winter 1968–69, *7*(1–2), pp. 1–168.

Stoleru, L. Investment Behaviour Rules and Practices of Public Enterprises. In *Margolis, J. and Guitton, H., eds.*, 1969, pp. 276–97.

Stolk, Leonard. Taxation of International Consolidations into a "European Corporation." *Bull. Int. Fiscal Doc.*, November 1969, *23*(11), pp. 521–44.

Stoll, Hans R. The Relationship between Put and Call Option Prices. *J. Finance*, December 1969, *24*(5), pp. 801–24.

Stolper, W. F. and Samuelson, Paul A. Protection and Real Wages. In *Bereday, G. Z. F., ed.*, 1969, pp. 245–68.

Stone, J. R. N. and Meade, James E. The Construction of Tables of National Income, Expenditure, Savings and Investment. In *Parker, R. H. and Harcourt, G. C., eds.*, 1969, pp. 329–46.

Stone, Lawrence M. A Comprehensive Income Tax Base for the U.S.?: Implications of the Report of the Royal Commission on Taxation. *Nat. Tax J.*, March 1969, *22*(1), pp. 24–38.

——— Tax Incentives as a Solution to Urban Problems. In *Tax Credits to Stimulate Job Opportunities in Rural Areas, SCH*, 1969, pp. 185–91.

Stone, Morris. Why Arbitrators Reinstate Discharged Employees. *Mon. Lab. Rev.*, October 1969, *92*(10), pp. 47–50.

Stone, Richard. Foreign Trade and Full Employment: An Input-output Analysis. *L'Industria*, October–December 1969, (4), pp. 431–43.

Stonehill, Arthur and Stitzel, Thomas. Financial Structure and Multinational Corporations. *Calif. Manage. Rev.*, Fall 1969, *12*(1), pp. 91–96.

Stonham, P. E. The Demand for Overseas Shipping in the Australian Export Trade. *J. Transp. Econ. Policy*, September 1969, *3*(3), pp. 333–49.

______ User Costs in Port: An Australian Study. *Australian Econ. Pap.*, December 1969, *8*(13), pp. 178–92.

Stout, Thomas T. Economics of Conglomerate Growth: Policy Implications for Agriculture. **In** *Garoian, L., ed.*, 1969, pp. 121–22.

Stover, Stephen L. The Government as Farmer in New Zealand. *Econ. Geogr.*, October 1969, *45*(4), pp. 324–38.

Strasma, John. Property Taxation in Chile. **In** *Becker, A. P., ed.*, 1969, pp. 187–200.

Straus, Robert. The Problem of Conceptualizing Poverty. **In** *Weaver, T. and Magid, A., eds.*, 1969, pp. 7–18.

Strauss, George. Union Bargaining Strength: Goliath or Paper Tiger. **In** *Wortman, M. S., Jr.*, 1969, pp. 315–22.

Street, James H. Latin American Economic Integration: Some Historic Guideposts. **In** *Hilton, R., ed.*, 1969, pp. 39–48.

Streeten, Paul. The Case for Export Subsidies. *J. Devel. Stud.*, July 1969, *5*(4), pp. 270–73.

______ Economic Development and Education. **In** *[Edding, Friedrich]*, 1969, pp. 183–98.

______ Keynes and the Classical Tradition. **In** *Williams, H. R. and Huffnagle, J. D., eds.*, 1969, pp. 21–37.

Streissler, Erich. Hayek on Growth: A Reconsideration of His Early Theoretical Work. **In** *[von Hayek, Friedrich A.]*, 1969, pp. 245–85.

______ Long Term Structural Changes in the Distribution of Income. *Z. Nationalökon.*, May 1969, *29* (1–2), pp. 39–110.

______ A Stochastic Model of International Reserve Requirements during Growth of World Trade. *Z. Nationalökon.*, December 1969, *29*(3–4), pp. 347–70.

______ Structural Economic Thought: On the Significance of the Austrian School Today. *Z. Nationalökon.*, December 1969, *29*(3–4), pp. 237–66.

Streit, M. E. Spatial Associations and Economic Linkages between Industries. *J. Reg. Sci.*, August 1969, *9*(2), pp. 177–88.

Striver, Herbert E. Toward a Fundamental Program for the Training, Employment, and Economic Equality of the American Indian. **In** *Indian Education, Pt. 2, SCH*, 1969, pp. 608–32.

Strnad, Vladimír. Structural Matrix Model of Energy Balance. *Czech. Econ. Pap.*, 1969, (11), pp. 113–26.

Stromberger, T. L. and McDonald, Howard E. Cost Control for the Professional Service Firm. *Harvard Bus. Rev.*, January–February 1969, *47*(1), pp. 109–21.

Stromsdorfer, Ernst W. Occupational Training Programs and Manpower Programs for the Disadvantaged: Discussion. **In** *Somers, G. G. and Wood, W. D., eds.*, 1969, pp. 152–59.

Stroup, Robert H. and Frazer, William J., Jr. The Demand for Money by Households in South Vietnam: The Evidence from Cross-Section Data. *J. Polit. Econ.*, Part I, July/August 1969, *77*(4), pp. 489–93.

______ **and Hargrove, Michael B.** Earnings and Education in Rural South Vietnam. *J. Human Res.*, Spring 1969, *4*(2), pp. 215–25.

Strout, Alan M. Korea's Use of Foreign and Domestic Resources: A Cross-Country Comparison. **In** *Adelman, I., ed.*, 1969, pp. 277–92.

Struble, Frederick M. Bank Credit Cards and Check Credit Plans in the Nation and the District. *Fed. Res. Bank Kansas City Rev.*, July–August 1969, pp. 3–9.

Strumilin, S. Industrial Crises in Russia 1847–67. **In** *Crouzet, F.; Chaloner, W. H. and Stern, W. M., eds.*, 1969, pp. 155–78.

Strümpel, Burkhard. The Contribution of Survey Research to Public Finance. **In** *Peacock, A. T., ed.*, 1969, pp. 13–32.

Struyk, Raymond J. Tax Structure and Regional Economic Growth: A Reply. *J. Reg. Sci.*, August 1969, *9*(2), pp. 327–28.

Strydom, P. D. F. Why Growth Rates Differ (A Review Note). *S. Afr. J. Econ.*, March 1969, *37*(1), pp. 76–80.

______ **and du Plessis, T. A.** Future Growth Patterns in South Africa—A Comment. *S. Afr. J. Econ.*, September 1969, *37*(3), pp. 252–59.

Stull, J. Warren and Angus, Robert C. Consumer Attitudes toward Milk Substitutes. *Amer. J. Agr. Econ.*, December 1969, *51*(5), pp. 1149–53.

Sturdivant, Frederick D. Business and the Mexican-American Community. *Calif. Manage. Rev.*, Spring 1969, *11*(3), pp. 73–80.

______ The Limits of Black Capitalism. *Harvard Bus. Rev.*, January–February 1969, *47*(1), pp. 122–28.

______ The Limits of Black Capitalism. **In** *Sturdivant, F. D., ed.*, 1969, pp. 257–68.

______ **and Wilhelm, Walter T.** Poverty, Minorities, and Consumer Exploitation. **In** *Sturdivant, F. D., ed.*, 1969, pp. 108–17.

Sturmthal, Adolf. Union-Management Cooperation Revisited: Discussion. **In** *Somers, G. G., ed. (II)*, 1969, pp. 93–95.

Sturrock, F. G. A Policy for British Sugar Supplies. *Nat. Westminster Bank Quart. Rev.*, August 1969, pp. 54–60.

Stýblo, Jan. The Socialist Entrepreneurship and the Investor's Risk. *New Trends Czech. Econ.*, July 1969, (4), p. 65–88.

Stykolt, Stefan. Anti-U.S. Trends in Canadian Economic Policy. **In** *Stykolt, S.*, 1969, pp. 154–57.

______ Economic Policy and Effective Competition in the Canadian Economy. **In** *Stykolt, S.*, 1969, pp. 3–8.

______ Enquiry into What? **In** *Stykolt, S.*, 1969, pp. 126–28.

______ Federal Government Policy Concerning Market Organization and Regulation. **In** *Stykolt, S.*, 1969, pp. 103–19.

______ In Defence of the Canadian Consumer. **In** *Stykolt, S.*, 1969, pp. 133–40.

______ A Note on Economic Activity in the Administrative State. **In** *Stykolt, S.*, 1969, pp. 193–95.

——— A Note on the Parametric Approach. **In** *Stykolt, S.,* 1969, pp. 196–98.

——— A Positive Monetary Policy. **In** *Stykolt, S.,* 1969, pp. 149–53.

——— Resale Price Maintenance and the New 'Escape Clause'. **In** *Stykolt, S.,* 1969, pp. 144–45.

——— A Rude Awakening. **In** *Stykolt, S.,* 1969, pp. 123–25.

——— **and Bladen, V. W.** Combines Policy and the Public Interest: An Economist's Evaluation. **In** *Stykolt, S.,* 1969, pp. 19–54.

——— **and Eastman, Harry C.** An Evaluation of Trading Stamp Schemes. **In** *Stykolt, S.,* 1969, pp. 141–43.

——— **and Eastman, Harry C.** Disturbing Prospects. **In** *Stykolt, S.,* 1969, pp. 129–32.

——— **and Eastman, Harry C.** The Economic Consequences of Mr. Coyne. **In** *Stykolt, S.,* 1969, pp. 146–48.

——— **and Eastman, Harry C.** The Performance of Two Protected Oligopolies in Canada. **In** *Stykolt, S.,* 1969, pp. 83–102.

Su, V. and Dutta, M. An Econometric Model of Puerto Rico. *Rev. Econ. Stud.,* July 1969, *36*(107), pp. 319–33.

Suavy, A. The Economic and Political Consequences of Selective Migrations from One Country to Another. **In** *Bechhofer, F., ed.,* 1969, pp. 43–56.

Subocz, V. The Cargo Cult, or the 'Cinderella' Cult, in Mineral Policy? *Econ. Rec.,* December 1969, *45* (112), pp. 596–606.

Subotnik, Abraham and Houck, James P. The U.S. Supply of Soybeans: Regional Acreage Functions. *Agr. Econ. Res.,* October 1969, *21*(4), pp. 99–108.

Sudman, Seymour; Bradburn, Norman M. and Gockel, Galen. The Extent and Characteristics of Racially Integrated Housing in the United States. *J. Bus.,* January 1969, *42*(1), pp. 50–92.

Sufrin, Sidney C. and Wagner, Abraham R. Disaggregate Employment: The Search for Short Run Demand and Labor Market Stability. *Rivista Int. Sci. Econ. Com.,* October 1969, *16*(10), pp. 965–92.

——— Interest Rate Manipulation, Employment and Output—A Disaggregated Suggestion. *Rivista Int. Sci. Econ. Com.,* April 1969, *16*(4), pp. 327–41.

Suits, Daniel B. Statement. **In** *The 1969 Economic Report of the President, Pt. 2, JECH,* 1969, pp. 497–500.

Sukhatme, B. V. and Sukhatme, P. V. On Some Methodological Aspects of Sample Surveys of Agriculture in Developing Countries. **In** *Johnson, N. L. and Smith, H., Jr., eds.,* 1969, pp. 528–61.

Sukhatme, P. V. The Dimensions of India's Food Problem in Economic Development. **In** *Bhuleshkar, A. V., ed.,* 1969, pp. 69–87.

——— **and Sukhatme, B. V.** On Some Methodological Aspects of Sample Surveys of Agriculture in Developing Countries. **In** *Johnson, N. L. and Smith, H., Jr., eds.,* 1969, pp. 528–61.

Šulc, Ota and Richta, Radovan. Forecasting and the Scientific and Technological Revolution. *Int. Soc. Sci. J.,* 1969, *21*(4), pp. 563–73.

Suleiman, A. A. and Osman, Omar. The Economy of Sudan. **In** *Robson, P. and Lury, D. A., eds.,* 1969, pp. 436–70.

Sulg, Madis. Individual Rights under Collective Agreements. *Mon. Lab. Rev.,* July 1969, *92*(7), pp. 40–42.

Sullivan, Gene D. Some Thoughts on Bargaining. *Amer. J. Agr. Econ.,* November 1969, *51*(4), pp. 960–61.

Summers, Clyde W. Collective Agreements and the Law of Contracts. *Yale Law J.,* March 1969, *78*(4), pp. 525–75.

Sun, I-Shuan. Trade Policies and Economic Development in Taiwan. **In** *Morgan, T. and Spoelstra, N., eds.,* 1969, pp. 99–123.

Sundquist, James L. Co-ordinating the War on Poverty. *Ann. Amer. Acad. Polit. Soc. Sci.,* September 1969, *385,* pp. 41–49.

Sunkel, Osvaldo. National Development Policy and External Dependence in Latin America. *J. Devel. Stud.,* October 1969, *6*(1), pp. 23–48.

Sunley, Emil M., Jr. The Present Value of Depreciation Allowances. *Quart. Rev. Econ. Bus.,* Winter 1969, *9*(4), pp. 77–79.

Sunoo, Don H. and Schooler, Robert D. Consumer Preceptions of International Products: Regional vs. National Labeling. *Soc. Sci. Quart.,* March 1969, *49*(4), pp. 886–90.

Surrey, Stanley S. Complexity and the Internal Revenue Code: The Problem of the Management of Tax Detail. *Law Contemp. Probl.,* Autumn 1969, *34*(4), pp. 673–710.

——— Statement. **In** *A Review of Balance of Payments Policies, JECH,* 1969, pp. 40–49.

——— **and Hellmuth, William F.** The Tax Expenditure Budget—Response to Professor Bittker. *Nat. Tax J.,* December 1969, *22*(4), pp. 528–37.

Sută, N. Comerțul exterior al României în anii construcției socialismului. (Foreign Trade of Romania in the Years of Socialist Construction. With English summary.) *Stud. Cercet. Econ.,* 1969, *3,* pp. 213–24.

Sută-Selejan, Sultana. Nicolae Bălcescu și curentele de gîndire economică din timpul său. (Nicolae Bălcescu and the Currents of Economic Thought of His Time. With English summary.) *Stud. Cercet. Econ.,* 1969, *1-2,* pp. 195–203.

Sutch, Richard and Modigliani, Franco. The Term Structure of Interest Rates: A Re-examination of the Evidence. *J. Money, Credit, Banking,* February 1969, *1*(1), pp. 112–20.

Sutcliffe, R. B. Debt-Servicing as an Aid to Promotion of Trade of Developing Countries: A Further Comment. *Oxford Econ. Pap.,* November 1969, *21*(3), pp. 420–23.

Sutter, Jean. The Effect of Birth Limitation on Genetic Composition of Populations. **In** *Behrman, S. J.; Corsa, L., Jr. and Freedman, R., eds.,* 1969, pp. 213–51.

Sutton, Anthony C. Statement. **In** *Export Expansion and Regulation, SCH,* 1969, pp. 420–25.

——— Technology, Trade and Peace with Communist Countries. **In** *To Extend and Amend the Export Control Act of 1949, HCH,* 1969, pp. 359–62.

Sutton, Willis A., Jr. Differential Perceptions of Impact of a Rural Anti-poverty Campaign. *Soc. Sci. Quart.*, December 1969, *50*(3), pp. 657–67.

Suykens, F. Containerization, the Unit Load, the Combination Ship. *Econ. Soc. Tijdschr.*, October 1969, *23*(5), pp. 455–70.

Sviatskaia, N. V. and Inosov, V. L. Some Problems in Optimal Inventory Control. *Matekon,* Fall 1969, *6*(1), pp. 44–56.

Swackhamer, Gene L. Agricultural Outlook: Approach of the 1970's. *Fed. Res. Bank Kansas City Rev.*, January 1969, pp. 3–11.

______ Concepts of Rural Economic Development. *Fed. Res. Bank Kansas City Rev.*, December 1969, pp. 3–10.

______ Synthetics and Substitutes: Challenge to Agriculture. *Fed. Res. Bank Kansas City Rev.*, March 1969, pp. 3–12.

Swadener, Paul. The Loss Ratio Method of Rating and the Feedback Control Loop Concept. *J. Risk Ins.*, December 1969, *36*(5), pp. 615–27.

Swamy, M. R. Kumara. An Econometric Analysis of Cost Curves and Supply Curves under Modern Dynamic Competitive Conditions. *Rivista Int. Sci. Econ. Com.*, March 1969, *16*(3), pp. 280–93.

______ The Paradox of Full Capacity *Vs.* Full Employment Growth. *Asian Econ. Rev.*, August 1969, *11*(4), pp. 446–51.

Swamy, Subramanian. Retail Price Index in the Peoples' Republic of China. *Rev. Econ. Statist.*, August 1969, *51*(3), pp. 309–19.

Swan, Craig and Tobin, James. Money and Permanent Income: Some Empirical Tests. *Amer. Econ. Rev.*, May 1969, *59*(2), pp. 285–95.

Swan, John E. Experimental Analysis of Predecision Information Seeking. *J. Marketing Res.*, May 1969, *6*(2), pp. 192–97.

Swann, D. Competition and Price Policies: Britain and the EEC. **In** *van Meerhaeghe, M. A. G., ed.*, 1969, pp. 33–57.

Swanson, Earl R. and Asopa, V. N. Profitability of Supplemental Irrigation of Corn. *Ill. Agr. Econ.*, January 1969, *9*(1), pp. 7–9.

______ **and Bretthauer, G. L.** Supplemental Irrigation of Corn: A Break-Even Analysis. *Ill. Agr. Econ.*, July 1969, *9*(2), pp. 19–24.

______ **and Dunlap, R. D.** Influence of Prices on Production Potential for Beef and Hogs on Farms with Fixed Acreages. *Ill. Agr. Econ.*, January 1969, *9*(1), pp. 10–17.

Swayambu, S. Role of H. E. L. in Power Development. **In** *Dagli, V., ed., Vol. II,* 1969, pp. 190–94.

Sweeney, Vernon E. and Goodfellow, Gordon P., Jr. Vertically Parallel Indifference Curves with a Non-Constant Marginal Utility of Money. *Amer. Econ.*, Fall 1969, *13*(2), pp. 81–86.

Sweeny, K. M.; Norton, W. E. and Jackson, G. H. A Demand Equation for Imports. *Econ. Rec.*, December 1969, *45*(112), pp. 589–95.

Sweet, Morris L. Decision Making and French Planning. **In** *Prybyla, J. S., ed.*, 1969, pp. 200–211.

Sweezy, Paul M. and Baran, Paul A. Economics of Two Worlds. **In** *Baran, P. A.*, 1969, pp. 68–91.

Swerdloff, Sol. How Good Were Manpower Projections for the 1960's. *Mon. Lab. Rev.*, November 1969, *92*(11), pp. 17–22.

Swidrowski, Jozef. Exchange Restrictions in 1969. *Finance Develop.*, December 1969, *6*(4), pp. 27–33.

Swinth, Robert L. and Pollay, Richard W. A Behavioral Simulation of the Agency-Client Relationship. *J. Marketing Res.*, May 1969, *6*(2), pp. 198–202.

Swoboda, Alexander. Vehicle Currencies and the Foreign Exchange Market: The Case of the Dollar. **In** *Aliber, R. Z., ed.*, 1969, pp. 30–40.

Sydsæter, Knut. Note on a Difference Equation Occurring in Growth Theory. *J. Econ. Theory,* June 1969, *1*(1), pp. 104–06.

Sykes, A. and Merrett, A. J. Return on Equities and Fixed Interest Securities: 1919–66. **In** *Carsberg, B. V. and Edey, H. C., eds.*, 1969, pp. 113–26.

Sykes, Z. M. Some Stochastic Versions of the Matrix Model for Population Dynamics. *J. Amer. Statist. Assoc.*, March 1969, *64*(325), pp. 111–30.

Sylla, Richard. Federal Policy, Banking Market Structure, and Capital Mobilization in the United States, 1863–1913. *J. Econ. Hist.*, December 1969, *29*(4), pp. 657–86.

Syroezhin, I. M. and Kolbin, V. V. Computer Analysis of a Business Game. *Matekon,* Fall 1969, *6*(1), pp. 57–74.

Syron, Richard and Greenwald, Carol S. Increasing Job Opportunities in Boston's Urban Core. *New Eng. Econ. Rev.*, January/February 1969, pp. 30–40.

Szabados, Joseph. Hungary's NEM: Reorganization or Basic Reform? **In** *Grub, P. D. and Holbik, K.*, 1969, pp. 194–98.

Szakolczai, György and Stahl, János. Increasing or Decreasing Returns to Scale in the Constant Elasticity of Substitution Production Function. *Rev. Econ. Statist.*, February 1969, *51*(1), pp. 84–90.

Szapary, Gyorgy; Quinn, Brian and Bhatia, Rattan J. Stabilization Program in Sierra Leone. *Int. Monet. Fund Staff Pap.*, November 1969, *16*(3), pp. 504–28.

Szerszewski, Robert. Some Features of the Economic Development of Tropical Africa. *J. Devel. Stud.*, July 1969, *5*(4), pp. 239–44.

______ **and Killick, A.** The Economy of Ghana. **In** *Robson, P. and Lury, D. A., eds.*, 1969, pp. 79–126.

Taagepera, Rein. National Differences within Soviet Demographic Trends. *Soviet Stud.*, April 1969, *20*(4), pp. 478–89.

Tabaček, Ján. Slovakia and the Development of Her Economy. *New Trends Czech. Econ.*, July 1969, (4), pp. 21–34.

______ Trade Relations Between Czechoslovakia and the Soviet Union. *New Trends Czech. Econ.*, November 1969, (7), pp. 37–64.

Tabah, L. Population Growth and Economic Development: Comment. **In** *Bechhofer, F., ed.*, 1969, pp. 165–69.

Tabb, William K. Government Incentives to Private Industry to Locate in Urban Poverty Areas. *Land Econ.*, November 1969, *45*(4), pp. 392–99.

Tadros, Mahfouz E. and Casler, George L. A Game Theoretic Model for Farm Planning under Uncertainty. *Amer. J. Agr. Econ.*, December 1969, *51*(5), pp. 1164–67.

Taeuber, Alma F. and Taeuber, Karl E. The Negro as an Immigrant Group: Recent Trends in Racial and Ethnic Segregation in Chicago. **In** *Kain, J. F., ed.*, 1969, pp. 100–111.

Taeuber, Conrad. Planning a New Inventory of the U.S.—Who Will Use the 1970 Census? *Univ. Missouri Bus. Govt. Rev.*, March–April 1969, *10*(2), pp. 5–13.

Taeuber, Irene B. Population Growth in Less-Developed Countries. **In** *Hauser, P. M., ed.*, 1969, pp. 34–58.

Taeuber, Karl E. Negro Population and Housing: Demographic Aspects of a Social Accounting Scheme. **In** *Katz, I. and Gurin, P., eds.*, 1969, pp. 145–93.

——— **and Taeuber, Alma F.** The Negro as an Immigrant Group: Recent Trends in Racial and Ethnic Segregation in Chicago. **In** *Kain, J. F., ed.*, 1969, pp. 100–111.

Taft, Philip. A Labor Historian Views Changes in the Trade Union Movement. *Mon. Lab. Rev.*, September 1969, *92*(9), pp. 8–11.

Tai, Janet and Bell, Peter F. Markets, Middlemen and Technology: Agricultural Supply Response in the Dualistic Economies of Southeast Asia. *Malayan Econ. Rev.*, April 1969, *14*(1), pp. 29–47.

Taira, Koji. Consumer Preferences, Poverty Norms, and Extent of Poverty. *Quart. Rev. Econ. Bus.*, Summer 1969, *9*(2), pp. 31–44.

Tait, Alan A. Deflation and Incomes Policy: The British Budget 1968/69. *Finanzarchiv*, October 1968, *28*(1), pp. 110–25.

——— Sensible Accounts and Control of Government Revenue and Expenditure. *Irish Banking Rev.*, December 1969, pp. 9–16.

Takayama, Akira. Behavior of the Firm under Regulatory Constraint. *Amer. Econ. Rev.*, June 1969, *59*(3), pp. 255–60.

——— On a 'Concave' Contract Curve. *Australian Econ. Pap.*, December 1969, *8*(13), pp. 232–38.

Takenaka, Yasukazu. Endogenous Formation and Development of Capitalism in Japan. *J. Econ. Hist.*, March 1969, *29*(1), pp. 141–62.

Talbot, Joseph E., Jr. An Analysis of 1968 Changes in Wages and Benefits. *Mon. Lab. Rev.*, July 1969, *92*(7), pp. 43–48.

Talwar, R. K. Public Sector Banking. **In** *Dagli, V., ed., Vol. II*, 1969, pp. 77–86.

Tambini, Luigi. Financial Policy and the Corporation Income Tax. **In** *Harberger, A. C. and Bailey, M. J., eds.*, 1969, pp. 185–222.

Tan, Edita Abella. Implications of Private Demand for Education on Manpower Planning. *Philippine Econ. J.*, Second Semester 1969, *8*(2), pp. 117–29.

Tanaka, Masaharu. The Narodniki and Marx on Russian Capitalism in the 1870's–1880's. *Kyoto Univ. Econ. Rev.*, October 1969, *39*(2), pp. 1–25.

Tănase, Gh. Perfecţionarea metodologiei de fundamentare a amplasării obiectivelor industriale. (Improvement of the Methodology in Substantiating the Location of Industrial Objectives. With English summary.) *Stud. Cercet. Econ.*, 1969, *1-2*, pp. 45–64.

Tanner, J. Ernest. Lags in the Effects of Monetary Policy: A Statistical Investigation. *Amer. Econ. Rev.*, December 1969, *59*(5), pp. 794–805.

Tanzi, Vito. Measuring the Sensitivity of the Federal Income Tax from Cross-Section Data: A New Approach. *Rev. Econ. Statist.*, May 1969, *51*(2), pp. 206–09.

——— Tax Incentives and Economic Development: The Ecuadorian Experience. *Finanzarchiv*, March 1969, *28*(2), pp. 226–35.

Taplin, J. and Ryan, W. The Prospects for Wine in Australia. *Quart. Rev. Agr. Econ.*, October 1969, *22*(4), pp. 198–209.

Tarascio, Vincent J. The Monetary and Employment Theories of Vilfredo Pareto. *Hist. Polit. Econ.*, Spring 1969, *1*(1), pp. 101–22.

——— Paretian Welfare Theory: Some Neglected Aspects. *J. Polit. Econ.*, January/February 1969, *77*(1), pp. 1–20.

——— **and Finkel, Sidney R.** A Theoretical Integration of Production and Wage Theory. *Western Econ. J.*, December 1969, *7*(4), pp. 371–78.

Tarbet, Joseph R. Present and Proposed Direct Federal, State, and Local Taxes in Washington Compared with Idaho and Oregon. *Univ. Wash. Bus. Rev.*, Autumn 1969, *29*(1), pp. 5–17.

——— Washington's 1969 Income Tax Proposal and Its Effect on Individuals and Families. *Univ. Wash. Bus. Rev.*, Summer 1969, *28*(4), pp. 18–24.

Tarnovskii, O. Price Formation on the World Socialist Market. *Prob. Econ.*, October 1969, *12*(6), pp. 42–57.

Tartara, Giovanni. Programmazione e sviluppo del prodotto. (Product Planning and Development. With English summary.) *L'Impresa*, July/October 1969, *11*(4–5), pp. 340–42.

Tarver, James D. Migration Differentials in Southern Cities and Suburbs. *Soc. Sci. Quart.*, September 1969, *50*(2), pp. 298–324.

Tasker, Antony. British Sugar Supplies: An Alternative View. *Nat. Westminster Bank Quart. Rev.*, November 1969, pp. 45–51.

Tatai, Z. Tools of Regional Development under the New System of Economic Control and Management. *Acta Oecon.*, 1969, *4*(4), pp. 417–22.

Taubman, Paul. Econometric Functions for Government Receipts. **In** *Duesenberry, J. S., et al.*, 1969, pp. 188–220.

——— **and Rasche, R. H.** Economic and Tax Depreciation of Office Buildings. *Nat. Tax J.*, September 1969, *22*(3), pp. 334–46.

——— **and Wales, Terence J.** Impact of Investment Subsidies in a Neoclassical Growth Model. *Rev. Econ. Statist.*, August 1969, *51*(3), pp. 287–97.

Tauchar, William F. Cross Elasticities of Collegiate Demand. *Rev. Soc. Econ.*, September 1969, *27*(2), pp. 222–32.

Tauchman, Josef and Novozámský, Jiří. The Nature of the International Division of Labour under Socialism. *Czech. Econ. Pap.*, 1969, (11), pp. 127–39.

Taussig, Michael K.; Pechman, Joseph A. and Aaron, Henry J. Improving Social Security Benefits and Financing: Brookings Research Report 94. **In** *Economics of Aging: Toward a Full Share in Abundance, Pt. 1, SCH*, 1969, pp. 253–63.

Tautscher, Anton. Die Entwicklung der österreichischen Staatswirtschaft. (The Development of the Austrian State Economy. With English summary.) *Schmollers Jahr.*, 1969, *89*(3), pp. 267–311.

Tauxe, G. W.; Yeh, W. W.-G. and Hall, Warren A. An Alternate Procedure for the Optimization of Operations for Planning with Multiple River, Multiple Purpose Systems. *Water Resources Res.*, December 1969, *5*(6), pp. 1367–72.

Tavis, Irene. Futurology and the Problem of Values. *Int. Soc. Sci. J.*, 1969, *21*(4), pp. 574–84.

Taylor, Basil. Investment: Art, Science or What? *Lloyds Bank Rev.*, January 1969, (91), pp. 10–21.

Taylor, Charles T. Meeting Seasonal Loan Demands. **In** *Jessup, P. F.*, 1969, pp. 89–100.

Taylor, David P.; Baitsell, John M. and Sprague, Christopher R. A Computer-Based Negotiation: Uses and Limitations as a Training Device. **In** *Siegel, A. J., ed.*, 1969, pp. 260–85.

Taylor, Gary C. Economic Issues in Controlling Agricultural Pollution. *Amer. J. Agr. Econ.*, December 1969, *51*(5), pp. 1182–88.

Taylor, James Stephen. The Mythology of the Old Poor Law. *J. Econ. Hist.*, June 1969, *29*(2), pp. 292–97.

Taylor, John. On the Economy of Mining. **In** *Burt, R., ed.*, 1969, pp. 31–48.

______ On the Economy of the Mines of Cornwall and Devon. **In** *Burt, R., ed.*, 1969, pp. 15–29.

Taylor, Lance J. Development Patterns: A Simulation Study. *Quart. J. Econ.*, May 1969, *83*(2), pp. 220–41.

______ **and Kendrick, David A.** A Dynamic Nonlinear Planning Model for Korea. **In** *Adelman, I., ed.*, 1969, pp. 213–37.

Taylor, Lester D. and Newhouse, Joseph P. On the Long-Run and Short-Run Demand for Money: A Comment. *J. Polit. Econ.*, September/October 1969, *77*(5), pp. 851–56.

Taylor, W. L. The Economy of Central Africa: Rhodesia, Malawi and Zambia. **In** *Robson, P. and Lury, D. A., eds.*, 1969, pp. 384–435.

Teeples, Ronald K. A Model of a Matching Grant-in-Aid Program with External Tax Effects. *Nat. Tax J.*, December 1969, *22*(4), pp. 486–95.

Teichova, Alice. The Development of Business in the United States during the Period of Early Industrialization: Inducements and Obstacles. **In** *Kennedy, C. J., ed.*, 1969, pp. 82–92.

Teigen, Ronald L. An Aggregated Quarterly Model of the U.S. Monetary Sector, 1953–1964. **In** *Brunner, K., ed.*, 1969, pp. 175–218.

______ Laidler's "Definition of Money": A Comment. *J. Money, Credit, Banking*, August 1969, *1*(3), pp. 531–34.

Tella, Alfred and Green, Christopher. Effect of Nonemployment Income and Wage Rates on the Work Incentives of the Poor. *Rev. Econ. Statist.*, November 1969, *51*(4), pp. 399–408.

di Tella, Guido. The Behavior of the Firm with a Financial Restriction. *J. Ind. Econ.*, April 1969, *17*(2), pp. 119–32.

Telser, Lester G. Another Look at Advertising and Concentration. *J. Ind. Econ.*, November 1969, *18*(1), pp. 85–94.

______ On the Regulation of Industry: A Note. *J. Polit. Econ.*, November/December 1969, *77*(6), pp. 937–52.

______ Theory of the Firm and of Market Structures: Discussion. *Amer. Econ. Rev.*, May 1969, *59*(2), pp. 121–23.

Tendulkar, Suresh D. Econometric Study of Monthly Consumption Expenditures in Rural Uttar Pradesh. *Amer. J. Agr. Econ.*, February 1969, *51*(1), pp. 119–37.

Tepicht, J. Problems of the Re-structuring of Agriculture in the Light of the Polish Experience. **In** *Papi, U. and Nunn, C., eds.*, 1969, pp. 534–47.

Tepping, Benjamin J. and Bershad, Max A. The Development of Household Sample Surveys. *J. Amer. Statist. Assoc.*, December 1969, *64*(328), pp. 1134–40.

______ **and Hansen, M. H.** Progress and Problems in Survey Methods and Theory Illustrated by the Work of the United States Bureau of the Census. **In** *Johnson, N. L. and Smith, H., Jr., eds.*, 1969, pp. 1–26.

Terborgh, George. The Inflation Dilemma. **In** *The 1969 Economic Report of the President, Pt. 4, JECH*, 1969, pp. 1066–1109.

Teresi, Salvatore. The Formation of Marketing Men. *Econ. Soc. Tijdschr.*, December 1969, *23*(6), pp. 555–65.

Terleckyj, Nestor E. Measuring Real Output for Industries Providing Services: OBE Concepts and Methods: Comment. **In** *Fuchs, V. R., ed.*, 1969, pp. 49–50.

______ The Service Industries in Canada, 1946–66: Discussion. **In** *Fuchs, V. R., ed.*, 1969, pp. 282–86.

______ **and Fabricant, Solomon.** Alternative Measures of the Real Output and Productivity of Commercial Banks: Comment. **In** *Fuchs, V. R., ed.*, 1969, pp. 195–99.

Terna, Pietro. Ricerca di uniformità di borsa di breve periodo: primi risultati. (Short Term Behaviour of Share Prices. With English summary.) *L'Industria*, October–December 1969, (4), pp. 493–505.

Terry, Edwin F. Public Finance and Regional Accounts. *Rev. Income Wealth*, June 1969, *15*(2), pp. 207–13.

Tesař, Jiří. The Development of the System of Economic Planning. *New Trends Czech. Econ.*, May 1969, (3), pp. 3–25.

Tévoédjré, Albert. A Strategy for Social Progress in Africa and the I.L.O.'s Contribution. *Int. Lab. Rev.*, January 1969, *99*(1), pp. 61–84.

Tew, Brian. Comments on the Papers by Oppenheimer and Mundell. *J. Money, Credit, Banking*, August 1969, *1*(3), pp. 666–67.

Tewes, Torsten. Exporthilfe oder Investitionshilfe —ein Problem der Entwicklungspolitik. (Export Aid or Investment Aid—a Problem of Development Policy. With English summary.) *Weltwirtsch. Arch.*, 1969, *103*(1), pp. 77–94.

Thage, Bent. Equilibrium and Stability in Harrod's Model. *Swedish J. Econ.*, December 1969, *71*(4), pp. 284–99.

Thakur, C. P. Obstacles to Productivity. **In** *Johri, C. K., ed.*, 1969, pp. 287–301.

Thal-Larsen, Margaret. Changing Employer Policies in a Large Urban Labor Market. **In** *Somers, G. G., ed. (II)*, 1969, pp. 248–56.

Theil, Henri. The Desired Political Entropy. *Amer.*

Polit. Sci. Rev., June 1969, 63(2), pp. 521–25.
——— How to Worry About Increased Expenditures. *Accounting Rev.*, January 1969, *44*(1), pp. 27–37.
——— A Multinomial Extension of the Linear Logit Model. *Int. Econ. Rev.*, October 1969, *10*(3), pp. 251–59.
Theiler, Donald F. Effects of Flood Protection on Land Use in the Coon Creek, Wisconsin, Watershed. *Water Resources Res.*, December 1969, *5*(6), pp. 1216–22.
Thernstrom, Stephan. Urbanization, Migration, and Social Mobility in Late Nineteenth-Century America. **In** *Bernstein, B. J., ed.*, 1969, pp. 158–75.
Thiesenhusen, William C. Population Growth and Agricultural Employment in Latin America, with Some U.S. Comparisons. *Amer. J. Agr. Econ.*, November 1969, *51*(4), pp. 735–52.
Thionet, P. Item Analysis and Reweighting. **In** *Johnson, N. L. and Smith, H., Jr., eds.*, 1969, pp. 282–304.
Thirlwall, A. P. Demand Disequilibrium in the Labour Market and Wage Rate Inflation in the United Kingdom (1) *Yorkshire Bull. Econ. Soc. Res.*, May 1969, *21*(1), pp. 66–76.
——— Okun's Law and the Natural Rate of Growth. *Southern Econ. J.*, July 1969, *36*(1), pp. 87–89.
——— Types of Unemployment: With Special Reference to 'Non Demand-Deficient' Unemployment in Great Britain. *Scot. J. Polit. Econ.*, February 1969, *16*(1), pp. 20–49.
——— Unemployment Compensation as an Automatic Stabilizer. *Bull. Oxford Univ. Inst. Econ. Statist.*, February 1969, *31*(1), pp. 23–37.
——— Weighting Systems and Regional Analysis: A Reply to Mr. Cunningham. *Oxford Econ. Pap.*, March 1969, *21*(1), pp. 128–33.
Thomas, Brinley. Brain Drain Again. **In** *Blaug, M., ed.*, 1969, pp. 250–80.
——— The Migration of Labour into the Glamorganshire Coalfield, 1861–1911. **In** *Minchinton, W. E., ed.*, 1969, pp. 37–56.
———**; Johnson, Harry G. and Scott, A. D.** Criticisms of Thomas's Analysis of Brain Drain. **In** *Blaug, M., ed.*, 1969, pp. 281–301.
Thomas, Clive Y. and Brewster, Havelock. Aspects of the Theory of Economic Integration. *J. Common Market Stud.*, December 1969, *8*(2), pp. 110–32.
Thomas, G. R. The Economics of Scale of Computing Systems. **In** *Hugh-Jones, E. M., ed.*, 1969, pp. 113–19.
Thomas, Jerry V. and Lyden, Fremont James. Citizen Participation in Policy-Making: A Study of a Community Action Program. *Soc. Sci. Quart.*, December 1969, *50*(3), pp. 631–42.
Thomas, Kenneth D. and Panglaykim, J. Indonesian Exports: Performance and Prospects. **In** *Morgan, T. and Spoelstra, N., eds.*, 1969, pp. 337–70.
Thomas, Morgan D. Regional Economic Growth: Some Conceptual Aspects. *Land Econ.*, February 1969, *45*(1), pp. 43–51.
Thomas, Roy. The Financial Benefits of Expanding in the Development Areas. *Bull. Oxford Univ. Inst. Econ. Statist.*, May 1969, *31*(2), pp. 77–87.
Thomas, V. J. A Stochastic Population Model Related to Human Populations. *J. Roy. Statist. Soc.*, Part 1, 1969, *132*, pp. 89–104.
Thomas, William C., Jr. Keeping the City Healthy. **In** *Connery, R. H. and Caraley, D., eds.*, 1969, pp. 121–32.
Thomason, George F. Industrial Relations. **In** *Kempner, T., ed.*, 1969, pp. 60–64.
Thompson, B. C. Recent Trends in the Coal Mining Industry. **In** *Coal Mine Health and Safety, Pt. 1, SCH*, 1969, pp. 510–14.
Thompson, Carey C. The Efficiency of Education in Economics: Discussion. *Amer. Econ. Rev.*, May 1969, *59*(2), pp. 242–43.
Thompson, Duane E. School Administration and Negotiations: Introduction. **In** *Sinicropi, A. V. and Gilroy, T. P., eds.*, 1969, pp. 32–33.
Thompson, Earl A. The Perfectly Competitive Production of Collective Goods: Reply. *Rev. Econ. Statist.*, November 1969, *51*(4), pp. 479–82.
Thompson, F. M. L. Landownership and Economic Growth in England in the Eighteenth Century. **In** *Jones, E. L. and Woolf, S. J., eds.*, 1969, pp. 41–60.
Thompson, Howard E. and Blakely, Edward J. Technological Change and Its Effects on Dollar-Value LIFO. *Manage. Account.*, August 1969, *51* (2), pp. 33–38.
Thompson, I. A. A. Galley Service and Crime in Sixteenth-Century Spain: Rejoinder. *Econ. Hist. Rev.*, August 1969, *22*(2), pp. 305–07.
Thompson, Proctor. Government and the Market. **In** *Starleaf, D. R., ed.*, 1969, pp. 179–95.
Thompson, Wilbur R. The Economic Base of Urban Problems. **In** *Chamberlain, N. W., ed.*, 1969, pp. 1–47.
——— Statement. **In** *Population Trends, Pt. 1, HCH*, 1969, pp. 565–96.
Thomsen, F. L. and Foote, R. J. Parity Price. **In** *Ruttan, V. W.; Waldo, A. D. and Houck, J. P., eds.*, 1969, pp. 90–95.
Thomson, Andrew W. J. The Next Step in Industrial Relations. *Scot. J. Polit. Econ.*, June 1969, *16*(2), pp. 212–24.
Thöni, Hanspeter. A Table for Estimating the Mean of a Lognormal Distribution. *J. Amer. Statist. Assoc.*, June 1969, *64*(326), pp. 632–36.
Thorbecke, Erik and Field, Alfred J. Relationships between Agriculture, Nonagriculture, and Foreign Trade in the Development of Argentina and Peru. **In** *Thorbecke, E., ed.*, 1969, pp. 165–213.
——— Relationships between Agriculture, Nonagriculture, and Foreign Trade in the Development of Argentina and Peru: Reply. **In** *Thorbecke, E., ed.*, 1969, pp. 217–18.
Thore, Sten. Credit Networks. *Economica, N.S.*, February 1969, *36*(141), pp. 42–57.
Thormann, Peter H. Employment and Earnings in Portugal, 1953–1967. *Int. Lab. Rev.*, June 1969, *99*(6), pp. 589–606.
Thornton, Thomas Perry. A View from Washington. *Ann. Amer. Acad. Polit. Soc. Sci.*, November 1969, *386*, pp. 19–30.
Thorp, Rosemary. A Note on Food Supplies, the Distribution of Income and National Income Accounting in Peru. *Bull. Oxford Univ. Inst. Econ. Statist.*, November 1969, *31*(4), pp. 229–41.

and Urban Unemployment in Less Developed Countries. *Amer. Econ. Rev.*, March 1969, *59*(1), pp. 138–48.

——— A Theoretical Note on Labour as an 'Inferior' Factor in Less Developed Economies. *J. Devel. Stud.*, July 1969, *5*(4), pp. 252–61.

——— **and Harris, John R.** Wages, Industrial Employment and Labour Productivity: The Kenyan Experience. *East Afr. Econ. Rev.*, June 1969, *1*(1), pp. 29–46.

——— **and Pack, Howard.** Technological Transfer, Labour Absorption, and Economic Development. *Oxford Econ. Pap.*, November 1969, *21*(3), pp. 395–403.

Todd, Jerry D. The Risk Management Function in Municipal Government. *J. Risk Ins.*, June 1969, *36*(2), pp. 285–95.

Tokman, Victor E. An Evaluation of Foreign Aid: The Chilean Case. *Bull. Oxford Univ. Inst. Econ. Statist.*, May 1969, *31*(2), pp. 89–103.

Tolkemitt, Georg. Volkswirtschaften mit unbeschränkt zunehmendem Konsumvorsprung gegenüber Golden-Rule-Konsumpfaden. (With English summary.) *Jahr. Nationalökon. Statist.*, March 1969, *182*(4–5), pp. 289–326.

Tolksdorf, Michael. Hoppmanns neoklassische Wettbewerbstheorie als grundlage der Wettbewerbspolitik. (Hoppmann's Neoclassic Theory of Competition as a Basis for Competition Policy. With English summary.) *Jahr. Nationalökon. Statist.*, June 1969, *183*(1), pp. 61–72.

Tollet, C. G. Exportfrämjandets mål och medel—diskussion om ett modeords innehåll. (The Ends and Means of Export Drives—A Discussion of the Content of a Fashionable Phrase. With English summary.) *Econ. Samfundets Tidskr.*, 1969, *22* (1), pp. 20–37.

Tolley, B. H. The Liverpool Campaign against the Order in Council and the War of 1812. **In** *Harris, J. R., ed.*, 1969, pp. 98–146.

Tolley, George S. Review Article: Mellor on Agricultural Development. *Econ. Develop. Cult. Change*, January 1969, *17*(2), pp. 254–61.

———**; Wang, Yi and Fletcher, R. G.** Reexamination of the Time Series Evidence on Food Demand. *Econometrica*, October 1969, *37*(4), pp. 695–705.

———**; Wang, Yi and Havlicek, Joseph, Jr.** "Solid Wastes"—A Resource? *Amer. J. Agr. Econ.*, December 1969, *51*(5), pp. 1598–1602.

Tollison, Robert and Ford, William Freithaler. Note on the Color of the Volunteer Army. *Soc. Sci. Quart.*, December 1969, *50*(3), pp. 544–47.

Tom, Franklin and Eiteman, David K. The New California Blue-Sky Law. *Calif. Manage. Rev.*, Winter 1969, *12*(2), pp. 5–12.

Tomasini, Luigi M. Funzioni di utilità, teoria del consumo e stima della domanda (II). (Utility Functions, Consumption Theories and Demand Estimation (II). With English summary.) *L'Industria*, October–December 1969, (4), pp. 444–74.

——— Funzioni di utilità, teorie del consumo e stima della domanda (I). (Utility Functions Consumption Theories and Demand Estimation (I). With English summary.) *L'Industria*, July–September 1969, (3), pp. 269–96.

——— Il valore dell'informazione nella teoria dell'impresa. (The Value of Information in the Theory of the Firm. With English summary.) *L'Industria*, January–March 1969, (1), pp. 17–34.

——— **and Kirman, Alan P.** A New Look at International Income Inequalities. *Econ. Int.*, August 1969, *22*(3), pp. 437–61.

——— **and Kirman, Alan P.** Teoria delle scelte sociali e relativi concetti. (Social Choice Theory and Related Concepts. With English summary.) *L'Industria*, April–June 1969, (2), pp. 176–96.

Tomek, William G. and Emerson, Peter M. Did Futures Trading Influence Potato Prices? *Amer. J. Agr. Econ.*, August 1969, *51*(3), pp. 666–72.

Topor, V. V. and Şotan, S. Determinarea influenţei nivelului de organizare şi conducere asupra rezultatelor economice ale I.A.S. (Determining the Influence of the Level of Organization and Management on the Economic Results of State Agricultural Enterprises. With English summary.) *Stud. Cercet. Econ.*, 1969, *1-2*, pp. 77–91.

Törnqvist, Erik. Nordek-planen. (The Nordek Plan. With English summary.) *Econ. Samfundets Tidskr.*, 1969, *22*(2), pp. 95–104.

Toro-Vizcarrondo, C. E. and Wallace, T. D. Tables for the Mean Square Error Test for Exact Linear Restrictions in Regression. *J. Amer. Statist. Assoc.*, December 1969, *64*(328), pp. 1649–63.

Toth, Barbara V. Labor in a Year of Expansion. *Mon. Lab. Rev.*, January 1969, *92*(1), pp. 11–19.

Toussaint, W. D. The Organization of Agriculture: Discussion. *Amer. J. Agr. Econ.*, December 1969, *51*(5), pp. 1283–85.

Townroe, P. M. Industrial Structure and Regional Economic Growth—A Comment. *Scot. J. Polit. Econ.*, February 1969, *16*(1), pp. 95–98.

Trabucchi, Romano and Santoro, Gaetano. Un'esperienza di addestramento mediante audiovisivi: il centro audiovisivi de la "rinascente-upim." (Training Experience through Audiovisual Methods. With English summary.) *L'Impresa*, November/December 1969, *11*(6), pp. 469–72.

Tracy, Derrick S. and Dwyer, Paul S. Multivariate Maxima and Minima with Matrix Derivatives. *J. Amer. Statist. Assoc.*, December 1969, *64*(328), pp. 1576–94.

Tracy, John A. Bayesian Statistical Methods in Auditing. *Accounting Rev.*, January 1969, *44*(1), pp. 90–98.

Traimond, Pierre. La capacité excéndentaire stratégique dans l'entreprise. (With English summary.) *Revue Écon.*, September 1969, *20*(5), pp. 830–50.

Trapeznikov, V. For Flexible Economic Management of Enterprises. **In** *Economic Concentration, Pt. 7A, SCH,* 1969, pp. 4412–16.

Trattner, Walter I. The First Federal Child Labor Law (1916). *Soc. Sci. Quart.*, December 1969, *50* (3), pp. 507–24.

Traylor, Harold D. and Gandy, Dewell R. Caloric Cost of Rice and Wheat Programs. *Amer. J. Agr. Econ.*, November 1969, *51*(4), pp. 962–63.

Treadway, Arthur B. On Rational Entrepreneurial Behaviour and the Demand for Investment. *Rev. Econ. Stud.*, April 1969, *36*(106), pp. 227–39.

——— What Is Output? Problems of Concept and

Measurement. In *Fuchs, V. R., ed.,* 1969, pp. 53–84.

Trebici, Vladimir. Metode moderne de analiză demografică. (Modern Methods of Demographic Analysis. With English summary.) *Stud. Cercet. Econ.,* 1969, *4,* pp. 165–71.

Trebilcock, Clive. "Spin-Off" in British Economic History: Armaments and Industry, 1760–1914. *Econ. Hist. Rev.,* December 1969, *22*(3), pp. 474–90.

Trebing, Harry M. Common Carrier Regulation—The Silent Crisis. *Law Contemp. Probl.,* Spring 1969, *34*(2), pp. 299–329.

_____ Government Regulation and Modern Capitalism. *J. Econ. Issues,* March 1969, *3*(1), pp. 87–109.

Treloar, D. W. G.; Mauldon, R. G. and Schapper, H. P. Operational Accounting for Farm Management. *Australian J. Agr. Econ.,* June 1969, *13*(1), pp. 47–57.

Treml, Vladimir G. Interaction of Economic Thought and Economic Policy in the Soviet Union. *Hist. Polit. Econ.,* Spring 1969, *1*(1), pp. 187–216.

_____ A Note on Soviet Input-Output Tables. *Soviet Stud.,* July 1969, *21*(1), pp. 21–34.

Trent, Robert H. and Young, William E. Geometric Mean Approximations of Individual Security and Portfolio Performance. *J. Financial Quant. Anal.,* June 1969, *4*(2), pp. 179–99.

Trenton, R. W. and Klos, Joseph J. The Effectiveness of Teaching Methods: One Semester or Two. *J. Econ. Educ.,* Fall 1969, *1*(1), pp. 51–55.

Trescott, Paul B. The Growth of Inputs and Output in Thailand, 1946–65. *Philippine Econ. J.,* First Semester 1969, *8*(1), pp. 75–84.

Trestrail, Richard W. Forests and the Property Tax —Unsound Accepted Theory. *Nat. Tax J.,* September 1969, *22*(3), pp. 347–56.

Trethewey, Richard J. The Economic Burden of the Sugar Act. *Amer. Econ.,* Spring 1969, *13*(1), pp. 63–71.

Trezza, Bruno. Produttività marginale del capitale e tasso di interesse nel modello keynesiano. (The Marginal Productivity of Capital and the Rate of Interest in the Keynesian Model. With English summary.) *L'Industria,* January–March 1969, (1), pp. 35–57.

Triffin, Robert. Neither Gold Nor the Dollar. In *Officer, L. H. and Willett, T. D., eds.,* 1969, pp. 3–11.

_____ On the Creation of a European Reserve Fund. *Banca Naz. Lavoro Quart. Rev.,* December 1969, (91), pp. 327–46.

_____ Statement. In *Linking Reserve Creation and Development Assistance, JECH,* 1969, pp. 37–42.

_____ The Thrust of History in International Monetary Reform. *Foreign Aff.,* April 1969, *47*(3), pp. 477–92.

Tripathi, B. N. Watchdog for Public Undertakings. In *Dagli, V., ed., Vol. II,* 1969, pp. 50–59.

Triplett, Jack E. Automobiles and Hedonic Quality Measurement. *J. Polit. Econ.,* May/June 1969, *77*(3), pp. 408–17.

Tritschler, Charles A. Statistical Criteria for Asset Valuation by Specific Price Index. *Accounting Rev.,* January 1969, *44*(1), pp. 99–123.

Trock, Warren L. Institutional Factors Affecting Land and Water Development, Lower Rio Grande Valley, Texas. *Water Resources Res.,* December 1969, *5*(6), pp. 1364–66.

Trotter, G. J. Personal Income Tax. *S. Afr. J. Econ.,* December 1969, *37*(4), pp. 306–44.

Troy, Leo. Trade Union Growth in a Changing Economy. *Mon. Lab. Rev.,* September 1969, *92*(9), pp. 3–7.

Troy, Patrick and Neutze, Max. Urban Road Planning in Theory and Practice. *J. Transp. Econ. Policy,* May 1969, *3*(2), pp. 139–51.

Truelove, A. J.; Mundle, P. B. and Blischke, W. R. On Non-Regular Estimation, I. Variance Bounds for Estimators of Location Parameters. *J. Amer. Statist. Assoc.,* September 1969, *64*(327), pp. 1056–72.

Truitt, George A. Participation as a Component of Integration: A Rationale for Regional Integration Centers. In *Hilton, R., ed.,* 1969, pp. 133–40.

Truman, Edwin M. The European Economic Community: Trade Creation and Trade Diversion. *Yale Econ. Essays,* Spring 1969, *9*(1), pp. 201–57.

Truman, Thomas C. Political Ideology, Belief Systems, and Parties: The Australian Labor Party. In *Preston, R., ed.,* 1969, pp. 255–91.

Tsaga, V. and Pavlov, P. The Marginalist Treatment of the Law of Value under Socialism. *Prob. Econ.,* July 1969, *12*(3), pp. 3–22.

Tsiang, S. C. A Critical Note on the Optimum Supply of Money. *J. Money, Credit, Banking,* May 1969, *1*(2), pp. 266–80.

_____ The Precautionary Demand for Money: An Inventory Theoretical Analysis. *J. Polit. Econ.,* January/February 1969, *77*(1), pp. 99–117.

Tsuchiya, Keizō. Economics of Mechanization in Small-scale Agriculture. In *Ohkawa, K.; Johnston, B. F. and Kaneda, H., eds.,* 1969, pp. 155–72.

Tu, Pierre N. V. The Classical Economists and Education. *Kyklos,* 1969, *22*(4), pp. 691–718.

_____ Externalities and Balanced Growth. *Australian Econ. Pap.,* June 1969, *8*(12), pp. 59–74.

Tucci, Giuseppe. Accostamenti economici tra Giappone e Italia; prospettive dell'esportazione calzaturiera in Giappone. (Economic Approaches between Japan and Italy. With English summary.) *Mondo Aperto,* October 1969, *23*(5), pp. 321–29.

Tucker, David M. Black Pride and Negro Business in the 1920's: George Washington Lee of Memphis. *Bus. Hist. Rev.,* Winter 1969, *43*(4), pp. 435–51.

Tucker, Donald P. Monetary Theory: Discussion. *Amer. Econ. Rev.,* May 1969, *59*(2), pp. 321–23.

Tuckwell, N. E. and Aggrey-Mensah, W. A Study of Banana Supply and Price Patterns on the Sydney Wholesale Market: An Application of Spectral Analysis. *Australian J. Agr. Econ.,* December 1969, *13*(2), pp. 101–17.

Tul'chinskii, L. I. Concerning Lecture Courses in the Economics of Education. In *Noah, H. J., ed.,* 1969, pp. 36–44.

Tull, Donald S. The Man in the President's Chair: Oregon and Elsewhere. *Oregon Bus. Rev.,* May 1969, *28*(5), pp. 1–4.

Urban, Glen L. A Mathematical Modeling Approach to Product Line Decisions. *J. Marketing Res.*, February 1969, *6*(1), pp. 40–47.

Urquidi, Victor L. International Trade and the Developing Countries: Comment. **In** *Samuelson, P. A., ed.*, 1969, pp. 41–45.

Urrila, Matti. Kommunikaatiopanos markkinoinnissa. (Communication Effort in Marketing. With English summary.) *Liiketaloudellinen Aikak.*, 1969, *18*(2), pp. 263–67.

Urwick, Lyndall F. The Function of Administration: With Special Reference to the Work of Henri Fayol. **In** *Gulick, L. and Urwick, L., eds.*, 1969, pp. 115–30.

______ Integration and Integrity. *Calif. Manage. Rev.*, Winter 1969, *12*(2), pp. 53–56.

______ Organization as a Technical Problem. **In** *Gulick, L. and Urwick, L., eds.*, 1969, pp. 47–88.

Usher, Abbott Payson. The Industrialization of Modern Britain. **In** *Scoville, W. C. and La Force, J. C., eds., Vol. III*, 1969, pp. 24–39.

______ The Origins of Banking: The Primitive Bank of Deposit, 1200–1600. **In** *Scoville, W. C. and La Force, J. C., eds., Vol. I*, 1969, pp. 81–110.

______**; Bowden, Witt and Karpovich, Michael.** Agrarian Reorganization and Reform in the Eighteenth Century. **In** *Scoville, W. C. and La Force, J. C., eds., Vol. III*, 1969, pp. 66–89.

Usher, Dan. Income as a Measure of Productivity: A Reply. *Economica, N.S.*, August 1969, *36*(143), pp. 317–20.

______ On the Social Rate of Discount: Comment. *Amer. Econ. Rev.*, December 1969, *59*(5), pp. 925–29.

Uvacek, Edward, Jr. A New Look at Demand Analysis for Beef: Reply. *Amer. J. Agr. Econ.*, November 1969, *51*(4), pp. 949–52.

Uzawa, H. Time Preference and the Penrose Effect in a Two-Class Model of Economic Growth. *J. Polit. Econ.*, Part II, July/August 1969, *77*(4), pp. 628–52.

Văcărel, Iulian. Finanţele—instrument activ în opera de edificare a socialismului în România. (Finance—An Active Instrument in the Work of Building up Socialism in Romania. With English summary.) *Stud. Cercet. Econ.*, 1969, *3*, pp. 131–41.

Vacha, S. Against Monopoly Administratively or by Economic Means? **In** *Economic Concentration, Pt. 7A, SCH*, 1969, pp. 4430–33.

Vachel, Jan. 50 Years of Czechoslovak Economic Development. *Czech. Econ. Pap.*, 1969, (11), pp. 141–51.

Vaivo, Fedi. Ajatuksia Euroopan integraatiokehityksestä ja suomalaisten yritysten strategiasta. (Impressions on the Development of European Integration and the Strategy of Finnish Firms. With English summary.) *Kansant. Aikak.*, 1969, *65*(2), pp. 82–90.

Vaizey, John. Keynes. *Irish Banking Rev.*, June 1969, pp. 10–19.

Vajda, Imre. The Problems of East-West Trade. **In** *Samuelson, P. A., ed.*, 1969, pp. 121–33.

______**; Khachaturov, T. S. and Nove, Alec.** Replies to Comments. **In** *Samuelson, P. A., ed.*, 1969, pp. 147–49.

Valarché, Jean. Innovations in Stock Farming: Information Flow from the Agricultural and Animal Food Industries. **In** *Papi, U. and Nunn, C., eds.*, 1969, pp. 344–56.

Valentei, D. Current Population Problems in the U.S.S.R. *Prob. Econ.*, November 1969, *12*(7), pp. 49–60.

Valentine, Thomas J. A Note on Multicollinearity. *Australian Econ. Pap.*, June 1969, *8*(12), pp. 99–105.

Valentini, Gilberto. Strategie di mercato. (Market Strategies. With English summary.) *L'Impresa,* July/October 1969, *11*(4–5), pp. 332–35.

Valticos, Nicolas. Fifty Years of Standard-Setting Activities by the International Labour Organisation. *Int. Lab. Rev.*, September 1969, *100*(3), pp. 201–37.

Van Arkadie, B. and Ghai, D. The East African Economies: Kenya, Uganda and Tanzania. **In** *Robson, P. and Lury, D. A., eds.*, 1969, pp. 316–83.

Van Cise, Jerrold G. A Franchise Contract. *Antitrust Bull.*, Summer 1969, *14*, pp. 325–46.

Van Cleef, Eugene. "Things Are Not Always What They Seem" for the Economic Geographer. *Econ. Geogr.*, January 1969, *45*(1), pp. 41–44.

Van Damme, G. De accountant in het Europa 1970. (The Accountant of the Seventies. With English summary.) *Econ. Soc. Tijdschr.*, April 1969, *23*(2), pp. 173–84.

Van de Ven, Petrus J. and Wolfson, Dirk J. Problems of Budget Analysis and Treasury Management in French-Speaking Africa. *Int. Monet. Fund Staff Pap.*, March 1969, *16*(1), pp. 140–58.

Van Horn, Richard. Validation. **In** *Naylor, T. H., ed.*, 1969, pp. 232–51.

Van Horne, James C. A Risk-Return Analysis of a Firm's Working-Capital Position. *Eng. Econ.*, January–February 1969, *14*(2), pp. 71–89.

______ **and Robichek, Alexander A.** Abandonment Value and Capital Budgeting: Reply. *J. Finance,* March 1969, *24*(1), pp. 96–97.

Van Houtte, J. B.T.W., een instrument van conjunctuur-politiek? (The Belgian V.A.T.-Bill and Economic Policy. With English summary.) *Econ. Soc. Tijdschr.*, February 1969, *23*(1), pp. 1–8.

______ De socialisering van het recht. (The Socialisation of the Law. With English summary.) *Econ. Soc. Tijdschr.*, June 1969, *23*(3), pp. 257–71.

Van Rompuy, P. Flexibility, Adaptability and Demand for Labour. *Tijdschr. Econ.*, 1969, *14*(3), pp. 436–48.

______ Note on the Optimum Period of Employment. *Tijdschr. Econ.*, 1969, *14*(4), pp. 584–86.

Van Roy, Edward and Cornehls, James V. Economic Development in Mexico and Thailand: An Institutional Analysis (Part I). *J. Econ. Issues,* September 1969, *3*(3), pp. 16–32.

______ Economic Development in Mexico and Thailand: An Institutional Analysis (Part II). *J. Econ. Issues,* December 1969, *3*(4), pp. 21–38.

Van Tatenhove, James M. Managing Indirect Costs in the Aerospace Industry. *Manage. Account.*, September 1969, *51*(3), pp. 36–42, 48.

Van Wickeren, A. C. and Klaassen, L. H. Interindustry Relations: An Attraction Model: A Progress Report. **In** *[Tinbergen, J.]*, 1969, pp. 245–68.

Vance, Jack O. Is Your Company a Take-Over Target? *Harvard Bus. Rev.*, May–June 1969, *47*(3), pp. 93–98.

Vance, Lawrence L. The Road to Reform of Accounting Principles. *Accounting Rev.*, October 1969, *44*(4), pp. 692–703.

Vandenhouten, F. De invoering van de B.T.W. in de ondernemingen. (The Value Added Tax in the Administration of the Firms. With English summary.) *Econ. Soc. Tijdschr.*, April 1969, *23*(2), pp. 159–71.

Vanderbeek, Robert E. Auto Insurance as a Fringe Benefit. *J. Risk Ins.*, September 1969, *36*(4), pp. 481–85.

Vanecko, James J. Community Mobilization and Institutional Change: The Influence of the Community Action Program in Large Cities. *Soc. Sci. Quart.*, December 1969, *50*(3), pp. 609–30.

Vanek, Jaroslav. Decentralization Under Worker's Management: A Theoretical Appraisal. *Amer. Econ. Rev.*, December 1969, *59*(5), pp. 1006–14.

——— **and Bertrand, T. J.** Growth with Technological Change, Variable Returns to Scale, and a General Saving Function. *Rivista Int. Sci. Econ. Com.*, August 1969, *16*(8), pp. 741–55.

Vaner, Josef and Koumarová, Miluše. Long-term Projection of the Sectoral Structure of the Czechoslovak National Economy on the Basis of an Input-Output Model. *Czech. Econ. Pap.*, 1969, (11), pp. 69–82.

Vanni, Lido. La direzione del personale: un primo bilancio italiano. (Personnel Management: A Preliminary Italian Survey. With English summary.) *L'Impresa*, November/December 1969, *11*(6), pp. 461–68.

Vanoli, Andre. Le Système Actuel de Comptabilité Nationale et la Planification. (With English summary.) *Rev. Income Wealth*, June 1969, *15*(2), pp. 171–84.

Vapnarsky, Cesar A. On Rank-Size Distributions of Cities: An Ecological Approach. *Econ. Develop. Cult. Change*, July 1969, *17*(4), pp. 584–95.

Varde, S. D. Life Testing and Reliability Estimation for the Two Parameter Exponential Distribution. *J. Amer. Statist. Assoc.*, June 1969, *64*(326), pp. 621–31.

Varshneya, J. S. Financing of Buffer Stock Operations: Role of Commercial Banks with Special Reference to the State Bank of India. **In** *Indian Society of Agricultural Economics*, 1969, pp. 128–33.

Vartiainen, Henri J. Kokonaistaloudellinen suunnittelu osallistumisen ja tavoitteiden ongelmana. (Economic Planning as a Problem of Participation and Aims. With English summary.) *Kansant. Aikak.*, 1969, *65*(2), pp. 95–101.

Vasconcellos, A. S. The French Plans: Character, Targets, Achievements. *Indian Econ. J.*, October–December 1969, *17*(2), pp. 172–204.

Vasilescu, Floarea and Stoichită, I. V. Analiza critică a metodologiei statistice de caracterizare a vitezei de rotaţie a fondurilor circulante. (Critical Analysis of the Statistical Methodology Used in Characterizing the Turnover Rate of the Circulation Means. With English summary.) *Stud. Cercet. Econ.*, 1969, *4*, pp. 137–58.

Vasilev, Dimitur. The International Socialist Division of Labor and Its Role in the Increased Profitability of Bulgaria's Foreign Trade. *Eastern Europ. Econ.*, Fall 1969, *8*(1), pp. 90–99.

Vasil'ev, N. The Distribution of Agricultural Enterprises and Increased Specialization of Agriculture. *Prob. Econ.*, April 1969, *11*(12), pp. 37–46.

Vasudevan, A. Deficit Financing and Economic Development. **In** *Bhuleshkar, A. V., ed.*, 1969, pp. 327–44.

——— The Portfolio Approach: Its Relevance to Under-Developed Economies. *Indian Econ. J.*, April–June 1969, *16*(4–5), pp. 520–31.

Vatter, Harold G. An Estimate of Import Substitution for Manufactured Products in the U.S. Economy, 1859 and 1899. *Econ. Develop. Cult. Change*, Part I, October 1969, *18*(1), pp. 40–43.

——— Capitalism without Accumulation. *J. Econ. Issues*, March 1969, *3*(1), pp. 110–25.

Vaughn, William M. and Holland, Daniel M. An Evaluation of Self-Assessment under a Property Tax. **In** *Lynn, A. D., Jr., ed.*, 1969, pp. 79–118.

Veblen, Thorstein. The Case of America: The Country Town. **In** *Minar, D. W. and Greer, S., eds.*, 1969, pp. 91–106.

Vecci, Giovanni. Il Planning-Programming-Budgeting-System—P.P.B.S. (The Planning-Programming-Budgeting-System—P.P.B.S. With English summary.) *L'Impresa*, November/December 1969, *11*(6), pp. 422–28.

Vechkanov, G. Raising the Effectiveness of the Territorial Redistribution of Labor Resources. *Prob. Econ.*, October 1969, *12*(6), pp. 58–67.

Veendorp, E. C. H. A Theorem on Non-tâtonnement Stability: A Comment. *Econometrica*, January 1969, *37*(1), pp. 142–43.

in't Veld, R. J. Stemmenhandel. (On Explicit Logrolling. With English summary.) *De Economist*, January/February 1969, *117*(1), pp. 24–72.

Veldkamp, Gerald M. J. A New Dimension for International Co-operation in Social Security. *Int. Lab. Rev.*, August 1969, *100*(2), pp. 131–39.

Velk, Thomas J. Chicago Campfires. *Quart. Rev. Econ. Bus.*, Winter 1969, *9*(4), pp. 39–45.

Venkateshwar Rao, H. Educational Costs: Concepts and Issues. **In** *Pandit, H. N., ed.*, 1969, pp. 46–56.

Ventriglia, Ferdinando. The Balance of Payments and Italian Economic Growth. *Rev. Econ. Cond. Italy*, September 1969, *23*(5), pp. 381–96.

Venturini, V. G. Monopolies and Restrictive Trade Practices in Italy. **In** *Economic Concentration, Pt. 7A, SCH*, 1969, pp. 4207–34.

Venugopal, Bhaskar and Ganguly, Swapan. International Crude Oil Prices after World War II. *Indian Econ. J.*, January–March 1969, *16*(3), pp. 382–87.

Venugopalacharyulu, N. Allocation Efficiency in Agriculture in Madras State. *Asian Econ. Rev.*, February 1969, *11*(2), pp. 216–20.

Vepa, Ram K. Planning of Resources. **In** *Dagli, V., ed., Vol. II*, 1969, pp. 153–60.

Vepřek, Jaromír. Lineární plánovací modely a podniková praxe. (Linear Planning Models in Business Practice. With English summary.) *Ekon.-Mat. Obzor,* 1969, *5*(3), pp. 273–94.

Verdoorn, P. J. and Post, J. J. Comparison of the Prewar and Postwar Business Cycles in the Netherlands: An Experiment in Econometrics. **In** *Bronfenbrenner, M., ed.,* 1969, pp. 436–66.

Vergé, Jean-Marie. Un modèle séquentiel de financement optimal à long terme dans l'entreprise. (With English summary.) *Revue Écon.,* March 1969, *20*(2), pp. 302–36.

Verhaegen, Jozef. Beleidsboekhouden. (Management Accounting. With English summary.) *Econ. Soc. Tijdschr.,* April 1969, *23*(2), pp. 113–28.

Verheirstraeten, A. Nominale tariefhoogte, effectieve bescherming en douane-opbrengsten met een toepassing op gegevens van het Beneluxdouanetarief. (Nominal Tarifflevel, Effective Protection and Customs Duties with an Application to data of the Benelux Customs Tariff. With English summary.) *Tijdschr. Econ.,* 1969, *14*(2), pp. 188–234.

Verma, Pramod. The Chemical Industry. **In** *Lerner, S. W.; Cable, J. R. and Gupta, S., eds.,* 1969, pp. 95–157.

______ Patents in British Industry: A Note. *Yorkshire Bull. Econ. Soc. Res.,* November 1969, *21*(2), pp. 114–18.

Vernon, John M.; Rives, Norfleet W., Jr. and Naylor, Thomas H. An Econometric Model of the Tobacco Industry. *Rev. Econ. Statist.,* May 1969, *51*(2), pp. 149–58.

Vernon, Raymond. Mexico: Public Planning and Private Initiative. **In** *Prybyla, J. S., ed.,* 1969, pp. 525–40.

______ Multinational Enterprise and the Nation State: Project Report from the Harvard Business School. *J. Common Market Stud.,* December 1969, *8*(2), pp. 160–70.

Verrill, Charles O., Jr. CATV's Emerging Role: Cablecaster or Common Carrier? *Law Contemp. Probl.,* Summer 1969, *34*(3), pp. 586–609.

Verschuur, Jan B. and Baker, James C. The Versatile Combination Export Manager. *Marquette Bus. Rev.,* Winter 1969, *13*(4), pp. 143–50.

Versluis, Jan and Cornelisse, Peter A. The Semi-Input-Output Method under Upper Bounds. **In** *[Tinbergen, J.],* 1969, pp. 175–99.

Vessillier, Elisabeth. L'instrument fiscal dans la politique française d'amenagement du territoire. (The Fiscal Instrument in the Regional Economic Policy of France. With English summary.) *Public Finance,* 1969, *24*(3), pp. 499–509.

Vickrey, William S. Congestion Theory and Transport Investment. *Amer. Econ. Rev.,* May 1969, *59*(2), pp. 251–60.

______ Current Issues in Transportation. **In** *Chamberlain, N. W., ed.,* 1969, pp. 185–240.

______ Decreasing Costs, Publicly Administered Prices, and Economic Efficiency. **In** *The Analysis and Evaluation of Public Expenditures: The PPB System, Vol. 1, JECP,* 1969, pp. 119–48.

______ Tax Simplification through Cumulative Averaging. *Law Contemp. Probl.,* Autumn 1969, *34*(4), pp. 736–50.

Videnov, Ivan. Theoretical Problems of Wholesale Prices. *Eastern Europ. Econ.,* Summer 1969, *7*(4), pp. 3–12.

Vigand, V. C. Once More on the World Price of Oil: A Comment. *Acta Oecon.,* 1969, *4*(2), pp. 211–14.

Viita, Pentti. Investoinnit ja maksutase. (Investments and the Balance of Payments. With English summary.) *Kansant. Aikak.,* 1969, *65*(3), pp. 233.

Villanueva, Javier. Inversión privada extranjera, desarrollo industrial y comercio internacional. (Direct Foreign Investment in Industry. With English summary.) *Económica,* May–August 1969, *15*(2), pp. 223–42.

Villard, Henry H. The Evaluation of Teaching Effectiveness: Where We Now Stand. *J. Econ. Educ.,* Fall 1969, *1*(1), pp. 60–66.

Vincens, Jean. Les prévisions par professions. (With English summary.) *Revue Écon.,* July 1969, *20*(4), pp. 561–600.

Vincent, Andre L.-A. La productivité globale clé de l'étude de la répartition. (With English summary.) *Revue Écon.,* September 1969, *20*(5), pp. 783–829.

Vincent, Phillip E. Reciprocal Externalities and Optimal Input and Output Levels. *Amer. Econ. Rev.,* December 1969, *59*(5), pp. 976–84.

Vind, Karl and Södersten, Bo. Tariffs and Trade in General Equilibrium: Reply. *Amer. Econ. Rev.,* June 1969, *59*(3), pp. 424–26.

Viner, Jacob. Power Versus Plenty as Objectives of Foreign Policy in the Seventeenth and Eighteenth Centuries. **In** *Coleman, D. C., ed.,* 1969, pp. 61–91.

Vingerhoets, J. The Kennedy Round and the Developing Countries. **In** *Alting von Geusau, F. A. M., ed.,* 1969, pp. 48–74.

Vining, Rutledge. On Two Foundation Concepts of the Theory of Political Economy. *J. Polit. Econ.,* March/April 1969, *77*(2), pp. 199–218.

Vinod, Hrishikesh D. Econometrics of Joint Production—A Reply. *Econometrica,* October 1969, *37*(4), pp. 739–40.

______ Integer Programming and the Theory of Grouping. *J. Amer. Statist. Assoc.,* June 1969, *64*(326), pp. 506–19.

Vinokur, R. and Atlas, M. The Economic Essence of Profit and Profitability under Socialism. *Prob. Econ.,* May 1969, *12*(1), pp. 3–32.

Vipond, M. J. Fluctuations in Private Housebuilding in Great Britain, 1950–1966. *Scot. J. Polit. Econ.,* June 1969, *16*(2), pp. 196–211.

Vladimirov, Iu. V. The Question of Soviet-Chinese Economic Relations in 1950–1966. *Chinese Econ. Stud.,* Fall 1969, *3*(1), pp. 3–32.

Vlasák, František. What Next in the Economic Policy? *New Trends Czech. Econ.,* September 1969, (5–6), pp. 3–89.

Vlček, Jaroslav. Systémová analýza a systémový přístup: Srovnavácí studie s návrhem metody. (System Analysis and System Approach. With English summary.) *Ekon.-Mat. Obzor,* 1969, *5*(4), pp. 409–22.

Vogel, Robert C. and Maddala, G. S. Estimating Lagged Relationships in Corporate Demand for

Liquid Assets. *Rev. Econ. Statist.*, February 1969, *51*(1), pp. 53–61.

Volcker, Paul A. Statement. **In** *The 1969 Economic Report of the President, Pt. 3, JECH,* 1969, pp. 732–37.

Volodarskii, L. and Eidel'man, M. Basic Results of Elaboration of the Interbranch Balance of Production and Distribution of Output throughout the National Economy of the U.S.S.R. for 1966. *Prob. Econ.*, September 1969, *12*(5), pp. 29–51.

Voorhis, Jerry. Statement. **In** *The 1969 Economic Report of the President, Pt. 4, JECH,* 1969, pp. 1189–97.

Vosloo, J. J. and Groenewald, J. A. An Analysis of the Demand for Apples in the Republic of South Africa. *Finance Trade Rev.*, June 1969, *8*(3), pp. 187–97.

Vosyka, Miroslav. Model vícefázové soustavy hromadné obsluhy s respektováním priority požadavků. (Model of a Multiple Parallel and Series Queueing System with Preemptive Priorities. With English summary.) *Ekon.-Mat. Obzor,* 1969, *5*(3), pp. 354–77.

Votaw, Dow and Sethi, S. Prakash. Do We Need a New Corporate Response to a Changing Social Environment? Part II. *Calif. Manage. Rev.*, Fall 1969, *12*(1), pp. 17–31.

——— Do We Need a New Corporate Response to a Changing Social Environment? Part I. *Calif. Manage. Rev.*, Fall 1969, *12*(1), pp. 3–16.

Votey, Harold L., Jr. The Optimum Population and Growth: A New Look. A Modification to Include a Preference for Children in the Welfare Function. *J. Econ. Theory,* October 1969, *1*(3), pp. 273–90.

———; Maxwell, Darold E. and Phillips, Llad. A Synthesis of the Economic and Demographic Models of Fertility: An Econometric Test. *Rev. Econ. Statist.*, August 1969, *51*(3), pp. 298–308.

Vraca, Alexandru and Pintilie, Constanti. Un concept nou: conducerea întegrată a întreprinderilor. (A New Conception: Integrated Management of Enterprises. With English summary.) *Stud. Cercet. Econ.*, 1969, *1-2,* pp. 65–75.

de Vries, Barend A. High Cost of Industry in Developing Countries—Causes and Remedies. *Finance Develop.*, December 1969, *6*(4), pp. 43–47.

de Vries, Margaret G. Exchange Restrictions: Progress Toward Liberalization. *Finance Develop.*, September 1969, *6*(3), pp. 40–44.

——— Fluctuating Exchange Rates: The Fund's Approach. *Finance Develop.*, June 1969, *6*(2), pp. 44–48.

Vyas, V. S. Integration of Farm and Non-Farm Employment, Part I: Farm and Non-Farm Employment in an Economically Backward Region. *Artha-Vikas,* January 1969, *5*(1), pp. 54–67.

——— and Pathak, Mahesh. A Case for Taxation of Agricultural Income. *Artha-Vikas,* July 1969, *5* (2), pp. 130–37.

Waardenburg, J. G.; Herman, B. and Mennes, L. B. M. Some Exercises with a Simple Model for World Development Planning. **In** *[Tinbergen, J.],* 1969, pp. 65–92.

van Waasdijk, T. The Budget and Economic Policy. *S. Afr. J. Econ.*, June 1969, *37*(2), pp. 98–104.

——— Some Thoughts on Indirect Tax Effects in South Africa. *S. Afr. J. Econ.*, December 1969, *37* (4), pp. 372–92.

Wabe, J. S. Commuter Travel into Central London. *J. Transp. Econ. Policy,* January 1969, *3*(1), pp. 48–68.

——— Labour Force Participation Rates in the London Metropolitan Region. *J. Roy. Statist. Soc.*, Part 2, 1969, *132,* pp. 245–64.

Wachter, Michael L. Wages and the Guideposts: Comment. *Amer. Econ. Rev.*, June 1969, *59*(3), pp. 354–58.

Wädekin, Karl-Eugen. Manpower in Soviet Agriculture—Some Post-Khrushchev Developments and Problems. *Soviet Stud.*, January 1969, *20*(3), pp. 281–305.

Wadhva, Charan D. Reserve Pooling in Asia and the Far East. *Pakistan Develop. Rev.*, Autumn 1969, *9*(3), pp. 309–29.

Waever, F. Stirton. The Dynamics of U.S. Investment in Latin America. *Sci. Soc.*, Winter 1969, *33* (1), pp. 20–24.

Wagner, Abraham R. and Sufrin, Sidney C. Disaggregate Employment: The Search for Short Run Demand and Labor Market Stability. *Rivista Int. Sci. Econ. Com.*, October 1969, *16*(10), pp. 965–92.

——— Interest Rate Manipulation, Employment and Output—A Disaggregated Suggestion. *Rivista Int. Sci. Econ. Com.*, April 1969, *16*(4), pp. 327–41.

Wagner, Carroll L., Jr. Deputization under Section 16(b): The Implications of *Feder v. Martin Marietta Corporation. Yale Law J.*, June 1969, *78*(7), pp. 1151–73.

Wagstaff, Thomas. Call Your Old Master—"Master": Southern Political Leaders and Negro Labor during Presidential Reconstruction. *Labor Hist.*, Summer 1969, *10*(3), pp. 323–45.

Wahba, Grace. Estimation of the Coefficients in a Multidimensional Distributed Lag Model. *Econometrica,* July 1969, *37*(3), pp. 398–407.

Waite, Charles A. and Wakefield, Joseph C. Federal Programs for Fiscal 1970. *Surv. Curr. Bus.*, February 1969, *49*(2), pp. 13–20.

Wakefield, Joseph C. and Waite, Charles A. Federal Programs for Fiscal 1970. *Surv. Curr. Bus.*, February 1969, *49*(2), pp. 13–20.

Waksberg, Joseph and Pritzker, Leon. Changes in Census Methods. *J. Amer. Statist. Assoc.*, December 1969, *64*(328), pp. 1141–49.

Wakstein, Allen M. The National Association of Manufacturers and Labor Relations in the 1920s. *Labor Hist.*, Spring 1969, *10*(2), pp. 163–76.

Wald, Haskell P. Information Requirements for Regulatory Decisions: Comment. **In** *Trebing, H. M. and Howard, R. H., eds.*, 1969, pp. 205–11.

Waldman, Elizabeth. Educational Attainment of Workers. *Mon. Lab. Rev.*, February 1969, *92*(2), pp. 14–22.

——— Employment Status of School Age Youth. *Mon. Lab. Rev.*, August 1969, *92*(8), pp. 23–32.

Waldo, Dwight. Reflections on Public Administration and National Development. *Int. Soc. Sci. J.*, 1969, *21*(2), pp. 294–309.

Wales, Terence J. and Taubman, Paul. Impact of

Investment Subsidies in a Neoclassical Growth Model. *Rev. Econ. Statist.*, August 1969, *51*(3), pp. 287–97.

______ **and Pollak, Robert A.** Estimation of the Linear Expenditure System. *Econometrica,* October 1969, *37*(4), pp. 611–28.

Walgreen, John A. Liner Nationality and Steamship Conference Rate-Making. *J. Ind. Econ.*, July 1969, *17*(3), pp. 205–09.

Walker, David A. A Two-Stage Decision Process to Estimate Functions with Collinear Independent Variables. *Jahr. Nationalökon. Statist.*, June 1969, *183*(1), pp. 48–60.

Walker, Douglas O. Economic Fluctuations: A Comparative Study: Comment. *Amer. Econ.*, Spring 1969, *13*(1), pp. 58–62.

Walker, Franklin V. The Restrictive Effect of the U.S. Tariff: Comment. *Amer. Econ. Rev.*, December 1969, *59*(5), pp. 963–66.

Walker, Geoffrey de Q. The Australian Plaintiff and the Sherman Act. *Antitrust Bull.*, Winter 1969, *14,* pp. 901–32.

Walker, Jack L. The Diffusion of Innovations among the American States. *Amer. Polit. Sci. Rev.*, September 1969, *63*(3), pp. 880–99.

Walker, James W. Forecasting Manpower Needs. *Harvard Bus. Rev.*, March–April 1969, *47*(2), pp. 152–64.

Walker, John E. The "Net Interest Cost" Method of Issuing Tax Exempt Bonds: Is It Rational?—A Comment. *Public Finance,* 1969, *24*(4), pp. 624–26.

Walker, Joseph E. A Comparison of Negro and White Labor in a Charcoal Iron Community. *Labor Hist.*, Summer 1969, *10*(3), pp. 487–97.

Wall, David. After UNCTAD II. **In** *Stewart, I. G., ed.*, 1969, pp. 181–84.

Wall, Kelvin A. Marketing to Low-Income Neighborhoods: A Systems Approach. *Univ. Wash. Bus. Rev.*, Autumn 1969, *29*(1), pp. 18–26.

Wallace, James P. and Beckmann, Martin J. Continuous Lags and the Stability of Market Equilibrium. *Economica, N.S.*, February 1969, *36*(141), pp. 58–68.

Wallace, Neil. Buse on Meiselman—A Comment. *J. Polit. Econ.*, Part I, July/August 1969, *77*(4), pp. 524–27.

______ **and McCall, John.** A Supply Function of First-Term Re-enlistees to the Air Force. *J. Human Res.*, Summer 1969, *4*(3), pp. 293–310.

Wallace, T. D. and Hussain, Ashiq. The Use of Error Components Models in Combining Cross Section with Time Series Data. *Econometrica,* January 1969, *37*(1), pp. 55–72.

______ **and Toro-Vizcarrondo, C. E.** Tables for the Mean Square Error Test for Exact Linear Restrictions in Regression. *J. Amer. Statist. Assoc.*, December 1969, *64*(328), pp. 1649–63.

Wallich, Henry C. In Defense of Fixed Exchange Rates. **In** *Starleaf, D. R., ed.*, 1969, pp. 392–95.

______ Instrumental Analysis and the Decisional Process: A Critique. **In** *Heilbroner, R. L., ed.*, 1969, pp. 155–65.

______ Keynesian Monetary Theories, Stabilization Policy, and the Recent Inflation: A Comment. *J. Money, Credit, Banking,* August 1969, *1*(3), pp. 590–99.

______ Money and Growth: A Country Cross-Section Analysis. *J. Money, Credit, Banking,* May 1969, *1* (2), pp. 281–302.

______ A Neo-Keynesian View of Monetary Policy: Discussion. **In** *Federal Reserve Bank of Boston,* 1969, pp. 127–131.

______ The Role of Money in National Economic Policy. **In** *Federal Reserve Bank of Boston,* 1969, pp. 31–36.

______ Round Table on Exchange Rate Policy. *Amer. Econ. Rev.*, May 1969, *59*(2), pp. 360–62.

______ Statement. **In** *Investment Company Amendments Act of 1969, SCH,* 1969, pp. 143–47.

______ Uses of Financial Accounts in Monetary Analysis. *Rev. Income Wealth,* December 1969, *15*(4), pp. 321–34.

Wallin, Michel. Labour Administration: Origins and Development. *Int. Lab. Rev.*, July 1969, *100*(1), pp. 51–110.

Wallis, George and Whitworth, Joseph. Overview of American Manufactures, 1854. **In** *Pursell, C. W., Jr.*, 1969, pp. 49–52.

Wallis, Kenneth F. Some Recent Developments in Applied Econometrics: Dynamic Models and Simultaneous Equation Systems. *J. Econ. Lit.*, September 1969, *7*(3), pp. 771–96.

Walls, Robert C. and Weeks, David L. A Note on the Variance of a Predicted Response in Regression. *Amer. Statist.*, June 1969, *23*(3), pp. 24–26.

Walmsley, David J. The Less Developed Country Exclusion from Subpart F. *Nat. Tax J.*, September 1969, *22*(3), pp. 425–30.

Walsh, Cornelius F. Professor Johnson's Hedges. *Miss. Val. J. Bus. Econ.*, Fall 1969, *5*(1), pp. 80–84.

Walsh, Richard G. and Araji, Ahmed A. Effect of Assembly Costs on Optimum Grain Elevator Size and Location. *Can. J. Agr. Econ.*, July 1969, *17*(2), pp. 36–45.

______ **and Madsen, Albert G.** Conglomerates: Economic Conduct and Performance. *Amer. J. Agr. Econ.*, December 1969, *51*(5), pp. 1495–1505.

Walsh, Robert E. Labor in Private Industry. **In** *Walsh, R. E., ed.*, 1969, pp. 5–12.

Walter, Emil J. Statistische Erhebungen über die Verbreitung von elektronischen Datenverarbeitungsanlagen (EDV) in der Schweiz. (Statistical Enquiries in Regard to the Diffusion in Switzerland of Electronic Installations for the Analysis of Information (IED). With English summary.) *Schweiz. Z. Volkswirtsch. Statist.*, December 1969, *105*(4), pp. 515–33.

Walter, Helmut. Bemerkungen zum gegenwärtigen Stand der Wettbewerbstheorie. (Remarks about the Present State of the Theory of Competition. With English summary.) *Schmollers Jahr.*, 1969, *89*(5), pp. 541–56.

______ Über einige Zusammenhänge zwischen Einkommensverteilung und globaler Beschäftigtenstruktur. (With English summary.) *Z. ges. Staatswiss.*, April 1969, *125*(2), pp. 248–60.

Walter, Ingo. Nontariff Barriers and the Free-Trade Area Option. *Banca Naz. Lavoro Quart. Rev.*, March 1969, (88), pp. 16–45.

______ **and Allen, Robert Loring.** Statement. **In** *Ex-*

port Expansion and Regulation, SCH, 1969, pp. 427–28.

——— **and Kramer, John E.** Political Autonomy and Economic Dependence in an All-Negro Municipality. *Amer. J. Econ. Soc.,* July 1969, *28*(3), pp. 225–48.

Walter, Jaromír. Modely obnovy. (Models of Renewal. With English summary.) *Ekon.-Mat. Obzor,* 1969, *5*(2), pp. 137–62.

Walters, A. A. The Cost of Using Roads. *Finance Develop.,* March 1969, *6*(1), pp. 16–22.

——— **and Bennathan, E.** Revenue Pooling and Cartels. *Oxford Econ. Pap.,* July 1969, *21*(2), pp. 161–76.

——— **and Dalton, George.** The Economy of Liberia. **In** *Robson, P. and Lury, D. A., eds.,* 1969, pp. 287–315.

Walters, J. Hart. Pressures of Growth on the Polish Marketing System. **In** *Grub, P. D. and Holbik, K.,* 1969, pp. 164–70.

Walton, Clarence C. The Role of Ethical Standards in Business. **In** *Burton, J. C., ed.,* 1969, pp. 59–69.

Walton, Gary M. and Shepherd, James F. Estimate of "Invisible" Earnings in the Balance of Payments of the British North American Colonies, 1768–1772. *J. Econ. Hist.,* June 1969, *29*(2), pp. 230–63.

Wang, Yi; Fletcher, R. G. and Tolley, George S. Reexamination of the Time Series Evidence on Food Demand. *Econometrica,* October 1969, *37* (4), pp. 695–705.

———**; Havlicek, Joseph, Jr. and Tolley, George S.** "Solid Wastes"—A Resource? *Amer. J. Agr. Econ.,* December 1969, *51*(5), pp. 1598–1602.

von Wangenheim, Eberhard. Developing Countries and Monetary Reform. *Weltwirtsch. Arch.,* 1969, *103*(1), pp. 95–109.

Wanner, Richard A. and Engelmann, Hugo O. Population Size and Industrial Technology. *Amer. J. Econ. Soc.,* July 1969, *28*(3), pp. 249–56.

Ward, Benjamin. Problems in the Theory of Public Choice: Discussion. *Amer. Econ. Rev.,* May 1969, *59*(2), pp. 214–16.

——— What is Distinctive about Contemporary Capitalism? *J. Econ. Issues,* March 1969, *3*(1), pp. 32–48.

Ward, Cordelia T. and Davis, William M. Negotiations and Wage Calendar for 1969. *Mon. Lab. Rev.,* January 1969, *92*(1), pp. 52–64.

Ward, Gordon H. The Structure and Organization of Cooperatives in Developing Nations. **In** *McGrath, M. J., ed.,* 1969, pp. 5–41.

Ward, Joe H., Jr. Synthesizing Regression Models —An Aid to Learning Effective Problem Analysis. *Amer. Statist.,* April 1969, *23*(2), pp. 14–20.

Ward, M. The Effects of the U.K. Devaluation of Sterling on the Fiji Economy. *Econ. Rec.,* March 1969, *45*(109), pp. 92–115.

Ward, Richard J. Absorbing More Labor in LDC Agriculture. *Econ. Develop. Cult. Change,* January 1969, *17*(2), pp. 178–88.

——— Alternative Means to Control Population Growth. *Rev. Soc. Econ.,* September 1969, *27*(2), pp. 121–38.

——— Two Views on Myrdal (I). *Indian Econ. J.,* July–September 1969, *17*(1), pp. 143–57.

Warford, J. J. and Ford, J. L. Cost Functions for the Water Industry. *J. Ind. Econ.,* November 1969, *18* (1), pp. 53–63.

Warner, Kenneth O. Cities at the Bargaining Table. **In** *Walsh, R. E., ed.,* 1969, pp. 34–41.

——— Financial Implications of Employee Bargaining in the Public Service. **In** *Walsh, R. E., ed.,* 1969, pp. 189–97.

Warrack, Allan A. The Challenge of Abundance: Comment. *Can. J. Agr. Econ.,* July 1969, *17*(2), pp. 118–23.

Warren, W. M. Urban Real Wages and the Nigerian Trade Union Movement, 1939–60: Rejoinder. *Econ. Develop. Cult. Change,* July 1969, *17*(4), pp. 618–33.

Wasowski, Stanislaw. The Fuel Situation in Eastern Europe. *Soviet Stud.,* July 1969, *21*(1), pp. 35–51.

Wasserman, Joseph J. Plugging the Leaks in Computer Security. *Harvard Bus. Rev.,* September–October 1969, *47*(5), pp. 119–29.

Wassom, John C. Inflation as a Tool for Promoting Growth. *Nebr. J. Econ. Bus.,* Winter 1968–69, *8* (1), pp. 34–43.

Wasson, Chester R. Le previsioni sulla moda e sugli altri aspetti del ciclo di vita del prodotto. (How Predictable Are Fashion and Other Product Life Cycles. With English summary.) *Mondo Aperto,* October 1969, *23*(5), pp. 357–70.

Watanabe, S. The Brain Drain from Developing to Developed Countries. *Int. Lab. Rev.,* April 1969, *99*(4), pp. 401–33.

Watanabe, Taro. The Economics of SDR's. *Osaka Econ. Pap.,* March 1969, *17*(32), pp. 1–20.

Waterman, Robert H., Jr. and Gee, Robert E. A New Tool for Bank Management: A Mathematical Model in Banking. **In** *Jessup, P. F.,* 1969, pp. 293–300.

Waters, Joseph B.; Bonin, Joseph M. and Finch, B. W. Alternative Tests of the "Displacement Effect" Hypothesis. *Public Finance,* 1969, *24*(3), pp. 441–56.

Waters, Judith A. Money Supply and Credit—Theory and Practice. *Nat. Westminster Bank Quart. Rev.,* November 1969, pp. 19–34.

Waterston, Albert. An Operational Approach to Development Planning. *Finance Develop.,* December 1969, *6*(4), pp. 38–42.

Watkins, Melville H. The Canadian Experience with Foreign Direct Investment. *Law Contemp. Probl.,* Winter 1969, *34*(1), pp. 126–34.

Watt, Melvin L. Tax Exemption for Organizations Investing in Black Businesses. *Yale Law J.,* June 1969, *78*(7), pp. 1212–27.

Watters, Elsie M. Fiscal Outlook for State and Local Government. **In** *[White, Charles P.],* 1969, pp. 112–23.

Watts, Donald. Time Series Analysis. **In** *Naylor, T. H., ed.,* 1969, pp. 165–79.

Watts, Harold W. Graduated Works Incentives: An Experiment in Negative Taxation. *Amer. Econ. Rev.,* May 1969, *59*(2), pp. 463–72.

——— Statement. **In** *Review of Federal Statistical Programs, JECH,* 1969, pp. 140–44.

Ways, Max. Labor Unions Are Worth the Price. **In** *Starleaf, D. R., ed.,* 1969, pp. 153–63.

Weale, W. Bruce. Creative Problem-Solving in Marketing. *Rivista Int. Sci. Econ. Com.,* January 1969, *16*(1), pp. 63–78.

Weaver, George L.-P. The ILO at 50: A Government Delegate's View. *Mon. Lab. Rev.*, May 1969, *92* (5), pp. 37–40.

Weaver, Mary F.; Fry, Edward R. and Beck, Darwin L. Revision of Money Stock Series. *Fed. Res. Bull.*, October 1969, *55*(10), pp. 787–803.

Webb, Bernard L. Collective Merchandising of Automobile Insurance. *J. Risk Ins.*, September 1969, *36*(4), pp. 465–71.

Webb, Kempton E. The Geography of Brazil's Modernization and Implications for the Years 1980 and 2000 A.D. **In** *Baklanoff, E. N., ed.*, 1969, pp. 142–56.

Webber, Melvin M. Statement. **In** *Panel on Science and Technology: Science and Technology and the Cities, HCH,* 1969, pp. 97–114.

Webbink, Douglas W. The Impact of UHF Promotion: The All-Channel Television Receiver Law. *Law Contemp. Probl.*, Summer 1969, *34*(3), pp. 535–61.

Weber, Arnold R. Paradise Lost; or Whatever Happened to the Chicago Social Workers? *Ind. Lab. Relat. Rev.*, April 1969, *22*(3), pp. 323–38.

Weber, Glen D. and Brown, Richard E. Tributary Area Development: TVA's Approach to Sub-Regional Development. *Land Econ.*, February 1969, *45*(1), pp. 141–46.

Wedderspoon, William M. Simplifying Taxes in East Africa. *Finance Develop.*, March 1969, *6*(1), pp. 51–56.

van der Wee, Herman. International Business Finance and Monetary Policy in Western Europe, 1384–1410. *Bus. Hist. Rev.*, Autumn 1969, *43*(3), pp. 372–80.

Weeks, David L. and Walls, Robert C. A Note on the Variance of a Predicted Response in Regression. *Amer. Statist.*, June 1969, *23*(3), pp. 24–26.

Weeks, John. Political Economy and the Politics of Economists. *Rev. Radical Polit. Econ.*, May 1969, *1*(1), pp. 1–10.

Wegge, Leon L. F. A Family of Functional Iterations and the Solution of Maximum Likelihood Estimating Equations. *Econometrica*, January 1969, *37*(1), pp. 122–30.

______ **and Kemp, Murray C.** Generalizations of the Stolper-Samuelson and Samuelson-Rybczynski Theorems in Terms of Conditional Input-Output Coefficients. *Int. Econ. Rev.*, October 1969, *10*(3), pp. 414–25.

______ **and Kemp, Murray C.** On the Relation between Commodity Prices and Factor Rewards. *Int. Econ. Rev.*, October 1969, *10*(3), pp. 407–13.

Weidenbaum, Murray L. Budget "Uncontrollability" as an Obstacle to Improving the Allocation of Government Resources. **In** *The Analysis and Evaluation of Public Expenditures: The PPB System, Vol. 1, JECP,* 1969, pp. 357–68.

______ The Effects of Government Contracting on Private Enterprise. **In** *Competition in Defense Procurement, SCH,* 1969, pp. 257–63.

______ Federal Aid to the States: An Analytical Examination of the Alternatives. *Amer. J. Econ. Soc.*, October 1969, *28*(4), pp. 367–83.

______ Fiscal Policy and the National Economy. *Univ. Missouri Bus. Govt. Rev.*, November–December 1969, *10*(6), pp. 24–32.

______ The Military/Space Market: The Intersection of the Public and Private Sectors. **In** *Competition in Defense Procurement, SCH,* 1969, pp. 883–916.

______ Statement. **In** *Competition in Defense Procurement, SCH,* 1969, pp. 3–32.

______ Statement. **In** *Unemployment Compensation, HCH,* 1969, pp. 221–25.

Weigel, Dale and Schutjer, Wayne. The Contribution of Foreign Assistance to Agricultural Development. *Amer. J. Agr. Econ.*, November 1969, *51* (4), pp. 788–97.

Weiller, Jean. Anti-Cyclical Policies in Relation to Foreign Trade Patterns and Tariffs (An Historical Approach). *Econ. Int.*, May 1969, *22*(2), pp. 225–44.

Weinberg, Edgar. Reducing Skill Shortages in Construction. *Mon. Lab. Rev.*, February 1969, *92*(2), pp. 3–9.

Weinschenck, G.; Henrichsmeyer, W. and Aldinger, F. The Theory of Spatial Equilibrium and Optimal Location in Agriculture: A Survey. *Rev. Marketing Agr. Econ.*, March 1969, *37*(1), pp. 3–70.

Weintraub, Robert. The Time Deposit-Money Supply Controversy. **In** *Brunner, K., ed.*, 1969, pp. 300–312.

Weinwurm, Ernest H. Discussion of Eugene L. Grant's "Tax Depreciation Restudied." *Eng. Econ.*, July–August 1969, *14*(4), pp. 237–38.

Weisbrod, Burton A. Benefits of Manpower Programs: Theoretical and Methodological Issues. **In** *Somers, G. G. and Wood, W. D., eds.*, 1969, pp. 3–15.

______ Collective Action and the Distribution of Income: A Conceptual Approach. **In** *The Analysis and Evaluation of Public Expenditures: The PPB System, Vol. 1, JECP,* 1969, pp. 177–97.

______ **and Hansen, W. Lee.** The Distribution of Costs and Direct Benefits of Public Higher Education: The Case of California. *J. Human Res.*, Spring 1969, *4*(2), pp. 176–91.

______ **and Hansen, W. Lee.** The Search for Equity in the Provision and Finance of Higher Education. **In** *the Economics and Financing of Higher Education in the United States, JECP,* 1969, pp. 107–23.

Weisenborn, David E. Allocation of Florida Orange Production among Alternative Product Forms and Market Sectors. *Amer. J. Agr. Econ.*, December 1969, *51*(5), pp. 1134–37.

Weiss, Jeffrey H. and Rivlin, Alice M. Social Goals and Federal Support of Higher Education—The Implications of Various Strategies. **In** *the Economics and Financing of Higher Education in the United States, JECP,* 1969, pp. 543–55.

Weiss, Leonard W. Advertising, Profits, and Corporate Taxes. *Rev. Econ. Statist.*, November 1969, *51*(4), pp. 421–30.

______ Conglomerate Mergers and Public Policy. **In** *Garoian, L., ed.*, 1969, pp. 88–95.

______ **and Kelley, Allen C.** Markov Processes and Economic Analysis: The Case of Migration. *Econometrica*, April 1969, *37*(2), pp. 280–97.

Weiss, Roger W. Mishan on Progress: A Review Note. *J. Polit. Econ.*, January/February 1969, *77* (1), pp. 138–40.

Weiss, Steven J. Bank Holding Companies and Public Policy. *New Eng. Econ. Rev.*, January/February 1969, pp. 3–29.

——— Commercial Bank Price Competition: The Case of "Free" Checking Accounts. *New Eng. Econ. Rev.*, September/October 1969, pp. 3–22.

——— Effects of Regulation, Branching, and Mergers on Banking Structure and Performance: Comment. *Southern Econ. J.*, October 1969, *36*(2), pp. 202–04.

——— Factors Affecting the Government Revenue Share in Less Developed Countries. *Soc. Econ. Stud.*, December 1969, *18*(4), pp. 348–64.

Weiss, Thomas J. and Gallman, Robert E. The Service Industries in the Nineteenth Century. **In** *Fuchs, V. R., ed.*, 1969, pp. 287–352.

——— The Service Industries in the Nineteenth Century: Reply. **In** *Fuchs, V. R., ed.*, 1969, pp. 372–81.

Weisskopf, Walter A. Mishan on Progress: A Rejoinder. *J. Polit. Econ.*, November/December 1969, *77*(6), pp. 1036–39.

Weitenberg, Johannes. The Incidence of Social Security Taxes. *Public Finance*, 1969, *24*(2), pp. 193–208.

von Weizsäcker, Carl Christian. Forschungsinvestitionen und makroökonomische Modelle—Ein wirtschaftstheoretisches Dilemma? (With English summary.) *Kyklos*, 1969, *22*(3), pp. 454–66.

Welch, Finis. Linear Synthesis of Skill Distribution. *J. Human Res.*, Summer 1969, *4*(3), pp. 311–27.

Welch, John M. Education for Institutional Food Service—On Wheels. *Amer. J. Agr. Econ.*, December 1969, *51*(5), pp. 1229–32.

Welch, Ronald B. Property Taxation: Policy Potentials and Probabilities. **In** *Lynn, A. D., Jr., ed.*, 1969, pp. 203–14.

Welden, William C. Milk Production and Utilization in the East. *Amer. J. Agr. Econ.*, November 1969, *51*(4), pp. 964–66.

Weller, Oren H. Touch-Tone Attendance and Labor Reporting. *Manage. Account.*, August 1969, *51* (2), pp. 27–28, 32.

Weller, Robert H. Role Conflict and Fertility. *Soc. Econ. Stud.*, September 1969, *18*(3), pp. 263–72.

Wellington, Donald. The Case of the Superfluous Railroads: A Look at Changing Transportation Patterns. *Econ. Bus. Bull.*, Fall 1969, *22*(1), pp. 33–38.

Wellington, Harry H. and Winter, Ralph K., Jr. The Limits of Collective Bargaining in Public Employment. *Yale Law J.*, June 1969, *78*(7), pp. 1107–27.

Wells, J. M. and Bates, W. R. Changes in Farm Business Organisation in Australia. *Quart. Rev. Agr. Econ.*, April 1969, *22*(2), pp. 53–65.

——— A Note on Some Implications of Family Partnership Formation for Farm Income Comparisons. *Quart. Rev. Agr. Econ.*, July 1969, *22*(3), pp. 140–46.

Wells, Louis T., Jr. Test of a Product Cycle Model of International Trade: U.S. Exports of Consumer Durables. *Quart. J. Econ.*, February 1969, *83*(1), pp. 152–62.

Wells, Oris V. Some Problems of Agricultural Development. *Amer. J. Agr. Econ.*, December 1969, *51* (5), pp. 1037–45.

Wells, Sidney. Paesi in sviluppo e commercio internazionale. (The Developing Countries, GATT and UNCTAD. With English summary.) *Mondo Aperto*, June–August 1969, *23*(3–4), pp. 189–204.

Welsh, Arthur L. and Fels, Rendigs. Performance on the New Test of Understanding in College Economics. *Amer. Econ. Rev.*, May 1969, *59*(2), pp. 224–29.

Wemelsfelder, J. The Theory of International Trade: Comment. **In** *Samuelson, P. A., ed.*, 1969, pp. 73–78.

Wendt, Paul F. The Determination of National Housing Policies. *Land Econ.*, August 1969, *45*(3), pp. 323–32.

Werner, Robert L. and Hill, John D. Corporate Expansion and the Law. **In** *Harvey, J. L. and Newgarden, A., eds.*, 1969, pp. 49–61.

Wert, James E. and Fredman, Albert J. Secondary Distributions of American Stock Exchange Securities. *Marquette Bus. Rev.*, Fall 1969, *13*(3), pp. 137–41.

Wertz, Kenneth; Wonnacott, Thomas H. and Naylor, Thomas H. Spectral Analysis of Data Generated by Simulation Experiments with Econometric Models. *Econometrica*, April 1969, *37*(2), pp. 333–52.

Wertz, Kenneth L. and Davis, Otto A. The Consistency of the Assessment of Property: Some Empirical Results and Managerial Suggestions. *Appl. Econ.*, May 1969, *1*(2), pp. 151–57.

Wesolowski, Zdzislaw P. An Inquiry into the Administration and Utilization of the Webb-Pomerene Act. *Marquette Bus. Rev.*, Winter 1969, *13* (4), pp. 174–88.

——— The Role of Marketing in a Soviet Type Economy. *Marquette Bus. Rev.*, Spring 1969, *13*(1), pp. 15–21.

Wessel, Robert H. What Is Producer's Surplus?—Comment. *Amer. Econ. Rev.*, Part I, September 1969, *59*(4), pp. 634–35.

West, David A. and Davids, Lewis E. Limited Market for Bank Data Processing—For the Medical and Dental Professions. *Univ. Missouri Bus. Govt. Rev.*, September–October 1969, *10*(5), pp. 11–16.

West, E. G. The Political Economy of Alienation: Karl Marx and Adam Smith. *Oxford Econ. Pap.*, March 1969, *21*(1), pp. 1–23.

——— Regional Planning: Fact and Fallacy. **In** *Task Force on Economic Growth and Opportunity*, 1969, pp. 249–68.

——— Welfare Economics and Emigration Taxes. *Southern Econ. J.*, July 1969, *36*(1), pp. 52–59.

West, Jude P. The Role of Public Officials and Administrators: Introduction. **In** *Sinicropi, A. V. and Gilroy, T. P., eds.*, 1969, pp. 45–46.

——— **and Sheriff, Don R.** The Changing Motivational Patterns of Professional Personnel. **In** *Gilroy, T. P., ed.*, 1969, pp. 9–17.

West, Richard R. The "Net Interest Cost" Method of Issuing Tax Exempt Bonds: Is It Rational?—A Reply to Professor Walker. *Public Finance*, 1969, *24*(4), pp. 627–30.

West, W. A. Planning. **In** *Ling, A. G., et al.*, 1969, pp. 38–42.

Westerman, P. A. Changes in the World Wheat Situation and the 1967 International Grains Arrangement. *Quart. Rev. Agr. Econ.*, January 1969, *22*(1), pp. 20–34.

Westoff, Charles F. and Ryder, Norman B. Recent Trends in Attitudes Toward Fertility Control and in the Practice of Contraception in the United States. **In** *Behrman, S. J.; Corsa, L., Jr. and Freedman, R., eds.,* 1969, pp. 388–412.

Weston, J. Fred. The Effects of Leverage and Corporate Taxes on the Shareholders of Regulated Utilities: Comment. **In** *Trebing, H. M. and Howard, R. H., eds.,* 1969, pp. 117–25.

______ Structure, Performance, and Behavior. **In** *Weston, J. F. and Peltzman, S., eds.,* 1969, pp. 67–78.

______ Summary of Discussions on Conglomerate Mergers. **In** *Weston, J. F. and Peltzman, S., eds.,* 1969, pp. 219–24.

______ **and Peltzman, Sam.** Issues in Public Policy Toward Mergers. **In** *Weston, J. F. and Peltzman, S., eds.,* 1969, pp. 3–9.

______ **and Peltzman, Sam.** Unresolved Issues and an Agenda for Future Research. **In** *Weston, J. F. and Peltzman, S., eds.,* 1969, pp. 227–31.

Westphal, Larry E. Multisectoral Project Analysis Employing Mixed Integer Programming. **In** *Adelman, I., ed.,* 1969, pp. 145–83.

______ **and Chenery, Hollis B.** Economies of Scale and Investment over Time. **In** *Margolis, J. and Guitton, H., eds.,* 1969, pp. 359–87.

van de Wetering, Hylke. Agricultural Planning: The Peruvian Experience. **In** *Thorbecke, E., ed.,* 1969, pp. 387–446.

Wetzel, James R. and Johnston, Denis F. Effect of the Census Undercount on Labor Force Estimates. *Mon. Lab. Rev.,* March 1969, *92*(3), pp. 3–13.

Weygandt, Jerry J. and Imdieke, Leroy F. Classification of Convertible Debt. *Accounting Rev.,* October 1969, *44*(4), pp. 798–805.

Weymar, Caroline S. and Goeke, Joseph R. Barriers to Hiring the Blacks. *Harvard Bus. Rev.,* September–October 1969, *47*(5), pp. 144–52.

Whalen, Edward L. On the Transactions Demand for Cash: Reply. *J. Finance,* December 1969, *24* (5), pp. 950–53.

Whan, R. B. and Richardson, R. A. A Simulated Study of an Auction Market. *Australian J. Agr. Econ.,* December 1969, *13*(2), pp. 91–100.

______ **and Willett, Helen E.** Price Variation within Wool Auction Sales. *Quart. Rev. Agr. Econ.,* April 1969, *22*(2), pp. 66–81.

Wharton, Clifton R., Jr. The Green Revolution: Cornucopia or Pandora's Box? *Foreign Aff.,* April 1969, *47*(3), pp. 464–76.

Wheatcroft, G. S. A. Inequity in Britain's Tax Structure. *Lloyds Bank Rev.,* July 1969, (93), pp. 11–26.

Wheatley, John J. and Randall, Gary B. Industrial Specialization in Washington. *Univ. Wash. Bus. Rev.,* Summer 1969, *28*(4), pp. 25–35.

Wheeler, James O. Some Effects of Occupational Status on Work Trips. *J. Reg. Sci.,* April 1969, *9*(1), pp. 69–77.

Whinston, Andrew; Colantoni, Claude S. and Manes, Rene P. Programming, Profit Rates and Pricing Decisions. *Accounting Rev.,* July 1969, *44*(3), pp. 467–81.

______ **and van De Panne, C.** The Symmetric Formulation of the Simplex Method for Quadratic Programming. *Econometrica,* July 1969, *37*(3), pp. 507–27.

______**; Graves, G. W. and Hatfield, G. B.** Water Pollution Control Using By-Pass Piping. *Water Resources Res.,* February 1969, *5*(1), pp. 13–47.

Whipple, William, Jr. Optimizing Investment in Flood Control and Floodplain Zoning. *Water Resources Res.,* August 1969, *5*(4), pp. 761–66.

______ Utility as a Surrogate for Value in Water Resources Analysis. *Eng. Econ.,* April–May 1969, *14* (3), pp. 159–67.

White, James H. The Supply Function in Agriculture Revisited: Discussion. *Amer. Econ. Rev.,* May 1969, *59*(2), pp. 187–88.

White, Kerr. Improved Medical Care Statistics and the Health Service System. **In** *Health Care in America, Pt. 1, SCH,* 1969, pp. 352–59.

______ Organization and Delivery of Personal Health Services. **In** *Health Care in America, Pt. 1, SCH,* 1969, pp. 203–36.

______ Statement. **In** *Health Care in America, Pt. 1, SCH,* 1969, pp. 181–202.

White, Lawrence J. Gains from Trade and Income Distribution: Some New Geometric Tools. *Rivista Int. Sci. Econ. Com.,* September 1969, *16*(9), pp. 837–58.

White, Lynn T., Jr. The Medieval Roots of Modern Technology and Science. **In** *Scoville, W. C. and La Force, J. C., eds., Vol. I,* 1969, pp. 60–75.

White, Rudolph A. Measuring Unemployment and Subemployment in the Mississippi Delta. *Mon. Lab. Rev.,* April 1969, *92*(4), pp. 17–23.

White, Sheila C. Work Stoppages of Government Employees. *Mon. Lab. Rev.,* December 1969, *92* (12), pp. 29–34.

White, T. Kelley and Boehlje, Michael D. A Production-Investment Decision Model of Farm Firm Growth. *Amer. J. Agr. Econ.,* August 1969, *51*(3), pp. 546–63.

White, W. James. Conventional Wisdom and Agricultural Policy. *Can. J. Agr. Econ.,* November 1969, *17*(3), pp. 175–80.

______ Farm Income Policy in Ontario: Review and Analysis. *Can. J. Agr. Econ.,* February 1969, *17*(1), pp. 132–40.

White, William H. How Useful Are Econometric Models? *Finance Develop.,* March 1969, *6*(1), pp. 23–29.

______ Lags between Actual and Reported Fixed Investment. *Int. Monet. Fund Staff Pap.,* July 1969, *16*(2), pp. 240–66.

______ The Usefulness of Econometric Models for Policymakers. *Finance Develop.,* September 1969, *6*(3), pp. 8–13.

Whitehead, Laurence. Basic Data in Poor Countries: The Bolivian Case. *Bull. Oxford Univ. Inst. Econ. Statist.,* August 1969, *31*(3), pp. 205–27.

Whitin, T. M. Optimal Plant under Conditions of Risk. *J. Ind. Econ.,* April 1969, *17*(2), pp. 81–85.

Whitman, Marina v. N. Economic Openness and International Financial Flows. *J. Money, Credit, Banking,* November 1969, *1*(4), pp. 727–49.

Whitmore, G. A. The Mathematical Structure of Investor Preferences. **In** *Association of Canadian Schools of Business,* 1969, pp. 196–218.

Whitney, Simon N. Ethical Drugs: Comments on

Means of Payments. *Rev. Econ. Statist.*, August 1969, *51*(3), pp. 373–74.

_____ The Influence of the Trade Balance and Export Financing on International Short-Term Capital Movements: A Theoretical Analysis. *Kyklos*, 1969, *22*(2), pp. 314–27.

_____ **and Officer, Lawrence H.** Reserve-Asset Preferences and the Confidence Problem in the Crisis Zone. *Quart. J. Econ.*, November 1969, *83*(4), pp. 688–95.

_____ **and Sherman, Roger.** Regional Development, Externalities and Tax-Subsidy Combinations. *Nat. Tax J.*, June 1969, *22*(2), pp. 291–93.

_____ **and Forte, Francesco.** Interest Rate Policy and External Balance. *Quart. J. Econ.*, May 1969, *83*(2), pp. 242–62.

Williams, Albert P., Jr. and Rowen, Henry S. Policy Analysis in International Affairs. **In** *The Analysis and Evaluation of Public Expenditures: The PPB System, Vol. 3, JECP*, 1969, pp. 970–1002.

Williams, Bill and Hall, Mildred. The Retailers, the Ghetto, and the Government. **In** *Sturdivant, F. D., ed.*, 1969, pp. 210–20.

Williams, C. Arthur, Jr. Insurer Views on Property and Liability Insurance Rate Regulation. *J. Risk Ins.*, June 1969, *36*(2), pp. 217–36.

Williams, D. M. Liverpool Merchants and the Cotton Trade 1820–1850. **In** *Harris, J. R., ed.*, 1969, pp. 182–211.

Williams, Donald B. Production Economics, Farm Management, and Extension. *Amer. J. Agr. Econ.*, February 1969, *51*(1), pp. 57–70.

Williams, Edward E. Selecting the Appropriate Form of Business Organization: A Decision Model. *Eng. Econ.*, July–August 1969, *14*(4), pp. 221–27.

Williams, F. A. Agricultural Price Policy in the Context of Economic Development: Discussion. *Amer. J. Agr. Econ.*, December 1969, *51*(5), pp. 1420–23.

Williams, G. D. V. Weather and Prairie Wheat Production. *Can. J. Agr. Econ.*, February 1969, *17*(1), pp. 99–109.

Williams, J. Allen, Jr. The Effects of Urban Renewal upon a Black Community: Evaluation and Recommendations. *Soc. Sci. Quart.*, December 1969, *50*(3), pp. 703–12.

Williams, L. J. and Morris, J. H. The South Wales Sliding Scale. **In** *Minchinton, W. E., ed.*, 1969, pp. 218–31.

Williams, R. J. and Baker, J. R. A Comparison of Response Surface and Factorial Designs in Agricultural Research: Reply. *Rev. Marketing Agr. Econ.*, June 1969, *37*(2), pp. 132–33.

Williams, Robert M. Statement. **In** *The 1969 Economic Report of the President, Pt. 2, JECH*, 1969, pp. 500–504.

Williams, Roger. Administrative Modernization in British Government. *Int. Soc. Sci. J.*, 1969, *21*(1), pp. 100–15.

Williams, T. David. Commodity Distribution in Malawi: A Case Study. **In** *Stewart, I. G., ed.*, 1969, pp. 83–103.

Williams, William Appleman. The Large Corporation and American Foreign Policy. **In** *Horowitz, D., ed.*, 1969, pp. 71–104.

Williamson, Harold F., Jr. and Mohring, Herbert. Scale and "Industrial Reorganisation" Economies of Transport Improvements. *J. Transp. Econ. Policy*, September 1969, *3*(3), pp. 251–71.

Williamson, Jeffrey G. Dimensions of Postwar Philippine Economic Progress. *Quart. J. Econ.*, February 1969, *83*(1), pp. 93–109.

_____ Income Growth and Savings. *Philippine Econ. J.*, First Semester 1969, *8*(1), pp. 54–74.

Williamson, Oliver E. Allocative Efficiency and the Limits of Antitrust. *Amer. Econ. Rev.*, May 1969, *59*(2), pp. 105–18.

_____ Corporate Control and the Theory of the Firm. **In** *Manne, H. G., ed.*, 1969, pp. 281–336.

_____ Economies as an Antitrust Defense: Reply. *Amer. Econ. Rev.*, December 1969, *59*(5), pp. 954–59.

Willis, E. S. and Kaimer, Fred R. Employee Benefit Options. **In** *Somers, G. G., ed. (II)*, 1969, pp. 317–25.

Willis, J. F.; Minden, A. J. and Snyder, James C. Monte Carlo Simulation of Management Systems. *Can. J. Agr. Econ.*, February 1969, *17*(1), pp. 42–49.

Willis, R. J. and Hawthorne, E. P. Forecasting the Market for Certain Machine Tools, 1974–1999. **In** *Arnfield, R. V., ed.*, 1969, pp. 241–52.

Wills, Gordon. Marketing. **In** *Kempner, T., ed.*, 1969, pp. 65–70.

Wilson, A. G. Developments of Some Elementary Residential Location Models. *J. Reg. Sci.*, December 1969, *9*(3), pp. 377–85.

_____ The Use of Entropy Maximising Models: In the Theory of Trip Distribution, Mode Split and Route Split. *J. Transp. Econ. Policy*, January 1969, *3*(1), pp. 108–26.

_____ **and Wood, A. W.** Regional Livestock Production and Feed Freight Assistance. *Can. J. Agr. Econ.*, February 1969, *17*(1), pp. 77–90.

Wilson, Aubrey. Industrial Marketing Research in Britain. *J. Marketing Res.*, February 1969, *6*(1), pp. 15–27.

Wilson, Charles. Canon Demant's Economic History. **In** *Wilson, C.*, 1969, pp. 128–39.

_____ Economics and Politics in the Seventeenth Century. **In** *Wilson, C.*, 1969, pp. 1–21.

_____ The Entrepreneur in the Industrial Revolution in Britain. **In** *Wilson, C.*, 1969, pp. 156–77.

_____ Government Policy and Private Interest in Modern English History. **In** *Wilson, C.*, 1969, pp. 140–55.

_____ History in Special and in General. **In** *Wilson, C.*, 1969, pp. 201–15.

_____ The Other Face of Mercantilism. **In** *Wilson, C.*, 1969, pp. 73–93.

_____ The Other Face of Mercantilism. **In** *Coleman, D. C., ed.*, 1969, pp. 118–39.

_____ Taxation and the Decline of Empires, an Unfashionable Theme. **In** *Wilson, C.*, 1969, pp. 114–27.

Wilson, Cyrus C. and Greenidge, Charles D. Classification Merchandising: An Overlooked Opportunity for Increasing Merchandising Profitability. *Calif. Manage. Rev.*, Fall 1969, *12*(1), pp. 53–61.

Wilson, George W. Transportation and Price Stability. *Amer. Econ. Rev.*, May 1969, *59*(2), pp. 261–69.

Wilson, J. S. G. Building the Financial System of a Developing Country. *Lloyds Bank Rev.*, July 1969, (93), pp. 36–48.

——— Regulation and Control of the United Kingdom Banking and Financial Structure. *Banca Naz. Lavoro Quart. Rev.*, June 1969, (89), pp. 128–45.

Wilson, James A. Motivation underlying the Brain Drain. **In** *Baier, K. and Rescher, N., eds.*, 1969, pp. 431–52.

Wilson, Robert. An Axiomatic Model of Logrolling. *Amer. Econ. Rev.*, June 1969, *59*(3), pp. 331–41.

Wilson, Ruth V. Public Treasurers' Money. **In** *Jessup, P. F.*, 1969, pp. 123–29.

Wilson, T.; Sinha, R. P. and Castree, J. R. The Income Terms of Trade of Developed and Developing Countries. *Econ. J.*, December 1969, *79*(316), pp. 813–32.

Wilson, Thomas A. and Comanor, William S. Advertising and the Advantages of Size. *Amer. Econ. Rev.*, May 1969, *59*(2), pp. 87–98.

Wimmer, Larry. Statement. **In** *Highway Beautification, SCH*, 1969, pp. 23–27.

Wimsatt, Genevieve B. 1969 Business Investment Programs and Sales—Strong Advances Expected. *Surv. Curr. Bus.*, March 1969, *49*(3), pp. 17–22.

Wind, Yoram and Frank, Ronald E. Interproduct Household Loyalty to Brands. *J. Marketing Res.*, November 1969, *6*(4), pp. 434–35.

Windal, Floyd W. Dynamic Programming: An Introduction. *Manage. Account.*, July 1969, *51*(1), pp. 47–49.

Winfield, Richard A. The Rising Cost of Mergers. **In** *Harvey, J. L. and Newgarden, A., eds.*, 1969, pp. 133–45.

Winger, Alan R. Regional Growth Disparities and the Mortgage Market. *J. Finance*, September 1969, *24*(4), pp. 659–62.

——— Trade-Offs in Housing. *Land Econ.*, November 1969, *45*(4), pp. 413–17.

van Winkel, E. G. F. Extrapolationen einer Zeitreihe durch exponentiell abnehmende Gewichtung. (Extrapolation of Time Series by Exponential Smoothing. With English summary.) *Ifo-Studien*, 1969, *15*(1/2), pp. 1–18.

Winn, Edward L., Jr. and Bacon, Peter W. The Impact of Forced Conversion on Stock Prices. *J. Finance*, December 1969, *24*(5), pp. 871–74.

Winokur, Herbert S., Jr. and Orcutt, Guy H. First Order Autoregression: Inference, Estimation, and Prediction. *Econometrica*, January 1969, *37* (1), pp. 1–14.

Winsberg, Morton D. Jewish Agricultural Colonization in Entre Rios, Argentina, III: Economic Problems of Townsmen Resettled on the Land. *Amer. J. Econ. Soc.*, April 1969, *28*(2), pp. 179–91.

Winston, Clement. Trade and Services Outlays Related to Income. **In** *Alexis, M.; Holloway, R. J. and Hancock, R. S., eds.*, 1969, pp. 33–38.

Winter, Ralph K., Jr. and Wellington, Harry H. The Limits of Collective Bargaining in Public Employment. *Yale Law J.*, June 1969, *78*(7), pp. 1107–27.

Winter, Sidney G., Jr. A Simple Remark on the Second Optimality Theorem of Welfare Economics. *J. Econ. Theory*, June 1969, *1*(1), pp. 99–103.

Winters, Stanley B. Trends in Labor Historiography in Czechoslovakia. *Labor Hist.*, Fall 1969, *10*(4), pp. 602–29.

Wipf, Larry J. and Bawden, D. Lee. Reliability of Supply Equations Derived from Production Functions. *Amer. J. Agr. Econ.*, February 1969, *51* (1), pp. 170–78.

Wippern, Ronald F. and Bower, Richard S. Risk-Return Measurement in Portfolio Selection and Performance Appraisal Models: Progress Report. *J. Financial Quant. Anal.*, December 1969, *4*(4), pp. 417–47.

Wise, John and Yotopoulos, Pan A. The Empirical Content of Economic Rationality: A Test for a Less Developed Economy. *J. Polit. Econ.*, November/December 1969, *77*(6), pp. 976–1004.

——— Epilegomena on Traditional Behavior Models. *Amer. J. Agr. Econ.*, November 1969, *51*(4), pp. 928–39.

——— On Testing Competing Hypotheses: Economic Rationality versus Traditional Behavior: Rejoinder. *Amer. J. Agr. Econ.*, February 1969, *51* (1), pp. 209–10.

——— On Testing Competing Hypotheses: Economic Rationality versus Traditional Behavior —A Further Development. *Amer. J. Agr. Econ.*, February 1969, *51*(1), pp. 203–08.

Wiseman, Jack and Peacock, Alan T. Principles of Educational Finance in Developed Countries. **In** *Blaug, M., ed.*, 1969, pp. 343–59.

——— **and Rees, Graham.** London's Commodity Markets. *Lloyds Bank Rev.*, January 1969, (91), pp. 22–45.

Witherell, William H. A Comparison of the Determinants of Wool Production in the Six Leading Producing Countries: 1949–1965. *Amer. J. Agr. Econ.*, February 1969, *51*(1), pp. 138–58.

——— **and Lynch, P. J.** The Carter Commission and the Saving Behavior of Canadian Corporations. *Nat. Tax J.*, March 1969, *22*(1), pp. 57–65.

Witney, Fred. The Era of Sophisticated Labor Relations. **In** *Wortman, M. S., Jr.*, 1969, pp. 442–48.

——— The Era of Sophisticated Labor Relations. **In** *Starleaf, D. R., ed.*, 1969, pp. 128–34.

Witt, Robert E. Informal Social Group Influence on Consumer Brand Choice. *J. Marketing Res.*, November 1969, *6*(4), pp. 473–76.

Witte, Eberhard. Organization of Management Decision-Making Processes: A Research Report. *Ger. Econ. Rev.*, 1969, *7*(3), pp. 256–62.

Wittmann, Walter. Die Staatsausgaben in der makroökonomischen Produktionsfunktion. (With English summary.) *Kyklos*, 1969, *22*(2), pp. 297–313.

Wojdak, Joseph F. A Theoretical Foundation for Leases and Other Executory Contracts. *Accounting Rev.*, July 1969, *44*(3), pp. 562–70.

Wold, Herman O. E. P. Mackeprangs fråga om val av regression. Ett nyckelproblem i ekonometrins utveckling. (E. P. Mackeprang's Question about the Choice of Regression: A Key Problem in the

Evolution of Econometrics. With English summary.) *Liiketaloudellinen Aikak.*, 1969, *18*(1), pp. 79–89.

_____ Econometrics as Pioneering in Nonexperimental Model Building. *Econometrica,* July 1969, *37*(3), pp. 369–81.

Wolf, Charles R. A Model for Selecting Commercial Bank Government Security Portfolios. *Rev. Econ. Statist.*, February 1969, *51*(1), pp. 40–52.

Wolf, E. Cartel and Monopoly Legislation: Its Application in the European Economic Community. **In** *Economic Concentration, Pt. 7A, SCH,* 1969, pp. 3944–56.

Wolf, Eleanor P. Community Control of Schools as an Ideology and Social Mechanism. *Soc. Sci. Quart.*, December 1969, *50*(3), pp. 713–22.

Wolf, Laurence G. The Metropolitan Tidal Wave in Ohio, 1900–2000. *Econ. Geogr.*, April 1969, *45*(2), pp. 133–54.

Wolf, S. K. Concepts and Measurement of Productivity in Developing Economies. **In** *Yesufu, T. M., ed.*, 1969, pp. 279–99.

Wolfe, Arthur C. Trends in Labor Union Voting Behavior, 1948–1968. *Ind. Relat.*, October 1969, *9*(1), pp. 1–10.

Wolfe, J. N. The Contribution of Demography to Physical and Spatial Planning: Comment. **In** *Bechhofer, F., ed.*, 1969, pp. 127–30.

_____ Problems of Federal Financial Arrangements. **In** *Wolfe, J. N., ed.*, 1969, pp. 92–107.

Wolff, Carole E. and Landis, Judson R. Dr. Irene Hickman and Tax Reform in Sacramento County, Calif. *Amer. J. Econ. Soc.*, October 1969, *28*(4), pp. 409–21.

de Wolff, Pieter. Experience with Econometric Analysis of the U.S. "Konjunktur" Position: Comment. **In** *Bronfenbrenner, M., ed.*, 1969, pp. 389–92.

Wolfson, Dirk J. and Van de Ven, Petrus J. Problems of Budget Analysis and Treasury Management in French-Speaking Africa. *Int. Monet. Fund Staff Pap.*, March 1969, *16*(1), pp. 140–58.

Woll, Artur. Die Theorie der Geldnachfrage: Analytische Ansätze und statische Ergebnisse für die Bundesrepublik Deutschland. (With English summary.) *Z. ges. Staatswiss.*, January 1969, *125*(1), pp. 56–81.

Wollett, Donald H. The Coming Revolution in Public School Management. *Mich. Law Rev.*, March 1969, *67*(5), pp. 1017–32.

Wolters, Raymond. Section 7a and the Black Worker. *Labor Hist.*, Summer 1969, *10*(3), pp. 459–74.

Wonnacott, Thomas H.; Naylor, Thomas H. and Wertz, Kenneth. Spectral Analysis of Data Generated by Simulation Experiments with Econometric Models. *Econometrica,* April 1969, *37*(2), pp. 333–52.

Wood, A. W. and Wilson, A. G. Regional Livestock Production and Feed Freight Assistance. *Can. J. Agr. Econ.*, February 1969, *17*(1), pp. 77–90.

Wood, Douglas. The Water Supply System up to A.D. 2001. *J. Ind. Econ.*, November 1969, *18*(1), pp. 64–75.

Wood, G. Donald, Jr. "Price" vs. "Tariff" Elasticities in International Trade: Comment. *Amer. Econ. Rev.*, March 1969, *59*(1), pp. 198–200.

Wood, Harold A. The Regional Implication of Economic Integration. **In** *Hilton, R., ed.*, 1969, pp. 141–48.

Wood, John H. Expectations and the Demand for Bonds. *Amer. Econ. Rev.*, Part I, September 1969, *59*(4), pp. 522–30.

Wood, Marshall and Labovitz, David E. The Korean Sectoral Model: Appendix. **In** *Adelman, I., ed.*, 1969, pp. 135–43.

Wood, Robert C. Statement. **In** *Public Facility Requirements over the Next Decade, JECH,* 1969, pp. 27–35.

Woodhall, Maureen and Blaug, Mark. Variations in Costs and Productivity of British Primary and Secondary Education. **In** *[Edding, Friedrich],* 1969, pp. 69–85.

Woodley, W. John R. Some Institutional Aspects of Exchange Markets in the Less-Developed Countries. **In** *Aliber, R. Z., ed.*, 1969, pp. 177–93.

Woodruff, A. M. Assessment Standards: Highest and Best Use as a Basis for Land Appraisal and Assessment. **In** *Lynn, A. D., Jr., ed.*, 1969, pp. 167–83.

_____ **and Ecker-Racz, L. L.** Property Taxes and Land-Use Patterns in Australia and New Zealand. **In** *Becker, A. P., ed.*, 1969, pp. 147–86.

Woodruff, Helga and Woodruff, William. The Role of the United States in Latin American Economic Integration. **In** *Hilton, R., ed.*, 1969, pp. 149–56.

Woodruff, William and Woodruff, Helga. The Role of the United States in Latin American Economic Integration. **In** *Hilton, R., ed.*, 1969, pp. 149–56.

Woods, M. J.; McKenzie, C. J. and Philpot, B. P. Price Formation in the Raw Wool Market. *Econ. Rec.*, September 1969, *45*(111), pp. 386–98.

Woods, W. Fred. A Basic Framework for Policy Education: Discussion. *Amer. J. Agr. Econ.*, December 1969, *51*(5), pp. 1367–68.

Woodside, Arch G. Analysis of General System Theory. *Marquette Bus. Rev.*, Summer 1969, *13*(2), pp. 45–64.

Woodward, V. H. and Brown, A. J. Regional Social Accounts for the United Kingdom. *Rev. Income Wealth,* December 1969, *15*(4), pp. 335–47.

Woodworth, Laurence N. Tax Simplification and the Tax Reform Act of 1969. *Law Contemp. Probl.*, Autumn 1969, *34*(4), pp. 711–25.

Woolf, Donald A. Labor Problems in the Post Office. *Ind. Relat.*, October 1969, *9*(1), pp. 27–35.

Woolf, S. J. and Jones, E. L. Introduction: The Historical Role of Agrarian Change in Economic Development. **In** *Jones, E. L. and Woolf, S. J., eds.*, 1969, pp. 1–21.

Woolwine, Phil C. The South Pacific as a Source of Timber. *Oregon Bus. Rev.*, August 1969, *28*(8), pp. 1–5.

Worcester, Dean A., Jr. Innovations in the Calculation of Welfare Loss to Monopoly. *Western Econ. J.*, September 1969, *7*(3), pp. 234–43.

_____ Optimal Pricing Policy for Public Utilities as Optimal Taxation: Electric Power and Water. *Philippine Econ. J.*, Second Semester 1969, *8*(2), pp. 145–65.

_____ Pecuniary and Technological Externality,

Factor Rents, and Social Costs. *Amer. Econ. Rev.*, December 1969, *59*(5), pp. 873–85.

Woroniak, Alexander. Industrial Concentration in Eastern Europe: The Search for Optimum Size and Efficiency. **In** *Salin, E.; Stohler, J. and Pawlowsky, P.*, 1969, pp. 265–84.

——— **and Spencer, Daniel L.** Valuing Transfer of Military-Acquired Skills to Civilian Employment. *Kyklos*, 1969, *22*(3), pp. 467–92.

Worswick, G. D. N. Fiscal Policy and Stabilization in Britain. *J. Money, Credit, Banking*, August 1969, *1*(3), pp. 474–95.

——— Postwar Business Cycles in the United Kingdom: Comment. **In** *Bronfenbrenner, M., ed.*, 1969, pp. 136–39.

Worthman, Paul B. Black Workers and Labor Unions in Birmingham, Alabama, 1897–1904. *Labor Hist.*, Summer 1969, *10*(3), pp. 375–407.

Wortman, Max S., Jr. Collective Bargaining Strategies and Tactics in the Federal Civil Service. **In** *Wortman, M. S., Jr.*, 1969, pp. 102–12.

——— National Policies and Programs for Human Resources Management. *Ohio State U. Bull. Bus. Res.*, December 1969, *44*(12), pp. 4–6.

Wortman, Sterling and Harrar, J. George. Expanding Food Production in Hungry Nations: The Promise, the Problems. **In** *Hardin, C. M., ed.*, 1969, pp. 89–135.

Worton, David A. The Service Industries in Canada, 1946–66. **In** *Fuchs, V. R., ed.*, 1969, pp. 237–82.

Wright, A. and Dent, J. B. The Application of Simulation Techniques to the Study of Grazing Systems. *Australian J. Agr. Econ.*, December 1969, *13*(2), pp. 144–53.

Wright, Albert W. Maintaining Balance in Financial Position. *Manage. Account.*, September 1969, *51*(3), pp. 14–16, 28.

Wright, Arthur W. Statement. **In** *Tax Reform Act of 1969, Testimony, Oct. 1, SCP*, 1969, pp. 347–68.

Wright, Colin. Estimating Permanent Income: A Note. *J. Polit. Econ.*, September/October 1969, *77*(5), pp. 845–50.

——— Saving and the Rate of Interest. **In** *Harberger, A. C. and Bailey, M. J., eds.*, 1969, pp. 275–300.

Wright, Deil S. The Politics and Economics of Intergovernmental Fiscal Relations: Federal Grants, Tax Credits, and Revenue Sharing. **In** *[White, Charles P.]*, 1969, pp. 63–87.

Wright, Frank K. Towards a General Theory of Depreciation. **In** *Parker, R. H. and Harcourt, G. C., eds.*, 1969, pp. 276–89.

Wright, J. C. G. Monopolistic Competition Theory. *Econ. Rec.*, June 1969, *45*(110), pp. 276–87.

——— 'Products' and Welfare. *Australian Econ. Pap.*, December 1969, *8*(13), pp. 134–53.

Wright, L. C. Some Fiscal Problems of Devolution in Scotland. **In** *Wolfe, J. N., ed.*, 1969, pp. 140–52.

Wright, Philip. Government Efforts to Facilitate Technical Transfer: The NASA Experience. **In** *Gruber, W. H. and Marquis, D. G., eds.*, 1969, pp. 238–51.

Wrightsman, Dwayne. Optimal Credit Terms for Accounts Receivable. *Quart. Rev. Econ. Bus.*, Summer 1969, *9*(2), pp. 59–66.

Wu, Chi-Yuen. Public Administration for National Development: An Analysis of the United Nations Public Administration Programme in the Past Two Decades and the Major Problems in the 1970s. *Int. Soc. Sci. J.*, 1969, *21*(1), pp. 116–34.

Wu, Hsiu-Kwang. Bank Examiner Criticisms, Bank Loan Defaults, and Bank Loan Quality. *J. Finance*, September 1969, *24*(4), pp. 697–705.

Wu, S. Y. A Multi-period Monopoly Model. *Tijdschr. Econ.*, 1969, *14*(4), pp. 497–518.

——— A Nonlinear Programming Production Model. *Western Econ. J.*, December 1969, *7*(4), pp. 319–33.

Wu, Ta-Yeh. Problems and Prospects of Economic Cooperation in Southeast Asia. **In** *Morgan, T. and Spoelstra, N., eds.*, 1969, pp. 15–36.

Wuchina, Stephen W. Program Control Network: A Tool for Month End Closing. *Manage. Account.*, July 1969, *51*(1), pp. 38–42.

Wueller, P. H. Concepts of Taxable Income: The German Contribution. **In** *Parker, R. H. and Harcourt, G. C., eds.*, 1969, pp. 141–60.

Wunderlich, Gene. A Concept of Property. *Agr. Econ. Res.*, January 1969, *21*(1), pp. 1–6.

——— The Organization of Agriculture: An Epilogue. *Amer. J. Agr. Econ.*, December 1969, *51*(5), pp. 1289–92.

Wurf, Jerry. The Use of Factfinding in Dispute Settlement. **In** *Walsh, R. E., ed.*, 1969, pp. 80–92.

Wyand, Robert R., II and Brandt, Harry. A Shift in Banking Philosophy? An Examination of Bank Investment Practices. **In** *Jessup, P. F.*, 1969, pp. 60–72.

Wynn, G. Richard and Jenny, Hans H. Expenditure Expectations for Private Colleges. **In** *the Economics and Financing of Higher Education in the United States, JECP*, 1969, pp. 440–64.

——— Short-Run Cost Variations in Institutions of Higher Learning. **In** *the Economics and Financing of Higher Education in the United States, JECP*, 1969, pp. 261–94.

Yaari, Menahem E. Some Remarks on Measures of Risk Aversion and on Their Uses. *J. Econ. Theory*, October 1969, *1*(3), pp. 315–29.

Yablonski, Steven K. and Scott, John C. Transnational Mergers and Joint Ventures Affecting American Exports. *Antitrust Bull.*, Spring 1969, *14*, pp. 1–36.

Yah, Lim Chong. West Malaysian External Trade, 1947–65. **In** *Morgan, T. and Spoelstra, N., eds.*, 1969, pp. 203–37.

Yamada, Hiroyuki and Ihara, Takeo. An Interindustrial Analysis of the Transportation Sector. *Kyoto Univ. Econ. Rev.*, October 1969, *39*(2), pp. 26–61.

Yamada, Saburō and Hayami, Yūjirō. Agricultural Productivity at the Beginning of Industrialization. **In** *Ohkawa, K.; Johnston, B. F. and Kaneda, H., eds.*, 1969, pp. 105–35.

Yamamoto, Hiromasa. A Note on Shorter Working Hours for Seamen. *Kobe Econ. Bus. Rev.*, 1969, *16*(1), pp. 39–45.

Yamamura, K. The Development of Anti-monopoly Policy in Japan: The Erosion of Japanese Antimonopoly Policy, 1947–1967. **In** *Economic Concentration, Pt. 7A, SCH*, 1969, pp. 4273–87.

Yamaoka, Ryoichi. The "Modernisation" of Agriculture at the Present Stage. *Kyoto Univ. Econ. Rev.*, April 1969, *39*(1), pp. 1–21.

Yamazawa, Ippei. Factor-Proportions Theory Reconsidered. *Hitotsubashi J. Econ.,* February 1969, *9*(2), pp. 43–60.

Yamey, B. S. and Stevens, R. B. The Justiciability of Restrictive Practices. **In** *Hunter, A., ed.,* 1969, pp. 183–201.

Ya-nan, Wang. The Marxist Population Theory and China's Population Problem. *Chinese Econ. Stud.,* Spring-Summer 1969, *2*(3–4), pp. 3–91.

Yance, Joseph V. Movement Time as a Cost in Airport Operations. *J. Transp. Econ. Policy,* January 1969, *3*(1), pp. 28–36.

______ Transportation and the Public Utilities: Discussion. *Amer. Econ. Rev.,* May 1969, *59*(2), pp. 274–76.

Yancey, William L. Intervention as a Strategy of Social Inquiry: An Exploratory Study with Unemployed Negro Men. *Soc. Sci. Quart.,* December 1969, *50*(3), pp. 582–88.

Yeager, Leland B. Fluctuating Exchange Rates in the Nineteenth Century: The Experiences of Austria and Russia. **In** *Mundell, R. A. and Swoboda, A. K., eds.,* 1969, pp. 61–89.

Yeh, M. H. and Lin, Leon. Technological Change in the Canadian Livestock Industry: An Input-Output Approach. *Can. J. Agr. Econ.,* July 1969, *17*(2), pp. 63–84.

Yeh, W. W.-G.; Hall, Warren A. and Tauxe, G. W. An Alternate Procedure for the Optimization of Operations for Planning with Multiple River, Multiple Purpose Systems. *Water Resources Res.,* December 1969, *5*(6), pp. 1367–72.

Yeh, Yeong-Her. A Note on the Marshall Condition: Reply. *Southern Econ. J.,* October 1969, *36*(2), pp. 215–16.

Yessian, Mark R. Statement. **In** *Usefulness of the Model Cities Program to the Elderly, Pt. 1, SCH,* 1969, pp. 78–82.

Yesufu, T. M. Forecasting Nigeria's Manpower Needs 1963–68: A Note on Methodology. **In** *Yesufu, T. M., ed.,* 1969, pp. 104–29.

______ Organization for Manpower Planning in Nigeria. **In** *Yesufu, T. M., ed.,* 1969, pp. 90–103.

Yeung, Patrick. Unifying Elements in the Theories of the Firm. *Quart. Rev. Econ. Bus.,* Winter 1969, *9*(4), pp. 21–28.

Yocum, James C. Recent Changes in Interstate and Interregional Population Flows. *Ohio State U. Bull. Bus. Res.,* May 1969, *44*(5), pp. 4–7.

Yohe, William P. and Karnosky, Denis S. Interest Rates and Price Level Changes, 1952–69. *Fed. Res. Bank St. Louis Rev.,* December 1969, *51*(12), pp. 18–38.

Yoingco, Angel Q. and Casem, Antonio O. Performance Budgeting in the Philippines. *Philippine Econ. J.,* Second Semester 1969, *8*(2), pp. 166–84.

Yoshihara, Hideki. A Note on the Behavioral Theory of Innovation. *Kobe Econ. Bus. Rev.,* 1969, *16*(1), pp. 55–61.

Yoshihara, Kunio. Demand Functions: An Application to the Japanese Expenditure Pattern. *Econometrica,* April 1969, *37*(2), pp. 257–74.

______ **and Forrest, Matthew D.** Japan's Dependence in Contrast with That of Six Other Nations. *Hitotsubashi J. Econ.,* June 1969, *10*(1), pp. 56–62.

Yossundara, Suparb and Huntrakoon, Yune. Some Salient Aspects of Thailand's Trade, 1955–64. **In** *Morgan, T. and Spoelstra, N., eds.,* 1969, pp. 127–50.

Yost, Larry and Foster, Phillips. A Simulation Study of Population, Education, and Income Growth in Uganda. *Amer. J. Agr. Econ.,* August 1969, *51*(3), pp. 576–91.

Yost, Robert C. and Childress, Robert L. An Investigation of the Determinants of Investment Expenditures in Large, Multiproduct Corporations. *Western Econ. J.,* June 1969, *7*(2), pp. 173–79.

Yotopoulos, Pan A. and Massell, Benton F. The Relationships between the Volume of Investment, Its Productivity and the Growth of the South American Countries. *Kyklos,* 1969, *22*(2), pp. 328–33.

______ **and Wise, John.** The Empirical Content of Economic Rationality: A Test for a Less Developed Economy. *J. Polit. Econ.,* November/December 1969, *77*(6), pp. 976–1004.

______ **and Wise, John.** Epilegomena on Traditional Behavior Models. *Amer. J. Agr. Econ.,* November 1969, *51*(4), pp. 928–39.

______ **and Wise, John.** On Testing Competing Hypotheses: Economic Rationality versus Traditional Behavior—A Further Development. *Amer. J. Agr. Econ.,* February 1969, *51*(1), pp. 203–08.

______ **and Wise, John.** On Testing Competing Hypotheses: Economic Rationality versus Traditional Behavior: Rejoinder. *Amer. J. Agr. Econ.,* February 1969, *51*(1), pp. 209–10.

Young, A. Patterns of Development in Zambian Manufacturing Industry since Independence. *East Afr. Econ. Rev.,* December 1969, *1*(2), pp. 29–38.

Young, Allan. Exchange Market Effects of Stock Repurchases through Tender Offers. *Miss. Val. J. Bus. Econ.,* Spring 1969, *4*(2), pp. 65–77.

Young, Allan H. and Harkins, Claudia. Alternative Measures of Price Change for GNP. *Surv. Curr. Bus.,* March 1969, *49*(3), pp. 47–52.

Young, Charles E. Statement. **In** *Timber Management Policies, SCH,* 1969, pp. 71–110.

Young, Edwin. Industrial Relations and University Relations: Discussion. **In** *Somers, G. G., ed. (II),* 1969, pp. 29–30.

Young, Jerry D. and Hilgert, Raymond L. Right-to-Work Legislation—Examination of Related Issues and Effects. **In** *Wortman, M. S., Jr.,* 1969, pp. 377–87.

Young, John H. Comments on the Papers by Goran Ohlin and André Marchal. **In** *Samuelson, P. A., ed.,* 1969, pp. 226–29.

Young, Kan Hua and Quandt, Richard E. Cross-sectional Travel Demand Models: Estimates and Tests. *J. Reg. Sci.,* August 1969, *9*(2), pp. 201–14.

Young, Ralph A. Making Peace with Gold. **In** *Starleaf, D. R., ed.,* 1969, pp. 401–12.

Young, Robert A.; Martin, William E. and Burdak, Thomas G. Projecting Hydrologic and Economic Interrelationships in Groundwater Basin Management. *Amer. J. Agr. Econ.,* December 1969, *51* (5), pp. 1593–97.

Young, William E. and Latané, Henry A. Test of Portfolio Building Rules. *J. Finance,* September 1969, *24*(4), pp. 595–612.

______ **and Trent, Robert H.** Geometric Mean Approximations of Individual Security and Portfolio Performance. *J. Financial Quant. Anal.*, June 1969, *4*(2), pp. 179–99.

Yu, S. C. A Flow-of-Resources Statement for Business Enterprises. *Accounting Rev.*, July 1969, *44* (3), pp. 571–82.

Yung, Shen. The Substance, Characteristics, and System of Socialist Public Finance. *Chinese Econ. Stud.*, Winter 1968/69, *2*(2), pp. 3–27.

Zabel, Edward. The Competitive Firm and Price Expectations. *Int. Econ. Rev.*, October 1969, *10* (3), pp. 467–78.

Zacharias, Jerrold R. Educational Opportunity through Student Loans: An Approach to Higher Education Financing. **In** *the Economics and Financing of Higher Education in the United States, JECP,* 1969, pp. 652–64.

Zaharescu, Barbu. On Some Theoretical Aspects of the Crisis of the World Monetary System. *Revue Roumaine Sci. Soc. Serie Sci. Econ.*, 1969, *13*(2), pp. 157–70.

Zaidan, George C. Population Growth and Economic Development. *Finance Develop.*, March 1969, *6*(1), pp. 2–8.

Zaidi, Mahmood A. The Determinants of Money Wage Rate Changes and Unemployment-Inflation "Trade-Offs" in Canada. *Int. Econ. Rev.*, June 1969, *10*(2), pp. 207–19.

——— Structural Unemployment, Labor Market Efficiency and the Intrafactor Allocation Mechanism in the United States and Canada. *Southern Econ. J.*, January 1969, *35*(3), pp. 205–13.

Zand, Dale E. and Steckman, William E. Resolving Industrial Conflict—An Experimental Study of the Effects of Attitudes and Precedent. **In** *Somers, G. G., ed. (II),* 1969, pp. 348–59.

Zandano, Gianni. The Heckscher-Ohlin Model and the Tariff Structures of the Industrial Countries. *Banca Naz. Lavoro Quart. Rev.*, March 1969, (88), pp. 46–65.

Zanetti, Giovanni and Filippi, Enrico. Il processo di sviluppo dell'impresa: Fattori endogeni ed esogeni esperienza italiana 1958–1963. (The Process of Firm Growth: Endogenous and Exogenous Factors in the Italian Experience 1958–1963. With English summary.) *L'Impresa,* January/February 1969, *11*(1), pp. 29–39.

Zangheri, R. The Historical Relationship between Agricultural and Economic Development in Italy. **In** *Jones, E. L. and Woolf, S. J., eds.*, 1969, pp. 23–39.

Zangwill, Willard I. Top Management and the Selection of Major Contractors at NASA. *Calif. Manage. Rev.*, Fall 1969, *12*(1), pp. 43–52.

Zarnowitz, Victor. The New ASA-NBER Survey of Forecasts by Economic Statisticians. *Amer. Statist.*, February 1969, *23*(1), pp. 12–16.

——— **and Mincer, Jacob.** The Evaluation of Economic Forecasts. **In** *Mincer, J., ed.*, 1969, pp. 3–46.

Zauberman, Alfred. The Rapprochement between East and West in Mathematical-Economic Thought. *Manchester Sch. Econ. Soc. Stud.*, March 1969, *37*(1), pp. 1–21.

——— **and Morton, George.** Von Neumann's Model and Soviet Long-Term (Perspective) Planning. *Kyklos,* 1969, *22*(1), pp. 45–61.

Zeckhauser, Richard J. Majority Rule with Lotteries on Alternatives. *Quart. J. Econ.*, November 1969, *83*(4), pp. 696–703.

——— Resource Allocation with Probabilistic Individual Preferences. *Amer. Econ. Rev.*, May 1969, *59*(2), pp. 546–52.

——— Uncertainty and the Need for Collective Action. **In** *The Analysis and Evaluation of Public Expenditures: The PPB System, Vol. 1, JECP,* 1969, pp. 149–66.

Zeidler, Frank P. Rethinking the Philosophy of Employee Relations in the Public Service. **In** *Walsh, R. E., ed.*, 1969, pp. 198–213.

Zeisel, Rose N. The Workweek for Production Workers in the Private Economy. *Surv. Curr. Bus.*, September 1969, *49*(9), pp. 21–26.

Zeitlin, Sherwin S. and Rosso, David J. United States Taxation of Foreign Enterprises—Structures for Doing Business in the United States and the Western Hemisphere. *Bull. Int. Fiscal Doc.*, December 1969, *23*(12), pp. 555–73.

Zelder, Raymond E. and Ross, Myron H. The Discount Rate: A Phantom Policy Tool? *Western Econ. J.*, December 1969, *7*(4), pp. 341–48.

Zellner, A. and Revankar, N. S. Generalized Production Functions. *Rev. Econ. Stud.*, April 1969, *36* (106), pp. 241–50.

Zelnik, Marvin. Age Patterns of Mortality of American Negroes: 1900–02 to 1959–61. *J. Amer. Statist. Assoc.*, June 1969, *64*(326), pp. 433–51.

Zepp, Glenn A. and McAlexander, Robert H. Predicting Aggregate Milk Production: An Empirical Study. *Amer. J. Agr. Econ.*, August 1969, *51*(3), pp. 642–49.

Zerbe, Richard. The American Sugar Refinery Company, 1887–1914: The Story of a Monopoly. *J. Law Econ.*, October 1969, *12*(2), pp. 339–75.

Zerby, J. A. An Econometric Model of Monetary Interaction in Australia. *Australian Econ. Pap.*, December 1969, *8*(13), pp. 154–77.

Zevering, K. H. and Mueller, P. Employment Promotion through Rural Development: A Pilot Project in Western Nigeria. *Int. Lab. Rev.*, August 1969, *100*(2), pp. 111–30.

Zhamin, V. A. Contemporary Problems of the Economics of Education. **In** *Noah, H. J., ed.*, 1969, pp. 3–19.

Zhil'tsov, E. N. Statistical Methods of Evaluating the Complexity of Labor. **In** *Noah, H. J., ed.*, 1969, pp. 75–86.

Ziderman, Adrian. Costs and Benefits of Adult Retraining in the United Kingdom. *Economica, N.S.*, November 1969, *36*(144), pp. 363–76.

Zieliński, Janusz G. Economics and Politics of Economic Reforms in Eastern Europe. *Econ. Planning,* 1969, *9*(3), pp. 279–95.

——— The Mechanism for Management of Socialist Industry. **In** *Margolis, J. and Guitton, H., eds.*, 1969, pp. 78–97.

Ziemba, William T. A Myopic Capital Budgeting Model. *J. Financial Quant. Anal.*, September 1969, *4*(3), pp. 305–27.

Zima, Petr. Řešení jedné modifikace řezného problému. (A Solution of One Modification of the "Cutting Problem." With English summary.) *Ekon.-Mat. Obzor,* 1969, *5*(1), pp. 72–76.

Zinam, Oleg. The Economics of Command Economies. **In** *Prybyla, J. S., ed.,* 1969, pp. 19–46.

Zinkin, Maurice. A Child's Guide to Planning. *Appl. Econ.,* May 1969, *1*(2), pp. 81–88.

Zinn, Karl Georg. Staatstätigkeit und Multiplikator in den Schriften Ludwig Galls—Eine dogmengeschichtliche Ergänzung zur Beschäftigungstheorie. (With English summary.) *Kyklos,* 1969, *22*(4), pp. 719–36.

Zlatin, V. and Rutgaizer, V. Comparison of the Levels of Economic Development of Union Republics and Large Regions. *Prob. Econ.,* June 1969, *12*(2), pp. 3–24.

Zoellner, John F. Bank Holding Companies—Tenth District States. *Fed. Res. Bank Kansas City Rev.,* February 1969, pp. 10–16.

Županov, Josip. The Producer and Risk. *Eastern Europ. Econ.,* Spring 1969, *7*(3), pp. 12–28.

Zusman, Pinhas. Welfare Implication and Evaluation of Buyers' Travel Inputs and Nonprice Offer Variations in Networks of Retail Food Stores. *Econometrica,* July 1969, *37*(3), pp. 439–56.

Zverev, A. Role of the State Budget in the Distribution of the Social Product and National Income. **In** *Yanowitch, M., ed.,* 1969, pp. 189–96.

Zweig, Michael. Political Economy and the "National Interest." *Rev. Radical Polit. Econ.,* May 1969, *1*(1), pp. 11–35.

Topical Guide
To Classification Schedule

TOPICAL GUIDE TO CLASSIFICATION SCHEDULE

This index refers to the subject index *group, category,* or *subcategory* in which the listed topic may be found. The subject index classifications include, in most cases, related topics as well. The term *category* generally indicates that the topic may be found in all of the *subcategories* of the 3-digit code; the term *group,* indicates that the topics may be found in all of the *subcategories* in the 2-digit code. The classification schedule (pp. xxviii) serves to refer the user to cross references.